International Dictionary of Theatre-2
PLAYWRIGHTS

International Dictionary of Theatre-2

Volume 1
PLAYS

Volume 2
PLAYWRIGHTS

Volume 3
ACTORS, DIRECTORS AND DESIGNERS

International Dictionary of Theatre-2
PLAYWRIGHTS

EDITOR
MARK HAWKINS-DADY

PICTURE EDITOR
HELEN OTTAWAY

St J
St James Press

Detroit   London   Washington DC

Front cover — **George Bernard Shaw**
(photo from the Mander and Mitchenson Theatre Collection)

Gale Research International Ltd.
PO Box 699
Cheriton House
North Way
Andover
Hants SP10 5YE
or
Gale Research Inc.
835 Penobscot Bldg.
Detroit MI 48226–4094

ST JAMES PRESS is an imprint of Gale Research
International Ltd.
An Affiliated Company of Gale Research Inc.

A CIP catalogue record for this book is available from
the British Library.

ISBN 1-55862-096-6

Typeset by Florence Type, Kewstoke, Avon
Printed in the United States of America

The paper used in this publication meets the minimum
requirements of American National Standard for
Information Sciences – Permanence Paper for printed
Library materials, ANSI Z39.48-1984 ⊗™

Published simultaneously in the United Kingdom and the
United States of America

The trade mark ITP is used under license   I⟨T⟩P

CONTENTS

EDITOR'S NOTE

The *International Dictionary of Theatre* is in three volumes: *Plays* (Volume 1), *Playwrights* (Volume 2), and Actors, *Directors and Designers* (Volume 3).

The selection of people and plays appearing in the *Dictionary* is based on the recommendations of the advisers listed on page xi, and its focus, as the titles of the individual volumes suggest, is primarily on the various genres of drama (both as literature and as performance) as distinct from the other performing arts such as opera, dance, mime, the musical, performance-art, and folk, ritual, and community theatre.

The scope of the *Dictionary* is historical (ranging from the theatre of Ancient Greece to that of the present day) and international, covering plays of some 20 languages, and playwrights, actors, directors, and designers of many nationalities. Many entries are illustrated with photographs of productions, designs, portraits, or engravings.

VOLUME 2: Playwrights

Volume 2 contains entries on 485 writers for the stage. Most are widely acknowledged as major dramatists in their country's and/or language's culture and beyond, and their plays are widely performed and studied today. Some of the writers, although their works are no longer considered stageworthy, have significance historically, while others have been "rediscovered" or have emerged as important dramatists in recent years.

A NOTE ON THE ENTRIES

Each entry contains: a summary of the writer's life and career; a list of works *by* the entrant; a list of publications (bibliographies and critical studies) *about* the entrant; a signed critical overview of the entrant's work for the stage by one of the *Dictionary*'s contributors. If any of an entrant's plays has an entry of its own in Volume 1 (*Plays*), a cross-reference make this explicit at the end of the entry in the present volume.

★

Each entry starts with a **Biographical Summary** of its subject. The summary begins with details (where known) of birth, education and training, and marriage(s), before giving a chronological resumé of the subject's life. Awards, honours, and honorary degrees are listed at the end.

The biographical summary is followed by a listing of the writer's **Works**. Here, titles are sometimes given in a "short" form, and publication dates refer to first publication in book form unless otherwise indicated. Titles are in italic, except for literal (i.e. non-published) English translations provided for some of the less familiar languages. This listing contains all or some of the following categories:

Collections: Includes editions of the subject's complete works (early and modern editions), along with other major collections that include plays, play-translations (for non English-language writers), screenplays, television plays, and radio plays. The order is chronological.

Stage Works: Includes original plays, adaptations, and other work for the stage (libretti, ballet scenarii, etc.). Titles are arranged chronologically, according either to *date of first performance or date of first publication—whichever is the earliest*. All information relating to performance appears within parentheses; otherwise, dates refer to publication (dates of composition are not given). For plays written in languages other than English, titles of published translations are given after dates of first publication: the intention here is to indicate the range of titles under which any particular play may have appeared in English rather than to approve or recommend any particular version. When the titles are indicated as being published in collections, very often these will be found in the Collections category.

There is considerable uncertainty in dating and locating the first performances of many plays, especially before the late 17th century, and therefore the practice here has been to provide locations only when known with reasonable certainty, and to offer conservative date estimates, leaning towards wider rather than narrower limits. Uncertainty about a particular date or date-span is indicated by the use of "c." before a date or "?" after it.

Unperformed plays existing only in manuscript and "lost" plays from before 1700 are not listed.

Screenplays; **Television Plays**; **Radio Plays**:   These categories include original works and adaptations for these media, normally listed chronologically by *date of release or first broadcast*. Relatively few works for these media get published, but any publication information appears within parentheses after the relevant title and release/broadcast date. Collections of published screenplays, television plays, or radio plays appear in the Collections category.

Fiction; **Verse**:   These categories include works published in book form, listed chronologically by date of publication.

Memoirs and Letters: Includes published diaries, autobiographies, personal recollections, and volumes of letters, listed chronologically by date of publication. Periodical publications are normally not included. Certain kinds of autobiographical works—anecdotal journalism, work journals, etc.—often appear in the category Other.

Other: Includes publications, normally in book form, that do not readily fit into the other categories—principally miscellanies and non-fictional writing, such as journalism, essays, theoretical works observations, etc., listed chronologically by date of publication. Excepting certain significant commentaries on theatre, publications in periodical form are excluded. Works by other authors which the subject has edited or translated appear at the end of this category.

★

The various categories of an entrant's works are then followed, where relevant, by the two categories of publications about the subject:

Bibliographies: Includes published reference works relating to primary and secondary literature. General bibliographies of literary/dramatic periods, genres, or countries are normally excluded.

Criticism: Includes critical studies and biographies of the subject, divided into the sub-categories of Books and Articles, and listed in chronological order of publication. This section concentrates on critical interest of the last 25 years (since the mid-1960's), although, in many cases, earlier material is also cited. Books in English, French, German, Italian, Spanish, and Portuguese are listed; books in the less familiar East- and Central-European languages and in languages using non-Roman alphabets are excluded. Articles (usually in English) are included when they are especially notable or when there is little material in English existing in book form. For reasons of space it has been the general policy to exclude the following categories from the lists of criticism:
> (a) General works on broad dramatic/literary periods, movements, and genres, and most general works on the literature of particular countries.
> (b) Books and articles dealing wholly with a subject's non-dramatic writing.
> (c) Most books and articles concentrating on an individual play—for specific commentary on many of the most prominent plays by the writers included here, the reader is referred to the entries in Volume 1 (*Plays*).
> (d) Articles of less than five pages in length.

★

Each entry concludes with the **Critical Overview** of the subject by one of the *Dictionary*'s contributors. Play-titles cited here are normally in italics (when they are original and/or published titles), but sometimes in Roman type—between inverted commas or in parentheses—when they are literal translations provided by the essayist or editor.

SOURCES

Several general works of reference have been proved extremely useful and I should like to record my debt to the following: *History of English Drama 1660–1900* (6 vols.), by Allardyce Nicoll, 1952–59; *Enciclopedia della spettacolo* (9 vols.), 1954–62; *McGraw-Hill Encyclopedia of World Drama* (5 vols.; 2nd edition), edited by Stanley Hochman, 1984; *Oxford Companion to the Theatre*, edited by Phyllis Hartnoll, 1985 (4th edition); *Modern Drama Scholarship and Criticism 1966–1980*, edited by Charles A. Carpenter, 1986; *Kindler's Neues Literatur Lexikon* (20 vols.), edited by W. Jens, 1988–92; *Annals of English Drama 975–1700*, edited by Alfred Harbage, revised by Sylvia Stoler Wagonheim, 1989;

Cambridge Guide to World Theatre, edited by Martin Banham, 1992 (revised edition). In addition, some entries are based on those in earlier St. James Press titles, notably *Reference Guide to English Literature* (3. vols.), 1992, *Contemporary Dramatists*, 1988 (4th edition), and *Guide to French Literature* (2 vols.), 1992–93.

ACKNOWLEDGEMENTS

I should like to thank the following for their help on this volume: all the advisers and contributors; John and Barbara Cavanagh; the staff of the British Library, Westminster Reference Library, the Goethe Institut (London), and several libraries of London University—notably Senate House, SSEES, SOAS, and the Latin American Institute; the late Jim Vinson for laying the foundations for the project; Daniel Kirkpatrick, for his editorial guidance and continuing support; Warren Cheshire; Tracy Chevalier; Sarah Hall; Comfort Jegede; Susan Mackervoy; and Martha Bremser, for her unpaid toil and for reminding me what's important in life.

ADVISERS

Arnold Aronson
Martin Banham
Eugene Benson
Michael Billington
David Bradby
James Brandon
John Russell Brown
Jarka M. Burian
Marvin Carlson
Ruby Cohn
Tish Dace
Daniel Gerould
Vera Gottlieb
Peter Holland
William D. Howarth

Christopher Innes
Bruce King
Felicia Hardison Londré
Frederick J. Marker
Walter J. Meserve
Michael Patterson
Kenneth Richards
Laurence Senelick
Peter Thomson
Stanley Wells
George E. Wellwarth
Margaret Williams
George Woodyard
Katharine Worth

CONTRIBUTORS

Asbjørn Aarseth
Elissa Adams
Gunilla Anderman
Richard Andrews
Chris Banfield
Martin Banham
Judith E. Barlow
Gene A. Barnett
Susan Bassnett
Richard C. Beacham
Jean Benedetti
Joss Bennathon
Susan Bennett
Eugene Benson
Renate Benson
Günter Berghaus
Gerald M. Berkowitz
Michael Billington
George Bisztray
Franz G. Blaha
Roy Booth
David Bradby
Gaynor F. Bradish
Philip Brady
Laurel Brake
Anthony D.P. Briggs
Christina Britzolakis
William Brooks
John Bull
Suzanne Burgoyne
Mark Thornton Burnett
Martin Butler
Denis Calandra
David Carnegie

Dennis Carroll
Anthony J. Cascardi
Ned Chaillet
Janet Clarke
Richard Corballis
Brian Corman
David Cottis
W.A. Coupe
T.W. Craik
Karen Cronacher
Brian Crow
Tish Dace
Jim Davis
Peter Davison
Terence Dawson
Barbara Day
Dennis Deletant
Maria M. Delgado
Elin Diamond
Maria DiCenzo
William Dolby
Leonard E. Doucette
Peter Doyle
Tony Dunn
Gwynne Edwards
Robert C. Egan
Stanislaw Eile
Peter Fitzpatrick
Kathy Fletcher
Helena Forsås-Scott
Verna A. Foster
Richard Foulkes
Steven H. Gale
Daniel Gerould

C.J. Gianakaris
Colin Gibson
Reid Gilbert
Don Gilman
George Gömöri
S.E. Gontarski
John Goodliffe
David G. Goodman
Robert Gordon
Lynn Carbón Gorell
Christopher Gossip
Anthony Graham-White
Peter Graves
Frances Gray
Valerie Grosvenor Myer
Maria Guterres
H. Gaston Hall
James Hansford
Michael Hattaway
Juan Carlos Hidalgo Ciudad
Marion Peter Holt
Marjorie L. Hoover
David Horton
Jane House
William D. Howarth
Derek Hughes
Hugh Hunt
John D. Hurrell
Naomi Iizuka
R.D.S. Jack
Christopher Johnson
Samantha Johnson
Robert Jordan
Brian Keith-Smith
Veronica Kelly
Burton S. Kendle
Dennis Kennedy
Adele King
Bruce King
Kimball King
Pamela M. King
A.V. Knowles
Manfred F. Kremer
Rosette C. Lamont
Bernd-Peter Lange
Paul Lawley
Ramon Layera
Robert Leach
Charles L. Leavitt
Peter Lewis
Tim Lewis
Ladislaus Löb
Derek W. Lomax
Felicia Hardison Londré
N.J. Lowe
Valerie Lucas
James MacDonald
Colin Mackerras
G. Jonathon Mallinson
John McCallum
Paul McGillick
Howard McNaughton
Gordon McVay
Anthony Meech
Ulrich Meissner
Walter J. Meserve
Patrick Miles

Ken Mills
Michael Mitchell
Christian H. Moe
Christopher Morash
Margery Morgan
J.R. Mulryne
Steve Nicholson
Ariadne Nicolaeff
Kirsten F. Nigro
Micheál Ó hAodha
R.J. Oakley
John Osborne
Dorothy Parker
Juliet Perkins
Andy Piasecki
Ludvika Popenhagen
Ron Popenhagen
Raphael Portillo
Karen Pratt
Leonard C. Pronko
David Ian Rabey
Colin Radford
Margaret Loftus Ranald
Donald Rayfield
Leslie du S. Read
Bonnie Hildebrand Reynolds
Francesca H.A. Richards
Kenneth Richards
Laura Richards
Sandra L. Richards
Hugh Rorrison
John Rothenberg
Donald Roy
Leslie C. Sanders
Robert K. Sarlós
Bernice Schrank
Claude Schumacher
Irene Scobbie
Virginia Scott
Robert Silvester
James Simmons
G. Singh
Robert Skloot
Peter Skrine
Christopher Smith
Noel Stanley
Paul Starkey
Mary E. Stewart
Ronald W. Strang
Elizabeth Swain
Elzbieta Szoka
Diana Taylor
Val Taylor
George Thaniel
Philip Thody
Bjarne T. Thomsen
Peter Thomson
James J. Troiano
Simon Trussler
Andrew T. Tsubaki
Paul Vincent
Colin Wills Visser
Carla Waal
Peter Walcot
David H. Walker
J. Michael Walton
Alan G. Waring

International Dictionary of Theatre-2
PLAYWRIGHTS

A-Z LIST OF PLAYWRIGHTS

Adam de la Halle
Arthur Adamov
Aeschylus
Ama Ata Aidoo
Edward Albee
Vittorio Alfieri
Maxwell Anderson
Robert Anderson
Jorge Andrade
Leonid Andreyev
Jean Anouilh
Solomon Ansky
Guillaume Apollinaire
Alexei Arbuzov
John Arden
Pietro Aretino
Ludovico Ariosto
Aristophanes
Roberto Arlt
Fernando Arrabal
W.H. Auden
Jacques Audiberti
Émile Augier
Alan Ayckbourn

Amiri Baraka (LeRoi Jones)
Jean Barbeau
Howard Barker
James Nelson Barker
Ernst Barlach
Peter Barnes
J.M. Barrie
Philip Barry
Pierre-Augustin Beaumarchais
Francis Beaumont
Samuel Beckett
Henri Becque
Brendan Behan
Aphra Behn
S.N. Behrman
Jacinto Benavente y Martínez
Alan Bennett
Hjalmar Bergman
Steven Berkoff
Thomas Bernhard
Ugo Betti
Isaac Bickerstaff(e)
Bjørnstjerne Bjørnson
Alexander Blok
Jean Bodel
George Henry Boker
Robert Bolt
Edward Bond
Wolfgang Borchert
Dion Boucicault
Volker Braun
Bertolt Brecht
Howard Brenton
James Bridie
Eugène Brieux
Harold Brighouse

Richard Brome
Georg Büchner
Antonio Buero Vallejo
Mikhail Bulgakov
Ed Bullins
Edward Bulwer-Lytton
Alexander Buzo
H.J. Byron

Pedro Calderón de la Barca
Albert Camus
Cao Yu
Karel Čapek
Ion Luca Caragiale
Emilio Carballido
Paul Vincent Carroll
Alejandro Casona
Susanna(h) Centlivre
Miguel de Cervantes
Aimé Césaire
George Chapman
Paddy Chayevsky
Anton Chekhov
Luigi Chiarelli
Chikamatsu Monzaemon
Alice Childress
Caryl Churchill
Colley Cibber
John Pepper Clark
Paul Claudel
Hugo Claus
Jean Cocteau
George Colman the Elder
George Colman the Younger
Padraic Colum
William Congreve
Marc Connelly
Michael Cook
Pierre Corneille
Thomas Corneille
John Coulter
Noël Coward
Fernand Crommelynck
Rachel Crothers
Richard Cumberland

Bernard Dadié
Stig Dagerman
Augustin Daly
Gabriele D'Annunzio
William Davenant
Eduardo De Filippo
Alma De Groen
Thomas Dekker
Shelagh Delaney
Jorge Díaz
Tankred Dorst
John Dryden
Marcel Dubé
Alexandre Dumas *fils*
Alexandre Dumas *père*

William Dunlap
Lord Dunsany
Christopher Durang
Marguerite Duras
Friedrich Dürrenmatt

José Echegaray
David Edgar
T.S. Eliot
Nikolai Erdman
Thomas Louis Esson
Sir George Etherege
Euripides

Diego Fabbri
George Farquhar
Rainer Werner Fassbinder
David Fennario
Leandro Fernández de Moratin
Georges Feydeau
Henry Fielding
Harvey Fierstein
Clyde Fitch
George Fitzmaurice
John Fletcher
Dario Fo
Denis Fonvizin
Samuel Foote
John Ford
María Irene Fornés
Dieter Forte
Michael Frayn
David French
Brian Friel
Max Frisch
Christopher Fry
Athol Fugard
Charles Fuller

Zona Gale
John Galsworthy
Griselda Gambaro
Federico García Lorca
João Baptista de Almeida Garrett
John Gay
Jack Gelber
Gratien Gélinas
Jean Genet
Michel de Ghelderode
Giuseppe Giacosa
W.S. Gilbert
Jean Giraudoux
Susan Glaspell
Reinhard Goering
Johann Wolfgang von Goethe
Nikolai Gogol
Carlo Goldoni
Oliver Goldsmith
Witold Gombrowicz
Alfredo Dias Gomes
Maxim Gorky
Carlo Gozzi
Christian Dietrich Grabbe
Harley Granville-Barker
Günter Grass
Simon Gray
Paul Green

Robert Greene
Lady Gregory
Alexander Griboyedov
Nordahl Grieg
Trevor Griffiths
Franz Grillparzer
Guan Hanqing
John Guare

Peter Hacks
Christopher Hampton
Peter Handke
Lorraine Hansberry
Alexandre Hardy
David Hare
Edward Harrigan
Walter Hasenclever
Gerhart Hauptmann
Václav Havel
Friedrich Hebbel
Ben Hecht
Herman Heijermans
Lillian Hellman
Beth Henley
Luis Josefina Hernández
James A. Herne
Dorothy Hewett
Thomas Heywood
Jack Hibberd
Rolf Hochhuth
Fritz Hochwälder
Hugo von Hofmannsthal
Ludvig Holberg
Thomas Holcroft
Israel Horovitz
Ödön von Horváth
Stanley Houghton
Sidney Howard
Hrotsvitha
Langston Hughes
Victor Hugo

Henrik Ibsen
Elizabeth Inchbald
William Inge
Eugène Ionesco
Vsevolod Ivanov

Alfred Jarry
Ann Jellicoe
Douglas Jerrold
Denis Johnston
Henry Arthur Jones
Ben Jonson

Georg Kaiser
Kalidasa
Kara Jūrō
Peter Karvaš
József Katona
George S. Kaufman
Nikos Kazantzakis
John B. Keane
Adrienne Kennedy
Thomas Kilroy
Sidney Kingsley
Kinoshita Junji

Heinar Kipphardt
Kishida Kunio
Heinrich von Kleist
Oskar Kokoschka
Arthur Kopit
August von Kotzebue
Zygmunt Krasiński
Franz Xaver Kroetz
Kubo Sakae
Milan Kundera
Thomas Kyd

Marie Laberge
Eugène Labiche
Pär Lagerkvist
František Langer
Arthur Laurents
Ray Lawler
D.H. Lawrence
John Howard Lawson
Nathaniel Lee
Mike Leigh
J.M.R. Lenz
Hugh Leonard
Mikhail Lermontov
Alain-René Lesage
Gotthold Ephraim Lessing
George Lillo
Charles Ludlam
John Lyly

Niccolò Machiavelli
James Steele Mackaye
Imre Madách
Maurice Maeterlinck
Antonine Maillet
Jean Mairet
David Mamet
F.T. Marinetti
Pierre Marivaux
Christopher Marlowe
René Marqués
John Marston
Edward Martyn
Bruce Mason
Philip Massinger
Somerset Maugham
Vladimir Mayakovsky
Greg McGee
John McGrath
Menander
David Mercer
Thomas Middleton
Arthur Miller
Langdon Mitchell
Molière
Ferenc Molnár
Henry de Montherlant
William Vaughn Moody
John Mortimer
Anna Cora Mowatt
Sławomir Mrożek
Heiner Müller
Kaj Munk
Thomas Murphy
T.C. Murray
John Murrell
Alfred de Musset

Johann Nepomuk Nestroy
Ngugi wa Thiong'o
Peter Nichols
Lars Norén
Marsha Norman
Louis Nowra

René de Obaldia
André Obey
Sean O'Casey
Clifford Odets
John O'Keeffe
Eugene O'Neill
István Örkény
Joe Orton
John Osborne
Alexander Ostrovsky
Thomas Otway

Stewart Parker
Eduardo Pavlovsky
George Peele
Lyudmila Petrushevskaya
Virgilio Piñera
Arthur Wing Pinero
Robert Pinget
Harold Pinter
Luigi Pirandello
René Guilbert de Pixérécourt
James Robinson Planché
Titus Maccius Plautus
Stephen Poliakoff
Sharon Pollock
Pandelis Prevelakis
J.B. Priestley
Stanisława Przbyszewska
Alexander Pushkin

Philippe Quinault

David Rabe
Jean Racine
Ferdinand Raimund
John Rastell
Terence Rattigan
Edward Ravenscroft
Charles Reade
James Reaney
José Régio
Jean-François Regnard
Elmer Rice
Jack Richardson
Gwen Pharis Ringwood
T.W. Robertson
Lennox Robinson
Nélson Rodrigues
John Romeril
Edmond Rostand
Ola Rotimi
Jean de Rotrou
Nicholas Rowe
Tadeusz Różewicz
David Rudkin
Juan Ruiz de Alarcón
Ruz(z)ante
George Ryga

Armand Salacrou

Bernardo Santareno
Victorien Sardou
William Saroyan
Natalie Sarraute
Jean-Paul Sartre
Alfonso Sastre
Satoh Makoto
James Saunders
Friedrich von Schiller
Arthur Schnitzler
Eugène Scribe
Georges de Scudéry
Seneca
Stephen Sewell
Thomas Shadwell
Peter Shaffer
William Shakespeare
Ntozake Shange
George Bernard Shaw
Sam Shepard
Richard Brinsley Sheridan
Martin Sherman
Robert Sherwood
George Shiels
James Shirley
Evgeny Shvarts
Antonio José da Silva
Neil Simon
N.F. Simpson
Fyodor Sologub
Carlos Solórzano
Sophocles
Reinhard Sorge
Thomas Southerne
Wole Soyinka
Martin Sperr
Sir Richard Steele
Carl Sternheim
Tom Stoppard
David Storey
Botho Strauss
August Strindberg
Hermann Sudermann
Alexander Sukhovo-Kobylin
Efua Sutherland
John Millington Synge

Rabindranath Tagore
Tang Xianzu
Jean Tardieu
Torquato Tasso
Nahum Tate
Tawfiq al-Hakim
Tom Taylor
Terayama Shūji
Terence
Megan Terry
Ludwig Tieck

Tirso de Molina
Ernst Toller
Alexei Konstantinovich Tolstoy
Leo Tolstoy
Josef Topol
Cyril Tourneur
Ben Travers
Michel Tremblay
Sergei Tretyakov
José Triana
Ivan Turgenev
Josef Tyl

Nicholas Udall
Rodolfo Usigli

Ramón del Valle-Inclán
Alexander Vampilov
John Van Druten
Jean-Claude van Itallie
Sir John Vanbrugh
Lope de Vega Carpio
Boris Vian
Gil Vicente
Alfred de Vigny
Michel Vinaver
Vsevolod Vishnevsky
Alexander Volodin
Voltaire

Derek Walcott
George F. Walker
Martin Walser
John Webster
Frank Wedekind
Peter Weiss
Timberlake Wertenbaker
Arnold Wesker
Patrick White
John Whiting
Oscar Wilde
Thornton Wilder
Paul Willems
Tennessee Williams
David Williamson
August Wilson
Lanford Wilson
Stanisław Witkiewicz
Charles Wood
William Wycherley
Stanisław Wyspiański

Kateb Yacine
W.B. Yeats

Zeami
Émile Zola
Carl Zuckmayer

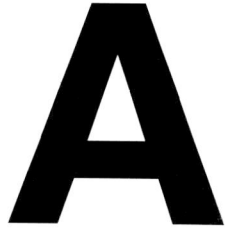

A

ADAM DE LA HALLE. Also known as Adan [*sic*] le Bossu [or Boscu] d'Arras. Born probably in Arras, France, c.1245. Probably studied in Paris. Cleric, poet, playwright, and musician; in the service of Robert II, Comte d'Artois, and made several trips to Italy with him, from 1274; entered the service of Robert's uncle, Charles d'Anjou, in Italy, 1283. Over 24 manuscripts survive, including his musical works—chansons, jeux-partis (often with Jehan Bretel), rondeaux, motets—and non-dramatic writing as well as the plays. Died in Naples, c.1288, or possibly in England, after 1306.

Works

Collections

Oeuvres complètes, edited by F. de Coussemaker. 1872.
Medieval French Plays (includes both plays), translated by Richard Axton and John Stevens. 1971.
Le Théâtre comique du Moyen Age (includes both plays), edited by Claude A. Chevallier. 1973.

Stage Works

Le Jeu de la feuillée (produced Arras, c.1276). In *Oeuvres complètes*, 1872; translated as *Le Jeu de la feuillée*, in *Medieval French Plays* (see Collections), 1971.
Le Jeu de Robin et Marion (possibly produced for the court of Comte d'Artois, c.1283). As *Li Gieus de Robin et de Marion*, edited by L.J.N. Monmerqué, 1822; with variants, in *Oeuvres complètes*, 1872; translated as *The Play of Robin and Marion*, 1928, and in *Five Comedies of Medieval France*, translated by Oscar Mandel, 1982; as *Le Jeu de Robin et Marion*, in *Medieval French Plays* (see Collections), 1971.

Other

Les Jeux-partis d'Adam de la Halle. 1917.
Les Congés d'Arras (includes works by others), edited by P. Ruelle. 1965.
The Lyric Works, edited by N. Wilkins. 1967.
The Chansons of Adam de la Halle, edited by J.H. Marshall. 1971.

*

Criticism

Books:
H. Guy, *Essai sur la vie et les oeuvres littéraires du trouvère Adan de la Hale*, Paris, 1898.
Grace Frank, *The Medieval French Drama*, Oxford, 1954.

Marie Ungureaunu, *La Bourgeoisie naissante: Société et littérature bourgeoise d'Arras aux XIIe et XIIIe siècles*, Arras, 1955.
A. Adler, *Sens et composition du "Jeu de la Feuillée"*, Ann Arbor, Michigan, 1957.
N.R. Cartier, *Le Bossu désenchanté*, Geneva, 1971.
Richard Axton, *European Drama of the Early Middle Ages*, London, 1974.
Jean-Claude Aubailly, *Le Théâtre médiéval profane et comique*, Paris, 1975.

Articles:
D.R. Sutherland, "Fact and Fiction in the *Jeu de la feuillée*", in *Romance Philology*, 13, 1959–60.
M. Zimmerman, "Controversies on *Le Jeu de la feuillée*", in *Studia Neophilologica*, 39, 1967.
E. Lance, "*Le Jeu de la feuillée* and the Poetics of Charivari", in *Modern Language Notes*, 100, 1985.
S. Huot, "Transformations of Lyric Voice in the Songs, Motets and Plays of Adam de la Halle", in *Romanic Review*, 78, 1987.

*　*　*

Experimentation in theatrical form, begun in Arras in the early 13th century by Jean Bodel, was further developed later in the century by fellow Arrageois Adam de la Halle, a bourgeois cleric who was an accomplished poet (author of love lyrics, debate poems, a *congé* and the epic *Roi de Sicile*) as well as an important musician. In fact, Adam's two plays *Le Jeu de la feuillée* and *Le Jeu de Robin et Marion* both contain music; in the former there is one short ditty sung by the fairies, in the latter several pastoral poems accompanied by their melodies. These plays, like much 13th-century French literature, are also experiments in genre, for the *Feuillée* is a dramatised *congé*, a poem in which the author adopts the persona of someone who bids farewell to friends and foes before leaving town, while *Robin et Marion* is an embryonic comic opera, in which Adam has given the lyric *pastourelle* and the *bergerie* dramatic form.

The order in which Adam composed his two plays is not known. Jean Dufournet argues that *Robin et Marion* was written before the *Feuillée*, hence while Adam was still in Arras, while other critics think his pastoral play was produced for the Count of Artois and his court while he was on campaign in Italy in the 1280's. While *Robin et Marion* lacks the satire on Arras and its inhabitants which is so prevalent in the *Feuillée*, its humorous presentation of an aristocratic, knightly lover and amusing rustic folk would probably have entertained an audience of bourgeois clerics of Arras just as much as the *Feuillée* would have done.

The *Jeu de Robin et Marion* begins by parodying the classic situation found in the lyric *pastourelle*: a knight attempts to seduce a young shepherdess whom he finds alone in the

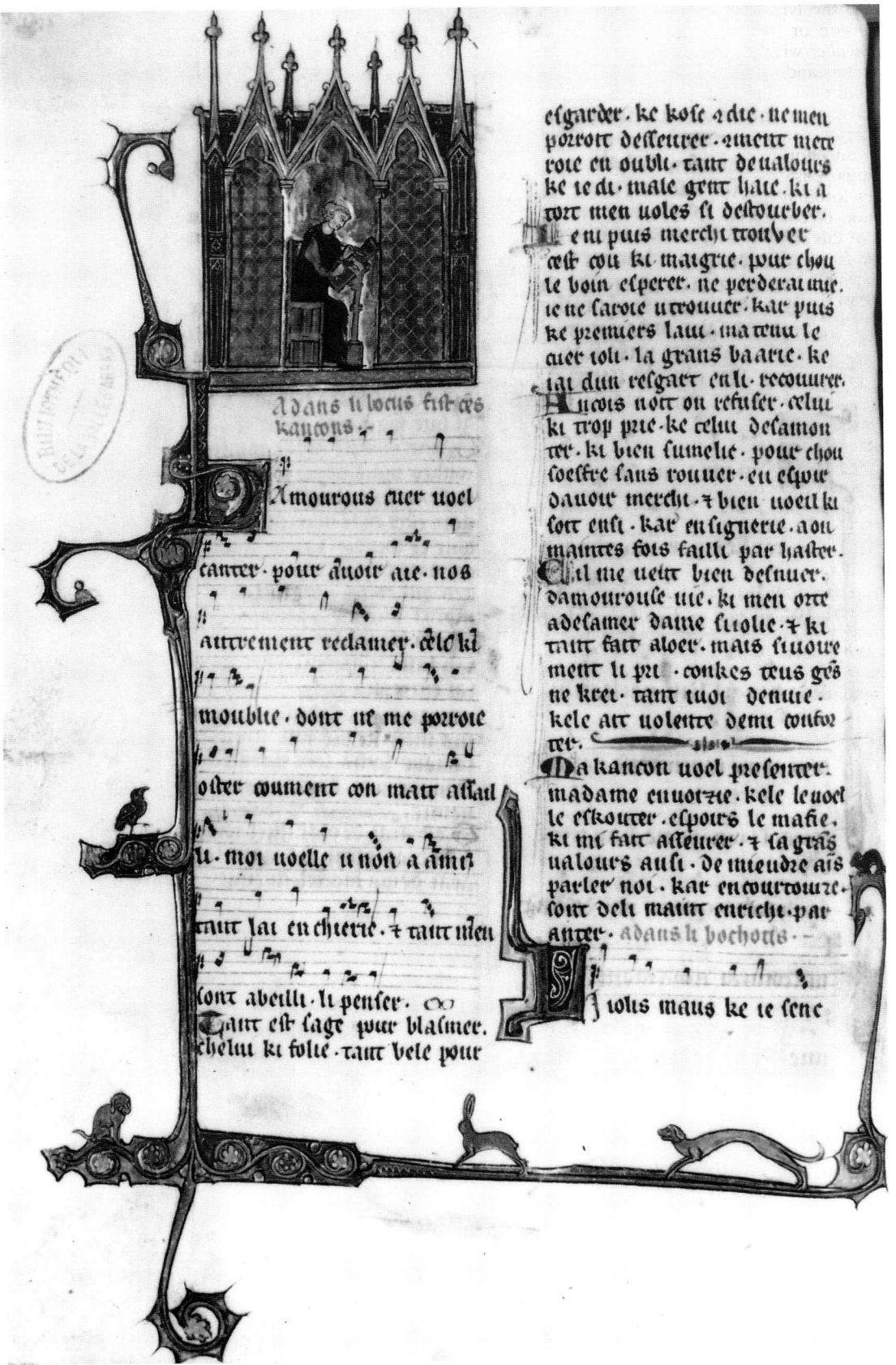

Page from the Arras *Chansonnier* (late 13th century) showing a miniature of **Adam de la Halle**.

forest. While in the lyric many girls succumb either to the knight's persuasion or to force, Adam's Marion is able to dismiss the *chevalier* wittily, though it is unclear whether or not her misunderstanding of the sexual undertones of his language is intentional. Her boyfriend Robin, learning of her narrow escape, goes to fetch peasant reinforcements and in his absence Marion again rebuffs the knight, who takes out his frustration on poor Robin. The second half of the play contains various pastoral entertainments, during which Marion teaches Robin how to treat a shepherdess like a lady, the juxtaposition of courtly ideals and everyday village life creating most of the humour.

The *Jeu de la feuillée*, whose title seems to refer to the leafy bower under which the Virgin's shrine would have been displayed on feast days, but which also alludes (by means of a Picard pun) to the play's main theme—folly in all its forms—was composed c.1276 and was probably performed on St. John's day (24th June) or another summer evening when fairies were traditionally expected to arrive. The play begins with a character called Adam (not necessarily representing the author himself) stating, in the manner of the *congé*, that he is leaving his wife and the materialistic town of Arras with its seductive pleasures of the flesh to resume his studies in Paris. Thus certain generic expectations are immediately raised: there will be satire on the dramatist's enemies and praise of his friends. Through a series of seemingly unconnected tableaux (nevertheless unified by Adam's project to leave Arras and the theme of folly), individuals (Adam's father, wife), professions (quack doctors and monks who peddle false relics), social groups (nagging wives and loose women), authority figures (fathers, clerics, the Pope, town councillors), and human vices and foibles (avarice, pride, gluttony, lechery, hypocrisy, superstition) are all ridiculed, much in the manner of a modern-day Cambridge Footlights revue. Even Adam himself does not escape ridicule, for despite his pretensions and the Parisian clerical garb he has donned somewhat prematurely, he does not escape from Arras and is to be found drinking in the tavern with his friends at the end of the play. He too is a victim of the madness endemic in Arras and which seems to affect even the fairies, whose visit forms the central section of the play. In this dream-like interlude, which seems in structure and theme to anticipate *A Midsummer Night's Dream*, madness runs riot as the clerics Adam and his friend Riquier set three places at a table and await the arrival of Morgan, Arsile, and Maglore (reminiscent of the Parcae or three Fates). The gifts and curse which they bestow on Adam and Riquier (the former doomed by the petulant Maglore to remain for ever in Arras in the arms of his wife) and the presence of fickle Fortune and her wheel (which provides further satire on the powerful of Arras), may be Adam's explanation as to why the character who bears his name is not successful in his project, for man's free will is limited by forces beyond his control. The fact, though, that the fairies are depicted as petty fallible women (Morgan has, after all, misguidedly fallen in love with a bourgeois braggart—Adam's rival Robert Sommeillon) may imply that their power is questionable and that man is not justified in blaming the supernatural for his own failures. Thus, a topical satirical revue, probably performed by bourgeois clerics (some of whom would have been playing themselves) succeeds not only in holding up a mirror of ridicule to the materialistic citizens of Arras and their crimes of foolish excess, but also in raising more universally relevant questions concerning fate, fortune, and individual free will.

Adam's two plays, the earliest examples of pure comedy to have survived, exploit a wide range of comic and dramatic techniques. The potentially serious theme of *Robin et Marion*

(the threatened rape of a defenceless girl, which the *pastourelle* often depicted) is quickly defused and the play turns into a light-hearted musical entertainment. In the *Feuillée* we find sophisticated verbal humour and mordant satire intermingling with the slapstick antics and scatological language of a madboy. However, manuscript evidence suggests that the two plays were rarely copied or performed and they seem to have had little influence on later theatrical traditions. We have to wait over 100 years for the next flowering of French comedy—the 15th-century farce.

—Karen Pratt

ADAMOV, Arthur. Born in Baku, Azerbaijan, 23 August 1908; lived abroad after 1912. Educated at Rosset School, Geneva; French lycée, Mainz, Germany, 1922–24; Lycée Lakanal, Paris, 1924–27. Married Jacqueline Trehet in 1961. Writer for the review *Discontinuité* in the late 1920's; editor of periodical *L'Heure nouvelle*, 1945–47; increasingly involved in left-wing politics during the 1950's; co-signatory of the "Manifeste des 121" opposing the war in Algeria, 1960; visiting lecturer, Cornell University, Ithaca, New York, 1964. Died in Paris from overdose of barbiturates, 15 March 1970.

Works

Collections

Théâtre 1 (includes *L'Invasion; Le Professeur Taranne; La Parodie; La Grande et la Petite Manoeuvre; Tous contre tous*). 1953.
Théâtre 2 (includes *Les Retrouvailles; Le Sens de la marche; Le Ping-Pong*). 1955.
Théâtre de société (includes *Intimité; Je ne suis pas français; La Complainte de ridicule*). 1958.
Théâtre 3 (includes *La Politique des restes; Sainte Europe; Paolo Paoli*). 1966.
Théâtre 4 (includes *M Le Modéré; Le Printemps 71*). 1968.

Stage Works

L'Arbitre aux mains vides (produced Studio des Ursulines, Paris, 1928).
Mains blanches (produced Studio des Ursulines, Paris, 1928).
La Mort de Danton, from a play by Büchner (produced by the Théâtre National Populaire, Avignon, 1948). In *Le Monde illustré, théâtral et littéraire*, 35, 1948; in book form, 1953.
La Parodie (produced Théâtre Lancry, Paris, 1952). With *L'Invasion*, 1950.
L'Invasion (produced Studio des Champs-Élysées, Paris, 1950). With *La Parodie*, 1950; translated as *The Invasion*, 1968.
La Grande et la Petite Manoeuvre (produced Théâtre des Noctambules, Paris, 1950). 1951.
Le Sens de la marche (produced Théâtre de la Comédie, Lyons, 1953). In *Théâtre 2*, 1955.
Tous contre tous (produced Théâtre de l'Oeuvre, Paris, 1953). In *Théâtre 1*, 1953.
Le Professeur Taranne (produced Théâtre de la Comédie, Lyons, 1953). 1953; translated as *Professor Taranne*, in *Two Plays*, 1962.

Comme Nous avons été (produced Théâtre de l'Oeuvre, Paris, 1954). In *La Nouvelle Revue Française 1*, 1953; translated as *As We Were*, in *Evergreen Review*, vol.1 no.4, 1957.

La Cruche cassée, from a play by Kleist (produced Théâtre de la Comédie, Lyons, 1954). In *Théâtre populaire*, March–April 1954.

Edward II, from the play by Marlowe (produced Festival de Lyon-Charbonnières, 1954).

Le Ping-Pong (produced Théâtre des Noctambules, Paris, 1955). In *Théâtre 2*, 1955; translated as *Ping Pong*, 1959

Les Retrouvailles. In *Théâtre 2*, 1955.

Le Pélican , from a play by Strindberg (produced Théâtre de l'Oeuvre, Paris, 1956). In *Théâtre populaire*, 17, 1956.

Les Ennemis, from a play by Gorky (produced Théâtre des Amandiers, Nanterre, 1965). In *Théâtre populaire*, 27, 1957.

Le Revizor, from a play by Gogol (produced Comédie de Saint-Etiènne, 1967). 1958.

Paolo Paoli (produced Théâtre de la Comédie, Lyon, 1957). 1957; translated as *Paolo Paoli*, 1959.

Vassa Geleznova, from a play by Gorky (produced Théâtre du Tertre, Paris, 1959). 1958.

Le Père, from a play by Strindberg. 1958.

Les Petits bourgeois, from a play by Gorky (produced Théâtre de l'Oeuvre, Paris, 1959). 1958.

Intimité. In *Théâtre de société*, 1958.

La Complainte du ridicule. In *Théâtre de société*, 1958.

Je ne suis pas français. In *Théâtre de société*, 1958.

Les Âmes mortes, from the novel *Dead Souls* by Gogol (produced Théâtre de la Cité, Villeurbanne, 1960). 1960.

La Sonate des spectres, with C.G. Bjürström, from a play by Strindberg (produced Théâtre des Nations Festival, Paris, 1962). In *Théâtre VI*, by Strindberg, 1961.

Le Printemps 71 (produced Unity Theatre, London, 1962; Théâtre Gerard-Philipe, Paris, 1963). 1961.

La Politique des restes (produced Unity Theatre, London, 1963). In *Théâtre 3*, 1966.

Sainte Europe. In *Théâtre 3*, 1966.

M Le Modéré (produced Théâtre des Mathurins, Paris, 1968). In *Théâtre IV*, 1968.

Off Limits (produced Théâtre de la Commune d'Aubervilliers, 1968). 1969.

La Grande Muraille, from a play by Frisch (produced Théâtre Populaire Romand, Lausanne, Switzerland, 1969). 1969.

Si l'Été revenait (produced Théâtre de la Cartoucherie, Vincennes, 1972). 1970.

Television Plays

La Parole est au prophète, with Bernard Hecht, 1952; *Tous contre tous*, 1956; *Les Trois Soeurs*, from *The Three Sisters* by Chekhov, 1958; *Le Ping-Pong*, 1958; *Paolo Paoli*, 1965; *Le Manteau*, from a story by Gogol, 1966; *Une Femme douce*, from a work by Dostoevsky, 1970; *La Mort de Danton*, from *Dantons Tod* by Büchner, 1970; *La Cigale*, from *The Seagull* by Chekhov, 1970; *Vassa Geleznova*, from a play by Gorky, 1971.

Radio Plays

L'Invasion, from the stage play, 1950; *La Logeuse*, from a work by Dostoevsky, 1950; *Polly*, from *The Beggar's Opera* by John Gay, 1951; *L'Éternel Mari*, from a work by Dostoevsky, 1952; *Le Potier politicien*, from a work by Holberg, 1952; *L'Agence universelle*, 1953; *Lady Macbeth au*

village, from a work by Leskov, 1953; *Parallèlement*, from a work by Kaiser, 1954; *Les Âmes mortes*, from the novel *Dead Souls* by Gogol, 1955; *Raillerie, satire, ironie et signification plus profonde*, from a play by Grabbe, 1957; *L'Autre Rive*, from a work by Goncharov, 1959; *Pierre et Jean*, from a work by Maupassant; *La Cruche cassée*, from a play by Kleist, 1962; *Le Temps vivant*, 1963; *En Fiacre*, 1963; *Finita la commedia*, 1964; *Du Matin à minuit*, from a play by Kaiser, 1966; *Le Professeur Taranne*, 1967; *La Politique des restes*, 1967; *Père*, from a play by Strindberg, 1967; *Si l'Été revenait*, 1970.

Memoirs and Letters

L'Aveu (autobiography). 1946; augmented edition, as *Je . . . ils . . .*, 1969; part translated as *The Endless Humiliation*, in *Evergreen Review*, vol.2 no. 8, 1959.

L'Homme et l'enfant (diaries). 1968; translated as *Man and Child*, 1992.

Other

Auguste Strindberg, dramaturge, with Maurice Gravier. 1955.

Ici et maintenant (essays). 1964.

Editor, *Le Commune de Paris*. 1959.

Translator, *Le Moi et l'inconscient*, by Jung. 1938.

Translator, with Marie Geringer, *Le Livre de la pauvreté et de la mort*, by Rilke. 1941.

Translator, *Crime et châtiment*, by Dostoevsky. 1956.

Translator, *Les Âmes mortes* (first part), by Gogol. 1956; both parts, 1964.

Translator, *La Mère*, by Gorky. 1958.

Translator, *Théâtre*, by Chekhov. 1958.

Translator, *Oblomov*, by Goncharov. 1959.

Translator, *Cinq récits*, by Gogol. 1961.

Translator, with Claude Sebisch, *Le Théâtre politique*, by Erwin Piscator. 1962.

*

Bibliographies

David Bradby, *Adamov*, London, 1975.

Criticism

Books:
Ezio M. Caserta, *Arthur Adamov*, Florence, 1971.
René Gaudy, *Arthur Adamov*, Paris, 1971.
Pierre Mélèse, *Arthur Adamov: Textes d'Arthur Adamov, points de vue critiques, témoignages, chronologie, bibliographie, illustrations*, Paris, 1973.
John H. Reilly, *Arthur Adamov*, New York, 1974.
John J. McCann, *The Theater of Adamov*, Chapel Hill, North Carolina, 1975.
Samia Asad Chahine, *Regards sur le théâtre de Adamov*, Paris, 1981.
Robert Abirachad, with others (eds.), *Lectures d'Adamov: Actes du colloque international Würzburg 1981*, Tübingen, 1983.
David Bradby, *Modern French Drama*, Cambridge, 1984; revised edition, 1991.
Elisabeth Hervic, *Lecture d'Adamov*, Brussels, 1984.

Articles:
Alfred Cismaru, "The Plays of Arthur Adamov", in *Serif: Quarterly of Kent State Universities*, vol. 5 no. 1, 1968.
Margaret Dietemann, "Departure from the Absurd: Adamov's Last Plays", in *Yale French Studies*, 46, 1971.

* * *

Adamov has been described by Roger Planchon, the theatre director with whom he collaborated regularly, as "a playwright's playwright". He never had a major public success to match that of Ionesco or Beckett, but is admired, especially in the theatrical profession, as an experimental writer who never tired of seeking new directions.

Adamov had an extraordinary childhood, being born in Baku in 1908 into a rich Armenian family, whose wealth was in oil, but was all lost through the father's passion for gambling. After the Russian Revolution the family joined thousands of others in exile and poverty, first in Switzerland, then Germany, finally settling in France on the outskirts of Paris. Adamov's father eventually committed suicide while his mother attempted to keep up appearances; the young Arthur was left to carry a burden of unresolved guilt for the rest of his life. He too committed suicide in 1970.

Adamov's earliest writings were surrealist poems, translations of Jung and Rilke, and a confessional autobiography, *L'Aveu* (The Confession), published in 1946 and described by Martin Esslin as a "Dostoevskian masterpiece". As a young man between the wars, Adamov frequented the same circles as Cocteau, Blin, Vilar, and Artaud. He also inherited the task of editing the posthumous papers of Roger Gilbert-Lecomte, an experience that was to form the basis of his second play, *L'Invasion* (The Invasion). Before this, he had written *La Parodie* (The Parody) in 1947, a bleak parable of the futility of all human endeavour. The experience of writing plays had a strongly therapeutic effect on the author, who had just turned 40 and felt that a new life was opening up: he completed six more plays in the next three years, most of which were staged in the small "pocket" theatres of the Parisian left bank in the early 1950's.

The most powerful influence on Adamov's early work was Strindberg (he published a monograph on the Swedish playwright) and his early plays are all dream plays employing techniques reminiscent of those used by Strindberg and the German Expressionists. But his chief originality lay in his insistence on the importance of the *performed* text: "Theatre as I understand it is linked utterly and absolutely to performance", he wrote in the preface to Volume II of his collected plays (1955). Following the lead of Artaud, he developed a theory of "literality" in the theatre. In the palpable, physical literality of the stage event, he saw the possibility of expressing the interpenetration of the conscious and the unconscious: "I believe that stage representation is no less than the projection into the world of the senses of the states and images that constitute its hidden motive springs". Because his theoretical elucidations fitted the early work of Ionesco and Beckett as well as his own, he was, for a while, considered as the chief spokesman for the new genre soon to become known as the "theatre of the absurd".

In the mid-1950's however, just as these new plays were beginning to achieve their first commercial successes, Adamov became convinced of the need for a more politically responsible approach to dramatic writing. In *Le Professeur Taranne* (Professor Taranne) Adamov had, for the first time, stepped out of the nightmarish no-man's-land of his early work and allowed himself to use a place name drawn from the real world. He began to see absurdist plays in a new light,

describing them as easy escapes from the real world, offering a convenient alibi to those who had an interest in obscuring the political scandals and absurdities of the capitalist system.

Beginning with *Paolo Paoli* (first produced by Planchon), he began a series of plays in which he attempted to investigate real historical and political situations using techniques learned from Brecht. *Paolo Paoli* is perhaps the most successful of these, charting the years leading up to World War I through the vicissitudes of a feather industrialist and a butterfly dealer. These apparently frivolous commodities represented very considerable commercial interests in the France of "*la belle époque*" and the story of their wheelings and dealings was able to stand as a model for the capitalist machine in which trade and war may be seen as two sides of the same coin. *Le Printemps 71* (*Spring 71*) was an attempt to improve on Brecht's *Days of the Commune*; *La Politique des restes* (The Rubbish Policy) was a *Lehrstück*, denouncing apartheid; *Sainte Europe* (Holy Europe) and *M Le Modéré* (M the Moderate) satirise the new European unity based on shared commercial interests.

In the early 1960's Adamov underwent a period of serious illness complicated by alcohol addiction. In his worst times he returned once more, as he had done in his youth, to autobiographical writing, producing a remarkable account of his life and obsessions entitled *L'Homme et l'enfant* (*Man and Child*). In the last two years of his life, he recovered sufficiently to write two of his best plays: *Off Limits*, about American society experiencing disintegration brought about by the pressures of the Vietnam War, and *Si l'Été revenait* (If Summer Came Again), a return to the Strindbergian dream play set in modern-day Sweden and successfully exploiting the contradictions of late-20th-century capitalism. In these late works he discovered ways of bringing together the strengths of both his early, nightmarish visions, and his later preoccupation with political realities. In fact, although he himself made much of his changes of manner, his work is united by its concentration on those aspects of life, whether social or individual, which are the cause of suffering or oppression in whatever form. He summed this up as a plea for a theatre linking the individual "not only with his own dreams and imaginings, but also with other men, and hence with their dreams, but set in a time that is emphatically not imaginary".

As well as plays and autobiography, Adamov left behind an impressive number of critical essays on the theatre of the post-war years, gathered together in 1964 in a volume entitled *Ici et maintenant* (Here and Now). Although his plays are only rarely performed, his work retains its exemplary importance because of the way it explores the territories of both the Artaudian and the Brechtian heritage.

—David Bradby

See also *Volume 1* entry on *Professor Taranne*.

———

ADDISON, Joseph. See *Volume 1* entry on *Cato*.

———

AESCHYLUS. Born in Eleusis, 525 or 524 BC. Fought in the Battle of Marathon, 490, and probably at Artemisium and

Aeschylus (bust in Museo Capitolino, Rome).

Salamis, 480. Wrote over 90 plays (we have the titles of 70): won his first playwriting prize in 484, 12 subsequent prizes, and some posthumously; also acted in his plays; visited Sicily to produce plays for Hieron I of Syracuse, soon after the foundation of the city of Aetna, 476, and again in 456. Died in 456 BC.

Works

Collections

The Tragedies, translated by Robert Potter.   1777.
Aeschylus: The Seven Plays, translated by L. Campbell. 1890; revised edition, 1906.
Tragoediae [Tragedies], edited by A. Sidgewick. 1895–1905.
Tragoediae [Tragedies], edited by Ulrich von Wilamowitz Möllendorf.   1914.
Four Plays of Aeschylus (includes *The Suppliant Maidens; The Persians; Seven Against Thebes; Prometheus Bound*), translated by G.M. Cookson.   1922.
Aeschylus (2 vols.; parallel texts), edited by H.W. Smyth. 1922–26 (Loeb Classical Library).
Aeschyli Septem Quae Supersunt Tragoediae [Tragedies], edited by Gilbert Murray.   1937.
Aeschylus 1 (*The Oresteia*), translated by Richmond Lattimore.   1953 (Complete Greek Tragedies series).
Aeschylus 2 (includes *The Persians; Seven Against Thebes; The Suppliant Maidens;* and *Prometheus Bound*), trans-lated by David Grene and S.G. Bernadette.   1956 (Complete Greek Tragedies series).
The Oresteia Trilogy, translated by Philip Vellacott.   1956.
Die Fragmente der Tragödien, edited by Hans Joachim Mette. 1959.
Prometheus Bound; The Suppliants; Seven Against Thebes; The Persians, translated by Philip Vellacott.   1961.
Aeschyli Septem Quae Supersunt Tragoediae [Tragedies], edited by Denys L. Page.   1972.
The Oresteia, translated by Richard Fagles.   1976.

Stage Works

Persae (produced Athens, 472 BC).   Translated in *The Tragedies*, 1777; several subsequent translations as *The Persians*.
Septem Contra Thebas (produced Athens, 467 BC). Translated in *The Tragedies*, 1777; several subsequent translations as *Seven Against Thebes*.
Prometheus Vinctus (produced Athens, c.466–459 BC). Translated in *The Tragedies*, 1777; several subsequent translations as *Prometheus Bound*; also translated as *Prometheus Chained*, 1823.
Supplices (produced Athens, c.463 BC).   Translated in *The Tragedies*, 1777; several subsequent translations as *The Suppliants, The Suppliant Women* (1930), and *The Suppliant Maidens*.
The Oresteia: trilogy includes *Agamemnon; Choephoroi; Eumenides* (produced 458 BC).   Translated in *The Tragedies*, 1777; several subsequent translations of the tri-logy as *The Oresteia*; several translations of the individual plays: *Agamemnon* as *Agamemnon; Choephoroi* as *The Choephoroe* or *The Libation Bearers; Eumenides* as *The Euemenides*.

*

Criticism

Books:
H.W. Smyth, *Aeschylean Tragedy*, Berkeley, California, 1924.
Gilbert Murray, *Aeschylus: The Creator of Tragedy*, Oxford, 1940.
G.D. Thomson, *Aeschylus and Athens: Study in the Social Origins of Drama*, London, 1941.
W.B. Stanford, *Aeschylus in His Style: A Study in Language and Personality*, 1942; reprinted 1972.
E. Fraenkl, *Aeschylus: New Texts and Old Problems*, New York, 1943.
F.R. Earp, *The Style of Aeschylus*, New York, 1948.
E.T. Owen, *The Harmony of Aeschylus*, Toronto, 1952.
J.H. Finley, *Pindar and Aeschylus*, Cambridge, Massachu-setts, 1955.
H.J. Rose, *A Commentary on the Surviving Plays of Aeschy-lus* (2 vols.), 1957–58.
Leon Golden, *Aeschylus and Ares: A Study in the Use of Military Imagery by Aeschylus*, Chicago, 1958.
R.D. Dawe, *Collation and Investigation of the Manuscripts of Aeschylus*, Cambridge, 1964.
R.D. Dawe, *Repertory of Conjectures on Aeschylus*, Leiden, 1965.
Leon Golden, *In Praise of Prometheus: Humanism and Rationalism in Aeschylean Thought*, 1966.
A.J. Podlecki, *The Political Background of Aeschylean Tragedy*, Ann Arbor, Michigan, 1966.

Marsh H. McCall Jr. (ed.), *Aeschylus: A Collection of Critical Essays*, Englewood Cliffs, New Jersey, 1972.

J.T. Sheppard, *Aeschylus: The Prophet of Greek Freedom*, New York, 1974 (reprint).

R.H. Beck, *Aeschylus: Playwright Educator*, The Hague, 1975.

D. Sansome, *Aeschylean Metaphors for Intellectual Activity*, Wiesbaden, 1975.

Michael Gagarin, *Aeschylean Drama*, Berkeley, California, 1976.

Oliver Taplin, *The Stagecraft of Aeschylus*, Oxford, 1977.

Thomas G. Rosenmeyer, *The Art of Aeschylus*, Berkeley, California, 1982.

R.P. Winnington-Ingram, *Studies in Aeschylus*, Cambridge, 1983.

Simon Goldhill, *Language, Sexuality, Narrative: The Oresteia*, Cambridge, 1984.

William C. Scott, *Musical Design in Aeschylean Theater*, Hanover, Massachusetts, and London, 1984.

* * *

Although Aeschylus was the first playwright whose work has survived, he was not the first Athenian playwright. Much can never be resolved about the origins and earliest form of Greek tragedy, but it is widely accepted that tragedies were first performed at the festival of the Great Dionysia in about 534 BC. This was several years before Aeschylus was born. What form such tragedies took is also largely a matter of conjecture but Aristotle was later to credit Aeschylus with introducing a second actor. If nothing else this confirms that previous tragedy had been performed by a single actor with a chorus and that Aeschylus' first work was of this nature. Aristotle goes on to state that Sophocles was the originator of the third actor and Aeschylus has clearly accepted the development by the time of the *Oresteia* in 458 BC.

No more than seven of Aeschylus' plays survive, a tiny proportion of those that are known by title. Of these seven, one, *Prometheus Bound*, is felt by some modern scholars to be wrongly attributed to him, though the grounds are circumstantial. The other six are from late in Aeschylus' career. *The Suppliant Women* was plausibly redated as a later work in the 1950's, which makes *The Persians* of 472 BC the earliest survivor. All seven, allowing *Prometheus Bound*, belong to connected trilogies. In the case of *The Persians*, *Seven Against Thebes*, *The Suppliant Women*, and *Prometheus Bound*, the other plays from the group are missing. *The Oresteia* (*Agamemnon*, *Libation Bearers* and *Eumenides*) lacks only the satyr afterpiece, *Proteus*. Even these seven complete plays have variant readings from different manuscripts and enough corrupt passages to create problems of interpretation and translation.

Such negative factors notwithstanding, the remaining texts combine to demonstrate a dramatist's instinct and a flair for the theatrical that are beyond challenge. When the playwright had only a single actor, his audience could only be the real audience or the chorus in attendance. A second actor makes possible not only dialogue between the two but the transfer of the whole dramatic action from the *orchestra*, where the chorus were positioned, to an exclusive stage area where the second actor was the person addressed and who contributed to the scene according to how he received the information. The third actor develops a triangular scene, used to powerful effect in *The Oresteia*, notably when one character remains silent for a time absorbing what is happening before joining in. Cassandra in *Agamemnon* and Pylades in *Libation Bearers* offer refined examples.

That this was a conscious device on the part of Aeschylus is established in Aristophanes' *Frogs* when the stage characters of Aeschylus and Euripides, both now dead, meet in Hades. In the ensuing slanging match, each dissects the dramatic tricks of the other. Comedy though the *Frogs* is, it guarantees that more than a modern perspective is involved in identifying theatrical effects and dramatic sophistication in the work of the two tragedians.

A common quality in all the Aeschylus plays is a dramatic language which is highly poetic and often original. Dialogue is in iambics, but there are lyric and choral passages which involve a variety of other rhythms. Verbal imagery is complex and is matched by a use of stage imagery to reinforce a situation through stage picture. The language of *Prometheus Bound* is full of the contrasts between restriction and freedom, a contrast visually conveyed by the differing states of Prometheus fettered to his rock and the visitors who pass in and out of his world. In *The Oresteia* there are numerous examples of the blend of word and picture, from the opening view of the solitary watchman waiting to see the beacon which will signify the fall of Troy, to the torchlit procession which concludes the trilogy, with the fearful Furies now transformed into benign deities.

The characters of Aeschylus have little of the subtlety of those of Sophocles or Euripides. They are closer to the world of myth and Olympian morality, but they do make it possible to investigate ideas about the relationship between men and gods, the risk of overreaching one's powers, the dangers of civil war, the need for, and nature of, justice and authority. Aeschylus' stage world is one of powerful forces of which the Olympian gods are not fully in control, since the gods are at odds with one another as well as with the elemental powers which preceded them.

In such a world the establishment of a proper order is the major priority and that is work for heroes. The gods are fallible and ultimately it is man who can and must find his own salvation. The Persians are defeated by a combination of Xerxes' *hubris* and Athenian bravery. The citizens of Thebes want an end to civil war with the fight between the fated sons of Oedipus. The chorus of suppliant women plead for the natural right to influence their own destiny. Prometheus is being punished for offering progress to mankind. And in *The Oresteia*, Aeschylus' major legacy to the world's stage, a son avenges a father, as he must, though it means he must kill his mother. When the Furies are roused in response, Orestes appeals to Apollo, then to Athena. The case proves to be one which even she cannot judge. Her solution is to return the case to a court of ordinary citizens for their verdict.

Aeschylus stood at a crossroads of Athenian political progress and much can be made of the political dimension of his work. With such a tiny proportion of his plays available, no convincing "throughline" can be drawn to give the full flavour of his message as the Athenians would have received it. Some things are sure, however. The world that he showed was a cruel and problematic one, and the solution to its problems resided finally, not with the gods, but with the Athenians themselves.

—J. Michael Walton

See also *Volume 1* entries on *The Oresteia; The Persians; Prometheus Bound; Seven Against Thebes; The Suppliants*.

AIDOO, (Christina) Ama Ata. Born in Abeadzi Kyiakor, Ghana, 1942. Educated at the University of Ghana, Legon (Institute of African Studies fellowship), BA (honours) 1964; Stanford University, California. Lecturer in English, University of Cape Coast, Ghana, 1970–82; PNDC Minister of Education for the Ghana Government, January 1982–June 1983; full-time writer, based in Harare, Zimbabwe, since 1983; Fulbright scholar-in-residence, Great Lakes Association, USA, 1988; writer-in-residence, University of Richmond, Richmond, Virginia, 1989. Recipient of several prizes for fiction, poetry, and radio drama.

Works

Stage Works

The Dilemma of a Ghost (produced Students' Theatre, Legon, Ghana, 1964). 1965.
Anowa. 1970.

Fiction

No Sweetness Here (short stories). 1970.
Our Sister Killjoy; or, Reflections From a Black-eyed Squint. 1977.
"The Eagle and the Chicken" and Other Stories (for children). 1986.
Changes. 1991.

Verse

"Birds" and Other Poems (for children). 1986.

Other

Dancing Out Doubts. 1982.
Someone Talking to Someone. 1985.

*

Criticism

Books:
Jane W. Grant, *Ama Ata Aidoo: The Dilemma of a Ghost*, London, 1980.

Articles:
Dap Adelugpa, "Language and Drama: Ama Ata Aidoo", in *African Literature Today*, 8, 1976; reprinted in *Ghanaian Literatures*, edited by Richard K. Priebe, New York, 1988.

* * *

Women playwrights are relatively rare in the African theatre. In Tanzania there is work by Penina (Mlama) Muhando and Amandina Lihamba, in Nigeria the plays of Zulu Sofola, and elsewhere on the continent a smattering of new and often radical playwriting by women. In Ghana, by contrast two of the leading dramatists of the post-1960's are women: Efua Sutherland and Ama Ata Aidoo. Sutherland is the more productive, but Ama Ata Aidoo merits special note for having written, in *Anowa*, one of the major plays to have come from the contemporary African theatre.

Both *Anowa* and her earlier *The Dilemma of a Ghost* make powerful reference to the impact of slavery upon future generations. *The Dilemma of a Ghost* is superficially a "clash-of-cultures" play—not uncommon in West African playwriting in the immediate post-independence years. The story it tells will not have been unfamiliar to many educated Ghanaians. A Ghanaian man brings back to Ghana his black American wife whom he married when he was studying in the United States. She arrives full of eagerness and optimism in the land of her ancestors, but soon encounters profound cultural and behavioural differences and becomes isolated and bewildered in her new home, and neglected and abused by her husband. She is rescued from her despair by her husband's mother, who overcomes the family's prejudice against the stigma of the "slave-tainted" stranger and creates a climate of care and understanding in which the Old World and the New can rediscover each other. This poignant tale is sympathetically presented from a woman's point of view, a feature of Aidoo's writing that is once again evident in *Anowa*.

The *Anowa* story is a familiar folk-tale in Ghana, and the basic story—that of a handsome stranger who takes a beautiful girl away from her parents and destroys her—occurs in many West African cultures. Aidoo's play is set in an indeterminate time that includes elements of pre-colonial Ghana (when it was the Gold Coast) and aspects of the present day. The plot is straightforward: Anowa marries her handsome stranger and sets off with him, against the wishes of her community, into an unknown world. What originates as an idealistic journey turns into disaster as her husband begins to seek power and wealth and to acquire slaves. Anowa's barrenness symbolises not *her* failure to be productive, but her husband's destructive infertility—the failure of men to create the future. In her despair she recalls a dream about the obscenity of slavery which turns on the reluctance of anyone in society to accept responsibility for their role in its horrors. As a retelling of the Anowa story the play is effective enough, but more pertinently it can be seen as a fierce allegory on the contemporary exploitation of man by man. In the long tradition of African storytelling, a familiar myth is elaborated to comment on present events. Aidoo writes in an English that reflects the decorative idiom of Ghanaian languages, and frames the play with chorus figures reinforcing the links between her powerful contemporary play and the intimate theatrical skills of the story-telling circle.

—Martin Banham

————————

ALBEE, Edward (Franklin, III). Born in Virginia, USA, 12 March 1928; adopted as an infant. Educated at Lawrenceville School; Valley Forge Military Academy, Pennsylvania; Choate School, Connecticut, graduated 1946; Trinity College, Hartford, Connecticut, 1946–47. Served in the US Army. Radio writer, WNYC, office boy, Warwick and Legler, record salesman, Bloomingdale's, book salesman, G. Schirmer, counterman, Manhattan Towers Hotel, messenger, Western Union, 1955–58, all in New York; first play, *The Zoo Story*, produced in Berlin, 1959; producer, with Richard Barr and Clinton Wilder, New Playwrights Unit Workshop, later Albarwild Theatre Arts, and Albar Productions, New York. Also a stage director. Founder, William Flanagan Center for Creative Persons, Montauk, Long Island, New York, 1971. US cultural exchange visitor to the USSR. Recipient of many awards, including Obie award, 1960, New York Drama Critics Circle award, 1964, Tony award, 1964, and Pulitzer Prizes, 1967 and 1975. Member, American Academy, 1966.

Works

Collections

The Zoo Story; The Death of Bessie Smith; The Sandbox: Three Plays. 1960; as *"The Zoo Story" and Other Plays* (includes *The American Dream*), 1962.
Plays 1 (includes *The Zoo Story; The Death of Bessie Smith; The Sandbox; The American Dream*). 1981.
Plays 2 (includes *Tiny Alice; A Delicate Balance; Box and Quotations from Chairman Mao Tse-tung*). 1982.
Plays 3 (includes *Seascape; Counting the Ways; Listening; All Over*). 1982.
Plays 4 (includes *Everything in the Garden; Malcolm; The Ballad of the Sad Café*). 1982.

Stage Works

The Zoo Story (produced Schiller-Theater Werkstatt, Berlin, 1959). In *The Zoo Story; The Death of Bessie Smith; The Sandbox*, 1960.
The Death of Bessie Smith (produced Schlosspark Theater, Berlin, 1960). Included in *The Zoo Story; The Death of Bessie Smith; The Sandbox*, 1960.
The Sandbox (produced White Barn Theatre, Westport, Connecticut, 1960). In *The Zoo Story; The Death of Bessie Smith; The Sandbox*, 1960.
Fam and Yam (produced White Barn Theatre, Westport, Connecticut, 1960). 1961.
The American Dream (produced York Playhouse, New York, 1961). 1961.
Bartleby, with James Hinton Jr., music by William Flanagan, from the story by Herman Melville (produced York Playhouse, New York, 1961).
Who's Afraid of Virginia Woolf? (produced Billy Rose Theatre, New York, 1962). 1962.
The Ballad of the Sad Café, from the story by Carson McCullers (produced Martin Beck Theatre, New York, 1963). 1963.
Tiny Alice (produced Billy Rose Theatre, New York, 1964). 1965.
Malcolm, from the novel by James Purdy (produced Shubert Theatre, New York, 1966). 1966.
A Delicate Balance (produced Martin Beck Theatre, New York, 1966). 1966.
Breakfast at Tiffany's, music by Bob Merrill, from the story by Truman Capote (produced Majestic Theatre, New York, 1966).
Everything in the Garden, from the play by Giles Cooper (produced Plymouth Theatre, New York, 1967). 1968.
Box and Quotations from Chairman Mao Tse-tung (as *Box-Mao-Box*, produced Arena Theatre Studio, Buffalo, New York, 1968; as *Box and Quotations from Chairman Mao Tse-tung*, produced 1968). 1969.
All Over (produced Martin Beck Theatre, New York, 1971). 1971.
Seascape (produced Shubert Theatre, New York, 1975). 1975.
Counting the Ways (produced National Theatre, London, 1976). In *Two Plays*, 1977.
Listening (produced Hartford Stage, Connecticut, 1977). In *Two Plays*, 1977.

The Lady from Dubuque (produced Morosco Theatre, New York, 1980). 1980.
Lolita, from the novel by Vladimir Nabokov (produced Boston, 1981).
The Man Who Had Three Arms (produced Goodman Theatre, Chicago, 1982).
Envy, in *Faustus in Hell* (produced Princeton, New Jersey, 1985).
Marriage Play (produced English Theatre, Vienna, 1987). 1987.
Three Tall Women (produced English Theatre, Vienna, 1992).

Screenplays

A Delicate Balance, 1976.

Radio Plays

Listening, 1976.

Fiction

Straight Through the Night. 1989.

*

Bibliographies

Richard E. Amacher and Margaret Rule, *Edward Albee at Home and Abroad: A Bibliography 1958–June 1968*, New York, 1970.
Charles Lee Green, *Edward Albee: An Annotated Bibliography 1968–1977*, New York, 1980.
Richard Tyce, *Edward Albee: A Bibliography*, Metuchen, New Jersey, 1986.
Scott Giantvalley, *Edward Albee: A Reference Guide*, Boston, 1987.

Criticism

Books:
Gillian Debusscher (translated by Anne D. Williams), *Edward Albee: Tradition and Renewal*, Brussels, 1967.
Richard E. Amacher, *Edward Albee*, New York, 1969; revised edition, 1982.
C.W.E. Bigsby, *Albee*, Edinburgh, 1969.
Ruby Cohn, *Edward Albee*, Minneapolis, 1969.
Michael E. Rutenberg, *Edward Albee: Playwright in Protest*, New York, 1969.
Ronald Hayman, *Edward Albee*, London, 1971.
Anne Paolucci, *From Tension to Tonic: The Plays of Edward Albee*, Cardondale, Illinois, 1972.
C.W.E. Bigsby (ed.), *Edward Albee: A Collection of Critical Essays*, New Jersey, 1975.
Anita M. Stenz, *Edward Albee: The Poet of Loss*, The Hague, 1978.
Forster Hirsch, *Who's Afraid of Edward Albee?*, Berkeley, California, 1978.
Julian N. Wasserman (ed.), *Edward Albee: An Interview and Essays*, Houston, Texas, 1983.
Harold Bloom (ed.), *Edward Albee: Modern Critical Views*, New York, 1987.
Gerald McCarthy, *Edward Albee*, London, 1987 (Macmillan Modern Dramatists Series).

Mathew C. Roudané, *Understanding Edward Albee*, Columbia, South Carolina, 1987.

Philip C. Kolin (ed.), *Conversations with Edward Albee*, Jackson, Mississippi, 1988.

* * *

The rise and fall of Edward Albee is one of the enigmas of modern American drama. When he burst unexpectedly onto the American theatrical scene in 1959 with a variety of plays which detailed the agonies and disillusionment of the 1950's and the transition from the placid Eisenhower years to the neo-Romantic 1960's, Albee was hailed as the successor to Arthur Miller, Tennessee Williams, and even Eugene O'Neill, and as the American Strindberg or Ionesco. His plays seemed to pierce American post-war complacency with surgical accuracy, and his summary of *The American Dream* could well serve as commentary on all of Albee's work:

> The play is an examination of the American Scene, an attack on the substitution of artificial for real values in our society, a condemnation of complacency, cruelty, emasculation and vacuity; it is a stand against the fiction that everything in this slipping land of ours is peachy-keen.

In his early work Albee demonstrated facility in a variety of theatrical styles. He conveyed the alienation and disillusionment of the existentialist drama in *The Zoo Story*, where a young drifter acts out (for it is finally a play within a play) a premeditated suicide with the unwitting aid of an upper-middle-class editor forced to defend his honor. But the anomaly of random violence which shocked the sensibilities of the late 1950's and early 1960's has since become commonplace, our quotidian reality.

Albee went on to explore American race relations in the southern Gothic atmosphere of *The Death of Bessie Smith*. In an attempt at *théâtre engagé*, Albee tried to deal with the complex question of race in America with his version of the "ugly episode" of Black-American blues legend Bessie Smith's death which resulted from the refusal of a "white" hospital to treat her. By the mid 1960's, however, racial tension had exploded into racial warfare in the United States, and Albee's analysis of racial issues paled before the theater of street violence or more direct theatrical confrontations of race such as Joseph Dolan Tuotti's *Big Time Buck White*.

When *The Zoo Story* was performed in Germany it shared the bill with Samuel Beckett's *Krapp's Last Tape*, and that same pair of plays was moved to the Provincetown Playhouse on 14 January 1960. Albee, in turn, tried his hand at developing an American absurdist drama (via Thornton Wilder and, perhaps, Elmer Rice) in *The Sandbox*, and then again, with the same characters, in his satire of American values "whose opening moments owe a great debt to Ionesco's *The Bald Soprano*", *The American Dream*. The play was paired with the first of Albee's adaptations, an operatic version of Herman Melville's story *Bartleby*, but it was replaced almost immediately by *The Death of Bessie Smith*.

Albee's defense of non-realistic theater was published in the *New York Times Magazine* as "Which Theater is the Absurd One?" Although satirically sharp, Albee's absurdist plays, however, never develop from the direct anguish of watching neighbors carted off to death camps or bombs explode in one's garden as the European absurdists did. Despite their incongruities and irrationalities, Albee's absurdist dramas retained the qualities of rational satire.

By the early 1960's Albee had shown himself adept at the existential drama of angst, the drama of social protest, and had tried to transplant the European sense of the irrational to the optimistic soil of the United States, but with each stylistic experiment, with each confrontation of social problems, history seems to have conspired against him, as social change outpaced the playwright's ability to keep up with it.

In 1962 Albee enjoyed critical and popular success with *Who's Afraid of Virginia Woolf?*, a realistic study of American family life which evoked comparisons with Eugene O'Neill's *Long Day's Journey into Night*. The play won the Drama Critics' Award, but in what was generally interpreted as a snub to Albee, the Pulitzer committee voted to award no prize for 1962. In *Tiny Alice*, a "metaphysical dream play", Albee explored his persistent theme of reality versus illusion in mystical, abstract, and even religious terms. Even Albee admitted that the play "is less opaque in reading than it would be in any single viewing". With *A Delicate Balance* Albee returned to the domestic realism that won him critical favor in *Who's Afraid of Virginia Woolf?*, and critics rewarded him with the Pulitzer Prize which eluded him earlier. But a series of ill-advised adaptations proved to be commercial and critical disasters: Carson McCullers's *The Ballad of the Sad Café*, a musical version of Truman Capote's *Breakfast at Tiffany's* (1966), James Purdy's *Malcolm*, which closed after seven performances, a rewrite of Giles Cooper's play *Everything in the Garden*, and the much anticipated adaptation of Vladimir Nabokov's *Lolita*, which *People* magazine dubbed "Broadway's Bomb of the Year".

With a pair of "interrelated plays", *Box* and *Quotations from Chairman Mao Tse-Tung*, Albee returned to theatrical experiment "having to do—in the main—with the application of musical form to dramatic structure, and the use of *Box* as a parenthesis around *Mao* is part of that experiment". In *All Over* Albee explored the responses of characters to the death of a famous man, in the process of which the betrayals and deceits of the living are revealed and their lives exposed as a death in life. Albee continued his combination of theatrical experiment and social commentary in *Seascape*, where a vacationing couple facing retirement, Nancy and Charlie, meets a pair of sea lizards, Sarah and Leslie, and, in a more directly Darwinian fashion, Albee develops a theme he introduced in *The Zoo Story* some 15 years earlier: "The way people exist with animals, and the way animals exist with each other, and with people too". With *Seascape* Albee won his second Pulitzer Prize.

After *Seascape*, Albee returned to the experimental one-act form, writing a play for BBC radio, *Listening*. With its external, shaping voice arranging the incidents, *Listening* recalled the radio experiments of Samuel Beckett. He paired it with "A Vaudeville", *Counting the Ways*, when he staged it at London's National Theatre.

Conceived in 1960 at the time of *Who's Afraid of Virginia Woolf?*, *The Lady from Dubuque* returns again to the style and themes of Albee's earlier work, including the theme of dying. In the play, although it is Joe who is dying from cancer, she generates more life than her husband Sam and the others at a suburban party, the malaise of which suggests it is another of Albee's images of death in life. The play, however, closed after 12 Broadway performances. In *The Man Who Had Three Arms* Albee seems almost to abandon artifice altogether in favor of a direct assault on his audience. In it he offers Himself, a character whose fame rose and fell as inexplicably as the growth of his third arm. One of Albee's more repulsive characters, Himself stands behind a podium and berates the audience for two acts.

In many respects, *The Man Who Had Three Arms* is Edward Albee's theatrical swan-song. He continues to direct his own work, but as a playwright Edward Albee seems to have lost his theater, at least temporarily. Despite the brilliant dialogue of his plays, Albee's theatrical reputation has declined to the point where Robert Brustein could say: "To be blunt about it Albee has nothing particularly urgent to communicate". Brustein's dismissal, may, however, be premature.

—S.E. Gontarski

See also *Volume 1* entries on *A Delicate Balance*; *Tiny Alice*; *Who's Afraid of Virginia Woolf?*; *The Zoo Story*.

ALARCÓN, Juan Ruiz de. See **RUIZ DE ALARCÓN, Juan.**

ALMEIDA GARRETT, João Baptista da Silva Leitão. See **GARRETT, João.** . . .

ALFIERI, Vittorio. Born in Asti, Italy, 16 January 1749. Educated at miltary academy in Turin, 1759–66. Joined local regiment, 1766 (resigned commission, 1774); travelled extensively in Europe, 1767–72; first play, *Cleopatra*, staged 1775; began life-long relationship with Luisa Stolberg, Countess of Albany, 1777; fled from revolutionary Paris with the Countess, 1792, and settled in Florence; left Florence during French occupation, 1799. Died in Florence, 8 October 1803.

Works

Collections

Tragedie (3 vols.). 1783–85.
Tragedie (6 vols.). 1787–89.
Opere postumi (13 vols.). 1804.
The Tragedies (3 vols.), translated by Charles Lloyd. 1815; augmented and revised edition (2 vols.), edited by E.A. Bowring, 1876.
Opere (5 vols.), edited by Francesco Maggini. 1926–33.
Opere (multi-volume, continuing series), edited by Luigi Fassò and others. 1971–.
Tragedie e scritti scelti, edited by Pietro Cazzani. 1975.

Vittorio Alfieri (portrait by Francesco Saverio Fabre).

Opere, edited by Mario Fabibi and Arnaldo DiBenedetto. 1977.

Stage Works

Cleopatra (produced Teatro Carignano, Turin, 1775). As *Antonio e Cleopatra*, in *Opere postumi*, 1804; translated as *Antony and Cleopatra*, in *Tragedies*, 1876.
Oreste (produced Teatro di Foligno, Rome, 1781). In *Tragedie*, 1783–85; translated as *Orestes*, in *Tragedies*, 1815 and 1876.
Antigone (produced Spanish Ambassador's Palace, Rome, 1782). In *Tragedie*, 1783–85; translated as *Antigone*, in *Tragedies*, 1815 and 1876.
Ottavia. In *Tragedie*, 1783–85; translated as *Octavia*, in *Tragedies*, 1815 and 1876.
Timoleone. In *Tragedie*, 1783–85; translated as *Timoleon*, in *Tragedies*, 1815 and 1876.
Merope. In *Tragedie*, 1783–85; translated as *Merope*, in *Tragedies*, 1815 and 1876.
Virginia (produced Teatro Carignano, Turin, 1784). In *Tragedie*, 1783–85; translated as *Virginia*, in *Tragedies*, 1815 and 1876.
Polinice (produced Teatro Carignano, Turin, 1824). In *Tragedie*, 1783–85; translated as *Polynices*, in *Tragedies*, 1815 and 1876.
Filippo (produced Teatro Carignano, Turin, 1825). In *Tragedie*, 1783–85; translated as *Philip*, in *Tragedies*, 1815 and 1876.
Rosmunda (produced Teatro Carignano, Turin, 1841). In

Tragedie, 1783–85; translated as *Rosmunda*, in *Tragedies*, 1815 and 1876.

Agamennone (produced Teatro Re, Milan, 1842). In *Tragedie*, 1783–85; translated as *Agamemnon*, in *Tragedies*, 1815 and 1876.

Don Garzia. In *Tragedie*, 1787–89; translated as *Don Garcia*, in *Tragedies*, 1815 and 1876.

Maria Stuarda. In *Tragedie*, 1787–89; translated as *Mary Stuart*, in *Tragedies*, 1815 and 1876.

Agide. In *Tragedie*, 1787–89; translated as *Agis*, in *Tragedies*, 1815 and 1876.

La congiura de Pazzi. In *Tragedie*, 1787–89; translated as *The Conspiracy of the Pazzi*, in *Tragedies*, 1815 and 1876.

Bruto primo. In *Tragedie*, 1787–89; translated as *The First Brutus*, in *Tragedies*, 1815 and 1876.

Saul (produced Teatro di Santa Maria, Florence, 1794). In *Tragedie*, 1787–89; translated as *Saul*, in *Tragedies*, 1815 and 1876.

Mirra (produced Arena del Sole, Bologna, 1819). In *Tragedie*, 1787–89; translated as *Myrrha*, in *Tragedies*, 1815 and 1876.

Sofonisba (produced Teatro Carignano, Turin, 1824). In *Tragedie*, 1787–89; translated as *Sophonisba*, in *Tragedies*, 1815 and 1876.

Bruto secondo (produced Teatro Carignano, Turin, 1848). In *Tragedie*, 1787–89; translated as *The Second Brutus*, in *Tragedies*, 1815 and 1876.

Alceste secundo, from Euripides' *Alcestis* (produced Teatro Carignano, Turin, 1831). In *Opere postumi*, 1804; translated as *Alcestis II*, in *Tragedies*, 1876.

Abele. In *Opere postumi*, 1804; translated as *Abel*, in *Tragedies*, 1876.

L'uno. In *Opere postumi*, 1804.

I pochi. In *Opere postumi*, 1804.

I troppi. In *Opere postumi*, 1804.

L'antidoto. In *Opere postumi*, 1804.

La finestrina. In *Opere postumi*, 1804.

Il divorzio. In *Opere postumi*, 1804.

Fiction

Le mosche e l'api. With *Panegirico di Plinio a Trajano* and *Parigi sbastigliata*, 1789.

Verse

L'America libera: Odi. 1784; translated as *America the Free: Five Odes*, 1975.

Parigi sbastigliata. With *Panegirico di Plinio a Trajano* and *Le mosche e l'api*, 1789.

Le Rime (first part). 1789.

L'Etruria vendicata. 1800.

Memoirs and Letters

Vita. In *Opere postumi*, 1804; translated (anonymously) as *Memoirs*, 1810 (revised 1961); as *The Autobiography of Vittorio Alfieri*, 1845; as *Life of Vittorio Alfieri*, 1877.

Lettere edite e inedite, edited by Giuseppe Mazzatinti. 1890.

Other

La virtù sconosciuta: Dialogo. 1786.

Della tirannide. 1789; translated as *Of Tyranny*, 1961.

Del principe e delle lettere. 1795; translated as *The Prince and Letters*, 1972.

Il misogalilo: Prose e rime. In *Opere postumi*, 1804.

Translator, *Panegirico di Plinio a Trajano*, by Pliny. 1787.

Translator, Works, by Sallust. 1826.

*

Bibliographies

G. Bustico, *Bibliografia di Vittorio Alfieri* (third edition), Florence, 1927.

W. Binni, *La critica alfieriana*, Florence, 1951.

Criticism

Books:

M. Porena, *Vittorio Alfieri e la tragedia*, Milan, 1904.

A. Mioli, *Jean Racine e Vittorio Alfieri*, Clusone, 1922.

P. Gobetti, *La filosofia politica di Vittorio Alfieri*, Turin, 1923.

M. Appolonio, *Alfieri*, Milan, 1930.

C.R.D. Miller, *Alfieri: A Biography*, 1936.

V. Branca, *Vittorio Alfieri e la ricerca dello stile*, Florence, 1948.

Massimiliano Boni, *Appunti per una tesi sulla teatralità del teatro alfieriano*, Bologna, 1963.

Riccardo Scrivano, *La natura teatrale dell'inspirazione alfieriana e altri scritti alfieriani*, Milan, 1963.

Vitilio Masiello, *L'ideologica tragica di Vittorio Alfieri*, Rome, 1965.

Mario Fubini, *Ritratto dell'Alfieri*, 1967.

Walter Binni, *Saggi alfieriani*, Florence, 1969.

Giuseppe Santarelli, *Studi e ricerche sulla genesi e le fonti delle commedie alfieriane*, Milan, 1971.

V. Placella, *Alfieri comico*, Bergamo, 1973.

Carmine Mensi, *Studi alfierani vecchi e nuovi*, Florence, 1974.

Pino Mensi, *Gli affeti nella tragedia di Vittorio Alfieri*, Padova, 1974.

Guido Nicastro, *Vittorio Alfieri*, Rome and Bari, 1974.

F. Portinari, *Di Vittorio Alfieri e della tragedia*, Turin, 1976.

Jacques Joly, *Le Désir et l'utopie: Études sur le théâtre d'Alfieri et de Goldoni*, Clermont-Ferrand, 1978.

Mario Travato, *Il messagio poetico dell'Alfieri: La natura del limite tragico*, Rome, 1978.

Giovanna Ioli (ed.), *Vittorio Alfieri e la cultura piemontese fra illuminismo e rivoluzione*, San Salvatore Monferrato, 1985.

* * *

For much of the 18th century in Italy, comic drama and opera, both *seria* and *buffa*, were the theatre forms most in the ascendent, and with the exception of one or two pieces of historical importance only, like Maffei's *Sofonisba*, there is little tragic drama of any note. The contribution of Alfieri to Italian drama is all the more important, then, in so far as it was to be in tragedy, rather than comedy, that Alfieri was to excel. Yet, notwithstanding that he was one of the most prolific and consistently able of Italian writers, none of his plays has secured a permanent place in the international repertory, although a handful, including *Oreste*, *Agamemnon*, *Saul*, and *Mirra*, are fairly regularly performed in Italy today.

Alfieri's drama is, in a sense, a drama of political commitment, for it is concerned with great issues of freedom versus tyranny, and the individual against the oppressive state, and is a drama the governing issues of which were rooted in the immediate Italian political situation and the struggle for national independence and political identity. These were issues to which he devoted, too, a considerable amount of his non-dramatic political and polemical writing. But while the political, social, and spiritual content of his drama is profoundly felt, most of the plays are curiously abstract, too much infused by a spirit of generalised egalitarianism and an overly academic and intellectualised classical regularity. The tone is often austerely aristocratic, and the dominant moods are those of a highly personal and rather melancholy anger and the assertion of an indomitable will.

Alfieri's theatre derived from the French, taking its main inspiration from the tradition of French classical tragedy, but reflecting, too, something of the strong sentimental dimension increasingly pronounced in French drama in the second half of the 18th century. It is, too, a highly personal drama, and many critics have remarked that Alfieri lacked the capacity to detach his passions from his work: he was a poet of emerging Romantic individualism, and his social and political assertions, while making much of the relationship between tyranny and the body politic, were ultimately more rooted in a concern with heroic individualism and the preoccupations of the self than with collective values and needs. Not surprisingly, his bent was more lyrical than dramatic, and many critics have had considerable reservations about the theatrical qualities of the plays, finding in them a self-conscious seriousness that does not fit well with the needs of the theatre.

Between 1790 and 1803 Alfieri wrote his autobiography, *La vita scritta da esso*, published posthumously. It is a lively account, and one of the most interesting and engaging autobiographies in Italian literature, but less a reliable record than a justification of his own literary mission. The care with which Alfieri composed his plays is evident from his description in the *Vita* of the three principles which for him governed the writing process: *ideare*, the outline of plot, characters and issues; *stendere*, the fleshing out of dialogue and situation in a fluent prose draft; and *verseggiare*, translating this draft into verse and refining the expression through a process of selection and substitution. It was an approach that served him well, as far as quantity of output is concerned, but perhaps tended to emphasise the academic quality that characterises so much of his work. Here reference can be made to only some of the most important of the tragedies, nearly all of which tend to be weak in characterisation, concentrating on the protagonist, and treating of conflicts in a highly schematic way.

An exception perhaps in these respects is *Agamemnon*, where the religious dimensions characteristic of Greek treatments of the story are marginalised, and emphasis is placed rather on the psychology and passions of the protagonists, making of the action a tale of love and adultery, somewhat akin to that found in the domestic entanglements of later-19th-century bourgeois drama. *Oreste*, by contrast, sets in opposition an impetuous, heroic protagonist (Orestes himself) and a confident, assertive tyrant (Aegistus), although rather than developing any persuasive tragic conflict, the play tends to traffic more in positional posture and grand gestures.

Saul and *Mira* rank as two of Alfieri's masterpieces. In the former, Saul, king of Israel, hates David, the husband of his daughter Micol, and exiles him, believing him to be a traitor. From the first act, the play underscores Saul's essentially divided nature: he can be kind and generous, yet suffers from a persecution mania that borders on paranoia, an instability that reaches its climax when, after being defeated by the Philistines, he commits suicide. The plot is simple, the protagonist's inner conflicts out-weighing external action. Saul is both tyrant and victim: a tyrant towards David, and a victim

of God's anger, and the usual conflict between tyranny and freedom becomes, here, an existential conflict. It is considered by many to mark the high point of Alfieri's dramatic work.

No less impressive is *Mirra*, written at about the same time, and Alfieri's last great work. The subject is taken from Ovid's *Metamorphoses*: Mirra, the daughter of Ciniro, king of Cyprus, conceives an incestuous love for her father, and is tormented by her passion and feelings of guilt. She tries to escape by hastening her marriage to Pereo, but during the ceremony faints, causing the wedding to be postponed. Pereo kills himself, and Mirra, unable to conceal her feelings from her father, commits suicide on his sword. *Saul* and *Mirra* are often taken to reflect two prominent elements in Alfieri's own temperament: a disposition to haughty, aristocratic disdain, and a tendency to melancholy and elegaic patrician resignation. The presence of such elements is one of the factors that has encouraged some recent commentary to contextualise Alfieri's work socially and to see in it tensions reflective of the decline of his social class.

Alfieri's tragic work includes several romantic tragedies, like *La congiura de Pazzi*, *Maria Stuarda*, and *Rosmunda*, which laid down a literary-dramatic fashion that was to attract many followers throughout the early decades of the 19th century, and a "tramelogedy", *Abele*, a curious mixed piece that is both tragedy and opera (in that it embraces music, chorus, and fantastic elements), a form that inspired few imitators. But the bulk of his drama was drawn from classical materials, whether a straight re-working of classical drama, like his re-orchestration of Euripides' *Alcestis*, *Alceste Secondo* and plays drawn from Roman history, particularly from Livy and Plutarch, like *Ottavia*, *Timoleone*, *Merope*, and *Sofonisba*, through to the final plays, *Bruto primo* and *Bruto secondo*. Alfieri was, too, a prolific non-dramatic poet and an able political satirist and polemicist.

Whatever Alfieri's limitations as a dramatist, his influence was profound. For much of the early and mid-19th century, little serious Italian drama escaped the Alfierian manner which, while it buoyed the mildly rebellious tone of drama committed, albeit often in veiled ways, to the cause of Italian independence, at its worst helped to entrench academicism, historicism, and weak rhetoric; it had, too, a profound effect on acting styles in serious drama, at least until the reaction against heavily formal styles set in with the strong romantic realism of Tommaso Salvini. But it is a measure of the quality of his best work that, while not establishing itself beyond Italy in translation, it held its place throughout the 19th century in the world-wide touring repertories of the great Italian touring "stars", like Adelaide Ristori, Ernesto Rossi, and Salvini himself.

—Laura Richards

See also *Volume 1* entry on *Oreste*.

———

ANDERSON, Maxwell. Born in Atlantic, Pennsylvania, 15 December 1888; grew up in North Dakota. Educated at Jamestown High School, North Dakota, graduated 1908; University of North Dakota, Grand Forks, 1908–11, BA 1911; Stanford University, California, 1913–14, MA in English 1914. Married 1) Margaret C. Haskett in 1911 (died

1931), three sons; 2) Gertrude Anthony in 1933 (died 1953), one daughter; 3) Gilda Oakleaf in 1954. Principal and English teacher, Minnewaukan High School, North Dakota, 1911–13; English teacher, Polytechnic High School, San Francisco, 1914–17; Professor and Head of the English Department, Whittier College, California, 1917–18; staff member, *New Republic* magazine, New York, 1918–19, New York *Evening Globe*, 1919–21, and New York *World*, 1921–24; founding co-editor, *Measure* magazine, New York, 1921–26; first play, *White Desert*, produced 1923; founder, with Robert E. Sherwood, Elmer Rice, S.N. Behrman, Sidney Howard, and John F. Wharton, Playwrights Company, 1938. Recipient: Pulitzer Prize, 1933; New York Drama Critics Circle award, 1936, 1937; American Academy Gold Medal, 1954. Litt.D.: Columbia University, New York, 1946; University of North Dakota, 1958. Member, American Academy, 1955. Died in Stamford, Connecticut, 28 February 1959.

Works

Collections

Three American Plays (includes *What Price Glory?; First Flight; The Buccaneer*) with Laurence Stallings.   1926.
Eleven Verse Plays 1929–1939.   1940.

Stage Works

White Desert (produced Princess Theatre, New York, 1923).
What Price Glory?, with Laurence Stallings (produced Plymouth Theatre, New York, 1924).   In *Three American Plays*, 1926.
First Flight, with Laurence Stallings (produced Plymouth Theatre, New York, 1925).   In *Three American Plays*, 1926.
The Buccaneer, with Laurence Stallings (produced Plymouth Theatre, New York, 1925).   In *Three American Plays*, 1926.
The Feud.   1925.
Outside Looking In, from a novel by Jim Tully (produced Greenwich Village Theatre, New York, 1925).   With *Gods of the Lightning*, 1928.
Forfeits (produced 1926).
Saturday's Children (produced Booth Theatre, New York, 1927).   1927.
Gods of the Lightning, with Harold Hickerson (produced Little Theatre, New York, 1928).   With *Outside Looking In*, 1928.
Gypsy (produced Klaw Theatre, New York, 1929). Shortened version in *The Best Plays of 1928–29*, edited by Burns Mantle, 1929.
Elizabeth the Queen (produced Guild Theatre, New York, 1930).   1930.
Night Over Taos (produced 48th Street Theatre, New York, 1932).   1932.
Sea-Wife (produced University of Minneapolis, Minnesota, 1932).
Both Your Houses (produced Royale Theatre, New York, 1933).   1933.
Mary of Scotland (produced Alvin Theatre, New York, 1933).   1933.
Valley Forge (produced Guild Theatre, New York, 1934).   1934.
Winterset (produced Martin Beck Theatre, New York, 1935). 1935.
The Masque of Kings (produced Shubert Theatre, New York, 1937).   1936.

The Wingless Victory (produced Empire Theatre, New York, 1936).   1936.
High Tor (produced Martin Beck Theatre, New York, 1937). 1937.
The Feast of Ortolans, from his radio play (produced 1938).   1938.
The Star-Wagon (produced Empire Theatre, New York, 1937).   1937.
Knickerbocker Holiday, music by Kurt Weill (produced Ethel Barrymore Theatre, New York, 1938).   1938.
Key Largo (produced Ethel Barrymore Theatre, New York, 1939).   1939.
Second Overture, from the radio play (produced 1940).   1940.
Journey to Jerusalem (produced National Theatre, New York, 1940).   1940.
Candle in the Wind (produced Shubert Theatre, New York, 1941).   1941.
The Eve of St. Mark (produced Cort Theatre, New York, 1942).   1942; revised edition, 1943.
Your Navy.   In *This Is War!*   1942.
Letter to Jackie.   In *The Best One-Act Plays of 1943*, edited by Margaret Mayorga.   1944.
Storm Operation (produced Belasco Theatre, New York, 1944).   1944.
Joan of Lorraine (produced Alvin Theatre, New York, 1946). 1946.
Truckline Cafe (produced Belasco Theatre, New York, 1946).
Anne of the Thousand Days (produced Shubert Theatre, New York, 1948).   1948.
Lost in the Stars, music by Kurt Weill, from a novel by Alan Paton (produced Music Box Theatre, New York, 1949).   1950.
Barefoot in Athens (produced Martin Beck Theatre, New York, 1951).   1951
Bad Seed, from a novel by William March (produced 46th Street Theatre, New York, 1954).   1955.
The Masque of Pedagogues.   In *North Dakota Quarterly*, Spring 1957.
The Day the Money Stopped, from the novel by Brendan Gill (produced Belasco Theatre, New York, 1958).
The Golden Six (produced York Theatre, New York, 1958).   1961.

Screenplays

All Quiet on the Western Front, with others, 1930; *Rain*, 1932; *We Live Again*, with others, 1934; *Death Takes a Holiday*, with Gladys Lehman and Walter Ferris, 1934; *So Red the Rose*, with Laurence Stallings and Edwin Justus Mayer, 1935; *Joan of Arc*, with Andrew Solt, 1948 (published 1948); *The Wrong Man*, with Angus MacPhail, 1957.

Television Play:

A Christmas Carol, music by Bernard Heerman, from the story by Dickens, 1954 (published 1955).

Radio Plays

The Feast of Ortolans, 1937; *Second Overture*, 1938; *The Bastion Saint-Gervais*, 1938; *The Miracle of the Danube*, 1941 (published in *The Free Company Presents*, edited by James Boyd, 1941); *The Greeks Remember Marathon*, 1944.

Fiction

Morning, Winter, and Night.   1952.

Verse

You Who Have Dreams.   1925.
Notes on a Dream, edited by Laurence G. Avery.   1971.

Memoirs and Letters

Dramatist in America: Letters 1912–1958, edited by Laurence
   G. Avery.   1977.

Other

*The Essence of Tragedy and Other Footnotes and
   Papers.*   1939.
The Bases of Artistic Creation: Essays, with Rhys Carpenter
   and Roy Harris.   1942.
Off Broadway: Essays About the Theatre.   1947.

*

Bibliographies

Laurence G. Avery, *A Catalogue of the Anderson Collection
   at the University of Texas*, Austin, Texas, 1968.
William Klink, *Maxwell Anderson and S.N. Behrman: A
   Reference Guide*, Boston, 1977; supplemented in *Resources
   for American Literary Study*, 12, 1982.
Alfred S. Shivers, *Maxwell Anderson: An Annotated
   Bibliography of Primary and Secondary Works*, Metuchen,
   New Jersey, 1985.
Nancy J. Doran Hazelton and Kenneth Krauss (eds.),
   Maxwell Anderson and the New York Stage, New York,
   1991.

Criticism

Books:
Barrett H. Clark, *Maxwell Anderson: The Man and His
   Plays*, New York, 1933.
Mabel Driscoll Bailey, *Maxwell Anderson: The Playwright as
   Prophet*, London, 1957.
John F. Wharton, *Life Among the Playwrights*, New York,
   1974.
Alfred S. Shivers, *Maxwell Anderson*, Boston, 1976.
Alfred S. Shivers, *The Life of Maxwell Anderson*, New York,
   1983.
Historical Society of Rockland County, *Maxwell Anderson
   (1888–1959) and the Playwrights' Producing Company*,
   New City, New York, 1988.
N.S. Sahu, *Theatre of Protest and Anger: Studies in Dramatic
   Works of Maxwell Anderson and Robert E. Sherwood*,
   Delhi, 1988.

Articles:
Esther M. Jackson, "Maxwell Anderson: Poetry and Morality
   in the American Drama", in *Educational Theatre Journal*,
   25, 1973.

*   *   *

Nine of Anderson's 12 Broadway plays were modern verse
dramas, spread over a long writing career—not just concentrated in periods when notions of an "art theatre" were in vogue. Some of them also use verse audaciously to accommodate vernacular language and down-to-earth material to a degree far beyond the experiments of Eliot and Fry. *Winterset* epitomises Anderson's achievement in this field, a contemporary murder drama set in the context of a gangster subculture. However, his commitment to blank verse in the theatre was established from his first play, *White Desert*, set in North Dakota with characters such as he himself had grown up with.

White Desert has some claim to being called a tragedy (Anderson's view of it), since its action has as its premise the austere puritanism of the main character whose instincts are finally in conflict with his understanding. Its failure led to a temporary abandonment of verse in favour of the tough military realism of *What Price Glory?*, co-authored with Laurence Stallings. By 1930, however, his confidence was sufficiently restored for him to attempt historical verse drama, which would come to be seen as his speciality. *Elizabeth the Queen* was derived from Strachey's *Elizabeth and Essex*, but pivots on Anderson's characteristic themes of the spirit of man and the quest for stature and power. It was followed by *Night Over Taos, Mary of Scotland, Valley Forge, The Masque of Kings, The Wingless Victory*, and *Anne of the Thousand Days*. In all of these, Anderson's respect for history is evidenced in substantial research, but his growing disrespect for historians is manifested in the way that his "historical" characters speak back against the way that "chroniclers" have represented them.

The tension between the conflicting perspectives of history in these works generates a counterpoint which is similar in kind to the ambivalence of tone and texture in numerous other plays. In his musicals with Kurt Weill, there is sometimes a Brechtian disparity between words and music. In some plays, like *Joan of Lorraine, Elizabeth the Queen*, and *The Wingless Victory*, the action overtly contains elements of another play. When he adapted novels or prose works for the stage, as in *Bad Seed* and *Lost in the Stars*, he reworked the original so thoroughly that his plays might be seen as answering the originals rather than illustrating them. The latter play, which has been undeservedly neglected because of the dismissive tendency of critics towards musicals, shows up well the complexity of his methods. Paton's *Cry, the Beloved Country*, on which it was based, is mainly subjective in its perspective, coming largely from one character's angle on events; but the musical objectifies this particularly through choruses which reduce individuality and sometimes work like a Greek chorus, giving the voice of the anonymous citizenry. At other times, though, the chorus is a projection of the main character's consciousness, a subconscious antagonist, a simple echo, or even possibly an authorial voice.

Ambivalence of attitude is not, however, integral to all of Anderson's work. *High Tor* is essentially a plea in verse for the conservation of the mountain which gives it its title, and near which the author lived. Basically set in the present, the play begins and ends with an old Indian trying to find a place to be buried; he speaks both in poetic soliloquy and in prose dialogue to a sympathetic young European. In the central action, invaders and exploiters appear in the form of miners, robbers, and officials, but there is also a diachronic perspective balancing that of the Indian in the ghosts of some Dutch mariners who were stranded there three centuries before. The convergence of these figures involves much that is comic or ludicrous, but Anderson's skilful management of these unlikely ingredients produced an ecological celebration which won him the prestigious New York Drama Critics' Circle Award.

After World War II. Anderson's verse drama output was less frequent, and he found several new directions, some of which took him away from the loosely Aristotelian axioms he had previously expounded with considerable precision and conviction. *Barefoot in Athens* is a prose reworking of the Socrates story which has often been called Shavian, but in its shrewd demythologising of Greek material is closer to the approach of Giraudoux. At another extreme, *Truckline Cafe* is a topical, realistic play about rehabilitation after the War. Its large spread of characters and thematic immediacy gave it a social relevance which is unusual in Anderson's plays, though it is also notable that the young Marlon Brando played a murderously jealous husband very similar to the main character in *White Desert*. This is more than the recurrent Anderson theme of female unfaithfulness; it is also a study of the aetiology of a passion that can lead to tragedy.

The Bad Seed, Anderson's last major play to be produced successfully, reads like a defiant epilogue constructed to undermine all generalisations about his work. If the human spirit—whether celebrated, questioned, or re-articulated—is the pervasive motif in his work, this play has to do with congenital evil, not just isolated in one villainous character, but liable suddenly to appear, contagiously, through the cast. The revelation of the three psychopathic characters has dimensions of the thriller or contemporary Gothic novel, but the malignant energy of these figures is allowed to protract itself through the play's resolution. However, when Reginald Denham read the play, with "a cartload of chips" on his shoulder because he himself had failed to secure the stage rights, he wrote in *Theatre Arts* that "Anderson had taken an extremely sprawling novel and reduced the story line to one of Grecian simplicity. Through it there burned the lit fuse of Sophoclean inevitability".

—Howard McNaughton

See also *Volume 1* entries on *What Price Glory?; Winterset*.

ANDERSON, Robert (Woodruff). Born in New York City, 28 April 1917. Educated at Phillips Exeter Academy, Exeter, New Hampshire, 1931–35; Harvard University, Cambridge, Massachusetts, 1935–42, BA (magna cum laude) 1939, MA 1940. Served in the United States Naval Reserve, 1942–46: Lieutenant; Bronze Star. Married 1) Phyllis Stohl in 1940 (died 1956); 2) the actress Teresa Wright in 1959 (divorced 1978). Actor, South Shore Players, Cohasset, Massachusetts, summers 1937 and 1938; first play, *Hour Town*, produced, 1938; Assistant in English, Harvard University, 1939–42; teacher, Erskine School, Boston, 1941; teacher of playwriting, American Theatre Wing, New York, 1946–51, and Actors Studio, New York, 1955–56; member of the faculty, Salzburg Seminar in American Studies, 1968; writer-in-residence, University of North Carolina, Chapel Hill, 1969, and University of Iowa Writers Workshop, Iowa City, 1976. Member of the Playwrights Producing Company, 1953–60; President, New Dramatists Committee, 1955–56, and Dramatists Guild, 1971–73; member of the Board of Governors, American Playwrights Theatre, 1963–79. Since 1965 member of the Council, and since 1980 Vice-President, Authors League of America. Recipient: National Theatre Conference Prize, 1945; Writers Guild of America award, for screenplay, 1970.

Works

Stage Works

Hour Town, music and lyrics by Anderson (produced Dunster House, Cambridge, Massachusetts, 1938).
Come Marching Home (produced Pasadena Playhouse, Iowa City, 1945).
The Eden Rose (produced Theatre Workshop, Ridgefield, Connecticut, 1949).
Sketches in *Dance Me a Song* (produced Royale Theatre, New York, 1950).
Love Revisited (produced Westport Country Playhouse, Westport, Connecticut, 1951).
All Summer Long, from novel by Donald Wetzel (produced Arena Theatre, Washington, D.C.).   1955.
Tea and Sympathy (produced Ethel Barrymore Theatre, New York, 1953).   1953.
Silent Night, Lonely Night (produced New Haven, Connecticut, and Morosco Theatre, New York, 1959).   1960.
The Days Between (produced Theatre Center, Dallas, 1965).   1965.
You Know I Can't Hear You When the Water's Running (produced Ambassador Theatre, New York, 1967).   1967.
I Never Sang for My Father (produced Philadelphia, 1967).   1968.
Solitaire/Double Solitaire (produced Long Warf Theatre, New Haven, Connecticut, 1971).   1972.
Free and Clear (produced New Haven, Connecticut, 1983).
The Last Act is a Solo.   1991.

Screenplays

Tea and Sympathy, 1956; *Until They Sail*, 1957; *The Nun's Story*, 1959; *The Sand Pebbles*, 1966; *I Never Sang for My Father*, 1970 (published 1970).

Radio and Television Plays

David Copperfield, Oliver Twist, Vanity Fair, The Glass Menagerie, Trilby, The Old Lady Shows Her Medals, The Petrified Forest, The Scarlet Pimpernel, A Farewell to Arms, Summer and Smoke, Arrowsmith, and other adaptations, 1946–52; *The Patricia Neal Story*, 1980; *Absolute Strangers*, 1991; *The Last Act is a Solo*, 1991.

Fiction

After.   1973.
Getting Up and Going Home.   1978.

Other

Editor, with others, *Elements of Literature* (6 vols.), New York.   1988.

*

Criticism

Books:
John F. Wharton, *Life Among the Playwrights*, New York, 1974.
Lewis Funke (ed.), *Playwrights Talk About Playwriting*, Chicago, Illinois, 1975.

Thomas Adler, *Robert Anderson*, Boston, 1978.
Samuel Bernstein, *The Strands Entwined*, Boston, 1980.

Articles:
Samuel Bernstein, "A Multi-Media Dramatist Explores Inner Space", in *Dramatists Guild Quarterly*, Spring 1979.
Robert Anderson and Jackson R. Bryer, "An Interview with Robert Anderson", in *Studies in American Drama*, 3, 1988.

*   *   *

Robert Anderson carved out a niche for himself in the popular American drama somewhat akin to that of William Inge, as a sort of domesticated, unspectacular Tennessee Williams, writing sensitively about the small but real pains of small people. His recurring theme is loneliness—the loneliness that can affect those who live in a crowd as well as those who live alone—and his recurring remedy, or hope of remedy, is simple human contact, however brief, incomplete, or morally ambiguous. Like those in the plays of Williams and Inge, his characters grasp at straws, gratefully accepting any interruption to the pain of disconnectedness.

Anderson's career and contribution are likely to be defined primarily by his first Broadway success, *Tea and Sympathy*, in which a sensitive schoolboy is suspected by his mates and teachers of homosexuality just because he is "different" in almost undefinable ways, and who is reassured of his normality by an older woman who offers herself to him sexually at the final curtain. Some critics read the play politically, as an attack on the mob mentality and fear of the different that were characteristic of McCarthyism. But Anderson's focus is always on the human story: on the pain of the boy, who is unformed enough to be confused by the attacks and in danger of being convinced that they are valid; on the teacher, whose rejection of the boy is actually a desperate attempt to escape his fears about his own sexuality; on his wife, whose own unhappiness helps her to understand the boy's pain at the same time that it makes her need to be needed by someone.

Tea and Sympathy is not above criticism: in Anderson's determination to focus audience sympathy on the boy and woman, he somewhat simplifies the moral issues, making the villains in particular one-dimensionally evil, and presenting the just-after-the-final-curtain sexual act as uncomplicatedly pure; and he allows the play to pretend that the one sexual experience will resolve all the boy's problems and most of the woman's. Still, these simplifications are the very things that made the play accessible to a mainstream audience, allowing them to see past the shocking subject to the play's empathy for its main characters.

Something of the same quality is in *Silent Night, Lonely Night*, about a woman whose marriage is collapsing and a man whose wife is in an asylum. Though both are good people, with no desire to be unfaithful, they are both in desperate need of comfort, and allow themselves to give in to a one-night affair. The whole thrust of the play is to justify their lapse on the basis that extreme situations override normal morality, and Anderson works hard to break down any audience resistance. The bulk of the play is devoted to establishing the ordinariness and goodness of both characters, to allow no hint of salaciousness in their motives. The Christmas Eve setting implicitly blesses the sin; and both are rewarded the next day, she with a reconciliation with her husband, he with news of his wife's partial improvement.

In *I Never Sang for My Father*, Anderson turns to another form of loneliness, as a middle-aged man coping with his elderly father is forced to deal with his own fears of aging, his unhappiness at being estranged from the man he wants to love, his guilt at the realization of his own contribution to the estrangement, and his discovery of the pains and insecurities behind his father's facade of strength. Once again Anderson demonstrates that almost any immoral, cruel, or merely inexplicable human behavior will, under patient and sensitive examination, prove to be a frantic and ultimately excusable attempt to cope with loneliness and fear.

The same themes run through Anderson's other plays. *The Days Between* and *Double Solitaire* both dissect unhappy marriages, while *Free and Clear* deals with the complex emotional bonds between parents and children; all discover the pains causing the pains, and accept and justify any sources of comfort. Even the trivial *You Know I Can't Hear You When the Water's Running*, a collection of four comic sketches, builds its sometimes sad humor on characters coping with unhappiness: an actor desperate to please, a father trying to explain loneliness to his son, a couple switching from a double bed to twins, an elderly couple who can't quite remember who the other other is.

Those critical of Anderson fault his moral oversimplifications, his hesitation about exploring psychological problems any deeper than he has solutions for, his inclination to find happy endings (or to label the endings he does find as happy), and the generally "safe" domestic tone of his plays. Those who admire him praise most of the same qualities, citing them as valid compromises necessary to make his ideas accessible to the Broadway audience.

—Gerald M. Berkowitz

ANDRADE, Jorge. Born Aluísio Jorge Andrade Franco in Barretos, São Paulo, Brazil, 21 March 1922. Educated at the Ginásio Municipal de Bebedouro; studied law at the Faculdade de Direito de São Paulo, but later abandoned studies; studied theatre at the Escola de Arte Dramática, São Paulo, 1951–54. Worked on his father's coffee plantation in the 1940's; became involved with the Teatro Brasiliero de Comédia; dramatist from 1951; in later years wrote for television, during the period of military government. Recipient of several theatre awards, including the Saci Prize, 1954; Radio Jornal do Brasil Prize, 1954; Brazilian Government Education and Culture Prize, 1964. Died in São Paulo, 13 March 1984.

Works

Collections

Marta, a Árvore e o Relógio (includes the "São Paolo cycle" of 10 plays and essays).   1970.

Stage Works

O Faqueiro de Prata.   Revised as *As Colunas do Templo*, 1954.
A Moratória (produced Teatro Moira Della Costa, São

Paulo, 1955). In *Teatro Brasiliero*, 9, 1956; in book form, in *Teatro Brasiliero Contemporâneo* (New York), edited by Wilson Martins and others, 1966.

O Telescópio (produced Teatro Nacional de Comédia, São Paulo, 1957). With *Pedreira das Almas*, 1960.

Pedreira das Almas (produced Teatro Brasileiro de Comédia, São Paulo, 1958). 1958.

A Escada (produced Teatro Brasileiro de Comédia, São Paulo, 1961). With *Os Ossos do Barão*, 1964.

Os Ossos do Barão (produced 1962). With *A Escada*, 1964.

A Vereda da Salvação (produced 1964). In *Marta . . .* (collection), 1970.

Rastro Atrás (produced 1965?). 1967.

Senhora na Bôca do Lixo (produced 1968). 1968.

O Sumidouro. In *Marta . . .* (collection), 1970.

As Confrarias. In *Marta . . .* (collection), 1970.

Milagre na Cela. 1977.

A Zebra. In *Feira Brasiliera de Opiniao*, 1978.

O Incêndio. 1979.

Television Plays

Os Ossos do Barão, 1973; *O Grito* (serial), 1975; *As Gaivotas*, 1979; *Ninho de Serpentes*, 1982.

Other

O Labirinto. 1978.

*

Criticism

Books:

Richard A. Mazzara, "The Theater of Jorge Andrade", in *Dramatists in Revolt: The New Latin American Theater*, edited by George Woodyard and Leon F. Lyday, Austin, Texas, 1976 (previously in *Latin American Theatre Review*, vol. 1 no. 1, 1967).

Anatol Rosenfeld, *O Mito e o Herói no Moderno Teatro Brasiliero*, São Paulo, 1982.

Articles:

Richard A. Mazzara, "Jorge Andrade's Newest Plays", in *Latin American Theatre Review*, 2, 1968.

Gerald Moser, "Jorge Andrade's São Paulo Cycle", in *Latin American Theatre Review*, 5, 1971.

Vicky Unruh, "Andrade's *Milgre na Cela*: Theatre Space and Body Movement", in *Latin American Theatre Review*, 15, 1981.

Paul Pinto, "Jorge Andrade's Three Enigmas", in *Hispania*, September 1984.

* * *

Jorge Andrade, the first successful modern Brazilian playwright, went on to become one of its most prize-winning dramatists, and his fame has extended far beyond Brazil. He contributed to the development of a truly contemporary Brazilian theatre, which was due in part to the flowering of theatre in Brazil beginning in the 1940's.

Andrade began his career studying law, then returned to the interior of Brazil, where he ran his father's estate until 1950. In 1951, during a performance by the Teatro Brasileiro de Comédia, he was smitten with all things theatrical and promptly enrolled in the Academy of Dramatic Art. By the

time he completed his degree in 1955, he had already developed an interest in writing for the theatre. While a student at the Academy, his one-act play, *O Telescópio* won the Fábio Prado Prize, and his entry for the Martins Pena Competition for Young Playwrights, *O Faqueiro de Prata*, received an honorable mention. Revised as *As Colunas do Templo*, it too won the Fábio Prado Prize. On May 6, 1955, his *A Moratória* opened at the Teatro Moira Della Costa, where it was awarded the Rádio Jornal do Brazil Prize and the Saci Prize of the Estado do São Paulo. He received a scholarship from the American government to visit American theatre centers and drama groups. While in the United States, *A Moratória* was translated into English and performed at Western Reserve University in Cleveland. He continued to win prizes for *Pedreira das Almas*, *A Escada*, *Vereda da Salvaçao*, and other plays.

Greatly influenced by Arthur Miller, Andrade recorded the abilities and aspirations of everyday people. His plays betray his own social roots, as he analyzes the changes in rural Brazil. *O Telescópio* charts the disintegration of a landowner's estate, destroyed by financial crisis and the conflict among the landowner's own children, who are pitted not only against their parents but against each other as they try to inherit the land. The father takes refuge in the study of astronomy and, through his telescope, visits other worlds which bring him peace—both intellectual and spiritual. The children are contemptuous of their father, and the conflicts seem irreconcilable. The telescope's destruction by the drunken older son symbolizes the tragic inevitability that the old ways pass on, and that the young will be victorious over the old.

Influenced by Miller's *Death of a Salesman*, *A Moratória* takes places between 1922 and 1932, which was a critical period for coffee plantations, as there were enormous drops in world prices. The plantation owners in the play, faced with ruin, make every attempt to survive, but to no avail. The subject matter is a continuation of *O Telescópio*, but clearly shows the author's growth as a playwright. The passage from one era to another is more sharply defined, and is supported by superior technical skills as Andrade uses two sets simultaneously, one the fazenda in the 1920's, and the other a city apartment in 1932. Physically and thematically the two levels are tightly interwoven, and there are many transitions between hope and despair which affect the audience both objectively and emotionally.

A more ambitious play artistically, *Pedreira das Almas* explores the pioneering spirit of Brazil, with its echoes of nostalgia for the past and its subtle pleas for a better world. Andrade experimented here with ancient tragedy and adapted it to Brazilian subjects. Ultimately the ancestors show the way forward for succeeding generations, with the implication that their sacrifices are worthy of respect.

In *A Vereda da Salvação*, modern man is seen in the context of labyrinth of social and political wrongs. Where in *O Telescópio* and *A Moratória* the emphasis is on the family, in *Vereda da Salvação* Andrade stresses the collective. The masses escape their misery through religious demagoguery, facing an even greater tragedy in the end, yet maintaining a note of triumph, even in defeat.

A Escada portrays a family divided and tormented, struggling in its insecurity to stay intact. Unlike the rural settings of his previous plays, Andrade places this one in an urban setting, with all its concomitant intolerance and betrayals. Andrade continues to explore contemporary socio-economic problems in *Os Ossos do Barão*, pitting two irreconcilable points of view—the traditional and the modern. Influenced by Molière's classical comedy, Andrade creates a slender plot, full of varied comedy, with comic types who are less indivi-dualized than in his previous plays.

Completed in 1963, *Senhora na Bôca do Lixo* was neither staged nor published until 1968. In it Andrade continues to trace the socio-economic history of São Paulo with characters who escape into the past seeking affluence and prestige. The lower classes, usually under-represented in Andrade's plays, act as a counterfoil to the principal character Noêmia, whose actions contribute to the *lixo* (garbage) or snobbish way of life.

Rasto Atrás marks the next step in Andrade's development as an accomplished playwright. The play is more frankly autobiographical than his other works, synthesizing the themes of his previous plays. The action, spanning the period from 1922 to 1965, represents a journey back in time to resolve conflicts with himself and with his father, through the use of flashbacks and audio-visual effects. The title refers literally and symbolically to the father's explanation of back-tracking in hunting, thus the *double entendre* of the title, and the symbolism of the hunted and the hunter.

The collection of plays, *Marta, a Árvore e o Relógio*, contains two new plays. Of importance is that Andrade places the plays not in order of writing, but in terms of the fictional chronology which creates a full cycle of São Paulo plays. *As Confrarias*, though the newest play, becomes the first play chronologically in the cycle, and *O Sumidouro*, the other new play, is the last. The plays are all unified through a poem by Andrade and a photograph before each play. The title rep-resents symbols that recur throughout the plays. Marta, a central figure who reappears in several plays, is symbolic of the strength of the nation. Martiniano, again a recurrent character, carries a clock which represents the passage of time. Andrade uses convertions such as the play-within-the-play, the flashback, and *trompe l'œil* techniques to create a world of semi-historical figures. Andrade frequently employs a narrator, whose voice and imagination move the action forward, and the playwright also effectively uses staging tech-niques which permit the audience to see two time frames unfolding. He adapts the conventions of epic theatre to pro-vide several perspectives at once, rather than the traditional linear and historical presentation.

Though not all of his plays are tragedies in the traditional sense, Andrade does posit conflicts between the values of the State and the individual, as well as the internal conflicts which the characters confront. In all cases Andrade's voice is evi-dent in the characters, as he has lived or studied experiences parallel to theirs in real life. His themes, representing local traditions and situations, are developed through a broad range of theatre techniques, all of which have contributed to making him one of the most influential of Brazilian play-wrights.

—Lynn Carbón Gorell

ANDREYEV, Leonid Nikolayevich. Born in Orel, Russia, 21 August [9 August, Old Style] 1871. Educated at Orel grammar school, from 1882; entered St. Petersburg Univer-sity, reading law, 1891; third suicide attempt, 1891, and aban-doned studies, resuming them at Moscow University, 1893, graduated 1897. Married 1) Alexandra [Shura] Vegligorskaya in 1902 (died 1906), a son and a daughter; 2) Anna Denisevich in 1908, two sons and one daughter. Gave up attempts to earn a living as a barrister, 1897; wrote short stories, articles, and court reports for the newspaper *Kuryor* [The Courier] in the 1890's; came under influence of Gorky's literary circle: Gorky's publishing house, Znanie, sub-sequently published many of his writings, 1901–07; first play, *K zvezdam* [*To the Stars*], published 1905; briefly imprisoned for his conncections with the Social Democratic Party, 1905; suffered emotional crisis following death of first wife, 1906; edited the arts journal *Shipovnik* [Sweetbriar], 1907–09; stayed with Gorky in Capri, 1907; settled in Terioki, Finland (then a Russian province), 1907; wrote mainly for the theatre, 1908–16; travelled to Hamburg and Amsterdam in 1909, Marseilles, Corsica, and Florence in 1910; travelled in Italy, 1913–14; editor of the patriotic newspaper *Russkaya Volya* [The Russian Will], 1916; opposed the 1917 Revolution, writ-ing anti-Bolshevik articles, most notably "S.O.S" [Russia's Call to Humanity: Save Our Souls] (1919) to encourage Western intervention. Also a painter and photographer. Died in Kuokkala, Finland, 12 September 1919.

Works

Collections

Sobranie sochineny [Collected Works] (7 vols.).   1901–09.
Sobranie sochineny [Collected Works] (17 vols.).   1911–17.
Polnoe sobranie sochineny [Complete Collected Works] (8 vols.).   1913.
Plays.   1915.
Pesy [Plays].   1959.
Sobranie sochineny [Collected Works] (6 vols.).   1990—

Stage Works

K zvezdam (produced Freie Volksbühne, Vienna, 1906). 1906; translated as *To the Stars*, 1907.
Savva: Ignis Sanat [Savva; or, Fire Cures] (produced Terioki Theatre, Finland, 1907).   1906; translated as *Savva*, 1914.
Zhizn cheloveka (produced Vera Kommissarzhevskaya's Theatre, St. Petersburg, 1907).   1907; translated as *The Life of Man*, in *Plays*, 1914.
Tsar golod (produced Proletkult Theatre, Moscow?, 1921). In *Shipovnik*, 1908; translated as *King Hunger*, in *Poet Lore*, 1912; in book form, 1973.
Lyubov k blizhnemu (produced Odessa Theatre, Odessa, 1909). 1908; translated as *Love of One's Neighbor*, 1914; as *The Dear Departing*, 1916; as *Love Thy Neighbour*, 1943.
Dni nashey zhizni [The Days of our Life] (produced Novy Theatre, St. Petersburg, 1908).   1908.
Chyornye maski (produced Vera Kommissarzhevskaya's Theatre, St. Petersburg, 1909).   1909; translated as *The Black Maskers*, in *Plays*, 1915.
Anatema (produced Moscow Art Theatre, 1909). In *Shipovnik*, 1909; translated as *Anathema*, 1910.
Anfisa [Anfisa] (produced Nezlobin's Theatre, Moscow, 1910).   1909.
Gaudeamus (produced Nezlobin's Theatre, Moscow, 1910). 1910.
Okean [The Ocean] (produced Drama and Comedy Theatre, Moscow, 1918).   In *Prometheus*, 1911.
Prekasnye sabinyanki.   1911; translated as *The Sabine Women*, in *Plays*, 1915.
Chest: Stary graf [Honour; or, The Old Count].   1912.
Yekaterina Ivanovna (produced Moscow Art Theatre, 1912). In *Shipovnik*, 1913; in book form, 1913 (Berlin); translated as *Yekaterina Ivanova*, 1923; as *Katerina*, 1924.

Professor Storitsyn (produced Alexandrinsky Theatre, St. Petersburg, 1913). 1913; translated as *Professor Storitsyn*, in *Masterpieces of the Russian Drama*, 1933.

Kainova pechat (Ne ubi) [The Mark of Cain (Thou Shalt Not Kill)] (produced Odessa, 1913). In *Shipovnik*, 1913; in book form, 1913 (Berlin).

Mysl [Thought], from his short story (produced Moscow Art Theatre, 1914). 1914.

Korol, zakon i svoboda [The King, the Law, and Freedom] (produced Dramatic Theatre, Moscow, 1914). 1915; translated as *The Sorrows of Belgium*, 1915.

Mladost [Youth]. 1915.

Tot, kto poluchayet poshchechiny (produced Dramatic Theatre, Moscow, 1915). In *Shipovnik*, 1916; translated as *He Who Gets Slapped*, 1921.

Monument [Monument] (produced Krivoye Zerkalo Theatre, Moscow, 1916). 1917.

Rekviem [Requiem] (produced Dramatic Theatre, Moscow, 1916). In *Strada* (miscellany), 1917.

Milye prizraki [Sweet Phantoms] (produced Alexandrinsky Theatre, Petrograd, 1917). 1917.

Kon v senate [The Horse in the Senate]. 1917.

Sobachy vals (produced Pokazatelny Theatre, Moscow?, 1920). In *Notes contemporains* (Paris), 1922; in book form, 1922 (USA); translated as *The Waltz of the Dogs*, 1922.

Dnevnik Satany [Satan's Diary] (produced Alexandrinsky Theatre, Leningrad, 1922). 1921.

Samson v okovakh. In *Epokha* (miscellany), 1923; translated as *Samson in Chains*, 1923.

Fiction

Yumoristichesky rasskazy [Humorous Stories], with Kuprin. 1909.

Sashka Zhegulev. 1911.

Rasskaz o semi poveshennykh [The Tale of the Seven Who Were Hanged]. 1918.

Nochnoi razgovor [A Night Conversation]. 1921.

Zapiski Satany [Satan's Journal]. 1921.

Izbrannye rasskazy [Selected Stories]. 1926.

Originalny chelovek; Lyubov k blizhnemy [An Original Person; Love for One's Fellow Man]. 1926.

Rasskazy [Stories]. 1930; later editions, 1956, 1957, 1959.

Povesti i rasskazy [Stories and Tales]. 1957; later editions, 1971 (2 vols.), 1979, 1982.

Selections of stories have been translated as *"The Little Angel" and Other Stories*, 1915, *"Seven That Were Hanged" and Other Stories*, 1958, *Selected Stories*, edited by M. Shotton, 1970, and other compilations.

Memoirs and Letters

The Letters of Gorky and Andreyev 1899–1912, edited by P. Yershov. 1958.

Other

Pod vpechatleniem Khudozhestvennogo teatra [An Impression of the Art Theatre], with S. Glagol. 1902.

Net smerti dlya togo, kto lyubit Rodinu [There Is no Death for One Who Loves His Country]. 1914.

O everyakh [About the Jews]. 1914.

Pervaya stupen [The First Step]. 1914.

V sei groznyi chas [At This Threatening Hour]. 1915.

Gibel [Ruin]. 1917.

Zemlya: Povesti, rasskazy i feletony [The Earth: Stories, Tales, and Articles]. 1982.

Photographs by a Russian Writer, edited by Richard Davies. 1989.

*

Criticism

Books:

D. Provenzal, *Una vittima del dubbio: Leonida Andreief*, 1921.

A. Kaun, *Leonid Andreyev: A Critical Study*, New York, 1924.

Maxim Gorky, *Reminiscences of Tolstoy, Chekhov, and Andreev*, New York, 1968.

James B. Woodward, *Leonid Andreyev: A Study*, Oxford, 1969.

Josephine M. Newcombe, *Leonid Andreyev*, Letchworth, Hertfordshire, 1972.

Rita Giuliani, *Leonid Andreev*, Florence, 1977.

Angela Martini, "The Syncretism of Dramatic Structure and the Failure of L.N. Andreev's Dramas", in *Theater and Literature in Russia 1900–1930*, edited by Lars Kleberg and Nils Å. Nilsson, Stockholm, 1984.

Articles:

James B. Woodward, "The Theme and Structural Significance of Leonid Andreyev's *Black Masks*", in *Modern Drama*, 10, 1967–68.

James B. Woodward, "Leonid Andreyev and 'Conventionalism' in the Russian Theatre", in *Modern Language Review*, 66, 1971.

Ludmilla B. Turkevich, "Andreev and the Mask", in *Russian Literature Triquarterly*, 7, 1973.

* * *

In the course of his 48 years Andreyev was associated with many "isms", such as symbolism, expressionism, and futurism, but he conformed to none, and both as an artist and an individual remained very much an outsider. He was rejected in turn by Gorky, who was committed to a realistic approach, and by the symbolists Bely and Blok.

Andreyev began his literary career as a writer of short stories, which were published between 1898 and 1901 in "The Courier". They attracted the attention of Gorky's circle, the "Znanie" group, but while Andreyev shared its antipathy to the Tsarist regime, his natural inclination was towards a more abstract representation of the human situation using types rather than individual characters. When he wished to deal with broad social issues he turned to prose rather than the theatre.

Like many writers of the period he was drawn to the works of Maeterlinck. His first play, *To the Stars*, contrasts an abstract, detached view of human destiny with the actual strivings of various revolutionary groups. He was considered sufficiently dangerous to be arrested in 1905. For the next two years he lived in exile and it was in Munich that he wrote his second play, *Savva*, and followed it with the play that brought him real success, *The Life Of Man*. The five acts represent the ages of man: 1) birth; 2) marriage and early struggles; 3) fame and its attendant falseness; 4) failure, loss, and the loss of a beloved son; 5) death. It was presented both in Moscow and St. Petersburg in productions by Russia's two greatest directors—by Stanislavsky for the Moscow Art Theatre and by Meyerhold for Vera Komissarzhevskaya's Theatre. The two productions provoked a public argument. Meyerhold gave a public lecture denouncing the Art Theatre's conservative "naturalistic" style, while the leading critic Nikolai Efros maintained that when it came to innovation Stanislavsky's production was unquestionably the more advanced. Stanislavsky directed the play unwillingly as he had no great opinion of its merits as a piece of theatre. He used his skills as a director to hide what he regarded as the poverty of the text, from an actor's point of view. He also used his newly discovered "black velvet" technique to make characters and sets appear and disappear, and the black-and-white designs were based on the drawings of Aubrey Beardsley. Andreyev approved of the production as a whole but commented that he would have preferred designs based on Goya, thus revealing a savage edge to his "cosmic" pessimism. When he saw the production in 1908 Gordon Craig declared that the sets and production were so oppressive as to make him feel physically sick.

After the death of his wife in December 1906 Andreyev abandoned his old life and settled in the Karelian isthmus. He appeared to have broken with his dissident past with his next play, *King Hunger*, which was interpreted as anti-revolutionary. He maintained that what he had attacked was mindless revolt not genuine revolution, but no one believed him. The play was intended to be the first part of a tetralogy which would have been completed by "War", "Revolution", and "God, the Devil and Man".

For the next few years Andreyev's writing consisted of plays which seemed closer to the tradition of psychological realism—the autobiographical "Days of Our Life", *Anfisa, Gaudeamus, Professor Storitsyn, Yekaterina Ivanovna*—and those which were more abstract—*Black Maskers*, and *Anathema*, which was presented at the Art Theatre in a production by Nemirovich-Danchenko with Kachalov in the leading role. But even the psychological plays, as with those of Ibsen, are tinged with symbolism.

Between 1911 and 1913 Andreyev developed his idea of "pan-psychism", the notion that each individual is part of a universal unconsciousness. He redefined his attitude towards the theatre of the future, in particular a theatre now faced by the challenge of the cinema. This he did in two articles, "Two Letters on the Theatre", published in 1912 and 1913. The cinema, in his view, was best suited to deal with the complexity of the external world, whereas the inner world of man belonged to the theatre. Thus in "Thought", the central character, Dr. Kerzhentsev, performs a series of experiments based on the hypothesis that a dark force exists behind the rational mind of man. The play was produced at the Art Theatre by Nemirovich-Danchenko.

At the same time, however, Andreyev was moving away from small, intimate drama and looking for a broader, noisier, more stylized form of presentation. In so doing he allied himself with those who were demanding a greater theatricalization of the theatre. It was in this spirit that he wrote his most significant success, *He Who Gets Slapped*. By setting the play in a circus, Andreyev was able to find a satisfactory form in which to combine theatrical action and inner significance. The actors no longer had to struggle with the problem of presenting abstractions, such as Death or Man, but were able to present living characters who, by their very nature, possessed symbolic meaning. Of all Andreyev's plays this is the one that has had the greatest international success. It had a long run in New York in 1922, and in 1924 was made into a silent film with Norma Shearer and Lon Chaney.

Andreyev's next play, *Samson in Chains*, was a biblical drama and his final play, "Sweet Phantoms", was a study of the young Dostoevsky.

Andreyev opposed the Revolution and sided with the invaders during the War of Intervention. In consequence his works disappeared from view and were not republished until the late 1950's. Yet even had he been favourable to the Revolution it is doubtful whether his popularity would have survived in the new society that was being created. His preoccupations and concerns belonged to a world that had vanished.

—Jean Benedetti

See also *Volume 1* entries on *He Who Gets Slapped; The Life of Man*.

————

ANOUILH, Jean (Marie Lucien Pierre). Born in Cérisole, Bordeaux, France, 23 June 1910. Educated at École Colbert, Bordeaux; Collège Chaptal; studied law at the Sorbonne, Paris, 1928–29. Military service during the 1930's. Married 1) the actress Monelle Valentin in 1931 (divorced 1953), one daughter; 2) the actress Nicole Lançon in 1953, two daughters and one son. Publicity and gag writer for films, and advertising copywriter for Publicité Damour, Paris, 2 years; secretary, Louis Jouvet's Comédie des Champs-Élysées, Paris, 1931–32; first play, *L'Hermine*, produced 1932; assistant to the director Georges Pitoeff; then full-time writer; collaborated with director André Barsacq, 1938–48; also a film director. Recipient: Grand Prize of French Cinema, 1949; Tony Award (USA), 1955; New York Drama Critics Award, 1957; Cino del Duca Prize, 1970; French Drama Critics award, 1970; Paris Critics Prize, 1971. Died in Lausanne, Switzerland, 3 October 1987.

Works

Collections

Pièces roses (includes *Le Bal des voleurs; Le Rendez-vous de Senlis; Léocadia*). 1942; augmented edition (includes *Humulus le muet*), 1958.
Pièces noires (includes *L'Hermine; La Sauvage; Le Voyageur sans bagage; Eurydice*). 1942.
Nouvelles pièces noires (includes *Jézabel; Antigone; Roméo et Jeannette; Médée*). 1946.
Pièces brillantes (includes *L'Invitation au château; Colombe; La Répétition; Cécile*). 1951.
Trois comédies (includes adaptations of *As You Like It; A Winter's Tale; Twelfth Night*, by Shakespeare). 1952.
Pièces grinçantes (includes *Ardèle; La Valse des toréadors; Ornifle; Pauvre Bitos*). 1956.
Five Plays (includes *The Ermine; The Restless Heart; Romeo and Jeannette; Ardele; The Rehearsal*). 1958
Pièces costuméess (includes *L'Alouette; Becket; La Foire d'empoigne*). 1960.
Collected Plays (2 vols.). 1966–67.
Seven Plays (includes *Thieves Carnival; Medea; Cecile, or The School for Fathers; Traveller Without Luggage; The Orchestra; Episode in the Life of an Author; Catch as Catch Can*). 1967.
Théâtre complet (9 vols.). 1968.

Jean Anouilh (self-portrait).

Nouvelles pièces grinçantes (includes *L'Hurluberlu; La Grotte; L'Orchestre; Le Boulanger, la boulangère, et le petit mitron; Les Poissons rouges*).   1970.
Pièces baroques (includes *Cher Antoine; Ne Réveillez pas Madame; Le Directeur de l'Opera*).   1974.
Pièces secrètes (includes *Tu étais si gentil quand tu étais petit; L'Arrestation; Le Scénario*).   1977.
Pièces farceuses (includes *Chers Zoiseaux; La Culotte; Episode de la vie d'un auteur; Le Nombril*).   1984.
Five Plays (includes *Antigone; The Lark; Poor Bitos; Leocadia; The Waltz of the Toreadors*).   1987.
Plays 2 (includes *The Rehearsal; Beckett; Eurydice; The Orchestra*).   1992.

Stage Works

L'Hermine (produced Théâtre de l'Oeuvre, Paris, 1932).   1934; translated as *The Ermine*, in *Plays of the Year 13*, 1956; in *Five Plays*, 1958.
La Mandarine (produced Théâtre de l'Athénée, Paris, 1933).
Y'avait un prisonnier (produced Théâtre des Ambassadeurs, Paris, 1935).   In *La Petite Illustration*, 18 May 1935.
Le Voyageur sans bagage (produced Théâtre des Mathurins, Paris, 1937).   In *Pièces noires*, 1942; translated as *Traveller Without Luggage*, 1959; in *Seven Plays*, 1967.
La Sauvage (produced Théâtre des Mathurins, Paris, 1938).   1938; translated as *The Restless Heart*, 1957; in *Five Plays*, 1958.
Le Bal des voleurs (produced Théâtre des Arts, Paris, 1938).   1938; translated as *Thieves' Carnival*, 1952.
Léocadia (produced Théâtre de la Michodière, Paris,

1940).   In *Pièces roses*, 1942; translated as *Time Remembered*, 1955.
Marie-Jeanne; ou, La Fille du peuple, from a play by Dennery and Mallain (produced Paris, 1940).
Le Rendez-vous de Senlis (produced Théâtre de l'Atelier, Paris, 1941).   In *Pièces roses*, 1942; translated as *Dinner with the Family*, 1958.
Eurydice (produced Théâtre de l'Atelier, Paris, 1942).   In *Pièces noires*, 1942; translated as *Point of Departure*, 1951; as *Legend of Lovers*, 1952.
Antigone, from the play by Sophocles (produced Théâtre de l'Atelier, Paris, 1944).   1946; translated as *Antigone*, 1946.
Roméo et Jeannette (produced Théâtre de l'Atelier, Paris, 1946).   In *Nouvelles pièces noires*, 1946; translated as *Romeo and Jeannette*, in *Five Plays*, 1958.
Jézabel.   In *Nouvelles pièces noires*, 1946.
Médée (produced Théâtre de l'Atelier, Paris, 1937).   In *Nouvelles pièces noires*, 1946; translated as *Medea*, in *Seven Plays*, 1967.
L'Invitation au château (produced Théâtre de l'Atelier, Paris, 1947).   1948; translated as *Ring Round the Moon*, 1950.
Ardèle; ou, La Marguerite with *Episode de la vie d'un auteur* (produced Comédie des Champs-Élysées, 1948).   1949; translated as *Ardele*, 1951; in *Five Plays*, 1958.
Les Demoiselles de la nuit (ballet scenario; produced 1948).
Épisode de la vie d'un auteur (produced Comédie des Champs-Élysées, 1948).   With *La Belle Vie*, 1980; translated as *Episode in the Life of an Author*, in *Seven Plays*, 1967.
Les Demoiselles de la nuit (ballet scenario; produced 1948).
Humulus le muet, with Jean Aurenche (produced Cité Universitaire, Paris, 1948).   N.d.
La Répétition; ou, L'Amour puni (produced Théâtre Marigny, Paris, 1950).   1950; translated as *The Rehearsal*, in *Five Plays*, 1958, and in *Plays 2*, 1992.
Colombe (produced Théâtre de l'Atelier, Paris, 1951).   In *Pièces brillantes*, 1951; translated as *Colombe*, 1952.
Cécile; ou, L'École des pères (produced Comédie des Champs-Élysées, Paris, 1954).   In *Pièces brillantes*, 1951; translated as *Cecile; or, The School for Fathers*, in *Seven Plays*, 1967.
La Valse des toréadors (produced Comédie des Champs-Élysées, Paris, 1952).   1952; translated as *Waltz of the Toreadors*, 1956.
La Nuit des rois, from the play *Twelfth Night* by Shakespeare (produced Paris, 1961).   In *Trois comédies*, 1952.
Le Loup (ballet scenario), with Georges Neveux, 1953.
L'Alouette (produced Théâtre Montparnasse-Gaston-Baty, Paris, 1953).   1953; translated as *The Lark*, 1955.
Ornifle; ou, Le Courant d'air (produced Comédie des Champs-Élysées, 1955).   1956; translated as *Ornifle*, 1970; as *It's Later Than You Think*, 1970.
Il est important d'être aimé, with Claude Vincent, from a play by Oscar Wilde (produced Paris, 1964).   In *L'Avant-scène*, 101, 1955.
Pauvre Bitos; ou, Le Dîner de têtes (produced Théâtre Montparnasse-Gaston-Baty, Paris, 1956).   In *Pièces grinçantes*, 1956; translated as *Poor Bitos*, 1964.
L'Hurluberlu; ou, Le Réactionnaire amoureux (produced Comédie des Champs-Élysées, 1959).   1959; translated as *The Fighting Cock*, 1960.
Becket; ou, L'Honneur de Dieu (produced Théâtre Montparnasse-Gaston-Baty, Paris, 1959).   1959; translated as *Becket; or, The Honor of God*, 1961, and in *Plays 2*, 1992.
Madame de . . . (in English; produced 1959).   1959.

La Petite Molière, with Roland Laudenback (produced Théâtre de France, Bordeaux, 1959). In *L'Avant-scène*, 15 December, 1959.

La Songe du critique (produced Paris, 1960). In *L'Avant-scène*, 143, 1959.

La Foire d'empoigne (produced Comédie des Champs-Élysées, Paris, 1962). In *Pièces costumées*, 1960; translated as *Catch as Catch Can*, in *Seven Plays*, 1967.

Tartuffe, from the play by Molière (produced Paris, 1960). In *L'Avant-scène*, 15 May 1961.

La Grotte (produced Théâtre Montparnasse-Gaston-Baty, Paris, 1961). 1961; translated as *The Cavern*, 1966.

Victor; ou, Les Enfants au pouvoir, from the play by Roger Vitrac (produced Paris, 1962). In *L'Avant-scène*, 15 November 1962.

L'Amant complaisant, with Nicole Anouilh, from a play by Grahame Greene (produced Paris, 1962). 1962.

L'Orchestre (produced Comédie des Champs-Élysées, 1962). 1970; translated as *The Orchestra*, (produced 1969), in *Seven Plays*, 1967; published separately, 1975.

Richard III from the play by Shakespeare (produced Paris, 1964). Nd.

L'Ordalie; ou, La Petite Catherine de Heilbronn, from a story by Kleist (produced Paris, 1966). In *L'Avant-scène*, 15 January 1967.

Le Boulanger, la boulangère, et le petit mitron (produced Comédie des Champs-Élysées, Paris, 1968). 1969.

Cher Antoine; ou, L'Amour raté (produced Comédie des Champs-Élysées, Paris, 1969). 1969; translated as *Dear Antoine; or, The Love That Failed*, 1971.

Le Théâtre; ou, La Vie comme elle est (produced Paris, 1970).

Ne Réveillez pas Madame (produced Comédie des Champs-Élysées, Paris, 1970). 1970.

Les Poissons rouges; ou, Mon père, ce héros (produced Théâtre de l'Oeuvre, Paris, 1970). 1970.

Tu étais si gentil quand tu étais petit (produced Théâtre Antoine, Paris, 1971). 1972.

Le Directeur de l'Opera (produced Comédie des Champs-Élysées, 1973). 1972; as *The Director of the Opera*, 1973.

Monsieur Barnett, (produced Café-Théâtre Le Fanal, Paris, 1974). In *L'Avant-scène*, 559, 1975.

L'Arrestation (produced Théâtre de l'Athénée, Paris, 1975). 1975; translated as *The Arrest*, 1978.

Le Scénario (produced Théâtre de l'Oeuvre, Paris, 1976). 1976.

Chers Zoizeaux (produced 1976). 1977.

Vive Henri IV. 1977.

La Culotte (produced Théâtre de l'Atelier, Paris, 1978). 1978.

Le Nombril (produced Théâtre de l'Atelier, Paris, 1981). 1981; translated as *Number One*, 1984.

Oedipe; ou, Le Roi boiteux from the play by Sophocles. 1986.

Screenplays

Les Dégourdis de la onzième, with Jean Aurenche, 1936; *Vous n'avez rien à déclarer*, with Jean Aurenche, 1937; *Les Otages*, with Jean Aurenche, 1939; *Cavalcade d'amour*, 1939; *Le Voyageur sans bagage (Identity Unknown)*, with Jean Aurenche, 1944; *Monsieur Vincent*, with Jean Bernard Luc, 1947 (published 1951); *Anna Karenina*, with Julien Duvivier and Guy Morgan, 1948; *Pattes blanches*, with Jean Bernard Luc, 1949; *Caroline chérie*, 1951; *Deux sous de violettes*, with Monelle Valentin, 1951; *Le Rideau rouge*, 1952; *Le Chevalier de la nuit*, 1953; *La Mort de belle (The Passion of Slow Fire)*, 1961; *La Ronde (Circle of Love)*, 1964;

Time for Loving, 1972; *Thomas More; ou, L'Homme libre* (published 1987).

Television Plays

Le Jeune Homme et le lion, 1976; *La Belle Vie*, 1979 (published with *Épisode de la vie d'un auteur*, 1980).

Memoirs and Letters

La Vicomtesse d'Eristal n'a pas reçu son balai mécanique: Souvenirs d'un jeune homme. 1987.

Other

Michel-Marie Poulain, with Pierre Imbourg and André Warnod 1953.

Fables 1962.

Robert Brasillach et la génération perdue, with others. 1987.

*

Bibliographies

Kathleen W. Kelly, *Anouilh: An Annotated Bibliography*, Metuchen, New Jersey, 1973.

Criticism

Books:

Marguerite Archer, *Anouilh*, New York, 1951.

Edward O. Marsh, *Anouilh, Poet of Pierrot and Pantaloon*, London and New York, 1953.

Leonard C. Pronko, *The World of Jean Anouilh*, Berkeley, California, 1961.

John Harvey, *Anouilh: A Study in Theatrics*, New Haven, Connecticut, 1964.

Clément Bargal, *Anouilh: La Peine de vivre*, Paris, 1966.

Philip Thody, *Jean Anouilh*, Edinburgh, 1968.

Alba della Fazia Amoia, *Anouilh*, New York, 1969.

Paul Ginestier, *Jean Anouilh: Textes d'Anouilh, points de vue critiques, témoignages, chronologie, bibliographie, illustrations*, Paris, 1969.

Bernard Beugnot, *Théâtre d'Anouilh*, Montreal, 1973.

Branko Lenski, *Jean Anouilh: Stages in Rebellion*, New York, 1975.

André F. Rombout, *La Pureté dans le théâtre de Jean Anouilh*, Amsterdam, 1975.

Jacques Vier, *Le Théâtre de Jean Anouilh*, Paris, 1976.

Elie de Comminges, *Anouilh, littérature et politique*, Paris, 1977.

Lewis W. Falb, *Anouilh*, New York, 1977.

Benito d'Ajetti, *Lecture d'Anouilh: Textes et réflexions critiques*, Naples, 1978.

Thérèse Malachy, *Jean Anouilh: Les Problèmes de l'Éxistence dans un théâtre de marionettes*, Paris, 1978.

H.G. McIntyre, *The Theatre of Anouilh*, London and New York, 1981.

Christopher Smith, *Jean Anouilh: Life, Work, and Criticism*, Fredericton, 1985.

Articles:

Dolores M. Burdick, "Anouilh Grows Middle-Aged: Evolution of Anouilh's Hero", in *Michigan Academician*, 7, 1974.

John Rothenberg, "Anouilh and His Directors", in *Nottingham French Studies*, vol. 29, no. 1, 1990.

* * *

Jean Anouilh is one of the major French dramatists of the 20th century. His lengthy career started with the production of *L'Hermine* (*The Ermine*) in 1932; his reputation was established with *Le Voyageur sans bagage* (*Traveller Without Luggage*) in 1937; his success was at its peak for over a quarter of a century following the wartime production of *Antigone*.

Although a dominant figure in France and abroad, Anouilh avoided publicity and stardom. When Hubert Gignoux was preparing the first critical study of his work in the 1940's, Anouilh refused an interview and sent the briefest of biographical notes which began: "I am happy to say I have no biography". This refreshing modesty persisted to the end of his life, so that even with the publication of some autobiographical material in *La Vicomtesse d'Eristal*, the reader is offered little more than a sketch of his early life in a series of entertaining, delightfully recounted anecdotes. He refused all encouragements to present himself for election to the Académie Française; and for many years after the end of his first marriage to Monelle Valentin, the actress who created the role of Antigone, even gossip-writers failed to discover that Anouilh had remarried. His reputation is therefore based almost exclusively on his plays.

Most of Anouilh's prolific output was published in collections with distinctive titles, starting with *Pièces roses* and *Pièces noires*: the former contains such delightful fantasies as *Bal des voleurs* (*Thieves' Carnival*) and *Léocadia*; in the latter collection are plays whose overall tonality is sad, grim and at times pessimistic, such as *La Sauvage*(*The Restless Heart*) and *Le Voyageur sans bagage*. And yet, even in these early collections, as in the corresponding *Pièces brillantes* and *Pièces grinçantes*, the division of mood is far from clear-cut. At the most poignant or tragic moments, Anouilh's humour is lurking in the wings, or in the next intervention, or in the latter half of a serious sentence, ready to deflate pomposity, destroy cant, and surprise the audience by a sudden change of gear.

Although Anouilh's themes, his characters, and even the idiosyncratic blend of pink and black were all discernible as far back as 1932 in *Bal des voleurs*, he was to renew and re-examine them in many varied contexts. In line with French theatre's traditional concern for classical subjects, he adapted and transposed into the 20th century a number of myths from Greek antiquity: *Eurydice*, *Antigone*, *Médée*, and the Orestes story in *Tu étais si gentil quand tu étais petit*.

Another source was history, sometimes medieval, as with his remarkable re-interpretation of the Joan of Arc legend, *L'Alouette* (*The Lark*), and with *Becket*; sometimes more modern in plays based on the French Revolution, such as *Pauvre Bitos* and *Le Boulanger, la boulangère et le petit mitron*. The choice of *Pièces costumées* as title for the volume into which some of his historical plays are grouped is doubly significant: it indicates that Anouilh's treatment of history is not a reversion to the realism or naturalism he had abandoned at the start of his career; it stresses that his re-interpretation of historical fact will be marked by a concern for the theatricality of life, a constant thematic preoccupation throughout his career.

From the early *Le Rendez-vous de Senlis*, whose hero hires an actor and actress to play the part of his parents, to *Colombe* which is set the theatre governed by a caricature of Sarah Bernhardt, and *L'Hurluberlu* (*The Fighting Cock*) where a retired general reluctantly agrees to the performance of a play in the grounds of his country house, Anouilh constantly uses the device of theatre within the theatre to comment upon theatre itself and on the blurred distinction between illusion and reality, between sincerity and pretence. This theme became a particularly prominent feature in later works: *Ne réveillez pas madame*, *Cher Antoine*, *Les Poissons rouges*, and *Le Directeur de l'Opéra* all have a playwright or theatre director as their hero, and provide Anouilh with an opportunity to explore the craft of comedy. In *La Grotte* (*The Cavern*), the author is himself one of the characters, inviting the audience to share in the creation of a play which, he claims, he has never managed to write.

Within Anouilh's theatre, there are other constants: the recurrent theme of revolt impelling heroines like Thérèse Tarde in *La Sauvage* and Joan of Arc, Antigone, and Médée, to say "No" to happiness and even to life itself; recurrent characters, in the array of eccentric noble women, peppery generals, egocentric thespians, and decrepit butlers; and even the occasional recurrence of dialogue, as one character echoes the words of someone in an earlier play. Inevitably, there were criticisms of repetition, by those who did not savour the pleasure of familiarity. For most theatre-goers, if not all academic critics, there was a sure attraction in Anouilh's personal style and theatrical craftsmanship: the blend of "pink" and "black", the carefully prepared effects, the precisely timed humour, the amazingly taut theatrical dialogue. Many academics were prepared initially to acknowledge this technical mastery, but then devoted the remainder of their work to criticising Anouilh for failing to propound a coherent philosophy.

Theatre audiences in France, England, and the USA were more perceptive, and his work enjoyed enormous popularity. Of 25 London theatres open in the early summer of 1962, five were playing Shakespeare, six had plays by Anouilh. It is to the theatre-goers' eternal advantage that Anouilh resolutely refused, as he put it, to take himself seriously enough to discuss philosophical principles and write serious plays. He examines serious subjects, but never in a manner that is pompous, dogmatic, or heavy-handed. He prefers to laugh at human folly in ways which range from a gentle mockery to a savage irony, reserving a particularly seething disdain for cant and hypocrisy.

There was one subject he often mocked, but never failed to take seriously: theatre itself. Yet, even there, he chose not to produce an *ars poetica*; his theories are contained in occasional observations, programme notes, and above all in skilfully crafted plays like *Antigone* and *La Grotte*, which explore the theory of drama and the processes of theatrical creativity.

—Colin Radford

See also *Volume 1* entries on *Antigone*; *Ring Round the Moon*.

————

ANSKY, Solomon. Also known as An-sky or An-ski. Born Shloyme Zanvil Rapaport [Solomon Seinwill Rapoport] in Vitebsk, White Russia (Belorussia, now Belarus), 8 November 1863. Received Hasidic education in the *Talmud*. Worked as blacksmith, bookbinder, factory labourer and tutor; began writing for the Russian *Narodniki* movement's periodical in St Petersburg; forced to leave Russia, on account of his progressive and socialist ideas, 1892; travelled to Germany, Switzerland, and settled in Paris, 1894–1904; secretary to the philosopher Peter Lavrov for six years; returned to Russia, 1905; led expedition, financed by Baron Horace Ginzburg, to study Jewish life and culture in Volhynia and Podolia, 1911–14; involved in organizing relief for Jewish communities in Russian and eastern Europe during World War I, and in Vilna after 1918; elected as a Socalist Revolutionary Deputy to the Constituent Assembly, 1917; moved to Warsaw, 1918; founder of a Jewish society of ethnography in Warsaw, 1919. Died in Warsaw, 8 November, 1920.

Works

Collections

Collected Works (15 volumes; writings in Yiddish, including the plays).   1920–25.

Stage Works

Foter und Zon [Father and Son].   In Collected Works, 1920–25.
Der Zeidah [The Grandfather].   In Collected Works, 1920–25.
Der Dybbuk (produced in Yiddish by the Vila Troupe, Warsaw, 1920; produced in Hebrew by the Habimah Company, Moscow, 1922).   In Collected Works, 1920–25; translated as *Between Two Worlds—The Dybbuk*, 1925?; as *The Dybbuk*, 1925 and 1953.
Tog und Nacht [Day and Night], completed by Alter Katzine (produced Warsaw, 1921).   In Collected Works, 1920–25.

*

Bibliographies

E.H. Jeshurin, bibliography in *Ilustrirte Yom-Toy Bleter*, Winter 1951.

Criticism

Books:
A.A. Roback, *The Story of Yiddish Literature*, New York, 1940.
M. Waxman, *A History of Jewish Literature 4*, New York, 1947.
N. Sandrow, *A World History of Yiddish Theater*, New York, 1986.

*   *   *

Solomon Ansky (his pen name also appears as An-sky, Anski, or An-ski) received a relatively narrow hasidic education, but at the age of 15 or 16 turned enthusiastically to the ideas of the Jewish Haskalah (Enlightenment) movement, which favoured a rapprochement with Western ideas and culture in contrast to religious obscurantism. Thus he sought experience outside his native Jewish community, learning Russian and working at various jobs in Russian villages. He was also attracted to socialism and the populism preached by the Narodniki group, leaving the southern Russian provinces

to write for the movement's periodical in St. Petersburg. His involvement with socialist politics brought him friction with the authorities, and for several years in the 1890's he lived abroad, mainly in Paris.

Ansky's writing was mainly in Russian until 1904. But from this date he reverted to Yiddish to document, in fictional and non-fictional forms, the imagination, folklore, social conditions, and material poverty of Jewish life in Russia and eastern Europe. Notable among his writings are the hymn of the Jewish-socialist Bund movement, "*Di Shvue*" (The Oath), and his observations of the chaos wrought on Jewish communities by World War I in the three-volume "The Destruction of the Jews of Poland, Galicia, and Bukovina" (contained in the 1920–25 collected edition).

Ansky is, however, chiefly remembered as the author of *The Dybbuk*, written in Yiddish, and inspired by his investigations into Jewish folklore and his observation of the social conditions of village life. In this play, the souls of a betrothed couple, whose marriage is prevented by the bride's father's greed, eventually unite when both souls are freed from earthly life. During the course of the play, the young man Khonen's wandering soul, the "dybbuk" of the title, enters Leah's (the bride's) body while she is still living. The history of the play, for one so apparently imbued with esoteric mysticism, has been remarkable. Although Ansky failed to get it staged during his lifetime, his death prompted its premiere, in Yiddish, 30 days later in Vilna, followed soon afterwards by its Hebrew premiere, staged by the Habimah company in Moscow. Very soon it was taken up in the rest of Europe, travelled across the Atlantic, and has held the stage ever since. At the time of writing, in 1993, Britain's Royal Shakespeare Company has completed a successful revival at its London theatre.

Ansky wrote also the one-act plays "Father and Son" and "The Grandfather", and the incomplete "Day and Night". The latter was finished by Alter Katzine and produced in 1921, but has had little impact. Ansky's various Yiddish writings, including the plays, poems, reportage, and social, political, and folkloric articles appeared in a posthumous collected edition (15 volumes) published in Warsaw, from 1920.

—Jeremy Weiner

See also *Volume 1* entry on *The Dybbuk*.

———

APOLLINAIRE, Guillaume. Born Guillaume Apollinaris de Kostrowitzky in Rome, 26 August 1880. Educated in Monaco, Cannes, and Nice, until 1897. Married Jacqueline Kolb in 1918. Moved to the Ardennes, 1899; first poetry appeared in *La Grande France*, 1901; began using name Apollinaire, 1901; in Germany, as French tutor to German family, 1901–02; co-founder of the Paris artistic review *Le Festin d'Ésope*, 1903; regular writer of art criticism for various publications, from 1907; moved to Montparnasse area of Paris, 1909; art critic for *L'Intransigeant*, 1910; columnist for *Mercure de France*, 1911–18; briefly imprisoned on suspicion of art theft, 1911; art critic for *Le Petit Bleu*, 1912; editor of the review *Les Soirées de Paris*, 1912–14; volunteered for infantry service, 1914, receiving promotion to lieutenant: wounded and underwent operation, 1916, subsequently returning to Paris; first play, *Les Mamelles de Tirésias*, produced, 1917. Died from influenza in Paris, 9 November 1918.

Works

Collections

Apollinaire: Selected Writings, edited by Roger Shattuck. 1950.
Oeuvres complètes (4 vols.), edited by Michel Décaudin. 1965–66.
Oeuvres en prose, edited by Michel Décaudin.   1977.
Oeuvres (5 vols.).   1983–84.

Stage Works

Les Mamelles de Tirésias (produced Conservatoire Renée Maubel, Paris, 1917).   1918.
Couleur du temps (produced 1918).   1949.
Casanova.   1952.
La Température, with André Salmon (produced 1975). In *Oeuvres en prose*, 1977.
A Quelle Heure un train partira-t-il pour Paris?.   1982.

Verse

Le Bestiare; ou, Cortège d'Orphée.   1911; translated as *Le Bestiare*, 1977; as *Bestiary; or, The Parade of Orpheus*, 1980.
Alcools.   1913; translated as *Alcools*, 1964.
Case d'armons.   1915.
Vitam impendere amori.   1917.
Calligrammes: Poèmes de la paix et de la guerre.   1918; translated as *Calligrammes: Poems of Peace and War 1913–1916*, 1980.
Le Cortège priapique.   1925.
Il y a.   1925.
Julie; ou, La Rose.   1927.
Le Condor et le morpion.   1931.
Ombre de mon amour.   1947; revised edition, as *Poèmes à Lou*, 1955.
Le Guetteur mélancolique.   1952.
Tendre comme le souvenir.   1952.
Oeuvres poétiques.   1956.
Selected Poems, edited by Oliver Bernard.   1956; expanded edition, 1986.

Fiction

Les Exploits d'un jeune Don Juan.   1907.
Les Onze mille verges.   1907; translated as *The Debauched Hospodar*, 1958; as *Les Onze Mille Verges*, 1976.
L'Enchanteur pourrissant.   1909.
L'Hérésiarque et Cie.   1910; selection translated as *Contes choisis*, 1922; also translated as *The Heresiarch and Company*, 1965.
La Fin de Babylone.   1914.
Les Trois Don Juan.   1915.
Le Poète assassiné.   1916; translated as *The Assassinated Poet*, 1923; as *The Poet Assassinated*, in *"The Poet Assassinated" and Other Stories*, 1985.
La Femme assise.   1920.
Les Épingles: contes.   1928.
Que faire?.   1950.
"The Wandering Jew" and Other Stories.   1965.

Memoirs and Letters

Lettres à sa marraine.   1948.
Correspondance, with André Level, edited by Brigitte Level. 1976.

Lettre à F.T. Marinetti, edited by P.A. Janini.   1978.
Correspondance: Guillaume Apollinaire, Jean Cocteau, edited by Pierre Caizergues and Michel Décaudin.   1991.

Other

Méditations esthétiques: LES PEINTRES CUBISTES. 1913; translated as *The Cubist Painters: Aesthetic Meditations 1913*, 1949.
Le Flâneur des deux rives.   1918.
Anecdotiques.   1926.
Contemporains pittoresques.   1929.
Oeuvres érotiques complètes (verse and prose; 3 vols.). 1934.
L'Esprit nouveau et les poètes.   1946.
Chroniques d'art 1902–1918, edited by Leroy C. Breunig, 1961; translated as *On Art*, 1972.
Petites flâneries d'art, edited by Pierre Caizergues.   1980.

Editor, *Chronique des grands siècles de la France*, 1912

*

Criticism

Books:
Francis J. Carmody, *Apollinaire's Politics 1901–1914*, 1963.
Scott Bates, *Guillaume Apollinaire*, New York, 1967.
Michel Décaudin (ed.), *Apollinaire, inventeur de langages*, Paris, 1973.
David Berry, *The Creative Vision of Apollinaire*, London, 1982.
Denis Bordat and Bernard Veck, *Apollinaire*, Paris, 1983.
Claude Schumacher, *Alfred Jarry and Guillaume Apollinaire*, London, 1985 (Macmillan Modern Dramatists series).

Articles:
Raymond C. and Virginia A. La Charite, "Guillaume Apollinaire: Poet of the Modern Theater", in *South Atlantic Bulletin*, vol.33 no.1, 1968.
Willard Bohn, "A New Play by Apollinaire", in *Comparative Drama*, 11, 1977.
Annabelle H. Melzer, "The Première of Apollinaire's *The Breasts of Tiresias*", in *Theatre Quarterly*, 27, 1977.
Scott Bates, "Erotic Propaganda in Apollinaire's *Les Mamelles de Tirésias*", in *French Literature Series*, 10, 1983.

*   *   *

Apollinaire's reputation as a playwright, such as it is, rests primarily on one play: *Les Mamelles de Tirésias* (Tiresias's Tits) which had a single Sunday matinée performance during the darkest days of World War I, at 4.30 p.m. on 24 June 1917, in the small theatre of a now-defunct drama school in Montmartre, the Conservatoire Renée Maubel. In the last months of his life Apollinaire wrote two verse dramas, *Casanova*, an opera buffa (never performed), and *Couleur du temps* (Mood of the Age) which was in rehearsals when he died: it had its first and only performance on 24 November 1918. Apollinaire was not a natural playwright and made no extravagant claims for his dramatic output. His fame rests firmly on his poetic writings (he is widely regarded as France's greatest poet of the 20th century) and, to a lesser extent, on his art criticism.

Les Mamelles de Tirésias is an important landmark in the history of theatre, a link between Jarry's *Ubu* and Ionesco's

The Bald Prima Donna, but that importance derives from the ideas contained in the preface and the prologue, not from the play itself. There is no record of a professional production of *Les Mamelles de Tirésias* in French, and the English "world premiere" was staged at the Crucible Studio, Sheffield, England, in December 1987. On that occasion, the publicity labelled it a "grotesque vaudeville"; the critical response was less than enthusiastic, although production and cast were generally praised. Apollinaire himself had called his play a "*drame surréaliste*", using the neologism which he had coined a month earlier in a programme note to Cocteau's *Parade*. In the preface, he explained his aims:

> In order to attempt, if not a renovation of the theatre, at least an original effort, I thought it necessary to come back to nature itself, but without copying it photographically. When man wanted to imitate walking, he created the wheel, which does not resemble a leg. In the same way he has created surrealism unconsciously [. . .] After all, the stage is no more the life it represents than the wheel is a leg.

More specifically, the prologue attacks the pre-war theatre (conventionally naturalistic and, more often than not, vacuous) as "slanderous and pernicious art". Apollinaire calls for a new vision and conception of form and content: "We are trying to bring a new spirit to the theatre", says the Theatre Director, "joyfulness voluptuousness". And he dreams of a new stage, "a circular theatre with two stages/One in the middle the other like a ring/Around the spectators permitting/The full unfolding of our modern art", on which all the performing arts (including the fine arts) would combine to create a total spectacle: "Sounds gestures colours cries noises/Music dance acrobatics poetry painting/Choruses actions and multiple sets". Such a vision of theatre is in complete opposition to naturalistic aesthetics since, for Apollinaire, "THE THEATRE MUST NOT BE 'REALISTIC'". Fascinated by cinema, Apollinaire had shrewdly sensed that the stage could not compete with the screen in the presentation of reality and he, therefore, urged dramatists to give free rein to their imagination.

Apollinaire certainly allowed his own imagination to run riot in *Les Mamelles de Tirésias*. The play not only defies definition but defeats any attempt to summarize it. "Surprise", said Apollinaire, "is the greatest source of what is new. It is by surprise, by the important position that has been given to surprise that the new spirit distinguishes itself from all literary and artistic movements which have preceded it". The play is indeed full of surprises. The main character of the farce, the young Thérèse, tells her astonished husband, "No Mr. my husband/You won't make me do what you want/I am a feminist and I do not recognize the authority of men". Cackling and imitating the sound of a train, she declares that she is to become soldier, artist, lawyer, senator, president, psychiatrist . . . and will no longer produce children. She then "sacrifices her beauty" by taking out two balloons from her blouse, the *mamelles* (tits) of the title, and she sets them alight; she grows a beard, undergoes a sex change, and becomes Tirésias. Now, a man, she sets off to war. But who is going to bring forth the cannon fodder? Well, men, of course! Thérèse-Tirésias's husband gets down to work and in a single night becomes mother and father to 40,049 brats. The story has a happy ending: Thérèse, still flat-chested, returns home to love her husband! Other characters include a one-man "People of Zanzibar", a singing and dancing newspaper kiosk, and two episodic figures who keep killing one another. Does the play, as Apollinaire maintained, contain a positive "message", namely that France needs more children?

Perhaps, but it is possible the message is just an extension of the joke.

Apollinaire's aim was to provoke and entertain his public, but he had also the ambition to influence and renew the art of theatre, wanting to rid the stage of the so-called "slice-of-life" drama, and dreaming of "new and striking aesthetics which would stress the characters' theatrical qualities and increase the pomp of the *mise en scène*". Apollinaire's new theatrical spirit shared the aspirations of men like Meyerhold, Evreinov, or Pirandello, and paved the way for the truly modern theatre that flourished in France in the late 1940's and early 1950's, not to mention the happenings of the 1960's, or today's performance art.

—Claude Schumacher

ARBUZOV, Alexei Nikolaievich. Born in Moscow, 13 May 1908. Received no formal schooling, and lost contact with both parents during the Revolution; eventually sent to aunt in Leningrad, where he entered the Palaestra acting school of the State Mobile Theatre, 1925. Married 1) Tatiana Alekseyevna in 1932 (divorced 1939), one son (died 1934) and one daughter; 2) Anna Nikiforovna in 1939 (divorced), one son and one daughter; 3) Margarita Ulianovna in 1965. Actor, stage-manager, and director with touring groups and the agitprop train, late 1920's; first play, *Klass* [*Class*], written and produced, 1930; became head of literary department, First Kolkhoz Theatre, 1933; created the Moscow Studio Theatre with V.N. Pluchek, 1939, which later performed at the Front during World War II: Studio closed, 1945; in later years ran theatrical studio for young playwrights, attended by Lyudmilla Petrushevskaya among others. Recipient: Order of the Red Banner of Labour, 1958, 1968, and 1987; State Award of the USSR, 1980; Order of People's Friendship, 1984. Died in Moscow, 20 April 1986.

Works

Collections

Pesy [Plays]   1957.
Teatr [Theatre]   1961.
Dramy [Drama]   1969.
Vybor: Sbornik piyes [Choice].   1976.
Izbrannoye [The Selection].   1981.
Selected Plays of Aleksei Arbuzov (includes *The Promise; Cruel Games; The Twelfth Hour; Lovely to Look At!; Once Upon a Time*), translated by Ariadne Nicolaeff.   1982.

Stage Works

Klass [Class] (produced Rybinsk Theatre, 1930; as *Bolishova zhizn* [Great Life], Leningrad, 1931).   1930 (stencil copies).
Trety Yan [Third Jan]; retitled *Sedtse* [Heart].   1932 (stencil copies).
Shestero lyubimykh [Six Favourites] (produced Venyovsky Kolkhoz Theatre, 1935).   In the Kolkhoz Theatre magazine, 1935?; revised version, 1958.
Dalnyaya doroga [The Distant Road] (produced by TRAM: the Central Theatre of the Working Youth, Moscow, 1936). 1936; revised edition, 1958.

Tanya (produced Red Torch Theatre, Novosibirsk, 1938). 1938; translated as *Tanya*, in *Classic Soviet Plays*, edited by Alex Miller, 1979.

Gorod na zare [Town at Dawn] (produced Studio Theatre, Moscow, 1940; revised version, produced Vakhtangov Theatre, Moscow, 1957). Revised version in *Teatr*, 11, 1957; in book form, 1957.

Bessmertny [The Immortal], with A. Gladkov (produced by the Red Army Theatre, Sverdlovsk, 1943). 1942.

Domik v Chernizove [The Little House in Cherzikov] (produced Studio Theatre, Moscow, 1943); revised version as *Domik na okraine* [The Little House on the Outskirts] (produced Mayakovsky Theatre, Moscow, 1954), 1956; further revised as *Vera, Nadezhda, Lyubov'* (produced Lenin Komsomol Theatre, Moscow, 1969).

Vstrecha s yunostyu [Meeting with Youth] (produced Comedy Theatre, Leningrad, 1948). 1948?

Yevropeyskaya khronika [European Chronicle] (produced Yermolova Theatre, Moscow, 1952). 1953.

Nakanune [On the Eve], from Turgenev's novel (produced Vakhtangov Theatre, Moscow, c.1952).

Gody stranstviya (produced Lenin Komsomol Theatre, Moscow, 1954). In *Teatr*, 3, 1954; translated as *Years of Wandering*, in *Soviet Literature* 9, 1954.

Dvenadtsaty chas (produced Ostrava Theatre, Ostrava, Czechoslovakia, 1959). In *Teatr*, 8, 1959; in book form, 1960; translated as *The Twelfth Hour*, in *Selected Plays*, 1982.

Irkutskaya istoriya (produced Vakhtangov Theatre, Moscow, 1959). In *Teatr*, 12, 1959; translated by Rosa Prokofieva as *It Happened in Irkutsk*, in *Three Soviet Plays*, 1962; as *An Irkutsk Story*, 1963.

Poteryanny syn [The Lost Son] (produced Regional Theatre of Drama, Khabarovsk, 1961). In *Teatr*, 3, 1961.

Nas gde-to zhdut [Somewhere Someone is Waiting for Us] (produced Maly Theatre, Moscow, 1963).

I vnov vstrecha s yunostyu [Another Meeting with Youth] (produced Kuibyshev Dramatic Theatre, 1964).

Moy bedny Marat (produced Lenin Komsomol Theatre, Moscow, 1965). In *Teatr*, 1, 1965; translated as *The Promise*, 1967.

Nochnaya ispoved (produced Moscow Arts Theatre, 1967). In *Teatr*, 5, 1967; translated as *Confession at Night*, 1971.

Schastlivye dni neschastlivogo cheloveka [The Happy Days of an Unhappy Man] (produced Bolshoi Dramatic Theatre, Leningrad, 1968). In *Teatr*, 4, 1968.

Skazki starogo Arbata [Tales of Old Arbat] (produced Drama Theatre ["Malaya Bronnaya" Theatre], Moscow, 1971). In *Teatr*, 9, 1970; translated as *Once Upon a Time*, in *Selected Plays*, 1982.

Vybor [The Choice] (produced in East Germany; first Soviet production, Lenin Komsomol Theatre, Moscow, 1972). In *Novy mir*, 9, 1971.

V etom milom starom dome [In This Dear Old House] (produced Comedy Theatre, Leningrad, 1972). In *Teatr*, 2, 1972.

Moe zaglyadenye (produced Russian Gorky Theatre of Drama, Daghestan, 1973). In *Moskva*, 5, 1972; translated as *Lovely to Look At!*, in *Selected Plays*, 1982.

Vecherny svet (produced Russian Theatre, Kiev, 1975). In *Teatr*, 6, 1974; translated as *Evening Light*, in *Nine Modern Soviet Plays*, 1977.

Staromodnaya komediya, with songs by Bella Akhmadulina (produced Lensovet Theatre, Leningrad, 1975). In *Teatr*, 6, 1975; translated as *Old World*, 1977; as *Do You Turn Somersaults?*, 1977.

Ozhidanie [Expectation] (produced Vakhtangov Theatre, Moscow, 1977). In *Teatr*, 7, 1977.

Zhestokiye igry (produced Griboyedov Theatre of Russian Drama, Tbilisi, 1978). In *Teatr*, 4, 1978; translated as *Cruel Games*, in *Selected Plays*, 1982.

Vospominanye (produced Red Torch Theatre, Novosibirsk, 1981). In *Teatr*, 5, 1981; translated as *Chance Visitor*, 1986.

Pobeditelnitsa [The Victorious Woman] (produced Theatre for Young Viewers, Riga, 1982). In *Teatr*, 4, 1983.

Vinovatye [The Guilty] (produced Mossovet Theatre, Moscow, 1984). In *Teatr*, 12, 1984.

Memoirs and Letters

Kakaya dolgaya zhizn: Aftoviografiya [What a Long Life: An Autobiography]. 1985.

Other

O trude dramaturga [On the Work of the Playwright], edited by Vladimir Fedorovich Pimenov. 1957.

*

Criticism

Articles:

Frederick I. Kaplan, "Love and Labor, Soviet Style: A Study of Alexei Arbuzov's *Irkutskaiia istoriia*", in *Proceedings of the Fifth National Convention of the Popular Cultural Association*, 1975.

Anna Stepanova, "Alexei Arbuzov's Theatre (Marking the Playwright's 75th Birthday)", in *Soviet Literature*, 4, 1983.

Ariadne Nicolaeff, "Aleksei Arbuzov Remembered", in *Plays and Players*, July 1986.

* * *

Aleksei Arbuzov was probably the most successful Russian playwright after Stalin's death in 1953. A man of the theatre, at first actor and director, he wrote more than 25 plays about Russian men and women living in the communist era. Most of his plays were produced and published from 1954 onwards though his first big success, *Tanya*, came in 1939 at the time of the Great Purges.

Briefly, *Tanya* has a cast of eighteen, two acts, eight scenes, and six sets. In Act I in Moscow, Tanya, a medical student drop-out, loses everything: her husband, on whom she dotes, to another woman, and then her child by him to diphtheria. In Act II, in the wilds of Siberia two years later, Tanya, now a practising doctor, saves the life of her ex-husband's child by his second wife and thereby finds herself. The last act takes place in 1938. The play was performed the same year in Novosibirsk, Siberia, and later in Moscow at the Theatre of Revolution.

It aroused a great deal of controversy because Tanya was such an unlikely, imperfect heroine in her private, domestic setting. Writing many years later about the first night, Victor Rozov, the dramatist, explained that anyone not involved in social activity at the time was considered unimportant, so Arbuzov's *Tanya* was the turning point of Soviet drama as it began to focus on the inner world, and related human behaviour to character and ethics. The audiences loved it. The critics described it as the theatrical event of the period and M. Babanova's performance as Tanya was called a supreme achievement.

To attract such attention in 1939 was, however, dangerous. But there was no hiding after the great success of *Tanya*. Arbuzov promptly founded the Moscow Studio Theatre with

Valentin Pluchek. A former pupil of Meyerhold, Pluchek later became a most distinguished director and administrator of the Theatre of Satire. At the Moscow Studio Theatre in 1939 the two men planned to create plays together with the actors as a collective. Their first play, *Gorod Na Zare* (The Town at Dawn) was staged in February 1941; it was dedicated to Maxim Gorky, the inspiration of the collective.

When Hitler's army invaded Russia, the Moscow Studio Theatre was reorganised to tour the troops. Before Stalin's death only one more of Arbuzov's plays, *Domik v Cherkizove* (The Little House in Cherkizov) was produced and only *Tanya* was published. An emergency operation in 1945 and the doctors' comments on his chances of survival, which Arbuzov overheard, made him realise how little he had achieved. The result was *Gody stranstviya* (Years of Wandering) which he wrote in 1950. It was not produced or published before 1954. No wonder that in his 70's when he was internationally famous he said: "It is extraordinary that I have survived".

There was a steady output of revised early plays and new plays from 1954. The plays are remarkably varied in form and content, giving multiple panoramas of Soviet life from many angles. Two very different plays, *Dvenadtsaty Chas* (The Twelfth Hour) and *Irkutskaya Istoria* (It Happened in Irkutsk) were published together in 1960 with an introduction by Arbuzov saying that they were linked by the same subject: time. *The Twelfth Hour* was first produced in Czechoslovakia the year before, while *It Happened in Irkutsk* was produced in three theatres in Moscow more or less simultaneously.

The Twelfth Hour has a cast of 13 guests in a naturalistic country house setting. Clive Barnes described the Oxford Playhouse production in 1964 as "pure Chekhov, 30 years later". The action takes place on 13th June, 1928, from 8 p.m. until 1 a.m. in Pavlovsk, outside Leningrad, while Nikolay Dor, his daughter, her husband and their friends and staff wait for news about whether the government will continue to subsidise Dor's factory and confectionery shops. 1928 was the end of the New Economic Policy started in 1921 to boost the economy during the post-revolutionary chaos by encouraging some private enterprise. The play's political content lies only in Arbuzov's contrast between community values and private interests in art as well as in industry and manufacture. With the news that the subsidy will not be renewed, the old bourgeois order comes to an end and the young potential new order, represented by Katenka, Ivan, and Seryozhka, led by Bezenchuk, goes striding out of *The Twelfth Hour* into the kind of world dramatised in *It Happened in Irkutsk*.

The latter, set in a Siberian town, near an industrial site, starts with a chorus and a cast of 19 standing on a platform on a revolving stage; members of the cast are prompted and directed by the Chorus in a quick succession of scenes which portray the development of a triangular love relationship in a close community: there are scenes on a small wooden bridge with a lamppost; outside the local store at closing time; next to the cinema in a public garden with a bench; and so on. It is the 1950's; Arbuzov's characters are mostly young, unpretentious, and shown going about their work and leisure with their problems and dreams.

Aleksei Arbuzov wrote in the introduction to *It Happened in Irkutsk*: "I am convinced that now, more than ever before, our life and therefore the steps we take, our thoughts and actions are our response to time and are defined by it. It is no longer the background against which humankind acts. Time is now the author of the steps man takes and therefore his destiny".

Frank Hauser, the director at the Oxford Playhouse, found that time was the subject of yet another play by Arbuzov, *Moy Bedny Marat* (The Promise). It has a cast of three. Again there is a threesome in love, but they are teenagers isolated in one room in Leningrad. The action starts during the Blockade and stays in the same room for 18 years.

Hauser wrote in *Plays and Players* (March 1967):

> Among modern great dramatists only Chekhov consistently deals with time passing . . . which may account for the haunting but impalpable kinship between Chekhov and Arbuzov. It is because Arbuzov wants to show the effect of the weeks and years on his three characters that the play is written in 14 short scenes. . . .
> The cumulative effect of the play is that we share in half a lifetime of three people.

People whose experience one shares is indeed how one thinks of Arbuzov's characters.

—Ariadne Nicolaeff

ARDEN, John. Born in Barnsley, Yorkshire, England, 26 October 1930. Educated at schools in Barnsley; Sedbergh School, Yorkshire, 1944–48; King's College, Cambridge, 1950–53, BA in architecture 1953; Edinburgh College of Art, 1953–55, diploma in architecture 1955. Served in the British Army Intelligence Corps, 1949–50: lance-corporal. Married the actress Margaretta Ruth D'Arcy in 1957; five sons. Architectural assistant, London, 1955–57; full-time writer from 1958; fellow in playwriting, Bristol University, 1959–60; visiting lecturer in politics and drama, New York University, 1967; Regents' lecturer, University of California, Davis, 1973; writer-in-residence, University of New England, Armidale, New South Wales, 1975. Founder, Committee of 100 anti-nuclear group, 1961; chairman, *Peace News* pacifist weekly, London, 1966–70; co-founder, Corrandulla Arts Centre, County Galway, Ireland, 1973; collaborated with Margaretta D'Arcy on plays for the Galway Theatre Workshop in the 1970's; founding member, Theatre Writers' Group (now Theatre Writers' Union), 1975. Recipient: *Evening Standard* award, 1960; Trieste Festival award, 1961; Vernon Rice award, 1966; John Whiting award, 1973.

Works

Collections

Three Plays (includes *The Waters of Babylon; Live Like Pigs; The Happy Haven*). 1964.
"Soldier, Soldier" and Other Plays (includes *When is a Door Not a Door?; Wet Fish; Friday's Hiding*). 1967.
Plays 1 (includes *Serjeant Musgrave's Dance; The Workhouse Donkey; Armstrong's Last Goodnight*). 1977.
The Non-Stop Connelly Show (includes *Boyhood, 1868–1889; Apprenticeship, 1889–1896; Professionals, 1896–1903; The New World, 1903–1910; The Great Lockout, 1910–1914; World War and the Rising, 1914–1916*). 1986.
John Arden and Margaretta D'Arcy: Plays 1 (includes *The Business of Good Government; The Royal Pardon; The Little Gray Home in the West; Ars Longa Vita Brevis; Friday's Hiding; Vandaleur's Folly; Immediate Rough Theatre: Sean O'Scrudu; The Hunting of the Mongrel Fox; No Room at the Inn; A Pinprick of History*). 1991.

Stage Works

All Fall Down (produced College of Art, Edinburgh, 1955).

The Waters of Babylon (produced Royal Court Theatre, London, 1957). In *Three Plays*, 1964.

When is a Door Not a Door? (produced Embassy Theatre, Central School of Speech and Drama, London, 1958). In *"Soldier, Soldier" and Other Plays*, 1967.

Live Like Pigs (produced Royal Court Theatre, London, 1958). In *Three Plays*, 1964.

Serjeant Musgrave's Dance: An Unhistorical Parable (produced Royal Court Theatre, London, 1959). 1960; revised version (produced 1972).

The Happy Haven, with Margaretta D'Arcy (produced Drama Studio, Bristol, 1960). In *Three Plays*, 1964.

The Business of Good Government: A Christmas Play, with Margaretta D'Arcy (as *A Christmas Play*, produced St. Michael's Church, Brent Knoll, Somerset, 1960; as *The Business of Good Government*, produced London, 1978). 1963.

The Workhouse Donkey: A Vulgar Melodrama (produced Festival Theatre, Chichester, 1963). 1964.

Ironhand, from a play by Goethe (produced Old Vic Theatre, Bristol, 1963). 1965.

Armstrong's Last Goodnight: An Exercise in Diplomacy (produced Glasgow Citizens' Theatre, Glasgow, 1964). 1965.

Ars Longa, Vita Brevis (for children), with Margaretta D'Arcy (produced by the Royal Shakespeare Company, at LAMDA, London, 1964). In *Eight Plays for Schools 1*, edited by Malcolm Stuart Fellows, 1965; also in *John Arden and Margaretta D'Arcy: Plays 1*, 1991.

Play Without Words (produced Glasgow, 1965).

Fidelio, from a libretto by Joseph Sonnleithner and Friedrich Treitschke, music by Beethoven (produced London, 1965).

Left-Handed Liberty: A Play about Magna Carta (produced Mermaid Theatre, London, 1965). 1965.

Friday's Hiding, with Margaretta D'Arcy (produced Royal Lyceum Theatre, Edinburgh, 1966). In *"Soldier, Soldier" and Other Plays*, 1967.

The Royal Pardon; or, The Soldier Who Became an Actor (for children), with Margaretta D'Arcy (produced Beaford Arts Centre, Devon, 1966). 1967.

The True History of Squire Jonathan and His Unfortunate Treasure (produced Ambiance Lunch Hour Theatre Club, London, 1968). In *Two Autobiographical Plays*, 1971.

The Hero Rises Up: A Romantic Melodrama, with Margaretta D'Arcy (produced The Roundhouse, London, 1968). 1969.

The Soldier's Tale, from a libretto by Ramuz, music by Stravinsky (produced Bath, 1968).

Harold Muggins is a Martyr, with Margaretta D'Arcy and the Cartoon Archetypical Slogan Theatre (produced Unity Theatre, London, 1968).

Two Hundred Years of Labour History, with Margaretta D'Arcy (produced London, 1971).

Granny Welfare and the Wolf, with Margaretta D'Arcy and Roger Smith (produced London, 1971).

My Old Man's a Tory, with Margaretta D'Arcy (produced London, 1971).

Rudi Dutschke Must Stay, with Margaretta D'Arcy (produced London, 1971).

The Ballygombeen Bequest, with Margaretta D'Arcy (produced St. Mary's College, Belfast, 1972). In *Scripts 9*, September 1972; revised version, as *The Little Gray Home in the West: An Anglo-Irish Melodrama* (produced Drama Department, Birmingham University, 1982), 1982.

The Island of the Mighty: A Play on a Traditional British

John Arden (photo by Longford)

Theme, with Margaretta D'Arcy (produced Aldwych Theatre, London, 1972). 1974.

The Devil and the Parish Pump, with Margaretta D'Arcy (produced Galway, Ireland, 1974).

The Crown Strike Play, with Margaretta D'Arcy (produced Galway, Ireland, 1975).

The Non-Stop Connolly Show: A Dramatic Cycle of Continuous Struggle in Six Parts, with Margaretta D'Arcy (produced Dublin, 1975). 1977–78 (5 vols.); 1-volume edition, 1986 (see Collections for contents).

Sean O'Scrudu, with Margaretta D'Arcy (produced Galway, Ireland, 1976). In *John Arden and Margaretta D'Arcy: Plays 1*, 1991.

The Mongrel Fox, with Margaretta D'Arcy (produced Galway, Ireland, 1976). In *John Arden and Margaretta D'Arcy: Plays 1*, 1991.

No Room at the Inn, with Margaretta D'Arcy (produced Galway, Ireland, 1976). In *John Arden and Margaretta D'Arcy: Plays 1*, 1991.

Silence, with Margaretta D'Arcy (produced Galway, Ireland, 1977).

Mary's Name, with Margaretta D'Arcy (produced Galway, Ireland, 1977).

Blow-in Chorus for Liam Cosgrave, with Margaretta D'Arcy (produced Galway, Ireland, 1977).

Vandaleur's Folly: An Anglo-Irish Melodrama, with Margaretta D'Arcy (produced Nuffield Studio Theatre, University of Lancaster, 1978). 1981.

The Mother, with Margaretta D'Arcy, from a play by Brecht (produced London, 1984).
The Making of Muswell Hill, with Margaretta D'Arcy (produced London, 1984).
A Pinprick of History. In *John Arden and Margaretta D'Arcy, Plays 1*, 1991.

Television Plays

Soldier, Soldier, 1960, and *Wet Fish*, 1961 (both published in *"Soldier, Soldier" and other Plays*, 1967) *Sean O'Casey: Portrait of a Rebel* (documentary), with Margaretta D'Arcy, 1973.

Radio Plays

The Life of Man, 1956; *The Bagman*, 1970 (published in *Two Autobiographical Plays*, 1971); *Keep These People Moving!* (for children), with Margaretta D'Arcy, 1972; *Pearl*, 1978 (published 1979); *To Put it Frankly*, 1979; *Don Quixote*, from the novel by Cervantes, 1980; *The Winking Goose* (documentary), 1982; *Garland for a Hoar Head*, 1982; *The Old Man Sleeps Alone*, 1982 (published in *Best Radio Plays of 1982*, 1983); *The Manchester Enthusiasts*, with Margaretta D'Arcy, 1984; *Whose is the Kingdom?*, with Margaretta D'Arcy, 1988 (published 1988).

Fiction

Silence Among the Weapons: Some Events at the Time of the Failure of a Republic. 1982; as *Vox Pop: Last Days of the Roman Republic*, 1983.
Books of Bale. 1988.

Other

To Present the Pretence: Essays on the Theatre and Its Public. 1977.
Awkward Corners: Essays, Papers, Fragments, with Margaretta D'Arcy. 1988.

*

Criticism

Books:
Ronald Hayman, *John Arden*, London, 1968.
John Russell Brown, *Theatre, Language: A Study of Arden, Osborne, Pinter, and Wesker*, London and New York, 1972.
Simon Trussler, *John Arden*, New York, 1973.
Albert Hunt, *Arden: A Study of His Plays*, London, 1974.
Glenda Leeming, *John Arden*, London, 1974.
Michael Anderson, *Anger and Detachment: A Study of Arden, Osborne, and Pinter*, London, 1976.
Frances Gray, *John Arden*, London and New York, 1982.
Malcolm Page, *John Arden*, Boston, 1984.
Malcolm Page (ed.), *Arden on File*, London, 1985.

* * *

A consciousness of society and politics as well as the individual informs John Arden's work as a playwright, critic, and actor. In almost any context one attempts to place him he appears, to his credit, abrasive and anomalous. Loosely implicated in the "angry young men" group of the 1950's, he

countered the commitment of their work with a resolute disengagement; as the universities have expanded to include modern drama in the syllabus of the academy, he observes the tyranny of the "literary" text of the play and the mistaken valuation of the "objective"; and as state subsidies have created a secure and, some might say, "entrenched" British theatre, Arden criticises a system where selection and production of plays are determined by a director-administrator whose policies are administrative rather than artistic. In an age where writers of all kind accept their isolation even when they do not prize it, Arden stresses collaboration—with other playwrights, and of playwrights with directors, actors, and production workers.

In an article reprinted in *To Present the Pretence*, Arden acknowledges a debt to Jonson rather than Shakespeare, distinguishing between Jonson's concrete and Shakespeare's impressionist language. But in its energy, catholicity, and virtuosity the achievement of Arden's plays is Shakespearian, while the richness of the worlds of his plays reveals a more general influence of Renaissance drama as a whole. Arden's own descriptions of this richness of content and form indicate other of its contexts: in the preface to *The Workhouse Donkey* he calls for "the old essential attributes of Dionysus" which include noise, disorder, generosity, corruption, fertility, and ease; and in *The Hero Rises Up* (about Nelson) he and Margaretta D'Arcy unfavourably contrast the rectilinear Romans with the curvilinear natives of ancient Britain who endearingly "muddle through"; both the Dionysiac and the curvilinear point to his marked preoccupation with natural man, and the modes of popular, and Brechtian, theatre.

Although the plays before 1970 share a similar kind of disengagement, and the plays afterwards show evident commitment, and though they all include prose and verse, there is no other single common language or style, as one finds in Pinter for example. A prodigious range of class, education, region, and historical period is manifest in the language of the plays. In the comedies set in the present, such as *The Waters of Babylon*, *Live Like Pigs*, and *The Workhouse Donkey*, the verse is balladic, the prose colloquial, and the mode at times melodramatic, but in some of the British history plays, such as *Left-Handed Liberty* (on the Magna Carta) and *Armstrong's Last Goodnight*, both the verse and prose are more poetic and in a high, literary style which is in part due to the strangeness to Arden's audience of medieval English and 16th-century Scots respectively. The fables, too, such as *Serjeant Musgrave's Dance* and *The Bagman*, share this poetic quality of language, which is conceived so as to be taken in on first hearing rather than only when read.

In several of his prefaces to the plays Arden links them to contemporary political situations (*Armstrong* with the Congo and *Musgrave* with Cyprus), in the way that Arthur Miller treats McCarthyism in *The Crucible*, but Arden's distance from all his characters in the earlier plays forces the audience to tolerate the more culpable characters along with the more innocent so that complete identification of the audience with the "good" is prevented; at the same time Arden provides a certain sympathy and room for imperfect men who verge on the repugnant such as Musgrave, and through this technique two recurring, rather sordid characters, Charlie Butterthwaite and Krank, take on Falstaffian proportions and complexity. But overall Arden curtails our interest in individual character and forces us to see the archetype, and the social and political implications of his characters' decisions.

The preface to *The Bagman* and the play itself chart the immediate circumstances of Arden's move from detachment to commitment in his life and work. Not surprisingly, however, even plays after this shift, *The Island of the Mighty* (on the Arthurian legends) and *The Ballygombeen Bequest* (on absentee landlordism and exploitation in Ireland) attest to Arden's virtuosity, the first being an epic of three very complex and poetic plays, and the latter a melodramatic but documented treatise.

In addition to these works, Arden has written several plays for children, opera libretti, drama for television and radio, and fascinating criticism—in the often ample prefaces to the plays and in *To Present the Pretence*.

Arden's removal to Ireland has resulted in a tendency to focus on the subject of Ireland, or subjects related to it; a further consequence of his decision to avoid English theatre productions for his plays is his curtailment of playwriting in the last decade, and his turn to fiction. Arden's portion of *Awkward Corners* is quite explicit about his and D'Arcy's decision to situate themselves in the tradition of radical literature, and to reject the (im)possibilities of "chained expression". The recent work in all its forms shows Arden's prodigious talent for language, his abiding interest in history, and his tough political vision.

—Laurel Brake

See also *Volume 1* entries on *Serjeant Musgrave's Dance; The Workhouse Donkey*.

ARETINO, Pietro. Born in Arezzo, Florentine Republic (now in Umbria), Italy, 20 April 1492. Moved to Perugia, 1508. Studied poetry and painting in Perugia. Had two daughters, the first by Caterina Sandella. First poetry published, 1512; moved to Rome, 1517, under protection of Agostino Chigi, and entered political and artistic circles; under protection of Pope Leo X and the Medici, wrote lampoons and "pasquinades" against influential and powerful contemporaries, often gaining their enmity; fled Rome on the election of Pope Hadrian VI, 1552, whom he had satirised; returned to Rome on election of Guilio de Medici as Pope Clement VII, 1523; following assault by servants of a Curia official, left Rome again; settled in Venice, 1527. Died in Venice, 21 October 1556.

Works

Collections

Teatro, edited by N. Macarrone.   1914.
The Works of Aretino (2 vols.), translated by S. Putnam.   1926.
Tutte le commedie, edited by G.B. de Sanctis.   1968.
Teatro (Volume 2 of *Tutte le opere*), edited by Giorgio Petrocchi.   1971.

Stage Works

Il marescalco (produced Mantua, 1526/27).   1533; translated as *The Stablemaster*, in *Five Italian Renaissance Comedies*, edited by Bruce Penman, 1978; as *The Marescalco*, 1986.
La cortigiana (produced Bologna, 1537).   In an edited version, 1534; in full, 1970.
La Talanta (produced Venice, 1542).   1542.

Lo ipocrito (produced Arezzo, 1545).   1542.
Il filosofo.   1546.
Orazia.   1546.

Fiction

Ragionamento della Nanna e della Antonia.   1534.
Dialogo nel quale la Nanna insegna a la Pippa.   1536.
Ragionamento de le Corti.   1538.
Le carte parlanti.   1543.
A Dialogue of Dying Well, translated by Richard Verstagen.   1603.
The Ragionamenti: The Lives of Nuns; The Lives of Married Women; The Lives of Courtesans, edited by Peter Stafford.   1971.
Aretino's Dialogues, translated by Raymond Rosenthal.   1972.
Sei giornate, edited by Guido Davico Bonino.   1975.

Verse

Opera nova del fecundissimo Giovene Pietro Pictore Aretino zoe strambotti sonetti capitoli epistole barzellette et una desperata.   1512.
Marfisa.   1532.
Stanze in loda de la Sirena.   1537.

Memoirs and Letters

Lettere (6 vols.).   Volume 1, 1537; Volume 2, 1542; Volume 3, 1546; Volume 4, c.1550; Volume 5, 1550; Volume 6, 1557.
Tutte le lettere, edited by Francesco Flora.   1960.
The Letters of Pietro Aretino, translated by Thomas C. Chubb.   1967.
Selected Letters, translated by George Bull.   1976.

Other

La Passione di Giesù.   1534.
I sette salmi della penitenzia di David.   1535.
Tre libri de La Humanità di Cristo.   1535.
Il Genesi (3 vols.).   1538.
Vita di Maria Vergine.   1539.
Vita di Caterina vergine e martire.   1540.
Orlandino.   1540.
Vita di san Tommaso signore d'Aguino.   1543.

*

Criticism

Books:
G.M Mazzuchelli, *La vita di Pietro Aretino*, Padua, 1741.
A. Luzio, *Pietro Aretino nei suoi primi anni a Venezia e la corte dei Gonzaga*, Turin, 1888.
D. Grasso, *L'Aretino e le sue commedie*, Palermo, 1900.
U. Fresco, *Le commedie di Pietro Aretino*, Camerino, 1901.
B. Stocchi, *Verga, l'Aretino, Scarlatti e Verdi*, 1941.
Edward Hutton, *Pietro Aretino: The Scourge of Princes*, 1947.
G. Petrocchi, *Pietro Aretino*, Milan, 1948.
J. Cleugh, *The Divine Aretino*, New York, 1966.
Johannes Hösle, *Pietro Aretinos Werk*, Berlin, 1969.
Paul Larivaille, *L'Aretin entre Renaissance et Maniérisme, 1492–1537* (2 vols.), Lille, France, 1972.

Giovanni Falaschi, *Progetto corporativo e autonomia dell'arte in Pietro Aretino*, Florence, 1977.

Giulio Ferroni, *Le voci dell'istrione: Pietro Aretino e la dissoluzione del teatro*, Naples, 1977.

Cesare Marchi, *L'Aretino*, Milan, 1980.

G. Petrocchi, "La fortuna europea dell'Aretino", in *Le Théâtre italien et l'Europe*, edited by C. Bec, Paris, 1983.

Christopher Cairns, *Pietro Aretino and the Republic of Venice: Researches on Aretino and His Circle in Venice, 1527–1556*, Florence, 1985.

Richard Adams, "Rhetoric and Drama: Monologues and Set Speeches in Aretino's Comedies", in *The Languages of Literature in Renaissance Italy*, edited by Peter Hainsworth and others, Oxford, 1988.

Angelo Romani, *Periegesi aretiniane: Testi, schede e note biografiche intorno a Pietro Aretino*, Rome, 1991.

* * *

Aretino rose from very humble origins in Arezzo to fame and eminence, simply by the calculated use of his pen. He operated mainly at the papal court in Rome until 1525; then, after a brief stay with the Duke of Mantua, he settled in Venice. He flattered and cajoled his chosen patrons, attacked their current adversaries, wrote outspoken letters to popes, kings and emperors, and earned from Ariosto the title of "Scourge of Princes" which has stuck with him ever since. His output ranged from Counter-Reformation devotional literature to outright pornography, everything being tackled, perplexingly, with equal apparent conviction and verbal skill.

His *Letters* tend to be seen as his crowning glory, but his comic drama is also of great significance. (He produced one tragedy, *Orazia*, printed in 1546.) He opened in 1525 with the absurd scurrilous *Cortigiana* (The Courtier's Play), combining two plots of elaborate practical jokes played on a naive Sienese who wants to become a courtier, and on a posturing Neapolitan gentleman who fancies himself as a lover. The play was clearly written for a specific audience at a specific time, and its vigorous verbal by-play is larded with topical jokes. It was not printed in its first version before 1970, and the edition which appeared in 1534 is toned down in its aspects of vaudeville performance, and re-written to fit the topicalities and preoccupations of Aretino and his readers at that later date. Meanwhile *Il marescalco* (The Stablemaster) was written for the court of Mantua, probably in 1527, and published in 1533: it is devoted to a single trick allegedly played by the Marquis of Mantua on his own homosexual stablemaster, by apparently forcing him to take a wife but in fact supplying a disguised page boy as the "bride" in Act V.

Both these early plays appear "un-classical" in structure, and owe little to Roman comedy in terms of plot. They seem to draw their inspiration more from the *beffa* tradition of practical joke in the medieval novella on the one hand; and from the harangues, dramatized dialogues, and sketches of street and court entertainment on the other. In fact a large part of both texts consists of one or two characters making speeches, to the audience or to each other: the content can be moralistic, satirical, sarcastic, celebratory, or just verbally fanciful, always supported by a level of language which is more dense and creative than that of most *commedia erudita*, though whether one would call it "poetic" is more debatable.

La Talanta and *Lo ipocrito* were both published in 1542, the former certainly being staged in Venice in the same year. The plays are named after a central character in each, Talanta being a rapacious prostitute, and the Hypocrite remaining named only by his principal characteristic. Both comedies have the surface function of detailing, in complex fictional plots, the dangers which prostitutes and religious hypocrites respectively pose to society and to individuals. But mixed in with these satirical aims, which continue to some extent the aggressive mockery of the first two plays, we find other elements sitting uneasily together for a modern reader, but foreshadowing quite separate developments in Italian theatre of the late 16th century. On the one hand, there are plots relating to marriages and family unity, traditional to classical comedy, but stretched by Aretino to such mannered lengths that one does not know whether they are to be taken at face value or as caricatures. The moral rhetoric is so stylized, the romantic misunderstandings and errors of identity so tortuous and implausible—and yet a couple of decades later plots very similar to these were to become the norm. On the other hand, Aretino cannot renounce (or knows that his audience cannot renounce) more scurrilous low-life scenes involving backchat and practical jokes. What is more, in *Talanta* in particular, there are clear hints of the nascent *commedia dell'arte*, both in certain stereotyped characters and in the dialogue structure of some scenes, which may well have been played by professional buffoons alongside the gentlemen amateurs who took the more dignified roles.

Romance and high-flown rhetoric disappear again in *Il filosofo* (published 1545), which, like *La cortigiana*, picks two fictional victims and submits them to humiliation: an unworldly scholar who pays more attention to his books than to his wife, and a young merchant who is just too gullible for his own good. The latter is given the name "Boccaccio", and both stories are reminiscent of formats in the *Decameron*: the Philosopher, Plataristotile, is like the impotent judge in Day II, Story 10, and "Boccaccio" is undoubtedly Andreuccio da Perugia in Day II, Story 5. It is against the Philosopher that the play devotes most of its aggressive satirical energy, both in the lunatic abstractions of that character's own speeches and in the comments of those who have to deal with him. Aretino's subversive relationship with Humanist and Neoplatonic culture comes out clearly, with a vigour that foreshadows Jonson's *The Alchemist*; but there is also, more unexpectedly, a plea which is both scurrilous and sympathetic for wives in general to be better treated by their husbands. This emerges, characteristically, in a long scene of harangues from female characters, again exploiting more a rhetorical relationship with the audience than a use of exemplary dramatic action.

Aretino's personal reputation was so bad by 1600 that his comedies were issued in a slightly re-written form, under altered titles and authorship. That they were reprinted at all at that period attests to their enduring influence. On the surface they are aimed firmly at a specific audience, and thus tend to date rapidly; their plots are fragmentary, and their structure over-leisurely; but their merciless satirical vein and their verbal creativity (the latter sadly rare in Italian, as opposed to English Renaissance comedy) seem to have made them hard to forget.

—Richard Andrews

ARIOSTO, Ludovico. Born in Reggio Emilio, Ferrara territory (now in Italy), 8 September 1474. Studied in the law faculty, University of Ferrara, 1489–94. Married Alessandra Benucci Strozzi in late 1520's; two earlier illegitimate children. Took a court post during the political unrest of the 1490's; captain of the garrison, Canossa, 1502–03; courtier, diplomat, and writer in service of Cardinal Ippolito d'Este until 1517; in service of Alfonso d'Este, Duke of Ferrara, 1518–33; Commissario of the Garfagnana, 1522–25. Died in Ferrara,6 July 1533.

Works

Collections

Le commedie (2 vols.), edited by Michele Catalano.   1933.
Commedie, edited by Cesare Segre.   1974.
The Comedies of Ariosto (includes *The Coffer* [prose and verse versions]; *The Pretenders; The Necromancer; Lena; The Students*), edited by Edmond M. Beame and Leonard G. Sbrocchi.   1975.
Satire e lettere, edited by Cesare Segre.   1976.
Opere, edited by Adriano Seroni.   1981.

Stage Works

La cassaria (produced Teatro Ducale, Ferrara, 1508).   1509; revised version, in verse (produced Teatro Ducale, Ferrara, 1531), 1546; translated as *The Coffer*, in *The Comedies*, 1975.
I suppositi (produced Teatro Ducale, Ferrara, 1509).   1509 or 1510; revised version, in verse, 1525; translated as *Supposes*, 1573; as *The Pretenders*, in *The Comedies*, 1975.
La lena (produced Ferrara, 1528).   1533 or 1536; translated as *Lena*, in *The Comedies*, 1976; as *La Lena*, in *Five Italian Renaissance Comedies*, edited by Bruce Penman, 1978.
Il negromante (produced 1529).   1535; translated as *The Necromancer*, in *The Comedies*, 1975.
La scolastica, completed by Gabriele Ariosto.   1547; translated as *The Students*, in *The Comedies*, 1975.

Verse

Orlando Furioso.   1515 (40 cantos); revised version, 1521; third edition, 1532 (46 cantos); additional *Cinque Canti* published in 1545 edition; translated as *Orlando Furioso*, 1591; as *The Frenzy of Orlando* (2 vols.), 1975.
Satire.   1534; translated as *Seven Planets Governing Italy*, 1611; as *The Satires*, 1976.
Two Satires.   1977.

Memoirs and Letters

Lettere, edited by A. Stella.   1965.
Lettera dalla Garfagnana, edited by Gianna Scalia.   1977.

Other

Opere minori, edited by Cesare Segre.   1954.

*

Bibliographies

Robert J. Rodini and Salvatore Di Maria, *Ludovico Ariosto: An Annotated Bibliography of Criticism, 1956–1980*, Columbia, Missouri, 1984.
Robert J. Rodini, "Selected Bibliography of Ariosto Criticism, 1980–87", in *Modern Language Notes*, January 1988.

Criticism

Books:
E.G. Gardner, *The King of the Court Poets*, New York, 1906.
C. Grabher, *Sul teatro dell'Ariosto*, Rome, 1947.
Guilio Natali, *Ludovico Ariosto*, Florence, 1966.
Walter Binni, *Ludovico Ariosto*, Turin, 1968.
Nino Borsellino, *Ludovico Ariosto*, Bari, 1973.
Robert Griffin *Ludovico Ariosto* (in English), New York, 1977.
Walter Moretti, *L'ultimo Ariosto*, Bologna, 1978.
C.P. Brand, "Disguise, Deception, and Concealment of Identity in Ariosto's Theatre", in *Renaissance and Other Studies: Essays Presented to Peter M. Brown*, Glasgow, 1988.

*   *   *

Born into a family of minor gentry in the Duchy of Ferrara and Modena, Ariosto has two claims to fame in Italian Renaissance culture. He was the author of one of Italy's uncontested masterpieces, the massive chivalric romance *Orlando Furioso*. Also, with his vernacular stage comedies modelled on Plautus and Terence, starting as early as 1508, he can fairly be said to have inaugurated modern European theatre.

The ground had been laid by Duke Ercole I of Ferrara (Este dynasty), who had systematically sponsored productions of Roman comedy in translation at court festivals, for a captive audience, from around 1486 onwards, mounting far more of such entertainments than any other Italian patron. There was a sustained avant-garde cultural policy involved, but the plays themselves, translated into very laborious verse, did not capture the audience's enthusiasm as much as was intended. Ariosto's first two original attempts, in 1508 and 1509, caused much more of a stir. They were in reasonably colloquial Italian prose, perhaps influenced by a single anonymous experiment (the brief five-act *Formicone*) produced by schoolboys in neighbouring Mantua in 1503. Their example was followed up elsewhere in Italy by Grasso and Bibbiena and Machiavelli. An initial model was thus established for *commedia erudita*, as critics now call it—a five-act secular comedy of intrigue, using a dramatic language which was mimetic rather than symbolic or poetic, in a fixed outdoor urban setting, and deriving its plot mechanisms and characters equally from Roman comedy and from scurrilous medieval *novella*. The effect on Italy and Europe was slow to begin with, but ultimately overwhelming.

After an interval due to political upheaval, Ariosto wrote and re-wrote two more comedies in the 1520's, and left a fifth unfinished at his death. He is known also to have involved himself in organizing performances of his own and other entertainments. His later comedies are all written in a kind of blank verse, and he was attached enough to this policy to re-write the first two prose ones into the same format. This is ironic, because he is responsible for establishing prose dramatic texts on the Italian stage, and the first English prose drama was George Gascoigne's *Supposes*, translated directly from Ariosto's 1509 *I suppositi*.

In the printed form which has come down to us, Ariosto's comedies show literary elegance and thoughtfulness, but also a good deal of satirical bite, and a potential for performance which has not been tested as it should have been in modern times. The first one, *La cassaria* (The Chest 1508), is set in the eastern Mediterranean (as Plautus' plays were set in Athens), and its plot is heavily derivative from Roman comedy—the basic situation of a pimp with two virgin slave

"Portrait of a Poet"— thought to be **Ariosto** (painting by Palma Vecchio, c.1515–16; National Gallery, London).

girls, whom two besotted young men want to buy from him if they can raise the cash, is based on Roman social patterns which were anachronistic. Ariosto was perhaps serving an apprenticeship here, with the ancient authors as his masters—but Plautus in particular was a good master, and the play shows enough comic and dramatic craftsmanship to stand as a creditable first attempt.

With *I suppositi* (The Substitutes) of the following year, both the central plot and the setting were brought closer to the audience's tastes and preoccupations. The "hero" has disguised himself as a servant in his mistress's house, and seduced her with a promise of marriage, while his place as a student in the community is taken by his own servant—we have, in fact, the sub-plot of *The Taming of the Shrew*, but also one much more in tune with both the romantic and the scurrilous elements in novella collections such as Boccaccio's well-read *Decameron*. Moreover, the setting was now contemporary Ferrara, where the play was being performed. This allowed room for topical jokes and satire on the one hand, and also stressed the contemporary relevance and "realism" of this new mode of drama with an explicitness not to be found in its Roman models. From that moment on, *commedia erudita* was firmly set in the world which its audience also inhabited, either in the home town or one near by; and the point was emphasized by the realistic perspective scenery which had actually been inaugurated for *La cassaria* in 1508, and which had turned the stage into an autonomous but coherent and plausible visual environment.

Il negromante (The Necromancer) was first drafted in 1520, but not performed until there was an improved version of 1528. There is a complex stylized web of forlorn loves and assumed identities (a foolish young lover determined to seduce a respectable virgin; a faithful young husband feigning impotence when "married" against his will to the same virgin), revolving round the figure of a charlatan magician whose help is enlisted by the gullible in various contrasting schemes. The plot is resolved in traditional fashion, by a series of farcical accidents and the discovery of a long-lost relative. The villainous figure at the centre gives the play more originality and spice, as Ariosto satirizes the fashion for what we would now call the "occult" (which we know from other sources he found particularly irritating). At the end of the second version, the magician is finally duped by his own servant in a way which dimly presages *Volpone*.

La lena is based more on social observation, and less on existing narrative and theatrical formats, than perhaps any other Italian comedy of the century. Lena herself is a working-class woman economically and sexually exploited by the middle-aged bourgeois Fazio, with the morally inert complaisance of her own husband, Pacifico. Acting as daily companion to Fazio's daughter, and increasingly resentful of her position, she intends cynically to allow the young man Flavio to seduce the girl in her house—provided he can pay. The accent on money-raising has links with standard Plautine plots, with Lena playing the part of the pimp. But Lena's relationships with her husband and her "protector" Fazio, which hold the stage on more than one occasion, provide a drama with no previous models and a severe implicit indictment of a corruption which was probably quite common at the time.

It is not too fanciful to see Ariosto the dramatist, in intention, as an embryonic Molière. He was formidably intelligent, had the same sharp eye for anti-social behaviour, and sometimes the same sense of fun. Inevitably he does not reach Molière's heights. He was only an occasional playwright, for all his enthusiasm, rather than a full-time professional. Most of all, in his position as initiator of a brand new mode of drama, he had to invent everything from scratch, and could not build as the Frenchman could on a well-established theatrical repertoire or on the quick response of a practised audience. This, together with his preference for a very measured verse form, makes some of his writing rather slow. In the context within which he had to operate, his comedies are, none the less, a respectable achievement, and his pioneering role should not be forgotten.

—Richard Andrews

See also *Volume 1* entry on *The Chest* (*La cassaria*).

———

ARISTOPHANES. Born in Athens, between 457 and 445 BC. May have lived or owned property on Aigina. First play produced c.428 BC; besides the 11 surviving plays, 32 other titles, some possible alternative titles, and nearly 1,000 fragments survive; known to have won several second prizes, and at least two first prizes (for *The Knights* and *The Frogs*) at the City Dionysia and Lenaea dramatic festivals; served on the *boule* (the Athenian Senate) in the early 4th century; his son, Araros, as well as producing two of Aristophanes' works, also wrote plays. Died c.385 BC.

Aristophanes (bust in Uffizi Gallery, Florence).

Works

Collections

[Comedies], edited by J. van Leeuwen. 1893–1906.

[Comedies] (2 vols.), edited by F.W. Hall and W.M. Geldart. 1901–02; second edition, 1906–07.

[Comedies; with translations], edited by B.B. Rogers. 1902–1915; texts subsequently appeared in the Loeb Classical Library series.

[Comedies], translated by William Arrowsmith and Douglass Parker. 1961–67 (Complete Greek Comedy series).

Four Comedies, translated by Dudley Fitts (includes *Lysistrata; The Birds; The Frogs; Thesmophoriazusae*). 1962.

Complete Plays, translated by Moses Hadas. 1962.

"The Frogs" and Other Plays (also includes *The Wasps; The Poet and the Women*), translated by David Barrett. 1964.

Plays (2 vols.), translated by Patric Dickinson. 1970.

Lysistrata; The Acharnians; The Clouds, translated by Alan H. Sommerstein. 1973.

The Knights; The Birds; The Assemblywomen; Wealth, translated by David Barrett and Alan H. Sommerstein. 1978.

Clouds; Women in Power; Knights, translated by Kenneth McLeish. 1979.

The Comedies of Aristophanes (parallel texts; titles published to 1990: *Acharnians; Knights; Clouds; Wasps; Birds; Peace; Lysistrata*), edited and translated by Alan H. Sommerstein. 1980—

Four Plays of Aristophanes (includes *The Birds; The Clouds; The Frogs; Lysistrata*), translated by James Mantinband. 1983.

Stage Works

Acharnes (produced Lenaea Festival, Athens, 425 BC). Translated as *The Acharnians*, in *Comedies*, 1820: several subsequent translations under same title.

Equites (produced Lenaea Festival, Athens, 424 BC). Translated as *The Knights*, in *Comedies*, 1820: several subsequent translations under same title.

Nubes (produced City Dionysia, Athens, 423 BC). Translated as *The Clouds*, in *Comedies*, 1820: several subsequent translations under same title.

Vespae (produced Lenaea Festival, Athens, 422 BC). Translated as *The Wasps*, in *Comedies*, 1820: several subsequent translations under same title.

Pax (produced City Dionysia, Athens, 421 BC). Translated as *Peace*, with *The Clouds*, 1840: several subsequent translations under same title.

Aves (produced City Dionysia, Athens, 414 BC). Translated as *The Birds*, 1830: several subsequent translations under same title.

Lysistrata (produced Lenaea Festival, Athens, 411 BC). Translated as *Revolt of the Women*, 1878; as *Lysistra*, 1911: several subsequent translations under same title.

Thesmophoriazusae [Women Celebrating the Thesmophoria] (produced City Dionysia, Athens, 411 BC). Translated as *The Thesmophoriazusae*, in *Eleven Comedies*, 1912: several subsequent translations under same title; also translated as *Ladies' Day* (1959), *The Poet and the Women* (1964).

Ranae (produced Lenaea Festival, Athens, 405 BC). Translated as *The Frogs* 1785: several subsequent translations under same title.

Ecclesiazusae (produced Athens, c.392 BC). Translated as *Ecclesiazusae*, 1833: several subsequent translations under same title; also translated as *Women in Parliament* (1929), *The Congresswomen* (1973), *The Assemblywomen* (1978), *Women in Power* (1979).

Plutus (produced Athens, 388 BC). Translated as *Plutus*, 1715: several subsequent translations under same title; also translated as *Wealth* (1978).

*

Criticism

Books:

Gilbert Murray, *Aristophanes: A Study*, New York, 1933.

C.C. Jernigan, *Incongruity in Aristophanes*, Greensboro, North Carolina, 1939.

K. Lever, *The Art of Greek Comedy*, London, 1956.

Victor Ehrenberg, *The People of Aristophanes: A Sociology of Old Attic Comedy*, New York, 1962; revised, 1974.

L.E. Lord, *Aristophanes: His Plays and His Influence*, New York, 1963.

C.H. Whitman, *Aristophanes and the Comic Hero*, Cambridge, Massachusetts, 1964.

F.M. Cornford, *The Origin of Old Attic Comedy* (edited by T.H. Gaster), Gloucester, Massachusetts, 1968.

G.M. Sifakis, *Parabasis and Animal Choruses*, London, 1971.

K.J. Dover, *Aristophanes' Comedy*, Berkeley, California, 1972.

A. Solomos, *The Living Aristophanes*, Ann Arbor, Michigan, 1974.

C.W. Dearden, *The Stage of Aristophanes*, London, 1976.

R.G. Ussher, *Aristophanes*, Oxford, 1979.

Kenneth McLeish, *The Theatre of Aristophanes*, London, 1980.

Jeffrey Henderson (ed.), *Aristophanes: Essays in Intrepretation*, Cambridge, 1981.

Carroll Moulton, *Aristophanic Poetry*, Göttingen, 1981.

Malcolm Heath, *Political Comedy in Aristophanes*, Göttingen, 1987.

Kenneth J. Reckford, *Aristophanes' Old and New Comedy*, Chapel Hill, North Carolina, and London, 1987.

* * *

The earliest comic dramatist extant, Aristophanes is our one surviving representative of what ancient critics distinguished as Old and Middle Comedy, in contrast to the New Comedy of Menander and his contemporaries from which the mainstream classical tradition of European comedy descends; but we should think rather of a single constantly and rapidly evolving genre tradition that comes to an abrupt crystallising halt around 320. He was a victim of the innovations of theatrical style and taste he pursued: his plays faded from the performance repertoire soon after his death, and their direct influence on later drama was minimal; but to modern taste their radical qualities of fantasy, topical satire, and verbal and theatrical exuberance place them among the most essential works in the genre.

Aristophanes' career was fitful, with three distinct periods: he seems to have written very little in the six years following the *Peace* (421) and the ten following the *Frogs* (405). The plays of the 420's are somewhat loosely constructed, but vigorously political and issue-centred, their satire often virulently personalised. Three particular targets recur: the impact of the war on the rural population (in *Acharnians, Peace*, the lost *Farmers*); the new radical politics of the "demagogue" Cleon and his disciples (especially in

Acharnians, Knights, Wasps); and on a more domestic level, the generation gap in lifestyle and values between Aristophanes' own contemporaries and their conservative parents (his lost debut *Banqueters*, the extant *Clouds* and *Wasps*). The fine middle plays, from *Birds* to *Frogs*, substitute new, less directly political obsessions (tragedy, myth, women) on a broader, more ambitious satirical canvas that generally resists single-issue interpretation; and they display a notably more confident handling of plot, pacing, and structure, with the parabasis shrivelling away to a ghost of its old self and the action building through a strong second half to a final climax and resolution signalled strongly in the opening minutes. The late plays are in some ways a puzzling pair, barely coherent in structure and action, with sharply reduced production values and a fast-disappearing chorus, yet intellectually among Aristophanes' most complex and sophisticated: both carefully worked-out thought-experiments in utopian social engineering, through the democratic redistribution of wealth.

Theatrically, Old Comedy differs fundamentally from the contemporary tragedy and the classical theatre tradition descended from it. Production values are higher, with a double-size chorus, spectacular costumes, and abundant props and mechanical effects. There is no overwhelming pressure towards unity and consistency in the treatment of space, time, or dramatic illusion. Characters, plot, and setting are generally contemporary rather than mythological; but realistic plots, and the naturalistic development of action and character, are squeezed out by fantastic plot premises and a dramatic logic based on thematic and comic development rather than classical cause and effect. Finally, the plays incorporate, and to a degree are constructed around, a uniquely complex repertoire of inherited formal patterns in musical, metrical, and dramatic structure. Along with the tragic prologue, *parodos* (or choral entry), and odes, we find the *agon* (or structured debate); the *parabasis* (an intricate choral medley in the middle of the play); the final *komos* (or revel); and the widespread and versatile *epirrhematic* structure of symmetrically patterned successive musical scenes.

However we categorise it, the range of humour in Aristophanic comedy is bewilderingly vast in both technique and sophistication. At one extreme we find comparatively naive visual, verbal, and conceptual types: slapstick, clowning, costume jokes; puns, bizarre coinages, punchline gags and repartee; obscenity, personal abuse, and wish-fulfilment fantasies of individual self-aggrandisement and the subversion of authority. But these jostle and combine with extremely complex, multi-layered ironic structures: elaborately extended conceits and comic metaphors; intertextual mischief and parody (particularly of tragedy, and sophistic rhetoric and thought); jokes about jokes, plays within plays, surrealistically inverted worlds within the world. Coherence is preserved partly by a generally tight concentration of theme and linear development, partly by careful attention to the timing principles of escalation and variation. Thus a frequent pattern is a series of variations on a single gag, rising progressively in both pace and absurdity, with the climax marking a transition to a new joke and a different escalating series.

Though Aristophanic comedy is strongly topical and satiric, the voice and thought of the "real" Aristophanes has proved controversially elusive. One, largely discredited, view sees a committed political and cultural conservative, ideologically pacifist and hostile to the new wave in artistic and intellectual life. Others argue for a faceless satirical opportunist who merely reflects and exploits his audience's prejudices, the pretence of *engagé* didacticism and commitment no more than an efficient genre conceit. The currently emerging compromise offers a more complex figure: politically and intellectually a Thucydidean figure, pro-Spartan and anti-demagogic by class background, but profoundly formed and fascinated by the art and thought of the sophistic enlightenment. But Aristophanes readily exploits the strong dialectical tendency in Old Comedy to explore the tensions between antagonistic forces in his society, without necessarily proclaiming a personal stance in the final verdict. An elite intellectual writer working in a genuinely popular medium, he mastered early on the versatile art of playing to all elements of the audience at once. Perhaps that is why individual critics today each find the Aristophanes they want.

—N.J. Lowe

See also *Volume 1* entries on *The Birds; The Clouds; The Frogs; Lysistrata*.

ARLT, Roberto.   Born Godfredo Christophersen in Buenos Aires, Argentina, 7 April 1900. Married 1) Carmen Antinucci in 1922 (died 1940), one daughter; 2) Elizabeth Mary Shine in 1940. Moved to Córdoba, 1920, returning to Buenos Aires, 1924; pursued career as journalist and writer; travelled to Uruguay and Brazil, 1930; first play, *Triscientos millones*, produced 1932; subsequent plays mostly produced by Leónidas Barletta's Teatro del Pueblo, Buenos Aires; visited Spain and Morocco, 1935, and Chile and Uruguay, 1941. Died in Buenos Aires, 26 July 1942.

Works

Collections

Obras (9 vols.).   1950–51.
Teatro completo, edited by Mirta Arlt.   1968.
Obras completas (2 vols.), edited by Julio Cortázar.   1981.

Stage Works

Trescientos millones (produced Teatro del Pueblo, Buenos Aires, 1932).   With *Prueba de amor*, 1932.
Prueba de amor.   With *Trescientos millones*, 1932.
Escenas de un grotesco.   In *La gaceta de Buenos Aires*, 2, 1934.
Saverio el cruel (produced Teatro del Pueblo, Buenos Aires, 1936).   1936.
El fabricante de fantasmas (produced Teatro del Pueblo, Buenos Aires, 1936).   1936.
La isla desierta (produced Teatro del Pueblo, Buenos Aires, 1937).   1938.
Africa (produced Teatro del Pueblo, Buenos Aires, 1938).   1938.
La fiesta del hierro (produced Teatro del Puebo, Buenos Aires, 1940).   1940.
El desierto entra en la ciudad (produced Teatro del Pueblo, Buenos Aires, 1942?).   1942.
La juerga de los polichinelas.   With *Trescientos millones*, edited by Mirta Arlt, 1980.
Un hombre sensible.   In *Obras completas*, 1981.

Fiction

El jugete rabioso.   1926.
Los siete locos.   1929.

Los lanzallamas.   1931.
El amor brujo.   1931.
El jorabadito (short story).   1933.
El criador de gorilas (short stories).   1941.
Novelas completas y cuentos (complete fiction; 3 vols.), edited by Mirta Arlt.   1963.

Other

Las ciencias ocultas en la ciudad de Buenos Aires.   1920.
Aguafuertes porteñas (journalism from *El Mundo*).   1933.
Aguafuertes españolas (journalism).   1936.
Nuevas aguafuertes porteñas (journalism).   1960.
Antología (includes *El jugete rabioso; El escritor fracasado; Aguafuertes porteñas; La isla desierta*), edited by David Viñas.   1967.
Un viaje terrible.   1968.
Entre crotos y sabihondos: aguafuertes porteñas.   1969.
Las muchachas de Buenos Aires: aguafuertes porteñas: Seguido de Pícaros sin historia.   1969.
El traje del fantasma.   1969.
Estoy cargada de muerte y otros borradores, edited by O. Borré.   1984.

*

Bibliographies

Horacio J. Becco, "Microbibliografía de Roberto Arlt", in *Macedonio*, 11, 1971.
Rita Gnutzmann, "Bibliografía selectiva sobre Roberto Arlt", in *Revista inter-americana de bibliografía*, 39, 1989.

Criticism

Books:
Raúl H. Castagnino, *El teatro de Roberto Arlt*, La Plata, Argentina, 1964; second edition, 1970.
Eduardo Lanunza González, *Roberto Arlt*, Buenos Aires, 1971.
Diana Guerrero, *Roberto Arlt: El habitante solitario*, Buenos Aires, 1972.

Articles:
James J. Troiano, "Pirandellism in the Theatre of Roberto Arlt", in *Latin American Theater Review*, 8, 1974.
Naomi E. Lindstrom, "The World's Illogic in Two Plays by Argentine Expressionists", in *Latin Literary Theater Review*, 4, 1976 (section on *El desierto entra en la ciudad*).
James J. Troiano, "The Grotesque Tradition and the Interplay of Fantasy and Reality in the Plays of Roberto Arlt", in *Latin American Literary Review*, 4, 1976.
David W. Foster, "Roberto Arlt's *La isla desierta*: A Structural Analysis", in *Latin American Theater Review*, 11, 1977.
James J. Troiano, "Social Criticism and the Fantastic in Roberto Arlt's *La fiesta del hierro*", in *Latin American Theater Review*, 13, 1979.
J.M. Flint, "Fantasy, the Absurd and the Gratuitous Act in the Works of Roberto Arlt", in *Neophilologus*, 68, 1984.
Jack Himmelblau, "The Argentine Avante-Garde Theatre", in *Symposium*, 39, 1985.
James J. Troiano, "Literary Traditions in *El fabricante de fantasmas*", in *Inti*, 24–25, 1986–87.

David P. Russi, "Metatheatre: Roberto Arlt's Vehicle Toward the Public's Awareness of an Art Form", in *Latin American Theatre Review*, 24, 1990.
James J. Troiano, "Love and Madness in Arlt's *La juerga de los polichinelas*", in *Confluencia*, vol. 6 no. 1, 1990.

* * *

Roberto Arlt's most significant plays are *Trescientos millones* (Three Hundred Million), *El fabricante de fantasmas* (The Creator of Phantoms), and *Saverio el cruel* (Saverio the Cruel). These works incorporate the intermingling of fantasy and reality, "Pirandellism", the world of the grotesque, social criticism, the relativity of madness, and an indebtedness to Dostoevsky. As seen in these plays, Arlt presents the fantasy world as bewitching in contrast to dull, prosaic reality. Nevertheless, to enter the realm of the imagination is to lose control and ultimately to encounter madness and death.

In *Trescientos millones* there is an intentional blending of "*fantasmas*"—phantoms or ghosts—and real characters. Arlt lists them separately, indicating that they represent different levels of reality, and then integrates them to such an extent that it becomes nearly impossible to distinguish between them. A poor servant creates a chimerical world in which innumerable phantoms are compelled to recreate the roles she conceives for them with her prolific imagination. There is considerable hostility exhibited against the servant girl, since the phantoms feel superior to her; they are repelled by her plebeian imagination. Only Rocambole, a Robin Hood-type character, originally from a series of novels by Ponson du Terrail, admires the melodramatic scenes she fabricates. Arlt juggles the various levels of reality, as he has ghosts communicating with each other and later interacting with the servant. The servant is continually pulled back to the real world by a service bell, which becomes increasingly more difficult to respond to as she is further lured into her reveries. At the end of the play, the protagonist commits suicide rather than submit herself to the sexual advances of her employer's drunken son. She is in the midst of an emotional fantasy with her imaginary daughter when this harsh interruption from the real world becomes too painful to endure.

Grotesque, dehumanized characters and the continuous confusion between what represents reality and fantasy are then major elements in the play. Death, for example, is presented as an almost comic character; everything is uncertain or perplexing in the grotesque world. Ghosts are presented as if they were more human than the supposed real characters. Arlt's social concerns are apparent in the way that the poor servant suffers degradation in both the fantasy and real worlds because of her low station in life. She is abused by her employer and sexually exploited by his son. Only the noble Rocambole admires and defends her, even after her death. Pirandello's influence is clearly evident in the play. There are rehearsals with the ghosts and the creator which echo scenes in *Six Characters in Search of an Author*, and there are parallels too with Pirandello's *Each in His Own Way*.

El fabricante de fantasmas concerns an egotistical playwright, Pedro, who, convinced of his superiority, proceeds to murder his wife, since he feels that she interferes with his creativity. He is then pursued and murdered by his own literary creations. The play is influenced by Dostoevsky's novel *Crime and Punishment*. The murderer has a "superman complex", as does Dostoevsky's Raskolnikov; he is later plagued by his conscience as is the protagonist of Dostoyevsky's novel; and the judge in Arlt's play represents Porfiry Petrovich in *Crime and Punishment* (Arlt's judge pursues Pedro after realizing that he did indeed kill his spouse).

The literary tradition of the grotesque is particularly evident in this play. The nightmarish characters created by Pedro represent his guilty conscience, which persecutes him despite his attempts to deny its existence. There is a bizarre masquerade in which the distraught protagonist unmasks a beautiful and seductive woman who suddenly is transformed into his dead wife, and then into a series of frightening creatures each time another mask is torn from her face.

The influence of Pirandello is clearly apparent in this drama too. Pedro creates a play reflecting a real-life situation which is a re-creation of his wife's murder. The inner play inspires the judge who had declared Pedro innocent to realize the playwright's guilt and consequently to pursue him. Arlt's confrontation is more subtle than Pirandello's, but the purposeful intermingling of the fictional and the real world remains similar. As in *Six Characters in Search of an Author*, the phantom characters in this play are autonomous, but only in their fixed roles.

Arlt's dramatic masterpiece is, however, *Saverio el cruel*. The play is a superb intermingling of fantasy and reality, an intriguing depiction of the relativity of madness; and the author once again exhibits his strong social awareness. A poor dairyman, named Saverio, is informed that a wealthy customer, Susana, has the insane illusion that she has been robbed of her kingdom and is being persecuted by a tyrannical colonel. The dairyman reluctantly agrees to play the role of the colonel in order to cure Susana. It becomes apparent that he has begun to accept his role as reality: he even buys a guillotine to execute his enemies. Saverio is returned to sanity when he is informed by Susana's sister that the farce has been a cruel joke intended to humiliate him. In the final moments of the play it becomes clear, however, that Susana is truly deranged: she murders the bewildered Saverio, exclaiming that he was indeed the colonel, who merely disguised himself as a dairyman.

Uncertainty and insecurity are fundamental components of the grotesque and play a major role in *Saverio el cruel*. The playwright continually dupes the spectators as the two central characters weave in and out of sanity. Arlt masterfully deceives everyone by providing spectators and characters with partial information and consequently giving them the (false) illusion of understanding the reality of the situation. The author can then startle with one astonishing revelation after another. Grotesque dream sequences intermingle with reality throughout the play.

This is the play most strongly influenced by Cervantes. Susana's derangement parallels that of Dorotea in *Don Quixote*. The Argentinean dramatist creates the same type of dubious distinction between rationality and lunacy which is apparent in Cervantes' characters such as Sanson Carrasco, Sancho Panza, and Don Quixote. There are clear parallels with the Duke and Duchess episode.

Saverio el cruel is also closely influenced by Pirandello's *Henry IV*. In Pirandello's play, Henry acquires the insane illusion that he is the King of Germany and, being wealthy, is able to surround himself with employees who act out his mad fantasy. When Henry regains his sanity, he finds that these followers become more dependent on his derangement than he. In Arlt's play, Susana's loyal friends accompany her in her supposed farce believing that she is sane. A play-within-a-play is created in Arlt's work in order to bring Susana back to sanity, and a similar inner play is fabricated in *Henry IV* to have the already sane Henry returned to rationality: the two authors create perplexing worlds in which no one can ever be sure of who is demented and who is sane.

There are, then, many influences in Roberto Arlt's plays. Nevertheless these plays are by no means pale imitations of other authors' works (indeed Arlt particularly denied the influence of Pirandello because he did not want to be compared to the many Pirandellian imitators who were inspired by the Italian's visits to Argentina in 1927 and 1933). Rather, Arlt incorporates ideas and techniques to create his own unique literary world of bizarre dream sequences and nightmarish characters, fuelled by a strong social conscience.

—James J. Troiano

See also *Volume 1* entry on *Saverio el cruel*.

———

ARRABAL (Terán), Fernando. Born in Melilla, Spanish Morocco, 11 August 1932. Educated at a school in Getafe; a military academy; Escuela Teórico-Práctica de la Industria del Papel, Valencia; studied law at the University of Madrid. Married Luce Moreau in 1958; one daughter and one son. Writer, and theatre and film director; moved to France in 1955; first-produced play, *Le Tricycle*, staged 1958; co-founder, Panic Movement, 1962; jailed for several months in 1967 during a trip to Spain; editor, *Le Théâtre*, 1968; taught at the University of California, Santa Cruz, 1971. Recipient: Lugné-Poë Prize, 1966; Society of Authors Prize, 1966; Grand Prix du Théâtre, 1967; World's Theatre Prize, 1984.

Works

Collections

Théâtre (18 vols. to 1990; vol.V published before vol.IV). 1958—
Four Plays (includes *Orison; The Two Executioners; Fando and Lis; The Car Cemetary*), translated by Barbara Wright. 1962.
Plays (includes *Guernica; The Labyrinth; The Tricycle; Picnic on the Battlefield; The Condemned Man's Bicycle*), translated by Barbara Wright. 1967.
"Guernica" and Other Plays (includes *The Labyrinth; The Tricycle; Picnic on the Battlefield*). 1969.
The Architect and the Emperor of Assyria; The Grand Ceremonial; The Solemn Communion, translated by Jean Benedetti and John Calder. 1970.

Stage Works

Oraison (produced London, 1961; produced as *Oraison*, Galerie Diogenes, Paris, 1965). 1958; translated as *Orison*, in *Four Plays*, 1962.
Les Deux Bourreaux (produced as *The Two Executioners*, New York, 1960). In *Théâtre I*, 1958; translated as *The Two Executioners*, with *The Automobile Graveyard*, 1960.
Fando et Lis (produced Paris 1961). In *Théâtre I*, 1958; translated as *Fando and Lis*, in *Four Plays*, 1962.
Le Cimetière des voitures (produced as *The Automobile Graveyard*, 41st Street Theatre, New York, 1961; produced as *Le Cimetière des voitures*, Dijon, 1966). In *Théâtre I*, 1958; translated as *The Automobile Graveyard*, with *The Two Executioners*, 1960; as *The Car Cemetery*, in *Four Plays*, 1962.

Le Tricycle (produced Teatro de Bellas Artes, Madrid, 1958). In *Théâtre II*, 1961; translated as *The Tricycle*, in *Plays*, 1967.

Pique-nique en campagne (produced Théâtre de Lutèce, Paris, 1959). In *Théâtre II*, 1961; translated as *Picnic on the Battlefield*, in *Plays*, 1967.

Dieu tenté par les mathématiques (produced as *Orchestration théâtrale*, Théâtre d'Alliance-Française, Paris, 1960). In *Théâtre VIII*, 1970.

Guernica (produced Schlosstheater, Celle, 1960). In *Théâtre II*, 1961; translated as *Guernica*, in *Plays*, 1967.

Le Labyrinthe (produced Théâtre Daniel-Sorano, Paris, 1967). In *Théâtre II*, 1961; translated as *The Labyrinth*, in *Plays*, 1967.

La Bicyclette du condamné (produced Paris, 1966). In *Théâtre II*, 1961; translated as *The Condemned Man's Bicycle*, in Plays, 1967.

La Communion solennelle (produced Dijon, 1964). In *Théâtre V*, 1967; translated as *The Solemn Communion*, in *The Architect and the Emperor of Assyria . . .* (collection), 1970.

Strip-tease de la jalousie (produced Centre Américain, Paris, 1964). In *Théâtre V*, 1967.

Le Couronnement (produced Théâtre Mouffetard, Paris, 1965). In *Théâtre III*, 1965; revised version, as *Le Lai de Barabbas*, in *Théâtre IV*, 1969.

Le Grand Cérémonial (produced Théâtre des Mathurins, Paris, 1966). In *Théâtre III*, 1965; translated as *The Grand Ceremonial*, in *The Architect and the Emperor of Assyria . . .* (collection), 1970.

Cérémonie pour un noir assassiné (produced Nancy, 1966). In *Théâtre III*, 1965.

Les Amours impossibles (produced Centre Américain, Paris, 1965). In *Théâtre V*, 1967; translated as *Impossible Loves*, in *The Drama Review*, Autumn 1968.

La Princesse (produced Paris, 1966).

L'Architecte et l'empereur d'Assyrie (produced Théâtre Montparnasse, Paris, 1967). In *Théâtre V*, 1967; translated as *The Architect and the Emperor of Assyria*, 1969.

Dieu est-il devenu fou?. In *Théâtre V*, 1967.

Les Quatres Cubes. In *Théâtre V*, 1967.

La Jeunesse illustrée (produced by the Théâtre Daniel-Sorano, Vincennes, 1967). In *Théâtre V*, 1967.

Une Chèvre sur un nuage (produced Théâtre du Bilboquet, 1966). In *Théâtre V*, 1967.

Concert dans un oeuf (produced Bordeaux, 1969). In *Théâtre IV*, 1969.

Le Jardin des délices. In *Théâtre VI*, 1969.

Bestialité érotique (produced Théâtre Alpha 347, Paris, 1969). In *Théâtre VI*, 1969.

Une Tortue nommée Dostoievski (produced Théâtre Alpha 347, Paris, 1969). In *Théâtre VI*, 1969.

Et ils passèrent des menottes aux fleurs (produced Théâtre de l'Épée, Paris, 1969). In *Théâtre VII*, 1969; translated as *And They Put Handcuffs on the Flowers*, 1973.

L'Aurore rouge et noire (produced Théâtre de Poche, Brussels, 1969). In *Théâtre VII*, 1969; part translated as *Groupuscule of My Heart*, in *The Drama Review*, Summer 1969.

La Contestation. In *Théâtre 1969*, 1969.

Le Grand Guignol. In *Théâtre 1969*, 1969.

Ars Amandi. In *Théâtre VIII*, 1970; translated as *Ars Amandi*, 1983.

Théâtre 1970: Théâtre en marge. 1970.

Théâtre 1971: Les Monstres. 1971.

Le Ciel et la merde. In *Théâtre IX*, 1972.

La Grande Revue du XXe siècle. In *Théâtre IX*, 1972.

Bella Ciao: La Guerre de mille ans (produced Théâtre du Palais de Chaillot, Paris, 1972). 1972; as *La Guerre de mille ans*, in *Théâtre X*, 1975.

La Marche royale (produced Palais des Sports, Paris, 1973). In *Théâtre XI*, 1976.

Sur le fils; ou, La Ballade du train fantôme (produced Paris, 1974). 1974.

Jeunes Barbares d'aujourd'hui (produced Théâtre Mouffetard, Paris, 1975). In *Théâtre X*, 1975.

La Gloire en images (ballet scenario; produced Bremen Opera, 1976). In *Théâtre XI*, 1976.

La Tour de Babel (produced São Paulo, Brazil, 1977). In *Théâtre XI*, 1976.

Une Orange sur le Mont de Vénus. In *Théâtre XI*, 1976.

Le Ciel et la merde II (produced Théâtre de Plaisance, Paris, 1976).

Vole-moi un Petit Milliard (produced Paris, 1977). In *Théâtre XII*, 1978.

La Pastaga des loufs. In *Théâtre XII*, 1978.

Ouverture orang-outan. In *Théâtre XII*, 1978.

Punk et punk Colégram. In *Théâtre XII*, 1978.

Le Roi de Sodome (produced Théâtre d'Edgar, Paris, 1979). In *Théâtre XIII*, 1981.

Baal Babylone, from the novel. 1980.

Mon Doux Royaume saccagé (produced Sala Villaroel, Barcelona, 1980). In *Théâtre XIII*, 1981.

Inquisición (produced Barcelona, 1980). As *Granada, Don Quichote*, 1982.

Lève-toi et Rêve. In *Théâtre XIV*, 1982.

L'Extravagante Réussite de Jésus-Christ, Karl Marx, et William Shakespeare. In *Théâtre XIV*, 1982.

Les Délices de la chair. In *Théâtre XV*, 1984.

La Ville dont le prince était une princesse. In *Théâtre XV*, 1984.

Tormentos y delicias de la carne: Homenaje a "La conjura de los necros" de John Kennedy Toole. 1985.

Bréviaire d'amour d'un haltérophile. In *Théâtre XVI*, 1986.

Apokalyptica. In *Théâtre XVI*, 1986.

La Charge de centaures. In *Théâtre XVI*, 1986.

Les "Cucarachas" de Yale. In *Théâtre XVII*, 1987.

Une Pucelle pour un gorille. In *Théâtre XVII*, 1987.

The Red Madonnna. In *Théâtre XVII*, 1987.

La Traversée de l'Empire. In *Théâtre XVII*, 1987.

La Nuit est aussi un soleil. In *Théâtre XVIII*, 1990.

Roues d'infortune. In *Théâtre XVIII*, 1990.

Screenplays

Viva la muerte!, 1971 (published with *Baal Babylone*, 1971); *The Tricycle*; *J'irai comme un cheval fou*, 1973; *L'Arbre de Guernica*, 1975; *L'Odysse de la Pacific* (*Odyssey of the Pacific*), 1982; *La Cimetière des voitures*.

Verse

La Pierre de la folie. 1963.
Le New York d'Arrabal. 1973.

Fiction

Baal Babylone. 1959; translated as *Baal Babylon*, 1961.

L'Enterrement de la sardine. 1961; translated as *The Burial of the Sardine*, 1965.

Arrabal celebrando la ceremonia de la confusion. 1966; French edition as *Fêtes et rites de la confusion*, 1967.

La torre herida por el rayo. 1983; French edition as *La Tour prends garde*, 1983; translated as *The Tower Struck by Lightning*, 1988.

La piedra de la locura.   1984.
La Reverdie.   1985.
La piedra iluminada.   1985; translated as *The Compass Stone*, 1987.
La Vierge rouge.   1986.
La Fille de King Kong.   1988; Spanish edition as *La hija de King Kong*, 1988.
L'Extravagante Croisade d'un castrat amoureux, ou, Comme un Lys entre les épines.   1989.
Humbles Paradis: Première anthologie poétique.   1985; Spanish edition as *Mis humildes paraísos*, 1985

Other

Lettre au General Franco.   1972.
Sur Fischer: Initiation aux échecs.   1973.
Carta a los militantes comunistas españoles.   1978.
Les Échecs féeriques et libertaires: Chronique de l'express. 1980.
Lettre à Fidel Castro.   1984.
Teatro, o seu demônio e beato, with Mariângela Alves de Lima.   1983.
Échecs et mythe.   1984.
Devoirs de vacances, été 85, with Jean Miotte.   1986.
La travesia del imperio, o, la guerra de las estrellas con Puerto Rico en las trincheras.   1988.
El Greco.   1991.

Editor, *Le "Panique"*.   1973.

*

Bibliographies

Joan P. Berenguer, *Bibliographie d'Arrabal*, Grenoble, 1978.

Criticism

Books:
Martin Esslin, "Fernando Arrabal", in *The Theatre of the Absurd*, New York, 1961; revised editions, 1968, 1980.
Bernard Gille, *Fernando Arrabal: Textes de Arrabal, points de vue critiques, témoignages, chronologie, bibliographie, llustrations*, Paris, 1970.
Jean Daetwyler, *Arrabal*, Lausanne, 1975.
Peter L. Podol, *Fernando Arrabal*, Boston, 1978.
Angel and Joan Berenguer, *Fernando Arrabal*, Madrid, 1979.
Thomas John Donahue, *The Theatre of Arrabal: A Garden of Earthly Delights*, New York, 1980.
Francisco Torres Monreal, *Introducción al teatro de Arrabal*, Murcia, 1981.
Luis Oscar Arata, *The Festive Plays of Arrabal*, Lexington, Kentucky, 1982.
Alain Schifres, *Entretiens avec Arrabal*, Belford, 1969.
Albert Chesneau, *Décors et décorum: Enquête sur les objets dans le théâtre d'Arrabal*, Sherbrooke, Quebec, 1984.
María S. Guiral Steen, *El humor en la obra de Arrabal*, Madrid, 1988.

Articles:
Janet Díaz Wincoff, "The Theater and Theories of Fernando Arrabal", in *Kentucky Romance Quarterly*, 16, 1969.
Alan Thiher, "Fernando Arrabal and the Theater of Obsession", in *Modern Drama*, 13, 1970.
R.L. Farmer, "Fernando Arrabal's Guerrilla Theatre", in *Yale French Studies*, 46, 1971.

John Killinger, "Arrabal and Surrealism", in *Modern Drama*, 14, 1971.
Dorothy Knowles, "Ritual Theatre: Fernando Arrabal and the Latin Americans", in *Modern Language Review*, 70, 1975.
Peter Norrish, "Farce and Ritual: Arrabal's Contribution to Modern Tragic Farce", in *Modern Drama*, 26, 1983.
David Whitton, "Arrabal's Guerrilla 'Politics'", in *Nottingham French Studies*, 22, 1983.

*   *   *

Arrabal's life and work are inextricably linked (he acknowledges the fact himself) and some biographical data are indispensable to the understanding of his plays. He was born in Melilla (Spanish Morocco) in 1932, four years before the outbreak of the Spanish Civil War. His father, a republican officer in the Spanish army, was arrested by the rebel forces on 17 July 1936, the day before Franco landed in the colony. Condemned to death, then reprieved, he was sent to a psychiatric institution from which he is said to have escaped and disappeared without trace. The son was never to see his father again, and Fernando's mother, a fervent Falangist, had denied her husband the right to kiss his children farewell, banned any reference to him, and cut his head out of all family photographs. Arrabal's theatre is a heart-rending response to the curse of having lost his father at the age of four and of having been betrayed by his mother. He then grew up in a country which cowered under a brutal military dictatorship where he witnessed corruption in the state and the army, and saw the wretchedness and poverty of the population. To these "bio-historical" circumstances, one must add the all-pervasive influence of the Catholic Church which instilled in the playwright an ever-present sense of guilt and led him to adopt an attitude of total revolt.

Arrabal's work is an exorcism, a creative effort to rid himself of his childhood obsessions, an attempt at coming to terms with the darker side of his personality by giving his obsessions an objective materialization. "Theatre", says Arrabal, "is a ceremony, a celebration bringing together the sacrilegious and the sacred, eroticism and mysticism, death and the exaltation of life". Of his dramaturgy he says, "I am obsessed by the idea of confusion, and I believe that nowadays only that which is confused is human. My theatre is realistic in the presentation of that confusion". For Arrabal the world has reached a stage of such corruption that art should try and accelerate the process of decomposition and, to help in that effort, he conceived of the "Panic Theatre", a theatre without rules, "presided over by confusion, humour, terror, chance and euphoria". "Panic" plays are a mixture of happening, tragedy, farce, sublime sentiments, and bad taste, bringing together real, sordid, magic, dreamlike characters in often nightmarish environments, "in order to provoke a sense of panic and to traumatize the spectator on the psychic as well as on the physical level".

Arrabal left Spain for France in 1955, having already written two plays in Spanish, *Picnic on the Battlefield* and *The Tricycle*. On arrival in Paris he was diagnosed as suffering from tuberculosis and was forced to spend some two years in a sanatorium. He had already met the woman who was to become his wife and collaborator, Luce Moreau, who inspired his next plays and helped him with his translation into French. According to him, he still needs her help—although he now writes directly in French—because his work is "conceived in Spanish". His first plays were published in French in 1958 and *Pique-nique en campagne* was staged in 1959, directed by Jean-Marie Serreau.

But Arrabal's career took off in earnest in the 1960's when a number of his plays were directed by the exiled Latin-American directors Victor Garcia, Jorge Lavelli, and Jérôme Savary. These three directors, and Arrabal himself, had their finger on the pulse of the period and were perfectly in tune with the upheaval that was taking place in French society, culminating with the events of 1968—an upheaval that was reflected in the theatre better than in any other art form and, most particularly, in Arrabal's plays. Garcia's *mise en scène* of *Le Cimetière des voitures* (*The Car Cemetery*) exploited the rich theatricality of the play to the full, by creating a chaotic environment for the spectators as well as the performers, with multiple stages and a broken-up seating arrangement, dotting spectators about the junkyard filled with cars reaching to the ceiling, with some even hanging from scaffolding in which most of the action took place. Arrabal has a positive attitude towards the work of his directors, urging them to "create something fabulous, even if it means betraying me".

Le Cimetière des voitures, "the Passion according to Arrabal", tells of Emanou's martyr, a 33-year-old trumpet player, whose kindness shines through the sordid rubbish dump. Betrayed by his friend Topé, he is "crucified" on the handlebar of his bicycle (a motorbike in Garcia's production) and taken away by the police. The theme of Christ's Passion is mocked, parodied, and subverted in scenes that "are alternately solemn, bizarre, tender, violent, scatological, sometimes pushed to the extreme limit of what is bearable", yet often ritualized and formalized. Such a play and such a production realize the ideal of Artaud's "theatre of cruelty".

Arrabal's published theatre includes many volumes, each one containing three or four plays, regularly performed all over the world: it would be futile to attempt to summarize them. But in transcending personal concerns, and treating with humour and derision the tragic events of the end of the 20th century, Arrabal's work testifies to post-modern man's bewilderment in a provocative and thought-provoking manner, holding up a broken mirror to our broken world.

—Claude Schumacher

See also *Volume 1* entry on *The Architect and the Emperor of Assyria*.

AUDEN, W(ystan) H(ugh). Born in York, England, 21 February 1907; emigrated to the USA, 1939; became US citizen, 1946. Educated at St. Edmund's School, Hindhead, Surrey, 1915–19; Gresham's School, Holt, Norfolk, 1920–25; Christ Church, Oxford (exhibitioner), 1925–28, BA in English 1928. Married Erika Mann, daughter of the writer Thomas Mann, in 1935. Lived in Berlin, 1928–29; private tutor in London, 1930; schoolmaster, Larchfield Academy, Helensburgh, Scotland, 1930–32, and Downs School, Colwall, Herefordshire, 1932–35 and Summer 1937; co-founder, Group Theatre, London, 1932; staff member, GPO Film Unit, London, 1935–36; travelled in Iceland with Louis MacNeice, 1936; ambulance driver with the Republican forces in Spanish Civil War, 1937; and in China with Christopher Isherwood, 1938; teacher, St. Mark's School, Southborough, Massachusetts, 1939; began long relationship with the writer Chester Kallman in 1939; served with the Strategic Bombing Survey for the US Army in Germany,

1945: major. Teacher; League of American Writers, New York, 1939, New School for Social Research, New York, 1940–41 and 1946–47, University of Michigan, Ann Arbor, 1941–42, Swarthmore College, Pennsylvania, 1942–45, Bryn Mawr College, Pennsylvania, 1943–45, Bennington College, Vermont, 1946, Barnard College, New York, 1947, and University of Virginia, Charlottesville, 1949; Neilson research professor, Smith College, Northampton, Massachusetts, 1953; professor of poetry, Oxford University, 1956–61; bought house in Kirchstetten, Austria, 1958; Ford Foundation artist-in-residence, Berlin, 1964–65; lived at Christ Church, 1972–73. Member of the editorial board, *Decision* magazine, 1940–41, and *Delos* magazine, 1968; editor, Yale Series of Younger Poets, 1947–62. Recipient: King's Gold Medal for Poetry, 1937; Guggenheim fellowship, 1942, 1945; American Academy Award of Merit Medal, 1945, and Gold Medal, 1968; Pulitzer Prize, 1948; Bollingen Prize, 1954; National Book award, 1956; Feltrinelli Prize, 1957; Guinness award, 1959; Poetry Society of America Droutskoy medal, 1959; Austrian State Prize, 1966; National Medal for Literature, 1967. D. Litt.: Swarthmore College, 1964; Oxford University, 1971; University of London, 1972; honorary degrees: Durham, Birmingham, and Kent universities, and Lafayette College, Easton, Pennsylvania. Member, American Academy, 1954; honorary student, Christ Church, 1962. Died in Vienna, 29 September 1973.

Works

Collections

The English Auden: Poems, Essays, and Dramatic Writings 1927–1939, edited by Edward Mendelson. 1977.
Plays and Other Dramatic Writings 1928–1938, with Christopher Isherwood, edited by Edward Mendelson. 1989 (volume 1 of *Complete Works*, 1989–).

Stage Works

Paid on Both Sides (produced Briarcliff College, New York, 1931). In *The Criterion*, January 1930.
The Dance of Death (produced privately, 1934; as *Come Out into the Sun*, produced Westminster Theatre, London, 1935). 1933.
The Dog Beneath the Skin; or, Where is Francis?, with Christopher Isherwood (produced Westminster Theatre, London, 1936; revised version produced Cherry Lane Theatre, New York, 1947). 1935.
No More Peace! A Thoughtful Comedy (lyrics only), book by Edward Crankshaw, from the play by Ernst Toller (produced 1936). 1937.
The Ascent of F6, with Christopher Isherwood (produced Mercury Theatre, London, 1937). 1936; revised version, 1937.
On the Frontier, with Christopher Isherwood (produced Arts Theatre, Cambridge, 1938). 1938.
Paul Bunyan, music by Benjamin Britten (produced Columbia University, New York, 1941). 1976.
The Duchess of Malfi, music by Benjamin Britten, from the play by John Webster (produced New York, 1946).
The Knights of the Round Table, from the work by Jean Cocteau (broadcast 1951; produced Salisbury, Wiltshire, 1954). In "*The Infernal Machine*" and Other Plays, by Cocteau, 1963.
The Rake's Progress, with Chester Kallman, music by Igor Stravinsky (produced Venice, 1951). 1951.

Delia; or, A Masque of Night (libretto) with Chester Kallman. In *Botteghe Oscure 12*, 1953.
The Punch Revue (lyrics only) (produced London, 1955).
The Seven Deadly Sins of the Lower Middle Class, with Chester Kallman, from the work by Brecht, music by Kurt Weill (produced City Center, New York, 1958). In *Collected Plays*, by Brecht, vol. 2, part 3, 1979.
The Play of Daniel (narration only) (produced New York, 1958). Editor, with Noah Greenberg, 1959.
The Caucasian Chalk Circle (lyrics only), with James and Tania Stern, from the play by Brecht (produced London, 1962). In *Plays*, by Brecht, 1960.
Elegy for Young Lovers, with Chester Kallman, music by Hans Werner Henze (produced Stuttgart, 1961). 1961.
Arcifanfarlo, King of Fools; or, It's Always Too Late to Learn, with Chester Kallman, from the libretto by Goldoni, music by Dittersdof (produced Town Hall, New York, 1965).
Die Bassariden (The Bassarids), with Chester Kallman, music by Hans Werner Henze (produced Salzburg Festival, 1966). 1966.
Moralities: Three Scenic Plays from Fables by Aesop, music by Hans Werner Henze (produced Cincinnati, Ohio, 1969). 1969.
The Ballad of Barnaby, music by Wykeham Rise School Students realized by Charles Turner (produced St. Johns Episcopal Church, Washington, Connecticut, 1969).
Love's Labour's Lost, with Chester Kallman, music by Nicolas Nabokov, from the play by Shakespeare (produced Edinburgh, 1971). 1972.
The Entertainment of the Senses, with Chester Kallman, music by John Gardner (produced London, 1974). In *Thank You, Fog*, 1974.
The Enemies of a Bishop; or, Die When I Say When, with Christopher Isherwood. In *Plays and other Dramatic Writings*, 1989.

Screenplays

Documentaries: *Night Mail*, 1936; *Coal Face*, 1936; *The Londoners*, 1938; *Runner*, 1962; *US*, 1968.

Television Plays

The Magic Flute, with Chester Kallman, from the libretto by Schikaneder and Giesecke, music by Mozart, 1956 (published 1956); *Don Giovanni*, with Chester Kallman, from the libretto by Lorenzo da Ponte, music by Mozart, 1960 (published 1961).

Radio Plays

Hadrian's Wall, 1937; *The Dark Valley*, 1940 (published in *Best Broadcasts of 1939–1940*, edited by Max Wylie, 1940); *The Rocking-Horse Winner*, with James Stern, from the story by D.H. Lawrence, 1941; *The Knights of the Round Table*, from a work by Jean Cocteau, 1951.

Verse

Poems. 1928.
Poems. 1930; revised edition, 1933.
The Orators: An English Study. 1932; revised edition, 1934, 1966.
Poem. 1933.
Two Poems. 1934.
Poems (includes *The Orators* and *The Dance of Death*). 1934.

Our Hunting Fathers. 1935.
Sonnet. 1935.
Look, Stranger! 1936; as *On This Island*, 1937.
Spain. 1937.
Letters from Iceland, with Louis MacNeice. 1937.
Selected Poems. 1938.
Journey to a War, with prose by Christopher Isherwood. 1939; revised edition, 1979.
Ephithalamion Commemorating the Marriage of Giuseppe Antonio Borghese and Elisabeth Mann. 1939.
Another Time (includes Spain). 1940.
Some Poems. 1940.
The Double Man. 1941; as *New Year Letter*, 1941.
Three Songs for St. Cecilia's Day. 1941.
For the Time Being. 1944.
The Collected Poetry. 1945.
Litany and Anthem for St. Matthew's Day. 1946.
The Age of Anxiety: A Baroque Eclogue. 1947.
Collected Shorter Poems 1930–1944. 1950.
Nones. 1951.
Mountains. 1954.
The Shield of Achilles. 1955.
The Old Man's Road. 1956.
Reflections on a Forest. 1957.
Goodbye to the Mezzogiorno (bilingual edition). 1958.
Auden: A Selection by the Author. 1958; as *Selected Poetry*, 1959.
Homage to Clio. 1960.
Auden: A Selection, edited by Richard Hoggart. 1961.
Elegy for J.F.K., music by Igor Stravinsky. 1964.
Half-Way. 1965.
About the House. 1965.
The Twelve, music by William Walton. 1966.
Marginalia. 1967.
Collected Shorter Poems 1927–1957. 1966.
River Profile. 1967.
Selected Poems. 1968.
Collected Longer Poems. 1968.
Two Songs. 1968.
A New Year Greeting, with *The Dance of the Solids*, by John Updike. 1969.
City Without Walls and Other Poems. 1969.
Natural Linguistics. 1970.
Academic Graffiti. 1971.
Epistle to a Godson and Other Poems. 1972.
Auden / Moore: Poems and Lithographs, edited by John Russell. 1974.
Poems, lithographs by Henry Moore, edited by Vera Lindsay. 1974.
Thank You, Fog: Last Poems. 1974.
Collected Poems, edited by Edward Mendelson. 1976.
Sue. 1977.
Selected Poems. 1979.

Other

Education Today—and Tomorrow, with T.C. Worsley. 1939.
The Intent of the Critic, with others, edited by Donald A. Stauffer. 1941.
Poets at Work: Essays Based on the Modern Poetry Collection at the Lockwood Memorial Library, University of Buffalo, with others, edited by Charles D. Abbott. 1948.
The Enchafèd Flood; or, The Romantic Iconography of the Sea. 1950.
Making, Knowing and Judging. 1956.
"The Dyer's Hand" and Other Essays. 1962.

Selected Essays.   1964.
Worte und Noten: Rede zur Eröffnung der Salzburger Festpiele 1968.   1968.
Secondary Worlds.   1969.
A Certain World: A Commonplace Book.   1970.
Forewords and Afterwords, edited by Edward Mendelson. 1973.
The Prolific and the Devourer (aphorisms), in *Antaeus 42*, Summer 1981.

Editor, with Charles Plumb, *Oxford Poetry 1926.*   1926.
Editor, with C. Day Lewis, *Oxford Poetry 1927.*   1927.
Editor, with John Garrett, *The Poet's Tongue: An Anthology* (2 vols.).   1935.
Editor, *The Oxford Book of Light Verse.*   1938.
Editor, *A Selection from the Poems of Alfred, Lord Tennyson.*   1944; as *Tennyson: An Introduction and a Selection*, 1946.
Editor, *The American Scene, Together with Three Essays from Portraits of Places*, by Henry James.   1946.
Editor, *Slick But Not Streamlined: Poems and Short Pieces*, by John Betjeman.   1947.
Editor, *The Portable Greek Reader.*   1948.
Editor, with Norman Holmes Pearson, *Poets of the English Language* (5 vols.).   1950.
Editor, *Selected Prose and Poetry*, by Edgar Allan Poe. 1950.
Editor, *The Living Thoughts of Kierkegaard.*   1952; as *Kierkegaard*, 1955.
Editor, with Chester Kallman and Noah Greenberg, *An Elizabethan Song Book: Lute Songs, Madrigals, and Rounds.*   1955.
Editor, *The Faber Book of Modern American Verse.*   1956; as *The Criterion Book of Modern American Verse*, 1956.
Editor, *Selected Writings of Sydney Smith.*   1956.
Editor, *Van Gogh: A Self-Portrait: Letters Revealing His Life as a Painter.*   1961.
Editor, with Louis Kronenberger, *The Viking Book of Aphorisms: A Personal Selection.*   1962; as *The Faber Book of Aphorisms*, 1964.
Editor, *A Choice of de la Mare's Verse.*   1963.
Editor, *The Pied Piper and Other Fairy Tales*, by Joseph Jacobs.   1963.
Editor, *Selected Poems*, by Louis MacNeice.   1964.
Editor, with John Lawlor, *To Nevill Coghill from Friends.* 1966.
Editor, *Selected Poetry and Prose*, by Byron.   1966.
Editor, *Nineteenth Century British Minor Poets.* 1966; as *Nineteenth Century Minor Poets*, 1967.
Editor, *G.K. Chesterton: A Selection from His Non-Fictional Prose.*   1970.
Editor, *A Choice of Dryden's Verse.*   1973.
Editor, *George Herbert: Poems and Prose.*   1973.
Editor, *Selected Songs of Thomas Campion.*   1973.

Translator, with Elizabeth Mayer, *Italian Journey 1786–1788*, by Goethe.   1962.
Translator, with Leif Sjöberg, *Markings*, by Dag Hammarskjöld.   1964.
Translator, with Paul B. Taylor, *Völupsá: The Song of the Sybil*, with an Icelandic text edited by Peter H. Salus and Paul B. Taylor.   1968.
Translator, with Paul B. Taylor, *The Elder Edda: A Selection*, edited by Peter H. Salus.   1969.
Translator, with Leif Sjöberg, *Selected Poems*, by Gunnar Ekelöf.   1971.
Translator, with Elizabeth Mayer and Louise Bogan, *The Sorrows of Young Werther, and Novella*, by Goethe. 1971.
Translator, with Leif Sjöberg, *Evening Land / Aftonland*, by Pär Lagerkvist.   1975.
Translator, *The Rise and Fall of the City of Mahagonny*, with Chester Kallman, from the libretto by Brecht, music by Kurt Weill.   1976.
Translator, with Paul B. Taylor, *Norse Poems.*   1981.

*

Bibliographies

B.C. Bloomfield and Edward Mendelson, *Auden: A Bibliography 1924–1969*, Charlottesville, Virginia, 1972.
Martin E. Gingerich, *Auden: A Reference Guide*, Boston, 1977.

Criticism

Books:
Monroe K. Spears (ed.), *Auden: A Collection of Critical Essays*, Englewood Cliffs, New Jersey, 1964.
George T. Wright, *W.H. Auden*, New York, 1969; revised edition, 1981.
John Fuller, *A Reader's Guide to Auden*, New York, 1970.
Samuel Hynes, *The Auden Generation: Literature and Politics in England in the 1930's*, New York, 1976.
Charles Osborne, *Auden: The Life of a Poet*, New York, 1979.
Humphrey Carpenter, *W.H. Auden: A Biography*, London, 1981.
Edward Mendelson, *Early Auden*, 1981.
Donald Mitchell, *Britten and Auden in the Thirties*, London, 1981.
Edward Callan, *Auden: A Carnival of Intellect*, New York, 1983.
John Haffenden (ed.), *Auden: The Critical Heritage*, London, 1983.
Michael J. Sidnell, *Dances of Death: The Group Theatre of London in the Thirties*, London, 1984.
Stan Smith, *W.H. Auden*, Oxford 1985.
Alan Bold (ed.), *Auden: The Far Interior*, London, 1985.
Katherine Bucknell and Nicholas Jenkins (eds.), *Auden: The Map of All My Youth: Early Works, Friends, and Influences*, Oxford, 1990.

Articles:
Edward Callan, "W.H. Auden's Plays for the Group Theatre: From Revalation to Revelation", in *Comparative Drama*, 12, 1978–79.
Robert Medley, "The Group Theatre 1932–39: Rupert Doone and W.H. Auden", in *London Magazine*, vol.20 no.10, 1980.

*   *   *

W.H. Auden and Christopher Isherwood were two of the most highly thought of young writers of the 1930's, Auden winning an immediate reputation with his first volumes of poetry, *Poems, The Orators*, and *Look, Stranger!*, and Isherwood attracting much attention with his highly autobiographical works, the early novel *All the Conspirators* (1932), the Sally Bowles stories, and, perhaps his finest novel, *Mr. Norris Changes Trains.*
    In the mid-1930's the two writers collaborated on several plays which appeared to signal that Renaissance of verse-drama for which critics were ever on the look-out. Most of their plays were produced by the Group Theatre, an avant-

garde independent theatre company formed in London in 1932 by Rupert Doone and a group of friends anxious to pioneer a more intellectually and socially committed theatre. The Group Theatre attracted the talents of artists like the director Tyrone Guthrie and the painter Robert Medley, and through to its closure in 1939 was to produce much of the most innovative literary drama of the inter-war years, particularly poetic drama.

The Group Theatre project was partly influenced by the European-wide revival of interest in poetic drama and by the example of German Expressionist theatre, but there was a strong wish too to treat political matters in a medium that enjoyed both immediacy and a large educated audience. The political sympathies of Auden and Isherwood at this time also lay with the left, and their plays have a broad socialist inclination. Their theatrical collaboration ceased with their departure to the United States shortly before the outbreak of World War II, and neither was to be significantly involved in playwriting again. In part, the switch of interest away from theatre may have coincided with political disillusionment; certainly Auden's experience in 1938 of the civil war in Spain helped rapidly to terminate his left-wing political enthusiasm.

Auden's early work reflected the influence of T.S. Eliot's poetry in its easy colloquial manner and disposition to the conversational, and his first playlet, *Paid on Both Sides*, was clearly shaped by the tone and language of pieces like Eliot's Sweeney poems. A short piece, with the left-wing slant that was a feature of nearly all his dramatic and non-dramatic verse in the 1930's, was not, however, a play intended for stage presentation. His first play proper was the one-act *The Dance of Death*, a satirical attack on the capitalism which Auden saw as responsible for the effects of the Depression. The play was a plea for solidarity in the socialist camp in order to mount effective opposition to capitalism. Auden deliberately chose highly theatrical means, like scenic colour, music, and dance, to give it strong audience appeal and to signal the novelty of the enterprise; indeed, Rupert Doone called it a political ballet, a charade with music. *The Dance of Death* was performed in a double bill with a mystery play about Noah, *The Deluge*, adapted from a 14th-century Chester play. In the programme notes Auden's experiment was called "a political-musical comedy", and a production note gave a brief explication of the action:

> DEATH appears as a dancer. THE ANNOUNCER is fate and also Death's mouthpiece. Death symbolises that decay which exists within a class of society. Always inspired and always betrayed by the death inside them, this class pursue at first one Utopia and then another without really wanting new life because secretly they desire the old.

Auden first began to collaborate with Isherwood in 1935. From later and incidental comments it would seem that Isherwood brought a theatrical sense and a knowledge of dramatic construction to their plays, while Auden contributed satirical wit, verbal fluency, and a skill at turning effective lyrics. Together their collaboration was to produce three plays of considerable importance.

The first piece they came up with was called, to begin with, *The Chase*, then *Where is Francis?*, and finally given the title it now bears, *The Dog Beneath the Skin*. Decidedly political, including mocking criticism of capitalism, Fascism, and materialism, the play owes a great deal, as do the later pieces, to contemporary German cabaret sketches: it consists of short, episodic scenes, crisp colloquial prose and verse dialogue, music, and comic antics. This first play was a satirical comedy, dealing with the search of a young man, Alan

Norman, for the missing explorer, Sir Francis, who had disappeared some years before. The parable shows the young man in pursuit of ethical, social, and political principles, in the course of which the proffered values of bourgeois society and its institutions are held up to ridicule. The play is a sharp intellectual satire on contemporary political and social abuses, but too often the tone smacks of a sixth-form *jeu d'esprit*. *The Dog* was directed by Rupert Doone, with a musical score by Herbert Murill, and some of the actors who appeared in it had previously been in Auden's *The Dance of Death*.

The second product of the collaboration was *The Ascent of F6*, a brilliantly cruel indictment of imperialism and opportunism in modern bourgeois, capitalist society, with the main motive, the exploration of the disputed mountain F6, giving the authors an opportunity to satirise press, media, government, the Church, and the sentimentality of the lower-middle class. Notwithstanding its experimental manner, it had a distinctly realistic flavour, not least in the details of a mountaineering expedition.

The play was very successful and produced several times, notably at the Maddermarket Theatre, Norwich, and the Birmingham Repertory Theatre, in 1938; and at the Old Vic Theatre, London, on 27 June, 1939, directed by Rupert Doone, with Alec Guiness playing the lead role of the mountaineer, Michael F. Ransom. Audiences found the play much easier to cope with than the structurally somewhat anarchic *Dog*: it was less bewilderingly pantomimic, its theme was more immediately related to the real world, its satire more readily perceptible, and its sentiments more in tune with current tastes. It was to be the most successful of the Auden and Isherwood plays.

While the production of *The Ascent of F6* was in preparation, Auden visited Spain; on his return he and Isherwood planned a new joint work—a revue. But what they actually wrote was their last play, *On the Frontier*, a serious drama, conspicuously less jokily satirical than their earlier work, warning of the futility of war in the absence of firm principles. It seems to reflect something of Auden's own disillusionment with Communism and the Spanish Civil War. But if more mature and considered than the earlier plays, it lacked their vitality and theatrical *brio*, and, although much rewritten, was the least successful of their plays. Part of the difficulty it seems, to judge from their own comments and those of their Group Theatre contemporaries, was that Auden and Isherwood merely flirted with the theatre: neither had much interest in it; both had other projects with which they were much more engaged. Isherwood wrote no more theatre plays, but turned his dramatic talents to scriptwriting in Hollywood; Auden did occasional literary work for the theatre, like *Paul Bunyan* (a choral operetta), a version of Webster's *The Duchess of Malfi* for the New York stage, and (with Chester Kallman) the libretto for Stravinsky's *The Rake's Progress*, but he, too, wrote no more plays. The Auden–Isherwood experiment with a new poetic drama petered out, but it remains one of several interesting "little theatre" attempts between the two world wars to give intellectual and artistic vitality to a British theatre verbally dead, scenically hidebound, and too much dominated by commercial considerations.

—Kenneth Richards

See also *Volume 1* entry on *The Ascent of F6*.

AUDIBERTI, Jacques.   Born in Antibes, France, 25 March 1899. Educated at the Collège d'Antibes. Worked as a journalist after leaving college; moved to Paris, 1924; wrote for *Le Journal* and *Le Petit Parisien*; first volume of verse, *L'Empire et la trappe*, published 1930; first-produced play, *Quoat-Quoat*, staged 1946; frequently collaborated with the stage director Georges Vitaly. Recipient: Prix Mallarmé, 1935; Académie Française Grand Prix de Littérature, 1964; Grand Prix des Lettres, 1965; Prix des Critiques, 1965. Died in Paris, 10 July 1965.

Works

Collections

Théâtre (5 vols.).   1948–62:
1. *Quoat-Quoat; L'Ampélour; Les Femmes de boeuf; Le Mal court.* 1948.
2. *Pucelle; La Fête noire; Les Naturels de Bordelais.* 1952.
3. *La Logeuse; Opéra parlé; Le Ouallou; Altanima.* 1956.
4. *Coeur à cuir; Le Soldat Dioclès: La Fourmi dans le corps; Les Patients; L'Armoire classique; Un Bel Enfant).* 1961.
5. *Pomme, pomme, pomme; Bâton et ruban; Boutique fermée; La Brigitta.* 1962.

Stage Works

La Fête noire (produced Théâtre de la Huchette, Paris, 1948). As *La Bête noire*, 1945; as *La Fête noire*, in *Théâtre 2*, 1952.
Quoat-Quoat (produced Théâtre de la Gaîte-Montparnasse, Paris, 1946). In *Théâtre 1*, 1948.
Sa Peau (produced Théâtre des Noctambules, Paris, 1947).
Le Mal court (produced Théâtre de Poche, Paris, 1947). 1947.
Les Femmes de boeuf (produced Comédie-Française, Paris, 1948). In *Théâtre 1*, 1948.
L'Ampélour (produced Théâtre des Noctambules, Paris, 1950). In *Théâtre 1*, 1948.
Pucelle (produced Théâtre de la Huchette, Paris, 1950). 1950.
Les Naturels de Bordelais (produced Théâtre La Bruyère, Paris, 1953). In *Théâtre 2*, 1952.
Opéra parlé (produced at the Festival des Nuits, Bourgogne, 1956). In *Théâtre populaire*, 10, 1954; in book form, in *Théâtre 3*, 1956; as *La Hoberaute*, 1959.
Le Cavalier seul (produced Compagnie du Cothurne, Lyon, 1964). 1955.
La Logeuse (produced Théâtre de l'Oeuvre, Paris, 1960). In *Théâtre 3*, 1956.
Le Ouallou (produced Théâtre La Bruyère, Paris, 1957). In *Théâtre 3*, 1956.
Altanima. In *Théâtre 3*, 1956.
La Mégère apprivoisée, from *The Taming of the Shrew* by Shakespeare (produced Théâtre de l'Athénée, 1957). 1957.
Les Carabiniers, from a play by Baniamino Joppolo (produced Théâtre d'Aujourd'hui, Paris, 1958).
L'Effet Glapion (produced Théâtre La Bruyère, 1959). 1959.
La Fourmi dans le corps (produced Landestheater, Darmstadt, 1961). In *Théâtre 4*, 1961.
Les Patients. In *Théâtre 4*, 1961.
L'Armoire classique. In *Théâtre 4*, 1961.
Un Bel Enfant. In *Théâtre 4*, 1961.
Coeur à cuir. In *Théâtre 4*, 1961.

Le Soldat Dioclès. In *Théâtre 4*, 1961.
Pomme, Pomme, Pomme (produced Théâtre La Bruyère, Paris, 1962). In *Théâtre 5*, 1962.
Boutique fermée. In *Théâtre 5*, 1962.
La Brigitta (produced Théâtre de l'Athénée, Paris, 1962). In *Théâtre 5*, 1962.
La Guérite (produced Frankfurt, 1967). In *Nouvelle Revue francaise*, 132, December 1963.
L'Opéra du monde, from the novel (produced Théâtre de Lutèce, Paris, 1965).
La Poupée (scenario with dialogues). 1962; revised version (produced Théâtre de Huitième, Paris, 1968), 1969.

Radio Plays

Bâton et ruban (published in *Théâtre 5*, 1961).

Verse

L'Empire et la trappe.   1930.
Race des hommes.   1937.
Des Tonnes de semence.   1941.
Toujours.   1943.
Vive Guitare.   1946.
La Pluie sur les boulevards.   1950.
Rempart.   1953.
Lagune hérissée.   1958.
Ange aux entrailles.   1964.
Poésies 1934–1943.   1976.

Fiction

Abraxas.   1938.
Septième.   1939.
Urujac.   1941.
Carnage.   1942.
Le Retour du divin.   1943.
La Nâ.   1944.
L'Opéra du monde.   1947.
Monorail.   1947.
Talent.   1947.
Le Victorieux.   1947.
Cent jours.   1950.
Le Maître de Milan.   1950.
Marie Dubois.   1952.
Les Jardins et les fleuves.   1954.
La Beauté et l'amour.   1955.
La Poupée.   1956.
Infanticide préconisé.   1958.
Les Tombeaux ferment mal.   1963.

Memoirs and Letters

Dimanche m'attend.   1965.

Other

La Nouvelle Origine.   1942.
La Fin du monde.   1943.
Les Médecins ne sont pas des plombiers.   1948.
Le Globe dans la main 1: L'Amour.   1950.
Le Globe dans la main 2: La Médicine.   1951.
L'Ouvre-Boîte, with Camille Bryen.   1952.
Molière dramaturge.   1954.
L'Abhumanisme.   1955.
Les Enfants naturels.   1956.
Le Sabbat ressuscité.   1957.

"La Fin du monde" et autres récits.   1984.

*

Criticism

Books:

André Deslandes, *Audiberti*, Paris, 1964.

George E. Wellwarth, "Jacques Audiberti: The Drama of the Savage God", in his *The Theater of Protest and Paradox* (revised edition), New York, 1971.

G.D. Farcy, *L'Oeuvre théâtrale d'Audiberti, dramaturgie et cosmogonie*, Paris, 1973.

Michel Giroud, *Jacques Audiberti*, Paris, 1973.

Jeanyves Guérin, *Le Théâtre d'Audiberti et le baroque*, Paris, 1976.

Constantin Toloudis, *Jacques Audiberti*, Boston, 1980.

Gérard-Denis Farcy, *Les Théâtres d'Audiberti*, Paris, 1988.

Articles:

"Hommage à Jacques Audiberti" in *Nouvelle Revue Française,* 156, 1965 (special edition).

Wolfgang F. Sohlich, "The Theater of Jacques Audiberti: The Player and the Playwright", in *Revue des langues vivantes*, 43, 1977.

Jacques Audiberti—Numéro spécial (Collection du Répertoire du Nouveau Théâtre National de Marseille, nos. 8–9), Marseilles, 1980.

*   *   *

Poet, novelist, essayist, and playwright, Jacques Audiberti preferred the theatre to the other forms of artistic expression that he practised. He felt that this was the medium through which it was the easiest for him to make contact with the public. He considered the theatre to be a courtroom, "le tribunal", where the audience judged what they saw on the stage.

Audiberti had a vision for the threatre—a theory—as did Antonin Artaud. Both authors had experience with surrealism, they were both attracted by the exotic, and both generally refused to be associated with any political faction or doctrine. However, whereas Artaud has influenced and revolutionized 20th-century theatre on an international scale, the vision of Jacques Audiberti and his work remain virtually unknown outside of France.

Audiberti's poems and novels received a lukewarm reception. His plays achieved a more positive recognition. Audiberti attempted to gather his entire literary work under the philosophical umbrella of "Abhumanism". Although Audiberti's first play, *Ampélour*, was written in 1937, he began to formulate his philosophical theory in the 1940's, and it eventually culminated in the essay entitled "Abhumanism". Audiberti's theory states that man is a part of nature, and that mankind exists in a world where there is a delicate balance between good and evil. For Audiberti the "good" is expressed by everything that has remained in a raw and unrefined state, and that is natural. This includes such things as mountains, forests, trees, lakes, and those living a peasant or provincial lifestyle. The "bad" is all that results from mankind's constant frustration with the human condition; all that is in opposition to nature. In his plays, Audiberti applied his theory by acutely focusing the themes of the dramas upon good and evil. In the 1960's he deduced that Abhumanism had failed, and to date Audiberti's "philosophy" has only been studied in an attempt to achieve insight into his literary works.

In his attempt to make an individual and innovative statement in the 20th-century theatre, Audiberti followed the example of other avant-garde playwrights by not restricting himself to any rules of formal structure. Using any quotidian place or event as a source of inspiration, Audiberti sought to present original themes with imaginative dialogue. Nevertheless, he perpetuated a long-standing tradition of rhetoric in the French theatre. Often the spectator or reader is conscious of long-winded passages of dialogue that are not integral to the essential propositions of the play.

In 1946 *Quoat-Quoat*, Audiberti's first play to be staged, was presented by the aspiring and ambitious young director André Reybaz. The prevailing theme is one of suffering and the desire to escape from this suffering. The central character, Amédée, a secret agent en route by ship to Mexico, becomes trapped in a complicated plot of intrigue, love, and spies. Amédée chooses death as an escape from his impossible situation. The production was unsuccessful, receiving small houses and poor reviews; Audiberti claimed that he wrote *Quoat-Quoat* as a playable short story with dialogue; he did not intend it to be staged. Postwar audiences were not appreciative of a philosophy with escapist overtones that proposed death as a release from suffering. Also, the left-wing intellectual audience was aware of the fact that Audiberti had continued his profession as journalist during the German Occupation of France. When the play was revived by Georges Vitaly in 1968, it received popular acclaim, not only due to Vitaly's energetic *mise-en-scène*, but also because the audience of a new generation could overlook the author's personal history and consider the play more calmly as escapist fantasy.

Both "Evil is Running Out" and "A Brief Evil" are utilized as English titles for Audiberti's next play, *Le Mal court*. In it an evil world of political intrigue and treachery pervades the 18th-century court of King Parfait. His daughter, Princess Alarica, who is both a moral and a physical virgin, is the sole "good" personage. Eventually she, too, succumbs to "evil" as she acquires experience and knowledge. In the end, there is no innocence left in the kingdom. In this near neoclassical structure, where a continuity of action, place, and time exist during the course of the three acts, the language is baroque and lyrical. The play is appropriately subtitled a "philosophical operetta".

Georges Vitaly directed *Le Mal court* for the first time in 1947 with the reknowned Suzanne Flon in the role of Alarica. Her interpretation was more subdued than the more wily and sexually provocative portrayal given in a subsequent revival in 1963 by Sylvia Montfort. Both interpretations, however, were valid and engaging: they illustrated the inherent flexibility and vitality of Audiberti's dramatic text, while remaining true to the initial theme of the constant struggle of evil over good.

Out of Audiberti's repertoire of plays, the third significant one is *La Fourmi dans le corps*. Here the Audibertian heroine, Pic Saint-Pop, is once again tempted and taunted by the diametrically opposed forces of good and evil. She transcends fundamental and quotidian desires, and takes evil and suffering upon herself so as to alleviate the burden for the rest of humanity. Her struggle takes on a universal dimension. The Comédie-Française mounted the initial production of *La Fourmi dans le corps*—a significant development in Audiberti's career. Now he was an author important enough to be considered part of the French theatrical establishment.

Audiberti's plays have entertained through their lyrical and poetic use of language, even though the style at times appears labored. His characterizations are developed and imaginative, and his philosophical propositions are original and provocative. Acclaim of his *oeuvre* came not without reservation and hesitation by the French public, but despite his now respected position in 20th-century French theatre, Jacques Audiberti has not been translated into English.

—Ludvika Popenhagen

AUGIER, (Guillaume-Victor-) Émile. Born in Valence, France, 17 September 1820. Family moved to Paris, 1828. Educated at the Lycée Louis-le-Grand; studied law, 1840–43. Married Laure Lambert, 1873; joined law firm, 1843; librarian for the Duc d'Aumale (a former schoolfriend), 1848; first play, *La Ciguë*, produced 1848; co-editor of *Le Specteur républicain*, from 1848; member of the regional government at Drôme, 1852–55. Elected to the Académie Française, 1857. Made Commandeur of the Légion d'Honneur, 1868. Died in Paris, 30 October 1889.

Works

Collections

Poésies complètes. 1852.
Théâtre complet (7 vols.). 1889.

Stage Works

La Ciguë (produced Théâtre de l'Odéon, Paris, 1844). 1844; translated as *The Love of Hyppolita*, 1881.

Émile Augier (portrait by Talabert, 1883).

Un Homme de bien (produced Comédie-Française, Paris, 1845). 1845.
L'Aventurière (produced Comédie-Française, Paris, 1848). 1848; translated as *Her Last Stake*, 1882; as *Home*, 1893.
L'Habit vert with Alfred de Musset (produced Théâtre des Variétés, Paris, 1849). 1849; translated as *The Green Coat*, 1914.
Gabrielle (produced Comédie-Française, Paris, 1849). 1850; translated as *Good for Evil* (as *Home Truths*, produced 1860), 1860.
Le Joueur de flûte (produced Comédie-Française, Paris, 1850). 1897.
Sapho (opera), with music by Gounod (produced Théâtre de l'Opéra, Paris, 1851). 1851.
La Chasse au roman, with Jules Sandeau. 1851.
Les Méprises de l'amour. 1852.
Diane (produced Comédie-Française, Paris, 1852). 1852.
Philiberte (produced Théâtre du Gymnase, Paris, 1853). 1853.
La Pierre de touche, with Jules Sandeau (produced Comédie-Française, Paris, 1853). 1854.
Le Gendre de M. Poirier, with Jules Sandeau (produced Théâtre du Gymnase, Paris, 1854). 1854; translated as *Monsieur Poirier's Son-in-Law*, 1915.
Le Mariage d'Olympe (produced Théâtre du Vaudeville, Paris, 1855). 1855; translated as *The Marriage of Olympe*, 1915.
La Ceinture dorée (produced Théâtre du Gymnase, Paris, 1855). 1855.
Les Lionnes pauvres, with Édouard Foussier (produced Théâtre du Vaudeville, Paris, 1858). 1858; translated as *A False Step*, 1879.
La Jeunesse (produced Théâtre de l'Odéon, Paris, 1858). 1858.
Un Beau Mariage, with Édouard Foussier. 1859.
Les Effrontés (produced Comédie-Française, Paris, 1861). 1861; translated as *Faces of Brass*, 1888.
Le Fils de Giboyer (produced Comédie-Française, Paris, 1862). 1863.
Maître Guérin (produced Comédie-Française, Paris, 1864). 1865.
La Contagion (produced Théâtre de l'Odéon, Paris, 1866). 1866.
Paul Forestier (produced Comédie-Française, Paris, 1868). 1868; translated as *Paul Forrester*, 1871.
Le Post-scriptum (produced Comédie-Française, Paris, 1869). 1869; translated as *The Post-Scriptum*, 1915.
Lions et renards (produced Comédie-Française, Paris, 1869). 1870.
Jean de Thommeray, with Jules Sandeau (produced Comédie-Française, Paris, 1873). 1874.
Madame Caverlet (produced Théâtre du Vaudeville, Paris, 1876). 1876.
Le Prix Martin, with Eugène Labiche (produced Théâtre du Palais-Royal, Paris, 1876). 1876.
Les Fourchambault (produced Comédie-Française, Paris, 1878). 1878; translated as *The House of Fourchambault*, 1915.

Verse

Les Pariétaires. 1855.

Other

La Question électorale (political pamphlet). 1864.

*

Criticism

Books:
P. Morillot, *Émile Augier*, Paris, 1901.
H. Gaillard, *Émile Augier et la comédie sociale*, Paris, 1910.

*   *   *

In the 18th century Denis Diderot wrote *Le Fils naturel* (1757) and *Le Père de famille* (1758) and argued that the theatre should concern itself with the social milieu and family relations. In this, as in many respects, he was ahead of his time. It took the French Revolution and its aftermath to bring about the right circumstances for the drama he had envisaged: but in Émile Augier he could hardly have wished for a better heir to his ideas. In the interval the bourgeoisie had established a hold on power and had come to constitute a theatre audience with its own particular tastes; and Eugène Scribe had brought the well-made play to such a pitch of technical sophistication that it provided an ideal instrument through which to articulate the middle-class experience of the mid-19th century.

Augier began writing plays in what was to prove a characteristic movement of reaction against the extravagance of Romanticism, ably seconding Ponsard and his "*école du bon sens*" with the verse drama *Gabrielle*, in 1849. It revolves around a feckless wife whose failure to replace a button missing from her husband's shirt is the first symptom of a slide towards marital infidelity in the pursuit of a romantic dream. Previously a pretext for laughter or angst, the theme is here treated as a matter of serious practical concern. The threatened couple is saved in the nick of time to lines such as "Oh père de famille! Oh poète! Je t'aime!" (Oh family man! Oh poet! I love you!).

Once he found his true *métier* in prose drama, Augier developed somewhat beyond such bathos, establishing himself as a staunch defender of the republican bourgeoisie which looked to the Revolution as its heroic achievement. His work can be seen to expound a moral vision justifying the social and political gains the bourgeoisie continued to make, despite the resistance of its political opponents, during the period which saw France move from Bourbon to Orleanist monarchy and thence, via the doomed Second Republic, to the Second Empire spanning the years 1852 to 1870.

The precepts and warnings which Augier's plays embody derive from the twin ideals of financial propriety and the sanctity of the family. His plots draw their dramatic force from the testing of these principles in encounters with what most threatens them. The lure of the courtesan is tackled in *Le Mariage d'Olympe* (*The Marriage of Olympe*); the dangers of financial greed, speculation and living beyond middle-class means are denounced in *La Ceinture dorée* (The Gilded Belt), *Les Lionnes pauvres* (Fine Ladies of Limited Means), and *Les Effrontés* (The Insolent); the temptation to share an aristocratic lifestyle and the aspiration to the status of the nobility are pilloried in *Le Gendre de M. Poirier* (*Mr. Poirier's Son-in-Law*) and *Le Fils de Giboyer* (Giboyer's Son). Above all, and most notably in this latter play, Augier pursues an uncompromising anti-clerical line, denouncing the machinations of catholics and monarchists, the chief bugbears of bourgeois republicans who saw them as constituting an infernal alliance seeking to halt the flow of history and drag the country back to a pre-revolutionary regime.

Though his portrayal of scheming villains is not without its successes, Augier's hallmark is perhaps his analysis of the enemy within the bourgeois citadel: he provides a gallery of characters drawn from the middle-class professions—lawyers, notaries, politicians, businessmen—whose onward progression brings them (and their wives and children) into contact with mentalities which are inimical to the convictions of moderate republicanism. Augier is concerned, like Molière before him, to teach the middle classes to know their place, since this is where their strength lies, and to cling to common-sense values in the face of all frivolity and contagion (*La Contagion*).

Though his outlook was deliberately less than elevated, Augier's technical skill as a dramatist enabled him to exploit to the full the theatrical potential of the material he made his own. *Le Gendre de M. Poirier* earned comparisons with *Le Bourgeois Gentilhomme*; *Le Fils de Giboyer* was described as the 19th century's *Mariage de Figaro*. Augier himself was undoubtedly one of the most successful dramatists of his era, dominating the Paris stage and influencing the wider European scene for some 30 years. Though in many respects he presents the perfect expression of contemporary social and political feeling, his popularity was due in no small measure to the fact that his solidarity with the bourgeoisie makes him an excessively accommodating portraitist, denouncing his clients' shortcomings but sugaring his criticisms rather too readily. In particular he over-exploits sentimentality and the device of marriage to resolve dramatic (and evade ideological) conflict; for the modern reader his plays often present convincing enough drama in the opening acts but all too frequently give way to facile emotion in the closing scenes.

Nonetheless, at its best his dialogue can be both natural and theatrically effective, while his ability to sustain a plot and manipulate dramatic interaction is outstanding, marred only by an occasional undue use of plot-twists at the expense of character portrayal. His concern for the shape of a play gives his works a balanced, harmonious structure which justifiably drew the admiration of his contemporaries. Moreover, during the 1850's his collaboration with the director Montigny at the Théâtre du Gymnase saw significant advances in methods of staging and approaches to acting. In thus developing a drama based on social issues which at the same time renewed theatrical techniques, he laid the foundations of realism and must be accounted a precursor of Ibsen, among others.

—David H. Walker

————

AYCKBOURN, Alan. Born in London, 12 April 1939. Educated at Haileybury, Hertford, 1952–56. Married Christine Roland in 1959; two sons. Stage manager and actor, Donald Wolfit's company, in Edinburgh, Worthing, Leatherhead, Scarborough, and Oxford, 1956–57; actor and manager, Stephen Joseph Theatre-in-the-Round Company, Scarborough, Yorkshire, 1957–62; first plays produced 1959; associate director, Victoria Theatre, Stoke-on-Trent, Staffordshire, 1962–64; last appearance as actor, 1964; drama producer, BBC Radio, Leeds, 1964–70; artistic director, Library Theatre, 1970–76, and Stephen Joseph Theatre-in-the-Round, from 1976 (both in Scarborough); associate director, National Theatre, London, 1986–87. Has directed productions of most of his own plays, as well as works by other authors. Recipient: five *Evening Standard* Awards; Olivier Award, 1985. CBE (Commander, Order of the British Empire), 1987.

Works

Collections

Three Plays (includes *Absurd Person Singular*; *Absent Friends*; *Bedroom Farce*). 1977.
Joking Apart; Ten Times Table; Just Between Ourselves. 1979; augmented edition, as *"Joking Apart" and Other Plays* (includes *Sisterly Feelings*), 1982.

Stage Works

The Square Cat (produced Library Theatre, Scarborough, 1959).
Love After All (produced Library Theatre, Scarborough, 1959).
Dad's Tale (for children; produced Library Theatre, Scarborough, 1960).
Standing Room Only (produced Library Theatre, Scarborough, 1961).
Xmas v. Mastermind (produced Victoria Theatre, Stoke-on-Trent, 1962).
Mr. Whatnot (produced Victoria Theatre, Stoke-on-Trent, 1963; revised version produced Arts Theatre, London, 1964).
Relatively Speaking (as *Meet My Father*, produced Library Theatre, Scarborough, 1965; as *Relatively Speaking*, produced Duke of York's Theatre, London, 1967). 1968.
The Sparrow (produced Library Theatre, Scarborough, 1967).
How the Other Half Loves (produced Library Theatre, Scarborough, 1969). 1972.
Countdown, in We Who Are about to . . ., later called *Mixed Doubles* (produced Hampstead Theatre Club, London, 1969). 1970.
Ernie's Incredible Illucinations (for children; produced 1971). 1969.
The Story So Far (produced Library Theatre, Scarborough, 1970; revised version, as *Me Times Me Times Me*, produced on tour, 1971; revised version, as *Family Circles*, produced 1978).
Time and Time Again (produced Library Theatre, Scarborough, 1971). 1973.
Absurd Person Singular (produced Library Theatre, Scarborough, 1972). In *Three Plays*, 1977.
Mother Figure, in Mixed Blessings (produced Library Theatre, Scarborough, 1973).
The Norman Conquests: Table Manners; Living Together; Round and Round the Garden (produced Library Theatre, Scarborough, 1973). 1975.
Absent Friends (produced Library Theatre, Scarborough, 1974). In *Three Plays*, 1977.
Confusions: Mother Figure; Drinking Companion; Between Mouthfuls; Gosforth's Fête; A Talk in the Park (produced Library Theatre, Scarborough, 1974). 1977.
Jeeves, music by Andrew Lloyd Webber, from works by P.G. Wodehouse (produced Her Majesty's Theatre, London, 1975).
Bedroom Farce (produced Library Theatre, Scarborough, 1975). In *Three Plays*, 1977.
Just Between Ourselves (produced Library Theatre, Scarborough, 1976). In *Joking Apart; Ten Times Table; Just Between Ourselves*, 1979.
Ten Times Table (produced Stephen Joseph Theatre, Scarborough, 1977). In *Joking Apart*: Ten Times Table; Just Between Ourselves, 1979.

Joking Apart (produced Stephen Joseph Theatre, Scarborough, 1978). In *Joking Apart; Ten Times Table; Just Between Ourselves*, 1979.
Men on Women on Men, music by Paul Todd (produced Stephen Joseph Theatre, Scarborough, 1978).
Sisterly Feelings (produced Stephen Joseph Theatre, Scarborough, 1979). With *Taking Steps*, 1981.
Taking Steps (produced Stephen Joseph Theatre, Scarborough, 1979). With *Sisterly Feelings*, 1981.
Suburban Strains, music by Paul Todd (produced Stephen Joseph Theatre, Scarborough, 1980). 1982.
First Course, music by Paul Todd (produced Stephen Joseph Theatre, Scarborough, 1980).
Second Helping, music by Paul Todd (produced Stephen Joseph Theatre, Scarborough, 1980).
Season's Greetings (produced Stephen Joseph Theatre, Scarborough, 1980; revised version produced 1982). 1982.
Way Upstream (produced Stephen Joseph Theatre, Scarborough, 1981). 1983.
Making Tracks, music by Paul Todd (produced Stephen Joseph Theatre, Scarborough, 1981).
Me, Myself, and I, music by Paul Todd (produced Stephen Joseph Theatre, Scarborough, 1981). 1989.
Intimate Exchanges (produced Stephen Joseph Theatre, Scarborough, 1982). 2 vols., 1985.
A Trip to Scarborough, from the play by Sheridan (produced Stephen Joseph Theatre, Scarborough, 1982).
Incidental Music (produced Stephen Joseph Theatre, Scarborough, 1983).
It Could Be Any One of Us (produced Stephen Joseph Theatre, Scarborough, 1983).
Seven Deadly Virtues, music by Paul Todd (produced Stephen Joseph Theatre, Scarborough, 1984).
The Westwoods (produced Stephen Joseph Theatre, Scarborough, 1984).
A Game of Golf (produced London, 1984).
A Chorus of Disapproval (produced Stephen Joseph Theatre, Scarborough, 1984). 1986.
Woman in Mind (produced Stephen Joseph Theatre, Scarborough, 1985). 1986.
Boy Meets Girl/Girl Meets Boy, music by Paul Todd (produced Stephen Joseph Theatre, Scarborough, 1985).
Mere Soup Songs, music by Paul Todd (produced Stephen Joseph Theatre, Scarborough, 1986).
A Small Family Business (produced National Theatre, London, 1987). 1987.
Henceforward (produced Stephen Joseph Theatre, Scarborough, 1987). 1988.
Man of the Moment (produced Stephen Joseph Theatre, Scarborough, 1988). 1990.
Mr. A's Amazing Maze Plays (for children; produced Stephen Joseph Theatre, Scarborough, 1988). 1989.
The Revengers' Comedies (produced Stephen Joseph Theatre, Scarborough, 1989). 1991.
Invisible Friends (produced Stephen Joseph Theatre, Scarborough, 1989). 1991.
Body Language (produced Stephen Joseph Theatre, Scarborough, 1990).
This is Where We Came in (for children; produced Stephen Joseph Theatre, Scarborough, 1990).
Callisto 5 (for children; produced Stephen Joseph Theatre, Scarborough, 1990).
My Very Own Story (for children; produced Stephen Joseph Theatre, Scarborough, 1991).
Wildest Dreams (produced Stephen Joseph Theatre, Scarborough, 1991).

Television Plays

Ernie's Incredible Illucinations, 1971 (published in *Playbill 1*, 1969); *Service Not Included (Masquerade* series), 1974; *A Cut in the Rates*, 1984 (published 1991).

Radio Plays

Events on a Hotel Terrace, 1988.

Criticism

Books:
Stephen Joseph, *Theatre in the Round*, London, 1967.
Michael Billington, *Alan Ayckbourn*, London, 1983; revised edition, 1990.
Simon Trussler (ed.), *File on Ayckbourn*, London, 1989.
Bernard F. Dukore (ed.), *Alan Ayckbourn: A Casebook*, New York, 1991.
Ian Watson and Alan Ayckbourn, *Conversations with Ayckbourn*, London, 1991.

* * *

In Germany, where they take writers seriously, Ayckbourn has been dubbed "the Molière of the middle-classes". Even in Britain the truth has begun to dawn: that Ayckbourn's prodigious comic output conceals a vision of life. He once said that, as a theatre director, he advised young writers "to say unpalatable things in a palatable manner". That is what Ayckbourn himself has been doing for the best part of 30 years.

The popular view is that Ayckbourn's comedies have, in recent years, become increasingly dark and sombre. But if one examines the early plays in detail one finds that Ayckbourn has always been a shrewd observer of marital pain, masculine insensitivity, and the hollowness of English social rituals. The sound that issues from *The Norman Conquests* is that of sexual and emotional desperation issuing from a rotten weekend family get-together. In *Absent Friends*, a tea-party thrown to console the recently bereaved hero turns into a display of fractious quarrelling and a revelation of our inability to express our sense of human belonging. *Just Between Ourselves* is a bleak and biting tragicomedy about what E.M. Forster called "the under-developed heart" and the way we casually destroy our nearest and dearest.

Thus, the darkness has always been there in Ayckbourn. What happened in the 1980's was that he started to use a wider-angled lens by relating personal pain to the moral decay of British society. He became a better and bigger writer not by stepping up the pain-quotient but by examining the foundations of a society where material reward was regarded as the ultimate symbol of success, where good and evil were regarded as faintly embarrassing concepts, and where God was not even part of the vocabulary.

Way Upstream in 1981 was the first sign of Ayckbourn's extended ambitions: it is a state-of-the-nation play in which moderation and reason finally triumph over fascist brutality, aristocratic decay, and capitalist arrogance in the course of a seven-day river journey. Less allegorically explicit, Ayckbourn's later plays of the 1980's were more successful at expressing his growing spiritual unease. *A Small Family Business*, written specifically for Britain's National Theatre, was a masterly study of the way a single compromise of basic moral principle leads to bribery, corruption, and ultimately

murder. But the saddest moment in the whole of this play was not the hero's descent into the abyss but his brother's revelation that he loved his car, his compact discs, his sailing boat and his digital wrist-computer far more than he loved his wife. The cardinal sin of elevating things above people also lay at the heart of Ayckbourn's dystopian comedy, *Henceforward*, in which the hero finally prefers to compose a "love" theme on ultra-sophisticated recording equipment than to save the lives of his wife and daughter. And *Man of the Moment* suggests that we, as viewers, passively and daily conspire in the distortion of reality on television.

Ayckbourn's comedies have, with time, become more profound, ambitious, and challenging: he is telling us, if we wish to hear, that we have become desensitised by political extremism, personal acquisitiveness, and technological advance. What makes him a first-rate dramatist, however, is that his comic pessimism is combined with a mastery of the techniques of theatre that dates back to his training as an assistant stage-manager and actor with Stephen Joseph's Theatre-in-the-Round at Scarborough. Many of Ayckbourn's contemporaries have started as message-bearers who have gradually learned the disciplines of their craft; Ayckbourn started by learning the basic theatrical skills and then discovered what he wanted to say.

There is, however, a fascinating and still unresolved contradiction in Ayckbourn's work. Part of the time he seems to argue that chance dictates human affairs: at other times, he suggests that we draw marked cards from birth. He even expresses both points of view in the mammoth *Intimate Exchanges*: eight separate plays that present the characters with different choices leading to a total of sixteen different versions. A chance decision as to whether or not to light a cigarette may determine a character's fate. But Ayckbourn also implies that it is impossible to escape from the cage of heredity, environment, and circumstances that we call character.

Only in his recent play, *Body Language*, does he suggest there may be a way out. The play is based on a grisly scenario wherein a topless model and an overweight local radio reporter find that their heads have been transplanted onto each other's bodies. Ayckbourn cynically pins down the way male attitudes to women are determined by surface attributes. But at the end the two women make common cause and decide that the body is the slave of the will rather than the other way round. It is the most optimistic piece Ayckbourn has yet written and suggests that he is still capable of striking out in new directions. Having gained a world-wide reputation as an analyst of suburban pain and social decay, he may now be breaking new ground as a challenger of fashionable determinism. As director of the Stephen Joseph Theatre-in-the-Round in Scarborough, he is also in the uniquely privileged position amongst modern British dramatists of being able to chart and steer his own future.

—Michael Billington

See also *Volume 1* entries on *Absurd Person Singular; The Norman Conquests.*

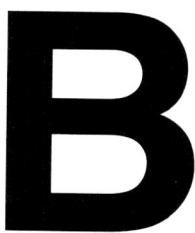

B

BARAKA, (Imamu) Amiri. Born Everett LeRoi Jones in Newark, New Jersey, USA, 7 October 1934; took name Amiri Baraka in 1968. Educated at Central Avenue School, and Barringer High School, Newark; Rutgers University, New Brunswick, New Jersey, 1951–52; Howard University, Washington, D.C., 1953–54, BA in English 1954. Served in the United States Air Force, 1954–57. Married 1) Hettie Roberta Cohen in 1958 (divorced 1965), two daughters; 2) Sylvia Robinson (now Amina Baraka) in 1967, five children; also two stepdaughters and one other daughter. First play, *A Good Girl is Hard to Find*, produced 1958; teacher, New School for Social Research, New York, 1961–64, and summers, 1977–79, State University of New York, Buffalo, Summer 1964, and Columbia University, New York, 1964 and Spring 1980; Visiting Professor, San Francisco State College, 1966–67, Yale University, New Haven, Connecticut, 1977–78, and George Washington University, Washington, DC, 1978–79. Assistant Professor, 1980–82, Associate Professor, 1983–84, and since 1985 Professor of Africana Studies, State University of New York, Stony Brook. Founder, *Yugen* magazine and Totem Press, New York, 1958–62; editor, with Diane di Prima, *Floating Bear* magazine, New York, 1961–63; founding director, Black Arts Repertory Theatre, Harlem, New York, 1964–66. Since 1966 founding director, Spirit House, Newark; involved in Newark politics: member of the United Brothers, 1967, and Committee for Unified Newark, 1969–75; chair, Congress of Afrikan People, 1972–75. Recipient: Whitney fellowship, 1961; Obie award, 1964; Guggenheim fellowship, 1965.

Works (earlier works were written as LeRoi Jones)

Collections

Four Black Revolutionary Plays. 1971.
"The Motion of History" and Other Plays (includes *S-1* and *Slave Ship*). 1978.
Selected Plays and Prose. 1979.

Stage Works

A Good Girl is Hard to Find (produced Sterington House, Montclair, New Jersey, 1958).
Dante (produced Off Bowery Theatre, New York, 1961; as *The 8th Ditch*, produced New Bowery Theatre, New York, 1964). In *The System of Dante's Hell*, 1965.
The Toilet (produced St. Mark's Playhouse, New York, 1964). With *The Baptism*, 1967.
Dutchman (produced Cherry Lane Theatre, New York, 1964). With *The Slave*, 1964.
The Slave (produced St. Mark's Playhouse, New York, 1964). With *Dutchman*, 1964.

The Baptism (produced Writers' Stage Theatre, New York, 1964). With *The Toilet*, 1967.
Jello (produced Black Arts Repertory Theatre, New York, 1965). 1970.
Experimental Death Unit 1 (produced St. Mark's Playhouse, New York, 1965). In *Four Black Revolutionary Plays*, 1969.
A Black Mass (produced Proctor's Theatre, Newark, 1966). In *Four Black Revolutionary Plays*, 1969.
Arm Yrself or Harm Yrself (produced Spirit House, Newark, 1967). 1967.
Slave Ship: A Historical Pageant (produced Spirit House, Newark, 1967). 1967.
Madheart (produced State College, San Francisco, 1967). In *Four Black Revolutionary Plays*, 1969.
Great Goodness of Life (A Coon Show) (produced Spirit House, Newark, 1967). In *Four Black Revolutionary Plays*, 1969.
Home on the Range (produced Spirit House, Newark and New York, 1968). In *Drama Review*, Summer 1968.
Police. In *Drama Review* (New York), Summer 1968.
The Death of Malcolm X. In *New Plays from the Black Theatre*, edited by Ed Bullins. 1969.
Rockgroup. In *Cricket*, December 1969.
Resurrection in Life (produced Harlem, New York, 1969).
Insurrection (produced New York, 1969).
Junkies Are Full of (SHHH . . .) (produced New Federal Theatre, New York, 1970). In *Black Drama Anthology*, edited by Woodie King and Ron Milner, 1971.
Bloodrites (produced New Federal Theatre, New York, 1970). In *Black Drama Anthology*, edited by Woodie King and Ron Milner, 1971.
BA-RA-KA. In *Spontaneous Combustion: Eight New American Plays*, edited by Rochelle Owens, 1972.
Black Power Chant. In *Drama Review* (New York), December 1972.
Columbia the Gem of the Ocean (produced Howard University, Washington, D.C., 1973).
A Recent Killing (produced New Federal Theatre, New York, 1973).
The New Ark's a Moverin (produced Spirit House, Newark, 1974).
The Sidnee Poet Heroical (produced New Federal Theatre, New York, 1975). 1979.
S-1 (produced Afro-American Studios, New York, 1976). In *"The Motion of History" and Other Plays*, 1978.
The Motion of History (produced New York City Theatre Ensemble, New York, 1977). In *"The Motion of History" and Other Plays*, 1978.
What Was the Relationship of the Lone Ranger to the Means of Production? (produced Ladies' Fort, New York, 1979).

At the Dim'crackr Convention (produced Columbia University, New York, 1980).
Boy and Tarzan Appear in a Clearing (produced New Federal Theatre, New York, 1981).
Weimar 2 (produced New York, 1981).
Money: A Jazz Opera, with George Gruntz, music by Gruntz (produced La Mama Experimental Theatre, New York, 1982).
Primitive World, music by David Murray (produced New York, 1984).

Screenplays

Dutchman, 1967; *Black Spring*, 1967; *A Fable* (from the play *The Slave*), 1971; *Supercoon*, 1971.

Fiction

The System of Dante's Hell (novel).   1965.
Tales.   1967.

Verse

April 13.   1959.
Spring and Soforth.   1960.
Preface to a Twenty Volume Suicide Note.   1961.
The Disguise.   1961.
The Dead Lecturer.   1964.
Black Art.   1966.
A Poem for Black Hearts.   1967.
Black Magic: Collected Poetry 1961–1967.   1969.
It's Nation Time.   1970.
In Our Terribleness: Some Elements and Meaning in Black Style, with Fundi (Billy Abernathy).   1970.
Spirit Reach.   1972.
Afrikan Revolution.   1973.
Hard Facts.   1976.
Selected Poetry.   1979.
AM/TRAK.   1979.
Spring Song.   1979.
Reggae or Not!   1982.
Thoughts for You!   1984.

Memoirs and Letters

The Autobiography of LeRoi Jones/Amiri Baraka.   1984.

Other

Cuba Libre.   1961.
Blues People: Negro Music in White America.   1963.
Home: Social Essays.   1966.
Black Music.   1968.
Trippin': A Need for Change, with Larry Neal and A.B. Spellman.   1969(?).
A Black Value System.   1970.
Gary and Miami: Before and After.   Nd.
Raise Race Rays Raze: Essays since 1965.   1971.
Strategy and Tactics of a Pan African Nationalist Party.   1971.
Beginning of National Movement.   1972.
Kawaida Studies: The New Nationalism.   1972.
National Liberation and Politics.   1974.
Crisis in Boston!!!!   1974.
Afrikan Free School.   1974.
Toward Ideological Clarity.   1974.
The Creation of the New Ark.   1975.

Daggers and Javelins: Essays 1974–1979.   1984.
The Artist and Social Responsibility.   1986.

*

Bibliographies

Letitia Dace, *LeRoi Jones (Imamu Amiri Baraka): A Checklist of Works By and About Him*, London, 1971.
Kimball King, *Ten Modern American Playwrights*, New York, 1982.

Criticism

Books:
Theodore Hudson, *From LeRoi Jones to Amiri Baraka: The Literary Works*, Durham, North Carolina, 1973.
Kimberly W. Benston, *Baraka: The Renegade and the Mask*, New Haven, Connecticut, 1976.
Kimberly W. Benston (ed.), *Imamu Amiri Baraka (LeRoi Jones): A Collection of Critical Essays*, Englewood Cliffs, New Jersey, 1978.
Werner Sollors, *Amiri Baraka/LeRoi Jones: The Quest for a Populist Modernism*, New York, 1978.
Lloyd W. Brown, *Amiri Baraka*, Boston, 1980.
Henry C. Lacey, *To Raise, Destroy, and Create: The Poetry, Drama, and Fiction of Imamu Amiri Baraka (LeRoi Jones)*, New York, 1981.
Alain Ricard, *Theatre and Nationalism: Wole Soyinka and LeRoi Jones*, Ife-Ife, Nigeria, 1983.
James B. Gwynne (ed.), *Amiri Baraka: The Kaleidoscopic Torch*, New York, 1985.

*   *   *

The leading voice in radical African-American theatre, Amiri Baraka has built a large and varied body of work that is revolutionary in both politics and form. In his quest to form a distinctly African-American voice from myth, reality, and visionary speculation, Baraka has undergone a multiplicity of transformations. From Beat poet to Black Nationalist, he has, over the past decades, held a range of ideological and aesthetic perspectives. His work in drama, as well as in poetry and political theory, has served as a mirror for his many transformations—it is an ongoing autobiographical narrative reflecting the evolution of a single African-American consciousness. Change seems to be the operative characteristic of Baraka's writings.

Yet, despite its dedication to continual, sometimes violent transformation, two common, intertwining threads link the body of his work. First, no matter what form it may take, whether it be the hard-edged naturalism of *The Toilet* or the Genet-inspired satire of *Great Goodness of Life*, Baraka's work evinces a tenacious effort at finding a voice capacious and supple enough to express the vast and varied landscape of the African-American experience. It is a voice that must include within its boundaries the myths of ancient Africa, the sounds of a slave ship, the clipped intonations of inner city speech, the inarticulate roar of armed revolt in an imagined future.

The second unifying thread throughout Baraka's work is inextricably related to the first. It is his fierce dedication to experimentation in writing. The very multiplicity of dramatic forms with which Baraka has experimented, from naturalism to surrealism, agitprop to multi-media pageant, attests to his hunger to find a new means of expression. In his continual stretching and reworking of dramatic forms, Baraka charts the contours of a revolutionary theatre, revolutionary not only in its political call to overthrow a dominant and oppressive culture, but revolutionary also in its insistent deconstruction of myth and language, those structural and linguistic conventions, those systems of thought and articulation by which a dominant culture exercises its most subtle and powerful control.

In his search for a single, unifying African-American voice, Baraka finds in theatre the ideal form by which to dramatize, in vivid detail, the haunting dissonant voices in his consciousness. Dramatic conflict between characters locked in often fatal struggles gives Baraka a vehicle with which to explore those oppositions between black and white, male and female, individual and community, master and slave, which recur again and again throughout his work.

Distilled to an essential identity, at times allegorical, his characters are larger-than-life archetypes at war with one another. In his most acclaimed play, *Dutchman*, for which he won an Obie award, the struggle is between a young African-American man, Clay, and an almost demonic female temptress, Lula. In a subway car filled with silent, ghost-like, white passengers, Lula challenges and taunts Clay with what it means to be an African-American male. As an educated, sexual, adventurous bohemian, Lula throws in Clay's face all the myths of African-American manhood. In his effort to keep secure the public mask he wears among whites, Clay tries to avoid and deflect Lula's verbal jabs. *Dutchman* consists of Lula probing and pushing at Clay's identity until he finally explodes in a powerful rush of words about what it is to be African-American:

They say, "I love Bessie Smith." And don't even unerstand that Bessie Smith is saying, "Kiss my ass, kiss my black unruly ass." Before love, suffering, desire, anything you can explain, she's saying, and very plainly, "Kiss my black ass." And if you don't know that, it's you that's doing the kissing.

Dutchman provides one of the clearest examples of Baraka's dramatic technique where dissonant voices battle for power, with one voice challenging, doubting, picking at the sorest points, and the other voice at last pushed to the brink, expressing its most repressed, inconceivable yearnings. The explosion often comes in the form of a soliloquy delivered by the African-American male protagonist who functions at once as hero and victim.

Whether it be Clay of *Dutchman*, Walker Vessels of *The Slave*, or Ray Foots of *The Toilet*, Baraka's hero/victim is engaged in the drama of finding and articulating a unified self beneath the public mask. The articulation of identity is, by nature, violent in Baraka's work. Brutal and at times profane, the language Baraka's heroes use to speak about themselves represents an effort to cut through the meaningless, wan chatter of the everyday, to scrape away the sanitized veneer of words to reveal the turmoil below. Like Walker Vessels who ceaselessly undermines, interrupts, and intentionally misinterprets the dialogue of the white couple in *The Slave*, Baraka subverts the language of the dominant culture, the English of a Western literary canon, in his search for a unique, genuine, African-American voice.

In his later work, Baraka turned to increasingly experimental forms. Abandoning the naturalism of his earlier work such as *Dutchman* and *The Toilet*, Baraka's post-1965 work moved in two distinct, but interrelated directions. On the one hand, he began to generate a body of agitprop skits. On the other, he began to experiment with the multi-media pageant incor-porating music and dance. Both types of work represent for Baraka a stretching of pre-existing theatrical forms to fit the dimensions of the African-American experience.

The agitprop skits constitute a significant portion of Baraka's work as teacher and activist. Like Brecht's *Lehrstücke*, these skits bring the audience together to teach a lesson by illustration. Aimed at an exclusively African-American audience, Baraka's agitprop skits such as *Arm Yrself, Or Harm Yrself* and *Junkies Are Full of (SHHH. . .)*, depict issues central to the African-American community. Whether the issue is drug abuse or police brutality, the plot action is simple and straightforward, oriented towards a single, powerful message. The language is pared down and colloquial. The characters are broadly sketched caricatures like the evil white policeman or the Judas-like traitor who betrays his own people.

In seemingly stark contrast to the urgent simplicity of the agitprop skits, Baraka's multi-media pageants such as *Slave Ship* and *The Motion of History* weave together text, sound, and image in a complex, multi-layered and self-consciously theatrical hybrid. In *The Motion of History*, Baraka tries to capture the whole history of the African-American experience from the period of slavery through the Civil War to the present day. In a series of tableaux within which characters perform symbolic actions, he draws upon a combination of history and mythology to articulate the African-American experience. From the sounds of the water against the sides of the ship and the human groans within, to the African drumming of the final celebratory dance sequence, the "Boogaloyoruba", Baraka's *Slave Ship* goes beyond the spoken word towards the realm of immediate visceral sensation. It is as though, having exhausted the expressive power of language, Baraka searches for a form of expression that blurs the distinction between experience and expression.

—Naomi Iizuka

See also *Volume 1* entry on *Dutchman*.

BARBEAU, Jean. Born in Saint-Romauld, Quebec, Canada, 10 February 1945. Received classical education at the Collège de Lévis; entered the Université Laval, Quebec City, studying literature: left without taking degree, 1969. Married Monique Oellet in 1972; one child. While at university, wrote and acted for the Troupe des Treize; co-founder of, and writer for, the Théâtre Quotidien de Québec, 1969; wrote for Quebec radio, 1970; his one-act plays inaugurated the Lunch-Time Theatre performances by the Théâtre du Nouveau Monde at the Comédie-Canadienne, Montreal, 1972; moved to Abitibi, in rural Amos, 1972.

Works

Stage Works

Caïn et Babel, with others (produced by the Troupe des Treize, Université Laval, Quebec City, 1966).
La Geôle, with others (produced by the Troupe des Treize, Université Laval, Quebec City, 1967).
Et caetera, with others (produced by the Troupe des Treize, Université Laval, Quebec City, 1968).

Les Temps tranquilles, with others (produced by the Troupe des Treize, Université Laval, Quebec City, 1969).

Le Frame all-dress, with others (produced by the Troupe des Treize, Université Laval, Quebec City, 1969).

Manon Lastcall (produced Conservatoire de Montréal, 1970). 1972.

Joualez-moi d'amour (produced by Théâtre Quotidien de Québec, Café Chantauteuil, Quebec City, 1970). 1972; translated as *Joualez-moi d'amour*, 1973.

Goglu (produced by the Théâtre Quotidien de Québec, Café Chantauteuil, Quebec City, 1970). 1971; translated as *Goglu*, 1976; as *Bobolink*, 1978.

Le Chemin de Lacroix (produced by the Théâtre Quotidien de Québec, Café Chantauteuil, Quebec City, 1970). Translated as *The Way of Lacross*, 1973.

Solange (produced by the Théâtre Quotidien de Québec, Café Chantauteuil, Quebec City, 1970). With *La Coupe stainless*, 1974; translated as *Solange*, 1976.

Tripez-vous Vous (produced Théâtre Quotidien de Québec, 1971).

Ben-Ur (produced by the Théâtre Populaire de Québec, Montreal, 1971). 1971; translated as *Ben-Ur*, 1974.

0–71 (produced Théâtre du Trident, Quebec City, 1971).

Le Chant du sink (produced by the Théâtre Populaire de Québec, Montreal, 1973). 1973.

La Coupe stainless (produced Piggery Theatre, North Hatley, Quebec, 1973). With *Solange*, 1974.

Le Théâtre de la maintenance (produced by the Nouvelle Compagnie Théâtrale, Montreal, 1973). 1978.

Une Brosse (produced Théâtre du Trident, Quebec City, 1975). 1975.

Citrouille (produced Théâtre du Nouveau Monde, Sherbrooke, 1975). 1975.

Dites-le avec les fleurs, with Marcel Dubé (produced by Le Bateau-Théâtre, 1976). 1976.

Émile et une nuit (produced Théâtre du Rideau Vert, Montreal, 1979). 1979.

Le Jardin de la maison blanche (produced by L'Atelier de la Nouvelle Compagnie Théâtrale, Collège Lionel-Groulx, Quebec, 1980). 1979.

Une Marquise de Sade et un lézard nommé King Kong (produced by the Théâtre de la Manufacture, 1980). 1979.

Le Vénus d'Emilio (produced Théâtre la Relève à Michaud, Calixa-Lavallée, Quebec, 1980). 1984.

Coeur de papa (produced Théâtre la Relève à Michaud, Calixa-Lavallée, Quebec, 1981). 1985.

Le Grand Poucet (produced by students, at the Salle Fred Barry de la Nouvelle Compagnie Théâtrale, Montreal, 1982). 1985.

Les Gars (produced by the Compagnie Jean Duceppe, Théâtre Port Royal, Place des Arts, Montreal, 1983). 1984; translated as *The Guys*, 1985.

L'Abominable Homme des sables (produced by the Théâtre de la Pudrière, Montreal, 1989). 1989.

Television Plays

Les Enfants de la rue (mini-series); *Coeur de Nylon*, 1989.

Radio Plays

Manon Lastcall, 1972.

*

Criticism

Books:

Jean Godin and Laurent Mailot, *Théâtre québécois II: Nouveaux auteurs, autres spectacles*, Quebec City, 1980; revised edition, 1988.

Jonathon M. Weiss, *French-Canadian Theater*, Boston, 1986.

Articles:

Yves Bolduc, "Jean Barbeau ou la mise à mort du héros vaincu", in *Livres et auteurs québécois*, 1972.

*   *   *

Jean Barbeau first took Quebec's theatrical world by storm in 1970–71, with no less than eight plays produced in a period of 16 months. Provocative, irreverent, satirical, his dramas are nonetheless generally serious in intent, often frankly political, and frequently tragic in resolution. Rabelaisian wordplay, visible in many of his titles, conceals an obsessive search for the meaning of language; pathos alternates or combines with reflexive, self-deprecating laughter; and coarse social satire masks an impassioned commitment to political and economic reform.

Only three years younger than Michel Tremblay, Barbeau nevertheless belongs, in a sense, to a different dramaturgical generation. The cathartic battle over the homely language of Tremblay's *Les Belles-Soeurs* in 1968 opened the way for Barbeau's less self-conscious use of *joual*, the heavily anglicized vernacular of francophone Quebec, just as the political crisis of 1970, culminating in the imposition by Ottawa of the War Measures Act and the murder of Quebec cabinet minister Pierre Laporte, legitimized his strong separatist political orientation. Thus Barbeau's characters converse in a colourful French resonant of Quebec City's working class, as they pursue, consciously or unconsciously, personal and societal ideals incompatible with Quebec's status as a cultural colony of France and an economic and social inferior in anglophone North America.

These are the two fundamental commitments of his work up to 1976. His one-act comedy, *Joualez-moi d'amour* (since *joual*, a rural deformation of the word *cheval*, is used to signify the popular French of working-class Quebec, thus *joualez=parlez*), expresses his rejection of European French language and culture, artificially imposed by a social and intellectual elite upon generations of Quebec students, writers, and readers. There are only two characters in this tightly structured play—the sexually impotent intellectual Jules, who has had to shed his Québécois diction and reject his working-class origins in order to achieve the social status he now enjoys, and the uncomplicated Parisian-born prostitute, Julie. Jules's impotence is eventually overcome only when "cousin" Julie learns, after an amusing linguistic lesson onstage, to play her role in *joual*. Visual and verbal metaphors operate at several levels, often in opposition to each other, and the Freudian basis of Barbeau's text is perhaps esoteric to many; but no spectator or reader can miss the play's message: the cultural sub-dependency that Quebec has so long accepted must be overcome if a healthy, mature, productive nationhood is to be achieved. This message had already been conveyed countless times by others, in serious reflective essays and speeches. Barbeau conveyed it more effectively, in this only apparently simple, apparently farcical drama.

The deleterious effect of European French cultural domination is a constant, but less central, feature of the rest of Barbeau's early works, which focus rather more on the cumulative effect on individuals (Bénoit-Urbain Théberge, the protagonist of *Ben-Ur*; Rodolphe Lacroix in *Le Chemin de Lacroix*; Goglu, in the play of the same name, and so on) of pervasive materialistic values in anglophone North America. Marginalized, culturally and linguistically schizoid, bitter, confused, and frustrated, these works are intended to represent the plight of contemporary Québécois at a critical point in their evolution.

Since the election of the independentist Parti Québécois in 1976, Barbeau, as most politically active dramatists in French Canada, has turned to more universal concerns in his plays, the quantity and quality of which has declined noticeably. He remains, however, one of the most original, most productive, and most catalytic dramatists of the 1970's in Quebec.

—Leonard E. Doucette

BARKER, Harley Granville. See **GRANVILLE-BARKER, Harley**

BARKER, Howard. Born in London, 28 June 1946. Educated at Battersea Grammar School, London, 1958–64; Sussex University, Brighton, 1964–68, MA in history 1968. Married Sandra Law in 1972; one son. First play, *Cheek*, produced 1970; resident dramatist, Open Space Theatre, London, 1974–75; The Wrestling School theatre company formed to produce Barker's plays, 1987.

Works

Collections

Collected Plays 1 (includes *Claw; No End of Blame; Scenes from an Execution; The Castle; Victory*). 1989.

Stage Works

Cheek (produced Royal Court Theatre Upstairs, London, 1970). In *New Short Plays 3*, 1972.
No One Was Saved (produced Royal Court Theatre Upstairs, London, 1971).
Edward: The Final Days (produced Open Space Theatre, London, 1971).
Faceache (produced Recreation Ground, London, 1971).
Alpha Alpha (produced Open Space Theatre, London, 1972).
Private Parts (produced Traverse Theatre, Edinburgh, 1972).
Skipper, and My Sister and I (produced Bush Theatre, London, 1973).
Rule Britannia (produced London, 1973).
Bang (produced London, 1973).
Claw (produced Open Space Theatre, London, 1975). With *Stripwell*, 1977.
Stripwell (produced Royal Court Theatre, London, 1975). With *Claw*, 1977.
Wax (produced Traverse Theatre, Edinburgh, 1976).
Fair Slaughter (produced Royal Court Theatre, London, 1977). 1978.

That Good Between Us (produced The Warehouse, London, 1977). With *Credentials of a Sympathizer*, 1980.
The Love of a Good Man (produced Crucible Theatre, Sheffield, 1978; revised version produced Playhouse, Oxford, 1980). With *All Bleeding*, 1980.
The Hang of the Gaol (produced The Warehouse, London, 1978). With *Heaven*, 1982.
Credentials of a Sympathizer (produced The Warehouse, London, 1979). With *That Good Between Us*, 1980.
All Bleeding (produced The Warehouse, London, 1979). With *The Love of a Good Man*, 1980.
The Loud Boy's Life (produced The Warehouse, London, 1980). In *Two Plays for the Right*, 1982.
Birth on a Hard Shoulder (produced Royal Dramatic Theatre, Stockholm, 1980). In *Two Plays for the Right*, 1982.
No End of Blame: Scenes of Overcoming (produced Playhouse, Oxford, 1981). 1981.
The Poor Man's Friend (produced Bridport, Dorset, 1981).
Victory: Choices in Reaction (produced Gardner Centre, Brighton, Sussex). 1983.
A Passion in Six Days (produced Crucible Theatre, Sheffield, 1983). With *Downchild*, 1985.
Crimes in Hot Countries (produced Essex University, Colchester, Essex, 1983). With *Fair Slaughter*, 1984.
The Power of the Dog (produced Lyceum Studio Theatre, Edinburgh, 1984). 1985.
Downchild (produced The Pit, Barbican Centre, London, 1985). With *A Passion in Six Days*, 1985.
The Castle (produced The Pit, Barbican Centre, London, 1985). With *Scenes from an Execution*, 1985.
Pity in History, from the television play (produced Edinburgh, 1986). With *Women Beware Women*, 1987.
Women Beware Women, from the play by Thomas Middleton (produced Royal Court Theatre, London, 1986). 1986.
The Possibilities (produced Almeida Theatre, London, 1988).
The Last Supper: A New Testament (produced Royal Court Theatre, London, 1988). 1988.
The Bite of the Night (produced The Pit, Barbican Centre, London). 1988.
Seven Lears: The Pursuit of the Good (produced Crucible Theatre, Sheffield, 1989). In *Seven Lears; Golgo*, 1990.
Golgo: Sermons on Pain and Privilege (produced Haymarket Theatre, Leicester, 1989). In *Seven Lears; Golgo*, 1990.
The Europeans: Struggles to Love. With *Judith*, 1990.
Judith: A Parting From the Body. With *The Europeans*, 1990.

Screenplays

Made, 1972; *Rape of Tamar*, 1973; *Aces High*, 1976 (published 1976).

Television Plays

Cows, 1972; *The Chauffeur and the Lady*, 1972; *Mutinies*, 1974; *Heroes of Labour* (published in *Gambit*, 29, 1976); *Pity in History*, 1985.

Radio Plays

One Afternoon on the North Face of the 63rd Level of the Pyramid of Cheops the Great, 1970; *Henry V in Two Parts*, 1971; *Herman, with Millie and Mick*, 1972; *Scenes from an Execution*, 1984 (published with *The Castle*, 1985); *The Early Hours of a Reviled Man*, 1990.

Howard Barker (1978).

Verse

Don't Exaggerate (*Desire and Abuse*).   1984.
Gary the Thief / *Gary Upright*.   1987.
Lullabies for the Impatient.   1989.
The Ascent of Monte Grappa.   1991.

Other

Arguments for a Theatre.   1989.

*

Criticism

Books:
Oleg Kerensky, *The New British Dramatists*, London, 1977,
    New York, 1979.
David Ian Rabey, *Howard Barker: Politics & Desire:
    Expository Study of His Poetry and Drama 1969–1987*,
    Basingstoke, 1989.

Articles:
"Howard Barker Issue" of *Gambit*, London, vol. 11, no. 41,
    1984.
Günther   Klotz,   "Howard   Barker: Paradigm   of
    Postmodernism", in *New Theatre Quarterly*, 25, 1991.

*   *   *

Initially grouped with the British political dramatists who

emerged during the 1970's, Howard Barker's uniquely challenging and ambitious dramatic styles and objectives are more
pertinently considered in the European context, where his
influence is increasing, and as the work of a major existential
dramatist.

Barker's drama and poetry demonstrate that the dominant
social terms of definition of possibilities are neither exhaustive nor complete. From the critiques of capitalism and the
failure of British social democracy in his 1970's plays,
Barker's work has transformed radically into a drama of
rupture, both external and internal, where sexual desire, the
compulsive imagination, and the drive towards the discovery
of personal knowledge together inform attempts to regenerate the individual self and thus defy all forms of prescriptive
ideology.

Even in Barker's plays of the 1970's, subsequent impulses
are identifiable: their savagely comic political expressionism
is characteristically based on language which springs from
individual   compulsion,   explored   through   extravagant
rhythms, imagery of wrenched and passionate physicality,
and a painful humour which alternately undermines and elevates. The sense of an unlived sexuality permeates many of
these images of social sterility and subordination through
shame (*That Good Between Us*, *The Hang of the Gaol*).
Indeed, the individual compulsion to express, and the terms
of its permission, are tensions in his early 1980's plays on art:
No End of Blame, *Pity in History*, *Scenes from an Execution*.

Victory marks the discovery of a particularly demanding
form of tragedy, in which the *Choices in Reaction* of the play's
subtitle are referred to the audience, without the restoration
of pre-existent moral values. The refusal of an identifiable

message creates an unassimilable complexity, from which audience members are encouraged to discover meaning, thus defining individual difference rather than celebrating solidarity. This presages Barker's identification of his own dramatic theory and form, "Theatre of Catastrophe", for which his collection of essays *Arguments for a Theatre* serves as an exposition.

With over 50 works for stage, radio, film and television to his name, Barker's achievements in the 1980's and 90's include reinventions of the dramatic poem as monologue (*Don't Exaggerate, The Breath of the Crowd, Gary the Thief/ Gary Upright*), painfully exhilarating explorations of the relationships between power and sexuality (*The Castle, Women Beware Women*), a huge, anti-systematic, mythic exploration of transgression (*The Bite of the Night*), and the insistence on self-definition as disruptive of corrupting social injunctions to reconciliation and order (*The Europeans*). 1988 saw the first production by The Wrestling School, a theatre company whose sole function is the performance of Barker plays. Their presentations of Barker's recent stage plays (*The Last Supper, Seven Lears, Golgo*) suggest that the keynotes of his writing are, increasingly, the individual reappraisal of morality, and the destabilisation of truth, conducted through language "as luscious and as spiteful as love, of which it is an expression".

—David Ian Rabey

See also *Volume 1* entry on *Victory*.

BARKER, James Nelson. Born in Philadelphia, Pennsylvania, USA, 17 June 1784; son of General George Barker. Educated at schools in Philadelphia. Married Mary Rogers in 1811; one daughter. First play, *Tears and Smiles*, produced 1807; studied government, Washington, D.C., 1809–10; returned to Philadelphia and resumed writing for the stage, 1812; commissioned Captain in the 2nd US Artillery, War of 1812; Assistant Adjutant-General, US Army, rising to the rank of Major, 1814–17; contributed "The Drama" series to *Dramatic Pieces*, 1816–17; member, Board of Aldermen, Philadelphia, 1817–19, 1822–29; Mayor, 1819–21; Collector of the Port of Philadelphia, 1829–38; controller, US Department of the Treasury, Washington, DC, 1838–41, and served various administrations as clerk in the office of the Chief Clerk of the Treasury, 1841–58. Died in Washington, DC, 9 March 1858.

Works

Stage Works

Tears and Smiles (produced Chestnut Street Theatre, Philadelphia, 1807). 1808; also edited by Paul H. Musser, in *James Nelson Barker*, 1929.
The Embargo; or, What News? (produced Chestnut Street Theatre, Philadelphia, 1808).
Travellers; or, Music's Fascination, from a work by Andrew Cherry (produced Chestnut Street Theatre, Philadelphia, 1808).
The Indian Princess; or, La Belle Sauvage, music by John Bray (produced Chestnut Street Theatre, Philadelphia,

1808). 1808; revised version, as *Pocahontas* (produced Chestnut Street Theatre, Philadelphia, 1820).
Marmion; or, The Battle of Flodden Field, from the poem by Scott (produced Chestnut Street Theatre, Philadelphia, 1813). 1816.
The Armourer's Escape; or, Three Years at Nootka Sound (produced 1817).
How to Try a Lover (as *A Court of Love*, produced Arch Street Theatre, Philadelphia, 1836). 1817.
Superstition; or, The Fanatic Father (produced Chestnut Street Theatre, Philadelphia, 1824). 1826.

Other

Delaplaine's Repository of the Lives and Portraits of Distinguished American Characters, vol. 1, part 2. 1817.
Sketches of the Primitive Settlements on the River Delaware. 1827.

*

Criticism

Books:
Paul H. Musser, *James Nelson Barker*, Philadelphia, 1929 (includes bibliography and *Tears and Smiles*).
Walter J. Meserve, *An Emerging Entertainment: The Drama of the American People to 1828*, Bloomington, Indiana, 1977.

Articles:
John W. Crowley, "James Nelson Barker in Perspective", in *Educational Theatre Journal*, 24, 1972.

*   *   *

More than any other playwright of his time, James Nelson Barker illustrates in his work the varied focus of themes, attitudes, and techniques in the drama that characterize the pre-Jacksonian years in America. He was also typical of one kind of dramatist of the early 19th century—a literary and political man whose talents were tempted to the theatre off and on during his mature life until he abandoned his dramatic muse altogether and went on to other things. As poet, drama critic, politican, and playwright, however, he consistently emphasized a patriotic interest in the new nation. In his best known play, *Superstition*, he not only used America's past more successfully than did any dramatist of his period but created a villain-hero without peer in early American drama.

Probably influenced by his father, a belligerent Patriot during the Revolution and a fierce politician who became mayor of Philadelphia, Barker was a strong patriot and supporter of America. *America*, although never produced, was essentially a patriotic effusion, a masque "consisting of poetic dialogue, and sung by the genius of America, Science, Liberty and attendant spirits". As a Democrat, Barker stoutly defended Jefferson's Embargo Act of 23 December 1807 with *The Embargo; or, What News?* which he wrote for the benefit performance for Blisset, a comedian with the Chestnut Street Theatre company who produced the play on 16 March 1808 as "a New Interlude written by a Gentleman of the City". *Cherry's Travellers; or, Music's Fascination*, advertised as "by a citizen of Philadelphia", was another patriotic spectacle by Barker, who also dramatized his national interests in a three-act "operatic melodrama" entitled *The Indian Princess; or,*

La Belle Sauvage, with John Bray, an actor-composer, providing the music for Barker's songs. Although Barker took his theme and many incidents of the play from John Smith's *General History of Virginia*, he was not constrained by historical detail, and he embellished the romance of Pocahontas and John Rolfe by manipulating history and creating an effective theatre piece with good change of pace, humor, and dramatic action.

Like other American dramatists who were sometimes reluctant to admit authorship of a play, Barker suffered the burden of his nationality during a period when theatre management was pointedly biased against American literary or theatrical talent. At one time he even consented to have his poetic melodrama, *Marmion*, produced under the pretense that it was written by the English playwright, Thomas Morton. This play, Barker's most successful in the American theatre, was written just before he enlisted his services in the War of 1812. Although it focused on England's attitude toward Scotland in the 16th century, the comparison with England's treatment of America in 1812 was unavoidable. During one performance in Philadelphia in January 1813, it sparked a ten-minute patriotic demonstration.

Tears and Smiles and *How To Try a Lover* demonstrated Barker's interest in love and romance. The earlier play takes place in Philadelphia and makes use of Restoration comic traditions with contemporary French, Irish, and Yankee characters. While revealing all the structural inadequacies of a work by a novice playwright, this play has a wit and comic temper suggesting the potential that was, in part, realized in *How To Try a Lover*, a play based on Pigault-Lebrun's novel, *La Folie espagnole*. In this instance, the usual conventions and intrigues of this type of comedy were enhanced by the development of individual characters and a lightness of action that was seldom found in early American comedy.

Barker's crowning achievement, yet one that neither he nor his contemporaries fully realized as such, was *Superstition; or, The Fanatic Father*. To his major theme of New England intolerance activated by the superstitious mind, Barker fused the incident of the Puritan refugee Goff leading the people against the Indians. The popularity of this historical story notwithstanding—it was one used later by James Fenimore Cooper in *The Wept of Wish-Ton-Wish* and by Nathaniel Hawthorne in the tale of "The Gray Champion"—it is the characterization of the villain, Ravensworth, that distinguishes this play. In spite of stiffness of dialogue, a conventional hero and heroine from romantic tragedy, and a weakness in plotting the climax which only the confusion of the moment makes believable, the character of Ravensworth controls the tragedy and makes it memorable in the history of American drama.

The fanaticism of Reverend Ravensworth is immediately revealed in his hatred of Isabella, the self-contained woman who will not bend to his authority, and in his declaration that his daughter, Mary, must not see Isabella's son, Charles, who will be later identified as the son of Charles I. Spiritually distorted by his belief in sorcery, Ravensworth determines that Isabella and Charles are the curse of the village, and will not desist in his persecution until he forces the court's decision regarding the execution of Charles: "It is accomplish'd", he exclaims, "Guided by Heaven's vengeance". A man of intelligence, eloquence, beliefs, and passions, Ravensworth is a true villain-hero. A clergyman who mistakes his own passion for the voice of God, he enjoys a powerful influence over his congregation and is able to mount a campaign of relentless revenge upon those who will not bow to his authority. From Ravensworth's first words, Barker does a remarkable job in delineating a fanatical father who

follows his god and destroys his daughter, the two objects of his consuming love.

Superstition was Barker's final play. In the presidential administrations of Andrew Jackson and Martin Van Buren he held political appointments and during these years he published the bulk of his poetry. Different conditions in the American theatre might have stimulated him to write more plays, but with only a few dramatic works he left his mark on a slowly developing American drama in his enthusiasm for patriotic drama and his creation of a superb villain-hero.

—Walter J. Meserve

BARLACH, Ernst (Heinrich). Born in Wedel, near Hamburg, Germany, 2 January 1870. Educated at Hamburg Gewerbeschule [Hamburg Industrial Art School], 1888–91; Dresden Academy of Fine Arts, 1891–95, studying sculpture and design; Académie Julian, Paris, 1895–96. Had one illegitimate son, born 1906; won custody battle, 1908. Sculptor in Paris, Hamburg, Altona, and Berlin, 1895–97; editor of *Jugend*, 1898–1902; taught at the Höhr School of Ceramics, Westerwald, 1904; visited Russia, 1906; illustrator for *Simplicissimus*, 1907–08; studied art in Florence, 1909; settled in Güstrow (near Lübeck), Mecklenburg, with his mother and son, 1910; first play, *Der tote Tag*, published 1912; volunteered for the home front at beginning of World War I, working in a children's nursery; first-produced play, *Der arme Vetter*, staged 1919; illustrated his published plays with his own lithographs; subjected to campaign of defamation under the Nazis: his exhibitions banned, works in the public domain destroyed, and he was threatened with house-searches; categorised by the Nazis as a "decadent" artist, 1937. Recipient: Kleist Prize, 1924. Elected to Berlin (1919) and Munich Academies for work as sculptor. Ritter der Friedensklasse des Ordens Pour le Mérite, 1933. Died in Güstrow, 25 October 1938.

Works

Collections

Das dichterische Werk (3 vols.).   1956–59.
Die Prosa.   1958.
Three Plays (includes *The Genuine Sedemunds; The Flood; The Blue Boll*), translated by Alex Page.   1964.

Stage Works:

Der tote Tag (produced Schauspielhaus, Leipzig, 1919). 1912.
Der arme Vetter (produced Kammerspiele, Hamburg, 1919). 1918.
Die echten Sedemunds (produced Kammerspiele, Hamburg, 1921). 1920; translated as *The Genuine Sedemunds*, in *Three Plays*, 1921.
Der Findling (produced Schauspielhaus, Königsberg, 1928). 1922.
Die Sündflut (produced Württembergisches Landestheater, Stuttgart, 1924). 1924; translated as *The Flood*, in *Three Plays*, 1964.

Der blaue Boll (produced Württembergisches Landestheater, Stuttgart, 1926).   1926; translated as *The Blue Boll*, in *Three Plays*, 1964; as *Squire Blue Boll*, in *Seven Expressionist Plays*, translated by J.M. Ritchie and H.F. Garten, 1968.
Die gute Zeit (produced Stadttheater, Gera, 1929).   1929.
Der Graf von Ratzeburg (produced Lessing –Theater, Nuremberg, 1951).   1951.

Fiction

Seespeck (novel).   1948.
Der gestohlene Mond (novel), edited by Friedrich Dross.   1948.

Memoirs and Letters

Ein selbsterzähltes Leben.   1928.
Aus seinen Briefen, edited by Friedrich Dross.   1947.
Ernst Barlach: Leben und Werk in seinen Briefen, edited by Friedrich Dross.   1952.
Frühe und späte Briefe, edited by Paul Schurek and Hugo Sieker.   1962.
Die Briefe 1888–1938 (2 vols.), edited by Friedrich Dross.   1968–69.
Berichte, Gespräche, Erinnerungen, edited by Elmar Jansen.   1972.

Other

Fragmente.   1939.
Barlach im Gespräch, edited by Friedrich Schult.   1948.
Sechs kleine Schriften zu besonderen Gelegenheiten, edited by F. Schult.   1950.
Güstrower Fragmente.   1951.
Drei Pariser Fragmente.   1952.

Illustrator, *Der Knopf: Ein Gedicht*, by Reinhold von Walter. 1919.

*

Criticism

Books:
Helmut Dohle, *Das Problem Barlach: Probleme, Charaktere seiner Dramen*, Cologne, 1957.
Willi Flemming, *Ernst Barlach: Wesen und Werk*, Bern, 1958.
Herbert Meier, *Der verborgene Gott: Studien zu den Dramen Barlachs*, Nuremburg, 1963.
Alfred Werner, *Barlach: His Life and Work*, New York, 1966.
Edson M. Chick, *Ernst Barlach*, New York, 1967.
Bernard R. Anderson, "The Grotesque in Barlach's Work", in *Essays on German Literature in Honour of G. Joyce Hallamore*, edited by Michael S. Batts and Marketa G. Stankiewicz, Toronto, 1968.
Wolfgang Paulsen, "Zur Struktur von Barlachs Dramen", in *Aspekte des Expressionismus*, edited by Paulsen, Heidelberg, 1968.
Karl Graucob, *Ernst Barlachs Dramen*, Kiel, 1969.
Herbert Kaiser, *Der Dramatiker Ernst Barlach: Analysen und Gesamtdeutung*, Munich, 1972.
Naomi Jackson Groves, *Ernst Barlach: Leben im Werk, Plastiken, Zeichnungen und Graphiken, Dramen, Prosawerke und Briefe*, Königstein im Taunus, 1975.

Henning Falkenstein, *Ernst Barlach*, Berlin, 1978.
Mannfred Durzak, *Das expressionistische Drama: Ernst Barlach; Ernst Toller; Fritz von Unruh*, Munich, 1979.
Margarethe Heukäufer, *Sprache und Gesellschaft im dramatischen Werk Ernst Barlachs*, Heidelberg, 1985.
Friedrich Schult, *Barlach im Gespräch*, Leipzig, 1985.
Kent W. Hooper, *Ernst Barlach's Literary and Visual Art: The Issue of Multiple Talent*, Ann Arbor, Michigan, 1987.

Articles:
Edson M. Chick, "Comic and Grotesque Elements in Ernst Barlach", in *Modern Language Quarterly*, 20, 1959.
Edson. M. Chick, "Ernst Barlach's *Der arme Vetter*", in *Modern Language Review*, 57, 1962.
Edson M. Chick, "Ernst Barlach and the Theater", in *German Quarterly*, 36, 1963.
W.I. Lucas, "*Der blaue Boll* and the New Man", in *German Life and Letters*, 16, 1963.
Heinz Beckmann, "Die metaphysische Tragödie in Ernst Barlachs Dramen", in *Veröffentlichungen der Ernst Barlach Gesellschaft*, 1964–65.
Ilhi Synn, "The Language in Barlach's Dramas", in *Revue des langues vivantes*, 37, 1971.
Ilhi Synn, "'Culpa Patris' in Barlach's Dramas", in *Litteratur in Wissenschaft und Unterricht*, 4, 1971.
Peter Meech, "The Frog and the Star: The Role of Music in the Dramatic and Visual Works of Ernst Barlach", in *Forum for Modern Language Studies*, 9, 1973.

*   *   *

Ernst Barlach was in his 40's before he wrote his first play *Der tote Tag*, (The Dead Day), in 1912. As well as two unfinished novels, he wrote in all seven plays ending with the fragmentary *Der Graf von Ratzeburg*, (The Duke of Ratzeburg), the 1927, unrevised, version of which was not published until 1951. Before 1912 Barlach had already established himself as a sculptor and graphic artist of international standing, a career he continued in parallel with his writing.

He was elected to membership of the Berlin and Munich academies for his work as a sculptor, while receiving the Kleist prize for his dramatic writing. He was awarded Prussia's highest honour "Pour le Mérite" in 1933. However, after the victory of the Nazis in Germany, his work was declared to be degenerate and removed from public exhibition—many pieces were destroyed. His plays, which had been staged with some success, but to mixed reviews from often incomprehending critics, were dropped from the German theatre repertoire until after World War II, since when they have been regularly revived. Barlach shared with a number of the artists of expressionism (most notably Oskar Kokoschka) a facility in more than one means of artistic expression, and much of the interest for students of Barlach lies in the transference of imagery from his sculpture and graphic work to his writing for the stage—the sculptor as dramatist. He also frequently illustrated the published versions of his plays.

Before he started writing he made two important overseas journeys. In 1906 he travelled to Russia, where the vastness of the countryside, and the stoicism with which the peasants endured their grinding poverty, shaped his portrayal of the human form for the rest of his career. In 1909 he was awarded a scholarship to study in Florence. There he was very unhappy, and returned as soon as practicable to settle in Güstrow, where he spent the rest of his life. It is the landscape and atmosphere of the north German coastal region which informs each of his plays.

Der tote Tag (The Dead Day) is an obscure allegory, perhaps inspired by Barlach's winning of custody over his illegitimate son. The play centres on sight and seeing. The Mother prefers the dark interior of the great hall in which the action is set. Inspired by the blind Kuhle, whose eyes refused to receive the complex images of reality and ceased to function, the Son wishes to see, but cannot through the thick mist around the hall.

In *Der arme Vetter* (The Poor Cousin) a choice is demanded of the heroine between her respectable fiancé, Siebenmark, and a suicide, Iver, whom they have met by chance on an Easter-Day boat trip to an island. Finally she chooses to associate herself with the corpse, as he has shown a sense of vision lacking in the fiancé—he has found life through a "higher death". Although allegorical, and written in Barlach's often difficult and obscure dialogue, the play is peopled with realistic and recognizable characters from the north German countryside, such as the self-satisfied bourgeois, Siebenmark, who does in fact achieve a new vision at the end of the play.

Die echten Sedemunds (The Genuine Sedemunds) is a grotesque comedy in which a father feigns mortal illness to force his too-radical son to return home in order to enter a mental asylum. The son compels the father to confess that he drove his mother to suicide, but in the confession of all his sins, the father shows his moral superiority over the son, who enters the asylum voluntarily. The central action is surrounded by a colourful collection of characters and sub-plots at a village shooting festival.

The play for which Barlach was awarded the Kleist Prize, *Die Sündflut* (The Flood) concerns a protracted argument between Noah and a tormentor, Calan, in which God is presented on stage in different guises—as a beggar and as a wealthy traveller. Calan's temptation of Noah, and Noah's faith in his vision of God, culminates in Calan's cutting off of a shepherd's hands, while challenging Noah's God to prevent him—which he does not. However, as Noah enters the ark as the waters rise, Calan is tied down hand and foot, the only person left to untie him being the handless shepherd. The play, which Barlach had intended as a simple debate, confused many of the critics and caused a good deal of discussion in religious groups.

Barlach's central themes of redemption, of new vision, and of characters' attempts to free themselves from "the flesh" find their most convincing expression in his most frequently revived play, *Der blaue Boll* (The Blue Boll). Boll, a wealthy and obese landowner, in search of a "new Boll", meets Grete, who intends to liberate her children from "the flesh" by poisoning them. Both characters are reconciled to their lives through a redemptive experience. Grete experiences a vision of Hell, and Boll (while watching over Grete one night in the church) before climbing the tower with the intention of committing suicide. Der Herr (The Lord), intervenes and declares that Boll is now ready for a new life, having overcome the "old Boll". Boll sees that through suffering and struggle he will attain self-realisation. The play has powerful allegorical elements, but is again peopled with realistically painted inhabitants of a small North German town, with its chapel, shops, and inn.

Barlach's central concern in his playwriting is to gain a perspective on two differing types of infinity, temporal and spatial, focusing not only on timelessness and eternity, but also on the contract between the minutiae of everyday life on earth and the infinity of limitless space. His central theme is that of "*werden*", of "becoming". Against recognizable backgrounds (Barlach could not understand people regarding his characters as anything other than realistic portrayals of real personalities), he presents different spiritual journeys undertaken by his protagonists in their search for their new selves—Barlach's interpretation of the Expressionists' concept of *Der neue Mensch* (The New Man).

—Anthony Meech

BARNES, Peter. Born in London, 10 January 1931. Educated at Stroud Grammar School, Gloucestershire. Served in the Royal Air Force, 1949–50. Married Charlotte Beck in 1961. Worked for the London County Council, 1948 and 1950–53; critic, *Films and Filming*, London, 1954; story editor, Warwick Films, 1956; first play, *The Time of the Barracudas*, produced 1963; has directed many of his own plays. Recipient: John Whiting Award, 1969; *Evening Standard* award, 1969; Olivier Award, 1985.

Works

Collections

Collected Plays (includes *The Ruling Class; Leonardo's Last Supper; Noonday Demons; The Bewitched; Laughter!; Barnes' People*). 1981.
Barnes' People II: Seven Duologues. 1984.
"The Real Long John Silver" and Other Plays: Barnes' People III (includes *After the Funeral; The Peace of Westphalia; The Real Long John Silver; The Heirs of Diogenes; Sisters; Dancing; The Perfect Pair; The Three Visions*). 1986.
Plays 1 (includes *The Ruling Class; Leonardo's Last Supper* and *Noonday Demons; The Bewitched; Laughter!; Barnes' People*). 1989.
"The Spirit of Man" and More Barnes' People (includes *The Spirit of Man* trilogy: *A Hand Witch of the Second Stage, From Sleep and Shadow,* and *The Night of the Sinhat Torah*; and the radio plays *Madame Zenobia, Slaughterman*; and *The Road to Strome*). 1990.

Stage Works

The Time of the Barracudas (produced San Francisco, 1963).
Sclerosis (produce Traverse Theatre, Edinburgh, 1965).
The Ruling Class: A Baroque Comedy (produced Playhouse, Nottingham, 1968). 1969.
Leonardo's Last Supper, (produced Open Space Theatre, London, 1969). With *Noonday Demons,* 1970.
Noonday Demons (produced *Open Space Theatre*, London, 1969). With *Leonardo's Last Supper,* 1970.
Lulu, from plays by Wedekind, translated by Charlotte Beck (produced Playhouse, Nottingham, 1970). 1971.
The Alchemist, with Trevor Nunn, from the play by Jonson (produced Playhouse, Nottingham, 1970; revised version produced The Other Place, Stratford-on-Avon, 1977).
The Devil is an Ass, from the play by Jonson (produced Playhouse, Nottingham, 1973; revised version produced Edinburgh, 1976).
The Bewitched (produced Aldwych Theatre, London, 1974). 1974.
The Frontiers of Farce, from plays by Feydeau and Wedekind (produced Old Vic Theatre, London, 1976).

For All Those Who Get Despondent (cabaret), from works by Brecht and Wedekind (produced Royal Court Theatre Upstairs, London, 1976).

Antonio, from plays by Marston (broadcast 1977; produced Playhouse, Nottingham, 1979).

Laughter! (produced Royal Court Theatre, London, 1978). 1978.

The Devil Himself (revue), from a play by Wedekind, music by Carl Davis and Stephen Deutsch (produced Lyric Theatre, Hammersmith, London, 1980).

Somersaults (revue; produced Haymarket Theatre, Leicester, 1981).

Red Noses (produced Barbican Theatre, London, 1985). 1985.

Scenes from a Marriage, from plays by Feydeau (produced Barbican Theatre, London, 1986).

The Real Long John Silver, from the radio play (produced London, 1989). In *"The Real Long John Silver" and other Plays*, 1986.

Sunsets and Glories (produced Leeds, 1990).   1990.

Screenplays

Violent Moment, 1959; *The White Trap*, 1959; *Breakout*, 1959; *The Professionals*, 1960; *Off-Beat*, 1961; *Ring of Spies (Ring of Treason)*, with Frank Launder, 1963; *Not with My Wife You Don't*, with others, 1966; *The Ruling Class*, 1972; *Leonardo's Last Supper*, 1977; *Enchanted April*, 1991.

Television Plays

The Man with a Feather in His Hat, 1960; *Revolutionary Witness*, 1989, and *Nobody Here But Us Chickens*, 1989 (published 1989); *More Than a Touch of Zen*, 1989; *Not as Bad as They Seem*, 1989; *The Spirit of Man* (published with *More Barnes People*, 1990).

Radio Plays

My Ben Jonson, 1973; *Eastward Ho!*, from the play by Jonson, Chapman, and Marston, 1973; *Antonio*, 1977; *The Two Hangmen: Brecht and Wedekind* (from the stage play *For All Those Who Get Despondent*), 1978; *A Chaste Maid in Cheapside*, from the play by Middleton, 1979; *Eulogy on Baldness*, from work by Synesius of Cyrene, 1980; *For the Conveyance of Oysters*, from a work by Gorky, 1981; *The Soldier's Fortune*, from the play by Thomas Otway, 1981; *The Atheist*, from the play by Thomas Otway, 1981; *Barnes' People*, 1981 (published in *Collected Plays*, 1981); *The Singer*, from a work by Wedekind, 1981; *The Magician*, from a work by Gorky, 1982; *The Dutch Courtesan*, from the play by Marston, 1982; *A Mad World, My Masters*, from the play by Middleton, 1983; *Barnes' People II*, 1984 (published 1984); *The Primrose Path*, from a play by Feydeau, 1984; *A Trick to Catch the Old One*, from the play by Middleton, 1985; *The Old Law*, from the play by Middleton and Rowley, 1986; *Woman of Paris*, from a play by Henri Becque, 1986; *Barnes' People III*, 1986 (published 1986); *No End to Dreaming*, 1987; *The Magnetic Lady*, from the play by Jonson, 1987; *The Devil is an Ass*, from the play by Jonson, 1987; *Don Juan and Faust*, from the play by Grabbe, 1987; *Madame Zenobia*, 1989, *Slaughterman*, 1990, and *The Road to Strome*, 1990 (all published in *"The Spirit of Man" and More Barnes People*, 1990).

*

Criticism

Books:

Bernard F. Dukore, *The Theatre of Peter Barnes*, London, 1981.

Articles:

Peter Barnes and Yvonne Schafer, "An Interview with Peter Barnes", in *Journal of Dramatic Theory and Criticism*, vol.2 no.1, 1987.

Peter Barnes and Clive Barker, "On Class, Christianity, and Questions of Comedy" (interview), in *New Theatre Quarterly*, 21, 1990.

*   *   *

Although he supports himself by his writing for radio and the screen, Peter Barnes' reputation as one of the most original and talented contemporary British playwrights is founded on a small number of major dramas, darkly comic and fiercely satirical in tone.

His earliest plays and a number of more recent works have a contemporary setting. *Sclerosis* dealt with the specious politics and brutalities of the recent civil war in Cyprus, but Barnes' chosen ground is a time of crisis in the history of earlier empires and other civilisations. The still unperformed *Heaven's Blessing* is set in Babylon; other plays have dealt with quarrelling Christian hermits in 4th-century Egypt, 14th-century France at the time of the Black Death, Leonardo da Vinci's death at Amboise, the reign of the last of the Hapsburgs in 17th-century Spain, the rise to power of Ivan the Terrible (paired with the administrators of Auschwitz), and the Victorian London of Jack the Ripper. Beyond their appeal to historical romanticism, such epochs are chosen for their demonstration of brutal or crazed authority in action, violent power struggles, hierarchical class conflict, religious fanaticism, and social intolerance.

Barnes delights in discovering bizarre facts, and surrealistic realities, and using anachronism as a deliberate technique to indicate that such sensational material is always a stalking horse for the main attack on the iniquities of contemporary British society. Frustrated by the reluctance of even major companies to mount his epically conceived major works, the dramatist has recently turned to writing what he calls historical footnotes, miniature pieces in which insignificant individuals report their critical and subversive view of history as seen from below.

A ruthless comic satirist, Barnes focuses passionately and obsessively on a narrow range of subjects. There is a Swiftian fascination with mortality in its cruellest and most violent forms: impalement, murder, torture, mutilation, mass execution—all treated in a way to raise wild laughter but going beyond even Jacobean catalogues of death. This is accompanied by an insistence on the grossest aspects of physicality, intended both to shock the audience into a response and to undercut the pretentions of oppressive greatness and authority. Leonardo da Vinci is drowned in "a bucket of excrement, urine and vomit"; in *The Bewitched*, the physical deformity and imbecility of Carlos II of Spain is emphasised as he leads his court dancing in a series of spastic lurches or collapses in epileptic fits.

Such assaults on human pride and vanity are accompanied by similar attacks on the tyrannical exercise of political and ecclesiastical power (usually linked, and typically ridiculed through association with impotence and insanity), the prudish repression of sexual desire, and the corrupting influence of capitalism (frequently characterised as literally and metaphorically murderous). Barnes offers little by way of solutions; his plays exist to expose ruthless authority and the inability to love or feel, rather than to advocate programmes of reform. Laughter and mockery is at once his prime means of bringing delight to such dark instruction and another powerful satirical weapon. However, the dramatist is well aware that it is a double-edged one, capable of making cruelty and injustice tolerable (*Laughter!* concludes with a group of Jewish prisoners joking their way through the Extermination Camp Christmas Concert), and this has led to the development of a serious debate on the nature and social function of comedy and laughter, running through much of his work and focused on the figure of the red-nosed clown.

Barnes offers the best description of his own theatre:

> The aim is to create, by means of soliloquy, formalized ritual, slapstick, songs and dances, a comic theatre of contrasting moods and opposites, where everything is simultaneously tragic and ridiculous. And we hope never to consent to the deadly servitude of naturalism, or lose our hunger for true size, weight and texture.

In using kaleidoscopic theatrical experiences, sudden and extreme contrasts of mood and subject, rapid shifts in location, radical compressions and movements of time, constant reorientation, and baroque juxtapositions of hilarity with horrific suffering, bizarre sensation with deadpan comic deflation, anarchic action with solemn ritual, he works both to detach the audience from the spectacle offered on the stage and to induce powerful emotional responses of astonishment, horror, delight, and exhilaration, in a manner analogous to the disorientating stream of video images projected to pop music film tracks.

Linguistic vividness is one of the most striking features of Barnes' drama. His language stands at the opposite pole to the deliberate understatement and economy of means of a writer such as Pinter. As with the Renaissance dramatists he admires (notably Jonson, Marston, and Middleton), copiousness, variety, untrammelled eclecticism, and richness of imagery are the hallmarks of his style. Barnes' people continually delight in talk. The monologues, duologues, and trios of his radio work seem the natural outworking of such excited and exciting garrulousness.

Each play displays the fresh invention of a carefully constructed and distinctive theatrical language; an artificial vernacular capable of suggesting a particular historical period, yet flexible enough to distinguish individual speakers and at the same time accommodate the harvest of Barnes' omnivorous reading and research (the parallel here is with John Webster). Characteristically the linguistic texture of a Barnes play is dense with quotation, allusion, and redrafting. Archaisms, dialectical forms, neologisms, and slang and arcane technical terms mingle with one-line gags, the lyrics of old American film musicals, Latin church ritual, nursery rhymes, outrageous punning, name-calling, and strikingly imaginative images, giving rise to an extraordinary variety of register and tone. Words are supplemented by an Artaudian language of inarticulate sounds, from screams to cries and animal noises, supported by stunning musical and aural effects.

Barnes' dramaturgy makes the most extreme demands on the technical resources of the theatre and his actors. The plays frequently call for astonishing and spectacular visual and aural effects, sudden *coups de théâtre*, large-scale scenes of courtly ritual and elaborate ceremonial; the Prologue to *The Bewitched* requires a grand processional entry of Queen Mariana with hooded monks singing the Magnificat, bearing candles and the skeleton of a saint on a bier, followed by a bedding and birth scene in which "the whole room shakes to a brutal thudding" and the skeleton jerks upright before collapsing in a heap. The Queen's birth cries are "drowned by a great tearing sound" and the floor slowly splits apart to emit a monstrous foetus in a cawl. In *Red Noses*, golden butterflies descend through the air as "a huge mountain of gold" is wheeled on stage. Expressionist effects, like the entry to a clap of thunder of an "eight-foot beast" in the shape of a gigantic guinea-pig dressed in top hat and morning coat, in *The Ruling Class*, or Pope Clement II howling like a wolf, in *Red Noses*, add to the baroque theatricality of the plays.

The actors are frequently called on to display circus skills of parodic movement, showmanship, and clowning, brought to a peak in *Red Noses* with its heroic troupe of blind jugglers, one-legged dancers, dumb musicians and stammering comedians. Beyond this they are required to perform virtuoso feats of vocalisation and lightning shifts of mood and mode, from slapstick action to stately ritual or naturalistic behaviour.

The experience of Barnes' theatre is one of enormous energy and delighted excess, of self-conscious theatricality and extravagant celebration; his comedy savages as it creates and affirms the vitality of his fools and monsters.

—Colin Gibson

See also *Volume 1* entry on *The Ruling Class*.

BARRIE, (Sir) J(ames) M(atthew). Born in Kirriemuir, Forfarshire (now Angus), Scotland, 9 May 1860. Educated at Misses Adam School, Kirriemuir; Glasgow Academy, 1868–70; Forfar Academy, 1870–72; Dumfries Academy, 1873–78; University of Edinburgh, 1878–82, MA 1882. Married the actress Mary Ansell in 1894 (divorced 1909). First play, *Bandolero, the Bandit*, staged 1877; drama and book critic, Edinburgh *Courant*, 1879–82; leader writer, Nottingham *Journal*, 1883–84; lived in London after 1885: journalist, contributing to the *St. James's Gazette* and *British Weekly*, 1885–90. President, Society of Authors, 1928–37, and Dramatists' Club, 1934–37. LL.D: University of St. Andrews, 1898; University of Edinburgh, 1909; D. Litt.: Oxford University, 1926; Cambridge University, 1930. Rector, University of St. Andrews. 1919–22; chancellor, University of Edinburgh, 1930–37. Created Baronet, 1913; Order of Merit, 1922. Died in London, 19 June 1937.

Works

Collections

The Works (Kirriemuir Edition; 10 vols.).   1913.
Half Hours (includes *Pantaloon; The Twelve-Pound Look; Rosalind; The Will*).   1914.
The Works (10 vols.).   1918.
Echoes of the War (includes *The Old Lady Show Her Medals; The New Word; Barbara's Wedding; A Well-Remembered Voice*).   1918.
Representative Plays (includes *Quality Street; The Admirable Crichton; What Every Woman Knows; Dear Brutus; The Twelve-Pound Look; The Old Lady Shows Her Medals*), edited by W.L. Phelps.   1926.

"What is genius? It is the power to be a boy again at will."

Cartoon of **J.M. Barrie** as Peter Pan.

The Works (Peter Pan Edition; 14 vols.). 1929–31.
The Plays (includes *Peter Pan; The Admirable Crichton; Alice Sit-by-the-Fire; What Every Woman Knows; A Kiss for Cinderella; Dear Brutus; Mary Rose; Pantaloon; Half an Hour; Seven Women; Old Friends; The Twelve-Pound Look; The New Word; A Well-Remembered Voice; Barbara's Wedding; The Old Lady Shows Her Medals; Shall We Join the Ladies?*). 1928; augmented edition, edited by A.E. Wilson (includes *Walker; London; The Professor's Love Story; The Little Minister; The Wedding Guest; The Boy David*), 1942.
Plays and Stories: edited by Roger Lancelyn Green. 1962.

Stage works

Bandolero, the Bandit (produced Dumfries Academy, Dumfries, Scotland, 1877).
Caught Napping. 1883.
Richard Savage, with H.B. Marriott Watson (produced Criterion Theatre, London, 1891). 1891.
Ibsen's Ghost; or, Toole Up-to-Date (produced Toole's Theatre, London, 1891). 1939.
Walker, London (produced Toole's Theatre, London, 1892). 1907.
Becky Sharp, from the novel *Vanity Fair* by Thackeray (produced Terry's Theatre, London, 1893).
Jane Annie; or, The Good Conduct Prize, with Arthur Conan Doyle, music by Ernest Ford (produced Savoy Theatre, London, 1893). 1893.
The Professor's Love Story (produced Comedy Theatre, London, 1894). In *Plays*, 1942.

The Little Minister, from the novel (produced Theatre Royal, Haymarket, London, 1897; as *Little Mary*, produced Wyndham's Theatre, London, 1903). In *Plays*, 1942.
A Platonic Friendship (produced Theatre Royal, Drury Lane, London, 1898).
The Wedding Guest (produced Garrick Theatre, London, 1900). 1900.
Quality Street (produced Vaudeville Theatre, London, 1902). 1913.
The Admirable Crichton (produced Duke of York's Theatre, London, 1902). 1914.
Peter Pan; or, The Boy Who Would Not Grow Up (produced Duke of York's Theatre, London, 1904; revised version, produced 1905). In *Plays*, 1928.
Pantaloon (produced Duke of York's Theatre, London, 1905). In *Half Hours*, 1914.
Alice Sit-by-the-Fire (produced Duke of York's Theatre, London, 1905). 1919.
Josephine (produced Comedy Theatre, London, 1906).
Punch (produced Comedy Theatre, London, 1906).
When Wendy Grew Up: An Afterthought (produced 1908). 1957.
What Every Woman Knows (produced Comedy Theatre, London, 1908). 1918.
Old Friends (produced Duke of York's Theatre, London, 1910). In *Plays*, 1928.
A Slice of Life (produced Duke of York's Theatre, London, 1910).
The Twelve-Pound Look (produced Duke of York's Theatre, London, 1910). In *Half Hours*, 1914.
Rosalind (produced Duke of York's Theatre, London, 1912). In *Half Hours*, 1914.
The Dramatists Get What They Want (produced Hippodrome Theatre, London, 1912; as *The Censor and the Dramatists*, produced 1913).
The Will (produced Duke of York's Theatre, London, 1913). In *Half Hours*, 1914.
The Adored One: A Legend of the Old Bailey (produced Duke of York's Theatre, London, 1913; as *The Legend of Leonora*, produced 1914; shortened version, as *Seven Women*, produced New Theatre, London, 1917). 1913; as *Seven Women* in *Plays*, 1928.
Half an Hour (produced Hippodrome Theatre, London, 1913). In *Plays*, 1928.
Der Tag (produced Coliseum Theatre, London, 1914; as *Der Tag; or, The Tragic Man*, produced 1914). 1914.
Rosy Rapture, The Pride of the Beauty Chorus, music by H. Darewski and Jerome Kern (produced Duke of York's Theatre, London, 1915).
The Fatal Typist (produced Her Majesty's Theatre, London, 1915).
The New Word (produced Duke of York's Theatre, London, 1915). In *Echoes of the War*, 1918.
The Real Thing at Last (produced Coliseum Theatre, London, 1916).
Irene Vanbrugh's Pantomime (produced Coliseum Theatre, London, 1916).
Shakespeare's Legacy (produced Duke of York's Theatre, London, 1916). 1916.
A Kiss for Cinderella (produced Wyndham's Theatre, London, 1916). 1920.
The Old Lady Shows Her Medals (produced New Theatre, London, 1917). In *Echoes of the War*, 1918.
Reconstructing the Crime (produced Palace Theatre, London, 1917).
Dear Brutus (produced Wyndham's Theatre, London, 1917). 1922.

La Politesse (produced Wyndham's Theatre, London, 1918).

A Well-Remembered Voice (produced Wyndham's Theatre, London, 1918).   In *Echoes of the War*, 1918.

Barbara's Wedding (produced Savoy Theatre, London, 1927).   In *Echoes of the War*, 1918.

The Truth About the Russian Dancers (ballet), music by Arnold Bax (produced Coliseum Theatre, London, 1920). 1962.

Mary Rose (produced Haymarket Theatre, London, 1920). 1924.

Shall We Join the Ladies? (produced Palace Theatre, London, 1921).   In *Plays*, 1928.

Neil and Tintinnabulum.   1925.

The Boy David (produced King's Theatre, Edinburgh, 1936). 1938.

Screenplays

The Little Minister, 1915; *The Real Thing at Last*, 1916; *As You Like It*, with Robert Cullen, 1936.

Fiction

Better Dead.   1887.
When a Man's Single: A Tale of Literary Life.   1888.
The Little Minister.   1891.
Two of Them.   1893.
A Tillyloss Scandal.   1893.
Sentimental Tommy: The Story of His Boyhood.   1896.
Tommy and Grizel.   1900.
The Boy Castaways of Black Lake Island.   1901.
The Little White Bird.   1902; as *The Little White Bird; or, Adventures in Kensington Gardens*, 1902; revised material for children, as *Peter Pan in Kensington Gardens*, 1906.
Peter and Wendy.   1911; as *Peter Pan and Wendy*, 1921.
Farewell Miss Julie Logan: A Wintry Tale.   1932.

Verse

Scotland's Lament: A Poem on the Death of Robert Louis Stevenson.   1895.

Memoirs and Letters

Letters, edited by Viola Meynell.   1942.

Other

The New Amphion.   1886.
Auld Licht Idylls.   1888.
A Window in Thrums.   1889.
An Edinburgh Eleven: Pencil Portraits from College Life. 1889.
My Lady Nicotine.   1890.
"A Holiday in Bed" and Other Sketches.   1892.
A Lady's Shoe.   1893.
"An Auld Licht Manse" and Other Sketches.   1893.
Allahakbarries C.C. (on cricket).   1893.
Margaret Ogilvy, by Her Son.   1896.
The Allahakbarrie Book of Broadway Cricket for 1899. 1899.
George Meredith 1909.   1909; as *Neither Dorking nor the Abbey*, 1910.
Charles Frohman: A Tribute.   1915.
Who Was Sarah Findlay? by Mark Twain, with a Suggested Solution of the Mystery.   1917.
The Greenwood Hat, Being a Memoir of James Anon 1885–1887.   1930; revised edition, 1937.

M'Connachie and J.M.B.: Speeches.   1938.

*

Bibliographies

B.D. Cutler, *Barrie: A Bibliography*, New York, 1931.
Carl Markgraf, *J.M. Barrie: An Annotated Secondary Bibliography*, Greensboro, North Carolina, 1989.

Criticism

Books:
H.M. Walbrook, *J.M. Barrie and the Theatre*, London, 1922.
Patrick Braybrooke, *J.M. Barrie*, London, 1924.
Thomas Moult, *Barrie*, London, 1928.
F.J. Harvey Darnton, *Barrie*, London, 1929.
Denis Mackail, *The Story of J.M.B. (Sir James Barrie)*, London, 1941.
Roger Lancelyn Green, *Barrie*, London, 1960.
Janet Dunbar, *Barrie: The Man Behind the Image*, Boston, 1970.
Harry M. Geduld, *Sir James Barrie*, New York, 1971.
Allen Wright, *Barrie: Glamour of Twilight*, Edinburgh, 1976.
Andrew Birkin, *Barrie and the Lost Boys*, London, 1979.
Leonee Ormond, *J.M. Barrie*, Edinburgh, 1987.
R.D.S. Jack, *The Road to the Never Land: A Reassessment of Barrie's Dramatic Art*, Aberdeen, 1990.

*   *   *

Barrie, almost universally accepted by his contemporaries as a genius, is now dismissed by most critics. Of his canon, only *Peter Pan*, *Mary Rose*, and *Dear Brutus* are regularly mentioned. The reference is brief, focusing on the children's audience of the first and the "whimsical fantasy" of the others. The reasons for such a volte-face are many and complex. Certainly, Barrie has suffered more than most from the vogue for Freudian criticism. His self-confessed mother-complex led some writers to isolate only the Oedipal themes in his work and others to attack the writer via the man. Surprisingly, he is even less popular in his homeland than elsewhere. In part this is because he provides a convenient anti-myth to pit against Burns. More fundamentally, he is still not forgiven for at least appearing to hold up comic Scottish stereotypes for the pleasure of English audiences. Like Harry Lauder he is viewed as a sort of literary traitor. Finally, he has been rejected as an artistically dishonest time-server of an undemanding, populist theatre. With the potential for greater things, he chose merely to charm. In this context he is set against Shaw and again found wanting.

Some recent criticism has begun to challenge the simplicity of these views. The stress on motherhood has been related also to Barrie's advanced literary theory, as advanced in his prose works *Sentimental Tommy* and *Tommy and Grizel*. Consistently—but especially in *Little Mary* and *Peter Pan*—he addresses the problem of artistic creation as compared to its divine and natural equivalents. *Little Mary* enacts, with subtlety, the idea that writing may be the male's egotistical substitute for childbearing. *Peter Pan* uses a flawed pagan creation myth to present the modern vision of Nietzsche's world without God. In its Dedication, Barrie claims sole authorship, joint authorship, and non-authorship; he grants the true creative power variously to his pen, to the youngest actress, to the boys whose adventures inspired it, to the audience, and to a cynical stage-hand.

The Scottish situation has been exacerbated by the need for a sub-culture to distinguish itself paradigmatically and ethnologically. As paradigms de-historicise, Barrie's anglicisation, upward social movement, and right-wing views have been unfavourably stressed in an age which values nationalism and left-wing radicalism as the distinguishing characteristics of the Scot. In fact, Barrie's competitive use of the more democratic opportunities and curriculum offered by 19th-century Scottish education was the defining distinctiveness of his own day. That it brought him more closely into line with Adam Smith than Hugh MacDiarmid may be a matter for ideological regret, but it is unsurprising and irrelevant to any specifically literary evaluation. Textual study reveals, further, that in only one play—*The Little Minister*—does he threaten to betray the Scottish character in the manner suggested. Usually, as in *Walker, London* or *Mary Rose*, any one national stereotype is comically balanced against another. Never—even with the bigoted elders in *The Little Minister*—does the hilarious naivety of the rural Scot lack matching satire of English high society; never is his simplicity seen as other than a necessary condition of dignity and merit.

A sentimental superficiality certainly does exist. The plots of Barrie's plays often end with cloyingly romantic scenes. But how does this evidence square with the playwright's claim to be so complex that he is only partially understood (*Sentimental Tommy*)? How does it sit with his admiration for, and professed imitation of, Ibsen? Jacqueline Rose's study of *Peter Pan* (*The Case of Peter Pan*, 1984) is the first major reassessment to claim this complexity while using the critical approach favoured by Barrie. It may well be that, like Ibsen, the Scot tells more than one story. Such a suggestion finds early confirmation in the (added) symbolism of the cuckoo in *Walker, London*. The serious associations introduced conflict with the light farcical tone, which elsewhere dominates. In *Quality Street*, there is a much more fully developed counterpointing. The basic story *is* sentimental. What could be more unlikely and romantic than a genteel spinster winning her soldier-lover by posing as her own niece at a ball? At the same time, many of the implications highlighted by fairytale technique, symbolism, imagery, and mime are tragic. Miss Phoebe is the only member of the spinsterhood to win her Valentine. To do this she has to escape, via a fantasy of her own making, from the dual impotence of social gentility and Christian submissiveness. The others remain determinedly blind to the conflict between their shuttered world of politeness and the cruel competitiveness of the Napoleonic wars outside. What Barrie implies is as important as what he states; usually the latter is as joyous as the former is bleak.

If highly sentimental conclusions such as the union of Babbie and Gavin around their rose-tree (in the 1942 text) can be shown to be part of a more complex structure of meaning derived from mythic Ibsenite techniques, the generative critic can usually reveal any individual Barrie ending to be one among alternatives. Anticipating one line in Postmodernist thinking, the Scottish playwright saw that any chosen denouement must represent a mimetic oversimplification. *The Little Minister* has two families of conclusions—one confirming Romance, the other stressing a darker sexual competitiveness symbolised by the cane. *The Admirable Crichton* presents more than ten substantial variations on the idea of the waiting hero whose final fate will be decided by social change. *Peter Pan* has as many endings as the potential of the human condition allows.

Retrospect teaches us that William Archer overstated his case in claiming Barrie to be *self-evidently* a genius. Sir James himself prophesied that he would have to endure the misinterpretation of ignorance before being welcomed on his own (often wilfully) obscure terms. Whether that, too, was overstatement may yet become a serious critical consideration.

—R.D.S. Jack

See also *Volume 1* entries on *The Admiral Crichton; Peter Pan*.

―――――――

BARRY, Philip. Born in Rochester, New York, 18 June 1896. Educated at East High School, Rochester; Yale University, New Haven, Connecticut (editor, *Yale Review*), 1913–17, 1919, AB 1919; studied with George Pierce Baker at Harvard University, Cambridge, Massachusetts, 1919–21. Married Ellen Semple in 1922; two sons and one daughter. Worked in the code department of the US Embassy, London, 1918–19; first play, *Autonomy*, produced 1919; worked in advertising, New York, 1921; full-time playwright from 1922; wrote for MGM, Hollywood, after 1934; lived in France, 1938–39. Member, American Academy. Died in New York, 3 December 1949.

Works

Collections

States of Grace: Eight Plays, edited by Brendan Gill.   1975.

Stage Works

Autonomy (produced Yale University, New Haven, Connecticut, 1919).
A Punch for Judy (produced Morosco Theatre, New York, 1921).   1922.
You and I (as *The Jilts*, produced 1923; as *You and I*, produced Belmont Theatre, New York, 1923).   1923.
God Bless Our Home.   1924.
The Youngest (produced Gaiety Theatre, New York, 1924).   1925.
In a Garden (produced Plymouth Theatre, New York, 1925).   1926.
White Wings (produced Booth Theatre, New York, 1926).   1927; revised version, music by Douglas Moore (produced 1935).
John (produced Klaw Theatre, New York, 1927).   1929.
Paris Bound (produced Music Box Theatre, New York, 1927).   1929.
Cock Robin, with Elmer Rice (produced 48th Street Theatre, New York, 1928).   1929.
Holiday (produced Plymouth Theatre, New York, 1928).   1929.
Hotel Universe (produced Martin Beck Theatre, New York, 1930).   1930.
Tomorrow and Tomorrow (produced Henry Miller's Theatre, New York, 1931).   1931.
The Animal Kingdom (produced Broadhurst Theatre, New York, 1932).   1932.
The Joyous Season (produced Belasco Theatre, New York, 1934).   1934.

Bright Star (produced Empire Theatre, New York, 1935).
Spring Dance, from a play by Eleanor Golden and Eloise Barrangon (produced Empire Theatre, New York, 1936). 1936.
Here Come the Clowns (produced Booth Theatre, New York, 1938). 1939.
The Philadelphia Story (produced Shubert Theatre, New York, 1939). 1939.
Liberty Jones (produced Shubert Theatre, New York, 1941). 1941.
Without Love (produced St. James Theatre, New York, 1942). 1943.
Foolish Notion (produced Martin Beck Theatre, New York, 1945). Abridged version in *The Best Plays of 1944–45*, edited by Burns Mantle, 1945.
My Name is Aquilon, from play by Jean Pierre Aumont (produced Lyceum Theatre, New York, 1949).
Second Threshold, completed by Robert E. Sherwood (produced Morosco Theatre, New York, 1951). 1951.

Fiction

War in Heaven. 1938.

Other

The Dramatist and the Amateur Public. 1927.

*

Criticism

Books:
Gerald Hamm, *The Drama of Philip Barry*, 1948.
Joseph Patrick Roppolo, *Philip Barry*, New York, 1965.
R.C. Reynolds, *Stage Left: The Development of the American Social Drama in the Thirties*, Troy, New York, 1986.
B.D. Joshi, *Major Plays of Barry and Behrman: A Comparative Study*, Jaipur, India, 1989.

Articles:
James M. Salem, "Philip Barry and the Spirituality of Love", in *Renascence*, 19, 1967.
David C. Gill, "Three Plays on Broadway: Three Plays of Psychodrama by Philip Barry", in *Markham Review*, 2, 1970.
Walter J. Meserve, "Philip Barry: A Dramatist's Search", in *Modern Drama*, 13, 1970.

*   *   *

Two such distinct images for theatre audiences were projected by the plays of Philip Barry that one critic dubbed him a "lightning bug—now he lights up, now he doesn't". In terms of Broadway, where Barry's plays achieved erratic success from 1923 to 1949, the metaphor was as apt as it was clever. A very precise and careful writer, Barry could create sparkling social comedy with thoroughly developed characters and witty dialogue. Influenced by his own substantial environment and the society of wealthy intellectuals, plus a Harvard education and the added experience of classes with Professor George Pierce Baker and his 47 Workshop, Barry viewed society and its problems with an intellectual detachment that allowed him to create several high comedies of distinctive

quality. He was also a man involved in a most serious spiritual search which he pursued throughout his life and for which he found an answer only in his final play. These two divergent approaches to drama underscore his entire output and give a truthful defense to his critic's observation. Theatre audiences enjoyed some of his plays tremendously; other plays, the ones he seemingly wanted to write, have seldom been properly appreciated.

In his sophisticated comedies Barry presented a scene of character and social conflict in which decisions are made from a sense of personal freedom. He felt very strongly that man must have the opportunity to find out about himself if he is to achieve some meaning in life. If Barry did not moralize—in fact, some critics thought him quite immoral, a view which disturbed him greatly—neither did he try to force solutions. Placed in certain situations, usually involving marriage, his characters invariably make discoveries about themselves, become more tolerant of humanity and take that first step—a decision for freedom—towards a discovery of truth. *Paris Bound* considered the significance of infidelity in modern marriage and suggested that the spiritual side of marriage was more important than the physical. In *Holiday* Barry contrasted the wealthy who lived for their business accomplishments with those who see something else in life. Tom Collier, a major character in *The Animal Kingdom*, is forced into a situation where he must choose between a stultifying life within a confining establishment and the freedom that honest individuality presents. *The Philadelphia Story* was one of Barry's most successful comedies. Against the sophisticated background of a country house near Philadelphia, Barry provides his heroine with a moment of self-realization which brings both delight and a sense of truth about human nature to the audience. In each play there was a social problem which Barry viewed in his distinctive manner, but within the slight framework of comedy he deliberately obscured the deeper significance of his constant theme in all of these plays—that man without freedom will suffer.

A very religious man, Barry was deeply troubled by questions concerning man, truth, and reality which his Catholicism left unanswered. It is the progress of this personal struggle and searching which his serious plays chart and finally resolve. First posing his questions about man and reality in *In a Garden*, Barry employed an egocentric dramatist who feels that he can understand, even control, everything, including his wife. He was, however, soon forced to discover, as Barry himself was doing, that there is a mystery to life. There is no guaranteed formula—no guiding idea. *White Wings* is more a farce-comedy than a search for truth; yet, the resolution through love (uniting the opposing families which illustrated the conflicting eras of the horse and the automobile) was one to which Barry would finally return years later.

In *Hotel Universe* he faced his question squarely. In a mysterious place where "time went sort of funny", he presented a group of people who found no value in life. "What's the answer to the whole works?" one of the group asks as they each reveal their problems to a mysterious person who is "supposed to have some kind of power" over people and can "set the hour-glass on its side". Even with the help of Freud, however, Barry found no solution in this play, but he did suggest an optimism and a process of thought. By dramatizing man as confined and defeated by society and by his own lost illusions, Barry was able to free him and show man's potential for knowing truth.

In a later play Barry questioned both the free will that he had allowed man and the inference that truth provided the answer to man's problems. The play was *Here Come the*

Clowns. In a complicated plot, Clancy, a Job character, searches for God and for the answer to the question of why there is so much misery in the world. At the final curtain Clancy is dying but still searching—yet of his "own free will". Curiously, the distinction in the play between God and the Devil is consciously vague, revealing man's confused ideas concerning both truth and God. Although the play is weak theatre, Clancy's search clearly exposes Barry's frame of mind.

From the production of *Here Come the Clowns* until his unexpected death, Barry worked on *The Second Threshold* which was posthumously produced with some "carpentry"-writing by Robert Sherwood. As the 42-year-old protagonist of this play feels that he has come to the end of "his soul's rope", he discovers that love makes life worthwhile. It is as simple as that and evidently the only satisfying conclusion that Barry could reach. In a play which seemed to combine more effectively than ever before his witty comedy with a serious statement, Barry answered the vagueness of *Hotel Universe* and the inconclusiveness of *Here Come the Clowns*.

Like any thoughtful dramatist, Barry was concerned with philosophical questions as well as social problems. He thought, he doubted, he questioned. Obviously, he was least effective in the theatre when he was most probing, intellectually, and this was his weakness. His successes, however, remain some of the best examples of high comedy produced in the history of American drama.

—Walter J. Meserve

See also *Volume 1* entry on *The Philadephia Story*.

BEAUMARCHAIS, Pierre-Augustin Caron de. Born Pierre-Augustin Caron, in Paris, 24 January 1732. Educated at L'École des métiers d'Alfort for three years, to age 13, then apprenticed to his clock-maker father. Married 1) Madeleine-Catherine Franquet in 1756 (died 1757); 2) Geneviève-Madeleine Warebled in 1768 (died 1770), one son (died 1772, aged three); 3) Marie-Thérèse Willermawlas in 1786 (divorced 1794; remarried 1797), one daughter. Became an innovative clockmaker, whose invention of a new system was recognised by the Academy of Sciences, 1754; entered and achieved popularity in Court circles; bought title of Clerk Controller in Royal Household, 1755; took name Beaumarchais from first wife's estate, 1757; also a harpist (improved the pedal system): gave lessons and organized concerts at Court; bought title of Secrétaire du Roi, 1761 (and consequently made a nobleman, 1761), and Lt.-General of hunting in the Varenne du Louvre, 1761; visited Spain, 1764–66; first full-length play, *Eugénie*, produced 1767; involved in several spectacular court cases in 1770's; government agent, 1774–75, and responsible for aid to American insurgents, 1775; involved in founding the Bureau de Legislation Dramatique (later Société des Auteurs et Compositeurs Dramatiques), 1777; arrested on suspicion of profiteering from arms, 1792; took refuge in London, but imprisoned there for debt, 1792; released on payment of ransom and returned to France, 1793; left for Holland, on mission to buy arms; family imprisoned, 1794; in exile in Holland and Germany, 1794; able to return to Paris, 1796; under scrutiny by various financial commissions for involvement in the Dutch arms affair. Died in Paris, the night of 17 May 1799.

Works

Oeuvres complètes, edited by Édouard Fournier.   1876.
Théâtres; Lettres relatives à son théâtre, edited by Maurice Allem and Paul Courant.   1957.
Le Trilogie de Figaro, edited by Gilbert Sigaux.   1966.
Oeuvres complètes, edited by Albert Demazière.   1973.
Théâtre, edited by Jean-Pierre de Beaumarchais.   1980.

Stage Works

Colin et Colette; Les Bottle de sept lieues; Les Députés de la Halle et du Gros-Caillou; Léandre marchand d'Agnus; Jean Bête à la foire (all short sketches, probably produced privately, c.1760–63).
Eugénie (produced Comédie-Française, Paris, 1767).   1767; translated as *The School for Rakes*, 1769.
Les Deux Amis; ou, Le Négociant de Lyon (produced Comédie-Française, Paris, 1770).   1770; translated as *The Two Friends*, 1800.
Le Barbier de Séville; ou, La Précaution inutile (produced Comédie-Française, Paris, 1775).   1775; various translations as *The Barber of Seville*.
La Folle Journée; ou, Le Mariage de Figaro (produced Comédie-Française, Paris 1784).   1785; translated as *The Follies of a Day; or, The Marriage of Figaro*, 1785; as *A Mad Day's Work; or, The Marriage of Figaro*, 1961; as *The Marriage of Figaro*, 1966: several subsequent translations under same title.
Tarare, music by Antonio Salieri (produced Académie Royale de Musique, Paris, 1787; revised version, produced 1790).   1790; translated as *Axur, King of Ormus*, 1813.
L'Autre Tartuffe; ou, La Mère coupable (produced Théâtre du Marais, Paris, 1792).   1794; translated as *Frailty and Hypocrisy*, 1804; as *A Mother's Guilt*, in *The Complete Figaro Plays*, 1983.

Memoirs and Letters

Mémoires contre M. Goëzman.   1775.
Mémoires, edited by J. Ravenal. (4 vols.).   1830.
Lettres inédites, edited by Gilbert Chinard.   1929.
Correspondance, edited by Brian N. Morton.   1969–.
For the Good of Mankind: Political Correspondence Relative to the American Revolution, edited and translated by Antoinette Shewmake.   1987.

*

Bibliographies

H. Cordier, *Bibliographie des oeuvres de Beaumarchais*, Paris, 1883.
Brian N. Morton and Donald C. Spinelli, *Beaumarchais: A Bibliography*, 1988.

Scene from *Le Mariage de Figaro* by **Beaumarchais**, with Mlle. Reichemberg as Chérubin, Mlle. Croizette as Suzanne, and Mlle. Broisat as the Countess (drawing in the Bibliothèque Nationale, Paris).

Criticism

Books:

G. Lemaître, *Beaumarchais*, Paris, 1949.

J.B. Ratermanis and W.R. Irwin, *The Comic Style of Beaumarchais*, Seattle, Washington, 1961.

Cynthia Cox, *The Real Figaro: The Extraordinary Career of Caron de Beaumarchais*, London, 1962.

René Thomasset, *Beaumarchais: Écrivain et aventurier*, Paris, 1966.

Frédéric Grendel, *Beaumarchais*, Paris, 1973.

Joseph Sungolowski, *Beaumarchais*, New York, 1974.

C. Janette Garry, *Beaumarchais sous la Révolution*, Leiden, 1976.

Elke Klein, *Kontinuität und Diskontinuität in der sogenannten Trilogie von Beaumarchais*, Bern, 1978.

Patrice Boussel, *Beaumarchais: Le Parisien universel*, Paris, 1983.

René Pomeau, *Beaumarchais ou la bizarre destinée*, Paris, 1987.

Articles:

Anthony R. Pugh, "Beaumarchais, the *Drame Bourgeois*, and the *Pièce Bien Faite*", in *Modern Language Review*, 61, 1966.

*   *   *

Beaumarchais's output was relatively slight—three *drames*, two comedies, some *parades*, and one opera libretto—but his contribution to French theatre is an important and varied one. His early plays, *Eugénie* and *Les Deux Amis*, and his last one, *L'Autre Tartuffe; ou, La Mère coupable*, were written in the tradition of the *drame bourgeois* as defined and embodied by Diderot in the 1750's. Beaumarchais was a modern and imaginative dramatist, and it is quite characteristic that he should have been attracted by the innovative aims and style of this new genre, characterised by its more modern settings, its attempt to bridge the gap between comedy and tragedy, its desire to engage the audience more closely in the dramatic experience, its experiments with different modes of theatrical expression, and its clear moral purpose. His preface to *Eugénie* is an important analysis of the principles and features of the genre, and his most important play in this mode is doubtless *La Mère coupable,* the third part of the Figaro trilogy. In this play Beaumarchais sets out to uplift the audience by the touching spectacle of the Countess, who looks back with nostalgia and regret on her adulterous love for Cherubin 20 years earlier, and he builds up an atmosphere of melancholy through powerful—at times melodramatic—scenes: expressions of lament, the discovery of love letters from the past, a tearful confrontation with the suspicious count. The play has weaknesses—lack of *vraisemblance,* simplistic characterisation, a tendency to moralise—but these are attributable to the very conception of the genre itself and its search for touching effects.

Beaumarchais is known principally, though, as the dramatist who re-introduced laughter to French comedy after a long absence. He began his career as a writer of *parades,* a popular, frequently obscene form of theatrical entertainment with rudimentary plots. By its very nature the *parade* was an essentially ephemeral genre, and yet it was to remain a vital part of the dramatist's style and inspiration.

It is his sense of the theatre, perceptible in these earliest works, which underlies the success of his two major comedies, *Le Barbier de Séville* and *Le Mariage de Figaro.* The first was originally written in the form of a *parade,* juxtaposing guile and authority in a battle of wits, and in its final version it blends many features of popular theatrical forms—*parade, farce, opéra-comique*—in a fast-moving and entertaining comedy; it brought back to the French theatre all the vivacity, wit, and excitement of the *comédie d'intrigue,* absent for nearly a century, and it restored to its centre the figure of the scheming valet, imbued now with an ingenuity and verve not seen since Molière's Scapin. In *Le Mariage de Figaro,* more boldly still, the dramatist brings together traditions as different as *vaudeville* and *drame bourgeois* to produce a highly original and complex play. Comedy of intrigue is shot through with sharp satirical observation, and traditional comic stereotypes are given deeper significance.

His most enduring and endearing achievement is perhaps the creation of Figaro, a clear descendant of the classical servant in his boundless energy and guile, but who also possesses now a sharp critical intelligence and a fierce pride in the independence of the individual. He grows out of the valet, whose identity is determined simply by the needs of the plot, and develops—notably in *Le Mariage de Figaro*—into a character as important for what he says as for what he does. It is through this character, above all, that Beaumarchais offers piercing judgements on contemporary society, from the moral complacency of the noble class to the arbitrary and cumbersome nature of judicial procedures, from the injustices of censorship to the evils of taxation. In *Le Barbier de Séville,* such comments exist largely at the level of epigrammatic asides and find little echo in the working-out of the main plot where the count is conceived as a *lover* rather than as a *noble.* This is not the case, though, in the later play where the count is associated directly or indirectly with the different abuses uncovered and the servant's satirical potency is thereby increased.

The versatility of Beaumarchais's talent is clear, but beneath the variety of his plays, there are significant areas of overlap; *drame* and comedy are not conceived as mutually exclusive genres. Comic characters inhabit his *drames* just as pathos hovers over the surface of his comedies, and in both genres similar situations or characters are to be found. Heroines made pregnant, then left by their lovers (*La Mère coupable, Jean-Bête à la foire*), or young heroes weary of courtly pleasures (*Eugénie, Le Barbier de Séville*) inhabit both worlds, just as the jealous Count Almaviva can move from *Le Mariage de Figaro* to *La Mère coupable;* in all these plays the same social and moral problems are apparent.

Beaumarchais's work brings together and resumes certain key features of 18th-century dramatic writing. He shared with the popular theatre a gift for comic entertainment, and blended with it the moral seriousness of the *drame* and the sharp satirical analysis of the *philosophes.* In so doing, he suggested the fragility of existing theatrical structures and sought, through his fertile and imaginative eclecticism, a new, more flexible mode of expression for his vision of the world.

—G. Jonathon Mallinson

See also *Volume 1* entries on *The Barber of Seville; The Marriage of Figaro.*

BEAUMONT, Francis. Born in Grace-Dieu, Leicestershire, England, in 1584 or 1585; brother of Sir John Beaumont. Educated at Broadgates Hall (now Pembroke College), Oxford, 1597–98; entered Inner Temple, London, 1600. Married Ursula Isley in 1613; two daughters. Lived in London from 1600; a friend of Drayton and Ben Jonson; met John Fletcher in 1605, and subsequently collaborated with him in writing plays; retired at the time of his marriage; lived in Kent from 1613. Died in London, 6 March 1616.

Works

Collections

Comedies and Tragedies, with Fletcher and others (includes many plays now not thought to be by Beaumont and Fletcher). 1647; revised edition, 1679.
Works of Beaumont and Fletcher, edited by A. Glover and A.R. Waller (10 vols.). 1905–12.
The Dramatic Works in the Beaumont and Fletcher Canon, edited by Fredson Bowers. 1966–.

Stage Works

The Noble Gentleman, with Fletcher, or possibly by Fletcher and another author (produced London, c.1606; revised version 1625–26?). Revised version in *Comedies and Tragedies,* 1647.
Love's Cure, with Fletcher, revised by Massinger (produced London, c.1606). In *Comedies and Tragedies,* 1647.
The Woman Hater, with Fletcher (produced London, 1606?). 1607.

The Knight of the Burning Pestle (produced London, c. 1607). 1613.

Philaster; or, Love Lies A-Bleeding, with Fletcher (produced by the King's Men, London, c.1608–10).   1620.

The Coxcomb, with Fletcher (produced London, c.1608–10). In *Comedies and Tragedies*, 1647.

The Maid's Tragedy, with Fletcher (produced by the King's Men, London, c.1608–11).   1619.

A King and No King, with Fletcher (produced by the King's Men, London, 1611).   1619.

Cupid's Revenge, with Fletcher (produced before 1612). 1615.

The Captain, with Fletcher, or possibly by Fletcher alone (produced by the King's Men, London, c.1609–12).   In *Comedies and Tragedies*, 1647.

The Masque of the Inner Temple and Gray's Inn (produced at Court, 1613).   1613.

The Scornful Lady, with Fletcher (produced London, 1613–17?).

Love's Pilgrimage, with Fletcher, or possibly by Fletcher alone (produced London, 1616?). In *Comedies and Tragedies*, 1647.

Thierry, King of France, and His Brother Theodoret, with Fletcher and Massinger, or possibly by Fletcher and Massinger alone (produced?).   1621.

Verse

Salmacis and Hermaphroditus.   1602.
Poems.   1640; revised editions, 1653, 1660.
Songs and Lyrics from the Plays of Beaumont and Fletcher, edited by E.H. Fellowes.   1928.

*

Bibliographies

S.A. Tannenbaum, *Beaumont and Fletcher: A Concise Bibliography*, New York, 1938; supplement, with D.R. Tannenbaum, 1946.

C.A. Pennell and W.F. Williams, *Elizabethan Bibliographies Supplements 8*, London, 1968.

Criticism

Books:

Charles M. Gayley, *Francis Beaumont Dramatist*, New York, 1914.

Arthur Colby Sprague, *Beaumont and Fletcher on the Restoration Stage*, Cambridge, Massachusetts, 1926.

J.H. Wilson, *The Influence of Beaumont and Fletcher on the Restoration Stage*, Columbus, Ohio, 1928.

R.C. Bald, *Bibliographical Studies in the Beaumont and Fletcher Folio of 1647*, London, 1938.

Baldwin Maxwell, *Studies in Beaumont, Fletcher and Massinger*, Chapel Hill, North Carolina, 1939.

L.B. Wallis, *Beaumont, Fletcher, and Company: Entertainers to the Jacobean Gentry*, New York, 1947.

Eugene Waith, *The Pattern of Tragicomedy in Beaumont and Fletcher*, New Haven, Connecticut, 1952.

W.W. Appleton, *Beaumont and Fletcher: A Critical Study*, London, 1956.

Ian Fletcher, *Beaumont and Fletcher*, London, 1967 (British Council pamphlet).

Philip J. Finkelpearl, *Court and Country Politics in the Plays of Beaumont and Fletcher*, Princeton, New Jersey, 1990.

Articles:

Cyrus Hoy, "The Shares of Fletcher and His Collaborators in the Beaumont and Fletcher Canon" in *Studies in Bibliography,* nos. 8–9 and 11–15, 1956–62.

*   *   *

See entry on **John Fletcher** for critical essay.

See also *Volume 1* entries on *The Knight of the Burning Pestle*; *The Maid's Tragedy*; *Philaster*.

———————

BECKETT, Samuel (Barclay). Born at Foxrock, near Dublin, Ireland, 13 April 1906. Educated at Ida Elsner's Academy, Stillorgan; Earlsfort House preparatory school; Portora Royal School, County Fermanagh; Trinity College, Dublin (foundation scholar), BA in French and Italian 1927, MA 1931. Married Suzanne Deschevaux-Dumesnil in 1961 (died 1989). French teacher, Campbell College, Belfast, 1928; lecturer in English, École Normale Supérieure, Paris, 1928–30; lecturer in French, Trinity College, Dublin, 1930–31; translator and writer in Paris in the 1920's and 1930's, and closely associated with James Joyce's circle; in Dublin and London, 1933–37; returned to Paris, 1937; joined French Resistance, 1940; fled to Roussillon in unoccupied France, where he remained 1942–45; worked at the Irish Red Cross Hospital, St. Lô, France, 1945; resumed literary activity in Paris after World War II; after 1945, published the majority of his work in both French and English versions; first professionally produced play, *En Attendant Godot*, staged 1953; in later years directed several productions of his own plays, especially for the Schiller-Theater, Berlin. Recipient: Croix de Guerre and Médaille de la Résistance for war service, 1945; many literary and artistic awards, including: Obie Award, 1958, 1960, 1962, 1964; Italia Prize, 1959; Nobel Prize for Literature, 1969; National Grand Prize for Theatre, 1975; New York Drama Critics Circle Citation, 1984. Member of the German Academy of Art; Companion of Literature, Royal Society of Literature, 1984; Member, Aosdána, 1986. Died in Paris, 22 December 1989.

Works

Collections

"Krapp's Last Tape" and Other Dramatic Pieces (includes *All That Fall; Embers; Act Without Words I and II*).   1960.

"Play" and Two Short Pieces for Radio (includes *Words and Music* and *Cascando*).   1964.

A Becket Reader.   1967.

"Eh Joe" and Other Writings (includes *Act Without Words II* and *Film*).   1967.

Samuel Beckett

"Cascando" and Other Short Dramatic Pieces (includes *Words and Music; Eh Joe; Play; Come and Go; Film*). 1968.

"Breath" and Other Shorts (includes *Come and Go; Act Without Words I and II*; and the prose piece *From an Abandoned Work*). 1971.

I Can't Go On: A Selection from the Work of Beckett, edited by Richard Seacver. 1976.

Ends and Odds: Eight New Dramatic Pieces (includes *Not I; That Time; Footfalls; Ghost Trio; Theatre I and II; Radio I and II*). 1976; as *Ends and Odds: Plays and Sketches* (includes *Not I; That Time; Footfalls; Ghost Trio; . . . but the clouds . . .; Theatre I and II; Radio I and II*), 1977.

"Rockaby" and Other Short Pieces (includes *A Piece of Monologue* and *Ohio Impromptu*). 1981.

Three Occasional Pieces (includes *A Piece of Monologue; Rockaby; Ohio Impromptu*). 1982.

"Catastrophe" et autres dramaticules: Cette fois; Solo; Berceuse; Impromptu d'Ohio. 1982.

Disjecta: Miscellaneous Writings and a Dramatic Fragment, edited by Ruby Cohn. 1983.

Collected Shorter Plays. 1984.

Ohio Impromptu; Catastrophe; What Where. 1984.

The Complete Dramatic Works. 1986.

Stage Works

Le Kid, with Georges Pelorson (produced Trinity College, Dublin, 1931).

En Attendant Godot (produced Théâtre de Babylone, Paris, 1953). 1952; translated by Beckett as *Waiting for Godot: Tragicomedy* (produced Arts Theatre, London, 1955), 1954.

Fin de partie (produced in French, Royal Court Theatre, London, 1957). With *Acte sans paroles*, 1957; translated by Beckett as *Endgame* (produced Cherry Lane Theatre, New York, 1958) with *Act Without Words*, 1958.

Acte sans paroles, with music by John Beckett (produced in French, Royal Court Theatre, London, 1957). With *Fin de partie*, 1957; translated by Becket as *Act Without Words*, with *Endgame*, 1958.

All That Fall, from the radio play (produced 1965). 1957.

From an Abandoned Work. 1958.

Krapp's Last Tape (produced Royal Court Theatre, London, 1958). With *Embers*, 1959.

Act Without Words II (produced Institute of Contemporary Arts, London, 1960). In *New Directions*, 1, Summer 1959; in book form in *"Krapp's Last Tape" and Other Dramatic Pieces*, 1960.

Happy Days (produced Cherry Lane Theatre, New York, 1961). 1961; translated by Beckett as *Oh Les Beaux Jours* (produced Odéon Théâtre de France, Paris, 1963), 1963; bilingual edition, edited by James Knowlson, 1978.

Play (in German, as *Spiel*, produced Ulmer Theater, Ulm-Donau, 1963; as *Play*, Cherry Lane Theatre, New York, 1964). As *Spiel*, in *Theater heute*, July 1963; as *Play*, in *"Play" and Two Short Pieces for Radio*, 1964.

Va et vient: Dramaticule (in German as *Kommen und Gehen*, produced Schiller-Theater Werkstatt, Berlin, 1966; as *Va et vient*, produced Odéon Théâtre de France, Paris, 1966). 1966; translated by Beckett as *Come and Go: Dramaticule* (produced Peacock Theatre, Dublin, 1968), 1967.

Breath (produced as part of Kenneth Tynan's *Oh! Calcutta!*, Eden Theatre, New York, 1969). In *"Breath" and Other Shorts*, 1971.

Not I (produced Lincoln Center, New York, 1972). 1973.

Fragment de Théâtre. 1974. translated by Beckett as *Theatre I and II*, in *Ends and Odds*, 1976.

That Time (produced Royal Court Theatre, London, 1976). 1976.

Footfalls (produced Royal Court Theatre, London, 1976). 1976.

A Piece of Monologue (produced La Mama Experimental Theatre Club, New York, 1980). In *"Rockaby" and Other Short Pieces*, 1981.

Rockaby (produced State University of New York, Buffalo, 1981). In *"Rockaby" and Other Short Pieces*, 1981.

Ohio Impromptu (produced Ohio State University, Columbus, Ohio, 1981). In *"Rockaby" and Other Short Pieces*, 1981.

Catastrophe (produced Avignon Festival, 1982). In *Collected Shorter Plays*, 1984.

What Where (in German, as *Was Wo*, produced 1983; as *What Where*, produced Harold Clurman Theatre, New York, 1983). In *Collected Shorter Plays*, 1984.

Screenplays

Film, 1965 (published in *"Eh Joe" and Other Writings*, 1967).

Television Plays

Eh Joe (broadcast BBC2, 1966). In *"Eh Joe" and Other Writings*, 1967.

Not I, from the stage play (broadcast BBC2, 1977).

Ghost Trio (broadcast BBC2, 1977). In *Ends and Odds*, 1976.

. . . but the clouds . . . (broadcast BBC2, 1977). In *Ends and Odds*, 1976.

Quad (broadcast as *Quadrat 1+2*, Süddeutscher Rundfunk, 1982). In *Collected Shorter Plays*, 1982.

Nacht und Träume (broadcast Süddeutscher Rundfunk, 1982). In *Collected Shorter Plays*, 1982.

Radio Plays

All That Fall (broadcast BBC Third Programme, 1957). 1957.

Embers (broadcast BBC Third Programme, 1959). In *Evergreen Review*, November–December, 1959; in book form, with *Krapp's Last Tape*, 1959.

The Old Tune, from Robert Pinget's *La Manivelle* (broadcast 1960). In *La Manivelle/The Old Tune*, by Pinget, 1960; also in *Plays 1*, by Pinget, 1963.

Words and Music (broadcast BBC Third Programme, 1962). In *Evergreen Review*, November–December 1962; in book form, in *"Play" and Two Short Pieces for Radio*, 1964.

Cascando, music by Marcel Mihalovici (broadcast in French, ORTF, 1963; in English, BBC Third Programme, 1964). In German, in *Dramatische Dichtungen*, 1, 1963; in English, in *Evergreen Review*, May–June, 1963; in book form, in *"Play" and Two Short Pieces for Radio*, 1964.

Rough For Radio I. Published as *Sketch for a Radio Play*, in *Stereo Headphones*, 7, 1976; as *Radio I*, in *Ends and Odds*, 1976; as *Rough for Radio I*, in *Collected Shorter Plays*, 1984.

Rough for Radio II (broadcast as *Rough for Radio*, BBC Radio 3, 1976). As *Radio II*, in *Ends and Odds*, 1976; as *Rough for Radio II*, in *Collected Shorter Plays*, 1976.

Fiction

More Pricks than Kicks. 1934.
Murphy. 1938.
Molloy. 1951; translated by Beckett and Patrick Bowles, 1955.
Malone meurt. 1951; translated by Beckett as *Malone Dies,* 1956.
L'Innommable. 1953; translated by Beckett as *The Unnamable,* 1958.
Watt (written in English). 1953.
Nouvelles et Textes pour rien. 1955; translated by Beckett and Richard Seaver as *Stories and Texts for Nothing,* 1967.
From an Abandoned Work. 1958.
Molloy; Malone Dies; The Unnamable. 1960.
Comment c'est. 1961; translated by Beckett as *How It Is,* 1964.
Imagination morte imaginez. 1965; translated by Beckett as *Imagination Dead Imagine,* 1965.
Assez. 1966; translated by Beckett as *Enough,* in *No's Knife,* 1967.
Bing. 1966; translated by Beckett as *Ping,* in *No's Knife,* 1967.
Têtes-Mortes (includes *D'Un Ouvrage abandonné; Assez, Bing; Imagination morte imaginez*). 1967; translated by Beckett in *No's Knife,* 1967.
No's Knife: Collected Shorter Prose 1945–1966 (includes *Stories and Texts for Nothing; From an Abandoned Work; Enough; Imagination Dead Imagine; Ping*). 1967.
L'Issue. 1968.
Sans. 1969; translated by Beckett as *Lessness,* 1971.
Mercier et Camier. 1970; translated by Beckett as *Mercier and Camier,* 1974.
Séjour. 1970.
Premier Amour. 1970; translated by Beckett as *First Love,* 1973.
Le Dépeupleur. 1971; translated by Beckett as *The Lost Ones,* 1972.
The North. 1972.
Abandonné. 1972.
Au loin un oiseau. 1973.
"First Love" and Other Shorts. 1974.
Fizzles. 1976.
For to End Yet Again and Other Fizzles. 1976.
All Strange Away. 1976.
Four Novellas (First Love; The Expelled; The Calmative; The End). 1977; as *"The Expelled" and Other Novellas,* 1980.
Six Residua. 1978.
Company. 1980.
Mal vu mal dit. 1981; translated by Beckett as *Ill Seen Ill Said,* 1982.
Worstward Ho. 1983.
Collected Shorter Prose 1945–1980. 1984.
Stirrings Still. 1988.
Nohow On (includes *Company; Ill Seen Ill Said; Worstward Ho*). 1989.
As the Story Was Told: Uncollected and Late Prose. 1990.

Verse

Whoroscope. 1930.
Echo's Bones and Other Precipitates. 1935.
Gedichte (collected poems in English and French, with German translations). 1959.
Poems in English. 1961.
Poèmes. 1968.

Collected Poems in English and French. 1977; revised edition, as *Collected Poems 1930–1978,* 1984.
Mirlitonnades. 1978.

Other

"Dante . . . Bruno. Vico . . . Joyce," in *Our Exagmination round His Factification for Incamination of Work in Progress.* 1929.
Proust. 1931; with *Three Dialogues with Georges Duthuit,* 1965.
Three Dialogues with Georges Duthuit. In *Transition 48,* 1949; in book form, with *Proust,* 1965.
Bram van Velde, with Georges Duthuit and Jacques Putman. 1958; translated by Beckett and Olive Classe, 1960.

Translator, *Negro: An Anthology,* compiled by Nancy Cunard. 1934.
Translator, *Seven Poems by Paul Éluard.* In *Thorns of Thunder,* 1936.
Translator, *Anthology of Mexican Poetry,* edited by Octavio Paz. 1958.
Translator, with others, *Selected Poems,* by Alain Bosquet. 1963.
Translator, *Zone,* by Guillaume Apollinaire. 1972.
Translator, *Drunken Boat,* by Arthur Rimbaud, edited by James Knowlson and Felix Leakey. 1977.
Translator, with others, *No Matter No Fact.* 1988.

*

Bibliographies

Raymond Federman and John Fletcher, *Samuel Beckett: His Works and His Critics: An Essay in Bibliography,* Berkeley, California, 1970.
Robin John Davis, *Samuel Beckett: Checklist and Index of His Published Works 1967–1976,* 1979.
Cathleen Culotta Andonian, *Samuel Beckett: A Reference Guide,* 1988.

Criticism

Books:
Hugh Kenner, *Samuel Beckett: A Critical Study,* New York, 1961, London, 1962; revised edition, Berkeley, California, 1968.
Ruby Cohn, *Samuel Beckett: The Comic Gamut,* New Brunswick, New Jersey, 1962.
William York Tindall, *Samuel Beckett,* New York, 1964.
Richard N. Coe, *Beckett,* Edinburgh, 1964; retitled as *Samuel Beckett,* New York, 1964.
Martin Esslin (ed.), *Samuel Beckett: A Collection of Critical Essays,* Englewood Cliffs, New Jersey, 1965.
John Calder (ed.), *Beckett at 60: A Festschrift,* London, 1967.
John Fletcher, *Samuel Beckett's Art,* London and New York, 1967.
Ronald Hayman, *Samuel Beckett,* London, 1968; revised edition, 1980.
Melvin J. Friedman (ed.), *Samuel Beckett Now: Critical Approaches to His Novels, Poetry, and Plays,* Chicago, 1970.
Colin Duckworth, *Angels of Darkness: Dramatic Effect in Samuel Beckett,* London, 1972.

John Fletcher and John Spurling, *Beckett: A Study of His Plays*, London and New York, 1972; revised as *Beckett the Playwright*, London and New York, 1985.

Hugh Kenner, *A Reader's Guide to Samuel Beckett*, New York and London, 1973.

Ruby Cohn, *Back to Beckett*, Princeton, New Jersey, 1974.

Ruby Cohn (ed.), *Samuel Beckett: A Collection of Criticism*, New York, 1975.

Hannah Case Copeland, *Art and the Artist in the Works of Samuel Beckett*, The Hague, 1975.

James Eliopulos, *Samuel Beckett's Dramatic Language*, The Hague, 1975.

Katharine J. Worth (ed.), *Beckett the Shape Changer*, London, 1975.

Clas Zilliacus, *Beckett and Broadcasting: A Study of the Works of Samuel Beckett for and in Radio and Television*, Abo, Finland, 1976.

John Pilling, *Samuel Beckett*, London, 1976.

Vivian Mercier, *Beckett/Beckett*, New York, 1977.

Deirdre Bair, *Samuel Beckett: A Biography*, New York and London, 1978.

Beryl S. Fletcher, *A Student's Guide to the Plays of Samuel Beckett*, London, 1978; revised edition, with John Fletcher, 1985.

Richard L. Admussen, *The Samuel Beckett Manuscripts: A Critical Study*, London, 1979.

Raymond Federman and Lawrence Graver (eds.), *Samuel Beckett: The Critical Heritage*, London, 1979.

James Knowlson and John Pilling (eds.), *Frescoes of the Skull: The Later Prose and Drama of Samuel Beckett*, London, 1979.

Frederick Busi, *The Transformations of Godot*, Lexington, Kentucky, 1980.

Ruby Cohn, *Just Play: Beckett's Theatre*, Princeton, New Jersey, 1980.

J.E. Dearlove, *Accommodating the Chaos: Samuel Beckett's Nonrelational Art*, Durham, North Carolina, 1982.

Morris Beja, S.E. Gontarski, and Pierre Astier (eds.), *Samuel Beckett: Humanistic Perspectives*, Columbus, Ohio, 1983.

Charles Lyons, *Samuel Beckett*, New York, 1983.

Sidney Homan, *Beckett's Theaters: Interpretations for Performance*, Lewisburg, Pennsylvania, 1984.

Lance St. John Butler, *Samuel Beckett and the Meaning of Being: A Study in Ontological Parable*, London and New York, 1984.

Harold Bloom (ed.), *Samuel Beckett: Modern Critical Views*, New York, 1985.

Virginia Cooke (ed.), *Beckett on File*, London, 1985.

S.E. Gontarski, *The Intent of Undoing in Samuel Beckett's Dramatic Texts*, Bloomington, Indiana, 1985.

As No Other Dare Fail: For Samuel Beckett on His 80th Birthday (essay collection), London and New York, 1986.

Linda Ben-Zvi, *Samuel Beckett*, Boston, 1986.

Enoch Brater (ed.), *Becket at 80/Beckett in Context*, New York, 1986.

Peter Gidal, *Understanding Beckett: A Study of Monologue and Gesture in the Works of Beckett*, London and New York, 1986.

S.E. Gontarski (ed.), *On Beckett: Essays and Criticisms*, New York, 1986.

James Acheson and Kateryna Arthur (eds.), *Beckett's Later Fiction and Drama: Texts for Company*, London, 1987.

Enoch Brater, *Beyond Minimalism: Beckett's Late Style in the Theatre*, New York, 1987.

Alan Warren Friedman, Charles Rossman, and Dina Sherzer (eds.), *Beckett Translating/Translating Beckett*, 1987.

Jane Alison Hale, *The Broken Window: Beckett's Dramatic Perspective*, Lafayette, Indiana, 1987.

Katherine H. Burkman, *Myth and Ritual in the Plays of Beckett*, Rutherford, New Jersey, 1988.

Brian T. Fitch, *Beckett and Babel: An Investigation into the Status of the Bilingual Work*, Toronto, 1988.

Sylvie Debevec Henning, *Beckett's Critical Complicity: Carnival, Contestation and Tradition*, Lexington, Kentucky, 1988.

Dougald McMillan and Martha Fehsenfeld, *Beckett in the Theatre: The Author as Practical Playwright and Director 1: From "Waiting for Godot" to "Krapp's Last Tape"*, New York, 1988.

Rosemary Pountney, *Theatre of Shadows: Beckett's Drama 1956–1976*, Gerrards Cross, Buckinghamshire, 1988.

Valerie Topsfield, *The Humour of Samuel Beckett*, New York, 1988.

Stanton B. Garner, *The Absent Voice: Narrative Comprehension in the Theater*, Urbana, Illinois, 1989.

Jonathan Kalb, *Beckett in Performance*, Cambridge, 1989.

Andrew K. Kennedy, *Beckett*, Cambridge, 1989.

Alan Astro, *Understanding Samuel Beckett*, Columbia, South Carolina, 1990.

Linda Ben-Zvi, *Women in Beckett: Performance and Critical Perspectives*, Urbana, Illinois, 1990.

Lance St. J. Butler and Robin J. Davis (eds.), *Rethinking Beckett: A Collection of Critical Essays*, New York, 1990.

Shimon Levy, *Beckett's Self-Referential Drama*, New York, 1990.

* * *

When Samuel Beckett's *En Attendant Godot* (*Waiting for Godot*) opened at the Théâtre Babylone in Paris on 5 January 1953, the French dramatist and critic Jean Anouilh compared the event to the historic opening of Pirandello's *Six Characters in Search of an Author* two decades earlier, and he astutely described this new work as "a music-hall sketch of Pascal's *Pensées* as played by the Fraterlini clowns". That combination of ontological enigma and vaudeville comedy (much of the latter indebted to the American silent films of Charlie Chaplin and Buster Keaton), combined, as Vivian Mercier observed, "in a play where nothing happens—twice", would become the hallmark of Beckett's assault first on naturalism and then on modernism itself.

The shock to English audiences schooled in the drawing-room comedies of Noël Coward, Somerset Maugham, and Arthur Wing Pinero was captured by the drama critic Harold Hobson: *Godot*

knocked the shackles of plot from off the English drama. It destroyed the notion that the dramatist is God, knowing everything about his characters and master of a complete philosophy answerable to all of our problems. It showed that Archer's dictum that a good play imitates the audible and visible surface of life is not necessarily true. It revealed that the drama approximates or can approximate the condition of music, touching chords deeper than can be reached by reason and saying things beyond the grasp of logic. It renewed the English theater in a single night.

The American premiere, however, generated something less than a theatrical renewal. Mistakenly promoted as "the laugh hit of two continents", *Waiting for Godot* opened at the Coconut Grove Playhouse in Miami Beach, Florida on January 3, 1956, to audiences of vacationers looking for easy diversion, and they, to say the least, were not amused. But

America also saw the most visceral production of *Godot* ever staged when, in 1957, the San Francisco Actors' Workshop brought its production into the maximum security prison of San Quentin. A group of America's most hardened criminals —sentenced, in a wonderfully Beckettian phrase, "to life"— seemed to have little difficulty with this tale of waiting which puzzled critics the world over. As the reviewer for *The San Quentin News* clearly saw on 28 November 1957: "We're still waiting for Godot, and shall continue to wait. When the scenery gets too drab and the action too slow, we'll call each other names and swear to part forever—but then there's no place to go". "That's how it is on this bitch of an earth", says Pozzo.

Thus with his first theatrical production Beckett managed to strip the theater of its conventions, to deal uncompromisingly with the philosophical enigmas of existence, and yet to appeal to audiences both cerebrally and viscerally by mixing the discourse of philosophy with the imagery of the music hall and the comic silent cinema.

The success of *Godot*, however, did not ensure future productions. When in 1957 French director Roger Blin attempted to stage Beckett's *Fin de partie* (*Endgame*) in Paris, he encountered so many difficulties that the play was finally produced in French at the Royal Court Theatre in London, before being moved to Paris. The interplay of the culinary characters, Hamm and Clov—chess pieces in a cosmic endgame, within the claustrophobic space of a bunker, pill box, or bomb shelter, Hamm blind and immobile, Clov sighted but tied to his master as tightly as Lucky is to Pozzo— is a dialectic of need and torment. More austerely than in *Godot*, Beckett developed in *Endgame* his unique sense of theater as a dialectic of mime and monologue.

In 1956 the BBC's Third Programme solicited a radio script from Beckett, and he was immediately intrigued with the possibilities of the medium; as he wrote to Nancy Cunard, he "got a nice gruesome idea full of cartwheels and dragging of feet and puffing and panting which may or may not lead to something". It did, and *All That Fall*, broadcast in January 1957, began Beckett's long association with the BBC and with media works in general. When the BBC sent Beckett a tape of the broadcast, he was again fascinated by the dramatic possibilities of a disembodied voice, this time captured on audio tape, and he set to work shortly thereafter to stage it, producing *Krapp's Last Tape*. This interplay of art and technology continued to fascinate Beckett, and he wrote a series of radio plays for the BBC: *Embers*, *Words and Music*, and *Cascando*. In 1963 Beckett's American publisher asked him to write a filmscript and Beckett responded with the generically entitled *Film*, the shooting of which he oversaw in New York in July of 1964. But it was television which would allow Beckett to reach yet a wider audience, and in 1966 Beckett wrote *Eh Joe*, which he directed himself for German television and then oversaw for the BBC production in June of 1966.

In the theatre proper, Beckett continued his preoccupation with the monologue, producing a female counterpart to *Krapp's Last Tape* (without the tapes), *Happy Days*, in 1961. Buried to her waist in scorched sand for the first act and to her neck in the shorter second, Winnie retains an optimism in the face of her post-nuclear calamity that evokes the sort of bitter irony and pathos that make the role one of the great female leads in the theatre. Actresses, however, have had difficulty memorizing the long, complex, repetitive, looping monologue. In the Lincoln Center (New York) Beckett festival in 1972, Jessica Tandy, for instance, needed a television monitor built into her mound which functioned as a teleprompter. That Lincoln Center festival also saw the world premiere of

another gruelling monologue, this time for a set of staged lips (reminiscent of the Man Ray painting and the Salvador Dali sofa), entitled *Not I*, and soon afterwards Beckett wrote another pair of monologues, *Footfalls* and *That Time*, both of which were produced as part of the 70th birthday celebration at the Royal Court Theater in 1976, the former directed by Beckett himself. In 1981 Beckett created another brace of monologues for symposia planned to celebrate his 80th birthday at American universities. *Rockaby* was performed at the State University at Buffalo in April and *Ohio Impromptu* had its premiere at the Ohio State University Beckett Symposium in May, with both staged by long-time Beckett director Alan Schneider.

In addition to becoming the modern period's dominant playwright, Beckett also developed into a complete theater man, serving an apprenticeship at first by attending rehearsals and advising directors and then taking full charge of his productions, beginning with *Va et vient* (*Come and Go*) in Paris in 1966. That same year Beckett directed, with full credit this time, the German television production of *Eh, Joe*. In 1967 the Schiller-Theater Werkstatt invited him to come to Berlin and direct any of his plays. He chose *Endspiel* (*Endgame*), "the favourite of my plays". Subsequently, from 1967 to 1985, Beckett directed some 16 other productions of his work in Berlin, Paris, and London, and beginning with *Endspiel*, kept detailed directorial notebooks for each staging. In the process of directing, Beckett also rewrote his texts. Publication of Beckett's theatrical notebooks, along with revised texts for his major plays, will make Beckett one of the most documented playwrights in the history of the theater.

—S.E. Gontarski

See also *Volume 1* entries on *Endgame*; *Happy Days*; *Krapp's Last Tape*; *Not I*; *Play*; *Waiting for Godot*.

BECQUE, Henry (-François). Born in Paris, 18 April 1837. Educated at the Lycée Condorcet, 1848–54, but did not complete studies. Worked for railway company, 1854–56; obtained clerical post, 1860, but left in the same year; possibly worked as private tutor; became private secretary to the Russian Count Patowsky; first work for the stage, *Sardanapale*, produced 1867; first drama, *L'Enfant prodigue*, published 1868; joined French army during the Franco-Prussian War, 1870; brief spell as a stockbroker; writer for newspaper *Le Peuple*, 1876–77, and for *Henri IV* and *L'Union républicaine*; lectured in Brussels and Paris, 1885–86; writer for *Le Gaulois*, *Le Figaro*, *Vie parisienne*, *Le Journal*, and *Gil Blas*; received state pension, 1894; injured in domestic fire, April 1899. Recipient: Légion d'Honneur, 1886. Died in Paris, 12 May 1899.

Works

Collections

Théâtre complet (2 vols.). 1890.
Théâtre complet (3 vols.). 1898.
The Vultures; The Woman of Paris; The Merry-Go-Round, translated by Freeman Tilden. 1913.
Oeuvres complètes (7 vols.). 1924–26.

Stage Works

Sardanapale (opera; produced Théâtre Lyrique, Paris, 1867).
  1867.
L'Enfant prodigue (produced Théâtre du Vaudeville, Paris,
  1868).   1868.
Michel Pauper (produced Théâtre de la Porte-Saint-Martin,
  Paris, 1871).   1870.
L'Enlèvement (produced Théâtre du Vaudeville, Paris,
  1871).   1871.
La Navette (produced Théâtre du Gymnase, Paris, 1878).
  1878; translated as *The Merry-Go-Round*, with *The
  Vultures* and *A Woman of Paris*, 1913.
Les Honnêtes Femmes (produced Théâtre du Gymnase,
  Paris, 1880).   1880.
Les Corbeaux (produced Comédie-Française, Paris, 1882).
  1882; translated as *The Crows*, in *The Drama*, 5, 1912; as
  The Vultures (with *The Woman of Paris* and *The
  Merry-Go-Round*; 1913), as *The Scavengers*, 1986.
La Parisienne (produced Théâtre de la Renaissance, Paris,
  1885).   1885; translated as *The Woman of Paris*, with *The
  Vultures* and *The Merry-Go-Round*, 1913.
Les Polichinelles (incomplete; first act produced Théâtre de
  l'Odéon, Paris, 1924).   1910.
Veuve (produced Théâtre de l'Odéon, Paris, 1914).   In
  Oeuvres complètes, 1924–26.
Le Départ (produced Théâtre de l'Odéon, Paris, 1924).   In
  Oeuvres complètes, 1924–26.
Une Exécution.   In *Oeuvres complètes*, 1924–26.
La Mère.   In *Oeuvres complètes*, 1924–26.

Memoirs and Letters

Souvenirs d'un auteur dramatique.   1895

Other

Le Frisson ("fantaisie rimée").   1884.
Molière et "L'École des Femmes".   1886.
Sonnets mélancoliques   1887–88.
Querelles littéraires   1890.

*

Criticism

Books:
A. Amaoutovitch, *Henri Becque* (3 vols.), Paris, 1927.
G. Möller, *Henry Becque and Eugène Brieux*, Breslau, 1937.
M. Descotes, *Henry Becque et son théâtre*, Paris, 1962.
Baldo Curato, *Il teatro di Henry Becque*, Cremona, Italy,
  1972.
Lois B. Hyslop, *Henry Becque*, New York, 1972.

* * *

Once described as "perhaps the most complete instance of splendid failure in the history of theatre", Henry Becque was chiefly a victim of accidents of history. His first play, *L'Enfant prodigue* (The Prodigal Son), was an attempt to emulate the box-office successes of Émile Augier, Dumas *fils*, and the like, who had perfected the formula of the well-made play as a means of providing popular, after-dinner entertainment for unreflective middle-class audiences. When Becque went on to attempt to stage *Michel Pauper*, a work dealing with what he referred to as "the demands being formulated by the socia-

lism of the time", he encountered flat refusals all round. A production he financed himself in 1870 was applauded but left him with considerable debts. A hastily-written imitation of Dumas *fils*, *L'Enlèvement* (The Kidnapping), flopped disastrously (and predictably) in 1871. For a period he turned his back on the theatre world and went to work in the Paris Stock Exchange; but he had no better fortune there and within a short while was once more contemplating a return to the fray.

He took time over the writing of what is perhaps his greatest play, *Les Corbeaux* (The Vultures), which was completed around 1874. Having it staged took even longer, however: over the next seven years, seven theatres and eleven directors turned it down. At length the Comédie-Française was persuaded to take it on, but the company were so afraid of its innovative techniques that the work was drastically cut, in the face of Becque's protests. Even so, the premiere in 1882 generated something of a tumult and the play's intrinsic qualities were more or less passed over in a rage of controversy. The arguments occasioned by Zola's campaign to introduce naturalism into the theatre were at their height, and *Les Corbeaux* was taken up as a stalking-horse by polemicists. The play, which ran for only 18 performances, nevertheless led to a commission for another work, but left Becque with more cause for bitterness than satisfaction.

Both sides in the controversy had assumed he was a naturalist—a misapprehension which has often occurred since. In fact he wrote *Les Corbeaux* before Zola's interventions, and was scathing about a stage version of Zola's *L'Assommoir* in 1881. He was repeatedly to complain about this new school, whose ringing manifestos, coupled as they were with inferior plays, made managers hostile to any and all innovative dramatists. Becque, for his part, was exploring techniques of realism in the theatre, but with no doctrinaire theories in mind. His story of a widow and her three daughters, who are swindled and driven from their home when the head of the household dies, says a great deal about sharp practice in business affairs and the vulnerability of women in a man's world; but the work is remarkably free from preaching or authorial intervention. In the place of the well-made play he sought to provide examples of the well-observed play. As a result his work is devoid of the features that were required of successful drama.

He was later to declare that he and the younger generation he subsequently inspired had invented a new form of drama in which nothing happened. The result is an orchestration of mood and rhythm, an unnervingly objective portrayal of character, minutely but mercilessly analysed. The simplicity and directness of his presentation are suffused with a detached irony which makes for a peculiar brand of black comedy. Both ruthless predators and hapless victims are shown to have foibles, so that much like Chekhov's characters, their behaviour is laughably incongruous because their perception of reality is coloured by their private obsessions.

As distractions from the struggle to have *Les Corbeaux* performed, Becque wrote two one-act comedies, *La Navette* (The Merry-Go-Round), and *Les Honnêtes Femmes* (Honest Women). These light but acerbic pieces underline Becque's special sympathy for women and his gift for creating female characters; they also stand as models of the closely circumscribed slice of life, and as such Strindberg was soon to acknowledge their importance in his own development.

When commissioned to write another play by the Comédie-Française, Becque embarked on the second great work with which his name is associated: *La Parisienne* (The Woman of Paris), which he completed in 1884. His witheringly lucid portrayal of a wife who, in the course of her infidelities, secures a government position for her husband, once more frightened off the old guard, and Becque found himself yet again unable to persuade any theatre to perform his work. The animosity and bad faith he had had to endure in the theatrical world had by now begun to take its toll of his creative energies. This, however, was the point at which the soon-to-be celebrated André Antoine, pioneer of new approaches to theatrical production, singled out Becque as the begetter and revered master of the rising generation. Antoine acted in a private performance of *La Parisienne*, and after hostile reviews greeted a professional production of this play in 1890, he publicly defended Becque's subtle innovations against the traditionalists who persisted in their refusal to see the value of what he was doing. it was Antoine who developed the acting style suited to Becque's realistic dialogue.

However, by the time Antoine opened his Théâtre Libre in 1887, Becque was no longer a young dramatist and in his place arose a new crop of playwrights who, nevertheless, acknowledged him as the originator of the so-called "*comédie rosse*" ("vicious comedy"). Becque was content to let them; during the 1890's he lectured, published collections of his journalistic writings, and wrote recollections of the swindles and betrayals he had suffered at the hands of theatrical luminaries. He spoke much about a great work he had planned, *Les Polichinelles* (The Puppets), which would expose the world of high finance. But while he was taken up by the society circles he regaled with malicious anecdotes, this projected play never advanced beyond a couple of acts and sketches and fragments of scenes. However, *Les Corbeaux* was revived to great acclaim in 1897, and on his death in 1899, Antoine's production of *La Parisienne* had just been launched—a production which was to run for over 100 performances.

The 20th century has been intermittently enthusiastic about Becque's work; *La Parisienne* has seen numerous productions throughout Europe, and *Les Corbeaux* has impressed regularly at anniversary revivals (particularly on its centenary at the Comédie-Française in 1982). In the English-speaking world two notable productions of *La Parisienne*, one by Ashley Dukes and another in a text by Peter Barnes, have made their mark. Becque's re-emergence from obscurity was signalled by BBC radio productions of *La Parisienne* and *Les Corbeaux* in 1987, while the British stage premiere of the latter play, directed by Alan Ayckbourn in 1989 (under the title of *Wolf at the Door*) was followed by a London revival of *La Parisienne* in 1990.

—David H. Walker

See also *Volume 1* entry on *The Vultures*.

BEHAN, Brendan (Francis). Born in Dublin, Ireland, 9 February 1923. Educated at the French Sisters of Charity School, Dublin, 1928–34; Christian Brothers School, Dublin, 1934–37; Day Apprentice School, 1937. Married Beatrice ffrench-Salkeld in 1955; one daughter. Joined the Irish Republican Army in 1937; apprentice housepainter, 1937–39; sent to Hollesley Bay Borstal, England, 1939–41, and deported; served terms in Mountjoy, Arbour Hill, and Curragh prisons, 1942–46; housepainter, journalist, and seaman, 1946–50; broadcaster, Radio Eireann, 1951–53; columnist, *Irish Press*, Dublin, 1954–55; first play, *The Quare Fellow*, produced 1954. Recipient: Obie award, 1958; Paris

An Giall (produced Gaelic League, Dublin, 1958). In *Poems and a Play in Irish*, 1981; translated by Richard Wall, 1987.
The Hostage, with Joan Littlewood, from *An Giall* (produced Theatre Royal, Stratford East, London, 1958). 1958; revised version, 1962.
The Big House, from his radio play (produced Pike Theatre Club, Dublin, 1958. In *Complete Plays*, 1978.
The New House, a two-act stage version of Behan's radio plays *Moving Out* and *A Garden Party* (produced Pike Theatre Club, Dublin, 1958). In *Best Short Plays of the World Theater 1958–1967*, edited by Stanley Richards, 1968.
Richard's Cork Leg, edited and completed by Alan Simpson (produced Peacock Theatre, Dublin, 1972). 1973.
Time for a Gargle (produced Haymarket Theatre, Leicester, 1973).

Radio Plays

Moving Out, 1952 (published in *Complete Plays*, 1978); *A Garden Party*, 1952 (published in *Complete Plays*, 1978); *The Big House*, 1957 (published in *Complete Plays*, 1978).

Fiction

The Scarperer.   1964.

Verse

Life Styles: Poems, with Nine Translations from the Irish of Brendan Behan, translated by Ulick O'Connor. 1973.
Poems and Stories, edited by Denis Cotter. 1978.
Poems and a Play in Irish. 1981.

Memoirs and Letters

Borstal Boy (autobiography).   1958.
Confessions of an Irish Rebel.   1965.

Other

Behan's Island: An Irish Sketch-Book. 1962.
Hold Your Hour and Have Another (articles). 1963.
Behan's New York. 1964.
The Wit of Behan, edited by Sean McCann. 1968.
After the Wake: Twenty-One Prose Works, edited by Peter Fallon. 1981.
Festival award, 1958; French Critics award, 1962. Died in Dublin, 20 March 1964.

Works

Collections

Complete Plays (includes *The Quare Fellow*; *The Hostage*; *The Big House*; *Moving Out*; *A Garden Party*; *Richard's Cork Leg*). 1978.
Poems and Stories, edited by Denis Cotter. 1978.
Poems and a Play [*An Giall*] in Irish. 1981.

Stage Works

The Quare Fellow (produced Pike Theatre Club, Dublin, 1954; revised version, Theatre Royal, Stratford East, London, 1956). 1956.

Brendan Behan (1952).

*

Bibliographies

E.H. Mikhail, *Brendan Behan: An Annotated Bibliography of Criticism*, New York, 1980.

Criticism

Books:
Alan Simpson, *Beckett and Behan and a Theatre in Dublin*, London, 1962.
Brian Behan, *With Breast Expanded*, London, 1964.
Dominic Behan, *My Brother Brendan*, London, 1965.
Sean McCann (ed.), *The World of Behan*, London, 1965.

Rae Jeffs, *Behan: Man and Showman*, London, 1966.
Ted E. Boyle, *Brendan Behan*, New York, 1969.
Ulick O'Connor, *Brendan Behan*, London, 1970; as *Brendan*, Englewood Cliffs, New Jersey, 1971.
Seamus de Burca, *Brendan Behan: A Memoir*, Newark, New Jersey, 1971.
Beatrice Behan, Des Hickey, and Gus Smith, *My Life with Brendan*, London, 1973.
Peter R. Gerdes, *The Major Works of Behan*, Bern, Switzerland, 1973.
Raymond Porter, *Brendan Behan*, New York, 1973.
Colbert Kearney, *The Writings of Behan*, Dublin, London, and New York, 1977.
E.H. Mikhail (ed.), *The Art of Behan*, London, 1979.
Peter Arthurs, *With Behan*, New York, 1981.
E.H. Mikhail (ed.), *Behan: Interviews and Recollections* (2 vols.), London, 1982.

*   *   *

The place of Behan in the pantheon of heroic drunks of 20th-century literature has long been secure, and with it the concomitant quality of masculine sexism. But, apart from alcohol dependence, numerous influences converge on the production of the plays which he may—loosely—be regarded as having written. His membership of the IRA, his experience of imprisonment, his collaboration with Alan Simpson and Joan Littlewood as director and dramaturg, and his proclivity towards the retrieval of a lost Gaelic identity—all of these factors merge in most of his work. Whatever the complexities of his personality, as a writer he was eagerly—and carelessly—eclectic, absorbing and distorting influences with what often looks like the swagger of literary vandalism but is probably closer to the workings of misprision. Scraps of Shaw and O'Casey surface surprisingly in *The Big House*, and the popular novels of Liam O'Flaherty are echoed in *An Giall* and its reworking as *The Hostage*. His journalistic curiosity meant that, in his sober years, any social situation seems to have stimulated his imaginative energy. His prose writings reflect his prison experience as a constant process of research, which included snatching at every opportunity to learn more Gaelic.

Behan's two major plays, *The Quare Fellow* and *The Hostage*, are stylistically antithetical, representing extremes of naturalism and Brechtian stylisation. However, their focusing methods are fundamentally the same. In each case, the on-stage characters represent the periphery of a more momentous public action, in that they have their attention fixed on another, off-stage drama in another arena: a person who is to be executed at dawn. In neither play is this person seen, but the reality of his predicament seems unquestionable, so that it governs the focus of both characters and audience; theatre-goers find themselves viewing reality through fictitious eyes. In each case, this ultimate focus has a high level of urgency, using a countdown process to generate tension both on stage and in the auditorium. For the characters, the condemned man represents a yardstick by which they measure themselves, whether in terms of normality, morality, or heroism. This is particularly clear in *The Hostage*, where one character brags about his impossible heroics with the IRA, subconsciously measuring himself against the Irish martyr in the background; but in the earlier play, also, the execution serves as a catalyst which makes the characters look hard at their own stature.

In neither play is it possible to isolate the text from the life and character of the author, and Behan's habit of writing himself into his plays means that they can have no pretension to objectivity. In the original production of *The Quare*

Fellow, Behan himself sang the part of the prisoner in the punishment cells, so that each act began or ended with the author's own voice, making its formal effect rather like that of a ballad: at times, there is just the voice of the singer, at other times the ballad is fleshed out and animated. In *The Hostage*, a similar effect is achieved by the presence of the pianist, who seems to be half a character in the play, half a function of the author. In that play, there is actually a reference to the author—"Brendan Behan, he's too anti-British". Coming immediately after the most inflammatory patriotic song in the play, the effect is of strong alienation, and it leads directly to the fulfilment of the play's parabolic form as the title character finds his name in a newspaper and reads that he is to be shot in reprisal.

Characteristically, Behan does not end his play at the point at which the parable realises itself, but adds a final act which works as a coda in which the reality of death is inescapable but the perception of it is blurred by the often ludicrous action in the brothel on stage.

The same absurd vision permeates Behan's last, incomplete play, *Richard's Cork Leg*, where one character echoes Donne: "The grave's a dark and silent place and none there are to there embrace". The setting, an Irish cemetery which is dominated by a chapel and a tomb, is the object of an annual pilgrimage by Irish prostitutes. The tomb, of Crystal Clear, a prostitute hero, broadly satirises Irish piety, especially as the pilgrims are met by a group of Open Brethren, an extreme form of puritanism, and there is an obvious parallel between their ethos and the grave. Every element in this play seems a travesty of what it initially appears to represent, a tendency which was already strong in the brothel of *The Hostage*, but here there is no off-stage referential focus to give the action urgency, and it frequently dissolves into the tone of a revue.

The prostitution theme in Behan may be seen as ambiguous. *An Giall*, the original Gaelic version of *The Hostage*, was much closer to the naturalism of *The Quare Fellow*, and Littlewood's involvement in reshaping it for the Theatre Workshop production obviously increased its stylisation very considerably. One Gaelic scholar has paradoxically termed *An Giall* a "naturalistic tragedy"—paradoxical because naturalism denies the attribution of blame—and it is not difficult to see the brothel as the context of a demonstration of the animalism of humanity. But it is also a more overtly ideological play than any of the plays in English, and although there seems little doubt that Littlewood did a lot of interpolation and rescripting, it is also arguable that Behan's choice of language reflected different senses of the function of theatre. All writing in Gaelic was essentially and inevitably political, but the English-speaking theatre was commonly the arena for Behan's imagined triumphs as a clown, vindicated by his perception of that theatre as culminating in music-hall.

—Howard McNaughton

See also *Volume 1* entries on *The Hostage*; *The Quare Fellow*.

———

BEHN, Aphra. Born probably in Kent, England, c.1640. Probably married a Mr. Behn c.1664 (died before 1666); lived with John Hoyle from c.1672. Possibly lived in the British colony Surinam, c.1663–64; English spy in Antwerp during second Dutch War, 1666; imprisoned for debt, late 1660's;

Aphra Behn (portrait by Sir Peter Lely).

first play, *The Forced Marriage*, produced 1670; arrested for alluding to the Duke of Monmouth's rebellion in a prologue, 1682. Died in London, 16 April 1689.

Works

Collections

Works, edited by Montague Summers (6 vols.).   1915.
Selected Writings, edited by Robert Phelps.   1950.
Five Plays (includes *The Lucky Chance; The Rover, Part One; The Widow Ranter; The False Count; Abdelazer*), edited by Maureen Duffy.   1990.

Stage Works

The Forced Marriage; or, The Jealous Bridegroom (produced Lincoln's Inn Fields Theatre, London, 1670).   1671.
The Amorous Prince; or, The Curious Husband (produced Lincoln's Inn Fields Theatre, London, 1671).   1671.
The Dutch Lover (produced Dorset Garden Theatre, London, 1673).   1673.
Abdelazar; or, The Moor's Revenge, from the play *Lust's Dominion* (produced Dorset Garden Theatre, London, 1676).   1677.
The Town Fop; or, Sir Timothy Tawdrey (produced Dorset Garden Theatre, London, 1676).   1677.
The Debauchee; or, The Credulous Cuckold, from a play by Richard Brome (produced Dorset Garden Theatre, London, 1677).   1677.

The Rover; or, The Banished Cavaliers (produced Dorset Garden Theatre, London, 1677). 1677.

Sir Patient Fancy (produced Dorset Garden Theatre, London, 1678). 1678.

The Feigned Courtesans; or, A Night's Intrigue (produced Dorset Garden Theatre, London, c.1679). 1679.

The Young King; or, The Mistake (produced Dorset Garden Theatre, London, 1679). 1683.

The Revenge; or, A Match in Newgate, from a play by Marston (produced Dorset Garden Theatre, London, 1680). 1680.

The Second Part of the Rover (produced Dorset Garden Theatre, London, 1681). 1681.

The Roundheads; or, The Good Old Cause, from a play by John Tatham (produced Dorset Garden Theatre, London, 1681). 1682.

The False Count; or, A New Way to Play an Old Game (produced Dorset Garden Theatre, London, 1681). 1682.

The City Heiress; or, Sir Timothy Treat-All, from a play by Middleton (produced Dorset Garden Theatre, London, 1682). 1682.

The Lucky Chance; or, An Alderman's Bargain (produced Dorset Garden Theatre, London, 1686). 1687.

The Emperor of the Moon (produced Dorset Garden Theatre, London, 1687). 1687.

The Widow Ranter; or, The History of Bacon in Virginia (produced Theatre Royal, Drury Lane, London, 1689). 1690.

The Younger Brother; or, The Amorous Jilt (produced Theatre Royal, Drury Lane, London, 1696). 1696.

Fiction

Love Letters Between a Nobleman and His Sister (3 vols.). 1683–87.

The Fair Jilt; or, The History of Prince Tarquin and Miranda. 1688.

Oroonoko; or, The Royal Slave. 1688.

The History of the Nun; or, The Fair Vow-Breaker. 1689.

The Lucky Mistake. 1689.

Histories and Novels. 1696; revised edition, 1697, 1700.

"Oroonoko" and Other Stories, edited by Maureen Duffy. 1986.

Verse

Poems upon Several Occasions, with A Voyage to the Island of Love. 1684.

A Pindaric on the Death of Our Late Sovereign. 1685.

A Pindaric Poem on the Happy Coronation of His Sacred Majesty James II and His Illustrious Consort Queen Mary. 1685.

A Poem to Catherine, Queen Dowager. 1685.

To Christopher, Duke of Albemarle, on His Voyage to Jamaica: A Pindaric. 1687.

To the Memory of George, Duke of Buckingham. 1687.

A Poem to Sir Roger L'Estrange. 1688.

A Congratulatory Poem to Her Majesty. 1688.

A Congratulatory Poem to the King's Most Sacred Majesty. 1688.

To Poet Bavius. 1688.

Lycidus; or, The Lover in Fashion, Together with a Miscellany of New Poems by Several Hands, with others. 1688.

A Congratulatory Poem to Her Sacred Majesty Queen Mary, upon Her Arrival in England. 1689.

A Pindaric Poem to the Rev. Dr. [Thomas] Burnet. 1689.

Uncollected Verse, edited by Germaine Greer. 1989.

Other

Editor, *Convent Garden Drollery.* 1672; edited by G. Thorn-Drury, 1928.

Editor, *Miscellany, Being a Collection of Poems by Several Hands* (includes Behn's translation of La Rochefoucauld). 1685.

Translator, *La Montre; or, The Lover's Watch*, by Balthasar de Bonnecorse. 1686.

Translator, *The Fatal Beauty of Agnes de Castro*, by J.B. de Brillac. 1688.

Translator, *A Discovery of New Worlds*, by Fontenelle. 1688; as *The Theory of New Worlds*, 1700.

Translator, *The History of Oracles, and the Cheats of the Pagan Priests*, by Fontenelle. 1688.

Translator, with others, *Cowley's Six Books of Plants.* 1689.

*

Bibliographies

Mary Ann O'Donnell, *Aphra Behn: An Annotated Bibliography of Primary and Secondary Sources*, New York and London, 1986.

Criticism

Books:

V. Sackville-West, *Behn: The Incomparable Astrea*, London, 1927.

George Woodcock, *The Incomparable Aphra: A Life of Behn*, London, 1948; retitled as *Behn, The English Sappho*, 1989.

W.J. Cameron, *New Light on Behn*, Auckland, New Zealand, 1961.

Frederick M. Link, *Aphra Behn*, New York, 1968.

Maureen Duffy, *The Passionate Shepherdess: Aphra Behn*, London, 1977.

Angeline Goreau, *Reconstructing Aphra: A Social Biography of Behn*, Oxford, 1980.

* * *

Aphra Behn's plays repeatedly storm against the sale of women on the marriage market, against the idea that money purchases freedom, against class oppression. The plays stand for sexual equality and real freedom. And most of them are bawdy, witty, and clever, with well-structured, complex plots and casts of memorable characters. Behn skilfully uses the classical devices of comic playwriting: disguise (particularly women in breeches roles), mistaken identity, physical farce, witty repartee, unexpected twists of plot, and a wide range of familiar character-types, from lascivious old men to tricky servants. Noticeably missing, however, are the passive, sweet young things. Most of Behn's women are intelligent, understand their options, and take action to improve their lot.

Behn's gift was for comedy, particularly comedy of intrigue. She did, however, experiment with other forms. Her first two plays were tragicomedies. The heroine of the comic plot of *The Forced Marriage* establishes Behn's future themes in her tart response to the terms of a marriage proposal:

> I will not purchase slavery
> At such a dangerous rate,
> But glory in my liberty
> And laugh at love and fate.

In *The Amorous Prince* Behn moves more confidently towards the comic elements of her plot, and shocked her contemporary audience with the daring opening scene in which two unmarried lovers are seen rising, still in their "night attire". *Abdelazar* and *The Young King* are tragedies, and not representative of her best writing. *Abdelazar* is about obsessive sexual passion, notable mainly because of Handel's overture and incidental music, and because it gave Elizabeth Barry her first Behn role (thereafter she was to play to acclaim in most of Behn's plays). *The Young King* pays debt to Calderón's *Life is a Dream* in its imprisonment of the young heir to the throne to subvert a prophecy. His sister, however, has been given a "masculine" education so that she may lead the army and succeed to the throne. She falls in love and all her "masculine courage" deserts her, only to return when she believes her lover dead. As she was to do again in later plays, Behn offers a keen dramatic exploration of gender stereotyping in this, her first-written play.

Behn's plays are almost always political. Sexual politics dominate, but she deals with many other issues. In the social satire *The False Count*, Behn debunks the myths of money and class. Young Isabella, daughter to a nouveau-riche tradesman-turned-gentleman, is only willing to be married to a count, but is tricked into marrying a disguised chimney-sweep. A sub-plot involves a young woman forced to marry an old lecher because her young lover is poor. His father's death changes matters and the old husband is persuaded to let young love thrive by granting an annulment. *The Forced Marriage* and *The Lucky Chance* also feature old men who relinquish their young wives to happier matches.

The Roundheads is an overtly political play about the 1660 dissolution of the Rump Parliament shortly before Charles II claimed the throne of England. Behn uses the names of the real people involved in the incident. She intended the play to stand as a warning about contemporary Whig policies and added a bawdy, comic sub-plot to lighten the tone. The blend of politics and humour is more successful in *The City Heiress* which includes a biting caricature of the Whig leader, Shaftesbury. *The Widow Ranter*, set in America during the Indian Wars, also mixes a delightfully comic plot with the tragic story of Sir Nathaniel Bacon's love for an Indian Queen. The play makes one of Behn's strongest statements about sexual equality.

The Rover is the quintessential Aphra Behn play, both in its comic spirit and the serious issues it raises: forced marriage, woman as commodity, woman as sexual object, the nature of sexual freedom and its implications for a woman. The writing is perhaps her most accomplished, particularly the passionate verse scenes between Angelica Bianca, the courtesan, and Willmore, the cavalier rover. In contrast is the sparkling repartee between Willmore and his ultimate bride, Hellena, the archetypal witty and enterprising Aphra Behn heroine. The intricate plot includes several boisterous sword fights, and characters in a variety of disguises causing mistaken identity and plot complications. There is a hilarious seduction scene in which the foolish cavalier, Blunt, is gulled by a "jilting wench". The play crackles with light-hearted fun, but Behn also includes some serious and dark tones to underscore her concerns. Angelica, cruelly spurned by Willmore, is roused to a passionate rage and sets out to shoot the man who was only too happy to bed her, but not to wed her. Hellena's sister, Florinda, is abused and nearly raped in two separate scenes. The way in which Behn brings about the marriages that end the play leaves serious questions about the future and the nature of wedded bliss.

The Rover was Aphra Behn's most produced play, and the one receiving most attention today. Many others are well worth modern production. *The Town Fop*, a comedy of manners and one of only three plays with London (or English) settings, cleverly uses (and thus advertised) a legal loophole to a forced marriage. The young lovers had exchanged vows in front of a witness, a marriage in the eyes of the law. *The Town Fop* has *The Rover*'s mixture of tones and blend of farce, high comedy and serious statement. Behn also shows that men may suffer under oppression of forced marriage too, though they always have alternatives not as safely available to women.

The Lucky Chance returns to the theme of rich old men preying on the poverty of desirable young women. Typical of Behn's heroines, the women take action to secure their integrity and freedom. Lady Fulbank says, "I'll not change my freedom and my humour to purchase the dull fame of being honest". The plot is blatantly but cleverly contrived and includes numerous scenes of physical and visual humour, particularly featuring various disguises. As are so many of Behn's aged suitors, the old men are modelled on *commedia dell'arte*'s Pantalone. *The Emperor of the Moon* employs *commedia* characters and techniques throughout, the first English play to do so, and is a delightful, fast-paced play about a mad scientist obsessed with his belief in life on the moon.

Aphra Behn's plays epitomise the spirit of the Restoration in their exuberance and sexual frankness. Despite contemporary accusations, Behn's plays are no "smuttier" than those written by her male colleagues. However, they do underscore and challenge the objectification of women, both in Restoration society and in their newly permitted roles on the Restoration stage. She went along with the game, putting heroine after heroine into breeches roles, but giving them the courage and wit to challenge their men.

In *The Rover* Behn dared to put a courtesan on the stage, one who advertised her price, and Angelica Bianca proved to be one of her most stunning and passionate characterisations. Behn dared to pair up lovers without the sanctity of marriage in *The Rover, Part II*, and *Sir Patient Fancy*. She defended her right to free expression in her prologues and epilogues, and in epistles to the readers of her published plays. In them she also railed against literary fashions, her critics, political and social hypocrisy, and, above all, she defended the rights of women to write, as for example in the epilogue to *Sir Patient Fancy*:

> To all the men of wit we will subscribe
> But for your half wits, you unthinking tribe,
> We'll let you see, whate'er besides we do,
> How artfully we copy some of you:
> And if you're drawn to th' life, pray tell me then,
> Why women should not write as well as men.

—Elizabeth Swain

See also *Volume 1* entry on *The Rover*.

BEHRMAN, S(amuel) N(athaniel). Born in Worcester, Massachusetts, USA, 9 June 1893. Educated at Providence Street School, and Classical High School, both Worcester; Clark College (now Clark University), Worcester, 1912–14; Harvard University, Cambridge, Massachusetts (in George

Pierce Baker's 47 Workshop), AB 1916 (Phi Beta Kappa); Columbia University, New York, MA 1918. Married Elza Heifetz in 1936; one son and two step-children. Advertising writer and book reviewer, *New York Times*, 1917–18; reviewer, *New Republic*, New York, and freelance publicist until early 1920's; first play, *Bedside Manners*, produced 1923; columnist, *New Yorker*, from 1927; founder, with Robert E. Sherwood, Elmer Rice, Maxwell Anderson, Sidney Howard, and John F. Wharton, Playwrights Company, 1938. Trustee, Clark University. Recipient: American Academy grant, 1943; New York Drama Critics Circle award, 1944; Writers Guild of America West award, for screenplay, 1959; Brandeis University Creative Arts Award, 1962. LL.D: Clark University, 1949. Member, American Academy, 1943, and American Academy of Arts and Sciences. Died in New York, 9 September 1973.

Works

Collections

Three Plays: Serena Blandish; Meteor; The Second Man. 1934.
Four Plays: The Second Man; Biography; Rain from Heaven; End of Summer. 1955.

Stage Works

Bedside Manners: A Comedy of Convalescence, with J. Kenyon Nicholson (produced Threshold Theatre, New York, 1923). 1924.
A Night's Work, with J. Kenyon Nicholson (produced Grand Theatre, Peekskill, New York, 1924). 1926.
The Man Who Forgot, with Owen Davis (produced Apollo Theatre, Atlantic City, Maryland, 1926).
The Second Man (produced Guild Theatre, New York, 1927). 1927.
Love is Like That, with J. Kenyon Nicholson (produced Cort Theatre, New York, 1927).
Serena Blandish, from the novel by Enid Bagnold (produced Morosco Theatre, New York, 1929). In *Three Plays*, 1934.
Meteor (produced Guild Theatre, New York, 1929). 1930.
Brief Moment (produced Belasco Theatre, New York, 1931). 1931.
Biography (produced Guild Theatre, New York, 1932). 1933.
Love Story (produced Walnut Street Theatre, Philadelphia, 1933).
Rain from Heaven (produced John Golden Theatre, New York, 1934). 1935.
End of Summer (produced Guild Theatre, New York, 1936). 1936.
Amphitryon 38, with Roger Gellert, from a play by Jean Giraudoux (produced Shubert Theatre, New York, 1937). 1938.
Wine of Choice (produced Guild Theatre, New York, 1938). 1938.
No Time for Comedy (produced Ethel Barrymore Theatre, New York, 1939). 1939.
The Talley Method (produced Henry Miller's Theatre, New York, 1941). 1941.
The Pirate, from a play by Ludwig Fulda (produced Martin Beck Theatre, New York, 1942). 1943.
Jacobowsky and the Colonel, from a play by Franz Werfel (produced Martin Beck Theatre, New York, 1944). 1944.

Dunnigan's Daughter (produced John Golden Theatre, New York, 1945). 1946.
Jane, from a story by W. Somerset Maugham (produced 1946; as *The Foreign Language*, produced Coronet Theatre, New York, 1952). 1952.
I Know My Love, from a play by Marcel Achard (produced Shubert Theatre, New York, 1949). 1952.
Let Me Hear the Melody (produced Walnut Street Theatre, Philadelphia, 1951).
Fanny, with Joshua Logan, music by Harold Rome, from a trilogy by Marcel Pagnol (produced Majestic Theatre, New York, 1954). 1955.
The Cold Wind and the Warm (produced Morosco Theatre, New York, 1958). 1959.
The Beauty Part (produced 1962).
Lord Pengo: A Period Comedy, based on his book *Duveen* (produced Royale Theatre, New York, 1962). 1963.
But for Whom Charlie (produced by ANTA, Washington Square Theatre, New York, 1964). 1964.

Screenplays

Liliom, with Sonya Levien, 1930; *Lightnin'*, with Sonya Levien, 1930; *The Sea Wolf*, with Ralph Block, 1930; *The Brat*, with others, 1931; *Surrender*, with Sonya Levien, 1931; *Daddy Long Legs*, with Sonya Levien, 1931; *Delicious*, 1931; *Rebecca of Sunnybrook Farm*, with Sonya Levien, 1932; *Tess of the Storm Country*, with others, 1932; *Brief Moment*, 1933; *Queen Christina*, with Salka Viertel and H.M. Harwood, 1933; *Cavalcade*, 1933; *Hallelujah, I'm a Bum* (*Hallelujah, I'm a Tramp, Lazy Bones*), with Ben Hecht, 1933; *My Lips Betray*, 1933; *As Husbands Go*, with Sonya Levien, 1934; *The Scarlet Pimpernel*, with others, 1934; *Anna Karenina*, with others, 1935; *A Tale of Two Cities*, with W.P. Lipscomb, 1935; *Conquest* (*Marie Walewska*), with others, 1937; *Parnell*, with John van Druten, 1937; *The Cowboy and the Lady*, with Sonya Levien, 1938; *Waterloo Bridge*, with others, 1940; *Two-Faced Woman*, with others, 1941; *Quo Vadis*, with others, 1951; *Me and the Colonel*, with George Froeschel, 1958; *Stowaway in the Sky* (English narration), 1962.

Fiction

The Burning-Glass. 1968.

Other

Duveen. 1952.
The Worcester Account (*New Yorker* sketches). 1954.
Portrait of Max: An Intimate Memoir of Sir Max Beerbohm. 1960; as *Conversation with Max*, 1960.
The Suspended Drawing Room. 1965.
People in a Diary: A Memoir. 1972; as *Tribulations and Laughter: A Memoir*, 1972.

*

Bibliographies

William Klink, *Maxwell Anderson and S.N. Behrman: A Reference Guide*, Boston, 1977.

Criticism

Books:
Urs. Kessely, *S.N. Behrmans Komödien: Spiel und Konflikt*, Bern, 1972.

Kenneth T. Read, *S.N. Behrman*, Boston, 1975.
William Klink, *S.N. Behrman: The Major Plays*, Amsterdam, 1978.
B.D. Joshi, *Major Plays of Barry and Behrman*, Jaipur, India, 1989.

* * *

S.N. Behrman's work encompasses more than 35 plays, most of which can be considered high comedy. Through his sophisticated social comedies walk an array of urbane, often intellectually articulate characters meeting in elegant surroundings on America's eastern seaboard, or abroad. The dramas convey Behrman's thematic concerns with the dangers of intolerance and the problems of success with its attendant moral questions and tensions arising when related to matrimony, money, politics, and love. The author's protagonists tend to be dispassionate observers of life rather than fighters for a cause. Frequently they confront fanatic or passionate points of view with an unheroic attitude of compromise. A tolerant, liberal humanistic view is the crux of Behrman's comic vision. Often at the center of his plays is a mature and radiant woman acting as a lodestone toward whom all the other characters are drawn. Forgiving and liberal in spirit, she clashes with more intense opponents to emerge triumphant, strengthened by her grace and magnanimity. Because Behrman's protagonists compromise rather than cope with issues, his plays are apt to seem inconclusive and are often faulted for structural looseness and insufficient plot progression. However, such shortcomings are redeemed in his best plays by lively, witty characters and incisive dialogue within which Behrman's humanistic vision is clearly implied.

In addition to finely-drawn female characters (providing vehicles for actresses the like of Ina Claire, Ruth Gordon, Katherine Cornell, and Lynn Fontanne), Behrman peopled his world with character-types bearing symbolic significance. These figures recur in his plays in different guises, such as the politically conservative man of power (commonly a financier or businessman); the failed, if modestly talented, artist; the emancipated woman; the success-motivated financial or professional genius; and the idealistic Marxist.

In *The Second Man*, the author's first major play, the limitedly talented writer Clark Storey is matrimonially desired by two women: an understanding rich woman offering financial security, and an emancipated young flapper who is beloved by an unexciting but talented and prosperous scientist. The plot's two love triangles are resolved when all characters prove true to themselves. Storey pragmatically chooses the wealthy lady, accepting his opportunistic nature, and the flapper agrees to marry her reliable scientist-suitor. The play is well realized with interesting characters surrounding a witty, unheroic protagonist.

Biography introduces Behrman's most masterfully created protagonist in Marion Froude, a charming and worldly portrait painter who views life and the many men she has loved with kindly detachment. Offered a lucrative commission to write her autobiography for a popular magazine by an intense and socially embittered young journalist named Richard Kurt, Marion accepts the offer and, soon, Kurt's developing love for her. When she learns, however, of Kurt's expectation that her memoirs scandalously expose her many celebrated acquaintances, Marion destroys her manuscript and, consequently, her relationship with Kurt who thinks her compromising attitude indulgent toward society's evils. Encountering this fanatic outlook, Marion refuses to abandon her own. Particular objects of Kurt's enmity are a pompous Senatorial candidate (a re-emerged former lover from Marion's youth) and his wealthy and powerful political

mentor who has exerted pressure to have the memoirs quashed. No other play of Behrman's so skillfully develops and interweaves character, story, and theme, emphasizing a protagonist embodying his humanistic beliefs.

Variations of Marion Froude appear in several subsequent Behrman comedies. *End of Summer* revolves around a wealthy and charming, but impressionable, divorcee who is infatuated with a fortune-hunting doctor. When she learns that the physician loves not her but her daughter, she sadly, but firmly, dismisses him, as does her daughter. Dealing with the often conflicting quests of love and money, the author draws a compelling portrait of his central woman in a social environment of interesting characters. In *Rain from Heaven* a liberal and wise English woman mediates a stormy debate of socio-political ideals among weekend guests at her country home. Among them are a German-Jewish music critic, an anti-semitic American aviator, and a dictatorial American millionaire bent on uniting youth in favor of Fascism. Accenting the world-wide turmoil of the 1930's, the author sharply raises and opposes the issues of political intolerance and racism.

In *No Time for Comedy*, an understanding actress wife temporarily accepts her playwright husband's affair with another woman while he attempts to turn from composing light comedies to serious drama in keeping with darkening times. Seeing his attempts are unsuccessful, she persuades him to write a comedy about his own love triangle which leads him to recover his true stylistic abilities and to return to his wife. That the secondary character of the wife emerges as a more forceful depiction than that of the writer-protagonist is a shortcoming in a play successfully dramatizing Behrman's self-admitted concern about a comic writer's proper path in a turbulent age.

Other noteworthy dramatic works in the latter portion of Behrman's career touch on problems of marriage, romance, and racism, and encompass several adaptations. *Amphitryon 38*, adapted from Giraudoux's play, is an entertaining bedroom farce employing the Amphitryon legend. *Jacobowsky and the Colonel*, an ironically amusing, if structurally diffuse, version of Franz Werfel's play, brings together a Jew and an anti-Semite fleeing from the Nazis in World War II. Based on Marcel Pagnol's trilogy and written in collaboration with Joshua Logan, *Fanny*—Behrman's only musical—charmingly treats the burdens of long-parted lovers. *The Cold Wind and the Warm* stands strongly as an affecting, semi-autobiographical memoir about a youthful friendship. Behrman did not continue to write for the theater after his last play, *But for Whom Charlie*, in 1964.

S.N. Behrman left a substantial legacy of social comedies, the best being notable for richly-drawn characters, dialogue filled with wit and the intelligent discussion of ideas, and a humanistic *Weltanschauung* advocating tolerance. As a dramatist, his comic view of the world greatly enriched the theater and its literature.

—Christian H. Moe

_____

BEKERDOMO, J.P. Clark. See **CLARK, John Pepper**.

_____

BENAVENTE Y MARTÍNEZ, Jacinto. Born in Madrid, 12 August 1866. Educated at San Isidro Institute; studied law,

University of Madrid, 1882–85. Never married. Impresario with a travelling circus, touring Europe; actor with Maria Tubau's company; first volume of plays, *Teatro fantástico*, published 1892; first book of poetry published in 1893; associated with the "Generation of '98" group of writers, which included Miguel de Unamuno and Valle-Inclán; wrote for the newspaper *El imparcial*, 1908–12; co-founder of a children's theatre, Teatro de los Niños, 1909; edited the magazine *La vida literaria*; supported Germany in World War I; made director of the Teatro Español, 1920; wrote no plays, 1920–24; lived in Valencia, during Spanish Civil War (possibly under house arrest), 1936–39; continued to write under the Franco regime. Recipient: Nobel Prize for Literature, 1922, and many honours under Franco. Elected to the Real Academia Española, 1912. Died in Madrid, 14 July 1954.

Works

Collections

Teatro fantástico.   1892.
Teatro (38 vols.), 1904–31.
Plays (4 vols.), translated by J.G. Underhill.   1917–24.
Obras completas (3 vols.).   1940; revised edition (7 vols.), 1941–42; further revised and augmented edition (10 vols.), 1947–69.

Stage Works

Where no publication date is given, plays appeared first in book form in the collected editions (see above).
Comedia italiana.   In *Teatro fantastico*, 1892.
El criado de Don Juan.   In *Teatro fantástico*, 1892.
La senda del amor.   In *Teatro fantástico*, 1892.
La blancura de Pierrot.   In *Teatro fantastico*, 1892.
Cuento de primavera.   In *Teatro fantástico*, 1892.
Amor de artista.   In *Teatro fantástico*, 1892.
Modernismo. In *Teatro fantastico*, 1892.
El encanto de una hora (produced Teatro de la Princesa, Madrid, 1905).   In *Teatro fantástico*, 1892; translated as *The Magic of an Hour*, in *Plays 4*.
El nido ajeno (produced Teatro de la Comedia, Madrid, 1894).   1894; translated as *Another's Nest*, in *Nineteenth Century Spanish Plays*, edited by L.E. Brett, 1935.
Gente conocida (produced Teatro de la Comedia, Madrid, 1896).
El marido de la Téllez (produced Teatro de Lara, Madrid, 1897).
De alivio (produced Teatro de la Comedia, Madrid, 1897).
Don Juan, from Molière's *Dom Juan* (produced Teatro de la Princesa, Madrid, 1897).
La farándula (produced Teatro de Lara, Madrid, 1897).
La comida de las fieras (produced Teatro de la Comedia, 1898).   1899.
Teatro feminista, music by D. Pablo Barbero (produced Teatro de la Comedia, Madrid, 1898).
Cuento de amor, from Shakespeare's *Twelfth Night* (produced Teatro de la Comedia, Madrid, 1899).
Operación quirúrgica (produced Teatro de Lara, Madrid, 1899).
Despedida cruel (produced Teatro de Lara, Madrid, 1899).
La gata de Angora (produced Teatro de la Comedia, Madrid, 1900).
Viaje de instrucción, with music by Amadeo Vives (produced Teatro Eslava, Madrid, 1900).
Por la herida (produced Teatro de Novedades, Barcelona, 1900).

Modas (produced Teatro de Lara, 1901).
Lo cursi (produced Teatro de la Comedia, Madrid, 1901).
Sin querer (produced Teatro de la Comedia, Madrid, 1901).
Sacrificios (produced Teatro de Novedades, Barcelona, 1901).
La gobernadora (produced Teatro de la Comedia, Madrid, 1901).   1901; translated as *The Governor's Wife*, in *Plays 2*, 1921.
El primo Román (produced Teatro Principal, Saragossa, 1901).
Amor de amar (produced Teatro de la Comedia, Madrid, 1902).   1902.
¡Liberdad!, from a play by Santiago Rusiñol y Prats (produced Teatro de la Comedia, 1902).
El tren de los maridos (produced Teatro de Lara, Madrid, 1902).
Alma triunfante (produced Teatro de la Comedia, Madrid, 1902).   1902.
El automóvil (produced Teatro de Lara, Madrid, 1902).
La noche del sábado (produced Teatro Español, Madrid, 1903).   1903; translated as *Saturday Night*, in *Plays 3*, 1923.
Los favoritos (produced Teatro de San Fernando, Seville, 1903).
El hombrecito (produced Teatro de la Comedia, Madrid, 1903).
Mademoiselle de Belle-Isle, from the play by Dumas *père* (produced Gran Teatro Calderón de la Barca, Valladolid, 1903).
Porque se ama (produced Teatro Español, Madrid, 1903).
Al natural (produced Teatro de Lara, Madrid, 1903).
La casa de la dicha (produced Teatro de las Artes, Barcelona, 1903).
En este Madrid (produced Teatro Español, 1903).   In *Catologo de la Sociedad de Autores*, 1913.
No fumadores (produced Teatro de Lara, Madrid, 1904). Translated as *No Smoking*, in *Plays 2*, 1921.
Richelieu, from the play by Edward Bulwer-Lytton (produced Mexico City, 1904).
El dragón de fuego (produced Teatro Español, Madrid, 1904).
Rosas de otoño (produced Teatro Español, Madrid, 1905). Translated as *Autumnal Roses*, in *Plays 2*, 1921.
Cuento inmoral (produced Teatro Novedades, Barcelona, 1905).
El susto de la condesa (Teatro Español, Madrid, 1905).
Los malhechores del bien (produced Teatro de Lara, Madrid, 1905).   Translated as *The Evil Doers of Good*, in *Plays 1*, 1917.
La sobresalienta, music by D. Ruperto Chapí (produced Teatro Español, Madrid, 1905).
Las cigarras hormigas (produced Teatro de la Comedia, Madrid, 1905).
Buena boda, from a play by Augier (produced Teatro de Sociedad, Madrid, 1905).
El encanto de una hora (produced Teatro de la Princesa, Madrid, 1905).
Manon Lescaut (produced Teatro Español, Madrid, 1906).
La princesa Bebé (produced Teatro Español, Madrid, 1906). Translated as *Princess Bebé*, in *Plays 2*, 1921.
Más fuerte que el amor (produced Teatro Español, Madrid, 1906).
El amor asusta (produced Teatro de Lara, Madrid, 1907).
Los buhos (produced Teatro de Lara, Madrid, 1907).
Abuela y nieta (produced Teatro de Lara, Madrid, 1907).
La copa encantada, from a story by Ariosto, music by Vicente Lleó (produced Teatro de la Zarzuela, Madrid, 1907).

Todos somos unos, music by Vicente Lleó (produced Teatro Eslava, Madrid, 1907).   1907.

Los ojos de los muertos (produced Teatro de la Princesa, Madrid, 1907).

La historia de Otelo (produced Teatro de Apolo, Madrid, 1907).

Los intereses creados (produced Teatro de Lara, Madrid, 1907).   Translated as *The Bonds of Interest*, in *Plays 1*, 1917.

La princesa sin corazón.   1908.

La sunrisa de Gioconda.   1908; translated as *The Smile of Mona Lisa*, 1915.

De pequeñas causas . . . (produced Teatro de la Princesa, Madrid, 1908).

Señora Ama (produced Teatro de la Princesa, Madrid, 1908).

El marido de su viuda (produced Teatro del Príncipe Alfonso, Madrid, 1908).   Translated as *His Widow's Husband*, in *Plays 1*, 1917.

La fuerza bruta (produced Teatro de Lara, Madrid, 1908).   Translated as *Brute Force*, 1935.

Hacia la verdad (produced Teatro del Príncipe Alfonso, Madrid, 1908).

Por las nubes (produced Teatro de Lara, Madrid, 1909).   Translated as *In the Clouds*, in *Plays 3*, 1923.

De cerca (produced Teatro de Lara, Madrid, 1909).   Translated as *At Close Range*, 1936.

La escuela de las princesas (produced Teatro de la Comedia, Madrid, 1909).   Translated as *The School of Princesses*, in *Plays 4*, 1924.

El último minué (produced Teatro Benavente, Madrid, 1909).

La señorita se aburre, from a poem by Tennyson (produced Teatro del Príncipe Alfonso, Madrid, 1909).

El príncipe que todo lo aprendió en los libros (produced Teatro del Príncipe Alfonso, Madrid, 1909).   Translated as *The Prince Who Learned Everything Out of Books*, in *Plays 3*, 1923.

¡A ver qué hace un hombre!.   In *Teatro, 18*, 1909.

Ganarse la vida (produced Teatro del Príncipe Alfonso, Madrid, 1909).

El Nietecito, from a story by Hermann Grimm (produced Teatro del Príncipe Alfonso, Madrid, 1910).

La losa de los sueños (produced Teatro de Lara, Madrid, 1911).

El criade de Don Juan (produced Teatro Español, Madrid, 1911).

El rey Lear, from Shakespeare's *King Lear*.   In *La lectura*, 1911.

La malquerida (produced Teatro de la Princesa, Madrid, 1913).   Translated as *The Passion Flower*, in *Plays 1*, 1917.

El destino manda, from a work by Paul Herrieu (produced Teatro de la Princesa, Madrid, 1914).

El collar de estrellas (produced Teatro de la Princesa, Madrid, 1915).   1915.

La verdad (produced Teatro Calderón de la Barca, Madrid, 1909).   1915; translated as *The Truth*, in *Plays 3*, 1923.

La propia estimación (produced Teatro de la Comedia, Madrid, 1915).

Campo de armiño (produced Teatro de la Princesa, Madrid, 1916).   Translated as *Field of Ermine*, in *Plays 4*, 1924.

La túnica amarilla, from a play by George C. Hazleton and Henry Benrimo (produced Teatro de la Princesa, Madrid, 1916).

La ciudad alegre y confiada (produced Teatro de Lara, Madrid, 1916).

El mal que nos hacen (produced Teatro de la Princesa, 1917).

Caridad (produced Teatro Real, Madrid, 1911).

Los cachorros (produced Teatro de la Princesa, Madrid, 1918).

La Mefistófela, with music by Prudencio Muñoz (produced Teatro de la Reina Victoria, Madrid, 1918).

La Inmaculada de los Dolores (produced Teatro de Lara, Madrid, 1918).

La ley de los hijos (produced Teatro de Zarzuela, Madrid, 1918).

Por ser con todos leal, ser para todos traidor (produced Teatro del Centro, Madrid, 1919).

La vestal de Occidente (produced Teatro de la Princesa, Madrid, 1919).

La honra de los hombres (produced Teatro de Lara, Madrid, 1919).

El Audaz, from a novel by D. Benito Pérez Galdós (produced Teatro Español, Madrid, 1919).

La Cenicienta (produced Teatro Español, Madrid, 1919).

Y va de cuento (produced 1919).

La fuerza bruta, with music by Federico Chaves (Teatro de Zarzuela, Madrid, 1919).

Una señora (produced Teatro del Centro, Madrid, 1920).   Translated as *A Lady*, in *Plays 4*, 1924.

Una pobre mujer (produced Teatro de la Princesa, Madrid, 1920).

Más allá de la muerte (produced Buenos Aires, Argentina, 1922).

Por que se quitó Juan de la bebida (produced Teatro Solis, Montevideo, 1922).

Lecciones de buen amor (produced Teatro Español, Madrid, 1924).

Un par de botas (produced Teatro de la Princesa, Madrid, 1924).

La otra honra (produced Teatro de Lara, Madrid, 1924).

La virtud sospechosa (produced Teatro Fontalba, Madrid, 1924).

Alfilerazos (produced Teatro Avenida, Buenos Aires, 1924).

Nadie sabe lo que quiere; o, El bailarín y el trabajador (produced Teatro Cómico, Madrid, 1925).

¡Si creerás tú que es por mi gusto!.   In *Teatro 30*, 1925.

El suicidio de Lucerito (produced Teatro Alcázar, Madrid, 1925).

Los nuevos yernos (produced Teatro Fontalba, Madrid, 1925).

La mariposa que voló sobre el mar (produced Teatro Fontalba, Madrid, 1926).

El hijo de Polichinela (produced Teatro de Lara, Madrid, 1927).

La noche iluminada (produced Teatro Fontalba, Madrid, 1927).

El demonio fué antes ángel (produced Teatro Calderón, Madrid, 1928).

¡No quiero, no quiero! (produced Teatro Fontalba, Madrid, 1928).

Pepa Doncel (produced Teatro Calderón, Madrid, 1928).

Para el cielo y los altares.   1929.

Vidas cruzadas (produced Teatro Reina Victoria, Madrid, 1929).

Los amigos del hombre (produced Teatro de la Avenida, Madrid, 1930).

Los andrajos de la púrpura (produced Teatro Muñoz Seca, Madrid, 1930).

De muy buena familia (produced Teatro Muñoz Seca, Madrid, 1931).

Literatura (produced Teatro Alcázar, Madrid, 1931).

La melodía del jazz-band (produced Teatro Fontalba, Madrid, 1931).

Cuando los hijos de Eva no son los hijos de Adán, from a

work by Margaret Kennedy (produced Teatro Calderón de la Barca, Madrid, 1931).
Santa Rusia (produced Teatro Beatriz, Madrid, 1932).
La duquesa gitana (produced Teatro Fontalba, Madrid, 1932).
La moral del divorcio (produced Teatro de la Avenida, Madrid, 1932).
Le verdad inventada (produced Teatro de Lara, Madrid, 1933).
El rival de su mujer (produced Teatro Odeón, Buenos Aires, 1933).
El pan comido en la mano (produced Teatro Fontalba, Madrid, 1934).
Ni al amor ni al mar (produced Teatro Español, Madrid, 1934).
Memorias de un madrileño (produced Teatro de Lara, Madrid, 1934).
La novia de nieve (produced Teatro Español, Madrid, 1934).
No juguéis con esas cosas (produced Teatro Esclava, Madrid, 1935).
Cualquiera lo sabe (produced Teatro de la Comedia, Madrid, 1935).
Lo increíble (produced Teatro de la Comedia, Madrid, 1940).
Aves y párajaros (produced Teatro de la Comedia, Madrid, 1940).
Abuelo y nieto (produced Teatro del Príncipe, San Sebastián, 1941).
Y amargaba . . . (produced Teatro de Zarzuela, Madrid, 1941).
La última carta (produced Teatro Alcázar, Madrid, 1941).
La honradez de la cerradura (produced Teatro Español, Madrid, 1942).
La culpa es tuya (produced Teatro del Príncipe?, San Sebastián, 1942).
Al fin, mujer (produced Teatro del Príncipe, San Sebastián, 1942).
¡Hija del alma! (produced Teatro de Lara, Madrid, 1942).
La enlutada (produced Teatro Principal, Saragossa, 1942).
El demonio del teatro (produced Teatro Cómico, Madrid, 1942).
Los niños perdidos en la selva (produced Teatro Infanta Beatriz, Madrid, 1944).
Don Magín él de las magias (produced Teatro Barcelona, Barcelona, 1944).
Espejo de grandes (produced Colonia Penitenciaria del Dueso, 1944).
Nieve en Mayo (produced Teatro de Zarzuela, Madrid, 1945).
La ciudad doliente (produced Teatro de la Comedia, Madrid, 1945).
Titania (produced Buenos Aires, 1945).
La infanzona (produced Buenos Aires, 1945).
Al servicio de Su Majestad Imperial. In *Obras completas 8*, 1947.
Abdicación (produced Teatro de Lara, Madrid, 1948).
Divorcio de almas (produced Teatro Fontalba, Madrid, 1948).
Adoración (produced Teatro Cómico, Madrid, 1948).
Al amor hay que mandarlo al colegio (produced Teatro de Lara, Madrid, 1950).
Su amante esposa (produced Teatro de la Infanta Isabel, Madrid, 1950).
Tú una vez y el diablo diez (produced Teatro Lope de Vega, Valladolid, 1950).
Mater Imperatrix (produced Teatro de la Comedia, Barcelona, 1950).
La vida en verso (produced Teatro de la Infanta Isabel, Madrid, 1951).
Ha llegado Don Juan (produced Teatro de la Comedia, Barcelona, 1952).
El lebrel del cielo, from the poem *The Hound of Heaven*, by Francis Thompson (produced Teatro Calderón de la Barca, Madrid, 1952).
El alfiler en la boca (produced Teatro de la Infanta Isabel, Madrid, 1953).
Almas prisioneras (produced Teatro Alvarez Quintero, Madrid, 1953).
Caperucita asusta al lobo (produced Teatro de la Infanta Isabel, Madrid, 1953).
Hijos padres de sus padres, (produced Teatro de Lara, Madrid, 1954).
El marido de bronce (produced Teatro Infanta Isabel, Madrid, 1954).
Por salvar el amor (produced Madrid, 1954).
El bufón de Hamlet (produced posthumously).

Verse

Versos. 1893.

Memoirs and Letters

Recuerdos y olvidos: Memorias. 1962.

Other

Cartas de mujeres (3 vols.). 1892–1902.
Figulinas. 1898.
Vilanos. 1905.
Teatro del pueblo (articles). 1909.
De sobremsa (6 vols.). 1910–16.
Acotaciones (notes). 1914.
Crónica y diálogos. 1916.
Conferencias (lectures). 1924.
Pensiamentos, edited by José M. Benavente. 1931.

*

Bibliographies

Federico C. Sáinz de Robles, *Jacinto Benavente: Apuntes para una bibliografía*, Madrid, 1974.

Criticism

Books:
Storm Jameson, "Benavente", in his *Modern Drama in Europe*, London, 1920.
F. de Onís, *Jacinto Benavente: Estudio literario*, New York, 1923.
Walter Starkie, *Jacinto Benavente*, Oxford, 1924.
C. Cienfuegos, *Benavente y la critica: Ensayos*, Covadonga, 1931.
J. Vila Selma, *Jacinto Benavente, fin de siglo*, Madrid, 1952.
I. Sánchez Estevan, *Jacinto Benavente y su teatro*, Barcelona, 1954.
A. Lázaro, *Vida y obra de Benavente*, Madrid, 1964.
José Montero Alonso, *Benavente: Su vida y su teatro*, Madrid, 1967.
Julio Mathias, *Jacinto Benavente*, Madrid, 1969.
M.C. Peñuelas, *Jacinto Benavente* (in English), New York, 1969.

Mariano Sánchez de Palacios, *Jacinto Benavente: Estudio y antología*, Madrid, 1969.

John E. Diall, *Jacinto Benavente and His Theatre*, Long Island, New York, 1972.

Julia Ortiz Griffin, *Drama y sociedad en la obra de Benavente (1894–1914)*, New York, 1974.

Robert L. Sheehan, *Benavente and the Spanish Panorama, 1894–1954*, Madrid, 1976.

Helene Tzitsikas, *La supervivencia existencial de la mujer en las obras de Benavente*, Barcelona, 1982.

Articles:

Julio Brouta, "Spain's Greatest Dramatist", in *Drama*, November 1915.

John Garrett Underhill, "Benavente as a Modern", in *Poet Lore*, 29, 1918.

Kessel Schwartz, "Benavente and Shakespearean Drama", in *Romance Notes*, 1960.

Kessel Schwartz, "Benavente on Shakespearean Characters", in *Modern Drama*, 1961.

Kessel Schwartz, "Shakespeare's Influence on Benavente's Plays", in *South Central Bulletin*, 1961.

Raymond A. Young, "The Heroines of Benavente and Martínez Sierra", in *Proceedings of the Pacific Northwest Conference on Foreign Languages*, 17, 1966.

Raymond A. Young, "Benavente and the Emancipation of Spanish Women", in *Modern Languages*, 49, 1968.

John E. Dial, "Benavente: The Dramatist on Stage", in *Revista de estudios hispánicos*, 8, 1974.

* * *

Benavente was the youngest son of a successful Madrid pediatrician, and as a wealthy bachelor lived a long and happy life, undisturbed by any serious financial, professional, or amorous setbacks. As a youth he studied law at Madrid University, travelled abroad, learned various languages, and read English and French classics in the original; he also became well known in the Madrid theatrical world and learned all he could about the commercial stage. Thus, by the mid-1890's he was very well prepared to succeed Echegaray as king of the Spanish theatre, and he created an image for himself to help in this. Richer, better educated, and more cosmopolitan than the other young writers (Azorín, Baroja, Machado), he dressed far more elegantly than they, always smoked a Havana cigar, and distinguished himself by caustic comments on people and things, "as much like Bernard Shaw as Spanish society would allow".

His early play, *El nido ajeno* (*Another's Nest*), used the same situation as Echegaray's *El gran Galeoto*, that is, the suspicion that a man living innocently with a married couple (in this case, the husband's brother) is really the wife's lover; but whereas Echegaray ended his play with a duel, disgrace, and death, Benavente lowered the emotional temperature and produced a reconciliation and the brother's amicable departure. *El nido ajeno* failed, because it so completely abandoned the violence of plot and language to which Echegaray had long accustomed Madrid audiences; but Benavente continued to write plays in the same low key, and by 1904 he had succeeded in totally reversing public taste. This was not because of any major concession on his part, "selling his soul to the devil" as Pérez de Ayala put it, for *El nido ajeno* already shows most of the virtues of Benavente's later plays, such as the technical skill, elegant language, and clever dialogue, and also their defects, such as the essential superficiality and the lack of poetry.

Of Benavente's over 200 plays, some are written for chil-

dren, with delightful lyricism and ironic wit, such as *El príncipe que todo lo aprendió en libros* (*The Prince Who Learned Everything Out of Books*), and others are dark rural tragedies, such as *La malquerida* (*The Passion Flower*), perhaps forming the link between Echegaray's tragedies and those of Lorca. The overwhelming majority are, however, light social satires, directed against the court aristocracy of Madrid in particular, and against the upper classes in general. They do not, of course, express working-class resentment at the Spanish social structure, or socialist condemnation of capitalism, like Dicenta; and they are uninterested in politics, economics, or history, except perhaps for *La ciudad alegre y confiada*. They criticise the upper classes on moral grounds for their materialism, prejudices, frivolity, and hypocrisy, but they do so precisely from the view-point of a member of the upper classes, judging his fellows according to their common standards of bourgeois, rather than specifically Christian, morality. Fond though Benavente was of preaching, it is difficult to see in his plays any lesson deeper than this; and outside the theatre, his statements and journalism seem totally opportunistic, aimed at shocking readers as Shaw did, but without Shaw's intellectual consistency. Really, Benavente was a conservative sceptic, without trust in man, or progress, or society, or anything, except, just possibly, the ennobling power of love.

He expressed his viewpoint most memorably at the end of his best play, *Los intereses creados*, a superb re-presentation of classical comedy, in which a confidence-trickster disguises himself as a servant, and his accomplice as his master, a great gentleman, and then wins for the latter prestige, wealth, and a desirable bride in a city where they arrive quite unknown. He achieves this success by incurring great debts, then persuading all the individual creditors that they will be repaid only if they persuade the heroine's father to marry her off to the pseudo-gentleman; and he explains to the latter, "What did I tell you, sir? That they would all join together to save us . . . Believe me, if you want to be successful, it is better to create vested interests than to arouse affection". And the heroine, addressing the audience, explains that the world is like the play, and that human beings are just puppets, moved by strings of greed, even if one string, delicate and golden, is the motive of love. She does not consider who in the world corresponds to the puppet-master; thus, though Benavente's plays continue the high comedy of Ayala and Tamayo, he lacks both their Romantic illusions and their religious beliefs; instead he has greater intelligence and technical skill.

In contrast to the grandiose plots, transcendent themes, and grandiloquent language of Echegaray, Benavente offers stories from daily life (sometimes lifted from newpaper items), a cool treatment, and a conversational tone. His plays are up-to-the-minute in their stories, characters, and phraseology; that is to say, they have dated badly in these respects, though keeping their value as social documents. Their plots are minimal, and most action takes place off stage; on stage there is narration, description, and what sometimes seems a series of tableaux, deriving from the *costumbrista* tradition. Though the characters often have strongly marked external characteristics, their personalities undergo little development, so that it has been claimed that their speeches could be interchanged without difficulty. The essence, and the true purpose of the plays is the dialogue: sparkling, witty, satirical and elegant, it is kept going by a master hand, no matter how many persons are participating, provided that the tone is kept light. Only when the story calls for serious feeling or passion does Benavente fail to produce adequate language, or to develop the situation or the characters. His characters are schematic, and sometimes no more than intellectual symbols, expressing their author's thoughts in turn, with witty comments not only on the plot, but also on recent events in real life outside the confines of the play.

Above all, Benavente is a master of irony—feline, malicious, sometimes biting, but never going for the jugular; and his plays are a literary creation presented for the entertainment, sometimes the nervous or scandalised enjoyment, of his own sort of people. So long as we can imagine ourselves to be among them, we too can continue to enjoy one of the most intelligent and entertaining, if not one of the most profound, of 20th-century dramatists.

—Derek W. Lomax

See also *Volume 1* entry on *Bonds of Interest*.

BENNETT, Alan. Born in Leeds, Yorkshire, England, 9 May 1934. Educated at Leeds Modern School, 1946–52; Exeter College, Oxford, 1954–57 (Open Scholar in History), BA (honours) 1957. National Service: Joint Services School for Linguists, Cambridge and Bodmin. Temporary junior lecturer in history, Magdalen College, Oxford, 1960–62; has subsequently pursued career as writer, actor, director, and broadcaster; first play, *Forty Years On*, produced 1968. Recipient: Tony Award, 1963; Royal Television Society Award, 1984 and 1986; Olivier Award, 1990.

Works

Collections

"Objects of Affection" and Other Plays for Television (includes *Objects of Affection: Our Winnie, A Woman of No Importance, Rolling Home, Marks;* and *Say Something Happened; A Day Out; Intensive Care; An Englishman Abroad*).   1982.
"Forty Years On" and Other Plays (includes *Habeas Corpus* and *Getting On*).   1985.
The Writer in Disguise (includes *Me, I'm Afraid of Virginia Woolf; Afternoon Off; One Fine Day; All Day on the Sands; The Old Crowd;* an essay).   1985.
"Single Spies" and "Talking Heads": Two Plays and Six Monologues.   1990.

Stage Works

Beyond the Fringe, with others (produced Edinburgh, 1960). 1963.
Forty Years On (produced Manchester, 1968).   1969.
Sing a Rude Song (additional material), book by Caryl Brahms and Ned Sherrin, music by Ron Grainer (produced London, 1969).
Getting On (produced Brighton, 1971).   1972.
Habeas Corpus (produced Playhouse, Oxford, 1973).   1973.
The Old Country (produced Playhouse, Oxford, 1977). 1978.
Enjoy (produced London, 1980).   1980.
Kafka's Dick (produced Royal Court Theatre, London, 1986).   In *Two Kafka Plays*, 1987.
An Englishman Abroad, from the television play (produced as part of the double-bill *Single Spies,* Royal National Theatre, London, 1988).   In *Single Spies,* 1989.

A Question of Attribution (produced as part of the double-bill *Single Spies,* Royal National Theatre, London, 1988).   In *Single Spies,* 1989.
The Wind in the Willows, from Kenneth Grahame's novel (produced Royal National Theatre, London, 1990).   1991.
The Madness of George III (produced Royal National Theatre, London, 1991).   1992.
Talking Heads (6 monologues, originally televised; produced Comedy Theatre, London, 1992).   With *Single Spies,* 1990.

Screenplays

A Private Function, 1984 (published 1984); *Prick Up Your Ears*, 1987 (published 1987).

Television Plays

On the Margin (series; broadcast 1966).
A Day Out (broadcast 1972).   In *"Objects of Affection" and other Plays,* 1982.
Sunset Across the Bay (broadcast 1977).
A Little Outing (broadcast 1977).
Green Forms (broadcast as *Doris and Doreen,* 1978).   In *Office Suite,* 1981.
A Visit from Miss. Prothero (broadcast 1978).   In *Office Suite,* 1981.
Me, I'm Afraid of Virginia Woolf (broadcast 1978).   In *The Writer in Disguise,* 1985.
All Day on the Sands (broadcast 1979).   In *The Writer in Disguise,* 1985.
One Fine Day (broadcast 1979).   In *The Writer in Disguise,* 1985.
The Old Crowd (broadcast 1979).   In *The Writer in Disguise,* 1985.
Afternoon Off (broadcast 1979).   In *The Writer in Disguise,* 1985.
Objects of Affection (includes *Our Winnie;* A *Woman of No Importance;* Rolling Home; Marks; Say Something Happened;* all broadcast 1982).   In *"Objects of Affection" and Other Plays,* 1982.
Intensive Care (broadcast 1982).   In *"Objects of Affection" and Other Plays,* 1982.
An Englishman Abroad (broadcast 1983).   In *"Objects of Affection" and Other Plays,* 1982.
The Insurance Man (broadcast 1986).   In *Two Kafka Plays,* 1987.
Talking Heads (6 monologues; broadcast 1988).   1987.
Down Cemetery Road: The Landscape of Philip Larkin (lecture broadcast 1991).
A Question of Attribution, from the stage play (broadcast 1991).   Stage version in *Single Spies,* 1988.
102 Boulevard Haussmann (broadcast 1991).

Radio Plays

Uncle Clarence, 1986; *The Lady in the Van,* 1990.

*

Criticism

Books:
Roland Bergan, *Beyond the Fringe . . . and Beyond: A Critical Biography of Alan Bennett, Peter Cooke, Jonathan Miller, and Dudley Moore,* London, 1990.

*   *   *

Bennett's television work as playwright and occasional actor is better known than his stage plays, which have suffered comparative critical neglect. Twenty-four television plays and two screenplays as against 8 stage plays may provide one explanation; but another might be Bennett's readiness to take risks with form and to escape the naturalism of his television plays, which, with few exceptions, are rooted in northern culture and exploit the observational intimacy of the medium. The stage plays are more southern, middle-class, and more obviously informed by cultural values accessible, if not always acceptable, to a West End audience.

It is tempting to read Bennett's stage plays as mediated autobiography, since their preoccupation with displaced characters—exiles, alienated sons, spies, the elderly and infirm, homosexuals—echoes divisions and contradictory cultural allegiances in their author. The son of a working-class butcher in Leeds, Bennett gained an Oxford degree in history. Early success in *Beyond the Fringe* led to writing and performing rather than an anticipated academic career. At once serious and jokey, Bennett's subsequent plays oscillate in tone and form. Social criticism jostles with farce and vulgar comedy, satire with sentiment. A fastidious literary stylishness, evidenced in linguistic playfulness and accurate parody, goes hand in hand with a taste for bluntness and smut. Bennett, poised between classes, cultures, and sensibilities, seems drawn to characters who are socially or sexually displaced. Often wryly aware of the ironies and embarrassments of their own lives and of public life in England, they struggle to define themselves or maintain their private identity in language shot through with feelings of guilt, nostalgia, ridicule, absurdity, and affection.

Bennett's comic armoury was forged in revue and television satire. The sketch, parody, monologue, bathetic utterance, absurd conversational juxtaposition, farce, pun, *double-entendre* and one-liner, all mockingly and affectionately deployed, form the constructional material of his plays, particularly *Forty Years On*. Little more than a string of sketches here forms an ingenious play-within-a-play depicting a minor public school whose Headmaster, mourning the passing of a culture vitiated by the two World Wars, presides over a touching and ridiculous allegory of Britain's decline.

Getting On is a more sombre well-made comedy portraying George Oliver, a Labour politician so self-absorbed and desperately jokey as to be blind to his family's needs. His wife commits adultery with a handyman, his mother-in-law is dying, and his teenage son feels neglected and sexually confused. Vigorous comic diatribe and social satire ultimately overshadow the painful education of family and friends, including a homosexual Conservative MP blackmailed into quitting politics. Each separate "getting on" is quietly and ironically observed but on the periphery of George's vision of an ordered socialist society.

Death and melancholy shadow *Habeas Corpus*, an uninhibited farce whose stereotypical characters are humanised by Bennett's exposure of the gap between their sexual desires and their unprepossessing bodies. Bennett masters the plot complications of farce but daringly jettisons its conventionally cluttered settings. The tangible presence of bodies is emphasised as a source of middle-class guilt, embarrassment, and betrayal, as the title implies.

Betrayal by the body gives way to treachery proper in three later plays. *The Old Country*, discursively witty, tricks its audience into believing initially that its setting is the Home Counties rather than Russia where Hilary, a Philby-like defector, contemplates the offer of a return to the old country which he knows to be utterly changed from the one he remembers and has recreated in exile. His real loyalties remain teasingly ambiguous. *An Englishman Abroad* dramatises the meeting in Moscow of flamboyant spy Guy Burgess and a visiting actress whom he persuades to obtain for him a new outfit from his London tailors. Two camp performers, one inebriated, the other imperious, spark high comedy and sympathy for another Bennett exile. *A Question of Attribution* has the as-yet-unexposed traitor Anthony Blunt, Keeper of the Queen's Pictures, engaging Her Majesty in a marvellously sly discussion mined by *double-entendre* on the subject of art, fakes, and attribution in a sketch elaborated in Stoppardian fashion by the added framework of Blunt's interrogation and his own detective work on a restored portrait which appropriately reveals a third, fourth, and fifth man.

Bennett's least commercially successful plays are his most challenging and personal. The painfully comic portrait of an elderly northern couple in *Enjoy* evokes Beckett, but turns Pinteresque in the tangled sexual relationship between parents and prostitute daughter and transvestite son. Veering towards farce before ending in a dream-like fantasy of son and daughter going their own ways, father hospitalised, and mother a living exhibit in a cultural museum, the play touches on the destruction and artificial preservation of culture, the emotional crippling of children, and the ethics of a dramatist's use of personal material for entertainment or therapeutic purposes.

Kafka's Dick, which has Kafka suddenly materialising in the home of a Leeds insurance clerk, develops cognate themes. That most abused of sons and anonymous of persons is put on trial in a farcical parody of his own novel, only to discover that his private parts have long been public property. Bennett again muses disturbingly on what it is to be a son, a writer, and a private/public person. An extraordinary final scene set in a heaven where God dances with Carmen Miranda and Wittgenstein parties with Betty Hutton finds Kafka more embarrassed and fearful than ever.

Dreams permeate Bennett's plays. The bodies of *Habeas Corpus* liberated from setting and inhibition assume dream-like form; the exiled and alienated create out-of-time dream-worlds. Hilary in *The Old Country* wakes from a nightmare of having killed his father, a fear or wish dramatised in *Enjoy*. Kafka's worst nightmare (and, one suspects, Bennett's) is to be known, while Anthony Blunt's is ironically the dream most frequently reported by the English middle classes, that of meeting the Queen. Bennett is perhaps at his most disturbing and amusing when he pushes comedy and language towards the surreal within unstable forms which dramatise anxious mental landscapes.

—Ronald W. Strang

See also *Volume 1* entry on *Forty Years On*.

BEOLCO, Angelo. See **RUZ(Z)ANTE**.

BERGMAN, Hjalmar (Frederick Elgerus). Born in Örebro, Närke, Sweden, 19 December 1883. Educated at high school in Örebro, to 1899, and privately in Västerås, 1899–1900; studied at the universities of Stockholm and

Uppsala, 1900–01, and in Florence, 1901–02. Married Stina Lindberg, daughter of actor August Lindberg, 1908. Travelled extensively in Europe and Asia Minor; first play, *Maria Jesu moder* [Mary, Mother of Jesus], published 1905; first-produced play, *Fru Wendla's kedja* [Mrs. Vendla's Necklace], staged 1908; lived in Rome, 1909–11; returned to Sweden, 1911, moving to Örebro, 1915, and then to Segelholmen, 1917; as screenwriter became associated with director Victor Sjöström, from 1919; travelled in Italy, Germany, and Austria, 1920–23; travelled to Hollywood, 1923, but returned after his screenplays were rejected, 1924. Died in Berlin, 1 January 1931.

Works

Collections

Marionettspel (includes *Dödens Arlekin; En skugga; Herr Sleeman kommer*).   1917.
Värvaren i Bagdad; Porton; Spelhuset.   1923.
Samlade skrifter [Collected Works] (30 vols.).   1949–58.
Four Plays (includes *The Markurells of Wadkoping; The Baron's Will; Swedenhielms; Mr. Sleeman is Coming*), edited by Walter Johnson.   1968.
"Arthur Maxglans" och andra filmmanuskript.   1989.

Stage Works

Maria, Jesu Moder [Mary, Mother of Jesus] (produced 1961).   1905.
Familjens renhet [The Purity of the Family].   In *Två skådespel*, 1907.
Det underbara leendet [The Wonderful Smile].   In *Två skådespel*, 1907.
Fru Vendlas kedja [Mrs. Vendla's Necklace] (produced 1908).   In *Samlade skrifter* (see Collections).
Savonarola [Savonarola] (produced 1908).
Lönggången [The Secret Passage].   1913.
Parisina [Parisina] (produced 1915).   1915.
Dödens Arlekin [Death's Harlequin] (produced 1917).   In *Marionettspel*, 1917.
En skugga [A Shadow] (produced 1917).   In *Marionettspel*, 1917.
Herr Sleeman kommer.   In *Marionettspel*, 1917; translated as *Mr. Sleeman is Coming*, in *Scandinavian Plays of the Twentieth Century 1*, 1944; also in *Four Plays*, 1968.
Ett experiment [An Experiment] (produced 1919).   1918.
Vävaren i Bagdad [The Weaver of Bagdad] (produced 1936).   With *Porton* and *Spelhuset*, 1923.
Porton [The Gateway].   With *Vävaren i Bagdad* and *Spelhuset*, 1923.
Spelhuset [The Gaming House].   With *Vävaren i Bagdad* and *Porton*, 1923.
Swedenhielms (produced 1925).   1925; translated as *The Swedenhielms*, in *Scandinavian Plays of the Twentieth Century 3*, 1951; as *Swiedenhielms*, in *Four Plays*, 1968.
Dollar [Dollar].   1926.
Patrasket [Joe and Co.] (produced 1928).   1928.
Markurells i Wadköping, from the novel (produced 1930).   1930; translated as *The Markurells of Wadkoping*, in *Four Plays*, 1968.
Hans nåds testamente [His Grace's Last Will], from the novel (produced 1931).   1930; translated as *The Baron's Will*, in *Four Plays*, 1968.
Andra upplagan.   1931.

Sagan [The Fairy Tale], completed by his wife (produced 1942).   1942; in *Samlade skrifter*, 1949–58.
Snödropparna [Snowdrops].   In *Samlade skrifter*, 1949–58.

Screenplays (selected)

Vem dömer (also released as *Love's Crucible* and *Mortal Clay*), 1922; *Makurells i Wadköping*, 1931; *Swedenhielms*, 1935; *Charles XII*.

Fiction

Solivro, Prins av Aeretanien [Solivro, Prince of Aetetania].   1906.
Blå blommer [The Blue Flowers].   1907.
Savonarola [Savonarola].   1909.
Amourer [Loves] (short stories).   1910.
Hans nåds testamente [His Grace's Last Testament].   1910.
Vi Bookar, Krokar och Rothar [We Books, Krooks, and Rooths].   1912.
Loewenhistorier [Stories of Loewen].   1913.
Fru Gunhild pa Hviskingeholm [Lady Gunhild at Hviskingeholm].   1913.
Komedier i Bergslagen [Comedies in Bergslagen]:
   Två släkter [Two Families].   1914; as *Klock eberga och Ryglinge*, 1927.
   Dansen på Frötjärn [Dance at Frötjärn].   1915.
   Knutsmässo marknad [St. Canute's Fair].   1916.
Mor i Sutre [Ma at Sutre].   1917.
En döds memoarer [Recollections of a Dead Man].   1918.
Markurells i Wadköping [The Markurells of Wadköping].   1919; translated as *God's Orchid*, 1924.
Herr von Hancken [Mr. Hancken].   1920.
Farmor och Vår Herre [Grandmother and the Good Lord].   1921; translated as *Thy Rod and Thy Staff*, 1937.
Eros' begraving [The Burial of Eros] (short stories).   1922.
Jag, Ljung och Medardus [Medardus, Ljung, and I].   1922.
Chefen fru Ingeborg.   1924; translated as *The Head of the Firm*, 1936.
Flickan i frack [The Girl in the Suit].   1925.
Jonas och Helen [Jonas and Helen].   1926.
Kerrmans i Paradiset [Kermanns in Paradise].   1927.
Lotten Brenners ferier [Lotten Brenner's Holidays].   1928.
Kärlek genom ett fönster [Love Through a Window] (short stories).   1929.
Clownen Jac [Jack the Clown].   1930.
Film (stories).   1940.

Memoirs and Letters

Brev [Letters], edited by J. Edfelt, Stockholm.   1964.

Other

Det har berättats mig (essays).   1935.

*

Bibliographies

Edgar Lund, "Hjalmar Bergman", in *Kortsa bibliografier 2*, Stockholm, 1939.
Eric Lilliehöök, "Hjalmar Bergman: Bibliografi 1938–1958", in *Hjalmar Bergman Samfundet Årsbok*, 1959.
Eric Lilliehöök, "Hjalmar Bergman bibliografi 1976–1980", in *Hjalmar Bergman Samfundet Årsbok*, 1985.

Criticism

Books:

E.H. Linder, *Hjalmar Bergman*, Boston, 1975.

Articles:
Evert Sprinchorn, "Hjalmar Bergman", in *Tulane Drama Review*, 6, 1961.
Stina Bergman, "Introductions", in *Hjalmar Bergman: Four Plays*, edited by Walter Johnson, Seattle, Washington, 1968.
Sarah A. Stevenson, "Comedy and Tragedy in *Makurells i Wadköping*", in *Edda*, 79, 1974.

Serials:
Hjalmar Bergman Samfundets Årsbok, 1959—.

* * *

Hjalmar Bergman's voluminous literary production began with a drama, though not an easily staged one. *Maria Jesu moder* (Mary, Mother of Jesus) is a Passion play with a difference: Mary is portrayed as a power hungry woman whose desire it is that her son shall be a leader and avenger here on earth rather than the gentle saviour he becomes. The play that followed, *Familjens renhet* (The Purity of the Family) came out of a radically different mould, owing a debt to Ibsen. Despite a documented childhood fascination with theatre, and despite close personal contacts with the theatre —he married into one of the leading theatrical families of the day and the director Per Lindberg was his brother-in-law— and the inherently dramatic technique of his novels, it took Bergman longer to find a firm and independent footing as a dramatist than as a prose-writer.

It is the three short plays *Dödens arlekin* (Death's Harlequin), *En skugga* (A Shadow) and *Herr sleeman kommer* (*Mr. Sleeman is Coming*), which Bergman collectively called his *Marionettspel* (Marionette Plays), that show his dramatic writing at its most powerful and original. Influenced to some extent by expressionism, and perhaps also by the Passion play, he works in a stylised manner in which the characters are reduced to puppets, since they are governed by forces over which they have no control. Thematically, then, they clearly reflect the tragic and deterministic philosophy of life that underlies much of Bergman's writing.

In *Dödens arlekin* the powerful dying Consul Broman, never present on the stage, has throughout his life played the tunes to which the characters dance, and now, at his death, they continue to dance—but to the bells of the harlequin of death described by one of their number. In *En skugga* the cleansing power of love proves unable to overcome the past, and, with the murder of her lover, the young bride is left to her ageing and hunchbacked bridegroom. In *Herr Sleeman kommer*, there is no hope for the young Anne-Marie as her aunts tie her into an arranged marriage with an old and world-weary man. Life is unforgiving, power is brutal, youth and innocence are sullied, and these "marionettes" are as unable to escape their strings as any other of Bergman's characters.

The influence of expressionism becomes more marked in the plays of the following years—*Porten* (The Gateway), *Vävaren i Bagdad* (The Weaver of Baghdad) and, especially, *Spelhuset* (The Gaming House), which is set throughout in the casino that symbolises a harsh, confused, and capricious world peopled once again by marionette-like characters. The few characters with human warmth and feelings, those who, so to speak, dare to bear individual names, can hope for no

more than the release that death brings. Nor is any greater hope expressed in the compelling *Sagan* (The Fairy Tale), not produced on the stage until 1942 and, in any case, better read than seen. It is a lyrical mixture of reality and fantasy, a fairytale examination of beauty and goodness set in a melancholy twilight world, concluding: "Every day is Judgement Day for the man who believes in fairy tales".

Swedenhielms, a comedy, and one of Bergman's most frequently produced plays, marks a conscious attempt to bring to the theatre the wit, colour, humour, and rich characterisation that find expression in his novels of the early 1920's. There is nothing experimental about the realistic setting and the rather old-fashioned plot of the play, centring, as it does, on misunderstandings about money in the family of the great, but stereotypically impractical, inventor Swedenhielm. It is on this title figure, representative of a certain open, honourable, and jovial type of Swede, and on its brisk and witty dialogue that the play's popularity rests. A less successful comedy is *Dollar*, in which Bergman attempts to satirise aspects of American society as he had observed it during his months in the USA in 1924.

Patrasket (Joe and Co.), however, is an altogether more vital work and the finest of Bergman's comedies. It has a relatively conventional plot, a convincingly real setting in a north German town, but, above all, a cast of characters with which the audience is quickly involved. The Meng family, poor Jews who have come to visit a rich relative in the hope of being given a start in business, are headed by Joe Meng, a role written as a vehicle for the actor Gösta Ekman. Joe—a mixture of Jewish stereotype, Ekman, and the playwright himself—is an incorrigible entrepreneur and fantasist, and through his words and behaviour Bergman proclaims his message:

> Imagination—what do you people want? Isn't it imagination that gives you your daily bread? That builds your houses? Drives your factories? What would wisdom and judicious consideration have to offer us if imagination had not existed first . . .?

The writing of drama in all its forms continued to fascinate Bergman to the end of his life. He was enthusiastic about the possibilities of both film and radio drama. But as a dramatist he never achieved the heights he occupies as a novelist. The unevenness and occasional banality and sentimentality that lurk in even his best novels emerge all too often in the plays, and the verbal dexterity can slide into verbosity. The comedies *Swedenhielms* and *Patrasket* survive well as playable, if lightweight, pieces; the *Marionettspel* give a truer reflection of the painful and ultimately tragic view of life that Bergman held; but perhaps only in his own dramatizations of his novels *Markurells i Wadköping* (The Markurells of Wadköping) and *Hans nåds testamente* (His Grace's Last Will) does the audience really have the opportunity of perceiving the bizarre and moving counterpoint between fantasy, irony, humour, and existential anguish that is the quintessential Hjalmar Bergman.

—Peter Graves

BERKOFF, Steven. Born in Stepney, London, 3 August 1937. Educated at schools in Stepney; Hackney Downs Grammar School, London; Webber-Douglas Academy of Dramatic Art, London, 1958–59; École Jacques Lecoq, Paris, 1965. Married Shelley Lee in 1976. Actor in repertory in

Steven Berkoff as Hamlet in a 1980 production of Shakespeare's play.

Nottingham, Liverpool, Coventry, and at Citizens' Theatre Glasgow, for six years; first play, *In the Penal Colony*, produced 1968; founding director, London Theatre Group, 1973, which has produced many of his plays; actor and director in own plays and other works and films.

Works

Collections

East; Agamemnon; The Fall of the House of Usher. 1978.
West; Lunch; Harry's Christmas. 1985.
The Trial; Metamorphosis; In the Penal Colony: Three Theatre Adaptations from Franz Kafka. 1988.
"Decadence" and Other Plays. 1989.

Stage Works

In the Penal Colony, adaptation of a story by Kafka (produced Arts Laboratory, London, 1968). In *The Trial; Metamorphosis; In the Penal Colony*, 1988.
Metamorphosis, from the story by Kafka (produced The Roundhouse, London, 1968). With *The Trial*, 1981.
The Trial, from a novel by Kafka (produced in the Netherlands, 1971; The Roundhouse, London, 1973). With *Metamorphosis*, 1981.
Agamemnon (produced The Roundhouse, London, 1971); revised version produced Greenwich Theatre, London, 1976). In *East; Agamemnon; The Fall of the House of Usher*, 1977.
Knock at the Manor Gate, from a story by Kafka (produced Falmer, Sussex, 1972).

Miss Julie Versus Expressionism, from a play by Strindberg (produced Institute of Contemporary Arts, London, 1973).
Lunch (as *Mr. Prufrock's Songs*, produced London, 1974; revised version, as *Lunch*, produced King's Head Theatre, London, 1983). In *West; Lunch; Harry's Christmas*, 1985.
The Fall of the House of Usher, from the story by Poe (produced Traverse Theatre, Edinburgh, 1974). In *East; Agamemnon; The Fall of the House of Usher*, 1977.
East (produced Traverse Theatre, Edinburgh, 1975; revised version produced Greenwich Theatre, London, 1976. In *East; Agamemnon; The Fall of the House of Usher*, 1977.
Greek (produced Arts Theatre, London 1980). With *Decadence*, 1982.
West (produced Donmar Warehouse, London, 1980). In *West; Lunch; Harry's Christmas*, 1985.
Decadence (produced New End Theatre, London, 1981). With *Greek*, 1982.
Harry's Christmas (produced Donmar Warehouse, London, 1985). In *West; Lunch; Harry's Christmas*, 1985.
The Tell-Tale Heart, from the story by Poe (produced Donmar Warehouse, London, 1985).
Kvetch (produced with *Acapulco*, Odyssey Theatre, Los Angeles, 1986). With *Acapulco*, 1986.
Acapulco (produced with *Kvetch*, Odyssey Theatre, Los Angeles, 1986). With *Kvetch*, 1986.
Sink the Belgrano! (produced Half Moon Theatre, London, 1986). With *Massage*, 1987.
Massage. With *Sink the Belgrano!*, 1987.

Fiction

"Gross Intrusion" and Other Stories. 1979.

Other

Steven Berkoff's America. 1988.
A Prisoner in Rio. 1989.
I Am Hamlet. 1989.
The Theatre of Steven Berkoff (mainly photographs; text by
    Berkoff). 1991.

* * *

Through his appearances in three of Hollywood's most successful motion pictures—*Octopussy, Beverly Hills Cop,* and *Rambo*—Steven Berkoff has become one of the cinema's favourite villains. For those who knew Berkoff through his stage work in Britain and Los Angeles it has been an unexpected transformation, as unlikely for a theatrical outsider as his recent embrace by Britain's National Theatre.

Long before the films were made, Berkoff had established his own dedicated following, an audience primed to admire the violent flow of his language as a dramatist and the physicality of his theatrical style. Where realism struggled to represent the inarticulacy of ordinary life, Berkoff gave his characters pages of poetic diatribe driven by profane imagery and obscene rhymes. He combined the street language of London's East End with Shakespearean grandiloquence. His visual images shared the urgent violence of his language, through the threatening presence of motorcycles and muscular actors in leather and denim.

His debt to classical theatre in his original plays is made clear by his productions of classics, ranging from Aeschylus to Shakespeare, and his adaptations of Kafka and Edgar Allan Poe. But his originality is also poured in great measure into those plays. In Berkoff's *Agamemnon,* for instance, the arrival of the watchman at the beginning of the play requires an actor to exhaust himself on a quarter-mile run before the play began, collapsing onto the stage with his message. When a chorus is required, in his original work or in his production of a classic, it is as organic as any of the leading characters.

Reassuringly, for those who cherished his iconoclasm, Berkoff reinvested much of his Hollywood earnings in stage projects that have remained faithful to his chosen theatrical prophets. Very early in his career he chose some difficult masters, admiring, for instance, the discipline and formal skills of Bertolt Brecht as playwright and director, and noting with particular interest the way in which Brecht was able to develop his technique and beliefs through his own company, the Berliner Ensemble. That was a lesson he applied when he formed his own company, the London Theatre Group, where a Berkoff school of acting and presentation was carefully developed. His next master was Antonin Artaud. All Berkoff's theatrical work demonstrates Artaud's dedication to using the theatre as a visceral art, drawing its energy from "the lower echelons of the body", from sexual and primal urges which can unleash profound feelings in actor and spectator. He once described his relationship with Artaud in clearly sexual terms when he said "since I started with Artaud I've never flirted with anyone else."

Like the Living Theatre of Julian Beck and Judith Malina, however, and rather unlike Artaud, he has found in the primal physicality of his theatre a means of expressing political ideas. His disgust at Britain's conduct during the Falklands War in 1982 was dramatized in his play *Sink the Belgrano!*, a diatribe in punk-Shakespearean verse. The play made no concessions to the sensibilities of his admirers who knew him only for his film work. He scourged the audience with typically violent language, and, as in his earliest work, demanded of his actors extreme physical acts, portraying the dying sailors of the Argentinian battleship Belgrano in screams and formalized agony while his indictment of the British government was expressed through coarse poetry and coarse comedy, burlesquing the conventions of polite society.

Having demonstrated with *Sink the Belgrano!* that success would not soften his theatre, Berkoff has consolidated the achievements of his earlier plays. His adaptation of Kafka's *Metamorphosis,* originally tailored to his own athletic performance as the man who is transformed into a giant insect, has proved exceptionally durable, and has been staged by Berkoff in several languages, including a notable French production starring Roman Polanski. That adaptation paved the way for his particular use of the human body and voice as the prime elements in his productions, powerfully demonstrating his concern for the expression of text through physical images which imprint themselves on the audience's memory. Visionary as his adaptations might be, however (his use of Poe is nightmarish in the extreme), it is the original writing which has proved most influential.

East, the play in which he first gave a violent representation to his vision of London life, has become a model for younger playwrights seeking to escape the limits of conversational drama. In that play he first mingled a Cockney corruption of Elizabethan-styled verse with sexual and aggressive prose speeches. Structured as a story of growing up in London's East End, with fights and fornication as major themes, the extreme imagery frequently grew into lyrical fantasias. "If I write a bit rationally, I know I fail. For instance, when I talk about a motorbike in *East,* it has to be the best, the shiniest. When I talk about a phallus, it is the largest . . . Everything has to be extreme". The extreme view of London working-class life continued with the sequel, *West,* a few years later.

His whole vision of drama is one of extremes, demonstrated again in his North London reworking of the *Oedipus Tyrannus* of Sophocles which he called *Greek.* "In *Greek* every speech is an extreme feeling; of tenderness, of passion, of hate". Typically, despite the extremity of feeling when his hero, Eddie, discovers he has married his mother, Berkoff dispenses with the tragic ending and lets Eddie continue as her husband. Love, wherever you find it, is something worth keeping. It is by using such sources as the Oedipus story and submitting them to his own vision that Berkoff achieves much of his intensity.

Decadence was his first full-scale assault on the ruling classes, though his distaste for middle-class values was earlier evident in his comically vulgar portrayal of the insect's family in *Metamorphosis.* Gluttony and the buggery practised in public schools were indulgences ideally suited to gross physical imagery, and the coarse poetry he provided for his couple in evening dress was potently expressed by the man as if the words were vomit. The theatricality of the play was enhanced by his demand that the same actors portray a complementary working-class couple, hopelessly in awe of decadence.

In *Harry's Christmas* Berkoff supplied a bitter corrective to the holiday spirit with his one-man play about a man whose loneliness leads him, each year, to recycle the few Christmas cards he has ever received. Like his other work, the play was designed for sharp physical interpretations of the world rather than representations. With the use of his dialogue and monologues, "acting becomes a compulsive medium because I can touch primeval forces and release them—madness and maybe enlightenment". Occasionally, he finds an inspiration for such expression in existing plays, such as his internationally successful version of Oscar Wilde's *Salomé,* first produced for Dublin's Gate Theatre.

His Hollywood and other American experiences have been absorbed into his writing, both dramatically and in prose, notably in his published imaginative "screenplay" *A Prisoner in Rio* and the plays *Kvetch* and *Acapulco*. The latter, in particular, demonstrates Hollywood's vulnerability to individuals such as Berkoff. In the process of turning him into a star, it allowed him to bear close-range witness to the movie-making megalomania of actors such as Sylvester Stallone in *Rambo*. Those experiences have been digested with customary bile to become the harsher entertainment of a Berkoff play.

—Ned Chaillet

See also *Volume 1* entry on *East*.

BERNHARD, Thomas. Born in Heerlen, near Maastricht, The Netherlands, 10 February 1931. Lived in Austria from 1932. Educated at Salzburg Gymnasium, 1943–47; studied singing, direction, and theatrical technique, 1952–55, and at the Salzburg Mozarteum, 1955–57. Grocer's assistant in Salzburg, 1947; contracted tuberculosis and spent two years in convalescence, 1951–52; journalist for the socialist *Demokratisches Volksblatt*, from 1952, and contributor to the newspaper *Die Furche*, 1953–55; first novella published, 1953; intermittent travel, to Italy and Yugoslavia, 1953–57, London, 1960, and Poland, 1962–63; settled on a farm in Ohlsdorf an Herzversagen, Upper Austria, 1965; first full-length play, *Ein Fest für Boris*, produced 1970: the first of several collaborations with the director Claus Peymann. Recipient of several awards, including Austrian State Prize, 1968; Büchner Prize, 1970; Grillparzer Prize, 1971; Premio Prato, 1982; Premio Mondello, 1983; Prix Medicis, 1988. Member, Deutsche Akademie für Sprache und Dichtung but withdrew 1979. Died in Ohlsdorf, 12 February 1989.

Works

Collections

Die Rosen der Einöde: Fünf Sätze für Ballett, Stimmen und Orchester (libretti). 1959.
Die Salzburger Stücke (includes *Der Ignorant und der Wahnsinnige* and *Die Macht der Gewohnheit*). 1975.
Die Stücke 1969–1981. 1984.
Stücke (4 vols.). 1988.
Histrionics: Three Plays (includes *A Party for Boris; Ritter, Dene, Voss; Histrionics*). 1991.

Stage Works

Die Rose (libretto). In *Die Rosen der Einöde*, 1959.
Der Kartenspieler (libretto; produced Deutsche Oper, Berlin, 1967). In *Die Rosen der Einöde*, 1959.
Unter den Pflaumenbäumen (libretto; produced Vienna, 1959). In *Die Rosen der Einöde*, 1959.
Der Kalbskopf (libretto). In *Die Rosen der Einöde*, 1959.
Phantasie (libretto). In *Die Rosen der Einöde*, 1959.
Köpfe (libretto; produced Theater am Tonhof, Maria-Saal, Austria, 1960). 1960.
Ein Fest für Boris (produced Deutsches Schauspielhaus, Hamburg, 1970). 1970; translated as *A Party for Boris*, in *Histrionics: Three Plays*, 1991.

Der Berg. In *Literatur und Kritik 5*, June 1970.
Der Ignorant und der Wahnsinnige (produced Festspiele, Salzburg, 1972). 1972.
Die Jagdgesellschaft (produced Burgtheater, Vienna, 1974).
Die Macht der Gewohnheit (produced Festspiele, Salzburg, 1974). 1974; translated as *The Force of Habit*, 1976.
Der Präsident (produced Akademietheater, Vienna, 1975). 1975; translated as *The President*, with *Eve of Retirement*, 1982.
Minetti: Ein Porträt des Künstlers als alter Mann (produced Württembergisches Staatstheater, Stuttgart, 1976). 1977.
Die Berühmten (produced Burgtheater, Vienna, 1976). 1976.
Immanuel Kant (produced Württembergisches Staatstheater, Stuttgart, 1978). 1978.
Vor dem Ruhestand (produced Württembergisches Staatstheater, Stuttgart, 1979). 1979; translated as *Eve of Retirement*, with *The President*, 1982.
Der Weltverbesserer (produced Schauspielhaus, Bochum, 1980). 1979.
Über allen Gipfeln ist Ruh: Ein deutscher Dichtertag um 1980. 1981.
Am Ziel (produced Festspiele, Salzburg, 1981). 1981.
Der Schein trügt (produced Schauspielhaus, Bochum, 1984). 1984.
Der Theatermacher (produced Landestheater, Salzburg, 1986). 1984; translated as *Histrionics*, in *Histrionics: Three Plays*, 1991.
Ritter, Dene, Voss (produced Landestheater, Salzburg, 1986).

Thomas Bernhard (1964).

1984; translated as *Ritter, Dene, Voss*, in *Histrionics: Three Plays*, 1991.
Einfach kompliziert (produced Schiller-Theater, Berlin, 1986). 1986.
Elisabeth II (produced Schiller-Theater, Berlin, 1989). 1987.
Heldenplatz (produced Burgtheater, Vienna, 1988). 1988.
Der deutsche Mittagstisch: Dramolette. 1988.
Claus Peymann kauft sich eine Hose und geht mit mir essen: *Drei Dramolette*. 1990.

Screenplays

Der Italiener, 1971 (published 1971).

Fiction

Ereignisse (short stories). 1963.
Frost. 1963.
Amras. 1964.
Vestörung. 1967; translated as *Gargoyles*, 1970.
Prosa. 1967.
Ungenach. 1968.
Watten: Ein Nachlass. 1969.
An der Baumgrenze. 1969.
Das Kalkwerk. 1970; translated as *The Lime Works*, 1970.
Gehen. 1971.
Midland in Stilfs: Drei Erzählungen. 1971.
Der Kulterer. 1974.
Korrektur. 1975; translated as *Correction*, 1979.
Der Wetterfleck. 1976.
Der Stimmenimitator. 1978.
Ja. 1978; translated as *Yes*, 1991.
Die Erzählungen, edited by Ulrich Greiner. 1979.
Die Billigesser. 1980; translated as *The Cheap-Eaters*, 1990.
Wittgensteins Neffe: Eine Freundschaft. 1982; translated as *Wittgenstein's Nephew: A Friendship*, 1987.
Beton. 1982; translated as *Concrete*, 1984.
Der Untergeher. 1983.
Holzfällen: Eine Erregung (novel). 1984; translated as *Cutting Timber: An Imitation*, 1988.
Alte Meister. 1985; translated as *Old Masters*, 1989.
Auslöschung: Ein Zerfall. 1986.
In der Höhe: Rettungsversuch. 1989.

Verse

Auf der Erde und in der Hölle. 1957.
Unter dem Eisen des Mondes. 1958.
In hora mortis. 1958.
Psalm. 1960.
Die Irren—Die Häftlinge. 1962.
Ave Vergil. 1981.
Gesammelte Gedichte, edited by Volker Bohn. 1991.

Memoirs and Letters

Die Ursache: Eine Andeutung. 1975.
Der Keller: Eine Entziehung. 1976.
Der Atem: Eine Entscheidung. 1978.
Die Kälte: Eine Isolation. 1981.
Ein Kind. 1982.
Gathering Evidence: A Memoir (translation of *Die Ursache, Der Keller, Der Atem, Die Kälte, Ein Kind*). 1987.

*

Bibliographies

Helen Chambers, "Theatre Checklist No. 12: Thomas Bernhard", in *Theatre Facts*, vol.3 no.4, 1976.
Jens Dittmar (ed.), *Bernhard Werkgeschichte*, Frankfurt, 1981.

Criticism

Books:
Anneliese Botond (ed.), *Über Thomas Bernhard*, Frankfurt, 1970.
Heinz Ludwig Arnold (ed.), *Thomas Bernhard*, Munich, 1974; third edition, 1991 (Text + Kritik series).
Herbert Gamper, *Thomas Bernhard*, Munich, 1977.
Bernard Sorg, *Thomas Bernhard*, Munich, 1977.
Denis Calandra, *New German Dramatists*, London, 1983 (Macmillan Modern Dramatists series).
Gerald Jurdzinski, *Leiden an der "Natur": Thomas Bernhards metaphysische Weltdeutung im Spiegel der Philosophie Schopenhauers*, Frankfurt, 1984.
Siegfried Steinmann, *Sprache, Handlung, Wirklichkeit im deutschen Gegenwartsdrama: Studien zu Thomas Bernhard, Botho Strauss und Bodo Kirchoff*, Frankfurt, 1985.
Rüdiger Görner, "The Excitement of Boredom: Thomas Bernhard", in *A Radical Stage: Theatre in Germany in the 1970s and 1980s*, edited by W.G. Sebald, Oxford, 1988.

Articles:
Alfred Barthofer, "The Plays of Thomas Bernhard: A Report", in *Modern Austrian Literature*, vol. 11 no. 1, 1978.
A.P. Dierick, "Bernhard's Austria: Neurosis, Symbol, or Expedient?", in *Modern Austrian Literature*, vol. 12, 1979.
Gerald A. Fetz, "The Works of Thomas Bernhard: 'Austrian Literature'?", in *Modern Austrian Literature*, vol. 17, nos. 3–4, 1984.
Nicholas Eisner, "Theatertheater/Theaterspiele: The Plays of Thomas Bernhard", in *Modern Drama*, 30, 1987.
"Thomas Bernhard Issue" of *Modern Austrian Literature*, vol. 20 nos. 3–4, 1988.
Gerald A. Fetz, "Life (and Death) after Life: The Portrayal of Old Age in the Works of Thomas Bernhard", in *University of Dayton Review*, vol. 20 no. 2, 1990.

* * *

Thomas Bernhard first attracted critical attention as a poet, but soon turned to fiction, and quickly came to be recognized as one of the most eminent Austrian novelists of the 20th century. In the late 1960's he shifted his interest to the stage and promptly became one of the most frequently performed contemporary playwrights in the German language. Thus Bernhard is among the most prolific and versatile post-war Austrian writers, and at the same time an extremely controversial figure on the contemporary Austrian artistic scene. His truculence toward his home country, his undisguised contempt for his audience and for the Austrian consumers and arbiters of culture, are in stark contrast to the honors his native country has heaped on him.

Like many of the modern authors with whom he is frequently associated (Antonin Artaud, Peter Handke, Samuel Beckett, and the playwrights of the "theatre of the absurd"), Bernhard de-emphasizes action and plot in his plays. His hostile treatment of his native country, his audiences, and of leading figures of politics and culture, particularly the presidium of the Salzburg Festival, is only a reflection of his existential malaise, probably dating back to his unhappy childhood and his nearly fatal bout with tuberculosis as a young man. Bernhard's opus is one long repetition of the same motif: modern man's agonized search for meaning, and sometimes for God, in a hostile Universe. Indeed, in his play *Die Berühmten*, Bernhard states that all great artists only create one single work which they vary and correct continuously throughout their creative life.

The world of Bernhard's stage is full of death, suffering, and mental and physical cruelty. His first play, *Ein Fest für Boris* (*A Party for Boris*), is a representative example of Bernhard's dramatic work. It is a bizarre, Beckett-inspired play, about legless, wheelchair-bound cripples dragged to a party from an asylum. Man is seen as trapped in a hopeless situation; interpersonal relationships and communication are impossible because of the monomania and egotism of individuals who will not engage in dramatic dialogue, but exhaust themselves in endless soliloquies. Indeed, much of the ennui and cruelty of the human condition is man-made and not caused by the indifference or total absence of a metaphysical authority.

In *Die Macht der Gewohnheit* (*The Force of Habit*), the travelling circus replaces the asylum as the central metaphor, with the monomaniacal circus director aspiring to train his hapless performers to play one perfect concert rendition of Schubert's *Forellenquintett* as a last spiritual defense against the repetitive daily circus routine in increasingly sordid places. Similarly, in *Minetti*, an aging actor hopes in vain for one last glorious engagement to play King Lear, a role for which he has practised all his life. But, like Godot in Beckett's play, the theatre director who would hire him for the role does not keep his appointment in the end, and the actor dons his Lear mask and freezes to death on a park bench.

Bernhard's preoccupation with death and the absurdity of life, his typically Austrian distrust of language as an effective means of communication, and his contempt for the cultural and political establishment are in many ways a reflection of a personal existential position which led to his hermit-like seclusion on his farm. The result of this stance is a literary opus which is the desperate, often sarcastic, cry of a tortured soul. In his early poems it is still God to whom the plea for solace is directed; in the fiction, and particularly in his dramatic work, the dominant theme is the inevitability of death and the fact that when confronted with the reality of death, all human endeavor becomes a bitter farce.

Bernhard's literary testament reveals the close connection between his personal convictions and the themes of his plays. His will stipulated that, for the next 70 years, none of his works may be performed or published in Austria, and that nothing of his unpublished work—manuscripts, notes, or letters—may be made public anywhere. Thus the pervasive misanthropy and anti-Austrianism of his last plays, *Elisabeth II* and, particularly, *Heldenplatz*, are a retrospect and a summary of his whole work: they are works of sadness, indignation, and resignation in the face of both the incorrigible arrogance of his countrymen and the absurdity of the human condition.

—Franz G. Blaha

See also *Volume 1* entry on *The Force of Habit*.

BETTI, Ugo. Born in Camerino, Italy, 4 February 1892. Educated in Parma, studying the classics; read law at Parma University, graduated 1914. Married Andreina Frosini in 1930. Artillery officer during World War I: captured by the Germans after the Italian defeat at Caporetto, 1917, and in prisoner-of-war camp, October 1917–December 1918; returned to Parma, 1919, becoming a magistrate; appointed as a judge, 1923; first play *La padrona*, produced 1926; judge in Rome, 1930–43; contributor to *Oggi*, 1933; retired to Camerino, 1943; officially cleared of charges of supporting Mussolini; appointed librarian at the Ministry of Justice, 1944; spent last years as legal advisor to the Coordinamento Spettacolo, a national association for writers and publishers. Recipient: Premio IDI (Italian Institute of Drama Prize), 1949, and other awards. Died in Rome, 9 June 1953.

Works

Collections

Teatro. 1955
Teatro postums. 1955.
Three Plays by Ugo Betti (includes *The Queen and the Rebels; The Burnt Flower-Bed; Summertime*), translated by Henry Reed. 1956.
Teatro completo. 1957.
Scritti inediti. 1964.
Three Plays on Justice (includes *Landslide; Struggle Till Dawn; The Fugitive*), translated by G.H. McWilliam. 1964.
Ugo Betti: Three Plays (includes *The Inquiry; The Gambler; Crime on Goat Island*), various translators. 1966.
Teatro completo. 1971.

Stage Works

La padrona (produced Teatro Politeama, Leghorn [Livorno], 1925). 1929.
La donna sullo scudo, with Osvaldo Gibertini (produced Teatro Valle, Rome, 1927). 1957.
La casa sull'acqua (produced Teatro Comunale, Salsomaggiore, 1929). In *Comoedia*, 11, 1929.
L'isola meravigliosa (produced Teatro Manzoni, Milan, 1930). In *Scenario*, 5, December 1936.
Un albergo sul porto (produced Teatro Alfieri, Turin, 1933). In *Il dramma*, August 1943.
Frana allo scalo Nord (produced Teatro Goldoni, Venice, 1936). In *Scenario*, 4, 1935, translated as *Landslide*, in *Three Plays on Justice*, 1964.
Una bella domenica di settembre (produced Teatro Margherita, Genoa, 1937). In *Via consolare*, May 1941.
I nostri sogni (produced Teatro Regio, Parma, 1937). In *Scenario*, July 1941.
Il cacciatore d'anitre (produced Teatro Manzini, Milan, 1940). In *Il dramma*, 1940.
Il paese delle vacanze (produced Teatro Odeon, Milan, 1942). In *Scenario*, May 1942; translated as *Summertime*, in *Three Plays by Ugo Betti*, 1956.
Notte in casa del ricco (produced Teatro Eliseo, Rome, 1942). In *Scenario*, December 1942.
Il diluvio (produced Teatro Argentina, Rome, 1943). In *Il dramma*, March 1943.
Il vento notturno (produced Teatro Olimpia, Milan, 1945). In *Il dramma*, September 1946.
Ispezione (produced Teatro Odeon, Milan, 1947). In *Sipario*, March–April 1947; translated as *The Inquiry,* in *Ugo Betti: Three Plays*, 1966.

Marito e moglie (produced Teatro delle Arti, 1947). In *Teatro*, November 1949.
Favola di Natale (produced Teatro Olimpia, Milan, 1948). In *Teatro*, 1955.
Corruzione al palazzo di giustizia (produced Teatro delle Arti, Rome, 1949). In *Sipario*, 4, March 1949; translated as *Corruption in the Palace of Justice*, in *The New Theatre of Europe, 1*, edited by Robert Corrigan, 1962.
Lotta fino all'alba (produced Teatro delle Arti, Rome, 1949). In *Sipario*, August–September 1949; translated as *Struggle Till Dawn*, in *Three Plays on Justice*, 1964.
Irene innocente (produced Teatro Quirino, Rome, 1950). In *Teatro*, 2, 1950.
Spiritismo nell'antica casa (produced Teatro di via Vittoria, Rome, 1950). In *Sipario*, 5, June 1950.
Delitto all'isola delle capre (produced Teatro delle Arti, Rome, 1950). In *Teatro*, vol.2 no.2, 1950; translated as *Goat Island*, 1961; as *Crime on Goat Island*, in *Ugo Betti: Three Plays*, 1966..
La regina e gli insorti (produced Teatro Eliseo, Rome, 1951). In *Sipario*, May 1951; translated as *The Queen and the Rebels*, in *Three Plays by Ugo Betti*, 1956.
Il giocatore (produced Teatro Valle, Rome, 1951). In *Teatro-Scenario*, vol.15 no.10, 1951; translated as *The Gambler*, in *Ugo Betti: Three Plays*, 1966.
Acque turbate; o, Il fratello protegge e ama. In *Teatro postumo*, 1955.
L'aiuola bruciata (produced Chiesa di San Francesco, San Miniato, 1953). 1953; translated as *The Burnt Flower-Bed*, in *Three Plays by Ugo Betti*, 1956.
La fuggitiva (produced Teatro La Fenice, Venice, 1953). 1953; translated as *The Fugitive*, in *Three Plays on Justice*, 1964.

Screenplays

I tre del pra' di sopra (published in *Scritti inediti*, 1964).

Fiction

Caino (stories). 1928.
Le case (stories). 1933.
Una strana serata (stories). 1948.
La piera alta, from the screenplay *I tre del pra' di sopra*. 1948.
Novelle (stories), edited by Mario Ortolani. 1968.

Verse

Le nozze di Teti e Peleo, from verse by Catullus. 1910.
Il Re pensieroso. 1922.
Canzonette—La morte. 1932.
Uomo e donna. 1937.
Poesie (includes poems written 1938–53). 1957.

Other

Considerazioni sulla forza maggiore come limite di responsabilità del vettore ferroviario (essay). 1920.
Religione e teatro. 1957; translated as *Religion and Theatre*, in *Tulane Drama Review*, 5, 1960.

*

Criticism

Books:
E. de Michelis, *La poesia di Ugo Betti*, Florence, 1937.
E. Barbetti, *Il teatro di Ugo Betti*, Florence, 1943.
N.D. Aloisio, *Ugo Betti*, Rome, 1952.
A. Fiocco, *Ugo Betti*, Rome, 1954.
Elettra Curetti, *Zu den Dramen von Ugo Betti*, Zurich, 1966.
Antonio di Pietro, *L'opera di Ugo Betti* (2 vols.), Bari, 1966–68.
Gildo Moro, *Il teatro di Ugo Betti*, Milan, 1973.
Elena F. Lo Cicero, *Ugo Betti: Teatro de la culpa y el rescate*, Buenos Aires, 1976.
Gianni Spera, *Coscienza e responsabilità nell'opera di Ugo Betti: Da "La padrona" a "Corruzione al palazzo di giustizia"*, Florida, 1977.
Giorgio Fontanelli, *Il teatro di Ugo Betti*, Rome, 1985.
Emanuele Licastro, *Ugo Betti: An Introduction*, Jefferson, North Carolina, 1985.

Articles:
G.H. McWilliam, "Interpreting Betti", in *Tulane Drama Review*, 5, 1960.
G. Rizzio, "Regression-Progression in Ugo Betti's Drama", in *Tulane Drama Review*, vol.8 no.1, 1963.
Ugo Betti, "Notes for the *Corruption in the Palace of Justice*", in *Tulane Drama Review*, vol.8 no.3, 1964.
Ugo Betti, "Notes for *Crime on Goat Island*", in *Tulane Drama Review*, vol.8 no.3, 1964.
Eric Salmon, "Ugo Betti's *Troubled Waters* [*Acque turbate*]", in *Modern Drama*, 11, 1968.
Harold H. Watts, "Ugo Betti: The Theater of 'Shame'", in *Modern Drama*, 12, 1969.
Robert Corrigan, "The Purgatorial Theatre of Ugo Betti, in his *The Theatre in Search of a Fix*, New York, 1973.
Antonio Illiano, "Ugo Betti's Last Plays", in *Perspectives on Contemporary Literature*, vol.1 no.1, 1975.
Lloyd A. Arnett, "Tragedy in a Postmodern Vein: Ugo Betti Our Contemporary?", in *Modern Drama*, 33, 1990.

*   *   *

Ugo Betti is widely considered one of the greatest Italian dramatists of the 20th century and is often ranked with Pirandello for the importance of his theatrical output. In 1914 Betti wrote a university thesis entitled "Revolution and the Law". In this thesis he argued that man's nature is essentially egotistical and that violent revolution is a necessary prerequisite for progress. These views reflected the general tenor of Italian youth in the pre-World-War-I period—views that were closely associated with the Futurist movement which was then exploding in Italy. His war experiences from 1915–18, however, made him reappraise his ideas. The influence of the "twilight" poets and symbolists can be seen in *Il Re pensieroso* (The Pensive King), a collection of poetry written in prison camp. In these early works Betti juxtaposes the fabulous world of childhood innocence with the adult world where death, disease, corruption, and poverty are components of reality. This became a recurring theme in his work.

While Betti continued to write in other modes throughout his career, it was as a playwright that he made his major contribution to world literature. He produced 26 plays (one of these in collaboration with Gibertini), of which the majority are tragedies. They may be separated into three periods: early, middle, and late. In the early period, comprising his first eight plays, Betti experimented with fairy-tales (*L'isola meravigliosa*, *La donna sullo scudo*), symbolic realism (*La casa sull'acqua*), animalistic naturalism (*Un albergo sul porto*), and surrealist farce (*Diluvio*). It is not until *Frana allo scalo nord* (*Landslide*), his first masterpiece, that his vision comes into focus. With this play critics recognized in Betti a great dramatic talent.

In the middle period, which fell in the late 1930's, Betti wrote four comedies in which he succeeded in his aim of creating diversions. They are conventional and stylized, peopled with stock characters. *Paese delle vacanze* is an idyllic love story full of warm spirits. Even here Betti presents a contrast between innocence and corruption. Alberto, a country boy, finds he is more deeply attached to his poor, sweet childhood girlfriend than to the rich girl who has been tainted by the urban world of power and money. It is the best known of Betti's comedies to English readers and has had the most success in Italy. During this time, one of the most escapist periods in Italian drama, Fascist Italy invaded Ethiopia, and Betti has been accused of writing these comedies in order to avoid important political issues.

The 14 plays which Betti wrote in his late period, 1940–53, have been described by Henry Reed as comprising one of "the greatest outbursts in dramatic literature". With the exception of his early masterpiece, *Frana allo scalo nord*, his best work belongs to this period (*Corruzione al palazzo di giustizia*, *Delitto all'isola di capre*, *La regina e gli insorti*, *Il giocatore*).

Betti's drama reflects his concerns with human motivations, the nature of evil, justice and the law, a career to which he devoted himself for over 20 years. These preoccupations carried Betti into an existential realm where he examined the spiritual aspirations of human beings and the "bewildering incongruity" between those aspirations and the actuality of human existence. Any attempt to place his drama exclusively in a socio-economic framework trivializes it. He is not concerned with a scientific investigation of reality, or with the influence of environment and heredity on people's lives (as were the 19th-century realists), but rather with mankind's never-ending quest for meaning.

Some critics have tried to link his drama with the tenets of fascism. Betti's work, however, transcends any particular political period. Moreover, the fascist authorities often censored his plays, and in 1938 he was charged with being both an anti-fascist and a Jew.

While none of his plays adopt orthodox Roman-Catholic tenets, they are metaphysical in nature, and the later plays are increasingly Christian in outlook. In *Religione e teatro* (*Religion and Theatre*), an essay which he wrote in 1953, the year of his death, Betti states that important contemporary theatre "draws its life from needs which, although variously expressed, are essentially religious". For him, religion was not a sugar-coated pill to ease man's conscience, but the "need for mercy, harmony, solidarity, immortality, trust, forgiveness, and above all, for love" that is found in all mankind. It is not surprising that at the time he wrote this essay, he himself had returned to Catholicism.

Betti moves easily between realistic and symbolic dimensions. The settings have no specific location and the time is vaguely contemporary. Many of the characters' names do not sound Italian, but the bureaucratic procedures, the familial relationships, the subordinate position of women in society, the descriptions of city and country life, are all recognizably Italian. Only two of the plays have political themes (*La regina e gli insorti* and *L'aiuola bruciata*).

Betti often reveals a dark perception of the human condition. In his drama, he plumbs the depths of human actions to their "tortuous roots" and the edges are often surrounded by shadow. Some of his favorite theatrical devices are the arrival of a stranger (*Delitto al'isola delle capre*, *Casa sull'acqua*), the return to the scene of action of a known person (*Padrona*, *Lotto fino all'alba*, *Fuggitiva*, *Spiritismo nell'antica casa*), and the trial or investigation (*Frana allo scalo nord*, *Corruzione*, *Ispezione*, *Giocatore*, *Irene innocente*). By means of these devices his main characters reach self-awareness which can take various forms. In *Acque turbate*, Giacoma's unconscious incestuous desire becomes conscious. In *Frana allo scalo nord* all of society realizes it bears responsibility for an accident that killed three workers. In *Corruzione al palazzo di giustizia*, Cust, obsessed by guilt, longs for atonement, and submits to a higher spiritual power. In *Casa sull'acqua*, Francesco accepts the impossibility of happiness.

Betti was never confined by the exigencies of realism. In *Frana allo scalo nord*, three characters come back from the dead. In *La fuggitiva*, the mountain becomes a character in the play. Betti enjoyed using sounds for emotional effect as can be seen from the thunder in *La fuggitiva* and the siren, dance music, and train whistle in *Frana allo scalo nord*. He had a wonderful sense of the theatrical. In the final moments of *Corruzione al palazzo di giustizia*, the staircase echoes with the sound of Cust's footsteps as he slowly ascends to confess to the Lord High Chancellor.

—Jane House

See also *Volume 1* entry on *Corruption in the Palace of Justice*.

BICKERSTAFF(E), Isaac (John). Born in Dublin, Ireland, 26 September 1733. Soldier: page to the Earl of Chesterfield, Lord Lieutenant of Ireland, 1745; commissioned ensign in the Fifth Regiment of Foot, 1745, and 2nd lieutenant, 1746 until he resigned, 1755; 2nd lieutenant, 91st Company, Plymouth Marine Corps, 1758–63. Wrote for the stage, 1756–72; first ballad opera, *Thomas and Sally*, produced 1760; fled England to avoid arrest for being homosexual, 1772, and spent the remainder of his life in exile abroad. Died c.1808.

Works

Collections

The Plays of Bickerstaff (3 vols.), edited by Peter A. Tasch. 1981.

Stage Works

Thomas and Sally; or, The Sailor's Return, music by Thomas Arne (produced Theatre Royal, Covent Garden, London, 1760). 1761; revised edition, 1780.
Judith (oratorio), music by Thomas Arne (produced Theatre Royal, Drury Lane, London, 1761). 1761.
Love in a Village, music by Thomas Arne and others (produced Theatre Royal, Covent Garden, London, 1762). 1763.
The Maid of the Mill, music by Samuel Arnold and others (produced Theatre Royal, Covent Garden, London, 1765). 1765.

Scene from *Love in a Village* by **Isaac Bickerstaff**, with Edward Shuter as Justice Woodcock (left), John Beard as Hawthorne (centre), and John Dunstall as Hodge (painting by Johann Zoffany).

Daphne and Amintor, from a work by Saint-Foix (produced Theatre Royal, Drury Lane, London, 1765).   1765.

The Plain Dealer, from the play by Wycherley (produced Theatre Royal, Drury Lane, London, 1765).   1766.

Love in the City, music by Charles Dibdin and others (produced Theatre Royal, Covent Garden, London, 1767). 1767; shortened version, as *The Romp* (produced Crow Street Theatre, Dublin, 1774), 1786.

Lionel and Clarissa, music by Charles Dibdin (produced Theatre Royal, Covent Garden, London, 1768). 1768; revised version, as *The School for Fathers* (produced Southwark Theatre, Philadelphia, 1770), 1770.

The Absent Man (produced Theatre Royal, Drury Lane, London,1768).   1768.

The Padlock, music by Charles Dibdin (produced Theatre Royal, Drury Lane, London, 1768).   1768.

The Royal Garland, music by Samuel Arnold (produced Theatre Royal, Covent Garden, London, 1768).   1768.

Queen Mab (cantata), music by Charles Dibdin (produced 1768).   1768.

The Hypocrite, from a play by Cibber (produced Theatre Royal, Drury Lane, London, 1768).   1769.

Doctor Last in His Chariot, from a play by Molière (produced Theatre Royal, Haymarket, London, 1769).   1769.

The Captive, music by Charles Dibdin, from the play *Don Sebastian* by Dryden (produced Theatre Royal, Haymarket, London, 1769).   1769.

The Ephesian Matron; or, The Widow's Tears, music by Charles Dibdin (produced Ranelagh House, followed by Theatre Royal, Haymarket, London, 1769).   1769.

Tis Well it's No Worse, from a play by Calderón (produced Theatre Royal, Drury Lane, London, 1770).   1770.

The Recruiting Serjeant, music by Charles Dibdin (produced Ranelagh House, followed by Theatre Royal, Drury Lane, London, 1770).   1770.

He Would if He Could; or, An Old Fool Worse Than Any, music by Charles Dibdin, from a play by G.A. Federico (as *The Maid the Mistress,* produced Ranelagh House, London, 1770; as *He Would if He Could,* produced Theatre Royal, Drury Lane, London, 1771).   1771.

The Brick-Dust Man and the Milk-Maid, music by Charles Dibdin (produced 1772).   In *St. James Chronicle,* 25 July 1772.

The Sultan; or, A Peep into the Seraglio, from a play by C.S. Favart, music by Charles Dibdin and others (produced Theatre Royal, Drury Lane, London, 1775; as *The American Captive,* produced 1794).   1787.

The Spoiled Child (produced Theatre Ulverstone, 1787; Theatre Royal, Drury Lane, London, 1790).   1792 (possibly not by Bickerstaffe).

Fiction

The Life and Adventures of Ambrose Gwinnet.   1770.

Verse

Leucothoë: A Dramatic Poem.   1756.

*

Criticism

Books:
Peter A. Tasch, *The Dramatic Cobbler: The Life and Works of Bickerstaff*, Lewisburg, Pennsylvania, 1971.
Roger Fiske, *English Theatre Music in the Eighteenth Century*, Oxford, 1973, revised edition, 1986.

Articles:
Ethel Macmillan, "The Plays of Isaac Bickerstaffe in America", in *Philological Quarterly*, 5, 1926.
Peter A. Tasch, "Bickerstaff, Colman and the Bourgeois Audience", in *Restoration and 18th Century Theatre Research*, 9, 1970.

* * *

Isaac Bickerstaffe undoubtedly possessed a genuine talent as a playwright, but he presumed too much on his innate abilities, preferring to display a certain facility rather than to make the effort needed to turn his opportunities to good account. With an eye for detail and some skill in the composition of dialogue he might well have continued and developed the 18th-century tradition in comedy. Instead he fell in too readily with the undemanding taste of his times, plundering earlier writers without adding anything significant to what he took from them, and accepting a high degree of stagey conventionality.

Bickerstaffe's earliest dramatic works were comic operas. After *Thomas and Sally: or, The Sailor's Return*, for which T.A. Arne arranged the music, he achieved a considerable success with *Love in a Village*. The plot, as the author freely admitted, was largely drawn from *The Village Opera* by Charles Johnson, with additional material from Wycherley's *The Gentleman Dancing-Master*, and its basis is a depiction of the unsophisticated delights of rural life in contrast to the knowing ways of the metropolis. The love stories, with all their talk of tyrannical fathers, elopements, disguises, and social inequalities, are rose-water stuff, and the stilted language of the lovers is no more convincing than the high-mindedness of the heroes. What is far more impressive is the liveliness of the presentation of manners of the age in the scenes where we see the older generation. The representatives of the 18th-century squirearchy express themselves with vigour, and though, admittedly, they do not do very much, they have a temperamental energy which contrasts with the emotional timidity of the tentative younger generation. There are times when even Bickerstaffe finds the love interest so artificial that he feels obliged to try and save the situation by comparing it openly with the sort of things one found in the romantic novels of the time. What is more surprising are occasional radical statements, forthright demands for respect for the rights of the ordinary man.

Love in a Village would, however, be nothing without the music for which ample opportunities are provided. Of the 40-odd musical items, only a small proportion, including the overture by Karl Friedrich Abel, were specially composed; as for the remainder of the songs, Bickerstaffe wrote new lyrics to existing tunes by such contemporaries as Boyce and Arne and Geminiani, with a few traditional airs thrown in for good measure. For the most part Bickerstaffe was content to create opportunities for solo singing. There are also a few ensembles, generally at the ends of acts. Even in the words for the songs, however, Bickerstaffe often shows himself too readily satisfied. In *Lionel and Clarissa*, for instance, with music this time arranged by Charles Dibdin, we find this:

> Come then, pining, peevish lover,
>   Tell me what to do and say;
> From your doleful dumps recover,
>   Smile, and it shall have its way.

Two of the lines are delightful in their balanced simplicity, but the other couplet is all-too-obviously a make-weight.

In the field of comedy proper too, Bickerstaffe combines a great readiness to adapt earlier works (as for instance in *The Hypocrite*, after Molière, by way of Cibber) adding only humour and close observation of the life of his times. *The Sultan: or, A Peep into the Seraglio* gives some idea of what he can do with material that is really very thin. Whether or not it can be seen as a source for Mozart's *Die Entführung aus dem Serail*, this little farce after Marmontel belongs to the same tradition that found a lot of fun in placing a pert English girl in the harem where she soon put the chief eunuch out of countenance and taught the Sultan to mind his manners. Though local colour is fairly rudimentary, there is enough to create the expected atmosphere, and the characters of the Turks belong to the well-established tradition of servants of vast proportions with terrifying manners and all-powerful masters with hearts of wax who are really prisoners of their own rank and situation. Turkish decadence and sensuality is set off against Roxalana's bracing self-confidence. In what appears at first to be a male-dominated world she pronounces some feminist views in ringing tones, and the action of the play serves to show their triumph.

Bickerstaffe's apparent feminism is, however, as hard to intepret as the radicalism that he puts into the mouths of some of his male characters. Taken out of context, the various statements could seem highly critical of life and manners in the 18th century. But, even when the development of the plot appears to bear them out, it is doubtful whether audiences at the time would hear them as anything other than cheeky comments made "in character", possibly containing a grain of truth, but not something that need to be given too serious attention.

—Christopher Smith

———

BJØRNSON, Bjørnstjerne Martinius. Born in Kvikne, Norway (then united with Sweden), 8 December 1832. Educated at Molde grammar school, from 1843; Christiania University, Christiana (now Oslo), from 1852. Married the actress Karoline Reimers. Contributed articles to newspapers while at university; theatre reviewer for *Morgenbladet*, 1854–56; editor, *Illusttreret Folkeblad*, from 1856, to which he contributed stories; first play, *Mellem slagene* [*Between the Battles*], published and produced, 1857; succeeded Ibsen as Director of the Norske Teatret [Norwegian Theatre], Bergen, 1857–59; editor, *Bergenposten*, Bergen; returned to Christiana to edit the newspaper *Aftenbladet*, 1859, but subsequently had to resign because of his political views; founded the Norwegian Cultural Society; spent two years in Rome, 1860–62; director of the Christiana Theatre, 1865–67; editor of *Norsk Folkeblad*, 1866–71; returned to Rome, 1873; became involved increasingly in political and social debate in the late 1870's; travelled and lectured in the USA, 1880–81; lived in Paris, 1882–1887; promoter of world peace and minority rights during the 1890's. Recipient: Nobel Prize for Literature, 1903. Died in Paris, 26 April 1910.

Works

Collections

Works, edited by Rasmus B. Anderson.   1894–99.
Samlede vaerker (12 vols.).   1910–11.
Gesammelte Werke (5 vols.).   1911.
Three Comedies (includes *The Newly Married Couple; Leonarda; A Gauntlet*), translated by R.F. Sharp.   1912.
Plays (2 vols.), translated by Edwin Björkman.   1913–14:
  1. *The Gauntlet; Beyond Our Power; The New System.*   1913.
  2. *Love and Geography; Beyond Our Might; Laboremus.*   1914.
Three Dramas (includes *The Bankrupt; The Editor; The King*), translated by R. Farquharson Sharp.   1914.
Samlede digter-verker [Collected Literary Works] (9 vols.), edited by Francis Bull.   1919–20.
Samlede verker (5 vols.).   1960.

Stage Works

Mellem slagene (produced Christiana Theatre, Christiana, 1857).   1857, translated as *Between the Battles*, in *The Nobel Prize Treasury*, 1948.
Halte Hulda [Limping Hulda] (produced Kongelige Teater, Copenhagen, 1858).   1858.
Kong Sverre [King Sverre] (produced Norske Teatret, Christiana, 1861).   1861.
Sigurd Slembe [Sigurd the Bad] (produced Trondheim Theatre, Trondheim, 1863).   1863; translated as *Sigurd Slembe*, 1888.
Maria Stuart i Skotland (produced Christiana Theatre, Christiana, 1867).   1864; translated as *Mary Stuart in Scotland*, 1912.
De nygifte (produced Kongelige Teater, Copenhagen, 1865).   1865; translated as *The Newly Married Couple*, 1868; as *A Lesson in Marriage*, 1911.
Sigurd Jorsalfer [Sigurd the Crusader].   1872.
En fallit (produced Nya Teatern, Stockholm, 1875).   1875; translated as *The Bankrupt*, in *Three Dramas*, 1914.
Redaktøren (produced Nya Teatern, Stockholm, 1875).   1875; translated as *The Editor*, in *Three Dramas*, 1919.
Kongen (produced Nationalteatret, Christiana, 1902).   1877; translated as *The King*, in *Three Dramas*, 1914.
Det ny system [The New System] (produced Residenztheater, Berlin, 1878).   1879; translated as *The New System*, in *Plays*, 1913.
Leonarda (produced Christiana Theatre, Christiana, 1879).   1879; translated as *Leonarda*, in *Three Comedies*, 1912.
En hanske (produced Stadttheater, Hamburg, 1883).   1883; translated as *A Gauntlet*, 1890.
Over Ævne I (produced Nya Teatern, Stockholm, 1886).   1883; translated as *Pastor Sang*, 1893; as *Beyond Our Power*, in *Plays 1*, 1913.
Geografi og kjaerlighed (produced Christiana Theatre, Christiana, 1885).   1885; translated as *Love and Geography*, in *Plays 2*, 1914.

Over Ævne II (produced Christiana Theatre, Christiana, 1895).   1895; translated as *Beyond Our Might*, in *Plays 2*, 1914.
Paul Lange og Tora Parsberg (produced Dagmar Teater, Copenhagen, 1901).   1898; translated as *Paul Lange and Tora Parsberg*, 1899.
Laboremus (produced Nationalteatret, Christiana, 1901).   1901; translated as *Laboremus*, 1901.
På Storhove [At Storhove] (produced Nationalteatret, Christiana, 1902).   1902.
Daglannet [Dag's Farm] (produced Nationalteatret, Copenhagen, 1905).   1904.
Naar den ny vin blomstrer [When the New Wine Blooms] (produced Nationalteatret, Christiana, 1909).   1909.
Kong Eystejn.   1933.

Fiction

Synnøve Solbakken.   1857; translated as *Trust and Trial*, 1858; as *Love and Life in Norway*, 1870; as *Betrothal*, in *Half Hours with Foreign Novelists*, 1880; as *Synnöve Solbakken*, 1881.
Arne.   1858; translated as *Arne*, 1861.
Smaastykker [Sketches].   1860.
En glad gut.   1860; translated as *Ovind*, 1869; as *The Happy Boy*, 1881; as *The Happy Lad*, in *"The Happy Lad" and Other Tales*, 1882; as *A Happy Boy*, 1892.
Fiskerjenten.   1868; translated as *The Fisher Maiden*, 1869; as *The Fishing Girl*, 1870; as *The Fisher Lass*, 1896; as *The Fisher Lassie*, with *Arne*, 1890.
Brudeslåtten.   1873; translated as *The Bridal March*, in *Life by the Fells and Fjords*, 1879.
Fortaelinger [Tales].   1872.
Magnhild.   1877; translated as *Magnhild*, 1883.
Kaptejn Mansana.   1879; translated as *Captain Mansana*, in *"Captain Mansana" and Other Tales*, 1882.
"The Bridal March" and Other Tales.   1884.
Det flayer i byen og på havnen.   1884; translated as *The Heritage of the Kurts*, 1890.
Støv.   1887.
På Guds veje.   1889; translated as *In God's Way*, 1908.
Nye fortaelinger [New Tales].   1893–94.
Mary.   1906; translated as *Mary*, 1910.
Novels (13 vols.; includes all the works of fiction listed above), edited by Edmund Gosse.   1895–1909.

Verse

Digte og sange [Poems and Songs].   1870.
Arnljot Gelline.   1870; translated as *Arnljot Gelline*, 1917.
Poems and Songs in the Original Metres, translated by A. Hubbell Palmer.   1915.

Memoirs and Letters

Gro-tid: Breve fra årene 1857–1870 (2 vols.), edited by Halvdan Koht.   1912.
Brytnings-år: Breve fra årene 1871–1878 (2 vols.), edited by Halvdan Koht.   1921.
Kamp-Liv: Breve fra årene 1879–1884 (2 vols.), edited by Halvdan Koht.   1932.
Brevveksling med danske 1875–1910 (2 vols.), edited by Anker Øyvind and others.   1953.
Brevveksling med danske 1854–1874 (3 vols), edited by Anker Øyvind and others.   1970–74.
Land of the Free: Bjørnson's American Letters, 1880–1881, translated by Eva Lund Haugen and Einar Haugen.   1978.
Briefwechsel mit Deutschen, edited by Aldo Keel.   1986.

Other

Udvalgte artikler og taler (2 vols.; articles and speeches), edited by C. Collin.   1912.

*

Bibliographies

Arthur Thuesen, *Bjørnson-bibliografi* (5 vols.), Oslo, 1948–57.

Criticism

Books:
G. Brandes, *Critical Studies of Ibsen and Bjørnson*, Copenhagen, 1899.
W.M. Payne, *Bjornstjerne Bjornson 1832–1910*, Chicago, 1910.
G. Neckel, *Ibsen und Bjornson*, Berlin, 1921.
Arthur Paulson, *The Norwegian-American Reaction to Ibsen and Bjørnson, 1850–1900*, Northfield, Minnesota, 1937.
B. Downs, "Bjornson", in his *Modern Norwegian Literature, 1860–1918*, Cambridge, 1966.

Articles:
Hjalmar Hjorth Boyesen, "Bjørnstjerne Bjørnson as a Dramatist", in *North American Review*, 116, January 1873.

* * *

Bjørnson was a poet, a novelist, and a public speaker with political ambitions, just as much as he was a dramatist. As both a poet and an orator, Bjørnson had a natural instinct for dramatic effects. His plays abound with stage directions, concerning the light, sounds off stage, music, the actors' use of the voice, costume, and so on. Like Ibsen, Bjørnson, in the 1850's and the 1860's, was an eager student of the Icelandic family sagas as well as the sagas of the old Norse kings. The sagas tell tragic stories of conflicts between close relatives, such as royal brothers, facing each other on the brink of civil war, of passionate and destructive women urging the men to take revenge for some strongly felt offense, and of ruthless men who value power and glory more than the love of a devoted woman.

In six plays Bjørnson exploited the dramatic potential of great ambitions and extreme passions involving old Norse saga characters—kings, queens, or local chieftains. His two earliest plays, both set in medieval Norway, end with the house sheltering the main characters being set on fire, a motif borrowed from *Njáls Saga*. It was one of the main tasks for mid-19th-century theatre in Norway to focus on national myths and to present on the stage heroic action and dignified, self-confident ways of expression in order to encourage in the audience a sense of national identity and pride. A couple of these plays, "Limping Hulda" and the first part of the trilogy *Sigurd Slembe*, were written in blank verse, revealing an influence from Shakespeare. And yet Bjørnson's history plays belong mainly to the Romantic tradition of the Danish playwrights of the early 19th century. The lyrical poet is never far away from the stage in this kind of dialogue, and Bjørnson frequently introduces a lyrical song or a ballad to develop an idyllic frame of mind, to suggest relief following a tense situation, or to conclude the drama on a note of harmony.

The age in which Bjørnson's plays were written witnessed a strong national revival in Norway and a growing demand for political independence from Sweden. Bjørnson was a courageous spokesman for the separatist interests, and the pathos of his drama, particularly in the plays about royal and aristocratic characters drawn from the medieval sagas, was inspired by, and gave strength to, some of the more radical attitudes in the contemporary political process. Also, some of the plays with a contemporary setting, such as *The King* and *Paul Lange and Tora Parsberg*, can be read as indirect comments on the situation of the country and what kind of men it would need.

The political debate of the age was dominated by constitutional issues rising from, for the most part, social conflicts. Bjørnson's drama rarely deals with social questions, and when it does, as in *Beyond Our Might, Part Two*, it is mostly the moral dimension of the action which is emphasized. Bjørnson's dramatic work, like the theatre of the 19th century as a whole, was created for the bourgeoisie and the intellectual elite, and not for the working classes. The plays with a contemporary setting bring forth representative attitudes, concerning the relationship between men and women, exposing human frailty and human folly, and exploring the possibilities of honest young people with radical ideas facing old, stubborn, or authoritarian ways of behaviour. There is often a conflict between civil servants or other representatives of the Establishment and newcomers in the political landscape, giving voice to a liberal or radical opposition, but the difference of opinion is mostly kept on a very general level. A dramatist facing an audience consisting of both left-wingers and right-wingers cannot be specific regarding political matters. Bjørnson knew this, and turned to moral questions involving Romantic ideals such as chastity, intellectual honesty, civil courage, and respect for truth.

From the 1870's on a number of newly established newspapers contributed to a certain change in the political institutions of Norway. An increasing part of the political debate took place in these newspapers, which were not merely channels for public information, but mouthpieces for party interests. Bjørnson attacked the reckless ways of the press in dealing with political opponents in his play *The Editor*, where the public voice interferes in the private lives of the characters. The action exposes the parental generation as cowardly and afraid of scandal, and shows the younger generation as strong and able to stand firm on their political course. The same year he published *The Bankrupt*, presenting the effects of economic crisis on a family and its associates, and revealing the true nature of a personal relationship when its material conditions are altered.

Thus, in turning to issues of the different interests operating in contemporary society, Bjørnson contributed to a significant change of direction in the dramatic writing of his time. Although much can be said as to the melodramatic character of the plots of these two plays, they no doubt did promote a closer contact between the theatre and the intellectual concerns of the audience. One may assume that Ibsen's development as a writer of contemporary drama, starting with *The Pillars of Society* in 1877, was influenced by Bjørnson's two 1875 plays in this respect.

In several of Bjørnson's plays the test of love is central to the development of the plot. In *Between the Battles*, *The Newly Married Couple*, and *The Editor*, a young girl is caught between her parents, who demand consideration and obedience, and the young man who loves her and whose attitudes point in a different direction. Not only the maturity and the love of the girl is being tested, but also the courage and the independence of the suitor. The conflict is solved through the triumph of love and a final reconciliation between the young couple and the parents.

Bjørnson is also the author of comedies, the most successful one being *Love and Geography*. In this play the satire is aimed against a selfish and tyrannical husband, and the wife, with the assistance of other women, is able to force him to change. Both in his dramatic work and in other writings Bjørnson was an incessant spokesman for the rights of women, and several of his female characters are strong and proud women facing weak and irresolute men. In his final comedy, *When the New Wine Blooms*, he explores with much humour a playful kind of relationship between modern young girls and middle-aged men, focusing on different views regarding marriage. Bjørnson's comedies frequently question traditional values, but always in a festive mood: the family crisis is never devastating, the final scene is invariably a heartfelt reconciliation, and the value of the family as an institution is not fundamentally questioned.

Bjørnson wrote several dramas where the action is a tragic. It is characteristic of his idea of the theatre, however, that tragedy does not exclude the use of comic elements. The best example of this is to be found in *Beyond Our Power, Part One*, arguably his best play. Dealing with the theme of religious excess, in the form of an attempt at healing by prayer, the play exposes the bewilderment among the clergy as to what policy the church should adopt regarding the possibility of miracles in modern times. This is done with much irony, and yet the mood of the concluding scene, focusing on the possible healing power of the protagonist, is definitely tragic.

In some of his plays he introduced easily recognizable public figures as models for important roles, and since the attitude of the playwright, in some cases, was imbued with a mixture of moral and political criticism, the result would invariably be the object of heated public debate. This was the case in particular with *The Editor*, where Christian Friele, who edited *Morgenbladet*, the leading conservative newspaper of the age, was the target of Bjørnson's scorn. The later and more successful drama, *Paul Lange and Tora Parsberg*, is based on the events leading up to the suicide of Ole Richter shortly after his resignation as Norwegian Prime Minister in Stockholm in 1888. Published ten years after the tragic incident, the play caused considerable resentment in some circles.

In his lifetime Bjørnson was a frequently disputed, but on the whole popular, writer. The afterlife of his dramatic work has not been anything like that of his contemporary, Ibsen. Still, a number of his plays have been produced in recent times by Norwegian theatres, although the saga plays are not among them—they definitely belong to the era of national Romanticism. Among the comedies, *Love and Geography* and *When the New Wine Blooms* have proved most resilient, while *Beyond Our Power, Part One* and *Paul Lange and Tora Parsberg* are the two tragedies most likely to appear on the contemporary stage. Since Bjørnson participated intensely in the intellectual debate of his age, both on and off stage, this may explain why so many of his plays appear to have lost their appeal for later audiences, and why he is remembered more as a prose-writer and poet than a dramatist.

—Asbjørn Aarseth

See also *Volume 1* entry on *Beyond Human Power*.

BLOK, Alexander Alexandrovich. Born in St. Petersburg, Russia, 28 November 1880. Educated at Vvedensky School,

St. Petersburg, 1891–98; entered St. Petersburg University, studying law, 1898–1901, but transferred to the Faculty of History and Philology, 1901–06; graduated 1906. Married Lyubov Dmitrievna Mendeleyeva, 1903. First poetry published in the Symbolist periodical *Novyi put'*, 1903; writer after 1906; travelled abroad, notably to Italy and Poland, 1909; kept records at the front during World War I, 1916–17; edited reports for the provisional government's Extraordinary Investigating Commission, 1917; following October Revolution, worked on various cultural commitees; member of the theatre department of the People's Commissariat for Education (and Chairman of Repertory section), 1918–19, and involved with Gorky's *Vsemirnaya Literatura* [World Literature] publishing house, 1918–21; helped administer the Free Philosophical Association; chairman of the Directorate of the Bolshoi Theatre, 1919–21; elected chairman of the All-Russian Union of Poets (Petrograd Section), 1920. Died in Petrograd 7 August 1921.

Works

Collections

Lyricheskiye dramy [Lyric Dramas].   1908.
Sobranie stikhotvoreny i teatr [Collected Poems and Plays].   1916.
Sobranie sochineny [Collected Works] (12 vols.)   1932–36.
Sobranie sochineny [Collected Works] (8 vols.)   1960–63.
Sobranie sochineny [Collected Works] (6 vols.).   1971; new edition, 1980—
Teatr edited by P.P. Gromova

Stage Works

Balaganchik (produced Vera Kommissarzhevskaya's Theatre, St. Petersburg, 1906).   In anthology [Torches], 1906; also in *Lyricheskiye dramy*, 1908; translated as *The Puppet Show*, in *Slavonic Review*, 28, 1949–50 and in *The Russian Symbolist Theatre*, edited by Michael Green, 1986.
Korol na ploshchadi [The King in the Square].   1907.
Olyubvi, poezy i gosudarstvennoy sluzhbe [About Love, Poetry, and the Civil Service].   1907.
Pesnya sudby [The Song of Fate].   1907; revised edition, 1919
Neznakomka [The Unknown Woman] (produced by Meyerhold's Studio at the Tenishev Academy, St. Petersburg, 1914).   In *Lyricheskiye dramy*, 1908.
Primater [The Ancestress], from a play by Grillparzer (produced Kommissarzhevskaya's Theatre, St. Petersburg, 1908).
Roza i krest (produced People's Theatre of Kostromsky, Kostroma, 1921).   1913; translated as *The Rose and the Cross*, in *The Russian Symbolist Theatre*, edited by Michael Green, 1986.
Ramzes [Ramses].   1921(?)

Verse

Stikhi o prekrasnoy dame [Verses About the Most Beautiful Lady].   1904.
Nechayannaya radost' [Unexpected Joy].   1906.
Snezhnaya maska [The Snow Mask].   1907.
Zemlya v snegu [The Earth in Snow].   1908.
Nochnye chasy [The Night-Watches].   1911.
Sobranie stikhotvoreny [Collected Poems] (3 vols.).   1911–12.
Skazki: Stikhi dlya detey [Fairy Tales: Poems for Children].   1913.

Krugly god: stikhotvoreniya dlya detey [All the Year Round: Poems for Children]. 1913.
Stikhi o Rossy [Poems About Russia]. 1915.
Soloviny sad [The Nightingale Garden]. 1918.
Dvenadtsat; Skify [The Twelve; The Scythians]. 1918; *Dvenadtsat* translated as *The Twelve*, in *"The Twelve" and Other Poems*, 1970 and 1971.
Yamby: Sovremennye stikhi (1907–1914) [Iambs: Contemporary Poems]. 1919.
Za grayu proshlykh dney [Beyond the Bounds of Days Gone By]. 1920.
Sedoye utro [The Grey Morning]. 1920.
Otrochesckye stikhi; Avtbiografiia [Adolescent Poems; Autobiography]. 1923.
"The Twelve" and Other Poems, translated by J. Stallworthy and P. France. 1970.
"The Twelve" and Other Poems, translated by A. Mollo, 1971.
Selected Poems, translated by Avril Peyman. 1972.
Selected Poems, translated by Alex Miller. 1981.

Memoirs and Letters

Otrochesckye stikhi; Avtbiografiya [Adolescent Poems; Autobiography]. 1923.

Other

Molny iskusstva [Lightning Flashes of Art] (essays). 1909?
Rossiya i intelligentsiya [Russia and the Intelligentsia] (essays). 1918; revised edition, 1919; some essays translated in *The Spirit of Music*, 1946.
Katilina. 1919.
The Journey to Italy, translated by Lucy E. Vogel. 1973.
An Anthology of Essays and Memoirs, edited by Lucy E. Vogel. 1982.

Editor, *Poslednie dni starogo rezhima* [The Last Days of the Old Regime]. 1919.

*

Criticism

Books:
Avril Pyman, *The Life of Aleksandr Blok* (2 vols.), Oxford, 1979–80.
Konstantin Mochulsky, *Aleksandr Blok*, Detroit, Illinois, 1983.

Articles:
Ewa M. Thomson, "The Development of Aleksandr Blok as Dramatist", in *Slavic and East European Journal*, 14, 1970.
Rochelle H. Stone, "Aleksandr Blok and Boleslaw Lesmian as Proponents and Playwrights of the New, Symbolist Drama: A Comparison", in *Theatre Journal*, 36, 1984.
Lucy Vogel, "Dichotomies in Blok's Drama *The King on the Square*", in *Slavic and East European Journal*, 31, 1987.

* * *

The symbolist movement's most interesting dramas were probably those of Alexander Blok, who was already established as an important poet when he wrote his first plays in 1906. He had always shown an interest in the theatre, and in his adolescence participated in amateur theatricals at various levels. His wife, Lyubov Dmitrievna, became an actress (her involvement with various companies, most notably Meyerhold's, caused Blok enormous anguish and jealousy). And after the Russian revolution he was an active member of the Theatrical Department of Narkompros, chairing the Repertory Section of this body, and an elected member of the presidium of the Commission for the Reorganization of Theatres and Public Performances.

His first play was the delightful, yet sombre, *Balaganchik* (*The Puppet Show*), which was staged by Vsevolod Meyerhold in an unforgettable production in 1906, and revived, with designs by Yuri Bondi, to accompany the 1914 premiere of *Neznakomka* (The Unknown Woman), also written in 1906, but banned until then. A third play written that year, *Korol na ploschadi* (The King in the Square),was never staged, though Fyodor Kommissarzhevsky was going to produce it in Petrograd in 1918, with designs by Yury Annenkov, and Meyerhold intended to present it at the Theatre of the Revolution in Moscow in 1923.

These plays deal with the tragedy of unattainable love, love which can be imagined but never achieved. *The Puppet Show* centres on the love triangle of Harlequin, Columbine, and Pierrot, among mystics and story-land lovers. It mixes symbolism and realism in unexpected and disconcerting ways through intrinsically theatrical devices, culminating in a remarkable finale when Pierrot's sad little song is interrupted by the scenery, props, and furniture being whisked off into the flies. Blok's curious mixture of romanticism, symbolism, cynicism, and black humour is established in this play, as is his lyric-dramatic form, unmatched by any writer except perhaps W.B. Yeats. Its originality lies in the creation of mood rather than the more usual dramatic conflict, so that the spectator is borne along on poetic rather than dramatic rhythms. Yet it is highly theatrical, and acknowledges the artificial conventions of the drama at every turn.

"The King in the Square" is considerably less successful as drama than *The Puppet Show*, since the level of intrinsic theatricality brought by the *commedia* characters is lacking. Nevertheless, it is typical of Blok in its conception and development. The King is a vast statue who dominates the square where the action is set and whose power is the predominant symbol of the play. Through a crowd of people wanders the Poet (a version of Pierrot, perhaps), yearning for the inexpressible. He is contrasted to the Clown of Common Sense and the Architect (in some respects equivalent to Blok's earlier Harlequin) who counsels him to learn from the workers. But he is in love with the Architect's daughter (a sort of Columbine), and he follows her up the steps towards the King, whom they destroy and by whom they are destroyed. The Poet's imagination and the eternal beauty of woman nullify and are nullified by the sterile power of the King. All that is left besides odd, but arresting, figure of the Clown of Common Sense, is the mundane organizer, the Architect, and the murmuring mob of working people. Beauty and imagination are incompatible with everyday life, the play implies.

In "The Unknown Woman", the focus has narrowed to the Poet figure and the Eternal Female. The poet here has three "Visions" which concern his ideal Beautiful Lady. In the first, she is a fantasy dreamed of in a tavern where the poet drinks; in the second, she is Maria, a falling star noted by an Astronomer on a bridge, but only valued by the poet; when she arrives at a society soiree in the third vision, again it is the poet who is aware of her reality, and soon she has melted away. "Where is Mary? Where is Mary?", cries the hostess, bustling the guests in for supper. But there is no-one by the window where she stood, through which now "a bright star shines". As a lyric drama of poetic loss, "The Unknown Woman" is unexpectedly powerful, as was shown when it was staged with sophisticated, almost Chinese, artistry by Meyerhold, with "proscenium servants", phantom twinkling lights on bamboo poles, and broad grotesquerie.

Blok's later plays are less successful. *Pesnya sudby* (The Song of Fate), unstaged in the author's lifetime, concerns another poet, Herman, whose cruel mistress, Faina, teaches him the song of Fate, which turns out to be the fate of Mother Russia. *The Rose and the Cross*, which Blok tried to persuade Stanislavsky or Nemirovich-Danchenko to stage at the Moscow Art Theatre, but which received its first performance, directed by Yuri Bondi, in Kostroma in 1921, was originally conceived as a ballet, then an opera, and only finally as a play. In it, the young and feather-brained Izora seeks love from exotic sources and fails to notice it in the self-sacrificing and noble retainer, Bertrand. Blok also wrote a dialogue *Olyubvi, poezy i gosudarstrennoy slu zhbe* (About Love, Poetry and the Civil Service) and he left unfinished *Ramses*, described as "Scenes from History" (1919). To these may be added his versions of the medieval *Miracle of Theophilus*, written for Nikolai Evreinov's "Ancient Theatre" season in 1908 and Grillparzer's *The Ancestress* for Vera Kommissarzhevskaya's theatre (1908).

Most of these plays, including *The Rose and the Cross* which is still produced occasionally in the former USSR, remain rather lifeless on stage, lacking the delicacy and the theatrical legerdemain which Blok achieved in *The Puppet Show* and "The Unknown Woman". For these two plays, in which he combines a rich feeling for what is theatrical with his essential poetic elegance, Blok remains the most interesting and innovative symbolist dramatist.

—Robert Leach

See also *Volume 1* entry on *The Puppet Show*.

BODEL, Jean. Born in late 12th century (c.1165?). Cleric to the civic magistrates, Arras, and member of the city guild, the "Confrérie des jongleurs et des bourgeois d'Arras"; contracted leprosy, preventing him from joining the 4th Crusade, and entered a lazar house, 1202. Died in Arras, c.1210.

Works

Stage Works

Le Jeu de Saint Nicolas (produced in Arras, c.1200). As *Li Jus de Saint Nicolai*, in *Misteriya et Miracula ad scenam ordinata*, edited by La Bouderie and L.J. N. Monmerqué, 1834; translated as *Le Jeu de Saint Nicolas*, in *Medieval French Plays*, translated by Richard Axton and John Stevens, 1971; as *The Play of Saint Nicolas*, in *Five Comedies of Medieval France*, translated by Oscar Mandel, 1982.

Other

Saxonlied [*Chanson des Saisnes*] (2 vols.), edited by E. Stengel and F. Menzel. 1906–09; French edition, as *Chanson des Saisnes*, edited by Annette Brasseur, 1991.

Fabliaux, edited by P. Nardin.   1965.
Les Congés d'Arras (includes works by others), edited by P. Ruelle.   1965.

Criticism

Books:
Grace Frank, *The Medieval French Drama*, Oxford, 1954.
Patrick Vincent, *The "Jeu de Saint-Nicolas" of Jean Bodel of Arras: A Literary Analysis*, Baltimore, Maryland, 1954.
Charles Foulon, *L'Oeuvre de Jehan Bodel*, Paris, 1958.
T.B.W. Reid, "On the Text of the *Jeu de Saint Nicolas*", in *Studies in Medieval French Presented to Alfred Ewert*, Oxford, 1961.
Richard Axton, *European Drama of the Early Middle Ages*, London, 1974.
Claude Aubailly, *Le Théâtre médiéval profane et comique*, Paris, 1975.
Henri Rey-Flaud, *Pour Une Dramaturgie du Moyen Age*, Paris, 1980.
Joseph Dane, *Res/Verba: A Study in Medieval French Drama*, Leiden, 1985.

Articles:
F.W. Marshall, "The Rhyme Schemes of the *Jeu de Saint Nicolas* as an Indication of Staging", in *Australian Journal of French Studies*, 1, 1964.
F.W. Marshall, "The Staging of the *Jeu de Saint Nicolas*: An Analysis of Movement", in *Australian Journal of French Studies*, 2, 1965.
P.R. Vincent, "Jean Bodel and the Fleury Play-Book", in *Symposium*, 20, 1966.
Tony Hunt, "The Authenticity of the Prologue of Bodel's *Jeu de Saint Nicolas*", in *Romania*, 97, 1976.
Joseph Dane, "Mythic Parody in Jean Bodel's *Jeu de Saint Nicolas*", in *Romance Notes*, 22, 1981.

* * *

The cleric Jean Bodel, author of lyric poems (*pastourelles* and *congés*) and of the epic *Chanson des Saisnes*, is best known for his innovatory and influential play *Le Jeu de Saint Nicolas*, which was written and performed around 1200 (perhaps on St Nicholas' Eve, December 5th) in the northern-French town of Arras. It represents the earliest surviving French miracle play, a genre comprising dramatic re-enactments of saints' lives. Nicholas, the patron saint of children, sailors and scholars, was especially popular in the Middle Ages and was the subject of two short plays which predate Bodel's: a Latin miracle found in the Fleury manuscript and the *Ludus super iconia Sancti Nicholai*, written by Hilarius in a mixture of Latin and Old French. Both plays concentrate on the episode in the Saint's life when his ability to protect treasure is put to the test by an unbeliever, who is eventually converted to Christianity. Although Hilarius's play already contains some slapstick humour, with the heathen beating the statue of Saint Nicholas when it at first fails to guard the treasure, it is Bodel's play which combines, in a sophisticated way, serious Christian truths with realistic comic scenes of Arras low life, thus invalidating the simplistic distinction made by critics between the sacred and the profane in medieval theatre.

Although the authenticity of the prologue spoken by a preacher at the beginning of the play has been questioned, it seems that the inconsistencies between it and the play proper are deliberate, for the preacher reminds the audience of the legend as related in the narratives of saints' lives and even alerts us to modifications made by Bodel in his dramatic reworking of the material. One such modification is that the traditional aggressors, the pagans, are presented in the first scene lamenting their defeat at the hands of Christian aggressors (a possible reflection of Bodel's hope that in the 4th Crusade the Christians would triumph in the Holy Land). Another is that the pagan king's messenger, Auberon, while journeying to summon help from the emirs, stops for a drink in a tavern, which is clearly located in Arras and where the customers drink wine from Auxerre, gamble, and cheat. We are then transported back to the Holy Land, where the combined pagan forces defeat the heroic Christians, whose reward, promised by an angel, is a seat in paradise. There is, however, one survivor, and his faith in Saint Nicholas and his statue are soon put to the test. The news that the king is leaving his treasure unguarded for the night reaches the tavern, where three thieves (one of whom was there when Auberon stopped earlier) assemble to drink and gamble before stealing the treasure. Needless to say, on their return God makes them sleepy, and Saint Nicholas, appearing in a dream, frightens them into returning the treasure. The pagan king, having threatened to kill the Christians when the treasure disappeared, is so impressed when it reappears that he destroys the image of his own god, Tervagan, and converts to Christianity, followed by all of his men save one emir, whose reluctance to abandon his faith is reminiscent of Christian steadfastness in some Old French epics.

Bodel's play is remarkable for its juxtaposition of literary scenes reminiscent of the epic or hagiography, with scenes reflecting observed reality, for switches in location between the geographically vague foreign lands and the immediately recognisable Arras tavern, for a use of time which is elastic when dealing with the holy wars but restricted to a mere 24 hours when depicting the thieves' activities, for his concentration on the viewpoint of the villains (pagans and thieves) and for the richness of his language and metre.

The play is not divided formally into scenes (an anachronistic concept), nor would there have been set-changes. The *Jeu* would probably have been performed in the round, with mansions (areas of the theatre representing specific locations) placed around the circle from which the amateur actors (probably male clerics) would step into the space centre-stage to utter their lines. It has been suggested that for the *Jeu* there would have been the following mansions: 1. the pagan palace (perhaps raised on scaffolding with the prison underneath and the statue of Tervagan in a prominent position); 2. the tavern; 3. Hell (Tervagan's statue would have been thrown in this direction); 4. Paradise (housing the statue of St Nicholas and the Christians who die in battle). Thus, through the use of simultaneous decor the audience would have been aware of the permanent conflict between good and evil, while the actors, who remained visible throughout the performance, would have provided a visual representation of man's choice between damnation and salvation. Changes in action and location or theme are marked by a change in versification, which ranges from the octosyllabic to Alexandrine line, organised in rhyming couplets or stanzas of four, six, or eight lines. Indeed, amongst Bodel's many innovations is the breaking of the couplet to provide a cue for the next speaker.

Li Jus de Saint Nicholai (its title in MS Paris BN fonds fr. 25566, a collection of Picard works copied around 1300) has survived in only one manuscript and may have been performed only once during Bodel's lifetime (though there is evidence that it was performed at Saint Omer on 6 December 1417). This does not, however, indicate a lack of popularity, for medieval vernacular plays were rarely written down or performed more than once. Besides, the *Jeu*'s influence on later playwrights is clear, for both the anonymous *Courtois d'Arras* and Adam de la Halle's *Jeu de la feuillée* have tavern scenes reminiscent of Bodel's play. Its combination of epic, saint's life, and raucous tavern behaviour, and its sudden changes in register and location, may seem incongruous to a modern audience, but medieval spectators seem to have revelled in such contrasts, while appreciating the play's unifying theme—chance. The message which emerges from the *Jeu* is that in the game of life we are all gamblers, but ultimately only those who place their bets on God and His saints will win.

—Karen Pratt

BOKER, George Henry. Born in Philadelphia, Pennsylvania, USA, 6 October 1823. Educated at the College of New Jersey, now Princeton University (one of the founders of the *Nassau Monthly*, 1842), graduated 1842; also studied law. Married Julia Mandeville Riggs in 1844; one son. Writer from 1845; playwright from 1848; first play, *Calaynos*, produced (without author's knowledge) in London, 1849; founding member, 1862, Secretary, 1862–71, and President, 1879, Union Club, later Union League, Philadelphia; US Ambassador to Turkey, 1871–75, and to Russia, 1875–78; President, Philadelphia Club, 1878; President, Fairmount Park Commission, Philadelphia, 1886–90. Died 2 January 1890.

Works

Collections

Plays and Poems (2 vols.).   1856.
"*Glaucus*" *and Other Plays* (includes *The World a Mask; The Bankrupt*), edited by Sculley Bradley.   1940.

Stage Works

Calaynos (produced Sadler's Wells Theatre, London, 1849). 1848.
Anne Boleyn (produced Walnut Street Theatre, Philadelphia, 1850).   1850.
The Betrothal (produced Walnut Street Theatre, Philadelphia, 1850).   In *Plays and Poems*, 1856.
The World a Mask (produced Walnut Street Theatre, Philadelphia, 1851).   1856.
The Widow's Marriage (produced 1852). In *Plays and Poems*, 1856.
Leonor de Guzman (produced Walnut Street Theatre, Philadelphia, 1853).   In *Plays and Poems*, 1856.
Francesca da Rimini (produced Broadway Theatre, New York, 1855).   In *Plays and Poems*, 1856.
The Bankrupt (produced Broadway Theatre, New York, 1855).   In "*Glaucus*" *and Other Plays*, 1940.
Königsmark.   With "*The Legend of the Hounds*" *and Other Poems*, 1869.
Nydia, edited by Sculley Bradley.   1929; revised version, as *Glaucus*, in "*Glaucus*" *and Other Plays*, 1940.

Verse

"The Lesson of Life" and Other Poems. 1848.
"The Podesta's Daughter" and Other Miscellaneous Poems.
   1852.
Poems of the War. 1864.
Our Heroic Themes. 1865.
Königsmark; "The Legend of the Hounds" and Other Poems.
   1869.
The Book of the Dead: Poems. 1882.
Sonnets: A Sequence of Profane Love, edited by Sculley
   Bradley. 1929.

*

Criticism

Books:
Sculley Bradley, *George Henry Boker: Poet and Patriot*,
   Philadelphia, 1927.
Oliver H. Evans, *George Henry Boker*, Boston, 1984.
Arthur Hobson Quinn, *A History of the American Drama
   from the Beginning to the Civil War* (second edition), New
   York, 1943.

Articles:
Joseph W. Krutch, "George Henry Boker: A Little Known
   American Dramatist", in *Sewanee Review*, 25, 1917.
Arthur Hobson Quinn, "The Dramas of George Henry
   Boker", in *Publications of the Modern Language Associa-
   tion* [*PMLA*], 32, 1917.
Kent G. Gallagher, "The Tragedies of George Henry Boker:
   The Measure of American Romantic Drama", in *Emerson
   Society Quarterly*, 20, 1974.

*   *   *

In *The Spirit of the Times* for 6 December 1856, there appeared a notice drawing attention to the recently published two-volume *Plays and Poems* by George Henry Boker. The plays were described as being "decidedly good, and those who admire this style of composition will be well pleased". By this time, however, Boker felt that his career as a playwright was a failure. He had been unable to satisfy theatre audiences to the degree he wished, and in his mind he had never been awarded the critical praise that his plays deserved. Even to this day, among historians of American drama, he is generally recognized for a single play: *Francesca da Rimini*.

A central problem for Boker was his failure to understand his relationship with his contemporary society. Associated with a group of writers of the "genteel tradition" who never quite justified their existence in the rapidly changing American world, Boker took his own advice as a writer to "get out of your age as far as you can". For a practising dramatist, however, this was a serious error. Largely ignorant of the demands of contemporary theatre, Boker was doomed to fail, although records indicate that he had greater success in the theatre in terms of fame and money than any of the many mid-century American writers who followed the romantic traditions of poetic drama.

From 1848 through 1857 Boker wrote nine plays, six of which were produced. *Calaynos*, first performed in London without his knowledge, eventually played in several American cities. As he would in the future, Boker dramatized the betrayal of innocence in this play and the corresponding

corruption of society. He also revealed his interest in character over other elements in drama, although he succeeded in this play only with his villain. In his second play, *Anne Boleyn*, he again treated the theme of the individual in conflict with society, but he explained too much in long soliloquies and expository dialogue and dramatized too little. The play was never produced.

Not realizing the success that he demanded for his art, Boker compromised his previous standards, abandoned his own advice, and attempted to write comedy. He was not, however, a comic writer. Neither in his approach to life nor in his approach to art did he show an appreciation of the comic spirit. It is an irony of the theatre of this period that the inadequacies of his artistry, revealed in the imitative and shallow quality of these plays, brought him some success on the stage.

The Betrothal is set in Renaissance Italy where an impoverished aristocrat agrees to marry his daughter to a physically and morally deformed, but wealthy, merchant rather than the handsome young man of her choice. With its happy ending, reviewers at the Broadway Theatre in New York found it a "distinguished" success. In *The World a Mask* Boker never extricated himself from a seriously tangled plot and showed clearly that his understanding of comedy apparently did not extend beyond the cleverness of a witty response. Twice more Boker tried to write comedy: *The Widow's Marriage* and *The Bankrupt*. Once, in *The Bankrupt*, he obviously tried to cater to popular tastes with topical references, currently popular characters such as the businessman and the detective, plus a hero and a heroine whose fortunes he saved in the melodramatic fashion of the day. Although the play received good reviews at the Broadway Theatre in 1855, Boker, by this time, had decided that he did not want to be a playwright.

Prior to this decision, however, Boker had written the two plays that give him a place in the history of American drama: *Leonor de Guzman*, completed in the fall of 1852 and produced in Philadelphia in October, 1853, and *Francesca da Rimini*, which he wrote during a torrid three-week period in 1853. In both plays Boker returned to his theme involving the nature of society and the demands placed upon certain individuals within it. In *Leonor de Guzman*, as mistress to King Alfonso XII of Spain (whose death from the plague has just been announced) Leonor must outwit Alfonso's queen in order to legitimize her eldest son and gain for him a strong political position. But the queen also has rights which Leonor de Guzman recognizes, and it is this feeling of ambiguity within the heroine, as well as the complexity of the entire situation, that intrigued Boker and in which his concept of tragedy lies.

The same is true of *Francesca da Rimini*, which Boker correctly considered his best work. It has the spectacle and a theatrical dimension that *Leonor de Guzman* lacked. It also has four well-defined characters. It tells the story of Francesca, who willingly accepts her role in an arranged marriage only to be deceived by the arrival of the bridegroom's handsome brother and who, in her subsequent life of deceit, finds herself doomed by circumstances worsened by the activity of a malicious villain. It was an impassioned story, first told by Dante, and well dramatized by Boker, whose major fault was the creation of four excellent characters for a theatre then controlled by the single touring star performer.

Boker received some satisfaction when acting techniques changed and Lawrence Barrett revived *Francesca da Rimini* in 1882 with considerable success (on 24 January 1885 the *New York Tribune* announced its 100th New York performance). Barrett made a great deal of money and Boker a little—enough to influence him to write two more plays: *Nydia* and *Glaucus* (a rewriting of *Nydia*). But neither play was performed, and Boker's interest in further playwriting was short-lived. Had the theatre of the 1850's been different, Boker might have enjoyed a greater reputation, and he is still remembered mainly for a single exceptional play.

—Walter J. Meserve

See also *Volume 1* entry on *Francesca da Rimini*

———

BOLT, Robert (Oxton). Born in Sale, Manchester, England, 15 August 1924. Educated at Manchester Grammar School, to 1940; Manchester University, 1943, 1946–49, BA (honours) in history 1949; Exeter University, 1949–50, teaching diploma 1950. Served in the Royal Air Force, 1943–44; in the Royal West African Frontier Force, 1944–46; Lieutenant. Married 1) Celia Ann Roberts in 1949 (marriage dissolved 1967), one son and two daughters; 2) the actress Sarah Miles in 1967 (divorced 1976), one son; 3) Ann, Lady Queensberry in 1980 (divorced 1985); 4) remarried Sarah Miles, 1988. Office boy, Sun Life Assurance Company, Manchester, 1942; schoolmaster, Bishopsteignton, Devon, 1950–51, and Millfield School, Street, Somerset, 1952–58; first play, *A Man for All Seasons*, produced 1960; concentrated on writing screenplays in the 1980's. Recipient: New York Drama Critics Circle Award, 1962, and a number of awards for screenplays, including Oscars, 1966 and 1967, and Golden Globe awards, 1967 and 1987. CBE (Commander, Order of the British Empire), 1972.

Works

Stage Works

A Man for All Seasons, from the radio play (produced Globe Theatre, London, 1960). 1960.
The Last of the Wine, from the radio play (produced London, 1956).
The Critic and the Heart (produced Playhouse, Oxford, 1957).
Flowering Cherry (produced Haymarket Theatre, London, 1957). 1958.
The Tiger and the Horse (produced Queen's Theatre, London, 1960). 1961.
Gentle Jack (produced Queen's Theatre, London, 1963). 1965.
The Thwarting of Baron Bolligrew (produced Aldwych Theatre, London, 1965). 1966.
Brother and Sister (produced Brighton, 1967; revised version produced Bristol, 1968).

Vivat! Vivat Regina! (produced Festival Theatre, Chichester, 1970). 1971.
State of Revolution (produced National Theatre, London, 1977). 1977.

Screenplays

Lawrence of Arabia, 1962; *Doctor Zhivago*, 1965 (published 1966); *A Man for All Seasons*, 1966; *Ryan's Daughter*, 1970; *Lady Caroline Lamb*, 1973; *The Bounty*, 1984; *The Mission*, 1986; *Thumbs Up: The James Brady Story*, 1991.

Radio Plays

The Master, 1953; *Fifty Pigs*, 1953; *Ladies and Gentlemen*, 1954; *A Man for All Seasons*, 1954; *Mr. Sampson's Sundays*, 1955; *The Last of the Wine*, 1955; *The Window*, 1958; *The Drunken Sailor*, 1958; *The Banana Tree*, 1961.

*

Criticism

Books:
Ronald Hayman, *Robert Bolt*, London, 1969.

* * *

Robert Bolt's works have enjoyed some very considerable successes, especially with those "middle-brow" audiences that alone in Britain can sustain the commercial theatre for any length of time. But Bolt has never been content simply to repeat a formula which has found favour. Something has always driven him on to further developments, and though these have not always worked out well for him, the very endeavour is something which commands respect.

With a run of 435 London performances, *Flowering Cherry*, after a number of radio plays and some stage adaptations of them, seemed to be a most promising start for Bolt. The manner is naturalistic, with a certain underpinning through symbolism, and, with its sharply observed characters, deft dialogue, and economy of presentation, the play stands within the tradition of Terence Rattigan's well-wrought drama. The plot revolves around an ageing insurance salesman who dreams of an idyllic future as a fruit farmer in Somerset, while in reality holding the horrors of his humdrum existence at bay only by heavy drinking. The remainder of the cast—his long-suffering wife, his children, three visitors to the house—are convincing as human beings, a little quirky, tending to quarrel, and representative of other ways of coping with the problems of life in circumstances that are none too prepossessing. In a play which establishes itself as a persuasive representation of English life in the 1950's, problems do, however, arise, as the tensions mount in the second act, and the conclusion is more melodramatic than powerful.

A similar criticism might be made of *The Tiger and the Horse*, a play offering fine acting roles in its depiction of the tensions that run wild in the eminently civilised situation of an Oxbridge college when the Master sees the opportunity of becoming Vice-Chancellor of the University. There is something artificial, or at any rate overprivileged, about this setting. The generation gap is a rather predictable secondary theme, and the use of an anti-nuclear petition as one of the major levers for the action is rather obvious too. Strong emotions reign at the end, but only at the cost of some violence to the tone of the play.

The stage play *A Man for All Seasons*, of which there were earlier versions for radio and television, and of which a fine film was made, gave Bolt his greatest triumph. It is an exploration of the attractive personality of Sir Thomas More, the witty, learned, and saintly chancellor to Henry VIII who forfeited everything, including his beloved family, rather than sully his Catholic conscience by expressing any approval of the King's divorce from Catherine of Aragon. Since More asserts that he should not be regarded as the King's enemy because he insists only on his right to remain silent on the "Great Matter", and then pleads that in English law silence means assent, the play is based on a quibble while pretending to examine a moral issue. But this is a point that seems to have worried few. Instead, audiences enjoyed the spectacle of the Tudor period on stage, the vivid characters expressing themselves in easily accessible English, and a human tragedy of the principled individual in conflict with the state. Bolt, moreover, forswears his naturalistic manner, opting instead for what he refers to as a "bastardised version" of Brecht. What this means, in this case, is a fast-moving action in settings which deliberately leave a lot to the imagination, and a character called the "Common Man" who acts, more or less, as a chorus to the drama. By these means Bolt economically presents an episode from history that is at least half-familiar to most of his audience, and the life and death of More provide him not only with a theme close to his own convictions, but the sort of story line moving from domestic scenes to a grand conclusion which he evidently feels to be the stuff of drama.

Vivat! Vivat Regina! is another chronicle play with swift dramatic action, though this time there is no direct counterpart of the "Common Man", which could be Bolt's response to earlier criticism of that character. The basis is the contrast between Queen Elizabeth and Mary Queen of Scots, with the latter, predictably, emerging as the moral victor from her defeat. The portrayal of the two queens as women of passion and frustration is gripping, but the historical scenes tend to become laborious.

In *State of Revolution* Bolt continues his experiment with historical drama, but sets the play not in 16th-century England, but in Russia in the days of the Bolshevik revolution. Lunacharsky, aptly enough, is the chorus figure, presenting the episodes as if in a lecture to a class of Young Communists. The play has Bolt's habitual virtues of careful research, imaginative reconstruction, and insightful characterisation, all presented with dialogue which is fast-moving, except in a few political speeches which are appropriately allowed to become expansive. But the human side of the drama is insufficiently brought out in a play whose historical framework is, besides, by no means so well-known to English-speaking audiences as is Tudor England. Since this play Bolt has devoted his considerable talent to the cinema, and the result has been some good films, but the loss to the stage is regrettable.

—Christopher Smith

See also *Volume 1* entry on *A Man For All Seasons*.

BOND, (Thomas) Edward. Born in London, 18 July 1934. Educated at Crouch End Secondary Modern School, 1944–49. Served in the British Army, 1953–55. Married Elisabeth Pablé in 1971. Member, English Stage Company Writers Group, Royal Court Theatre, London, from 1958; first-produced play, *The Pope's Wedding*, staged 1962; founding member, Theatre Writers' Group (now Theatre Writers' Union), 1975; Northern Arts literary fellow, universities of Newcastle upon Tyne and Durham, 1977–79; resident writer, University of Essex, Colchester, 1982; visiting professor, University of Palermo, Italy, 1983. Recipient: George Devine award, 1968; John Whiting award, 1968; Obie award, 1976. D.Litt: Yale University, New Haven, Connecticut, 1977.

Works

Collections

The Pope's Wedding (collection; includes the plays *The Pope's Wedding* and *Sharpeville Sequence*, and the stories "Mr. Dog" and "The King with Golden Eyes").   1971.
Plays 1 (includes revised versions of *Saved; Early Morning; The Pope's Wedding*).   1977.
Plays 2 (includes revised versions of *Lear; The Sea; Narrow Road to the Deep North; Black Mass; Passion*).   1978.
The Woman (includes the play *The Woman*, the stories "In Praise of Bad Times" and "Black Animal, We're Free", poems, and essays).   1979.
The Activists Papers; The Worlds (includes the play *The Worlds*, the stories "The Team" and "A Story", and poetry).   1980.
"Summer", With Fables and "Service": A Story, 1983.
The War Plays: A Trilogy (2 vols; includes *Red, Black and Ignorant; The Tin Can People; Great Peace*).   1985.
Plays 3 (includes *Bingo; The Fool; The Woman*).   1987.
Two Post-Modern Plays (includes *Jackets* (play); *The Company of Men* (play); *September*).   1990.
Plays 4 (includes *The Worlds; The Activists Papers; Restoration; Summer*).   1992.

Stage Works

The Pope's Wedding (produced Royal Court Theatre, London, 1962).   In *Plays and Players*, April 1969; in book form, in *The Pope's Wedding* (collection), 1971.
Saved (produced Royal Court Theatre, London, 1965).   In *Plays and Players*, January 1966; in book form, 1966.
A Chaste Maid in Cheapside, from the play by Middleton (produced Royal Court Theatre, London, 1966).
Three Sisters, from a play by Chekhov (produced Royal Court Theatre, London, 1967).   In programme for the 1967 production.
Narrow Road to the Deep North (produced Belgrade Theatre, Coventry, 1968).   1968.
Early Morning (produced Royal Court Theatre, 1968). 1968; revised version in *Plays, 1*, 1977.
Sketch in *The Enoch Show* (produced 1969).
Black Mass, part of *Sharpeville Sequence: A Scene, A Story, and Three Poems* (produced Lyceum Theatre, London, 1970).   In *Gambit*, vol.5 no.17, 1970; in book form in *The Pope's Wedding* (collection), 1971.
Passion (produced Alexandra Park, 1971).   In *Plays and Players*, June 1971; in book form, with *Bingo*, 1974.
Lear (produced Royal Court Theatre, London, 1971).   1972.
The Sea (produced Royal Court Theatre, London, 1973).   1973.
Bingo: Scenes of Money and Death (and Passion) (produced Northcott Theatre, Exeter, 1973).   1974.

Edward Bond (1981).

Spring Awakening, from a play by Wedekind (produced by the National Theatre, 1974).   1979.

The Fool: Scenes of Bread and Love (produced Royal Court Theatre, London, 1975).   With *We Come to the River*, 1976.

We Come to the River: Actions for Music, music by Hans Werner Henze (produced Royal Opera House, Covent Garden, London, 1976).   With *The Fool*, 1976.

The White Devil, from the play by Webster (produced Old Vic Theatre, London, 1976).

A-A-America: Grandma Faust, and The Swing (produced Almost Free Theatre, London, 1976).   With *Stone*, 1976; revised edition, 1981.

Stone (produced Institute of Contemporary Arts, London, 1976).   With *A-A-America*, 1976; revised edition, 1981.

The Woman: Scenes of War and Freedom (produced National Theatre, London, 1978).   1979 (includes stories).

The Bundle: Scenes of Right and Evil; or, New Narrow Road to the Deep North (produced The Warehouse, London, 1978).   1978.

Orpheus (ballet scenario; produced Würtembergisches Staatstheater, Stuttgart, 1979).

The Worlds (produced Playhouse, Newcastle, 1979).   With *The Activists Papers*, 1980.

Restoration: A Pastoral, music by Nick Bicât (produced Royal Court Theatre, London, 1981).   1981; revised version, with *The Cat*, 1982.

Summer: A European Play (produced National Theatre, London, 1982).   1982.

Derek (produced The Other Place, Stratford-upon-Avon,

1982).   With *Choruses from After the Assassinations*, 1983.

The Cat (opera libretto), music by Hans Werner Henze, from a work by Balzac (as *Die englische Katze*, produced Schloss Schwetzingen, Germany, 1983; as *The English Cat*, 1985).   With *Restoration*, 1982; as *The English Cat: A Story for Singers and Instrumentalists*, 1983.

After the Assassinations (produced University of Essex, Colchester, 1983).   Choruses published with *Derek*, 1983.

Red, Black and Ignorant (produced The Pit, Barbican Centre, London, 1984).   In *The War Plays*, 1985.

The Tin Can People (Midland Arts Centre, Birmingham, 1984).   In *The War Plays*, 1985.

The War Plays: A Trilogy (includes *Red, Black and Ignorant*; *The Tin Can People; Great Peace*; trilogy produced 1985).   2 vols., 1985.

Human Cannon (produced National Theatre, London, 1986).   1985.

Burns (for children; produced 1986).

Jackets 1 (produced Nuffield Studio Theatre, University of Lancaster).   In *Two Post-Modern Plays*, 1990.

Jackets 2 (produced Nuffield Studio Theatre, University of Lancaster, 1989).   In *Two Post-Modern Plays*, 1990.

In the Company of Men (produced Avignon, France, 1992).

Olly's Prison.   1993.

Screenplays

Blow-up, with Michelangelo Antonioni and Tonino Guerra, 1967; *Laughter in the Dark*, 1969; *Michael Kohlhaas*, with others, 1969; *The Lady of Monza* (English dialogue), 1970;

Walkabout, 1971; *Nicholas and Alexandra*, with James Goldman, 1971; *Fury*, with Antonio Calenda and Ugo Pirro, 1973.

Television Plays

Olly's Prison, 1993.

Verse

The Swing Poems. 1976.
Theatre Poems and Songs, edited by Malcolm Hay and Philip Roberts. 1978.
Poems 1978–1985. 1987.

*

Criticism

Books:

Richard Scharine, *The Plays of Edward Bond*, Lewisburg, Pennsylvania, 1976.
Simon Trussler, *Edward Bond*, London, 1976.
Tony Coult, *The Plays of Edward Bond: A Study*, London, 1977; revised edition, 1979.
Malcolm Hay and Philip Roberts, *Edward Bond: A Companion to the Plays* (includes bibliography), London, 1978.
Delia Donahue, *Edward Bond: A Study of His Plays*, Rome, 1979.
Malcolm Hay and Philip Roberts, *Bond: A Study of His Plays*, London, 1980.
David L. Hirst, *Edward Bond*, London, 1985 (Macmillan Modern Dramatists series).
Philip Roberts (ed.), *Bond on File*, London, 1985.
Lou Lappin, *The Art and Politics of Edward Bond*, New York, 1987.
Detlef Buhmann, *Edward Bond: Theater zwischen Psyche und Politik*, Frankfurt, 1988.

* * *

Edward Bond first came to public notice with *Saved* in 1965, and this play, together with his first, *The Pope's Wedding*, gives a good sense of where his roots lay as a writer. Both are powerfully dramatic pieces in which the emphasis on ordinary colloquial speech in a context of heightened naturalism proclaims a theatre more interested in the presentation of things as they are than as they might be, or as they can wittily be ordered in the model of most contemporary offerings. *Saved* attracted considerable controversy, not to mention the attentions of the police, and to this day attention has been concentrated absurdly on the single scene in which the baby is stoned to death in its pram, in a way that has made proper discussion of the play very difficult and has brought accusations of "violence" upon the author.

The controversial potential of the writer was increased by *Early Morning*, an unwieldly and technically awkward experiment in surrealism, in which all the sacred cows of Victorian nostalgia come under attack in a play whose action culminates in Heaven. It is not an easy play to come to terms with, but the most important theme in the play is one that recurs over and over in Bond's work: the relationship between past and present, and the tracing of the current social malaise back to its historical roots.

Bond found critical favour the same year with *New Narrow Road to the Deep North*, based on a Japanese story about a baby found abandoned next to a river. Its classic stripped-

down simplicity was in stark contrast to the excesses of *Early Morning*, and Bond was to return to the story with *The Bundle* of 1977, transferring the action from Japan in an unlocatable past to modern Asia, producing a more directly political consideration of the dilemmas offered by the story line. *The Bundle* was to be the first of a series of plays in which Bond attempted to give "answers" to the political questions asked by all his works, and it came after three quite remarkable plays (themselves preceded by the strange and frequently highly comic post-Chekhovian piece *The Sea*, about the symbolic rise of fascism in a small fishing-village before World War II) which dealt with what Bond has described as the burden of the past.

Bingo dealt with the last days of William Shakespeare, and his attempts to reconcile the bleak analysis of society made in *King Lear* with his organised retirement into the life of the rich and landed in Stratford: a tension that results in his suicide. *The Fool* uses the figure of the displaced poet John Clare as another way of linking the present with the past in terms of the long history of capitalistic exploitation, and continues the theme of the responsibility of the writer to take a political position. The third play, *The Woman*, was directed by Bond himself: a vast epic re-examination of Greek mythology, it properly utilised for the first time the potential of the Olivier stage at the British National Theatre. These plays, together with the massively conceived *Lear* of 1971, confirmed Bond's stature as a major international playwright—one who, indeed, probably has a higher reputation on the continent of Europe than in Britain where critics have continued to carp at the political commitment of his work.

Bond's work in the 1980's was more varied than in the 1970's, when his was clearly the most consistently exciting theatrical voice to be heard in Britain. In 1981 his *Restoration* was first produced at the Royal Court, the theatre which had done so much to aid his early efforts and where so much of his earlier work, including *Saved*, had been first performed. In this play Bond yoked his disgust at the 1979 assumption to power of the Thatcher administration with a savagely comic account of the politics of 18th-century England as partially mediated through the re-examined conventions and stereotypes of Restoration and post-Restoration comedy. *Summer* and *Derek* followed the next year, but it was not until 1985 and the post-nuclear holocaust *War Play* that anything of the power of the plays of the previous decade emerged.

Since then Bond has moved away from the major subsidised theatrical venues, working instead with students and touring companies. *Jackets*, a two-part piece that connects the politics of 18th-century Japan with an only slightly futuristic urban Europe in which the dispossessed fight the army on the streets, was first performed at Lancaster University, and the second part later toured around the English Midland's theatre-in-education circuit. Bond continues to enjoy a massive reputation abroad, but his work is increasingly rarely found either in the London theatre or in provincial repertory. This is much to be regretted for never has a British theatre largely devoid of content needed his work more. Currently then, Bond remains something of a paradox, a playwright with a world-wide reputation dealing with political debate on a global scale, but one with far less than the honour due him in his own country.

—John Bull

See also *Volume 1* entries on *Bingo*; *Lear*; *Saved*.

BORCHERT, Wolfgang. Born in Hamburg, Germany, 20 May 1921. Educated at the Hamburg Gymnasium, 1932–38; also trained as an actor, until 1940. Worked at a Hamburg bookstore, 1940; published some poems in newspapers; joined touring theatre company, performing in Lower Saxony; drafted into the German army, June 1941; sent to the Russian Front, November 1942; sustained a hand wound, and, suspected of inflicting it himself, imprisoned in Nuremburg, May 1942: acquitted of the charge, but sentenced to six-weeks' imprisonment for anti-war statements; returned to Russian Front; after suffering frostbite and jaundice, granted leave in Hamburg; appeared in cabaret performances in Hamburg, September 1943; imprisoned in Berlin, awaiting trial for satirizing Goebbels in the cabaret: sentenced to nine-months' imprisonment; returned to the Russian Front, September 1944; captured by Allies near Frankfurt, Spring 1945, but escaped, arriving in Hamburg, 10 May; bedridden, 1945–47, and concentrated on writing during this period; his only play, *Draussen vor der Tür*, broadcast by Nordwest-deutsche Rundfunk, February 1947; sent to Swiss hospital, September 1947. Died in Basle, 20 November 1947.

Works

Collections

Das Gesamtwerk. 1949.
"Draussen vor der Tür" und ausgewählte Erzählungen. 1956.
The Man Outside: The Prose Works of Wolfgang Borchert (translations). 1971.

Stage Works

Draussen vor der Tür (broadcast Nordwestdeutsche Rundfunk, 1947; produced Kammerspiele, Hamburg, 1947). 1947; translated as *The Man Outside*, 1952; as *The Outsider*, in *Postwar German Theatre*, translated by M. Benedikt, 1967.

Radio Plays

Draussen vor der Tür, 1947.

Fiction

An diesem Dienstag: Neunzehn Geschichten. 1947.
Die Hindeblume. 1947.
"Die Traurigen Geranien" und andere Geschichten aus dem Nachlass. 1962; translated by K. Hammett as *"The Sad Geraniums" and Other Stories.* 1973.

Verse

Laterne, Nacht und Sterne. 1946.

*

Bibliographies

Claus B. Schröder, *Wolfgang Borchert: Bibliografie*, Hamburg, 1985.

Criticism

Books:
Anna Maria Darboven, *Wolfgang Borchert: Der Rufer in einer Zeit der Not*, 1957.
P. Rühmkopf, *Wolfgang Borchert in Selbstzeugnissen und Bilddokumenten*, Reinbek bei Hamburg, 1962.
K. Migner, *Interpretationen zu Wolfgang Borchert*, Munich, 1966.
M. Schmidt, *Wolfgang Borchert: Analysen und Aspekte*, Halle, 1970.
K.J. Fickert, *Signs and Portents: Myth in the Work of Wolfgang Borchert*, 1980.
Bernd Balzer, *Wolfgang Borchert: "Draussen vor der Tür"*, Frankfurt, 1983.
Rudolf Wolff (ed.), *Wolfgang Borchert: Werk und Wirkung*, Bonn, 1984.
Gordon J.A. Burgess and others, *Wolfgang Borchert*, Hamburg, 1985 (contains bibliography).

Articles:
A. Klarmann, "Wolfgang Borchert: The Lost Voice of a New Germany", in *Germanic Review*, 27, 1952.
Joseph Mileck, "Wolfgang Borchert: *Draussen vor der Tür*: A Young Poet's Struggle With Guilt and Despair", in *Monatshefte für den deutschen Unterricht, Sprache, und Literatur*, 1959.
A.L. Wilson, "The Drowning Man: *Draussen vor der Tür*", in *Texas Studies in Literature and Language*, 10, 1968–69.
Donald F. Nelson, "To Live or Not to Live: Notes on Archetypes and the Absurd in Borchert's *Draussen vor der Tür*", in *German Quarterly*, 48, 1975.
Wulf Koepke, "German Writers After 1945: Wolfgang Borchert", in *German Studies Review*, 2, 1979.
J.H. Reid, "*Draussen vor der Tür* in Context", in *Modern Languages*, 61, 1980.

*   *   *

Wolfgang Borchert began writing poetry at the age of 15, very much under the influence of G. Trakl and R.M. Rilke—for a time he even called himself Wolff Maria Borchert in honour of Rilke. However, these poems were typical products of youthful exuberance, and Borchert later destroyed most of them. His first prose work, a sketch called *Die Blume* (The Flower), resulted from his 1942 incarceration in the prison of Nuremberg. But not until he returned to Germany in 1945, and after his illness prevented him from pursuing a career as an actor and director, did Borchert take up writing again. The common theme of his *oeuvre* is the War and its devastating effect on the simple soldier who was forced to fight it, and on its innocent victims. Borchert's pacifist aim is most clearly displayed in his last prose work *Dann gibt es nur eins!* (There's only One Thing.), where he challenges the professions to disobey any order to prepare for another war; the ensuing vision of what would happen if people did not reject war is the most apocalyptic of German anti-war literature, comparable to that of G. Kaiser's *Gas II*.

In the last two years of his life Borchert produced almost forty short stories, a number of poems, a sketch for a novel, and his only drama, *Draussen vor der Tür*. This play, written in a few days in the fall of 1946, was first produced as a radio play on 13 February 1947. The theatre premiere took place at the Hamburg Kammerspiele on 21 November 1947, and a film adaptation was made in 1947 by Wolfgang Liebeneiner; the play immediately entered the repertoire of theatres all over Germany.

Borchert had subtitled *Draussen vor der Tür* "a play no theatre will produce and no public will want to see". The play's contemporary success was based on the fact that the public found it easy to identify with the figure of Beckmann, "one of many" who returned after the war only to find himself an outcast. Borchert said of these outcasts, "there's no home for them any more. And their home is outside the door. Their Germany is outside in the rain at night in the street". Beckmann, guilt-ridden about his wartime role as a German soldier, and about being the lover of a girl who betrayed her husband just as his own wife had forgotten him, is left without any support; society as he once knew it and accepted it now shows its ugly face. This is best demonstrated in the scenes with the Colonel who dismisses the War as merely "this spot of warfare", and with the insensitive Cabaret Producer who puts Beckmann off with fair words: "Positive! Positive, my friend! Think of Goethe! Think of Mozart! The Maid of Orleans, Richard Wagner, Schmeling, Shirley Temple!". Beckmann's tragedy is the tragedy of one man's awareness of the truth which others do not see or do not want to see. This is why Beckmann rejects The Other, a kind of optimistic alter ego, who wants him to believe in the goodness of people, while Beckmann sees nothing but man's hypocrisy, ignorance, and shallow materialism. Beckmann's final cry—a cry of existential loneliness—for an answer as to *how* to continue living in this world of betrayal remains unheard.

Draussen vor der Tür is the best example of the kind of German post-war literature known as *Trümmerliteratur* ("rubble-literature"). Its aim was twofold: to tell its German audience of the horrors of war and to point to a new direction—philosophically as well as artistically. While German writers after World War I indulged in an ecstatic, expressionist vision of a new dawn, German writers after 1945 denounced radically their country's military and Nazi past. For this, a new, unsentimental, true language was needed. Borchert's "This is Our Manifesto" expresses best the artist's credo at that time: "We have no further use for a poet's good grammar. We lack patience for good grammar. We need those with the hot hoarse-sobbed emotion. Who call a tree a tree and a woman a woman and say yes and say no: loud and clear and triply and without subjunctives". Borchert's own style is succinct, often laconic, and important statements are repeated in rhythmic monotony.

Borchert's language, however, is also marked by a richness of original metaphors and imagery. One of the best examples is Beckmann's recurring dream about a fat, blood-stained general, playing on a giant xylophone made of the bones of thousands of dead soldiers. Equally impressive in *Draussen vor der Tür* are the personifications of the river Elbe, of Death as a street-sweeper, and of an Undertaker "belching" from his rich harvest of corpses: "Why, yes, I've put on a bit of weight this century. Business has been good. One war after another. Like flies! Like flies the dead hang on the walls of the century. Like flies they lie stiff and dried up on the windowsill of the times". While *Draussen vor der Tür* is the best example of post-war Germany's *Trümmerliteratur*, it transcends mere *aktuelles Theater* to become an important European 20th-century drama.

—Renate Benson

————

BOUCICAULT,   Dion. Born   Dionysius   Lardner Boursiquot in Dublin, Ireland, 27(?) December 1820; became US citizen, 1873. Educated at schools in London, 1828–34; University College School, London, 1834–35; Brentford Collegiate School, 1836; a school in Dublin, 1837. Married 1) Anne Guiot in 1845 (died c.1848); 2) the actress Agnes Robertson in 1853 (separated 1872, divorced 1888), four sons and two daughters; 3) bigamously the actress Louise Thorndyke in 1885, two children. Apprenticed as civil engineer to Dionysius Lardner (probably his father), London, 1837; actor (as Lee Moreton) and playwright from 1838; on US tour, 1853–55; leased Gaiety Theatre, New Orleans, 1855–56, and Wallack's Theatre, New York, 1856–58; manager of a theatre in Washington, DC, 1858; joint manager, Winter Garden Theatre, New York, 1859; returned to London, 1860; manager, New Royal Theatre, London, 1862–63; on provincial tour, 1864; moved to New York, 1872, and lived with the actress Katherine Rogers, 1872–74; lived in England, 1875–76; on US tour, 1876–79; leased Booth's Theatre, New York, 1879; on Australia tour, 1885, and US tour, 1886–88. Died in New York, 18 September 1890.

Works

Collections

"Forbidden Fruit" and Other Plays (includes *Louis XI; Dot; Robert Emmett; Flying Scud; Mercy Dodd*), edited by Allardyce Nicoll and F.T. Clark.   1940.
The Dolmen Boucicault (includes *The Colleen Bawn; Arragh-na-Pogue; The Shaughraun*), edited by David Krause.   1964.
Plays (includes *Used Up*; *Old Heads and Young Hearts; Jessie Brown; The Octoroon; The Shaughraun*), edited by Peter Thomson.   1984.
Selected Plays, edited by Andrew Parkin.   1985.

Stage Works

The Old Guard (as *Napoleon's Old Guard*, produced Collegiate School, Brentford, 1836; revised version, as *The Old Guard*, produced Theatre Royal, Brighton, 1840). 1900(?).
A Legend of the Devil's Dyke (produced Theatre Royal, Bristol, 1838).   1898.
Lodgings to Let (produced Theatre Royal, Bristol, 1839).
Jack Sheppard, from the novel by William Harrison Ainsworth (produced Theatre Royal, Hull, 1839).
London Assurance (produced Covent Garden Theatre, London, 1841).   1841; edited by James L. Smith, 1984.
The Irish Heiress (produced Covent Garden Theatre, London, 1842; also produced as *West End*).   1842.
A Lover by Proxy (produced Theatre Royal, Haymarket, London, 1842).   1845(?).
Alma Mater; or, A Cure for Coquettes (produced Theatre Royal, Haymarket, London, 1842).   1842(?).
Curiosities of Literature (produced Theatre Royal, Haymarket, London, 1842).   1842(?).
The Bastille (produced Theatre Royal, Haymarket, London, 1842).
Woman (produced Theatre Royal, Haymarket, London, 1843).
Victor and Hortense; or, False Pride (produced Theatre Royal, Haymarket, London, 1843; revised version, as *Paul Lafarge*, produced Princess's Theatre, London).
Laying a Ghost (produced Theatre Royal, Haymarket, London, 1843).
Sharp's the Word (produced London, 1843).

Act 2, final scene, of *The Corsican Brothers* by **Dion Boucicault**, at the Princess's Theatre, London, 1852, showing a vision of Louis dei Franchi in Corsica behind the set for the forest of Fontainbleu.

Old Heads and Young Hearts (produced Theatre Royal, Haymarket, London, 1844).   1845.

Used Up, with Charles Mathews, from a play by F.A. Duvert and A.T. de Lauzanne de Vauxroussel (produced Theatre Royal, Haymarket, London, 1844).   1848(?).

The Confederacy, from the play by Vanbrugh (produced Theatre Royal, Haymarket, London, 1844).

The Fox and the Goose; or, The Widow's Husband, with Ben Webster, music by Ambroise Thomas (produced Adelphi Theatre, London, 1844).   1844.

Don Caesar de Bazan; or, Love and Honour, with Ben Webster, from a play by P.F. Dumanoir and Adolph Dennery (produced Adelphi Theatre, London, 1844). 1844.

Lolah; or, The Wreck-Light (produced Theatre Royal, Haymarket, London, 1844).

Love in a Sack (produced Theatre Royal, Haymarket, London, 1844).

Mother and Son (produced Adelphi Theatre, London, 1844).

A Soldier of Fortune; or, The Irish Settler, with Ben Webster (produced Adelphi Theatre, London, 1845).

Peg Woofington (produced Adelphi Theatre, London, 1845).

Enquire Within (produced Lycam Theatre, London, 1845).

Who Did It?, with Charles Kenney (produced Adelphi Theatre, London, 1846; also produced as *Up the Flue; or, What's in the Wind*).

The Old School (produced Theatre Royal, Haymarket, London, 1846).

Mr. Peter Piper; or, Found Out at Last (produced Theatre Royal, Haymarket, London, 1846).

The Wonderful Water Cure, with Ben Webster (produced Theatre Royal, Haymarket, London, 1846).   Nd.

Shakespeare in Love (produced 1846).

The School for Scheming (produced Theatre Royal, Haymarket, London, 1847; revised version produced as *Love and Money*).   1847(?).

La Salamandrine (ballet scenario; produced Royal Opera House, Covent Garden, London, 1847).

A Confidence (produced Theatre Royal, Haymarket, London, 1848).

The Knight of Arva (produced Theatre Royal, Haymarket, London, 1848).   1868(?).

The Willow Copse, with Charles Kenney, from a play by Frédéric Soulié (produced Adelphi Theatre, London, 1849).   1856(?).

A Radical Cure (produced 1850).

La Garde Nationale (produced Queen's Theatre, London, 1850; also produced as *The Garde Mobile*).

Giralda; The Invisible Husband, from a play by Scribe (produced Olympic Theatre, London, 1850); revised version, as *A Dark Night's Work* (produced Princess's Theatre, London, 1870).

Belphegor, with Ben Webster, from a play by Adolph Dennery (produced Adelphi Theatre, London, 1851).

Sixtus V; or, The Broken Vow, with John Bridgeman, from a play by Dinaux and Lemoine (produced Olympic Theatre, London, 1851).   1851; as *The Pope of Rome*, nd.

Love in a Maze (produced Princess's Theatre, London, 1851).   1851.

The Dame of Spades, from a play by Scribe (as *The Queen of*

Spades, produced Theatre Royal, Drury Lane, London, 1851). 1851.

O'Flannigan and the Fairies (produced Adelphi Theatre, London, 1851).

The Corsican Brothers; or, The Vendetta, from a French play based on a story by Dumas *père* (produced Princess's Theatre, London, 1852). 1852.

The Phantom, from a play by Carmouche, de Jouffrey, and Charles Nodier (as *The Vampire,* produced Princess's Theatre, London, 1852; as *The Phantom,* produced 1862). 1852(?).

The Prima Donna (produced Princess's Theatre, London, 1852). 1852(?).

The Sentinel, music by Roberth Stöpel (produced Strand Theatre, London, 1853).

Genevieve; or, The Reign of Terror, from a play by Dumas *père* and Auguste Maquet (produced Adelphi Theatre, London, 1853).

The Young Actress, from the work *The Manager's Daughter* by Edward Lancaster (produced Theatre Royal, Montreal, 1853).

The Fox Hunt; or, Don Quixote II (produced Burton's Theatre, New York, 1853; as *The Fox Chase,* produced St. James's Theatre, London, 1864).

To Parents and Guardians, from the play by Tom Taylor (produced Burton's Theatre, New York, 1853).

Faust and Margaret, from a play by Michel Carré (produced Princess's Theatre, London, 1854). 1854.

Janet Pride (produced Metropolitan Theatre, Buffalo, New York, 1854).

Andy Blake; or, The Irish Diamond, from a play by Bayard and Vanderburch (produced Boston Museum, Boston, 1854; also produced as *The Dublin Boy* and *The Irish Boy*). 1884.

The Devil's in It, from a play by Scribe (produced Chestnut Street Theatre, Philadelphia, 1854).

The Fairy Star (produced Broadway Theatre, New York, 1854).

Apollo in New York (produced Walnut Street Theatre, Philadelphia, 1854).

Pierre the Foundling, from a play by Mme. Dudevant (produced Adelphi Theatre, London, 1854).

Eugénie; or, A Sister's Vow (produced Theatre Royal, Drury Lane, London, 1855).

Louis XI, King of France, from a play by Casimir Delavigne (produced Princess's Theatre, London, 1855). 1855.

Agnes Robertson at Home (produced Pelican Theatre, New Orleans, 1855).

There's Nothing in It (produced Walnut Street Theatre, Philadelphia, 1855).

Grimaldi; or, Scenes in the Life of an Actress, from a play by Anicet-Bourgeois and Théodore Barrière (produced National Theatre, Cincinnati, 1855; as *Violet,* produced 1856; also produced as *The Life of an Actress).* 1856.

The Cat Changed into a Woman, from a play by Scribe (produced National Theatre, Washington D.C., 1855).

Rachel is Coming (produced St. Louis Theatre, St. Louis, 1855).

The Chameleon (produced Gaiety Theatre, New Orleans, 1855).

Azael; or, The Prodigal Son, from a play by Scribe (produced Gaiety Theatre, New Orleans, 1856).

Una (produced Gaiety Theatre, New Orleans, 1856).

Blue Belle, from a play by Adolphe de Leuven and Mazilier, music by Adolphe Adam (produced Burton's Theatre, New York, 1856).

George Darville (produced Boston Theatre, Boston, 1857).

Wanted a Widow, with Immediate Possession, with Charles Seymour, from a play by Theanlon and Choquart (produced Wallack's Theatre, New York, 1857). Nd.

The Streets of New York, with others, from a play by Brisebarre and Nus (as *The Poor of New York,* produced Wallack's Theatre, New York, 1857; as *The Streets of London,* produced 1857; as *The Poor of Liverpool,* produced Royal Amphitheatre, Liverpool, 1864; numerous later revisions for touring). 1857(?).

Jessie Brown; or, The Relief of Lucknow (produced Wallack's Theatre, New York, 1858). 1858.

Brigham Young; or, The Revolt of the Harem (produced Wallack's Theatre, New York, 1858).

Pauvrette, from a play by Desnoyer and Adolph Dennery (produced Niblo's Garden, New York, 1858; also produced as *The Snow Flower* and *The Maid of the Alps*). 1858(?).

The Octoroon; or, Life in Louisiana (produced Winter Garden Theatre, New York, 1859). 1859.

Dot, from the story *The Cricket and the Hearth* by Dickens (produced Winter Garden Theatre, New York, 1859; as *A Christmas Story,* produced Gaiety Theatre, London, 1870). In *"Forbidden Fruit" and Other Plays,* 1940.

Chamooni III, from a play by Scribe (produced Winter Garden Theatre, New York, 1859).

Smike; or, Scenes from Nicholas Nickleby, from the novel by Dickens (produced Winter Garden Theatre, New York, 1859).

The Colleen Bawn; or, The Brides of Garryowen, from the novel *The Collegians* by Gerald Griffin (produced Keene's Theatre, New York, 1860). 1860(?); opera version, as *The Lily of Killarney,* with John Oxenford, music by Jules Benedict (produced Royal Opera House, Covent Garden, London, 1862), 1863.

Vanity Fair, from a French play (produced Keene's Theatre, New York, 1860).

Jeanie Deans; or, The Heart of Midlothian, from the novel by Scott (produced Keene's Theatre, New York, 1860; also produced as *The Trial of Effie Deans*).

Lady Bird; or, Harlequin Lord Dundreary (produced simultaneously at Astley's Amphitheatre, London, and Wallack's Theatre, New York, 1862).

How She Loves Him! (produced Prince of Wales's Theatre, Liverpool, 1863). 1868.

Omoo; or, The Sea of Ice, from a play by Adolph Dennery and Dugue (produced Royal Amphitheatre, Liverpool, 1864).

Arrah-na-Pogue; or, The Wicklow Wedding (produced Old Theatre Royal, Dublin, 1864; revised version produced Princess's Theatre, London, 1864). 1865.

Rip Van Winkle, from the play by Joe Jefferson based on the story by Washington Irving (produced Adelphi Theatre, London, 1865).

The Two Lives of Mary Leigh (produced Prince's Theatre, Manchester, 1866; as *Hunted Down,* produced 1866).

The Parish Clerk (produced Prince's Theatre, Manchester, 1866).

The Long Strike, from works by Elizabeth Gaskell (produced Lyceum Theatre, London, 1866). 1870(?); as *The Strike* (produced 1896).

Flying Scud; or, A Four Legged Fortune (produced Holborn Theatre, London, 1866). In *"Forbidden Fruit" and Other Plays,* 1940.

Wild Goose, with Lester Wallack, from the work *Rosedale* by Wallack (produced Theatre Royal, Haymarket, London, 1867).

Foul Play, with Charles Reade, from their novel (produced Holborn Theatre, London, 1868; revised version, produced

1868). 1871(?); revised version, as *Our Seamen* (produced 1874); as *The Scuttled Ship* (produced 1877).

After Dark: A Tale of London Life (produced Princess's Theatre, London, 1868). Nd.

Presumptive Evidence, from a play by Moreau, Siraudin, and Delacour (produced Princess's Theatre, London, 1869; as *Mercy Dodd,* produced 1874). In *"Forbidden Fruit" and Other Plays,* 1940.

Seraphine; or, A Devotee, from a play by Sardou (produced Queen's Theatre, London, 1869).

Formosa; or, The Railroad to Ruin (produced Theatre Royal, Drury Lane, 1869). 1869; revised version (produced 1891).

Lost at Sea: A London Story, with H.J. Byron (produced Adelphi Theatre, London, 1869).

Dreams, from the play *My Lady Clara* by Tom Robertson (produced 5th Avenue Theatre, New York, 1869).

The Rapparee; or, The Treaty of Limerick (produced Princess's Theatre, London, 1870). Nd.

Jezebel; or, The Dead Reckoning, from a play by Anicet-Bourgeois and Michel Masson (produced Holborn Theatre, London, 1870). 1870.

Elfie; or, The Cherry-Tree Inn (produced Theatre Royal, Glasgow, 1871). Nd.

Night and Morning, from a play by Emile de Girardin (produced Prince's Theatre, Manchester, 1871). Nd; revised version, as *Kerry* (produced 1893).

John Bull; or, The Gentleman's Fireside, from the play by George Colman the Younger (produced Prince's Theatre, Manchester, 1871).

Babil and Bijou; or, The Lost Regalia, songs by J.R. Planché (produced Royal Opera House, Covent Garden, London, 1872).

Led Astray, from a play by Octave Feuillet (produced Union Square Theatre, New York, 1873). 1873(?).

The O'Dowd; or, Life in Galway, from a play by Cormon Grange (as *Daddy O'Dowd,* produced Booth's Theatre, New York, 1873; as *The O'Dowd,* produced 1880; also produced as *Suil-a-mor*). 1909.

Mora; or, The Golden Fetters (produced Wallack's Theatre, New York, 1873).

Mimi, from a play by Théodore Barrière and Henry Murger (produced Wallack's Theatre, New York, 1873).

A Man of Honor, from a play by Dumas *fils* (produced Wallack's Theatre, New York, 1873).

The Shaughraun (produced Wallack's Theatre, New York, 1874). 1880.

Boucicault in California (produced San Francisco Theatre, San Francisco, 1874).

Venice Preserved, from the play by Otway (produced Booth's Theatre, New York, 1874).

Belle Lamar (produced Booth's Theatre, New York, 1874; revised version, as *Finn Maccoul,* produced 1887; also produced as *Fin MacCool of Skibbereen*).

Forbidden Fruit (produced Wallack's Theatre, New York, 1876). In *"Forbidden Fruit" and Other Plays,* 1940.

A Bridal Tour (produced Wallack's Theatre, New York, 1877; as *Marriage,* produced 1877).

The Dead Secret, from the novel by Wilkie Collins (produced Fifth Avenue Theatre, New York, 1878).

Clarissa Harlowe, from the novel by Samuel Richardson (produced Wallack's Theatre, New York, 1878).

The School for Scandal, from the play by Sheridan (produced Wallack's Theatre, New York, 1878).

Spell-Bound (produced Wallack's Theatre, New York, 1879).

Rescued; or, A Girl's Romance (produced King's Cross Theatre, London, 1879).

Contempt of Court (produced Wallack's Theatre, New York, 1879).

Therese; or, The Maid of Croissey (produced Adelphi Theatre, London, 1880).

Vice Versa, from a play by Duru and Chivot (produced Springfield, Massachusetts, 1883).

The Amadan (produced Boston Museum Theatre, Boston, 1883).

Robert Emmett, from a play by Frank Marshall (produced Prince of Wales's Theatre, Greenwich, London, 1884). In *"Forbidden Fruit" and Other Plays,* 1940.

The Jilt (produced Elephant and Castle Theatre, London, 1885). 1904.

The Spae Wife, from a novel by Scott (produced Elephant and Castle Theatre, London, 1886; revised version, as *Cuishla-Ma-Chree,* produced Hollis Street Theatre, Boston, 1888).

Phryne; or, The Romance of a Young Wife (produced Baldwin Theatre, San Francisco, 1887).

Captain Swift, from a play by Haddon Chambers (produced Madison Square Theatre, New York, 1888).

Jimmy Watt (produced Elephant and Castle Theatre, London, 1890; as *The Tale of a Coat,* produced 1890).

Lend Me Your Wife, from a play by Maurice Desvallières (produced Boston Museum Theatre, 1890).

99, possibly not by Boucicault (produced Standard Theatre, London, 1891).

Fiction

Foul Play, with Charles Reade. 1868.

Other

The Story of Ireland. 1881.
The Art of Acting. 1926.

*

Criticism

Books:
Townsend Walsh, *The Career of Boucicault,* New York, 1915.
G.C. Duggan, *The Stage Irishman,* Dublin, 1937.
Robert Hogan, *Dion Boucicault,* New York, 1969.
Richard Fawkes, *Dion Boucicault,* London, 1979.
Sven Eric Molin and Robin Goodfellowe (eds.), *Boucicault: A Documentary Life,* Newark, New Jersey, 1979.
John McCormick, *Boucicault,* Cambridge, 1987.

* * *

"I localise it for each town, and hit the public between the eyes, so they see nothing but fire. *Et voilà.* I can spin out these rough and tumble dramas as a hen lays eggs. It's a degrading occupation, but more money has been made out of guano than poetry". Boucicault's celebrated excursion into dramaturgic theory may trivialise his stage artistry, but it rightly acknowledges that throughout his career he fought to see that playwrights should get a fair financial return for their work, a cause which he termed an *argumentum ad pocketum.* In addition, he was constantly researching new markets in Europe, Britain, America, and even Australasia, and although most of his output may be loosely located within the parameters of melodrama the totality of his work was not formulaic, and his dramaturgy showed several major innovations in accordance with his perception of potential new audiences.

It was in farcical comedy, however, that Boucicault leapt to prominence. *London Assurance* was, by his own account, written before his 18th birthday, and was almost immediately recognised as being among the best English comedies since the Restoration. It has been his most frequently revived play this century, which has meant that his reputation has, misleadingly, pivoted on an apprentice work which lacks the ingenuity of his maturity; its popularity led to several similar, though less successful, works written under the ambivalent patronage of Charles Mathews.

A regression to *ad pocketum* thinking, the first of many in a highly fluctuating career, led the playwright to several years in Paris, prompted by debate among the Bohemians of Percy Street about the system of royalties. Bankruptcy in 1848 developed into prosperity by 1852, when he began to gather the profits of exploiting the French stage for his own canon, notably with *The Vampire* and *The Corsican Brothers*, the former so popular that Queen Victoria saw it twice, and the latter (which she saw five times) introducing the form of "gentlemanly" or "cloak-and-sword" melodrama to the London stage. Both plays were written for the Oxford Street theatre of Charles Kean, who had salaried Boucicault specifically to pirate and adapt French scripts. It was probably Kean's stagecraft that generated Boucicault's later scrupulous realism in production, a principle which he would, in turn, pass on to David Belasco. *The Corsican Brothers*, with a single actor playing both title roles, with simultaneous action in Corsica and Paris generating the factor of telepathy, and with a complicated trap required for a ghost scene, posed challenges of stage management which fascinated producers and audiences through the age of Henry Irving and beyond.

Eloping to New York with Agnes Robertson, Kean's Scottish *ingénue*, Boucicault recalled that he spent "three years in study of the American people, their tastes, and the direction of their intellectual appetites". It was while reading a newspaper that it occurred to him "that the stage might be employed in a similar manner to embody and illustrate the moving events of the period". In fact, his plays with such a documentary basis were so topical that they reflected the events of the day rather than the period: *Jessie Brown* was first performed while the siege of Lucknow was still in progress, and *The Octoroon* opened four days after John Brown's execution. The racial themes of the latter work would still be sensitive when O'Neill approached them over 60 years later, but the play also flaunted the axioms of melodrama by ending with the death of the heroine of the title. The dramaturgy in fact proved more controversial than the theme, to the extent that Boucicault, after stubbornly mounting his original script on both sides of the Atlantic, eventually wrote a happy ending for London audiences. In these plays, he had discovered the stage marketability of "actuality", and he would continue intermittently to exploit it until late works such as *Robert Emmet*, which uses, in only slightly modified form, the historical speech from the scaffold. This unfairly neglected work defied the introduction of a happy ending for the hero, and its use of well-known patriotic speeches provided a model for Sean O'Casey.

It was two months before *Jessie Brown* that Boucicault had produced the original version of the work which he had specifically termed "guano". *The Poor of New York* had a social topicality that matched that of the Lucknow play, but he kept it locally topical by writing at least ten versions to please the parochialism of particular audiences. The play was also revolutionary on a technical level in that it marked his first full-scale use of the "sensation scene", which would

quickly become a trademark of his work, and that of his numerous imitators. Until now, his plays had always reflected his own profession as actor—usually in his own plays—to the extent that their meticulous exploitation of the performance resources of the stock company could justly label them "actors' plays". But with the sensation scene, performance would take a decidedly second place behind a spectacular display of the stage pyrotechnics which the technologically sophisticated American theatre was particularly able to provide. Exploding steamboats, snowstorms and avalanches, duels and massacres, urban conflagrations—these and dozens of other sensations kept audiences at a high level of tension, especially as Boucicault began to use them nearly 20 years before he finally perfected the invention of fireproof scenery.

Boucicault's recurrent complaint that actors made more money than authors was obviously a significant factor in keeping him on the stage. However, his broad Irish accent which persisted through his life, coupled with Agnes's Scottish voice, inevitably determined the character range in his plays. If it was plausible that *Jessie Brown* should have a Scottish heroine turning up at the Sepoy Mutiny, it was less so that the Nana Sahib should have a thick Irish accent. Boucicault was in fact finding the constraints of the stock company system increasingly problematic, and for the first of his Irish plays, *The Colleen Bawn*, he defied professional tradition and simply hired four comedians for touring companies. This, and the remaining Irish plays—*Arrah-na-Pogue* and *The Shaughraun*—are distinct from his other plays on Irish themes such as the historical documentary *Robert Emmet* in that they transcend the nationalism that was normal to melodrama and which Boucicault had exploited through his policy of localisation. Irishness is certainly an amiable commodity in these plays, but not at the expense of generating other antagonisms: in *The Shaughraun*, Molineux, the English officer, is—remarkably for melodrama with a political theme—established as likeable from his first appearance.

The diversity of Boucicault's achievements and the fecundity of his writings cannot be summarised briefly and have led some critics into the inflation of his stature in dramatic history, a tendency which his recent editor, Peter Thomson, has rightly challenged. However, one aspect of his work has been neglected. In his long career he did stage versions of novels by Dickens, Reade, Gaskell, Scott (Irishised), Collins, and numerous others. Such adaptation has sometimes been dismissed as a failure of his own imagination but, occurring in a century in which the low literary status of drama disinclined most novelists from the stage, Boucicault's role may be seen as both that of interventionist and mediator, who by traversing genres greatly expanded the English-speaking world's perception of the boundaries of dramatic representation.

—Howard McNaughton

See also *Volume 1* entries on *London Assurance*; *The Shaughraun*.

———

BRAUN, Volker. Born in Dresden, Germany, 7 May 1939. Remained in East Germany after World War II. Left school with *Abitur*, 1957; attended Leipzig University, studying philosophy, 1960–64. Has one daughter. Machine operator in the printing industry, construction worker in the mining industry, 1957–60; travelled to Siberia, 1964; dramaturgical adviser,

Berliner Ensemble, East Berlin, 1965–66; travelled to France, 1971; first-produced play, *Hans Faust* (subsequently revised as *Hinze und Kunze*), staged 1968; other early plays not produced in the DDR until 1972, after the cultural liberalisation under Erich Honecker; employed with the Leipzig Städtische Bühnen, 1971–72; associated with the Deutsches Theater, Berlin, since 1972, often in the capacity of reader or assistant director; excluded from the board of the East German Writers Organization for supporting exiled author Wolf Biermann; travelled to Cuba, Peru, and Italy, 1976; toured England, 1980, giving readings. Recipient: Heinrich Heine Prize, 1971; Heinrich Mann Prize, 1980; Berlin Prize for German Literature, 1989. Member, Academy of Arts, Berlin, and Academy of Sciences and Literature, Mainz.

Works

Collections

Stücke 1 (includes *Die Kipper; Hinze und Kunze; Tinka*). 1975.
Stücke 2 (includes *Schmitten; Guevara oder Der Sonnenstaat; Grosser Frieden; Simplex Deutsch*). 1981.
Stücke (2 vols.). 1983.
Gesammelte Stücke (2 vols.). 1989.
Texte (7 vols.). 1989–91.

Stage Works

Die Kipper. As *Kipper Paul Bauch*, in *Forum*, 18, 1966; revised as *Die Kipper* (produced Städtische Bühnen, Leipzig, 1972), 1972.
Hinze und Kunze (produced as *Hans Faust*, Nationaltheater, Weimar, 1968; produced as *Hinze und Kunze*, Städtisches Theater, Karl-Marx-Stadt, 1973). In *Spectaculum 19*, 1971; revised version in *Theater der Zeit*, 2, 1973; in book form, in *Stücke 1*, 1975.
Tinka (produced Städtisches Theater, Karl-Marx-Stadt, 1976). In *Stücke 1*, 1975.
Guevara; oder, Der Sonnenstaat (produced Nationaltheater, Mannheim, 1977). In *Spectaculum 27*, 1977; also in *Stücke 2*, 1981.
Grosser Frieden (produced by the Berliner Ensemble, Berlin, 1979). In *Theater der Zeit*, 7, 1979; in book form, in *Stücke 2*, 1981.
Simplex Deutsch (produced Berliner Ensemble's Experimental Theatre, Berlin, 1980). In *Theater der Zeit*, 7, 1980; in book form, in *Stücke 2*, 1981.
Schmitten (produced Kellertheater der Oper, Leipzig, 1982). In *Stücke 2*, 1981.
Dmitri, from Schiller's *Demetrius* (produced Badisches Staatstheater, Karlsruhe, 1982). 1982.
Siegfried Frauenprotokolle deutsche Furor (produced Nationaltheater, Weimar, 1986). 1987.
Die Übergangsgesellschaft (produced Bremen, 1987). 1987.
Lenins Tod, with the prologue "Der Eisenwagen" (produced by the Berliner Ensemble, Berlin, 1988). In *Sinn und Form*, 1, 1988; in book form, in *Gesammelte Stücke 1*, 1989.
Transit Europa, from a novel by Anna Seghers (produced Berliner Ensemble, Berlin, 1988). 1988.
T. In *Gesammelte Stücke 1*, 1989.
Totleben. In *Gesammelte Stücke 1*, 1989.
Das Denkmal. In *Texte, 6*, 1991.

Fiction

Das ungezwungene Leben Kasts: Drei Berichte (includes *Der Schlamm; Der Hörsaal; Die Bretter*). 1972; augmented edition (also containing *Die Tribüne*), 1979.
Unvollendete Geschichte. In *Sinn und Form*, 5, 1975; in book form, with *Arbeit für Morgen*. 1988.
Berichte von Hinze und Kunze. Parts in *GDR Monitor*, 3, 1980; complete, 1983.
Hinze-Kunze-Roman. 1985.
Bodenloser Satz. 1990.

Verse

Provokation für mich. 1965.
Kriegserklärung. 1967.
Wir und nicht sie. 1970; augmented edition, 1979.
Gedichte. 1972; expanded edition, 1976.
Der Stoff zum Leben. 1977.
Gegen die symmetrische Welt. 1974.
Posiealbum 115. 1977.
Zeit Gedichte. 1977.
Gedichte. 1979.
Training des aufrechten Gangs. 1979.
Rimbaud: Ein Psalm der Aktualität. 1985.
Langsamer knirschender Morgen. 1987.
Anatomie. 1989.

Other

Es genügt nicht die einfache Wahrheit: Notate. 1975.
Im Querschnitt Volker Braun: Gedichte, Prosa, Stücke, Aufsätze. 1978.
Anekdoten. 1988.
Arbeit für Morgen. With *Unvollendete Geschichte*, 1988.
Verheerende Folgen mangelnden Anscheins innerbetriebliche Demokratie. 1988.

*

Bibliographies

Winifried Hönes, "Bibliographie Volker Braun", in *Text und Kritik*, 55, 1977.
Ian Wallace, *Volker Braun: Forschungsbericht*, Amsterdam, 1986.

Criticism

Books:
Ludwig Arnold (ed.), *Volker Braun*, Munich, 1977.
Karl Heinz Schmidt, *"Grosser Frieden" von Volker Braun: Eine Dokumentation der Aufführung des Berliner Ensembles 1979*, Berlin, 1982.
Jay Rosselini, *Volker Braun*, Munich, 1983.
Ian Wallace, "Volker Braun's *Tinka*", in *The Writer and Society in the GDR*, edited by Wallace, Tayport, Fife, Scotland, 1984.
Ulrich Profitlich, *Volker Braun: Studien zu seinem dramatischen und erzählerischen Werk*, Munich, 1985.
Julian Hilton, "Back to the Future: Volker Braun and the German Theatrical Tradition", in *A Radical Stage*, edited by W.G. Sebald, Oxford and New York, 1988.

Articles:
Margaret E. Ward, "Volker Braun's *Tinka*: Two Views", in *University of Dayton Review*, vol.13 no.2, 1978.

Christine Cosentino, "Theater of Provocation: The Plays of Volker Braun", in *West Virginia University Philological Papers*, 25, 1979.

Christine Cosentino, "Volker Braun's 'Geschichten von Hinze und Kunze': A New Look at an Old Problem", in *Studies in GDR Culture and Society*, 4, 1984.

* * *

Volker Braun has established himself in the last 20 years as one of the leading playwrights of the former East Germany. A Saxon, born in Dresden, he is a committed socialist, a fact reflected in his writing, but by no means was he an uncritical apologist for the government of East Germany. He sees writing as a political act, as an active intervention in the development of socialism in a spirit of positive criticism. This attitude placed him in the public eye, and led to his featuring in political, as well as artistic, discussions in the East German media.

In his criticism of the system, however, he was not seeking to replace socialism by Western capitalism; he was critical of the East German regime for not *itself* being truly socialist.

His plays, from *Die Kipper* onwards, have shown a growing mastery of the theatrical form, and a broadening of his themes, but they generally reflect the development of the East German state from its uncertain and utopian beginnings in the 1950's, through the problems it experienced in its attempts at the application of practical socialism, to the disillusion and insecurities of a society about to embark on the change to a market economy.

In *Die Kipper* and *Hinze und Kunze* (both set in the 1950's), the physical labour involved in mining and construction work is equated with the political effort needed to build the ideology of the newly established State. *Tinka* confronted the problems of female emancipation in East Germany. The heroine may have trained as an engineer, but on her return to the factory with her new qualifications she is still seen by male fellow workers primarily as a sex object. Unable, herself, to come to terms with the situation, she finally provokes the man she loves into an act of violent domination over her. The problems of the establishment of genuine socialism in society as a whole lie in each individual's attitude to, and interaction with, his fellows. But the conflict between the individual and the collective may, Braun suggests, be the result of the State's inability to accommodate the aspirations of the individual, as much as the lack of recognition on the part of that individual of the personal changes necessary for the successful building of the socialist State.

Grosser Frieden (The Great Peace) marks a development away from a specific social milieu into a China reminiscent of Brecht's Setzuan. In this play Braun uses a tradition which, through Brecht and Büchner, stretches back to Shakespeare. In *Grosser Frieden* we are shown a great peasant revolution, which, after a period of struggle and turmoil, replaces the autocracy of the aristocratic rulers with a regime of equal tyranny—surely a powerful indictment of the state of affairs in East Germany at the time. At the end of the play the character Wang mirrors the epilogue in Brecht's *Der Gute Mensch von Setzuan* (*The Good Person of Setzuan*) in handing the responsibility for action to the audience. But Braun remains more optimistic than Brecht: re-education is essential, but improvements are possible.

In *Dmitri*, Braun stakes a claim to a different tradition. By finishing Schiller's fragment *Demetrius*, Braun shows his confidence as a playwright in a study of power and who has the right to wield it. But in completing *Demetrius* he changes Schiller's aim, reflecting the changes in European history in the intervening years. We see Demetrius as the pretender, who, it is claimed, has more right to power—as the people's choice—than the true ruler. The resonances through history are also pointed up by an agitprop presentation of the events of 1918. Throughout Braun exploits the stage as a forum for moral and political debate, perhaps as the only true forum for such debate in his society at that time.

In *Die Übergangsgesellschaft* (Society in Transition), Braun returns to a contemporary setting. Having worked on a production of Chekhov's *Three Sisters* in Berlin, he wrote in *Die Übergangsgesellschaft*, a modern parallel piece played originally by the company with whom he had worked on *Three Sisters*. Thus, the characterisation was already familiar to the audience, as was the atmosphere of disillusion and dissatisfaction. Braun suggests that the socialism which has created the state in which the play is set needs rethinking, and new forms and means of expression must be sought to prevent a decline into unproductive attitudes.

Braun views his writing as a craft and prides himself on his skill as a wordsmith. His plays are marked by a strong sense of irony and frequent punning. His language is at once colloquial and allusive. He has been an unforgiving critic of a state which he sees as unreceptive to its people's needs and demands, but has kept faith with socialism throughout despite his critique of its failings.

—Anthony Meech

BRECHT, Bertolt. Born Eugen Berthold Friedrich Brecht in Augsburg, Germany, 10 February 1898. Educated at elementary school, 1904–08, and Gymnasium, Augsburg, 1908–17; University of Munich, 1917–18, 1919. Served as medical orderly during World War I. Married 1) Marianne Zoff in 1922 (divorced 1927), one daughter; 2) the actress Helene Weigel in 1929, one son and one daughter; also had one son by Paula Banholzer. Drama critic, *Der Volkswille*, Augsburg, 1919–21; dramaturg, Munich Kammerspiele, 1923–24; in Berlin, 1924–33: dramaturg, Deutsches Theater; following Hitler's assumption of power, left Germany, 1933; based in Denmark, 1933–39; stripped of German citizenship, 1935; editor, with Lion Feuchtwanger and Willi Bredel, *Das Wort*, 1936–39; moved to Sweden, 1939; fled Sweden, 1941, arriving in USA via Moscow and Vladivostock; based in California, 1941–47; called before the House Un-American Activities Committee, 1947: flew to Europe immediately after testifying; in Switzerland, 1947–48; moved to East Berlin and founded (with his wife) the Berliner Ensemble, 1949; became Austrian citizen, 1950; Berliner Ensemble given the Theater am Schiffbauerdamm as a permanent home, 1954. Recipient: Kleist Prize, 1922; Stalin Peace Prize, 1954. Died in East Berlin, 14 August 1956.

Works

Collections

Versuche (15 vols.). 1930–32, 1949–57.
Gesammelte Werke (2 vols.). 1938.
Stücke (13 vols.). 1957–66.
Seven Plays by Bertolt Brecht (includes *Jungle of Cities; A Man's a Man; St. Joan of the Stockyards; Mother Courage*

Bertolt Brecht

and Her Children; *Galileo*; *The Good Woman of Setzuan; The Caucasian Chalk Crcle*), translated by Eric Bentley. 1961.
Plays (2 vols.; includes *The Threepenny Opera; Lucullus; Galileo; The Caucasian Chalk Circle; Mother Courage; Saint Joan of the Stockyards; The Good Person of Setzuan*). 1960–62.
Baal; A Man's a Man; The Elephant Calf, translated by Eric Bentley and Martin Esslin.   1964.
"Jungle of Cities" and Other Plays, translated by Frank Jones. 1966.
Gesammelte Werke (20 vols.: divided into *Stücke*, *Prosa*, *Gedichte*, and *Schriften*).   1967; supplemented with: *Texte für Filme* (2 vols.), 1969; *Arbeitsjournal* (2 vols.), 1974; *Gedichte aus dem Nachlass* (2 vols.), 1983.
Collected Plays (multi-volume series; US and UK versions have a slightly different arrangement and sometimes different translations), edited by John Willett and Ralph Mannheim.   1970—; some translations reprinted as *Plays* (4 vols.).

Stage Works

Baal (produced Altes Theater, Leipzig, 1922; revised version, Deutsches Theater, Berlin, 1926).   1922; revised version, in *Stücke 1*, 1955; translated as *Baal*, in *Baal; A Man's a Man; The Elephant Calf*, 1964.
Trommeln in der Nacht (produced Kammerspiele, Munich, 1922).   1922; revised version, in *Stücke 1*, 1955; translated as *Drums in the Night*, in *"Jungle of Cities" and Other Plays*, 1966.
Im Dickicht der Städte (produced as *Im Dickicht*,

Residenztheater, Munich, 1923; revised version produced Hessisches Landestheater, Darmstadt, 1927).   1927; translated as *In the Jungle of Cities*, in *Seven Plays*, 1961; as *Jungle of Cities*, in *"Jungle of Cities" and Other Plays*, 1966.
Pastor Ephraim Magnus, with Arnolt Bronnen, from the work by Hans Henry Jahn (produced 1923).
Leben Eduards des Zweiten von England, with Lion Feuchtwanger, from Christopher Marlowe's *Edward II* (produced Kammerspiele, Munich, 1924).   1924; translated as *Edward II*, 1966.
Gösta Berling, from E. Karin's adaptation of the novel by Selma Lagerlöf.   In *Das Kunstblatt*, January 1944.
Die Hochzeit (produced Schauspielhaus, Frankfurt, 1926). As *Die Kleinbürgerhochzeit*, in *Stücke 13*, 1966; translated as *A Respectable Wedding*, in *Collected Plays 1*, 1970.
Mann ist Mann, with others (produced Landestheater, Darmstadt, 1926; revised version, produced Staatstheater, Berlin, 1931).   1927; revised version, in *Stücke 2*, 1957; translated as *Man Equals Man*, in *Seven Plays*, 1961; as *A Man's a Man*, in *Baal; A Man's a Man; The Elephant Calf*, 1964.
Das Elefantkalb.   Included with *Mann ist Mann*, 1927; translated as *The Elephant Calf*, in *Wake* (Cambridge, Massachusetts), Autumn 1949; also in *Baal; A Man's a Man; The Elephant Calf*, 1964.
Kalkutta 4 Mai, with Lion Feuchtwanger, from Feuchtwanger's play *Warren Hastings: Gouverneur von Indien*.   In *Drei angelsächsische Stücke*, 1927; translated as *Warren Hastings*, in *Two Anglo-Saxon Plays*, 1928.
Die Dreigroschenoper, music by Kurt Weill (produced Theater am Schiffbauerdamm, Berlin, 1928).   1929; translated as *The Threepenny Opera*, in *From the Modern Repertoire*, edited by Eric Bentley, 1949.
Happy End, with Elizabeth Hauptmann (produced Theater am Schiffbauerdamm, Berlin, 1929).   Translated as *Happy End*, 1982.
Lindberghflug, with Elizabeth Hauptmann and Kurt Weill (produced Deutsche Kammermusik, Baden-Baden, 1929). 1929; retitled *Der Ozeanflug*.
Aufstieg und Fall der Stadt Mahagonny, music by Kurt Weill (produced Leipzig Opera, Leipzig, 1930).   1929; translated as *The Rise and Fall of the City of Mahagonny*, 1976.
Das Badener Lehrstück vom Einverständnis, music by Paul Hindemith (produced Music Festival, Baden-Baden, 1929).   In *Versuche 2*, 1930; translated in *Harvard Advocate*, vol.134 no.4, February 1951; as *The Didactic Play of Baden-Baden on Consent*, in *Tulane Drama Review*, May 1960.
Der Jasager / Der Neinsager, from Arthur Waley's translation of the Japanese play *Taniko*, music by Kurt Weill (*Der Jasager* produced Zentralinstitut für Erziehung und Unterricht, Berlin, 1930; both versions produced together, Comenius-Gymnasium, Düsseldorf, 1958).   In *Versuche 4*, 1931; translated in *Accent* (Urbana), vol.7 no.2, 1946; as *He Who Said Yes; He Who Said No*, in *"The Measures Taken" and Other Lehrstücke*, 1977.
Die Massnahme, music by Hanns Eisler (produced Grosses Schauspielhaus, Berlin, 1930).   In *Versuche 4*, 1931; translated as *The Measures Taken*, in *Colorado Review* (Fort Collins), vol.1 no.1, Winter 1956–57, and reprinted in *The Modern Theatre 6*, edited by Eric Bentley.
Die heilige Johanna der Schlachthöfe, from the radio play, music by Paul Dessau (produced Deutsches Schauspielhaus, Hamburg, 1959).   In *Versuche 5*, 1932; translated as *St. Joan of the Stockyards*, in *From the Modern Repertoire*, edited by Eric Bentley, 1956.
Die Mutter, music by Hanns Eisler, from the novel by Gorky

(produced Theater am Schiffbauerdamm, Berlin, 1932). In *Versuche 7*, 1932; revised version in *Gesammelte Werke 2*, 1938; translated as *The Mother*, 1965.

Die Sieben Todsünden der Kleinbürger, music by Kurt Weill, choreography by George Balanchine and Boris Kochno (produced as *Les Sept Péchés capitaux*, Théâtre des Champs-Élysées, 1933). 1959; translated as *The Seven Deadly Sins of the Petty Bourgeoisie*, in *Tulane Drama Review*, vol.6 no.1, 1961.

Die Rundköpfe und die Spitzköpfe, music by Hanns Eisler (produced in Danish translation, Riddersalen Theatre, Copenhagen, 1936). In *Gesammelte Werke 2*, 1938; translated in *International Literature* (Moscow), 5, 1937; as *Roundheads and Peakheads*, in *"Jungle of Cities" and Other Plays*, 1966.

Die Gewehre der Frau Carrar (produced Salle Adyar, Paris, 1937). In *Gesammelte Werke, 2*, 1938; translated in *Theatre Workshop* (New York), April–June, 1938; as *The Guns of Carrar*, 1971; as *Señora Carrar's Rifles*, in *Collected Plays 4, iii*, 1983.

Furcht und Elend des Dritten Reiches (produced as *99%*, Paris, 1938). As *Deutschland: Ein Greuelmärchen*, 1941 (Moscow edition, 13 scenes); 1945 (24 scenes); translated as *Fear and Misery in the Third Reich* (12 scenes); as *The Private Life of the Master Race* (17 scenes), 1944; as *Fear and Misery of the Third Reich* (24 scenes), in *Collected Plays 4, iii*, 1983.

Die Ausnahme und die Regel (produced Givath Chajim, Palestine, 1938). In *Gesammelte Werke, 2*, 1938; translated as *The Exception and the Rule*, in *Chrysalis* (Boston), nos. 11–12, 1954; also in *"The Jewish Wife" and Other Short Plays*, 1965.

Die Horatier und die Kuratier (produced Theater der Jungen Garde, 1958). In *Gesammelte Werke, 2*, 1938; translated as *The Horatians and the Curatians*, in *Accent* (Urbana), vol.7 no.1, Autumn 1947.

Mutter Courage und ihre Kinder (produced Schauspielhaus, Zurich, 1941; revised version, Deutsches Theater, Berlin, 1949). In *Versuche 9*, 1949; revised edition, 1950; translated as *Mother Courage and Her Children*, 1941.

Der gute Mensch von Setzuan (produced Schauspielhaus, Zurich, 1943). In *Versuche, 12*, 1953; revised edition, 1958; translated as *The Good Woman of Setzuan*, in *Parables for the Theatre*, 1948; as *The Good Person of Setzuan*, in *Plays 2*, 1962.

Leben des Galilei (produced as *Galileo*, Schauspielhaus, Zurich, 1943; version revised with Charles Laughton, produced 1947; further revised version, produced Cologne, 1955). In *Versuche 14*, 1955; with more revisions, in *Stücke, 2*, 1957; translated by Brecht and Charles Laughton as *Galileo*, in *From the Modern Repertoire, Series 2*, edited by Eric Bentley, 1953; as *Life of Galileo*, in *Collected Plays 5, i*, 1980.

Der kaukasische Kreidekreis (produced in English, Nourse Little Theatre, Northfield, Minnesota, 1948; produced in German, Theater am Schiffbauerdamm, Berlin, 1954). In *Sinn und Form—Sonderheft*, 1949; translated as *The Caucasian Chalk Circle*, in *Two Parables for the Theatre*, 1948.

Herr Puntila und sein Knecht Matti (produced Schauspielhaus, Zurich, 1948). In Finnish translation, 1946; in *Versuche 10*, 1950; translated as *Mr. Puntila and His Man Matti* (=*Collected Plays 6, iii*), 1977.

Die Antigone des Sophokles, from Hölderlin's translation of Sophocles' play (Stadttheater, Chur, Switzerland, 1948). As *Antigonemodell* (a *Modellbuch*), 1949; revised edition, 1955; translated as *Antigone*, 1989.

Der Hofmeister, from the play by J.M.R. Lenz (produced by theBerliner Ensemble, Theater am Schiffbauerdam, East Berlin, 1950). In *Versuche 11*, 1951; translated as *The Tutor*, in *Collected Plays 9*, 1973 (US only); also translated by Pip Broughton, 1988 (UK).

Herrnburger Bericht, music by Paul Dessau (produced Deutsches Theater, East Berlin, 1951). 1951.

Das Verhör des Lukullus, from his radio play, music by Paul Dessau (produced Staatsoper, Berlin, 1951: subsequently retitled *Die Verurteilung des Lukullus*). 1951.

Der Prozess der Jeanne d'Arc zu Rouen 1431, from his radio play (produced by the Berliner Ensemble, East Berlin, 1952). In *Stücke 12*, 1959; translated as *The Trial of Joan of Arc*, in *Collected Plays 9*, 1973 (US only).

Don Juan, from Molière's *Dom Juan* (produced by the Berliner Ensemble, East Berlin, 1953). In *Stücke, 12*, 1959; translated as *Don Juan*, in *Collected Plays 9*, 1973 (US only).

Der Gesichte des Simone Machard, with Lion Feuchtwanger (produced Frankfurt, 1957). In *Sinn und Form*, 5–6, 1956; in *Stücke 9*, 1957; translated as *The Visions of Simone Machard*, 1965.

Die Tage des Kommune, music by Hanns Eisler (produced Stadttheater, Karl-Marx-Stadt, East Germany, 1956). In *Versuche 15* and *Stücke 10*, both 1957; translated as *The Days of the Commune*, in *Dunster Drama Review*, vol.10 no.2, 1971; in book form, 1978.

Pauken und Trompeten, from a play by Farquhar (produced 1956). In *Stücke 12*, 1959; translated as *Trumpets and Drums*, in *Collected Plays 9*, 1973 (US only).

Der aufhaltsame Aufstieg des Arturo Ui (produced Stuttgart, 1958). In *Sinn und Form: Zweites Sonderheft Bertolt Brecht*, 1957; in book form, in *Stücke 9*, 1957; translated as *The Resistable Rise of Arturo Ui* (=*Collected Plays 6, ii*), 1976.

Schweik im zweiten Weltkrieg, music by Hanns Eisler (produced Teatr Dramatyczny, Warsaw, 1957). In *Stücke 10* 1957; translated as *Schweik in the Second World War*, in *Collected Plays 7*, 1976.

Coriolan, from Shakespeare's *Coriolanus* (produced Schauspielhaus, Frankfurt, 1962). In *Stücke 11*, 1959; translated as *Coriolanus*, in *Collected Plays 9*, 1973 (US only).

Der Bettler oder der tote Hund. In *Stücke 13*, 1966; translated as *The Beggar or the Dead Dog*, in *Collected Plays 1*, 1970.

Er treibt den Teufel aus. In *Stücke 13*; translated as *Driving Out a Devil*, in *Collected Plays 1*, 1970.

Lux in Tenebris. In *Stücke 13*, 1966; translated as *Lux in Tenebris*, in *Collected Plays 1*, 1970.

Der Fischzug. In *Stücke 13*, 1966; translated as *The Catch*, in *Collected Plays 1*, 1970.

Was kostet das Eisen. In *Stücke 13*, 1966.

Dansen. In *Stücke 13*, 1966.

Turandot; oder, Der Kongress der Weisswäscher, music by Hanns Eisler (produced Schauspielhaus, Zurich, 1969). In *Gesammelte Werke*, 1967.

The Duchess of Malfi, with others, from Webster's play. In *Collected Plays 7*, 1976.

Screenplays

Kühle Wampe, 1932 (published in *Kühle Wampe; oder, Wem gehört die Welt: Protokoll des Films und Materialien*, edited by W. Gersh and W. Hecht, 1969); *Hangmen Also Die*, with John Wexley and Fritz Lang, 1942; *Texte für Filme* (published as part of *Gesammelte Werke*, 1967).

Radio Plays

Macbeth, from Shakespeare's play, 1927; *Hamlet*, from Shakespeare's play, 1931; *Die heilige Johanna der Schlachthöfe*, 1932; *Das Verhör des Lukullus*, 1940 (published in *Internationale Literatur* [Moscow], 3, 1940; augmented version, in *Versuche 11*, 1951; translated as *The Trial of Lucullus*, 1943; as *Lucullus*, in *Plays 1*, 1960); *Der Prozess der Jeanne d'Arc zu Rouen 1431* (published in *Stücke 12*, 1959).

Fiction

Der Dreigroschenroman.   1934; translated as *A Penny for the Poor*, 1937; as *The Threepenny Novel*, 1956.
Kalendergeschichten.   1948; translated as *Tales from the Calendar*, 1961.
Flüchtlingsgespräche.   1960.
Die Geschäfte des Herrn Julius Caesar.   1957; parts translated in *Nimbus*, February 1958.
Short Stories 1921–1946.   1983.

Verse

Taschenpostille.   1926.
Hauspostille.   1927; translated as *Manual of Piety*, 1966.
Lieder Gedichte Chöre, with Hanns Eisler.   1934.
Svenborger Gedichte.   1939.
Poems on the Theatre, translated by John Berger and Anya Bostock.   1961.
Poems 1913–1956 [translations], edited by John Willett and Ralph Mannheim, 1976; revised edition, 1979; corrected, 1979.
Gedichte aus dem Nachlass (2 vols.), edited by Herta Ramthun.   1983.
Poems and Songs from the Plays, translated by John Willett.   1990.

Memoirs and Letters

Arbeitsjournal (2 vols.).   1973.
Tagebücher 1920–1922; Autobiographische Aufzeichnungen 1920–1954.   1975.
Diaries 1920–1922.   1979.
Briefe (2 vols.), edited by Günter Gläser.   1981.
Letters 1913–1956.   1990.

Writings On Theatre

Theaterarbeit, with others.   1952.
Antigonemodell 1948 [play-text and commentary].   1955.
Couragemodell 1949 [play-text and commentary].   1958.
Aufbau einer Rolle: Galilei, with others.   1958.
Schriften zum Theater, 1918–1956 (7 vols.).   1963–64.
Brecht on Theatre, translated by John Willett.   1964.
The Messingkauf Dialogues, translated by John Willett.   1965.

Other

Schriften zur Literatur und Kunst [part of the *Gesammelte Werke*].   1967.
Schriften zur Politik und Gesellschaft [part of the *Gesammelte Werke*].   1967.

Editor, with Lion Feuchtwanger and Willi Bredel, *Das Wort* (Moscow), 1936–39.

*

Bibliographies

Klaus D. Petersen, *Bertolt-Brecht-Bibliographie*, Bad Homburg, 1968.
Darko Suvin and others, "A Selected Brecht Bibliography", in *Tulane Drama Review*, vol.12 no.2, 1968.
Reinhold Grimm, *Bertolt Brecht* (third edition), Stuttgart, 1971.
Maritta Rost, *Brecht-Bücher der DDR: Eine Bibliographie*, Leipzig, 1977.
Stephan Bock, *Brecht, Bertolt: Auswahl- und Ergänzungsbibliographie*, Bochum, 1979.

Criticism:

Books:
Martin Esslin, *Brecht: A Choice of Evils*, London, 1959; revised editions, 1969, 1980, 1984.
John Willett, *The Theatre of Brecht*, London, 1959; revised editions, 1967, 1977.
Peter Demetz (ed.), *Brecht: A Collection of Critical Essays*, Englewood Cliffs, New Jersey, 1962.
Ernst Wendt and others (eds.), *Bertolt Brecht*, Bad Godesberg, 1966.
Camille Demange, *Bertolt Brecht: Textes, points de vue critiques, témoignages, chronologie, bibliographie, illustrations*, Paris, 1967.
Frederick Ewen, *Bertolt Brecht: His Life, His Art and His Times*, New York, 1967.
Agnes Hüfner, *Brecht in Frankreich 1930–1963*, Stuttgart, 1968.
Werner Hecht, with others (eds.), *Bertolt Brecht: Sein Leben und Werk*, Berlin, 1969.
Helmut Jendreiek, *Bertolt Brecht: Drama der Veränderung*, Düsseldorf, 1969.
Rodney T.K. Symington, *Brecht und Shakespeare*, Bonn, 1970.
Julian Wulbern, *Brecht and Ionesco: Commitment in Context*, Urbana, Illinois, 1971.
Arnold L. Heinz, *Bertolt Brecht: Sonderband aus der Reihe Text + Kritik* (2 vols.), Munich, 1971–72.
John Fuegi, *The Essential Brecht*, Los Angeles, 1972.
Reinhold Grimm, *Bertolt Brecht: Die Struktur seines Werkes* (sixth edition), Nuremberg, 1972.
Werner Hecht, *Sieben Studien über Brecht*, Frankfurt, 1972.
Werner Mittenzwei, *Brechts Verhältnis zur Tradition*, Berlin, 1972.
Erika Munk (ed.), *Brecht*, New York, 1972.
Walter Benjamin, *Understanding Brecht* (from the German), New York, 1973.
Claude Hill, *Bertolt Brecht*, New York, 1974.
Paul Kussmaul, *Bertolt Brecht und das englische Drama der Renaissance*, Bern, 1974.
Siegfried Mews and Herbert Knust (eds.), *Essays on Brecht: Theater and Politics*, Chapel Hill, North Carolina, 1974.
Hubert Witt (ed.), *Brecht—As They Knew Him* (translated from the German), New York, 1974.
Arnolt Bronnen, *Tage mit Bertolt Brecht* (second edition), Berlin, 1975.
Karl H. Ludwig, *Bertolt Brecht: Philosophische Grundlagen und Implikationen seiner Dramaturgie*, Bonn, 1975.
Arrigo V. Subiotto, *Bertolt Brecht's Adaptations for the Berliner Ensemble*, London, 1975.
Klaus Völker, *Brecht Chronicle* (translated from the German), New York, 1975.
Heinz Brüggemann, *Literarische Technik und soziale*

Revolution: Versuche über das Verhältnis von Kunstproduktion, Marxismus und literarischer Tradition in den theoretischen Schriften Bertolt Brechts (second edition), Reinbek, 1976.

Annemarie Christiansen, *Brecht: Einführung in das Werk*, Stuttgart, 1976.

Ronald Gray, *Brecht the Dramatist*, Cambridge, 1976.

Herbert Claas, *Die politische Ästhetik Bertolt Brechts: Vom Baal zum Ceasar*, Frankfurt, 1977.

Anthony Tatlow, *The Mask of Evil: Brecht's Response to the Poetry, Theatre and Thought of China and Japan*, Bern, 1977.

Keith A. Dickson, *Towards Utopia: A Study of Brecht*, Oxford, 1978.

Werner Hecht (ed.), *Brecht: Vielseitige Betrachtungen*, Berlin, 1978.

Karl H. Schoeps, *Bertolt Brecht*, New York, 1978.

Alfred D. White, *Bertolt Brecht's Great Plays*, London, 1978.

Ralph J. Ley, *Brecht as Thinker: Studies in Literary Marxism and Existentialism*, Normal, Illinois, 1979.

Klaus Volker, *Brecht: A Biography* (from the German), London, 1979.

Wolfgang F. Haug and others (eds.), *Aktualisierung Brecht*, Berlin, 1980.

James K. Lyon, *Bertolt Brecht in America*, Princeton, New Jersey, 1980.

Betty N. Weber and Hubert Heinen (eds.), *Bertolt Brecht: Political Theory and Literary Practice*, Athens, Georgia, 1980.

Ute Baum, *Bertolt Brechts Verhältnis zu Shakespeare*, Berlin, 1981.

Eric Bentley, *The Brecht Commentaries 1943–1980*, New York, 1981.

Monika Hähnel, *Partei und Volk im Verständnis Brechts*, Berlin, 1981.

Jan Needle and Peter Thomson, *Brecht*, Chicago, 1981.

Patty L. Parmalee, *Brecht's America*, Columbus, Ohio, 1981.

Graham Bartram and Anthony Waine (eds.), *Brecht in Perspective*, Harlow (Essex) and New York, 1982.

Ronald Spiers, *Brecht's Early Plays*, London, 1982.

Anthony Tatlow and Tak-Wai Wong (eds.), *Brecht and East Asian Theatre*, Hong Kong, 1982.

Bruce Cook, *Brecht in Exile*, New York, 1983.

John Fuegi and others (eds.), *Beyond Brecht/Über Brecht hinaus* (*Brecht Yearbook 11*), Detroit, 1983.

Ronald Hayman, *Brecht: A Biography*, New York, 1983.

Ule Wedel, *Die Rolle der Frau bei Bertolt Brecht*, Frankfurt, 1983.

John Willett, *Brecht in Context*, London, 1983.

Ronald Hayman, *Bertolt Brecht: The Plays*, London, 1984.

Eric Bentley, *The Brecht Memoir*, New York, 1985.

John Fuegi and others (eds.), *Brecht: Women and Politics* (*Brecht Yearbook 12*), Detroit, 1985.

David Pike, *Lukács and Brecht*, Chapel Hill, North Carolina, 1985.

John Fuegi, *Brecht: Chaos, According to Plan*, Cambridge, 1986.

Hans M. Ritter, *Das gestische Prinzip bei Bertolt Brecht*, Cologne, 1986.

Ruth Berlau, *Living for Brecht: The Memoirs of Ruth Berlau*, New York, 1987.

Werner Mittelzwei, *Das Leben des Bertolt Brecht; oder, Der Umgang mit den Welträtseln* (2 vols.), Frankfurt, 1987.

John Rousse, *Brecht and the West German Theatre: The Practice and Politics of Interpretation*, Ann Arbor, Michigan, 1989.

Matthias J. Fischer, *Brechts Theatertheorie: Forschungsgeschichte, Forschungsstand, Perspektiven*, Frankfurt, 1989.

Elizabeth Wright, *A Modern Brecht: A Re-presentation*, London, 1989.

Pia Kleber and Colin Visser (eds.), *Re-interpreting Brecht: His Influence on Contemporary Drama and Film*, Cambridge, 1990.

Serials:
Brecht heute/Brecht Today: Jahrbuch der Internationalen Brecht-Gesellschaft, 1971–73; as *Brecht Jahrbuch*, 1974–80, then published irregularly.

* * *

Bertolt Brecht, as dramatist, theorist, and director, is one of the seminal figures in 20th-century theatre. Born in Augsburg, he made his name in the Weimar Republic, challenging Max Reinhardt's theatre of illusion and the breast-beating pathos of the Expressionists alike.

His first play, *Baal*, was a dramatic biography of a bohemian poet who flouts convention and exploits man and woman alike in his ruthless drive for self-realisation through sensuality. It is lyrical and episodic, crudely imagined but vigorously expressed and located in the provinces Brecht knew, where town meets country under the open sky. *Drums in the Night*, which is set in Berlin, followed. Kragler, a soldier long missing in colonial Africa, returns to find a revolution in progress and his fiancée Anna pregnant by a war-profiteer. This powerful evocation of the seedy underbelly of the post-war capital ends with Kragler turning his back on revolution to take up Anna's offer of sexual reconciliation in a great, white, wide bed.

In the Jungle of Cities, with its inscrutable, self-destructive duel in Chicago between the Malayan timber-merchant Schlink and the hick librarian Garga, is even more redolent of the ruthless struggle for survival Brecht experienced in Berlin. These three plays all have expressionist features. *Man Equals Man*, set, in homage to Kipling, in colonial India, is a knockabout comedy in which the docile porter Galy Gay is roughly brainwashed and converted into a fighting machine in the service of the British Raj. It is Brecht's first demonstration that a man is what circumstances make him.

The early anarchic plays culminated in his collaboration with Kurt Weill on the sexy, cynical, and revolutionary (if only in terms of musical theatre) *Threepenny Opera*, which was a hit with the bourgeois audiences whose entertainment Brecht had been trying to subvert since he draped the auditorium with banners telling them not to "gawp so romantically" at *Drums in the Night* in 1922.

Brecht joined Reinhardt's team of dramaturgs in Berlin in 1924. He also began to develop a collective mode of writing, getting his friends in to discuss work in progress. Dedicated women friends like Elisabeth Hauptmann, Margarete Steffin, and later Ruth Berlau did his research and typing. Brecht watched everybody's rehearsals, including Erwin Piscator's. It was his inability to find a politically coherent dramatic form for *Wheat*, a play about the Chicago grain exchange for the communist Piscatorbühne, that drew him to Marxism. The sight of policemen firing on unarmed May Day marchers in 1929 made him a convinced, but not a card-carrying, communist. He accepted the Party line that fascism signalled the death throes of capitalism and, in contrast to Piscator's heavily documentary and technically complex type of political play, he devised the *Lehrstück* (or teaching play) for amateurs as his contribution to the political education of the workers. These *Lehrstücke*, mainly choral pieces set to music by Weill (*He Who Said Yes/He Who Said No*), Hanns Eisler

(*The Measures Taken*), and Paul Hindemith (*Der Ozeanflug*), were pared-down, highly formalised exercises in role-playing. In *The Exception and the Rule* for example, a businessman is tried for shooting a coolie after their water has run out in the desert. The coolie had been reaching for his secret water reserve, but the judge rules that the businessman's assumption that he had a hidden weapon was reasonable and acquits him. Identifying the real mistake—the coolie should have suppressed any fellow-feeling for the class enemy—was the consciousness-raising exercise for spectators and performers alike. Close in spirit to the *Lehrstücke*, although conceived for an audience, is *The Mother*, adapted from Maxim Gorky's novel, which demonstrates how a mother is persuaded that her true loyalty is to her class, not her family, in the Russia of 1905.

The term "epic theatre" originated in Germany in the 1920's in the context of the dissemination of political ideas. Brecht made the term his own when he tabulated the results of his work in this field in *Notes on the Opera "The Rise and Fall of the City of Mahagonny"* in 1930. These listed the salient features of epic (or non-Aristotelian) theatre opposite the corresponding features of dramatic (or Aristotelian) theatre. He dismissed the standard dramatic theatre of his time as "culinary"—fancy fare for mindless audiences. Epic theatre was to provide challenging fare for thinking audiences. Dramatic theatre relied on empathy, absorbed the audience into a comforting illusion, drained their emotions, and left them predisposed to accept the world as they found it. Epic theatre would appeal to the intellect, control and limit empathy, and demand critical appraisal of the story. To achieve this, the seamless, interlocking scenes that made up dramatic illusion would give way to a montage of independent incidents that demonstrated a process taking place. The jumps and curves that led from scene to scene would compel the audience to judge what they saw. Brecht liked to think his plays were akin to scientific experiments which submitted human beings to various tests to identify the principles governing their behaviour and indicate socially beneficial improvements. The fixed hero who imposed his will on the world would be replaced by characters conditioned by their social environment who change when it changes, though they can also impose social change, so that there is a constant dialectic or process of reciprocal transformation. These principles were implemented by a range of techniques known as alienation effects.

Brecht went into exile the day after the Reichstag fire in 1933, settling in Skovbostrand in Denmark. In 1935 he was stripped of his German citizenship. Only in Zurich were his new plays performed in German until after the War. Brecht involved himself in the anti-fascist cause and in 1938 wrote *Fear and Misery of the Third Reich*, a string of naturalistic scenes from life under Hitler, and then the equally naturalistic *Señora Carrar's Rifles* as a boost for Republican morale in the Spanish Civil War. Brecht had been branded as a formalist in Moscow where Socialist Realism was the officially approved style, so reverting to realism was partly an act of self-defence.

Having lost the working-class audience at whom the *Lehrstücke* were targeted, Brecht turned to bigger plays with historical or exotic plots and produced a series of masterpieces in which the political message is more general and oblique and the Communist premises are integrated unobtrusively into the structure: *Life of Galileo*, *Mother Courage and her Children*, *The Caucasian Chalk Circle*, and *The Good Person of Setzuan*. These are full of colour and incident and, in Galileo, Courage, Grusha, and Azdak, have some of the most memorable figures in modern theatre.

In 1940, with invasion imminent, Brecht left for Finland where he dramatised a quirky tale of Finnish life as *Mr Puntila and his Man Matti* and wrote *The Resistable Rise of Arturo Ui* and *The Good Person of Setzuan*. In 1941 he travelled via the Soviet Union to the USA where he settled in Santa Monica. Hollywood employed him as an occasional scriptwriter, but, apart from his work on *Galileo* with Charles Laughton, the American theatre rejected him. In 1947, after deviously outwitting the committee on Un-American Activities at the height of McCarthyism, Brecht returned to Europe and settled in East Berlin. He retained an Austrian passport, a Swiss bank account, and a West German publisher. He was a private critic but never an open opponent of the Ulbricht regime, which for its part subsidised his work lavishly. He and his wife Helene Weigel founded the Berliner Ensemble in 1949, and in 1954 took over the Theater am Schiffbauerdamm.

Brecht now concentrated on directing, producing meticulously rehearsed stagings of *Mother Courage*, *Puntila*, *The Mother*, and *The Caucasian Chalk Circle*, which were carefully documented to serve as models for others. He introduced many techniques that became standard in the decades that followed—revealed lights and full white, un-atmospheric lighting, the half-curtain, uncluttered sets with sparse but well-made props, well-worn costumes, visible scene changes, demonstrative, unhistrionic acting, captions between scenes, songs interrupting the action—all carefully tested in rehearsal and handled with a freedom that made for startling freshness and conviction. His alienation effects were designed to defamiliarize the familiar and stimulate critical appraisal. In 1954 the Berliner Ensemble took the prizes for the best play and best production at the Paris Théâtre des Nations festival. In 1956 Brecht died while preparing the Ensemble's visit to London, which went ahead and changed the course of British theatre.

In recent years there has been a tendency in West Germany to revive Brecht's earlier plays. Dramatists like David Hare have pronounced his solutions too easy, and Botho Strauss has contended that Hitchcock's film *The Birds* will outlast *Mother Courage*, because the former is mythical whereas the latter is only instructive. Brecht indeed found he could not control the effect his plays had on audiences, and one must wonder whether directors will now find quite new readings of the plays, following the collapse of communism in the USSR and eastern Europe.

—Hugh Rorrison

See also *Volume 1* entries on *Baal*; *The Caucasian Chalk Circle*; *The Good Person of Setzuan*; *Life of Galileo*; *Man Equals Man*; *The Measures Taken*; *Mother Courage and Her Children*; *The Resistable Rise of Arturo Ui*; *The Threepenny Opera*.

BRENTON, Howard. Born in Portsmouth, Hampshire, England, 13 December 1942. Educated at Chichester High School; St. Catharine's College, Cambridge, BA (honours) in English 1965. Married Jane Fry in 1970; two sons. First plays produced 1965; stage manager in several repertory companies; resident dramatist, Royal Court Theatre, London, 1972–73. Recipient: Arts Council bursary, 1969, 1970; John Whiting Award, 1970; *Evening Standard* award, 1977, 1985.

Howard Brenton (mid-1980's)

Works

Collections

"Christie in Love" and Other Plays (includes *Heads; The Education of Skinny Spew*).   1970.
Plays for the Poor Theatre (includes *The Saliva Milkshake; Christie in Love; Heads; The Education of Skinny Spew; Gum and Goo*). 1980.
Plays 1 (includes *Christie in Love; Magnificence; The Churchill Play; Weapons of Happiness; Epsom Downs; Sore Throats*). 1986.
Plays 2 (includes *The Romans in Britain; Thirteenth Night; The Genius; Bloody Poetry; Greenland*). 1989.
Three Plays (includes *Measure for Measure; How Beautiful with Badges; A Sky-Blue Life*), edited by John Bull. 1989.

Stage Works

Ladder of Fools (produced University of Cambridge, Cambridge, 1965).
Winter, Daddykins (produced Playhouse, Nottingham, 1965).
It's My Criminal (produced Royal Court Theatre, London, 1966).
A Sky-Blue Life, adaptation of stories by Gorky (produced Little Theatre, London, 1966; revised version produced Open Space Theatre, London, 1971).   In *Three Plays*, 1989.
Gargantua, adaptation of the novel by Rabelais (produced Brighton, 1969).
Gum and Goo (produced Brighton, 1969).   In *Plays for Public Places*, 1972.

Revenge (produced Royal Court Theatre Upstairs, London, 1969).   1970.
Heads (produced University of Bradford, Bradford, 1969).   In *"Christie in Love" and Other Plays*, 1970.
The Education of Skinny Spew (produced University of Bradford, Bradford, 1969).   In *"Christie in Love" and Other Plays*, 1970.
Christie in Love (produced Brighton, 1969).   In *"Christie in Love" and Other Plays*, 1970.
Fruit (produced Royal Court Theatre Upstairs, London, 1970).
Wesley (produced Eastbrook Hall Methodist Church, Bradford, 1970).   In *Plays for Public Places*, 1972.
Scott of the Antarctic; or, What God Didn't See (produced Mecca Ice Rink, Bradford, 1971).   In *Plays for Public Places*, 1972.
Lay By, with others (produced, Edinburgh, 1971).   1972.
Hitler Dances (produced Traverse Theatre, Edinburgh, 1972).   1982.
How Beautiful with Badges (produced Open Space Theatre, London, 1972).   In *Three Plays*, 1989.
England's Ireland, with others (produced Mickery Theatre, Amsterdam, 1972).
Measure for Measure, from the play by Shakespeare (produced Northcott Theatre, Exeter, 1972).   In *Three Plays*, 1989.
A Fart for Europe, with David Edgar (produced London, 1973).
The Screens, from a play by Jean Genet (produced New Vic Studio, Bristol, 1973).

Brassneck, with David Hare (produced Playhouse, Nottingham, 1973). 1974.
Magnificence (produced Royal Court Theatre, London, 1973). 1973.
Mug (produced at the Inter-Cities Conference, Manchester, 1973).
The Churchill Play: As It Will Be Performed in the Winter of 1984 by the Internees of Churchill Camp Somewhere in England (produced Playhouse, Nottingham, 1974; revised version produced The Other Place, Stratford-upon-Avon, 1978; further revised version produced Barbican Theatre, London, 1988). 1974; revised version in *Plays 1*, 1986.
Jedefrau, from a play by Hofmannsthal (produced Mozart Festival Fringe, Salzburg, Austria, 1974).
The Saliva Milkshake, adaptation of the novel *Under Western Eyes* by Conrad (produced London, 1975). 1977.
Government Property (produced Aarhus, Denmark, 1975).
Weapons of Happiness (produced National Theatre, London, 1976). 1976.
Epsom Downs (produced The Roundhouse, London, 1977). 1977.
Deeds, with others (produced Playhouse, Nottingham, 1978). In *Plays and Players* (London), May and June 1978.
Sore Throats (produced The Warehouse, London, 1979) With *Sonnets of Love and Opposition,* 1979.
The Life of Galileo, from a play by Brecht (produced National Theatre, London, 1980). 1980.
The Romans in Britain (produced National Theatre, London, 1980). 1980; revised version, 1982.
A Short Sharp Shock!, with Tony Howard (produced Theatre Royal, Stratford East, London, 1980). With *Thirteenth Night*, 1981.
Thirteenth Night (produced The Warehouse, London, 1981). With *A Short Sharp Shock!*, 1981.
Danton's Death, from a play by Büchner (produced National Theatre, London, 1982). 1982.
The Thing (for children; produced Brackley, Northamptonshire, 1982).
Conversations in Exile, from a work by Brecht (produced 1982). In *Yale/Theatre,* Spring 1986.
The Genius (produced Royal Court Theatre, London, 1983). 1983.
Sleeping Policemen, with Tunde Ikoli (produced Hemel Hempstead, 1983). 1984.
Bloody Poetry (produced Haymarket Theatre, Leicester, 1984). 1985.
Pravda: A Fleet Street Comedy, with David Hare (produced National Theatre, London, 1985). 1985; revised edition, 1986.
Greenland (produced Royal Court Theatre, London, 1988). 1988.
H.I.D. (Hess is Dead) (produced Almeida Theatre, London, 1989). 1989.
Iranian Nights, with Tariq Ali (produced Royal Court Theatre, London, 1989). 1989.
Moscow Gold, with Tariq Ali (produced Barbican Theatre, London, 1990). 1990.
Berlin Bertie (produced Royal Court Theatre, London, 1992). 1992.

Screenplays
Skin Flicker, 1973.

Television Plays
Lushly, 1972; *The Saliva Milkshake,* 1975 (published 1975);

The Paradise Run, 1976; *A Desert of Lies,* 1984; *Dead Head* serial, 1986 (published 1987).

Fiction

Diving for Pearls. 1989.

Verse

"*Notes from a Psychotic Journal*" and *Other Poems.* Privately printed, 1969.
Sonnets of Love and Opposition. With *Sore Throats,* 1979.
Nail Poems. 1981.

*

Bibliographies

Tony Mitchell, "Theatre Checklist No.5: Howard Brenton", in *Theatre Facts,* vol.2 no.1, 1975.

Criticism

Books:
John Bull, *New British Political Dramatists,* London and New York, 1984; revised edition, 1990.
Tony Mitchell (compiler), *File on Brenton,* London, 1988.
Richard Boon, *Howard Brenton,* London, 1992.

Articles:
Interview with Peter Ansorge, in *Plays and Players,* London, February, 1972.
Howard Brenton and Tony Mitchell, "The Red Theatre Under the Bed" (interview), in *New Theatre Quarterly,* 11, 1987.
Susan Bennett, "At the End of the Great Radical Tradition? Recent Plays by Howard Brenton", in *Modern Drama,* 33, 1990.
Richard Boon, "Retreating to the Future: Brenton in the Eighties", in *Modern Drama,* 33, 1990.
Judy L. Oliva, "Howard Brenton's Dramaturgy of the Nineties: Eclipsing Utopia", in *Theater Three,* 9, 1990.

*   *   *

Howard Brenton's considerable body of work for the theatre—some 15 full-length plays since 1969 plus translations and adaptations of Shakespeare, Büchner, and Brecht—has consistently explored the pathology of power. Private spaces are invaded by public worlds, and intimacy is impossible.

The setting for *Sore Throats* is a bare room. In it lives a divorcée in her late 30's. To it come her husband, a policeman, and a younger woman as lodger. The man communicates mainly through physical violence, but his (and the play's) central speech is a long, horrifying account of his girlfriend giving birth in the wilds of Canada. The most domestic of acts is located on the broadest possible stage. A barely articulate man is inexplicably given language of great evocative power. The spectator's imagination soars out and away beyond the sordid South London flat. It is as if Brenton has suddenly seen the naturalist trap he is constructing for himself and escapes through an evocation of primitive space.

Sex in Brenton's plays can never exist for itself because free and equal exchange is impossible. It is rather a situation, or a metaphor, exemplifying larger relations of power. Heroes of the Left are censured. Shelley's advocacy of free love in *Bloody Poetry* is, perhaps unfairly, shown as hypocritical through his aristocratic philandering with powerless women such as Mary Shelley and Claire Clairemont. Christie's "love" in *Christie in Love* is with women he has killed, but the necrophiliac's history is mediated by a brutal police-inspector and a limerick-reciting constable. Christie's notorious private life is a vivid means for dramatising Brenton's main concern, the unequal relations between interrogator and suspect. The constable's limericks are a measure of Brenton's distance from the erotic; they are all about sex, but they are not sexy.

It is ironic that *The Romans in Britain* should have been prosecuted under the Sexual Offences Act because of simulated buggery between actors playing Romans and Celts. Rape was Brenton's metaphor for colonialism and the play parallels the Roman occupation of Britain with the British occupation of Ireland. Brenton would argue that the prosecution was maliciously political. It could equally be argued that the crazed imaginations of the prosecution detected far more intimate intercourse between sex and politics than Brenton would allow. But he was certainly right to separate them for his principal characters in *The Genius*. We expect Leo and Gilly, brilliant scientist and research assistant, to sleep together as well as work together. But they have no sexual relations, and not through caution or prudery. The play proposes that the lust for knowledge can transcend divisions of gender and that it is the impersonal, despite the feminist ending at Greenham Common, that is political. No surprise, then, to find that Brenton had already translated Brecht's *Galileo* for a National Theatre production in 1980. Brecht's hero indulges in food, not women. *The Romans in Britain* is a *tour de force* which not only links two totally different time-periods but also invents a language for Celts which is both comprehensible and alien.

From the mid-1970's Brenton's major works have deliberately pushed against the limits of contemporary theatre's finance and structure. He has obtained large theatrical spaces and casts to play out a series of epic statements about the state of Britain. An internment camp and a factory are the settings for *The Churchill Play* and *Weapons of Happiness*. Prisoners and workers try to subvert their rulers through wit and random violence, but power always reasserts itself. The icon of ancient rule is Churchill himself, who rises from his coffin and forces everyone to participate in a replay of his history and paranoias. His watchwords are blood and heritage and his obsession is with the unity of "the Island Race".

Epsom Downs provides a panoramic view of that race at play on Derby Day, a "carnival" day for the workers which finishes by reinforcing the class relations between owners and jockeys. Only the ghost of Emily Davison, who threw herself in front of a horse to publicise women's suffrage, disturbs the apolitical fun, but she is a ghost. The jockey Lester Pigott is the working-class hero invoked by the sane and the mad (he would, as Brenton did not then know, later be jailed for tax evasion). This is a kind of heroism within capitalist criteria but not according to Brenton's socialist perspectives. His instinct, to debunk this figure in 1977, has been proven right.

In his two best-known, recent works, *Pravda* and *Moscow Gold*, Brenton continues his large-scale analysis of power-mania, but he would appear to have decided that farce, rather than tragedy, is the appropriate genre for our times. Both plays are collaborations (with David Hare and Tariq Ali respectively) so the problem arises of attribution. *Pravda* pits a megalomaniac newspaper proprietor, Lambert Le Roux against a wimpish liberal editor, Andrew May, who is backed in his stand for integrity by his teacher-historian wife, Rebecca. The tortured young liberal is found elsewhere in Hare's work, Lambert descends from Churchill and any of the Romans, and Rebecca seems the composite figure of virtuous feminism created by so many left-wing male imagin-

ations in the 1980's. The very public nature of all the power-plays, including a hilarious scene where Le Roux practises his samurai techniques in front of his wife in their bedroom, can be related to Brenton's disbelief in any politics of intimacy. When Andrew gives in to Le Roux's tyranny and money and agrees to work for his "foundry of lies", Rebecca leaves him, so power is now uninterrupted by sex.

Moscow Gold could be said to draw up a balance-sheet between socialism and power at the end of the Russian Revolution and the Cold War. Andropov, Gorbachev, and Yeltsin argue on and around a huge table-revolve as Stalin's statue cracks and the nationalities rise. Lenin and Gorbachev hold an angelic conversation in mid-air during a break in the Rekyjavik negotiations. A Moscow food-queue winds on and off-stage, a posse of female Kremlin cleaners acts as a contemptuous chorus to the Politburo machinations around the table, and the pathetic domestic tale of an ex-KGB man and his horrified son counterpoints the lives of the great. This is the weakest strand in this work of "living history" and could stand as further evidence of Brenton's unease at any separation of private trauma from public events. By contrast, two scenes of cunning political farce show Gorbachev and Raisa in bed discussing the Politburo, and Raisa massaging Gorbachev after a work-out where his back, neck, and buttocks come to stand for troublesome republics and knotty members of the Politburo. If this is Brenton's scene then it confirms his determination to consider the body as always politic. Politics in the 1990's will produce even more bizarre bedfellows and alliances than in the 1980's. Brenton's switch from tragedy to farce makes very good Marxist sense.

—Tony Dunn

See also *Volume 1* entries on *The Churchill Play*; *The Romans in Britain*.

BRIDIE, James. Born Osborne Henry Mavor in Glasgow, Scotland, 3 January 1888. Educated at Glasgow Academy; Glasgow High School; University of Glasgow, 1905–13 (editor, *University Magazine*); qualified as physician: fellow, Royal Faculty of Physicians and Surgeons, Glasgow. Served in the Royal Army Medical Corps, 1914–19 and 1939–42: major. Married Rona Bremner in 1923; two sons, including the writer Ronald Mavor. Staff member, Glasgow Royal Infirmary, 1913; practising physician from 1919; consulting physician from 1923, and governor, Victoria Infirmary, Glasgow: professor of medicine, Anderson College, Glasgow; first play, *The Sunlight Sonata*, produced 1928; used pseudonym James Bridie from 1929; founder, with Paul Vincent Carroll, Glasgow Citizens' Theatre, based in the former Royal Princess's Theatre, 1943; founder, Glasgow College of Drama, 1950; member of the Council, League of Dramatists; Scottish chairman, Arts Council of Great Britain. LL.D: University of Glasgow, 1939. Fellow, Royal Society of Literature. CBE (Commander, Order of the British Empire), 1946. Died in Edinburgh, 29 January 1951.

Works

Collections

The Switchback; The Pardoner's Tale; The Sunlight Sonata. 1930.

"The Anatomist" and Other Plays (includes *Tobias and the Angel* and *The Amazed Evangelist*).   1931.

"Colonel Wotherspoon" and Other Plays (includes *What it is to Be Young; The Dancing Bear; The Girl Who Did Not Want to Go to Kuala Lumpur*).   1934.

Moral Plays: (includes *Marriage is No Joke; Mary Read; The Black Eye*).   1936.

"The King of Nowhere" and Other Plays (includes *The Last Trump* and *Babes in the Wood*).   1938.

"Susannah and the Elders" and Other Plays (includes *What Say They?; The Golden Legend of Shults; The Kitchen Comedy*).   1940.

Plays for Plain People (includes *Lancelot; Holy Isle; Mr. Bolfry; Jonah 3; The Sign of the Prophet Jonah; The Dragon and the Dove*).   1944.

"John Knox" and Other Plays (includes *Dr. Angelus; It Depends What You Mean; The Forrigan Reel*).   1949.

Stage Works

The Sunlight Sonata; or, To Meet the Seven Deadly Sins (produced Lyric Theatre, Glasgow, 1928).   In *The Switchback . . .*, 1930.

The Switchback (produced Birmingham Repertory Theatre, Birmingham, 1929).   In *The Switchback . . .*, 1930; revised version (produced 1931).

What it is to Be Young (produced Birmingham Repertory Theatre, Birmingham, 1929).   In *"Colonel Wotherspoon" and Other Plays*, 1934.

The Anatomist: A Lamentable Comedy of Know, Burke, and Hare, and the West Port Murders (produced Lyceum Theatre, Edinburgh, 1930).   In *"The Anatomist" and Other Plays*, 1931.

The Girl Who Did Not Want to Go to Kuala Lumpur (produced Lyric Theatre, Glasgow, 1930).   In *"Colonel Wotherspoon" and Other Plays*, 1934.

Tobias and the Angel (produced Festival Theatre, Cambridge, 1930).   In *"The Anatomist" and Other Plays*, 1931.

The Dancing Bear (produced Lyric Theatre, Glasgow, 1931).   In *"Colonel Wotherspoon" and Other Plays*, 1934.

The Amazed Evangelist (produced Westminster Theatre, London, 1932).   In *"The Anatomist" and Other Plays*, 1931.

Jonah and the Whale: A Morality (produced Westminster Theatre, London, 1932).   1932; revised version, as *The Sign of the Prophet Jonah* (broadcast 1942), in *Plays for Plain People*, 1944.

The Proposal, from a story by Chekhov (produced Lyric Theatre, Glasgow, 1932).

A Sleeping Clergyman (produced Festival Theatre, Malvern, 1933).   1933.

Marriage is No Joke (produced King's Theatre, Glasgow, 1934).   1934.

Colonel Wotherspoon; or, The Fourth Way of Greatness (produced Lyric Theatre, Glasgow, 1934).   In *"Colonel Wotherspoon" and Other Plays*, 1934.

Mary Read, with Claud Gurney (produced Her Majesty's Theatre, London, 1934).   1935.

The Black Eye (produced Shaftesbury Theatre, London, 1935).   1935.

Mrs. Waterbury's Millennium.   1935.

The Tragic Muse. In *Scottish One-Act Plays*, edited by J.M. Reid, 1935.

Storm in a Teacup, from a play by Bruno Frank (produced Lyceum Theatre, Edinburgh, 1936; as *Storm over Patsy*, produced Theatre Guild, New York, 1937).   1936.

Susannah and the Elders (produced Duke of York's Theatre, London, 1937).   In *"Susannah and the Elders" and Other Plays*, 1940.

Roger—Not So Jolly, with Ronald Mavor.   1937.

The King of Nowhere (produced Old Vic Theatre, London, 1938).   In *"The King of Nowhere" and Other Plays*, 1938.

Babes in the Wood (produced Embassy Theatre, London, 1938).   1938.

The Last Trump (produced Festival Theatre, Malvern, 1938).   In *"The King of Nowhere" and Other Plays*, 1938.

The Letter-Box Rattles.   1938.

The Starling. In *London Mercury*, December 1938.

The Golden Legend of Shults (produced Repertory Theatre, Perth, Scotland, 1939).   In *"Susannah and the Elders" and Other Plays*, 1940.

What Say They? (produced Festival Theatre, Malvern, 1939).   1939.

The Niece of the Hermit Abraham (produced Lyric Theatre, Glasgow, 1942; revised version, as *The Dragon and the Dove; or, How the Hermit Abraham Bought the Devil for His Niece*, produced Lyric Theatre, Glasgow, 1942).

Jonah 3 (produced Manchester, 1942).   In *Plays for Plain People*, 1944.

Holy Isle (produced Arts Theatre, London, 1942).   In *Plays for Plain People*, 1944.

A Change for the Worse (produced Lyric Theatre, Glasgow, 1942).   In *Tedious and Brief*, 1944.

Mr. Bolfry (produced Westminster Theatre, London, 1943).   In *Plays for Plain People*, 1944; edited by J.T. Low, 1978.

It Depends What You Mean: An Improvisation for the Glockenspiel (produced Westminster Theatre, London, 1944).   1948.

The Forrigan Reel (produced Glasgow Citizens' Theatre, 1944; revised version produced Sadler's Wells Theatre, London, 1945).   In *"John Knox" and Other Plays*, 1949.

Lancelot (produced Glasgow Citizens' Theatre, 1945).   In *Plays for Plain People*, 1944.

Hedda Gabler, from the play by Ibsen (produced Glasgow Citizens' Theatre, 1945).

The Pyrate's Den (produced 1946).

The Wild Duck, from a play by Ibsen (produced Glasgow Citizens' Theatre, 1946).

John Knox (produced Glasgow Citizens' Theatre, 1947).   In *"John Knox" and Other Plays*, 1949.

Dr. Angelus (produced Lyceum Theatre, Edinburgh, 1947).   In *"John Knox" and Other Plays*, 1949.

Gog and Magog (produced Arts Theatre, London, 1948).

Daphne Laureola (produced Wyndhams Theatre, London, 1949).   1949.

The Tintock Cup, with others (produced Glasgow Citizens' Theatre, 1949).

Paradise Enow. In *One-Act Plays for the Amateur Theatre*, edited by M.H. Fuller, 1949.

Mr. Gillie (produced Theatre Royal, Glasgow, 1950).   1950.

The Queen's Comedy: A Homeric Fragment (produced Lyceum Theatre, Edinburgh, 1950).   1950.

Red Riding Hood, with others (produced Glasgow Citizens' Theatre, 1950).

The Baikie Charivari; or, The Seven Prophets (produced Glasgow Citizens' Theatre, 1952).   1953.

Meeting at Night, edited by Archibald Batty (produced 1956).   1956.

Screenplays

Under Capricorn, with Hume Cronyn, 1949; *Stage Fright*, with Alma Reville and Whitfield Cook, 1950.

Radio Plays

The Kitchen Comedy, 1938 (published in *"Susannah and the Elders" and Other Plays*, 1940); *The Sign of the Prophet Jonah*, 1942 (published in *Plays for Plain People*, 1944).

Fiction

The Christmas Card (story).   1949.

Memoirs and Letters

One Way of Living (autobiography).   1939.

Other

Some Talk of Alexander: A Revue with Interludes in the Antique Mode. 1926.
The Perilous Adventures of Sir Bingo Walker of Alpaca Square (for children).   1931.
Alphabet for Little Glasgow Highbrows (essays).   1934.
Tedious and Brief (miscellany).   1944.
The British Drama.   1945.
A Small Stir: Letters on the English, with Moray McLaren. 1949.

*

Criticism

Books:
Winifred Bannister, *Bridie and His Theatre: A Study of Bridie's Personality, His Stage Plays, and His Work for the Foundation of a Scottish National Theatre*, London, 1955.
U. Gerber, *James Bridies Dramen: Versuch einer Analyse*, Bern, 1961.
Helen L. Luyben, *Bridie: Clown and Philosopher*, Philadelphia, 1965.
Ernest G. Mardon, *The Conflict Between the Individual and Society in the Plays of James Bridie*, Glasgow, 1972.
Michael Nentwich, *Der schottische Shaw: Untersuchungen zum dramatischen Werk von James Bridie*, Bern, 1977.
Terence Tobin, *James Bridie*, Boston, 1980.
J.T. Low, *Doctors, Devils, Saints, and Sinners: A Critical Study of the Major Plays of James Bridie*, Edinburgh, 1980.

Articles:
H.L. Luyben, "The Dramatic Method of Bridie", in *Educational Theatre Journal*, 15, 1963.

* * *

A practising doctor for many years, James Bridie came late to the theatre: his first play, *The Sunlight Sonata*, appeared under the pseudonym of Mary Henderson in 1928 when he was 40: a year later he attracted critical attention with a play on a medical theme, *The Switchback*; and he had his first real success in 1930 with perhaps the best known of his pieces, *The Anatomist*. The latter was again a play with a medical theme, although this time medicine was mingled with murder and an Edinburgh period setting in what was a highly successful, emotionally powerful, and intellectually engaging piece of melodrama that reworked the Burke and Hare tale of body-snatching. Yet, notwithstanding his late start, Bridie's output was prodigious, amounting in all to some 40 plays, although many were hastily written and their quality distinctly uneven.

He worked mainly in the Scottish theatre and had several modest successes in London, and for many years several of his plays were frequently performed on repertory stages throughout Britain. Despite the fact that few of his plays are revived at all regularly today outside Scotland, he must be acknowledged a dramatist of no mean achievement.

Like Shaw, whose example exercised great influence on his work, Bridie had a particular flair for the comico-satiric mode, for crafting persuasive stage characters, and for fashioning strong, polemical, often witty and always theatrically engaging dialogue. Perhaps nowhere in his work are these qualities better in evidence than in *The Anatomist*. But in that play too, as in much of his other work, certain structural deficiencies are equally evident: while the opening and central scenes are impressively handled, the dialogue vigorous, and the characterisations persuasive, the orchestration of the final scenes is rather weak. This was not uncharacteristic: Bridie was as adept as Shaw at establishing and developing dramatically engaging situations, but his dramatic resolutions, unlike those of Shaw, were all too frequently either botched or contrived. Perhaps because he is less abstract in his treatment of subjects than Shaw, Bridie's plays have not worn as well as those of the Irishman.

Nor, in the main, do audiences today favour the kinds of subject matter to which he was inclined. He had a particular liking for various kinds of religious and biblical material, predilections which underpinned plays in other respects as different as the whimsical *Tobias and the Angel*, the wry *Jonah and the Whale*, a curious mixture of fairytale and symbolic satire, the overly ambitious *The Amazed Evangelist*, and one of his finest plays, *A Sleeping Clergyman*, which is an exploration of the destructive and regenerative impulses in life through the adventures of three generations of a representative family.

Other pieces with a certain religious emphasis include *Suzannah and the Elders*, *The Last Trump*, and the archly amusing *The Devil and Mr. Bolfry*, a play which put the Devil in a modern setting. In the latter play, a group of rather disparate young people comes together in the house of a Calvinist minister in the Scottish Highlands, dabbles in witchcraft, and summons up the Devil in the guise of a minister of the Church of Scotland. The play reveals Bridie's strengths and weaknesses as a playwright: the first half is witty and well-engineered, and the situation set up is engaging, but the promise of a searching exploration of issues like good and evil, the authority of religion, and the ultimate purpose of things is not realised, and the piece degenerates into mere vapid talk.

Bridie's best plays engage with themes of moral responsibility, although their ultimate high seriousness is underpinned, and occasionally, as with Shaw, undermined, by a sharp sense of the comic: in Bridie this ranges from trenchant irony to rather mawkish whimsy. Bridie's talents were various however, and he could script some decidedly curious fare, like, for example, *Mary Read*, a costume melodrama written in 1934 in collaboration with Claude Gurney, that recounts the story of a celebrated female pirate: with Robert Donat and Flora Robson in the lead roles, it might have been conceived more for the popular cinema than the 1930's stage. Bridie's *forte* however was humour of an intellectual, combative kind. The didactic note is never wholly absent from his work, and in some respects that penchant for debate, which helped make the plays appealing in their time, accounts now for their neglect: too many of the issues treated seem somewhat *passé*.

Part of Bridie's success lay, too, in the fact that he was a reliable professional writer, a craftsman who always kept the needs of players and managements in mind as he shaped his plays. In that respect he was not uncharacteristic of many playwrights between the two World Wars: like much of the more serious theatre of that decade, most of his work seems to have been crafted for the taste of a middle-class, liberal, and humane intelligentsia, providing an entertainment for the educated that turned on amiable and urbane discussion, spiced with a satirical edge and a touch of wry humour. The best of the plays are never less than interesting. But they are, too, distinctly limited, more ruminative than challenging, and more inclined to toy with than to confront the major social, political, and philosophical issues of the time. In these regards also, perhaps Bridie's plays were all too characteristic of English drama in the 1930's.

—Kenneth Richards

————————

BRIEUX, Eugène. Born in Paris, 19 January 1858. Attended elementary school; learned cabinet-making in his father's workshop; also studied Italian and Greek. Journalist in Rouen, becoming editor of the *Nouvelliste de Rouen*; first play, *Bernard Palissy*, produced 1879; returned to Paris, and worked on *Le Figaro* and other newspapers, until 1908; moved to Agay, near Cannes, 1908, and subsequently lived on a farm. Elected to the Académie-Française, 1910. Died in Nice, 6 December 1932.

Works

Collections

Three Plays (includes *Damaged Goods*; *Maternity*; *The Three Daughters of Monsieur Dupont*).   1911.
The Woman on Her Own; False Gods; The Red Robe.   1916.
Théâtre complet (9 vols.).   1921–30.

Stage Works

Bernard Palissy, with Gaston Salandri (produced Théâtre Cluny, Paris, 1879).   1880.
Le Bureau des divorces, with Gaston Salandri.   1880.
Stenio, music by Frédéric Le Roy (produced Théâtre des Arts, Rouen, 1881).   1881.
Ménages d'artistes (produced Théâtre Libre, Paris, 1890). 1890; revised edition, 1898; translated as *Artists' Families*, 1918.
La Fille de Duramé (produced Théâtre Français, Rouen, 1890).   1890.
Monsieur de Réboval (produced Théâtre de l'Odéon, Paris, 1892).   1892.
Blanchette (produced Théâtre Libre, Paris, 1892; revised version produced Comédie-Française, Paris, 1903).   1892; translated as *Blanchette*, with *The Escape*, 1913.
La Couvée (produced privately, Rouen, 1893; produced publicly, Université Populaire du Faubourg Saint-Antoine, 1903).   1904.
L'Engrenage (produced Théâtre de la Comédie-Parisienne, Paris, 1894).   1894.
La Rose bleue (produced Grand Théâtre, Geneva, 1895). 1895.
Les Bienfaiteurs (produced Théâtre de la Porte-Saint-Martin, Paris, 1896).   1897.

L'Évasion (produced Comédie-Française, Paris, 1896). 1897; translated as *The Escape*, with *Blanchette*, 1913.
Les Trois Filles de M. Dupont (produced Théâtre du Gymnase, Paris, 1897).   1899; translated as *The Three Daughters of Monsieur Dupont*, in *Three Plays*, 1911.
L'École des belles-mères, from his *La Couvée* (produced Théâtre du Gymnase, Paris, 1898).   1898; translated as *The School for Mothers-in-Law*, in *The International*, 3, 1911.
Résultat des courses! (produced Théâtre Antoine, Paris, 1898).   1898.
Le Berceau (produced Comédie-Française, Paris, 1898). 1898.
La Robe rouge (produced Théâtre du Vaudeville, Paris, 1900).   1900; translated as *The Red Robe*, 1915.
Les Remplaçantes (produced Théâtre Antoine, Paris, 1901).   1901.
Les Avariés (produced Théâtre du Gymnase, Liège, 1902). 1902; translated as *Damaged Goods*, in *Three Plays*, 1911
La Petite Amie (produced Comédie-Française, Paris, 1902). 1902.
Maternité (produced Théâtre Antoine, Paris, 1903).   1904; translated as *Maternity*, 1907.
La Déserteuse (produced Théâtre de l'Odéon, Paris, 1904). 1904.
L'Armature, from a novel by Paul Hervieu (produced Théâtre du Vaudeville, Paris, 1905).   1905.
Les Hannetons (produced Théâtre de la Renaissance, Paris, 1906).   1906.
La Française (produced Théâtre de l'Odéon, Paris, 1907). 1907.
Simone (produced Comédie-Française, Paris, 1908).   1908.
Suzette (produced Théâtre du Vaudeville, Paris, 1909).   In *L'Illustration théâtrale*, 1909; revised as *La Plus Forte*, 1909.
La Foi (produced Théâtre de Monte Carlo, 1909).   1912; translated as *False Gods*, in *The Woman on Her Own; False Gods; The Red Robe*, 1916.
La Femme seule (produced Théâtre du Gymnase, Paris, 1912).   1913; translated as *The Woman on Her Own*, in *The Woman on Her Own; False Gods; The Red Robe*, 1916.
Le Bourgeois aux champs, with Gaston Salandri (produced Théâtre de l'Odéon, Paris, 1914).   In *L'illustration théâtrale*, May 1914.
Les Américains chez nous (produced Théâtre de l'Odéon, Paris, 1920).   1920.
Trois Bons Amis (produced Théâtre de l'Odéon, Paris, 1921). 1921.
L'Avocat (produced Théâtre de Vaudeville, Paris, 1922).   1922.
L'Enfant (produced Théâtre de Vaudeville, Paris, 1923).   In *La Petite Illustration théâtrale*, 1923; retitled, as *Pierette et Galaor*, 1923.
La Famille Lavolette (produced Théâtre des Nouveautés, Paris, 1926).   1926.
La Régence.   In *Les Oeuvres libres*, 67, 1927.
Puisque Je t'aime (produced Comédie-Française, Paris, 1929).   In *Revue des deux mondes*, June 1929.

Fiction

Les Remplaçantes, from the stage play, with Marcel Luguet.   1901.

Verse

Mi-Ki-Ka.   1893.

Other

Voyage aux Indes et en Indo-Chine.   1910.
Tunisie.   1912.
Algérie.   1912.
Au Japon, par Java, la Chine, la Corée.   1914.
Nos soldats aveugles.   1916.
Lettres aux soldats blessés aux yeux.   1918.

*

Bibliographies

E. F. Santavicca, *Four French Dramatists: A Bibliography of Criticism of the Works of Eugène Brieux, F. de Curel, E. Fabre, and P. Hervieu*, Metuchen, New Jersey, 1974.

Criticism

Books:
Antoine Benoist, *Le Théâtre de Brieux*, Toulouse, 1907.
Adrien Bertrand, *Eugène Brieux: Biographe critique*, Paris, 1910.
P. Vaughan Thomas, *The Plays of Eugène Brieux*, London, 1913.
W. H. Scheifley, *Brieux and Contemporary French Society*, Boston, 1915.
G. Möller, *Henry Becque and Eugène Brieux*, Breslau, 1937.
Malcolm P. Byrnes, *Eugène Brieux: Humanitaire et patriote méconnu*, London, 1967.

* * *

One of the new young authors discovered and promoted by Antoine, Brieux was a victim of ritual critical slaughter when his first play, *Ménages d'artistes* (Artists' Households), featured in the third (1889–1890) season of the Théâtre Libre. This did not stop the author going on to become a prominent dramatist of his day.

Blanchette, in 1892, was to be one of his most successful works and set something of a pattern for the rest of his career. The eponymous heroine is the victim of an education which estranges her from the humble provincial milieu her family inhabits and leads to her uprooting and corruption by the alien environment of Paris. The first two acts make the principal point of the play. Brieux wrote two versions of the last act, his first impulse being to follow the trend of the *comédie rosse* ("vicious comedy") with its cynical stance on the ways of the world. But his worthy nature intervened and, reluctant to be a doctrinal pessimist, as he put it, he wrote a bitter conclusion, giving expression to his disapproval of the social malady he had portrayed. All of Brieux is contained in this episode. He later confessed that, in the final analysis, he was not much concerned with the way his play ended: the essential thing for him was the exposure of the problem.

His was to be a social theatre, and he was prepared to concede something to the audience's sensibilities, to sugar the pill if need be, as a means of ensuring that his point came across. He freely admitted that he spent his life writing thesis plays. *La Robe rouge* (The Red Robe) highlighted abuses in the exercise of justice; *Les Remplaçantes* (The Substitutes) pointed out the risks run by mothers who hand over the care of their infants to nurses. A stream of similar works was to follow, concerning political corruption, charitable institutions, divorce, horse-racing, and betting.

In the main these plays are worth what the author's reflections are worth: he sets them out forthrightly and honestly and compels a certain moral respect, but rarely captures the theatrical imagination. On the more controversial or sensational topics, the drama often takes the form of an onstage debate which can function as a fairly effective displaced rendering of the author's struggle with an audience's hypocrisy and reluctance even to face up to issues. Syphilis in *Les Avariés* (*Damaged Goods*), and abortion in *Maternité* (*Maternity*), are presented with a directness faintly prefiguring later styles of agitprop. The former play comes with a prologue scripted for the theatre manager who is required to declare that the subject is "the disease of syphilis in its effect on marriage" but that it contains nothing to provoke scandal or arouse disgust. The latter play was originally accompanied by an epilogue setting out the budget of the poverty-stricken household afflicted with unwanted pregnancies.

Les Avariés became a *cause célèbre* when it was banned by the censor while being rehearsed at the Théâtre Antoine. Its first performance had to be in Belgium in 1902, and Parisian audiences were not allowed to see it until 1905. Similar difficulties befell Brieux's texts in England, where Charlotte Shaw, wife of George Bernard Shaw, found her translation of *Maternité* refused permission for performance by the censor in 1907. Publishers on both sides of the Atlantic proved unwilling to bring out a volume containing this play and *Damaged Goods* until 1911, following Brieux's elevation to the Académie Française. By this time, the book had acquired a preface by George Bernard Shaw who was prepared to liken Brieux to Sophocles and announced that the French dramatist's achievements placed him on a par with Ibsen. The real purpose of this intemperate praise was to defy the censor and English social hypocrisy, which still stood in the way of a production of *Damaged Goods* (and numerous other modern plays); however much it enhanced Brieux's reputation, a reading of the plays following such hyperbole could only disappoint.

Among Brieux's chief admirers since this time appear to have been those with a concern for public health: copies of *Damaged Goods* were recommended as appropriate reading for American college youth, especially at Yale University; and subsequent editions have been produced for distribution to soldiers stationed in foreign parts. It is possible that Brieux would not have been displeased with such an outcome.

—David H. Walker

BRIGHOUSE, Harold. Born in Eccles, Lancashire, England, 26 July 1882. Educated at Manchester Grammar School. Served in the Royal Air Force, attached to the Air Ministry Intelligence Staff, during World War I. Married c.1905. Assistant buyer in his father's cotton business, Eccles, 1899–1901, and London, 1902–04: lived in Withington, Cheshire, from 1905; first play, *The Doorway*, produced 1909; associated with Gilbert Cannan and Stanley Houghton in the repertory theatre movement and the so-called "Manchester school" of playwrights in England from 1909; reviewer, Manchester *Guardian*, 1913–49; lived in Hampstead, London, from 1919; published some works jointly with John Walton, under the pseudonym Olive Conway, from the mid-1920's; London columnist for New York's *Drama* magazine, early 1930's; director of a cotton mill, Swinton,

Lancashire. Chairman, Author's Society Dramatic Committee (later British Drama League), 1930–31. Died in London, 25 July 1958.

Works

Collections

Three Lancashire Plays (includes *The Game; The Northeners; Zack*). 1920.
Plays for the Meadow and Plays for the Lawn (includes *Maypole Morning; The Paris Doctor; The Prince Who Was a Piper; The Man About the Place*). 1921.
Open Air Plays (includes *The Laughing Mind; The Oracles of Apollo; The Rational Princess; The Ghosts of Windsor Park; How the Weather is Made*). 1926; revised version (includes *Maypole Morning* and *The Prince Who Was a Piper*), 1926.
Costume Plays, with John Walton (includes *Becky Sharp; Mimi; Prudence Corner; The King's Waistcoat*). 1927.
Four Fantasies for the Open Air (includes *The Exiled Princess; The Ghost in the Garden; The Romany Road; Cupid and Psyche*). 1931; augmented edition, as *Six Fantasies* (also includes *The Ghosts of Windsor Park* and *The Oracles of Apollo*), 1931.
Modern Plays in One Act, with John Walton (includes *One of Those Letters; Dux; When the Bells Rang; The Bureaucrats; The Desperationist; Wireless Can't Lie; Women Do Things Like That*). 1937.

Stage Works

The Doorway (produced Gaiety Theatre, Manchester, 1909). 1913.
Dealing in Futures (produced Royalty Theatre, Glasgow, 1909). 1913.
The Price of Coal (produced Royalty Theatre, Glasgow, 1909). 1911.
Graft (as *The Polygon*, produced Court Theatre, London, 1911; as *Graft*, Lyric Theatre, London, 1911). 1913.
Lonesome-like (produced Royalty Theatre, Glasgow, 1911). 1914.
Spring in Bloomsbury (produced Gaiety Theatre, Manchester, 1911). 1913.
The Oak Settle (produced Theatre Royal, Dalston, 1911). 1911.
The Scaring Off of Teddy Dawson (produced Theatre Royal, Dalston, 1911). 1911.
The Odd Man Out (produced Royalty Theatre, London, 1912). 1912.
Little Red Shoes (produced Prince of Wales' Theatre, London, 1912). 1925.
The Game (produced Playhouse, Liverpool, 1913). In *Three Lancashire Plays*, 1920.
Garside's Career (produced Gaiety Theatre, Manchester, 1914). 1914.
The Northerners (produced Gaiety Theatre, Manchester, 1914). In *Three Lancashire Plays*, 1920.
Followers: A Cranford Sketch (produced Prince's Theatre, Manchester, 1915). 1922.
The Hillarys, with Stanley Houghton (produced Kelly's Theatre, Liverpool, 1915).
Converts (produced Gaiety Theatre, Manchester, 1915). 1920.
Hobson's Choice (produced Poughkeepsie, New York, 1915). 1916.
The Road to Raebury (produced Prince's Theatre, Manchester, 1915). 1921.

Zack: A Character Comedy (produced Syracuse Theatre, Syracuse, New York, 1916). In *Three Lancashire Plays*, 1920.
The Clock Goes Round (produced Devonshire Park Theatre, Eastbourne, 1916).
Maid of France (produced Metropolitan Theatre, New York, 1917). 1917.
The Bantam V.C. (produced St. Martin's Theatre, London, 1920). 1925.
Other Times (produced Little Theatre, London, 1920).
The Starlight Widow, with John Walton. 1920.
Plays for the Meadow and Plays for the Lawn (includes *Maypole Morning, The Paris Doctor, The Prince Who Was a Piper, The Man About the Place;* all produced Cripplegate Institute, London, 1922). 1921.
Once a Hero (produced Ambassador's Theatre, Southend, 1922). 1922.
The Happy Hangman: A Grotesque (produced Cripplegate Institute, London; then Court Theatre, London, 1925). 1922.
Once a Year (produced Playhouse, Liverpool, 1923).
The Apple Tree; or, Why Misery Never Dies. 1923.
A Marrying Man (produced Playhouse, Liverpool, 1924). 1924.
Mary's John (produced Playhouse, Liverpool, 1924). 1925.
Becky Sharp, with John Walton, from a novel by Thackeray (produced Playhouse, Liverpool, 1924). 1924.
Open Air Plays (includes *The Laughing Mind; The Oracles of Apollo; The Rational Princess; The Ghosts of Windsor Park; How the Weather is Made*). 1926; revised version (includes *Maypole Morning* and *The Prince Who Was a Piper*), 1926.
What's Bred in the Bone (produced Playhouse, Liverpool, 1927). 1927.
The Little Liberty. 1927.
Fossie for Short, from his novel. 1927.
The Night of Mr. H.: A Charles Lamb Pastiche. 1927.
When Did They Meet Again? (produced Grand Theatre, Leicester, 1927). 1927.
Mimi, with John Walton. In *Costume Plays*, 1927.
Prudence Corner, with John Walton. In *Costume Plays*, 1927.
The King's Waistcoat, with John Walton. In *Costume Plays*, 1927.
The Witch's Daughter. In *One-Act Plays for Stage and Study 4*, 1928.
It's a Gamble (produced Playhouse, Liverpool, 1928).
Safe Amongst the Pigs (produced Birmingham Repertory Theatre, 1929). 1930.
Behind the Throne. 1929.
Coincidence. 1929.
The Sort-of-a-Prince. 1929.
The Stoker. 1929.
Four Fantasies for the Open Air (includes *The Exiled Princess; The Ghost in the Garden; The Romany Road; Cupid and Psyche*). 1931; augmented edition, as *Six Fantasies* (includes *The Ghosts of Windsor Park* and *The Oracles of Apollo*), 1931.
A Bit of War. 1933.
Smoke-Screens. 1933.
Exhibit C. In *The Best One-Act Plays of 1933*, edited by J.W. Marriott, 1934.
Tip and Run. In *Three Sections*, with John Walton, in *The One-Act Theatre 1*, 1934.
The Dye-Hard. In *One-Act Plays of Today 6*, edited by J.W. Marriott, 1934.
The Great Dark, from a play by Don Totheroh. 1934.

The Boy: What Will He Become?. In *The Best One-Act Plays of 1934*, edited by J.W. Marriott, 1935.
The Friendly King. 1935.
Back to Adam: A Glimpse of Three Periods. 1935.
The Wish Shop. 1936.
Mr. Somebody, from a play by Molnár (produced Fine Arts Center, Colorado Springs, Colorado, 1936).
Modern Plays in One Act, with John Walton (includes *One of Those Letters; Dux; When the Bells Rang; The Bureaucrats; The Desperationist; Wireless Can't Lie; Women Do Things Like That*). 1937.
Below Ground. In *Eight One-Act Plays of 1936*, edited by William Armstrong, 1937.
New Leisure. In *The Best One-Act Plays of 1936*, edited by J.W. Marriott. 1937.
Passport to Romance. 1937.
Under the Pylon. In *One-Act Plays for Stage and Study 9*, 1938.
The Funk-Hole: A Farce of the Crisis. 1938.
British Passport. 1939.
The Man Who Ignored the War. 1940.
Golden Ray: An Idealistic Melodrama. 1941.
London Front. 1941.
Hallowed Ground. In *The Best One-Act Plays of 1941*, edited by J.W. Marriott, 1942.
Sporting Rights. 1943.
Albert Gates. 1945.
The Inner Man. 1945.
Let's Live in England. In *The Best One-Act Plays of 1944–1945*, edited by J.W. Marriott, 1946.
Alison's Island. In *The Best One-Act Plays of 1946–1947*, edited by J.W. Marriott, 1948.
Above Rubies. In *The Best One-Act Plays of 1952–1953*, edited by Hugh Miller, 1954.
Disclosure Day. In *The Best One-Act Plays of 1954–1955*, edited by Hugh Miller, 1956.

Fiction

Fossie for Short. 1917.
Hobson's, with Charles Forrest. 1917.
The Silver Lining. 1918.
The Marbeck Inn. 1920.
Hepplestall's. 1922.
Captain Shapely. 1923.
The Wrong Shadow: A Romantic Comedy. 1923.
Hindle Wakes. 1927.

Memoirs and Letters

What I Have Had: Chapters in Autobiography. 1953.

Other

Editor, *The Works of Stanley Houghton* (3 vols.). 1914.

*

Criticism

Books:
Rex Pogson, *Miss Horniman and the Gaiety Theatre, Manchester*, London, 1952.

* * *

Brighouse was one of the so-called "Manchester School" of playwrights, the development of which was largely furthered by the patronage of Miss Annie Horniman. After assisting the Abbey Theatre in Dublin, she helped to establish the Manchester Repertory Theatre, initially at the little theatre in the prestigious Midland Hotel, then in the refurbished Comedy Theatre, renamed the Gaiety. Impressively innovative, the Gaiety, under young directorial talents like Lewis Casson and Basil Dean, bred a number of new acting talents, and nurtured the skills of several new dramatists, including Stanley Houghton, celebrated for his social problem drama, *Hindle Wakes*, and Alan Monkhouse, who won a considerable reputation with full-length plays like *Mary Braine: A Comedy*.

Brighouse was perhaps the most prolific dramatist of this "School", and is always associated with it, although, as he himself pointed out, his repertory activities were a mere "ante-room" to his work as a whole, and indeed the Glasgow Repertory at the Royalty Theatre under Alfred Wareing might have a greater claim to fostering his talent, for it staged some of his best early work. Important in the later development of Brighouse's career were American productions of his work, for he was very consciously a dramatist who sought to write for a wide theatrical market.

However, it was the Gaiety at Manchester that staged several of his early plays: he sent its first director, Ben Iden Payne, three one-act plays, one of which, *The Doorway*, Payne staged in 1909. Brighouse was an accomplished craftsman in the one-act form, and although these plays served as a means to hone his talent as a playwright, he continued to produce them throughout his writing life. Payne took up more of his work in the 1910 season, putting on his *Dealing in Futures*, and then *Spring in Bloomsbury*, *The Polygon*, and *Garside's Career*.

Brighouse was a versatile writer, capable of writing in a variety of kinds and moods—serious drama of distinctly realistic emphasis, romantic drama, comedy, and farce. Some of his earliest plays, like *The Price of Coal* and *The Northerners*, the latter a dramatisation of the Luddite riots of the 1820's, are particularly powerful treatments of working-class life. Many of his plays through to the late 1920's are marked by a distinctively ironic humour and neat observation of the details of everyday working-class life, and some have a powerful, socially critical edge in their handling of domestic trials, industrial disputes, and the complexities of class relations. Distinctly innovative for its kind of subject matter was *The Game*, concerned with professional football. Too many of his later plays, however, handle their subject matter in sentimental and unchallenging ways, and Brighouse perhaps became a victim of his commitment as a professional playwright, too heavily dependent upon the established actor-manager system of his day to treat his subjects in the fresh, perceptive, independent, and engaging way we find in the best of his early plays.

By far the best known of his plays, and the only one to receive fairly regular revival, is his comedy of working- and lower-middle-class life, *Hobson's Choice*, an engaging domestic comedy that amiably, but firmly, challenged traditional assumptions about patriarchal rule and the place of women in the home. It concerns the progressive worsting of a hard-headed boot- and shoe-maker, Hobson, by his level-headed and skilfully manipulative daughter, Maggie. Quietly confident of her own judgement, and determined to control her own life, she manipulates her father, marries his best workman, Willie Mossop, sets up a shoe shop of her own, and demonstrates her good judgement and sharp business sense by capturing, gradually, her father's trade. The play makes its points the more effectively by eschewing polemic, the action moves easily and is persuasive in its depiction of Lancashire domestic life, and the dialogue is light and witty, firmly tied to a characterization comically the more effective in that it does not wholly avoid caricature.

It underscores how deceptive the term "Manchester school" can be when we note that neither of the two best plays of the "school", *Hobson's Choice* and Stanley Houghton's *Hindle Wakes*, was actually premiered at the Gaiety. Brighouse's play, indeed, was first done by Iden Payne in New York, after being turned down by Oscar Asche and other London actor-managers. A brilliant film version was made in 1954, with Charles Laughton and Wendy Hiller in the leading roles. The play was revived in 1970's at the National Theatre, and his comedy *Zack* was turned into a musical.

—Kenneth Richards

BROME, Richard.   Born in England, c.1590. Servant or secretary to Ben Jonson c.1614, and was afterward Jonson's friend and protégé; wrote for the King's Men, (1629–33), Prince Charles's Men (c.1633–34), the King's Revels (1635), and Beeston's Boys (1637–42); involved in lawsuit over a contract, 1640. Died in London (?), 1652.

Richard Brome (engraving)

Works

Collections

Five New Plays.   1653.
Five New Plays, edited by Alexander Brome.   1659.
Dramatic Works (3 vols.), edited by R.H. Shepherd.   1873.

Stage Works

The Northern Lass (produced by the King's Men, Globe or Blackfriars Theatre, London, 1629).   1632.
The Queen's Exchange (produced Blackfriars Theatre, London, 1629–32?).   1657; as *The Royal Exchange*, 1661.
The City Wit; or, The Woman Wears the Breeches (produced London, 1630–31?).   In *Five New Plays*, 1653.
The Novella (produced by the King's Men, Blackfriars Theatre, London, 1632).   In *Five New Plays*, 1653.
The Weeding of the Covent Garden; or, The Middlesex Justice of Peace (produced London, 1632).   In *Five New Plays*, 1659.
The Love-Sick Court; or, The Ambitious Politique (produced 1633–34?).   In *Five New Plays*, 1659.
The Late Lancashire Witches, with Thomas Heywood (produced by the King's Men, Globe Theatre, London, 1634).   1634.
The Sparagus Garden (produced by the King's Revels, Salisbury Court Theatre, London, 1635).   1640.
The New Academy; or, The New Exchange (produced by the King's Revels, Salisbury Court Theatre, London, 1635?).   In *Five New Plays*, 1959.
The Queen and Concubine (produced by the King's Revels, Salisbury Court Theatre, London, 1635–36?).   In *Five New Plays*, 1659.
The English Moor; or, The Mock Marriage (produced by the Queen's Men, Salisbury Court Theatre, London, 1637).   In *Five New Plays*, 1659.
The Damoiselle; or, The New Ordinary (produced London, 1637–38).   In *Five New Plays*, 1653.
The Antipodes (produced by the Queen's Men, Salisbury Court Theatre, London, 1638).   1640.
A Mad Couple-Well Matched (produced before 1639).   In *Five New Plays*, 1653.
The Court Beggar (produced by Beeston's Boys, Cockpit/Phoenix Theatre, London, 1640).   In *Five New Plays*, 1653.
A Jovial Crew; or, The Merry Beggars (produced by Beeston's Boys, Cockpit/Phoenix Theatre, London, 1641).   1652.

Other

Editor, *Monsieur Thomas*, by John Fletcher.   1639.
Editor, *Lachrymae Musarum: The Tears of the Muses* (elegies on the death of Henry, Lord Hastings).   1649.

*

Criticism

Books:
Herbert F. Allen, *A Study of the Comedies of Brome, Especially as Representative of Dramatic Decadence*, London, 1912.
Clarence E. Andrews, *Richard Brome: A Study of His Life and Works*, New York, 1913; reprinted, 1972.

R.J. Kaufmann, *Richard Brome, Caroline Playwright*, New York, 1961.

Catherine M. Shaw, *Richard Brome*, 1980.

Martin Butler, *Theatre and Crisis 1632–1642*, Cambridge, 1984.

Articles:

Alwin Thaler, "Was Richard Brome an Actor?", in *Modern Language Notes*, 32, 1921.

Joe Lee Davis, "Richard Brome's Neglected Contribution to Comic Theory", in *Studies in Philology*, 40, 1943.

*   *   *

Richard Brome was the last major dramatist before the English Civil War on whom the impact of traditions of popular Elizabethan theatre can still be felt. Although he began his career quite literally under the eye of Ben Jonson, and although the bulk of his writing was done for the principal "private" playhouses of his day, he had associations with dramatists of an older generation such as Dekker and Heywood, he spent a period writing for the popular Red Bull playhouse, and he was the one Caroline playwright who made sustained use of the festive and carnivalesque devices of Elizabethan popular comedy. The nostalgia and playfulness of the style which he cultivated enabled the legacy of an earlier dramatic manner still to be felt on the eve of the closing of the playhouses, and while his plays were not out of place on the more fashionable Caroline stages, they still stood in some antithesis to the ruling tastes of London's literary elites. In *The Court Beggar* (1640), which lampoons William Davenant and John Suckling, and in *The Lovesick Court*, which burlesques the posturings and inflated rhetoric of courtly romance, Brome overtly parodied the current vogue for a precious and heroic drama written by gentlemanly amateur playwrights.

A writer who "never spilt ink, except in comedy", Brome's output ranges from frivolous farce through comedies of humours to panoramas of his times freighted with an anxious social concern. Perhaps his most characteristic pieces are comedies such as *The Weeding of the Covent Garden, The Sparagus Garden*, and *A Mad Couple Well Matched*, which treat matters of topical interest under the veil of a lightly subversive comic anarchy.

Brome's typical territory was the follies and foibles of citizen and gentry classes interacting in contemporary London, though he brought to his subject a somewhat more disenchanted eye than that of his competitiors, Shirley and Davenant. For example, in *The Weeding of the Covent Garden*, the central figure is Crosswill, a patriarch who obsessively contradicts his children's wishes. Crosswill eventually relinquishes his humour, but not until it has become clear that quarrelsomeness is rife in society at large, and that it will be necessary to curb the irresponsible wilfulness of more than just one individual. As a comment on the problems plaguing the London of Charles I this analysis has some force, not least because of its relevance to the crown's own perpetual paternalistic interference in economic life, to which the play repeatedly alludes.

The tendency of the comedy to involve reflections on contemporary worries is characteristic of this playwright who became increasingly politicized under the pressure of the decade's events. In *The Queen and Concubine*, Brome used a seemingly innocent tragicomedy of love and exile to explore an ideological contest between responsible and irresponsible styles of royal will, and *The Court Beggar* (1640), which satirized monopolies, wardships, and sycophantic courtiers, was deemed sufficiently offensive to get its playhouse closed down and its actors imprisoned. Brome's final plays are poised uncomfortably between a rejection of arbitrary political authority and forebodings about the consequences of a loss of political consensus.

Brome's two major achievements are *The Antipodes* and *A Jovial Crew*. *The Antipodes*, set against the background of a plague visitation which had closed the playhouses, counterpoints the cure of individual sickness with the cure of the sick state. The play follows the therapy devised for the gentleman Peregrine, who has run mad with extravagant thoughts of travelling; but all his family and friends need psychiatric attention too. Their communal cure is a pretended voyage to the Antipodes where the norms of Caroline England are provocatively inverted. In Antipodean London, poets are rich, lawyers are honest, churchmen are usurers, courtiers are beggars, and beggars gallants. In some cases anti-London seems worse than real London but in others it is distinctly to be preferred, and the cure enacts a teasing interplay between what is to be desired and what is to be averted. As Brome's stage Londoners slough off their old selves through a confrontation with their opposites, the play provides a therapy for its audience too: the way to wholeness is through laughter and a renewed commitment to a properly integrated society.

In *A Jovial Crew*, on the other hand, the laughter is far less buoyant and is counterpointed with intimations of social breakdown. With the closing of the playhouses and the plunge into civil war only a year away, *A Jovial Crew* follows the fortunes of four young lovers who seek to escape from the oppressive melancholy of their patriarch, Oldrents, by embarking on a carefree life with a covey of beggars. But far from proving a means of escape, the four have their romantic illusions shattered by the unpleasant realities of beggary, and return home chastened and newly persuaded of the benefits of prosperity. Meanwhile, Oldrents has dispelled his melancholy by throwing care to the wind and embarking on his own career of irresponsibility. He is rewarded for his playfulness by the recovery of a lost son; but it is clear too that commitments cannot be shirked forever, and the play invokes a powerful sense of the social and historical continuity of the English countryside, as well as making a sympathetic plea for concern about England's vagrant classes. It was uniquely appropriate that, as Brome later claimed, this was the play being performed at the Drury Lane Cockpit on the very day that civil war brought on the 18-year closure of the London theatres.

—Martin Butler

———————

BÜCHNER, Georg. Born in Goddelau, Duchy of Hesse Darmstadt, 17 October 1813. Educated at Carl Weitershausen's school, 1822–25, and Gymnasium in Darmstadt, 1825–31; studied zoology and anatomy at University of Strasbourg, 1831–33, and University of Giessen, 1833–34. Politically active as student in Darmstadt, founding the "Society of Human Rights", and writing the political pamphlet *Der hessische Landbote* [*The Hessian Courier*]; fled Germany to escape impending arrest for sedition, 1835, and sought refuge in Strasbourg; undertook biological research, earning membership of the Strasbourg Societé d'Histoire Naturelle and a doctorate from the

University of Zurich, 1836; took up post as lecturer in comparative anatomy, University of Zurich, 1836. Died of typhus in Zurich, 19 February 1837.

Works

Collections

Nachgelassene Schriften, edited by Ludwig Büchner.   1850.
Sämtliche Werke, edited by Karl Emil Franzos.   1879.
Gesammelte Werke und Briefe, edited by Fritz Bergemann. 1922.
Sämtliche Werke und Briefe (2 vols.), edited by Werner R. Lehmann.   1967–71.
The Plays of Georg Büchner, translated by Victor Price. 1971.
The Complete Plays (includes *Danton's Death*; *Leonce and Lena*; *Woyzeck*; the prose works *The Hessian Courier*, *Lenz*, *On Cranial Nerves*; and selected letters).   1987.

Stage Works

Dantons Tod (produced Belle Alliance Theater, Berlin, 1902).   1835 (incomplete version); complete, in *Nachgelassene Schriften*, 1850; translated as *Danton's Death*, 1939: several subsequent translations under same title.
Leonce und Lena (produced Intimes Theater, Biederstein, Germany, 1895).   In the journal *Telegraph für Deutschland*, edited by Karl Gutzkow, 1838; translated as *Leonce and Lena*, in *From the Modern Repertoire 3*, edited by Eric Bentley, 1956: several subsequent translations under same title.
Woyzeck (produced Residenztheater, Munich, 1913).   As *Wozzeck*, in the journal *Mehr Licht*, 1875; in book form, in *Sämtliche Werke*, 1879; as *Woyzeck*, in *Gesammelte Werke und Briefe*, 1922; "accurate" version in *Sämtliche Werke und Briefe*, 1967–71; translated as *Woyzeck*, 1927; several subsequent translations under same title.

Fiction

Lenz.   In *Telegraph für Deutschland*, January 1839; translated as *Lenz*, in *The Complete Plays*, 1987.

Other

Der hessische Landbote, with Pastor Weidig.   1834 (private printing); translated as *The Hessian Courier*, in *The Complete Plays*, 1987.

*

Bibliographies

Werner Schlick, *Das Büchner Schrifttum bis 1965*, Hildesheim, 1968.
Marianne Beese, *Georg Büchner*, Leipzig, 1983.

Gerhard P. Knapp, *Georg Büchner* (second edition), Stuttgart, 1984.

Criticism

Books:
Max Zobel von Zabelitz, *Georg Büchner: Sein Leben und sein Schaffen*, Berlin, 1912.
L. Marcuse, *Georg Büchner und seine besten Bühnenwerke*, Berlin, 1921.
Walter Hoyer, *Stoff und Gestalt bei Georg Büchner*, Leipzig, 1922.
Heinz Lipmann, *Georg Büchner und die Romantik*, Munich, 1923.
Rudolf Majut, *Studien um Büchner: Untersuchungen zur Geschichte der problematischen Natur*, Berlin, 1932.
Peter Schmid, *Georg Büchner: Versuch über die tragische Existenz*, Bern, 1940.
Hans Mayer, *Georg Büchner und seine Zeit*, Wiesbaden, 1946; revised edition, Frankfurt, 1972.
Ludwig Büttner, *Georg Büchner: Revolutionär und Pessimist*, Nuremberg, 1948.
Karl Viëtor, *Politik, Dichtung, Wissenschaft*, Bern, 1949.
Arthur Knight, *Georg Büchner*, Oxford, 1951.
Ernst Kreuder, *Georg Büchner: Existenz und Sprache*, Mainz, 1955.
Ingeborg Strudthoff, *Die Rezeption Georg Büchners durch das deutsche Theater*, Berlin, 1957.
Donald Brinkmann, *Georg Büchner als Philosoph*, Zurich, 1958.
Ernst Johann, *Georg Büchner in Selbstzeugnissen und Bilddokumenten*, Hamburg, 1958.
Gerhart Baumann, *Georg Büchner: Die dramatische Ausdruckswelt*, Göttingen, 1961.
H. Lindenberger, *Georg Büchner*, Carbondale, Illinois, 1964.
Ludwig Büttner, *Büchners Bild von Menschen*, Nuremburg, 1967.
Henry J. Schmidt, *Satire, Caricature, and Perspectivism in the Works of Büchner*, The Hague and Paris, 1970.
Heinz Fischer, *Georg Büchner: Untersuchungen und Marginalien*, Bonn, 1972.
Ronald Hauser, *Georg Büchner*, 1974.
Maurice B. Benn, *The Drama of Revolt: A Critical Study of Büchner*, Cambridge, 1976.
David G. Richards, *Büchner and the Birth of Modern Drama*, Albany, New York, 1977.
Heinz L. Arnold (ed.), *Georg Büchner* (3 vols.), 1979–81.
William C. Reeve, *Georg Büchner*; 1979.
Julian Hilton, *Georg Büchner*, London, 1982.
Albert Meier, *Georg Büchners Ästhetik*, Munich, 1983.
Henri Poschmann, *Georg Büchner: Dichtung der Revolution und Revolution der Dichtung*, Berlin, 1983.
Walter Grab, *Georg Büchner und die Revolution von 1848: Der Büchner-Essay von Wilhelm Schulz aus dem Jahr 1851: Text und Kommentar*, Königstein, 1985.
Reinhold Grimm, *Love, Lust, and Rebellion: New Approaches to Georg Büchner*, Madison, Wisconsin, 1985.
Jan C. Hauschild, *Georg Büchner: Studien und neue Quellen zu Leben, Werk und Wirkung*, Königstein, 1985.
Brian Keith-Smith and Ken Mills (eds.), *Büchner in Britain: A Passport to Georg Büchner*, Bristol, 1987.
Rudolf Loch, *Georg Büchner: Das Leben eines Frühvollendeten: Biografie*, Berlin, 1988.
Hans G. Werner (ed.), *Studien zu Georg Büchner*, Berlin, 1988.
U-Tag Yang, *Reflexion und Desintegration: Zur*

Identitätskrise der Protagonisten im Werk Georg Büchners, Frankfurt, 1989.

Burghard Dedner (ed.), *Der widerständige Klassiker: Einleitungen zu Büchner vom Nachmärz bis zur Weimarer Republik*, Frankfurt, 1990.

Dietmar Goltschnigg, *Büchner im Dritten Reich*, Bielefeld, 1990.

Serials:
Georg Büchner Jahrbuch, 1981—

* * *

None of Georg Büchner's plays was staged during his lifetime. There is, in fact, no evidence that Büchner had any experience of the theatre. When he died of typhus at the age of 24, he was known by some as a brilliant lecturer in anatomy at the University of Zurich, and by others as an active revolutionary on the run from the authorities in Hesse after having written the inflammatory pamphlet *Der hessische Landbote* (*The Hessian Courier*).

His first play, *Dantons Tod* (*Danton's Death*), was written in 1835, while he was under investigation for his political involvement. Written in secret in five weeks, it is a remarkable first play. That is should have been written by someone himself active in revolutionary politics is astonishing. Its objectivity and clarity in presentation of character and historical material, perhaps one sixth of which comes directly from his sources, is unparalleled by any writer before the documentary-drama writers of the 1960's. Himself disillusioned by the failure of the populace of Hesse to respond to calls for an uprising, and disheartened by the arrest of his collaborators, Büchner presents, in Danton, a study of a man who has withdrawn from the Revolution convinced that no man can change the course of events, and has given himself over to an epicurean lifestyle. Confident that the tribunal will not dare to sentence him to death, he denounces Robespierre and St. Just; but the people side with Robespierre against him. The play's positive force is to be found in the humanity of Danton at the end, as he awaits execution, calm in the acceptance of his fate. The receptivity Büchner shows in the play to all he found in his historical characters upset many of his readers. He, however, refused to compromise by sanitising his material of overt sexual reference, or to diminish the brutality and apparent pointlessness of his characters' existences. Not until the Naturalist movement, some 50 years after Büchner's death, would such a vision of history become acceptable.

In the fragmentary *Woyzeck*, Büchner presents an equally uncompromising picture of the human condition. He used as his source a report on the trial and execution of Johann Christian Woyzeck in 1824 for the murder of a widow (a case remarkable for the investigations into Woyzeck's mental condition at the time of the crime). In his play *Woyzeck* Büchner presents the first tragedy of the working class in the history of German theatre. Woyzeck, working as a barber in the army, is abused by caricatured figures in authority over him. The Doctor subjects him to inhuman experimentation, and the Drum Major seduces his wife, Marie, for whose love Woyzeck was prepared to suffer the experiments. When he discovers the betrayal, he stabs Marie to death. His world collapses utterly when Karl, the idiot, runs off with his son.

Both plays show the strong influence Shakespeare had over Büchner's freedom of style, his epic "snap-shot" presentation of scenes, and various accurately observed levels of language. But, above all, Büchner learns from Shakespeare not to judge his characters, but to present them as truthfully as possible, without attempting to misquote them or to improve them. In so doing he sought to give a clearer view of history than either the account of an academic historian, or the distorted, idealised picture painted by a Schillerian historical dramatist. Büchner regarded Schiller's heroes and heroines as lifeless, cold, and essentially unsympathetic. He did not consider suffering to be either ennobling or liberating, rather as brutalising and demeaning. Büchner did not see his role as a dramatist as the interpreting of history, but as the "charting of the irresistible and inscrutable necessity in historical events", and his highest duty to "come as close to history as it actually happened as he can". He rejected any idea of progress, of theodicy, and utopianism, replacing them with an objective fatalism, seeing even important historical characters as "mere foam on the wave". He fearlessly faces a world without hope of a divine redemptive force, and portrays a bleak landscape whether of those active in the vanguard of revolution, or those at the very bottom of the social ladder.

In 1836 Büchner submitted a script in a competition for the best German comedy run by the publisher Cotta. He had missed the submission date, and the play, *Leonce und Lena* (*Leonce and Lena*),was returned to him. It was not performed until 1895. In the play, a fairy-tale prince and princess escape from their respective kingdoms to avoid an arranged marriage to each other. In their flight they meet and fall in love with one another (unaware of each other's identity). In the last scene they marry, and are reconciled together. The play is a comedy of great charm and lightness of touch in places, but it also contains an indictment of the fickle autocracy of the petty German states, and, although couched in humour, strong censure of the rulers' lack of concern for the ruled. Büchner, however, reserves his most biting ridicule for the differing manifestations of idealism shown by the philosopher king (whose attempts at abstract thinking serve no good end other than to confuse him) and the indolent, vacuous prince (whose concepts of the unattainable ideal render him incapable of action, or constructive thinking).

Büchner's motive for writing was the same as his motive for political involvement: his refusal to accept the current rationalisation of the suffering in the world. This is as true of his rejection of Schiller's concept of the ideal state achieved by his major historical characters, as it is of the apparently arbitrary distress of the working class. It is the objective expression of this concern in theatre which has served as a major inspiration for subsequent theatre writers.

—Anthony Meech

See also *Volume 1* entries on *Danton's Death*; *Woyzeck*.

———

BUERO VALLEJO, Antonio. Born in Guadalajara, Spain, 29 September 1916. Educated at the Instituto de Segunda Enseñanza, Guadalajara; studied painting at San Fernando School of Fine Arts, Madrid, 1934–35. Married Victoria Rodríguez in 1959; two sons. Served as medical corpsman in the Loyalist (Republican) forces during the Spanish Civil War, 1937–39; imprisoned for five years at end of war by the Franco government (released 1946); first-produced play, *Historia de una escalera*, staged 1949. Recipient of many awards, including the Lope de Vega Prize

Scene from the Philadelphia Wilma Theatre's 1986 production of *The Sleep of Reason* by **Antonio Buero Vallejo**, with Roger Serbagi as Goya, directed by Blanca Ziska.

for new playwrights, 1949, and the Cervantes Prize for Literature, 1986. Elected to the Real Academia Española 1971.

Works

Collections

Teatro (2 vols.: Volume 1 includes *En la ardiente oscuridad; Madrugada; Hoy es fiesta; Las cartas boca abajo;* Volume 2 includes *Historia de una escalera; La tejedora de sueño; Irene; o, El tesoro; Un sonador para un pueblo*). 1959–62.
Buero Vallejo: Antologia teatral. 1966.
Teatro selecto (includes *Historia de una escalera; Las cartas boca abajo; Un sonador para un pueblo; Las meninas; El concierto de San Ovidio*). 1966.
Marginalia (includes *La señal que se espera; Diana; Poemas*). 1984.
Three Plays (includes *The Sleep of Reason; The Foundation; In the Burning Darkness*), translated by Marion Peter Holt. 1985.

Stage Works

Historia de una escalera (produced Teatro Español, Madrid, 1949). 1950.
Las palabras en la arena (produced Teatro Español, Madrid, 1949). With *Historia de una escalera*, 1952.
En la ardiente oscuridad (produced Teatro María Guerrero, Madrid, 1950). 1951; translated as *In the Burning Darkness*, in *Three Plays*, 1985.

La tejedora de sueños (produced Teatro Español, Madrid, 1952). 1952; translated as *The Dream Weaver*, in *Masterpieces of the Modern Spanish Theatre*, edited by Robert W. Corrigan, 1967.
La señal que se espera (produced Teatro Infanta Isabel, Madrid, 1952). 1953.
Casi un cuento de hadas: Una glosa de Perrault (produced Teatro Alcázar, Madrid, 1953). 1953.
Madrugada (produced Teatro Alcázar, Madrid, 1953). 1954.
El terror inmóvil. 1954; complete version, 1979.
Irene; o, El tesoro (produced Teatro María Guerrero, Madrid, 1954). 1955.
Aventura en lo gris. 1955; revised version (produced Teatro Club Recoletos, Madrid, 1963), 1964.
Hoy es fiesta (produced Teatro Nacional María Guerrero, Madrid, 1956). 1957; translated as *Today's a Holiday*, 1987.
Las cartas boca abajo (produced Teatro Reina Victoria, Madrid, 1957). 1958.
Un sonador para un pueblo (produced Teatro Español, Madrid, 1958). 1959.
Las Meninas (produced Teatro Español, Madrid, 1960). 1961; translated as *Las Meninas*, 1987.
Hamlet, from the play by Shakespeare (produced Teatro Español, Madrid, 1961). 1962.
El concierto de San Ovidio (produced Teatro Goya, Madrid, 1962). 1963; translated as *The Concert at Saint Ovide*, in *The Modern Spanish Stage*, edited by Marion Peter Holt, 1970.

Madre Coraje y sus hijos, from a play by Brecht (produced Teatro Bellas Artes, Madrid, 1966).   1967.
La doble historia del Doctor Valmy (produced in English as *The Double Case History of Doctor Valmy*, Gateway Theatre, Chester, 1968; in Spanish, Madrid, 1976).   Both Spanish and English versions published in *Artes hispánicas* vol 1 no. 2, 1967; in book form, 1970.
El tragaluz (produced Teatro Bellas Artes, Madrid, 1967). In *Primer acto*, November 1967; in book form, 1968; translated as *The Basement Window*, in *Plays of Protest from the Franco Era*, edited by Patricia W. O'Connor, 1981.
Mito: Libro para una ópera.   1968.
El sueño de la razón (produced Teatro Reina Victoria, Madrid, 1970).   In *Primer acto*, February 1970; in book form, 1970; revised edition, 1985; translated as *The Sleep of Reason*, in *Three Plays*, 1985.
Llegada de los dioses (produced Teatro Lara, Madrid, 1972). In *Primer acto*, November 1971; in book form, in *Teatro español 1971–72*, 1973.
La fundación (produced Teatro Figaro, Madrid, 1974).   In *Primer acto*, April 1974; in book form, with *El concierto de San Ovidio*, 1974; translated as *The Foundation*, in *Three Plays*, 1985.
La detonación (produced Teatro Bellas Artes, Madrid, 1977). In *Estreno*, Spring 1978; in book form, 1979; translated as *The Shot*, 1989.
Jueces en la noche (produced Teatro Lara, Madrid, 1979).   1979.
Caimán (produced Teatro Reina Victoria, Madrid, 1981). With *Las cartas boca abajo*, 1981.
El pato Silvestre, from a play by Ibsen (produced Teatro María Guerrero, Madrid, 1982).   1990.
Diálogo secreto (produced Teatro Victoria Eugenia, San Sebastián, 1984).   1985.
Lázaro en el laberinto (produced Teatro Maravillas, Madrid, 1986).   1987.
Música cercana (produced Bilbao, 1989).   1990.

Fiction

Diana. In *Marginalia*, 1984.

Verse

Poemas. In *Marginalia*, 1984.

Other

García Lorca ante el esperpento (address).   1972.
Tres maestros ante el público (Valle-Inclán, Velázquez, Lorca).   1973.

*

Bibliographies

John W. Kronik, "Buero Vallejo: A Bibliography (1949–70)", in *Hispánia*, December 1971.
Marsha Forys, *Antonio Buero Vallejo and Alfonso Sastre: An Annotated Bibliography*, Metuchen, New Jersey, 1988.

Criticism

Books:
José R. Cortina, *El arte dramatica de Antonio Buero Vallejo*, Madrid, 1969.

Emilio F. Bejel, *Buero Vallejo: Lo moral, lo social y lo metafísico*, Montevideo, 1972.
Robert L. Nicholas, *The Tragic Stages of Buero Vallejo*, Chapel Hill, North Carolina, 1972.
Joelyn Roeple, *Buero Vallejo: The First Fifteen Years*, New York, 1972.
Martha T. Halsey, *Buero Vallejo*, New York, 1973.
Ricardo Domenech, *El teatro de Buero Vallejo*, Madrid, 1973.
Marion Peter Holt, *The Contemporary Spanish Theatre (1949–1972)*, Boston, 1975.
Julio Mathías, *Buero Vallejo*, Madrid, 1975.
Carmen Gonzalez-Cobos Davila, *Buero Vallejo: El hombre y su obra*, Salamanca, 1979.
Luis Iglesias Feijoo, *La trayectoria dramatica de Buero Vallejo*, Santiago, 1982.
Mariano de Paco (ed.), *Estudios sobre Buero Vallejo*, Murcia, 1984.
Enrique Pajón Mecloy, *Buero Vallejo y el antihéroe: Una crítica de la razón creadora*, Madrid, 1986.
Antonio Buero Vallejo: Premio de Literatura en Lengua Castellana Miguel de cervantes, 1986 (collection of essays), Barcelona, 1987.

Articles:
Wallace Woolsey, "Buero Vallejo: Versatile Spanish Dramatist", in *South Central Bulletin*, 26, 1966.
Kenneth Brown, "The Significance of Insanity in Four Plays by Antonio Buero Vallejo", in *Revista de estudios hispánicos*, 8, 1974.
Ida Molina, "The Dialectical Structure of Buero Vallejo's Multi-Faceted Definition of Tragedy", in *Kentucky Romance Quarterly*, 22, 1975.
Francis Donahue, "Spain's Tragic Voice: Antonio Buero Vallejo", in *Revista/Review interamericana*, 9, 1979.
Martha T. Halsey, "Dictatorship to Democracy in the Recent Theater of Buero Vallejo (*La fundación* to *Diálogo*)", in *Estreno*, vol. 13 no. 9, 1987.

* * *

Spain's pre-eminent post-Lorcan dramatist was virtually unknown in 1949 when the production of his second play, *Historia de una escalera*, brought him critical and popular acclaim. Although this realistic social drama, set on a stairway in a drab Madrid tenement, represents an important turning-point in the modern Spanish theatre, and is frequently cited as a major example of Buero's writing, it lacks the inventive scenic transformations and complementary aural effects characteristic of his finest plays.

Shortly after his release from prison in 1946, Buero had written his first play, *En la ardiente oscuridad* (*In the Burning Darkness*), and this seminal work, set in a school for the blind where the students' comfortable but rigidly structured society is threatened by a young nonconformist, reached the stage in 1950. During production revisions Buero created a scenic effect that would prove startling: while the messianic youth proclaims to his antagonist a quixotic desire to see, the stage-and house-lights fade momentarily to total darkness, compelling the audience to experience the blindness of the characters on stage. It was this single departure from the play's symbolic realism that was to be the keystone of Buero's developing dramatic mode and of his increasing innovative techniques to bridge the proscenium and bring his audiences into closer physical or psychological identity with a character or dramatic situation. In 1973 the Spanish critic Ricardo Doménech coined the term *"efectos de inmersión"* ("immersion-effects") for Buero's techniques, viewing them as almost the antithesis of Brecht's *Verfremdungseffekte*—though both playwrights were attempting to challenge conventional ways of viewing a performance.

Both *Aventura en lo gris* and *Irene; o, el tesoro* are early plays in which Buero experimented successfully with new dramatic forms; but his finest and most characteristic works followed his turn to historical drama in 1958 and his move from a closed, to a more flexible or unrestricted, scenic environment. In *Las Meninas* he experiments boldly with form, allowing a narrator to move in and out of the frame of action, employing simultaneous scenes, and mingling the arts by using a musical motif to suggest, synesthetically, a visual object. At the same time the dual themes of social injustice and the struggle of the creative person (the painter Velazquez) against religious bigotry and authoritarianism suggest parallels with contemporary social and political inequities.

Early critical attention to Buero's theatre focused on his concept of a modern tragedy in which hope prevails in the face of death or irreversible loss and his recourse to dramatic situations in which individuals struggle against their own physical limitations. An outstanding example of Buerian tragedy is *El concierto de San Ovidio* (*The Concert at Saint Ovide*), in which the idealistic blind violinist, David, is driven by the cruelty and insensivity of an ambitious impresario to murder him. While David must go to his execution, his dream for the blind to read and play serious music is carried on by the historical character Valentin Haüy. For the first time Buero presents extreme brutality and violence on stage; in the terrifying dressing scene, the confused blind musicians are forced to don ridiculous costumes; the following "concert scene" ends in a cacaphony of jeers and mockery from an onstage audience. Later, David kills his oppressor on stage but in total darkness, after he has snuffed out the single light to plunge both victim and audience into his world of blindness.

Buero's concepts of total theatre as well as his most urgent personal concerns are best illustrated in *El sueño de la razón* (*The Sleep 0f Reason*) and *La fundación* (*The Foundation*). The protagonist of the former is the aged and deaf painter Francisco de Goya who has covered the walls of his country house with the phantasmagoric "Black Paintings". Threatened by the despotic Fernando VII, he is also troubled by the sexual frustration of his young mistress, Leocadia. His ultimate humiliation is to watch her violent rape by an officer in the king's militia. Buero employs sound and the absence of sound in the same way he had used light and darkness in earlier plays. None of the words spoken in the deaf man's presence are audible, though the audience does share the sounds that Goya imagines he hears and the sounds of his heartbeats, speeded up and made louder at times to signal his growing terror. To complete the effect, the "Black Paintings" are projected singly or in orchestrated combinations to underscore the painter's mental turmoil.

La fundación, staged in 1974 after a prolonged delay by the censors, draws directly on Buero's own painful experiences in prison. The work is pointedly set in an unidentified country to make a universal statement about the recurring cruelty spawned by ideological conflicts. Up to this point in his career Buero had used immersion-effects to draw audiences into the special situation of characters from a base of reality which exists onstage before the scenic transformation. In *La fundación* he reverses the process, initiating the action within the fantasy of the young prisoner who believes he is working in a comfortable research center, and gradually disclosing the harsh reality of a dank prison cell where he and his com-

panions await the summons to execution. A brief segment from Rossini's *William Tell* serves as a motif for the young man's fictional world, and the theme returns at the end of the play, signalling a potential renewal of the delusion of "the Foundation" for the next occupants of the cell. Whether it is apparent to every spectator or not, the Rossini fragment makes its own metatheatrical statement about yet another drama dealing with political conflict.

Buero's later plays, with the exception of his final historical drama (*La detonación*), focus directly on contemporary political, social, or ethical problems. The protagonist of *Diálogo secreto* is a colour-blind art critic who is tormented by the lifelong deception he believes his father has forced upon him; yet he denies that his insensitive negative review may have provoked the suicide of a young artist. Buero's scenic concept for this play is among his most consummate. As a focal point throughout is a large reproduction of Velazquez's "The Spinners", and, as in *El sueño de la razón*, live characters relate to figures in the painting—in effect making these icons of art subsidiary characters within the play. The audience is led into the inner world of the art critic through a series of interior conversations with the father, and at these moments the Velazquez painting and the set are drained of colour. As a musical motif the Spinning Chorus from Wagner's *The Flying Dutchman* is heard played on a glockenspiel, reiterating the spinning theme of the painting as well as suggesting the Dutchman's search for redemption in the opera.

The existentialist angst of Buero's alienated protagonists has its roots in Unamuno's "tragic sense of life". However, it is the presence of Ibsen, Buero's acknowledged master, that is most frequently evident in his characters and dramatic conflicts. His Goya echoes both Brand and Rubek, and repeatedly he confronts a character bent on defining truth with another who survives through his "life-lie"—though Buero's point of view may differ greatly in plays as distinct as *En la ardiente oscuridad* and the more recent *Lázaro en el laberinto*.

Like Lorca, Buero envisions his plays in the totality of their performance, pointedly describing the scenic environment, lighting effects, characters' attire, stage movement and tempos. His precepts for a theatre that unites the arts are uniquely his; he has merged the plastic and the tonal to a remarkable degree, employing painting, music, and nonverbal sound to achieve a melding of dialogic drama with a theatre of images.

—Marion Peter Holt

See also *Volume 1* entry on *The Sleep of Reason*.

———

BULGAKOV, Mikhail (Afanasevich). Ukraine, Russian Empire, Born in Kiev, 2 May (14 May, New Style) 1891. Educated at First Kiev High School, 1900–09; Medical Faculty, Kiev University, 1909–16, degree 1916. Served as doctor in front-line and district hospitals, 1916–18. Married 1) Tatyana Nikolayevna Lappa in 1913; 2) Lyubov Yevgenievna Belozerskaya in 1924; 3) Yelena Sergeyevna Shilovskaya in 1932. Doctor in Kiev, 1918–19, but abandoned medicine in 1920; organized a "sub-department of the arts", Vladikavkaz, 1920–21; in Moscow from 1921: journalist for various groups and papers (including *Nakanune*); associated with the Moscow

Art Theatre from 1925: assistant producer, 1930–36; librettist and consultant, Bolshoi Theatre, Moscow, 1936–40. Much of his writing only published posthumously. Died in Moscow, 10 March 1940.

Works

Collections

Pesy [*Plays*].   1962; revised edition, as *Dramy i komedy*, 1965.
Early Plays (includes *Days of the Turbins; Zoia's Apartment; The Crimson Island; A Cabal of Hypocrites*), edited by Ellendea Proffer.   1972.
Sobraniye sochineny, edited by Ellendea Proffer (10 vols.).   1982–
Pesy [*Plays*].   1986.
Six Plays (includes *The White Guard; Madam Zoyka; Flight; Molière; Adam and Eve; The Last Days*).   1991.

Stage Works

Dni Turbinykh from his novel (produced Moscow Art Theatre, Moscow, 1926).   With *Poslednie dni* (*Pushkin*), 1955; translated as *The Days of the Turbins*, in *Six Soviet Plays*, translated by Eugene Lyons, 1935; as *The White Guard*, 1979.
Zoykina kvartira (produced Vakhtangov Theatre, Moscow, 1926).   In *Novy Zhurnal* (New York), 97–98, 1969–70; in book form, edited by Ellendea Proffer, 1971; translated as *Zoia's Apartment*, in *Early Plays*, edited by Proffer, 1972; as *Madame Zoyka*, in *Six Plays*, 1991.
Bagrovy ostrov (produced Kamerny Theatre, Moscow, 1928).   In *P'esy*, 1971; translated as *The Crimson Island*, in *Early Plays*, edited by Ellendea Proffer, 1972.
Myortvye dushi [*Dead Souls*], from the novel by Gogol (produced Moscow Art Theatre, Moscow, 1932).   With *Ivan Vasilevich*, 1964.
Kabala sviatosh (as *Molier*, produced Moscow Art Theatre, Moscow, 1936).   In *Pesy*, 1962; translated as *A Cabal of Hypocrites*, in *Early Plays*, edited by Ellendea Proffer, 1972; translated as *Molière*, 1983.
Skupoy [*The Miser*], from *L'Avare* by Molière, in *Polnoe sobranie sochineny 4*, by Molière.   1939.
Don Kikhot [*Don Quixote*] from the novel by Cervantes (produced Pushkin Theatre, Leningrad, 1940).   In *Pesy*, 1962.
Posledniye dni (*Pushkin*) (produced Moscow Art Theatre, Moscow, 1943).   With *Dni Turbinykh*, 1955; translated as *The Last Days (Pushkin)*, in *Russian Literature Triquarterly 15*, 1976; also in *Six Plays*, 1991.
Rakhel edited by Margarita Aliger, music by R.M. Glière, from a story by Maupassant (produced 1947).   Edited by A. Colin Wright, in *Novy zhurnal 108*, September 1972.
Beg (produced Gorky Theatre, Volgagrad, 1957).   In *Pesy*, 1962; translated as *Flight*, 1970; as *On the Run*, 1972.
Ivan Vasilevich (produced Film Actors' Studio, Moscow, 1966).   With *Myortvye dushi*, 1964.
Poloumnyi Zhurden, from *Le Bourgeois Gentilhomme* by Molière (produced 1972).   In *Dramy i komedy* 1965.
Blazhenstvo.   In *Zvezda vostoka*, 7, 1966;
Adam i Eva.   In *Pesy*, 1971; as *Adam and Eve*, in *Russian Literature Triquarterly*, 1, 1971; also in *Six Plays*, 1991.
Minin i Pozharski, music by Boris Asafiev, edited by A. Colin Wright.   In *Russian Literature Triquarterly 15*, 1976.
Voina i mir [*War and Peace*], from the novel by Tolstoy, edited by A. Colin Wright.   In *Canadian-American Slavic Studies 15*, Summer-Fall 1981.

Fiction

Dyavoliada: Rasskazy.   1925; as *"Diaboliad" and Other Stories*, edited by Ellendea and Carl Proffer, 1972.
Rasskazy [Stories].   1926.
Dni Turbinykh (Belaya gvardiya).   In *Rossiya*, 1924; as book, 2 vols., 1927–29; translated as *Day of the Turbins*, 1934; as *The White Guard*, 1971.
Sbornik rasskazov (short stories).   1952.
Zapiski yunogo vracha.   1963; augmented edition, as *A Country Doctor's Notebook*, 1975.
Izbrannaya proza.   1966.
Teatralny roman.   In *Novy mir*, 8, 1965; in book form, in *Izbrannaya proza*, 1966; translated as *Black Snow: A Theatrical Novel*, 1967.
Master i Margarita.   1967; complete version, 1969; translated as *The Master and Margarita*, 1967; complete version, 1967.
Sobache serdtsa.   1969; translated as *The Heart of a Dog*, 1968.
Zapiski gunogo vracha (short stories).   1970.

Memoirs and Letters

Manuscripts Don't Burn: A Life in Letters and Diaries, edited by J.A.E. Curtis.   1991.

Other

Rokovye yaytsa.   1925.
Zhizn gospodina de Moliera.   1962; translated as *The Life of Monsieur de Molière*, 1970.

*

Bibliographies

Judit Bálint, "Theatre Checklist No. 11: Mikhail Bulgakov", in *Theatrefacts*, vol.3 no.3, 1976.
Ellendea Proffer, *An International Bibliography of Works By and About Bulgakov*, Ann Arbor, Michigan, 1976.

Criticism

Books:
A. Colin Wright, *Bulgakov: Life and Interpretations*, Toronto, 1978.
Rita di Meo Giuliani, *Michail Bulgakov*, Florence, 1981.
Ellendea Proffer, *Bulgakov: Life and Work*, Ann Arbor, Michigan, 1984.
Nadine Natov, *Mikhail Bulgakov*, Boston, 1985.
Julie Curtis, *Bulgakov's Last Decade: The Writer as Hero*, Cambridge, 1987.
Robert Russell, *Russian Drama of the Revolutionary Period*, Totowa, New Jersey, 1988.
Articles:
Konstantin Rudnitsky, "Bulgakov's Plays", in *Russian Literature Triquarterly*, 15, 1978.
Peter Doyle, "Bulgakov's *Ivan Vasil'evich*: Light-Hearted Comedy or Serious Satire?", in *Journal of Russian Studies*, 43, 1982.
"Bulgakov Issue" of *Canadian-American Slavic Studies*, 15, Summer-Fall 1981.

* * *

When Bulgakov died, in 1940, he left behind a total of some 20 plays, including translations and adaptations. Some of these exist in more than one version, as a result of re-writings dictated, either by his complicated working relationship with the Moscow Art Theatre, or by the equally contrary demands of the state censorship body. At the time of his death, many of his plays were still either unperformed or unpublished, something which remained true, until 1966, of the work for which he is probably best known—the novel, *The Master and Margarita*. A fantastic tale, drawing on the Bible, the Faust legend, and the literary and theatrical worlds of contemporary Moscow, the novel also lent itself to theatrical adaptation, in Yuri Lyubimov's famous version at the Taganka Theatre (1977). This, in itself, was in a tradition of adaptation to which Bulgakov made significant contributions, having adapted major works of fiction for the stage. Similarly, his political fantasy, *Heart of a Dog*, has also lent itself to successful stage adaptation, during the 1980's.

It is interesting to note the way in which Bulgakov's dramatic imagination seems preoccupied with the past and with the future, viewed from a present which is the site of fantasy or nightmare. He shares with Mayakovsky and Zamyatin an interest in science-fiction, which surfaces in both his 1920's prose-writing and in the plays written during the 1930's. There is also a sense in which his imagination is constantly being invaded by literary and historical figures from the distant, or not-so-distant, past. These include Lenin, Trotsky, and Jules Verne (*The Crimson Island*), Ivan the Terrible (*Bliss* and *Ivan Vasilevich*), Gogol (*Dead Souls*), Napoleon and Tolstoy (*War and Peace*), Pushkin (*Last Days*), Don Quixote (*Don Quixote*) and the young Stalin (*Batum*). First and foremost among the literary figures is Molière with whom, and with whose work, Bulgakov became obsessed during the 1930's. In addition to writing a play, *A Cabal of Hypocrites*, based on Molière's work in the theatre and his relationship with Louis XIV, he also wrote a fictional interpretation of Molière's life, translated *The Miser*, and re-wrote *Le Bourgeois Gentilhomme* as "Half-witted Jourdain".

His first play, *The Days of the Turbins*, is a re-working in recognisable, but significantly altered, dramatic form of his own Civil War novel set in Kiev, *The White Guard*. Accused at the time of being over-sympathetic to the "White" cause (the "Reds" never appear), in fact, the play testifies to Bulgakov's abiding fascination with the notion of life as theatre. Drawing on theatrical metaphors from farce, comic opera, pantomime, and the puppet show, the play concludes with the anticipation that the unreal costume play of the past will now give way to the "historical drama" of a new epoch heralded by the Revolution.

His next play, the satirical comedy, *Zoia's Apartment*, deals with the shady underworld of the period of the New Economic Policy, the "apartment" in question serving as a front for a brothel where aspects of reality begin to take on a hellish, phantasmagorical aura. The same is true, in more serious and tragic vein, of his Civil War drama *Flight*, conceived as a series of "dreams", at the centre of which is the figure of Khludov, a "White" officer, haunted by visions, who inhabits a sleepless, nightmare world of violence and chaotic transition.

The theme of revolution is also dealt with, satirically, in *The Crimson Island*, which contains a play-within-the-play. It begins on a desert island, where an anti-colonial revolt has broken out, the revolutionary explosion at the beginning being contrasted, ironically, with a natural volcanic explosion on the island. It is in this contrasting key that the drama is played out, culminating in an attempt by a member of the censorship body to have the play banned. The attempt is circumvented within the play itself, but was not reflected in reality, Tairov's production at the Kamerny Theatre being taken off after only a few performances.

Having obtained employment at the Moscow Art Theatre,

with the unexpected help of Stalin, Bulgakov set to work adapting *Dead Souls* for his new employers. Stanislavsky tended to disapprove of the more original elements in Bulgakov's dramatisation, with the result that crucial elements were either jettisoned altogether or suffered drastic alteration during rehearsal. Bulgakov's working relationship with Stanislavsky proved a difficult one—a fact not helped by the latter's illness following a heart attack. It proved especially aggravating when it came to staging *A Cabal of Hypocrites*, especially since the work was close to Bulgakov's heart, dealing as it did with his hero, Molière, as well as mirroring his own difficult relationship with the Soviet state. The upshot was that Stanislavsky got his own way with the production, but Bulgakov exacted his revenge in the shape of his *Theatrical Romance* (the work of fiction sometimes translated as *Black Snow*), in which the figure of Stanislavsky, and his rehearsal methods, are caricatured unmercifully. At the time Bulgakov noted that work on this play had cost him four years of his life, and to little avail. Meanwhile, his country had managed to construct the Moscow metro and emerge, through rapid industrialisation, as a major world power.

Adam and Eve, *Bliss*, and *Ivan Vasilevich*, all belong to the world of Bulgakov's early science-fiction. In the first of the plays, he foresees a devastating world war in which the population of Leningrad is wiped out by fascists using a solar nerve gas. The plot owes something to H.G. Wells, while some of the characters and themes belong to *The Master and Margarita*. The soviet literary scene is satirised in the person of one Ponchik–Nepobeda, who seems to be related to the Englishman, Pont-Kitch, and the "Chief Co-ordinator", Pobedonosikov, of Mayakovsky's *The Bathhouse*. At the end of the play, the Soviet Union emerges victorious and the "General Secretary" is left in control of a world government.

The debt to Mayakovsky is also apparent in *Bliss* (the first version of *Ivan Vasilevich*). As in *The Bathhouse*, there is an inventor and a time-machine. However, whereas in *Bliss* time-travel is into the future, in *Ivan Vasilevich* it is back to the past—to 16th-century Muscovy and the court of Ivan the Terrible. Bulgakov also exploits the idea of dream in both plays, in an apparent attempt to provide a realistic framework for the unlikely events, but this "explanatory" device is not very successful. More successful is the comic exploitation, in *Ivan Vasilevich*, of contrasting linguistic styles, ranging from pseudo-Old Slavonic to contemporary cliché and bureaucratic jargon. It is also interesting to note a line of development from the serious tragi-farce, *Zoia's Apartment*, through the intellectual utopian problem play, *Adam and Eve*, to the serio-comic utopian *Bliss* and, thence, to the almost exclusively comic *Ivan Vasilevich*.

Bulgakov's last play, *Batum*, was written to celebrate Stalin's 60th birthday and, to date, has neither been published nor performed in the former Soviet Union. Those who have read it in manuscript tend to describe it as a mediocre and uninspired work written as an act of expediency, possibly in order to gain a more favourable reception for some of Bulgakov's other plays. The plot deals with the revolutionary exploits of the young Stalin, beginning with his period of training for the priesthood, continuing with his work for the Bolshevik "underground" and concluding with his imprisonment, exile and subsequent escape.

—Nick Worrall

See also *Volume 1* entry on *The White Guard*.

BULLINS, Ed. Born in Philadelphia, Pennsylvania, USA, 2 July 1935. Educated in Philadelphia public schools; William Penn Business Institute, Philadelphia; Los Angeles City College; San Francisco City College (B.Ed.). Served in the US Navy, 1952–55. Married to Trixie Bullins. Founding director, Black Arts/West, San Francisco, 1965–67; playwright-in-residence and associate director, New Lafayette Theatre, Harlem, New York, 1967–73; editor, *Black Theatre* magazine, 1969–74; teacher of playwriting on various college and university programs, 1971–79; producing director, The Surviving Theatre, New York, 1974–; writers' unit co-ordinator, Shakespeare Festival Public Theatre, New York, 1975–82; Mellon lecturer in dramatic literature, Amherst College, Amherst, Massachusetts, from 1977; in charge of publicity and promotion at various theatres in San Francisco, 1982–83; teacher of drama, City College, San Francisco, 1984–88; producer and writer for the BMT Theater, Emeryville, California, 1988; earned BA, Antioch University, San Francisco, 1989, and has also pursued postgraduate research; lecturer, University of California, Berkeley, 1989–. Recipient: Vernon Rice Award, 1968; Obie Award, 1971 and 1975.

Works

Collections

Five Plays (includes *Clara's Ole Man; In the Wine Time; A Son, Come Home; The Electronic Nigger; Goin' a Buffalo*). 1969; as *"The Electronic Nigger" and Other Plays*, 1970.
The Theme is Blackness: "The Corner" and Other Plays (includes *Dialect Determinism, or The Rally; It Has No Choice; The Helper; A Minor Scene; The Theme is Blackness; The Man Who Dug Fish; Street Sounds;* and the scenarios and short plays *Black Commercial No. 2, The American Flag Ritual, State Office Bldg. Curse, One-Minute Commercial, A Street Play, A Short Play for a Small Theatre,* and *The Play of the Play*). 1973.

Stage Works

Clara's Ole Man (produced Firehouse Repertory Theatre, San Francisco, 1965). In *Five Plays*, 1969.
How Do You Do? (produced Firehouse Repertory Theatre, San Francisco, 1965). 1965.
Dialect Determinism; or, The Rally (produced Firehouse Repertory Theatre, San Francisco, 1965). In *The Theme is Blackness*, 1973.
The Theme is Blackness (produced State College, San Francisco, 1966). In *The Theme is Blackness*, 1973.
It Has No Choice (produced West Repertory Theatre School, San Francisco, 1966). In *The Theme is Blackness*, 1973.
A Minor Scene (produced West Repertory Theatre School, San Francisco, 1966). In *The Theme is Blackness*, 1973.
The Game of Adam and Eve, with Shirley Tarbell (produced Playwrights Theatre, Los Angeles, 1966).
In New England Winter (produced New York, 1967). In *New Plays from the Black Theatre*, edited by Bullins, 1969.
In the Wine Time (produced New Lafayette Theatre, New York, 1968). In *Five Plays*, 1969.
A Son, Come Home (produced American Place Theatre, New York, 1968). In *Five Plays*, 1969.

The Electronic Nigger (produced American Place Theatre, New York, 1968). In *Five Plays*, 1969.
Goin' a Buffalo: A Tragifantasy (produced American Place Theatre, New York, 1968). In *Five Plays*, 1969.
The Gentleman Caller (produced Chelsea Theater Center, Brooklyn, New York, 1969). In *Illuminations 5*, 1968.
The Corner (produced Boston, 1968). In *The Theme is Blackness*, 1973.
We Righteous Bombers, from a play by Camus (produced New Lafayette Theatre, New York, 1969).
The Man Who Dug Fish (produced Boston, 1969). In *The Theme is Blackness*, 1973.
Street Sounds (produced La Mama Experimental Theatre, New York, 1970). In *The Theme is Blackness*, 1973.
The Helper (produced New Dramatists Workshop, New York, 1970). In *The Theme is Blackness*, 1973.
A Ritual To Raise the Dead and Foretell the Future (produced New Lafayette Theatre, New York, 1970). In *The Theme is Blackness*, 1973.
The Fabulous Miss Marie (produced New Lafayette Theatre, New York, 1970). In *The New Lafayette Theatre Presents*, edited by Bullins, 1974.
It Bees Dat Way (produced Ambiance Lunch Hour Theatre Club, London, 1970). In *Four Dynamite Plays*, 1971.
Death List (produced Theatre Black, New York, 1970). In *Four Dynamite Plays*, 1971.
The Pig Pen (produced American Place Theatre, New York, 1970). In *Four Dynamite Plays*, 1971.
Night of the Beast. In *Four Dynamite Plays*, 1971.
The Duplex: A Black Love Fable in Four Movements (produced New Lafayette Theatre, New York, 1970). 1971.
The Devil Catchers (produced New Lafayette Theatre, New York, 1970).
The Psychic Pretenders (produced New Lafayette Theatre, New York, 1972).
You Gonna Let Me Take You Out Tonight, Baby? (produced Shakespeare Festival Public Theatre, New York, 1972).
Next Time, in *City Stops* (produced Bronx Community College, New York, 1972).
House Party, music by Pat Patrick, lyrics by Bullins (produced American Place Theatre, New York, 1973).
[Short plays and scenarios]: *Black Commercial No. 2; The American Flag Ritual; State Office Bldg. Curse; One Minute Commercial; A Street Play; A Short Play for a Small Theatre;* and The *Play of the Play*. In *The Theme is Blackness*, 1973.
The Taking of Miss Janie (produced New Federal Theatre, New York, 1975). In *Famous American Plays of the 1970's*, edited by Ted Hoffman, 1981.
The Mystery of Phyllis Wheatley (produced New Federal Theatre, New York, 1976).
I Am Lucy Terry (produced American Place Theatre, New York, 1976).
Jo Anne!!! (produced Riverside Church, New York, 1976).
Home Boy, music by Aaron Bell, lyrics by Bullins (produced Perry Street Theatre, New York, 1976).
Daddy (produced New Federal Theatre, New York, 1977).
Sepia Star; or, Chocolate Comes to the Cotton Club, music and lyrics by Mildred Kayden (produced Stage 73, New York, 1977).
Storyville, music and lyrics by Mildred Kayden (produced Mandeville Theatre, La Jolla, California, 1977; revised version, produced Washington DC, 1979).
Michael (produced New Heritage Repertory, New York, 1978).
C'mon Back to Heavenly House (produced Amherst College Theatre, Amherst, Massachusetts, 1978).

Leavings (produced by Syncopation, New York, 1980).
Steve and Velma (produced by the New African Company, Boston, 1980).
American Griot (produced La Mama Experimental Theatre, New York, 1990).
I Think it's Gonna Turn Out Fine, with others (produced La Mama Experimental Theatre, New York, 1991).
Salaam, Huey Newton, Salaam (produced New York, 1991). In *The Best Short Plays of 1990*, 1991.

Screenplays

Night of the Beast, 1971; *The Ritual Masters*, 1972.

Fiction

The Hungered One: Early Writings.   1971.
The Reluctant Rapist.   1973.

Verse

To Raise the Dead and Foretell the Future.   1971.

Other

Editor, *New Plays from the Black Theatre.*   1969.
Editor, *The New Lafayette Theatre Presents: Plays with Aesthetic Comments by 6 Black Playwrights.*   1974.

*

Bibliographies

Kimball King, *Ten Modern American Playwrights*, New York, 1982.

Criticism

Books:
Peter Bruck, "Ed Bullins: The Quest and Failure of an Ethnic Community Theatre", in *Essays on Contemporary American Theatre*, edited by Hedwig Bock and Albert Wertheim, Munich, 1981.
Geneviève Fabre (translated by Melvin Dixon), *Drumbeats, Masks, and Metaphor: Contemporary Afro-American Theatre*, Cambridge, Massachusetts, 1983.
William Herman, *Understanding Contemporary American Drama*, Columbia, South Carolina, 1987.
Arlene A. Elder, "Ed Bullins: Black Theatre as Ritual", in *Connections: Essays on Black Literatures*, edited by Emmanuel S. Nelson, Canberra, Australia, 1988.
Leslie C. Sanders, *The Development of Black Theater in America: From Shadows to Selves*, Baton Rouge, Louisiana, 1988.

Articles:
Ed Bullins and Marvin X, "Black Theater: An Interview With Ed Bullins", in *Negro Digest*, vol. 8 no. 6, 1969.
Ed Bullins and Erika Munk, "Up from Politics: An Interview With Ed Bullins", in *Performance*, vol. 1 no. 2, 1972.
Lance Jeffers, "Bullins, Baraka, and Elder: The Dawn of Grandeur in Black Drama", in *College Language Association Journal*, 16, 1972.
Don Evans, "The 'Theater of Confrontation': Ed Bullins Up Against the Wall", in *Black World*, vol. 23 no. 6, 1974.

Robert L. Tener, "Pandora's Box: A Study of Ed Bullins' Dramas", in *College Language Association Journal*, 19, 1976.
Warren R. True, "Ed Bullins, Anton Chekhov, and the Drama of Mood", in *College Language Association Journal*, 20, 1977.
W.D.E. Andrews, "Theater of Black Reality: The Blues Drama of Ed Bullins", in *Southwest Review*, 65, 1980.
Nicholas Canaday, "Toward Creation of a Collective Form: The Plays of Ed Bullins", in *Studies in American Drama*, 1, 1986.

*   *   *

Although Ed Bullins wrote some "revolutionary" plays in the manner of Amiri Baraka in the late 1960's, his best and most characteristic works are pictures of the daily life of working-class or criminal-class blacks (the distinction not always being a clear one). His recurring subject is the very thin line that separates ordinary, day-to-day events from despair, violence, or madness, and how very little it takes to push an individual, a group, or a whole society over that line. His usual mode is a seemingly plotless slice of life that meanders like a jazz improvisation, spiraling back on itself until an unexpected moment of violence focuses the play and forces the audience to redefine everything that went before. (The comparison to jazz is not forced; music plays an important role in Bullins' scripts, which often call for specific songs, even specific recordings, to be played at key moments.)

In *Clara's Ole Man*, a young man calls on a girl and spends the play drinking and chatting with her masculine friend. It isn't until he repeats a joking remark about "Clara's ole man" that he realizes it is a disparaging reference to the lesbian in front of him. He has, without intending to, violated a taboo everyone recognizes, and the lesbian's friends take him out and beat him up. In *Goin' a Buffalo*, a group of petty criminals and their girls in Los Angeles dream of the big project that will give them the money to leave town and start fresh in Buffalo. But events defeat them: a quarrel with a bartender over back-pay turns into murder, and a newcomer brought into the gang informs on them, stealing both the money and the girls. The play's central metaphor is the chess game that the men (improbably) play, without realizing that the same kinds of strategy and exploitation of weaknesses are being used against them in life.

In the Wine Time is almost plotless through most of its length. A black family living at the edge of respectability go through their usual round of lounging, drinking, arguing, and making up. But as the play progresses, a benign sitting-around-doing-nothing slides into dead-end unemployment and vagrancy, social drinking into chronic public drunkenness, teasing and trading of insults into violence. Without warning, the one boy who seems to have a future is attacked by a gang, and his uncle has to kill to save him. Suddenly nothing will be as it was before, but just as suddenly we realize that this or some other hope-destroying event was inevitable.

In New England Winter, a sequel to *In the Wine Time*, revisits Cliff Dawson, the uncle, after he has gotten out of prison, having lost his family in the interim. He and his half-brother, Steve Benson, plan a robbery with two friends, but individual and group tensions get in their way. Where Cliff is sometimes uncontrollably emotional and impulsive, Steve is obsessed with order and meticulous planning. Steve is driven by the memory of a girl he once knew in New England and wants to return to, and it is as if he is channeling all his emotional resources into that dream; but flashbacks show that his memories are false and his fantasy of reunion impossible. A sudden argument ends with Steve killing one of the others, putting an end to the whole plan and any hope of escape.

A recurring sub-theme of Bullins's work is the acceptance of open emotionalism as part of the black heritage. The immediate motive for the murder in *In New England Winter* is Steve's hope of keeping Cliff from learning that Steve had slept with his wife while he was in prison, helping to break up the marriage. But Cliff knew all along; in his undisciplined and passionate way he was more able to accept and deal with the pains of loss and betrayal than the more controlled Steve was. In *The Electronic Nigger*, a pretentious and egotistical black student steals control of a creative writing class from its bookish black teacher; his unfettered black energy, however crude and foolish-looking, is superior to the teacher's imitation of white culture.

Another repeated theme is the limited vision and imaginative horizon that contributes to his characters' doom. Though Steve in *In New England Winter* has a controlling fantasy, and Ray, the boy in *In the Wine Time*, has vague stirrings of ambition toward something better, the former is self-deluding and the latter too innocent and unformed to survive. Meanwhile, virtually all the other characters, from the gang in *Goin' a Buffalo* to Cliff Dawson, are trapped by an inability to see beyond their immediate lives to any meaningful alternatives. Yet, at the same time, this lack of vision saves them from the despair that would come from recognizing lost or unavailable alternatives.

The Taking of Miss Janie focuses on this paradox by presenting a group of black and white college students at a party in the early 1960's, and then allowing each a soliloquy or flash-forward in which he sees what will happen to him in the next decade. Some don't alter much, others decay or sell out, others make radical changes. At the play's center, a black man who has maintained an idealized platonic romance with a white woman finally rapes her. What the characters all have in common is the inability to imagine (in the "then" of the party) that life would affect them in any way, and the inability (in the "now" of the future) to see any surprises or contradictions in their subsequent lives. On one level the play is a dirge for the energy and idealism of the 1960's; on another it is an acceptance of the losses and compromises (the central couple stay together after the rape); on another, it is an acknowledgement of the degree to which life, particularly for American blacks, is ruled by forces outside their control and imagination.

—Gerald M. Berkowitz

BULWER-LYTTON, Edward (George Earle); 1st Baron Lytton of Knebworth. Born in London, 25 May 1803. Educated at Dr. Ruddock's School, Fulham, London; Dr. Hooker's School, Rottingdean, Sussex; with Charles Wallington, Ealing, London, 1819–21; Trinity College, Cambridge (pensioner), 1822, and Trinity Hall, Cambridge (fellow-commoner; chancellor's medal for verse, 1825), 1822–25, BA 1826, MA 1835. Married Rosina Doyle Wheeler in 1827 (separated 1836); one daughter and one son. Travelled, 1824–26; lived at Woodcot House, near Pangbourne, Berkshire, and wrote for various magazines, including *Quarterly Review, Keepsakes*, and *Books of Beauty*, 1827–29; moved to London, 1829; editor, *New Monthly*, London, 1831–32; Radical member of Parliament for St. Ives, Huntingdonshire, 1831, and for Lincoln, 1832–41: active supporter of stronger copyright laws and of the removal of taxes on literature; first play, *The Duchess of Vallière*, produced 1837; publisher, with others, the *Monthly Chronicle*, London, 1841; succeeded to the family estate at Knebworth, Hertfordshire, 1843; travelled, 1849; Conservative member of Parliament for Hertford, 1852 until his elevation to the peerage, 1866: secretary of state for the colonies in Lord Derby's administration, 1858–59. Rector, University of Glasgow, 1856, 1858. LL.D.: Cambridge University, 1864. Created Baron Lytton, 1866; member, Order of St. Michael and St. George, 1869. Died in Torquay, Devon, 18 January 1873.

Works

Collections

Poetical and Dramatic Works (5 vols.).   1852–54.
Works (Knebworth Edition; 37 vols.).   1873–77.

Stage Works

The Duchess de la Vallière (produced Covent Garden Theatre, London, 1837).   1836.
The Lady of Lyons; or, Love and Pride (produced Covent Garden Theatre, London, 1838).   1838.
Richelieu; or, The Conspiracy (produced Covent Garden Theatre, London, 1839).   1839.
The Sea Captain; or, The Birth Right (produced Theatre Royal, Haymarket, London, 1839).   1839
Money (produced Theatre Royal, Haymarket, London, 1840).   1840.
Not So Bad as We Seem; or, Many Sides to a Character (produced Devonshire House, London, 1851).   1851.
The Rightful Heir (produced Lyceum Theatre, London, 1868).   1868.
Walpole; or, Every Man Has His Price.   1869.
The House of Darnley Court, revised by Charles F. Coghlan (produced Court Theatre, London, 1877).
Junius Brutus; or, The Household Gods (produced Princess's Theatre, London, 1885).

Fiction

Falkland.   1827.
Pelham.   1828; revised edition, 1839.
The Disowned.   1828.
Devereux.   1829.
Paul Clifford.   1830.
Eugene Aram.   1832.
Asmodeus at Large.   1833.
Godolphin.   1833.
The Last Days of Pompeii.   1834; revised edition, 1835.
The Pilgrims of the Rhine.   1834.
Rienzi, The Last of the Roman Tribunes.   1835.
Ernest Maltravers.   1837.
Leila; or, The Siege of Granada.   1837.
Alice; or, The Mysteries.   1838.
Night and Morning.   1841.
Zanoni.   1842.
The Last of the Barons.   1843.
Lucretia; or, The Children of Night.   1846.
Harold, The Last of the Saxon Kings.   1848.
The Caxtons: A Family Picture.   1849.

My Novel; or, Varieties in English Life.   1852.
The Haunted and the Haunters.   1857.
What Will He Do with It?   1859.
A Strange Story.   1862; revised edition, 1863.
The Coming Race.   1871; as *Vril: The Power of the Coming Race*, edited by Paul Allen, 1972.
Kenelm Chillingly: His Adventures and Opinions.   1873.
The Parisians.   1873.
Pausanias the Spartan, edited by Bulwer-Lytton's son.   1876.

Verse

Ismael: An Oriental Tale with Other Poems.   1820.
Delmour; or, A Tale of a Sylphid and Other Poems.   1823.
Sculpture.   1825.
Weeds and Wild Flowers.   1826.
O'Neill; or, The Rebel.   1827.
The Siamese Twins: A Satirical Tale.   1831.
Eva, The Ill-Omened Marriage, and Other Poems.   1842.
Poems, edited by C.D. Macleod.   1845.
The New Timon.   1846.
King Arthur: An Epic Poem (2 vols.).   1849; revised edition, 1870.
Poetical Works.   1859; revised editions, 1865, 1873.
St. Stephen's.   1860.
The Boatman.   1864.
Lost Tales of Miletus.   1866.

Memoirs and Letters

A Letter to a Late Cabinet Minister on the Present Crisis.   1834.
Letters to John Bull Esquire.   1851.
Letters to His Wife, edited by Louisa Devey.   1884.
Letters to Macready.   1911.

Other

England and the English (2 vols.).   1833; edited by Standish Meacham, 1970.
The Student: A Series of Papers (2 vols.).   1835.
Athens: Its Rise and Fall (2 vols.).   1837.
Critical and Miscellaneous Works (2 vols.).   1841.
Confessions of a Water-Patient.   1846.
A Word to the Public.   1847.
Caxtoniana: A Series of Essays on Life, Literature, and Manners (2 vols.).   1863.
Miscellaneous Prose Works (3 vols.).   1868.
Speeches (2 vols.).   1874.
Quarterly Essays.   1875.
Pamphlets and Sketches.   1875.
Bulwer and Macready: A Chronicle of the Early Victorian Theatre, edited by Charles H. Shattuck.   1958.

Editor, *Literary Remains of William Hazlitt* (2 vols.).   1836.

Translator, *The Poems and Ballads of Schiller* (2 vols.).   1844.
Translator, *The Odes and Epodes of Horace.*   1869.

*

Criticism

Books:
Earl of Lytton (ed.) (2 vols.), *The Life, Letters, and Literary Remains*, London, 1883.

V.A.G.R.B. Lytton (2 vols.), *The Life of Lytton*, 1913.
V.A.G.R.B. Lytton, *Bulwer-Lytton*, London, 1948.
Charles H. Shattuck (ed.), *Bulwer and Macready: A Chronicle of the Early Victorian Theatre*, Urbana, Illinois, 1958.
Sibylla Jane Flower, *Bulwer-Lytton: An Illustrated Life*, 1973.
Richard A. Zipser, *Bulwer-Lytton and Germany*, 1974.
James L. Campbell Sr., *Edward Bulwer-Lytton*, Boston, 1986.

Articles:
Charles H. Shattuck, "E.L. Bulwer and Victorian Censorship", in *Quarterly Journal of Speech*, 34, 1948.

*   *   *

Bulwer-Lytton's reputation was founded on his work as a Liberal politician and novelist. By the time he turned to the theatre he was already the author of ten novels in a variety of genres ranging from "fashionable" life (*Pelham*), reforming "Newgate" melodramas (*Eugene Aram*, originally conceived as a stage play and later adapted for the stage by W. G. Wills as a vehicle for Henry Irving), and historical works (*The Last Days of Pompeii* and *Rienzi*, also popular in stage versions).

Bulwer-Lytton first revealed his interest in the theatre in his capacity as a politician. In 1832 he caused the setting up of a Select Committee of Enquiry into the condition of the theatre, and in 1833 he introduced bills aimed at addressing the worst evils which the Committee had identified. Lytton had three objectives: to establish effective copyright for stage-authors (resulting in the Dramatic Copyright Act of 1833, familiarly known as Bulwer-Lytton's Act); the removal of the "Patent Theatres" monopoly (achieved in 1843); and the abolition of the Lord Chamberlain's function as play-censor (not realised until 1967).

That Lytton's thoughts were concurrently turning to the practicalities of playwriting is indicated in *England and the English* (1833) in Book IV of which, as well as discussing legal aspects of the theatre, he analysed the strengths and weaknesses of the contemporary stage and advanced some precepts for aspiring dramatists:

> By a bold and masterly adaptation of modern materials to modern taste will an author revive the glories of drama. In this he will in reality profit by the study of Shakespeare . . . Byron and Scott, Goethe and Schiller, all took the germ of popular impulse . . . [they] cultivated that taste to the highest, and so at once conciliated and exalted the public mind.

In 1836 Bulwer-Lytton invited the leading actor of the day, William Charles Macready, to visit him at his chambers in the Albany to inform him that he had written a play designed for Macready. Macready advised Bulwer-Lytton on the construction and production of the play, but despite this, and the actor's performance as the Marquis de Bragelone, *The Duchess de la Vallière* was not a success. Another play called *Cromwell* did not reach fruition.

Despite these set-backs, Bulwer-Lytton and Macready, who saw the involvement of such established authors as part of his strategy to reform the stage, persevered. The correspondence between the dramatist and the actor (collected together by Charles H. Shattuck) illustrates the earnestness of the two men and the nature of their co-operation. In November 1837 Bulwer-Lytton wrote to Macready, "I have been considering deeply the elements of Dramatic art, and I think I see the secret". Again he turned to a French subject, a story by Helen Marie Williams entitled *The History of*

Perourov; or, The Bellows Mender (1801). Bulwer-Lytton reshaped the tale, setting it in Napoleonic times, chronicling the snobbish aspirations of Madame Deschappelles to marry her daughter, Pauline, into the aristocracy. She is duped into marrying Claude Melnotte, a gardener's son who genuinely loves her, but, the trick discovered, Melnotte leaves to serve in Napoleon's Italian Campaign. Two years later he returns—rich and disguised—just in time to rescue Pauline from a forced marriage to the villainous Beauseant: "I have a prior claim. Before the face/Of man and Heaven I urge it; I outbid/Yon sordid hickster for your priceless/Jewel . . ./The stain is blotted from my name./I have redeem'd mine honour".

Pauline welcomes Claude with relief and Madame Deschappelles (arguably the prototype for many a snobbish mother in Victorian drama) finds him "wondrously improved!". Audiences also found Bulwer-Lytton's dramaturgy improved. Such was his apprehensiveness about its reception that *The Lady of Lyons* (the title was Macready's suggestion) was first performed as the work of an anonymous author. However after its success (thanks in no small measure to Macready's performance as Melnotte and Helen Faucit's as Pauline) Bulwer-Lytton promptly revealed his authorship.

Bulwer-Lytton's predilection for French subjects was evident in his next play, *Richelieu*. In retrospect, he postulated that his three French plays constituted a trilogy depicting the movement of political power from one autocratic figure (*Richelieu*) via "the old provincial chivalry" (*The Duchess de la Vallière*) to the new order of "the People" (*The Lady of Lyons*). The evolution of *Richelieu* was painstaking. Bulwer-Lytton researched his subject thoroughly, sending to Macready (17 November 1838) a list of "Books relative to Richelieu". The most influential source was Alfred de Vigny's novel *Cinq Mars*. Despite this, Bulwer-Lytton's *Richelieu* played freely not only with historical fact, but also with the generally accepted view of the Cardinal. In fact, initially, the central character (Macready's) was one of Richelieu's secretaries, Marillac. As the focus inevitably shifted to Richelieu a tension developed between the dramatist's and the actor's concept of the character and the actor confided to his *Diaries* that he was being forced to "resort to low jest, which outrages one's notions of the ideal of Cardinal Richelieu, with all his vanity, and suppleness, and craft".

Bulwer-Lytton regarded comedy as an essential (presumably popular) ingredient, writing to Macready (23 October 1838): "It [*Richelieu*] is written on the plan of a Historical Comedy". In fact Bulwer-Lytton relied on stock melodramatic devices: a conspiracy against Richelieu, the cardinal's protection of his ward Julie de Mortemar (Helen Faucit) and consequent misunderstandings with her suitor the Chevalier de Mauprat, and reliance on the custody of an incriminating packet, of which Charles Shattuck wrote: "This is melodrama mechanics at its shoddiest". In the theatre the emphasis of Macready's performance was idealised and domestic; he achieved one of his high points in the delivery of the "Curse of Rome" speech (Act IV, Scene 2):

Then wakes the power which in the age of iron
Bursts forth to curb the great, and raise the low . . .
Set but a foot within that holy ground,
And on thy head—yea though it wore a crown—
I launch the curse of Rome!

Bulwer-Lytton's next play, *Money*, was a social comedy set in contemporary London. It tells of Alfred Evelyn (played by Macready), secretary to Sir John Vesey, who suddenly inherits great wealth. He becomes engaged to Sir John's daughter, Georgina, but suspects her motives, which he tests by pretending to have lost his fortune. Georgina abandons

him and he marries her poor relative, Clare (Helen Faucit). The plot hinges upon a stock situation, but the tone, with its bitter satire on Victorian commercialism, over-steps the bounds of comedy.

Although he struggled to complete other plays, Bulwer-Lytton's dramatic career was effectively confined to a short span (1836–40). Nevertheless he wrote three plays (*The Lady of Lyons*, *Richelieu*, and *Money*) which remained in the theatrical repertoire until the close of the century and beyond. *Richelieu* attracted many interpreters (Samuel Phelps, Edwin Booth, Henry Irving, Frank Benson, and—on film—George Arliss). Not surprisingly it is his contemporary prose comedy *Money* that has appealed to modern interest, receiving a BBC radio broadcast in 1969, and a creditable revival by the Royal Shakespeare Company in 1981.

—Richard Foulkes

See also *Volume 1* entry on *Money*.

BUZO, Alexander (John). Born in Sydney, New South Wales, Australia, 23 July 1944. Educated at the Armidale School, New South Wales, 1956–60; International School of Geneva, 1962; University of New South Wales, Sydney, 1963–65, BA 1965. Married Merelyn Johnson in 1968; two daughters. Salesman, David Jones Ltd., Sydney, 1960; messenger, E.L. Davis and Company, Sydney, 1961; storeman-packer, McGraw-Hill Book Company, Sydney, 1967; first play, *The Revolt*, produced 1967; clerk, New South Wales Public Service, Sydney, 1967–68; resident playwright, Melbourne Theatre Company, 1972–73; writer-in-residence, Sydney Teachers College, 1980; writer-in-residence, James Cook University, 1985, and University of Wollongong, 1989. Recipient: Australian Literature Society Gold Medal, 1972.

Works

Collections

Norm and Ahmed; Rooted; The Roy Murphy Show: Three Plays. 1973.

Stage Works

The Revolt (produced Sydney, 1967).
Norm and Ahmed (produced Old Tote Theatre, Sydney, 1968). In *Norm and Ahmed; Rooted; The Roy Murphy Show*, 1973.
Rooted (produced Jane Street Theatre, Canberra, 1969). In *Norm and Ahmed; Rooted; The Roy Murphy Show*, 1973.
The Front Room Boys (produced Perth, 1970). In *Plays*, 1970.
The Roy Murphy Show (produced by Nimrod Theatre, Sydney, 1971). In *Norm and Ahmed; Rooted; The Roy Murphy Show*, 1973.
Macquarie (produced Melbourne, 1972). 1971.
Tom (produced by the Melbourne Theatre Company, Melbourne, 1972). 1975.
Batman's Beach-head, from a play by Ibsen (produced Melbourne, 1973).

Coralie Lansdowne Says No (produced by Nimrod Theatre, Adelaide, 1974).   1974.
Martello Towers (produced by Nimrod Theatre, Sydney, 1976).   1976.
Vicki Madison Clocks Out (produced Adelaide, 1976).
Makassar Reef (produced by the Melbourne Theatre Company, Melbourne).   1978.
Big River (produced Adelaide Festival, 1980).   With *The Marginal Farm*, 1985.
The Marginal Farm (produced by the Melbourne Theatre Company, Melbourne, 1983).   With *Big River*, 1985.
Stingray (produced Sydney, 1987).   1987.
Shellcove Road (produced Sydney, 1989).   1989.

Screenplays

Rod, 1972.

Television Plays (animated films):

A Christmas Carol, 1982, *Great Expectations*, 1983, *David Copperfield*, 1984, and *The Old Curiosity Shop*, 1985, all from works by Dickens.

Radio Plays

File on Rod, 1972; *Duff*, 1980; *In Search of the New Class*, 1982; *East of Singapore*, 1986.

Fiction

The Search for Harry Allway.   1985.

Other

Tautology: I Don't Want to Sound Incredulous But I Can't Believe It.   1981; revised edition, as *Tautology Too*, 1982.
Meet the New Class.   1981.
Glancing Blows.   1987.
The Young Person's Guide to the Theatre and Almost Everything Else.   1988.

Editor (Australian edition), *Real Men Don't Eat Quiche*, by Bruce Feirstein.   1982.

*

Criticism

Books:
Peter Fitzpatrick, *After "The Doll": Australian Drama Since 1955*, Melbourne, 1979.
T.L. Sturm, *Alexander Buzo's "Rooted" and "Norm and Ahmed": A Critical Introduction*, Sydney, 1980.
Rosyln Arnold, "Aggressive Vernacular", in *Contemporary Australian Drama*, Sydney, 1981.
T.L. Sturm, "Alexander Buzo: An Imagist with a Personal Style of Surrealism" in *Contemporary Australian Drama*, Sydney, 1981.
Dennis Carroll, *Australian Contemporary Drama 1909–1982*, New York, 1985.

Articles:
Alexander Buzo and Geoffrey Sirmai, "An Interview with Alex Buzo", in *Southerly*, Sydney, March 1986.

* * *

Alexander Buzo came to prominence in the late 1960's in Australia, but his theatrical beginnings lie not so much in the "rough" techniques of the "alternative" nationalist theatre of that time as they do in the earlier, European-based "theatre of the absurd".

Throughout Buzo's career so far the major dramatic theme has been the way the idiosyncratic individual can "fit in", or not, with the the wider sociological pattern in which she or he must function—and the absurdist "alienation" that is both the cause and the result of this dichotomy. This "outsider" theme, as it has been called, is a classic preoccupation of Australian drama, and is probably congenial and important to Buzo because of his own experience as a first-generation son of an Albanian-American father and Australian mother, educated at Armidale in New South Wales, and Geneva.

Buzo's early plays are primarily absurdist allegories rather than quasi-naturalist exposés, though some early critics were misled by Buzo's colorfully accurate reconstitutions of Australian vernacular and geography. A central individual, by design or default a non-conformist, is destroyed by the "system", the coercive power of which is seen as not only social, but metaphysical and absurdist in origin. *Norm and Ahmed*, Buzo's first short play, is a two-character encounter between a middle-aged, white, slightly drunk Australian and a young Pakistani student at a late-night bus stop. Norm is free with his self-disclosure and attempts to draw Ahmed out in return—but finally, sensing reserve and superiority, bashes him senseless. The play appears to be naturalistic, but in fact here the "system" is internalized in Norm, the aggressor—the "normic" attitudes of xenophobic, circa 1940's white Australian prejudice operate viciously, and have nullified the more positive and generous impulses, which are sufficiently on view to put Ahmed, and the audience, off their guard.

Rooted and *The Front Room Boys* are more clearly stylized into allegories. There are surreal rituals and heightened verbal liturgies which concurrently suggest the specifics of the vernacular. In *Rooted*, the victim Bentley is a pathetic little civil servant undone by a "system" headed by a super-achiever and predator named Simmo, who leaves the hero bereft of wife, home, "mates", job, and all means of support. Bentley has a Chaplinesque pathos about him some of the time—Buzo alludes to silent film comedy in several episodes where his hero is undone by objects such as hoses and cash-registers—but he lacks the Tramp's resource, courage, and cunning.

The Front Room Boys focuses on a young man of stronger mettle who works in an office of "front room boys", at the beck and call of the "back room boys", the bosses who appear only briefly. But the results are similar. The hero's idiosyncratic behavior and lack of tact increasingly alienate his co-workers, who gang up on him and ostracize him; at a Christmas party he is sacked, vilified, and physically abused. A new Australian colleague, on the other hand, progresses up the scale and into the backroom by ignoring the hypocritical professions of "mateship" which keep the "old Australians" tied to their front-room status but give them no compensating spiritual bonds.

After *Macquarie*, a quasi-Brechtian play comparing the dilemma of the 19th-century liberal governor Lachlan Macquarie with those of so called "liberals" in the polarized Australia of the early 1970's, Buzo launched a second phase of his career in which a more fully-inflected realism predominates. As in the earlier plays, a central character is at odds with the trends and norms of a social context—but that context is now dramatized with greater realism, and the protagonist is able to make an equivocal compromise with it, and so survive.

The most impressive of this group is probably the second—*Coralie Lansdowne Says No*, in part because of the vitality of the central non-conformist character and her brilliantly aggressive dialogue. After the wife of a former lover commits suicide while her guest, Coralie, decides that her life of superficial liaisons has failed as an avenue to some possibly apocryphal, totally communicating and involving sexual relationship, she chooses a husband—a prosaic published poet who will "do" as the lesser of two evils.

Martello Towers deals with the dilemma of an Italian-Australian son and his father adjusting their ingrained patriarchal traditions of the older society to a modern Australian context. *Makassar Reef* presents Australians who are "in transit" in an alien South-East Asian city which is itself in a state of cultural flux, but which proves a catalyst for their accommodation to Australia and to each other.

In his plays of the 1980's, Buzo is more sociologically and historically precise in showing the way that an individual must compromise with a society at a crucial point of historical transition. In *Big River*, the society is Australia, and the epoch that of Federation; the heroine essentially opts for a compromise based on past rather than present realities, but the compromise involves its rewarding elements. In *The Marginal Farm*, the society is Fiji in the late 1950's, but the pattern is more complicated in that there are two characters who have to compromise, the Australian governess Toby, and her eventual husband Illy, an Indian-Fijian who is an outsider in his own land. Illy is the more interesting character. In a way he is a reprise of the character of *The Front Room Boys'* New Australian; when he shows signs of being a "trouble-maker", as a potential strike leader, he is bribed by a job-offer to opt into the "sugar company" colonial old-boy network which is already being abandoned by the Whites who set it up. These two later plays do not have the verbal or imagist verve of the earlier works, though they are consistently intelligent and eschew obvious and superficially effective theatrical gestures, in fact, at times, parodying them.

Buzo's stylistic signature is most apparent in two dramaturgical areas: the witty, idiosyncratic, and expertly rhythmic dialogue with its different spheres and classes of colloquialism; and a scenography based on startling and near-surreal juxtapositions of disparate images. Both of these elements stand forth in bold relief in the early plays, where they operate more independently of realism. *Rooted*, for example, ranges through all-mates-together public school talk, the jargon of bureaucratic officialdom, middle-class politesse, and the "poetry" beloved of advertising copywriters. In the later, more realistic plays, the idioms expand to include American, South-East Asian, and various "historical" modes of English. The scenography is seen at its most sparse and unsettling in the early plays; in the later ones, unusual objects and juxtapositions—such as the tree growing through the roof of a modern apartment in *Coralie Lansdowne Says No*—are justified "realistically", but are still very arresting; and as critics have shown, there is a careful and symbolically loaded use of color in much of the imagery.

—Dennis Carroll

See also *Volume 1* entry on *Norm and Ahmed*.

————————

BYRON, H(enry) J(ames). Born in Manchester, England, 8 January 1835. Educated at a school in Essex; St. Peter's College, London; with a private tutor to 1849; articled to the surgeon Miles Morley in London, and to his grandfather, Dr. Bradley, in Buxton, 1849–53; studied law at the Middle Temple, London, 1858. Married 1) Martha Foulkes in 1856 (died 1876); 2) Eleanor Mary Joy in 1876. Actor in provincial company, Colchester, Oldham, and Rochester, 1853–58; first burlesque, *Richard of the Lionheart*, produced 1857; wrote burlesques for the Strand Theatre, London, 1858–65; editor, *Fun* weekly, from 1861, and *Comic News*, 1863–64; manager, with Marie Wilton, Prince of Wales's Theatre, London, 1865–67; manager, Theatre Royal, Liverpool, 1866; leased Royal Amphitheatre, 1866, and Royal Alexandra Theatre, 1867, both Liverpool: petitioned for bankruptcy and relinquished management, 1868; London debut as professional actor, 1869, and thereafter appeared in the London productions of his own comedies (*Our Boys* had record-breaking run, 1875–79); became joint manager, Criterion Theatre, London, 1874; editor, *Mirth*, 1877–78. Died 12 April 1884.

Works

Collections

Sensation Dramas for the Back Drawing Room.   1864.
Bits of Burlesque.   1877
Plays (includes *The Babes in the Wood; The Lancashire Lass; Our Boys; The Gaiety Gulliver*), edited by Jim Davis. 1984.

Stage Works

Richard of the Lion Heart (produced Strand Theatre, London, 1857).
The Lady of Lyons; or, Twopenny Pride and Penny-tence (produced Strand Theatre, London, 1858).   1858.
Fra Diavolo Travestie; or, The Beauty and the Brigands (produced Strand Theatre, London, 1858).   1858.
The Bride of Abydos; or, The Prince, The Pirate, and the Pearl (produced Strand Theatre, London, 1858).   1858.
The Maid and the Magpie; or, The Fatal Spoon (produced Strand Theatre, London, 1858).   1859.
Mazeppa (produced Olympic Theatre, London, 1858).   1865.
The Very Latest Edition of The Lady of Lyons (produced Strand Theatre, London, 1859).   Nd.
The Babes in the Wood and the Good Little Fairy Birds (produced Adelphi Theatre, London, 1859).   1859; also in *Plays*, 1984.
Jack the Giant Killer; or, Harlequin King Arthur and Ye Knights of Ye Round Table (produced Princess's Theatre, London, 1859; revised version produced Gaiety Theatre, London, 1878).   1859.
The Nymph of the Lurleyburg; or, The Knight and the Naiads (produced Adelphi Theatre, London, 1859).   1859.
The Pilgrim of Love (produced Theatre Royal, Haymarket, London, 1860).   1860.
The Miller and His Men, with Francis Talfourd (produced Strand Theatre, London, 1860).   1860.
The Garibaldi Excursionists (produced Princess's Theatre, London, 1860).   1861.
Blue Beard from a New Point of Hue (produced Adelphi Theatre, London, 1860).   1861.
Cinderella; or, The Lover, The Lackey, and the Little Glass Slipper (produced Strand Theatre, London, 1860).   1861.
Robinson Crusoe; or, Harlequin Friday and the King of the

Caribee Islands, music by W.H. Montgomery (produced Princess's Theatre, London, 1860). 1861.

The Rival Othellos (produced Strand Theatre, London, 1861).

Aladdin; or, The Wonderful Scamp (produced Strand Theatre, London, 1861). 1861.

The Old Story (produced Strand Theatre, London, 1861). 1861.

Esmeralda; or, The Sensation Goat! (produced Strand Theatre, London, 1861). 1862.

Miss Eily O'Connor (produced Theatre Royal, Drury Lane, London, 1861). 1862; as *The Colleen Bawn* (produced 1870).

Puss in a New Pair of Boots, music by F. Musgrave (produced Strand Theatre, London, 1861). 1862.

Whittington and His Cat; or, Harlequin King Kollywobbol and the Genius of Good Humour, music by W.H. Montgomery (produced Princess's Theatre, London, 1861). 1862.

The Rosebud of Stinging-Nettle Farm; or, The Villainous Squire and the Virtuous Villager (produced Crystal Palace, London, 1862; revised version, as *The Villainous Squire and the Village Rose*, produced Toole's Theatre, London, 1882). 1867.

Goldenhair the Good (produced St. James's Theatre, London, 1862).

Harlequin Beauty and the Beast; or, The Gnome Queen and the Good Fairy (produced Covent Garden Opera House, London, 1862). 1862.

George de Barnwell; or, Harlequin Folly in the Realms of Fancy (produced Adelphi Theatre, London, 1862). 1863.

Ivanhoe, in Accordance with the Spirit of the Times, music by F. Musgrave (produced Strand Theatre, London, 1862). 1864.

Ali Baba; or, The Thirty-Nine Thieves, in Accordance with the Author's Habit of Taking One Off (produced Strand Theatre, London, 1863). 1864.

Beautiful Haidée; or, The Sea Nymph and the Sallee Rovers (produced Princess's Theatre, London, 1863). 1863.

Ill-Treated Il Trovatore; or, The Mother, The Maiden, and the Musician (produced Adelphi Theatre, London, 1863). 1863(?).

The Motto: I Am All There (produced Strand Theatre, London, 1863). 1864.

Harlequin St. George and the Dragon; or, The Seven Champions and the Beautiful Princess (produced Covent Garden Opera House, London, 1863). 1863.

Lady Belle Belle; or, Fortunio and His Seven Magic Men (produced Adelphi Theatre, London, 1863). 1864.

Orpheus and Eurydice; or, The Young Gentleman Who Charmed the Rocks (produced Strand Theatre, London, 1863). 1864; revised version, as *Eurydice* (produced Strand Theatre, London, 1871), 1872; revised version, as *Pluto* (produced Royalty Theatre, London, 1881).

1863; or, The Sensations of the Past Season (produced St. James's Theatre, London, 1863). 1864.

Mazourka; or, The Stick, The Pole, and the Tartar (produced Strand Theatre, London, 1864). 1865.

Timothy to the Rescue (produced Strand Theatre, London, 1864). 1865; as *How to Tame Your Mother-in-Law*, nd.

Lord Dundreary Married and Done For (produced Theatre Royal, Haymarket, London, 1864).

The Grin Bushes; or, The Mrs. Brown of the "Missis"-sippi (produced Strand Theatre, London, 1864). 1865.

The Lion and the Unicorn Were Fighting for the Crown (produced Her Majesty's Theatre, London, 1864). 1864.

Princess Springtime; or, The Envoy Who Stole the King's Daughter (produced Theatre Royal, Haymarket, London, 1864). 1866.

Pan; or, The Loves of Echo and Narcissus (produced Adelphi Theatre, London, 1865). 1866.

La Somnambula! or, The Supper, The Sleeper, and the Merry Swiss Boy (produced Prince of Wales's Theatre, London, 1865). 1866.

War to the Knife (produced Prince of Wales's Theatre, London, 1865). 1866.

Lucia di Lammermoor; or, The Laird, The Lady, and the Lover (produced Prince of Wales's Theatre, London, 1865). 1867.

Little Don Giovanni; or, Leperello and the Stone Statue (produced 1865). 1867.

A Hundred Thousand Pounds (produced Prince of Wales's Theatre, London, 1866). 1868.

Der Freischutz; or, The Bill! the Belle!! and the Bullet!!! (produced Prince of Wales's Theatre, London, 1866). 1869.

Pandora's Box; or, The Young Spark and the Old Flame (produced Princess's Theatre, London, 1866). 1875.

Little Dick Whittington, Thrice Lord Mayor of London; or, Harlequin Hotpot and the Fairies of the Elfin Grot (produced Theatre Royal, Liverpool, 1866).

Harlequin Bluebeard (produced Royal Amphitheatre, Liverpool, 1866).

The Wonderful Travels of Gulliver (produced Theatre Royal, Manchester, 1867; as *Gulliver*, produced Theatre Royal, Manchester, 1867). 1867.

Robinson Crusoe; or, The Injun Bride and the Injured Wife, with W.S. Gilbert (produced Theatre Royal, Haymarket, London, 1867). In *English Plays of the Nineteenth Century 5*, edited by Michael Booth, 1976.

William Tell, with a Vengeance; or, The Pet, The Patriot, and the Pippin (produced Alexandra Theatre, Liverpool, 1867). 1868.

The Lancashire Lass; or, Tempted, Tried, and True (produced Alexandra Theatre, Liverpool, 1867; revised version produced Queen's Theatre, London, 1868). 1879; in *Plays*, 1984.

Dearer Than Life (produced Alexandra Theatre, Liverpool, 1867).

Blow for Blow (produced Holborn Theatre, London, 1868). 1875.

Lucrezia Borgia, M.D.; or, La Grande Doctresse (produced Holborn Theatre, London, 1868). 1871.

Cyril's Success (produced Globe Theatre, London 1868). 1870.

Not Such a Fool as He Looks (produced Theatre Royal, Manchester, 1868). 1884.

Robinson Crusoe; or, Friday and the Fairies (produced Covent Garden Opera House, London, 1868). 1868.

Lost at Sea: A London Story, with Dion Boucicault (produced Adelphi Theatre, London, 1869).

Minnie; or, Leonard's Love (produced Globe Theatre, London, 1869).

The Corsican "Bothers"; or, The Troublesome Twins (produced Globe Theatre, London, 1869). 1871.

Uncle Dick's Darling (produced Gaiety Theatre, London, 1869). 1907.

Lord Bateman; or, The Proud Young Porter and the Fair Sophia (produced Globe Theatre, London, 1869). 1871.

The Yellow Dwarf; or, Harlequin Cupid and the King of the Gold Mines (produced Covent Garden Opera House, London, 1869). 1869.

The Prompter's Box: A Story of the Footlights and the Fireside (produced Adelphi Theatre, London, 1870; as *Two Stars*, produced Strand Theatre, London, 1872; as *The Crushed Tragedian*, produced Theatre Royal, Haymarket, London, 1878). 1884.

Robert Macaire; or, The Roadside Inn Turned Inside Out (produced Globe Theatre, London, 1870). 1872.

The Enchanted Wood; or, The Three Transformed Princes (produced Adelphi Theatre, London, 1870). 1874.

The English Gentleman; or, The Empty Pocket (produced Theatre Royal, Bristol, 1870; also produced as *The Squire's Last Shilling*). 1887.

Wait and Hope (produced Gaiety Theatre, London, 1871).

Daisy Farm (produced Olympic Theatre, London, 1871). 1879.

The Orange Tree and the Humble Bee; or, The Little Princess Who Was Lost at Sea (produced Vaudeville Theatre, London, 1871). 1872.

Not If I Know It (produced Theatre Royal, Haymarket, London, 1871).

Giselle; or, The Sirens of the Lotus Lake (produced Olympic Theatre, London, 1871). 1872.

Partners for Life (produced Globe Theatre, London, 1871). 1878.

Camaralzaman and the Fair Badoura; or, The Bad Djinn and the Good Spirit (produced Vaudeville Theatre, London, 1871). 1872.

Blue Beard (produced Covent Garden Opera House, London, 1871). 1871.

Haunted Houses; or, Labyrinths of Life: A Story of London and the Bush (produced Princess's Theatre, London, 1872).

The Spur of the Moment (produced Globe Theatre, London, 1872).

Time's Triumph (produced Gaiety Theatre, London, 1872).

Good News (produced Gaiety Theatre, London, 1872).

The Lady of the Lane (produced Strand Theatre, London, 1872).

Mabel's Life; or, A Bitter Bargain (produced Adelphi Theatre, London, 1872).

Old Soldiers (produced Strand Theatre, London, 1873). 1879.

Fine Feathers (produced Globe Theatre, London, 1873). 1884.

Chained to the Oar (produced Prince of Wales's Theatre, Liverpool, 1873).

La Fille de Mme. Angot, from the opera by L.F.N. Clairville, P. Siraudin, and V. Koning, music by A.C. Lecocq (produced Philharmonic Theatre, Islington, London, 1873).

Sour Grapes (produced Olympic Theatre, London, 1873). 1887.

Don Juan (produced Alhambra Palace, London, 1873).

The Thumbscrew (produced Holborn Theatre, London, 1874).

Guy Fawkes (produced Gaiety Theatre, London, 1874).

An American Lady (produced Criterion Theatre, London, 1874).

Normandy Pippins (produced Criterion Theatre, London, 1874).

The Pretty Perfumeress, from an opera by H. Crimieux and E. Blum, music by Offenbach (produced Alhambra Palace, London, 1874).

The Demon's Bride, music by Georges Jacobi (produced Alhambra Palace, London, 1874).

Old Sailors (produced Strand Theatre, London, 1874). 1880.

Oil and Vinegar (produced Gaiety Theatre, London, 1874).

Our Boys (produced Vaudeville Theatre, London, 1875). 1880; also in *Plays*, 1984.

Weak Women (produced Strand Theatre, London, 1875). 1878.

Married in Haste (produced Theatre Royal, Haymarket, London, 1875). 1879.

Tottles (produced 1875).

Wrinkles: A Tale of Time (produced Prince of Wales's Theatre, London, 1876). 1879.

£20 a Year—All Found (produced Folly Theatre, London, 1876). 1880.

The Bull by the Horns (produced Gaiety Theatre, London, 1876).

Little Don Caesar de Bazan (produced Gaiety Theatre, London, 1876).

Widow and Wife (produced Theatre Royal, Bristol, 1876).

Old Chums (produced Opera Comique, London, 1876).

Pampered Menials (produced Opera Comique, London, 1876). 1876.

The Bohemian G'yurl and the Unapproachable Pole (produced Opera Comique, London, 1877).

Guinea Gold; or, Lights and Shadows of London Life (produced Princess's Theatre, London, 1877).

Little Doctor Faust (produced Gaiety Theatre, London, 1877).

A Fool and His Money (produced Globe Theatre, London, 1878).

Ali Baba and the Forty Thieves, with others (produced Gaiety Theatre, London, 1878). 1878.

Il Somnambulo and the Lively Little Alessio (produced Gaiety Theatre, London, 1878).

A Hornet's Nest (produced Theatre Royal, Haymarket, London, 1878).

Conscience Money (produced Theatre Royal, Haymarket, London, 1878).

Uncle (produced Gaiety Theatre, London, 1878). 1880.

Young Fra Diavolo, The Terror of Terracina (produced Gaiety Theatre, London, 1878).

Pretty Esmeralda and Captain Phoebus of Ours (produced Gaiety Theatre, London, 1879).

Handsome Hernani; or, The Fatal Penny Whistle (produced Gaiety Theatre, London, 1879).

Courtship; or, The Three Caskets (produced Court Theatre, London, 1879). 1884.

The Gaiety Gulliver (produced Gaiety Theatre, London, 1879). 1880.

The Girls (as *Our Girls*, produced Vaudeville Theatre, London, 1879). 1887.

The Upper Crust (produced Folly Theatre, London, 1880).

Il Trovatore; or, Larks with a Libretto (produced Olympic Theatre, London, 1880).

Without a Home (produced Theatre Royal, Cardiff, Wales, 1880).

Bow Bells (produced Royalty Theatre, London, 1880). 1881.

The Light Fantastic (produced Folly Theatre, London, 1880).

Michael Strogoff (produced Adelphi Theatre, London, 1881).

Punch (produced Vaudeville Theatre, London, 1881). 1887.

New Brooms (produced Gaiety Theatre, Dublin, 1881).

Fourteen Days (produced Criterion Theatre, London, 1882).

Auntie (produced 1882).

Frolique, with H.B. Farnie (produced Strand Theatre, London, 1882).

Open House (produced Vaudeville Theatre, London, 1885).

The Shuttlecock, completed by J.A. Sterry (produced Toole's Theatre, London, 1885).

Fiction

Paid in Full (3 vols.).   1865.

Other

The Slang Dictionary, with W.C. Hazlitt.   1864.

*

Criticism

Books:
Introduction, in *Plays by H.J. Byron*, edited by Jim Davis, Cambridge, 1984.

*   *   *

H.J. Byron was one of the most prolific writers of burlesques during the mid-19th century. The excesses of melodrama and grand opera, in particular, were mercilessly parodied in high-spirited burlesques replete with songs, dances, and a seemingly unstoppable artillery of puns. Byron was particularly associated with the Strand and later with the Gaiety theatres, both popular centres of burlesque performance. These theatres catered for an adult, middle-class audience and it was for such a public that Byron first created such pantomime perennials as Buttons and Widow Twankay. He also wrote Christmas pantomimes, usually in the traditional Harlequinade format, although *The Gaiety Gulliver* of 1879, an innovative Christmas burlesque in 3-act form, is closer in spirit to modern pantomime than the Harlequinades. Byron and his contemporaries so undermined melodrama by constantly burlesquing it that its popularity began to decline; so too did the burlesque itself, which had depended on the melodramatic form to feed it.

Byron also demonstrated competence in other dramatic forms. Melodrama, which he so derided, was one of these: *The Lancashire Lass*, for instance, with its sensation scene (a drowning at a Liverpool pier, as the night ferry steams on stage), its sensational climax in the Australian outback, and its adventurer-villain, Robert Redburn (played by a young Henry Irving), was a classic example of the sort of melodramatic fare taken seriously in the 1860's. *Blow for Blow*, *Haunted Houses*, and *Lost at Sea* (a collaboration with Dion Boucicault) were among the dramas in which Byron used the form seriously rather than as fodder for burlesque.

Byron was at his best, perhaps, in the composition of comedy. He wrote many original works, at a time when translations were still a dominant force in British drama, and scored a number of successes. Part of his strength lay in his ability to write for specific actors: this had already been apparent in the burlesque roles he wrote for Marie Wilton and Ada Swanborough, not to mention Nelly Farren, Kate Vaughan, Edward Royce, and Edward Terry at the Gaiety; it was equally true of the roles he wrote for J.L. Toole in *Dearer than Life*, *Uncle Dick's Darling*, *A Fool and His Money*, *The Upper Crust*, and many more comedies, not to mention the parts he created for himself.

Domestic themes predominated in many of Byron's comedies: marriage, money and class; marital difficulties; the notion that "the quality of a man is in an inverse ratio to that of his coat"; all are among his major concerns. Some critics found Byron's plotting simplistic and contrived and his characters nothing more than mouthpieces for witty retorts. William Archer commented that Byron's comedies "do not contain a thought worth thinking, a lesson worth learning, a scene worth remembering or a character worth loving and hating". Such a judgement is unfair: the comedies are witty, original, representative of the tastes and lives of the middle-class audiences they attracted, and highly moralistic, if rather conventionally so. Byron does not eschew criticism of the greed and self-interest of his contemporaries: one of his best comedies, *Not Such a Fool as He Looks*, exposes human selfishness, but less forcefully than W.S. Gilbert was to do. The wit to be found in many of these plays anticipates the wit of both Gilbert and Wilde later in the century. However artificial and sentimental such plays as *Cyril's Success* (Byron's own favourite), *Married in Haste*, or *Partners for Life* seem today, they certainly helped prepare the ground for the work of later dramatists.

Byron's most successful comedy was the record-breaking *Our Boys*. It ran at the Vaudeville Theatre for over four years, with David James as the vulgar ex-butterman, Perkyn Middlewick, and Thomas Thorne as the foppish Talbot Champneys. In this play Charles Middlewick and Talbot Champneys return from travels abroad; both defy the wishes of their fathers, when they fall in love with women of whom their parents disapprove. The sons depart to London, to make their own livings, but are pursued by their fathers and reconciliation takes place, as well as the marriages the sons desire. Although not the best of Byron's plays, *Our Boys* perfectly exemplifies the sort of concerns at the heart of his plays and also the fare required by his audiences. A travelling production of the play through the English provinces proved equally successful as did subsequent productions in America and Europe.

Prolific, witty, and, for a time (between the demise of Robertson and the ascendancy of Gilbert, Pinero, and Jones) the most prominent of British dramatists, Byron fills a unique place in the history of 19th-century British drama. The announcement of a new play by Byron frequently drew crowded houses, and his skills at character-building, as in Perkyn Middlewick (*Our Boys*), Mould or Sir Simon (*Not Such a Fool as He Looks*), Michael Garner and Bob Gassett (*Dearer Than Life*), together with his moral and domestic concerns, earned him a reputation as the Dickens of the stage. His plays were not the most literary of works, but they catered most effectively for the theatrical tastes of the time.

—Jim Davis

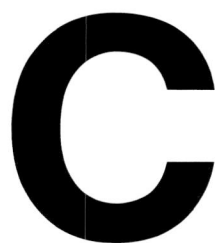

C

CALDERÓN (DE LA BARCA), Pedro. Born in Madrid, Spain, 17 January 1600. Educated at the Jesuit Colegio Imperial; studied canon law at the University of Alcalá, 1614–15, and University of Salamanca, 1615–c.1621, no degree. Entered the household of the Constable of Castille, Don Bernardino Fernández de Velasco, 1621; began writing plays for the court from 1623; most of his plays produced in public theatres, 1623–40; entered order of St. James, 1637; served in the campaign against the Catalans, 1640–42; served in the household of the Duke of Alba from 1645; became a priest in 1651, but continued to write plays as court dramatist for Philip IV; also wrote two *autos sacramentales* each year for the city of Madrid; Chaplain of the Chapel of Reyes Nuevos, Toledo, from 1653, but lived in Madrid after 1657: Honorary Chaplain to the King, 1663. Died in Madrid, 25 May 1681.

Pedro Calderón de la Barca (engraving).

Works

Collections

Obras (5 vols.), edited by Joseph Calderón. Volume 1, 1636; Volume 2, 1637; Volume 3, 1664; Volume 4, 1672; Volume 5 ("unauthorised"), 1677.

Obras (9 vols.), edited by J. de Vera Tassis y Villarroel. 1682–91.

Dramas of Calderón: Tragic, Comic and Legendary (2 vols.; includes *Love After Death*; *The Scarf and the Flower*; *The Physician of His Own Honour*; *The Constant Prince*; *The Purgatory of St. Patrick*), translated by Denis Florence McCarthy. 1853.

Six Dramas of Calderón, translated by Edward Fitzgerald. 1865; revised and expanded as *Eight Dramas* (includes *Beware of Smooth Water*; *Gil Pérez the Galician*; *Keep Your Own Secret*; *The Painter of His Own Dishonour*; *Three Judgements at a Blow*; *The Mighty Magician*; *Such Stuff as Dreams Are Made of*), 1906.

Mysteries of Corpus Christi (includes *Belshazzar's Feast*; *The Divine Philothea*; part of *The Poison and the Antidote*), translated by Denis Florence McCarthy. 1867.

Three Dramas of Calderón (includes *Love is the Greatest Enchantment*; *The Sorceries of Sin*; *The Devotion of the Cross*), translated by Denis Florence McCarthy. 1870.

Calderón's Dramas (includes *The Wonderworking Magician*; *Life is a Dream*; *The Purgatory of St. Patrick*), translated by Denis Florence McCarthy. 1873.

Obras escogidas. 1940.

Obra lírica, edited by M. de Montoliu. 1943.

Obras completas (3 vols: *Dramas*; *Comedias*; *Autos sacramentales*), edited by Angel Valbuena Briones and Angel Valbuena Prat. 1952–60.

Four Plays (includes *Secret Vengeance for Secret Insult*; *The Mayor of Zalamea*; *The Phantom Lady*; *The Devotion of the Cross*), translated by Edwin Honig. 1961.

Four Comedies (includes *From Bad to Worse*; *The Secret Spoken Aloud*; *The Worst is Not Always Spoken*; *The Advantages and Disadvantages of a Name*), translated by Kenneth Muir. 1980.

Three Comedies (includes *A House with Two Doors*; *Mornings of April and May*; *No Trifling with Love*), translated by Kenneth Muir and Ann L. MacKenzie. 1985.

Teatro cómico breve, edited by María-Luisa Lobato. 1989.

Plays 1 (includes *The Surgeon of Honour*; *Life is a Dream*; *Three Judgements in One*), translated by Gwynne Edwards. 1990.

Stage Works

Alphabetical lists of plays and *autos sacramentales*, based on the standard *Obras completas*, 1952–60. Most plays first published in the 17th-century collected editions.

A secreto agravio, secreta vengenza. Translated as *Secret Vengeance for Secret Insult*, in *Four Plays*, 1961.

El acaso y el error.

Afectos de odio y amor.

Agradecer y no amar.

El alcaide de sí mismo.

El Alcalde de Zalamea (produced 1636?). Translated as *The Mayor of Zalamea*: several subsequent translations under same title; as *The Mayor of Zalamea; or, The Best Garrotting Ever Done*, 1981.

Amado y aborrecido.

Amar después de la muerta. Translated as *Love After Death*, in *Dramas of Calderón*, 1853, and in *Classic Theatre 3*, edited by Eric Bentley, 1960.

Amigo amante y leal.

Amor, honor y poder, from a work by Matteo Bandello (produced 1623).

Antes que todo es mi drama.

Apolo y Climene (first part of *El hijo del sol Faetón*).

Argenis y Poliarco.

Las armas de la hermosura.

El astrólogo fingido.

Auristela y Lisidante.

La aurora en Copacabana.

La banda y la flor. Translated as *The Scarf and the Flower*, in *Dramas of Calderon*, 1853.

Basta callar.

Bien vengas, mal si vienes solo.

Los cabellos de Absalón, partly from a work by Tirso de Molina.

Cada uno para si.

Las cadenas del demonio.

Casa con dos puertas malas es de guardar. Translated as *A House with Two Doors is Difficult to Guard*, in *Tulane Drama Review*, 1963, and in *Three Comedies*, 1980.

El castillo de Lindabridis.

Celos aún de aire matan. Translated as *Even Baseless Jealousy Can Kill*, 1981.

La cisma de Inglaterra. Translated as *The Schism in England*, 1990.

El conde Lucanor.

Con quien vengo, vengo.

¡Cuál es mayor perfección.

La dama duende. Translated as *The Phantom Lady*, in *Four Plays*, 1961.

Darlo todo y no dar nada.

Dar tiempo al tiempo.

De una causa, dos efectos.

De un castigo, tres venganzas.

La desdicha de la voz.

La devoción de la cruz. Translated as *The Devotion of the Cross*, in *Three Dramas of Calderón*, 1870, and in *Four Plays*, 1961.

Dicha y desdicha del nombre. Translated as *The Advantages and Disadvantages of a Name*, in *Four Comedies*, 1980.

Los dos amantes del cielo.

Duelos de amor y lealtad.

Eco y Narciso.

Los empeños de un acaso.

En esta vida todo es verdad y todo mentira.

El encanto sin encanto.

El escondido y la tapada.

La estatua de Prometeo.

La exaltación de la cruz.

La fiera, el rayo y la piedra.

Fieras afemina amor.

Fineza contra fineza.

Fortunas de Andrómeda y Perseo.

Fuego de Dios en el querer bien.

El galán fantasma.

El golfo de las sirenas.

La gran Cenobia.

El gran principe de Fez.

Guárdate del agua mansa. Translated as *Beware of Smooth Water*, in *Eight Dramas*, 1906.

Gustos y disgustos son no más que imaginación.

Hado y divisa de Leonido y Marfisa.

La hija del aire (parts 1 and 2; produced 1653).

El hijo del sol, Faetón.

Los hijos de la fortuna: Teágenes y Cariclea.

El hombre pobre todo es trazas.

El jardín de Falerina, from *Orlando innamorato*, by Matteo Maria Boiardo.

El José de las mujeres.

Judas Macabeo.

Lances de amor y fortuna.

El laurel de Apolo (produced 1658).

Luis Pérez el gallego. Translated as *Gil Pérez the Galician*, in *Eight Dramas*, 1906.

El maestro de danzar.

El magico prodigioso. Translated as *The Wonderworking Magician*, in *Calderón's Dramas*, 1873, and 1982; as *The Prodigious Magician*, 1982.

Mañanas de abril y mayo. Translated as *Mornings of April and May*, in *Three Comedies*, 1985.

Mañana será otro día.

Las manos blancas no ofenden.

El mayor encanto, amor. Translated as *Love is the Greatest Enchantment*, in *Three Dramas of Calderon*, 1870.

El mayor monstruo los celos.

El medico de su honra. Translated as *The Physician of His Own Honour*, in *Dramas of Calderón*, 1853; as *The Surgeon of His Honour*, 1960; as *The Surgeon of Honour*, in *Plays 1*, 1990.

Mejor está que estaba. Translated as *Fortune Mends*, in *The Theatrical Recorder*, 2, 1806.

El monstruo de los jardines.

Mujer, llora y vencerás.

Nadie fie su secreto. Translated as *Keep Your Own Secret*, in *Eight Dramas*, 1906.

Ni Amor de libra de amor.

La niña de Gómez Arias.

No hay burlas con el amor.

No hay cosa como callar.

No siempre lo peor es cierto. Translated as *The Worst is Not Always Certain*, in *Four Comedies*, 1980.

Origen, pérdida y restauración de la Virgin del Sagrario.

Para vencer amor, querer vencerle (produced 1650).

Peor está que estaba. Translated as *From Bad to Worse*, in *Four Comedies*, 1980.

El pintor de su deshonra. Translated as *The Painter of His Own Dishonour*, in *Eight Dramas*, 1906.

El postrer duelo de España.

Primero soy yo.

El principe constante. Translated as *The Constant Prince*, in *Dramas of Calderon*, 1853.

La puente de Mantible.

El purgatorio de San Patricio. Translated as *The Purgatory of St. Patrick*, in *Dramas of Calderon*, 1853.

La púrpura de la rosa, with music by Tomás de Torrejón (produced 1660).

Saber del mal y del bien.

El secreto a voces. Translated as *The Secret Spoken Aloud*,

in *Four Comedies*, 1980.
El segundo Escipión.
La señora y la criada.
La síbila de Oriente.
El sitio de Bredá.
También hay duelo en las damas.
Los tres afectos de amor.
Las tres justicias en una.   Translated by Edwin Honig as
  Three Judgements at a Blow, in *Eight Dramas*, 1960; by
  Gwynne Edwards, as *Three Judgements in One*, in *Plays 1*,
  1990.
Los tres mayores prodigios.
La vida es sueño (produced 1635).   Translated as *Life is a
  Dream* in *Calderón's Dramas*, 1873: several subsequent
  translations under same title; also translated by E.
  Fitzgerald as *Such Stuff as Dreams Are Made of*, 1865; as
  Life's a Dream, in *The Classic Theatre 3*, edited by Eric
  Bentley, 1960.

Autos sacramentales

A Dios por razón de estado.
Los alimentos del hombre.
A María el corazón
Amar y ser amado; divina Filotea.   Translated as *The Divine
  Philothea*, in *Mysteries of Corpus Christi*, 1867.
Andrómeda y Perseo.
El año santo en Madrid.
El árbol del mejor fruto.
El arca de Dios cautiva.
La cena de Baltazar.   Translated as *Belshazzar's Feast*, in
  Mysteries of Corpus Christi, 1867.
El cordero de Isaías.
El cubo de la Almudena.
La cura y la enfermedad.
La devoción de la misa.
El diablo mundo.
El día mayor de los días.
El divino Jasón.
El divino Orfeo.
Los encantos de la culpa.   Translated as *The Sorceries of Sin*,
  in *Three Dramas of Calderón*, 1870.
En valle de la zarzuela.
Las espigas de Ruth.
El gran duque de Gandía.
El gran mercado del mundo.
El gran teatro del mundo.   Translated by Richard C. Trench
  as *The Great Theatre of the World*, in *The Life and Genius
  of Calderón*, 1856; as *The Great World-Theatre*, 1955; as
  The Great Stage of the World, 1976.
La hidalga del valle.
La humildad coronada de las plantas.
La iglesia sitiada.
El indulto general.
La immunidad del sagrado.
El jardín de Falerina.
El laberinto del mundo.
La lepra de Constantino.
El lirio y la azucena.
Llamados y escogidos.
Lo que va del hombre a Dios.
El maestrazgo del Toisón.
Los misterios de la misa.
Mistica y real Babilonia.
La nave del mercader.
No hay instante sin milagro.
No hay más fortuna que Dios.

No hay que creer ni en la verdad.
El nuevo hospicio de pobres.
El nuevo palacio del Retiro.
El orden de Melchisedech.
Las órdenes militares.
El pastor fido.
La piel Gedeón.
El pleito matrimonial del cuerpo y el alma.
La primer flor del Carmelo.
Primero y segundo Isaac.
El primer refugio del hombre y probático piscina.
La protestación de la fe.
Psiquis y Cupido.
¿Quién hallará mujer fuerte?.
La redención de cautivos.
El sacro Parnaso.
El santo rey Don Fernando (2 parts).
La segunda esposa y triunfar muriendo.
La semilla y la cizaña.
La serpiente de metal.
La siembra del Señor.
El socorro general.
Sueños hay que verdad son.
El tesoro escondido.
La torre de Babilonia.
Tu prójimo como a ti.
La vacante general.
El veneno y la triaca.   Part translated as *The Poison and the
  Antidote*, in *Mysteries of Corpus Christi*, 1867.
El verdadero Dios Pan.
El viático cordero.
La vida es sueño
La viña del Señor.

Verse

Psalle et sile, edited by Leopoldo Trenor.   1936.

Other

Obras menores, edited by A. Pérez Gómez.   1969.

*

Bibliographies

H.W. Bilborn, *A Chronology of the Plays of Calderón de la
  Barca*, 1928.
Warren T. McCready, *Bibliografia tematica de estudios sobre
  el teatro espanol antiquo*, 1966.
Jack H. Parker and Arthur M. Fox, *Calderón de la Barca
  Studies*, Toronto, 1971.

Criticism

Books:
F. de S. MacGarry, *The Allegorical and Metaphorical
  Language in the Autos Sacramentales of Calderón*,
  Washington, DC, 1937.
Alexander A. Parker, *The Allegorical Drama of Calderón*,
  Oxford, 1943.
Albert E. Sloman, *The Dramatic Craftmanship of Calderón:
  His Use of Earlier Plays*, Oxford, 1958.
Harry Lund, *Pedro Calderón de la Barca: A Biography*,
  Edinburgh, Texas, 1964.

A. Valbuena-Briones, *Perspectiva crítica de los dramas de Calderón*, Madrid, 1965.

B.W. Wardropper (ed.), *Critical Essays on the Theatre of Calderón*, 1965.

Osvaldo B. Dalmasso, *Calderón de la Barca*, Buenos Aires, 1969.

Edwin Honig, *Calderón and the Seizures of Honor*, Cambridge, Massachusetts, 1972.

E.M. Wilson and D.W. Cruikshank, *The Textual Criticism of Calderón's Comedias*, London, 1973.

Manuel Durán and Roberto González Echevarría (eds.), *Calderón y la crítica: Historia y antología* (2 vols.), Madrid, 1976.

John V. Bryans, *Calderón de la Barca: Imagery, Rhetoric, and Drama*, London, 1977.

Angel L. Cilverti, *El demonio en el teatro de Calderón*, Valencia, 1977.

A.J. Valbuena-Briones, *Calderón y la comedia nueva*, Madrid, 1977.

Gwynne Edwards, *The Prison and the Labyrinth: Studies in Calderónian Tragedy*, Cardiff, 1978.

James E. Maraniss, *On Calderón*, Columbia, Missouri, 1978.

Barbara Louise Mujica, *Calderón's Characters: An Existential Point of View*, Barcelona, 1980.

Frederick A. De Armas and others (eds.), *Critical Perspectives on Calderón de la Barca*, Lincoln, Nebraska, 1981.

W. Richard Tyler and Sergio D. Elizondo, *The Characters, Plots and Settings of Calderón's Comedias*, Lincoln, Nebraska, 1981.

P. Sydney Cravens (ed.), *Calderón de la Barca at the Tercentenary: Comparative Views*, Lubbock, Texas, 1982.

Michael McGaha (ed.), *Approaches to the Theater of Calderón*, Washington, D.C., 1982.

David Jonathon Hildner, *Reason and the Passions in the Comedias of Calderón*, Amsterdam, 1982.

Robert Ter Horst, *Calderón: The Secular Plays*, Lexington, Kentucky, 1982.

Luciano García Lorenzo, *Calderón: Actas del Congresso internacional sobre Calderón y el teatro español del Siglo de Oro* (3 vols.), Madrid, 1983.

Henry W. Sullivan, *Calderón in the German Lands and the Low Countries: His Reception and Influence 1654–1780*, Cambridge, 1983.

Kurt Levy with others (eds.), *Calderón and the Baroque Tradition*, Waterloo, Ontario, 1985.

Frederick A. De Armas, *The Return of Astraea: An Astral-Imperial Myth in Calderón*, Lexington, Kentucky, 1986.

Dian Fox, *Kings in Calderón: A Study in Characterization and Political Theory*, London, 1986.

Thomas Austin O'Connor, *Myth and Mythology in the Theater of Pedro Calderón de la Barca*, San Antonio, 1988.

Alexander A. Parker, *The Mind and Art of Calderón: Essays on the Comedias*, Cambridge, 1989.

María Alicia Amadei-Pulice, *Calderón y el barroco*, Amsterdam, 1990.

Margaret Rich Greer, *The Play of Power: Mythological Court Dramas of Calderón de la Barca*, Oxford, 1991.

* * *

Rivalled only by Lope de Vega, Calderón is one of the most important dramatists of Golden-Age Spain. Although his plays follow closely in the Lopean model, some of Calderón's early comedies, like *La dama duende* (*The Phantom Lady*), resemble the situational dramas of Tirso de Molina, and are characterized by their rapid dialogue and quick pace. The later works are increasingly intricate in their style, and tend to draw characters in more symbolic and allegorical fashion than the earlier plays. In his later years, Calderón developed a series of elaborate mythological themes that reflected the tastes and interests of the Spanish Court during the waning years of the Golden Age. But Calderón is perhaps best known for his plays of honor and revenge, of which *El médico de su honra* (*The Surgeon of His Honour*) is doubtless the most important. Although Calderón did not write many of these works, they have so impressed successive generations of theatregoers that they have come to be perceived as his most characteristic plays. It is on this basis that Calderón is sometimes regarded as an exceptionally stern and merciless dramatist, one who upholds the standards of social and divine justice regardless of how rigorous these might seem.

In the honor plays like *El médico* and *El pintor de su deshonra* (*The Painter of His Own Dishonour*), Calderón engages the problems of suspicion, guilt, justice, and revenge in a context of potential marital infidelity. The characters in these plays are preoccupied with the notion of "cleanliness of blood" on which the system of social castes in Golden-Age Spain relied. The honor-conscious husbands of these plays are provoked to jealousy and violent revenge by the mere suspicion of the infidelity of their wife. As an extraordinary but strikingly theatrical measure, the resolution of these plays turns on the cold-blooded murder of the wife, which is seen as the price of social justice and reconciliation.

Precisely because of the harshness of revenge in these plays, much critical ink has been spilled in attempts to determine Calderón's motives in writing these plays. To what extent does Calderón reflect social practice in Golden-Age Spain? To what degree does Calderón himself condone such brutal revenge? These questions bear directly on the generic status of the works in question, and have prompted critics to place Calderón's bloody honor plays within the field of tragedy. But because Calderón is also a profoundly Christian dramatist, it seems more reasonable to say that the works reflect a set of social and religious tensions at work within Golden-Age Spain, and that Calderón neither recommends nor condemns the symbolic "honor code" of his society, but rather takes it as the occasion for dramatic conflict.

Because of his profound exploration of intellectual themes and because of the speculative and sometimes disputational style in which many of his characters speak, Calderón is often regarded as a philosophical dramatist. Works like *La vida es sueño* (*Life is a Dream*) adopt a distinctively philosophical attitude toward their subject matter. Calderón is thus often compared, in his explorations of the problem of reality and illusion, to his close contemporary in France, René Descartes. And yet there is an enormous contrast in the responses of these two figures to the question of illusion. Whereas Descartes answers skepticism through the development of a rationalist philosophy based on the powers of the *ego cogitans*, Calderón denies the primacy of the rational subject and locates the response to skepticism in faith. He revives a confidence in the neo-scholastic philosophy that elsewhere in Europe had come under fierce attack, and uses this philosophy in order to sustain the vision of social order necessary to the successful resolution of his plays.

Calderón's mythological plays and allegorical *autos* are among his most distinctive works and yet remain quite alien to modern tastes. It is easy to regard these works as symptomatic of an empire in decline, but it is also possible to detect an important theatrical sensibility at work in them. Calderón demonstrates his talents as a man of the theatre in these plays, and confidently integrates the most important advances in staging, scenery, and set design brought by Cosme Lotti from Italy to Spain.

The allegorical impulse in Calderón is deep, and extends well beyond the explicitly allegorical plays. Allegory in Calderón does not depend on the possibility of establishing direct correspondence between worldly signs and a fixed order of meaning, or on the possibility of drawing universally valid moral conclusions from the interpretations we may in fact give to signs. Instead, it takes as its point of departure the worry that the commanding authority of nature may be inaccessible to human intelligence. In the plays that best reflect Calderón's allegorical tendency, epitomized by *La vida es sueño*, we discover an initial reversion to the conditions of nature's brutishness; yet, at the same time we encounter in the actions of Basilio, the astrologer-king, the search for a meaning—an attempt to read nature's signs—that would, in turn, secure the order of the secular-political realm.

In these and other ways, Calderón's work has close alliances with the power of the absolutist state in Golden-Age Spain. Calderón was, for a number of years, the official dramatist of the Spanish Court, and so it is only natural to find that the theme of secular power is prominent in his work. In particular, Calderón is concerned with the legitimation of power and with the consequences that ensue when the forces of history preclude the establishment of just rule. Insofar as these concerns are brought into relief by the task of reconciling secular power with the ever-present demands of faith, it can be said that the principal dramatic force in his courtly work reflects the alliance of Church and State power in Golden-Age Spain.

—Anthony J. Cascardi

See also *Volume 1* entries on *The Great Theatre of the World*; *Life is a Dream*; *The Mayor of Zalamea*.

CAMUS, Albert. Born in Mondovi, Algeria, 7 November 1913. Educated at the University of Algiers, graduated 1936. Married 1) Simone Hié in 1934 (divorced); 2) Francine Faure in 1940 (died 1979), twin son and daughter. Worked as meteorologist, ship-broker's clerk, automobile parts salesman, clerk in the automobile registry division of the prefecture, actor and amateur theatre producer for the Théâtre de L'Équipe, Algiers, 1935–39; member of Communist Party, 1935–39; staff member, *Alger-Républicain*, 1938–39, and editor, *Soir-Républicain*, 1939–40, both Algiers; sub-editor for lay-out, *Paris-Soir*, 1940; teacher, Oran, Algeria, 1940–42; convalescent in central France, 1942–43; joined Resistance in Lyons region, 1943; journalist, Paris, 1943–45; reader, and editor of Espoir series, Gallimard publishers, Paris, 1943–60; first play, *Le Malentendu*, produced 1944; Co-founding editor, *Combat*, 1945–47. Recipient: Critics Prize (France), 1947; Nobel Prize for Literature, 1957. Died in car crash, Villeblevin, 4 January 1960.

Works

Collections

"*Caligula*" *and Three Other Plays* (includes *Cross Purpose; State of Siège; The Just Assassins*), translated by Stuart Gilbert and others.   1958.

Théâtre; récits; nouvelles; Essais, edited by Roger Quilliot (2 vols.).   1962–65.
The Collected Plays of Albert Camus.   1965.
Caligula; Cross Purpose; The Just; The Possessed, translated by Stuart Gilbert, Henry Jones, and Justin O'Brien. 1984.

Stage Works

Le Malentendu (produced Théâtre des Mathurins, Paris, 1944).   With *Caligula*, 1944; translated by Stuart Gilbert, as *Cross Purpose*, with *Caligula*, 1948.
Caligula (produced Théâtre Hébertot, Paris, 1945).   With *Le Malentendu*, 1944; 1941 version (produced 1983), 1984; translated as *Caligula*, with *Cross Purpose*, 1948.
L'État de siège (produced Théâtre Marigny, Paris, 1948). 1948; translated as *State of Siege*, in "*Caligula*" *and Three Other Plays*, 1958.
Les Justes (produced Théâtre Hébertot, Paris, 1949).   1950; translated as *The Just Assassins*, in "*Caligula*" *and Three Other Plays*, 1958; as *The Just*, 1984.
La Dévotion à la croix, from a play by Calderón (produced Château d'Angers, Angers, 1953).   1953.
Les Esprits, from the work by Pierre de Larivey (produced Château d'Angers, Angers, 1953).   1953.
Un Cas intéressant, from the work by Dino Buzzati (produced Théâtre de la Bruyère, Paris, 1955).   1955.
Requiem pour une nonne, from a work by William Faulkner (produced Théâtre des Mathurins, Paris, 1956).   1956.
Le Chevalier d'Olmedo, from a play by Lope de Vega (produced 1957).   1957.
Les Possédés, from the novel by Dostoevsky (produced Théâtre Antoine, Paris, 1959).   1959; translated as *The Possessed*, 1960.

Fiction

L'Étranger.   1942; translated as *The Stranger*, 1946; as *The Outsider*, 1946.
La Peste.   1947; translated as *The Plague*, 1948.
La Chute.   1956; translated as *The Fall*, 1957.
L'Exil et le royaume.   1957; translated as *Exile and the Kingdom*, 1958.
La Mort heureuse.   1971; translated as *A Happy Death*, 1973.

Memoirs and Letters

Correspondance 1932–1960, with Jean Grenier, edited by Marguerite Dobrenn.   1981.

Other

L'Envers et l'endroit.   1937.
Noces.   1939.
Le Mythe de Sisyphe.   1942; translated as "*The Myth of Sisyphus*" *and Other Essays*, 1955.
Lettres à un ami allemand.   1945.
L'Existence.   1945.
Le Minotaure; ou, La Halte d'Oran.   1950.
Actuelles 1–3: Chroniques 1944–1948, Chroniques 1948–1953, Chronique algérienne 1939–1958 (3 vols.).   1950–58.
L'Homme révolté.   1951; translated as *The Rebel: An Essay on Man in Revolt*, 1954.
L'Été.   1954.
Réflexions sur la guillotine, in *Réflexions sur la peine capitale*, with Arthur Koestler.   1957; translated as *Reflections on the Guillotine*, 1960.

Discours de la Suède. 1958; translated as *Speech of Acceptance upon the Award of the Nobel Prize for Literature*, 1958.
Resistance, Rebellion, and Death (selection). 1961.
Méditation sur le théâtre et la vie. 1961.
Carnets: Mai 1935–février 1942. 1962; translated as *Carnets 1935–1942*, 1963; as *Notebooks 1935–1942*, 1963.
Lettres à Bernanos. 1963.
Carnets: Janvier 1942–mars 1951. 1964; translated as *Notebooks 1942–1951*, 1970.
Lyrical and Critical Essays, edited and translated by Philip Thody. 1968.
Le Combat d'Albert Camus, edited by Norman Stokle. 1970.
Selected Essays and Notebooks, edited by Philip Thody. 1970.
Le Premier Camus. 1973; translated as *Youthful Writings*, 1976.
Journaux de voyage, edited by Roger Quilliot. 1978.
Fragments d'un combat 1938–1940: Alger-Républicain, Le Soir-Républicain, edited by Jacqueline Lévi-Valensi and André Abbou. 1978.
American Journals. 1987.
Carnets: Mars 1951–décembre 1959. 1989.

Translator, *La Dernière Fleur*, by James Thurber. 1952.

*

Bibliographies

Robert F. Roeming, *Camus: A Bibliography*, Madison, Wisconsin, 1968.
Peter C. Hoy, *Camus in English: An Annotated Bibliography of Albert Camus's Contributions to English and American Periodicals and Newspapers* (second edition), Paris, 1971.
R. Gay-Crosier, *A Critical Bibliography of French Literature*, 6, 1980.

Criticism

Books:
Philip Thody, *Camus: A Study of His Work*, London, 1957.
Germaine Bree, *Albert Camus*, New Brunswick, New Jersey, 1959.
Philip Thody, *Albert Camus 1913–1960*, London, 1961.
Germaine Bree (ed.), *Camus, A Collection of Critical Essays*, Englewood Cliffs, New Jersey, 1962.
Germaine Bree, *Albert Camus*, New York and London, 1964; revised edition, 1972.
Emmett Parker, *Albert Camus: The Artist in the Arena*, Madison, Wisconsin, 1965.
Ilona C. Coombs, *Camus, homme du théâtre*, Paris, 1968.
Robert de Luppé, *Albert Camus*, New York, 1968.
Christa Melchinger, *Albert Camus*, Velber, 1969.
Philip H. Rhein, *Albert Camus*, New York, 1969.
Conor Cruise O'Brien, *Albert Camus*, 1970.
Jacqueline Lévi-Valensi, *Les Critiques de notre temps et Camus*, Paris, 1970.
Edward Freeman, *The Theatre of Camus*, London, 1971.
Albert Maquet, *Albert Camus: The Invincible Summer*, 1972.
Monique Crochet, *Les Mythes dans l'oeuvre de Camus*, Paris, 1973.
Pol Gaillard, *Albert Camus*, Paris, 1973.
Donald Lazere, *The Unique Creation of Camus*, 1973.
Lev Braun, *Witness of Decline: Albert Camus: A Moralist of the Absurd*, Rutherford, New Jersey, 1974.
Herbert R. Lottman, *Camus: A Biography*, Garden City, New York, 1979.
Anthony Rizzuto, *Camus' Imperial Vision*, 1981.
Patrick McCarthy, *Albert Camus: A Critical Study of His Life and Work*, London, 1982.
Roger Grenier, *Albert Camus, soleil et ombre: Une Biographie intellectuelle*, Paris, 1987.
Fernande Bartfeld, *L'Effet tragique: Essai sur le tragique dans l'oeuvre de Camus*, Paris, 1988.
David Sprintzen, *Albert Camus: A Critical Examination*, Philadelphia, 1988.
Alba Amoia, *Albert Camus*, New York, 1989.

*   *   *

Albert Camus is known for his novels, particularly *The Outsider* (*L'Étranger*) and *The Plague* (*La Peste*), and for his defence of liberal values and his attack on abstract systems of thought (including both Christianity and Marxism) in *The Rebel* (*L'Homme révolté*). He was also a man of the theatre—an actor, director, and translator of plays, as well as the author of four plays produced in France in the late 1940's. Before he came to France during World War II, he was active in the theatre in his native Algiers, founding two small theatre companies (Théâtre du Travail and Théâtre de l'Équipe), for which he adapted a number of works by Malraux, Gide, Dostoevsky, Aeschylus, Shakespeare, and others. He also was the guiding spirit behind a collective play (of which he probably wrote half), *Revolt in Asturia* (*Révolte dans les Asturies*), based on the Spanish Civil War, but never allowed to be performed by the Algerian authorities. Camus said that working in the theatre and playing soccer were the only collective activities in which he could be happy.

He early planned his work to consist of several phases. The first phase—which includes *The Outsider* and *The Myth of Sisyphus*—is an exploration of the individual's awareness of what Camus defined as "the absurd": the tense confrontation between our desire for happiness and clarity and the lack of meaning and the inevitability of death. This phase includes his first two plays, *Caligula* and *Cross Purpose* (*Le Malentendu*).

In *Caligula*, the young Roman emperor, having discovered the lack of transcendent meaning in the world, destroys all social bonds, and revolts by allying himself with the "logic" of a universe hostile to humankind, killing indiscriminately (if you are a subject of Caligula, or if you are an individual in the universe, you are condemned to death). Caligula performs a dance in the figure of Venus, whom he transforms into a goddess of the absurd. After realizing that individual rebellion fails, he courts his own assassination.

Cross Purpose, Camus's second play, is the story of a man who returns to his central European village after 20 years abroad. His mother and sister keep an inn where they murder and rob rich travellers. Unable to find the right words to identify himself, Jan decides to spend one night in the inn posing as a stranger, and thus becomes the next victim. When his mother discovers whom she has killed, she commits suicide. His sister, who feels that she has been rejected in favour of the returned prodigal son, also kills herself. *Cross Purpose* is more bitter and nihilistic than Camus's other early work, offering no hope, as did *Caligula*, that a valid revolt is possible. Like *Caligula*, it is written in a stylized, highly poetic diction. For Camus, the language of theatre was always to be elevated above that of everyday speech. The language of tragedy, he said, should be natural enough to be spoken by modern actors, and yet different enough from contemporary speech to have a tragic resonance. In a 1989 Paris production of *Cross Purpose*, the director changed the formal mode of address (*vous*) used between the mother and the daughter to the informal (*tu*) form. Camus might not have approved.

The later plays, *State of Siege* (*L'État de siège*) and *The Just* (*Les Justes*) belong to Camus's second phase, which also includes *The Plague* and *The Rebel*. It is the phase of rebellion in solidarity with others against the injustice of the world and presents a more positive ethic of revolt. *State of Siege* is the story of a community's reaction to the plague, which is personified and appears as a political dictator; the play seems almost an allegory of the German Occupation. It lacks the complexity and ambiguity of Camus's novel *The Plague*.

The Just is based on the history of the Russian revolutionaries of 1905, whom Camus praises in *The Rebel* for the purity of their rebellion, in contrast to abstract ideological movements which have lost a sense of humanity. The hero, Ivan Kaliayev, is romantic and idealistic. His hatred of oppression has not destroyed his belief that men must conduct themselves with honour even when opposing tyranny. Ordered to bomb the Grand-Duke's carriage, Kaliayev refuses because of the unexpected presence of two children in the carriage. When he succeeds in a later assassination attempt, Kaliayev rejects an offer of pardon because he feels that his death will restore a moral balance; it will make the assassination an act of justice and not a crime: "If I did not die, then I would be a murderer". As another revolutionary comments, however, after she has heard a detailed account of Kaliayev's bravery on the scaffold, "it is easy, it is so much easier to die from one's inner conflicts than to live with them". The play shows the ambiguity of their ideal of revolt, and avoids the moralism that detracts from *State of Siege*.

The themes of Camus's dramatic work are confrontation with the "absurd" and revolt against the universe and against all forms of injustice. Psychology, he felt, was secondary to the metaphysical. His plays are not static or philosophical, but use theatrical techniques to dramatize forcefully the anguish of a world without transcendent meaning. He remained, however, within the French tradition of presenting articulate, perceptive characters who can express their torments in elevated language. Even Jan in *Cross Purpose*, who cannot find the words to reveal his identity to his mother, can express this inability clearly. Camus's dramatizations of the "absurd" are far from the "theatre of the absurd" of such playwrights as Ionesco or Beckett.

After these plays, but especially after the bitter polemic in the early 1950's following the publication of *The Rebel* (when many accused Camus of moving to the political right), Camus went through a period of depression and crisis, during which he wrote little and turned to translating or adapting works of foreign literature for the stage. The theatre was, for him, a place in which working with others did not present the conflicts of political action, and by all accounts he was an excellent director. He directed his own translation from the Spanish of Calderón's *Devotion to the Cross* (*La Dévotion à la Croix*) for the Angers Festival in 1953. His adaptations of two novels—Faulkner's *Requiem for a Nun* (*Requiem pour une nonne*) and Dostoevsky's *The Devils* (*Les Possédés*)—are the high points of this part of Camus's theatrical career.

While most critics agree that Camus's fiction and essays are superior to his work for the stage, his plays (with the exception of *State of Siege*) continue to be performed, as they provide striking images of the moral and metaphysical dilemmas of the contemporary world.

—Adele King

See also *Volume 1* entries on *Caligula*; *Cross-Purpose*.

CAO Yu. Also known as Tsao Yu or Ts'ao Yū. Born Wan Jiaobao [Wan Chia-pao] in Qianjian, Hubei Province, China, 24 September 1910. Educated at American-supported Nankai Middle School, Tianjin, 1922–28; Nankai University, reading economics and politics, 1928–30; American-founded Qinghua University, Beijing, studying Western languages and literature, 1930–33. Married 1) Zheng Xia in 1939 (divorced 1951), two daughters; 2) Deng Yisheng in 1951 (died 1980), two daughters; 3) Li Yuru. Taught English at Women's Normal College in Hubei Province, 1934; first play, *Leiyu* [*Thunderstorm*], produced 1934; co-founder, teacher, then Dean at the National Drama Training School, in Namjing [Nanking], 1936–38; lecturer, Fudan University, first in Shanghai, then in Chongqing, during World War II; after 1941, performances of plays often banned; lectured with Lao She in USA and Canada, 1946; travelled to Hong Kong, 1948; screenwriter and drama teacher in Shanghai, 1948–49; after the Chinese Communist victory in 1949, held various offical posts: deputy director, Central Institute of Drama, 1949–53; director, Beijing People's Art Theatre, 1953–55; vice-chairman, Beijing Literary and Artistic Association, 1955–66; director, Beijing People's Art and Drama Institute, 1956; vice-chairman, Chinese Dramatists Association, 1960–66; frequent traveller abroad as member of cultural delegations; joined Chinese Communist Party, 1956; denounced as a counter-revolutionary, 1966: nothing heard of him during the Cultural Revolution, 1966–76, after he was sent to a country reform school; restored to literary and theatrical prominence after 1976; deputy at the Party congress, 1978–83, and elected to Presidium, 1983; reappointed director, Beijing People's Art Theatre, 1979; elected chairman of Chinese Dramatists' Association, 1979; headed delegations to: Switzerland, 1979; Great Britain, 1980; Japan, 1982; North Korea, 1985. Awarded the Légion d'Honneur by the French government, 1987.

Works

Collections

Xuan-ji (selections).   1951–52.
Juben xuan (selections).   1954.
Xuan-ji (selections).   1962.
Xiji zinshang (works).   1989.

Stage Works

Leiyu (produced by Liuyi jushe group, 1934; produced professionally, Shanghai and Beijing, 1935).   In *Weixue jikan*, vol.1 no.3, 1934; in book form, 1936; translated as *Thunderstorm*, 1958.
Richu (produced Carlton Theatre, Shanghai, 1937).   1936; revised edition, 1982; translated as *Sunrise*, 1960.
Yuanye [*The Wilderness*] (produced by Yingren xiehui group, Shanghai, 1937).   1937.
Quanmin zongdongyuan, with Song Zhidi.   1938.
Zheng zai xiang [*Just Thinking*].   1940.
Shuibian [*Metamorphosis*] (produced National Institute of Dramatic Art, Chongqing, 1939).   1940.
Beijing Ren (produced Chongqing, 1940).   1941; translated as *Peking Man*, 1946.
Jia [*The Family*], from a novel by Pa Chin.   1942.
Qiao [*The Bridge*].   1946.
Heizi ershiba, with Song Zhidi.   1947.
Minglangde tian (produced People's Art Theatre, Beijing).   1956; translated as *Bright Skies*, 1960.

Jian-dan pian [Gall and Sword Piece], with others.   1962.
Wang Zhaojun [Wang, Resplendent Lady].   1978; translated
   as *The Consort of Peace*, 1989.

Screenplays

Janyangtian [A Sunny Day], 1948 (published 1948); *Richu*,
1978.

Other

Ying-chun ji [Welcome, Spring] (collected essays).   1958.

Editor, *Hunagxiuqui*, by I-so chu.   1987.

Translator, *Jou-mi-ou yü yiu-li-yeh*, from Shakespeare's
   Romeo and Juliet.   1949.

*

Criticism

Books:
David Y. Ch'en, "The Trilogy of Ts'ao Yü and Western
   Drama", in *Asia and the Humanities*, edited by Horst
   Frenz, 1959.
John Y. Hu, *Ts'ao Yü*, New York, 1972.
J.S.M. Lau, *Ts'ao Yü: The Reluctant Disciple of Chekhov and
   O'Neill: A Study in Literary Influence*, Hong Kong, 1970.

Articles:
Cao Yu and Yang Yu, "Interview", in *Chinese Literature*,
   November 1963.
David Y. Chen, "Two Chinese Adaptations of Eugene
   O'Neill's *The Emperor Jones*, in *Modern Drama*, 9, 1967.
Walter J. and Ruth I. Meserve, "Ts'ao Yü: Dramatist in
   Communist China", in *Comparative Drama*, 2, 1968.

* * *

The most prominent playwright of *huaju* ("speech
drama"), China's modern Western-style drama, Cao Yu was
also the dramatist who first solidly established the genre with
his *Leiyu* (*Thunderstorm*) in the early 1930's, although *huaju*
has never really replaced traditional Chinese styles of theatre
in general popularity, much of its appeal having been to
urban intellectuals. From a typical wealthy, old-style
mandarin-status family, he was, in his early childhood, heavily exposed to the traditional literature of China. Then, at
secondary school and university, he developed a fondness for
Western drama, focusing on such dramatists as Aeschylus,
Sophocles, Euripides, Shakespeare, Ibsen, Chekhov, O'Neill
and Galsworthy. He also acted, in both male and female
roles, in such plays as Hauptmann's *The Weavers*, Ibsen's *An
Enemy of the People* and *A Doll's House*, Ding Xilin's
Oppression (*Yapo*), Galsworthy's *Strife*, and Molière's *The
Miser*.
   Cao Yu's early plays, such as *Leiyu*, *Bejingren* (*Peking
Man*), and *Jia* (The Family), are often concerned chiefly with
the titanic clash between tradition and modernity as witnessed in the explosive battles and tensions between generations within the family; and *Richu* (*Sunrise*) and *Qiao* (The
Bridge) depict the unstable, internecine situation of modern
capitalism in China. Almost inevitably, in the turbulent
1930's and 1940's, especially during the war of resistance
against the Japanese invaders (1937–1945), he was drawn

increasingly into patriotic and political causes, and this is
reflected in some of his work. He maintained his love of
Western theatre, however, and, for instance, produced a
translation of Shakespeare's *Romeo and Juliet*. *Zheng zai
xiang* (Just Thinking), based on a Mexican play, is a sparkling
and humorous study of the clash between traditional and
modern Chinese theatre.
   In Communist China, after 1949, he was accorded high
honours but was creatively unproductive for a number of
years. His *Minglangde tian* (*Bright Skies*) was a propagandis-
tic piece. In 1961, in co-operation with two other writers, he
brought out his drama *Jian-dan pian* (Gall and Sword Piece),
based on a famous revenge tale of the first millennium BC
After the blank years of the Cultural Revolution, his *Wang
Zhaojun* (Wang Resplendent Lady) turns, once again, back
to ancient Chinese literature and events of nearly 2000 years
ago, and depicts the fate of a Chinese woman forced to end
her life among the barbarians. The wheel, in some ways, had
turned full circle, with Cao Yu the painter of wealthy and
middle-strata families and society, now plunged back as in
infancy into the wealth of Chinese antiquity, and claiming
that the latter allowed him more creative depth.

—William Dolby

See also *Volume 1* entry on *Thunderstorm*.

———————

ČAPEK, Karel.   Born in Malé Svatoňovice, Bohemia, 9
January 1890. Studied art history, aesthetics, and philosophy
at the Czech University, Prague, 1909–15, with one year at
the universities of Paris and Berlin, 1909–10, doctorate in
philosophy 1915. Married the actress Olga Scheinpflugová in
1935. Wrote for the periodical *Lidové noviny*; collaborated
on a number of plays (and their productions) with his older
brother, the writer and scene-designer Josef Čapek; co-
founder, with Josef, František Langer, and Edmond Konrad,
of the avant-garde circle "The Pragmatists"; stage director
and dramaturg, Vinohrady Theatre, Prague, 1921–23. Died
in Prague, 25 December 1938.

Works

Collections

Spisy bratři [Collected Works](51 vols.).   1928–47.

Stage Works

Lásky hra osudná [The Fateful Play of Love], with Josef
   Čapek (produced by an amateur group, Ceske Budejovice,
   Bohemia, 1919; produced professionally, 1922).   1910.
Loupežník [The Robber] (produced National Theatre,
   Prague, 1921).   1920.
RUR (Rossum's Universal Robots) (produced National
   Theatre, Prague, 1920).   1920; translated as *R.U.R. (Ros-
   sum's Universal Robots)*, 1923.
Ze života hmyzů, with Josef Čapek (produced National
   Theatre, Brno, 1922).   1921; translated as *The Life of the
   Insects*, 1923; as *The Insect Play*, 1923; as *The World We
   Live In (The Insect Comedy)*, 1933.

Scene from the Prague National Theatre's 1968 production of *Bílá nemoc* [White Plague, translated as *Power and Glory*] by **Karel Čapek**, directed by Evžen Sokolovský, designed by Ladislav Vychodil.

Věc Makropoulos (produced Vinohrady Theatre, Prague, 1922).   1922; translated as *The Makropoulos Secret*, 1925.
Adam Stvořitel, with Josef Čapek (produced National Theatre, Prague, 1927).   1927; translated as *Adam the Creator*, 1929.
Bílá nemoc (produced National Theatre, Brno, and National Theatre, Prague, 1937).   1937; translated as *Power and Glory*, 1938.
Matka (produced National Theatre, Prague, 1938).   1938; translated as *The Mother*, 1939.

Fiction

Zářivé hlubiny [The Luminous Depths], with Josef Čapek. 1916.
Boźí muka [Wayside Crosses].   1917.
Krakonošova zahrada [The Garden of Krakonos], with Josef Čapek.   1918.
Trapné povídky.   1921; translated as *"Money" and Other Stories*, 1929.
Továrna na Absolutno.   1922; translated as *The Absolute at Large*, 1927.
Krakatit.   1924; translated as *Krakatit*, 1925; as *An Atomic Fantasy*, 1948.
Povidky z jedné kapsy [Tales from One Pocket], *Povidky z druhé kapsy* [Tales from the Other Pocket] (2 vols.).   1929; translated in part as *Tales from Two Pockets*   1932.
Apokryfy; Kniha apokryfu (2 vols.).   1932–45; translated as *Apocryphal Stories*, 1949.
Hordubal.   1933; translated as *Hordubal*, 1934.
Povětrón.   1934; translated as *Meteor*, 1935.
Obyčejný život.   1934; translated as *An Ordinary Life*, 1936.

Válka s mloky.   1936; translated as *War with the Newts*, 1937.
První parta.   1937; translated as *The First Rescue Party*, 1939.
Zivot a dílo skladatele Foltýna.   1939; translated as *The Cheat*, 1941.

Memoirs and Letters

Dopisy ze Zasuvky [Letters Out of a Drawer] (letters to Vera Hruzová), edited by Jiří Opelik.   1980.

Other

Pragmatismus; čili, Filosofie praktického života.   1918.
Kritika slov.   1920.
Italské listy.   1923; translated as *Letters from Italy*, 1929.
Anglické listy.   1924; translated as *Letters from England*, 1925.
O nejbližšich věcech.   1925; translated as *Intimate Things*, 1935.
Jak vzniká divadelní hra a pruvodce po zákulisí.   1925; translated as *How a Play is Produced*, 1928.
Skandální afera Josefa Holouška.   1927.
Hovory s T.G. Masarykem (3 vols.).   1928–35; translated as *President Masaryk Tells His Story*, 1934, and *Masaryk on Thought and Life*, 1938.
Zahradníkuv rok.   1929; translated as *The Gardener's Year*, 1931.
Výlet do Spanél.   1930; translated as *Letters from Spain*, 1932.

Minda; čili, Ochova psu.   1930; translated as *Minda; or, On Breeding Dogs*, 1940.
Devatero pohádek.   1932; translated as *Fairy Tales*, 1933.
Obrazky z Holandska.   1932; translated as *Letters from Holland*, 1933.
O věcech obecných; čili, Zoon politikos.   1932.
Dasěnka.   1933; translated as *Dashenka*, 1940.
Legenda o člověku zahradníkovi.   1935.
Cesta na sever.   1936; translated as *Travels in the North*, 1939.
Jak se co dělá.   1938; translated as *How They Do It*, 1945.
Kalendář.   1940.
O lidech.   1940.
Vzrušené tance.   1946.
Bajky a prdpovídky.   1946.
Sedm rozhlásku.   1946.
Ratolest a vavřín.   1947.
"In Praise of Newspapers" and Other Essays on the Margin of Literature.   1951.
Obrázky z domova.   1953.
Sloupkový ambit.   1957.
Poznámky o tvorbě.   1959.
Na břehu dnu.   1966.
Divadelníkem proti své vuli.   1968.
V zajetí slov.   1969.
Ctení o T.G. Masarykovi.   1969.
Místo pro Janathana!   1970.
Listy Olze 1920–38.   1971.
Drobty pod stolem doby.   1975.

*

Criticism

Books:
William E. Harkins, *Karel Čapek*, London, 1962.
Alexander Matuska, *Karel Čapek: An Essay*, London, 1964.
Eckehard Thiele, *Karel Čapek* (in German), Leipzig, 1988.

*   *   *

The Čapek brothers were not first and foremost playwrights; Karel, internationally the better-known of the two, produced a large body of work which included short stories, essays, novels, and a collection of "conversations" with the first President of Czechoslovakia, T.G. Masaryk. Josef, who is often considered to have been intellectually the more original of the brothers, was a painter who also designed for the theatre, illustrated books, and drew caricatures; his literary work included poetry, journalism, and editing. Both died prematurely: Karel just after the Munich agreement, seriously ill and under attack from the Czech fascists; Josef in Bergen-Belsen at the end of World War II, after six years in the concentration camps.

Karel followed his brother to Prague in 1907. Much of his early writing was undertaken in collaboration with his brother; they were among the avant-garde of the period, and together with František Langer and Edmond Konrad formed the group known as the "Pragmatists". Karel, like Josef, did not serve in World War I, in his case because of a suspected disease of the spine. From autumn 1921 he was employed for 18 months as a dramaturg and director at the Vinohrady Theatre, Prague, out of which experience came the collection of essays "*How a Play is Produced*", entertaining in its *faux naif* observations of backstage life.

Altogether (jointly and individually) Josef and Karel

Čapek wrote only ten plays over 20 years; two of them, however, attracted international interest and were translated and played all over the world: *R.U.R (Rossum's Universal Robots)* and *The Insect Play* (also known as *From the Life of the Insects* and *And So on ad infinitum*).

Their first (joint) attempt was based on the Italian *commedia dell'arte*: "The Fateful Play of Love", written in 1910, was not performed until 1919, by an amateur group in the southern Bohemian town of Ceske Budejovice. It did not reach Prague until 1922, and then only on the cabaret stage of the Seven of Hearts. It is deliberately artificial in style; the characters frequently remind the audience that they are only actors, and the jokes arise from the wry awareness that they are all sitting in a theatre.

After "The Fateful Play of Love" (and during their term together in Paris) the brothers embarked on a version of the play which Karel was to rewrite as "The Robber". This had its premiere at the National Theatre in 1920, directed by Vojta Novák. Combining romantic drama with farcical elements, Čapek championed the cause of iconoclastic youth against conventional middle age. "The Robber" was followed by the allegorical drama *R.U.R*, which, after a production by the South Bohemian amateurs, was staged in 1921 by Novák at the National Theatre. Within a few months *R.U.R* had made Karel Čapek internationally famous; and although, in these post-war years, the Čapeks could no longer claim to be the avant-garde of Czech culture, it was a valuable triumph for the young Republic.

In February of the following year, *The Insect Play* was given its premiere by the National Theatre in Brno; in April, it was directed by Karel Hilar for the National Theatre in Prague, with sets and costumes by Josef Čapek. In November 1922 Karel's own production of *The Macropoulos Secret* opened at the Vinohrady Theatre. *The Macropoulos Secret* is better known today through Leos Janacek's adaptation of it as an opera, made between 1923 and 1925. As in *R.U.R* and *The Insect Play*, the theme of *The Macropoulos Secret* is the brevity of an individual life and its meaning within the continuity of human life as a whole. Čapek expresses this dramatically by making the central character, Emilia Marty, a woman who has already lived 300 years and who must now reconcile herself to death. The culmination of the play is the destruction of the formula for longevity by the person who has inherited it; not only Marta but also her successor has come to terms with the brief meaning of life.

The following year Josef Čapek's first independent play, "The Land of Many Names", was staged, and the next joint production by the brothers was *Adam the Creator*, directed by Hilar at the National Theatre in 1927. It is a similar fantasy: Adam, dissatisfied with the world, challenges God and is given the opportunity to recreate it. But both Adam and his alter ego fail: the worlds they create are grotesque and pitiful, and turn against their own creators. *Adam the Creator* has never been a success in the theatre; it fails dramatically, the political intention—criticism of "progressive" movements—being overly didactic.

After this play, Josef wrote only one more, and Karel intended to leave the theatre for good. But in the 1930's the threat of fascism—both from neighbouring Germany and Austria, and from potentially powerful groups within Czechoslovakia—gave Karel the determination to use the theatre again for political purposes. His last two plays, "The White Plague" (produced in Great Britain and translated under the title *Power and Glory*) and *The Mother* were written as warnings against passivity in the face of evil.

The White Plague, first produced simultaneously in Brno and Prague in January 1937, is about a world, not unlike the contemporary world, of escalating conflict between the principles of democracy and of dictatorship; many people wrongly identified the model of the character of the Marshal as Hitler. As an image of the total breakdown which threatens civilisation, Čapek postulates an epidemic, the "white plague". The only cure is in the hands of the seemingly insignificant Dr. Galen, thus giving him unprecedented powers. The play ends with his death at the hands of the crowd and the exposure of the world to disaster and ruin.

The Mother, said to have been based on an idea from Olga Scheinpflugová, opened in Prague in February 1938. The opening gives the audience the misleading impression that it is watching a conventional family drama; but in reality the household represents the state of the nation, with all its ambitions and conflicts. "To create order means to put things where they feel right", says the Mother in the opening scene; but at the close of the play she reluctantly orders her last remaining son to go out in defence of his country.

The Čapek brothers' reputation in the international theatre is based on *R.U.R* and *The Insect Play*. They had, however, comparatively little influence on the future development of the Czech theatre, and Karel's practical involvement as dramaturg and director was brief and undistinguished (far more significant in Czechoslovakia was the work of Josef as a theatre designer, giving impetus to the Czech theatre's later achievements in this field).

—Barbara Day

See also *Volume 1* entries on *The Insect Play; R.U.R.*

CARAGIALE, Ion Luca. Born in Haimanale, near Ploeşti, Principality of Wallachia (united with Moldavia as Romania, 1877), 30 January 1852. Educated in Ploeşti, 1859–68; studied in his uncle Costache Caragiale's acting and mime classes, Conservatoire, Bucharest, 1868–70. Married Akexandrina Burelly in 1889; one son and three daughters (two died in infancy); also had an illegitimate son in 1885. Court-copyist, Ploeşti, 1870; prompter, National Theatre, Bucharest, 1870; also proofreader for newspapers; contributor, *Ghimpele* [Thorn], 1875; publisher, the humorous periodical *Clapomul* [Capon], 1877; theatre critic, *Româniă libera* [Free Romania], 1877; contributor, *Timpul* [Time], 1878–81; became associated with the conservative literary and political group Junimea [Youth], from the late 1870's until he broke with it, 1892: many of his works first published in the group's journal, *Convorbire literare* [Literary Conversations]; first original play, *O noapte furtunoasă; sau, Numarul 9* [*A Stormy Night; or, Number Nine*], produced and published 1879; schools inspector, northern Moldavia, 1881, Wallachia, 1882–84; worked in tobacco factory, 1884; contributor, *Voinţa naţională* [National Will], 1885; Director of the National Theatre, Bucharest, 1888–89; wrote mainly sketches and stories from the late 1880's; contributor, *Constituţionalul* [The Constitutionalist], 1889; tavern manager, Bucharest, in the 1890's; founder and editor, the humorous magazine *Motful roman* [Romanian Nonsense], 1893: closed, 1893, but briefly revived, 1901; co-publisher, *Vatra* [Hearth], 1894, but left the same year; joined Conservative Party, 1895; civil servant, Department of State Monopolies, 1899–1901; travelled with his family in Western Europe, 1905, and settled in Berlin,

1904; continued to contribute to Romanian newspapers and periodicals in his last years. Died in Berlin, 9 June 1912.

Works

Collections

Teatru [Theatre]. 1889.
Opere [Works] (7 vols.). 1930–42:
1–2. *Nuvele şi schiţe*. 1930–31.
  3. *Reminiscenţe şi not critice*. 1932.
  4. *Notiţe critice, literatură şi versuri*. 1938.
  5. *Articole politice şi cronici dramatice*. 1938.
  6. *Teatru*. 1939.
  7. *Corespondenţă*. 1942.
"The Lost Letter" and Other Plays (includes *Carnival Scenes; A Stormy Night; Mr. Leonida and the Reactionaries*), translated by F. Knight. 1956.
Opere [Works] (4 vols.), edited by Al. Rosetti, S. Cioculescu, and Liviu Calin. 1959–65:
  1. *Teatru*. 1959.
  2. *Momente; Schiţe; Notiţe critice*. 1960.
  3. *Nuvele; Povestiri; Amintiri; Versuri; Parodii; Varia*. 1962.
  4. *Publicistică*. 1965.

Stage Works

Rome vaincue, from a play by A. Parodi (produced National Theatre, Bucharest, 1878).
O noapte furtunoasă; sau, Namarul 9 (produced National Theatre, Bucharest, 1879). In *Convorbiri literare*, 1879; in book form, in *Teatru*, 1889; translated as *A Stormy Night*, in *"The Lost Letter" and Other Plays*, 1956.
Conul Leonida faţă cu reacţiunea (probably produced before 1885; produced National Theatre, Bucharest, 1912). In *Convorbiri literare*, 1880; in book form, in *Teatru*, 1889; translated as *Mr. Leonida and the Reactionaries*, in *"The Lost Letter" and Other Plays*, 1956.
O soacră [A Mother-in-Law] (produced as *Soacra mea Fifina*, National Theatre, Bucharest, 1883). 1894.
Hatmanul Baltaq, with Iavcob Negruzzi, music by Eduard Caudell, from a story by N. Gane (produced National Theatre, Bucharest, 1884).
O scrisoare pierdută (produced National Theatre, Bucharest, 1884). 1885; translated as *The Lost Letter*, in *"The Lost Letter" and Other Plays*, 1956.
D'ale carnavalului (produced National Theatre, Bucharest, 1885). In *Convorbiri literare*, May 1885; in book form, in *Teatru*, 1889; translated as *Carnival Scenes*, in *"The Lost Letter" and Other Plays*, 1956.
Năpasta [Injustice] (produced National Theatre, Bucharest, 1890). In *Convorbiri literare*, January 1890.
1 Aprilie [1 April] (produced National Theatre, Bucharest, 1912). 1896.
Incepem! [We're Beginning!] (produced Leon Popescu Theatre, Bucharest, 1909). 1909.

Fiction

O făclie de Paşte; Păcat; Om cu noroc [An Easter Candle; Sin; The Fortunate Man]. 1892.
Momente (stories). 1901.
Schiţa nuoă [New Sketches] (stories). 1910.
Fiction collected in editions of *Opere* (see Collections).

Memoirs and Letters

Corespondenţă [Correspondence] (Volume 7 of *Opere*). 1942.
Scrisori şi acte (letters).   1962.

Other

Note şi schiţe [Notes and Sketches].   1892.
1907, Din primăvară în toamnă [1907, From Spring to Autumn] (articles).   1907; part translated as "Causes of the Peasant Revolt, 1907", in *Contrasts in Emerging Societies*, edited by D. Warriner, 1965.
Miscellaneous writings collected in editions of *Opere* (see Collections).

*

Criticism

Books:
H.P. Petrescu, *Ion Luca Caragiales Leben und Werke*, Leipzig, 1911.
A. Colombo, *Vita e opere di Ion Luca Caragiale*, Rome, 1934.
Şerban Ciculescu, *Caragiale: Leben und Werke* (in German), Bucharest, 1971.
Eric D. Tappe, *Ion Luca Caragiale*, New York, 1972.

Articles:
Ileana Popovici, "Two Visions of *A Lost Letter*", in *Romanian Review*, vol. 26 no.3, 1972.
Eliza M. Ghil, "Ideological Parody in Eugene Ionesco's *Rhinoceros* and in *A Lost Letter* by I.L. Caragiale", in *Yearbook of Romanian Studies*, 7, 1982.

*   *   *

Generally regarded as Romania's most accomplished comic playwright and humorist, and unquestionably its most enduring author, Caragiale encapsulates in his work the typical traits of the Romanian character. As a journalist Caragiale perfected a talent for observing the manners and behaviour of his fellow citizens and these observations he incorporated into his comedies. Such is the perennality of the attitudes displayed by his characters, and the vivid colloquiality of his language, that Caragiale's comedies possess a timelessness which ensures their continuing popularity with Romanian audiences.

His work became an antidote to the bleakness and harshness of the Ceauşescu regime until performances of his comedies were banned by the dictator's censors in the 1980's. Today, it has resumed that role amidst the impoverishment engendered by economic reform. "Cargialean" has become a byword to describe the posturings, the verbiage, the vacuousness, and the insincerity of contemporary political life where actions of an ignominious nature are regarded with admiration and worthy of emulation. The embodiment of these attitudes is represented by the figure Caţavencu in Caragiale's *O scrisoare pierdută* (*The Lost Letter*) whose name has been given to the most popular satirical journal to appear in Romania since the revolution in December 1989.

The hallmarks of Caragiale comedies are frenzy and agitation; characters often mill around incessantly in unbridled commotion. The agitation is reflected in the dialogues where people do not just talk, they chatter and prattle, gossip and jabber, scream and shout, rant and rage, protest and ridicule, taunt and tease, cajole and threaten. They speak endlessly, sometimes incoherently, often without making a point, but always with boundless energy. These features are present in Caragiale's first play *O noapte furtunoasă* (*A Stormy Night*), based on the theme of the deceived husband, naively confident in the good faith of his younger assistant who is his wife's lover.

The theme is repeated in *O scrisoare pierdută* where the lower middle-class triangle of the earlier comedy is replaced by three figures from the upper-middle class: Trahanache, the chairman of the local electoral committee; Zoe, his wife, and Tipătescu, the prefect and Zoe's lover. The setting is a county town in the run-up to parliamentary elections. Trahanache is shown a love letter from Tipătescu to his wife by Caţavencu, a local newspaper editor, in an attempt to blackmail Trahanache into supporting him for election. Trahanache dismisses the letter as a forgery and Caţavencu threatens to publish. Zoe is thrown into despair by this threat and enlists Tipătescu's help in an effort to recover the lost letter which, after several mishaps, she does.

Such is the ingenuity of the plot that the audience's attention is constantly maintained and the exits and entrances admirably contrived. Yet, as numerous critics have pointed out, the notable aspect about this satire is the unattractive nature of the principal characters. Except for Trahanache, who has an unshakable trust in Tipătescu, not one them is appealing. Tipătescu and Zoe are selfish, Caţavencu is unscrupulous and unprincipled, and Dandanache, whose surprise entrance at the last moment as the officially sponsored and ultimately successful candidate, is a blackmailer and an ass. The cynical reconciliation of all at the end of the play remains a caustic comment on Romanian political life which has lost none of its validity for Romanian audiences today.

D-ale carnavalului (*Carnival Scenes*) has the perpetual motion of a farce. It was withdrawn after its second performance because the intellectual elite of the time regarded it as violent and crude. Today, however, audiences find its low-life characters amusing and see little to shock them in their behaviour. Caragiale's last play, his only serious drama, *Năpasta* (*Injustice*) fared equally badly with contemporary audiences, undoubtedly because they found it difficult to sympathize with any of the characters. It is study of the psychological aberration of a woman whose well-planned revenge is reminiscent of the murder carried out by Raskolnikov in Dostoevsky's *Crime and Punishment*. Caragiale's preoccupation with the monstrous and the macabre typifies a number of his short stories and in these, as in *Năpasta*, he attempts to explain his characters' behaviour by probing their minds.

Set in an inn in a mountain village the play opens with a discussion between the innkeeper Dragomir, his wife Anca, and the village schoolmaster Gheorghe, about a newspaper report that Ion, a forester convicted nine years earlier for the murder of Anca's first husband, Dumitru, has escaped from the salt mines. Anca is the catalyst for the entire drama. It is she who is the reason for Dumitru's murder by Dragomir; it is she who taunts Dragomir without mercy to make him confess his guilt; it is she who is partly to blame for Ion's death since she prevented his departure with Dragomir. Her desire to see Dragomir confess his guilt and die for it provides the dramatic tension in the play, but the depth of her vindictiveness, well illustrated by her reflections on how she would like to kill Dragomir ("shall I wake him first, so that he knows that death is coming, from whom and why?"), seems improbable. However, it was precisely this abnormal behaviour that attracted Caragiale, and *Năpasta* reveals as much of his extraordinary perceptiveness as does his comic writing.

—Dennis Deletant

CARBALLIDO, Emilio. Born Emilio Carballido Fentanes, in Córdoba, Veracruz, Mexico, 22 May 1925. Family moved to Mexico City, 1926. Studied English literature and drama at the Universidad Nacional Autónoma de México, 1945–49. Has one son. Appointed assistant director at the University of Veracruz's theatre school, Xalapa, 1954, becoming professor in the Faculty of Philosophy and Letters, 1960–61; professor at the theatre school, National Institute of Fine Arts, Mexico City, from 1955; literary adviser, Mexican National Ballet, from 1957, and public relations adviser for the Ballet's tours of Europe and Asia, 1957–58; staff member, department of culture and media, Instituto Politécnico Nacional, Mexico City, 1960–74; travelled to Cuba, 1963; visiting professor at Rutgers University, New Jersey, 1965; professor of dramatic theory and composition, Universidad Nacional Autónoma, Mexico City, 1965–68; visited Germany, 1966, and Spain, 1968; director, Workshop for Dramatic Composition, 1969–74; visiting professor, University of Pittsburgh, 1970; director of the Faculty of Arts, University of Veracruz, Xalapa, 1974–76; editor of the theatre journal *Tramoya*, 1974—. Also theatre director, and has directed productions of his own works. Recipient of many Latin-American theatre awards since 1957.

Works

Collections

D.F. (includes 9 one-act plays: *Misa primera; Selaginela; El censo; Escribo, por ejemplo; El espejo; Hipólito; Tangentes; Parásitas; La medalla*). 1957; expanded, second edition (13 one-act plays: all the above, except *Hipólito; La perfecta casada; Paso de Madraguda; El solitario en octobre; Un cuento de Navidad; Pastores de la ciudad*), 1962; revised, third edition (without *El espejo* and *La medalla*; with *Delicioso domingo* and *Una rosa, con otro nombre*), 1973; expanded, fourth edition, as *D.F.: 26 obras en un acto*, 1978.
Teatro (includes *El relojero de Córdoba; Medusa; Rosalba y los llaveros; El día que soltaron los leones*). 1960.
"The Golden Thread" and Other Plays (includes *The Mirror; The Time and the Place: Dead Love, The Glacier, and The Wine Cellar; The Golden Thread; The Intermediate Zone; The Clockmaker from Cordoba; Theseus*), translated by Margaret Peden Sayers. 1971.
Tres comedias (includes *Un vals sin fin por el planeta; La danza que sueña la tortuga; La felicidad*). 1981.
Teatro 2 (includes *Un vals sin fin por el planeta; La danza que sueña la tortuga; Las estatuas de marfil*). 1988.
Ceremonia en el tiempo del tigre; Rosa de dos aromas; Un pequeño día de ira. 1986.

Stage Works

El triángulo sutil (produced Mexico City, 1948).
La triple porfía (produced Escuela de Arte Teatral, Mexico City, 1948). In *México en el arte*, 8, 1949; in book form, with *La zona intermedia* and *Escribo, por ejemplo*, 1951.
La zona intermedia (produced Teatro Latino, Mexico City, 1950). In *América*, November-December 1948; in book form, with *La triple porfía* and *Escribo, por ejemplo*, 1951; translated as *The Intermediate Zone*, in *"The Golden Thread" and Other Plays*, 1971.
El suplicante (produced Concurso de Primavera del Instituto Nacional de Bellas Artes, Mexico City, 1950). In *Universidad de México*, 13, 1958.
Rosalba y los llaveros (produced Palacio de Bellas Artes, Mexico City), 1950. In *Novedades* ("Mexico en la cultura" supplement), 1950; in book form, in *Teatro*, 1960.
Escribo, por ejemplo (produced Teatro del Caracol, Mexico City, 1950). In book form, with *La zona intermedia* and *La triple porfía*, 1951.
Ermesinda (ballet scenario; produced Academia de la Danza Mexicana, Palacio de Bellas Artes, Mexico City, 1952).
El invisible (ballet scenario; produced Academia de la Danza Mexicana, Palacio de Bellas Artes, Mexico City, 1952).
El pozo (libretto; produced by the Opera Nacional, Mexico City, 1953).
La sinfonía doméstica (produced Teatro Ideal, Mexico City, 1953).
El viaje de Nocresida, with Sergio Magaña (produced Palacio de Bellas Artes, Mexico City, 1953).
Las palabras cruzadas (produced as *La danza que sueña la tortuga*, Teatro de la Comedia, Mexico City, 1955). In *Teatro mexicano del siglo XX, 3*, 1956.
Felicidad (produced Auditorio Reforma, Mexico City, 1955; produced professionally, Teatro Ródano, Mexico City, 1957). In *Concurso nacional de teatro: Obras premiadas 1954–55*, 1955.
La hebra de oro (produced Auditorio Reforma del Seguro Social, Mexico City, 1956). With the trilogy *El lugar y la hora*, 1957; translated as *The Golden Thread*, in *"The Golden Thread" and Other Plays*, 1971.
Misa primera. In *Estaciones* by Elías Nandino, vol.1 no.4, 1957.
El lugar y la hora (trilogy including *La bodega, El amor muerto*, and *El glacier*). With *La hebra de oro*, 1957; as *Tangentes*, in *D.F.*, 1957; translated as *The Time and the Place*, in *"The Golden Thread" and Other Plays*, 1971.
Selaginela (produced Teatro de la Feria del Libro, Mexico City, 1959). In *D.F.*, 1957.
El censo (produced Teatro de la Feria del Libro, Mexico City, 1959). In *La palabra y el hombre*, January-March, 1957.
Cinco pasos al cielo, with Luisa Bauer and Fernando Wagner (produced Palacio de Bellas Artes, Mexico City, 1959). As *Las lámparas del cielo y de la tierra*, in *El arca de Noé*, 1974.
Parásitas (produced in German as *Die Parasiten*, Kiel, West Germany, 1963). In *D.F.*, 1957.
Pastores de le ciudad, pastorela, with Luisa Josefina Hernandez (produced Teatro Universitario de Puebla, Mexico City, 1972). In *La palabra y el hombre*, October-December 1959; in book form, in *D.F.* (second edition), 1962.
Las estatuas de marfil (produced Teatro Ofelia, Mexico City, 1960). 1960.
Guillermo y el nahua (produced Teatro Orientación, Mexico City, 1960).
El jardinero y los párajos (produced Teatro Orientación, Mexico City, 1960).
La lente maravillosa (produced Teatro Orientación, Mexico City, 1960).
Homenaje a Hidalgo, music by Rafael Elizondo (produced

Palacio de Bellas Artes, Mexico City, 1960; revised version produced Plaza de la Alhóndiga, Mexico City, 1965).

El rejolero de Córdoba (produced Teatro del Bosque, Mexico City, 1960). In *Teatro*, 1960; translated as *The Clockmaker from Cordoba* in *"The Golden Thread" and Other Plays*, 1971.

Medusa (produced Cornell University, Ithaca, New York, 1966). In *Teatro*, 1960.

La perfecta casada (produced Teatro del Estado, Xalapa, Mexico, 1963). In *La palabra y el hombre*, October-December, 1961; in book form, in *D.F.* (second edition), 1962.

Paso de Madraguda. In *D.F.* (second edition), 1962.

El solitario en octobre. In *D.F.* (second edition), 1962.

Un cuento de Navidad. In *D.F.* (second edition), 1962.

Un pequeno día de ira (broadcast Cuban television, 1969; produced Mexico City, 1976). 1962; translated by Margaret Sayers Peden, as *A Short Day's Anger*, in *Drama and Theatre*, 1975.

Teseo (produced Teatro Xola, Mexico City, 1962). In *La palabra y el hombre*, October-December 1962; translated as *Theseus*, in *"The Golden Thread" and Other Plays*, 1971.

El día que se soltaron los leones (produced Teatro del Sótano, Havana, 1963). Translated as *The Day They Let the Lions Loose*, in *Voices of Change in Latin American Theatre*, translated by William Oliver, 1971.

¡Silencio, pollos pelones, ya les van a echar su maíz . . .! (produced Teatro de Seguro Social, Ciudad Juárez, Mexico, 1963). In *La palabra y el hombre*, July-September 1964.

Los hijos del capitán Grant, from a work by Jules Verne (produced by the Compañia Estudianti de la Preparatoria 5, Mexico City, 1964). 1972.

Te juro, Juana, que tengo ganas (produced Monterrey, Mexico, 1967). In *La palabra y el hombre*, July-September, 1965; in book form, with *Yo también hablo de la rosa*, 1970.

Yo también hablo de la rosa (produced Teatro Jiménez Rueda, Mexico City, 1966). In *Revista de bellas artes*, November-December, 1965; in book form, with *Te juro, Juana, que tengo ganas*, 1970; translated by William Oliver, as *I, Too, Speak of the Rose*, in *Drama and Theatre*, 8, 1969; also in *The Modern Stage in Latin America: Six Plays*, edited by George Woodyard.

Antes cruzaban ríos (monologue). In *Revista de bellas artes*, March-April, 1967.

¡Tianquis! (produced Auditorio Nacional, Mexico City, 1968).

Almanaque de Juárez (produced Teatro del Bosque, Mexico City, 1968). In *Colección "Poesía en el Mundo"* (special edition), 1972.

La fonda de las siete cabrillas, from a work by M. Eduardo de Gorostiza (produced Mexico City, 1970). In *Revista de bellas artes*, 19, 1975.

Las noticias del día. In *Colección teatro mexicano*, edited by Alvaro Arauz, 1968.

Acapulco, los lunes (produced Teatro San Antonio Caso, Mexico City, 1970). In *Colección "Poesía en el mundo"*, 1969.

Un vals sin fin por el planeta (produced Teatro Orientación, Mexico City, 1970). In *Tres comedias*, 1981.

El final de un idilio. In *Revista de la Universidad de México*, vol.25 no.6, 1971.

Conversación entre las ruinas (produced in English as *Conversation Among the Ruins*, Kalamazoo College, Kalamazoo, Michigan, 1971).

Una rosa, con otro nombre. In *La palabra y el hombre*,

January–March, 1972; in book form, in *D.F.* (third edition), 1973.

Delicioso domingo. In *Sagitario*, February 1972; in book form, in *D.F.* (third edition), 1973.

Las cartas de Mozart (produced Teatro Jiménez Rueda, Mexico City, 1975). In *La palabra y el hombre*, September 1974.

Una mujer de malas. In *Textos* (Department of Fine Art, Guadalajara), 1975.

Numancia, from the play by Cervantes (produced Festival de Guanajuato, Mexico, 1975).

Nahui Ollin (produced Caracas, Venezuela, 1977).

Orinoco (produced Teatro Gorostiza, Mexico City). 1982.

Fotografía en la playa (produced 1984).

Ceremonia en el tiempo del tigre. With *Rosa de dos aromas* and *Un pequeño día de ira*, 1986.

Rosa de dos aromas. With *Rosa de dos aromas* and *Un pequeño día de ira*, 1986.

Screenplays

Macario, 1968; *La adoración de los magos* (published in *Revista de bellas artes*, 1968); *Los novios*, 1970.

Television Plays

El relojero de Córdoba and *Un pequeño día de ira* (Cuban television), 1967; *La danza que sueña la tortuga*, 1975;

Verse

Eso es todo. 1972.

Fiction

La veleta oxidada. 1956.

El norte. 1958; translated as *The Norther*, 1968.

La caja vacía (short stories). 1962.

Las vistaciones del diablo. 1965; second edition, 1969.

El sol. 1970.

Los zapatos de fiero (for children). 1977.

Tiempo de ladrones: La historia de Chucho el Roto. 1983.

Other

Editor, *Tramoya* (theatre journal). 1974—
Editor, *Avanzada: Más teatro joven*. 1985.

Compiler, *Teatro joven de México*. 1973.
Compiler, *El arca de Noé* (children's anthology). 1974.
Compiler, *Nueve obras jóvenes*. 1985.

*

Bibliographies

Margaret Sayers Peden, "Emilio Carballido: Curriculum Operum", in *Texto crítico*, vol.2 no.3, January–April, 1976.

Criticism

Books:
Mary Vasquez Amaral, *El teatro de Emilio Carballido (1950–1965)*, Mexico City, 1974.

Frank N. Dauster, *Ensayos sobre teatro hispanoamericano,* Mexico City, 1975.

Eugen R. Skinner, "The Theater of Emilio Carballido: Spinning a Web", in *Dramatists in Revolt: The New Latin American Theater,* edited by Leon F. Lyday and George Woodyard, Austin, Texas, 1976.

Margaret Sayers Peden, *Emilio Carballido,* Boston, 1980.

Articles:

Karen Peterson, "Existential Irony in Three Carballido Plays", in *Latin American Theatre Review,* vol.10 no.2, 1977.

Jacqueline Lee Bixler, "A Theatre of Contradictions: The Recent Works of Emilio Carballido", in *Latin American Theatre Review,* 18, 1985.

* * *

Emilio Carballido is one of Mexico's most prolific and important playwrights. Since 1948, when he published his one-act play *La zona intermediar (The Intermediate Zone),* Carballido has written over 100 plays. His most notable work include plays such as *Rosalba y los llaveros, La hebra de oro (The Golden Thread),* a collection of one-act plays about Mexico City, entitled *D.F.* (Federal District), *El día que se soltaron los leones (The Day They Let the Lions Loose), El relojero de Córdoba, Yo también hablo de la rosa (I, Too, Speak of the Rose), Orinoco,* and *Ceremonia en el templo del tigre.*

Carballido's particular strength lies in his theatrical and playful examination of some of Mexico's most profound and urgent problems—conquest, colonization, and neo-colonialism; the hegemonic socio-political infrastructure that allows the controlling elite to marginalize its many "others" on the grounds of gender, race, class, and educational training; the role of culture in maintaining or subverting hegemony. Yet, unlike much didactic and politically committed theatre in Latin America, Carballido's plays seem marvellously funny, almost frivolous. A glance at plays such as *El día que se soltaron los leones* or *Yo también hablo de la rosa* with their immense casts and spectacular sets is enough to illustrate that this is no "poor theatre" in either aesthetic or economic terms. His plays burst with a sense of humor and vitality that underlines, rather than eclipses, his socio-political concerns.

El día que se soltaron los leones (The Day They Let the Lions Loose), for example, seems a light-hearted and extravagant play. Ana, a 65-year-old spinster, has waited on her domineering aunt all her adult life. After they have a confrontation over her cat, Ana impetuously leaves the repressive home and runs away to Mexico's famous Chapultepec Park. There she meets a man, a down-and-out poet, and together they cook a meal and discuss the systems—familial, social, ideological—that have denied them freedom. Meanwhile, some children from a military academy visiting the park zoo, with their authoritarian teacher, open the lions' cage, thus provoking the disruption that brings in the police. After their initial fear on seeing the lions loose, Ana and the man befriend them, and they swim out to the island in the middle of Chapultepec lake to escape the police. The police hunt the lions and, by extension, Ana and the man as accomplices. In the confusion of police activity, the school teacher is killed. It becomes clear that Ana and the poet are surrounded. She realizes that her choice is not between freedom and captivity but between two kinds of captivity; she opts to live in the cage with the lions. The man chooses to participate with the corrupt and violent system by claiming *he* caught the lions; he is

rewarded with a job as a zoo keeper and the promise of bounty money.

Set in modern Mexico City, *Lions,* for all its farcical features, evokes centuries of destructive displays of power. The area of Chapultepec, where most of the action takes place, has, historically, been the scene of brutal confrontation; it indicates not only the sacrifice of the individual in modern Mexico, but sacrifice as a persistent theme in Mexican history. Ana and the man realize that the ground they sit on is "slightly rotten". The ground, the leaves, the air, the water itself retain the memory of violent, unnatural deaths. The absurd attack by the police on the island that harbors the fugitives, though staged in a highly theatrical, fanciful manner, recalls the Spaniards' siege of the island of Tenochtitlán, approximately on the same spot, in 1521. It recalls the bitter "Battle of Chapultepec" when school-age children (military cadets like the children in Carballido's play) died defending Chapultepec hill from the invading United States army in 1847. Moreover, Chapultepec Castle, overlooking the park, symbolizes the French domination of Mexico, inhabited as it was by the French appointed imperial couple, Maximiliano and Carlota, in 1864. The domination of Ana by her aunt or the violence suffered by the school children do not constitute isolated acts of silencing and annihilation. Rather, they indicate the perennial sacrifice of individuals trapped in a violent history.

One of Carballido's principal concerns throughout his career is the role of culture—specifically of theatre as a cultural subsystem—in sustaining or subverting a political system. From early works, such as *Yo también hablo de la rosa,* to his recent *Ceremonia en el templo del tigre,* he explores the theatrical arena as a highly politicized and contested space. In *Rosa,* characters from diverse socio-political backgrounds —a peasant woman, a Marxist economist, a Freudian psychologist—vie to tell the story of the two lower-class children who derail a train. The various discourses reflect the experience of the speaker within language (orality/literacy), and illustrate how the interpretations compete for hegemony. The professors, who use Cartesian logic to expound European theories of consciousness and being-in-the-world, have traditionally dominated Mexico's center stage. By confronting their views with the peasant woman's, a representative of Mexico's *mestizo,* semi-literate population, Carballido does not mean to suggest that they are wrong, but that European theories alone cannot explain Mexico's complex cultural diversity. His strategy lies not in replacing but displacing the hegemonic discourse. By bringing the peasant woman to stage center, he automatically marginalizes those who have previously enjoyed the limelight.

In *Templo,* the confrontation is far more overt and violent. The ruins of the pre-Hispanic culture serve as the stage setting for the tension, which soon escalates to open aggression between the oppressors and the oppressed. The ruling elite not only asserts economic power over its exploited fellow Mexicans; it has also destroyed or co-opted its indigenous and *mestizo* cultural manifestations. The pre-Hispanic figures unburied near the ruins are given away to influential foreigners or shattered in target practice. The ritual at the temple, handed down since before the Conquest from one generation to another in keeping with the indigenous tradition, has been taken over by the sons of the rulers. The women, now wearing miniskirts, cheer on their men from the sidelines.

The oppressed realize, however, that defending their culture is fundamental to their sense of identity as well as to their communal cohesion and survival. The Singer, who invents verses of a traditional Mexican *corrida* (epic song) as he sings along to his audience, explicitly refers to his people's oppression and names the corrupt officials responsible for their predicament. Art forms, Carballido implies, can effectively address and even redress some of the violence done to the dominated. Although the powerful members of the community threaten to kill the Singer who exposes them, and although it is clear that they can get away with murder, the situation in which the Singer is forced to sing to his enemies allows him to kill them before they can kill him. The battle, far more explicitly than in Carballido's earlier plays, is now a matter of life or death. Unlike his earlier pieces, such as *Rosa*, where changing the cultural relationships and perspectives was sufficient to remedy historical imbalances, in the early 1980's (after the US invasion of Grenada, Carballido specifies), the dominated must defend themselves, and their culture, with weapons as well as songs.

Over 40 years of playwrighting have established Emilio Carballido as one of the most important dramatists not only in Mexico, but in Latin America. He also directs, runs playwrighting workshops, encourages young playwrights by staging and publishing their works, and edits Mexico's most prestigious theatre journal, *Tramoya*.

—Diana Taylor

See also *Volume 1* entry on *I, Too, Speak of the Rose*.

————

CARON DE BEAUMARCHAIS, Pierre-Augustin. See BEAUMARCHAIS, Pierre-Augustin.

————

CARROLL, Paul Vincent. Born in Blackrock, Dundalk, County Louth, Ireland, 10 July 1900. Educated at St. Mary's College, Dundalk, 1913–16; St. Patrick's Training College, Dublin, 1916–20. Married 1) Helena Reilly in 1923 (died), three daughters; 2) second marriage in 1944 (wife died 1955), one son. Teacher of mathematics and English in state schools in Glasgow, 1921–37; first play, *The Watched Pot*, produced 1930; a founder, Curtain Theatre, Glasgow, 1933; resident dramatist, Molly Urquhart's theatre, Rutherglen, Lanark, 1939; gave lecture tour of USA, 1939–40; columnist ("Standing on the Corner"), Scottish newspapers, 1940's; founder, with James Bridie, 1943, director and productions adviser, 1943–50, and honorary director, 1950–68, Glasgow Citizens' Theatre; moved to England, 1945, and lived for 20 years in Bromley, Kent. Council member, British League of Dramatists, 1943–68. Recipient: Abbey Theatre Prize, 1931; New York Drama Critics Circle Award, 1938, 1939; Irish Academy of Letters Casement Award, 1939. Died 20 October 1968.

Works

Collections

Plays for My Children (includes *The King Who Could Not Laugh*; *His Excellency—the Governor*, from *Don Quixote*

by Cervantes; *St. Francis and the Wolf*; *Beauty is Fled*; *Death Closes All*; *Maker of Roads*). 1939.
Three Plays (includes *The White Steed*; *Things That Are Caesar's*; *The Strings, My Lord, Are False*). 1944.
Irish Stories and Plays (includes *The Conspirators*; *Beauty is Fled*; *Interlude*; *The Devil Came from Dublin*). 1958.

Stage Works

The Watched Pot (produced Peacock Theatre, Dublin, 1930).
Things That Are Caesar's (produced Abbey Theatre, Dublin, 1932). 1934; revised version in *Three Plays*, 1944.
Coggerers (produced Abbey Theatre?, Dublin, 1934). With *The White Steed*, 1939; as *The Conspirators*, 1947.
Shadow and Substance (produced Abbey Theatre, Dublin, 1937). 1937.
Kindred (produced Abbey Theatre, Dublin, 1939).
The White Steed (produced Cort Theatre, New York, 1939). With *Coggerers*, 1939.
Plays for Children (see Collections for contents). 1939.
The Strings, My Lord, Are False (produced Olympia Theatre, Dublin, 1942). In *Three Plays*, 1944.
The Old Foolishness (produced Arts Theatre, London, 1943). 1944.
The Wise Have Not Spoken (produced London, 1944). 1947.
Interlude. 1947.
Green Cars Go East (produced Glasgow Citizens' Theatre, 1951). 1947.
Goodbye to the Summer (earlier version, as *Weep for Tomorrow*, produced Glasgow Citizens' Theatre, 1948). 1970.
The Devil Came from Dublin (as *The Chuckeyhead Story* produced Pavilion Theatre, Bournemouth, 1950; revised version, as *The Border Be Damned*, produced 1951; further revised version, as *The Devil Came from Dublin*, produced John Drew Memorial Theatre, East Hampton, New York, 1951). In *Irish Stories and Plays*, 1958.
The Wayward Saint (produced Cort Theatre, New York, 1955). 1955.
We Have Ceased to Live. In *Journal of Irish Literature*, January 1972.

Screenplays

Saints and Sinners, with Leslie Arliss, 1949.

Television Plays

Farewell to Greatness!, 1956 (published 1966).

*

Criticism

Books:
Robert Hogan, *After the Irish Renaissance: A Critical History of Irish Drama Since "The Plough and the Stars"*, Minneapolis, Minnesota, 1967.
Paul A. Doyle, *Paul Vincent Carroll*, Lewisburg, Pennsylvania, 1971.
Marion Sitzmann, *Indomitable Irishery: Carroll: Study and Interview*, Salzburg, 1975.

Articles:
John D. Conway, "The Satires of Paul Vincent Carroll", in *Eire*, vol. 7 no. 3, 1972.

John D. Conway, "Paul Vincent Carroll's Major Dramatic Triumphs", in *Connecticut Review*, vol. 6 no. 2, 1973.

* * *

After O'Casey's departure from Ireland, the supply of new plays at the Abbey began to dry up. Constant repetition of well-worn comedies alienated the more intelligent audiences. At the same time the Censorhip of Publications Act of 1929, combined with a rigid and dominant Catholic hierarchy, had a baleful influence on literary creativity. Carroll was the first of the bolder spirits to venture onto the dangerous ground of anti-clerical criticism; he was also the most persistent. In five out of his six full-length plays, he dealt with clerical influence on provincial Ireland. As a Catholic himself he did not attack the universal values of the Church, but its parochial manifestations. By adhering to the realistic form familiar to Irish audiences, and by liberally spicing his plays with humour, he managed to win their confidence and at the same time avoid the label of anti-clericalism by pitting the clergy against each other. At his best, he is a powerful dramatist, reflecting much of Ibsen's strength in his criticism of social and marital ills; but he lacks Ibsen's genius of transforming the parochial into the universal. His work is exemplified by his first three plays.

In *Things That Are Caesar's* he deals with one of the evils of Irish provincial life: the marriage of convenience. Eilish Hardy is trapped into a loveless marriage by her avaricious mother. The parish priest, Father Duffy, gives his consent, but Eilish's father condemns the materialism of his wife and the "huckstering" of the priest. His untimely death leaves Eilish to fight alone. Like Ibsen's Nora (of *A Doll's House*) she defies convention and the condemnation from the Church by abandoning her marriage and her child. Carroll is careful not to side with Eilish to the extent of denying the sanctity of the marriage vow. His attack is directed against the greed and hypocrisy of a society that condones and encourages marriage merely as a means of acquiring financial profit.

In his most successful play, *Shadow and Substance*, Carroll attacks the Church's domination of the Free State's educational system. Carroll himself was a schoolmaster who chose to work in Glasgow rather than in his native country. In this play the schoolmaster, O'Flingsley, writes a book under a pseudonym attacking a system he calls "the sewer of European culture". His main target is the proud and unyielding Canon Skerritt, more at home with his grandee friends in Spain than isolated among his ignorant curates and bourgeois parishioners. His only friend is his young housekeeper, Brigid. Brigid's claim to be visited and instructed by her patron saint, St. Brigid, is rejected by the Canon as an example of the emotional credulity of the "spiritual rowdies willing to sell themselves to anything that can produce signs and wonders to please their vanity". Carroll drives his two themes—the Church's domination of the schools and Brigid's belief in her visions of reconciliation and humility—with considerable skill. When O'Flingsley is revealed as the author of the book an angry mob descends on his house intent on beating him up. Brigid is killed in an attempt to intervene, leaving the Canon alone, his pride humbled, and O'Flingsley free to walk out.

The title of Carroll's next play, *The White Steed*, is derived from the legend of Ossian returning to Ireland after 300 years in Tír na nog to find the land "swarming with priests and little black men". The "little black men" in this parable of contemporary Ireland are a fanatical zealot, Father Shaughnessy, and the vigilante he recruits to enforce hell-fire morality. Father Shaughnessy is the new incumbent called in to replace the paralysed Canon Matt Lavelle, a humane, broadminded priest who confesses to liking "a little sugar in my tea, a little soda in my whiskey, a wee bit of coaxing in my dogma and a hot bottle in my bed on a frosty night". His puritanical successor is determined to make his parish a model of strict morality. Nora Phintry, another Ibsenesque young woman, is dismissed from the hockey team for "going with a boy". The weak and timid schoolmaster, Denis Dillon, is forced to abandon his Protestant girlfriend and only plucks up courage when he is drunk. Sanity returns when the Canon is miraculously restored to health and the play ends in an unlikely scene with Dillon throwing himself into Nora's arms after an orgy of smashing crockery. Despite its sentimentalised conclusion the play succeeded in New York and London, but in 1938 it proved too strong for the timid directors of the Abbey Theatre.

Carroll's contribution to Irish theatre, and indeed the success of his plays overseas, acted as a spur to other playwrights to venture upon controversial issues facing Ireland in the 1930's and 1940's. If at times he fails to live up to the tensions he created in his savage attacks on an autocratic clergy and the hypocritical piety of middle-class provincial society, his plays must be seen against the background of Irish sensibilities of his time. His problem was his inability to free himself from the pattern of priest-ridden provincial life. Constant repetition of his limited types, however differentiated the characters, eventually cramped the range of his imagination and diminished the considerable impact his early plays had on Irish audiences.

—Hugh Hunt

See also *Volume 1* entry on *Shadow and Substance*.

———

CASONA, Alejandro. Born Alejandro Rodríguez Álvavrez, in Besullo, Asturia, Spain, 23 March 1903. Studied at the Instituto Jovellanos, Gijón, and the Instituto de Palencia; passed baccalaureate in Murcia, 1919; University of Murcia, 1920–22 (left for financial reasons) and the Escuela Superior del Magisterio, Madrid, 1922–26. Married Rosalía Martín Bravo in 1928; one daughter. First volume of poetry, *El peregrino de la barba florida*, published 1926; director of an elementary school in the Pyrenees, 1928–30, where he founded a children's theatre; director of elementary school in León, and subsequently superintendent of all schools in Madrid, 1931; director of the Teatro del Pueblo for the government Misiones Pedagógicas, 1931–36; left for France, 1936; director of a Paris-based Spanish-language touring theatre company, 1937: travelled to Venezuela, Puerto Rica, Cuba, and Mexico, 1937–38; settled in Buenos Aires, Argentina, 1939; works banned in Spain under Franco's regime; began directing films, 1941; worked for Radio Belgrano, Buenos Aires, 1956; travelled to Europe, 1956 and 1960; resettled in Spain, 1963. Recipient: Lope de Vega Prize, 1933. Died in Madrid, 17 September 1965.

Works

Collections

Retablo jovial. 1949.
Teatro (includes *La sirena varada; La barca sin pescador; Los árboles mueren de pie*). 1951.

Obras completas (2 vols.). 1954 and 1959; several revised and augmented editions since 1960.
Teatro selecto (includes *La sirena varada; Prohibido suicidarse en primavera; Los árboles mueren de pie; La casa de los siete balcones; El caballero de las espuelas de oro; Nuestra Natacha*). 1966.

Stage Works

El crímen de Lord Arturo, from a work by Oscar Wilde (produced Zaragoza, 1929). 1951.
Sancho Panza en la insula, from *Don Quixote* by Cervantes (produced by Teatro del Pueblo, Madrid, early 1930's). In *Retablo jovial*, 1949.
El entremés del mancebo que se casó con mujer brava, from A work by Infante don Juan Manuel (produced by Teatro del Pueblo, Madrid, c.1933). 1941.
La sirena varada (produced Teatro Español, Madrid, 1934). 1934.
El misterio de María Celeste, with A. Hernández Catá (produced Valencia, 1935).
Otra vez el diablo (produced Teatro Español, Madrid, 1935). 1935.
Nuestra Natacha (produced Barcelona, 1935). 1936.
Prohibido suicidarse en primavera (produced Teatro Arbeu, Mexico City, 1937). 1941; translated as *Suicide Prohibited in Springtime*, in *Modern Spanish Theater*, edited by Michael Benedikt and George E. Wellwarth, 1968.
Romance de Dan y Elsa / Romance en tres noches (produced Teatro Nacional, Caracas, Venezuela, 1938). In *Obras completas*, 1954.
Sinfonía inacabada (produced Teatro Solís, Montevideo, Bolivia, 1940). With *La Molinera de Arcos*, 1949.
María Curia, with Francisco Madrid (produced Teatro Smart, Buenos Aires, 1940).
Las tres perfectas casadas, from a play by Arthur Schnitzler (produced Teatro Avenida, Buenos Aires, 1941). 1943.
La dama del alba (produced Teatro Avenida, Buenos Aires, Argentina, 1944). 1945; translated as *The Lady of the Dawn*, 1949; as *Lady of the Dawn*, with *Love, Death and a Crown*, 1972.
La barca sin pescador (produced Teatro Liceo, Buenos Aires, 1947). In *Teatro*, 1951; translated as *The Boat Without a Fisherman*, 1970.
La molinera de Arcos (produced Teatro Argentino, Buenos Aires, 1947). With *Sinfonía inacabada*, 1949.
Fablilla del secreto bien guardado. In *Retablo jovial*, 1949.
Farsa del cornudo apaleado, from *The Decameron* by Bocaccio. In *Retablo jovial*, 1949.
Farsa y justicia del corregidor. In *Retablo jovial*, 1949.
Los árboles mueren de pie (produced Teatro Ateneo, Buenos Aires, 1949). In *Teatro*, 1951.
La llave en el desvan (produced Teatro Ateneo, Buenos Aires, 1951). 1959.
¡A Belén, pastores! (for children; produced Parque Rodó, Montevideo, Bolivia, 1951). In *Obras completas*, 1954.
Siete gritos en el mar (produced Teatro Politeama, Madrid, 1952). In *Obras completas*, 1954.
La tercera palabra (produced Teatro Odéon, Buenos Aires, 1953). In *Obras completas*, 1954.
El lindo Don Gato (for children). In *Obras completas*, 1954.
Corona de amor y muerte (produced Teatro Odéon, Buenos Aires, 1955). In *Obras completas*, 1960; translated as *Love, Death and a Crown*, with *Lady of the Dawn*, 1972.
Carta de una desconocida, from a story by Stefan Zweig (produced Teatro São Pedro, Porto Alegre, Brazil, 1957). In *Obras completas*, 1960.

La casa de los siete balcones (produced Teatro Liceo, Buenos Aires, 1957). In *Obras completas*, 1960.
El anzuelo de Fenisa, from a play by Lope de Vega (produced Buenos Aires, 1958). In *Obras completas*, 1966.
El caballero de las espuelas de oro (produced Teatro Bellas Artes, Madrid, 1964). 1965.
Tres diamantes y una mujer (produced Teatro Ateneo, Buenos Aires, 1961). In *Obras completas*, 1966.
El burlador de Sevilla, from the play by Tirso de Molina (produced Buenos Aires, 1961). In *Obras completas*, 1966.
Peribañez y el Comendador de Ocaña, from the play by Lope de Vega (produced Buenos Aires, 1962). In *Obras completas*, 1966.
Cartas de amor de una monja portuguesa (produced Buenos Aires, 1963).
El sueño de una noche de verano, from Shakespeare (produced 1963?). In *Obras completas*, 1966.
Don Rodrigo, music by Ginastera (libretto; produced Madrid, 1964).
La Celestina, from the work by Rojas (produced Teatro Bellas Artes, Madrid, 1965). In *Obras completas*, 1966.
Ricardo III, from *Richard III* by Shakespeare. In *Obras completas*, 1966.

Screenplays

Veinte años y una noche, 1940; *El viaje Buenos Aires*, 1941; *La Maestrita de los obreros*, 1941; *Ceniza al viento*, 1942; *Nuestra Natacha*, 1943; *El María Celeste*, 1944; *Casa de muñecas*, from a play by Ibsen, 1943; *Le fruit mordu*, with Jules Superville, 1945; *Margarita la tornera*, 1946; *El Abuelo*, from the work by Benito Pérez Galdos, 1946; *La dama del alba*, 1950.

Verse

El peregrino de la barba florida. 1926.
La flauta del sapo. 1930.

Other

Flor de leyendas; Lecturas y literaturas para niños. 1933.
Una misión pedagógico-social en Sanabria: Teatro estudiantil. 1941.
Vida de Francisco Pizarro. 1969.

Translator, *Los placeres y los tormentos del opio*, by Thomas de Quincey. 1926.
Translator, *Novelas selectas de Voltaire*. 1928.
Translator, *Cuatro dramas en un acto de Strindberg*. 1929.
Translator, *Los fracasados; La loca del cielo; La inocente*, by Lenormand. 1943.
Translator, *Sombra querida*, by Jacques Deval. 1952.

*

Bibliographies

Arturo Sánchez-Rojas, "Bibliografía de Alejandro Casona", in *Boletín del Instituto de Estudios Asturianos*, 27, 1972.
Marsha Foys, "Alejandro Casona: A Bibliography of Criticism Through 1987", in *Hispania*, 73, 1990.

Criticism

Books:
J. Rodríguez Richart, *Vida y obra de Alejandro Casona,* Oviedo, 1963.

Esperanza Gurza, *La realidad caleidoscópia de Alejandro Casona,* Oviedo, 1968.

Hilda Bernal Labrada, *Simbolo, mito, y leyenda en el teatro de Casona,* Madrid, 1972.

Harold Kay Moon, *Alejandro Casona,* Boston, 1985.

Articles:
Marina Villalba Alvarez, "Alejandro Casona: Datos biográficos, producción literaria (1962–1965): El autor y la crítica", in *Boletín del Instituto de Estudios,* 40, 1986.

A. Wallace Woolsey, "Illusion Versus Reality in Some of the Plays of Alejandro Casona", in *Modern Languages,* 38, 1954.

Kessel Schwartz, "Reality in the Works of Alejandro Casona", in *Hispania,* 40, 1957.

Frank L. Toms, "The Reality-Fantasy Technique of Alejandro Casona", in *Hispania,* 44, 1961.

Charles H. Leighton, "Alejandro Casona and the Significance of Dreams", in *Hispania,* 95, 1962.

Charles H. Leighton, "Alejandro Casona and Suicide", in *Hispania,* 55, 1972.

John A. Moore, "Death as a Theme in Casona's Plays", in *South Atlantic Bulletin,* vol.39 no.2, 1974.

Thomas C. Turner, "Eyes in the Drama of Alejandro Casona", in *Hispanófila,* 61, 1977.

Phyllis Zatlin, "Alejandro Casona and Nikolai Evreinov: Life as Theater", in *Modern Drama,* 22, 1979.

* * *

Although not particularly well known in English-speaking countries, Alejandro Casona produced, over a period of 38 years, a prolific and varied body of work which has confirmed his unquestionable position, alongside Valle Inclán and García Lorca, as a major innovator in the otherwise moribund, commercialized Spanish theatre of the first half of the 20th century.

Criticized in recent years for the ideological naivety prevalent in much of his work, Casona was never concerned with a realistic or logical theatre; his skills as a dramatist lay, rather, in the exploration of the poetic potential of the stage. Drawing on the mythical and pagan folklore of his native Asturias and the allegorical tradition of the 17th-century dramatist Calderón, Casona produced a series of lyrical and haunting plays characterized by an almost surreal poetic compression, a gentle humour, and a dream-like aura, which exploited the stage's visual and aural possibilities in a manner unforeseen by pseudo-naturalistic dramatists of the Generation of '98.

Seeking to explore what he perceived as the indefinable boundaries of fantasy and reality, he brought characters from the real world into conflict with those from beyond. In *Romance de Dan y Elsa* (Ballad of Dan and Elsa), it is the city's slums which become a horrifically surreal world of vice and degeneracy, populated by figures with no concept of the rural world Dan comes from. Those who prove to have lost touch with the moral, social, and ethical values which Casona, like Lope de Vega, saw embodied in the rural way of life, can provide no defenses against the Gothic-like figures of death and the devil. Thus, Angelica is lured to her death by the beautiful comforting pilgrim of *La dama del alba* (Lady of the Dawn). Unable to perceive death's all-engulfing dimen-

sion, she allows herself to fall into the mysterious woman's clutches, thereby losing any possibility of a much-desired reconciliation with her family. Ricardo, too, in *La barca sin pescador* (*The Boat Without a Fisherman*) is trapped in a single-minded pursuit of wealth and power and signs away the life of another human being in the cold, detached manner of a business transaction. In this mechanized society where friendship, like human life, can be bought and sold, Satan represents man's conscience in turmoil and can often triumph unperceived, as *Otra vez el diablo* (The Devil Again) and *¡A Belén, pastores!* (To Bethlehem, Shepherds!) also suggest.

It is against such a dehumanized society that Casona's work, from the early children's plays like *El lindo Don Gato* (Beautiful Mr Cat) to the later historical and comic works like the unpublished *María Curia* (produced 1940) and *Tres diamantes y una mujer* (Three Diamonds and One Woman, produced 1961), is most sharply focused. The world of fantasy into which his characters retreat in their attempts to come to terms with a society in which they feel ever less significant, is physicalized by Casona in a manner which highlights the futility of such escapism. In time, the patients of the asylum for suicides in *Prohibido suicidarse en primavera* (*Suicide Prohibited in Springtime*) and the home for sick souls in *Los árboles mueren de pie* (Trees Die Standing), come to realize that the truth cannot be harboured by the dreams and illusions which appear so much more attractive than the mundane, and often lonely, reality of one's day-to-day existence. Ricardo and Daniel in *La sirena varada* (Mermaid Aground), achieve what can best be termed a compromise with reality when they come to realize that imaginative energy must be channelled into positive sources. For Casona, as for Goya before him, the sleep of reason has the capacity to produce monsters in the mind.

The role of dreams in the human unconscious became an increasing preoccupation in Casona's later plays, pointing to his acquaintance with the theories of Freud, Jung, and Adler. *Siete gritos en el mar* (Seven Cries at Sea), for instance, is constructed within a dream framework, while in *La llave en el desvan* (The Key in the Attic), an interpretation of Mario's dreams holds the key to the mystery at the heart of the play.

Despite the many years spent in self-imposed exile in Argentina, Casona's plays retain various Iberian traits, in particular that interpenetration of the real and unreal so characteristic of the work of Calderón, Cervantes, and Rafael Alberti. In addition, the recognizably Asturian settings of *La barca sin pescador, La casa de los siete balcones* (The House with the Seven Balconies) and *La dama del alba*—the latter dedicated to the region itself—betray a nostalgia for his homeland which in many respects pre-empts his return there in 1963.

Although some of Casona's adaptations—*El crimen de Lord Arturo,* based on Oscar Wilde's *Lord Arthur Savile's Crime,* and *Carta de una desconocida* (Letter from an Unknown Woman), derived from Stefan Zweig's short story of the same name—had their origins in non-Hispanic sources, the majority betray his debt to Spain. Perhaps the best known is *La molinera de Arcos* (The Miller's Wife), a reworking of Pedro de Alarcon's popular novel *El sombrero de tres picos* (The Three Cornered Hat) but other theatrical adaptations include versions of Fernando de Rojas' *La Celestina,* Lope de Vega's *El anzuelo de Fenisa* (Fenisa's Bait) and Tirso de Molina's *El burlador de Sevilla* (*The Trickster of Seville*), and all testify to this Spanish influence.

His historical dramas—*Sinfonía inacabada* (Unfinished Symphony), a theatrical homage to Schubert, is the only conspicuous exception—also display Hispanic resonances. *Corona de amor y muerte* (*Love, Death and a Crown*) is based on the ill-fated relationship between Ines de Castro and Prince Pedro of Portugal, and *El caballero de las espuelas de oro* (The Knight with the Golden Spurs) on the life of the 16th-century satirist, Francisco de Quevedo.

Although primarily known as a dramatist, Casona's prolific work as an essayist and columnist, his libretto for Alberto Ginastera's opera, *Don Rodrigo*, and his work for the radio and film industries in Buenos Aires are evidence of his diverse talents. Although a small number of Casona's plays have been translated into English, it is in France, Italy and Portugal that his work has been most widely produced outside Spain and Argentina.

—Maria M. Delgado

CENTLIVRE, Susanna(h). Born in or near Holbeach, Lincolnshire, England, c.1669. Possibly married a nephew of Sir Stephen Fox, c.1684, and an officer named Carroll, c.1685; married Joseph Centlivre, yeoman of the mouth (i.e., principal cook) to Queen Anne and George I, in 1707 (died c.1722). First play, *The Perjured Husband*, produced 1700; actress in the provinces, often appearing in her own works, written as S. Carroll; wrote prologues, epilogues, and some poems in support of Whig politicians. Died in London, 1 December 1723.

Works

Collections

Works (3 vols.).   1760–61; as *Dramatic Works*, 1872.

Stage Works

The Perjured Husband; or, The Adventures of Venice (produced Theatre Royal, Drury Lane, London, 1700).   1700.
The Beau's Duel; or, A Soldier for the Ladies (produced Lincoln's Inn Fields Theatre, London, 1702).   1702.
The Stolen Heiress; or, The Salamanca Doctor Outplotted (as *The Heiress*, produced Lincoln's Inn Fields Theatre, London, 1702).   1703.
Love's Contrivance; or, Le Médecin Malgré Lui (produced Theatre Royal, Drury Lane, London, 1703).   1703.
The Gamester, from a play by J.F. Regnard (produced Lincoln's Inn Fields Theatre, London, 1705).   1705.
The Basset-Table (produced Theatre Royal, Drury Lane, London, 1705).   1705.
Love at a Venture (produced New Theatre, Bath, 1706?).   1706.
The Platonic Lady (produced Queen's Theatre, Haymarket, London, 1706).   1707.
The Busy Body (produced Theatre Royal, Drury Lane, London, 1709).   1709.
The Man's Bewitched; or, The Devil to Do about Her (produced Haymarket Theatre, London, 1709).   1709.
A Bickerstaff's Burying; or, Work for the Upholders (produced Theatre Royal, Drury Lane, London, 1710).   1710; as *The Custom of the Country* (produced 1715).
Mar-Plot; or, The Second Part of The Busy Body (produced Theatre Royal, Drury Lane, London, 1710).   1711.
The Perplexed Lovers (produced Theatre Royal, Drury Lane, London, 1712).   1712.

The Wonder! A Woman Keeps a Secret (produced Theatre Royal, Drury Lane, London, 1714).   1714.
The Gotham Election (produced Haymarket Theatre, London, 1724).   1715; as *The Humours of Elections*, 1737.
A Wife Well Managed (produced Haymarket Theatre, London, 1715).   1715.
The Cruel Gift; or, The Royal Resentment (produced Theatre Royal, Drury Lane, London, 1716).   1717.
A Bold Stroke for a Wife (produced Lincoln's Inn Fields Theatre, London, 1718).   In *A Collection of Plays 3*, 1718.
The Artifice (produced Theatre Royal, Drury Lane, London, 1722).   1723.

Verse

A Trip to the Masquerade; or, A Journey to Somerset House.   1713.
A Poem to His Majesty upon His Accession to the Throne.   1715.
An Epistle to Mrs. Wallup, Now in the Train of the Princess of Wales.   1715.
A Woman's Case, in an Epistle to Charles Joye.   1720.
An Epistle to the King of Sweden, in *Charles XII of Sweden: A Character and Two Poems*, edited by Eveline Cruickshanks.   1983.

*

Bibliographies

Jane E. Norton, "Some Uncollected Authors 14", in *Book Collector*, 6, 1957.

Criticism

Books:
John Bowyer, *The Celebrated Mrs. Centlivre*, Durham, North Carolina, 1952.
F.P. Lock, *Susanna Centlivre*, Boston, 1979.

*   *   *

Susanna Centlivre's success and productivity as a comic playwright in the early 18th century is matched only by Colley Cibber's. Both were masters of an intrigue comedy that could easily accommodate doses of farce and sentiment. Both produced plays that were extremely popular with actors and audiences; neither has pleased many critics. Both attempted tragedies without success; both were ardent Whigs who allowed their political views to enter their plays. But they are not without striking differences, most notably in their relationships to the power structures of the 18th-century stage.

Cibber wrote his first plays to help establish his acting career. Once established, he worked his way up to becoming a manager with control of access to the stage; he had no trouble seeing his own plays performed. Centlivre met with considerable resistance as a young playwright, much of it because women playwrights were not readily welcomed. After the hostile reception of her first plays, she chose to see her next few performed and published anonymously. Only after several successes was it possible for her to be taken seriously as a professional writer with a marketable name. And even then, Cibber turned down her seventh play, *Love at a Venture*, only to plagiarise it shamelessly for his very popular *The Double Gallant*.

A number of common elements are evident in Centlivre's comedies. She rarely wrote without a source, usually foreign. Her favorite sources were French (early in her career) and (later) Spanish comedies. They provided her with plot elements and character types which she always naturalised and made her own. Even *Love's Contrivance, or, Le Médecin Malgré Lui*, to take the extreme case with its acknowledged source in Molière, had minimal resemblance to the original by the time Centlivre had added material from two other Molière plays and transposed the whole to England. The plot of Centlivre's play focuses on the successful scheming of Lucinda and her lover, Bellmein, to prevent Lucinda's father from forcing her to marry Sir Toby Doubtful, a lecherous and foolish old city knight. The lovers, predictably, succeed through comic trickery and are rewarded with the marriage to each other they so strongly desire. The theme of marriage by choice and its key corollary, that young women should not be forced to marry against their will by older men, remains central throughout the Centlivre canon.

Centlivre wrote 16 full-length plays and three afterpiece-length farces in her 22-year career as a playwright. Though few were outright failures, only four entered the repertory. *The Gamester* (1705) was her first success to hold the stage well beyond its initial run. It is an unusual play for Centlivre in that the obstacle to the marriage of the young lovers, Angelica and Valere, is Valere's compulsive gambling rather than an obstructing elder. The play's popularity seems to have come largely from its realistic representation of contemporary gambling and its concomitant social problems. Centlivre followed *The Gamester* with a play in which a woman has a gambling problem to be corrected, but *The Basset-Table* (1706) did not match the success of its predecessor. Recent critics, however, often prefer it, and it is generally seen as the most unjustly neglected of her plays.

Centlivre's critical reputation is based on her three final successful comedies, all in the tradition of Spanish intrigue comedy. *The Busy Body* was her most successful play, with over 400 performances in the 18th century. Though it is set in London, the plot is structured around the attempt of the Iberophile Sir Jealous Traffick to impose Spanish rule on his daughter Isabinda. Sir Jealous plans to marry her to a Spanish merchant, but is outwitted by Charles Gripe, the son of Sir Francis Gripe, a miser whose greed informs the second plot, which revolves around his ward Valeria's endeavors to marry Sir George Airy rather than her guardian. Sir Francis's other ward, Marplot, provides the play with its title as he interferes good-naturedly, but compulsively, in the affairs of his friends, providing an additional obstacle to their marriage. It is the loveable meddler Marplot who seems to have been the great crowd-pleaser in *The Busy Body*.

The Wonder! A Woman Keeps a Secret was performed over 200 times in the 18th century, as was *A Bold Stroke for a Wife*. Set in Lisbon, *The Wonder* follows *The Busy Body* in focusing on the successful attempts of two young women to marry the men of their choice. Violante wishes to marry the jealous Don Felix rather than succumb to her father's desire that she should enter a nunnery (he could then keep her fortune). Felix's sister, Isabella, escapes an arranged marriage, falls in love with Colonel Britton, and hides at Violante's until she can decide her own fate. Violante's ability to protect Isabella—even from the determined inquiries of her lover—gives the play its title and provides much of the action. Felix was one of Garrick's favorite roles and the last he performed on the London stage.

A Bold Stroke is built around a single plot, the schemes of Fainwell to win the consent of his intended's four guardians—a beau, a virtuoso, a stock jobber, and a Quaker. Several attempts and multiple disguises are required before Fainwell ultimately succeeds.

At her best, as in *The Busy Body*, *The Wonder*, and *A Bold Stroke*, Centlivre writes fast-moving, action-filled, farcical intrigues, with well-oiled plots, characters in the humours tradition who provide splendid vehicles for actors, and a range of highly allusive dialects appropriate for such humours characters. The popularity of these three plays continued well into the 19th century, and spread to British colonies throughout the world. She was one of the best comic playwrights of her time, and the best woman playwright of the early 18th century. Like Aphra Behn, her counterpart a generation earlier, "the celebrated Mrs. Centlivre" was an accomplished professional who could provide her audiences with the entertainment they demanded.

—Brian Corman

CERVANTES, (Saveedra) Miguel de. Born in Alcalá de Henares, Spain, October 1547. Grew up in Córdoba, Cabra, and Seville. Educated at the Estudio de la Villa, Madrid, 1567–68, and studied under the Erasmian Humanist, López de Hoyos. Married Catalina de Salazar y Palacios, 1584; had one daughter by Ana Franca de Rojas. Went to Rome, 1569, entering service of Cardinal Guilio Acquaviva; enlisted as soldier, 1571; fought with the Spanish fleet at the Battle of Lepanto, 1571, sustaining injury; on expeditions to Corfu and Navarino, 1572, and to Tunis, 1573, and served in garrisons at Palermo, Sardinia, and Naples; was captured and imprisoned by Turks in Algiers, 1575: ransomed, 1580; returned to Spain, and held posts as diplomat to North Africa (1581), tax inspector, and purchasing agent; briefly excommunicated for financial zeal, 1587; suffered bankruptcy and two short prison terms (1597 and 1602) for financial irregularities; application for administrative post in America denied; lived mainly in Seville, 1596–1600, and Madrid from 1606. Died in Madrid, 23 April 1616.

Works

Collections

Ocho comedias y ocho entremeses nuevos.   1615.
La Numancia; El trato de argel (with *Viage al Parnaso*). 1784.
Numantia; The Commerce of Algiers; together with "The Voyage to Parnassus", translated by Gordon W.J. Gyll. 1870.
Complete Works, edited by James Fitzmaurice-Kelly.   1901–03.
Obras completas, edited by R. Schevill and A. Benilla y San Martin (16 vols.).   1914–41.
Entremeses, edited by Miguel Herrero Garcia.   1945.
The Interludes of Cervantes (includes *The Judge of the Divorce Court; Trampagos the Widower Bully; The Election of the Daganzo Alderman; The Picket of Love; The Sham Biscayan; The Marvellous Pageant; The Cave of Salamanca; The Jealous Old Man*), translated by S. Griswold Morley.   1948.
Interludes, translated by E. Honig (includes *Choosing a*

Miguel de Cervantes (engraving after an allegorical drawing by Monnet).

Councilman in Daganzo; The Vigilant Sentinel; The Divorce Court Judge; The Wonder Show; The Jealous Old Husband; The Basque Imposter).   1964.

Obras completas, edited by Angel Valbuena Prat (2 vols.). 1967.

Entremeses, edited by E. Asensio.   1984.

Stage Works

Los baños de Argel (comedia).   In *Ocho comedias y ocho entremeses nuevos*, 1615.

La casa de los celos y selvas de Ardenia (comedia).   In *Ocho comedias y entremeses nuevos*, 1615.

La Entretenida (comedia).   In *Ocho comedias y ocho entremeses nuevos*, 1615.

El gallardo español (comedia).   In *Ocho comedias y ocho entremeses nuevos*, 1615.

La gran sultana, doña Catalina de Oviedo (comedia).   In *Ocho comedias y ocho entremeses nuevos*, 1615.

El laberinto de amor (comedia).   In *Ocho comedias y ocho entremeses nuevos*, 1615.

Pedro de Urdemalas (comedia).   In *Ocho comedias y ocho entremeses nuevos*, 1615; translated as *Pedro the Artful Dodger*, in *Eight Spanish Plays of the Golden Age*, edited by W. Starkie, 1964.

El rufián dichoso, Cristóbal de Lugo (comedia).   In *Ocho comedias y ocho entremeses nuevos*, 1615.

La cueva de Salamanca (entremes).   In *Ocho comedias y ocho entremeses nuevos*, 1615; translated as *The Cave of Salamanca*, in *World Drama 2*, edited by B.H. Clark, 1933, and in *The Interludes of Cervantes*, 1948.

La elección de los alcaldes de Daganzo (entremes).   In *Ocho comedias y ocho entremeses nuevos*, 1615; translated as *The Election of the Daganzo Aldermen*, in *The Interludes of Cervantes*, 1948; as *Choosing a Councilman in Daganzo*, in *Interludes*, 1964.

La guarda cuidadosa (entremes).   In *Ocho comedias y ocho entremeses nuevos*, 1615; translated as *The Picket of Love*, in *The Interludes of Cervantes*, 1948; as *The Vigilant Sentinel*, in *Spanish Drama*, edited by A. Flores, 1961.

El juez de los divorcios (entremes).   In *Ocho comedias y ocho entremeses nuevos*, 1615; translated as *The Judge of the Divorce Court*, in *The Interludes of Cervantes*, 1948; as *The Divorce Court Judge*, in *Interludes*, 1964.

El retablo de las maravillas (entremes).   In *Ocho comedias y ocho entremeses nuevos*, 1615; translated as *The Marvellous Pageant*, in *The Interludes of Cervantes*, 1948; as *The Wonder Show*, in *Interludes*, 1964.

El rufián viudo llamado Trampagos (entremes).   In *Ocho comedias y ocho entremeses nuevos*, 1615; translated as *Trampagos the Widower Bully*, in *The Interludes of Cervantes*, 1948.

El viejo celoso (entremes).   In *Ocho comedias y ocho entremeses nuevos*, 1615; translated as *The Jealous Old Man*, in *The Interludes of Cervantes*, 1948; as *The Jealous Old Husband*, in *Interludes*, 1964.

El vizcaíno fingido (entremes).   In *Ocho comedias y ocho entremeses nuevos*, 1615; translated as *The Sham Biscayan*, in *The Interludes of Cervantes*, 1948; as *The Basque Imposter*, in *Interludes*, 1964.

El cerco de Numancia (comedia).   With *El trato de argel* and *El viaje al Parnasso*, 1784; translated as *Numantia*, with *The Commerce of Algiers* and *Voyage to Parnassus*, 1870; as *The Siege of Numancia*, 1959.

El trato de Argel (comedia).   With *El cerco de Numancia* and *El viaje al Parnasso*, 1784; translated as *The Commerce of Algiers*, with *Numantia* and *Voyage to Parnassus*, 1870.

Los habladores, possibly not by Cervantes.   Translated as *Two Chatterboxes*, in *Spanish One-Act Plays in English*, edited by W.K. Jones, 1934.

Fiction

La Galatea.   1585; translated as *La Galatea*, 1867.

El ingenioso hidalgo Don Quixote de la Mancha (2 vols.).   1605–15; translated as *Don Quixote*, 1612: several subsequent translations under same title.

Novelas ejemplares.   1613; translated as *Exemplary Novels*, 1972.

Los trabajos de Persiles y Sigismunda.   1617; translated as *The Travels of Persiles and Sigismunda*, 1619.

Verse

El viage al Parnasso.   1614; translated as *Voyage to Parnassus*, with *Numantia* and *The Commerce of Algiers*, 1870.

*

Bibliographies

Alberto Sanchèz, *Cervantes: Bibliografía fundamental (1900–59)*, Madrid, 1961–62.

R.L. Grismer, *Cervantes: A Bibliography*, New York, 1946.

Criticism

Books:

R. Schevill, *Cervantes*, New York, 1919.

J.B. Trend, *Cervantes in Arcadia*, 1954.

Teresa Aveleyra Arroyo de Anda, *El humorismo de Cervantes en sus obras menores*, Mexico City, 1962.

Joaquín Casalduero, *Sentido y forma del teatro de Cervantes*, Madrid, 1966.

L. Nelson, Jr. (ed.), *Cervantes: A Collection of Critical Essays*, Englewood Cliffs, New Jersey, 1969.

Arnaldo Mondadori (ed.), *Cervantes: His Life, His Times, His Works*, New York, 1970.

Gregorio Mayans y Siscar, *Vida de Miguel de Cervantes*, Madrid, 1972.

Francisco Navarro y Ledesma, *Cervantes, The Man and the Genius*, New York, 1973.

Manuel Durán, *Cervantes*, New York, 1974.

William Byron, *Cervantes: A Biography*, London, 1978.

Manuel Criado de Val (ed.), *Cervantes: Su obra y su mundo: Actas del I Congreso internacional sobre Cervantes*, Madrid, 1981.

Edward H. Friedman, *The Unifying Concept: Approaches to the Structure of Cervantes' Comedias*, York, South Carolina, 1981.

Jean Canavaggio, *Cervantes*, Paris, 1986.

Harold Bloom (ed.), *Cervantes: Modern Critical Views*, New York, 1987.

Articles:

Edward H. Friedman, "Cervantes' Dramatic Development: From *Los tratos de Argel* to *Los baños de Argel*", in *Revista de estudios hispánicos*, 10, 1976.

* * *

Cervantes' career as a dramatist can be divided into two

periods, during the first of which he wrote primarily trage-dies, and the second of which was dominated by comedies and farcical interludes written mostly in prose, known as *entremeses*. Cervantes's tragedies are composed in four acts and reflect his ambition to produce works of classical stature, combining historical and moral elements. His comedies and farces are generally thought more successful as theatrical works, in part because of their more natural language and tone and because of the more accessible subjects they treat.

The most important of Cervantes's earlier theatrical works is *El cerco de Numancia*, conceived as a tragedy. The work is set in Roman Iberia, and tells of the heroic self-sacrifice of an entire city. Although Cervantes attempts by allusion to relate the historical events of Numancia to those of contemporary Spain, the period remains remote and Cervantes was not able to draw the necessary literary connections with the past to make the events seem compelling. The work uses a number of allegorical characters (including that of Spain herself) in order to press its moral message. But perhaps most important of all, the work is less successful dramatically than some of Cervantes's later works because of its essentially static struc-ture. Events in the play occur on one side or the other of the wall that encircles the city, and there is little other movement. In addition, the central dramatic action of the work is the suffering or *pathos* of the city, which is not in the strict sense an "action" at all. In drawing the picture of the suffering of this city, Cervantes tries to ennoble the action and raise it to heroic proportions through the use of stage effects calculated to produce wonder or awe (*admiratio*) in the audience. But these are offset by a series of pathetic characterizations that may gain our sympathy but that ultimately lower the status of the events.

Cervantes's later works, and in particular the comic *entre-meses* published after Lope de Vega came to dominate the stage, are more successful theatrically. Particularly in the *entremeses* Cervantes uses rapid dialogue, colloquial speech, highly stylized characterizations, and the tricks of self-conscious theatrical illusion in order to ridicule the common illusions and self-deceptions of ordinary life. His figures in-clude jealous husbands and wives, self-deceiving old men, and deluded town officials.

In one of the most important *entremeses*, *El retablo de las maravillas* (*The Marvellous Pageant*), Cervantes takes as the object of his criticism the (illusory) belief in the myth of "cleanliness of blood" held by a majority of the Spaniards of his day. This *entremés* is a version of the "emperor's new clothes" deception, except that in this case the self-deceived "emperor" is the entire public, and the illusion consists in the belief that each of them is of pure lineage. It is said that only those of pure blood will be able to witness the play to be put on by a travelling troupe, and while there is no play all claim to witness it. In this work, as in others, Cervantes seems to be criticizing the link between the myth of cleanliness of blood and the dramatic illusions sustained by the theatre of Lope de Vega and his followers. In particular, Cervantes sees that the wish to represent oneself as of pure (i.e. "old Christian") lineage is reinforced in potentially damaging ways by the illusory practices of the *comedia*.

Cervantes held a lifelong ambition to be a successful dra-matist, but this ambition was never fully realized or reflected by audiences. On Cervantes' own account, his modest thea-trical talents were overshadowed by the genius of Lope de Vega, whose work became enormously popular toward the end of the 16th century. In addition, Cervantes' talents as a writer of verse—the all-but obligatory form for a writer of *comedias* in Golden-Age Spain—were slim. He himself remarked in the *Viaje al Parnaso* that "one could expect a

great deal from my prose, but little from my verse". At its worst, the language of a work like *Numancia* tends to be pretentious and overblown. But even in the *comedias*, Cervantes' verse does not demonstrate the supple dramatic incorporation of imagery and metre that one could find in the works of Lope de Vega.

Cervantes also wrote theatrical criticism, some of which can be found in the prologue to his *Ocho comedias y entremeses*—which gives a thumbnail account of the gen-ealogy of theatrical practice in Spain—and some of which is to be found in the form of dialogue among the characters in *Don Quixote*. In Part One of *Don Quixote*, the Canon of Toledo, the Barber, and the Priest hold a series of discussions about literary practice in Spain and criticize the theatre for its lack of verisimilitude, its unselfconscious use of illusion, and the moral injury its deceptions might cause for the public. In these criticisms, Cervantes seems to be thinking principally of the theatre of Lope de Vega and its tendency to create the illusion of a vital link between the Spain of the present day and the epic culture of the medieval past.

—Anthony J. Cascardi

CÉSAIRE, Aimé (Fernand). Born in Basse-Pointe, Martinique, West Indies, 25 June 1913. Educated at Lycée Schoelcher, Fort-de-France, Martinique, 1924–31; Lycée Louis-le-Grand, Paris, 1931–35; École Normale Supérieure, Paris, 1935–39, licencié ès lettres 1936. Married Suzanne Roussy in 1937 (died 1966); four sons and two daughters. Founder, with Léopold Senghor and Léon Damas, *L'Étudiant noir*, Paris, 1934; teacher, Lycée Schoelcher, Fort-de-France, 1939–45; editor, *Tropiques*, Fort-de-France, 1941–45; member of the two French constituent assemblies, 1945–46, and since 1946 Deputy for Martinique in the French National Assembly; founding member, later President, Parti Progressiste Martiniquais; Mayor of Fort-de-France, 1945–83: re-elected, but result invalidated by Tribunal, 1983; Councillor for 4th canton, Fort-de-France, 1956–70; President, Conseil régional Martinique, 1983–86; President, Society of African Culture, Paris. Recipient: Laporte Prize, 1960; Viareggio-Versilia Prize for Literature, 1968; Grand Prix National de Poésie, 1982.

Works

Collections

Oeuvres complètes (3 vols.).   1976.

Stage Works

Et les chiens se taisaient.   1956.
La Tragédie du roi Christophe (produced Salzburg, 1964). 1963; revised edition, 1970; translated as *The Tragedy of King Christophe*, 1970.
Une Saison au Congo (produced by the Théâtre Vivant, Brussels, 1966). 1966; translated as *A Season in the Congo*, 1968.
Une Tempête: Adaptation pour un théâtre nègre, from *The Tempest by* Shakespeare (produced Hammamet, Tunisia, 1969). 1969; translated as *A Tempest*, 1985.

Verse

Les Armes miraculeuses.   1946; revised edition, 1970.
Cahier d'un retour au pays natal.   1947; revised edition 1956; translated as *Memorandum on My Martinique*, 1947; as *Return to My Native Land*, 1968; as *Notebook of a Return to the Native Land*, 1979.
Soleil cou-coupé.   1948; revised version, in *Cadastre*, 1961.
Corps perdu, with illustrations by Picasso.   1950; revised version, in *Cadastre*, 1961; translated as *Lost Body*, 1986.
Ferrements.   1960.
Cadastre.   1961; translated as *Cadastre*, 1973.
State of the Union, translated by Clayton Eshleman and Denis Kelly.   1966.
Aimé Césaire: Écrivain martiniquais (selected poems).   1977.
Moi, laminaire.   1982.
Collected Poetry, translated by Clayton Eshleman and Annette Smith.   1983.
Non-Vicious Circle: Twenty Poems, translated by Gregson Davis.   1984.
Lyric and Dramatic Poetry 1946–82, translated by Clayton Eshleman and Annette Smith.   1990.

Other

Discours sur le colonialisme.   1950; 5th edition, 1970; translated as *Discourse on Colonialism*, 1972.
Lettre ouverte à Maurice Thorez.   1956; translated as *Letter to Maurice Thorez*, 1957.
Toussaint Louverture: La Révolution française et le problème colonial.   1960; revised edition, 1962.
Culture and Colonization.   1978.

*

Bibliographies

Frederick I. Case, *Aimé Césaire: Bibliographie*, Toronto, 1973.
Thomas A. Hale, "Les Écrits d'Aimé Césaire, in *Études Littéraires*, 14, October 1978.

Criticism

Books:
Henock Trouillot, *L'Itinéraire d'Aimé Césaire,* Port au Prince, Haiti, 1968.
Rodney E. Harris, *L'Humanisme dans le théâtre d'Aimé Césaire,* Sherbrooke, Quebec, 1973.
Lilyan Kesteloot and Barthélémy Kotchy, *Césaire: L'Homme et l'oeuvre,* Paris, 1973.
Susan Frutkin, *Césaire, Black Between Worlds,* Florida, 1973.
M. a M. Ngal, *Césaire: Un Homme à la recherche d'une patrie,* Senegal, 1975.
Clément Mbom, *Le Théâtre d'Aimé Césaire ou la primauté de l'universalité humaine,* Paris, 1979.
Jacqueline Leiner (ed.), *Soleil éclaté: Mélanges offerts à Aimé Césaire,* Tübingen, 1984.
Aliko Songolo, *Aimé Césaire: Une Poétique de la découverte,* Paris, 1985.

Aimé Césaire ou l'Anthano d'un alchimiste (collection of essays), Paris, 1987.
Rémy S. Boulet, *Espaces et dialectique du héros césairien,* Paris, 1987.

Articles:
Seth L. Wolitz, "The Hero of Negritude in the Theater of Aimé Césaire", in *Kentucky Romance Quarterly,* 16, 1969.
Robert P. Smith, "The Misunderstood and Rejected Black Hero in the Theatre of Aimé Césaire", in *College Language Association Journal,* 16, 1972.

Serial:
Cahiers Césairiens, 1974–

*   *   *

The theatre of Aimé Césaire is replete with fascinating paradoxes. Striking on the one hand for the diversity and eclecticism of its author's art, on the other it is marked by the recurrence of a small number of central themes, largely associated with colonialism and its aftermath. It is a *théâtre engagé*. But Césaire the dramatist draws freely on the skills of Césaire the poet to explore complex political issues in a succinct and memorable way. And in addressing the present, he is more than ready to make telling use of a historical, mythic, or legendary past. Finally, Césaire's theatre exudes formidable erudition yet has popular appeal for a third-world public.

Both chronologically and stylistically, Césaire's first play, *Et les chiens se taisaient*, stands apart from the rest of his work for the theatre. In fact it might be more accurately described as a dramatic poem than as a play (indeed it was first published in an anthology of Césaire's poetry, *Les Armes miraculeuses*, before being adapted for the stage in 1956). It is a half-mythic, half-allegorical work, largely inspired by Césaire's reading of Nietzsche's *The Birth of Tragedy*, but in which such disparate influences as French surrealism and the tragedies of Aeschylus are also discernible. It is a cry of protest at the inhumanity of the colonial condition and an expression of man's need for freedom, whatever the cost. The action of the play is minimal. The protagonist has killed his white master in a slave revolt (recalled in Act II) and is awaiting death in prison. This comes in Act III and provides the play with its climax and resolution. Characterization is couched in terms of roles or functions (e.g. La Mère, L'Amante, Le Geôlier) rather than individual identities.

The text of the play is dense with allusion, aimed at reinforcing its symbolism. Le Rebelle, Césaire's hero, is subjected to a series of attempts to weaken his resolve. Clear parallels are discernible between these and the various temptations undergone by Christ. Elsewhere he is equated with Oedipus and Don Juan. Césaire's title itself rests upon a multiplicity of allusions: "les chiens" evoke the guard dogs used by white colonists to hunt down escaped slaves and by extension symbolize the colonists themselves. Moreover, some Martiniquais are said to believe that the dead may be reincarnated in canine form. The silence of the dogs may therefore signify white indifference to the fate of "Le Rebelle" (who actually asks the dogs to bark), but may also be intended to indicate that even those who are familiar with the pain of death are overawed by the intensity of his suffering. To European audiences, *Et les chiens se taisaient* has seemed a difficult work. But to a Caribbean public, its allusions have an altogether more familiar resonance.

Césaire's remaining three plays were all written within the

space of a decade and have more in common with each other than with *Et les chiens se taisaient*. All are written in an epic manner, though in the last of them this is coloured by a self-consciousness that may owe as much to Barthes as to Brecht. In all of them Césaire makes effective use of poetry, pageant, music, and song.

La Tragédie du roi Christophe is set in Haiti at the beginning of the 19th century and takes as its protagonist the hotel-servant turned soldier who became that country's second post-revolutionary ruler. *Une Saison au Congo* focuses on the turbulent last six months of 1960, during which the elected leader of the independent Congo, Patrice Lumumba, was deposed and met his death at the hands of Katangese rebels, manipulated by neo-colonialist interests.

Despite the difference in geographical and temporal setting, both works deal with problems facing black leaders in the immediate aftermath of independence and have a clear contemporary resonance. Henry Christophe is depicted as a man whose desperate drive to secure the foundations of an independent black nation leads him into brutality, tyranny, and murder. His best-remembered work is the *Citadelle de la Ferrière*, the construction of which he is seen supervising in the play. While he intends it as a manifest expression of the ability of a free black nation to withstand external aggression, the *Citadelle* becomes, in fact, not a monument to his people, who are forced to build it, but a symbol of their oppression. Césaire successfully reinterprets Christophe as a Promethean figure, with whose vision and determination it is impossible not to identify and by whose demise one cannot but be saddened. But his play is also an account of political failure. Christophe's inability to free his people from the alienation induced by centuries of colonialism sounds a warning to the leaders of newly independent Africa. Césaire eschews facile didacticism, however. The dilemma he explores is a complex one: how are we to judge a political regime which is at once totalitarian and progressive?

Une Tempête differs from Césaire's other works in that it is an adaptation of a previously existing text. Césaire modifies Shakespeare's *The Tempest* in a number of ways, to produce subtle, thought-provoking reversals at almost every turn. *Une Tempête* shares the three-act structure characteristic of Césaire's plays, and which has been held to reflect his attachment to dialectical reasoning. A New-World setting replaces Shakespeare's consciously Old-World one. Prospero becomes a smug tyrant who, selfishly, refuses to communicate his knowledge to the other inhabitants of the island, the better to dominate them. Caliban is a negro slave, while Ariel is a mulatto. These ethnic divisions have, historically, been a feature of Caribbean society; but they are also used symbolically by Césaire to examine differences in the political stances of black liberals and black radicals in 1960's America. Césaire's most significant change to Shakespeare's play is found at the end. Here a visibly decrepit Prospero remains on the island, in order—as he puts it—to save civilization. His enfeeblement, which contrasts strikingly with Caliban's growing exuberance, reflects the discredit into which the racism he represents has fallen. But Césaire's central point is that in modern America (and by extension the modern world) blacks and whites will inevitably have to live together. Today this realization is so commonplace as to seem trite. But this fact emphasizes the timeliness and accuracy of Césaire's vision.

Contemporaneity is one of the great strengths of Césaire's theatre. But the contemporary is ephemeral. Even the traumas of decolonization will fade from the collective memory, if they have not already done so. Those of Césaire's plays which deal exclusively with this period of history will, perhaps, have less appeal for a broad public, despite the fact that they are accessible and attractive as theatre. *Une Tempête*, which addresses the broader and more enduring question of cultural relativity, may consequently prove to be Césaire's most durable play.

—Tim Lewis

See also *Volume 1* entry on *A Season in the Congo*.

CHAPMAN, George. Born near Hitchin, Hertfordshire, England, in 1559 or 1560. Educated probably at Oxford University, possibly at Cambridge University; may have studied law at the Inner Temple, London. Lived on the Continent, 1585–91, and may have served with the forces of Sir Francis Vere in the Low Countries; returned to London and wrote for Philip Henslowe until 1599, then for the Children of the Queen's Revels until 1608; thereafter worked mainly on his translations; server-in-ordinary to Prince Henry, 1603–12; imprisoned in Tower of London for satirical references to James I in *Eastward Ho!*, 1605 (Jonson also imprisoned); given patronage by Earl of Somerset. Died in London, 12 May 1634.

Works

Collections

The Tragedies, edited by T.M. Parrot.   1910.
The Comedies, edited by T.M. Parrot.   1914.
Plays: The Comedies; The Tragedies, edited by Allan Holaday (2 vols.).   1970–87.

Stage Works

The Blind Beggar of Alexandria (produced by the Admiral's Men, Rose Theatre, London, 1956).   1598.
An Humorous Day's Mirth (produced by the Admiral's Men, Rose Theatre, London, 1597).   1599.
May Day (produced by the Children of the Queen's Revels, London, c.1601).   1611.
Sir Giles Goosecap, Knight (produced by the Chapel Children, Blackfriars Theatre, London, 1602).   1606.
The Gentleman Usher (produced by the Chapel Children, Blackfriars Theatre, London, 1602?).   1606.
All Fools (produced by the Children of the Queen's Revels, Blackfriars Theatre, London, 1604?).   1605.
Monsieur D'Olive (produced by the Children of the Queen's Revels, Blackfriars Theatre, London, 1604).   1606.
Bussy D'Ambois (produced by the Children of St. Paul's, London, 1604).   1607.
The Wars of Caesar and Pompey (produced before 1605?).   1631.
The Widow's Tears (produced by the Children of the Queen's Revels, Blackfriars Theatre, London, c. 1605).   1612.
Eastward Ho!, with Jonson and Marston (produced by the Children of the Queen's Revels, Blackfriars Theatre, London, 1605).   1605.
The Conspiracy and Tragedy of Charles, Duke of Byron, Marshal of France (produced by the Children of the Queen's Revels, Blackfriars Theatre, London, 1608).   1608.

The Revenge of Bussy D'Ambois (produced by the Children of the Queen's Revels, Whitefriars Theatre, London, 1610?). 1613.

Chabot, Admiral of France (produced London, c.1613). 1639, in a revision by Shirley (produced by Queen Henrietta's Men, Cockpit/Phoenix Theatre, London, 1635).

The Memorable Masque of the Middle Temple and Lincoln's Inn (produced at Court, Whitehall Palace, London, 1613). 1613.

Verse

The Shadow of Night, Containing Two Poetical Hymns. 1594.

Ovid's Banquet of Sense, a Coronet for His Mistress Philosophy, and His Amorous Zodiac. 1595; edited by Elizabeth Story Donno, in *Elizabethan Minor Epics*, 1963.

Seven Books of the Iliad of Homer. 1598; *Achilles' Shield*, 1598; *Twelve Books*, 1609(?); complete work, as *The Iliads of Homer*, 1611.

Hero and Leander, Begun by Marlowe, Finished by Chapman. 1598.

Euthymiae Raptus; or, The Tears of Peace, with Interlocutions. 1609.

An Epicede or Funeral Song on the Death of Henry Prince of Wales. 1612.

Petrarch's Seven Penitential Psalms, Paraphrastically Translated with Other Philosophical Poems and a Hymn to Christ upon the Cross. 1612.

Andromeda Liberata; or, The Nuptials of Perseus and Andromeda. 1614.

Eugenia; or, True Nobility's Trance for the Death of William Lord Russell. 1614.

Homer's Odyssey (12 books). 1614(?); complete work, 1615(?).

The Divine Poem of Musaeus. 1616.

The Whole Works of Homer (*Iliad* and *Odyssey*). 1616.

The Georgics of Hesiod. 1618.

Pro Vere Autumni Lachrymae, Inscribed to the Memory of Sir Horatio Vere. 1622.

The Crown of All Homer's Works, Batrachomyomachia, or, The Battle of Frogs and Mice, His Hymns and Epigrams. 1624(?).

A Justification of a Strange Action of Nero, Being the Fifth Satire of Juvenal Translated. 1629.

Poems, edited by Phyllis Brooks Bartlett. 1941.

Chapman's Homer: The Iliad, The Odyssey, and the Lesser Homerica (2 vols.), edited by Allardyce Nicoll. 1956; revised edition, 1967.

Selected Poems, edited by Eirian Wain. 1978.

Chapman's Minor Translations: A Critical Edition of His Renderings of Musaeus, Hesiod, and Juvenal, edited by Richard Corballis. 1984.

Other

A Free and Offenceless Justification of Andromeda Liberata. 1614.

*

Bibliographies

S.A. Tannenbaum, *George Chapman: A Concise Bibliography*, New York, 1938, supplement, 1946.

Charles A. Penel and W.P. Williams, *Elizabethan Bibliographies Supplements 4*, London, 1968.

Akihiro Yamada, "George Chapman: A Checklist of Editions, Biography, and Criticism, 1946–1965", in *Research Opportunities in Renaissance Drama*, vol. 10, 1967; "addenda", compiled by George W. Ray, in vol. 11, 1968.

Criticism

Books:

Paul V. Kreider, *Elizabethan Comic Character Conventions as Revealed in the Comedies of George Chapman*, Ann Arbor, Michigan, 1935.

John W. Wieler, *George Chapman: The Effects of Stoicism upon His Tragedies*, New York, 1949.

Jean Jacquot, *George Chapman: Sa vie, sa poésie, son théâtre, sa pensée*, Paris, 1951.

Ennis Rees, *The Tragedies of Chapman: Renaissance Ethics in Action*, Cambridge, Massachusetts, 1954.

Millar MacLure, *George Chapman: A Critical Study*, Toronto, 1966.

Charlotte Spivak, *George Chapman*, New York, 1967 (Twayne World Authors Series).

Peter Bement, *George Chapman: Action and Contemplation in His Tragedies*, Salzburg, 1974.

Derek Crawley, *Character in Relation to Action in the Tragedies of George Chapman*, Salzburg, 1974.

Leonard Goldstein, *George Chapman: Aspects of Decadence in Early Seventeenth-Century Drama*, Salzburg, 1975.

M.C. Bradbrook, *George Chapman*, London, 1977.

Richard S. Ide, *Possessed with Greatness: The Heroic Tragedies of Chapman and Shakespeare*, Chapel Hill, North Carolina, 1980.

Gerald Snare, *The Mystification of Chapman*, Durham, North Carolina, 1989.

* * *

The inscription on Inigo Jones's monument to Chapman in St Giles-in-the-Fields is now obliterated, but we are told that it once celebrated his old friend as *"philosophus verus"*. Anthony a Wood, however, gives a very different portrait. He records that Chapman studied at Oxford, where "he was observed to be most excellent in the *Lat.* and *Greeke* Tongues but not in Logic or Philosophy, and . . . that was the reason why he took no degree here".

From these two 17th-century accounts two conflicting traditions may be said to descend. The first stresses not only the breadth of Chapman's learning but also the coherence with which it is deployed. The second denies this coherence and concludes, with F.L. Schoell, that "la pensée reste amorphe et ne progresse selon aucune règle". Of today's two pre-eminent Chapman scholars one (Jean Jacquot) adheres to the former tradition, the other (Millar MacLure) to the latter.

If a man may be known by the company he keeps, then Chapman's close association with Ben Jonson should indicate his capacity for coherent thought. The two probably collaborated on the stage version of *Sejanus* and were certainly both involved—along with Marston—in the composition of *Eastward Ho!*. (Both plays landed them in trouble with the authorities.) Earlier they had traded recipes for comedy. Chapman first exploited "humours" as the basis for comic characterization in *An Humorous Day's Mirth*. Jonson promptly picked up the idea and, in *Everyman in His Humour* grafted it onto the four-part plot structure—*protasis, epitasis, katastasis, katastrophe*—derived ultimately from Terence. Chapman, in turn, adopted this structure in *All*

Fools, which is actually an adaptation of Terence's *Heautontimoroumenos*.

All Fools and the excellent later comedy *The Widow's Tears*, which is also "Terentian" in structure, prove that Chapman was capable of pressing his intellect into the service of content as well as form. Indeed he has some claim to be considered the foremost political playwright of his age. These two plays, along with the tragedy *Caesar and Pompey*, find him—like Jonson in the plays which he wrote at this time, *Sejanus* and *Volpone*—in a Machiavellian phase.

Most of Chapman's contemporaries—Marlowe (in *The Jew of Malta*), Shakespeare (in *Henry VI, Part Three* and *Richard III*) were content to caricature Machiavelli. *All Fools*, too, contains a caricatured "Machiavel" (Gostanzo), but alongside him we find an authentic Machiavellian (Rinaldo). Both are discredited in the end. In *Caesar and Pompey* and *The Widow's Tears*, however, the Machiavellian heroes (Caesar and Tharsalio respectively) triumph.

Once James I had established himself on the throne, Chapman set aside such provocative ideas, and was rewarded with a court appointment, as server-in-ordinary to Prince Henry. (This position no doubt helped him to secure the commission to compose a masque for the wedding of the Princess Elizabeth in 1613.) His new orthodoxy is evident in the sprawling *Byron* diptych, where the eponymous hero (who in some respects resembles the Earl of Essex) is tempted by the Machiavellian La Fin into challenging the enlightened rule of Henri IV of France. The King exhibits exemplary patience, but finally orders Byron's execution, and, although Byron gets a few fine speeches, there can be little doubt that he is rightfully condemned.

Some details of the portrait of Henri IV (the current French monarch) ruffled the feathers of the French Ambassador. Chapman found himself in trouble with the authorities once again, and the published text (especially Act IV of *The Conspiracy*) shows obvious signs of interference by the censor. But all this did not deter Chapman from depicting recent French history again in his last two tragedies.

The Revenge of Bussy D'Ambois confirms a tendency towards closet drama which can be found in all Chapman's tragedies; it is a spectacularly esoteric and undramatic celebration of a hero (Clermont D'Ambois) who turns his back on politics in order to cultivate "learning", friendship (with the Duke of Guise) and private virtue. Ironically it anticipates Chapman's own retreat from Court following the death of Prince Henry (1612).

Pressure from importunate creditors forced him to stay in the country (where he worked on his translation of Homer) until 1619. When he returned to the stage in 1621 (?), he had evidently mellowed, for *Chabot, Admiral of France* is a more human work than any of the other tragedies—a study of errors of judgement rather than of competing philosophical systems. This change of tone is no doubt attributable in part to the influence of James Shirley, who worked over the play before it was published in 1639. It may also have something to do with Chapman's affection for Robert Carr, Earl of Somerset, whose ill-fated career is reflected in Chabot's.

If *Chabot* is Chapman's most underrated work, his first tragedy—*Bussy D'Ambois* (another study of recent French history)—is certainly his most overrated. It is a controversial play; even estimates of its date of composition vary widely, from 1596 to 1604. Since the hero "neglects the light, and shuns obscure abodes", it is tempting to accept a date near the beginning of this spectrum—close to Chapman's earliest published work, the two-part poem *The Shadow of Night*, which celebrates "imperiall Night" at the expense of "shame-lesse Day". If we adopt the poem's frame of reference, Bussy can be seen as a consummate hero, a latter-day version of that Hercules who, in the closing lines of "Hymnus in Noctem" (the first part of *The Shadow of Night*) is urged to "fall . . . from heaven in tempestes hurld,/ And cleanse this beastly stable of the world".

Bussy is compared to Hercules on several occasions, and the King (Henri III), who hires him as an avenging "eagle", describes him as a specimen of prelapsarian man—"man in his native noblesse". Unfortunately, however, there seems to be a discrepancy between this rhetoric and many of Bussy's actions. His adultery with Tamyra and his conjuring of the spirit Behemoth in particular look decidedly postlapsarian, and most critics have concluded that, though Bussy may begin the play as a consummate hero, he is rapidly corrupted by the "policy" which he encounters at Court. The evocation of this atmosphere of corruption was perhaps the most memorable feature of Jonathan Miller's brave revival of the play at London's Old Vic in 1988.

The rhetorical flourishes on Bussy's behalf nevertheless persist to the end of play (where he is said to have undergone apotheosis). Thus *Bussy D'Ambois* brings us back to the question of Chapman's coherence. In fact, if we take Chapman's early worship of darkness seriously, there is a way of making sense of the play. The adultery, of course, takes place at night, and a close reading of the scenes in question suggest that this gave it special significance in Chapman's eyes. And Behemoth describes himself as "Emperor/ Of that inscrutable darkness where are hid/ All deepest truths, and secrets never seen". Thus—at least to Chapman personally—the play was probably coherent. His problem, here, as always, was to create an adequate public vehicle for these private convictions. The difficulty that this caused him is indicated in the moving poem prefixed to his 1598 translation of *Achilles' Shield*, where he wishes that Thomas Harriot had "organs to pierce/ Into that Chaos whence this stifled verse/ By violence breaks", where "genuine forms struggle for birth". Throughout Chapman's *oeuvre* the "forms" are "genuine", but the reader must usually labour hard to discern them.

—Richard Corballis

See also *Volume 1* entries on *Bussy D'Ambois*; *Eastward Ho!*

CHAYEFSKY, Paddy. Born Sidney Chayefsky in the Bronx, New York, USA, 29 January 1923. Educated at DeWitt Clinton High School, Bronx, graduated 1939; City College, New York, BS in social science 1943. Served in the US Army, 1943–45: private; Purple Heart. Married Susan Sackler in 1949; one son. Worked for a printer, New York, 1946; writer in Hollywood, late 1940's; gag writer for Robert Q. Lewis, New York, 1950; President, Sudan Productions, 1956, Carnegie Productions, 1957, SPD Productions after 1959, Sidney Productions after 1967, and Simcha Productions after 1971, all New York; council member, Dramatists Guild, from 1962. Recipient: Screen Writers Guild Award, 1954, 1971; Oscar, for screenplay, 1955, 1971, 1976; New York Film Critics Award, 1956, 1971, 1976; British Academy Award, 1976. Died in New York, 1 August 1981.

Works

Collections

Television Plays (includes *The Bachelor Party; The Big Deal; Holiday Song; Marty; The Mother;* and *Printer's Measure*). 1955.

Stage Works

No T.O. for Love, music by Jimmy Livingston (produced on services tour, 1945).
Middle of the Night (televised 1954; revised version, produced ANTA Theatre, New York, 1956). 1957.
The Tenth Man (produced Booth Theatre, New York, 1959). 1960.
Gideon (produced Plymouth Theatre, New York, 1961). 1962.
The Passion of Josef D. (produced Ethel Barrymore Theatre, New York, 1964). 1964.
The Latent Heterosexual (produced Dallas Theater Center, Dallas, Texas, 1968). 1967.

Screenplays

The True Glory (uncredited), with Garson Kanin, 1945; *As Young as You Feel*, with Lamar Trotti, 1951; *Marty*, 1955; *The Bachelor Party*, 1957 (published 1957); *The Goddess*, 1958 (published 1958); *Middle of the Night*, 1959; *The Americanization of Emily*, 1964; *Paint Your Wagon*, with Alan Jay Lerner, 1969; *The Hospital*, 1971; *Network*, 1975; *Altered States*, 1979.

Television Plays

Scripts for *Danger* and *Manhunt* series; *Holiday Song*, 1952 (published in *Television Plays*, 1955); *The Reluctant Citizen*, 1952; *Printer's Measure*, 1953, *Marty*, 1953, *The Big Deal*, 1953, and *The Bachelor Party*, 1953 (all published in *Television Plays*, 1955); *The Sixth Year*, 1953; *Catch My Boy on Sunday*, 1953; *The Mother*, 1954 (published in *Television Plays*, 1955); *Middle of the Night*, 1954; *The Catered Affair*, 1955; *The Great American Hoax*, 1957.

Radio Plays

The Meanest Man in the World, Tommy, and *Over 21* (all in *Theater Guild of the Air* series), 1951–52; scripts for *Cavalcade of America.*

Fiction

Altered States. 1978.

*

Criticism

Books:
John M. Clum, *Paddy Chayefsky*, Boston, 1976.

* * *

The Broadway drama of the 1950's was dominated by Arthur Miller and Tennessee Williams, the one focussing on ordinary people and using their stories to make political and social comment, and the other writing about the very human psychological and spiritual pains of society's outcasts and freaks. Almost every other playwright of the period can be placed somewhere on a continuum between the two giants; and one way of defining the early work of Paddy Chayefsky is as giving the Williams treatment to Miller characters. That is, in his most successful early plays, for television and film as well as for theatre, Chayefsky dissects the ordinary lives of ordinary people and finds tiny but moving drama within.

Among his theatrical plays, only *Middle of the Night* is as successful as his television play, *Marty*, in blending an accurate and intermittently satiric depiction of a milieu with the serious treatment given to the central story. The play is about a 53-year-old widower who falls in love with an unhappily married woman who is 30 years younger. She appreciates and returns his devotion, but friends and family on both sides are shocked by the mismatch, which seems to violate basic cultural taboos, and the lovers themselves are led to doubt their right to happiness. As in *Marty*, the very small question of whether these unremarkable people will stay together and have an ordinary chance of happiness is made a meaningful one through an unpatronizing respect for the reality of their emotions.

The careful balance of social reportage, satire, and sentimentality begins to break down in Chayefsky's next play, *The Tenth Man*, as he moves from what had been his area of strength—the characterization of ordinary people—toward a more abstractly philosophical focus. The play is about a congregation of elderly Jews who decide that the schizophrenic grand-daughter of one of them is really possessed by a demon and decide to exorcise it. They actually affect the dead-spirited young man they dragged off the street to participate in the ceremony; with renewed faith and love, he proposes to the girl. But the human story of the damaged young people reaching toward each other is buried in vague discussions about the nature of sanity and faith, and theatrically overpowered by the string of easy and patronizing jokes at the expense of the bored and confused old men.

That this movement away from small melodrama and toward philosophy mixed with social satire was deliberate is made obvious in the biblical play *Gideon*, which has almost no real human interaction, but rather builds to an interesting and challenging debate between Gideon and God about how man finds belief in an omnipotent deity too difficult and frightening because it leaves no place and dignity for humans. The ideas are not fully integrated into the play, coming almost as afterthoughts, and one must wade through too much easy humor built on the demythologized characterizations—God as a petulant old man, Gideon as a dim country hick—to get to them. Still, they are there, and give what would otherwise be a trivial play some weight.

After two commercial failures—*The Passion of Josef D.*, a misguided attempt to tell the story of Stalin through Brechtian devices which Chayefsky had not mastered, and *The Latent Heterosexual*, a satire on the dehumanizing power of success—Chayefsky left the theatre to concentrate on his parallel career as a screenwriter, where his best work resembled *Gideon* in placing thought-provoking ideas in otherwise unremarkable contexts.

Except for those who know him only from such late filmscripts as *The Hospital* and *Network*, Paddy Chayefsky will probably be remembered primarily as the author of *Marty*, a 1953 television play later expanded into a film. The title character is a New York butcher in his 30's, overweight and socially awkward, who is stuck in an extended adolescence of living with his mother and idly hanging out with his buddies. He meets an equally plain schoolteacher at a dance, and they clumsily begin a small courtship—and that is just about it. The material is obviously very fragile, and Chayefsky's skill lies in making the small story seem meaningful while still acknowledging its comic aspects, and without lapsing into preciousness.

Such films as *The Bachelor Party*, *The Americanization of Emily* and *Network* have in common the fact that they are all very conventional formula pieces into which Chayefsky was able to squeeze one or two scenes, discussions, or characterizing touches of unexpected depth. And that, indeed, might be the summation of Chayefsky's accomplishment on stage and screen: while less ambitious and talented writers settled for convention, and more ambitious writers stretched or challenged it, Paddy Chayefsky wrote little plays and films that were just a little deeper and better than one expected them to be.

—Gerald M. Berkowitz

CHEKHOV, Anton (Pavlovich). Born in Taganrog, Russia, 17 January 1860. Educated at a school for Greek boys, Taganrog, 1867–68; Taganrog grammar school, 1868–79; Moscow University Medical School, 1879–84, graduated as doctor 1884. Married the actress Olga Knipper in 1901. Practising doctor in Moscow, 1884–92, Melikhovo, 1892–99, and in Yalta after 1899; freelance writer while still in medical school, especially for humorous magazines, and later for serious ones; first-produced play, *Ivanov*, staged 1887; travelled to Sakhalin Island, 1890; suffered severe haemorrhage of the lungs, 1897; first collaborated with Nemirovich-Danchenko, Stanislavsky, and the Moscow Art Theatre, on a revival of *Chayka* [*The Seagull*], 1898; moved for reasons of ill-health to Yalta, 1899. Recipient: Pushkin Prize, 1888. Member, Imperial Academy of Sciences, 1900 (resigned 1902). Died in Badenweiler, Germany, 2 July 1904.

Works

Collections

Sobranie sochineny [Collected Works] (11 vols.). 1899–1906.
Plays (includes *Ivanov*; *The Sea Gull*; *Swan Song*; *Uncle Vanya*), translated by Marian Fell. 1912.
Plays by Anton Tchekhov (includes *The Anniversary; The Bear; The Cherry Orchard; On the High Road; The Proposal; The Three Sisters; A Tragedian in Spite of Himself; The Wedding*), translated by Julius West. 1916.
"The Cherry Orchard" and Other Plays includes *The Bear; The Proposal; The Sea Gull; Uncle Vanya*), translated by Constance Garnett. 1923.
The Plays of Anton Chekhov (includes *The Anniversary; The Cherry Orchard; On the High Road; The Sea Gull; Three Sisters; Uncle Vanya; The Wedding*), translated by Constance Garnett. 1929; supplemented with *The Bear*

Anton Chekhov reading *Chayka* [*The Seagull*] to the company of the Moscow Art Theatre, 1898: Konstantin Stanislavski is seated on Chekhov's right, and Vladimir Nemirovich-Danchenko is standing far left.

and *On the Harmfulness of Tobacco*, 1935; retitled *Nine Plays*, 1946.

Polnoe sobranie sochineny i pisem [Complete Works and Letters] (20 vols.), edited by S.D. Balukhaty and others. 1944–51; new edition (26 vols.), 1974–80.

"The Brute" and Other Farces (includes *The Brute; The Celebration; The Harmfulness of Tobacco; Marriage Proposal; Summer in the Country; Swan Song; A Wedding*), translated by Eric Bentley and Theodore Hoffman. 1958.

Plays, translated by Elisaveta Fen. 1959 (two earlier volumes reissued as one; includes *Ivanov; The Cherry Orchard; The Seagull; Uncle Vanya; Three Sisters; The Bear; The Proposal; A Jubilee*).

Six Plays of Chekhov (includes *The Cherry Orchard; Ivanov; The Sea Gull; The Three Sisters; Uncle Vanya; The Wood Demon*), translated by Robert Corrigan. 1962.

The Major Plays, translated by Ann Dunnigan. 1964.

The Oxford Chekhov (9 vols.), edited and translated by Ronald Hingley. 1964–80; excerpts as *Five Major Plays*, 1977, and various volumes of stories (see Fiction). Original volumes:
1: *On the High Road; Swan Song; The Bear; The Proposal; Tatyana Repin; A Tragic Role; The Wedding; The Anniversary; Smoking is Bad for You; The Night Before the Trial.*
2: *Platonov; Ivanov; The Seagull.*
3: *Uncle Vanya; Three Sisters; The Cherry Orchard; The Wood Demon.*
4–9: *Stories.*

Ten Early Plays (includes *The Anniversary; The Bear; On the Harmfulness of Tobacco; On the High Road; The Proposal; The Reluctant Tragedian; Swan Song; The Wedding; The Wood Demon; Ivanov*), translated by Alex Szogyi. 1965.

Four Plays (includes *The Cherry Orchard; The Sea Gull; The Three Sisters; Uncle Vanya*), translated by David Magarshack. 1969.

Plays (includes *The Cherry Orchard; Impure Tragedians and Leprous Playwrights; On the Injurious Effects of Tobacco* (1886 and 1902 versions)*; The Seagull; The Three Sisters; Uncle Vanya*), edited and translated by Eugene K. Bristow. 1977 (Norton Critical Editions).

Shutki [Farces]. 1978.

Collected Works (5 vols.; published in Moscow). 1987—

Plays (includes *The Seagull; Uncle Vanya; Three Sisters; The Cherry Orchard;* four vaudevilles), translated by Michael Frayn. 1988.

The Sneeze: Plays and Stories, translated by Michael Frayn. 1989.

Stage Works

O vrede tabaka. In *Peterburgskaya gazeta* [Petersburg Gazette], 1886; several revisions: final version in *Sobranie Sochineniy 14*, 1903; translated by Constance Garnett (in *Plays*, 1935) and others as *On the Harmfulness of Tobacco*; as *The Harmfulness of Tobacco*, in *"The Brute" and other Farces*, 1958; as *Smoking is Bad for You*, in *The Oxford Chekhov 1*, 1968; as *On the Injurious Effects of Tobacco*, in *Plays*, 1977.

Ivanov (produced Korsch's Theatre, Moscow, 1887; revised version, produced 1889). In *Pesy*, 1897; translated as *Ivanov*, in *Plays*, 1912; several subsequent translations under same title.

Lebedinaya pesnya (produced Korsch's Theatre, Moscow, 1888). In *Sezon* [The Season], 1, 1887; revised version in *Pesy*, 1897; translated as *Swan Song*, in *Plays*, 1912: several subsequent translations under same title.

Medved (produced Korsch's Theatre, Moscow, 1888). In *Novoye vremya* [New Time], 30 August 1888; revised version in *Pesy*, 1897; translated as *The Bear*, in *Plays*, 1916: several subsequent translations under same title; also translated as *The Boor*, 1915, and *The Brute*, in *"The Brute" and Other Farces*, 1958.

Leshy (produced Abramova Theatre, Moscow, 1889). 1890; translated as *The Wood Demon*, in *Calendar of Modern Letters*, 2, December 1925–January 1926: several subsequent translations under same title.

Predlozheniye (produced Artists' Club, St. Petersburg, 1889). 1889; revised version in *Pesy*, 1897; translated as *A Marriage Proposal*, 1914; as *The Proposal*, in *Plays*, 1916: several subsequent translations under same title.

Tragik ponevole (produced St. Petersburg, 1889). 1890; revised version in *Artist* [Artist], April 1890; translated as *A Tragedian in Spite of Himself*, in *Poet Lore*, Autumn 1922; as *An Unwilling Martyr*, in *"The Three Sisters" and Other Plays*, 1923; as *The Reluctant Tragedian*, in *Ten Early Plays*, 1965; as *A Tragic Role*, in *The Oxford Chekhov 1*, 1968.

Svadba (produced Moscow, 1900). 1890; translated as *The Wedding*, in *New Age*, nos. 16–17, 1915: several subsequent translations under same title (see Collections).

Yubiley (produced Society of Art and Literature, Moscow, 1900). 1892; revised version in *Svadba; Yubiley; Tri Sestry*, 1902; several translations as *The Anniversary* (see Collections); as *A Jubilee*, in *"The Sea Gull" and Other Plays*, 1953, as *The Celebration*, in *"The Brute" and Other Plays*, 1958.

Dyadya Vanya (produced in the Russian provinces, 1897). In *Pesy*, 1897; translated as *Uncle Vanya*, in *Plays*, 1912: several subsequent translations under same title.

Chayka (produced Alexandrinsky Theatre, St. Petersburg, 1896). In *Russkaya mysl* [The Russian Idea], December 1896; in book form, in *Pesy* [Plays], 1897; revised version, in *Sobranie sochineny* [Collected Works], 1901; translated as *The Sea Gull*, in *Plays*, 1912: several subsequent translations under same title.

Tri sestry (produced Moscow Arts Theatre, Moscow, 1901). In *Russkaya mysl* [The Russian Idea], 1901; in book form, 1901; revised version as supplement to *Sobranie sochineny* [Collected Works], 1902; translated as *The Three Sisters*, in *Plays*, 1916: several subsequent translations under same title, or as *Three Sisters*.

Vishnevy sad (produced Moscow Arts Theatre, Moscow, 1904). 1904; translated as *The Cherry Orchard*, 1908: several subsequent translations under same title.

Neizdannaya pesa, edited by N.F. Belchikov. 1923; translated as *That Worthless Fellow Platonov*, 1930; as *Don Juan (in the Russian Manner)*, 1952; as *Platonov*, 1964; as *Wild Honey*, 1984.

Tatyana Repin. In *Polnoe sobranie . . .*, 1944–51; translated as *Tatyana Repin*, 1927, and in *The Oxford Chekhov 1*, 1968.

Na bolshoy doroge. In *Polnoe sobranie . . .*, 1944–51; translated as *On the Highway*, in *Drama* (Chicago), 22, 1916; as *On the High Road*, in *Plays*, 1929: several subsequent translations under same title.

Fiction

Peostrye rasskazy [Motley Tales]. 1886; revised edition, 1891.

V sumerkakh [In the Twilight]. 1887.

Nevinnye rechi [Innocent Tales]. 1887.

Rasskazy [Tales]. 1889.
Khmurye lyudi [Gloomy People]. 1890.
Duel [The Duel]. 1892.
Palata No. 6 [Ward No. 6]. 1893.
Tales, translated by Constance Garnett (13 vols.). 1916–22.
The Unknown Chekhov: Stories and Other Writings Hitherto Untranslated, edited by A. Yarmolinsky. 1954.
Early Stories. 1960.
The Oxford Chekhov 4–9, translated by Ronald Hingley; excerpts as *Seven Stories*, 1974; *Eleven Stories*, 1975; *"The Russian Master" and Other Stories*, 1984; *"Ward Number Six" and Other Stories*, 1988; *"A Woman's Kingdom" and Other Stories*, 1989; *"The Princess" and Other Stories*, 1990; *"The Steppe" and Other Stories*, 1991.
Chuckle with Chekhov: A Selection of Early Stories. 1975.
The Early Stories 1883–1888, edited and translated by Patrick Miles and Harvey Pitcher. 1982.
"The Kiss" and Other Stories, translated by R. Wilks. 1982.
"The Duel" and Other Stories, translated by R. Wilks. 1984.
"The Party" and Other Stories, translated by R. Wilks. 1985.
"The Black Monk" and Other Stories, translated by Alan Sutton. 1985.
"The Fiancée" and Other Stories, translated by Alan Sutton. 1986.

Memoirs and Letters

Pisma [Letters]. 1909; *Sobraniye pisma*, 1910; *Pisma*, 1912–16, and later editions.
Zapisnye knizhki. 1914; as *The Note-Books*, 1921.
Letters to Olga Knipper. 1925.
Literary and Theatrical Reminiscences, edited by S.S. Koteliansky. 1927.
Personal Papers. 1948.
Selected Letters, edited by Lillian Hellman. 1955.
Letters, edited by Simon Karlinsky. 1973.

Other

Ostrov Sakhalin [Sakhalin Island]. 1895; translated as *The Island: A Journey to Sakhalin*, 1967.

*

Bibliographies

Anna Heifetz and A. Yarmolinsky (eds.), *Chekhov in English: A List of Works by and About Him*, New York, 1949.
Rissa Yachnin, *The Chekhov Centennial: Chekhov in English: A Selective List of Works by and About Him 1949–1960*, New York, 1960.
K.A. Lantz, *Anton Chekhov: A Reference Guide to Literature*, Boston, 1985.
Charles W. Meister, *Chekhov Bibliography: Works in English by and About Anton Chekhov*, Jefferson, North Carolina, 1985.

Criticism

Books:
William Gerhardie, *Anton Chekhov: A Critical Study*, London, 1923; revised edition, 1972.

Ronald Hingley, *Chekhov: A Bibliographical and Critical Study,* London, 1950; revised edition, 1966.
David Magarshack, *Chekhov the Dramatist*, New York, 1960.
Ernest J. Simmons, *Chekhov: A Biography*, London, 1962.
Maurice Valency, *The Breaking String: The Plays of Anton Chekhov*, Oxford, 1966.
Robert Louis Jackson (ed.), *Chekhov: A Collection of Critical Essays*, Englewood Cliffs, New Jersey, 1967.
J.L. Styan, *Chekhov in Performance: A Commentary on the Major Plays*, Cambridge, 1971.
David Magarshack, *The Real Chekhov: An Introduction to Chekhov's Last Plays*, London, 1972.
Siegfried Melchinger, *Anton Chekhov* (translated from the German), New York, 1972.
Harvey Pitcher, *The Chekhov Plays: A New Interpretation*, London, 1973.
Donald Rayfield, *Chekhov: The Evolution of His Art*, New York, 1975.
Ronald Hingley, *A New Life of Chekhov*, New York, 1976.
Beverly Hahn, *Chekhov: A Study of the Major Stories and Plays*, Cambridge, 1977.
Henry Urbanski, *Chekhov as Viewed by His Russian Literary Contemporaries*, Wrocław, Poland, 1979.
Irina Kirk, *Chekhov*, Boston, 1981.
Victor Emeljanow (ed.), *Chekhov: The Critical Heritage*, London, 1981.
Jean P. Barricelli (ed.), *Chekhov's Great Plays: A Critical Anthology*, New York, 1981.
Peter Urban, *Čechov Chronik: Daten zu Leben und Werk*, Zurich, 1981.
Vera Gottlieb, *Chekhov and the Vaudeville: A Study of Chekhov's One-Act Plays*, Cambridge, 1982.
Richard Peace, *Chekhov: A Study of the Four Major Plays*, New Haven, Connecticut, 1983.
Vera Gottlieb, *Chekhov in Performance in Russia and Soviet Russia* (book and slides), Cambridge, 1984.
René and Nonna D. Wellek (eds.), *Chekhov: New Perspectives*, Englewood Cliffs, New Jersey, 1984.
Toby W. Clyman (ed.), *A Chekhov Companion*, Westport, Connecticut, 1985.
Laurence Senelick, *Anton Chekhov*, London, 1985 (Macmillan Modern Dramatists series).
Henri Troyat, *Chekhov: A Biography* (translated from the French), New York, 1986.
Nick Worrall (compiler), *File on Chekhov*, London, 1986.
Carolina de Maegd-Soëp, *Chekhov and Women: Women in the Life and Work of Chekhov*, Columbus, Ohio, 1987.
V.S. Pritchett, *Chekhov: A Spirit Set Free*, New York, 1988.
Thomas A. Eekman (ed.), *Critical Essays on Anton Chekhov*, Boston, 1989.

*   *   *

If, as Dr. Chekhov once said, medicine was his wife and literature his mistress, what was his relationship with playwriting and the theatre? Perhaps he simply subsumed all of his literary work under the non-conjugal heading. Author of over 600 short stories, most of which are not published outside the Soviet Union, while only a handful are widely available in translation, Chekhov has acquired an international reputation as the writer of four full-length plays (if you include *Uncle Vanya*) written towards the end of his life when he was an increasingly sick man. Early plays such as *Ivanov* have had a mixed reputation and are rarely performed. *The Wood Demon* has hardly ever been performed at all, whilst *Platonov* has been staged infrequently and in severely cut versions or "adaptations". The one-act "jokes" (*shutki*)

Chekhov claimed to have dashed off in spare moments and, of the 12 one-acters, only two, *The Bear* and *The Proposal*, are performed with any degree of frequency and then, usually, by amateurs. Whence, then, Chekhov's reputation as a major European dramatist challenging comparison with Ibsen, Strindberg, Brecht, and Pirandello?

A great deal is made of Chekhov's "objectivity" as a dramatist and his sense of moral detachment, despite Gorky's claim that he was something of a didactic moraliser concerned to point out that people "lived badly". The famous productions staged by Stanislavsky and Nemirovich-Danchenko at the Moscow Art Theatre between 1898 and 1904 conceived of Chekhov's plays, in the main, as falling within the 19th-century naturalistic tradition, preoccupied with the surface detail of life viewed from a perspective where, in Chekhov's terms, dungheaps occupied just as respectable a place in the landscape as flower beds. This naturalistic approach characterised the Art Theatre productions from *The Seagull* to *The Cherry Orchard*, despite Chekhov's disapproval of the manner in which these two of his plays, in particular, were staged. Meyerhold, in a famous essay, criticised the Art Theatre's approach to Chekhov and emphasised the latter's "abstract" quality, linking him more with the symbolists.

Over the years, East and West have sought to enlist Chekhov to serve in their ideological struggles. This has found expression in differing approaches to the plays, veering from the revolutionary-cum-sociological, on the one hand, to one which draws its strength from notions of a "theatre of the absurd", on the other. In this battle, the "Moscow" to which the three sisters in their play hope to go, can be seen either as somewhere metaphorically and historically attainable, or merely as a site for regressive childhood fantasies, representing the unattainable and the chimerical. Within the terms of this ideological struggle, characters in *The Cherry Orchard*, for example, can be viewed either as sympathetic human beings with a meaningful past and future, or as meaningless puppets no longer supported by their metaphysical and social strings, the noise of whose sundering reverberates throughout that play. It is, perhaps, precisely this point of tension between approaches which points to a tension between opposites in Chekhov's drama and which makes his plays appear so interesting and apposite to this century. The interpretative oppositions can be seen to be based on tensions within the plays themselves, between tragedy and farce, the individual and the group, between realistically imagined human characters and dehumanised puppets, between drama and vaudeville, and between an indifferent, self-renewing natural world and the self-conscious, self-justifying, and self-destructive world of human beings.

In the scheme of Chekhov's work it is important not to neglect the significance of the so-called "vaudevilles" as well as his "apprentice" full-length plays when it comes to a consideration of his more "serious" work. It could, and perhaps should, be argued that plays such as *The Wedding* and *Platonov* are essential prerequisites to an understanding of Chekhov's development as a dramatist and that his "great" plays cannot be fully understood without reference to these earlier, neglected, works. Like the later plays, most of Chekhov's *shutki* have their (farcical) basis in the relationships between the sexes, focusing specifically on courtship and marriage. His best-known one-acters are either about unusual methods of courtship, or getting married, whilst others are about the awfulness of the married state and the mutual hostility, as well as the inevitable attraction, that exists between men and women. Love as farce could equally be said to fuel the plots of *Uncle Vanya* and *The Seagull*, whilst *Platonov* (which might more appropriately be titled

"The Platonist", "Platon" being the Russian for Plato) is a tragi-farce on the theme of love, ranging from the platonic to the passionate.

Ivanov, (whose stress falls on the "a" rather than the "o", making of him a Smythe rather than a Smith) is another tragi-farce on the theme of love, where the protagonist's grotesque sense of his own individual significance finds its parodied self-projection in Turgenev's universal prototypes of Hamlet and Don Quixote. Hamlet might also be said to be the "alter ego" of Konstantin, the playwright manqué in *The Seagull*, a play which is itself about love, mother love, and lovelessness as well as being about the relationship between life and art. The other figure to be sacrificed on the altar of realism in this play, and who identifies with the poetic symbol of the seagull, Nina, is also someone incapable of conceiving of the bird as a predator.

Chekhov's interest in ecology, in the relationship between unnatural man and a natural world, finds expression both in *The Wood Demon* and in *Uncle Vanya*; but even the ecological enthusiast is, like the others, contaminated by passions which are all-too-human and which can only find expression in frustrated or parodied forms. In *Three Sisters*, the characters appear to be caught in a tug-of-war between versions of the world seen, on the one hand, as naturalistically determined or, on the other, as infected by a sense of the absurd, where waiting for "Moscow" can be seen merely to anticipate waiting for Godot.

Finally, in *The Cherry Orchard*, the dying Chekhov appears to contemplate a world in which humanity itself is exhausted, reduced to a futile pattern of physical gestures, squeaky boots, pratfalls, and conversations with bookcases or with the setting sun. Here the very absence of humanity—an empty stage, sunlight and birdsong—can seem a consummation devoutly to be wished and even the party scene in Act III can appear, as it did to Meyerhold, symbolic of a dance of death. In Vershinin's famous philosophical soliloquies (in *Three Sisters*) he contemplates what the world will be like a millenium hence. One cannot help thinking that Chekhov's own dying mind contained the prospect of a future world which, as in Turgenev's "poem in prose", *The Conversation*, had returned, thankfully and peacefully, to a pristine state of nature.

—Nick Worrall

See also *Volume 1* entries on *The Cherry Orchard*; *Ivanov*; *The Seagull*; *The Three Sisters*; *Uncle Vanya*.

CHIARELLI, Luigi. Born in Trani (Bari), Italy, 7 July 1880. Brought up in Rome. Became a journalist, contributing regularly to *L'Alfieri* and *La patria* and publishing some poetry; moved to Milan, 1911, and edited *Il secolo*; two one-act plays, *Una notte d'amore* and *Er gendarme*, produced 1912; editor of the literary magazine *Armi e politica*; drafted into Italian army, 1915, but permitted to continue theatrical activites, and became director of Rome's Dramatic Theatre; co-founder, with Virgilio Talli, Ars Italica theatre company, Rome, 1918; became theatre critic for *Corriere italiano*, 1923; elected President of the Dramatists Union, 1925, and attended many conferences; film critic for *Il tempo* in the 1940's; adviser to the Italian Theatre Corporation, 1941–45. Died in Rome, 20 December 1947.

Works

Collections

Varietà (2 vols.).   1934.

Stage Works

Una notte d'amore (produced Teatro Verdi, Bologna, 1912).
Er gendarme [The Policeman] (produced Teatro Fossati, Milan, 1912).
Extra Dry (produced Teatro Olimpio, Milan, 1914).   1926.
La maschera e il volto (produced Teatro Argentina, Rome, 1916).   1917; translated as *The Mask and the Face*, in *International Modern Plays* (Everyman's Library), 1950.
La scale di seta (produced Teatro Argentina, Rome, 1917). 1922.
La portantina (produced Teatro Manzoni, Milan, 1917).
Le lacrime e le stelle (produced Teatro Argentina, Rome, 1918).   1918.
Chimere (produced Teatro Carignano, Turin, 1920).   1923.
Le gaie spose di Windsor, from *The Merry Wives of Windsor* by Shakespeare (produced Teatro Argentina, Rome, 1921). 1939.
Fuochi d'artificio (produced Teatro Alfieri, Turin, 1923). 1923.
La morte degli amanti (produced Teatro Valle, Rome, 1921). 1924.
Les Tripes à la mode de Caen (produced Teatro Arcimboldi, Milan, 1925).   1925.
Ciclo delle noci di cocco.   In *Il secolo*, April 1926.
Il libre nero.   In *La lettura*, April 1928.
La providente Lucilla.   In *Il secolo*, June 1928.
Jolly (produced Teatro Manzoni, Milan, 1928).   1929.
Don Juan.   In *Le grandi firme*, 1 May 1929.
La reginetta (produced Teatro Arcimboli, Milan, 1931). 1929.
Legger e scriveree (produced Teatro Arcimboldi, Milan, 1931).   1929.
K.41 (produced Teatro Politeama, Como, 1929).   1930.
L.E.F..   In *La lettura*, May 1930.
L'errore necessario.   In *Giovedi*, 15 May 1930.
Scaramanzia (produced Teatro Arcimboldi, Milan, 1931). 1931.
Un uomo da rifare (produced Teatro Manzoni, Milan, 1932). 1932.
Clara ha ragione.   In *Commedia*, 6, 1932.
Carne bianca.   1934.
La follia dell'oro.   In *Le grandi firme*, 15 April 1935.
Una più due (produced San Remo Casino, 1935).   1935.
Il cerchio magico (produced San Remo Casino, 1937).   1937.
Enea come oggi (produced San Remo Casino, 1937).   1937.
L'Aulalaria, from the play by Plautus (produced Teatro Romano, Ostia, 1938).   1938.
I Menaechmi, from the play by Plautus (produced Teatro Romano, Ostia, 1938).   1938.
Asmodeo, from a work by Mauriac (produced Teatro Manzoni, Milan, 1939).
Pulchinella.   1939.
Ninon.   1940.
Enrico VIII.   1941.
Il teatro in fiamme (produced Teatro Quirino, Rome, 1945).
Don Giovanni Tenorio, from a play by Zorilla.   1946.
Essere (produced Teatro Pirandello, Rome, 1953).   1953.

Radio Plays

L'anello di Teodosio, 1929.

*

Criticism

Books:
G. Gori, *Il grottesco nell'arte e nella letteratura*, Rome, 1926.
M. Lo Vecchio Musti, *L'opere di Luigi Chiarelli*, Rome, 1942.
Lander McLintock, *The Age of Pirandello*, Bloomington, Indiana, 1951.
Claudia Terzi, "Le poetiche del grottesco", in *L'idea del teatro e la crisa del naturalismo: Studi di poetica della spettacolo*, edited by L. Anceschi, Bologna, 1971.

Articles:
M. Vena, "Luigi Chiarelli (1880–1947): Profile of a Playwright", in *Connecticut Review*, vol. 7 no. 2, 1974.

* * *

Luigi Charelli's reputation, both inside and outside Italy, rests almost entirely on one play: *The Mask and the Face*. This play, which he himself designated as a "grotesque" in three acts, established what came to be called the "Grotesque" school or movement in Italian theatre, a tendency that has its clearest expression in some of Pirandello's earlier plays.

Chiarelli wrote the play around 1913 as a tragedy, for the plot revolves around the story of adultery, loss of face, and bitter ironic reversals. An unfaithful wife is sent away forever by her husband, who then claims he has killed her to avenge his honour. He is arrested, but declared innocent, and becomes a local hero for this supposed act of bravery. When a decomposing body is found in the nearby lake, the whole community assumes it is his wife, and a funeral takes place. The wife, meanwhile, turns up at the funeral and the play ends with husband and wife reconciled, running away together to start a new life. It has been pointed out that there are strong resemblances between this play and Synge's *Playboy of the Western World* (1907), and it is not impossible that there might have been a direct influence.

Nevertheless, when the play was first written, Chiarelli was unable to find any company willing to perform it, and in an article attacking the Grotesque in 1920, Marco Praga claimed that the problem was that the play which Chiarelli had written as a tragedy was in fact so funny that it could only be played as comedy. Praga suggests that Chiarelli realized that there was more money to be made by comedy than badly written realist tragedy, and so the concept of the grotesque was born. Chiarelli himself admits that Virgilio Talli found the play extremely funny on first reading, and when it was eventually performed in 1916 (in May in Rome and in August in Milan) it was a huge success. Italy had entered World War I, and the tone of the play, with its bitterness and cynicism, had great public appeal.

Pirandello's essay on the Grotesque (1920) uses the image of a tree apparently covered in beautiful blossom that turns out, on closer inspection, to be a dead tree covered with little white snails. The illusion of beauty that is created by the horrible is what constitutes the grotesque, and so in Chiarelli's play, the nobility of tragedy is actually a squalid piece of play acting, and the behaviour of the unfaithful wife, the vain husband, and the hypocritical neighbours, is equally despicable. There is, however, a hint of a solution, something that we would never find in a Pirandello play: the final stage directions show Paolo and his wife reunited in love, and as they leave the stage there is a message of hope for a new future.

The vogue for the Grotesque was short-lived, which is not surprising, given its limitations. The Grotesque was principally a movement (if indeed it can even be termed such) that relied on shock effects of plot, while still utilizing the conventional form of the well-made play. Chiarelli's grotesque is a mood rather than a genre, and once that mood was no longer fashionable, with the end of the War and Mussolini's rise to power, the Grotesque dwindled away, and by the mid-1920's it had virtually disappeared. Chiarelli continued to write plays, though with diminished success, because he was not a particularly skilful dramatist, and in consequence his style barely developed at all.

Both in tone and content, Chiarelli's plays can be compared to the work of Jean Anouilh in France, who also deals with love triangles and the relativity of truth and perception in a somewhat lightweight manner. In fact, although Chiarelli has been hailed as a prominent name in the Italian theatre around the time of World War I, he left no lasting impact on the Italian theatre. Compared to Pirandello, his dramatic skills are negligible. Walter Starkie, who recognizes the importance of *The Mask and the Face* as a play of its time, mentions the parallels with Synge and comments aptly that Chiarelli is "a dweller in the plain". He does, however, give Chiarelli credit for being a skilful parodist.

Luigi Chiarelli was a man with a passion for the theatre, who worked hard and had some good critical insights into theatre, but who did not have any great originality, for the Grotesque was certainly not his own invention. What Chiarelli did was to take a term in vogue and apply it specifically to his own play, distinguishing it from traditional genres, and making it appeal to the soul of the age.

—Susan Bassnett

See also *Volume 1* entry on *The Mask and the Face*.

CHIKAMATSU Monzaemon. Born Sugimori Jirokichi (adult name Nobumori) into a samurai family, in Echizen Province (now in Fukui district), Japan, 1653. Family moved to Kyoto, c.1667. Married (wife died 1734); two sons. In the service of Ichijo Zenkakuekan, a nobleman, until c.1671–72; began writing plays, at first for Uji Kadayū [Kaga-no-jō] and other chanters of the *jōruri* (puppet) theatre; first signed play was *Yotsugi soga* [The Soga Heir], 1683; wrote for the chanter Takemoto Gidayū's theatre, Takemoto-za, in Osaka; also wrote kabuki plays, from 1684; house writer for Sakata Tōjūrō I's theatre, Miyako-za, in Kyoto, 1695–1703; following Tōjūrō's retirement, c.1703, resumed collaboration with Gidayū, in Osaka; wrote solely for the puppet theatre, chiefly in the genres of the domestic drama (*sewamono*) and historical play (*jidaimono*), after c.1705; moved back to Osaka, and became staff writer for the Takemoto-za, 1706; wrote last plays, c.1723. Died in Osaka, 1725.

Works

Collections

Works (10 vols.), edited by Takam Tatsuyuki and Kuroki Kanzo. 1924.

Works (16 vols.), edited by Kitano Hogi. 1925.
Chikamatsu zenshū [Complete Works] (12 vols.) edited by Fujii Otoo. 1927.
Masterpieces of Chikamatsu (includes *The Courier for Hades; The Love Suicide at Amijima; The Adventures of the Hakata Damsel; The Tethered Steed*), translated by Asatoro Miyamori. 1926.
Major Plays of Chikamatsu (includes *The Love Suicides at Sonezaki; The Drum of the Waves of Horikawa; Yosaku from Tamba; The Love Suicides in the Women's Temple; The Courier for Hell; Gonza the Lancer; The Uprooted Pine; The Girl from Hakata*), translated by D. Keene. 1961.

Stage Works (selected *jōruri* plays)

Yotsugi Soga [The Soga Heir] (produced 1683).
Shusse Kagekiyo [Kagekiyo Victorious] (produced 1686).
Semimaru (produced 1686). Translated as *Semimaru*, in *The Legend of Semimaru*, by S. Matisoff, 1978.
Sonezaki Shinjū (produced 1703). Translated as *The Love Suicides at Sonezaki*, in *Major Plays of Chikamatsu*, 1961.
Yomei Tenno Shokunin Kagami (produced 1705).
Horikawa Nami no tsuzami (produced 1706). Translated as *The Drum of the Waves of Horikawa*, in *Major Plays of Chikamatsu*, 1961.
Shinjū nimai ezōshi [Love Suicide and the Double Folded Picture Books] (produced 1706).
Shinjū Kasaneizutsu [Love Suicide at the Sunken Well] (produced 1707).
Tamba Yosaku (produced 1708). Translated as *Yosaka from Tamba*, in *Major Plays of Chikamatsu*, 1961.
Shinjū Mannensō (produced 1708). Translated as *The Love Suicides in the Women's Temple*, In *Major Plays of Chikamatsu*, 1961.
Keisei Hangoko (produced 1708).
Imamiya shinjū [Love Suicide at Imamiya] (produced 1711).
Meido no Hikyaku (produced 1711). Translated as *The Courier for Hades*, in *Masterpieces of Chikamatsu*, 1926; as *The Courier for Hell*, in *Major Plays of Chikamatsu*, 1961.
Yugiri Awa no Naruto (produced 1712). Part translated as *Love Letter from the Licensed Quarter*, in *Kabuki*, by James R. Brandon, 1975.
Kokusenya Kassen (produced 1715). Translated as *The Battles of Coxinga*, in *Major Plays of Chikamatsu*, 1961.
Ikudama shinjū [Love Suicide at Ikudama] (produced 1715).
Yari no Gonza (produced 1717). Translated as *Gonza the Lancer*, in *Major Plays of Chikamatsu*, 1961.
Nebiki no Kadomatsu (produced 1718). Translated as *The Uprooted Tree*, in *Major Plays of Chikamatsu*, 1961.
Soga Kaikeizan (produced 1718). Translated as *The Soga Revenge*, in *Outline History of the Japanese Drama*, by F.A. Lombard, 1928.
Heike Nyogo no shima (produced 1719). Part translated in *The Art of Kabuki: Famous Plays in Performance*, by Samuel L. Leiter, 1979.
Hakata Kojorō Namimakura (produced 1719). Translated as *The Adventures of the Hakata Damsel*, in *Masterpieces of Chikamatsu*, 1926; as *The Girl from Hakata*, in *Major Plays of Chikamatsu*, 1961.
Shinjū Ten no Amijima (produced 1721). Translated as *The Love Suicide at Amijima*, in *Masterpieces of Chikamatsu*, 1926; as *The Love Suicides at Amijima*, 1953.
Onnagoroshi Abura Jigoku (produced 1721). Translated as *The Woman Killer and the Hell of Oil*, in *Major Works of Chikamatsu*, 1706.

Pages from the 1703 text of *Sonezaki shinjū* [*Love Suicides at Sonezaki*] by **Chikamatsu**.

Kwan-Hasshu Tsunagi.   Translated as *The Tethered Steed*, in
    Masterpieces of Chikamatsu, 1926.
Kaoyo Utragaruta.   Translated as *Fair Ladies at a Game of
    Poem-Cards*, in *Masterpieces of Chikamatsu*, 1926.
Koi Hakkée Hashiragoyomi.   Translated as *The Almanac of
    Love*, in *Masterpieces of Chikamatsu*, 1926.

*

Criticism

Books:

Detlef Schauwacker, *Studien zu Chikamatsu Monzaemon*,
    Kyoto, 1975.
Donald Keene, *World Within Walls*, 1976.
Andrew C. Gerstle, *Circles of Fantasy*: *Convention in the
    Plays of Chikamatsu*, Cambridge (Massachusetts) and
    London, 1986.

*   *   *

Chikamatsu, sometimes referred to as the "Japanese
Shakespeare" (as in the subtitle to Asatoro Miyamori's 1926
collection of translations, *Masterpieces of Chikamatsu*), is
widely considered Japan's most notable dramatist. Born in
1653, he became a major writer of the end of the 17th century

and beginning of the 18th, producing plays for the puppet
theatre (*ningyo jōruri*) and, in the middle period of his career,
for the kabuki stage.

In Chikamatsu's day, the puppet theatre consisted of relatively simple puppets, operated from beneath the stage, with
music provided by a *shamisen* player, and the dialogue, scenic
evocations, and commentary delivered by a chanter. The
plots drew largely on traditional forms and subject matter,
including semi-historical stories of war and scenes of allegorical journeys (*michiyuki* scenes), but, as with any great dramatist, Chikamatsu is notable for his distinctive use of, and
modifications to, existing conventions. Thus, the first play to
which Chikamatsu's name is attached, *Yotsugi Soga* (The
Soga Heir), based its plot on a traditional revenge tale concerning the Soga brothers, but introduces two courtesans who
imbue the play with a level of pathos through their discussions
of the pitfalls of love with the mother of the dead Soga
brothers. Though this play is often considered crude and
clumsy in many respects, already evident in it is the increased
sophistication of emotional content brought about through
the use of the mistress/courtesan figure — a figure that was to
become characteristic of Chikamatsu. In his next important
play, *Shusse Kagekiyo* (Kagekiyo Victorious), the mistress of
Kagekiyo is, according to one critic, "a believable woman
with the contradictions and complexities that distinguish human beings from puppets", and possesses a "genuine tragic
intensity".

Shusse Kagekiyo was written for the famous chanter Takemoto Gidayū, with whom Chikamatsu was collaborating from 1686. But (and perhaps logically, considering his increasing "humanization" of character-types), Chikamatsu turned increasingly towards the kabuki theatre of live actors, and wrote almost exclusively for the kabuki stage from 1693 to 1703, becoming a contracted writer for the actor Sakata Tōjūrō I in Kyoto. He probably wrote about 30 kabuki plays, but those that have survived (rarely in complete forms) are not regarded as highly as the puppet plays by most commentators. Above all, and perhaps to Chikamatsu's disappointment, kabuki theatre was one in which the actor was pre-eminent, and the writer's scripts, often produced in collaboration, were more bases for histrionic improvisation than structured, literary products.

Whether because of any artistic limitations of the kabuki stage, the retirement of Tōjūrō, the resurgence in popularity of Gidayū's puppet theatre, or other reasons (an open biographical question which has intrigued scholars and theatre historians), Chikamatsu returned to writing puppet plays in the early 1790's, and wrote almost wholly in this form after 1795. It is from this period that those works generally considered his masterpieces derive. The later puppet plays fall into two categories—the *sewamono* form (domestic tragedies, also described as 'dramas of contemporary life') and the *jidaimono* form (historical plays).

In the *sewamono* category are the "love suicide" plays, notably *The Love Suicides at Sonezaki* and *The Love Suicides at Amijima*. The former of these drew on actual reports of the suicide of a pair of lovers, a shop-assistant and a prostitute, and formed the basis for this entire genre of puppet plays. Chikamatsu wrote more than 11 "love suicide" plays, whose plots were usually based on the efforts of the male lover to buy his beloved from the brothel where she has been sent by her father, with the tragic element often involving the destitution brought about thereby. The characters' heroism does not derive from any innate "superhuman" qualities or attributes, but emerges through their struggles, sacrifices, and depth of their love—elements brought out particularly in the *michiyuki* scenes. Chikamatsu was able to make extensive use of irony, tragic pathos, social and economic realism, to produce an extremely popular dramatic concoction—indeed one so popular that the plays increased the rate of such suicides in real life, causing consternation for the authorities and new legislation criminalizing such suicide attempts.

Most of the plays of the *jidaimono* category, the historical plays, have faded into relative obscurity, although Chikamatsu composed around 50 of them, and they were given higher priority in the theatre of his time. Nevertheless, the category does contain the play sometimes cited as his greatest achievement—*The Battles of Coxinga*. It was certainly his greatest popular success, achieving an extraordinary run of around 17 months. Its treatment of history is highly fantastic—it presents the story of the almost single-handed rescue of the Ming dynasty in China from the Tartar tyranny by a half-Chinese, half-Japanese fisherman—and its contrasts are stark in tone, including broad humour, heroic and sensational feats, vivid exploitation of the audience's unfamiliarity with a foreign setting, and, by virtue of the hero's semi-Japanese lineage, patriotic appeal.

Such a play as *The Battles of Coxinga* is a world away from the concerns of the *sewamomo* works, and it is the latter which tend to be the better known today, particularly in the West. The Japanese theatre director Yukio Ninagawa recently visited Britain's National Theatre with his own highly successful synthesis of themes and scenes from several of Chikamatsu's "love suicide" plays.

—Noel Stanley

See also *Volume 1* entry on *The Battles of Coxinga*.

CHILDRESS, Alice. Born in Charleston, South Carolina, USA, 12 October 1920. Educated at schools in Harlem, New York; Radcliffe Institute for Independent Study (scholar), 1966–68, graduated 1968. Married 2) the musician Nathan Woodard; one daughter by first marriage. Actress and director, American Negro Theatre, New York, 1941–52; first play, *Florence*, produced 1949; columnist ("Here's Mildred"), Baltimore *Afro-American*, 1956–58; has collaborated with her husband on some works; contributor of articles on Afro-American literature and theatre to various publications; artist-in-residence, University of Massachusetts, Amherst, 1984. Recipient: Obie Award, 1956, and several other prizes.

Works

Stage Works

Florence (produced American Negro Theatre, New York, 1949). In *Masses and Mainstream*, October 1950.
Just a Little Simple, adaptation of stories by Langston Hughes (produced Club Baron Theatre, New York, 1950).
Gold Through the Trees (produced Club Baron Theatre, New York, 1952).
Trouble in Mind (produced Greenwich Mews Theatre, New York, 1955). In *Black Theatre: A Twentieth-Century Collection of the Work of Its Best Playwrights*, edited by Lindsay Patterson, 1971.
Wedding Band (produced University of Michigan, Ann Arbor, Michigan, 1966). 1974.
The World on a Hill. In *Plays to Remember*, 1968.
Young Martin Luther King, music by Nathan Woodard (produced by Performing Arts Repertory Theatre, on tour, 1969).
String, from a story by Maupassant (produced St. Mark's Playhouse, New York, 1969). With *Mojo*, 1971.
Mojo (produced New Heritage Theatre, New York, 1970). With *String*, 1971.
When the Rattlesnake Sounds (for children), illustrated by Charles Lilly. 1975.
Let's Hear it for the Queen (for children), illustrated by Loring Eutemey. 1976.
Wine in the Wilderness, from the television play (produced New York, 1976).
Sea Island Song (produced Stage South, Charleston, South Carolina, 1977; produced as *Gullah*, Amherst, Massachusetts, 1984).
Moms: A Praise Play for a Black Comedienne, music and lyrics by Childress and Nathan Woodard (produced Art Awareness, New York, 1987).

Screenplays

A Hero Ain't Nothin' But a Sandwich (from the novel), 1977.

Television Plays

Wine in the Wilderness, 1969 (published 1970); *Wedding Band*, 1973; *String*, 1979.

Fiction

A Hero Ain't Nothin' But a Sandwich (for children).   1973.
A Short Walk.   1979.
Rainbow Jordan (for children).   1981.
Those Other People (for children).   1989.

Other

Like One of the Family: Conversations from a Domestic's Life.   1956.
Editor, *Black Scenes: Collections of Scenes from Plays Written by Black People about Black Experience*.   1971.

*

Criticism

Books:
Janet Brown, *Feminist Drama: Definition and Critical Analysis,* Metuchen, New Jersey, 1979.
Samuel A. Hay, "Alice Childress's Dramatic Structure", in *Black Women Writers (1950–1980)*, edited by Mari Evans, Garden City, New York, 1984.
Elizabeth Brown-Guillory, *Their Place on Stage: Black Women Playwrights in America*, New York, 1988.

Articles:
Gayle Austin, "Alice Childress: Black Woman Playwright as Feminist Critic", in *Southern Quarterly*, vol. 25 no. 3, 1987.

* * *

Alice Childress's contribution to 20th-century American theatre is remarkable. She came to playwriting after 11 years as an actor with the American Negro Theatre and, in her writing career, has many achievements which mark her importance as a playwright.

Her 1952 play, *Gold Through the Trees*, was the first by a black woman to be produced professionally. The Obie award she won for *Trouble in Mind* was the first for a woman playwright. *Wedding Band* was the first play to show an inter-racial relationship on the stage. Indeed, Childress's commitment to develop her playwriting in the context of a theatre for, and of, black people has been often demonstrated. Alongside the many plays, she has edited a book of scenes for black actors and has written for young audiences too.

Childress's plays invariably deal with emotional relationships and the tensions within them. Sometimes the cause of such tension is overt as in the inter-racial relationship of Julia and Herman (in *Wedding Band*). Other times it is caused by fears which are provoked by the inevitable insecurity of being black in a white person's world. In her history-drama *When The Rattlesnake Sounds* (based on the life of escaped slave and underground railway-worker Harriet Tubman), Celia reveals a very real fear of being found working with Harriet for whom there is a $40,000 reward outstanding. In *Mojo* Irene faces an imminent hospital treatment where she sees herself lying on a white sheet in a white room where a white man with a white mask will put her to sleep so that another white man in a white suit can cut her open.

Childress shows again and again in her drama how marginalized position breeds fear and tension within a community. This is perhaps best portrayed in the action of *String*, a play set at an annual block association picnic. Here, Joe is sus-pected of stealing a wallet for two simple reasons: first, because he was seen picking something up (in fact a piece of string that one of the women had dropped), and second, because of his unconventional appearance and behaviour. L.V. Craig, the owner of the lost wallet, has all the power and credibility because of his appearance—he is wearing a suit—and his ownership of a bar. The action shows Joe to be the most honest and also the most misunderstood person in the community. Everyone recognizes the deceit of Craig—he cheats his customers and has apparently shot a man some time previously—but nevertheless respects him because of his economic position. Like much of her writing, *String* demonstrates that justice is determined both in terms of race and class.

Childress's work contributed significantly to a developing black women's theatre and her texts foreground her own personal experience. Childress was born in South Carolina, where her great-grandmother had been a slave, and raised in Harlem. The importance of her roots was acknowledged when the South Carolina Commission for the Arts asked her to prepare a play to tour in the state's schools and in response Childress wrote *Gullah*, a musical play for which her husband, Nathan Woodard, wrote the score. "Gullah" is a language spoken only on some of the islands off the South Carolina coast and Childress wanted to capture the poetry of these people (which included her stepfather). The South Carolina Commission for the Arts, however, objected to the title, because of its sometime use to disparage country people, and substituted *Sea Island Song*. This act was itself a testament to Childress's sense that her work is inevitably read out of context (in other words, in the context of the dominant white culture and its prejudices and sensitivities). *Gullah*, as does much of Childress's writing, recoups and celebrates black American history for black Americans.

Perhaps the most significant contribution of Childress's playwriting, however, is her creation of many major female characters. Cynthia in *Wine in the Wilderness* leads Tommy (Tommorrow Marie) away from idealized (male) notions of the women's role towards a sense of her own self. As Tommy projects her new-found confidence, she not only attracts the artist, Bill, but becomes the model to represent the future in the triptych of past, present, and future that he is painting. In the two-hander *Mojo*, it is Irene who shows her ex-husband, Teddy, how his success has been conceived in "white" terms. It is not coincidental that Teddy's girlfriend (never seen on stage) is a white woman. Here, as in other Childress plays, the events which touch the characters' lives are those which affect the working-class black community in America—drugs, family violence, teenage pregnancy, exploitation by white consumerism. Against such a background, however, Childress creates characters who behave with dignity and humanity. There are no easy solutions in Childress's plays, but realistic, honest, and brave ways of coping.

The plays achieve Childress's aim to present the experience of black Americans. She intends to present ordinary people in their everyday world; she looks not to the extraordinary few winners, but to the many and commonplace losers. Her plays show a keen awareness, too, of class and of gender. Childress has acknowledged that in many ways she has been doubly disadvantaged because she writes both as a black and as a woman. She has commented that it is not that critics have always and necessarily dealt with her work unfairly, but that their criteria are always theirs (thus primarily white and male). Hers, then, is a theatre of resistance. The plays have been successful in the mainstream (perhaps particularly marked by the translation of some into television productions), but Childress has apparently never compromised her aims in order to gain that success. For this reason, she has been a remarkable role model for other black and women writers.

—Susan Bennett

See also *Volume 1* entry on *Wedding Band*.

CHURCHILL, Caryl.   Born in London, 3 September 1938. Educated at Trafalgar School, Montreal, 1948–55; Lady Margaret Hall, Oxford, 1957–60, BA in English 1960. Married David Harter in 1961; three sons. First play, *Downstairs*, produced 1958; collaborated with Monstrous Regiment and Joint Stock theatre companies in the 1970's and 1980's; resident dramatist, Royal Court Theatre, London, 1974–75. Recipient: Obie Award, 1982, 1983, and 1988; Society of West End Theatre Award, 1988.

Works

Collections

Plays 1 (includes *Owners; Vinegar Tom; Traps; Light Shining in Buckinghamshire; Cloud Nine*).   1985.
Plays 2 (includes *Softcops; Top Girls; Fen; Serious Money*).   1990.

Caryl Churchill

Shorts (includes *Lovesick; Abortive; Not, Not, Not, Not, Not Enough Oxygen; Schreber's Nervous Illness; The Hospital at the Time of the Revolution; The Judge's Wife; The After-Dinner Joke; Seagulls; Three More Sleepless Nights; Hot Fudge*).   1990.

Stage Works

Downstairs (produced Oxford, 1958).
Having a Wonderful Time (produced Oxford, 1960).
Easy Death (produced Oxford, 1962).
Schreber's Nervous Illness (produced King's Head Theatre, London, 1972).   In *Shorts*, 1990.
Owners (produced Royal Court Theatre Upstairs, London, 1972).   1973.
Perfect Happiness (produced Soho Poly Theatre, London, 1974).
Moving Clocks Go Slow (produced Royal Court Theatre Upstairs, London, 1975).
Objections to Sex and Violence (produced Royal Court Theatre Upstairs, 1975).   In *Plays by Women 4*, edited by Michelene Wandor, 1985.
Light Shining in Buckinghamshire (produced Traverse Theatre, Edinburgh, 1976).   1978.
Vinegar Tom (produced Arts Centre, Hull, 1976).   1978.
Traps (produced Royal Court Theatre Upstairs, London, 1977).   1978.
Floorshow, with others (produced North London Poly Centre, London, 1978).
Cloud Nine (produced Royal Court Theatre, London, 1979).   1979.
Three More Sleepless Nights (produced Soho Poly Theatre, London, 1980).   In *Shorts*, 1990.
Top Girls (produced Royal Court Theatre, London, 1982).   1982; revised version, 1984.
Fen (produced University of Essex, Colchester, then Almeida Theatre, London, 1983).   1983.
Softcops (produced The Pit, Barbican Centre, London, 1984).   1984.
Midday Sun, with Geraldine Pilgrim, Pete Brooks, and John Ashford (produced 1984).
A Mouthful of Birds, with David Lan (produced Royal Court Theatre, London 1986).   1987.
Serious Money (produced Royal Court Theatre, London, 1987).   1987.
Icecream (produced Royal Court Theatre, London, 1989).   1989.
Mad Forest (produced Royal Court Theatre, London, 1990).
The Hospital at the Time of the Revolution.   In *Shorts*, 1990
Seagulls.   In *Shorts*, 1990.
Hot Fudge.   In *Shorts*, 1990.
The Lives of the Great Poisoners, music by Orlando Gough (dance libretto; produced Arnolfini Arts Centre, Bristol, 1991).   1993 ("production dossier").

Television Plays

The Judge's Wife, 1972 (published in *Shorts*, 1990); *Turkish Delight*, 1974; *The After-Dinner Joke*, 1978 (published in *Shorts*, 1990); *The Legion Hall Bombing*, 1978; *Crimes*, 1982.

Radio Plays

The Ants, 1962 (published in *New English Dramatists 12*, 1968); *Lovesick*, 1967 (published in *Shorts*, 1990); *Identical Twins*, 1968; *Abortive*, 1971 (published in *Shorts*, 1990); *Not, Not, Not, Not, Not Enough Oxygen*, 1971 (published in

Shorts, 1990); *Schreber's Nervous Illness*, 1972; *Henry's Past*, 1972; *Perfect Happiness*, 1973.

*

Criticism

Books

Phyllis R. Randall (ed.), *Caryl Churchill: A Casebook,* New York, 1988.
Linda Fitzsimmons (ed.), *File on Churchill,* London, 1989.
Geraldine Cousin, *Churchill the Playwright,* London, 1989.
Amelia Howe Kritzer, *The Plays of Caryl Churchill,* London, 1991.

* * *

Caryl Churchill's professional career as a playwright started in her 20's, with radio plays. These facts are important for an understanding of the unique strengths of her stage output. Her male contemporaries, such as Brenton and Hare, largely served their apprenticeship in the fringe theatre and their plays tended to articulate the romantic socialism of the late 1960's through bold theatrical effects which could be achieved with small casts and few financial resources. Radio—far easier to break into than the theatre for a young woman in an era so much less egalitarian than it looked—demanded different virtues. It works in short scenes; it has the intimacy of a story-teller's fireside; it can make ambitious leaps in time and space as long as the mind's eye of the listener is sufficiently engaged to follow them; and it can play upon that same mind's eye to create scenes of great imagined visual beauty. On the other hand, it cannot cope with clutter; redundant images can lead the imagination to give up on the job, and our closeness to the characters (they are, after all, made of pure sound, a substance which literally enters us) means that we are almost painfully alive to subtext; an attempt to spell things out too overtly will irritate. The radiophonic virtues may be summed up in a single word: concentration.

Churchill has the almost unique gift of concentrating layers of meaning in a simple, economical, and striking image. In one of her earliest plays for the Royal Court Theatre, *Light Shining in Buckinghamshire*, an account of the upheavals of the 1640's, there is a short scene in which two women look in a mirror. On one level this is a scene about poverty and revolution: the mirror has been looted from one of the great country houses, and the woman who took it embodies the attitudes of the poor energised by Puritanism. She speaks of burning the "Norman" deeds to the land they found in the house, the symbol of an oppressive aristocracy, but of preserving the corn "because it's our corn now". She speaks of "choosing" from the array of possessions there, as if this act must be done responsibly and without greed. But this is also a scene about identity, and in particular female identity. "They must know what they look like all of the time", she says of the rich. "And now we do". To have a sense of one's own identity is to take power for oneself. The impact of the scene is increased by its juxtaposition with other scenes in which women begin to speak in church, to acquire a sense of themselves in other ways, and also by the fact that it inverts all the usual clichés of self-absorption and narcissism that adhere to the idea of a woman looking in a mirror. The woman who takes the mirror at once goes to share it with another; together they see new selves in a new world.

Churchill's economy allows her to make bold shifts in convention. Sometimes she will use the techniques of natural-

ism: in *Fen*, for instance, the harshness of rural East-Anglian life is seen subtextually in a scene where Val, torn between her lover Frank and her children, encounters her daughter who is living with her mother because Frank's tied cottage cannot hold them all. They swap elephant jokes. Underneath the jokes, however, we track Val's awareness that her child is slipping away from her and that she cannot hold on to her love the way things are. By the next scene she will have decided to die. But in the same play we see a ghost, casually walking in the fields and articulating her hatred of the landowner. "I live in your house", she says, "I watch television with you". She too lost her child. Nothing has changed. But the way that this surreal image integrates with the texture of everyday experience enables us to make connections and perceive Val's world in a new way.

A similar combination of the naturalistic and the surreal is employed in two plays exploring the world of the rich. *Serious Money* paints a black picture of corruption in the Stock Exchange at the time of the "big bang": it is generous with sheer information, in the style of many thrillers which use a near-documentary mode, but the slick verse spoken by the characters shifts them into the realm of the grotesque. In *Top Girls* two sisters quarrel in a realistic scene where passions are both personal and political: Marlene, who has made it as a successful executive, has left Joyce to rear her unwanted child for her, and they fight as she comes back on a visit. Their personal differences are given a political perspective by the opening scene, a banquet in which Marlene is toasted by famous women from history and hears their own stories of sexual oppression—notably that of Pope Joan, perhaps the most "successful" woman in history in terms of wielding power, albeit briefly, who was, according to legend, stoned to death for bearing a child. The play also makes leaps in time, a device explored with more complexity in her first Broadway success, *Cloud Nine*. Here the sexual and colonial oppressions of the 19th century are shown in a satirical, almost clowning spirit; but when the characters leap into the 20th century it becomes apparent that we have no right to laugh at our Victorian legacy: the same characters struggle with their sexuality and their place in the world and only one of them, Betty, achieves any kind of personal harmony, a moment symbolised by her embrace with her Victorian self.

The multi-layered style and concentration of ideas make Churchill a difficult dramatist on the page; this has perhaps impeded or slowed up her recognition as a dramatist of major stature, but the clarity and power of her work in performance cannot be missed.

—Frances Gray

See also *Volume 1* entries on *Cloud Nine*; *Top Girls*.

———————

CIBBER, Colley.   Born in London, 6 November 1671; son of the sculptor Caius Cibber. Educated at the Free School, Grantham, Lincolnshire, 1682–87. Served in the Earl of Devonshire's Volunteers, 1688, and remained in the service of the Earl, 1689–90. Married Katherine Shore in 1693 (died 1734); 12 children. Actor, United Company at Theatre Royal, Drury Lane, 1691–1706, and adviser to Christopher Rich, the manager, after 1700; imprisoned, probably for unpaid gambling debts, 1697; actor, Haymarket Theatre,

London, 1706 until the two theatres consolidated, 1708; co-owner/manager, Theatre Royal, Drury Lane, 1710–32; largely retired as actor, 1733, but appeared occasionally until 1745: acted more than 130 roles. Poet laureate, 1730–57. Died in London, 11 December 1757.

Works

Collections

Plays (2 vols.). 1721.
Dramatic Works (5 vols.). 1736.
Dramatic Works (4 vols.). 1760; revised edition (5 vols.), 1777.
Three Sentimental Comedies (includes *Love's Last Shift; The Careless Husband; The Lady's Last Stake*), edited by Maureen Sullivan. 1973.

Stage Works

Love's Last Shift; or, The Fool in Fashion (produced Theatre Royal, Drury Lane, London, 1696). 1696.
Woman's Wit; or, The Lady in Fashion (produced Theatre Royal, Drury Lane, London, 1697). 1697.
Xerxes (produced Theatre Royal, Drury Lane, London, 1699). 1699.
King Richard III, from the play by Shakespeare (produced Theatre Royal, Drury Lane, London, 1699). 1700.
Love Makes a Man; or, The Fop's Fortune (produced Theatre Royal, Drury Lane, London, 1700). 1701.
She Would and She Would Not; or, The Kind Imposter (produced Theatre Royal, Drury Lane, London, 1702). 1703.
The Schoolboy; or, The Comical Rival, from his own play *Woman's Wit* (produced Theatre Royal, Drury Lane, London, 1702). 1707.
The Careless Husband (produced Theatre Royal, Drury Lane, London, 1704). 1705.
Perolla and Izadora (produced Theatre Royal, Drury Lane, London, 1705). 1706.
The Comical Lovers (produced Haymarket Theatre, London, 1707). 1707; as *Marriage la Mode* (produced Haymarket Theatre, London, 1707; as *Court Gallantry*, produced 1715).
The Double Gallant; or, The Sick Lady's Cure (produced Haymarket Theatre, London, 1707). 1707.
The Lady's Last Stake; or, The Wife's Resentment (produced Haymarket Theatre, London, 1707). 1708.
The Rival Fools (produced Theatre Royal, Drury Lane, London, 1709). 1709.
The Rival Queens (produced Haymarket Theatre, London, 1710). 1729.
Hob; or, The Country Wake, from a play by Thomas Dogget (produced Theatre Royal, Drury Lane, London, 1711). 1715.
Ximena; or, The Heroic Daughter, from a play by Pierre Corneille (produced Theatre Royal, Drury Lane, London, 1712). 1719.
Bulls and Bears (produced Theatre Royal, Drury Lane, London, 1715).
Myrtillo, music by J.C. Pepusch (produced Theatre Royal, Drury Lane, London, 1715). 1715.
Venus and Adonis, music by J.C. Pepusch (produced Theatre Royal, Drury Lane, London, 1715). 1715.
The Non-Juror, from a play by Molière (produced Theatre Royal, Drury Lane, London, 1717). 1718.
The Refusal; or, The Ladies' Philosophy, from a play by Molière (produced Theatre Royal, Drury Lane, London, 1721). 1721.
Caesar in Egypt (produced Theatre Royal, Drury Lane, London, 1724). 1725.
The Provoked Husband; or, A Journey to London, completion of a play by Vanbrugh (produced Theatre Royal, Drury Lane, London, 1728). 1728.
Love in a Riddle, possibly not by Cibber (produced Theatre Royal, Drury Lane, London, 1729). 1729; shortened version, as *Damon and Phillida* (produced Haymarket Theatre, London, 1729), 1729; revised version, 1730.
Polypheme, from an opera libretto by Paul Rolli, music by Nicholas Porpora (produced 1734).
Papal Tyranny in the Reign of King John, from *King John* by Shakespeare (produced Covent Garden Theatre, London,). 1745.

Verse

A Poem on the Death of Queen Mary. 1695.
The Sacred History of Arlus and Odolphus. 1714.
An Ode to His Majesty for the New Year. 1731.
An Ode for His Majesty's Birthday. 1731.
A Rhapsody upon the Marvellous Arising from the First Odes of Horace and Pindar. 1751.
Verses to the Memory of Mr. Pelham. 1754.

Memoirs and Letters

An Apology for the Life of Mr. Colley Cibber, Comedian. 1740; revised editions, 1750, 1756.
A Letter to Mr. Pope. 1742; *Second Letter*, 1743; *Another Letter*, 1744.
The Egoist; or, Colley upon Cibber. 1743.

Other

The Character and Conduct of Cicero Considered. 1747.
The Lady's Lecture: A Theatrical Dialogue Between Sir Charles Easy and His Marriageable Daughter. 1748.

*

Bibliographies

Leonard R.N. Ashley, bibliography in *Restoration and 18th-Century Theatre Research*, 6–7, 1967–68.

Criticism

Books:
D.M.E. Habbema, *An Appreciation of Colley Cibber, Actor and Dramatist* (includes text of *The Careless Husband*), Amsterdam, 1928; reprinted, 1967.
F. Dorothy Senior, *The Life and Times of Colley Cibber*, London, 1928.
R.H. Barker, *Mr. Cibber of Drury Lane*, New York, 1939.
Leonard R.N. Ashley, *Colley Cibber*, New York, 1965; revised edition, 1989.
Helene Wickham Koon, *Colley Cibber: A Biography*, Lexington, Kentucky, 1986.

* * *

Colley Cibber was arguably the dominant force in the

Colley Cibber as Lord Foppington in Sir John Vanbrugh's *The Relapse* (engraving by J. Simon, after the portrait by Grisoni).

English theatre in the first half of the 18th century. He was an accomplished actor, a powerful manager whose responsibilities included the selection of new plays for production at Drury Lane, and a highly productive playwright of above-average competence. There were better playwrights and more charismatic actors, but it is difficult to find a rival to match either Cibber's achievement in all the major areas of theatrical activity or his longevity—55 seasons on the London stage.

Cibber began his acting career in September 1690, in a servant's role in Southerne's *Sir Anthony Love*. Minor successes in plays like Otway's *The Orphan* and Congreve's *The Old Bachelor* and *The Double-Dealer* could support neither his ambition nor his growing family. In his autobiography, Cibber explains that having failed to secure important roles any other way, he was "reduc'd to write a character" for himself. The result, *Love's Last Shift*, established Cibber as a playwright, and his role, Sir Novelty Fashion, signalled what was to become Cibber's most important line as an actor, the fop. When Vanbrugh produced *The Relapse* soon after, a sequel to *Love's Last Shift*, and expanded and ennobled Cibber's character as Lord Foppington, Cibber's acting career was made.

Although Cibber considered playwriting a sideline to his career as actor and manager, he still wrote 12 comedies, six tragedies, a tragicomedy, a farce, and several musical entertainments. He wrote original plays and adaptations (the majority) and had equal success with each. Cibber's most important plays are his comedies. *Love's Last Shift* is typical in that it includes his favorite subject (marital discord), his favorite setting (fashionable London society), a prominent fop's role for himself (Sir Novelty Fashion), an exemplary character (Amanda) who helps correct an erring mate (Loveless), mild social satire mitigated by the near-tearful closure provided by reform, reconciliation, and (in the subplot) marriage. The combination of witty dialogue laced with both *double entendre* and *sententiae*, of titillation and reform, and of bedroom farce and exemplary comedy, confirm Cibber's claims in his epilogue that he tried to include something for everyone in his plays. One of the prices he was prepared to pay was the sacrifice of unity and consistency in favor of more local effects.

Cibber's next play was his only successful attempt at tragedy, his adaptation of Shakespeare's *Richard III*. Again his choice was made in part to advance his acting career, establishing himself as a heavy villain. Like other Shakespeare adaptations, Cibber's *King Richard III* cuts, simplifies, and "purifies" its original. Cibber's Richard is more villainous than Shakespeare's, and his adaptation focusses more narrowly on the title character. The initial production met with a lukewarm reception, but its revival in 1710 established it as the acting version for 150 years. Cibberian accretions are often found even in 20th-century productions. Cibber subsequently attempted adaptations of tragedies by Boyle, Corneille, and, late in his career, Shakespeare again (*King John*), but he was never again to match the success of his *King Richard III*.

Cibber's skill at pleasing audiences with his comedies, however, more than compensated for his ineptness at tragedy. He had a long series of successes in the first decade of the 18th century, including several long-running adaptations. A list reveals the eclecticism of Cibber's taste: *Love Makes a Man* from Fletcher and Massinger's *The Elder Brother* and *The Custom of the Country*; *She Would and She Would Not* from John Leanerd's *The Counterfeits*; *The Rival Queens*, a burlesque of Lee's *The Rival Queens*; *The Comical Lovers*, an amalgam of the comic plots of Dryden's tragicomedies *Secret Love* and *Marriage à-la-Mode*; *The Double Gallant* from William Burnaby's *The Reformed Wife* and *The Lady's Visiting Day* and Susanna Centlivre's *Love at a Venture*. As an actor-manager, Cibber was familiar with an enormous range of plays, and was able to draw on that familiarity in the service of his playwrighting.

The same period also saw Cibber produce two of his better original comedies. *The Careless Husband* is usually considered Cibber's finest play, and its plots allow him to include most of his favorite elements. In the main plot, Sir Charles Easy, the title character, is a rake who is reformed by his kind and loving wife. The most famous scene—a crowd-pleaser for the rest of the century—consists of Lady Easy discovering her husband asleep with her maid. Rather than disturbing them, she covers his head with her steinkirk (neck cloth) to prevent his catching cold. When he awakes, reform follows quickly. The subplot portrays the taming of the coquette, Lady Betty Modish, by the good-natured but serious-minded Lord Morelove. His main rival is provided by Cibber's old favorite, Lord Foppington. *The Lady's Last Stake* is a more serious comedy with a clearly didactic assault on the evil effects of gambling, a popular subject in the early 18th century. Cibber, as always, could sense literary trends and help form them through his writing.

After he became a full-time manager in 1710, Cibber had less time for writing. His next important play was *The Non-Juror*, his adaptation of Molière's *Tartuffe*. It was Cibber's most overtly political comedy. Molière's Tartuffe becomes Dr. Wolf, a Jesuit disguised as a non-juring Anglican priest. Cibber created the role himself, drawing on his portrayal of characters like Richard III. Dr. Wolf is an unusually dangerous and vicious villain for a comedy, representing, as he does, the threat of radical Jacobitism. An unusually partisan play, *The Non-Juror* made Cibber strongly committed friends and enemies. The enemies henceforward made it difficult for him to stage a new play of his own. The only important success thereafter for Cibber as playwright was his reworking of Vanbrugh's unfinished comedy, *A Journey to London*, into a typically Cibberian play, *The Provoked Husband*. Vanbrugh's challenging, open-ended social comedy becomes an exemplary comedy that reassures its audience with the triumph of middle-class values and matrimony.

Among the rewards Cibber received for his ardent support of Whig causes was the poet laureateship. The result was 27 years of undistinguished verse. His most important late work was his autobiography, *An Apology for the Life of Mr. Colley Cibber, Comedian*, a lively, engaging narrative of his professional life, which remains, despite its factual unreliability, one of the most important accounts of the 18th-century English stage.

—Brian Corman

See also *Volume 1* entry on *Love's Last Shift*.

CLARK, John Pepper. Now writes as J.P. Clark Bekederemo. Born in Kiagbodo, Warri Province, Nigeria, 6 April 1935. Educated at Warri Government College, Ughelli, 1948–54; University of Ibadan, 1955–60, BA (honours) in English 1960, and graduate study (Institute of African Studies fellowship), 1963–64; Princeton University, New Jersey (Par-vin fellowship). Married to Ebun Odutola Clark; three daughters and one son. Founding editor, *Horn* magazine, Ibadan, 1957; information officer, Government of Nigeria, 1960–61; first play, *Song of a Goat*, produced 1961; head of features and editorial writer, Lagos *Daily Express*, 1961–62; research fellow, 1963–64, lecturer, 1964–72, and Professor of English, 1972–80, University of Lagos; co-editor, *Black Orpheus*, Lagos, from 1968; visiting fellow, Wesleyan University, Middletown, Connecticut, 1975–76; founder, PEC Repertory Theatre, Lagos, 1982; founding member, Society of Nigerian Authors.

Works

Collections

Three Plays (includes *Song of a Goat; The Masquerade; The Raft*). 1964.
The Bikoroa Plays (includes *The Boat; The Return Home; Full Circle*). 1985.
Collected Plays 1964–1988. 1992.

Stage Works

Song of a Goat (produced Mbari Theatre Club, Ibadan, 1961). 1961.
The Masquerade (produced London, 1965). In *Three Plays*, 1964.
The Raft (produced New York, 1978). In *Three Plays*, 1964.
Ozidi. 1966.
The Bikoroa Plays (includes *The Boat; The Return Home; Full Circle*; all produced Lagos, 1981). 1985 (under pen name J.P. Clark Bekederemo).

Screenplays

The Ozidi of Atazi.

Radio Plays

The Raft, 1966 (published in *Three Plays*, 1964).

Verse

Poems. 1962.
A Reed in the Tide: A Selection of Poems. 1965.
Casualties: Poems 1966–1968. 1970.
Urhobo Poetry. 1980.
A Decade of Tongues: Selected Poems 1958–1968. 1981.
State of the Union. 1985.

Other

America, Their America. 1964.
The Example of Shakespeare: Critical Essays on African Literature. 1970.
The Hero as a Villain. 1978.

Editor and Translator, *The Ozidi Saga*, by Okabou Ojobolo. 1977.

*

Criticism

Books:
Margaret Laurence, *Long Drums and Cannons: Nigerian Dramatists and Novelists 1952–1966*, London, 1968.

Wilfred Cartey, *Whispers from a Continent: The Literature of Contemporary Black Africa*, London, 1971.
Anthony Graham-White, *The Drama of Black Africa*, New York, 1974.
Albert O Ashaolo, "J.P. Clark: His Significance as Dramatist", in *Theatre in Africa*, edited by Oyin Ogunba and Abiola Irele, Ibadan, Nigeria, 1978.
Martin Owusu, *Drama of the Gods: A Study of Seven African Plays*, Roxbury, Massachusetts, 1983.
Robert M. Wren, *J.P. Clark*, Boston, 1984.
Martin Banham, *A Critical View of John Pepper Clark's Three Plays*, London, 1985.

* * *

In John Pepper Clark's many-sided career, he has written plays less consistently than he has written poems. His *Three Plays* was followed closely by *Ozidi*, but almost 20 years passed before the trilogy *The Bikoroa Plays* appeared in 1985.

His first play, *Song of a Goat*, has been produced in various countries, and is probably the most successful artistically. Masseur, in its opening lines, states the theme to his daughter, Ebiere: "Your womb/ Is open and warm as a room:/ It ought to accomodate many/ . . . An empty house, my daughter, is a thing/ Of danger". Ebiere's husband, Zifa, refuses to think of his sterility as permanent or of following the Masseur's suggestion that the claims of fertility be honored by his brother Tonye. When Ebiere in her frustration seduces Tonye, Zifa perverts the ritual which would legitimize that surreptitious union: he makes Tonye force the head of the sacrificed goat into a pot, which shatters. This is, by analogy (as they all realize) an assault upon Ebiere's womb. Tonye hangs himself, Zifa drowns himself, and Ebiere is left pregnant. The intensity of this conflict, in which each of the trio is both victim and aggressor, sustains this short play and sweeps us through the trappings of Greek tragedy—a chorus of neighbors, a Cassandra-like aunt, a messenger-speech telling of the final disaster—in which Clark dresses the story. Despite some self-conscious writing (evident also in the etymological reference of the title) overall there is an extraordinary assurance in this play.

Clark seems to have designed *The Masquerade* to offer relief from the intensity of *Song of a Goat*. He offers us "a real dance of the dragon-flies", the high-spirited wooing of Titi by a stranger, Ebiere's son Tufa. Since Clark makes Tufa innocent of any knowledge of the tragedy surrounding his conception, the wooing can be lyrically joyful, somewhat in the spirit of Romeo and Juliet. Only as Tufa's father investigates rumor, and the past is revealed, do we return to tragedy. Unfortunately, one senses that the play's style and its denouement were willed into being. The language is full of echoes of Shakespeare and conceits in the manner of Christopher Fry. Tufa has done nothing culpable, and even with the intransigent hostility to the marriage of Titi's father it takes a combination of misprision and accident to bring about the lovers' deaths.

The third of the *Three Plays, The Raft*, presents four men drifting down a river on a raft of logs. Differences between the characters are subordinated to an atmosphere of drift through the fog, and to the intent to convey, in Clark's phrase, the "human condition". Civil war overtook Nigeria not long after the play appeared and some read it as a prescient allegorical vision. The raft does split and carry off one of the four men, but if the work bears such meaning it is only as one metaphor among others and cannot be pushed into the precision of an allegory.

Clark's recent trilogy, *The Bikoroa Plays*, again traces the fate of a family through successive generations. This time the focus is not on sexual relationships but on the differing ambitions of two brothers of contrasting character. They alternate in the use of the family boat, month by month, and irritations mount to the point where there is a fatal quarrel. One is shot, the other condemned to death and, ironically, the boat is split to carry each to his grave. The other two plays present the fatal quarrels of their two sons and two grandsons. This is so precise a repetition that the action becomes predictable. Yet there is less sense of the author's self-conscious control of the action. As one character says, "Fate is what we say after the event, not what we see before it". The treatment is more relaxed and less relentlessly tragic than in his first plays, in part because these were Clark's first plays in prose, but more because the brothers' behavior is seen—as the action in the earlier plays is not—from the viewpoint of the community, within whose life they seek their fulfilment. Climactic scenes are trials and ceremonies. The prose easily incorporates praise-names and metaphors seem the language of the community—as when the hasty exit of an angry man evokes the comment "There goes a whirlwind with a lot of dust in its eye"—rather than a poet's invention. Beyond the community are the pressures of a changing colonial society that offers new opportunities but which has destroyed the traditional ideal of "the man, the fish, the vessel, all brought together in the one act of quest by man for fish over waters spilling into the sun".

Based on an Ijaw epic that is narrated and performed over seven days, *Ozidi* is unlike Clark's other plays in length, scope, and staging demands. It too deals with blood honor and the curse on a family, worked out in this case by a son revenging his father through his own strength, abetted by his grandmother's magic. But the traditional society is refracted through Clark's ironic consciousness. Ozidi is presented as a figure trapped in his destined role of warrior-avenger but at a loss to find himself and, like Goethe's Götz von Berlichingen, increasingly an outsider exemplifying anachronistic values. It has been suggested that Clark created a "parable of the talented individual in Africa today", and, indeed, Clark the modern storyteller changes Ijaw tradition in his play to have the storyteller take on the role of Ozidi.

—Anthony Graham-White

CLAUDEL, Paul (Louis Charles Marie) Born in Villeneuve-sur-Fère, France, 6 August 1868. Educated at schools in Bar-le-Duc, 1870–75, Nogent-sur-Seine, 1876–79, and Wassy-sur-Blaise, 1879–81; Lycée Louis-le-Grand, Paris, 1882–85; law school, and École des Sciences Politiques. Married Reine Sainte-Marie-Perrin in 1906; five children. First play, *Tête d'or*, published 1890; in the French diplomatic service from 1890: commercial department, Paris, 1890–92, New York, 1893, Boston, 1894, China, 1895–1909, Prague, 1909–11, Frankfurt, 1911–14, Berlin, 1914, Rome and Brazil during World War I; ambassador to Japan, 1921–25, to the United States, 1926–31, and to Belgium, 1933–35; retired 1935; served in the Ministry of Propaganda during World War II. Elected to the Académie Française, 1946. Died in Paris, 23 February 1955.

Works

Collections

Théâtre (4 vols.). 1911–12; revised edition (2 vols.), 1947–48.
Oeuvres complètes (26 vols.). 1950–67; supplement, 1990.
Théâtre (2 vols.), edited by Jacques Madaule and Jacques Petit. 1956; revised edition, 1965–67.

Stage Works

Tête d'or. 1890; revised version (produced Théâtre du Gymnase, Paris, 1924), in *L'Arbre*, 1901; translated as *Tête d'or*, 1919.
La Ville. 1893; revised version (produced Vlaamse Volkstoonell, Brussels, 1931), in *L'Arbre*, 1901; translated as *The City*, 1920.
L'Agamemnon, from the play by Aeschylus (produced 1963). 1896.
L'Échange (produced Théâtre du Vieux-Colombier, Paris, 1914). In *L'Arbre*, 1901; revised version (produced 1951), 1954.
La Jeune Fille Violaine. In *L'Arbre*, 1901; revised version, as *L'Annonce faite à Marie* (produced Théâtre de l'Oeuvre, Paris, 1912), 1912; revised version (produced 1948), 1948; translated as *The Tidings Brought to Mary*, 1916.
Le Repos du septième jour (produced Narodny Theatre, Warsaw, 1928). In *L'Arbre*, 1901.
Partage de midi. 1906; revised version (produced Théâtre Marigny, Paris, 1948), 1914, 1949; translated as *Break of Noon*, 1960.
L'Otage (produced Théâtre de l'Oeuvre, Paris, 1914). 1911; translated as *The Hostage*, 1917.
Protée. In *Deux poèmes d'été*, 1914; revised version (produced Municipal Theatre, Amsterdam, 1933) in *Deux farces lyriques*, 1927.
La Nuit de Noël 1914. 1915.
Le Pain dur (produced in German, Landestheater, Oldenburg, 1926; produced in French, Théâtre d'Atelier, Paris, 1949). 1918; translated as *Crusts*, in *Three Plays*, 1945.
L'Ours et la lune (produced 1948). 1919.
Le Père humilié (produced in German, Schauspielhaus, Dresden, 1928). 1920; translated as *The Humiliation of the Father*, in *Three Plays*, 1945.
Les Choéphores, music by Darius Milhaud, from the play by Aeschylus (produced Théâtre de la Monnaie, Brussels, 1935). 1920.
Les Euménides, music by Milhaud, from the play by Aeschylus (produced Brussels, 1949). 1920.
L'Homme et son désir, with music by Darius Milhaud (ballet; produced Théâtre des Champs-Élysées, Paris, 1921). In *Le Livre de Christophe Colomb*, 1929.
La Femme et son ombre (produced Imperial Theatre, Tokyo, 1923). In *Le Livre de Christophe Colomb*, 1929.
Sous le rempart d'Athènes, with music by Germaine Taillefer (produced Comédie-Française, Paris, 1929). 1928.
Le Livre de Christophe Colomb, with music by Darius Milhaud (produced Staatsoper unter den Linden, Berlin, 1930). 1929; translated as *The Book of Christopher Columbus*, 1930.
Le Soulier de satin. 1928–29; stage version (produced Comédie-Française, Paris, 1943), 1944; translated as *The Satin Slipper*, 1931.
Jeanne d'Arc au bûcher, with music by Arthur Honegger (produced Théâtre Municipal, Orléans, 1939). 1939.

L'Histoire de Tobie et de Sara (produced Verger d'Urbain V, Avignon, 1947).   1947.

La Sagesse; ou, La Parabole du festin, from the radio version, with music by Darius Milhaud (produced Perugia, Italy, 1949).   1939.

L'Endormie.   1947.

La Lune à la recherche d'elle-même.   In *Théâtre 2*, 1948.

Le Ravissement de Scapin.   In *Opéra*, 55, 1952.

Radio Plays

La Sagesse; ou, La Parabole du festin, 1945 (published 1939).

Verse

Vers d'exil.   1895.

Cinq grandes odes suivies d'un processional pour saluer le siècle nouveau.   1910; translated as *Five Great Odes*, 1967.

Cette heure qui est entre le printemps et l'été.   1913; as *La Cantate à trois voix*, 1931.

Corona benignitatis anni dei.   1915; translated as *Coronal*, 1943.

Trois Poèmes de guerre.   1915; translated as *Three Poems of the War*, 1919.

Autres poèmes durant la guerre.   1916.

Poèmes et paroles durant la guerre.   1916.

La Messe là-bas.   1919.

Poèmes de guerre.   1922.

Feuilles de saints.   1925.

Écoute, ma fille.   1934.

La Légende de Prakriti.   1934.

Poèmes et paroles durant la guerre de trente ans.   1945.

Visages radieux.   1946.

Oeuvres poétiques, edited by Stanislas Fumet.   1957.

Sainte Agnès et poèmes inédites.   1963.

Psaumes: traductions 1918–1959, edited by Renée Nantet and Jacques Petit.   1966.

Memoirs and Letters

Correspondance 1907–1914, with Jacques Rivière.   1926; translated as *Letters to a Doubter*, 1929.

Correspondance 1899–1926, with André Gide, edited by Robert Mallet.   1949; translated as *Correspondence*, 1952.

Correspondance 1904–1938, with André Suarès.   1951.

Mémoires improvisés, edited by Jean Amrouche.   1954.

Correspondance 1918–1953, with Darius Milhaud, edited by Jacques Petit.   1961.

Journal (2 vols.), edited by Jacques Petit and François Varillon.   1968–69.

Correspondance 1908–1914, with Louis Massignon, edited by Michel Malicet.   1973.

Correspondance, with Jean-Louis Barrault, edited by Michel Lioure.   1974.

Chroniques du Journal de Clichy, with François Mauriac (includes Claudel-Fontaine correspondence), edited by François Morlot and Jean Touzot.   1978.

Other

Connaissance de l'est, 1st series (1895–1900).   1900; 2nd series (1900–05), 1907; translated as *The East I Know*, 1914.

Art poétique.   1907; translated as *Poetic Art*, 1948.

Positions et propositions (2 vols.).   1928–34.

L'Oiseau noir dans le soleil levant.   1929.

Ways and Crossways.   1933.

Introduction à la peinture hollandaise.   1935.

Conversations dans le Loir-et-Cher.   1935.

Toi, qui es-tu? Tu quis es?.   1936.

Figures et paraboles.   1936.

Vitraux des cathédrales de France.   1937.

L'Aventure de Sophie.   1937.

Un poète regarde la croix.   1938; translated as *Poet Before the Cross*, 1958.

L'Épée et le miroir.   1939.

Contacts et circonstances.   1940.

La Rose et le rosaire.   1946.

L'Oeil écoute.   1946; translated as *The Eye Listens*, 1950.

Chine, with photographs by Hélène Hoppenot.   1946.

Présence et prophétie.   1947.

Lord, Teach Us to Pray.   1947.

Sous le signe du dragon.   1948.

Paul Claudel interroge la Cantique des Cantiques.   1948.

Accompagnements.   1949.

Emmaüs.   1950.

L'Évangile d'Isaïe.   1951.

J'aime la Bible.   1955.

Oeuvres en prose, edited by Jacques Petit and Charles Galperine.   1965.

I Believe in God: A Commentary on the Apostles' Creed, edited by Agnes du Sarment.   1965.

Au milieu des vitraux de l'Apocalypse, edited by Pierre Claudel and Jacques Petit.   1966.

Mes idées sur le théâtre, edited by Jacques Petit and Jean-Pierre Kempf.   1966.

Translator, *Poèmes*, by Coventry Patmore.   1912.

*

Bibliographies

Jacques Petit, *Bibliographie des oeuvres de Claudel*, Paris, 1973.

Jacquéline de Labriolle, *Claudel and the English-Speaking World: A Critical Bibliography*, London, 1973.

Criticism

Books:

J. Madaule, *Le Génie de Paul Claudel*, Paris, 1933.

Jacques Madaule, *Le Drame de Paul Claudel*, Paris, 1936; revised edition, 1947.

C. Chonez, *Introduction à Paul Claudel*, Paris, 1947.

Rayner Heppenstall, *The Double Image: Mutations of Christian Mythology in the Work of Four French Catholic Writers*, London, 1947.

Joseph Chiari, *The Poetic Drama of Claudel*, Harvell, 1954.

Ernest Beaumont, *The Theme of Beatrice in the Plays of Claudel*, London, 1954.

Wallace Fowlie, *Paul Claudel*, London, 1957.

Richard Griffiths (ed.), *Claudel: A Reappraisal*, London, 1963.

William H. Matheson, *Claudel and Aeschylus*, Ann Arbor, Michigan, 1965.

Richard Berchan, *The Inner Stage: An Essay on the Conflict of Vocations in the Early Works of Claudel*, East Lancing, Michigan, 1966.

Edwin M. Landau, *Paul Claudel*, Velber, 1966.

Léon Emery, *Claudel*, Lyons, 1967.

André Alter, *Paul Claudel: Textes de Claudel, points de vue critiques, témoignages, bibliographie, illustrations*, Paris, 1968.

Georges Cattaui and Jacques Madaule (eds.), *Entretiens sur Paul Claudel*, Paris, 1968.

Gilbert Gadoffre, *Claudel et l'univers chinois*, 1968.

Richard M. Griffiths, *Claudel: A Reappraisal*, London, 1968.

Jacques Madaule, *Claudel et le langage*, Paris, 1968.

Marianne Mercier-Campiche, *Le Théâtre de Claudel, ou la puissance du grief et de la passion*, Paris, 1968.

Jacques Madaule, *Claudel et le Dieu caché*, Paris, 1969.

André Blanc (ed.), *Les Critiques de notre temps et Claudel*, Paris, 1970.

Harold A. Waters, *Paul Claudel*, New York, 1970.

Pierre Brunel, *Claudel et Shakespeare*, Paris, 1971.

Michel Lioure, *L'Esthétique dramatique de Paul Claudel*, Paris, 1971.

Jacques Petit, *Claudel et l'usurpateur*, Paris, 1971.

Harold Watson, *Claudel's Immortal Heroes: A Choice of Deaths*, New Brunswick, New Jersey, 1971.

André Blanc, *Claudel*, Paris, 1973.

Aimé Becker, *Claudel et l'interlocuteur invisible: Le Drame de l'appel*, Paris, 1974.

Joy Nachod Humes, *Two Against Time: A Study of the Very Present Worlds of Claudel and Charles Péguy*, Chapel Hill, North Carolina, 1978.

Jean B. Barrère, *Claudel: Le Destin et l'oeuvre*, Paris, 1979.

Lynne L. Gelber, *In/stability: The Shape and Space of Claudel's Art*, Ann Arbor, Michigan, 1980.

Bettina L. Knapp, *Paul Claudel*, New York, 1982.

Marie J. Legros-Guers, *Tableau généalogique de Paul Claudel*, Paris, 1983.

Aimé Becker, *Claudel et S. Augustin, une parenté spirituelle*, Paris, 1984.

Paul A. Lesort, *Claudel*, Paris, 1985.

Marie J. Guers, *Paul Claudel: L'Homme intérieur*, Paris, 1986.

Edwin M. Landau, *Paul Claudel auf deutschsprachigen Bühnen*, Munich, 1986.

Albert Lorranquin, *Claudel et la terre*, Paris, 1987.

Pierre Brunel and Anne Ubersfeld, *La Dramaturgie claudelienne*, Paris, 1988.

Antoine Gérald, *Paul Claudel ou l'enfer du génie*, Paris, 1988.

Serials:
Bulletin de la Société Paul Claudel, 1966—
Claudel Newsletter, 1968–72 (9 issues).
Claudel Studies, 1973—

*   *   *

Claudel's youth was largely an unhappy one—he found family life repressive, was profoundly marked by his grandfather's death from cancer in 1881, and disliked Paris where the family moved in 1882 leaving his father in the provinces. He also found the scientific positivism which pervaded the instruction at the Lycée Louis-le-Grand deeply depressing. Indeed, he was later to reject almost all he was taught there, preferring private study, particularly of Shakespeare and Aeschylus. These authors, together with his later study of the Psalms and Proverbs, were to have a significant effect upon the development of his distinctive non-rhyming verse form, known as the "verset claudelien". The only break in the gloom of these years came with Claudel's discovery of the poetry of Rimbaud in 1886, whom he perceived as a kindred spirit.

He was, however, to find two means of escape: via religion and his career. On Christmas Day 1886, while attending vespers in Notre Dame, Claudel experienced a sudden conversion, regaining the faith he had earlier lost. It was, however, only four years later, after a struggle regarding the reconciliation of his poetic vocation with his religious belief, that Claudel was finally accepted into the Catholic Church. From then on, religion, and particularly the representation of man's often unknowing struggle towards God, was to provide the dynamic for the whole of his theatrical creation. Moreover, Catholic liturgy, combining with other influences, was to direct him towards the creation of what Michel Lioure describes as "an eminently ceremonial and sacred theatre, at once poetic, pathetic and invested with a high symbolic and mystical meaning" (in *L'Esthétique dramatique de Paul Claudel*). More specifically, the representation of divine wisdom as a woman in Proverbs 8 was significantly to influence his depiction of women, who represent either "the human soul, the Church, the Holy Virgin, or sacred Wisdom" (*Mémoires improvisées*).

The second way in which Claudel escaped from his restrictive upbringing was by his choice of a career in the diplomatic service. Here he was highly successful, if not always happy (*L'Échange* was written as an expression of his unhappiness in materialistic America, and Mesa in *Partage de midi* feels that he is wasting time in China when he should be serving God). Nevertheless, Claudel prided himself on being a good civil servant, and his travels had the advantage of bringing him into contact with the theatres of different cultures, and Japanese theatre in particular was to have a great influence on those works written in the latter part of his career, notably *Le Soulier de satin*.

Claudel's playwriting career can be divided into three phases. Plays in the first phase are, for the most part, expressions of the author's personal problems and preoccupations, composed with no intention of performance. Of these, *Tête d'or* represents the fervour with which Claudel defended himself against faith, and *La Ville* addresses the question of a conflict between poetic and religious vocations, as well as expressing Claudel's hatred of Paris. The central theme of *La Jeune Fille Violaine*, the most obviously Christian of Claudel's plays to that point, is that of sacrifice to the will of God. This play and *L'Échange* mark a change, for in them the dramatist abandons his former "ultra-poetic" style in favour of a vigorous, although still highly lyrical, realism. They also suggest a desire for a more coherent ordering of material, and *L'Échange* is, in fact, a "classical" play. This may also have motivated the series of revisions of earlier works which followed, although it is doubtful that Claudel seriously contemplated their production.

The religious and emotional crisis which triggered the composition of *Partage de midi* marks the beginning of the second phase of Claudel's career. Other works from this period included the historical trilogy, *L'Otage*, *Le Pain dur*, and *Le Père humilié*, in which Claudel attempted to suppress his personal voice in favour of an exterior, objective viewpoint. These were the years which saw the first productions of Claudel's plays, notably of *L'Annonce faite à Marie* (*Tidings Brought to Mary*), directed by Lugné-Poe at the Théâtre de l'Oeuvre, 1912, and of the same play at Hellerau, 1913, *L'Échange* directed by Jacques Copeau at the Théâtre du Vieux-Colombier, 1914, and *L'Otage* at the Théâtre de l'Oeuvre, 1914. This phase of Claudel's career concludes with the composition of *Le Soulier de satin*, in many ways the synthesis of all Claudel's previous experience both theatrical and personal. Originating in the same crisis as *Partage de midi*, *Le Soulier de satin* illustrates the Augustinian thesis that even sin may be instrumental in bringing man to God.

The plays of the final phase of Claudel's career for the most part consist of experiments in theatrical form and modes of presentation, the most successful being *Le Livre de Christophe Colomb*. In this work, given for the first time at the Berlin Grand Opera in 1930 with music by Darius Milhaud, Claudel experimented with the use of cinematic projection, allowing a single scene to be seen from several perspectives simultaneously.

The religious aspect of Claudel's works, together with their frequently proseletyzing nature, has the disadvantage of making difficult any impartial assessment of his power as a playwright. Spectators and commentators are frequently either alienated or else fear that an unfavourable comment implies a criticism of the Church itself. Similarly problematic is Claudel's representation of women, for although his female characters are strong and sensitively drawn, when not purely symbolic, they frequently perform the essentially subservient Beatrician role of providing the means of bringing the hero to God. Nevertheless, they are often even more mature and more in touch with both practical and spiritual reality (as seen by Claudel) than the men they exist to save.

Appreciation of Claudel's work is further complicated by the fact that he professed the view that "in art nothing is definitive", and so constantly reworked his plays, whether in preparation for production, as a reaction to seeing them performed, or under the influence of new theories of staging. This did not make him an easy collaborator. Having early in his career declared that production of his works was quite impossible, he later insisted on full participation, rewriting dialogue as he saw fit, issuing instructions as to props and decor, and frequently confusing actors with the abstruse nature of his suggestions. Nevertheless, despite this passion for the practical side of the theatre, it was only towards the end of his life that Claudel finally agreed to allow certain of his more personal works to be produced by Jean-Louis Barrault (*Le Soulier de satin*, 1943; *Partage de midi*, 1948; *L'Échange*, 1951; *Le Livre de Christophe Colomb*, 1953; *Tête d'or*, 1959). The success of this collaboration says as much of Barrault's tact and forbearance as it does of their individual skills as director and playwright.

—Janet Clarke

See also *Volume 1* entries on *Break of Noon*; *The Satin Slipper*.

CLAUS, Hugo (Maurice Julien). Born in Bruges, Belgium, 5 April 1929. Educated at schools in Eke, Aalbeke, Kortrijk, Deinze, Ghent. Married Elly Overzier in 1955; one son. Worked as housepainter, agricultural worker, actor, then later became full-time writer: editor, *Tijd en Mens*, 1949–55; first-produced play, *De getuigen* [The Witnesses], staged 1955. Recipient: Krijn Prize, 1951; Lugné-Poë Prize (France), 1955; Triennial Belgian State Prize, for drama, 1955, 1967, 1973, and for verse, 1971; Roland Holst Prize, 1965; Huygens Prize, 1979; Dutch Literature Prize, 1986.

Works

Collections

Acht toneelstukken [Eight Stageplays] (includes *De getuigen; Een bruid in de morgen; (M)oratorium; In een haven; Het* *lied van de moordencear; Suiker; Mama. . . ; De dans van de reiger*). 1966.
Toneel [Theatre] (3 vols.). 1988–91.
  1. Contents as *Acht toneel stukken*.
  2. *Monturi; Vrijdag; Tand om tand; Het leven en de werken van Leopold II; Interieur; Pas de deux*.
  3. *Blauw blauw; Thius; Jessica!; Met haar van de hond; Serenade; Blindeman*.

Stage Works

De gelieven [The Loved Ones]. In *Nieuw Vlaams Tijdschrift*, 1953.
De getuigen [The Witnesses] (produced Brussels, 1955).
Een bruid in de morgen [A Bride in the Morning] (produced Rotterdam, 1955). 1955.
Het lied van de moordenaar [The Song of the Murderer] (produced Rotterdam, 1957).
Dantons dood, from a play by Büchner. 1958.
Suiker [Sugar]. 1958.
Onder het Melkewoud [Under Milkwood], from a play by Dylan Thomas. 1958.
Mama, kijk, zonder Handen! [Look, Ma, No Hands] (produced Brussels, 1960). 1959.
Het Mes (scenario). 1961.
De dans van de reiger [The Heron's Dance]. 1962.
Tijl Uilenspiegel, adaptation of a work by Charles De Cooster (produced Leiden, 1965). 1965.
Thyestes, from the play by Seneca (produced 1966). 1966.
Het Goudland [The Gold Country], from a novel by Henrik Conscience (produced Antwerp, 1966). 1966.
(M)oratorium. In *Acht toneelstukken*, 1966.
In een haven. In *Acht toneelstukken*, 1966.
Masscheroen (produced Knokke, 1967). 1968.
Wrrraak!, from *The Revenger's Tragedy* by Cyril Tourneur or Thomas Middleton (produced Eindhoven, 1968). 1968.
Morituri (produced as *Hyperion en het geweld*, Brussels, 1968). 1968.
Motet (produced Ghent, 1969).
Reconstructie, with others (libretto; produced Amsterdam, 1969). 1969.
Vrijdag (produced Amsterdam, 1969). 1969; translated as *Friday*, 1972.
Tand om tand [Eye for an Eye]. 1970.
Het leven en de werken van Leopold II: 29 taferelen uit de Belgische oudheid [The Life and Works of Leopold II: 29 Scenes from Belgian Antiquity]. 1970.
De Spaanse hoer [The Spanish Whore], from *La Celestina* by Fernando de Rojas (produced Eindhoven, 1970). 1970.
Interieur, from the novel *Omtrent Deedee* (produced Amsterdam, 1971). 1971.
Oedipus, from the play by Seneca. 1971.
De vossejacht, from a play by Ben Jonson. 1972.
Blauw blauw [Blue Blue], from a play by Noël Coward. 1973.
Pas de deux. 1973.
Thuis [Home]. 1975.
Orestes, from the play by Euripides. 1976.
Jessica! 1977.
Het huis van Labdakos [The House of Labdakos], from a scenario by Frans Marijnen. 1977.
Phaedra, from the play by Seneca. 1980.
Het haar van de hond [The Hair of the Dog]. 1982.
Lysistrata, from the play by Aristophanes. 1982.
Hamlet, from the play by Shakespeare. 1984.
Serenade [Serenade]. 1984.
Blindeman [Blindman]. 1985.

Georg Faust, music by Konrad Boehmer.   1985.
In Kolonos, from a play by Sophocles.   1986.
Het schommelpaard [The Rocking Horse].   1988.
Gilles! (produced Brussels, 1988).   1988.

Screenplays

De dans van de reiger [The Heron's Dance] (published 1966);
De vijanden [The Enemies] (published 1967).

Verse

Kleine reeks [Small Series].   1947.
Registreren [Registration].   1948.
Zonder vorm van proces [Without Trial].   1950.
De blijde en onvoorziene week [The Happy, Unexpected Week], illustrated by Karel Appel.   1950.
Tancredo infrasonic.   1952.
Een Huis det tussen nacht en morgen staat [A House Between Night and Morning].   1953.
Paal en perk [Limits].   1955.
De Oostakkerse gedichten [Poems from Oostakker].   1955.
Een geverfde ruiter [A Painted Horseman].   1961.
Love Song, illustrated by Karel Appel.   1963.
Oog om oog [An Eye for an Eye], photographs by Sanne Sannes.   1964.
Gedichten [Poems].   1965.
Relikwie [Relic].   1967.
Heer Everzwijn [Lord Boar].   1970.
Van horen zeggen [On Hearsay].   1970.
Dag, jij [Hello, Love].   1971.
Figuratief.   1973.
Het Jansenisme [Jansenism].   1977.
De wangebeden [No-Good Prayers].   1977.
Van de koude grond [Outdoor Grown].   1978.
Het teken van de hamster [The Sign of the Hamster].   1979.
Gedichten 1969–1978 [Poems].   1980.
Claustrum: 222 knittelverzen [Claustrum: 222 Doggerel Verses].   1980.
Dertien manieren om een fragment van Alechinsky te zien [Thirteen Ways of Looking at a Fragment of Alechinsky's].   1980.
Jan de Lichte.   1981.
Almanak: 366 knittelverzen.   1982.
Alibi.   1985.
Een weerzinwekkend bezoek.   1985.
Wyckaert, with Freddy de Vree.   1986.
Bewegen, photographs by Willy Legendre.   1986.
Selected Poems 1953–1973, edited by Theo Hermans, translated by Hermans, Paul Brown, and Peter Nifmeijer.   1986.
Gedichten van Hugo Claus (series; 22 pamphlets).   1986–90.
Evergreens.   1986.
Het verschijnsel.   1986.
Voor Pierre.   1987.
Hymen.   1987.
Sporen.   1987.
Mijn honderd gedichten.   1987.
Sonnetten.   1988.

Fiction

De Metsiers.   1950; translated as *The Duck Hunt*, 1965; as *Sister of Earth*, 1966.
De hondsdagen [The Dog Days].   1952.
Natuurgetrouw: Schetsen, verhalen, fabels. . . [True to Life: Sketches, Stories, Fables. . .].   1954.

De koele minnaar [The Cool Lover].   1956.
De zwarte keizer [The Black King].   1958.
Omtrent Deedee [About Deedee].   1963.
De verwondering [Wonderment].   1963.
Het jaar van de kreeft [The Year of the Cancer].   1972.
Schaamte [Shame].   1972.
Gebed om geweld: verhalen.   1972.
In het wide westen.   1973.
Aan de evenaar [At the Equator].   1973.
De groene ridder en de paladijnen [The Green Knight and the Paladins].   1973.
Jessica!   1977.
De vluchtende Atalanta [Atalanta in Flight].   1977.
Het verlangen [Longing].   1978.
De verzoeking [The Temptation].   1980.
Het verdriet van België.   1983; translated as *The Sorrow of Belgium*, 1990.
Een overtreling.   1985.
De mensen hiernaast: verhalen.   1985.
Een zachte vernieling.   1988.
Gilles en de nacht.   1989.

Other

Over het werk van Corneille [On the Work of Corneille].   1951.
Karel Appel, Schilder.   1964; as *Karel Appel, Painter*, 1962.
De man van Tollund: Schilderijen 1962–1963 [The Tollund Man: Paintings].   1963.
Louis Paul Boon.   1964.
De schilderijen van Roger Raveel [The Paintings of Roger Raveel].   1965.
Het landschap [The Landscape] (on Maurice Wyckaert).   1965.
De avonturen van Belgman I [The Adventures of Belgman I] (strip cartoon), drawings by Hoguké.   1967.
Schola Nostra (as Dorothea van Male).   1971.
Mexico vandaag: land van Posada, with Freddy de Vree.   1982.
Beelden.   1988.
De zwaardvis.   1989.
Kort dagboek.   1989.
Perte totale.   1989.

Translator, *Als een jonge hond* [Portrait of the Artist as a Young Dog], by Dylan Thomas.   1958.
Translator, *Het Hooglied* [The Song of Solomon].   1982.
Translator, with Freddy de Vree, *De anderehand*, by Pierre Alechinsky.   1987.

*   *   *

Hugo Claus is indisputably the most prolific, protean, and celebrated dramatist writing in Dutch today, which makes him the playwright laureate of both his native Flanders, in Belgium, and the Netherlands. Claus's theatre is as difficult to categorize as the man himself. An abiding curiosity, playfulness, vast erudition, love of mystification, and impatience with complacency have all contributed to an *oeuvre* of multiple facets. And despite his recent forays into cinema and frequent avowals that theatre is an outmoded art-form which he stoutly intends to foreswear, Claus's instinct for showmanship gets the better of him, and he continues to write regularly for the theatre.

Just as his poetry and prose bear the disparate stamps of Eliot and Pound, as well as those of Breton and the surrealists, Faulkner, and Dada, so his theatre is equally eclectic.

One has but to cull through the long list of classic works which he has adapted into modern Dutch (and significantly altered in the process) to get a feeling for his aspirations when it comes to his original works. Having tackled *Hamlet, A Midsummer Night's Dream, Richard III*, he is evidently, first of all, enamored with Shakespeare's works, although the Elizabethan structure and heterogeneity in his work is over-shadowed by the Jacobean (he has also adapted *The Revenger's Tragedy*). Claus's propensity for the overblown, the baroque, the iconoclastic, and perverse, find another spiritual ancestor in Seneca, whose *Thyestes, Oedipus*, and *Phaedra* he has also adapted.

But Claus shares the fate of Ibsen, who, though he wrote such far-ranging epics as *Peer Gynt* and *Emperor and Galilean*, is better remembered for his domestic dramas into which he crammed the mythic sub-structure of the larger works. *Een bruid in de morgen* [A Bride in the Morning], which was later produced by the Pitoëffs in Paris, and in English off-off Broadway in 1960, is about a girl's (Andrea) incestuous love for her brother Thomas. This successful early work introduces both Claus's Jacobean penchant for the dark underside of forbidden longing and a critical vision of the narrow-minded, petit-bourgeois milieu of present-day Flanders—both recurrent tendencies in his theatre.

Een bruid in de morgen was the first of a group of naturalis-tic dramas, which includes *Suiker* (Sugar), a melodrama about seasonal farm workers in the North of France, *Vrijdag* (Friday), and *Thuis* (*Back Home*). While Claus, himself, denies the naturalism of these works, preferring to describe them as "black-poetic", they all treat the day-to-day lives of the "little man".

Vrijdag, generally considered Claus's best play (he also directed his own film version of it), is about George Vermeersch's return home from a stint in prison, where he was serving a sentence for an incestuous relationship with his daughter, Christine. His wife, Jean, in the meantime has given birth to a baby by George's best friend, Eric. This triangle of wronged souls try to purge themselves of their resentment, and seek to forgive the unforgivable. The play's sober naturalistic structure is intercut with a series of cinema-tic flashbacks to George's past relationship with Christine, supported by a sub-structure that derives from the New Testament.

More grotesque is the Breughelian *Thuis*, in which a son brings a casual girlfriend to visit his mother and butcher-father, who are providing lodging for an incontinent, dodder-ing old woman, Mrs. Vergote. The butcher, a colorfully lusty but impotent figure, prevails on his son to let him bed down for a night with his nubile girlfriend, Sonya, who goes along agreeably with Pa's fantasy fulfilment. Through a Scribean turn of plotting, they trick Ma into leaving the house and render the field free for Pa's tryst with Sonya. The grotesque and farcical facets of *Thuis* come to the fore as Pa, faced with pressure to perform well sexually, fakes a spectacular heart attack, after which he nestles into Mrs. Vegote's crapulous but platonic lap, preferring a return to the womb to the more daunting option of a sexual romp with his son's girlfriend.

Interieur, an adaptation of Claus's novel *Omtrent Deedee* (Regarding Deedee), is yet another domestic drama which debunks Flemish mores and manners. Deedee is a priest who receives a visit from his entire family on the occasion of the anniversary of their mother's death. While the adults make the most of the occasion to get drunk and disport themselves in erotic abandon, Deedee's troubled nephew, Claude, turns to his uncle for wise counsel regarding his homosexuality and consequent guilt. The churchman, who puts himself across as broadminded and emphathetic, fails to provide either wisdom or solace, and the evening of frolics ends as Claude hangs himself.

Claus's Elizabethan/Jacobean *esprit* is unleashed from its domestic fetters in a series of panoramic romps based on social subjects. These include *Tijl Uilenspiegel, Tand om Tand* (Eye for an Eye), *Het leven en de werken van Leopold II* (The Life and Works of Leopold II), and *Serenade*. These works are as epic, in the Brechtian sense, as they are are Artaudian. Divided into a plethora of short scenes, each crafted to reveal a discrete aspect of societal corruption, these works have large casts and range freely through time and place, and in the case of *Leopold* wreak havoc with historical fact.

Tijl is a personal adaptation of Charles DeCoster's classic novel about the impish Flemish rebel who stood up to the Spanish conquerors in the 15th century. Claus harbors a special fondness for this archetypal outlaw, who shows up the restrictive tyranny of the establishment, which is enemy to individual expression: by implication a critique of modern society. Whereas *Tijl* penetrates Belgium's fictionalized his-torical past, *Tand om Tand* imagines a futuristic society, whose mechanized, technocratic ways suck the life from hu-man existence. Just as Claus's *Tijl* refracts present-day Belgium from a far distant past, so *Tand om Tand* is but an extension into the future of a situation Claus sees as already rampant.

Leopold II, the most successful of these episodic pageant plays, uses the grandiose figure, the Belgian king who col-onized the Congo, as a fulcrum for revealing the hypocrisy and overweaning pride which led to one people's subjugation by another. The play, enveloped in the atmosphere of a clown-show, moves wildly and capriciously through the monarch's career. Leopold's inexaustive appetite for land is equated with his lust for flesh, and his sado-masochistic han-kering for possession of a perfect black body which would reflect, in negative, his own white one back to him, is offered as an explanation for imperialism. The tone shifts drastically between low farce and music hall to a theatrical language which surely rivals W.S. Gilbert for wit and dexterity.

The last in this series of epics, *Serenade*, consists of a series of black-out sketches, whose oneiric mood betrays the play's sources—the dreams of the actors who collaboratively devel-oped the play with Claus. Wish-fulfillment and dread alter-nate as a dizzying series of perverse vignettes unfurl: a sexual molester's penis stretches elastically across the stage, pulled and ultimately snapped off by his victim; an august cardinal takes time out from his procession to sodomize a duckling that crosses his path; and so on. While wildly zany, *Serenade* throws down a defiant gauntlet against any restriction on sexual imagination society could impose.

The vast canvasses of these pageants do not preclude Claus from providing a smaller, more intimate focus. Although written as a prose work, *De verzoeking* (The Temptation) has been performed often as a one-woman show. With the hundred-year-old, three-hundred-pound, carbunkle-covered Sister Mechtild at its center, this work, like *Interieur*, makes a frontal assault on organized religion. A *tour-de-force* acting opportunity, Sister Mechtild converses freely with angels and Christ; in recognition of this gift, the Catholic Church pre-pares to beatify her. But she, inured to primitive mysticism and self-mortification, endures this honor as though it were her Golgotha (which reaches its climax in the toilet room she is dragged off to by the ashamed nuns after she urinates on the red carpet rolled out for her), providing a source for much dark humor and grotesquery, not to mention brilliant poetic language. Claus further explores the one-character form of play in his *Gilles!*, a work concerning the French Bluebeard,

Gilles de Rais—sadistic, bloody, and the quintessential Jacobean hero.

In *Het haar van de hond* (The Hair of the Dog), Claus synthesizes many of his stylistic and thematic fetishes. Ostensibly a thriller in which a small-time prostitute's murderer is on the loose, menacing other prostitutes in the vicinity, Claus constructs a reworking of the Christ story through the character of Mira Davids, friend to the dead hooker. While small in scale, and often darkly comic in tone, Claus manages to interweave a subtext of great significance into the framework of the story.

Claus's theatre language needs a word of comment. While he virtually creates a new, stately, stripped-down Dutch for his classic adaptations, in his domestic works he fuses standard Dutch with Flemish dialect. The result is a personal language, which no one, in real life, actually speaks, but which is eminently stageworthy. Erudite and crude, calculated and paroxysmic, grounded in the European theatrical heritage yet also boldly modernist, his plays make Claus a major figure among contemporary playwrights.

—David Willinger

COCTEAU, Jean (Maurice Eugène Clément). Born in Maisons-Lafitte, Paris, 5 July 1889. Educated at the Lycée Condorcet, Paris, and privately. Entered Parisian theatrical and literary circles, giving readings and attending functions; co-founder of the literary magazine, *Shéhérezade*, 1909; collaborated with Diaghilev's Ballets Russes as librettist, designer, and painter, from c.1911; joined the Red Cross, 1914; co-editor of the patriotic magazine, *Le Mot*, 1914–15; contributor, *Paris-Midi*, 1919; first play, *Antigone*, produced 1922; travelled around the world, under commission to write articles for *Paris-Soir*, 1936–37; travelled to USA, 1949. Recipient: Louions-Delluc Prize, 1946; Avant-garde Film Grand Prix, 1950. D. Litt: Oxford University, 1956. Member, Académie Française, 1955, and Royal Academy of Belgium; Honorary Member, American Academy and German Academy. Commandeur, Légion d'Honneur, 1961. Died in Milly-la-Forêt, 11 October 1963.

Works

Collections

Oeuvres complètes (11 vols.). 1946–57.
Théâtre de poche (includes scenarios, sketches, and radio works). 1949.
Théâtre complet (2 vols.). 1957.
Five Plays (includes *Orphée; Antigone; Intimate Relations; The Holy Terrors; The Eagle with Two Heads*). 1961.
"The Infernal Machine" and Other Plays (includes *Bacchus; Orpheus; The Eiffel Tower Wedding Party; The Knights of the Round Table*), translated by Albert Bermel. 1963.
Three Screenplays (*L'Éternel Retour; Orphée; La Belle et la bête*). 1972.

Stage Works

Le Dieu bleu, with Frédérick de Madrazo, music by Reynaldo Hahn (ballet scenario; produced Théâtre du Châtelet, Paris, 1912).

Jean Cocteau: illustration for *Le Chiffre* (drawing in the Bibliothèque Littéraire Jacques Doucet).

Parade, music by Erik Satie (ballet scenario; produced Théâtre du Châtelet, Paris, 1917).
Le Boeuf sur le toit, music by Darius Milhaud (ballet scenario; produced Théâtre des Champs-Élysées, Paris, 1920).
Les Mariés de la tour Eiffel (ballet scenario; produced Théâtre des Champs-Élysées, Paris, 1921). 1924; translated, as *The Eiffel Tower Wedding Party*, in *"The Infernal Machine" and Other Plays*, 1963.
Antigone (produced Théâtre de l'Atelier, Paris, 1922; revised version, with music by Arthur Honegger, produced 1927). 1927; translated as *Antigone*, in *Five Plays*, 1962.
Le Train bleu, music by Milhaud (ballet scenario, produced Théâtre des Champs-Élysées, Paris, 1924).
Roméo et Juliette, from the play by Shakespeare (produced Théâtre de la Cigale, Paris, 1924). 1926.
Orphée (produced Théâtre des Arts, Paris, 1926). 1927; translated as *Orpheus*, 1933.
Le Pauvre Matelot, with music by Milhaud (produced 1927). 1927.
Oedipus Rex, with music by Stravinsky (produced Théâtre Sarah-Bernhardt, Paris, 1927). 1949.
Oedipe-roi (produced Nouveau Théâtre Antoine, Paris, 1937). 1928.
La Voix humaine (produced Comédie-Francaise, Paris, 1930). 1930; translated as *The Human Voice*, 1951.
La Machine infernale (produced Comédie des Champs-Élysées, Paris, 1934). 1934; translated as *The Infernal Machine*, 1936.
Les Chevaliers de la table ronde (produced Théâtre de l'Oeuvre, Paris, 1937). 1937; translated as *The Knights of*

the Round Table, in "The Infernal Machine" and Other Plays, 1963.
Les Parents terribles (produced Théâtre des Ambassadeurs, Paris, 1938). 1938; translated as Intimate Relations, in Five Plays, 1961.
Les Monstres sacrés (produced Théâtre Michel, Paris, 1940). 1940; translated as The Holy Terrors, in Five Plays, 1961.
La Machine à écrire (produced Théâtre Hébertot, Paris, 1941). 1941; translated as The Typewriter, 1947.
Renaud et Armide (produced Comédie-Française, Paris, 1943). 1943.
L'Aigle à deux têtes (produced Théâtre des Galeries, Paris, 1946). 1946; translated as The Eagle Has Two Heads, 1948.
Un Tramway nommé désir, from a play by Tennessee Williams (produced Théâtre Édouard VII, Paris, 1949). 1949.
Phèdre (ballet scenario; produced Opéra, Paris, 1950).
Bacchus (produced Théâtre Marigny, Paris, 1951). 1952; translated as Bacchus, in "The Infernal Machine" and Other Plays, 1963.
La Dame à la licorne (ballet scenario; produced Theater am Gärtnerplatz, Munich, 1953).
Le Poète et sa muse (ballet scenario; produced 1959).
Cher menteur, from a play by Jerome Kilty (produced 1960). 1960.
L'Impromptu du Palais-Royal (produced by the Comédie-Française, Japan, 1962). 1962.

Screenplays

Le Sang d'un poète, 1930 (published 1948; translated as The Blood of a Poet, 1949); La Comédie du bonheur, 1940; Le Baron fantôme, with Serge de Poligny, 1943; L'Éternel Retour, 1943 (published in Three Screenplays, 1972); Les Dames du Bois du Boulogne, with Robert Bresson, 1945; La Belle et la bête, 1946 (published 1958; translation in Three Screenplays, 1972); Ruy Blas, 1947; L'Aigle à deux têtes, 1947; Les Parents terribles, 1948; Noces de sable, 1949; Les Enfants terribles, 1950; Orphée, 1950 (published 1951; translation in Three Screenplays, 1972); La Villa Santo-Sospiro, 1952; La Corona negra, 1952; Le Testament d'Orphée, 1960 (published 1961; translation in Two Screenplays, 1968); La Princesse de Clèves, 1961; Thomas l'imposteur, 1965.

Fiction

Le Potomak. 1919; revised edition, 1934.
Le Grand Écart. 1923; translated as The Grand Ecart, 1925; as The Miscreant, 1958.
Thomas l'imposteur. 1923; translated as Thomas the Imposter, 1925; as The Imposter, 1957.
Le Livre blanc. 1928; translated as The White Paper, 1957.
Les Enfants terribles. 1929; translated as Enfants Terribles (in English), 1930; as Children of the Game, 1955; as The Holy Terrors, 1957.
Le Fantôme de Marseille. 1936.
La Fin du Potomak. 1940.
Deux travestis. 1947.

Verse

La Lampe d'Aladin. 1909.
Le Prince frivole. 1910.
La Danse de Sophocle. 1912.
Le Cap de Bonne-Espérance. 1919.
Ode à Picasso. 1919.

Discours du grand sommeil. 1920.
Escales, with André Lhote. 1920.
Poésies 1917–20. 1920.
Vocabulaire. 1922.
Plain-chant. 1923.
La Rose de François. 1923.
Poésie 1916–23. 1924.
Cri écrit. 1925.
Prière mutilée. 1925.
L'Ange Heurtebise. 1926.
Opéra: oeuvres poétiques 1925–1927. 1927.
Morceaux choisis. 1932.
Mythologie. 1934.
Allégories. 1941.
Les Poèmes allemands. 1944.
Léone. 1945; translated as Leoun, 1960.
La Crucifixion. 1946.
Poèmes. 1948.
Le Chiffre. 1952.
Appogiatures. 1953.
Dentelle d'éternité. 1953.
Clair-obscur. 1954.
Poèmes 1916–1955. 1956.
Gondole des morts. 1959.
Cérémonial espagnol du phénix; La Partie d'échecs. 1961.
Le Requiem. 1961.
Faire-part. 1969.

Memoirs and Letters

Journals, edited by Wallace Fowlie. 1956.
Professional Secrets: An Autobiography, edited by Robert Phelps. 1970.
Lettres à André Gide, edited by Jean-Jacques Kihm. 1970.
Lettres à Milorad, edited by Milorad. 1975.

Other

Le Coq et l'arlequin: notes autour de la musique. 1918; translated as Cock and Harlequin, 1921.
Dans Le Ciel de la patrie. 1918.
Carte blanche. 1920.
Visites à Maurice Barrès. 1921.
Les Mariés de la tour Eiffel. 1921.
Le Secret professionnel. 1922.
Dessins. 1923.
Picasso. 1923.
Ferat. 1924.
Le Mystère de Jean l'oiseleur, monologues. 1925.
Lettre à Jacques Maritain. 1926; translated as Art and Faith, 1948.
Le Rappel à l'ordre. 1926; translated as A Call to Order, 1926.
Maison de santé: dessins. 1926.
Le Mystère laïc. 1928.
Une Entrevue sur la critique avec Maurice Rouzaud. 1929.
25 dessins d'un dormeur. 1929.
Essai de critique indirecte. 1932; translated as An Essay of Indirect Criticism, 1936.
Opium. 1932; translated as Opium, 1932.
Portraits-souvenir 1900–1914. 1935; translated as Paris Album 1900–1914, 1956.
60 Dessins pour "Les Enfants terribles". 1935.
Mon Premier Voyage: Tour du monde en 80 jours. 1936; translated as Round the World Again in Eighty Days, 1937.
Énigme. 1939.

Dessins en marge du texte des "Chevaliers de la table ronde,". 1941.
Le Greco. 1943.
Serge Lifar à l'opéra. 1944.
Portrait de Mounet-Sully. 1945.
La Belle et la bête: Journal d'un film. 1946; translated as *Beauty and the Beast: Diary of a Film*, 1950.
Poésie critique. 1946.
La Difficulté d'être. 1947; translated as *The Difficulty of Being*, 1966.
Le Foyer des artistes. 1947.
Drôle de ménage. 1948.
Reines de France. 1948.
Lettre aux américains. 1949.
Maalesh: Journal d'une tournée de théâtre. 1949; translated as *Maalesh: A Theatrical Tour in the Middle-East*, 1956.
Dufy. 1949.
Orson Welles, with André Bazin. 1950.
Modigliani. 1950.
Jean Marais. 1951.
Entretiens autour de la cinématographie, edited by André Fraigneau. 1951; revised edition, edited by André Bernard and Claude Gauteur, 1973; as translated *On Film*, 1954.
Journal d'un inconnu. 1952; translated as *The Hand of a Stranger*, 1956.
Gide vivant, with Julien Green. 1952.
La Nappe du Catalan. 1952.
Aux Confins de la Chine. 1955.
Lettre sur la poésie. 1955.
Le Dragon des mets. 1955.
Adieu à Mistinguett. 1956.
L'Art est un sport. 1956.
Impression: Arts de la rue. 1956.
Cocteau chez les sirènes, edited by Jean Dauven. 1956.
Témoignage. 1956.
Entretiens sur la musée de Dresde, with Louis Aragon. 1957; as *Conversations in the Dresden Gallery*, 1983.
Erik Satie. 1957.
La Chapelle Saint-Pierre, Villefranche-sur-Mer. 1957.
La Corrida du premier mai. 1957.
Comme un miel noir (in French and English). 1958.
Paraprosodies, précédées de 7 dialogues. 1958.
La Salle des mariages, Hôtel de Ville de Menton. 1958.
La Canne blanche. 1959.
Poésie critique: monologues. 1960.
Notes sur "Le Testament d'Orphée". 1960.
Le Cordon ombilical: souvenirs. 1962.
Hommage. 1962.
Anna de Noailles oui et non. 1963.
Adieux d'Antonio Ordonez. 1963.
La Mésangère. 1963.
Entretien avec Roger Stéphane. 1964.
Entretien avec André Fraigneau. 1965.
Pégase. 1965.
My Contemporaries, edited by Margaret Crosland. 1967.
Entre Radiguet et Picasso. 1967.
Cocteau's World (selections), edited by Margaret Crosland. 1972.
Cocteau, poète graphique, edited by Pierre Chanel. 1975.

Editor, *Almanach du théâtre et du cinéma.* 1949.
Editor, *Choix de lettres de Max Jacob à Jean Cocteau 1919–1944.* 1949.
Editor, *Amadeo Modigliani: quinze dessins.* 1960.

*

Criticism

Books:
Margaret Crosland, *Cocteau*, New York, 1956.
N. Oxenhandler, *Scandal and Parade: The Theatre of Cocteau*, London, 1957.
Wallace Fowlie, *Cocteau: The History of a Poet's Age*, Bloomington, Indiana, 1966.
Frederick Brown, *An Impersonation of Angels: A Biography of Cocteau*, New York, 1968.
Jean M. Magnan, *Cocteau*, Bruges, Belgium, 1968.
Elizabeth Sprigge and Jean-Jacques Kihm, *Jean Cocteau: The Man and the Mirror*, New York, 1968.
Francis Steegmuller, *Jean Cocteau: A Biography*, Boston, 1970.
Bettina L. Knapp, *Jean Cocteau*, New York, 1970; revised edition, 1989.
William Fifield, *Jean Cocteau*, New York, 1974.
Irena Filipowska, *Éléments tragiques dans le théâtre de Jean Cocteau*, Poznan, Poland, 1976.
Lydia Crowson, *The Esthetic of Cocteau*, Hanover, New Hampshire, 1978.
Frank W.D Ries, *The Dance Theatre of Jean Cocteau*, Ann Arbor, Michigan, 1985.
Arthur K. Peters, *Jean Cocteau and His World*, London, 1987.
Monique Lange, *Cocteau: Prince sans royaume*, Paris, 1989.
Jean Touzot, *Jean Cocteau*, Lyons, 1989.

Serials:
Cahiers Jean Cocteau, 1969— (published irregularly)

*   *   *

Jean Cocteau's prodigious output extended to literary criticism, cinema, ballet-scenarios, recordings, and murals as well as drama, fiction, and poetry. But in attempting to capture the elusive qualities of a deeper consciousness reflective of a universal reality, he blurs generic boundaries. In his first significant work, *Le Potomak* (*The Potomak*), he combined poems, dialogues, letters, confessions, and drawings. His novel, *Les Enfants terribles* (*Children of the Game*), touches upon autobiography; and, by incorporating episodes of his childhood fears, anxieties, frustrations, cruelties, and pleasures into his film *Le Sang d'un poète* (*The Blood of a Poet*), he experimented with different fictions to re-create a unified, unchanging vision.

In presenting varied perspectives of a single insight, Cocteau drew upon numerous narratives, settings, and situations. Greek myth serves as the plot for *Orphée* (*Orpheus*), *Antigone*, and *La Machine infernale* (*The Infernal Machine*), and for his opera-oratorio *Oedipe-roi* (Oedipus-Rex); Arthurian legend and medieval lore inform the stories and personages of *Les Chevaliers de la Table Ronde* (*The Knights of the Round Table*), the film *L'Éternel Retour* (Eternal Return), and the ballet *La Dame à la licorne* (*The Lady and the Unicorn*); melodramatic intrigues are enacted in *Les Parents terribles* (*Intimate Relations*) and *L'Aigle à deux têtes* (*The Eagle with Two Heads*); farcical entertainment characterizes his ballet *Les Mariés de la Tour Eiffel* (*The Eiffel Tower Wedding Party*); the neo-classical plays of Racine and Molière inspire respectively *Renaud et Armide* (Renaud and Armide) and *L'Impromptu du Palais-Royal* (The Impromptu of the Royal Palace); and the cult of Dionysus, the theological turmoil of Reformation Germany, polemical explanations of philosophy, and the protagonist's political martyrdom inform *Bacchus*.

In spite of these contrasts, a sense of shock identifies the style of Cocteau. Working with Diaghilev, the choreographer, Eric Satie, the composer, and Picasso, the artist, Cocteau wrote the scenario for the ballet *Parade* which, through its disparate music, dialogues, and staging, scandalized its audience. Recurring relationships (couples, families, intimate friends) and familiar images (rooms, letters, mirrors) evoke the ordinary. But by endowing these expected interactions with conflict and these recognizable objects with supernatural attributes, he rebelled against accepted structures and traditions. This diversity, then, represents an iconoclasm consistent throughout his drama which, in form, disrupts the conventional, but which, in theme, broaches the instinctual.

Incongruities intensify astonishment, suggest disorder, and call for an explanation that leads to an insight into the human situation. In *Orphée* (*Orpheus*), for example, Cocteau presents a horse whose tapping hoof conveys cosmic secrets, a mirror that serves as an entrance to Hades, and Orpheus's decapitated speaking head that is identified as Cocteau's. These images of the fantastic deviate from the expected but reflect a fixed reality. By accepting the validity of these impressions, or by attempting to resolve their disparities, Cocteau's characters transcend the delusions of their individual perceptions and penetrate the fearful truth of their existence. The horse communicates the correct message. But Orpheus misconstrues the code, thereby offending the Bacchantes and triggering his downfall. Freedom, too, is illusory. Love for Eurydice incites Orpheus to descend to Hades to redeem his wife. Self-love, however, overpowers his affections for her, and, in glancing backwards, he condemns her to the Underworld. Egoism, passion, and blindness characterize Orpheus; and, in spite of his efforts to overcome these limitations, he is trapped in a predicament that results in pain and death. Through his poetic ambitions he neglects Eurydice, incurs insults and suspicions, and provokes violence. In yielding to his personal feelings, he loses his wife and undergoes stoning and death. Self-deception, though, results in a glimpse into the unrelenting suffering and meaninglessness of life. Structurally, the play is cyclical, beginning and ending with lunch. But if the tensions of the opening scene on earth evolve into a tranquillity in the final setting in heaven, the conclusion denotes death and oblivion and connotes, for personage and spectator, the agony and absurdity of the human condition.

Through irony and paradox, Cocteau dramatizes the role of fate that compels protagonists to confront conflict and to become resigned to the torment and futility of their situation. In *La Machine infernale* (*The Infernal Machine*), Oedipus intends to avoid murder and incest. By announcing the solution to the riddle provided by the Sphinx, he believes to have resisted the curse. But he cannot escape destiny. His repetition of the answer masks ignorance, and the fame and happiness derived from this delusory triumph disguise disgrace and despair which, inherent in human existence, drive Oedipus to shame, blindness, and exile. Reality is a monstrosity; and, like the paradox of the double-headed eagle in *L'Aigle à deux têtes* (*The Eagle with Two Heads*), an "infernal machine" imprisons man in a struggle between illusion and truth. Initially, Cocteau's characters confuse peace and self-dignity with pain and death. An inevitable reconciliation of apparent contradictions, though, reveals the terrifying recognition of the emptiness and annihilation that constitute the duality of earthly existence.

In theme and form, Cocteau creates a theatre of shock and spectacle that concretizes, in narrative, image, and set, the horror of reality. Unlike his fifth-century Athenian or 17th-

century French predecessors, he does not analyze intentions and emotions. Rather, he presents a situation of changing illusions that hide, but eventually illuminate, the persistent presence of destruction and damnation. Destiny impels the discovery of this reality. Like the personages in the plays of Artaud, Beckett, and Genet, Cocteau's characters are victims who must meet defeat and despair. Through the unravelling of inconsistencies, they encounter, and reveal for the spectator, the absurdity of a universal predicament realized by the struggle of human endeavor or marked by the doom of inevitable death.

—Donald Gilman

See also *Volume 1* entry on *The Infernal Machine*.

COLMAN, George, the Elder. Born in Florence, Italy, where his father was an envoy, 15(?) April 1732; returned to London, and brought up by his uncle William Pulteney (later Earl of Bath), from 1733. Educated at Westminster School, London (king's scholar), 1741–51; Christ Church, Oxford, 1751–55, BA 1755, MA 1758; Lincoln's Inn, London, 1755–57; called to the bar, 1757. Married the actress Sarah Ford in 1767 (died 1771); children include the playwright George Colman the Younger. Founding editor, with Bonnell Thornton, *Connoisseur*, 1754–56; lawyer on the Oxford circuit, 1758–61; first play, *Polly Honeycombe*, produced 1760; soon began collaborating with David Garrick; performance director, Theatre Royal, Drury Lane, 1763–65; bought one quarter of the Covent Garden Theatre, 1767: manager, 1767–74; lived in Bath, 1775–76; contributor, *London Packet*, 1775; owner and manager, Theatre Royal, Haymarket (the Summer Theatre), succeeding Samuel Foote, 1776–89; paralysed by a stroke, 1785: pronounced insane by the Commission of Lunacy, and succeeded at the Haymarket by his son, 1789. Member of Samuel Johnson's literary Club from 1768. Died in London, 14 August 1794.

Works

Collections

Dramatic Works (4 vols.).   1777.
Plays by David Garrick and Colman (includes *The Jealous Wife; The Clandestine Marriage;* and three plays by Garrick), edited by E.R. Wood.   1982.

Stage Works

Polly Honeycombe: A Dramatic Novel (produced Theatre Royal, Drury Lane, London, 1760).   1760.
The Jealous Wife, from the novel *Tom Jones* by Fielding (produced Theatre Royal, Drury Lane, London, 1761).   1761.
The Musical Lady (produced Theatre Royal, Drury Lane, London, 1762).   1762.
Philaster, from the play by Beaumont and Fletcher (produced Theatre Royal, Drury Lane, London, 1763).   1763.
The Deuce is in Him (produced Theatre Royal, Drury Lane, London, 1763).   1763.

A Fairy Tale, from *A Midsummer Night's Dream* by Shakespeare (produced Theatre Royal, Drury Lane, London, 1763).   1763.

The Clandestine Marriage, with David Garrick (produced Theatre Royal, Drury Lane, London, 1766).   1766.

The English Merchant, from a play by Voltaire (produced Theatre Royal, Drury Lane, London, 1767).   1767.

The Oxonion in Town (produced Covent Garden Theatre, London, 1767).   1769.

King Lear, from the play by Shakespeare (produced Covent Garden Theatre, London, 1768).   1768.

Man and Wife; or, The Shakespeare Jubilee (produced Covent Garden Theatre, London, 1769).   1770.

The Portrait, music by Samuel Arnold, from a play by Louis Anseaume, music by Grétry (produced Covent Garden Theatre, London, 1770).   1770.

Mother Skipton, music by Samuel Arnold (produced Covent Garden Theatre, London, 1770).   Songs published 1771.

The Fairy Prince, music by Thomas Arne, from the masque *Oberon* by Jonson (produced Covent Garden Theatre, London, 1771).   1771.

Comus, music by Thomas Arne, from the masque by Milton (produced Covent Garden Theatre, London, 1772).   1772.

An Occasional Prelude (produced Covent Garden Theatre, London, 1772).   1776.

Achilles in Petticoats, music by Thomas Arne, from a work by John Gay (produced Covent Garden Theatre, London, 1773).   1774.

The Man of Business (produced Covent Garden Theatre, London, 1774).   1774.

The Spleen; or, Islington Spa (produced Theatre Royal, Drury Lane, London, 1776).   1776.

Epicoene; or, The Silent Woman, from the play by Jonson (produced Theatre Royal, Drury Lane, London, 1776).   1776.

New Brooms! An Occasional Prelude, with David Garrick (produced Theatre Royal, Drury Lane, London, 1776).   1776.

Polly, from the play by John Gay (produced Theatre Royal, Haymarket, London, 1777).   1777.

The Sheep Shearing, music by Thomas Arne and others, from the play *The Winter's Tale* by Shakespeare (produced Theatre Royal, Haymarket, London, 1777).   1777.

The Spanish Barber; or, The Fruitless Precaution, music by Samuel Arnold, from a play by Beaumarchais (produced Theatre Royal, Haymarket, London, 1777).

The Female Chevalier, from a play by William Taverner (produced Theatre Royal, Haymarket, London, 1778).

The Suicide (produced Theatre Royal, Haymarket, London, 1778).

Bonduca, music by Samuel Arnold, from the play by Fletcher (produced Theatre Royal, Haymarket, London, 1778).   1778.

The Tailors: A Tragedy for Warm Weather, revision of a play by Samuel Foote.   1778.

The Separate Maintenance (produced Theatre Royal, Haymarket, London, 1779).

The Manager in Distress (produced Theatre Royal, Haymarket, London, 1780).   1780?.

The Genius of Nonsense, music by Samuel Arnold (produced Theatre Royal, Haymarket, London, 1780).   Songs published, 1781.

The Beggar's Opera Reversed (produced Theatre Royal, Haymarket, London, 1781).

Harlequin Teague; or, The Giant's Causeway, with John O'Keeffe, music by Samuel Arnold (produced Theatre Royal, Haymarket, London, 1782).   Songs published 1782.

The Fatal Curiosity, from the play by Lillo (produced Theatre Royal, Haymarket, London, 1782).   1783.

The Election of the Managers (produced Theatre Royal, Haymarket, London, 1784).

Tit for Tat; or, The Mutual Deception, from a play by Marivaux (produced Theatre Royal, Haymarket, London, 1786).   1788.

Ut Pictura Poesis! or, The Enraged Musicians: A Musical Entertainment Founded on Hogarth, music by Samuel Arnold (produced Theatre Royal, Haymarket, London, 1789).   1789.

Verse

Two Odes, with Robert Lloyd.   1760.
Poems on Several Occasions (3 vols.).   1787.

Memoirs and Letters

Some Particulars of the Life of George Colman, Written by Himself.   1795.

Other

The Connoisseur, with Bonnell Thornton (4 vols.).   1757.
A Letter of Abuse to D–d G–k.   1757.
A True State of the Differences (on Covent Garden Theatre).   1768.
An Epistle to Dr. Kenrick.   1768.
T. Harris Dissected.   1768.
Prose on Several Occasions (3 vols.).   1787.

Editor, with Bonnell Thornton, *Poems by Eminent Ladies* (2 vols.).   1755.
Editor, *The Works of Beaumont and Fletcher* (10 vols.).   1778.

Translator, *The Comedies of Terence.*   1765; revised edition, 1766.
Translator, *The Merchant*, in *Comedies of Plautus.*   1769.
Translator, *Epistola de Arte Poetica*, by Horace.   1783.

*

Criticism

Books:
Richard Brinsley Peake, *Memories of the Colman Family, Including Their Correspondence* (2 vols.), London, 1841.
Eugene R. Page, *George Colman the Elder: Essayist, Dramatist, and Theatrical Manager, 1732–1794*, New York, 1935.
Richard Bevis, *The Laughing Tradition: Stage Comedy in Garrick's Day*, Athens, Georgia, 1980.

Articles:
Peter A. Tasch, "Bickerstaff, Colman, and the Bourgeois Audience" in *Restoration and 18th Century Theatre Research*, 9, 1970.

*   *   *

George Colman the elder's first play, *Polly Honeycombe*, was a satirical afterpiece, which mocked the harmful effects of circulating libraries and sentimental fiction (its influence can be observed in Sheridan's *The Rivals*). Colman also criticised the mercantile principles behind Polly's father's intention to match her with a ludicrous suitor, Mr Ledger. "Your head's so full of trade and commerce", says Polly, "that you would dispose of your daughter like a piece of merchandise—but my heart is my own property, and at nobody's disposal but my own". Nothing is resolved at the end of the play, a factor which strengthens its impact and satirical thrust.

Colman was to continue to satirise the foibles of the time, mocking a preoccupation with Italian music in *The Musical Lady* and the vogue for opera at the King's Theatre in *New Brooms*. "We have nothing but wind, wire, rosin and catgut", complains Crotchet in this *Occasional Prelude*, "Operas are the only real entertainment. The plain unornamented drama is too flat . . .". *The Manager in Distress* satirised the vogue for debating societies, in particular the Belle Assemblée, which met at Mrs Theresa Cornely's rooms in Carlisle House, whilst *The Genius of Nonsense* made fun of the quack Doctor Graham and his "Temple of Health". Representatives of the press were targeted in a number of plays, including *The English Merchant*, *The Spleen* and *New Brooms*. *The Oxonian in Town*, however, provoked opposition on the grounds that Colman's satire was levelled at the Irish.

Colman's satirical afterpieces, preludes, and farces were doubtless composed with a managerial eye as to what would draw audiences. At Covent Garden he was in competition with Garrick's Drury Lane management: *Man and Wife; or, The Shakespearean Jubilee* was rapidly brought out to capitalise on Garrick's ill-fated Stratford Jubilee just prior to a similar piece written by Garrick for Drury Lane. Adaptations and revivals were similarly motivated by his managerial needs: Beaumont and Fletcher's *Philaster* was adapted to provide a vehicle for William Powell; versions of Milton's *Comus* and Jonson's masque *Oberon* (restaged as *The Fairy Prince*) proved theatrically effective, as did a revision of *King Lear*, which removed Nahum Tate's interpolated love affair between Edgar and Cordelia, but retained his happy ending and omission of the Fool. Colman adapted and translated assiduously: *The Spleen* was partially based on Molière's *Le Malade imaginaire*, whilst *The Spanish Barber* was a version of Beaumarchais' *The Barber of Seville*; echoes of many other writers are also to be found in his work. Originality is not an important feature of Colman's plays, whether in regard to sources or to the dramatic structures adopted.

Colman, however, proved himself adept in his use of some of the conventional forms of the time. *The English Merchant*, based on Voltaire's *L'Écossaise*, is, according to Allardyce Nicoll, one of the best examples of sentimental comedy in the 18th-century English repertoire. *The Man of Business*, which has been dismissed as "a weakly sentimental thing", also belongs to this genre. Dwelling as it does on the supposed ruin, remorse, and happy marriage of its profligate hero, Beverley, its possible debts to Holcroft, Plautus, Terence, Beaumarchais and others led to its being designated "a very confused miscellany of several plays and tales". More successful were two plays belonging to the comedy of manners genre, *The Jealous Wife* and *The Clandestine Marriage*, both of which owe something to Garrick and both of which have sustained revivals during the present century. The former play is largely Colman's work; the extent of each author's contribution to the second play has been disputed, but recent scholarship has attributed the lion's share to Garrick.

The Jealous Wife retains something of the energy of Wycherley's and Vanbrugh's plays, whilst also anticipating the anti-sentimental strain of Sheridan's comedies. The characters are sharply drawn, the plot moves steadily forward, and the morals are succinctly pointed. The absurd jealousy of Mrs. Oakly, the superficial "city" values of Lady Freelove and Lord Trinkett, and the transactional attitude of Mr. Russet (determined to marry off his daughter to the absurdly horse-loving Sir Harry Beagle) are all delineated forcefully and effectively; the play retains its satirical edge without degenerating into sermonising or sentimentality.

The Clandestine Marriage, partially inspired by the first plate in Hogarth's series "Marriage à-la-Mode", intertwined plots concerning a transactional marriage and a secret marriage between two lovers, whilst also introducing the elderly and absurdly comic character of Lord Ogleby. Garrick's refusal to play the amorous Lord in the first production was to lead to a temporary rift between him and Colman.

George Colman the elder was as significant a theatre manager as he was a dramatist. It was he who was responsible for the first stagings of Goldsmith's *The Good-Natured Man* and *She Stoops to Conquer* at Covent Garden. When he took over the Haymarket Theatre from Samuel Foote his management proved as effective as it had been at Covent Garden. Together with Garrick he succeeded in establishing strong management in the mid-18th century London theatre and sustaining a strong and vigorous repertory in the theatre of his time.

—Jim Davis

See also *Volume 1* entry on *The Clandestine Marriage*.

COLMAN, George, the Younger. Born in London, 21 October 1762; son of George Colman the Elder, dramatist. Educated at Marylebone Seminary, London, 1770–71; Westminster School, London, 1772–79; Christ Church, Oxford, 1780–81; King's College, Aberdeen, 1781–84; Lincoln's Inn, London. Married 1) Catherine Morris in 1784 (separated 1801); 2) the actress Maria Gibbs in 1809. First play, *The Female Dramatist*, produced 1782; manager (succeeding his father), Theatre Royal, Haymarket, 1789–1813 (bought Haymarket patent, 1794; sold half his shares, 1805, and the remainder, 1818); arrested for debt, 1806, and kept under King's Bench restrictions, 1806–17; appointed Lieutenant of the Yeoman Guard by George IV, 1820 (sold commission, 1831); examiner of plays, Lord Chamberlain's Office, 1824–36. Died in London, 26 October 1836.

Works

Collections

Dramatic Works (4 vols.).   1827.
Broad Grins, My Night-Gown and Slippers, and other Humorous Works, edited by G.B. Buckstone.   1872.
Plays by Thomas Morton and George Colman the Younger (includes *Inkle and Yarico; The Surrender of Calais; Blue Beard;* and two plays by Morton), edited by Barry Sutcliffe.   1983.

Stage Works

The Female Dramatist, from a novel by Tobias Smollett (produced Theatre Royal, Haymarket, London, 1782).

Two to One, music by Samuel Arnold (produced Theatre Royal, Haymarket, London, 1784). 1785.

Turk and No Turk, music by Samuel Arnold (produced Theatre Royal, Haymarket, London, 1785). Songs published 1785.

Inkle and Yarico, music by Samuel Arnold (produced Theatre Royal, Haymarket, London, 1787). 1787.

Ways and Means; or, A Trip to Dover (produced Theatre Royal, Haymarket, London, 1788). 1788.

The Family Party (produced Theatre Royal, Haymarket, London, 1789). 1789.

The Battle of Hexham, music by Samuel Arnold (produced Theatre Royal, Haymarket, London, 1789). 1790.

The Surrender of Calais, music by Samuel Arnold (produced Theatre Royal, Haymarket, London, 1791). 1792.

Poor Old Haymarket; or, Two Sides of the Gutter (produced Theatre Royal, Haymarket, London, 1792). 1792.

The Mountaineers, music by Samuel Arnold (produced Theatre Royal, Haymarket, London, 1793). 1794.

New Hay at the Old Market (produced Theatre Royal, Haymarket, London, 1795). 1795; abridged version, as *Sylvester Daggerwood* (produced 1796), 1796.

The Iron Chest, music by Stephen Storace, from a novel by William Godwin (produced Theatre Royal, Drury Lane, London, 1796). 1796.

My Nightgown and Slippers; or, Talks in Verse (produced Theatre Royal, Drury Lane, London, 1797). 1797; revised version, as *Broad Grins*, 1802.

The Heir at Law (produced Theatre Royal, Haymarket, London, 1797). 1798.

Blue Beard: or, Female Curiosity! A Dramatic Romance, music by Michael Kelly, from a play by Michel Jean Sedaine (produced Theatre Royal, Drury Lane, London, 1798). 1798.

Blue Devils, from a play by Patrat (produced Theatre Royal, Drury Lane, London, 1798). 1808.

The Castle of Sorrento, with Henry Heartwell, music by Thomas Attwood, from a French play (produced Theatre Royal, Haymarket, London, 1799). 1799.

Feudal Times; or, The Banquet-Gallery, music by Michael Kelly (produced Theatre Royal, Drury Lane, London, 1799). 1799.

The Review; or, The Wags of Windsor, music by Samuel Arnold (produced Theatre Royal, Haymarket, London, 1800). 1801.

The Poor Gentleman (produced Covent Garden Theatre, London, 1801). 1802.

John Bull; or, An Englishman's Fireside (produced Covent Garden Theatre, London, 1803). 1803.

No Prelude! (produced Theatre Royal, Haymarket, London, 1803).

Love Laughs at Locksmiths, music by Michael Kelly, from a play by J.N. Bouilly (produced Theatre Royal, Haymarket, London, 1803). 1803.

The Gay Deceivers; or, More Laugh Than Love, music by Michael Kelly, from a play by Theodore Hell (produced Theatre Royal, Haymarket, London, 1804). 1808.

Who Wants a Guinea? (produced Covent Garden Theatre, London, 1805). 1805.

We Fly by Night; or, Long Stories (produced Covent Garden Theatre, London, 1806). 1806.

The Forty Thieves, with Charles Ward, music by Michael Kelly (produced Theatre Royal, Drury Lane, London, 1806). 1808; as *Ali Baba*, 1814.

The Africans; or, War, Love, and Duty, music by Michael Kelly (produced Theatre Royal, Haymarket, London, 1808). 1808.

X.Y.Z. (produced Covent Garden Theatre, London, 1810). 1820.

The Quadrupeds of Quedlinburgh; or, The Rovers of Weimar (produced Theatre Royal, Haymarket, London, 1811).

Doctor Hocus Pocus; or, Harlequin Washed White (produced Theatre Royal, Haymarket, London, 1814).

The Actor of All Work; or, First and Second Floor (produced Theatre Royal, Haymarket, London, 1817).

The Gnome King (produced Covent Garden Theatre, London, 1819). 1819.

A Figure of Fun (produced Covent Garden Theatre, London, 1821).

The Law of Java, music by Henry Bishop (produced Covent Garden Theatre, London, 1822). 1822.

Stella and Leatherlungs; or, A Star and a Stroller (produced Theatre Royal, Drury Lane, London, 1823).

Five Minutes Too Late (produced Theatre Royal, Drury Lane, London, 1825).

Verse

Poetical Vagaries. 1812.
Vagaries Vindicated; or, Hypocritic Hypercritics. 1813.
Eccentricities for Edinburgh. 1816.
Poetical Works. 1840.

Memoirs and Letters

Random Records (autobiography; 2 vols.). 1830.

Other

Editor, *Posthumous Letters Addressed to Francis Colman and George Colman the Elder*. 1820.

*

Criticism

Books:

Richard Brinsley Peake, *Memories of the Colman Family, Including Their Correspondence* (2 vols.), London, 1841.

Walther Steinwender, *Colman the Younger als Dramatiker*, Königsberg, 1913.

Jeremy F. Bagster-Collins, *George Colman the Younger*, New York, 1946.

Articles:

Peter Thomson, "The Early Career of Colman" in *Essays on Nineteenth-Century British Theatre*, 1971.

*   *   *

The younger Colman was not intended by his socially ambitious father for a theatrical career, but, owing to a blend of inheritance and temperamental drift, he slipped into it. 43 years separated his first play, *The Female Dramatist* (1782), from his last, light-hearted musical interlude, *Five Minutes Too Late* (1825). For all of 30 years he was involved in the management of the Haymarket Theatre and, for the last 12 years of his life, he was an unimpressive Examiner of Plays. It was not to the advantage of the English drama that these two functions gave Colman a significant influence over theatrical taste. There was no malice in him, but neither did he have a sense of direction. Where public preferences were concerned, he was a weathervane, quite unable to hold steady in the critical years during which English society assimilated the impact of the French Revolution. It was a period that witnessed the collapse of traditional dramatic genres and the emergence of melodrama. Colman's contribution to the collapse was primarily a matter of carelessness, confessed in his description of *The Quadrupeds of Quedlinburgh* as a "tragico-comico-anglo-germanico-hippo-ono-drama-tico romance". It was a characteristically good-humoured surrender.

Most of Colman's plays were written for his own company at the Haymarket, creating parts to suit the talents of the actors who were regular favourites during the theatre's summer seasons. In two occasional pieces, *Poor Old Haymarket* and *New Hay at the Old Market*. Colman makes specific claims for the superiority of this comparatively small theatre over the vast stages and auditoria of Drury Lane and Covent Garden. Certainly he could display there the lightness of touch which was his greatest asset. His facility as a writer of comic verse was recognised by his contemporaries and exploited by his friend, the sentimental comedian Jack Bannister. Colman's was the major contribution to the writing of the first substantial one-man show since Samuel Foote's *Diversions*, *Bannister's Budget*.

It was also Bannister who created the character of Inkle in Colman's first successful piece, *Inkle and Yarico*. Based on a cautionary tale from Steele's *Spectator*, which tells how a young Bristol merchant was saved by a dark-skinned island princess when his boat was wrecked, fell in love with her, took her with him when they were rescued, and then sold her into slavery in the West Indies, this so-called "opera" is, in fact, a comedy enlivened by songs and given a sufficiently sentimental turn to render it innocuous in the debate about slavery. It is the songs, set to music by Samuel Arnold, that distinguish it. Like many writers of modern musicals, Colman used them to shift or establish a mood rather than to advance the narrative. The shameless mixture of high romance and low farce, of archaic rhetoric and contemporary colloquialism, was a challenge to the 18th-century values of pure form and chaste diction. Colman was protected by the new taste for the gothic, which remained his chief resource for the rest of his career.

The next significant development was what James Boaden would soon call "a sort of Colman drama in three acts", of which *The Battle of Hexham* was the first, and *The Surrender of Calais* probably the best example. These history plays take a serious theme, dress it in blank verse which steals from, or imitates, Shakespeare, and conscientiously trivialise it by importing low-life buffoons and lively but irrelevant songs. Rigorous critics of the drama hated them, but audiences applauded, and Colman was sufficiently confident to carry the technique straight into the world of the contemporary gothic. John Philip Kemble triumphed as the gloomy hero of *The Mountaineers*, and although Colman's subsequent adaptation of William Godwin's novel *Caleb Williams* as *The Iron Chest* crashed to disaster on its first night at Drury Lane, it survived to become a popular favourite until well into the 19th century.

Celebrated, on such slender evidence, as the leading playwright of the day, Colman dug Drury Lane out of a Christmas crisis by providing it with *Blue Beard*, not so much a pantomine as a gothic extravaganza for actors, singers, dancers, and stage-machines. Under pressure to justify his inflated reputation, he also wrote for Covent Garden three five-act comedies, of which the second, *John Bull*, is sufficiently robust to suggest a greater potential than he had the stamina to realise. Financial problems at the Haymarket cannot have helped. From 1806 to 1817, Colman was confined as a debtor under the rules of the King's Bench, a sufficient inconvenience to impede the development of a writer who valued present ease above posthumous glory.

—Peter Thomson

COLUM, Padraic. Born in Longford, Ireland, 8 December 1881. Educated at Glasthule National School, Sandycove, County Dublin. Married the writer Mary Catherine Gunning Maguire in 1912 (died 1957). Clerk, Irish Railway Clearing House, Dublin, 1898–1904; member of the National Theatre Society and associated with the founding of the Abbey Theatre, Dublin; founder, with others, 1911, and editor, 1912–13, *Irish Review*, Dublin; moved to the USA, 1914, and lived in Pittsburgh, Connecticut, and New York; lived in France, 1930–33; lecturer, Columbia University, New York, from 1939. President, James Joyce Society, New York, and Poetry Society of America, 1938–39. Recipient: Academy of American Poets fellowship, 1952; Irish Academy of Letters Gregory medal, 1953. Litt.D: Columbia University, 1958; Trinity College, Dublin, 1958. Member, Irish Academy of Letters, and American Academy. Died 11 January 1972.

Works

Collections

Three Plays: The Fiddler's House; The Land; Thomas Muskerry. 1916; revised edition, 1925.
Selected Plays (includes *The Land; The Betrayal; Glendalough; Monasterboice*), edited by Sanford Sternlicht. 1986.

Stage Works

The Children of Lir. In *Irish Independent*, 1902.
Brian Boru. In *Irish Independent*, 1902.
The Kingdom of the Young (produced 1902). In *United Irishman*, 1903.
The Foleys. In *United Irishman*, 1903.
Eoghan's Wife. In *United Irishman*, 1903.
The Saxon Shillin' (produced by the Irish National Theatre Society, Molesworth Hall, Dublin, 1903). In *Lost Plays of the Irish Renaissance*, edited by Robert Hogan and James Kilroy, 1970.
The Broken Soil (produced by the Irish National Theatre Society, Molesworth Hall, Dublin). In *United Irishman*, 1903; revised version, as *The Fiddler's House* (produced by the Theatre of Ireland Company, Large Concert Hall, Rotunda, Dublin, 1907), 1907.
The Land (produced Abbey Theatre, Dublin, 1905). 1905.
The Miracle of the Corn: A Miracle Play (produced Abbey Theatre, Dublin, 1908). In *Studies*, 1907.
Thomas Muskerry (produced Abbey Theatre, Dublin, 1910). 1910.
The Destruction of the Hostel (for children; produced St. Enda's School, Dublin, 1910).
The Desert. 1912; as *Mogu the Wanderer; or, The Desert: A Fantastic Comedy*, 1917 (produced as *Mogu of the Desert*, Gate Theatre, Dublin, 1931).

The Betrayal (produced Carnegie Institute, Pittsburgh, Pennsylvania, 1914). 1917.
The Grasshopper, with F.E. Washburn-Freund, from a play by Count Keyserling (produced Abbey Theatre, Dublin, 1922).
Balloon (produced Ogunquit, Maine, 1929). 1929.
The Show-Booth, from a play by Alexander Blok (produced Dublin, 1948).
Moytura: A Play for Dancers (produced Dublin Festival, 1962). 1963.
The Challengers: Monasterboice, Glendalough, Cloughoughter (produced Lantern Theatre, Dublin, 1966). *Monasterboice* and *Glendalough* in *Selected Plays*, 1986.
The Road Round Ireland, with Basil Burwell, from works by Colum (produced Norwalk, Connecticut, 1967; as *Carricknabauna*, produced New York, 1967).

Radio Plays

Monasterboice; *Glendalough*; *Cloughoughter*; *Kilmore*.

Fiction

Castle Conquer. 1923.
Three Men: A Tale. 1930.
The Flying Swans. 1957.
Selected Short Stories, edited by Sanford Sternlict. 1985.

Verse

Heather Ale. 1907.
Wild Earth. 1907; revised edition, as *"Wild Earth" and Other Poems*, 1916.
"Dramatic Legends" and Other Poems. 1922.
The Way of the Cross: Devotions on the Progress of Our Lord Jesus Christ from the Judgement Hall to Calvary. 1926.
Creatures. 1927.
Old Pastures. 1930.
Poems. 1932; revised edition, as *The Collected Poems*, 1953.
The Story of Lowry Maen. 1937.
Flower Pieces: New Poems. 1938.
The Jackdaw. 1939.
The Vegetable Kingdom. 1954.
Ten Poems. 1957.
Garland Sunday. 1958.
Irish Elegies. 1958; revised edition, 1961, 1966.
The Poet's Circuits: Collected Poems of Ireland. 1960.
Images of Departure. 1969.
Selected Poems, edited by Sanford Sternlicht. 1989.

Other (for children)

A Boy in Eirinn. 1913.
The King of Ireland's Son. 1916.
The Boy Who Knew What the Birds Said. 1918.
The Adventures of Odysseus and the Tale of Troy. 1918; as *The Children's Homer*, 1946.
The Girl Who Sat by the Ashes. 1919.
The Children of Odin: A Book of Northern Myths. 1920.
The Boy Apprenticed to an Enchanter. 1920.
The Golden Fleece and the Heroes Who Lived Before Achilles. 1921.
The Children Who Followed the Piper. 1922.
The Six Who Were Left in a Shoe. 1923.
The Peep-Show Man. 1924.
Tales and Legends of Hawaii: At the Gateways of the Day, and *The Bright Islands* (2 vols.). 1924–25; as *Legends of Hawaii*, 1937.
The Island of the Mighty, Being the Hero Stories of Celtic Britain Retold from the Mabinogion. 1924.
The Voyagers, Being Legends and Romances of Atlantic Discovery. 1925.
The Forge in the Forest. 1925.
The Fountain of Youth: Stories to Be Told. 1927.
Orpheus: Myths of the World. 1930; as *Myths of the Old World*, nd.
The White Sparrow. 1933; as *Sparrow Alone*, 1975.
The Big Tree of Bunlahy: Stories of My Own Countryside. 1933.
Where the Winds Never Blew and the Cocks Never Crew. 1940.
The Frenzied Prince, Being Heroic Stories of Ancient Ireland. 1943.
"The Stone of Victory" and Other Tales. 1966.

Editor, *Gulliver's Travels*, by Swift. 1917.
Editor, *The Arabian Nights, Tales of Wonder and Magnificence*. 1953.

Other

Studies (miscellany). 1907.
My Irish Year. 1912.
The Irish Rebellion of 1916 and Its Martyrs: Erin's Tragic Easter, with others, edited by Maurice Joy. 1916.
The Road round Ireland. 1926.
Cross-Roads in Ireland. 1930.
Ella Young: An Appreciation. 1931.
A Half-Day's Ride; or, Estates in Corsica. 1932.
The Legend of Saint Columba. 1935.
Our Friend James Joyce, with Mary Colum. 1958.
Arthur Griffith. 1959; as *Ourselves Alone! The Story of Arthur Griffith and the Origin of the Irish Free State*, 1959.
Story Telling Old and New. 1961.

Editor, *Oliver Goldsmith*. 1913.
Editor, *Broad-Sheet Ballads, Being a Collection of Irish Popular Songs*. 1913.
Editor, with Edward J. O'Brien, *Poems of the Irish Revolutionary Brotherhood*. 1916; revised edition, 1916.
Editor, *Anthology of Irish Verse*. 1922; revised edition, 1948.
Editor, *A Treasury of Irish Folklore: The Stories, Traditions, Legends, Humor, Wisdom, Ballads, and Songs of the Irish People*. 1954; revised edition, 1962, 1967.
Editor, with Margaret Freeman Cabell, *Between Friends: Letters of James Branch Cabell and Others*. 1962.
Editor, *The Poems of Samuel Ferguson*. 1963.
Editor, *Roofs of Gold: Poems to Read Aloud*. 1964.

*

Criticism

Books:
Zack R. Bowen, *Padraic Colum: A Biographical-Critical Introduction*, Carbondale, Illinois, 1970.

Articles:
Zack R. Bowen, "Padraic Colum and Irish Drama", in *Eire*, vol.5 no.4, 1970.

Padraic Colum issue of *Journal of Irish Literature*, vol.2, no.1, 1973 (includes interviews and articles).
Zack R. Bowen, "The Theatre of Padraic Colum", in *Threshold*, 29, 1978.

* * *

In his youth, Padraic Colum was a formative influence in the development of a native school of Irish playwrights. In the first decade of the century he wrote of the peasant in *The Land*, of the artist in *The Fiddler's House*, and of the public official in *Thomas Muskerry*. This notable trilogy owed little to the influence of J.M. Synge who largely shaped the form and content of what became known as an "Abbey play". To a large extent, Colum dispensed with plot and relied on the gradual unfolding of character and motive. The quiet and gentle folk in his plays were a sharp contrast to the more flamboyant of Synge's creations. Colum's lovers whisper like doves cooing, while Synge's Playboy and Pegeen Mike storm the gates of Paradise with their mighty talk.

"The passion for the land that motivates the first play", wrote Colum in later life, "is not likely to be responded to in days when farms are being abandoned and when men who knew the oppression of landlordism . . . are not to be met with in the flesh. If staged nowadays, *The Land* would have to be played as a historical piece and for character parts". In the second play of the trilogy, *The Fiddler's House* (first produced under the title *Broken Soil*), it is the artist who rebels against the tyranny of life on the land. The principal character, Conn Hourican, is a folk-musician and a rambler by inclination. He has tramped the roads of Ireland as free as the birds, and cannot settle down to the humdrum life of a small farmer. Despite family ties, he must answer the call of the road, for "those who have the gift must follow the gift".

In the preface to the first edition of *Thomas Muskerry*, Colum stated that he intended to tackle a major task, the writing of a comedy of Irish life through all the social stages. What he achieved was a study, in the Ibsen manner, of an official in a small country town, brought to ruin by the inordinate demands on him by his relatives. Through the greed and insensitivity of his family, Thomas Muskerry, once the Master of the Workhouse, dies in a pauper's bed in the institution over which he once ruled. Although the picture of small-town life is unconvincing, there are moments in the last act as fine as anything in Balzac's *Père Goriot*.

After the production of *Thomas Muskerry* in 1910, Colum wrote nothing of significance for the Irish theatre for over 50 years. He became better known as a poet and as a collector of folk-tales. He abandoned the realism of his early plays and experimented with German expressionism in the 1920's in plays like *Balloon*, in an American setting. When he was in his 80's, he planned a cycle of plays, on Irish historical subjects, in the Japanese Noh manner, which Yeats had adopted some 30 years earlier in his *Plays for Dancers*. Four of these symbolic plays were produced on radio, and one, *Moytura*, dealing with the archaeologist Sir William Wilde and the legendary battle site, was staged during the Dublin Theatre Festival in 1962. *Monasterboice* underlined the link between Celtic Art and the intricacies of Joyce's *Finnegans Wake*. *Glendalough*, a monastic site, is the setting for an evocation of the fall of Parnell, Ireland's "uncrowned king". *Cloughoughter* links Owen Roe O'Neill with Sir Roger Casement and *Kilmore* sounds a requiem for Archbishop Bedell and Edward Bunting who, in different times and ways, tried to bring about a union of Irish people of different religious beliefs through a resurgence of Irish art and culture.

There was but a limited audience for Colum's imaginative leap into the historic past. As a dramatist, he never quite fulfilled the great promise of his youth. Today he is best known as a poet who wrote lyrically of the quiet pastures and gentle people of the Irish midlands.

—Micheál Ó hAodha

CONGREVE, William. Born in Bardsey, Yorkshire, England, 24 January 1670; moved with his family to Youghal, Ireland, 1674. Educated at Kilkenny College, 1682–86; Trinity College, Dublin, 1686–89, MA 1696; Middle Temple, London, 1691. Had affair with Henrietta, Duchess of Marlborough; one daughter. First play, *The Old Bachelor*, produced 1693; held several government posts: commissioner for licensing hackney coaches, 1696, manager, Malt Lottery, 1697, customs officer, Poole, Dorset, 1700–03, commissioner for wines, 1705, secretary for Jamaica from 1714; manager, with John Vanbrugh, Queen's Theatre, London, 1705–06. Died in London, 19 January 1729.

William Congreve (engraving after a portrait by Godfrey Kneller).

Works

Collections

Works (3 vols.).   1710.
Complete Works, edited by Montague Summers (4 vols.)
    1923.
Comedies, edited by Bonamy Dobrée.   1925.
Works, edited by F.W. Bateson.   1930.
Complete Plays, edited by Herbert J. Davis.   1967.
The Comedies, edited by Anthony G. Henderson.   1982.
The Comedies, edited by Eric S. Rump.   1985.

Stage Works

The Old Bachelor (produced Theatre Royal, Drury Lane,
    London, 1693).   1693.
The Double-Dealer (produced Theatre Royal, Drury Lane,
    London, 1693).   1694; edited by J.C. Ross, 1981.
Love for Love (produced Lincoln's Inn Fields Theatre,
    London, 1695).   1695.
The Mourning Bride (produced Lincoln's Inn Fields Theatre,
    London, 1697).   1697.
The Way of the World (produced Lincoln's Inn Fields
    Theatre, London, 1700).   1700.
The Judgement of Paris (produced Dorset Garden Theatre,
    London, 1701).   1701.
Semele (opera libretto; produced Covent Garden Theatre,
    London, 1744).   In *Works*, 1710.
Squire Trelooby, with Vanbrugh and William Walsh, from a
    play by Molière (produced Lincoln's Inn Fields Theatre,
    London, 1704).   Revised version by James Ralph pub-
    lished as *The Cornish Squire*, 1734.

Fiction

Incognita; or, Love and Duty Reconciled.   1692.
An Impossible Thing: A Tale.   1720.

Verse

The Mourning Muse of Alexas: A Pastoral.   1695.
A Pindaric Ode to the King.   1695.
The Birth of the Muse.   1698.
A Hymn to Harmony.   1703.
The Tears of Amaryllis for Amyntas.   1703.
A Pindaric Ode to the Queen.   1706.

Memoirs and Letters

Letters and Documents, edited by John C. Hodges.   1964.

Other

Amendments of Mr. Collier's False and Imperfect Citations.
    1698.
A Letter to the Viscount Cobham.   1729.
Last Will and Testament.   1729.

Editor, *The Dramatic Works of Dryden* (6 vols.).   1717.

*

Bibliographies

Laurence Bartlett, *William Congreve: A Reference Guide*,
    Boston, 1979.

Criticism

Books

D. Crane Taylor, *William Congreve*, Oxford, 1931.
John C. Hodges, *Congreve the Man: A Biography*, New
    York, 1941.
Kathleen Lynch, *A Congreve Gallery*, Cambridge,
    Massachusetts, 1951.
E.L. Avery, *Congreve's Plays on the Eighteenth-Century
    Stage*, New York, 1951.
Bonamy Dobrée, *William Congreve*, New York, 1963.
William Van Voris, *The Cultivated Stance: The Designs of
    Congreve's Plays*, Dublin and London, 1966.
Maximillian E. Novak, *William Congreve*, New York, 1971.
Brian Morris (ed.), *William Congreve: A Collection of
    Critical Studies*, London, 1972.
Harold Love, *William Congreve*, 1974.
Audrey L. Williams, *An Approach to Congreve*, New Haven,
    Connecticut, 1974.
Ursula Jantz, *Targets of Satire in the Comedies of Etherege,
    Wycherley, and Congreve*, Salzburg, 1978.
Patrick Lyons (ed.), *Congreve: Comedies—A Casebook*,
    London, 1982.
Robert Markley, *Two-Edg'd Weapons: Style and Ideology in
    the Comedies of Etherege, Wycherley and Congreve*,
    Oxford, 1988.
Alexander Lindsay and Howard Erskine-Hill, *Congreve: The
    Critical Heritage*, London, 1989.
Julie Stone Peters, *Congreve, The Drama, and the Printed
    Word*, 1990.

*   *   *

Congreve's career as a dramatist was early and brief: he
began at 23 in 1693 and effectively stopped in 1700, before he
was 30. But in that short period he was recognized as the
leading comic playwright of his generation and as a respected
writer of tragedy. And though his reputation as a tragedian
subsided long ago, his stature as a comic writer has, if anything, risen in the 20th century. He is generally recognized as
the best playwright of the late 17th century, almost exclusively for his work in comedy.

The young Congreve gained the attention of Dryden and
his circle soon after his arrival in London. Dryden considered
The Old Bachelor the best first play he had ever seen, and,
along with Southerne, helped revise and promote it. In the
poem "To My Dear Friend Mr. Congreve", written for the
publication of *The Double-Dealer*, Dryden proclaimed
Congreve his successor; Congreve could count on Dryden's
friendship and support until his death, and his return tribute
to his mentor included his 1717 edition of Dryden's *Dramatic
Works*. But his success with his peers did not ensure popular
acceptance. *The Old Bachelor* was followed by the far less
successful *The Double-Dealer*; *Love for Love*, Congreve's
second major success, was equalled by *The Mourning Bride*,
but *The Way of the World* met a lukewarm initial reception.

The comedies share a number of thematic and structural
elements. Like most plays in the tradition of Greek New
Comedy as it developed in England, particularly those of
John Fletcher, Congreve's plays focus on the attempts of
young lovers to overcome obstacles—usually parental—to
their marrying. And like most lovers, his, ultimately, are
successful. But what distinguishes Congreve in his handling of
this standard plot material is that after *The Old Bachelor*, his
largely derivative as well as brilliant first play, he includes
increasingly serious and thoughtful analyses of the difficulties
in achieving fulfilling, happy marriages. In *The Double-*

Dealer, the obstacles are largely external, in the persons of villains who are unusually forceful for love comedy. In *Love for Love*, Congreve partially internalizes the comic barriers: Valentine must convince Angelica that his love is genuine and that their marriage has a better chance than those of the other characters who inhabit their world. Mirabell, similarly, must convince Millamant that the risk involved in entering into marriage is sufficiently small to warrant the gamble. *The Way of the World* is filled with negative examples who serve as warnings; marriage goes wrong more often than not in these plays and the few couples like Mirabell and Millamant who seem likely to overcome the odds have relationships all the more special for their rarity. Congreve's one serious play, *The Mourning Bride*, also focuses on the attempts of lovers to overcome parental opposition, but in the mode of tragicomedy (in the sense of tragedy with a happy ending). It was his most popular play in the 18th century, but its popularity has not survived the eclipse of the genre of the late heroic play it so well represents.

Congreve was an accomplished, if not prolific, literary critic. His "uncommonly judicious" (Samuel Johnson) preface to his first published work, the short novel *Incognita*, contains a thoughtful discussion of the problems involved in writing prose fiction; his model is the drama. He also wrote the first critical treatise in English on the Pindaric ode. His most important piece of dramatic criticism, his letter to John Dennis "Concerning Humour in Comedy" (1965), reveals his familiarity with the other major tradition of English comedy, the humours comedy of Ben Jonson. Congreve helped redefine the humour by insisting that it is "a singular and unavoidable manner of doing, or saying any thing, peculiar and natural to one man only". By making the humour an essential component of the individual psyche, Congreve implied that it could not change or be changed. If characters cannot be driven from their humours, the purpose of criticizing them is no longer corrective. Humours characters accordingly become more complex and three-dimensional, less the targets of unmixed comic satire. Such is the case with most of the humours who are found in Congreve's own comedies.

Congreve's thoughts about humour evolved alongside his thoughts about wit which, he points out, "is often mistaken for humour". Wit in the theatre should always be "adapted to the humour" of the character who speaks it. The same principle applies to non-humours characters, and one of Congreve's most generally admired talents as a playwright is his ability to provide an appropriately distinctive and colloquial language for his characters. He requires his audience to be unusually sensitive to subtle differences in language use among his characters, a requirement audiences have not always been willing or able to meet. The wit of his comic heroes and heroines, always recognized as his greatest glory, not only reflects their characters, but embodies a complex set of cultural and moral values representing the best their society can offer.

Congreve's other extended piece of dramatic criticism came in response to Jeremy Collier's attack on his plays in *A Short View of the Immorality and Profaneness of the English Stage* (1698). Congreve's *Amendments of Mr. Collier's False and Imperfect Citations* seen by Collier's admirers as a specious, cynical, and weak piece of self-defense, in fact offers a thoughtful alternative to Collier's anti-theatrical polemic. Congreve did not believe that comedy should present the world as it should be; he was not prepared to apply a comic analogue to poetic justice to his plays; he insisted that passages should be quoted in context and that not all statements in a play reflect the beliefs of their author. But in part because of Collier and in part because of the relative failure of *The*

Way of the World, Congreve abandoned his career as a playwright in 1700.

He remained involved in the management of the theatre in Lincoln's Inn Fields, and was one of the partners in Vanbrugh's new Queen's Theatre in the Haymarket, but he quickly—and wisely—terminated his involvement when it became clear that the new theatre was a financial as well as dramatic liability. Though most of Congreve's later writing was non-dramatic, he did not entirely abandon the theatre. His masque, *The Judgement of Paris*, was written for a contest in 1701 between the composers John Eccles, Godfrey Finger, Daniel Purcell, and John Weldon (the surprise winner). It was later choreographed by John Weaver (1733) to great success at Drury Lane. He joined Vanbrugh and William Walsh in contributing an act to *Squire Trelooby* (1704), an unpublished adaptation of Molière's *Monsieur de Pourceaugnac*. And he wrote the libretto for John Eccles' opera *Semele*, later immortalised in Handel's setting (1744).

—Brian Corman

See also *Volume 1* entries on *The Double-Dealer*; *Love For Love*; *The Way of the World*.

CONNELLY, Marc(us Cook). Born in McKeesport, Pennsylvania, USA, 13 December 1890. Educated at Trinity Hall, Washington, Pennsylvania, 1902–07. Married Madeline Hurlock in 1930 (divorced, 1935). Reporter and drama critic, Pittsburgh *Press* and *Gazette-Times*, 1908–15; moved to New York, 1915: freelance writer and actor, 1915–33; reporter, New York *Morning Telegraph*, 1918–21; helped found the *New Yorker*, 1925; wrote screenplays and directed in Hollywood, 1933–44; Professor of Playwriting, Yale University Drama School, New Haven, Connecticut, 1947–52; US Commissioner to Unesco, 1951; adviser, Equity Theatre Library, 1960. Council member, Dramatists Guild, from 1920; member of the Executive Committee, US National Committee for Unesco. Recipient: Pulitzer Prize, 1930; O. Henry Award, for short story, 1930. President, Authors League of America; President, National Institute of Arts and Letters, 1953–56. Died in New York, 21 December 1980.

Works

Stage Works

$2.50 (produced Pittsburgh, Pennsylvania, 1913).
The Lady of Luzon (lyrics only), book by Alfred Ward Birdsall, music by Zoel Parenteau (produced Pittsburgh, Pennsylvania, 1914).
Follow the Girl (lyrics only, uncredited; produced New York, 1915).
The Amber Empress, music by Zoel Parenteau (produced New York, 1916; as *The Amber Princess*, produced 1917).
Dulcy, with George S. Kaufman (produced Frazee Theatre, New York, 1921). 1921.
Erminie, revised version of the play by Henry Paulton (produced 1921).
To the Ladies!, with George S. Kaufman (produced Liberty Theatre, New York, 1922). 1923.

No, Sirree!, with George S. Kaufman (produced 49th Street Theatre, New York, 1922).

The 49ers, with George S. Kaufman (produced Punch and Judy Theatre, New York, 1922).

West of Pittsburgh, with George S. Kaufman (produced 1922; revised version, as *The Deep Tangled Wildwood*, produced Frazee Theatre, New York, 1923).

Merton of the Movies, with George S. Kaufman, from the story by Harry Leon Wilson (produced Cort Theatre, New York, 1922).   1925.

A Christmas Carol, with George S. Kaufman, from the story by Dickens.   In *Bookman*, December 1922.

Helen of Troy, New York, with George S. Kaufman, music and lyrics by Harry Ruby and Bert Kalmar (produced Selwyn Theatre, New York, 1923).

Beggar on Horseback, with George S. Kaufman, music by Deems Taylor, from a play by Paul Apel (produced Frazee Theatre, New York, 1924).   1925.

Be Yourself, with George S. Kaufman, music and lyrics by Lewis Genzler and Milton Schwarzwald, additional lyrics by Ira Gershwin (produced Sam H. Harris Theatre, New York, 1924).

The Wisdom Tooth: A Fantastic Comedy (produced Little Theatre, New York, 1926).   1927.

The Wild Man of Borneo, with Herman J. Mankiewicz (produced Bijou Theatre, New York, 1927).

How's the King? (produced New York, 1927).

The Green Pastures: A Fable Suggested by Roark Bradford's Southern Sketches "Ol' Man Adam an' His Chillun" (produced Mansfield Theatre, New York, 1930).   1929.

The Survey (skit).   In *New Yorker*, 1934.

The Farmer Takes a Wife, with Frank B. Elser, from a novel by Walter D. Edmonds (produced 46th Street Theatre, New York, 1934).   Abridgement in *Best Plays of 1934–1935*, edited by Burns Mantle, 1935.

Little David: An Unproduced Scene from "The Green Pastures."   1937.

Everywhere I Roam, with Arnold Sundgaard (produced National Theatre, New York, 1938).

The Traveler.   1939.

The Flowers of Virtue (produced Royale Theatre, New York, 1942).

A Story for Strangers (produced Royale Theatre, New York, 1948).

Hunter's Moon (produced Winter Garden, London, 1958).

The Portable Yenberry (produced Purdue University, Lafayette, Indiana, 1962).

The Stitch in Time (produced New York, 1981).

Screenplays

Whispers, 1920; *Exit Smiling*, with others, 1926; *The Bridegroom, The Burglar, The Suitor,* and *The Uncle* (film shorts), 1929; *The Unemployed Ghost* (film short), 1931; *The Cradle Song*, 1933; *The Little Duchess* (film short), 1934; *The Green Pastures*, 1936 (edited by Thomas Cripps, 1975); *The Farmer Takes a Wife*, 1937; *Captains Courageous*, with John Lee Mahin and Dale Van Emery, 1937; *The Good Earth*, with others, 1937 (published in *Twenty Best Film Plays*, edited by John Gassner and Dudley Nichols, 1943); *I Married a Witch*, with Robert Pirosh, 1942; *Reunion (Reunion in France)*, with others, 1942; *The Imposter* (additional dialogue), 1944; *Fabiola* (English dialogue), 1951; *Crowded Paradise* (additional scenes), 1956.

Radio Plays

The Mole on Lincoln's Cheek, 1941 (published in *The Free Company Presents*, edited by James Boyd, 1941).

Fiction

A Souvenir from Qam.   1965.

Memoirs and Letters

Voices Off-Stage: A Book of Memoirs.   1968.

*

Criticism

Books:
Paul T. Nolan, *Marc Connelly*, New York, 1969.

* * *

Marc Connelly attracted attention between 1920 and 1924 as co-author with George S. Kaufman of several popular social comedies about contemporary America, beginning with *Dulcy*. *To the Ladies!* seems more original in apparently celebrating the business acumen of women, but, for all its mockery of male superiority, it is unregenerately chauvinistic. The woman's role, except for one improbably successful impromptu after-dinner speech, is as the supportive wife, winning advancement for her husband by what is presented as persuasive advocacy, but in fact is an opportunist piece of near-blackmail, reinforced by sentimentality. That the husband seems congenitally unlikely to succeed in the post she secures for him is ignored entirely, as is the unlikelihood of the employer's gullible blindness to the man's manifestly inept mediocrity. Described once as "a hilarious American counterpart to Barrie's *What Every Woman Knows*" (written 14 years earlier), the play's greatest merit is having brought Helen Hayes into starring prominence. It was followed by *Merton of the Movies* and the unpublished musical *Helen of Troy*, both equally popular.

In *Beggar on Horseback* a less ambivalent satiric aim comes at least nearer to realisation. The authors' established association with the smart set of New York humorists known as the Algonquin Wits gave the dialogue a sharper edge and guaranteed a receptive audience, but the preface to the published text, by one of the best-known of the group, Alexander Woollcott, is over-generous. The most inventive of their joint plays, though based on a German original, it contrasts the impecunious insecurity of the artist's integrity with the monied attractions of a capitalist business world. It contains a dream-sequence with elements of surrealism and expressionism which gave it, in 1924, an avant-garde interest, but which could have been more tightly controlled and better exploited. Like two Sinclair Lewis novels, *Main Street* and *Babbitt*, the play promises a vigorous satire on the "booster" American business ethic of the 1920's and has the necessary witty acuteness of observation. Had Connelly accepted Lewis's invitations to partner him in play-writing, however, their joint products would have been as limited as their individual works: both writers are among what Lewis revealingly called "those of us who hesitated about being drafted into the army of complacency". Satire cannot be satisfactorily based on mere hesitation. Neither, for all its imaginative vitality, can *Beggar on Horseback* be claimed, as it sometimes is, to be an important progenitor of the "theatre of the absurd": here again, it tries to ride on the backs of two different horses at once.

The Kaufman-Connelly partnership ended amicably in 1924, after they had followed *Beggar on Horseback* with *Be*

Yourself, their second musical. Connelly wrote on his own, between 1925 and 1930, two more comedies, a musical comedy, a series of ten one-act plays, and numerous short stories, including some for the *New Yorker*, which he helped to found. He also acted in and directed the plays of others. The only readily-accessible piece of his writing of this period is an undistinguished one-acter, *The Traveler*. Its hero is seen leaving Grand Central Station on the Twentieth Century Limited, the Chicago express. After brief but enthusiastic conversations with two of the train's staff he alights with his luggage at its first stop, 125th Street, still in New York City. We are to see his short trip home as invested with a glamour that will sustain him until he can afford to repeat it in a year's time, but the suburban little man's pathetic zest for new experience is neither comic nor moving.

For the small-town Pennsylvanian grandson of an Irish Catholic immigrant to be remembered primarily for an all-black play based on the unsophisticated religion of the ethnic minority in the American South seems wildly improbable, yet it was as the author of *The Green Pastures* that Connelly became known internationally. That it is hard to imagine a successful revival of the play now is less a sign of progress than a matter of regret. Its artless translation of Old Testament stories into the idiom and ethic of a race but lately itself delivered from slavery is neither as patronising, as *faux-naif*, nor as reactionary as it would be judged today. To Connelly it was "an attempt to present certain aspects of a living religion in the terms of its believers". He acknowledged the "terrific spiritual hunger and the greatest humility" with which "these untutored black Christians . . . have adapted the contents of the Bible to the consistencies of their everyday lives", and 1930's audiences accepted it in that spirit. Comparisons have been drawn with the medieval English mystery plays when, for example, a heavenly celebration resembling a Louisiana Sunday School treat is initiated by "de Lawd God Jehovah", incarnate as a black minister, solemnly pronouncing, "Let de fish fry proceed". Major critics compared it favourably with its acknowledged source, Roark Bradford's original fiction *Ol' Man Adam an' His Chillun*, and responded warmly to the integrity of its concept and its sympathetic image of the blacks. The humour, the inventiveness, the interweaving of text with serio-comic spectacle and the music of the spirituals, and the directness of the piece, however sentimental and over-long, sufficiently explain its original popularity but would probably embarrass today's audiences.

It is inevitable, if less than wholly fair, to remember Connelly only as the author of *The Green Pastures*. His most carefully researched work, it is undeniably his greatest artistic achievement. Easy-going and enthusiastic, he continued to spread his energy over an area too wide for the good of his reputation, and there is less social philosophy than nostalgic complacency in his work. The small-town attitude to life that underlay the Algonquin wit was symbolised in his acting success in the 1940's in the role of the Stage Manager in the New York and London productions of Thornton Wilder's *Our Town*.

—Dennis Welland

See also *Volume 1* entry on *The Green Pastures*.

COOK, Michael. Born in London, 14 February 1933. Educated at boarding schools near London to age 15;

Nottingham University College of Education, 1962–66, TTC (honours) in English 1966. Served in the Royal Electrical and Mechanical Engineers, and later in the Intelligence Corps, 1949–61: Staff Sergeant. Married 1) Muriel Horner in 1951 (marriage dissolved 1966), eight children; 2) Janis Jones in 1967 (divorced 1973), two children; 3) Madonna Decker in 1973, four children. Farm worker and waiter, 1948–49; steel-worker and farm worker, 1961–62; emigrated to Canada, 1966, and became Canadian citizen, 1971; schoolteacher, 1966; specialist in Drama, 1967–70, Lecturer, 1970–74, Assistant Professor, 1974–79, and since 1979 Associate Professor of English, Memorial University, St. John's, Newfoundland; drama critic, St. John's *Evening Telegram*, 1967–77; artistic director, St. John's Summer Festival, 1969–76; host of the weekly television review *Our Man Friday*, St. John's, 1973; playwright-in-residence, Banff Festival, Alberta, 1978, and Stratford Festival, Stratford, Ontario, 1987. Member of the Editorial Board, *Canadian Theatre Review*, from 1973; Governor, Canadian Conference of the Arts, Ottawa, 1975–79; Vice-President, Guild of Canadian Playwrights, 1978–80; member of the Newfoundland and Labrador Arts Council, 1979–82. Also actor on stage, radio, and television, mainly in character roles. Recipient: Labatt Award, 1974, 1975, 1978, 1979; Queen's Silver Jubilee Medal, 1979; Newfoundland and Labrador Government Award, 1985.

Works

Collections

"Tiln" and Other Plays (includes *Quiller* and *Therese's Creed*). 1976.
Three Plays (includes *On the Rim of the Curve; The Head, Guts, and Soundbone Dance; Therese's Creed*). 1977.

Stage Works

The J. Arthur Prufrock Hour (revue; produced St. John's, Newfoundland, 1968).
Tiln, from the radio play (produced Toronto, 1972). With *Quiller*, 1975.
Colour the Flesh the Colour of Dust (produced St. John's, Newfoundland, 1971). 1972.
The Head, Guts, and Soundbone Dance (produced Arts and Culture Centre, St. John's, Newfoundland, 1973). 1974.
Jacob's Wake (produced St. John's, Newfoundland, 1974; produced professionally, Festival Lennoxville, Lennoxville, Quebec, 1975). 1975.
Quiller (produced Memorial University, St. John's, Newfoundland, 1975). With *Tiln*, 1975.
Therese's Creed (produced Centaur Theatre, Montreal, 1977). In *"Tiln" and Other Plays*, 1976.
The Fisherman's Revenge (for children; produced by Newfoundland Travelling Theatre, Trinity Bay, Newfoundland, 1976). 1985.
Not as a Dream (produced Dalhousie University, Halifax, Nova Scotia, 1976). 1976.
On the Rim of the Curve (produced by the Avion Players, Gander, Newfoundland, 1977). In *Three Plays*, 1977.
The Gayden Chronicles (produced Festival Lennoxville, Lennoxville, Quebec, 1977). In *Canadian Theatre Review*, 13, 1977; in book form, 1979.
The Apocalypse Sonata (produced Globe Theatre, Regina, Saskatchewan, 1980).
The Deserts of Bohemia (produced San Francisco, 1980).

Of the Heart's Cold (produced Globe Theatre, Regina, Saskatchewan, 1982).
The Great Harvest Festival (produced Stratford, Ontario, 1986).

Television Plays

In Search of Confederation, 1971; *Daniel My Brother, The C.F.A.*, and *The Course of True Love* (all in *Up at Ours* series), 1979–80.

Radio Plays

How to Catch a Pirate, 1966; *A Walk in the Rain*, 1967; *No Man Can Serve Two Masters*, 1967; *The Concubine*, 1968; *Or the Wheel Broken*, 1968; *The Truck*, 1969; *A Time for Doors*, 1969; *The Iliad* (for children), from the poem by Homer, 1969; *A Midsummer Night's Dream*, from the play by Shakespeare, 1970; *To Inhabit the Earth Is Not Enough*, 1970; *Journey into the Unknown*, 1970; *Ballad of Patrick Docker*, 1971; *Tiln*, 1971 (published in *Encounter: Canadian Drama in Four Media*, 1973); *Apostles for the Burning*, 1972; *There's a Seal at the Bottom of the Garden*, 1973; *An Enemy of the People*, from a play by Ibsen, 1974; *Love is a Walnut*, 1975; *Travels with Aunt Jane* series (1 episode), 1975; *The Producer, The Director*, 1976; *Knight of Shadow, Lady of Silence*, 1976; *Ireland's Eye* (*The Best Seat in the House* series), 1977; *The Gentleman Amateur*, 1978; *All a Pack o' Lies*, 1979; *The Hunter*, 1980; *The Preacher*, 1981; *The Terrible Journey of Frederick Dunglass*, 1982 (published in *Canadian Theatre Review*, 36, 1986); *The Sweet Second Summer of Kitty Malone*, from the novel by Matt Cohen, 1983; *This Damned Inheritance*, 1984; *The Bailiff and the Women*, 1984; *The Ocean Ranger*, 1985; *The Saddest Barn Dance Ever Held*, 1985; *The Hanging Judge*, 1985; *The Moribundian Memorandum*, 1986.

Fiction

The Island of Fire.

*

Bibliographies

Don Rubin, "Biographical Checklist: Michael Cook", in *Canadian Theatre Review*, 16, 1977.

Criticism

Books:
Robert Wallace and Cynthia Zimmerman, *The Works: Conversations with English-Canadian Playwrights*, Toronto, 1982.
Richard Perkyns (ed.), *Major Plays of the Canadian Theatre 1934–1984*, Toronto, 1984 (includes bibliography).

Articles:
Brian Parker, "On the Edge: Michael Cook's Newfoundland Trilogy" in *Canadian Literature*, 85, 1980.

* * *

Although Michael Cook continues to be best known for the so-called Newfoundland Trilogy (*Colour the Flesh the Colour of Dust*; *The Head, Guts and Sound Bone Dance*; and *Jacob's Wake*), he has written some 50 radio plays (only two of which have been published— *Tiln* and *The Terrible Journey of Frederick Dunglas*. He has lately returned to radio writing. It is not incidental that this form suits Cook: he is, in his own words, a "literary playwright" interested in language in general and the rich, local dialect of Newfoundland in particular. His plays display his fascination with sound patterns; he has said he is "unable to disassociate the sounds of words from the action that goes with them". He is also concerned with large concepts elaborately described in stage directions which can emerge imaginatively within the dialogue, but are hard to replicate on stage. Additionally, he prefers large casts which are easier to manage in text and on radio than on stage. It is not surprising that his stage plays are often subject to literary analysis but rarely performed.

Cook's protagonists are often trapped in an existential dilemma, caught between a desire for order and the apparent chaos of the external world. In his historical work—three of the seven major stage plays—Cook explores the plight of the rebel and the outsider caught in this struggle. In *The Gayden Chronicles* he presents William Gayden (executed for mutiny, murder, and desertion in 1812, and upon whose diary the action is based) as such a figure. Gayden's thoughts on rebellion and his own psychology allow Cook to introduce the ideology of the French Revolution, Tom Paine, and William Blake, as well as a critical assessment of the 19th-century British Navy. In his struggle to comprehend meaning within his society and to come to terms with authority, Gayden is a hero typical of Cook.

The same questions are raised in *Colour the Flesh the Colour of Dust* where the brief rule of a captured St. John's by the French in 1762 prompts Cook to contrast officials who are corrupt and cynical with the common people who survive the occupation largely unchanged, albeit in a bleak environment and cheerless society. Central images of birth and death frame the play but in reverse order, suggesting hope as the images move from a corpse to a baby. It is, however, hope of a universal, mythical kind; there is no individual salvation for the citizens of this time and place. Such a vision can be seen in all of Cook's writing and especially in the plays of contemporary Newfoundland where characters struggle and fail in an essentially tragic manner while the great forces of the sea and the land endure. In this regard, Cook shares as much with Synge as with Beckett (whom he claims as a major influence on his writing).

In a number of plays, Cook narrows this view of the human predicament to explore family relationships and family politics within the larger landscape of Newfoundland. In *The Head, Guts and Sound Bone Dance* he introduces the figure of the tyrannical skipper, an Old Testament allusion who appropriately inhabits "the rock" of Newfoundland's hard, formative terrain and who, here and in *Jacob's Wake*, rails against modern society, the decline of traditional industry and values, and the loss of a patriarchal society, while he symbolizes a stoic human fight against the power of Nature and mutability. Cook's picture of the loss of an old way of life is movingly presented in the contest between a young man and his powerful father-in-law, Skipper Pete. Like the detritus of the fish they clean (the head, back bone, and guts, of the title) three drunken old men dance to a folk song that sums up their decline. A version of the figure appears even in Cook's children's play, *The Fisherman's Revenge*, though the skipper has become a town merchant against whom the fisherfolk fight for economic survival.

In *Jacob's Wake* the figure is at once most completely

drawn and most abstract. The play was developed through a number of preliminary versions by Newfoundland's Open Group with Cook's collaboration; the published script arises from these early productions and from the first professional performance at the 1975 Festival Lennoxville. The difficulties of production have not been solved by this revision process: in his stage directions Cook admits to the practical difficulties of portraying a convincing apotheosis of Newfoundland culture on a naturalistic set. The play is essentially expressionistic, as the National Arts Centre production in 1986 attempted to convey.

The old master lies dying upstairs in the two-level set while his presence dominates the household: his failed son (the existential victim locked between his sense of failure and his rebellion against his father's values), his repressed daughter and exploited daughter-in-law, and his three amoral grandsons. As the story of Jacob, the favoured son with all his Biblical associations, proceeds, the story of a modern Newfoundland of unemployment, alcoholism, welfare, empty religious values, and destructive gender roles unfolds. Over a symbolic Easter weekend the family fights out its rivalries as the wind mounts over an archetypal sea. Skipper mourns the loss of his firstborn and, with him, any hope for a continuation of the sealing industry and the old way of life. As the family tensions reach crisis, the storm intrudes onto the stage, the soul (or force) of the Skipper appears at the door blown open by a "cosmic disaster", and the outport house transforms itself into a ship at sea. As the women are sent below, the ruined son attempts too late to steer a new course for his generation while "a ripping and rending and smashing" destroys the human world.

The play is an excellently crafted literary piece with inter-related images and allusions, some well drawn characterizations (especially of the protagonist son), and a compelling vision of catastrophe. It brings together themes and characters common in Cook's work and illustrates the rich sonorities of his language. The vision it presents, like that in all Michael Cook's plays, is fundamentally tragic: Newfoundland is seen as a classic testing ground for the struggle of a trapped humankind against its own authoritarian traditions and the awesome power of a dispassionate Nature.

—Reid Gilbert

See also *Volume 1* entry on *Jacob's Wake*.

CORNEILLE, Pierre. Born in Rouen, France, June 1606; elder brother of the dramatist Thomas Corneille. Educated in Jesuit College, Rouen, 1615–22; studied law, 1622–24, licensed lawyer, 1624. Married Marie de Lampérière in 1641; seven children. Member of the Rouen *Parlement*, 1629–50; held offices as King's advocate in water and forests court and in Rouen port Admiralty court; lived in Paris after 1662; first play, *Mélite*, produced 1629/30; collaborated with Montdory's company, and later with Molière's company; publication of *Le Cid*, 1637, initiated intense literary controversy, the "Querelle du *Cid*". Elected to the Académie Française, 1647. Died in Paris, 1 October 1684.

Works

Collections

Oeuvres. 1644.
Oeuvres (2 vols.). 1648.
Oeuvres (3 vols.). 1652.
Oeuvres de Corneille (3 vols.). 1654–57.
Le Théâtre de P. Corneille (3 vols.). 1660; later expanded editions, 1663, 1664, 1668, and 1682.
Oeuvres (12 vols.). 1862–68.
Six Plays by Corneille and Racine (includes *Le Cid*; *Cinna*; and four plays by Racine), various translators, edited by Paul Ladis. 1931.
Théâtre complet (3 vols.). 1941.
The Chief Plays of Corneille (includes *Horace*; *Le Cid*; *Cinna*; *Polyeucte*; *Rodogune*; *Nicomède*), translated by Lacy Lockert, 1952; revised edition, 1956.
Moot Plays of Corneille (includes *La Mort de Pompée*; *Héraclius*; *Don Sanche d'Aragon*; *Othon*; *Sertorius*; *Attila*), translated by Lacy Lockert. 1959.
The Cid; Cinna; The Theatrical Illusion, translated by John Cairncross. 1975.
Polyeuctus; The Liar; Nicomedes, translated by John Cairncross. 1980.
Oeuvres complètes (3 vols.), edited by Georges Couton. 1980–87.

Stage Works

Mélite; ou, Les Fausses Lettres (produced by Montdory's Company, Berthault Tennis Court, Paris, 1629/30). 1633; translated as *Melite*, 1776.
Clitandre; ou, L'Innocence délivrée (produced by Montdory's Company, Berthault Tennis Court, Paris, 1630/31). 1632.
La Veuve; ou, Le Traitre trahi (produced by Montdory's Company, Berthault Tennis Court, Paris, 1631/32). 1634.
Le Château de Bicêtre (ballet; produced at court, 1632).
La Galerie du Palais; ou, L'Amie rivale (produced by Montdory's Company, Berthault Tennis Court, Paris, 1632/33). 1637.
La Suivante (produced Fontaine Tennis Court, Paris, c.1633/34). 1637.
La Place Royale; ou, L'Amoureux extravagant (produced Fontaine Tennis Court, Paris, c.1633/34). 1637.
Médée (produced Paris, c.1634/35). 1639; edited by André de Leyssac, 1978.
La Comédie des Tuileries, with Rotrou and others (produced Théâtre du Marais, Paris, 1635). 1638.
L'Illusion comique (produced Théâtre du Marais, Paris, 1635/36). 1639; translated as *The Theatrical Illusion*, with *The Cid* and *Cinna*, 1975; as *The Illusion*, with *The Liar*, 1989.
Le Cid (produced Théâtre du Marais, Paris, 1636/1637). 1637; revised version, 1682; translated as *The Cid*, 1637: several subsequent translations under same title, and as *Le Cid*.
L'Aveugle de Smyrne, with Rotrou and others (produced Palais Cardinal, Paris, 1637). 1638.
Horace (produced Théâtre de l'Hôtel de Bourgogne, Paris, 1640). 1641; translated as *Horatius*, 1656; as *Horace*, in *The Chief Plays of Corneille*, 1952, and 1962.
Cinna; ou, La Clémence d'Auguste (produced Théâtre de L'Hôtel de Bourgogne, Paris, 1642). 1643; translated as *Cinna's Conspiracy*, 1713; also translated as *Cinna* (see Collections).
Polyeucte, Martyr (produced Théâtre du Marais, Paris 1642/

Pierre Corneille reading aloud his *Polyeucte* at the Hôtel de Rambouille, Paris (19th-century engraving, after Philippoteau).

43).   1643; translated as *Polyeuctes*, 1655; as *Polyeucte*, in *The Chief Plays of Corneille*, 1952; as *Polyeuctus*, with *The Liar* and *Nicomedes*, 1980.

La Mort de Pompée (produced Théâtre du Marais, Paris, 1643/44).   1644; translated as *Pompey the Great*, 1664; as *La Mort de Pompée*, in *Most Plays of Corneille*, 1959.

Le Menteur (produced Théâtre du Marais, Paris, 1643/44).   1644; translated as *The Mistaken Beauty; or, The Liar*, 1685; as *The Lying Lover*, 1717; as *The Liar*, with *Polyeuctus* and *Nicomedes*, 1980.

La Suite du Menteur (produced Théâtre du Marais, Paris 1644/45).   1645.

Rodogune, Princesse des Parthes (produced Théâtre du Marais, Paris 1644/45).   1645; translated as *Rodogune*, 1765; also in *Chief Plays of Corneille*, 1952.

Théodore, vierge et martyre (produced Théâtre du Marais, Paris, 1645/46).   1646 or 1647.

Héraclius, Empereur d'Orient (produced Théâtre du Marais?, Paris, 1646/47).   1647; translated as *Heraclius, Emperor of the East*, 1664; also in *Moot Plays of Corneille*, 1959.

Don Sanche d'Aragon (produced Théâtre du Marais?, Paris, 1649/50).   1650; translated as *The Conflict*, in *Plays and Poems*, 1798; translated as *Don Sanche* in *Moot Plays of Corneille*, 1959.

Andromède (produced Théâtre du Petit-Bourbon, Paris, 1650).   1650.

Nicomède (produced Théâtre de l'Hôtel de Bourgogne?, Paris, 1651).   1651; translated as *Nicomede*, 1671; as *Nicomède*, in *The Chief Plays of Corneille*, 1952; as *Nicomedes*, with *Polyeuctus* and *The Liar*, 1980.

Pertharite, Roi des Lombards (produced Paris, 1651/52).   1653.

Oedipe (produced Théâtre de l'Hôtel de Bourgogne, Paris, 1659).   1659.

La Conquête de la toison d'or (produced Théâtre du Marais, Paris, 1660).   1661.

Sertorius (produced Théâtre du Marais, Paris, 1662).   1662; translated as *Sertorius*, in *Moot Plays of Corneille*, 1959.

Sophonisbe (produced Théâtre de l'Hôtel de Bourgogne?, Paris, 1663).   1663.

Othon (produced Fontainebleu, 1664).   1665; translated as *Othon*, in *Moot Plays of Corneille*, 1959.

Agésilas (produced Théâtre de l'Hôtel de Bourgogne, Paris, 1666).   1666.

Attila, Roi des Huns (produced Palais-Royal, Paris, 1667).   1667; translated as *Attila*, in *Moot Plays by Corneille*, 1959.

Tite et Bérénice (produced Palais-Royal, Paris, 1670).   1671.

Psyché, with Molière and Quinault, music by Lully (produced the Tuileries, Paris, 1671).   1671.

Pulchérie (produced Théâtre du Marais, Paris, 1672).   1673.

Suréna, Général des Parthes (produced Théâtre de l'Hôtel de Bourgogne, Paris, 1674).   1675; translated as *Surenas*, 1969.

Others

Oeuvres diverses. 1738.
Writings on the Theatre, edited by H.T. Barnwell. 1965.
Translator, *L'Imitation de Jésus-Christ*, by Thomas à Kempis. 1651–56.
Translator, *Louanges de la Sainte Vierge*, by St. Bonaventure. 1665.
Translator, *L'Office de la Sainte Vierge*, by St. Bonaventure. 1670.

*

Criticism

Books:

Martin Turnell, *The Classical Moment: Studies of Corneille, Molière, and Racine*, London, 1947.

O. Nadal, *Le Sentiment de l'amour dans l'oeuvre de Pierre Corneille*, 1948.

Georges Couton, *La Vieillesse de Corneille (1658–1684)*, Paris, 1949; revised editions, 1958 and 1969.

Bernard Dort, *Corneille dramaturge*, Paris, 1957; revised edition, 1972.

Robert Brassilach, *Pierre Corneille*, Paris, 1961.

Georges Couton, *Corneille et la Fronde: Théâtre et politique il y a trois siècles*, Paris, 1963.

Marie-Odile Sweetser, *Les Conceptions dramatiques de Corneille d'après ses écrits théoretiques*, Geneva, 1963.

Robert J. Nelson, *Corneille: His Heroes and Their Worlds*, Philadelphia, 1963.

P.J. Yarrow, *Corneille*, London and New York, 1963.

Albert West, *The Cornelian Hero*, Auckland, New Zealand, 1963.

Jacques Maurens, *La Tragédie sans tragique: Le Néostoïcisme dans l'oeuvre de Pierre Corneille*, Paris, 1966.

Robert J. Nelson (ed.), *Corneille and Racine: Parallels and Contrasts*, Englewood Cliffs, New Jersey, 1966.

Herbert Fogel, *The Criticism of Cornelian Tragedy: A Study of Critical Writing from the Seventeenth Century to the Twentieth Century*, New York, 1967.

Claude K. Abraham, *Corneille*, New York, 1972.

Gordon Pocock, *Corneille and Racine: Problems of Tragic Form*, Cambridge, 1973.

Marie-Odile Sweetser, *La Dramaturgie de Corneille*, Geneva, 1977.

A.S.M. Goulet, *L'Unité théâtral de Corneille: Paradoxe et subtilité historique*, Cambridge, Massachusetts, 1978.

Joseph Martin, *Le Vieillard amoureux dans l'oeuvre corné-lienne*, Paris, 1979.

Carlo François, *Raison et déraison dans le théâtre de Pierre Corneille*, York, South Carolina, 1980.

Cynthia B. Kerr, *L'Amour, l'amitié et la fourberie: Une Étude des premières comédies de Corneille*, Saratoga, California, 1980.

Théodore A. Litman, *Les Comédies de Corneille*, Paris, 1981.

Han Verhoeff, *Les Grandes Tragédies de Corneille: Une Psycholecture*, Paris, 1982.

Milorad R. Margitíc (ed.), *Corneille comique*, 1983.

G.J. Mallinson, *The Comedies of Corneille*, Manchester, 1984.

Germain Poirier, *Corneille et la vertu de prudence*, Geneva, 1984.

H.T. Barnwell, *The Tragic Drama of Corneille and Racine: An Old Parallel Revisited*, Oxford, 1982.

I.D. McFarlane, *The Liar and the Lieutenant in the Plays of Pierre Corneille*, Oxford, 1984.

Alain Niderst (ed.), *Pierre Corneille*, Paris, 1985.

Michel Prigent, *Le Héros et l'État dans la tragédie de Pierre Corneille*, Paris, 1985.

Mitchell Greenberg, *Corneille, Classicism and the Ruses of Symmetry*, Cambridge, 1986.

Josephine A. Schmidt, *If There Are No More Heroes, There are Heroines: A Feminist Critique of Corneille's Heroines 1637–1644*, Lanham, Maryland, 1987.

Michel Barreau (ed.), *Pierre Corneille: Ambiguïtés*, Liège, 1990.

Albert Gérard, *Pierre Corneille ou la sénilité lucide*, Liège, 1990.

* * *

Earliest and most versatile of the three famous French "classical" dramatists, Corneille is chiefly remembered for his tragedies, often contrasted with those of Racine. His scarcely less innovative comedies have less well withstood comparison with Molière, who not only performed and sometimes parodied Corneille's tragedies, but maintained *Le Menteur* (*The Liar*)—adapted from Alarcón's *Verdad sospechosa* (*Suspect Truth*)—in his repertory. Of some 33 five-act plays in verse (collaborative playwriting as one of Cardinal Richelieu's Five Authors recruited to renovate French theatre 1635–38 precludes greater precision), 20 performed between 1636 and 1674 represent some sort of *tragédie*—tragedy more heroic than Aristotelian, because the hero more often astounds with exceptional energy than he elicits terror and compassion. Compassion is more often associated, in Corneille's theatre, with female roles.

His *tragédies* include *Le Cid* (*The Cid*) (performed and published as a tragicomedy in 1637, republished as a *tragédie* in 1648), two martyr plays or *tragédies chrétiennes*, *Polyeucte* and *Théodore*, and two mythological machine plays or semi-operas, *Andromède* (*Andromeda*) and *La Conquête de la toison d'or* (*The Conquest of the Golden Fleece*). They are based mainly on historical or mythical royal subjects involving bloodshed and are elevated throughout in sentiment and style. Corneille normally used alexandrines, the 12-syllable rhyming couplets favoured by contemporary French dramatists and writers of epic poems. However, he sometimes heightens emotion with soliloquy stanzas in other metres, and in *Agésilas* and *Psyché* he uses the *vers mêlés* or mixed metres familiar to readers of La Fontaine's *Fables*, long used in court ballets and in such devotional poems as Corneille's *Louange de la Sainte Vierge* (*Praise of the Holy Virgin*).

Corneille's skill in spectacular theatre is already evident in much earlier works, notably his first tragedy *Médée*, adapted from Seneca, where the witch Medea makes her final exit borne aloft by a dragon-drawn chariot. Sorcerers dominate the action in his court ballet *Le Château de Bicêtre* (1632), which used ornamental backdrops and special lighting effects evoking a haunted castle at different times of day and night to combine changing spectacle with a strict observance of the unities of time and place (which Corneille later admits only reluctantly in tragedy). *L'Illusion comique* (*The Theatrical Illusion*) used sorcery to celebrate the dramatic genres in a structured "anthology" at a time when commercial acting (legally dishonouring in France until 1641) and the small theatre in the Palais-Cardinal (later Palais-Royal) had only recently been established (it was the first in France equipped with a forestage curtain). In the *tragicomédie-ballet*, *Psyché*, written in collaboration with Molière for the reopening of the great Palais-Royal theatre in 1671, he returns to the mythological and the marvellous.

Corneille's reputation rests more solidly upon *Le Cid*, adapted from Guillén de Castro's *comedia* on the youthful love and exploits of the Spanish Crusader Rodrigo, and a number of other plays: *Horace*, (on the legendary Horatii and Curiacii), *Cinna* (concerning a conspiracy against the emperor Augustus as an ideal monarch who, through self-mastery and clemency, wins dominion over the rebellious hearts of disaffected subjects), *Polyeucte* (on an exemplary martyrdom), and *La Mort de Pompée* (*The Death of Pompey the Great*), adapted and, in part, translated from Lucan's epic *Pharsalia*. Corneille develops highly emotive dilemmas arising from conflicting demands: politics or reason of state on the one hand, for example, with love and other loyalties (those of dynasty in *Le Cid*, family in *Horace*, conjugal love and Christianity in *Polyeucte*) on the other.

In *Le Cid* conflicts between the three centres of the hero's passionate commitment (to family honour, to the state, and to Chimène) are poetically expressed through assimilation of lyric topoi and symmetries between the thwarted lovers. *Le Cid*, the subject of fierce controversy, was the first work judged by the Académie-Française, whose judgement (in the light of Corneille's own later critical appreciations) highlights the aesthetic basis of Corneille's stagecraft in the emotive effects which its structure, characterization, and dilemmas produce. The energy, sentiments, and deeds of exceptional beings are dramatized not because they are morally improving, but because they are theatrically exciting. For Corneille versimilitude involved fewer expectations of normality than it did for some critics among his contemporaries; and he was satisfied to draw upon striking historical accounts, sometimes published with his later plays. *Nicomède*, which presents a magnanimity or *grandeur de courage* equal to Polyeucte's, lacks the influential blend of love and politics in *Le Cid* and his earlier Roman tragedies. In contrast with other later tragedies, including *Rodogine* (in which a widowed Syrian Cleopatra is prepared to sacrifice her twin sons to retain power, and the twins are ready to sacrifice all for love of Rodogune), the first Roman tragedies share a relative simplicity of plot. Only in *Suréna*, Corneille's last tragedy, is the hero defeated. Corneille's education by Jesuits and training as a lawyer is considered evident in the way that passions are manipulated through insight, and in his highly articulated rhetoric.

Marivaux is the most obvious heir to Corneille's early comedies—*Mélite* (which the Marais troupe discovered in Rouen and brought to Paris), *La Veuve* (*The Widow*), *La Galerie du Palais* (*The Courthouse Mall*), *La Suivante*, and *La Place Royale*. These were urbanized, as it were, from Hardy's pastorals and depicted the conversations and equivocations of youthful contemporary French gentry. Corneille also wrote three "heroic comedies", critical prefaces, three *Discourses* on drama (to which John Dryden's essay *Of Dramatic Poesy* is clearly much indebted), critical correspondence, and numerous poems both profane and sacred, including translations of *The Imitation of Christ* and the *Officium parvum* (*L'Office de la Sainte Vierge*).

—H. Gaston Hall

See also *Volume 1* entries on *El Cid*; *Cinna*; *Horatius*; *The Theatrical Illusion*.

CORNEILLE, Thomas. Born in Rouen, France, 20 August 1625; younger brother of the dramatist Pierre Corneille (and sometimes referred to as Corneille d'Isle to distinguish him from Pierre). First play, *Les Engagements du hasard*, produced 1649; first tragedy, *Timocrate*, produced 1658; member of Rouen *Parlement*, before travelling with Pierre to Paris, 1662; co-editor, with J. Donneau de Visé, *Le Mercure galant*, founded by de Visé, 1672; collaborated with de Visé on a number of plays. Also a grammarian. Assumed Pierre's membership of the Académie Française, following Pierre's death, 1685. Died in Les Andelys, Normandy, 8 October 1709.

Works

Collections

Oeuvres complètes (5 vols.).   1682; revised editions, 1692, 1706, and 1722.
Théâtre complet. 1881.
The Chief Rivals of Corneille and Racine (includes *Laodice; Le Comte d'Essex*), translated by Lacy Lockert.   1956.
More Plays by Rivals of Corneille and Racine (includes *Timocrate*; *Maximian*; *Ariane*), translated by Charles Lacy Lockert.   1968.

Stage Works

Les Engagements du hasard (produced Théâtre de l'Hôtel de Bourgogne, Paris, 1649).   1657.
Le Feint astrologue (produced Théâtre de l'Hôtel de Bourgogne, Paris, 1650).   1651.
Dom Bertrand de Cigarral (produced Théâtre de l'Hôtel de Bourgogne, Paris, c.1651).   1651.
L'Amour à la mode (produced Théâtre de l'Hôtel de Bourgogne, Paris, 1651).   1653; translated as *Amorus Orontus; or, The Fool in Fashion*, 1665; as *The Amorous Gallant*, 1675.
Le Berger extravagant (produced Théâtre de l'Hôtel de Bourgogne, Paris, 1652). 1653; translated as *The Extravagant Shepherd*, 1654.
Les Illustres ennemis (produced Théâtre du Marais, Paris, 1655).   1657.
Le Geôlier de soi-même (produced Théâtre du Marais, Paris, 1655).   1656.
Le Charme de la voix (produced Théâtre de l'Hôtel de Bourgogne, Paris, c.1656).   1658.
Timocrate (produced Théâtre du Marais, Paris, 1656).   1658; translated as *Timocrate*, in *More Plays by Rivals of Corneille and Racine*, 1968.
Bérénice (produced Théâtre du Marais, Paris, 1657).   1659.
La Mort de l'empereur Commode (produced Théâtre du Marais, Paris, 1657).   1659.
Darius (produced Théâtre de l'Hôtel de Bourgogne, Paris, 1659).   1659.
Stilicon (produced Théâtre de l'Hôtel de Bourgogne, Paris, 1660).   1660.
Le Galant doublé (produced Théâtre de l'Hôtel de Bourgogne, Paris, 1660).   1660.
Camma, Reine de Galatie (produced Théâtre de l'Hôtel de Bourgogne, Paris, 1661).   1661.
Maximian (produced Théâtre de l'Hôtel de Bourgogne, Paris, 1662).   1662; translated as *Maximian*, 1800, and in *More Plays by Rivals of Corneille and Racine*, 1968.
Persée et Démétrius (produced Théâtre de l'Hôtel de Bourgogne, Paris, 1662).   1665.
Pyrrhus, Roy d'Empire (produced Théâtre de l'Hôtel de Bourgogne, Paris, c.1663).   1665.
Antiochus (produced Théâtre de l'Hôtel de Bourgogne, Paris, 1666).   1666.
Le Baron d'Albikrac (produced Théâtre de l'Hôtel de Bourgogne, Paris, 1667).   1669.
Laodice, Reine de Cappadoce (produced Théâtre de l'Hôtel de Bourgogne, Paris, 1668).   1668; translated as *Laodice*, in *The Chief Rivals of Corneille and Racine*, 1956.
La Mort d'Annibal (produced Théâtre de l'Hôtel de Bourgogne, Paris, 1669).   1670.
La Comtesse d'Orgueil (produced Théâtre de l'Hôtel de Bourgogne, Paris, 1670).   1671.
Ariane (produced Théâtre de l'Hôtel de Bourgogne, Paris, 1672).   1672; translated as *The Labyrinth; or, The Fatal Embarrassment*, 1795; as *Ariane*, in *More Plays by Rivals of Corneille and Racine*, 1968.
Théodat (produced Théâtre de l'Hôtel de Bourgogne, Paris, 1672).   1673.
Le Comédien poète, with Montfleury (produced Théâtre Guénégaud, Paris, 1673).   1674.
La Mort d'Achille (produced Théâtre Guénégaud, Paris, 1673).   1674.
Don César d'Avalos (produced Théâtre Guénégaud, Paris, 1674).   1676.
Circé, with J. Donneau de Visé (produced Théâtre Guénégaud, Paris, 1675).   1675.
L'Inconnu, with J. Donneau de Visé (produced Théâtre Guénégaud, Paris, 1675).
Le Triomphe des dames, with J. Donneau de Visé (produced Théâtre Guénégaud, Paris, 1676).   Libretto in *Histoire du théâtre française 11*, by Claude and François Parfaict, c.1745.
Le Festin de Pierre, from Molière's *Dom Juan* (produced Théâtre Guénégaud, Paris, 1677).   1683.
Le Comte d'Essex (produced Théâtre de l'Hôtel de Bourgogne, Paris, 1678).   1678; translated as *Le Comte d'Essex*, in *The Chief Rivals of Corneille and Racine*, 1956.
Psyché, music by Lully (produced Académie Royale de Musique, Paris, 1678).   1678.
Bellerophon, with B. le Bovier de Fontanelle and N. Boileau-Despréaux, music by Lully (produced Académie Royale de Musique, Paris, 1679).   1679.
La Devineresse, with J. Donneau de Visé (produced Théâtre Guénégaud, Paris, 1679).   1680.
La Pierre philosophale, with J. Donneau de Visé (produced Théâtre Guénégaud, Paris, 1681).   Libretto in *Histoire du théâtre français 12*, by Claude and François Parfaict, c.1746.
Médée, music by Charpentier (produced Académie Royale de Musique, Paris, 1693).   1693.
Les Dames vengées, with J. Donneau de Visé (produced Comédie-Française, Paris, 1695).   1695.
Bradamante (produced Comédie-Française, Paris, 1695).   1696.

Other

Le Dictionnaire des arts et des sciences (2 vols.).   1694.

*

Criticism

Books:
J. Carlez, *Pierre et Thomas Corneille: Librettistes*, Caen, 1881.
G. Regnier, *Thomas Corneille: Sa vie et son théâtre*, Paris, 1892.
David A. Collins, *Thomas Corneille: Protean Dramatist*, The Hague, 1966.
Alex de Pino, "Male and Female Roles and the Quest for Power in Four Tragedies by Thomas Corneille", in *Actes de Davis (1988): Madame de Lafayette, La Bruyère, la femme et le théâtre au pouvoir*, edited by Claude Abraham, Paris, 1988.

Articles:
Christopher J. Gossip, "*Timocrate* Reconsidered", in *Studi francesi*, 50, 1973.
June Moravcevich, "Thomas Corneille's *Ariane* and Its Racinian Models", in *Romance Notes*, 15, 1974.

Marcel Oddon, "Les Tragédies de Thomas Corneille: Structures de l'univers des personnages", in *Revue d'histoire du théâtre*, vol.37 no.3, 1985.

* * *

Thomas Corneille is an author who, despite recent critical work on him, still requires the rehabilitation of a fresh, in-depth study. Even today he lives in the shadow of his elder, more famous, and more talented brother Pierre, who shared adjoining accommodation with him in Rouen for over 35 years and who, then and later in Paris, exerted a literally incalculable influence on both him and his art. A prolific dramatist, Thomas moved with apparent ease between different types of play, adept at following fashion rather than anticipating it. But such flexibility need not be synonymous with mediocrity; it reflects, rather, the taste and interests of the average playgoer and thus provides a more accurate gauge of what theatre life was like in France in the second half of the 17th century.

Like Pierre Corneille 20 years before, Thomas started by writing comedies—in his case, however, Spanish-inspired ones given initially to the long-established Hôtel de Bourgogne theatre in Paris. One of his earliest successes (the dates of first performance are still uncertain) was *Dom Bertrand de Cigarral*, published in December 1651, a tightly-constructed comedy centred on a miser not unlike the Harpagon whom Molière created later in *The Miser*. The younger Corneille was already aware of the advantages of focusing on a central figure, avoiding the diffuseness of his previous plots. Four years later he achieved even greater success with *Le Geôlier de soi-même*, played at the Marais theatre and featuring the famous actor Jodelet in a story which combines slapstick, burlesque, death, hidden identity, and considerable suspense. The paradox of allying humour to potential tragedy was one which matched the mood of the mid-1650's, in the immediate aftermath of the civil disturbances of the Fronde.

Thomas Corneille exploited the vogue for tragicomedy and braggart heroism in his first "tragedy", *Timocrate*, staged in the autumn of 1656 and destined to have what appears to be the longest initial run of any 17th-century French play. The 80 or so performances are proof that a highly contrived, romanesque plot—in which the title-character plays two personages simultaneously—can be both a money-spinning crowd-puller and a source of not inconsiderable psychological interest. Disguise, melodrama, misunderstanding, and a certain lack of verisimilitude may dominate much of the action, but the outcome is a genuinely serious situation in which the Queen of Argos must reconcile two mutually incompatible promises and choose between life and death.

This and other rather similar plays, among them *Bérénice*, *Darius* and *Pyrrhus*, drawn from contemporary prose fiction or reproducing the atmosphere to be found in the mid-century novels, aimed to present and analyse the various stages in the progression of gallant love, with concealed identity seen as a means both to interest the audience and to provide a framework for characters to test and express their emotions. But by the late 1650's the mood in France was turning to more serious matters, with the conclusion of the wars with Spain and the prospect of a new young king on the throne. From 1657 to 1669 Thomas brought out a series of half-a-dozen tragedies based on Roman subjects, where political intrigue, ambition, and alliances of convenience took precedence over personal passion. These plays are often described as "Cornelian", but they differ notably in atmosphere and aim from the tragedies of Pierre Corneille staged in the late 1630's and the 1640's, such as *Horace* and *Cinna*. The concepts of public duty, honour, and glory, used—but already devalued—in a plot like *Timocrate*'s, are replaced, in the case of *Camma* by what Geoffrey Brereton has summed up as "murder and suicide, the attempted assassination scene on the stage, ambition, revenge, jealousy, emotional blackmail, political intrigue, a popular rising, a tyrant ruthlessly in love, chivalrous, self-sacrificial love in Sostrate, the apparent treachery of a trusted friend, the nominal marriage, the poisoned cup". This melodramatic mixture, to be found also in *Laodice* contrasts with the relative simplicity of plot in *Stilicon*, where overweening personal ambition results in the truly tragic realisation by a father that he has killed the son he loves, and in *La Mort d'Annibal*, where, unlike Pierre Corneille in *Nicomède*, Thomas rightly focuses attention on the dignified last hours and death of the Carthaginian general and the proud defiance of his daughter Élise.

By the late 1660's Racine, with his minimal plots and higly charged emotions, was established as the greatest French writer of tragedy, dominating his older rival Pierre Corneille. By inclination or design, Thomas, too, turned to simpler tragedies of love and betrayal, and in the plot of *Ariane* (1672) gave dramatic shape to characters whom Racine was to stage five years later in *Phèdre*. The jealous figure in the eternal-triangle plot is the title-character Ariane, abandoned by Thésée in favour of her sister Phèdre. Six years later Thomas moved from Greek legend to English history and mounted a version of the Essex/Elizabeth I story in *Le Comte d'Essex*, other versions of which had appeared on the Paris stage earlier in the century. In Thomas's treatment the earl's treason can be pardoned if he responds to the jealously passionate love which the Queen feels for him, but there is no room for manoeuvre and after his execution Elizabeth is left to regret her indecisiveness and lost opportunities.

Among over 40 dramatic productions extending to 1695, including operas and machine-plays written largely on a collaborative basis and a verse version (*Le Festin de Pierre*) of Molière's banned comedy *Dom Juan*, Thomas could boast several notable successes. *Camma*, for instance, required extra performances on Thursdays, to supplement those given on the normal three performance days each week. Many of his works are drawn from easily identified sources, but that should not be seen as a defect, since adaptation of, and improvement on, existing plays was common practice at a time when copyright laws did not exist. He had a strong sense of plot, a fondness for comedies of intrigue and for more serious plays where complex storylines could be mixed with sharply-drawn, forceful characters. Not all of these were realistic, but the patent artificiality of some may be interpreted as deliberate and successful parodies of the conventional hero/heroine. In other cases, he achieves a true sense of tragedy, as in Stilicon's admission that he has brought about his own downfall and the very opposite of what he desired. The tragic emotions of fear and pity, and that of *admiratio* or wonder, are certainly not absent from his repertoire.

In between these extremes there are more run-of-the-mill offerings, with simply-drawn good and evil characters lacking the psychological depth or ambivalence of great dramatic characters. Even in his best work his sense of stagecraft is stronger than his literary style, and while surprise and reversals of fortune can often be best served by ambiguous language, Thomas Corneille's dialogue lacks the rhetorical force of Pierre's or the poetic clarity of Racine's. Yet its frequent banality perhaps only serves to underline the readiness of this workaday yet enterprising dramatist to give his potential audiences and readers what they wanted: fanciful, highly-coloured plots and gripping characters, often divorced from the everyday, yet paradoxically couched in slack, wordy language akin to that of ordinary life. The mix may be unconventional or apparently unpromising, but it worked, and the playwright should be given credit for this considerable sucess.

—Christopher Gossip

COULTER, John. Born in Belfast, Ireland, 12 February 1888. Educated at Model School and the School of Art and Technology, Belfast, and at Manchester University's Institute of Art and Technology. Married Olive Clare Primrose in 1936; two daughters. Taught at Coleraine Academic Institute, Ulster; also taught at Wesley College, Dublin, 1914–19; returned to Belfast, 1919, then travelled to London, 1920, where he began writing radio plays; editor, *Ulster Review*, 1924; managing editor, *The Adelphi*, 1927–30; after marriage in 1936, emigrated to Canada; wrote for CBS radio in New York, 1938–40; settled in Toronto. Died 1 December 1980.

Works

Stage works

Conochar.   1917.
The House in the Quiet Glen, from the radio play *Sally's Chance* (produced Hart House Theatre, Toronto, 1937). With *The Family Portrait*, 1937.
Father Brady's New Pig (produced Arts and Letters Club Theatre, Toronto, 1937).
The Family Portrait (produced Hart House Theatre, Toronto, 1938).   With *The House in the Quiet Glen*, 1937.
Holy Manhattan (produced Arts and Letters Club Theatre, Toronto, 1940).
Mr. Churchill of England (produced Arts and Letters Club Theatre, Toronto, 1942).
Transit Through Fire, music by Healey Willan; from the radio opera (produced Convocation Hall, University of Toronto, Toronto, 1943).   1942.
Oblomov, from the novel by Ivan Goncharov (produced Arts and Letters Club Theatre, Toronto, 1946).
The Drums Are Out (produced Abbey Theatre, Dublin, 1948).   1971.
Riel (produced Royal Ontario Museum Theatre, Toronto, 1950).   1962.
Sleep My Pretty One (produced St. James's Theatre, London, 1961).
The Crime of Louis Riel (produced Dominion Drama Festival, London, Ontario, 1966).   1976.
The Trial of Louis Riel (produced Saskatchewan House, Regina, Saskatchewan, 1967).   1968.
A Capful of Pennies (produced Central Library Theatre, Toronto, 1967).
François Bigot: A Rediscovery in Dramatic Form of The Fall of Quebec.   1978.

Radio plays

Sally's Chance, 1925; *A Tale of Old Quebec*, 1935; *The Family Portrait*, 1935 (as *Stars of Brickfield Street*, 1938);

Pigs, 1940 (as *Clogherbann Fair*, Belfast, 1948); *Quebec in 1670*, 1940; *This is My Country*, 1941; *Holy Manhattan*, 1941; *This Great Experiment*, 1942; *The Trial of Joseph Howe*, 1942; *Transit Through Fire*, music by Healey Willan, 1942 (opera; published 1942); *Mr. Churchill of England*, 1943; *Deirdre of the Sorrows*, music by Healey Willan, 1946 (opera; published 1944; revised as *Deirdre*, 1965); *Oblomov*, 1946; *The Drums Are Out*, 1950; *While I Live*, 1951; *Riel*, 1951; *A Capful of Pennies*, 1967; *The Crime of Louis Riel*, 1968; *The Red Hand of Ulster*, 1974.

Television Plays

Come Back to Erin, 1955; *Transit Through Fire*, 1955; *Riel*, 1961; *Mr. Oblomov*, 1962; *The Drums Are Out*, 1969.

Fiction

Turf Smoke.   1945; retitled as *Turf Smoke on Manhattan*, 1949.

Verse

The Blossoming Thorn.   1946.

Memoirs and Letters

Prologue to a Marriage: Letters and Diaries of John Coulter and Olive Clare Primrose.   1979.
In My Day: Memoirs.   1980.

Other

Radio Drama is Not Theatre, with Ivor Lewis.   1937.
Churchill.   1944.

*

Criticism

Books:
Geraldine Anthony, *John Coulter*, Boston, 1976.
Geraldine Anthony, "John Coulter", in *Stage Voices*, Toronto, 1978.

Articles:
Anton Wagner, "John Coulter: Death of a Griot", in *Canadian Theatre Review*, 30, 1981.
Kathleen Gray, "Highest Hopes and Deepest Disappointments: John Coulter's London Diaries", in *Canadian Drama*, 10, 1984.

*   *   *

Coulter's early plays deal mostly with Irish themes since it was his avowed aim to do for Ulster theatre what playwrights like J.M. Synge and Sean O'Casey had done for theatre in Dublin. *The House in the Quiet Glen*, produced by the Toronto Masquers in 1937, was first produced on BBC radio, Belfast, in 1925, as *Sally's Chance*, directed by Tyrone Guthrie. It is a one-act comedy about Sally, whose parents arrange to marry her to Robert, not knowing that she loves his son. *The Family Portrait* is a three-act comedy about a young Belfast playwright whose play becomes a hit in London. Tensions arise when his family discover they are the subject of the play. The three-act *Holy Manhattan* evokes the nostalgia of an Irishman, exiled in New York, for his homeland. The best of these Irish plays is *The Drums Are Out*, a three-act play which was first produced at Dublin's Abbey Theatre. It dramatizes with sympathy and understanding the dilemma facing an Ulster police officer whose daughter's wounded IRA husband is finally cornered in his home. The action takes place against a backdrop of sectarian violence in Belfast in the 1920's.

When Coulter settled in Canada he turned his attention to Canadian themes in the many plays he wrote for radio, dramatizing incidents in the lives of such historical figures as François Bigot, an Intendant of New France, and Joseph Howe, a 19th-century Premier of Nova Scotia. But it was Coulter's stage trilogy—*Riel*, *The Trial of Louis Riel*, and *The Crime of Louis Riel*—dramatizing the life and execution of Louis Riel that has earned him an important place in Canadian drama. Sensitized by his experience of the violence, bloodshed, and religious intolerance of Belfast in the early 1920's, Coulter was drawn to the enigmatic figure of the Métis leader, Riel, the founder of Manitoba, whom he saw as representing the tensions inherent in Canadian society—tensions between English and French, between Protestant and Catholic, between the idealistic west and the manipulative east (represented by Prime Minister Sir John A. Macdonald who ordered the execution of Riel). The trilogy, and especially *Riel*, is notable for the way in which it fuses myth, history, and epic while creating a larger-than-life hero who, in his *hubris* and tragic fall, touches a responsive nerve in the Canadian psyche. The one-act *Trial of Louis Riel* is offered annually each year in Regina, the city where Riel was hanged, in a courtroom-theatre built to resemble the original courtroom. Based on transcriptions of the original trial, it still has a striking theatricality which is enriched by historical verisimilitude.

Coulter's work is notable for its poetic character which is best seen in two verse-dramas or libretti—*Transit Through Fire*, reflections by a young Canadian soldier and his wife, in 1942, on their trials in the Depression years and how those trials tempered them for the struggle against Nazism, and *Deirdre of the Sorrows*, a retelling of the ancient Irish story of Deirdre, fated to bring destruction on herself and the Sons of Usna. But his major contribution to Canadian drama is the lesson he taught other aspiring playwrights—that they did not need to seek foreign models, that Canadian history and legend and myth could provide the stuff of indigenous drama.

—Eugene Benson

See also *Volume 1* entry on *The Riel Trilogy*.

COWARD, (Sir) Noël (Pierce). Born in Teddington, Middlesex, England, 16 December 1899. Educated at Chapel Road School, Clapham, London, and privately. Actor, producer, and director: made London stage debut with Charles Hawtrey's company, 1911, and thereafter appeared on the London and New York (from 1925) stage, often in productions of his own works; also composer, lyricist, night-club and cabaret entertainer, and, from 1917, film actor; served in the Artists Rifles, British Army, 1918; head of the British Information Service propaganda bureau, Paris, 1939–40; entertained troops, 1943–44; built house at Blue Harbour, Jamaica, 1948; lived in Bermuda, 1956–59, and part of the

time in Switzerland from 1959. President, Actors' Orphanage, 1934–56. Recipient: New York Drama Critics Circle Award, 1942; Tony Award, 1971. D.Litt: University of Sussex, Brighton, 1972. Fellow, Royal Society of Literature. Knighted, 1970. Died Port Maria, Jamaica, 26 March 1973.

Works

Collections

Three Plays: The Rat Trap; The Vortex; Fallen Angels; With the Author's Reply to His Critics. 1925.
The Collected Sketches and Lyrics. 1931.
Play Parade:
  1. *Cavalcade; Bitter-Sweet; The Vortex; Hay Fever; Design for Living; Private Lives; Post-Mortem.* 1933.
  2. *This Year of Grace!; Words and Music; Operette; Conversation Piece.* 1939; augmented edition including *Fallen Angels* and *Easy Virtue*, 1950.
  3. *The Queen Was in the Parlour; I'll Leave It to You; The Young Idea; The Rat Trap; Sirocco; This Was a Man, Home Chat; The Marquise.* 1950.
  4. *Tonight at 8:30; Present Laughter; This Happy Breed.* 1954.
  5. *Pacific 1860; Peace in Our Time; Relative Values; Quadrille; Blithe Spirit.* 1958.
  6. *Point Valaine; South Sea Bubble; Ace of Clubs; Nude with Violin; Waiting in the Wings.* 1962.
Short Stories, Short Plays, and Songs, edited by Gilbert Millstein. 1955.
Cowardy Custard: The World of Coward, edited by John Hadfield. 1973.
Plays:
  1. *Hay Fever; The Vortex; Fallen Angels; Easy Virtue.* 1979.
  2. *Private Lives; Bitter-Sweet; The Marquise; Post-Mortem.* 1979.
  3. *Design for Living; Cavalcade; Conversation Piece; Tonight at 8.30 (I).* 1979.
  4. *Blithe Spirit; This Happy Breed; Present Laughter; Tonight at 8.30 (II).* 1983.
  5. *Relative Values; Look After Lulu; Waiting in the Wings; Suite in Three Keys.* 1983.

Stage Works

Ida Collaborates, with Esmé Wynne (produced Theatre Royal, Aldershot, 1917).
Sketches in *Tails Up!* (produced London, 1918).
Woman and Whisky, with Esmé Wynne (produced Wimbledon Theatre, Wimbledon, 1919).
I'll Leave it to You (produced Gaiety Theatre, Manchester, 1920). 1920.
Bottles and Bones (produced for the Newspaper Press Fund, Theatre Royal, Drury Lane, London, 1922).
The Better Half (produced Little Theatre, London, 1922).
Sketches in *The Co-Optimists: A Pierrotic Entertainment* (produced London, 1922; revised version produced 1924).
The Young Idea: A Comedy of Youth (produced Prince's Theatre, Bristol, 1922). 1924.
London Calling!, with Ronald Jeans (revue: produced Duke of York's Theatre, London, 1923; revised versions produced 1923, 1924). Some items in *The Collected Sketches and Lyrics*, 1931, and *The Noël Coward Song-Book*, 1953.

Noël Coward as Elyot and Gertrude Lawrence as Amanda in Coward's *Private Lives*, 1930.

The Vortex (produced Everyman Theatre, Hampstead, London, 1924). 1925.

Sketches in *Charlot's London Revue of 1924* (produced New York, 1924).

The Rat Trap (produced Everyman Theatre, Hampstead, London, 1926). 1924.

Sketches in *Yoicks!* (produced Kingsway Theatre, London, 1924).

Sketches in *Charlot's Revue of 1926* (produced London, 1925).

On with the Dance, music by Philip Braham (revue: produced Palace Theatre, Manchester, 1925). Some items in *The Collected Sketches and Lyrics*, 1931, and *The Noël Coward Song-Book*, 1953.

Hay Fever (produced Ambassador's Theatre, London, 1925). 1925.

Fallen Angels (produced Globe Theatre, London, 1925; revised version produced London, 1967). 1925.

Easy Virtue (produced Empire Theatre, New York, 1925). 1926.

The Queen Was in the Parlour (produced St. Martin's Theatre, London, 1926). 1926.

This Was a Man (produced Klaw Theatre, New York, 1926). 1926.

The Marquise (produced Criterion Theatre, London, 1927). 1927.

Home Chat (produced Duke of York's Theatre, London, 1927). 1927.

Sirocco (produced Daly's Theatre, London, 1927). 1927.

Sketches in *White Birds* (produced London, 1927).

This Year of Grace! (revue: produced Palace Theatre, Manchester, 1928). In *Play Parade 2*, 1939.

Bitter-Sweet, music by Coward (produced His Majesty's Theatre, London, 1929). 1929.

Private Lives: An Intimate Comedy (produced King's Theatre, Edinburgh, 1930). 1930.

Sketches in *Charles B. Cochran's 1931 Revue* (produced Palace Theatre, Manchester, 1931).

Sketches in *The Third Little Show* (produced New York, 1931). 1931.

Parody of Private Lives (as *Some Other Private Lives*, produced Hippodrome, London, 1931). In *The Collected Lyrics and Sketches*, 1931.

Post-Mortem (televised 1967). 1931.

Cavalcade (produced Theatre Royal, Drury Lane, London, 1931). 1932.

Weatherwise (produced Festival Theatre, Malvern, 1932). In *The Collected Sketches and Lyrics*, 1931.

Words and Music (revue; produced Opera House, Manchester, 1932; revised version, as *Set to Music*, produced New York, 1939). In *Play Parade 2*, 1939.

Design for Living (produced Ethel Barrymore Theatre, New York, 1933). 1933.

Conversation Piece (produced His Majesty's Theatre, London, 1934). 1934.

Point Valaine (produced Ethel Barrymore Theatre, New York, 1935). 1935.

Tonight at 8:30 (includes *We Were Dancing, The Astonished Heart, Red Peppers: An Interlude with Music, Hands Across the Sea, Fumed Oak: An Unpleasant Comedy, Shadow Play, Family Album: A Victorian Comedy with Music, Star Chamber, Ways and Means, Still Life*) (produced in three programmes, Opera House, Manchester, 1936). 3 vols., 1936 (*Star Chamber* unpublished).

Operette, music by Coward (produced Opera House, Manchester, 1938). 1938.

Sketches in *All Clear* (produced London, 1939).

Blithe Spirit: An Improbable Farce (produced Opera House, Manchester, 1941). 1941.

Present Laughter (produced Grand Theatre, Blackpool, 1942). 1943.

This Happy Breed (produced Grand Theatre, Blackpool, 1942). 1943.

Sign No More (revue; produced Opera House, Manchester, 1945). Some items in *The Noël Coward Song-Book*, 1953.

Pacific 1860: A Musical Romance, music by Coward (produced Theatre Royal, Drury Lane, London, 1946). In *Play Parade 5*, 1958.

Peace in Our Time (produced Theatre Royal, Brighton, 1947). 1947.

Ace of Clubs, music by Coward (produced Palace Theatre, Manchester, 1950). In *Play Parade 6*, 1962.

Relative Values (produced Theatre Royal, Newcastle, 1951). 1952.

Sketches in *The Lyric Revue* (produced London, 1951).

South Sea Bubble (as *Island Fling*, produced Country Playhouse, Westport, Connecticut, 1951; as *South Sea Bubble*, produced Dublin, 1956). 1956.

Quadrille (produced Opera House, Manchester, 1952). 1952.

Sketches in *The Globe Revue* (produced London, 1952).

After the Ball, music by Coward, from a play by Wilde (produced Royal Court Theatre, Liverpool, 1954). 1954.

Nude with Violin (produced Olympia Theatre, Dublin, 1956). 1957.

Look after Lulu, from a play by Feydeau (produced Royal Court Theatre, London, 1959). 1959.

London Morning (ballet scenario; produced 1959).

Waiting in the Wings (produced Duke of York's Theatre, London, 1960). 1960.

Sail Away, music by Coward (produced Broadhurst Theatre, New York, 1961).

The Girl Who Came to Supper, music and lyrics by Coward, from play *The Sleeping Prince* by Rattigan (produced Broadway Theatre, New York, 1963).

Suite in Three Keys: A Song at Twilight, Shadows of the Evening, Come into the Garden Maud (produced in two programmes, Queen's Theatre, London, 1966). 1966.

Semi-Monde (produced Glasgow Citizens' Theatre, Glasgow, 1977).

Screenplays

In Which We Serve, 1942; *This Happy Breed*, 1944; *Blithe Spirit*, with others, 1945; *Brief Encounter*, with others, 1946 (published in *Three British Screenplays*, edited by Roger Manvell, 1950); *The Astonished Heart*, with others, 1949; *Meet Me Tonight*, 1952.

Radio Plays

The Kindness of Mrs. Redcliffe, 1951.

Fiction

To Step Aside: Seven Short Stories. 1939.
Star Quality: Six Stories. 1951.
Pomp and Circumstance. 1960.
The Collected Short Stories. 1962.
Seven Stories. 1963.
"Pretty Polly Barlow" and Other Stories. 1964; as *"Pretty Polly" and Other Stories*, 1965.
"Bon Voyage" and Other Stories. 1967.

Verse

Poems by Hernia Whittlebot. 1923.
Chelsea Buns (as Hernia Whittlebot). 1925.
Spangled Unicorn: An Anthology. 1932.
The Coward Song-Book. 1953.
The Lyrics of Coward. 1965.
"Not Yet the Dodo" and Other Verses. 1967.
Collected Verse, edited by Graham Payn and Martin Tickner. 1984.

Memoirs and Letters

Autobiography (includes the unfinished *Past Conditional*). 1986.
Present Indicative. 1937.
Future Indefinite. 1954.
Diaries, edited by Graham Payn and Sheridan Morley. 1982.

Other

A Withered Nosegay: Imaginary Biographies. 1922; augmented edition, as *Terribly Intimate Portraits*, 1922.
Australian Broadcast. 1941; as *Australia Visited 1940*, 1941.
Middle East Diary, July to October 1943. 1944.
The Wit of Coward, edited by Dick Richards. 1968.
Out in the Midday Sun: The Paintings of Coward, text by Sheridan Morley. 1988.

Editor, *The Last Bassoon: From the Diaries of Fred Bason*. 1960.

*

Criticism

Books:
Robert Greacen, *The Art of Coward*, London, 1953.
Raymond Mander and Joe Mitchenson, *Theatrical

Companion to Coward: A Pictorial Record of the First Performances of the Theatrical Works of Coward, London, 1957.

Milton Levin, *Noël Coward*, New York, 1968.

Sheridan Morley, *A Talent to Amuse: A Biography of Coward*, Garden City, New York, 1969.

Charles Castle, *Noël*, London, 1972.

William Marchant, *The Privilege of His Company: Coward Remembered*, London, 1975.

Cole Lesley, *The Life of Coward*, London, 1976; as *Remembered Laughter*, New York, 1976.

Cole Lesley, *Coward and His Friends*, London, 1979.

John Lahr, *Coward the Playwright*, London, 1982.

Robert F. Kiernan, *Noël Coward*, New York, 1986.

Frances Gray, *Noël Coward*, Basingstoke, 1987.

Jacqui Russell (ed.), *File on Coward*, London, 1987.

*   *   *

Perhaps the most prolific and uniformly successful of the English dramatists who wrote between the two World Wars. Noël Coward was more than a dramatist, he was an *homme de théâtre* of great versatility, being author, dramatist, actor, producer, director, scenarist, cinema director, and composer. Even as a dramatist he was remarkably versatile in terms of the kinds of material he produced, his *opus* including farce, social, domestic, and manners comedy, serious bourgeois drama, satire, revue, musical and historical drama, lyrics and sketches, and scenarios for documentary and fiction films. So various were his talents that even those sceptical of their depth would not begrudge him the title he bestowed on himself, and which later came to be worn as his of right, "the Master".

Coward first came to prominence with a piece that was, for the generation of the 1920's, what 30 years later John Osborne's *Look Back in Anger* was to be for the late 1950's. The play was *The Vortex*, which Coward not only wrote, but starred in. It was a society domestic drama treating what, for its time, was strong subject matter—promiscuity and drug addiction. Particularly effective was the denouement, which brought together the mother, heartbroken at losing her young lover to the girlfriend of her son, and the son, himself a drug addict: the scene between them, first of mutual recrimination, then of reconciliation, was brilliantly played by Coward and Lillian Braithwaite, and was the highlight of a play that even today retains considerable power. Coward's stage dialogue was neither profound nor rich, but he had a brilliant theatrical sense, and was a master at manipulating situations to effect surprise or shock. His command of stagecraft was turned to fine account in *The Vortex*, as too was his skill at making the superficial and sentimental appear profound and moving.

The skills evident in such early work were capitalised on with particular effect in his light and sophisticated high-life social comedies of the 1920's, like *Hay Fever* and *Easy Virtue*. These were, in effect, social dramas translated into manners comedy for satirical purpose; in them, bourgeois society is castigated for its immorality, hypocrisy, and lack of tolerance, and the manners-comedy tone is qualified by a melodramatic note derived from 1890's and Edwardian society drama, for these pieces stand in a tradition of comic *drame* Coward took over from the early Wilde and the more astringent Maugham.

With *Private Lives*, however, produced in 1930, Coward's own very distinctive voice sounds unmistakably. Modern, debonaire, mildly astringent manners comedy in the vein of this play was henceforth to be his *forte*. *Private Lives* is a comedy of social and sexual relations, with engaging character psychology, witty dialogue, and a humorous satirical def-

lation of the pretentions of smart socialite living of the 1920's and 1930's. Its patterned plot-line indicates the degree of its artificiality: Elyot Chase and his second wife, Sybil, are in the south of France on their honeymoon. But staying at the same hotel with them, and in adjacent rooms, is Elyot's first wife, Amanda, and her new husband, Victor. Elyot and Amanda meet, when on their respective balconies, are attracted to one another again, and elope together to Amanda's flat in Paris. But ensconced there, they argue as of old, as too do Sybil and Victor, who pursue them to Paris and who are soon in the flat with them, quarrelling with all the gusto of a married couple. Elyot and Amanda, amused by the irony of this recurring love-hate situation, slip quietly away together. The manners comedy Coward evolved here is essentially a domestic drama: many of the principals are married or engaged, but the comedy is firmly in the manners tradition in that the emphasis in relationships is on individual freedom of action, and the ways in which emotional self-absorption and pursuit of self-gratification run counter to socially imposed restraints. It is a light, slick, poised comic drama of impressive durability, as is evidenced by recent restagings in London and elsewhere.

Much of Coward's best work, then, was done in varieties of sophisticated comedy, and his drama is nearly always informed by a confident and assured social style, a fine theatrical sense, brittle wit, and a dialogue rich in neat epigrams and engaging one-liners. But his talents were various. *Conversation Piece*, written in both French and English, was a brittle sophisticated comedy more of sentiment than manners, but a quasi-historical drama too, set in the fashionable Brighton of 1811. Coward was no less successful with several kinds of quasi-naturalistic drama: in *Cavalcade*, popular on both stage and screen, he presented a panoramic overview of English domestic and public life from the Boer War through to the Armistice night of World War I, and in *In Which We Serve*, a semi-documentary film, expressly conceived as part of the war effort, he recounted the story of a British destroyer and her personnel, and the fortunes of the crew's families ashore. In both he mined an engaging, and at the time very appropriate, vein of patriotism and sentiment. The latter emotion was marked, too, in his one-act piece, *Still Life*, later the inspiration for an outstanding British film, *Brief Encounter*. This piece reminds one that Coward was a master of the one-act form: notable was his 1935 *Tonight at 8:30*, a collection of short pieces including *Red Peppers*, *Hands Across the Sea*, and *Fumed Oak*, written for himself and Gertrude Lawrence.

There is no doubt some truth in the charge that Coward wrote too much and too fast, was too anxious to capitalise on his early success, and that he too frequently sacrificed quality for quick commercial returns. But given the degree and range of his success, and the length of time he worked in the theatre, the number of his plays still holding a place in the repertory is impressive. Add the range and quality of his performing talent, and the combination makes of Coward one of the most interesting creative figures to have worked in the 20th-century English theatre.

—Kenneth Richards

See also *Volume 1* entries on *Design For Living*; *Hay Fever*; *Private Lives*.

———

CROMMELYNCK, Fernand.   Born in Paris, 19 November 1885. Left school at age 12. Married the actress Anna-Marie

Letellier in 1908 (separated 1932); one son. Stockbroker's assistant after leaving school; stage debut as actor, at Théâtre des Bouffes-Parisiennes, Paris, 1899; followed his parents to Brussels; first poetry published in *La Libre Critique*, 1903; first play published 1906; moved to Ostend after marriage, and then lived in Paris, 1909–13; founded his own theatre company, *Le Théâtre Volant* [The Flying Theatre] in Brussels, 1916, acting with his wife in its productions: company broke up due to financial pressure, 1917; writer for *L'Homme libre*, 1919; during World War II was director of the Théâtre des Galeries in occupied Brussels; theatre critic for *XXe Siècle*, 1945–46; founder, with Maurice Kaplan, the periodical *Les Belles Lectures*, 1946. Recipient: L'Ordre de Léopold, and several literary awards. Died in Saint-Germain-en-Laye, 17 March 1970.

Works

Collections

Théâtre (3 vols.). 1967–68.

Stage Works

Le Sculpteur de masques (produced Théâtre du Gymnase, Paris, 1911). In *En Art*, 1906 (in verse); in book form, 1908; revised prose version, 1918.
Nous n'irons plus au bois (produced Théâtre du Parc, Brussels, 1906). 1906.
Chacun pour soi. 1907.
Le Marchand de regrets (produced Théâtre du Parc, Brussels, 1913). In *La Vie intellectuelle*, 1913.
Les Contes de la grand-mère (for children; produced by the Théâtre Volant, 1916).
Le Cocu magnifique (produced Théâtre de l'Oeuvre, Paris, 1920). 1921.
Les Amants puérils (produced Comédie-Montaigne, Paris, 1921). 1921.
Jeanne d'Arc, from a work by Péguy (produced 1924).
Tripes d'or (produced Comédie des Champs-Élysées, Paris, 1925). 1930.
Carine; ou, La Jeune Fille folle de son âme (produced Théâtre de l'Oeuvre, Paris, 1929). 1930
Une Femme qui a le coeur trop petit (produced by the Théâtre de l'Oeuvre, Palais des Beaux-Arts, Brussels, 1934). 1934.
Chaud et froid; ou, L'Idée de Monsieur Dom (produced Comédie des Champs-Élysées, Paris, 1934). 1936.
Le Chevalier à la lune; ou, Sir John Falstaff. 1954.

Screenplays

Le Sculpteur de masques, 1911; *Je suis avec toi*, 1943.

Verse

Les Alternances. 1945.

Fiction

Miroir de l'Enfance (stories). 1933.
Monsieur Larose est-il l'assassin?. 1950.

*

Bibliographies

Charles Diereck, *Fernand Crommelynck 1866–1970: Catalogue*, Brussels, 1980.

Criticism

Books:
M. Arland, *À La Rencontre de Fernand Crommelynck*, Liège, 1947.
Jeanine Moulin, *Textes inconnus et peu connus de Fernand Crommelynck: Étude critique et littéraire*, Brussels, 1974.
G. Feal, *Le Théâtre de Fernand Crommelynck: Érotisme et spiritualité*, Paris, 1976.
Bettina L. Knapp, *Fernand Crommelynck*, Boston, 1978.
Jeanine Moulin, *Fernand Crommelynck, ou le théâtre du paroxysme*, Brussels, 1978.
Jean P. de Cruvanaere, *Fernand Crommelynck*, Brussels, 1988.

Articles:
Bettina L. Knapp, "Crommelynck's Farcical and Myth-Making Expressionism", in *Comparative Drama*, 10, 1976–77.

* * *

Farce with tragic undercurrents and drama depicting human folly typify the style of Fernand Crommelynck. Crommelynck encountered early 20th-century drama through his father and uncle, both actors, and regarded it disapprovingly. He felt the characters that he saw spoke endlessly, and he set out to create plays in which dramatic action would supersede exposition, where characterization and situation would go beyond the limitations of naturalism, and where text and silence would be of equal value. In Crommelynck's *oeuvre*, humor and a poetic command of language prevail over all other dramatic techniques. Crommelynck's plays show us how human behavior can be dominated and even determined by extreme expressions of passion and emotion.

From the repertoire of Crommelynck's plays the following six have attracted the greatest amount of attention and analysis: *Le Sculpteur des masques* (The Sculptor of Masks)—where there is an eternal love triangle existing in a world where the lifestyle and work of the artist is not tolerated by the general community; *Tripes d'or* (Golden Guts)—where a miser decides that the best way to retain his fortune is to ingest it, even if it leads ultimately to his death; *Carine; ou La Jeune Fille folle de son âme* (Carine or the Young Girl in Love with Her Soul)—in which the purist attitudes of a young woman lead to disastrous consequences; *Une Femme qui a le coeur trop petit* (A Woman Whose Heart is Too Small)—where the tortuous constraints of excessive virtue imprison an entire household; *Chaud et froid; ou L'Idée de Monsieur Dom* (Hot and Cold, or Mr. Dom's Idea)—where outrage and humiliation are succeeded by obsession, which is eventually transformed into submission; and *Le Cocu magnifique* (The Magnificent Cuckold)—in which the idealization of love leads to ridicule and estrangement.

Le Cocu magnifique is the most widely acclaimed of Crommelynck's plays, and achieved international recognition shortly after its creation. The most famous production to date has been Vsevelod Meyerhold's in Moscow (1922). Meyerhold captured the essence of the situation—the humorous portrayal of the unrelenting obsessive love of Bruno for the naive and obedient Stella—through innovative and imaginative staging techniques. The wheel of the converted windmill was the centre of a multi-level set. The designer, L.P. Popova, a constructivist, used geometric shapes, ladders, and doors, to provide scenic elements essential to the business of the actor, and created a world that illustrated both the internal and external action of Crommelynck's drama.

Crommelynck's plays recurrently pose the question: is marital bliss possible? In his plays infidelity constantly causes stress, sometimes to the point of death. Bruno in *Le Cocu magnifique* suspects his wife's infidelity and sets out to reveal it. He can be compared to Shakespeare's Othello, overpowered by the destructive and overwhelming forces of jealousy. However, Bruno does not require an Iago to incite him, his own imagination is sufficient. Pascal in *Le Sculpteur des masques*, in an attempt to recapture his youth, makes advances to his wife Louison's adolescent sister. The pain of her husband's unfaithfulness causes Louison's insidious illness and finally her death. It is possible that the turbulence in the relationship of Crommelynck's own parents and his father's constant infidelity inspired the playwright to treat this theme.

Crommelynck's characters become obsessed in their quest for satisfaction. Bruno is insensitive to the truth, and obsession—he believes Stella has a secret lover—provokes his actions. Léona in *Chaud et froid* cannot suppress her desire for exclusivity. She coerces her dead husband's mistress into the arms of her own lover, Odillon. By the end of the play Léona feels she is the sole possessor of her husband's love. Pierre-Auguste, the miserly bachelor in *Tripes d'or*, comparable to Molière's Harpagon, trusts no one, not even his fiancée, and goes to the point of swallowing his gold coins to secure their safe-keeping.

These potentially pathetic and melodramatic situations are rendered sublime and grotesque at various moments in the plays. Crommelynck's prose style is full of sensuous and poetic imagery, and it was this sublime element that often inspired spontaneous reactions of applause during performances. The masks, which are an integral part of Crommelynck's plays, establish the sense of the grotesque. They create an atmosphere that is carnivalesque, and the effect is simultaneously entertaining and menacing. When the revelers arrive at Pascal's shop in *Le Sculpteur des Masques*, their activity, at first, creates a comic relief from the preceding dramatic tension. However, the non-life-sized features of the masks and the antagonistic intentions of the mummers then create mounting suspense and amplify the existing tension. The swooping down of the chorus of masks is reminiscent of classical tragedy in the sense that it criticizes and comments upon the motives of the protagonists. Some of the unmasked characters are transformed beyond normal physical proportions, and their faces take on the qualities of masks. This metamorphosis is within the reality of the situation, but does not belong to naturalistic conventions: with each ensuing scene of the last act, Bruno becomes more haggard and aged; he loses his hair with worry; he groans and grimaces in tortuous anguish.

Each of Crommelynck's plays is a carefully constructed three-act farce. Crommelynck typically starts out from a realistic situation, then introduces a twist in the psyche of the character that launches the rest of the action—for example, in *Le Cocu magnifique* a suspected glimmer of lust in Petrus' eye suffices to incite Bruno and to subjugate the other personages to his expression of his folly—and the realistic is soon overtaken by the obsessional and the absurd.

—Ludvika Popenhagen

See also *Volume 1* entry on *The Magnificent Cuckhold*.

CROTHERS, Rachel. Born in Bloomington, Illinois, USA, 12 December 1878. Educated at Illinois State University Normal High School, Bloomington, graduated 1891; New England School of Dramatic Instruction, certificate 1892; Stanhope-Wheatcroft School of Acting, New York, 1897. Elocution teacher, Bloomington, 1892–96; teacher, Stanhope-Wheatcroft School, 1897–1901; directed and staged her own plays; first play, *Elizabeth*, produced 1919; founder, Stage Women's War Relief Fund, 1917; President, Stage Relief Fund, 1932–51; founder and first President, American Theatre Wing, and organized American Theatre Wing for War Relief, 1940. Recipient: Megrue Prize, 1933; Chi Omega Award, 1939. Died in Danbury, Connecticut, 5 July 1958.

Works

Collections

Mary the Third; Old Lady 31; A Little Journey: Three Plays. 1923.
Expressing Willie; Nice People; 39 East: Three Plays. 1924.
Six One-Act Plays (includes *The Importance of Being Clothed; The Importance of Being Nice; The Importance of Being Married; The Importance of Being a Woman; What They Think; Peggy*). 1925.

Stage Works

Elizabeth (produced Madison Square Theatre, New York, 1899).
Criss-Cross (produced Madison Square Theatre, New York, 1899). 1904.
Mrs. John Hobbs (produced Madison Square Theatre, New York, 1899).
The Rector (produced Madison Square Theatre, New York, 1902). 1905.
Nora (produced Savoy Theatre, New York, 1903).
The Point of View (produced Manhattan Theatre, New York, 1904).
The Three of Us (produced Madison Square Theatre, New York, 1906). 1916.
The Coming of Mrs. Patrick (produced Madison Square Theatre, New York, 1907).
Myself, Bettina (produced Powers Theatre, Chicago, 1908).
Kiddie. 1909.
A Man's World (produced National Theatre, Washington, DC, 1910). 1915.
He and She (produced Poughkeepsie, Washington, 1911; as *The Herfords*, produced 1912). In *Representative American Plays*, 1917; revised edition, 1925.
Young Wisdom (produced Criterion Theatre, New York, 1914). 1913.
Ourselves (produced Lyric Theatre, New York, 1913).
The Heart of Paddy Whack (produced Baltimore, Maryland, 1914). 1925.
Old Lady 31, from the novel by Louise Forsslund (produced Schenectady, New York, 1916). In *Mary the Third. . .*, 1923.
Mother Carey's Chickens, with Kate Douglas Wiggin, from the novel by Wiggin (produced Cort Theatre, New York, 1917). 1925.
A Little Journey (produced Little Theatre, New York, 1918). In *Mary the Third . . .*, 1923.
Once upon a Time (produced Atlantic City, New Jersey, 1917). 1925.
39 East (produced Broadhurst Theatre, New York, 1919). In *Expressing Willie . . .*, 1924.

Everyday (produced Atlantic City, New Jersey, 1921). 1930.
Nice People (produced Atlantic City, New Jersey, 1921).   In *Expressing Willie . . .*, 1924.
Mary the Third (produced 39th Street Theatre, New York, 1923).   In *Mary the Third . . .*, 1923.
Expressing Willie (produced 48th Street Theatre, New York, 1924).   In *Expressing Willie . . .*, 1924.
A Lady's Virtue (produced Selwyn Theatre, Chicago, 1925). 1925.
Venus (produced Masque Theatre, New York, 1927).   1927.
Let Us Be Gay (produced Little Theatre, Chicago, 1929). 1929.
As Husbands Go (produced John Golden Theatre, New York, 1931).   1931.
Caught Wet (produced John Golden Theatre, New York, 1931).   1932.
When Ladies Meet (produced Royale Theatre, New York, 1932).   1932.
The Valiant One.   1937.
Susan and God (produced Plymouth Theatre, New York, 1937).   1938.

Screenplays

Splendor, 1935.

*

Criticism

Books:
Lois C. Gottlieb, *Rachel Crothers*, Boston, 1979.

Articles:
Lois C. Gottlieb, "Obstacles to Feminism in the Early Plays of Rachel Crothers", in *University of Michigan Papers in Womens Studies*, June 1975.

*   *   *

Rachel Crothers was America's most successful woman playwright during the early decades of the 20th century. From the turn of the century until the late 1930's her plays were a staple of the New York stage, with productions of two dozen full-length works. Her career was made still more astonishing by the fact that she usually directed her own plays and sometimes produced, designed, and (in the case of the 1920 revival of *He and She*) starred in them. In an era when women directors were even rarer on Broadway than women playwrights, Brooks Atkinson of the *New York Times* called Crothers "one of the best directors we have".

Crothers was among the first American dramatists to attempt the problem play, already popular in Europe. These dramas comprise her most important early works and, in fact, may be her most enduring legacy to American drama. *A Man's World* is a perceptive look at the double standard of morality—an issue Crothers would continue to explore throughout her career. The heroine of the play is Frank Ware, an independent "New Woman", who is a writer, social activist, and single mother of an adopted son. When Frank eventually renounces her suitor, she does so not because he had impregnated a young single woman but because he fails to acknowledge that he, a man, shares equal responsibility for the consequences of their affair. Critics compared her rejection of him to Nora's slamming the door of her "doll's house" in Ibsen's play.

Also powerful, in different ways, is *He and She*, which presents the dilemma of a talented woman artist caught between her desires for a career and the needs of her teenage daughter. Although Crothers resolves the play along conventional lines—family taking priority over career—she is sensitive enough to present the difficulty of the choice involved, a choice being faced by more and more women of the period.

After a spate of cloyingly sentimental comedies like *Old Lady 31* (based on Louise Forsslund's novel) and *39 East*, Crothers turned to the form that would dominate the last two decades of her career and earn her great commercial success: social comedies about women of the upper and upper-middle classes. The action is typically set in an opulent house, and the dialogue—particularly toward the end of Crothers' career—is the witty repartee of high comedy. Although the works of the early 1920's tend to focus on flappers at odds with their parents, while the later ones center on more experienced women, they share a concern with the choices and challenges facing women in a world of shifting moral values.

Among the most effective of the plays of the 1920's is a dark comedy entitled *Mary the Third*. While Crothers' comedies usually end with that most conventional of conclusions, the uniting of hero and heroine, her picture of marriage is often so bleak that the traditional ending scarcely qualifies as a happy one. Young Mary has seen the flaws in her grandmother's marriage, a union based on wheedling and deception, as well as her parents' marriage, an angry clash of disparate personalities that her mother says went sour after only five years. Mary is an articulate spokeswoman for what Crothers believed was wrong with the American marriage: young people wed before they had a chance to know their prospective mates, and women's economic dependence kept them hostages to their husbands. When Mary finally accepts the proposal of her conservative suitor, responding to much the same urges that her mother and grandmother did, her decision can only be viewed with deep irony.

Numerous characters in Crothers' later plays comment on the prevalence of sexual affairs and divorce, reflecting the changing social climate in post-World-War-I America, but none of Crothers' heroines seems to find a satisfying alternative to the flawed institution of marriage. Kitty Brown, in *Let Us Be Gay*, divorces her unfaithful husband and then tries a life of sexual adventure herself, only to discover that neither free love nor a budding business career can replace the husband she still misses.

Crothers' last produced play was also her most successful: *Susan and God*, a satirical portrait of a woman infected by a European religious enthusiasm much like the Oxford Movement. A better effort—both more substantial and wittier—is *When Ladies Meet*. Ringing still one more change on the love triangle that is a virtual constant throughout her canon, the playwright presents talented, self-sufficient Mary Howard, a novelist in love with her married publisher, Rogers Woodruff. When Mary meets his wife, the two discover both empathy for each other and a realization of how badly he has treated all women. Instead of forgiving him one more time, as conventional comedy would demand, Claire Woodruff abandons her husband because of his cruelty to Mary.

Rachel Crothers was very much a Broadway playwright: she considered the art theaters of the 1910's and 1920's a "very grave menace" to the New York stage, and her plays of the 1930's largely ignored the economic disaster that had struck the nation and the theatrical world. The author of well-crafted plays that are rarely structurally innovative, she proclaimed that "realism at its best . . . is the highest form of dramatic writing". Crothers' critique of a society that treats women unfairly comes from an often traditional point of view likely to alienate many late 20th-century audiences. Her "answer" to the question of the double standard is to hold both sexes to a rigid code of morality and, along with most of her generation, Crothers seems unable to imagine women successfully synthesizing career and family.

But if Crothers is scarcely the daring artist and feminist some defenders would claim her to be, neither is she simply a prolific crafter of conventional comedies. Like her character Mary Howard, who hoped in her writing to "say something *new* and *honest*—from a woman's standpoint", Crothers saw her work as a "*Comédie Humaine de la Femme*" that traces women's "evolution" in modern society. The best of her problem plays and comedies combine a genuine sense of what works on stage with a thoughtful investigation of such serious issues as the double standard, the conflict between career and domestic responsibility, the challenges of the new sexual freedom, the loneliness of the career woman, and the hollowness of many marriages—problems that time and the slow currents of social change have still not resolved.

—Judith E. Barlow

See also *Volume 1* entry on *He and She*.

————————

CUMBERLAND, Richard. Born in Cambridge, England, 19 February 1732. Educated at a school in Bury St. Edmunds, Suffolk, 1738–43; Westminster School, London, 1744–47; Trinity College. Cambridge, 1747–51, BA 1751. Married Elizabeth Ridge in 1759; four sons and three daughters. Fellow of Trinity College, 1751; private secretary to Lord Halifax, president of the Board of Trade, from 1751, and Ulster secretary under Halifax, 1761–62: also crown agent for Nova Scotia and provost marshal of South Carolina; clerk of reports, 1762–75, and secretary, 1775–80, Board of Trade; peace negotiator in Spain, 1780–81: retired to Tunbridge Wells, Kent, after negotiations failed. DCL: University of Dublin, 1771. Died in Tunbridge Wells, Kent, 7 May 1811.

Works

Collections

Posthumous Dramatic Works (2 vols.).   1813.

Stage Works

The Banishment of Cicero.   1761.
The Summer's Tale, music by Thomas Arne (produced Covent Garden Theatre, London, 1765).   1765; revised version, as *Amelia* (produced Covent Garden Theatre, London, 1768), 1768; revised version, music by Charles Dibdin (produced 1771), 1771.
The Brothers (produced Covent Garden Theatre, London, 1769).   1770.
The West Indian (produced Theatre Royal, Drury Lane, London, 1771).   1771.
Timon of Athens, from the play by Shakespeare (produced Theatre Royal, Drury Lane, London, 1771).   1771.
The Fashionable Lover (produced Theatre Royal, Drury Lane, London, 1772).   1772.

The Squire's Return (produced 1773).
The Note of Hand; or, *The Trip to Newmarket* (produced Theatre Royal, Drury Lane, London, 1774).   1774.
The Choleric Man (produced Theatre Royal, Drury Lane, London, 1774).   1775.
The Princess of Parma (produced Kelmarsh, Northamptonshire, 1774).
The Election (produced Kelmarsh, Northamptonshire, 1774).
The Battle of Hastings (produced Theatre Royal, Drury Lane, London, 1778).   1778.
Calypso: A Masque, in *Miscellaneous Poems*.   1778; revised version, music by Thomas Butler (produced Covent Garden Theatre, London, 1779), 1779.
The Bondman, from the play by Massinger (produced Covent Garden Theatre, London, 1779).
The Duke of Milan, from the play by Massinger (produced Covent Garden Theatre, London, 1779).
The Widow of Delphi; or, The Descent of the Deities, music by Thomas Butler (produced Covent Garden Theatre, London, 1780).   Songs published 1780.
The Walloons (produced Covent Garden Theatre, London, 1782).   In *Posthumous Dramatic Works*, 1813.
The Mysterious Husband (produced Covent Garden Theatre, London, 1783).   1783.
The Carmelite (produced Theatre Royal, Drury Lane, London, 1784).   1784.
The Natural Son (produced Theatre Royal, Drury Lane, London, 1784).   1785; revised version (produced 1794).
Alcanor (as *The Arab*, produced Covent Garden Theatre, London, 1785).   In *Posthumous Dramatic Works*, 1813.
The Country Attorney (produced Theatre Royal, Haymarket, London, 1787; as *The School for Widows*, produced 1789).
The Imposters (produced Theatre Royal, Drury Lane, London, 1789).   1789.
An Occasional Prelude (produced Covent Garden Theatre, London, 1792).
The Clouds, from the play by Aristophanes.   1793.
The Armourer (produced Covent Garden Theatre, London, 1793).   Songs published 1793.
The Box-Lobby Challenge (produced Theatre Royal, Haymarket, London, 1794).   1794.
The Jew (produced Theatre Royal, Drury Lane, London, 1794).   1794.
The Wheel of Fortune (produced Theatre Royal, Drury Lane, London, 1795).   1795; edited by T.J. Campbell, 1787.
First Love (produced Theatre Royal, Drury Lane, London, 1795).   1795.
The Dependent (produced Theatre Royal, Drury Lane, London, 1795).
The Days of Yore (produced Covent Garden Theatre, London, 1796).   1796.
Don Pedro (produced Theatre Royal, Haymarket, London, 1796).   In *Posthumous Dramatic Works*, 1813.
The Last of the Family (produced Theatre Royal, Drury Lane, London, 1797).   In *Posthumous Dramatic Works*, 1813.
The Village Fete (produced Covent Garden Theatre, London, 1797).
False Impressions (produced Covent Garden Theatre, London, 1797).   1797.
The Eccentric Lover (produced Covent Garden Theatre, London, 1798).   In *Posthumous Dramatic Works*, 1813.
The Passive Husband (as *A Word for Nature*, produced 1798).   In *Posthumous Dramatic Works*, 1813.
Joanna of Montfaucon, music by Thomas Busby, from a work by Kotzebue (produced Covent Garden Theatre, London, 1800).   1800.

Lovers' Resolutions (produced Theatre Royal, Drury Lane, London, 1802). In *Posthumous Dramatic Works*, 1813.

The Sailor's Daughter (produced Theatre Royal, Drury Lane, London, 1804). 1804.

The Death and Victory of Lord Nelson (produced Theatre Royal, Drury Lane, London, 1805). 1805.

A Hint to Husbands (produced Covent Garden Theatre, London, 1806). 1806.

The Jew of Mogadore, music by Michael Kelly (produced Theatre Royal, Drury Lane, London, 1808). 1808.

The Robber (produced Tunbridge Wells, Kent, 1809).

The Widow's Only Son (produced Covent Garden Theatre, London, 1810).

The Confession. In *Posthumous Dramatic Works*, 1813.

Torrendal. In *Posthumous Dramatic Works*, 1813.

Tiberius in Capreae. In *Posthumous Dramatic Works*, 1813.

The False Demetrius. In *Posthumous Dramatic Works*, 1813.

The Sybil; or, The Elder Brutus (produced Theatre Royal, Drury Lane, London, 1818). In *Posthumous Dramatic Works*, 1813.

Fiction

Arundel. 1789.
Henry. 1795.
John de Lancaster. 1809.

Verse

An Elegy Written on Saint Mark's Eve. 1754.
Odes. 1776.
Miscellaneous Poems. 1778.
Calvary; or, The Death of Christ. 1792.
A Poetical Version of Certain Psalms of David. 1801.
The Exodiad, with J.B. Burges. 1807.
Retrospection: A Poem in Familiar Verse. 1811.

Memoirs and Letters

Memoirs (2 vols.). 1806–07; edited by Henry Flanders, 1856.
Letters, edited by Richard J. Dircks. 1988.

Other

A Letter to the Bishop of O–d. 1767.
Anecdotes of Eminent Painters in Spain During the Sixteenth and Seventeenth Centuries (2 vols.). 1782.
A Letter to Richard, Lord Bishop of Llandaff. 1783.
Character of the Late Viscount Sackville. 1785.
An Accurate Catalogue of the Paintings in the King of Spain's Palace at Madrid. 1787.
The Observer (5 vols.). 1788; edited by A. Chalmers, in *British Essayists 38–40*, 1817.
A Few Plain Reasons Why We Should Believe in Christ. 1801; as *The Anti Carlile*, 1826.

Editor, *Pharsalia*, by Lucan. 1760.
Editor, *The London Review*. (2 vols.). 1809.
Editor, *The British Drama*. (14 vols.). 1817.

*

Criticism

Books:
Stanley T. Williams, *Richard Cumberland: His Life and Dramatic Works*, New Haven, Connecticut, 1917.
Louis I. Newman, *Richard Cumberland, Critic and Friend of the Jews*, New York, 1919.
Joseph Donohue, *Dramatic Character in the English Romantic Age*, Princeton, New Jersey, 1970.
Richard J. Dircks, *Richard Cumberland*, Boston, 1976.

Articles:
S.T. Williams, "The Early Sentimental Dramas of Richard Cumberland", in *Modern Language Notes*, 36, 1921.
S.T. Williams, "The Dramas of Richard Cumberland, 1779–85", in *Modern Language Notes*, 36, 1921.

* * *

Richard Cumberland is better remembered as the original of Sir Fretful Plagiary in Sheridan's *The Critic* than for his own prolific output, although *The West Indian* gets a mention in most theatrical histories as an archetype of sentimental comedy. Yet Cumberland was the author of around 50 plays in most contemporary forms, including a new version of *Timon of Athens* and, in *The Jew*, an enlightened plea for its time on behalf of a persecuted people. Sensitive to criticism though Cumberland was (and as his own *Memoirs* affirms), Sheridan's satire did nothing to discourage a dramatic career which began with *The Banishment of Cicero* in 1761 and ended with *The Widow's Only Son* just a year before his death, 50 years later.

Goldsmith, in his posthumous *Retaliation*, describes him as: "A flattering painter who made it his care / To draw men as they ought to be, not as they are". And it is true that his comedies too often tended to be the "bastard tragedies" Goldsmith elsewhere dubbed them. Yet Cumberland's first play was a true tragedy, and he also tried his hand at comic opera before attempting his first comedy, *The Brothers*, in 1769. Presumably it was the relatively favourable reception accorded this play that encouraged him to continue in this vein with *The West Indian*, whose titular hero, Belcour, blunders his good-natured but untutored way through London society, a sort of diluted, colonial version of Tom Jones.

The plot of the play is convoluted even by the standards of its time, and few of the characters do more than exemplify their required vice or virtue: but Belcour himself is strong enough to sustain a certain interest through the twists and turns of the plotting, and the Irish Major O'Flaherty, an honest soldier of fortune, serves occasionally to deflate the more sententious exchanges. If Cumberland lacked much originality, his work remains nevertheless an interesting link between sentimental comedy and melodrama, and the moral code enshrined in the one is often expressed in the exclamatory style of the other in his later work.

—Simon Trussler

See also *Volume 1* entry on *The West Indian*.

D

DADIÉ, Bernard Binlin. Born in Assinie, Ivory Coast, 1916. Educated at Grand Bassam, 1928–30; École Primaire Supérieure, Bingerville, 1930–33; École Normale William-Ponty in Gorée, Senegal, from 1933, studying administration. Married Rosa Assamala Koutoua in 1950; nine children. Librarian, Institut Français d'Afrique Noire (IFAN), University of Dakar, 1936–47; co-founder, Théâtre Indigène de Côte d'Ivoire, which operated 1938–46; became press secretary for the Comité Directeur of the Parti Démocratique, 1947; arrested, 1949, and imprisoned for 16 months; after release, continued work for IFAN in Abidjan; founded the Cercle Culturel et Folklorique de Côte d'Ivoire, 1953; Chef de Cabinet in the Ministry of Education, 1957–59; Director of the Government Information Service, 1959–61; Director of Culture (Service des Beaux Arts et des Traditions Populaires) for the Ministry of Education, since 1961; vice president of executive council, Unesco, 1964–72; director, Commission Nationale de la Fondation Félix Houphouet-Boigny; member, Conseil Économique et Social, 1976–77; president, Conférence Générale de l'Agence de Coopération Culturelle et Technique, 1977–79; president, Association Internationale pour le Développement de la Documentation des Bibliothèques et des Archives en Afrique, Association Générale des Arts et Lettres de la Côte d'Ivoire, Association Internationale pour le Développement de la Documentation des Bibliothèques, des Archives, et des Musées de la Côte d'Ivoire, and Société Africaine de Culture (Ivory Coast chapter). Recipient of numerous awards and honours, including: Lauréat du Grand Prix Littéraire de l'Afrique Noire, 1965; Ville de Paris Silver Medal; Unesco Gold Medal; Haute Académie Internationale de Lutèce Gold Medal. Commandeur de l'Ordre National de la Côte d'Ivoire; Commandeur de l'Ordre du Mérite de l'Éducation Nationale; Commandeur de Pleiade de l'Ordre de la Francophonie et du Dialogue des Cultures; Commandeur de l'Ordre National de la Légion d'Honneur (France); Grand Officier de l'Ordre de Léopold (Belgium); Grand Officier de l'Ordre National du Mérite (France).

Works

Collections

Sidi maître escroc; Situation difficile; Serment d'amour. 1968.

Stage Works

Les Villes (produced at festival in Abijan, Ivory Coast, 1933).
Assémien Déhylé, roi du Sanwi (produced École Normale William-Ponty, Senegal, 1936; produced professionally, at the Théâtre des Champs-Élysées, Paris, 1937). In *Album officiel de la Mission Pontificale*, 1936.
Min adja-o (C'est mon héritage!) (produced 1960). In *Le Théâtre populaire en République de Côte d'Ivoire*, 1965.
Sidi maître escroc (produced 1960). In *Sidi maître escroc; Situation difficile; Serment d'amour*, 1968.
Serment d'amour (produced Théâtre Populaire, Abidjan, Ivory Coast, 1965). In *Le Théâtre populaire en Republique de Côte d'Ivoire*, 1965.
Situation difficile (produced Théâtre Populaire, Abidjan, Ivory Coast, 1965). In *Le Théâtre populaire en Republique de Côte d'Ivoire*, 1965.
Monsieur Thôgô-gnini (produced Institut National des Arts, Abidjan, 1967). 1970; translated as *Monsieur Thôgô-gnini*, 1986.
Les Voix dans le vent (produced 1969). 1970.
Béatrice du Congo (produced 1969). 1970.
Îles de tempête. 1973.
Mhoi-Ceul. 1979.

Fiction

Légendes africaines (short stories). 1954.
La Pagne noire: Contes africains. 1955; translated as *The Black Cloth*, 1987.
Climbié. 1956; translated as *Climbié*, 1971.
Un Nègre à Paris. 1959.
Les Belles Histoires de Kacou Ananzé, l'araignée. 1963.
Commandant Taureault et ses nègres. 1980.
Les Jambes du fils de Dieu (novellas). 1980.
Les Contes de Koutou-as-samala (stories). 1982.

Verse

Afrique debout. 1950.
La Ronde des jours. 1956.

Other

Hommes de tous les continents (stories and poems). 1957.
Patron de New York. 1964.
Legendes et poèmes (includes *Afrique debout; Légendes africaines; Climbié; La Ronde des jours*). 1967.
La Ville où nul ne meurt. 1968.
Opinions d'un nègre: Aphorismes 1934–1946. 1980.
Carnet de Prison. 1981.

*

Bibliographies

Bernard Magnier, "Bibliographie de Bernard Binlin Dadié",
in *Présence Francophone*, 13, 1976.

Criticism

Books:
C. Quillateau, *Bernard Binlin Dadié: L'Homme et l'oeuvre*,
Abidjan, Ivory Coast, 1962.
M. and S. Battestini, and Roger Mercier, *Bernard Dadié:
Écrivain ivoirien*, Paris, 1964.
C. Quillateau (ed.), *Bernard Binlin Dadié*, Paris, 1968.
Martin Banham, *African Theatre Today*, London, 1976.
Barthélémy Kotchy, *La Critique sociale dans l'oeuvre de
Bernard Binlin Dadié*, Paris, 1984.
Nicole Vincileoni, *Comprendre l'oeuvre de Bernard B. Dadié*,
Issy les Moulineaux, 1986.

Articles:
Robert P. Smith, "History and Tragedy in Bernard Dadié's
Béatrice du Congo", in *French Review*, 55, 1982.
John Conteh-Morgan, "History or Literature: A Critical
Study of Bernard Dadié's *Béatrice de Congo*", in *Canadian
Journal of French Studies*, 19, 1985.

* * *

Bernard Dadié is unique among African playwrights in the length of his career. The first non-traditional drama in francophone Africa developed at the upper primary school in Bingerville, Ivory Coast. The first play performed there seems to have been Dadié's *Les Villes*. The principal of the school moved to the École Normale William-Ponty, in Senegal, which functioned as a kind of college, since the students were at least 18 years old when they entered. There Dadié wrote *Assémien Déhylé, roi du Sanwi*, which has been called the one play of the period to treat pre-colonial Africa with respect. With two other graduates of the school, he founded the Théâtre Indigène de Côte d'Ivoire, active from 1938 to 1946, and then the Cercle Culturel et Folklorique de Côte d'Ivoire in 1953. With independence in 1960, Dadié and his colleagues moved into busy government careers, but in 1966 some of their plays—mostly didactic comedies—were anthologized in *Le Théatre populaire en République de Côte d'Ivoire*.

After writing a number of other kinds of works, including the classic autobiographical novel *Climbié*, Dadié returned to the drama with *Monsieur Thôgô-gnini*, a satiric comedy whose central character is a combination of Monsieur Jourdain and Tartuffe, and like Tartuffe ultimately discomfited by the ruler's intervention. Thôgô-gnini means "seeker after fame", and he is the first of several Black entrepreneurs who are "short of patience, long on greed, and brutal" in Dadié's plays. Dazzled by the chance to enrich themselves and ignorantly imitative of Western ways—Thôgô-gnini wears an elegant suit made of gunnysacks—it is they who help to establish colonial rule and, by becoming the exploiters of their own people, make it work on a day-to-day basis.

Apart from a farce reworked from earlier in his career (*Sidi maître escroc*), his subsequent plays have been large-scale historical tragedies. *Les Voix dans le vent* presents the overturning of the traditional order by Nahoubou, who perverts the idea of a chief's authority into a megalomaniac reign, but is haunted by the voices in the wind of the title. It is not just that Nahoubou is grossly insensitive and cruel, but that power

renders him blind to his own faults: "power intoxicates and leads one to death" is the theme. Both this play and *Monsieur Thôgô-gnini* are set in undefined countries in the 19th century, but their contemporary applications are clear.

These tragedies aim at total theatre in their use of crowds, mime, and music. *Béatrice du Congo*, for example, begins with a virtual overture:

Western music dominating Arab music.
The calls of the muezzins intercut with the intermittent and feeble sound of bells; hand-clapping; the Arab music wanes and the Western music grows; the muted bells increase in frequency to become a tocsin.
Many gunshots; noise of a crowd, neighing of horses.
The curtain rises on the end of a battle . . . the dead of both sides.

Béatrice was a Congolese who led a revolt against the Portuguese and was burnt at the stake. Yet the play begins with the defeat of the Moors at Ceuta and Henry the Navigator's call for expansion:

Henry: The lesson of Ceuta? It is simple. No tyrants, however powerful, can oppress a whole people for centuries.
Diogo: Away with abductions, imprisonments, insecurity . . .
Henry: Liberty recovered . . . All these are our benefits, ours alone. The earth . . .
Diogo: Ours.
Henry: The sky . . .
Diogo: Ours . . . At last we work for ourselves, labor for our own families and not for others and their children . . .
Henry: Reverse the course of history . . .
Diogo: Dance for ourselves, for our families and not for the entertainment of an oppressor; plant flowers for our pleasure and not for that of a master. At last, to work, to suffer, and even to die for our country and not to increase the fortune of another.

Even the dialogue has a musical rhythm. Furthermore, as Henry goes on to speak of spreading Christianity and of mastering the world, church bells and the sound of the sea in each case precede his words. The scale of the work is evident in this scene; ironically, the Portuguese will become the oppressors in the Congo and the sentiments of liberation will be expressed, toward the end of the play, by the rebels.

The reiterated idealism of the Portuguese is wilfully hypocritical. So Henry declares:

It is imperative for us to tear out the disdain these infidels have for women, so great that they shut them up in harems; jealousy is so great among these barbarians that they veil that sublime creature, woman; it is imperative, I say, to tear out their monopoly on the sale of cinnamon, of ginger, of cloves, of silk, of incense, of musk, of ivory . . . .

The conversion of the indigenous king to Christianity leads to Portuguese control of his kingdom, but his conversion also leads to its destruction, for, since each wife represents an alliance, when he renounces polygamy he loses his hegemony.

The first mention of Béatrice is not until the second act, with the line "a girl surrounded by flames rekindles dawn in our hearts", and her rebellion is not introduced until two-thirds of the way through the play. That initial metaphor for Béatrice becomes visible onstage in the flaming torches of the rebels, and so, though she is burned at the end, her burning becomes the enactment of the metaphor. Though tragedies, these plays end in a muted optimism, implicitly inviting their audiences to change history.

Îles de tempête, a play about Toussaint L'Ouverture's revolt against the French in Haiti, is even more ambitious in its inclusion of the common man in the drama (sometimes in crowd scenes and sometimes as a vivid background to the dialogue) and in its counterpoint of black government in Haiti with white government in France, and of Toussaint with Napoleon as men who overturn the status quo and end their lives in exile.

In writing on such a scale, with an emphasis on the cycles of history, there is a loss of individuality in the characters, who tend to be written to represent something larger than themselves. But the sense of dramatic control, of the structural balance of one scene and character against another, of the integration of the resources of theatre to serve a vision of history, has great power.

—Anthony Graham-White

* * *

DAGERMAN, Stig (Halvard). Born in Älvkarleby, Sweden, 5 October 1923. Studied literature and art at the University of Stockholm. Married twice, the second time to the actress Anita Björk. Writer, from 1941, and arts editor, 1944–46, for the syndicalist newspaper *Arbetaren*; contributor to *40-tal*, 1946–47, and *Prisma*, 1948–50; first-produced play, *Den dödsdömde* [*The Comdemned*], staged 1947. Committed suicide in Stockholm, 4 November 1954.

Works

Collections

Dramer om dömda (includes *Den dödsdömde; Skuggen av Mart*).   1948.
Judasdramer (includes *Streber; Ingen går fri*).   1949.
Samlede skrifter [Complete Works].   1959.
Processen; Anarkismen; Vär nattliga badort; Den dödsdömde. c.1980.
Samlede skrifter [Complete Works] (11 vols.).   1981–83.

Stage Works

Den dödsdömde (produced Dramaten, Stockholm, 1947). In *Dramer om dömda*, 1948; translated as *The Condemned*, in *Scandinavian Plays of the Twentieth Century* (third series), 1951.
Upptäcktsresanden [The Explorer] (produced Stadsteater, Hälsinborgs, 1950). In *40-tal*, 4, 1947.
Skuggen av Mart [The Shadow of Mart] (produced Dramaten, Stockholm, 1948). In *Dramer om dömda*, 1948.
Streber [The Go-Getter] (produced by the Bioteatern Amiralen at the Stadsteater, Malmö, 1948). In *Judasdramer*, 1949.
Ingen går fri [No One Goes Free], from the novel *Bränt barn* (produced Stadsteater, Malmö, 1949). In *Judasdramer*, 1949.
Den yttersta dagen [The Day of Judgement], from the radio play (produced Stadsteater, Gothenburg, 1952).

Radio Plays

Vår lilla sommar, 1951 (published in *Samlede skrifter*, 1951); *Den yttersta dagen* [The Day of Judgement], 1952 (published 1952); *En spelmans mössa* [A Musician's Cap], 1955 (published in *Samlede skrifter*, 1951).

Fiction

Ormen [The Serpent].   1945.
De dömdas ö [The Isle of the Damned].   1946.
Nattens lekar (short stories).   1947; translated as *Games of the Night*, 1959.
Bränt barn.   1948; translated as *A Burnt Child*, 1950.
Bröllopsbesvär [Wedding Trouble].   1949.

Verse

Dagsedlar [Comments on Daily Events].   1954.

Other

Tysk höst.   1947; translated as *German Autumn*, 1988.
Vårt behov av tröst (prose and verse), edited by O. Lagercrantz.   1955;   translated   as   *Our   Need   of Consolation*, 1958.
Dikter, noveller, prosafragment [Poems, Stories, Fragments] (Volume 10 of *Samlede skrifter*).   1983.
Essäer och journalistik [Essays and Journalism] (Volume 11 of *Samlede skrifter*).   1983.

*

Bibliographies

Hans Sandberg, *Stig Dagerman—forfättare och journalist: En bibliografi*, Stockholm, 1975.

Criticism

Books:
Olaf Lagercrantz, *Stig Dagerman*, Stockholm, 1958.
L.A. Thompson, *Stig Dagerman*, Boston, 1983.

Articles:
S.A. Bergman, "Blinded By Darkness: A Study of the Novels and Plays of Stig Dagerman", in *Delta: The Cambridge Literary Magazine*, 11, 1957.
L.A.   Thompson,   "Stig   Dagerman   and   Politics",   in *Scandinavica*, vol.19 no.1, 1980.

* * *

In Stig Dagerman's hectic literary career, the proportion of it devoted to drama—essentially 1947—is even more hurried. In spite of that, in drama as in prose, he established himself as the foremost Swedish figure of the 1940's. His first play, *Den dödsdömde* (*The Condemned*), was based on a short story he had written some months earlier, and in Alf Sjöberg's production at the Dramatic Theatre in Stockholm it brought him immediate acclaim.

Its action is simple: a man condemned to death for the murder of his wife is reprieved when another man confesses to the murder. He is taken from the prison by a group of men, all of whom have had close escapes from death in some way ("the Reprieved Club") and treated to a celebration dinner. At the dinner they provide him with a whore whom, rather than make love to, he kills. He is returned to prison and presumably to execution. The play is in the expressionistic mode, in which the atmosphere is that of a nightmare heavy with symbols—many of them obscure and many suggestive of the influence of Kafka—and in which the majority of the characters are unnamed types: the Condemned Man, the Duellist, and so on. Dagerman himself suggested that we should interpret the figure of the Condemned Man as representative of the post-war generation as a whole: that is, reprieved in a superficial sense but so burdened by guilt and memories that it is, in any case, doomed.

The interesting short play *Upptäcktsresanden* (The Explorer) centres on one of the members of the Reprieved Club in *Den dödsdömde*. Again we are in an expressionistic world: each act ("In the desert", "In the jungle", etc.) being preceded by a stage direction of the type *"A jungle corresponding to every spectator's idea of a jungle"*, and the five characters being known only as The Guide, The Camel-Driver, and so on. In the first two acts the Explorer himself seems to be asleep while his servants bicker among themselves, sometimes about travel, sometimes about the possible unfaithfulness of the women left at home, and sometimes make cryptic reference to the camel-driver's knife. In Act III the Explorer wakes and expresses his doubts about the meaning and purpose of exploration—there is the fear of arriving somewhere you have already been, and the depressing fact that each undiscovered country is already familiar to its inhabitants. By Act IV the Explorer has been murdered by his servants who, unafflicted by the malaise of exploration, merely desire the ordinary pleasures of home. It is left to the Guide—not a party to the murder—to berate them for cowardice and to suggest tentatively the value of the Explorer's search.

If "The Explorer" offers a statement about the situation of modern man (and perhaps the modern writer, in particular) and his attempt to make the search itself a meaningful response to an existentialist perception of the world, *Streber* (The Go-Getter) is a simple piece of political propaganda in a realistic setting. Throughout his life Dagerman remained a committed anarcho-syndicalist, and Blom (the "Go-Getter" of the title) is a man who betrays both his anarcho-syndicalist beliefs and his colleagues in a garage run on collectivist principles in order to feather his own nest. As a drama it is weak and flawed by its contrivance, simplistic psychology, and wordiness.

Skuggan av Mart (The Shadow of Mart) is usually considered to be Dagerman's finest play. It is a family drama set in an unnamed country (though France or Belgium are obvious candidates) after liberation from wartime occupation. A mother constantly makes unfavourable comparisons between her surviving son Gabriel, a shy and not very courageous weakling, and his dead brother Mart who had been a hero of the resistance. Driven beyond the limits of endurance, Gabriel shoots his mother with Mart's gun as the shadow of Mart looms ever larger across the stage. Here, Dagerman has captured the post-war atmosphere of recrimination mixed with hero-worship and distilled it within the claustrophobic setting of the family. More effectively conveyed, because more concrete, are the same pessimistic tidings of the doom of post-war man that we heard in *Den dödsdömde*.

Ingen går fri (No One Goes Free) is a competent dramatisation of Dagerman's most successful novel, *Bränt barn* (A Burnt Child). Once again the setting is the closed and intense space of the family, in which Bengt discovers that his exaggerated loyalty to his dead mother and his hatred for his widowed father's mistress, Gun, hides both lust for her and, ultimately, passion and love. The play, the theme of which is to be found in the compromising of youthful purity, lacks the psychological subtlety with which the novel probes the mother/mistress nexus; nor does it posit so forcefully the existential questioning of conventional morality that the novel offers as justification for such a quasi-incestuous relationship. It is, however, a powerful and moving drama.

Deep problems of creativity and the inability to carry work through to its conclusion haunted Dagerman from 1949 onwards and the radio play *Den yttersta dagen* (The Day of Judgement) was, in fact, the last piece of work he completed. It has also been performed on stage. Superficially a realistic drama set on an Uppland farm, more mysterious elements emerge as the characters react to the strange behaviour of an unknown troublemaker who pesters the farm with petty theft and mild nuisance-making. In each of the people on the farm, the stranger awakens specific perceptions of guilt hidden within themselves.

Thus, like most of Dagerman's other plays, this final play is a drama of revelation rather than action, and therein, perhaps, lies a general limitation in Dagerman's dramatic approach. And although his dialogue can often be compressed, nuanced, and suggestive (as, for instance, in *Upptäcktsresanden*), it can also too often lapse into verbosity at the expense of other dramatic possibilities—the final monologue in *Skuggan av Mart* is reckoned to take 28 minutes. Despite this weakness, Dagerman's theatre speaks with the genuine and powerful voice of its period.

—Peter Graves

DALY, (John) Augustin. Born in Plymouth, North Carolina, USA, 20 July 1838; grew up in New York City. Educated in local schools. Married Mary Dolores Duff in 1869; two sons. Worked for house furnishers in mid-1850's; writer, New York *Sunday Courier*, 1859–67; drama critic, *Express*, 1864–67, *Sun*, 1866–67, *Citizen*, 1867, and *Times*, 1867–69, all New York; professional playwright from 1862; manager for Batemans, Philadelphia, 1863; manager of the Fifth Avenue Theatre, New York, where he established his own company of actors, 1869, until the theatre burned down in 1873; took over the New York Theatre and reopened it as Daly's Broadway Theatre, 1873; also formed the first professional organization of theatrical managers in New York, 1873; managed the Grand Opera House, New York, 1873, and the New Fifth Avenue Theatre, 1873–77; visited Italy and England, 1878–79; returned to New York and converted Wood's Museum into Daly's Theatre, where he assembled a new company of actors, and subsequently became internationally known for his productions of Shakespeare: managed the theatre and company, 1879–99; toured London, 1884, 1886 (also Germany and Ireland), 1888, 1890, 1891, 1896, 1897, and Paris, 1888, 1891; ran Daly's Theatre, London, 1893–95. Died in Paris, France, 7 June 1899.

Works

Collections

"Man and Wife" and Other Plays (includes *Divorce; The Big Bonanza; Pique; Needles and Pins*), edited by Catherine Sturtevant. 1942.

Poster advertising the "sensation scene" from *Under the Gaslight* by **Augustin Daly**, 1867.

Plays (includes *A Flash of Lightning; Horizon; Love on Crutches*), edited by Don B. Wilmeth and Rosemary Cullen.   1984.

Stage Works

Leah the Forsaken, from a play by S.H. von Mosenthal (produced Howard Atheneum, Boston, 1862).   1863.

Taming a Butterfly, with Frank Wood, from a play by Sardou (produced Olympia Theatre, New York, 1864).   1867; revised version, as *Delmonico's; or, Larks up the Hudson* (produced 1871).

Lorlie's Wedding, from a play by C. Birchpfeiffer (produced Boston Theatre, Boston, 1864).

Judith, The Daughter of Merari, with Paul Nicholson (produced Winter Garden Theatre, New York, 1864).

The Sorceress (produced 1864).

Griffith Gaunt; or, Jealousy, from the novel by Charles Reade (produced New York Theatre, New York, 1866).   1867(?).

Hazardous Ground, from a play by Sardou (produced Park Theatre, Brooklyn, New York, 1867).   1868.

Under the Gaslight; or, Life and Death in These Times (produced New York Theatre, New York, 1867).   1867; revised version (produced 1881).

A Legend of "Norwood"; or, Village Life in New England, with Joseph W. Howard, from the novel *Norwood* by Henry Ward Beecher (produced New York Theatre, New York, 1867).   1867.

The Pickwick Papers, from the novel by Dickens (produced Worrell Sisters' Theatre, New York, 1868).

A Flash of Lightning (produced Broadway Theatre, New York, 1868).   1885.

The Red Scarf; or, Scenes in Aroostock (produced Bowery Theatre, New York, 1868).

Fernanda, with Hart Jackson, from a play by Sardou (produced Fifth Avenue Theatre, New York, 1870).

The Red Ribbon (produced Fifth Avenue Theatre, New York, 1870).

Frou-Frou, from a play by Henri Meilhac and Ludovic Halévy (produced Fifth Avenue Theatre, New York, 1870).   1870(?).

Man and Wife, from the novel by Wilkie Collins (produced Fifth Avenue Theatre, New York, 1870).   1885.

Come Here; or, The Debutante's Test, from a play by F. von Elsholtz (produced Academy of Music, New York, 1870).

Divorce, from the novel *He Knew He Was Right* by Trollope (produced Fifth Avenue Theatre, New York, 1871).   1884.

Horizon (produced Olympic Theatre, New York, 1871).   1885.

No Name, from the novel by Wilkie Collins (produced Fifth Avenue Theatre, New York, 1871).

Article 47, from a play by Adolphe Belot (produced Fifth Avenue Theatre, New York, 1872).

King Carrot, from a play by Sardou, music by Offenbach (produced 1872).

Round the Clock; or, New York by Dark (produced Grand Opera House, New York, 1872).

Alixe, from a play by Théodore Barrière and A. Régnauld de Prébois (produced New Fifth Avenue Theatre, 1873).

Roughing It! (produced New Fifth Avenue Theatre, 1873).

Uncle Sam; or, The Flirtation, from a play by Sardou (produced New Fifth Avenue Theatre, 1873).

Madelaine Morel, from a play by S.H. von Mosenthal (produced Fifth Avenue Theatre, New York, 1873).   1884.

The Parricide, from a play by Adolphe Belot (produced 1873).

Folline, from a play by Sardou (produced 1874).

Monsieur Alphonse, from a play by Dumas *fils* (produced Fifth Avenue Theatre, New York, 1874).   1886.

What Should She Do? or, Jealousy, from a novel by E. About (produced New Fifth Avenue Theatre, New York, 1874).

The Two Widows, from a play by F. Mallefille (produced New Fifth Avenue Theatre, New York, 1874).

The Critic, from the play by Sheridan (produced New Fifth Avenue Theatre, New York, 1874; as *Rehearsing the Tragedy*, produced 1888).   1889.

Yorick, from a play by M. Tamayo y Baus (produced New Fifth Avenue Theatre, New York, 1874).

The School for Scandal, from the play by Sheridan (produced New Fifth Avenue Theatre, New York, 1874; revised version produced 1891).   1891.

The Big Bonanza; or, Riches and Matches, from a play by Gustav von Moser (produced New Fifth Avenue Theatre, New York, 1875).   1884.

Pique (produced New Fifth Avenue Theatre, New York, 1875; as *Only a Woman*, produced 1882; as *Her Own Enemy*, produced 1884).   1884.

Life (produced New Fifth Avenue Theatre, New York, 1876).

The American, from a play by Dumas *fils* (produced New Fifth Avenue Theatre, New York, 1876).

Lemons; or, Wedlock for Seven, from a play by Julius Rosen (produced New Fifth Avenue Theatre, New York, 1877).   1877.

Blue Grass, from a play by J.B. von Schweitzer (produced New Fifth Avenue Theatre, New York, 1877).

The Princess Royal, from a play by J. Adenis and J. Rostaing (produced New Fifth Avenue Theatre, New York, 1877).

Vesta, from a play by D.A. Parodi (produced New Fifth Avenue Theatre, New York, 1877).

The Dark City! and Its Bright Side, from a play by T. Cogniard and L.F. Nicolaïe (produced New Fifth Avenue Theatre, New York, 1877).

The Assommoir, from a novel by Zola (produced Olympic Theatre, New York, 1879).

Love's Young Dream, from a French play (produced New York, 1879).   In *Three Preludes to the Play*, nd.

An Arabian Night in the Nineteenth Century, from a play by Gustav von Moser (produced Daly's Theatre, New York, 1879).   1884.

Needles and Pins, from a play by Julius Rosen (produced Daly's Theatre, New York, 1880).   1884.

The Royal Middy, with Frederick Williams, from an opera by F. Zell, music by R. Genée (produced Daly's Theatre, New York, 1880).

The Way We Live, from a play by A. L'Arronge (produced Daly's Theatre, New York, 1880).

Tiote; or, A Young Girl's Heart, from a translation by Frederick Williams of a play by M. Drach (produced Daly's Theatre, New York, 1880).

Zanina; or, The Rover of Cambaye, from an opera by A. West and F. Zell, music by R. Genée (produced Daly's Theatre, New York, 1880).

The Passing Regiment, from a play by Gustav von Moser and Franz von Schönthan (produced Daly's Theatre, New York, 1880).   1884.

Quits; or, A Game of Tit for Tat (produced Daly's Theatre, New York, 1881).

Royal Youth, from a play by Dumas and *fils* (produced Daly's Theatre, New York, 1881).

Odette, from a play by Sardou (produced Daly's Theatre, New York, 1882).

Mankind, from the play by P. Merritt and G. Conquest (produced Daly's Theatre, New York, 1882).

Our English Friend, from a play by Gustav von Moser (produced Daly's Theatre, New York, 1882).   1884.

She Would and She Would Not, from the play by Colley Cibber (produced Daly's Theatre, New York, 1883).   1884.

Serge Panine, from a play by G. Ohnet (produced 1883).

7–20–8; or, Casting the Boomerang, from a play by Franz von Schönthan (produced Daly's Theatre, New York, 1883).   1886.

Dollars and Sense; or, The Heedless Ones, from a play by A. L'Arronge (produced Daly's Theatre, New York, 1883).   1885.

The Country Girl, from Garrick's adaptation of the play *The Country Wife* by Wycherley (produced Daly's Theatre, New York, 1884).   1898.

Red Letter Nights; or, Catching a Croesus, from a play by E. Jacobson (produced Daly's Theatre, New York, 1884).

A Woman Won't, from a play by M. Röttinger (produced 1884).

A Wooden Spoon; or, Perdita's Penates, from a play by Franz von Schönthan (produced Daly's Theatre, New York, 1884).

Love on Crutches, from a play by H. Stobitzer (produced Daly's Theatre, New York, 1884).   1885.

Nancy and Company, from a play by Julius Rosen (produced Daly's Theatre, New York, 1886).   1884.

A Night Off; or, A Page from Balzac, from a play by Franz and P. von Schönthan (produced Daly's Theatre, New York, 1885).   1885.

The Recruiting Officer, from the play by Farquhar (produced Daly's Theatre, New York, 1885).   1885.

Denise, from a play by Dumas *fils* (produced 1885).

Living for Show, from a German play (produced 1885).

The Merry Wives of Windsor, from the play by Shakespeare (produced Daly's Theatre, New York, 1886).   1886.

A Wet Blanket, from a play by P. Bilhaud and J. Lévy (produced Daly's Theatre, New York, 1886).   In *Three Preludes to the Play*, nd.

A Sudden Shower, from a play by F. Beissier (produced Daly's Theatre, New York, 1886).   In *Three Preludes to the Play*, nd.

After Business Hours, from a play by Oscar Blumenthal (produced Daly's Theatre, New York, 1886).   1886.

Love in Harness; or, Hints to Hymen, from a play by Albin Valabrègue (produced Daly's Theatre, New York, 1886).   1887.

The Taming of the Shrew, from the play by Shakespeare (produced Daly's Theatre, New York, 1887).   1887.

The Railroad of Love, from a play by Franz von Schönthan and G. Kadelburg (produced Daly's Theatre, New York, 1887).   1887(?).

A Midsummer Night's Dream, from the play by Shakespeare (produced Daly's Theatre, New York, 1888).   1888.

The Lottery of Love, from a play by A. Bisson and A. Mars (produced Daly's Theatre, New York, 1888).   1889.

The Undercurrent (produced 1888).

The Inconstant; or, The Way to Win Him, from the play by Farquhar (produced Daly's Theatre, New York, 1889).   1889.

An International Match, from a play by Franz von Schönthan (produced Daly's Theatre, New York, 1889). 1890.

Samson and Delilah, from a play by A. Bisson and J. Moineaux (produced Daly's Theatre, New York, 1889).

The Golden Widow, from a play by Sardou (produced Daly's Theatre, New York, 1889).

Roger la Honte; or, A Man's Shadow, from the play by R. Buchanan (produced Daly's Theatre, New York, 1889).

The Great Unknown, from a play by Franz von Schönthan and G. Kadelburg (produced Daly's Theatre, New York, 1889). 1890.

As You Like It, from the play by Shakespeare (produced Daly's Theatre, New York, 1889). 1890.

Miss Hoyden's Husband, from a play by Sheridan (produced Daly's Theatre, New York, 1890).

The Last Word, from a play by Franz von Schönthan (produced Daly's Theatre, New York, 1890). 1891.

The Prodigal Son, from a play by M. Carré *fils*, music by A. Wormser (produced Daly's Theatre, New York, 1891).

Love's Labour's Lost, from the play by Shakespeare (produced Daly's Theatre, New York, 1891). 1891.

A Sister's Sacrifice. In *Werner's Readings and Recitations 4*, edited by Elsie M. Wilbor. 1891.

Love in Tandem, from a play by H. Bocage and C. de Courcy (produced Daly's Theatre, New York, 1892). 1892.

Little Miss Million, from a play by Oscar Blumenthal (produced Daly's Theatre, New York, 1892). 1893.

A Test Case; or, Grass Versus Granite, from a play by Oscar Blumenthal and G. Kadelburg (produced Daly's Theatre, New York, 1892). 1893.

The Hunchback, from the play by Sheridan Knowles (produced Daly's Theatre, New York, 1892). 1893.

The Belle's Stratagem, from the play by Hannah Cowley (produced Daly's Theatre, New York, 1892). 1892.

The Foresters, from the play by Tennyson, music by Arthur Sullivan (produced Daly's Theatre, New York, 1892).

Twelfth Night, from the play by Shakespeare (produced Daly's Theatre, New York, 1893). 1893.

The Wonder, from a play by Susanna Certilevre (produced Daly's Theatre, New York, 1893). In *Two Old Comedies*, 1893.

The Orient Express, from a play by Oscar Blumenthal and G. Kadelburg (produced Daly's Theatre, New York, 1895).

Two Gentlemen of Verona, from the play by Shakespeare (produced Daly's Theatre, New York, 1895). 1895.

A Bundle of Lies, from a play by K. Laufs and W. Jacoby (produced Daly's Theatre, New York, 1895).

The Transit of Leo, from a play by B. Köhler and Oscar Blumenthal (produced Daly's Theatre, New York, 1895).

The Countess Gueki, from a play by Franz von Schönthan and F. Koppel-Ellfeld (produced Daly's Theatre, New York, 1896). 1894?

Much Ado About Nothing, from the play by Shakespeare (produced Daly's Theatre, New York, 1896). 1897.

The Tempest, from the play by Shakespeare (produced Daly's Theatre, New York, 1897). 1897.

Number Nine; or, The Lady of Ostend, with F.C. Burnand, from a play by Oscar Blumenthal and G. Kadelburg (produced Daly's Theatre, New York, 1897).

Cyrano de Bergerac, from a translation by G. Thomas and M.F. Guillemard of a play by Rostand (produced Daly's Theatre, New York, 1898).

The Merchant of Venice, from the play by Shakespeare (produced Daly's Theatre, New York, 1898). 1898.

Other

Woffington: A Tribute to the Actress and the Woman. 1888.

*

Criticism

Books:
Edward A. Dithmar, *Memories of Daly's Theatres*, New York, 1897 (private printing).
Joseph F. Daly, *The Life of Daly*, New York, 1917.
D.F. Winslow, *Daly's: The Life of a Theatre*, 1944.
Marvin Felheim, *The Theatre of Augustin Daly*, Cambridge, Massachusetts, 1956.

* * *

Many of the better-known American dramatists of the latter part of the 19th century started out as men of the theatre. Daly reversed the formula. He began his theatrical career as a drama critic in New York, wrote his first successful play, *Leah the Forsaken,* in 1862, and soon went into theatre management where he made a distinctive contribution to American theatre as a *régisseur*, an autocratic director of his theatre. To provide for his theatre, he wrote or adapted dozens of plays which, consistent with the extravagant times of the Gilded Age, contributed more to the individuality of the American theatre than to a developing American drama.

Daly became involved in theatre management before the end of the Civil War but entered the profession in earnest in 1869 when he leased the Fifth Avenue Theatre in New York and began to hire actors and actresses without regard for "lines of business". At this time and throughout his career, his major objective was financial success, and his particular technique was to establish absolute and dictatorial control over all aspects of his theatre. Devoted to his theatre, he expected from others a similar degree of concentrated effort and professionalism. Members of his acting companies, for example, had to follow his rules of conduct or pay heavy fines. Utterly opposed to the "star system", he was concerned with cultivating the talents of his chosen performers in order to create a first-class acting company, which, in well-designed productions, would enjoy long runs in the theatre.

With the various melodramas he produced, he was always interested in a high degree of realism in scenic design as well as in acting; yet, he produced Shakespearean plays using bastard texts mainly to display the talents of his leading performers. Both approaches—the realistic and the spectacular—responded, however, to expressed desires of audiences. With the opening of Daly's Theatre in New York on 18 September 1879 he reached a certain point in his march toward theatrical autocracy, but his successes continued to mount as he toured his companies across America and to England and Europe, establishing the first company to tour Germany and France in 1886. In 1893 he opened Daly's Theatre in London which, although not a lasting success, was a considerable achievement for an American theatre manager in the 19th century.

Daly's basic philosophy of giving audiences exactly what he believed they wanted was not advantageous for the development of native drama in America. Although it is true that, as society advanced and tastes changed, Daly wisely changed his bills with the result that he was generally successful, he could never be considered a leader in avant garde theatre and drama. He did not, for example, produce the plays of George

Bernard Shaw, nor those of Henrik Ibsen, whose *Ghosts* created an adverse sensation in New York in the late 1880's. On the other hand, he was ready to take avantage of the popularity of such contemporary writers as W.D. Howells, Mark Twain, and Bret Harte; he produced some of Howells' plays as well as *Ah Sin*, that singular attempt of Mark Twain and Bret Harte which convinced most people of their ineffectiveness in the theatre. Although in an excellent position to do so, Daly did not attempt to encourage the work of American dramatists, as another successful manager, A. M. Palmer, did with his author's matinees. Instead, as a strong-minded individual and theatrical impresario, Daly followed the economic, social, and political changes of his day and then, alone or with others, wrote or adapted plays that would be acceptable to audiences.

From his first success in 1862, Daly built much of his playwriting career upon adaptations, part of the time with collaborators or with his brother, Joseph. Daly himself relied completely on translations, while the significance of Joseph's role in Daly's playwriting career remains something of a mystery. Because Daly understood the requirements of the theatre, however, he was able to inject just the right ingredients into his adaptations and please audiences throughout his career of playwriting which lasted nearly four decades. Both as an adapter and as a writer of original plays, however, Daly's reputation is deservedly limited.

Daly was able to vary his subject matter and to reflect something of contemporary society—the western movement and the popular interest in local color in *Horizon*; the business world in *The Big Bonanza*; and social themes in *Divorce* and *Pique*. He was at his best, however, with the sensational melodramas, such as *A Flash of Lightning* with its water and fire spectacles; *The Red Scarf*, in which the hero was tied to a log and sent to a sawmill; or *The Undercurrent*, which dealt with the seamy side of big-city life.

With its four acts and 11 scenes carefully arranged for sensational effect, no melodrama reveals Daly's skills better however than *Under the Gaslight*. Comments on social conditions, the system of justice in America, and the current battle for women's rights are carefully worked into the seemingly undefeatable villainy. Act II, employing a police court scene with all of the identifiable devices of melodrama, is immediately contrasted with vaudeville acts and a fight on the pier before the heroine jumps into a river to escape the villain. It would appear difficult to build upon such a climax, but Daly did it with ease in his famous railroad scene in the next act. The play ends, as did many sentimental melodramas of this period, satisfactorily for the audience: everything happens "just in time", and there is always hope for tomorrow where one may find the "long sought sunlight of our lives".

Daly made his major contributions to American theatre under two titles: the autocrat of the theatre and the master of sensational melodrama.

—Walter J. Meserve

See also *Volume 1* entry on *Under the Gaslight*.

———

D'ANNUNZIO, Gabriele. Born in Pescara, Italy, 12 March 1863. Educated at a secondary school, Prato, 1874–81; University of Rome, 1881. Married Duchess Maria Hardouin di Gallese in 1883, three children; had romance with the actress Eleonora Duse, 1895–1904. Staff member, *Tribuna*, Rome, in the 1880's; elected to Chamber of Deputies, 1897–1900 (defeated 1900); lived in Tuscany, 1899–1910; forced by debts to live in France, 1910–15; served in the Italian infantry, navy, and air force during World War I: injury led to loss of sight in one eye; after the Treaty of Versailles, seized Fiume with other patriots and held the city, 1919–20; supported the Fascists: granted a title by Mussolini; spent last years at his home, the Vittoriale, on Lake Garda. Died in Gardone, 1 March 1938.

Works

Collections

Tutte le opere, edited by Angelo Sodini (49 vols.). 1927–36.
Tutte le opere, edited by Egidio Bianchetti (10 vols.). 1939–50.
Poesie; Teatro; Prose, edited by Mario Praz. 1966.

Stage Works

Sogno d'un mattino di primavera (produced Théâtre de la Renaissance, Paris, 1897, then Teatro Valle, Rome, 1898). 1897; translated as *The Dream of a Spring Morning*, 1911.
La città morta (produced as *La Ville morte*, Théâtre de la Renaissance, Paris, 1898). 1898; translated as *The Dead City*, 1900.
La Gioconda (produced Teatro Bellini, Palermo, 1899). 1898; translated as *Gioconda*, 1901.
Sogno di un tramonto d'autunno (produced Teatro Rossi, Leghorn, 1905). 1898; translated as *The Dream of an Autumn Sunset*, 1903.
La gloria (produced Teatro Mercadante, Naples, 1899). 1899.
Francesca da Rimini (produced Teatro Costanzi, Rome, 1901). 1901; revised version, music by Riccardo Zandonai (produced 1914), 1914; translated as *Francesca da Rimini*, 1902.
La figlia di Iorio (produced Teatro Lirico, Milan, 1904). 1904; revised version, music by Alberto Franchetti (produced 1906), 1906; translated as *The Daughter of Jorio*, 1907.
La fiaccola sotto il moggio (produced Teatro Manzoni, Milan, 1905). 1905.
Più che l'amore (produced Teatro Constanzi, Rome, 1906). 1907.
La nave (produced Teatro Argentina, Rome, 1908). 1908; translated as *La Nave*, 1919.
Fedra (produced Teatro Lirico, Milan, 1909). 1909.
Le Martyre de Saint Sébastien, music by Debussy (produced Théâtre du Châtelet, Paris, 1911). 1911.
Il ferro (produced as *Le Chèvrefeuille*, Théâtre du Châtelet, Paris, 1913; revised version, as *Il ferro*, produced Teatro Valle, Rome, Teatro Carignano, Turin, and Teatro Manzoni, Milan—simultaneously in 1914). 1914; translated as *The Honeysuckle*, 1911.
La Pisanelle (produced Théâtre du Châtelet, Paris, 1913). In *Tutte le opere*, 1935.
La Parisina, music by Mascagni (produced La Scala, Milan, 1913). 1913.
Cabiria. 1914.

Screenplays

La crociata degli innocenti, 1911.

Fiction

Terra vergine (short stories). 1882.
Il libro delle vergine. 1884.
Il piacere. 1889; translated as *The Child of Pleasure*, 1898.
L'innocente. 1892; translated as *The Intruder*, 1898; as *The Victim*, 1915.
Giovanni Episcopo. 1892; translated as *Episcopo and Company*, 1896.
Trionfo della morte. 1894; translated as *The Triumph of Death*, 1896.
Le vergini delle rocce. 1896; translated as *The Maidens of the Rocks*, 1898; as *The Virgins of the Rocks*, 1899.
Il fuoco. 1900; translated as *The Flame of Life*, 1900; as *The Flame*, 1906.
Le novelle della Pescare. 1902; translated as *Tales of My Native Town*, 1920.
Forse che sì, forse che no. 1910.
La leda senza cigno. 1916.
Prose, edited by Federico Roncoroni. 1983.

Verse

Primo vere. 1879; revised edition,1880.
Canto novo. 1882.
Intermezzo di rime. 1883.
San Pantaleone. 1886.
Isaotta Guttadàuro ed altre poesie. 1886; revised edition, as *L'Isottèo, La Chimera*, 1890.
Elegie romane 1887–1891. 1892.
Odi navali. 1893.
L'Allegoria dell'autunno. 1895.
La canzone di Garibaldi. 1901.
Laudi del cielo, del mare, della terra, e degli eroi: Anno 1903—Maia; Anno 1904—Elettra Alcyone; Libro IV—Merope (3 vols.). 1903–12; *Alcyone* translated as *Halcyon*, 1988.
L'orazione e la canzone in morte di Giosuè Carducci. 1907.
Canto novo. 1907.
Le città del silenzio. 1926.
Poesia, edited by Federico Roncoroni. 1978.

Memoirs and Letters

Carteggio D'Annunzio—Duse: Superstiti missive: Lettere, cartoline, telegrammi, dediche 1898–1923, edited by Piero Nardi. 1975.
Lettere a una donna. 1975.
Lettere inedite. In *Quaderni del Vittoriale*, July–August 1980.

Other

Scritti politici, edited by Paolo Alatri. 1980.

*

Bibliographies

Anna Baldazzi, *Bibliografia della critica dannunziana nei periodici italiani dal 1880 al 1938*, Rome, 1977.
Mario Vacchioni, *Bibliografia critica di Gabriele D'Annunzio*, Rome, 1970.
"Bibliografia dannunziana", in issues of *Quaderni vittoriale*.

Criticism

Tom Antongini, *D'Annunzio*, London, 1938.
Bertita Harding, *Age Cannot Whither: The Story of Duse and D'Annunzio*, London, 1949.
Frances Winwar, *Wings of Fire: A Biography of Gabriele D'Annunzio and Eleonora Duse*, London, 1957.
Walter Fogliani, *Il teatro francese di Gabriele D'Annunzio*, Udine, 1968.
Giovanni Gullace, *Gabriele D'Annunzio in France: A Study in Cultural Relations*, Syracuse, New York, 1966.
Ettore Paratore, *Studi dannunziana*, Naples, 1966.
Giuseppe Pecci, *D'Annunzio e il mistero*, Milan, 1966.
Nicola Ciarletta, *D'Annunzio; Pirandello*, Aquila, 1967.
Philippe Julian, *D'Annunzio*, New York, 1973.
G.B. Squarotti, *Il tragico nel mondo borghese*, Turin, 1974.
Maria T.M. Moevs, *Gabriele D'Annunzio e le estetiche della fine del secolo*, Aquila, 1976.
Piero Chiara, *Vita di Gabriele D'Annunzio* (third edition), Milan, 1979.
Ricardo Scrivano, *Finzioni teatrali*, Messina, 1982.
G.B. Squarotti, *Invito alla lettura di D'Annunzio*, Milan, 1982.
Franco Robecchi, *Il teatro di poesie di Gabriele D'Annunzio*, Milan, 1984.
Piero Chiara, *Prato: nella vita e nell'arte di Gabriele D'Annunzio*, Prato, 1985.
Charles Klopp, *Gabriele D'Annunzio*, Boston, 1988.
Andrea Bisicchia, *D'Annunzio e il teatro: Tra cronaca e letteratura dramatica*, Milan, 1991.

Articles:
R. Hastings, "D'Annunzio's Theatrical Experiment", in *Modern Language Review*, 66, 1971.
Lynn M. Gunzberg, "*La figlia di Iorio, La lupa* and the Locus of Patriarchy", in *Annali d'Italianistica*, 5, 1987.
Louis Kibler, "Myth and Meaning in D'Annunzio's *La figlio di Iorio*", in *Annali d'Italianistica*, 5, 1987.

*   *   *

Assessing the contribution of Gabriele D'Annunzio to the theatre is very difficult, both on account of his aesthetics and his politics. Romain Rolland once commented on D'Annunzio's destructive drive, an aspect of his character that led him into all kinds of excesses, from the sexual to the military. He saw his role as that of a great Italian patriot, leading Italian letters from the doldrums and then extolling the greatness of Italy in his writing and his speeches; but this vision led him to elitism, racism, and finally commitment to fascism.

He was romantically involved with large numbers of women, most notably with Eleonora Duse; but his novels and plays are full of tortured, dead, and mutilated women. *La Gioconda*, which he wrote for Duse, involves the female protagonist in a particularly nasty mutilation, when her hands are crushed beneath a statue carved by her unfaithful husband. If we consider that Duse was so famed for the use of her hands on stage (extant photographs show the way in which her costumes were designed to accentuate them), that reviewers continually praised this feature and D'Annunzio himself dedicated *La città morta* to "Eleonora Duse with the beautiful hands", then the extent of D'Annunzio's destructive sadism in *La Gioconda* becomes clear.

D'Annunzio's venture into theatre was initially bound up with his relationship with Duse. He wrote his first play for her, and then wrote several more which she took on tour for some years, even though they continued to fail at the box office in Italy and overseas. Nevertheless, despite the dedication of *La città morta* to Duse, the play opened in Paris with Sarah Bernhadt playing the lead, because D'Annunzio negotiated behind Duse's back with her great French rival. Again, in this anecdote we can see the way in which D'Annunzio unscrupulously manipulated anyone and everyone in his quest for the greater glory of himself and of the new Italian writing that he claimed to embody.

He achieved commercial success in the theatre only finally with his sixth play, *La figlia di Iorio*, written again for Duse but given, despite Duse's bitter resentment, to Irma Gramatica. This was the last play he wrote for Duse, who left him shortly after this second great betrayal in 1904, and some critics have argued that his writing declined once she was no longer part of his life. Much as one may wish to believe this, it does not have much basis in fact. He was never a particularly good playwright, and after 1904, although some of his plays were failures, he also discovered his strength as a librettist. He collaborated with Debussy in 1911 on *Le Martyre de Saint Sébastien*, and Ida Rubinstein, who played the role of the martyred saint, claimed that it was D'Annunzio who had finally given her a voice in the theatre, after years as a dancer and mime artist. *La Pisanelle* was also written for Ida Rubinstein. His last work, *La Parisina*, was in collaboration with Mascagni and was first performed at La Scala in 1913. It was received coldly, but was a success when revived in a considerably shortened version directed by Virgilio Talli in Rome in 1921.

The initial failure of *La Parisina*, like the initial failure of *Francesca da Rimini* in 1901 (the two plays were originally intended to be part of a trilogy that was never completed) reveals much about D'Annunzio as a playwright. The first versions of both plays were hopelessly long (*La Parisina* ran for six hours on the first night) because D'Annunzio was so reluctant to cut any of his text. Debussy, endeavouring tactfully to help him with the cumbersome *La Pisanelle*, wrote asking why he continued to place such attention on empty visual effects and rhetorical flourishes which neither actors nor audiences could adequately cope with; but the advice went unheeded. Having been allowed backstage, as it were, through his relationship with Duse, D'Annunzio saw himself also as a director, and a major reason for the failure both in financial and in aesthetic terms of *Francesca da Rimini* was D'Annunzio's extravagance regarding sets, costumes, and lighting and his total inability to conduct a rehearsal. That so many major actors went along with him throughout his career is evidence of the strength of his personality, not of his ability to work well in the theatre.

Despite the negative value judgements of his work in the theatre, some credit must be given to D'Annunzio as a man of his own time who started out at least with a vision of where the Italian theatre ought to go. He and Duse shared a sense of disillusionment and contempt for the feebleness of the Italian repertoire at the turn of the century and for the inadequacies of the touring system. Duse believed passionately that the Italian theatre needed a new repertoire, and her life was a search for exactly that. The relationship with D'Annunzio, a prominent literary figure when the affair began in 1897, promised a great deal to both of them: she had the prospect of a writer who could give her the plays she needed and he had the chance of working with the greatest actress the Italian theatre possessed. In the early heady days of the relationship they dreamed about a great festival theatre, along the same lines as those articulated by Rolland or Wagner, that would be built on the shores of Lake Albano outside Rome. D'Annunzio and Duse planned to set up a group of share-holders and form their own company. The date of the first performance was set for the first day of Spring in 1899, and D'Annunzio announced that he would write a play for Duse entitled *Persefone*. The play was never written, though significantly the protagonist of D'Annunzio's autobiographical novel *Il fuoco* has written just such a work and it has been his greatest success.

The line between real life and fiction is very narrow when we come to D'Annunzio. It can be argued that his entire life was theatrical to an extraordinary degree, and in old age he took to wearing a monk's habit at home in the Vittoriale (a more stagy construction than any purpose-built theatre). His plays are verse dramas of their time, and some of the language is very beautifully constructed. What he failed to understand was the difference between the poetic and the dramatic, and his idea of theatre always involved excess—large casts, huge sets, many costume and set changes, rhetorical speeches, melodramatic set pieces. The plays have not been revived, nor have they been exported, which has as much to do with the impracticalities of staging them as with D'Annunzio's subsequent disgrace on account of his sympathies with Mussolini's fascism. At the end of the 20th century they can be fairly seen as period pieces, and although a strong case can be made for D'Annunzio as a major poet and novelist, as a playwright he must be located among the many others who, at the turn of the century, dreamed about making a new kind of lyric theatre that would simultaneously be modern and classical, but never actually managed to do so effectively.

—Susan Bassnett

See also *Volume 1* entry on *Francesca da Rimini*.

DAVENANT (or D'Avenant), **Sir William.** Born in Oxford, England, in February 1606. Educated at Oxford Grammar School; Lincoln College, Oxford, 1620–21. Married 1) Mary c.1624, two children; 2) Dame Anne Cademan in 1652 (died 1655); 3) Henrietta-Maria du Tremblay in 1655, seven sons. Page to the Duchess of Richmond from 1621, then clerk in household of Fulke Greville, Lord Brooke, until Greville's murder, 1628; with Duke of Buckingham's unsuccessful siege of Isle of Rhé, 1627, and possibly on second expedition, 1628; convicted of murder and fled to Holland, c.1629; seriously ill with syphilis, 1630–32; allowed to return to England, 1633 (pardoned 1638); entered service of Queen Henrietta Maria and presented masques at court from 1634; given annuity by Charles I as unofficial poet laureate, 1638; manager, Cockpit Theatre, Drury Lane, 1640–41; arrested for treason and fled to France, 1641; fought for the royalists at the siege of Gloucester, and knighted by the king, 1643; negotiator on numerous royal missions in the Netherlands and France, 1643–49; after execution of Charles I served Charles II as treasurer of Virginia and lieutenant-governor of Maryland; led colonizing expedition bound for America, 1650: intercepted by the parliamentarians, and imprisoned in Cowes Castle, 1650, and the Tower of London, 1651–52; pardoned by Cromwell, 1654; gave theatrical performances (which he styled "operas" to avoid puritan restrictions) at Rutland House, 1656, and transferred to the Cockpit Theatre, 1658; after the Restoration given patent by

William Davenant (engraving)

Charles II to open the Duke's Playhouse, Lincoln's Inn Fields, and to form the Duke's Company, 1661–68: frequently presented adaptations of Shakespeare's plays; built Dorset Garden Theatre. Died in London, 7 April 1668.

Works

Collections

Works. 1673.
Dramatic Works, edited by James Maidment and W. H. Logan (5 vols.) 1872–74.

Stage Works

The Cruel Brother (produced Blackfriars Theatre, London, 1627). 1630.
The Siege (as *The Colonel*, produced Cockpit Theatre, London, 1629?). In *Works*, 1673.
Albovine, King of the Lombards. 1629.
The Just Italian (produced Blackfriars Theatre, London, 1629). 1630.
The Wits (produced Blackfriars Theatre, London, 1634). 1636.
Love and Honour (produced Blackfriars Theatre, London, 1634). 1649.
The Platonic Lovers (produced Blackfriars Theatre, London, 1635). 1636.
The Temple of Love (produced Whitehall Palace, London, 1635). 1635.

News from Plymouth (produced Globe Theatre, London, 1635). In *Works*, 1673.
The Triumphs of the Prince d'Amour, music by William Lawes (produced Middle Temple, London, 1636). 1636.
Luminalia; or, The Festival of Light (produced Whitehall Palace, London, 1638). 1637.
The Fair Favourite (produced Blackfriars Theatre, London, 1638). In *Works*, 1673.
Britannia Triumphans (produced Whitehall Palace, London, 1638). 1638.
The Unfortunate Lovers (produced Blackfriars Theatre, London, 1638). 1643.
The Spanish Lovers (The Distresses) (produced Blackfriars Theatre, London, 1639). In *Works*, 1673.
Salmacida Spolia, music by Lewis Richard (produced Whitehall Palace, London, 1640). 1640.
The First Day's Entertainment at Rutland House (produced Rutland House, London, 1656). 1657.
The Siege of Rhodes, music by Henry Lawes and others (produced Rutland House, London, 1656). 1656; revised version (produced 1657–59), 1663.
The Preparation of the Athenians for the Reception of Phocion. 1657.
The Cruelty of the Spaniards in Peru (produced Cockpit Theatre, London, 1658). 1658.
The History of Sir Francis Drake (produced Cockpit Theatre, London, 1658–59?). 1659.
Hamlet, possibly by the actor Thomas Betterton, from the play by Shakespeare (produced 1661). 1676
The Law Against Lovers (produced Lincoln's Inn Fields Theatre, London, 1662). In *Works*, 1673.
The Play House to Be Let (produced Lincoln's Inn Fields Theatre, London, 1663). In *Works*, 1673.
The Rivals, from the play *The Two Noble Kinsmen* by Fletcher and Shakespeare (produced Lincoln's Inn Fields Theatre, London, 1664). 1668.
The Tempest; or, The Enchanted Island, with Dryden, from the play by Shakespeare (produced Lincoln's Inn Fields Theatre, London, 1667). 1670.
The Man's the Master, from a play by Paul Scarron (produced Lincoln's Inn Fields Theatre, London, 1668). 1669.
Macbeth, from the play by Shakespeare (produced Dorset Garden Theatre, London, 1673). 1674.

Verse

"Madagascar", with Other Poems. 1638.
London, King Charles His Augusta or City Royal. 1648.
Gondibert: An Heroic Poem. 1651; *Seventh and Last Canto*, 1685.
Poem upon His Majesty's Return. 1660.
Poem to the King's Most Sacred Majesty. 1663.
Shorter Poems and Songs from the Plays and Masques, edited by A.M. Gibbs. 1972.
Selected Poems, edited by Douglas Bush. 1943.

Other

A Discourse upon Gondibert. 1650.

*

Bibliographies

Sophia B. Blaydes, *Davenant: An Annotated Bibliography 1629–1985*, New York, 1986.

Criticism

Books:

John David Ellis Williams, *Sir William Davenant's Relation to Shakespeare*, Strasbourg, 1905.

Friedrich Wilhelm Laig, *Englische und französische Elemente in Sir William Davenants dramatischer Kunst*, Emsdatten, 1934.

Alfred Harbage, *Sir William Davenant, Poet, Venturer 1606–1668*, Philadelphia, 1935.

Arthur H. Nethercot, *Davenant: Poet Laureate and Playwright-Manager*, Chicago, 1939; reprinted as *Sir William D'Avenant, Poet Laureate and Playwright-Manager*, 1967.

Lothar Hoennighausen, *Der Stilwandel im Dramatischen Werk Davenants*, Cologne, 1965.

Howard S. Collins, *The Comedy of Sir William Davenant*, Paris and The Hague, 1967.

Mongi Raddadi, *Davenant's Adaptations of Shakespeare*, 1979.

Philip Bordinat and Sophia B. Blaydes, *Davenant*, Boston, 1981.

Mary Edmond, *Rare Davenant: Poet Laureate, Playwright, Civil War General, Restoration Theatre Manager*, Manchester, 1987.

*   *   *

Davenant's uncorroborated claims that he was Shakespeare's illegitimate son and that his family name was of French origin (hence to be written in the ennobling form D'Avenant) reveal his taste for grandeur. Hardly surprizing then, that he should come into his own during the Restoration, a time renowned for its sense of elevated style. Even the titles of his early plays *The Wits* and *Love and Honour* (both first performed in 1634) would seem to epitomize the spirit of that age.

Indeed, many of the stylistic and formal features commonly associated with Restoration Comedy are to be found in *The Wits*. This intrigue comedy has many plots and numerous farcical elements, and contains the town-country conflict. The eponymous wits are headed by Young Pallatine, who marries Lucy and gulls his elder brother into wedlock with the supposedly good catch Lady Ample. Characteristically, the two independent-minded women are equal to their partners in wisdom and wit. The king himself had to save Davenant's play from censorship, because Henry Herbert, the Master of the Revels, had taken exception against some mild expletives.

The serious play *Love and Honour*, on the other hand, contains the most high-flown heroic language and characters who are the purest representations of virtue, and thus is, in many ways, a precursor to the rhymed heroic play of the Restoration. An established playwright by the mid-1630's, Davenant was frequently commissioned to write semi-theatrical court entertainments, the so-called masques, such as *The Temple of Love*. He also continued writing for the theatre: *The Unfortunate Lovers* is a revenge play, a genre he had already exploited with his earlier work, *Albovine*.

Davenant was appointed to the post of poet laureate under Charles I in 1638, and knighted in 1643 for his services against the Parliamentarian onslaught, but he only made theatre history with his much cited, though rarely praised, proto-opera *The Siege of Rhodes*, which is sometimes taken to be the first rhymed heroic play. In its final version this drama had gala presentation in the summer of 1661 at the new theatre in Lincoln's Inn Fields. King Charles II paid the first of many visits to the public playhouse, accompanied by all the nobility

and his brother James, patron of the Duke of York's Company which Davenant headed as director. All these facts would seem to make the author an arch-Cavalier and the embodiment of the supposedly decadent and cynical "Restoration spirit".

However, in its first form *The Siege of Rhodes* had already been produced under the protectorate of Oliver Cromwell. The plot, with Knights of the Cross, led by the chivalrous Sicilian Alphonso, fighting against the honourable Ottoman Emperor Solyman, is a startlingly impartial metaphor for the English Civil Wars. Alphonso is full of suspicion when his wife, Ianthe, having pawned her jewellery in aid of the Christian war effort, is unconditionally released by Solyman, who had captured her on her way to her husband. Solyman's motives are entirely honourable and he emerges as a good ruler who wages war mainly because his greedy subjects are looking for spoils of war. Neither side is perfect, though. Alphonso being on the "right" (that is Christian) side is guilty of "jealousy", a term which was current in describing human relationships on a public, as well as on a private, level: Royalists and Parlamentarians accused each other of just this political vice. The Ottoman Emperor, on the other hand, being a Muslim and thus the conventional villain, behaves in an admirable fashion and he would seem to be the representation of the Protector Oliver Cromwell, to whose government Davenant had reconciled himself and his art.

The true heroine of the play, however, is Ianthe, who very obviously resembles Henrietta Maria, Charles's influential consort. The Queen had indeed tried to help the Royalists' war efforts by exchanging the crown jewels against military supplies, and she was also seen by some as a moderating influence in the conflict between Crown and Parliament. Davenant had not only helped Henrietta Maria in procuring material aid for the Royalist cause, but had also worked for her in her French exile. The connection is not simply a political one, as the poet had also been the Queen's artistic protegé. In the late 1630's he had written lead parts for her in the court masques designed by Inigo Jones. These splendid entertainments were highly controversial celebrations of the monarchy, and the puritan Member of Parliament William Prynne had been punished for his attack on the stage mainly because his remarks on actresses were taken to be a reflection on Henrietta Maria's taking part in the masques. 20 years later, in September 1656, the first recorded performance of a professional actress in Britain must have been a great *coup de théâtre*: Ianthe, veiled, entered the stage, her face being revealed only after some time. The allusion to the exiled Queen could hardly have been lost on the audience.

For *The Siege of Rhodes* Inigo Jones's pupil John Webb designed moveable scenes, another first on the professional and public stage. Both music and dance gained a more important place in Davenant's representations of the Protectorate than they had held on the Caroline stage. All four innovations—actresses, scenery, music, and dance—are generally, and mistakenly, associated with the Restoration theatre, the exaltedness and celebratory character of which is often explained as a backlash against the restrictive puritanism of the Interregnum.

The Siege of Rhodes remained his most ambitious attempt at a *Gesamtkunstwerk*, synthesizing the arts of sung drama, music, dance, and impressive scenery. This was an expensive venture, and therefore Davenant tried to set off the costs with the more popular and less costly comedy. Indeed, one of his other claims to fame is that, with his mock-heroic burlesque *The Play House to Be Let*, he introduced the play-about-the-theatre to the London stage.

For the same reason, the poet laureate perseveringly

worked towards a theatre monopoly that would allow him to maintain his enterprise in a controlled environment. As is apparent from an anonymous play of the late 1650's, *The Alimony Lady*, he nearly succeeded in his project under Cromwell. After the Restoration he managed to repeat this feat by sharing the legitimate London stage with only one other company, that of the returned king's favourite and groom of the bedchamber, Sir Thomas Killigrew. They shared a duopoly which survived until the licensing act of 1735.

The author demonstrated his literary versatility by writing a number of poems, and a romantic verse epic, *Gondibert*, which was never finished. But he was truly at home in the theatre, even though he did not write another complete play after the Restoration. His adaptations of Shakespeare, which are frequently dismissed by modern critics, were highly successful, and his *Tempest* with Dryden (as revised by Thomas Shadwell) held the stage for centuries—in preference to Shakespeare's original.

—Ulrich Meissner

DE FILIPPO, Eduardo. Born in Naples, Italy, 24 May 1900; illegitimate son of playwright and actor-manager Eduardo Scarpetta. Educated at Isituto Chierchia, Naples, 1911. Married 1) the actress Dorothy Pennington in 1928 (marriage annulled in San Marino, 1952, recognized in Italy, 1956); 2) Thea Prandi in 1956 (separated 1959; died 1960), one son and one daughter before marriage; 3) Isabella Quarantotti in 1977. Child actor with family troupe: stage debut as infant in his father's play *Geisha*, 1904; actor with the theatre company of Vincenzo Scarpetta, 1914–20; military service, 1920–22; actor with Francesco Corbinci's troupe, 1922, Peppino Villani's troupe, 1922–27, the Carini-Falconi company, 1927–28, the Riviste Molinari company, 1930–31; co-founder, with his brother Peppino and sister Titino, Il Teatro Umoristico, 1929, and toured with it until Peppino's departure in 1945; first-produced play, *Sik-Sik, l'artefice magico*, staged 1929; co-founder, with Titina, Il Teatro di Eduardo, 1945–54, in which Eduardo and Titina usually acted the leading roles; director and owner, the rebuilt Teatro San Fernando, Naples, from 1954; toured Austria, Belgium, Hungary, Poland, and Russia, 1962; underwent heart surgery to implant a pacemaker, 1974. Also film actor, and director of films and operas. Recipient: Institute of Italian Drama Prize, 1951; Simoni Prize, 1969; Feltrinelli Prize, 1972; Pirandello Prize, 1975. D.Litt: University of Birmingham, England, 1977; University of Rome, 1980. Named Senator for life of the Italian Republic, 1981. Died in Rome, 31 October 1984.

Works

Collections

Cantata dei giorni dispari:
1. *Napoli milionaria!*, *Questi fantasmi!*; *Filumena Marturano*; *Le bugie con le gambe lunghe*; *La grande magia*; *Le voci di dentro*.   1951; revised edition, 1971.
2. *Non ti pago!*; *Occhiali neri*; *La paura numero uno*; *I morti non fanno paura*; *Amicizia*; *Mia famiglia*; *Bene mio e core mio*; *De Pretore Vincenzo*.   1958; revised edition, 1971.
3. *Il figlio di Pulcinella*; *Dolore sotto chiave*; *Sabato, domenica e lunedì*; *Il sindaco del Rione Sanità*; *Tommaso D'Amalfi*; *L'arte della commedia*; *Il cilindro*.   1966; revised edition, 1971.

Cantata dei giorni pari (includes *Farmacia di turno*; *Uomo e galantuomo*; *Filosoficamente*; *Sik-Sik*; *Quei figuri di trent'anni fa*; *Chi è cchiù felice 'e me!* . . .; *Natale in casa Cupiello*; *Gennariniello*; *Il dono di Natale*; *Ditegli sempre di sì*; *Quinto piano, ti saluto!*; *Uno coi capelli bianchi*; *L'Abito nuovo*; *Pericolosamente*; *La parte di Amleto*; *Io, l'erede*).   1959.

I capolavori (2 vols.).   1973.

Three Plays (includes *The Local Authority*; *Grand Magic*; *The Best House in Naples—Filumena Marturano*), translated by Carlo Ardito.   1976.

Stage Works

Sik-Sik, l'artefice magico (produced Teatro Kursaal, Naples, 1929).   1932; translated as *Sik-Sik, The Masterful Magician*, in *Italian Quarterly 11*, 1967.

Natale in casa Cupiello (produced Teatro Kursaal, Naples, 1931; revised version produced Teatro Quirino, Rome, 1942).   In *Cantata dei giorni pari*, 1959.

Farmacia di turno (produced Teatro Nuovo, Naples, 1931).   In *Cantata dei giorni pari*, 1959.

Ogni anno punto e da capo (produced Teatro Kursaal, Naples, 1931).   1971.

Quei figuri di trent'anni fa (produced Teatro Kursaal, Naples, 1932).   In *Cantata dei giorni pari*, 1959.

Chi è cchiù felice 'e me! . . . (produced Teatro Sannazzaro, Naples, 1932).   In *Cantata dei giorni pari*, 1959.

Gennariniello (produced Teatro Kursaal, Naples, 1932).   In *Cantata dei giorni pari*, 1959.

Ditegli sempre di sì (produced Teatro Nuovo, Naples, 1932).   In *Cantata dei giorni pari*, 1959.

I morti non fanno paura (as *Requie all'anima soia*, produced Teatro Kursaal, Naples, 1932; revised version, as *I morti non fanno paura*, produced Ridotto del Teatro Eliseo, Rome, 1952).   In *Cantata dei giorni dispari 2*, 1958.

L'ultimo bottone (produced Teatro Kursaal, Naples, 1932).

Cuoco della mala cucina, with Maria Scarpetta (produced Teatro Sannazzaro, Naples, 1932).

Uomo e galantuomo (produced Teatro Sannazzaro, Naples, 1933).   In *Cantata dei giorni pari*, 1959.

Parlate al portiere, with Maria Scarpetta (produced Teatro Sannazzaro, Naples, 1933).

Scorzetta di limone, from play by Gino Rocca (produced Naples, 1933).

Il dono di Natale (produced Teatro Sannazzaro, Naples, 1934).   In *Cantata dei giorni pari*, 1959.

Tre mesi dopo (produced Naples, 1934).

Sintetici a qualunque costa (produced Teatro Sannazzaro, Naples, 1934).

Il berretto a Sonagli, from a play by Pirandello (produced Teatro Fiorentini, Naples, 1936).

Quinto piano, ti saluto! (produced Teatro Elises, Rome, 1936).   In *Cantata dei giorni pari*, 1959.

L'abito nuovo, from story by Pirandello (produced Teatro Manzoni, Milan, 1937).   In *Cantata dei giorni pari*, 1959.

Uno coi capelli bianchi (produced Teatro Quirino Rome, 1938). In *Cantata dei giorni pari*, 1959.

Si salvi chi può, from work by Gino Rocca (produced Teatro Politeama, Naples, 1940).

Non ti pago! (produced Teatro Quirino, Rome, 1940). 1943.

La parte di Amleto (produced Teatro Odeon, Milan, 1940). In *Cantata dei giorni pari*, 1959.

In licenza, from work by Eduardo Scarpetta (produced Teatro Quirino, Rome, 1941).

La fortuna con l'effe maiuscola, with Armando Curcio and R. De Angelis (produced Teatro Alfieri, Turin, 1942).

Io, l'erede (produced Teatro La Pergola, Florence, 1942). In *Cantata dei giorni pari*, 1959.

Il diluvio, from play by Ugo Betti (produced Teatro Argentina, Rome, 1943).

Napoli milionaria! (produced Teatro San Carlo, Naples, 1945). 1946.

Occhiali neri (produced Naples, 1945). In *Cantata dei giorni dispari 2*, 1958.

Questi fantasmi! (produced Teatro Eliseo, Rome, 1946). In *Cantata dei giorni dispari 1*, 1951; translated as *Oh, These Ghosts*, 1963.

Filumena Marturano (produced Teatro Politeama, Naples, 1946). In *Cantata dei giorni dispari 1*, 1951; translated as *The Best House in Naples*, in *Three Plays*, 1976; as *Filumena*, 1978.

Pericolosamente (produced Teatro Carignano, Turin, 1947). In *Cantata dei giorni pari*, 1959.

Le bugie con le gambe lunghe (produced Teatro Eliseo, Rome, 1948). In *Cantata dei giorni dispari 1*, 1951.

Le voci di dentro (produced Teatro Nuovo, Naples, 1948). In *Cantata dei giorni dispari 1*, 1951; translated as *Inner Voices* in *Italian Theatre Review*, vol. 6 no. 2, 1957, and as single edition, 1983.

La grande magia (produced Teatro Mercadente, Naples, 1949). In *Cantata dei giorni dispari 1*, 1951; as *Grand Magic*, in *Three Plays*, 1976.

La paura numero uno (produced Teatro La Fenice, Venice, 1950). In *Cantata dei giorni dispari 2*, 1958.

Amicizia (produced Ridotto del Teatro Eliseo, Rome, 1952). In *Cantata dei giorni dispari 2*, 1958.

Miseria e nobiltà, from a play by Eduardo Scarpetta (produced Teatro della Mostre d'Oltre Mare, Naples, 1953).

Bene mio e core mio (produced Teatro Eliseo, Rome, 1955). 1956.

Mia famiglia (produced Teatro Morlacchi, Perugia, 1955). 1955.

Il medico dei pazzi, from work by Eduardo Scarpetta (produced Teatro Eliseo, Rome, 1957).

De Pretore Vincenzo (produced Rome, 1957). 1957.

Tre cazune furtunate, from a play by Eduardo Scarpetta (produced Teatro Odeon, Milan, 1958).

La fortuna in cerca di tasche, from a play by Eduardo Scarpetta (produced Teatro Odeon, Milan, 1958).

Sabato, domenica e lunedi (produced Teatro Quirino, Rome, 1959). 1960; translated as *Saturday, Sunday, Monday*, 1974.

Il sindaco del Rione Sanità (produced Teatro Quirino, Rome, 1960). 1961; translated as *The Local Authority*, in *Three Plays*, 1976.

Il figlio di Pulcinella (produced Teatro Quirino, Rome, 1962). In *Cantata dei giorni dispari 3*, 1966.

Dolore sotto chiave (produced Teatro San Ferdinando, Naples, 1964). With *L'arte della commedia*, 1965.

L'arte della commedia (produced Teatro San Ferdinando, Naples, 1965). With *Dolore sotto chiave*, 1965.

Tommaso D'Amalfi. In *Cantata dei giorni dispari 3*, 1966.

Il cilindro (produced Teatro Quirino, Rome, 1966). In *Cantata dei giorni dispari 3*, 1966.

Il contratto (produced Teatro La Fenice, Venice, 1967). 1967.

Cani e gatti, from work by Eduardo Scarpetta (produced Teatro Piccinni, Bari, 1970).

Il monumento (produced Teatro La Pergola, Florence, 1970). 1971.

'Na santarella, from work by Eduardo Scarpetta (produced Teatro Eliseo, Rome, 1972).

Gli esami non finiscono mai (produced Teatro La Pergola, Florence, 1973). 1973.

Lu curaggio de nu pumpiere napulitano, from work by Eduardo Scarpetta (produced Teatro La Pergola, Florence, 1974).

L'erede di Shylock, from Shakespeare. 1984.

La Tempesta, from *The Tempest* by Shakespeare. 1984.

Screenplays

"Adelina" episode, with Isabella Quarantotti, of *Ieri, oggi e domani (Yesterday, Today and Tomorrow)*, 1963; *Matrimonió all'italiana (Marriage Italian Style)*, 1964; *Spara forte, più forte . . . non capisco (Shoot Loud, Louder . . . I Don't Understand)*, with Suso Cecchi D'Amico, 1966.

Television Plays

Peppino Girella, with Isabella Quarantotti, 1963 (published 1964); *Li nepute de lu sinneco*, from work by Eduardo Scarpetta, 1975; *'O Tuono 'e marzo*, from work by Vincenzo Scarpetta, 1975; and adaptations of about 20 of his own plays.

Verse

Il paese di Pulcinella. 1951.
'O canisto. 1971.
Le poesie. 1975.

Other

Editor, *Manzù: Album inedito*. 1977.

*

Criticism

Books:
Laura C. Pizer, *L'esperienza comica di Eduardo De Filippo*, Assisi, 1972.
Federico Frascani, *Eduardo*, Naples, 1974.
Fiorenza Di Franco, *Il teatro de Eduardo*, Rome, 1975.
Fiorenza Di Franco, *Eduardo De Filippo*, Rome, 1978.
Isabella De Filippo (ed.), *Eduardo nel mondo*, Rome, 1978.
Carla Filosa, *Eduardo De Filippo: Poeta comico del tragico quotidiano*, Casamari, 1978.
Giovanni Antonucci, *Eduardo De Filippo: Introduzione e guida allo studio dell'opera eduardiana, storia e antologia della critica*, Florence, 1980.
Federico Frascani, *Eduardo segreto*, Naples, 1982.
Fiorenza Di Franco, *La commedie di Eduardo*, Bari, 1984.
Mario Mignone, *Eduardo De Filippo* (in English), Boston, 1984.
Anna Barsotti, *Eduardo drammaturgo*, Rome, 1988.

Articles:

Robert G. Bander, "A Critical Estimate of Eduardo De Filippo", in *Italian Quarterly*, vol.11 no.3, 1967.

Robert G. Bander, "The Neapolitan Scene in De Filippo's Theatre", in *Italian Quarterly*, vol.13 no.3, 1970.

* * *

Eduardo the playwright cannot readily be separated from Eduardo the comic actor and acting-company director, for he wrote his plays invariably with himself, his sister Titina, and the members of his company in mind as their interpreters. From the late 1920's until his death he was a prolific dramatist, and the best of his plays rank as the most vital in the modern Italian theatre. They attest to the enduring invention of the Neapolitan dialect "prose" stage, are very much of the theatre, are essentially of the popular meridian, have elements in common with the *commedia dell'arte*, and delight in their own artifice. At the same time, character and situation are handled in what are basically naturalistic ways, and the plays are firmly placed in the language, life, and attitudes of the Neapolitan petty bourgeoisie and working class. They contain, too, many strong literary and dramatic influences, notably the work of Pirandello.

Eduardo's view of the world is essentially tragicomic: in his work confusions and misunderstandings abound, ambitions are frustrated, life is confusing and hazardous; in many of the plays the action turns on the ultimately futile attempts of a good-natured, even naïve, individual to change a rapacious and materialistic society. The emphasis ultimately, however, is on the comic, and any darker tones tend eventually to be overlaid by a genial acceptance of the nature of men and societies.

Some of the early plays, like *Napoli milionaria* and *Filumena Marturano* certainly tackle very real social and political problems, and their mood impressively reflects the mood of the immediate post-war years in which they were written. But they are not underpinned by any firm socio-political stance, and the biss is towards acceptance, and the resolution of social and personal conflicts by recourse to a vague concept of the the enduring values of the local community. Other pieces are even more bland and locally oriented, like *Sabato, domenica e lunedi* (*Saturday, Sunday, Monday*), a manifestly light piece reflecting the Italy of the "economic miracle": here the domestic upheavals are no more than a storm in a teacup, the misunderstandings contrived and the issues superficially examined. A darker, more melancholy tone is ever more prominent in his later work. At the centre of nearly all Eduardo's plays, however, is the idea of the family, and even in his darkest comedy familial ties and obligations remain the one certainty in an otherwise unstable world. Indeed, at times this emphasis on the domestic, and on familial and community relationships, is treacherous subject-matter, and some of the plays are marred by a rather mawkish sentimentality and a simplistic moral didacticism; however apparently vigorous the challenges made to the social status quo, received values invariably prevail.

But such strictures are perhaps more evident when the plays are encountered as words on the page; in the theatre they have countervailing strengths, and are invariably crafted with an eye to satisfying the taste of Neapolitan audiences for bravura performances from lead and character actors alike. For Eduardo's plays are of the theatre in another sense than that remarked above: they are manifestly the work of a practitioner, as can be seen in the detailed stage directions. They are accommodated specifically to Eduardo's own economic, realistic style of humane, comic playing, and at the same time give ample scope too for the other leads to exploit their playing strengths and, in the eccentric figures with which they abound, allow support players to display their performer skills in traditional character-type roles so long beloved of the Neapolitan stages. The plays are very much rooted in the Neapolitan theatrical ambience, and appeal most to those informed of its particular traditions and conventions; they are equally of the Neapolitan social ambience, locale and dialect being crucial to their stage effect: their Neapolitan orientation, indeed, in part accounts for the fact that they are not frequently performed outside Italy, for they are cultural artefacts which do not easily travel or translate.

—Laura Richards

See also *Volume 1* entry on *Saturday, Sunday, Monday*.

———

DE GROEN, Alma. Born Alma Mathers in Foxton, New Zealand, 5 September 1941. Educated at Mangakino District High School, Waikoto, 1954–57. Married Geoffrey De Groen in 1965; one daughter. Library Assistant, National Library Service, Wellington and Hamilton, 1958–64; settled in Australia, 1964; librarian, New Zealand Trade Commission, Sydney; spent 4 years abroad, in Britain, France, and Canada, 1969–72; first-produced play, *The Joss Adams Show*, produced 1970: the play won the Canadian Playwriting Competition of that year; writer-in-residence, Western Australian Institute of Technology, Perth, 1986; dramaturg, Griffin Theatre Company, Sydney, 1987; writer-in-residence, University of Queensland, St. Lucia, 1989, and Rollins College, Florida, USA, 1989. Recipient: Australian Writers Guild Award, 1985; New South Wales Premier's Award, 1988; Victoria Premier's Award, 1988.

Works

Collections

"Going Home" and Other Plays (includes *The Joss Adams Show*; *Perfectly All Right*).   1977.

Stage Works

The Joss Adams Show (produced Festival Theatre, Stratford, Ontario, 1970).   In *"Going Home" and Other Plays*, 1977.

Perfectly All Right (produced as *The Sweatproof Boy*, Nimrod Street Theatre, Sydney, 1972; revised version, as *Perfectly All Right*, produced Adelaide, 1973).   In *"Going Home" and Other Plays*, 1977.

The After-Life of Arthur Cravan (produced Jane Street Theatre, Sydney, 1973).

Going Home (produced Melbourne, 1976).   In *"Going Home" and Other Plays*, 1977.

Chidley (produced by Hoopla Productions, Melbourne, 1976).   In *Theatre Australia*, January-February 1977.

Vocations (produced Melbourne, 1981).   1983.

The Rivers of China (produced Wharf Theatre, Sydney, 1987).   1988.

The Girl Who Saw Everything (produced Melbourne, 1991).

Television Plays

Going Home 1980; *Man of Letters*, from the novel by Glen Tomasatti, 1985; *Chris* (episode of *Singles*), 1986; *After*

Marcuse, 1986; *The Women* (episode of *Rafferty's Rules*), 1987.

Radio Plays

Available Light, 1992.

*

Criticism

Articles:
Elizabeth Perkins, "Form and Transformation in the Plays of Alma De Groen", in *Australasian Drama Studies*, 11, 1987.
Alma De Groen and Helen Gilbert, "'Walking Around in Other Times': An Interview", in *Australasian Drama Studies*, 15–16, 1989–90.

* * *

Alma De Groen began writing for the theatre in 1968. Today she describes herself as a feminist playwright, recently commenting that "I think I started out as one without knowing I was one".

Nonetheless, her first overtly feminist play was only produced in 1981—*Vocations*. The ambivalent prominence of feminism in her work, together with the importance of form, makes De Groen what might be termed a "sceptical feminist" —she is concerned with feminist issues, but not at the expense of artistic integrity. Moreover, her highly developed sense of the ironic and her aversion to the didactic—both evident in her recent play, *The Rivers of China*, which is set in a feminist dystopia—always save her from becoming earnest.

Her early play, *The Joss Adams Show*, written in Canada, reflects the kinds of influences and preoccupations which have since shaped her work. A desperate young mother batters her baby to death. The play begins with her appearing on a television talk show, ostensibly carrying her dead baby in a bag. The nature of television as a medium inevitably trivialises Joss's predicament and the horror of her case is distanced for the audience. Given that the theatre audience is familiar with the TV talk show and that it is also used to having its perceptions of the world shaped by media like TV, this device is highly ironical and disjunctive.

The same device re-appears, albeit in a different form, in *The Rivers of China* where, in a flashback to pre-feminist times, two men are seen setting up for a pornographic "snuff" video in which a girl is to be sexually assaulted and murdered. Simulating a filmic dissolve, the lights come up on two other characters in the present watching that very video. This ironical foregrounding of perception is a feature of De Groen's writing. It is also a practice which has its origins as much in the visual arts as it does in theatrical precedents (such as non-didactic, social-conscience British writers like Howard Brenton). De Groen was married for some time to the abstract painter, Geoffrey De Groen, and her experience of abstract and pop art of the late 1960's (and the Western tradition of painting generally) became assimilated into her writing. Indeed, she claims that most of her plays begin with a visual image, often a work of art.

The Joss Adams Show and its parody of television is a pop idea. However, at a more subtle level, it is the way abstract and pop art foreground the process and context of perception (together with the notion that "the medium is the message") which De Groen applies in her work.

She has described her artistic objectives as a kind of "thea-trical quietism, a feeling of psychic wholeness which I think you cannot get through naturalism. In the audience's experience of the play, they enter into it in a way that is absolutely paralleled in what is happening on stage and what the message of the play is".

De Groen's 1973 play *The After-Life of Arthur Cravan* also uses a disjunctive device as a "defamiliarising" tactic. Here she sets up four audiences to witness the re-enactment of the life of Cravan, the exotic nephew of Oscar Wilde. The basic motivation of the play is a lecture on Cravan by André Gide, who based the character of Lafcadio in *Les Caves du Vatican* on Cravan. Hence, we have Cravan acting out his life to the real audience, to Gide, to Gide's stage audience and to Oscar Wilde who, at the beginning and end of the play, exhorts Cravan to "lay it out for me, all of it, like a map of China".

Generally, De Groen eschews naturalistic conventions (her 1976 play *Going Home* being an exception), especially in her more explicitly feminist plays. She has commented that "women's theatre is so often about transcending the barriers of time and place, and naturalism is of very little help there". This comment is germane to *Vocations*, De Groen's first explicitly feminist play, which introduces the theme of reconciling the sexes by dissolving the polarisation of gender roles, a theme further explored in *The Rivers of China*.

Vocations is also a subtle exploration of the notion of form as the bearer of content. De Groen makes multiple use of a single stage setting when two adjoining apartments (one occupied by novelist Joy and her husband Godfrey, the other by actress Vicki and her scientist boyfriend, Ross) are served by the same space. This device sets up uncertainty in the minds of the audience, reinforced by uncertainty about the sequence of events; in turn, the device reflects the uncertainty of the characters. The two women not only share a space, but also the fact that they have allowed their lives to be dictated by their men. Likewise, the two men share a space and a common sense of insecurity. In the end, the two men share the experience of raising Ross and Vicki's child, while the two women share in the making of a script. Not only are traditional roles inverted, but De Groen has her characters beginning to speak and act like the opposite sex.

In ways such as these, the audience is regularly surprised as familiar things are presented in an unfamiliar way and within an overall structure that keeps the audience always a little off balance. By using such devices, De Groen has become one of the most sophisticated playwrights on the Australian stage. Apart from the variety of other themes explored in her work, De Groen's writing is also intriguingly reflexive in that it is a continuing re-evaluation of the nature and role of art itself: her formal choices are integral to her subject matter.

—Paul McGillick

See also *Volume 1* entry on *The Rivers of China*.

DEKKER, Thomas. Born probably in London, c.1572. Married: 1) Mary (died 1616); 2) Elizabeth. Playwright for Philip Henslowe, c.1595–1602: mentioned in documents as having worked on more than 50 plays; lived in poverty: imprisoned for debt in 1598 and 1599, and in King's Bench Prison, London, 1613–19. Died (buried) in London, 25 August 1632.

Works

Collections

Non-Dramatic Works, edited by Alexander B. Grosart (5 vols.). 1884–86.
Dramatic Works, edited by Fredson Bowers (4 vols.). 1953–61; revised edition of vols. 2–3, 1964–66; *Introductions, Notes, and Commentaries* by Cyrus Hoy (4 vols.), 1980–81.

Stage Works

Old Fortunatus (produced by the Admiral's Men, London, 1598/99). 1600.
The Shoemaker's Holiday; or, The Gentle Craft (produced by the Admiral's Men, London, 1599–1600?). 1600.
Patient Grissel, with Henry Chettle and William Haughton (produced by the Admiral's Men, London, 1600). 1603.
Lust's Dominion; or, The Lascivious Queen (as *The Spanish Moor's Tragedy*, produced 1600). 1657.
Satiromastix; or, The Untrussing of the Humorous Poet, possibly with John Marston (produced London, 1601). 1602.
Blurt, Master Constable; or, The Spaniard's Night-Walk (produced by the Children of St. Paul's, London, 1601–02). 1602.
Sir Thomas Wyatt, with Thomas Heywood and Webster (produced London, 1602–07?). 1607.
King James His Royal and Magnificent Entertainment, with Jonson and others (produced London, 1604). Dekker's part published separately, 1604.
The Honest Whore, part 1, with Middleton (produced by Prince Henry's Men, London, 1604). 1604; as *The Converted Courtesan*, 1604.
Westward Ho, with Webster (produced by the Children of St. Paul's, London, 1604). 1607.
The Honest Whore, part 2 (produced by Prince Henry's Men, London, 1604-05?). 1630.
Northward Ho, with Webster (produced by the Children of St. Paul's, London, 1605). 1607.
The Whore of Babylon (produced by Prince Henry's Men, London, 1606–07?). 1607.
If It Be Not Good the Devil is in It (produced by Queen Anne's Men, London, 1611–12?). 1612.
The Roaring Girl; or, Moll Cut-Purse, with Middleton (produced by Prince Henry's Men, London, 1611). 1611.
Match Me in London (produced London, 1611–13?). 1631.
Troia-Nova Triumphans, London Triumphing (pageant; produced London, 1612). 1612.
The Virgin Martyr, with Massinger (produced by the Red Bull Company, Red Bull Theatre, London, 1620). 1622.
The Witch of Edmonton, with William Rowley and John Ford (produced by Prince Charles' Men, Cockpit/Phoenix Theatre, 1621). 1658.
The Noble Soldier; or, A Contract Broken, Justly Revenged (as *The Noble Spanish Soldier*, produced London, 1622). 1634.
The Welsh Ambassador, with Ford (produced c.1623). Edited by H. Littledale and W.W. Greg, 1920.
The Wonder of a Kingdom (produced 1623–31?). 1636.
The Sun's Darling: A Moral Masque, with Ford (produced by Lady Elizabeth's Men, London, 1624). 1656.
Britannia's Honour (pageant; produced London, 1628). 1628.
London's Tempe; or, The Field of Happiness (pageant; produced London, 1629). 1629.

Verse

The Artillery Garden. 1616.
Wars, Wars, Wars. 1628.

Other

The Wonderful Year, Wherein Is Shown the Picture of London Lying Sick of the Plague. 1603.
News from Gravesend, Sent to Nobody. 1604.
The Meeting of Gallants at an Ordinary; or, The Walks in Paul's. 1604.
The Double PP: A Papist Encountered by the Protestant. 1606.
News from Hell. 1606; revised edition, as *A Knight's Conjuring, Done in Earnest, Discovered in Jest*, 1607.
The Seven Deadly Sins of London. 1606.
Jests to Make You Merry, with George Wilkins. 1607.
The Dead Term; or, Westminster's Complaint for Long Vacations and Short Terms. 1608.
The Bellman of London, Bringing to Light the Most Notorious Villainies. 1608.
Lantern and Candle-Light; or, The Bellman's Second Night's Walk. 1608; revised edition, 1609; as *O Per Se O; or, A New Crier of Lantern and Candle-Light*, 1612; revised edition, as *Villainies Discovered by Lantern and Candle-Light*, 1616, 1620; revised edition, as *English Villainies*, 1632.
Four Birds of Noah's Ark. 1609.
The Gull's Horn-Book. 1609.
The Raven's Almanac Foretelling of a Plague, Famine, and Civil War. 1609.
Work for Armourers; or, The Peace is Broken. 1609.
A Strange Horse Race. 1613.
Dekker His Dream. 1620.
A Rod for Runaways. 1625; revised edition, 1625.
London Look Back at That Year of Years 1625. 1630.
The Black Rod and the White Rod, Justice and Mercy, Striking and Sparing London. 1630, edited by F.P. Wilson, in *Plague Pamphlets*, 1925.
Penny-Wise Pound-Foolish; or, A Bristow Diamond Set in Two Rings and Both Cracked. 1631, in *Selected Prose Works*, 1967.
The Plague Pamphlets, edited by F.P. Wilson. 1925.
Selected Prose Works, edited by E.D. Pendry. 1967.

*

Bibliographies

S.A. Tannenbaum, *Dekker: A Concise Bibliography*, New York, 1939; supplement, with Dorothy R. Tannenbaum, 1945; further supplement in *Elizabethan Bibliographies Supplements 2*, by Dennis G. Donovan, London, 1967.
Antony F. Allison, *Thomas Dekker: A Bibliographical Catalogue of the Early Editions (to 1700)*, Folkestone and London, 1972.
Doris Ray Adler, *Thomas Dekker: A Reference Guide*, Boston, 1983.

Critism

Books:
K. L. Gregg, *Dekker: A Study in Economic and Social Backgrounds*, Seattle, Washington, 1924.
Normand Berlin, *The Base String: The Underworld of Elizabethan Drama*, Rutherford, New Jersey, 1968.
George R. Price, *Thomas Dekker*, New York, 1968.
James H. Conover, *Thomas Dekker: An Analysis of Dramatic Structure*, The Hague, 1969.
Suzanne K. Blow, *Rhetoric in the Plays of Dekker*, Salzburg, 1972.
L. M. Michael, *The Sports of Art: Convention and Theme in the Plays of Thomas Dekker*, Salzburg, 1972.

Peggy F. Shirley, *Serious and Tragic Elements in the Comedy of Dekker*, Salzburg, 1975.

Frederick O. Waage, *Dekker's Pamphlets 1603–1609 and Jacobean Popular Literature* (2 vols.), Salzburg, 1977.

Tirthankar Bose, *The Gentle Craft of Revision in Dekker's Last Plays*, Salzburg, 1979.

Larry S. Champion, *Dekker and the Traditions of English Drama*, Frankfurt and Bern, 1985.

Julia Gasper, *The Dragon and the Dove: The Plays of Thomas Dekker*, 1990.

*   *   *

Critical esteem has only come recently to Dekker's plays. Once out of favour for his homely wisdom and prosaic style, Dekker is now recognized as a complex dramatist and a shrewd political spokesman, deft at collaboration and skilled in manipulating a range of literary genres. Variety is the keynote of his dramatic *oeuvre*. His works span several categories and might be defined as moral allegories, professional statements, satirical comedies, political discussions, and social commentaries.

A number of his plays have allegorical dimensions and concern themselves with the tribulations of virtuous individuals in corrupt societies. *Patient Grissel*, written with Henry Chettle and William Haughton, dramatizes the troubles of Grissel who is tested by her untrusting husband, the Marquess of Salucia. The play develops into a sophisticated investigation of patience, and its different narratives elaborate upon this theme; the subplot involving a Welsh knight and his shrewish wife broaches, in a comic fashion, the subject of marital responsibilities. A further moral element can be detected in *Old Fortunatus*. This work (which was presented at Court) shows Dekker drawing upon German folktales to lend weight to an economic analysis. Sparkling with displays of magic and elaborate spectacles and presenting the feuding brothers, Andelocia and Ampedo, in stylized terms, the play delineates the dangers of improvidence.

The Virgin Martyr, written with Philip Massinger, the last of the dramas which might be characterized as a moral allegory, sets the martyrdom of the Christian Dorothea against Roman venality. Portrayed in the play are symbolic manifestations of the torments of martyrdom (in Angelo and Harpax, the good and evil angels), the consequences of temptation, the operations of divine grace and, in Dorothea, the achievement of salvation.

It would be misleading, however, to suggest that Dekker was a conservative dramatist who employed conventions unquestioningly and who endorsed establishment attitudes. Many of his works reveal the playwright adopting a critical stance, launching satirical barbs at enemies or social abuses. The so-called "War of the Theatres" was a phenomenon in which Dekker took an active part. A response to *Poetaster* in which Ben Jonson attacks his theatrical rivals, Dekker's *Satiromastix* lampoons Jonson in the form of Horace, figured as a bitter, insulting, and sycophantic pedant. The climax is particularly vitriolic as Crispinus (John Marston) is sick with Horace's words: vocabulary is transformed into vomit.

The critical aspect of Dekker's work is seen again in his city comedies. Most of the plays belonging to this group treat middle-class foibles and mores satirically, mocking London citizens while also remaining indulgent and sympathetic. With John Webster, Dekker produced *Westward Ho* and *Northward Ho*, boisterous comedies which focus upon the successes of citizens' wives in repelling the advances of their gallant suitors. One reason for the popularity of *The Roaring Girl*, by Dekker and Thomas Middleton, was its basis in the "real-life" career of Mary Frith who came to the attention of 17th-century authorities for dressing in male attire. In the play, Moll Cutpurse (Mary Frith) delights and terrifies Londoners with her underworld speech, dazzling sword-play, intrigue, songs, and nimble verbal pyrotechnics. Of the same year, *If This Be Not Good the Devil is in It* develops Dekker's social preoccupations, the devils which people the play are infernal versions of the Jacobean professions.

More interrogative still are the political dramas. While staunchly Protestant, *Sir Thomas Wyatt*, written with Thomas Heywood and John Webster, reflects ambivalently upon Essex's rebellion even as it seems to defend the concept of divine right. *The Whore of Babylon* would appear to be a reply to and a condemnation of the Gunpowder Plot as it recalls the glories of the Elizabethan period; simultaneously, though, the play implicitly questions the excesses of Jacobean monarchical authority. *Match Me in London* is in a similar vein: the overweening behaviour of the tyrannical King of Spain (who attempts to seduce Tormiella, a shopkeeper's wife) encourages speculation about how easily royal power is abused.

All of the characteristics of Dekker's dramatic abilities are displayed in the plays for which he is usually praised. His most powerful dramas are marked by an economy of style, a probing social commentary, a sensitivity to the plight of marginalized individuals, and a responsiveness to issues of political importance. A good example of this combination of features is in the rumbustious comedy *The Shoemaker's Holiday*. The uses and misuses of money, social mobility, and the flexibility of the class structure are among the play's thematic imperatives. Dominating the action is Simon Eyre, the eloquent and magnanimous shoemaker, and his bubbling linguistic dexterity lends the play its holiday mood of buoyancy, conviviality, and vitality.

The intricate dovetailing of plots in *The Shoemaker's Holiday* anticipates a similar knitting together of narratives in the two parts of *The Honest Whore* . The first part, written with Thomas Middleton, contrasts the patience (which is sorely tested) of Candido, the linen-draper, with the trials of the lovers, Infelice and Hippolito, who endeavour to come together against their parents' wishes. Contrast is the chief dramatic strategy in the second part, too, which Dekker seems to have written unaided. While Bellafront, the courtesan of the title, regrets her former life, ironic commentaries are provided in the lusty prose of Matheo and the bawdy jokes of Bryan, the Irish footman.

One of Dekker's final collaborations was *The Witch of Edmonton*; John Ford and William Rowley were the co-playwrights. An acute exploration of the prejudices that rule a narrow and superstitious community, the play charts the ways in which a powerless woman (Mother Sawyer) is forced to become a witch by the gossiping, competitive society she inhabits. A social indictment, the play is a fine instance of Dekker's craft, of his collaborative talents, of his perceptive reading of social conditions, of his equanimity and understanding—the qualities that constitute his dramatic achievement.

—Mark Thornton Burnett

See also *Volume 1* entries on *The Shoemaker's Holiday*; *The Witch of Edmonton*.

DELANEY, Shelagh. Born in Salford, Lancashire, England, 25 November 1939. Educated at Broughton Secondary School. Has one daughter. Worked as salesgirl, usherette, and photographer's laboratory assistant; first play, *A Taste of Honey*, produced 1958. Recipient: New York Drama Critics Circle Award, 1961; BAFTA Award, 1962; Robert Flaherty Award, for screenplay, 1962; Writers Guild Award, for screenplay, 1969; Cannes Film Festival Award, 1985. Fellow, Royal Society of Literature, 1985.

Works

Stage Works

A Taste of Honey (produced Theatre Royal, Stratford East, London, 1958).   1959.
The Lion in Love (produced Belgrade Theatre, Coventry). 1961.
The House That Jack Built (televised 1977; produced New York, 1979).
Don't Worry About Matilda, from the radio play (produced London, 1987).

Screenplays

A Taste of Honey, with Tony Richardson, 1961; *The White Bus*, 1966; *Charlie Bubbles*, 1968; *Dance with a Stranger*, 1985.

Television Plays

Did Your Nanny Come from Bergen?, 1970; *St. Martin's Summer*, 1974; *The House That Jack Built* series (published 1977), 1977; *Find Me First*, 1981.

Radio Plays

So Does the Nightingale, 1981; *Don't Worry about Matilda*, 1983.

Other

Sweetly Sings the Donkey.   1963.

*

Judged solely on the plots, Shelagh Delaney's first two plays would seem to place her with her hands firmly in the kitchen-sink world of working-class life: all penny-in-the-slot and gasworks-in-view, northern grime and vowel sounds. *A Taste of Honey* takes place in a seedy bedsit. Helen, a "semi-whore", leaves with her latest fancy man, abandoning her teenage daughter. The girl, Jo, is an embarrassment: old enough to undermine Helen's perpetual youth, and pregnant by a black sailor. Jo and Geoffrey (a homosexual art student) care for each other, but he leaves when Helen returns, her latest romance in ruins. The two women are left alone, together. There is no suggestion that life will be much different for the unborn child.

Less well known, *The Lion in Love* features a larger cast coping with the same lack of choices. Frank is forever about to leave Kit who, typically, has been arrested for drunk and disorderly behaviour just as the play opens. Both their children dream of a better life. One is set to emigrate, the other is falling in love. Not much hope is suggested for either. A street corner prophet appears from time to time, predicting change. The action demonstrates the unlikeliness of this. Social determinism reigns.

Obviously Delaney was influenced by what came before, but it is a mistake to regard her plays as part of any continuum of social realism. Delaney must take some responsibility for this distorted view of her work, given that she wrote the screenplay for *A Taste of Honey* and so transformed it into an archetypal early 1960's black-and-white film.

John Osborne's *Look Back in Anger* is popularly held to have hurled stones through the drawing-room windows of British theatre in the mid-1950's, and a comparison of the depiction of female characters in that play with the protagonists of *A Taste of Honey* and *The Lion in Love* is revealing. Constantly Delaney presents women toughened by circumstance. Frustrated, trapped, and dissatisfied, they are offered only momentary sweetness in a bleak world. Economic dependency is stressed, whether in marriage or prostitution, which Delaney depicts without sentiment or moral judgements. The unsatisfactory nature of sexual relationships is revealed again and again. Peg's careless rapture in *The Lion in Love* is undercut by her mother and father's tormented marriage and the life of Nell, the local street-corner tart. Sex results in unwanted pregnancy. The only tenderness displayed between men and women (other than siblings) is between the pregnant Jo and the homosexual Geoffrey. Even that relationship is doomed; unfortunately, Delaney is of her time in her stereotypical depiction of the feminised and unhappy gay outsider.

Delaney's women's lives and actions are responsive to male behaviour. (Ruth Ellis, the heroine of Delaney's notable screenplay for *Dance with a Stranger*, is perhaps the ultimate example of this.) Nevertheless the very act of representing such lives, of celebrating the strength and endurance of these women, of declaring that such things are an appropriate subject to place centre-stage, is a proto-feminist gesture.

In the same way that Delaney began the reclamation of women's domain that is seen in the work of later, feminist playwrights, her plays anticipate the concern with how a story is told, as much as with what is said. On both sides of the Atlantic, writers such as Megan Terry, Caryl Churchill, and Pam Gems have abandoned traditional (male) theatrical structures in the belief that form *and* content must change to reflect different concerns. Joan Littlewood, who was attempting to establish a new, populist form of theatre saw the potential and significance of the expressionistic, non-naturalistic style of *A Taste of Honey*. The play—first staged by Littlewood's Theatre Workshop—has no fourth wall. A jazz trio accompany and heighten the action. Characters turn from each other mid-sentence, and address the audience directly. In *The Lion in Love*, music is again integral. The structure is episodic, following the various related but separate stories, while the location shifts accordingly between home and street market. (All in all, the play is probably unstageable. Certainly, it met nowhere near the acclaim of *A Taste of Honey* nor has it been revived in the same way.)

It is beyond the brief of this piece to speculate why, after only two plays for the stage and just turned 20 years old, Delaney gave up writing for the theatre in favour of other media. It is tempting to imagine that she was already weary of the patronising amazement of much contemporaneous criticism, which constantly marvelled that a teenage, Northern shop girl could produce art. With hindsight, it is easy to dismiss Delaney's plays as minor period pieces. Like most work which resolutely addresses and reflects the social mores of its time, the plays have not worn well. But Delaney's plays were unique, not to say isolated at the time. Her concern with form and the emphasis she places on working-class women's experience means that Delaney's true significance lies beyond her plays, in her influence.

—Joss Bennathon

See also *Volume 1* entry on *A Taste of Honey*.

DIAS GOMES, Alfredo.   See GOMES, Alfredo Dias.

DÍAZ (GUTIERREZ), Jorge. Born in Rosario, Argentina, 20 February 1930. Family moved to Chile, 1934, and took Chilean citizenship. Studied architecture at the Catholic University, Santiago. Architect and painter, until 1965; travelled in Europe, 1958; joined the Chilean theatre company Ictus as actor and stage designer, 1959, becoming its president, 1963–64; first plays produced by Ictus, 1961; emigrated to Spain, 1965; founder and director, Teatro del Nuevo Mundo, 1969–71; director, Teatro Trabalenguas, 1972–81; began writing for radio and television in 1980. Recipient: many theatre awards in Chile and Spain; two prizes for fiction.

Works

Collections

Tres obras.   1967.
Ceremonias de la soledad.   1978.

Stage Works (for adults)

Un hombre llamado Isla (produced Sala Talía, Santiago, 1961).
El cepillo de dientes (one-act version produced Sala Talía, Santiago, 1961; two-act version produced Teatro Valle Inclán, Madrid, 1966).   1967.
Réquiem por un girasol (produced Teatro Petit Rex, Santiago, Chile, 1961).   In *Tres obras*, 1967.
La orgástula.   In *Latin American Theatre Review*, vol. 14 no. 1, 1970.
El velero en la botella (produced Teatro La Comedia, Santiago, Chile, 1962).   In *Mapocho*, vol.1 no.1, then in *Primer acto* (Madrid), 69, 1965; in book form, with *El cepillo de dientes*, 1972.
El lugar donde mueren los mamíferos (produced Teatro La Comedia, Santiago, 1963).   In *Mapocho*, vol.3 no.3, 1965; in book form, 1972; translated as *The Place Where the Mammals Die*, in *The Modern Stage in Latin America: Six Plays* edited by George Woodyard, 1971.
Variaciones para muertos de percusión (produced Teatro La Comedia, Santiago, 1964).   In *Conjunto* (Havana), 1, 1964.
El nudo ciego (produced Teatro La Comedia, Santiago, 1965).

Topografía de un desnudo (produced Teatro Camilo Henríquez, Santiago, 1967).   1967.
La vispera del degüello [earlier title, *El Génesis fue mañana*] (produced Sala Puente Cultural, Madrid, 1970).   1967; translated as *The Eve of Execution; or, Genesis Was Tomorrow*, in *Modern One Act Plays from Latin America*, edited by Gerardo Luzuriaga and Robert S. Rudder, 1974.
Liturgia para cornudos (produced Sala Mozart, Santiago, 1970).   Revised as *Ceremonia ortopédica* (produced Teatro Lebrel Blanco, Pamplona, Spain, 1976), 1978.
La pancarta; o, Esta estrictamente prohibido todo lo que no es obligatorio (produced Club Pueblo, Madrid, 1971).   In *Teatro difícil*, 1971.
Americaliente (produced Latin American Festival, San Juan, Puerto Rico, 1971).
Algo para contar en Navidad (produced Barcelona, 1972).   1974.
Los alacranes (produced with *Las hormigas*, Club Pueblo, Madrid, 1973).
Las hormigas (produced with *Los alacranes*, Club Pueblo, Madrid, 1973).
Antropofagia de salón; o, Electroshock para gente de orden (produced Teatro Alfil, Madrid, 1973).
Amaos los unos sobre los otros.   In English translation, as *Love Yourself Above All Others*, in *Selected Latin American One Act Plays*, edited by Francesca Colecchia and Julio Matas, 1973.
Mear contra el viento, with Francisco Javier Uriz (produced Lisbon, 1976).   In *Conjunto*, 21, 1974.
El locuturio (produced Aula de Teatro, Universidad de Valladolid, Valladolid, 1979).   In *Teatro . . .* (anthology), with others, 1976.
Mata a tu prójimo como a ti mismo (produced Teatro Quart 23, Valencia, 1976).   1977; revised as *Esplendor carnal de la ceniza* (produced Teatro El Conventillo, Santiago, Chile, 1984).
La puñeta (produced Teatro Lebrel Blanco, Pamplona, Spain, 1977).
Un día es un día; o, Los sobrevivientes (produced Centro Cultural de la Villa, Madrid, 1978).
Ecuación (produced Café-Teatro, Zaragoza, Spain, 1979).   1983.
El espantajo (produced Théâtre du Midi, Nimes, France, 1979).
El generalet.   1979.
La manifestación (produced Caja des Ahorros Provincial, Valladolid, 1979).   1980.
Toda esta larga noche (produced Theater 44, Munich, 1981).
Estuias o trabajas?, with Rafael Herrero (produced Centro Cultural de la Villa, Madrid, 1981).
Un ombligo para dos (produced Café-Teatro El Pavo Real, Madrid, 1982).
"Piel contra piel" (produced Teatro Pedro Valdivia, Santiago, Chile, 1982).
Oscuro vuelo compartido (produced Spain, 1982).
Ligeros de equipaje (produced International Festival, Sitges, Spain, 1982).   In *Primer acto*, 1985.
Desde la sangre y el silencio; o, Fulgor y muerte de Pablo Neruda (produced Volkstheater, Rostock, East Germany, 1984).   1982.
Introducción al elefante y otras zoologías (produced Chile, 1986).   One scene translated as *Man Does Not Die By Bread Alone*, in *Tulane Drama Review*, vol.14 no.2, 1970.
Dicen que la distancia es el olvido (produced Sala Cadarso, Madrid, 1986).   1987.
Los tiempos oscuros (produced Théâtre La Barraca, Montreal, Canada, 1986).

Las cicatrices de la memoria (Finale: Allegro ma non troppo). (produced 1987). 1986.
Muero, luego existo (produced Spain, 1990).
Un corazón lleno de lluvia (produced Spain, 1991).
A imagen y semeijanza (produced Spain, 1991).
Pablo Neruda viena volando (produced Chile, 1991).

Stage Works (for Children)

Chumingo y el pirata de lata, with Mónica Echeverría (produced Teatro La Comedia, Santiago, 1963; revised version, as *El pirata de hojalata*, produced Huelva, Spain, 1972).
Serapio y Yerbabuena (produced Teatro La Comedia, Santiago, 1964). 1975.
La mala nochebuena de don Etcétera (produced Cine-Teatro Astor, Santiago, 1964).
Los ángeles ladrones (produced Teatro La Comedia, Santiago, 1970).
Pirueta y Voltereta (produced Léon, Spain, 1970).
Rascatripa (produced Teatro Alfil, Madrid, 1973).
La barraca de Jipi Japa (produced Teatro Alfil, Madrid, 1974).
Cuentos para armar entre todos (produced Teatro Alfil, Madrid, 1975).
El supercoco (produced Lucena, Córdoba, Spain, 1975).
Rinconete y Cortadillo, from Cervantes (produced Vigo, Spain, 1976).
La ciudad que tiene la cara sucia (produced Teatro Alfil, Madrid, 1977).
El mariscalito; o, El generalito (produced Plaza del Valle Suchil, Madrid, 1979).
Séneca, ratón de biblioteca (produced Lucena, Córdoba, Spain, 1979).
La dragonera (produced Teatro La Trepa, Barcelona, 1980).
El imperio del humo (produced Teatro Tilingo, Caracas, Venezuela, 1980).
Los juguetes olvidados (produced by the Campaña de la Caixa, Barcelona, 1981).
Viaje alrededor de un pañuelo (produced Auditorium del Centro Cultural de la Villa, Madrid, 1983).
La ciudad al revés (produced 1983). 1985.
El guirigay; o, Zambacanuta (produced Teatro Dante, Santiago, 1983).
Entre pícaros (produced 1983).
Ulises en el titirimundo (produced by the Grupo Taormina, Madrid, 1985).

Screenplays

La rosa de los vientos, 1984.

Television Plays

El próximo verano, 1984; *Cosas de dos* (series), 1986.

Radio Plays

Contrapunto para dos voces cansadas, 1987; *El abrazo del Winnipeg*, 1989; *Lugares*, 1989; *Los habitantes de la memoria*, 1990.

Other

"Reflections on the Chilean Theatre", in *The Drama Review*, vol.14 no.2, 1970.

*

Criticism

Books:
Mario Cánepa Guzmán, *Gente de teatro: Desde Camilo Henríquez hasta Jorge Díaz*, Santiago, 1969.
George Woodyard, "Jorge Díaz and the Liturgy of Violence", in *Dramatists in Revolt: The New Latin American Theater*, edited by Leon F. Lyday and George Woodyard, Austin, Texas, 1976.
George Woodyard, "Jorge Díaz", in *Latin American Writers, 3*, edited by Carlos A. Solé and María Isabel Abrue, New York, 1989.

Articles:
Gerardo Claps, "Jorge Díaz, dramaturgo chileno", in *Comunidad*, 17, 1969.
George Woodyard, "Ritual as Reality in Díaz's *Mata a tu prójimo como a ti mismo*", in *Estreno: Cuadernos del teatro español contemporáneo*, vol.9 no.2, 1983.
Kirsten F. Nigro, "Stage and Audience: Jorge Díaz's *El lugar donde mueren los mamíferos* and *Topografía de un desnudo*", in *Estreno: Cuadernos del teatro español contemporáneo*, vol.9, no.2, 1983.
Leon F. Lyday, "Inversion in the Absurdist Plays of Jorge Díaz", in *Romance Notes*, vol.27 no.1, 1986.

* * *

Jorge Díaz's early work is illustrative of the kind of experimentation to come out of independent theatre groups in Chile and elsewhere in Latin America during the 1960's. A pervasive influence at that time was the theatre of the absurd, of which Díaz's now-classic *El cepillo de dientes* (The Toothbrush) is a prime example. The two characters, Him and Her, engage each other in an extended dialogue that consists of clichés, non sequiturs, and at times, plain nonsense. He ends by killing her, but she returns as the maid, and their games continue, *ad infinitum* it would seem, as the play ends essentially where it began. This kind of absurdist playfulness and rejection of traditional proscenium theatre are characteristic of Díaz's work with the theatre group Ictus up until 1965, when he departed Chile for Spain, where he has since resided.

Díaz's first plays were sharp barbs at middle-class values and hypocrisy. *El cepillo de dientes* pokes fun at crass consumerism; *El lugar donde mueren los mamíferos* (The Place Where the Mammals Die) is a dark comedy about charitable organizations which ultimately cannot afford to be successful for fear of losing their clientele. In later texts, like *Topografía de un desnudo* (Topography of a Nude), Díaz's playwriting assumes an even more pointed socio-political purpose. Like other talented contemporary Latin-American playwrights, however, Díaz expresses that purpose through a constantly changing theatrical vocabulary, one which each time pushes the stage closer to the edges of its traditional limits. *Topografía de un desnudo*, for example, deals with the massacre of slum dwellers in Brazil by having one of the victims come back from the dead to investigate his own murder, a process that is aided by the onstage use of film sequences, slides, and other electronic devices. In *La orgástula* Díaz underscores his concern with verbal and sexual violence in a plot involving homicide and eroticism, with characters who speak an aggressive pseudo-language that mixes Spanish syntax with made-up words.

In the 1970's Díaz formed the Teatro del Nuevo Mundo (the New World Theatre), which focused mostly on plays of political protest whose targets were class and economic oppression, nuclear war, racism, and particularly the United States' imperialism and meddling in Latin American domestic affairs. *Mear contra el viento* (Piss Against the Wind) was written for Swedish television and is a fierce critique of the US role in the destabilization of Salvador Allende's government in Chile. Not surprisingly, the 1973 *coup d'état* that toppled Allende's Popular Front was the theme for various of Díaz's plays. *Desde la sangre y el silencio, o Fulgor y muerte de Pablo Neruda* (From Blood and Silence; or, Splendor and Death of Pablo Neruda) commissioned by the Oxford Playhouse, deals with the last months of Neruda's life, which sadly coincided with political chaos in Chile and the military take-over. The themes of torture and the disappeared are also evident in plays that Díaz wrote during this period.

Most of Díaz's work since 1965 has had its premiere in Madrid, which makes him a considerable figure in the Spanish theatre. Since Franco's death in 1975, along with all Spanish playwrights Díaz has been freer to touch on more local themes; *Las cicatrices de la memoria* (Scars of Memories), winner of the Tirso de Molina Prize in 1985, explores the extreme stress placed on society with Spain's rapid democratization. Other recent plays have dealt with problems of drug addiction and family disintegration. As if to bridge the painful past of his two homelands, in his *Ligeros de equipaje* (Traveling Lightly), Díaz creates the character of an actress who has suffered and survived both the Spanish Civil War and the 1973 Chilean *coup*.

Although Díaz's playwriting is varied, it does show a continuous concern with violence, be it individual or collective, verbal or physical. Following a paradigm popular in much recent Spanish-language theatre, Díaz often structures dramatic action as dangerous game-playing; for example, in *Mata a tu prójimo como a ti mismo* (Kill Thy Neighbor as Thyself), two sisters and a young man enact a sadomasochistic recreation of the past. In a world where violence has been ritualized and institutionalized, it is not surprising that Díaz's characters should play their own variations on this theme.

Despite this penchant for the violent in his theatre, Jorge Díaz is also an accomplished and prolific writer of children's dramas. These are playful in the traditional sense, filled with the magic of and nostagia for childhood. His group Trabalenguas (Tongue Twisters) was formed specifically to produce these plays.

Although summaries of Latin-American and Chilean theatre claim Jorge Díaz as their own, his many years of work in Spain and elsewhere in Europe should assure him an important place in histories of world theatre. However, like many other dramatists who write in the Spanish language, his work has not been translated sufficiently into English, thereby denying too many theatregoers access to an extraordinary talent and an acute social critic.

—Kirsten F. Nigro

See also *Volume 1* entry on *Elcepillo de dientes*.

DORST, Tankred. Born in Oberland bei Sonneberg, Thuringia, Germany, 19 December 1925. Educated at Volkschule and Gymnasium. Drafted into the German army, 1942; on the Western front, 1944; prisoner-of-war in England, USA, and Belgium, 1945–47. Finished school

studies, 1950; studied German and art history in Bamberg, 1950–52; history and drama at the University of Munich, 1952–56 (did not take final examinations). Began working at the Munich student puppet theatre Das Kleine Spiel, 1953, for which he wrote six plays by 1959; worked for a number of publishing companies during the 1960's and 1970's; first play for legitimate stage, *Die Kurve*, produced 1960; first collaboration with the director Peter Zadek, 1960; achieved international recognition with *Grosse Schmährede an der Stadtmauer*, produced in 1961; in Rome on a fellowship, 1962; travelled to Algeria, 1964; writer in residence, Oberlin College, USA, 1970; visited Australia and New Zealand, 1973, India, 1978, Brazil, 1984, Mexico, 1985; visiting professor, Gesamthochschule, Kassel, 1986–87; travelled extensively in South America, 1984–85, and 1989. Recipient: Mannheim Nationaltheater Prize, 1959; Gerhart Hauptmann Prize (Berlin Volksbühne), 1964; Adolf Grimme Prize, 1969, 1970; Prix Italia, 1970; Bavarian Academy of Fine Art Literature Prize, and the Belgian Prix de l'Age d'Or for the film *Eisenhans*; Rhineland Palatinate Carl Zuckmayer Medal, 1987; Carl Schaeffer Playwrights Award (New York), 1987; Mulheim Drama Prize, 1989. Fellow of the German Academy of Language and Literature, Darmstadt, 1978; Fellow of Academy of Science and Literature, Mainz.

Works

Collections

Grosse Schmährede an der Stadtmauer; Freiheit für Clemens; Die Kurve. 1962.
Stücke (2 vols.), edited by Gerhart Menschling. 1978.
Werkausgabe (4 vols.). 1985–87:
  1. *Dorothea Merz; Klaras Mutter; Heinrich; oder, Die Schmerzen der Phantasie; Die Villa; Mosch: Ein Film; Auf dem Chimborazo.*
  2. *Merlin; oder, Das wüste Land*, with Ursula Ehler.
  3. *Frühe Stücke* (includes *Der Kater; Gesellschaft im Herbst; Die Kurve; Grosse Schmährede an der Stadtmauer; Rameaus Neffe; Der Richter von London*).
  4. *Politische Stücke* (includes *Toller; Sand; Kleiner Mann, was nun; Eiszeit; Goncourt, oder, Die Abschaffung des Todes; "Ergänzungen zu Toller"*).

Stage Works

Aucussin und Nicolette (puppet play; produced by Das Kleine Spiel, Munich, 1953).
Rhampsinit (puppet play; produced by Das Kleine Spiel, Munich, 1954).
Der gestiefelte Kater, from the play by Tieck (puppet play; produced by Das Kleine Spiel, Munich, 1955). In *Auf kleiner Bühne*, 1959; stage version (produced Max Reinhardt Seminar, Schönbrunner Schlosstheater, Vienna, 1962), 1963; revised version, as *Der Kater; oder, Wie man das Spiel spielt* (produced Stadttheater, Bad Godesberg, 1979), in *Stücke 1*, 1978; operatic version, with music by Günter Bialas (produced by the Hamburgische Staatsoper, Schwetzingen, 1975).
Eugen (puppet play; produced by Das Kleine Spiel, Munich, 1956). In *Auf kleiner Bühne*, 1959.
La Ramée, music by Wilhelm Killmayer (puppet play; produced by Das Kleine Spiel, Munich 1957). In *Auf kleiner Bühne*, 1959.
A Trumpet for Nap, music by Wilhelm Killmayer (puppet play; produced by Das Kleine Spiel, Munich, 1959). In *Auf kleine Bühne*, 1959.

Die Kurve (produced Bühnen der Hansestadt, Lübeck, 1960). 1959 ("Bühnenmanuskript"); in *Modernes deutsches Theater*, edited by Paul Pörtner, 1961; translated as *The Curve*, in *New Theatre of Europe 3*, edited by Robert W. Corrigan, 1968.

Gesellschaft im Herbst (produced Nationaltheater, Mannheim, 1960; revised version, produced Kammerspiele, Hamburg, 1961). 1960 ("Bühnenmanuskript"); revised version, in *Junges deutsches Theater von heute*, edited by Joachim Schöndorff, 1961.

La Buffonata, music by Wilhelm Killmayer (produced Liederhalle, Stuttgart, 1960). 1961.

Freiheit für Clemens (produced by the Städtische Bühnen, Studio am alten Markt, Bielefeld, 1960). 1960 ("Bühnenmanuskript"); in *Grosse Schmährede an der Stadtmauer. . .* (collection), 1962.

Grosse Schmährede an der Stadtmauer (produced Bühnen der Hansestadt, Lübeck, 1961). In *Theater heute*, December 1961; in book form, in *Grosse Schmährede an der Stadtmauer . . .* (collection), 1962.

Rameaus Neffe, from a novel by Diderot (produced Städtische Bühnen, Nuremberg, 1963). 1963.

Philemon (produced Schiller-Theater, Berlin, 1963).

Die Mohrin, music by Wilhelm Killmayer, from the puppet play *Aucussin und Nicolette* (produced Städtische Bühnen, Frankfurt, 1964). 1964; operatic version, as *Die Geschichte von Aucassin und Nicolette*, music by Günter Bialas (produced Bayerische Staatsoper, Munich, 1975).

Yolimba; oder, Die Grenzen der Magie, music by Wilhelm Killmayer (produced Hessische Staatstheater, Wiesbaden, 1964; revised version produced Theater am Gärtnerplatz, Munich, 1970). 1965.

Der Richter von London, from Thomas Dekker's *The Shoemaker's Holiday* (produced Städtische Bühnen, Essen, 1966). 1966 ("Bühnenmanuskript"); in *Stücke 1*, 1978.

Der Geizige, from Molière's *L'Avare* (produced Württembergisches Staatstheater, Stuttgart, 1967). 1967 ("Bühnenmanuskript"); in *Molière: Drei Stücke*, 1978.

Wittek geht um (produced Stadttheater, Düsseldorf, and Stadttheater, Bern, 1967).

Der Pott, lyrics by Karl Wessler, from O'Casey's *The Silver Tassie* (produced Schauspielhaus, Wuppertal, 1967). In *Sean O'Casey: Stücke 1920–1940*, 1973.

Toller (produced Württembergisches Staatstheater, Stuttgart, 1968). 1968.

Der eingebildete Kranke, from Molière's *Le Malade imaginaire* (produced Kassel, 1969). 1968 ("Bühnenmanuskript"); in *Molière: Drei Stücke*, 1978.

Dem Gegner den Daumen aufs Auge und das Knie auf die Brust (produced Westfälisches Landestheater, Castrop-Rauxel in Soest, 1969).

Kleiner Mann, was nun?, with Peter Zadek, from the novel by Hans Fallada (produced Schauspielhaus, Bochum, 1972). 1972.

Eiszeit, with Ursula Ehler (produced Schauspielhaus, Bochum, 1973). 1972 ("Bühnenmanuskript"); 1973.

Auf dem Chimborazo, with Ursula Ehler (produced Schlosspark Theater, Berlin, 1975). 1974 ("Bühnenmanuskript"); 1975.

Goncourt; oder, Die Abschaffung des Todes, with Horst Laube (produced Schauspielhaus, Frankfurt, 1977). In *Stücke 1*, 1978.

George Dandin, from Molière's play (produced Festspiele, Bad-Hersfeld, 1977). 1977 ("Bühnenmanuskript"); in *Molière: Drei Stücke*, 1978.

Die Villa, with Ursula Ehler (produced Württembergisches Staatstheater, Stuttgart, and Schauspielhaus, Düsseldorf, 1980). 1979 ("Bühnenmanuskript"); in *Theater* (*Theater heute* yearbook), 1979; in book form, 1980.

Merlin; oder, Das wüste Land (produced Schauspielhaus, Düsseldorf, 1981). 1981.

Ameley, der Biber und der König auf dem Dach (for children; produced Burgtheater, Vienna, 1982). 1982 ("Bühnenmanuskript").

Der verbotene Garten: Fragmente über D'Annunzio, with Ursula Ehler (produced St. Gallen, 1987). 1983.

Heinrich; oder, Die Schmerzen der Phantasie, with Ursula Ehler, from the radio play *Fragmente einer Reise nach Stettin* (produced Schauspielhaus, Düsseldorf, 1985; revised version produced Residenztheater, Munich, 1986). 1984 ("Bühnenmanuskript"); in *Spectaculum*, 40, 1985; also in *Werkausgabe 1*, 1985.

Der Bürger als Edelmann, from Molière's *Le Bourgeois Gentilhomme* (produced Deutsches Schauspielhaus, Hamburg, 1986). 1985 ("Bühnenmanuskript").

Ich, Feuerbach, with Ursula Ehler (produced Residenztheater, Munich, 1986). 1986.

Grindkopf, with Ursula Ehler (libretto; produced Schülerklub des Schauspiels, Frankfurt, 1988). 1986.

Wie im Leben wie in Traum, with Ursula Ehler. 1987 ("Bühnenmanuskript").

Korbes, with Ursula Ehler (produced Deutsches Schauspielhaus, Hamburg, 1987). 1987 ("Bühnenmanuskript"); 1988.

Parzifal: Auf der anderen Seite des Sees, with Robert Wilson and Ursula Ehler (produced Thalia Theater, Hamburg, 1987). In *Programmheft 21* (booklet accompanying premiere), 1987; in book form, 1990.

Screenplays

Eisenhans, 1983.

Television Plays

A Trumpet for Nap, 1961; *Die Kurve*, 1961; *Die Schelminnen*, from the play *La Buffonata*, 1962; *Grosse Schmährede an der Stadtmauer*, 1961; *Der Richter von London*, 1966; *Aucussin und Nicolette*, 1967; *Rotmord; oder, I Was a German*, from the play *Toller*, 1969; *Piggies*, 1970; *Der Pott*, 1971; *Sand*, 1971 (published 1971); *Kleiner Mann, was nun?*, 1973; *Die scharlachrote Buchstabe*, from a story by Nathaniel Hawthorne, 1973; *Eiszeit*, 1975; *Dorothea Merz*, with Ursula Ehler, 1976 (published 1976); *Auf dem Chimborazo*, 1977; *Klaras Mutter*, with Ursula Ehler, 1978 (published 1978); *Mosch*, with Ursula Ehler, 1980 (published 1980); *Eisenhans*, with Ursula Ehler, 1983 (published 1983); *Ameley, der Biber und der König auf dem Dach*, 1985; *Heinrich; oder, Die Schmerzen der Phantasie*, 1986.

Radio Plays

Die Kurve, 1963; *Grosse Schmährede an der Stadtmauer*, 1963; *Toller*, 1969; *Sand*, 1973; *Auf dem Chimborazo*, 1974; *Fragmente einer Reise nach Stettin*, with Ursula Ehler, 1981; *Ameley, der Biber und der König auf dem Dach*, 1982; *Der verbotene Garten*, 1984; *Ich, Feuerbach*, 1986; *Korbes*, 1987; *Grindkopf*, 1989.

Fiction

Die mehreren Zauberer (children's stories). 1966.
Dorothea Merz, with Ursula Ehler (fragment of novel). 1976.

Klaras Mutter.   1978.
Die Reise nach Stettin, with Ursula Ehler.   1984.
Der nackte Mann, with Ursula Ehler.   1986.

Other

Geheimnis der Marionette.   1957.
Auf kleine Bühne: Versuche mit Marionetten.   1959.
Rotmord; oder, I was a German (materials relating to television production).   1969.

Editor, *Die Münchener Räterepublik: Zeugnisse und Kommentar.*   1966.

*

Criticism

Books:
Cesare Cases and Claudio Magris, *L'anarchismo al bivio: Intellectuale e politica nel teatro di Dorst*, Turin, 1974.
Horst Laube (ed.), *Werkbuch über Tankred Dorst*, Frankfurt, 1974.
Rainer Taëni, *Tankred Dorst*, Frankfurt, 1977.
Monika Schattenhofer, *Eine Modellwirklichkeit: Literarisches Theater der 50er und 60er Jahre—Tankred Dorst schreibt "Toller"*, Frankfurt, Bern, and New York, 1985.
Günther Erken (ed.), *Tankred Dorst*, Frankfurt, 1989.
Richard Sheppard, *Tankred Dorst's "Toller": A Case-Study in Reception*, New Alyth, 1989.

* * *

There have been many attempts to map out the course of post-war German theatre, whether according to shifts of political concern and unconcern or according to some kind of tidy chronology of changing styles. But, whatever the shifts and whatever the chronology, there seems to be no clear place for Tankred Dorst. On occasion he seems, during some 30 years of writing for the theatre, to have converged with a prevailing trend, but the convergence has proved to be unplanned, if not, indeed, illusory.

Toller, an early success, looked like a response to political upheavals in and around 1968, and the note of scepticism about the artist's role in revolution looked like Dorst's contribution to a current debate; but work on the play had started years earlier—and the question of the artist's role was—and has remained—a matter of enduring urgency for Dorst rather than a topical issue. Similarly *Merlin*, the eight-hour reworking of Arthurian legend, seemed in the early 1980's to be part of a general retreat from political theatre, but Dorst himself has emphasised the links with his own lifelong interest in myth and fairy tale. And there are in *Korbes*, a recent succes, hints of plays and films set in dour, brutalised, rural German backwoods, but Dorst had begun to sketch out the play some ten years earlier and in his hands that harsh world faces a different, visionary world on stage.

Dorst's singular and singularly undefinable position in German theatre arises, in part, from the fact that he crosses familiar boundaries, exploring the complementarity and the interactive role of differing media commonly kept apart. He adapts and re-adapts the same material for different forms: *Toller* was first heard as a radio-documentary, was worked up simultaneously as a play and, with Peter Zadek, as a television documentary (*Rotmord*), and was subsequently re-arranged for radio and excerpted as a reading on stage. At a

certain level, moreover, different media interact within a single multi-media project. In 1973 Dorst began to plan a seven-stage extended family chronicle, overlapping with his own life, in particular his early years in a village in Thuringia. The project, not yet completed, has produced six works published together as *Deutsche Stücke* (*Werkausgabe 1*, 1985), in which linked personal histories are chronicled through the contrasting perspectives of three plays, a film-script, a novel, and a prose sketch. In a sense, then, Dorst is not an orthodox writer for the theatre because theatrical, televisual, cinematic, and radiophonic possibilities may be being pursued in parallel. The text may, on occasion, be more a vehicle for performance than an independent entity.

Dorst has, indeed, never underestimated the role of performance, the extent to which words are provisional until enacted. Nevertheless—and despite his manifest love of film-making and stage-production—Dorst's plays in print are not verbal artefacts bereft of a visual dimension. Visible performance is written into the printed word. Thus his most elaborate work, *Merlin*, appeared in book form before it was staged, but the spectacle, the palpable decline of Arthur's world, is vividly present in the book. More simply, the collision between an other-wordly vision and the meticulously described frenzies of Korbes, the wretched peasant blinded overnight, is at the heart of Dorst's text.

If an Arthurian panorama is, for all its unwieldiness, celebrating physical, visible theatre, it is also expressing a theme to which Dorst has frequently returned. Merlin the magician, whose central importance is reflected in the title, fails to create a valid communal Utopia. His failure is that of an artist unable to reshape reality and of a social engineer sceptical about social engineering. That scepticism has deep roots in Dorst's writing. Years earlier it had informed the insights and the failure of the artist-turned-politician Toller who, in Dorst's play (and Dorst has admitted to a close sympathy with his central figure), confronts and distances himself from the "professional" revolutionaries in the abortive Munich uprising of 1919.

The artist, creating realities as well as being in reality, is a character in conflict, a conflict which the stage can make visible. Thus *Eiszeit* and *Der verbotene Garten* centre on creative artists whose creativity has proved suspect and dangerous. The Old Man in *Eiszeit*, withdrawn into his own "Ice Age", is clearly modelled on Knut Hamsun, Nobel-prizewinner-turned-Nazi-collaborator; in *Der verbotene Garten* Gabriele D'Annunzio, decadent-turned-fascist, is presented through his own grotesque visions. Both plays withhold from condemnation (critics have repeatedly charged Dorst with being non-commital, a charge he has not sought to rebut other than by doubting the dramatist's right or duty to superior judgement). Both plays are structured according to what Dorst, with regard to *Der verbotene Garten*, has called a dramaturgy of pictures rather than a dramaturgy of plot.

In a recent, much-performed play, *Ich, Feuerbach*, Dorst has retained the figure of the artist but shifted the ground nearer to home, as it were, and onto a psychological plane. It is a play about theatre, a monologue-play in which an actor, seven years without an engagement, faces a last-chance audition which never materialises, and he uses the long wait to reflect bitterly on the perils and paradoxes of his profession.

Dorst's scepticism about solutions and his aversion to labels are not negative virtues because they are inseparable from an experiment in the form (the "pictures" rather than the "plot") and in the expressive resources of theatre. The variety that results is striking: there can be few greater contrasts than that between the eight-hour panorama of *Merlin* and the monologue-drama *Ich, Feuerbach*. Nor is the variety in

Dorst's work exhausted by that particular contrast. The six parts of the *Deutsche Stücke* exhibit what Dorst has called a hard-won realism, a realism against the grain of his own temperament. Here the experiment lies not in the use of theatre but in the juxtaposition of different media, each exploited for its own brand of close-up, undemonstrative observation. Here too there is no finalised verdict on people —as early as 1972 Dorst expressed a strong preference for the open-ended portrayals of Chekhov and Gorky—and there is no commitment to a single form of drama. As Dorst once observed, "a play is always unfinished".

—Philip Brady

DRUTEN, John van.   See **VAN DRUTEN, John**.

DRYDEN, John. Born in Aldwincle All Saints, Northamptonshire, England, 9 August 1631. Educated at Westminster School, London (king's scholar), c.1644–50; Trinity College, Cambridge (pensioner), 1650–55, BA 1654. Married Lady Elizabeth Howard in 1663; three sons. Moved to London, 1657; possibly held minor clerical post in Cromwell's government, 1657; first-produced play, *The Wild Gallant*, staged 1663; shareholder, King's Company, 1668–77; joined Roman Catholic church, c.1685, at accession of James II; lost his royal offices at accession of William and Mary, 1689. Member, Royal Society, 1660. Poet Laureate, 1668–88; Historiographer Royal, 1670–88. Died in London, 1 May 1700.

Works

Collections

Works (4 vols.).   1695
Comedies, Tragedies, and Operas (2 vols.).   1701.
The Works, edited by Sir Walter Scott (18 vols.).   1808; revised edition, edited by George Saintsbury, 1882–93.
Dramatic Works, edited by Montague Summers (6 vols.). 1931–32.
Works (Clark Edition). edited by Edward N. Hooker, H.T. Swedenberg Jr., and others.   1956–
Four Comedies, Four Tragedies (2 vols.; includes *Secret Love; Sir Martin Mar-All; An Evening's Love; Marriage à-la-Mode; The Indian Emperor; Aureng-Zebe; All for Love; Don Sebastian)*, edited by L.A. Beaurline and Fredson Bowers.   1967.
A Selection, edited by John Conaghan.   1978.
(Selections), edited by Keith Walker.   1987.

Stage Works

The Wild Gallant (produced Theatre Royal, Vere Street, London, 1663).   1669.
The Indian Queen, with Sir Robert Howard (produced

John Dryden (portrait by James Maubert).

Theatre Royal, Bridges Street, London, 1664).   In *Four New Plays*, by Howard, 1665.
The Rival Ladies (produced Theatre Royal, Bridges Street, London, 1664).   1664.
The Indian Emperor; or, The Conquest of Mexico by the Spaniards, Being the Sequel of The Indian Queen (produced Theatre Royal, Bridges Street, London, 1665). 1667.
Secret Love; or, The Maiden Queen (produced Theatre Royal, Bridges Street, London, 1667).   1668.
Sir Martin Mar-All; or, The Feigned Innocence, from a translation by William Cavendish of a play by Molière (produced Lincoln's Inn Fields Theatre, London, 1667).   1668.
The Tempest; or, The Enchanted Island, with William Davenant, from the play by Shakespeare (produced Lincoln's Inn Fields Theatre, London, 1667).   1670.
An Evening's Love; or, The Mock Astrologer (produced Theatre Royal, Bridges Street, London, 1668).   1671.
Tyrannic Love; or, The Royal Martyr (produced Theatre Royal, Bridges Street, London, 1669).   1670.
The Conquest of Granada by the Spaniards, 2 parts (produced Theatre Royal, Bridges Street, London, 1670, 1671). 1672.
Marriage à-la-Mode (produced Lincoln's Inn Fields Theatre, London, 1672).   1673.
The Assignation; or, Love in a Nunnery (produced Lincoln's Inn Fields Theatre, London, 1672).   1673.
Amboyna (produced Lincoln's Inn Fields Theatre, London, 1673).   1673.
The Mistaken Husband, one scene by Dryden (produced Theatre Royal, Drury Lane, London, 1674).   1675.

Aureng-Zebe (produced Theatre Royal, Drury Lane, London, 1675).   1676.
The State of Innocence and Fall of Man.   1677.
All for Love; or, The World Well Lost from *Antony and Cleopatra* by Shakespeare (produced Theatre Royal, Drury Lane, London, 1677).   1678.
The Kind Keeper; or, Mr. Limberham (produced Dorset Garden Theatre, London, 1678).   1680.
Oedipus, with Nathaniel Lee (produced Dorset Garden Theatre, London, 1678).   1679.
Troilus and Cressida; or, Truth Found Too Late, from the play by Shakespeare (produced Dorset Garden Theatre, London, 1679).   1679.
The Spanish Friar; or, The Double Discovery (produced Dorset Garden Theatre, London, 1680).   1681.
The Duke of Guise, with Nathaniel Lee (produced Theatre Royal, Drury Lane, London, 1682).   1683.
Albion and Albanius, music by Lewis Grabu (produced Dorset Garden Theatre, London, 1685).   1685.
Don Sebastian, King of Portugal (produced Theatre Royal, Drury Lane, London, 1689).   1690.
Amphitryon; or, The Two Socias (produced Theatre Royal, Drury Lane, London, 1690).   1690.
King Arthur; or, The British Worthy, music by Henry Purcell (produced Dorset Garden Theatre, London, 1691).   1691.
Cleomenes, The Spartan Hero, completed by Thomas Southerne (produced Theatre Royal, Drury Lane, London, 1692).   1692.
Love Triumphant; or, Nature Will Prevail (produced Theatre Royal, Drury Lane, London, 1694).
The Secular Masque, in *The Pilgrim*, by Vanbrugh (produced Theatre Royal, Drury Lane, London, 1700).   1700.

Verse

Heroic Stanzas to the Memory of Oliver, Late Lord Protector, in *Three Poems upon the Death of His Late Highness Oliver, Lord Protector*, with Waller and Sprat.   1659.
Astraea Redux: A Poem on the Happy Restoration and Return of His Sacred Majesty Charles the Second.   1660.
To His Sacred Majesty: A Panegyric on His Coronation.   1661.
To My Lord Chancellor, Presented on New Year's Day.   1662.
Annus Mirabilis, The Year of Wonders 1666: An Historical Poem.   1667.
Ovid's Epistles, with others.   1680.
Absalom and Achitophel.   1681; *Second Part*, with Nahum Tate, 1682.
The Medal: A Satire Against Sedition.   1682.
Mac Flecknoe; or, A Satire upon the True-Blue-Protestant Poet T[homas] S[hadwell].   1682.
Religio Laici; or, A Layman's Faith.   1682.
Miscellany Poems, with others.   1684; *Sylvae; or, The Second Part*, 1685; *Examen Poeticum, Being the Third Part*, 1693; *The Annual Miscellany, Being the Fourth Part*, 1694; *Fifth Part*, 1703, and *Sixth Part*, 1709, edited by Nicholas Rowe.
Threnodia Augustalis: A Funeral-Pindaric Poem Sacred to the Happy Memory of King Charles II.   1685.
The Hind and the Panther.   1687.
A Song for St. Cecilia's Day 1687.   1687.
Britannia Rediviva: A Poem on the Birth of the Prince.   1688.
Eleonora: A Panegyrical Poem Dedicated to the Memory of the Late Countess of Abingdon.   1692.
The Satires of Juvenal, with others, *Together with the Satires of Persius.*   1693.

An Ode on the Death of Henry Purcell.   1696.
The Works of Virgil, Containing His Pastorals, Georgics, and Aeneis.   1697.
Alexander's Feast; or, The Power of Music: An Ode in Honour of St. Cecilia's Day.   1697.
Fables Ancient and Modern.   1700.
Ovid's Art of Love, Book 1, translated.   1709.
Hymns Attributed to Dryden, edited by George Rapall and George Reuben Potter.   1937.
Prologues and Epilogues, edited by William B. Gardner.   1951.
Poems (4 vols.), edited by James Kinsley.   1958.

Memoirs and Letters

Letters, edited by Charles E. Ward.   1942.

Other

Of Dramatic Poesy: An Essay.   1668; revised edition 1684.
Notes and Observations on the Empress of Morocco by Settle, with John Crowne and Thomas Shadwell.   1674.
His Majesty's Declaration Defended.   1681.
The Vindication.   1683.
A Defence of An Essay of Dramatic Poesy.   1688.
Critical and Miscellaneous Prose Works, edited by Edmond Malone (4 vols.).   1800.
Essays, edited by W.P. Ker. (2 vols.).   1900.
"Of Dramatic Poesy" and Other Essays, edited by George Watson.   1962.
Literary Criticism, edited by A.C. Kirsch.   1966.

Editor, *The Art of Poetry*, by Nicolas Boileau, translated by William Soames, revised edition.   1683.

Translator, *The History of the League*, by Louis Maimbourg.   1684.
Translator, *The Life of St. Francis Xavier*, by Dominick Bouhours.   1688.
Translator, with Knightly Chetwood, *Miscellaneous Essays*, by Saint-Evremond.   1692.
Translator, *De arte graphica: The Art of Painting*, by C.A. De Fresnoy.   1695.
Translator, with others, *The Annals and History of Tacitus*, (vol. 1).   1698.

*

Bibliographies

Hugh Macdonald, *John Dryden: A Bibliography of Early Editions and of Drydeniana*, Oxford, 1939.
John A. Zamonski, *An Annotated Bibliography of John Dryden: Texts and Studies 1949–1973*, New York and London, 1975.
David J. Latt and Samuel Holt Monk, *John Dryden: A Survey and Bibliography of Critical Studies 1895–1974*, Minneapolis, 1976.
James M. Hall, *John Dryden: A Reference Guide*, Boston, 1984.

Criticism

Books
Margaret Sherwood, *Dryden's Dramatic Theory and Practice*, London, 1898; reprinted, 1966.

Bevin John Pendlebury, *Dryden's Heroic Plays: A Study of the Origins*, London, 1923.

T.S. Eliot, *Dryden: The Poet, The Dramatist, The Critic*, New York, 1932.

Ned Bliss Allen, *The Sources of John Dryden's Comedies*, Ann Arbor, Michigan, 1935; reprinted, 1967.

J.M. Osborn, *John Dryden: Some Biographical Facts and Problems*, New York, 1940; revised edition, Gainesville, Florida, 1965.

William Frost, *Dryden and the Art of Translation*, New Haven, Connecticut, 1955.

Bonamy Dobrée, *John Dryden*, London, 1956.

Charles E. Ward, *The Life of John Dryden*, Raleigh, North Carolina, 1961.

John M. Aden, *The Critical Opinions of Dryden: A Dictionary*, 1963.

Frank Harper Moore, *The Nobler Pleasure: Dryden's Comedy in Theory and Practice*, Chapel Hill, North Carolina, 1963.

B.N. Schilling (ed.), *John Dryden: A Collection of Critical Essays*, Englewood Cliffs, New Jersey, 1963.

A.W. Verrall, *Lectures on Dryden*, New York, 1963.

Arthur C. Kirsch, *Dryden's Heroic Drama*, Princeton, New Jersey, 1965.

George R. Wasserman, *John Dryden*, New York, 1965.

Selma Assir Zebouni, *John Dryden: A Study in Heroic Characterization*, Baton Rouge, Louisiana, 1965.

H.T. Swedenberg, Jr. (ed.), *Essential Articles for the Study of Dryden*, London, 1966.

Bruce King, *John Dryden's Major Plays*, Edinburgh and London, 1966.

Bruce King (ed.), *John Dryden's Mind and Art*, London, 1969.

Earl Miner (ed.), *John Dryden*, London, 1972.

Dennis Davison, *John Dryden*, London, 1968.

Phillip Harth, *Contexts of Dryden's Thought*, Chicago and London, 1968.

Anne T. Barbeau, *The Intellectual Design of Dryden's Heroic Plays*, New Haven, Connecticut, 1970.

Robert D. Hume, *Dryden's Criticism*, Ithaca (New York) and London, 1970.

James Kinsley and Helen Kinsley (eds.), *John Dryden: The Critical Heritage*, New York, 1971.

William Myers, *John Dryden*, London, 1973.

Joan Carroll Grace, *Tragic Theory in the Critical Works of Thomas Rymer, John Dennis, and Dryden*, 1975.

Richard Leslie Larson, *Studies in Dryden's Dramatic Technique*, 1975.

E. Pechter, *Dryden's Classical Theory of Literature*, London, 1975.

David Wykes, *A Preface to Dryden*, London, 1977.

George McFadden, *John Dryden: The Public Writer 1660–1685*, Princeton, New Jersey, 1978.

G. Douglas Atkins, *The Faith of Dryden: Change and Continuity*, Lexington, Kentucky, 1980.

Derek Hughes, *Dryden's Heroic Plays*, London, 1981.

Ruth Salvaggio, *Dryden's Dualities*, Victoria, British Columbia, 1983.

Judith Sloman, *Dryden: The Poetics of Translation*, Toronto, 1985.

David Hopkins, *John Dryden*, Cambridge, 1986.

James Anderson Winn, *John Dryden and His World*, New Haven, Connecticut, 1987.

*   *   *

John Dryden was the towering figure among English play-wrights between the Restoration and his death in 1700. He may not have written the best plays in all the prominent dramatic genres in that period, but he certainly tried his hand successfully at most of them. In the 28 plays which he either wrote by himself or in collaboration with other authors, as original dramatic pieces or adaptations from classical drama-tists and Shakespeare, he was always in the forefront of theatrical and literary developments. Dryden's status as a professional writer in the widening public sphere of the later 17th century may now have come to rest more on his political satire or his poetry, or even his translations from Chaucer and Greek and Roman authors. But his writing for the English stage of his time covered most of his literary career during three decades, from the production of his first comedy, *The Wild Gallant*, to his last, *Love Triumphant*, with which he took his leave of an unsympathetic audience after his fall from royal and popular favour at the Glorious Revolution.

Dryden's prolific output for the theatre significantly in-cluded the first English sketch of a theory of the drama—in numerous dedications, prefaces, prologues and epilogues to his plays, and, most importantly, in his essay *Of Dramatic Poesy*, the first major document of neoclassical drama criti-cism in Britain. Though much of this criticism was occasional in scope, it still added up to a consistent theory of plays as images of "nature" as well as of some representative forms of late 17th century English theatre, especially the heroic play.

As a professional playwright, Dryden started off in the fashionable new genres of the early Restoration era, in the comedy of manners, heroic plays, and operas. His reliance on audience taste was a more serious matter than for most other playwrights of his day, since in his social status he was placed ambiguously on the periphery of the Court Wits' circle under Charles II. He came from a Puritan family and only estab-lished a personal link with the gentry by marrying Sir Robert Howard's sister after the Restoration, rising quickly in royal favour to become poet laureate and Historiographer Royal and converting to the Duke of York's (the later James II's) Roman Catholic faith. Dryden's identification with the Court Wits had to survive various controversies with "the mob of gentlemen who wrote with ease" (as Pope described them) that affected his success on the two stages in London.

His comic plays spanned most of his career in drama, while he wrote heroic plays for only a decade, afterwards changing over to Shakespearean adaptations and neoclassical trage-dies. Thus, he produced most plays in the field that came lowest on the scale of normative classicist poetics to which, in theory, he subscribed, like most of his contemporaries. In the preface to his comedy *An Evening's Love* Dryden did his best to sound casual about his favourite genre: "Neither . . . do I value a reputation gain'd from Comedy, . . . for I think it, in it's own nature, inferior to all sorts of Dramatick writing". In view of this attitude, the range of Dryden's comedies is as surprising as their considerable, if uneven, achievement. He contributed to almost all popular kinds of Restoration com-edy, basing his comic theory on a redefinition of Ben Jonson's idea of humour, seeing it as a "ridiculous extravagance of conversation, wherein one man differs from all others".

From the first comedy onwards, it was the comic dialogue and the skilful manipulation of a great variety of idiosyncratic characters that defines Dryden's comic art more justly than the strict plotting of French neoclassical drama. In the central loving couple in *Secret Love*, Florimell and Celadon, Dryden transformed the sexual antagonism of some Elizabethan com-edies into the (heterosexual) "gay couple" of Restoration comedy with its witty repartee as well as its libertinism. But perhaps only *Sir Martin Mar-All* and *Marriage à-la-Mode* came close to the standard of the comedy of manners with its genteel setting in fashionable contemporary life and a hierarchy of easily differentiated characters. Dryden's penchant went more towards the juxtaposition of high idealized passion and the routine cynical naturalism that was the striking characteristic of early Restoration comedy. In his plays *Secret Love* and *Marriage à-la-Mode* there are double plots that express this complementary view of human nature. These plays could be called high farce, at least in their anti-romantic plots, whereas in comedies like *The Kind Keeper; or, Mr. Limberham* Dryden approached pure farce.

Dryden established another positive relationship to earlier English drama in tragicomedies on the model of Fletcher. His adaptations were from divergent sources. He rewrote Shakespeare's *The Tempest* as a tragicomic opera and adapted *Amphitryon* from Plautus' Latin. *The Spanish Friar* was a more highly original tragicomedy among Dryden's later plays.

In tune with the received hierarchy of dramatic forms, Dryden's most consistent work for the stage concerned the new heroic drama based on Renaissance and modern prose romances and French classical tragedy. Ever since *The Indian Queen*, written jointly with his brother-in-law Sir Robert Howard, Dryden was the pre-eminent author in this short-lived but long-lasting dramatic mode. This play, like its successor *Tyrannic Love*, employs all the familiar conventions of the genre: the central conflict of love and valour, the black-and-white *dramatis personae* who are either villains or walking ideals, the elevated imagery, often turning into rant in the heroes' monologues, the neatly rhymed heroic couplets, and the appeal to a taste for romance and projective identification.

In this kind of writing, *The Conquest of Granada* is Dryden's most sustained attempt at asserting heroic values in distinctly non-heroic times, the price for the idealized abstraction being paid by a heightening of rhetorical expression that always threatened to fall into the absurdities its detractors noticed and that paved the way for later demotic kinds of literary wish-fulfilment. Undeterred by hostile criticism and popular parodies of his heroic writing, Dryden wrote a final rhymed heroic play, *Aureng-Zebe*, where he curbed some of the declamatory exuberance of his earlier ventures while following the familiar pattern in its stock characters, its adherence to poetic justice, and the complications suffered by the noble lovers. Dryden's final transition from heroic drama to neoclassical tragedy proper was marked by an unperformed adaptation of Milton's epic *Paradise Lost*, rewritten as a rhymed opera, *The State of Innocence*.

It seems a fair measure of Dryden's stature as a playwright that his most ambitious tragedies should be his adaptations of Shakespeare's *Troilus and Cressida* and *Antony and Cleopatra* (the latter as *All for Love*). While here he departed from the strict artificialities of his earlier heroic verse and adopted Shakespeare's blank verse, the general drift of his adaptations was still towards the regularization of what seemed to Dryden the poetic effusions of a less civilized age. He imposed, most of all, the three unities of French neoclassical criticism on Shakespeare's originals and elevated their central characters to heroic level; but he did not deprive them of their tragic dimension. Mainly for this reason, *All for Love* is the only one of Dyrden's serious plays, and of the tragedies of his period, to have held the stage until the 20th century. In these tragedies, Dryden tried to adjust the rulés of the ancients to an English audience, and he did this without any of the neoclassical didacticism favoured by most tragic writers of his time.

None of the later efforts by Dryden in the field of tragedy—neither his adaptations of *Oedipus* (written with Nathaniel Lee) nor his *Don Sebastian*—met with any success. His libretti for the operas *Albion and Albanius* and *King Arthur* also did not survive as texts in themselves. They demonstrate, however, that Dryden shared in most of the dominant literary and aesthetic developments in the English theatre as a professional craftsman, even if his fame now rests on other achievements.

—Bernd-Peter Lange

See also *Volume 1* entries on *All for Love*; *The Conquest of Granada, Parts One and Two*; *Marriage à-la-Mode*.

DUBÉ, Marcel. Born in Montreal, Canada, 3 January 1930. Educated at local Catholic Schools Le Jardin de l'Enfance and L'École Champlain; Jesuit Collège Saint-Marie, 1943–51; Université de Montréal, 1951–52 (studies not completed). Married Nicole Fontaine in 1956. Co-founder, the theatre group La Jeune Scène, 1950: disbanded, 1956; first play, *Le Bal triste*, produced 1950; began writing for Canadian radio, 1950; military service with the Canadian army 1951–52; achieved national recognition with the prize-winning play *Zone*, produced 1953; studied theatre in France on a scholarship, 1953–55; on return to Montreal embarked on career as professional playwright, scriptwriter, and journalist; wrote mainly for radio and television, mid 1950's–early 1960's; joined editorial board, *Écrits du Canada français*, 1958; speech-writer for Quebec Premier, Jean Lesage, c.1960; contributor, *Perspectives*, 1962–63; resident dramatist, Théâtre du Nouveau Monde, Montreal; member of the Conseil de la Langue Française (created after the election of the separatist Parti Québécois), 1976–79. Recipient of many awards, including: Dominion Drama Festival best play award, 1953; Prix Victor Morin, 1966; Prix David, 1973; Medal of the Académie Canadienne-Française, 1987. Elected to the Royal Society of Canada, 1959; member of the Académie Canadienne-Française.

Works

Collections

"De l'Autre Côté du mur" suivi de cinq courtes pièces (includes *Les Frères ennemis; L'Aiguillage; Le Père idéal; Rendez-vous du lendemain; Le Visiteur*). 1973.

Stage Works

Le Bal triste (produced by La Jeune Scène, Montreal, 1950).
De l'Autre Côté du mur (produced by La Jeune Scène, Dominion Drama Festival, Victoria, British Columbia, 1952). In *"De L'Autre Cote du mur" suivi de cinq courtes pièces*, 1973.
Zone (produced Théâtre des Compagnons, Montreal, 1953). In *Écrits du Canada français*, 2, 1955; in book form, 1956; translated as *Zone*, 1982.
Chambres à louer (produced by La Jeune Scène, Montreal, 1954).
Le Barrage (produced by the Théâtre-Club, Montreal, 1954).
Le Naufragé (produced by the Théâtre-Club, Montreal, 1955). 1971.

Un Simple Soldat, from the television play (produced Comédie-Canadienne, Montreal, 1957).   With *Le Temps des lilas*, 1958; revised version (produced Comédie-Canadienne, Montreal, 1967), 1967.

Octobre (produced Théâtre de l'Essai, Montreal, 1959).   In *Écrits du Canada français*, 17, 1964; in book form, 1977.

Florence, from the television play (produced Comédie-Canadienne, Montreal, 1960).   1960.

Le Temps des lilas (produced Théâtre Orphéum, Montreal, 1958)   With *Le Simple Soldat*, 1958; revised edition, 1967.

Bilan, from the television play (produced Comédie-Canadienne, Montreal, 1965).   1968.

Les Beaux Dimanches (produced Comédie-Canadienne, Montreal, 1965).   1968.

Au Retour des oies blanches (produced Comédie-Canadienne, Montreal, 1966).   1969; translated as *The White Geese*, 1972.

Équation à deux inconnus, from the television play (produced Théâtre de l'Égregore, Montreal, 1967).

Pauvre Amour (produced Comédie-Canadienne, Montreal, 1968).   1969.

Un Matin comme les autres (produced Comédie-Canadienne, Montreal, 1968).   1971.

Virginie (produced by Compagnie Jean Duceppe, Montreal, 1968).   1968.

La Vie quotidienne d'Antoine X (produced Congrès des Notaires, Montreal, 1968).

Hold-Up, with Louis-George Carrier (produced Théâtre de la Marjolaine, Eastman, Quebec, 1969).   1969.

Le Coup de l'étrier (produced Théâtre du Rideau Vert, Montreal, 1969).   With *Avant de t'en aller*, 1970.

Avant de t'en aller (produced Théâtre du Rideau Vert, Montreal, 1969).   With *Le Coup d'étrier*, 1970.

Paradis perdu.   With the television play, *L'Échéance du vendredi*, 1972.

Le Père idéal.   In *"De l'Autre Côté du mur" suivi de cinq courtes pièces*, 1973.

Jérémie (ballet scenario; produced Sir George Williams University, Montreal, 1973).   1973 (with English translation).

L'Aiguillage.   In *"De l'Autre Côté du mur" suivi de cinq courtes pièces*, 1973.

Les Frères ennemis.   In *"De l'Autre Côté du mur" suivi de cinq courtes pièces*, 1973.

Rendez-vous du lendemain.   In *"De l'Autre Côté du mur" suivi de cinq courtes pièces*, 1973.

Le Visiteur.   In *"De l'Autre Côté du mur" suivi de cinq courtes pièces*, 1973.

L'Impromptu de Québec; ou, Le Testament (produced by Théâtre de la Marjolaine, Eastman, Quebec, 1974).   1974.

L'Été s'appelle Julie (produced 1975).   1975.

C'était le fil de la vie (produced 1975).   1976.

Dites-le avec des fleurs, with Jean Barbeau (produced 1976).   1976.

Le Réformiste; ou, L'Honneur des hommes (produced by the Théâtre du Nouveau Monde, Montreal, 1977).   1977.

L'Amérique à sec (produced Théâtre de l'Écluse, Saint-Jean-sur-Richelieu, Quebec, 1986).   1986.

Television Plays

L'Étranger, 1953; *Zone*, 1953; *La Lettre*, 1954; *Chambres à louer*, 1954; *La Bicyclette*, 1954; *Pour Cinq Sous d'amour*, with Louis-Georges Carrier, 1955; *Florence*, 1957 (published 1970); *Un Simple Soldat*, 1957; *La Fin du rêve*, 1958; *Médée*, 1958 (published 1973); *La Cellule*, 1959 (published 1973); *Équation à deux inconnus*, 1959; *Bilan*, 1960; *La Côte de sable* (series), 1960–62; *L'Échéance du vendredi*, 1962 (published with *Paradis perdu*, 1972); *Le Temps des lilas*, 1962; *De 9 à 5* (series), 1963–65; *Entre Midi et Soir* (series), 1968–72 (extracts published as *Le Monde de Marcel Dubé*, 1971).

Radio Plays

Pleure, pauvre Guillaume, 1951; *Cartes postales*, 1951; *Pivart, le malin*, 1951; *L'Anneau*, 1952; *La Randonée fantastique*, 1953; *Un Bord de la rivière*, 1954; *Zone*, 1954; *Chambres à louer* (series), 1955–56; *Un Bouquet d'immortelles*, 1956; *La Cage*, from a work by Mac Shoub, 1959; *Octobre*, 1964; *Manuel*, 1968 (published 1973).

Verse

Poèmes de sable.   1974.

Fiction

Le Train du nord.   1961.

Other

Textes et documents.   1968; revised edition, 1973.
La Tragédie est un acte de foi (essays).   1973.

*

Bibliographies

Philippe Houyoux and others, *Théâtres québécois*, Université de Québec Centre Bibliographique, 1975.

Criticism

Books:
Edwin C. Hamblett, *Marcel Dubé and French-Canadian Drama*, New York, 1970.
Laurent Mailhot and Jean-Cléo Godin, *Le Théâtre québécois 1*, Montreal, 1970.
Maximilien Laroche, *Marcel Dubé*, Montreal, 1970.

Articles:
Edwin C. Hamblet, "The North American Outlook of Marcel Dubé and William Inge", in *Queen's Quarterly*, 77, 1970.
Claude Pelletier (ed.), *Marcel Dubé: Dossier de presse, 1965–1987*, Sherbrooke, 1988.

*   *   *

The most prolific playwright in the history of French Canada, and one of its most popular, Marcel Dubé was the first to earn his living exclusively from the dramatic scripts he has composed for stage, radio, and television. He began to write for radio in 1950 and for national television as soon as it was established, two years later. His talent for incorporating televisual techniques into stage plays soon became his signature, and throughout his career he has continued to move with great ease from one medium to the other.

Original music and songs, short cinematic sequences, and astute use of lighting characterize his theatre, most of which is tragic in atmosphere and theme. But realistic techniques and sombre settings are frequently counterbalanced by oneiric sequences, and by the interpolation of poetic speech and compelling visual symbols. Critics have generally grouped Dubé's dramatic texts into two periods, with the year 1960 representing their demarcation. Thus the first period deals with young, culturally deprived, and economically disadvantaged characters in urban, proletarian settings, whereas the second period, paralleling Dubé's own socio-economic evolution, focuses on middle-class characters, values, and concerns. If not followed slavishly, this grouping is useful. But a third period is now evident as well, covering the lighter, satirical texts he has favoured since the mid-1970's.

Dubé's third play, *Zone*, first brought him to national attention, winning the prize for best play at the Dominion Drama Festival in Victoria, British Columbia. Produced on radio and television within a short time, it marked, as surely as Gélinas' *Tit-Coq* had five years previously, a new direction in French-Canadian dramaturgy. It was a period when Quebec was beset by worsening social problems and obsessed by its own search for identity. The difficult transition from the closed, provincial society of the pre-war period to the more liberal, internationalist world of the 1950's brought unfamiliar tensions to conservative, Catholic Quebec—tensions exacerbated by the reactionary political regime of Maurice Duplessis, premier of Quebec from 1944. In Tarzan, the youthful protagonist of *Zone*, many concerned Québécois saw a symbol of their own dissatisfaction.

Un Simple Soldat, Dubé's most influential work, added dimension and nuance to his portrayal of the combined effects of heredity and milieu, of social reaction and political repression. Ironically, the playwright who was perceived in the 1950's as an iconoclastic model for his generation is now almost universally regarded in Quebec as outdated, far too tame in his demands and too muted in his indignation.

Un Simple Soldat and *Florence* are representative also of a major problem posed for retrospective critical assessment of Dubé's work: the former was televised in one version in 1957, considerably reworked for stage performance in 1958, published in the stage version the same year, then in a radically different one in 1967. Similarly, *Florence* was produced on television in 1957, published in one version in 1958, adapted for stage in 1960 and published in a second, significantly different version in 1970. To varying degrees, all of his plays which have travelled from stage to screen or vice-versa (and this includes most of them) exhibit similar reworking, for Dubé refuses to accept a text as static.

Le Temps des lilas marks the end of his first period; *Bilan* marks the beginning of the second, in which *nouveau-riche* adults display the vilest of human qualities in their amoral pursuit of power and status. *Les Beaux Dimanches* and *Au Retour des oies blanches* are the most important works of this period. The latter, translated and performed in English as *The White Geese*, is generally considered Dubé's finest drama, classic in theme, in form, and in atmosphere. Since the election of the separatist Parti Québécois in 1976, Dubé, like many another Quebec playwright, has composed nothing to equal his earlier successes, turning instead to light comedy, social satire, and romantic drama, some of it written in collaboration. His recent play, *L'Amérique à sec*, is illustrative of this third vein.

As Dubé appears, despite his relative youth, to be nearing the end of his creative period, a critical re-assessment of his role in the establishment of a modern, self-confident Québécois dramaturgy seems essential. Such reassessment will surely assign him a smaller, but still central role in the creation of that dramatic tradition.

—Leonard E. Doucette

See also *Volume 1* entry on *The White Geese*.

DUMAS *fils*, Alexandre. Born in Paris, 28 July 1824, the illegitimate son of the writer Alexandre Dumas *père*. Educated at the Pension Goubaux and the Collège Bourbon. Had daughter by Nadejda Naryschkine, 1860; married: 1) Nadejda Knorring (maiden name of Nadejda Naryschkine) in 1864 (died 1895), one more daughter; 2) Henriette Régnier de la Brière, 1895. Lived with father in Saint-Germain-en-Laye, 1843–51; travelled with father to Spain and Algeria, 1846–47; first-produced play, *La Dame aux camélias*, staged 1852; wrote for the Théâtre du Gymnase, and later in career, for the Comédie-Française. Elected to the Académie Française, 1875. Died in Marly-le-Roi, 28 November 1895.

Works

Collections

Théâtre complet (7 vols.).   1868–92.
Théâtre des autres (2 vols.; includes collaborative works). 1894.
Théâtre complet (10 vols.).   1923.

Stage Works

Atala, music by P. Varney.   1848.
La Dame aux camélias (produced Théâtre du Vaudeville, Paris, 1852).   1852; translated as *The Lady of the Camellias*, 1930; as *Camille*, 1931.
Diane de Lys (produced Théâtre du Gymnase, Paris, 1853). 1853.
Éva, with A. Montjoye and R. Deslandes (produced Théâtre du Vaudeville, 1854).   1854.
Le Bijou de la reine (produced Théâtre de l'Hôtel Castellane, Paris, 1855).   In *Théâtre complet*, 1868.
Le Demi-monde (produced Théâtre du Gymnase, Paris, 1855).   1855; translated as *The Outer Edge of Society*, 1921.
Comment la trouves-tu?, with others (produced Théâtre du Vaudeville, Paris, 1857).   1857.
La Question d'argent (produced Théâtre du Gymnase, Paris, 1857).   1857; translated as *The Money Question*, 1915.
Le Fils naturel (produced Théâtre du Gymnase, Paris, 1858). 1858; translated as *Le fils naturel*, 1879.
Un Père prodigue (produced Théâtre du Gymnase, Paris, 1859).   1859.
Un Mariage dans un chapeau, with Auguste Vivier (produced Théâtre du Gymnase, Paris, 1859).   1859.
L'Ami des femmes (produced Théâtre du Gymnase, Paris, 1864).   1864; translated as *The Friend of Women*, nd.
Le Supplice d'une femme, with Émile de Girardin (produced Comédie-Française, Paris, 1865).   1865.

Héloïse Paranquet, with Anne-Adrien-Armand Durantin (produced Théâtre du Gymnase, Paris, 1866).   1866.
Les Idées de Madame Aubray (produced Théâtre du Gymnase, Paris, 1867).   1867.
Le Filleul de Pompignac, with A. de Jolin and N. Fournier (produced Théâtre du Gymnase, Paris, 1869).   1869.
Une Visite de noces (produced Théâtre du Gymnase, Paris, 1871).   1872.
La Princesse Georges (produced Théâtre du Gymnase, Paris, 1871).   1872; translated as *La Princesse Georges*, 1881.
La Femme de Claude (produced Théâtre du Gymnase, Paris, 1873).   1873; translated as *Claude's Wife*, nd.
Monsieur Alphonse (produced Théâtre du Gymnase, Paris, 1873).   1874; translated as *M. Alphonse*, 1886.
Les Danicheff, with Pyotr Korvin-Krukovsky (produced Théâtre de l'Odéon, Paris, 1876).   1879.
La Comtesse Romani, with Gustave-Eugène Fould (produced Théâtre du Gymnase, Paris, 1876).   1878.
L'Étrangère (produced Comédie-Française, Paris, 1876).   1877; translated as *The Foreigner*, 1881.
La Princesse de Bagdad (produced Comédie-Française, Paris, 1881).   1881.
Denise (produced Comédie-Française, Paris 1885).   1885; translated as *Denise*, 1885.
Francillon (produced Comédie-Française, Paris, 1887).   1887.

Fiction

Aventures de quatre femmes et d'un perroquet (6 vols.).   1846–47.
La Dame aux camélias (2 vols.).   1848; translated as *The Lady of the Camelias*, nd.
Césarine.   1848.
Le Docteur Servans (2 vols.).   1848–49.
Le Roman d'une femme (4 vols.).   1849.
Antonine (2 vols.).   1849.
La Vie à vingt ans (2 vols.).   1850.
Tristan le roux (3 vols.).   1850; translated as *The Beggar of Nimes*, 1988.
Trois Hommes forts (4 vols.).   1850.
Diane de Lys et Grangette (3 vols.).   1851.
Le Régent Mustel (2 vols.).   1852 (originally published as *Les Revenants* as offprint from *Le Pays*, 1852).
Contes et nouvelles.   1853.
La Dame aux perles (4 vols.).   1853.
Sophie Printems (2 vols.).   1854.
Un Cas de rupture.   1854.
L'Affaire Clemenceau.   1866; translated as *The Clemenceau Case*, nd.

Verse

Péchés de jeunesse.   1847.

Other

Histoire de la loterie.   1851.
Histoire du "Supplice d'une femme".   1865.
Les Madeleines repenties.   1869.
Nouvelle Lettre de Junius à son ami A.D..   1871.
La Révolution plébéienne: lettres à Junius.   1871.
Une Lettre sur les choses du jour.   1871.
Nouvelle Lettre sur les choses du jour.   1871.
L'Homme-femme.   1872; translated as *Man-Woman*, 1873.
Entr'actes (3 vols.).   1878–79.
Les Femmes qui tuent et les femmes qui votent.   1880.

La Question du divorce.   1880.
Lettre à M. Naquet.   1882.
La Recherche de la paternité.   1883.
Nouveaux Entr'actes.   1890.

*

Criticism

Books:
R. Hörner, *Die Erstlingsdramen des jungen Dumas*, Tübingen, 1910.
C.M. Noël, *Les Idées sociales dans le théâtre de Dumas*, Paris, 1912.
O. Cheorgiu, *Le Théâtre de Dumas fils et la société contemporaine*, Nancy, 1931.
F.A. Taylor, *The Theatre of Alexandre Dumas fils*, Oxford, 1937.
André Maurois, *Les Trois Dumas*, Paris, 1957.
A. Lebois, *Alexandre Dumas fils*, Paris, 1969.

* * *

"To give the impression of being original when one is nothing of the sort, that is Dumas *fils*'s greatest achievement", wrote Émile Zola. To give the impression of honesty and sincerity while leading by one's own bigoted standards the kind of immoral life that every moralistic page of his novels and plays condemns is an even greater achievement. Dumas *fils*'s hypocrisy, pomposity, and "sacerdotal gravitas" perfectly illustrate the double standards and the twisted notions of "Victorian morality" of the French (male) establishment of the second half of the 19th century.

In 1846–47 Dumas *fils* published his first works: a book of poems and a novel closely modelled on his father's style. They both failed to make a mark and the young author abandoned the path of imaginative writing to pursue what was then called a more realistic style, establishing his name most firmly with the runaway success of *La Dame aux camélias* (*The Lady of the Camellias*), an autobiographical novel retelling the story of his recent affair with a prostitute (Alphonsine Plessis, otherwise Marie Duplessis, now immortalized as Marguerite Gautier). The stage adaptation became the box-office success of the century with an initial run of 200 performances. In the late 1840's and early 1850's Dumas *fils* had written some ten novels, but following his triumph he wrote almost exclusively for the stage. Regarded as one of the leading dramatists of his day, his posthumous reputation, in France and abroad, rests solely on *The Lady of the Camellias*. The remainder of his *œuvre* is neither read nor performed. In effect, his plays sank into oblivion in his own lifetime and were forgotten by the time of his death.

As a dramatist Dumas *fils* is credited with bringing a new realism to the stage, but *The Lady of the Camellias* is rather more a titillating well-made play, tailor-made to appeal to the jaded tastes of the Second-Empire audiences. Yet Dumas *fils* was writing for the theatre as a moral reformer! He was society's self-appointed scourge. He saw immorality everywhere, but particularly in women and in their depraved sexuality. According to him, society was in mortal danger, because of the disintegration of the sacrosanct family. The theatre was to become the pulpit from which true Christian values would be preached. Dumas *fils* had only contempt for the "apostles of art for art's sake" and he was happy to declare that art as such had no meaning for him and that "any literature whose aim is not perfectibility, moralization, idealization, usefulness is suffering from rickets, is unhealthy and stillborn". The playwright's task is to dramatize "a world divided between good and evil in which good always triumphs".

Additionally, Dumas *fils*'s special mission was to be the champion of women's rights. It would appear, from the numerous pamphlets that he wrote, that the dramatist genuinely believed in his mission and that he saw no contradiction between his public pronouncements and his private life. He is, after all, the man who was notorious for his numerous affairs, with prostitutes as well as with married women, the man who seduced Nadejda Knorring, wife of a Russian aristocrat and mother of a little girl, who lived maritally with her, who fathered a daughter whom he did not, at first, recognize, the man who—having married his widowed mistress—was distressed when she gave birth to another daughter instead of a son and finally complained bitterly, publicly, and in print, that life with her was Hell.

Still, in 1875, Dumas *fils* was elected to the Académie Française and in his reception speech he was proud of his achievements. He crowed: "Our duty—to speak the truth; our art—to speak it well; our aim—to impose it". But such truth is for men only (although it concerns mainly women and women are the true target of his invectives). He warned his fellow academicians not to take their daughters to the theatre to see classical heroines like Agnès (of Molière's *School for Wives*), Rosine (*Figaro*), Juliet, or Desdemona: the experience would be fraught with dangers. Nor should frail females see his own plays for he claims "to respect what is respectable", adding, "I have too much respect for young women [*jeunes filles*] to invite them to listen to what I have to say, and I have too much respect for my art to reduce it to what they can hear". Dumas *fils*'s double-talk and double-think knows no bounds: in *Tue-la* (Kill Her), a pamphlet written to castigate *female* adultery, he advocated the murder of the adulterous woman by the aggrieved husband; but he later denied any responsibility when a real-life murderer tried to defend himself by claiming that he had found justification for his action in the famous author's writings. To be fair, in 1880, in *Les Femmes qui tuent et les femmes qui votent* (Women Who Kill and Women Who Vote) he called for a more liberal divorce law and for a change in the law to give women the right to vote. But he could not hide his chauvinistic and paternalistic attitude when he affirmed that woman is "the creation" of man and her freedom can only be bestowed on her by her creator, not conquered by her.

The theses defended by Dumas *fils* were often seen by his contemporaries as daring, yet they are commonplace in the extreme. If *The Lady of the Camellias* insinuates that true love can erase the past, the dramatist still refuses his heroine the right to live and sanctimoniously kills her off. *Diane de Lys* castigates the adulterous woman who is guilty of having caused the death of her lover shot by her husband: the wife is the personification of feminine duplicity and wile; the husband the embodiment of virile nobility; and the lover is that irresponsible but so lovable creature, the artist! *Le Demi-Monde* (The Demi-Monde) parades as an exposé of Parisian society, yet condones the sexual double standard, blaming on women the promiscuity that is forced on them by men. *La Question d'argent* (A Question of Money) and *Le Fils naturel* (The Illegitimate Son) examine the link between money and morality and the plight of the illegitimate child. Money, Dumas *fils* concludes, must be earned by the sweat of one's brow and family ties must be tightly knotted! *Un Père prodigue* (A Prodigal Father) is a mean and nasty attack by the son against the father (Dumas *père* was then 57): the "old" man is guilty of still enjoying life in his late fifties. The son resented

his father's easy-going and care-free lifestyle and the play pleads for paternal respectability and responsibility.

Dumas *fils*'s thesis plays failed to bring any real characters to life; his *dramatis personae* are mere abstractions: they are either the dramatist's whipping boys (or rather girls) or his moralizing mouthpieces; and the "theses" offered to the consideration of the public were terribly narrow-minded and vitiated by the author's lack of intellectual integrity and his unimaginative conception of the art of theatre. As Zola said, Dumas *fils*'s work is "a philosophical carnival", not deserving too much consideration from a theatrical point of view, but essential reading for anyone interested in the history of ideas and in the psychology of men.

—Claude Schumacher

See also *Volume 1* entry on *The Lady of the Camelias*.

––––––––––

DUMAS *père*, Alexandre (Davy de la Pailleterie). Born in Villers-Cotterêts, France, 24 July 1802. Attended local school. Married Ida Ferrier in 1840 (separated, 1844; died, 1861); had one son, the writer Alexandre Dumas *fils*, by Catharine Labay, a daughter by Mélanie Serre, a son by Anna Bauër, and a daughter by Émilie Cordier. Articled at age 14 to a solicitor in Villers-Cotterêts, and one in Crépy, until 1822; employed in the secretariat of the Duc d'Orléans, 1822–29, and entered literary circle of Charles Nodier; first play, the vaudeville *La Chasse et l'amour*, produced 1825; librarian, Palais Royal, 1829; successful and prolific playwright and historical novelist, often publishing fiction first in serialised form, and often developing and revising plots written by others; founder and editor, *Le Mois*, 1848–50, and *La France nouvelle*, 1848; declared bankrupt and moved to Brussels, 1852, returning to Paris in 1853; founder and editor, *Le Mousquetaire*, 1853–57, and the weekly *Le Monte-Cristo*, 1857–60; aided Garibaldi's invasion of Sicily, 1860; director of excavations and museums, Naples, 1860–61, and editor, *L'indipendente*, Naples, 1860–64; returned to France, 1864; revived *Le Mousquetaire*, 1866–67, and edited the newspapers *Le D'Artagnan*, 1868, and *Théâtre-Journal*, 1868–69. Recipient: Chevalier, Légion d'Honneur, 1837; Order of Isabella the Catholic (Brussels); Cross of Gustavus Vasa (Sweden); Order of St. John of Jerusalem. Died in Puys, Normandy, 5 December 1870.

Works

Collections

Théâtre complet (15 vols.). 1863–74.
Oeuvres complètes (301 vols.). 1885–88.

Stage Works

La Chasse et l'amour, with Adolphe de Leuven and Pierre-Joseph Rousseau (produced Théâtre de l'Ambigu-Comique, Paris, 1825).
La Noce et l'enterrement, with E.H. Lassagne (produced Théâtre de la Porte-Saint-Martin, Paris, 1826).
Henri III et sa cour (produced Comédie-Française, Paris, 1829). 1829.

ALEXANDRE DUMAS

Alexandre Dumas *père* caricatured as "The Musketeer" by A. Gill in *La Lune*, c.1867–68, (Musée Carnavalet, Paris).

Christine (produced Théâtre de l'Odéon, Paris 1830).   1830.

Antony (produced Theatre de la Porte-Saint-Martin, Paris, 1831).   1831.

Napoléon Bonaparte (produced Théâtre de l'Odéon, Paris, 1831).   1831.

Richard Darlington, with Dinaux (produced Théâtre de la Porte-Saint-Martin, Paris, 1831).   1832.

Charles VII chez ses grands vassaux (produced Théâtre de l'Odéon, Paris, 1831).   1831.

La Tour de Nesle, from play by Frédéric Gaillardet (produced Théâtre de la Porte-Saint-Martin, Paris, 1832).   1832.

Térésa, with Anicet Bourgeois (produced Opéra-Comique, Paris, 1832).   1832.

Perinet Leclerc; ou, Paris en 1418 (produced Théâtre de la Porte-Saint-Martin, Paris, 1832).   1832.

Le Fils de l'émigré, with Anicet Bourgeois (produced Theatre de la Porte-Saint-Martin, Paris, 1832).

Le Mari de la veuve, with Anicet Bourgeois and Eugène Durieu (produced Comédie-Française, Paris, 1832).   1832.

Angèle, with Anicet Bourgeois (produced Théâtre de la Porte-Saint-Martin, Paris, 1833).   1834.

La Vénitienne, with Anicet Bourgeois (produced Théâtre de la Porte-Saint-Martin, Paris, 1834).   1834.

Catherine Howard (produced Théâtre de la Porte-Saint-Martin, Paris, 1834).   1834; translated as *Catherine Howard*, 1859.

La Tour de Babel, with others (produced Théâtre des Variétés, Paris, 1834).   1834.

Cromwell et Charles Ier, with Cordellier Delanoue (produced Théâtre de la Porte-Saint-Martin, Paris 1835).   1835.

Don Juan de Marana (produced Théâtre de la Porte-Saint-Martin, Paris, 1836).   1836.

Kean; ou, Désordre et génie, with Théaulon (produced Théâtre des Variétés, Paris, 1836).   1836; translated as *Edmund Kean*, 1847.

Le Marquis de Brunoy, with others (produced Théâtre des Variétés, Paris, 1836).   1836.

Caligula (produced Comédie-Française, Paris, 1837).   1838.

Piquillo, with Gérard de Nerval, music by Hippolyte Monpou (produced Opéra-Comique, Paris, 1837).   1837.

Paul Jones (produced Théâtre du Panthéon, Paris, 1838).   1838.

Le Bourgeois de Gand; ou, Le Secrétaire du Duc d'Albe, with Hippolyte Romand (produced Théâtre de l'Odéon, Paris, 1838).   1838.

Mademoiselle de Belle-Isle (produced Comédie-Française, Paris, 1839).   1839; translated as *The Lady of Belle Isle*, 1872; as *The Great Lover*, 1979.

Bathilde, with Auguste Maquet (produced Théâtre de la Renaissance, Paris, 1839).   1839.

L'Alchimiste, with Gérard de Nerval (produced Théâtre de la Renaissance, Paris, 1839).   1839.

Léo Burckart, with Gérard de Nerval (produced Théâtre de la Porte-Saint-Martin, Paris, 1839).   1839.

Jarvis l'honnête homme, with Charles Lafont (produced Théâtre du Gymnase, Paris, 1840).   1840.

Un Mariage sous Louis XV (produced Comédie-Française, Paris, 1841).   1841; translated as *A Marriage of Convenience*, 1899.

Jeannil le Breton; ou, Le Gérant responsable, with Eugène Bourgeois (produced Théâtre de la Porte-Saint-Martin, Paris, 1841).   1842.

Le Séducteur et le mari, with Charles Lafont (produced Théâtre des Délassements Comiques, Paris, 1842).   1842.

Halifax, with Adolphe d'Ennery (produced Théâtre des Variétés, Paris, 1842).   1842.

Lorenzino (produced Comédie-Française, Paris, 1842).   1842.

Les Demoiselles de Saint-Cyr (produced Comédie-Française, Paris, 1843).   1843; translated as *The Ladies of Saint-Cyr*, 1870.

Le Laird de Dumbicky, with Adolphe de Leuven and Léon Lhérie (produced Théâtre de l'Odéon, Paris, 1843).   1844.

Louise Bernard, with Adolphe de Leuven and Léon Lhérie (produced Théâtre de la Porte-Saint-Martin, Paris, 1843).   1843.

L'École des princes (produced Théâtre de l'Odéon, Paris, 1843).   1843.

Le Mariage au tambour (produced Théâtre des Variétés, Paris, 1843).   1843.

Le Garde-Forestier, with Adolphe de Leuven and Léon Lhérie (produced Théâtre des Variétés, Paris, 1845).   1845.

Un Conte de fées, with Adolphe de Leuven and Léon Lhérie (produced Théâtre des Variétés, Paris, 1845).   1845.

Sylvandire, with Adolphe de Leuven and Léon Lhérie, from the novel by Dumas and Maquet (produced Théâtre du Palais-Royal, Paris, 1845).   1845.

Les Mousquetaires, with Auguste Maquet, from their novel *Vingt ans après* (produced Théâtre de l'Ambigu-Comique, Paris, 1845).   1845.

Une Fille du régent, from the novel by Dumas and Maquet (produced Théâtre de l'Odéon, Paris, 1846).   1846.

Échec et Mat, with Octave Feuillet and Paul Bocage (produced Théâtre Historique, Paris, 1846).   1846.

Intrigue et amour, from a play by Schiller (produced Théâtre Historique, Paris, 1847).   In *Théâtre complet*, 1864.

Hamlet, with Paul Meurice, from the play by Shakespeare (produced Théâtre Historique, Paris, 1847). 1848.

La Reine Margot, with Auguste Maquet, from their novel (produced Théâtre Historique, Paris, 1847). 1847.

Le Chevalier de Maison-Rouge, with Auguste Maquet, from their novel (produced Théâtre Historique, Paris, 1847). 1847; translated as *The Chevalier de Maison-Rouge*, 1859.

Catalina, with Auguste Maquet (produced Théâtre Historique, Paris, 1848). 1848.

Monte-Cristo, parts 1–2, with Auguste Maquet, from their novel *Le Comte de Monte-Cristo* (produced Théâtre Historique, Paris, 1848). 2 vols., 1848.

Le Cachemire vert, with Eugène Nus (produced Théâtre du Gymnase, Paris, 1849). 1850.

Le Comte Hermann (produced Théâtre Historique, Paris, 1849). 1849.

La Jeunesse des mousquetaires, with Auguste Maquet, from their novel *Les Trois Mousquetaires* (produced Théâtre Historique, Paris, 1849). 1849; translated as *The Three Musketeers*, 1855; as *The Musketeers*, 1898.

Le Chevalier d'Harmental, with August Maquet, from their novel (produced Théâtre Historique, Paris, 1849). 1849.

La Guerre des femmes, with Auguste Maquet, from their novel (produced Théâtre Historique, Paris, 1849). 1849.

Le Connétable de Bourbon; ou, L'Italie au seizième siècle, with Eugène Grangé and Xavier de Montépin (produced Théâtre de la Porte-Saint-Martin, Paris, 1849). 1849.

Le Testament de César, with Jules Lacroix (produced Comédie-Française, Paris, 1849). 1849.

Pauline, with Eugène Grangé and Xavier de Montépin (produced Théâtre Historique, Paris, 1850). 1850.

Les Frères corses, with Eugène Grangé and Xavier de Montépin, from the novel (produced Théâtre Historique, Paris, 1850).

Trois Entr'actes pour l'amour médecin (produced Comédie-Française, Paris, 1850). 1850.

La Chasse au Chastre, from his own novel (produced Théâtre Historique, Paris, 1850). 1850.

Les Chevaliers du Lansquenet, with Eugène Grangé and Xavier de Montépin (produced 1850). 1850.

Urbain Grandier, with Auguste Maquet (produced Théâtre Historique, Paris, 1850). 1850.

Le Vingt-quatre février (produced Théâtre de la Gaîté, Paris, 1850). 1850.

La Barrière de Clichy (produced 1851). 1851.

Le Vampire, with Auguste Maquet (produced 1851). 1851.

Le Comte de Morcerf, with Auguste Maquet, from their novel *Le Comte de Monte-Cristo* (produced Théâtre de l'Ambigu-Comique, Paris, 1851). 2 vols., 1851.

La Jeunesse de Louis XIV (produced Théâtre du Vaudeville, Brussels, 1854). 1854; translated as *Young King Louis*, 1979.

Le Marbrier, with Paul Bocage (produced Théâtre du Vaudeville, Paris, 1854). 1854.

Romulus (produced Comédie-Française, Paris, 1854). 1854; translated as *Romulus*, 1969.

La Conscience, with E. Lockroy, (produced Théâtre de la Porte-Saint-Martin, Paris 1854). 1854.

L'Orestie (produced Théâtre de la Porte-Saint-Martin, Paris, 1856). 1856.

La Tour Saint-Jacques, with Xavier de Montépin (produced Théâtre Impérial du Cirque, Paris, 1856). 1856.

Le Verrou de la reine (produced Théâtre du Gymnase, Paris, 1856). In *Théâtre complet*, 1865.

Samson, music by E. Duprez (produced Paris, 1857). Parts published, 1856.

L'Invitation à la valse with P. Bocage (produced Théâtre du Gymnase, Paris, 1857). 1857; translated as *Childhood's Dreams*, 1881.

La Bacchante (Thais), with Adolphe de Leuven and A. de Beauplan, music by Eugène Gautier (produced 1858).

L'Honneur est satisfait, with others (produced Marsiglia Grand Théâtre, Paris, 1858). 1858.

Les Forestiers, from his novel *Catherine Blum* (produced Marsiglia Grand Théâtre, Paris, 1858). In *Théâtre complet 13*, 1865.

L'Envers d'une conspiration, with E. Lockroy (produced Théâtre du Vaudeville, Paris, 1860). 1860.

Le Roman d'Elvire, with Adolphe de Leuven, music by Ambroise Thomas (produced Opéra-Comique, Paris, 1860). 1860.

Le Gentilhomme de la montagne, from his novel *El Salteador* (produced Théâtre de la Porte-Saint-Martin, Paris, 1860). 1860.

La Dame de Monsoreau, with Auguste Maquet, from their novel (produced Théâtre de l'Ambigu-Comique, Paris, 1860). 1860.

Le Prisonnier de la Bastille: Fin des Mousquetaires, with Auguste Maquet, from their novel *Le Vicomte de Bragelonne* (produced Théâtre-Imperial du Cirque, Paris, 1861). 1861.

La Veillée Allemande, with Bernard Lopez (produced Théâtre Belleville, Paris, 1863).

Les Mohicans de Paris, from the novel by Dumas and Bocage (produced Théâtre de la Gaîté, Paris, 1864). 1864.

Gabriel Lambert, with Amédée de Jallais, from the novel by Dumas (produced Théâtre de l'Ambigu-Comique, Paris, 1866; as *Gabriel le Faussaire*, produced 1868). 1866.

Madame de Chamblay, from his own novel (produced Salle Ventadour, Paris, 1868). 1869.

Les Blancs et les bleus, from his own novel (produced Théâtre du Châtelet, Paris, 1869). 1874.

Ivanhoë. With *Fiesque de Lavagna*, 1974.

Fiesque de Lavagne. With *Ivanhoë*, 1974.

Fiction

Nouvelles contemporaines. 1826.

Souvenirs d'Antony. 1835; translated as *The Reminiscences of Antony*, 1905.

Guelfes et Gibelins. 1836; translated as *Guelphs and Ghibellines*, 1905.

Isabelle de Bavière. 1836; translated as *Isabel of Bavaria*, 1846.

La Main droite du Sire de Giac. 1838; translated as *The King's Favorite*, 1906.

Le Capitaine Paul. 1838; translated as *Captain Paul*, 1848; as *Paul Jones*, 1889.

La Salle d'Armes (includes *Pauline, Pascal Bruno, Murat*). 1838; translated as *Pascal Bruno*, 1837, and *The Sicilan Bandit*, 1859; as *Pauline*, 1844.

Acté. 1839; translated as *Acté*, 1904.

Les Crimes célèbres, with others. 1839–40; translated as *Celebrated Crimes*, 1896.

La Comtesse de Salisbury. 1839.

Monseigneur Gaston Phoebus. 1839.

Mémoires d'un maître d'armes. 1840; translated as *The Fencing-Master*, 1850.

Aventures de John Davys. 1840.

Maître Adam le Calabrais. 1840.

Othon l'archer. 1840; translated as *Otho the Archer*, 1860.

Praxède. 1841.

La Chasse au Chastre.   1841; translated as *The Bird of Fate*, 1906.

Aventures de Lyderic.   1842; translated as *Lyderic, Count of Flanders*, 1903; as *Adventures of Lyderic*, 1981.

Jehanne la Pucelle.   1842; translated as *Joan the Heroic Maiden*, 1847.

Albine.   1843; translated as *Le Château d'Eppstein*, 1844; as *The Spectre Mother*, 1864; as *The Castle of Eppstein*, 1903.

Le Chevalier d'Harmental, with Auguste Maquet.   1843; translated as *The Chateau d'Harmental*, 1856; as *The Orange Plume*, 1860; as *The Conspirators*, 1910.

Georges.   1843; translated as *George*, 1846.

Ascanio.   1843–44; translated as *Francis I*, 1849; as *Ascanio*, 1861.

Le Comte de Monte-Cristo, with Auguste Maquet.   1844–45; translated as *The Count of Monte Cristo*, 1846.

Amaury.   1844; translated as *Amaury*, 1854.

Une Âme à naître [*Histoire d'une âme*].   1844.

Cécile.   1844; as *La Robe de noces*, 1844; translated as *Cecile*, 1904.

Fernande.   1844; translated as *Fernande*, 1904.

Une Fille du régent, with Auguste Maquet.   1844; translated as *The Regent's Daughter*, 1847.

Les Frères corses.   1844; translated as *The Corsican Brothers*, 1880.

Les Trois Mousquetaires, with Auguste Maquet.   1844; translated as *The Three Musketeers*, 1846.

Trois Maîtres (on Michelangelo, Titian, and Raphael).   1844.

Gabriel Lambert.   1844; translated as *The Galley Slave*, 1849; as *Gabriel Lambert*, 1904.

Invraisemblance [*Histoire d'un mort*].   1844.

Sylvandire, with Auguste Maquet.   1844; translated as *The Disputed Inheritance*, 1847; as *Beau Tancrede*, 1861; as *Sylvandire*, 1907.

La Guerre des femmes, with Auguste Maquet.   1845–46; translated as *Nanon*, 1847; as *The War of Women*, 1895.

La Reine Margot, with Auguste Maquet.   1845; translated as *Margaret de Navarre*, 1845; as *Marguerite de Valois*, 1846; as *Queen Margot*, 1885.

Vingt ans après, with Auguste Maquet.   1845; translated as *Twenty Years After*, 1846; as *Cromwell and Mazarin*, 1847.

La Dame de Monsoreau, with Auguste Maquet.   1846; translated as *Chicot the Jester*, 1857; as *La Dame de Monsoreau*, 1894; as *Diane*, 1901.

Mémoires d'un médecin: Joseph Balsamo.   1846–48; translated as *Memoirs of a Physician*, 1847.

Le Chevalier de Maison-Rouge, with Auguste Maquet.   1846; translated as *Marie Antoinette*, 1846; as *Chateau-Rouge*, 1859; as *The Chevalier de Maison-Rouge*, 1895.

Le Bâtard de Mauléon, with Auguste Maquet.   1846; translated as *The Bastard of Mauleon*, 1849; as *The Half Brothers*, 1858; as *Agenor de Mauleon*, 1897.

Les Quarante-cinq, with Auguste Maquet.   1848; translated as *The Forty-Five Guardsmen*, 1847.

Le Vicomte de Bragelonne; ou Dix ans plus tard, with Auguste Maquet.   1848–50; translated as *The Vicomte de Bragelonne*, 1857; as *The Man in the Iron Mask*, 1893.

Les Mille et un fantômes.   1848–51; translated as *Tales of the Supernatural* [*Strange Adventures, Terror*], 1907–09.

Le Collier de la Reine, with Auguste Maquet.   1849–50; translated as *The Queen's Necklace*, 1855.

Le Trou de l'enfer.   1850–51; translated as *The Mouth of Hell*, 1906.

La Tulipe noire.   1850; translated as *Rosa; or, The Black Tulip*, 1854.

La Colombe.   1851; translated as *The Dove*, 1906.

Dieu dispose.   1851–52; translated as *God's Will Be Done*, 1909.

La Comtesse de Charny.   1852–55; translated as *The Countess of Charny*, 1858.

Un Gil-Blas en Californie.   1852; translated as *A Gil Blas in California*, 1933.

Isaac Laquedem.   1852–53.

Conscience l'innocent.   1852; translated as *The Conscript*, nd; as *Conscience*, 1905.

Olympe de Clèves.   1852; translated as *Olympe de Cleves*, 1894.

Emmanuel Philibert.   1852–54; as *Le Page du duc de Savoie*, 1855; translated as *Emmanuel Philibert*, 1854; as *The Page of the Duke of Savoy*, 1861.

Ange Pitou.   1853; translated as *Taking the Bastille*, nd; translated as *Ange Pitou*, 1907.

Le Pasteur d'Ashbourne.   1853.

El Saltéador.   1854; translated as *The Brigand*, 1897.

Ingénue.   1854; translated as *Ingenue*, 1855.

Les Mohicans de Paris; Salvator le Commissionnaire, with Paul Bocage.   1854–59; translated as *The Mohicans of Paris*, 1875.

Catherine Blum.   1854; as *The Foresters*, 1854; translated as *Catherine Blum*, 1861.

Les Compagnons de Jéhu.   1857; translated as *Roland of Montreval*, 1860; as *The Company of Jehu*, 1894.

Charles le téméraire.   1857; translated as *Charles the Bold*, 1860.

Le Meneur de loups.   1857; translated as *The Wolf Leader*, 1904.

Black.   1858; translated as *Black*, 1895.

Le Capitaine Richard.   1858; translated as *The Twin Captains*, 1861; as *The Young Captain*, 1870.

Herminie.   1858.

L'Horoscope.   1858; translated as *The Horoscope*, 1897.

Les Louves de Machecoul.   1859; translated as *The Last Vendee*, 1894; as *The She Wolves of Machecoul*, 1895.

Ammalet Beg.   1859; translated as *Sultanetta*, in *Tales of the Caucasus*, 1895.

La Boule de neige.   1859; translated as *The Ball of Snow*, in *Tales of the Caucasus*, 1895.

L'Histoire d'un Cabanon et d'un chalet.   1859; translated as *Monsieur Coumbes*, 1860; as *Le Fils de Forçat*, 1864; as *The Convict's Son*, 1905.

La Princesse Flora.   1859.

Jane.   1859; translated as *Jane*, with *Crop-Ear Jacquot*, 1903.

Le Chasseur de Sauvagine.   1859; translated as *The Wild Duck Shooter*, 1906.

Le Médecin de Java.   1859(?); as *L'Île de feu*, 1870; translated as *Doctor Basilius*, 1860.

Madame de Chamblay.   1859; translated as *Mme. de Chamblay*, nd.

Une Aventure d'amour.   1860.

Le Père la Ruine, with de Cherville.   1860; translated as *Père la Ruine*, 1905.

La Maison de glace.   1860; translated as *The Russian Gipsy*, 1860.

Jacquot sans oreilles.   1860; translated as *Crop-Ear Jacquot*, with *Jane*, 1903.

Les Drames galants, La Marquise d'Escoman.   1860.

Une Nuit à Florence.   1861.

La San-Felice [*Emma Lyonna*].   1864–65; translated as *The Lovely Lady Hamilton*, 1903; as *The Neapolitan Lovers; Love and Liberty*, 1916–18.

Memoirs and Letters

Mes Mémoires (22 vols.). 1852–54; annotated edition (5 vols.), 1954–68; selections as *Memoirs* (2 vols.), 1890; translated as *My Memoirs* (6 vols.), 1907–09.

Other

La Vendée et Madame. 1833; translated as *The Duchess of Berri in La Vendée*, 1833.
Gaule et France. 1833.
Impressions de Voyage: En Suisse (5 vols.). 1833–37; translated as *Adventures in Switzerland*, 1960.
Quinze jours à Sinaï (2 vols.). 1839.
Napoléon. 1840; translated as *Napoleon*, 1894.
Le Capitaine Pamphile (juvenile). 1840; translated as *Captain Pamphile*, 1850.
Les Stuarts (2 vols.). 1840.
Excursions sur les bords du Rhin (3 vols.). 1841.
Une Année à Florence (2 vols.). 1841.
Midi de la France (3 vols.). 1841.
Le Speronare (4 vols.). 1842; translated as *The Speronara*, 1902.
Le Capitaine Arena (2 vols.). 1842.
Le Corricolo (4 vols.). 1843.
La Villa Palmieri (2 vols.). 1843.
Filles, lorettes, et courtisanes. 1843.
Louis XIV et son siècle (2 vols.). 1844–45.
Histoire d'un casse-noisette (juvenile; 2 vols.). 1845; translated as *The Story of a Nutcracker*, 1846; as *The Nutcracker of Nuremberg*, 1930.
La Bouillie de la Comtesse Berthe (juvenile). 1845; translated as *Good Lady Bertha's Honey Broth*, 1846; as *The Honey Feast*, 1980.
Italiens et Flamands. 1845.
Les Médicis (2 vols.). 1845.
De Paris à Cadix (5 vols.). 1848; translated as *Adventures in Spain*, 1959.
Le Véloce; ou, Tanger, Alger, et Tunis (4 vols.). 1848–51; translated as *Tales of Algeria*, 1868; as *Adventures in Algeria*, 1959.
Louis XV et sa cour (4 vols.). 1849.
La Régence (2 vols.). 1849.
Montevideo; ou, Une Nouvelle Troie. 1850.
Histoire de Louis XVI et la révolution (3 vols.). 1850–51.
Mémoires de Talma (3 vols.). 1850.
Le Drame de '93 (7 vols.). 1851–52.
Les Drames de la mer (2 vols.). 1852.
Histoire de Louis-Philippe. 1852; translated as *The Last King; or, The New France*, 1915.
Une Vie d'artiste (2 vols.). 1854; translated as *A Life's Ambition*, 1924.
La Jeunesse de Pierrot (juvenile). 1854; translated as *When Pierrot Was Young*, 1975.
La Dernière Année de Marie Dorval. 1855.
Isabel Constant (2 vols.). 1855.
Les Grands Hommes en robe de chambre: Henri IV, Louis XIII, et Richelieu; César (12 vols.). 1856–57.
L'Homme aux contes (juvenile). 1857.
Le Lièvre de mon grand-père (juvenile), with de Cherville. 1857.
Marianna. 1859.
Les Baleiniers, with Félix Meynard (3 vols.). 1860.
Le Caucase. 1859; translated as *Adventures in Caucasia*, 1962.
L'Art et les artistes contemporains au salon de 1859. 1859.

Contes pour les grands et les petits enfants (juvenile; 2 vols.). 1859.
Causeries (2 vols.). 1860.
La Route de Varennes. 1860.
Les Garibaldiens: Révolution de Sicile et du Naples. 1861; translated as *The Garibaldians in Sicily*, 1861; complete version, as *On Board the "Emma": Adventures with Garibaldi's "Thousand" in Sicily*, edited by R.S. Garnett, 1929.
Bric-à-Brac (2 vols.). 1861.
Les Morts vont vites (2 vols.). 1861.
Le Pape devant les évangiles. 1861.
I Borboni di Napoli. (10 vols.). 1862–64.
Impressions de voyage: En Russie (4 vols.). 1865; translated as *Voyage en Russie*, edited by Jacques Suffel, 1960; excerpts as *Celebrated Crimes of the Russian Court*, 1906; as *Adventures in Czarist Russia*, 1960.
Bouts-rimés. 1865.
Étude sur "Hamlet" et sur William Shakespeare. 1867.
Histoire de mes bêtes. 1868; translated as *My Pets*, 1909; as *Adventures with My Pets*, 1960.
Souvenirs dramatiques (2 vols.). 1868.
Le Grand Dictionnaire de cuisine. 1873; translated as *Dictionary of Cuisine*, 1958; selection as *Dumas on Food*, 1978.
Propos d'art et de cuisine. 1877.
The Dumas Fairy Tale Book, edited by H.A. Spurr. 1924.

Editor, *Un Pays inconnu.* 1845.
Editor, *Pierre précieuse*, by Saphir. 1854.
Editor, *L'Arabie heureuse.* 1855.
Editor, *Le Journal de Madame Giovanni* (4 vols.). 1856; translated as *The Journal of Madame Giovanni*, 1944.
Editor, *Pélerinage de Hadji-abd-el-Hamid-Bey (à la Mecque)* (6 vols.). 1856–57.

Translator, *Mémoirs de Garibaldi* (2 vols.). 1860; revised edition (5 vols.), 1860–61; (3 vols.), 1861; translated as *Garibaldi: An Autobiography*, 1860; revised edition, as *The Memoirs of Garibaldi*, 1931.

*

Bibliographies

F.W. Reed, *A Bibliography of Alexandre Dumas père*, London, 1933.
Douglas Munro, *Dumas père: Works Published in French; Works Translated into English* (2 vols.), 1978–81.

Criticism

Books:
H. Wilke, *Alexandre Dumas als Dramatiker*, Munich, 1927.
André Maurois, *Les Trois Dumas*, Paris, 1957.
Fernande Basson and Sylvie Chevalley, *Alexandre Dumas père et la Comédie-Française*, Geneva, 1972.
Jean de Lamaze, *Alexandre Dumas*, Paris, 1972.
Richard S. Stowe, *Alexandre Dumas père*, Boston, 1976.
F.W.J. Hemmings, *The King of Romance: A Portrait of Alexandre Dumas*, New York, 1979.
Michael Ross, *Alexandre Dumas*, 1981.
C. Schopp, *Le Génie de la vie*, Paris, 1985.

Articles:

Jennifer Robin Goodman, "To Display a Clearly Dramatic Talent: The *Théâtre historique* of Alexandre Dumas", in *Harvard Library Bulletin*, 26, 1978.

Anne Ubersfeld, "Alexandre Dumas *père* et le drame bourgeois", in *Cahiers de l'Association Internationale des Études Françaises*, 35, 1983.

Claude Schopp, "Dumas, critique dramatique", in *Nineteenth-Century French Studies*, vol. 18 nos. 3–4, 1990.

* * *

The son of a mulatto general in Napoleon's armies, Alexandre Dumas received a patchy education, but was to find clerical employment in the household of the Duc d'Orléans. He read voraciously in his early 20's, developing an interest in Shakespeare and other authors who helped to determine the rejection of neo-classical traditions by a new generation of writers, and frequenting the company of Hugo and other young Romantics. Dumas was much influenced, like other aspiring playwrights of his generation, by the visit of the English actors who brought Shakespeare (and a style of acting unknown to the French) to Paris in 1827, an influence to which the following lyrical passage bears eloquent witness:

> Imagine someone blind from birth whose sight is suddenly restored, and who discovers a whole new world; imagine Adam waking after his creation and discovering at his feet the earth spangled with flowers, overhead the brilliant sky . . . and at his side his young, chaste companion, and you will have some idea of the magical Eden on which this performance opened the door. . . .

His own theatrical career began with historical dramas: *Henri III et sa cour* (Henry III and His Court), followed by *Christine* and *La Tour de Nesle*. Even though the first of these was played at the Comédie-Française, as a prose play it was decidely less provocative than Hugo's *Hernani* was to prove. *Christine*, though in verse, was performed at the Odéon; generally speaking the relative lack of literary ambition (particularly evident in a play like *La Tour de Nesle*) meant that Dumas's historical dramas were given an easier passage by the critics, at the same time as they appealed to audiences because of their technical craftsmanship and sense of theatre.

A similar blurring of the distinction between literary drama and popular melodrama is to be seen in some of the plays on modern subjects which this prolific playwright turned out through the 1830's. However, *Antony*, the first of these, owed its tremendous success with contemporary audiences to the challenging way in which it dealt with the quintessential Romantic theme of the relationship between the individual—in this instance the heroine Adèle d'Hervey, drawn into an adulterous relationship with the Byronic Antony—and an uncomprehending and hostile society. This was a true drama of ideas, which presented a powerful contrast between the "authentic" personality of the heroine and a highly conventional society whose values are based on hypocrisy and compromise.

The play had been accepted by the Comédie-Française in 1830, but an administrative crisis at that theatre, combined with a lukewarm attitude on the part of certain actors there, led to Dumas withdrawing it and offering it to the Porte-Saint-Martin, where, with the leading parts played by Bocage and Marie Dorval, it became one of the great successes of the Romantic decade. Théophile Gautier's account of the first night deserves to stand beside that of the première of *Hernani* as an outstanding expression of the nostalgia of his generation for the heroic days of their youth:

The burning passion of the play had set every heart on fire. All the young women adored Antony, and there was not a young man who would not have given his life for Adèle. Never was there such identification of actor and role: Bocage was truly Antony, and Adèle was inconceivable without Mme Dorval.

Dumas was never to equal the success of *Antony*, and several of his other plays on modern subjects—*Richard Darlington*, *Térésa*, *Angèle*—were little more than melodramas written to a formula. One play which does stand out, however, is his *Kean* of 1836. Edmund Kean had died in 1833, and not only had he become a legend in his lifetime in England, but French audiences had been able, in 1827, to compare the conventional acting style of the Comédie-Française with the uninhibited, dynamic style of Kean and his colleagues. By 1836 Frédérick Lemaître, now in his mid-30's and at the height of his reputation, was beginning to be the subject of a similar legend based not only on his theatrical achievements but also on his sexual exploits, his capacity for wine, and his flamboyant life-style. Dumas's incarnation of the Romantic idea of unruly genius was a role tailor-made for Frédérick, while the part of Anna Danby, who is represented as Kean's guardian angel, was given to the playwright's mistress Ida Ferrier. The play was one of Dumas's more notable successes, though nowadays it tends to be known for having provided the vehicle for an adaptation by Jean-Paul Sartre, who saw in the subject an interesting possibility for a study of self-awareness in the existentialist manner.

From the middle of the 1830's onwards, Dumas ceased to count as a challenging exponent of Romantic ideas who appealed to the sensibilities and enthusiasms of his young contemporaries; and for the rest of his life he was to be content with commercial success, pursuing this with extraordinary energy. His plays number over 90: a large number of these were popular historical dramas, many written in collaboration with others. Dumas's collaboration with Auguste Maquet, from the middle of the 1840's onwards, produced the historical novels by which he is best known today: *The Three Musketeers*, *The Count of Monte Cristo*, *The Chevalier de Maison-rouge*, and many others, usually first published in serial form. These novels were regularly turned into dramatic form, normally with Maquet's collaboration; and Dumas's acquisition of his own theatre, the Théâtre Historique, in 1847, gave further impetus to the staging of these and similar works.

—William D. Howarth

See also *Volume 1* entry on *Antony*.

DUNLAP, William.   Born in Perth Amboy, colony of New Jersey, now USA, 19 February 1766. Educated in local schools until his family moved to New York in 1777; then studied painting with a New York artist. Married Elizabeth Woolsey in 1789; one son and one daughter. Clerk in his father's store, then portrait painter, New York, 1782–84; studied art with Benjamin West in London, 1784–87; first plays produced 1789; returned to New York and abandoned painting to write for the stage; manager and part owner, Old American Company, at the John Street Theatre, later at the Park Theatre, New York, presenting his own plays as well as current French and German plays in translation, from 1796 until he went bankrupt, 1805; itinerant painter of miniatures, 1805–06; general assistant to the new manager of the Park

Theatre, 1806–11; freelance writer and editor, 1811–15; founder, *Monthly Record*, New York, 1813; Assistant Paymaster-General, New York Militia, 1814–16; painter of miniatures, portraits, and religious commissions, 1816–mid-1830's. Founder member, 1826, and Vice-President, 1831–38, National Academy of Design. Died in New York, 28 September 1839.

Works

Collections

Dramatic Works (3 vols.). 1806–16.
Dunlap's "False Shame" and "Thirty Years", edited by Oral Sumner Coad. 1940.
Four Plays (1789–1812) (includes *The Father of an Only Child; Leicester; The Italian Father; Yankee Chronology*), edited by Julian Mates. 1976.
Musical Works (includes *Darby's Return; The Archers; The Wild-Goose Chase; The Glory of Columbia*), edited by Julian Mates. 1980.

Stage Works

The Father; or, American Shandy-ism (produced John Street Theatre, New York, 1789). 1789; revised version, as *The Father of an Only Child*, in *Dramatic Works*, 1806.
Darby's Return (produced John Street Theatre, New York, 1789). 1789.
The Miser's Wedding (produced John Street Theatre, New York, 1793).
Leicester (as *The Fatal Deception; or, The Progress of Guilt*, produced John Street Theatre, New York, 1794). In *Dramatic Works*, 1806.
Shelty's Travels (produced John Street Theatre, New York, 1794).
Fountainville Abbey (produced John Street Theatre, New York, 1795). In *Dramatic Works*, 1806.
The Archers; or, Mountaineers of Switzerland, music by Benjamin Carr (produced John Street Theatre, New York, 1796). 1796; in *Musical Works*, 1980.
Ribbemont; or, The Feudal Baron (as *The Mysterious Monk*, produced John Street Theatre, New York, 1796). 1803.
The Knight's Adventure (produced John Street Theatre, New York, 1797). 1807.
The Man of Fortitude, with John Hodgkinson (produced John Street Theatre, New York, 1797). 1807.
Tell Truth and Shame the Devil, from a play by A.L.B. Robineau (produced John Street Theatre, New York, 1797). 1797.
The Stranger, from a play by Kotzebue (produced Park Theatre, New York, 1798). 1798.
André (produced Park Theatre, New York, 1798). 1798; revised version, as *The Glory of Columbia–Her Yeomanry!* (produced Park Theatre, New York, 1803), 1817.
False Shame; or, The American Orphan in Germany, from a play by Kotzebue (produced Park Theatre, New York, 1798). Edited by Oral Sumner Coad, with *Thirty Years*, 1940.
The Natural Daughter (produced Park Theatre, New York, 1799).
The Temple of Independence (produced Park Theatre, New York, 1799).
Don Carlos, from the play by Schiller (produced Park Theatre, New York, 1799).
Indians in England, from a play by Kotzebue (produced Park Theatre, New York, 1799).
The School for Soldiers, from a play by L.S. Mercier (produced Park Theatre, New York, 1799).

The Robbery, from a play by Boutet de Monval (produced Park Theatre, New York, 1799).
The Italian Father, from a play by Dekker (produced Park Theatre, New York, 1799). 1810.
Graf Benyowsky, from a play by Kotzebue (produced Park Theatre, New York, 1799).
Sterne's Maria; or, The Vintage (produced Park Theatre, New York, 1799).
Lovers' Vows, from a play by Kotzebue (produced Park Theatre, New York, 1799). 1814.
The Force of Calumny, from a play by Kotzebue (produced Park Theatre, New York, 1800).
The Stranger's Birthday, from a play by Kotzebue (produced Park Theatre, New York, 1800).
The Knight of Guadalquiver (produced Park Theatre, New York, 1800).
The Wild-Goose Chase, music by J. Hewitt, from a play by Kotzebue (produced Park Theatre, New York, 1800). 1800; in *Musical Works*, 1980.
The Virgin of the Sun, from a play by Kotzebue (produced Park Theatre, New York, 1800). 1800.
Pizarro in Peru; or, The Death of Rolla, from a play by Kotzebue and the version by Sheridan (produced Park Theatre, New York, 1800). 1800.
Fraternal Discord, from a play by Kotzebue (produced, Park Theatre, New York, 1800). 1809.
The Soldier of '76 (produced Park Theatre, New York, 1801).
Abée de l'Epée, from a play by Jean Bouilly (produced Park Theatre, New York, 1801).
Where is He?, from a German play (produced Park Theatre, New York, 1801).
Abaellino, The Great Bandit, from a play by J. H. D. Zschokke (produced Park Theatre, New York, 1801). 1802.
The Merry Gardener, from a French play (produced Park Theatre, New York, 1802).
The Retrospect; or, The American Revolution (produced Park Theatre, New York, 1802).
Peter the Great; or, The Russian Mother, from a play by J. M. Babo (produced Park Theatre, New York, 1802). 1814.
The Good Neighbor: An Interlude, from a work by A. W. Iffland (produced Park Theatre, New York, 1803). 1814.
Blue Beard: A Dramatic Romance, from the play by George Colman the Younger. 1803.
The Voice of Nature, from a play by L.C. Caigniez (produced Park Theatre, New York, 1803). 1803.
The Blind Boy, from a play by Kotzebue (produced Park Theatre, New York, 1803).
Bonaparte in England (produced Park Theatre, New York, 1803).
The Proverb; or, Conceit Can Cure, Conceit Can Kill (produced Park Theatre, New York, 1804).
Lewis of Monte Blanco; or, The Transplanted Irishman (produced Park Theatre, New York, 1804).
Nina, from a play by Joseph Marsollier (produced Park Theatre, New York, 1804).
Chains of the Heart; or, The Slave of Choice, from a play by Prince Hoare (produced ?). 1804.
The Wife of Two Husbands, from a play by Pixérécourt (produced Park Theatre, New York, 1804). 1804.
The Shipwreck, from a play by Samuel James Arnold (produced?). 1805.
Alberto Albertini; or, The Robber King (produced Park Theatre, New York, 1811).
Yankee Chronology; or, Huzza for the Constitution! (produced Park Street Theatre, New York, 1812). 1812.
The Flying Dutchman (produced 1827).

A Trip to Niagara; or, Travellers in America (produced Park
Theatre, New York, 1828).   1830.
Thirty Years; or, The Gambler's Fate, from a play by Prosper
Goubaux and Victor Ducange (produced Park Theatre,
New York, 1828).   Edited by Oral Sumner Coad, with
False Shame, 1940.

Memoirs and Letters

*Diary: The Memoirs of a Dramatist, Theatrical Manager,
Painter, Critic, Novelist, and Historian*, edited by Dorothy
C. Barck (3 vols.).   1930.

Other

Memoirs of the Life of George Frederick Cooke (2 vols.).
1813; revised edition, as *The Life of Cooke*, 1815.
*A Record, Literary and Political, of Five Months in the Year
1813*, with others.   1813.
*The Life of the Most Noble Arthur, Marquis and Earl of
Wellington*, with Francis L. Clarke.   1814.
*A Narrative of the Events Which Followed Bonaparte's
Campaign in Russia*.   1814.
The Life of Charles Brockden Brown, with Selections (2
vols.).   1815; as *Memoirs of Charles Brockden Brown*,
1822.
A History of the American Theatre.   1832.
*History of the Rise and Progress of the Arts of Design in the
United States* (2 vols.).   1834; revised edition, edited by
Alexander Wyckoff, 1965.
Thirty Years Ago; or, The Memoirs of a Water Drinker (2
vols.).   1836.
A History of New York, for Schools (2 vols.).   1837.
*History of the New Netherlands, Province of New York, and
the State of New York* (2 vols.).   1839–40.

*

Bibliographies

Oscar Wegelin, *A Bibliographical Checklist of Plays and
Miscellaneous Writings of William Dunlap*, New York,
1916.
Oral Sumner Coad (ed.), "Bibliography", in *"False Shame"
and "Thirty Years"*, 1940.

Criticism

Books:
Oral Sumner Coad, *William Dunlap: A Study of His Life and
Works and of His Place in Contemporary Culture*, New
York, 1917.
Arthur Hobson Quinn, *A History of American Drama: From
the Beginning to the Civil War*, New York, 1923.
Edward Southern Hipp, *Drama's Father in America: William
Dunlap*, Newark, New Jersey, 1934.
William Carroll McGinnis, *William Dunlap* (biography),
Perth Amboy, New Jersey, 1956.
Harold E. Dickson, *Arts of the Young Republic: The Age of
Dunlap*, Chapel Hill, North Carolina, 1968.
David Grimsted, *Melodrama Unveiled: American Theatre
and Culture 1800–1850*, Chicago, 1968.
Robert H. Canary, *William Dunlap*, New York, 1970.
Walter J. Meserve, *An Emerging Entertainment: The Drama
of the American People to 1828*, Bloomington, Indiana,
1977.

J. Martin, "William Dunlap: The Documentary Vision", in
Theater und Drama in Amerika, edited by E. Lohner and
R. Haas, Berlin, 1978.

Articles:
Fred Moramarco, "The Early Dramatic Criticism of William
Dunlap", in *American Literature*, 40, 1968.
A. Behrman, "Kotzebue and the American Stage", in
Arcadia, 4, 1969.
J. Zapes, "Dunlap, Kotzebue, and the Shaping of American
Theater: A Re-evaluation from a Marxist Perspective", in
Early American Literature, 8, 1974.

*   *   *

Dunlap wrote some 70 plays. That he is called the "Father
of the American Stage" rightly suggests that his influence was
not narrowly or exclusively as a dramatist and that his historical significance outweighs the intrinsic merits of his dramas.
There was an American theatre before Dunlap, and he is less
original than he claims, but as playwright, translator, dramatic critic, theatre manager, impresario, and historian of the
theatre he was unique in his own time.

His father was an English emigrant whose colonially-made
fortune enabled his son to spend three years in England
studying painting. Dunlap thus knew and responded sympathetically to two cultural traditions, but was energetically
single-minded in his commitment to America, politically and
artistically, and in his enthusiasm for establishing in his
newly-independent country a comparably wide and independent indigenous culture. At the same time he assiduously
introduced American audiences to the best in contemporary
European drama, often in his own translations. His admiration for George Washington, whose portrait he painted in
1783 and who was himself a keen theatre-goer, is reflected in
many of his plays, some of which Washington is known to
have enjoyed in performance. Dunlap's veneration for "the
Father of his Country" may be another facet of the preoccupation with paternity and paternalism so prominent among
his dramatic themes. (This has also been linked with his
position as an only child in an age of large families.)

His first two plays to be produced, *The Father* and *Darby's
Return*, in 1789, established him at once in two genres, comedy and patriotic drama. A prologue to the former pledges to
"rear on our blest shore a 'moral stage'", in contrast to that of
Europe which prefers to see "with wanton arts sweet Modesty
opprest". This, and the play itself, are more analogous to the
sentimental comedy of Richard Cumberland than to
Goldsmith and Sheridan who were already moving away from
it. English influence is also present in the subtitle, "American
Shandyism", referring to two characters complimentarily
modelled on Laurence Sterne's Uncle Toby and Corporal
Trim. Dunlap is known to have attended performances at
Drury Lane of Sheridan's *The School for Scandal* and *The
Critic*; in his own work, however, we are reminded of the
latter more by his excessive reliance on themes, situations,
and techniques parodied in Mr. Puff's play about the Armada
than by any originality or virtuosity comparable to
Sheridan's. Nevertheless, an epilogue, with clever irony,
allows the heroine to mock the "thumps by battledores of
Fate" in a self-styled comedy of which she is sure the audience
is unlikely to approve because it is American and not
imported from London.

American audiences did, however, approve, and Dunlap
claimed it (erroneously) as "the first and only American play"
to have been published. In 1806 he re-published it in a revised
form as *The Father of an Only Child*. The most original

character is certainly the garrulously self-important physician, and the dialogue often has a liveliness and accuracy of observation that mitigate the moralistic sentimentality.

Darby's Return is slighter, a comic sketch with music, mocking the amazement of Irish rustics hearing a former villager recount his adventures as a mercenary and praise the democracy of America to which he is determined to return. During the War of 1812 between America and Britain, Dunlap reworked and updated this theme in *Yankee Chronology*; its subtitle, *Huzza for the Constitution!*, epitomises the chauvinistic intention of both pieces.

Equally topical but more ambitious and substantial is the blank verse tragedy, *André*, a dramatisation of the capture and execution in 1780 of the eponymous British officer to whom Benedict Arnold had traitorously given the plans of the fort at West Point. Its attempt to be fair to the English, its use of Washington as a character at once heroic and human, and its dramatic unity are impressive. That it was later rewritten in a less sophisticated form and with music, as *The Glory of Columbia*, reflects Dunlap's theatre manager's eye for the market.

In an earlier blank verse tragedy, *The Fatal Deception*, (renamed *Leicester* when published), Dunlap used the material Scott was to use for *Kenilworth*. It was not, as he claimed, "the first American tragedy produced upon the stage" (Thomas Godfrey's *The Prince of Parthia* was professionally performed in 1767; and in 1765 it was the first American play to be published), and his insistence that the heroine is closer to Clytemnestra than to Lady Macbeth suggests an uneasy awareness of his literary debts. The prologue defines the function of the tragic muse as "in Virtue's ways to fix the mind", and again moral romanticisation has good triumphing over evil in the best sentimental tradition. It is still, however, an interesting example of the range of his dramatic ability.

In *André* one liberty he took with historical fact was in bringing an Englishwoman to whom André had once been engaged to visit him in America (her historical counterpart had died four months before his arrest). What interested Dunlap may have been the termination of their engagement by her parents; a breach between over-rigorous parents and their offspring is a recurrent theme from *The Father* to his own favourite among his plays, *The Italian Father*. Another sentimental comedy, this draws on Thomas Dekker's *The Honest Whore*. The good characters are insipidly idealised, the bad undergo instantaneous conversions, and the play culminates in the customary glow of lachrymose and complete reconciliation; but pace, dialogue and humour are well maintained. That it was popularly attributed, when produced anonymously, to the contemporary German playwright Kotzebue illustrates the extent to which Dunlap's own translations and productions of Kotzebue's domestic comedies had familiarised American audiences with them.

Dunlap was also a lecturer on historical painting, a poet, novelist, and magazine editor; he published histories of New York and of the American Theatre, as well as the definitive work *The Rise and Progress of the Arts of Design in the United States*. His lifelong interest in the pictorial arts is reflected in his emphasis on scenery in all the many productions in his long theatrical career.

—Dennis Welland

———

DUNSANY, Lord; Edward John Moreton Drax Plunkett, 18th Baron Dunsany. Born in London, 24 July 1878; succeeded to the barony, 1899. Educated at Cheam School, Surrey; Eton College, Berkshire; then privately tutored; Royal Military Academy, Sandhurst, Surrey. Married Lady Beatrice Child-Villiers in 1904; one son. Served as a 2nd lieutenant in the Coldstream Guards in Gibraltar and in the Boer War, 1899–1902; first play, *The Glittering Gate*, produced 1909; captain in the Royal Inniskilling Fusiliers during World War I; wounded in the Dublin Easter Rebellion, 1916; served in the Home Guard during World War II. Lived at Dunstall Priory, Kent, and Dunsany Castle, County Meath, Ireland. Byron professor of English literature, University of Athens, 1940–41. D.Litt: University of Dublin, 1939. Fellow, Royal Society of Literature, and Royal Geographical Society; Member, Irish Academy of Letters. Died in Dublin, 25 October 1957.

Works

Collections

Five Plays (includes *The Glittering Gate; The Gods of the Mountain; King Argimenes and the Unknown Warrior; The Golden Doom; The Lost Silk Hat*). 1914.
Plays of Gods and Men (includes *The Text of Arabs; The Queen's Enemies; The Laughter of the Gods*).
Plays of Near and Far (includes *The Compromise of the King of the Golden Isles; The Flight of the Queen; Cheezo; A Good Bargain; If Shakespeare Lived Today; Fame and the Poet*). 1922.
"Alexander" and Three Small Plays (includes *The Old King's Tale; The Evil Kettle; The Amusements of Khan Kharuda*). 1925.
Seven Modern Comedies (includes *Atalanta in Wimbledon; The Raffle; The Journey of the Soul; In Holy Russia; His Sainted Grandmother; The Hopeless Passion of Mr. Bunyon; The Jest of Hahalaba*). 1928.
Plays for Earth and Air (includes *Fame Comes Late; A Matter of Honour; Mr. Sliggen's Hour; The Pumpkin; The Use of Man; The Bureau de Change; The Seventh Symphony; Golden Dragon City; Time's Joke; Atmospherics*). 1937.

Stage Works

The Glittering Gate (produced Abbey Theatre, Dublin, 1909). In *Five Plays*, 1914.
The Gods of the Mountain (produced Theatre Royal, Haymarket, London, 1911). In *Five Plays*, 1914.
King Argimenes and the Unknown Warrior (produced Abbey Theatre, Dublin, 1911). In *Five Plays*, 1914.
The Sphinx at Gizeh. In *Tripod*, May 1912.
The Golden Doom (produced Theatre Royal, Haymarket, London, 1913). In *Five Plays*, 1914.
The Lost Silk Hat (produced Gaiety Theatre, Manchester, 1913). In *Five Plays*, 1914.
The Tents of the Arabs (produced Playhouse, Liverpool, 1914). In *Plays of Gods and Men*, 1917.
A Night at an Inn (produced Neighborhood Playhouse, New York, 1916). 1916.
The Queen's Enemies (produced Neighborhood Playhouse, New York, 1916). In *Plays of Gods and Men*, 1917.
The Laughter of the Gods (produced Punch and Judy Theatre, New York, 1919). In *Plays of Gods and Men*, 1917.
The Murderers (produced Shubert Murat, Indianapolis, 1919).

The Prince of Stamboul (produced USA, 1919?).
If (produced Ambassador's Theatre, London, 1921).   1921.
Cheezo (produced Everyman Theatre, London, 1921).   In *Plays of Near and Far*, 1922.
The Flight of the Queen.   1922.
The Compromise of the King of the Golden Isles.   In *Plays of Near and Far*, 1922.
A Good Bargain.   In *Plays of Near and Far*, 1922.
If Shakespeare Lived Today.   In *Plays of Near and Far*, 1922.
Fame and the Poet (produced Albert Hall, Leeds, 1924).   In *Plays of Near and Far*, 1922.
Lord Adrian (produced Prince of Wales Theatre, Birmingham, 1923).   1933.
Alexander (produced 1938).   1925.
The Old King's Tale.   In *"Alexander" and Three Small Plays*, 1925.
The Evil Kettle.   In *"Alexander" and Three Small Plays*, 1925.
The Amusements of Khan Kharuda.   In *"Alexander" and Three Small Plays*, 1925.
His Sainted Grandmother (produced Fortune Theatre, London, 1926).   In *Seven Modern Comedies*, 1928.
The Jest of Hahalaba (produced Playroom 6, London, 1927).   In *Seven Modern Comedies*, 1928.
Mr. Faithful (produced Queens Theatre, London, 1927).   1935.
Atlanta in Wimbledon.   In *Seven Modern Comedies*, 1928.
The Raffle.   In *Seven Modern Comedies*, 1928.
The Journey of the Soul.   In *Seven Modern Comedies*, 1928.
In Holy Russia.   In *Seven Modern Comedies*, 1928.
The Hopeless Passion of Mr. Bunyon.   In *Seven Modern Comedies*, 1928.
The Old Folks of the Centuries.   1930.
Fame Comes Late.   In *Plays for Earth and Air*, 1939.
A Matter of Honour.   In *Plays for Earth and Air*, 1939.
Mr. Sliggen's Hour.   In *Plays for Earth and Air*, 1939.
The Pumpkin.   In *Plays for Earth and Air*, 1939.
The Use of Man.   In *Plays for Earth and Air*, 1939.
The Bureau de Change.   In *Plays for Earth and Air*, 1939.
The Seventh Symphony.   In *Plays for Earth and Air*, 1939.
Golden Dragon City.   In *Plays for Earth and Air*, 1939.
Time's Joke.   In *Plays for Earth and Air*, 1939.
Atmospherics.   In *Plays for Earth and Air*, 1939.
The Strange Lover.   1939.

Fiction

The Gods of Pegāna.   1905.
Time and the Gods.   1906.
"The Sword of Welleran" and Other Stories.   1908.
A Dreamer's Tales.   1910.
The Book of Wonder: A Chronicle of Little Adventures at the Edge of the World.   1912.
Fifty-One Tales.   1915; as *The Food of Death*, 1974.
Tales of Wonder.   1916; as *The Last Book of Wonder*, 1916.
Tales of War.   1918.
Tales of Three Hemispheres.   1919.
The Chronicles of Rodriguez.   1922; as *Don Rodriguez: Chronicles of Shadow Valley*, 1922.
The King of Elfland's Daughter.   1924.
The Chairwoman's Shadow.   1926.
The Blessing of Pan.   1927.
The Travel Tales of Mr. Joseph Jorkens.   1931.
The Curse of the Wise Woman.   1933.
Jorkens Remembers Africa.   1934; as *Mr. Jorkens Remembers Africa*, 1934.

Up in the Hills.   1935.
Rory and Bran.   1936.
The Story of Mona Sheehy.   1939.
Jorkens Has a Large Whiskey (stories).   1940.
Guerrilla.   1944.
The Fourth Book of Jorkens.   1948.
The Man Who Ate the Phoenix.   1949.
The Strange Journeys of Colonel Polders.   1950.
The Last Revolution.   1951.
His Fellow Men.   1952.
The Little Tales of Smethers.   1952.
Jorkens Borrows Another Whiskey.   1954.
At the Edge of the World, edited by Lin Carter.   1970.
Beyond the Fields We Know, edited by Lin Carter.   1972.
Gods, Men, and Ghost: The Best Supernatural Fiction of Dunsany, edited by E.F. Bleiler.   1972.
Over the Hills and Far Away, edited by Lin Carter.   1974.
The Ghosts of the Heaviside Layer.   1980.

Verse

Fifty Poems.   1929.
Mirage Water.   1938.
War Poems.   1941.
A Journey.   1943.
Wandering Songs.   1943.
The Year.   1946.
"To Awaken Pegasus" and Other Poems.   1949.

Memoirs and Letters

My Ireland.   1937.
Patches of Sunlight (autobiography).   1938.
While the Sirens Slept (autobiography).   1944.
The Sirens Wake (autobiography).   1945.

Other

Selections.   1912.
Nowadays.   1918.
Unhappy Far-Off Things.   1919.
If I Were Dictator: The Pronouncements of the Grand Macaroni.   1934.
My Talks with Dean Spanley.   1936.
The Donellan Lectures 1943.   1945.
A Glimpse from a Watchtower: A Series of Essays.   1945.

Editor, *Modern Anglo–Irish Verse*.   1914.

Translator, *The Odes of Horace*.   1947.

*

Bibliographies

H. Danielson, bibliography in *Bibliographies of Modern Authors 1*, 1925.

Criticism

Books:
Edward Hale Bierstadt, *Dunsany the Dramatist*, London, 1917, revised 1919.
Hazel Smith, *Dunsany, King of Dreams: A Personal Portrait*, London, 1959.

Mark Amory, *Biography of Lord Dunsany*, London, 1972.

* * *

Edward Bierstadt, writing in 1917, reckoned that Dunsany—along with Yeats and Synge—was one of "the three great contemporary dramatic poets of Ireland". He looks less great today. He also looks less Irish. He had no sympathy with Irish nationalism, and once the nationalist cause took root he did most of his living (and writing) in England. No play of his is set in Ireland (though some of his fiction is, including what is perhaps his best work, *The Curse of the Wise Woman*). And as early as 1916 he began to dissociate himself explicitly from the Irish Literary Revival; in that year he wrote to the American Stuart Walker, "*Argimenes* [*and the Unknown Warrior*] was the first play I ever wrote about my own country. *The Glittering Gate* I had already written partly to please Yeats, but that play never interested me. *Argimenes* was the first play ever in the native land of my spirit". His "own country" was, then, a country of the mind, not the Ireland of Yeats.

But of course, as this same letter grudgingly concedes, it was Yeats who got him started as a playwright by commissioning *The Glittering Gate* in 1909. Though he gently mocked the Abbey Theatre in *If Shakespeare Lived Today*, his first plays were performed there. A selection of his works was published by Yeats in 1912. ("It is my way of claiming you for Ireland", Yeats wrote.) And he was friendly with several prominent figures of the Irish Literary Revival—especially A.E., Gogarty, Yeats, and Lady Gregory.

It is possible to see the Irish Literary Revival as a mutation of the orientalism that was fashionable in Britain and France at the turn of the century. Most of the writers associated with the movement supplemented their contemplation of Ireland with admiring glances at the Orient and its myths (Wilde's *Salomé*, Lady Gregory's *The Deliverer*), its history and politics (Lady Gregory's agitation on behalf of Arabi Bey), its art-forms (Yeats's experiments with Noh drama), and its religions (the mysticism of A.E. and Yeats, the exotic associations of Shaw's "Life Force"). Dunsany's full-blooded orientalism can thus be seen as a reversion to the stock on which the Irish Literary Revival had been grafted.

His best known plays all pit Western logic and restraint against the workings of the inscrutable East. In his first full-length play, *Alexander*, for example, the eponymous hero is torn between Greek decorum and Persian excess. Much the same tension is evident in the better-known *If*, where John Beal, a conventional City businessman, experiences the lure of despotic power during a brief experiment in time-travel.

Dunsany's most celebrated one-acters follow the same pattern. The glittering gate in his first play may be, technically, the entrance to a Christian heaven; but when the two burglars finally succeed in prising open the gate and find that "there ain't no heaven", only "blooming great stars", the "cruel and violent" laughter that mocks them seems to belong to some harsher creed. In *A Night at an Inn* a "hideous idol" finally wreaks its vengeance on a band of English thieves whose leader (The Toff) has had the wit to "foresee" everything else. And in *The Gods of the Mountain*—arguably Dunsany's finest play—a band of beggars, who have assumed the identity of the Gods, are outflanked by the Gods in an ironic and chilling climax.

In Dunsany's later (and less remarkable) plays the Other which confronts his heroes and heroines usually assumes less exotic forms—ghosts in *His Sainted Grandmother* and *The Seventh Symphony*; a Turandot-style heroine in *Atalanta in Wimbledon*; unscrupulous capitalists in *Cheezo* and *Time's*

Joke; the Devil in *The Raffle*, *Mr Sliggen's Hour*, *The Bureau de Change* and *The Evil Kettle*; the goddess of fame in *Fame and the Poet* and *Fame Comes Late*; animals in *The Use of Man*, *Mr Faithful* and (at least by analogy) *The Flight of the Queen*; and extreme aestheticism in *The Lost Silk Hat*. Ordinary mortality—especially *youthful* mortality—is sometimes allowed to triumph over these alien forces. "Fight the gods! They cannot stand against youth", advises the eponymous hero of *The Old King's Tale*.

According to Mark Amory, "Dunsany had an intellect but did not care to use it in his work". It is true that the content of his plays is (as Rebecca West put it in her review of *If*) "intellectually negligible", but the best of them are beautifully constructed, which surely argues an intellectual input of some kind. He was a master of that rather old-fashioned genre, the well-made or "plotted" one-acter—a brief play of intrigue with a twist in the tail. He could—and sometimes did—toss off effective plays of this kind in a few hours.

But full-length plays required more thought and extra ingredients—either a more convoluted plot or characters of some complexity. Both of these solutions eluded Dunsany. In *Alexander* the hero does not develop; rather, he undergoes a series of oscillations—one per act—between Greek and Persian values. The play's two principal women (Thais and the Queen of the Amazons) look as though they are intended to make an important contribution to these oscillations, but they are so thinly drawn that their function is hard to define. *If*, though better known, is not more successful. John Beal's travel through space and time amounts to little more than a rather wayward yarn. The perfunctory denouement is full of loose ends. (It is also extremely difficult to stage.) And the characterization is so rudimentary that we cannot even be sure whether wish-fulfilment or Eastern magic is the principal cause of his journeyings.

Lord Adrian is more carefully constructed. In effect Dunsany placed one one-acter inside another, like a letter in an envelope. The inner play—about the life and grisly death of a young man whose elderly father has (like Yeats) had a monkey gland implanted to restore his youth—works well enough, though the long time-span causes some technical problems. (Dunsany shows an amusing awareness of these problems when he has characters comment from time to time on the way time has flown.) The outer play—about the father—is less successful. The ending is particularly unconvincing, largely because of weak characterization.

It is on the one-acters that Dunsany's reputation—such as it is—must rest. On the whole the early, exotic ones are the best, but one quality that stands out even in the more conventional later ones is his remarkable ear. This guarantees that the dialogue is always effective; indeed the inspired banality of some of the exchanges—as in the first two scenes of *If*—almost anticipates the absurdists. Dunsany's ear inevitably made him quick to perceive the possibilities of radio. The "plays for air" in *Plays for Earth and Air* are for this medium. He thus paved the way which many Irish writers have since trod with distinction. Moreover, as early as 1937 (in the preface to *Plays for Earth and Air*) he was capable of seeing that "probably the future of plays for the air lies with television". Unfortunately he died before he could pioneer this field as well.

—Richard Corballis

DURANG, Christopher (Ferdinand). Born in Montclair, New Jersey, USA, 2 January 1949. Educated at Harvard University, Cambridge, Massachusetts, 1967–71, AB in English 1971; Yale University School of Drama, New Haven, Connecticut, 1971–74, MFA in playwriting 1974. Drama teacher, Southern Connecticut College, New Haven, 1975, and Yale University, 1975–76. Recipient: Obie Award, 1980; Dramatists Guild Hull-Warriner Award, 1985.

Works

Collections

The Nature and Purpose of the Universe; Death Comes to Us All, Mary Agnes; 'dentity Crisis: Three Short Plays. 1979.
Christopher Durang Explains it All for You (includes *The Nature and Purpose of the Universe; 'dentity Crisis; Titanic; The Actor's Nightmare; Sister Mary Ignatius Explains it All for You; Beyond Therapy*). 1982.

Stage Works

The Nature and Purpose of the Universe (produced Northampton, Massachusetts, 1971). In *The Nature and Purpose of the Universe; Death Comes to Us All, Mary Agnes; 'dentity Crisis*, 1979.
'dentity Crisis (as *Robert*, produced Harvard College, Cambridge, Massachusetts, 1971; as *'dentity Crisis*, produced Yale Repertory Theatre, New Haven, Connecticut, 1975). In *The Nature and Purpose of the Universe; Death Comes to Us All, Mary Agnes; 'dentity Crisis*, 1979.
Better Dead Than Sorry, music by Jack Feldman, lyrics by Durang (produced Yale University, New Haven, Connecticut, 1972).
I Don't Generally Like Poetry But Have You Read "Trees"?, with Albert Innaurato (produced Yale University, New Haven, Connecticut, 1972).
The Life Story of Mitzi Gaynor; or, Gyp, with Albert Innaurato (produced Yale University, New Haven, Connecticut, 1973).
The Marriage of Bette and Boo (produced Yale University, New Haven, Connecticut, 1973; revised version produced New York, 1979; further revised version produced New York, 1985). Revised version in *Yale/Theatre*, 1973; further revised version, 1985.
The Idiots Karamazov, with Albert Innaurato, music by Jack Feldman, lyrics by Durang (produced Yale Repertory Theatre, New Haven, Connecticut, 1974). In *Yale/Theatre*, 1974; augmented edition, 1981.
Titanic (produced Yale University, New Haven, Connecticut, 1974). 1983.
Death Comes to Us All, Mary Agnes (produced Yale Repertory Theatre, New Haven, Connecticut, 1975). In *The Nature and Purpose of the Universe; Death Comes to Us All, Mary Agnes; 'dentity Crisis*, 1979.
When Dinah Shore Ruled the Earth, with Wendy Wasserstein (produced Yale University, New Haven, Connecticut, 1975).
Das Lusitania Songspiel, with Sigourney Weaver, music by Mel Marvin and Jack Gaughan (produced Van Dam Theatre, New York, 1976; revised version produced New York, 1976; further revised version produced New York, 1980).
A History of the American Film (produced by the Hartford Stage Company, Hartford, Connecticut, 1976). 1978.

The Vietnamization of New Jersey (produced Yale Repertory Theatre, New Haven, Connecticut, 1977). 1978.
Sister Mary Ignatius Explains it All for You (produced Ensemble Studio Theatre, New York, 1979). 1980.
Beyond Therapy (produced Phoenix Theatre, New York, 1981; revised version produced New York, 1982).
The Actor's Nightmare (produced Playwright's Horizons, New York, 1981). With *Sister Mary Ignatius Explains it All for You*, 1982.
Baby with the Bathwater (produced Cambridge, Massachusetts, 1983). 1984.
Sloth, in *Faustus in Hell* (produced Princeton University, Princeton, New Jersey, 1985).
Laughing Wild (produced Playwrights' Horizons, New York, 1987). With *Baby with the Bathwater*, 1989.
Naomi in the Living Room (produced Ensemble Studio Theatre, New York, 1991).

Screenplays

Beyond Therapy, with Robert Altman, 1987.

Television Plays

Comedy Zone series; Carol Burnett Special.

*

Bibliographies

Philip C. Kolin, *American Playwrights Since 1945: A Guide to Scholarship, Criticism, and Performance*, New York, 1989.

Criticism

Books:
Interview in *In Their Own Words: Contemporary American Playwrights*, edited by David Savran, New York, 1988.

Articles:
Interview in *Dramatists Guild Quarterly*, vol.26 no.4, 1990.

* * *

Christopher Durang's reputation as a powerful black humorist was clinched with two major plays, *Sister Mary Ignatius Explains it All for You* and *The Marriage of Bette and Boo*. Earlier, critics tended to dismiss his work as "sophomoric", partly because of his bourgeois-baiting shock humor, and partly because of his beginnings at the Yale Cabaret; and two plays somewhat more restrainedly designed to please Broadway tastes—*A History of the American Film* and *Beyond Therapy*—did little to change that view.

The outrageous and often verbally dexterous humor, literate and sardonic, often conceals rage, but is central to Durang's distinctiveness as a comic playwright. David Savran has rightly commented that the comedy harks back to various models of drama familiar to the audience—soap-opera, situation comedy, the "well-made" play. Durang satirizes those forms, and the structure devolves into a well-paced series of revue sketches which accumulate into an experience of considerable impact.

A major theme in Durang is the way that various systems, both societal and metaphysical, promise the individual more than they can deliver. They do not provide a sense of personal fulfilment in exchange for the discipline they exact; worse, they promise a satisfying meaning and "order" for life, which it does not possess. The most powerful and funny Durang plays are those which deal with Roman Catholicism as the "system" in question. *The Nature and Purpose of the Universe*, Durang's earliest published play, already presents a castigation of Roman Catholicism.

In *Sister Mary Ignatius Explains it All for You*, apparently gouged out of the playwright by the devastating experience of his mother's death from cancer, the situation centers on a paranoid nun whose ex-students interrupt her class to re-enact a passion play, but then confront her with her rigidity and the cruel and demanding authoritarianism which both she and her religion embody to them. She responds to their accusations by shooting two of them dead and humiliating the rest; she remains fully in control and safe from legal or any other retribution as the play ends. The central statement of the play—and perhaps the clearest example of Durang's seminal preoccupation—comes in the long monologue in which the ex-student ringleader, Diane, challenges Sister Mary: she relates how her mother's death and her rape by an intruder in her home happened on the same day, and that this *"randomness seemed intolerable. I found I grew to hate you, Sister, for making me once expect everything to be ordered and to make sense"*.

The Marriage of Bette and Boo, expanded from a one-acter in the 1970's to its definitive form in 1985, recounts the progression of a marriage in which a Roman-Catholic couple can produce only one child, the others being stillborn. She becomes more apathetic and hermeticized; he more alcoholic; and after the inevitable divorce there is a slight rapprochement in hospital before her death. Matt, the only son, serves as narrator and commentator on the scenes, some of which are "flash-forwards" out of sequence with the rest, dictated in their sequence by his urgency and guilt at his own strange detachment from their anguish. But, at the end, there are signs that he can overcome this and accept his insight into the apparent randomness of the blows which God seems to deal to people.

In other plays, Durang investigates constricting systems other than Roman Catholicism: in *Titanic* and *'dentity Crisis*, it is the family unit, and the way that, when its proprieties are too rigidly endorsed, its members will indulge in a farrago of eccentric and destructively deviant behavior. In *The Vietnamization of New Jersey*, a satire on David Rabe's over-praised *Sticks and Bones*, a "WASP" family disintegrates under the pressure of assimilating their Vietnam veteran son and the son's Asian wife, who later turns out to be a Caucasian in disguise. In *Baby with the Bathwater* a mother and father raise their son as a daughter for 15 years.

Beyond Therapy examines the constrictions of the nuclear family at greater length and specificity. There is also a satire on psychiatry in the form of two grotesquely imcompetent mentor-psychiatrists who bring their respective patients to the brink of disaster. The major point, partly made through the bisexual confusions of the main character, is that "primary relationships" have become intimidating because they promise more than they can deliver, and require more discipline than modern adult New Yorkers, at least, can muster.

Two other plays deal with the stimulating, but ultimately constricting, effects that literary and film genres and artistic masterworks can have on individualism and creative imagination. In the short *The Actor's Nightmare*, an actor finds himself rehearsing and playing in roles he doesn't know and in plays he hasn't read, and finally is dispatched in a "real" replay of the execution scene from Robert Bolt's *A Man for All Seasons*. In *A History of the American Film* it is filmic

genre that is both lure and target. Durang begins by unrolling a series of sappy and amusing film scenes from the palmiest days of the various genres. But, as the years go by and present reality looms closer, the genres become increasingly scrambled and threatening, and at the end the Loretta Young archetype character is stuck half-way up in the flies above a littered stage, with apocalypse seemingly just around the corner.

Formally, Durang uses two major stylistic devices to embody his major themes. One is an extensive use of various kinds of ritual, both social and religious; and the other is the use of the long self-contained monologue or "aria". In *Sister Mary Ignatius*, the rituals are those of the classroom lesson, and later the enactment of the passion play; in *The Marriage of Bette and Boo*, it is the wedding itself, and later family meals (such as Thanksgiving dinner), Christmas celebrations, and visits to hospitals for births that turn out to be deaths. Generic rituals of Hollywood films, psychoanalytic sessions, and restaurant dinners are some of the other kinds that Durang relies on, and in all the plays the intimations of a progressive breakdown and looming apocalypse are often manifested in the subversion of these rituals or ceremonies. The "arias" are used in two contrasting ways. Sometimes, as in the Sister's early speeches in *Sister Mary Ignatius*, they indicate a hermetically sealed paranoia on the part of the character uttering them; at other times there is some kind of protective indulgence or fantasy in which whatever sense of selfhood that is left is shored up against the forces ranged against the individual, as occurs with Diane in *Sister Mary*, or with Bette in *The Marriage of Bette and Boo*.

—Dennis Carroll

DURAS, Marguerite. Born Marguerite Donnadieu in Giadinh, near Saigon, French Indochina (now Vietnam), 4 April 1914. Educated at Lycée de Saigon, baccalauréat, 1931; the Sorbonne, Paris, 1933–34; licence in law and political science, 1935. Married Robert Antelme in 1939; had a son by Dionys Mascolo. Moved to France, 1932. Secretary, Ministry of Colonies, Paris, 1935–41; full-time writer and journalist after 1943; expelled from the Communist Party, 1950; first play, *Le Square*, produced 1957: this, and many subsequent plays, adapted from her own fiction; writer of screenplays, especially in the 1970's and 1980's; also director. Recipient: Prix Jean Cocteau, 1954–55; Ibsen prize, 1970; Grand Prix de l'Académie du Cinéma (for *India Song*), 1975; Grand Prix du Théâtre de l'Académie Française, 1983; Prix Goncourt, 1984.

Works

Collections

Théâtre 1 (includes *Les Eaux et fôrets; Le Square; La Musica*). 1965.
Three Plays (includes *Days in the Trees; The Square; The Viaducts of Seine-et-Oise*). 1965.
Théâtre 2 (includes *Suzanna Andler; Yes, peut-être; Le Shaga; Des Journées entières dans les arbres; Un homme est venu me voir*). 1968.
Suzanna Andler; La Musica; L'Amante Anglaise (translations). 1975.

Marguerite Duras (1955).

Théâtre 3 (includes *La Bête dans la jungle*; *Les Papiers d'Aspern*; *La Danse de mort*). 1984.

Stage Works

Le Square, with Claude Martin, from her novel (produced Studio des Champs-Élysées, Paris, 1957; revised version, produced 1965). In *Théâtre 1*, 1965; translated as *The Square*, in *Three Plays*, 1967.
Les Viaducs de la Seine-et-Oise (produced Théâtre de Poche, Paris, 1960). 1960; translated as *The Viaducts of Seine-et-Oise*, in *Three Plays*, 1967.
Les Papiers d'Aspern, with Robert Antelme, from the play *The Aspern Papers* by Michael Redgrave, based on the story by Henry James (produced Théâtre des Mathurins, Paris, 1961). 1970.
Miracle en Alabama, with Gérard Jarlot, from a play by William Gibson (produced 1961). 1962.
La Bête dans la jungle, with James Lord, from a story by Henry James (produced Théâtre de l'Athénée, Paris, 1962).
Les Eaux et fôrets (produced Théâtre Mouffetard, Paris, 1965). In *Théâtre 1*, 1965; translated as *The Rivers and Forests*, with *The Afternoon of Monsieur Andesmas*, 1964.
La Musica (produced Studio des Champs-Élysées, Paris). In *Théâtre 1*, 1965.
Des Journées entières dans les arbres, from her novel (produced Odéon Théâtre de France, Paris, 1965). In *Théâtre 2*, 1968; translated as *Days in the Trees*, in *Three Plays*, 1967; as *Whole Days in the Trees*, 1984.
Yes, peut-être (produced Théâtre Gramont, Paris, 1968). In *Théâtre 2*, 1968.

Un Homme est venu me voir. In *Théâtre 2*, 1968.
Le Shaga (produced Théâtre Gramont, Paris, 1968). In *Théâtre 2*, 1968.
Susanna Andler (produced Théâtre des Mathurins, Paris, 1969). In *Théâtre 2*, 1968; translated as *Suzanna Andler*, in *Suzanna Andler; La Musica; L'Amante Anglaise*, 1975.
L'Amante anglaise, from her novel (produced by Théâtre National Populaire, Salle Gémier, Paris, 1969). 1968; translated as *Suzanna Andler*, in *Suzanna Andler; La Musica; L'Amante Anglaise*, 1975.
La Danse de mort, from a play by Strindberg (produced Théâtre du Palais de Chaillot, Paris, 1970). In *Théâtre 3*, 1984.
India Song (in French). 1973; translated as *India Song*, 1976.
Home (in French), from the play by David Storey. 1973.
L'Eden cinéma (produced Théâtre d'Orsay, Paris, 1977). 1977; bilingual edition, 1988.
Savannah Bay (produced London, 1984). 1982; revised edition, 1983.
La Maladie de la mort. 1983.
La Musica deuxième (produced Théâtre du Rond-Point, Paris, 1985). 1985.
La Mouette, from a play by Chekhov. 1985.
Véra Baxter; or The Atlantic Beaches from her screenplay. In *Drama Contemporary: France*, edited by Philippa Wehle, 1988.

Screenplays

Hiroshima mon amour, 1959 (published 1960; translated, 1961); *Moderato Cantabile*, with Gérard Jarlot and Peter

Brook, 1960; *Une Aussi Longue Absence (The Long Absence)*, with Gérard Jarlot, 1961 (published 1961; translated, with *Hiroshima mon amour*, 1966); *10:30 P.M. Summer*, with Jules Dassin, 1966; *La Musica*, 1966; *Détruire, dit-elle (Destroy, She Said)*, 1969; *Les Rideaux blancs*, 1966; *Jaune le soleil*, 1971; *Nathalie Granger*, 1972 (published with *La Femme du Gange*, 1973); *La ragazza di Passaggio/La Femme du Gange*, 1973 (published with *Nathalie Granger*, 1973); *Ce que savait Morgan*, with others, 1974; *India Song*, 1975; *Des journées entières dans les arbres*, 1976; *Son nom de Venises dans Calcutta désert*, 1976; *Baxter—Vera Baxter*, 1977 (published as *Vera Baxter*, 1980); *Le Camion*, 1977 (published 1977); *Le Navire Night*, 1978, and *Césarée; Les Mains négatives; Aurélia Steiner* (all published together, 1979); *L'Homme assis dans le couloir*, 1980 (published 1980); *Agatha et les lectures illimitées*, 1981 (published as *Agatha*, 1981); *L'Homme atlantique*, 1981 (published 1982); *Dialogue de Rome*, 1982; *Les Enfants*, 1985.

Television Plays

Sans merveille, with Gérard Jarlot, 1964.

Fiction

Les Impudents.   1943.
La Vie tranquille.   1944.
Un barrage contre le Pacifique.   1950; translated as *The Sea Wall*, 1952; as *A Sea of Troubles*, 1953.
Le Marin de Gibraltar.   1952; translated as *The Sailor from Gibraltar*, 1966.
Les Petits Chevaux de Tarquinia.   1953; translated as *The Little Horses of Tarquinia*, 1960.
Des Journées entières dans les arbres.   1954; translated as *Whole Days in the Trees*, 1981.
Le Square.   1955; translated as *The Square*, 1959.
Moderato Cantabile.   1958; translated as *Moderato Cantabile*, 1960.
Hiroshima mon amour.   1960; translated as *Hiroshima mon amour*, 1961.
Dix Heures et demie du soir en été.   1960; translated as *10.30 on a Summer Night*, 1962.
L'Après-midi de Monsieur Andesmas.   1962; translated as *The Afternoon of Mr Andesmas*, 1964.
Le Ravissement de Lol V. Stein.   1964; translated as *The Ravishing of Lol V. Stein*, 1967; as *The Rapture of Lol V. Stein*, 1967.
Le Vice-consul.   1965; translated as *The Vice-Consul*, 1968.
L'Amante anglaise.   1967; translated as *L'Amante Anglaise*, 1968.
Détruire, dit-elle.   1969; translated as *Destroy, She Said*, 1970.
Abahn Saban David.   1970.
L'Amour.   1972.
Ah! Ernesto, with Bernard Bonhomme.   1971.
La Maladie de la mort.   1983; translated as *The Malady of Death*, 1986.
L'Amant.   1984; translated as *The Lover*, 1985.
Les Yeux bleus cheveux noirs.   1986; translated as *Blue Eyes, Black Hair*, 1987.
Emily L.   1987; translated as *Emily L.*, 1989.
La Pluie d'été.   1990; translated as *Summer Rain*, 1992.
L'Amant de la Chine du Nord.   1991.

Other

Les Parleuses (interviews), with Xavière Gauthier.   1974; translated as *Woman to Woman*, 1987.

Étude sur l'oeuvre littéraire, théâtrale, et cinématographique de Marguerite Duras, with Jacques Lacan and Maurice Blanchot.   1975.
Territoires du féminin, with Marcelle Marini.   1977.
Les Lieux de Marguerite Duras (interview), with Michelle Porte.   1978.
L'Été 80.   1980.
Les Yeux ouverts (special "Marguerite Duras Issue").   In *Cahiers du Cinéma*, 312–313, June 1980.
Outside: Papiers d'un jour.   1981; revised edition, 1984; translated as *Outside: Selected Writings*, 1986.
Marguerite Duras à Montréal (interviews and lectures), edited by Suzanne Lamy and André Roy.   1981.
La Douleur.   1985; translated as *The War*, 1986.
La Pute de la côte normande.   1986.
La Vie matérielle: Marguerite Duras parle à Jérôme Beaujour.   1987; translated as *Practicalities: Marguerite Duras Speaks to Jérôme Beaujour*, 1990.
Les Yeux verts.   1987; translated as *Green Eyes*, 1990.
Marguerite Duras (interview).   1987.

*

Criticism

Books:
Alfred Cismaru; *Marguerite Duras* (in English), New York, 1971.
Jean Pierrot, *Marguerite Duras*, Mayenne, 1986.
Mary K. Martin, "Space Invasions: Voice-Overs in Works by Samuel Beckett and Marguerite Duras", in *The Theatrical Space*, edited by James Redmond, Cambridge, 1987 (Themes in Drama series).
Helga Fintner, "Vom Theater des Wortes, das fehlt. . . .", in *Marguerite Duras*, edited by Ilma Rakusa, Frankfurt, 1988.
Liliane Papin, *L'Autre Scène: Le Théâtre de Marguerite Duras*, Saratoga, California, 1988.

Articles:
Janice B. Gross, "Women Writing Across Purpose: The Theater of Marguerite Duras and Nathalie Sarraute", in *Modern Drama*, 32, 1989.
Liliane Papin, "Staging Writing or the Ceremony of the Text in Marguerite Duras", in *Modern Drama*, 34, 1991.

* * *

Marguerite Duras is a prolific novelist, dramatist, scriptwriter, filmmaker, and journalist. Her childhood in French Indochina (now Vietnam) taught her how individuals are often trapped, through no fault of their own, in a mysterious world of forces greater than they can cope with or even hope to understand—a notion that lies behind much of her work.

Her first two novels appeared in wartime Paris, and made little impact. Her first works to be critically admired were *Le Square, Moderato Cantabile*, and, especially, her filmscript for Alain Resnais' *Hiroshima mon amour*. But it was not until *L'Amant (The Lover)* won the Prix Goncourt in 1984 that she achieved a really popular success.

One of the most remarkable aspects of her writing is how closely every work is interrelated with every other. She picks up characters and motifs from previous ideas, and reworks them (notably in the so-called "cycle" of five works which include *The Ravishing of Lol V. Stein, The Vice-Consul, L'Amour* [Love], *La Femme du Gange* [The Woman from the Ganges], and *India Song*). She is always exploring different genres: *India Song*, for example, is a "text", a play, and a film. She adapts her novels into plays (*Whole Days in the Trees*). She adapted one play (*The Viaducts of Seine-et-Oise*) into a novel (*L'Amante anglaise*) and then turned it into another play. 20 years after her success with *La Musica*, she returned to write a continuation. Nothing could better illustrate her belief that her work is only a tentative exploration of a theme, to be refashioned whenever she discovers the technical "means" to explore a further facet of an issue which she sees as implicit in the earlier work.

If her novels can be compared with the *nouveaux romans* which began to appear in France in the mid-1950's, her plays owe much to Beckett and Ionesco. A striking feature of them is how many are set in public places of one kind or another: a street in *Les Eaux et forêts* (*The Rivers and Forests*), a hotel lobby in *La Musica*, an empty villa in an off-season resort (*Suzanna Andler*), an embassy (*India Song*), or an indefinite space in *Shaga* and *Yes, peut-être* (Yes, Perhaps). The characters are similarly a-personal. Some are anonymous, others have foreign names. They have no past, or only one that informs their present, and no future: they can only be imagined in the situation in which they are depicted.

One of Duras's major themes is an interest in motivation. This is perhaps most obvious in her first play, which is based on a true incident reported in the papers, and in which an elderly couple who have committed a murder reflect on their deed while waiting for their arrest. But more typically it takes the form of an open-ended presentation of a meeting between two protagonists in which it is never quite clear what each of them wants. Why does a relationship fall apart, as in *Suzanna Andler*? Or why are relationships founded on such flimsy grounds as those described in *The Square*?

Germaine Brée is surely right to describe love as the principal theme in Duras' work. The young nanny and young man of *The Square* begin to converse. In spite of some fundamental differences of character, she is clearly interested in him. She more or less invites him to a ball. Will he go? "Perhaps". Much of the dramatist's work is involved with a similar "perhaps". *La Musica* looks at a couple who meet by chance in a hotel immediately following their divorce. They are still drawn towards one another. Will they get back together? Probably not; but the point is that perhaps they should. These questions are not simply a dramatic trick; they are the very stuff of Duras's style. She probes an issue for all its possibilities, but comes to no conclusions. She invites the audience to ask questions, but not to settle for any answers.

Her male characters are rarely well defined. The emphasis is almost always on the female characters and yet, strangely, they are types rather than individuals. The nanny in *The Square* represents any young woman who would like to escape from work which imprisons her, even if it be to a relationship that will allow her no greater freedom. Claire, in *The Viaducts of Seine-et-Oise*, who is haunted by the overture to Verdi's *Traviata*, represents any middle-aged woman who has experienced only one exquisite pleasure in her life, and that only very indirectly related to sex. Anne Marie Stretter, the bored wife of the ambassador in *Le Vice-Consul* and who eventually ends the way that so many of Duras's heroines do, by drowning, represents any woman in search of a pleasure that evades her. It is because they are types that they make such a powerful impression on an audience. We feel for them in their suffering precisely because their suffering involves and indicts us all, men and women alike.

Given the markedly visual emphasis in many of her novels, it was perhaps inevitable that Duras should have wanted to experiment with both theatre and film, and found the latter better suited to her talent. Paradoxically, however, it was not the visual possibilities that attracted her so much as the opportunity offered to explore sound and tempo. Perhaps the most distinctive feature of her work is the way in which a theme is explored in almost musical terms. In her plays in particular, the words rise and fall in cadences and silences are made pregnant. It is this quality which gives them that unique emotional intensity which distinguishes all that she has written. In the mid 1960's, it looked as if Duras was just a fringe member of the new novelists. Since then, partly prompted by the interest shown in her work by feminist critics, the claims of her individual voice have been winning increasing critical acclaim.

—Terence Dawson

DÜRRENMATT, Friedrich. Born in Konolfingen bei Bern, Switzerland, 5 January 1921. Educated at Grosshöchstetten school; Freies Gymnasium and Humboldtianum, Bern; University of Zurich, one term; University of Bern. Married 1) the actress Lotti Geissler in 1946 (died 1983), a son and two daughters; 2) Charlotte Kerr in 1984. First play, *Es steht geschrieben*, produced 1947; drama critic, *Die Weltwoche* (Zurich), 1951; co-director, Basler Theater, 1968–69; co-owner, *Züricher Sonntags-Journal*, 1969–71; writer-in-residence, University of Southern California, Los Angeles, March-June 1981; travelled to Greece and South America, 1983–84; and to Egypt, 1985. Also television director. Recipient: City of Bern Prize, 1954, 1979; Radio Play Prize (Berlin), 1957; Italia Prize, for radio play, 1958; Schiller Prize (Mannheim), 1959; New York Drama Critics Circle Award, 1959; Schiller Prize (Switzerland), 1960; Grillparzer Prize, 1968; Kanton of Bern Prize, 1969; Buber-Rosenzweig Medal, 1977; Austrian State Award, 1983; Carl Zuckmayer Medal (Rhineland Palatinate), 1984; Bavarian Literature Prize, 1985. Honorary doctorate: Temple University, Philadelphia, 1969; Hebrew University, Jerusalem, 1977; University of Nice, 1977; University of Neuchâtel, 1981. Honorary Fellow, Modern Language Association (USA). Died in Neuchâtel, Switzerland, 14 December 1990.

Works

Collections

Komödien (3 vols.).   1957–72.
Gesammelte Hörspiele (radio plays; includes *Abendstunde im Spätherbst; Der Doppelgänger; Herkules und der Stall des Augias; Nächtliches Gespräch mit einem verachteten Menschen; Die Panne, Der Prozess um des Esels Schatten; Stranitzky und der Nationalheld; Das Unternehmen der Wega*).   1961.
Four Plays 1957–62 (includes *Romulus the Great; The Marriage of Mr. Mississippi; An Angel Comes to Babylon; The Physicists*), translated by Gerhard Nellhaus and others.   1964; retitled as *Four Plays* (New York), 1965.
Werkausgabe (30 vols.).   1980–86.
Plays and Essays, edited by Volkmar Sander.   1982.
Versuche.   1988.

Stage Works

Es steht geschrieben (produced Schauspielhaus, Zurich, 1947).   1947; revised version, as *Die Wiedertäufer* (produced Schauspielhaus, Zurich, 1967), 1967.

Scene from the 1959 Zurich Schauspielhaus production of *Frank V* by **Friedrich Dürrenmatt** and Paul Burkhard, designed by Teo Otto.

Der Blinde (produced Stadttheater, Basle, 1948).   1960; revised edition, 1965.

Romulus der Grosse (produced Stadttheater, Basle, 1949).   1956; revised version (produced Schauspielhaus, Zurich, 1957), 1958; translated as *Romulus*, 1962.

Die Ehe des Herrn Mississippi (produced Kammerspiele, Munich, 1952).   1952; revised version, 1957; translated as *The Marriage of Mr. Mississippi*, 1966.

Ein Engel kommt nach Babylon (produced Kammerspiele, Munich, 1953; operatic version, with music by Rudolf Kelterborn, produced Opernhaus, Zurich, 1977).   1954; revised version (produced Schauspielhaus, Zurich, 1957), 1958; translated as *An Angel Comes to Babylon*, with *Romulus the Great*, 1964.

Der Besuch der alten Dame (produced Schauspielhaus, Zurich, 1956).   1956; translated as *The Visit*, 1958.

Frank V, music by Paul Burkhard (produced Schauspielhaus, Zurich, 1959).   1960.

Abendstunde im Spätherbst, from his radio play (produced Berlin, 1959).   1959; translated as *Episode on an Autumn Evening*, 1959; as *Incident at Twilight*, in *Postwar German Theatre*, edited by Michael Benedikt and George E. Wellwarth, 1968.

Die Physiker (produced Schauspielhaus, Zurich, 1962).   1962; translated as *The Physicists*, 1963.

Herkules und der Stall des Augias,, from his radio play (produced Schauspielhaus, Zurich, 1963).   1960; translated as *Hercules and the Augean Stables*, nd.

Der Meteor (produced Schauspielhaus, Zurich, 1966).   1966; translated as *The Meteor*, 1973.

König Johann, from *King John* by Shakespeare (produced Stadttheater, Basle, 1968).   1968.

Play Strindberg: Totentanz nach August Strindberg (produced Komödie, Basle, 1969).   1969; translated as *Play Strindberg: The Dance of Death* 1972.

Titus Andronicus, from the play by Shakespeare (produced Schauspielhaus, Düsseldorf, 1970).   1970.

Porträt eines Planeten (produced Schauspielhaus, Düsseldorf, 1970; revised version, produced Schauspielhaus, Zurich, 1971).   1971.

Urfaust, from the play by Goethe (produced Schauspielhaus, Zurich, 1970).   1980.

Der Mitmacher (produced Schauspielhaus, Zurich, 1973).   1973; augmented edition, *Der Mitmacher—Ein Komplex* (includes notes, essays, narratives), 1976.

Die Frist (produced Schauspielhaus, Zurich, 1977).   1977.

Die Panne, from the novel (produced Theatre le Carré Silvia Montfort, Paris).   In *Die Panne: Ein Hörspiel und eine Komödie*, 1980.

Dichterdämmerung.   In *Werkausgabe 1*, 1980.

Nachgedanken.   In *Werkausgabe 1*, 1980.

Achterloo (produced Schauspielhaus, Zurich, 1983; revised version, produced Festspiele, Schwetzingen, 1988).   1983.

Screenplays

Es geschah am hellichten Tag [*It Happened in Broad Daylight*], 1960 (published 1960); *Die Ehe des Herrn Mississippi*, 1961 (published 1961); *Der Besuch der alten Dame*, 1963 (published 1963).

Radio plays

Der Prozess um des Esels Schatten, 1951 (published 1959); *Stranitzky und der Nationalheld*, 1952 (published 1959); *Nächtliches Gespräch mit einem verachteten Menschen*, 1952 (published 1957; translated as *Conversation at Night with a*

Despised Chatacter, nd); *Herkules und der Stall des Augias*, 1954 (published 1954); *Das Unternehmen der Wega*, 1954 (published 1958); *Die Panne*, 1956 (published 1961; translated as *The Deadly Game*, 1966); *Abendstunde im Spätherbst*, 1958 (published 1959; see Stage Works for translations); *Der Doppelgänger*, 1961 (published 1960).

Fiction

Pilatus.   1949.

Der Nihilist.   1950; reprinted as *Die Falle*.

Der Richter und sein Henker.   1952; translated as *The Judge and His Hangman*, 1954.

Die Stadt: Prosa 1–4.   1952.

Das Bild des Sisyphos.   1952.

Der Verdacht.   1953; translated as *The Quarry*, 1961.

Grieche sucht Griechin.   1955; translated as *Once a Greek . . .*, 1965.

Das Versprechen: Requiem auf den Kriminalroman.   1958; translated as *The Pledge*, 1959.

Die Panne: Eine noch mögliche Geschichte.   1960; translated as *Traps* (New York), 1960; as *A Dangerous Game* (London), 1960.

Der Sturz.   1971.

The Judge and His Hangman; The Quarry: Two Hans Barlach Mysteries, translated by George Stade.   1983.

Dürrenmatt: His Five Novels (includes *The Judge and the Hangman; The Quarry; Once a Greek . . .; A Dangerous Game; The Pledge*).   1985.

Justiz.   1985; translated as *The Execution of Justice*, 1989.

Minotaurus: Eine Ballade, with drawings by Dürrenmatt.   1985.

Der Auftrag; oder, Vom Beobachten des Beobachters der Beobachter.   1986; translated as *The Assignment; or, On the Observing of the Observer of the Observers*, 1988.

Durcheinanderthal.   1989.

Other

Theaterprobleme.   1955; translated as *Problems on the Theatre*, with *The Marriage of Mr. Mississippi*, 1966.

Friedrich Schiller: Rede (address).   1960.

Der Rest ist Dank (addresses), with Werner Weber.   1961.

Die Heimat im Plakat: Ein Buch für Schweizer Kinder (drawings).   1963.

Theater-Schriften und Reden (2 vols.), edited by Elisabeth Brock-Sulzer.   1966–72; translated in part as *Writings on Theatre and Drama*, edited by H.M. Waidson, 1976.

Monstervortrag über Gerechtigkeit und Recht.   1968.

Sätze aus Amerika.   1970.

Zusammenhänge: Essay über Israel.   1976.

Gespräch mit Heinz Ludwig Arnold.   1976.

Frankfurter Rede.   1977.

Lesebuch.   1978.

Bilder und Zeichnungen, edited by Christian Strich. 1978.

Albert Einstein: Ein Vortrag.   1979.

Literatur und Kunst: Essays, Gedichte und Reden.   1980.

Philosophie und Naturwissenschaft: Essays, Gedichte und Reden.   1980.

Politik: Essays, Gedichte und Reden.   1980.

Kritik: Kritiken und Zeichnungen.   1980.

Stoffe 1–3: Winterkrieg in Tibet; Mondfinsternis; Der Rebell.   1981.

Hildi Hess, text by Dorothea Christ and Dürrenmatt, edited by Daniel Keel.   1981.

Uber Jef Verheyen: Eine Rede.   1982.

Denken mit Dürrenmatt, edited by Daniel Keel.   1982.

Rollenspiele: Protokoll einer fiktiven Inszenierung und "Achterloo III" (includes text of play *Achterloo III*).   1986.

*

Bibliographies

Johannes Hansel, *Friedrich Dürrenmatt Bibliografie*, Bad Homburg, 1968.
Gerhard B. Knapp, *Friedrich Dürrenmatt*, Stuttgart, 1980.

Criticism

Books:
Peter Schneider, *Die Fragwürdigkeit des Rechts im Werke von Friedrich Dürrenmatt*, Karlsruhe, 1967.
Murray B. Peppard, *Friedrich Dürrenmatt*, New York, 1969.
Edgar Neis, *Erläuterungen zu Friedrich Dürrenmatt*, Hollfeld, 1970.
Elizabeth Brock-Sulzer, *Dürrenmatt in unserer Zeit* (revised edition), 1971.
Arnold Armin, *Friedrich Dürrenmatt*, New York, 1972.
Kurt J. Fickert, *To Heaven and Back: The New Morality in the Plays of Friedrich Dürrenmatt*, Lexington, Kentucky, 1972.
Ulrich Profitlich, *Friedrich Dürrenmatt: Komödienbegriff und Komödienstruktur: Eine Einführung*, Stuttgart, 1973.
Hans Bänziger, *Frisch und Dürrenmatt* (seventh edition), Bern, 1976.
Gerhard P. Knapp, *Friedrich Dürrenmatt: Studien zu seinem Werk*, Heidelberg, 1976.
Timo Tiusanen, *Dürrenmatt: A Study in Plays, Prose and Theory*, Princeton, New Jersey, 1977.
Urs Jenny, *Dürrenmatt: A Study of His Plays*, London, 1978.
Hansueli Beusch, *Die Hörspiele Friedrich Dürrenmatts*, Zurich, 1979.
Bodo Fritzen and H. F. Taylor (eds.), *Friedrich Dürrenmatt: A Collection of Critical Essays*, Normal, Illinois, 1979.
Daniel Keel (ed.), *Über Friedrich Dürrenmatt*, Zurich, 1980 (volume 30 of the *Werkausgabe*).
Jan Knopf, *Friedrich Dürrenmatt* (third edition), Munich, 1980.
Kenneth S. Whitton, *The Theatre of Dürrenmatt: A Study in the Possibility of Freedom*, London, 1980.
Arnold Armin (ed.), *Zu Friedrich Dürrenmatt*, Stuttgart, 1982.
Moshe Lazar (ed.), *Play Dürrenmatt*, Malibu, California, 1983.
Flora Sotiraki, *Friedrich Dürrenmatt als Kritiker seiner Zeit*, Frankfurt, 1983.
Hannes Gertner, *Das Komische im Werk Friedrich Dürrenmatts*, Frankfurt, 1984.
Hans Bänziger, *Frisch und Dürrenmatt: Materialien und Kommentare*, Tübingen, 1987.
Jan Knopf, *Der Dramatiker Friedrich Dürrenmatt*, Berlin, 1987.
Kenneth S. Whitton, *Dürrenmatt: Reinterpretation in Retrospect*, New York, 1990.

* * *

Friedrich Dürrenmatt was one of the *enfants terribles* of the German-speaking stage. After bursting like a meteor on to that stage—on 19 April 1947—with his drama of the Anabaptist rising in Münster in 1534 (*Es steht geschrieben*)

Dürrenmatt delighted and exasperated his audiences and critics with a series of comic, grotesque, and provocative plays, all of which however (in retrospect) show a deep concern for the future of humanity and a hatred of oppression. If he will be chiefly remembered for his two masterpieces *Der Besuch der alten Dame* (The Visit of The Old Lady) and *Die Physiker* (*The Physicists*) Dürrenmatt has produced other fine plays, notably *Romulus der Grosse* (Romulus the Great), a satire on the last Roman Emperor whose actual name and status, Romulus Augustulus (i.e. "the small"), Dürrenmatt comically enlarges in order to reduce his and Rome's power to absurdity, and *Der Meteor* (*The Meteor*), in which a Dürrenmattian self-portrait, Wolfgang Schwitter, weary of literary cant and hypocrisy, finds himself, however, unable to die, but—meteor-like—paradoxically brings dramatic and sudden death to those around him.

The Visit (the title of the published translation of *Der Besuch*) has been performed all over the world in many languages. Its brilliant *Einfall* (original idea), taken from Dürrenmatt's own short story *Mondfinsternis* (*Eclipse of the Moon*) and its subsequent re-working, never fails to strike a contemporary audience in the theatre. Claire Zachanassian, the main character—the name is a satirical compound of 20th-century power and greed, from Zacharoff, Onassis, and Gulbenkian—who has been made pregnant by the village shop-keeper, Alfred Ill, and driven out of the equally satirically named village, Güllen ("liquid cattle dung" in Swiss German), now returns as the wealthiest woman in the world to wreak revenge on both Alfred and her village. By promising the villagers "eine Milliarde" (a thousand million or a million million in the USA or the UK), she turns the villagers against their friend while, hypocritically, they maintain they are keeping their loyalty to him. He is ritually strangled by the villagers who are then left with the money, but also with the awful thought that, one day, "an old lady" might visit *them* too.

Guilt and retribution for 20th-century mores are also the themes of *The Physicists*, where an atomic scientist, Möbius, has fled to an asylum and faked insanity in order to preserve the awful secret of "the bomb", only to find that his two closest inmates are likewise fakes, the one a US agent, the other a Soviet agent, both bent on stealing his secret. The typical Dürrenmattian denouement comes when the female director of the asylum, a Dr. Mathilde von Zahnd, is shown to be the only *true* mad person of the group—a grotesque, power-crazy hunchback who has already stolen and photocopied Möbius's secret plans.

Dürrenmatt's last play, *Achterloo* (which is untranslateable), exists in four versions (1983–1988), none of which proved attractive to critics or audiences; it was after the failure of the last version at the Schwetzingen Festival in 1988 that Dürrenmatt announced that "the theatre has no future" and he did not publish a play subsequently, although he was working on the theme of "The Death of Socrates" shortly before his death.

The publication of what then became two volumes of autobiographical reminiscences (*Stoffe I-III*) and later essays in the same vein, allowed Dürrenmatt-watchers to reform earlier opinions and to suggest that much of what he had written had been, in part, a protest at his own physical and geographical condition—a diabetic for over 40 years; a citizen of a tiny, politically and morally powerless, neutral country tied to economic capitalism and individualism, but also a citizen whose philosophical belief in an enlightened idealistic socialism had driven him away from the doctrinal Calvinism of his clergyman father; and a writer whose works had always met with as much critical opposition as public praise. All this led him to see himself in later years as the "minotaur" imprisoned in a glass-walled enclosure shut off from an uncomprehending world.

Dürrenmatt's vast *oeuvre* comprises almost every literary genre — his fame in schools, for example, rests on his three "*Krimis*" (thrillers) *Der Richter und sein Henker* (*The Judge and His Hangman*), *Der Verdacht* (literally "The Suspicion"), and *Das Versprechen* (*The Pledge*). Later he made himself a considerable reputation as a painter and sketcher with several exhibitions to his name; his style owed much to the cataclysmic art of medieval painters such as Hieronymus Bosch, but also to the wit and point of cartoonists like Ronald Searle.

Dürrenmatt, who always considered himself to be a *zoon politikon*, a political animal, applied his philosophy of theatre to real life and commented with much insight on the political happenings of the day in his many trenchant essays. "Tragedy", he proclaimed many years ago, "is no longer a valid art form for today", for this "mess of an age". "Only the *Komödie* can reach us now", and he wrote about untrustworthy politicians, money-grabbing crooked financiers, and sensation-hungry press moguls in the same penetrating way as he conjured up absurd guilt-ridden characters for his stage.

Why did he continue to write at all? "To warn", he told his second wife, Christine Kerr, in a film which she made about him in 1984. "That is the only way to avoid the avalanche — not to fall into it. . .".

—Kenneth S. Whitton

See also *Volume 1* entries on *The Physicists*; *The Visit*.

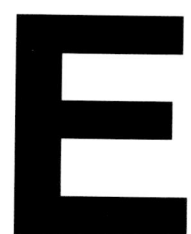

E

ECHEGARAY (Y EIZAGUIRRE), José. Born in Madrid, 19 April 1832. Spent childhood in Murcia. Studied engineering (especially of roads) and mathematics in Madrid, from 1848. Engineer in Almería and Granada; returned to Madrid, 1858, and held various academic positions at his old school; professor of mathematics, University of Madrid; admitted to the Academia de Ciencas Exactas, Físicas y Naturales [Academy of Science], 1865, subsequently becoming its president: wrote a number of scientific and mathematical works. Also pursued career of public service: following the end of the rule of Isabella II, became Minister of Commerce and Director of Public Works, 1868; subsequently elected to Parliament; Minister of Public Education, 1873, and Minister of Finance, 1874; founded the Bank of Spain. First-produced play, *El libro talonario*, staged 1874; achieved theatrical success with *La esposa del vengador*, 1874, and wrote prolifically for the stage thereafter; occupied a seat in the Academia de la Langua, 1884. Returned to government for brief time as Chief of the Treasury, 1904. Elected to the Royal Spanish Academy 1894. Recipient: Nobel Prize for Literature, jointly with Frédéric Mistral, 1904. Died in Madrid, 15 September 1916.

Works

Collections

Obras dramáticas escogidas (2 vols.; includes *La esposa del vengador; En el puño de la espada; O locura o santidad; En el seno de la muerte; La muerte en los labios; El gran Galeoto*). 1884.
Obras dramáticas escogidas (12 vols.). 1884–1905.
Teatro escogido. 1955; second edition, 1965.

Stage Works

Some have appeared in book form in the collections *Obras drámaticas escogidas* and *Teatro escogido* (see above).

El libro talonario (produced Teatro de Apolo, Madrid, 1874).
La esposa del vengador (produced Teatro Español, Madrid, 1874).
La última noche (produced Teatro Español, Madrid, 1875). 1875.
En el puño de la espada (produced Teatro de Apolo, Madrid, 1875).
Un sol que nace y un sol que muere (produced Teatro del Circo, Madrid, 1876).
Cómo empieza y cómo acaba (produced Teatro Español, Madrid, 1876).
El gladiador de Ravena, from a play by Friedrich Halm (produced Teatro de Novedades, 1876).

José Echegaray

O locura o santidad (produced Teatro Español, Madrid, 1877). Translated as *Folly or Saintliness*, with *The Great Galeoto*, 1895; as *Madman or Saint*, in *Poet Lore*, 1912.
Iris de paz (produced Teatro Español, Madrid, 1877).
Para tal culpa tal pena (produced Teatro Español, Madrid, 1877).
Lo que no puede decirse (produced Teatro Español, Madrid, 1877).
En el pilar y en la cruz (produced Teatro Español, Madrid, 1878).
Correr en pos de un ideal (produced Teatro Español, Madrid, 1878).
Algunas veces aqui (produced Teatro de Apolo, Madrid, 1878).
Morir por no despertar (produced Teatro de Apolo, Madrid, 1879).

En el seno de la muerte (produced Teatro Español, Madrid, 1879).

Bodas trágicas (produced Seville, 1879).

Mar sin orillas (produced Teatro Español, Madrid, 1879).

La muerte en los labios (produced Teatro Español, Madrid, 1880).

El gran Galeoto (produced Teatro Español, Madrid, 1881). Translated as *The Great Galeoto*, with *Folly or Saintliness*, 1895; as *The World and His Wife*, 1908; several subsequent translations as *The Great Galeoto*.

Los dos curiosos impertinentes (produced Teatro Español, Madrid, 1881).

Haroldo el Normando (produced Teatro Español, Madrid, 1881).

Conflicto entre dos deberes (produced Teatro Español, Madrid, 1882).

Un milagro en Egipto (produced Teatro Español, Madrid, 1882).

Piensa mal . . . y acertarás (produced Teatro Español, Madrid, 1884).

María Rosa, from a work by Angel Guiméra (produced 1884).

La peste de Otranto (produced Teatro Español, Madrid, 1884).

Vida alegre y muerte triste (produced Teatro Español, Madrid, 1885).

El bandido Lisandro (produced Madrid?, 1886).

De mala raza (produced Teatro Español, Madrid, 1886).

El conde Lotario (produced Valencia, 1887).

Los dos fanatismos (produced Teatro Español, Madrid, 1887).

La realidad y el delirio (produced Teatro Español, Madrid, 1887).

El hijo de hierro y el hijo de carne (produced Teatro de la Princesa, 1888).

Lo sublime en lo vulgar (produced Teatro Calvo-Vico, Barcelona, 1888).

Los rígidos (produced Barcelona, 1888).

Manantial que no se agota (produced Teatro Español, Madrid, 1889).

El prólogo de un drama (produced Valladolid, 1890).

Siempre en ridículo (produced Teatro Español, Madrid, 1890). Translated as *Always Ridiculous*, in *Poet Lore*, 27, 1916.

Irene de Otranto (produced Teatro Real, Madrid, 1891).

Un crítico incipiente (produced Teatro de la Comedia, Madrid, 1891).

Comedia sin desenlace (produced Teatro de la Comedia, Madrid, 1891).

El hijo de Don Juan (produced Teatro Español, Madrid, 1892). Translated as *The Son of Don Juan*, 1895.

Sic vos no vobis; o, La última limosna (produced Teatro de la Comedia, Madrid, 1892).

Mariana (produced Teatro de la Comedia, Madrid, 1892). Translated as *Mariana*, 1895.

El poder de la impotencia (produced Teatro de la Comedia, Madrid, 1893).

A la orilla del mar (produced Teatro de la Comedia, Madrid, 1893).

La rencorosa (produced Teatro de la Comedia, Madrid, 1894).

Mancha que limpia (produced Teatro Español, Madrid, 1895).

El primer acto de un drama (produced Teatro de Novedades, Madrid, 1895).

El estigma (produced Teatro Español, Madrid, 1895).

La cantante callejera (produced Teatro Español, Madrid, 1896). Translated as *The Street Singer*, in *The Drama*, vol.7 no.25, 1917; also in *Twenty Five Short Plays*, edited by Frank Shay, 1925.

La calumnia por castigo (produced Teatro Español, Madrid, 1897).

Semíramis; o, La hija del aire, from *La hija del aire* by Calderón (produced Teatro Español, Madrid, 1897).

Tierrabaja, from a work by Angel Guiméra (produced 1897).

La duda (produced Teatro Español, Madrid, 1898).

El hombre negro (produced Teatro Español, Madrid, 1898). Translated as *The Man in Black*, in *Universal Anthology* 27, 1899.

Silencio de muerte (produced Barcelona, 1898).

Amor salvaje (produced Teatro de la Comedia, Madrid, 1899).

El loco Dios (produced Teatro Español, Madrid, 1902).

Malas herencias (produced Teatro Español, Madrid, 1902).

La escalinata de un trono (produced Teatro Español, Madrid, 1903).

La desequilibrada (produced Teatro Español, Madrid, 1903).

Los tres sueños de Colilla (produced Teatro Español?, Madrid, 1903).

A fuerza de arrastrarse (produced Teatro Español, Madrid, 1905).

El preferido y los cenicientos (produced Teatro Español, Madrid, 1908).

Fiction

Cuentos.   1912.

Verse

Monologos en verso (includes *Entre dolore y cuento; El moderno Endymión; El canto de la sirena*).   1906.

Memoirs and Letters

Recuerdos (memoirs; 3 vols.).   1917.

Scientific Works

Elementos de agricultura teórico-práctica (2 vols.).   1852–57.
Cálculo de variaciones.   1858.
El túnel de los Alpes.   1863.
Discursos leidos, with L. del Valle.   1866.
Teorías modernas de la Física, unidad de las fuerzas materiales (5 vols.).   1883–89.
Observaciones y teorias sobre la afinidad química.   1901.
Navegación aérea.   1902.
Ciencia popular (2 vols.).   1905.
La ciencia y la crítica.   1905.
Conferencias sobre fisica matemática, with others (9 vols.). 1905–14.
Problemas de geometría analítica.   Nd.
Problemas de geometría plana.   Nd.
Muestras.   Nd.

Other

Algunas reflexiones generales sobre la crítica y el arte literario. 1894.
La poesia en la crisis literaria actuel, with Emilio V. Ferrari. Nd.

*

Criticism

Books:
F. Herrán, *Echegaray: Su tiempo y su teatro*, Madrid, 1880.
F. Pi y Arsuaga *Echegaray, Sellés y Cano*, Madrid, 1884.
H. de Curzon, *Le Théâtre de José Echegaray: Étude analytique*, Paris, 1912.
A. Gallego y Burín, *Echegaray: Su obra dramática*, Granada, 1917.
Y.R. Young, *José Echegaray: A Study of His Dramatic Technique*, Urbana, Illinois, 1936.
R.W. Kuykendall, *A Study of Echegaray's Popularity Through His Dramatic Technique*, 1937.
A. Martínez Olmedilla, *José Echegaray: Su vida, su obra, su ambiente*, Madrid, 1946.
Julio Mathias, *Echegaray*, Madrid, 1970.

Articles:
E. Mérimée, "José Echegaray et son oeuvre dramatique", in *Bulletin hispanique*, 1916.
José M. Cabrales Arteaga, "El teatro neorománico de Echegaray", in *Revista de literatura*, 101, 1989.

* * *

Paradoxically, Echegaray is at once the most neglected and the most vilified of Spain's major dramatists. Historians of literature fill many pages reiterating how bad his plays are, without explaining why such an allegedly worthless writer should deserve such attention. At the same time, many of the basic facts of Echegaray's life and works are unknown: there is no complete bibliography of his writings, and no serious research on them has been done for over 40 years.

Yet he would seem to deserve careful study. He was the most brilliant mathematician and science-teacher in 19th-century Spain; he was an effective politician, and as Minister of Finance he founded the Bank of Spain and began to open up the Spanish economy for many decades of growth. From being a sensational anti-Catholic agitator in 1869, he grew into a tolerant pragmatist who could present moral problems on the stage, without bringing forth religious implications, but without offending his largely Catholic audience. Probably no playwright anywhere has ever been so popular for so long within his own country and his own lifetime.

Echegaray himself said that the theatre was his second love, coming after mathematics, but before politics: throughout his life he was fascinated by the theatre, never missing a first night in Madrid. He wrote his first plays in order to support his family, in political exile; but he clearly enjoyed writing them (as well as the wealth and colossal prestige which they brought him), and although he was occasionally tempted to use the stage as a pulpit, he can best be understood as a simple professional entertainer, with no doctrinal axe to grind.

Of his more than 60 plays which were actually performed in the commercial theatre, about 18 were on historical subjects, particularly those made popular by the Romantic writers of the 1830's—subjects such as the Crusades, the Vikings, and Spanish history of the period 1252–1598. The rest of his plays were set in his own time, and almost always concerned the upper and upper-middle classes of Madrid, whether in the capital itself, or in the Cantabrian region where they spent their summer holidays.

Most of the plays have as their subject a secret conflict within a protagonist's conscience, between duty and self-interest or, more often, between two competing duties. Thus in *Mancha que limpia* the foundling Matilde is torn between love for Fernando and gratitude to her foster-family; and in *O locura o santidad* (*Folly or Saintliness*) Lorenzo is torn between the financial welfare of his family and that of the heirs of his foster-father, whose property he believes himself to be usurping. The title of *Conflicto entre dos deberes* would apply to most of the other plays, too.

The theatrical origins of such conflicts went back to Calderón and Lope de Vega, whose Golden Age of the Spanish theatre Echegaray was seen by many to be reviving. However, there is a gulf between Calderón and Echegaray. The former's plays treat moral problems from the point of view of Catholic moral theology, and these problems almost always concern (as theatrical convention then demanded) real or suspected adultery in relation to family honour or shame. When the Spanish Romantic dramatists tried to revive this tradition in the 1830's, they omitted the moral theology and concentrated on the purely emotional aspect of the conflicts, and on the spectacular accessories of Baroque theatre—storms, castles, feudal barons, outlaws, minstrels, duels, disguises, secret letters, and misunderstandings. Echegaray draws on both the Baroque and the Romantic tradition, but makes changes: he reverts to the Baroque tradition of moral problems, but omits their religious framework (which perhaps he did not see in Calderón); and he replaces, in his contemporary dramas, the late medieval paraphernalia with the trappings of upper-class life in Restoration Spain: secret letters, disguises, and misunderstandings survive as plot-machinery, but barons, outlaws, minstrels, and castles are replaced by bankers living in elegant flats, or "Segismundos in frock-coats". Thus, although Echegaray showed that he could outdo his Romantic predecessors in writing the older type of medieval melodrama, as in *En el puño de la espada*, his contemporary plays were usually more successful, and he naturally tended to write more of them and fewer of the historical ones.

Some critics have claimed that after about 1890 Echegaray felt the influence of Ibsen, and began to write problem plays which reflected this influence. This seems an exaggeration. In his plays, ideas are usually as unimportant as theme, dialogue, or characterisation. What is primary is the plot and the ways by which it can be brought to a spectacular conclusion, with one or more murders or suicides. Indeed, Echegaray was said to have often chosen a striking title or spectacular dénouement first, and then to have worked out the steps needed in order to reach it, displaying the skill of the engineer or the mathematician, and treating his characters rather as if they were mere constructional components or abstract concepts. Thus his characterisation is usually very limited. His personages have only such personal characteristics as are necessary for the working out of the plot, and these characteristics develop but little, if at all, in the course of the play. Of course, the same comment could be made about many Golden Age plays; but whereas in the latter the plot itself subserves a greater theme, in Echegaray the plot subserves little, except the need to produce a conclusion that will leave the audience thunderstruck and applauding frenetically.

Only in his best play, *El gran Galeoto* (*The Great Galeoto*) does the plot subserve a theme of universal relevance, the evil of malicious gossip. In this play, a young poet lives innocently as a guest with a banker and his wife, until city gossip suggests that the poet is the wife's lover; as a result, the three become self-conscious, distrustful, and doomed to death and disgrace. The play was a colossal success, in Spain and other countries, and was widely translated.

Echegaray wrote almost half his plays in verse, and was a fluent versifier; but he rarely rose to poetry, and frequently fell back on mere jingles or bombast. That the latter aroused tumultuous applause was, in part, due to the skill of the actors, but also to Echegaray's skill in tailoring the speeches to the talents of the specific actors who would play the roles in the first performances, such as Matilde Díez, María Guerrero, and Antonio and Manuel Calvo. As a result he achieved not only unprecedented popular success and the Nobel Prize for Literature (shared with Mistral in 1904), but also the approval of excellent critics like Menéndez Pelayo and Ciarín. Despite his posthumous poor reputation, he deserved the encomium "the Spanish author with least vanity and greatest love for his art", and at least a favourable judgement as a skilful story-teller of demonic daring and energy.

—Derek W. Lomax

EDGAR, David. Born in Birmingham, England, 26 February 1948. Educated at Oundle School, Northamptonshire, 1961–65; Manchester University, 1966–69, BA (honours) in drama 1969. Married Eve Brook. Reporter, Bradford *Telegraph and Argus*, Yorkshire, 1969–72; Yorkshire Arts Association Fellow, Leeds Polytechnic, 1972–73; resident playwright, Birmingham Repertory Theatre, 1974–75; lecturer in Playwriting, Birmingham University, 1974–78; literary adviser, Royal Shakespeare Company, 1984–88. Honorary senior research fellow, University of Birmingham, England, since 1988. Recipient: John Whiting Award, 1976; Society of West End Theatre Award, 1980; New York Drama Critics Circle Award, 1982; Tony Award, 1982.

Works

Collections

Plays 1 (includes *The Jail Diary of Albie Sachs; Mary Barnes; Saigon Rose; O Fair Jerusalem; Destiny*).
Shorts (includes *Blood Sports* with *Ball Boys; Baby Love; The National Theatre; The Midas Connection*).   1989.
Plays 2 (includes *Ecclesiastes; Nicholas Nickleby, Parts 1 and 2; Entertaining Strangers*).   1990.
Plays 3 (includes *Teendrams; Our Own People; That Summer; Maydays*).   1991.

Stage Works

Two Kinds of Angel (produced Bradford University, Bradford, 1970).   In *The London Fringe Theatre*, edited by V.E. Mitchell, 1975.
A Truer Shade of Blue (produced Bradford University, Bradford, 1970).
Still Life: Man in Bed (produced Pool Theatre, Edinburgh, 1971).
The National Interest (produced by General Will Theatre Company on tour, 1971).
Tedderella (produced Pool Theatre, Edinburgh, 1971).
Bloody Rosa (produced Edinburgh, 1971).
Acid (produced Bradford University, Bradford, 1971).
Conversation in Paradise (produced Edinburgh University, 1971).

The Rupert Show (produced by General Will Theatre Company on tour, 1972).
The End (produced Bradford University, Bradford, 1972).
Excuses, Excuses (produced Belgrade Theatre Studio, Coventry, 1972; as *Fired*, produced Birmingham, 1975).
Rent; or, Caught in the Act (produced by General Will Theatre Company on tour, and Unity Theatre, London, 1972).
State of Emergency (produced by General Will Theatre Company on tour).
Not with a Bang But a Whimper (produced The Polytechnic, Leeds, 1972).
Death Story (produced Birmingham Repertory Studio Theatre, Birmingham, 1972).
The Road to Hanoi, in *Point 101* (produced London, 1972).
England's Ireland, with others (produced Mickery Theatre, Amsterdam, 1972).
A Fart for Europe, with Howard Brenton (produced Royal Court Theatre Upstairs, London, 1973).
Gangsters (produced Soho Poly Lunchtime Theatre, London, 1973).
Up Spaghetti Junction, with others (produced Birmingham Repertory Studio Theatre, 1973).
Baby Love (produced Playhouse, Leeds, 1973).   In *Shorts*, 1989.
The Case of the Workers' Plane (produced New Vic Theatre, Bristol, 1973; shorter version, as *Concorde Cabaret*, produced on tour, 1975).
Operation Iskra (produced by the Paradise Foundry on tour and London, 1973).
Liberated Zone (produced Bingley, Yorkshire, 1973).
The Eagle Has Landed (televised 1973; produced Liverpool University, 1973).
Man Only Dines (produced The Polytechnic, Leeds, 1974).
The Dunkirk Spirit (produced by General Will Theatre Company on tour, 1974).
Dick Deterred (produced Bush Theatre, London, 1974). 1974.
The . . . Show (produced Bingley, Yorkshire, 1974).
O Fair Jerusalem (produced Birmingham Repertory Studio Theatre 1975).   In *Plays 1*, 1987.
The National Theatre (produced Open Space Theatre, London, 1975).   In *Shorts*, 1989.
Summer Sports: Beaters, Cricket, Shotputters, Cross Country, Ball Boys (produced Arts Lab, Birmingham, 1975; as *Blood Sports*, produced Bush Theatre, London, 1976; revised version of *Ball Boys* produced London, 1977).   *Ball Boys* published 1978; *Blood Sports* in *Shorts*, 1989.
Events Following the Closure of a Motorcycle Factory (produced Birmingham Repertory Studio Theatre, 1976).
Destiny (produced The Other Place, Stratford-on-Avon, 1976; revised version produced London, 1985).   1976; revised version, 1986.
Welcome to Dallas, J.C., from a play by Alfred Jarry (produced London, 1976).
The Perils of Bardfrod, with Richard Crane (produced Theatre in the Mill, Bradford University, Bradford, 1976).
Saigon Rose (produced Traverse Theatre, Edinburgh, 1976). In *Plays 1*, 1987.
Wreckers (produced by 7:84 theatre company, Exeter, 1977). 1977.
Our Own People (produced by Private Jennie, on tour, 1977). With *Teendreams*, 1988.
Mary Barnes (produced Birmingham Repertory Studio Theatre, 1978).   1979; revised version, 1984.
The Jail Diary of Albie Sachs, from the work by Sachs (produced The Warehouse, London, 1978).   1978.

Teendreams, with Susan Todd (produced Vandyck Theatre, Bristol, 1979).

The Life and Adventures of Nicholas Nickleby, from the novel by Dickens (produced Aldwych Theatre, London, 1980).

Maydays (produced Barbican Theatre, London, 1983). 1983; revised version, 1984.

Entertaining Strangers: A Play for Dorchester (produced Dorchester, Dorset, 1985; revised version produced National Theatre, London, 1987). 1986.

That Summer (produced Hampstead Theatre, London, 1987). 1987.

Heartlanders, with Stephen Bill and Anne Devlin (produced Birmingham, 1989).

The Shape of the Table (produced National Theatre, London, 1990). 1990.

The Strange Case of Dr. Jekyll and Mr. Hyde (produced Barbican Theatre, London, 1991). 1991.

Screenplays

Lady Jane, 1986.

Television Plays

The Eagle Has Landed, 1973; *Sanctuary*, from his play *Gangsters*, 1973; *I Know What I Meant*, 1974; *The Midas Connection*, 1975 (published in *Shorts*, 1989); *Censors*, with Hugh Whitemore and Robert Muller, 1975; *Vote for Them*, with Neil Grant, 1989 (published 1989).

Radio Plays

Ecclesiastes, 1977 (published in *Plays 2*, 1990); *A Movie Starring Me*, 1991.

Other

The Second Time as Farce: Reflections on the Drama of Mean Times. 1988.

The Shape of the Table. 1990.

*

Criticism

Books:

John Bull, *New British Political Dramatists*, London, 1984 (Macmillan Modern Dramatists series).

Elizabeth Swain, *David Edgar, Playwright and Politician*, New York, 1986.

Raimund Schaffner, *Politik und Drama bei David Edgar: Eine Studie zum politischen Gegenwartstheater in England*, Essen, 1988.

Malcolm Page and Simon Trussler (compilers), *File on Edgar* (includes bibliography), London, 1991.

* * *

David Edgar is a political playwright, one of the group who emerged after the 1968 lifting of censorship of the British stage, and one who was affected profoundly by the political events of that same year.

The substance of Edgar's plays provides a mini-history of Britain's economic and political climate since World War II. The plays present a record and analysis of Britain's weakening left and the growth of right-wing extremism. They show the impact of specific pieces of legislation. They are concerned with industrial action. They portray people in the process of change, becoming political. For example, among Edgar's agitprop plays, *The Dunkirk Spirit* focuses on Britain's economic decline since the war, *The Rupert Show* is about pornography and sexual politics, *Not With a Bang But a Whimper* is about ecology, *The End* about nuclear disarmament, and *The Case of the Workers' Plane* about the aerospace industry. While Edgar's socialist point of view informs and colours his plays, his strength is his incisive social analysis, particularly of the impulses he ultimately condemns.

David Edgar is also a skilled craftsman. He has written in a variety of forms, from the agitprop of the early plays, written for touring companies, to the more mimetic social realism of his later plays, which have been produced in large establishment theatres. He has also written parody, burlesque, docudrama, and three remarkable adaptations from other forms. Linguistically, he is equally versatile, writing in iambic pentameter (in the clever *Richard III*/Richard Nixon burlesque, *Dick Deterred*), nonsense (in *Blood Sports*), song lyrics, dialects, and realistic, character-rooted dialogue. Edgar's plays always include irony and humour, serving to counterbalance the deep seriousness of his topics.

Many of Edgar's early plays were, as he notes, "self-combustible" because of their immediate and specific political purpose, such as *Rent; or, Caught in the Act*, a Victorian melodrama illustrating the evils of a Housing Act, and *Tedderella*, a pantomime parody, quite unsympathetic to Britain's entry into the Common Market. As Edgar became more and more politically active his plays became less polemical and the dramaturgy more complex. Perhaps the first major landmark in his career was *Destiny*, a masterly realist social analysis of the growth of the political right in Britain, examining its roots and its implications. Edgar's thesis here is that neo-fascism has sprung from colonialism and its aftermath. He opens the play with Nehru's 1947 speech on Indian Independence, followed by a scene in which members of different ranks in the British Army, along with an Indian servant (all of whom reappear later in the play, in England), dismantle a barracks in preparation for the British departure. All the attitudes that will emerge in 1970's Britain, particularly about race and class, are aired in this scene.

The main thrust of the plot of *Destiny* concerns the efforts of the Labour Party, the Conservatives, and the neo-fascists to organize an election campaign. The election is the catalyst to the key issues of the play: discriminatory labour practices, unions and politics, the corporate world and politics, immigration policies, and the rule of law. These issues all contribute to the main investigation of the play, the question of why Britain is moving politically to the right. Only one of the play's 20 scenes is not set in the public sphere. Possibly the most powerful and terrifying scene is one in which a patriotic league meeting is manipulated into commitment to the fascist cause.

Like *Destiny*, *Maydays* depends on a historical perspective for its political analysis. The play traces several lives, spanning the period from the election of Clement Attlee's radical socialist government in 1945 to the time immediately after the election of Margaret Thatcher's equally radical right-wing government. Edgar's focus this time is on British socialism—on its splintering, factionalism, and resultant weakening. Edgar analyzes the phenomena of political change in 35 scenes which range from Hungary during the 1956 Soviet invasion, to a Soviet labour camp, to a 1960's anti-draft demonstration in California. The lives of the foreign characters bring them to Britain either as exiles, students, or goodwill ambassadors, and Edgar skillfully weaves an international dimension into his analysis of British political life. In a noticeable change from the technique of *Destiny*, Edgar repeatedly includes in *Maydays* scenes which take place in the private sphere, and so grapples with the implications of characters' private lives for their political behaviour.

That Summer, Edgar's next play, quite unexpectedly has a small cast and one setting—a summer home. An Oxford don, his son, and his chiropractor wife offer a two-week holiday to two teenage daughters of a striking Welsh miner, as some form of social gesture. The atmosphere crackles as assumptions are demolished and all—including the married couple, their homosexual friend, and the don's son—learn some humbling human and political lessons.

Edgar's next project was an entirely new one for him, a vast community play for the people of Dorchester. In fact, it may be seen as a natural evolution of his other huge epic pieces, and before long *Entertaining Strangers* appeared at the National Theatre with a reduced cast and some textual changes. The meat of the play is the legendary 19th-century conflict between the staunch individualist female owner of the local brewery and the town's new fundamentalist minister, Moule. The minister is despised for his religious fanaticism, but becomes a hero after his demonstrations of courage and compassion during a cholera epidemic. The scale of the production is vast, requiring a steam locomotive (*Maydays* demands a train too), multiple and sometimes simultaneous locations, a circus parade, and a horse race. What impresses is that Edgar writes his "big" plays on the scale of an epic film and assumes the theatre will contain it.

Such extraordinary confidence in the possibilities of theatre clearly underscores his now legendary adaptation of *Nicholas Nickleby* into a two-play, nearly nine-hour theatrical event. Edgar saw that the pursuit of money was the key issue in the novel and made this the unifying theme of the play, taking only minor liberties with Dickens to make it work. His earlier adaptations were of Albie Sachs' account of his solitary confinement in South African prisons, and the artist Mary Barnes' and her therapist's account of her treatment and cure for schizophrenia in one of R.D. Laing's therapeutic communes. Both are powerful pieces of theatre that effectively maintain the integrity of the original works while allowing Edgar's own political voice to resonate in a fully theatrical way.

It is not possible to refer to all of Edgar's more than 40 plays, but some of the subject matter will suggest their scope: *Baby Love* is about the treatment of psychological disorders as criminal behaviour, *O Fair Jerusalem* draws a parallel between the medieval bubonic plague and the modern atomic bomb, *Wreckers* is about the 1972 dock strike and the rule of law, *Teendreams*, written with Susan Todd, attempts an analysis of some of the problems and contradictions of feminism, *Blood Sports*, comprising five short plays, is about violence and class hatred. *Ball Boys*, perhaps the most powerful of these playlets, is often produced separately.

Edgar's plays are marked by assiduous research. The lists of facts of the agitprop work has evolved into the rich social and historical backgrounds of the later plays. Edgar's ability to collaborate with other theatre artists has also been a strength, beginning with the early touring work, then moving to such plays as *Teendreams* with Monstrous Regiment and the development of the *Nicholas Nickleby* script with the Royal Shakespeare Company, and most recently shown in *Entertaining Strangers*, made in collaboration with the Dorchester community. Michael Billington aptly summed up the import of David Edgar's plays when he likened him to Balzac, "a secretary for our times".

—Elizabeth Swain

See also *Volume 1* entry on *Destiny*.

EDUARDO.   See **DE FILIPPO, Eduardo**.

ELIOT, T(homas) S(tearns).   Born in St. Louis, Missouri, USA, 26 September 1888; became British citizen, 1927. Educated at Mrs. Lockwood's school, St. Louis; Smith Academy, St. Louis, 1898–1905; Milton Academy, Massachusetts, 1905–06; Harvard University, Cambridge, Massachusetts (board member, *Harvard Advocate*, 1909–10; Sheldon travelling fellowship, 1914), 1906–10, 1911–14, AB 1909, AM in English 1910; the Sorbonne, Paris, 1910–11; Merton College, Oxford, 1914–15. Married 1) Vivien (born Vivienne) Haigh-Wood in 1915 (separated 1933; died 1947); 2) Esmé Valerie Fletcher in 1957. Teacher, High Wycombe Grammar School, Buckinghamshire, 1915–16, and Highgate Junior School, London, 1916; tutor, University of London Extension Board, Southall, 1916–19; clerk in the Colonial and Foreign Department, then in charge of the Foreign Office Information Bureau, Lloyd's Bank, London, 1917–25; assistant editor, the *Egoist*, London, 1917–19; regular contributor, *Times Literary Supplement*, London, from 1919; founding editor, the *Criterion*, London, 1922–39; editor, later director, Faber and Gwyer, 1925–28, and Faber and Faber, publishers, London, 1929–65; Clark lecturer, Trinity College, Cambridge, 1926; Charles Eliot Norton professor of poetry, 1932–33, and Theodore Spencer memorial lecturer, 1950, Harvard University; Page-Barbour lecturer, University of Virginia, Charlottesville, 1933; member of the editorial board, *New English Weekly*, London, 1934–44, and *Christian News Letter*, Oxford, 1939–46; visiting fellow, Institute for Advanced Studies, Princeton University, New Jersey, 1948. Joined Church of England, 1927. Recipient: Nobel Prize for Literature, 1948; New York Drama Critics Circle Award, 1950; Hanseatic-Goethe Prize (Hamburg), 1954; Dante Gold Medal (Florence), 1959; Order of Merit (Bonn), 1959; Emerson-Thoreau Medal, 1960; US Medal of Freedom, 1964. Numerous honorary doctorates from US and European universities. OM (Order of Merit), 1948; Officer, Légion d'Honneur, and Commander, Order of Arts and Letters (France), 1950; honorary member, American Academy; foreign member, Accademia dei Lincei (Rome) and Akademie der schönen Künste. Died in London, 4 January 1965.

Works

Collections

The Complete Poems and Plays.   1952.
Collected Plays: Murder in the Cathedral; The Family

T.S. Eliot (bust by Sir Jacob Epstein, 1951).

Reunion; The Cocktail Party; The Confidential Clerk; The Elder Statesman. 1962; as The Complete Plays, 1969.

Stage Works

Sweeney Agonistes: Fragments of an Aristophanic Melodrama (produced Vassar College, Poughkeepsie, New York, 1933). 1932.
The Rock: A Pageant Play (produced Sadler's Wells Theatre, London, 1934). 1934.
Murder in the Cathedral (produced Canterbury Cathedral, Canterbury, 1935). 1935; subsequent editions 1936, 1937, 1938.
The Family Reunion (produced Westminster Theatre, London, 1939). 1939.
The Cocktail Party (produced Edinburgh Festival, 1949). 1950; revised edition, 1950.
The Confidential Clerk (produced Edinburgh Festival, 1953). 1954.
The Elder Statesman (produced Edinburgh Festival, 1958). 1959.

Verse

"Prufrock" and Other Observations. 1917.
Poems. 1919.
Ara Vos Prec. 1920; as Poems, 1920.
The Waste Land. 1922; A Facsimile and Transcripts of the Original Drafts Including the Annotations of Ezra Pound, edited by Valerie Eliot, 1971.
Poems 1909–1925. 1925.
Journey of the Magi. 1927.
A Song for Simeon. 1928.
Animula. 1929.
Ash-Wednesday. 1930.
Marina. 1930.
Triumphal March. 1931.
Words for Music. 1935.
Two Poems. 1935.
Collected Poems 1909–1935. 1936.
Old Possum's Book of Practical Cats. 1939.
"The Waste Land" and Other Poems. 1940.
East Coker. 1940.
Later Poems 1925–1935. 1941.
The Dry Salvages. 1941.
Little Gidding. 1942.
Four Quartets (includes Burnt Norton; East Coker; The Dry Salvages; Little Gidding). 1943.
A Practical Possum. 1947.
Selected Poems. 1948.
The Undergraduate Poems. 1949.
Poems Written in Early Youth, edited by John Hayward. 1950.
The Cultivation of Christmas Trees. 1954.
Collected Poems 1909–1962. 1963.

Memoirs and Letters

Letters, edited by Valerie Eliot. 1990—

Other

Ezra Pound: His Metric and Poetry. 1918.
The Sacred Wood: Essays on Poetry and Criticism. 1920.
Homage to John Dryden: Three Essays on Poetry in the Seventeenth Century. 1924.
Shakespeare and the Stoicism of Seneca. 1927.

For Lancelot Andrewes: Essays on Style and Order. 1928.
Dante. 1929.
Charles Whibley: A Memoir. 1931.
Thoughts after Lambeth. 1931.
Selected Essays 1917–1932. 1932; revised edition, 1950.
John Dryden: The Poet, The Dramatist, The Critic. 1932.
The Use of Poetry and the Use of Criticism: Studies in the Relation of Criticism to Poetry in England. 1933.
After Strange Gods: A Primer of Modern Heresy. 1934.
Elizabethan Essays. 1934; as Elizabethan Dramatists. 1963; selection, as Essays on Elizabethan Drama, 1956.
Essays Ancient and Modern. 1936.
The Idea of a Christian Society. 1939.
Points of View, edited by John Hayward. 1941.
The Classics and the Man of Letters. 1942.
The Music of Poetry. 1942.
Reunion by Destruction: Reflections on a Scheme for Church Unity in South India Addressed to the Laity. 1943.
What is a Classic? 1945.
Die Einheit der Europäischen Kultur. 1946.
On Poetry. 1947.
Milton. 1947.
From Poe to Valéry. 1948.
A Sermon Preached in Magdalene College Chapel. 1948.
Notes Towards the Definition of Culture. 1948.
The Aims of Poetic Drama. 1949.
Poetry and Drama. 1951.
The Value and Use of Cathedrals in England Today. 1952.
An Address to the Members of the London Library. 1952.
Selected Prose, edited by John Hayward. 1953.
American Literature and the American Language. 1953.
The Three Voices of Poetry. 1953.
Religious Drama, Mediaeval and Modern. 1954.
The Literature of Politics. 1955.
The Frontiers of Criticism. 1956.
On Poetry and Poets. 1957.
Geoffrey Faber 1889–1961. 1961.
George Herbert. 1962.
Knowledge and Experience in the Philosophy of F.H. Bradley (doctoral dissertation). 1964.
To Criticize the Critic and Other Writings. 1965.
Selected Prose, edited by Frank Kermode. 1975.

Editor, Selected Poems, by Erza Pound. 1928; revised edition, 1949.
Editor, A Choice of Kipling's Verse. 1941.
Editor, Introducing James Joyce. 1942.
Editor, Literary Essays of Ezra Pound. 1954.
Editor, The Criterion 1922–1939 (18 vols.). 1967.

Translator, Anabasis: A Poem, by Saint-John Perse. 1930; revised edition, 1938, 1949, 1959.

*

Bibliographies

Donald Gallup, T.S. Eliot: A Bibliography, 1952; revised edition, New York, 1969.
Bradley Gunter, The Merrill Checklist of Eliot, 1970.
Mildred Martin, A Half-Century of Eliot Criticism: An Annotated Bibliography of Books and Articles in English, 1916–1965, Lewisburg, Pennsylvania, 1972.
Beatrice Ricks, T.S. Eliot: A Bibliography of Secondary Works, Metuchen, New Jersey, 1980.

Criticism

Books:

George Williamson, *A Reader's Guide to Eliot*, London, 1953; revised edition, 1966.

Grover Smith, *Eliot's Poetry and Plays: A Study in Sources and Meaning*, Chicago, 1956; revised edition, Chicago, 1974.

David Jones, *The Plays of T.S. Eliot*, Toronto, 1961.

Hugh Kenner (ed.), *Eliot: A Collection of Critical Essays*, Englewood Cliffs, New Jersey, 1962.

Carol H. Smith, *Eliot's Dramatic Theory and Practice*, Princeton, New Jersey, 1963.

Northrop Frye, *T.S. Eliot*, Edinburgh and London, 1963, revised 1968.

Philip R. Headings, *T.S. Eliot*, New York, 1964; revised edition, 1982.

Helen Gardner, "The Comedies of T.S. Eliot", in *T.S. Eliot: The Man and His Work*, edited by Allen Tate, New York, 1966.

Leonard Unger, *T.S. Eliot: Movements and Patterns*, Minneapolis, Minnesota, 1966.

William V. Spanos, *The Christian Tradition in Modern British Verse Drama*, New Brunswick, New Jersey, 1967.

E. Martin Browne, *The Making of Eliot's Plays*, London, 1969.

A.G. George, *T.S. Eliot: His Mind and Art* (second edition), New York, 1969.

Katharine J. Worth, "Eliot and the Living Theater", in *Eliot in Perspective: A Symposium*, edited by Graham Martin, New York, 1970.

Joseph Chiari, *T.S. Eliot: Poet and Dramatist*, New York, 1972; revised edition, 1979.

Russel Kirk, *Eliot and His Age: T.S. Eliot's Moral Imagination in the Twentieth Century*, New York, 1972.

Franz Kuna, *T.S. Eliot* (second edition), Munich, 1972.

Douglas B. Kurdys, *Form in the Modern Verse Drama*, Salzburg, 1972.

John D. Margolis, *Eliot's Intellectual Development 1922–1939*, Chicago, 1972.

Subhas Sarkar, *T.S. Eliot the Dramatist*, Calcutta, 1972.

Kristian Smidt, *The Importance of Recognition: Six Chapters on T.S. Eliot*, Tromso, Norway, 1973.

David Ward, *T.S. Eliot Between Two Worlds: A Reading of T.S. Eliot's Poetry and Plays*, London, 1973.

Andrew K. Kennedy, "T.S. Eliot", in his *Six Dramatists in Search of a Language*, Cambridge, 1979.

Stephen Spender, *T.S. Eliot*, London, 1975.

Lyndall Gordon, *Eliot's Early Years*, Oxford, 1977.

Arnold P. Hinchcliffe, *Modern Verse Drama*, London, 1977.

K.S. Misra, *The Plays of T.S. Eliot: A Critical Study*, San'a, Yemen, 1977.

Bernard Bergonzi, *T.S. Eliot* (second edition), London, 1978.

Subhas Sarkar, *Eliot and Yeats: A Study*, Calcutta, 1978.

A.D. Moody, *T.S. Eliot, Poet*, Cambridge, 1979.

Brian Lee, *Theory and Personality: The Significance of Eliot's Criticism*, London, 1979.

M.K. Naik, *Mighty Voices: Studies in T.S. Eliot*, New Delhi, 1980.

Michael Grant (ed.), *T.S. Eliot: The Critical Heritage* (2 vols.), London, 1982.

Eloise Knapp Hay, *T.S. Eliot's Negative Way*, Cambridge, Massachusetts, 1982.

Caroline Behr, *T.S. Eliot: A Chronology of His Life and Works*, London, 1983.

Peter Ackroyd, *T.S. Eliot: A Life*, London, 1984.

Harold Bloom (ed.), *T.S. Eliot: Modern Critical Views*, New York, 1985.

Arnold P. Hinchcliffe (ed.), *T.S. Eliot: Plays: A Casebook*, London, 1985.

F.B. Pinion (ed.) *A T.S. Eliot Companion: Life and Works*, Basingstoke and London, 1986.

Robert Crawford, *The Savage and the City in the Work of Eliot*, Oxford, 1987.

Angus Calder, *T.S. Eliot*, Brighton, 1987.

S.S. Deo, *T.S. Eliot: Philosophical Themes in Drama*, Delhi, 1987.

Jewel S. Brooker (ed.), *Approaches to Teaching Eliot's Poetry and Plays*, New York, 1988.

Lyndall Gordon, *T.S. Eliot's New Life*, Oxford, 1988.

Glenda Leeming, *Poetic Drama*, London, 1989 (Macmillan Modern Dramatists series).

Parwati Singh, *Character and Symbol in the Plays of T.S. Eliot*, Delhi, 1989.

* * *

T.S. Eliot became known as a dramatist when his fame as a poet was already well established. In a certain sense, he had always been seen as a "dramatic" poet, and from the outset his criticism was preoccupied with the relation between drama and poetry. His early dramatic theory was anti-naturalist and Symbolist, taking as its models the ballet and the liturgy. After his conversion to Anglicanism in 1927, however, he came to consider the question, "Is the poetic drama possible for our century?" in different terms. In the essay "A Dialogue on Dramatic Poetry", the theatre is proposed not as an aestheticist substitute for orthodox religion but as a medium for the conscious life of a community, a force for cultural cohesion ancillary to religion.

Eliot's first dramatic effort, *Sweeney Agonistes*, subtitled *Fragments of an Aristophanic Melodrama*, was a coda, in parody music-hall rhythms, to the despairing diagnosis of cultural decline in *The Waste Land*. The characters epitomize a terminal and paralyzing boredom and horror at the heart of life. For all the brilliant vernacular vitality of the language, *Sweeney* represents a static, anti-dramatic spectacle, an imaginative stalemate in Eliot's career as a writer. The use of classical Greek drama as a structural analogy, however, was to remain a constant in his stagecraft.

It was perhaps the writing of choruses for the pageant-play *The Rock* that led to the experiment of *Murder in the Cathedral*, an imaginative reconstruction of the martyrdom of Thomas à Becket. The plot is not theatrical in any usual sense, centred as it is on the spiritual conflict of one character who is almost completely defined by the sanctity for which he is destined. The events of the play do not follow a temporal dramatic logic but an "eternal design" of "action as suffering" which admits of little development; in his preparation for martyrdom Thomas is assailed by personified temptations, while the instinctive rhythms of human response to the religious mystery are voiced by the chorus of the women of Canterbury.

The surprising success of *Murder in the Cathedral*, written for a small church audience at the Canterbury Festival, encouraged Eliot in his belief that the theatre might offer a solution to the problem of communication between poet and audience, if existing forms of theatrical entertainment were utilized. In the essay "John Marston" he applauded the Jacobean dramatists for managing to operate simultaneously on the level of the groundlings and on that of the sensitive minority who could appreciate the quality of the poetry. This "doubleness in the action, as if it took place on two planes at once", is the strategy adopted in *The Family Reunion*, as in the plays that followed. A modern, naturalistic outer plot (a matriarch's attempt to install her son as master of the family estate) is superimposed on an inner, timeless plot (the spiritual ordeal and conversion of the son, who has murdered his wife), signalled by the otherworldly presence of the Eumenides. What appears to the largely unconscious chorus of uncles and aunts to be a drama of "crime and punishment" is revealed to the conscious protagonist as a drama of "sin and expiation".

In Eliot's first two plays, surface naturalism is violated by the protagonist's calling to religious attainment. With *The Cocktail Party*, however, he made a bid for a larger audience by turning to drawing-room comedy in the Noël Coward mode. In keeping with the dictum of *Murder in the Cathedral* that "humankind cannot bear very much reality", the religious message is, as it were, conveyed in a sugar-coated pill. "Poetry and Drama" concludes that poetic drama is possible for our century, as long as the poetic element in the language is strictly subordinated to dramatic utility, muted to the point of invisibility or "transparence" except at moments of exceptional intensity. Crucially, the effect of the verse rhythm ought to be largely unconscious; the vulgar substance of conventional plot would thus satisfy the demands of the mass of the audience, while the poetic spirit would work on their emotions without their awareness.

A frequent criticism of the later plays is that the conventional or prosaic dilution of Eliot's poetic style, though highly successful on its own terms, entails a corresponding loss of dramatic power and conviction. In *The Cocktail Party*, for example, the martyrdom of the spiritual aspirant Celia Coplestone is relegated to offstage status, but the gruesome details of her suffering return to haunt the reconciling final scene, where they sound harshly dissonant against the prevailing note of light entertainment.

The vestiges of ritual choreography in *The Cocktail Party*, such as the libation of the Guardians, are entirely dispensed with in *The Confidential Clerk*, a farce of mistaken identity in which the higher, analogical level dealing with vocation and spiritual fatherhood is all but submerged. In spite of box-office success, many reviewers noted that the cost of a determination to sanctify the average in human experience is a bloodlessness of character and feeling, unredeemed by the rather self-regarding morality—exemplified by the obscure and homely Eggerson—of cultivating individual small gardens in accordance with our sphere in life, the duties of our station, and our paternal inheritance of values. Much the same criticisms were applied to *The Elder Statesman*, where Lord Claverton has to come to terms with his own imperfect past, detach himself from his public persona, and learn to love his children before he can find happiness in old age.

Any discussion of Eliot's success as a dramatist must confront the attitudes of patronage and paternalism towards the audience implicit in his theories. In their desire to avoid the élitism of the avant-garde "anti-theatre", his plays did not avoid the dangers of viewing the community in terms of mass civilization and minority culture—the few conscious and the many unconscious—and thus cannot be said to have given expression, as he had hoped, to the ethical awareness of a people. They did, however, significantly further the debate about the possibility of poetic drama in the 20th century.

—Christina Britzolakis

See also *Volume 1* entries on *The Cocktail Party; The Family Reunion; Murder in the Cathedral.*

ERDMAN, Nikolai Robertovich. Born in Moscow, 16 November (New Style) 1902. Educated at the School of Peter and Paul, Moscow. Brief military service with the Red Army during the Russian Civil War. In Moscow, wrote songs and sketches for revues; associated with the Imaginist Group, 1919–24; wrote sketches for the opening production of the Theatre of Satire, Moscow, in 1924; first play, *Mandat* [*The Mandate*], produced 1925; next play, *The Suicide*, banned; collaborated on theatre and film projects, from 1927; a lost play, *Zasedaniye o smekhe* [Conference on Laughter] was probably the cause of his arrest in 1933: exiled to Yeniseysk and Tomsk in Siberia, 1933–c.1937, and subsequently allowed to live in Kalinin; collaborated on film adaptations and animation scripts, often with Mikhail Volpin, for the state film company, Mosfilm, from 1942; eventually allowed to return to Moscow. Recipient: two Stalin prizes for screenplays. Died in Moscow, 10 August 1970.

Works

Collections

"The Mandate" and "The Suicide", translated by George Genereux Jr., Marjorie Hoover, and Jacob Volkov. 1975.

Stage Works

Interludes in *Lev Gurych Sinichkin*, by D. Lensky (produced Vakhtangov Theatre, Moscow, 1924).
Sketches in *Moskva s tochki zreniya* [Moscow from a Perspective] (produced Theatre of Satire, Moscow, 1924).
Mandat (produced Meyerhold Theatre, Moscow, 1925). 1976 (Munich); translated as *The Mandate*, with *The Suicide*, 1975.
Samoubytsa (produced in Swedish, Malmö, Sweden, 1969; produced in Russian, Theatre of Satire, Moscow, 1982). In *Novy Zhurnal* (New York), 112–14, 1973–74; translated as *The Suicide*, in *Russian Literature Triquarterly*, 7, 1973; translation reprinted, with *The Mandate*, 1975; also translated, 1979.

Screenplays

Include: *Prints i nishchy;* the animated film *Bratya Lyu* (published in *Filmy Skazki*, 1952).

Verse

Selections in *Russian Imagism 1919–1924*, edited by V. Markov. 1980.

*

Criticism

Books:
Robert Russell, *Russian Drama of the Revolutionary Period*, Totowa, New Jersey, 1988.

Articles:
Marjorie Hoover, "Nikolai Erdman: A Soviet Dramatist Rediscovered", in *Russian Literature Triquarterly*, 2, 1972.
John Freedman, "Nikolaj Erdman: An Overview", in *Slavic and East European Journal*, 28, 1984.

* * *

Nikolai Robertovich Erdman was a typical victim of Stalin's dictatorship. Born in Moscow in 1902 of Russified German stock, he attended Moscow's Peter and Paul School before serving briefly in the Red Army during the Civil War. After demobilisation, Erdman plunged precociously into the hectic literary-bohemian life of post-revolutionary Moscow. A poet since his schooldays, he became a minor member of the enterprisingly experimental, anarchic, self-advertising Imaginist group, participating in Imaginist declarations and publications between 1919 and 1924. Erdman's real fame, however, came in the theatre, thanks to two satirical comedies: *Mandat* (*The Mandate*), staged by Meyerhold in 1925, and *Samoubytsa* (*The Suicide*), banned by the Stalinist censor in 1932 while in rehearsal by both Meyerhold and the Moscow Arts Theatre. Erdman's brilliantly promising career as Russia's new Gogol was further curtailed when, as he put it, he "wrote some fables in 1933", as a result of which he was "exiled from Moscow for three years" to Yeniseysk and Tomsk, returning in 1937. Thereafter he worked chiefly as a script-writer for the cinema, usually collaborating with Mikhail Volpin for Mosfilm. Nadezhda Volpin (Mikhail's sister) describes Erdman as "very witty and very gifted", while Anna Nikritina (widow of the Imaginist Anatoly Mariengof) characterises him as "charming, intelligent and witty, a good friend . . . very talented, very open-hearted, and benevolent".

The Stalin years, however, had taken their toll. In *Hope Against Hope*, Nadezhda Mandelstam paints a tragic picture of the suppressed artist: "Erdman himself chose to fall silent —anything just to stay alive . . . Very occasionally he would put his head close to mine and tell me the plot of a new play he had just thought of but would never write . . . Erdman just sat and drank, without saying a word". Erdman subsequently earned a living by devising scenarios for the music-hall, libretti for operettas, and numerous film-scripts, as well as a drama, *Geroi nashego vremeni* (*A Hero of our Time*), based on Lermontov's works, which was staged by his co-author Yury Lyubimov in Moscow in 1964. Nevertheless, in *The Times* of 2 September 1970, a correspondent aptly remarked: "The death in Moscow of Nikolai Erdman removes from the Russian stage one of its most gifted, if almost forgotten, writers . . .".

Erdman's theatrical immortality is guaranteed by his two original plays of the 1920's. *The Mandate* is a delicious soufflé, a delightfully exuberant satire-farce. The play presents an absurd array of impotent bourgeois reactionaries, nostalgic monarchists, and dispossessed capitalists yearning for a restoration of the old order and ancient privilege. Imposture and mistaken identity abound, with the nonentity Pavel Gulyachkin pretending to be a powerful Party functionary, and the dreamy cook Anastasia Nikolaevna mistaken for her illustrious namesake, the daughter of the late Tsar. *The Mandate* contains numerous farcical moments when characters are subjected to physical indignity, such as having their heads stuck in a pot, or being hidden in a trunk or obliged to sit on a loaded pistol. Of greater significance, however, is Erdman's amazing verbal dexterity, as he reels off a sparkling series of puns and *double entendres*, while also subtly deflating contemporary clichés and Communist slogans.

The Mandate's plot is lightweight, with its characters mainly caricatures and its situations basically traditional (concerning obstacles to marriage and the need for a suitable dowry). Yet the play still lives as something more than a youthful bagatelle. It is a highly literate work, containing comical allusions to Dostoevsky and to Pushkin's *Boris Godunov*, while its exclusively negative characters and emphasis on imposture and mistaken identity echo Gogol's *Government Inspector*. Above all, *The Mandate* evokes the atmosphere of the mid-1920's, with its dénouement indicating the relative innocence of the first post-revolutionary years. Although Erdman alludes to party privilege, house-searches, arrests, and fear, he chooses to end his play with the counter-revolutionary dupes metaphorically suspended in mid-air, mocked by the audience's laughter but untouched by the Bolshevik police. Such satirical irreverence was still officially tolerated, and Meyerhold hastened to produce *The Mandate*, deploying large concentric revolves and tall wooden screens as a setting for his actors' sudden freezes and pantomime. Meyerhold's inventive production of a topical Soviet comedy was greatly appreciated.

Erdman's masterpiece, however, is *The Suicide*, a satire far too daring to secure public performance in Stalin's Russia. Both Meyerhold and the Moscow Arts Theatre eagerly rehearsed the play in 1931–32, before their efforts were thwarted by the censor's prohibition. Stalin had written ominously to Stanislavsky in November 1931: "I do not have a very high opinion of the play *The Suicide*. My closest comrades consider it rather empty and even harmful . . .". *The Suicide* is a brilliant work, risqué, farcical, linguistically dazzling, wickedly subversive. It broaches issues of major political and metaphysical import—the primacy of the individual, the dehumanisation inherent in Marxist collectivity, the riddle of death, God, and an after-life. Yet Erdman's writing is never pretentious or portentous: it sparkles with wit, youth, and intelligence. The hero, Semen Semenovich Podsekalnikov, is a comic-pathetic "little man", whose happiness has been blighted by a year's unemployment, and a cloying spouse and mother-in-law. When Podsekalnikov's life no longer seems worth living, a mighty chorus of malcontents endeavours to encourage and exploit his likely suicide, in order to advertise their own grievances and discredit the Soviet state. Amidst all the absurdity and ambiguity, serious overtones are discernible in the fervent complaints of intellectual, writer, and priest, and in Podsekalnikov's plea to be allowed to whisper that life is hard. Ten years later, at the height of Stalin's Terror, such whispers would prove fatal.

Erdman's international renown has been posthumously established by recent productions of *The Suicide*. Two portrayals stand out: the virtuoso performance of Roger Rees, gaunt, haggard and wild-eyed, for the Royal Shakespeare Company in 1980, and R.D. Tkachuk's magnificent Podsekalnikov at Moscow's Satire Theatre in 1989—rubber-faced, bullet-headed, genuinely tragi-comic, a hero in spite of himself.

—Gordon McVay

See also *Volume 1* entry on *The Suicide*.

ESSON, (Thomas) Louis (Buvelot). Born in Leith, near Edinburgh, Scotland, 10 August 1878. Family moved to Australia, 1881. Educated at Carlton Grammar School; Scotch College, Melbourne; Melbourne University, from 1896: left without taking final examinations. Married 1) Madeleine Tracy in 1906 (divorced 1911), one son; 2) Hilda Wager Bull in 1913, one son. Librarian, Melbourne Public Library; contributor, the *Bulletin*, from 1904; staff-member, *Table Talk* magazine; travelled widely in Europe and the Far

East, 1905–08: reporter for *Lone Star* in India and Japan; founder member, Victorian Socialist Party, 1906, and contributor to their publication, *The Socialist*; first-produced play, *The Woman Tamer*, staged 1909; lived as a journalist in New York and London, 1916–21; co-founder, with Stewart Macky and Vance Palmer, the Pioneer Players, Melbourne, 1922: company disbanded in 1926; had difficulties getting his later plays produced, eventually abandoning playwriting in the later 1920's; drama critic, *New Triad*, 1924–27; settled in Sydney in later years. Died in Sydney, 27 November 1943.

Works

Collections

Three Short Plays (includes *The Woman Tamer; Dead Timber; The Sacred Place*).   1911
"Dead Timber" and Other Plays (includes *The Woman Hater; The Drovers; The Sacred Place*).   1920.
"The Southern Cross" and Other Plays (includes *The Bride of Gospel Place; Mother and Son*), edited by Hilda Bull. 1946.
Ballades of Old Bohemia (includes verse, short stories, and the plays *Terra Australis; The Sacred Place; The Woman Tamer; Dead Timber; Australia Felix; Vagabond Camp*), edited by Hugh Anderson.   1980.

Stage Works

The Woman Tamer (produced Melbourne, 1909).   In *Three Short Plays*, 1911.
Dead Timber (produced Melbourne Repertory Theatre, 1911).   In *Three Short Plays*, 1911.
The Sacred Place, from the short story.   In *Three Short Plays*, 1911.
The Time is Not Yet Ripe (produced Melbourne, 1912). 1912.
The Drovers (produced by the Pioneer Players, Melbourne, 1923).   In *"Dead Timber" and Other Plays*, 1920.
The Battler (produced by the Pioneer Players, Melbourne Playhouse, Melbourne, 1922).
Mother and Son (produced by the Pioneer Players, Melbourne, 1923).   In *"The Southern Cross" and Other Plays*, 1946.
The Bride of Gospel Place (produced by the Pioneer Players, Melbourne, 1926).   In *"The Southern Cross" and Other Plays*, 1946.
Andenagora.   In *Best Australian One-Act Plays*, 1937.
The Southern Cross.   In *"The Southern Cross" and Other Plays*, 1946.
Terra Australis.   In *Ballades of Old Bohemia*, 1980.
Australia Felix.   In *Ballades of Old Bohemia*, 1980.
Vagabond Camp.   In *Ballades of Old Bohemia*, 1980.

Verse

Bells and Bees.   1910.
"Red Guns" and Other Verses.   1912.

*

Criticism

Books:
Vance Palmer, *Louis Esson and the Australian Theatre*, Sydney, 1948.

Leslie Rees, *The Making of Australian Drama: From the 1830s to the Late 1960s*, Sydney, 1973; revised edition, Sydney, 1978.
David Walker, *Dream and Disillusion: A Search for Australian Cultural Identity*, Canberra, 1976.
John McCallum, "'Something with a Cow in It': Louis Esson's Imported Nationalism", in *Australian Drama 1920–1955: Papers Presented to a Conference at the University of New England, Armidale, 1984*, Armidale, New England, 1986.

Articles:
Keith Macartney, "Louis Esson and Australian Drama", in *Meanjin Quarterly*, 6, 1947.

* * *

Louis Esson's career in the theatre is commonly seen as a story of romantic disillusionment. As the most distinguished Australian playwright of the first half of the 20th century, he is seen as the most conspicuous casualty of a cultural insecurity which ensured that imported plays and performers dominated the stage. Moreover, Esson's association with the Pioneer Players offers a particularly poignant instance of the failure of heroic enterprise. The Pioneers, with their commitment to a wholly Australian repertoire, began with high hopes in April 1922, presenting Esson's *The Battler*; however, from the beginning, they struggled for funds and audiences, and in 1926 closed with a season of Esson's *The Bride of Gospel Place*. They had produced 18 new plays, five of them full-length, but the whole experience seemed to demonstrate how depressingly inhospitable to pioneers and local plays the Australian theatre could be. It was an experience that was confirmed still more bitterly for Esson by the years of almost total neglect which followed.

There is a good deal of obvious truth in this legend, but the stereotype of a doomed idealist simplifies not only the matter of Esson's achievement, but also the nature of the difficulties that he faced. The first of Esson's plays to attract attention was the four-act political satire *The Time is Not Yet Ripe*, which deflated the pomposities of all its ideologues, whatever their persuasions; there is still a good deal of freshness in its wit, and the third act very successfully takes the risk of moving outside the drawing-room walls to stage a street-corner political squabble. But Esson had already decided that such a play was an irrelevance to his vision of a vital indigenous theatre, and he came to be increasingly dismissive of this early exercise in Shavianism.

Instead Esson sought to develop myths of Australian cultural distinctiveness. *The Battler*, and the one-acters *The Drovers* and *Dead Timber*, reflect the influence of the Abbey Theatre model in their attempt to locate their images of Australian uniqueness in the outback. *The Drovers* and *Dead Timber* centre on the archetypal conflict between man and a hostile environment, and find there the materials for tragedy. Both plays testify to Esson's eye for the compelling visual image, and his assured sense of what will work on stage. But, despite their power, these plays run into some dramatic obstacles which make their brevity a necessity. Not only are the plot catalysts (respectively a stampede and a flood) unstageable within the conventions of Esson's naturalism, but the phlegmatic bushman stereotype leaves most of the emotional responses to such events unexpressed. The spareness of action and dialogue is potent, but the possibilities for development are limited. The contrast with the sophisticated talk and playful ironies of *The Time is Not Yet Ripe* could hardly have been more marked.

The other avenue explored by Esson in his attempt to construct a distinctively Australian mythology in the theatre involved the experience of the urban working and criminal classes, and this proved rather more fruitful. The rich vernacular of the larrikins who people the one-act *The Woman Tamer* and the full-length *The Bride of Gospel Place* provides a good deal of local colour, while the spectre of actual or potential violence gives a certain guaranteed momentum to the plots. There is also some room in these plays for Esson's considerable talents as a comic writer, though their dialogue has more vigour than wit.

Esson's standing in Australian theatre involves more than the quality of his plays themselves. His output, in the end, was fairly modest, and much of his writing seems to reflect a conscious constriction of his abilities in the interests of a programmatic approach to the development of a nationalist theatre. Esson was a fine writer in a number of forms: his verse, his journalism, and his literary criticism are among the most impressive of the period. He had a great fondness for the bohemian intellectual life. The quest for a theatre of the people led him away from those things, and away too from the suburban reality which, for most audiences, was the source of an identifiable Australian-ness; ironically the search ended in the marginalization that so often is the fate of the self-conscious pioneer. His last play, the Eureka chronicle *The Southern Cross*, took him into the area of popular historical myth. It remained unperformed in his lifetime. It is in the representative nature of his disappointments, as well as in the strengths and pioneering concerns of his writing, that Esson is justly regarded as the "father" of Australian drama.

—Peter Fitzpatrick

See also *Volume 1* entry on *The Time is Not Yet Ripe*.

ETHEREGE, Sir George. Born in Maidenhead, Berkshire, England, in 1636. Possibly educated at a school in Thame, Oxfordshire, and at Cambridge University; apprenticed to George Gosnall, an attorney in Beaconsfield, 1654–58; admitted to Clement's Inn, London, 1659. Married Mary Arnold c.1677; may have had a daughter by the actress Elizabeth Barry. Possibly travelled in France and Flanders, c.1660–63; first play, *The Comical Revenge*, produced 1664; gentleman of the privy chamber, 1668; diplomat: secretary to Sir Daniel Harvey, the ambassador to Constantinople, 1668–71; envoy in the Hague, 1671; ambassador to the imperial court at Ratisbon (Regensburg), Bavaria, 1685–89; possibly served in Paris, 1691. Knighted, c.1679. Died in Paris, c. May 1692.

Works

Collections

Works, edited by A. Wilson Verity. 1888.
Dramatic Works (2 vols.), edited by H.F.B. Brett-Smith. 1927.
Plays, edited by Michael Cordner. 1982.

Stage Works

The Comical Revenge; or, Love in a Tub (produced Lincoln's Inn Fields Theatre, London, 1664).

She Would if She Could (produced Lincoln's Inn Fields Theatre, London, 1668). 1668.
The Man of Mode; or, Sir Fopling Flutter (produced Dorset Garden Theatre, London, 1676). 1976.

Verse

Poems, edited by James Thorpe. 1963.

Memoirs and Letters

Letters, edited by Frederick Bracher. 1974.

Other

The Letterbook, edited by Sybil Rosenfeld. 1928.

*

Bibliographies

David D. Mann, *Sir George Etherege: A Reference Guide*, Boston, 1981.

Criticism

Books:
Vincenz Meindl, *Sir George Etherege: Sein Leben, seine Zeit, und seine Dramen*, Leipzig, 1901.
Frances S. McCamic, *Etherege: A Study in Restoration Comedy*, 1931.
Thomas H. Fujimura, *The Restoration Comedy of Wit*, Princeton, New Jersey, 1952.
Dale Underwood, *Etherege and the Seventeenth-Century Comedy of Manners*, London and New Haven, Connecticut, 1957.
Norman L. Holland, *The First Modern Comedies: The Significance of Etherege, Wycherley and Congreve*, Cambridge, Massachusetts, 1959.
Jocelyn Powell, "George Etherege and the Form of a Comedy", in *Restoration Theatre*, edited by John Russell Brown and Bernard Harris, London and New York, 1965.
Ursula Jantz, *Targets of Satire in the Comedies of Etherege, Wycherley, and Congreve*, Salzburg, 1978.
Arthur R. Huseboe, *Sir George Etherege*, Boston, 1987.
Robert Markley, *Two-Edg'd Weapons: Style and Ideology in the Comedies of Etherege, Wycherley, and Congreve*, London, 1988.

* * *

Along with those of William Wycherley, the plays of Sir George Etherege define the "first wave" of Restoration comic drama: comedies of manners reflecting the styles and concerns of the narrow stratum of society attached to the newly established court of King Charles II. If Wycherley views that world and its frankly Hobbesian pursuit of social and sexual self-interest with a satirist's eye, Etherege writes from a viewpoint largely within the order of things he depicts. His great achievement lies in capturing and conveying to his audience (and preserving for subsequent audiences) a dynamic image of its cultural codes and vital energies. A gentleman-amateur, he wrote only three plays, separated by intervals of four and eight years. They reflect a progressive mastery of comic form and a shift in technique from reliance on broad action, dancing, and song (Etherege being a celebrated lyricist) to a kind of leisure-class realism with emphasis on character, language, and social situation.

In form, *The Comical Revenge* is a Restoration "tragicomedy", its action neatly divisible between a rhymed couplet quasi-tragedy of four star-crossed lovers, joyfully concluded, and a prose comedy of intrigue, manners, and farce. It is in the latter, centering on the true-wit and rake Sir Frederick Frollick, that we encounter what will be the distinctive elements of Etherege's drama. Sir Frederick is a normative figure, a model of stylishness and wit in the pursuit of pleasure. His wildness makes him the more attractive to the wealthy Widow Rich, with whom he engages in a kind of courtship dance involving witty attempts at seduction on his part and witty evasion on hers. At length, after much verbal combat, they agree to marry. The antithesis to Sir Frederick is Sir Nicholas Cully, who fulfills what will become the standard pattern of the fop in Restoration comedy. A pretender to wit and grace who is utterly without such qualities, he attempts to replicate Sir Frederick's exploits with ridiculous results, finally marrying the other's cast-off wench under the delusion that she is his sister. Knighted by Cromwell during the Interregnum, Sir Nicholas can never be a true Cavalier, endowed by nature with the aristocratic graces which Sir Frederick commands. Etherege clearly means not only to entertain his audience but to define the boundaries and behavioral standards of its new, Court-centered social world.

The borders of that world are sufficiently secure by the time of *She Would if She Could* for its stable existence to be taken for granted. There are no real victims in this play, and even its fools are treated evenhandedly. All the principal characters are equally committed to the game of sexual pursuit, with varying degrees of success. Hunting for new quarry, the two rakes Courtall and Freeman encounter Ariana and Gatty, two country heiresses on the ramble. The action that follows comprises a game of pursuit and evasion in which the young men exercise their intelligence and charm to the fullest, while the ladies encourage interest, repel seduction, mock their suitors, and finally reward them with profitable marriages. This pattern, echoing the Frollick-Widow relationship and repeated in *The Man of Mode*, amounts to a kind of competition of manners, in which paradigmatic types of male and female wit emerge and are celebrated as winners.

On the other hand, the country couple Sir Oliver and Lady Cockwood are clumsy players at the game of London high-life. His attempts at libertine debauchery miscarry woefully, and her determined pursuit of both Freeman and Courtall (described in the play's title) while mouthing furious defenses of her honor, comes to little better. Yet no real onus is attached to his attempted infidelities or to her hypocrisy. Most of the play's characters are capable of falsehood—Courtall and Freeman deceive one another with alacrity—and while this gives the plot a level of intrigue and error at times foreshadowing a Feydeau comedy, it bears little moral weight other than as the characters' successful or unsuccessful strategies for getting what they want.

The question of judgement has dominated critical response to Etherege's masterpiece, *The Man of Mode*, for three centuries. Critics continue to ask how we should judge Dorimant, the play's rake-hero, and how, if we cannot judge the character, we should judge the playwright himself. Dorimant fulfills absolutely the Restoration image of aristocratic maleness: he is witty and attractive by nature, effortlessly brilliant in conversation and fashionable in taste, and so a conqueror of women. In the two days' exploits which the play chronicles, he accomplishes the public humiliation of his former mistress Mrs. Loveit, the easy seduction of Bellinda, and betrothal to the rich country heiress Harriet. Like Sir Frederick Frollick, he is further defined by a foppish foil, artificially pretending to the graces inherent in Dorimant. Yet Sir Fopling Flutter, in his energetic self-display and unshakeable self-delight, achieves a dynamic comic presence of his own, making him surely the richest version of this character type.

Harriet proves Dorimant's match in more than one sense. Without a doubt his counterpart in wit and will, she plays the social-sexual game with "temper", keeping her emotions in check and leading him through a mocking ordeal-by-courtship which culminates in his commitment to marriage, if not necessarily to fidelity. The problem of judgment arises with the distinct relish Dorimant takes in the pain of his discarded conquests, especially the energy with which he plots the public revelation of Mrs. Loveit's anger and grief. Etherege provides no clear moral perspective here. With a sociologist's dispassion he presents the rules of the game, the skill of its winners, and the suffering of its losers.

More, he allows us to glimpse strains and contradictions within the game itself, such as when Loveit, in revenge, briefly convinces the Town that Fopling has replaced Dorimant in her affections. The marked anxiety this causes in Dorimant with regard to his reputation suggests a deeper anxiety, perhaps ingrained in the social order Etherege represents, as to whether a secure distinction between true-wit and fop actually exists. By such means Etherege renders present to us the complex illusion of a complete world, making *The Man of Mode* one of the great comedies of manners in the European canon.

—Robert G. Egan

See also *Volume 1* entries on *The Man of Mode*; *She Would if She Could*.

EURIPIDES. Born probably on the island of Salamis (Athenian territory), 480 or 485 BC. Married to Melito; three sons. Held a local priesthood at Phyla; not prominent politically, but went on an embassy to Syracuse; also travelled to court of King Archelaus, Macedonia, c.408 BC; first competed at the City Dionysia festival, 455 BC; won four dramatic prizes during his lifetime, and one posthumously; emigrated to Macedonia, c.407–408 BC. The titles of 80 of his plays are known. Died in Macedonia, before February or March 406 BC.

Works

Collection

The Tragedies (2 vols.), translated by R. Potter. 1781–83.
The Nineteen Tragedies, and Fragments (4 vols.), edited by M. Woodhull. 1782.
Euripides (3 vols.; Greek texts), edited by F.A. Paley. 1857–60; revised edition, 1872–80.
Plays (2 vols.), translated by Edward P. Coleridge. 1891; reprinted 1956.
[Works] (5 vols.), translated by A.S. Way. 1894–98; parallel texts as *Euripides* (4 vols.), edited by W.H.D. Rouse, 1912 (Loeb Classical Library).
The Plays (2 vols.), translated by Gilbert Murray. 1931; as *Collected Plays*, 1954.

Ten Plays, translated by Moses Hadas and J.M. McLean. 1936.

[Works], edited by L. Méridier and others. 1947–61.

Three Plays (includes *Hippolytus; Iphigenia in Tauris; Alcestis*), translated by Philip Vellacott. 1953; revised edition, 1974.

"The Bacchae" and Other Plays (includes *Ion; Women of Troy; Helen*), translated by Philip Vellacott. 1954; second edition, 1972.

"The Complete Greek Tragedies" series contains translations as follows (by various translators):

   Euripides 1 (includes *Alcestis; The Medea; The Heracleidae; Hippolytus*). 1955.

   Euripides 2 (includes *Cyclops; Heracles; Iphigenia in Tauris; Helen*). 1956

   Euripides 3 (includes *Hecuba; Andromache; The Trojan Women; Ion*). 1958.

   Euripides 4 (includes *Rhesus; The Suppliant Women; Orestes; Iphigenia in Aulis*). 1958.

   Euripides 5 (includes *Electra; The Phoenecian Women; The Bacchae*). 1959.

Three Great Plays (includes *Medea; Hippolytus; Helen*), translated by Rex Warner. 1958.

"Medea" and Other Plays (includes *Hecabe; Electra; Heracles*), translated by Philip Vellacott. 1963.

"Orestes" and Other Plays (includes *The Children of Heracles; Andromache; The Suppliant Women; The Phoenecian Women; Orestès; Iphigenia in Aulis*), translated by Philip Vellacott. 1972.

Fabulae (2 vols.), edited by James Diggle. 1981–84.

Plays 1 (translations; includes *Medea; The Phoenecian Women; The Bacchae*), introduced by J. Michael Walton. 1988.

The War Plays (includes *Iphigenia at Aulis; The Women of Troy; Helen*), translated by Don Taylor. 1990.

Plays 2 (translations; includes *Hecuba; The Women of Troy; Iphigenia at Aulis; Cyclops*), introduced by J. Michael Walton. 1991.

Stage Works

Alcestis (produced Athens, 438 BC). Several translations as *Alcestis* since 1782.

Medea (produced Athens, 431 BC). Several translations as *Medea* since 1782.

Heracleidae (produced Athens, c.430–428 BC). Several translations as *Heracleidae* since 1782; also translated as *The Children of Heracles*, in *"Orestes" and Other Plays*, 1972.

Hippolytus (produced Athens, 428 BC). Several translations as *Hippolytus* since 1782.

Andromache (produced Athens, c.426–425 BC). Several translations as *Andromache* since 1782.

Hecuba (produced Athens, c. 424 BC). Several translations as *Hecuba* since 1782; also translated as *Hecabe*, in *"Medea" and Other Plays*, 1963.

Supplices (produced Athens, 423–422 BC). Several translations as *The Suppliant Women*; also translated as *The Suppliants*, 1957.

Electra (produced Athens, 422–416 BC). Several translations as *Electra* since 1782.

Heracles (produced Athens, c.417–415 BC). Several translations as *Heracles* since 1782; also translated as *The Madness of Heracles*, 1969.

Troades (produced Athens, 415 BC). Several translations as *The Trojan Women* since 1782; also translated as *The Women of Troy*, in *"The Bacchae" and Other Plays*, 1954, and in *The War Plays*, 1990.

Iphigeneia Taurica (produced Athens, c.414–413 BC). Several translations as *Iphigenia in Tauris* since 1782.

Ion (produced Athens, c.414–413 BC). Several translations as *Ion* since 1782.

Helena (produced Athens, 412 BC). Several translations as *Helen* since 1782.

Phoenissae (produced Athens, c.412–408 BC). Translated as *Jocasta*, 1572; several translations as *The Phoenecian Women* since 1782; as *The Phoenecian Virgins*, 1823.

Orestes (produced Athens, 408 BC). Several translations as *Orestes* since 1782.

Bacchae (produced Athens, c.405 BC). Several translations as *The Bacchae* since 1782.

Iphigeneia Aulidensis, completed by another writer (produced Athens, c.405 BC). Several translations as *Iphigenia in Aulis* since 1782; also translated as *Iphigenia at Aulis*, in *The War Plays*, 1990.

Rhesus, possibly not by Euripides (production date unknown). Several translations as *Rhesus* since 1782.

Cyclops (production date unknown). Several translations as *Cyclops* since 1782.

Fragments (including *Hypsiple* and *Phaethon*). Translated in *The Nineteen Tragedies, and Fragments*, 1782; some translated in *The Macedonian Tetralogy of Euripides*, edited by Richard Johnson Walker, 1920.

*

Criticism

Books:

G.M.A. Grube, *The Drama of Euripides*, London, 1941; reprinted New York, 1973.

Euripides (bust in the Museo Capitolino, Rome).

Gilbert Murray, *Euripides and His Age*, London, 1946.

E.M. Blaiklock, *Male Characters of Euripides*, Wellington, New Zealand, 1952.

G. Norwood, *Essays on Euripidean Drama*, Berkeley, California, 1954.

Gunther Zuntz, *The Political Plays of Euripides*, Manchester, 1955.

W.N. Bates, *Euripides*, Cranbury, Connecticut, 1961.

Gunther Zuntz, *An Inquiry into the Transmission of the Plays of Euripides*, Cambridge, 1965.

F.L. Lucas, *Euripides and His Influence*, New York, 1963.

Desmond J. Conacher, *Euripidean Drama: Myth, Theme, and Structure*, Toronto, 1967.

A.W. Verrall, *Euripides the Rationalist: A Study in the History of Art and Religion*, New York, 1967.

T.B.L. Webster, *The Tragedies of Euripides*, London, 1967.

P. Decharme, *Euripides and the Spirit of His Dramas*, Port Washington, New York, 1968.

Erich Segal (ed.), *Euripides: A Collection of Critical Essays*, Englewood Cliffs, New Jersey, 1968.

S.A. Barlow, *The Imagery of Euripides*, London, 1970.

W.H. Salter, *Essays on Two Moderns: Euripides and Samuel Butler*, Port Washington, New York, 1970.

A.P. Burnett, *Catastrophe Survived: Euripides' Plays of Mixed Reversal*, Oxford, 1971.

R.B. Appleton, *Euripides the Idealist*, Freeport, New York, 1972.

L.H.G. Greenwood, *Aspects of Euripidean Tragedy*, New York, 1972.

S. Melchinger, *Euripides*, New York, 1973.

C.H. Whitman, *Euripides and the Full Circle of Myth*, Cambridge, Massachusetts, 1974.

Philip Vellacott, *Ironic Drama: A Study of Euripides: Method and Meaning*, Cambridge, 1975.

W. Sale, *Existentialism and Euripides* (on *Medea*, *Hippolytus*, and *The Bacchae*), Berwick, Victoria, 1977.

James Diggle, *Studies on the Text of Euripides*, Oxford, 1981.

Anton Powell, *Euripides: Women and Sexuality*, London, 1990.

* * *

By the time that Euripides was presenting his plays in Athens, the fashion for the connected trilogy had passed. Playwrights still offered groups of four at the festival of the Great (or City) Dionysia, but the link between the plays was at most thematic. Dating is difficult for all but a handful of Euripides' plays, but of the 19 extant, no two can be claimed to belong to the same year—with the exception of *Iphigenia in Aulis* and *The Bacchae*, both performed posthumously. Of the 19, one, *Cyclops*, is a satyr play, while *Alcestis* occupied the fourth, or satyr, position in a submission. The other 17, including *Rhesus*, whose authenticity as by Euripides is in some doubt, are all tragedies.

The surviving tragedies of Aeschylus and Sophocles possess a certain uniformity of tone, for all their differences of emphasis and approach. Under the umbrella heading of tragedy, Euripides offers a series of plays whose differences outweigh their similarities. They range in mood from the stark horror of war plays, such as *Hecuba* and *Trojan Women*, to the romantic comedy with serious overtones of *Helen* and *Iphigenia in Tauris*. Several, *Electra* and *Phoenician Women* among them, draw attention to a previous version of the same story by Aeschylus, reaching on occasion a level of parody. *The Bacchae* features Dionysus, god of the theatre, in a play as full of illusion as one by Pirandello. *Ion* looks forward to

the New Comedy of Menander in a play of foundling and birth tokens. Euripides' range could be described as Shakespearean in its breadth.

Behind such versatility may well lie Euripides' solid belief in the theatre as a place to flout expectation and illuminate through shock. Despite the Delphic precept of "learning through suffering", which appears as a major theme in Aeschylus and Sophocles, few of their characters change in the course of a play. The Orestes of *The Oresteia* never regrets murdering his mother. Oedipus' only discovery in *Oedipus Tyrannus* is that he was ignorant of the truth. In Euripides, characters are capable of radical change. Declared motives are often suspect. Scenes can be pervaded by a sense of sub-text. In 19th-century terms, realism has supplanted romanticism.

This new approach to character and situation can reach the point where it must have seemed perverse to the first audiences to encounter *Medea*, *Hippolytus*, *Electra*, *Orestes*, or *Helen*. What were they expecting of Medea? She was a witch who murdered her children. What is she for Euripides? —a woman driven to that extremity by the behaviour of Jason. What was the relationship between Clytemnestra, Electra, and Orestes? Clytemnestra had murdered her husband and was properly done to death by her children. What do they become in Euripides' *Electra*?—Clytemnestra, apologetic and repentant; Electra, sex-starved and manic; Orestes, cowardly and reluctant. In *Orestes* the brother and sister are something else again, Bonnie and Clyde let loose in a world with a legal system capable of dealing with any crimes of Clytemnestra. And Helen—what of Helen, scourge of the Greeks, cause of the Trojan War? In *Orestes* Euripides makes her a vain and frivolous thing, but in *Helen* she is a respectable matron who never went to Troy. The gods supplied a lookalike while the real Helen languished in Egypt, waiting for Menelaus to come and rescue her.

The refusal to take characters or situations at face value leads to a much more prosaic style and a direct approach to the real problems of everyday existence, despite being couched in the terms of myth. Most of his plays were written during the Peloponnesian War which broke out in 431 BC and lasted for the rest of his life. There are moments of patriotic sentiment, even jingoism, but in none is war glorified. The effects of war on victors no less than vanquished leave honour a poor third to wanton cruelty and cynical expediency. Alongside this savage assessment of human motive, Euripides reveals a black humour which throws light on his own view of the human condition. Dionysus' taunting of Pentheus in *The Bacchae* or the terrified messenger stammering out his rudimentary Greek in *Orestes* increase tension by contrast. There are moments of great pathos too, often over the fate of women or children. Evadne flings herself on to her husband's funeral pyre. The murdered baby Astyanax is carried in on his father's enormous shield. The majesty of Aeschylus and Sophocles is replaced by personal pain.

Aeschylus and Sophocles were innovators in their own time, no less than was Euripides, but the dramatic structure and performance conditions of all three playwrights was largely the same. Euripides did make more use of the frame plot and the expository prologue. As the familiar version of the myth was so often to be overturned, it was is his interest to declare his opening position. Established characters from myth proceed to act "out of character", in the sense in which Strindberg uses the phrase to mean contrary to stereotype but psychologically sound. With human motive directing the action, the plots seem at times to reach the point at which the ending prescribed by myth is no longer feasible. Critics of Euripides (and in the face of such innovation there have been many) have seen this as a failing, a confession that he had written himself into a corner from which only a *deus ex machina* could extricate him. In over half of the plays a god or goddess does appear at the end to sort out the human muddle. Far from being a defensive device, this is a positive dramatic statement, serving in part to offer ironic comment on what has happened, in part to force the stubborn to see sense, and in part to restore the myth to the position from which human reaction has deflected it.

Ever the experimenter and professional iconoclast, Euripides is justly represented to posterity by more plays than have survived from Aeschylus or Sophocles. Whether or not he merits more than the other two combined is a different matter, and it has to be confessed that there is a body of decidedly minor Euripides plays. But if Aeschylus and Sophocles invented the rules of the stage, Euripides was the playwright who first saw the potential in breaking those rules.

—J. Michael Walton

See also *Volume 1* entries on *Alcestis*; *The Bacchae*; *Electra*; *Hippolytus*; *Iphigenia in Tauris*; *Medea*; *The Trojan Women*.

EVREINOV, Nikolai.   See *Volume 3* entry.

F

FABBRI, Diego. Born in Forli, Emilia-Romagna, Italy, 2 July 1911. Studied economics and business sciences at the University of Bologna, graduated 1936. Married in 1937. First play, *I fiori del dolore*, published 1931; writer for various Catholic newspapers and periodicals, 1936–40; moved to Rome, 1939; Secretary-General, Centro Cattolico Cinematografico [Catholic Film Centre], 1940–50; first professionally produced play, *Orbite*, staged 1941; gave lectures during the German occupation of Rome in World War II; co-founder, with Ugo Betti and others, Sindacato Nazionale degli Autori Drammatici, 1945; co-editor, 1945, co-manager, 1949, and manager, 1959–68, *La fiera litteraria*; director, Teatro la Cometa, Rome, 1960–62; chairman, Confédération Internationale des Sociétés des Auteurs et des Compositeurs, 1973–75; editor, *Il dramma*, 1977. Recipient: National Prize, 1950; Marzotto International Prize; Théâtre des Nations Prize (Paris), 1959; Feltrinelli Prize for theatre, 1977. Died in Riccione, 14 August 1980.

Works

Collections

Teatro (3 vols.). 1959–64.
Tre commedie d'amore (includes *Non è per scherzo che ti ho amato*; *Area fabbricabile*; *Lascio alle mie donne*). 1972.
Tutto il teatro (2 vols.). 1984.
Mastro Don Gesualdo; I vicere. 1988.

Stage Works

I fiori del dolore. In *Controcorrente*, 5, 1931; revised version in *Controcorrente*, 1933.
Ritorno. 1933.
I loro peccati. 1935.
Il fanciullo sconosciuto. 1935.
Il nodo. In *Controcorrente*, 5–6, 1936; revised as *Paludi* (produced Teatro dell'Arti, Rome, 1942), in *Spettacolo*, 2–3, 1942; in book form, in *Teatro 1*, 1959.
Ricordo. 1937.
Rifiorirà la terra. 1937.
Miraggi. 1937.
Orbite (produced Teatro Quirino, Rome, 1941). In *Palcoscenico*, 21, 1950; in book form, in *Teatro 1*, 1959.
Il prato, from his radio play (produced Rome, 1943). In *Teatro 1*, 1959.
La libreria del sole (produced Teatro Quirino, Rome, 1943). 1943.
Rancore (produced Teatro della Soffita, Bologna, 1950). In *Sipario*, April 1950; in book form, in *Teatro 2*, 1960.
Inquisizione (produced Teatro Nuovo, Milan, 1950). 1950.

Il seduttore (produced Teatro La Fenice, Venice, 1951). In *Scena*, 19, 1951; in book form, in *Teatro 3*, 1964.
Processo di famiglia (produced Teatro Carignano, Turin, 1953). In *Il Dramma*, 197, 1954; in book form, in *Tutti il teatro*, 1984.
Processo a Gesù (produced Piccolo Teatro, Milan, 1955). In *Il Dramma*, 223, 1955; in book form, 1956; translated as *Between Two Thieves*, 1967.
La bugiarda (produced Teatro Manzoni, Milan, 1956). In *Dramma*, 236, 1956; in book form, in *Tutti il teatro*, 1984.
Veglia d'armi (produced Istituto del Dramma Popolare, San Miniato, 1956). 1957.
Delirio, from his radio play *Trio* (produced Teatro Nuovo, Milan, 1958). 1958.
I demoni, from a work by Dostoevsky (produced Genoa, 1957). With *Processo Karamazov*, 1960.
Processo Karamazov: La leggenda del Grande Inquisitore, from a work by Dostoevsky (produced Rome, 1960). With *I demoni*, 1960; revised as opera libretto, *Leggenda del ritorno*, with music by Renzo Rossellini (produced 1966).
Figli d'arte (produced Teatro Eliseo, Rome, 1959). 1960.
Divertimento. In *Teatro 2*, 1960.
Contemplazione. In *Teatro 2*, 1960.
I testimoni. In *Teatro 2*, 1960.
Teresa Desqueyroux, from the work by Mauriac (produced Teatro Quirino, Rome, 1961). In *Il dramma*, 296, 1961; in book form, in *Tutti il teatro*.
Ritratto d'ignoto (produced Teatro della Cometa, Rome, 1962). 1962.
Lo scoiattolo (produced Milan, 1963). In *Teatro 3*, 1964.
A tavola non si parla d'amore (produced Florence, 1963). In *Teatro 3*, 1964.
Il confidente (produced Teatro La Fenice, Venice, 1964). 1964.
L'avvenimento (produced Teatro Duse, Genoa, 1967). 1968.
Lascio all mie donne (produced Piacenza, 1969). In *Il dramma*, 11–12, 1971; in book form, in *Tre commedie d'amore*, 1972.
Non è per scherzo che ti ho amato (produced Teatro Politeama, Naples, 1977). In *Tre commedie d'amore*, 1972.
Area fabbricabile (produced Teatro San Babila, Milan, 1973). In *Tre commedie d'amore*, 1972; revised version, as *Il cedro del Libano* (produced 1976), in *Tutti il teatro*, 1984.
Il vizio assurdo (produced Teatro Verdi, Padua, 1974). 1974.
Il commedione di Giuseppe Gioacchino Belli poeta e impiegato pontificio (produced Cesena, 1978). 1978.
L'hai mai vista in scena . . . ? (produced Teatro Duse, Bologna, 1979). In *Tutto il teatro*, 1984.

Al Dio ignoto (produced by the Campagnia del Capronica, Piazza del Duomo, San Miniato, 1980). In *Tutto il teatro*, 1984.
Gli assenti, with Guido Chiesa. In *Tutti il teatro*, 1984.
L'avventuriero. In *Tutti il teatro*, 1984.
Incontro al parco delle terme (produced Forli, 1985). In *Tutto il teatro*, 1984.
Mastro Don Gesualdo. With *I vicere*, 1988.
I vicere. With *Mastro Don Gesualdo*, 1988.

Screenplays

La porta del cielo, with others, 1945; *Un giorno nella vita*, with others 1946; *Il testimone*, with others, 1946; *Daniele Cortis*, with others, 1947; *Guerra alla guerra*, 1948; *Fabiola*, 1950; *La Belleza del diavolo*, 1950; *Verginita*, 1952; *Processa alla città*, 1952; *Europa '51*, 1952; *Il mondo le Condanna*, 1953; *La passeggiata*, 1953; *I vinti*, 1953; *Il seduttore*, 1954.

Television Plays

Pane vivo, adapted from a work by Mauriac, 1952; *Qualcuno fra voi*, 1963 (published 1963).

Radio Plays

Il prato, 1941 (published 1941); *Trio*, 1949 (published in *Tutti il teatro*, 1984).

Other

Christo tradito, 1949.
Ambiguità cristiana, 1954.

*

Criticism

Books:
Antonio Alessio, *Il teatro di Diego Fabbri*, Savona, 1970.
Giovanni Cappello, *Invito all lettura di Diego Fabbri*, Milan, 1979.
Giovanni Marchi, "Diego Fabbri", in *Teatro italiano*, edited by Mario Verdone, Rome, 1981.
Federico Doglio and Wanda Raspilini (eds.), *Atti del Convegno Internazionale Diego Fabbri*, Rome, 1986.

* * *

Diego Fabbri acquired his love for liberty, spirituality, and literature from his family environment. His republican father, a factory worker, instilled in him a taste for freedom that precluded any accommodation with the Fascism which prevailed in Italy from the early 1920's to the end of World War II. From his mother, a profoundly religious woman who had acted in her youth, he inherited a passion for the theatre, and at an early age he was a member of a Forlinese amateur company, "Ricreativo di S. Luigi".

Fabri's career as a playwright began while he was still in his adolescence; his first play, *I fiori del dolore*, was written when he was only 17 years old. Even at this young age, Fabbri showed a strong predisposition to tackle serious themes. *Il nodo* was banned because its outlook was too pessimistic for the Fascists. Fabbri chose not to include these early plays in the first collection of his work, but they are incorporated into Volume 1 of the 1984 collection.

After graduating from university, Fabbri opened his own private school for several years; he was reluctant to pursue a public career under Mussolini's regime. In 1939, he moved to Rome ostensibly to work in a Catholic publishing house; in reality, he was aiming to get ahead as a playwright and he brought three scripts with him. His anti-Fascist views, his intellectual and spiritual involvement with Catholicism, and his commitment to social reform continued to inform his work.

Fabbri was a leading dramatist of Catholic Christianity. His attitudes were unconventional, however; his views were in conflict with orthodox doctrine and conservative critics accused him of irreverence. From 1940–50, as one of the leaders of the Catholic Film Centre, he devoted himself to liberalizing Catholic attitudes, including censorship of film and theatre. Towards the end of World War II he made a speech, "Cristo Tradito", in which he advocated a rapprochement between Marxism and Christianity, thereby arousing heated debate. He habitually questioned the Catholic Church's official doctrines and positions and found himself anticipating important Church controversies, especially those preceding the reforms of Pope John XXIII and Vatican Council II. He suggested, for instance, that the Roman Catholic Church should cease blaming Jews for the death of Christ (*Processo a Gesú*); that it needed to get closer to the lives of ordinary people (*Libreria del sole*); that a rapprochement should be made with the East (*Veglia d'armi, Ritratto d'ignoto*).

In his plays he also investigated the role religion might play in the lives of modern man. His answers were not facile ones. His tragic view—that man's life is basically lonely, painful, and unhappy, and that salvation only comes in a union with God in the afterlife—is ameliorated by a belief that some relief from metaphysical anxiety can be found in spiritual strivings expressed through faith in God, the love of others, and through artistic expression.

Fabbri came to public attention as a playwright in the early 1940's with *Orbite*, *Paludi*, and *La libreria del sole*. *Orbite* suggests that man can escape from his essential solitude and his isolated, individual orbit through sacrifice and through his yearnings for poetry, music, and study. *Paludi*, a direct comment on dictatorship, is clearly anti-fascist. The ending is pessimistic. Carlo attempts to free himself by rebelling against the corrupt system and is killed by his fellow workers, who cannot understand a man's desire for freedom and can only attribute Carlo's rebellion to greed. The anguish inherent in the play calls to mind the work of Ugo Betti, who was present at the opening and who, along with Pirandello, had a strong influence on the younger Fabbri.

In *La libreria del sole* Fabbri investigates the relationship between the Church and ordinary men through the character of Anselmo, a priest, who in the midst of a spiritual crisis pays a visit to his family. He realizes that the priestly vocation entails more than the private joys of religious devotion he experienced as a young seminarian. He must go out into the world of real people and accept them as they are.

After the end of the War, Fabbri moved into a second artistic phase. It was in this period that he wrote his trial plays, of which the major ones are *Inquisizione, Processo di famiglia*, and *Processo a Gesú*. It was also in this period that he came to international attention and began to spend part of every year in Paris. He achieved great success in France, where his plays have been widely performed and published.

Fabbri has stated in an introductory note to *I demoni* that the heart of his work lies in the depth of his characters. "Are they innocent or guilty? Will they save themselves or not? If it were up to me, I would not hesitate to call all my works 'trials'". These "trials" have a didactic component. In

Rancore, the cold, intellectual, egotistical Renato, proudly convinced of the superiority of his ideas about living, attempts to dominate and control his effervescent, spontaneous wife. He is doomed to disappointment and suffering because he does not love her as she is and has no compassion for human nature.

Inquisizione was successful not only in Italy but also elsewhere in Europe and in Latin America. It contains subtle arguments and brilliant dialogue. Renato Simoni contrasted it with Sartre's *No Exit* as "the most anti-existentialist play on the Italian stage". It involves the catharsis of three characters undergoing emotional crises. A disillusioned and cynical Don Sergio, who is thinking of giving up the priesthood, is persuaded to counsel a couple on their marriage. The wife, Angela, feels guilty about having entrapped Renato in marriage while he was a novitiate. Through the intervention of an older priest all three are forced into facing their self-deception and the web of lies they have created.

Processo a Gesù is Fabbri's most famous play. Inspired by the news that a trial of Jesus was publicly solemnized by some English-speaking jurists in Jerusalem, Fabbri created a play within a play. The cast consists of two groups. The first is the travelling family troupe of German-Jewish actors who re-enact the trial of Jesus, impersonating the judge and the witnesses—Caiaphas, Pilate, Mary, Joseph, three disciples, Judas, Mary Magdalene—to redetermine the innocence or guilt of Christ and the innocence or guilt of society. The second group comprises the spectators—an intellectual, a prostitute, a prodigal, a blind man, a priest—who represent modern man and express their current opinions. Giancarlo Vigorelli has pointed out that Mary Magdalena provides the key to *Processo a Gesù* and to all Fabbri's plays, when she emphasizes that Christ returns among men only if they come together in his name; that Christianity does not celebrate the individual experience but its opposite: the communal, social, and ecclesial.

Fabbri has written a number of secular plays. With *Il seduttore* and *La bugiarda* he showed himself particularly adept at writing comedy, and these plays show a more flexible attitude towards human nature. In the former, which was directed by Luchino Visconti, Eugenio has affairs with three women at the same time. Fabbri denied that his character was a Don Juan since Eugenio has not an ounce of cruelty in him and lets himself be seduced by the women. What brings him close to Don Juan, said Fabbri, is "the love of the game. I believe that human relationships are dominated by play; one wants to win—right up to the moment when one can no longer play—because one reaches the point when one must be sincere." The comedy had two different endings. In the 1951 version, when Eugenio revealed the truth to the women and they rejected him, he renounced life. In the 1956 version, Eugenio only simulated his death.

La bugiarda continues the theme of the lie. Fabbri proves his mastery of light, amusing, and aggressive comedy with the story of the strong and artful Isabella, a courtesan, who keeps two men on a string. Vito Pandolfi wrote that *La bugiarda* "is perhaps the Italian comedy with the most brilliant language to appear after the war". He points out that Fabbri has learned from the dialect texts of Peppino and Eduardo De Filippo and understands the appeal to the public of language that is flavored with popular expressions and intonations. In responding to accusations (from the conservatives) of irreverence, Fabbri wrote that the play was the fruit of pure invention, that it bewildered him how people could "confuse serious discussions of Faith with a defense of a low-class prostitute" whom he only meant "benevolently to ridicule and unmask".

Fabbri's passion for the theatre extended to his work within theatrical institutions, and his interest in bringing theatre to the people can be seen in, for example, the 1943 "Manifesto per un teatro del popolo", which he signed with Vito Pandolfi and others, calling for a national and popular theatre.

—Jane House

FARQUHAR, George. Born in Londonderry, Ireland, 1677 or 1678. Educated at a school in Londonderry; Trinity College, Dublin (sizar), 1694–95. Married Margaret Pemell c.1703; two daughters. Press corrector for a bookseller in Dublin, 1696; actor, Smock Alley Theatre, Dublin, 1696–97, but gave up acting after accidentally wounding a fellow-actor; moved to London c.1697; first play, *Love and a Bottle*, staged 1698; travelled in the Netherlands, 1700; lieutenant in the Grenadiers, 1704: recruiting officer in Shrewsbury and Lichfield, 1705; also garrisoned in Dublin. Died in London, May 1707.

Works

Collections

George Farquhar (includes *The Constant Couple; The Twin Rivals; The Recruiting Officer; The Beaux' Stratagem*), edited by William Archer.   1906; reprinted 1959.

Clamp Sculp.

George Farquhar (engraving).

The Complete Works (2 vols.), edited by Charles Stonehill. 1930.
Works (2 vols.), edited by Shirley Strum Kenny. 1988.

Stage Works

Love and a Bottle (produced Theatre Royal, Drury Lane, London, 1698). 1699.
The Constant Couple; or, A Trip to the Jubilee (produced Theatre Royal, Drury Lane, London, 1699). 1700.
Sir Harry Wildair, Being the Sequel of The Trip to the Jubilee (produced Theatre Royal, Drury Lane, London, 1701). 1701.
The Stage Coach, from a play by Jean de la Chapelle (produced 1701–02). 1704; with variants, 1705.
The Inconstant; or, The Way to Win Him, from the play *The Wild Goose Chase* by Fletcher (produced Theatre Royal, Drury Lane, London, 1702). 1702.
The Twin-Rivals (produced Theatre Royal, Drury Lane, London, 1702). 1703.
The Recruiting Officer (produced Haymarket Theatre, London, 1706). 1706.
The Beaux' Stratagem (produced Haymarket Theatre, London, 1707). 1707.

Verse

Love and Business in a Collection of Occasionary Verse and Epistolary Prose, A Discourse Likewise upon Comedy in Reference to the English Stage. 1702.
Barcelona; or, The Spanish Expedition. 1710.

Fiction

The Adventures of Covent Garden. 1698.

*

Bibliographies

Eugene Nelson James, *George Farquhar: A Reference Guide*, Boston, 1986.

Criticism

Books:
Willard Connely, *Young Farquhar: The Restoration Drama at Twilight*, London, 1949.
A.J. Farmer, *George Farquhar*, London, 1966 (British Council booklet).
Eric Rothstein, *George Farquhar*, New York, 1967.
Eugene N. James, *The Development of George Farquhar as a Comic Dramatist*, The Hague, 1972.
Raymong A. Anselment (ed.), *Farquhar: "The Recruiting Officer" and "The Beaux' Stratagem": A Casebook*, London, 1977.

* * *

The wits and critics of Farquhar's own age were less than impressed with him. He was a writer of farce, his dialogue lacked polish, his plotting was irregular, and many of his characters were unnatural. Farquhar himself professed no great concern about this criticism. He was frequently, and cheekily, dismissive of the "rules", and could nonchalantly point out that, whatever the critics might say, many of his plays were extremely successful, and the one which was a particular target for critical venom, *The Constant Couple*, was a runaway smash hit. Farquhar's success with the public, moreover, was not short-lived. Four of his comedies went on to become staples of the 18th-century theatre, and two, *The Recruiting Officer* and *The Beaux' Stratagem*, are among the handful of Restoration plays that have a secure place in the modern repertoire.

A particular target of the critics was Farquhar's "low dialogue". This may well be one of his modern selling points. Instead of the lapidary sentences of a Wycherley or a Congreve, with their extended similes developed through elaborately wrought clauses, Farquhar tends to favour rattle and dash. His verbal high points are often rapid-fire catalogues of objects or events, short snappy phrases succeeding one another, often making use of parallelism or antithesis and mounting to a crescendo. This is nowhere more evident than in *The Constant Couple* and *The Beaux' Stratagem*, and it gives a sense of vitality and liveliness, as opposed to the cool and measured control of an Etherege or a Congreve.

Another of Farquhar's selling points is his alleged "realism". Thus there are the suggestions of a relationship between the plays and the author's own life experience. The raffish hero of *Love and a Bottle*, like Farquhar himself, is an impecunious Irish gentleman newly come to town; *The Recruiting Officer* is explicitly connected with his own activities in that trade; and *The Beaux' Stratagem* draws its setting from a visit made to Lichfield. Beyond that is the very fact that he has chosen to set the last two plays neither in a capital city (the usual convention) nor in a fashionable resort (the usual alternative), but in the workaday world of country towns. He is not unique in the social range of his characters, but he has a broader spread than most Restoration playwrights, and while the concerns of the plays are very much those of the gentry, his lower-class characters (such as Bullfinch the landlady, Tom Jolt the coachman, Midnight the Midwife, Kite the recruiting sergeant, and Scrub the country servant) are far from being ciphers. The way in which a few of his plays, however notionally, are touched by the social concerns of the day, such as the recruiting act, or the problems of divorce, further enhances this sense of proximity to the "real" world.

Another source of Farquhar's appeal is the air of amiability that pervades most of his plays, the conspicuous exception being the self-consciously moral near-melodrama, *The Twin-Rivals*. A significant part of this amiability comes from Farquhar's readiness to handle his fools gently, so that in *The Beaux' Stratagem*, highwaymen remain unpunished, an Irish traitor unhanged, and a boorish husband is revealed to have some right on his side, as well as a slightly redeeming puppy-like friendliness. Even the French officer, instead of being grossly humiliated by the heroine's trickery of him, is allowed a thoroughly witty retort and a stylish exit.

The same easy tolerance could be said to have been extended, by Farquhar, to his rakish heroes. Thus in his first play, *Love and a Bottle*, the heroine says of the wild Roebuck that "his behaviour can add a Grace to the unseemliness of Vice". This encapsulates Farquhar's basic strategy with most of his heroes, to rely on their raffish charm and liveliness to excuse, or even distract attention from, the darker sides of their behaviour. It is a strategy by no means unique to Farquhar and, by and large, it succeeds; but at times the darkness comes through, and the results can be disturbing. The examples that are likely to unsettle a modern audience are not so much manifestations of licentiousness as of an almost aggressive callousness: Roebuck's attitude to his bastards, Sir Harry's attitude to his wife's death, Plume's ultimate indifference to his recruits, Archer's cold demand for his share of the booty at the end of *The Beaux' Stratagem*. It is not clear whether this is simple insensitivity on Farquhar's part, or a calculated effort to add a touch of abrasiveness to the mixture.

In Farquhar's most extravagant comic creation, the Sir Harry Wildair of *The Constant Couple*, the problem does not arise. Any harshness in this Sir Harry (though not in the Sir Harry of the play's sequel) is totally smothered by his ebullience. As Vizard has it, he turns "all Passion into Gaiety of Humour, by which he chuses to rejoice his Friends, than be hated by any". Sir Harry is irrepressibly cheerful, distinctly lacking in seriousness, and unable to take offence even at the sort of insult that would have propelled any other Restoration hero into a duel. The result is a carnival figure, who is as released from the constraints of a machismo honour as he is from the inhibitions of the moral order. In all of this he comes curiously close to that prince of fops, Vanbrugh's Lord Foppington, and like him he has the problem of floating through a play otherwise encumbered with a great deal of mechanical plotting and wooden sentiment. *The Recruiting Officer* and *The Beaux' Stratagem* are undoubtedly Farquhar's finest plays, but one can only regret that the freewheeling Sir Harry was not given a more adequate context in which to disport himself.

—Robert Jordan

See also *Volume 1* entries on *The Beaux' Stratagem*; *The Recruiting Officer*.

FASSBINDER, Rainer Werner. Born in Bad Wörishofen, Bavaria, West Germany, 31 May 1946. Educated at the Rudolf Steiner School and secondary schools in Augsburg and Munich until 1964; studied acting at Fridl-Leonhard Studio, Munich. Married Ingrid Caven, 1970 (divorced). Worked as decorator and in archives of Süddeutsche Zeitung, Munich, 1964–66; failed entrance exam to West Berlin Film and Television Academy, 1965; joined Action-Theater, Munich, 1967: group disbanded May 1968; first original play, *Katzelmacher*, produced 1968; co-founder, theatre group antiteater, 1968; began making films with members of antiteater, 1969; founder, Tango Film, independent company, 1971; with Kurt Raab and Roland Petri, took over Theater am Turm (TAT), Frankfurt, 1974; TAT project failed, so returned to Munich to concentrate on film work, 1975. Frequently writer, director, and actor in his film work. Recipient: Golden Bear, Berlin Festival, for *Die Sehnsucht der Veronika Voss*, 1982. Died, probably from overdose of sleeping pills and cocaine, in Munich, 10 June 1982.

Works

Collections

Antiteater (includes *Katzelmacher*; *Preparadise Sorry Now*; *Die Bettleroper*).   1970.
Antiteater 2 (includes *Das Kaffeehaus*; *Bremer Freiheit*; *Blut am Hals der Katze*).   1972.
Stücke 3.   1976.

"*Anarchie in Bayern*" *und andere Stücke* (includes *Tröpfen auf heisse Steine*; *Der amerikanische Soldat*; *Werwolf*).   1985.
Antiteater: Fünf Stücke nach Stücken (includes *Ajax*; *Die Bettleroper*; *Das Kaffeehaus*; *Das brennende Dorf*; *Iphigenie auf Tauris*).   1986.
Plays, translated by Denis Calandra.   1986.
Die Kinofilme (5 vols.), edited by Michael Töteberg.   1987–90:
1. *Der Stadtstreicher*; *Das kleine Chaos*; *Liebe ist kälter als der Tod*; *Katzelmacher*; *Götter der Pest*.   1987.
2. *Warum läuft Herr R. Amok?*; *Rio das Mortes*; *Whitty*; *Die Niklashauser Fahrt*; *Der amerikanische Soldat*; *Warnung vor einer heiligen Nutte*.   1990.
3. *Händler der vier Jahreszeiten*; *Angst essen Seele auf*; *Fontane Effie Briest*.   1990.
4–5. *Acht Stunden sind kein Tag*.   1990.
Sämtliche Stücke (includes all the stage plays and adaptations).   1991.

Stage Works

Katzelmacher (produced by Action-Theater, Munich, 1967). In *Antiteater*, 1970.
Ajax, from the play by Sophocles (produced by antiteater, Munich, 1968).   In *Antiteater*, 1986.
Iphigenie auf Tauris, from the play by Goethe (produced by antiteater, Munich, 1968).   In *Antiteater*, 1986.
Der amerikanische Soldat (produced by antiteater, Munich, 1968).   In "*Anarchie in Bayern*" *und andere Stücke*, 1985.
Die Bettleroper, from a work by John Gay (produced by antiteater, Munich, 1969).   In *Antiteater*, 1970.
Preparadise Sorry Now (produced by antiteater, Munich, 1969).   In *Antiteater*, 1970.
Anarchie in Bayern (produced by antiteater, Werkraum-Theater, Munich, 1969).   1969.
Werwolf, with Harry Baer (produced by antiteater, Forum Theater, Berlin, 1969).   In "*Anarchie in Bayern*" *und andere Stücke*, 1985.
Das Kaffeehaus, from a play by Goldoni (produced Theater der Freien Hansestadt, Bremen, 1969).   In *Antiteater 2*, 1972.
Das brennende Dorf, from a play by Lope de Vega (produced Theater der Freien Hansestadt, Bremen, 1970).   1970.
Bremer Freiheit (produced Theater der Freien Hansestadt, Bremen, 1971).   In *Antitheater 2*, 1972; translated as *Bremen Coffee*, in *Wolfgang Bauer: "Shakespeare the Sadist"; Rainer Werner Fassbinder: "Bremen Coffee"; Peter Handke: "My Foot My Tutor"; Franz Xaver Kroetz: "Stallerhof"*, 1977.
Blut am Hals der Katze (produced Städtische Bühnen, Nuremberg, 1971). In *Antitheater 2*, 1972; translated as *Blood on the Neck of the Cat*, with *The Bitter Tears of Petra von Kant*, 1984.
Die bitteren Tränen der Petra von Kant (produced by Landestheater, Darmstadt, in Frankfurt, 1971).   1973; translated as *The Bitter Tears of Petra von Kant*, with *Blood on the Neck of the Cat*, 1984.
Der Müll, die Stadt und der Tod (produced Schauspielhaus, Frankfurt, 1985).   In *Stücke 3*, 1976; revised version, with *Die bitteren Tränen der Petra von Kant*, 1986.
Tröpfen auf heisse Steine (produced Internationales Theaterfestival, Munich, 1985).   In "*Anarchie in Bayern*" *und andere Stücke*, 1985.

Screenplays

Der Stadtstreicher, 1965, *Das kleine Chaos*, 1966, *Liebe ist kälter als der Tod*, 1969, *Katzelmacher*, 1969, *Götter der Pest*,

1969: all published in *Die Kinofilme 1*, 1987; *Warum läuft Herr R amok?*, with others, 1969 (published in *Die Kinofilme 2*, 1990); *Fernes Jamaica*, 1969; *Rio das Mortes*, 1970 (published in *Die Kinofilme 2*, 1990); *Whitty*, 1970 (published in *Die Kinofilme 2*, 1990); *Die Niklashauser Fahrt*, with others, 1970 (published in *Die Kinofilme 2*, 1990); *Der amerikanische Soldat*, 1970 (published in *Die Kinofilme 2*, 1990); *Warnung vor einer heiligen Nutte*, 1970 (published in *Die Kinofilme 2*, 1990); *Pioniere in Ingolstadt*, 1971; *Das Kaffeehaus*, 1971; *Der Händler der vier Jahreszeiten*, 1971 (published in *Die Kinofilme 3*, 1990); *Die bitteren Tränen der Petra von Kant*, 1972; *Wildwechsel*, 1972; *Welt am Draht* (in 2 parts), 1973; *Angst essen Seele auf*, 1973 (published 1978); *Martha*, 1973; *Fontane Effi Briest*, 1974 (published in *Die Kinofilme 3*, 1990); *Faustrecht der Freiheit*, with others, 1974; *Mutter Küsters Fahrt zum Himmel*, with others, 1975; *Angst vor der Angst*, 1975; *Ich will doch nur, dass Ihr mich liebt*, 1976; *Chinesisches Roulette*, 1976; *Schatten der Engel*, 1976; *Bolwieser*, 1977; *Die Ehe der Maria Braun*, 1978 (published as *The Marriage of Maria Braun*, 1986); *In einem Jahr mit dreizehn Monden*, 1978; *Die dritte Generation*, 1979; *Lili Marleen*, 1980; *Lola*, 1981; *Die Sehnsucht der Veronika Voss*, 1982; *Querelle*, 1982 (published 1982).

Television Plays

Acht Stunden sind kein Tag (in 5 episodes), 1972 (published in *Die Kinofilme 4–5*, 1990); *Bremer Freiheit*, 1972; *Nora Helmer*, 1973; *Wie ein Vogel auf dem Draht*, 1974; episode of *Deutschland im Herbst*, 1978; *Berlin Alexanderplatz* (in 13 episodes), 1980; *Theater in Trance*, 1981.

Radio Plays

Preparadise Sorry Now, 1970; *Ganz in Weiss*, 1970; *Iphigenie auf Tauris*, from the play by Goethe, 1971; *Keiner ist böse und keiner ist gut*, 1972 (published in *Sämtliche Stücke*, 1991).

Other

Der Film 'Berlin Alexanderplatz' (work journal), with Harry Baer. 1980.
Film Befreien den Kopf: Essays und Arbeitsnotizen, edited by Michael Töteberg. 1984.
Die Anarchie der Phantasie: Gespräche und Interviews, edited by Michael Töteberg. 1986.

*

Criticism

Books:
Karl H. Assenmacher, "Das engagierte Theater Rainer Werner Fassbinders", in *Sprachnetze*, edited by Gerhart C. Rump, Hildesheim, 1976.
Günther Rühle (ed.), *Fassbinder ohne Ende: Eine Dokumentation anlässlich der Aufführung von . . . "Der Müll, die Stadt und der Tod".* . . . Frankfurt, 1985.
Robert Kotz and Peter Berling, *Love is Colder than Death: The Life and Times of Rainer Werner Fassbinder*, London, 1987.

Articles:
Fritz Rumler, "Rainer Werner Fassbinder" (in English), in *Gambit*, 21, 1972.
Denis Calandra, "Politicised Theatre: The Case of Rainer Werner Fassbinder's *Garbage, the City and Death*", in *Modern Drama*, 31, 1988.
Fassbinder issue of *Text und Kritik* (includes several articles and a bibliography), 103, 1989.
Erik MacDonald, "Rainer Werner Fassbinder and the Politics of Simulation", in *Journal of Dramatic Theory and Criticism*, vol.5 no.1, 1990.
Reinhold Grimm, "The Jew, the Playwright, and Trash: West Germany's Fassbinder Controversy", in *Monatshefte*, vol.83 no.1, 1991.

*   *   *

In a very short span of time Rainer Werner Fassbinder made about 40 films and either wrote or adapted 15 stage plays. He also wrote for radio and television and acted in his own and other directors' work. Though he was to abandon the theatre in the mid-1970's, in a sense it never left him, and a feature of his films to the very last was his use of distinctly theatrical groupings and tableaux.

Fassbinder's first experience in theatre was in Munich in the mid-1960's with the "Action Theater". He then provided leadership for a loosely organized collective called the "anti-teater", some of whose actors went on to work with Fassbinder until his death in 1982. The "antiteater" group offered audiences "vehemently passionate acting, and a light, nonchalant kind of aggressiveness", according to critic Peter Iden. They cavalierly adapted classics by Sophocles, Büchner, John Gay and others, and also had a hand in reviving interest in the folk-play tradition associated with Ödön von Horvath and Marie Luise Fleisser. (Franz Xaver Kroetz, the important exponent of the modern folk play, played the part of the young officer in Fassbinder's production of Fleisser's *Pioneers in Ingolstadt*.)

Loneliness is a common theme in Fassbinder's work, together with the Strindbergian idea that power becomes a determining factor in all human relationships. His characters yearn for love, but then seemed condemned to exert an often violent control over those around them. In *Die bitteren Tränen der Petra von Kant* (*The Bitter Tears of Petra von Kant*) the titular character describes what she had hoped was possible in marriage: "We didn't want that stuffy sort of marriage which grinds along in the same old routine. We wanted always to be fully conscious, always to decide for ourselves anew. . . .". The relationship fails, as does the homosexual one which follows, because, in Fassbinder's world, love turns inevitably to possessiveness.

Bremer Freiheit (translated as *Bremen Coffee*), inspired by an actual 19th-century case, tells the story of Geesche Gottfried, who systematically eliminates anyone who tries to "keep her in her place". In revenge for the humiliation she suffers in the male-dominated society, she cheerfully sets about serving poisoned coffee to husbands, father, brother, even a best friend—a woman she wants to save from "the kind of life [she's] having to lead". By the time she is caught at the end, the alienation is absolute.

A zany sort of comedy characterizes *Blut am Hals der Katze* (*Blood on the Cat's Neck*). Cartoon-strip character Phoebe Zeitgeist arrives from another planet to study "human democracy". Witness to the usual environment of Fassbinder lowlife and institutionalized mean-spiritedness, she assimilates human behavior only too well, plunging her teeth into each of the characters in turn and reducing them to a state of torpor. The play ends with this vampire from outer space reciting Immanuel Kant on the faculty of human understanding.

The "fascistoid underpinnings of everyday life" set the tone for *Preparadise Sorry Now*, a play Fassbinder based in part on the infamous Moors murderers, Ian Brady and Myra Hindley. Fassbinder alternates sections of the murder story with a series of Christian liturgical passages, stressing their "cannibalism", and with brutal everyday vignettes between teachers and students, parents and children, pimps and whores, and so on. He leaves the choice of order of all but the Brady/Hindley scenes to the director, with the result that the beginning, middle, and end of the central plot drive towards a gruesome conclusion propelled by the other two individually chosen structures.

Xenophobia and perverse jealousy, fed by economic and social pressures in suburban working-class Munich, lead to violence against the Greek "guest laborer" Jorgos in *Katzelmacher*. Exploited as cheap labor, Jorgos also functions as hate-object for the men and sexual fantasy for the women in the play. In one of his first internationally acclaimed films, *Angst essen Seele auf* (*Fear Eats The Soul*), Fassbinder was to explore the theme again, focusing on the relationship between a Moroccan laborer and a cleaning woman.

Fassbinder consistently sympathized with the victims and outcasts of society, though he was not sentimental when it came to describing their capacity to be cruel when given the chance. Typically, he did much to demystify homosexuality by treating it as a given, as ordinary complex human behavior. His penchant for melodrama and lurid detail, however, has led some critics to accuse him of perpetuating myths about gay sexuality. Fassbinder's own ruthless honesty managed to alienate him from virtually every political or ideological group at one time or another. He had a knack of going for the open wound, of forcing people to confront themselves. His last play, *Der Müll, die Stadt und der Tod* (*Garbage, the City, and Death*), written in 1975, is a good example.

Heiner Müller, as incisive a writer as Fassbinder, describes "Garbage, the City and Death" as using "a victim's revenge to describe the devastation of a city in huge, harsh images. The city is Frankfurt. The means of revenge is property speculation and its consequences". The victim in this play is one of the few characters without a proper name, the Rich Jew, and the symbolic revenge is an act of love, his murder of the lonely abused whore, Roma B. "Love, and you blow your rights", exclaims the dwarf Little Prince. The Rich Jew seems to have expressed Fassbinder's feelings with an earlier line, "It all evens out in the end". "Garbage" is rambling in form, concocted out of kitschy music, ballads, sleazy drag routines, 1950's rock and roll, and arias from operas of the great Romantic tradition—*La Traviata*, *Tristan und Isolde*, and others. The plot line and dialogue owe something to hard-boiled American detective fiction, as hustlers, pimps, speculators, and city officials vie for advantage over each other. The heart of the controversy over "Garbage" has to do with the accusations of anti-semitism and the counter charge that banning production is an infringement of the Basic Law (*Grundgesetz*) guarantee of free expression. Fassbinder claimed his Rich Jew was the only one who could feel and express love in the play, and that his profiteering was simply to make use of conditions he did not create. Heiner Müller quoted Fassbinder in his response to the controversy: "There are anti-semites in this play. But then they exist in other places too—in Frankfurt for instance". Fassbinder could be counted on to choose taboo material, and to treat it in an aggressively extreme manner, giving rise to the most disparate responses.

—Denis Calandra

FENNARIO, David. Born David William Wiper in Montreal, Canada, in 1947. Educated at Dawson College, Montreal, 1969–71. Married Elizabeth Fennario in 1976; one child. Did various casual jobs in the late 1960's playwright-in-residence, Centaur Theatre, Montreal, from 1973. Co-founder, Cultural Workers Association. Recipient: Chalmers Award, 1979.

Works

Stage Works

On the Job (produced Centaur Theatre, Montreal, 1975). 1976.
Nothing to Lose (produced Centaur Theatre, Montreal, 1976). 1977.
Toronto (produced Centaur Theatre, Montreal, 1978).
Without a Parachute, from his journal (produced Theatre Pass Muraille, Toronto, 1978).
Balconville (produced Centaur Theatre, Montreal, 1979). 1980.
Changes, from his journal *Without a Parachute* (produced Ottawa, 1980).
Moving (produced Centaur Theatre, Montreal, 1983).
Blue Mondays, with poems by Daniel Adams. 1984.
Joe Beef (produced Black Rock Theatre, Verdun, Quebec, 1984).
Neil Cream (produced McGill University, Montreal, 1985).
The Murder of Susan Parr (produced 1989).

Memoirs and Letters

Without a Parachute (journal). Privately printed, 1972; 1974.

*

Criticism

Articles:
Paulette Collet, "Fennario's *Balconville* and Tremblay's *En pièce détachées*: A Universe of Backyards and Despair", in *Canadian Drama*, 10, 1984.
Jim Desson and Bruce K. Filson, "Where is David Fennario Now?", in *Canadian Theatre Review*, 46, 1986.
Robert C. Nunn, "The Interplay of Action and Set in the Plays of David Fennario", in *Theatre History in Canada*, 9, 1988.

* * *

It is impossible to separate David Fennario's biography from his writing. Born in the working-class Montreal district of Pointe-St-Charles, Fennario [David Wiper] lived the life of poverty and disenfranchisement which has become his recurrent *mise en scène* and developed the Marxist ideology which motivates his plays. His first published work, *Without a Parachute* (dramatized in 1978 and again, as *Changes*, in 1980), reveals the conditions which shaped his political vision; his attitudes have remained aggressively those of his formative years. As he says, "Because of my background, just the fact that I'm writing plays is a political thing". His vision of life in the Pointe is most personal in *Nothing to Lose*, where a protagonist returns to his district to discuss with his buddies what it is like to become a popular playwright and media personality. When Fennario moves away from his sociological roots, his own extended self, and the Quebec which he understands, as he did in *Toronto*, the results are less successful.

On the Job establishes the tone and themes central to Fennario's major plays. Set in the shipping room of a clothing factory on Christmas Eve, the action is incited by a rush order from a Canadian department store chain which symbolizes the bourgeois Establishment. Emboldened by alcohol and responding to feelings of exploitation and powerlessness, three workers refuse to work into the holiday. They organize a wildcat strike, only to be fired. The characters represent types of the milieu: the broken, old worker hopes only to keep his job until retirement; the Québécois foreman who has risen to power in a hierarchy dominated by the Anglophones sells out to retain his position; the young punk wants only to drink and avoid responsibility; the young radical attempts to politicize his fellows. That his call to action finally ends in defeat reflects Fennario's cynical vision of compromise and negotiation and his repeated call for a revolutionary solution.

The dialogue in which Fennario's workers argue is realistic and highly effective on stage. Credible dialogue in an authentic vernacular is Fennario's chief dramatic talent, one which gives strength to his portrayals and contributes, in considerable measure, to his popular success. He has attempted to bring working-class audiences into the essentially bourgeois theatre; his unremitting language and honest characters probably facilitate peer acceptance. Certainly *On the Job* reflects this sense of language and shows, with fights, props, and a fast pace, an equally lively command of the stage.

Balconville is Fennario's most popular play. Showing growth in his craft, it provides more fully developed characterizations (including female characters for the first time), a clever use of both French and English, and a more layered plot. (The creation, for example, of the traditional figure of the Clown in Thibaud shows Fennario moving outside the confines of political naturalism.) The play dramatizes ghetto life in a hot, urban summer. Unlike the wealthy who flee the heat, the residents of the Pointe "holiday" in Balconville—on their tenement verandas. Here they play out their own empty lives and witness similar desperation in the lives of their neighbours. The play centres on three families. The francophone antagonist toils in a stifling job which he loses at the climax of the play; the anglophone protagonist wastes his days waiting for an unemployment insurance cheque and dreaming about his past as a local rock star. Their wives, and the mother of another aimless son downstairs, struggle to keep their homes together; it is the realistic women who perceive both the seriousness of their situation and the need for communal action.

A second generation is shown in the more sympathetic but equally futile lives of a francophone student whose drunken father fondles her but who must quit her education when he loses his job, and a young anglophone who dreams of escaping to New York to be a musician but who plays his guitar badly and will end in a boring factory job. Even these two cannot communicate, however, partly because the strong gender definitions of this milieu make them awkward with one another, and partly because they cannot understand one another's language. The play uses both languages without translation and has been billed as Canada's first bilingual play; its comment on language as a force of tension within the community attracted much popular and critical comment in the first production.

The symbolic comment on Canadian society is obvious, but, in Fennario's vision, misunderstanding also becomes a metaphor for the lack of communication among unorganized workers. Not only do these people fail to connect in political action (despite the call for a protest demonstration by a female character); they fail to connect in any personal way. Despite their compressed living space, each is isolated and lonely. Any attempt at intimacy is interpreted as sexual aggression or ignored by people so bitter and alienated that feelings are mistrusted. Alcohol again exacerbates the pent-up anger. In a well structured motif, the heat fuels their hopelessness and linguistic rivalry even as the threat of arson encroaches. At the conclusion, the tenement begins to burn down (perhaps in a fire set by the landlord/politician to collect the insurance), and the families collide in an attempt to save their few possessions and to come together as a community in crisis. The language barrier intrudes and is partly overcome in the face of the emergency, but the final question of the play, "What are we going to do?", and its French echo, "Qu'est-ce qu'on va faire?", suggest that no solution can be found within this system. The ending has been criticized as an easy solution for the playwright, but the burning down of a worthless world by common people struggling toward a sense of association is also a clear Marxist message.

Disillusioned with mainstream theatre, Fennario began to work with an amateur community group. *Joe Beef* and *Neil Cream*, written for this group, continue his Marxist reading of Montreal history, and have been poorly received. *The Murder of Susan Parr*, which concerns the splintering of the Pointe-St-Charles community, returns Fennario to an established playhouse and to his familiar subject. Fennario invariably demonstrates keen observation and an ear for dialogue; he also creates situations of genuine conflict and, especially in his female characters, shows a growing complexity of character. Where his plays ultimately fail to satisfy, however, is in the repetition of context and the overly predictable polemic.

—Reid Gilbert

FERNÁNDEZ DE MORATÍN, Leandro. Born in Madrid, Spain, 10 March 1760, son of the writer Nicolás Fernández de Moratín. Educated at home by his father. Goldsmith's apprentice, 1780–86; private secretary to the Count of Cabarrús on trip to Paris, 1787–88; took orders as abbé, 1789; under patronage of the King's favourite, Manuel de Gody, his first play, *El viejo y la niña*, produced 1790; travelled to Paris, 1792, England, 1792–93, Germany and Switzerland, 1793, and Italy, 1793–96; on return to Spain, became Secretary for Language Interpretation, 1796; settled in Pastrana, 1796; abandoned playwriting after attacks on him by the Spanish Inquisition; French sympathiser during Peninsular War: following French invasion of Spain, appointed Librarian at the National Library, 1811, but left Madrid for Valencia with the French forces, 1812, and was besieged with them in the Castle of Peñiscola; lived in Barcelona, 1814–17; after further investigations by the Inquisition, moved to France and Italy, 1817–20; briefly returned to Barcelona, 1820, but lived in France after 1821. Died in Paris, 21 June 1828.

Works

Collections

Obras dramáticas y líricas (3 vols.).   1825.
Obras (4 vols.).   1830–31.
Obras póstumas (3 vols.).   1867–68.
Teatro, edited by F. Ruiz Morcuende.   1924.
Teatro completo.   1944.
Teatro completo (2 vols.).   1977.

Stage Works

El viejo y la niña (produced Teatro del Príncipe, Madrid, 1790).   1795.
La comedia nueva; o, El café (produced Teatro del Príncipe, Madrid, 1792).   1792.
Hamlet, from the play by Shakespeare (produced Madrid, 1798).   1798.
El barón (produced Teatro de la Cruz, Madrid, 1803).   1804; translated as *The Baron*, in *Theatrical Review* (London), vol.2 no.11, 1805.
La mojigata (produced Teatro de la Cruz, Madrid, 1804).   1804.
El sí de las niñas (produced Teatro de la Cruz, Madrid, 1806).   1805; translated as *Fanny's Consent*, in *Poet Lore*, 40, 1929; as *When a Girl Says Yes*, in *Spanish Drama*, edited by Angel Flores, 1962; as *The Maiden's Consent*, 1963.
La escuela de maridos, from a play by Molière (produced Teatro del Príncipe, Madrid, 1812).   1812.
El médico a palos, from a play by Molière (produced Barcelona, 1814).   1814.

Memoirs and Letters

Diario (Mayo 1780 – Marzo 1808).   1967.

Other

La derrota de los pedantes.   1789.
Orígenes del teatro español.   In *Obras*, 1830–31.

Translator, *Cándido; o, El optimismo*, by Voltaire.   1838.

*

Bibliographies

Francisco Aguilar Piñal, "Bibliografía de Leandro Fernández de Moratín", in *Cuadernos bibliográficos*, 40, 1980.

Criticism

Books:
F. Ruiz Morcuende, *Vocabulario de Leandro Fernández de Moratín*, Madrid, 1945.
A. Lefebvre, *El teatro de Moratín*, Santiago, 1958.
A. Papell, *Moratín y su época*, Mallorca, 1958.

John A. Cook, *Neo-Classic Drama in Spain: Theory and Practice*, Dallas, Texas, 1959.
Fernando Lázaro Carreter, *Moratín y su teatro*, Oviedo, 1961.
Juis Felipe Vivanco, *Moratín y la ilustración*, Madrid, 1963.
S. Melón R. de Gordejuela, *Moratín por dentro*, Oviedo, 1964.
R. Andioc, *Sur la querelle du théâtre au temps de Leandro Fernández de Moratín*, Toulouse, 1970.
John C. Dowling, *Leandro Fernández de Moratín* (in English), New York, 1971.
L.F. Vivanco, *Moratín y la ilustración mágica*, Madrid, 1972.
Hidehito Higashitani, *El teatro de Leandro Fernández de Moratín*, Madrid, 1973.
Giuseppe Carlo Rossi, *Leandro Fernández de Moratín: Introducción a su vida y obra*, Madrid, 1974.
Coloqui internacional sobre Leandro Fernández de Moratín en Bologna, Abano Terme, 1980.
P. Ortiz Armengol, *El año que vivío Moratín en Ingleterra*, Madrid, 1985.

*   *   *

Moratín is a notable figure among the major dramatists that Spain has produced for two reasons: first, he composed the comedies for which he is famous at a time of exceptional mediocrity in the Spanish theatre; and second, his important position in the history of Spanish drama was won by writing a mere five plays.

Late 18th-century Bourbon Spain certainly seemed to offer an intellectual and aesthetic ambience propitious for the development and prosperity of neo-classical drama; but the Spanish theatre of the period threw up no dramatist with the discipline and genius to make the neo-classical rules beloved of 17th- and 18th-century France work on the stage until the young Moratín composed his *El viejo y la niña* in 1786. This indeed was the case in France itself from the close of the *grand siècle*; but Moratín faced further obstacles. Imbued with French ideas in politics as well as in aesthetics, he was therefore what was known in Spain at the time as an *afrancesado*; and the *afrancesados* enjoyed but a precarious ascendance in a francophile Court that ruled a xenophobic and conservative nation. It is significant that the indigenous three-act *comedia* of Spain's Golden Age still held sway on the Spanish stage, albeit in a sorry and decadent state. Revivals and adaptations of Lope de Vega and Calderón were still popular, but no playwright of their stature had appeared in upward of 100 years. Also popular were absurdly melodramatic pseudo-historical extravaganzas without an ounce of dramatic force or sense.

It is therefore not surprising that Moratín, as one of the most ardent would-be regenerators and reformers of the Spanish theatre, should choose as the subject of one of his five original plays this theatrical decadence and ineptitude. *La comedia nueva*, as its title suggests, is a play within a play that ridiculed the pretensions of dramatists who confused true drama with garish, overblown, and grotesque dramatic devices. In this and his four other comedies, Moratín shows how single-mindedly and skilfully he embraced the essential tenet of neo-classicism in the drama, the three unities. In the prologue to his collected plays, he later defined thus his ideal comedy: "Imitation in dialogue (in prose or verse) of an event occurring in one place and within a few hours among middle-class people, by means of which, and through the appropriate expression of emotions and character, the vices and errors common to society are ridiculed, while truth and virtue are in consequence exalted". These words express, of course, other tenets of neo-classicism in the drama, and in particular, a strong mimetic thrust whereby the work of art endeavours to imitate nature by means of a close observation of reality and an attention to verisimilitude at all times.

No less a figure than one of the censors of the Inquisition examining Moratín's greatest play, *El sí de las niñas* (*When a Girl Says Yes*), testified to the power of its language: "This comedy is all the more harmful because the language and witticisms in which it abounds are taken from the purest elements of the Castilian tongue and are accompanied by a charming naturalness in the characters who speak". Moratín was also innovative in writing two of his five comedies in prose. Modern critics give witness to the freshness and naturalness of his dialogue, whether in prose or verse, and go so far as to say that no Spanish dramatist before the 20th century has matched Moratín's capacity for catching the exact flavour of everyday Madrid speech and reproducing it convincingly on the stage. This is not the least of the reasons why his plays have withstood the passage of time.

Moratín essayed no tragedy. This, too, is singular in an age obsessed with the tragic muse but bereft of tragic genius. His temperament was against it, and he was too interested in the foibles and frailties of the middle-class society in which he moved to want to write of anything else. The reality and naturalness of everyday life was the material with which he worked. It was also his message: honourable and honest conduct prompted by sincere, authentic, human emotion is the constant ideal in all his plays. In *El viejo y la niña*, the heroine's duty to her aged husband triumphs, but the cause of all her suffering is seen to be a totally inappropriate marriage. Again, in *El sí de las niñas*, marriage of convenience to an older man threatens social tragedy. Here Moratín strikes an optimistic blow for freedom for women. In *La mojigata*, the liberal education of Isabel is set beside the oppressive, forced, and therefore unnatural education received by her cousin, Clara, who has grown up devious, scheming, and self-absorbed.

Moratín has been frequently and loosely compared with Molière, whom he certainly admired greatly. He did distinguished translations of *L'École des maris* and *Le Médecin malgré lui*. *La mojigata* and *El barón* (*The Baron*) have both put people in mind of Molière's *Tartuffe*, for they deal with the themes of religious hypocrisy, greed, fraud, and dissembling. Fermina, Aunt Mónica's maid-servant in *El barón*, and Calamocha and Rita in *El sí de las niñas* are notable examples of the witty, earthy, and often forceful servants one encounters in the plays of Molière, but who derive ultimately from the *graciosos* of the Spanish Golden Age *comedia*.

Moratín lacks, however, Molière's thematic and dramatic richness of texture, as well as his rumbustious humour. His satire is gentle and discreet. At its best, in his last play, *El sí de las niñas*, the characters are bathed in a gentle and humane irony. But like Molière, he was undoubtedly a crusader. For Moratín, literature was an educator, an instrument to put the world to rights. Thus he reflected the ideals of the 18th-century *philosophes* and *littérateur*. His works also look forward to the crusading ideals of 19th-century realism. This also may have contributed to his enduring reputation as playwright.

—R.J. Oakley

FEYDEAU, Georges (-Léon-Jules-Marie). Born in Paris, 8 December 1862; son of the writer Ernest-Aimé Feydeau.

Educated at boarding schools, 1871–79. Married Marianne Duran in 1889 (divorced 1914); a son, Jacques, and other children. Lawyer's clerk, 1879; began writing and reciting monologues in the early 1880's; military service, 1883–84; first play, *Amour et piano*, produced 1883; established career with the long run of *Champignol malgré lui*, from 1892; lived at the Hôtel Terminus, Paris, 1909–19; suffered declining mental health, due to syphilis, after 1916: committed by his family to a sanatorium in Rueil-Malmaison, 1919. Died in Rueil-Malmaison, 5 June 1921.

Works

Collections

Théâtre complet (9 vols.).   1948–56.
Four Farces (includes *Wooed and Viewed; On the Marry-Go-Wrong; Not By Bed Alone; Going to Pot*), translated by Norman Shapiro.   1970.
Three Farces (includes *Love By the Bolt; All My Husband; That's My Girl*), translated by J. Paul Marcoux.   1976.
Feydeau, First to Last: Eight One-Act Comedies (includes *Ladies' Man; Wooed and Viewed; Romance in A Flat; Fit to be Tried; or, Stepbrothers in Crime; Mixed Doubles; The Boor Hug; Caught with His Trance Down; Tooth and Consequences; or, Hortense Said: "No Skin Off My Ass!"*), translated by Norman Shapiro.   1982.
Georges Feydeau: Three Boulevard Farces (includes *The Lady From Maxim's; A Flea in Her Ear; A Little Hotel on the Side*), translated by John Mortimer.   1985.

Stage Works

La Petite Révoltée (monologue).   1880.
Le Mouchoir (monologue).   1881.
Par la fenêtre (produced Rosendaël, 1881).   1887; translated as *Wooed and Viewed*, in *Four Farces*, 1970.
Un Coup de tête (monologue).   1882.
J'ai mal aux dents (monologue).   1882.
Un Monsieur qui n'aime pas les monologues (monologue).   1882.
Trop vieux! (monologue).   1882.
Notre Futur (produced Salle de Géographie, Paris, 1894).   1882; translated as *Ladies' Man*, in *Feydeau First to Last*, 1982.
Le Diapason.   1883.
Le Potache.   1883.
Aux Antipodes (monologue).   1883.
Patte-en-l'air (monologue).   1883.
Le Petit Ménage (monologue).   1883.
Amour et piano (produced Théâtre de l'Athénée, Paris, 1883).   1887; translated as *Call Me Maestro*, 1973; as *Romance in A Flat*, in *Feydeau First to Last*, 1982.
Gibier de potence (produced Cercle Volney, Paris, 1884).   1885; translated as *Before We Were So Rudely Interrupted*, 1973; as *Fit to Be Tried; or, Stepbrothers in Crime*, 1982.
Les Célèbres (monologue).   1884.
Le Volontaire (monologue).   1884.
Le Billet de mille (monologue).   1885.
Le Colis (monologue).   1885.
L'Homme économe (monologue).   1885.
Les Réformes (monologue).   1885.
L'Homme intègre (monologue).   1886.
Fiancés en herbe (produced Salle Kriegelstein, Paris, 1886).   1886; translated as *Budding Lovers*, 1969.

Georges Feydeau (portrait by Charles Durand, 1899).

Tailleur pour dames (produced Théâtre de la Renaissance, Paris, 1886).   1888; translated as *A Gown for His Mistress*, 1969; as *Fitting for Ladies*, 1974; as *Love by the Bolt*, in *Three Farces*, 1976.
Les Enfants (monologue).   1887.
La Lycéenne, music by G. Serpette (produced Théâtre des Nouveautés, Paris, 1887).   1887.
Les Fiancés de Loches, with Maurice Desvallières (produced Théâtre Cluny, Paris, 1888).   1888.
Le Chat en poche (produced Théâtre Déjazet, Paris, 1888).
Un Bain de ménage (produced Théâtre de la Renaissance, Paris, 1888).   1889.
L'Affaire Édouard, with Maurice Desvallières (produced Théâtre des Variétés, Paris, 1889).   1889.
Tout à Brown-Séquart! (monologue).   1890.
Monsieur Nounou, with Maurice Desvallières (produced Brussels, 1890).
C'est une femme du monde!, with Maurice Desvallières (produced Théâtre de la Renaissance, Paris, 1890).   1890; translated as *Mixed Doubles*, 1982.
Le Mariage de Barillon, with Maurice Desvallières (produced Théâtre de la Renaissance, Paris, 1890).   1890; translated as *On the Marry-Go-Wrong*, in *Four Farces*, 1970; as *All My Husband*, in *Three Farces*, 1976.
Madame Sganarelle (produced Spa, Belgium, 1891).
Champignol malgré lui, with Maurice Desvallières (produced Théâtre des Nouveautés, Paris, 1892).   1925; translated as *A Close Shave*, 1974.
Monsieur chasse (produced Théâtre du Palais-Royal, Paris, 1892).   1896; translated as *13, Rue de l'Amour*, 1972; as *The Happy Hunter*, 1973; as *The Chaser and the Chaste*, 1975; as *A-Hunting We Will Go*, 1976.

Le Système Ribadier (produced Théâtre du Palais-Royal, Paris, 1892).   1925.
Un Fil à la patte (produced Théâtre du Palais-Royal, Paris, 1894).   1899; translated as *Cat Among Pigeons*, 1970; as *Not by Bed Alone*, in *Four Farces*, 1970; as *Get Out of My Hair!*, 1973; as *On a String*, 1975.
L'Hôtel du Libre-Échange, with Maurice Desvallières (produced Théâtre des Nouveautés, Paris, 1894).   1928; translated as *Hôtel Paradiso*, 1957; as *A Little Hotel on the Side*, in *Three Boulevard Farces*, 1985.
Le Ruban, with Maurice Desvallières (produced Théâtre de l'Odéon, Paris, 1894).   In *Théâtre complet*, 1948–56.
Le Dindon (produced Théâtre du Palais-Royal, Paris, 1896).   In *Théâtre complet*, 1948–56; translated as *There is One in Every Marriage*, 1970; as *Sauce for the Goose*, 1974; as *Paying the Piper*, 1975.
Les Pavés de l'ours (produced Théâtre Montpensier, Versailles, 1896).   In *Théâtre complet*, 1948–56; translated as *A Little Bit to Fall Back On*, 1973; as *The Boor Hug*, 1982.
Séance de nuit (produced Théâtre du Palais-Royal, Paris, 1897).   In *Théâtre complet*, 1948–56.
Dormez, je le veux! (produced Théâtre de l'Eldorado, Paris, 1897).   In *Théâtre complet*, 1948–56; translated as *Caught with His Trance Down*, in *Feydeau, First to Last*, 1982.
La Bulle d'amour, music by F. Thomé (ballet scenario; produced Théâtre Marigny, Paris, 1898).
Le Juré (monologue).   1898.
Un Monsieur qui est condamné à mort.   1899.
La Dame de chez Maxim (produced Théâtre des Nouveautés, Paris, 1899).   1914; translated as *The Lady from Maxim's*, 1971.
Le Billet de Joséphine, with J. Méry and A. Kaiser (produced Théâtre de la Gaîté, Paris, 1902).
La Duchesse des Folies-Bergères (produced Théâtre des Nouveautés, Paris, 1902).   In *Théâtre complet*, 1948–56.
La Main passe (produced Théâtre des Nouveautés, Paris, 1904).   1907; translated as *Chemin de Fer*, 1968.
L'Age d'or, with Maurice Desvallières, music by L. Varney (produced Théâtre des Variétés, Paris, 1905).   In *Théâtre complet*, 1948–56.
Le Bourgeon (produced Théâtre du Vaudeville, Paris, 1906).   1907.
La Puce à l'oreille (produced Théâtre des Nouveautés, Paris, 1907).   1909; translated as *A Flea in Her Ear*, 1966 and 1968; as *Caught in the Act!*, 1975.
Feu la mère de Madame (produced Théâtre de la Comédie-Royale, Paris, 1908).   1923; translated as *A Good Night's Sleep*, 1973; as *Better Late*, 1976.
Occupe-toi d'Amélie (produced Théâtre des Nouveautés, Paris, 1908).   1911; translated as *Keep an Eye on Amélie*, in *"Let's Get a Divorce" and Other Plays*, edited by Eric Bentley, 1958, and 1973 as *Look after Lulu*, 1959; as *That's My Girl*, in *Three Farces*, 1976.
Le Circuit, with Francis Croisset (produced Théâtre des Variétés, Paris, 1909).   In *Théâtre complet*, 1948–56.
On purge bébé (produced Théâtre des Nouveautés, Paris, 1910).   1910; translated as *Going to Pot*, in *Four Farces*, 1970; as *The Purging*, 1977.
Mais n'te promène donc pas toute nue! (produced Théâtre Fémina, Paris, 1911).   1912.
Léonie est en avance; ou, Le Mal joli (produced Théâtre de la Comédie-Royale, Paris, 1911).   1920.
Cent Millions qui tombent (produced Théâtre des Nouveautés, Paris, 1911).
On va faire la cocette (produced Théâtre Michel, Paris, 1913).   In *Théâtre complet*, 1948–56.

Je ne trompe pas mon mari, with René Peter (produced Théâtre de l'Athénée, 1914). 1921.
Complainte du pauvr' propriétaire. 1915.
Hortense a dit: "Je m'en fous!" (produced Théâtre du Palais-Royal, Paris, 1916). In *Théâtre complet*, 1948–56; translated as *Tooth and Consequence; or, Hortense Said: "No Skin Off My Ass!"*, in *Feydeau, First to Last*, 1982.

*

Bibliographies

Bibliography in *Théâtre complet 1*, 1988 (see Collections).

Criticism

Books:
Jacques Lorcey, *Georges Feydeau*, Paris, 1972.
Arlette Shenkan, *Georges Feydeau: Textes de Feydeau, points de vue critiques, témoignages, chronologie, bibliographie, illustrations*, Paris, 1972.
Leonard C. Pronko, *Georges Feydeau*, New York, 1975.
Henry Gidel, *Le Théâtre de Georges Feydeau*, Paris, 1979.
Stuart E. Baker, *Georges Feydeau and the Aesthetics of Farce*, Ann Arbor, Michigan, 1981.
Leonard C. Pronko, *Eugène Labiche and Georges Feydeau*, London, 1982 (Macmillan Modern Dramatists Series).
James Redmond (ed.), *Farce*, Cambridge, 1988 (*Themes in Drama*, 10).

Articles:
Norman R. Shapiro, "Suffering and Punishment in the Theatre of Georges Feydeau", in *Tulane Drama Review*, vol.5 no.1, 1960.
Cahiers du théâtre, numéro spécial: Georges Feydeau, edited by Jacques Lorcey, 1973.
Henry Gidel, "Feydeau 1862–1921: Dossier", in *Comédie-Française*, 139–140, 1985.

*   *   *

Considered by many to be the greatest French comic dramatist after Molière, Feydeau, by his structural mastery, his deep grasp of reality, and the relentless energy of his plays, reduces virtually all competitors to the stature of pygmies. Writing at a time when the bourgeoisie had finally consolidated its victories in the Third Republic, he recreates to perfection the life of the *Belle Époque*. Selfish, egotistical, lying men bent on pleasure; suspicious, resentful wives, bent on revenge; frivolous women of easy virtue set on finding the easiest way—these are the major characters of Feydeau's world, reflecting the hedonistic world of turn-of-the-century Paris, alive with the bustle of new shops, stylish theatres and cafés, and entertainments of all kinds, a world that saw life as a performance.

What gives this picture depth and universality is the keen power of observation that Feydeau brought to his work. No matter how fanciful his Byzantine inventions, they are always solidly based in observed reality. Indeed, Feydeau claimed that every word of a play must arise logically from the situation, and his last collaborator described Feydeau's aesthetic as originating in his love of truth.

Feydeau once described the farce-writer's job as that of taking a story that would make an undertaker shudder and treating it from a comic perspective. Despite its brilliant surface, Feydeau's period, like our own, had its seamy underside, and the constant scandals in high places, strikes, terrorist attacks, and other events of the day suggested the instability of a world that the bourgeoisie would have liked to believe solid and eternal. It was Feydeau's genius to paint this brilliant, frivolous world in such a way that we can feel, beneath the glamorous surface, the seething, disagreeable reality.

Heir to the perfected *vaudeville* that Labiche had left at his death, Feydeau took up the form made popular by that master's *Italian Straw Hat*, wound it up tighter, and set it off at a more insane pace than Labiche had ever conceived. Actually this "clockwork" *vaudeville* was not Feydeau's invention, but a legacy from a Belgian engineer turned dramatist, Alfred Hennequin, whose mastery Feydeau acknowledged when he experienced several failures early in his career and turned to the great *vaudevillistes* of the past to learn his craft. In Labiche he studied the sense of truth, in Hennequin the flawless construction, and in Henri Meilhac the naturalness of the dialogue. Feydeau learned his lessons well, for in all his major works he blends truth with the wildest fantasy, perfection of structure, and liveliness of dialogue.

Feydeau's work falls into three categories. Most characteristic are the long plays with large casts and complex structures, driven mercilessly by some demonic force that invariably topples characters into the least desired situations. Most of the plays which have become popular in English-speaking countries fall into this category, like *L'Hôtel du Libre-Échange* (*Hotel Paradiso*) and *La Puce à l'oreille* (*A Flea in Her Ear*). Typically, this kind of play begins with a man (occasionally a woman) lying, or not telling the whole truth, in order to get out of an unpleasant situation, or to seek some illicit pleasure. Like a subtle moralist, Feydeau seems to suggest that the demonic force tumbling characters into unpleasant fixes may often be found in the characters themselves, and the fundamental dishonesty of their ways may be responsible for much of their suffering. By Act II, usually set in a public place, all hell breaks loose as all the major characters from Act I find themselves brought together in a hotel, at a bachelor apartment, or at some social event. Feydeau made it a rule always to bring face to face, as soon as possible, those characters who least wished to encounter each other, and Act II is where we see this phenomenon in its most terrifying form, resulting in horrifying complications. A lengthy third act is usually required to unravel all the complexities of the second, and in his most successful plays, like *A Flea in Her Ear*, the unravelling can be as amusing, eventful, wild, and fantastic as the ravelling.

Even in these extravagant pieces Feydeau is a master of reality. Despite his dislike for Naturalism and its rejection of conventions which he believed essential to the theatrical form, Feydeau often deals in subject matter that the Naturalists were treating in less amusing ways. *A Flea in Her Ear*, for example, treats in some physiological detail the problem of impotence—indeed, it is this problem that sets the whole play in motion. The life of the prostitute, prime territory for the Naturalists, is shown in piquant detail in a number of plays, most notably in *Occupe-toi d'Amélie* (which Noël Coward adapted as *Look After Lulu*). In these pieces we see not only the frivolity and pleasures of the *demi-monde*, but the tedium, the tawdry hangers-on, the would-be lovers, and the ex-husbands who come by for hand-outs. Amélie, by the end of the play, is perhaps no wiser; but we, the audience, are more aware of the solitude of this kind of woman, tossed from man to man like an object, yet somehow more likeable than any of the selfish males or most of the acrid, if more respectable, married women.

A second group of plays are those that are somewhat more realistic, less extravagant in their developments. Most of these have fewer characters than the above plays, thus allowing for fewer cases of mistaken identity, misunderstanding, or unwished-for encounters. They normally begin more slowly than the first group, allowing more time for the author to establish character, and above all to paint a picture of married life and contemporary manners. *Monsieur chasse* (*The Happy Hunter*) and *La Main passe* (*Chemin de fer*) belong in this group. The frantic second act is set in a less public place, a bedroom usually, and, while all the characters may finally show up there, they are fewer than in the first group of plays.

One of Feydeau's masterpieces, *Le Dindon* (variously translated as *There is One in Every Marriage* and *Sauce for the Goose*) belongs to both groups, for its first act, though full of wild implausibities, offers a relatively realistic picture of married life, and its last act almost concludes with a tearful reunion of husband and wife. But Act II belongs firmly in the other tradition; one of the maddest of all hotel scenes brings together mistaken hotel guests, husbands, wives, *cocottes*, men about town, an old military doctor and his deaf wife, and numerous other characters, appearing and disappearing vertiginously through several doors and, in some cases, leaping in and out of bed, while hidden bells ring furiously. When the actors of the Comédie-Française decided to take a full-length Feydeau play into their repertoire, it was no accident that they chose this play, which brings together all of Feydeau's most characteristic virtues. Performances of *Le Dindon* at the Comédie in the 1950's established Feydeau as a major French writer. He has since become a staple of the house and three or four of his major plays have received stunning productions there.

Even before they performed *Le Dindon*, the actors of the Comédie-Française had accorded their approval to several of Feydeau's one act plays. In 1908, when his own marriage had clearly failed, Feydeau began a series of four one-act plays which he intended to publish under the title "From Marriage to Divorce". The most famous of these are *Feu la Mère de madame* (*Madame's Late Mother*), and *On purge bébé* (*Going to Pot*), plays that show Feydeau at his most bitter and acrimonious, painting a picture of married life that, in its biting humor and misanthropy (he is not merely misogynistic, for man and woman alike are seen with a cool, unkind eye) remind one of the most terrible moments of Strindberg. Although there is an unfamiliar realism in these plays (hence, no doubt, their early acceptance at the Comédie), and a lack of fireworks of coincidence, reversal, and discovery we have come to expect in Feydeau, they display still his dazzling inventiveness of situation, and reveal more clearly than any of his other works his clear-sighted understanding of the human heart and his ability to portray its darker aspects with lucidity and humor.

While Feydeau was recognized during his lifetime as an ingenious entertainer, and was even occasionally lauded for the realism of his characters, it remained for critics after World War II to become aware of deeper values in his plays. When *La Main passe* was revived after the war, Jean Cocteau wrote, "It's a veritable nightmare—pure Kafka!". This new sensitivity to a metaphysical note in Feydeau set the tone for much post-war criticism. After the horrors of Nazi Germany, the dehumanization of contemporary man in a world that seems indeed to have gone mad, after the new perspectives of existentialism, and, above all, after the new sensibilites revealed by the "theatre of the absurd", it is impossible to read or see Feydeau without finding in him some of the terror that Antonin Artaud found at the base of all great art—a terror arising from the discovery that "the sky can still fall on our

heads". Artaud recognized his ancestor, Feydeau, as did Ionesco and other absurdists.

Today Feydeau has found an international audience, and apparently speaks as meaningfully to contemporary spectators today as he did to the *Belle Époque*, perhaps because we have lost the brilliance of that period and are living only the seamy underside which he suggested through his extravagances. In any case, Feydeau is assured his place in world drama at the dazzling peak of comic invention and, perhaps, as a bitterly lucid moralist.

—Leonard C. Pronko

See also *Volume 1* entry on *A Flea in Her Ear*.

FIELDING, Henry. Born at Sharpham Park, near Glastonbury, Somerset, England, 22 April 1707; older brother of the writer Sarah Fielding. Educated at Eton College, Berkshire, 1719–24; University of Leyden, 1728–29; Middle Temple, London, 1737–40, called to the bar, 1740. Married 1) Charlotte Cradock in 1734 (died 1744), four daughters and one son; 2) Mary Daniel in 1747, two sons and three daughters. Lived mainly in East Stour, Dorset, to 1739, then in London; first play, *Love in Several Masques*, produced 1728; successful playwright until advent of the Theatrical Licensing Act, 1737; regular contributor, the *Craftsman*, 1734–38; writer/manager, Haymarket Theatre (or Little Theatre in the Hay), 1736–37 (theatre closed by Theatrical Licensing Act); editor, with James Ralph, the *Champion*, 1739–40; lawyer and novelist from 1740; editor, the *True Patriot*, 1745–46, the *Jacobite's Journal*, 1747–48, and the *Covent Garden Journal*, 1752; appointed high steward of the New Forest, Hampshire, 1746; ran a puppet theatre, 1748; principal magistrate, City of Westminster, 1748, and County of Middlesex, 1749: drafted a plan for reorganizing the constabulary and helped establish London's first organized police force; chairman, Westminster Quarter Sessions, 1749–52; travelled to Portugal in hope of improving his health, 1754. Died in Lisbon, 8 October 1754.

Works

Collections

Dramatic Works (2 vols.).   1745.
Works, edited by Arthur Murphy (4 vols.).   1762.
Complete Works, edited by W.E. Henley (16 vols.).   1903.
Works (Wesleyan Edition), edited by W.B. Coley and others. 1967—
Burlesque Plays of the Eighteenth Century (includes *Tom Thumb* and *The Covent Garden Tragedy* by Fielding, and works by other authors), edited by Simon Trussler.   1969.

Stage Works

Love in Several Masques (produced Theatre Royal, Drury Lane, London, 1728).   1728.
The Temple Beau (produced Goodman's Fields Theatre, London, 1730).   1730.
The Author's Farce, and The Pleasures of the Town (produced Haymarket Theatre, London, 1730).   1730; revised version (produced Haymarket Theatre, London, 1734), 1750.
Tom Thumb (produced Haymarket Theatre, London, 1730).

1730; revised version, as *The Tragedy of Tragedies; or, The Life and Death of Tom Thumb the Great* (produced Haymarket Theatre, London, 1731), 1731.

Rape upon Rape; or, The Justice Caught in His Own Trap (produced Haymarket Theatre, London, 1730). 1730; revised version, as *The Coffee House Politician* (produced Haymarket Theatre, London, 1730), 1730.

The Letter Writers; or, A New Way to Keep a Wife at Home (produced Haymarket Theatre, London, 1731). 1731.

The Welsh Opera; or, The Grey Mare the Better Horse (produced Haymarket Theatre, London, 1731). 1731; as *The Genuine Grub Street Opera*, 1731; as *The Grub Street Opera*, 1731.

The Lottery (produced Theatre Royal, Drury Lane, London, 1732). 1732.

The Modern Husband (produced Theatre Royal, Drury Lane, London, 1732). 1732.

The Covent Garden Tragedy (produced Theatre Royal, Drury Lane, London, 1732). 1732.

The Old Debauchees (produced Theatre Royal, Drury Lane, London, 1732). 1732; as *The Debauchees; or, The Jesuit Caught*, 1745.

The Mock Doctor; or, The Dumb Lady Cured, from a play by Molière (produced Theatre Royal, Drury Lane, London, 1732). 1732.

The Miser, from a play by Molière (produced Theatre Royal, Drury Lane, London, 1733). 1733.

Deborah; or, A Wife for You All (produced Theatre Royal, Drury Lane, London, 1733). 1733.

The Intriguing Chambermaid, from a play by J.F. Regnard (produced Theatre Royal, Drury Lane, London, 1734). 1734.

Don Quixote in England (produced Haymarket Theatre, London, 1734). 1734.

An Old Man Taught Wisdom; or, The Virgin Unmasked (produced Theatre Royal, Drury Lane, London, 1735). 1735.

The Universal Gallant; or, The Different Husbands (produced Theatre Royal, Drury Lane, London, 1735). 1735.

Pasquin: A Dramatic Satire on the Times, Being the Rehearsal of Two Plays, Viz. A Comedy Called The Election and a Tragedy Called The Life and Death of Common Sense (produced Haymarket Theatre, London, 1736). 1736.

Tumble-Down Dick; or, Phaeton in the Suds (produced Haymarket Theatre, London, 1736). 1736.

Eurydice (produced Theatre Royal, Drury Lane, London, 1737). In *Miscellanies*, 1743.

The Historical Register for the Year 1736 (produced Haymarket Theatre, London, 1737). With *Eurydice Hissed*, 1737; revised version, 1737.

Eurydice Hissed; or, A Word to the Wise (produced Haymarket Theatre, London, 1737). With *The Historical Register*, 1737; revised version, 1737.

Plutus, The God of Riches, with William Young, from a play by Aristophanes. 1742.

Miss Lucy in Town: A Sequel to The Virgin Unmasqued, music by Thomas Arne (produced Theatre Royal, Drury Lane, London, 1742). 1742.

The Wedding Day (produced Theatre Royal, Drury Lane, London, 1743). In *Miscellanies*, 1743.

The Fathers; or, The Good-Natured Man (produced Theatre Royal, Drury Lane, London, 1778). 1778.

Fiction

An Apology for the Life of Mrs. Shamela Andrews. 1741.
The History of the Adventures of Joseph Andrews and of His Friend Mr. Abraham Adams. 1742; revised edition, 1742.

The Life of Mr. Jonathan Wild the Great, in *Miscellanies 3*. 1743; revised edition, 1754.

A Journey from This World to the Next, in *Miscellanies 2*. 1743.

The History of Tom Jones, A Foundling. 1749; revised edition, 1749.

Amelia. 1751; revised version, in *Works*, 1762.

Verse

The Masquerade. 1728.
The Vernon-iad. 1741.
Of True Greatness: An Epistle to George Dodington, Esq. 1741.

Other

The Champion (2 vols.). 1741.
The Opposition: A Vision. 1741.
A Full Vindication of the Duchess Dowager of Marlborough. 1742.
Some Papers Proper to Be Read Before the Royal Society. 1743.
Miscellanies (3 vols.). 1743.
An Attempt Towards a Natural History of the Hanover Rat. 1744.
The Charge to the Jury. 1745.
A Serious Address to the People of Great Britain, in Which the Certain Consequences of the Present Rebellion Are Fully Demonstrated. 1745.
The History of the Present Rebellion in Scotland. 1745.
A Dialogue Between the Devil, The Pope, and the Pretender. 1745.
The Female Husband; or, The Surprising History of Mrs. Mary, Alias Mr. George Hamilton, Taken from Her Own Mouth since Her Confinement. 1746.
Ovid's Art of Love, Paraphrased and Adapted to the Present Time. 1747; as *The Lover's Assistant*, 1759.
A Dialogue Between a Gentleman of London, Agent for Two Court Candidates, and an Honest Alderman of the Country Party. 1747.
A Proper Answer to a Late Scurrilous Libel, Entitled An Apology for the Conduct of a Late Celebrated Second-Rate Minister. 1747.
A Charge Delivered to the Grand Jury. 1749.
A True State of the Case of Bosavern Penlez, Who Suffered on Account of the Late Riot in the Strand. 1749.
An Enquiry into the Causes of the Late Increase of Robbers. 1751.
A Plan of the Universal Register Office, with John Fielding. 1751.
Examples of the Interposition of Providence in the Detection and Punishment of Murder. 1752.
A Proposal for Making an Effectual Provision for the Poor. 1753.
A Clear State of the Case of Elizabeth Canning. 1753.
The Journal of a Voyage to Lisbon. 1755.
Criticism, edited by Ian Williams. 1970.
New Essays by Fielding: His Contributions to the "Craftsman" (1734–1739) and Other Early Journalism, edited by Martin C. Battestin and Michael G. Farringdon. 1989.

Translator, *The Military History of Charles XII, King of Sweden*, by M. Gustavus Alderfeld (3 vols.). 1740.

*

Bibliographies

H. George Hahn, *Henry Fielding: An Annotated Bibliography*, Metuchen, New Jersey, 1979.

L.J. Morrissey, *Henry Fielding: A Reference Guide*, Boston, 1980.

John A. Stoler and Richard Fulton, *Henry Fielding: An Annotated Bibliography of Twentieth Century Criticism 1900–1977*, New York and London, 1980.

Criticism

Books:

G. M. Godden, *Henry Fielding*, London, 1910.

Wilbur L. Cross, *The History of Henry Fielding* (3 vols.), New Haven, Connecticut, 1918.

H.K. Banerji, *Henry Fielding, Playwright, Journalist, and Master of the Art of Fiction*, Oxford, 1929.

Erwin Weide, *Henry Fieldings Komödien und die Restaurationskomödie*, Hamburg, 1944.

F. Holmes Dudden, *Henry Fielding: His Life, Works, and Times* (2 vols.), 1952.

John Butt, *Henry Fielding*, 1954; revised edition, 1959.

Ronald Paulson (ed.), *Henry Fielding: A Collection of Critical Essays*, Englewood Cliffs, New Jersey, 1962.

Andrew Wright, *Henry Fielding: Mask and Feast*, London, 1965.

Morris Golden, *Fielding's Moral Psychology*, Amherst, Massachusetts, 1966.

Michael Irwin, *Henry Fielding: The Tentative Realist*, Oxford, 1967.

Glenn W. Hatfield, *Henry Fielding and the Language of Irony*, Chicago, 1968.

Ronald Paulson and Thomas Lockwood (eds.), *Henry Fielding: The Critical Heritage*, London and New York, 1969.

C.J. Rawson (ed.), *Henry Fielding: A Critical Anthology*, Harmondsworth, 1973.

Jean Ducrocq, *Le Théâtre de Fielding, 1728–1737, et ses prolongements dans l'oeuvre romanesque*, Paris, 1975.

J. Paul Hunter, *Occasional Form: Henry Fielding and the Chains of Circumstance*, Baltimore, Maryland, 1975.

Pat Rogers, *Henry Fielding: A Biography*, London, 1979.

Brian McCrea, *Fielding and the Politics of Mid-Eighteenth-Century England*, Athens, Georgia, 1981.

Richard J. Dircks, *Henry Fielding*, Boston, 1983.

Thomas R. Cleary, *Henry Fielding, Political Writer*, Waterloo, Ontario, 1984.

K.G. Simpson (ed.), *Henry Fielding: Justice Observed*, London, 1985.

Simon Varey, *Henry Fielding*, Cambridge, 1986.

Peter Lewis, *Fielding's Burlesque Drama: Its Place in the Tradition*, Edinburgh, 1987.

Robert D. Hume, *Fielding and the London Theatre 1728–1737*, London, 1988.

Martin C. Battestin and Ruthe R. Battestin, *Henry Fielding: A Life*, London, 1989.

Albert J. Rivero, *The Plays of Henry Fielding: A Critical Study of His Dramatic Career*, 1989.

Donald Thomas, *Henry Fielding*, London, 1990.

*   *   *

Fielding's achievement as one of the great innovators of the novel in the 18th century so overshadows his earlier work for the stage between 1728 and 1737 that his short, but prolific and enterprising, career as a playwright and a man of the theatre is often neglected. Yet, in the years before the Licensing Act of 1737 imposed a strict political censorship on the stage and closed the non-patent theatres in London, thus stifling the most innovative dramatic developments in the wake of Gay's *The Beggar's Opera*, Fielding became one of the leading figures in the city's theatrical life. In about ten years he wrote (or adapted) over 20 plays and afterpieces, and even though these are rarely performed today, he ranks as an outstanding dramatist of the Augustan period. If the Licensing Act had not brought his theatrical activities to an abrupt end when he was still only 30, Fielding might never have made the transition from playwright to novelist.

Although Fielding attempted a variety of forms, he did not write a tragedy, preferring to burlesque contemporary versions of the genre with the exception of George Lillo's unusual and comparatively realistic "bourgeois" tragedies, which he admired. As one would expect from his two best-known novels, *Joseph Andrews* and *Tom Jones*, Fielding was much at home with comedy, farce, and ballad opera, but his most original and exciting works for the theatre can be found among his irregular satires and burlesques. Fielding's first two plays to be staged, *Love in Several Masques* and *The Temple Beau*, are orthodox comedies of wit and intrigue in the manner of Congreve. They give no indication of the startling individuality of his third, *The Author's Farce* (1730, substantially revised 1734), an ambitious and wide-ranging satire of Grub Street hacks, booksellers, theatre managers, a number of well-known individuals, and "the pleasures of the town", including most of the theatrical entertainments on offer, such as Italian opera and pantomine. The climax is the play-within-a-play section of the third and final act, supposedly a performance at the Theatre Royal in Drury Lane of an eccentric "puppet show" performed by human actors.

The Author's Farce has been called a partial dramatization of Pope's *The Dunciad*, and by issuing his play as the work of Scriblerus Secundus, Fielding was affirming his debt to the first Scriblerians, such as Gay, Pope, and Swift. Fielding used this pseudonym when publishing several other plays in 1730 and 1731, although not for his lively satirical comedy *Rape upon Rape*, a title that caused some offence and was consequently replaced by *The Coffee-House Politician*.

A few weeks after the first performance of *The Author's Farce*, it was staged with a new afterpiece by Fielding, *Tom Thumb*, a superb burlesque of Restoration and Augustan tragedy and the play for which he is best remembered today. Nearly a year later in March 1731, the considerably expanded third and final version of the play with a new title, *The Tragedy of Tragedies*, was staged in a double bill with a three-act farce by Fielding, *The Letter Writers*. Within weeks, however, he supplied an alternative afterpiece, *The Welsh Opera*, which was an instant success because of its daring and almost scurrilous caricatures of the Royal Family and the leading politicians of the nation, including Sir Robert Walpole. Fielding's response was to expand this satirical ballad opera into three acts for performance in June as *The Grub Street Opera*, but the production was abandoned as a result of political pressure.

Fielding's first play for Drury Lane after becoming its resident playwright later in 1731 was another satirical ballad opera, *The Lottery*, exposing the corrupt practices of dealers in State Lotteries who made fortunes for themselves at the expense of the public. He quickly followed this with his most serious and morally earnest play thus far, *The Modern Husband*, which, like his later *The Universal Gallant*, is formally a comedy but in fact is no laughing matter. With its diagnosis of the moral corruption and perverted values in the high society of Walpole's England, *The Modern Husband* comes close to being a melodramatic problem play.

Fielding's next play, the anti-Catholic comedy *The Old Debauchees*, is much less sombre and appealed strongly to audiences when it opened in June 1732, but the mock-tragic afterpiece that accompanied it, *The Covent Garden Tragedy*, met a hostile reception and was withdrawn. The astonishingly fertile Fielding replaced it almost immediately with a more lightweight afterpiece, *The Mock Doctor*, his one-act adaptation of Molière's *Le Médecin malgré lui*. After Fielding's earlier mock tragedy, the exuberant *Tom Thumb*, *The Covent Garden Tragedy* must have come as a shock, because it concentrates almost exclusively on prostitutes and their clients in a brothel. Yet despite the dark tone and black humour of the play, the sustained inventiveness of Fielding's burlesque of the language and rhetoric of contemporary tragedy, in particular of Ambrose Philip's *The Distrest Mother*, makes it one of the few masterpieces of English burlesque drama.

Fielding was somewhat less productive and adventurous in the next couple of years, mainly working as a professional dramatist for a known market. His main production in 1733 was *The Miser*, a good stage comedy based on Molière's *L'Avare*, but much more freely adapted from the French than *The Mock Doctor* had been. His only other theatrical work in 1733 was an ephemeral piece, *Deborah*, a brief ballad opera conceived especially for the benefit night of the actress Kitty Clive. It was performed once and never published. To accompany the revised version of *The Author's Farce* at the beginning of 1734, Fielding provided a sparkling comic afterpiece, *The Intriguing Chambermaid*, adapted from a French comedy by Regnard, Molière's most gifted disciple. Later in the year he staged his farcical ballad opera *Don Quixote in England*, a reworking of a comedy written at the beginning of his career, but rejected for production in 1729. Another farcical ballad opera, *An Old Man Taught Wisdom*, appeared early in 1735, and was shortly followed by *The Universal Gallant*, a most ambitious "sentimental" play which, like *The Modern Husband*, is labelled "A Comedy" but is more tedious than humorous and lives up to its generic description in form only. Audiences found Fielding's seriousness hard to take, and *The Universal Gallant* failed on the stage.

The final phase of Fielding's theatrical career in 1736–37 is certainly the most fascinating. In 1735 he wrote *Pasquin*, by far his most original play since *The Author's Farce*, and even more comprehensive in its satire. After its rejection by the two main theatres, Fielding formed his "Great Mogul's Company of English Comedians", took over the non-patent New Haymarket (Little Theatre), and staged the play there. Its success can be compared only with that of the record-breaking *The Beggar's Opera* in 1728. *Pasquin* takes the form of a double rehearsal, but the two inner plays are not primarily burlesques in the style of Buckingham's influential *The Rehearsal* (1671), but part of Fielding's overall satirical attack on the social, political, moral, and cultural condition of Walpole's England. The first deals with electoral malpractices and political corruption, while the second, *The Life and Death of Common Sense*, is more allegorical and *Dunciad*-like. The afterpiece that Fielding soon added to *Pasquin* during its long run, *Tumble-Down Dick*, is without precedent in being an integrated continuation of the main piece rather than a totally independent play. Nevertheless, *Tumble-Down Dick*, also using a rehearsal format, does differ somewhat from *Pasquin* in being a more truly burlesque work, so that its social and political satire is less central. Fielding's main targets are English pantomime, a popular variety of afterpiece largely devoid of literary interest and heavily dependent on

spectacle, and its chief exponent, John "Harlequin" Rich. Fielding's mock-pantomime follows William Pritchard's popular *The Fall of Phaeton* closely, but is a deftly sustained parodic travesty of it.

1737 opened badly for Fielding when his new afterpiece, *Eurydice*, a satirical ballad-farce, was abandoned in mid-performance on its opening night because of uproar at the Drury Lane theatre. As in the case of *The Covent Garden Tragedy*, this fate was undeserved because the play, although lightweight, is a sophisticated comic treatment of a classical myth. Fielding's last two plays for his own theatre are very different. Even before their appearance, the New Haymarket was becoming a thorn in the side of Walpole's government, and *The Historical Register for the Year 1736* and *Eurydice Hissed* added insult to injury. *The Historical Register* is shorter and more episodic than *Pasquin*, but in its unorthodox use of the rehearsal method and its satirical survey of English morals and manners, especially in high society and political circles, it is a kind of sequel to *Pasquin*, though more acerbic and fierce. Fielding paints defamatory portraits of several well-known figures, especially Walpole.

Eurydice Hissed, a highly ingenious play about a play about a play, was designed to follow *The Historical Register* as a rehearsal afterpiece in much the same way as *Tumble-Down Dick* did *Pasquin*, although both afterpieces are capable of standing alone. On the surface, *Eurydice Hissed* is about the failure of his own *Eurydice*, but, as in several plays of 1736–37, Fielding employs the theatre as a metaphor for politics. The real target of the inner tragedy is not contemporary drama but Walpole, and government accusations that the non-patent theatres were little more than platforms for anti-government propaganda inevitably followed.

Fielding had made himself an intolerable nuisance, and the popularity of his plays, containing the most audacious political satire that had ever appeared on the English stage, provoked government retaliation. On the pretext of a supposedly obscene, libellous, and seditious play, the anonymous *The Golden Rump*, which was neither performed nor published, Parliament quickly passed the Licensing Act, which virtually put an end to political satire by closing the non-patent theatres and by ensuring that all plays intended for performance were licensed in advance by the Lord Chamberlain.

Fielding could have continued as a dramatist, writing innocuous plays for the two patent theatres, but he decided to make a complete break and follow a different path. Three previously unperformed plays were eventually staged and published, but these were largely written before 1737: *Miss Lucy in Town*, a sequel to *An Old Man Taught Wisdom*; *The Wedding Day*, a very early comedy; and another comedy, *The Good-Natured Man*, which did not see the light of day until 1778 when it appeared as *The Fathers*.

—Peter Lewis

See also *Volume 1* entry on *Tom Thumb*.

FIERSTEIN, Harvey (Forbes). Born in Brooklyn, New York, 6 June 1954. Educated at Pratt Institute, Brooklyn, BFA 1973. Drag performer and actor from 1970: professional debut at Club 82 and La Mama Experimental Theatre Club, New York, 1971; roles in more than 60 plays and in several films. Recipient: Obie Award, 1982; Tony Award, 1983 (for writing and acting), 1984; Oppenheimer Award, 1983; Drama Desk Award, 1983 (for writing and acting); Dramatists Guild

Hull-Warriner Award, 1983; Los Angeles Drama Critics Circle Award, 1984.

Stage Works

In Search of the Cobra Jewels (produced New York, 1972).
Freaky Pussy (produced New York, 1973).
Flatbush Tosca (produced by the New York City Theatre Ensemble, New York, 1975).
Torch Song Trilogy (as trilogy, first produced Richard Allen Center, New York, 1981). 1981. Separate plays as follows:
    The International Stud (produced La Mama Experimental Theatre, New York, 1978).
    Fugue in a Nursery (produced La Mama Experimental Theatre, New York, 1979).
    Widows and Children First! (produced La Mama Experimental Theatre, New York, 1979).
Spookhouse (produced off Broadway, New York, 1982; London, 1987). In *Plays International*, July 1987.
La Cage aux Folles, music and lyrics by Jerry Herman, from the play by Jean Poiret (produced Colonial Theatre, Boston, 1983).
Manny and Jake (produced New York, 1987).
Safe Sex (trilogy: includes *Manny and Jake, Safe Sex, On Tidy Endings;* produced La Mama Experimental Theatre, New York, 1987).
Forget Him (produced St. Clement's Church, New York, 1988).
Legs Diamond, with Charles Suppon, music and lyrics by Peter Allen (produced Mark Hellinger Theatre, New York, 1988).

Screenplays

Torch Song Trilogy, 1988.

Television Plays

Tidy Endings, 1988.

*

Criticism

Articles:
William Green, "*Torch Song Trilogy*: A Gay Comedy with a Dying Fall", in *Maske und Kothurn*, 30, 1984.

*   *   *

Harvey Fierstein is probably America's most prominent gay male playwright and certainly the most popular among heterosexuals; Anne Bancroft's reaction to his best-known play *Torch Song Trilogy* is very typical:

> In 1982, when I saw *Torch Song Trilogy* off-Broadway, it was revolutionary . . . the play *relieved* us, it made us relax. I don't know about the homosexual world, but in the heterosexual world it felt like some kind of barrier had come down. And I think this is because *Torch Song* made us laugh so much. Through the laughter, we could cry.

As well as the humour (Fierstein is a master of the one-liner), this popularity has a lot to do with his use of forms already familiar from heterosexual romance. *Torch Song Trilogy* itself draws not only on the torch song as sung by Helen Morgan or Ruth Etting, but also on the Hollywood melodramas of the 1930's and 1940's, the television sitcom (the third play, *Widows and Children First!*, takes place in a kitchen, a locale beloved of American television writers), and the theatrical comedy of manners; this last form is most obvious in the central *Fugue in a Nursery* in which a female character remarks, "imagine being hostess to your lover's ex and his new boyfriend. . . . It's downright Noël Coward", referring, presumably, to *Private Lives*.

Fierstein uses situations that would, but for the sexuality of the protaganists, be the most bewhiskered of clichés, such as the reunion with an old lover that closes *Torch Song Trilogy* (the plot of which can roughly be summarised as boy meets boy, boy loses boy, boy gets boy), and the confrontation between the two lovers of a dead man (in *On Tidy Endings*, the final play in the *Safe Sex* trilogy). His morality, which focuses on stability, fidelity, monogamy, and truthfulness, is self-consciously old-fashioned, as if in direct opposition to the stereotype of the promiscuous gay male; his overall statement seems to be that homosexuals are just like heterosexuals, only rather more so.

This use of existing heterosexual forms and clichés is nothing new—it's a staple of the vast area called camp. The word "camp", sometimes used simply as a synonym for homosexual, has a wider application, to describe an attitude that uses and appropriates heterosexual iconography in a way that combines parody and sincerity. A drag artiste performing the songs of Judy Garland or Billie Holiday is archetypal camp, sending up the song's depiction of love and femininity, while also implying a genuine identification with the singer. The words also come to be used in a non-homosexual context, to describe anything that takes this ambivalent attitude towards itself.

This goes some way towards explaining why Fierstein is both loved and hated within the gay community. He has presented homosexual life to a larger audience than any other writer (except possibly Armistead Maupin), but in such a way that immediately undercuts it; no sooner is a point made, an emotion shown, than it is parodied. (At one point in the film of *Torch Song Trilogy*, Fierstein, playing Arnold Beckoff, comments on his own actions: "How Alice Faye!") This isn't simply to do with camp; Fierstein also comes from the New York Jewish tradition (epitomised among heterosexuals by Woody Allen) wherby you disarm your adversaries by insulting yourself before they can do it. (Fierstein's Jewishness is very important in his writing; his own stage persona evokes the stereotype of the Jewish mother.)

The best summary of Fierstein's appeal was written by the man himself, in the introduction to *Torch Song Trilogy*:

> Like a gaudy East India purse, outrageous in color, embroidered in cliché design, the worth of these plays lies ultimately in the tiny mirrors woven into the fabric wherein we catch our reflections . . . Not one of the characters you'll meet is "right". There are no answers forthcoming. But you might just catch a line, like, an old familiar half-heard song playing on a juke-box that reaches out and touches something inside of you. And for that moment you are relieved of the isolation.

Fierstein's method is to put real, recognizable characters into clichés, almost archetypal situations. He is essentially a mass-market writer who, because of the relative smallness of his potential audience, works in a non mass-market medium. To measure him against agitprop gay writers like Martin Sherman or Larry Kramer is to miss the point; his plays should be compared not with other plays, but with television series, films, and popular novels. His world-view is limited; it doesn't include much physical passion or any truly dislikeable characters, and it can get cloying, as in his book for Jerry Herman's musical version of *La Cage aux Folles* (not helped by Herman's rather banal songs). But it is an honest one, and to see *Torch Song Trilogy* with an almost entirely gay audience is know the meaning of "laughter of recognition".

—Frances Gray

See also *Volume 1* entry on *Torch Song Trilogy*.

———

FILIPPO, Eduardo de.   See DE FILIPPO, Eduardo.

———

FITCH, (William) Clyde. Born in Elmira, New York, USA, 2 May 1865. Educated at Hartford Public High School, Connecticut; Holderness School, New Hampshire; Amherst College, Massachusetts (editor, *Student*), 1882–86, BA 1886, MA 1902. Freelance writer and tutor, New York, 1886: wrote for *Life* and *Puck*; visited Paris and London, and met writers in the aesthetic movement, 1888; returned to New York, and wrote children's stories for *Churchman, Independent,* and other magazines; first plays produced 1890; full-time playwright and producer/director of his own plays from 1898. Died 4 September 1909.

Works

Collections

Plays (includes *Beau Brummell; Lovers' Lane; Nathan Hale; Barbara Frietchie; Captain Jinks of the Horse Marines; The Climbers; The Stubbornness of Geraldine; The Girl with the Green Eyes; Her Own Way; The Woman in the Case; The Truth; The City*), edited by Montrose J. Moses and Virginia Gerson (4 vols.).   1915.

Stage Works

Beau Brummell (produced Madison Square Theatre, New York, 1890).   1908; in *Plays*, 1915.
Frédérick Lemaitre (produced Tremont Theatre, Boston, 1890).   Edited by Oscar Cargill, in *The Social Revolt*, 1933.
Betty's Finish (produced Boston Museum, Boston, 1890).
Pamela's Prodigy (produced Royal Court Theatre, London, 1891).   1893.
A Modern Match (produced Union Square Theatre, New York, 1892; as *Marriage*, produced 1892).
The Masked Ball, from a play by Alexandre Bisson and Albert Carré (produced Palmer's Theatre, New York, 1892).
The Moth and the Flame (as *The Harvest*, produced Fifth

Avenue Theatre, New York, 1893; revised version, as *The Moth and the Flame*, produced Chestnut Street Theatre, Philadelphia, 1898).   1908.
April Weather (produced Daly's Theatre, New York, 1893).
A Shattered Idol, from a novel by Balzac (produced Globe Theatre, St. Paul, Minnesota, 1893).
The Social Swim, from a play by Sardou (produced Alvin Theatre, Pittsburgh, 1893).
An American Duchess, from a play by Henri Lavedan (produced Lyceum Theatre, New York, 1893).
Mrs. Grundy, Jr., from a French play (produced 1893).
His Grace de Grammont (produced Rockford, Illinois, 1894).
Gossip, with Leo Ditrichstein, from a play by Jules Claretie (produced Palmer's Theatre, New York, 1895).
Mistress Betty (produced Garrick Theatre, New York, 1895; revised version, as *The Toast of the Town*, produced Broad Street Theatre, Philadelphia, 1905).
Bohemia, from a play by Théodore Barrière and Henri Murger (produced Empire Theatre, New York, 1896).
The Liar, from a play by Alexandre Bisson (produced Walnut Street Theatre, Philadelphia, 1896).
A Superfluous Husband, with Leo Ditrichstein, from a play by Ludwig Fulda (produced Fifth Avenue Theatre, New York, 1897).
The Head of the Family, with Leo Ditrichstein, from a play by Adolph L'Arronge (produced Knickerbocker Theatre, New York, 1898).
Nathan Hale (produced Hooley's Theatre, Chicago, 1898).   1899.
The Merry-Go-Round, with F. Kinsey Peile (produced 1898).
The Cowboy and the Lady (produced Broad Street Theatre, Philadelphia, 1899).   1908.
Barbara Frietchie, The Frederick Girl (produced Broad Street Theatre, Philadelphia, 1899).   1900; in *Plays*, 1915.
Sappho, from the play by Daudet and Belot, based on the story by Daudet (produced Powers Theatre, Chicago, 1899).
Captain Jinks of the Horse Marines (produced Walnut Street Theatre, Philadelphia, 1901).   1902.
The Climbers (produced Bijou Theatre, New York, 1901). 1906; in *Plays*, 1915.
Lovers' Lane (produced Manhattan Theatre, New York, 1901).   In *Plays*, 1915.
The Marriage Game, from a play by Émile Augier (produced Broad Street Theatre, Philadelphia, 1901).
The Last of the Dandies (produced Her Majesty's Theatre, London, 1901).
The Way of the World (produced Hammerstein's Victoria Theatre, New York, 1901).
The Girl and the Judge (produced Lyceum Theatre, New York, 1901).
The Stubbornness of Geraldine (produced Garrick Theatre, New York, 1902).   1906; in *Plays*, 1915.
The Girl with the Green Eyes (produced Savoy Theatre, New York, 1902).   1905; in *Plays*, 1915.
The Bird in the Cage, from a play by Ernst von Wildenbruch (produced Bijou Theatre, New York, 1903).
The Frisky Mrs. Johnson, from a play by Paul Gavault and Georges Beer (produced Princess Theatre, New York, 1903).   1908.
Her Own Way (produced Star Theatre, Buffalo, New York, 1903).   1907; in *Plays*, 1915.
Algy (produced 1903).
Major André (produced Savoy Theatre, New York, 1903).
Glad of It (produced Savoy Theatre, New York, 1903).
The Coronet of the Duchess (produced Garrick Theatre, New York, 1904).

Granny, from a play by Georges Michell (produced Lyceum Theatre, New York, 1904).

Cousin Billy, from a play by Labiche and Martin (produced Criterion Theatre, New York, 1905).

The Woman in the Case (produced Herald Square Theatre, New York, 1905). In *Plays*, 1915.

Her Great Match (produced Criterion Theatre, New York, 1905). Edited by Arthur Hobson Quinn, in *Representative American Plays*, 1917.

Wolfville, with Willis Steell, from a novel by Alfred Henry Lewis (produced Broad Street Theatre, Philadelphia, 1905).

Toddles, from a play by Godferneaux and Bernard (produced Duke of York's Theatre, London, 1906).

The House of Mirth, with Edith Wharton, from the novel by Wharton (produced Opera House, Detroit, Illinois, 1906). Edited by Glenn Loney, 1981.

The Girl Who Has Everything (produced Hollis Street Theatre, Boston, 1906).

The Straight Road (produced Astor Theatre, New York, 1907).

The Truth (produced 1907).   1907; in *Plays*, 1915.

Miss McCobb, Manicurist (produced 1907).

Her Sister, with Cosmo Gordon-Lennox (produced Hudson Theatre, New York, 1907).

The Honor of the Family, from a play by Émile Fabre based on a novel by Balzac (produced Hudson Theatre, New York, 1908).

Girls, from a play by Alexander Engel and Julius Horst (produced Belasco Theatre, Washington DC, 1908).

The Blue Mouse, from a play by Alexander Engel and Julius Horst (produced Hyperion Theatre, New Haven, Connecticut, 1908).

A Happy Marriage (produced Garrick Theatre, New York, 1909).

The Bachelor (produced Hyperion Theatre, New Haven, Connecticut, 1909).

The City: A Modern Play of American Life (produced Lyric Theatre, New York, 1909).   In *Plays*, 1915.

Fiction

"The Knighting of the Twins" and Ten Other Tales (for children).   1891.

A Wave of Life.   1909.

Memoirs and Letters

Some Correspondence and Six Conversations.   1896.

The Smart Set: Correspondence and Conversations.   1897.

Fitch and His Letters, edited by Montrose J. Moses and Virginia Gerson.   1924.

*

Criticism

Books:
Archie Bell, *The Fitch I Knew*, New York, 1909.

*   *   *

The contribution of Clyde Fitch to the development of drama in America is generally acknowledged to be that of a theatre craftsman who combined excellent powers of observation with skills in drawing character to produce faithful representations of American society. Much more a man of the commercial theatre than a literary figure in his own right, Fitch wrote easily and rapidly, turning out over 30 original plays and over 20 adaptations of foreign works or dramatizations of novels during a 20-year period. Undoubtedly, his membership of the "Syndicate School" of dramatists helped assure him the success which made him the first millionaire dramatist in America, but his 1901 record of four plays running in New York theatres at one time indicates something more than a favored position with the Theatrical Trust. By this time America's signature on the 1891 international copyright accord had helped a playwright's situation in America considerably. He now had some stature, and Fitch's remarkable success in England obviously increased his reputation in America.

Although something of a dandy and a very colorful figure in the New York theatre world, Fitch was far from being a fraud. He reflected a sensitivity toward life and tried constantly to present truthfully and realistically the people whom he watched daily and the environment in which they lived. With such detail he was at his best, but he lacked the larger perspective of life and the meaningful ideas that might have distinguished his plays. When he carried his enthusiasm for realistic particulars to excess (as he sometimes did) the result was either a caricature or an overabundance of what critics termed "Fitchian detail".

Very much a man-about-town, Fitch enjoyed picturing the social scene in and around New York and the favorite "watering holes" of New York Society. The problems of married life, the peculiarities of individuals, the faults and foibles of a fast-changing society—these were the aspects of life that fascinated Fitch. His first attempt at a full-length social comedy was *A Modern Match*, a thin play which tells of a flippant and selfish wife who refuses to assume the responsibilities of marriage. True to the laws of Victorian dramatists in America, Fitch did not allow his heroine to be redeemed after her fall from purity. Fitch's satire on aspects of New York social life, *The Climbers*, is a better play, with a spectacularly frank opening scene that shocked many theatregoers because it ridiculed the hypocrisy and unfeeling materialism of a family immediately after the funeral of the father. *The Stubbornness of Geraldine* and *Her Great Match* revealed Fitch's interest in the international scene, particularly the problems inherent in a marriage involving an American woman and an Englishman. Although in these plays and in others he created some fine scenes, such as the dinner scene at the beginning of *A Happy Marriage*, Fitch never wrote a completely effective comedy, either on society in general or on the theme of marriage.

Instead, he seemed more comfortable writing melodrama and farce, which were in the mainstream of American drama at the turn of the century. From the plays of Augustin Daly and Edward Harrigan through the works of William Dean Howells to the triumphant successes of Charles Hoyt and George Ade, farce held a great appeal for the American theatregoers. Fitch showed his skills in this genre with such plays as *The Blue Mouse*, an adaptation from the German. Melodrama—social melodrama—was, however, Fitch's great strength, although two of his historical melodramas, *Nathan Hale* and *Barbara Frietchie*, were also stage successes along with *Captain Jinks of the Horse Marines*, a period piece about an opera singer in New York in the early 1870's which gave Ethel Barrymore her first major role in the theatre.

In his best social melodrama Fitch concerned himself with character idiosyncrasies and resulting conflicts and struggles within a sophisticated society. The individual social vice that overwhelms *The Girl with the Green Eyes* is, of course, jealousy. Jenny Tillman seems to have inherited her weakness and nearly ruins her marriage when she misunderstands her husband's concern for another woman. Actually, he has been trying to help Jenny's brother out of a marital mess, but circumstances cloud the truth for Jenny, who then attempts suicide. Fortunately, however, she is saved by Fitch's manipulation of time in the honored way for melodrama, and the happy ending required by the "Syndicate School" provides an appropriate climax. *The Truth* dramatizes the problem of a pathological liar married to a man who is as naively honest as Jenny Tillman's husband is incapable of understanding a jealous person. Such contrived characters, however, as exciting as they were in melodrama, limited the development of Fitch's heroines and created an artificiality in his plays that detracted from the wit of his dialogue and his use of dramatic irony.

Only in his final play, *The City*, did Fitch attempt to combine a contemporary issue and the co-existing struggles among individuals with a larger view of society, and this was not completely successful. With the death of their father, the members of the Rand family move from their small-town home to New York City, where the son develops political aspirations only to have them thwarted by a scandal within the family. Presumably there is a thematic solution in the family's decision to leave the "evils" of the city and return to their small town, but the issue is clouded by the fact that the major source of corruption is a blackmailing, degenerate, illegitimate son spawned in that same small town. Produced after Fitch's death, *The City* showed his typical melodramatic techniques and platitudinous moral assertions but with the added strength of a realistic presentation of an advancing society's problems.

Fitch was never a profound thinker, but he helped prepare the way for an established social comedy in America, and deserves attention for that achievement. He was, above all, a man of that society, and a craftsman of the commercial theatre whose interest in truthfulness in drama helped him create some believable characters and memorable social scenes against a background of melodrama.

—Walter J. Meserve

FITZMAURICE, George. Born near Listowel, County Kerry, Ireland, 28 January 1877. Served in the British Army, 1914–18. Clerk in the Irish civil service, 1901–42; wrote newspaper sketches of Kerry peasant life, 1900–07; first-produced play, *The Country Dressmaker*, staged 1907; several plays published posthumously. Died in Dublin, 12 May 1963.

Works

Collections

Five Plays (includes *The Country Dressmaker; The Moonlighter; The Pie-Dish; The Magic Glasses; The Dandy Dolls*). 1914.
Plays (3 vols.). 1967–70.

Stage Works

The Country Dressmaker (produced Abbey Theatre, Dublin, 1907). In *Five Plays*, 1914.

The Pie-Dish (produced Abbey Theatre, Dublin, 1908). In *Five Plays*, 1914.
The Magic Glasses (produced Abbey Theatre, Dublin, 1913). In *Five Plays*, 1914.
The Dandy Dolls (produced by the Lyric Theatre Company, Abbey Theatre, Dublin, 1945). In *Five Plays*, 1914.
The Moonlighter (produced by the Earlsfort Players, Peacock Theatre, Dublin, 1948). In *Five Plays*, 1914.
'Twixt the Giltinans and the Carmodys (produced Abbey Theatre, Dublin, 1923). In *The Dublin Magazine*, July-March 1949; in book form, in *Plays 3*, 1970.
The Linnaun Shee (produced by the Lyric Theatre Company, Abbey Theatre, Dublin, 1949). In *The Dublin Magazine*, October 1924; in book form, in *Plays 1*, 1967.
The Green Stone. In *The Dublin Magazine*, January-March 1926; in book form, in *Plays 1*, 1967.
There Are Tragedies and Tragedies (produced St. Mary's College, Dublin, 1952). In *The Dublin Magazine*, July-September 1948; in book form, in *Plays 2*, 1970.
One Evening Gleam (produced Studio Theatre Club, Dublin, 1952). In *The Dublin Magazine*, January-March 1949; in book form, in *Plays 3*, 1970.
The Coming of Ewn Andzale. In *The Dublin Magazine*, July-September 1954; in book form, In *Plays 3*, 1970.
The Terrible Baisht. In *The Dublin Magazine*, October-December 1954; in book form, in *Plays 2*, 1970.
The Enchanted Land. In *The Dublin Magazine*, March 1957; in book form, in *Plays 1*, 1967.
The Waves of the Sea. In *Plays 1*, 1967.
The Toothache (produced 1973). In *Malahat Review*, January 1967; in book form, in *Plays 3*, 1970.
The Ointment Blue; or, The King of the Barna Men (as *The King of the Barna Men*, produced Peacock Theatre, Dublin, 1967). In *Plays 2*, 1970.
The Simple Hanrahans. In *Plays 3*, 1970.
The Wonderful Wedding, with John Guinan. In *Journal of Irish Literature*, September 1978.

Fiction

"The Crows of Mephistopheles" and Other Stories, edited by Robert Hogan. 1970.

*

Bibliographies

Joanne L. Henderson, "Checklist of Four Kerry Writers", in *Journal of Irish Literature*, vol.1 no.2, 1972.

Criticism

Books:
Howard K. Slaughter, *George Fitzmaurice and His Enchanted Land* (with bibliography), Dublin, 1972.
Arthur E. McGuinness, *George Fitzmaurice*, Lewisburg, Pennsylvania, 1974.
Carol W. Gelderman, *George Fitzmaurice*, Boston, 1979.

Articles:
John P. Conbere, "The Obscurity of George Fitzmaurice", in *Eire*, vol.6 no.1, 1971.
Jochen Achilles, "George Fitzmaurice's Dramatic Fantasies: Wicked Old Children in a Disenchanting Land", in *Irish University Review*, 15, 1985.

Jochen Achilles, "'The Glame from That Old Lamp': The Unity of George Fitzmaurice's Plays", in *Eire*, vol.20 no.4, 1985.

* * *

In the 1960's and 1970's, productions of *The Magic Glasses*, *The King of the Barna Men*, *The Dandy Dolls* and *The Pie-Dish* revived the interest of Abbey Theatre audiences in the long neglected plays of George Fitzmaurice. Playgoers, somewhat belatedly, have come to recognise the unique quality of this Kerry playwright in the realm of fantasy and the grotesque.

Earlier in the century, after the death of Synge in 1909, George Fitzmaurice seemed destined to become one of the outstanding dramatists of the Irish theatre. His first play, *The Country Dressmaker*, had won him instant recognition as a purveyor of kitchen-comedy. His second play, the one-act *The Pie-Dish*, although less popular, impressed the more discerning as a richly symbolic piece with overtures of what would today be described as "black" comedy. The play concerns a Kerry farmer who has spent 20 years moulding a pie-dish. He intends it to be the masterpiece of a long lifetime. A farmer who has spent his days and nights moulding such a useless article could hardly expect the sympathy of his family and neighbours, and he has become the laughing-stock of seven parishes. Now he is dying, and his family, concerned for his eternal salvation, send for the priest. But the farmer's only prayer is for more time to finish the pie-dish. The priest begs him to prepare his soul; but his soul is in the pie-dish—his little unfinished masterpiece. The artist in the old man refuses to surrender. If God will not give him time, the Devil will, and so he dies with a prayer to the Devil on his lips, and the pie-dish is smashed to smithereens on the floor. There were many who regarded the little play as blasphemous, sacrilegious, and grotesque.

The Magic Glasses, produced in 1913, tells of another artist manqué, Shanahan, who retires to the loft in order to enjoy the unearthly music of the magic glasses and to forget the workaday world. Fitzmaurice's next play, *The Dandy Dolls*, was rejected for no good reason. Some critics have attributed this to the jealousy of Yeats and Lady Gregory. It is an interesting but implausible theory. A more likely explanation is that Fitzmaurice was uncertain and thin-skinned in the face of harsh Dublin criticism. He had neither the inclination nor the temperament to stand in the limelight.

Fitzmaurice had a mastery of the Kerry idiom. His dialogue owes little to Synge or other folk-dramatists. His characters also leap on stage with a wild abandon, as if they had suddenly broken loose from the mind of their creator. Roger Carmody in *The Dandy Dolls* makes puppets that take on a life of their own. One can no more analyse or paraphrase the plots of such pieces than describe exactly a haunting dream or a violent nightmare. On one level the plots are as nonsensical as *Alice's Adventures in Wonderland* but we are left with a similar impression of wild tomfoolery hiding a share of common sense. One detects also a sub-stratum of pagan belief beneath the topsoil of conventional Christianity. Modern critics may resort to a Freudian interpretation of what are, essentially, dream plays. There is nothing quite like them in modern theatre except, perhaps, the trolls in *Peer Gynt*.

Fitzmaurice was more conventional and unconvincing when he attempted a realistic treatment of the land war in *The Moonlighter*. Agrarian disturbers are harried by the police until the four acts expire in unrelieved tragedy. Another less ambitious piece, *'Twixt the Giltinans and the Carmodys*, was staged without much success at the Abbey Theatre in 1923. Fitzmaurice continued to publish short plays in *The Dublin Magazine*. These show occassional flashes of inspiration, but there is also an ominous note of self-parody; his best work had been completed before 1914.

—Micheál Ó hAodha

———

FLETCHER, John. Born in Rye, Sussex, England, in December 1579. Possibly educated at Benet College (now Corpus Christi College), Cambridge, possibly BA 1595, MA 1598. Met Francis Beaumont in 1605, and collaborated with him in writing plays until Beaumont retired c.1613; thereafter wrote for the King's Men, on his own and in collaboration with others, particularly Massinger. Died in London, August 1625.

Works

Collections

Comedies and Tragedies, with Beaumont and others.   1647; revised edition, 1679.
Works of Beaumont and Fletcher, edited by A. Glover and A.R. Waller (10 vols.).   1905–12.
Variorum Edition, edited by A.H. Bullen (4 vols.; incomplete).   1904–12.
The Dramatic Works in the Beaumont and Fletcher Canon, edited by Fredson Bowers.   1966–

Stage Works

The Noble Gentleman, with Beaumont or another author (produced London, c.1606; revised version produced, 1625–26?).   Revised version in *Comedies and Tragedies*, 1647.
Love's Cure, with Beaumont, revised by Massinger (produced London, 1606?).   In *Comedies and Tragedies*, 1647.
The Woman Hater, with Beaumont (produced London, 1606?).   1607.
Philaster; or, Love Lies A-Bleeding, with Beaumont (produced by the King's Men, London, c.1608–10).   1620.
The Faithful Shepherdess (produced by the Children of the Queen's Revels, Blackfriars Theatre, London, 1608–09).   1609(?).
The Coxcomb, with Beaumont (produced London, c.1608–10).   In *Comedies and Tragedies*, 1647.
The Maid's Tragedy, with Beaumont (produced by the King's Men, London, c.1608–11).   1619.
The Captain, possibly with Beaumont (produced by the King's Men, London, c.1609–12).   In *Comedies and Tragedies*, 1647.
Valentinian (produced by the King's Men, London, c.1610–14).   In *Comedies and Tragedies*, 1647.
Monsieur Thomas (produced c.1610–16).   Edited by Richard Brome, 1639; as *Father's Own Son*, 1661(?).
The Night Walker; or, The Little Thief (produced c.1611).
A King and No King, with Beaumont (produced by the King's Men, London, 1611).   1619.
Bonduca (produced by the King's Men, London, c. 1611–14).   In *Comedies and Tragedies*, 1647.
Cupid's Revenge, with Beaumont (produced before 1612).   1615.

Henry VIII (attributed), with Shakespeare (produced by the King's Men, Globe Theatre, London, 1612). 1613.

The Two Noble Kinsmen, with Shakespeare (produced by the King's Men, Blackfriars Theatre, London, c. 1613). 1634.

The Honest Man's Fortune, with Nathan Field (produced c.1613). In *Comedies and Tragedies*, 1647.

The Scornful Lady, with Beaumont (produced London, 1613–17?).

Wit Without Money (produced c.1614–16). 1639.

The Nice Valour, with Middleton (produced c.1615–16). In *Comedies and Tragedies*, 1647.

Love's Pilgrimage, possibly with Beaumont (produced Blackfriars Theatre, London, 1616?). In *Comedies and Tragedies*, 1647.

The Mad Lover (produced by the King's Men, 1616?). In *Comedies and Tragedies*, 1647.

The Bloody Brother; or, Rollo Duke of Normandy, with Massinger, possibly also with Jonson (produced by the King's Men, London, c.1616). 1639.

The Queen of Corinth, possibly with Massinger and Nathan Field (produced by the King's Men, Blackfriars Theatre, London, c.1616–18). In *Comedies and Tragedies*, 1647.

The Knight of Malta, with Massinger and Nathan Field (produced by the King's Men, Blackfriars Theatre, London, 1616–19). In *Comedies and Tragedies*, 1647.

The Chances (produced by the King's Men, Blackfriars Theatre, London, c.1617). In *Comedies and Tragedies*, 1647.

The Loyal Subject; or, The Faithful General (produced by the King's Men, Blackfriars Theatre, London, 1618). In *Comedies and Tragedies*, 1647.

The Humourous Lieutenant (produced by the King's Men, Blackfriars Theatre, London, 1619 or after). In *Comedies and Tragedies*, 1647.

Sir John van Olden Barnavelt, with Massinger (produced by the King's Men, Globe Theatre?, London, 1619). In *A Collection of Old English Plays 2*, 1883.

The Custom of the Country, with Massinger (produced by the King's Men, Blackfriars Theatre, London, 1619–20?). In *Comedies and Tragedies*, 1647.

The Little French Lawyer, with Massinger (produced by the King's Men, Blackfriars Theatre, London, 1619–23). In *Comedies and Tragedies*, 1647.

Women Pleased (produced by the King's Men, c. 1619–23). In *Comedies and Tragedies*, 1647.

The Double Marriage, with Massinger (produced by the King's Men, Blackfriars Theatre, London, 1619–23). In *Comedies and Tragedies*, 1647.

The False One, with Massinger (produced by the King's Men, Blackfriars Theatre, London, 1619–23). In *Comedies and Tragedies*, 1647.

Thierry, King of France, and His Brother, Theoderet, with Beaumont and Massinger (produced ?). 1621.

The Island Princess (produced by the King's Men, Blackfriars Theatre, London, c.1621). In *Comedies and Tragedies*, 1647.

The Pilgrim (produced by the King's Men, Blackfriars Theatre, London, 1621?). In *Comedies and Tragedies*, 1647.

The Wild Goose Chase (produced by the King's Men, Blackfriars Theatre, London, 1621?). 1652.

The Spanish Curate, with Massinger (produced by the King's Men, Blackfriars Theatre, London, 1622). In *Comedies and Tragedies*, 1647.

The Prophetess, with Massinger (produced by the King's Men, Blackfriars Theatre, London, 1622). In *Comedies and Tragedies*, 1647.

The Sea Voyage, with Massinger (produced by the King's Men, London, 1622). In *Comedies and Tragedies*, 1647.

The Beggars' Bush, with Massinger (produced by the King's Men, 1622). In *Comedies and Tragedies*, 1647.

The Lover's Progress (produced by the King's Men, 1623; revised version by Massinger, as *Cleander*, produced 1634). In *Comedies and Tragedies*, 1647.

The Maid in the Mill, with Rowley (produced by the King's Men, 1623). In *Comedies and Tragedies*, 1647.

Rule a Wife and Have a Wife (produced by the King's Men, Blackfriars Theatre, London, 1624). 1640.

A Wife for a Month (produced by the King's Men, Blackfriars Theatre, London, 1624). In *Comedies and Tragedies*, 1647.

The Elder Brother, with Massinger (produced by the King's Men, Blackfriars Theatre, London, 1625?). 1637.

The Fair Maid of the Inn, with Massinger and others (produced by the King's Men, Blackfriars Theatre, London, 1626). In *Comedies and Tragedies*, 1647.

A Very Woman, with Massinger (produced in a revised version by Massinger, 1634). In *Three New Plays*, by Massinger, 1655.

*

Bibliographies

S.A. Tannenbaum, *Beaumont and Fletcher: A Concise Bibliography*, New York, 1938; supplement, with D.R. Tannenbaum, 1946; further supplement in *Elizabethan Bibliographies Supplements 8*, by C.A. Pennell and W.P. Williams, 1968.

Criticism

Books:

Arthur Colby Sprague, *Beaumont and Fletcher on the Restoration Stage*, Cambridge, Massachusetts, 1926; revised edition, 1965.

E.C. Oliphant, *The Plays of Beaumont and Fletcher*, New Haven, Connecticut, 1927.

John H. Wilson, *The Influence of Beaumont and Fletcher on Restoration Drama*, Columbus, Ohio, 1928.

R.C. Bald, *Bibliographical Studies in the Beaumont and Fletcher Folio of 1647*, London, 1938.

D.M. Keithlan, *The Debt to Shakespeare in the Beaumont and Fletcher Plays*, New York, 1938.

Baldwin Maxwell, *Studies in Beaumont, Fletcher, and Massinger*, Chapel Hill, North Carolina, 1939.

L.B. Wallis, *Beaumont, Fletcher, and Company: Entertainers to the Jacobean Gentry*, Oxford, 1947.

E.M. Smith, *The Pattern of Tragicomedy in Beaumont and Fletcher*, New Haven, Connecticut, 1952.

W.W. Appleton, *Beaumont and Fletcher: A Critical Study*, London, 1956.

Clifford Leech, *The John Fletcher Plays*, London, 1962.

Ian Fletcher, *Beaumont and Fletcher*, London, 1967 (British Council booklet).

Nancy C. Pearse, *John Fletcher's Chastity Plays: Mirrors of Modesty*, Lewsiburg, Pennsylvania, 1973.

Bertha Hensman, *The Shares of Fletcher, Field, and Massinger in Twelve Plays of the Beaumont and Fletcher Canon*, Salzburg, 1974.

Mary Cone, *Fletcher Without Beaumont: A Study of the Independent Plays of Fletcher*, Salzburg, 1976.

Philip J. Finkelpearl, *Court and Country Politics in the Plays of Beaumont and Fletcher*, Princeton, New Jersey, 1990.

Articles:

Cyrus Hoy, "The Shares of Fletcher and His Collaborators in the Beaumont and Fletcher Canon" in *Studies in Bibliography*, 8–9, 1956, and 11–15, 1962.

* * *

Although the names of Francis Beaumont and John Fletcher are customarily bracketed together, their collaboration lasted only until about 1615 after which time Fletcher continued, until his death in 1625, to write plays on his own or in collaboration with Nathan Field, William Shakespeare, William Rowley (possibly), John Webster, John Ford, and, particularly, Philip Massinger. He is associated with over 50 titles, of which around 15 are probably by him alone. Nevertheless, it is for his collaboration with Beaumont that he tends to be chiefly remembered.

Fletcher was a gentleman, the son of a bishop, and educated at Cambridge. He and Beaumont (who came from the gentry) both wrote with Court audiences in mind, and show the signs of an academic concern with the humour theory that Jonson had utilized so successfully as a means of characterization, and with dramatic form.

Like Marston, Beaumont began his dramatic career by writing texts for revels at the Inns of Court. His most well known play, *The Knight of the Burning Pestle*, which was probably performed by the Children of the Revels at the private Blackfriars playhouse, gives signs of having been written for a coterie audience of intellectuals and professionals. It draws its energy from its parodying of the dramatic fare of the amphitheatre playhouses frequented by citizens and by lampooning a group of their number, the nameless Citizen and his Wife, who, as members of the "audience" in the play, interrupt the action. Their prentice Rafe takes heroic roles in the episodes which are inserted, at the Citizens' request, into a conventional and dreary play, *The London Merchant*, which purports to be the advertised entertainment for the Blackfriars audience. However, Rafe's episodes prove in performance to be as delightful as naive and thus serve not only to parody romance but to endorse it: "The Knight" becomes the true hero of the play, and the work's carnivalized atmosphere makes it impossible to read it simply as a satire on the citizenry and their literary taste.

Fletcher's first solo work was an elegant if somewhat academic tragi-comic pastoral, *The Faithful Shepherdess*, written in imitation of Guarini. Like *The Knight of the Burning Pestle*, it is pre-eminently theatrical, drawing attention to itself as a play and to the way that plays are a species of games. The first collaboration with Beaumont was probably *The Woman Hater*, a comedy of intrigue with a cluster of Jonsonian humour characters who are used to satirize gluttony and greed. Beaumont and Fletcher then turned to the writing of a series of romances or tragicomedies which followed the pattern set by Shakespeare in *Pericles* and *Cymbeline*, and which bore titles like *Philaster; or, Love Lies A-Bleeding*, and *A King and No King*. Dryden considered, however, that they "understood and imitated the conversation of gentlemen much better" than Shakespeare and, unlike Shakespeare, they moved away from myth towards the depiction of strong feeling and passion.

These romances, designed for the fashionable spectators at the Blackfriars Theatre, but also performed at the Globe, are notable for their smooth eloquence, their romantic treatment of Court intrigue, their avoidance of the resolution of the action through death—a characteristic of tragicomedy, according to the epistle to *The Faithful Shepherdess*, is that it "wants deaths"—and, occasionally, for choric moments that offer a muted critique of monarchical absolutism. (*Henry VIII; or, All is True*, which Fletcher wrote in collaboration with Shakespeare, may have failed to achieve the honour of performance at the wedding of the Princess Elizabeth with the Elector Palatine because, in the words of a contemporary, it made "greatness familiar".)

Heroes and heroines of the plays undergo tests of virtue and constancy of the sort familiar from medieval chivalric literature (the women, often in disguise, have a habit of being wounded by their lovers' swords). There is the frisson of incest in *A King and No King* which is allayed when it is revealed that the "sister" of King Abaces, with whom he had made love, is not his sister after all. Consistency of character is often thus sacrificed to resolution of plot, morality to effect, so that wonder predominates over woe, with some comic servants or bawds establishing appropriate social perspectives. Although the plays seem to be suffused in nostalgia for a vanished Arcadian world (Sidney's pastoral romance, the *Arcadia*, was frequently reprinted during the years of Fletcher's popularity), the morality of these plays can be subtle: like the plays of Ford, they suggest that there are no easy remedies for passion, even if we feel that the romantic scenes cater to a kind of voyeurism rather than to a critique of conventional social morality. (Modern revivals of *The Maid's Tragedy*, a play which centres on the destruction of a marriage by the adulterous love of a king, have exploited the eroticism of the text.)

The plays were also self-consciously artful: Beaumont and Fletcher's fellow dramatist, James Shirley, wrote in an epigraph to a collection of their works:

> You may here find passions raised to that excellent pitch, and by such insinuating degrees, that you shall not choose but consent and go along with them, finding yourself at last grown insensibly the very same person you read; and then stand admiring the subtle tracks of your engagement.

This kind of refined dramatic fare, which looks back to Sidneyean romance and forward to Dryden, and even to the comedies of manners popular after the Restoration (*A Wild Goose Chase* is a Restoration comedy before its time), became immensely popular, not only at Blackfriars, but at Court, and was the staple of the King's Men, the leading company of the period. The savage indignation of a dramatist like Jonson disappeared from the Court's theatrical diet and from the playhouses frequented by courtiers: what supplanted it was not quite mere entertainment—there is an implicit insistence on independence for women in the Fletcherian drama—but it lacks the robustness and profound political and moral scepticism for which we value the earlier dramatists of the English Renaissance.

—Michael Hattaway

See also *Volume 1* entries on *The Maid's Tragedy; Philaster; The Two Noble Kinsmen*.

FO, Dario.   Born in San Giano, Lombardy, Italy, 24 March 1926. Educated at the Academy of Fine Arts, Milan; Brera Art Academy, studying set design, and Milan Polytechnic, studying architecture, 1945–51. Married the writer and performer Franca Rame in 1954; one son. Wrote and performed for cabarets and theatres, including Piccolo Teatro, Milan; wrote and performed *Poer nano* radio programme, RAI radio network, from December 1951; co-founder, I Dritti revue company, 1953: disbanded 1954; screenwriter, Rome, 1956–58; artistic director, *Chi l'ha visto?* weekly television musical revue, 1959; co-founder, with Rame, Compagnia Dario Fo-Franca Rame, 1959: disbanded 1967; travelled to USA, Cuba, and Eastern Europe, 1966; co-founder, with Rame, Nuova Scena theatre co-operative, linked to the Italian Communist Party: company split from the Party, 1969; co-founder, with Rame, Il Collettivo Teatrale La Comune, 1970, based at the Capannone di via Coletta, Milan, until 1972: disbanded 1973; briefly under arrest for police obstruction in Sardinia, 1973; toured Germany and Scandinavia, with Rame, 1974; was refused entry to USA on account of left-wing links, 1980 and 1983, but gained entry, 1984, and subsequently toured eastern states, 1986. Recipient: Sonning Award (Denmark), 1981; Obie Award, 1987.

Works

Collections

Teatro comico (includes *La Marcolfa; Gli imbianchini non hanno ricordi; I tre bravi; Non tutti i ladri vengono per nuocere; Un morto da vendere; I cadaveri si spediscono e le donne si spogliano; L'uomo nudo e l'uomo in frak*).   1962; re-issued as *Le commedie VI*, 1984.
Le commedie (9 vols. to 1991):
1. *Gli arcangeli non giocano a flipper; Aveva due pistole con gli occhi bianchi e neri; Chi ruba un piede è fortunato in amore.*   1966.
2. *Isabella, tre caravelle e un cacciaballe; Settimo, ruba un po' meno; La colpa è sempre del diavolo.*   1966.
3. *Grande pantomima con bandiere e pupazzi piccoli e medi; L'operaio conosce 300 parole, il padrone 1000: Per questo lui è il padrone; Legami pure che tanto io spacco tutto lo stesso.*   1975.
4. *Vorrei morire anche stasera se dovessi pensare che non è servito a niente; Tutti uniti! Tutti insieme! Ma scusa, quello non è il padrone?; Fedayn).*   1977.
5. *Mistero buffo; Ci ragiono e canto 2.*   1977.
6. *La Marcolfa; Gli imbianchini non hanno ricordi; I tre bravi; Non tutti i ladri vengono per nuocere; Un morto da vendere; I cadaveri si spediscono e le donne si spogliano; L'uomo nudo e l'uomo in frak; Canzoni e ballate).* 1984.
7. *Morte accidentale di un anarchico; La signora è da buttare.*   1988.
8. *25 monologhi per una donna*, subdivided into: *Tutta casa, letto e chiesa; Altre storie; Giullarate religiose; Fabulazioni della resistenza; Discorsi sur terrorismo e la repressione*; all with Franca Rame.   1989.
9. *Coppia aperta, quasi spalancata; Un giornata qualunque*; and the short plays: *La casellante, Il papazzo giapponese, L'uomo incinto, I piatti; Il problema deo vecchi; Il black-out; Previsioni meteorologiche movimenti di stupro in Italia; Voce amica; Ho fatto la plastica; La nonna incinta; Il figlia in provetta; Parigi-Dakar; Lettera dalla Cina*; with Franca Rame.   1991.
Campagni senza cesura 1 (includes *Mistero Buffo; L'operaio conosce 300 parole, il padrone 1000: Per questo lui è il padrone; Il Telaio; Il funerale del padrone).*   1970.
Compagni senza cesura 2 (includes *Morte accidentale di un anarchico; Vorrei morire anche stasera se dovessi pensare che non è servito a niente; Morte e resurrezione di un pupazzo; Tutti uniti! Tutti insieme! Ma scusa, quello non è il padrone?; Fedayn).*   1972.
Il teatro politico di Dario Fo (includes *Mistero Buffo; Isabella, tre caravelle e un cacciaballe).*   1977.
Female Parts: One Woman Plays, with Franca Rame (includes *Waking Up; A Woman Alone; The Same Old Story*). 1981.
"A Woman Alone" and Other Plays, with Franca Rame (includes the series of short plays *All Home, Bed, and Church; More Stories; Tales of the Resistance; Questions of Terrorism and Repression*), translated by Christopher Cairns, Ed Emery, and Gillian Hanna.   1991.
Plays 1 (includes *Mistero Buffo; Accidental Death of an Anarchist; Trumpets and Raspberries; The Virtuous Burglars; One was Nude and One Wore Tails*), edited by Stuart Hood.   1992.

Stage Works

Poer nano ed altre storie, from the radio series (produced Teatro Odeon, Milan, 1952).   As *Poer Nano*, 1976.
Il dito nell'occhio (produced Piccolo Teatro, Milan, 1953). In *Teatro d'oggi*, vol.2 no.3, 1954.
I Sani da legare (produced Piccolo Teatro, Milan, 1954).   In *Sipario*, 1955.
L'uomo nudo e l'uomo in frak (produced as part of *Ladri, manichini e donne nude*, Piccolo Teatro, Milan, 1957).   In *Teatro comico*, 1962; translated as *One Was Nude and One Wore Tails*, 1985.
I cadaveri si spediscono e le donne si spogliano (produced as part of *Ladri, manichini e donne nude*, Piccolo Teatro, Milan, 1957).   In *Teatro comico*, 1962.
Non tutti i ladri vengono per nuocere (produced as part of *Ladri, manichini e donne nude*, Piccolo Teatro, Milan, 1957).   In *Teatro comico*, 1962; translated as *The Virtuous Burglars*, in *Plays 1*, 1992.
Gli imbianchini non hanno ricordi (produced as part of *Ladri, manichini e donne nude*, Piccolo Teatro, Milan, 1975).   In *Teatro comico*, 1962.
Quando sarai povero sarai re (produced in *Comico finale*, Teatro Stabile, Turin, 1958).
La marcolfa (produced in *Comico finale*, Teatro Stabile, Turin, 1958).   In *Teatro comico*, 1962.
Un morto da vendere (produced in *Comico finale*, Teatro Stabile, Turin, 1958).   In *Teatro comico*, 1962.
I tre brevi (produced in *Comico finale*, Teatro Stabile, Turin, 1958).   In *Teatro comico*, 1962.
Gli arcangeli non giocano a flipper (produced Teatro Odeon, Milan, 1959).   In *Le commedie 1*, 1966; translated as *Archangels Don't Play Pinball*, 1987.
Aveva due pistole con gli occhi bianchi e neri (produced Teatro Odeon, Milan, 1960).   In *Le commedie 1*, 1966.
Chi ruba un piede è fortunato in amore (produced Teatro Odeon, Milan, 1961). In *Le commedie 1*, 1966.
Isabella, tre caravelle e un cacciaballe (produced Teatro Odeon, Milan, 1963).   In *Le commedie 2*, 1966.
Settimo, ruba un po' meno (produced Teatro Odeon, Milan, 1964).   In *Le commedie 2*, 1966.
La colpa è sempre del diavolo (produced Teatro Odeon, Milan, 1965).   In *Le commedie 2*, 1966.
[The Sunday Walk], from a play by Georges Michel (produced Teatro Durini, Milan, 1967).

Dario Fo in his *Mistero Buffo*

Ci ragione e canto (produced Teatro Carignano, Turin, 1966). 1966.

La Signora è da buttare (produced Teatro Manzoni, Italy, 1967). 1976.

Grande pantomima con bandiere e pupazzi piccoli e medi (produced Sala di Vittorio, Milan, 1968). In *Le commedie 3*, 1975.

L'operaio conosce 300 parole, il padrone 1000: Per questo lui è il padrone (produced Teatro della Gioventù, Genoa, 1969). In *Compagni senza censura 1*, 1970.

Legami pure che tanto io spacco tutto lo stesso (produced Teatro della Gioventù, Genoa, 1969). In *Le commedie 3*, 1975.

Mistero Buffo (produced Sestri Levanti, Milan, 1969). In *Compagni senza censura 1*, 1970; translated as *Mistero Buffo*, 1988.

Ci ragiono e canto 2 (produced Camera del Lavoro, Milan, 1969). 1972.

Morte accidentale di un anarchico (produced Capannone di via Colletta, Milan, 1970). 1970; translated as *Accidental Death of an Anarchist*, 1980.

Vorrei morire anche stasera se dovessi pensare che non è servito a niente (produced Capannone di via Colletta, Milan, 1970). 1970.

Tutti uniti! Tutti insieme! Ma scusa, quello non è il padrone? (produced Casa del Popolo, Varese, 1971). 1971.

Morte e resurrezione di un pupazzo (produced Capannone di via Colletta, Milan, 1971). 1971.

Fedayn (produced Capannone di via Colletta, Milan, 1972). 1972.

Pum pum! Chi e? La polizia! (produced Circolo Quarticciolo La Comune, Rome, 1972). 1972; revised edition, 1974.

Ordine! Per Dio.OOO.OOO.OOO (produced Capannone di via Colletta, Milan, 1972). 1972.

Ci ragiono e canto 3 (produced Teatro della Gioventù, Genoa, 1973). 1973.

Basta con i fascisti (produced on tour, Northern Italy, 1973).

Guerra di popolo in Cile (produced Palazzo dello Sport, Bolzano, 1973). 1973.

Non si paga, non si paga (produced Palazzina Liberty, Milan, 1974). 1974; translated as *We Can't Pay? We Won't Pay!*, 1978; revised as *Can't Pay? Won't Pay*, 1982; as *We Won't Pay? We Won't Pay!*, 1984.

Canzoni e ballate (produced 1974). In *Le commedie 6*, 1984.

Il fanfari rapito (produced Palazzina Liberty, Milan, 1975). 1975.

La giullarata (produced Palazzina Liberty, Milan, 1975). 1975.

La marjuana della mamma è la più bella (produced Palazzina Liberty, Milan, 1976). 1976.

Tutta casa, letto e chiesa, with Franca Rame (short plays; produced Palazzina Liberty, Milan, 1977). 1978; three plays translated as *Waking Up, A Woman Alone*, and *The Same Old Story*, in *Female Parts*, 1981; five plays translated as *A Woman Alone, Rise and Shine, Bless Me Father for I Have Sinned, The Same Old Story*, and *Medea*, all under the title *All Home, Bed, and Church*, in *"A Woman Alone" and Other Plays*, 1991.

La storia di un soldato, music by Stravinsky (produced Teatro Ponchielli, Cremona, 1978). 1979.

Storia delle tigre et altre storie (produced Palazzina Liberty, Milan, 1979). 1980; translated as *The Tale of a Tiger*, 1984.

Clacson, trombette e pernacchi (produced Cinema-Teatro Cristallo, Milan, 1980). 1981; translated as *About Face*, in *Theater*, Summer-Fall 1983; in book form, 1989; also translated as *Trumpets and Raspberries*, 1984.

L'opera dello sghignazzo, with Franca Rame, from a ballad opera by John Gay (produced Teatro Il Fabbricone, Prato, 1981). 1982.

Storia vera di Piero d'Angera: Che alla crociata non c'era (produced Teatro Stabile, Genoa, 1984). 1981.

Una madre (produced 1982). In *Le commedie 8*, 1989; translated as *The Mother*, 1984; as *A Mother*, in *"A Woman Alone" and Other Plays*, 1991.

Fabulazzo osceno, with Franca Rame (monologues; produced Cinema Smeraldo, Milan, 1982). 1982.

Coppia aperta, quasi spalancata, with Franca Rame (produced Teatro Comunale di Monfalcone, Milan, 1983). In *Le commedie 9*, 1991; translated as *The Open Couple*, 1984.

Quasi per caso una donna: Elisabetta (produced Riccione, 1984). In *Ridotto* (Rome), 1984; translated as *Elizabeth: Almost by Chance a Woman*, 1987.

Diario di Eva (produced northern Italy, 1984).

Hellequin, Harlekin, Arlechino (produced Palazzo del Cinema, Venice, 1985).

Una giornata qualunque (produced Teatro Nuovo, Milan, 1986). Translated as *An Ordinary Day*, with *The Open Couple*, 1990.

Il ratto della Francesca (produced Teatro Sloveno, Trieste, 1986). 1986.

[The Barber of Seville], from the opera by Rossini (produced Musiktheater, Amsterdam, 1987).

La parte del Leone (produced Bologna, 1987).

Lettera dalla cina (produced 1989).

Il papa e la strega (produced Italy, 1989). Translated as *The Pope and the Witch*, 1992.

25 monologhi per una donna, with Franca Rame (includes the play-groups *Tutta casa, letto e chiesa; Altre storie; Giullarate religiose; Fabulazioni della resistenza; Discorsi sul terrorismo e la repressione*; produced 1989). In *Le commedie 8*, 1989; all except *Giullarate religiose* translated as *"A Woman Alone" and Other Plays*, 1991.

Zitti! Stiamo precipitando! (produced Italy, 1990).

Johan Padan a la descoverta de le Americhe (produced Italy, 1991). 1991.

Parliamo di donne: L'eroina—grassa e'bello, with Franca Rame (produced Italy, 1991).

Screenplays

Lo svitato, 1956; *Musica per vecchi animali*, 1989.

Television Plays

Monetine da 5 lire, 1956; *Chi l'ha visto?*, 1961; *Il teatro di Dario Fo*, with Franca Rame, 1977; *Parliamo di donne*, 1978; *La professione della Signora Warren*, 1981; *Trasmissione forzata* (variety), 1988; *Una lepre con la faccia da bambina*, with Franca Rame, 1989; *Parti femminili*, 1989; *Promessi sposi*, 1989; *Coppia aperta*, with Franca Rame, 1990; *Settimo ruba un po'meno*, 1991; *Mistero Buffo*, 1991.

Other

Manuale minimo dell'attore. 1987; translated as *The Tricks of the Trade*, 1991.

Dialogo provacatorio sul comico, il tragico, la follia e la ragione (interviews), with Luigi Allegri. 1990.

*

Criticism

Books:

Lanfranco Binni, *Attento te . . .! Il teatro politico di Dario Fo*, Verona, 1975.

Erminia Artese (ed.), *Dario Fo parla di Dario Fo*, Cosenca, 1977.

Lanfranco Binni, *Dario Fo*, Florence, 1977.

Chiara Valentini, *La storia di Fo*, Milan, 1977.

Helga Jungblut, *Das politische Theater Fos*, Frankfurt, 1978.

Claudio Meldolesi, *Su un comico in rivolta: Dario Fo, il bufalo, il bambino*, Rome, 1978.

Paolo Puppa, *Il teatro di Fo: Dalla scena alla piazza*, Venice, 1978.

Tony Mitchell, *Fo: People's Court Jester*, London and New York, 1984; revised edition, 1986.

R.C. McAvoy (ed.), *Dario Fo and Franca Rame: The Theatre Workshops at Riverside Studios*, London, 1983.

David L. Hirst, *Dario Fo and Franca Rame*, London, 1989 (Macmillan Modern Dramatists series).

Tony Mitchell (compiler), *File on Fo*, London, 1989.

Articles:

Suzanne Cowan, "The Throw-Away Theatre of Fo", in *Drama Review*, 1975.

Mimi D'Aponte, "From Italian Roots to American relevance: The Remarkable Theatre of Dario Fo", in *Modern Drama*, 32, 1989.

* * *

Notwithstanding the great presence of Pirandello, modern Italian drama has, in the main, been undistinguished; the strength of Italian theatre today, as invariably in the past, lies in the work of its actors, directors, and designers. In this regard at least, Dario Fo, in his highly individual way, is characteristic of the Italian theatrical tradition: he is performer before he is playwright, a versatile mime, improviser, and satirist, who began his career as a writer and performer in comic sketches and political cabaret, and who remains a director and interpreter of much of his own work. A difficulty, then, in discussing his work, is that Fo the playwright and Fo the performer are inseparable. An allied problem is that Fo has, too, a performer's attitude to text: it is not sacrosanct, but there to serve the needs of performers.

In the late 1950's Fo and his wife, Franca Rame, herself from a family of popular entertainers, formed a company that worked a comic repertory of materials whose inspiration was largely drawn from 19th-century farce and the techniques and strategies of popular street, fair, and club theatre. This traditional popular entertainment, as much of the streets as of the institutional theatre, has remained the dominant influence on Fo's plays and styles of performance. It underpinned the work he did in the 1960's in theatre and television, where he established a national reputation as a writer and performer of satires which were mocking, irreverent, and anarchic, but essentially amiable: pieces like *Aveva due pistole dagli occhi bianchi e neri* (Had Two Pistols with White and Black Eyes), and *Settimo: ruba un po' meno* (Seventh Commandment: Steal a Bit Less).

In the later 1960's, however, his satire became increasingly sharp in its digs at capitalism, imperialism, and the scandals and abuses of a succession of Italian governments, finally leading Fo to abandon what he called his role of jester for the bourgeoisie, and to turn almost wholly to theatre work. He took to this the same armoury of traditional, popular performance means as had served him in television, but along with them an increased appreciation, too, of the ways in which the response of modern audiences had been conditioned by film and television images: if Fo's drama draws on the methods of the *giulliari* and the *commedia dell'arte*, it is no less indebted to film comedians, from Buster Keaton to Jacques Tati, and to television comedy and spectacle. Drawing on a wide variety of comic materials, Fo fashioned an overtly political drama for the two companies which, between them, produced most of his work from the late 1960's through to the mid 1970's, *Nuova Scena* (New Stage), and La Comune. Most of the Fo plays best known to audiences and readers outside Italy were written for one or other of these two companies.

Fo's search for a genuinely political theatre has issued in many formal experiments, all drawing on popular means: quasi-Brechtian didactic pieces like *L'operaio conosce 300 parole, il padrone 1000: Per questo lui è il padrone* (The Worker Knows 300 Words, the Boss 1000: That's Why He's the Boss); pantominic spectaculars like *Grande pantomima*, traditionally structured quasi-naturalistic farces like *Non si paga! Non si paga!* (Can't Pay? Won't Pay!) and one-man *tours de force* like *Mistero Buffo*. This last is one of Fo's most original pieces, crafted in the manner of a medieval morality drama and exploiting the comic techniques of the *guillari*, it provided him with a flexible satirical vehicle with which to address modern Italian social, political, and cultural ills. Some of Fo's best, and more readily transferable, work dramatises topical political issues and seeks to expose the corruption, oppression, and incompetence of bourgeois capitalist government: an obvious instance is his most successful play to date abroad, *Morte accidentale di un anarchico* (*Accidental Death of an Anarchist*), where the satirical edge is the more cutting for the tone of "honest-man" reasonableness that permeates the comic action.

In its appropriation of the voice of the common man for satirical purposes, as well as in the firm social and political stances adopted, and in the delight in farcical extravagance, Fo's work has much in common with the satirical comedy of Aristophanes. Fo is Aristophanic, too, in the way his comic wit works to scourge the arrogance and pomposity of the Italian socio-political establishment and its dependents. He has written more than 40 plays, and in many respects his comedy, by virtue of its topical relevance and the extent to which it is bedded in observation of, and comment on, Italian life, is difficult to translate. But given this specific cultural dependency, a surprisingly large number of the plays has been acted abroad, and some, notably *Morte accidentale*, have been enormously successful. In his best work Fo has put his devastating comic ridicule to the service of an ideological engagement that transcends merely local and national political concerns, and is of universal human relevance: certainly no one in the contemporary theatre has more effectively wedded comedy and savage political comment.

—Laura Richards

See also *Volume 1* entry on *Accidental Death of an Anarchist*.

———————

FONVIZIN, Denis Ivanovich. Born in Moscow, 3 April 1745. Educated at Moscow University Gymnasium, 1755–60; Moscow University, 1760–62. Married Yekaterina Khlopova,

1774. After university, moved to St. Petersburg and entered the civil service: secretary to Ivan Yelagin in the Foreign Ministry, 1763–69, and secretary to the statesman Count Nikita Ivanovich Panin, from 1769; received an estate, 1773; travelled to France and Germany, 1777–78; achieved dramatic success with the St. Petersburg production of *The Minor*; retired from public life, 1783, following the death of Panin (1783) and after incurring the displeasure of Catherine the Great; a founding member of the Russian Academy, 1783; his works temporarily banned in the early 1780's; travelled to Germany and Italy, 1784–85; suffered stroke, 1785; planned to launch a periodical, *Starodum* [Old Thought], which eventually never appeared owing to censorship; travelled to Austria for health reasons, 1786–87. Died in St. Petersburg, 1 December 1792.

Works

Collections

Polnoe sobranie sochineny [Complete Collected Works] (4 vols.). 1830.
Pervoe polnoe sobranie sochineny [Complete Collected Works]. 1888.
Sobranie sochineny [Collected Works] (2 vols.), edited by G. Makogonenko. 1959.
Sochineniya [Works], edited by A.I. Vredinsky. 1983.
The Dramatic Works (includes *The Minor; The Brigadier; The Selection of a Tutor;* and the fragment *A Good Mentor*), translated by Marvin Kantor. 1974.
Komedy. 1976.

Stage Works

Alzir; ili, Amerikantsey [Alzire; or, The Americans], from a play by Voltaire. In *Pervoe polnoe sobranie sochineny*, 1888.
Korion [Korion], from a play by Jean-Baptiste Gresset (produced St. Petersburg, 1764).
Brigadir (produced St. Petersburg, 1780). In *Polnoe sobranie sochineny*, 1830; translated as *The Brigadier*, in *The Literature of Eighteenth-Century Russia 2*, edited by Harold B. Segel, 1968, and in *The Dramatic Works*, 1974.
Nedorosl (produced Knipper's Theatre, St. Petersburg, 1782). 1783; translated as *The Young Hopeful*, in *Masterpieces of the Russian Drama*, edited by G.R. Noyes, 1933; as *The Minor*, in *Anthology of Russian Plays 1*, 1961, and *The Dramatic Works*, 1974; as *The Infant*, in *Four Russian Plays*, translated by J. Coulson, 1972.
Vybor guvernyova (produced 1790). In *Polnoe sobranie sochineny*, 1830; translated as *The Choice of a Tutor*, in *Five Russian Plays with One from the Ukrainian*, edited by C.E.B. Roberts, 1916; as *The Selection of a Tutor*, in *The Dramatic Works*, 1974.

Memoirs and Letters

Lettres de France de D.I. von Vizine à sa soeur à Moscou, edited by E.M. de Vogüé. 1888.

Other

Zhizn grafa N.I. Panina [The Life of Count N.I. Panin]. 1784 (in French); 1786 (in Russian).

Translator, *Basni nravouchitel nye s iz iasnenyami*, from Holberg's fables. 1761; augmented edition, 1765.

Translator, *Geroiskaya dobrodetel; ili, zhizn Sifa* (4 vols.), by Jean Terrasson. 1762–68.
Translator, *Lyubov Karity i Polidora* [The Love of Carita and Polydore], by Jean-Jacques Barthélémy. 1763.
Translator, *Torguyushchee dvorianstvo* [The Commercial Nobility], by Gabriel-François Coyer. 1766.
Translator, *Sidny i Silly* [Sidney and Silly], by François-Thomas Baculard d'Arnaud. 1769.
Translator, *Joseph*, by Paul-Jérémie Bitaube. 1769.
Translator, *Rassuzhdenie o natsionalynom lyubochesty* [An Essay on National Patriotism], by Johann Zimmermann. 1785.

*

Bibliographies

L. Savoj, *Saggio di una bibliografia del Fonvizin*, Rome, 1935.

Criticism

Books:
D. Walsh, *Russian Comedy 1765–1823*, The Hague, 1966.
Alexis Strychek, *Denis Fonvizine*, Paris, 1976.
Charles A. Moser, *Denis Fonvizin*, Boston, 1979.
Simon Karlinsky, *Russian Drama from Its Beginnings to the Age of Pushkin*, Berkeley, California, 1985.

Articles:
M. Kantor, *Fonvizin and Holberg: A Comparison of "The Brigadier" and "Jean de France"*, in *Canadian Slavic Studies*, 7, 1973.

*   *   *

Fonvizin is the only 18th-century Russian writer whose plays are still performed on occasion in the former Soviet Union today. A well-educated, cultured and widely-travelled man, his work as a dramatist was not central to his career, and he always remained something of a dilettante of the theatre. Entering government service after his graduation from university, he spent his leisure time translating from French and German; this gave him a taste for the theatre and provided a good preparation for his own plays. His first attempt in the genre was a Russian version of Gresset's *Sidney* (1764) to which he gave the "Russian" title of *Korion*. It is written in not incompetent verse but is of no great account, although it is an adequate example of the travesty which was very much in vogue at the time.

The Russian theatre before Fonvizin, since its official foundation by Tsar Alexei in 1672, had had a checkered career and produced little of lasting interest. The middle of the 18th century did, however, witness some important developments when some largely original plays in Russian were written (notably by Alexander Sumarokov, albeit in an imitative and neo-classical style), and then, especially during the reign of Catherine the Great, when the theatre was given State support and encouragement.

The high-water-mark of the period is marked by Fonvizin's plays *The Brigadier*, and, especially, *The Minor*, which are undoubtedly the best Russian plays before Griboyedov's *Woe from Wit*. They are both written in prose and follow the rules of neo-classical comedy. They are social satires with a marked didactic element. *The Brigadier* was a notable success when it first appeared at the end of the 1760's. Its plot concerns a young couple whose respective families are meeting in order to get to know one another. The comedy revolves around the two fathers' attempted liaisons with each other's wives, while the young man in question also courts his prospective mother-in-law, thus becoming a rival to his own father. Ultimately, such behaviour is given its just reward and the elders are ridiculed, while the young girl finds her true love in someone else. Thus the sanctity of marriage is upheld and love based on true feeling and respect is encouraged. The main object, though, of Fonvizin's ridicule was the then current "Gallo-mania", especially rife at court and imitated throughout society. Fonvizin was not specifically anti-French but wished his countrymen to show a sense of proportion. The play is amusing in both its action and its dialogue, which was the most natural-sounding yet to be heard on the Russian stage, and is neatly constructed.

Fonvizin's best-known play of the time, and the one for which he is remembered, is *The Minor*, even though it is less well constructed than *The Brigadier*, and is more blatantly didactic and true to the tenets of neo-classicism. It has a pair of virtuous lovers who, although the plot revolves about them, are conventional and uninteresting. The central targets of the satire are the brutal, crude, uneducated, unthinking country landowners and their equally uninspiring entourages of servants and tutors. The negative characters, with hardly a redeeming characteristic among them, are wonderfully comic creations with a language that is lively, idiomatic, and individualized, in stark contrast to the positive and somewhat preaching representatives of the good and true, whose words are stiff and formal. Fonvizin was putting forward the claims of social justice and virtuous behaviour, suggesting they could be achieved through a proper education, with the State doing all it could to foster these attitudes among its citizens. Even Empress Catherine approved of the play, despite some dark hints that Fonvizin had reached the limits of the allowable.

Fonvizin was always interested in political matters and how best society might be organized. In his "Essay on National Patriotism" of 1785 he propounded the idea that to be anything of worth the individual must rise above personal concerns and promote the general good. In the play *Selection of a Tutor*, written in the aftermath of the French Revolution, he developed this idea. Politics, he asserted, is far more complicated than, say, mathematics because in the latter one may go forward from established criteria. Politics is a different matter because it has to deal with questions of freedom and equality and, according to him, the former is far more important, for equality between people is an illusion: one class will always predominate. Consequently he believed that there would always be differences between the various social classes and therefore inequalities between them would always exist. This might well go towards an explanation of his general view that it was not the institutions of Russia that were at fault but their procedures.

Fonvizin also wrote in forms other than the dramatic, most successfully in his "Travel Letters", which originally were, quite literally, his correspondence with his friends. He made two extensive journeys abroad, to France, Germany, and Italy, and his recollections of the countries he visited—a common literary form of the period—are among the best. But his reputation today rests quite justly on his plays.

—A.V. Knowles.

FOOTE, Samuel. Born in Truro, Cornwall, England; baptized 27 January 1721. Educated at Truro Grammar School; Worcester College, Oxford, 1737–40; Inner Temple, London, 1740. Married Mary Hickes in 1741; had two illegitimate sons. Imprisoned for debt in Fleet Prison, London, 1742–43; actor in London, Dublin, and elsewhere, 1744–77; received an inheritance, 1749, and travelled in Europe, 1749–53; operated an unlicensed "lecture" theatre, London, 1759–66; lost a leg in a riding accident, 1766; granted a patent to present a summer theatre season: manager, Theatre Royal, Haymarket London, 1766–77; charged with and acquitted of indecent assault, 1776. Died in Dover, 21 October 1777.

Works

Collections

Dramatic Works (2 vols.).   1809; reprinted, 1963.
Works, edited by John Badcock (3 vols.).   1830.
Plays by Samuel Foote and Arthur Murphy (includes *The Minor; The Nabob*; and three plays by Murphy), edited by George Taylor.   1984.

Stage Works

The Diversions of the Morning (produced Haymarket Theatre, London, 1747; revised versions produced as *A Dish of Chocolate and A Cup of Tea*).   Act 2 of 1758 version in *The Wandering Patentee 4* by Tate Wilkinson, 1795.
An Auction of Pictures (produced Haymarket Theatre, London, 1748).
The Knights (produced Theatre Royal, Drury Lane, London, 1749; revised version produced 1754).   1754.
Taste (produced Theatre Royal, Drury Lane, London, 1752). 1752; revised version (produced 1758 and regularly thereafter), in *Works*, 1830.
An Englishman in Paris (produced Covent Garden Theatre, London, 1753).   1753.
A Writ of Inquiry on the Inquisitor General (produced Haymarket Theatre, London, 1754).
The Englishman Returned from Paris (produced Covent Garden Theatre, London, 1756).   1756.
The Author (produced Theatre Royal, Drury Lane, London, 1757).   1757.
The Minor (produced Haymarket Theatre, London, 1760; revised version produced 1760).   1760.
Tragedy a la Mode (alternative act 2 of *The Diversions of the Morning*) (produced Theatre Royal, Drury Lane, London, 1760; as *Modern Tragedy*, produced 1761).   In *The Wandering Patentee 1* by Tate Wilkinson, 1795; as *Lindamira*, in *Thespian Gleanings* by Thomas Matthews, 1805.
The Liar, from a play by Corneille (produced Covent Garden Theatre, London, 1762).   1764.
The Orators (produced Haymarket Theatre, London, 1762).   1762.
The Young Hypocrite, from a French play.   In *The Comic Theatre*, 1762.
The Mayor of Garret (produced Haymarket Theatre, London, 1763).   1764.
The Trial of Samuel Foote for a Libel on Peter Paragraph (produced Haymarket Theatre, London, 1763).   In *The Wandering Patentee 4* by Tate Wilkinson, 1795.
The Patron (produced Haymarket Theatre, London, 1764).   1764.
The Commissary (produced Haymarket Theatre, London, 1765).   1765.

The Tailors: A Tragedy for Warm Weather (produced 1767). Revised by Colman the Elder, 1778.

An Occasional Prologue (produced Theatre Royal, Haymarket, London, 1767). In *Memoirs of Foote* by William Cooke, 1805.

The Devil upon Two Sticks (produced Theatre Royal, Haymarket, London, 1768). 1778.

The Lame Lover (produced Theatre Royal, Haymarket, London, 1770). 1770.

The Maid of Bath (produced Theatre Royal, Haymarket, London, 1771). 1771; revised version, 1778.

The Nabob (produced Theatre Royal, Haymarket, London, 1772). 1778.

Piety in Pattens (produced Theatre Royal, Haymarket, London, 1773). Edited by Samuel N. Bogorad and Robert G. Noyes, in *Theatre Survey*, Fall 1973.

The Bankrupt (produced Theatre Royal, Haymarket, London, 1773). 1776.

The Cozeners (produced Theatre Royal, Haymarket, London, 1774). 1778.

A Trip to Calais (as *The Capuchin*, produced Theatre Royal, Haymarket, London, 1776). 1778.

Other

A Treatise on the Passions, So Far as They Regard the Stage. 1747.

The Roman and English Comedy Considered and Compared, with Remarks on The Suspicious Husband. 1747.

A Letter to the Author of The Remarks Critical and Christian on The Minor. 1760.

Wilkes: An Oratorio. 1769.

Apology for The Minor, in a Letter to Mr. Baine. 1771.

Editor, *The Comic Theatre* (French plays; 5 vols.). 1762.

*

Criticism

Books:

Percy H. Fitzgerald, *Samuel Foote: A Biography*, London, 1910.

Mary M. Belden, *The Dramatic Work of Samuel Foote* (with bibliography), New Haven, Connecticut, 1929; reprinted 1969.

Gregory Sinko, *Samuel Foote: The Satirist of a Rising Capitalism*, Breslau, 1950.

Simon Trefman, *Samuel Foote, Comedian*, New York, 1971.

Elizabeth N. Chatten, *Samuel Foote*, Boston, 1980.

*   *   *

Samuel Foote was doubly improvident. The wasting of two inheritances caused him to turn to the stage in the first place and, after spending the second in extravagant living in Paris in his late 20's, he returned to London where, by dint of hard work, natural talent, and enterprise, he made a name for himself as an actor, theatre manager, and playwright. Two of his early plays, *An Englishman in Paris* and *The Englishman Returned from Paris*, might, at first sight, seem to stem from that experience, and although the former was suggested by de Boissy's *Frenchman in London* (which Foote may have seen in Paris), it was written to show off the Macklin family, whereas the second was an idea of Arthur Murphy's which Foote plagiarised.

Foote was a remarkably gifted mimic, an excellent comic actor, a capable theatre manager, and a competent playwright. As a dramatist he had a fine turn of satire but his plays depended for their undoubted liveliness in their day on their topical references and on the audience's knowledge of those he mimicked. For example, in *The Minor* he mocked the Methodists and George Whitefield, and in *The Orators* his targets were Thomas Sheridan (Richard Brinsley Sheridan's father) and his lectures.

Despite some good—indeed, some brilliant—moments, his plays lack those qualities that might have enabled them to maintain a place in the repertoire. As Mary Belden puts it, "there was a curious lack of sureness in his literary sense; he recognised easily the germ of popular appeal in a character or an incident, but he seemed to need the public's verdict before he could put the material into an entirely satisfactory form" (*The Dramatic Works of Samuel Foote*). But revision, even to the extent of turning *The Minor* from a two- to a three-act play as a result of its first production in Ireland, was not enough to transform thin plots and repetitive characters into drama of genius. *The Orators* began life as a series of mock lectures in imitation of Sheridan's, and hardly recovers from that, though it is often very amusing, for example in the indictment of Fanny Phantom, a ghost. Excerpts can still work extremely well, but a complete performance is unsustainable.

The Minor illustrates at the extreme the difference between Foote's great success in his day and the unlikelihood of his plays holding the stage in the 20th century. Quite apart from its theatrical success, it sparked off a lengthy controversy in print—pamphlets, verse and prose, dramatic sketches, and correspondence in the press (even John Wesley writing in defence and in explication of Methodism). The story is a rather ramshackle account of the attempt to strip a young man of his inheritance, the youth being himself not particularly likeable, his interests being mainly the less salubrious aspects of life. That he ends up betrothed to Lucy, his cousin, gives little satisfaction. What gave *The Minor* its vitality when first performed was that the models for nearly all the principal characters could be identified. Further, Foote played several parts, including that of Mrs Coles, the bawd, because, as explained in a Prologue in which he appeared as himself, Mrs O'Schohnesy had returned the part because to play it would reflect on her family.

The Liar, based on Corneille's *Le Menteur* (itself drawn from a Spanish original), was frequently revived, at least until the end of the 19th century. It is lively and, as usual with Foote, has its brilliant moments (such as Papillion's description, early in the first scene, of how book reviewers operate). Perhaps the liveliest of Foote's plays, from the point of view of a modern audience, is *The Mayor of Garret*. This play retains its humour, though the mock election it satirises has itself long since been swept away. As often with Foote, two of his favourite butts reappear—Thomas Sheridan as Peter Primmer, a schoolteacher, one of the candidates for Mayor (rejected on the ground that he is Irish), and the Methodists ("what a deal of mischief those rascals do in this country").

If Foote's plays cannot claim a place on the stage today, with the possible exception of *The Mayor of Garret*, he is still worthy of our attention for he had two qualities of lasting significance which have been influential in drama and the theatre. In the first place he had an outstanding gift for breaking and then refashioning dramatic illusion. Second, he stood up to government in a way that greater writers, such as Fielding, failed to.

There are many examples of his breaking dramatic illusion. After Foote had lost a leg when thrown from a horse, he wrote plays for one-legged actors—which, of course, he played—and there are marvellous moments when real life (the fact of his amputation) and dramatic circumstance are both simultaneously "in play", as when, in *The Lame Lover*, Charlotte complains that it would be "A pretty thing truly, for a girl, at my time of life, to be tied to a man with one foot in the grave".

But perhaps most important was the way that Foote refused to be put out of business by the attempts of those (under Sir Robert Walpole) who would restrain dramatic performance. His early "plays", the most ephemeral of all his works, were presented as rehearsals, or sessions for training actors. A kind of revue was offered—but not as a theatrical entertainment. An audience was invited to join Foote in a dish of chocolate or a cup of tea, for a diversion of the morning, so getting around the need to licence performance. If the content was of little moment (though, as ever, there were superb moments), Foote's enterprise in the face of hostile authority is well worthy of being borne in mind.

—Peter Davison

FORD, John.   Born in Ilsington, Devon, England; baptised 17 April 1586. Probably educated at Exeter College, Oxford, 1601–02; Middle Temple, London, 1602–05, 1608–17, but probably never practised law. Some early plays written in collaboration with others, notably Thomas Dekker; wrote for the King's Men and Beeston's Boys in the late 1620's and early 1630's. Died after 1639.

Works

Collections

Works, edited by William Gifford, revised by Alexander Dyce (3 vols.).   1869.
John Ford (includes *The Lover's Melancholy; 'Tis Pity She's a Whore; The Broken Heart; Love's Sacrifice; Perkin Warbeck*), edited by Havelock Ellis.   1888; reprinted, 1957.
Selected Plays (includes *The Broken Heart; 'Tis Pity She's a Whore; Perkin Warbeck*), edited by Colin Gibson.   1986.

Stage Works

The Witch of Edmonton, with Rowley and Dekker (produced by Prince Charles' Men, Cockpit/Phoenix Theatre, London, 1621).   1658.
Perkin Warbeck: A Strange Truth (produced by Queen Henrietta's Men, Cockpit/Phoenix Theatre, London, 1622–33?).   1634.
The Welsh Ambassador, with Dekker (produced c.1623). Edited by H. Littledale and W.W. Greg, 1920.
The Sun's Darling. A Moral Masque, with Dekker (produced by Lady Elizabeth's Men, London, 1624).   1656.
The Broken Heart (produced by the King's Men, London, 1627–33?).   1633.
The Lover's Melancholy (produced by the King's Men, Blackfriars Theatre, London, 1628).   1629.
'Tis Pity She's a Whore (produced by Queen Henrietta's Men, Cockpit/Phoenix Theatre, London, 1629–33?).   1633.

Love's Sacrifice (produced by Queen Henrietta's Men, Cockpit/Phoenix Theatre, London, 1632?).   1633.
The Fancies, Chaste and Noble (produced 1635–36?).   1638.
The Lady's Trial (produced by Beeston's Boys, London, 1638).   1639.
The Queen; or, The Excellency of Her Sex (produced?).   1653.

Verse

Fame's Memorial; or, The Earl of Devonshire Deceased.   1606.
Christ's Bloody Sweat.   1613.

Other

Honour Triumphant; or, The Peers' Challenge.   1606.
The Golden Mean.   1613; revised editions, 1614 and 1638.
A Line of Life, Pointing at the Immortality of a Virtuous Name.   1620.

*

Bibliographies

S.A. Tannenbaum, *John Ford: A Concise Bibliography*, New York, 1914; supplement in *Elizabethan Bibliographies Supplements 8*, by C.A. Pennell and W.P. Williams, London, 1968.
Kenneth Tucker, *A Bibliography of Writings by and About John Ford and Cyril Tourneur*, Boston, 1977.

Criticism

Books:
M.J. Sargeaunt, *John Ford*, Oxford, 1935.
S. Blaine Ewing, *Burtonian Melancholy in the Plays of John Ford*, Princeton, New Jersey, 1940.
George F. Sensabaugh, *The Tragic Muse of John Ford*, Stanford (California), and London, 1944.
R. Davril, *Le Drame de John Ford*, Paris, 1954.
H.J. Oliver, *The Problem of John Ford*, Melbourne, 1955.
Clifford Leech, *John Ford and the Drama of His Time*, London, 1957.
Mark Stavig, *John Ford and the Traditional Moral Order*, Madison (Wisconsin), and London, 1968.
Donald K. Anderson Jr., *John Ford*, New York, 1972.
Tucker Orbison, *The Tragic Vision of John Ford*, Salzburg, 1971.
Florence Ali, *Opposing Absolutes: Conviction and Convention in John Ford's Plays*, Salzburg, 1974.
Ronald Huebert, *John Ford: Baroque English Dramatist*, Montreal, 1977.
Dorothy M. Farr, *John Ford and the Caroline Theatre*, London, 1979.
Ian Robson, *The Moral World of John Ford's Drama*, Salzburg, 1983.
Donald K. Anderson Jr. (ed.), *Concord and Discord: The Plays of John Ford 1586–1986*, New York 1986.
Michael Neill (ed.), *John Ford: Critical Re-Visions*, Cambridge, 1988.

*   *   *

John Ford is generally considered the last great dramatist

of the English Renaissance. Of his eight plays of sole author-ship, three—'Tis Pity She's a Whore, The Broken Heart, and Perkin Warbeck—are major achievements. Ford's strengths include psychological insight, especially into unusual states of mind and feeling, and the ability to create, through his use of multiple plots, the sense of a whole community. In all of his plays Ford experimented with the dramatic forms and con-ventions of his predecessors.

'Tis Pity She's a Whore transforms the star-crossed romance of Romeo and Juliet into the incestuous love of Giovanni and Annabella. Drawing on the conventions of both Jacobean tragedy and city comedy and employing his characteristic multiple-plot structure, Ford has constructed what might be termed a city tragedy. The play's three sub-plots vividly create the society of Parma, which, through its vice and folly, both contributes to the lovers' tragedy and is destroyed with them. Ford's use of incest is not merely a piece of decadent sensationalism, as early critics believed, but, as a transgression of divine law and social inhibition, the basis for the play's metaphysical, psychological, and sociological complexity.

If in 'Tis Pity Ford manipulates the conventions and motifs of his predecessors to extraordinarily original ends, The Broken Heart is the least derivative of Ford's tragedies, though even in this play Ford has reworked earlier dramatic situations for his own purposes. For example, Calantha's refusal to interrupt her dance when she receives news of three deaths echoes a similar situation in Marston's The Malcontent, though to very different effect. The Broken Heart's unusual Spartan setting provides the play with its unifying theme and structure. The main characters, who have been variously pursuing their goals of love or vengeance, are united by their ritualistic deaths as sacrifices that symbolically enable the preservation of the Spartan aristocratic code of behaviour and of the state itself. Princess Calantha's death, in particular ("They are the silent griefs which cut the heart-strings; / Let me die smiling") underscores the Spartan ideal of the repression of self for the sake of public duty.

The scope of Love's Sacrifice is narrower than that of the other two tragedies. In this play Ford unsuccessfully com-bines Shakespearean and Fletcherian models of tragedy, a version of Othello with an emotionally convoluted tale of Platonic lovers. Though determining to be chaste, the lovers, Biancha and Fernando, behave amorously and are reported by D'Avolos, the Iago-figure, to Biancha's husband, who, Othello-like, kills his wife and then, upon discovering her innocence, himself. The psychological interest of the play lies in Biancha's self-temptations and increasingly rash ex-pressions of affection for Fernando, but Ford's blending of the Fletcherian psychological tragedy of sex with a clever adaptation of Othello—the wife is guilty in spirit if not in fact—blurs moral issues and makes it difficult to take any of the characters' dilemmas seriously.

For Perkin Warbeck Ford looked back to the English his-tory plays of the 1590's, especially Richard II. Like Shakespeare, Ford contrasts different styles of kingship: the chivalrous, poetic, ineffectual Pretender, Perkin; slippery, dishonest, showy James of Scotland; and successful, pragma-tic, Machiavellian Henry VII. In making Perkin a pretender who never admits that he is not the rightful king and who may, indeed, believe in his supposed identity, Ford adds a further metatheatrical and psychological dimension to Shakespeare's exploration of kingly role-playing.

Ford's four plays that end happily can be distinguished as romantic tragicomedies (The Lover's Melancholy and The Queen) and serious comedies (The Fancies, Chaste and Noble and The Lady's Trial). The finest of these plays is The Lover's

Melancholy, which deals in the manner of Shakespeare's romances with the tragic experience of loss subsumed in the joy of reunion—the restoration of Eroclea to her suffering lover and father. The Queen is more like Fletcherian tragico-medy, constructed to produce its happy ending by averting the danger of death (three times). In both The Lover's Melancholy and The Queen Ford draws on Robert Burton's psychological work The Anatomy of Melancholy for some of his characters' mental afflictions and their cures.

The Fancies and The Lady's Trial are less exotic in their action and more ordinary in their urban environments than the tragicomedies. The Lady's Trial presents yet another version of Othello. This time the wife is virtuous, the infor-mant genuinely mistaken, and the husband trusting in his wife's honesty. Ford handles Auria and Spinella's resolution of their marital difficulty with delicacy and discrimination. The Fancies is Ford's worst play. The main plot toys with the audience, making us suppose that the heroine, Castamela, is in real danger of abuse by the elderly Octavio when, in fact, the ladies in his bower of fancies turn out to be his nieces. Only one of the two subplots is interesting. In it Ford nicely captures the feelings of a woman who has been sold by her husband to a richer man, again displaying his ability to pres-ent with delicacy and psychological acuity a character who is in an unusual situation.

Ford's fondness for multiple plotting assists him, in 'Tis Pity and The Lady's Trial, for example, in creating coherent social communities whose values impinge on the actions of the protagonists, but it can also lead him into tediousness. Ford's attempts at low comedy, in particular, are rarely suc-cessful. The superb Bergetto subplot in 'Tis Pity, which com-bines farce and pathos, is exceptional in Ford's plays.

In his best plays, and at times in his weaker ones, Ford displays a mastery of blank verse that can be either lyrical or incisively expressive of a character's state of mind. He has an eye, too, for the striking and symbolically significant stage image—Calantha's uninterrupted dance, Annabella's heart impaled on Giovanni's dagger. Though most of Ford's plays are no longer performed, there have been 20th-century pro-ductions of The Broken Heart and Perkin Warbeck, while the frequent stagings of 'Tis Pity She's a Whore testify to the dramatic excellence of Ford's best-known play.

—Verna A. Foster

See also Volume 1 entries on The Broken Heart; 'Tis Pity She's a Whore; The Witch of Edmonton.

FORNÉS, María Irene. Born in Havana, Cuba, 14 May 1930; emigrated to USA, 1945: became citizen, 1951. Educated in Havana public schools. Lived in Europe, 1954–57; painter and textile designer, New York, 1957–60; costume designer, Judson Poets Theatre and New Dramatists Committee productions, 1965–70; teacher and collaborator with the Teachers and Writers Collaborative (New York), the Theatre for the New City (New York), 1972–73, Padua Hills Festival (Claremont, California), from 1978, International Arts Relations [INTAR], from 1981, and various workshops at universities and other institutions; co-founder and President, New York Theatre Strategy, 1973–80. Recipient of several awards and fellowships, including: Obie Award, 1965,

1977, 1979, 1982, 1984, 1985, 1988; American Academy Award, 1985.

Works

Collections

"Promenade" and Other Plays (includes *Tango Palace; The Successful Life of Three; A Vietnamese Wedding; Dr. Kheal; The Red Burning Light; Molly's Dream*) 1971; revised edition, 1987.
Plays (includes *Mud; The Danube; Sarita; The Conduct of Life*). 1986.

Stage Works

The Widow (produced Actors' Studio, New York, 1961). As *La Viuda*, in *Teatro Cubano* (Havana), 1961.
Tango Palace (as *There! You Died*, produced Actors' Workshop, San Francisco, 1963; as *Tango Palace*, produced Actors' Studio, New York, 1964; revised version produced Firehouse Theatre, Minneapolis, 1965). In *"Promenade" and Other Plays*, 1971.
The Successful Life of Three: A Skit for Vaudeville (produced Firehouse Theatre, Minneapolis, 1965). In *"Promenade" and Other Plays*, 1971.
Promenade, music by Al Carmines (produced Judson Poets Theatre, New York, 1965; revised version produced Promenade Theatre, New York, 1969). In *"Promenade" and Other Plays*, 1971.
The Office (produced Henry Miller's Theatre, New York, 1966).
A Vietnamese Wedding (produced Washington Square Methodist Church, New York, 1967). In *"Promenade" and Other Plays*, 1971.
The Annunciation (produced Judson Poets Theatre, New York, 1967).
Dr. Kheal (produced Judson Poets Theatre, New York, 1968). In *"Promenade" and Other Plays*, 1971.
The Red Burning Light; or, Mission XQ3 (produced Open Theatre, Zurich, 1968; La Mama Experimental Theatre, New York, 1969). In *"Promenade" and Other Plays*, 1971.
Molly's Dream, music by Cosmos Savage (produced Boston University Workshop, Lenox, Massachusetts, 1968). In *"Promenade" and Other Plays*, 1971.
The Curse of the Langston House, in *Baboon!!!* (produced Playhouse in the Park, Cincinnati, 1972).
Dance, with Remy Charlip (produced London, 1972).
Aurora, music by John FitzGibbon (produced Riverside Church, New York, 1974).
Cap-a-Pie, music by José Raúl Bernardo (produced by INTAR, New York, 1975).
Lines of Vision (lyrics only), book by Richard Foreman, music by George Quincy (produced New York, 1976).
Washing (produced New York, 1976).
Fefu and Her Friends (produced by New York Theatre Strategy, New York, 1977). In *Wordplays 1*, 1980.
Lolita in the Garden, music by Richard Weinstock (produced by INTAR, New York, 1977).
In Service (produced Padua Hills Festival, Claremont, California, 1978).
Eyes on the Harem (produced by INTAR, New York, 1979).
Blood Wedding, from a play by García Lorca (produced by INTAR, New York, 1980).
Evelyn Brown: A Diary (produced Theatre for the New City, New York, 1980).
Life is Dream, from a play by Calderón, music by George Quincy (produced by INTAR, New York, 1981).
A Visit, music by George Quincy (produced Padua Hills Festival, Claremont, California, 1981).
The Danube (produced Padua Hills Festival, Claremont, California, 1982). In *Plays*, 1986.
Mud (produced Padua Hills Festival, Claremont, California, 1983; revised version produced Omaha, 1985). In *Plays*, 1986.
Sarita, music by Leon Odenz (produced by INTAR, New York, 1984). In *Plays*, 1986.
Abingdon Square (produced Seattle, Washington, 1984).
No Time (produced Padua Hills Festival, Claremont, California, 1984).
The Conduct of Life (produced Theatre for the New City, New York, 1985). In *Plays*, 1986.
Cold Air, from a play by Virgilio Piñera (produced by INTAR, New York, 1985).
Drowning, from a story by Chekhov, in *Orchards* (produced Urbana, Illinois, 1985). 1986.
The Trial of Joan of Arc on a Matter of Faith (produced New York, 1986).
Lovers and Keepers, music by Tito Puente and Ferrando Rivas, lyrics by Fornés (produced by INTAR, New York, 1986).
Art. In *Box Plays* (produced Theatre for the New City, New York, 1986).
The Mothers (produced Padua Hills Festival, Claremont, California, 1986; as *Charlie*, produced as part of *And What of the Night*, Milwaukee Repertory, Milwaukee, Wisconsin, 1989).
Uncle Vanya, from a play by Chekhov (produced by the Classic Stage Company, New York, 1987).
Hunger (produced by En Garde Productions, New York, 1989).
And What of the Night (includes *Hunger; Springtime; Lust; Charlie*; produced Milwaukee Repertory, Milwaukee, Wisconsin, 1989).

*

Criticism

Books:
Bonnie Marranca, "The Real Life of María Irene Fornés" in *Theatre Writings*, New York, 1984.
Gayle Austin, "The Madwoman in the Spotlight: The Plays of María Irene Fornés", in *Making a Spectacle: Feminist Essays on Contemporary Women's Theatre*, Ann Arbor, Michigan, 1989.

Articles:
Bonnie Marranca and María Irene Fornés, "Interview", in *Performing Arts Journal*, vol.2 no.3, 1978.
Lurana D. O'Malley, "Pressing Clothes/ Snapping Beans/ Reading Books: María Irene Fornés Women's Work", in *Studies in American Drama 1945–Present*, 4, 1989.
Deborah R. Geis, "Wordscapes of the Body: Performative Language as *Gestus* in María Irene Fornés' Plays", in *Theatre Journal*, 42, 1990.

* * *

María Irene Fornés is one of the most prolific and bold playwrights in contemporary American theatre, with a voice that expresses uniquely her Caribbean roots and her experimental aesthetic. In a career that spans nearly 30 years, Fornés has created a large and multi-textured body of work. A self-taught emigrée from Cuba who lives and writes in the United States, she is committed to a theatre in which modernist experiments in form and language are inextricably intertwined with questions of politics and philosophy: in short those central questions "about . . . the conduct of life" (Susan Sontag, Preface to *María Irene Fornés: Plays*). The issues she grapples with are political in the broadest sense of the word. The questions animating her plays are nothing less than the origin of evil and the site of salvation, the nature of societies and of the individual soul.

From Isidore's bullfight with Leopold in *Tango Palace* to Mae's murder in *Mud*, Fornés' plays locate themselves at that place where the mystery of the human condition and the enigma of human relationships reveal themselves in sudden, elusive, and often violent spasms. Desire and fear form the poles of the complex universe she recreates in her work. It is a world where lovers and cripples, convicts and dictators struggle to articulate themselves. It is a world where the threat of torture, rape, and nuclear war are palpable constants. And yet it is also a world of slapstick, dancing, and song.

Fornés' 1965 play *Promenade* embodies many of the functional paradoxes of her work. From the plaintive cries of the Mother who has lost her babies to the Ionesco-inspired hilarity of Miss I, O, U and Mr. R, S, T, tragedy mingles with comedy, and fear rubs up against desire. At that point where these oppositions meet and bleed into one another is that moment of instant, inexplicable revelation. Whether it be that moment when the gunshot sounds and Julia falls in *Fefu and Her Friends* or the sudden bright light of a nuclear holocaust at the close of *The Danube*, Fornés' plays find meaning in that moment when the disparate and seemingly irreconcilable collide and fuse in an unexpected marriage. The union is at once beautiful and horrific, like a Goya painting where ivory-skinned maidens and bug-eyed devils dance side by side.

Fornés' theatre borrows from traditions and conventions outside of theatre, weaving them together with dramatic forms to create works that are vibrant and multi-faceted responses to a contemporary world. She began her career not as a playwright, but as a painter. Over and over again, this early training in painting is evident in her written work. Her conception of time and space alludes to both cubist and surrealist traditions. Modernist experiments from Braque and Picasso onwards shaped her conception of fractured narrative as well as shifting character. Like the room in *Tango Palace* with its whip, toy parrot, and "two masks in the form of beetles' faces", where "an androgynous clown" and "an earnest youth" engage in mortal combat, the dramatic situations of most of Fornés' work are warped and dream-like, peppered with vivid, mysterious images. Like the instantaneous jump cuts across years and locations in *The Successful Life of Three*, the transitions and movements across time are disjunctive, subject to conflation, expansion and unexpected upheaval, echoing not only cubism and surrealism, but also the neo-expressionist experiments in representing a lived reality on canvas. From her beginnings in the Judson Poet Theatre in the early 1960's to her recent work at INTAR where she writes, directs, and teaches a new generation of Hispanic-American playwrights, Fornés is engaged in the constant stretching of dramatic form. Whether it be the freeze frames

of *Mud* or the musical interludes of *Sarita*, the result is a dramatic synthesis of genres ranging from poetry and painting to music and film.

Despite their varied influences from other art forms, Fornés' plays are very much of and about theatre. Indeed, her work is informed by an acute awareness of the context and constraints of theatre—the frame of the black box, the fact of live performers, the effect of light and sound within a confined space and within a delimited period of time. In almost all of her work there is an aspect of ritual as though Fornés were trying to get at some essential underpinning in the theatrical experience. In some instances, the component of ritual is explicit, as in *A Vietnamese Wedding*, an actual re-enactment of the marriage ceremony involving audience and actors alike. Yet even when ritual plays a less explicit role, primal relationships and essential conflicts animate Fornés' drama. The struggle between dominant and submissive, male and female, teacher and student—these are the operative power dynamics that fuel the action of her plays.

Whether the play is a dissection of a love triangle, as in *Mud* and *The Successful Life of Three*, or the examination of women's lives, as in *Sarita* and *Fefu and Her Friends*, Fornés' gift is to strip away the surface peculiarities layer by layer until she reaches the bedrock conflicts structuring individual human lives. Her work detects and dramatizes these universals. Beneath the specifics of gender, race, and social class, Fornés' characters are archetypes fated to act the way they do with an almost primitive, unwavering, unavoidable necessity. Whether it is the mad savant in *Dr. Kheal* who is compelled to articulate, with compulsive detail, his theory of the universe to an audience of strangers and skeptics, or the tragic Fefu who shoots and kills her weaker friend, Julia, a casualty of years of misogyny and abuse as much as of a single bullet, Fornés' characters move with the fatalism of characters from a classical Greek drama. Their expressions of love, their violent explosions aimed at one another and at circumstance, and the sudden silence following their extinction, represent the rituals of living where struggle and loss are necessary trials in some mysterious initiation.

—Naomi Iizuka

FORTE, Dieter. Born in Düsseldorf, Germany, 14 June 1935. Trained in business and commerce. Worked first as photographer, painter, and advertising consultant; began working in theatre in the early 1960's; employed at NDR television, 1960–63; subsequently a freelance writer, living in Düsseldorf; first-broadcast radio play, *Die Wand*, produced 1965; first-produced stage play, *Martin Luther und Thomas Münzer; oder, Die Einführung der Buchhaltung*, performed 1970; resident playwright at the Basler Theater, Basle, 1971–75; based in Basle since 1971. Recipient: Gerhard Grünholz Prize, 1968.

Works

Collections

Fluchtversuche: 4 Fernsehspiele (includes the television plays *Sonntag; Achsensprung; Gesundheit!; Der Aufstieg: Ein Mann geht verloren*). 1980.

Stage Works

Martin Luther und Thomas Münzer; oder, Die Einführung der Buchhaltung (produced Basler Theater, Basle, 1970). 1971, translated as *Luther, Münzer, and the Bookkeepers of the Reformation*, 1973.
Weisse Teufel, from a play by John Webster (produced Basler Theater, Basle, 1972).
Cenodoxus, from a work by Jakob Bidermann (produced Festspiele, Salzburg, 1972).
Jean Henry Dunant; oder, Die Einführung der Zivilisation (produced Staatstheater, Darmstadt, 1978).   1978.
Kaspar Hausers Tod (produced Hessisches Staatstheater, Wiesbaden, 1979).   1979.
Das Labyrinth der Träume; oder, Wie man den Kopf vom Körper trennt (produced Basler Theater, Basle, 1983). 1983.
Der Artist im Moment seines Absturzes.   1988.

Television Plays

Nachbarn, 1970; *Sonntag*, 1975 (published in *Fluchtversuche*, 1980); *Achsensprung*, 1977 (published in *Fluchtversuche*, 1980); *Gesundheit!*, 1979 (published in *Fluchtversuche*, 1980); *Der Aufstieg: Ein Mann geht verloren*, 1980 (published in *Fluchtversuche*, 1980).

Radio Plays

Die Wand, 1965 (published 1973); *Porträt eines Nachmittags* 1965 (published 1973); *Bergerstrasse 8* broadcast 1967; *Sprachspiel: Ein Kommunikationstraining*, 1980 (published 1981); *Wach auf, wach auf, du deutsches Land*, 1983; *Martin Luther und Thomas Münzer*, 1983; *Schalltoter Raum*, 1984; *Die eingebildeten Gesunden; oder, Die Fahrt nach Jerusalem*, 1987.

*

Criticism

Articles:
Georg Hensel, "Dieter Forte : Das dämonisierte Portemonnaie", in his *Theater der Zeitgenossen: Stücke und Autoren*, 1972.
Guy Stern, "*Luther, Münzer, and the Bookkeepers of the Reformation*—or, the Difficulties of Writing Historical Truth", in *Michigan Germanic Studies*, 10, 1984.

* * *

After an apprenticeship in radio, Forte achieved a sensational success with his controversial first stage-drama, *Martin Luther und Thomas Münzer; oder, die Einführung der Buchhaltung* (*Luther, Münzer, and the Bookkeepers of the Reformation*), in 1970. This montage of 82 short scenes was produced on some of the most prestigious German stages, and was voted joint "play of the year" by the jury of the authoritative theatre journal *Theater heute*. Forte was universally hailed as a major new talent. His subsequent works, however, have not been able to emulate this initial success.

In the 1970's, while the German stage was dominated by the neo-realistic popular dramas of Kroetz and the emerging post-modernism of Handke, Bernhard, and Strauss, Forte turned to the reconstruction of history for his plays. In keeping with the intellectual climate in the aftermath of the 1968 unrest, he engaged in a radically materialistic reinterpretation of the past with a view to a critical illumination of the present.

Martin Luther, conceived in the spirit of documentary theatre, remains an impressive example of the subversive potential of theatre which challenges established ideologies. Thoroughly researched and, according to its author, factually accurate, it amounts to nothing less than a scurrilous deconstruction of the Luther figure, a polemical reassessment of the entire Reformation period. As its subtitle suggests, the play bypasses the abstract theological basis of Luther's conflict with the Church of Rome, and seeks to establish a purely political and economic causation behind events. Through the character of the omnipotent financier, Fugger, a connection is drawn between the Reformation and early monopoly capitalism. Luther is no longer the autonomous man of conscience, but the servile and corrupt lackey of his secular and ecclesiastical masters. He attacks the Catholic trade in indulgences not out of religious conviction, but on the instruction of his paymasters, and produces theses to order. Religion is degraded to an instrument of power politics. The positive counterbalance to the opportunist Luther in the play is the social-revolutionary Münzer, a hero of the 1968 movement. At the end of the play, as Münzer is executed, Luther, Fugger, and the Princes pray to their new god: capital.

The extraordinary success of Forte's first play was due no doubt in part to the controversy it aroused, which was reminiscent of that surrounding Hochhuth's *Der Stellvertreter* seven years earlier. But the play is theatrically very effective and shows, in its dialogue, exceptional wit and ingenuity. In his concern to amplify the topical relevance of his historical material, Forte employs blatant anachronisms and heavy irony, mixing historically authentic passages with 1970's slang and jargon. Despite its great length and, at times, somewhat clichéed schematism, it remains a fascinating experiment in political theatre.

In subsequent works Forte has continued to explore the mechanics of bourgeois ideology, power, and exploitation through a re-examination of history, with clearly didactic intentions. None of his later works, though, has been able to establish itself on the stage.

Jean Henry Dunant; oder, Die Einführung der Zivilisation offers, through its loose plot based on the career of its eponymous hero, the founder of the Red Cross, a panoramic view of the 19th century. Character psychology, by which Forte, on the whole, sets little store, is again sacrificed to the demonstration of ideas, as the economic, political, and intellectual forces of the age are unfolded. Dunant's humanitarian mission is hijacked by the military apparatus of the modern imperialist state, his idealism crushed by the purely economic interests of an immoral and dehumanized machine. He is dumped unceremoniously and ends up penniless. The ironic subtitle points to the process of history as Forte sees it: a relentless movement away from civilized values.

A similar denunciation of bourgeois capitalist society is evident in *Kaspar Hausers Tod*. This short, and much more strictly controlled, play uses the murder, in 1833, of its titular hero, the famed foundling of Nuremberg, as the focal point for an analysis of the reactionary politics of post-Napoleonic Germany, again intended as an analogue of modern West-German society. Peter Handke, in 1968, had exploited the Kaspar Hauser legend as an abstract metaphor for the manipulative power of language. Forte's play, typically, is historically more specific and politically explicit. Metternich's regime, with its repression and censorship, is seen to lead to profound insecurity and alienation among the liberal bourgeoisie. The Hauser story stands as a testimony to the perversity of both the Biedermeier age and the modern one. While the activities of political dissenters (such as Feuerbach's son) are declared taboo, the uneducated Hauser becomes a folk-hero.

After these materialistic reinterpretations of historical material (and, indeed, of older dramatic texts in *Weisse Teufel* and *Cenodoxus*), Forte turned to the world of imagination for his next play, *Das Labyrinth der Träume; oder, Wie man den Kopf vom Körper trennt*. This work represents a new departure in as far as it moves away from the preoccupation with carefully documented socio-economic analysis towards a visionary exploration of individual and collective consciousness. It is, in Forte's own words, "a nocturnal play about the inner world of Man". But Forte's underlying concern with the relationship between the aberrations of the past and the present (in this case fascism) is evident here, too. The careers of Adolf Hitler and the mass murderer Peter Kürten are juxtaposed in an effort to demonstrate the perversity of popular reaction to pathological evil: while Kürten was demonized, Hitler was greeted as a messiah. At the centre of Forte's labyrinth is the evil in man, held in check by a veneer of civilization, but always ready to re-emerge when reason is suspended.

—David Horton

FRAYN, Michael.   Born in Mill Hill, London, 8 September 1933. Educated at Sutton High School for Boys; Kingston Grammar School, Surrey; Emmanuel College, Cambridge, BA 1957. Served in the Royal Artillery and Intelligence Corps, 1952–54. Married Gillian Palmer in 1960 (divorced 1990), three daughters. Reporter, 1957–59, and columnist, 1959–62, the *Guardian*, Manchester and London; columnist, the *Observer*, London, 1962–68. Recipient: Maugham Award, 1966; Society of West End Theatre award, 1977, 1982; British Theatre Association Award, 1981, 1983; Olivier Award, 1985; New York Drama Critics Circle Award, 1986; Emmy Award, 1990. Honorary Fellow, Emmanuel College, 1985.

Works

Collections

Plays 1 (includes *Alphabetical Order; Donkeys' Years; Clouds; Make and Break; Noises Off*). 1986.
Plays 2 (includes *Benefactors; Balmoral; Wild Honey*). 1992.

Stage Works

Zounds!, with John Edwards, music by Keith Statham (produced Cambridge, 1957).
The Two of Us (includes *Black and Silver; The New Quixote; Mr. Foot; Chinamen;* produced Garrick Theatre, London, 1970). 1970.
The Sandboy (produced Greenwich Theatre, London, 1971).
Alphabetical Order (produced Hampstead Theatre, London, 1975). With *Donkeys' Years*, 1977.
Donkeys' Years (produced Globe Theatre, London, 1976). With *Alphabetical Order*, 1977.

Michael Frayn

Clouds (produced Hampstead Theatre, London, 1976). 1977.
The Cherry Orchard, from the play by Chekhov (produced National Theatre London, 1978). 1978.
Balmoral (produced Guildford, Surrey, 1978; revised version, as *Liberty Hall*, produced Greenwich Theatre, London, 1980; revised version, as *Balmoral*, produced Bristol, 1987). 1987.
The Fruits of Enlightenment, the play play by Tolstoy (produced National Theatre, London, 1979).
Make and Break (produced Lyric Theatre, Hammersmith, London, 1980). 1980.
Noises Off (produced Lyric Theatre, Hammersmith, London, 1981). 1982.
Three Sisters, from the play by Chekhov (produced Royal Exchange Theatre, Manchester, 1985). 1983.
Benefactors (produced Vaudeville Theatre, London, 1984). 1884.
Wild Honey, from a play by Chekhov (produced National Theatre, London, 1984). 1984.
Number One, from a play by Anouilh (produced Queen's Theatre, London, 1984).
The Seagull, from the play by Chekhov (produced Palace Theatre, Watford, Hertfordshire, 1986). 1986.
Uncle Vanya, from the play by Chekhov (produced Vaudeville Theatre, London, 1988). 1987.
The Sneeze, from works by Chekhov (produced Newcastle-upon-Tyne, 1988. 1989.
Exchange, from a play by Yuri Trifonov (produced Southampton, Hampshire, 1989). 1990.

Look Look (produced as *Spettattori*, Rome, 1989; as *Look Look*, produced London, 1990).   1990.
Here (produced Donmar Warehouse, London, 1993).   1993.

Screenplays

Clockwise, 1986 (published 1986).

Television Plays (and documentaries)

Second City Reports, with John Bird, 1964; *Jamie, on a Flying Visit*, 1968 (published with *Birthday*, 1990); *One Pair of Eyes*, 1968; *Birthday*, 1969 (published with *Jamie, on a Flying Visit*, 1990); *Beyond a Joke* series, with John Bird and Eleanor Bron, 1972; *Laurence Sterne Lived Here* (*Writers' Houses* series), 1973; *Imagine a City Called Berlin*, 1975; *Making Faces*, 1975; *Vienna: The Mask of Gold*, 1977; *Three Streets in the Country*, 1979; *The Long Straight* (*Great Railway Journeys of the World* series), 1980; *Jerusalem*, 1984; *First and Last*, 1989 (published 1989).

Radio Plays

Exchange, from a play by Yuri Trifonov, 1986.

Fiction

The Tin Men.   1965.
The Russian Interpreter.   1966.
Towards the End of the Morning.   1967; as *Against Entropy*, 1967.
A Very Private Life.   1968.
Sweet Dreams.   1973.
The Trick of It.   1989.
A Landing in the Sun.   1991.

Other

The Day of the Dog (*Guardian* columns).   1962.
The Book of Fub (*Guardian* columns).   1963; as *Never Put Off to Gomorrah*, 1964.
On the Outskirts (*Observer* columns).   1967.
At Bay in Gear Street (*Observer* columns).   1967.
Constructions (philosophy).   1974.
Great Railway Journeys of the World, with others.   1981.
The Original Michael Frayn: Satirical Essays, edited by James Fenton.   1983.

Editor, *The Best of Beachcomber*, by J.B. Morton.   1963.

Translator, *Plays*, by Chekhov.   1988.

*

Criticism

Books:
Albert R. Glaap, "Order and Disorder on Stage and in Life: Farce majeure in Frayn's Plays", in *Studien zur Ästhetik des Gegenwartstheaters*, edited by Christian W. Thomsen, Heidelberg, 1985.

*   *   *

As with many British mainstream writers of his generation, Frayn's earliest stage writing consisted of short sketches for the sort of revue that was so prevalent in the 1950's and early 1960's prior to the success of *Beyond the Fringe*. Indeed, his first full-length presentation, *The Two of Us* consisted of four short two-handers linked largely by the use of the same two actors throughout—Lynn Redgrave and Richard Briers in the original production. Frayn first achieved real success on stage, however, in 1975 with *Alphabetical Order*, a witty comedy in which the mechanics of farce are directly linked to the narrative thread of attempts to maintain order in a newspaper cuttings library. His use of his own journalistic experience was more seriously in evidence in *Clouds* of the following year, in which he drew directly from a professional visit to Cuba.

A mild flirtation with global political issues is to be found in a number of his plays, including *Balmoral* (and in a slightly revised version as *Liberty Hall*). This play is set in a Britain in which World War II has been averted because the country has become a Soviet satellite state. The royal palace of Balmoral has become a state home for authors, among whom are to be found Enid Blyton and Godfrey Winn, and Frayn is able to play fairly harmlessly with a rather jokey debate about the comparative attractions of communism and capitalism. Generally, Frayn has seemed at his best when he has concentrated on the mechanics of the plot rather than on any particularly serious attempt to invest it with any great depth of meaning, and in this way he has become one of the most successful providers of material for the serious end of London's West End theatres, as just one of the extremely mixed stable of talents brought together by the important impresario Michael Codron (for whom he produced the screenplay for *Clockwise*, starring John Cleese, in 1986).

Undoubtedly, his most successful play has been *Noises Off*, the three acts of which move from onstage, to behind stage, to onstage again, while a parody of a dreadful farcical romp moves from dress rehearsal into performance. The problems of the performed piece, *Nothing On*, are revealed as nothing compared to those of the actors attempting to fulfil the obligations of the seasonal run in the teeth of rapidly disintegrating, and no less farcically treated, personal lives.

Frayn has more recently followed this popularly light-hearted bow towards Pirandello's "box of tricks" with another play in which the theatre becomes the subject of, as well as the venue for, the performance—*Look Look*. The first act places the action and the drama within an actual theatre audience watching a play, and then, in a similar reversal to that offered in *Noises Off*, the second act places the real audience (us) behind the back of the stage to watch the play that the other audience is supposedly watching. There was a grave suspicion that what had been offered fairly frivolously in the earlier play was now turning into a rather more philosophical debate and the play flopped commercially.

Elsewhere Frayn had already shown an interest in a discussion that was apparently more political in its location. In *Make and Break* there is the usual West End box-set, consisting of walls and doors, all of which are movable. The action is located on and around a trade stand at an international exhibition, and the movable set is both the product to be sold and the source of much comic business. That the action should culminate in the revelation of the corpse of a dead salesman from behind a revolving wall might suggest the possibility of some questioning of the values of a consumerist society; but Frayn is at pains to prevent the process being pushed too far. As he said, "Could anyone really think I am advocating a world without walls and doors? . . . [my] plays are attempts to show something about the world, not to change it or to promote any particular idea of it".

Benefactors represents something of a development, in

that, although ultimately still relying on its wit to retain audience interest, it also presents an authorial voice prepared to discuss serious social issues. The action involves the tangled relationships between two married couples during the protracted efforts to build a massive high-rise building development in the face of an opposition that, significantly, never includes any of the people who might be affected by the plans. Instead the play relies on the potential for heterosexual permutations between the two couples, given the added bite that one husband is the architect of the plan and the other becomes its chief opposer.

Despite his immense popularity, possibly only second to Ayckbourn amongst contemporaries, Frayn has yet to make the transition from commercial to subsidised theatre made by Ayckbourn—except as a translator whose main interest lies in a Chekhov whose bitter-sweet comic voice has yet to find a real counterpart in his own work.

—John Bull

FRENCH, David. Born in Coley's Point, Newfoundland, Canada, 18 January 1939. Educated at Harbord Collegiate High School; Oakwood Collegiate High School, Toronto, graduated 1958; studied acting at Al Saxe Studio, Toronto, 1958, Pasadena Playhouse, California, 1959, and Lawlor School of Acting, Toronto, 1960. Married Leslie Grey in 1978. Actor in Toronto, 1960–65; post-office worker, 1971–72; first play, *Leaving Home*, produced 1972. Recipient: Chalmers Award, 1973; Lieutenant-Governor's Award, 1974; Dora Award, 1985; Canadian Authors Association Award, 1986.

Works

Stage Works

Leaving Home (produced Tarragon Theatre, Toronto, 1972). 1972.
Of the Fields, Lately (produced Tarragon Theatre, Toronto, 1973). 1973.
One Crack Out (produced Tarragon Theatre, Toronto, 1975). 1975.
The Seagull, from the play by Chekhov (produced Tarragon Theatre, Toronto, 1977). 1977.
Jitters (produced Tarragon Theatre, Toronto, 1979). 1980.
The Riddle of the World (produced Tarragon Theatre, Toronto, 1981).
Salt-Water Moon (produced Tarragon Theatre, Toronto, 1984). 1985.
1949 (produced Tarragon Theatre, Toronto, 1988).

Television Plays

Beckons the Dark River, 1963; *The Willow Harp*, 1964; *A Ring for Florrie*, 1964; *After Hours*, 1964; *Sparrow on a Monday Morning*, 1966 (USA); *A Token Gesture*, 1970; *A Tender Branch*, 1972; *The Happiest Man in the World*, from a short story by Hugh Garner, 1972; scripts for *Razzle Dazzle* children's series.

Radio Plays

Angeline, 1967; *Invitation to a Zoo*, 1967; *Winter of Timothy*, 1968.

*

Criticism

Articles:
Anne Nothof, "David French and the Theatre of Speech", in *Canadian Drama*, 13, 1987.
Brian F. Tyson, "'Swallowed Up in Darkness': Vision and Division in *Of the Fields, Lately*", in *Canadian Drama*, 16, 1990.

*   *   *

David French is regarded by many as one of Canada's most significant playwrights. While not a technical innovator, he is a meticulous craftsman with considerable poetic gifts, and is often credited with the establishment of a "neo-realistic" school of Canadian playwriting in the 1970's, while the enormous success of his first play, *Leaving Home*, was an important step in the development of a Canadian audience for Canadian plays.

French's reputation rests largely on the four "Mercer" plays: *Leaving Home; Of the Fields, Lately; Salt-Water Moon*; and *1949*, the saga of a Newfoundland family that immigrated to Toronto in the 1940's, when the island province was still an independent country.

Leaving Home began its life as a TV script, but French offered it to Bill Glassco, then Artistic Director of the Tarragon Theatre in Toronto, after being impressed by that theatre's production of David Freeman's *Creeps*. The centre of the play is the father/son conflict between Jacob Mercer, a carpenter who brought with him to Toronto his Newfoundland outport traditional values, and his eldest son, Ben, a rather bookish young man, urban and contemporary, with a late 1950's outlook. Mary Mercer struggles to keep the peace between her husband and her son, observing that the similarities between the two men, especially their pride, contribute as much to the conflict as do their differences. The play's crisis is precipitated by the imminent marriage of younger son Billy, and the apparently pregnant Kathy Jackson, whose antagonistic relationship with her blunt, high-spirited mother, also a Newfoundlander, parallels the father/son conflict of the Mercers. In the course of the play, everyone "leaves home", the sons physically, and the father in spirit, as the break with his sons leaves him no one to whom he can pass on "old country" values which he must consequently abandon in some measure.

Leaving Home is a well-made, often claustrophobic play, but its acutely observed domestic tension is well leavened with comedy; the soundscape is especially rich, the lilting dialogue of the parental generation contrasting sharply with the flatter generic North American speech of the young people and giving theatrical presence to the conflict of values therein embodied. The play resonated strongly with Canadian audiences, whose national sense of self is so permeated with the immigrant experience, and *Leaving Home* was produced to great acclaim by over 30 other theatres across the country in the season after its Tarragon premiere. The Tarragon production was the beginning of French's long association with that theatre, and also of his collaboration with Glassco, forming arguably the most significant playwright/director team in contemporary English Canadian theatre.

Of the Fields, Lately picks up the story a few years later; Ben has returned to Toronto for an aunt's funeral, and learning that his father is in ill-health, he attempts a reconciliation, but also sides with his mother in her attempt to dissuade Jacob from returning to a dangerous high-rise construction site while not yet himself. Finally understanding the extent to which Jacob's sense of self depends on his work, Ben achieves a fleeting, heavily veiled moment of communication with his father, and leaves home again, letting events take their course; in the closing framing speech, "bookending" the one which began the play, we are told that Jacob dies of a heart attack shortly afterwards.

As the sequel is a more tightly focused, cleaner play than is *Leaving Home*, less given to slackening the tension with comic relief, there are those who consider it the finer work; the rich subtext of the three central father/son scenes is especially gripping, and does something to correct the imbalanced favouring of the son's perspective which some felt marred *Leaving Home*. While not quite as commercially successful as his first, French's second play consolidated his reputation.

French did not return to the Mercers until 1984, after a number of intervening plays. Set in 1926, *Salt-Water Moon* is a "prequel" to the two previously written; Jacob comes home to Coley's Point after a year in Toronto to court his former sweetheart, Mary Snow, now engaged to another young man, a bookish scion of the merchant class. He finds her looking through a telescope at the stars from the porch of the house where she works as a domestic, and in the course of the warm August evening that follows, wins her back. Along the way, we are given some insight into the social conditions of the working class in Newfoundland at the time, and while the play stands on its own, it gives substance and additional resonance to the earlier Mercer plays. The long one-act play is celebrated by many for its lyricism, condemned by some as a perpetuation of patriarchal values.

The last of the Mercer plays thus far, *1949*, is set in the year Newfoundland entered the Canadian confederation; the events depicted thus follow those of *Salt-Water Moon*. In some respects the most ambitious of the Mercer plays, *1949* uses a cast of 14 and several sub-plots to provide a multi-generational portrait of the Mercers, their in-laws, and Toronto neighbours. The highly charged emotional debate on the question of whether Newfoundland should join Canada splits generations, and is reflected in marital strife and jealousies, tentative courtships, and personal regrets, all giving French the opportunity to present the universal tension between past and present in a very specific Canadian context. While some feel that the play sprawls, and that some of the sub-plots verge on situation comedy, few English-Canadian plays have explored in a personal dimension the ever-relevant tension between national and regional loyalties with as much detailed care.

Those of French's plays which are not devoted to the Mercer saga are generally less highly regarded, but *Jitters* has been celebrated as Canada's most successful comedy about theatre, and the best exploitation of the play-within-a-play device. Setting his play in a small, alternative theatre much like the Tarragon, during the premiere of a new Canadian play, *The Care and Treatment of Roses*, French uses the ironic counterpoint of play and production to comment on and satirize Canadian cultural institutions and insecurities. The three acts depict a disastrous dress rehearsal, an even more disastrous opening night, and the morning after, complete with the reading of representative reviews, a fine opportunity for the playwright (the real one) to retaliate against pompous reviewing through wicked parody. In the play's central conflict, an ageing former star attempts to use the play as the vehicle for her come-back, while her cynical co-star sabotages the attempt, evidently fearful that the play's transfer to New York would expose his own artistic and personal inadequacies.

French's third play, *One Crack Out*, explores male sexual insecurity in the context of Toronto's *demi-monde* of hustlers, gamblers, prostitutes, and pool halls; while it achieves some Runyanesque pungency, the play gets lost in a profusion of short, choppy scenes. *The Riddle of the World*, thus far unpublished, is also about male sexual insecurity; the central character attempts to rebuild his life after his live-in girlfriend goes to India to join an ashram. While the play often succeds at the level of farce and social satire, quotations from Scripture and from T.S. Eliot too often substitute for dramatic action.

—Christopher Johnson

See also *Volume 1* entry on *Leaving Home*.

FRIEL, Brian. Born Bernard Patrick Friel in Killyclogher, County Tyrone, Northern Ireland, 9 January 1929. Educated at St. Columb's College, Derry, 1941–46; St. Patrick's College, Maynooth, 1946–49, BA 1949; St. Mary's Training College (now St. Joseph's College of Education), Belfast, 1949–50. Married Anne Morrison in 1954; four daughters and one son. Schoolteacher in primary and intermediate schools in Derry, 1950–60; first play, *The Francophile*, produced 1960, and from 1960 full-time writer; founder, with the actor Stephen Rea, Field Day Theatre Company, Northern Ireland, 1980. Recipient: Irish Arts Council Macauley fellowship, 1963; Christopher Ewart-Biggs Memorial Award, 1982; Writers' Guild of Great Britain Award, 1991; Olivier Award, 1991. D. Lit: Rosary College, Chicago, 1979; University of Ulster, Coleraine, 1986; D.Litt: National University of Ireland, Dublin, 1983; Queen's University, Belfast, 1992; Trinity College, Dublin, 1992. Member, Irish Academy of Letters, 1972, Aosdana, 1983, and Irish Senate, 1987.

Works

Collections

Selected Plays (includes *Philadelphia, Here I Come!*; *The Freedom of the City*; *Living Quarters*; *Aristocrats*; *Faith Healer*; *Translations*). 1984.

Stage Works

The Francophile (produced 1960; as *The Doubtful Paradise*, produced Group Theatre, Belfast, Northern Ireland, 1960).
The Enemy Within (produced Abbey Theatre, Dublin, 1962). 1979.
The Blind Mice (produced Eblana Theatre, Dublin, 1963).
Philadelphia, Here I Come! (produced Gaiety Theatre, Dublin, 1964). 1965.
The Loves of Cass McGuire (broadcast 1966; produced Helen Hayes Theatre, New York, 1966). 1967.
Lovers: Part One: Winners; Part Two: Losers (produced Gate Theatre, Dublin, 1967). 1968.
Crystal and Fox (produced Gaiety Theatre, Dublin, 1968). 1970.
The Mundy Scheme (produced Olympia Theatre, Dublin, 1969). With *Crystal and Fox*, 1970.

The Gentle Island (produced Olympia Theatre, Dublin, 1971).   1974.
The Freedom of the City (produced Abbey Theatre, Dublin, 1973).   1974.
Volunteers (produced Abbey Theatre, Dublin, 1975).   1979.
Living Quarters (produced Abbey Theatre, Dublin, 1977).   1978.
Faith Healer (produced Longacre Theatre, New York, 1979).   1980.
Aristocrats (produced Guildhall, Londonderry, Northern Ireland, 1979).   1980.
Translations (produced Guildhall, Londonderry, Northern Ireland, 1980).   1981.
American Welcome (produced 1980). In *The Best Short Plays 1981*, edited by Stanley Richards, 1981.
Three Sisters, from a play by Chekhov (produced Guildhall, Londonderry, Northern Ireland, 1981).   1981.
The Communication Cord (produced Guildhall, Londonderry, Northern Ireland, 1982).   1983.
Fathers and Sons, from a novel by Turgenev (produced National Theatre, London, 1987).   1987.
Making History (produced Guildhall, Londonderry, Northern Ireland, 1988).   1989.
Dancing at Lughnasa (produced Abbey Theatre, Dublin, 1990).   1990.
The London Vertigo, from a play by Charles Macklin (produced Gate Theatre, Dublin, 1992).
A Month in the Country, from the play by Turgenev (produced Gate Theatre, Dublin, 1992).

Screenplays

Philadelphia, Here I Come!, 1970.

Radio Plays

A Sort of Freedom, 1958; *To This Hard House*, 1958; *The Founder Members*, 1964; *The Loves of Cass McGuire*, 1966.

Fiction

The Saucer of Larks.   1962.
The Gold in the Sea.   1966.
A Saucer of Larks: Stories of Ireland (selection).   1969.
Selected Stories.   1979.
The Diviner.   1983.

Other

Editor, *The Last of the Name*, by Charles McGlinchey.   1986.

*

Bibliographies

Kimball King, *Ten Modern Irish Playwrights*, New York, 1979.

Criticism

Books:
Desmond E.S. Maxwell, *Brian Friel*, Lewisburg, Pennsylvania, 1973.
Ulf Dantanus, *Brian Friel: The Growth of an Irish Dramatist*, Gothenburg, Sweden, 1985.
George O'Brien, *Brian Friel*, Boston, 1990.

Richard Pine, *Brian Friel and Ireland's Drama*, London, 1990.

* * *

Brian Friel emerged during the 1980's as the leading Irish playwright of his generation. His *Translations* made an equally strong impact on Irish and English audiences, almost immediately acquiring the status of a modern classic. It was the first play produced by the Field Day Theatre Company, which he and the actor, Stephen Rea, set up in 1980. Like all Field Day's new plays (including *The Communication Cord* and *Making History*) it had its premiere in Derry (Londonderry), where Friel was born and bred, before moving to Dublin and London. Northern Ireland became a breeding ground for a new Irish dramatic movement, one which aimed to make audiences re-think the myths and stereotypes built into Irish issues.

Critics have observed a dichotomy in Friel's drama which seems to reflect deep divisions in his own attitude to his subjects as well as in the subjects themselves. On the one hand, his commitment to Field Day suggests an optimistic, Shavian kind of belief in the power of drama to revise old, fixed attitudes. The hedge schoolmaster, Hugh, in *Translations*, could be speaking for the author, as for Field Day, when he argues the necessity of renewing "the images of the past embodied in language"; otherwise "we fossilise". Despite the atmosphere of pain and loss at the close of the play, following the disappearance of the young English officer, Yolland, with whom the Irish-speaking Maire is in love, some such "renewing" has been achieved. In the play's most poignant scene the young lovers manage to break through the barrier of language, she using her few words of English, he reciting like a love song the Irish place names he has learnt in the course of his army duties. Friel skilfully creates the illusion that Irish is being spoken, even when, as mostly happens, all the characters use English. It is a powerful means of dissolving the audience's linguistic estrangement, giving them a liberating sense of understanding—and of hope for reconciliation of the alien cultures.

Yet the illusion is loaded with ironies. The lovers' moment of communion is real but so are their failures to understand each other: Maire does not see how inextricably Yolland's feeling for her is bound up with the passion he has developed for the West of Ireland. It is a double irony, since the British reason for being in Donegal is to anglicise Irish place names like Baile Beag (Friel has conferred mythological status on the place, which figures in earlier plays under the name conferred in *Translations*, Ballybeg).

The movements of hopeful change in the play are shadowed by a sense of human life as intrinsically lonely and tragic. Friel is deeply preoccupied with the separateness of people's inner experience. Father and son in *Philadelphia, Here I Come!* cannot express their feelings for each other: even their memories of happy times they remain separate and alone.

The metaphysical aspects of this aloneness are to the fore in one of Friel's strongest and strangest plays, *Faith Healer*. Frank Hardy's "gift" of healing allows him, from time to time, a mystical communion with those he heals; but he has no control over this disconcerting faculty. Mostly it condemns him to a life apart from his kind, travelling the British Isles, with his wife and manager, in an old van, offering his "performance" in barns and halls, endlessly making stories of his life in which other people can live (Grace feels herself so much dependent on his fictive power that she commits suicide when he dies, unable to "sustain" herself alone).

344   **FRIEL**

Faith Healer has been taken as a paradigm of the playwright's fate, in which Ireland plays a crucial role. Frank returns there from his nomadic "exile", to be murdered in an inn yard by farmers whose crippled friend he has failed to cure: it is a death he appears to expect. Seamus Deane sees it as a metaphor for the self-healing which the healer can only find by "dying back into the place out of which his healing came in the first place". The ambiguous event, however, remains open to interpretation. The tension between "public" and "private" readings, here as in Friel's other plays, is a major source of their power.

Friel's bold experiments with dramatic form are part of his originality. He often takes historical subjects (the 1833 Survey of Ireland in *Translations*, Derry's civil rights marches in *The Freedom of the City*) and constructs his plays in the gap between history and myth, deliberately breaking the illusion in a variety of artful ways. In *The Loves of Cass McGuire*, Cass sweeps through the audiorium to interrupt the stage action, insisting that her story be told her way. By contrast, in *Making History*, the subject of the story fails to control how it is told. In Act II, the exiled O'Neill has to stand chafing while an ecclesiastical historian writes his history from an official angle which irons out the human variety and inconsistencies shown in Act I. The spirited Yorkshire wife, who has enlivened the earlier scenes with her independent, forthright ways, vanishes from the history under relentless pressure from the need for an all-Irish patriotic myth.

Friel is even-handed in his choice of subjects: Irish or English "stories" may serve the purpose of provoking the audience into re-thinking received ideas. In *The Freedom of the City* it is the account promulgated by the British Army which is seen to distort the truth of events and feelings. A skilful double narrative is set in a time framework which starts with the catastrophe (the shooting of three Derry citizens during a civil rights march), then backtracks to trace what happens in the brief period between their taking shelter in the Guildhall and their deaths. The audience see for themselves the humble, ordinary lives which, from the outside military view (relayed by devices like the public address system) become terrorist activity. Characteristically, Friel relieves the dark political irony with humour and human tenderness, as Lily struggles to explain why she comes on marches (and Skinner supplies a bitter answer: "It's about us—the poor—the majority—stirring in our sleep!").

Faith Healer is set in some void where the sense of place is created through language (we "see" what happens entirely through narrative, laid out in four monologues). Other plays by Friel are more naturalistic, but always, as in *Aristocrats*, there are resonances beyond the ordinary. Friel conveys sympathy both for the backward- and forward-looking characters, a capacity which, like much else in his work, draws comparisons with Chekhov. He has written an "Irished" *Three Sisters*, and shown, in his adaptation of Turgenev's *Fathers and Sons*, his understanding of people's devotion to the status quo (which prevails at the end of the play) while applying a sharp irony to their readiness to turn away from radicals like Bazarov, the man who, like Friel himself, "sees everything critically".

—Katharine Worth

See also *Volume 1* entries on *Philadelphia, Here I Come!*; *Translations*.

FRISCH, Max (Rudolf). Born in Zurich, Switzerland, 15 May 1911. Educated at the Realgymnasium, Zurich, 1924–30; University of Zurich, studying arts and philosophy, 1930–33; Technische Hochschule, Zurich, studying architecture, 1936–41, diploma, 1941. Married 1) Gertrud Anna Constance von Meyenburg in 1942 (divorced 1959), two daughters and one son; 2) Marianne Oellers in 1968. Freelance journalist, from 1933; intermittent Swiss military service, 1939–45; began own architectural firm in Zurich, 1942; first-produced play, *Nun singen wir wieder*, staged 1945; visited Germany, France, and Italy, in 1946, Poland and Czechoslovakia in 1948, Spain in 1950; spent a year in the USA and Mexico, 1951–52; architectural firm closed, 1954, and he became full-time writer thereafter; travelled to the USA, Mexico, and Cuba in 1956, Greece and the Middle East in 1957; based in Rome, 1960–65; travelled to Israel in 1965, the USSR in 1968, Japan in 1969; in the USA, travelling and lecturing, in the early 1970's; visited China, 1975; lived briefly in New York, 1981. Recipient of numerous awards, including: Raabe Prize, 1954; Schleussner Schüller Prize, for radio play, 1955; Büchner Prize, 1958; Zurich Prize, 1958; Veillon Prize, 1958; Nordrhein-Westfalen Prize, 1962; Jerusalem Prize, 1965; Schiller Prize (Baden-Württemberg), 1965; Schiller Prize (Switzerland), 1974; Neustadt International Prize, 1986; Heine Prize (Düsseldorf), 1989. Honorary doctorate: University of Marburg, 1962; Bard College, Annandale-on-Hudson, New York, 1980; City University of New York, 1982; University of Berlin, 1987. Honorary Member, American Academy, 1974. Died in Zurich, 4 April 1991.

Works

Collections

Stücke (2 vols.).   1962; augmented edition (2 vols.), 1972.
Three Plays (includes *The Fire Raisers; Count Öderland; Andorra*), translated by Michael Bullock.   1962.
Three Plays (includes *When the War Was Over; Don Juan; The Great Rage of Philip Hotz*), translated by James L. Rosenberg, 1967.
Four Plays (includes *The Great Wall of China; Philip Hotz's Fury; Biography; Don Juan*), translated by Michael Bullock.   1969.
Gesammelte Werke (12 vols.).   1976; same texts also published in 6 volumes, 1976, with supplementary volume in 1987.
Gesammelte Werke ("Jubiläum" edition; 7 vols.).   1986.

Stage Works

Nun singen sie wieder: Versuch eines Requiems (produced Schauspielhaus, Zurich, 1945).   1946.
Santa Cruz (produced Schauspielhaus, Zurich, 1946).   1947.
Die chinesische Mauer (produced Schauspielhaus, Zurich, 1946).   1947; revised version, 1955; "Paris version", 1972; translated as *The Chinese Wall*, 1961; as *The Great Wall of China*, in Four Plays, 1969.
Als der Krieg zu Ende war (produced Schauspielhaus, Zurich, 1948).   1949; translated as *When the War Was Over*, in Three Plays, 1967.
Graf Öderland (produced Schauspielhaus, Zurich, 1951).   1951; translated as *Count Oderland*, in Three Plays, 1962.
Don Juan; oder, Die Liebe zur Geometrie (produced Schauspielhaus, Zurich, 1953).   1953; revised version, in *Stücke 2*, 1962; translated as *Don Juan*, in *Three Plays*, 1967.

Scene from the Zurich Schauspielhaus's 1961 production of *Andorra* by **Max Frisch**, directed by Kurt Hirschenfeld, designed by Teo Otto.

Biedermann und die Brandstifter, from the radio play (produced Schauspielhaus, Zurich, 1958).   1958; translated as *The Fire Raisers*, 1962; as *The Firebugs*, 1963.
Die grosse Wut des Philipp Hotz (produced Schauspielhaus, Zurich, 1958).   1958; translated as *The Great Fury of Philipp Hotz*, in *Three Plays*, 1967; as *Philip Hotz's Fury*, in *Four Plays*, 1969.
Andorra (produced Schauspielhaus, Zurich, 1961).   1962; translated as *Andorra*, in *Three Plays*, 1962.
Biografie (produced Schauspielhaus, Zurich, 1968).   1967; translated as *Biography*, 1969.
Triptychon (produced Théâtre Municipal, Lausanne, Switzerland, 1979).   1978; translated as *Triptych*, 1981.

Television Plays

Zurich Transit, 1966 (published 1966); *Blaubart*, with Krzysztof Zanussi, 1984 (published 1985).

Radio Plays

Rip van Winkle, 1953 (published 1969); *Herr Biedermann und die Brandstifter*, 1955 (published 1955).

Fiction

Jürg Reinhart: Eine sommerliche Schicksalsfahrt.   1934.
Antwort aus der Stille: Eine Erzählung aus den Bergen.   1937.
J'adore ce qui me brûle; oder, Die Schwierigen.   1943; revised version, as *Die Schwierigen*, 1957.
Bin; oder, Die Reise nach Peking.   1945.
Marion und die Marionotten: Ein Fragment.   1946.
Stiller.   1954; translated as *I'm Not Stiller*, 1958.
Homo Faber. 1957; translated as *Homo Faber*, 1959.
Mein Name sei Gantenbein.   1964; translated as *A Wilderness of Mirrors*, 1965; as *Gantenbein*, 1982.
Wilhelm Tell für die Schule.   1971.
Montauk.   1975; translated as *Montauk*, 1976.
Der Traum des Apothekers von Locarno (stories from *Tagebuch 1966–1971*).   1978.
Der Mensch erscheint im Holozän.   1979; translated as *Man in the Holocene*, 1980.
Blaubart.   1982; translated as *Bluebeard*, 1983.

Other

Blätter aus dem Brotsack.   1940.
Tagebuch mit Marion.   1947; revised edition, as *Tagebuch 1946–1949*, 1950; translated as *Sketchbook 1946–1949*, 1977.
Achtung: Die Schweiz.   1955.
Die neue Stadt: Beitrage zur Diskussion.   1956.
Ausgewählte Prosa.   1961.
Öffentlichkeit als Partner.   1967.
Tagebuch 1966–1971.   1972; translated as *Sketchbook 1966–1971*, 1974.
Dienstbüchlein.   1974.
Stich-Worte (selection), edited by Uwe Johnson.   1975.
Kritik, Thesen, Analysen.   1977.
Schweiz ohne Armee: Ein Palaver.   1989.

Schweiz als Heimat?: Versuche über 50 Jahre, edited by Walter Obschlager.   1990.

*

Criticism

Books:
Carol Petersen, *Max Frisch* (third edition), Berlin, 1966.
Ulrich Weisstein, *Max Frisch*, New York, 1967.
Adelheid Weise, *Untersuchungen zur Thematik und Struktur der Dramen von Max Frisch*, Göppingen, 1969.
Thomas Beckermann (ed.), *Über Max Frisch*, Frankfurt, 1971.
Albrecht Schau (ed.), *Max Frisch: Beiträge zur Wirkungsgeschichte*, Freiburg, 1971.
Heinrich Geisser, *Die Enstehung von Max Frischs Dramaturgie der Permutation*, Bern, 1973.
Marianne Biedermann, *Das politische Theater von Max Frisch*, Lampertheim, 1974.
Hellmuth Karasek, *Max Frisch* (fifth edition), Velber, 1974.
Annemarie Schnetzler-Suter, *Max Frisch: Dramaturgische Fragen*, Bern, 1974.
Tildy Hanhart, *Max Frisch: Zufall, Rolle und literarische Form: Interpretationen zu seinem Werk*, Kronberg, 1976.
Manfred Jürgensen, *Max Frisch: Die Dramen* (second edition), Bern, 1976.
Walter Schmitz (ed.), *Über Max Frisch 2*, Frankfurt, 1976.
Manfred Jürgensen (ed.), *Frisch: Kritik, Thesen, Analysen*, Bern, 1977.
Hans Mayer, *Über Friedrich Dürrenmatt und Max Frisch*, Pfullingen, 1977.
Jürgen Petersen, *Max Frisch*, Stuttgart, 1978.
Gertrud B. Pickar, *The Dramatic Works of Max Frisch*, Bern, 1978.
Gerhart P. Knapp (ed.), *Max Frisch: Aspekte des Bühnenwerks*, Bern, 1979.
Malcolm Pender, *Max Frisch: His Work and Its Swiss Background*, Stuttgart, 1979.
Manfred E. Schuchmann, *Der Autor als Zeitgenosse: Gesellschaftliche Aspekte in Max Frischs Werk*, Frankfurt, 1979.
Gerhard F. Probst and Jay F. Bodine (eds.), *Perspectives on Max Frisch*, Lexington, Kentucky, 1982.
Volker Hage, *Max Frisch*, Reinbek, 1983.
Theo Rosebrock, *Erläuterungen zu Max Frisch* (tenth edition), Hollfeld, 1984.
Michael Butler, *The Plays of Max Frisch*, London, 1985.
Walter Schmitz, *Max Frisch: Das Spätwerk (1962–1982): Eine Einführung*, Tübingen, 1985.
Hans Bänziger, *Frisch und Dürrenmatt: Materialien und Kommentare*, Tübingen, 1987.
Heinz Gockel, *Max Frisch: Drama und Dramaturgie*, Munich, 1989.

*   *   *

Born at the start of the 20th century, Swiss novelist and playwright Max Frisch bore constant witness to the agony of world war and the diminishing importance of the individual. But his plays respond not to the large-scale moral horror of Europe in this century, but to what he sees as the heart of the problem—the difficult interaction between the individual and society. He explored this clash through a kaleidoscope of theatrical styles, sometimes narrowing his scope to examine marriage as a microcosm of the larger struggle, in *Santa Cruz* and *Biografie: Ein Spiel* specifically, and sometimes widening his scope to examine entire societal models like the one he creates in *Andorra*. In all cases the themes are the same—the societal hypocrisies which suppress individuality; the fissure between society's technical, political power and the moral strength of the individual; and always, the ceaseless quest for a definition of self.

The plays *Don Juan; oder, Die Liebe zur Geometrie* (*Don Juan; or, The Love of Geometry*) and *Biedermann und die Brandstifter* (*The Fire Raisers*) both illustrate brilliantly how the weight of social norms can petrify the individual. In *Don Juan* Frisch portrays the title character on the eve of his wedding. The persona of Don Juan as lover and rogue has been created through countless legends. Frisch shows him searching for his true identity. Don Juan's nemesis is the glittering city of Seville where identities are defined through false heroics and the enactment of empty social rituals. Don Juan attempts to discover himself through the "unique" emotion of true love but discovers that love is also a social construct. He fakes a descent into Hell in an attempt to escape the pressures of society, but after his "death" the citizens of Seville simply reconstruct the legend of Don Juan, thereby regaining control over the persona Don Juan has tried to wrest from them.

In *Biedermann und die Brandstifter*, the middle-class Biedermann cannot escape from the prison of socialized behaviour. This weakness leads to the destruction of his home and to his own death. This play, like *Don Juan*, offers a dramatic analysis of social behaviour and its ability to co-opt personality. In *Biedermann und die Brandstifter* homes, are being destroyed all over Biedermann's neighborhood by peddlars who infiltrate the houses and set fires in the attics. The play's black humor is fueled by Biedermann's inability, when a peddlar appears at his door, to respond with anything but the semantics of bourgeois decency. His individuality submerged behind the mask of middle-class niceties, Biedermann plays the perfect host to his own destruction.

When individuality and behavior are defined so completely by a hypocritical society, moral muscles atrophy. In response to an age of wars and particularly the atom bomb, Frisch began to explore the fissure between technical prowess and moral strength. In his early play *Nun singen sie weider* (*And Then They Were Singing Again*), this imbalance is embodied in the character of the Nazi officer, Herbert. As an officer, Herbert has been given the power to interrogate and kill. Under the stress of war his morality wavers. His decisions and the spiritual crises that follow are those of a man replete with physical/political power and devoid of the moral power to temper it.

The imbalance between physical/political power and the puny moral resources people possess surfaces again in *Die chinesische Mauer* (*The Chinese Wall*) in which Frisch sees the Wall itself as a symbol of the imbalance. This "wonder of the world" was produced by tremendous energy and technical skill in an absurd effort to halt the march of time.

Seeking the genesis of the problems he saw in society, Frisch examined the most intimate of political relationships— that of husbands and wives. In *Biografie: Ein Spiel* and the early *Santa Cruz* the protagonists find themselves suddenly middle-aged, complacent, and unhappy. Within the theatrical structure of memory plays they explore their pasts, re-enact the decisions that have shaped them, and realize that they cannot overcome the weaknesses and compromises that have led to the present. The moral fiber that fails the individual in his struggle against society also fails him in his struggle against himself.

Andorra is Frisch's most accomplished play. In it, all of the interpersonal and political relationships he has explored in his other work are played out in the town square of the fictional Andorra. A young man, Andri, who the Andorrans believe is a Jew, is at first condescendingly tolerated and finally persecuted by the citizens of Andorra whose fear of change, personal deficiencies, and corrosive prejudices trap them in moral paralysis. The characters are a gallery of easily recognizable "types". But Frisch carefully details their behavior, dramatizing each of their deceits, hypocrisies, and rationalizations. The inevitability of the play's tragic end in no way lessens the discomfort of watching Andri's persona corrode beneath the pressure of the Andorrans' prejudice.

The messages of Frisch's plays are those of a philosopher. The purpose of his work, like that of Brecht's, is the presentation of ideas to a public that has anesthetized itself against thinking. What keeps Frisch's plays from becoming didactic is the marvelous theatricality of their forms. Frisch's best plays are as much about their existence on a stage as they are about their content. *Santa Cruz* and *Biografie: Ein Spiel* step away from a natural, mimetic style into the synchronic world of dream plays, interweaving levels of time, and juxtaposing reality and supposition. *Die chinesische Mauer* is labeled a "farce" and exploits this genre's presentational style, verbal dexterity, and absurd humor. The action of the play is constantly framed by the sardonic commentary of a Master of Ceremonies in the tradition of the German cabaret. *Biedermann und die Brandstifter* is a parable play but incorporates the convention of a Greek chorus and undermines its own style by being, as Frisch calls it, "a morality play without a moral". *Andorra* begins as a parable but evolves the stylistic feel of a nightmare.

In *Don Juan* Frisch's message and style merge. The consciously created stage fiction of the "theatrical Seville in a period of good costumes" stipulated in the stage directions establishes the theatrical model as the ideal metaphor for contemporary society. Both are arenas of masks and role-playing, hollow surfaces, and lines spoken by rote.

This fusion of style and message is the grand paradox of Frisch's work and the root of its fascination. His plays are at once delightful in their theatricality and devastating in their depiction of the world as a play in which the roles have consumed the actors and meaning is obscured by glittering sets and empty prose.

—Elissa Adams

See also *Volume 1* entry on *The Fire Raisers*.

FRY, Christopher. Born Christopher Fry Harris in Bristol, England, 18 December 1907. Educated at Bedford Modern School, 1918–26. Married Phyllis Marjorie Hart in 1936 (died 1987); one son. Teacher, Bedford Froebel Kindergarten, 1926–27; actor and office worker, Citizen House, Bath, 1927; schoolmaster, Hazelwood School, Limpsfield, Surrey, 1928–31; secretary to H. Rodney Bennett, 1931–32; founding director, Tunbridge Wells Repertory Players, 1932–35; lecturer and editor of schools magazine, Dr. Barnardo's Homes, 1934–39; first play, *Youth and the Peregrines*, produced 1934; director, 1939–40, and visiting director, 1945–46, Oxford Playhouse; served in the Non-Combatant Corps, 1940–44; visiting director, 1946, and staff dramatist, 1947, Arts Theatre

Club, London. Also composer. Recipient: New York Drama Critics Circle Award, 1951, 1952, 1956; Queen's Gold Medal for Poetry, 1962; Royal Society of Literature Heinemann Award, 1962. DA: Manchester Polytechnic, 1966; DL: "Lambeth" (awarded by Archbishop of Canterbury) 1988; Oxford University, 1988. Honorary fellow, Manchester Polytechnic, 1988; fellow, Royal Society of Literature.

Works

Collections

Selected Plays (includes *The Boy with a Cart; A Phoenix Too Frequent; The Lady's Not for Burning; A Sleep of Prisoners; Curtmantle*). 1985.

Stage Works

Youth and the Peregrines (produced at the Pump Room, Tunbridge Wells, Kent, 1934).
She Shall Have Music (lyrics only, with Ronald Frankau), book by Frank Eyton, music by Fry and Monte Crick (produced Saville Theatre, London, 1934).
To Sea in a Sieve (revue; produced Reading, Berkshire, 1935).
Open Door (produced London, 1936).   Nd.
The Boy with a Cart: Cuthman, Saint of Sussex (produced Coleman's Hatch, Sussex, 1938).   1939.
The Tower (produced Tewkesbury, Gloucestershire, 1939).
Thursday's Child: A Pageant, music by Martin Shaw (produced Albert Hall, London, 1939).   1939.
A Phoenix Too Frequent (produced Mercury Theatre, London, 1946).   1946.
The Firstborn (broadcast 1947; produced Gateway Theatre, Edinburgh, 1948)   1946; revised version (produced Winter Garden Theatre, London, 1952), 1952, 1958.
The Lady's Not for Burning (produced Arts Theatre, London, 1948).   1949; revised version, 1950, 1958.
Thor, with Angels (produced Chapter House, Canterbury, Kent, 1948).   1948.
Venus Observed (produced St. James's Theatre, London, 1950).   1950.
Ring round the Moon: A Charade with Music, from *L'Invitation au château* by Jean Anouilh (produced Globe Theatre, London, 1950).   1950.
A Sleep of Prisoners (produced Oxford University Church, Oxford, 1951).   1951.
The Dark is Light Enough: A Winter Comedy (produced Edinburgh, 1954).   1954.
The Lark, from the play by Jean Anouilh (produced 1955). 1955.
Tiger at the Gates, from a play by Jean Giraudoux (produced Apollo Theatre, London, 1955).   1955; as *The Trojan War Will Not Take Place*, 1983.
Duel of Angels, from *Pour Lucrèce* by Jean Giraudoux (produced Apollo Theatre, London, 1958).   1958.
Curtmantle (produced Stadsschouwburg, Tilburg, Holland, 1961).   1961.
Judith, from the play by Jean Giraudoux (produced Her Majesty's Theatre, London, 1962).   1962.
Peer Gynt, from the play by Ibsen (produced Festival Theatre, Chichester, 1970).   1970.
A Yard of Sun: A Summer Comedy (produced Playhouse, Nottingham, 1970).   1970.
Cyrano de Bergerac, from the play by Edmond Rostand (produced Festival Theatre, Chichester, 1975).   1975.

Paradise Lost, music by Penderecki, from the poem by Milton (produced Chicago, 1978).   1978.
One Thing More; or, Caedmon Construed (produced Chelmsford, Essex, 1986).   1987.

Screenplays

The Beggar's Opera, with Denis Cannan, 1953; *A Queen is Crowned* (documentary), 1953; *Ben Hur*, 1959; *Barabbas*, 1962; *The Bible: In the Beginning*, 1966 (published, 1966).

Television Plays

The Canary, 1950; *The Tenant of Wildfell Hall*, 1968; *The Brontës of Haworth* (four plays), 1973 (published in 2 vols., 1974); *The Best of Enemies*, 1976; *Sister Dora*, from the book by Jo Manton, 1977.

Radio Plays

Material for *Children's Hour* series, 1939–40; *The Firstborn*, 1947; *Rhineland Journey*, 1948.

Verse

Root and Sky: Poetry from the Plays of Fry, edited by Charles E. Wadsworth and Jean G. Wadsworth.   1975.

Memoirs and Letters

Can You Find Me: A Family History.   1978.

Other

An Experience of Critics, with *The Approach to Dramatic Criticism* by W.A. Darlington and others, edited by Kaye Webb.   1952.
The Boat That Mooed (for children).   1966.
Death is a Kind of Love (lecture).   1979.
Genius, Talent and Failure (lecture).   1987.
Looking for a Language (lecture).   1992.

Editor, *Charlie Hammond's Sketchbook*.   1980.

Translator, *The Boy and the Magic*, by Colette.   1964.

*

Bibliographies

B.L. Schear and E.G. Prater, bibliography in *Tulane Drama Review*, March 1960.

Criticism

Books:
Derek Stanford, *Christopher Fry: An Appreciation*, London, 1950.
Derek Stanford, *Christopher Fry*, London, 1954; revised edition, 1962.
Nelson Vos, *The Drama of Comedy: Victim and Victor*, Virginia, 1965.
W.M. Merchant, *Creed and Drama*, London, 1965.
William V. Spanos, *The Christian Tradition in Modern British Verse*, New Jersey, 1967.

Emil Roy, *Christopher Fry*, Carbondale, Illinois, 1968.
Mahendra P. Sangal, *Christopher Fry and T.S. Eliot*, Meerut, India, 1968.
Stanley M. Wiersma, *Christopher Fry: A Critical Essay*, Grand Rapids, Michigan, 1970.
S. Krishna Sarma, *Imagery in the Plays of Christopher Fry*, Vijayawada, India, 1972.
Stanley M. Wiersma, *More Than the Ear Discovers: God in the Plays of Christopher Fry*, Chicago, 1983.
Glenda Leeming, *Poetic Drama*, London, 1989 (Macmillan Modern Dramatists series).
Glenda Leeming, *Christopher Fry*, Boston, 1990.

*   *   *

Although he began to write before the World War II, Fry first came to wide attention in the post-war period with plays like *A Phoenix Too Frequent*, and reached a high point of commercial and critical success in 1948 with his light and witty costume verse drama, *The Lady's Not For Burning*, in which John Gielgud and Pamela Brown played the leading roles. He followed this success two years later with the almost equally successful *Venus Observed*, starring Laurence Olivier, and then, in 1954, with the reflective *The Dark Is Light Enough*, written for Edith Evans. Indeed in the late 1940's and early 1950's Fry was remarkably prolific. There was also a strong religious strain in his work, most evident in the austere and manifestly Christian pieces of these years, like *Thor, With Angels* and *A Sleep of Prisoners*. And his translations from the French dramatists Anouilh and Giraudoux justifiably won considerable box office success, notably the former's *Ring Round the Moon*, directed by Peter Brook.

Together with Terence Rattigan, a dramatist of very different interests and emphases, Fry became the most discussed playwright of the decade following World War II. The revival of English verse drama had been long awaited, and not least because the century had already seen several false starts, in the short-lived popularity of the dramas of Stephen Philips, or the later fashionable but côterie work of avant-garde writers like Auden and Isherwood, and Ronald Duncan. Fry's plays appeared to mark a more genuine, theatrically accessible revival. In part, what dazzled critics and public alike was the way in which Fry linked engaging plot materials, intellectually serious subject matter, and colourful settings, to a verbally rich and exciting poetic dialogue. Fry's language, in particular, seemed to herald a new dawn for poetic drama.

One of Fry's finest plays was his first London success, *The Lady's Not for Burning*. Labelled a comedy, its action takes place in the house of the mayor of a small medieval town about the year 1400, where a young woman, Jennet Jourdemayne, condemned to be burned at the stake for witchcraft, meets a cynical and world weary discharged soldier, Thomas Mendip, in the house of the local mayor. He demands that he be hanged. The relative attractions of life and death are debated. Thomas is saved from the gallows, Jennet from the stake, and both depart together, back into life. The plot line is slight, a mere peg on which to hang discussion, but it has a certain freshness; Fry describes the play as a comedy, and it is, indeed, a comic fantasy, providing opportunity for engaging and civilised, if not particularly profound, discussion of life and moral responsibility.

A motive prominent in this play recurs in other plays by Fry: life is not ordered and explicable; on the contrary it is confused, inchoate, and random. Reflective of this randomness is the incident in which, after her father's death, and while in his study, Jennet accidentally knocks over several bottles, confusing their contents, and in the process turns

copper into gold; thus she discovers the great secret her father and others had spent their lives searching for in vain. But of course this was just an accident, and she has no formula that will secure the discovery.

Life, for Fry, is a tissue of such hazards; they may all be, ultimately, part of a great design, but what that design is remains unknowable, and we are confronted only with the apparent arbitrariness and absurdity of things. For Fry, however, unlike many existentialist writers of the 1940's and 1950's, this is a cue not for existential *angst*, but for delight in the rich confusion of existence: life is indeed bewilderingly inexplicable, and therein lies wonder and delight. Unfortunately, expressions of amazement at the great mystery of creation are rather too insubstantial a response on which to build significant drama.

The language of this play, like that of Fry's other work, has a great comic gusto, and in its trafficking in conceits, quibbles, and verbal paradoxes, and in its delight in long rhetorical set-pieces, it might almost have been modelled on that of *Love's Labour's Lost*. But it betrays, too, deficiencies which later criticism highlighted: Fry's is too much an artificial, fabricated quasi-poetic idiom, too little a discourse rooted in common speech; the rich, exotic language, and "Elizabethan" word-play came increasingly to be seen by critics and audiences alike as an excessive delight in the verbal for its own sake. Again, the plays' general concerns were increasingly felt to be artificial—contrived, like the language in which they are couched, and remote from contemporary society and its social and political realities.

As remarked above, underpinning many of Fry's plays too, and not only the specifically Christian pieces like *The Boy with a Cart* and *A Sleep of Prisoners*, was a keenly felt religious faith. But that was concern shared by only a minority of Fry's audiences, and unfortunately he seemed unable to turn it to persuasive dramatic or philosophical account. Fry's success was short-lived, and even before John Osborne's *Look Back in Anger* of 1956 signalled the arrival of a more gritty, naturalistic prose drama of youthful characters, social issues, and "kitchen sink" locales, the initial enthusiasm for his drama had begun to wane. Since the later 1950's such concerns as Osborne's have perhaps overly dominated British drama, and the more appealing philosophical and ruminative emphases that are characteristic of Fry's plays at their best have had little appeal.

Yet it cannot be denied that Fry's was a distinctive talent. Notwithstanding that the substance of his plays is, at times, thin, their dramatic conflicts rather contrived, and their language and sentiments often overblown, he wrote with an undeniable ease and panache, could turn a delightfully witty phrase, and had a keen sense of the theatrically effective. The mid-1950's reaction against his work has probably been too extreme, and although it is unlikely they will recover the high repute they once enjoyed, the plays now stand in need of critical and theatrical reassessment.

—Kenneth Richards

See also *Volume 1* entry on *The Lady's Not for Burning*.

———

FUGARD, (Harold) Athol (Lannigan). Born near Middleburg, Cape Province, South Africa, 11 June 1932. Educated at Marist Brothers College, Port Elizabeth, 1938–45; Port Elizabeth Technical College, 1946–50; University of Cape Town, 1950–53. Married Sheila Meiring in 1956; one

Athol Fugard (1988).

daughter. Seaman, *S.S. Graigaur*, 1953–54; journalist, Port Elizabeth *Evening Post*, 1954; reporter, South African Broadcasting Corporation, Port Elizabeth and Cape Town, 1955–57; co-founder, Circle Players theatre workshop, Cape Town, 1957; clerk, Fordsburg Native Commissioner's Court, Johannesburg, 1958; first play, *No-Good Friday*, produced 1958; stage-manager and publicity agent, National Theatre Organization, 1958; co-founder, African Theatre Workshop, Sophiatown, 1958–59, New Africa Group, Brussels, 1960; worked as cleaner in London, 1960; co-founder, Ijinle Company, London, 1966, and The Space experimental theatre, Cape Town, 1972; director, Serpent Players, Port Elizabeth, from 1963. Director of, and actor in, many of his own plays. Recipient: *New York Times* Award, 1965; Obie Award, 1971; London Theatre Critics Award, 1974; Locarno Film Festival Ernest Artaria Award, 1977; Berlin Film Festival Golden Bear, 1980; Yale University fellowship, 1980; New York Drama Critics Circle Award, 1981; London *Evening Standard* Award, 1984; Common Wealth Award, 1984; Drama League Award, 1986. D.Litt: University of Natal, Durban, 1981; Rhodes University, Grahamstown, 1983; University of Cape Town, 1984; University of Witwatersrand, 1989. DFA: Yale University, New Haven, Connecticut, 1983; DHL: Georgetown University, Washington, DC, 1984.

Works

Collections

Three Port Elizabeth Plays: The Blood Knot; Hello and Goodbye; Boesman and Lena. 1974.

Statements: Three Plays (includes *Statements After an Arrest . . .; Sizwe Bansi is Dead; The Island*). 1974.
"Dimetos" and Two Early Plays (includes *No-Good Friday; Nongogo*). 1977.
"Boesman and Lena" and Other Plays (includes *The Blood Knot; People Are Living There; Hello and Goodbye*). 1978.
Selected Plays (includes *"Master Harold" . . . and the Boys; The Blood Knot* (revised version); *Hello and Goodbye; Boesman and Lena*). 1987.

Stage Works

No-Good Friday (produced Bantumens Social Centre, Cape Town, 1958). In *"Dimetos" and Two Early Plays*, 1977.
Nongogo (produced Trades Hall, Johannesburg, 1959). In *"Dimetos" and Two Early Plays*, 1977.
The Blood Knot (produced The Rehearsal Room, Johannesburg, 1961). 1963; revised version, in *Selected Plays*, 1987.
Hello and Goodbye (produced Library Theatre, Johannesburg, 1965). 1966.
The Coat (produced Theatre Club, Port Elizabeth, 1966). With *The Third Degree*, by Don MacLennan, 1971.
People Are Living There (produced Close Theatre, Glasgow, 1968). 1969.
The Occupation: A Script for Camera. In *Ten One Act Plays*, edited by Cosmo Pieterse, 1968.
Boesman and Lena (produced Rhodes University Little Theatre, Grahamstown, 1969; revised version produced Circle in the Square Theatre, New York, 1970). 1969.
Orestes (produced 1971). In *Theatre One: New South African Drama*, edited by Stephen Gray, 1978.
Statements After an Arrest under the Immorality Act (produced Royal Court Theatre, London, 1972). In *Statements*, 1974.
Sizwe Bansi is Dead, with John Kani and Winston Ntshona (as *Sizwe Banzi is Dead*, produced The Space, Cape Town, 1972; as *Sizwe Bansi is Dead*, produced 1973). In *Statements*, 1974.
The Island, with John Kani and Winston Ntshona (as *Die Hodoshe Span*, produced The Space, Cape Town, 1973; as *The Island*, produced 1974). In *Statements*, 1974.
Dimetos (produced Edinburgh Festival, 1975; revised version produced Playhouse, Nottingham, 1976). In *"Dimetos" and Two Early Plays*, 1977.
The Guest: An Episode in the Life of Eugène Marais, with Ross Devenish (as *The Guest at Steenkampskraal*, televised 1977). 1977.
A Lesson from Aloes (produced Market Theatre, Johannesburg, 1978). 1981.
The Drummer (produced Actors' Theatre, Louisville, Kentucky, 1980).
"Master Harold" . . . and the Boys (produced Yale Repertory Theatre, New Haven, Connecticut, 1982). 1982.
The Road to Mecca (produced Yale Repertory Theatre, New Haven, Connecticut, 1984). 1985.
A Place with the Pigs: A Personal Parable (produced Yale Repertory Theatre, New Haven, Connecticut, 1987). 1988.
My Children! My Africa! (produced Market Theatre, Johannesburg, 1989). 1990.

Screenplays

Boesman and Lena, 1973; *Marigolds in August*, with Ross Devenish, 1980 (published 1982).

Television Plays

Mille Miglia, 1968; *The Guest at Steenkampskraal*, with Ross Devenish, 1977.

Fiction

Tsotsi.   1980.

Other

Notebooks 1960–1977, edited by Mary Benson.   1983.

*

Bibliographies

Russell Vandenbroucke, *Athol Fugard: A Bibliography, Biography, Playography*, London, 1977.
Temple Hauptfleisch, *Athol Fugard: A Source Guide*, Johannesburg, 1982.

Criticism

Books:
Stephen Gray (ed.), *Athol Fugard*, Johannesburg, 1982.
Dennis Walder, *Athol Fugard*, London, 1984 (Macmillan Modern Dramatists series).
Russell Vandenbroucke, *Truths the Hand Can Touch: The Theatre of Athol Fugard*, New York, 1985.
Margarete Seidenspinner, *Exploring the Labyrinth: Athol Fugard's Approach to South African Drama*, Essen, 1986.
Stephen Gray (compiler), *File on Fugard*, London, 1991.

* * *

Although his work is deeply rooted in the specific conditions of his native South Africa, Athol Fugard today enjoys a large international reputation, his plays being regularly produced and read in many countries. Interest in his writing for the stage has inevitably been closely linked with the world-wide focus on and protest against the apartheid system. Where normal political forms of opposition are ruthlessly silenced, art—and perhaps especially the theatre—may become a means of resistance, however enfeebled by censorship and harrassment. Fugard consistently sought to defy apartheid through his work in the theatre: in practical ways—for example by collaborating with black actors even when legislation made such multi-racial theatrical activity very difficult; but also through the writing itself, which as an entry in his *Notebooks* makes apparent, is inspired by his perception "that my life's work was possibly just to witness as truthfully as I could, the nameless and destitute (desperate) of this one little corner of the world".

Not that Fugard is a political dramatist in the obvious sense of using the stage to articulate a particular ideological viewpoint, which he seeks to convince his audience also to adopt. He has rejected the description of himself as "political" and seems to accept that he is a "liberal"—a pejorative term as used by militant critics within South Africa, but one which seems to square with the humanist spirit of his commitment both to the theatre and to the larger society which he sees it as serving.

This humanism is apparent in Fugard's concern, from the beginning of his career, with ordinary, often marginalised,

South Africans—black, white, and coloured—whose relationships and sufferings are the product of the racial and racist political forces operating in their country. Characters such as Zach and Morris in *The Blood Knot*, Boesman and Lena in the play of that name, or Philander and his white lover Frieda in *Statements after an Arrest under the Immorality Act*, are not in any sense heroic, or even always capable of acquiring a privileged awareness of their situations. They do not usually make discoveries which permit the audience to develop its own social analysis, or be energised by positive images of ultimately triumphant struggle. Their power lies primarily in the empathy they are able to arouse as the audience becomes imaginatively and emotionally involved in their sad, often desperately bleak, lives. The characters may be no wiser or more empowered at the end than they were at the beginning; but the audience may well have experienced intense compassion and outrage—feelings which are not political in themselves but which are the source of raised awareness and resistance to injustice and oppression.

In pursuit of what Fugard believes to be the revelatory and liberating experiences of which theatre is capable, he has always been willing to depart from conventional practice and to work collaboratively with his actors, often through improvisation, to create powerful images of life among the oppressed in South Africa. From his earliest prentice pieces, *No-Good Friday* and *Nongogo*, which were created in and about the now demolished township of Sophiatown, to the far more assured "Statements" plays (*Sizwe Bansi is Dead*, *The Island*, and *Statements After an Arrest*), Fugard has worked with actors such as Zakes Mokae, John Kani, and Winston Ntshona in ways which allowed his work to include experiences beyond those of a white South African, however imaginative, but familiar to black performers who might otherwise not have the literary skills to give effective dramatic expression to them. At its best, this method has produced plays which combine acute and detailed perceptions of the lives of ordinary black South Africans, the energy of African performance styles and conventions, and the ultimately controlling personal vision of Fugard the writer.

In *Sizwe Bansi Is Dead*, for example, which enjoyed critical and popular acclaim when it was performed in London in the early 1970's, Kani and Ntshona evoked the community of New Brighton (an African township of Port Elizabeth) on a stage furnished only with a few pieces of furniture and simple props. The action is centred upon Styles's photographic studio, the "strong-room of dreams" where the photographer, like the artist, puts down on paper the dreams and hopes of people who would otherwise be forgotten. With wit and humour the audience is given an insight into the everyday travails and dreams of ordinary black people through theatre which is, at the same time, simple, richly resonant, and strikingly effective, as Fugard focuses attention on what has been one of his perennial themes: the problem of defining identity for people who have been systematically denied any.

In *Sizwe Bansi is Dead* a black man "solves" his immediate dilemma of not being able to stay in Port Elizabeth to work by assuming the identity of another, a man called Robert Zwelinzima, whom he has found dead in the street. At first he is horrified by the idea, but he is finally won over by the argument that names are of no importance in a society where, for the white rulers, blacks are "ghosts" anyway. In other plays, too, Fugard returns to the ways in which the workings of the apartheid system threaten identity and basic human dignity. In *Statements After an Arrest* humiliation is shown as extending into even the most intimate areas of sexual relationship and destroying the sense of dignity of the self as a loving sexual being which is crucial to personal identity.

In pursuit of these concerns Fugard's later plays have returned to Port Elizabeth, the scene of earlier work such as *The Blood Knot* and *Hello and Goodbye*. The most successful, artistically and critically, is also the most directly autobiographical. *"Master Harold"* . . . *and the Boys* is based on an incident in Fugard's youth, when he spat in the face of his own best friend, a black waiter in his mother's tea-room in Port Elizabeth. With devastating honesty Fugard dramatizes the power of racism to invade and influence the behaviour of the individual, and to negate the identity and dignity of another person.

Occasionally Fugard's dramatic writing has sought its subject matter outside South African realities, for example in his allegorical play *Dimetos*, which is based on a passage in Camus's notebooks. Even here Fugard is faithful to his basic impulse to "bear witness", through arguably less powerfully and successfully than in some of the plays set in South Africa. Ultimately, it is in the unique quality of his "testimony" that Fugard's importance as a contemporary dramatist rests, for in his best work he has achieved what so many playwrights seek but only occasionally find—the means of bringing into relationship private and personal experience with some of the momentous political and social forces of our time.

—Brian Crow

See also *Volume 1* entries on *Boesman and Lena; The Island; "Master Harold"* . . . *and the Boys; Sizwe Bansi is Dead.*

FULLER, Jr. Charles (H.).   Born in Philadelphia, Pennsylvania, USA, 5 March 1939. Educated at Villanova University, 1956–58, and La Salle College, 1965–67, both Philadelphia. Served as a petroleum lab technician in the United States Army in Japan and Korea, 1959–62. Married Miriam A. Nesbitt in 1962; two sons. Bank loan collector, counsellor at Temple University, and city housing inspector, all Philadelphia, 1960's; co-founder and co-director, Afro-American Arts Theatre, Philadelphia, 1967–71; writer and director, *The Black Experience* programme, WIP Radio, Philadelphia, 1970–71. Recipient: Obie Award, 1981; Audelco Award, 1981, 1982; Pulitzer Prize, 1982; New York Drama Critics Circle Award, 1982; Outer Circle Award, 1982. DFA: La Salle College, 1982; Villanova University, 1983.

Works

Stage Works

The Village: A Party (produced McCarter Theater, Princeton, New Jersey, 1968; as *The Perfect Party*, produced Tambellini's Gate Theater, New York, 1969).
The Rise. In *New Plays from the Black Theatre*, edited by Ed Bullins. 1969.
In My Many Names and Days (one-act plays; produced New Federal Theatre, New York, 1972).
Candidate (produced New Federal Theatre, New York, 1974).
In the Deepest Part of Sleep (produced St. Mark's Playhouse, New York, 1974).

First Love (produced Billie Holiday Theatre, Brooklyn, New York, 1975).
The Lay Out Letter (produced Freedom Theatre, Philadelphia, 1975).
The Brownsville Raid (produced Waterford, Connecticut, 1975).
Sparrow in Flight, music by Larry Garner, based on a concept by Rosetta LeNoire (produced AMAS Repertory Theatre, New York, 1978).
Zooman and the Sign (produced Theater Four, New York, 1980).
A Soldier's Play (produced Theater Four, New York, 1981). 1982.

Screenplays

A Soldier's Story, 1984.

Television Plays

Roots, Resistance, and Renaissance series, 1967; *Mitchell*, 1968; *Black America* series, 1970–71; *The Sky is Gray*, from the story by Ernest J. Gaines (*American Short Story* series), 1980.

*

Criticism

Books:
Interview in *In Their Own Words: Contemporary American Playwrights*, edited by David Savran, New York, 1988.
Esther Harriott (ed.), *American Voices: Five Contemporary Playwrights in Essays and Interviews*, Jefferson, North Carolina, 1988.

* * *

An angry, consuming energy which propels the protagonist towards violence, an irony which humanizes him while depriving the viewer of easy categorizations: these elements characterize Charles Fuller's style. Within an American theatre tradition Fuller's work both acknowledges the seminal position of Amiri Baraka and extends the vision of the tumultuous 1960's beyond a rigid, racial schematization which, in conferring upon blacks the status of victims of oppression, seemingly robbed them of any responsibility for or power over the circumstances in which they found themselves.

A former bank loan collector, college counsellor, and city housing inspector, Fuller initially gained a measure of national recognition in 1976 with *The Brownsville Raid*. Though presently out of circulation, the play is of interest because it prefigures the approach adopted in the later *A Soldier's Play*. *The Brownsville Raid* is a dramatization of the investigation into a 1906 shooting spree which culminated in President Teddy Roosevelt's unwarranted, dishonorable discharge of an entire black infantry brigade. With historical accounts as his starting point, Fuller skilfully interweaves a "whodunnit" plot with a compelling portrait of a black corporal who has his faith in the Army shattered when he refuses to comply with his officers' demand for a scapegoat. Both black and white men are presented with strengths and faults; what emerges is a composite picture of men and a society whose vision is distorted by racism.

In both *Zooman and the Sign* and *A Soldier's Play* racism

appears not as a specific, external event to which the black protagonists must react; rather, its negative values have been so internalized that, propelled by their own frantic despair, the characters move relentlessly towards self-destruction. In the first play, about a father's search for his daughter's killer, a knife-toting, drug-running 15-year-old casually admits to the audience at the outset that he is the killer. Although Zooman attempts to mask a mounting sense of entrapment with calculated bravado, his direct conversations with the audience about familial disintegration, unwanted homosexual encounters, and detention for uncommitted crimes characterize him as an alienated youth whose experiences have taught him that "niggahs can't be heroes", that blacks seemingly have no control over the atrophy engulfing their families and communities. These monologues, delivered in a street-wise, frenetic style which is nonetheless reminiscent of black toast traditions and Muhammad Ali's alliterative poetry, have the effect of humanizing Zooman, of placing him in a context where his asocial behavior becomes more understandable, and his affinity to the larger society more apparent.

Just as Zooman believes that blacks are helpless, so too do the neighbors of the slain girl, for no one will come forth as witnesses to the crime. The father's erecting a sign accusing them of moral complicity triggers only hostile recriminations from the neighbors and argument within the family itself. Symbolic of a community's failure to foster a more active, ennobling sense of its own possibilities, the sign occasions the final violence wherein Zooman is accidentally killed in his attempt to tear it down. Another black child lies dead in the street, another family grieves, and another sign goes up as momentary monument to incredible waste.

An ultimately pervasive irony, which empties the landscape of possible victors and reveals instead a society maimed by racism, is equally evident in *A Soldier's Play*. Unlike Zooman, Sergeant Waters espouses the black middle-class values of hard work, education, and racial pride as the means of self-advancement. Like Zooman, Waters, in seeking a sphere in which to exercise a masculine sense of control and dignity, has had only limited success, for he operates within the segregated Army of World War II. The search for his killer triggers a series of flashbacks which reveal him as a vicious, petty tyrant bent upon literally ridding the race of all those blues-singing, hoodoo-oriented men who he says prevent advancement; yet they also create a measure of sympathy for this ambitious man, consumed by misplaced faith, self-hatred, and guilt.

The eventual identification of two black recruits as Waters's murderers defies the expectation, carefully nurtured by the playwright, that overt white hostility is the motivating factor. Additionally, it raises questions concerning the definition of justice, for the infantrymen have just received their long-awaited orders to ship out, in effect being granted license to kill in Europe a tyranny similar to what Waters represents at home. Compounding the irony further, Fuller provides a postscript which subverts the dramatic experience: the investigating officer reveals that the entire incident is recorded in military documents as meaningless black-on-black crime; Waters is inadvertently listed as a heroic war casualty; and the entire company is destroyed in combat. Thus, the Army learns nothing from this sorry episode.

Fuller's dramatic world is dominated by driven, destructive men trying to carve out a viable place within a hostile environment. Though his characters inhabit a bleak landscape, his audiences need not: through the dramatic experience they can appreciate how racism distorts an entire society and choose to stop the human destruction.

—Sandra L. Richards

See also *Volume 1* entry on *A Soldier's Play*.

G

GALE, Zona. Born in Portage, Wisconsin, 26 August 1874. Educated Portage public schools, and at the University of Wisconsin, Madison, 1891–95, BL 1895, ML 1899. Married William L. Breese in 1928; one adopted daughter. Reporter, Milwaukee *Evening Wisconsin*, 1895–96, Milwaukee *Journal*, 1896–1901, and New York *Evening World*, 1901–03; returned to Portage, 1904; thereafter a full-time writer; first play, *The Neighbours*, produced 1912. Member, Wisconsin Library Commission, 1920–32; member, Board of Regents, 1923–29, and Board of Visitors, 1936–38, University of Wisconsin; Wisconsin delegate, International Congress of Women, Chicago, 1933. Recipient: Butterick Prize, 1911; Pulitzer Prize, for drama, 1921. D.Litt: Ripon College, Wisconsin, 1922; University of Wisconsin, 1929; Rollins College, Winter Park, Florida, 1930. Died in Chicago, 27 December 1938.

Works

Stage Works

The Neighbours (produced 1912).   1926.
Miss Lulu Bett, from her novel (produced Belmont Theatre, New York, 1920).   1921.
Uncle Jimmy.   1922.
Mister Pitt, from her novel *Birth* (produced 1925).   1925.
Evening Clothes.   1932.
Faint Perfume, from her novel.   1934.
The Clouds.   1936.

Radio Plays

Neighbors, with Marian de Forest, from stories in *Friendship Village*, 1933.

Fiction

Romance Island.   1906.
The Loves of Pelleas and Etarre (stories).   1907.
Friendship Village (stories).   1908.
Friendship Village Love Stories.   1909.
Mothers to Men.   1911.
Christmas: A Story.   1912.
Neighborhood Stories.   1914.
Heart's Kindred.   1915.
A Daughter of the Morning.   1917.
Birth.   1918.
Peace in Friendship Village (stories).   1919.
Miss Lulu Bett.   1920.
Faint Perfume.   1923.
Preface to a Life.   1926.
Yellow Gentians and Blue (stories).   1927.

Borgia.   1929.
Bridal Pond (stories).   1930.
Papa La Fleur.   1933.
Old-Fashioned Tales.   1933.
Light Woman.   1937.
Magna.   1939.

Verse

The Secret Way.   1921.

Other

Civic Improvement in Little Towns.   1913.
When I Was a Little Girl.   1913.
What Women Won in Wisconsin.   1922.
Portage, Wisconsin, and Other Essays.   1928.
Frank Miller of Mission Inn.   1938.

*

Bibliographies

Harold P. Simonson, "Zona Gale", in *American Literary Realism*, 3, 1968.

Criticism

Books:
August Derleth, *Still Small Voice: The Biography of Zona Gale*, 1940.
Harold P. Simonson, *Zona Gale*, 1962.

Articles:
Judith L. Stephens, "The Compatability of Traditional Dramatic Form and Feminist Expression", in *Theatre Annual*, 40, 1985.

* * *

"Neither version is very impressive, but she has secured the humor which springs from a clever reproduction of dullness". Arthur Hobson Quinn's assessment of *Miss Lulu Bett*, Gale's most famous play, has met with surprisingly little challenge, and probably partly explains why she still receives little attention in a period committed to the retrieval of neglected women writers. That Gale was also extremely active in numerous social and political causes—such as women's suffrage, pacifism, and the status of women within the journalistic profession—further compounds the irony of her continuing obscurity.

Gale was well known as a writer of fiction before the appearance of her first—and possibly only—major play in 1920. The quality of this early fiction is, admittedly, scarcely memorable, and infects her first, short play, *The Neighbors*, as well as her later one-acter, *Uncle Jimmy*. Both of these works generate the cloying ambiance of her "Friendship Village" stories, with a sentimental, superficial complacency that appears to celebrate the average while denying the abnormal an existence. If it seems difficult to reconcile such a tone with Gale's non-literary championing of socially disadvantaged groups, it should also be observed that Gale was anything but a single-issue fanatic, and that the element common to most of her diverse ideologies was an optimism in humanity. The balance between this optimism and the apparent naivety of her early writings is a fine one.

Eugene O'Neill has long been forgiven the domestic sentiment of *Ah, Wilderness!*, since it was followed by *Long Day's Journey Into Night*, and a similar tolerance should be granted to Gale's eventual move from naivety to ironic under-writing in *Miss Lulu Bett*. A reading of the first pages of that novel beside those of the exactly contemporary work of Sinclair Lewis, with whom she has always been compared, leaves no doubt that both writers deployed an apparently laconic satire of small-town manners in a way that contrasts strongly with more florid styles then in vogue in much American writing. As a novelist using multi-personal narration, Gale also allows her authorial voice to intrude to further prune back her characters' postures and pretensions, and if her primary target is an oppressively boorish patriarch very like Lewis's, she is also merciless to most of the female characters.

In the years around 1920, many other women writers were producing studies of female entrapment and loneliness which have deservedly out-lived Gale's novel. In transmuting such material to the stage, however, Gale achieved a feat which was, for the period, remarkable. With overt authorial commentary no longer available, Gale radically redrafted it, with a sensitivity to the theatre that belied her inexperience, so that almost every line pivots on the characters' self-exposure. Figures who are minor or incidental in the novel are more amply fleshed out on the stage, so that the spasmodically senile old Mrs. Bett is both a vital instrument to the plot in her blundering and obtuseness, but is also, through her very presence, a warning that a malaise that infects three generations may be self-perpetuating.

Though it could seem specious to extract a thesis from the play, the fact that early in its Pulitzer Prize-winning season Gale was pressured to re-write the sombre ending in terms of marital concord has overshadowed the values that the play articulates. Lulu's adult life is perceived by tribal wisdom as a saga of failure beside that of her married sister with whom she lives as a domestic help. When it appears that the marriage, through which Lulu has escaped this condition, may be bigamous, discussion turns to the specific totems and taboos that have been violated as well as to how reputations in the face of gossip might be preserved. For Lulu, however, there is no ambiguity once it is established that the bigamy motif was not invented to throw her off; whatever the experience is called, she does not regret it. She has established herself as her own person, and she has transcended the inter-generational modelling that is the family's real entrapment. However the dramatic action is resolved, Lulu's stature is intact in these terms.

Gale dealt with similar issues in several of her other works, but never with comparable success on stage. Her other major play, *Mister Pitt*, was, through its brevity, sharply reductive of *Birth*, the relatively complex novel on which it was based—though in this case Quinn, perversely, preferred the play. The novel's title announces the fateful pressures of conditioning, drawing attention to the fact that Gale's mature work is always complex in its polemics. In her overt broadsides against patriarchy, she clearly establishes herself as a pioneer feminist, but she is also often sharply critical of the female function of domesticity, as in one of her collected essays: "Maternity is less a relationship than an extra-physical force, to which shocking violence has been done by children, through sentimentality, and by mothers, through monarchy".

—Howard McNaughton

GALSWORTHY, (John). Born at Parkfield, Kingston Hill, Surrey, England, 14 August 1867. Educated at Saugeen School, Bournemouth, 1876–80; Harrow School, Middlesex, 1881–86; New College, Oxford, 1886–89, BA 1889; Lincoln's Inn, London, 1889–90; called to the bar, 1890. Married Ada Cooper in 1905. Travelled in North America, Australia, New Zealand, and the Pacific (met Conrad, 1892), then briefly practised law until 1895; thereafter full-time writer; first-produced play, *The Silver Box*, staged 1906; worked in a military hospital in France, 1916–17; editor, *Reveille* magazine for soldiers, 1918; first president, International PEN Club, 1921–33; Romanes lecturer, Oxford University, 1931. Recipient: Nobel Prize for Literature, 1932. LL.D: University of St. Andrews, Fife, 1922; Litt.D: University of Manchester, 1927; University of Dublin, 1929; University of Sheffield, 1930; Cambridge University, 1930; Oxford University, 1931; Princeton University, New Jersey, 1931. Fellow, Royal Society of Literature, 1912; honorary fellow, New College, Oxford, 1926; honorary member, American Academy of Arts and Sciences, 1926. Order of Merit, 1929. Died in London, 31 January 1933.

Works

Collections

Six Short Plays (includes *The First and the Last; The Little Man; Hallmarked; Defeat; The Sun; Punch and Go*). 1921.
Works (Grove Edition, 26 vols.). 1927–34.
Plays. 1928.
The Galsworthy Reader, edited by Anthony West. 1967.
Five Plays (includes *Strife; Justice; The Eldest Son; The Skin Game; Loyalties*). 1984.

Stage Works

The Silver Box (produced Royal Court Theatre, London, 1906). 1909.
Joy: A Play on the Letter I (produced Savoy Theatre, London, 1907). 1909.
Strife (produced Duke of York's Theatre, London, 1909). 1909.
Justice (produced Duke of York's Theatre, London, 1910). 1910.
The Little Dream: An Allegory (produced Gaiety Theatre, Manchester, 1911). 1911; revised edition, 1912.
The Pigeon: A Fantasy (produced Royalty Theatre, London, 1912). 1912.

The Eldest Son: A Domestic Drama (produced Kingsway Theatre, London, 1912).   1912.
The Fugitive (produced Royal Court Theatre, London, 1913). 1913.
The Mob (produced Gaiety Theatre, Manchester, 1914). 1914.
The Little Man (produced Birmingham Repertory Theatre, 1915).   In *Six Short Plays*, 1921.
A Bit o' Love (produced Kingsway Theatre, London, 1915). 1915.
The Foundations: An Extravagant Play (produced Royalty Theatre, London, 1917).   1920.
Defeat (produced Lyric Theatre, Hammersmith, London, 1920).   In *Six Short Plays*, 1921.
The Skin Game (produced St. Martin's Theatre, London, 1920).   1920.
A Family Man (produced Comedy Theatre, London, 1921). 1922.
The First and the Last (produced Aldwych Theatre, London, 1921).   In *Six Short Plays*, 1921.
Hallmarked.   In *Six Short Plays*, 1921.
The Sun (produced Playhouse, Liverpool, 1922).   In *Six Short Plays*, 1921.
Punch and Go (produced Mary Ward Settlement, London, 1924).   In *Six Short Plays*, 1921.
Loyalties (produced St. Martin's Theatre, London, 1922). 1922.
Windows: A Comedy for Idealists and Others (produced Royal Court Theatre, London, 1922).   1922.
The Forest, from his story "The Stoic" (produced St. Martin's Theatre, London, 1924).   1924.
Old English (produced Theatre Royal, Haymarket, London, 1924).   1924.
The Show (produced St. Martin's Theatre, London, 1925). 1925.
Escape: An Episodic Play (produced Ambassador's Theatre, London, 1926).   1926.
Exiled: An Evolutionary Comedy (produced Wyndham's Theatre, London, 1929).   1929.
The Roof (produced Vaudeville Theatre, London, 1929). 1929.
Carmen, with Ada Galsworthy, from the opera by Henri Meilhac and Ludovic Halévy, music by Bizet.   1932.
The Winter Garden: Four Dramatic Pieces (includes *Escape—Episode VII, The Golden Eggs, Similes, The Winter Garden*).   1935.

Fiction

From the Four Winds (stories).   1897.
Jocelyn.   1898.
Villa Rubein.   1900; revised edition, 1909.
A Man of Devon.   1901; revised edition, with *Villa Rubein*, 1909.
The Island Pharisees.   1904; revised edition, 1908.
The Forsyte Saga.   1922; parts individually published:
    The Man of Property.   1906.
    In Chancery.   1920.
    Awakening.   1920.
    To Let.   1921.
The Country House.   1907.
Fraternity.   1909.
The Patrician.   1911.
The Dark Flower.   1913.
The Freelands.   1915.

John Galsworthy (c.1920).

Beyond.   1917.
Five Tales.   1918; as *The First and the Last* and *The Stoic* (2 vols.), 1920; as *"The Apple Tree" and Other Tales*, 1965.
The Burning Spear, Being the Adventures of Mr. John Lavender in Time of War.   1919.
Saint's Progress.   1919.
Tatterdemalion (stories).   1920.
Captures (stories).   1923.
A Modern Comedy.   1929; parts individually published:
    The White Monkey.   1924.
    The Silver Spoon.   1926.
    Swan Song.   1928.
Caravan: The Assembled Tales.   1925.
Two Forsyte Interludes: A Silent Wooing, Passers By.   1927.
On Forsyte 'change.   1930.
Soames and Flag.   1930.
End of the Chapter.   1934; parts individually published:
    Maid in Waiting.   1931.
    Flowering Wilderness.   1932.
    Over the River.   1933; as *One More River*, 1933.
Corduroys.   1937.
The Rocks.   1937.
'Nyasha.   1939.

Verse

Moods, Songs, and Doggerels.   1912.
Five Poems.   1919.
Verses New and Old.   1926.
Collected Poems, edited by Ada Galsworthy.   1934.

Memoirs and Letters

Autobiographical Letters: A Correspondence with Frank Harris. 1933.
Letters 1900–1932, edited by Edward Garnett. 1934.
Letters to Leon Lion, edited by Asher Boldon Wilson. 1968.

Other

A Commentary. 1908.
A Justification of the Censorship of Plays. 1909.
A Motley. 1910.
The Inn of Tranquillity: Studies and Essays. 1912.
"The Little Man" and Other Satires. 1915; as *"Abracadabra" and Other Satires*, 1924.
A Sheaf. 1916.
The Land: A Plea. 1917.
Addresses in America. 1919.
Another Sheaf. 1919.
International Thought. 1923.
Memorable Days. 1924.
Castles in Spain and Other Screeds. 1927.
Two Essays on Conrad. 1930.
Author and Critic. 1935.
Forsytes, Pendyces, and Others, edited by Ada Galsworthy. 1935.
Glimpses and Reflections. 1937.
My Galsworthy Story (includes letters), by Margaret Morris. 1967.

Editor, with Ada Galsworthy, *Ex Libris John Galsworthy*. 1933.

*

Bibliographies

H.V. Marrot, *A Bibliography of the Works of John Galsworthy*, London, 1928.
G.H. Fabes, *John Galsworthy: His First Editions*, 1932.
E.H. Mikhail, *John Galsworthy the Dramatist: A Bibliography of Criticism*, Troy, New York, 1971.
Earl E. Stevens and H. Ray Stevens, *John Galsworthy: An Annotated Bibliography of Writings about Him*, De Kalb, Illinois, 1980.

Criticism

Books:
R.H. Coats, *John Galsworthy as Dramatic Artist*, London, 1926.
L.L. Scalit, *John Galsworthy: A Survey*, Nework, 1929.
H.L. Ould, *John Galsworthy*, London, 1934; reprinted 1974.
H.V. Marrot, *The Life and Letters of John Galsworthy*, London, 1935.
M.E. Reynolds, *Memories of John Galsworthy by His Sister*, London, 1936.
R.H. Mottram, *John Galsworthy*, 1953.
R.H. Mottram, *For Some We Loved: An Intimate Portrait of Ada and John Galsworthy*, 1956.
A.D. Choudhuri, *John Galsworthy's Plays: A Critical Survey*, Calcutta, 1961.
Dudley Barker, *The Man of Principle: A View of Galsworthy*, London, 1963.
Rudolf Sauter, *Galsworthy the Man*, London, 1967.
David Holloway, *John Galsworthy*, London, 1968.

Catherine Dupré, *John Galsworthy: A Biography*, London, 1976.
James Gindin, *The English Climate: An Excursion into a Biography of John Galsworthy*, London, 1979.
S.B. Shulka, *Social and Moral Ideas in the Plays of John Galsworthy*, Salzburg, 1979.
Alec Fréchet, *John Galsworthy: A Reassessment*, London, 1982.
M. Radhamani Gopalakrishnan, *Galsworthy's Plays: A Thematic Study*, Madras, 1982.
Jan McDonald, *The New Drama 1900–1914*, London, 1986 (Macmillan Modern Dramatists series).
James Gindin, *John Galsworthy's Life and Art: An Alien's Fortress*, Ann Arbor, Michigan, 1987.
Sanford Sternlicht, *John Galsworthy*, Boston, 1987.
Ian Clarke, *Edwardian Drama*, London, 1989.

Articles:
G.J. Scrimgeour, "Naturalist Drama and John Galsworthy", in *Modern Drama*, 7, 1964.

* * *

Best known in the second half of the 20th century as author of the series of novels known as *The Forsyte Saga*, John Galsworthy has an assured place in dramatic history as the leading English representative of naturalism in its original philosophic sense. A prolific writer, he was the one serious dramatist who held the London West End stage with play following play from 1906 to 1930, when at times even Bernard Shaw was relegated to the provinces or had plays premiered abroad. As a humanitarian liberal, he holds a place in the English theatre corresponding to that of Arthur Miller in the American.

His first play, *The Silver Box*, was instantly successful when produced at the Court Theatre under the management of Granville Barker and J.E. Vedrenne, who were soliciting new plays in order to demonstrate that the art of playwriting was not dead in England and that a non-commercial theatre could nurture it with performances of high quality. This was part of the campaign for a National Theatre, and plays on public issues had a special place in the repertoire. *The Silver Box* demonstrates the thesis of one law for the rich and another for the poor with a heavy-handed insistence that suggests Edwardian audiences were less sophisticated, slower to pick up unspoken implications than modern audiences have become.

Galsworthy's next play, *Joy*, was disappointing, marred by an Edwardian whimsy that recurs occasionally in his later work. Then came Granville Barker's production of *Strife* and, most sensational, *Justice*, generally accepted as the high point of naturalistic acting and direction in the first quarter of the century. The titles claim kinship with the work of T.W. Robertson, the author of *Caste* (the play being rehearsed in *The Eldest Son*), in the British tradition.

The bleak determinism of naturalist philosophy shows in the acceptance of men and women of their circumstances (the result of heredity and environment), unable to change or be changed by the efforts of themselves or others. The ne'er-do-wells, and equally their rash benefactor, in *The Pigeon*, can only live out what they are until they die. Bly, in *Windows*, a character faintly reminiscent of Doolittle in Shaw's *Pygmalion* (although *Windows* is in dialectical opposition to Shaw's play), recognises his daughter to be unchangeable; at best, by cleaning the windows of the better-off, he can enable them to see the less fortunate more clearly and care for them a little.

Strife is set in a mining area during a long and bitter strike. Although it had some topicality in England, Zola's *Germinal* also presides over Galsworthy's view of his subject. The confrontation between labour and capital (the terms in which old Anthony, Chairman of the Directors, thinks and speaks) is presented in social Darwinist form as a struggle to the death between groups whose natural interests are utterly opposed. That, at least, is how the strong men see it, the leaders who confront each other like dominant beasts in herds disputing prey or territory. What turns the play into tragedy is the throwing-over of the heroic figures by smaller men with no breadth of view, an alliance of cowards, soft-minded liberals, and those who see only their own private interests; and the death through starvation of Mrs. Roberts, wife of the miners' leader, deepens the ironic sense of waste when the settlement eventually agreed proves to be the same as was proposed before the strike began. Galsworthy never wrote a play about the Forsytes, but old Anthony (and, indeed, Sylvanus Heythorp in *Old English*) belongs to the same stock, Galsworthy's own: figures of a previous generation of City men whom, ambivalently, he admires and deplores.

Galsworthy's attack on the inhumanity of social institutions, particularly the legal system, in *Justice*, was part of his general campaign for prison reform. This had involved much visiting of prisons, interviewing staff and convicts, writing letters to the press, lobbying politicians, as if he were a self-appointed one-man commission. Winston Churchill, as Home Secretary, went to see the play, and it was referred to in the debate on his Prison Reform Bill, certainly influencing the provisions governing solitary confinement. As a tragedy, *Justice* belongs to the uneasy category of plays, containing also *Death of a Salesman*, which have a weak, rather unattractive character at the centre of the dramatic action. Pathos is the dominant emotion, controlled by a clear, dispassionate disposition of characters and arguments within an artificially balanced structure (the formula tried first in *The Silver Box* and which came into its own by matching the theme in *Strife*). The most powerful scene in performance is wordless, yet so placed that it releases the protest smothered by the bare conventional dialogue, and answers the formal rhetoric of the court scene.

The Fugitive is another tragedy concerned with one of society's victims, but this time the tragic character, Clare Dedmond, is paradigmatic, representing the cultural ideal of "the lady": beautiful, sensitive, refined—indeed, over-bred, over-refined, too weak and vulnerable to be able to survive adverse circumstances outside the circle of privilege she was brought up to grace. Like Irene, in *The Forsyte Saga*, Clare is sympathetically treated; but the same cannot be said of all the ladies in Galsworthy's plays. They are deadlier than the male of the species in *The Skin Game* (it is Mrs. Hillcrist who plays dirty in fighting for the traditional interests of the gentry against the advance of a new class of wealthy industrialists) and *The Mob* (in which Katherine More's attempt at sexual bribery is the last, worst betrayal of her husband's stand against a bullying colonial war in the face of "patriotic" hysteria). The robust working-girl, Madge Thomas, in *Strife*, is distinctly less repellant when she bargains with her sexual favours to bring the strike to an end. Indeed, Galsworthy's robuster women characters, especially younger women, such as the girls in the anti-patriarchal comedy, *A Family Man*, or Mabel Dancy in *Loyalties* (a play concerning anti-semitism and class solidarity against outsiders) tend to be the most perceptive and fair-minded figures in the plays. D.H. Lawrence identified an unpleasant quality in Galsworthy's treatment of sex, and this may well be sustainable by less partial criticism. It is also worth keeping in mind that Galsworthy showed and discussed all his writing with his wife Ada, the model for Irene, if not Clare, whom he married after her painful divorce from his cousin.

The strong moral themes, lucid presentation of the issues, firm construction, ease and simplicity of dialogue, and competence in drawing comprehensible characters just emergent from type, add up to a "middle-brow" drama, never devoid of interest, expertly handled to amuse or excite, as well as to provoke thought. The tradition was to be continued in the serious plays of Terence Rattigan, who also chose to run with the fox rather than the hunters.

—Margery Morgan

See also *Volume 1* entries on *Justice*; *Strife*.

GAMBARO, Griselda.   Born in Buenos Aires, Argentina, 28 July 1928. Left high school, 1943. Married Juan Carlos Distéfano; two sons. Publisher's clerical asistant, 1943; clerical worker with sports club, 1947–56; published first volume of short stories, 1963; first play, *Viejo matrimonio*, produced 1965; worked closely with the avant-garde arts organisation Centro de Experimentación Audiovisual del Instituto Torcuatro Di Tella (founded 1958, closed 1971), which also published some of her plays; drama teacher, Universidad Nacional del Litoral, c.1969; spent a year in Rome, 1970; lecturer in contemporary drama for National Endowments for the Arts, 1973; her novel *Ganarse la muerte* banned in Argentina, and, under increasing persecution from Argentine authorities, she moved to Europe, and lived in Barcelona, 1977–80; returned to Argentina, 1980; collaborated with the "vanguardist" Teatro Abierto, 1981. Recipient: Premio de la Asociación de Teatros, 1964; Fondo Nacional de las Artes Prize, 1964; Premio Emecé, 1965; Premio Argentores, 1968, 1976, and 1980.

Works

Collections

Teatro: Las paredes; El desatino; Los siameses.   1979.
Teatro (3 vols.).   1984–89:
  1. *Real envido; La malasangre; Del sol naciente.*   1984.
  2. *Dar la vuelta; Información para extranjeros; Puesta en claro; Sucede lo que pasa.*   1987.
  3. *Viaje de invierno; Solo un aspecto; La gracia; El miedo; Decir sí; Antígona furiosa;* and short plays.   1989.

Stage Works

Viejo matrimonio (produced Instituto Torcuatro Di Tella, Buenos Aires, 1965).
Las paredes (produced Instituto Torcuatro Di Tella, Buenos Aires, 1966).   In *Teatro*, 1979.
El desatino, from her novel (produced Instituto Torcuatro Di Tella, Buenos Aires, 1966).   1965.
Los siameses (produced Instituto Torcuatro Di Tella, Buenos Aires, 1967).   1967.
El campo (produced Instituto Torcuatro Di Tella, Buenos Aires, 1968).   1967; translated as *The Camp*, in *Voices of*

Change in the Spanish American Theater, translated by William Oliver, 1971.

La gracia. In *El Urogallo*, 1972; in book form, in *Teatro 3*, 1989.

Nada que ver, from her novel *Nada que ver con otra historia* (produced Buenos Aires, 1972). With *Sucede lo que pasa*, 1983.

Sólo un aspecto (produced Palacia de San Luis, Buenos Aires, 1974). In *La palabra y el hombre*, 8, 1973; in book form, in *Teatro 3*, 1989.

Información para extranjeros (produced 1978). In Italian translation, 1975; in Spanish, in *Teatro 2*, 1987; translated as *Information for Strangers*, in *Literary Review*, Summer 1989.

El nombre (produced Buenos Aires, 1976).

Sucede lo que pasa (produced Buenos Aires, 1976). With *Nade que ver*, 1983.

Decir sí (produced Teatro Abierto festival, Buenos Aires, 1981). In *Hispamérica*, vol.7 no. 21, 1978; in book form, in *Antologia Teatro Abierto*, 1981, and in *Teatro 3*, 1989.

El despojamiento (produced 1983). In *Tramoya: Cuaderno de teatro*, 21–22, 1981.

La malasangre (produced Buenos Aires, 1982). In *Teatro 1*, 1984.

Real envido (produced Buenos Aires, 1984). In *Teatro 1*, 1984.

Del sol naciente (produced Buenos Aires, 1984). In *Teatro 1*, 1984.

Nosferatu (produced Buenos Aires, 1985).

Viaje de invierno (produced Buenos Aires, 1985). In *Teatro 3*, 1989.

Antígona Furiosa (produced 1986). In *Teatro 3*, 1989.

Dar la vuelta. In *Teatro 2*, 1987.

Pestro en claro. In *Teatro 2*, 1987.

Morgon (produced 1988).

El miedo. In *Teatro 3*, 1989.

Penas sin importancia (produced 1990).

Screenplays

La infancia de Petra, 1966.

Fiction

Madrigal en ciudad (stories). 1963.
El desatino. 1965.
Un felicidad con menos pena. 1968.
Nada que ver con otra historia. 1972.
La cola mágica (stories for children). 1975.
Ganarse la muerte. 1976.
Dios no nos quiere contentos. 1979.
Lo impenetrable. 1984.

Other

Conversaciones con chicos: Sobre la sociedad, los padres, los afectos, la cultura. 1977.

*

Criticism

Books:

Sandra Meissinger Cypess, "The Plays of Griselda Gambaro", in *Dramatists in Revolt: The New Latin American Theatre*, edited by Leon F. Lyday and George Woodyard, Austin, Texas, 1976.

Kathleen Betsko and Rachel Koening (eds.), *Interviews with Contemporary Women Playwrights*, New York, 1987.

Nora Mazziotti (ed.), *Poder, deseo y marginación: Aproximaciones a la obra de Griselda Gambaro*, Buenos Aires, 1989.

Diana Taylor (ed.), *Ensayos críticos sobre Griselda Gambaro*, Ottowa, 1989.

Diana Taylor, *Theatre of Crisis: Drama and Politics in Latin America*, Lexington, Kentucky, 1991.

Articles:

Tamara Holzapfel, "Griselda Gambaro's Theatre of the Absurd", in *Latin American Theatre Review*, vol.4 no.1, 1970.

Sandra Messinger Cypress, "Physical Imagery in the Plays of Griselda Gambaro", in *Modern Drama*, vol.18 no.4, 1975.

Joan Rea Boorman, "Contemporary Latin American Women Playwrights", in *Rice University Studies*, vol.64 no.1, 1978.

David W. Foster, "The Texture of Dramatic Action in the Plays of Griselda Gambaro", in *Hispanic Journal*, vol.1 no.2, 1979.

*   *   *

Griselda Gambaro has focused on victimized protagonists trying to survive in a violent, criminal society since her first play, *Las paredes*. While she notes that her plays are variations on the theme of violence, the modulations reflect the radical change which has affected the Argentine society during her 25-year career. The political situation in Argentina has shifted violently during these years from an on-going Peronism, through a military dictatorship and its atrocious "dirty war" against its own population which left an estimated 15,000 Argentines "missing" between 1976 and 1983, to a new democracy under Raúl Alfonsín and a revamped Peronism under Menem. The attitudes of Gambaro's protagonists have also changed as they struggle to survive and as they gradually come to understand Argentina's constant crisis, as well as whose interests that crisis serves. Gambaro's dramatic style, too, has undergone transformation. The intensifying stages of socio-political violence beg new ways of addressing the atrocities artistically, resulting in new stages in the aesthetic representation of violence. While the thematic concern with violence remains constant throughout Gambaro's work, certain changes in perspective, resulting in innovative artistic strategies, make it possible for us to distinguish three major phases in her playwriting, coinciding roughly with the three decades in which it was produced.

First, there are the plays of the 1960's: paradigms of crisis both in themes and models, such as *Las paredes* (The Walls), *El desatino* (The Blunder), *El campo* (*The Camp*), *Los siameses* (Siamese Twins). Gambaro's early plays study the various manifestations of social crisis and the progressive decomposition of all social and judicial structures and systems devised to contain violence. The recurring images in her plays include the general collapse of boundaries separating inner from outer, private from public, self from other. The seemingly private room in *Las paredes* becomes a prison cell, and the walls physically move in on the inmate; the twins' individual desires for self-definition in *Siameses* crumbles into a self/other undifferentiation that destroys both. The violence practised in the inner, familial spheres proves as devastating, as systematic, as that carried out in concentration camps. Yet, the causes for the collapse remain unexamined, for one of the immediate responses to crisis involves denial of its existence or true significance and, consequently, displacement of responsibility. One of the constant ironies running throughout

Gambaro's early work is that her victims star in dramas of persecution which they fail to recognize as their own. They make up explanations, and their language, completely out of sync with the reality we see onstage, seems to belong to other scripts. Unable to fathom the causes of the aggression which threatens to exterminate them, they expend most of their energy convincing themselves that it does not really exist, or that a reasonable solution will be found. The passive, unrealistic response to a very real danger leaves the protagonist defenseless and, ultimately, dead.

Throughout these plays contradictions and confusion multiply, the known universe becomes unknowable, the familiar becomes strange and threatening as the world melts into a terrifying, unknowable void whose parameters recede and contract. Monsters—bizarre as Siamese twins or mundane as husband and wife—populate this grotesque sphere of apparently inexplicable violence.

Then there are the plays of the 1970's, which could be described as demythifications of models, dramas of erasure, stages of naked violence, such as *Decir sí* (Saying Yes), *El despojamiento* (Strip-Tease), and *Información para extranjeros* (*Information for Foreigners*). Gambaro's drama in the 1970's continued to explore the effects of social crisis, returning repeatedly to the themes of violence and victimization. The victims keep stumbling into the wrong plays: while innocently seeking a haircut (*Decir sí*), an audition (*El despojamiento*), or diversion (*Información para extranjeros*) they meet with the most degrading cruelty. Again the victims, unable to accept their predicaments, continue elaborating fictions in the face of gruesome fact. The collapse of barriers separating inner from outer and private from public characterizes this period as well. Scenes of institutional, objective cruelty are staged in a home in *Información*. In *Decir sí*, a seemingly personal desire for domination is acted out in the neutral professional space associated with barber shops.

Aesthetically, however, this period was one of intense experimentation for Gambaro. She observed that people have been blinded to violence in "real" life. Theatre must therefore attempt to recover the reality of violence in the symbolic order. The task became one of transposing violence from the realm of the real to the symbolic without distorting, simplifying, or mythologizing it. Towards this end, her drama of this period strips the onstage world of any remaining vestiges of rationality or coherence. Gone is the psychological and mythic framework of her earlier pieces, and by extension, any basis from which to explain or justify the crime. Gone is the characterization, exposition, complication, and again conflict normally associated with theatricality. Gambaro places the spectators in the naked contradiction of their historical moment. In *Información* she suggests no one should be exposed to the grotesque display of atrocity so prevalent in Argentina: "No one under 18 will be admitted. Or under 35 or over 36. Everyone else can attend with no problem. No obscenity or strong language. The play speaks to our lifestyle: Argentine, Western and Christian. We are in 1971".

Fragmentation-as-theme finds reflection in a marked formal fragmentation during this period, whether in the very short one-act plays like *Decir sí* and *El despojamiento*, or the episodic *Información*, "a chronicle in 20 scenes". These are no "well-made" plays. Gambaro's theatre stages atrocity, and by so doing, she addresses the question posed by all literature of atrocity: how can we speak about the unspeakable? Gambaro's plays of the 1970's are the drama of the "missing" —they do not explain or fill in the gaps. There is no reason, no justification, nothing to identify with—only terror.

The anti-theatricality of Gambaro's plays during this period should not imply that they afford no theatrical interest. On the contrary, these works are Gambaro's most riveting pieces. The audience plays a major role in the drama. Confronted with the crisis, with the inexplicable ruptures and lacunae that the plays themselves refuse to link or inscribe with meaning, the audience must make the connections. Gambaro's pieces, like the historic moment producing them, challenge us to make sense of crazed contradiction.

The plays of the 1980's can be summed up as an analysis of crisis, of a differentiation between victims and victimizers. They include *Real envido* (Royal Gambit), *La malasangre* (Bitter Blood), *Del sol naciente* (From the Rising Sun), *Antígona Furiosa* (Antigone Enraged), and *Morgon*. Gambaro's theatre of the 1980's continued examining the victim/victimizer relationship, but with important differences that reflected the changing socio-political climate. The victims have now differentiated themselves from their oppressors. While they remain as powerless as before in the face of absolute brutality and stupidity, they no longer deceive themselves about what is happening to them. The victims have moved from the passive acceptance of catastrophe in the early theatre to an acute awareness that their passivity has disempowered them and that they have contributed to their own annihilation. During their victimization, and after their deaths, they keep denouncing authority. Their dead voices are heard, not as absence, but as presence.

Though the victims no longer participate in the fictionalization of reality, the fictions keep proliferating, thus portraying the elaborate process of legitimation necessary to keep the criminal authorities in power. The authority figures behind the crumbling socio-political structure (personified by the King in *Real envido*, the Father in *La malasangre*, and Obán in *Del sol naciente*) attempt to mask the economic and moral bankruptcy of their regimes and try to fill the void left by multiple disappearances with some socially acceptable meaning. The Father in *La malasangre* does not like cutting off heads, we are told, but the elimination of the "savages" and "undesirables" proves necessary in order to maintain peace. The King in *Real envido* tries to fill a bankrupt state with "things", money and meaning. The question posed by the work is how to produce things and engender meaning in an empty realm ruled by a windbag full of "hot air" surrounded by self-regarding counsellors and yes-men. In this closed economy, within which nothing new can be created, everything, every sign, every name has to be rediscovered and recycled. The King forever picks up the same leaf: "Where do they come from? There aren't any trees". His daughter, the disobedient Margarita, gives place to Margarita 2, product of the counsellor's bed.

While this theatre continues to represent the effects of social crisis, Gambaro's main concern at this point lies in dismantling the fictions of power designed to justify and normalize the abusiveness by those in control. The problem, as Dolores makes clear in *La malasangre*, lies in the contradiction that that which benefits the rulers goes against the general good. The rulers must devise new strategies to justify their malpractice. In the failure to justify their position in terms of power and wealth—both suspect now that the powerful can no longer claim legitimate right to either— leaders must divert attention from the pitiful, dead-end situation in which those they rule find themselves. Engaging in war functions as a worthy diversion in *Real envido* and *Del sol naciente*, as much as it did for the military junta in the Falkland Islands in 1982. As Ama notes in *Del sol naciente*, people dare not even look at the reality of warriors: "they marched before a congregation of blindmen! No one dared look at them!".

During a 25-year period, Gambaro's plays have reflected

the evolving social consciousness of crisis, from the initial experience of social collapse to the critical understanding of how and why crisis becomes cemented into the disintegrating social fabric; continual crisis justifies the existence of an active military and makes necessary ever-escalating acts of social control.

—Diana Taylor

See also *Volume 1* entry on *Los Siameses*.

GARCÍA LORCA, Federico. Born in Fuentevaqueros, near Granada, Spain, 5 June 1898. Educated at Colegio de Sagrado Corazón de Jesús, Granada; Granada conservatory, studying piano; University of Granada, 1914–19; University of Madrid, from 1919: graduated in law, 1923. First play, *El maleficio de la mariposa* [*The Butterfly's Evil Spell*], produced 1920; first collection of poems, *Libro de poemas*, published 1921; edited artistic review, *El gallo*, 1928; travelled to Paris, London, New York, and Havana (Cuba), 1929–30; founder, touring theatre company, La Barraca (sponsored by the newly established Republican government), 1931: he adapted and directed plays for the company until its grant was withdrawn, 1935; travelled to Buenos Aires, 1933; following outbreak of the Spanish Civil War, was captured by Franco supporters near Granada, August 1936. Executed (shot) at Viznar, c.19 August 1936.

Works

Collections

Obras completas (7 vols.), edited by Guillermo de Torre. 1938–42.
From Lorca's Theatre: Five Plays (includes *If Five Years Pass; Yerma; The Love of Don Perlimpín; Doña Rosita the Spinster; The Shoemaker's Prodigious Wife*), translated by James Graham-Luján and Richard L. O'Connell. 1941.
Three Tragedies (includes *Blood Wedding; Yerma; The House of Bernarda Alba*), translated by James Graham-Luján and Richard L. O'Connell. 1947.
Obras completas, edited by Arturo del Hoyo. 1954; revised edition (2 vols.), 1973.
Five Plays: Comedies and Tragedies (includes *The Butterfly's Evil Spell; The Billy-Club Puppets; The Shoemaker's Prodigous Wife; The Love of Don Perlimpín; Doña Rosita the Spinster*), translated by James Graham-Luján and Richard L. O'Connell. 1963.
Collected Plays (includes the texts of *Three Plays*, 1947, and *Five Plays*, 1963), translated by James Graham-Luján and Richard L. O'Connell. 1976.
Three Tragedies (includes *Blood Wedding; Yerma; Bernarda Alba*), translated by Sue Bradbury. 1977.
Obras (6 vols.), edited by Miguel Garcia Posada. 1980.
Three Plays (includes *Blood Wedding; Doña Rosita the Spinster; Yerma*), translated by Gwynne Edwards and Peter Luke. 1988; subsequently retitled *Plays 1*, 1991.
Plays 2 (includes *The Shoemaker's Wonderful Wife; The Love of Don Perlimpín; The Puppet Play of Don Cristóbal; The Butterfly's Evil Spell; When Five Years Pass*), translated by Gwynne Edwards. 1990.

Stage Works

El maleficio de la mariposa (produced Teatro Eslava, Madrid, 1920). In *Obras completas*, 1954; translated as *The Butterfly's Evil Spell*, in *Five Plays*, 1963.
Mariana Pineda (produced Teatro Goya, Barcelona, 1927). 1928; translated as *Mariana Pineda*, 1987.
Quimera. In *Gallo*, May 1928; in book form, in *Teatro breve*, 1954.
El paseo de Buster Keaton (produced Teatro Maria Guerrero, Madrid, 1986). In *Gallo*, May 1928; in book form, in *Teatro breve*, 1954; translated as *Buster Keaton's Promenade*, in *Accent*, vol.17 no.3, 1967.
La doncella, el marinero y el estudiante (produced Teatro María Guerrero, Madrid, 1986). In *Gallo*, May 1928; in book form, in *Teatro breve*, 1964.
La zapatera prodigiosa (produced Teatro Español, Madrid, 1930; revised version produced Teatro Avenida, Buenos Aires, 1933). In *Obras completas*, 1938; translated as *The Shoemaker's Prodigious Wife*, in *From Lorca's Theatre*, 1941; as *The Shoemaker's Wonderful Wife*, in *Plays 2*, 1990.
El amor de Don Perlimpín con Belisa en su jardín (produced Teatro Español, Madrid, 1933). In *Obras completas*, 1938; translated as *The Love of Don Perlimpín and Belisa in the Garden*, in *From Lorca's Theatre*, 1941, and in *Three Plays*, 1988.
Bodas de sangre (produced Teatro Beatriz, Madrid, 1933). 1935; translated as *Blood Wedding*, 1939 in *Three Tragedies*, 1947, and in *Three Plays*, 1988.
La dama boba, from a play by Lope de Vega (produced Buenos Aires, 1934).
Yerma (produced Teatro Español, Madrid, 1934). 1937; translated as *Yerma*, 1947; several subsequent translations under same title.
Doña Rosita la soltera (produced Teatro Principia Palace, Barcelona, 1935). In *Obras completas*, 1938; translated as *Doña Rosita the Spinster*, in *From Lorca's Theatre*, 1941; and in *Three Plays*, 1988.
Retablillo de Don Cristóbal (produced La Feria del Libro, Madrid, 1935). In *Obras completas*, 1938; translated as *The Puppet Play of Don Cristóbal*, in *Plays 2*, 1990.
Los títeres de Cachiporra: Tragicomedia de Don Cristóbal y la señoritza Rosita (produced Teatro de la Zarzuela, Madrid, 1937). In *Obras completas*, 1954; translated as *The Billy-Club Puppets: Tragicomedy of Don Cristobál and Miss Rosita*, in *Five Plays*, 1963.
Así que pasen cinco años (produced Provincetown Playhouse, New York, 1945; first produced in Spanish, Teatro Eslava, Madrid, 1978). In *Obras completas*, 1938; translated as *If Five Years Pass*, in *From Lorca's Theatre*, 1941; as *When Five Years Pass*, in *Plays 2*, 1990.
La casa de Bernarda Alba (produced Teatro Avenida, Buenos Aires, 1945). 1945; translated as *The House of Bernarda Alba*, in *Three Tragedies*, 1947.
El público (produced in English, University of Texas, Austin, 1972; produced in Spanish, Piccolo Teatro studio, Milan, 1986). With *Comedia sin título*, 1978; translated as *The Public*, with *Play Without a Title*, 1983.
Comedia sin título (produced Teatro María Guerrero, Madrid, 1989). With *El público*, 1978; translated as *Play Without a Title*, with *The Public*, 1983.

Screenplays

Trip to the Moon (published in translation, in *New Directions*, 18, 1964).

Verse

Libro de poemas.   1921.
Canciones.   1927; as *Canciones*, translated by Philip Cummings, edited by Daniel Eisenberg, 1976.
Primer romancero gitano.   1928; as *Gypsy Ballads*, translated by Rolfe Humphries, 1963.
Poema del canto jondo.   1931.
Oda a Walt Whitman.   1933.
Llanto por la muerte de Ignacio Sánchez Mejías.   1935.
Primeras canciones.   1936.
Seis poemas gallegos.   1936.
"Lament for the Death of a Bullfighter" and Other Poems, translated by A.L. Lloyd, 1937.
Poems, translated by Stephen Spender and J.L. Gili.   1939.
Poeta en Nueva York.   1940; translated as *Poet in New York*, 1940; several subsequent translations under same title.
Diván del Tamarit.   1940; translated as *Divan*, in *"Divan" and Other Writings*, 1974.
Poemas sueltos.   1954.
Cantares populares.   1954.
Selected Poems, translated by J.L. Gili.   1960.
Lorca and Jiménez, translated by Robert Bly.   1973.
"Divan" and Other Writings, translated by Edwin Honig.   1974.
Poesía I, edited by Miguel Garcia-Posada.   1980.
The Towers of Cordova: Selected Poems, translated by Merryn Williams.   1990.

Memoirs and Letters

Cartas a sus amigos, edited by S. Gasch.   1950.
Selected Letters, edited and translated by David Gershator.   1983.

Other

Impresiones y paisajes.   1918.
Cartas; postales; poemas y dibujos, edited by A. Gallego Morell.   1968.
"Deep Song" and Other Prose, edited by Christopher Maurer.   1980.

*

Bibliographies

Joseph L. Laurenti, *Federico García Lorca y su mundo: Ensayo de una bibliografía general*, Metuchen, New Jersey, 1974.
Francesca Colecchia, *García Lorca: A Selectively Annotated Bibliography of Criticism*, New York, 1979.
Francesca Colecchia, *García Lorca: An Annotated Primary Bibliography*, New York and London, 1982.
Everett E. Larson, *Federico García Lorca: A Bibliography*, Washington, DC (Library of Congress), 1987.

Criticism

Books:
Arturo Barea, *Lorca: The Poet and His People*, London, 1944.
Edwin Honig, *Federico García Lorca*, Norfolk, Connecticut, 1944.
A. del Rio, *Vida y obra de Federico García Lorca*, Zaragoza, 1952.

J. Mora Guarnido, *Federico García Lorca y su mundo*, Buenos Aires, 1958.
C. Morla Lynch, *Con Federico en España*, Madrid, 1958.
Manuel Durán (ed.), *Lorca: A Collection of Critical Essays*, Englewood Cliffs, New Jersey, 1962.
Robert Lima, *The Theatre of García Lorca*, New York, 1963.
Rafael Alberti, *García Lorca*, Milan, 1966.
Marie Laffranque, *Federico García Lorca: Textes et propos de Lorca, points de vue critiques, témoignages, bibliographie, illustrations*, Paris, 1966.
Ferruccio Massini, *Federico García Lorca e La Barraca*, Bologna, 1966.
A. Sopena Ibáñez, *El concepto de la mujer española en la obra de García Lorca*, Madrid, 1966.
Carl W. Cobb, *Federico García Lorca*, New York, 1967.
M. Laffranque, *Les Idées esthétiques de Federico García Lorca*, Paris, 1967.
Rolf Michaelis, *Federico García Lorca*, Velber, 1969.
Manuel Vicent, *García Lorca*, Madrid, 1969.
Cedric Busettem, *Obra dramática de García Lorca: Estudio de su configuración*, New York, 1971.
Rupert Allen, *The Symbolic World of García Lorca*, Albuquerque, New Mexico, 1972.
Brenda Frazier, *La mujer en el teatro de Federico García Lorca*, Madrid, 1973.
Ildefonso M. Gil (ed.), *Federico García Lorca*, Madrid, 1973.
Rupert Allen, *Psyche and Symbol in the Theatre of García Lorca*, Austin, Texas, 1974.
Suzanne W. Byrd, *La Barraca and the Spanish National Theater*, New York, 1975.
Carlos Rincón, *Das Theater García Lorcas*, Berlin, 1975.
Antonina Rodrigo, *García Lorca en Cataluña*, Barcelona, 1975.
Maria T. Babin, *Estudios lorquianos*, Rio Pedras, Puerto Rico, 1976.
Virginia Higginbotham, *The Comic Spirit of Federico García Lorca*, Austin, Texas, 1976.
Mildred Adams, *García Lorca, Playwright and Poet*, New York, 1977.
Gregorio Prieto (ed.), *Lorca y la Generación del 27*, Madrid, 1977.
Paola Ambrosi and Maria Grazia Profeti, *Federico García Lorca: La frustrazione erotica maschile*, Rome, 1979.
Gwynne Edwards, *Lorca: The Theatre Beneath the Sands*, London, 1980.
Francisco García Lorca, *Federico y su mundo*, edited by Mario Hernández, Madrid, 1980.
Rafael Utrera, *García Lorca y el cinema*, Seville, 1982.
Antonio F. Cao, *Federico García Lorca y las vanguardia: Hacia el teatro*, London, 1984.
Gwynne Edwards, *Dramatists in Perspective: Spanish Theatre in the Twentieth Century*, Cardiff, 1985.
Felicia H. Londré, *Federico García Lorca*, New York, 1985.
Miriam Balboa-Echeverria, *Lorca: El espacio de la representación*, Barcelona, 1986.
Eutimio Martin, *Federico García Lorca, heterodoxo y mártir: Análisis y proyección de la obra juvenil inédita*, Madrid, 1986.
C. Grant McCurdy, *Federico García Lorca: Life, Work, and Criticism*, Fredricton, New Brunswick, 1986.
Ian Gibson, *Federico García Lorca: A Life* (from the 2-volume Spanish edition), London, 1989.

Serials

García Lorca Review, 1973—
FGL: Bolétin de la Fundación Federico García Lorca, 1987–

* * *

Undoubtedly Spain's greatest dramatist of the 20th century, Federico García Lorca produced, in 16 years, a body of work that was at once highly personal, often intensely Spanish, consistently experimental, and, in its style, excitingly European. Unrivalled in his own time for the intense poetic quality of his theatre, he has not been equalled since by any other Spanish dramatist.

The themes of Lorca's plays are largely autobiographical, rooted in the reality of his life, in particular in his homosexuality. Passion, frustration, passing time, and death link *El maleficio de la mariposa* (*The Butterfly's Evil Spell*) to *La casa de Bernarda Alba* (*The House of Bernarda Alba*) in a way that points to the personal and obsessive nature of Lorca's concerns within a range of subject matter marked by its variety. Abandoning the cockroaches of his first play for the persecuted liberal heroine of his second, *Mariana Pineda*, he then focused on the traditional stories of an old man married to a young wife—*La zapatera prodigiosa* (*The Shoemaker's Wonderful Wife*), *El amor de Don Perlimpín* (*The Love of Don Perlimpín*), and *Retablillo de Don Cristóbal* (*The Puppet Play of Don Cristóbal*)—before giving vent to strong personal feelings in the more obviously confessional *El público* (*The Public*) and *Así que pasen cinco años* (*When Five Years Pass*). In the subsequent rural trilogy—*Bodas de sangre* (*Blood Wedding*), *Yerma*, and *La casa de Bernarda Alba*—those issues again acquire fictional forms as Lorca projects the anguish of frustrated love into his tragic heroines.

The Spanishness of Lorca's work reveals itself in many ways. His Andalusian background lies at the heart of a view of life in which men's lives are ruled by fate, and sorrow is never far away. It explains, too, the strongly traditional elements in the plays, in particular the songs, ballads, and lullabies (an interest which Lorca shared with another notable inhabitant of Granada, Manuel de Falla), as well as the pervasive influence of that most characteristic form of Andalusian song and dance, flamenco. The tradition of the puppet-play, much loved by earlier writers like Cervantes, is a key element, and so is the reality of the Spanish countryside, its small villages and its vibrant people so in evidence in the farces and puppet-plays and, in particular, in the rural tragedies.

On the other hand, Lorca's interest in the European avant-garde, stimulated by his experience at the Residencia de Estudiantes in Madrid, and by his friendship with Luis Buñuel and Salvador Dalí, is evident throughout his work: in the strongly symbolist elements of the early *El maleficio de la mariposa*, reminiscent of Maeterlinck; in the markedly surrealist *El público* and *Así que pasen cinco años*; and in the cinematic qualities evident both in the latter and in the black-and-white tonalities of *La casa de Bernarda Alba*. In addition the legacy of traditional Spanish dance should not be allowed to obscure Lorca's interest in modern ballet.

Opposed to the unimaginative, bourgeois, and largely naturalistic theatre of his day, Lorca sought to confront his audience with uncomfortable truths expressed in an arresting, non-naturalistic style. His intention, embodied in such phrases as "my characters . . . burn the curtain" and his wish "to inaugurate the true theatre, the theatre beneath the sand", was combined with a theatrical technique that, in the manner of Maeterlink, Adolph Appia, and Edward Gordon Craig, brought together different elements of stage-performance—setting, costume, lighting, movement, music, and speech—and integrated them imaginatively, a process facilitated both by Lorca's natural instinct for the stage and by his practical experience, in particular as the director of the touring theatre company La Barraca. The uncompromising truthfulness of his plays' themes, together with their fresh and vigorous style, have ensured that they have survived the test of time.

The characters of Lorca's theatre have both a generic quality—they are named la Madre, el Padre, el Novio, la Novia, Martirio, Angustias, and so on—and a concentrated power that make them at once universal and consistently memorable: they are images less of Spain, than of humanity at large. The effect is enhanced, moreover, by Lorca's imaginative conception of his plays as "total theatre" in which the close integration of visual, verbal, and musical elements not only intensifies the emotional colouring of a particular scene but also involves the audience deeply. Stage-settings, invariably stylised in form and colour, mirror and communicate to the audience the optimism, joy, grief, and despair of the on-stage characters. The particular mood is further deepened by movement and posture, from seated figures immobilised by despair, to running, leaping, dancing figures expressing the fullness of life. Effects of lighting are crucial too: darkness evoking despair or the blind force of passion; sunlight flooding the stage, suggesting a new beginning or a joy close at hand; or the icy light of the moon announcing the approach of death. And frequently, of course, music underpins these moments, be it in the form of a melancholy violin, or the vibrant and vigorous songs of approaching wedding-guests.

For the most part, however, the music of Lorca's theatre lies in the language itself. The rhythms of poetry, pulsating and vibrant, encapsulate moments of happiness, or, flat and heavy, the dullness of despair, while Lorca's prose, itself highly stylised, is equally expressive. No dramatist of the 20th century engages his audience more intensely than Lorca or seems more distant from Brechtian alienation.

The general view of Lorca as a tragic dramatist—the author of *Bodas de sangre*, *Yerma*, *La casa de Bernarda Alba*—needs to be countered by an appreciation of his delightful comic gifts, exemplified in the farces and puppet-plays. His theatre as a whole, embracing the extremes of joy and despair, bears witness to his own capacity to experience life in all its immense variety.

—Gwynne Edwards

See also *Volume 1* entries on *Blood Wedding*; *The House of Bernarda Alba*; *Yerma*.

———

GARRETT, João Baptista da Silva Leitão de Almeida. Born in Oporto, Portugal, 4 February 1799. Family moved to the Azores following the French Invasion of Portugal, 1809. Studied law at Coimbra University, 1816–20. Married Luisa Midosi in 1821 (separated 1836); had a daughter by Adelaide Pastor, c.1841. Served in the Ministry of Home Affairs in the early 1820's; became known as a prominent liberal; went into exile in England after the restoration of the absolutist monarch João VI, 1823; moved to France; returned to Portugal after publication of the Constitutional Charter, 1826, and was re-employed by the Ministry; wrote political journalism, 1826–28; fled to England following the return of absolutism, 1828; joined the Constitutional forces in the Azores, 1832: took part in occupation of Oporto, 1832; Portuguese *chargé d'affaires* in Belgium, 1834–36: dismissed from post; returned to Lisbon, and was made Inspector of Theatres, entrusted by Prime Minister Passos Manuel with the planning of a national theatre: founded the Maria II Theatre and the National Drama School, and wrote plays for the national repertoire; following coup of Costa Cabral, was dismissed from public office, but continued in Parliament with the opposition; appointed Minister of Foreign Affairs, 1852. Following revolution of 1851, was made a Viscount. Died in Lisbon, 9 December 1854.

Works

Collections

Obras (24 vols.).   1839–77.
Obras Completas (2 vols.), edited by Teófilo Braga.   1904.
Obras Postúmas, edited by Gomes de Amorim.   1914.
Obras (2 vols.).   1966.
Obras Completas (3 vols.), edited by J. Prado Coelho. 1972–73.

Stage Works

Mérope.   1841.
Lucrécia (produced Coimbra, 1819).   In *Obras postúmas*, 1914.
Catão. (produced Lisbon, 1821).   1822.
Um Auto de Gil Vicente (produced Teatro da Rua-dos-Condes, Lisbon, 1838).   1841.
O Alfageme de Santarém (produced Lisbon, 1842).   1842.
Filipa de Vilhena (produced Teatro do Salitre, Lisbon, 1840). 1846.
Frei Luís de Sousa (produced Teatro do Pinheiro, Laranjeiras, 1843).   1844; translated as *Brother Luiz de Souza*, 1909.
Tio Simplício (produced 1844).   1844.
Falar Verdade a Mentir (produced 1844).   1844.
As Profecias de Bandarra (produced 1845).   1848.
Camões no Rossio (produced 1846).   1852.
Um Noivado no Dàfundo (produced 1847).   1848.
O Conde de Novion (produced 1852).   In *Obras Postúmas*, 1914.
A Sobrinha do Marquês.   1861.

Verse

O retrato de Vénus.   1821
O roubo das Sabinas.   1968.
Camões.   1825.
Dona Branca.   1826.
Adozinda.   1828.
Lirica de João Minimo.   1829.
Flores sem Fruto.   1845.
Folhas Caídas.   1853.
Lirica Completa.   1963.
Poesias Dispersas, edited by Luis Augusto Costa Dias. 1985.

Other

Da Educação.   1829.
Portugal na Balança da Europa.   1830.
O Romanceiro (3 vols.).   1843 (vol.1) and 1851 (vols. 2–3).
O Arco de Sant'Ana (2 vols.).   1845–51.
Viagens na Minha Terra.   1846; translated as *Travels in My Homeland*, 1987.

Discursos Parlementares, edited by Manuel Mendes.   Nd.
Doutrinas de Estética Literaria, edited by Agostinho da Silva. 1961 (second edition).
Magico; ou, Os Doze de Inglaterra, edited by Alberto Pimenta.   1978.
Os Papelinhos, edited by Luís Augusto Costa Dias.   1988.

*

Criticism

Books:
Otto Antscherl, *J.B. de Almeida Garrett und seine Beziehungen sur Romantik*, Heidelberg, 1927.
Andrée Crabbé Rocha, *O Teatro de Garrett*, Coimbra, 1944.
João Gaspar Simoes, *Almeida Garrett*, Lisbon, 1964.
R.A. Lawton, *Almeida Garrett: L'Intime contrainte*, Paris, 1966.
Ofélia Paiva Monteiro, *A Formaçao de Almeida Garrett* (2 vols.), Coimbra, 1971.
Lia Noémia R.C. Raitt, *Garrett and the English Muse*, London, 1983.

* * *

Almeida Garrett's wide-ranging literary achievements and his political activity earn him a place among the greatest Portuguese figures of the 19th century. Throughout his varied and distinguished career in the fields of politics, oratory, public administration, journalism, history, philosophy, literary criticism, poetry and fiction, runs his contribution to the theatre. Although he himself declared that his dominating passion was the theatre, it is arguable that politics was the stronger motivation in his life. His early education in the classics was complemented, at university, by his acquisition of liberal beliefs and Romantic leanings and, during his periods of exile, by wide exposure to English, French, and German literature and culture.

The tension between his classical training and his Romantic nationalistic fervour can be seen almost from the beginning of his writing career. His debut as a playwright, in 1818, was with *Xerxes*, a neoclassical piece, the text of which has been lost. Also during his student years, he sketched out, or half-completed, plays on other classical figures, such as Iphigenia and Oedipus. In *Lucrécia*, he depicts a heroine of the stock of Racine and Corneille, and attacks despotism and tyranny. In *Catão* (based on Addison's *Cato*) he found a theme that responded to the Portuguese situation in 1821. The disinterested patriotism displayed in *Cato* was of relevance to Garrett's belief in a national theatre, one that reflected the concerns of its audience, be the characters and theme Portuguese or not. In *Catão*, the appeal to patriotism, and the primacy of civic responsibility over the individual's emotions or actions, points the way to Garrett's later elevation of the *povo* (folk) as the custodians of national identity.

After the September Revolution of 1836, Garrett threw himself into the task of restructuring Portugal's theatre. In order to educate and refine the public's taste, to inculcate the habit and necessity, as he saw it, of theatre, he had to provide a national repertory. His first play of a national stamp, *Um Auto de Gil Vicente* (An Auto by Gil Vicente), set in the 16th century at the Court of D. Manuel, brings together on stage the founding father of Portuguese theatre, the plebeian Gil Vicente, and his contemporary, the courtly lyric poet Bernardim Ribeiro, thereby uniting the satiric comic Vicentine tradition with the intensely emotional and nostalgic spirit of Ribeiro who, as legend had it, loved the Portuguese Princess Maria Beatrice, the betrothed of the Duke of Savoy. Abandoning classical rules, form, and diction, Garrett forsook the lofty poetry of *Catão* for naturalistic and often comic dialogue. He did not, however, escape some of the clichés or defects of Romantic drama, such as lack of psychological subtlety, hackneyed declamations, and the reliance on the picturesque and local colour.

The next two plays, *Filipa de Vilhena* and *O Alfageme de Santarém* (The Armourer from Santarém) are historical dramas, the first set towards the end of the Spanish Occupation in 1640, the second during 1383–85, when Portuguese independence was under threat from Castille. As a playwright, Garrett needed a story, plot, or episode from which to depart; he lacked imagination in creating original characters and stories. He never lacked seriousness of purpose, however; but this very quality makes these plays sometimes too literal, too zealously conscious of nationhood. Appealing to patriotic sentiments, their very defined locality and timescale work against a universal application, and the characters, though motivated by the universal passions of love and jealousy, as well as patriotism, fail to cross their national dramatic boundaries.

O Alfageme de Santarém suffers from a confusing plot, some over-idealized characters, and the rather intrusive insertion of ballads, sung by choruses of village maidens and craftsmen, to stress the rich oral tradition that Garrett, as a Romantic, saw as the essence of the nation. In textual terms, these ballads act as comment on and echo of the events and emotions experienced in the play, but in dramatic terms they hold up the action. Garrett's desire to make his audience react emotionally to the action, rather than deliberate over the meaning of the story, may have been the justification for the many about-turns and contrasts in situation—for example, the class conflict between the nobles and the folk, and their respective loyalties to Spain and Portugal; the individual conflicts arising from love, jealousy, honour, public duty; the conflict of interests engendered by the political opportunist and his manipulation of the common people. The play is a political one, reflecting much of Garrett's thinking and his experience of civil war and exile, as well as his interpretation of recent historical events in Portugal.

Garrett's belief that in a historical drama the truth of the past offers a mirror to present society lay equally behind his greatest play, *Frei Luís de Sousa* (*Brother Luis de Souza*). Although not wishing to call the play a tragedy, Garrett considered it as such, comparing its purity, severity, passion, and energy to Greek tragedy, yet further elevated by its Christian spirit of contrition and absolution. Around the central domestic tragedy concerning a noble and fiercely patriotic Portuguese family, whose existence is shattered when the wife's first husband (believed dead in battle at the hands of the Moors, along with King Sebastian, some 20 years before) returns to Portugal, revolve many interconnecting historical, political, personal, and psychological themes. With great economy of plot and character, parallels are established between the past and the present, suggesting the tragic outcome for Portugal, were the return of the messianic King Sebastian to happen, or, in other words, if the old figures of history were called upon to be more than memories. The balance created between the classical and the Romantic is only broken by the melodramatic last scene, in which the daughter of the family loses her reason and dies of shame in the arms of her parents. The crises of guilt and conscience, the interpretation of the wife's sin as adultery rather than bigamy, the way that first or previous claims on affection are supplanted by later loves, the stigma of illegitimacy falling

upon the innocent offspring of the union—all are aspects also of Garrett's own personal and emotional life.

After *Frei Luís de Sousa*, Garrett turned his talents to comedy. Most of the six comedies that he wrote during the last ten years of his life are quite forgotten today. Three of these are mere imitations of French plays; one was constructed on a farce written by his brother-in-law and former collaborator; and of the other two, *As Profecias de Bandarra* (Bandarra's Prophecies) is a burlesque complement to the Sebastianism of *Frei Luís de Sousa*, and *A Sobrinha do Marquês* (The Niece of the Marquis), although praised for its acute observation of manners and class, in no way reflects Garrett's great literary talent. In spite of a feeble end to his career as a dramatist, this does not detract from the overall picture of a complete man of the theatre, in his roles as playwright, critic, educator, and administrator.

—Juliet Perkins

GARRICK, David.   See *Volume 3* entry.

GAY, (John).   Born in Barnstaple, Devon, England, c.30 June 1685. Educated at Barnstaple Grammar School; apprentice to a silk mercer in London. Returned to Barnstaple after leaving apprenticeship, then moved to London, 1707; secretary to Aaron Hill, 1708–12, in the household of Anne Scott, Duchess of Monmouth, 1712–14, and to the Earl of Clarendon on his diplomatic mission to Hanover, 1714; with Pope, Swift, John Arbuthnot, and others formed the Scriblerus Club, 1713–14; accompanied William Pulteney, later Earl of Bath, to Aix, 1717; lived at Lord Harcourt's estate in Oxfordshire, 1718; earned considerable income from publication of his collected poems, 1720, and made and lost a fortune in South Sea funds speculation; commissioner for the Public Lottery, 1722–31; recovered much of his fortune from the success of *The Beggar's Opera*, 1728; lived with his patrons the Duke and Duchess of Queensberry, 1728–32. Died in London, 4 December 1732.

Works

Collections

Poetical, Dramatic, and Miscellaneous Works (6 vols.). 1795.
Selected Works, edited by Samuel Joseloff.   1976.
Dramatic Works, edited by John Fuller (2 vols.).   1983.

Stage Works

The Mohocks.   1712.
The Wife of Bath (produced Theatre Royal, Drury Lane, London, 1713).   1713; revised version (produced Lincoln's Inn Fields Theatre, London, 1730), 1730.

Satirical engraving interpreting *The Beggar's Opera*, by **John Gay**, at Lincoln Inn Fields Theatre (after the 1728 etching attributed to William Hogarth).

The What D'ye Call It (produced Theatre Royal, Drury Lane, London, 1715).   1715.

Three Hours After Marriage, with Pope and Arbuthnot (produced Theatre Royal, Drury Lane, London, 1717).   1717; revised version in *Supplement to the Works of Pope*, 1757.

Acis and Galatea, music by Handel (produced Oxford? c.1718).   1732.

Dione.   In *Poems on Several Occasions*.   1720.

The Captives (produced Theatre Royal, Drury Lane, London, 1724).   1724.

The Beggar's Opera (produced Lincoln's Inn Fields Theatre, London, 1728).   1728.

Polly, Being the 2nd Part of The Beggar's Opera (version revised by Colman the Elder produced Theatre Royal, Haymarket, London, 1777).   1729.

Achilles (produced Lincoln's Inn Fields Theatre, London, 1733).   1733.

The Distressed Wife (produced Covent Garden Theatre, London, 1734).   1743; as *The Modern Wife* (produced 1771).

The Rehearsal at Goatham.   1754.

Verse

Wine.   1708.

Rural Sports.   1713; revised edition, 1720; edited by O. Culbertson, 1930.

The Fan.   1714.

The Shepherd's Week.   1714.

A Letter to a Lady.   1714.

Two Epistles, One to the Earl of Burlington, The Other to a Lady.   1715(?).

Trivia; or, The Art of Walking the Streets of London.   1716.

Horace, epode iv, Imitated.   1717(?).

The Poor Shepherd.   1720(?).

Poems on Several Occasions (2 vols.).   1720.

A Panegyrical Epistle to Mr. Thomas Snow.   1721.

An Epistle to Her Grace Henrietta Duchess of Marlborough.   1722.

A Poem Addressed to the Quidnunc's.   1724.

Blueskin's Ballad.   1725.

To a Lady on Her Passion for Old China.   1725.

Daphnis and Cloe. 1725(?).

Molly Mog.   1726.

Fables (2 vols.).   1727–38.

Some Unpublished Translations from Ariosto, edited by J.D. Bruce.   1910.

Poetical Works, edited by G.C. Faber.   1926.

Selected Poems, edited by Marcus Walsh.   1979.

Memoirs and Letters

Letters, edited by Chester F. Burgess.   1966.

Other

The Present State of Wit.   1711.

An Argument Proving That the Present Mohocks and Hawkubites Are the Gog and Magog Mentioned in the Revelations.   1712.

Poetry and Prose (2 vols.), edited by Vinton A Dearing and Charles Beckwith.   1976.

*

Bibliographies

Bibliography in *Poetical Works*, 1926.
Julie T. Klein, *John Gay: An Annotated Checklist of Criticism*, New York, 1974.

Criticism

Books:
E.M. Gagey, *Ballad Opera*, New York, 1937.
William H. Irving, *John Gay, Favorite of the Wits* (biography), Durham, North Carolina, 1940.
Sven M. Armens, *John Gay, Social Critic*, New York, 1954.
Oliver Warner, *John Gay*, 1964.
Patricia M. Spacks, *John Gay*, New York, 1965.
Yvonne Noble (ed.), *Twentieth-Century Interpretations of "The Beggar's Opera"*, Englewood Cliffs, New Jersey, 1975.
Peter Lewis, *John Gay: The Beggar's Opera*, London, 1976.
Peter Lewis and Nigel Wood (eds.), *John Gay and the Scriblerians*, 1988.

*   *   *

As a member of the small but influential Scriblerus Club, which included Pope and Swift, Gay is usually linked with literary rather than theatrical figures, and ranks as a major Augustan poet. But alone among the Scriblerians, he possessed a strong dramatic gift and was attracted by the potential of the theatre. He wrote regular (five-act) comedies and tragedies, but he was more successful in irregular plays, such as burlesques, satires, and ballad operas (a form he invented), because they allowed him much greater imaginative freedom.

His first ballad opera, and also his masterpiece, *The Beggar's Opera*, has proved to be one of the most enduring and popular plays in English theatre. After its highly successful first production in 1728, it was performed in London every year for the rest of the 18th century, and held the stage throughout the 19th century. Since the 1920's, following Nigel Playfair's famous and long-running postwar production at the Lyric Theatre, Hammersmith, and the innovative imitation by Bertolt Brecht with music by Kurt Weill, *Die Dreigroschenoper* (*The Threepenny Opera*), *The Beggar's Opera* has enjoyed regular theatrical revivals, several television productions, and a film version.

Gay wrote *The Beggar's Opera* towards the end of his relatively short life, by which time he was a highly accomplished dramatist. He first tried his hand at playwriting in 1712 with *The Mohocks*, not long after publishing his first poetic and prose works. This short farcical comedy in three scenes failed to reach the stage, but it prefigures some of his later plays in that it contains ingredients recognizable as typical of Gay, such as the influence of Shakespearean comedy. The fine burlesque (limited to the first scene) of the bombastic verse used by many contemporary tragic dramatists is a precursor of the important burlesque elements in several of Gay's plays, including *The Beggar's Opera*. Both his playfully ironic description, "A Tragi-Comical Farce", and his satirical dedication in the published version, claiming that *The Mohocks* closely follows one of John Dennis's sombre neo-classical tragedies, point forward to the more elaborate ironies of some later works.

Gay's first attempt at a regular play was *The Wife of Bath*, an energetic though technically unpolished comedy based on Chaucer, who was popular at the time. After the success of *The Beggar's Opera*, Gay radically revised *The Wife of Bath* for performance in 1730 in the hope that the comedy would win more acclaim than in 1713; but what the second version (almost a new play) gains in skilful organization, it loses in dramatic verve.

His first theatrical success was his afterpiece *The What D'ye Call It*, the best dramatic burlesque since Buckingham's *The Rehearsal* (1671). This immediately became a firm favourite with audiences, remaining in the repertory for many years. The generic mixture announced by Gay's ironic description, "A Tragi-Comi-Pastoral Farce", is more complex than in *The Mohocks*, and the subtle burlesque method of the inner play, contained within a small comic frame, is more fully sustained. Gay gently mocks the high-flown rhetoric of contemporary tragedy, especially the "pathetic" variety, by incongruously putting it into the mouths of peasants who undergo experiences comparable to those endured by the stereotyped heroes and heroines of Rowe's "she-tragedies" and similar works. Yet Gay's mock-heroic irony is double-edged. By applying an elevated idiom to those at the bottom of the social scale, Gay paradoxically succeeds in giving his burlesque characters an unexpected dignity. The element of non-literary satire is not highly developed, but Gay shows how the mock-heroic method of ironic burlesque can be exploited as an effective weapon of personal, social, and political satire, a technique he brings to perfection in *The Beggar's Opera*. Gay adds a further dimension of satire in the published version by prefacing *The What D'ye Call It* with a Scriblerian introduction that ironically demolishes its supposed author, a Swiftian Modern, from within.

Three Hours After Marriage, a satire in the form of an irregular (three-act) farcical comedy, is a truly Scriblerian enterprise in which Gay collaborated with Pope and Arbuthnot. Not surprisingly, it was extremely controversial when staged in 1717. The blend of burlesque, caricature, and bizarre comic situations results in a highly eccentric, yet fast-moving and punchy, play, characteristically Scriblerian in its assault on misplaced scientific curiosity, bogus intellectuality, and bad writing.

In the following year Gay provided Handel with a libretto for an "English Pastoral Opera" based on a mythological story, *Acis and Galatea*, performed privately at the time but not publicly until 1731. Gay's two attempts at tragedy followed. *Dione*, a sententious and undramatic "Pastoral Tragedy" written in couplets, is a very literary work, which failed to reach the stage. The far more theatrical *The Captives* was produced in 1724, but with its grandiloquent style it exhibits some of the weaknesses of contemporary "heroic" and "pathetic" tragedy diagnosed in *The What D'ye Call It*.

After working on his poetic *Fables*, Gay returned to the theatre triumphantly in 1728 with *The Beggar's Opera*. Burlesque of Italian opera and wide-ranging social and political satire are seamlessly integrated by means of irony in this original work of genius. None of his other dramatic works embodies so completely his uniquely ambiguous blend of the satirical and the emotional, detached amusement and involved feeling.

The reception of *The Beggar's Opera* encouraged Gay to write a sequel, *Polly*, but the production scheduled for 1729 was officially banned. This was an act of retaliation for Gay's oblique yet incisive satire on Sir Robert Walpole's government in *The Beggar's Opera*, in which it is implied that politicians differ from criminals only in escaping punishment for their misdeeds. By setting *Polly* in the West Indies, complete with noble savages, rather than London, Gay shifted the balance of the play towards sentimentalism, and although it is not lacking in social satire, it is much less of an anti-Walpole and anti-government satire than *The Beggar's Opera*.

Polly eventually reached the stage in 1777, but a short dramatic satire Gay wrote after the banning of *Polly*, *The Rehearsal at Goatham*, did not reach the stage at all. Despite its title, this is not a "rehearsal" play of the usual burlesque kind, but an adaptation of an episode in *Don Quixote*, transformed by Gay into an allegory about the fate of *Polly*. It specifically lampoons Walpole and the Poet Laureate Colley Cibber, but at a general level it is a full-blooded attack on the philistinism of censors and the paranoid stupidity of petty officials, who can find subversive propaganda even in the most innocuous works of art.

Gay wrote two other plays towards the end of his life, his third ballad-opera, *Achilles*, and a serious, or "dark", regular comedy, *The Distress'd Wife*, both of which were produced posthumously. *Achilles* retells, in a comic and burlesque manner, the story of the eponymous Greek hero's sojourn on Scyros when disguised as a girl by his goddess mother to prevent him from going to the Trojan War. Usually dismissed as considerably inferior to *The Beggar's Opera*, *Achilles* is, in fact, a totally different kind of play, and its preoccupation with gender, sexual identity, and cross-dressing makes it particularly relevant to the late 20th century. Like Fielding's exactly contemporary *The Modern Husband*, *The Distress'd Wife* is an attempt to expand comedy in the direction of the problem play, and as in some late 19th-century examples of the type, both Gay's and Fielding's plays focus on marriage, sexual morality, and the corruption of social values. The weakness of *The Distress'd Wife* is that it is too static and tract-like to be effective theatrically, and it confirms the view that Gay's forte as a playwright was not regular, but irregular, drama.

—Peter Lewis

See also *Volume 1* entry on *The Beggar's Opera*.

GELBER, Jack. Born in Chicago, Illinois, USA, 12 April 1932. Educated at the University of Illinois, Urbana, BS in journalism 1953. Married Carol Westenberg in 1957; one son and one daughter. Writer-in-residence, City College, New York, 1965–66; adjunct professor of Drama, Columbia University, New York, 1967–72; professor of Drama, Brooklyn College, City University of New York, 1972–. Recipient: Obie Award, 1960, for directing, 1972; Vernon Rice Award, 1960.

Works

Stage Works

The Connection (produced by the Living Theatre, New York, 1959). 1961.
The Apple (produced by the Living Theatre, New York, 1961). 1961.

Square in the Eye (produced Theatre de Lys, New York, 1965). 1966.
The Cuban Thing (produced Henry Miller's Theatre, New York, 1968). 1969.
Sleep (produced American Place Theatre, New York). 1972.
Barbary Shore, from the novel by Norman Mailer (produced New York, 1973).
Farmyard, from a play by Franz Xaver Kroetz (produced Yale Repertory Theatre, New Haven, Connecticut, 1975). In *"Farmyard" and Four Other Plays*, by Kroetz, 1976.
Rehearsal (produced American Place Theatre, New York, 1976).
Starters (produced Yale Repertory Theatre, New Haven, Connecticut, 1980).

Screenplays

The Connection, 1962.

Fiction

On Ice. 1964.

*

Bibliographies

Kimball King, *Ten Modern American Playwrights*, New York, 1982.
Philip C. Colin (ed.), *American Playwrights Since 1945: A Guide to Scholarship, Criticism, and Performance*, New York, 1989.

* * *

Jack Gelber is among the more innovative 20th-century American dramatists. Among the theater-going public, his acclaim derives primarily from one play, *The Connection*; among theater scholars, his reputation rests on his attempts to expand the limits of contemporary American theater.

In the first act of *The Connection* a group of jazz musicians wait for a heroin pusher, their "connection", to arrive with their fix. While they wait they talk and play jazz. In the second act the supplier arrives. By the end of the play Gelber has established his two major points: first, that all people need a connection of some sort; and second, that innovative theater is an excellent medium for expressing this theme.

The concept of form reflecting content is illustrated in *The Connection*. There is little plot development, since all of the action centers on the group of addicts waiting for Cowboy to appear with their dope. Likewise, there is only one set— Teach's room where they are waiting. Furthermore, since waiting is their primary activity, the characters' concentration is narrowly focused; any action that takes place appears unplanned and unstructured. This provides a sense of aimlessness and creates an atmosphere of tension in the audience, who are frustrated by the randomness and tedium of what is happening on stage.

The playwright reinforces the resultant tension through the structure of the action and dialogue as well as through the jazz music that the actors play. Jazz is improvisational, and the music emphasizes Gelber's theme by paralleling the characters' moods rather than relating to specific actions. It enhances the audience's anxiety because it seems to signal movement or transitions that never take place. Besides being popular enough to warrant a motion-picture adaptation, *The Connection* earned Gelber the Obie, the Vernon Rice Award, and the New York Drama Critics Poll Award for the most promising playwright for the 1959–1960 season.

Gelber's second play, *The Apple*, extends some of the innovative devices employed in *The Connection*. By presenting the action in the first act from the audience's point of view, as they observe a madman, then presenting the madman's perspective in the second act, and finally returning to the audience's perspective in the third act, Gelber comments on the death of individuality, art, society, and intellectuality —all killed by prejudice and a lack of understanding and human sympathy.

Square in the Eye utilizes experimental techniques such as those used by Bertolt Brecht, Thornton Wilder, and Tennessee Williams to portray an "instant replay, about art and artists, marriage and death". Flashbacks, movies, still photographs, and similar devices are used throughout. In a sense, these devices are more conventional than those used in *The Connection* and *The Apple* because they are part of mainstream drama tradition.

Sleep is an even more conventional play that revolves around experiments into the nature of sleep, conducted by two scientists, and one of the subjects of their experimentation. *Sleep* is not about art or the theater, but with *Rehearsal* the dramatist returns to the subject of the theater.

Like John Osborne in England, who burst on the theatrical scene with a startling, innovative first play, *Look Back in Anger*, Gelber's contribution to the theater, particularly in America, has been substantial. In exposing the theater-going public to a dreary, desolate new world, Gelber has constantly tried to expand theatrical boundaries. He has also been active as a director, both of his own works and the works of some of his contemporaries (he received an Obie Award for his direction of Robert Coover's *The Kid*), and his work as a director has been useful in helping him understand the possibilities and limitations inherent in drama—an understanding he has taken into account in his own writing.

—Steven H. Gale

GÉLINAS, Gratien. Born in Saint-Tite, Quebec, Canada, 8 December 1909. Educated at the Collège de Montréal, 1924–29. Married 1) Simone Lalonde in 1935 (died 1967), six children; 2) the actress Huguette Oligny, 1973. Worked for an insurance company, 1929–37; began acting on radio, and performed monologues at various venues in Montreal, in the early 1930's; became full-time writer, actor, and director, 1937; devised and performed the annual revues *Fridolinons*, based on his radio character Fridolin, 1938–46; first full-length play, *Tit-Coq*, produced 1948; founder, the Comédie-Canadienne, for the purpose of producing Canadian plays, 1958: directed productions at the theatre until 1972; Chairman, Canadian Film Development Corporation, 1969–78. Recipient: several artistic awards and honorary degrees. Fellow, Royal Society of Canada, 1959. Medal of the Order of Canada, 1967.

Works

Collections

Les Fridolinades 1945 et 1946.   1980.
Les Fridolinades 1943 et 1944.   1981.
Les Fridolinades 1941 et 1942.   1981.
Les Fridolinades 1938, 1939, 1940.   1988.

Stage Works

Télévise-moi ça (monologues; produced Montreal, 1932–37).
Fridolinons (satirical revues; staged annually, Monument National, Montreal, 1938–46 and 1956). As *Les Fridolinades* (3 vols. for 1941–46), 1980–81, and *Les Fridolinades 1938, 1939, 1940*, 1988.
Tit-Coq (produced Monument National, Montreal, 1948). 1950; translated as *Tit-Coq*, 1967.
Bousille et les justes (produced Comédie-Canadienne, Montreal, 1959). 1960; translated as *Bousille and the Just*, 1961.
Le Diable à quatre (revue; produced 1964).
Hier, Les Enfants dansaient (produced Comédie-Canadienne, Montreal, 1966). In translation, as *Yesterday the Children Were Dancing*, 1967; as *Hier, Les Enfants dansaient*, 1968.
La Passion de Narcisse Mondoux (produced Théâtre du P'tit Bonheur, Toronto, 1986). 1987.

Television Plays

Les Quat'Fers en l'air (series), 1954.

Radio Plays

Le Train de plaisir (series), 1937–41.

*

Criticism

Books:
Margaret A. Primeau, "Gratien Gélinas et le théâtre populaire au Canada français", in *Dramatists in Canada*, edited by W.H. New, Vancouver, 1972.
Mavor Moore, *Four Canadian Playwrights: Robertson Davies, Gratien Gélinas, James Reaney, George Ryga*, Toronto, 1973.
Renate Usmiani, *Gratien Gélinas*, Toronto, 1977.
Gratien Gélinas: Dossiers de presse, 1940–1980, Sherbrooke, Quebec, 1981.

Articles:
Yves Bolduc, "Gratien Gélinas", in *Archives des lettres canadiennes*, 5, 1976.
Donald Smith, "Gratien Gélinas rénovateur du théâtre québécois", in *Lettres québécois*, 36, 1984–85.
Renate Usmiani, "Gélinas' Fridolin Rides Again: *La Passion de Narcisse Mondoux*", in *Canadian Drama*, 15, 1989.

*   *   *

A major pioneer, usually considered the progenitor of

modern Quebec theatre, Gratien Gélinas has left an indelible mark on Canadian dramaturgy, acting, and directing.

Experienced in college theatre, he began working in radio in Montreal in the early 1930's, when that medium's unparalleled hegemony in French Canada had just begun. By 1937 he had his own weekly radio series, starring as his most famous creation, Fridolin, a subtly nuanced character which he always played, on stage and on the air. Over the next decade Fridolin evolved into a quintessential Québécois everyman: youthful, ingenuous, poor, semi-literate, he spoke in a popular Canadian French which exuded wit, humour (mostly unconscious), pathos, humane compassion, and a wry wisdom far beyond his years. In the worst years of the pre-war decade, Fridolin made his countrymen laugh at politics, the Depression, at their own society and themselves. By the end of World War II Gélinas-Fridolin had become a national cultural hero, the best-known personality in French Canada.

His first full-length stage play, *Tit-Coq*, consolidated Gélinas's fame. From its premiere, in 1948, at Montreal's historic Monument National, is generally dated the birth of modern French-Canadian theatre. The titular character (the name means "Little Rooster") was again played by the author, who also directed the production. Tit-Coq is an older, more sober Fridolin, a foundling whose tragic destiny seemed ill-served in this case by the comic identity his predecessor had acquired, but whose credibility was also reinforced by familiarity. The play was a striking success, with more than 300 performances in its first two years. It has not become part of the Canadian repertory, however, being apparently too solidly anchored in the preoccupations of its time.

His second stage play, on the other hand, has been revived regularly, with reasonable success. Produced in 1959, at the very end of the most repressive era in modern Quebec's political history (conservative Premier Maurice Duplessis died that year), *Bousille* is less indulgent than *Tit-Coq*, and much less the vehicle for a single dominant role. After more than 100 performances in French in its first year, it was translated into English, performed on the CBC, BBC, and other European television networks, and staged in the USA, Germany, Poland, Finland, and Czechoslovakia. Although it is as deeply rooted in the Quebec society of the day as *Tit-Coq*, its resolution is less timid, its tone less respectful of religious and civil authority than its predecessor. In Quebec, it is generally considered his best work.

Significantly, English-Canadian criticism has been more favourable to *Hier, Les Enfants dansaient*, particularly after its English-language premiere in Charlottetown, Prince Edward Island, in 1967—the centenary of Canadian Confederation—with Gélinas and his son, Yves, playing the two major roles, as they had in the French production the previous year. Dealing with the violent anti-federalist activity which shook Quebec in the early and mid-1960's, it seeks to portray impartially both sides in the intensifying conflict. But Quebec audiences and readers have frequently judged the play more sympathetic to the federal cause than to the increasingly popular independentist option. It continues to be revived more often than any other of Gélinas's works—mainly in English Canada.

Gélinas remained inactive as a playwright for 20 years thereafter, concentrating on his duties as director, actor, Chair of the Canadian Film Corporation, and general spokesman for scenic arts in Canada. Semi-retired since 1978, he returned to the stage in 1986 with a play he wrote for himself and his actress wife, *La Passion de Narcisse Mondoux*. Reviews have been respectfully generous, but this superficial romantic comedy is not likely to endure. Gratien Gélinas will be remembered, much less for the plays he wrote, than for his

unique role in salvaging theatre in Quebec almost single-handedly from the marginal, commercial destiny it seemed to accept for itself before he arrived on the scene.

—Leonard E. Doucette

See also *Volume 1* entry on *Tit-Coq*.

GENET, Jean. Born in Paris, 19 December 1910; took mother's surname. Abandoned by parents, and reared by foster parents in Le Moravan area. Sent to reformatory, Mettray, for petty crimes, 1926–29; enlisted in the Foreign Legion, but deserted; lived an itinerant life of crime in various European countries, 1930–42, and began his writing in prison; met Jean-Paul Sartre and Jean Cocteau in the early 1940's; began publishing his works in the mid-1940's; sentenced to life imprisonment for recurrent theft, 1948: intervention by writers (organized by Sartre and Cocteau) and the review *Combat* secured a presidential pardon; first-produced play, *Les Bonnes* [*The Maids*], produced 1954; largely ceased literary activity after 1966, and subsequently espoused various radical causes, supporting the Black Panthers in the USA (lecturing on their behalf, 1970), Palestinian liberation groups, and the Baader-Meinhof group in West Germany. Died in Paris, 15 April 1986.

Early photograph of **Jean Genet**

Works

Collections

Oeuvres complètes (5 vols.).   1951–79.

Stage Works

Les Bonnes (produced Théâtre de l'Athénée, Paris, 1947; revised version produced Théâtre de la Huchette, Paris, 1954).   1948; revised versions, 1954, 1958; the 1958 version translated as *The Maids*, with *Deathwatch*, 1954.
'Adame Miroir (ballet scenario), music by Darius Milhaud.   1948.
Haute Surveillance (produced Théâtre des Mathurins, Paris, 1949).   1949; revised version, 1965; further revised version, in *Oeuvres complètes 4*, 1968; the 1965 version translated as *Deathwatch*, with *The Maids*, 1954.
Le Balcon (produced Arts Theatre, London, 1957; first French production, Théâtre du Gymnase, Paris, 1960).   1956; revised editions, 1960, 1962; translated as *The Balcony*, 1958; revised translation, 1966.
Les Nègres (produced Théâtre de Lutèce, Paris, 1959).   1958; translated as *The Blacks*, 1960.
Les Paravents (abridged version produced in German, Schlosspark Theater, Berlin, 1961; complete version produced Stadsteater, Stockholm, Sweden, 1964; first French production, Théâtre de France, Paris, 1966).   1961; revised version, 1976; translated as *The Screens*, 1963.

Screenplays

Un Chant d'amour, 1950; *Goubbiah*, 1955; *Mademoiselle*, 1966.

Fiction

Notre-Dame des Fleurs.   1944; revised version, in *Oeuvres complètes 2*, 1951; translated as *Our Lady of the Flowers*, 1949; translated as *Gutter in the Sky*, 1956.
Miracle de la rose.   1946; revised version, in *Oeuvres complètes 2*, 1951; translated as *Miracle of the Rose*, 1965.
Pompes funèbres.   1947; revised version, in *Oeuvres complètes 3*, 1953; translated as *Funeral Rites*, 1969.
Querelle de Brest.   1947; revised version, in *Oeuvres complètes 3*, 1953; translated as *Querelle of Brest*, 1966.

Verse

Chants secrets.   1947.
La Galère.   1947.
Poèmes.   1948; revised edition, 1966.
Poems.   1980.
Treasures of the Night: Collected Poems, translated by Steven Finch.   1981.

Other

Journal du voleur.   1949; translated as *The Thief's Journal*, 1954.
L'Enfant criminel, 'Adame Miroir.   1949.
Lettres à Roger Blin.   1966; as *Letters to Roger Blin: Reflections on the Theatre*, 1969.
May Day Speech.   1970.
Reflections on the Theatre and Other Writings.   1972.

*

Bibliographies

Richard C. and Suzanne A. Webb, *Jean Genet and His Critics: An Annotated Bibliography 1943–1980*, Metuchen, New Jersey, 1982.

Criticism

Books:
Jean-Paul Sartre, *Saint-Genet, Actor and Martyr* (translated from the French), New York, 1963.
Joseph H. McMahon, *The Imagination of Genet*, New Haven, Connecticut, 1963.
Tom F. Driver, *Jean Genet*, New York, 1966.
Werner Kleiss, *Genet*, Hanover, 1967.
Bettina L. Knapp, *Jean Genet*, New York, 1968; revised edition, 1989.
Philip Thody, *Jean Genet: A Study of His Novels and Plays*, London, 1968.
Richard N. Coe, *The Vision of Jean Genet*, London and New York, 1968.
Richard N. Coe (ed.), *The Theater of Jean Genet: A Casebook*, New York, 1970.
Jean M. Magnan, *Jean Genet: Un Essai* (second edition), Paris, 1971.
Odette Aslan, *Jean Genet: Textes de Genet, points de vue critiques, témoignages, chronologie, bibliographie, illustrations*, Paris, 1973.
Lewis T. Cetta, *Profane Play, Ritual, and Jean Genet: A Study of His Drama*, University of Alabama, 1974.
Peter Brooks and Joseph Halpern (eds.), *Genet: A Collection of Critical Essays*, Englewood Cliffs, New Jersey, 1979.
Jeannette L. Savona, *Jean Genet*, London, 1983 (Macmillan Modern Dramatists series).
Una Chaudhuri, *No Man's Stage: A Semiotic Study of Jean Genet's Major Plays*, Ann Arbor, Michigan, 1986.
Laura Oswald, *Jean Genet and the Semiotics of Performance*, Bloomington, Indiana, 1989.
Harry E. Stewart and Rob R. McGregor, *Jean Genet: A Biography of Deceit, 1910–1951*, New York, 1989.

*   *   *

With his death in 1986, the legend of Jean Genet began to give way to documented fact. The delinquent who, allegedly, started writing in prison as an act of defiance against authority, is gradually emerging as already a highly-cultured, widely-read artist at a very early phase in his life. However, none of the details unearthed by scholars make his work any the less challenging or provocative. Arising at first out of the fantasies inspired by his experience of prison and originally elaborated in the controversial novels *Our Lady of the Flowers* and *Miracle of the Rose*, Genet's plays were to penetrate to the core of the West's cultural mythology. Precisely because it is grounded in the experience of deviants, marginals, outcasts, and the oppressed, his theatre provides a searching portrayal of power-structures at work in society and, more especially, in the collective imagination.

His first-written play, *Deathwatch*, provided the basis for much that was to follow. It features three inmates of a prison cell who struggle with their conflicting phantasms and aspirations, influenced by evocations of an unseen fourth prisoner who embodies all that is most powerful and compelling about the murderer as hero. In this closed world of criminals, conventional value-systems are turned upside down and the greatest crime is the greatest good, while the vilest act prompts ideas of beauty.

Though originally staged as a more-or-less realistic piece, the play has had most success when, as Genet indicates in a stage direction, it unfolds "as in a dream". The setting is deliberately claustrophobic, the plot is systematically blurred, gestures are ritualistic, the action includes a balletic display of erotic anguish, and the language is poetry shot through with vulgarisms. What is enacted is a contest for domination within the criminal hierarchy; what is revealed is a collusion between oppressed and oppressor which was to become a hallmark of all Genet's plays.

The dramatic structure of *Deathwatch* is transposed into the setting of an upper-class interior in *The Maids*, written at the invitation of Louis Jouvet and first produced by him in a manner designed to highlight its apparently conventional features. But within the triangular relationship of two maids and their mistress in the shadow, this time, of the latter's unseen lover, Genet explores undercurrents which present a stark challenge to convention. The resentful servants take turns to act as "Madame" in her absence, and to abuse each other either as servant or as employer, for their hatred has as its target not only the woman they see as their domineering mistress, but also themselves for their craven collusion in the hierarchy which places them at the bottom of the social ladder. Their plan to denounce Madame's criminal lover misfires and the play ends with one servant, dressed again in her mistress's clothes, taking poison at the instigation of the other servant: the ritual enacts both the maids' revolt against authority and their hatred of themselves. Indeed, the ritual aspect of this play is its most telling feature. While providing a vehicle for exploring the ambiguities of homosexual desire and related psychoanalytical fantasies, the work's ritualistic elements, which Genet was prompted to underline by his dissatisfaction with the naturalistic premiere it received, situate it in the lineage of Artaud, whom Genet's subsequent theatre constantly calls to mind.

After a break of some nine years, due to a crisis in his attitude to his creative career, Genet returned to the stage with a vengeance, extending the themes and techniques of the earlier works on a vastly more ambitious scale, embracing politics and revolution in *The Balcony*, racism and oppression of the Third World in *The Blacks*, and colonial war in *The Screens*. These plays all dramatize the struggle between rebellious oppressed groups and the figures of authority, who appear in more or less the same form in each work: a queen, a judge, a representative of the Church, a figure embodying the police state and/or military authority, and a political manipulator or diplomatic go-between. These figures, costumed grotesquely, with hugely-padded shoulders and high platform shoes, are placed in contexts which deliberately evoke scandal and controversy: a brothel which doubles as a royal palace in *The Balcony*; a performance of the assassination of a white girl by a black murderer in *The Blacks*; the Algerian war in *The Screens*.

From these ingredients alone we can see that Genet is deliberately courting scandalized visceral reactions while simultaneously challenging his audiences with intellectual paradoxes. His plays are a glorification of the image and the reflection, he says, and indeed it is impossible to unravel the fabric of fantasy, pretence, and simulation which is the stuff of Genet's theatre. We cannot take seriously the caricatures he confronts us with—the more so as his plays constantly point to their own artificiality, through the use of masks, mime, and self-conscious theatre simultaneously cultivating and denouncing the stage illusion. Yet Genet's images of eroticism, violence, and torture operate on the senses all the more effectively precisely because they represent a concentration of what, in reality, is imperfect and fragmented. To experience Genet's plays is to have the intellect pursue the evidence of the senses to discover the existential void at the heart of reality.

These works had their socio-political impact. *The Balcony* was first staged at a private club in London because it was considered too scandalous for Paris audiences. *The Blacks* made a significant contribution to the Civil Rights movement in the USA during its three-year off-Broadway run. *The Screens* provoked threats of military demonstrations in the streets of the French capital and had to wait for five years (during which time it was staged in several other European countries) and the end of the Algerian war before receiving its Paris premiere. However, with the passing of the immediate sources of scandal, Genet's plays come into their own for their sheer theatrical inventiveness, complexity, and for the creative challenges they present to practitioners. They have features in common with the "theatre of the absurd", with which they coincide chronologically: eschewing the logic of plot and character, they proceed by fragmentation and frequent shifts between different levels of represented reality. But above all, they embody the urge towards stage poetry in which all the resources of language and production, as well as a vast range of genres and techniques, are exploited, producing outstanding examples of "total theatre".

—David H. Walker

See also *Volume 1* entries on *The Balcony*; *The Blacks*; *The Maids*.

GENNE-HŌIN. See *Volume 1* entry on *Suehirogari*.

GHELDERODE, Michel de. Born Adémar-Adolphe-Louis Martens, in Ixelles, Belgium, 3 April 1898. Educated at the Institut St. Louis, Brussels, 1910–14; Conservatoire de Bruxelles, 1915–17; suffered partial paralysis after an illness, and had to give up education. Married Jeanne-Françoise Gérard in 1924. First play, *La Mort regarde à la fenêtre*, produced 1918; professor, Institut Dupuich, 1921–22: resigned for reasons of poor health; bookseller, 1922–23; worked for local government in the Communale de Schaerbeek, Brussels, 1923–45; secretary, the Cabinet Maldoror art gallery, 1923; contributor, *La Flandre littéraire*, *La Renaissance d'Occident*, and other publications, from 1924; wrote for the puppet theatre Les Marionnettes de la Renaissance d'Occident, 1924–25; became co-editor of *La Flandre littéraire*, 1925; collaborated in staging his plays with the Dutch producer Johan de Meester, 1925–30; officially adopted Flemish name Michel de Ghelderode, 1930; abandoned playwriting, 1939; remained in Belgium during World War II; a prominent contributor to *Le Journal de Bruges*, 1946–53. Wrote his plays in French, although they were sometimes first produced in Dutch or Flemish translations.

Recipient: Prix du Brabant, 1928; Prix Picard, 1928; Prix Rubens de la Fondation Franco-Belge des Artistes, 1929; Prix Triennal de Littérature Dramatique, 1939 and 1954; Belgian Society of Authors Award, 1945; Malpertuis Prize, 1951; Prix Italia, 1957. Elected to the Académie Picard, 1932. Died in Schaerbeek, 1 April 1962.

Works

Collections

Théâtre.   1943.
Théâtre complet (2 vols.).   1943 (but showing date 1942).
Théâtre (5 vols.).   1950–57.
Théâtre d'écoutes (radio plays: includes *Le Singulier Trépas de Messire Ulenspiegel; Le Perroquet de Charles V; La Folie d'Hugo van der Goes*).   1951.
Seven Plays (includes *The Women at the Tomb; Barabbus; Three Actors and Their Drama; Pantagleize; The Blind Men; Chronicles of Hell; Lord Halewyn*), translated by G. Hauger.   1960.
Seven Plays (includes *Red Magic; Hop Signor!; The Death of Doctor Faust; Christopher Columbus; A Night of Pity; Piet Bouteille; Miss Jairus*) translated by G. Hauger.   1964.
"The Strange Rider" and Other Plays (includes *The Blind Men; The Women at the Tomb; Red Magic; Christopher Columbus; Evening Lament; The Old Men; Pantagleize*), translated by S. Draper.   1967 (private printing).

Stage Works

La Mort regarde à la fenêtre (produced La Bonbonnière, Brussels, 1918).
Le Repas des fauves (produced La Bonbonnière, Brussels, 1919).
Têtes de bois.   In *La Flandre littéraire*, November 1924.
Les Vieillards (broadcast on radio, 1942).   1924; translated as *The Old Men*, in *"The Strange Rider" and Other Plays*, 1967.
Piet Bouteille (produced by Les Ouvriers de la Renaissance d'Occident, Antwerp, 1925).   As *Oude Piet*, 1925; as *Piet Bouteille*, in *Théâtre 5*, 1957; translated as *Piet Bouteille*, in *Seven Plays*, 1964.
Le Mystère de la Passion de Notre Seigneur Jésus-Christ (produced Théâtre des Marionnettes de Toone IV, Brussels, 1934).   1925.
La Tentation de St. Antoine (produced Théâtre de Toone VII, Brussels, 1967).   In *La Renaissance d'Occident*, June 1925.
La Farce de la mort qui faillit trépasser (produced Vlaamsche Volkstooneel, Brussels, 1925).   1952.
La Mort du Docteur Faust (produced Théâtre Art et Action, Paris, 1928).   1926; translated as *The Death of Doctor Faust*, in *Seven Plays*, 1964.
Vénus.   In *La Flandre littéraire*, 1927.
Beeldekens uit het leven van Sint Franciskus van Assisi (produced Vlaamsche Volkstoneel, Malines, 1927).   1927.
Le Miracle dans le faubourg (produced Brussels, 1928).
Christophe Colomb (produced Théâtre Art et Action, Paris, 1929).   1928; translated as *Christopher Columbus*, in *Seven Plays*, 1964.
Don Juan; ou, Les Amants chimériques (produced Théâtre National, Brussels, 1962).   1928.
Escurial (produced in Flemish translation, Théâtre Royal Flamand, Brussels, 1929; in French, Conservatoire, Liège, 1930).   1928; translated as *Escurial*, in *The Modern Theatre 5*, edited by Eric Bentley, 1957, and in *An Anthology of Belgian Literature*, edited by Bettina L. Knapp, 1981.

La Transfiguration dans le cirque (produced Rotterdams Toneel, Rotterdam, 1959).   In *Théâtre 2* (La Renaissance d'Occident edition), 1928.
Barabbas (produced Vlaamsche Volkstoneel, Brussels, 1928; produced in French, Théâtre Residence, Brussels, 1934).   1932; translated as *Barabbus*, in *Seven Plays*, 1960.
Un Soir de pitié (produced Théâtre Expérimental am Lichtenwerd, Vienna, 1959).   1929; translated as *Evening Lament*, in *"The Strange Rider" and Other Plays*, 1967.
Fastes d'enfer (produced Théâtre de l'Atelier, Paris, 1949).   1929; translated as *Chronicles of Hell*, in *Seven Plays*, 1960.
Atlantique (produced Vlaamsche Volkstoneel, Brussels, 1930).
Noyade des songes.   In *La Revue mosane*, 1930.
Het Meisje met de houten handen [The Little Girl with Wooden Hands], with Jean Barleig (broadcast on radio, 1934).   1930.
Pantagleize (produced Vlaamsche Volkstoneel, Saint-Trond, Belgium, 1930; produced in French, Théâtre du Parc, Brussels, 1934).   1934; translated as *Pantagleize*, in *Seven Plays*, 1960.
Trois Acteurs, un drame (produced Théâtre du Parc, Brussels, 1931).   1931(?); translated as *Three Actors and Their Drama*, in *Seven Plays*, 1960.
Duvelor; ou, La Farce de diable vieux.   In *Le Rouge et le noir*, 27 May 1931; in book form, in *Marionnettes de tradition populaire*, edited by R. Guiette, 1950.
De Sterrendief [The Star Thief] (produced Vlaamsche Volkstoneel, Brussels, 1932).   1931.
Le Sommeil de la raison (produced in Dutch, Oudenaarde, 1934; produced in French, Korbach, Germany, 1968).   As *De Zeren Hoofzonden*, 1931; as *Le Sommeil de la raison*, in *Marginales*, May 1967.
Godelieve (produced Ostend, 1932).   1934.
Le Chagrin d'Hamlet ("dialogue").   In *Le Rouge et le noir*, March 1933.
Arc-en-ciel (produced Compagnie de la Rose, Paris, 1939).   1933.
Les Femmes au tombeau (produced Compagnie théâtrale de la Cité, Paris, 1953).   1934; translated as *The Women at the Tomb*, in *Seven Plays*, 1960.
Le Vieux Soudard, music by René Defosset (produced 1935).
Adrian et Jusémina (produced de la Rose, Paris, 1939).   1935.
Masques ostendais (produced Théâtre de l'Étuve, Liège, 1954).   1935.
Le Ménage de Caroline (produced Théâtre de l'Exposition, Brussels, 1935).   1935.
Magie rouge (produced Estaminet Barcelone, Brussels, 1934).   1935; translated as *Red Magic*, in *Seven Plays*, 1964.
La Balade du grand macabre (produced Théâtre de la Comédie, Lyons, 1953).   1935.
Les Aveugles (broadcast on radio, 1933; produced Théâtre de Poche, Paris, 1956).   In Flemish, 1936; as *Les Aveugles*, 1943; translated as *The Blind Men*, in *Seven Plays*, 1960.
Le Cavalier bizarre (produced by the Cercle Paul Valery, Paris, 1953).   1938; translated as *The Strange Rider*, in *"The Strange Rider" and Other Plays*, 1967.
Sire Halewyn (produced Théâtre Communal, Brussels, 1938).   1943; translated as *Lord Halewyn*, in *Seven Plays*, 1960.
Hop Signor! (produced Théâtre du Parc, Brussels, 1942).   1938; translated as *Hop Signor!*, in *Seven Plays*, 1964.
La Pie sur le gibet (broadcast on radio, 1939; produced

Théâtre de Marionnettes de Toone VII, Brussels, 1969).
1938; translated as *The Magpie on the Gallows*, in *An
Anthology of Belgian Literature*, edited by Bettina L.
Knapp, 1981.
L'École des bouffons (produced Théâtre de l'Oeuvre, Paris,
1953). 1942 translated as *School for Buffoons*, 1968.
Mademoiselle Jaïre (produced Théâtre de l'Atelier, Paris,
1949). In *Théâtre complet 1*, 1943; translated as *Miss
Jairus*, in *Seven Plays*, 1964.
La Farce des ténébreux (produced Théâtre du Grand
Guignol, Paris, 1952). In *Théâtre complet 1*, 1943.
Sortie de l'acteur (produced in Polish translation, Teatr 38,
Cracow, Poland, 1960; first produced in Belgium,
Kelderteater Arca, Toneelstudio 58, Ghent, 1961). In
Théâtre complet 2, 1943.
Le Soleil se couche (produced Théâtre Royal Flamand,
Brussels, 1951). In *Théâtre complet 2*, 1943.
D'Un Diable qui prêcha merveilles (produced Grenier aux
Chansons, Brussels, 1964). In *Théâtre complet 2*, 1943.
Le Club des menteurs (broadcast on radio, 1954; produced
University of Frankfurt, 1958). 1943.
Marie le Misérable (produced outside the Church of St.
Lambert, Woluwé-St.-Lambert, 1952). In *Théâtre 4*,
1955.
La Vie publique de Pantagleize. In *Audace*, January 1954.

Radio Plays

Le Cavalier bizarre, 1932; *Le Coeur révélateur*, from a work
by Edgar Allen Poe, 1932; *Plaisir d'amour*, 1933; *Les
Aveugles*, 1933; *Le Perroquet de Charles Quint*, 1934 (published in *Théâtre d'écoutes*, 1951); *Het Meisje met de houten
handen* [The Little Girl with Wooden Hands], 1934; *Payül
reporter*, 1934; *Payül champion*, 1934; *Payül dans le beffroi*,
1934; *Payül lauréat*, 1934; *Payül au paradis*, 1935; *Cinq Mai
1835*, 1935; *De Dood van Ulenspiegel*, 1935 (published in
Volk, December 1937–January 1938; as *Le Singulier trépas de
Messire Ulenspiegel*, in *Théâtre d'écoutes*, 1951); *La Folie
d'Hugo van der Goes*, 1935 (published in *Théâtre d'écoutes*,
1951); *Le Massacre des innocents*, 1937 (published in *La
Renaissance d'Occident*, November 1926); *L'Oiseau chocolat*,
from the stage-play *Atlantique*, 1938; *La Pie sur le gibet*, 1939;
Comment L'Empereur Charles devint voleur de chiens, 1941;
D'un Fou qui se croyait empereur, from the stage play *La
Couronne de fer-blanc*, 1941; *Scènes de la vie d'un bohème:
Franz Schubert*, 1941; *Il fiammingo*, 1942; *Jeudi Saint*, from
the stage-play *Les Vieillards*, 1942; *Le Club des menteurs*,
1954; *La Grande Tentation de Saint Antoine*, 1957 (published
in *Cahiers d'étude de radio-télévision*, June 1958).

Fiction

Sortilèges (short stories). 1941.
"Sortilèges" et autres contes crépusculaires. 1962.
Contes et dicts hors du temps. 1975.

Verse

La Corne d'abondance. 1925.
Ixelles, mes amours. . . ., under the pseudonym P.
Costenoble. 1928.

Memoirs and Letters

"Lettres à Catherine Toth et André Reybaz, René Dupuy,
Roger Iglésias, Jean Le Poulain, Marcel Lupovici, Gilles
Chancrin, Georges Goubert", in *Revue d'histoire du*

théâtre, vol.14 no.2, 1962; partly translated as "To
Directors and Actors: Letters 1948–1959", in *Tulane
Drama Review*, vol.9 no.4, 1965.
Correspondance: Autour d'une amitié naissante, with Henri
Vandeputte. 1964.
Autour d'Une Amitié littéraire: Correspondance 1932–1934,
with Henri Vandeputte, edited by Guy Descamps. 1984.

Other

*L'Histoire comique de Keizer Karel telle que la perpétuèrent
jusqu'à nos jours les sens gens de Brabant et de
Flandre*. 1922.
La Halte catholique. 1922.
L'Homme sous l'uniforme. 1923.
Kwiebe-Kwiebus. 1926; in French, as *Voyage autour de ma
Flandre*, 1947.
Choses et gens de chez nous. 1943.
Mes Statues. 1943.
La Flandre est un songe. 1953.
Le Siège d'Ostende. 1980.

*

Bibliographies

Roland Beyen, *Bibliographie de Michel de Ghelderode*,
Brussels, 1987.

Criticism

Books:
J. Francis, *Michel de Ghelderode: Dramaturge des pays de
par-deçu*, Brussels, 1949.
R. Inglésas and A. Trutat, *Michel de Ghelderode: Les
Entretiens d'Ostende*, Paris, 1956.
P. Vandromme, *Michel de Ghelderode*, Paris, 1963.
Élisabeth Deberdt-Malaquais, *La Quête de l'identité dans le
théâtre de Ghelderode*, Paris, 1967.
J. Francis, *L'Éternel aujourd'hui de Michel de Ghelderode:
Spectographie d'un auteur*, Brussels, 1968.
J. Decock, *Le Théâtre de Michel de Ghelderode: Une
Dramaturgie de l'anti-théâtre et de la cruauté*, Paris, 1969.
Alice Santt, *Michel de Ghelderode*, Vieux-Virton, 1970.
Roland Beyen, *Michel de Ghelderode ou la hantise du mas-
que: Essai de biographie critique*, Brussels, 1971.
George E. Wellwarth, *The Theater of Protest and Paradox*
(revised edition), New York, 1971.
Adrien Jans, *La Vie de Michel de Ghelderode, ange et démon*,
Paris, 1972.
Roland Beyen, *Michel de Ghelderode: Présentation, choix de
textes, chronologie, bibliographie*, Paris, 1974.
Albert Lepage, *L'Énigme Ghelderode*, Brussels, 1976.
Nadine B. Castro, *Le Théâtre de Michel de Ghelderode*,
Lausanne, 1979.
Raymond Trousson (ed.), *Michel de Ghelderode:
Dramaturge et conteur*, Brussels, 1983.
Anne M. Beckers, *Michel de Ghelderode*, Brussels, 1985.
Bettina L. Knapp, *French Theatre 1918–1939*, London, 1985
(Macmillan Modern Dramatists series).
Jacqueline Blancart-Cassou, *Le Rire de Michel de
Ghelderode*, Paris, 1987.
Anne M. Beckers, *Michel de Ghelderode*, 1988.

Articles:

Paul M. Levitt, "Ghelderode and Puppet Theatre", in *French Review*, 48, 1975.

Gillan Farish, "Michel de Ghelderode: The Theatre of the Swerving Dream", in *University of Windsor Review*, vol.13 no.2, 1978.

Serials

Ghelderode: Bulletin de la Fondation Internationale Michel de Ghelderode, 1980–

* * *

Michel de Ghelderode, with his incantatory poetic use of language, his stage images often inspired by the works of Renaissance painters, and his obsessive themes created an intensely personal theatre which does not fit into any established tradition. In some ways it prefigured the new French theatre of the 1950's. Like Ionesco and Beckett, Ghelderode mingled farce and tragedy, and showed reason and logic as powerless in an inexplicably cruel world. He can be seen as a link in the chain between Jarry, Artaud, and the "theatre of the absurd". He accepted that his plays embodied Artaud's ideas for a "theatre of cruelty", but, in his own words, laughed "like a drain" when he heard critics suggesting that he took part in the intellectual experimentation of the 1920's, complaining that they missed the essentially popular, direct appeal of his work.

In fact, some early plays do experiment extensively with new techniques, such as the use of film, expressionist decor, multiple staging and simultaneous dialogue—plays such as *La Mort du Docteur Faust* (*The Death of Doctor Faust*) and *Images de la vie de Saint François d'Assise* (Images of the Life of Saint Francis of Assisi). The "Saint Francis", written for the Vlaamsche Volkstoneel (Popular Theatre of Flanders), began a successful collaboration with the company, which certainly encouraged the dramatist to discipline his style and make his theatre accessible to a wider public.

Barabbas is typical of this period. Ghelderode was asked by the director Johan de Meester for a play to be performed at Eastertide, and wrote what he called "a popular Flemish Passion-play". It is a very unconventional version of the Crucifixion, seen from the point of view of the rabble and their criminal hero, Barabbas. First seen behind the massive bars of his cell, Barabbas is a violent, anti-social animal, who is nonetheless presented as a heroic anarchist figure. Like Jean Genet's criminal characters, he has chosen to live to the full the role society has given him. His rejection of traditional social values and beliefs is paralleled with Christ's call for a new order, and he explains Christ's despair on the Cross by His realisation that man's injustice to man will never change.

Barabbas is converted to a Christian belief in non-violent revolt, but in later versions the author attempted to strip the play of its Catholic elements, and we now have an ambiguous ending where Barabbas is stabbed to death in the slum streets while Christ is being crucified. The Crucifixion itself is offstage, but is presented to the crowd by a fairground barker and his clown, in a bitterly ironic mode which we find again in many later works.

Pantagleize, another success with the Flemish company, and one of the few play set in modern times, also contains a violent attack on capitalist society; but its overall message is less political than cynical and bitterly pessimistic. The anti-hero Pantagleize is a Chaplinesque "little man"—the author admired Chaplin and had him in mind as a model. He is a poet, a dreamer, caught up in events he does not understand when he accidentally gives the password to start a revolution, and finds himself hailed as the clandestine leader who planned the great day. The action takes place on May 1, with all its socialist and utopian associations, and, despite the clowning, this caricature of a hopeful revolution betrayed by the incompetence and dishonesty of its leaders, and ending with the innocent dying before the firing squad of the old regime, has a relevance which makes it probably the most frequently performed of Ghelderode's plays world-wide.

Ghelderode felt that his culture was Flemish, although his language was French, and his work draws on the folklore and legends of Flanders. The fact that the early successes were first performed under the mask of a Flemish translation and by a Flemish company must have strengthened this feeling. This may explain why the problem of identity and the mask are important themes in his plays. The mask may be a personal disguise, or part of the ceremonial and ritual which conceals ugly social realities.

Escurial uses these themes to powerful effect. Like many of the plays, it is set in the early Renaissance, as seen through the eyes of its great painters, in this case El Greco and Velasquez. The scene is a crumbling Spanish throne-room, where a half-mad King forces his deformed Flemish jester, Folial, to make him laugh, while his Queen lies dying in the palace that "stinks of Death". As King and jester swap places in a sinister game, both reveal truths about themselves, and their laughter, "full of the gnashing of teeth", does not hide their mutual hatred. The role-playing and the doubts about who is truly master, and who servant, are more important than the rather melodramatic revelations that the jester has been the Queen's lover and that the King has poisoned her. The play ends with the King ordering his executioner to strangle Folial when the jester refuses to return the crown.

Most of the plays written after 1930 continue in this vein, presenting extreme situations and characters that represent the author's obsessions. Hiéronymous, in *Magie Rouge* (*Red Magic*), who loves the yellow candle-light which turns his room into a cube of gold, and refuses to make love to his virgin wife for fear of squandering his strength, deserves a place beside Harpagon in the gallery of great stage misers. He, too, is a ridiculous yet tragic figure, but this tragedy involves frenzied sexual betrayal and a violently bloody ending. The linking of sexuality and death is a recurring theme in Ghelderode's work. In *Mademoiselle Jaïre* the frustrated wife wills the death of her husband and dreams of a masochistic sexual satisfaction at the hands of the executioner.

The nightmarish world of some of these plays seems so extreme as to invite rejection, but the best works are comparable to the great artistic portrayals of our inner monsters which inspired the dramatist. They bring to life the worlds of Goya and Hieronymous Bosch, while echoing the violence and alienation of our own times, and have earned themselves a permanent place in the repertoire.

—John Rothenberg

———

GIACOSA, (Giuseppe). Born in Collerato Parella (now Collerato Giacosa), near Ivrea, Val d'Aosta, Piedmont (now in Italy), 21 October 1847. Educated in Ivrea, Modena, Brescia; University of Turin, studying law, 1865–68. Married Maria Bertola in 1877; three daughters. Worked in his father's law firm, 1868–73; professional writer from 1873; first play, *Una partita a scacchi*, produced 1873; travelled to Sicily, 1876, and France and Germany, 1878; Professor of History and Fine Arts, Academy of Fine Arts, Turin, 1885–88; moved to Milan, 1888; Director of the School of Acting, Milan Academy of Philodramatics, 1888–89; professor of dramatic literature and acting, Milan Conservatory, 1888–92; travelled to the USA to work with the actress Sarah Bernhardt, for whom he had written *La signorina di Challant*, 1891; director, Society of Authors, 1895; collaborated with Luigi Illica on opera libretti, 1893–1901; director of *La lettura*, a monthly supplement to *Corriere della serca*, and contributor to various other periodicals. Died in Ivrea, 2 September 1906.

Works

Collections

Scene e commedie. 1873.
Teatro in versi (6 vols.). 1875–88.
Teatro in prosa (3 vols.). 1877–90.
The Stronger; Like Falling Leaves; Sacred Ground, translated by E. and A. Updegraff. 1916.
Teatro (2 vols.; includes fragments), edited by P. Nardi. 1948.
Scritti scelti. 1960.
Puccini Librettos (includes texts and translations of *La Bohème; Tosca; Madame Butterfly*). 1973.

Stage Works

Una partita a scacchi (produced by the company of the Accademia Filarmonica, Naples, 1873). In *Nuova antologia*, March 1872; translated as *The Wager*, 1914.
A can che lecca cenere nongli fidar farina (produced Teatro Gerbino, Turin, 1872). In *Nuova antologia*, June 1872.
Al pianoforte. In *Scene e commedie*, 1873.
Chi lascia la via per la nuova sa quel che lascia, non sa quel que trova In *Scene e commedie*, 1873.
Non dir quattro se non l'hai nel sacco. In *Scene e commedie*, 1873.
La scuola del matrimonio (produced Trieste, 1881). In *Scene e commedie*, 1873.
Affari di banca (produced Teatro del Corso, Bologna, 1873).
Storia vecchia (produced Teatro Gerbino, Turin, 1872). In *Serate italiene*, January-February 1874.
Sorprese notturne (produced Teatro Gerbino, Turin, 1875). In *Serate italiene*, December 1875.
Il trionfo d'amore (produced Teatro Gerbino, Turin, 1875). 1875.
Luisa (produced as *Teresa*, Teatro Rossini, Venice, 1875; revised version, as *Luisa*, produced Teatro Manzoni, Milan, 1879). 1881.
Il marito amante della moglie (produced Teatro Manzoni, Milan, 1876). 1876.
Acquazzoni in montagne (produced Teatro Valle, Rome, 1876). In *Teatro in prosa 1*, 1877.
Il Fratello d'armi (produced Teatro Gerbino, Turin, 1877). 1877.
Il Conte Rosso (produced Teatro Carignano, Turin, 1880). 1880.
Il filo: Scene filosofico-morale per marionette (produced Turin, 1883). 1883.
La zampa del gatto (produced Arena Nazionale, Florence, 1883). 1888.
La sirena (produced Teatro Valle, Rome, 1883). 1888.

Resa a discrezione (produced Teatro Filodrammatico, Milan, 1886). 1888.
Le tardi ravveduta (produced Villa Visconti di Modrone, Cernobbio, 1886). 1888.
Tristi amori (produced Teatro Valle, Rome, 1887). 1890; translated as *Unhappy Love*, in *Poet Lore*, 27, 1916; in book form, in *Poet Lore Plays*, 1916.
La Dame de Challant (produced Stand Theatre, New York, 1891; revised version, as *La signora di Challant*, produced Turin, 1891). 1891.
I diritti dell'anima (produced Teatro Nuovo, Verona, 1894). 1900; translated as *Sacred Ground*, in *The Stronger; Like Falling Leaves; Sacred Ground*, 1916; as *The Rights of the Soul*, in *Drama*, 10, 1918.
Come le foglie (produced Teatro Manzoni, Milan, 1900). In *Teatro*, 1900–06; translated as *As the Leaves*, in *Drama*, 1, 1911; as *Like Falling Leaves*, in *The Stronger; Like Falling Leaves; Sacred Ground*, 1916.
Il più forte (produced Teatro Alfieri, Turin, 1904). In *Teatro*, 1900–06. translated as *The Stronger*, in *The Stronger; Like Falling Leaves; Sacred Ground*, 1916.
Intrighi eleganti (produced Teatro Gerbino, Turin, 1874). In *Teatro*, 2, 1948.
I figli del Marchese Arturo (produced Teatro Manzoni, Milan, 1873). In *Teatro 2*, 1948.
L'onorevole Ercole Mallardi (produced Teatro Manzoni, Milan, 1885). In *Teatro 2*, 1948.
La gente di spirito. In *Teatro 1*, 1948.
Gli annoiati (produced Teatro Gerbino, Turin, 1878). In *Teatro 2*, 1948.
La Bohème, with Luigi Illica, music by Puccini (produced Teatro Regio, Turin, 1896).
Tosca, with Luigi Illica, music by Puccini (produced Teatro Constanzi, Rome, 1900).
Madame Butterfly, music by Puccini (produced La Scala, Milan, 1904).

Fiction

Novelle e paesi valdostani. In periodicals, 1880–85; in book form, 1886.
Genti e cose della montagna: Novelle e capitoli. 1986.

Other

Castelli valdostani e canavesani. 1898.
Impressioni d'America. 1898.
Conferenze e discorsi. 1909.

*

Criticism

Books:
Piero Nardi, *Vita e tempo di Giacosa*, Milan, 1948.
Anna Barsotti, *Giuseppe Giacosa*, Florence, 1973.

Articles:
Stanley Astredo Smith, "Giuseppe Giacosa", in *The Drama*, 10, 1913.
Donatella Ravanello, "Inizio di Giacosa drammaturgo", in *Lettere italiane*, 39, 1987.

* * *

Giuseppe Giacosa grew to maturity in Turin, at a time of

political and artistic ferment. Turin remained one of the most progressive cultural centers of northern Italy (the other being Milan) where the bourgeoisie attempted to overcome their provincialism and become more refined and European; although it must be said that Turin was not as open-minded as Milan and tended to retain a more conservative and conformist attitude despite the changes that followed the revolution.

As a young man, Giacosa showed a penchant for writing and the artistic life. He was part of a group of young Piedmontese poets, writers, painters, and sculptors. Artistic debates, characteristic of the bohemian *scapigliatura* movement in Milan and Piedmont, nourished his imagination. His interests extended beyond literature. At an early age he was an art critic for the Turin periodical *L'arte in Italia*. From the artists who belonged to the Rivara school of painters and who spent the summers near Ivrea, he absorbed the neo-romantic nostalgia for medieval archeology. The effects of these diverse influences can be seen in his first three plays.

The monologue of the one scene sketch, *Al pianoforte*, takes on a tone which, falling as it does between ironic scepticism and decadent sentimentalism, is characteristic of *scapigliatura*. *Chi lascia la via . . .*, a dramatic proverb, upholds the traditional values of domestic life over worldliness. The 14th-century setting of *Una partita a scacchi* reflects the passion for medievalism he had learned from the neo-romantics and the Rivara school.

His success as a playwright was not always assured. Early in his career Giacosa admired the thesis plays of Paolo Ferrari, an important Italian dramatist of the earlier generation who had fallen under the influence of Augier and Dumas *fils*. Giacosa wrote some plays of this type himself in the 1870's— *Affari di banca*, *I figli del Marchese Arturo*—but they were not successful.

His reputation was made with four kinds of play that fall generally into two periods. The medieval romantic plays and light comedies and proverbs of his first period were primarily escapist and conservative, and did not question society's values, or probe the psychology of character. In his second period, which began in 1880 but only came into focus with *Tristi amori* and his last three plays (all four in prose), one can see his growing commitment to social commentary. This change has been attributed to the influence of *verismo* writers, particularly of Verga, Capuana, and the Venetian, Fogazzaro.

It was *Una partita a scacchi* (*The Wager*), based on a scene from the *chanson de geste*, *Huon de Bordeaux*, that first made artistic circles pay attention to Giacosa as a playwright. The setting is the Valley of Aosta in the 14th century. The prologue explains that the work is the product of a daydream brought on by a reading of the legend. Unlike the humorous original, where the victor in the chess game, a penniless page, prefers a sack of gold to marrying a beautiful princess, Giacosa's version idealizes the characters and the romantic notion of love: Princess Iolande purposefully forfeits the game, and the boastful Fernando marries her. As in his other medieval plays, the sonorous and soft 12-syllable Martelliano verse is well suited to the dreamy atmosphere and increases the charm of the piece.

The second medieval legend, *Il trionfo d'amore*, was inspired by Gozzi's *Turandot*. Whereas the latter is set in China, *Il trionfo d'amore*, like *Una partita a scacchi*, takes place in the picturesque and wild Valley of Aosta also during the 14th century. The characters are more fully developed than those in *Partita*.

In *Il fratello d'armi*, set in the 13th century in Piedmont's Valley of Soana, Giacosa presents a darker view of medieval life. It is the story of two knights, Valfrido and Ugone, a beautiful woman, and Ugone's fierce and masculine sister, Bona. Through excessive passion the tale ends in tragedy. Certain elements heighten the horror: prophecies of mad women, dark and terror-filled dungeons, and hidden passages whose secret entrances are suddenly discovered by hostile forces.

Il Conte Rosso, a drama of a man's struggle with his mother, ends in his death by poison. It shows the influence of *verismo* and is the only one of his verse dramas to be written in hendecasyllables. After *Il Conte Rosso* Giacosa produced no more medieval romantic dramas until *La Dame de Challant*, which he wrote in French 11 years later for Sarah Bernhardt.

Giacosa wrote many light comedies and proverbs. Among his best are *Il marito amante della moglie*, which sparkles with witty dialogue and is often considered his best comedy, *La tardi ravveduta*, which fuses Goldoni's simple plot, humor, and lively dialogue with Musset's grace and whimsy, and *Acquazzoni in montagne*, a rollicking farce which has been compared to Labiche. Of all comic writers Giacosa admired Goldoni for his good humor and good sense.

Giacosa began to commit himself more and more in his drama to research on the social, psychological, and moral aspects of contemporary life. Traces of his new approach can be seen in polemical papers such as "Della morale nell'arte" and "Del vero in teatro", in criticism of upper-class frivolity (*Resa a discrezione*), in the influence of *verismo* on *Il Conte Rosso*, *L'onorevole Ercole Mallardi*, and on the narrative of *Novelle e paesi valdostani*. But *Tristi amori* (*Unhappy Love*) was a turning point and marks the beginning of his second period, 1887–1906. It is the four plays that he wrote during this time that are remembered today: *Tristi amori*, *I diritti dell'anima* (*Sacred Pleasure*), *Come le foglie*, and *Il più forte* (*The Stranger*). Each is an intimate drama set within the home of a bourgeois family in a small provincial city. There is a strong sense of the influence of environment on the characters' lives. They perform domestic duties as part of their action, and the dialogue is full of realistic detail about provincial life. Except for *Come le foglie*, each play focusses on the impact of a wife's adultery, in action or in thought, on a marital relationship. *Come le foglie* takes as its subject the way different members of a bourgeois family react when they are forced to adjust to a lower standard of living, and this is one of Giacosa's most successful plays. It was acclaimed in Paris in the 1900 French production directed by André Antoine.

Giacosa had many friends among the artistic elite. It was Arrigo Boito who introduced him to Eleonora Duse. While theirs was not always a happy relationship, she performed in six of his plays between 1883 and 1891, when she was leading actress for the Rossi Company and when she managed her own company. It was Duse, through the power of her artistry, who turned *Tristi amori* from a terrible failure into a resounding success.

Giacosa was involved in a multitude of activities besides playwriting. Most importantly he collaborated on the librettos of Puccini's three best operas. But he also wrote short stories and works demanding serious historical research, and he was a prominent lecturer, teacher, and journalist.

—Jane House

GILBERT, (Sir) W(illiam) S(chwenck).   Born in London,
18 November 1836. Educated at a school in Boulogne, 1843–
46; Western Grammar School, Brompton, London, 1846–50;
Great Ealing School, London, 1850–55; King's College,
London, 1855–57, BA 1857; Inner Temple, London, from
1855; called to the bar, 1863. Married Lucy Agnes Turner in
1867. Commissioned in the militia in the 3rd Battalion of the
Gordon Highlanders, 1857: captain, 1867; retired with the
rank of major, 1883; clerk in the Education Department of
the Privy Council Office, London, 1857–61; regular contributor, as writer and artist, to *Fun*, London, 1861–71; first-
produced play, *Uncle Baby*, staged 1863; lawyer in London
and on the northern circuit, 1864–68; playwright from 1860's,
in partnership with the composer Arthur Sullivan, 1871–96:
wrote operas with Sullivan for Richard D'Oyly Carte at the
Royalty Theatre, 1875, the Opera Comique, 1877–81, and the
Savoy Theatre (specially built for them by D'Oyly Carte),
from 1881; built the Garrick Theatre, London, 1889; bought
Grims' Dyke estate, Middlesex, 1890; justice of the peace and
deputy-lieutenant of Middlesex, 1891–1911. Knighted, 1907.
Died in Harrow Weald, Middlesex, 29 May 1911.

Works

Collections

Original Plays (4 vols.).   1876–1911; revised edition, 1920.
New and Original Extravaganzas (includes *Dulcamara; La
    Vivandière; The Merry Zingara; Robert the Devil; The
    Pretty Druidess*), edited by Isaac Goldberg.   1931.
The First Night Gilbert and Sullivan, edited by Reginald
    Allen.   1958; revised edition, 1975.
The Savoy Operas (2 vols.).   1962–63.
Gilbert Before Sullivan: Six Comic Plays (includes *No Cards;
    Ages Ago; Our Island Home; A Sensation Novel; Happy
    Arcadia; Eyes and No Eyes*), edited by Jane W. Stedman.
    1967.
Final Curtain: The Last Gilbert and Sullivan Operas (includes
    Utopia (*Limited*); *The Grand Duke*; and lyrics), edited by
    John Wolfson.   1976.
The Annotated Gilbert and Sullivan (includes *H.M.S.
    Pinafore; The Pirates of Penzance; Iolanthe; The Mikado;
    The Gondoliers*), edited by Ian Bradley.   1982.
Plays (includes *The Palace of Truth; Sweethearts; Princess
    Toto; Engaged; Rosencrantz and Guildenstern*), edited by
    George Rowell.   1982.

Stage Works

Uncle Baby (produced Lyceum Theatre, London, 1863).
    Edited by Terence Rees, 1968.
Ruy Blas.   In *Warne's Christmas Annual*.   1866.
Dulcamara; or, The Little Duck and the Great Quack (pro-
    duced St. James's Theatre, London, 1866).   1866.
Hush-a-Bye Baby on the Tree Top, with Charles Millward
    (produced Astley's Amphitheatre, London, 1866).
La Vivandière; or, True to the Corps, from a work by
    Donizetti (produced St. James's Hall, Liverpool, 1867).
    1867.
Robinson Crusoe; or, The Injun Bride and the Injured Wife,
    with H.J. Byron (produced Theatre Royal, Haymarket,
    London, 1867).   In *English Plays of the Nineteenth
    Century 5*, edited by Michael Booth, 1976.
Harlequin Cock-Robin, and Jenny Wren (produced Lyceum
    Theatre, London, 1867).   1867.
Allow Me to Explain (produced Prince of Wales Theatre,
    London, 1867).

W.S. Gilbert (cartoon by Spy)

Highly Improbable (produced Royalty Theatre, London, 1867).

The Merry Zingara; or, The Tipsy Gipsy and the Pipsy Wipsy: A Whimsical Parody on The Bohemian Girl (produced Royalty Theatre, London, 1868). 1868.

Robert the Devil; or, The Nun, The Dun, and the Son of a Gun (produced Gaiety Theatre, London, 1868). 1868.

No Cards, music by L. Elliott (produced Royal Gallery of Illustration, London, 1869). 1869.

The Pretty Druidess; or, The Mother, The Maid, and the Mistletoe Bough (produced Charing Cross Theatre, London, 1869). 1869.

An Old Score (produced Gaiety Theatre, London, 1869). 1869.

Ages Ago, music by Fred Clay (produced Royal Gallery of Illustration, London, 1869). 1869.

The Princess: A Whimsical Allegory, Being a Respectful Perversion of Tennyson's Poem (produced Olympic Theatre, London, 1870). 1870.

The Gentleman in Black, music by Fred Clay (produced Charing Cross Theatre, London, 1870). 1870.

Our Island Home, music by German Reed (produced Royal Gallery of Illustration, London, 1870). In *Gilbert Before Sullivan*, 1967.

The Palace of Truth (produced Theatre Royal, Haymarket, London, 1870). 1870.

A Medical Man (produced St. George's Hall, London, 1872). In *Drawing-Room Plays and Parlour Pantomimes*, edited by C.W. Scott, 1870.

Randall's Thumb (produced Court Theatre, London, 1871). 1871.

A Sensation Novel, in Three Volumes, music by German Reed (produced Royal Gallery of Illustration, London, 1871). 1871.

Creatures of Impulse, music by Alberto Randegger (produced Court Theatre, London, 1871). 1871.

The Brigands, from a work by Meilhac and Halévy, music by Offenbach (produced Theatre Royal, Plymouth, Devon, 1889). 1871.

Great Expectations, from the novel by Dickens (produced Court Theatre, London, 1871).

On Guard (produced Court Theatre, London, 1871). 1871.

Pygmalion and Galatea (produced Theatre Royal, Haymarket, London, 1871). 1872.

Thespis; or, The Gods Grown Old: A Grotesque Opera, music by Arthur Sullivan (produced Gaiety Theatre, London, 1871). 1871.

Happy Arcadia, music by Fred Clay (produced Royal Gallery of Illustration, London, 1872). 1872.

The Wicked World (produced Theatre Royal, Haymarket, London, 1873). 1873.

The Happy Land, with Gilbert à Beckett (produced Court Theatre, London, 1873). 1873.

The Wedding March: An Eccentricity, from a play by Eugène Labiche and Marc-Michel (produced Court Theatre, London, 1873). 1873; revised version, music by George Grossmith, Jr., as *Haste to the Wedding* (produced Criterion Theatre, London, 1892), 1892.

The Realm of Joy (produced Royalty Theatre, London, 1873). Edited by Terence Rees, 1969.

Ought We to Visit Her?, from the novel by Annie Edwardes (produced Royalty Theatre, London, 1874). 1874.

The Blue-Legged Lady (produced Court Theatre, London, 1874). Edited by Jane W. Stedman, in *Nineteenth Century Theatre Research*, Spring 1975.

Charity (produced Royal Opera House, London, 1874). 1874.

Topsy-Turvydom (produced Criterion Theatre, London, 1874). 1931.

Sweethearts (produced Prince of Wales Theatre, London, 1874). 1874.

On Bail, from a play by Meilhac and Halévy (as *Committed for Trial*, produced Globe Theatre, London, 1874; revised version, as *On Bail*, produced Criterion Theatre, London, 1877). 1877.

Trial by Jury, music by Arthur Sullivan (produced Royalty Theatre, London, 1875). 1875.

Tom Cobb; or, Fortune's Toy (produced St. James's Theatre, London, 1875). 1875.

Eyes and No Eyes; or, The Art of Seeing, music by German Reed (produced St. George's Hall, London, 1875). 1896; in *Gilbert Before Sullivan*, 1967.

Broken Hearts (produced Court Theatre, London, 1875). 1875.

Princess Toto, music by Fred Clay (produced Nottingham, 1876). 1876.

Dan'l Druce, Blacksmith (produced Theatre Royal, Haymarket, London, 1875). 1876.

Engaged (produced Theatre Royal, Haymarket, London, 1877). 1877.

The Sorcerer, music by Arthur Sullivan, from the story "An Elixir of Love" by Gilbert (produced Opera Comique, London, 1877). 1877; revised version (produced 1884), 1884.

Ali Baba and the Forty Thieves, with others (produced Gaiety Theatre, London, 1878). 1878.

The Ne'er-Do-Weel (produced Olympic Theatre, London, 1878). 1878; revised version, as *The Vagabond* (produced Olympic Theatre, London, 1878).

H.M.S. Pinafore; or, The Lass That Loved a Sailor, music by Arthur Sullivan (produced Opera Comique, London, 1878). 1878.

Gretchen (produced Olympic Theatre, London, 1879). 1879.

The Pirates of Penzance; or, The Slave of Duty, music by Arthur Sullivan (produced Bijou Theatre, Paignton, Devon, 1879). 1879.

Patience; or, Bunthorne's Bride!, music by Arthur Sullivan (produced Opera Comique, London, 1881). 1881.

Foggerty's Fairy, from his own story (produced Criterion Theatre, London, 1881). 1881.

Iolanthe; or, The Peer and the Peri, music by Arthur Sullivan (produced Savoy Theatre, London, 1882). 1882.

Princess Ida; or, Castle Adamant, music by Arthur Sullivan, from the poem *The Princess* by Gilbert, based on the poem by Tennyson (produced Savoy Theatre, London, 1884). 1884.

Comedy and Tragedy (produced Lyceum Theatre, London, 1884). 1884.

The Mikado; or, The Town of Titipu, music by Arthur Sullivan (produced Savoy Theatre, London, 1885). 1885.

Ruddigore; or, The Witch's Curse!, music by Arthur Sullivan (as *Ruddygore*, produced Savoy Theatre, London, 1887). 1887.

The Yeomen of the Guard; or, The Merryman and His Maid, music by Arthur Sullivan (produced Savoy Theatre, London, 1888). 1888.

Brantinghame Hall (produced St. James's Theatre, London, 1888). 1888.

The Gondoliers; or, The King of Barataria, music by Arthur Sullivan (produced Savoy Theatre, London, 1889). 1889.

A Stage Play. 1890.

Rosencrantz and Guildenstern (produced Vaudeville Theatre, London, 1891). 1892.

The Mountebanks, music by Alfred Cellier (produced Lyric Theatre, London, 1892).   1892.
Utopia (Limited); or, The Flowers of Progress, music by Arthur Sullivan (produced Savoy Theatre, London, 1893).   1893.
His Excellency, music by Osmond Carr (produced Lyric Theatre, London, 1894).   1894.
The Grand Duke; or, The Statutory Duel, music by Arthur Sullivan (produced Savoy Theatre, London, 1896).   1896.
The Fortune Hunter (produced Birmingham, 1897).   1897.
The Fairy's Dilemma, from his own story (produced Garrick Theatre, London, 1904).   1911.
Fallen Fairies; or, The Wicked World, music by Edward German (produced Savoy Theatre, London, 1909).   1909.
The Hooligan (produced Coliseum, London, 1911).   In *Century Illustrated Magazine*, November 1911.
Trying a Dramatist.   1911.
A Colossal Idea.   1932.

Fiction

"Foggerty's Fairy" and Other Tales.   1890.
Lost Stories, edited by Peter Haining.   1982.

Verse

The Bab Ballads: Much Sound and Little Sense, illustrated by the author.   1869.
More Bab Ballads, illustrated by the author.   1873.
Fifty Bab Ballads.   1877.
Songs of a Savoyard, illustrated by the author.   1890.
Songs of Two Savoyards.   1892.
Lost Bab Ballads, edited by Townley Searle.   1932.
The Bab Ballads, edited by James Ellis.   1970.

Other

The Pinafore Picture Book: The Story of "H.M.S. Pinafore".   1908.
The Story of The Mikado.   1921.

*

Bibliographies

Townley Searle, *A Bibliography of W.S. Gilbert*, London, 1931.
Reginald Allen, *W.S. Gilbert: An Anniversary Survey and Exhibition Checklist*, 1963.

Criticism

Books:
Isaac Goldberg, *Sir William Schwenk Gilbert: A Study in Modern Satire*, Boston, 1913.
Sidney Dark and Rowland Greay, *Gilbert: His Life and Letters*, London, 1923.
A.H. Godwin, *Gilbert and Sullivan: A Critical Appreciation of the Savoy Operas*, London, 1926.
Isaac Goldberg, *The Story of Gilbert and Sullivan*, New York, 1928.
Hesketh Pearson, *Gilbert and Sullivan: A Biography*, London, 1935; revised edition, 1947.
Hesketh Pearson, *W.S. Gilbert: His Life and Strife*, London, 1957.

Leslie W.A. Bailey, *The Gilbert and Sullivan Book*, London, 1952; revised edition, 1956.
Audrey Williamson, *Gilbert and Sullivan Opera*, London, 1953; revised edition, 1982.
Raymond Mander and Joe Michenson, *A Picture History of Gilbert and Sullivan*, London, 1962.
Terence Rees, *Thespis: A Gilbert and Sullivan Enigma*, London, 1964.
John Bush Jones (ed.), *W.S. Gilbert: A Century of Scholarship and Commentary*, New York, 1970.
James Helyar (ed.), *Gilbert and Sullivan Papers*, Lawrence, Kansas, 1970.
George E. Dunn, *A Gilbert and Sullivan Dictionary*, New York, 1971.
James Helyar (ed.), *Gilbert and Sullivan: Papers Presented at the International Conference*, Lawrence, Kansas, 1971.
Leslie Ayre, *The Gilbert and Sullivan Companion*, London, 1972.
Max K. Sutton, *W.S. Gilbert*, Boston, 1975.
Caryl Brahms, *Gilbert and Sullivan: Lost Chords and Dischords*, London, 1975.
William Cox-Ife, *W.S. Gilbert, Stage Director*, London, 1977.
Andrew Goodman, *Gilbert and Sullivan at Law*, Rutherford, New Jersey, 1983.
Geoffrey Smith, *The Savoy Operas: A New Guide to Gilbert and Sullivan*, London, 1983.
Robin Wilson and Frederic Lloyd, *Gilbert and Sullivan: The D'Oyly Carte Years*, London, 1984.
David Eden, *Gilbert and Sullivan: The Creative Conflict*, Rutherford, New Jersey, 1986.
Charles Hayter, *W.S. Gilbert and Arthur Sullivan*, London, 1987.

Serials

The Savoyard, London, 1962–82.
W.S. Gilbert Society Journal, edited by Brian Jones, 1985–

*   *   *

So institutionalised have the Gilbert and Sullivan operas become in the 20th century that it is difficult, now, to see in Gilbert one of the most original, innovative, and at times subversive British dramatists of the mid- to late-19th century. Nevertheless, his significance is well worth reassessing.

Gilbert's work bore evidence of many influences, but it was never merely imitative. At a time when the output of many dramatists relied heavily on translation (even such innovators as Tom Robertson did their fair share of hack work), Gilbert invariably created something new. Apart from the comic operas, he also wrote melodramas, burlesques, pantomimes, and farces, but often seemed more intent on breaking away from, or parodying, the form he adopted rather than merely emulating it. He certainly absorbed all the lessons of dramatic structure that such masters as Scribe could teach him, becoming adept at handling the coincidences, reversals, discoveries, and witheld secrets so common in drama at the time. Robertson's more subdued and realistic tones left their marks on such plays as *Sweethearts*, whilst Byron, Talfourd, and Burnard provided initial models for burlesque. Gilbert was particularly influenced by fairy tales and by the whimsical extravaganzas of J.R.Planché, although his own compositions are easily differentiated from Planché's in tone and style. The lightly critical stance of a writer such as H.J.Byron, targeting greed and selfishness in such comedies as *Not Such a Fool as He Looks* and *A Fool and His Money*, was also to emerge in Gilbert's comedy. He could not have written as he did without such diverse influences; but he transmuted them all into something fresh.

Gilbert's work is often critical of the smugness and complacency of the Victorian society to which he belonged. The difference between the way people are and the way they actually appear is at the centre of much of his work. In *The Palace of Truth*, when all constraints are lifted so that nobody hides their thoughts or feelings, the selfishness underlying most human motivation is quickly highlighted. In *Engaged* the time-honoured pecuniary motives behind love and marriage are treated with a candour usually absent in everyday life. Truth is often shocking—by implication society works more effectively through condoning deception. Such views were often considered heartless and cynical by Gilbert's contemporaries, but they were at the heart of his philosophy. The irony is absolute: it is in the eye of the beholder rather than in any touchstone provided by the dramatist.

Victorian values, institutions, and even individuals are often satirised in Gilbert's works. The notion of self-help is shown up as absurd in *H.M.S. Pinafore* through the elevation of Sir Joseph Porter to First Lord of the Admiralty; the problems that occur when a Victorian sense of duty becomes entangled with self-interest are explored in *The Pirates of Penzance*; Gladstone's cabinet is satirised in *The Happy Land*; Oscar Wilde and aestheticism are the butts of *Patience*; *Charity* implicity criticises the double standards of Victorian morality, whilst *Iolanthe* uses fantasy to stress the absurdity of the British parliamentary system. The later Gilbert and Sullivan operas, although less localised and more exotic in setting, provide further opportunities for Gilbertian subversion. *The Mikado* reveals the absurdities of the law, of social hierarchy, and of petty officialdom, whilst *The Gondoliers* gently endorses the virtues of republicanism. British institutions are also the target of Gilbert's irony at the conclusion of *Utopia Ltd*, when Utopia prepares to remodel itself on the British pattern.

Gilbert's Britain is, in fact, a heartless, selfish, grasping, hierarchical, hypocritical, jingoistic nation; although mellowed by wit and humour, the reflection from the mirror he holds up is not a pleasant one. Using the relentless logic derived from his lawyer's training, Gilbert created an absurd yet credible universe in which the most unlikely sequence of events is held together in a totally convincing manner. Like Dickens and Shaw, Gilbert's satire and criticism seem less astringent with time. Nevertheless, for his contemporaries he provided unpalatable truths wrapped within a highly palatable form.

The effectiveness of Gilbert's work was enhanced by the care he took over its presentation on stage. He was a relentless stage manager, with no time for the excesses of Victorian actors; he stated that *Engaged* could only succeed if played with "perfect earnestness and gravity throughout", as he knew to his cost after the play had initially been ruined by the exaggerated low-comedy performance of George Honey in the role of Cheviot Hill. Jessie Bond later recalled how, under Gilbert's direction, "the actors were trained to get their effects by doing and saying absurd things in a matter-of-fact way, without obvious burlesque of the characters they were representing". Gilbert would make the actors go over a scene again and again until they had achieved what he required. He was equally meticulous about setting—indeed, prior to *H.M.S. Pinafore* he travelled to Portsmouth to make sketches of exactly what he would require for the play's sets. He was a great admirer of Robertson's meticulous methods of rehearsing and staging, claiming that Robertson had practically invented stage-management.

Less successful as a writer of melodrama and as an adaptor (his version of *Great Expectations*, for example, actually omits Miss Haversham), uneasy with conventional burlesque, Gilbert effectively used comic opera, farce, and comedy to reveal the dishonest ways by which his contemporaries sometimes lived their lives. Called the "English Aristophanes" on account of his satirical thrust, he also revealed an ability to probe beneath the surface of things, rather as Ibsen had done. Beneath the wit, humour, and nonsense that characterise his work lies a seriousness of purpose that also deserves credit.

—Jim Davis

GIRAUDOUX, Jean (Hippolyte). Born in Bellac, France, 29 October 1882. Educated at a school in Pellevoisin; lycée, Chateauroux, 1893–1900; Lycée Lakanal, Paris, 1900–02; École Normale Supérieure, Paris, 1903–05. Military service, 1902–03. Married Suzanne Boland 1918; one son. French-language assistant, Harvard University, Cambridge, Massachusetts, 1906–7; took civil service examinations, and entered the diplomatic service, 1910; worked in the press office, Ministry of Foreign Affairs, 1910–14; mission to Russia and the East, 1911; rejoined former regiment at outbreak of World War I, 1914: wounded in the leg, 1914, recuperated in Bordeaux, then served in the Dardanelles campaign, and was wounded again; military instructor in Portugal, 1916, and liaison officer with the US Army in USA and Paris, 1917–18; Director, "Service des oeuvres françaises à l'étranger" [Foreign Cultural Service], 1920–24; secretary, French Embassy, Berlin, 1924; appointed chief government press officer, 1924; mission to Turkey, 1926; first play, *Siegfried*, produced 1928; appointed director general of information services, 1939: resigned following establishment of Vichy regime, 1940. Died in Paris, 31 January 1944.

Works

Collections

Théâtre complet (16 vols.). 1945–53.
Oeuvre romanesque; oeuvres littéraires diverses (3 vols.). 1955–58.
Four Plays (includes *The Madwoman of Chaillot; The Apollo of Bellac; The Enchanted; Ondine*), adapted by Maurice Valency. 1958.
Plays (includes *Judith; Tiger at the Gates; Duel of Angels*), translated by Christopher Fry. 1963.
Three Plays (includes *Siegfried; Amphitryon 38; Electra*), translated by Phyllis La Farge and Peter H. Judd. 1964.
Plays (includes *Amphitryon 38; Intermezzo; Ondine*), translated by Roger Gellert. 1967.
Théâtre complet. 1971.

Stage Works

Siegfried (produced Théâtre des Champs-Élysées, Paris, 1928). 1928; translated as *Siegfried*, 1930.
Amphitryon 38 (produced Comédie des Champs-Élysées, Paris, 1929). 1929; translated as *Amphitryon 38*, 1938.
Judith (produced Théâtre Pigalle, Paris, 1931). 1931; translated as *Judith*, in *Drama*, 1, 1963.

Intemezzo (produced Comédie des Champs-Élysées, Paris, 1933).   1933; translated as *The Enchanted*, 1950.
Tessa, from a play by Margaret Kennedy and Basil Dean (produced Théâtre de l'Athénée, Paris, 1934).   In *Théâtre 2*, 1958.
La fin de Siegfried.   1934.
Supplément au voyage de Cook (produced Théâtre de l'Athé-née, Paris, 1935).   1937; translated as *The Virtuous Island*, 1956.
La Guerre de Troie n'aura pas lieu (produced Théâtre de l'Athénée, Paris, 1935).   1935; translated as *Tiger at the Gates*, 1955; as *The Trojan War Will Not Take Place,* 1983.
Electre (produced Théâtre de l'Athénée, Paris, 1937).   1937; translated as *Electra*, 1957.
L'Impromptu de Paris (produced Théâtre de l'Athénée, Paris, 1937).   1937.
Cantique des cantiques (produced Comédie-Française, Paris, 1938).   1939.
Ondine (produced Théâtre de l'Athénée, Paris, 1939).   1939; translated as *Ondine*, 1954.
L'Apollon de Bellac (as *L'Apollon de Marsac*, produced Rio de Janeiro, Brazil, 1942).   In *Théâtre 4*, 1959; translated as *The Apollo of Bellac,* in *Four Plays*, 1958.
Sodome et Gomorrhe (produced Théâtre Hébertot, Paris, 1943).   1943.
La Folle de Chaillot (produced Théâtre de l'Athénée, Paris, 1945).   1945; translated as *The Madwoman of Chaillot,* 1949.
Pour Lucrèce (produced Théâtre Marigny, Paris, 1953).   1954; translated as *Duel of Angels,* 1958.
Les Gracques, edited by R.M. Albérès and Jean-Pierre Giraudoux.   1958.

Screenplays

La Duchesse de Langeais, 1942; *Les Anges du péché,* with R.-L. Bruckberger and Robert Bresson, 1943 (published as *Le Film de Béthanie: Texte du "Les Anges du péché"*, 1944).

Fiction

Provinciales.   1909.
Simon le pathétique.   1918.
Elpénor.   1919.
Adorable Clio.   1920.
Suzanne et le Pacifique.   1921; translated as *Suzanne and the Pacific,* 1923.
Siegfried et le Limousin.   1922.
Juliette au pays des hommes.   1924.
Bella.   1926; translated as *Bella,* 1927.
Eglantine.   1927.
Les aventures de Jérôme Bardini.   1930.
La France sentimentale.   1932.
Combat avec l'ange.   1934.
L'École des indifférents.   1934.
Choix des élues.   1938.
Les Contes d'un matin.   1952.
La Menteuse.   1958; translated as *Lying Woman*, 1972.
Oeuvres romanesques complètes.   1990.

Other

Retour d'Alsace, août 1914.   1916.
Lectures pour une ombre.   1917.
Amica America.   1919.
Visite chez le prince.   1924.
Le Sport.   1928.

Racine.   1930; translated as *Racine,* 1938.
Fugues sur Siegfried.   1930.
Fontrages au Niagara.   1932.
De Pleins Pouvoirs à sans pouvoirs.   1935.
Les Cinq Tentations de La Fontaine.   1938.
Le Futur armistice.   1939.
Pleins Pouvoirs.   1939.
Littérature.   1941.
Ecrits dans l'ombre.   1944.
Armistice à Bordeaux.   1945.
Sans Pouvoirs.   1946.
Pour Une Politique urbaine.   1947.
La Française et la France.   1951.
Visitations.   1952.
Portugal, suivi de Combat avec l'image.   1958.
Or dans la nuit: Chroniques et préfaces 1910–1943.   1969.
Carnets des Dardanelles, edited by Jacques Body.   1969.
Souvenir de deux existences.   1975.

*

Bibliographies

Brett Dawson, *Bibliographie de l'oeuvre de Giraudoux 1899–1982*, Bellac, 1982.

Criticism

Books:
Donald Inskip, *Jean Giraudoux: The Making of a Dramatist*, London, 1958.
Laurence LeSage, *Jean Giraudoux: His Life and Works*, University Park, Pennsylvania, 1959.
Agnes G. Raymond, *Jean Giraudoux: The Theatre of Victory and Defeat* (from the French), Amherst, Massachusetts, 1966.
Gilbert Van de Louw, *La Tragédie grecque dans le théâtre de Giraudoux*, Nancy, 1967.
Robert Cohen, *Giraudoux: Three Faces of Destiny*, Chicago, 1968.
Claude E. Magny, *Précieux Giraudoux* (revised edition), Paris, 1968.
Georges Lemaitre, *Jean Giraudoux: The Writer and His Work*, New York, 1971.
Paul A. Mankin, *Precious Irony: The Theatre of Giraudoux*, The Hague, 1971.
Charles Mauron, *Le Théâtre de Giraudoux: Étude psychocri-tique*, Paris, 1971.
Jean C. Sertelon, *Giraudoux et le moyen âge*, Paris, 1974.
Jacques Body, *Giraudoux en Allemagne*, Paris, 1975.
Charles P. Marie, *La Réalité humaine chez Jean Giraudoux*, Paris, 1975.
Jacques Robichez, *Le Théâtre de Giraudoux*, Paris, 1975.
Adela Porwol, *Le Comique dans l'oeuvre dramatique de Jean Giraudoux*, Poznan, Poland, 1977.
Étienne Brunet, *Le Vocabulaire de Jean Giraudoux*, Geneva, 1978.
Chris Marker, *Giraudoux* (revised edition), Paris, 1978.
John H. Reilly, *Jean Giraudoux*, Boston, 1978.
Renée Zénon, *Le Traitement des mythes dans le théâtre de Jean Giraudoux*, Washington, DC, 1981.
Lise Gauvin, *Giraudoux et le thème d'Electre*, Paris, 1982.
Michel Raimond, *Sur Trois Pièces de Giraudoux: La Guerre de Troie n'aura pas lieu; Electre; Ondine*, Paris, 1982.
Arthur C. Buck, *Jean Giraudoux and Oriental Thought: A Study of Affinities*, New York, 1984.

Jacques Body, *Jean Giraudoux: La Légende et le secret*, Paris, 1986.

Serials

Cahiers Jean Giraudoux, 1972–1989.

* * *

In the relatively short period between 1928 and the outbreak of World War II, Jean Giraudoux became the leading French dramatist. If judged by its varied choice of subject, his theatre would seem remarkable for its range and diversity. In reality, it is above all notable for its constancy of theme and for its highly individual style which, together, served to introduce a more intellectual and literary flavour into French theatre in the inter-war years.

Starting with *Siegfried*, Giraudoux's collaboration with Louis Jouvet was particularly timely, as the theatre-going public had become increasingly dissatisfied with realism and, turning in the 1920's from the "well-made play", was prepared for Giraudoux's re-introduction of the "well-written play". His popularity continued into the immediate post-war years, not only in Paris, but also in London where several plays were performed in translation; and many dramatists (notably Jean Anouilh) were influenced by the freshness of Giraudoux's approach, his poetic dialogue, and his imaginative and even fanciful treatment of serious subjects. Tastes have changed, with the result that his theatre tends now to be seen as belonging decisively to the first half of the 20th century.

Classical antiquity provided the basic story and characters for some of Giraudoux's best-known plays: *Amphitryon 38*— the 38th version, according to Giraudoux, of Alcmène's seduction by Jupiter—*La Guerre de Troie n'aura pas lieu* (*The Trojan War Will Not Take Place*), and *Electre*. Biblical antiquity was the starting point for such plays as *Judith* and *Sodome et Gomorrhe*. And yet, in these plays, as in *Ondine* (a fairy story set in medieval Germany), Giraudoux's principal concern is with the 20th century, which he presents more directly in *Intermezzo* and *La Folle de Chaillot*. Indeed, there is much of Giraudoux's theatrical method implied in the title alone of his first play, *Siegfried*: by its reference to a legendary German warrior, it evokes the past and the poetry of a neighbouring culture with which Giraudoux was permanently enthralled; and yet, by his treatment, it examines the 20th-century conflicts and hostilities between two traditional enemies, starting with World War I from which both countries were still recovering. In a similar way, the debates between Hector and Ulysees in *La Guerre de Troie* resemble the summit meetings of national leaders prior to World War II. Ultimately, of course, the Trojan War was not averted: the warmongers of antiquity were as powerful as those in modern times, but the fault was not exclusively theirs.

In Giraudoux's plays a fatal flaw in human nature seems to create a form of tragic destiny for mankind, perverting and subverting the endeavours of men and women of good will. It needs the eccentricity of the madwoman of Chaillot to thwart the money-grubbing capitalists, the captains of industry, and the magnates of modern France. It needs the integrity of Isabelle in *Intermezzo* to prevent an excessively regulated educational system from damaging its pupils.

Indeed, it is frequently, but not exclusively, the heroines of Giraudoux's theatre who represent the positive ethic: not those like Helen of Troy whose love was insincere, but those like Hecuba and Andromaque, like the faithful Alcmène, who offered Jupiter friendship instead of an adulterous liaison, like Ondine, the water sprite, who was able to bring a powerful love into the human orbit . . . but only briefly.

In almost every play by Giraudoux, a devoted and courageous woman represents the simple, uncomplicated pleasures of life. Giraudoux's heroines still retain a human link with nature: they are the elemental and uncorrupted in societies where men are quadrupeds who have learned to stand on their hind legs merely to pin medals on their chests.

Another constant is Giraudoux's idiosyncratic style. His dialogue is invariably polished and elegant, subtle and refined. Imagery, paradox, and irony fuse with wit, humour, and puns to form a distinctively poetic language, studded with literary and classical allusions, which all his characters, regardless of rank and class, employ.

Giraudoux has not escaped criticism: artificiality, verbal glitter, and *préciosité* are the terms frequently applied by those who would prefer more realistic modes of speech; his intellect and intelligence have created detachment and coolness to the detriment of emotional depth; frivolity and even flippancy reveal a dramatist who is clever, but shallow. Giraudoux's answer was to point out that art is not a slavish imitation of reality, and that the theatre should not be confused with a classroom, nor the stage with a pulpit. "Theatre" said one of his characters in *L'Impromptu de Paris*, "is not a theorem, but an entertainment; not a lesson, but a filter". It will be interesting to see whether Giraudoux's choice of filter, and what has been called the "permanent topicality" of his work, enable his plays to survive beyond the century in which they have formed an important landmark. Perhaps today, more than ever, there is a need for Giraudoux's condemnation of violence, his plea for integrity, and his refinement.

—Colin Radford

See also *Volume 1* entry on *The Trojan War Will Not Take Place*.

GLASPELL, Susan (Keating). Born in Davenport, Iowa, USA, 1 July 1882 (possibly 1876). Educated at schools in Davenport; Drake University, Des Moines, Iowa, Ph.D. 1899; University of Chicago, 1902. Married 1) the writer George Cram Cook in 1913 (died 1924); 2) the writer Norman Matson in 1925 (divorced 1932). Reporter, Des Moines *Daily News* and *Capital*, 1899–1901; freelance writer in Davenport, 1901–11; founder, with George Cram Cook, Provincetown Players, 1915, and wrote for the company in Provincetown, Massachusetts, and New York, 1915–22; lived in Greece, 1922–24; abandoned playwriting in the early 1930's; director, Midwest Play Bureau of the Federal Theater Project, Chicago, 1936–38. Recipient: Pulitzer Prize, 1931. Died in Provincetown, 27 July 1948.

Works

Collections

Plays (includes *Suppressed Desires; Trifles; The Outside; Woman's Honor; Tickless Time; Bernice*). 1920; retitled *"Trifles" and Other Short Plays*, 1926.
Plays (includes *Trifles; The Outside; The Verge; The Inheritors*), edited by C.W.E. Bigsby. 1987.

Stage Works

Suppressed Desires, with George Cram Cook (produced Wharf Theatre, Provincetown, Massachusetts, 1915). In *Plays*, 1920.
Trifles (produced Wharf Theatre, Provincetown, Massachusetts, 1916). In *Plays*, 1920.
The People (produced Provincetown Playhouse, New York, 1917). With *Close the Book*, 1918.
Close the Book (produced Provincetown Playhouse, New York, 1917). With *The People*, 1918.
The Outside (produced Provincetown Playhouse, New York, 1917). In *Plays*, 1920.
Woman's Honor (produced Provincetown Playhouse, New York, 1918). In *Plays*, 1920.
Tickless Time, with George Cram Cook (produced Provincetown Playhouse, New York, 1918). In *Plays*, 1920.
Bernice (produced Provincetown Playhouse, New York, 1919). In *Plays*, 1920.
Inheritors (produced Provincetown Playhouse, New York, 1921). 1921.
The Verge (produced Provincetown Playhouse, New York, 1921). 1922.
Chains of Dew (produced Provincetown Playhouse, New York, 1922).
The Comic Artist, with Norman Matson (produced Strand Theatre, London, 1928; revised version produced Morosco Theatre, New York, 1933). 1927.
Alison's House (produced Civic Repertory Theatre, New York, 1930). 1930.

Fiction

The Glory of the Conquered. 1909.
The Visioning. 1911.
Lifted Masks: Stories. 1912.
Fidelity. 1915.
A Jury of Her Peers (stories). 1927.
Brook Evans. 1928; as *The Right to Love*, 1930.
Fugitive's Return. 1929.
Ambrose Holt and Family. 1931.
The Morning is near Us. 1940.
Cherished and Shared of Old. 1940.
Norma Ashe. 1942.
Judd Rankin's Daughter. 1945; as *Prodigal Giver*, 1946.

Other

The Road to the Temple (on George Cram Cook). 1926.

Editor, *Greek Coins* (verse), by George Cram Cook. 1925.

*

Bibliographies

Gerhard P. Bach, "Susan Glaspell (1876–1948): A Bibliography of Dramatic Criticism", in *Great Lakes Review*, vol. 3 no. 2, 1977.

Criticism

Books:
Arthur E. Waterman, *Susan Glaspell*, New York, 1966.
Gerhard P. Bach, *Susan Glaspell und die Provincetown Players: Die Anfänge des modernen amerikanischen Dramas und Theaters*, Frankfurt, 1979.
Articles:
Gerhard P. Bach, "Susan Glaspell: Provincetown Playwright", in *Great Lakes Review*, vol. 4 no. 2, 1978.
Beverly A. Smith, "Women's Work—*Trifles*? The Skill and Insight of Playwright Susan Glaspell", in *International Journal of Women's Studies*, 5, 1982.
Ann Larabee, "Death in Delphi: Susan Glaspell and the Companionate Marriage", in *Mid-American Review*, vol. 7 no. 2, 1987.
Christine Dymkowski, "On the Edge: The Plays of Susan Glaspell", in *Modern Drama*, 31, 1988.
Yvonne Shafer, "Susan Glaspell: German Influence, American Playwright", in *Zeitschrift für Anglistik und Amerikanistik*, 36, 1988.
Linda Ben-Zvi, "Susan Glaspell's Contributions to Contemporary Women Playwrights", in *Feminine Focus: The New Women Playwrights*, edited by Enoch Brater, New York, 1989.

* * *

Susan Glaspell was an established journalist, novelist, and author of short stories before co-founding the Provincetown Players with her husband, George Cram Cook. This experimental theatre group, envisioned as a community of artists working together but maintaining amateur status, dedicated itself to encouraging new playwrights and sought to create a more meaningful theatrical experience than the commercial Broadway fare. Glaspell proved to be a successful actress in its productions and sometimes directed her own work, but writing was clearly her greatest contribution. All but the last two of her plays were written for the Provincetown Players and reflect the idealism and theatrical innovation characteristic of that organization.

Trifles, her best known play, is a one-act play which maintains a realistic style but twists traditional expectations of the murder mystery. In the kitchen of a bleak Midwestern farmhouse, two women piece together the motive and events leading up to a murder, while the men responsible for the investigation are unsuccessful at finding clues in the expected places. Belittled by their husbands for attending to "trifles", the women can interpret the domestic detail—a disorderly room, uneven stitching on a quilt block, a dead canary carefully laid in a delicate box—and are able to reconstruct, emotionally, the isolation and despair of a woman who murdered her abusive husband. Glaspell quietly builds suspense as the women come to understand and identify with the suspect, ultimately deciding to conceal their evidence. Along with its careful construction, the play is noteworthy for its examination of traditional spheres of experience related to gender and for its concentration on the psychological and emotional life of a woman who is never seen.

Glaspell returned to the device of an off-stage central character in *Bernice*, a play about coming to terms with the death of an extraordinary woman, and in the Pulitzer Prize-winning *Alison's House*. Based on Emily Dickinson, the poet Alison has been dead for 18 years, but her family has gathered to dismantle the house where she lived. In the process, the characters explore the position of the artist as private individual, family member, and contributor to society, and face questions about the ownership of artistic creation, as well as responsibility to social contracts in the face of intense, consuming love. Glaspell treated issues of the artist and family less successfully in *Chains of Dew* (which was not published) and *The Comic Artist*, a collaboration with her second husband, Norman Matson.

In a more light-hearted vein, Glaspell wrote several brief social satires, including *Close the Book*, which depicts the snobbery of upper-middle-class Midwestern society, as well as the extravagant behavior of a rebel who scorns respectability. She treated a feminist issue comically in *Woman's Honor*, as men's chivalrous protection of women is presented as a means of creating male importance and control. *Suppressed Desires* and *Tickless Time*, both written with Cook, and set in Greenwich Village where they lived at the time, are humorous looks at the vogue for Freudian analysis and at idealism carried to a ludicrous extreme.

In both her personal and creative life, however, the relationship between the idealist and society was an important concern, and she treated the topic seriously in *The People*, a rather contrived and sentimental one-act play which illustrates the disillusionment and revitalization of the editor of a radical newspaper. Glaspell's respect for the pioneers who settled the interior of the country is manifest in the four-act play *Inheritors*, which tells the story of three generations. As it follows the degeneration of commitment to freedom of thought to xenophobic and conservative "Americanism", the play also explores the difficult path of those who act from conviction in the face of negative public opinion.

Fascinated with extreme psychological states, Glaspell created *The Outside*, a one-act play which explores the withdrawal from life by two women. The setting, a former life-saving station on the furthest tip of land as it meets the sea, is a good example of the playwright's symbolic use of surroundings. The constant struggle of stunted plant life to survive the encroaching sand is interpreted by the major character as a heroic battle between the forces of life and death, and she herself comes to embrace living, once again.

The Verge, Glaspell's greatest experiment stylistically, and her most interesting dramatic work, presents the story of Claire, a woman on the edge of normality and sanity, using expressionistic techniques in set, light, and sound to help portray the character's inner state. Determined to reject all that is commonplace, Claire creates plants designed to break through the boundaries of known species. As she becomes increasingly obsessed with exploding limits and frustrated by her own ties to mundane reality, she rejects the traditional roles of mother, wife, and mistress, pursues the one man who has some appreciation for her vision, and finally kills him. Claire is caustic and unkind in her rejection of those around her, yet Glaspell gives her an intelligence and eloquence which set her apart from the others, making her a problematic and intriguing protagonist.

Often cited as the second most important playwright to be nurtured by Provincetown after Eugene O'Neill, Glaspell helped to bring the examination of important ideas to the indigenous American theatre. For the most part these issues still retain their interest and relevance. She was able to handle material from both a serious and comic viewpoint, and created important women characters who were not simply extensions of more fully developed male figures. There is little overt physical action in the plays; they tend to focus on intellectual exploration or psychological and emotional change. While she was adept at creating and maintaining mood, her dialogue is sometimes repetitious, particularly in the full-length plays, and in allowing characters to express specific ideas or explain symbols she was often left with self-conscious or overly literary speech. Certainly, however, the searching quality of thought and intensity of imagery make Glaspell's plays worthy of study and performance in today's theatre.

—Kathy Fletcher

See also *Volume 1* entry on *The Verge*.

GOERING, Reinhard.   Born in Schloss Bieberstein, Fulda, Hesse, Germany, 23 June 1887. Both parents committed suicide. Studied medicine in Jena, Munich, Berlin, and Bonn, 1905–14; took degree, 1926. Married 1) Helene Gurowitsch in 1912 (divorced 1926), two daughters; 2) Marlene Holzapfel in 1935, two sons previous to marriage. Army physician, 1914; contracted tuberculosis; spent four years in sanatorium, Davos, 1914–18; first play, *Seeschlacht* [*Naval Encounter*], produced 1918; travelled throughout Europe; spent six weeks in a mental asylum, 1923; attempted, unsuccessfully, to start a medical practice; contracted cancer, 1933. Recipient: Kleist Prize, 1918 and 1930. Committed suicide near Jena, 7 November 1936.

Works

Collections

Dramen der Zeit. 1954.
Prosa; Dramen; Verse. 1961.
"Die Retter" und "Die Südpolexpedition des Kapitän Scott". 1966.

Stage Works

Seeschlacht (produced Königliches Schauspielhaus, Dresden, 1918). 1917; translated as *Naval Encounter*, in *Vision and Aftermath: Four Expressionist Plays*, edited by J.M. Ritchie, 1969; as *Sea Battle*, in *Seeschlacht/Sea Battle* (parallel text), 1977.
Der Erste. 1918.
Die Retter. 1918.
Scapa Flow. 1919.
Der Zweite. 1919.
Die Südpolexpedition des Kapitän Scott (produced Staatstheater, Berlin, 1930). 1929; operatic version, music by V.W. Zillig (produced 1937).

Fiction

Jung Schuk. 1913.

Verse

Poems in *Prosa; Dramen; Verse.* 1961.

*

Bibliographies

Michael C. Eben, "A Bibliography of Secondary Literature Concerning Reinhard Goering (1887–1936)", in *Modern Language Notes*, 92, 1977.

Criticism

Books:
H. Schlötermann, *Das deutsche Weltkriegsdrama*, 1944.
Robert C. Davis, *Final Mutiny: Reinhard Goering, His Life and Art*, New York, 1987.

Articles:

W.J. Lillyman, "Reinhard Goering's *Seeschlacht*: The Failure of the Will", in *German Life and Letters*, 22, 1969.

Sigrid Mayer, "Reinhard Goerings *Seeschlacht*: 'Klassisches' Drama des Expressionismus", in *Seminar: A Journal of Germanic Studies*, 14, 1978.

W.R. Elwood, "Reinhard Goering's *Seeschlacht* and the Expressionistic Vision", in *To Hold a Mirror to Nature*, edited by K.V. Hartigan, Washington, DC, 1982.

* * *

Goering's first writings—a small volume of lyrics and an autobiographical novel—have their roots in German classicism and display little of the dynamics which characterize the style and themes of his dramatic output. His first drama, *Seeschlacht* (*Sea Battle*), is based on the sea battle between the German and British fleets on 31 May and 1 June 1916 at Skagerrak. The play contributed to the establishment of German expressionist drama which was seeking a radical renewal of traditional thought and form.

In *Seeschlacht* the true action takes place in the minds of seven sailors who are nameless types; they include a religious believer, a cynical freethinker, and a mutineer. Imprisoned in the gun turret of a battleship they realize that they have no power over their fate, that they are mere pawns in the game of war. In their dialogues and laments they express their dreams, hopes, and fears. Goering condemns the notion of patriotism as senseless and ultimately destructive:

Voice: Fatherland, Fatherland, O dear Fatherland. We are pigs waiting for the butcher. We are calves being slaughtered. Our blood stains the fish! . . . Fatherland, Fatherland, Death devours us like rice. Look at us lying here, Fatherland. Give us Death, Death! Death!

Apart from the shortened, exclamatory expressionist language—the play opens with a scream—Goering employed conventions drawn from classical drama, especially that of the choric lament, in order to convey the inexorability of the sailors' fate. However, in contrast to Greek tragedy, their fate is not caused by the gods but by men; their sacrifice is senseless because the battle goes on; and their only guilt is their love for life. The play clearly bears existentialist traits in that it transcends the events of the historical battle, depicting, in fact, the battle for survival in the "turret" of man's existential isolation. The writer Karl Otten justifiedly points out that Goering anticipated Sartre's *Huis-Clos* and Beckett's *Endgame*.

Seeschlacht, which was first produced in Dresden in 1918, in a carefully prepared production by director E. Lewinger and designer A. Linnebach, provoked a scandal because of its outspoken pacifism and anti-patriotism. Furthermore it shocked the audience with its realistic details, especially in the battle scenes and in the depiction of the crew's painful dying. Lewinger's direction highlighted the play's inherent realism, which distinguishes *Seeschlacht* from pure expressionist drama like Toller's *Wandlung* (*Transfiguration*) and Kaiser's *Gas* plays. The Reinhardt production in the same year in Berlin proved to be highly successful, and Goering was hailed by critics as a new dramatic genius.

Scapa Flow, another anti-war play, is based on a true incident—the scuttling of the German naval fleet on 21 June 1919 by Admiral von Reuter. The play is in two short acts, the first taking place on the ship of the German Admiral, the second—after the fleet's destruction—on the ship of the British Admiral. As in *Seeschlacht*, there is little action, but here again the sailors express their despair about the fruitlessness of their action, and again the play conveys their feelings of total isolation; the ships have turned into cages from which the only escape is death:

O sea, a cemetery
O you ships—coffins
Which have been forgotten.
O we, the ghosts
Tied to our ships
Which are coffins . . .

The German Admiral justifies his action in scuttling the fleet as a humane one; the war was a deadly error which must not be repeated. His vision is that of a united "holy" fatherland harbouring a regenerated mankind. This vision is typical of expressionist drama, as is the concise, often telegram-like, language. However, while in general this style is used to convey a sense of breathlessness and to portray events occurring in rapid succession, Goering slowed the speed of the action through the balladesque form into which he moulded the dialogue; in fact, the whole play conveys the melancholy of an old ballad.

Goering did not take up the war theme again. The three remaining plays written between 1918 and 1919 deal with various aspects of love. *Der Erste* depicts a debauched priest, Antonio, who kills the young girl who loves him. The girl's bridegroom is wrongly accused of her murder and hanged. Antonio, having undergone a character change, admits his guilt and decides to hang himself. In *Der Zweite*, Goering portrays two couples trying to come to terms with marriage. Both plays are rather conventional in structure and language while their content, especially that of *Der Erste*, displays unfortunate melodramatic traits.

The most interesting of the three, and also Goering's most experimental play, is *Die Retter*. In it, two old dying men encounter a man without an arm, a seriously wounded man, two armed men, a man covered in blood—all symbolic of the destructive elements in mankind. A young couple express (through dance) their love for one another and for life, in which all that counts is an unrestrained surrender to the moment. As the Young Woman proclaims:

Light, shortlived,
Without pain,
Without want.
We dance,
We exist
And don't exist
Nothing troubles us.
We live, we live.

However, both are killed. It has been said that the play displays evidence of Goering's interest in Buddhist philosophy, but it is more likely that *Die Retter* is, in part, a projection of his psychopathic mentality, which made it impossible for him to maintain a sustained love-relationship, and of his preoccupation with death. The play's action and imagery display fascinating surrealist elements that were much ahead of the time.

Goering's last play, *Die Südpolexpedition des Kapitän Scott*, is once more based on an actual event. It is one of the best examples of "New Realism", and the 1930 production at the Staatstheater, Berlin, directed by Leopold Jessner, and designed by Caspar Neher, underlined this aspect. The play depicts the last days in the lives of Scott and his men, and Amundsen's successful expedition to the South Pole. Goering again introduces the classical Chorus which describes—almost in the style of a news reporter—the background to each scene, which is then enacted by the *dramatis personae*;

through the voice of the Chorus, Goering also dramatizes, once again, the existential loneliness of man, which is impressively depicted against a backdrop of an Antarctic ice and storm, and Lady Scott's widowhood. Yet while in his early plays Goering displays a nihilistic attitude, which is reflected in his characters dying lonely and senseless deaths, the fate of Scott, as well as that of his wife, is tempered through their friendship and love for each other. Goering's 1930 comments on the play demonstrate his new attitude, which entailed a renewed creativity. He planned a drama about Peter the Great, drafted the libretto for an opera based on *Die Südpolexpedition*, and wrote a novel (with Robert Büschgens). In a poem entitled "Tanzetanz" ("Dance-dance"), 1928, Goering reveals clearly and cynically how much death was part of his life—and of his *oeuvre*: "Our Father who thou art in Heaven/Give us our daily Death".

—Renate Benson

GOETHE, Johann Wolfgang von. Born in Frankfurt, 28 August 1749. Studied law at Leipzig University, 1765–68, and drawing with Adam Oeser; after a period of illness, resumed his studies in Strasbourg, 1770–71, Licentiate in Law 1771. Lived with Christiane Vulpius from 1788; married her in 1806 (died 1816); one son. Practised law in Frankfurt, 1771–72, and Wetzlar, 1772; then writer: contributor, *Frankfurter Gelehrte Anzeigen*, 1772–73; at invitation of Duke Karl August, joined the small court of Weimar in 1775: Member of the Council, 1776, President, War Commission, 1779, Director of Roads and Services, 1779, granted degree of nobility, 1782, took over much of the financial affairs of the court; after a visit to Italy, 1786–88, released from day-to-day government business: became general supervisor for arts and sciences, 1788; Director of the Court Theatres, 1791–1817: as artistic director of the recently formed professional Court theatre company, developed a repertory of plays, partly in collaboration with Schiller (1799–1805), and strengthened the company with leading German actors, such as August Wilhelm Iffland and Friedrich Ludwig Schröder. Editor of a variety of yearbooks and magazines, including, with Schiller, *Xenien*, 1796–97; with J.H. Meyer, *Die Propyläen*, 1798–1800; *Kunst und Altertum*, 1816–32; and *Zur Naturwissenschaft*, 1817–24. Chancellor of the University of Jena. Died in Weimar, 22 March 1832.

Works

Collections

Schriften. 8 vols., 1787–90; 13 vols., 1806–10.
Werke (40 vols.). 1827–30.
Complete Works (Bohn Standard Library translations; 14 vols.). 1848–90.
Werke ("Weimar" or "Sophie" edition; 134 vols.). 1887–1919.
Sämtliche Werke (Jubiläumsausgabe; 40 vols.), edited by Eduard von der Hellen. 1902–07.
Werke ("Hamburg" edition; 14 vols.), edited by Erich Trunz and others. 1948–69.
Gedenkausgabe der Werke, Briefe und Gespräche ("Artemis" edition; 27 vols.), edited by Ernst Beutler. 1984–71.
Werke ("Akademie" edition). 1952—
Plays (includes *Götz von Berlichingen; Fellow Culprits; The Lover's Whim; Iphigenia in Tauris; Egmont; Torquato Tasso; Faust*), translated by Charles E. Passage. 1980.
Collected Works (12 vols.) edited by Victor Lange, Eric A. Blackall, Cyrus Hamlin, and others. 1983—
Sämtliche Werke ("Munich" edition). 1985—

Stage Works

Götz von Berlichingen mit der eisernen Hand (produced Berlin, 1774). 1773; translated as *Goetz of Berlichingen with the Iron Hand*, 1799; as *Ironhand*, 1965; as *Götz von Berlichingen*, in *Plays*, 1980.
Clavigo (produced Hamburg, 1774). 1774; translated as *Clavigo*, in *Collected Works* 7, 1987.
Götter, Helden, und Wieland. 1774.
Das Jahrmarktsfest zu Plundersweilern (produced Ettersburg, 1778). In *Neueröffnetes moralisch-politisches Puppenspiel*, 1774; revised version, in *Schriften* 8, 1789.
Erwin und Elmire, music by Jean André (produced Liebhabertheater, Frankfurt, 1775). 1775; revised version, in verse, in *Schriften* 5, 1788.
Stella (produced Nationaltheater, Hamburg). 1776; revised version (produced 1806), in *Werke* 6, 1816; translated as *Stella*, in *Collected Works* 7, 1987.
Claudine von Villa Bella (produced Herzogliches Liebhabertheater, Weimar, 1776). 1776; revised version (produced 1789), in *Schriften* 5, 1788.
Die Geschwister (produced Herzogliches Liebhabertheater, Weimar, 1776). In *Schriften* 1, 1787; translated as *Brother and Sister*, in *Collected Works* 7, 1987.
Die Mitschuldigen (produced Herzogliches Liebhabertheater, Weimar, 1777). In *Schriften* 2, 1787; translated as *Fellow Culprits*, in *Plays*, 1980.
Lila, music by Sigmund von Seckendorff (produced Herzogliches Liebhabertheater, Weimar, 1777). In *Schriften*, 1790.
Der Triumph der Empfindsamkeit (produced Herzogliches Liebhabertheater, Weimar, 1778). In *Schriften* 4, 1787; revised version, as *Proserpina*, music by Sigmund von Seckendorf (produced Herzogliches Liebhabertheater, Weimar, 1779), in *Werke*, 1808; translated as *Proserpina*, in *Collected Works* 7, 1987.
Die Laune des Verliebten (produced Herzogliches Liebhabertheater, Weimar, 1779). In *Werke* 4, 1806; translated as *The Lover's Whim*, in *Plays*, 1980.
Iphigenie (produced Ettersburg, 1779; revised version, in verse, as *Iphigenie auf Tauris*, produced Vienna, 1800). In *Schriften* 3, 1787; translated as *Iphigenia in Tauris*, 1793, in *Plays*, 1980 and *Collected Works* 8, 1987.
Die Vögel, from the play by Aristophanes (produced 1780). 1787.
Jery und Bätely, music by Sigmund von Seckendorff (produced Weimar, 1780). 1790; translated as *Jery and Betty*, in *Collected Works* 7, 1987.
Die Fischerin, music by Corona Schröter (produced Tiefurt Park, Weimar, 1782). 1782.
Egmont (produced Deutsche Schauspielgesellschaft, Weimar, 1791). 1788; translated as *Egmont*, in *Five German Tragedies*, translated by F.J. Lamport, 1969; also translated in *Plays*, 1980.
Torquato Tasso (produced Hoftheater, Weimar, 1807). 1790; translated as *Torquato Tasso*, in *Plays*, 1980, and *Collected Works* 8, 1987.

Goethe "in the Roman Countryside" (by J.H.W. Tischbein; Kunstinstitut und Städtische Gallerie, Frankfurt).

Scherz, List und Rache (libretto; produced Seefeld, 1790).   In *Schriften 7*, 1790.
Der Gross-Cophta (produced Hoftheater, Weimar, 1791). 1792.
Der Bürgergeneral (produced Hoftheater, Weimar, 1793). 1793.
Mahomet, from the play by Voltaire (produced Hoftheater, Weimar, 1799).   1802.
Paläophron und Neoterpe (produced Hoftheater, Weimar, 1800; revised version, produced 1803).   In *Werke*, 1808.
Tancred, from the play by Voltaire (produced Hoftheater, Weimar, 1801).   1802.
Die natürliche Tochter (produced Hoftheater, Weimar, 1803).   1804; translated as *The Natural Daughter*, in *Collected Works 8*, 1987.
Pandora.   As *Pandoras Wiederkunft*, in *Prometheus*, 1808; in book form, as *Pandora*, 1810; translated as *Pandora*, in *Collected Works 8*, 1987.
Faust, Part 1 (produced complete, Nationaltheater, Brunswick, 1829).   In *Werke 8*, 1808; numerous translations, sometimes with Part 2, as *Faust*; also translated as *Faustus*, 1821.
Romeo und Juliet, from *Romeo and Juliet* by Shakespeare (produced Hoftheater, Weimar, 1812).
Des Epimenides Erwachen (produced Nationaltheater, Berlin, 1815).   1815.
Satyros; oder, Der vergötterte Waldteufel.   In *Werke 9*, 1817.
Prometheus (2-act fragment).   In *Werke 33*, 1827–30; translated as *Prometheus*, in *Collected Works 7*, 1987.

Faust, Part 2 (produced Schauspielhaus, Hamburg, 1854).   In *Werke: Ausgabe letzter Hand 41* (first complete publication), 1832; numerous translations with Part 1 as *Faust*.
Urfaust.   As *Goethes Faust in ursprünglicher Gestalt nach der hochhausenschen Abschrift*, edited by Erich Schmidt 1887; revised edition, 1897; translated as *The Urfaust*, c.1958.

Verse

Neue Lieder mit Melodien, music by Bernhard Breitkopf.   1770.
Gedichte, in *Schriften 8*.   1789; and subsequent editions.
Römische Elegien.   1789; translated as *Roman Elegies*, 1977.
Reineke Fuchs.   1794; translated as *Reynard the Fox*, 1886.
Hermann und Dorothea.   1798; translated as *Herman and Dorothea*, 1801.
West-östlicher Divan.   1819.
Selected Verse (bilingual edition), edited by David Luke.   1964.
Selected Poems (bilingual edition), edited by Christopher Middleton.   1983.

Fiction

Die Leiden des jungen Werthers.   1774; revised edition, 1787; translated as *The Sorrows of Werter*, 1780; several subsequent translations under same title.
Wilhelm Meisters Lehrjahre.   1795; early version, *Wilhelm Meisters theatralische Sendung*, translated as *Wilhelm Meister's Apprenticeship*, 1824; also translated, 1977–79.

Die Wahlverwandtschaften. 1809; translated as *Elective Affinities*, in *Works*; as *Kindred by Choice*, 1960; as *Elective Affinities*, 1971.
Wilhelm Meisters Wanderjahre. 1821; translated as *Wilhelm Meister's Travels*, 1827 and 1977–79.
Novelle. 1826.

Memoirs and Letters

Aus meinem Leben: Dichtung und Wahrheit (4 vols.). 1811–33.
Tag- und Jahreshefte. In *Werke 31–32*, 1830; translated as *Annals*, 1901.
Correspondence with Goethe, by Carlyle. 1887.
Briefe und Gespräche (4 vols.), edited by K.R. Mandelkow and B. Morawe. 1962–67.

Other

Beiträge zur Optik. 1790.
Versuch, die Metamorphose der Pflanzen zu erklären. 1790.
Winckelmann und sein Jahrhundert. 1805.
Zur Farbenlehre. 1810.
Italienische Reise. 1816–17; translated as *Travels in Italy*, 1849; as *Italian Journey*, 1962.
Gespräche mit Goethe, by Johann Peter Eckermann. 1836; translated as *Conversations with Goethe*, 1839.
Die Schriften zur Naturwissenschaft. 1947—
Amtliche Schriften (3 vols.), edited by Willy Flach and Helma Dahl. 1950–72.
Gespräche, edited by W.F. and F. von Biedermann, revised by Wolfgang Herwig (3 vols.). 1965–72.
Goethe on Art, edited by John Gage. 1980.

*

Bibliographies

Hans Pyritz, Heinz Nicolai, and Gerhard Burckhardt, *Goethe-Bibliographie*, Heidelberg, 1954; supplement, 1968.
W. Hagen, *Die Drucke von Goethes Werken* (2 vols.), Berlin, 1966–82.

Criticism

There is a vast amount of general critical literature on Goethe; the following selection of books includes only works devoted to Goethe as dramatist.

Books:
H.-J. Schifferdecker, *Das mimische Element in Goethes Dramen*, Berlin, 1928.
E. Kästner, *Wahn und Wirklichkeit im Drama der Goethe-Zeit*, Leipzig, 1929.
F. Sengle, *Goethes Verhältnis zum Drama: Die theoretischen Bemerkungen im Zusammenhang mit seinem dramatischen Schaffen*, Berlin, 1937.
W. Flemming, *Goethes Gestaltung des klassischen Theaters*, Cologne, 1949.
H.U. Voser, *Individualität und Tragik in Goethes Dramen*, Zurich, 1949.
J. Paris, *Johann Wolfgang Goethe, Dramaturge*, Paris, 1956.
R. Peacock, *Goethe's Major Plays*, Manchester, 1959.

Ronald. D. Miller, *The Drama of Goethe*, Harrogate, Yorkshire, 1966.
S. Burckhardt, *The Drama of Language: Essays on Goethe and Kleist*, Baltimore (Maryland) and London, 1970.
J. Prudhoe, *The Theatre of Goethe and Schiller*, Oxford, 1973.
J. Müller, *Der Begriff des "Pathologischen" im Drama Goethes und Kleists*, Berlin, 1974.
Marvin Carlson, *Goethe and the Weimar Theatre*, Ithaca, New York, 1978.
W.K. Stewart, *Time Structure in Drama: Goethe's Sturm und Drang Plays*, Amsterdam, 1978.
W. Hinderer (ed.), *Goethes Dramen: Neue Interpretationen*, Stuttgart, 1980.
T.J. Reed, *The Classical Centre: Goethe and Weimar 1775–1832*, London, 1980.
W. Hinck, *Goethe, Mann des Theaters*, Göttingen, 1982.
J.D. Prandi, *Sprites Woman Heroes: Major Female Characters in the Dramas of Goethe, Schiller and Kleist*, New York, 1983.
R. Brandmeyer, *Heroik und Gegenwart: Goethes klassische Dramen*, Frankfurt, 1987.

Serials

Goethe Jahrbuch, 1880–1913.
Jahrbuch der Goethe-Gesellschaft (Weimar), 1914–35.
Goethe Vierteljahrsschrift der Goethe Gesellschaft (Weimar), 1936–71.
Goethe Jahrbuch (Weimar), 1972—
Goethe Yearbook (USA)

*   *   *

Alongside Goethe's major achievements as a novelist and writer of short prose-forms, his astonishing range of lyric poetry, scientific research (especially on plants and colours), autobiographical works (*Poetry and Truth*), and administrative work as minister for the Grand Duke of Weimar, his contributions to drama and the theatre are of singular importance.

His "Storm und Stress" dramas, especially *Götz of Berlichingen with the Iron Hand* and *Urfaust*, defined the ideal of the titanic man of power—thus Götz, "the model of a knight, bold and noble in his freedom, and calm and loyal in misfortune"—and perfected a colloquial dramatic language suited to the local, historical nature of their subjects. In *Egmont*, the struggle in the central character between historical role and daemonic individual personalizes the search for political freedom. *Torquato Tasso* portrays the insufficiencies and tragically cast isolations of the artist-figure in a small Court clinging to autocracy, and fearing social revolution. In *Iphigenie auf Tauris*, Goethe points up the relationship between man and the gods, using a virtuous priestess from ancient Greek legend. In these last two dramas he developed an intense, richly textured, classical blank-verse style that raised the author's autobiographical concerns to a more universal level. The final achievement of world theatre came in *Faust*, where the central character's pact with the devil eventually wins him redemption as the human being ever struggling for richer experience, despite being torn apart by the continuous struggle within his soul.

In Goethe's dramas final tragedy seems to be avoided by the attainment of a more critical self-awareness, often the result of closer involvement with the fates of others. This, among other features, shows that his interest as a dramatist lay primarily with the implications of his material and less with effective presentation on the stage. Nevertheless, as with all his work, Goethe's dramatic achievements were put to the test in public performance or discussion. His work as Director of the Weimar Court Theatre and elsewhere within the Grand Duchy was of a more local, private, prestigious importance than developments taking place in such theatrical centres as Hamburg, Mannheim, and Vienna. His dramas sought an ideal resolution of the problems concerning the individual and society, and were thus representations of noble ideals— partly consciously seeking to further the social, psychological, and political awareness of his time, partly experiments in exploring the potentials of his central characters to their limits.

Incipient in this dual aim was a tendency towards allegory and a reduction in vital living experience. The plays depend on the creative, imaginative force of their poetic imagery rather than the dramatic clash of personalities in unavoidable set scenes. Formally, his "Storm and Stress" dramas imitated, in *Götz*, the unfettered expression and open form of Shakespeare's historical dramas, in *Urfaust* the leaps and bounds of balladic story-telling, leaving much to the imagin- ation, and, in *Egmont*, a kaleidoscopic construction of the central character. In the two classical plays *Torquato Tasso* and *Iphigenie auf Tauris*, the unrhymed iambic pentameters of English drama (already found in Lessing's *Nathan the Wise* and Schiller's *Don Carlos*) grew naturally from the 1779 prose version of *Iphigenie*, whose iambic rhythms hark back to passages at the end of *Egmont*.

His masterpiece, *Faust*, written in instalments, grew in aim and scope from a personal tragedy (the Gretchen story) until the original network of symbols and myths began to be re- placed by a personal world grafted onto Christian tradition (the Faust wager). This found full form in *Faust, Part II* where restless striving for more intense experience and, at times, frenzied activity set against the cynical Mephistopheles expand into a representation of most of the themes found elsewhere in Goethe's works. These are given universal and lasting significance through their interlinking by symbolic patterns, providing a cosmic view over all activity and a vision of unity in diversity.

Astounding contrasts in Goethe's range of dramas emerge when one takes into account, for instance, the early spirited satires *Götter, Helden, und Wieland* (Gods, Heroes, and Wieland) and *Satyros*, the domestic tragedies *Clavigo* and *Stella*, and the musical entertainments *Elmira, Claudine von Villa Bella, Jery und Bätely*, and *Die Fischerin* (The Fisherwoman) of his "Storm and Stress" and early Weimar days; the mainly ephemeral quality of the set of comedies inspired by the French Revolution—*Der Gross-Cophta, Der Bürgergeneral* (The Citizen General), and the fragmentary "Agitation"; and the experiments just before Schiller's death in 1805—*Die natürliche Tochter* (The Natural Daughter) and *Pandora*.

Taken as a whole, the range of Goethe's dramas is baffling. Individually, in the major examples, the intensity of ex- pression and depth of vision are remarkable. Each is a crea- tive writer's response to a series of challenges—often immediate, short-lived, and quickly answered, sometimes demanding years of thought and rewriting. In all of them the characters exist as suffering human beings with, however, a vision of meaning to their lives. They all, finally, show a dramatist who wrote truthfully about the complexities of his vivid imagination, who had lasting concern for the develop- ment of humanity standing against tyranny of all sorts, who followed an urge to represent individual problems, and ex- tend these representations towards an allegorical view of life. Goethe's dramas measure the limitations implied once the

discrepancy between individual weakness and mortality and the demands of an absolute spiritual existence are recognized. The redemption of Faust comes because he continually strives for greater awareness—Goethe's major dramas celebrate different varieties of that struggle and their creator's endless quest for new forms.

—Brian Keith-Smith

See also *Volume 1* entries on *Faust*; *Götz von Berlichingen mit der eisernen Hand*.

———————

GOGOL (Yanovsky), Nikolai (Vasilevich). Born in Sorochintsy, Poltava, Ukraine, 19 March 1809. Educated at Poltava boarding school, 1819–21, and Nezhin high school, 1821–28. Civil servant in St. Petersburg, 1828–31; history lecturer, Patriotic Institute, St. Petersburg, and private tutor, 1831–34; first-produced play, *Revizor* [*The Government Inspector*], staged 1836; visited Germany, Switzerland, and France, 1836; in Rome, 1837–39; travelled throughout Western Europe, returning intermittently to Russia, 1839–48; began association with the "spiritual adviser" Father Konstantinovsky, 1847; visited Holy Land, 1848; re-settled in Russia, 1849. Destroyed several manuscripts of his own works, including the sequel to *Dead Souls*. Died in Moscow, 21 February 1852.

Works

Collections

Sochineniya [Works] (4 vols.).   1842.
Collected Works (6 vols.), translated by Constance Garnett.   1922–27.
"The Government Inspector" and Other Plays (includes *Marriage; The Gamblers*; Dramatic Sketches and frag- ments: *An Official's Morning, A Lawsuit, The Servants' Hall, A Fragment*), translated by Constance Garnett. 1926.
"The Gamblers" and "Marriage", translated by A. Berkman. 1927.
Polnoe sobranie sochineny [Complete Collected Works] (14 vols.).   1940–52.
The Collected Tales and Plays (translations), edited by Leonard J. Kent.   1969.
The Theater of Nikolay Gogol: Plays and Selected Writings (includes *Marriage; The Government Inspector; The Gamblers*; extracts from Gogol's notes, letters, and essays) edited by Milton Ehre, translated by Ehre and Fruma Gottschalk.   1980.

Stage Works

Utro delovogo cheloveka (produced Alexandrinsky Theatre, St. Petersburg, 1871).   1836; translated as *An Official's Morning*, in *"The Government Inspector" and Other Plays*, 1926.
Revizor (produced Alexandrinsky Theatre, St. Petersburg, 1836).   1836; revised version, 1841; further revised version (produced Alexandrinsky Theatre, St. Petersburg, 1870) in

Scene from Vsevolod Meyerhold's 1926 production of *Revizor* [*The Government Inspector*] by **Nikolai Gogol**.

Sochineniya, 1842; translated as *The Government Inspector*, in *"The Government Inspector" and Other Plays*, 1926: several subsequent translations under same title; as as *The Inspector General*, 1892 and 1937.

Zhenitba (produced Alexandrinsky Theatre, St. Petersburg, 1842). 1841; translated as *The Marriage*, in *"The Government Inspector" and Other Plays*, 1926; several subsequent translations under the same title.

Igroki (produced Bolshoi Theatre, Moscow, 1843). In *Sochineniya*, 1842; translated as *The Gamblers*, in *"The Government Inspector" and Other Plays*, 1926.

Tyazhba (produced Alexandrinsky Theatre, St. Petersburg, 1844). In *Sochineniya*, 1842; translated as *A Lawsuit*, in *"The Government Inspector" and Other Plays*, 1926.

Otyrok (produced Alexandrinsky Theatre, St. Petersburg, 1860). In *Sochineniya*, 1842; translated as *A Fragment*, in *"The Government Inspector" and Other Plays*, 1926.

Lakeyskaya (produced Alexandrinsky Theatre, St. Petersburg, 1863). In *Sochineniya*, 1842; translated as *The Servants' Hall*, in *"The Government Inspector" and Other Plays*, 1926.

Teatralny razyezd posle predstavleniya novoy komedy. In *Sochineniya*, 1842; part translated as *Leaving the Theater After a Performance of a New Comedy*, in *The Theater of Nikolay Gogol*, 1980.

Fiction

Vechera na khutore bliz Dikanki (stories; 2 vols.). 1831–32; translated as *Evenings on a Farm Near Dikanka*, 1926.

Mirgorod (stories). 1835; translated as *Mirgorod, Being a Continuation of Evenings in a Village Near Dikanka*, 1928.

Arabeski (stories). 1835; translated as *Arabesques*, 1982.

Myortvye dushi. 1842; translated as *Home Life in Russia*, 1854; as *Tchitchikoff's Journeys*, 1886; as *Dead Souls*, 1887, and several subsequent translations under this title.

Rome [Rome]. In *Sochineniya*, 1842.

The stories have subsequently appeared in various collections of translations, including: *Cossack Tales*, 1860; *"St. John's Eve" and Other Stories from "Evenings at the Farm" and "St. Petersburg Stories"*, 1886; *Taras Bulba; also "St. John's Eve" and Other Stories*, 1887; *"The Mantle" and Other Stories*, 1915; *"Taras Bulba" and Other Tales*, 1917; *"The Overcoat" and Other Stories*, 1923, and *Tales*, 1926, both translated by Constance Garnett; *Tales*, translated by R. Portnova, 1945; *Tales of Good and Evil*, translated by David Magarshack, 1949; *"Diary of a Madman" and Other Stories*, translated by Ronald Wilks, 1972.

Memoirs and Letters

Vybrannye mesta iz perepiski s druz'yami. 1847; translated by Jesse Zeldin as *Selected Passages from Correspondence with Friends*, 1968.

Letters of Nikolai Gogol (translations), edited by Carl R. Proffer. 1967.

*

P. Franz, *Gogol Bibliography*, Ann Arbor, Michigan, 1983.

Books:
Vladimir Nabokov, *Gogol*, New York, 1944.
J. Lavrin, *Nikolay Gogol*, London, 1951.
N. Gourfinkel, *Nikolay Gogol, Dramaturge*, Paris, 1956.
David Magarshack, *Gogol: A Life*, London, 1957.
Vsevolod Setchkarev, *Gogol: His Life and Works*, New York, 1965.
Victor Ehrlich, *Gogol*, New Haven (Connecticut) and London, 1969.
Henri Troyat, *Gogol: The Biography of a Divided Soul* (from the French), New York, 1973.
T.S. Lindstrom, *Nikolay Gogol*, New York, 1974.
Robert A. Maguire (ed.), *Gogol from the Twentieth Century*, Princeton, New Jersey, 1974; with corrections, 1976.
Simon Karlinsky, *The Sexual Labyrinth of Gogol*, Cambridge, Massachusetts, 1976.
William Woodin Rowe, *Through Gogol's Looking Glass: Reverse Vision, False Focus, and Precarious Logic*, New York, 1976.
Donald Fanger, *The Creation of Gogol*, Cambridge, Massachusetts, 1979.
Richard Peace, *The Enigma of Gogol*, Cambridge, 1981.
G. Daniel, *Gogol et le théâtre*, Troyes, 1982.
Nick Worrall, *Nikolai Gogol and Ivan Turgenev*, London, 1982 (Macmillan Modern Dramatists series).
Jane Grayson and Faith Wigzell (eds.), *Nikolay Gogol: Text and Context*, London, 1989.

* * *

Gogol is the Ben Jonson of Russian dramatists. Although ignorant of Jonson's work, and by no means a follower of the neo-classical school, Gogol looked back nostalgically from the unsettled, rapidly changing time in which he lived, to one of order, nobility, and stability. Like Jonson, Gogol's attachment to an idealised feudal past and his hostility towards an encroaching capitalist present might be described as "reactionary". Gogol's "reactionariness", identified by the critic Belinsky in his famous "Letter to N.V. Gogol", consisted in his conservative view of Russia and his allegiance to Russia's monarchy, as well as to her Orthodox Church. This went hand in hand with Slavophile sympathies and antagonism towards Westernising tendencies in contemporary Russian thought, of a kind espoused by Belinsky, himself, and other radicals. Seeking further parallels, Gogol's Volpone can be seen in his Chichikov, the capitalist trader in human souls who charts a comic-epic odyssey through the novel *Dead Souls*. His Mosca (or Face) can be seen in the archetypal "chancer" Khlestakov, from *The Government Inspector*. Jonson's world of foxes, vultures, ravens, and gorcrows is transformed into the visionary one composed of "pigs' snouts" identified by the semi-demented mayor at the conclusion of *The Government Inspector*.

Gogol emerged on the artistic scene when there was little in the way of an indigenous literary or dramatic tradition in Russia. There was, of course, the towering example of Pushkin, who was an important influence on Gogol, and who is said to have given him the idea for the plot of *The Government Inspector*. However, there is little evidence of Pushkin's influence in Gogol's own fiction-writing, and even

less in his dramatic work. Gogol, like Pushkin, was a great original and, despite the fact that his main claim to fame rests on his fictional output—chiefly the St. Petersburg stories and the novel *Dead Souls*—his contribution to the development of the theatre in Russia, though slight in terms of output, was great in terms of its historical importance.

Quite apart from contributing one major play to the international repertoire, Gogol was the first Russian dramatist to establish theoretical claims for the significance of the theatre. In his "Petersburg Notes of 1836", in *Selected Passages from Correspondence with Friends*, and in his short dramatic piece, *Leaving the Theater . . .*, Gogol established himself as an important theorist of drama, in addition to being a considerable practitioner. He wished for a Russian theatre which served as a means of education for the nation. He wrote of the importance of laughter and the significance of the comic genre and, in many respects, saw the theatre as having a distinctly religious mission. It was a platform from which good could be preached to the world at large.

Gogol's influence on the subsequent history of Russian theatre is such that, without him, much that came after is unimaginable. He initiated an attitude towards realistic acting which affected his contemporary, Mikhail Shchepkin (the Garrick of the Russian stage) and, via Shchepkin, Stanislavsky. If, according to Dostoevsky, the whole of Russian literature emerged from under Gogol's *Overcoat*, then the entire satirical tradition of both the Russian and Soviet theatre can be traced to Gogol. The line extends through the work of Turgenev, Ostrovsky, Sukhovo-Kobylin, Chekhov, Bulgakov, Erdman, to Zoschenko and beyond. In addition, Russian definitions of realism have always needed to take account of Gogol's deployment of bizarre fantasy and, to this extent, he may also be said to have had an effect in restraining some of the more extreme ways in which "socialist realism" sought to define itself, especially during the 1930's. Such definitions always needed to accommodate Gogol who, just as much as Kafka, belonged to the then current, and hotly disputed, debate between the "modernists" and the "realists".

Gogol's reputation as a dramatist rests effectively on a single play, *The Government Inspector* (*Revizor*), which manages to survive better in translation than do his other dramatic works, although this has not prevented some of his English translators from taking on the role of "adaptors", sometimes with regrettable consequences. The two other plays on which his reputation rests, *Marriage* and *The Gamblers*, depend on punning and word-play to an extent which renders their essence difficult to convey in a foreign language. The connection between fantasy and reality in Gogol's work is, in any case, always a puzzle. In his fiction, dead souls assume a seemingly animate life, as do noses and overcoats. The world often begins to assume phantasmagoric proportions, as if illuminated by a devilish lamplighter, like the one who lights the lamps on Nevsky Prospect at the end of the story of that name.

If illusion and reality are difficult to disentangle, so are form and substance. One thing can very easily be mistaken for another, as in *The Government Inspector*, where the mayor mistakes a hatbox for a hat before mistaking an insignificant clerk for a high-ranking Petersburg official. Fuelling these errors and fantasies is an all-pervading sense of fear—fear of the unknown (the government inspector is travelling "incognito"), or fear of change. Podkolesin in *Marriage* is fearfully hesitant before the sacred grove of Hymen. He is terrified of embarking on what a character in Vanbrugh's *The Provoked Wife* calls "Hobbes's Voyage" which involves "a great leap in the dark". The pun is itself Gogolian—a grosser notion of the sexual underlying a genuine intuition of the unknown, an imaginative leap into mystery and infinity, into a genuine union of opposites. All Podkolesin can manage at the end is a leap out of the window.

The government inspector himself emerges out of the darkness of the human subconscious in ways which anticipate some of the discoveries of Freud, terrifying us with our fears and seducing us with our unacknowledged desires. Khlestakov is a devil himself, but one born of our imaginative poverty, of our inertia, our triviality, our petty dissatisfactions, our snobberies. The government inspector represents, momentarily, for a god-forsaken town, a visitation from a tin god—a vicarious association with the mystique of power, authority, and glamour. A "nobody" metamorphoses, under the power of impoverished human fantasy, into a "somebody". Khlestakov's sense of neglected inferiority is transmuted into a grotesque sense of self-importance and invested with an awesome authoritarian power, one which is prophetically anticipatory of historical events in our own century. This latter sense of Gogol's prophetic power has probably best been realised by the great director Vsevolod Meyerhold, whose production of *The Government Inspector*, in 1926, gave intense embodiment to the play's tragi-comic potential.

—Nick Worrall

See also *Volume 1* entry on *The Government Inspector*.

GOLDONI, Carlo. Born in Venice, 25 February 1707. Educated in Venice; at a Jesuit school in Perugia; with Domenicans in Rimini; studied law at Papal College in Pavia, 1723–25. Married Nicoletta Conio in 1736. Assistant to his physician father in Chioggia, 1721–23, and in other towns; clerk in criminal court, Chioggia, 1728–29, and Feltre, 1729–30; passed law examinations in Padua in 1731, and called to the Venetian bar, 1732; wrote plays for amateur companies as early as 1729–30, and for Giuseppe Imer's company, 1734–44, beginning with bare scenarios and gradually working towards completely written scripts; by 1737, director of the Teatro San Giovanni Crisostomo (an opera house), Venice; obliged to leave Venice, and practised law in Pisa, 1744–47; house dramatist for Girolamo Medebac's acting company at the Teatro San Samuele, Venice, 1747–53; wrote for the Vendramin family's Teatro San Luca, Venice, 1753–62; increasingly drawn into theatrical rivalry with playwrights Carlo Gozzi and Pietro Chiari in the late 1740's; moved to France, 1761, and wrote in French and Italian for the Comédie-Italienne, Paris; Italian tutor to the daughter of Louis XV, Princess Adelaide, 1764–65, and to royal children, 1768–80, in Versailles; in Paris after 1780. Also a prolific librettist for *intermezzi*, *opera buffa*, and *opera seria*. Died in Paris, 6 February 1793.

Works

Collections

Commedie. Successive editions: 1750–55, 1753–57, 1757–63, 1761–78.
Opere teatrali (first complete edition; 44 vols.). 1788–95.
The Comedies (includes *The Beneficent Bear; A Curious Mishap; The Fan; The Spendthrift Miser*), edited by Helen Zimmern. 1892.
Opere complete (40 vols.), edited by Giuseppe Ortolani, E. Maddalena, and C. Musatti. 1907–60.

Four Comedies (includes *Mine Hostess; The Good Girl; The Impresario from Smyrna; The Fan*), translated by Clifford Bax. 1922.
Tutte le opere (14 vols.; includes letters), edited by Giuseppe Ortolani. 1935–56.
Opere, edited by Filippo Zampieri. 1954.
Three Comedies (includes *The Boors; The Fan; Mine Hostess*), translated by Clifford Bax. 1961.
Four Comedies (includes *The Superior Residence; The Venetian Twins; Mirandolina; The Artful Widow*), translated by Frederick H. Davies. 1968.

Stage Works (Plays)

For a list of Goldoni's libretti and the composers of their musical settings, see the Goldoni entry in *Enciclopedia dello spettacolo*, 1954–64.

Belisario (produced Teatro San Samuele, Venice, 1734). 1798.
Rosmonda (produced Teatro San Samuele, Venice, 1734). 1793.
Don Giovanni Tenorio; o, Sia il dissoluto (produced Teatro San Samuele, Venice, 1736). 1754.
Rinaldo di Montalbano (produced Teatro San Samuele, Venice, 1736). 1774.
Enrico, Re di Sicilia (produced Teatro San Samuele, Venice, 1736). 1740.
Momolo cortesan, o, L'uomo di mondo (produced Teatro San Samuele, Venice, 1738). 1757.
Il prodigo, also known as *Momolo sulla Brenta* (produced Teatro San Samuele, Venice, 1739). 1757.
La bancarotta (produced Teatro San Samuele, Venice, 1740).
La donna di garbo (produced Teatro San Samuele, Venice, 1743). 1747.
Il figlio d'Arlecchino perduto e ritrovato (produced Teatro San Samuele, Venice, c.1745).
Il servitore di due padroni (produced Teatro San Samuele, Venice, 1745). 1753; translated as *The Servant of Two Masters*, 1928.
Tonin Bella Grazie; o, Il frappatore (produced 1748). 1757.
I due gemelli Veneziani (produced Teatro Sant'Angelo, Venice, 1748). 1750; translated as *The Venetian Twins*, in *Four Comedies*, 1968.
L'uomo prudente (produced Teatro Sant'Angelo, Venice, 1748). 1750.
La vedova scaltra (produced Modena, 1748). 1750; translated as *The Artful Widow*, in *Four Comedies*, 1968.
La putta onorata (produced Teatro Sant'Angelo, Venice, 1749). 1751.
La buona moglie (produced Teatro Sant'Angelo, Venice, 1749). 1751.
Il cavaliere e la dama; o, I cicisbei (produced Teatro Sant'Angelo, Venice, 1749). 1751.
La famiglia dell'Antiquario (produced Teatro Sant'Angelo, Venice, 1750). 1752.
L'avvocato veneziano (produced Teatro Sant'Angelo, Venice, 1750). 1752.
Il padre di famiglia (produced Teatro Sant'Angelo, Venice, c.1750). 1751; translated as *The Father of a Family*, 1757.
Il teatro comico (produced Milan, 1750). 1751; translated as *The Comic Theatre*, 1969.
La femme puntigliose (produced Teatro Sant'Angelo, Venice, 1750). 1753.
La bottega del caffè (produced Mantua, 1750). 1753; translated as *The Coffee House*, 1925.
Il bugiardo (produced Mantua, 1750). 1753; translated as *The Liar*, 1922.

L'adulatore (produced Mantua, 1750).   1753.

Il poeta fanatico (produced Milan, 1750).

La Pamela, from a novel by Samuel Richardson (produced Milan, 1750).   1753; translated as *Pamela*, 1756.

Il cavaliere di buon gusto (produced Teatro Sant'Angelo, Venice, 1750).   1753.

Il giuocatore (produced Teatro Sant'Angelo, Venice, 1750). 1754.

Il vero amico (produced Teatro Sant'Angelo, Venice, 1750). 1753.

L'erede fortunata (produced Teatro Sant'Angelo, 1750). 1752.

La finta ammalata (produced Teatro Sant'Angelo, Venice, 1751).   1753.

La dama prudente (produced Teatro Sant'Angelo, Venice, 1751).   1753.

L'incognita persequitata (produced Teatro Sant'Angelo, Venice, 1751).   1754.

L'avventuriere onorato (produced Teatro Sant'Angelo, Venice, 1751).   1753.

La donna volubile (produced Teatro Sant'Angelo, Venice, 1751).   1755.

I pettigolezzi delle donne (produced Teatro Sant'Angelo, Venice, 1751).   1753.

Il Moliere (produced Teatro Sant'Angelo, Venice, 1751).

L'amante militare (produced Teatro Sant'Angelo, Venice, 1751).   1755.

La castalda (produced Teatro Sant'Angelo, Venice, 1751). 1753.

Il tu tare (produced Teatro Sant'Angelo, Venice, 1752). 1753.

La moglie saggia (produced Teatro Sant'Angelo, Venice, 1752).   1753.

Il feudatario (produced Teatro Sant'Angelo, Venice, 1752).   1753.

La figlia obbediente (produced Teatro Sant'Angelo, Venice, 1752).   1754; translated as *The Good Girl*, in *Four Comedies*, 1922.

La serva amorosa (produced Bologna, 1752).   1753.

Le donne gelose (produced Teatro Sant'Angelo, Venice, 1752).   1753; translated as *The Good-Humoured Ladies*, 1922.

I puntigli domestici (produced Milan, 1752).   1754.

I mercatanti (produced Teatro Sant'Angelo, Venice, 1752). 1754.

Le donne curiose (produced Teatro Sant'Angelo, Venice, 1753).   1753.

Il contrattempo; o, Il chiaccherione imprudente (produced Teatro Sant'Angelo, Venice, 1753).   1754.

La Locandiera (produced Teatro Sant'Angelo, Venice, 1753).   1753; several translations as *The Mistress of the Inn*; also translated as *Mine Hostess*, in *Four Comedies*, 1922; as *Mirandolina*, in *Four Comedies*, 1968.

La donna vendicativa (produced Teatro Sant'Angelo, Venice, 1753).   1754.

Il geloso avaro (produced Livorno, 1753).   1757.

La donna di testa debole (produced Teatro San Luca, Venice, 1753).   1757.

La sposa persiana (produced Teatro San Luca, Venice, 1753). 1757.

La cameriera brillante (produced Teatro San Luca, Venice, 1754).   1757.

Il filosofo inglese (produced Teatro San Luca, Venice, 1754). 1757.

Il vecchio bizzarro (produced Teatro San Luca, Venice, 1754).   1757.

Il festino (produced Teatro San Luca, 1754).   1757.

Terenzio (produced Teatro San Luca, Venice, 1754).   1758.

L'impostore (produced Modena, 1754).   1754.

La peruviana (produced Teatro San Luca, Venice, 1754). 1757.

La madre amorosa (produced Genoa, 1754).   1757.

Le massere (produced Teatro Sant'Angelo, Venice, 1755). 1758.

Il cavaliere giocondo (produced Teatro San Luca, Venice, 1755).   1758.

Le donne di casa soa (produced Teatro San Luca, Venice, 1755).   1758.

Ircana in Julfa (produced Teatro San Luca, Venice, 1755). 1758.

Torquato Tasso (produced Teatro San Luca, Venice, 1755). 1757.

I malcontenti (produced Teatro San Luca, Venice, 1755). 1755.

La buona famiglia (produced Teatro San Luca, Venice, 1755).   1758.

La villeggiatura (produced Teatro San Luca, Venice, 1755). 1758.

Il medico olandese (produced Teatro San Luca, Venice, 1756).   1760.

Il campiello (produced Teatro San Luca, Venice, 1756).   1758; translated as *Il Campiello*, 1976.

Ircana in Ispahan (produced Teatro San Luca, Venice, 1756). 1760.

La dalmatina (produced Teatro San Luca, Venice, 1756). 1763.

La donna capricciosa.   1760.

Il raggiratore (produced Teatro San Luca, Venice, 1756). 1758.

La donna stravagante (produced Teatro San Luca, Venice, 1756).   1760.

L'avaro (produced Bologna, 1756).   1762.

Il buon compatriotto (produced Teatro San Luca, Venice, 1756).   1790.

Il padre per amore (produced Teatro San Luca, Venice, 1757).   1763.

L'amante di se medesimo (produced Milan, 1757).   1760.

La vedova spiritosa (verse version produced Teatro San Luca, Venice, 1757; prose version produced Teatro Tordinona, Rome, 1758).   Prose version, 1759; verse version, 1761.

Un curioso accidente (produced Teatro San Luca, Venice, 1757).   1768; translated as *A Curious Mishap*, in *Comedies*, 1892.

Le donne di buonmore (produced Teatro Tordinona, Rome, 1759).   1789.

La donna sola (produced Teatro San Luca, Venice, 1757).

Il cavaliere di spirito (produced Zola, 1757).   1764.

L'impresario delle Smirne (produced Teatro San Luca, Venice, 1757).   1774; translated as *The Impresario from Smyrna*, in *Four Comedies*, 1922.

La bella selvaggia (produced Teatro San Luca, Venice, 1758). 1761.

Il ricco insidiato (produced Teatro San Luca, Venice, 1758). 1761.

La donna di governo (produced Teatro San Luca, Venice, 1758).   1761.

La sposa sagace (produced Teatro San Luca, Venice, 1758). 1761.

Lo spirito di contraddizione (produced Teatro San Luca, Venice, 1758).   1761.

Pamela maritata (produced Teatro Capranica, Rome, 1759). 1761.

Le morbinose (produced Teatro San Luca, Venice, 1758). 1761.

La donna bizzarra (produced Zola, 1758). 1760.
L'apatista; o, Sia l'indifferente (produced Zola, 1758). 1760.
Gl'innamorati (produced Teatro San Luca, Venice, 1759). 1761.
La scuola di ballo (produced Bologna, 1759). 1792.
Artemisia (produced Teatro San Luca, Venice, 1759). 1793.
La buona madre (produced Teatro San Luca, Venice, 1759). 1764.
La guerra (produced Teatro San Luca, Venice, 1760). 1764.
I rusteghi (produced Teatro San Luca, Venice, 1760). 1761; translated as *The Boors*, in *Three Comedies*, 1961.
Eneo nel Lazi (produced Teatro San Luca, Venice, 1760). 1793.
Zoroaster (produced Teatro San Luca, Venice, 1760). 1793.
La donna forte. 1761.
Le smanie della villegiatura (produced Teatro San Luca, Venice, 1761). 1768.
Le avventure della villegiatura (produced Teatro San Luca, Venice, 1761). 1768.
Il ritorno dalla villegiatura (produced Teatro San Luca, Venice, 1761). 1768.
La casa nova (produced Teatro San Luca, Venice, 1761). 1768; translated as *The Superior Residence*, in *Four Comedies*, 1968.
Sior Todero Brontolon (produced Teatro San Luca, Venice, 1761). 1774.
La scozzese (produced Comédie-Italienne, Paris, 1761). 1774.
La bella Giorgiana (produced Teatro San Luca, Venice, 1761). 1792.
Le baruffe chiozzote (produced Teatro San Luca, Venice, 1762). 1774; translated as *The Squabbles of Chioggia*, in *Drama*, 15, 1914; as *It Happened in Venice*, 1965.
Una della ultime sere di carnevale (produced Teatro San Luca, Venice, 1762). 1777.
L'osteria della posta (produced Bologna, 1762). Translated as *The Post-Inn*, in *The Drama 5*, edited by A. Bates, 1902.
L'amor paterno; o, La serva riconscente (produced Comédie-Italienne, Paris, 1763).
Il ventaglio (produced Comédie-Italienne, Paris, 1763). 1789; translated as *The Fan*, in *Comedies*, 1892.
Il matrimonio per concorso (produced Teatro San Luca, Venice, 1763). 1778.
Il ritratto d'Arlecchino (produced Comédie-Italienne, Paris, 1764). 1777.
Chi la fa l'aspetta (produced Teatro San Luca, Venice, 1765). 1789.
Le Bourru bienfaisant (produced Comédie-Italienne, Paris, 1771). Translated as *The Times*, 1780; as *The Beneficent Bear*, in *Comedies*, 1892.
L'Avare fasteaux (produced Fontainebleu, 1776). 1789; translated as *The Spendthrift Miser*, in *Comedies*, 1892.
I metempsicosi. 1793.
Gli amori di Alessandro Magno. 1793.

Memoirs and Letters

Mémoirs, pour servir à l'histoire de sa vie, et à celle de son théâtre (3 vols.). 1787; translated as *Memoirs* (2 vols.), 1814.

Other

On Play-Writing, edited by F.C.L. van Steenderen. 1919.

*

Bibliographies

A. Della Torre, *Saggio di una bibliografia delle opere intorno a Carlo Goldoni (1793–1907)*, Florence, 1908.
N. Mangini, *Bibliografia goldoniana (1958–1967)*, Venice, 1961; supplemented in the journal *Studi goldoniani*, 1968–79.

Criticism

Books:
D. Mantovani (ed.), *Carlo Goldoni e il teatro di San Luca*, Milan, 1885; new edition, revised by N. Mangini, Venice, 1979.
H.C. Chatfield-Taylor, *Goldoni* (biography), New York, 1913.
E. Rho, *La missione teatrale di Carlo Goldoni: Storia del teatro goldoniano*, Bari, 1936.
E. Caccia, *Carattere e caratteri nella commedia del Goldoni*, Venice and Rome, 1959.
A. Momigliano, *Saggi goldoniani*, edited by V. Branca, Venice and Rome, 1959; second edition, 1968.
V. Branca and N. Mangini, *Studi goldoniani: Atti del Convegno Internazionale di Studi Goldoniani* (2 vols.), Venice and Rome, 1960.
L. Ferrante, *I comici goldoniani (1721–1960)*, Bologna, 1961.
Heinz Riedt, *Carlo Goldoni*, Velber, 1967.
P.E. Weiss, *Carlo Goldoni, Librettist: The Early Years*, New York, 1970.
L. Ferrante, *Carlo Goldoni*, Milan, 1971.
G. Cavallini, *Le commedie del Goldoni*, Turin, 1972.
G. Nicastro, *Goldoni e il teatro del secondo Settecento*, Rome and Bari, 1974.
S. Ferrone, *Carlo Goldoni*, Florence, 1975.
Timothy Holme, *A Servant of Many Masters: The Life and Times of Goldoni*, London, 1976.
M. Petrini, *Le commedie popolari del Goldoni*, Padua, 1976.
Franco Fido, *Guida a Goldoni: Teatro e società nel Settecento*, Turin, 1977.
Jacques Joly, *Le Desir et l'utopie: Études sur le théâtre d'Alfieri et de Goldoni*, Clermont-Ferrand, 1978.
P. Bosisio, *Carlo Gozzi e Goldoni: Una polemica letteraria con versi inediti e rari*, Florence, 1979.
Gastone Geron, *Goldoni libertino*, Milan, 1979.
K. Hecker, *La concezione dell'educazione in Carlo Goldoni*, Venice, 1980.
Linda L. Carroll, *Language and Dialect in Ruzante and Goldoni*, Ravenna, 1981.
Eugene Steel, *Carlo Goldoni*, Ravenna, 1981.
N. Borsellino (ed.), *L'interpretazione goldoniana, critica e messinscena*, Rome, 1982.
B. Anglani, *Goldoni: Il mercato, la scena, l'utopia*, Naples, 1983.
G. Nicastro, *Goldoni: Riformatore*, Catania, 1983.
F. Fido, *Da venezia all'Europa: Prospettive sull'ultimo Goldoni*, Rome, 1984.
G. Cavallini, *La dimensione civile e sociale del quotidiano nel teatro comico di Carlo Goldoni*, Rome, 1986.
G. Petronio (ed.), *Il punto su Goldoni*, Rome and Bari, 1986.
Pamela D. Stewart, *Goldonif fra letteratura e teatro*, Florence, 1989.

Serials

Studi goldoniani, 1968–1986.

* * *

Perhaps the greatest Italian dramatist, Goldoni was certainly one of the most prolific, for in addition to the comedies, tragedies, and tragi-comedies listed above, he wrote a large number of *scenarii* for improvising players in the Italian and French theatres, and libretti for intermezzi and opera *seria* and *buffa*. His historical importance is considerable, for he sought to effect a reform of the Italian comic stage that would issue in a fully scripted drama, comparable to that triumphant in France and England, thereby supplanting the traditional improvisation, masked figures, and unbridled physical knockabout of the *commedia dell'arte*. In this attempt he was successful, but his reforms helped to bring about even greater changes in the Italian theatre, leading, in due course, to the development of the role of the professional dramatist, and to the introduction of certain bourgeois emphases, the general tone of which may be associated with those Enlightenment ideas beginning to circulate in his native Venice by the middle years of the early 1750's; indeed, Goldoni's play, *Il padre di famiglia*, was later imitated by Diderot.

But the evolution of Goldoni's reform of the Italian comic drama was long and, at least in its earlier stages, less deliberate than he came later to claim in his play prefaces and *Memoirs*. Pivotal, perhaps, was the period between the no-longer extant first version of his play *Momolo cortesan*, written in 1738 for the actor Golinetti, and crafted to include a mixture of scripted and improvised dialogue, and *La donna di garbo*, a fully scripted piece written 1742–43, and perhaps the first of his plays to carry the distinctively Goldonian comic tone.

More substantial, because it was more regular, was the work he did at the Teatro Sant' Angelo with a company led by one of the most versatile actor-managers of the period, Girolamo Medebach, and it was in 1748 that he began the first steps of his reform of comedy with *La vedova scaltra* (*The Artful Widow*). By 1750 he was vigorously attacking, in some of his scripted pieces, the crudities and excesses of the old form, as he did in *Pamela nubile*, his popular stage adaptation of Samuel Richardson's novel, and in his dramatised comic discourse on the ills of the stage, regular and musical, *Il teatro comico*. Again, from the early 1750's his plays may be described as significantly more "naturalistic", conspicuously dealing with Italian, and particularly Venetian, issues, especially those of the working and professional and business classes. They reflected, too, something of the values of the Enlightenment. Goldoni was not an intellectual dramatist, however, but pre-eminently a professional entertainer, skilled at providing acting companies with performable work: in the 1750–51 season, for example, he upheld a promise to produce 16 comedies in a single season.

In his plays of social observation, Goldoni developed a kind of refined poetic realism that, while rooted in the depiction of the familiar and everyday in Venetian life, never lost the artifice appropriate to the theatre. Venice had fallen considerably from its Renaissance authority as *La Serenissima*, and the city in which most of his plays were set was essentially a quiet and provincial one, notwithstanding its new *settecento* reputation as the playground of Europe. In Goldoni's comedy at its best, there is, in addition to a prevailing bourgeois tone, a new emphasis on niceties of conduct and the pointing of fine moral discriminations. Characteristic of the new forces and attitudes emerging in mid-18th century society is the prominent mercantile spirit in the plays, an attitude somewhat similar to that found in Lessing and Lillo. For the first time in Italian drama there was a focus on economic considerations, middle-class domestic issues, and the complexities of human relationships, as well as a marked reaction against aristocratic theatre forms.

But although Goldoni's reform furthered the demise of the improvised drama, he acquired much of his dramaturgical skill, during his apprentice years in the theatre, working with the improvising comedians, and rarely in any of his mature comedies does he abandon, altogether, the example of fast, physical, choreographic performance provided by those players. Goldoni wrote either in Italian (Tuscan) or in the Venetian dialect, and very often combined the two in the same dramatic piece. Nevertheless, he earned the disgust of his rival, Carlo Gozzi, defender of social, literary, and linguistic tradition, and champion of the improvised *commedia dell'arte* supposedly undermined by the Goldonian reforms.

Goldoni was a professional writer, and hence the amount, and the variable quality, of his output. Of the theatre forms available to him, the musical was, financially, by far the most rewarding, and throughout his career he looked to opera, more particularly opera *buffa*, to supplement the income from his playwriting. In his early years he attempted to write for the more lucrative opera *seria*, and sought advancement as a literary director in this highly fashionable field. With little support from patronage, the need to earn money was ever an imperative. The success of Gozzi's *fiabe*, fantasy spectacles which exploited the talents of the improvising comedians, encouraged Goldoni to leave Venice for a post with the Comédie-Italienne in Paris. His move was probably inspired mainly by the attractions of the salary and relative security he hoped to obtain there, and the possibility of gaining the patronage of the French monarch and those about the court. In the event, he obtained, in Paris, a comfortable living, and in the longer term obtained a pension for his services as Italian tutor; but for these benefits he cut the tap roots of his stage inspiration, and little of his later work in France stands comparison with his Venetian output.

—Kenneth Richards

See also *Volume 1* entries on *The Mistress of the Inn*; *The Servant of Two Masters*.

––––––––––

GOLDSMITH, Oliver. Born probably in Pallas, near Ballymahon, County Longford, Ireland, 10 November 1730 (possibly 1728 or 1731). Educated at a village school in Lissoy, West Meath, 1734–37; Elphin School, 1738; schools in Athlone, 1739–41, and Edgeworthstown, Longford, 1741–44; Trinity College, Dublin (sizar; Smyth exhibitioner, 1747), 1745–49, BA 1750; studied medicine at the University of Edinburgh, 1752–53, and University of Leyden, 1754; travelled in France, Germany, Switzerland, and Italy, 1755–56, and may have obtained a medical degree (failed examination at the College of Surgeons, 1758). Moved to London, 1756; practised unsuccessfully as physician in Southwark; usher, Dr. Milner's classical academy, Peckham, 1756, 1758; writer for Ralph Griffiths, proprietor of the *Monthly Review*, 1757, and for Smollett's *Critical Review*, 1759, and *British Magazine*, 1760; editor, the *Bee*, 1759, and the *Lady's Magazine*, 1761; proof-reader and preface-writer for the publisher John Newbery, and contributed the "Chinese Letters" to Newbery's *Public Ledger*, 1760–61; prepared *Compendium of Biography* (7 vols.), 1762; founder member, with Burke and Reynolds, Samuel Johnson's literary Club, 1764. Died in London, 4 April 1774.

Works

Collections

Collected Letters, edited by Katharine C. Balderston. 1928.
Collected Works, edited by Arthur Friedman (5 vols.). 1966.
Poems and Plays, edited by Tom Davis. 1975.
Selected Writings, edited by John Lucas. 1988.

Stage Works

The Good Natured Man (produced Covent Garden Theatre, London, 1768). 1768.
Threnodia Augustalis, Sacred to the Memory of the Princess Dowager of Wales, music by Mattia Vento (produced 1772). 1772.
The Captivity (oratorio). In *Miscellaneous Works*, 1820.
The Grumbler, from a translation by Charles Sedley of a work by Brueys (produced Covent Garden Theatre, London, 1773). Edited by Alice I. Perry Wood, 1931.
She Stoops to Conquer; or, The Mistakes of a Night (produced Covent Garden Theatre, London, 1773). 1773.

Fiction

The Vicar of Wakefield. 1766.

Verse

The Traveller; or, A Prospect of Society. 1764.
The Deserted Village. 1770.
Retaliation. 1774.
The Haunch of Venison: A Poetical Epistle to Lord Clare. 1776.

Other

An Enquiry into the Present State of Polite Learning in Europe. 1759.
The Bee. 1759.
The Mystery Revealed. 1762.
The Citizen of the World; or, Letters from a Chinese Philosopher Residing in London to His Friends in the East (2 vols.). 1762.
The Life of Richard Nash of Bath. 1762.
An History of England in a Series of Letters from a Nobleman to His Son (2 vols.). 1764.
An History of the Martyrs and Primitive Fathers of the Church. 1764.
Essays. 1765; revised edition, 1766.
The Present State of the British Empire in Europe, America, Africa, and Asia. 1768.
The Roman History, from the Foundation of the City of Rome to the Destruction of the Western Empire (2 vols.). 1769; abridged edition (for children), 1772.
The Life of Thomas Parnell. 1770.
The Life of Henry St. John, Lord Viscount Bolingbroke. 1770.
The History of England, from the Earliest Times to the Death of George II (4 vols.). 1771; abridged edition, 1774.
The Grecian History, from the Earliest State to the Death of Alexander the Great (2 vols.). 1774.
An History of the Earth and Animated Nature (8 vols.). 1774.
A Survey of Experimental Philosophy, Considered in Its Present State of Improvement (2 vols.). 1776.

Editor, Poems for Young Ladies in Three Parts, Devotional, Moral, and Entertaining. 1767.
Editor, The Beauties of English Poesy (2 vols.). 1767.

Translator, The Memoirs of a Protestant, by Jean Marteilhe (2 vols.). 1758; edited by A. Dobson, 1895.
Translator, Plutarch's Lives (7 vols.). 1762.
Translator, A Concise History of Philosophy and Philosophers, by Jean Formey. 1766.
Translator, The Comic Romance of Scarron (2 vols.). 1775.

*

Bibliographies

Temple Scott, *Goldsmith Bibliographically and Biographically Considered*, New York, 1928.
Samuel H. Woods, *Oliver Goldsmith: A Reference Guide*, Boston, 1982.

Criticism

Books:
R.W. Jackson, *Goldsmith: Essays Towards an Interpretation*, Dublin, 1951.
Ralph M. Wardle, *Oliver Goldsmith*, London, 1957.
A. Norman Jeffares, *Oliver Goldsmith*, London, 1959.
Clara M. Kirk, *Oliver Goldsmith*, New York, 1967.
Ricardo Quintana, *Oliver Goldsmith: A Georgian Study*, London and New York, 1967.
Robert H. Hopkins, *The True Genius of Goldsmith*, Baltimore, Maryland, 1969.
E. Lehmann, *"Not Merely Sentimental": Studien zu Oliver Goldsmiths Komödien*, Munich, 1974.
A. Lytton Sells, *Goldsmith: His Life and Works*, London, 1974.
G.S. Rousseau (ed.), *Oliver Goldsmith: The Critical Heritage*, London, 1974.
Munro MacLennan, *The Secret of Oliver Goldsmith*, New York, 1975.
John Ginger, *The Notable Man: The Life and Times of Oliver Goldsmith*, London, 1977.
Marlies Danziger, *Oliver Goldsmith and Richard Brinsley Sheridan*, New York, 1978.
Sean Lucy (ed.), *Oliver Goldsmith: The Gentle Master*, Cork, Eire, 1984.
Andrew Swarbrick (ed.), *The Art of Goldsmith*, London, 1984.
Harold Bloom (ed.), *Oliver Goldsmith*, New York, 1987.

* * *

Goldsmith won his special place in the English theatre on the strength of one comedy, *She Stoops to Conquer*. His first and only other play, *The Good Natured Man*, though well worth a modern director's attention, was received rather tepidly in his own day and has attracted relatively few revivals. *She Stoops to Conquer*, however, was an instant success. Dr. Johnson delighted in it, and even Horace Walpole, who considered it a mere farce lacking in "edification", had to admit that it made him laugh. There has been general agreement ever since that it is a masterpiece which strikes an unusual balance between robust farce and comedy of a more delicate and profound kind: it has provided actors with rich opportunities for psychological finesse as well as high-spirited fun.

Goldsmith was already celebrated as a writer before he turned to the theatre. His immensely popular novel *The Vicar of Wakefield* (itself later dramatised) gave him a reputation which should have allowed easy access to the Theatre Royal in Drury Lane, where he had hoped to have his first play performed. He knew David Garrick through their membership of Dr. Johnson's Club, the most exclusive literary and artistic circle of the day; and Johnson himself supported Goldsmith's theatrical ambitions (he wrote the prologue for *The Good Natured Man*). Goldsmith may have alienated Garrick by his frank criticism of current theatre practices. In his essay, *An Enquiry into the Present State of Polite Learning in Europe*, for example, he accused the theatre managers of being too addicted to Shakespeare and too ready to resurrect the "lumber" of the past rather than risk new plays. When he did take the risk, a playwright would suffer from seeing his text at the manager's mercy: the "histrionic daemon" ruled the stage. Garrick must have thought himself targeted: at any rate he made difficulties about accepting *The Good Natured Man* for Drury Lane and instead it was produced at the rival establishment, Covent Garden, by George Colman.

Colman had his own reservations about the play: he was nervous (as Goldsmith said of his reaction to *She Stoops to Conquer*) at it's being "not merely sentimental". The fashion for sentimental comedy was abhorrent to Goldsmith. He frequently attacked the genre, complaining in his "Essay on the Theatre; or, a Comparison between Laughing and Sentimental Comedy" that it flattered the audience by focusing on the "virtues" and "distresses" of refined characters in polite society whereas comedy had traditionally satirised "the absurdities of the vulgar". Such satire had now become "low", he mocked. Garrick had chosen a classical example of the sentimental genre, Hugh Kelly's *False Delicacy*, in preference to *The Good Natured Man* (compounding the injury by rushing through its first night to beat Covent Garden's production of Goldsmith's play). This could only confirm Goldsmith in his view that the bastard sentimental comedy was driving "true" comedy off the stage.

The reception of *The Good Natured Man* provided further evidence that public taste had "grown of late, perhaps, too delicate". It enjoyed a fair run, but the audience rejected as "low" one of its funniest scenes — Young Honeywood's attempt to pass off the bailiffs as his friends. Goldsmith took revenge in *She Stoops to Conquer*, reducing the dreaded epithet to absurdity by assigning it to Tony Lumpkin's vulgar drinking companions: "I loves to hear him sing, bekeays he never gives us nothing that's *low*".

The Good Natured Man was Goldsmith's first, partially successful, attempt to mix "humours" characters, like the name-dropping Lofty, and farcical episodes such as Mr Croker's misreading of the "incendiary letter" (both much enjoyed by the first audiences) with more realistic scenes. At the centre is the "education" of the good natured man, a study in a curious psychology. Honeywood is beset by debts and bailiffs, generous, vain and extravagant, kind (except to tradesmen), over-anxious to be liked; he is characterised by Goldsmith with a subtle mixture of irony and sympathy beyond the reach of most English playwrights of that time. Though, as contemporary reviewers said, not wholly successful in its "fable", the play strikes some lively sparks and may have influenced Sheridan. Croker's attempt to make his son propose more enthusiastically seems echoed in Sir Anthony Absolute's tetchy encouragement to a provocatively cool Jack in *The Rivals*.

In *She Stoops to Conquer; or, The Mistakes of a Night* (produced at Covent Garden after more pressure, "nay, a kind of force", from Dr. Johnson) Goldsmith succeeded in creating not just an effective comic plot but a true "fable". Though so preposterous, the practical joke Tony Lumpkin plays on Marlow, in directing him to Mr. Hardcastle's house and convincing him it is an inn, works with remarkable naturalness, perhaps because it had a distant source in a similar embarrassment experienced by Goldsmith as a youth in Ireland. The authenticity of that "memory" has been doubted, and several other sources for the plot have been suggested, including Isaac Bickerstaffe's comic opera, *Love in a Village* (whose rustic, Hodge, is a possible prototype for Tony Lumpkin) and Marivaux's *Le Jeu de l'amour et du hasard*, in which a young couple disguise themselves as their respective servants in order to learn more about their proposed partners: a situation with obvious relevance to that of Kate Hardcastle and Marlow.

Whatever Goldsmith drew on, there is no doubt that the great naturalness of *She Stoops to Conquer* comes in part from his putting so much of himself into its characters. The awkward genius, who "wrote like an angel and talked like poor Poll" is projected, with comic distortion, in Marlow, the divided personality, easy with barmaids but humiliatingly ill at ease with women such as Kate Hardcastle. It has been conjectured that Goldsmith went deeper still into his unconscious to release the anarchic figure of Tony Lumpkin, locked in a relationship with a mother who spoils and harasses him in equal measure. Like Shakespeare's Puck, or some pagan spirit of misrule, Tony upsets the benignly repressive order against which all the young lovers are rebelling. He gives Kate her chance of free choice: by acting the barmaid, she finds her way to the true Marlow and displays him to the baffled fathers hidden behind the screen in Act V (another hint here for Sheridan). Tony's final piece of mischief, the journey which ends with a bedraggled and distraught Mrs. Hardcastle discovering that she has been deceived into thinking herself on Crackskull Common, beset by highwaymen, is a true comic nemesis: "All the parish says you have spoilt me, and so you may take the fruits on't".

Goldsmith wrote no more plays, dying in 1744, still in his early 40's, just when theatre doors were swinging open to him: Garrick was to have revived *The Good Natured Man* and produced his projected new comedy. Nevertheless *She Stoops to Conquer* has kept its author a place in the repertoire, with its warm and genial presence.

—Katharine Worth

See also *Volume 1* entry on *She Stoops to Conquer*.

GOMBROWICZ, Witold. Born in Maloszyce, Poland, 4 August 1904. Educated at Warsaw University, 1922–27, degree in law 1927; studied philosophy and economics in Paris, 1927–29. Married Marie Labrosse in 1969. Bank employee, Argentina, 1939–63; first play, *Iwona* [*Princess Ivona*], produced 1957; Ford Foundation Fellow, Berlin, 1963–64; lived in Vence, France, 1964–69. Recipient: International Literary Prize, 1967. Died in Vence, 25 July 1969.

Works

Stage Plays

Iwona, Księżniczka Burgunda (produced Teatr Dramatyczny, Warsaw, 1957). 1935; translated as *Princess Ivona*, 1969; as *Ivona, Princess of Burgundy*, 1969.

Ślub (produced Théâtre Récamier, Paris, 1963). In *Kultura*, 1950; in book form, with *Trans-Atlantyk*, 1953; translated as *The Marriage*, 1969.

Operetka (produced Teatro Stabile, Aquila, Mexico, 1969). 1966; translated as *Operetta*, 1971.

Historia [History] (unfinished). In *Kultura*, 1975.

Fiction

Pamietnik z okresu dojrzewania [Memoir from Adolescence]. 1933.

Ferdydurke. 1937; translated as *Ferdydurke*, 1961.

Trans-Atlantyk [Trans-Atlantic]. With *Ślub*, 1953.

Bakakaj (selections). 1957.

Pornografia. 1960; translated as *Pornografia*, 1966.

Kosmos. 1965; translated as *Cosmos*, 1966.

Opetani. 1973; translated as *Possessed; or, The Secret of Myslotch*, 1980.

Memoirs and Letters

Dziennik 1953–1966 [Journal]. In *Kultura* (Paris), 1953–69; in book form (3 vols.), 1957–66; translated as *Diary*, 1988; as *Diaries* (2 vols.), 1988–89.

Entretiens avec Gombrowicz, edited by Dominique de Roux. 1968; translated as *A Kind of Testament*, 1973.

Wspomnienia polskie [Polish Reminiscences]. 1977.

*

Bibliographies

Zofia Bilek-Dabrowska, "Bibliograph", in *Literary Studies in Poland*, 10, 1983.

Criticism

Books:

Dominique de Roux (ed.), *Entretiens avec Gombrowicz*, Paris, 1968.

Dominique de Roux and Konstantin A. Jelénski, *Gombrowicz* (essay collection, in French), Paris, 1971.

Jacques Volle, *Gombrowicz: Bourreau-martyr*, Paris, 1972.

François Bondy and Konstantin Jelénski, *Witold Gombrowicz* (in German), Velber, 1977.

Rosine Georgin, *Gombrowicz* (in French), Lausanne, 1977.

Ewa M. Thompson, *Witold Grombrowicz*, Boston, 1979.

Rita Gombrowicz, *Gombrowicz en Europe: Témoignages et documents 1963–1969*, Paris, 1988.

Manuel Carcassone and others (eds.), *Gombrowicz, vingt ans après*, Paris, 1989.

Articles:

George Gömöri, "The Antinomies of Gombrowicz", in *Modern Language Review*, 73, 1978.

Timothy J. Wiles, "History as Fashion in Gombrowicz's *Operetta*", in *Perspectives on Contemporary Literature*, vol.4 no.1, 1978.

David Brodsky, "Witold Gombrowicz and the 'Polish October' ", in *Slavic Review*, 39, 1980.

Czesław Milosz, "Who is Gombrowicz?", in *Performing Arts Journal*, 18, 1982.

Mari Barniecki, "Gombrowicz's Drama Within and Without the Absurd", in *Canadian Slavonic Papers*, 27, 1985.

Beth Holmgren, "Witold Gombrowicz in the United States", in *Polish Review*, 33, 1988.

*   *   *

Witold Gombrowicz wrote three plays and started but never finished a fourth one. The first of these, written before World War II and first published in the elite Warsaw review *Skamander*, but staged only in 1957, is *Iwona, Ksieżniczka Burgunda* (*Princess Ivona*). It is a four-act play described by the author as a "tragifarce". It takes place in a mythical kingdom, which has many modern features (the King plays bridge and makes "democratic" gestures such as walking amongst the people), and where the young heir to the throne decides to exercise his individual freedom to the full. This amounts to the inexplicable choice of a particularly ugly and uncommunicative girl as a bride: the Prince chooses Ivona on an absolute whim. Ivona, by her sheer presence, acts as a catalyst for the suppressed guilt and anxiety of everybody, and by Act IV the entire royal family is eager to kill her, whether by poison, knife, or a staged accident. This last stratagem, devised by the King, is ultimately successful and Ivona chokes on a fishbone. The play can be interpreted as a manifestation of Gombrowicz's revolt against convention and family ties.

Family again, and an unreal "royal" one, is at the centre of Gombrowicz's second, and philosophically most ambitious play, *Ślub* (*The Marriage*), completed in 1947. At the time of its writing Gombrowicz lived in Argentina, isolated from Polish "reality", but grappling with problems of authenticity, and of tradition and deviation. *The Marriage* uses World War II as a starting point: it shattered the old value-system, which now can be restored only by a kind of "magic". The plot takes place in an imaginary space created in Henry's mind. As in a dream, Henry returns home, that is to his parents' house in Poland now transformed into an inn of ill repute, and finds his father is now an innkeeper and his fiancée, Molly, a barmaid. This situation depresses him, but he soon realizes his power to shape events when the act of kneeling before his father transforms the old man into a "king", and the seedy inn into a royal court.

The act of Father's "enthronement", however, is followed by his being dethroned. All Henry has to do is to touch Father, and through this magic (and implicitly sexual) act he destroys the Father's "royal" power. Following this deed, Henry decides to "give himself a wedding"; after all he does not need any divine or paternal sanction to get married. His plans are eventually thwarted by the crafty Drunkard who manages to make Henry jealous of his best friend, Johnny (in the original, Władzio). Jealousy and a wish to assert his power make Henry drive his friend to suicide. This, however, creates an impasse—Henry realizes that individual will, however "creative", can never be absolute. The marriage will not take place—it will not make sense if it cannot restore innocence, which is, of course, impossible.

In *Ślub*, "the constant presence of form on the stage is the moving spirit of the play", as Gombrowicz noted. One thing creates another, one single gesture or word can have unforeseeable consequences. People are the creators of forms, but they themselves are manipulated by the discreet terror of form. In a sense, *The Marriage* is a parody of Shakespeare's

Hamlet, but it is a parody informed by the savage humour of Alfred Jarry and by the excesses of modern totalitarianism.

Between *The Marriage* and Gombrowicz's third and last play, *Operetka (Operetta)*, there is a fragment of a play called *Historia* (History), first published in the Paris *Kultura* (1975). Here Gombrowicz goes back to the root of all modern conflicts, the dominance of form over people. World wars break out because leaders cannot discard their traditional roles; they cannot "step out" of their shoes, or more appropriately, boots.

The "brotherhood of feet" camouflaged by a variety of footwear is one of the leitmotifs of *Operetta* too. This tragicomedy, in three acts, opens with a highly stylish parody of the "ancien régime", symbolized by Prince Himalay's castle. While the young rake Count Charmant plans the seduction of lovely (but bourgeois) Albertine (Albertynka), Prince Himalay is visited by Master Fior, "the universal dictator of fashion". At the suggestion of Count Hufnagel, a grand masquerade ball is planned, at the culmination of which the participants, masking themselves with sacks, will reveal their designs—the fashion of the future. Hufnagel, in fact, is no Count but Joseph, the Prince's former valet in disguise, whose aim is to sow confusion and bring about a revolution.

At the ball, Count Charmant's rivalry with Baron Firulet causes disaster. In an attempt "to awake" Albertine (who is overdressed and dreams of nudity, so keeps falling asleep) they unleash their respective pickpockets on the unsuspecting guests. The "uninhibited touch" of the pickpockets creates panic and anarchy, and finally Hufnagel takes off his mask and gallops forth at the head of the lackeys. Revolution sweeps away the old order. Its results become frighteningly clear in Act III: the cold wind of history is blowing, and people dress up in the weirdest ways. People are distorted and reified—they are turned into things by the "gallopers" of history, by fascism and communism.

The change of tone here is radical: Offenbach giving way to something nearer the world of Beckett. Yet Gombrowicz's historically justified pessimism is mitigated by his belief in man's biological brotherhood. *Operetta* ends with the apotheosis of the naked Albertine. She is believed to be dead and her coffin is carried about by two gravediggers who at one point throw off their masks and are identified as the pickpockets of the previous acts. Now she steps out of her coffin and shows herself in her brilliant nudity while the Choir sings: "O nudity eternally youthful, hail!". In conclusion, Gombrowicz expresses his faith in mankind's eternal capacity to start anew in spite of successive cataclysms that shake and ruin his world. *Operetta* received its first French production by Theâtre National Populaire, and has since been staged many times in Europe and the USA.

—George Gömöri

See also *Volume 1* entry on *Marriage*.

GOMES, Alfredo (de Freitas) Dias. Born in Salvador, Bahia, Brazil, 19 October 1922. Studied law in Rio de Janeiro, but did not complete studies. Married novelist Janette Clair. Began writing plays at the age of 15; wrote for radio and television during the 1950's; returned to playwriting in the 1960's; television producer in São Paulo and Rio de Janeiro. Recipient of many awards, including: Prêmio Nacional de Teatro, 1960; Palme d'Or (France), 1960; Prêmio Cláudio Souza, 1961 and 1962; Prêmio Padre Ventura, 1962.

Works

Collections

Teatro (2 vols.; includes *O Pagador de Promessas; A Invasão; A Revolução dos Beatos; Odorico, o Bem-Amado; O Berço do Herói; O Santo Inquérito; Dr. Getúlio, Sua Vida e Sua Glória; O Túnel; Vamos Soltar os Demonios*).   1972.

Stage Works

Pé-de-Cabra (produced 1942?).
Amanha Será Outro Dia (produced Teatro Brasileiro de Comédia, São Paulo, 1943).
João Cambão (produced 1943).
Doutor Ninguém (produced as *Sulamita*, 1945).
Zeca Diabo.   1944?
Cinco Fugitivos do Juizo Final.   1944?
O Pagador de Promessas (produced Teatro Brasileiro de Comédia, São Paulo, 1960).   1960; in *Teatro*, 1972; translated as *Payment as Pledged*, in *The Modern Stage in Latin America: Six Plays*, 1971, edited by George Woodyard.
A Invasão (produced Teatro do Rio, Rio de Janeiro, 1962). In *Teatro*, 1972.
A Revolução dos Beatos (produced Teatro Brasileiro de Comédia, São Paulo, 1962).   1962; in *Teatro*, 1972.
O Berço de Herói (produced Teatro Princesa Isabel, Rio de Janeiro, 1965?).   1965.
O Santo Inquérito (produced Teatro Jovem, Rio de Janeiro, 1966).   1966; second edition, 1976.
Dr. Getúlio, Sua Vida e Sua Glória, with Ferreira Gullar (produced Teatro Leopoldina, Pôrto Alegre, Brasil, 1968). 1968; second edition, as *Vargas; ou, Dr. Getúlio, Sua Vida e Sua Glória*, 1983.
Odorico, o Bem-Amado; ou, Uma Obra do Govêrno (produced Teatro Santo Isabel, Recife, Brasil, 1969). In *Teatro*, 1972.
O Túnel.   In *Teatro*, 1972.
Vamos Soltar os Demônios.   In *Teatro*, 1972.
As Primícias.   1978.
Campeões do Mundo.   1980.
O Re de Ramos.   1980.
Amor em Campo Minado.   1984.

Screenplays

Um Caso de Polícia, 1959; *O Pagador de Promessas*, 1962; *O Marginal*, 1974.

Television Plays

O Bem-Amado, 1980.

Radio Plays

Sinhazinha, 1945 (published 1945); *O Homen que Não Era Seu*, 1948 (published 1948).

Fiction

Sucupira, Ame-a ou Deixa (stories).   1982.
Odorico na Cabeça (stories).   1983.

*

Criticism

Books:
Décio de Almeida Prado, *Teatro em Progresso*, Sao Paulo, 1964.
Leon F. Lyday, "The Theater of Alfredo Dias Gomes", in *Dramatists in Revolt: The New Latin American Theater*, edited by Leon F. Lyday and George Woodyard, Austin, Texas, 1976.
Anatol Rosenfeld, *O Mito e o Herói no Moderno Teatro Brasiliero*, Rio de Janeiro, 1982.

Articles:
Richard A. Mazzara, "Alfredo Dias Gomes, Social Commentator and Artist", in *Latin American Theatre Review*, 2, 1969.
Dale S. Bailey, *O Pagador de Promessas*: A Brazilian Morality", in *Latin American Theatre Review*, 6, 1972.
Leon F. Lyday, "*O Pagador de Promessas* and *Berço do Herói*: Variations on a Theme", in *Romance Notes*, 14, 1972.
Fred Clark, "Society and the Alienated Man in Two Plays of Alfredo Dias Gomes [*O Pagador de Promessas; O Berço do Herói*]", in *Romance Notes*, 16, 1975.

*   *   *

Alfredo Dias Gomes stands as one of the most prominent contemporary social commentators of Brazilian theatre, whose writing demonstrates a clear cultural and political mission. Beginning with *O Pagador de Promessas*, Dias Gomes presents the evil forces in society revealed through caricature-like types. The play, with its classical approach and artistic interest, demonstrates the social appeal for which it won so many international awards. Dias Gomes uses elements of popular culture and employs many theatrical structures and styles. Many of his plays are adaptations of historical subjects to portray human truths and social preoccupations. The inability of the protagonists to communicate comes across as cruel and pathetic in Dias Gomes's theatre. He sees language, not as a thread which connects human beings, but rather as an invisible wall of misunderstanding and possible destruction.

The anti-clericalism in his theatre is seen most effectively in *O Pagador de Promessas* and *O Santo Inquérito*. In *O Pagador de Promessas* society serves as the dehumanizing force which sets up the conflict between the individual and the church, which, while professing to be accessible to its parishioners, ultimately denies them their freedom. The main protagonist, Zé-do-burro, unwittingly becomes the hero who refuses to budge in his firm belief that truth will win. Despite the forces that destroy him, he is victorious in death, achieving what was denied him in life.

If *O Pagador* suggests popular mysticism through its dialogue and religious syncretism, *A Revolução dos Beatos* presents a vision of religious fanaticism. A more impressionistic and complex drama, *A Revolução* combines epic, chronicle, and documentary contexts with personal episodes; it is light in tone with occasional farce and satire throughout. Dias Gomes has departed from the realism of previous plays and leaned towards a more expressionistic style. In both works, an animal plays an important part. In *Revolução*, the donkey of *O Pagador* is replaced by an ox, whose personalized behaviour and antics form the thread that holds the play together. Dias Gomes presents a negative mental and moral picture of Father Cícero, a man who hesitates, incapable of making decisions, easily led by a political character who manipulates

not only the priest, but the people too. Basing the play on historical fact, Dias Gomes interweaves reality and fantasy to create an imaginative interpretation of real events. Where in *O Pagador* the main character achieves salvation through death, it is unclear whether the protagonists in *A Revolução* can reform either themselves or their society.

Dias Gomes refers to *Odorico, o Bem Amado* as a socio-politico-pathological farce. A black comedy, the play concerns the political fortunes of Odorico, the town's newly elected mayor, who has won with a campaign to build a cemetery. No one in the town dies; even those on the brink recover or reform, and the one person murdered is buried in her home town rather than in Odorico's cemetery. In an attempt to regain his political clout, he fakes an attack on his life, accidentally killing himself, thus becoming the cemetery's first inhabitant. As in previous plays, the individual is always subordinate to the larger collective, yet in this play the theme is treated much more lightly, providing a basis for political satire and farce.

In *Berço de Herói*, Dias Gomes blends a more pessimistic view with the political satire and expressionistic techniques seen in his previous plays. Influenced by Ibsen's *An Enemy of the People*, and not unlike *O Pagador* in its theme, *Berço de Herói* presents the conflict of a man defending the truth and faced with compromises forced upon him by the town. Its attacks on both the church and the military have served to ensure that the play has been banned from production to date. Nevertheless, the play demonstrates Dias Gomes's technical mastery, as he uses multiple staging and mixed media to drive home his satirical point of view, evident in his use of the classical chorus to comment on the plot and the concept of heroism.

Later plays, such as *O Santo Inquérito* and *Dr. Getúlio, Sua Vida e Sua Glória*, make use of surrealistic innovations, as Dias Gomes has experimented with structure and techniques, mixing verse and prose. His two later works, *O Túnel* and *Vamos Soltar os Demônios*, are not as well written as his earlier plays, even though Dias Gomes continues to experiment with technical aspects. The latter play includes game-playing and other techniques popularized in the theatre of the 1960's.

Dias Gomes's recurring theme of the individual seeking freedom in a continually oppressive society is presented in a variety of ways: *O Pagador de Promessas* is realistic in style; *O Berço do Herói* is expressionistic and satirical; *O Santo Inquérito* is a historical drama in surrealistic manner; and *Dr. Getúlio*, also based on history and legend, is lighthearted, presented as a play-within-a-play. Considered along with Jorge Andrade as among Brazil's foremost playwrights, Dias Gomes continues to grow as a playwright, experimenting in style and technique with each new work.

—Lynn Carbón Gorell

GORKY, Maxim. Born Alexei Maximovich Peshkov in Nizhny Novgorod (now Gorky), Russia, 16 March 1868 (28 March, New Style). Educated in parish school, Nizhny Novgorod; Kumavino elementary school, 1877–78. Married Yekaterina Pavlovna Volzhina in 1896 (separated); one son and one daughter. Apprenticed to a shoemaker at age 12; various jobs, including apprentice to icon painter, and cook's boy on a

Volga steamer; arrested for involvement in revolutionary politics, 1889; travelled to the Caucasus, 1891, and worked there on the railways; published first story in the Tbilisi newspaper *Kavkaz*, 1892; began publishing in prominent journals by the mid 1890's; literary editor, *Zhizn'* [Life], St. Petersburg, from 1899; worked for the publishing house Znanie, 1900, and was subsequently its leading editor; exiled to Arzamas, central Russia, for involvement with a covert printing press, 1901; first-produced play, *Na dne* [*The Lower Depths*], staged 1902; joined the Bolshevik party, 1905; travelled to the USA, 1906; lived in Capri, 1906–13; following the declaration of a general amnesty, returned to Russia, 1913; founding editor, *Letopis* [Chronicles], 1915–17; contributed observations on the October Revolution to Menshevik newspaper *Noyaya zhizn* [New Life], 1917–18; co-founder, the publishing house Vsemirnaya Literatura [World Literature]; left Russia, 1921, partly for health reasons, and lived in Germany and Czechoslovakia, before settling in Sorrento, Italy; visited Russia, 1928 and 1929, and re-settled there, 1931; editor, of the periodical "Literary Apprenticeship", 1933; helped set up the Biblioteka Poeta [Poet's Library] publishing project; travelled widely throughout the USSR; took a leading role at the All-Union Congress of Soviet Writers, 1934, and was associated with the implementation of Socialist Realism as the artistic orthodoxy. Recipient: Order of Lenin. Gorky Literary Institute established in his honour. Died in Moscow, 18 June 1936.

Works

Collections

The Last Plays (translations; includes *Yegor Bulichoff and Others; Dostigaeff and the Others*).   1937.
Seven Plays (includes *Barbarians; Enemies; Vassa Zheleznova (Mother); The Lower Depths; Queer People; The Zykovs; Yegor Bulychov and Others*), translated by A. Bakshy and Paul Nathan.   1945.
Polnoe sobranie sochineny [Complete Collected Works] (25 vols.).   1968–76.
Sobranie sochineny [Collected Works] (16 vols.).   1979.
Collected Works (translations; 10 vols.; Volume 4, *Plays*, includes *The Petty Bourgeois; The Lower Depths; Summer Folk; Enemies; Yegor Bulychov and Others; Vassa Zheleznova*—second version).   1978–82 (Moscow).
Five Plays (includes *The Lower Depths; Summerfolk; Children of the Sun; Barbarians; Enemies*), translated by Jeremy Brooks and Kitty Hunter-Blair, edited by Edward Braun.   1988.

Stage Works

Meshchane (produced Moscow Art Theatre, 1902).   1902; translated as *The Smug Citizens*, 1906; as *The Courageous One*, 1958; as *The Petty Bourgeois*, in *Collected Works 4*, 1979.
Na dne (produced Moscow Art Theatre, 1902).   1903; translated as *A Night's Lodging*, 1905; as *The Lower Depths*, 1912; as *Submerged*, 1914; as *At the Bottom*, 1930.
Dachniki (produced Vera Komissarzhevskaya's Theatre, St. Petersburg, 1904).   1904; translated as *Summerfolk*, 1975.
Varvary (produced Berlin, 1906).   1905; translated as *Barbarians*, in *Seven Plays*, 1945.
Deti solntsa (produced Vera Kommissarzhevskaya's Theatre, St. Petersburg, 1905).   1905; translated as *Children of the Sun*, 1912.

Vragi (produced Reinhardt's Theatre, Berlin, 1907; first Russian production, State Academic Theatre, Leningrad, 1933).   1906; translated as *Enemies*, in *Seven Plays*, 1945.
Poslednie [The Last Ones] (produced in the Russian provinces, 1908).   1908.
Vstrecha [The Meeting] (produced 1910).   1910.
Vassa Zheleznova (produced 1911).   1910; revised version, 1935; translated as *Vassa Zheleznova*, in *Seven Plays*, 1945.
Chudaki (produced 1910).   1910; translated as *Queer People*, in *Seven Plays*, 1945.
Zykovy (produced 1918).   1913; translated as *The Zykovs*, in *Seven Plays*, 1945.
Starik (produced Maly Theatre, Moscow, 1919).   1915; translated as *The Judge*, 1924; as *The Old Man*, 1956.
Somov i drugiye [Somov and the Others].   1931.
Yegor Bulychov i drugiye (produced 1932).   1932; translated as *Yegor Bulichoff and Others*, in *The Last Plays*, 1937; as *Yegor Bulychov and Others*, in *Seven Plays*, 1945.
Dostigayev i drugiye (produced 1934).   1933; translated as *Dostigaeff and the Others*, in *The Last Plays*, 1937.

Fiction

Ocherki i rasskazy (3 vols.).   1898–99; translated as *Tales*, 1902.
Foma Gordeyev.   1899; translated as *Foma Gordeyev*, 1902; as *The Man Who Was Afraid*, 1905; as *Foma*, 1945.
Troye.   1900; translated as *Three of Them*, 1902; as *Three Men*, 1902; as *The Three*, 1958.
"Orloff" and His Wife: Tales of the Barefoot Brigade.   1901.
"Chelkash" and Other Stories.   1902.
"The Outcasts" and Other Stories.   1902.
"Twenty-Six Men and a Girl" and Other Stories.   1902.
Mat'.   1906; translated as *Mother*, 1907; as *Comrades*, 1907.
Zhizn nenuzhnovo cheloveka.   1907–08; translated as *The Spy: The Story of a Superfluous Man*. 1908; as *The Life of a Useless Man*, 1971.
Ispoved.   1908; translated as *A Confession*, 1909.
Gorodok Okurov [Okurov City].   1909.
Leto [Summer].   1909.
Zhizn Matveya Kozhemyakina.   1910–11; translated as *The Life of Matvei Kozhemyakin*, 1959.
Tales of Two Countries.   1914.
Creatures That Once Were Men.   1918.
Zhizn Klima Samgina. 1925–36; translated as *The Bystander, The Magnet, Other Fires*, and *The Spectre* (4 vols.).   1938.
A Book of Short Stories, edited by A. Yarmolinsky and M. Bulberg.   1939.
Delo Artamonovykh.   1925; translated as *Decadence*, 1927; as *The Artamanov Business*, 1948; as *The Artamanovs*, 1952.
"Unrequited Love" and Other Stories.   1949.
Selected Stories (Volume 1 of *Collected Works*).   1978.

Verse

Pesnya o Burevestnike.   1901.
Chelovek.   1902.
Devushka i smert.   1917.

Memoirs and Letters

Detstvo V lyudakh, Moi universitety.   1913–22; translated as *My Childhood In the World [My Apprenticeship], My University Days [My Universities]*, 1915–23; as *Autobiography*, 1949.

Vospominaniya. 1923; translated as *Reminiscences*, 1946.
Zametki iz dnevnika. 1924; as *Fragments from My Diary*, 1924.
Letters of Gorky and Andreev 1899–1912, edited P. Yerschov. 1958.

Other

A.P. Chekhov. 1905; translated as *Anton Tchekhov: Fragments of Recollections*, 1921.
Vospominaniya o Tolstoi. 1919; translated as *Reminiscences of Tolstoy*, 1920.
Revolyutsiya i kultura [Revolution and Culture]. 1920.
O russkom krestyanstve [On the Russian Peasantry]. 1922.
On Guard for the Soviet Union. 1933.
V.I. Lenin. 1924; translated as *V.I. Lenin*, 1931; as *Days with Lenin*, 1933.
Reminiscences of Leonid Andreyev. 1928.
O literature. 1933; revised edition, 1935, 1955; translated as *On Literature: Selected Articles*, 1958.
Culture and the People. 1940.
Creative Labour and Culture. 1945.
Literature and Life: A Selection from the Writings, edited by E. Bone. 1946.
History of the Civil War in the USSR, volume 2: The Great Proletarian Revolution, October-November 1917. 1947.
F.I. Chaliapin (2 vols.). 1957–58; translated as *Chaliapin: An Autobiography*, edited by Nina Froud and James Hanley, 1967.
Nesvoyevremennye mysli. 1971; translated as *Untimely Thoughts*, edited and translated by Herman Ermolaev, 1968.

*

Bibliographies

E. Czikowsky, Ilse Idzikowski, and G. Schwartz, *Maxim Gorky in Deutschland: Bibliographie 1899 bis 1965*, Berlin, 1968.
Garth M. Terry, *Maxim Gorky in English: A Bibliography, 1868–1986*, Cotgrave, England, 1986.
Edith W. Clowes, *Maksim Gorky: A Reference Guide*, Boston, 1987.

Criticism

Books:
Alexander Kaun, *Maxim Gorky and His Russia*, 1931.
F. Holtzman, *The Young Maxim Gorky*, New York, 1948.
N. Gourfinkel (ed.), *Maxim Gorky in Selbstzeugnissen und Bilddokumenten*, Reinbek, 1958.
Richard Hare, *Maxim Gorky: Romantic Realist and Conservative Revolutionary*, London, 1962.
Dan Levin, *Stormy Petrel: The Life and Work of Maxim Gorky*, New York, 1965.
I. Weil, *Gorky: His Literary Development and Influence on Soviet Intellectual Life*, New York, 1966.
Bertram D. Wolfe, *The Bridge and the Abyss: The Troubled Friendship of Maxim Gorky and V.I. Lenin*, New York, 1967.
F.M. Borras, *Maxim Gorky, The Writer: An Interpretation*, Oxford, 1967.
Ralf Schröder (ed.), *Mit der Menschheit auf du und du: Schriftsteller der Welt über Gorky*, Berlin, 1968.
Ilse Stauche (ed.), *Maxim Gorki: Drama und Theater* (essay collection), Berlin, 1968.

Gerhard E. Habermann, *Maxim Gorky* (from the German), New York, 1971.
Henning Rischbieter, *Maxim Gorki*, Velber, 1973.
Nadeshda Ludwig, *Maxim Gorki: Leben und Werk*, Berlin, 1984.
Robert Russell, *Russian Drama of the Revolutionary Period*, Totowa, New Jersey, 1988.
Barry P. Scherr, *Maxim Gorky*, Boston, 1988.
Galina Belaya (ed.), *Gorky and His Contemporaries: Memoirs and Letters*, Moscow, 1989.
Henri Troyat, *Gorky* (biography, from the French), New York, 1989.

Articles

Nicholas Moravcevich, "Gorky and the Western Naturalists: Anatomy of a Misalliance", in *Comparative Literature*, 21, 1969.
Daniel C. Gerould, "Gorky, Melodrama, and the Development of Early Soviet Theatre", in *Yale/Theatre*, vol. 7 no. 2, 1976.
Yael Harussi, "Realism in Drama: Turgenev, Chekhov, Gorky and Their Summer Folk", in *Ulbandus Review*, vol. 2 no. 2, 1982.

* * *

A true assessment of Gorky the writer has long been vitiated by the legend of Gorky the man. An autodidact emerging from Russia's lower depths, he survived the poverty and barbarity of a provincial childhood, and the precarious wanderings of a rootless adolescence, to become a national celebrity at 30. His collected short stories revealed a new literary and social phenomenon, personifying romantic revolt. Gorky's pre-revolutionary reputation was rapidly clouded by his increasing commitment to radical politics, which earned him imprisonment and exile, crucially dividing his readers according to their political sympathies. This polarisation persisted after the 1917 October Revolution, and was complicated by Gorky's ambivalence towards Bolshevism. Following his death in Stalin's Russia in 1936, Gorky was virtually canonised in the Soviet Union as an unassailable writer of classics, the father of Soviet literature and founder of Socialist Realism. In the West, by contrast, critics approached his works warily, suspecting an artificially inflated mediocrity. Only recently did Gorbachovian *glasnost* and greater Western objectivity allow a more dispassionate evaluation.

These biographical and historical factors must be borne in mind when considering the nature of Gorky's plays. A writer with his life's experience and political leanings was incapable of producing drama akin to that of the Russian symbolists, with their emphasis on the illusory and the transcendental, on musicality, theatricality, and stylisation. The psychological and atmospheric subtlety of Chekhov's theatre, multi-faceted, tragi-comic, and undidactic, was likewise unsuited to Gorky's intentions. Although he frequently borrowed the outer format of Chekhov's plays (a four-act family drama with numerous characters and a realistic setting), Gorky focused the dramatic interest on socio-political problems, instead of the vaguer, more "universal" yearnings of Chekhov's characters. Whereas Chekhov posed questions, Gorky tended to propose, or even impose, solutions.

The result was a sequence of predominantly topical plays, written between 1901 and 1935, treating serious socio-political issues in a forthright and forceful manner. As with many "political plays", however, where the revolutionary content is not matched by formal innovation, the explicit didactic message and somewhat two-dimensional characters (villains, heroes, and waverers—black, white, and grey) may appear predictable and dated with the passage of time. Nevertheless, if not a master of literary style, psychological nuance, and metaphysical profundity, Gorky did portray personalities, ideas, and aspirations powerfully.

Gorky's theatrical debut in 1902 was a direct result of encouragement from Chekhov and Stanislavsky. His first play, *Meshchane* (Philistines, or *The Petty Bourgeois*) received its premiere at the Moscow Arts Theatre in March 1902, after preliminary mutilation by the censor. A savage indictment of narrow-minded petty-bourgeois provincialism, "Philistines" highlights the conflict between Vasily Bessemenov, an energetic, prosperous, but blinkered house-painter, and his dispirited, disaffected children—the aimlessly drifting Petr, and suicidally despondent Tatyana. Gorky's hope for Russia's future is embodied in the hearty engine-driver, Nil, and his virtuous sweetheart, Polya. Nil's man-size love of life and socialistic slogans are tediously schematic, but the drama is enlivened by the ambivalently depicted Vasily (Gorky admired strong men, even if they came from the "wrong" class), incessant quarrels, and colourful cameo roles, such as Perchikhin and Teterev. Chekhov, who found the play "very interesting", despite the "conservatism of its form", credited Gorky with being "the first in Russia, and in the world at large, to express disdain and disgust towards philistinism".

In December 1902 the Moscow Arts Theatre staged Gorky's most famous play, *Na dne* (*The Lower Depths*), a philosophical drama about truth and lies, reality and illusion, featuring tramps in a seedy dosshouse. The "consoling lie" of Luka, an enigmatic, elderly wanderer, is opposed to the grandiloquent humanist hymn of Satin ("Man is the truth!"). Although Gorky's political sympathies lay with Satin, he was fascinated by the escapist lure of Luka, and audiences ever since have responded freely to the play's central ambiguity.

Gorky was never able to repeat the phenomenal success of *The Lower Depths*. His next plays—*Dachniki* (*Summerfolk*), *Deti solntsa* (*Children of the Sun*), and *Varvary* (*Barbarians*) —are undoubtedly of historical interest, in depicting, for instance, the intelligentsia's confusion around the time of the 1905 revolution, but their large casts, fragmented plots, and inconsequential dialogue render them unsatisfactory as theatrical experiences.

Gorky fared little better when displaying the class conflict between factory owners and socialist workers in *Vragi* (*Enemies*), which was banned from the Tsarist stage. The ruthless capitalist, Mikhail Skrobotov, and pseudo-liberal, Zakhar Bardin, are predictably negative types, while the united socialists remain insubstantial shadows. Greater dramatic potential resides in the undeveloped drifters, Yakov and Tatyana. In his denunciatory article "The End of Gorky", the critic Dmitri Filosofov blamed "success and naive, ill-considered socialism" for the writer's decline in such works as *Barbarians* and *Enemies*. Certainly, when produced at Moscow's Malaya Bronnaya Theatre in 1981, *Enemies* resembled a ritual exhumation rather than a dramatic performance.

The plays of Gorky's middle period (1908–17) have been largely ignored in the West, although Barry P. Scherr has recently indicated their originality. *Zykovy* (*The Zykovs*), a historical and philosophical morality, reveals Gorky's admiration for a strong self-made businessman, Antipa Zykov.

Throughout the 1920's Gorky neglected the theatre, and the theatre neglected Gorky. Only in the 1930's did Soviet companies rediscover his early works, and Gorky resumed writing plays. Two of his better efforts belong to this final period. *Yegor Bulychov i drugie* (*Yegor Bulychov and Others*) powerfully presents, in its title figure, a vigorous merchant dying of cancer, his terminal illness coinciding symbolically with the last days of capitalism and the Tsarist regime. While relatives vie for his inheritance, the sympathetically portrayed Yegor regrets his mis-spent life, and routs various quacks and shady representatives of the church. *Yegor Bulychov*, with its major central role and colourful minor parts, is an impressive evocation of individual and historical death. In 1935 Gorky reworked his earlier play *Vassa Zheleznova* into a stark, unsubtle melodrama, exposing the depravity of the Zheleznov family and business. Vassa herself completes Gorky's gallery of misguided individuals admired for their strength; her dream of a capitalist dynasty is defeated by her daughter-in-law, the schematic socialist, Rachel.

Although scarcely to be ranked among Russia's greatest playwrights, Gorky should not be dismissed (in D.S. Mirsky's words) as "nothing but a bad disciple of Chekhov". The scholarly investigations of Barry P. Scherr and Robert Russell, and the pioneering productions of Britain's Royal Shakespeare Company, have demonstrated the vitality of his best creations.

—Gordon McVay

See also *Volume 1* entries on *The Lower Depths*; *Summerfolk*.

GOZZI, Carlo . Born in Venice, 13 December 1720. Educated privately. Military service in Dalmatia, 1741–44. Began literary career as writer of poetry and satire; co-founder, with his brother, the conservative literary group Accademia degli Granelleschi in the 1740's; began polemical campaign against the bourgeois, realistic drama of fellow Venetian playwright Carlo Goldoni in the 1750's; the first of his *fiabe*, *Il corvo*, performed by Antonio Sacchi's company, 1761; wrote ten *fiabe* for Sacchi's company, 1761–76; in later years, worked chiefly on his memoirs. Also wrote adaptations, mainly of Spanish plays by Calderón, Agustín de Moreto y Cabaña, Tirso de Molina, and other authors. Died in Venice, 4 April 1806.

Works

Collections

Opere (8 vols.).   1772–74.
Opere edite e unedite (14 vols.).   1801–02.
Scritti, edited by Ettore Bonora.   1951; second edition, 1977.
Opere: Teatro e polemiche teatrali, edited by G. Petronio.   1962.
Fiabe teatrali, edited by Paulo Bosisio.   1984.
The Love of Three Oranges; Turandot; The Snake Lady, translated by John L. Di Gaetani.   1988.
Five Tales for the Theatre (includes *The Raven; The King Stag; Turandot; The Serpent Woman; The Green Bird*), translated by Albert Bermel and Ted Emery.   1989.

Stage Works

Gozzi's plays were published in the collected editions *Opere*, 1772–74 (includes all the *fiabe*), and *Opere edite e unedite*, 1801–02.

Carlo Gozzi (engraving).

Doride; ossia, La rassegnata, from a play by A. Firenzuola (produced Mantua, 1762).

L'amore delle tre melarance (produced Teatro San Samuele, Venice, 1761). Translated as *The Love of Three Oranges*, in *The Love of Three Oranges . . .* (collection), 1988.

Il corvo (produced Teatro Regio, Milan, 1761). Translated as *The Raven*, in *Five Tales for the Theatre*, 1989.

Il cavaliere; ossia, Il trionfo dell'amicizia (produced Mantua, 1762). 1774.

Il re cervo (produced Teatro San Samuele, Venice, 1762). In *Opere*, 1772–74; translated as *The King Stag*, in *The Classic Theatre, 1*, edited by Eric Bentley, 1958, and in *Five Tales for the Theatre*, 1989.

Turandot (produced Teatro San Samuele, Venice, 1762). Translated as *Turandot*, 1836: several subsequent translations under same title.

La donna serpente (produced Teatro Sant'Angelo, Venice, 1762). Translated as *The Snake Lady*, in *The Love of Three Oranges . . .* (collection), 1988; as *The Serpent Woman*, in *Five Tales for the Theatre*, 1989.

La Zobeide (produced Turin, 1763).

I pitocchi fortunati (produced Parma, 1763).

Il mostro turchino (produced Teatro Sant'Angelo, Venice, 1764). Translated as *The Blue Monster*, 1951.

L'augellin belverde (produced Teatro Sant'Angelo, Venice, 1765). Translated as *The Green Bird*, in *Five Tales for the Theatre*, 1989.

Zeim, re dei genii (produced Teatro Sant'Angelo, Venice, 1765).

La donna vendicativa disarmata dall'obbligazione, from a work by Diego and José Figueroa de Córdova (produced Teatro Sant'Angelo, Venice, 1767).

La caduta di donna Elvira, regina di Navarra, from a work by J. de Matos Fragoso (produced Teatro Sant'Angelo, Venice, 1768).

La punizione nel precipizio, from a work by J. de Matos Fragoso (produced Teatro Sant'Angelo, Venice, 1768).

Il pubblico secreto, from a play by Calderón (produced Modena, 1769).

La vedova del Malabar; ossia, L'impero de'costumi, from a play by Antoine-Marin Le Mière (produced by the Sacchi company, 1770).

Le due notti affannose; ossia, Gl'inganni dell'immaginazione, from a play by Calderón (produced Teatro San Salvatore, Venice, 1771).

La donna innamorata davvero, from a play by Cervantes (produced Mantua, 1771).

La principessa filosofa; ossia, Il contravvelno, from a play by Agustín de Moreto (produced Teatro San Salvatore, Venice, 1772).

I due fratelli nimici, from a play by Agustín de Moreto y Cabaña (produced Teatro San Salvatore, Venice, 1773).

La malia della voce, from a play by Agustín de Moreto y Cabaña (produced Teatro San Samuele, Venice, 1774).

Il moro di corpo bianco; ossia, Lo schiavo del proprio onore (adaptation; produced Teatro San Luca, Venice, 1775).

Le droghe d'amore, from a play by Tirso de Molina (produced Venice, 1777).

Il metafisico; ossia, L'amore e l'amicizia alla prova, from a play by Tirso de Molina (produced Teatro San Salvatore, Venice, 1778).

Bianca contessa di Melfi; ossia, Il maritaggio per vendetta, from a play by Ferando de Rojas Zorilla (produced Teatro San Luca, Venice, 1779).

Amore assottiglia il cervello, from a play by Caninarez (produced Teatro San Giovanni Crisostomo, Venice, 1781).

La figlia dell'aria; ossia, L'innalzamento di Semiramide, from a play by Calderón (produced Teatro San Salvatore, Venice, 1786).

Cimene Pardo (adaptation; produced Teatro San Giovanni Crisostomo, Venice, 1786).

Annibale duca d'Atene, from a play by Agustín de Moreto y Cabaña (produced Teatro Sant'Angelo, Venice, 1799).

La donna contraria al consiglio (produced by the Pellandi company, Trieste, 1800).

Verse

Marfisa bizzarro. 1772.

Memoirs and Letters

Memorie inutile della vita di C.G. (3 vols.). 1797; translated as *The Useless Memoirs of Count Carlo Gozzi* (2 vols.), 1890.

*

Bibliographies

G. Perale, "Bibliografia essenziale critica di Carlo Gozzi", in *Ateneo veneto*, 131, 1940.

Criticism

Books:

G.B. Magrini, *I tempi, la vita e gli scritti di Carlo Gozzi*, Benevento, 1883.

E. Borghesani, *Carlo Gozzi e l'opera sua*, Udine, 1904.

B. Cestaro, *Carlo Gozzi*, Turin, 1932.

H. Feldmann, *Die Fiabe Carlo Gozzis: Die Entstehung einer Gattung und ihre Transposition in das System der deutschen Romantik*, Cologne and Vienna, 1971.

G. Luciani, *Carlo Gozzi: L'Homme et l'oeuvre* (2 vols.; includes bibliography), Paris, 1977.

P. Bosisio, *Carlo Gozzi e Goldoni: Une polemica letteraria con versi inediti e rari*, Florence, 1979.

A. Beniscelli, *La finzione del fiabesco*, Casale Monferrato, 1986.

Kenneth and Laura Richards, *The Commedia dell'Arte: A Documentary History*, Oxford, 1990.

*   *   *

Although engaged in literary activities in Venice from the mid 1740's when he left the army, it was not until some 10 years later that Gozzi began to emerge as a writer of significance. His early forte was verse satire, expressing his hostility to the bourgeois, realistic, and reformist tendencies of contemporary writers, for he was vigorously hostile to Enlightenment ideas, and a champion of aristocratic decorum and linguistic purity. Gozzi's conservative views were formed early and they conditioned virtually all his literary output, but notably his early non-dramatic literary polemics: in 1757, for example, he produced a long satirical poem "The Tartane: An Almanack of Influences for the Leap Year 1756", aimed broadly at new-fangled movements, but directed more particularly at two of the most popular and influential dramatists of the day, Pietri Chiari and Carlo Goldoni. He disliked their preference for scripted drama over the improvised, the natural over the artistically contrived, the values of the bourgeoisie over those of the aristocracy. The intense literary imbroglios with which he was engaged were bitter and hard-fought, and the Venetian government was finally obliged to intervene.

In the early 1760's Gozzi very deliberately sought to counter the influence of Goldoni by devising a drama of his own concerned to restore to the stage the masks and improvisation of the traditional *commedia dell'arte*, supposedly undermined by the Goldonian reform of comedy. Gozzi deplored this Goldonian reform, and against Goldoni's stylised, yet often quasi-realistic, depictions of Venetian society, family, and street life, he set his highly imaginative *fiabe*. They are fantastic and scenically spectacular romances, which wedded the comic strategies and masked figures of the improvised drama to the fairy-tale materials of exotic oriental stories. Goldoni had capitalised in the mid-1750's on the Venetian taste for tales of the mysterious East; in a sense, then, he had prepared the way for Gozzi's highly exotic theatrical concoctions, which proved equally successful in the 1760's—so much so, it is said, that they helped to drive Goldoni from Venice.

Underpinning Gozzi's work was his hostility to the local realism, the scenographic simplicity, and the idiomatic language of Goldoni's new comedy, which, in his eyes, breached artistic decorum by mingling characters of high and low social condition, extolled the virtues and values of the Venetian bourgeoisie, indulged in mere sentimentality, and, in banishing the techniques and figures of the improvised drama, banished, too, imagination and invention from the stage. Oddly, however, notwithstanding that his plays championed the improvised drama, they are very wordy pieces, replete with rather heavy and rhetorical dialogue, the more evident in Gozzi's delight in exploiting a wide variety of Italian dialects, notably Venetian and Begamask, in addition to the formal Tuscan.

The best of his comedies undeniably have a certain charm, both in the fanciful story-lines as well as in the rather engaging mingling of exotic figures and the masks of the *commedia dell'arte*, and in the curious mixture of satire, imaginative fantasy, farcical "business", and whimsical comedy. But unfortunately there is little that is profound in this drama, and Gozzi was quite simply not sufficiently a poet of the theatre to carry off effectively his ambitious project.

Much of Gozzi's work was a product of his 25-year association with one of the best Venetian acting companies of the 18th century, the troupe of Antonio Sacchi. For them he composed the most enduring of his works, the *fiabe*, ten of which he wrote between 1761 and 1776, including *L'amore delle tre melarance* (*The Love of Three Oranges*), *Il corvo* (*The Raven*), *Il re cervo* (*The King Stag*), *Turandot*, and *La donna serpente* (*The Snake Lady*): pieces in which he translated the masked figures to a courtly world of kings, aristocrats, and *magi*. His plays enjoyed an immediate vogue, were later to be taken up as precursors of the Romantic movement, and as libretti were set by many opera composers. But, as plays in their own right, they have little depth, and although Gozzi was certainly a champion of theatricalism in the theatre, it was largely in the service of decoration, and the picturesqueness and grotesquerie of his plays are in many respects an extension of elements latent in some of the depictions of *commedia dell'arte* figures found in contemporary paintings and ceramics. Gozzi did not succeed in restoring the improvised drama. He later wrote tragicomedies, which drew plot materials and inspiration from Spanish drama, and which seem to have been an unavailing attempt to reassert the courtly values of the aristocratic past.

Gozzi's witty and waspish memoirs, *Memorie inutile*, are a mine of information on the 18th-century Venetian theatre and provide an invaluable, if one-sided, account of his dispute with Goldoni and his association with the actors and actresses of Sacchi's company.

—Kenneth Richards

See also *Volume 1* entry on *Turandot*.

———————

GRABBE, Christian Dietrich. Born in Detmold, Westphalia (now in Germany), 11 December 1801. Educated at Gymnasium, Detmold; Leipzig University, studying law, 1820–22; also studied law in Berlin. Married Luise Clostermeier (separated). Attempted, unsuccessfully, to become an actor, 1823; established a legal practice in Detmold, 1824; military legal officer, 1826–1834: resigned under pressure because of his dissolute lifestyle; first works published in 1827; the only one of his plays to be performed in his lifetime, *Don Juan und Faust*, staged 1829; quarrelled with Heinrich Heine and Ludwig Tieck, losing their friendship and support; lived in Düsseldorf, 1835; contracted a spinal illness, and returned to Detmold. Died in Detmold, 12 September 1836.

Works

Collections

Dramatische Dichtungen.   1827.
Werke und Briefe (4 vols.).   1960.
Werke.   1961.
Werke (3 vols.), edited by Roy C. Cowen.   1975–77.

Stage Works

Herzog Theodor von Gothland (produced Deutsches Volkstheater, Vienna, 1892). In *Dramatische Dichtungen*, 1827.
Scherz, Satire, Ironie und tiefere Bedeutung (produced privately, Akademietheater, Vienna, 1876; produced publicly, Schauspielhaus, Munich, 1907). In *Dramatische Dichtungen*, 1827; translated as *Comedy, Satire, Irony and Deeper Meaning*, 1955.
Marius und Sulla (produced Stadttheater, Münster, 1936). In *Dramatische Dichtungen*, 1827.
Nanette und Maria (produced Bergtheater, Kettwig, 1914). In *Dramatische Dichtungen*, 1827.
Don Juan und Faust (produced Hoftheater, Detmold, 1829). 1829.
Hohenstaufen I: Kaiser Friedrich Barbarossa (produced Hoftheater, Schwerin, 1875). 1829.
Hohenstaufen II: Kaiser Heinrich der Sechste (produced Hoftheater, Schwerin, 1875). 1830.
Aschenbrödel (produced Landestheater, Detmold, 1937). 1835.
Napoleon; oder, Die hundert Tage (produced in a shortened version, Theater an der Wien, Vienna, 1869; complete version produced Opernhaus, Frankfurt, 1895). 1831.
Kosciuszko (produced Stadttheater, Münster, 1940). 1835.
Alexander (incomplete; produced Deutsches National-theater, Mannheim, 1929).
Hannibal (produced Nationaltheater, Munich, 1918). 1835.
Die Hermannsschlacht (produced Freilichtbühne, Nettel-stadt, 1934). 1838.

*

Bibliographies

A. Bergmann, *Grabbe Bibliographie*, Amsterdam, 1973.

Criticism

Books:
R. von Gottschall, *Christian Dietrich Grabbe*, Leipzig, 1901.
O. Nieten, *Christian Dietrich Grabbe: Sein Leben und seine Werke*, Dortmund, 1908; reprinted 1978.
A. Bergmann, *Die Glaubwürdigkeit der Zeugnisse für den Lebensgang und Charakter Christian Dietrich Grabbes*, Berlin, 1933; reprinted 1967.
A. Bergmann, *Christian Dietrich Grabbe: Chronik seines Lebens*, Detmold, 1954.
A. Bergmann (ed.), *Grabbes Werke in der zeitgenössischen Kritik* (6 vols.), Detmold, 1958–66.
F. Böttger, *Grabbe: Glanz und Elend eines Dichters*, Berlin, 1963.
A. W. Hornsey, *Idea and Reality in the Dramas of Christian Dietrich Grabbe*, New York, 1966.
W. Steffens, *Christian Dietrich Grabbe*, Velber bei Hannover, 1966; revised edition, 1972.

A. Bergmann (ed.), *Grabbe in Berichten seiner Zeitgenossen*, Stuttgart, 1968.
R. A. Nicholls, *The Dramas of Christian Dietrich Grabbe*, The Hague, 1969.
W. Hegele, *Grabbes Dramenformen*, Munich, 1970.
R. C. Cowen, *Christian Dietrich Grabbe*, New York, 1972.
Hans Werner Nieschmidt, *Deutung und Dokumentation: Studien zum Geschichtsdrama Christian Dietrich Grabbes*, Detmold, 1973.
M. Schneider, *Destruktion und utopische Gemeinschaft: Zur Thematik und Dramaturgie des Heroischen im Werk Christian Dietrich Grabbes*, Frankfurt, 1973.
Alfred Lang, *Grabbe-Studien*, Detmold, 1977.
Ulrich Wesche, *Byron und Goethe: Ein geistesgeschichtlicher Vergleich*, Detmold, 1978.
Hans-Werner Nieschmidt, *Brecht und Grabbe: Rezeption eines dramatischen Erbes*, Detmold, 1979.
David Horton, *Grabbe und sein Verhältnis zur Tradition*, Detmold, 1980.
Detlev Kopp, *Geschichte und Gesellschaft in den Dramen Christian Dietrich Grabbes*, Frankfurt, 1982.
Lothar Ehrlich, *Christian Dietrich Grabbe: Leben, Werk, Wirkung*, Berlin, 1983.
M. Vogt, *Literaturrezeption und historische Krisenerfahrung: Die Rezeption der Dramen Christian Dietrich Grabbes 1827–1945*, Frankfurt, 1983.
Karl Ziegler, *Grabbes Leben und Charakter*, Horn am Externsteine, 1984.
Antonio Cortesi, *Die Logik von Zerstörung und Grössenphantasie in den Dramen Christian Dietrich Grabbes*, Berne and New York, 1986.
W. Freund, *Grabbes Gegenentwürfe: Neue Deutungen seiner Dramen*, Munich, 1986.
W. Broer and D. Kopp, *Christian Dietrich Grabbe: Ein Symposium*, Tübingen, 1987.

Serials

Grabbe Jahrbuch, Emsdetten, 1982.

*   *   *

Heine called him "a drunken Shakespeare", Immermann remembered him as "a great nature in ruins, but ruins made of granite and porphyry", and Freud described him as "an original and rather peculiar poet". The notion of a remarkable talent marred by grave flaws, which haunted Grabbe for most of his life, still persists, although he is now also regarded as one of Germany's major dramatists. This mixed response is due no less to his eccentric personality than to the contradictions in his writing.

Born the only child of the local jailer, Grabbe felt oppressed and alienated in Detmold, his provincial home town, where, as he put it, "an educated person is looked upon as an inferior kind of fattened ox". Physically frail and emotionally unstable, torn between sullen shyness and aggressive self-assertion, noisily demanding recognition but unwilling to please or to conform, boorish in company, erratic in his post as army legal officer, embroiled in a disastrous marriage, and precipitating an early death by heavy drinking, he appeared as the model of the dissolute bohemian artist. While it is difficult to tell how far his notorious "bizarreness" was natural or assumed in order to shock, the "Grabbe legend" soon became confused with, and has often overshadowed, his work. More recently, however, his plays have been appreciated in their own right and their irregularities accepted as part of their orginality.

After his death, Grabbe was consigned by the prevailing classically-oriented criticism to oblivion, until both the nationalists and naturalists of the late 19th century rediscovered him as a kindred spirit. In the 20th century, the expressionists hailed him as a fellow-outcast of bourgeois society, the Dadaists and Surrealists welcomed him as another rebel against reason, the Nazis exalted him as a prophet of "blood and soil", and Brecht placed him alongside Büchner in the "non-Aristotelian" tradition leading from the Elizabethans to his own Marxist "epic theatre". On the German stage he was first adopted in the 1870's, revived in the early 1920's and late 1930's, and finally included in the established repertory—chiefly with *Scherz, Satire, Ironie und tiefere Bedeutung* (*Comedy, Satire, Irony and Deeper Meaning*) and *Napoleon; oder, Die hundert Tage* (*Napoleon; or, The Hundred Days*)—in the 1950's, although he is still all but unknown in other countries.

In philosophical terms Grabbe is generally regarded—together with Byron, Lamartine, Leopardi, and Heine—as the product of an age in which idealism gave way to materialism, leaving young intellectuals in a spiritual void and delivering them to post-Romantic scepticism and melancholy. His early plays, notably the sado-masochistic melodrama *Herzog Theodor von Gothland* and the black comedy *Scherz, Satire, Ironie*, reflect, in his own words, the despair of "intellect spent and emotion shattered". A similar disillusionment fuels superhuman desires in *Don Juan und Faust*—his only play to be performed while he was alive—which "glorifies the tragic fall of the sensualist and the metaphysician" alike. Nihilistic moods also underlie his later plays, particularly *Napoleon* and *Hannibal*, which blend the longing for powerful heroes with a sense of the vanity of all human effort in the face of impermanence and the "immeasurable chaos of baseness".

Current social and political affairs were of little interest to him. Thus, although he began a fashionably patriotic *Hohenstaufen* cycle, he abandoned it after two instalments on Barbarossa and Heinrich VI, while his last play, *Die Hermannsschlacht* (*Arminius's Battle*), was inspired by his "best childhood memories" of its setting in the nearby Teutoburg Forest, rather than by the nationalism traditionally associated with the topic. Nevertheless, his cynicism, pessimism, and iconoclasm can be interpreted together as an oblique indictment of the constricting socio-political conditions of the era of "Restauration".

By common consent Grabbe's supreme achievement consists in his innovations in historical drama. Unlike the historical plays of Schiller and his disciples, which were classical in style and idealistic in content, Grabbe's are prosaic in language, episodic in structure, and realistic in outlook. Above all, they present history as determined not by abstract ideas or outstanding individuals but by mass movements and the contingencies of time, place, and circumstance. Foreshadowed in *Marius und Sulla*, carried further in the two *Hohenstaufen* pieces, and culminating in *Napoleon* and *Hannibal*, Grabbe's ability to recreate the broad sweep of history itself has been much admired. He was hardly exaggerating when, with direct reference to *Napoleon*, but with historical drama as a whole in mind, he claimed to have accomplished "a dramatic-epic revolution".

Grabbe's "revolution" in historical drama was accompanied by a revolutionary treatment of drama as such. Dismissed in the past as signs of incompetence, waywardness, or a pathological disposition, his methods now seem eminently modern. Rife with incongruities and distortions, studiously avoiding any appearance of harmony or beauty, his disjointed actions, ambiguous characters, and dissonant dialogues not only expressed his conflicts in his own age but anticipated the "open" form and "absurd" content favoured by many dramatists in ours.

Commenting on *Napoleon* Grabbe once declared: "I have not taken any trouble over its shape as a drama. The present stage doesn't deserve it". On another occasion, however, he observed: "Drama is not bound to the stage . . . the proper theatre is—the imagination of the reader". We cannot be sure whether Grabbe's refusal to compromise with the stage was a protest against the specific theatrical conventions of his period or the result of more fundamental doubts about theatrical production as a medium for any literary creation. If the latter is true, then it is perhaps the paradox of a born dramatist who does not believe in the theatre that explains both the failures and the successes of this maverick in the evolution of German drama.

—Ladislaus Löb

See also *Volume 1* entry on *Comedy, Satire, Irony and Deeper Meaning*.

GRANVILLE(-)BARKER, Harley. Born Harley Granville Barker (no hyphen) in London, 25 November 1877. Married 1) the actress Lillah McCarthy in 1906 (divorced 1917); 2) Helen Huntington Gates in 1918. Child entertainer with his mother, then stage actor: London debut, 1892; actor and director, Stage Society, London, 1900–04; campaigned for a National Theatre, and successfully ran a pilot scheme for such a theatre at the (Royal) Court Theatre (Vedrenne-Barker management), London, 1904–07; helped to establish Shaw's reputation as a dramatist; producer of repertory theatre seasons at the Little Theatre, 1911, Kingsway Theatre, 1912, Savoy Theatre, 1912–14 (Shakespeare productions), and St. James's Theatre, 1913 (all in London); toured USA, 1915; during World War I served in the Red Cross, 1916, and British Army Intelligence, 1917–18; after his second marriage began to hyphenate his name; worked only intermittently in the theatre after 1918; lived in Paris after 1930; Clark lecturer, Cambridge, 1930; Romanes lecturer, Oxford, 1937; director, British Institute of the University of Paris, 1937–39; visiting professor, Yale University, New Haven, Connecticut, 1940; worked for British Information Services, New York, 1940–42; visiting professor, Harvard University, Cambridge, Massachusetts, 1941–42 and 1944–45. Member of the Executive Committee, Fabian Society, 1907–12; chairman, British Drama League, 1919–32. LL.D: University of Edinburgh, 1930; Litt.D: University of Reading, 1937; D.Litt: Oxford University, 1937. Fellow, and president, 1929, Royal Society of Literature. Died in Paris, 31 August 1946.

Works

Collections

Three Plays (includes *The Marrying of Ann Leete; The Voysey Inheritance; Waste*). 1909.
Rococo; Vote by Ballot; Farewell to the Theatre. 1917; as *Three Short Plays*, 1917.
Four Plays, with Helen Granville-Barker, from plays by S. and J. Alvarez Quintero (includes *A Hundred Years Old; Fortunato; The Lady from Alfaqueque; The Women Have Their Way*). 1927.

Harley Granville Barker (chalk drawing by John Singer Sargent, 1900).

Four Comedies, with Helen Granville-Barker, from plays by S. and J. Alvarez Quintero (includes *Love Passes By; Don Abel Wrote a Tragedy; Peace and Quiet; Doña Clarines*). 1932.
Collected Plays 1 (includes *The Marrying of Ann Leete; Rococo; The Voysey Inheritance*), edited by C.B. Purdom. 1967 (1 vol. only published).
Plays (includes *The Marrying of Ann Leete; The Voysey Inheritance; Waste*), edited by Dennis Kennedy. 1987.
Plays (2 vols.; includes *The Voysey Inheritance; Waste; The Secret Life; Rococo; Vote by Ballot; The Marrying of Ann Leete; The Madras House; His Majesty; Farewell to the Theatre*), edited by Margery Morgan. 1993.

Stage Works

The Weather-Hen, with Berte Thomas (produced Terry's Theatre, London, 1899).
The Marrying of Ann Leete (produced Royalty Theatre, London, 1902). In *Three Plays*, 1909.
Prunella; or, Love in a Dutch Garden, with Laurence Houseman (produced Royal Court Theatre, London, 1904). 1906; revised version, 1930.
The Voysey Inheritance (produced Royal Court Theatre, London, 1905). In *Three Plays*, 1909; revised version, 1913, 1934.
Waste (produced Imperial Theatre, London, 1907). In *Three Plays*, 1909; revised version (produced Westminster Theatre, London, 1936), 1926.
A Miracle (produced Terry's Theatre, London, 1907).
The Madras House (produced Duke of York's Theatre, London, 1910). 1910; revised version, 1925.

Rococo (produced Little Theatre, London, 1911). In *Rococo . . .*, 1917.
Anatol, from the play by Schnitzler (produced Little Theatre, London, 1911). 1911.
Das Märchen, with C.E. Wheeler, from the play by Schnitzler (produced 1912).
The Morris Dance, from a novel by Robert Louis Stevenson and Lloyd Osbourne (produced Little Theatre, New York, 1913).
The Harlequinade: An Excursion, with D.C. Calthrop (produced St. James's Theatre, London, 1913). 1918.
The Dynasts, from the play by Thomas Hardy (produced Kingsway Theatre, London, 1914).
Vote by Ballot (produced Royal Court Theatre, London, 1917). In *Rococo . . .*, 1917.
Farewell to the Theatre. In *Rococo . . .*, 1917.
Deburau, from a play by Sacha Guitry (produced Belasco Theatre, New York, 1920). 1921.
The Romantic Young Lady, with Helen Granville-Barker, from a play by G. Martínez Sierra (produced Royalty Theatre, London, 1920). In *The Plays of Martínez Sierra*, 1923.
The Two Shepherds, with Helen Granville-Barker, from a play by G. Martínez Sierra (produced Birmingham Repertory Theatre, 1921). In *The Plays of Martínez Sierra*, 1923.
The Kingdom of God, with Helen Granville-Barker, from a play by G. Martínez Sierra (produced Strand Theatre, London, 1923). In *The Plays of Martínez Sierra*, 1923.
Wife to a Famous Man, with Helen Granville-Barker, from a play by G. Martínez Sierra (produced Aldwych Theatre, London, 1924). In *The Plays of Martínez Sierra*, 1923.
The Secret Life (produced 1988). 1923.
Doctor Knock, from a play by Jules Romains (produced 1926). 1925; edited by Eric Bentley, in *From the Modern Repertory 3*, 1956.
Six Gentlemen in a Row, from a play by Jules Romains (produced 1927). 1927.
The Women Have Their Way, with Helen Granville-Barker, from a play by S. and J. Alvarez Quintero (produced Playhouse, Oxford, 1928). In *Four Plays*, 1927.
A Hundred Years Old, with Helen Granville-Barker, from a play by S. and J. Alvarez Quintero (produced Glasgow, 1928). In *Four Plays*, 1927.
Fortunato, with Helen Granville-Barker, from a play by S. and J. Alvarez Quintero (produced Royal Court Theatre, London, 1928). In *Four Plays*, 1927.
The Lady from Alfaqueque, with Helen Granville-Barker, from a play by S. and J. Alvarez Quintero (produced Royal Court Theatre, London, 1928). In *Four Plays*, 1927.
His Majesty. 1928.
Take Two from One, with Helen Granville-Barker, from a play by G. Martínez Sierra. 1931.
Love Passes By; Don Abel Wrote a Tragedy; Peace and Quiet; Doña Clarines, with Helen Granville-Barker, from plays by S. and J. Alvarez Quintero. As *Four Comedies*, 1932.

Fiction

Souls on Fifth (stories). 1916.

Memoirs and Letters

Granville Barker and His Correspondents: A Selection of Letters by Him and to Him, edited by Eric Salmon. 1986.

Other

Scheme and Estimates for a National Theatre, with William
    Archer.   1904; revised edition, 1907.
The Red Cross in France.   1916.
The Exemplary Theatre.   1922.
Prefaces to Shakespeare (5 vols.).   1927–47; revised edition
    (2 vols.), 1946–47.
A National Theatre.   1930.
On Dramatic Method (lectures).   1931.
The Use of the Drama.   1945; revised edition, 1946.

Editor, *The Players' Shakespeare* (7 vols.).   1923–27 (pre-
    faces later revised and published separately).
Editor, *The Eighteen-Seventies*.   1929.
Editor, with G.B. Harrison, *A Companion to Shakespeare
    Studies*.   1934.
Editor, *Eight Letters from T.E. Lawrence*.   1939.

*

Criticism

Books:
Desmond MacCarthy, *The Court Theatre 1904–1907*,
    London, 1907; edited by Stanley Weintraub, 1966.
P.P. Howe, *The Repertory Theatre*, London, 1910.
W. Bridges Adams, *The Lost Leader*, London, 1954.
C.B. Purdom, *Harley Granville Barker, Man of the Theatre,
    Dramatist, and Scholar*, London, 1955.
C.B. Purdom (ed.), *Bernard Shaw's Letters to Granville
    Barker*, London, 1956.
Margery Morgan, *A Drama of Political Man: A Study in the
    Plays of Harley Granville Barker*, London, 1961.
Manmohan Mehra, *Granville Barker: A Critical Study of the
    Major Plays*, 1981.
Elmo Selenius, *Granville Barker*, Boston, 1982.
Eric Salmon, *Granville Barker: A Secret Life*, London, 1983.
Dennis Kennedy, *Granville Barker and the Dream of Theatre*
    (includes bibliographies), Cambridge, 1985.
Christine Dymkowski, *Harley Granville Barker: A Preface to
    Modern Shakespeare*, Washington, D.C., and London,
    1986.
Jan McDonald, *The "New Drama" 1900–1914*, London, 1986
    (Macmillan Modern Dramatists series).
Ian Clarke, *Edwardian Drama*, London, 1989.

Articles:
George Bernard Shaw, "Harley Granville Barker: Some
    Particulars" in *Drama*, Winter 1946; reprinted in *Shaw on
    Theatre*, edited by E.J. West, New York, 1958.
Anthony Jackson, "Harley Granville Barker as Director of
    the Court Theatre", in *Theatre Research International*, 12,
    1972.
Richard Nicksen, "Granville-Barker as Playwright", in
    Theatre Annual, 27, 1971–72.
Cary M. Mazer, "Finders Keepers: Recent Scholarship on
    Granville Barker", in *Nineteenth Century Theatre*, 15,
    1987.

*   *   *

Actor, playwright, director, manager, critic, theorist,
Harley Granville Barker was one of the most versatile and
most influential artists of the British stage. From his first work
as an actor and playwright he attempted to create a climate
hospitable to revitalized acting and advanced drama; this
struggle became the major narrative of his life, as he fought
against an ingrained theatrical system and against English
insularity for a theatre concerned with ideas and art instead of
conventional responses and conventional entertainment.
With the almost paternal help of his great friend Bernard
Shaw, Barker abandoned Victorian commercialism for a
modernist approach to acting, production, and dramatic writing. As a result, much of his effort was subversive and relatively slow in its effect, and he was always in danger of
appearing elitist. Yet his accomplishments were major and his
dreams anticipated many of the features of contemporary
theatre.

The difficult fate of his own plays indicates the extent of the
challenge Barker faced as a reformer. Subtle in manner and
highly nuanced in thought, they did not much appeal to
Edwardian audiences, who sometimes found them incomprehensible. Like Chekhov, who was writing at the same time,
Barker's plays are more concerned with the delicate overtones of human existence than in big dramatic moments or
resounding resolutions. Shaw, equally insistent upon ideas in
drama, provided melodramatic structures and operatic
characters to gain attention and win audiences, while Barker
forced the action to occur under the surface and often indirectly; indeed Shaw liked to compare his own plays to
Verdi, and Barker's to Debussy. Yet Barker did not avoid
important contemporary issues.

Waste, for example, ran foul of the censor because its
twinned subjects of abortion and political corruption were too
sensitive for an age which believed in controlling official
morality; Barker refused to make the required changes and
the work could be given but two private performances. *The
Madras House*, which is a brilliant analysis of sex and the
economic domination of women by men, fared little better
when exposed to the rigours of the open market, lasting for
ten performances. Only recently have Barker's plays begun to
attract serious attention, at least partly because they prefigure
subjects and styles congenial to the late-20th century. Their
large casts, however, still make them risky ventures for any
but heavily subsidized theatres.

As an actor Barker's qualities were similar. From the time
he played Richard II for William Poel in 1899, he excelled in
roles that combined intelligence with romantic dreaminess,
and his subtle but natural playing was particularly suited to
contemporary scripts. Shaw saw him as the ideal young lead
for his own lover-poets, and Barker had great success in the
premiere roles of Marchbanks in *Candida*, Tanner in *Man
and Superman*, Cusins in *Major Barbara*, and Dubedat in *The
Doctor's Dilemma*, among others.

Acting did not greatly appeal to him, however, especially
as it usually meant touring, and in 1911, when he was well
established as a director, he gave it up. At the turn of the
century in England the stage director was barely distinguishable from the stage manager on the one hand, or the actor-
manager on the other; building on the models of André
Antoine in Paris and Max Reinhardt in Berlin, Barker almost
singlehandedly transformed the authority of the director and
the quality of production in London. His first assignments
were under the limited auspices of the Stage Society, but it
was at the (Royal) Court Theatre in Sloane Square that he
established himself as the dominant force behind the "New
Drama" of Shaw as the leader of the campaign to reform the
Edwardian stage. Together with his business manager, J.E.
Vedrenne, he mounted in three seasons 32 plays by 17
authors for a total of 988 performances. Most were new works
(or new translations of Euripides by Gilbert Murray); 701 of
the performances were of 11 plays by Shaw. Barker collabor-

ated with Shaw in staging his plays, and directed all the others himself.

Finances were heavily restricted, and on principle even highly successful plays were not permitted to crowd other works off the rotating schedule. Barker secured a new standard of production by accenting the ensemble rather than a star, by an almost perfectionist attention to detail, and by choosing plays that offered roles that were socially and aesthetically substantial. The artistic success of the Vedrenne-Barker venture did not mean financial stability, however, and the managers failed when they tried to extend their operation on a more permanent basis at a larger theatre. A second repertory experiment at the Duke of York's theatre in 1910 reinforced for Barker that the only hope for a revitalized theatre was an endowed repertory company, and he spent the rest of his life trying to achieve it. In 1904 he wrote a book with William Archer (published in 1907) which outlined, in practical terms, the need for a national theatre, and he continued to champion such an institution, both in print and through his example, that would be free of the pressures of the box office and of censorious minds, where actors could learn their craft assiduously, and where the public could see the best dramatic art of the past and the present on a regular basis. Though he did not see its creation in his lifetime, his persistent advocacy encouraged the growth of the regional repertory movement in Britain and ultimately influenced the founding of the subsidized Royal Shakespeare Company and the National Theatre.

His directing reached its height in the years just prior to World War I, most notably in the famous productions of Shakespeare at the Savoy in 1912 and 1914, in which he revoked the Victorian traditions of staging Shakespeare in a pictorial manner and for the benefit of a star actor. Producing nearly complete texts, Barker accented the power of the verse, speed of vocal delivery, and stylization in design (the fairies in *A Midsummer Night's Dream*, for example, looked like Indian temple idols, gold from head to foot). Despite the visual shock, Barker's Shakespeare was both respectful and interpretative; he did not offer a violent substitution of the director's mind for the dramatist's.

The War effectively brought an end to his directing, however; he chose thereafter to devote himself to the study, where he said he always wanted to be. A second marriage in 1918 to a wealthy American allowed him this freedom, but to his allies in the reform of the theatre Barker had abandoned the battle for a life of luxury, and for many years his reputation declined. Though he continued his attention to the stage, he did so in a reflective mode; even the two plays he wrote in this period—*The Secret Life* and *His Majesty*—seem to many observers over-literary. Nonetheless his *Prefaces to Shakespeare*, the first extended critical attention to the plays from an experienced theatrical perspective, remained highly influential. In recent years Barker's own plays have been revived and his general contributions re-evaluated, so that his stature as a crucial figure in the modern theatre is now secure.

—Dennis Kennedy

See also *Volume 1* entries on *The Madras House*; *The Voysey Inheritance*.

GRASS, Günter (Wilhelm). Has also written as Artur Knoff. Born in Danzig, Germany (now Gdansk, Poland),

16 October 1927. Educated at Volksschule and Gymnasium, Danzig; trained as stone-mason and sculptor; attended Academy of Art, Düsseldorf, 1948–52, and State Academy of Fine Arts, Berlin, 1953–55. Served in World War II: prisoner of war, Marienbad, Czechoslovakia, 1945–46. Married 1) Anna Margareta Schwarz in 1954, three sons and one daughter; 2) Ute Grunert in 1979. Worked as farm labourer, miner, apprentice stonecutter, jazz musician; speechwriter for Willy Brandt when Mayor of West Berlin; first play, *Noch zehn Minuten nach Buffalo* [*Only Ten Minutes to Buffalo*], produced 1954; writer-in-residence, Columbia University, New York, 1966. Co-editor, *L*, since 1976, and the publishing house Verlag L'80, since 1980. Also artist and illustrator. Recipient: Gruppe 47 Prize, 1959; Berlin Critics Prize, 1960; Bremen Prize, 1960 (withdrawn); Prix du Meilleur Livre Étranger, 1962; Büchner Prize, 1965; Fontane Prize, 1968; Theodor Heuss Prize, 1969; Mondello Prize (Palermo), 1977; International Literature Prize, 1978; Alexander Majkowski Medal, 1978; Vienna Literature Prize, 1980; Feltrinelli Prize, 1982. Honorary doctorate: Kenyon College, Gambier, Ohio, 1965; Harvard University, Cambridge, Massachusetts, 1976; Adam Mickiewicz University, Poznań. Member, 1963, and President, 1983–86 (resigned), Deutsche Akademie der Künste, Berlin; member, American Academy of Arts and Sciences.

Works

Collections

Four Plays (includes *Flood*; *Onkel, Onkel*; *Only Ten Minutes to Buffalo*; *the Wicked Cooks*). 1967.
Theaterspiele (includes *Noch zehn Minuten nach Buffalo*; *Hochwasser*; *Onkel, Onkel*; *Die Plebejer proben den Aufstand*; *Davor*). 1970.
Werkausgabe (10 vols.). 1987.

Stage Works

Noch zehn Minuten nach Buffalo (produced Schauspielhaus, Bochum, 1954). In *Theaterspiele*, 1970; translated as *Only Ten Minutes to Buffalo*, in *Four Plays*, 1967.
Hochwasser (produced Neue Bühne, Frankfurt, 1957). 1963; translated as *Flood*, in *Four Plays*, 1967.
Onkel, Onkel (produced Bühnen der Stadt, Cologne, 1958). 1965; translated as *Onkel, Onkel*, in *Four Plays*, 1967.
Fünf Köche (ballet scenario; produced Aix-Les-Bains and Bonn, 1959).
Stoffreste, with A. Reimann (ballet scenario; produced Stadttheater, Essen, 1959). 1960.
Beritten hin und zurück (produced Neue Bühne, Frankfurt, 1959).
Die bösen Köche (produced Schiller-Theater Werkstatt, Berlin, 1961). In *Theaterspiele*, 1970; translated as *The Wicked Cooks*, in *Four Plays*, 1967.
Goldmäulchen (produced Kammerspiele Munich, 1964).
Die Plebejer proben den Aufstand (produced Schiller-Theater, Berlin, 1966). 1966; translated as *The Plebeians Rehearse the Uprising*, 1966.
Davor (produced Schiller-Theater, Berlin, 1969). In *Theaterspiele*, 1970; translated as *Max*, 1972.
Die Vogelscheuchen (ballet scenario; produced Berlin, 1970).

Screenplays

Katz und Maus, 1967; *Die Blechtrommel*, with Volker Schlöndorff, 1979 (published as *Die Blechtrommel als Film*, 1979).

Radio Plays

Zweiunddreissig Zähne, 1959; *Noch zehn Minuten nach Buffalo*, 1962; *Eine öffentliche Diskussion*, 1963; *Die Plebejer proben den Aufstand*, 1966; *Hochwasser*, 1977.

Fiction

Danziger Trilogie.   1980; translated as *The Danzig Trilogy*, 1987; includes:
  Die Blechtrommel.   1959; translated as *The Tin Drum*, 1962.
  Katz und Maus.   1961; translated as *Cat and Mouse*, 1963.
  Hundejahre.   1963; translated as *Dog Years*, 1965.
Geschichten (as Artur Knoff).   1968.
Örtlich betäubt.   1969; translated as *Local Anaesthetic*, 1969.
Aus dem Tagebuch einer Schnecke.   1972; translated as *From the Diary of a Snail*, 1973.
Der Butt.   1977; translated as *The Flounder*, 1978.
Das Treffen in Telgte.   1979; translated as *The Meeting at Telgte*, 1981.
Kopfgeburten; oder, Die Deutschen sterben aus.   1980; translated as *Headbirths; or, The Germans Are Dying Out*, 1982.
Die Rättin.   1986; translated as *The Rat*, 1987.
Unkenrufe: Erzählung.   1992.

Verse

Die Vorzüge der Windhühner.   1956.
Gleisdreieck.   1960.
Selected Poems, translated by Michael Hamburger and Christopher Middleton.   1966; as *Poems*, 1969; as *Selected Poems*, 1980.
März.   1966.
Ausgefragt.   1967; translated as *New Poems*, translated by Michael Hamburger, 1968.
Danach.   1968.
Die Schweinekopfsülze.   1969.
Gesammelte Gedichte.   1971.
Mariazuehren/Hommageàmarie/Inmarypraise.   1973; translated as Inmarypraise, 1974.
Liebe geprüft.   1974.
Mit Sophie in die Pilze gegangen: Lithographien und Gedichte.   1976; revised edition, 1987.
"In the Egg" and Other Poems, translated by Michael Hamburger and Christopher Middleton.   1977.
Kinderlied: Verse and Etchings.   1982.
Nachruf auf einen Handschuh: Sieben Radierungen und ein Gedicht.   1982.
Ach, Butt, dein Märchen geht böse aus.   1983.
Mädchen, pfeif auf den Prinzen!, with Sarah Kirsch.   1984.
Aua, zum Fürchten, mannomann, illustrated by Arik Brauer.   1985.
Gedichte.   1985.
Die Rättin: 3 Radierungen und 1 Gedicht.   1985.
Die Gedichte 1955–1986.   1988.
Tierschutz.   1990.

Other

O Susanna: Ein Jazzbilderbuch: Blues, Balladen, Spirituals, Jazz, with H. Geldmacher and H. Wilson.
Die Ballerina.   1963.
Rede über das Selbstverständliche.   1965.
Dich singe ich Demokratie (pamphlets; 5 vols.).   1965.
Der Fall Axel C. Springer am Beispiel Arnold Zweig.   1967.
Briefe über die Grenze: Versuch eines Ost-West-Dialogs, with Pavel Kohout.   1968.

Über meinen Lehrer Döblin und andere Vorträge.   1968.
Über das Selbstverständliche: Reden, Aufsätze, Offene Briefe, Kommentare.   1968; revised and enlarged edition, as *Über das Selbstverständliche: Politische Schriften*, 1969; translated in part as *Speak Out! Speeches, Open Letters, Commentaries*, 1969.
Dokumente zur politischen Wirkung, edited by Heinz Ludwig Arnold and Franz Josef Görtz.   1971.
Der Schriftsteller als Bürger—eine Siebenjahresbilanz.   1973.
Der Bürger und seine Stimme.   1974.
Denkzettel: Politische Reden und Aufsätze 1965–76.   1978.
Aufsätze zur Literatur.   1980.
Zeichnen und Schreiben: das bildnerische Werk des Schriftstellers Günter Grass (2 vols.):
  1. *Zeichnungen und Texte 1954–1977*.   1982; translated as *Drawings and Words 1954–1977*, 1983.
  2. *Radierungen und Texte, 1972–1982*.   1984; translated as *Etchings and Words, 1972–1982*, 1985.
Günter Grass: Lithographien: 19. Juni bis 24. Juli 1983 (exhibition catalogue).   1983.
Die Vernichtung der Menschheit hat begonnen.   1983.
Widerstand Lernen: Politische Gegenreden, 1980–1983.   1984.
Vatertag (lithographs).   1984(?).
Geschenkt Freiheit: Rede zum 8. Mai 1945.   1985.
On Writing and Politics 1967–1983.   1985.
Erfolgreiche Musterreden für den Bürgermeister.   1986.
In Kupfer, auf Stein.   1986.
Es war einmal ein Land: Lyrik und Prosa, Schlagzeug und Perkussion, with Günter "Baby" Sommer.   1987.
Zunge Zeigen (travel).   1988; translated as *Show Your Tongue*, 1989.
Skizzenbuch.   1989.
Meine grüne Wiese: Kurzprosa.   1989.
Wenn wir von Europa sprechen: ein Dialog, with Françoise Giroud.   1989.
Alptraum und Hoffnung: zwei Reden vor dem Club of Rome, with T. Aitmatow.   1989.
Deutscher Lastenausgleich: Wider das dumpfe Einheitsgebot: Reden und Gespräche.   1990; translated as *Two States—One Nation? The Case Against German Reunification*, 1990.
Totes Holz: ein Nachruf.   1990.
Deutschland, einig Vaterland? Ein Streitgespräch, with Rudolph Augstein.   1990.
Erfolgreiche Mustergrussworte und Musterbriefe für Bürgermeister und Kommunalpolitiker.   1990.
Droht der deutsche Einheitstaat?   1990.
Ein Schnäppchen namens DDR: Letzte Reden vorm Glockengeläut.   1990.
Schreiben nach Auschwitz: Frankfurter Poetik-Vorlesung.   1990.
Gegen die verstreichende Zeit: Reden, Aufsätze und Gespräche 1989–1991.   1991.
Vier Jahrzehnte: Ein Werkstattbericht.   1991.

Editor, with Elisabeth Borchers and Klaus Roehler, *Luchterhands Loseblatt Lyrik: Eine Auswahl* (2 vols.).   1983.

*

Bibliographies

George A. Everett, *A Select Bibliography of Günter Grass (from 1956 to 1973)*, New York, 1974.

Patrick O'Neill, *Günter Grass: A Bibliography 1955–1975*, Toronto, 1976.

Ray Lewis White (ed.), *Günter Grass in America: The Early Years*, Hildesheim, 1981.

Criticism

Books:

Gerd Loschütz, *Von Buch zu Buch: Günter Grass in der Kritik: Eine Dokumentation*, Neuwied, 1968.

W. Gordon Cunliffe, *Günter Grass*, New York, 1969.

Kurt Lothar Tank, *Günter Grass*, New York, 1969.

A. Leslie Willson (ed.), *A Günter Grass Symposium*, Austin, Texas, 1971.

Irene Leonard, *Günter Grass*, Edinburgh, 1974.

Manfred Jürgensen, *Über Günter Grass: Untersuchungen zur sprachbildlichen Rollenfunktion*, Bern, 1974.

Keith Miles, *Günter Grass*, London, 1975.

Hanspeter Brode, *Günter Grass*, Munich, 1979.

Michael Hollington, *Günter Grass: The Writer in a Pluralist Society*, London, 1980.

Franz J. Görtz (ed.), *Günter Grass: Auskunft für Leser*, Darmstadt, 1984.

Richard H. Lawson, *Grass*, New York, 1984/85.

Ronald Hayman, *Günter Grass*, London, 1985.

Norbert Honsza, *Günter Grass: Werk und Wirkung*, Wroclaw, 1987.

Alan Frank Keele, *Understanding Günter Grass*, New York, 1988.

*   *   *

Günter Grass's artistic talents are truly universal. He has been successful as a sculptor, but even more so with his drawings and etchings which often have been published together with his poems. Although world-renowned for his monumental novels and his political, social, ecological and human rights activism, his dramatic works have received comparatively little attention.

In common with so many other Germans of his generation, Grass experienced the totalitarian Nazi state, and has suffered from it; but, unlike many German writers, especially those in previous eras, he has decided that it is not only the right but the duty of the intellectual to become involved in politics. Thus, he could be labelled an "engaged" artist, which, of course, would be saying little. While his inclination (like that of many other engaged writers) is towards democratic socialism, his political philosophy is more precisely defined by his anti-fascism and his commitment to non-violence. Closely associated with the liberal Left over the years, he has nevertheless sometimes taken a stance that has been at odds with the majority of that group.

As early as 1969, in his stage play *Davor*, and in his novel *Örtlich betäubt* (which is based on the same theme), Grass discussed the legitimacy of using violence against political and social oppression. His conclusion was that human progress should be sought without resorting to violence, even if, as a result, that progress arrives at a mere snail's pace. What he demonstrated artistically he had already practised politically since 1962 by supporting the Social Democratic Party (SPD) and the future chancellor, Willy Brandt.

His commitment to non-violence also lay behind his notorious confrontation with the late playwright and stage director Heinar Kipphardt who had produced a Wolf Biermann play in Munich in 1972 that appeared to advocate political assassinations. Grass's fears were borne out with the appearance of the infamous terrorist group the Red Army Faction (ARF) which, despite its violent actions, engendered a certain sympathy among liberal writers of the Left, most prominently Heinrich Böll.

The early plays by Grass, such as *Onkel, Onkel*, in which a murderer is finally killed by a group of children, and *Die bösen Köche* (*The Wicked Cooks*), which ends in suicide and murder, were indebted to the "theatre of the absurd". Grass moved on to the political play with *Die Plebejer proben den Aufstand* (*The Plebeians Rehearse the Uprising*) and *Davor*, so far his last play. Both deal with contemporary themes. *Die Plebejer* attempts to analyze the role of Bertolt Brecht in the popular uprising led by construction workers in East Berlin in 1953. The play creates a pertinent situation: the "Boss" (Brecht) is rehearsing Shakespeare's *Coriolanus*, while in front of his theatre the protest is erupting. The striking workers ask the famous revolutionary author for his support. But although in his stage directing he is emphasizing the victory of the plebeians over the oppressor, in real life his support is not forthcoming and the uprising is crushed with the help of Russian tanks. The only reaction of the *theoretical* revolutionary is to incorporate the actuality into his interpretation of the play! Rather than being merely an attack on Brecht, the play also implies a justification for Grass's own political activism and his conviction that the artist can no longer withdraw into the make-believe world of his art.

Davor explores the other tenet of the playwright's philosophy: non-violence. At the height of the protests against the US involvement in Vietnam and the indiscriminate use of napalm, a Berlin high-school student plans to immolate his beloved dog, "Max", by burning him in front of the "furry animals"—rich bourgeois women in their fur coats, who are having their coffee and cake on Berlin's famous Kurfürstendamm. The young man (and the author) in the end eschew the radical solution and opt for a moderate, but by necessity slower approach in their attempt to cure society's ills. The play is considered by most critics to be a failure dramatically, since much more weight is put on dialectic discussion rather than on action. It is hardly surprising, then, that the small novel *Örtlich betäubt*, which Grass based on the same topic, was more successful. Here he presents his political argument in the literary medium that has become his real forte.

—Manfred K. Kremer

See also *Volume 1* entry on *The Plebeians Rehearse the Uprising*.

GRAY, Simon (James Holliday). Born on Hayling Island, Hampshire, England, 21 October 1936. Educated at a school in Montreal; Westminster School, London; Dalhousie University, Halifax, Nova Scotia, 1954–57, BA (honours) in English 1957; Trinity College, Cambridge, 1958–61, BA (honours) in English 1961, MA. Married Beryl Mary Kevern in 1965; one son and one daughter. Harper-Wood Student, 1961–62, and research student, 1962–63, Trinity College; lecturer in English, University of British Columbia, Vancouver, 1963–64; supervisor in English, Trinity College, 1964–66; lecturer in English, Queen Mary College, London, 1965–85; first-produced play, *Wise Child*, staged 1967. Recipient: *Evening Standard* Award, 1972, 1976; New York Drama

Critics Circle Award, 1977. Honorary fellow, Queen Mary College, 1985.

Works

Collections

"Otherwise Engaged" and Other Plays.   1975.
"The Rear Column" and Other Plays.   1978.
"The Rear Column", "Dog Days", and Other Plays.   1979.
Plays 1 (includes *Butley; Otherwise Engaged; The Rear Column; Quartermaine's Terms, The Common Pursuit*). 1986.
The Definitive Simon Gray 1 (includes *Butley; Wise Child; Dutch Uncle; Spoiled; The Caramel Crisis; Sleeping Dog*). 1991.
The Definitive Simon Gray 2 (includes *Otherwise Engaged; Dog Days; Molly; Pig in a Poke; Man in a Side-Car; Plaintiffs and Defendants; Two Sundays*).   1991.

Stage Works

Wise Child (produced Wyndham's Theatre, London, 1967). 1972.
Molly (as *Death of a Teddy Bear*, televised 1967; revised version, as *Molly*, produced Palace Theatre, Watford, 1977).   In *"The Rear Column" and Other Plays*, 1978.
Spoiled (televised 1968; produced Close Theatre Club, Glasgow, 1970).   1971.
Dutch Uncle (produced Theatre Royal, Brighton, 1969). 1969.
The Idiot, from a novel by Dostoevsky (produced Old Vic, London, 1970).
Butley (produced Playhouse, Oxford, 1971).   1971.
Otherwise Engaged (produced Queen's Theatre, London, 1975).   In *"Otherwise Engaged" and Other Plays*, 1975.
Dog Days (produced Playhouse, Oxford, 1976).   1976.
The Rear Column (produced Globe Theatre, London, 1978). In *"The Rear Column" and Other Plays*, 1978.
Close of Play (produced National Theatre, London, 1979). With *Pig in a Poke*, 1980.
Stage Struck (produced Vaudeville Theatre, London, 1979). 1979.
Quartermaine's Terms (produced Queen's Theatre, London, 1981).   1981; revised version, 1983.
Chapter 17 (produced 1982).
Tartuffe, from the play by Molière (produced Kennedy Center, Washington, DC, 1982).   With *The Holy Terror (Melon Revised)*, 1990.
The Common Pursuit: *Scenes from Literary Life* (produced Lyric Theatre, Hammersmith, London, 1984; revised version produced 1987).   1984.
Melon (produced Yvonne Arnaud Theatre, Guildford, 1987; revised version produced New York, 1990).   1987.
Hidden Laughter (produced Vaudeville Theatre, London, 1990).   1990.

Screenplays

Butley, 1976; *A Month in the Country*, 1987 (published with *Old Flames*, 1990).

Television Plays

The Caramel Crisis, 1966 (published in *The Definitive Simon Gray 1*, 1991); *Death of a Teddy Bear*, 1967; *A Way with the Ladies*, 1967; *Sleeping Dog*, 1967 (published 1968); *Spoiled*, 1968 (published 1971); *Pig in a Poke*, 1969 (published with *Close of Play*, 1980); *The Dirt on Lucy Lane*, 1969; *Style of the Countess*, 1970; *The Princess*, 1970; *Man in a Side-Car*, 1971 (published in *"The Rear Column" and Other Plays*, 1978); *Plaintiffs and Defendants*, 1975, and *Two Sundays*, 1975 (both published in *"Otherwise Engaged" and Other Plays*, 1975); *After Pilkington*, 1987 (published 1987); *They Never Slept*, 1991; *The Common Pursuit*, 1992.

Radio Plays

Up in Pigeon Lake, from his novel *Colmain*, 1963; *The Holy Terror*, 1989.

Fiction

Colmain.   1963.
Simple People.   1965.
Little Portia.   1967.
A Comeback for Stark.   1968.

Others

An Unnatural Pursuit and Other Pieces: A Playwright's Journal.   1985.
How's That for Telling 'em, Fat Lady? A Short Life in the American Theatre.   1988.

Editor, with Keith Walker, *Selected English Prose.*   1967.

*

Criticism

Books:
Rüdiger Imhof, "Simon Gray", in *Essays on Contemporary British Drama*, edited by Hedwig Bock and Albert Wertheim, Munich, 1987.
Katherine H. Burkman (ed.), *Simon Gray: A Casebook*, New York and London, 1992.

Articles:
Anne Nothof, "Simon Gray's Comedy of Bad Manners", in *Essays in Theatre*, 6, 1988.

* * *

Beth: In otherwords, you do know.
Simon: In otherwords, can't we confine ourselves to the other words?

In Simon Gray's early plays his characters, often non-U types, wear actual disguises or construct elaborate verbal facades to hide their unacknowledged frustrations; these characters convey their unhappiness with contemporary England through a nostalgia for the art and supposedly superior values of the past; and though they are usually married, they attempt to lead unconventional sex lives. Gray's more recent plays concentrate on the linguistic disguises. Increasingly, his characters tend to be the publishers and educators, often second-rate, who shape what passes for England's intellectual life.

Wise Child, Gray's first play, depicts a heterosexual criminal whose female clothing helps him elude the police, while his young associate's wigs and games reveal a desire to revert to childhood and make the criminal his "Mum". Murder, and a sexual tangle that plays like a grim parody of *As You Like It* justify the criminal's indictment of modern England ("the beggars of Europe as we are now"), however skewed his perspective. In *Wise Child* and his next play, *Dutch Uncle*, Gray's witty dialogue seems too polished for his characters, a possible sign of his unfamiliarity with their milieu, and he uneasily mixes cartoon-like farce with grim comedy.

Spoiled confronts what the stage directions call "*the comfortable middle-class, intellectual*" world of his best plays. In Gray's most complex writing so far, a married male French teacher tutors a working-class youth while courting him obliquely, with verses from Mallarmé. The teacher's Pygmalion-like role foreshadows Ben Butley's attempt to shape the tastes and life of his former student Joey, while the soured vulnerability of middle-class marriage prefigures Simon Hench's adventures with young girls in *Otherwise Engaged*.

Butley, which established Gray both critically and commercially, creates a verbally dazzling university lecturer whose untiring wit gives the illusion of order to the messy reality of his life and disguises his confused sexuality. He purposefully forgets names, pretending to confuse his protégé Joey's new lover, Reg, with his predecessor, presumably to deny Reg meaning in Joey's life. Though both Joey and the audience get trapped by Ben's power to transform reality, ultimately reality triumphs when Reg persuades Joey to leave both Ben's office and flat. And Ben's Wildean phrase "After all, a man's bound to be judged by his wife's husband" will prove more painfully true than he intends. His estranged wife *will* marry "the most boring man in London", whose novel Reg will publish, while Ben's book on Eliot remains unfinished. Though Ben tries to hide behind the ambiguity of his "marriage", probably non-sexual, to Joey, Reg says, "our Joey will be moving out of figures of speech into matters of fact. Ours will be too much like a marriage to be a metaphor".

The homosexuality in Gray's "middle-class" plays is obviously an important part of the London-Oxbridge world they chronicle, but homosexuality pervades the non-U *Wise Child* as well. The theme connects with Gray's disguise motif: Joey and his lover apparently fool Reg's family and friends in the hearty masculine world of Reg's northern home town. That sexual identity can assume convincing disguises raises questions about its real nature, and about other forms of behavior or belief, like the obsession with England's past. Helped immeasurably in the original production by the deceiving warmth of Alan Bates's performance, Ben (like Simon in *Otherwise Engaged*) tricks the audience into equating wit with strength, until the movement of the play forces a negative reevaluation of his character. Ben refuses to repeat the Joey pattern with a new student: "You're not what I mean at all, not what I mean at all. I'm too old for the likes of you". But Ben articulates this break with the past in language with echoes of Eliot and a tradition that has provided only verbal strength and a false sense of intellectual superiority.

In *Otherwise Engaged* publisher Simon Hench prefers to ignore his wife's infidelity, though even his epigrammatic wit cannot disguise her pregnancy. Like Ben, he focuses on verbal ambiguities to trivialize or distance real problems, like the loss of his wife. He acknowledges romantic passion only through a new recording of *Parsifal* and spends the entire play trying to listen to the music. When, just before the final curtain, the opening bars "*fill the theatre*", they mock his reduction of disorderly passion to pre-recorded sounds on a disc. The audience shares Simon's ridicule of the unhygienic, uneducated student, Dave, but gradually learns that Simon's obsession with elegant surfaces allows no attention to moral content (Simon, like other Gray adulterers, washes off the

"stench" of his affairs with quick showers at his club). Since one of Simon's authors is writing a book on British sadism in colonial Africa (the subject of *The Rear Column*), even Simon may no longer be able to retreat into a belief in the British past.

The Rear Column is Gray's venture into the heart of darkness to test the legend of Stanley, who appears only briefly in the final scene to thwart the expectations the play has developed. The atmosphere is, at times, authentically Conradian, as various cultivated Englishmen attempt, with generally negative results, to follow their concept of "honour": "When I see them lying about in the compound, in their sickness, as if they were the image of sickness itself. Or while they stand there, heads lolling, while I supervise one of them flogging another of them to death. That makes me hate them". The characters' frequent witty exchanges remind the audience that 19th-century empire builders were surely the intellectual equals of Gray's 20th-century publishers and educators, an insight which emphasizes the extent of their moral collapse. And the mute "Native Woman" foreshadows the almost mute central figure of *Close of Play*.

This central figure, a distinguished classical scholar named Jaspar (portrayed originally by Sir Michael Redgrave), with only an-end-of-first-act groan and an-end-of-second-act "The door is open!", repeated once, creates a desperate need in an audience to define the character as either a teasing oracle or a collapsed villain responsible for the disastrous personal lives of his grown sons. After the play's final revelation that Jasper *can* speak, his earlier silence seems especially ominous, whether he is failed oracle, ineffectual parent, or ailing actor. *Close of Play*, which has not achieved the popularity it merits, treats its tormented characters with a compassion rare at this stage of Gray's work, and the dialogue rivals anything in *Butley*.

Stage Struck also has a theatrical title and continually tricks the viewer about the "reality" he watches and the amount of control the stage-manager-protagonist can exert over characters who may be following their own scripts. This venture into Anthony Shaffer territory provides lively, if frantic, entertainment. Much of its limited success stemmed from the by now overripe handsomeness of actor Alan Bates, whose compulsive charm implied a contrast with easy past conquests. Bates displayed this same quality in *Melon*, a relatively unsuccessful return to the publishing world of *Otherwise Engaged*. The wit in *Melon* seems forced, perhaps to suggest the protagonist's desperation. But since the play fails to provide the fullness of characterization that might justify such desperation, the character's perpetual irony seems less the result of profound pain than of bad temper.

Quartermaine's Terms, *The Common Pursuit*, and *Hidden Laughter* seem much fresher thematically and technically than their immediate predecessors. Though all three plays explore relationships among the publishers, writers, and educators of Gray's familiar world, we see these characters develop over time (a number of years in the last two) before they have hardened into compulsively witty armadillos like Butley and Melon. Unlike his earlier star vehicles, Gray's recent plays are primarily ensemble pieces exploring complex interrelationships adroitly.

Quartermaine's Terms is set in a Cambridge language school for foreign students. Quartermaine, a socially inept bachelor, unsuccessfully attempts to live off the anguished lives of his fellow teachers without even understanding the depth of this anguish, and he misses, among other lurid events, a colleague's murder of her ailing mother. Unlike the wit of Gray's typical protagonists, Quartermaine's humor is inadvertent and unpolished, as he blunders apologetically towards his final rejection from the school, a failure both as teacher and colleague. Grateful for invitations to babysit, he innocently suggests his hosts' real feelings about parenthood: "They suddenly remembered there was a film at The Arts, some old um, um German classic that they seem very fond of, about—about a child-murderer as far as I could make out . . . .". Gray's willingness to modify his signature of polished dialogue helps create an atmosphere that is both authentically seedy and compassionate.

The Common Pursuit follows the careers of a number of Cambridge graduates, followers of Leavis, into the "real" world of publishing and literary journalism, and tests the meaning of university friendships in the context of professional successes and failures. The play traces the friends over 15 years and movingly returns in the epilogue to a scene set, chronologically, minutes after the opening. This renewed glimpse of youthful promise acquires tremendous pathos because of our knowledge of the characters' fates and of the relationship between their love of literature and their limited talents.

Like *The Common Pursuit*, *Hidden Laughter* takes its title from Eliot, a frequent source of allusion in Gray, and follows the lives of a publisher, his would-be novelist wife, and their family over a 10-year period. The couple share the spotlight with a clergyman neighbour, whose quirky religious and sexual problems play against the perpetual turmoil of the publisher's family in their edenic country retreat. The play generates increasing anxiety, even terror, about the possible fates of the couple's children, a theme developed less effectively in *Melon*. While children in Gray's earlier plays are primarily sources of humor or frustration, they now suggest man's vulnerability to both his own unstable nature and to a universe of threatening accidents from which there is no escape. Thus, Gray's recent work has suggested an apparent desire to go beyond the themes and techniques of his past successes.

—Burton Kendle

See also *Volume 1* entry on *Butley*.

GREEN, Paul (Eliot). Born near Lillington, North Carolina, USA, 17 March 1894. Educated at Buies Creek Academy (now Campbell College), North Carolina, graduated 1914; University of North Carolina, Chapel Hill, 1916–17 and 1919–21, AB 1921 (Phi Beta Kappa), graduate study, 1921–22; Cornell University, Ithaca, New York, 1922–23. Married Elizabeth Atkinson Lay in 1922: one son and three daughters. School principal, Olive Branch, North Carolina, 1914–17; served in the US Army Engineers, 1917–19, partly in France and Belgium: Lieutenant; lecturer, then Associate Professor of Philosophy, 1923–39, Professor of Dramatic Art, 1939–44, and Professor of Radio, Television, and Motion Pictures, 1962–63, University of North Carolina; editor, *Reviewer* magazine, Chapel Hill, 1925; president, National Folk Festival, 1934–45, National Theatre Conference, 1940–42, and North Carolina State Literary and Historical Association, 1942–43; created large-scale "symphonic dramas" on historical themes, from late 1940's; member, US Executive Committee, and National Commission, Unesco, 1950–52; Rockfeller Foundation lecturer in Asia,

1951; director, American National Theatre Company, 1959–61; delegate, International Conference on the Performing Arts, Athens, 1962. Recipient of several prizes, including: Pulitzer Prize, 1927; Yale School of Drama Award, 1964; Susanne M. Davis Award, 1966; National Theatre Conference citation, 1974; American Theatre Association Award, 1978. Litt.D: Western Reserve University, Cleveland, 1941; Davidson College, North Carolina, 1948; University of North Carolina, 1956; Berea College, Kentucky, 1957; University of Louisville, Kentucky, 1957; Campbell College, Buies Creek, North Carolina, 1969; Duke University, Durham, North Carolina, 1980; DFA: North Carolina School of the Arts, Winston-Salem, 1976. Member, American Academy, 1941. Died in Chapel Hill, 4 May 1981.

Works

Collections

"The Lord's Will" and Other Carolina Plays (includes *Blackbeard; Old Wash Lucas (The Miser); The No 'Count Boy; The Old Man of Edenton; The Last of the Lowries*). 1925.
Lonesome Road: Six Plays for the Negro Theatre (includes *In Abraham's Bosom*, one-act version; *White Dresses; The Hot Iron; The Prayer Meeting; The End of the Row; Your Fiery Furnace*). 1926.
"In the Valley" and Other Carolina Plays (includes *Quare Medicine; Supper for the Dead; Saturday Night; The Man Who Died at Twelve O'Clock; In Aunt Mahaly's Cabin; The No 'Count Boy; The Man on the House; The Picnic; Unto Such Glory; The Goodbye*). 1928.
Wings for to Fly: Three Plays of Negro Life, Mostly for the Ear But Also for the Eye (includes *The Thirsting Heart; Lay This Body Down; Fine Wagon*). 1959.
Out of the South: The Life of a People in Dramatic Form (includes *The House of Connelly; The Field God; In Abraham's Bosom; Potter's Field; Johnny Johnson; The Lost Colony; The No 'Count Boy; Saturday Night; Quare Medicine; The Hot Iron; Unto Such Glory; Supper for the Dead; The Man Who Died at Twelve O'Clock; White Dresses; Hymn to the Rising Sun*). 1939.
Five Plays of the South (includes revised versions of *The House of Connelly; In Abraham's Bosom; Johnny Johnson; Hymn to the Rising Sun; White Dresses*). 1963.

Stage Works

Surrender to the Enemy (produced University of North Carolina, Chapel Hill, 1917).
Souvenir (produced 1919).
The Last of the Lowries (produced University of North Carolina, Chapel Hill, 1920). In *"The Lord's Will" and Other Carolina Plays*, 1925.
The Long Night. In *Carolina Magazine*, 1920.
Granny Boling. In *Drama*, August–September 1921.
Old Wash Lucas (The Miser) (produced University of North Carolina, Chapel Hill, 1921). In *"The Lord's Will" and Other Carolina Plays*, 1925.
The Old Man of Edenton (produced University of North Carolina, Chapel Hill, 1921). In *"The Lord's Will" and Other Carolina Plays*, 1925.
The Lord's Will (produced University of North Carolina, Chapel Hill, 1922). In *"The Lord's Will" and Other Carolina Plays*, 1925.
Blackbeard, with Elizabeth Lay Green (produced University of North Carolina, Chapel Hill, 1922). In *"The Lord's Will" and Other Carolina Plays*, 1925.

White Dresses (produced White Plains, New York, 1923). In *Lonesome Road*, 1926.

Wrack P'int (produced University of North Carolina, Chapel Hill, 1923).

Sam Tucker. In *Poet Lore*, Summer 1923; revised version, as *Your Fiery Furnace*, in *Lonesome Road*, 1926.

Fixin's, with Erma Green (produced University of North Carolina, Chapel Hill, 1924). 1934.

The No 'Count Boy (produced Little Theatre, Chicago, 1925). In *"The Lord's Will" and Other Carolina Plays*, 1925; revised (white) version, 1953.

In Aunt Mahaly's Cabin: A Negro Melodrama (produced by the Vagabond Players, Baltimore, Maryland, 1925). 1925.

Quare Medicine (produced University of North Carolina, Chapel Hill, 1925). In *"In the Valley" and Other Carolina Plays*, 1928.

The Man Who Died at Twelve O'Clock (produced High School, Thermopolis, Wyoming, 1925). 1927.

The Prayer Meeting. In *Lonesome Road*, 1926.

The End of the Row. In *Lonesome Road*, 1926.

In Abraham's Bosom (produced Greenwich Village Theater, New York, 1926). With *The Field God*, 1927.

The Hot Iron. In *Lonesome Road*, 1926; revised version as *Lay This Body Down* (produced College Theater, Berea, Kentucky, 1972), in *Wings for to Fly*, 1959.

The Field God (produced Greenwich Village Theater, New York, 1927). With *In Abraham's Bosom*, 1927.

Bread and Butter Come to Supper. 1928; as *Chair Endowed* (produced in *Salvation on a String*, 1954).

Saturday Night. In *"In the Valley" and Other Plays*, 1928.

The Man on the House. In *"In the Valley" and Other Plays*, 1928.

The Picnic. In *"In the Valley" and Other Plays*, 1928.

Supper for the Dead (produced in *Salvation on a String*, Theatre de Lys, New York, 1954). In *"In the Valley" and Other Carolina Plays*, 1928.

Unto Such Glory (produced 1936). In *"In the Valley" and Other Carolina Plays*, 1928.

The Goodbye (produced 1954). In *"In the Valley" and Other Carolina Plays*, 1928.

Blue Thunder; or, The Man Who Married a Snake. In *One Act Plays for Stage and Study*, 1928.

Old Christmas. In *Wide Fields*, 1928.

The House of Connelly (produced Martin Beck Theatre, New York, 1931). In *"The House of Connelly" and Other Plays*, 1931; revised version (produced 1959), in *Five Plays of the South*, 1963.

Potter's Field (produced Plymouth Theatre, Boston, 1934). In *The House of Connelly and Other Plays*, 1931; revised version, as *Roll Sweet Chariot: A Symphonic Play of the Negro People*, music by Dolphe Martin (produced Cort Theatre, New York, 1934), 1935.

Tread the Green Grass, music by Lamar Stringfield (produced University of Iowa, Iowa City, 1932). In *"The House of Connelly" and Other Plays*, 1931.

Shroud My Body Down (produced University of North Carolina, Chapel Hill, 1934). 1935; revised version, as *The Honeycomb*, 1972.

The Enchanted Maze: The Story of a Modern Student in Dramatic Form (produced University of North Carolina, Chapel Hill, 1935). 1939.

Hymn to the Rising Sun (produced New York, 1936). 1939.

Johnny Johnson: The Biography of a Common Man, music by Kurt Weill (produced 44th Street Theatre, New York, 1936). 1937; revised version, 1972.

The Southern Cross (produced Dallas, Texas, 1936). 1938.

The Lost Colony (produced Waterside Amphitheatre, Roanoke Island, North Carolina, 1937). 1937; revised versions, 1939, 1946, 1954, 1980.

Alma Mater. In *The Best One-Act Plays of 1938*, edited by Margaret Mayorga, 1938.

The Critical Year: A One-Act Sketch of American History and the Beginning of the Constitution. 1939.

Franklin and the King. 1939.

The Highland Call: A Symphonic Play of American History (produced La Fayette Opera House, Fayetteville, North Carolina, 1939). 1941; revised version, 1975.

Native Son (The Biography of a Young American), with Richard Wright, from the novel by Wright (produced St. James Theatre, New York, 1941). 1941; revised version, 1980.

The Common Glory: A Symphonic Drama of American History (produced Lake Mataoka Amphitheatre, Williamsburg, Virginia, 1947). 1948; revised version, 1975.

Faith of Our Fathers (produced Carter Barron Amphitheatre, Washington, DC, 1950).

Peer Gynt, from the play by Ibsen (produced ANTA Playhouse, New York, 1951). 1951.

The Seventeenth Star (produced Columbus, Ohio, 1953).

Serenata, with Josefina Niggli (produced Santa Barbara, California, 1953).

Carmen, from the libretto by H. Meilhac and L. Halévy, music by Bizet (produced 1954).

This Declaration. 1954.

Salvation on a String (includes *Chair Endowed*; *The No 'Count Boy*; *Supper for the Dead*; produced Theatre de Lys, New York, 1954).

Wilderness Road: A Symphonic Outdoor Drama (produced Indian Fort Amphitheatre, Berea, Kentucky, 1955; revised version produced 1972). 1956.

The Founders: A Symphonic Outdoor Drama (produced Cove Amphitheatre, Williamsburg, Virginia, 1957). 1957.

The Confederacy: A Symphonic Outdoor Drama Based on the Life of General Robert E. Lee (produced Lee Amphitheatre, Virginia Beach, Virginia, 1958). 1959.

The Stephen Foster Story: A Symphonic Drama Based on the Life and Music of the Composer (produced J. Dan Talbott Amphitheatre, Bardstown, Kentucky, 1959). 1960.

Fine Wagon, from the radio play *A Start in Life*. In *Wings for to Fly*, 1959.

The Thirsting Heart (produced Orangeburg, South Carolina, 1971). In *Wings for to Fly*, 1959.

Cross and Sword: A Symphonic Drama of the Spanish Settlement of Florida (produced Anastasia Island Amphitheatre, St. Augustine, Florida, 1965). 1966.

The Sheltering Plaid. 1965.

Texas: A Symphonic Outdoor Drama of American Life (produced Pioneer Amphitheatre, Palo Duro Canyon, Texas, 1966). 1967.

Sing All a Green Willow (produced University of North Carolina, Chapel Hill, 1969).

Trumpet in the Land (produced Tuscarawas Valley Amphitheatre, New Philadelphia, Ohio, 1970). 1972.

Drumbeats in Georgia: A Symphonic Drama of the Founding of Georgia by James Edward Oglethorpe (produced Jekyll Island Amphitheatre, Jekyll Island, Georgia, 1973).

Louisiana Cavalier: A Symphonic Drama of the 18th Century French and Spanish Struggle for the Settling of Louisiana (produced Grand Encore Amphitheatre, Natchitoches, Louisiana, 1976).

We the People: A Symphonic Drama of George Washington

and the Establishment of the United States Government (produced Merriweather Post Pavilion, Columbia, Maryland, 1976).

The Lone Star: A Symphonic Drama of Sam Houston and the Winning of Texas Independence from Mexico (produced Mary Moody North Amphitheatre, Galveston, Texas, 1977).

Palo Duro: A Sound and Light Drama (produced Palo Duro, Texas, 1979).

Screenplays

Cabin in the Cotton, 1932; *State Fair*, with Sonya Levien, 1933; *Dr. Bull*, 1933; *Voltaire*, with Maude T. Howell, 1933; *The Rosary*, 1933; *Carolina*, 1934; *David Harum*, 1934; *Time Out of Mind*, 1947; *Roseanna McCoy*, 1949; *Red Shoes Run Faster*, 1949.

Radio Plays

A Start in Life, 1941 (published in *The Free Company Presents*, edited by James Boyd, 1941).

Fiction

Wide Fields (stories). 1928.
The Laughing Pioneer: A Sketch of Country Life. 1932.
This Body the Earth. 1935.
"Salvation on a String" and Other Tales of the South. 1946.
Dog on the Sun: A Volume of Stories. 1949.
Words and Ways: Stories and Incidents from My Cape Fear Valley Folklore Collection. 1968.
Home to My Valley (stories). 1970.
Land of Nod and Other Stories: A Volume of Black Stories. 1976.

Verse

Trifles of Thought. 1917.
The Lost Colony Song-Book. 1938.
The Highland Call Song-Book. 1941.
Song in the Wilderness, music by Charles Vardell. 1947.
The Common Glory Song-Book. 1951.
Texas Song-Book. 1967.
Texas Forever. 1967.

Other

Contemporary American Literature: A Study of Fourteen Outstanding American Writers, with Elizabeth Lay Green. 1925; revised edition, 1927.
The Hawthorn Tree: Some Papers and Letters on Life and the Theatre. 1943.
Forever Growing: Some Notes on a Credo for Teachers. 1945.
Dramatic Heritage (essays). 1953.
Challenge to Citizenship (address). 1956.
Drama and the Weather: Some Notes and Papers on Life and the Theatre. 1958.
The University in a Nuclear Age (address). 1963.
Plough and Furrow: Some Essays and Papers on Life and the Theatre. 1963.

*

Bibliographies

Joseph M. Flora and Robert Bain, *Fifty Southern Writers after 1900: A Bio-Bibliographical Sourcebook*, New York, 1987.

Criticism

Books:
Barrett H. Clark, *Paul Green* New York, 1928.
Agatha Boyd Adams, *Paul Green of Chapel Hill*, edited by Richard Walser, Chapel Hill, North Carolina, 1951.
Walter S. Lazenby, *Paul Green*, Austin, Texas, 1970.
Vincent Kenny, *Paul Green*, New York, 1971.

Articles:
Howard D. Pearce, "Transcending the Folk: Paul Green's Use of Folk Materials", in *Mosaic*, vol.4 no.4, 1971.
Paul Green issue of *Pembroke Magazine*, 10, 1978.

*   *   *

North Carolinian Paul Green became noted nationally as a dramatist in the 1920's for plays depicting the harsh existence of the whites and blacks of the rural South. He won particular attention as a white writer with an uncommon understanding of the black experience. Many of his full-length plays were produced on Broadway from 1926 to 1941. Later in his career, Green translated a love of country into national themes in regionally-produced historical dramas. Often criticized for flaws in dramaturgical craftsmanship, Green nevertheless was a distinctive American playwright with a keen understanding of man's delicate, often despairing relationship to the earth, and to his fellow man.

The playwright's early one-act plays, designed for small regional theatres and published in anthologies, deal with Southern poor folk wrestling with the often insurmountable hostility of nature and neighbor, deceived by religion as panacea, with few characters surviving the frustration or suffering. Several representative works can be cited. *The Lord's Will* introduces a self-appointed preacher who ignores his family's crushing ills to "preach the Word". *Unto Such Glory* looks farcically at a religious zealot justifiably tricked by a shrewd layman. Notably focusing on the black culture is *The No 'Count Boy*, whose title-character is a shiftless, persuasive young dreamer who nearly succeeds in enticing a girl with similar dreams to abandon her hard-working suitor and take to the open road.

In *White Dresses* a pretty Mulatto interprets a Christmas gift to mean her beloved white employer-lover will marry her, until she realizes that his father has arranged her marriage to a black admirer. These plays are compactly structured, employ details of folklore and local color well known by the author, and sensitively display compassion for society's downtrodden and humor toward its fools.

An outstanding one-act play, *Hymn to the Rising Sun*, was first produced in New York in 1936. Set in a Southern prison camp on 4th July, the play relates a chain gang's brutal treatment. The sadistic warden whips a young white prisoner who is tormented by a black fellow prisoner's punishment, suffering, and death in a "sweat box". Telling characterizations, graphic stage images, and irony effectively expose the brutality inherent in incarceration.

Three full-length plays about the black experience, presented in New York, reflect a similar mood of anger and indictment. *Abraham's Bosom*, Green's first full-length work, was produced in 1926 by the Provincetown Players. Despite critical surprise and controversy it won the Pulitzer Prize. It is the story of a self-educated black man who wishes to raise the lot of the Negro through education, and with the aid of his white father opens a school in rural North Carolina against white planters' opposition and blacks' apathy. Frustrated in continuing his school after his father's death, he kills his deceiving white half-brother and consequently is killed by a Klan posse. While flawed in construction and in stereotypical characterizations of secondary figures, the folk tragedy holds power in its despairing compassion for the plight of blacks and in its portrait of a relentlessly driven protagonist.

Roll, Sweet Chariot delivers a trenchant indictment in depicting a marginally-existing black community that is facing callous severance by road construction. Green termed the play a "symphonic drama" because it synthesizes such elements as sound, music, dance, and pantomime—an influence of expressionistic and Brechtian techniques studied during a European stay. Neither commercially nor artistically successful, this ambitious work's form came to be better realized in his subsequent history-dramas.

Continuing his concern with the fate of blacks in America, Green collaborated with Richard Wright in dramatizing Wright's novel *Native Son*, in which a black chauffeur's unintentional killing of a white woman leads to his trial and conviction. The 1941 Mercury Theatre production, directed by Orson Welles, projected a sterner attitude toward repression of blacks than Green had intended. Flawed, but dramatically powerful, it achieved commercial success despite mixed critical reviews.

Green wrote sympathetically about white people too. *The Field God*, an early drama, concerns a rural Southern farmer driven to conform to his neighbors' puritanical Christianity, which he ultimately rejects to find God in his own creative existence. The play failed in New York in 1927, with critically observed deficiencies of plot and character, but it underlines Green's distrust of the inflexible, uncharitable ways of so-called "Christians."

In 1931 *The House of Connelly*, patterned after Chekhov's *The Cherry Orchard*, proved more significant than *The Field God*, chronicling the decay of a landed Southern aristocratic family. Originally a tragedy, the 1931 Group Theatre production interpolated a marriage of the weak surviving son to a poor white woman, thereby providing a hopeful note of redemption and continuation of the family estate. Commercially unsuccessful, the play nonetheless earned attention for its poignant treatment of a dying white aristocracy amidst the anguish of blacks.

In *Johnny Johnson*, a 1936 Group Theatre production, Green enlisted expressionism and Kurt Weill's music to create a powerful anti-war play centering on a pacifist soldier in World War I who is wounded and suffers consequent disillusionment. His attempts, with laughing gas, to force the military high command to decree war's end result in arrest and committal to an asylum for the insane, where he consolidates his pacifist beliefs before returning home to be ignored as a peace-promulgating toy peddler. Satirizing jingoism and the military, Green offers an international theme proving his ability to extend beyond regional themes and subjects.

In 1937, Green began the last decades of his career with *The Lost Colony*, a "symphonic drama" about the first British settlement in North America, which continues to thrive in summertime amphitheatre performances on North Carolina's Roanoke Island, near the subject's historical site. Green subsequently wrote other outdoor epic dramas of the American heritage, several of which also enjoy continuity in similar regional theatres from Virginia to Texas.

Paul Green's canon of history-dramas, contributing to an awareness of American history, represents a significant achievement. Furthermore, his plays treating the themes of the biracial South reflect a compassionate understanding rarely expressed by other dramatists of his time. His place as a distinctive voice in American theatre is secure.

—Christian H. Moe

See also *Volume 1* entries on *In Abraham's Bosom*; *Johnny Johnson*.

GREENE, Robert. Born in Norwich, Norfolk, England; baptized 11 July 1558. Probably educated at St. John's College, Cambridge, from 1575, BA 1580; Clare Hall, Cambridge, MA 1583; incorporated MA at Oxford University, 1588. Married c.1581 (separated c.1586); one illegitimate son. Travelled in Italy and Spain, 1579–80; moved to London c. 1586. Died in London, 3 September 1592.

Works

Collections

Life and Complete Works in Prose and Verse, edited by Alexander B. Grosart (15 vols.).   1881–86.
Plays and Poems, edited by J.C. Collins (2 vols.).   1905.
Complete Plays, edited by T.H. Dickinson.   1909.

Stage Works

Alphonsus, King of Aragon (produced London, 1587?).   1599.
George à Greene, The Pinner of Wakefield (produced London, c. 1587–93).   1599.
A Looking Glass for London and England, with Thomas Lodge (produced London, c.1587–89).   1594.
Friar Bacon and Friar Bungay (produced London, 1589?).   1594.
Orlando Furioso, One of the Twelve Peers of France (produced London, 1591?).   1594.
The Scottish History of James the Fourth (produced London, 1591?).   1598.
John of Bordeaux; or, The Second Part of Friar Bacon, possibly not by Greene, probably revised by Henry Chettle (produced London, c. 1590–94).
I Selimus, possibly not by Greene (produced London, c.1591–94).   1594.

Fiction

Mamillia: A Mirror of Looking Glass for the Ladies of England.   1583; part 2, as *The Triumph of Pallas*, 1583(?).
Arbasto: The Anatomy of Fortune.   1584.
Gwydonius: The Card of Fancy.   1584.
Morando the Tritameron of Love.   1584; augmented edition, 1587.
The Mirror of Modesty.   1584.
Planetomachia.   1585.
Euphues His Censure to Philautus.   1587.
Penelope's Web.   1587.

Pandosto: The Triumph of Time. 1588; as *Dorastus and Fawnia*, 1636.
Perimedes the Blacksmith. 1588.
Ciceronis Amor: Tullie's Love. 1589.
The Spanish Masquerado. 1589.
Menaphon: Camilla's Alarum to Slumbering Euphues. 1589; as *Greene's Arcadia*, 1610.
Greene's Never Too Late. 1590.
Greene's Mourning Garment. 1590.
Greene's Farewell to Folly. 1591.
The Black Book's Messenger: The Life and Death of Ned Browne. 1592.
Philomela: The Lady Fitzwater's Nightingale. 1592.
Greene's Groatsworth of Wit, Bought with a Million of Repentance (possibly not by Greene), edited by Henry Chettle. 1592.
Greene's Vision, Written at the Instance of His Death (possibly not by Greene). 1592.
Greene's Orpharion, Wherein is Discovered a Musical Concord of Pleasant Histories. 1599 (first extant edition).
Alcida: Greene's Metamorphosis. 1617 (first extant edition).

Verse

A Maiden's Dream: Upon the Death of Sir Christopher Hatton. 1591.

Other

A Notable Discovery of Cozenage. 1591; *The Second Part of Cony-Catching*, 1591; *Third and Last Part*, 1592.
A Disputation Between a He Cony-Catcher and a She Cony-Catcher. 1592; as *Thieves Falling Out, True Men Come by Their Goods*, 1615.
A Quip for an Upstart Courtier. 1592.
The Repentance of Robert Greene, Master of Arts (possibly not by Greene). 1592.

Translator, *An Oration at the Burial of Gregory the 13th*, from the French. 1585.
Translator, *The Royal Exchange*, by Orazio Rinaldi. 1590.

*

Bibliographies

Tetsumaro Hayashi, *Robert Greene Criticism: A Comprehensive Bibliography*, Metuchen, New Jersey, 1971.
A.F. Allison, *Robert Greene: A Bibliographical Catalogue of the Early Editions in English to 1640*, Folkestone, England, 1975.
James Seay Dean, *Robert Greene: A Reference Guide*, Boston, 1984.

Criticism

Books:
J.C. Jordan, *Robert Greene*, New York, 1915.
E.C. Petit, "The Comedies of Greene", in his *Shakespeare and the Romance Tradition*, London, 1949.
Norman Sanders, "The Comedy of Greene and Shakespeare", in *Early Shakespeare*, edited by John Russell Brown and Bernard Harris, London, 1961.
Kenneth Muir, "Robert Greene as Dramatist", in *Essays on Shakespeare and Elizabethan Drama in Honor of Hardin*

Craig, edited by Richard Hosley, Columbia, Missouri, 1962.
Werner Senn, *Studies in the Dramatic Construction of Robert Greene and George Peele*, Bern, 1973.
W. Chapman, *William Shakespeare and Robert Greene: The Evidence*, London, 1974.
R.G. Helgerson, *The Elizabethan Prodigals*, Berkeley, California, 1976.
Charles W. Crupi, *Robert Greene*, Boston, Massachusetts, 1986.

*   *   *

Satire, fantasy and romance are the most successful features of Greene's work, much of which now appears overladen with decorative literary allusions. Greene exploited his education as an ironic commentary on, and defence of, the "natural" life of the streets, alehouses, brothels, and theatres of Elizabethan London: an environment in which he was, for a brief period, a notorious celebrity. His fame was built on some 36 prose pamphlets—"Glad was that Printer that might be so blest to pay him deare for the very dregs of his wit"—and his publicly raffish life—"the Patriarch of shifters" as described by Gabriel Harvey in *Four Letters*.

His work for the theatre belongs to the final four years of this life, and appears to have been prompted by the publicity surrounding him. His prose ranges from the euphuistic style of *Mamilia* to the colloquial realism of *A Notable Discovery of Cozenage*, and his plays, likewise, vary in style. Just as in publication he began by imitating the fashion set by Lyly, so in theatre he seems to have begun by trying to emulate the success of Marlowe's *Tamburlaine*. Throughout *Alphonsus, King of Aragon* there are extravagant imitations of Marlowe's "mighty line". Amurack's blasphemous defiance of Mahomet in Act III, for example, mirrors the outburst in Act V, Scene 1 of *Tamburlaine, Part Two*. However, Greene's handling of blank verse is inept and, compared with his other plays, lacks variety (just as the plot lacks dramatic coherence).

Although all his dramas were published posthumously (and when they were written or first performed is not definitely known), it seems certain that *Alphonsus* was his earliest work for the theatre and must have been composed and performed in or soon after 1587. It was clearly not a success and he appears to have been derided for being unable to make his verses "jet upon the stage in tragical buskins". However, he did not forsake tragedy and bombast immediately, and in *Orlando Furioso* he proved more adept both with the blank verse and the stagecraft. This play is only loosely based on Ariosto's poem, Orlando's madness being the closest parallel, and still shows the influence of Marlowe, especially in the character of Sacripant. Its success on the stage must have derived from the "personation" of the title-role by the great actor Edward Alleyn, and its interest today rests on the existence of the original roll in Alleyn's handwriting, which can be compared with the printed text to give a valuable insight into Elizabethan theatre practice.

Greene's finest plays are *The Honourable History of Friar Bacon and Friar Bungay* and *The Scottish History of James the Fourth*. Neither are, in fact, historical dramas, but hybrid compositions which, like the best of his prose romances, are a blend of myth, history, and fairy-tale. Unlike the earlier hybrid plays of the 1560's and 1570's, Greene's comedies harmonize the heterogeneous elements to unify and sustain the illusion of a specific play-world. This world, though fanciful and romantic, is recognizably Elizabethan both in its cheerful celebration of the countryside and its realistic city tone. It is a world Shakespeare was to make his own in such comedies as *The Two Gentlemen of Verona* and *As You Like It*. Dramatic illusion is strengthened by Greene's use of reflective characters and situations to blur the audience-actor barrier. In *James the Fourth*, not only do Bohan and Oberon frame the action as spectators, but Bohan's sons, Slipper and Nano, slip from this fictional framework and its present time to the play-world and its fictional time, deepening the audience's sense of involvement and unsettling a too confident distinction between the real and the imaginary.

In *Friar Bacon and Friar Bungay*, Bacon's "glass prospective wherein men might see / Whatso their thoughts or hearts' desire could wish" allows stage characters to witness events taking place elsewhere which affect them inwardly in ways that the spectators in the theatre can also witness and experience, as it were, alongside them. Use of a play-within-a-play structure, of inductions and framework devices, choric interludes and dances, is not particular or special; but where Greene does appear to have been original is in using such techniques to strengthen belief in the present time and coherence of the play-world, in the consistent atmosphere of celebratory "magic" which supports the bitter-sweet optimism of the love-interest central to the comedy. It was an achievement that Shakespeare, among others, was quick to learn from and develop.

It is ironic then that a writer from whom Shakespeare gained much should now be so often remembered as one of the bard's jealous detractors. In his last semi-autobiographical pamphlet, *Greene's Groats-Worth of Wit*, the educated professional writer warns his fellow "university wits" of this player turned playwright:

> There is an upstart crow, beautified with our feathers that, with his "Tyger's heart wrapped in a player's hide", supposes he is as well able to bombast out a blank verse as the best of you: and being an absolute *Iohannes fac totum*, is in his own conceit the only Shake-scene in a country.

Greene's own quotation parodies York's attack on Margaret just before his death at her hand in *Henry VI* (a trilogy in which, some have argued, Greene's signature is apparent). It is a pastiche that marks an important shift in Elizabethan theatre for, from this moment on, Shakespeare stood alone ahead of a younger generation of playwrights, many of whom, like him, had experience as professional actors. However, Shakespeare's debt to Greene goes beyond any reworking of the repertoire which was the property of the adult companies, and beyond the rhymed couplets and blank verse of his early comedies. His fascination with the distinctive world created by Greene persisted throughout his career as his transformation of the prose fiction *Pandosto* into *The Winter's Tale* shows. Although Greene's clowns and heroines no longer hold the stage, their lineaments can be discerned in the Touchstones or Imogens that do.

—Leslie du S. Read

See also *Volume 1* entry on *Friar Bacon and Friar Bungay*.

GREGORY, Lady (Isabella Augusta). Born Isabella Augusta Persse in Roxborough, County Galway, Ireland, 5 March 1852. Educated privately. Married Sir William Gregory in 1880 (died 1892); one son. Co-founder, with Edward Martyn, George Moore, and William Butler Yeats, Irish Literary Theatre, 1899, which became the Irish National Theatre Society, eventually based at the Abbey Theatre, Dublin, 1904: director, with Yeats, and with Synge (to 1909), until 1932; toured the US with the Abbey Players, 1911–13. Lived at Coole Park, County Galway. Died at Coole Park, 22 May 1932.

Works

Collections

Spreading the News; The Rising of the Moon; and The Poorhouse, with Douglas Hyde. 1906.
Seven Short Plays (includes *Spreading the News; Hyacinth Halvey; The Rising of the Moon; The Jackdaw; The Workhouse Ward; The Travelling Man; The Gaol Gate*). 1909.
Irish Folk-History Plays (2 vols.; includes *Grania; Kincora; Dervorgilla; The Canavans; The White Cockade; The Deliverer*). 1912.
New Comedies (includes *The Bogie Men; The Full Moon; Coats; Damer's Gold; McDonough's Wife*). 1913.
"The Image" and Other Plays (includes *The Wrens; Hanrahan's Oath; Shanwalla*). 1922.
Three Wonder Plays (includes *The Dragon; Aristotle's Bellows; The Jester*). 1922.
Three Last Plays (includes *Sancho's Master; Dave; The Would-Be Gentleman*). 1928.
Selected Plays, edited by Elizabeth Coxhead. 1962.
Works (Coole Edition; vols. 5–9, *Plays*, edited by Ann Saddlemyer), edited by T.R. Henn and Colin Smythe. 1970—

Stage Works

The Twisting of the Rope, from the Gaelic version by Douglas Hyde (produced Gaiety Theatre, Dublin, 1901). In *Samhain*, October 1901.
A Losing Game. 1902; revised version, as *Twenty-Five* (produced Molesworth Hall, Dublin, 1903), in *Lost Plays of the Irish Renaissance*, edited by Robert Hogan and J.F. Kilroy, 1970; further revised version, as *On the Racecourse*, 1926 (as *Galway Races*, produced 1913).
The Lost Saint. In *Samhain*, October 1902.
Spreading the News (produced Abbey Theatre, Dublin, 1904). In *Spreading the News . . .*, 1906.
The Poorhouse, with Douglas Hyde (produced 1904). In *Spreading the News . . .*, 1906.
The Rising of the Moon (produced Abbey Theatre, Dublin, 1906). In *Samhain*, December 1904; in book form, in *Spreading the News . . .*, 1906.
Kincora (produced Abbey Theatre, Dublin, 1905). 1905; revised version, in *Irish Folk-History Plays*, 1912.
The White Cockade (produced Abbey Theatre, Dublin, 1905). 1905.
Hyacinth Halvey (produced Abbey Theatre, Dublin, 1906). 1906.
The Doctor in Spite of Himself, from *Le Médecin malgré lui* by Molière (produced Abbey Theatre, Dublin, 1906). In *The Kiltartan Molière*, 1910.
The Canavans (produced Abbey Theatre, Dublin, 1906). In *Irish Folk-History Plays*, 1912.
The Gaol Gate (produced Abbey Theatre, Dublin, 1906). In *Seven Short Plays*, 1909.

The Unicorn from the Stars, with W.B. Yeats, from the play *Where There is Nothing* by Yeats (produced Abbey Theatre, Dublin, 1907).   1908.

The Jackdaw (produced Abbey Theatre, Dublin, 1907).   In *Seven Short Plays*, 1909.

Dervorgilla (produced Abbey Theatre, Dublin, 1907).   In *Irish Folk-History Plays*, 1912.

The Workhouse Ward (produced Abbey Theatre, Dublin, 1908).   In *Seven Short Plays*, 1909.

Teja, from a play by Sudermann (produced Abbey Theatre, Dublin, 1908).

The Rogueries of Scapin, from a play by Molière (produced Abbey Theatre, Dublin, 1908).   In *The Kiltartan Molière*, 1910.

The Miser, from a play by Molière (produced Abbey Theatre, Dublin, 1909).   In *The Kiltartan Molière*, 1910.

The Travelling Man, with W.B. Yeats (produced Abbey Theatre, Dublin, 1910).   In *Seven Short Plays*, 1909.

The Image (produced Abbey Theatre, Dublin, 1909).   1910.

Mirandolina, from a play by Goldoni (produced Abbey Theatre, Dublin, 1910).   1924.

Coats (produced Abbey Theatre, Dublin, 1910).   In *New Comedies*, 1913.

The Full Moon (produced Abbey Theatre, Dublin, 1911).   1911.

The Nativity Play, from a Gaelic play by Douglas Hyde (produced Abbey Theatre, Dublin, 1911).

The Deliverer (produced Abbey Theatre, Dublin, 1911).   In *Irish Folk-History Plays*, 1912.

Grania.   In *Irish Folk History Plays*, 1912.

The Bogie Men (produced Royal Court Theatre, London, 1912).   In *New Comedies*, 1913.

Damer's Gold (produced Abbey Theatre, Dublin, 1912).   In *New Comedies*, 1913.

McDonough's Wife (produced Abbey Theatre, Dublin, 1912).   In *New Comedies*, 1913.

The Marriage, from a Gaelic play by Douglas Hyde (produced Abbey Theatre, Dublin, 1913).

The Wrens (produced Royal Court Theatre, London, 1914).   In *"The Image" and Other Plays*, 1922.

Shanwalla (produced Abbey Theatre, Dublin, 1915).   In *"The Image" and Other Plays*, 1922.

The Golden Apple: A Play for Kiltartan Children (produced Abbey Theatre, Dublin, 1920).   1916.

Hanrahan's Oath (produced Abbey Theatre, Dublin, 1918).   1918.

The Dragon: A Wonder Play (produced Abbey Theatre, Dublin, 1919).   1920.

Aristotle's Bellows (produced Abbey Theatre, Dublin, 1921).   In *Three Wonder Plays*, 1922.

The Old Woman Remembers (produced Abbey Theatre, Dublin, 1923).

The Story Brought by Brigit: A Passion Play (produced Abbey Theatre, Dublin, 1924).   1924.

The Would-Be Gentleman, from a play by Molière (produced Abbey Theatre, Dublin, 1926).   In *Three Last Plays*, 1928.

Sancho's Master (produced Abbey Theatre, Dublin, 1927).   In *Three Last Plays*, 1928.

Dave (produced Abbey Theatre, Dublin, 1927).   In *Three Last Plays*, 1928.

My First Play: Colman and Guaire.   1930.

Memoirs and Letters

Our Irish Theatre: A Chapter of Autobiography.   1913; revised edition, in *Works*, 1972.

Journals 1916–1930, edited by Lennox Robinson.   1946; revised edition (2 vols.), edited by Daniel J. Murphy, in *Works*, 1978–87 (part of *Works*, 1970–).

Seventy Years (1852–1922), edited by Colin Smythe.   1974.

Theatre Business: The Correspondence of the First Abbey Theatre Directors: William Butler Yeats, Gregory, and J.M. Synge, edited by Ann Saddlemyer.   1982.

Other

Arabi and His Household.   1882.

Poets and Dreamers: Studies and Translations from the Irish.   1903.

A Book of Saints and Wonders.   1906.

The Kiltartan History Book.   1909.

The Kiltartan Wonder Book.   1910.

Hugh Lane's Life and Achievement.   1921; as *Sir Hugh Lane: His Life and Legacy*, in *Works*, 1973.

Case for the Return of Sir Hugh Lane's Pictures to Dublin.   1926.

Coole.   1931; in *Works*, 1971.

Editor, *The Autobiography of Sir William Gregory*.   1894.

Editor, *Mr. Gregory's Letter Box 1813–1830*.   1898.

Editor, *Ideals in Ireland*.   1901.

Editor, *Visions and Beliefs in the West of Ireland* (2 vols.).   1920; in *Works*, 1970.

Translator, *Cuchulain of Muirthemne: The Story of the Men of the Red Branch of Ulster*.   1902; in *Works*, 1970.

Translator, *Gods and Fighting Men: The Story of the Tuatha De Danaan and of the Fianna of Ireland*.   1904; in *Works*, 1970.

Translator, *The Kiltartan Poetry Book: Prose Translations from the Irish*.   1918.

*

Bibliographies

E.H. Mikhail, *Lady Gregory: An Annotated Bibliography of Criticism*, Metuchen, New Jersey, 1982.

Criticism

Books:

Elizabeth Coxhead, *Lady Gregory: A Literary Portrait*, London, 1961, revised edition, London, 1966.

Elizabeth Coxhead, *J.M. Synge and Lady Gregory*, London, 1962.

Ann Saddlemyer, *In Defence of Lady Gregory, Playwright*, Dublin, 1966.

Ann Dedio, *Das dramatische Werk von Lady Gregory*, Bern, 1967.

Augusta Anne Gregory, *Me and Nu: Childhood at Coole*, Gerrards Cross, 1970.

Hazard Adams, *Lady Gregory*, Lewisburg, Pennsylvania, 1973.

Michèle Dalmasso, *Lady Gregory et la renaissance irlandaise*, Aix-en-Provence, 1982.

Edward A. Kopper Jr., *Lady Isabella Persse Gregory*, Boston, 1976.

E.H. Mikhail (ed.), *Lady Gregory: Interviews and Recollections*, London, 1977.

Mary Lou Kohfeldt, *Lady Gregory: The Woman Behind the Irish Renaissance*, New York, 1984.

Ann Saddlemyer and Colin Smythe (ed.), *Lady Gregory, Fifty Years After*, Gerrards Cross, 1987.

* * *

Lady Gregory's fame rests securely on the part she played, with W.B. Yeats, in creating the Irish dramatic movement. Without her influential and vigorously practical support, Yeats's vision of an Irish theatre could scarcely have been realised, as he acknowledged when receiving his Nobel prize in 1923. She should have been standing beside him, he said, along with the ghost of Synge.

Augusta Gregory was also a playwright—"a first-class one, and a prolific one too", said Sean O'Casey, one of those whose talents she fostered. She discovered her talent relatively late, when she and Yeats set themselves the task of building up "a Celtic and Irish school of dramatic literature" for the Irish Literary Theatre they had founded, with others, in 1899. Lady Gregory had access, through her knowledge of the Irish language and her long-standing interest in folklore, to the legends, myths, and stories which made up the "matter of Ireland". Initially she put these riches entirely at the disposal of others, notably Yeats (who drew heavily on her *Cuchulain of Muirthemne*). She provided Yeats with myths from Gaelic, and Douglas Hyde with scenarios to enrich with Gaelic: one of her first exercises in dramatic writing was her translation of Hyde's *Casad-an't-Sugan* as *The Twisting of the Rope*.

She served her playwriting apprenticeship as collaborator on plays which called for her special knowledge of peasant ways. Her experience as a widowed Anglo-Irish landowner, living on her estate, Coole Park, in the Kiltartan district of Galway, had brought her close to the cultural life of her Irish-speaking tenants. Many of the situations in her plays are based on local lore or real-life incidents concerning local people; her own favourite, *The Gaol Gate*, derived from three such strands. She invented an Irish version of English based partly on Gaelic syntax and enlivened with colourful colloquialisms from everyday speech around Coole. "Kiltartan" became a new stage language. It greatly influenced Synge, and was sometimes heard on the Abbey stage in an unexpected context, as when Molière's Sganarelle and the rest spoke with a brogue through Lady Gregory's translations. It is an idiom easy to parody, but at its best brings a freshness and colour into the humdrum lives Lady Gregory often chose to dramatise. *The Workhouse Ward*, a potentially grim play about two old men with only their quarrels to make life bearable, announces itself as vivacious and high-coloured from its opening line: "Isn't it a hard case, Mike McInery, myself and yourself to be left here in the bed, and it the feast day of Saint Colman, and the rest of the ward attending on the mass".

Wherever peasant characters appear in the early plays of the movement, the hand of Lady Gregory may be suspected. Critics have credited her with a large, if not dominant share in Yeats's peasant comedy *The Pot of Broth*, and his patriotic folk play, *Cathleen ni Houlihan*. She certainly provided important help in 1902 with *Where There is Nothing*, a play about a middle-class visionary who takes to the road with a band of tinkers, a scenario where Lady Gregory's ear for common speech was indispensable. When she collaborated with Yeats in revising the play (as *The Unicorn From the Stars*), it became, he said, "almost wholly hers in handiwork". He included it, however, in his *Collected Plays*, showing how difficult it had become, by then, to draw the line between collaboration and single authorship.

Augusta Gregory ventured into authorship on her own account in 1901 when she wrote (but kept to herself) a play for children, *Colman and Guaire*, based on local legend: she strongly believed in using drama as an educational tool. Her style of writing really needed Irish actors and it was, in fact, only when the talented Fay brothers joined the movement (which became the Abbey Theatre in 1904) that the first play to appear under Lady Gregory's name alone was produced in Dublin. *Twenty-Five*, a comedy in her preferred one-act form, was well received but overshadowed by Synge's *The Shadow of the Glen* which figured in the same programme.

This was to be Lady Gregory's fate with the critics, if not with the audiences, who developed a taste for her plays, especially her folk comedies. She herself contributed to the "modest" version of her achievement. Of one of her most popular comedies, *Spreading the News*, she said that its initial idea—a rumour spreading at a fair till it turned truth upside down—came to her as a tragedy, but "comedy and not tragedy was wanted at our theatre to put beside the high poetic work". Sean O'Casey fumed at her tendency, as he saw it, to give too much time to helping others, which "loosened the tautness of her own work". She was, he said, "a better playwright than most of them", and yet "acted the part of a charwoman", though "one with a star on her breast".

Misunderstandings and ironic reversals, comic or poignant, are a staple of Augusta Gregory's drama. Bartley Fallon is reported as running after a man with a hayfork (in fact, simply to return it to him) and rumour soon has him committing a murder: the play ends with the "victim" in handcuffs. A different kind of reversal occurs in *The Rising of the Moon*, when a policeman encounters, without at first recognising, the escaped Fenian prisoner he is looking out for and is persuaded to let him go, because, as Yeats put it, "the prisoner has aroused with some old songs the half-forgotten patriotism of his youth".

Lady Gregory's more ambitious plays on Irish legend and history, such as *Kincora* (about Brian Boru), were respectfully received in their time: she consistently maintains some homely realism, even in the folk history form. Unusually among the playwrights of her day, she offered a feminine perspective on heroic material. *Grania*, an intimate three-act treatment of the legendary love story, using only three characters, was unproduced in her lifetime, perhaps because she felt it revealed too much about the feelings of a young woman committed (as she herself had been) to marriage with a much older husband. *Dervorgilla* also presents a romantic tragedy from a woman's viewpoint, that of the aged Dervorgilla. Even in her late 60's she continued to experiment, writing fantastic or "wonder" plays (often with children in mind), such as *The Golden Apple*, and plays on religious themes, like *The Story Brought by Brigit*.

It is probably for her short folk plays, especially her comedies, however, that Augusta Gregory will be best remembered. She may often have written in haste to provide plays for the Abbey repertoire, but she had a genuine inspiration. She invented a language and a landscape and demonstrated in her drama the truth of her saying about Irish writers and their "incorrigible genius for myth-making".

—Katharine Worth

————

GRIBOYEDOV, Alexander Sergeyevich. Born in Moscow, 15 January 1795. Educated at the University of

Moscow, 1806–08, studying humanities, law, and natural sciences: graduated in law; education interrupted by Napoleon's invasion of Russia, 1812. Joined the Moscow hussars (General Kologryvov's reserve), but saw no military action. Married daughter of the poet Prince Alexander Chavchavadze in 1828. Joined Ministry of Foreign Affairs in St. Petersburg, 1816; diplomat in Tehran, 1819–21; diplomatic secretary to General A.P. Yermolov, in Tiflis, 1821–23; returned to Georgia, 1825; under arrest for four months on suspicion of involvement in the Decembrist uprising, 1825: returned to Caucasus after release, 1826; prepared the text of the Treaty of Turkmanchai, concluding the Russian-Persian war; was promoted to Resident Russian Minister in Persia. Killed during the storming of the Russian embassy, Tehran, by a mob of insurgents, 11 February 1829.

Works

Collections

Polnoe sobranie sochineny [Collected Works].   1911–17.
Sochineniya v stikhakh [Works], edited by I.N. Medvedeva.   1967.
Izbrannoe [Selections], edited by S.A. Fomicheva.   1978.

Stage Works

Molodye suprugi [The Young Married Couple], from a play by Creuzé de Lesser (produced St. Petersburg, 1815). 1815.
Pritvornaya nevernost [False Infidelity], with A.A. Gendre, from a play by Nicholas Barthe (produced St. Petersburg, 1818).   1818.
Student [The Student], with Pavel A. Katenin (produced Alexandrinsky Theatre, St. Petersburg, 1904).   1817.
Svoya semya; ili, Zamuzhnyaya nevesta [All in the Family; or, The Married Fiancée], with A.A. Shakovskoy and Nikolay Khmelnitsky (produced Maly Theatre, St. Petersburg, 1818).
Proba intermedy [Test of an Interlude] (produced Bolshoi Theatre, St. Petersburg, 1819).   In *Polnoe sobranie sochineny*, 1911–17.
Kto brat, kto sestra; ili, Obman za obmanom [Who's the Brother, Who's the Sister; or, Deception for Deception], with Prince Peter Vyazemsky and others (libretto; produced St. Petersburg, 1824).
Gore ot uma [Woe from Wit] (produced St. Petersburg Theatre, St. Petersburg, 1825; complete version produced Kive Theatre, Kiev, 1831).   1825 (partial version); 1833 (censored version); 1875 (uncensored version); translated as *Intelligence Comes to Grief*, in *Anthology of Russian Literature 2*, edited by Leo Wiener, 1902; as *The Misfortune of Being Clever*, 1914; as *Wit Works Woe*, in *Masterpieces of Russian Drama, 1*, edited by G.R. Noyes, 1933; as *Chatsky*, in *Four Russian Plays*, translated by Joshua Cooper, 1972.

*

Criticism

Books:
J. Bonamour, *Griboedov et la vie littéraire de son temps*, Paris, 1965.
Evelyn J. Harden, *The Murder of Griboedov: New Materials*, Birmingham, 1979.

Alexander Griboyedov (1827).

Articles:
D.P. Costello, "The Murder of Griboedov", in *Oxford Slavonic Papers*, 1958.

* * *

Although nothing like as well known outside Russia as Chekhov, Griboyedov is the classic dramatist of the Russian theatre, and playing the part of his his principal character, Chatsky, is like playing Hamlet in the English-speaking world.

The barrier to the reception of Griboyedov's work away from home has been its form and language. He is the author of one work which is not only the cornerstone of the Russian theatre but a landmark in Russian culture. This comedy, *The Misfortune of Being Clever* (also known as "Woe from Wit"), is written in richly idiomatic verse. It is a monument of lapidary language which not merely shows, in an unrivalled way, the speech of the society of the time; but like the language of Pushkin fixes the standard language which had been so agonizingly unsettled and so exotic in foreign influences throughout the preceding century and before. Griboyedov reaches back into the age-old resources of the native language, brought into focus by Krylov in his folk fables, and creates on stage a panoply of Moscow personages (each with matching speech), binds them in dramatic conflict and comic confusion, infuses the whole with insight and perception, and brings forth a tone poem of Russian high society caught in the crossfire of ancient traditions under threat from modern innovation. Translations are but pale reflections of the original, those in prose sounding like opera without the music.

What is beyond dispute is that he found the civil service irksome and longed to devote himself to literature. His writing career began in 1814 with two adaptions of lightweight French salon comedies in literary verse. In 1817 he collaborated on two plays, this time closer to Russian traditions and more colloquial in language. After *The Misfortune of Being Clever* Griboyedov turned his back on comedy and declared his intention to write tragedy. There remain fragments of several works of a historical nature from events of old Russian history to a grandiose epic of the Napoleonic war, but he had no time in his remaining few years to bring them to fruition. Thus he left completed only his single masterpiece, *The Misfortune of Being Clever*, which, as often happens with writers, is a happy amalgam of the best of his talent and formative influences, whereas the time of great tragedies such as he had in mind to write had probably gone.

In the play he brings together knowledge of West European theatre—Shakespeare, Molière, Beaumarchais—and the best of Russian 18th-century satirical theatre, creating a work not derivative or imitative, however, but uniquely different. It has none of Shakespeare's ebullience. Unlike Molière, Griboyedov gives portraits, not types, though the portraits are so finely drawn that they have come to have universal validity. Unlike Beaumarchais, he has not written a political play, although the clash of values in the play has readily been seen as political in the context of revolutionary Europe and reactionary Russia.

There is a significant difference too, between *The Misfortune of Being Clever* and the comedy of manners which takes its comic effects from the contrast between the hero who is wrong, and society which is right. In Griboyedov's play the same is true in Russian society's own terms, but society itself is clearly the object of the author's satire. Yet the hero, Chatsky, is no mere catalyst. Like Hamlet, but without the tragedy, he is alienated by the dramatic argument of the play. His frustration he pours out in tirades in which he hits out at everything and everyone. He is the ageless champion of the individual against the establishment, of youth against age, of new ideas against old ways, of the patriot against foreign fashions, and, at base, of idealism against society's indifference (an extension of the heroine's indifference to him).

Griboyedov holds a unique place in Russian literature and has been many things to many men. For some he has portrayed a fossilized society, for others his has been a clarion call, the voice of his generation. For most, he has entered the lists of dramatists of world stature rising above their national background. He is the sole representative in Russian literature of a writer of sophisticated timeless charm and wit, albeit already tinged with a poignancy prefiguring the yawning rift between letters and society so characteristic of 19th-century Russia.

—Alan G. Waring

See also *Volume 1* entry on *The Misfortune of Being Clever*.

GRIEG, (Johan) Nordahl (Brun). Born in Bergen, Norway, 1 November 1902. Educated at University of Oslo, 1920 (studies interrupted by his travels, but graduated 1925); two terms at Wadham College, Oxford, 1923–24. Married the actress Gerd Egede-Nissen in 1940. Seaman, 1920–21; returned to Europe, 1922, and travelled throughout Italy, France, Germany; journalist in China, reporting on the civil war: experiences published in *Kinesiske dage*, 1927; first play, *En ung mands kjærlighet* [A Young Man's Love], produced 1927; lived in Finnmark, 1929; returned to Oxford, 1931; in the Soviet Union, observing Russian theatre and culture, 1933–34; founded the anti-fascist magazine *Veien frem*, 1936; reported on the Spanish Civil War, and published experiences in *Spansk sommer*, 1937; military service on the Finnish border, 1939–40; following the German invasion of Norway, participated in the evacuation of gold from the Norwegian treasury to England, 1940; served with the Norwegian government-in-exile, London, making many BBC radio broadcasts to Norway. Was shot down and killed while accompanying an Allied bombing mission over Berlin, 2 December 1943.

Works

Collections

Samlede verker [Collected Works] (7 vols.). 1947.
Skuespill [Plays]. 1948.

Stage Works

En ung mands kjærlighet [A Young Man's Love] (produced Nationale Scene, Bergen, 1927). 1927.
Barabbas [Barabbas] (produced Nationalteatret, Oslo, 1927). 1927.
Atlanterhavet [The Atlantic] (produced Nationalteatret, Oslo, 1932). 1932.
Vår ære og vår makt (produced Nationalteatret, Oslo, 1935). 1935. translated as *Our Power and Our Glory*, 1971.
Men imorgen [But Tomorrow] (produced Nationale Scene, Bergen, 1936). 1936.
Nederlaget (produced Nationalteatret, Oslo, 1937). 1936; translated as *The Defeat*, 1944.

Fiction

Skibet gaar videre. 1924; translated as *The Ship Sails On*, 1927.
Ung må verden ennu være [May the World Stay Young]. 1948.

Verse

Rundt Kap det gode haab. 1922.
Stene i strømmen. 1925.
Norge i våre hjerter. 1929.
Digte i utvalg. 1932.
Friheten. 1943; translated as *All That is Mine Demand: War Poems*, 1944.
Håbet. 1946.
Samlede dikt [Collected Poems]. 1948.

Memoirs and Letters

Graeske breve (letters). 1952.
Et varig vennskap: 46 brev fra Nordahl Grieg til Nils Lie (letters). 1981.

Other

Kinesiske dage [Chinese Days]. 1927.
De unge døde [The Young Dead]. 1932.

Spansk sommer [Spanish Summer].   1937.
Flagget (war experiences).   1946.
Veien frem (journalism), edited by Odd Hølaas.   1947.
Morgen over Finnmarksvidden.   1967.

*

Bibliographies

Bibliography in *Nordahl Grieg: En dikter og hans tid*, by F. J. Hasluund, Oslo, 1962.

Criticism

Books:
J. Mawby, *Writers and Politics in Modern Scandinavia*, London, 1978.

Articles:
Halvdan Koht, "Nordahl Grieg", in *American-Scandinavian Review*, vol. 30 no. 1, 1942.
Martin Nag, "Nordahl Grieg und Bertolt Brecht", in *Études germaniques*, 22, 1967.
Miluse Jurickova, "Das dramatische Werk von Nordahl Grieg im Kampf gegen Krieg und Faschismus", vol. 29 no. 5, 1981.
Bien Horst, "Zehn Thesen zur literaturhistorischen Stellung Nordahl Griegs", in *Nordeuropa*, 15, 1982.

*   *   *

Nordahl Grieg has become a hero whose life and works are inseparable. His dedication to causes, enthusiasm for Stalinist Marxism, and achievements as a writer have been evaluated differently as historical perspective has changed. In addition to novels and poems, Grieg wrote six plays, each inspired by an intense desire to express personal experiences, artistic vision, and social problems in theatrical terms. The extent to which Grieg is appreciated as a political activist and author varies, but no one can deny the vitality of his concern about international issues and his devotion to Norway.

Grieg's first work for the stage has traditional dramatic form. *En ung mands kjærlighet* [A Young Man's Love] is a somewhat melodramatic piece showing the entanglements and cruelty of love affairs and the sacrifice of innocent people. Suspense builds as the young man of the title must choose between an innocent young girl and an attractive divorcée, who is anguished by the death of her child. Grieg would continue to explore the dualism presented here, the contrast between the vulnerability of gentle, good people and the attractiveness of those who are dangerous and strong. All Grieg's later plays are more innovative in craftsmanship and broader in their social vision.

Inspired by his observations in China, Grieg explored the concept of the necessity of revolution by using Biblical characters in *Barabbas* and the contrast of goodness and violence symbolized by Barrabas and Christ. Grieg wrote this expressionistic drama to show that in any epoch, in any country, people face choices, the most pervasive being that between pacifism and force. Presented in short scenes that are lyrical or bitterly ironic, the allegorical play shows why Jesus's gospel of liberation through love is rejected and Barrabas is chosen to lead the fight against imperialism. The weak character of Jesus and the unfamiliarity of form limited the play's appeal, but it is significant for foreshadowing the technique Grieg would use in his major works.

The playwright made a brave attempt at expressionism with *Atlanterhavet* [The Atlantic], inspired by his experiences as a journalist. Trying to use the latest scenic, lighting, and sound effects to create the tense and hectic atmosphere of the newspaper world, Grieg directed the play for Den Nationale Scene in Bergen. *Atlanterhavet* satirizes the public's appetite for hero worship and sensational news and the willingness of the press to feed that appetite with stories of danger and death. A young reporter on the rebound from an unhappy love-affair betrays his ideals and dares to experience a fatal transatlantic flight. Machines—whether the airplane or the rotary press—symbolize the restlessness, escapism, and cynicism that Grieg saw as characteristic of the period. The play's exciting action builds to a powerful final scene.

In 1935 *Vår ære og vår makt* [Our Power and Our Glory], a successful and controversial play, was produced in Bergen and Oslo, bringing the conflict of class interests and the suffering of war on stage in sharply contrasting images. Using an anti-Aristotelian epic technique reminiscent of Noël Coward's *Cavalcade*, the playwright alternates between the profiteering shipowners and the seamen whom they send into torpedo-strewn waters. Grieg showed that he could combine the panoramic staging techniques he had admired in London and Moscow with charming and poignant vignettes drawn from an intimate understanding of life in Bergen. He was well acquainted with the educated, privileged leaders of society, but his heart was with the humble seamen and their families. While writing the play Grieg interviewed seamen who could tell him of the dangerous voyages they survived during World War I, and the neglect and poverty they were suffering in the 1930's. Grieg was not only looking back to the years when commercial speculators and foreign spies were operating in Bergen, he was looking ahead to the horrors of the approaching war. With striking dramatic episodes, a speech that seemed to be a spontaneous outburst from an audience member, and symbolic tableaux, he hoped to awaken compassion and a sense of responsibility to work for peace.

Grieg's next play, *Men imorgen* [But Tomorrow] was inspired by his continuing foreboding about war. Within the framework of a domestic psychological drama, he explored ethical problems by having, as the major character, a Norwegian industrialist involved with the German munitions industry. Reminiscent of Ibsen's drama, the action presents the protest of factory workers who are endangered by exposure to hazardous poison gas, but emphasizes, still more, the family of the industrialist. That the capitalistic system depends on war for profits is asserted through the decisions of members of the board of the company and of the central characters. Despite his sincere exploration of serious issues in terms of Marxist theory, Grieg did not succeed here in creating an effective dramatic work.

Grieg's travels—whether to Greece, England, the Soviet Union, China—always had an impact on his thinking and writing. In 1937 he completed an epic masterpiece, his most ambitious and international play, *Nederlaget* [The Defeat]. The playwright planned to establish rhythm by alternating quiet two-character scenes with tumultuous crowd scenes, and emphasizing the effect with a musical score by Sparre Olsen. While Grieg demonstrated that he had done research on the history of the Paris Commune of 1879, he also wanted audiences to be aware of the complexities of contemporary civil wars and socialist experiments. Drawing upon his poetic gifts, Grieg created numerous characters who are vivid even though they appear briefly, and pictured them caught in the clash of opposing forces and ambitions. Whether dramatizing desperate hunger, slaughter, arrogant governance, or noble courage, *Nederlaget* evokes a sense of the futility of the people's struggle, the cruelty of war, and faith in the eventual triumph of human rights.

Nordahl Grieg lived his brief life intensely, expressing his beliefs and transforming his observations into vigorous poetic images and daring actions. Serving his country took all his energy after Norway was invaded and occupied in 1940. The manuscript of his last play, about the poet Henrik Wergeland, was lost. The extant plays reflect the period of history in which they were written, while at the same time touching our hearts and consciences because of the universality of their concern with world peace and the welfare of humanity. No other Norwegian dramatist in the 1930's tried as Grieg did to use the technical and expressive means of contemporary theatre and film or to present the urgent ethical and political issues of the day.

—Carla Waal

GRIFFITHS, Trevor. Born in Manchester, Lancashire, England, 4 April 1935. Educated at St. Bede's College, Manchester, 1945–52; Manchester University, 1952–55, BA in English 1955; studied for external MA from 1961. Served in the British Army, Manchester Regiment, 1955–57: infantryman. Married Janice Elaine Stansfield in 1960 (died 1977); one son and two daughters. Teacher of English and games in a private school, Oldham, Lancashire, 1957–61; Lecturer in Liberal Studies, Stockport Technical College, Cheshire, 1962–65; co-editor, *Labour's Northern Voice*, 1962–65, and series editor for Workers Northern Publishing Society; further education officer, BBC, Leeds, 1965–72; first stage play, *The Wages of Thin*, produced 1969; first television plays, the *Adam Smith* series, broadcast 1972. Recipient: BAFTA Writer's Award, 1982.

Works

Collections

Collected Plays for Television. 1988.

Stage Works

The Wages of Thin (produced Stables Theatre, Manchester, 1969).
The Big House, from his radio play (produced Newcastle upon Tyne, 1975).
Occupations (produced Stables Theatre, Manchester, 1970). With *The Big House*, 1972; revised version, published separately, 1980.
Apricots (produced Basement Theatre, London, 1971). With *Thermidor*, 1978.
Thermidor (produced Edinburgh Festival Fringe, 1971). With *Apricots*, 1978.
Lay By, with others (produced Traverse Theatre, Edinburgh, 1971). 1972.
Sam, Sam (produced Open Space Theatre, London, 1972; revised version produced London, 1978). In *Plays and Players*, April 1972.
Gun (produced Pool Theatre, Edinburgh, 1973).
The Party (produced by the National Theatre Company, Old Vic, London, 1973; revised version produced Coventry, 1974). 1974.
Comedians (produced Playhouse, Nottingham, 1975). 1976; revised version, 1979.
All Good Men from the television play (produced Young Vic Theatre, London, 1975).
The Cherry Orchard, from a play by Chekhov, translated by Helen Rappaport (produced Playhouse, Nottingham, 1977). 1978.
Deeds, with others (produced Playhouse, Nottingham, 1978). In *Plays and Players*, May and June 1978.
Oi for England (produced Royal Court Theatre Upstairs, London, 1982). 1982.
Real Dreams, from the story "Revolution in Cleveland" by Jeremy Pikser (produced Williamstown, Massachusetts, 1984). 1987 (includes "Revolution in Cleveland" by Pikser).
Piano (produced National Theatre, London, 1990). 1990.
The Gulf Between Us: The Truth and Other Fictions (produced West Yorkshire Playhouse, Leeds, 1992). 1992.

Screenplays

Reds, with Warren Beatty, 1981; *Fatherland*, 1987 (published 1987).

Television Plays

Adam Smith series (as Ben Rae), 1972; *The Silver Mask*, from a story by Horace Walpole (*Between the Wars* series), 1973; *All Good Men*, 1974 (published with *Absolute Beginners*, 1974); *Absolute Beginners* (*Fall of Eagles* series), 1974 (published with *All Good Men*, 1974); *Don't Make Waves* (*Eleventh Hour* series), with Snoo Wilson, 1975; *Through the Night*, 1975 (published with *Such Impossibilities*, 1977); *Bill Brand* series, 1976; *Such Impossibilities* (published with *Through the Night*, 1977); *Comedians*, 1979; *Sons and Lovers*, 1981 (published 1981); *The Cherry Orchard*, from a play by Chekhov, 1981; *Country: A Tory Story*, 1981 (published 1981); *Oi for England*, 1982; *The Last Place on Earth*, from a book by Roland Huntford, 1985 (published as *Judgement Over the Dead: The Screenplay of the Last Place on Earth*, 1986); *The Party*, 1988.

Radio Plays

The Big House, 1969 (published with *Occupations*, 1972); *Jake's Brigade*, 1971.

Other

Tip's Lot (for children). 1972.

*

Bibliographies

Malcolm Hay, "Theatre Checklist No.9: Trevor Griffiths", in *Theatre Facts*, vol.3 no.1, 1976.

Criticism

Books:
Oleg Kerensky, *The New British Drama*, London, 1977.
Janet Wolff and others, "Problems of Radical Drama: The

Plays and Productions of Trevor Griffiths", in *Literature, Society and the Sociology of Literature*, edited by Francis Barker and others, Colchester, Essex, 1977.

John Bull, *New British Political Dramatists*, London, 1984.

Mike Poole and John Wyver, *Powerplays: Trevor Griffiths in Television*, London, 1984.

Richard A. Cave, *New British Drama in Performance*, Gerrards Cross, 1987.

* * *

Though a prolific writer for television in the 1970's, Griffiths has never abandoned the theatre, and as opportunities for serious and politically committed work on television have decreased, he has also turned to film. All his work is directly informed by his socialist convictions, and even his translation of *The Cherry Orchard* revealed a text which found the destruction of the old order to be less an elegy for those losing power than a positive recognition of the necessity of the decline of the old order. Politics frequently constitute the actual subject matter of Griffiths' plays, which may focus on historical moments of rebellion and revolution (for example, *Occupations* and *Absolute Beginners*), on more recent attempts to overthrow the state, (*The Party*, *Real Dreams*), or on the politics of the Right (*Country*, *Oi for England*). Even where the subject may not seem, at first, to be political, as in *Comedians*, similar discussions and issues lie just below the surface.

The decision to channel work into television is itself consciously political; recognising that talking to small and probably converted audiences in fringe venues permits little chance to contribute meaningfully to society's political debates, Griffiths advocates television as the medium for reaching the largest possible audience, and for engaging wholeheartedly with "the popular imagination". While other socialist playwrights of his generation moved from fringe into mainstream theatres, Griffiths describes television as our true National Theatre, and compares writing for the major middle-class theatrical institutions to watching sport "from the covered stand; you stay dry but there's a pitch dividing you from another possible, and possibly decisive, action on the terraces". Though conceding that the television writer must hand control of his text over to producers whose responsibility is to advertisers or to a hierarchy that may well be deeply antagonistic towards the play's message, Griffiths believes it is possible to exploit a basic "leakiness" in the way television operates, and describes as "strategic penetration" his subversive attempts to infiltrate an essentially conservative medium.

A similar choice, between preserving the purity of one's ideas and compromising them in order to gain power and influence, occurs as a crucial focus of debate within several of Griffiths' plays; it is embodied in the 12-part series about a Labour Member of Parliament, *Bill Brand*, and in *All Good Men*, both of which question whether to work within the parliamentary Labour Party for socialist change is a betrayal of ideals and principles or a necessary sacrifice which allows actual advances to be made. Pragmatism and idealism are central to the debate between the purist Gramsci and the realistic Kabak in *Occupations*, and to the discussions of *The Party*, which also asks whether socialist television writers and producers can use television effectively, or whether it simply uses them.

Superficially naturalistic, Griffiths' plays have rarely broken new stylistic ground; he himself describes his writing as "critical realism", indicating that though it may seem simply to reproduce real life, it is actually honed and shaped

to a precise degree. The format of a recognisably well-made play is used to counterpoint the difficulty of the arguments with which Griffiths is confronting his audience; since he is specifically aiming to introduce a broad, rather than a university-educated, audience to what he acknowledges to be "unfamiliar, dense and complex arguments", it is, he says, "an overwhelming imposition to present those arguments in unfamiliar forms". Some critics have found this to be either too restrictive or simply invalid, complaining, for example, that audiences of *Bill Brand* identified with the central character irrespective of, rather than because of, his politics.

Nevertheless more than most contemporary political playwrights, Griffiths chooses to build his debates around character, while subtly undermining and challenging the view that personal lives inevitably take priority over political actions: in *Real Dreams*, for example, we are asked to admire two young revolutionaries who sacrifice their long-term relationship in order to make the movement stronger and more effective, while in *Comedians* we have to accept that the vicious and unfunny anger of Price is more likely to change society than the much pleasanter liberal humanism of the older comedian. Griffiths argues that his characterisation "is not basically psychological, but social, sociological and political", and that he provides audiences with opportunities for both empathy and critical distance from all the characters.

Certainly, the plays never offer easy conclusions or resolve the conflicts they set up, for Griffiths aims "to occupy the space of all the people I'm talking about". His characters engage in a genuine debate, and the result is a level of political dialectic which is sophisticated and complex, nowhere more so than in *The Party* which, like several other plays, explores the views of differing factions on the Left. Typically, audiences may well be successively persuaded by the viewpoints and auguments of different characters and forced to reach their own conclusions, for Griffiths insists that "people have to make choices".

The frequent use of history allows Griffiths both to reveal incidents which are forgotten or suppressed, and to offer alternative perspectives on those which are more familiar. He thus consciously reclaims and de-mythologises the past, arguing that history is traditionally presented from a particular class perspective and that a socialist playwright has a duty to counterbalance this. History also provides Griffiths with a new way of looking at the present: "Sometimes it's difficult to see today, and so you look for . . . an historical correlative that will illuminate today much more sharply".

Griffiths' plays have deliberately avoided spending their energies attacking capitalism or arguing the need for socialism, which he takes as given; it will be interesting to see whether the combination of more than a decade of right-wing British Government and the collapse of communism, with the consequent crisis of socialism, in Eastern Europe will allow him to continue working from the same assumptions, or how these events may influence his writing.

—Steve Nicholson

See also *Volume 1* entry on *Comedians*.

———

GRILLPARZER, Franz. Born in Vienna, 15 January 1791. Educated at Anna-Gymnasium, Vienna, 1800–07; studied

Franz Grillparzer (1841).

law at University of Vienna, 1807–11. Tutor in law studies to nephew of Graf von Seilern, 1812; unpaid assistant in Court library, 1813; civil servant from 1814: appointed Theater-dichter, 1818; his plays produced at Vienna's Burgtheater, under the artistic direction of Joseph Schreyvogel from 1818; assistant to Count Stadin, the finance minister, 1823–24; Director of Court Archives, 1832: retired 1856, as Hofrat; became a member of the Herrenhaus (upper house of the Austrian parliament), 1861. Founder-member, Austrian Academy of Sciences, 1847. Honorary Doctorate: University of Leipzig, 1859. Died in Vienna, 21 January 1872.

Works

Collections

Sämmtliche Werke (10 vols.), edited by Heinrich Laube and Josef Weilen. 1872.
Dramatische Meisterwerke. 1901.
Sämtliche Werke, edited by August Sauer and Reinhold Backmann (42 vols.). 1909–48.
Sämtliche Werke; Ausgewählte Briefe; Gespräche; Berichte (4 vols.), edited by Peter Frank and Karl Pörnbacher. 1960–65.

Stage Works

Die Ahnfrau (produced Theater an der Wien, Vienna, 1817). 1817; translated as *The Ancestress*, 1938.
Sappho (produced Burgtheater, Vienna, 1818). 1819; trans-lated as *Sappho*, 1820: several subsequent translations under same title.
Das goldene Vlies (trilogy; produced Burgtheater, Vienna, 1821). 1822; translated as *The Golden Fleece*, 1942; as *The Guest-Friend* and *The Argonauts* (2 vols.), 1947; final part translated as *Medea*, 1879.
König Ottokars Glück und Ende (produced Burgtheater, Vienna, 1825). 1825; translated as *King Ottokar, His Rise and Fall*, 1932.
Ein treuer Diener seines Herrn (produced Burgtheater, Vienna, 1828). 1830; translated as *A Faithful Servant of His Master*, 1941.
Des Meeres und der Liebe Wellen (produced Burgtheater, Vienna, 1831). 1839; translated as *Hero and Leander*, 1938; as *The Waves of Sea and Love*, 1969.
Melusina, music by Konradin Kreutzer (produced Burgtheater, Vienna, 1833). 1833.
Der Traum ein Leben (produced Burgtheater, Vienna, 1834). 1840; translated as *A Dream is Life*, 1946.
Weh dem, der lügt (produced Burgtheater, Vienna, 1838). 1840; translated as *Thou Shalt Not Lie*, 1939.
Esther (produced Burgtheater, Vienna, 1868). In *Dichterbuch aus Östreich*, 1863; revised edition, 1877; translated as *Esther*, with *The Jewess of Toledo*, 1953.
Ein Bruderzwist in Habsburg (produced Stadttheater, Vienna, 1872). In *Sämmtliche Werke*, 1872; translated as *Family Strife in Hapsburg*, 1940.
Die Jüdin von Toledo (produced Prague, 1872). In *Sämmtliche Werke*, 1872; translated as *The Jewess of Toledo*, 1913.
Libussa (produced Burgtheater, Vienna, 1874). In *Sämmtliche Werke*, 1872; translated as *Libussa*, 1941.

Fiction

Das Kloster bei Sendomir. In *Aglaja*, 1828; in book form, in *Sämtliche Werke*, 1930.
Der arme Spielmann. In *Iris*, 1848; in book form, in *Sämtliche Werke*, 1930; translated as *The Poor Musician*, 1914: several subsequent translations under same title; as *The Poor Fiddler*, 1929.

Verse

Tristia ex Ponto. In *Vesta*, 1827.

Memoirs and Letters

Selbstbiographie. 1872.

Other

Grillparzers Gespräche und die Charakteristiken seiner Persönlichkeit durch die Zeitgenossen (6 vols.), edited by August Sauer. 1904–16; supplementary volume, edited by Reinhold Backmann, 1941.
Tagebücher und Reiseberichte, edited by Klaus Geissler. 1981.

*

Criticism

Books:
Fred O. Nolte, *Grillparzer, Lessing, and Goethe in the Perspective of European Literature*, 1938.

Douglas Yates, *Grillparzer: A Critical Biography* (vol. 1 only), 1946.

Gisela Stein, *The Inspiration Motif in the Works of Grillparzer*, The Hague, 1955.

U. Helmensdorfer, *Grillparzers Bühnenkunst*, Bern, 1960.

J. Kaiser, *Grillparzers dramatischer Stil*, Munich, 1961.

J. Müller, *Franz Grillparzer*, Stuttgart, 1963.

G. Kleinschmidt, *Illusion und Untergang: Die Liebe im Drama Franz Grillparzers*, Lahr, 1967.

G. Baumann, *Zu Franz Grillparzer: Versuche zur Erkenntnis*, Heidelberg, 1969.

George A. Wells, *The Plays of Grillparzer*, Oxford, 1969.

H.F. Schafroth, *Die Entscheidung bei Grillparzer*, Bern, 1970.

F. Hoesch, *Der Gestus des Zeigens: Wirklichkeitsauffassung und Darstellungsmittel in den Dramen Franz Grillparzers*, Bonn, 1972.

H. Kindermann (ed.), *Grillparzer-Bild des 20. Jahrhunderts*, Vienna, 1972.

A. Viviani, *Grillparzer-Kommentar 1*, Munich, 1972.

W.E. Yates, *Grillparzer: A Critical Introduction*, Cambridge, 1972.

Toni Ghirelli, *Goethes Entwicklung zum Dramatiker*, Zurich, 1974.

Friedrich Keinz, *Grillparzer als Denker*, Vienna, 1975.

Zdenko Skreb, *Grillparzer: Eine Einführung in das dramatische Werk*, Kronberg, 1976.

Bruce Thompson, *A Sense of Irony: An Examination of the Tragedies of Franz Grillparzer*, Bern, 1976.

Bruce Thompson and Mark Ward (eds.), *Essays on Grillparzer*, Hull, England, 1978.

S. Hitchman, *The World as Theatre in the Works of Franz Grillparzer*, Bern, 1979.

William N.B. Mullan, *Grillparzer's Aesthetic Theory*, Stuttgart, 1979.

H. Bachmaier, *Franz Grillparzer*, Salzburg, 1980.

Bruce Thompson, *Franz Grillparzer*, Boston, 1981.

Dagmar C.G. Lorenz, *Grillparzer, Dichter des sozialen Konflikts*, Vienna, 1986.

Grillparzer und die europäische Tradition (symposium), Vienna, 1987.

Ian F. Rose, *An Introduction to the Major Works of Franz Grillparzer*, Lewiston, Maine, 1991.

Serials

Jahrbuch der Grillparzer-Gesellschaft, Vienna.

*   *   *

Most of the serious German dramatists of the 18th and 19th centuries, working in small provincial towns, were essentially writers of literary drama. Grillparzer, working in the one cosmopolitan capital in German-speaking Europe was, by contrast, a genuinely theatrical dramatist. "I was", he recalled in his autobiography, "an Austrian to the core, and with every one of my plays had in mind its performance—and indeed its performance in my native city". But in his work, the vigorous theatrical tradition of his Vienna, with its fondness for visual symbolism and vivid action, is coloured by his receptive reading of the German classics (Goethe and Schiller), of Shakespeare, and of Lope de Vega. The result is a corpus of dramatic writing of unusual range and variety.

The rather melodramatic play that first made his name, *Die Ahnfrau* (*The Ancestress*), was too easily classified by the critics as a Romantic tragedy of fate for Grillparzer to be pleased with its success, and in reaction his next work,

Sappho, modelled partly on Goethe's *Torquato Tasso*, was a tragedy of classical simplicity. In contrast to the trochaic verse of his first play, this work is written in the iambic pentameters that were thereafter his normal verse form. The theme, the contrast between Sappho's poetic duty and the temptations of pleasure in love, is a recurrent motif in Grillparzer's work.

After one further work on a classical subject, the trilogy *Das goldene Vlies* (*The Golden Fleece*), Grillparzer turned to the manner of the Shakespearian history-play, using material from the history of the Austro-Hungarian empire. This was sensitive territory in Metternich's Austria; the powerful tragedy about the defeat of the ambitious Bohemian King Ottokar by the Habsburg Rudolf I, ran into difficulties with the ever-cautious censor and was temporarily banned in 1824, while *Ein treuer Diener seines Herrn* (*A Faithful Servant of His Master*), treating a Hungarian subject, and showing loyalty as a quality having tragic consequences, was withdrawn under court pressure after five performances.

The influence of the Viennese popular stage is strongest in the libretto *Melusina* (intended for Beethoven, who was a friend) and *Der Traum ein Leben* (*A Dream is Life*), a dreamplay in which Grillparzer reverts to trochaic verse. Recognisably adapting a form of popular comedy that had been in vogue in the suburban theatres from about 1818 onwards, *Der Traum ein Leben* achieved the greatest success of all his plays in box-office terms. But in the meantime he had also tasted failure with another classical love-tragedy, *Des Meeres und der Liebe Wellen* (*The Waves of Sea and Love*). This work, in which the illicit love of Hero for Leander is set against the severe requirements of her duty as a priestess of Aphrodite, is judged by many to be his finest play. But the delicate psychology of the characterisation, especially the portrayal of Hero's burgeoning love, made it vulnerable to insensitive performance. Nevertheless Grillparzer had always placed faith in the authority of the theatre public as "jury"; he repeatedly argued that while a dramatist must not be dictated to by popular taste he must make his work accessible to that common humanity which is represented in the theatre by the audience.

Four years later, another failure brought his active career as a dramatist to an end, when his only comedy also fell victim to a poor performance (and to cliquish criticism). It was such disappointments that led him to withhold his last three plays from the theatre. (When Heinrich Laube took over the direction of the Burgtheater in 1849, he quickly reinstated Grillparzer's plays in their rightful place at the heart of the repertory of the Austrian national theatre—albeit, as Grillparzer ironically observed, "too late!").

The late plays are again in contrasting forms: one is a love-tragedy after Lope de Vega, the other two treating material from the Austro-Hungarian past. Especially in *Ein Bruderzwist in Habsburg* (*Family Strife in Hapsburg*), which deals with the events leading up to the outbreak of the Thirty Years' War and is recognised as one of the finest historical tragedies in German, Grillparzer shows his concern about the political developments in the 1840's, the time when the play was completed. A liberal in sympathy, he feared the disruption that revolution might bring, and the central figure of the play, the Emperor Rudolf II, perceives his function as being to preserve the peaceful order of things; but he is helpless to achieve this.

Despite their thematic, formal, and generic diversity, Grillparzer's plays are consistent in their vivid use of action, gesture, and scenic effects, supported by a vigorous gestural language—the ideal of "word and image working together", as he formulated it in a diary note in 1817. There is no parallel, in the German-speaking theatre, to the combination of these effects with the range and complexity of his characterisation. It has rightly been observed (by Ronald Peacock) that he was one of the first European dramatists, "for whom psychology does not primarily support the picture of the actions of a particular character, as in Shakespeare, but becomes in increasing degree itself the object of portrayal" (*The Poet in the Theatre*, 1948).

—W. E. Yates

GROEN, Alma de.   See DE GROEN, Alma.

GUAN Hanqing.   Also known as Huan Han-ching or Kuan Han-ch'ing. Born in the vicinity of Dadu [Tatu] (now Beijing), China, c.1220-30. Possibly a physician or teacher at the imperial school of medicine, during the Mongolian Yuan dynasty. Reputedly wrote over 60 plays, of which c.20 survive, although correct attribution of titles and texts remains problematic; also wrote *qu* songs. Died probably late 13th century.

Works

Collections

Guan Hanqing xiqu ja (complete works, collating surviving texts).   1958.
Selected Plays (includes *Snow in Midsummer; The Wife-Snatcher; The Butterfly Dream; Rescued by a Coquette; The Riverside Pavilion; The Jade Mirror-Stand; Lord Kuan Goes to the Feast; Death of the Winged-Tiger General*) translated by Yang Hsien-yi and Gladys Yang.   1958.
Guan Hanqing xiqu ja (works).   1976.
Plays by Kuan Han-ching (includes *Single-Sword Parley; Wrong Clothes Dream*), translated by William Dolby. 1984 (private printing).

Stage Works

Bai-yue ting [Moon Prayer Pavilion].
Chen-mu jiao-zi [Mother Chen Teaches Her Son].
Dan-bian duo-shuo [Snatching Lances Armed Only with a Mace].
Dan dao hui.   Translated as *Lord Kuan Goes to the Feast*, in *Selected Plays*, 1958; *Single-Sword Parley*, in *Plays by Kuan Han-ching*, 1984.
Dou E yuan.   Translated as *Snow in Midsummer*, in *Selected Plays*, 1958; as *Injustice to Tou O* (with study), 1972; as *The Injustice Done to Tou O*, in *Six Yüan Plays*, translated by Liu Jung-en, 1972; as *Tou O Was Wronged*, in *Four Plays of the Yuan Drama*, translated by Richard F.S. Yang, 1972.
Fei-yi-meng.   Translated as *Wrong Clothes Dream*, in *Plays by Kuan Han-ching 1*, 1984.
Hu-die meng.   Translated as *The Butterfly Dream*, in *Selected Plays*, 1958.

Jin-xian chi [The Pond of Gold Thread].
Jiu feng-chen.   Translated as *Rescued by a Coquette*, in *Selected Plays*, 1958.
Ku Cun-xio [Crying Over Cunxiao].   Translated as *Death of the Winged-Tiger General*, in *Selected Plays*, 1958.
Lu Zhai-lang [Lu Zhai-lang].   Translated as *The Wife-Snatcher*, in *Selected Plays*, 1958.
Pei Du huan-dai [Pei Du Returns the Belt].
Qie-kuai dan [Slicing Fish].   Translated as *The Riverside Pavilion*, in *Selected Plays*, 1958.
Shuang-fu meng [Dream of the Two on a Journey].
Tiao feng-yue [Arranging the Romance].
Xie Tianxiang [Xie Tianxiang].
Wu-hou-yan [Feast of the Five Nobles].
Yu jing-tai.   Translated as *The Jade Mirror-Stand*, in *Selected Plays*, 1958.

Verse

San-ch'o Poems, translated by William Dolby.   1990.

*

Criticism

Books:
J.P. Seaton, "*Mother Ch'en Instructs Her Sons*: A Yüan Farce and Its Implications", in *Critical Essays on Chinese Literature*, edited by W.H. Nienhauser, Hong Kong, 1976.
William Dolby, *Father of Chinese Drama: A Sketch of the Life and Works of Guan Hanqing*, Edinburgh (private printing), c.1983.
Werner Oberstenfeld, *Guan Hanqing: Chinas bedeutende Dramatiker der Mongolenzeit*, Frankfurt, 1983.
William Dolby, *Editions of Kuan Han-ch'ing's Plays: A Comparative Study*, Edinburgh, 1986.
William Dolby, *Kuan Han-ch'ing: A Detailed Study*, Edinburgh, 1986.

Articles:
William Dolby, "Kuan Han ch'ing" (biographical study), in *Asia Major* (new series), 16, 1971.

*   *   *

Guan Hanqing (Kuan Han-ch'ing) was probably the greatest, and certainly the most prolific, exponent of the style of Chinese drama termed *zaju* (literally "variety drama"), which reached its apogee in north China during the Mongolian Yuan dynasty (1234–1368) in the second half of the 13th century and the first three decades of the 14th. From a literary point of view the *zaju* is often considered the high point of the Chinese theatre. Not very much is known of its performance and theatrical aspects, and although the texts of about 170 dramas have survived, none of the music has done so.

The variety drama had a strict structure. There were four, or occasionally five, acts. The function of the four acts were, respectively, to introduce the plot, to develop it, to bring it to a climax, and to resolve the conflicts and restore harmony. This structure was in sharp contrast to most of traditional Chinese narrative literature, which was episodic. In a variety drama there was both prose and poetry, the latter being sung. Within each act only one character sang. Even if more than one character sang, there was only one singer, the main performer of the troupe, who sang both singing roles, irrespective of gender.

Guan Hanqing was a director, troupe-manager, and actor as well as dramatist. Most of his intimate friends were also in the theatre, including some well known prostitutes who were also actresses. Apart from his dramas, Guan wrote many love songs, some of them highly erotic.

About 60 plays are attributed to Guan Hanqing, of which about 20 survive, 15 of them complete. The plays can be divided roughly into two categories, according to content. The majority are social dramas in which the lead characters are female: they are mainly prostitutes or noble widows. Courtroom dramas featuring righted injustice are common both among Yuan variety dramas in general, and Guan Hanqing's in particular. The other category is historical or military plays, with heroes especially from the Three Kingdoms period of the third century AD.

The most famous of Guan Hanqing's plays is *Injustice to Tou O* (*Dou E yuan*), an excellent representative example of the social, courtroom dramas. Dou E is a young widow who rejects the advances of the wicked Donkey Zhang. He plots to poison her mother-in-law, but his own father drinks the poisoned soup by mistake. He then threatens to take Dou E to court unless she accepts him. When she persists in refusing him, he accuses her of murdering his father. In the trial a corrupt judge has her beaten in an unsuccessful attempt to force her to confess, but his threat to beat her mother-in-law makes Dou E take responsibility for the crime and she is executed. In the final act, her ghost visits her father, a virtuous judge, who holds a re-trial. Dou E is cleared posthumously, Donkey Zhang is executed in the market-place, and the corrupt judge is beaten and dismissed.

A representative of the historical plays is *Single Sword Parley* (*Dan dao hui*). The play is set in the third century AD, and the lead character is Guan Yu, a historical military hero. He is invited to a feast by an enemy who is intent on killing him and thus capturing the place which he rules. Out of loyalty to his overlord, Guan Yu is determined to thwart this plan and succeeds in doing so through the fearlessness with which he attends the feast and the courage with which he brandishes his single sword. Though the characterization of Guan Yu is effective, he can seem a bit self-righteous in his undue consciousness of his own Confucian virtues of loyalty and courage. Moreover, the drama lacks action until the last act, and it is only then that any actual confrontation between Guan Yu and his crafty enemy is shown. The drama does not result in the death either of the hero or his adversary.

Guan Hanqing's social plays show a very much greater appreciation of women than those of most other Chinese dramatists. In the first place, it is not typical of variety drama that the main characters should be mostly female. Second, the female heroes are shown as intelligent, courageous, and willing to fight for what they think is right. They may be idealized, but they do not offer the traditional image of the Chinese woman who simply acts the dutiful servant to her father, husband, or sons.

Dou E is a good example of Guan Hanqing's female characters, and it is her characterization which is the core of *Injustice to Tou E*. She is portrayed in a very idealized way, as utterly loyal to her moral principles, as courageous, committed to justice, and chaste. Her moral values are Confucian. It is filial piety which makes her willing to face execution rather than see her mother-in-law beaten. There is added irony in the portrayal of the mother-in-law as a silly and opportunistic woman, a widow who, by being willing to remarry, is prepared to ignore one of the very moral principles for which Dou E is prepared to sacrifice herself. Although she is a tragic figure in the sense that the dramatist does not bring her back to life, the final act does restore harmony because her father

avenges the injustice she has suffered and has the immoral characters suitably punished.

Guan Hanqing shows a strong ability to create a tense and dramatic atmosphere. For example, in *Single Sword Parley*, the hero Guan Yu does not actually appear on stage until the beginning of Act III, but the tension is built through many awe-inspiring references to him: he is a tiger or like a god so powerful that his enemies turn white at the sight of him (Act I). In the 13th century, Guan Yu was on the verge of deification in popular lore.

Guan Hanqing's greatness in the history of Chinese drama lies not only in his productiveness and in the literary and theatrical skills with which his plays are crafted, but in their unusually wide range of dramatic expression. Apart from tragedy, suspense, and social protest, he was able to turn his hand to light-hearted comedy and plays of foreboding.

Guan Hanqing has been termed "the father of Chinese drama". It is not an accurate title, since the drama was already about a century old in south China at the time of his birth. But he is certainly the first of the truly distinguished known creators of drama in China.

—Colin Mackerras

GUARE, John (Edward). Born in New York City, 5 February 1938. Educated at Joan of Arc Elementary School, and St. John's Preparatory School, New York; Georgetown University, Washington, DC, 1956–60, AB 1960; Yale University School of Drama, 1960–63, MFA 1963. Married Adele Chatfield-Taylor in 1981. Assistant to the manager, National Theatre, Washington, DC, 1960; served in the US Air Force Reserve, 1963; member, Barr/Wilder/Albee Playwrights Unit, New York, 1964; founding member, Eugene O'Neill Playwrights Conference, Waterford, Connecticut, 1965; playwright-in-residence, New York Shakespeare Festival, 1976–77; Adjunct Professor of Playwriting, Yale University, 1978. Council member, Dramatists Guild, 1971; Vice-President, Theatre Communications Group, 1986. Recipient: ABC-Yale University fellowship, 1966; Obie award, 1968, 1971; *Variety* award, 1969; Cannes Film Festival Award, for screenplay, 1971; New York Drama Critics Circle Award, 1971, 1972; Tony Award, 1972, 1986; Joseph Jefferson Award, 1977; Venice Film Festival Golden Lion, National Society of Film Critics Award, New York Film Critics Circle Award, and Los Angeles Film Critics Award, all for screenplay, 1980; American Academy Award of Merit Medal, 1981.

Collections

Cop-Out; Muzeeka; Home Fires.   1971.
Three Exposures (includes *The House of Blue Leaves; Landscape of the Body; Bosoms and Neglect*).   1982.
"The House of Blue Leaves" and Two Other Plays (includes *Landscape of the Body* and *Bosoms and Neglect*).   1987.

Stage Works

Thirties Girl (produced Georgetown University, Washington, DC, 1959).
The Toadstool Boy (produced Georgetown University, Washington, DC, 1960).

The Golden Cherub (produced Yale University, New Haven, Connecticut, 1962?).

Did You Write My Name in the Snow? (produced Yale University, New Haven, Connecticut, 1963).

To Wally Pantoni, We Leave a Credenza (produced New Dramatists' Community Workshop, New York, 1965).

The Loveliest Afternoon of the Year (produced with *Something I'll Tell You Tuesday*, Caffe Cino, New York, 1966). With *Something I'll Tell You Tuesday*, 1968.

Something I'll Tell You Tuesday (produced with *The Loveliest Afternoon of the Year*, Caffe Cino, New York, 1966). With *The Loveliest Afternoon of the Year*, 1968.

Muzeeka (produced Eugene O'Neill Theatre, Waterford, Connecticut, 1967). In *Off-Broadway Plays*, 1970; also in *Cop-Out; Muzeeka; Home Fires*, 1971.

Cop-Out (produced Eugene O'Neill Theatre, Waterford, Connecticut, 1968). In *Off-Broadway Plays*. 1970; also in *Cop-Out; Muzeeka; Home Fires*, 1971.

Home Fires (produced Cort Theatre, New York, 1969). In *Cop-Out; Muzeeka; Home Fires*, 1971.

A Day for Surprises (produced Caffe Cino, New York, 1970). With *Kissing Sweet*, 1971.

The House of Blue Leaves (produced Truck and Warehouse Theatre, New York, 1971). 1972.

Two Gentlemen of Verona, with Mel Shapiro, music by Galt MacDermot, lyrics by Guare, from the play by Shakespeare (produced Delacorte Theatre, New York, 1971). 1973.

Optimism; or, The Misadventures of Candide, with Harold Stone, based on a novel by Voltaire (produced Eugene O'Neill Theatre, Waterford, Connecticut, 1973).

Rich and Famous (produced Academy Festival Theatre, Lake Forest, Illinois, 1974). 1977.

Marco Polo Sings a Solo (produced Cyrus Pierce Theatre, Nantucket, Massachusetts, 1976; revised version produced Shakespeare Festival Public Theatre, New York, 1977). 1977.

Landscape of the Body (produced Academy Festival Theatre, Lake Forest, Illinois, 1977). 1978.

Take a Dream (produced Delacorte Theatre, New York, 1978).

Bosoms and Neglect (produced Goodman Theatre, Chicago). 1980.

In Fireworks Lie Secret Codes (produced in *Holidays*, Actor's Theatre, Louisville, 1979; produced separately, Vivian Beaumont Theatre, New York, 1981). 1981.

Lydie Breeze (produced American Place Theatre, New York, 1982). 1982.

Gardenia (produced Manhattan Theatre Club, New York, 1982). 1982.

Women and Water (produced Actors' Theatre, Los Angeles, 1984; revised version produced Arena Stage, Washington, DC, 1985).

Hey, Stay a While, music by Galt MacDermot, lyrics by Guare (produced Goodman Theatre, Chicago, 1984).

Gluttony, in *Faustus in Hell* (produced Princeton, New Jersey, 1985).

The Talking Dog, from a story by Chekhov (produced as part of *Orchards*, Krannert Center, Urbana, Illinois, 1985). In *Orchards*, 1986.

Six Degrees of Separation (produced Lincoln Center, New York, 1990). 1990.

Screenplays

Taking Off, with others, 1971 (published 1971); *Atlantic City*, 1980.

Television Plays

Kissing Sweet (*Foul!* series), 1969 (published with *A Day for Surprises*, 1971).

*

Bibliographies

John Harrop, "*NTQ* Checklist No. 3: John Guare", in *New Theatre Quarterly*, 10, 1987.

Philip C. Kolin (ed.), *American Playwrights Since 1945: A Guide to Scholarship, Criticism, and Performance*, New York, 1989.

Criticism

Books:

Bonnie Marranca and Gautam Dasgupta, *American Playwrights: A Critical Survey*, New York, 1981.

John Guare, interview in *In Their Own Words: Contemporary American Playwrights*, edited by David Savran, New York, 1988.

Articles:

John Harrop, "'Ibsen Translated By Lewis Carroll': The Theatre of John Guare" (includes interview), in *New Theatre Quarterly*, 10, 1987.

*   *   *

John Guare's development as a playwright spans the heady experimentation of the late 1960's to the more sober and self-reflexive drama of the 1980's. While he has adapted to the changing theatrical climate of the period, he has maintained the integrity of his signature—a very literate, very irreverent outrageousness epitomised in sudden "turns" from farce to brutal violence. The plays of the late 1960's and early 1970's bear this signature very heavily; they, especially, disconcerted critics because of the "turns" and because of the profusion of ingenious presentational devices, many rooted in the "transformational" and "rough theatre" techniques of the late 1960's theatre.

At the same time, these early plays boldly etch in a moral dilemma which Guare has consistently explored in all his plays. The protagonist is tempted with the lure of materialism, "success", and celebrity, and the glitzy "freedom" they promise, and finds that the "limiting" sobrieties of family, aestheticism, hard work, and the consolations of religion, are usually no substitute. The dilemma is compounded because authentic self-definition is often inhibited by the various role models, not only of celebrities, but fictional or theatrical characters as well.

Home Fires and *Muzeeka* are both responses to the link between power politics and the materialist "success" myth in the context of the Vietnam era, though the former is ostensibly set in 1918 and the latter functions as a metaphorical cartoon-fable for much of the time. *Cop-out* is more direct in its commentary, at least in that part of it which deals with the attraction between an Establishment-co-opted cop and an anti-war activist. At the climax, the cop shoots the activist as she runs down the aisle, forcing the audience to step around the "body" to leave the theatre—the latter event the most notorious example of Guare's flirtation with "audience participation" at this time. Guare's best-known play, *The House of Blue Leaves*, is narrower in its focus and explores the poisonous way that the cult of celebrity invades the spheres of family and religion, at times with a near-farcical carapace which can suddenly break into violence.

Guare's four major plays of the 1970's, though somewhat bemusedly received, now seem exciting works ahead of their time. *Rich and Famous* is a satire on the cult of celebrity in the form of a story of the "world's oldest promising young playwright", upstaged by a childhood friend who has become a movie star. A telling central episode shows the playwright rejected by his parents because he is not yet successful. During this funny "morality" of disintegration, there are some scabrously irreverent references to musical and theatrical New York celebrities. *Marco Polo Sings a Solo* is even more prodigiously inventive—a look at the consequences of too much freedom rather than too little. Set in 1999, it spoofs the egomania of the celebrity-myth, which gets some characters into outer space, the "limiting" weight of the 20th-century cultural inheritance, and much else besides.

In the late 1970's, Guare's work became somewhat more restrained, and he focused more consistently on the family, its failure to nurture, and its unreasonable expectations of some of its members. In *Landscape of the Body*, a mother has to face up to her partial responsibility for the murder of her 14-year-old son, without ever discovering either the motive or the identity of the killers. In *Bosoms and Neglect*, a middle-aged man's failure to be close to his dying mother poisons his ability to "connect" with a younger woman in his life. Both these plays have Guare's characteristic signature, but strike deeper and suggest a greater self-disclosure on the part of the playwright.

With the "Lydie Breeze" plays, the family becomes an extended rather than a nuclear one—and a metaphor also for the failure of the commune ideal, as well as the politics, of the late 1960's. These three plays take place at three time-periods just after the American Civil War. A group of ex-soldiers and the nurse Lydie Breeze form a commune on Nantucket island called Aipotu—Utopia spelled backwards. Hickman, the would-be-writer and legal husband of Lydie, becomes the pivotal character. An early manuscript is rejected, and the commune collapses when he kills his friend, Dan, also Lydie's lover, in a jealous rage over a triviality. Jailed, he writes a great manuscript charting his torment; but the third male member of the commune (and now a powerful politican) persuades Hickman, over Lydie's objections, to destroy it as a trade for his physical freedom. Lydie kills herself in consequence. Reunited with his young daughter, Hickman achieves religious transcendence after his agony—but at a terrible cost to himself and others. The plays so far completed form a complex metaphor for the failure of American ideals, then and now.

Techniques of dialogue and scenic image, often functioning together, stress the restrictive effects of role models and received cultural norms on the development of real feeling and individuality. For example, in *Marco Polo Sings a Solo*, the characters flounder on an iceberg off the Norwegian coast amid the intimidating detritus of Grieg's grand piano, heat-lamps, a work-bench, an elegantly set dining table, and a bouquet of lush flowers; and their awareness of 20th-century literature and theatre, especially of Ibsen and Tennessee Williams, epitomises the hilarious intimidation they face from literary artefacts and role-models. And in *Bosoms and Neglect*, an episode of violent yet authentic intimacy between the two lovers is initiated with the man's attempt to break beyond these literary role models by cutting up his partner's books. But at the same time, especially through the technique of extended monologues, like arias, Guare suggests that his people are partly to blame for their failure to achieve some kind of authenticity, for the dreams and the sensitivity they exhibit in their monologues are often incommunicable and irrelevant to the other people in their lives.

The surprising twists and turns in a Guare plot are not signs of a lack of discipline or incompetence, as some critics have charged, but are a function of Guare's highly individual approach to dramatic structure; he wishes to have the density and texture of a novel. Consequently there are devices—such as Brechtian commentary and narrative, which place the audience in a "privileged" position over certain characters (knowing information that the characters do not know), and narratives within narratives—that give novelistic density or variety to the enacted story, or there is a deliberate flouting of the conventional, realist "well-made" play technique—high-profiled action occurs offstage so that only its more important refractions and reverberations are seen onstage (as in the "Lydie Breeze" series). All this makes Guare, formally, a highly adventurous playwright.

Guare' recent play, *Six Degrees of Separation*, is a return to the major themes of the 1970's plays, and again examines the destructive lure of celebrity, as well as sexual novelty, on the precarious stability of family structures.

—Dennis Carroll

See also *Volume 1* entry on *The House of Blue Leaves*.

GUARINI, Giovanni Battista. See *Volume 1* entry on *The Faithful Shepherd*.

H

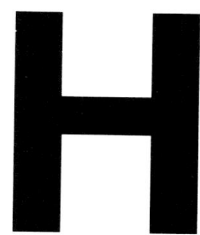

HACKS, Peter. Born in Breslau, Germany (now Wrocław, Poland), 21 March 1928. Educated at the University of Munich, Ph.D 1951. Married Anna Elizabeth Wiede in 1955. Emigrated to East Germany (DDR), 1955. First-produced play, *Eröffnung des indischen Zeitalters*, produced 1954; a number of subsequent plays produced at the Deutsches Theater, East Berlin, where he was dramaturg, 1960–63. Has written for both adults and children. Recipient: DDR Ministry of Culture Lessing Prize, 1956; Weisskopf Prize, 1965; German Critics Prize, 1972; DDR National Prize, 1974 and 1977; Heinrich Mann Prize, 1981.

Works

Collections

Theaterstücke (includes *Das Volksbuch vom Herzog Ernst; Eröffnung des indischen Zeitalters; Die Schlacht bei Lobositz*). 1957.
Fünf Stücke (includes *Das Volksbuch vom Herzog Ernst; Eröffnung des indischen Zeitalters; Die Schlacht bei Lobositz; Der Müller von Sanssouci; Die Sorgen und die Macht*). 1965.
Stücke nach Stücken (includes *Der Frieden; Die Schöne Helena; Die Kindermörderin; Polly*; oder, *Die Bataille am Bluewater Creek*). 1965.
4 Komödien (includes *Moritz Tassow; Margarete in Aix; Amphitryon; Omphale*). 1972.
Ausgewählte Dramen (3 vols.). 1972–81:
  1. *Columbus; Die Schlacht bei Lobositz; Moritz Tassow; Amphitryon; Omphale*. 1972.
  2. *Das Volksbuch vom Herzog Ernst; Die Sorgen und die Macht; Margarete in Aix; Prexaspes; Ein Gespräch im Hause. . .* 1976.
  3. *Der Müller von Sanssouci; Adam und Eva; Die Fische; Senecas Tod; Musen*. 1981.
Oper (includes the essays "Geschichten meiner Oper" and "Versuch über das Libretto", and the libretti *Noch einen Löffel Gift, Liebling?; Die Vögel*). 1975.
Sechs Dramen (includes *Numa; Prexaspes; Adam und Eva; Ein Gespräch im Hause . . .; Die Fische; Senecas Tod*). 1978.
Stücke nach Stücken 2. 1985.

Stage Works

Die Eröffnung des indischen Zeitalters (produced Kammerspiele, Munich, 1954). In *Theaterstücke*, 1957; revised version, as *Columbus*; oder, *Die Weltidee zu Schiffe* (produced Zaragoza, Spain, 1975), in *Ausgewählte Dramen 1*, 1972.

Die Schlacht bei Lobositz (produced Deutsches Theater, Berlin, 1956). In *Theaterstücke*, 1957.
Der Held der westlichen Welt, with Anna Wiede, from a play by J.M. Synge (produced Deutsches Theater, Berlin, 1956). In *Stücke*, by Synge, 1972.
Der Müller von Sanssouci (produced Deutsches Theater, Berlin, 1958). In *Fünf Stücke*, 1965.
Das Volksbuch vom Herzog Ernst; oder, *Der Held und sein Gefolge* (produced Nationaltheater, Mannheim, 1967). In *Theaterstücke*, 1957.
Die Kindermörderin, from a play by H.L. Wagner (produced Wuppertaler Bühnen, Wuppertal, 1959). In *Zwei Bearbeitungen*, 1963.
Die Sorgen und die Macht (produced Theater der Bergarbeiter, Senftenberg, 1960; revised version produced Deutsches Theater, Berlin, 1962). In *Fünf Stücke*, 1965.
Der Frieden, from a play by Aristophanes (produced Deutsches Theater, Berlin, 1962). In *Zwei Bearbeitungen*, 1963.
Die schöne Helena, from the operetta libretto by Meilhac and Halévy (produced Deutsches Theater, Berlin, 1964). In *Stücke nach Stücken*, 1965.
Polly; oder, *Die Bataille am Bluewater Creek*, from a play by John Gay (produced Halle, 1966). In *Stücke nach Stücken*, 1965.
Moritz Tassow (produced Volksbühne, Berlin, 1965). In *Vier Komödien*, 1971.
Der Schuhu und die fliegende Prinzessin (produced Staatliche Schauspielschule, Berlin, 1966).
Amphitryon (produced Deutsches Theater, Göttingen, 1968). 1969.
Margarete in Aix (produced Basler Theater, Basle, 1969). In *Vier Komödien*, 1971.
Omphale (produced Städtische Bühnen, Frankfurt, 1970). In *Vier Komödien*, 1971; revised version, music by S. Matthus (produced Oper, Berlin, 1975).
Numa (produced 1971). In *Sechs Dramen*, 1978.
Noch einen Löffel Gift, Liebling?, music by S. Matthus (produced Komische Oper, Berlin, 1972). In *Oper*, 1975.
Adam und Eva (produced Staatstheater, Dresden, 1973). 1976.
Die Vögel, from the play by Aristophanes (produced Staatstheater, Dresden, 1981). In *Oper*, 1975.
Prexaspes (produced Staatstheater, Dresden, 1975). In *Ausgewählte Dramen 2*, 1976.
Das Jahrmarktsfest zu Plundersweilern, from the play by Goethe (produced Deutsches Theater, Berlin, 1975). With *Rosie träumt*, 1976.
Rosie träumt, from plays by Hrotsvitha (produced Maxim-Gorki-Theater, Berlin, 1975). With *Das Jahrmarktsfest zu Plundersweilern*, 1976.
Ein Gespräch im Hause Stein über den abwesenden Herrn von

435

Goethe (produced Staatstheater, Dresden, 1976). In *Ausgewählte Dramen 2*, 1976.
Die Fische (produced Göttingen, 1978). In *Sechs Dramen*, 1978.
Senecas Tod (produced Deutsches Theater, Berlin, and Staatstheater, Dresden, 1980). In *Sechs Dramen*, 1978.
Armer Ritter (for children; produced Deutsches Theater, Göttingen, 1978). In *Märchendramen*, 1980.
Pandora, from a play by Goethe (produced Deutsches Theater, Göttingen, 1982). 1981.
Musen (produced Magdeburg, 1983). In *Ausgewählte Dramen 3*, 1981.
Barby, from a play by R. Strahl (produced Halle, 1983).
Die Kinder (for children; produced Greifswald, 1984).
Die Binsen (produced Berlin, 1985). With *Fredegunde*, 1985.
Fredegunde (produced Braunschweig, 1989). With *Die Binsen*, 1985.
Maries Baby (for children; produced Nordhausen, 1987). 1985.
Jona. 1989.

Television Plays

Die unadlige Gräfin, 1957–58; *Falsche Bärte und Nasen*, 1961.

Radio Plays

Der gestohlene Ton, 1953; *Das Fell der Zeit*, 1954; *Geschichte eines alten Wittibers in Jahre 1637*, 1957.

Fiction

Der Schuhu und die fliegende Prinzessin. 1966.
Die Dinge in Buta. 1974.
Magister Knauerhase. 1985.

Verse

Lieder zu Stücken. 1968.
Poesiealbum. 1972.
Historien und Romanzen. 1985.
Der blaue Hund, with Anne Heseler. 1987.
Die Gedichte. 1988.

Other (for children)

Das Windloch. 1956.
Das Turmverlies. 1962.
Der Flohmarkt. 1965.
Der Bär auf dem Försterball. 1972.
Kathrinchen ging spazieren. 1973.
Die Katze wäscht den Omnibus. 1975.
Meta Morfoss. 1975.
Das musikalische Nashorn. 1978.
Leberecht am schiefen Fenster. 1979.
Der Mann mit dem schwärzlichen Hintern. 1980.
Jules Ratte. 1981.
Onkel Mo. 1986.
Kinderkurzweil. 1986.
Liebkind im Vogelnest. 1987.

Other

Das Poetische: Ansätze zu einer postrevolutionären Dramaturgie. 1972.
Die Massgaben der Kunst: Gesammelte Aufsätze (essays). 1977.
Essais. 1983.
Historien und Romanzen. 1985.
Schöne Wirtschaft: Ästhetisch-ökonomische Fragmente. 1988.
Ascher gegen Jahn: Ein Freiheitskrieg. 1991.

Translator, *Gedichte*, by Attila Jozsef. 1960.
Translator, *Gedichte*, by Carl M. Bellman. 1965.
Translator, *Gedichte*, by Sean O'Casey. 1966.

*

Bibliographies

Raymond Heitz, "Situation de la recherche sur Peter Hacks", in *Revue d'Allemagne*, 16, 1984.

Criticism

Books:
Horst Laube, *Peter Hacks*, Velber, 1972.
Winfried Schleyer, *Die Stücke von Peter Hacks: Tendenzen, Themen, Theorien*. Stuttgart, 1976.
Peter F. Schütze, *Peter Hacks: Ein Beitrag zur Ästhetik des Dramas*, Kronberg, 1976.
Judith R. Scheid, *"Enfant Terrible" of Contemporary East German Drama: Hacks in His Role as Adaptor and Innovator*, Bonn, 1977.
Gertrud Schmidt, *Peter Hacks in BRD und DDR: Ein Rezeptionsvergleich*, Cologne, 1980.
Christoph Trilse, *Das Werk des Peter Hacks*, Berlin, 1980.
Judith R. Scheid, *Zum Drama in der DDR: Heiner Müller und Peter Hacks*, Stuttgart, 1981.
Michael Mitchell, "Peter Hacks" in *The Writer and Society in the GDR*, edited by Ian Wallace, Tayport, Fife, 1983.
Raymond Heitz, *Peter Hacks: Théâtre et socialisme*, Bern, 1984.
Andrea Jäger, *Der Dramatiker Peter Hacks: Vom Produktionsstück zur Klassizität*, Marburg, 1986.

Articles:
Margy Gerber, "After the Revolution—What Then? Peter Hacks' Theory of Socialist Classicism", in *University of Dayton Review*, vol.13 no.2, 1978.
Peter Graves, "Utopia in Mecklenburg: Peter Hacks' Play *Moritz Tassow*", in *Modern Language Review*, 75, 1980.
Michael Mitchell, "Peter Hacks: Drama for a Socialist Society", in *Scottish Papers in Germanic Studies*, 10, 1990.

* * *

Before the reunification of Germany, Peter Hacks was one of the most important East German playwrights and was also widely performed in West Germany, particularly in the later 1960's and 1970's. His popularity came from a renewal of poetic drama with larger-than-life characters as images of a future state of society which he saw as developing from the basic liberation he believed had taken place through the common ownership of the means of production under socialism. That it proved a false dawn does not invalidate his best plays, which are a glorious celebration of creative humanity.

His first four plays, written both before and after he emigrated from West to East Germany in 1955, follow, although not slavishly, the Brechtian method of epic theatre, using historical figures to present models of the historical process seen from a Marxist perspective, at the same time uncovering the workings of a class society. In them, his commitment to Marxist theory is shown both through an intellectual wit that has become the hallmark of his use of language, and through an awareness of the possibilities, especially comic, of the stage.

In his next two plays he attacked the contemporary subject-matter that the cultural functionaries were calling for. The theme of *Die Sorgen und die Macht* (The Cares of Power) is the conflict between the demands for quality and for quantity during the reconstruction period. With its positive moral, it looks like the kind of play the socialist authorities were trying to encourage; but it ran into criticism, in particular for the excessively subjective motivation of the hero, whose exemplary development is fuelled by the energy of his own temperament rather than by class consciousness. Hacks' insistence that social emancipation included sexual emancipation always irritated the prudish socialist establishment, and he also drew criticism for his treatment of the contrast between the ideal (a future Communist society) and reality (the drab East Germany).

It is this contrast, in a more generalised, and therefore less objectionable, form, that is the central theme of his later "classical" plays. In the early 1960's Hacks rejected epic theatre for a "socialist classicism" which he saw as the aesthetic correlation of the official view of the DDR as a "mature socialist society": now that the majority accepted socialism there was no need to preach to them and, therefore, no need for epic theatre. This view has been criticised in the West as conformism and a retreat from the dangers inherent in contemporary subjects. In fact, although it seemed to follow Ulbricht's proclamation of the coming of age of the DDR, it did not bring Hacks immediate acceptance in the East, and in the late 1960's and early 1970's a number of his plays received their first performances in the West. Although he accepted the authority of the State as necessary in politics, he insisted on his own control in aesthetic matters.

Hacks' classical plays can be divided into two groups—those which observe the unities of time, place, and action, and are written throughout in verse (*Amphitryon, Adam und Eva, Senecas Tod, Fredegunde, Jona*) and those with complex plots, a multiplicity of characters, and a mixture of prose and verse (*Margarete in Aix, Prexaspes, Numa, Die Binsen*). The former group concentrates on great characters as exemplars of human potential, whilst the latter category focuses on society, history, and politics. All of Hacks' plays are, basically, in the comic mode which, together with the socialist classicism and poetic theatre he revived, he sees as an expression of the "self-confidence of the [working] class".

As well as writing his own plays on classical subjects, Hacks has been active as an adaptor. His version of Aristophanes' *Peace* (*Der Frieden*) was, in the production by Bruno Besson in 1962, one of the great events in East German theatre history, and his "Operetta for Actors", *Die schöne Helena*, was by far the most popular of his plays in the East. His main concern in the 1970's was with Goethe, who is the subject of several of his major essays; he clearly sees Goethe's rejection of the Romantics as a model for his own attitude to left-wing Marxists. He has adapted unfinished plays by Goethe, and *Adam und Eva* and *Rosie träumt* (Rosie Dreams) have echoes of *Faust*. But the most enduring expression of his admiration for Goethe is the one-hander, *Ein Gespräch im Hause Stein Über den abwesenden Herrn von Goethe* (A Conversation in the Stein Household About the Absent Mr. Goethe), his most widely-performed play in the West. It is not dramatised literary history, but through a portrait of Goethe and his patroness of the Weimar years, Frau von Stein, Hacks illuminates the situation both of women and of the artist in society.

Apart from this *tour de force*, Hacks seemed to lose his way in the 1970's, producing witty romps, such as *Rosie träumt*, and minor plays, such as *Senecas Tod*. However *Die Binsen* and *Fredegunde* in the 1980's showed a renewed vigour in Hacks' writing, in their portrayal of two women who know what they want and make things happen, rather than passively respond to society. In *Die Binsen*, Hacks did, finally, but too late, what he has often been criticised for failing to do: he placed one of his active characters within the context of (an admittedly extremely generalised) DDR society.

In spite of the disappearance of the society on which his view of man is predicated, there may still come a time when the theatre will turn to Hacks as a writer who, in his vigorously active characters, has given expression to the creative side of mankind.

—Michael Mitchell

HAMPTON, Christopher (James). Born in Fayal, the Azores, 26 January 1946. Educated at schools in Aden and Alexandria, Egypt; Lancing College, Sussex, 1959–63; New College, Oxford, 1964–68, BA in modern languages (French and German) 1968, MA. Married Laura Margaret de Holesch in 1971; two daughters. First play, *When Did You Last See My Mother?*, produced 1966; resident dramatist, Royal Court Theatre, London, 1968–70. In addition to his original plays, has adapted a number of works by European dramatists for the stage and screen. Recipient: *Evening Standard* award, 1970, 1984, 1986; *Plays and Players* award, 1970, 1973, 1985; Los Angeles Drama Critics Circle Award, 1974, 1989; Olivier Award, 1986, 1989; BAFTA Award, 1987, 1990; New York Drama Critics Circle Award, 1987; Writers Guild of America Award, 1989; Prix Italia, 1989; Oscar (for screenplay), 1989. Fellow, 1976, and since 1984 council member, Royal Society of Literature.

Works

Collections

"*The Philanthropist*" *and Other Plays* (includes *Total Eclipse; Treats*). 1991.

Stage Works

When Did You Last See My Mother? (produced Oxford University, 1966; professionally produced Royal Court Theatre, London, 1966). 1967.
Marya, from a play by Isaak Babel, translated by Michael Glenny and Harold Shukman (produced Royal Court Theatre, London, 1967). In *Plays of the Year 35*, 1969.
Total Eclipse (produced Royal Court Theatre, London, 1968). 1969; revised version (produced Lyric Theatre, Hammersmith, London, 1981), 1981.
Uncle Vanya, from a play by Chekhov, translated by Nina Froud (produced Royal Court Theatre, London, 1970). In *Plays of the Year 39*, 1971.
The Philanthropist: A Bourgeois Comedy (produced Royal Court Theatre, London, 1970). 1970; revised version, 1985.

Christopher Hampton

Hedda Gabler, from the play by Ibsen (produced National Theatre, Stratford, Ontario, 1970). 1971.

A Doll's House, from a play by Ibsen (produced Playhouse Theatre, New York, 1971). 1972.

Don Juan, from a play by Molière (broadcast 1972; produced Theatre Royal, Bristol, 1972). 1974.

Savages (produced Royal Court Theatre, London, 1973). 1974; revised version, 1976.

Treats (produced Royal Court Theatre, London, 1976). 1976.

Signed and Sealed, from a play by Georges Feydeau and Maurice Desvallières (produced Comedy Theatre, London, 1976).

Tales from the Vienna Woods, from a play by Ödön von Horváth (produced National Theatre, London, 1977). 1977.

Ghosts, from a play by Ibsen (produced on English tour, 1978). 1983.

Don Juan Comes Back from the War, from a play by Ödön von Horváth (produced National Theatre, London, 1978). 1978.

The Wild Duck, from a play by Ibsen (produced National Theatre, London, 1979). 1980.

After Mercer, based on works by David Mercer (produced London, 1980).

The Prague Trial, from a work by Patrice Chéreau and Ariane Mnouchkine (produced Paris, 1980).

A Night of the Day of the Imprisoned Writer, with Ronald Harwood (produced London, 1981).

The Portage to San Cristobal of A.H., from the novel by

George Steiner (produced Mermaid Theatre, London, 1982). 1983.

Tales from Hollywood (produced Mark Taper Forum, Los Angeles, 1982). 1983.

Tartuffe; or, The Impostor, from the play by Molière (produced The Pit, Barbican Centre, London, 1983). 1984.

Les Liaisons Dangereuses, the novel by Choderlos de Laclos (produced The Other Place, Stratford-on-Avon, 1985). 1985.

Faith, Hope and Charity, from a play by Ödön von Horváth (produced Lyric Theatre, Hammersmith, London, 1989). 1989.

White Chameleon (produced National Theatre, London, 1991). 1991.

Sunset Boulevard. with Don Black, music by Andrew Lloyd Webber, from the screenplay by Charles Brackett, Billy Wilder, and D. M. Marsham Jr. (produced Adelphi Theatre, London, 1993).

Screenplays

A Doll's House, 1973; *Geschichten aus dem Wiener Wald* (*Tales from the Vienna Woods*), with Maximilian Schell, 1981 (published 1979); *Beyond the Limit* (*The Honorary Consul*), 1983; *The Good Father*, 1986; *Dangerous Liaisons*, 1989 (published 1989).

Television Plays

Able's Will, 1977 (published 1979); *The History Man*, from the novel by Malcolm Bradbury, 1981; *Hotel du Lac*, from the novel by Anita Brookner, 1986; *The Ginger Tree*, from the novel by Oswald Wynd, 1989 (published 1989).

Radio Plays

2 Children Free to Wander (documentary), 1969; *Don Juan*, 1972; *The Prague Trial 79*, from a work by Patrice Chereau and Ariane Mnouchkine, 1980.

Criticism

Books:

Robert Gross (ed.), *Christopher Hampton: A Casebook* (includes bibliography), New York, 1990.

*   *   *

Christopher Hampton is an exceptionally literate playwright. Several of his dramatic subjects derive from the works and lives of continental European writers: he calls *The Philanthropist* "a riposte to Molière's *Le Misanthrope*"; *Les Liaisons Dangereuses* is based upon the 18th-century epistolary novel by Choderlos de Laclos; *Total Eclipse* interprets the relationship between the French symbolist poets Verlaine and Rimbaud; *Tales from Hollywood*, a flight of fancy grounded in thorough research, brings together writers Ödön von Horváth, Thomas Mann, Bertolt Brecht, Leon Feuchtwanger, and others in the California of the 1940's. Even those plays without a literary touchstone—*When Did You Last See My Mother?*, *Treats*, *Savages*, and *Able's Will*—might be characterized as stylistically witty and intelligent treatments of exceptionally articulate characters in finely tuned plots. Hampton manages this, John Russell Taylor notes, "without being drily intellectual".

Hampton's fairly limited canon of original plays—only

seven in 24 years—hints at the time he spends researching his subjects. *Total Eclipse* was researched in Paris. His four years of preparation for writing *Savages* included a fact-finding and interview trip to Brazil. He flew to California to research his first commissioned play, *Tales from Hollywood*, for which he credits several institutes as well as access to taped interviews with wartime emigrés. Such efforts were interspersed with his adaptations of plays from French, Russian, Norwegian, and Austrian sources. His dramatization of George Steiner's novel, *The Portage to San Cristobal of A.H.*, about the various political forces that come into play surrounding the capture of the elderly Hitler deep in an Amazonian jungle, resembles *Savages*, not only in the centrality of the Brazilian setting, but also in its use of simultaneous action. In both of these plays, what appear to be separate strands of narrative or levels of action actually comment upon and reinforce one another.

Several recurring themes may be discerned in Hampton's work, perhaps most importantly an examination of what is meant by civilized society. His treatment is especially ironic in *Savages*, in which the supposedly savage Amazon Indians are systematically exterminated by representatives of presumably civilized Western culture. The picture is complicated by the West's metaphorically being held hostage by Marxist terrorists who profess their idealism, but whose methods are ruthless. *Les Liaisons Dangereuses* depicts the highly codified social interactions of civilization at the peak of its pre-revolutionary development, and at the same time exposes the decadence beneath the surface. In *Tales from Hollywood*, Hampton evokes a reality set apart from the reality of wartime. Hampton presents contemporary civilization as a context for aberrant attitudes and flawed behavior in plays like *When Did You Last See My Mother?*, *Treats*, *The Philanthropist*, and *Able's Will*. The intelligence of his characters, especially the academic and literary figures in *The Philanthropist*, makes their irresponsible attitudes all the more reprehensible.

Ruby Cohn has pointed out the presence of a strong erotic element in all of Hampton's original plays except *Savages*. His translation/adaptations include two Don Juan plays. For the most part, his characters indulge in seduction games motivated by a need for ego gratification rather than by romantic love. This impetus is demonstrated, to striking effect, at the end of the triangle play, *Treats*: David looks worried when he thinks that Ann is leaving him for Patrick, but Ann's return to him is greeted with a cold stare.

The critical reception of Hampton's plays has been mixed. *Savages* especially elicited strongly divided opinions. However, he captured a mainstream audience with the extremely successful *Les Liaisons Dangereuses*.

—Felicia Hardison Londré

See also *Volume 1* entry on *The Philanthropist*.

HANDKE, Peter. Born in Griffen, Carinthia, Austria, 6 December 1942. Educated at a school in Griffen, 1948–54; Marianum Catholic Boys School, Tanzenberg bei Klagenfurt, 1954–59; Klagenfurt Gymnasium, 1959–61; University of Graz, studying law, 1961–65. Married Libgart Schwarz in 1966 (separated 1972), one daughter. Full-time writer since 1966; first-produced play, *Publikumsbeschimpfung* [*Offending the Audience*], produced 1966; co-founder, the publisher Verlag der Autoren, 1969; published no new plays, 1974–82. Has collaborated with directors Claus Peymann (in the theatre) and Wim Wenders (in the cinema). Recipient: Hauptmann Prize (Berlin), 1967; Schiller Prize (Mannheim), 1972; Steiermark Prize, 1972; Büchner Prize, 1973; Kafka Prize (refused), 1979; Salzburg Literary Prize, 1986.

Works

Collections

"Publikumsbeschimpfung" und andere Sprechstücke.   1966.
Hörspiele (2 vols.).   1968–69.
Prosa, Gedichte, Theaterstücke, Hörspiel, Aufsätze.   1969.
Hörspiel Nr. 2, 3, und 4.   1970.
Wind und Meer: 4 Hörspiele.   1970.
"Kaspar" and Other Plays (includes *Offending the Audience* and *Self-Accusation*), translated by Ralph Mannheim. 1969.
Stücke 1–2 (2 vols.).   1972–73.
"The Ride Across Lake Constance" and Other Plays (includes *Prophecy; Calling for Help; My Foot My Tutor; Quodlibet; They Are Dying Out*).   1976.

Stage Works

Publikumsbeschimpfung (produced Theater am Turm, Frankfurt, 1966). In *"Publikumsbeschimpfung" und andere Sprechstücke*, 1966; translated as *Tongue-Lashing*, in *Dimension*, vol. 1 no. 1, 1968; as *Offending the Audience*, in *"Kaspar" and Other Plays*, 1969.
Selbstbezichtigung (produced Städtische Bühnen Oberhausen, 1966). In *"Publikumsbeschimpfung" und andere Sprechstücke*, 1966; translated as *Self-Accusation*, in *"Kaspar" and Other Plays*, 1969.
Weissagung (produced Städtische Bühnen, Oberhausen, 1966). In *"Publikumsbeschimpfung" und andere Sprechstücke*, 1966; translated as *Prophecy*, in *"The Ride Across Lake Constance" and Other Plays*, 1976.
Hilferufe (produced by Städtische Bühnen Oberhausen, Stockholm, 1967). In *Stücke 1*, 1972; translated as *Calling for Help*, in *"The Ride Across Lake Constance" and Other Plays*, 1976.
Kaspar (produced Theater am Turm, Frankfurt, and Städtische Bühnen, Oberhausen, 1968).   1968; translated as *Kaspar*, in *"Kaspar" and Other Plays*, 1969.
Das Mündel will Vormund sein (produced Theater am Turm, Frankfurt, 1969). In *Prosa, Gedichte, Theaterstücke, Hörspiel, Aufsätze*, 1969; translated as *My Foot My Tutor*, in *"The Ride Across Lake Constance" and Other Plays*, 1976.
Quodlibet (produced Basler Theater, Basle, 1970).   1970; translated as *Quodlibet*, in *"The Ride Across Lake Constance" and Other Plays*, 1976.
Der Ritt über den Bodensee (produced Schaubühne am Halleschen Ufer, Berlin, 1971).   1970; translated as *The Ride Across Lake Constance*, 1973; also in *"The Ride Across Lake Constance" and Other Plays*, 1976.
Die Unvernünftigen sterben aus (produced Theater am Neumarkt, Zurich, 1974).   1973; translated as *They Are Dying Out*, 1975; also in *"The Ride Across Lake Constance" and Other Plays*, 1976.
Über die Dörfer: Dramatisches Gedicht (produced Salzburg Festspiele, 1982).   1981.
Das Spiel vom Fragen; oder, Die Reise zum sonoren Land (produced Burgtheater, Vienna, 1989).   1989.

The Long Way Round (produced National Theatre, London, 1989). 1989.

Screenplays

Die Angst des Tormanns beim Elfmeter/The Goalie's Fear of the Penalty Kick, 1971; *Der kurze Brief zum langen Abschied; Falsche Bewegung* (published 1975); *Die linkshändige Frau*, 1977; *Der Himmel über Berlin/Wings of Desire*, with Wim Wenders, 1987 (published 1987).

Radio Plays

Hörspiel, 1968, *Hörspiel Nr. 2*, 1968, *Geräusch eines Geräusches*, 1969, and *Wind und Meer*, 1970 (all published together in *Wind und Meer: Hörspiele*, 1970); *Hörspiel 3* and *Hörspiel 4* (published in *Hörspiel Nr. 2, 3, und 4*, 1970).

Fiction

Die Hornissen. 1966.
Der Hausierer. 1967.
Begrüssung des Aufsichtsrats: Prosatexte. 1967.
Die Angst des Tormanns beim Elfmeter. 1970; translated as *The Goalie's Anxiety at the Penalty Kick*, 1972.
Der kurze Brief zum langen Abschied. 1972; translated as *Short Letter, Long Farewell*, 1974.
Wünschloses Unglück. 1972; translated as *A Sorrow Beyond Dreams*, 1975.
Die Stunde der wahren Empfindung. 1975; translated as *A Moment of True Feeling*, 1977.
Die linkshändige Frau. 1976; translated as *The Left-Handed Woman*, 1978.
Langsame Heimkehr. 1979; translated as *The Long Way Around*, in *Slow Homecoming*, 1983.
Die Lehre der Sainte-Victoire. 1980; translated as *The Lesson of Mont Sainte Victoire*, in *Slow Homecoming*, 1985.
Kindergeschichte. 1981; translated as *Child's Story*, in *Slow Homecoming*, 1985.
Phantasien der Wiederholung. 1983.
Der Chinese des Schmerzes. 1983; translated as *Across*, 1986.
Slow Homecoming (includes *The Long Way Around; Child's Story; The Lesson of Mont Saine Victoire*). 1985.
Die Wiederholung. 1986; translated as *Repetition*, 1988.
Die Abwesenheit. 1987; translated as *Absence*, 1990.
Nachmittag eines Schriftstellers. 1987; translated as *The Afternoon of a Writer*, 1989.
3 × Handke (includes *The Goalie's Anxiety at the Penalty Kick; Short Letter, Long Farewell; A Sorrow Beyond Dreams*). 1988.

Verse

Die Innenwelt der Aussenwelt der Innenwelt. 1969; translated as *The Innerworld of the Outerworld of the Innerworld*, 1974.
Deutsche Gedichte. 1969.
Das Ende des Flanierens. 1976.
Gedichte, 1962–1963. 1983.
Gedichte an die Dauer. 1986.

Other

Chronik der laufenden Ereignisse. 1971.
Ich bin ein Bewohner des Elfenbeinturms. 1972.

Wiener Läden, photographs by Didi Petrikat. 1974.
Als das Wünschen noch geholfen hat. 1974; translated as *Nonsense and Happiness*, 1976.
Der Rand der Wörter: Erzählungen, Gedichte, Stücke, edited by Heinz F. Schafroth. 1975.
Das Gewicht der Welt: Ein Journal (November 1975–März 1977). 1977; translated as *The Weight of the World*, 1983.
Die Geschichte des Bleistifts. 1982.
Aber ich lebe nur von den Zwischenräumen. 1987.
Versuch über die Müdigkeit. 1989.
Versuch über die Jukebox. 1990.
Noch einmal für Thukydides. 1990.
Versuch über den geglückten Tag. 1991.

Editor, *Der gewöhnliche Schrecken: Neue Horrorgeschichten.* 1969.
Editor, *Charakter; Der Schwur des Martin Krist, Dokument: Frühe Erzählung*, by Franz Nabl. 1975.

Translator, *Der Spiegeltag*, by Georges-Arthur Goldschmidt. 1982.
Translator, *Gedichte 1962–1983*, by Gustav Janus. 1983.
Translator, *Bécon-les-Bruyères eine Vorstadt*, by Emmanuel Bove. 1984.
Translator, *Prometheus, gefesselt*, by Aeschylus. 1986.
Translator, *Das Wintermärchen*, by William Shakespeare. 1991.

*

Bibliographies

June Schlueter and Ellis Finger, *Handke: An Annotated Bibliography*, New York, 1982.

Criticism

Books:
Nicholas Hern, *Peter Handke: Theatre and Anti-Theatre*, London, 1971; as *Peter Handke*, New York, 1972.
Michael Scharang (ed.), *Über Handke.* Frankfurt, 1972.
Uwe Schultz, *Peter Handke*, Velber, 1973.
Henning Falkenstein, *Peter Handke*, Berlin, 1974.
Manfred Mixner, *Peter Handke*, Kronberg, 1977.
Hartmut König, *Peter Handke: Sprachkritik und Sprachverwendung: Anmerkungen zu ausgesuchten Texten*, Hollfeld, 1978.
Rainer Nägele and Renate Voris, *Peter Handke*, Munich, 1978.
Heinz Ludwig Arnold (ed.), *Handke*, Munich, 1978.
Manfred Jurgensen (ed.), *Handke: Ansätze, Analysen, Anmerkungen*, Bern, 1979.
Gunther Segooris, *Peter Handke und die Sprache*, Bonn, 1979.
June Schlueter, *The Plays and Novels of Peter Handke*, Pittsburgh, 1981.
Hugh Rorrison, "The 'Grazer Gruppe': Handke and Wolfgang Bauer" in *Modern Austrian Writing*, edited by Alan Best and Hans Wolfschutz, London, 1990.
Manfred Durzak, *Peter Handke und die deutsche Gegenwartsliteratur. Narziss auf Abwegen*, Stuttgart, 1982.
Denis Calandra, *New German Dramatists*, London, 1983 (Macmillan Modern Dramatists series).
Norbert Gabriel, *Peter Handke und Österreich*, Bonn, 1983.
Jerome Klinkowitz and James Knowlton, *Handke and the*

Postmodern Transformation: The Goalie's Journey Home, Columbia, Missouri, 1983.

Thomas K. Thornton, *Die Thematik von Selbstauslöschung und Selbsterwahrung in den Werken von Peter Handke*, Frankfurt, 1983.

Christoph Bartmann, *Suche nach Zusammenhang: Handkes Werk als Prozess*, Vienna, 1984.

Renate Voris, *Peter Handke*, 1984.

Raimund Fellinger (ed.), *Peter Handke* (essay collection), Frankfurt, 1985.

Gerhard Melzer and Jale Tinkel (eds.), *Handke: Die Arbeit am Glücke*, Konigstein, 1985.

Rolf G. Renner, *Peter Handke*, Stuttgart, 1985.

Michael Linstead, *Outer World and Inner World: Socialisation and Emancipation in the Works of Peter Handke, 1964–1981*, Frankfurt, 1988.

Articles:

Bonnie Marranca, "The *Sprechstücke*: Peter Handke's Universe of Words", in *Performing Arts Journal*, vol.1 no.2, 1976.

Jeanette R. Malkin, "'Think What You're Saying': Verbal Politics in the Early Plays of Handke and Kroetz", in *Modern Drama*, 33, 1990.

*   *   *

Austrian Peter Handke is one of the most highly-regarded contemporary German authors. He is a poet, essayist, novelist, translator, film director, and screenwriter, as well as a playwright. He has also been a controversial figure through much of his career. Since his famous public attack in the 1960's on his literary elders for their adherence to the dead tradition of "descriptive writing", Handke has consistently challenged the artistic *status quo*. *Offending the Audience*, the best known of his early plotless, characterless "speech plays", directed an irritating torrent of sentences at the audience and declared its independence from all previous drama. The aim seemed to be to wrest the post-war stage from the stranglehold of naturalism and its most significant challengers, including Brecht. His argument with politically engaged contemporaries like Franz Xaver Kroetz set him apart as an unabashedly subjective writer in quest of a personal poetic harmony. An unrelenting self-criticism in his work seems to answer detractors' rebukes of Handke for his alleged "narcissism".

Handke's interest in Ludwig Wittgenstein informs much of the language critique that is central to his work. Language is the declared subject and substance of the short pieces *Self-Accusation*, *Calling for Help*, and *Prophecy*. In considering his theatre work, the idea of language must be extended to include the various sign systems operating simultaneously during live performance. For example, in *My Foot My Tutor*, a short play without words in which a ward and warden are locked in a power struggle, every movement is carefully described. Into the prescribed movements, however, Handke introduces a cat, which "does what a cat does". By using the arbitrary movements of a cat to foreground the chance aspect of any live performance, Handke wryly celebrates unmediated, pure moments on stage.

Pure "epiphanic" moments in life, and their direct expression in, and even causation by, works of art, are recurring subjects for Handke. In the "speech torture" play, *Kaspar*, inspired by the mythical quality of the Kaspar Hauser story, Handke explores the tension between "states of feeling" and the utterances which express or record them. Kaspar faces the world with one sentence, as did the boy found in the public

square in Nuremberg in the early 19th century. His sentence is then stripped from him as a prelude to his transformation into a "rational" human being by the end of the play, at which point he is mad. In *Kaspar*, Handke's focus is the paradox of language: on the one hand it is a tool the Prompters (disembodied voices) use to socialize, and thus victimize, Kaspar; on the other it is a medium to transform or transcend reality. At one point in the play Kaspar cries out in despair, but the words he uses are from the playwright Ödon von Horváth: they form an irrational sentence in defiance of the Prompters, and therefore a muted poetic victory. When Peter Brook directed a much pared-down version of the play, the author was delighted by the "movement, dancing, songs", and perhaps by the kind of liberation the performative language itself afforded.

Twenty years after *Kaspar*, in *Das Spiel vom Fragen; oder, Die Reise zum sonoren Land* [Question Play; or, A Voyage to the Sonorous Country], a boy named Parzival accompanies a group of people under the guidance of a native mystic (Der Einheimische) on a strange pilgrimage to "the most distant of distant lands" in pursuit of the "basic questions". When Parzival joins them he is mute, then he manages to stammer, and by the end of the play he can speak. The character is a later incarnation of Kaspar, but the balance has tipped from scepticism about the powers of language toward faith in the constructive powers of words.

Handke's two plays of the 1970's are characterized by a quirky sense of humor. The title *The Ride Across Lake Constance* refers to another "language myth", the knight who rides safely on horseback across the frozen lake, only to drop dead when told the ice is barely an inch thick. The main characters, named in the printed text for classical film stars such as Elizabeth Bergner and Erich von Stroheim, wander through different states of consciousness. The older Wittgenstein seems the model here, the one who published very little but uttered cryptic statements about the whole area of experience beyond logic and language. The odd grammar of gesture in the play, at times literally connecting the figures to one another, makes for a farcical extension of Handke's interest in the web of human communication. The characters find themselves caught in the interstices between thought, speech, and action, and are alternately ecstatic at "knowing where they are", and terrified at their victimization by illusion and their impotence in the face of the intractable, incomprehensible world around them. Thematically relevant and entertaining sequences, such as magic tricks and an attack by a ferocious doll right out of a B-movie, are typical of Handke's use of elements from pop culture.

The consistent importance attached to private experience, which has led critics to associate Handke with writers like Botho Strauss as exponents of the "new subjectivity", is apparent in *They Are Dying Out*, albeit in arch comedic form. The successful advertising executive, Hermann Quitt, throws off his old life in order to refine and indulge his emotions. The satire in the characterization is droll: the play has an entrepreneurial priest, a Marxist businesswoman, a dwarfish stockholder, a "sensitive" millionaire. Handke does, however, seem to credit the hero's yearning for "moments of true feeling" with sincerity. An extended passage from Adalbert Stifter, the 19th-century Austrian romantic writer, read by Quitt's servant Hans as a kind of spiritual sauna for his master, signals a homage to Handke's roots. And in *Das Spiel vom Fragen* a "character" actually reveals himself to be the 19th-century Austrian playwright Ferdinand Raimund, exponent of the *Zauberstück* (magical folk play).

Handke's most recent plays have something of a *Zauberstück* and fairy-tale quality to them. *Slow Homecoming* is the general title for the tetralogy comprising three works of fiction and *Über die Dörfer* [Beyond the Villages]. In this play Handke also reveals his interest in Greek drama, which later led to his translation of Aeschylus's *Prometheus Bound* for a Claus Peymann production. A sermon on nature, art and the value of self by a character named Nova, through whom the "spirit of the new age" speaks, is the climax of the play. The poet Gregor, the "man with the writ", and Nova, who accompanies him, bring about the opportunity for people to transform themselves, to recognize joy as the "only legitimate power" and to see artists as those capable of "creating the people".

Karl Ernst Hermann created a stunning image for the premiere of "Question Play"—a stage luxuriantly green set off the diminutive hut the pilgrims had been travelling towards. Fittingly for a writer like Handke the hut, like the destination, is called the "Palace of Questions"—an appropriate description, which could be applied to Handke's *oeuvre* as a whole

—Denis Calandra

See also *Volume 1* entries on *Kaspar*; *Offending the Audience*.

HANSBERRY, Lorraine (Vivian). Born in Chicago, Illinois, USA, 19 May 1930. Educated at the Art Institute, Chicago; University of Wisconsin, Madison, 1948–50. Married Robert Nemiroff in 1953 (divorced 1964). Journalist, 1950–51, and associate editor after 1952, *Freedom*, New York; first play, *A Raisin in the Sun*, produced 1959. Recipient: New York Drama Critics Circle Award, 1959. Died from cancer in New York, 12 January 1965.

Works

Collections

Les Blancs: The Collected Last Plays (includes *Les Blancs; The Drinking Gourd; What Use Are Flowers?*), edited by Robert Nemiroff.   1972.

Stage Works

A Raisin in the Sun (produced Ethel Barrymore Theatre, New York, 1959).   1959.
The Sign in Sidney Brustein's Window (produced Longacre Theatre, New York, 1964).   1965.
To Be Young, Gifted, and Black: A Portrait of Hansberry in Her Own Words, adapted by Robert Nemiroff (produced Cherry Lane Theatre, New York, 1969).   1971.
Les Blancs, edited by Robert Nemiroff (produced Longacre Theatre, New York 1970).   In *Les Blancs: The Collected Last Plays*, 1972.
The Drinking Gourd.   In *Les Blancs: The Collected Last Plays*, 1972.
What Use Are Flowers?.   In *Les Blancs: The Collected Last Plays*, 1972.

Screenplay

A Raisin in the Sun, 1961.

Other

The Movement: Documentary of a Struggle for Equality. 1964; as *A Matter of Colour*, 1965.
To Be Young, Gifted, and Black: A Portrait of Hansberry in Her Own Words, edited by Robert Nemiroff.   1969.

*

Criticism

Books:
Anne Cheney, *Lorraine Hansberry*, Boston, 1984.

Articles:
Edward W. Farrison, "Lorraine Hansberry's Last Dramas", in *College Language Association Journal*, 16, 1972.
"Lorraine Hansberry Issue" of *Freedomways* (New York), vol.19 no.4, 1979.
Margaret B. Wilkerson, "Diverse Angles of Vision: Two Black Women Playwrights", in *Theatre Annual*, 40, 1985.

*   *   *

In her short life, Lorraine Hansberry completed two plays and left three others uncompleted; a sixth theatre piece was assembled by others out of excerpts from her dramatic and nondramatic writing. But her reputation must rest on her first produced play, *A Raisin in the Sun*, the first play by a black woman to be staged on Broadway, and one of the very few plays by black authors to be mainstream successes before the 1960's.

A Raisin in the Sun is the story of the Younger family: matriarch Lena, her adult son and daughter, Walter Lee and Beneatha, and Walter Lee's wife Ruth and son Travis, all living in a Chicago slum apartment. The father's death has left the family with $10,000 in insurance money, and much of the first act is devoted to a debate on what to do with the windfall, Walter Lee wanting to invest it in a liquor store and Lena holding out for buying a house in a better part of town. As the head of the family, Lena wins, and uses some of the money as a down payment on a house in a white neighborhood, only to be visited by a representative of the neighbors offering to buy back the house, to prevent the black family from moving in. He is sent away, but called back when Walter Lee impulsively loses the rest of the money in a swindle. In the play's climax, Walter Lee finds the strength to send the man away again, and the family prepares for the move.

There are two plot lines to *A Raisin in the Sun*. The more obvious one concerns the family's attempt to raise itself, and its encounter with one more example of racial prejudice. Curiously, while that plot is built on the fact that the Youngers are black, it does not really *depend* on it. It would take very little rewriting to make the play one about Jews, the Irish, Italians, or any working-class group unwelcome in a restricted neighborhood; and probably much of the play's power and success comes from white audiences' recognition of an experience not very foreign to their own.

The second, more subtle, story line of the play is built on the conflicts within the family, particularly between Lena and Walter Lee, which expose one of the tragic paradoxes of black family life in America: generations of prejudice have limited the potential and weakened the will of black men, forcing the women (who, for various reasons, have not been quite as broken in spirit) to be strong; yet the women know that every step they take to help their men is an addition to their emasculation. The argument between Walter Lee and his mother over how to spend the insurance money is not just monetary; it is a contest for the role as head of the family. By all objective considerations Lena's plan is far superior; but her insisting on it is also a slap in the face for her son, and she knows it. When Walter Lee loses his share, he is clearly in the wrong, and yet too much of his manhood is at stake to allow the women to condemn him too harshly.

The play dramatizes the delicate balance and subtle adjustments the women must constantly make in the very real and vital struggle to protect their men from further indignities. Having won the first-act battle, Lena makes a point of giving Walter Lee the rest of the money, to make use of (implicitly, to make foolish use of) as he sees fit, because the act of respect in giving him this authority is worth more than the money. When Walter Lee calls the white man back to sell him the house, the women see that this is not just a financial setback, but a final capitulation to failure, and unite to save his soul. And when Walter Lee finds in himself the strength to reject the racists a second time, and the white man turns to Lena for help, she can reply, "My son said we was going to move and there ain't nothing left for me to say", as a joyous abdication of power. It is in these, and similar, quiet insights into the dynamics of family life, more than in the conflict with racism, that *A Raisin in the Sun* offers its greatest insights into the American black experience.

The Sign in Sidney Brustein's Window, Hansberry's only other completed play, was a commercial and critical failure, though it did attract some passionate supporters. It is a sympathetic study of the plight of the white liberal. The title character, a right-thinking but apolitical man, is slowly drawn into action, working to support a reform candidate in a city election; the titular sign is a banner declaring his political commitment. But dedication, and even victory, does not change the world, and Sidney discovers that people who believe the right things can be personally corrupt or weak in ways that invalidate their theoretical commitment: the candidate sells out, a black friend proves to be prejudiced, a homosexual friend is sexually manipulative. Driven to the point of despair, Sidney regains his determination to fight for the good in spite of all the obstacles and defections along the way.

The play is excessively talky, and secondary characters are either underwritten (such as the politician) or overwritten (as with Sidney's conservative sister-in-law, too complexly developed for the minor role she plays). A character on whom the plot turns does not even appear until Act III, while the important subplot of Sidney's marital problems is never integrated with the other action or themes. Still, it is a failure of accomplishment rather than of conception, and one can see the core of a play that might have been stronger had Hansberry (who was terminally ill at the time of production) been able to work on it more.

—Gerald M. Berkowitz

See also *Volume 1* entry on *A Raisin in the Sun*.

HARDY, Alexandre. Born in Paris, c.1570–75. Probably educated in the classics. Possibly an actor; under protection of the Prince de Condé, associated with various touring theatre companies from the mid 1590's; dramatist with the company of Valleran le Conte, by 1611, and with Bellerose's Comédiens du Roi, c.1622–26. Claimed to have written over 600 plays: only 34 surviving plays positively attributed to him. Died in Paris, c.1631.

Works

Collections

Théâtre (5 vols.).   1624–28.
Théâtre (5 vols.), edited by E. Stengel.   1883–84.

Stage Works

Premiere dates and locations remain uncertain; publication dates for all plays except *Théagène et Chariclée* and *Les Ramonneurs* refer to Hardy's five-volume *Théâtre*, 1624–28.

Théagène et Chariclée (cycle of tragicomedies).   1623.
Méléagre.   1624.
Panthée.   1624.
Scédase; ou, L'Hospitalité violée.   1624.
Alceste.   1624.
Ariadne ravie.   1624.
Procris.   1624.
Alphée; ou, La Justice d'amour.   1624.
Didon se sacrifiant.   1624.
Coriolan.   1625.
Mariamne.   1625.
La Mort d'Achille.   1625.
Arsacomé.   1625.
Cornélie.   1625.
Alcée.   1625.
La Mort d'Alexandre.   1626.
La Mort de Daïre.   1626.
Aristoclée.   1626.
Dorise.   1626.
Félismène.   1626.
La Force du sang.   1626.
Frégonde.   1626.
Gésippe; ou, Les Deux Amis.   1626.
La Gigantomachie.   1626.
Phraarte, from a play by G.G. Cinthio.   1626.
Le Ravissement de Proserpine.   1626.
Corine; ou, Le Silence.   1626.
Triomphe d'amour.   1626.
Alcméon; ou, La Vengeance féminine.   1628.
Lucrèce.   1628.
Timoclée.   1628.
La Belle Égyptienne, from a story by Cervantes.   1628.
Elmire; ou, L'Heureuse bigamie.   1628.
L'Amour victorieux ou vengé.   1628.
Les Ramonneurs, possibly not by Hardy.   Edited by A. Gill, 1957.

*

Bibliographies

Michael G. Paulson and T. Alvarez-Detrell, *Alexandre Hardy: A Critical and Annotated Bibliography*, Paris, 1985.

Criticism

Books:

K. Nagel, *Alexandre Hardys Einfluss auf Pierre Corneille*, Marburg, 1884.

E. Rigal, *Alexandre Hardy et le théâtre français*, Paris, 1889.

H.R. Kranzfelder, *Die Hirtendichtung und die dramatischen Pastoralen Alexandre Hardys*, Würzburg, 1933.

E. Forsyth, *La Tragédie française de Jodelle à Corneille*, Paris, 1962.

K. Garscha, *Hardy als Barockdramatiker*, Frankfurt, 1971.

T.J. Reiss, *Toward Dramatic Illusion: Theatrical Technique and Meaning from Hardy to Horace*, New Haven (Connecticut) and London, 1971.

S.W. Deierkauf-Holsboer, *Vie d'Hardy*, Paris, 1972.

Geoffrey Brereton, *French Tragic Drama in the Sixteenth and Seventeenth Centuries*, London, 1973.

Carla Federici, *Réalisme et dramaturgie: Étude de quatre écrivains: Garnier, Hardy, Rotrou, Corneille*, Paris, 1974.

Articles:

F.K. Dawson, "Alexandre Hardy and 17th-century French Tragedy", in *Renaissance and Modern Studies*, 3, 1959.

* * *

Alexandre Hardy was the most prolific and arguably the most important French playwright during the reign of Henri IV and regency of Marie de Médicis. Like Shakespeare, he was also an actor. Like Lope de Vega, he wrote a very large number of plays. Protected by the Prince de Condé, and associated at various times with the early troupes led by Valleran le Conte, Claude Husson, Bellerose, Gros-Guillaume, and Du Villiers, Hardy helped as much as anyone to establish modern commercial theatre in France by providing newly formed French troupes with a copious supply of actable scripts. J.-F. Sarazin credited Hardy with having brought tragic drama in from the "middle of the streets and street-corner platforms"—that is, into the rectangular, artificially lit, indoor playing places already typical of French theatre early in the 17th century.

In the "*Au lecteur*" of the fifth volume of his *Théâtre* (1628), Hardy claims to have written over 600 dramatic poems in the genre of *tragédie*. The figure is assumed to include the tragicomedies which were evidently his most popular form of play. It probably includes adaptations and may include interludes. However, only some 41 plays survive in print, and few, if any, are performed today. More than half of those extant are tragicomedies, a variable, often novelistic, and sometimes heroic or pastoral modern genre which went out of fashion shortly after Hardy's death. Eight tragicomedies form a cycle adapted from a Greek romance, Heliodorus's *Theagenes and Charicleia*, Hardy's first and now most neglected volume of plays. 12 tragedies, five pastorals, two mythological machine plays—*Proserpine (The Abduction of Proserpina by Pluto)* and *La Gigantomachie (The Battle of Gods and Giants)*—and 14 tragicomedies are contained in the five volumes of Hardy's *Théâtre* (1624–28). Ten additional titles are known from Mahelot's *Mémoire*. Deierkauf-Holsboer has identified two more, including *Le Jaloux (The Jealous Male)*, which she considers a comedy, together with documents (such as a contract dated 16 March 1598) which specify "comedy, tragedy, tragicomedy, pastorals etc". Scholars are not agreed upon attribution to Hardy of the bawdy anonymous prose comedy *Les Ramonneurs (The Chimneysweeps)*, published in 1957.

Regarding the dramatic subject as the "soul" of tragic drama, Hardy adapted plays from a wide variety of ancient, and then popular modern, authors, including Homer, Euripides, Xenophon, Apollodorus, Diodorus Siculus, Lucian, Pausanias, Virgil, Ovid, Seneca, Quintus Curtius, Boccaccio, Ariosto, Tasso, Giraldi Cinthio, Lope de Vega, Montemayor, and Robert Greene. Hardy's pastorals are the most obvious models for the comedies with which Corneille began writing for the stage. His tragic drama is characterized by extreme physical and/or emotional violence, and by an astonishing theatrical energy not easily transmitted through a casual reading of the difficult scripts. Hardy affected a rugged style, creating a generally elevated stage language somewhat reminiscent of the lofty Renaissance epics of Ronsard and of Du Bartas.

The young Racan is said to have been highly excited by Hardy's plays in performance. Numerous other contemporary writers, including the playwrights Théophile de Viau and Tristan L'Hermite, expressed appreciation of Hardy's *Théâtre*. But the style of his stagecraft was already out of fashion by the time the plays were published. It stands in sharp contrast with the smoother diction of Court poets then associated with Malherbe's reform of versification, already introduced to the French stage around 1618 by Racan in *Les Bergeries (Arthenice)*. Latinate, allusive, and often somewhat obscure through frequent ellipsis, archaism, and hypallage, Hardy's dialogue was probably never fully understood by his audiences. Nor is his language made easier for readers by misprints in editions of his *Théâtre*. However, any attempt to understand the differences between the tragic dramaturgies developing in either Elizabethan England or Golden Age Spain and the basic characteristics of French tragic drama until the end of the *Ancien Régime* might well begin with Hardy's assertion that "true tragic style must be totally distinct from everyday language".

Among the tragedies, the more memorable include *Didon se sacrifiant (The Death of Dido)*, *Scédase (Scédase; or, Hospitality Violated)*, *La Mort d'Achille (The Death of Achilles)*, *Coriolan (Coriolanus)*, *Mariamne*, and *Lucrèce (Lucretia; or, Adultery Punished)*. *Scédase*, based on Plutarch's account of two Boeotian village girls raped and murdered by two aristocratic Spartan guests, and of their father's failure to obtain justice in Sparta and his final suicide, may represent domestic tragedy, which soon disappeared in France. In comparison with Shakespeare's *Coriolanus*, *Coriolan* is more Senecan in structure; and its chorus is relatively less developed into crowd scenes. *Mariamne*, based on Josephus's narrative of Herod's jealousy and execution of the captive princess he married against her will, is perhaps Hardy's finest tragedy, remaining in the repertory until the end of the *Ancien Régime* through adaptations by Tristan L'Hermite (who reduced such supernatural features as the ghost of Aristobulus) and Voltaire.

Among the tragicomedies, *Ariadne ravie (The Abduction of Ariadne)* includes a lamentation reminiscent of Renaissance tragedy (Ariadne's soliloquy throughout Act IV) in a modern tragicomic form. *La Belle Égyptienne (The Fair Gypsy)*, adapted from one of Cervantes' *Exemplary Tales*, may also represent Hardy's baroque stagecraft through retention of the richly theatrical, often scarcely plausible, incident, ambiguity, illusion, passion, and surprise of a typical Renaissance tale. Hardy's debt to the "total theatre" stagecraft of Guarini's *The Faithful Shepherd* is acknowledged in *Proserpine*.

—H. Gaston Hall

HARE, David. Born in Bexhill, Sussex, England, 5 June 1947. Educated at Lancing College, Sussex; Jesus College, Cambridge, MA 1968. Married Margaret Matheson in 1970 (divorced 1980); two sons and one daughter. Founding director, Portable Theatre, Brighton and London, 1968–71; literary manager, 1969–70, and resident dramatist, 1970–71, Royal Court Theatre, London; resident dramatist, Nottingham Playhouse, 1973; director and co-founder, Joint Stock Theatre Company, 1975–80; founder, Greenpoint Films, 1982. Since 1984 associate director, National Theatre, London. Since 1981 member of the Council, Royal Court Theatre. Has directed several of his own plays for stage and screen, as well as works by other authors. Recipient: BAFTA Award, 1979; New York Drama Critics Circle Award, 1983; Berlin Film Festival Golden Bear, 1985; Olivier Award, 1990; London Theatre Critics' Award, 1990.

Works

Collections

The History Plays (includes *Knuckle; Licking Hitler; Plenty*). 1984.
The Asian Plays (includes *Fanshen; Saigon: Year of the Cat; A Map of the World*). 1986.
"Heading Home", with "Wetherby" and "Dreams of Leaving". 1991.

David Hare (1990).

The Early Plays (includes *Slag; Teeth 'n' Smiles; Dreams of Leaving*). 1992.

Stage Works

Inside Out, with Tony Bicât, from the diaries of Kafka (produced Arts Lab, London, 1968).
How Brophy Made Good (produced Brighton Combination, Brighton, 1969). In *Gambit 17* (London), 1971.
What Happened to Blake? (produced Royal Court Theatre Upstairs, London, 1970).
Slag (produced Hampstead Theatre, London, 1970). 1971.
The Rules of the Game, from a play by Pirandello (produced New Theatre, London, 1971).
Deathsheads, in *Christmas Present* (produced Traverse Theatre, Edinburgh, 1971).
Lay By, with others (produced Traverse Theatre, Edinburgh, 1971). 1972.
The Great Exhibition (produced Hampstead Theatre, London, 1972). 1972.
England's Ireland, with others (produced Mickery Theatre, Amsterdam 1972).
Brassneck, with Howard Brenton (produced Playhouse, Nottingham, 1973). 1974.
Knuckle (produced Playhouse, Oxford, 1974). 1974; revised version, 1978.
Fanshen, from the book by William Hinton (produced Crucible Theatre Studio, Sheffield, 1975). 1976.
Teeth 'n' Smiles, music by Nick Bicât, lyrics by Tony Bicât (produced Royal Court Theatre, London, 1975). 1976.
Plenty (produced National Theatre, London, 1978). 1978.
Deeds, with others (produced Playhouse, Nottingham, 1978). In *Plays and Players*, May and June 1978.
A Map of the World (produced Adelaide Festival, Adelaide, Australia, 1982). 1982; revised version, 1983.
The Madman Theory of Deterrence (sketch), in *The Big One* (produced London, 1983).
Pravda: A Fleet Street Comedy, with Howard Brenton (produced National Theatre London, 1985).
The Bay at Nice (produced National Theatre, London, 1986). With *Wrecked Eggs*, 1986.
Wrecked Eggs (produced National Theatre, London, 1986). With *The Bay at Nice*, 1986.
The Knife (opera), music by Nick Bicât, lyrics by Tim Rose Price (produced New York, 1987).
The Secret Rapture (produced National Theatre, London, 1988). 1988.
Racing Demon (produced National Theatre, London, 1990). 1990.
Murmuring Judges (produced National Theatre, London, 1991). 1991.
The Absence of War (produced National Theatre, London, 1993).

Screenplays

Wetherby, 1985 (published 1985); *Plenty*, 1985; *Paris by Night*, 1989 (published 1988); *Strapless*, 1990 (published 1990); *Damage*, 1992.

Television Plays

Man Above Men, 1973; *Licking Hitler*, 1978 (published 1978); *Dreams of Leaving*, 1980 (published 1980); *Saigon: Year of the Cat*, 1983 (published 1983); *Heading Home* (published with *Wetherby* and *Dreams of Leaving*, 1991).

Other

Writing Left-Handed.   1991.

*

Criticism

Books:

Oleg Kerensky, *The New British Drama*, London, 1977, New York, 1979.
Gunther Klotz, *Britische Dramatiker der Gegenwart*, Berlin, 1982.
John Bull, *New British Political Dramatists*, London, 1984.
David Ian Rabey, *British and Irish Political Drama in the Twentieth Century*, Basingstoke and London, 1986.
Richard A. Cave, *New British Drama in Performance on the London Stage*, Gerrards Cross, 1987.
Colin Chambers and Mike Prior, *Playwrights' Progress: Patterns of Postwar British Drama*, Oxford, 1987.
Gaetano D'Elia and Christopher Williams, *La scrittura multimediale di David Hare*, Fasano, 1989.
Joan F. Dean, *David Hare*, Boston, 1990.
Judy I. Oliva, *David Hare: Theatricalizing Politics*, Ann Arbor, Michigan, 1990.
Malcolm Page (compiler), *File on Hare* (includes bibliography), London, 1990.

* * *

Since co-founding Portable Theatre in the late 1960's, Hare has worked as a professional director in theatre and, more recently, in film. He is best known, however, as a playwright, and is frequently linked with a generation of socialist writers including Howard Brenton, with whom he has twice collaborated on major plays. The label of "political playwright" perhaps fits Hare less obviously, since his plays are usually set within middle-class establishments and contain sophisticated cultural references and a psychological approach to characterisation, while relying heavily on witty dialogue and intellectual argument. However, though never flaunting their socialist allegiances, Hare's plays explore the relationship between the political and personal worlds. Contemptuous of the easy sloganising often associated with political theatre, he has consistently refused to simplify the complex moral issues which his plays debate; if theatre is a political weapon, he argues, then its power lies not in a playwright's message, but in "the interaction of what you are saying and what the audience is thinking".

Hare is sometimes seen as a lapsed socialist writer by those who view his play for Joint Stock about the Chinese Revolution, *Fanshen*, as the highlight of his career. In fact, *Fanshen* is far from a simplistic endorsement of that revolution, and concentrates largely on its difficulties, mistakes, and corruption; but ultimately the play offers a positive perspective, focusing on the learning process of those most directly involved, and showing them learning from their mistakes and opting to continue the struggle for a better society rather than discard their ideals. In his introduction to the published text, Hare warns of the danger of becoming trapped in "a culture of dissent", where artists make only negative criticisms of society; and the later play, *A Map of the World*, derives its title from Oscar Wilde's observation that "A map of the world that does not include Utopia is not worth even glancing at". Hare's continuing belief in the possibility of creating a more just and moral society than that of modern capitalism underpins the recurring debate in his work between idealism and cynicism; sometimes this is addressed within the play itself, and sometimes audiences are required to explore the gap between the characters' conclusions and their own views.

Hare's work is noteworthy for its exploration of female psychology, and it is within the female characters that idealism frequently resides, though they are largely unable to put their ideals into practice. Hare avoids the trap of equating women simplistically with virtue in a male-dominated world, and in writing *The Secret Rapture* and the screenplay *Paris by Night* at a time when Britain had, on three successive occasions, elected a female-led right-wing government, Hare has also focused on women whose political ideology he detests. His own belief that society could be changed easily was dented by the betrayals and failures of Harold Wilson's Labour government—failures which he explored in *The Great Exhibition*—and Hare has consistently depicted the existing order as resistant, rather than susceptible, to attack. *Slag*, for example, showed the failure of three women in a girls' school to establish an alternative society, while the anarchic impulses of the rock band in *Teeth 'n' Smiles* succeed only in destroying themselves while leaving the establishment, as represented by a Cambridge University Ball, unscathed. *Knuckle* offers a trenchant critique of capitalist society, but Sarah's idealistic beliefs and actions are seen by everyone else as the hopelessly naive gestures of someone who doesn't understand the real world; since she does not appear in the play herself, it is left to audiences to measure this against their own views. Similarly, Susan in *Plenty* loses her sanity because of the discrepancy between her belief in a better society, which inspires the wartime fight against fascism, and the betrayal of those ideals in a declining post-war Britain.

Later plays have concentrated more on the necessity and survival of ideals. *A Map of the World*, set at a conference on poverty in a luxury Bombay hotel, contrasts the cynicism of a successful Indian novelist with the initially aggressive and unquestioning idealism of a young British left-wing journalist who, though accidentally killed after discovering a new strength in his convictions, succeeds in penetrating the cynicism of others. The novelist's final rediscovery of an idealism he has long since discarded expresses a crucial Hare statement: "This feeling, finally, that we may change things—this is at the centre of everything we are. Lose that . . . lose that, lose everything".

The Secret Rapture follows a similar pattern by contrasting two sisters: Marion is a hard-headed and selfish Tory cabinet minister whose materialism embodies the ethos of Britain in the 1980's, while the saint-like Isobel lives by alternative and idealistic values. Again, though Isobel fails professionally because of her refusal to work within the commercial values of the business world, and is murdered because she cannot accept the compromise her lover has made with that world, even the cynical Marion finally acknowledges the worth of her sister's beliefs. This occurs in a scene which was enhanced in the original production when the house interior vanished to reveal a sunlit vision of lawns, across which the spirit of Isobel approached Marion in a gesture of reconciliation.

Recently, *Racing Demon* dealt with conflicts of moral and political ideology within a Church of England unable to unite on how to help society's oppressed. The final scene shows Frances, who has discarded orthodox religious beliefs while retaining both her ideals and the determination to put them into practice, symbolically penetrating the clouds of Europe and flying towards the sun to work for a better society elsewhere.

Repeatedly, Hare reveals the difficulty of actualising ideals and the impossibility of living a good life in a bad world. His refusal to make definitive moral statements or to fit characters and events into an ideologically pre-determined pattern has led to accusations from the Left of irrelevance and of pandering to middle-class audiences; but if the apparently comfortable qualities of his plays have sometimes been more palatable to such audiences than the more direct assaults of his contemporaries, then the questions which he raises may be equally subversive.

—Steve Nicholson

See also *Volume 1* entries on *Plenty*; *Pravda*; *Teeth 'n'*; *Smiles*.

HARRIGAN, Edward. Born in New York, 26 October 1844. Received little schooling. Married Annie T. Braham in 1876; seven children. Left home for San Francisco, and appeared in vaudeville in the west, 1867–70; returned to New York, and appeared on stage, with Sam Rickey, as a vaudeville comic team, 1870; first appeared with Anthony J. Cannon (stage name: Tony Hart), as Harrigan and Hart, 1871, and with him managed and appeared at the Theatre Comique, New York, 1871 until the theatre was torn down, 1881: during this period wrote more than 80 sketches, music by David Braham, which developed into the complete plays of his later career in which he always acted the leading part; with Hart, opened the New Theatre Comique, 1881, and managed it until it was destroyed by fire, 1884; partnership with Hart ended, 1885; leased Harrigan's Park Theatre, 1884–88; built Harrigan's, later the Garrick, Theatre, 1891–95; retired, 1908. Died in New York, 6 June 1911.

Works

Collections

The Famous Songs of Harrigan and Hart, edited by Edward B. Marks. 1938.

Stage Works

Unless otherwise indicated, productions between 1871 and 1880 were at the Theatre Comique, and those between 1881 and 1884 were at the New Theatre Comique, both New York.

The Mulcahey Twins (produced Pacific Melodeon, San Francisco, 1870). Songs published 1872.
The Little Fraud (produced 1871). Songs published 1870.
The Big and Little of It (produced 1871).
The Day We Went West (produced 1871).
The German Emigrants (produced 1871).
The Irish Emigrant (produced 1871).
You 'spute Me (produced 1871).
Ireland vs. Italy (also called *Who Owns the Line?*) (produced 1872).
Shamus O'Brien at Home (produced 1872).
Sing Sing (produced 1872).
The Mulligan Guard (produced 1873). Songs published 1873.
St. Patrick's Day Parade (also called *The Day We Celebrate*) (produced 1873; revised 1874 and thereafter). Songs published 1884.

The Absent-Minded Couple (produced 1873).
An Editor's Troubles (produced 1873). 1875.
The Mixed Couple (produced 1873).
Eureka, with John Woodard (produced 1874).
Muldoon, The Solid Man (produced 1874).
The Raffle for Mrs. Hennessey's Clock (produced 1874).
The Regular Army, O! (produced 1874).
A Terrible Example (produced 1874).
Who Stole the Monkey? (produced 1874).
The Skidmores (produced 1874).
The Invalid Corps (produced 1874).
Going Home Again (produced 1874).
The Night Clerk's Troubles; or, The Fifth Avenue Hotel (also called *The Porter's Troubles*) (produced 1875). 1875.
The Blue and the Gray (produced 1875). 1875.
Fee-Gee (produced 1875).
The Doyle Brothers, with John Woodard (produced 1875).
April Fool (produced 1875).
Innocence at Home (produced 1875).
No Irish Wanted Here (produced 1875).
The Donovans (produced 1875).
King Calico's Body Guard (produced 1875).
The Two Awfuls (produced 1875).
Behind the Scenes (produced 1875).
Slavery Days (produced 1875). Songs published 1875.
Down Broadway; or, From Central Park to the Battery (produced 1875). Songs published 1878.
The Bradys (produced 1876).
The Italian Ballet Master (produced 1876).
Malone's Night Off (produced 1876).
The Bold Hibernian Boys (produced 1876).
S.O.T. (Sons of Temperance) (produced 1876). Songs published 1876.
Iascaire (produced 1876).
Walkin' for Dat Cake (produced 1876). Songs published 1877.
Bar Ber Ous (produced 1876).
Down in Dixie (produced 1876).
Matrimonial Ads (produced 1877).
The Rising Star (produced 1877).
The Telephone (produced 1877).
Christmas Joys and Sorrows (produced 1877). 1877.
The Grand Duke's Opera House (produced 1877).
Old Lavender (also called *Old Lavender Water* and *Around the Docks*) (produced 1877; revised versions produced 1878 and 1885). 1877.
My Wife's Mother (produced 1878). 1877.
Callahan the Detective (produced 1877).
The Crushed Actors (produced 1877).
The Pillsbury Muddle (produced 1877).
Sullivan's Christmas (produced 1877).
Our Irish Cousins (produced 1877).
The Two Young Fellows and Her Majesty's Marines (produced 1877).
Love vs. Insurance (produced 1878).
A Celebrated Hard Case (produced 1878). 1878.
The Lorgaire (produced 1878; revised 1888). 1878.
The Mulligan Guard Picnic (produced 1878). 1880.
Coloured Baby Show (produced 1878).
The Italian Junkman (produced 1878).
The Lady of Lions (produced 1878).
Our Law Makers (produced 1878).
O'Brien, Counselor-at-Law (produced 1879).
The Great In-Toe-Natural Walking Match (produced 1879).
The Mulligan Guard Ball (produced 1879). 1879.
The Mulligan Guard Chowder (produced 1879). 1879.
The Mulligan Guards' Christmas (produced 1879). 1879.

The Mulligan Guard Nominee (produced 1880).   1880.
The Mulligan Guards' Surprise (produced 1880).   1880.
The Major (produced 1881).   1881.
The Mulligans' Silver Wedding (produced 1881).   1881.
Squatter Sovereignty (produced 1882).   1881.
Our Cranks, with G.L. Stout (produced 1881).
Mordecai Lyons (produced 1882).   1882.
McSorley's Inflation (produced 1882).   1882.
The Muddy Day (also called *Bunch o' Berries*) (produced 1883).   Songs published 1883.
Cordelia's Aspirations (produced 1883).
Dan's Tribulations (also called *Tribulations*) (produced 1884).   Songs published 1893.
Investigation (produced 1884).   Songs published 1884.
McAllister's Legacy (produced Harrigan's Park Theatre, New York, 1885).
Are You Insured? (produced Harrigan's Park Theatre, New York, 1885).
The Grip (produced Harrigan's Park Theatre, New York, 1885).
The O'Reagans (produced Harrigan's Park Theatre, New York, 1886).
The Leather Patch (produced Harrigan's Park Theatre, New York, 1886).   Songs published 1886.
McNooney's Visit (produced Harrigan's Park Theatre, New York, 1887).
Pete (produced Harrigan's Park Theatre, New York, 1887).
Waddy Googan (produced Harrigan's Park Theatre, New York, 1888).   Songs published 1893.
Reilly and the Four Hundred (produced Harrigan's Theatre, New York, 1890).   Songs published 1890.
The Last of the Hogans (produced Harrigan's Theatre, New York, 1891; shortened version, as *Sergeant Hickey*, produced Proctor's 23rd Street Theatre, New York, 1897).   Songs published 1891.
The Woollen Stocking (produced Harrigan's Theatre, New York, 1893).   Songs published 1893.
Notoriety (produced Harrigan's Theatre, New York, 1894).   Songs published 1894.
The Blue Ribbon (produced Harrigan's Theatre, New York, 1894).
My Son Dan (produced Brooklyn, New York, 1896).
Marty Malone (produced Bijou Theatre, New York, 1896).
Low Life (produced 1897).
An Old New Yorker (produced 1899).
Under Cover (produced Murray Hill Theatre, New York, 1903).
The Simple Life (produced 1905).

Fiction

The Mulligans.   1901.

Verse

Songs for the Banjo.   1888.
Songs.   1893.

Other

Comique Joker, with Tony Hart.   1870(?).
Pictorial History of the Mulligan Guard Ball.   1879.

*

Criticism

Books:
E.J. Kahn Jr., *The Merry Partners: The Age of Harrigan and Hart*, 1955.
Richard Moody, *Ned Harrigan: From Corlear's Hook to Herald Square*, Chicago, 1980.

Articles:
Philip K. McLaughlin, "'H-A-R-R-I-G-A-N': Glimpses of the Irish on stage in the Late Nineteenth Century", in *Eire/Ireland*, vol.23 no.1, 1988.

*   *   *

The enthusiastic comparisons which contemporary critics applied to Harrigan's plays would seem to have assured him of an international reputation. During the last quarter of the 19th century, William Dean Howells described him as the American Goldoni in *Harper's Monthly* (1886) and a playwright who created "the spring of a true American comedy", while others compared Harrigan to Hogarth, Balzac, Zola, and Dickens. At a time when American literature and art were firmly caught up in the rise of realism, Harrigan deserved this critical attention through his successful depiction of Lower-East Side New York life. As a comedian and a playwright, he believed in "holding the mirror up to nature", as he explained in an essay in *Pearson's Magazine* (1903) and providing a "series of photographs of life today in the Empire City" (*Harper's Weekly*). By using authentic scenes, character types, speech patterns, dress, and gestures, he provided a vaguely realistic farce-comedy into which he infused his own belief in the kindness and good nature of the majority of people. As riotous fun, his plays and performances were both a reflection of the serious artistic and social movements of his generation and an antidote for the grimness which they frequently unveiled.

Harrigan began his acting career in 1871 with Anthony J. Cannon, a young singer and female impersonator who soon changed his name to Hart, and as "Harriganandhart" the two performed together for 14 years. During this time Harrigan started writing the sketches that they performed, finally creating the Mulligan plays for which he is best known. The setting of these plays was Mulligan's Alley in New York City's Sixth Ward, where one of the major characters, Dan Mulligan, lived. Modelled on the Lower-East Side of New York which Harrigan knew so well, his characters, dialogue, and scene presented a jumbled population of Germans, Italians, Negroes, and Irish as they faced their everyday problems in ward politics, the policy rackets, and the battle of the sexes. There was the Wee Drop Saloon run by Walfingham McSweeney, an Italian junk shop, a Chinese laundry-lodging combination, Lockmuller's butcher shop, and a Negro social club called the Full Moon Union. Whatever issues— economic, social, emotional, political—bothered New York City and its residents, Harrigan would create a play about them in record time, just as American playwrights had been doing since early in the 19th century. With realistic sets and costumes supported by carefully worked-out "business" on stage, Harrigan dramatized an international community at Harrigan and Hart's Theatre Comique. Additionally, a comedian's enthusiasm for the "general mêlée" characterized the evening's entertainment.

The Mulligans seemed to focus Harrigan's theatrical formula, and *The Mulligan Guard Ball* was one of his best plays. Tommy Mulligan and Katy Lochmuller are in love. As the Mulligan Guards celebrate in the Harp and Shamrock Ballroom, which is directly below the Red Man's Hall where a Negro group called the Skidmore Guards is having a dance, Tommy and Katy elope. One of the grand "mêlées" for which Harrigan was popular occurs when the ceiling collapses with a grand crash and the Irish and Negro parties are unceremoniously merged. There is another fight when the two sets of parents discover that the marriage they both opposed has taken place. But it all ends happily as the action did in the other Mulligan plays, such as *The Mulligan Guard Picnic, The Mulligan Guard Chowder, The Mulligan Guards' Surprise,* and *The Mulligan Guard Nominee.* For three seasons, with these and other plays by Harrigan, no other dramatist ever presented a more truthful or exciting panorama of New York's Lower East Side.

Harrigan opened his new Harrigan and Hart's Theatre Comique in late August 1881 with *The Major,* in which he played Major Gilfeather, a happy rogue, whose escapades at Caleb Jenkin's policy shop in Coney Island—the poor man's Saratoga—result in an explosion in which the front of a factory sinks through the stage, the roof crashes to the stage amidst smoke and fire, with "*heads, limbs, and bodies of omnes seen by audience descending from sky*". The scene of *Squatter Sovereignty* is the shanty towns on the west side of Central Park and along the upper stretches of Fifth Avenue. It is again a confrontation between the Irish and the Dutch as Nellie Nolan elopes with the son of the wealthy Kline family, who live in a mansion. *Cordelia's Aspirations* takes place after Cordelia and Rebecca have returned from the Grand Tour, and it shows her attempt to change the men of the family, auction the furniture, and move uptown to Madison Avenue. Cordelia's aggressivness is one of the features of the sketch, against which Dan Mulligan reacts by saving "my dad's dinner pail", and being himself as he drinks from a fish tank and combs his hair with a crumb brush.

The astute critic, Nym Crinkle, maintained that Harrigan's sketches were a new order of entertainment, an American order. The acting style and the management of the production were clearly central to the success of these works. It was comedy of a very distinct and individual kind. In fact, Harrigan once stated that he did not allow anyone to play his sketches, that he could not conceive of anyone else doing them. He wrote them for himself, for his company, and for his theatre. It was a one-person venture, in which the truthfulness and validity of the plays depended upon the intelligence and observant mind of one person, Harrigan. If the people in these plays were slight, they were also real, and the spectators came to see something of themselves on stage. Trying always to be truthful to the society he observed, Harrigan confessed to being both provincial and optimistic. Although he did not fulfill the potential that some critics saw in him, and he did not stimulate followers for his theory of American comedy, he was a major favorite as an actor and as a playwright for a generation or more of New York theatregoers, and created a form of comedy that contributed to the development of American drama.

—Walter J. Meserve

HART, Moss. See entry on **KAUFMAN, George,** and *Volume 1* entries on *Once in a Lifetime* and *You Can't Take It with You.*

HASENCLEVER, Walter. Born in Aachen, Westphalia, Germany, 8 July 1890. Studied law at the universities of Oxford and Lausanne, 1908–09. Married for the first time, 1925 (divorced 1925); 2) Edith Schäfer in 1934. Left for Leipzig after break with his father, 1909; first play, *Nirwana,* published 1909; published a pacifist magazine, *Der jüngste Tag,* with Kurt Ointhus and Franz Werfel, 1913–21; drafted into the army as a staff orderly in Macedonia, 1914; interpreter in the postal censorship department, Ghent, 1915; first-produced play, *Der Sohn,* staged 1916; in a military sanatorium after receiving a wound, 1916–17; lived in Berlin, 1917–24; Paris correspondent for the Berlin newspaper *Berliner 8-Uhr Abendblatt,* 1924–30; travelled to the USA; following Nazi rise to power, 1932, went into exile: travelled to England, Italy, Yugoslavia, before settling in France; stripped of German citizenship, 1933, and his works banned by the Nazis; following invasion of France, interned by the French Vichy government at Les Milles, 1940. Recipient: Kleist Prize, 1917. Committed suicide (drug overdose), Les Milles, 21 June 1940.

Works

Collections

Gedichte; Dramen; Prosa, edited by K. Pinthus.   1963.

Stage Works

Nirwana.   1909.
Der Sohn. (produced Kammerspiele des Deutschen Landestheaters, Prague, 1916).   1914.
Antigone, from the play by Sophocles (produced Stadttheater, Leipzig, 1917).   1917; translated by J.M Ritchie and J.D. Stowell as *Antigone,* in *Vision and Aftermath: Four Expressionist Plays,* 1969.
Die Menschen (Kammerspiele des Deutschen Landestheaters, Prague, 1920).   1918.
Der Retter (produced Tribüne, Berlin, 1919).   1919.
Die Entscheidung (produced Tribüne, Berlin, 1919).   1919.
Jenseits (produced Schauspielhaus, Leipzig, 1920).   1919.
Gobseck (produced Schauspielhaus, Dresden, 1922).   1921.
Mord (produced Deutsches Theater, Berlin, 1926).   1926.
Ein besserer Herr (produced Schauspielhaus, Frankfurt, 1927).   1926.   1927.
Ehen werden im Himmel geschlossen (produced Kammerspiele des Deutschen Theaters, Berlin, 1928).   1928.
Bourgeois bleibt Bourgeois, with Ernst Toller, from a play by Molière (produced Lessingtheater, Berlin, 1929).
Napoleon greift ein (produced Neues Theater, Frankfurt, 1930).   1929.
Kommt ein Vogel geflogen (produced Komödietheater, Berlin, 1931).   1931.
Christoph Columbus; oder, Die Entdeckung Amerikas, with Kurt Tucholsky (produced Schauspielhaus, Leipzig, 1932). Published in translation, as *Christopher Columbus,* in *German Drama Between the Wars,* edited by George A. Wellwarth, 1974.
Ehekomödie, with Robert Klein and Hubert Griffith (produced as *What Should a Husband Do?,* London, 1937).
Skandal in Assyrien; oder, Konflikt in Assyrien (produced as *Esther,* International Theatre Club, London, 1937; in German, Deutsches Theater, Göttingen, 1937).
Münchhausen (produced Schauspielhaus, Leipzig, 1948).   1963.

Screenplays

Die Pest, 1920; *Anna Christie*, 1930.

Fiction

Die Rechtlosen.   1963.
Irrtum und Leidenshaft.   1969.

Verse

Der Jüngling.   1913.
Tod und Auferstehung.   1917.
Gedichte an Frauen.   1922.

Other

Ihr werdet Deutschland nicht wiedererkennen: Erinnerungen.   1975.
Saul Bellow: Eine Monographie.   1978.
Hasenclever Archiv (includes four-volume *Gemischtes Copierbuch* and two-volume *Amerikanische Korrespondenz*), edited by Michael P. Zerres.   1978.
Denken als Widerspruch: Plädoyers gegen die Irrationalität, oder ist Vernunft nicht mehr gefragt?.   1982.

Translator, *Himmel, Hölle, Geisterwelt*, by Swedenborg.   1925.

*

Criticism

Books:
W. Paulsen, "Walter Hasenclever", in *Expressionismus als Literatur*, edited by W. Rothe, Bern and Munich, 1969.
Miriam Raggam, *Walter Hasenclever: Leben und Werk* (includes bibliography), Hildesheim, 1973.
James M. Ritchie, *German Expressionist Drama*, Boston, 1976.
A. Hoelzel, *Walter Hasenclever's Humanitarianism: Themes of Protest in His Work*, New York, 1983.
Ania Wilder, *Die Komödien Walter Hasenclevers*, Frankfurt, 1983.

Articles:
Alfred Hoezel, "Hasenclever's Satiric Treatment of Religion", in *German Quarterly*, 41, 1968.
Alfred Hoezel, "Walter Hasenclever's Political Satire", in *Monatshefte*, 61, 1969.

* * *

Walter Hasenclever is today best known for his drama *Der Sohn*, the first expressionist drama to be staged, whose subject matter voiced what was felt by many of the young generation. The Son seeks a new life and freedom from his arch-conservative father who symbolizes the oppressive, outlived literary and political tradition against which the young revolt. The Friend, representing the life force, becomes the Son's mentor: "You must recognize that the battle against the father is similar to the revenge a hundred years ago on sovereign Princes. Today right is on our side". Hasenclever's popularity began with the publication of *Der Sohn* in 1914, which sold an astonishing 20,000 copies. His fame followed him throughout the various stages of his dramatic develop-

ment and began to decline only with his exile from Germany in 1932.

That Hasenclever's dramas of his first period are classified as expressionist is due mostly to their content and less to their style and structure, which are rather conventional. The three plays of this period, *Der Sohn*, *Der Retter*, and *Antigone*, are also examples of Hasenclever's politically inspired period. (The theatre as platform for political activism had been called for as early as 1910, by F. Pfemfert in his journal *Die Aktion*, as well as by K. Hiller and L. Rubiner.) *Antigone*, Hasenclever's purest political drama, has little in common with the Sophoclean original; Hasenclever's Antigone fights for the rights of the poor and for world peace, while preaching a gospel of love for mankind. In *Der Retter* Hasenclever proclaims the same ideas through the voice of the Poet. Both protagonists believe ecstatically and uncompromisingly in their mission to regenerate mankind—a typical topic of expressionist drama.

However, as early as 1917, Hasenclever began to see that "the realization of political ideals in Germany was impossible". The proletariat, at whom these plays were aimed, had no understanding of their ecstatic pathos and futuristic visions; the reality of World War I and its aftermath defeated these high ideals quickly, and from 1919 the message of expressionist drama was often obscured by the technical brilliance of the staging in theatres whose seat prices, ironically, were out of reach of blue-collar workers.

Two main factors contributed to Hasenclever's declining interest in political drama. In the wake of the 1920 Kapp *coup d'état* he witnessed bloody street fights which caused him to lose his faith in his role as a saviour of the people. In two plays, *Die Entscheidung* and *Der Retter*, Hasenclever expressed his deep disillusionment with Germany's political system. Ironically, the two plays were first performed at the newly opened Tribüne theatre under Karlheinz Martin, whose aim was to promote expressionist/activist drama in Berlin; the reviews reflected the disappointment with the playwright who had lost his political "bite".

In Hasenclever's next plays, *Die Menschen* and *Jenseits*, his decreased interest in political drama was reinforced by his growing interest in the occult and in mysticism, influenced by the writings of Swedenborg. Hasenclever wrote of *Die Menschen* that its "only purpose was to link the world of the living with that of the dead . . . it depicts the tragic world of the spirits gathered in a magical play". His new philosophy, to which he remained faithful for the rest of his life, was based on his belief in an immanent cosmic order, where man is able to gain a spiritual renewal through the mystical experience of his death and rebirth. Interestingly, Hasenclever also experimented with a new style like that of A. Stramm's expressionist telegram style, combining dialogue and dramatic gesture into one integral whole:

Alexander opens the bag
The Head falls out
Alexander (taken aback): My head!!
The Head: My body.
Alexander: I have been killed?!
The Head: The murderer lives.
Alexander: He is forgiven.
    Gust of wind
Alexander: He lies in his grave.
The Head: Atonement!
Alexander: I live for him.

This second period of Hasenclever's dramatic accomplishment is relatively weak, as his withdrawal into the world of the transcendental took its toll on his creativity. He moved to

Paris where, for three years, he translated and adapted Swedenborg's works. He also became fascinated with French comedy, and consequently he changed his dramatic style decisively. Between 1926 and 1934 he wrote five successful comedies, the most notable of which were *Ein besserer Herr* and *Ehen werden im Himmel geschlossen*. In one season alone both received some 100 performances. In these plays Hasenclever attacks superficial bourgeois values, political megalomania, and religious hypocrisy with wit and humour; in contrast to his earlier plays, the dialogue is realistic, flows with great ease, and is free of overblown symbolism and metaphor. While in these comedies Hasenclever demonstrates a mastery of a genre that is rarely found in German literature, his satire drew protests. For example the delightful *Ehen werden im Himmel geschlossen*, which depicts Mary Magdalene as an elegant, emancipated young woman who bargains with her jeweller over the price of a new golden halo, and in which God appears dressed like an English Lord, was plagued by lawsuits from both the Catholic and Protestant church.

In 1934 Hasenclever wrote his last and most mature comedy, *Münchhausen*, which was first produced in 1948 in Leipzig and Vienna (with Curt Jürgens in the role of the Prince Ernst August). In 1935, Hasenclever turned to prose, writing two novels: *Die Rechtlosen*, which depicts the life of Germans in exile, and *Irrtum und Leidenschaft*, in part an autobiography, and in part a biting satirical statement on German society and politics of the 1920's.

Between 1914 and 1932 Hasenclever was one of Germany's best and most popular dramatists, and his plays were translated and performed all over the world. His exile and untimely death, however, and especially the banning of much of his *oeuvre* by the Nazis, are major factors accounting for the decline of his fame, a fate which he shared with many of Germany's most talented modern writers of the pre-Nazi period.

—Renate Benson

See also *Volume 1* entry on *Der Sohn*.

HAUPTMANN, Gerhart (Johann Robert). Born in Ober-Salzbrunn, Silesia (now in Poland), 15 November 1862. Educated at a school in Breslau; studied sculpture at Royal College of Art, Breslau, 1880–82; also studied at University of Jena, 1882–83. Married 1) Marie Thienemann in 1884 (divorced), three sons; 2) Margarete Marschalk in 1905, one son. Sculptor in Rome, 1883–84; also worked as actor in Berlin, before becoming a full-time writer; co-founder of literary group *Durch*; first play, *Vor Sonnenaufgang*, produced 1889; became identified as a major playwright of the Naturalist movement; frequent collaborator with Otto Brahms Freie Bühne, and with the director Max Reinhardt, who produced over 20 of his plays. Recipient: Grillparzer Prize, 1896, 1899, 1905; Goethebünde Schiller Prize, 1905; Nobel Prize for Literature, 1912; Goethe Prize (Frankfurt), 1932. Honorary degrees: Oxford University, 1905; University of Leipzig, 1909; University of Prague, 1921; Columbia University, New York, 1932. Ordre pour le Mérite, 1922. Died in Agnetendorf, Silesia, 8 June 1946.

Works

Collections

Gesammelte Werke (6 vols.). 1906; revised editions, 1912, 1921 (8 vols.), 1922 (12 vols.).
Dramatic Works (translations; 9 vols.). 1913–29.
Atridentetralogie (4 vols.; includes *Iphigenie in Aulis; Agamemnons Tod; Elektra; Iphigenie*). 1941–48.
Gesammelte Werke (17 vols.), edited by C.F.W. Behl and F.A. Voigt. 1942.
Five Plays (includes *The Weavers* and other plays), translated by Theodore H. Lustig. 1961.
Sämtliche Werke, edited by Hans-Egon Hass (11 vols.). 1962–74.

Stage Works

Vor Sonnenaufgang (produced by the Freie Bühne, Lessing-Theater, Berlin 1889). 1889; translated as *Before Dawn*, in *Dramatic Works 1* (see Collections); as *Before Daybreak*, 1978; as *Before Sunrise*, 1978.
Das Friedenfest (produced by the Freie Bühne, Ostendtheater, Berlin 1890). 1890; translated as *The Coming of Peace*, 1900; as *The Reconciliation*, in *Dramatic Works*, 1941.
Einsame Menschen (produced by the Freie Bühne, Residenz-theater, Berlin, 1891). 1891; translated as *Lonely Lives*, 1898.
Die Weber (produced by the Freie Bühne, Neues Theater, Berlin, 1893). 1892; translated as *The Weavers*, 1899: several subsequent translations under same title.
Kollege Crampton (produced Deutsches Theater, Berlin, 1892). 1892; translated as *Colleague Crampton*, in *Dramatic Works*, 1914.
Der Biberpelz (produced Deutsches Theater, Berlin, 1893). 1893; translated as *The Beaver Coat*, 1912.
Hanneles Himmelfahrt (produced Königliches Schauspiel-haus, Berlin, 1893). 1893; translated as *Hannele*, 1894.
Florian Geyer (produced Deutsches Theater, Berlin, 1896). 1896; translated as *Florian Geyer*, in *Dramatic Works*, 1929.
Die versunkene Glocke (produced Deutsches Theater, Berlin, 1896). 1896; translated as *The Sunken Bell*, 1898.
Fuhrmann Henschel (produced Deutsches Theater, Berlin, 1898). 1898; translated as *Drayman Henschel*, in *Dramatic Works*, 1913.
Schluck und Jau (produced Deutsches Theater, Berlin, 1900). 1900; translated as *Schluck and Jau*, in *Dramatic Works*, 1919.
Michael Kramer (produced Deutsches Theater, Berlin, 1900). 1900; translated as *Michael Kramer*, in *Dramatic Works*, 1914.
Der rote Hahn (produced Deutsches Theater, Berlin, 1901). 1901; translated as *The Conflagration*, in *Dramatic Works*, 1913.
Der arme Heinrich (produced Hofburgtheater, Vienna 1903). 1902; translated as *Henry of Auë*, in *Dramatic Works*, 1914.
Rose Bernd (produced Deutsches Theater, Berlin, 1903) 1903; translated as *Rose Bernd*, in *Dramatic Works*, 1913.
Elga (produced Lessingtheater, Berlin, 1905). 1905; translated as *Elga*, in *Dramatic Works*, 1919.
Und Pippa tanzt! (produced Lessingtheater, Berlin, 1906). 1906; translated as *And Pippa Dances*, 1907.
Die Jungfrau vom Bischofsberg (produced Lessingtheater, Berlin, 1907). 1907; translated as *Maidens of the Mount*, in *Dramatic Works*, 1919.
Kaiser Karls Geisel (produced Lessingtheater, Berlin, 1908).

Gerhart Hauptmann

1908; translated as *Charlemagne's Hostage*, in *Dramatic Works*, 1919.
Griselda (produced Lessingtheater, Berlin, 1909). 1909; translated as *Griselda*, in *Dramatic Works*, 1919.
Die Ratten (produced Lessingtheater, Berlin, 1911). 1911; translated as *The Rats*, in *Dramatic Works*, 1913.
Gabriel Schillings Flucht (produced Goethe-Theater, Bad Lauchstadt, 1912). 1912; translated as *Gabriel Schilling's Flight*, in *Dramatic Works*, 1919.
Festspiel in deutschen Reimen (produced Jahrhunderthalle, Breslau, 1913). 1913; translated as *Commemoration Masque*, in *Dramatic Works*, 1919.
Der Bogen des Odysseus (produced Deutsches Künstlertheater, Berlin, 1914). 1914; translated as *The Bow of Ulysses*, in *Dramatic Works*, 1919.
Winterballade (produced Deutsches Theater, Berlin, 1917). 1917; translated as *A Winter Ballad*, in *Dramatic Works*, 1925.
Der weisse Heiland (produced Grosses Schauspielhaus, Berlin, 1920). 1920; translated as *The White Savior*, in *Dramatic Works*, 1925.
Indipohdi (produced Staatliches Schauspielhaus, Dresden, 1920). 1920; translated as *Indipohdi*, in *Dramatic Works*, 1925.
Peter Bauer (produced Lustspielhaus, Berlin, 1921). 1921.
Veland (produced Deutsches Schauspielhaus, Hamburg, 1925). 1925; translated as *Veland*, in *Dramatic Works*, 1929.
Dorothea Angermann (produced simultaneously, Theater in der Josefstadt, Vienna, and 16 German theatres, 1926). 1926.

Spuk, oder Die Schwarze Maske und Hexenritt (produced Burgtheater, Vienna, 1929). 1929.
Vor Sonnenuntergang (produced Deutsches Theater, Berlin 1932). 1932.
Die goldene Harfe (produced Kammerspiele, Munich, 1933). 1933.
Hamlet in Wittenberg (produced Altes Theater, Leipzig, Stadttheater, Altona, and (Dutch) Nationaltheater, Osnabrück, 1935). 1935.
Ulrich von Lichtenstein (produced Burgtheater, Vienna, 1939). 1939.
Die Tochter der Kathedrale (produced Staatiches Schauspielhaus, Berlin, 1939). 1939.
Iphigenie in Delphi (produced Staatliches Schauspielhaus, Berlin, 1941). 1941.
Magnus Garbe (produced Schauspielhaus, Düsseldorf, 1942). 1942.
Iphigenie in Aulis (produced Burgtheater, Vienna, 1943). 1944.
Agamemnons Tod (broadcast 1946; produced Deutsches Theater, Berlin, 1947). 1948.
Elektra (produced Deutsches Theater, Berlin, 1947). 1948.
Die Finsternisse (produced Studio, Göttingen, 1952). 1947.
Herbert Engelmann, completed by Carl Zuckmayer (produced Akademie-Theater, Vienna, 1952). 1952.

Fiction

Fasching. 1887.
Bahnwärter Thiel. 1888.
Der Apostel. 1890.
Der Narr in Christo, Emanuel Quint. 1910; translated as *The Fool in Christ, Emanuel Quint*, 1911.
Atlantis. 1912; translated as *Atlantis*, 1912.
Lohengrin. 1913.
Parsival. 1914.
Der Ketzer von Soana. 1918; translated as *The Heretic of Soana*, 1923.
Phantom. 1922; translated as *Phantom*, 1923.
Die Insel der grossen Mutter. 1924; translated as *The Island of the Great Mother*, 1925.
Wanda. 1928.
Buch der Leidenschaft. 1930.
Die Hochzeit auf Buchenhorst. 1931.
Das Meerwunder. 1934.
Im Wirbel der Berufung. 1936.
Der Schuss im Park. 1939.
Das Märchen. 1941.
Mignon. 1944.
"Lineman Thiel" and Other Tales, translated by Stanley Radcliffe. 1988.

Verse

Promethidenlos. 1885.
Das bunte Buch. 1888.
Anna. 1921.
Die blaue Blume. 1924.
Till Eulenspiegel. 1928.
Ährenlese. 1939.
Der grosse Traum. 1942.
Neue Gedichte. 1946.

Memoirs and Letters

Das Abenteuer meiner Jugend. 1937.
Diarium 1917 bis 1933, edited by Martin Machatzke. 1980.

Gerhart Hauptmann—Ludwig van Hofmann: Briefwechsel 1894–1944, edited by Merta Hesse-Frielinghaus. 1983.
Otto Brahm—Gerhart Hauptmann: Briefwechsel 1889–1912, edited by Peter Sprengel. 1983.

Other

Um Volk und Geist. 1932.
Gespräche, edited by Josef Chapiro. 1932.
Griechischer Frühling. 1908.
Ausblicke. 1922.
Notiz-Kalender 1889 bis 1891. 1982.
Tagebuch 1892 bis 1894. 1985.
Tagebücher 1897 bis 1905, edited by Martin Machatzke. 1987.

*

Bibliographies

W. Requardt, *Gerhart-Hauptmann-Bibliographie* (3 vols.), Berlin, 1931.
V. Ludwig, *Gerhart Hauptmann: Werke von ihm und über ihn (1881–1931)*, Neustadt, 1932.
W.A. Reichart, *Gerhart-Hauptmann-Bibliographie*, Bad Homburg, 1969.
Heinz D. Tschörtner, *Gerhart-Hauptmann-Bibliographie*, Berlin, 1971.
Siegfried Hoefert, *Gerhart Hauptmann*, Stuttgart, 1974.
Siegfried Hoefert, *Internationale Bibliographie zum Werk Gerhart Hauptmanns* (2 vols.), Berlin, 1986–89.

Criticism

Books:
C.F.W. Behl and F.A. Voigt, *Chronik zum Gerhart Hauptmanns Leben und Werk*, Munich, 1957.
Frederick A. Klemm, *The Death Problem in the Life and Works of Hauptmann*, 1939.
H. Schreiber, *Gerhart Hauptmann und das Irrationale*, Aichkirchen, Vienna, and Leipzig, 1946.
S.H. Muller, *Gerhart Hauptmann und Goethe*, New York, 1949.
J.J. Weisert, *The Dream in Gerhart Hauptmann*, New York, 1949.
J. Gregor, *Gerhart Hauptmann: Das Werk und unsere Zeit*, Vienna, 1951.
R. Fiedler, *Die späten Dramen Gerhart Hauptmanns: Versuch einer Deutung*, Munich, 1954.
Hugh F. Garten, *Hauptman*, Cambridge, 1954.
C.F.W. Behl, *Hauptmann: His Life and Works*, Würzburg, 1956.
Margaret Sinden, *Hauptmann: The Prose Plays*, Toronto, 1957.
K.S. Guthke and H.M. Wolff, *Das Leid im Werke Gerhart Hauptmanns: Fünf Studien*, Bern, 1958.
L.R. Shaw, *Witness of Deceit: Hauptmann as a Critic of Society*, Berkeley, California, 1958
K.L. Tank, *Gerhart Hauptmann in Selbstzeugnissen und Bilddokumenten*, Reinbek, 1959; fifth edition, 1980.
N.E. Alexander, *Studien zum Stilwandel im dramatischen Werk Gerhart Hauptmanns*, Stuttgart, 1964.
K.G. Knight and F. Norman (eds.), *Hauptmann: Centenary Lectures*; 1964.
F.A. Voigt, *Gerhart Hauptmann und die Antike*, Berlin, 1965.

H. Mayer, *Gerhart Hauptmann*, Velber, 1967.
K. Hilderbrandt, *Gerhart Hauptmann und die Geschichte*, Munich, 1968.
Hans Daiber, *Gerhart Hauptmann, oder der letzte Klassiker*, Vienna, 1971.
Rolf Goetze, *Von "Sonnenaufgang" bis "Sonnenuntergang": Gerhart Hauptmanns Berliner Beziehungen*, Berlin, 1971.
John Osborne, *The Naturalist Drama in Germany*, Manchester, 1971.
Albert A. Kipa, *Gerhart Hauptmann in Russia, 1889–1917: Reception and Impact*, Hamburg, 1974.
Ladislaus Löb, *From Lessing to Hauptmann: Studies in German Drama*, London, 1974.
Ronald Hayman (ed.), *The German Theatre: A Symposium*, London, 1975.
P.A. Mellen, *Gerhart Hauptmann und Utopia*, Stuttgart, 1976.
Hans J. Schrimpf (ed.), *Gerhart Hauptmann* (essay collection), Darmstadt, 1976.
Carolyn Thomas Sussere, *The Image of the Primitive Giant in the Works of Hauptmann*, Stuttgart, 1979.
K.S. Guthke, *Gerhart Hauptmann: Weltbild im Werk* (second edition), 1980.
W. Requardt und M. Machatzke, *Gerhart Hauptmann und Erkner: Studien zum Berliner Frühwerk*, Berlin, 1980.
R.C. Cowen, *Hauptmann: Kommentar zum dramatischen Werk*, Munich, 1980.
Martin Machatzke (ed.), *Gerhart Hauptmann: Notiz-Kalender 1889 bis 1891*, Frankfurt, 1982.
A. Marshall, *The German Naturalists and Gerhart Hauptmann: Reception and Influence*, Frankfurt, 1982.
W.R. Maurer, *Gerhart Hauptmann*, Boston, 1982.
K. Hildebrandt, *Naturalistische Dramen Gerhart Hauptmanns*, Munich, 1983.
Philip Mellen, *Gerhart Hauptmann: Religious Syncretism and Eastern Religions*, New York, 1984.
Peter Sprengel, *Gerhart Hauptmann: Epoche, Werk, Wirkung*, Munich, 1984.
R. Mittler, *Theorie und Praxis des sozialen Dramas bei Gerhart Hauptmann*, Hildesheim, 1985.
Eberhard Hillscher, *Gerhart Hauptmann: Leben und Werk*, Frankfurt, 1986.
W. Leppman, *Gerhart Hauptmann: Leben, Werk und Zeit*, Bern, 1986.
Philip Mellen and Peter Sprengel (eds.), *Hauptmann-Forschung: Neue Beiträge/Hauptmann Research: New Directions*, Frankfurt and Bern, 1986.
Heinz D. Tschörtner, *Ungeheures erhofft: Zu Gerhart Hauptmann, Werk und Wirkung*, Berlin, 1986.
Peter Skrine, *Hauptmann, Wedekind and Schnitzler*, London, 1989 (Macmillan Modern Dramatists series).

* * *

Gerhart Hauptmann is one of the most prolific and versatile playwrights of the modern period. The young dramatist who excited and provoked the Berlin public of 1889 with a naturalist drama of contemporary society, *Vor Sonnenaufgang (Before Dawn)*, ended his career over 50 years later with a classical tetralogy devoted to the Orestes-myth. In between, he explored a full range of realist, historical, visionary, fantastic, and symbolist styles and subjects without ever becoming closely associated with any of the various literary movements which succeeded Naturalism.

Despite the scope of his ambition, the enduring reputation of Hauptmann rests almost exclusively on the realist plays of his early period up to *Die Ratten (The Rats)*. This corresponds to the years during which he had the support of the theatre director Otto Brahm, who discovered Hauptmann and, until his own death in 1912, was principally responsible for the production of Hauptmann's plays in Berlin. Hauptmann's first four dramas, written and first produced in a very short space of time, introduced Naturalism to the German stage and rapidly brought it to a climax in its most successful realisation and Hauptmann's own masterpiece, *Die Weber* (*The Weavers*).

Although overloaded with the topical problems and shock effects associated with the naturalist style, and in certain respects technically clumsy in its use of the stage, *Vor Sonnenaufgang* immediately revealed the enduring concerns of Hauptmann and the qualities which would come to inform his best work. Using the analytical form familiar from the social dramas of Ibsen, Hauptmann introduced an idealistic newcomer into an environment whose barely concealed tensions are rapidly brought into the open by his presence. The directness with which the dramatist drew attention to economic exploitation, marital and family strife, sexual depravity, cruelty, and alcoholism caused one indignant member of his first audience to ask whether he were not in a brothel. Analysis of the central character, the fanatical social reformer Alfred Loth, reveals however a shallowness in the portrayal which compares unfavourably with Ibsen's treatment of the superficially similar Gregers Werle in *The Wild Duck*. It is, nevertheless, neither here nor in the schematic treatment of the play's teetotalist-eugenicist thesis that its real qualities lie, but in the breadth of characterisation, particularly of the minor characters, which extends the range of naturalist drama beyond the articulate, self-torturing heroes and heroines of Ibsen's tragedies.

If Hauptmann's next two plays, *Das Friedenfest* (*The Coming of Peace*) and *Einsame Menschen* (*Lonely Lives*) appear to enter the territory of Ibsen—and O'Neill, a later admirer of Hauptmann—the purpose of this is to pursue, with greater intensity, problems related to heredity, the family, and the position of women in society: problems which had been raised but not fully explored in the earlier play. In fact these plays confirm Hauptmann's compassionate interest in characters who suffer because they do not understand their own predicament, who fall without attaining lucidity, and who assume increasingly the roles of desperate, hunted victims.

In *Die Weber* Hauptmann successfully brings together a clear and rational analysis of the causes and the course of a revolt among the weaving community of his native Silesia and the sense that his characters are the uncomprehending victims of some grand, malevolent, and arbitrary power.

The same skilful preservation of the naturalist surface, beneath which there are intimations of fatalist determination, is evident in the best plays of Hauptmann's post-naturalist period: *Fuhrmann Henschel* (*Drayman Henschel*) and *Rose Bernd*, in which Hauptmann builds on the success of *Die Weber* by drawing his inspiration from the intimately-known setting and language of his native Silesia. He was also able to repeat this success in a Berlin setting with *Die Ratten*, and his comedy, *Der Biberpelz* (*The Beaver Coat*). This latter play, a sharply satirical attack on the foolish blindness and political prejudice of Prussian bureaucracy during the Wilhemine period, contains Hauptmann's most famous stage character, Waschfrau Wolff, an affectionately portrayed scoundrel who has certain features in common with Brecht's Mother Courage. Here, however, it should be said that it was precisely the lack of higher political and historical insight vouchsafed to Hauptmann's characters that lay at the root of Brecht's critique of the naturalist style, and which prompted

him to re-write Hauptmann's play before directing it himself with the Berliner Ensemble.

As early as 1893 Hauptmann had made a fairly decisive break with strict Naturalism in the two-part play, *Hanneles Himmelfahrt* (*Hannele*), which presents both the material suffering of an impoverished adolescent girl and her subjective dream of transcendent release from earthly misery. In *Die versunkene Glocke* (*The Sunken Bell*), Hauptmann wrote a play entirely in the neo-romantic style, which nevertheless looked back to *Einsame Menschen* in its theme of the artist placed between different kinds of women. This play enjoyed great public success in the 1890's, but like the later, and almost equally successful, fantastic drama, *Und Pippa tanzt!*, it has acquired a certain following among Hauptmann enthusiasts without ever establishing itself as a canonical work.

The remainder of Hauptmann's considerable *oeuvre* has been largely neglected. Apart from the classical tetralogy of the 1940's, *Die Atriden*, which received a notable production by Piscator as a political drama, expressing Hauptmann's last words to the German people during the barbarism of the National Socialist state, it has been the realist dramas from various periods of the dramatist's life, such as *Michael Kramer* and *Vor Sonnenuntergang*, that have been seen most frequently in German theatres, confirming his pre-eminence among German playwrights in this field of early-modern drama.

—John Osborne

See also *Volume 1* entries on *Before Dawn*; *The Weavers*.

HAVEL, Václav. Born in Prague, Czechoslovakia (now the Czech Republic), 5 October 1936. Educated at a technical college, 1955–57; Academy of Arts, Prague, 1962–66. Married Olga Šplíchalová in 1964. Chemical laboratory technician, 1951–55; served in the Czechoslovak army, 1957–59; stagehand, ABC Theatre, Prague, 1959–60; stagehand, 1960–61, assistant to the artistic director, 1961–63, literary manager, 1963–68, and resident playwright, 1968, Theater Na Zábradlí [Theatre on the Balustrade], Prague; first-produced play, *Autostop* [The Hitchhike], produced 1961; member of editorial board, *Tvář*, 1965; following the Soviet invasion of Czechoslovakia, 1968, his works declared subversive; passport confiscated, 1969; worker at Trutnov Brewery, North Bohemia, 1974; co-founder, 1977, and spokesman, 1978, 1989, Charter 77 human rights group; imprisoned for brief terms, 1977, 1978–79; co-founder, Committee for the Defence of the Unjustly Prosecuted (VONS), 1978; sentenced to 4½ years imprisonment for subversion, 1979: released because of illness, 1983; member of editorial board, and regular contributor, *Lidové noviny* samizdat newspaper, 1987–89; arrested and sentenced to nine months imprisonment for incitement and resisting arrest, January 1989: released May 1989; co-founder and leader, Občanské Fórum [Civic Forum] political party, 1989; elected by Parliament as President of the Czech and Slovak Federal Republic, December 1989, re-elected July 1990: stood down, having failed re-election from Parliament, 1992; elected by Parliament as President of the Czech Republic, 1993. Recipient of many awards for literary and human rights achievements, including: Obie Award, 1968, 1970; Austrian

Václav Havel in Prague (1989).

State Prize, 1969; Prix Plaisir du Théâtre (France), 1981; Palach Prize, 1981; Erasmus Prize, 1986; Olof Palme Prize, 1989; UNESCO Bolívar Prize, 1990; Malaparte Prize, 1990; Legion of Honour Grand Cross, 1990; UNESCO Prize for the teaching of human rights, 1991; Charlemagne Prize, 1991; Sonning Prize, 1991; Freedom Award (USA), 1991; Raoul Wallenberg Human Rights Award (USA), 1991; International Book Award, 1991. Honorary doctorate: York University, Toronto, 1982; Le Mirail University, Toulouse, 1982; Columbia University (New York), Hebrew University (Jerusalem), Bayreuth University; University of F. Palacký (Olomouc), Charles University (Prague), and University of J.A. Komenský (Bratislava), all 1990; Free University of Brussels, St. Gallen University, LeHigh University (Bethlehem, Pennsylvania), and New York University, all 1991.

Works

Collections

Hry 1970–1976 (includes *Spiklenci; Zebrácká opera; Horský hotel; Audience; Vernisáž*).   1977 (Toronto).
Sorry (two one-act plays: *Audience* and *A Private View*).   1978.
Three Vanek Plays (includes *Audience; Protest; Unveiling*), translated by Jan Novak and Vera Blackwell.   1990.
Selected Plays 1963–1983 (includes *The Garden Party; The Memorandum; The Increased Difficulty of Concentration; Audience/Conversation; Private View; Protest; The Mistake*).   1991.

Stage Works

Autostop [The Hitchhike], with Ivan Vyskočil (produced Theatre on the Balustrade, Prague, 1961).   1961.
Nejlepši rocky paní Hermanové [The Best "Rock" of Mrs. Herman], with Miloš Macourek (produced Theatre on the Balustrade, Prague, 1962).
Zahradni slavnost (produced Theatre on the Balustrade, Prague, 1963).   1964; translated as *The Garden Party*, 1969.
Vyrozuměni (produced Theatre on the Balustrade, Prague, 1965).   1965 (cyclostyed edition); in *Protokoly*, 1966; translated as *The Memorandum*, 1967.
Ztížená možnost soustředění (produced Theatre on the Balustrade, Prague, 1968).   1968; translated as *The Increased Difficulty of Concentration*, 1972.
Spiklenci [The Conspirators] (produced Theater der Stadt, Baden-Baden, 1974).   In *Hry*, 1977.
Audience (produced Akademietheater, Vienna, 1976).   1975 ("samizdat" edition); in *Hry*, 1977; translated as *Conversation*, in *Index*, Autumn 1976; as *Audience*, in *Sorry*, 1978.
Vernisáž (produced Akademietheater, Vienna, 1976).   1975 ("samizdat" edition); in *Hry*, 1977; translated as *A Private View*, in *Sorry*, 1978; as *Unveiling*, in *Three Vanek Plays*, 1990.
Zebrácká opera [The Beggar's Opera] (produced Teatro Stabile, Trieste, 1976).   In *Hry*, 1977.
Horsky hotel [A Mountain Hotel] (produced Burgtheater, Vienna, 1981).   In *Hry*, 1977.
Protest (produced Burgtheater, Vienna, 1979).   1979 ("samizdat" edition); translated as *Protest*, in *Three Vanek Plays*, 1990.
Chyba (produced Dramaten, Stockholm, 1983).   In *Svědectví*, 18, 1983; translated as *The Mistake*, in *Selected Plays 1963–1983*, 1991.
Pokoušení (produced Burgtheater, Vienna, 1986).   1985 ("samizdat" edition); 1986; translated as *Temptation*, 1988.
Largo Desolato (produced Burgtheater, Vienna, 1985).   1984 ("samizdat" edition); 1985 (Munich); translated as *Largo Desolato*, 1987.
Asanace (produced Zurich, 1989).   1987 ("samizdat" edition); 1988 (Munich); translated as *Redevelopment; or, Slum Clearance*, 1990.

Television Plays

Motýl na anteně [Butterfly on the Antenna], 1975 (Germany).

Radio Plays

Andél Strážý [The Guardian Angel], 1969 (Germany); *Sorry: Two Plays*, 1978–79.

Memoirs and Letters

Hérmanické úvahy (correspondence). 1981 ("samizdat" edition).
Šestnáct dopisů (correspondence). 1982 ("samizdat" edition).
Dopisy Olze. 1983; translated as *Letters to Olga June 1979 to September 1982*, 1988.

Other

Josef Čapek, with Vera Ptáčková. 1963.
Protokoly [Minutes] (miscellany). 1966.
Moc bezmocných. 1979 (London).
O Lidskou identitu: úvahy, fejetony, protesty, polemiky, prohlášení a rozhovory z let 1969–1979. 1984 (London).
Výzva k transcendenci, with *Consolatio philosophiae hodeivna*, by Sidonius. 1984 (London).
The Anatomy of a Reticence: Eastern European Dissidents and the Peace Movement in the West. 1985 (Stockholm).
Václav Havel; or, Living in Truth, edited by Jan Vladislav. 1986 (Amsterdam).
Ztížené možnosti: (tři hry z šedesátých let). 1986 (London).
Politics and Conscience. 1986 (Stockholm).
Acceptance Speech Written on the Occasion of the Award of the Erasmus Prize 1986. 1986 (Amsterdam).
Dálkový výslech: rozhovor s Karlem Hvížd'alou. 1986 ("samizdat" and London editions); translated as *Disturbing the Peace: A Conversation with Karel Hvížďala*, 1990.
Do různých stran: Eseje a články z let 1983–1989 [Different Destinations]. 1989 (Scheinfeld-Schwarzenberg).
Projevy: Leden-červen 1990 (speeches). 1990.
Open Letters: Selected Writings. 1991 (New York); as *Open Letters: Selected Prose 1965–1990*, 1991 (London).
Letní přemítaní. 1991; translated as *Summer Meditations*, 1992.

Editor, *Přirozený svět jako politický problém*, by Václava Bělohradského and others. 1984 ("samizdat" edition).
Editor, *Hostina: filozofický sborník*. 1985 ("samizdat" edition); 1989 (Toronto).

*

Bibliographies

Bibliography in *Slovnik ceskych spisovatelu*, Toronto, 1982.

Criticism

Books:
Antonin J. Liehm, *The Politics of Culture*, New York, 1970.
Paul I. Trensky, *Czech Drama since World War II*, White Plains, New York, 1978.
Marketa Goetz-Stankiewicz, *The Silenced Theatre: Czech Playwrights Without a Stage*, Toronto, 1979.
A. French, *Czech Writers and Politics 1945–1969*, New York, 1982.
Eda Kriseova, *Václav Havel: The Authorized Biography*, Boston, 1991.

Articles:
Paul I. Trensky, "Václav Havel and the Language of the Absurd", in *Slavic and East European Journal*, 13, 1969.

Marketa Goetz-Stankiewicz, "Havel, A Writer for Today's Season", *World Literature Today*, Summer 1981.
Muriel C. Bradbrook, "Václav Havel's Second Wind", in *Modern Drama*, 27, 1984.
Marketa Goetz-Stankiewicz, "Variations of Temptation: Václav Havel's Politics of Language", in *Modern Drama*, 33, 1990.

*   *   *

Václav Havel has had one of the most remarkable careers experienced by a playwright, culminating in his election, at the end of 1989, as President of the former Czechoslovakia. Nevertheless, he had assembled a respectable body of work, even if one were to suppose then that in future he would lack either time or inclination to return to the theatre.

His work in the theatre can, so far, be divided into three periods: the plays written with Ivan Vyskočil and Jan Grossman for the Theatre on the Balustrade in Prague, from 1961–68; those written during the early years of his exclusion from public life, from 1970 until his imprisonment in 1979; and those written after his release in 1983, when he had become internationally known as a political dissident.

The Theatre on the Balustrade had been founded towards the end of the conformist years of the 1950's, and many of the company had originally worked without pay for the excitement of creating a new kind of theatre. Havel, because of his "bourgeois" background, had for years been excluded from any form of higher education; he came to the Theatre on the Balustrade as scene shifter, electrician, and dramaturg, for it was the kind of theatre where anyone could turn his hand to anything. During the theatre's early years, productions—often musical—were devised for the performers who were taking part, and Havel collaborated on these before writing his first "straight" play, *The Garden Party*; over the next few years he completed *The Memorandum* and *The Increased Difficulty of Concentration*. These formed part of a dramaturgical programme devised by Jan Grossman in response to the times, and included works by Beckett, Ionesco, Kafka, and Jarry, as well as by new Czech writers.

The Garden Party opened in December 1963, directed by Otomar Krejča. It is a play in which characters exercise control over each other by the mechanical manipulation of language. The central character, the featureless Hugo Pludek, progresses from the clichés of his conventional home background, through the bureaucratic jargon used by the secretaries running the garden party and the liberalised phraseology of a more advanced functionary, to the point where until he challenges the Director of the Inauguration Office, a master of dialectics. In the final act, the previously monosyllabic youth proves that through an understanding of linguistic conventions one can gain control of the whole system.

The Memorandum and *The Increased Difficulty of Concentration* similarly take as their theme the absurdity of a world in which man's life is subordinated to the operation of a mechanical system. When the translated versions of the plays were seen in the West, they were immediately allocated to the recently-defined genre, "the theatre of the absurd". The title is, however, only applicable if it is realised that the "absurd" in Western eyes was all too real in the East. One of the leading theatre critics, Sergej Machonin, wrote of how passages in Havel's plays reminded him of the way people had conformed both as a whole and in their personal lives, and of the all-too-recent history of the loss of feeling, reason, and character.

Within a few years, that all-too-recent history was repeating itself. In the early years of normalisation, Václav Havel, banned from publication because of his outspoken denunciations of President Husak's regime, wrote three long plays, only one of which was performed in Czechoslovakia. This was *The Beggars' Opera*, whose single performance by an amateur group set off a massive police operation. Neither this, nor *Spiklenci* (Conspirators) nor *Horsky hotel* (A Mountain Hotel; has been well-received abroad; for Western audiences, the themes appeared to be too intellectual and the structures too complex.

On the other hand, the short plays which Havel wrote for performance by his friends gained great popularity abroad. There are three of them, *Audience, A Private View*, and *Protest*, together known as the Vaněk plays, after their leading character. Their popularity lies in the deceptive simplicity of their form: the unsophisticated Vaněk, an ironic version of the author, is confronted with the deformation of contemporary life in Czechoslovakia, personified in convincing characterisations. A brewer, required to inform on his new employee, begs the writer to supply the information himself; a married couple display the tedious round of their material possessions; an "official" writer uses his contorted conscience to manipulate both Vaněk and himself.

Havel's involvement in the human rights organisations Charter 77 and VONS led him, in 1979, to a prison sentence. On his release in 1983 he wrote, in response to Samuel Beckett's *Catastrophe*, the brief sketch *Mistake*. It was followed by two of his best plays, *Largo Desolato*—essentially an extended Vaněk play—and *Temptation*. In *Largo Desolato*, the writer-hero is waiting for the arrival of the secret police who, when they do arrive, tease him with a dilemma which, at the end, they remove with the dexterity of conjurors. It is this play which shows, most clearly, Havel's fascination with the world of the popular small-stage theatre and the early film, which he wrote about in his essay "The Anatomy of the Gag" (included in *Protokoly*, 1967). The underlying seriousness of the play is constantly deflated by the use of double-acts, double-takes, and wordplay.

Temptation was based on a theme which had preoccupied Havel for many years, and which his years in prison had given him time to dwell on. It concerns the nature of truth, and our active relationship towards it: "Truth is not merely what we are thinking, but also why, to whom and under what circumstances we say it". Dr Foustka ("Faust") is a research worker in an institute which bears a close resemblance to Czechoslovak socialist society: the employees busy themselves with making coffee and doing their shopping, whilst tolerating periodic visits from the Director and his sinister shadow, the Secretary. Out of boredom, Foustka calls up Mephistopheles—Fistula—and, under the illusion that he is living a "free" life, contorts his conscience until he does not know when he is speaking truth and when pretence. In the final Walpurgisnacht he discovers that Fistula, too, is a secret agent of the regime he thought he had defied. Fistula's words are Havel's challenge to the complacency of the times: "Did I not, throughout, let you know that you had a range of choices and that you alone could decide your fate?"

Havel had time to write only one more play before political events absorbed him completely. *Redevelopment* treats the subject of sweeping away the past on two levels: first, the realistic level of the environmental damage caused by pretentious rebuilding schemes (as in Bratislava); and second, as an image of the self-deception practised by even the most "human" characters when colluding in the destruction of human values.

Twenty years after Havel's plays were banished from the Czech theatre, they were performed there again—as the work, not of an aspiring stagehand, but of the country's President. The reversal is far more absurd than anything to be found in the plays themselves, and reinforces the view that the "theatre of the absurd" is the true realist theatre.

—Barbara Day

See also *Volume 1* entry on *The Memorandum*.

HEBBEL, (Christian) Friedrich. Born in Wesselburen, Holstein, Denmark (now in Germany), 18 March 1813. Educated in a dame's school, 1817–19; primary school, Wesselburen, 1819–25; servant and clerk for local official, 1827–35; in Hamburg a group of benefactors supported him in his studies, and helped send him to University of Heidelberg, 1836; doctorate, University of Erlangen, 1844. Married the actress Christine Enghaus in 1846, two children; also had two sons before marriage by Elise Lensing. Freelance writer in Munich, 1836–39, Hamburg, 1839–43; first play, *Judith*, produced 1840; travel allowance from the Danish king allowed him to live in Paris, 1843–44, and Rome, 1844–45; lived in Vienna from 1845; honorary Court Librarian, Weimar, 1863. Recipient: Schiller Prize, 1863. Died in Vienna, 13 December 1863.

Works

Collections

Sämmtliche Werke (12 vols.), edited by Emil Kuh. 1865–67.
Sämtliche Werke (includes the 12-volume *Werke*, the 4-volume *Tagebücher*, and the 8-volume *Briefe*), edited by Richard Maria Werner. 1904–22.
Three Plays (includes *Maria Magdalena; Herod and Mariamne; Gyges and His Ring*), translated by L.H. Allen and Barker Fairley. 1914.
Werke (5 vols.), edited by Gerhard Fricke, Werner Keller, and Karl Pörnbacher. 1963–67.

Stage Works

Judith (produced Hoftheater, Berlin, 1840). 1840; translated as *Judith*, 1914.
Genoveva (produced Burgtheater, Vienna, 1849). 1843.
Maria Magdalena (produced Stadttheater, Königsberg, 1846). 1844; translated as *Maria Magdalene*, in *Poet Lore*, 25, 1914; as *Maria Magdalena*, in *Three Plays*, 1914: several subsequent translations under same title.
Der Diamant (produced Kremsier, 1852). 1847.
Julia (produced Schauspielhaus, Munich, 1903). 1848.
Herodes und Mariamne (produced Burgtheater, Vienna 1849). 1850; as *Herod and Mariamne*, in *Three Plays*, 1914.
Der Rubin (produced Hofburgtheater, Vienna, 1849). 1851.
Michel Angelo (produced Quaitheater, Vienna, 1861). 1851.
Ein Trauerspiel in Sizilien (produced Deutsches Schauspielhaus, Hamburg, 1907). 1851.
Agnes Bernauer (produced Hoftheater, Munich, 1852). 1852; translated as *Agnes Bernauer*, in *Poet Lore*, 1909.
Gyges und sein Ring (produced Burgtheater, Vienna, 1889). 1856; translated as *Gyges and His Ring*, in *Three Plays*, 1914.

Die Nibelungen: trilogy includes *Der gehörte Siegfried; Siegfrieds Tod; Kriemhilds Rache* (*Der gehörte Siegfried* and *Siegfrieds Tod* produced Hoftheater, Weimar, 1861). 2 vols., 1862; translated as *The Nibelungs*, 1921.
Demetrius, from an uncompleted play by Schiller (produced Berlin, 1869). 1864
Ein Steinwurf. 1883.

Fiction

Schnock: Ein niederländisches Gemälde.   1850.
Erzählungen und Novellen.   1855.

Verse

Gedichte.   1842.
Neue Gedichte.   1848.
Gedichte.   1857.
Mutter und Kind.   1859.

Memoirs and Letters

Tagebücher (2 vols.), edited by F. Bamberg.   1885–87.
Briefe (8 vols.).   In *Sämtliche Werke*, 1904–22.
Neue Hebbel-Briefe, edited by Anni Meetz.   1963.
Der einsame Weg (diaries), edited by Klaus Geissler.   1966.
Briefe (2 vols.), edited by U. Henry Gerlach.   1975–78.

Other

Mein Wort über das Drama!   1843.
Über den Stil des Dramas.   1857.
Hebbels Dramaturgie, edited by Wilhelm von Scholz.   1907.

*

Bibliographies

Ulrich H. Gerlach, *Hebbel-Bibliographie 1910–1970*, Heidelberg, 1973; supplements: *1970–1980*, in *Hebbel-Jahrbuch*, 1983; *1981–1984*, in *Hebbel-Jahrbuch*, 1986.

Criticism

Books:
O. Walzel, *Friedrich Hebbel und seine Dramen: Ein Versuch*, Leipzig, 1913; third edition, 1927 (reprinted 1973).
E. Dosenheimer, *Das zentrale Problem in der Tragödie Hebbels*, Halle, 1925; reprinted, Hildesheim, 1976.
Edna Purdie, *Hebbel: A Study of His Life and Work*, London, 1932.
K. Ziegler, *Mensch und Welt in der Tragödie Hebbels*, Berlin, 1938; reprinted, Darmstadt, 1963.
W. Thomas (ed.), *Friedrich Hebbel: Leben und Werk in Einzeldarstellungen*, Vienna, 1942.
William F. Oechler, *Motivation in the Drama of Hebbel*, Glencoe, Illinois, 1948.
Sten G. Flygt, *Friedrich Hebbel's Conception of Movement in the Absolute and History*, Chapel Hill, North Carolina, 1952.
H. Frisch, *Symbolik und Tragik in Hebbels Dramen* (second edition), Bonn, 1963.
H. Kreuzer, *Hebbel in neuer Sicht*, Stuttgart, 1963.
C. Kleinschmidt, *Die Person in frühen Drama Hebbels*, Lahr, 1965.
A. Meetz, *Friedrich Hebbel* (second edition), Stuttgart, 1965.
M. Schaub, *Friedrich Hebbel*, Velber, 1967.
Sten G. Flygt, *Friedrich Hebbel* (in English), New York, 1968.
H. Matthiesen, *Friedrich Hebbel in Selbstzeugnissen und Bilddokumenten*, Reinbek, 1970; revised edition, 1979.
Ulrich H. Gerlach, *Hebbel as a Critic of His Own Works*, Göppingen, 1972.
Mary Garland, *Hebbel's Prose Tragedies*, Cambridge, 1973.
Ladislaus Lob, *From Lessing to Hauptmann: Studies in German Drama*, London, 1974.
H. Grundmann (ed.), *Friedrich Hebbel: Neue Studien zu Werk und Wirkung*, Heide in Holstein, 1982.
H. Kaiser, *Friedrich Hebbel*, Munich, 1983.
W.J. Niven, *The Reception of Friedrich Hebbel in Germany in the Era of National Socialism*, Stuttgart, 1984.
H. Kreuzer, *Friedrich Hebbel*, Darmstadt, 1989.

Serials

Hebbel-Jahrbuch, 1939—

*   *   *

It has become something of a cliché in Hebbel criticism to characterise his dramas as plays of ideas, coolly formulated presentations of his own highly abstract and often somewhat obscure speculative philosophy. Hebbel himself contributed, in large measure, to this image by his theoretical statements about the nature of art, culminating in his comment that a prime function of art is the "realisation of philosophy". Yet, as with most clichés, this one both highlights and oversimplifies a potential truth.

Hebbel's works are indeed heavily dependent upon his philosophic musings, but equally they draw upon an intensity of personal emotions, and much of their undoubted power derives from personal experiences, from actual, as well as perceived, suffering. Born into a harsh family situation, and exposed for much of his early life to poverty, Hebbel quickly became embittered with his contemporary society, in which his conviction of his own intellectual and artistic abilities saw itself frustrated by prevailing circumstances. His enforced dependence on (and, some might say, exploitation of) his relationships with women did little to alleviate that frustration—small wonder, perhaps, that he became obsessively preoccupied with the man-woman relationship, presenting it as a relentless and unending battle between the sexes. All of his major tragedies centre on such a conflict, which invariably ends in the destruction of both male and female protagonist.

The world-view dominant in Hebbel's plays is fundamentally tragic, and even those he designated as comedies reveal a darker edge, tending more towards the tragicomic mode. Much of the early work, in particular, shows strong affinities with the thinking of the first major pessimistic German philosopher, Arthur Schopenhauer (although he did not actually meet him until very late on): human life is characterised by suffering, the very individuation which is inherent in life leads individuals into conflict with one another, and the course of history itself is determined by such factors. As he developed and refined his philosophy, Hebbel became convinced that the principle of contradiction leading to conflict encompassed even those qualities which traditionally would be regarded as good and positive, since each quality inevitably calls forth its opposite: thus purity provokes evil, and beauty brings ugliness to the fore, whether or not this be a conscious desire on the part of the individuals involved (as in, for example, *Genoveva, Agnes Bernauer, Gyges und sein Ring*).

In pursuing such a line of thought, Hebbel is very much representative of a widespread philosophic trend of his times, manifested also in the contemporary dramatists Büchner and Grabbe (and, to some extent, Nestroy), a trend which perceives a fundamental flaw in Creation, so profound that it calls into question the very existence of a benevolent and omnipotent God. Indeed, God Himself (now at best a "deus absconditus"—a hidden God) is called to account by his own Creation, and Hebbel is led to replace the concept of moral guilt by that of tragic guilt, whereby the individual is compelled into tragedy as the internally consistent product of his own circumstances, rather than by the exercise of his free will to choose good or evil. History irresistibly moves on through a succession of conflicts, manifesting, ever-recurrently, the ultimate helplessness of the individual before the force of the universal. Hebbel wrote arguably his finest work, the political drama *Agnes Bernauer*, precisely to document the truth that the individual—regardless of personal qualities—is crushed when he comes into conflict with society or the State.

Yet paradoxically, Hebbel insists, the course of history reveals itself most clearly at its crucial turning-points in the fates of great individuals, "world-historical personages"; historical dramas thus acquire a "dual historical significance", for their content-matter should be relevant both to the actual historical setting of the play and to the contemporary setting of the playwright. An important function of the tragedy is to effect a reconciliation of the individual to his fate within the concept of the universal (society, the State, history, and, ultimately, God), both for the central characters within the play and the audience outside of it.

If Hebbel, from an early stage, shows affinities with Schopenhauer, then the maturing Hebbel seems to become steadily affected by the ideas of Hegel—unlikely as such a combination might seem. Hebbel himself on occasions denied the direct influence of Hegel, and certainly he never achieves a comparably optimistic, rationalist stance. Yet if one tabulates the kinds of characterisation in the major tragedies especially, it is possible to trace an ever more significant appearance of a third character, who completes a dialectical triangle, with the man and woman destroyed at the climax. It would be an exaggeration to suggest that this third character represents progress in the full Hegelian sense; but he does at least seem to imply continuity, in an ever more overtly political, and indeed religious, sense, offering a positive element amid the tragic gloom (Titus in *Herodes und Mariamne*, Gyges in *Gyges und sein Ring*, and Dietrich in *Die Nibelungen*). This may to some extent reflect Hebbel's own situation, settling down after the disappointments of his early itinerant life to personal and artistic success in Vienna, following his marriage to the leading Burgtheater actress Christine Enghaus.

Within the broad terms of literary history, Hebbel is often portrayed as standing on the threshold between German idealism and the nascent realist movement. In a work such as *Maria Magdalena* he certainly does display astute observation of realistic detail, even if he fails quite to achieve his aim of producing convincingly realistic dialogue. Throughout his works he demonstrates perceptive psychological insight, and the dignity of his verse-forms does not negate the emotional intensity of his characters. Yet, to his dying day, he acknowledged his indebtedness to the tradition of German classicism: his last, unfinished tragedy was *Demetrius*, an attempt to complete a play by Friedrich Schiller. Hebbel's death in 1863 signals the end of an era, and it is perhaps revealing that

it is difficult to trace direct influence on subsequent leading dramatists: not until the emergence of the German Naturalist movement, a full quarter of a century later, did the German drama receive a radically new impulse.

—Ken Mills

See also *Volume 1* entry on *Maria Magdalena*.

HECHT, Ben.   Born in New York City, 28 February 1894; moved with his family to Chicago, then to Racine, Wisconsin. Educated at Racine High School, graduated 1910. Married 1) Marie Armstrong in 1915 (divorced 1925), one daughter; 2) Rose Caylor in 1925, one daughter. Reporter, Chicago *Journal*, 1910–14; reporter, 1914–18, correspondent in Berlin, 1918–19, and columnist, 1919–23, Chicago *News*; founding editor and publisher, Chicago *Literary Times*, 1923–24; thereafter a full-time writer for the stage, and for films from 1933; formed a production company with Charles MacArthur, 1934–36; columnist ("1001 Afternoons in Manhattan"), *PM* newspaper, Long Island, New York, 1940–41. Active Zionist from 1946: Co-Chairman, American League for a Free Palestine. Recipient: Oscar, 1928, 1936. Died in New York, 18 April 1964.

Ben Hecht

Works

Collections

"The Wonder Hat" and Other One-Act Plays (includes *The Two Lamps, An Idyll of the Shops, The Hand of Siva, The Hero of Santa Maria*), with Kenneth Sawyer Goodman. 1925.

Stage Works

The Wonder Hat: A Harlequinade, with Kenneth Sawyer Goodman (produced Arts and Crafts Theatre, Detroit, 1916). 1920.

The Hero of Santa Maria, with Kenneth Sawyer Goodman (produced Comedy Theatre, New York, 1917). 1920.

The Master Poisoner, with Maxwell Bodenheim, in *Minna and Myself*, by Bodenheim. 1918.

The Hand of Siva, with Kenneth Sawyer Goodman. 1920.

The Egotist (produced 39th Street Theatre, New York, 1922).

An Idyll of the Shops, with Kenneth Sawyer Goodman. In *"The Wonder Hat" and Other One-Act Plays*, 1925.

The Stork, from a play by Laszlo Fodor (produced Cort Theatre, New York, 1925).

Man Eating Tiger (produced Allentown, Pennsylvania, 1927).

Christmas Eve: A Morality Play (produced 1939). 1928.

The Front Page, with Charles MacArthur (produced Times Square Theatre, New York, 1928).

Twentieth Century, with Charles MacArthur (produced Broadhurst Theatre, New York, 1932). 1932.

The Great Magoo, with Gene Fowler (produced Selwyn Theatre, New York, 1932). 1933.

Jumbo, with Charles MacArthur, music by Richard Rodgers, lyrics by Lorenz Hart (produced Hippodrome, New York, 1935). 1935.

To Quito and Back (produced Guild Theatre, New York, 1937). 1937.

Ladies and Gentlemen, with Charles MacArthur, from a play by Ladislas Bus-Fekete (produced Martin Beck Theatre, New York, 1939). 1941.

Fun to Be Free: Patriotic Pageant, with Charles MacArthur (produced Madison Square Garden, New York, 1941). 1941.

Lily of the Valley (produced Windsor Theatre, New York, 1942).

We Will Never Die (produced Madison Square Garden, New York, 1943). 1943.

A Tribute to Gallantry (produced The Waldorf, New York, 1943). In *The Best One-Act Plays of 1943*, edited by Margaret Mayorga. 1943.

Miracle on the Pullman (broadcast 1944). In *The Best One-Act Plays of 1944*, edited by Margaret Mayorga, 1945.

The Common Man (produced 1944).

Swan Song, with Charles MacArthur, from a story by Ramon Romero and Harriett Hinsdale (produced Booth Theatre, New York, 1946). In *Stage Works of MacArthur*, 1974.

A Flag is Born, music by Kurt Weill (produced Alvin Theatre, New York, 1946). 1946.

Hazel Flagg, music by Jule Styne, lyrics by Bob Hilliard, from a story by James Street and the screenplay *Nothing Sacred* (produced Mark Hellinger Theatre, New York, 1953). 1953.

Winkelberg (produced Renata Theatre, New York, 1958). 1958.

Simon, from play by Bertolt Brecht and Lion Feuchtwanger (produced 1962).

Screenplays

Underworld (Paying the Penalty), with others, 1927; *The Big Noise*, with George Marion, Jr., and Tom Geraghty, 1928; *The Unholy Night*, with others, 1929 (also French version, *Le Spectre vert*, 1930); *The Great Gabbo*, with Hugh Herbert, 1929; *Roadhouse Nights (The River Inn)*, with Garrett Fort, 1930; *The Unholy Garden*, with Charles MacArthur, 1931; *Scarface, The Shame of the Nation*, with others; 1932; *Turn Back the Clock*, with Edgar Selwyn, 1933; *Design for Living*, 1933; *Hallelujah, I'm a Bum (Hallelujah, I'm a Tramp, Lazy Bones)*, with S.N. Behrman, 1933; *Viva Villa!*, with Howard Hawks, 1934; *Twentieth Century*, with Charles MacArthur, 1934; *Crime Without Passion*, with Charles MacArthur, 1934; *Upperworld*, with others, 1934; *The Scoundrel*, with Charles MacArthur, 1935; *Barbary Coast*, with Charles MacArthur, 1935; *Once in a Blue Moon*, with Charles MacArthur, 1935; *Soak the Rich*, with Charles MacArthur, 1936; *Nothing Sacred*, 1937; *The Goldwyn Follies*, with others, 1938; *Gunga Din*, with others, 1939; *Lady of the Tropics*, 1939; *Wuthering Heights*, with Charles MacArthur, 1939 (published in *Twenty Best Film Plays*, edited by John Gassner and Dudley Nichols). 1943.; *It's a Wonderful World*, with Herman J. Mankiewicz, 1939; *Let Freedom Ring (Song of the West)*, 1939; *Angels over Broadway*, 1940; *Comrade X*, with Charles Lederer and Walter Reisch, 1940; *Lydia*, with others, 1941; *Tales of Manhattan*, with others, 1942; *The Black Swan*, with Seton I. Miller, 1942; *China Girl*, with Melville Crossman, 1942; *Spellbound*, with Angus MacPhail, 1945 (published in *Best Film Plays 1945*, edited by John Gassner and Dudley Nichols), 1946; *Watchtower over Tomorrow* (short), 1945; *Specter of the Rose*, 1946; *Notorious*, 1946; *Her Husband's Affairs*, with Charles Lederer, 1947; *Kiss of Death*, with Charles Lederer and Eleazar Lipsky, 1947; *Ride the Pink Horse*, with Charles Lederer, 1947; *The Miracle of the Bells*, with Quentin Reynolds, 1948; *Whirlpool*, with Andrew Solt, 1950; *Where the Sidewalk Ends*, with others, 1950; *Actors and Sin*, 1951; *Monkey Business*, with Charles Lederer and I.A.L. Diamond, 1952; *The Indian Fighter*, with Frank Davis and Ben Kadish, 1955; *Ulisse (Ulysses)*, with others, 1955; *Miracle in the Rain*, 1956; *The Iron Petticoat*, 1956; *Legend of the Lost*, with Robert Presnell, Jr., 1957; *A Farewell to Arms*, 1957; *Queen of Outer Space*, with Charles Beaumont, 1958; *Circus World (The Magnificent Showman)*, 1964; uncredited collaborations (selection)—*The Front Page*, 1931; *Back Street*, 1932; *Topaze*, 1933; *The President Vanishes (The Strange Conspiracy)*, 1934; *The Hurricane*, 1937; *His Girl Friday*, 1939; *The Shop Around the Corner*, 1940; *Roxie Hart*, 1942; *Gilda*, 1946; *Dishonored Lady*, 1947; *Rope*, 1948; *Love Happy*, 1949; *The Thing (The Thing from Another World)*, 1951; *The Secret of Convict Lake*, 1951; *Roman Holiday*, 1953; *John Paul Jones*, 1959; *Mutiny on the Bounty*, 1962; *Casino Royale*, 1967.

Television Plays

Light's Diamond Jubilee, 1954; *Hello Charlie*, from his book *Charlie*, 1959; *The Third Commandment*, 1959.

Radio Plays

Miracle on the Pullman, 1944 (published in *The Best One-Act Plays of 1944*, edited by Margaret Mayorga, 1945); *Miracle of a Bum*, 1945.

Fiction

Erik Dorn. 1921.
Fantazius Mallare: A Mysterious Oath. 1922.
A Thousand and One Afternoons in Chicago (stories). 1922.
Gargoyles. 1922.
The Florentine Dagger. 1923.
Humpty Dumpty. 1924.
The Kingdom of Evil: A Continuation of the Journal of Fantazius Mallare. 1924.
Cutie, A Warm Mamma, with Maxwell Bodenheim. 1924.
"Broken Necks" and Other Stories. 1924.
Tales of Chicago Streets. 1924.
Broken Necks, Containing More 1001 Afternoons (stories). 1926.
Count Bruga. 1926.
"Infatuation" and Other Stories of Love's Misfits. 1927.
"Jazz" and Other Stories of Young Love. 1927.
"The Unlovely Sin" and Other Stories of Desire's Pawns. 1927.
"The Policewoman's Love-Hungry Daughter" and Other Stories of Chicago Life. 1927.
"The Sinister Sex" and Other Stories of Marriage. 1927.
A Jew in Love. 1931.
The Champion from Far Away (stories). 1931.
Actor's Blood (stories). 1936.
A Book of Miracles (stories). 1939.
1001 Afternoons in New York. 1941.
Miracle in the Rain. 1943.
I Hate Actors! 1944; as *Hollywood Mystery!*, 1946.
The Collected Stories. 1945.
"Concerning a Woman of Sin" and Other Stories. 1947.
The Cat That Jumped Out of the Story (for children). 1947.
The Sensualists. 1959.
In the Midst of Death. 1964.

Memoirs and Letters

A Child of the Century (autobiography). 1954.
Gaily, Gaily (autobiography). 1963.
Letters from Bohemia. 1964.

Other

Charlie: The Improbable Life and Times of Charles MacArthur. 1957.
A Treasury of Hecht. 1959.
Perfidy. 1961.
A Guide for the Bedevilled. 1944.

*

Criticism

Books:
Arthur Dorlag and John Irvine (eds.), *The Stage Works of Charles MacArthur*, Tallahasse, Florida, 1974.
James T. Farrell, "The Mind of Ben Hecht", in *Literary Essays 1954–74*, edited by Jack Robbins, Port Washington, New York, 1976.
Doug Fetherling, *The Four Lives of Ben Hecht*, 1977.
Jeffrey Brown, *Ben Hecht: Hollywood Screenwriter*, Ann Arbor, Michigan, 1985.

Articles:
Marvin Felheim, "Tom Sawyer Grows Up: Ben Hecht as a Writer", in *Journal of Popular Culture*, 9, 1976.

*   *   *

"O admirable *Front Page!*", wrote Walter Kerr in *God on the Gymnasium Floor.* "Plays that perfectly represent their own times never have to worry about what time it is." Kerr, writing of a revival in the late 1960's, went on to explain that he was not referring to "historical time" but to "playwriting time"—when it was "thought to be good" when a play "lives right smack up to its aspirations and meets of all its own demands, it is beautiful". Remarkably, when this 44-year-old play had its very successful London premiere in 1972, Alan Brien was also absorbed into the adolescent nostalgia of Hecht's newspaper world-cum-brothel, and advised Arnold Wesker to try to inject some of its "sleazy excitement" into his own work.

Hecht was too busy an author to try to write the same play twice, and none of his many other dramatic works bears any resemblance to *The Front Page*, his only play to have had a significant stage life. He continued to collaborate intermittently with Charles MacArthur for 18 years, but none of their subsequent plays repeats any of the techniques which Kerr analysed in admiring detail as "a meticulously careful combination of vigorous melodrama and cynical comedy" and—perhaps more accurately—as "broad farce, gamy farce, hollering farce, exquisitely mechanized farce, and therefore beautiful". For contrast, one need only look at their last collaboration, *Swan Song*, a domestic murder melodrama about an unsuccessful musician set in Long Island, which had 155 performances in 1946–47. The same New York season also included a 78-night revival of *The Front Page*, as well as 120 performances of Hecht's *A Flag is Born*, with music by Kurt Weill.

A Flag is Born may be taken as the other polarity in Hecht's work: it is a very earnest, musical spectacular play on heavily Zionist themes. The young Marlon Brando—nose as yet unbroken—played the Jewish King David in an ambitiously stylised expressionistic drama with an action generated in a Jewish cemetery in wartime Europe. Statesmen and soldiers of four nations converge here, and the action leaps back to the courts of the first three kings of Israel, as well as forward to the road to Zion, in an explicit plea for a new Jewish homeland. Hecht's commitment, which is reflected in this play, had become obvious only during World War II, and he expressed it primarily through his prose writings, rather than on the stage. This particular Broadway production was presented by the American League for a Free Palestine, but Hecht's position was more radical than this may suggest: he was by now a member of Irgun Zvai Leumi.

Most of Hecht's pre-war work had been mainstream Broadway shows in which unpretentious entertainment sometimes hovers on the verge of banality. Even *To Quito and Back*, the most serious in tone of his plays of that period, almost fulfils his late, approving pronouncement in *Theatre Arts* that during this period playwrights were not "concerned with denouncing the world or improving it, or even noticing it". Although this play received warm critical applause for its assumed implications about the Spanish Civil War, it is actually a fictional account of an American author caught up in a South American coup. In this respect, the margins between Hecht's journalism and his play-writing parallel the writing practice of Hemingway, whose *A Farewell to Arms* he adapted for the screen.

World War II was a watershed for Hecht's writing. Some of his most pronounced dramatic failures—notably *Lily of the Valley*—occurred then, and his alignment with Zionism was developing. But by this time his output of screenplays was beginning to diminish, and his subsequent work seems less concerned to address a popular audience. With MacArthur, he had formed his own producing company in New York in 1934 and, altogether, wrote scripts for more than 60 films, mainly approximating to the 1930's genre of "screwball comedy", but also including *Design for Living* and *Wuthering Heights*. The cinema historian Richard Corliss has noted the extension of *The Front Page* into *Nothing Sacred*, which he terms "the definitive Hecht newspaper picture", and has also astutely observed that "Hecht manages both to congratulate journalism for its importance and to chastise it for its chicanery, by underlining the newspapers' complicity in promoting the underworld image" in films like *Underworld* and *Scarface*.

After the War, Hecht seems to have distinguished much more sharply between writing for screen and for stage. *Winkelberg*, his last play, is also his most puzzling. It was immediately recognised as being based on the life of his writer friend Maxwell Bodenheim (whom Hecht had already fictionalised in his 1926 novel *Count Bruga*), who died in 1954 without having written much for two decades. However, the name Hecht gave him derives from his own early novel *Humpty Dumpty*, and the two Winkelbergs seem deliberately antithetical, so that his play not only focuses on Bodenheim and the flamboyant gestures of the "Chicago Renaissance", but also seems to subvert his own earlier literary posture. The play is stylistically complex, too, presenting in its most developed form the expressionism that had been intermittent in Hecht's plays for 20 years; in Gerald Weales' succinct analysis, the dead poet is sent back in search of the "sweet dream" of his life, "a device that allows him to use brief scenes, to telescope time, and to abstract character (one actor plays The Enemy in five incarnations) in a way that suggests the combination of techniques from television and the twenties avant-garde that are currently [1962] popular off Broadway".

The sophistication of this play makes it ironic that within a year of his death Hecht would lament in *Theatre Arts* the constrictions of modernism, and perhaps the imminence of post-modernism: "I have no criticism of any modern artists, except this one—that they seem to create artistic audiences more than works of art. . . They reveal often more than our dramatic surfaces. I have detected in some of them the story of our discarded sanity as we sit in the shadow of salesmanship and statesmanship, wooing us to bankruptcy or global destruction".

—Howard McNaughton

See also *Volume 1* entry on *The Front Page*.

———

HEIJERMANS, Herman. Born in Rotterdam, The Netherlands, 3 December 1864. Educated at Ringlever school and Hogere Burgerschool. Married 1) Marie Peers in 1898 (divorced 1918), one daughter; 2) the actress Annie Jurgens in 1918, one daughter and one son. After failed attempts at a business career, left Rotterdam for Amsterdam, 1892, to pursue literary and journalistic activities; journalist and critic for the satirical *De Clown*, and for *De Telegraaf* until 1895; first play, *Dora Kremer*, produced 1893; achieved international success with next play, *Ahasverus*, 1893; under the pen name Samuel Falkland wrote the so-called *"Falklandjes"* (sketches) for *De Telegraaf*, *Algemeen Handelsblad*, and *Berliner Tageblatt*, 1894–1917; founder, the socialist period-

ical *De Jonge Gids* [The Young Guide], 1897; wrote for the Socialist Party's *De Nieuwe Tijd*; moved to Berlin, 1907; returned to Amsterdam, 1912; co-founder and director, Nederlandsche Tooneelvereniging [Netherlands Stage Society], 1912: acquired the Théâtre Carré, but Society disbanded, 1922; returned to journalism after 1922. Also directed many productions of his own plays. Died in Zandvoort, 22 November 1924.

Works

Collections

Drie tooneelstukjes. 1899.
Kinderen: Drie tooneelspelen. 1903.
Tooneel-studies (4 vols.). 1904–05.
Verzamelde tooneelspelen en opstellen over tooneel (2 vols.). 1909–11.
Drie éénakters. 1921.
Tooneelwerken [Complete Works] (3 vols.), edited by S. Carmiggelt and others. 1965.

Stage Works

Dora Kremer [Dora Kremer] (produced Groote Schouwburg, Rotterdam, 1893). 1893.
Ahasverus (produced Salon des Variétés, Amsterdam, 1893). 1894; translated as *Ahasverus*, in *Drama*, February 1929, and in book form, 1934; as *A Knock at the Door*, in *American Hebrew*, 110, 1922.
Ego. As *Vorstendroom, fantasie door Herm*, in *Nederland*, 1896.
Puntje [The Dot] (produced Conference of Social Democratic Workers, Amsterdam, 1898). In *De Jonge Gids*, 1, 1897–98; in book form, in *Drie Tooneelstukjes*, 1899.
Ghetto (produced Hollandsche Schouwburg, Amsterdam, 1898). 1899; revised version, 1911; translated as *The Ghetto*, 1899.
Het antwoord [The Answer]. In *De Jonge Gids*, 1, 1897–98; in book form, in *Drie Tooneelstukjes*, 1899.
Nummer tachtig [Number Eighty] (produced Tivoli Schouwburg, Rotterdam, 1903). In *De Jonge Gids*, 2, 1898-99; revised version, 1903.
De onbekende [The Unknown Woman]. In *Drie Tooneelstukjes*, 1899.
De machien [The Machine]. In *De Jonge Gids*, 3, 1899–1900; in book form, in *Tooneel-Studies 1*, 1904.
Het zevende gebod [The Seventh Commandment] (produced Hollandsche Schouwburg, Amsterdam, 1899). 1900.
Eén mei [May Day] (produced 1900). 1900.
Het pantser [The Suit of Armour]. In *De Jonge Gids*, 1900–01; in book form, 1902.
Op Hoop van Zegen (produced Hollandsche Schouwburg, Amsterdam, 1900). 1901; translated as *The Good Hope*, 1928.
Ora et labora [Pray and Work] (produced Hollandsche Schouwburg, Amsterdam, 1902). 1903.
Het kind [The Child] (produced Groote Schouwburg, Rotterdam, 1903). In *Kinderen: Drie tooneelstudies*, 1903.
Het kamerschut [The Screen] (produced Tivoli Schouwburg, Rotterdam, 1903). In *Kinderen: Drie tooneelstudies*, 1903.
In de Jonge Jan [At "De Jonge Jan" Café] (produced as *Brand in "De Jonge Jan"*, Hollandsche Schouwburg, Amsterdam, 1903). In *Kinderen: Drie tooneelstudies*, 1903.

Schakels (produced Paleis voor Volksvlijt, Amsterdam, 1903). In *Tooneel-Studies 2*, 1905; translated as *Links*, 1927.

Buren [Neighbours] (produced Hollandsche Schouwburg, Amsterdam, 1904).   In *Tooneel-studies 1*, 1904.

Bloeimaand [The Time of May] (produced Hollandsche Schouwburg, Amsterdam, 1904). 1905.

Saltimbank. (produced Centraal-Theater, Amsterdam, 1922). In *Tooneel-studies 1*, 1904; translated as *Saltimbank* in *The Drama*, August-September 1923.

Allerzielen [All Souls] (produced Hollandsche Schouwburg, Amsterdam, 1904). In *Tooneel-studies 4*, 1905.

Artikel 188 [Article 188] (produced Hollandsche Schouwburg, Amsterdam, 1905). In *Schetsen 10*, 1906.

De dasspeld [The Stick Pin] (produced Theater De Appel, Scheveningen, 1980). In *Schetsen 11*, 1907.

Verloving [Engagement]. In *Algemeen Handelsblad*, 1906; in book form, in *Schetsen 13*, 1909.

Feest (produced Hollandsche Schouwburg, Amsterdam, 1908). In *Algemeen Handelsblad*, December 1906; in book form, 1912; translated as *Jubilee*, in *Twenty-Five Short Plays*, edited by Frank Shay, 1926, and in a single edition, 1928.

Uitkomst [The Way Out] (produced Hollandsche Schouwburg, Amsterdam, 1907). In *Verzamelde tooneelspelen . . .* (collection), 1909.

Vreemde jacht [Strange Pursuit] (produced Hollandsche Schouwburg, Amsterdam, 1907). In *Verzamelde tooneelspelen . . .* (collection), 1909.

De groote vlucht [The Great Flight] (produced Hollandsche Schouwburg, Amsterdam, 1908). 1908.

De meid [The Maid] (produced Hollandsche Schouwburg, Amsterdam, 1908). 1911.

De opgaande zon (produced Hollandsche Schouwburg, Amsterdam, 1908). 1911; translated as *The Rising Sun*, 1926.

De schoone slaapster [The Sleeping Beauty] (produced Hollandsche Schouwburg, Amsterdam, 1909). In *Verzamelde Tooneelspelen . . . 2* (collection), 1911.

Nocturne [Nocturne] (produced Hollandsche Schouwburg, Amsterdam, 1914). In *Schetsen 14*, 1910.

Verveling [Boredom] (produced Theater De Appel, Scheveningen, 1980). In *Schetsen 16*, 1910.

Beschuit met muisjes [Blessed Occasion] (produced Hollandsche Schouwburg, Amsterdam, 1910). 1911.

Glück auf! [Good Luck!] (produced Hollandsche Schouwburg, Amsterdam, 1911). 1912.

Brief in de schemer [Letter at Twilight] (produced Grand Théâtre, Amsterdam, 1914). In *Algemeen Handelsblad*, August 1914; in book form, in *Drie éénakters*, 1921.

Een heerenhuis te koop [A Mansion House for Sale] (produced Grand Théâtre, Amsterdam, 1914). In *Drie éénakters*, 1921.

De buikspreker [The Ventriloquist]. In *Algemeen Handelsblad*, August 1914; in book form, in *Drie éénakters*, 1914.

Robert, Bertram & Comp [Robert, Bertram & Co.], from a work by Gustav Raeder (produced Grand Théâtre, Amsterdam, 1914). 1914.

Eva Bonheur [Eva Bonheur] (produced Grand Théâtre, Amsterdam, 1917). 1919.

De wijze kater [The Wise Tomcat] (produced Grand Théâtre, Amsterdam, 1917). 1919.

Dageraad [Dawn] (produced Stadsschouwburg, Amsterdam, 1918). 1921.

Pitten [Slumbering] (produced Grand Théâtre, 1918). In *Tooneelwerken 3*, 1965.

De vliegende Hollander; of, Het groote weddenschap [The Flying Dutchman; or, The Great Wager] (produced Théâtre Carré, Amsterdam, 1920). 1924.

Van Ouds "De Morgenster" [Good Old "Morning Star"] (produced Groote Schouwburg, Rotterdam, 1923). 1924.

Fiction

Kamertjeszonde: Herinneringen van Alfred Speer [Sin in a Furnished Room], under pseudonym Koos Habbema. 1898.

Diamantstad [Diamond City]. 1904.

Joep's wonderlijke avonturen [Joep's Strange Adventures]. 1909.

Droomkoninkje [Little Dream King] (for children). 1924.

Vuurvlindertje [The Flame-Coloured Butterfly] (for children). 1925.

Duczika [Duczika]. 1926.

Other

Fleo (includes *'n Jodenstreek?; Ahasverus; Fleo*). 1893.

Trinette [Trinette]. 1893.

Interieurs [Interiors]. 1897.

Schetsen (18 vols.), under pseudonym Samuel Falkland. 1897–1914.

Sabbath. 1903.

'n Jodenstreek? . . . Tweede druk [A Jewish Trick]. 1904.

Kleine Verschrikkingen [Small Terrors]. 1904.

Gevleugelde daden, zijnde de historie van eenige onthutsende, hart-be-klemmende, duizelingwekkende . . . familie-avonturen. 1905.

Biecht eener schuldige: Aanteekeningen van een getrouwde vrouw, verzameld, geordend, overigens niet veranderd [Confessions of a Guilty Woman]. 1906.

Kleine vertelsels [Small Narratives]. 1906

Wat niet kon [The Impossible]. 1908.

Een wereldstand: Berlijnsche impressies en schetsen [A Metropolis: Berlin Impressions and Sketches]. 1908.

Berliner Skizzenbuch. 1908.

Drijvende klompjes [Floating Clogs]. 1909.

24 Stunden in der Irrenstalt [24 Hours in the Lunatic Asylum]. 1910.

De roode flibustier [The Red Filibusterer]. 1911.

Korte verhalen uit de "Wereldbibliotheek" [Short Stories from the "World Library"]. 1923.

Camera (collection). 1924–25.

Levensschetsen [Life Drawings]. 1925.

De moord in den trein [Murder on the Train]. 1925.

Een bundel Falkland-schetsen [A Collection of Falkland Sketches], edited by A.C. Bouman. 1931.

Keur uit de beste vertellingen van Samuel Falkland [A Selection of the Best Tales of Samuel Falkland], edited by Henri Dekking and Frans Mijnssen. 1934.

Translator, *Kok & Springer: Advocaten en procureurs*, by Adolf Eisler. 1936.

*

Criticism

Books:

Seymour L. Flaxman, *Herman Heijermans and His Dramas*, New York, 1954.

H. van Neck-Yoder, *Dramatizations of Social Change:*

Herman Heijermans' Plays Compared with Selected Dramas by Ibsen, Hauptmann and Chekhov, The Hague, 1978.

* * *

The versatile and prolific Herman Heijermans graduated to literature from journalism (his father's profession) after an early failure in business. Besides three-act and one-act plays, he produced many volumes of fiction and other prose and 18 volumes of vivid sketches of everyday life (*Schetsen*) published under the pseudonym Samuel Falkland. The success of his best-known play, *Op Hoop van Zegen* (produced in English as *The Good Hope*), a moving indictment of the exploitation of fishermen, won him an international reputation as a socially committed dramatist.

Heijermans was sensitive both to important currents in European drama (having first encountered the work of Ibsen, Tolstoy, and Hauptmann through the Dutch tour of André Antoine's Théâtre Libre in 1892, by which he had been profoundly influenced) and to political and social injustice (he joined the infant Dutch Socialist party in 1895). However, his work remains resolutely individual, and his theatrical craftsmanship and feeling for character, authentic dialogue, and mood usually helped him avoid crude propaganda. Though at first attracted to the linguistic inventiveness and aestheticist iconoclasm of the Dutch literary generation of 1880, he came to see its often hermetic products as self-indulgent, elitist, and bourgeois. In theatre he rejected not only the innovation of the Gordon Craig type as lacking social awareness, but also dogmatic Naturalism's abandonment of plot and insistence that the action should simply "drain away into the sand".

His Ibsenesque *Dora Kremer*, whose heroine walks out on an unsatisfactory marriage, was a critical flop, but Heijermans took swift revenge by presenting his one-act play *Ahasverus*, a study of Jewish persecution, as the translated work of a Russian writer: it won praise from the same pundits who had savaged his debut. In *Ghetto*, the young Rafaël, who denounces the inward-looking mentality of his Jewish father, is the first of a series of lonely rebel figures created by Heijermans. However, their author's socialism was more evolutionary than revolutionary, and in his one-act drama *Het antwoord* (The Answer), where a strike for a small wage-increase results in the death of a number of workers, he denounced violence as a political weapon. Heijermans was moving towards a Spinozan belief in cosmic harmony and the essential goodness of human nature as exemplified particularly in children, the hope of the future.

Heijermans was first and foremost a practical man of the theatre. Both of his wives were actresses and he numbered distinguished actors and directors, including Willem Royaards, among his friends. From 1912 until 1922 he headed the Nederlandsche Tooneelvereniging (Netherlands Stage Society) company, and when it was forced into liquidation took personal responsibility for its debts. From 1907 to 1912 he was based in Berlin, partly for copyright reasons (the Netherlands did not sign the Berne Convention until 1911 and offered no protection to authors). In Germany he was active both as a playwright and an investigative journalist.

In *Het zevende gebod* (The Seventh Commandment), a father ruthlessly destroys his son's extra-marital relationship with a "liberated" woman. The play's exposure of domestic hypocrisy takes up a theme explored in his outspoken novel *Kamertjeszonde* (Sin in a Furnished Room) of two years earlier, based loosely on the author's own cohabitation with his later-wife Marie Peers.

Op Hoop van Zegen, which centres on the sinking of an unseaworthy fishing boat and poignantly depicts exploitation by its owners, eventually led to protective legislation in the Netherlands. Nevertheless it is far from black-and-white in its presentation. The shipowner Bos, for example, is a victim of his own brutal struggle for self-betterment, while the matriarchal fisherwoman Kniertje (played by Ellen Terry in the first English production) can be seen as over-deferential and fatalistic. The play's third act, where a chorus of women await their menfolk's fate, is a classic example of Heijermans' "static" drama. The play's masterly characterisation was praised by Max Beerbohm, despite its "pamphlet" elements, and its evocation of atmosphere and communal suffering may have influenced J.M. Synge's *Riders to the Sea*. In *Het pantser* (The Suit of Armour), the anti-militarism of a young officer leads to his dishonourable discharge and suicide. *Ora et labora* (Pray and Work) is a harrowing evocation of rural poverty and despair in Friesland, while *Schakels* (*Links*) focuses on the betrayal of a rich father by his children. The heroine of *Bloiemaand* (The Time of May) is forced by poverty into prostitution.

Uitkomst (The Way Out) represented a new departure, juxtaposing a naturalistic scene of a child's death in squalor with fairytale sequences which are finally exposed as a delusion. *Glück Auf!* (Good Luck!) is a well-researched study of industrial unrest and disaster in a coal mine; significantly the play is one of Heijermans' few direct depictions of contemporary industrial society (both *Op Hoop van Zegen* and *Ora et labora* are set in pre-industrial communities), and the common reaction to disaster overrides the partisan confrontation of views and aims. In the ambitious symbolist drama *Dageraad* (Dawn), written in iambic free verse, the creativity of the central inventor figure provokes the short-sighted workers to attack him and his machine, instead of welcoming the release from drudgery it offers—hardly a heroic picture of the proletariat. The message of *Eva Bonheur* seems a gloomy one: the taxidermist Jasper applauds his daughter's refusal to make a "good" marriage, and sees retreat from society into the security of the family as the only way of maintaining one's integrity. Heijermans' last years, in which he was handicapped by protracted illness, saw a similar retreat from the theatrical limelight into prose fantasies written for children, like *Droomkoninkje* (Little Dream King) and its uncompleted sequel *Vuurvlindertje* (The Flame-Coloured Butterfly), where his indomitable optimism is expressed with childlike energy and innocence.

Heijermans' is virtually the only drama from the turn of the 20th century to have survived in the contemporary Dutch repertoire, and though his brand of unashamed theatricality is not very fashionable at present, the best of his work retains its appeal and merits revival.

—Paul Vincent

See also *Volume 1* entry or *The Good Hope*.

————

HELLMAN, Lillian (Florence). Born in New Orleans, Louisiana, USA, 20 June 1905 (some sources give 1906). Educated at New York University, 1924–25; Columbia University, New York, 1925. Married the writer Arthur Kober in 1925 (divorced 1932). Reader, Horace Liveright publishers, New York, 1924–25; reviewer, New York *Herald-*

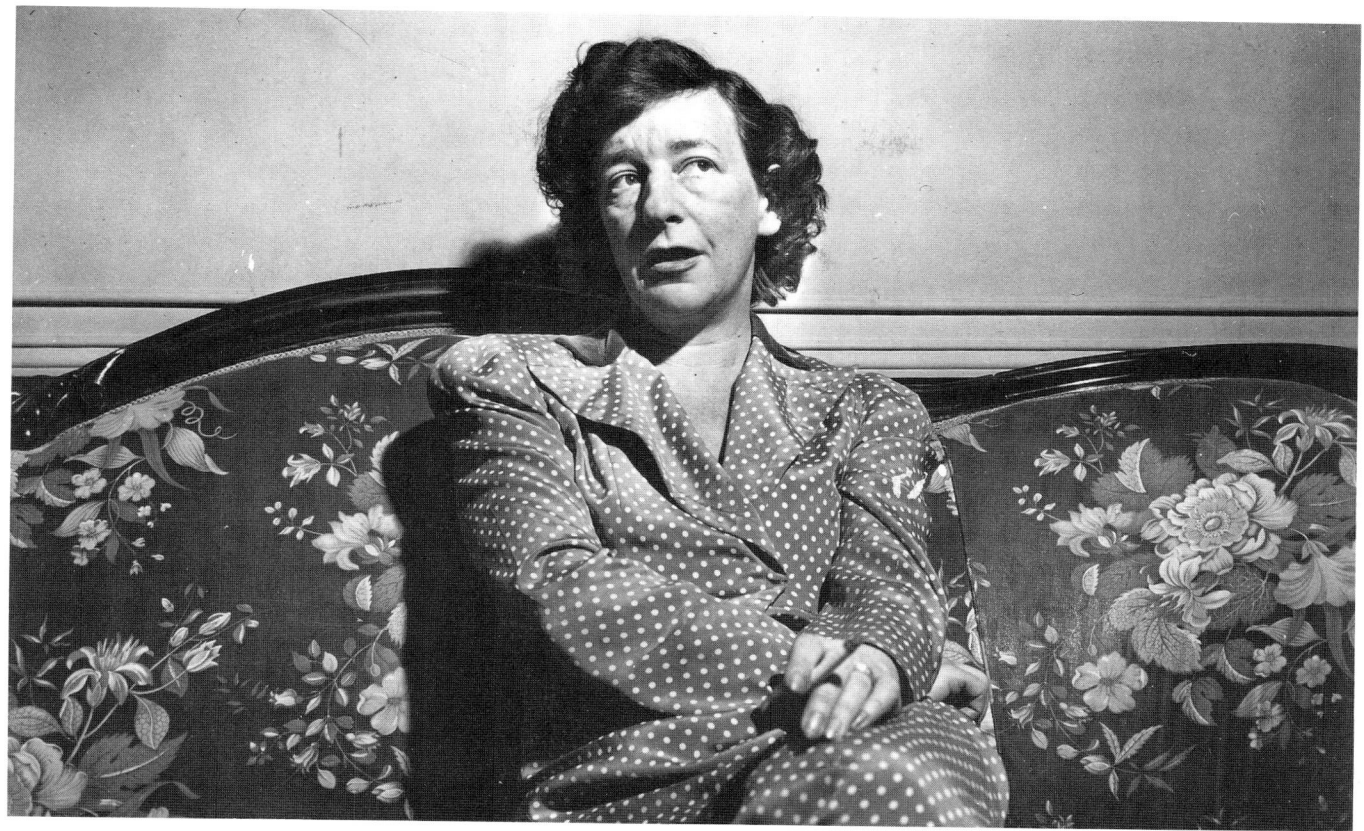

Lillian Hellman, interviewed at her home in New York City (1949).

Tribune, 1925–28; theatrical play reader, 1927–30; reader, Metro-Goldwyn-Mayer, 1930–32; began long relationship with Dashiell Hammett in 1930; first play, *The Children's Hour*, produced 1934; teacher at Yale University, New Haven, Connecticut, 1966, and at Harvard University, Cambridge, Massachusetts, Massachusetts Institute of Technology, Cambridge, and University of California, Berkeley. Recipient: New York Drama Critics Circle Award, 1941, 1960; American Academy Gold Medal, 1964; Paul Robeson Award, 1976; MacDowell Medal, 1976. MA: Tufts College, Medford, Massachusetts, 1940; Litt.D: Wheaton College, Norton, Massachusetts, 1961; Rutgers University, New Brunswick, New Jersey, 1963; Brandeis University, Waltham, Massachusetts, 1965; Yale University, New Haven, Connecticut, 1974; Smith College, Northampton, Massachusetts, 1974; New York University, 1974; Franklin and Marshall College, Lancaster, Pennsylvania, 1975; Columbia University, 1976. Vice-President, National Institute of Arts and Letters, 1962; Member, American Academy of Arts and Sciences, 1960, and American Academy, 1963. Died in Martha's Vineyard, Massachusetts, 30 June 1984.

Works

Collections

Four Plays (includes *The Children's Hour; Days to Come; The Little Foxes; Watch on the Rhine*). 1942.
Six Plays. 1960.
The Collected Plays (includes *The Children's Hour; Days to Come; The Little Foxes; Watch on the Rhine; The Searching Wind; Another Part of the Forest; Montserrat; The Autumn Garden; The Lark; Candide; Toys in the Attic; My Mother, My Father and Me*). 1972.

Stage Works

The Children's Hour (produced Maxine Elliott Theatre, New York, 1934). 1934.
Days to Come (produced Vanderbilt Theatre, New York, 1936). 1936.
The Little Foxes (produced National Theatre, New York, 1939). 1939.
Watch on the Rhine (produced Martin Beck Theatre, New York, 1941). 1941.
The Searching Wind (produced Fulton Theatre, 1944). 1944.
Another Part of the Forest (produced Fulton Theatre, 1946). 1947.
Montserrat, from a play by Emmanuel Roblès (produced Fulton Theatre, 1949). 1950.
Regina, music by Marc Blitzstein (produced 46th Street Theatre, New York, 1949).
The Autumn Garden (produced Coronet Theatre, New York, 1951). 1951.
The Lark, from a play by Jean Anouilh (produced Longacre Theatre, New York, 1955). 1956.
Candide, music by Leonard Bernstein, lyrics by Richard Wilbur, John LaTouche, and Dorothy Parker, from the novel by Voltaire (produced Martin Beck Theatre, New York, 1956). 1957.

Toys in the Attic (produced Hudson Theatre, New York, 1960).   1960.
My Mother, My Father and Me, from a novel by Burt Blechman (produced Plymouth Theatre, New York, 1963).   1963.

Screenplays

The Dark Angel, with Mordaunt Shairp, 1935; *These Three,* 1936; *Dead End,* 1937; *The Little Foxes,* with others, 1941; *Watch on the Rhine,* with Dashiell Hammett, 1943 (published in *Best Film Plays of 1943–44,* edited by John Gassner and Dudley Nichols, 1945); *The North Star,* 1943 (published 1943); *The Searching Wind,* 1946; *The Children's Hour* (*The Loudest Whisper*), with John Michael Hayes, 1961; *The Chase,* 1966.

Memoirs and Letters

An Unfinished Woman: A Memoir.   1969.

Other

Three.   1979; contents separately published as:
   An Unfinished Woman: A Memoir.   1969.
   Pentimento: A Book of Portraits.   1973.
   Scoundrel Time.   1976.
Maybe: A Story.   1980.
Eating Together: Recollections and Recipes, with Peter Feibleman.   1984.
Conversations with Hellman (interviews), edited by Jackson R. Bryer.   1986.

Editor, *Selected Letters,* by Chekhov, translated by Sidonie K. Lederer.   1955.
Editor, *The Big Knockover: Selected Stories and Short Novels,* by Dashiell Hammett.   1966; as *The Hammett Story Omnibus,* 1966; as *The Big Knockover* and *The Continental Op* (2 vols.), 1967.

*

Bibliographies

Steven H. Bills, *Lillian Hellman: An Annotated Bibliography,* New York, 1979.
Mary M. Riordan, *Lillian Hellman: A Bibliography 1926–1978,* Metuchen, New Jersey, 1980.

Criticism

Books:
Jacob H. Adler, *Lillian Hellman,* Austin, Texas, 1969.
Richard Moody, *Lillian Hellman: Playwright,* New York, 1972.
Lorena Ross Holmin, *The Dramatic Works of Lillian Hellman,* Stockholm, 1973.
Doris V. Falk, *Lillian Hellman,* New York, 1978.
Katherine Lederer, *Lillian Hellman,* Boston, 1979.
Mark W. Estrin, *Lillian Hellman: Plays, Films, Memoirs: A Reference Guide,* Boston, 1980.
Jackson R. Bryer, *Conversations with Lillian Hellman,* Jackson, Mississippi, 1986.
R.C. Reynolds, *Stage Left: The Development of the American Social Drama in the Thirties,* Troy, New York, 1986.
William Wright, *Lillian Hellman: The Image, the Woman,* New York, 1986.

Peter Feibleman, *Lilly: Reminiscences of Lillian Hellman,* New York, 1988.
Carl Rollyson, *Lillian Hellman: Her Legend and Her Legacy,* New York, 1988.

* * *

Lillian Hellman is one of America's major dramatists. She entered a male-dominated field when she was nearly thirty and wrote some dozen plays in three decades. Her early model was Ibsen, and she shared his love of tightly knit plots and emphasis on sociological and psychological forces. Her best plays, like Ibsen's, are those in which a powerful character cuts loose and transcends the limitations of the play's rigid symmetry and plot contrivance. Along with Clifford Odets, the other significant writing talent of the 1930's, Hellman showed a keen interest in Marxist theory and explored the relationship between the nuclear family and capitalism. Hellman, more than Odets, held ambiguous views of man and society. Her antagonists are not wholly the products of environment but seem at times innately malicious. The quest for power fascinated the author and her characters became famous for their ruthlessness and cunning. Most of her plays verge on melodrama but are admired for their energetic protagonists and swift-moving plots.

In her first play, *The Children's Hour,* Hellman showed how the capricious wielding of power could ruin innocent people. Two young women at a girl's school are falsely accused of having a lesbian relationship by a disturbed child. They are brought to trial by outraged parents and eventually lose their case—and their school. One of the teachers commits suicide and, too late, the child's treachery is discovered. The homosexual motif, though discreetly handled, accounted for the play's notoriety in 1934; but the abuse of power by an arrogant elite is its enduring theme.

Usurping power is also the motivating force in Hellman's best-known play, *The Little Foxes,* at once a political statement and a complex study of family dynamics. The rapacious Hubbard family represents a new brand of southern capitalist who subordinates all traditions and human values to the goal of acquiring wealth and property. The strength of the play lies in Hellman's implicit comparison of the Hubbard siblings' rivalries with the competitiveness of Americans in the free enterprise system. The role of Regina Hubbard, who withholds her dying husband's heart medicine and who outwits her equally greedy brothers in a major business coup, has become a favorite vehicle for American actresses.

At the beginning of World War II Hellman wrote *Watch on the Rhine* and *The Searching Wind,* both of which dealt with the fascist menace. The former play contains some witty repartee and suspenseful moments; but its solutions to the international crisis are simplistic, and it is better described as an adventure story than a thesis play.

When the War ended, Hellman returned to the easy-to-hate Hubbard family in *Another Part of the Forest.* Unfortunately the exaggerated spitefulness and hysteria of the characters and the unrelieved high-tension atmosphere of this play become nearly ludicrous. The concept of personal manipulation had become an obsession with the author, and a correlation seemed to have developed between her studies of social and societal exploitation and her own excessive control over plot characterization and stage effects. Perhaps the playwright realized this, because in her last plays she turned from Ibsen to Chekhov for inspiration. Both *The Autumn Garden* and *Toys in the Attic* recall the mood and ambiguous moral judgments of Chekhov. Neither of these plays has a truly pernicious villain, and most of the characters seem to be suffering from a Chekhovian paralysis of will. The atmosphere is deterministic and the plots are truer to life. What has changed is that all bids for personal power prove self-defeating—the predatory are caught in traps of their own making and hardly struggle before acknowledging defeat. Nevertheless these plays also include sharp, amusing verbal exchanges and the famous blackmail scenes associated with Hellman. Blackmail, present in all of her plays, is Hellman's favorite metaphor for personal manipulation; but in the later works she uses blackmail and other devices with greater subtlety, and presents a somewhat blurred but more convincing vision of stumbling modern man and his society.

Hellman's dramatic mode, based on her adherence to continental models, was bound to an earlier era. Most of her experiments with screenwriting proved frustrating. Her best later works were autobiographical sketches: in *An Unfinished Woman*, *Pentimento*, and *Scoundrel Time* she revealed her penetrating intelligence but tacitly acknowledged that her insights and talents were better suited to the historical memoir.

—Kimball King

See also *Volume 1* entries on *The Children's Hour*; *The Little Foxes*.

HENLEY, Beth. Born Elizabeth Becker Henley in Jackson, Mississippi, USA, 8 May 1952. Educated at Southern Methodist University, Dallas, BFA 1974; University of Illinois, Urbana, 1975–76. Actress, Theatre Three, Dallas, 1972–73, with Southern Methodist University Directors Colloquium, 1973, and with the Great American People Show, New Salem, 1976; teacher, Dallas Minority Repertory Theatre, 1974–75. Recipient: Pulitzer Prize, 1981; New York Drama Critics Circle Award, 1981; Oppenheimer Award, 1981.

Works

Collections

Four Plays (includes *The Miss Firecracker Contest*; *The Wake of Jamey Foster*; *The Lucky Spot*; *Abundance*). 1992.

Stage Works

Am I Blue? (produced Southern Methodist University, Dallas, 1973; revised version produced Hartford, Connecticut, 1981).
Crimes of the Heart (produced Actors' Theatre, Louisville, Kentucky, 1979). 1982.
The Miss Firecracker Contest (produced Victory Theatre, Los Angeles, 1980). 1985.
The Wake of Jamey Foster (produced Hartford Stage Company, Hartford, Connecticut, 1982). 1983.
The Debutante Ball (produced South Coast Repertory, Costa Mesa, California, 1985). 1991.
The Lucky Spot (produced Williamstown, Massachusetts, 1986). 1987.
Abundance (produced Costa Mesa, California, 1989). In *Four Plays*, 1992.
Control Freaks (produced Chicago, 1992).

Screenplays

The Moon Watcher, 1983; *True Stories*, with Stephen Tobolowsky, 1986; *Crimes of the Heart*, 1987; *Nobody's Fool*, 1987; *Miss Firecracker*.

*

Criticism

Books:
Interview, in *Mississippi Writers Talking*, edited by John G. Jones, Jackson, Mississippi, 1982.

Articles:
Nancy D. Hargrove, "The Tragicomic Vision of Beth Henley's Drama", in *Southern Quarterly*, vol.22 no.4, 1984.
Billy J. Harbin, "Familial Bonds in the Plays of Beth Henley", in *Southern Quarterly*, vol.25 no.3, 1987.
Lisa J. McDonnell, "Diverse Similitude: Beth Henley and Marsha Norman", in *Southern Quarterly*, vol.25 no.3, 1987.

*   *   *

Herself a former actor, Beth Henley writes substantial roles for other women. Her eccentric southerners, sharply sketched and spouting dialogue penned in Mississippi dialect, comprise a huge collection of oddballs and misfits with whom we sympathize.

As Henley's exotics pursue their unfulfilled dreams, they inhabit a Southern, gothic, whimsical world likely to make us laugh and wince in about equal measure. When she appears primed to veer into pathos, Henley generally undercuts sentimentality with eccentric characters or grotesque action. Although generally optimistic in response to adversity, even as she makes us care about her independent outsiders and generates suspense about what will happen to them, the playwright employs human idiosyncrasy or the macabre to humorous effect.

Death claims more characters than we might expect in comedy: Aunt Ronelle and Turnip (*The Miss Firecracker Contest*), Jamey and the arson victims (*The Wake of Jamey Foster*), Violet's brother, dead by his own hand, and the murdered man (*The Debutante Ball*), Sue Jack's mother and Cassidy's parents (*The Lucky Spot*), and Bess's Indian chief (*Abundance*). Henley's most famous play, *Crimes of the Heart*, kills off Billy Boy, Old Granddaddy, and the sisters' mother, as well as her cat. Meg exhibits a death wish, and Babe attempts suicide hours after shooting her abusive husband Zachery. Several sets of offstage parents have died leaving orphans. Even when not lethal, violence—physical as well as psychological—occurs in nearly every Henley play.

The gentlest of these, her early *Am I Blue?*, dramatizes an encounter between 16-year-old hippie, Ashbe, and college freshman John Polk, her preppy, awkward, overweight new friend. When they meet in New Orleans in 1968, Ashbe encourages John to avoid going along mindlessly with his frat brothers' values. Yet hope for their future must be tempered by the pressures John will experience to conform and by Ashbe's parental neglect.

For *The Lucky Spot* Henley goes further back, to Christmas Eve 1934, and to the Depression in Pigeon, a Louisiana bayou village. Reed Hooker aims to cheer up the local rural folk and turn a profit by converting the ramshackle house he won in a poker game into a taxi-dance hall, despite its location far from anyone likely to have the price of a dance. He's joined in this enterprise by untidy, 15-year-old Cassidy Smith, whom he also won in that card game, and whom he has impregnated. Reed unleashes violence against men and women alike, but then so does his wife, released from prison for Christmas through Cassidy's contrivance, because she hopes Sue Jack and Reed will divorce; of course, that's not what happens. The happy ending (as close to sentimentality as Henley comes) proves simultaneously predictable and implausible. Yet the play does amuse intermittently, while it suggests that in this lucky spot dreams sometimes come true, indeed that happiness need not elude us. These are losers, but—without any of O'Neill's irony in *The Iceman Cometh*—hopeful losers, still, appropriately, looking at life through rose-colored glasses.

In *The Wake of Jamey Foster*, a more bitter play, the disillusioned dreamer has already died from a kick in the head by a cow, leaving to his survivors their own disappointed dreams, rage, humiliation, depression, and, ironically, hope. When we meet the newly widowed Marshael Foster in her dilapidated, rural home in Mississippi, she is gnawing on a chocolate Easter rabbit and reading a ladies' magazine. Her wild sister Collard (nicknamed Collard Greens) arrives wearing a muddy red evening gown and cowboy boots and without a change of clothes for the funeral. Collard's dreams of becoming a lawyer have been dashed by the I.Q. test she took, aged 12, so she has consoled herself (or tried to destroy herself) by caressing "death and danger with open legs". Marshael's backward brother, Leon, jerks out turkey innards for a living, while his 17-year-old girlfriend, Pixrose, aims to become a dog bather, and Marshael's friend Brocker unsuccessfully tried to raise hogs. Henley conveys such salient details about her hilarious human menagerie's dreams in exposition composed of stunning *non sequiturs*.

Like other Henley characters, these wage war with their relatives: Jamey's mean brother, Wayne, offends his priggish wife, Kathy, so badly that she locks herself in the bathroom. And Jamey had left Marshael for a young baker, who sends a pie to the wake, giving Marshael a chance to hurl it to the floor from the upstairs landing. Naturally, Pixrose and Marshael and her siblings are orphans, while Jamey's parents project off-stage malevolence. Marshael neglects her own bereaved children. Pixrose recounts the funniest, and yet most pathetic familial discord: her pyromaniac mother and father had committed suicide separately while nearly killing her and her brother as well.

The somewhat more lighthearted *The Miss Firecracker Contest* also mixes pain with our pleasure. Again, Mississippi relatives have failed to nurture each other. Mean Aunt Ronelle, who grew furry after a monkey's pituitary gland was substituted for hers, raised orphaned Carnelle along with her own children—beautiful but egocentric Elain and difficult Delmount—but she instilled little self-esteem in her niece. Siding with those who fail to achieve perfection, popularity, and success, Henley directs our compassion towards insecure Carnelle, while keeping us laughing at her hopeless hope of winning the beauty contest. While Cousin Elain, a former winner who dislikes her husband and children, prepares her speech on "My Life as a Beauty", Carnelle practises baton-twirling and tap-dancing, setting herself up for humiliation. Born into a culture with little tolerance of difference and which prefers women to boast beauty rather than brains, spunky Carnelle wins respect not only for her tenacity in pursuing her goal, but for her indomitable spirit after she has endured one indignity too many. "I'll always remember you",

comments a friend, "as the one who could take it on the chin".

Pulitzer Prize-winning *Crimes of the Heart*, another Mississippi comedy, dramatizes all the themes which Henley considers, a few at a time, in other plays: hope, loneliness, respect, control, domestic violence, and death. The three sisters (echoes of Chekhov probably intended) as well as their four men suffer from their own crimes of the heart: two pairs—Lenny and Charlie, Meg and Doc—have languished and anguished because the women lacked the courage to remain in the relationships, while Babe has shot husband Zachery and got young Willie Jay in trouble. Yet the women also have been damaged by others' crimes of the heart, for Zachery abused Babe, and the Magrath sisters were orphaned by their mother's suicide. Although initially having little self-esteem and courage, however, they take control of their lives by making affirmative choices. Even Lenny, in one of several expertly written farcical scenes, chases a tormenting cousin out of the house with a broom.

Two less well-known, but also bizarrely amusing plays, *The Debutante Ball* and *Abundance*, likewise portray gutsy women coping with a world in which men abuse their women. The former, set in the present in Hattiesburg, ostensibly concerns the preliminaries to a pregnant, guilt-ridden, suicidal teenager's ignominious debut, overseen by a mother intent upon re-establishing her reputation after she was found innocent of murdering her daughter's father. Both lighter and darker than such a synopsis suggests, the play unfolds the cause of their troubles in some of Henley's funniest scenes. By the play's end, the debutante appears bound for happiness, as does her neglected half-sister, who heads into the sunset with her step-father's deaf-mute niece.

The more pessimistic *Abundance* concerns two men and their two mismatched mail-order brides, living during the last quarter of the 19th-century in the Wyoming Territory, where they have less to fear from the Wild West than they do from each other. Romantic Bess and pragmatic Macon all but trade places. After Bess is abducted by Indians, they betray their own values and each other's trust, and Bess fulfills Macon's dream. Their power struggles and dashed hopes—Bess's for domestic bliss and Macon's for adventures she can turn into a novel—constitute familiar Henley themes. But the play especially resembles *The Debutante Ball*; both dramatize the love/hatred within families that erupts in violence. Their effective poignancy combined with humor in dramatizing abused women's shaky self-esteem contributes significantly to late 20th-century drama.

—Tish Dace

HERNÁNDEZ, Luisa Josefina. Born in Mexico City, 1928. Educated at the Universidad Nacional Autónoma de México [UNAM], Mexico City, initially studying law, then languages, finally graduating in English literature and theatre; MA, UNAM, 1955; also studied at Columbia University, New York. Succeeded the teacher and playwright Rodolfo Usigli, under whom she had studied, as professor of drama at UNAM in the late 1950's; first-produced play, *Aguardiente de caña*, staged 1951; many of her plays produced under the auspices of the drama section of Mexico's Instituto Nacional de Bellas Artes (founded 1946). Recipient of several prizes, including Magda Donato Award, 1971.

Works

Stage Works (selected)

El ambiente jurídico. In *América (Revista antológica)*, 64, 1950.
Aguardiente de caña (produced Fiesta de Primavera, Mexico City, 1951).
Agonía. In *América*, 65, 1951.
Afuera lleuve. In *Prometeus*, 4, 1952.
Los sordomudos (produced Sala Chopin, Mexico City, 1953). In *América*, 69, 1954.
Botica modelo (produced Sala del Seguro Social, Mexico City, 1954). In *El Nacional*, 1954.
Los frutos caídos (produced Teatro Granero, Mexico City, 1957). In *Teatro mexicana del siglo XX, 3*, edited by Celestino Gorostiza, 1956.
Los duendes (produced Sala Villaurrutia, Mexico City, 1958). In *Teatro mexicano 1963*, edited by Antonio Magaña Esquivel, 1965.
Arpas blancas, conejos dorados (produced Orientación, Mexico City, 1959). In *La palabre y el hombre*, 28, 1963.
Los huéspedes reales (produced National Festival, Mexico City, 1959). In *La palabre y el hombre*, 2, 1957; in book form, in *Teatro mexicano del siglo XX, 4*, edited by Antonio Magaña Esquivel, 1970.
El hija del rey. In *Mexico en la cultura: Novedades*, 518, 1959.
La paz ficticia (produced Teatro del Bosque, Mexico City, 1960). In *Mexico en la cultura: Novedades*, 598, 1960.
La historia de un anillo. In *La palabra y el hombre*, 20, 1961.
Escándalo en Puerto Santo, from the novel *La Plaza de Puerto Santa* (produced ?).
La calle de la gran ocasión (one act plays). 1962; second series, 1985; selections translated as *Dialogues*, in *Selected Latin American One-Act Plays*, edited by Francesca Colecchia and Julio Matas, 1973.
Clemencia. In *Cuadernos de Bellas Artes*, March 1963.
Popul-Vuh. In *La palabra y el hombre*, 40, 1966; in book form, in *Teatro popular mexicano*, 1974.
Cuetzalcóatl. In *Cuadernos de lectura popular*, 1968.
La danza del Urogallo múltiple (produced 1971). In *Teatro mexicano 1971*, edited by Antonio Magaña Esquivel, 1974.
Apostasía (produced 1974.). In *Revista de Bellas Artes*, 17, 1974.
La Pavana de Aranzazú (produced 1975). In *Tramoya*, 1, 1975.
Hecuba (produced 1976). In *Tramoya*, 5, 1976.
La fieste del mulato. In *Tramoya*, 17, 1979; translated as *The Mulatto's Orgy*, in *Voices of Change in the Spanish American Theater*, translated by William I. Oliver, 1971.
Apocrypha. In *Consenso*, 2, 1978.
Ciertas cosas. In *Tramoya*, 18, 1980.
El orden de los factores (produced 1983). 1988.

Fiction

El lugar donde crece la hierba. 1959.
La Plaza de Puerto Santo. 1961.
Los palacios desiertos. 1963.
La coléra secreta. 1964.
La noche exquisita. 1965.
La primera batalla. 1965.
El valle que elegimos. 1965.
La memoria de Amadís. 1967.
Nostalgia de Troya. 1970.

Los trovadores. 1973.
Apostasía. 1978.
Las fuentes ocultas. 1980.
Apocalipsis cum figuris. 1982.
Carta de navegaciones submarinas. 1987.
La cabalgata. 1988.

Other

Caprichos y disparates de Francisco Goya. 1979.

Translator, *El doctor y los demonios*, by Dylan Thomas. 1960.

*

Criticism

Books:
John K. Knowles, "Luisa Josefina Hernández: The Labyrinth of Form", in *Dramatists in Revolt: The New Latin American Theater*, edited by Leon F. Lyday and George Woodyard, Austin, Texas, 1976.

* * *

The beginning of Luisa Josefina Hernández's career as a playwright coincides with the heyday of stage realism in Mexico. As a student in the 1950's of Rodolfo Usigli, Mexico's foremost playwright and most vocal champion of realism, Hernández wrote her first plays which are notable for their almost perfect (although sometimes contrived) three-act structure, their insistence on psychological verisimilitude, and on believable social types. *Los frutos caídos* (The Fallen Fruit) was her first major stage success, under the very talented Japanese director Seki Sano, who had introduced Mexican theatre artists to Stanislavsky as well as to method acting. The play deals with the conservative values of a Mexico that, in the 1950's, could not tolerate a woman like Celia, the protagonist, who is twice married and on the verge of taking on a young lover. She returns from Mexico City to the provincial town where she still owns a house that is rented to other family members. This homecoming provides the catalyst for the highly charged confrontations and dramatic revelations so typical of realism, and which clearly echo the example of Eugene O'Neill's *Long Day's Journey into Night*. Also reminiscent of O'Neill is *Los huéspedes reales* (The Royal Guests), which explores a daughter's rancor towards her mother and subliminal sexual attraction for her father.

Although *Los frutos caídos* remains one of Hernández's better-known plays in the United States, inside Mexico she is noted for many of the more experimental plays she wrote in the 1960's and 1970's. It is during this period also that she began to write on a commission basis only, very often for educational institutions or agencies. No longer so interested in individual psychology, Hernández's plays began to focus on collective social issues, which she has often explored through the reconstruction of Mexico's past, and through a variety of theatrical techniques. Works like *Popol Vuh* and *Quetzalcóatl* deal with pre-Colombian Mexico; *La paz ficticia* (The Fictitious Peace) recreates an incident in which Yaqui Indians were duped and robbed of their land; *La historia de un anillo* (The History of a Ring) tells the true story of a rural school teacher who was fired for having taught her students about their constitutional rights. *La fiesta del mulato* (*The Mulatto's Orgy*) is the finest of this group of plays and reveals the strong, positive influence of Brechtian theatre on Mexican and Latin American playwrights at that time. Based on the journal of a friar who, in 1799, witnessed the trial of a mulatto accused of embezzling funds from the rich silver mines of Guanajuato, *La fiesta del mulato* denounces a colonial regime, or any class system, based on purity of race and the exploitation of the poor. In contrast to her early realistic technique, Hernández makes the action here fast-moving and episodic; the stage is nearly bare, with only a few key props, and the characters are highly stylized and dressed in period costumes. *La fiesta del mulato*, however, is not a traditional historical play; rather, and following Brecht, Hernández uses alienation techniques to frame the past in relationship to the present.

Through the 1960's and 1970's Hernández's playwriting continued to evolve and absorb a variety of influences or models; for example, *La danza del urogallo múltiple* (The Dance of the Multiple Woodcock) is an experiment in the kind of actor-centered theatre associated with Jerzy Grotowski. Yet in recent years, Hernández seems to have come back to her earlier realism in plays like *El orden de los factores* (The Order of Factors), which deals again with middle-class mores, but with a significant difference— between the 1950's and the 1980's Mexican society had radically changed, having gone through the tumultuous 1960's, the economic boom of the 1970's, and the devastating bust of the 1980's. In Mexico today, divorce may still be frowned upon, but drugs, violence, economic instability, and political corruption—all themes that Hernández touches on in her latest plays—are much more of a threat to the middle class. According to Hernández, her return to realism is logical, if not inevitable, given the failure of the artistic and political programs of the two previous decades.

Luisa Josefina Hernández holds a special position in Mexico, for she is recognized not only as a playwright but also as an award-winning novelist, with over a dozen prose works to her credit. She has also been a major influence in the training of playwrights and actors, in her capacity as a professor of drama at the National Autonomous University and the National Institute of Fine Arts in Mexico City. Her collection of short sketches, *La calle de la gran ocasión* (The Street of the Great Occasion), has been a standard in acting classes and workshops in Mexico; some of these brief pieces have also been used in classes in the United States. And although she does not consider herself a feminist, Luisa Josefina Hernández's early and continued concern with the position of women in Mexico, and her own success, cannot help but serve as an example to other aspiring women playwrights.

—Kirsten F. Nigro

HERNE, James A. Born James Ahern in Cohoes, New York, USA, 1 February 1839. Educated in local schools to age 13. Married 1) Helen Western in 1866 (divorced); 2) the actress Katherine Corcoran in 1878, three daughters. Debut as an actor, in repertory, Troy, New York, 1859; appeared with John Ford's company in Baltimore and Washington, DC, during the American Civil War; leading man in the Lucille Western Company, touring USA, 1865–67; thereafter managed the Grand Opera House, New York; stage director,

Lucky Baldwin's Academy of Music, San Francisco, 1875–80; began writing for the stage by collaborating with his associate David Belasco in 1879; starred in *Hearts of Oak* for the next seven years, a success which allowed him to retire to Dorchester, Massachusetts, and become full-time writer; lost his fortune on his next play: forced to move back to New York and work as stage manager for Klaw and Erlanger, 1891; appeared in his own play *Shore Acres*, 1892–98, the success of which restored his fortunes; retired to Southampton, Long Island. Died in New York, 2 June 1901.

Works

Collections

"Shore Acres" and Other Plays (includes *Sag Harbor* and *Hearts of Oak*), edited by Mrs. James A. Herne.   1928.
The Early Plays (includes *The Minute Men of 1774–1775; Drifting Apart; The Reverend Griffith Davenport; Within an Inch of His Life*), edited by Arthur Hobson Quinn.   1940.

Stage Works

Within an Inch of His Life, with David Belasco, from a play by Emile Gaboriau (produced Grand Opera House, San Francisco, 1879).   In *The Early Plays*, 1940.
Marriage by Moonlight, with David Belasco, from a play by Watts Phillips (produced Baldwin Theatre, San Francisco, 1879).
Hearts of Oak, with David Belasco (as *Chums*, produced Baldwin Theatre, San Francisco, 1879; as *Hearts of Oak*, produced 1879).   In *"Shore Acres" and Other Plays*, 1928; revised version by Herne, as *Sag Harbor* (produced Park Theatre, Boston, 1900), in *"Shore Acres" and Other Plays*, 1928.
The Minute Men of 1774–1775 (produced Chestnut Street Theatre, Philadelphia, 1886).   In *The Early Plays*, 1940.
Drifting Apart (produced People's Theatre, New York, 1888).   In *The Early Plays*, 1940.
Margaret Fleming (produced Lynn Theatre, Lynn, Massachusetts. 1890).   1890; revised version in *"The Black Crook" and other 19th-Century American Plays*, 1967.
My Colleen (produced People's Theatre, New York, 1892).
Shore Acres (produced McVicker's Theatre, Chicago, 1893).   In *"Shore Acres" and Other Plays*, 1928.
The Reverend Griffith Davenport, from a novel by Helen H. Gardener (produced Herald Square Theatre, New York, 1899).   In *The Early Plays*, 1940; Act III edited by Arthur Hobson Quinn, in *American Literature 24*, 1952.

*

Bibliographies

John Perry, "Selected Bibliography of James A. Herne", in *Bulletin of Bibliography*, 31, 1974.
Barbara C. Gannon, "James A. Herne: A Bibliography", in *American Literary Realism*, 16, 1983.

Criticism

Books:
Herbert J. Edwards and Julia A. Herne, *James A. Herne; The Rise of Realism in the American Drama*, Orono, Maine, 1964.

John Perry, *James A. Herne: The American Ibsen*, Chicago, 1978.

Jack A. Vaughn, *Early American Dramatists: From the Beginnings to 1900*, New York, 1981.

Articles:

Alice M. Robinson, "James A. Herne and His 'Théâtre Libre' in Boston", in *Players*, 48, 1973.

Patti P. Gillespie, "James A. Herne: A Reassessment", in *Players*, 51, 1976.

Bruce McConachie, "Herne's *Shore Acres* and the Family in the Tradition of the Irish-American Theatre", in *Theatre Studies*, 30, 1983–84.

*   *   *

In the history of American drama, the career of James A. Herne is an obvious milepost of importance. Like other theatre people in the latter part of the nineteenth century, he was a theatre manager and an actor of some distinction, as well as a playwright; but more than his peers he felt the impact of the twin forces of science and democracy that challenged all sensitive life in America during this period. Breaking out of the confining network of theatre people, he became friends with William Dean Howells, Hamlin Garland, and Stephen Crane, whose interests in literary realism stimulated Herne to move away from traditional melodrama. With the further influence of writers such as Henrik Ibsen, Thomas Hardy, and Émile Zola, Herne was moved to create his own theory of drama which he expressed in an essay entitled "Art for Truth's Sake in the Drama" (in *Arena*, 1897). In this essay he pronounced *truthfulness* to be the "supreme quality" of all drama, which must "interest" and "instruct". Art for truth's sake, Herne asserted, emphasizes "humanity", is "serious", and works "to perpetuate the life of its time". With his most realistic play, *Margaret Fleming*, which was as unacceptable to American audiences as Ibsen's *Ghosts*, Herne illustrated his theory and truly initiated the period of modern drama in America.

Writing with David Belasco, or in the Belasco manner, during the first two decades of his theatre career, Herne gave little evidence of his later accomplishments as a theorist and playwright. *Within an Inch of His Life*, which he and Belasco adapted from a French novel, was a traditional melodrama of the young wife/old husband type with stereotyped characters and typical sensations and spectacles. *The Minute Men of 1774–75*, Herne's first original play, emphasized a typical love story against a war background in which the lovers discover their true parents. Tableaux, a little Yankee dialect, and a charming and witty *ingénue* did not compensate for an awkward and loosely knit plot. With *Drifting Apart*, however, Herne attracted the attention of Howells and Garland. Concerned with the temperance theme, this play combined an effective melodramatic plot with the realistic scene and dialect of a New England fishing village.

Herne's real impact on the development of American drama occurred in 1891 when *Margaret Fleming* was performed in Boston's Chickering Hall, which was rented for the occasion by Howells and Garland, among others. Taken to a New York theatre after its three-week run in Boston, the play was not successful, undoubtedly because, as more than one critic noted, it did not "give pleasure". The plot of *Margaret Fleming* tells of a sensual and faithless husband, Philip, whose motto of "live and let live" underlines his business activities as well as his personal life with wife and child. The contrasting emotional sensitivity of his wife, Margaret, is dramatized by a disease which may blind her if she receives a great shock. This shock comes when Margaret discovers that the unmarried sister of her own child's nurse has died giving birth to Philip's baby. In the last act Margaret has lost her sight while Philip shamefully returns to a home with two children and a wife whose mysterious smile at the final curtain reveals her own sense of moral superiority as well as hope for the future.

An early version of *Margaret Fleming* ended with a melodramatic confrontation in Boston and, consistent with Victorian conventions of this period, did not allow for a reconciliation between husband and wife. The plot of *Margaret Fleming*, however, does not fully explain the epoch-marking quality that criticism has attached to this play. Although the moralizing of Margaret's doctor is extremely heavy-handed, the truthfulness of the dialect, scenes, and characters is everywhere emphasized. Symbolism is effective in a song that Margaret sings as well as in the comments on the care of roses. The concept that Margaret reveals through her cry that truth has killed her is a reference to Ibsen's work, and it appears again in Herne's commentary on the double standards, the medical practices, and in the scene during which Margaret unbuttons her blouse to nurse the newborn child. This scene was the shocking event for audiences. A strong reference to social determinism also discloses Herne's interest in Darwin and Henry George. Essentially, the play suggested a new objective for the drama and shows the absorption of the dramatist in the ideas that eventually were to shape modern America.

If *Margaret Fleming* is meaningful for drama historians, *Shore Acres*, was, perhaps, more memorable for Herne, who realized a million dollars for his effort. The central character in this play is Uncle Nat Berry, a kindhearted, tolerant man of selfless character and a spirit of overwhelming sentimental goodness. There is additional appeal in a spectacular lighthouse scene and in the effective quality of real life revealed in the odds and ends of daily activity, which culminate in the play's final scene, as Uncle Nat wanders through the house-making sure that everything is safe before he goes to bed.

Herne's final play, *The Reverend Griffith Davenport*, was less successful, but once again illustrates the dramatist's serious objectives in writing plays. When the Civil War begins, one Davenport son chooses to fight for the North, the other for the South. Davenport himself, with strong anti-slavery theories which are opposed by his neighbors, is finally prevailed upon by Lincoln to lead Union troops to his home, where he is captured by his own son and led away to prison. Like Margaret Fleming and Uncle Nat, Davenport is a strong character who faces up to a crisis and makes a meaningful decision.

Like Steele Mackaye, Bronson Howard, and William Gillette (each in his own way), Herne was an apostle of realism in that movement which swept into the American theatre on the heels of European influence. Unlike his peers in the theatre, however, Herne associated with literary people and social thinkers and asserted his views in theoretical writing. In this writing, and in several of his plays, Herne focused upon a new emphasis in American drama which, unfortunately, took many years to become fully realized.

—Walter J. Meserve

See also *Volume 1* entry on *Margaret Fleming*.

HEWETT, Dorothy (Coade). Born in Perth, Western Australia, 21 May 1923. Educated at Perth College;

Dorothy Hewett

University of Western Australia, Perth, 1941–42, 1959–63, BA 1961. Married Lloyd Davies in 1944 (marriage dissolved 1949), one son; lived with Les Flood, 1949–58, three sons; married Merv Lilley in 1960, two daughters. Millworker, 1950–52; advertising copywriter, Sydney, 1956–58; Senior Tutor in English, University of Western Australia, Perth, 1964–73; writer-in-residence, Monash University, Melbourne, 1975, University of Newcastle, New South Wales, 1977, Griffith University, Nathan, Queensland, 1980, La Trobe University, Bundoora, Victoria, 1981, and Magpie Theatre Company, Adelaide, 1982. Member of the editorial board, *Westerly* magazine, Nedlands, Western Australia, 1972–73, and *Overland* magazine, Melbourne, since 1970. Member of the Communist Party, 1943–68. Recipient: Australian Broadcasting Commission Prize, 1945, 1965; Australian Writers Guild award, 1974, 1982; and a number of Australia Council grants. AO (Member, Order of Australia), 1986.

Works

Collections

Collected Plays 1 (includes *This Old Man Comes Rolling Home; Mrs. Porter and the Angel; The Chapel Perilous; The Tatty Hollow Story*). 1992.

Stage Works

Time Flits Away, Lady (produced 1941).
This Old Man Comes Rolling Home (produced Perth, 1966; revised version produced Sydney, 1968). 1976.

Mrs Porter and the Angel (produced Sydney, 1969). In *Collected Plays 1*, 1992.
The Chapel Perilous; or, The Perilous Adventures of Sally Banner, music by Frank Arndt and Michael Leyden (produced Perth, 1971). 1972.
Bon-Bons and Roses for Dolly (produced Perth, 1972). With *The Tatty Hollow Story*, 1976.
Catspaw (produced Perth, 1974).
Miss Hewett's Shenanigans (produced Canberra, 1975).
Joan, music by Patrick Flynn (produced Canberra, 1975). 1984.
The Tatty Hollow Story (produced Sydney, 1976). With *Bon-Bons and Roses for Dolly*, 1976.
The Beautiful Miss Portland. In *Theatre Australia* (Sydney), November–December and Christmas 1976.
The Golden Oldies (produced by Hoopla Productions, Melbourne, 1976). With *Susannah's Dreaming*, 1981.
Pandora's Cross (produced Sydney, 1978). In *Theatre Australia*, September–October 1978.
The Man from Mukinupin (produced Perth, 1979). 1980.
Golden Valley (for children; produced Adelaide, 1981). With *Song of the Seals*, 1985.
The Fields of Heaven (produced Perth, 1982).
Song of the Seals (for children), music by Jim Cotter (produced Adelaide, 1983). With *Golden Valley*, 1985.
Christina's World (opera libretto; produced Sydney, 1983).
The Rising of Pete Marsh (produced Perth, 1988).

Screenplays

For the First Time, with others, 1976; *Journey Among Women*, with others, 1977; *The Planter of Malata*, with Cecil Holmes, 1983; *Song of the Seals*, 1984; *Catch the Wild Fish*, with Robert Adamson, 1985.

Radio Plays

Frost at Midnight, 1973; *He Used to Notice Such Things*, 1974; *Susannah's Dreaming*, 1980 (published with *The Golden Oldies*, 1981).

Fiction

Bobbin Up. 1959; revised edition, 1985.
The Australians Have a Word for It. 1964.

Verse

What About the People, with Merv Lilley. 1962.
Windmill Country. 1968.
The Hidden Journey. 1969.
Late Night Bulletin. 1970.
Rapunzel in Suburbia. 1975.
Greenhouse. 1979.
Journeys, with others, edited by Fay Zwicky. 1982.
Alice in Wormland: Selected Poems. 1987.
A Tremendous World in Her Head: Selected Poems. 1989.

Memoirs and Letters

Wild Card: An Autobiography 1923–1958. 1990.

Other

Editor, *Sandgropers: A Western Australian Anthology*. 1973.

*

Criticism

Books:
Peter Fitzpatrick, *After "The Doll"*, Melbourne, 1979.
Jennifer Palmer (ed.), *Contemporary Australian Playwrights*, Adelaide, 1979.
Peter Holloway (ed.), *Contemporary Australian Drama: Perspective Since 1955*, Sydney, 1981.

Articles:
Alrene Sykes, "Dorothy Hewett: Playwright of Splendid Moments", in *World Literature Written in English*, 17, 1978.
Dorothy Hewett and Jim Davidson, interview in *Meanjin*, 1979.
May B. Akerholt, "Female Figures in the Plays of Dorothy Hewett and Patrick White", in *Westerly*, vol.29 no.1, 1984.
Dorothy Hewett and Paul Kavanagh, "An Interview with Dorothy Hewett", in *Southerly*, 44, 1984.

* * *

Since her first play *This Old Man Comes Rolling Home*, a relatively realistic comedy-drama of working-class life based on her Redfern experience, Dorothy Hewett's work has fallen into two broad periods, with the early plays focusing on female sexuality and intimate relationships, and the later "pastoral" plays, as she has called them, on the Australian landscape and cultural heritage. All her plays are eclectic in style, and make use of heightened language, music and song, and sometimes spectacular, even brash, theatrical effects. Her part-autobiographical play *The Chapel Perilous*, with its quasi-expressionist set, large chorus, music, song and dance, and abrupt shifts in place and time (as well as style and tone) epitomises the "epic" theatricality for which she is best known, though her styles in various plays also encompass Ibsenite melodrama, expressionistic psychodrama, and a reflective lyricism.

The earlier plays explore female sexuality and its compulsive hold over both men and women through the recurrent figure of the *femme fatale* in its various manifestations of girlish innocence, legendary beauty, and vampishness. In *Bon-Bons and Roses for Dolly*, a musical set in a 1930's-style picture palace, the central figure Dolly Garden, seen as a series of personae from adored child to ageing spinster, is both seduced and destroyed by the escapist fantasies of Hollywood. *The Tatty Hollow Story*, a surreal piece in which certainties are constantly undermined, depicts its central character through the fantasies of Tatty's lovers, who destroy her dummy image though the real Tatty eludes them to become a cheerful old eccentric. *The Golden Oldies* recreates, through two actresses, several generations of mother-daughter-sister relationships in the shadow of the unconforming and sexually liberated Becca, a disturbing presence long after her death.

With their fusing of styles, ranging from lyrical to grotesque, and explicit references to abortion and menopause, Hewett's earlier plays have often polarised both audiences and critics. The more conservative have reacted with outrage, while the more radical have seen her fascination with the seductress image as validating stereotyped views of femininity. The plays are more complex than either of these views suggests, with the ideal-unreal figure of the *femme fatale* presented as a highly ambivalent image—a nostalgic celebration of female seductive power, but satirically undermined as an illusion or delusion which imprisons the real self.

The more recent Hewett plays assert the necessity of cher-

ishing Australia's imaginative heritage, seen as intrinsically linked to the unspoiled landscape. Two rock operas, *Catspaw* and *Pandora's Cross*, bring to life an eccentric collection of artistic bohemians, sexual misfits, and old-timers drawn from Australian history, fusing elements of artistic tradition and popular legend. The musical play *The Man From Mukinupin* sets the daytime routines of commerce and courtship in a mythical country town against "dark" night rituals of sexuality and guilt which reveal the inhabitants' secret desires, and link the township with the timeless harvest and fertility rites of much older societies. *The Fields of Heaven* chronicles the decline of a beautiful property over a generation through its commercial exploitation, a betrayal of the land's beauty as well as of its fertility.

Two children's plays, *Golden Valley* and *Song of the Seals*, develop the theme of humans' need for harmony with the natural world, and the power of the imagination to prevent and heal the destruction of nature through greed and cruelty. The pastoral plays all share a simplicity reminiscent of naïve painting, with a reflective calm overlaying the disruptive sexual and psychic tensions always present in her work.

If Dorothy Hewett is among the most prominent Australian playwrights, she has also been, until recently, the most controversial, paradoxically too confrontational for some people and too conservative for others. Today, her explicitiness about female sexuality is much less provocative than in the 1970's, though her freewheeling associative style can still disconcert audiences in the mainstream theatres in which her work is increasingly performed. But her reputation has been consolidated throughout the 1980's, and she is now generally regarded as one of the most adventurous and imaginative Australian dramatists in both subject-matter and style. Her wide-ranging use of language from lyrical poetry to satirical wit and colloquialism, and her juxtaposition of symbolic and psychic rituals with "show-biz" celebration and gutter vulgarity, challenge the polarity between high and popular cultures, while her uncensored exploration of sexual and family relationships from a female perspective has paved the way for a new generation of women playwrights.

—Margaret Williams

See also *Volume 1* entries on *The Chapel Perilous*; *The Man from Mukinupin*.

———

HEYWOOD, Thomas. Born in Rothwell or Ashby, Lincolnshire, England, in 1573 or 1574. Probably educated at Emmanuel College, Cambridge, c. 1591–93. Married 1) Anne Buttler in 1603 (died); 2) Jane Span in 1633. Playwright for Philip Henslowe from 1596; actor and possibly a shareholder in Henslowe's company, the Admiral's Men, from 1598; later wrote for the Earl of Worcester's company, Queen Anne's Men, and Lady Elizabeth's Men; wrote mayoral pageants for the City of London, 1631–39; claimed to have written over 200 plays, most now lost. Died in Clerkenwell, August 1641 (buried 16 August).

Works

Collections

Pleasant Dialogues and Dramas, from Lucian, Erasmus, Ovid (contains short plays and fragments, some possibly from

lost plays, including *Amphrisa; Apollo and Daphne; Jupiter and Io).* 1637.
Dramatic Works, edited by R.H. Shepherd (6 vols.). 1874.
Pageants (includes all the pageants), edited by David M. Bergeron. 1986.

Stage Works

The Four Prentices of London (produced London, 1594–1600). 1615.
King Edward the Fourth, 2 parts, possibly not by Heywood or possibly with others (produced by Derby's Men, before 1599). 1599.
How a Man May Choose a Good Wife from a Bad (produced by Worcester's Men, 1602?). 1602.
The Royal King and the Loyal Subject (produced by Worcester's Men, Curtain Theatre, London, 1602?). 1637.
Sir Thomas Wyatt, with Dekker and Webster (produced London, 1602–07?). 1607.
A Woman Killed with Kindness (produced by Worcester's Men, Curtain Theatre, London, 1603). 1607.
The Wise Woman of Hogsdon (produced by Queen Anne's Men, Red Bull Theatre, London, 1604?). 1638.
If You Know Not Me, You Know Nobody; or, The Troubles of Queen Elizabeth (produced by Queen Anne's Men, Red Bull Theatre, London, 1604–05). 1605.
The Second Part of If You Know Not Me, You Know Nobody (produced by Queen Anne's Men, Red Bull Theatre, London, 1604–05). 1606; as *The Second Part of Queen Elizabeth's Troubles,* 1609.
The Rape of Lucrece (produced by Queen Anne's Men, Red Bull Theatre, London, 1606–08). 1608.
The Miseries of Enforced Marriage, with George Wilkins; possibly by Wilkins alone (produced by the King's Men, Globe Theatre, London, c. 1606). 1607.
Fortune by Land and Sea, with William Rowley (produced Queen Anne's Men, Red Bull Theatre, London, 1607?). 1655.
The Fair Maid of the West; or, A Girl Worth Gold (2 parts; produced before 1610?). 1631.
The Golden Age; or, The Lives of Jupiter and Saturn (produced by Queen Anne's Men, Red Bull Theatre, London, 1609–11). 1611.
The Silver Age (produced by Queen Anne's Men, Red Bull Theatre, London, 1610–12). 1613.
The Brazen Age (produced by Queen Anne's Men, Red Bull Theatre, London, 1610–13). 1613.
The Iron Age, 2 parts (produced by Queen Anne's Men, Red Bull Theatre, London, c. 1613). 1632.
The Martyred Soldier, with Henry Shirley (produced before 1619). 1638.
The Captives; or, The Lost Recovered (produced Lady Elizabeth's Men, Cockpit/Phoenix Theatre, London, 1624). Edited by A.H. Bullen, in *A Collection of Old English Plays 4,* 1885.
The Escapes of Jupiter (produced London, c. 1625). Edited by Henry D. Janzen. 1978.
A Maidenhead Well Lost (produced Queen Henrietta's Men, Cockpit/Phoenix Theatre, London, 1625–34?). 1634.
The English Traveller (produced Queen Henrietta's Men, Cockpit/Phoenix Theatre, London, 1627?). 1633.
London's Jus Honorarium, Expressed in Sundry Triumphs, Pageants, and Shows (pageant; produced London, 1631). 1631. 1986.
Londini Artium et Scientiarum Scaturigo; or, London's

Fountain of Arts and Sciences (pageant; produced London, 1632). 1632.
Londini Emporia; or, London's Mercatura (pageant produced London, 1633). 1633.
The Late Lancashire Witches, with Richard Brome (produced by the King's Men, Globe Theatre, 1634). 1634.
Love's Mistress; or, The Queen's Masque (produced by Queen Henrietta's Men, Cockpit/Phoenix Theatre, London, 1634). 1636.
A Challenge for Beauty (produced by the King's Men, London, 1634–35?). 1636.
Londini Sinus Salutis; or, London's Harbour of Health and Happiness (pageant; produced London, 1635). 1635.
Londini Speculum; or, London's Mirror (pageant; produced London, 1637). 1637.
Porta Pietatis; or, The Port or Harbour of Piety (pageant; produced London, 1638). 1638.
Londini Status Pacatus; or, London's Peaceable Estate (pageant; produced London, 1639). 1639.

Verse

Oenone and Paris. 1594.
Troia Britannica; or, Great Britain's Troy. 1609.
A Marriage Triumph. 1613.
A Funeral Elegy upon King James. 1625.
The Hierarchy of the Blessed Angels. 1635.
The Life and Death of Queen Elizabeth, in Heroical Verse. 1639.
Reader, Here You'll Plainly See Judgement Perverted by These Three: A Priest, A Judge, A Patentee. 1641.

Other

An Apology for Actors. 1612; as *The Actors' Vindication,* 1658.
Nine Books of Various History Concerning Women. 1624; as *The General History of Women,* 1657.
England's Elizabeth: Her Life and Troubles During Her Minority. 1631.
Philocothonista; or, The Drunkard Opened, Dissected, and Anatomized. 1635.
The Wonder of This Age. 1635.
The New Year's Gift. 1636.
The Three Wonders of This Age. 1636.
A True Discourse of the Two Prophets, Richard Farnham, Weaver, and John Bull, Weaver. 1636.
A Curtain Lecture, as it is Read by a Country Farmer's Wife to Her Good Man. 1637.
The Phoenix of These Times; or, The Life of Mr. Henry Welby. 1637.
A True Description of His Majesty's Royal Ship Built This Year 1637 at Woolwich in Kent. 1637; revised edition, 1638.
A True Relation of the Lives and Deaths of the Two Most Famous English Pirates, Purser and Clinton. 1639.
The Exemplary Lives and Memorable Acts of Nine of the Most Worthy Women of the World. 1640.
The Black Box of Rome Opened. 1641.
Brightman's Predictions and Prophecies. 1641.
A Dialogue Betwixt Mr. Alderman Abell and Richard Kilvert. 1641.
The Life of Merlin, Surnamed Ambrosius, His Prophecies and Predictions Interpreted. 1641.
Machiavel's Ghost. 1641; as *Machiavel, as He Lately Appeared,* 1641.
A New Plot Discovered. 1641.

The Rat Trap; or, The Jesuits Taken in Their Own Net. 1641.
A Revelation of Mr. Brightman's Revelation. 1641.
Sir Richard Whittington. 1656.

Translator, *De Arte Amandi; or, The Art of Love*, by Ovid. 1600(?).
Translator, *The Two Most Worthy and Notable Histories of Catiline and Jugurtha*, by Sallust. 1608.

*

Bibliographies

S.A. Tannenbaum, *Thomas Heywood: A Concise Bibliography*, New York, 1939; supplement in *Elizabethan Bibliographies Supplements 2*, by Dennis G. Donovan, London, 1967.
Michael Wentworth, *Thomas Heywood: A Reference Guide*, Boston, 1986.

Criticism

Books:
Mowbray Velte, *The Bourgeois Elements in the Dramas of Thomas Heywood*, Mysore, 1924, revised edition, 1966.
Otelia Cromwell, *Thomas Heywood: A Study in the Elizabethan Drama of Everyday Life*, London, 1928.
Arthur M. Clark, *Thomas Heywood, Playwright and Miscellanist*, Oxford, 1931.
F.S. Boas, *Thomas Heywood*, London, 1950.
Marilyn L. Johnson, *Images of Women in the Work of Thomas Heywood*, Salzburg, 1974.
Barbara J. Baines, *Thomas Heywood*, Boston, 1984.

*   *   *

In his preface to *The English Traveller*, Heywood refers to 220 plays in which he had "either an entire hand, or at the least a main finger". He was indeed prolific and enjoyed a long career as an actor, collaborator, pamphleteer, and playwright. The axiom he usually followed was "aut prodesse solent, aut delectare", and the impulse behind his works does seem to be to teach and to please. The less privileged audiences at the Cockpit (or Phoenix) in Drury Lane, the Curtain, the Red Bull, and the Rose were the chief consumers of his plays, but this is not to argue that his work was unsubtle. Far from being crudely popular, Heywood wrote for a range of audiences, was adept in manipulating many genres, responded to changing fashions, and produced several plays of particular distinction.

The sequence known as *The Ages* is the least known of Heywood's dramatic endeavours. *The Golden Age, The Silver Age, The Brazen Age*, and the two parts of *The Iron Age* recount the story of the Fall of Troy and the founding of London, a new Troy; despite the familiar material, the plays are not without merit. They were applauded by popular and aristocratic audiences and they provided Heywood with opportunities to display his expertise in the staging of masques and spectacles (linked by the choric figure of Homer) and the employment of a variety of elaborate theatrical devices.

A deeper level of interest can be found in the historical dramas. *The Four Prentices of London*, sensitive to the tastes of the city apprentices, dramatizes the fantastic exploits of

four apprentices who become soldiers to demonstrate their patriotic allegiances, and to be revenged upon foreign enemies. While the two parts of *Edward IV* might appear merely to celebrate the values of London citizens, they also respond to rebellions in the metropolis during this period and display a sophistication of dramatic design. In the first part, the lust for material possessions of Falconbridge's rebels parallels Edward's sexual desire for Jane Shore; by extension, the rebellion implicitly indicts Edward for failing to meet his royal responsibilities. The second part is similarly structurally successful; as Jane Shore falls from a position of favour, the future Richard III rises to claim ascendancy. Another two-part historical drama was *If You Know Not Me, You Know Nobody*. An exercise in Elizabethan nostalgia, the play praises Elizabeth's virtues, transforms her into a saintly figure and, through John Gresham, a young spendthrift, suggests the necessity for the wealthier classes to develop more charitable consciences.

The comedies reveal Heywood's talents to particular advantage. Such is the integrity of Mistress Arthur in *How a Man May Choose a Good Wife from a Bad* that she resists the attentions of her suitor, Anselme, and wins back her errant husband, thus ensuring the stability of her family and the local community. Again concerned with the role of the family and its social importance, *Fortune by Land and Sea*, written with William Rowley, explores the conflict between a desire for revenge and social obligations; reliance upon Fortune resolves the difficulties the play delineates. A social dimension is present, too, in *The Wise Woman of Hogsdon* in which Heywood passes a censorious judgement upon the gulls who flock to hear the advice of a white witch. And Heywood's flexibility within the comic medium is shown in *A Maidenhead Well Lost*, a play that engages with the contemporary vogue for aristocratic, Fletcherian romances.

In the tragicomedies, Heywood's preoccupation with social questions is elaborated into a discussion of royal authority, 17th-century abuses, and the dangers of materialism. The answering fidelity of the marshal in *The Royal King and the Loyal Subject* reflects favourably upon the King of England's trust in his servants. More critical of the political system is *The Captives*, in which Heywood pleads for the abolition of the contemporary practice of chattel slavery. Money is the key concern of *The English Traveller*; in a mock-heroic vein, the play portrays the effects of money on two families and the ways in which a dedication to material considerations disrupts father-and-son relations.

Two plays stand out as among Heywood's best. The abilities of the dramatist are abundantly evident in these productions which span the period of his professional activity. *The Fair Maid of the West* is a play whose first and second parts can be approximately dated 1597–1603 and 1630 respectively. An adventure or romance, it contains patriotic elements and betrays a fascination (as do many of Heywood's dramas) with honour: all of the characters feel impelled to define themselves in honourable terms. Prominent is the virtuous and courageous Bess (a version of Elizabeth I), and through her Heywood dispels the misogynistic sentiments the male characters articulate.

A Woman Killed with Kindness, Heywood's domestic tragedy, also focuses upon the position of women: in the play, jokes and songs signify male attempts to contain women and to control their sexuality. A question urgently posed is the nature of Frankford's kindness. When he discovers his wife, Anne, is unfaithful, he exiles her to a pleasant retirement rather than reject her completely. However, simultaneously he dwells on his situation in maudlin terms and regards himself (possibly self-indulgently) as a martyred figure in a fallen paradise. These contradictory images of Frankford are clearly drawn, and *A Woman Killed with Kindness* offers no easy means of effecting their reconciliation. A subplot involves the trials of the Mountford family and provides another perspective on the theme of the loss of reputation. The earthy commentaries of Nicholas, Frankford's servant, the images of gates, the counterpointing of characters, and the emphasis on hospitality all enhance the treatment of the relationship between sexuality and morality in a play that well attests to Heywood's poetic skills, thematic versatility, and technical accomplishment.

—Mark Thornton Burnett

See also *Volume 1* entries on *The Fair Maid of the West, Parts One and Two*; *A Woman Killed with Kindness*.

HIBBERD, Jack. Born John Charles Hibberd in Warracknabeal, Victoria, Australia, 12 April 1940. Educated at Marist Brothers College, Bendigo, Victoria; University of Melbourne, MD 1964. Married 1) Jocelyn Hibberd in 1969 (divorced 1977), one daughter and one son; 2) Evelyn Krape in 1978, one son. Practising physician, 1965–66, 1970–73, and since 1986; co-founder, La Mama Theatre Company, Melbourne; member, Australian Performing Group, Melbourne, 1970–77. Also wine columnist, Melbourne *Age*. Member, Australia Council Theatre Board, 1977–79; first president, Melbourne Writers' Theatre.

Works

Collections

Three Popular Plays (includes *One of Nature's Gentlemen; The Les Darcy Show; A Toast to Melba*).   1976.
Squibs: A Collection of Short Plays (includes selections from *Brain Rot* and *Asian Oranges; A League of Nations; The Three Sisters; Death of a Traveller*).   1984.

Stage Works

Three Old Friends (produced by La Mama Theatre Company, Melbourne, 1967).
Below the Belt (produced as part of revue, University of Melbourne, 1967).
Just Before the Honeymoon (produced by La Mama Theatre Company, Melbourne, 1967). In *Kosmos II* (Clayton, Victoria), 1972.
O! (produced by La Mama Theatre Company, Melbourne, 1967).
This Great Gap of Time (produced by La Mama Theatre Company, Melbourne, 1967).
White with Wire Wheels (produced University of Melbourne, 1967). In *Four Australian Plays*, 1970.
No Time Like the Present (produced University of Melbourne, 1968).
Who? (produced University of Melbourne, 1968). In *Four Australian Plays*, 1970.
Jack Juan (produced University of Melbourne, 1968).
One of Nature's Gentlemen (produced University of Melbourne, 1968). In *Three Popular Plays*, 1976.
Commitment (produced by the Melbourne Theatre Company, 1968).

Dimboola: A Wedding Reception Play (produced by La Mama Theatre Company, Melbourne, 1969).   1978.
Customs and Excise (produced by La Mama Theatre Company, Melbourne, 1970; augmented version, as *Proud Flesh*, produced Carlton, Victoria, 1972).
Klag (produced University of Melbourne, 1970).
Marvellous Melbourne, with John Romeril (produced by the Australian Performing Group, Melbourne, 1970). In *Theatre Australia*, July-September, 1977.
Aorta (produced University of Melbourne, 1971).
A Stretch of the Imagination (produced by the Australian Performing Group, Melbourne, 1972).   1973.
Captain Midnight V.C., music by Lorraine Milne (produced on tour in Victoria, 1972).   1984.
Women!, from a play by Aristophanes (produced Carlton, Victoria, 1972).
See You Tomorrow at Maxim's (produced by the Australian Performing Group as part of the Earth, Air, Fire and Water Show, Melbourne, 1973).
Peggy Sue; or, The Power of Romance (produced by the Australian Performing Group, Melbourne, 1974; revised version produced Melbourne, 1983).   1982.
The Architect and Emperor of Assyria, from a play by Fernando Arrabal (produced Carlton, Victoria, 1974).
The Les Darcy Show (produced Flinders University, Adelaide, 1974). In *Three Popular Plays*, 1976.
Goodbye Ted, with John Timlin (produced 1975).   1983.
A Toast to Melba (produced by the Australian Performing Group, Adelaide, 1976). In *Three Popular Plays*, 1976.
The Overcoat, music by Martin Friedel, from a story by Gogol (produced Carlton, Victoria, 1976).   With *Sin*, 1981.
Memoirs of a Carlton Bohemian (produced by La Mama Theatre Company, Melbourne, 1977). In *Meanjin*, 3, 1977.
Sin (opera libretto), music by Martin Friedel (produced Victorian State Opera, Melbourne, 1978). With *The Overcoat*, 1981.
A Man of Many Parts (produced Perth, 1980).
Mothballs (produced Universal Theatre, Melbourne, 1981). In *Meanjin* (Melbourne), 4, 1980.
Breakfast at the Windsor. In *Meanjin*, 40, 1981; in book form in *Squibs*, 1984.
Liquid Amber (produced Wodonga, Victoria, 1982). In *A Country Quinella*, 1984.
Lavender Bags. In *Aspect*, 25, 1982.
Glycerine Tears (produced by the Melbourne Theatre Company, Melbourne, 1983). In *Meanjin*, 4, 1982; revised version (produced Melbourne Writers' Theatre, Melbourne, 1989), in *Duets*, 1989.
Asian Oranges. In *Squibs*, 1984.
A League of Nations (produced Wagga Wagga, Victoria, 1985). In *Squibs*, 1984.
The Three Sisters. In *Squibs*, 1984.
Death of a Traveller (produced by the Melbourne Writers' Theatre, Melbourne, 1985). In *Squibs*, 1984.
Death Warmed Up. In *Scripsi* (Melbourne), vol.2, no.4, 1984.
Odyssey of a Prostitute. (produced The Church, Melbourne). In *Outrider* (Indooroopilly, Queensland), 1985.
The Old School Tie (produced Melbourne Writers' Theatre, Melbourne, 1989). In *Duets*, 1989.

Fiction

Memoirs of an Old Bastard.   1989.
The Life of Riley.   1991.

Other

The Barracker's Bible: A Dictionary of Sporting Slang, with Garrie Hutchinson.   1983.

Translator, *Le vin des amants: Poems from Baudelaire*.   1977.

Editor, "Performing Arts in Australia" issue of *Meanjin*, 1984.

*

Criticism

Books:
Alrene Sykes, "Jack Hibberd and the New Wave Drama", in *Bards, Bohemians, and Bookmen: Essays in Australian Literature*, edited by Leon Cantrell, St. Lucia, Queensland, 1976.
Leslie Rees, *Australian Drama in the 1970s: A Historical and Critical Survey*, Sydney, 1978.
Peter Fitzpatrick, *After "The Doll": Australian Drama Since 1955*, London, 1979.
Peter Holloway (ed.), *Contemporary Australian Drama: Perspectives Since 1955*, Sydney, 1981.
Paul McGillick, *Jack Hibberd* (in English), Amsterdam, 1988.

Articles:
Interview with Elizabeth Perkins, in *Literature in North Queensland*, vol.2 no.1, 1983.
Interview with Geoff Sirmai, in *Southerly*, 45, 1985.
Interview in *Australasian Drama Studies*, 10, 1987.
John Tittensor, "Jack Hibberd and Australian Popular Theatre", in *Commonwealth Essays and Studies*, vol.12 no.1, 1989.

*   *   *

Jack Hibberd occupies a special place in the recent history of the Australian theatre. First, he was one of a small group of playwrights who provided material for the rebirth of the Australian theatre which took place in the late 1960's. He was a founding member of the La Mama Company in Melbourne, the core of which went on, in 1970, to form the Australian Performing Group, for the ten years of its life the most dynamic source of new directions in the Australian theatre.

This rebirth was characterised by a preference for Australian plays (usually set locally), an acceptance of Australian English as a valid stage voice (where previously British English was *de rigeur*), and a challenging of theatrical conventions—in particular, the "well-made" play of the English repertoire. There was great emphasis on reassessing performance values, especially actor-audience relationships. As a result, a new kind of theatre began to emerge which was "rough" and direct, which brought actors and audience closer together, and which had deliberately set out to assimilate the lessons of modernist theatre, embodied in the work of people like Brecht, Beckett, and the post-1956 British playwrights.

Hibberd worked as a member of the company, providing performable texts for a permanent ensemble of actors. These texts would be worked over in rehearsal and revised even during performance runs. In other words, Hibberd was not (at least until he left the APG in 1977) the kind of playwright who wrote in his study and delivered a finished product. He

was an active participant in the whole process of theatrical production, and his plays have always been marked by the constraints and possibilities of performance.

Hibberd is also special in another way: he has consistently produced anti-naturalistic theatre in the face of the entrenched naturalism of the Australian stage. His anti-naturalism is, in turn, related to another characteristic which tends to set him apart from his Australian contemporaries: he has a highly refined notion of theatrical practice and of the role of the theatre in society. Not only has Hibberd directed and designed a number of his own plays, but he has also written extensively about the theatre.

He expressed his views on the function and practice of the theatre when he commented that:

> The theatre must redefine or rediscover, then demonstrate forcefully its unique and incomparable attributes —the intimate black magic yet sun-drenched volatility of live performance in the context of social occasion. If unencumbered in its instincts yet intrinsic to a sense of community, the theatre tends naturally to evocations and signs rather than statements and maps. It encourages a more active, less supine, range of creative audience response.

Hibberd sees the theatre as a social institution with the two-fold function of both expressing and challenging the values of society. It is a communal ritual, a kind of social drama in which the participants are constantly redefining the character of their society. This implies that the audience has an active role to play. In turn, this implies a rejection of naturalism because naturalism suggests that men and the world are fixed and knowable entities. It, therefore, tends to endorse an established world-view. Hibberd rejects naturalism because, no matter how challenging the themes of a play might be, the theatrical means will always subvert those ends.

Significantly, Hibberd has been strongly influenced by German Expressionist theatre and art. The Expressionists maintained that the way people behaved could not be changed until people changed the way they perceived the world. Hence, Hibberd's theatre has always emphasised the fusion of form and content, seeing form (as the Expressionists did) as the bearer of content.

In his early work, Hibberd explored literal audience participation at the same time as exploring Australian myths and archetypes. In *Dimboola*, for example, the audience are guests at a country wedding reception. Similarly, *One of Nature's Gentlemen* and *The Les Darcy Show* both imply direct audience participation, with the former taking place in a pub, and the latter in a boxing gym. These plays, along with *A Toast to Melba*, he termed "Popular Plays" because of their "mythological" subject-matter and because of their informal, almost burlesque, formal character.

These plays also had a consciously theatrical quality and, in his later work, Hibberd has consistently used the theatre as a metaphor for life itself, thus supporting his generally relativist credo which sees the world as an absurd and unpredictable place. "In one sense", he says, "God is dead, but in another sense we are free in an absurd world. That is the great existentialist contradiction. Therefore, audiences have to partake of that contradiction too and that's why they must take a creative role in the theatre performance".

This credo is particularly evident in his adaptations of Gogol's *The Overcoat* and Maupassant's *Odyssey of a Prostitute*, two of his best plays, which evince a sure use of a loose "Brechtian" style. His use of the theatre as a metaphor is best seen in the seven monodramas. Sometimes, the metaphor is explicit as in *Mothballs* and *Lavender Bags* where the protagonist is an actress. In plays like *A Stretch of the Imagination* and later monodramas it is implicit in the way the sole character performs for himself.

Apart from plays and critical writing, Hibberd has written a novel and a book of translations from Baudelaire, and has collaborated on other books and plays. He is a doctor who has now returned to medical practice, having temporarily given up writing plays because

> ... of the sheer pointlessness of the activity in the Australian context, because of a sequence of shoddy productions of new plays, the mounting artistic depravity of our clique-ridden theatre, the indifference to almost everything except fashion of our theatre public and, lastly, because critical standards have fallen by the wayside.

—Paul McGillick

See also *Volume 1* entry on *A Stretch of the Imagination*.

HOCHHUTH, Rolf. Born in Eschwege, Germany, 1 April 1931. Educated at Realgymnasium, Eschwege, until 1948; studied bookselling at a technical school; universities of Heildelberg and Munich, 1952–55. Married to Dana Pavic; three sons. Worked for mayor of Eschwege, after World War II; staff member, Verlag C. Bertelsmann, Gütersloh, from 1955; resident dramatist, Municipal Theatre, Basle, 1963; founder, with Martin Walser, Meersburg summer theatre festival; since 1989 chief cultural correspondent, *Die Welt*. Recipient: Hauptmann Prize, 1962; Young Generation Prize, 1963; Berlin Prize, 1963; Melcher Prize, 1965; Basler Prize, 1976; Stadt München und des Verbandes Bayerischer Verlager Prize, 1980; Geschwister-Scholl Prize, 1980; Lessing Prize, 1981.

Works

Stage Works

Der Stellvertreter (produced Freie Volksbühne, Berlin, 1963). 1963; translated as *The Representative*, 1963; as *The Deputy*, 1964.
Die Berliner Antigone, from his story (produced Volkstheater, Vienna, 1966).
Soldaten: Nekrolog auf Genf (produced Freie Volksbühne, Berlin, 1967). 1967; translated as *Soldiers: An Obituary for Geneva*, 1968.
Guerillas (produced Württembergisches Staatstheater, Stuttgart, 1970). 1970.
Die Hebamme (produced Schauspielhaus, Zurich, 1972). 1971.
Lysistrate und die NATO (produced Bühne der Stadt, Essen, and Volkstheater, Vienna, 1974). 1973.
Tod eines Jägers (produced Festspiele Salzburg, 1977). 1976.
Juristen (produced: Ernst-Deutsch-Theater, Hamburg, Städtische Bühne, Heidelberg, and Deutsches Theater, Göttingen, 1980). 1979.
Ärztinnen (produced Nationaltheater, Mannheim, 1980). 1980.

Judith (produced in English, Citizens' Theatre, Glasgow; produced in German, Bühne der Landeshauptstadt, Kiel, 1985).
Unbefleckte Empfängnis: Ein Kreidekreis. 1988.

Fiction

Zwischenspiel in Baden-Baden. 1959.
Die Berliner Antigone. 1964.
Eine Liebe in Deutschland. 1978; translated as *A German Love Story*, 1980.
Atlantik-Novelle: Erzählung. 1985.
Alan Turing: Erzählung. 1987.
Jede Zeit baut Pyramiden: Erzählungen und Gedichte. 1988.

Other

Krieg und Klassenkrieg: Studien. 1971.
Die Berliner Antigone: Prose und Verse. 1975.
Dokumente zur politischen Wirkung, edited by Reinhart Hoffmeister. 1980.
Räuber-Rede: drei deutsche Vorwürfe: Schiller, Lessing, Geschwister Scholl. 1982.
Spitze des Eisbergs: ein Reader. 1982.
Tell '38. 1984.
Schwarze Segel: Essays und Gedichte. 1986.
War hier Europa? Reden, Gedichte, Essays. 1987.
Täter und Denker: Profile und Probleme von Cäsar bis Jünger. 1987.
Sommer 14: ein Totentanz. 1989.

Editor, *Sämtliche Werke*, by Wilhelm Busch. 1959.
Editor, *Lustige Streiche in Versen und Farben*, by Wilhelm Busch. 1961.
Editor, *Liebe in unserer Zeit: 16 Erzählungen.* 1961.
Editor, *Die Deutschen*, by Otto Flake. 1962.
Editor, *Am grauen Meer: Gesammelte Werke*, by Theodor Storm. 1963.
Editor, *Dichter und Herrscher*, by Thomas Mann. 1964.
Editor, *Die grossen Meister.* 1966.
Editor, with Peter Härting, *Werke*, by Otto Flake. 1973.
Editor, with Hans Heinrich Koch, *Kaisers Zeiten: Bilder einer Epoche aus dem Archiv der Hofphotographen Oscar und Gustav Tellgmann.* 1973.
Editor, *Die Gegenwarf. 79 deutschsprachige Erzähler der Jahrgänge 1900–1963* (2 vols.). 1981.
Editor, *Die Zweite Klassik: deutschsprachige Erzähler der Jahrgänge 1850–1900.* 1983.

*

Bibliographies

Günter Peters, "Auswahlbibliographie zu Rolf Hochhuth", in *Text und Kritik*, 58, 1978.

Criticism

Books:
Edgar Neiss, *Erläuterungen zu Rolf Hochhuth: Der Stellvertreter; Soldaten*, Hollfeld, 1974.
Margaret E. Ward, *Rolf Hochhuth* (in English), Boston, 1977.
Arnold Blumer, *Das dokumentarische Theater der sechziger Jahre in der Bundesrepublik Deutschland*, Meisenheim, 1977.

Rainer Taëni, *Rolf Hochhuth* (translated from the German), London, 1977.

Rosemarie von dem Knesbeck (ed.), *In Sachen Filbinger gegen Hochhuth: Die Geschichte einer Vergangenheitsbewältigung*, Reinbek, 1980.

Walter Hinck (ed.), *Rolf Hochhuth: Eingriff in die Zeitgeschichte*, Reinbek, 1981.

Ferdinand Fasse, *Geschichte als Problem von Literatur: Das "Geschichtsdrama" bei Howard Brenton und Rolf Hochhuth*, Frankfurt, 1983.

Manfred Durzak, "American Mythologies: Rolf Hochhuth's Plays *Guerillas, Tod eines Jägers*, and *Judith*", in *Amerika! New Images in German Literature*, edited by Heinz Osterle, New York, 1989.

* * *

Rolf Hochhuth is one of the most controversial German playwrights of the 1960's. His first play, *Der Stellvertreter* (*The Representative*), was severely criticised by the Catholic Church, while his second, *Soldaten* (*Soldiers*), was banned by the British Lord Chancellor in 1967/8. Later plays have brought the accusation of fascism (*Die Hebamme*, The Midwife) and have led to court proceedings (*Juristen*, Lawyers). Apart from controversies brought about by Hochhuth's choice of subject-matter, his whole *oeuvre* has sometimes been dismissed an anachronistic by academic and professional theatre critics alike. Despite this, the plays have enjoyed great popularity with the theatre-going public, and even Hochhuth's severest critics have to take his work seriously.

Unusually for a German playwright in the early 1960's, Hochhuth set his early plays in specific, clearly defined locations and times, and brought controversial contemporary or near-contemporary issues directly on to the stage. Thus, *Der Stellvertreter* deals with Hitler's "Final Solution" and suggests that Pope Pious XII chose, for political and economic reasons, not to intervene, while *Soldaten* accuses Churchill of conniving in the murder of the Free Polish leader General Sikorsky, because he endangered the alliance with Stalin. The presentation of such subject-matter, especially in productions by Erwin Piscator, marked a radical break with Brechtian "parables", absurdist or grotesque theatre, and also such symbolic plays as Max Frisch's *Andorra*.

Hochhuth's earlier plays present named historical characters (together with fictional characters) in specific historical circumstances. In later plays the relation to reality is more indirect, so that *Lysistrate und die NATO* (which takes place on a fictitious Greek island) could even be considered a parable. Yet other plays (*Guerillas, Judith*) are completely fictional, but are set in recognisable historical-political situations and present possible political developments.

Even though he increasingly used fictional subject-matter, Hochhuth always emphasised the importance of documentary material, and the printed versions of his texts include detailed stage directions, background information, and character descriptions which resemble critical essays, as well as newspaper cuttings which relate the plot directly to current events. Despite this emphasis on documentary material, Hochhuth always insisted that his plays were not "documentary" or "naturalistic" and, following Schiller, emphasised the role of imagination, subordinating facts to the presentation of ideas. His works cannot, therefore, be directly related to the "documentary theatre" of the 1960's, even though they helped inaugurate it, and indeed, in order to underline their anti-naturalism, Hochhuth has generally written them in a form of free verse.

The dramatic form of Hochhuth's plays is mostly unexperimental, with forms related to the conventional five acts of classical tragedy repeated with variations in about half the works, while *Die Hebamme* is divided into eight "*Bilder*", and *Tod eines Jägers* (Death of a Hunter) has just two acts. Earlier plays bear the conventional generic subtitles "Tragedy" or "Comedy", although in plays after the *Lysistrate* comedy, these are occasionally replaced by less conventional descriptions such as "five acts for seven players" (*Ärztinnen*, Doctors) or the ironic "A Chalk-circle" for *Unbefleckte Empfängnis* (Immaculate Conception), a play dealing with bureaucratic responses to a surrogate pregnancy.

Despite these developments, a number of factors have remained constant. These include, in particular, Hochhuth's political inclinations, a well as his image of mankind and the relation between man, history, and society. Central to the former is Hochhuth's socialistically-orientated but anti-dogmatic humanism, while the latter is characterised by his often-repeated conviction that man is a responsible being, capable of independent decisions which may affect historical developments. It is, for Hochhuth, the task of the drama to emphasise at least the potential for this independence. Such a belief in individual responsibility is rare in serious post-war German theatre where, for the 1950's, it was axiomatic that historically or politically significant events could not be presented as the result of individual choice or of the conventional "clash of personalities". Through his belief in the reality of choice and individual responsibility, Hochhuth can present conflicts of principle as theatrically effective verbal and personal clashes. He can then condemn historical characters such as Pope Pius XII and Churchill for the decisions they take, but can also present Churchill as a character embodying a grandeur commensurate with classical notions of tragedy.

In Hochhuth's purely fictional plays, too, he has chosen subjects that illustrate the possibility of free choice in characters enjoying privileged positions. Sophie, a town councillor in *Die Hebamme*, and Heinemann, the judge in *Unbefleckte Empfängnis*, retain the ability to take decisions for good (even if such decisions break the written law), while in *Ärztinnen*, one of the doctors, Lydia, is initially able to choose to tell the truth while others prevaricate. Lysistrate, an island representative, employs means fair and foul to save her island from becoming a NATO base. On the other hand, in *Tod eines Jägers* the suicide of the "hunted hunter", Hemingway, another privileged individual, is treated as the result of his own decision to refuse to use his position to contribute to society. Finally, in *Juristen*, Hochhuth examines the problem of ex-Nazi judges who are re-established in Western Germany and pass judgement on left-wing activists. Here, too, Hochhuth pursues his theme of choice: even under National Socialism judges could still choose between leniency and the full rigour of the law.

With the growing significance of the "*Neues Volksstück*" during the 1970's, and with Peter Handke's experiments in language drama, Hochhuth's influence has now declined. It is, however, to his lasting credit that he continued for over 20 years to write plays that initiated public debate and discussion on significant contemporary social issues, and that while doing this he continued, following Schiller, to uphold the concept of the stage as a form of moral institution.

—John P. Wieczorek

See also *Volume 1* entry on *The Representative*.

Fritz Hochwälder

HOCHWÄLDER, Fritz. Born in Vienna, Austria, 28 May 1911. Educated at Reform-Realgymnasium, Vienna; evening classes at the Volkshochschule. Married 1) Ursula Buchi in 1951; 2) Susanne Schreiner in 1960, one daughter. Apprentice upholsterer in Vienna; first-produced play, *Jehr*, staged 1933; escaped from the Nazis to Switzerland, 1938; freelance writer in Zurich, from 1945. Recipient: Vienna Prize, 1955, and Ehrenring, 1972; Grillparzer Prize, 1956; Wildgans Prize, 1963; Austrian State Prize, 1966; Austrian Ehrenkreuz für Kunst und Wissenschaft, 1971. Named Professor by Austrian government, 1963. Died in Zurich, 20 October 1986.

Works

Collections

Dramen 1 (includes *Das heilige Experiment; Die Herberge; Donnerstag*). 1959.
Dramen 2 (includes *Der öffentliche Ankläger; Der Unschuldige; 1003*). 1964.
Dramen (*Das heilige Experiment; Die Herberge; Der Himbeerpflücker*). 1968.
Stücke (*Das heilige Experiment; Die Herberge; Der Unschuldige; Der Himbeerpflücker*). 1968.
Dramen (4 vols.). 1975–85.
"The Public Prosecutor" and Other Plays (includes *The Strong Are Lonely; The Raspberry Picker; Lanzaretti*), introduced by Martin Esslin. 1980.

Stage Works

Jehr (produced Kammerspiele, Vienna, 1933).
Liebe in Florenz; oder, Die unziemliche Neugier (produced Theater für 49, Vienna, 1936).
Das heilige Experiment (produced Städtebundtheater, Biel-Solothurn, Switzerland, 1943). 1947; translated as *The Strong Are Lonely*, 1954.
Der Flüchtling, from a play by Kaiser (produced Städtebundtheater, Biel-Solothurn, Switzerland, 1945). 1954.
Hôtel du commerce (produced Theater des 5 Mai, Prague, 1946). 1954.
Meier Helmbrecht (produced Theater in der Josefstadt, Vienna, 1947). 1956.
Der öffentliche Ankläger (produced Neues Theater, Stuttgart, 1948). 1954; translated as *The Public Prosecutor*, 1958.
Virginia (produced Grosses Schauspielhaus, Hamburg, 1951).
Der Unschuldige (produced Akademietheater, Vienna, 1958). 1949 (private printing); 1958.
Virginia (produced Deutsches Schauspielhaus, Hamburg, 1951).
Donadieu (produced Burgtheater, Vienna, 1953). 1953.
Die Herberge (produced Burgtheater, Vienna, 1957). 1956; translated as *The Inn*, 1962.
Donnerstag (produced Landestheater, Salzburg, 1959). In *Dramen 1*, 1959.
Esther. 1960.
1003 (produced Theater in der Josefstadt, Vienna, 1964).
Der Himbeerpflücker (televised, 1965; produced Schauspielhaus Zurich, 1965). 1965; translated as *The Raspberry Picker*, in *"The Public Prosecutor" and Other Plays*, 1979.
Der Befehl (televised 1967; produced Burgtheater, Vienna, 1968). 1967; translated as *The Order*, in *Modern International Drama 3*, no. 2, 1970.
Lazaretti; oder, Der Säbeltiger (produced Festspiele, Salzburg, 1975). 1975; translated as *Lazaretti; or, the Saber-Toothed Tiger*, in *"The Public Prosecutor" and Other Plays*, 1979.
Die Prinzessin von Chimay. 1982.
Der verschwundene Mond. 1985.
Die Burgschaft. 1985.

Television Plays

Der Himbeerpflücker, 1965; *Der Befehl*, 1967.

Radio Plays

Der Reigen, from the play by Schnitzler; *Weinsberger Ostern 1525*, 1939.

Other

Im Wechsel der Zeit: Autobiographische Skizzen und Essays. 1980.

*

Bibliographies

James Schmitt, "Fritz Hochwälder Bibliography", in *Modern Austrian Literature*, vol.11 no.1, 1978.

Criticism

Books:
George E. Wellwarth, *The Theatre of Protest and Paradox*, New York and London, 1964.
Wilhelm Bortenschlager, *Der Dramatiker Fritz Hochwälder*, Innsbruck, 1979.
Alan Best and Hans Wolfschütz (eds.), *Modern Austrian Writing: Literature and Society After 1945*, London, 1980.

Articles:
Anthony J. Harper, "Tradition and Experiment in the Work of Fritz Hochwälder", in *New German Studies*, 5, 1977.
James Schmitt, "The Theater of Fritz Hochwälder: Its Background and Development", in *Modern Austrian Literature*, vol.11 no.1, 1978.
Donald G. Daviau, "Fritz Hochwälder's Range of Theme and Form", in *Modern Austrian Literature*, vol.18 no.2, 1985.
Edward R. McDonald, "The Classical Theater-of-Illusion Modernized: The Conflicting Messages of the Moral Imperative in Fritz Hochwälder's Drama *Das heilige Experiment*", in *Maske und Kothurn*, 31, 1985.

*   *   *

Although Hochwälder, after World War II, voluntarily remained in the Swiss exile he chose in 1938, he claimed that his Austrian heritage endowed him with the three key components for his success as a playwright: clarity of thought, a sense of form, and theatre in his blood. These ingredients define very clearly the essence of his dramatic work and identify him as one of the few modern representatives of the classical tradition of Austrian drama. Contrary to the anti-illusionist, absurdist influence so evident in the plays of Peter Handke, Thomas Bernhard, and Wolfgang Bauer, Hochwälder's dramatic precursors are the masters of the well-made *pièce-à-thèse*—Dumas *fils*, Scribe, Ibsen, Hauptmann—and the Viennese *Volkstheater* of Ferdinand Raimund and Johann Nestroy. From the well-made play, his plays have inherited a terse, clearly-defined plot, a strict adherence to the unities of time, place, and action, a strong *scène-à-faire*, and archetypal characters; the Viennese popular stage is responsible for the playwright's use of dialect, satire, and techniques of Raimund's "magic theatre".

Hochwälder's work, like that of other German exile writers, was informed by his own fate during the Hitler years, and it is not surprising that the dominant themes are the effects of totalitarianism, individual and collective guilt, and the—rarely grasped—opportunity to learn from history. Although he claimed that there was little of the "great, burning, topical issues" in *Das heilige Experiment* (*The Strong Are Lonely*), the play clearly discusses the imposition of a political, economic, and social order on an initially unwilling populace. Such a totalitarian order must fail, even if it is based on the noblest motives, as in the case of the Jesuits in Paraguay.

In his early creative period, Hochwälder wrote mainly historical plays, with strong references to contemporaneous events; after the fall of the Nazi regime he could permit himself to lighten the high moral tone of *Das heilige Experiment*, even when alluding to the horrors of the recent past. Thus, *Der öffentliche Ankläger* (*The Public Prosecutor*) is an adaption of the Oedipus motif to a very topical issue: Fouquier-Tinville, one of the most feared prosecutors during the years of terror in the French Revolution, is tricked into using the nefarious techniques he has employed against so many innocent people to condemn himself. In addition, Hochwälder attempted to answer the question asked repeatedly at the Nuremberg trials: what is it that turns intelligent, basically decent human beings into ferocious instruments of totalitarian terror? Hochwälder saw Fouquier-Tinville and people of his ilk as sincerely committed to a revolutionary social ideal; even when they see that their utopia is changing into a nightmare, they will do anything in their power to uphold the system, for without this ideological base, however tainted it may have become, they would stare into an existential void. The machine of the system that turned them into bureaucratic puppets signing death warrants and deportation orders has simultaneously given them an excuse for their behaviour and a *raison d'être*. Order, as the judge in *Die Herberge* (The Hospice) recognizes, has replaced justice.

In his third creative period, Hochwälder dealt more directly with the aftermath of the National Socialist era in Austria than in his earlier historical plays. *Der Befehl* (*The Order*) is yet another variation on the Oedipus theme, with an Austrian police officer discovering that he, himself, is the war criminal he has been asked to ferret out. Like Oedipus, Inspector Mittermayer, whose whole life is "following orders, obedience, service", refuses to blame the system or the times for his crimes and commits ritual suicide to atone for his sins. In *Der Himbeerpflücker* (*The Raspberry Picker*), described by the playwright himself as a "nasty farce on a topical theme", Hochwälder transposes Nikolai Gogol's *The Government Inspector* to a small Austrian town. In an ingenious variation on Gogol's theme, a petty criminal is mistaken for an infamous Nazi war criminal and showered with honours and favours. The unmasking of their "hero" as a petty thief, and the arrest and death of the real war criminal, rob the townspeople of their nostalgia for their "dream of blood and loyalty".

Hochwälder's dramatic output after *Der Befehl* has not been accorded the same critical acclaim as his earlier plays. Only *Lazaretti*, a play about terrorism and the fallacy of trying to combat violence with violence, has been moderately successful. Thus the playwright's reputation will rest mainly on the uncompromising humanism of his historical plays and on the biting satire of *Der Himbeerpflücker*; his mastery of the tightly constructed three-act play in an era dominated by the anti-illusionist "theatre of the absurd" is an anachronism much appreciated by audiences as nostalgic for order and logic on stage as in their daily lives.

—Franz G. Blaha

———

HOFMANNSTHAL, Hugo (Laurenz August Hofmann, Edler) von. Born in Vienna, Austria, 1 February 1874. Educated at Akademisches Gymnasium, Vienna, 1884–92; studied law, 1892–94, and romantic philology: dissertation on Pléiade poets, 1897, and habilitation work on Victor Hugo, 1900–01, University of Vienna. Served with 6th Dragoon Regiment in Göding, 1894–95. Married Gertrud Schlesinger in 1901; one daughter, and two sons. First plays produced in the late 1890's; full-time writer, from 1901; collaborated with Richard Strauss on operas, from 1909; undertook propaganda work for the Austrian government during World War I; editor with the Österreichische Bibliothek, 1915–17; co-founder, with Max Reinhardt, the Salzburg Festival, 1919. Died in Rodaun (now Wien-Rodaun), 15 July 1929.

Works

Collections

Theater in Versen. 1899.
Kleine Dramen (2 vols.). 1906–07.
Vorspiele. 1908
Die Gedichte und kleinen Dramen. 1911.
Gesammelte Werke (6 vols.). 1924; 5 vols., 1934.
Dramatische Entwürfe aus dem Nachlass, edited by Heinrich Zimmer. 1936.
Gesammelte Werke in Einzelausgaben, edited by Herbert Steiner (15 vols.). 1945–59.
Selected Writings: Prose, Plays and Libretti, Poems and Verse Plays (3 vols.; various translators). 1952–63.
Sämtliche Werke, edited by Heinz Otto Burger and others. 1973—

Stage Works

Gestern (produced Vienna, 1928). In *Moderne Rundschau*, 1891.
Der Tod der Tizian (produced Künstlerhaus, Munich, 1901). In *Blätter für die Künst*, 1892.
Das kleine Welttheater; oder, Die Glücklichen (produced Residenztheater, Munich, 1929). In *Pan*, 1897; in book form, 1903; translated as *The Little Theatre of the World*, in *Selected Writings*, 1961.
Der Thor und der Tod (produced Theater am Gärtnerplatz, Munich, 1898). In *Moderne Musen Almanach*, 1894; as *Der Tor und der Tod*, in *Kleine Dramen 1*, 1906; translated as *Death and the Fool*, 1914 and 1961.
Der weisse Fächer (produced Akademietheater, Vienna, 1927). In *Die Zeit*, 1898; in book form, 1907.
Die Frau im Fenster (produced as *Madonna Dianora*, Deutsches Theater, Berlin, 1898). In *Theater in Versen*, 1899; translated as *Dianora*, 1916.
Der Abenteurer und die Sängerin (produced Deutsches Schauspielhaus, Berlin, 1899). In *Theater in Versen*, 1899; revised version (produced Kammerspiele, Berlin, 1921), 1909.
Die Hochzeit der Sobeide (produced as *Sobeide, Abenteurer*, Deutsches Theater, Berlin, and Burgtheater, Vienna, 1899). In *Theater in Versen*, 1899; translated as *The Marriage of Sobeide*, 1916; as *The Marriage of Zobeide*, in *Selected Writings*, 1961.
Das Bergwerk zu Falun, from a story by E.T.A. Hoffmann (partial version produced Deutsches Theater, Konstanz, 1899). 1933; complete version (produced Konstanz, 1949), in *Gedichte und lyrische Dramen*, 1946; translated as *The Mine at Falun*, in *Selected Writings*, 1961.
Der Kaiser und die Hexe (produced Urania-Schattenspiele, Vienna, 1926). In *Die Insel*, 1900; translated as *The Emperor and the Witch*, in *Selected Writings*, 1961.
Der Triumph der Zeit. In *Die Insel*, 1900.
Der Schüler. In *Neue Rundschau*, 1901.
Elektra (produced Kleines Theater, Berlin, 1903). 1904; revised version, music by Strauss (produced Hofoper, Dresden, 1909), 1908; translated as *Electra*, 1908: several subsequent translations under same title.
Das gerettete Venedig, from a play by Otway (produced Lessingtheater, Berlin, 1905). 1905 (complete version).
Vorspiel für ein Puppentheater. In *Neue Rundschau*, 1906.
Ödipus und die Sphinx (produced Deutsches Theater, Berlin, 1905). 1906.
König Ödipus, from a play by Sophocles (produced Munich, 1910). In *österreichische Rundschau*, 1907; in book form, 1910.
Die Begegnung mit Carlo. 1909.
Florindo und die Unbekannte (produced Kammerspiele, Berlin, 1921). In *Süddeutsche Monatshefte*, 1909; in book form, 1923.
Alkestis, from a play by Euripides, music by Egon Wellesz (produced Kammerspiele, Munich, 1916). 1909 (complete version).
Lucidor. 1910.
Die Heirat wider Willen, from a play by Molière. 1910.
Christinas Heimreise (produced Deutsches Theater, Berlin, 1910). 1910; translated as *Christina's Journey Home*, 1916.
Amor und Psyche. 1911.
Das fremde Mädchen. 1911.
Der Rosenkavalier, music by Strauss (produced Königliches Opernhaus, Dresden, 1911). 1911; translated as *The Rose Bearer*, 1912; as *The Knight of the Rose*, 1926; as *The Cavalier of the Rose*, in *Selected Writings*, 1963.
Jedermann: Das Spiel vom Sterben des reichen Mannes (produced Zirkus Schumann, Berlin, 1911). 1911; translated as *The Play of Everyman*, 1917; as *The Salzburg Everyman*, 1930.
Ariadne auf Naxos, music by Strauss (produced Königliches Hoftheater, Stuttgart, 1912). 1912; revised version (produced 1916), 1916; translated as *Ariadne on Naxos*, 1912.
Josephs Legende (ballet scenario), with Harry Graf Kessler, music by Strauss (produced Opéra, Paris 1914). 1914.
Die Frau ohne Schatten, music by Strauss (produced Hofoper, Vienna, 1919). 1916; translated as *The Woman Without a Shadow*, 1927.
Die grüne Flöte (ballet scenario), music by Mozart (produced Deutsches Theater, Berlin, 1916). 1925.
Die Lästigen, from a play by Molière (produced 1916). In *Marsyas*, 1917.
Der Bürger als Edelmann, from a play by Molière, music by Strauss (produced Deutsches Theater, Berlin, 1918). 1918.
Dame Kobold, from a play by Calderón (produced Deutsches Theater, Berlin, 1920). 1920.
Der Schwierige (produced Residenztheater, Munich, 1921). 1921; translated as *The Difficult Man*, in *Selected Writings*, 1963.
Das Salzburger grosse Welttheater, from a play by Calderón (produced Kollegien Kirche, Salzburg, 1922). 1922; translated as *The Salzburg Great Theatre of the World*, in *Selected Writings*, 1963.
Prima Ballerina (ballet scenario). 1923 (?).
Der Unbestechliche (produced Raimundtheater, Vienna, 1923). In *Gesammelte Werke: Lustspiele 4*, 1956.
Die Ruinen von Athen (produced Operntheater, Vienna, 1924). 1925.
Der Turm, from a play by Calderón (produced in a revised version, Staatstheater, Munich, and Deutsches Schauspielhaus, Hamburg, 1928; original version produced Burgtheater, Vienna, 1948). In *Neue deutsche Beiträge*, 1925–27; revised version, 1927; translated as *The Tower*, in *Selected Writings*, 1963.
Die ägyptische Helena, music by Strauss (produced Staatsoper, Dresden, 1928). 1928; translated as *Helen in Egypt*, 1928.
Semiramis: Die beiden Götter. 1933.
Arabella, music by Strauss (produced Staatsoper, Dresden, 1933). 1933; translated as *Arabella*, in *Selected Writings*, 1963.
Silvia im "Stern". In *Corona*, 1935.

Alexanderzug. In *Dramatische Entwürfe aus dem Nachlass*, 1936.
Alexander—Die Freunde. In *Dramatische Entwürfe aus dem Nachlass*, 1936.
Leda und der Schwan. In *Dramatische Entwürfe aus dem Nachlass*, 1936.
Pentheus. In *Dramatische Entwürfe aus dem Nachlass*, 1936.
Der Priesterzögling. In *Dramatische Entwürfe aus dem Nachlass*, 1936.
Danae; oder, Die Vernunftheirat. 1952.

Fiction

Prinz Eugen der edle Ritter. 1905.
"Das Märchen der 672. Nacht" und andere Erzählungen (includes "Ein Brief" [The Chandos Letter]). 1905.
Die Frau ohne Schatten. 1919.
Andreas; oder, Die Vereinigten. 1932; translated as *Andreas; or, The United*, 1936.
Four Stories, edited by Margaret Jacobs. 1968.

Verse

Ausgewählte Gedichte. 1903.
Die gesammelten Gedichte. 1907.
Lyrical Poems, translated by Charles Wharton Stork. 1918.
Gedichte. 1922.
Nachlese der Gedichte. 1934.

Memoirs and Letters

Briefe 1890–1901. 1935.
Briefe 1900–1909. 1937.
Briefwechsel, with Anton Wildgans, edited by Joseph A. von Bradish. 1935.
Briefwechsel, with Stefan George, edited by Robert Boehringer. 1938; revised edition, 1953.
Briefwechsel, with Richard Strauss, edited by Franz and Alice Strauss. 1952; revised edition, edited by Willi Schuh, 1954; translated as *Correspondence*, 1961.
Briefe der Freundschaft, with Eberhard von Bodenhausen, edited by Dora von Bodenhausen. 1953.
Briefwechsel, with Rudolf Borchardt, edited by Marie Luise Borchardt and Herbert Steiner. 1954.
Briefwechsel, with Carl J. Burckhardt, edited by Burckhardt. 1956.
Briefwechsel, with Arthur Schnitzler, edited by Theresa Nickl and Heinrich Schnitzler. 1964.
Briefwechsel, with Helene von Nostitz, edited by Oswalt von Nostitz. 1965.
Briefwechsel, with Edgar Karl von Bebenburg, edited by Mary E. Gilbert. 1966.
Briefwechsel, with Leopold von Andrian. 1968.
Briefwechsel, with Willy Haas. 1968.
Briefwechsel, with Harry Graf Kessler. 1968.
Briefwechsel, with Josef Redlich. 1971.
Briefwechsel, with Richard Beer-Hofmann. 1972.
Briefwechsel, with Max Rycher, Samuel and Hedwig Fischer, Oscar Bie, and Moritz Heimann, edited by Claudia Mertz-Rycher and others. 1973.
Briefwechsel, with Ottonie Gräfin Degenfeld, edited by Marie Therese Miller-Degenfeld. 1974.
Briefwechsel 1899–1925, with Rainer Maria Rilke, edited by Rudolf Hirsch and Ingeborg Schnack. 1978.
Briefwechsel, with Max Mell, edited by Margaret Dietrich and Heinz Kindermann. 1982.

Briefwechsel, with Ria Schmujlow-Claasen. 1982.
Briefwechsel, with Paul Zifferer. 1983.

Other

Stüdie über die Entwickelung des Dichters Victor Hugo. 1901; as *Versuch über Victor Hugo*, 1925.
Unterhaltungen über literarische Gegenstände. 1904.
Victor Hugo. 1904.
Die prosaischen Schriften gesammelt (3 vols.). 1907–17.
Hesperus: Ein Jahrbuch, with Rudolf Borchardt and Rudolf Alexander Schröder. 1909.
Grete Wiesenthal in Amor und Psyche und Das Fremde Mädchen. 1911.
Die Wege und die Begegnungen. 1913.
Rodauner Nachträge (3 vols.). 1918.
Reden und Aufsätze. 1921.
Buch der Freunde. 1922; edited by Ernst Zinn, 1965.
Gesammelte Werke (6 vols.). 1924; revised edition (3 vols.), 1934.
Augenblicke in Griechenland. 1924.
Früheste Prosastücke. 1926.
Grillparzers politisches Vermächtnis. 1926.
Loris: Die Prosa des Jungen Hoffmansthals. 1930.
Die Berührung der Sphären. 1931.

General editor, "Die österreichische Bibliothek" series (26 vols.). 1915–17.

*

Bibliographies

Horst Weber, *Hugo von Hofmannsthal: Bibliographie des Schrifttums 1892–1963*, Berlin, 1966.
Horst Weber, *Hugo von Hofmannsthal: Bibliographie: Werke, Briefe, Gespräche, Übersetzungen, Vertonungen*, Berlin, 1972.
H.-A. and U. Koch, *Hugo von Hofmannsthal Bibliographie 1964–1976*, Freiburg, 1976.
C. Köttelwesch, "Hofmannsthal Bibliographie", in *Hofmannsthal Blätter*, from 1979.

Criticism

Books:
W. Jens, *Hofmannsthal und die Griechen*, Tübingen, 1955.
Hans Hammelmann, *Hugo von Hofmannsthal*, London, 1957.
R. Alewyn, *Über Hugo von Hofmannsthal*, Göttingen, 1958; fourth edition, 1978.
W.H. Rey, *Weltentzweiung und Weltversöhnung in Hugo von Hofmannsthals Dramen*, Philadelphia, 1962.
E. Rösch, *Die Komödien Hofmannsthals*, Marburg, 1963; third edition, 1975.
B. Coughlin, *Hofmannsthals Festival Dramas*, 1964.
M. Hamburger, *Hofmannsthal: Zwei Studien*, Göttigen, 1964.
W. Nehring, *Die Tat bei Hofmannsthal: Eine Untersuchung zu Hofmannsthals grossen Dramen*, Stuttgart, 1966.
L. Wittmann, *Sprachthematik und dramatische Form im Werke Hofmannsthals*, Stuttgart, 1966.
G. Erken, *Hofmannsthals dramatischer Stil*, Tübingen, 1967.
Frederick Ritter, *Hugo von Hofmannsthal und Österreich*, Heidelberg, 1967.

S. Bauer (ed.), *Hugo von Hofmannsthal*, Darmstadt, 1968.

M. Hoppe, *Literatentum, Magie und Mystik im Frühwerk Hugo von Hofmannsthals*, Berlin, 1968.

G. Pickerodt, *Hofmannsthals Dramen: Kritik ihres historischen Gehalts*, Stuttgart, 1968.

W. Volke, *Hugo von Hofmannsthal in Selbstzeugnissen und Bilddokumente*, Reinbek, 1968.

K.G. Esselborn, *Hofmannsthal und der antike Mythos*, Munich, 1969.

Heinz Kindermann, *Hofmannsthal und die Schauspielkunst*, Vienna, 1969.

Erwin Kobel, *Hugo von Hofmannsthal*, Berlin, 1970.

Benno Rech, *Hofmannsthals Komödie: Verwirklichte Konfiguration*, Bonn, 1971.

Michael Hamburger, *Hugo von Hofmannsthal: Three Essays*, Princeton, New Jersey, 1972.

G. Wunberg, *Hofmannsthal im Urteil seiner Kritiker: Dokumente zur Wirkungsgeschichte*, Frankfurt, 1972.

Steven P. Sondrup, *Hofmannsthal and the French Symbolist Tradition*, Bern and Frankfurt, 1976.

Lowell A. Bangerter, *Hugo von Hofmannsthal* (in English), New York, 1977.

W. Mauser, *Hugo von Hofmannsthal: Konfliktbewältigung und Werkstruktur*, Munich, 1977.

W.E. Yuill and Patricia Howe (ed.), *Hugo von Hofmannsthal: Commemorative Essays*, London, 1981.

G. Briese-Neumann, *Ästhet-Dilettant-Narziss: Untersuchung zur Reflexion der Fin-de-siècle-Phänomene im Frühwerk Hugo von Hofmannsthals*, Frankfurt, 1985.

Thomas A. Kovach, *Hofmannsthal and Symbolism: Art and Life in the Work of a Modern Poet*, New York, 1985.

Donna C. van Handle, *"Das Spiel vor der Menge": Hugo von Hofmannsthals Bemühungen um Bühnenwirksamkeit am Beispiel ausgewählter Dramen*, New York, 1986.

Helen Frink, *Animal Symbolism in Hofmannsthal's Works*, New York, 1987.

Benjamin Bennett, *Hofmannsthal: The Theatres of Consciousness*, Cambridge, 1988.

Friedrich Schröder, *Die Gestalt des Verführers im Drama Hugo von Hofmannsthals*, Frankfurt, 1988.

H.-A. Koch, *Hugo von Hofmannsthal*, Darmstadt, 1989.

Ronald Gray, "The Success and Failure of Poetic Drama in Austria and Britain: Hugo von Hofmannsthal and T.S. Eliot", in *Patterns of Change: German Drama and the European Tradition*, edited by Dorothy James and Others, New York, 1990.

Articles:

W.E. Yates, "Hofmannsthal and the Austrian Comic Tradition", in *Colloqui Germanica*, 15, 1982.

Serials

Hofmannsthal Blätter, 1968—
Hofmannsthal Forschungen, 1971—

*   *   *

Phenomenally precocious, Hofmannsthal established his literary reputation with his verse playlet *Gestern* (Yesterday) when he was still a schoolboy of 17, and was quickly recognised as the outstanding poet of *fin-de-siècle* Vienna. His early work, which expresses a clear rejection of art for art's sake, is fundamentally lyrical in character. Though three of his short plays were produced by Otto Brahm at the Deutsches Theater in Berlin (1898–99), the reception was disappointing, and Hofmannsthal distinguished his early "theatre in verse" from his later dramatic work by publishing it in separate collections (*Theater in Versen* and *Kleine Dramen*) and together with his lyrical poems (*Die Gedichte und kleinen Dramen*, 1911).

A change of direction, coinciding with his decision not to pursue an academic career, is signalled in the so-called "Chandos letter" of 1902, which is widely regarded as a seminal document of the modernist "language crisis". The fictional Chandos, who is giving up writing altogether, is quite different from Hofmannsthal, who remained very prolific; what the fiction reflects is rather his dissatisfaction with the predominantly lyrical idiom of his work in the 1890s and his resolve to devote himself to more socially-orientated forms of writing.

His first breakthrough to public success came with Max Reinhardt's production in Berlin of *Elektra*, a torrid post-Freudian reworking of Sophocles's tragedy, with Gertrud Eysoldt in the title role. This was the start of Hofmannsthal's long association with Reinhardt, who produced no fewer than 19 of his plays. It was also through *Elektra* that he came into contact with Richard Strauss, for whom he recast the play as a libretto, so beginning their collaboration on their operas, from *Der Rosenkavalier* (the most successful of all) to *Arabella*, which Hofmannsthal did not live to see performed. Hofmannsthal was a very prolific letter-writer (over 11,000 letters have survived), and his collaboration with Strauss, in which they strove to achieve a perfect match of music and text ("fitting like hand and glove", as Hofmannsthal put it in 1928) is documented in their remarkable published correspondence.

One of the attractions of music for Hofmannsthal was that (like dance) it added a further expressive dimension to verbal language. Hence, too, his interest in visual effects, developed by his association with Reinhardt, but misleadingly traced back by Hofmannsthal to Austrian baroque tradition. He absorbed a huge range of influences, translating and adapting not only from Greek but also from Spanish (Calderón, from 1901 onwards), English (Otway's *Venice Preserved*), and French (intensive study of Molière). But from about 1907 he finally settled into two main styles of dramatic work: high comedy and morality plays. The first major products in these two styles were the Casanova comedy *Christinas Heimreise* (*Christina's Journey Home*) and the morality *Jedermann* (*The Play of Everyman*) respectively, both works given their first performances under Reinhardt in Berlin.

Jedermann, adapted from the English *Everyman*, reflects the dramatist's sense of disintegrating values in a materialist world—his attempt, as he put it in an essay of 1911, "to contrast an intact world order with the infinitely fragmented conditions" of the time. His sense of a disintegrating world order was intensified by the War, during which he became convinced of the cultural mission of Catholic Austria as a repository of traditional values in Europe. After the War, he remained committed to the idea of a cosmopolitan "conservative revolution"; and these cultural concerns inform his later dramatic work.

In 1917 he turned again to comedy. He first completed *Der Schwierige* (*The Difficult Man*), by common consent his masterpiece, and one of the greatest (and certainly the most urbane) of German comedies: it is a comedy about language and moral development set in an idealised aristocratic setting. The final comedy, *Der Unbestechliche*, centres on a role (that of a masterful servant) that was written for Max Pallenberg. It is generally seen as a more lightweight piece; but the action, which is set in pre-war Austria, treats a restoration of the moral order, enacted on the domestic front.

Hofmannsthal's continuing connection with Reinhardt was

one of the reasons why his work did not establish itself in the repertory of the Burgtheater during his lifetime. It was a failure that rankled as he came, increasingly, to regard himself as "primarily a Viennese dramatist" (letter of 2 October 1918 to Leopold von Andrian). Instead, his energies were invested in the Salzburg Festival, of which, together with Reinhardt, he was one of the principal guiding spirits. At the first Festival in August 1920, *Jedermann* was performed in front of the cathedral, and it has remained an annual focal point thereafter. Hofmannsthal followed it up with a further morality play, *Das Salzburger grosse Welttheater* (*The Salzburg Great Theatre of the World*), after Calderón, which was performed in the baroque Kollegienkirche, with a cast headed by Alexander Moissi, the original Jedermann. The social concerns underlying the moralities are also reflected in the tragedy *Der Turm* (The Tower), another play derived from Calderón, which depicts a society dominated by material values and violence—the darker side of the world-view that is merely hinted at in the graceful comedies which, together with his comic libretti, are Hofmannsthal's supreme artistic achievement.

—W. E. Yates

See also *Volume 1* entry on *The Difficult Man*.

HOLBERG, Ludvig. Born in Bergen, Norway (then part of the Kingdom of Denmark and Norway), 3 December 1684. Studied at school and university in Bergen; University of Copenhagen, 1702–04; travelled in Holland and Germany, 1704–06; travelled in England, and studied in Oxford and London, 1706–08; tutor in Germany, 1708–09; at Borch's College, Copenhagen, 1709–14; appointed unpaid associate professor at University of Copenhagen, 1714, but spent the time of the appointment travelling in the Low Countries, Paris, and Rome, 1714–16; professor of metaphysics, 1717, professor of Latin, 1720, member of the University Council, 1720, professor of History and Geography, 1730, and University bursar (*quaestor*), 1737–51, University of Copenhagen; wrote for Montaigu's troupe at the newly organized Danish theatre, the Lille Grønnegade Theatre, Copenhagen, from 1722 until its closure in 1728; first-produced play, *Den politiske Kandestøber* [*The Political Tinker*], staged 1722; ceased writing plays during the reign of Christian VI, 1730–46, who banned all theatrical activity in Denmark and Norway; unofficial adviser and writer for the Kongelige Teater [Royal Theatre], Copenhagen, established shortly after the succession of Frederik V, in 1748. Made a baron, 1747. Died in Copenhagen, 28 January 1754.

Works

Collections

Comoedier (3 vols.). 1723–25.
Den danske Skue-Plads (5 vols.). 1731–54.
Udvalgte Skrifter (21 vols.), edited by Knud Lyne Rahbek. 1804–14.
Samlede Skrifter (18 vols.), edited by Carl S. Petersen. 1913.

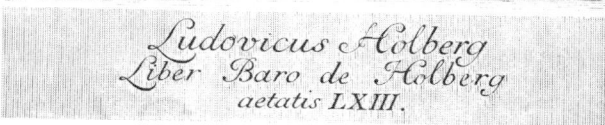

Ludwig Holberg (engraving).

Three Comedies (includes *Captain Bombastes Thunderton; Heinrich and Pernille; Scatterbrains*), translated by H.W.L. Hime. 1912.
Comedies 1 (includes *Jeppe of the Hill; The Political Tinker; Erasmus Montanus*), translated by O.J. Campbell and F. Schenck. 1914.
Four Plays (includes *Masquerade; The Fussy Man; The Masked Ladies; The Weathercock*), translated by H. Alexander. 1946.
Seven One-Act Plays (includes *The Talkative Barber; The Arabian Powder; The Christmas Party; Diderich the Terrible; The Peasant in Pawn; Sganarel's Journey to the Land of the Philosophers; The Changed Bridegroom*), translated by H. Alexander. 1950.
Three Comedies (includes *The Healing Spring; The Transformed Peasant; The Arabian Powder*), translated by R. Spink. 1957.
Samtlige Komedier (3 vols.), edited by Wilhelm Martsrands Tegninger. 1976.

Stage Works

The plays were published in the collections *Comoedier*, 1723–25, and *Den danske Skue-Plads*, 1731–54 (see above).

Den politiske Kandstøber (produced Lille Grønnegade Theatre, Copenhagen, 1722). 1723; translated as *The Blue-Apron Statesman*, 1885; as *The Political Tinker*, in *Comedies*, 1914.
Den Vaegelsindede (produced Lille Grønnegade Theatre, Copenhagen, 1722). 1724; translated as *The Weathercock*, in *Four Plays*, 1946.

Jean de France; *eller*, *Hans Fritz* [Jean de France; or, Hans Fritz] (produced Lille Grønnegade Theatre, Copenhagen, 1722). 1731.

Jeppe på Bierget; *eller*, *Den forvandlede Bonde* (produced Lille Grønnegade Theatre, Copenhagen, 1722). 1723; translated as *Jeppe of the Hill*, in *Comedies*, 1914; as *Barney Brie*, 1980.

Mester Gert Westphaler; *eller*, *Den meget talende Barbeer* (produced Lille Grønnegade Theatre, Copenhagen, 1722). 1723; translated as *Mester Gert Westphaler; or, The Very Loquacious Barber*, in *The Drama 17*, edited by A. Bates, 1903–04; as *The Talkative Barber*, in *Seven One-Act Plays*, 1950.

Nye-Aars Prologus [New Year's Prologue] (produced Lille Grønnegade Theatre, Copenhagen, 1723).

Erasmus Montanus (produced Laederstraede Theatre, Copenhagen, 1748). 1723; translated as *Erasmus Montanus*, 1885, and in *Comedies 1*, 1914; also translated in *The Chief Modern Dramatists*, edited by B. Mathews, 1916.

Den ellefte Juni [The Eleventh of June] (produced Lille Grønnegade Theatre, Copenhagen, 1723). 1724.

Barselstuen [Room of the Child's Birth] (produced Lille Grønnegade Theatre, Copenhagen, 1723). 1731.

Det arabiske Pulver (produced Lille Grønnegade Theatre, Copenhagen, 1724). 1724; translated as *The Arabian Powder*, in *Seven One-Act Plays*, 1950.

Jule-stue (produced Lille Grønnegade Theatre, Copenhagen, 1724). 1724; translated as *The Christmas Party*, in *Seven One-Act Plays*, 1950.

Mascarade (produced Lille Grønnegade Theatre, Copenhagen, 1724). 1724; translated as *Masquerade*, in *Four Plays*, 1946.

Ulysses von Ithacia; *eller*, *En tysk Comoedie* [Ulysses of Ithaca; or, A German Comedy] (produced Lille Grønnegade Theatre, Copenhagen, 1724). 1725.

Diderich Menschenskraeck (produced Lille Grønnegade Theatre, Copenhagen, 1724). 1731; translated as *Captain Bombastes Thunderton*, in *Three Comedies*, 1912; as *Diderich the Terrible*, in *Seven One-Act Plays*, 1950.

Henrik og Pernille (produced Lille Grønnegade Theatre, Copenhagen, 1724). 1731; translated as *Heinrich and Pernille*, in *Three Comedies*, 1912.

Jacob von Tyboe; *eller*, *Den stortalende Soldat* [Jacob von Tyboe; or, The Braggart Soldier]. 1725.

Uden Hoved og Hale [Without Head or Tail]. 1725.

Melampe [Melampe] (produced Lille Grønnegade Theatre, Copenhagen, 1724). 1725.

Kilde-reysen (produced Lille Grønnegade Theatre, Copenhagen, 1724). 1725; translated as *The Healing Spring*, in *Three Comedies*, 1957.

Den Stundesløse (produced Lille Grønnegade Theatre, Copenhagen, 1726). 1731; translated as *Scatterbrains*, in *Three Comedies*, 1912; as *The Fussy Man*, in *Four Plays*, 1946.

Den Pantsatte Bondedreng (produced 1726). 1731; translated as *The Peasant in Pawn*, in *Seven One-Act Plays*, 1950; as *The Transformed Peasant*, in *Three Comedies*, 1957.

Den danske Comoedies Liigbegiaengelse [The Danish Drama's Funeral] (produced 1727). 1746.

Hexerie; *eller*, *Blind Allarm* [Witchcraft; or, False Alarm] (produced Kongelige Teater, Copenhagen, 1750). 1731.

Det lykkelige Skibbrud [The Fortuitous Shipwreck] (produced Kongelige Teater, Copenhagen, 1754). 1731.

De Usynlige (produced 1747). 1731; translated as *The Masked Ladies*, in *Four Plays*, 1946.

Pernilles korte Frøikenstand [Pernille's Short Ladyship] (produced Laederstraede Theatre, 1747). 1731.

Den honnete Ambition [Social Aspiration] (produced Laederstraede Theatre, 1747). 1731.

Don Ranudo de Colibrados; *eller*, *Fattigdom og Hoffaerdighed* [Don Ranudo de Colibrados; or, Poverty and Pride]. 1745.

Sganarels Reyse til de philosophiske Land (produced c.1751–53). 1751; translated as *Sganarel's Journey to the Land of the Philosophers*, in *Seven One-Act Comedies*, 1950.

Plutus (produced Kongelige Teater, Copenhagen, 1751). 1753.

Abracadabra; *eller*, *Huus-Spøgelse* [Abracadabra; or, The House-Ghost] (produced Kongelige Teater, Copenhagen, 1752).

Den forvandlede Brudgrom (produced Kongelige Teater, Copenhagen, 1882). 1753; translated as *The Changed Bridegroom*, in *Seven One-Act Plays*, 1950.

Republiqven; *eller*, *Det gemene Bedste* [The Republic; or, The General Good] (produced 1754). 1754.

Philosophus udi egen Indbilding (produced 1754). 1754.

Fiction

Nicolai Klimii iter subterraneum [Niels Klim] (in Latin). 1741; translated as *A Journey to the World Under-Ground*, 1742; as *Niels Klim's Journey under the Ground*, 1845.

Memoirs and Letters

Memoirs (translation based on various sections of works). 1827.

Memoirer, edited by F.J. Billeskov Jansen. 1943.

Other

Introduction til de formemste Europaeiske Rigers Historier. 1711; revised edition, 1728.

Introduction til Natur- og Folke-Retten [Introduction to Natural Law]. 1715; revised edition, 1734.

Epistola ad virum perillustrem. 1728.

Dannemarks og Norges Beskrivelse. 1729; translated in part as *The History of Norway*, 1817.

Dannemarks Riges Historie [History of the Kingdom of Denmark]. 1732–35.

Synopsis Historiae Universalis. 1733; translated as *An Introduction to Universal History*, 1755.

Bergens Beskrivelse [Description of Bergen]. 1737.

Almindelig Kirkehistorie [General Church History]. 1738.

Heltehistorier [Achievements of Great Men]. 1739.

Jødiske Historie [History of the Jews](2 vols.). 1742.

Moralske Tanker [Moral Thoughts]. 1744; edited by F.J. Billeskov Jansen, 1943.

Heltindehistorier [Comparative History of Famous Women]. 1745.

Epistler(2 vols.). 1748–54; translated in part as *Selected Essays*, edited by P.M. Mitchell, 1955.

Moralske Fabler [Moral Fables]. 1751.

Remarques sur quelques positions qui se trouvent dans l'Esprit des lois (written in French). 1753.

Den radikale Holberg, edited by Thomas Bredsdorff. 1984.

Moral Reflections and Epistles, translated by P.M. Mitchell. 1991.

Translator, *Herodiani historie*. 1746.

*

Bibliographies

H. Ehrencron-Müller, *Bibliografi over Holbergs Skrifter* (3 vols.), Copenhagen, 1933–35.
Holberg-Ordbog, Copenhagen, 1981–

Criticism

Books:
Oscar James Campbell Jr., *The Comedies of Holberg*, Cambridge, Massachusetts, 1914.
G. Brandes, *Ludwig Holberg*, Frankfurt, 1926.
F.J. Billeskov Jansen, *Ludwig Holberg* (in English), New York, 1974.
A. Bamberger, *Ludwig Holberg und das erste dänische Nationaltheater*, Frankfurt, 1983.
K. Jensen, *Moral und Politik: Gesellschaftsbild und Komödienkonzeption in Ludwig Holbergs Frühwerk*, Frankfurt, 1986.

* * *

When, in 1721, the Danish King Frederik IV decided to dismiss his royal company of French actors, a public theatre in Copenhagen was established instead. It opened in 1722. For the first time in the cultural history of Denmark, an institution came into existence in which comical and critical drama was performed in the Danish language. The opportunities offered by this new public theatre were exploited brilliantly by the Danish-Norwegian playwright Ludvig Holberg.

In 1719, the 35-year-old Holberg—who had made himself an academic career and was then a Professor of Philosophy at the University of Copenhagen—was hit by what has been described as a "poetic fit". The fit lasted for a few years, and during these few years Holberg not only made an astonishing literary debut, but also wrote the bulk of his comedies. Holberg's debut-work was a comic epic called *Peder Paars*. It is a parody of the classical epic as well as a topical satire on classes and social conditions in the absolutist state of Denmark. Satire, with its combination of humour and criticism, is a characteristic of almost all Ludvig Holberg's literary works, including his comedies.

Holberg set to work on writing comedies in the summer of 1722. His energy and productivity were immense. By the end of the year, five of Holberg's comedies had been performed in the newly established public theatre in Copenhagen. In the autumn of 1723, when little more than a year had passed, Holberg had written 15 comedies, including all the best-known ones. In 1723 he also published the first of several volumes of plays.

Holberg's comedies were inspired by Roman comedy, particularly the plays of Plautus, by the Italian *commedia dell'-arte* tradition, and by the French classicists, first and foremost Molière. Holberg's comedies are in stark contrast to the mainstream of Danish baroque literature, which saw as its aim the glorification of society and its elite, and which was often very personal. In Holberg's comedies a general moral reason and a general moral criticism are expressed.

Holberg's comedies are almost always portrayals of fallible character types. They explore typically an individual's ridiculous one-sidedness. By depicting the absurd affectation and deviation of the main character, and often by opening the character's eyes to these defects towards the end of the play, Holberg developed an ideal picture of balanced reason: passion and reason are like body and soul, and Holberg's ideal was the golden balance between the two. This view distances

Holberg from the religious orthodoxy of his time, which saw the human body and soul as clouded and darkened, and it also distances him from the affectations of the aristocracy.

Much easier for Holberg to identify with was the growing group of public servants and officials connected to the absolutist state. This was a social group in which Holberg conscientiously fulfilled his role, as a university professor and administrator as well as playwright. When a moral message is expressed explicitly in Holberg's comedies, it is usually voiced by one of the many servants of the absolutist state (by a military officer in *Erasmus Montanus*, for example). The ideology of Holberg's comedies resembles the rationalistic philosophy of the 17th century and can be traced back to Holberg's pioneer philiosophical work *Natur- og Folke-Retten*, in which he declared human reason, rather than religion, the foundation of ethics.

Holberg's dramatic ridicule and laughter are directed against foolishness in all its social and psychological manifestations. In *Jeppe paa Bierget* (*Jeppe of the Hill*), a poor tyrannized peasant, who drinks excessively, is made to believe that he has become a baron. The peasant, Jeppe, immediately responds by behaving even more tyranically than the real tyrants, the baron and the wife. *Jean de France* depicts the self-importance of a young man—Hans, or Jean as he prefers to call himself—who has visited Paris and, on returning to his native Copenhagen, can hardly speak Danish any longer. In *Den Politiske Kandstøber* (*The Political Tinker*), Holberg's first comedy, the target of the ridicule is the arrogance of a craftsman who sees it as his vocation to involve himself in politics.

Thus, the view expressed directly or indirectly in Ludvig Holberg's comedies is that everyone should strive to fulfil his role within the social hierarchy to the best of his abilities, but should *not* strive beyond his role. Holberg was an enlightened humanist and rationalist, not a modern democrat.

In 1727, the public comedy house in Copenhagen was closed down. The audiences did not turn up in great numbers any longer. The great Copenhagen fire in 1728, and the accession to the throne of the pietistic Christian VI in 1730, changed the atmosphere in Denmark. The cultural climate became more sombre. Comedies were not in vogue any longer, and a decree in 1738 banned the performance of them throughout the kingdom of Denmark. Not until 1747, one year after Christian VI had been succeeded by the less pious Frederik V, were comedies performed in Copenhagen again.

Ludvig Holberg did not write any comedies during these two dark decades. In 1751, however, he renewed his interest in the theatre with a new of set plays. Holberg's later comedies, though, do not possess the same irresistible combination of social insight, satirical power, and linguistic energy as did the earlier ones.

—Bjarne Thorup Thomsen

HOLCROFT, Thomas. Born in London, 10 December 1745. Self-educated. Married four times, in 1765, c. 1772, and 1778 (first three wives died), and to Louisa Mercier in 1789; one son and two daughters. Stableboy, Newmarket, Suffolk, 1757–58; shoemaker, apprenticed to his father, London, 1758–64; schoolteacher in Liverpool, 1764; shoemaker in London, 1764–69, and contributor to *Whitehall Evening Post*; tutor in the family of Granville Sharpe, 1769; prompter, Haymarket Theatre, London, 1770, and at a theatre in Dublin, 1770–71; actor in companies touring England and

Scotland, 1771–78: took mainly comic roles; returned to London, 1778; contributor, *Westminster Magazine, Town and Country*, 1778–79, and *English Review*; actor and playwright, Theatre Royal, Drury Lane, 1778–83; Paris correspondent, London *Morning Herald*, 1783; founding editor, *Wit's Magazine*, 1784; member, Society for Promoting Constitutional Information, 1792: indicted for high treason, imprisoned, then discharged, 1794; lived in Hamburg, 1799–1800, and attempted to establish the *European Repository*; lived in Paris, 1801–02; started printing business with his brother-in-law, London, 1803 (business failed); editor *The Theatrical Recorder*, 1805. Died in London, 23 March 1809.

Works

Collections

Sacred Dramas Written in French by la Comtesse de Genlis (translated). 1786.
Plays (2 vols.), edited by Joseph Rosenblum. 1980.

Stage Works

The Crisis; or, Love and Fear (produced Theatre Royal, Drury Lane, London, 1778).
Duplicity (produced Covent Garden Theatre, London, 1781). 1781; as *The Masked Friend* (produced 1796).
The Noble Peasant, music by William Shield (produced Theatre Royal, Haymarket, London, 1784). 1784.
The Follies of a Day; or, The Marriage of Figaro, from a play by Beaumarchais (produced Covent Garden Theatre, London, 1784). 1785.
The Choleric Fathers, music by William Shield (produced Covent Garden Theatre, London, 1785). 1785.
Seduction (produced Theatre Royal, Drury Lane, London, 1787). 1787.
The German Hotel, possibly not by Holcroft (produced Covent Garden Theatre, London, 1790). 1790.
The School for Arrogance, from a play by Destouches (produced Covent Garden Theatre, London, 1791). 1791.
The Road to Ruin (produced Covent Garden Theatre, London, 1792). 1792.
Love's Frailties (produced Covent Garden Theatre, London, 1794). 1794.
The Rival Queens; or, Drury Lane and Covent Garden (produced Covent Garden Theatre, London, 1794).
The Deserted Daughter, from a work by Diderot (produced Covent Garden Theatre, London, 1795). 1795.
The Man of Ten Thousand (produced Theatre Royal, Drury Lane, London, 1796). 1796.
The Force of Ridicule (produced Theatre Royal, Drury Lane, London, 1796).
Knave or Not?, from plays by Goldoni (produced Theatre Royal, Drury Lane, London, 1798). 1798.
He's Much to Blame (produced Covent Garden Theatre, London, 1798). 1798.
The Inquisitor (produced Theatre Royal, Haymarket, London, 1798). 1798.
The Old Clothesman, music by Thomas Attwood (produced Covent Garden Theatre, London, 1799). Songs published 1799(?).
Deaf and Dumb; or, The Orphan Protected, from a play by J.N. de Bouilly (produced Theatre Royal, Drury Lane, London, 1801). 1801.
The Escapes; or, The Water-Carrier, music by Thomas Attwood, songs by T.J. Dibdin, from an opera by J.N.

Nouilly, music by Cherubini (produced Covent Garden Theatre, London, 1801).
A Tale of Mystery, from a play by Pixérécourt (produced Covent Garden Theatre, London, 1802). 1802.
Hear Both Sides (produced Theatre Royal, Drury Lane, London, 1803). 1803.
The Lady of the Rock (produced Theatre Royal, Drury Lane, London, 1805). 1805.
The Vindictive Man (produced Theatre Royal, Drury Lane, London, 1806). 1806.

Fiction

Alwyn; or, The Gentleman Comedian. 1780.
The Family Picture; or, Domestic Dialogues on Amiable Subjects. 1783.
An Amorous Tale of the Chaste Loves of Peter the Long and His Most Honoured Friend Dame Blanche Bazu. 1786.
Anna St. Ives. 1792.
The Adventures of Hugh Trevor. 1794.
Memoirs of Bryan Perdue. 1805.

Verse

Elegies. 1777.
Human Happiness; or, The Sceptic. 1783.
Tales in Verse, Critical, Satirical, Humorous. 1806.

Memoirs and Letters

Memoirs, completed by William Hazlitt (3 vols.). 1816; as *The Life of Holcroft* (2 vols.), edited by Elbridge Colby, 1925.

Other

A Plain and Succinct Narrative of the Late [Gordon] *Riots*. 1780.
The Trial of the Hon. George Gordon. 1781.
Memoirs of Baron de Toth, Containing the State of the Turkish Empire and the Crimea, possibly not by Holcroft (2 vols.). 1785.
The Secret History of the Court of Berlin, possibly not by Holcroft (2 vols.). 1789.
A Narrative of Facts Relating to a Prosecution for High Treason (2 vols.). 1795.
A Letter to William Windham on the Intemperance and Danger of His Public Conduct. 1795.
Travels from Hamburg Through Westphalia, Holland, and the Netherlands (2 vols.). 1804.

Editor, *Letter on Egypt*, by Mr. Savary (2 vols.). 1786.
Editor, and translator, *Posthumous Works of Frederick, King of Prussia* (13 vols.). 1789.
Editor, *The Theatrical-Recorder* (2 vols.). 1805–06.

Translator, *Philosophical Essays with Observations on the Laws and Customs of Several Eastern Nations*, by Foucher d'Osbornville. 1784.
Translator, *Tales of the Castle*, by la Comtesse de Genlis (5 vols.). 1785.
Translator, *Caroline of Lichtfield*, by Baroness de Montolieu (2 vols.). 1786.
Translator, *Historical and Critical Memoirs of the Life and Writings of Voltaire*, by Chaudon. 1786.
Translator, *The Present State of the Empire of Morocco*, by Chenier (2 vols.). 1788.

Translator, *The Life of Baron Frederick Trenck* (3 vols.). 1788.

Translator, *Essays on Physiognomy*, by J.C. Lavater (3 vols.). 1789.

Translator, *Travels Through Germany, Switzerland, and Italy*, by Frederick Leopold, Count Stolberg (2 vols.). 1796–97.

Translator, *Herman and Dorothea*, by Goethe. 1801.

*

Bibliographies

Elbridge Colby, "A Bibliography of Thomas Holcroft", in *Bulletin of the New York Public Library*, 26, 1922.

Criticism

Articles:
Elbridge Colby, "Thomas Holcroft, Translator of Plays", in *Philological Quarterly*, 3, 1924.
Virgil R. Stallbaumer, "Thomas Holcroft: A Satirist in the Stream of Sentimentalism", in *English Literary History*, 3, 1936.

*   *   *

Holcroft's contribution to English drama has sometimes been dismissed as negligible, yet he provided his contemporaries with one of the best comedies of the period, *The Road to Ruin*, along with the first English version of Beaumarchais's *The Marriage of Figaro*, and the first English melodrama, *A Tale of Mystery*. In all his works, whether originals or translations and adaptations, there is a strong moral and social concern and a sense that mankind is ever capable of improvement.

Holcroft was quite open about his intentions. In his preface to *Duplicity* he wrote that he "would rather have the merit of driving one man from the gaming-table than of making a whole theatre merry". Just as *Duplicity* is a warning about the dangers of gaming (but with a happy ending), so *The Road to Ruin* is concerned with the improvidence of Harry Dornton, who has ruined himself and is about to bring his father's bank to disaster. Out of remorse he is about to marry an elderly woman with a fortune, rather than the woman he loves, but is saved from such an eventuality at the last minute—once again Holcroft provides an optimistic ending after the moral has been conveyed. *The School for Arrogance* exposes the weakness of pride, whether founded on birth or wealth, a theme which recurs in *Love's Frailties*, a play which offended its original audiences when one of the characters claimed that the profession of gentleman was one of the most worthless and useless of occupations. Holcroft's libertarian principles, as embodied in his plays and other writings, are given full expression in his prologue to *The Road to Ruin*:

. . . Frenchman, and Polishman, and every man is our
    brother:
And that all men, ay, even poor negro men, have a
    right to be free; one as well as another!
Freedom at length, said he, like a torrent is spreading
    and swelling,
To sweep away pride and reach the most miserable
    dwelling:
To ease, happiness, art, science, wit, and genius to give
    birth;
    Ay, to fertilize a world, and renovate all earth!

Such preoccupations demonstrate why Holcroft should have been attracted to Beaumarchais's revolutionary comedy. *The Follies of a Day* proved a popular piece in theatres throughout England and even formed the basis of Henry Bishop's adaptation of Mozart's opera for Covent Garden in 1818. No doubt Holcroft was equally attracted to the revolutionary characteristics of early French melodrama, with its emphasis on wicked nobility and the ultimate triumph of moral justice. *Deaf and Dumb*, based on a French play by M. Bouilly, concerns the plight of a deaf and dumb orphan, Julio, deprived of his rightful inheritance by his wicked uncle, Darlemont. Ultimately, the former is restored to his usurped inheritance. Darlemont provided an excellent "heavy" role, whilst Julio, as played by Miss De Camp at Drury Lane, allowed for a virtuoso performance in which a credible impact had to be made through gesture without benefit of speech. *A Tale of Mystery* provided more virtuoso roles in the form of the villainous Romaldi, who finally shows penitence and is forgiven, and Francisco, his brother, whose dumbness enabled Charles Farley to give a performance in which speech was totally absent. Farley was also responsible for the staging of this piece, which relied heavily on music for dramatic and atmospheric effect. In both plays, virtue is rewarded and vice repentent. In many ways *A Tale of Mystery* provided stereotypes for much of the melodrama that was to follow throughout the 19th century, together with the moral and social thrust that would often characterise it.

It has been suggested that Holcroft recognised in Pixérécourt's plays something that he, Morton, and other dramatists of the period had been working towards. Hence, the introduction of Pixérécourt's melodrama was a culmination rather than an innovation, an embodiment of a trend already in existence. Moreover, a number of Gothic plays, such as "Monk" Lewis's *The Castle Spectre*, had already been performed in England; *A Tale of Mystery* was a popular and logical addition to the contemporary dramatic repertoire.

Much of Holcroft's work was derivative, even though his influence on the drama was so often unique and original. *Duplicity* was partially based on a German play by Brandes and also contained echoes of Moore's *The Gamester*. *The School for Arrogance* was, in part, influenced by *Le Glorieux* of Destouches, whilst *Seduction* owed something to *Les Liaisons Dangereuses*. Nevertheless, Holcroft provided the English theatre with much that was new and much that consistently utilised the moral and didactic possibilities of the drama. It was Holcroft who complained of Sheridan's *The School for Scandal* that it never transcended (in its social satire) mere entertainment. Holcroft, on the other hand, believed the stage could be "a very efficient school of morality".

Holcroft also wrote good roles for actors, not only in the melodramas discussed above, but also in plays like *The Road to Ruin*: Harry Dornton and his father, Old Dornton, are never mere types, but drawn with a touch of truth, whilst the play also contains several strong character parts, especially that of Goldfinch, originally played by the comedian Lewis. Goldfinch is a mercurial, high-spirited figure, much given to catch-phrases such as "that's your sort". He is the forerunner of many similar characters in the 19th century, including Jingle in *The Pickwick Papers*. The use of a catch-phrase by which to identify a character was novel when Holcroft introduced it—it was to become a characteristic of many subsequent farces and comedies.

Holcroft may not have been one of the greatest of English dramatists; nevertheless, he was of transitional importance in introducing new forms and new plays to the English stage. He also possessed a serious vision of the social and moral role the theatre could fulfil within society, although such a vision was not altogether realised in the years that immediately followed.

—Jim Davis

————————

HONG SHENG. See *Volume 1* entry on *The Palace of Eternal Youth*.

————————

HOROVITZ, Israel (Arthur). Born in Wakefield, Massachusetts, USA, 31 March 1939. Educated at the Royal Academy of Dramatic Art, London, 1961–63; City College, New York, MA in English 1972. Married 1) Elaine Abber in 1959 (marriage annulled 1960); 2) Doris Keefe in 1961 (divorced 1972), one daughter and two sons; 3) Gillian Adams in 1981, twin daughter and son. Stage manager, Boston and New York, 1961–65; playwright-in-residence, Royal Shakespeare Company, London, 1965; Instructor in Playwriting, New York University, 1967–69; professor of English, City College, 1968–73; columnist, *Magazine Littéraire*, Paris, 1971–77; Fanny Hurst Professor of Theatre, Brandeis University, Waltham, Massachusetts, 1973–75; founder, New York Playwrights Lab, 1977; founder, 1980, and producer and artistic director, Gloucester Stage Company, Massachusetts. Recipient: Obie Award, 1968, 1969; Vernon Rice Award, 1969; Drama Desk Award, 1969; Cannes Film Festival Jury Prize, 1971; National Endowment for the Arts fellowship, 1974, 1977; American Academy Award, 1975; Emmy Award, 1975; Christopher Award, 1976; French Critics Prize, 1977; Los Angeles Drama Critics Circle Award, 1980; Goldie Award, 1985; Eliot Norton Prize, 1986.

Work

Collections

First Season: Line; The Indian Wants the Bronx; It's Called the Sugar Plum; Rats. 1968.
The Wakefield Plays (includes The Wakefield Plays trilogy: *Alfred the Great, Our Father's Failing,* and *Alfred Dies;* and *Hopscotch; Stage Directions; Spared*). 1979.

Stage Works

The Comeback (produced Emerson College, Boston, 1958).
The Death of Bernard the Believer (produced Café Cabaret Theatre, South Orange, New Jersey, 1960).
This Play is About Me (produced Café Cabaret Theatre, South Orange, New Jersey, 1961).
The Hanging of Emanuel (produced Café Cabaret Theatre, South Orange, New Jersey, 1962).
Hop, Skip, and Jump (produced Café Cabaret Theatre, South Orange, New Jersey, 1963).
The Killer Dove (produced Theatre on the Green, West Orange, New Jersey, 1963).

The Simon Street Harvest (produced Café Cabaret Theatre, South Orange, New Jersey, 1964).
The Indian Wants the Bronx (produced Waterford, Connecticut, 1966; Astor Place Theatre, New York, 1968). In *First Season*, 1968.
Line (produced La Mama Experimental Theatre, New York, 1967; revised version produced Theatre de Lys, New York, 1971). In *First Season*, 1968.
It's Called the Sugar Plum (produced Waterford, Connecticut, 1967). In *First Season*, 1968.
Acrobats (produced New York, 1968). 1971.
Rats (produced New York, 1968). Included in *First Season*, 1968.
Morning (in *Chiaroscuro*, produced Festival of Two Worlds, Spoleto, Italy, 1968; in *Morning, Noon, and Night*, produced Henry Miller's Theatre, New York, 1968). Published in *Morning, Noon and Night*,
The Honest to God Schnozzola (produced Provincetown, Massachusetts, 1968). 1971.
Leader (produced Gramercy Theatre, New York, 1969). With *Play for Trees*, 1970.
Shooting Gallery (produced Players' Art Theatre Workshop, New York, 1971). With *Play for Germs*, 1973.
Dr. Hero (as *Hero*, produced Shakespeare Festival Public Theatre, New York, 1971; revised version, as *Dr. Hero*, produced Great Neck, New York, 1972). 1973.
Alfred the Great (produced Théâtre du Centre Culturel Américain, Paris, and Great Neck, New York, 1972). 1974.
Our Father's Failing (produced Eugene O'Neill Memorial Theatre, Waterford, Connecticut, 1973). In *The Wakefield Plays*, 1979.
Hopscotch (produced Paris and Manhattan Theatre Club, New York, 1974). With *The 75th*, 1977.
Spared (produced Paris and Manhattan Theatre Club, New York, 1974). With *Stage Directions*, 1977.
Turnstile (produced Dartmouth College, Hanover, New Hampshire, 1974).
The First, The Last, and the Middle: A Comedy Triptych (produced Cubiculo Theatre, New York, 1974).
The Primary English Class (produced Waterford, Connecticut, 1975). 1976.
Uncle Snake: An Independence Day Pageant (produced New York, 1975). 1976.
Stage Directions (produced Actors' Studio, New York, 1976). With *Spared*, 1977.
The Reason We Eat (produced Hartman Theatre, Stamford, Connecticut, 1976).
Alfred Dies (produced New York, 1976).
The 75th (produced as part of *The Quannapowitt Quartet*, Yale University, New Haven, Connecticut, 1976). With *Hopscotch*, 1977.
The Lounge Player (produced Actors' Studio, New York, 1977).
Man with Bags, from a play by Eugène Ionesco, translated by Marie-France Ionesco (produced Towson State University, Baltimore, Maryland, 1977). 1977.
The Former One-on-One Basketball Champion (produced Actors' Studio, New York, 1977). With *The Great Labor Day Classic*, 1982.
Cappella, with David Boorstin, from Horovitz's novel (produced Off-Centre Theatre, New York, 1978).
The Widow's Blind Date (produced Actors' Studio, New York, 1978). 1981.
Mackerel (produced Hartford Stage, Hartford, Connecticut, 1978; revised version produced Folger Theatre Group, Washington, DC, 1978). 1979.

A Christmas Carol: Scrooge and Marley, from of the story by Dickens (produced Center Stage, Baltimore, Maryland, 1978).   1979.

The Good Parts (produced Actors' Theatre, Louisville, Kentucky, 1979).   1983.

The Great Labor Day Classic (in *Holidays*, produced Actors' Theatre, Louisville, Kentucky, 1979; produced separately, New York, 1984).   With *The Former One-on-One Basketball Champion*, 1982.

Sunday Runners in the Rain (produced New York, 1980).

Park Your Car in Harvard Yard (produced New York, 1980).

Henry Lumper (produced Gloucester, Massachusetts, 1985).

Today, I am a Fountain Pen, from stories by Morley Torgov (produced New York, 1986).

A Rosen by Any Other Name, from a novel by Morley Torgov (produced New York, 1986).

The Chopin Playoffs, adaptation of stories by Morley Torgov (produced New York, 1986).

North Shore Fish (produced Gloucester, Massachusetts, 1986).

Year of the Duck (produced Portland, Maine, 1986).   1987.

Screenplays

Machine Gun McCain (English adaptation), 1970; *The Strawberry Statement*, 1970; *Believe in Me (Speed is of the Essence)*, 1970; *Alfredo*, 1970; *The Sad-Eyed Girls in the Park*, 1971; *Camerian Climbing*, 1971; *Acrobats*, 1972; *Fast Eddie*, 1980; *Fell*, 1982; *Berta*, 1982; *Author! Author!*, 1982–83; *Light Years*, 1985; *A Man in Love*, with Diane Kurys, 1988.

Television Plays

Play for Trees, 1969 (published with *Leader*, 1970); *VD Blues*, with others, 1972 (part published as *Play for Germs*, with *Shooting Gallery*, 1973); *Start to Finish*, 1975; *The Making and Breaking of Splinters Braun*, 1976; *Bartleby the Scrivener*, from the story by Melville, 1978; *A Day with Conrad Green*, from a story by Ring Lardner, 1978; *The Deer Park*, from the novel by Norman Mailer, 1979.

Fiction

Capella.   1973.
Nobody Loves Me.   1975.

*

Bibliographies

Philip C. Kolin (ed.), *American Playwrights Since 1945: A Guide to Scholarship, Criticism, and Performance*, New York, 1989.

Criticism

Articles:
Liliane Kerjan, "Un jeune premier du théâtre américain: Israel Horovitz", in *Études anglaises*, 28, 1975.

*   *   *

A prolific and talented contemporary American dramatist, Israel Horovitz has written over 50 plays in the last 30 years.

His plays have been produced on and, more regularly, off-Broadway (*Line* is, in fact, one of off-Broadway's longest-running plays), and he has also been successfully produced outside the USA. In addition, his plays have been translated and produced in 20 languages.

It is difficult to fit Horovitz's work into the operational categories of modern drama. He is too flamboyant a playwright to be considered a realist, but he is too realistic to be labelled an experimentalist. He is thoroughly eclectic. His work ranges in mood and in content from melodrama (*The Indian Wants the Bronx, Henry Lumper*) to farce (*The Primary English Class*). His subjects include studies of capitalist competition (*Mackerel, Line*), urban alienation and violence (*Rats, The Indian Wants the Bronx*), marital discord (*Acrobats, The Alfred Trilogy* including *Alfred the Great, Our Father's Failing*, and *Alfred Dies*), racism (*Morning*), Jewish domestic life (*Growing Up Jewish*), and the problems of the Atlantic fishery (*North Shore Fish, Henry Lumper*). What unifies such dramatic diversity is Horovitz's intense theatricality, his cunning exploitation of the resources of the theatre.

Horovitz's work from 1961 to about 1975 has, as its hallmark, a concentrated dramatic symbolism. Typical of Horovitz's dramatic style in this early phase are such plays as *Acrobats, Line*, and *Shooting Gallery*. Each is a short one-acter. In *Acrobats*, the entire action consists of a husband and wife angrily discussing their marital breakdown while they perform delicate acrobatic feats, thus symbolically suggesting the complexities and ironies of human interdependence. In *Line*, the stage is empty except for a "*fat, white strip of adhesive tape that is fixed to the stage floor*". Five characters appear and, using subterfuge, sex, and violence, jockey for position at the front of this line, even though neither standing in the line nor being first on the line has any apparent purpose. In so doing, they act out the dysfunctions of a highly competitive society in which meaningful goals have been subordinated to an amorphous notion of "winning".

In *Shooting Gallery*, a young man, accompanied by his wife, tries to shoot a mechanical bear to win a goldfish. He has been at this game so long his wife has forgotten the names of their children. Despite his sacrifices of time, money, and peace of mind, he runs out of ammunition before he can accumulate enough points to win the goldfish. Like *Line*, *Shooting Gallery* suggests, through its symbolic action, the vacuity and silliness of the goals to which our competitive society is addicted.

By the mid-1970's, Horovitz's work had changed direction. Instead of short symbolic statements, his plays became more expansive and inclusive. They have more characters, they are longer, and/or they are linked together as cycles using umbrella titles to underline their thematic connection. What emerges in *The Wakefield Plays* (made up of *The Alfred Trilogy* and "The Quannapowitt Quartet": *Hopscotch, The 75th, Stage Directions*, and *Spared*), *Growing Up Jewish* (consisting of *Today I Am a Fountain Pen, A Rosen by Any Other Name*, and *The Chopin Playoffs*) and the Gloucester cycle (including *North Shore Fish, Henry Lumper, The Widow's Blind Date, Park Your Car in Harvard Yard*) is narrative in the form of drama.

Taken together, *The Wakefield Plays*, like the other of Horovitz's cycles, tell a story. The three Alfred plays at the center of this cycle dramatize the often incestuous and violent domestic inter-relationships that, in Horovitz's view, characterize old New England towns. When Alfred returns to Wakefield, he is forced to confront the confused and overlapping family ties that show his wife to be his sister and his former friends, his near relatives. The sequence is organized around the principle of progressive revelation: each of the three plays uncovers a little more of the complex puzzle, until the whole terrifying truth is known. The two short plays which Horovitz suggests should be produced at the beginning (*Hopscotch* and *The 75th*) and the two which he suggests for the end (*Stage Directions* and *Spared*) are emblematic anticipations and recapitulations of the thematic concerns of the central three plays.

Whether they are concentrated dramatic symbols or expansive cycles, three themes run through Horovitz's plays: first, the fragility of communication; second, the destructiveness of competition; and third, the inter-relatedness of humanity. When communication breaks down, as it invariably does in his plays, the results can be comic. Such is the case in *The Primary English Class*, in which all the characters share the same condition of radical loneliness, yet because only the teacher speaks English, no dialogue is possible. A series of farcical misunderstandings ensue, as when the Polish-speaking janitor is mistaken for a rapist. But beneath the superficial hilarity of this play is the sad recognition of failed connections. Most often in Horovitz's plays, when communication breaks down, the results are tragic and violent. In *The Indian Wants the Bronx*, for example, Joey and Murph are angry and unintelligent losers, unable to fashion from their adolescent posturings and macho rituals a language expressive of their frustrations and aspirations. So when circumstances offer them a helplessness more profound than their own in the form of a lost Indian who cannot speak English, they turn to the only form of communication that they command, violence.

Through the dramatic permutations of his second theme, in plays as diverse as *Mackerel* and *Henry Lumper*, Horovitz isolates one of the root causes of the violence and discontent that afflicts so many of his characters. In Horovitz's plays, competition is the most pervasive means for preventing and/or disrupting human relationships. Competition exacerbates the difficulties the characters already face because their lines of communication are so tenuous.

Horovitz dramatizes the third theme, the inter-relationship of humanity, through the topic of incest, common in his plays. Because of social taboos, as well as the difficulties of communication and the ideology of competition, these incestuous relationships are denied, concealed, ignored, or forgotten, so that the offspring of such unions often have no idea to whom they are related. The dramatic logic of Horvitz's plays works to reveal these connections, and by so doing, Horovitz gives specific, literal, and often violent meaning to that cozy metaphor, the human family.

—Bernice Schrank

See also *Volume 1* entry on *The Indian Wants the Bronx*.

HORVÁTH, Ödön (Josef) von. Born in Fiume, then part of the Austro-Hungarian Empire (now in Croatia), 9 December 1901. Educated at Episcopal School, Budapest, 1909–13; Wilhelmsgymnasium and Realschule, Munich, 1913–16; school in Pressburg, 1916; Realgymnasium, Vienna, 1916–19; University of Munich, 1919–22. Married Maria Elsner in 1933 (divorced 1934). Contributor to various newspapers and journals; settled in Berlin, 1926; freelance writer, with contract from a publisher, from 1929; increasingly attacked by the Nazis, from 1931; writer of dialogue for the German film industry, 1934; left Germany for final time, 1934, becoming Hungarian citizen; moved to Austria until the German annexation, then emigrated to Zurich, Switzerland. Recipient: Kleist Prize, 1931. Killed by a falling branch in Paris, 7 June 1938.

Works

Collections

Stücke, edited by Traugott Krischke. 1961.
Gesammelte Werke, edited by Traugott Krischke, Walter Huder, and Dieter Hildebrandt (4 vols.). 1970; 8 vols., 1972; 14 vols., 1988.
Kasimir and Karoline; Hope and Charity; Figaro Gets a Divorce; Judgement Day. 1986.
Gesammelte Werke (4 vols.), edited by Traugott Krischke. 1988.

Stage Works

Das Buch der Tanze (libretto; produced Steinicke-Saal, Munich, 1922). 1922.
Revolte auf Cote 3018 (produced Kammerspiele, Hamburg, 1927). 1927; as *Die Bergbahn* (produced Theater am Bülowplatz, Berlin, 1929), 1928.
Zur schönen Aussicht (produced Schauspielhaus, Graz, 1969). 1927.
Sladek; oder, Die schwarze Armee (produced Kammerspiele, Munich, 1972). 1928; revised version, as *Sladek, der schwarze Reichswehrmann* (produced Lessingtheater, Berlin 1929), 1929.
Rund um den Kongress (produced Theater im Belvedere, Vienna 1959). 1929.
Italienische Nacht (produced Theater am Schiffbauerdamm, Berlin, 1931). 1930.
Geschichten aus dem Wiener Wald (produced Deutsches Theater, Berlin, 1931). 1931; translated as *Tales from the Vienna Woods*, 1977.
Kasimir und Karoline (produced Schauspielhaus, Leipzig, 1932). In *Stücke*, 1961; translated as *Kasimir and Karoline*, in *Kasimir and Karoline . . .* (collection), 1986.
Glaube, Liebe, Hoffnung (produced as *Liebe, Pflicht und Hoffnung*, Theater für 49 am Schottentor, Vienna, 1936). 1932; translated as *Faith, Hope and Charity*, in *Kasimir and Karoline. . . .* (collection), 1986.
Die Unbekannte aus der Seine (produced Studio in der Kolingasse, Vienna, 1949). 1933.
Hin und Her (produced Schauspielhaus, Zurich, 1934). In *Gesammelte Werke*, 1970.
Mit dem Kopf durch die Wand (produced Scala Theater, Vienna, 1935). 1935.
Figaro lässt sich scheiden (produced Deutsches Theater, Prague, 1937). 1959; translated as *Figaro Gets a Divorce*, in *Kasimir and Karoline . . .* (collection), 1986.
Himmelwärts (produced in revised version, Komödie Theater, Vienna, 1937; original version produced Kleines Theater im Konzerthaus, Vienna, 1953). In *Gesammelte Werke*, 1970.
Der jüngste Tag (produced Deutsches Theater, Moravská, Ostrava, Czechoslovakia, 1937). 1955; translated as *Judgement*, in *Kasimir and Karoline . . .* (collection), 1986.
Ein Dorf ohne Männer, from a novel by Koloman van Mikszáth (produced Neues Deutsches Theater, Prague, 1937). In *Gesammelte Werke*, 1970.

Don Juan kommt aus dem Krieg (produced as *Don Juan kommt zurück*, Theater der Courage, Vienna, 1952). In *Stücke*, 1961; translated as *Don Juan Comes Back from the War*, 1978.
Pompeji (produced Tribüne, Vienna, 1959). In *Stücke*, 1961.

Fiction

Der ewige Spiesser. 1930.
Ein Kind unserer Zeit; Jugend ohne Gott. 2 vols., 1938; as *Zeitalter der Fische*, 1953; translated as *A Child of Our Time*, 1938; as *The Age of the Fish*, 1939.

*

Criticism

Books:
M. Kesting, *Ödön von Horváth: Leben und Werk aus ungarischer Sicht*, Freiburg, 1969.
R. Hummel, *Die Volksstücke Horváths*, Baden-Baden, 1970.
Traugott Krischke (ed.), *Materialien zu Horváth*, Frankfurt, 1970.
Dieter Hildebrandt and Traugott Krischke, *Über Ödön von Horváth*, Frankfurt, 1972.
H. Kuzenberger, *Horváths Volksstücke: Beschreibung eines poetischen Verfahrens*, Munich, 1974.
Kurt Bartsch (ed.), *Horváth-Diskussion*, Kronberg, 1976.
Symposium on Ödön von Horváth (1901–1938), London, 1976.
W. Nolting, *Der totale Jargon: Die dramatischen Beispiele Ödön von Horváths*, Munich, 1976.
Traugott Krischke, *Ödön von Horváth: Kind seiner Zeit*, Munich, 1980.
Dieter Hildebrandt, *Ödön von Horváth in Selbstzeugnissen und Bilddokumenten*, Reinbek, 1975; revised edition, 1987.
Austrian Institute, *Symposium on Horváth*, 1977.
Krishna Winston, *Horváth Studies: Close Readings of Six Plays (1926–1931)*, Bern, 1977.
Jean G, François, *Histoire et fiction dans le théâtre d'Ödön von Horváth*, Grenoble, 1978.
Teodoro Scamardi, *Ödön von Horváth: Teatro popolare nella Republica di Weimar*, Bari, 1980.
Traugott Krischke (ed.), *Ödön von Horváth*, Frankfurt, 1981.
Belinda H. Carstens, *Prostitution in the Work of Ödön von Horváth*, Sttutgart, 1982.
M. Hell, *Kitsch als Element der Dramaturgie Ödön von Horváths*, Bern, 1983.
S. Kienzle, *Ödön von Horváth* (second edition), Berlin, 1984.
Christopher B. Balme, *The Reformation of Comedy: Genre Critique in the Comedies of Ödön von Horváth*, Dunedin, Australia, 1985.
H. Gamper, *Horváths komplexe Textur: Dargestellt an frühen Stücken*, Zurich, 1987.
Traugott Krischke, *Horváth-Chronik: Daten zu Leben und Werk*, Frankfurt, 1988.
Traugott Krischke (ed.), *Horváths Stücke* (essay collection), Frankfurt, 1988.
Angelika D. Mildenberger, *Motivkreise in Ödön von Horváths dramatischen Werk*, Zurich, 1988.

Articles:
Ian C. Loram, "Ödön von Horváth: An Appraisal", in *Monatshefte*, 59, 1967.
Margaret M. Stoljar, "The Drama as Metaphor: Meaning and Structure in Ödön von Horváth's *Volkstücke*", in *AUMLA*, 48, 1977.
Stuart Parkes, "The Dramatic Art of Ödön von Horváth", in *New German Studies*, 5, 1977.
Dirk Bruns, "Horváth's Renewal of the Folk Play and the Decline of the Weimar Republic", in *New German Critique*, 18, 1979.
Violet B. Ketels, "The World of Ödön von Horváth", in *Performing Arts Journal*, vol.3 no.3, 1979.
David Midgley, "Ödön von Horváth: The Strategies of Audience Enticement", in *Oxford German Studies*, 14, 1983.
James L. Rosenberg, "*NTQ* Checklist No.2: Ödön von Horváth", in *New Theatre Quarterly*, 8, 1986.

Serials:

Horváth Blätter, 1983—

*   *   *

Ödön von Horváth was one of the most significant playwrights in the German language from the period between the two world wars. Coming from an old Austro-Hungarian family, he was confronted during a period spent in Berlin in the later Weimar Republic with the Great Depression and the rise of National Socialism, historical events which provided the background to many of his works.

A prolific writer, he wrote three novels and a number of short stories as well as, more famously, his plays. Of his works for the theatre, it is the "folk plays" that are most impressive, combining elements from the older Austrian tradition, epitomised by Nestroy and Anzengruber, with contemporary subject-matter, and demonstrating a particular fascination with the language of the characters presented.

Horváth's primary interest lies with these characters and their interaction, rather than with dramatic plots, and in general his plays are episodic rather than conventionally dramatic. They are generally economical in construction, with few events and characters, and his plots revolve around frequently sordid events in the milieu of the lower-middle classes.

Thus, in *Glaube Liebe Hoffnung* (*Faith, Hope and Charity*), a girl whose life is ruined because she lacks a trading permit eventually commits suicide, out of hunger, while her ex-lover, a policeman, simply complains of his bad luck. In *Geschichten aus dem Wiener Wald* (*Tales from the Vienna Woods*), a young girl breaks off her respectable engagement to live with a ne'er-do-well, by whom she has a child which is then killed by her lover's grandmother. At the end of the play the girl returns to her fiancé, who has finally accepted the child, only to discover that it is now dead.

In *Kasimir und Karoline* (*Kasimir and Karoline*), a couple break off their engagement at the Munich Octoberfest because Kasimir has become unemployed and his fiancée cannot stand his bitterness and jealousy. By the end of the play, Karoline has narrowly avoided virtual prostitution, and both she and Kasimir have entered into new fragile relationships which promise, at most, material comfort. In *Italienische Nacht* (Italian Night), some National Socialists wish to disrupt the Republicans' Italian celebrations. They are stopped only after the courageous intervention of the otherwise totally downtrodden wife of the town mayor and the arrival of a group of left-wing activists who have just been expelled from the party for indiscipline.

Although strongly individualised, Horváth's characters have much in common: his young men, behind their expressions of moral rectitude, loyalty, and so forth, are frequently dishonest, womanising, brutally ambitious, and apparently not even aware of their own callousness; his young women, who most often, are the "victims", are not sentimentalised (although Horváth shows his sympathy for them), but simply lack the strength to survive physically, emotionally, or morally under the circumstances of inhumanity produced by economic tensions.

Even more than earlier writers, Horváth avoided idealising these people (who, after all, represented the social group that voted Hitler into power) and aimed, instead, to show their true nature, to unmask their consciousness. A number of theatrical devices helps audiences maintain a critical distance similar to that intended by Brecht. Thus Horváth insisted on a stylised stage set, avoiding exact replication of milieu. He frequently made ironic use of music to underline false pathos, to highlight ironic contrasts, or to create false expectations. His "romantic" titles and settings (Viennese woods, the Munich Octoberfest) stand in marked contrast to the sordid and petty events presented on stage.

Horváth's most thorough-going unmasking devices are, however, linguistic. As one device to indicate the pretensions of his characters, he insisted that his actors use standard German while at the same time suggesting that the natural language of these characters would be dialect. This already "false" language is additionally shot through with "*Bildungsjargon*", an unnatural, acquired language of clichés, proverbs, slogans, and second-hand wisdom, producing a mixture of linguistic levels which is amusing, but at the same time revealing. At moments of decision or emotional intensity, the incongruity or inappropriateness of this unnatural language is particularly evident. The characters appear unable to say what they really think, and communication is lost. An essential part of this linguistic unmasking is the dramatic pause, long enough to interrupt the flow of the dialogue and maintain the audience's distance.

After leaving Berlin, Horváth abandoned these generally realistic folk plays for a series of dramas and comedies of uneven quality, frequently making satirical use of literary or stereotypical figures such as Don Juan, in *Don Juan kommt aus dem Krieg*, (*Don Juan Comes Back from the War*), and Figaro, in *Figaro lässt sich scheiden* (*Figaro Gets a Divorce*). These new works raise, with less specifically drawn characters, more general themes, such as guilt, exile, revolution, and love. They also employ a wider range of non-realistic theatrical devices, such as ghosts, in *Der jüngste Tag* (*The Last Judgement*), or scenes set in Heaven and Hell, in *Himmelwärts* (*Heavenwards*). They continue, however, to display Horváth's critical concern with language.

After his death in 1938, Horváth's plays were virtually ignored. In the later 1960's, however, interest in him and in Marieluise Fleisser was revived, as a younger generation of playwrights, including Martin Sperr and Franz Xaver Kroetz, took up the realistic critical folk play again, while Peter Handke, with a very different style, further pursued Horváth's investigations into the deforming possibilities of language. Although this revival has now receded, Horváth has remained significant as a politically unaligned chronicler of the Weimar scene and as an observer and critic of the eternal human disposition towards self-deception through language. Together, these factors constitute the main reasons why even a writer of the stature of Peter Handke has been able to argue in the essay "Horváth und Brecht", "Ich ziehe Ödön von Horváth . . . vor" ("I prefer Ödön von Horváth").

—John Wieczoreck

See also *Volume 1* entry on *Tales From the Vienna Woods*.

HOUGHTON, (William) Stanley. Born in Ashton-upon-Mersey, Cheshire, England, 22 February 1881. Educated at Bowdon College; Stockport Grammar School; Wilmslow Grammar School, Cheshire; Manchester Grammar School, 1896–97. Worked in his father's cotton business, Manchester, 1897–1912; amateur actor, 1901–12; theatre reviewer, Manchester *City News*, 1905–06; feature writer and literary and drama critic, Manchester *Guardian*, 1905–13; first-produced play, *The Intriguers*, written with Frank Naismith, staged 1906; associated with Harold Brighouse and Gilbert Cannan in the repertory theatre movement in England from 1909; lived in Paris, 1913, then returned to Manchester. Died in Manchester, 11 December 1913.

Works

Collections

Works, edited by Harold Brighouse (3 vols.).   1914.

Stage Works

The Intriguers, with Frank G. Naismith (produced Athanaeum, Manchester, 1906).
The Reckoning, with Frank G. Naismith (produced Queen's Theatre, Manchester, 1907; as *The Day of Reckoning*, produced Crown Theatre, Eccles, 1912).
The Dear Departed (produced Gaiety Theatre, Manchester, 1908).   1910.
Independent Means (produced Gaiety Theatre, Manchester, 1909).   1911.
The Master of the House (produced Gaiety Theatre, Manchester, 1910).   1913.
The Younger Generation (produced Gaiety Theatre, Manchester, 1910).   1910.
Fancy Free (produced Gaiety Theatre, Manchester, 1911). 1912; revised version, as *Partners* (produced Prince's Theatre, Manchester, 1915), in *Works 2*, 1914.
Hindle Wakes (produced Aldwych Theatre, London, 1912). 1912.
Phipps (produced Garrick Theatre, London, 1912).   1913.
Pearls (produced Pavilion, Glasgow, 1912).
Trust the People (produced Garrick Theatre, London, 1913).
The Fifth Commandment (produced Little Theatre, Chicago, 1913).   1913; revised version, as *The Perfect Cure* (produced Apollo Theatre, London 1913), in *Works 2*, 1914.
Ginger (produced Halifax, 1913).
The Old Testament and the New (produced Gaiety Theatre, Manchester, 1914).   In *Works 3*, 1914.
Marriages in the Making.   In *Works 1*.   1914.
The Hillarys, with Harold Brighouse (produced Kelly's Theatre, Liverpool, 1915).

Criticism

Books:
Rex Pogson, *Miss Horniman and the Gaiety Theatre, Manchester*, Manchester, 1952.
Marcel Gaberthuel, *William Stanley Houghton 1881–1913: Eine Untersuchung seiner Dramen*, Solothurn, 1973.

Articles:
Paul Mortimer, "W. Stanley Houghton: An Introduction and a Bibliography", in *Modern Drama*, 28, 1985.

* * *

The most successful of the so-called Manchester school of playwrights, Houghton was born and raised in the world he wrote about in his plays. Keenly interested in the theatre from an early age, he acted in his youth with amateur groups, and wrote drama criticism for Manchester newspapers. The opportunity for him to develop as a playwright came with the establishment in Manchester of a repertory theatre under the aegis of Miss A.E.F. Horniman, who had been responsible for backing some early experimental production work in London (such as that of Florence Farr) and for helping to fund the Abbey Theatre, Dublin. The Manchester school included dramatists like Allan Monkhouse and Harold Brighouse, but Houghton is generally considered to be the most significant, as he was, too, the most successful.

Like a number of Edwardian dramatists, Houghton treated serious subject-matter pertinent to the society of his day in an essentially naturalistic style, in which discussion of social and moral issues was a prominent feature. But where those dramatists, among them Shaw, Galsworthy, Hankin, and Granville Barker, employed Ibsenite kinds of material, dealt with the concerns pertaining to upper-middle-class characters, and invariably set their plays in comfortable bourgeois metropolitan or southern county environments, Houghton had a more local and provincial slant to his work.

His first long play at the Gaiety Theatre was *Independent Means*, produced in August 1909 to open the 1909–10 season. This was a fairly typical piece, a discussion and social problem play, concerned in part with women's suffrage, although according to *The Manchester Guardian* (31 August 1909) not noticeably contentious and disputative in its treatment of this then topical subject. In fact it is rather flat and lifeless, and gives little indication of the qualities Houghton was to display in his next piece, *The Younger Generation*, in which a wastrel son discovers that the rectitude of his formidably moral father is a sham concealing a far from blameless youth. The play is psychologically plausible, inventive, and witty, and its governing themes are neatly handled: the older generation is reproved for hypocrisy, and the social plea is for understanding and tolerance between the age groups, a recurring theme in Houghton's plays.

Unquestionably his most celebrated play was *Hindle Wakes*, written in three months at the end of 1911. Notwithstanding its local Lancashire setting, it had a theme that proved popular not only in England, but in America and elsewhere: a young working-class woman revolts against the mores and restrictions of traditional society and affirms female independence. Its subject-matter was of a kind to invite melodramatic and sentimental treatment, but Houghton handles it with restraint; his depiction of the "misalliance" of a strong-willed factory girl is not only powerful and persuasive, but altogether without that attitude of social condescension that mars much serious drama of the period. First produced under the auspices of the Stage Society at London's Aldwych Theatre in June 1912, it was an outstanding success, triumphing first in London, then in Manchester and on tour, and finally in Canada and the United States.

The great success of *Hindle Wakes* gave Houghton freedom to pursue his intellectual and artistic interests: he went first to London, and became caught up in literary and theatrical life, then moved on to Paris in 1913 (as was the vogue of the times). But his enjoyment of this freedom, and of literary and theatrical life, was to be short-lived. In 1913 he went on holiday to Venice, where he was taken ill. He returned eventually to Manchester, to die there in the same year. Of course his return brought new work. In the first instance it led to commissions from London actor-managers. But in the short time vouchsafed him, Houghton was not to repeat the success of *Hindle Wakes*, and his later pieces made very little stir, in part perhaps because he turned from writing plays about issues which particularly appealed to him to preparing pieces as vehicles for a star player. Such were *The Perfect Cure*, written for Charles Hawtrey, and produced in June 1913, and *Trust the People*, written for Arthur Bouchier. He also produced five one-act plays in 1913, which included the well-known and highly accomplished *The Dear Departed*. These plays are rather loosely structured, are rather short on theatrical high moments, and tend to be talk-pieces.

A strain of realism dominates his plays, but it is of a very particular kind: Houghton was brilliant at depicting the domestic relations, the psychological tensions, and the social hypocrisies and deceptions of the north-country world he knew. The main impetus to his work, like that of others in the Manchester school, was provided by the example of Ibsen's drama; contributive too was much recent native dramatic writing concerned with social issues, like that of John Galsworthy, St John Hankin, and Harley Granville Barker, whose plays treated the conflict between the individual and society, and directed attention to injustices. But Houghton was no mere imitator. Nor was he, as those English and Anglo-Irish dramatists were, self-consciously reformist. His was, perhaps, a modest talent, and his dialogue lacks the solidity of Galsworthy's or the mercurial fluent wit of Shaw's, but he portrayed Lancastrian life not just with the trenchant understanding of the north-country world he depicted, but in accents at once locally authentic and yet of universal appeal.

—Kenneth Richards

See also *Volume 1* entry on *Hindle Wakes*.

———

HOWARD, Sidney (Coe). Born in Oakland, California, USA, 26 June 1891. Educated at the University of California, Berkeley (editor, *Occident*), 1911–15, BA 1915; studied with George Pierce Baker at Harvard University, Cambridge, Massachusetts, 1915–16, AM 1916. Served in the American Ambulance Corps, and later in the US Army Air Corps, during World War I: Captain; Silver Star. Married 1) the actress Clare Jenness Eames in 1922 (divorced 1930), one daughter; 2) Leopoldine Blaine Damrosch in 1931, one daughter and one son. Member of the editorial staff, 1919–22, and literary editor, 1922, *Life* magazine, New York; special investigator and feature writer, *New Republic* and *Hearst's International Magazine*, New York, 1923; full-time playwright from 1923; founder, with Robert E. Sherwood, Elmer

Rice, Maxwell Anderson, S.N. Behrman, and John F. Wharton, Playwrights Company, 1938. Member, Board of Directors, American Civil Liberties Union; President, Dramatists Guild, 1935–37. Recipient: Pulitzer Prize, 1925; Oscar, for screenplay, 1940. Litt.D: Washington and Jefferson College, Washington, Pennsylvania, 1935. Member, American Academy. Died in Tyringham, Massachusetts, 23 August 1939.

Works

Stage Works

The Sons of Spain (produced Carmel, California, 1914).
Swords (produced National Theatre, New York, 1921). 1921.
S.S. Tenacity, from a work by Charles Vildrac (produced Belmont Theatre, New York, 1922).
Sancho Panza, from play by Melchior Lengyel (produced Hudson Theatre, New York, 1923).
Casanova, from a play by Lorenzo de Azertis (produced Empire Theatre, New York, 1923). 1924.
They Knew What They Wanted (produced Garrick Theatre, New York, 1924). 1925.
Bewitched, with Edward Sheldon (produced National Theatre, New York, 1924).
Lexington (produced Lexington, Massachusetts, 1925). 1924(?).
Michel Auclair (produced Provincetown Playhouse, New York, 1925). In *Plays for College Theater*, edited by Garrett H. Leverton, 1932.
The Last Night of Don Juan, from a play by Edmond Rostand (produced Greenwich Village Theatre, New York, 1925).
Morals, from a play by Ludwig Thoma (produced Comedy Theatre, New York, 1925).
Lucky Sam McCarver (produced Playhouse, New York, 1925). 1926.
Ned McCobb's Daughter (produced John Golden Theatre, New York, 1926). 1926.
The Silver Cord (produced John Golden Theatre, New York, 1926). 1927.
Salvation with Charles MacArthur (produced Empire Theatre, New York, 1928). In *Stage Works of MacArthur*, 1974.
Olympia, from a play by Ferenc Molnár (produced Empire Theatre, New York, 1928). 1928.
Half Gods (produced Plymouth Theatre, New York, 1929). 1930.
Lute Song, with Will Irwin (as *Pi-Pa-Ki*, produced Berkshire Playhouse, Stockbridge, Massachusetts, 1930); revised version, as *Lute Song*, music by Raymond Scott, lyrics by Bernard Hanighen (produced Plymouth Theatre, New York, 1946). 1955.
President, from a play by Ferenc Molnár (as *One, Two, Three*, produced Henry Miller's Theatre, 1930). In *Romantic Comedies*, by Molnar, 1952.
Marseilles, from a work by Marcel Pagnol (produced Henry Miller's Theatre, 1930).
The Late Christopher Bean, from a play by René Fauchois (produced Henry Miller's Theatre, 1932). 1933.
Alien Corn (produced Belasco Theatre, New York, 1933). 1933.
Gather Ye Rosebuds, with Robert Littell (produced 1934).
Ode to Liberty, from a play by Michel Duran (produced Lyceum Theatre, New York, 1934).
Dodsworth, from the novel by Sinclair Lewis (produced Shubert Theatre, New York, 1934). 1934.

Yellow Jack, with Paul de Kruif, from a work by de Kruif (produced Martin Beck Theatre, New York, 1934). 1934.
Paths of Glory, from the novel by Humphrey Cobb (produced Plymouth Theatre, New York, 1935). 1935.
The Ghost of Yankee Doodle (produced Guild Theatre, New York, 1937). 1938.
Madam, Will You Walk? (produced Phoenix Theatre, New York, 1953). 1955.

Screenplays

Bulldog Drummond, with Wallace Smith, 1929; *Condemned*, 1929; *A Lady to Love*, 1930; *Raffles*, 1930; *One Heavenly Night*, with Louis Bromfield, 1930; *Arrowsmith*, 1931; *The Greeks Had a Word for Them*, 1932; *Dodsworth*, 1936; *Gone with the Wind*, 1939 (published 1980); *Raffles*, with John van Druten, 1940.

Fiction

Three Flights Up (stories). 1924.

Other

The Labor Spy: A Survey of Industrial Espionage, with Robert Dunn. 1921; revised edition, 1924.
Professional Patriots, with John Hearley, edited by Norman Hapgood. 1927.

*

Criticism

Books:
Joseph Wood Krutch, *American Drama Since 1918*, New York, 1939.
Sidney H. White, *Sidney Howard*, Boston, 1977.

Articles:
Edith J.R. Isaacs, "Sidney Howard", in *Theatre Arts*, 23 October 1939.
Walter J. Meserve, "Sidney Howard and the Social Drama of the Twenties", in *Modern Drama*, 1963; reprinted in *Discussions of American Drama*, edited by Meserve, Boston, 1966.

* * *

In his preface to *Lucky Sam McCarver*, Sidney Howard admitted that, as a thinker, he was neither profound nor original. Such modesty, however, should not be misinterpreted. Although his plays do not illustrate great intellectual depth or imaginative development, Howard emerged during the 1920's as a major writer of social drama in a line of development leading from James A. Herne to Tennessee Williams. A potent force in a movement in American drama, his best plays transcend the limitations of his contemporary drama and reveal something essential about the human condition.

Although Sidney Howard wrote or adapted more than 25 plays over a period of nearly 20 years, his reputation rests largely on a few original works, mainly written during the 1920's. During this period he also wrote fiction and published articles as an investigative reporter. After these very productive years for the stage, he devoted much of his time to writing screenplays, primarily for Samuel Goldwyn's studio.

His adaptation to the screen of two novels by Sinclair Lewis, *Arrowsmith* and *Dodsworth*, illustrates his interest in people and society and uses the same skills in the dramatization of character that made his plays successful; but he is best remembered for his film adaptation of Margaret Mitchell's *Gone with the Wind*, for which he received an Academy Award.

Guided by the realistic patterns of stage presentation established by his predecessors in the American theatre, Sidney Howard wrote plays that gave social drama a new dignity and position in the eyes of audiences and critics, both in America and abroad. Dispite the playwright's tendency to sermonize throughout his career, *They Knew What They Wanted* is an epoch-marking play for its sense of humanity and its insight into social morality. In Tony, Howard created his most successful character, a 60-year-old Italian wine-grower who successfully proposes by mail to Amy, a young and discouraged waitress, but jeopardizes his suit by sending a photograph of his handsome young helper, Joe. Shocked by her discovery on her wedding day, and confused by an auto accident which incapacites the husband she has met for the first time, Amy momentarily succumbs to the wayward Joe. When she realizes that she is pregnant and confesses to her husband, Tony's immediate anger is soon tempered by the mature realization that he knows what he wants. Joe is a wanderer and will be on his way; Amy wants security and a life with a man she can admire and love; and Tony can become, not the most miserable of men, but a "most happy fella".

Strong people, knowing what they want, dominate Howard's plays in which psychological interpretation of character is fundamental to plot. In *The Silver Cord*, Howard dramatizes the conflict between a "professional mother", Mrs. Phelps, and Christina, an independent and ambitious woman who is the wife of her older son, David. In her struggle to possess the love of her sons, Mrs. Phelps destroys the love of her younger son, Robert, and his fiancée, Hester, but fails to break up the marriage of David and Christina. Through Christina, a research biologist, who declares that "an embryological accident is no ground for honor", Howard expresses his antipathy toward filial duty demanded by pathological dependence, and concentrates the violence of the conflict in Mrs. Phelps, who is singularly diabolical in ways that invite comparisons with Laura in Strindberg's *The Father*.

Both *Lucky Sam McCarver* and *Ned McCobb's Daughter* dramatize strong characters who face a series of frustrating social situations and react powerfully to those conditions and frustrations. *Lucky Sam McCarver* begins as an analysis of Sam McCarver, a cold and materialistic man, but becomes more effective as the story of a woman who desperately wants love from a man who has only money to give. Hardened by the worship of money, Sam frankly uses his wife and her name and sees nothing beyond his growing empire. Having lost human compassion and the ability to feel, he can only think and contrive. Social conditions also provide the background for Ned McCobb's daughter, Carrie, to show the superiority of her character as a shrewd woman motivated by the heart rather than the head, who has a Yankee determination to get what she wants.

The dominant idea in Howard's plays, as presented in the title of his first popular success, reflects the distinctive and positive individualism of the social drama of the 1920's, and distinguishes this period of social drama from what came before and what eventually followed. To create this drama, Howard mixed realistic melodrama with expertly contrived scenes of fast-moving action. The wedding scene in *They Knew What They Wanted*, the festive scene in Venice, in Act

III of *Lucky Sam McCarver*, the final scene of *Ned McCobb's Daughter* which forms the climax of the melodramatic cops-and-robbers plot, and a number of scenes such as Mrs. Phelps tearing the telephone from the wall in *The Silver Cord*—all suggest Howard's concern for strong emotional episodes of theatrical effectiveness. Consequently, and in the tradition of melodrama, violence is a major part of the social life he portrays, while the frequently rapid emotional changes in his characters sometimes suggest the contrivance that haunts melodrama. If so, it is overshadowed by Howard's spectacular use of dramatic irony, both in character development and in situations. The irony in the titles of *Lucky Sam McCarver* and *They Knew What They Wanted*, for example, is extended to the dramatic situation as well as to the character development. *The Silver Cord* is a mass of irony, ending with the double irony of Mrs. Phelps left once again with the younger son.

Although the independence of Howard's spirit may be traced in the theme of individual freedom that distinguishes his plays, his independence never tempted him to experiment with dramatic forms. He was interested, he once explained, only in creating "satisfactory" plays that would be worthy vehicles for actors—and in this endeavor he had success.

—Walter J. Meserve

See also *Volume 1* entry on *They Knew What They Wanted*.

HROSVIT.   See HROTSVITHA.

HROTSVITHA (of Gandersheim).   Also known as Hrosvit or Roswitha. Born in Saxony, c.935. Noblewoman and member of a Benedictine order in Gandersheim. Wrote verse and six plays in Latin, first published in 1501. Died in Kloster Gandersheim, c.973.

Works

Collections

Opera, edited by C. Celtis.   1501.
Opera, edited by Paul von Winterfeld.   1902.
Plays (includes all six plays), translated by Christopher St. John.   1923.
Plays (includes all six plays), translated by H.J.W. Tillyard.   1923.
Opera, edited by K. Strecker.   1930 (second edition).
Opera, edited by Helena Homeyer.   1970.
Plays, translated by L. Bonfante.   1979.
The Dramas of Hrosvit, translated by Katharina M. Wilson.   1985.

Stage Works

Abraham.   In *Opera*, 1501; translated as *Abraham*, 1922; as *The Fall and Repentence of Mary*, in *The Dramas of Hrosvit*, 1985.

Callimachus. In *Opera*, 1501; translated as *Callimachus*, 1923; as *The Resurrection of Drusiana and Callimachus*, in *The Dramas of Hrosvit*, 1985.

Dulcitius. In *Opera*, 1501; translated as *Dulcitius*, 1916 (private printing), and in *Plays* (St. John), 1923; as *Dulcitius; or, The Martyrdom of the Holy Virgins Irene, Agape and Chionia*, in *Plays* (Tillyard), 1923; as *The Martyrdom of the Holy Virgins Agape, Chionia, and Hirena*, in *The Dramas of Hrosvit*, 1985.

Gallicanus. In *Opera*, 1501; translated as *Gallicanus*, in *Plays* (St. John), 1923; as *Gallicanus: First Part* and *Gallicanus: Second Part*, in *Plays* (Tillyard), 1923; as *The Conversion of General Gallicanus*, in *The Dramas of Hrosvit*, 1985.

Paphnutius. In *Opera*, 1501; translated as *Paphnutius*, in *Plays* (St. John), 1923; as *Paphnutius; or, The Conversion of the Thais, the Harlot*, in *Plays* (Tillyard), 1923; as *The Conversion of the Harlot Thais*, in *The Dramas of Hrosvit*, 1985.

Sapientia. In *Opera*, 1501; translated as *Sapientia*, in *Plays* (St. John), 1923; as *Sapientia; or, The Martyrdom of the Holy Virgins Faith, Hope and Charity*, in *Plays* (Tillyard), 1923; as *The Martyrdom of the Holy Virgins Fides, Spes, and Karitas*, in *The Dramas of Hrosvit*, 1985.

Verse

Pelagius. In *Opera*, 1501.
Theophilus. In *Opera*, 1501.
Passio Gongolphi. In *Opera*, 1501.

Other

Gesta Oddonis (chronicles), edited by Justus Reuber. 1584.
Carmen de primordiis et fundatoribus coenobii Gandersheimensis. Fragments in *Annalium Paderbonnensium 11 Partes*, edited by Nicolaus Schaten, 1693; complete, in *Antiquitates Gandersheimenses*, edited by Johan G. Leuckfeld, 1709.

*

Bibliographies

Edwin Zeydel, "A Chronological Hrotsvitha Bibliography Through 1700, with Annotations", in *Journal of English and Germanic Philology*, 46, 1947.

Anne Lyon Haight (ed.), *Hrotsvitha of Gandersheim: Her Life, Times, and Works and a Comprehensive Bibliography*, New York, 1965.

Criticism

Books:
Rudolph Kopke, *Hrotsvitha von Gandersheim*, Stuttgart, 1869; reprinted, 1965.
Otto Pilz, *Die Dramen der Hrotsvitha von Gandersheim*, Leipzig, 1925.
Hans Walther, *Hrotsvit von Gandersheim*, Bielefeld, 1931.
M. Rigobon, *Il teatro e la latinità di Hrotsvitha*, Padua, 1932.
Sister Mary Marguerite Butler, *Hrotsvitha: The Theatricality of Her Plays*, New York, 1960.
K. Kronenberg, *Roswitha von Gandersheim: Leben und Werk*, Bad Gandersheim, 1962.
Bert Nagel, *Hrotsvit von Gandersheim*, Stuttgart, 1965.

Helena Homeyer, *Hrotsvitha von Gandersheim*, Munich, 1973.

Articles:
Cornelia C. Coulter, "The Terentian Comedies of a Tenth Century Nun", in *Classical Journal*, 24, 1929.
Zoltan Haraszti, "The Works of Hrotsvitha", in *More Books*, 20, 1945.
Rosemary Sprague, "Hroswitha: Tenth Century Margaret Webster", in *Theatre Annual*, 13, 1955.
Kenneth de Luca, "Hrotsvit's Imitation of Terence", in *Classical Folia*, 28, 1974.

*   *   *

"Look! I am playfully swimming, unhurt, in this boiling pitch and wax!". For centuries, such lines have raised doubts about the stage practicability of Hrotsvitha's plays, with some justification according to modern notions of realisation. Hrotsvitha has also become one of the jokes of dramatic history, a playwright whom few people read except perhaps in clumsily pious translation, the victim of her own deferential admiration for the Roman Terence. Yet her six extant Latin plays are of monumental importance in world drama: one may look several centuries in either direction without finding a comparable corpus by a single dramatist, and women playwrights have always been a rarity in the Western theatre. Moreover, she is a much better Latin stylist than her apologetic prefaces would have us believe: her copious non-dramatic poetry has an obvious competence in hexameters and elegiacs, and her plays have an impish use of sardonic understatement and sometimes crisp dialogue.

Hrotsvitha (sometimes anglicised as Roswitha) wrote in 10th-century Saxony, primarily for the entertainment of the Benedictine circles to which she belonged. Some episodes in the plays, like two long didactic speeches on mathematics and cosmic harmony, are puzzling in their dramatic function; but elsewhere there is enough broad situational comedy and vicarious sensationalism to make their entertainment appeal obvious. Their classification as comedies, however, probably rests on the acceptably Christian resolution to which they all develop: they are "lost sheep" dramas in which a saintly man retrieves a female prostitute and guides her through an appropriate penance towards a state of grace, or gruesome dramas of stoical female martyrdom at the hands of a sadistic but slow-witted Roman emperor. Hrotsvitha did not invent these stories, but she did take many liberties with her main source (the Latin and Greek *Patrologiae*), including extensive interpolation of slapstick and historically impossible conjunctions of characters.

The prostitution plays, *Abraham* and *Paphnutius*, are blatantly exemplary pieces which do little to question the pervasive tradition of medieval misogyny, and focus on a character type that is the antecedent of the late medieval obsession with Magdalene. The title characters are the male retrievers who are presented as showing considerable courage and self-sacrifice in venturing outside the sphere of asceticism, risking contamination from the larger world. Abraham is by far the more resourceful, and that play contains copious internal evidence of performance: asides, disguises, dramatic irony, and a stratagem-type central action not unlike those of Terence.

The martyrdom plays are more interesting in terms of both gender issues and dramaturgy. The title character of *Sapientia* gives spiritual support to her three daughters, Faith, Hope, and Charity, as they are tortured to death by Hadrian's men; it is, in fact, Faith who swims across the cauldron of boiling fluids. Sapientia is perceived as an "alien", subverting the women of Rome to the extent that they will neither eat nor sleep with their men. The emperor, advised that the most effective way to control women is to exploit their frailty through flattery, offers himself as surrogate father to the daughters, a proposal which he reiterates between torture scenes, only to be told by Hope, in the Roman language of divorce, "I repudiate your paternity!". In the final scene, Hrotsvitha develops a chorus of Matrons (scarcely mentioned in the source) to attend Sapientia in the funeral, without on-stage male commiseration or sanction—though she can announce that she has the consolation of being crowned and glorified by her daughters' virginity and martyrdom.

In *Dulcitius*, the martyrdom of three sisters (Love, Purity, and Peace) under Diocletian is fused with a heavy element of slapstick and situational comedy which even imbues the pieties of the final scene. The play begins formally, as the women are interrogated by the emperor in Court Record style and ordered to renounce both their Christianity and their celibacy. The next scene is one entirely of comic irony in which the title character, the Roman governor, is discredited; inanely, he chats with his men about his prospects of sexual success with the women, an absurdity not only to the audience, but to everyone else on stage. In central scenes, he gropes around lustfully in the dark, in search of the sisters, and with a brilliant stroke of theatricality Hrotsvitha gives us a brief scene in the cell with the women, from which perspective we hear Dulcitius becoming entangled in a variety of kitchenware. Frustrated, he goes to the emperor for sympathy, and—with even less success—to his wife. He then responds to the crisis by blustering himself to sleep and is left snoring on stage. The imperial rapist-cum-inquisitor having been turned into a figure of comic contempt, the more phlegmatic Sisinnius is introduced to effect the martyrdoms (by fire and arrows), but even he is left walking round in circles in the last scene.

Within the context of Hrotsvitha's ideology, the ambiguities of oppression and resistance in these plays are considerable. Sapientia seems to have been successful in her religious colonisation of Rome, just as Hrotsvitha's religion had overrun Saxony. But in addition, Frankish imperialism had introduced the death penalty for numerous "pagan" practices, and a local inquisition continued for several centuries. Hrotsvitha's tone could afford to be triumphant, because not only had the persecution of Christians stopped locally, but Christianity was now doing the persecuting; the colonised had become the colonisers. Nonetheless, it is important to bear in mind the fragility and variety of Hrotsvitha's cultural and religious milieu; when she wrote her plays she was possibly very close to another, anonymous scribe who was preserving our only extant manuscript of *Beowulf*, a poem written in the not-too-distant past and grounded in Hrotsvitha's immediate world.

—Howard McNaughton

———

HUAN Han-ching.   See GUAN Hanqing

———

HUGHES, (James) Langston.   Born in Joplin, Missouri, USA, 1 February 1902. Educated at Central High School, Cleveland, 1916–20; Columbia University, New York, 1921–22; Lincoln University, Pennsylvania (Witter Bynner Award, 1926), 1926–29, BA 1929. English teacher in Mexico, 1920–21; seaman, 1923–24; busboy, Wardman Park Hotel, Washington, DC, 1925; first play, *Mulatto*, produced in adapted version, 1935; Madrid correspondent, Baltimore *Afro-American*, 1937; founder, Harlem Suitcase Theatre, New York, 1938, New Negro Theatre, Los Angeles, 1939, and Skyloft Players, Chicago, 1941; during World War II, member of the Music and Writers war boards; columnist ("Simple"), Chicago *Defender*, 1943–67, and New York *Post*, 1962–67; based in New York after 1947; visiting professor of creative writing, Atlanta University, 1947; poet-in-residence, University of Chicago Laboratory School, 1949. Recipient: Anisfield-Wolf Award, 1953; NAACP Spingarn Medal, 1960. D.Litt: Lincoln University, 1943; Howard University, Washington, DC, 1963; Western Reserve University, Cleveland, 1964. Member, American Academy, 1961, and American Academy of Arts and Sciences. Died in New York, 22 May 1967.

Works

Collections

Five Plays (includes *Mulatto; Soul Gone Home; Little Ham; Simply Heavenly; Tambourines to Glory*), edited by Webster Smalley.   1963.

Stage Works

The Gold Piece.   In *Brownies' Book*, July 1921.
Mulatto (produced Vanderbilt Theatre, New York, 1935; original version produced Karamu House, Cleveland, Ohio, 1939).   In *Five Plays*, 1963.
Little Ham (produced Karamu House, Cleveland, Ohio, 1935).   In *Five Plays*, 1963.
Troubled Island (produced Karamu House, Cleveland, Ohio, 1935; revised version, music by William Grant Still, produced City Center, New York, 1949).   1949.
When the Jack Hollers, with Arna Bontemps (produced Karamu House, Cleveland, Ohio, 1936).
Joy to My Soul (produced Karamu House, Cleveland, Ohio, 1937).
Soul Gone Home (produced Federal Theatre, Cleveland, Ohio, 1937?).   In *Five Plays*, 1963.
Don't You Want to Be Free?, music by Carroll Tate (produced Harlem Suitcase Theatre, New York, 1937).   In *One Act Play Magazine*, October 1938.
Front Porch (produced Karamu House, Cleveland, Ohio, 1938).
The Organizer, music by James P. Johnson (produced Harlem Suitcase Theatre, New York, 1939).
The Sun Do Move (produced Good Shepherd Community House, Chicago, 1942).
Street Scene (lyrics only), book by Elmer Rice, music by Kurt Weill (produced Adelphi Theatre, New York, 1947). 1948.
The Barrier, music by Jan Meyerowitz (produced Columbia University, New York, 1950).
Just Around the Corner (lyrics only), book by Abby Mann and Bernard Drew, music by Joe Sherman (produced Ogunquit Playhouse, Ogunquit, Maine, 1951).
Simply Heavenly, music by David Martin (produced 85th Street Playhouse, New York, 1957).   1959.

Esther, music by Jan Meyerowitz (produced University of Illinois, Urbana, 1957).
Shakespeare in Harlem, with James Weldon Johnson (produced 1959).
Port Town, music by Jan Meyerowitz (produced Lenox, Massachusetts, 1960).
The Ballad of the Brown King, music by Margaret Bonds (produced Clark Auditorium, YMCA, New York, 1960).
Black Nativity (produced 41st Street Theatre, New York, 1961).
Gospel Glow (produced Brooklyn, New York, 1962).
Let Us Remember Him, music by David Amram (produced 1963).
Tambourines to Glory, music by Jobe Huntley, from the novel by Hughes (produced Little Theatre, New York, 1963).   In *Five Plays*, 1963.
Jerico-Jim Crow (produced Greenwich Mews Theatre, New York, 1963).
The Prodigal Son (produced Greenwich Mews Theatre, New York, 1965).
Mule Bone, with Zora Neale Hurston (produced Ethel Barrymore Theatre, New York, 1991).

Screenplays

Way Down South, with Clarence Muse, 1939.

Television Plays

The Big Sea, 1965; *It's a Mighty World*, 1965; *Strollin' Twenties*, 1966.

Radio Plays

Jubilee, with Arna Bontemps, 1941; *Brothers*, 1942; *Freedom's Plow*, 1943 (published 1943); *John Henry Hammers it Out*, with Peter Lyons, 1943; *In the Service of My Country*, 1944; *The Man Who Went to War*, 1944 (UK); *Booker T. Washington at Atlanta*, 1945 (published in *Radio Drama in Action*, edited by Eric Barnouw, 1945); *Pvt. Jim Crow* (published in *Negro Story*, May-June 1945); *Swing Time at the Savoy*, with Noble Sissle, 1949.

Fiction

Not Without Laughter.   1930.
The Ways of White Folks (stories).   1934.
Simple Speaks His Mind.   1950.
Laughing to Keep from Crying (stories).   1952.
Simple Takes a Wife.   1953.
Simple Stakes a Claim.   1957.
Tambourines to Glory.   1958.
The Best of Simple.   1961.
Something in Common and Other Stories.   1963.
Simple's Uncle Sam.   1965.

Verse

The Weary Blues.   1926.
Fine Clothes to the Jew.   1927.
Dear Lovely Death.   1931.
"The Negro Mother" and Other Dramatic Recitations.   1931.
"The Dream-Keeper" and Other Poems.   1932.
Scottsboro Limited: Four Poems and a Play in Verse.   1932.
A New Song.   1938.
Shakespeare in Harlem.   1942.
Jim Crow's Last Stand.   1943.

"Lament for Dark Peoples" and Other Poems, edited by H. Driessen.   1944.
Fields of Wonder.   1947.
One-Way Ticket.   1949.
Montage of a Dream Deferred.   1951.
Selected Poems.   1959.
Ask Your Mama: 12 Moods for Jazz.   1961.
The Panther and the Lash: Poems of Our Times.   1967.
Don't You Turn Back (for children), edited by Lee Bennett Hopkins.   1969.

Memoirs and Letters

The Big Sea: An Autobiography.   1940.
I Wonder as I Wander: An Autobiographical Journey.   1956.
Arna Bontemps-Hughes: Letters 1925–1967, edited by Charles H. Nichols.   1980.

Other

Popo and Fifina, Children of Haiti (for children), with Arna Bontemps.   1932.
The First Book of Negroes (for children).   1952.
The First Book of Rhythms (for children).   1954.
Famous American Negroes (for children).   1954.
Famous Negro Music-Makers (for children).   1955.
The First Book of Jazz.   1955 (for children): revised edition, 1962.
The Sweet Flypaper of Life (on Harlem), with Roy De Carava.   1955.
A Pictorial History of the Negro in America, with Milton Meltzer.   1956; revised edition (for children), 1963, 1968; as *A Pictorial History of Black Americans*, 1973.
The First Book of the West Indies (for children).   1956; as *The First Book of the Caribbean*, 1965.
The Hughes Reader.   1958.
Famous Negro Heroes of America (for children).   1958.
The First Book of Africa (for children).   1960; revised edition, 1964.
Fight for Freedom: The Story of the NAACP.   1962.
Black Magic: A Pictorial History of the Negro in American Entertainment, with Milton Meltzer.   1967.
Black Misery.   1969.
Good Morning, Revolution: Uncollected Social Protest Writings, edited by Faith Berry.   1973.
Hughes in the Hispanic World and Haiti, edited by Edward J. Mullen.   1977.

Editor, *Four Lincoln University Poets*.   1930.
Editor, with Arna Bontemps, *The Poetry of the Negro 1746–1949: An Anthology*.   1949; revised edition, 1970.
Editor, with Waring Guney and Bruce M. Wright, *Lincoln University Poets*.   1954.
Editor, with Arna Bontemps, *The Book of Negro Folklore*.   1958.
Editor, *An Africa Treasury: Articles, Essays, Stories, Poems by Black Africans*.   1960.
Editor, *Poems from Black Africa*.   1963.
Editor, *New Negro Poets: USA*.   1964.
Editor, *La Poésie negro-américaine* (bilingual edition).   1966.
Editor, *Anthologie africaine et malgache*.   1966.
Editor, *The Best Short Stories by Negro Writers: An Anthology from 1899 to the Present*.   1967.

Translator, with Mercer Cook, *Masters of the Dew*, by Jacques Roumain. 1947.
Translator, with Ben Frederic Carruthers, *Cuba Libre*, by Nicolás Guillén. 1948.
Translator, *Gypsy Ballads*, by Federico García Lorca. 1951.
Translator, *Selected Poems of Gabriela Mistral*. 1957.

*

Bibliographies

Donald C. Dickinson, *A Bio-Bibliography of Langston Hughes 1902–1967* (second edition), Hamden, Connecticut, 1972.
R. Baxter Miller, *Langston Hughes and Gwendolyn Brooks: A Reference Guide*, Boston, 1978.

Criticism

Books:
James A. Emmanuel, *Langston Hughes*, New York, 1967.
Milton Melzer, *Langston Hughes: A Biography*, New York, 1968.
Therman B. O'Daniel (ed.), *Langston Hughes: Black Genius*, New York, 1971.
Edward J. Mullen (ed.), *Critical Essays on Langston Hughes*, Boston, 1986.
Leslie C. Sanders, *The Development of Black Theater in America*, Baton Rouge, Louisiana, 1988.
Arnold Rampersad, *The Life of Langston Hughes* (2 vols.), New York, 1986–88.

Articles:
Arthur P. Davis, "The Tragic Mulatto Theme in Six Works by Langston Hughes", in *Phylon*, 16, 1955.

*   *   *

Known primarily as a poet, Langston Hughes is by far the most loved of African-American writers, and his influence on black letters is immeasurable. First published in 1921, he also wrote for the theatre throughout his career: his theatrical work includes not only plays, but also libretti, lyrics, revue material, and ballet choreography, as well as scripts for radio and television. Hughes began writing plays in the late 1920's. His first, *Mulatto*, rendered sensational by the producer's alterations, opened on Broadway in 1935, ran for one year, and toured for another two seasons. Broadway was not, however, Hughes's usual venue; more typically, his plays were produced by community theatres, some of which he himself founded. Notably, Karamu House in Cleveland, Ohio, the settlement house he attended as a boy, staged the premieres of five of his works.

As with his poetry, Hughes grounded his theatrical endeavours in the language and forms of African-American culture. Some of his plays depend on conventional stage realism; most, however, derive from African-American cultural forms, principally the arts of story-telling and preaching. Even the more formally conventional plays, such as *Mulatto*, *Emperor of Haiti*, *Little Ham*, *Front Porch*, *Soul Gone Home*, *Simply Heavenly*, and *Tambourines to Glory*, contest American theatre tradition by addressing black audiences, probing and celebrating black experience, and creating authentic portraits of black life.

The oppositional quality of his dramatic work is most obvious in early plays: *Mulatto*, for example, proposes a counter-statement to the racist presuppositions of the portrait of the mulatto in the 1927 Pulitzer Prize-winning play *In Abraham's Bosom*, by the white playwright Paul Green. Comedies, such as *Little Ham*, *Simply Heavenly*, *Joy to My Soul*, and his co-written *When the Jack Hollers*, similarly challenge assumptions by grounding themselves in black humor, rather than in blackness as source of humour, the convention of the dominant stage tradition.

Hughes's formal experiments were influenced by the agit-prop theatre he encountered both in the USSR and in the United States, and evolved from techniques he developed for his poetry readings. His first experiment with the agitprop form, the verse play *Scottsboro Limited*, protested the conviction of nine black boys imprisoned in Alabama for the alleged rape of two white prostitutes, a case that received international attention. In 1938, when Hughes founded the Harlem Suitcase Theatre, the first of three community theatres he would found over the next four years (in Los Angeles, the New Negro Theatre, 1939, and in Chicago, the Skyloft Players, 1942), he created the first of a series of dramatic works in which a representative black character told the history of black America through poetry, song, and skit. *Don't You Want to Be Free?*, updated several times, inspired his later off-Broadway hit about the Civil Rights Movement, *Jericho-Jim Orow*.

The chronicle plays, as well as his loosely constructed dramatization of a slave's escape to freedom, *The Sun Do Move*, in which black religious music is used to articulate the slave community's pain and longing, gave rise to what many regard as his most perfectly realized theatrical work: the gospel play. *Black Nativity*, *The Gospel Glory*, and *The Prodigal Son* recreate a black church service, in sermon and song. A celebration of black faith and its typical forms of expression, the plays brought into the theatre black gospel music, just then gaining popularity with white audiences. In part, the plays expressed Hughes's determination, mindful of the historical appropriation by white artists of black music in particular, to retain black control of indigenous forms.

Hughes's principal contribution to the theatre lies in the originality of his project: to provide black theatre audiences with material truly about them. In fact, at Karamu, and later at Broadway and off-Broadway theatres, Hughes's audiences were racially mixed, and his comedy, which sometimes played on, and with, traditional stereotypes, occasionally caused embarrassment and confusion. His formally conventional plays depend on predictable plots, and his comedies on sentimental conclusions, but Hughes's inventiveness lies in setting rather than story. In the comedies, it lies in his authentic portrayal of black life, particularly urban life; in the serious dramas, it lies in history seen from a black perspective.

At his best, particularly in his poetry, but also in his plays, Hughes created language that depended on common expressions, rhythms, and lyric concreteness typical of African-American speech. His formal experiments showed how African-American folk-forms might be translated into formal theatrical art.

For 30 years Hughes was among the most productive of the African-American dramatists. By the early 1960's, however, he was overshadowed by younger playwrights, who were inclined to an explicitly political theatre, and interested in galvanizing the audiences that Hughes sought to instruct and entertain. Yet few have surpassed him, and all depend on his legacy, his successful challenge of the stereotypical and racist stage tradition of mainstream American theatre, and his myriad suggestions regarding what black theatre might accomplish.

—Leslie K. Sanders

HUGO, Victor (Marie). Born in Besançon, France, 26 February 1802. Educated at Cordier and Decotte's school, Paris, 1814–18. Married Adèle Foucher in 1822 (died 1868), three sons and two daughters; lived with Juliette Drouet from 1868 (his mistress since 1833; died 1883). Co-founder, with his brother Abel, *Le Conservateur littéraire*, 1819, and its editor, 1819–21; received first royal pension, 1822; first play, *Amy Robsart*, produced 1827; travelled in Europe, 1837–40; increasingly involved in politics, from the mid 1840's; founded newspaper *L'Événement* (later *L'Événement du peuple*), 1848; elected to legislative assembly, 1849; went into exile following the *coup d'état* by Louis-Napoleon, 1851; lived in Brussels, Jersey (1853), and settled in Guernsey; following proclamation of the Third Republic, 1870, returned to France, and was elected to the Assemblée Nationale: resigned, 1871; expelled from Paris for speaking out on behalf of the Communards, 1872; elected to Senate, 1876; suffered stroke, 1878. Elected to Académie Française, 1841. Chevalier, Légion d'Honneur, 1825. Ennobled as Vicomte Hugo, 1845. Died in Paris, 22 May 1885.

Works

Collections

Théâtre en liberté (short plays).   1886.
Dramatic Works (includes *Hernani; The King's Diversion; Ruy Blas*), translated by Frederick L. Slous and Mrs. Newton Crosland.   1887.
Dramas (4 vols.), translated by I.G. Burnham.   1895.
Théâtre de jeunesse.   1934.
Théâtre complet (2 vols.), edited by Roland Purnal.   1963–64.
Oeuvres complètes (18 vols.), edited by Jean Massin.   1967–70.

Stage Works

Amy Robsart, from a novel by Sir Walter Scott (produced Théâtre de l'Odéon, Paris, 1827); translated as *Amy Robsart*, 1933.
Cromwell (produced Palais du Louvre, Paris, 1956).   1827.
Marion Delorme (produced Théâtre de la Porte-Saint-Martin, Paris, 1831).   1829; translated as *The King's Edict*, 1872.
Hernani (produced Comédie-Française, Paris, 1830).   1830; translated as *Hernani*, 1830.
Le Roi s'amuse (produced Comédie-Française, Paris, 1832).   1832; translated as *Le Roi s'amuse*, 1843; as *The King's Diversion*, in *Dramatic Works*, 1887.
Marie Tudor (produced Théâtre de la Porte-Saint-Martin, Paris, 1833).   1833.
Lucrèce Borgia (produced Théâtre de la Porte-Saint-Martin, Paris, 1833).   1833; translated as *Lucretia Borgia*, 1847.

Angelo, Tyran de Padoue (produced Comédie-Française, Paris, 1835).   1835; translated as *Angelo*, 1855(?).
La Esméralda, music by Louise Bertin, from *Notre-Dame de Paris* by Hugo (produced Académie Royale de Musique, Paris, 1836).   1836.
Ruy Blas (produced Théâtre de la Renaissance, Paris, 1838).   1838; translated as *Ruy Blas*, 1860(?): several subsequent translations under the same title.
Les Burgraves (produced Comédie-Française, Paris, 1843).   1843.
Inez de Castro.   In *Victor Hugo raconté par un témoin de sa vie*, 1863.
Welf, Castellan d'Osbor.   In *La Légende des siècles*, 1877.
Les Deux Trouvailles de Gallus.   In *Les Quatres Vents de l'esprit*, 1881.
Magarita.   In *Les Quatre Vents de l'esprit*, 1881.
Torquemada.   1882.
La Forêt mouillée.   In *Théâtre en liberté*, 1886.
La Grand' Mère (produced Théâtre de l'Odéon, Paris, 1898). In *Théâtre en liberté*, 1866.
L'Épée.   In *Théâtre en liberté*, 1886.
Mangeront-ils? (produced Théâtre du Parc, Brussels, 1907). In *Théâtre en liberté*, 1886.
Esca (produced Comédie-Française, Paris, 1923).   In *Théâtre en liberté*, 1886.
Les Jumeaux.   1889.
L'Intervention.   In *Théâtre de jeunesse*, 1934.
Irtamène.   In *Théâtre de jeunesse*, 1934.
Mille Francs de récompense (produced Théâtre Municipal, Metz, 1961).   In *Théâtre de jeunesse*, 1934.
À Quelque Chose malheur est bon (libretto).   In *Théâtre de jeunesse*, 1934.
Le Château du diable.   In *La Nouvelle Revue française*, March 1939.
Sur la Lisière d'un bois (produced Théâtre Municipal, Brive, 1945).

Fiction

Han d'Islande.   1823; translated as *Han of Iceland*, 1825; as *The Demon Dwarf*, 1847; as *The Outlaw of Iceland*, 1885.
Bug-Jargal.   1826; translated as *The Slave King*, 1833; as *The Noble Rival*, 1845; as *Jargal*, 1866.
Le Dernier jour d'un condamné.   1829; translated as *The Last Day of a Condemned*, 1840.
Notre-Dame de Paris.   1831; translated as *The Hunchback of Notre-Dame*, 1833; as *La Esmeralda*, 1844.
Les Misérables.   1862; translated as *Les Misérables*, 1862.
Les Travailleurs de la mer.   1866; translated as *Toilers of the Sea*, 1866.
L'Homme qui rit.   1869; translated as *By Order of the King*, 1870; as *The Laughing Man*, 1887.
Quatre-vingt-treize.   1874; translated as *Ninety-Three*, 1874.
Novels (28 vols.).   1895.
Romans, edited by Henri Guillemin (3 vols.).   1963.

Verse

Odes et poésies diverses.   1822.
Nouvelles Odes.   1824.
Odes et ballades.   1826.
Les Orientales.   1829.
Les Feuilles d'automne.   1831.
Les Chants du crépuscule.   1835; translated as *Songs of Twilight*, 1836.
Les Voix intérieures.   1837.
Les Rayons et les ombres.   1840.

(Thé artistique assaisonné de grands hommes.)

"Thé artistique assaisonné de grands hommes": 1845 drawing from *L'Illustration* showing **Victor Hugo** (right) with George Sand, Dumas *père* (above left), Balzac (left), and Liszt (at the piano).

Le Rhin. 1842; translated as *Excursions along the Banks of the Rhine*, 1843.
Les Châtiments. 1853.
Les Contemplations. 1856.
La Légende des siècles (3 vols.). 1859–83.
Les Chansons des rues et des bois. 1865.
L'Année terrible. 1872.
L'Art d'être grand-père. 1877.
Le Pape. 1878.
La Pitié suprême. 1879.
Religions et religion. 1880.
L'Âne. 1880.
Les Quatre vents de l'esprit. 1881.
La Fin de Satan. 1886.
Toute la lyre (2 vols.). 1888–93.
Dieu. 1891.
Oeuvres poétiques, edited by Pierre Albouy. 1964—
Poésies, edited by Bernard Leuilliot (3 vols.). 1972.
The Distance, The Shadows: Selected Poems, translated by Harry Guest. 1981.

Memoirs and Letters

Memoirs. 1899.
Correspondance (4 vols.). 1947–52.
Lettres à Juliette Drouet 1833–1883, edited by Jean Gaudon. 1964.
Correspondance, with Pierre-Jules Hetzel, edited by Sheila Gaudon. 1979—

Other

Littérature et philosophie mêlées. 1834.
Lettres sur le Rhin. 1846.
Napoléon le Petit. 1852; translated as *Napoleon the Little*, 1852.
Dessins de Hugo (art). 1862,
L'Archipel de la Manche. 1863.
Hugo raconté par un témoin de sa vie. 1863.
William Shakespeare. 1864; translated as *William Shakespeare*, 1864.
Actes et paroles. (3 vols.). 1875–76.
Choses vues (2 vols.). 1887–1900; translated in part as *Things Seen*, 1887; revised edition, edited by David Kimber, 1964.
Alpes et Pyrénées. 1890; translated as *The Alps and Pyrenees*, 1896.
France et Belgique. 1892.
Les Années funestes. 1896.
Post-scriptum de ma vie. 1901. translated as *Hugo's Intellectual Biography*, 1907.
Dernière gerbe. 1902.
Océan, Tas de Pierres. 1942.
Pierres: Vers et prose, edited by Henri Guillemin. 1951.
Carnets intimes, edited by Henri Guillemin. 1953.
Journal 1830–1848, edited by Henri Guillemin. 1954.
Hugo dessinateur, edited by Roger Cornaille and Georges Herscher. 1963.

*

Bibliographies

Elliott M. Grant, *Victor Hugo: A Select and Critical Bibliography*, Chapel Hill, North Carolina, 1967.
Ruth Lestha Doyle, *Victor Hugo: His Drama: An Annotated Bibliography 1900–1980*, Westport, Connecticut, 1981.

Criticism

Books
E. Gregh, *Victor Hugo: Sa Vie, son oeuvre*, Paris, 1954.
J. Gaudon, *Victo Hugo, dramaturge*, Paris, 1955.
Elliott M. Grant, *The Career of Hugo*, Cambridge, Massachusetts, 1945.
André Maurois, *Victor Hugo*, 1956.
André Maurois, *Victor Hugo and His World*, 1966.
P. Van Tieghem, *Dictionnaire de Victor Hugo*, Paris, 1970.
Charles Affron, *A Stage for Poets: Studies in the Theatre of Hugo and Musset*, Princeton, New Jersey, 1971.
S. Chahine, *La Dramaturgie de Victor Hugo, 1816–1843*, Paris, 1971.
M. Lebreton-Savigny, *Victor Hugo et les Américains, 1825–1885*, Paris, 1971.
John Porter Houston, *Victor Hugo*, New York, 1974.
Annie Ubersfeld, *Le Roi et le buffon: Étude sur le théâtre de Hugo de 1830 à 1839*, Paris, 1974.
Samuel Edwards, *Victor Hugo: A Biography*, London, 1975.
Patricia A. Ward, *The Medievalism of Hugo*, University Park, Pennsylvania, 1975.
Joanna Richardson, *Victor Hugo*, London, 1976.
P. Seghers, *Victor Hugo visionnaire*, Paris, 1983.
H. Wentzlaff-Eggebert, *Zwischen komischer Offenbarung und Wortoper: Das romantische Drama Victor Hugos*, Erlangen, 1984.
J. Gaudon, *Victor Hugo et le théâtre: Stratégie et dramaturgie*, Paris, 1985.
O. Krakovitch, *Hugo censuré: La Liberté au théâtre au 19e siècle*, Paris, 1985.
Anne Ubersfeld, *Paroles de Hugo*, Paris, 1985.

* * *

Born in 1802, the son of one of Napoleon's generals, Victor Hugo achieved early distinction in various branches of literature—lyric poetry (*Odes et ballades*, *Lest Orientales*, and *Les Feuìlles d'automne*) and the novel (*Notre-Dame de Paris*), as well as in the theatre (*Cromwell* and its preface, and *Hernani*); and by the time he was 30 he was the recognised leader of the Romantic movement in literature and the arts.

The conflict between the new ideas and the old was particularly violent in the theatre, where the "battle of *Hernani*" was a well-prepared assault by Hugo and the young partisans of Romantic drama on the Comédie Française as the citadel of reactionary conservatism: the first three performances in particular took on the character of a pitched battle, and although *Hernani* ran for 39 performances, this sustained, hard-fought campaign was hardly proof of durable success.

Other plays by Hugo followed, at the Comédie Française and other Paris theatres: *Marion de Lorme*, *Le Roi s'amuse* (The King's Diversion) *Ruy Blas*, and *Les Burgraves* (The Burgraves) in verse—Hugo's colourful and vigorous "reformed" Alexandrine metre, in place of the traditional neo-classical verse-form; and *Lucrece Borgia*, *Marie Tudor*, and *Angelo, Tyran de Padoue* (Angelo, Tyrant of Padua) in prose. The most successful of these plays was *Ruy Blas* (performed at the Théâtre de la Renaissance), in which Frédérick Lemaître, trained in *boulevard* melodrama, played the title role; the role of the Queen was written with Hugo's mistress, Juliette Drouet (who had already failed badly as Jane in *Marie Tudor*), in mind, but fortunately for the success of the play, she was replaced at the last minute by Frédérick's own mistress, Atala Beauchêne.

Throughout this period of intense theatrical activity, Hugo

and his plays were not only subject to adverse criticism from a generally hostile press, but also suffered from the censor's activities, as well as from machinations on the part of rival authors, unreliable managements, and performers with personal jealousies. However, he did slowly succeed in converting Paris audiences (especially those outside the Théâtre-Français) to acceptance of a new style of historical drama based on the formula set out in the preface to *Cromwell*, and owing much more to the Shakespearean example than to the neo-classical drama still in vogue in France in the 1820's.

With *Les Burgraves*, set in Germany in the Dark Ages, Hugo adopted an epic conception of history, with characters much larger than life and a quasi-mythical subject-matter. The play ran for 33 performances, a very respectable total at the Théâtre Française, but it was received with indifference, and the reception given to *Les Burgraves* is generally reckoned to have been the final factor discouraging Hugo from further activity in the theatre. Indeed, he was to complete only one more play, *Torquemada* (written in 1869, but not performed) in the idiom of Romantic historical drama, and half-a-dozen other works in dramatic form, mostly written to be read rather than performed, though *Mangeront-ils?* (Shall They Eat?), written in mid-century—a play owing something to the fantasy of Shakespeare's comedies—was admitted to the repertoire of the Comédie-Française in 1919.

From the break with the theatre in 1843 onwards, Hugo's inspiration became more epic and visionary than dramatic. It was to find expression in major collections of verse such as *Contemplations* and *La Légende des siècles*; while a similarly powerful, large-scale imagination can also be seen in novels like *Les Misérables*, *Les Travailleurs de la mer* (Toilers of the Deep), *L'Homme qui rit* (The Laughing Man) and *Quatre-vingt-treize* (Ninety-Three). At the time of his early successes, Hugo had belonged to the Royalist wing of the Romantic movement; but by the end of the 1840's he had become a firm Republican, and after the 1848 Revolution he was elected to the Legislative Assembly. His political ambitions were dashed, however, when he was not offered an important office on Louis Napoleon's becoming President; and after the *coup d'état* of 1851 he became the most outspoken critic of Napoleon III as Emperor. His campaign of opposition was waged from exile—Hugo settled in Guernsey in 1855 after two years in Jersey—and received its most powerful expression in the scathing satire of the verse collection, *Les Châtiments* (1853). The years of exile by the sea intensified Hugo's growing belief in the poet as a visionary leader of his fellow men, coupled with the interpretation of his grandiose (and highly personal) conception of a universe controlled by occult forces.

Although Hugo's career as a dramatist accounted for a relatively small proportion of his prodigious output, and was confined for practical purposes to a mere 15 years or so of his long life, the preface to *Cromwell* still has considerable importance as a major aesthetic manifesto, while his revitalised, imaginative form of historical drama can be seen to have influenced the work of later playwrights, not only in France, but right across the range of Western dramatic literature.

—William D. Howarth

See also *Volume 1* entries on *Hernani*; *Ruy Blas*.

I

IBSEN, Henrik (Johan). Born in Skien, Norway (then united with Sweden), 20 March 1828. Educated at local schools, including private school in Skien; attended Heltberg's school, Christiana (now Oslo), 1850–51, but failed matriculation to the University of Christiana. Married Suzannah Thoresen in 1858, one son; also had son by Else Jonsdatter in 1848. Pharmacist's assistant, Grimstad, 1844–50; first-produced play, *The Warrior's Barrow*, staged 1850; drama critic, *Manden*, later *Andhrimmer*, 1851; contributor to the radical newspaper *Arbejderforeningernes blad*, until it was shut down by the police, 1851; house dramatist, Norske Teater [Norwegian Theatre], Bergen, 1851–57; visited Copenhagen and Dresden, 1852; artistic director, Norske Teater in Christiana, 1857–62: theatre declared bankrupt, 1862; travelled in northern Norway on grant to collect folk tales, 1862; last production as a director, his play *The Pretenders*, at the Christiana Theatre, 1864; left Norway, 1864; lived in Italy, 1864–68; awarded annual pension by Norwegian government, 1866; visited Egypt, 1869; lived in Dresden, 1868–75 (with summer visit to Norway, 1874), Munich, 1875–78, Rome, 1878–85 (with brief visit to Norway, 1885), Munich, 1885–91; returned to Norway and settled in Christiana, 1891–1906. Doctor of Letters: Uppsala University, 1877. Died in Christiana, 23 May 1906.

Works

Collections

Samlede verker [Collected Works] (10 vols.).   1898–1902.
The Collected Works (12 vols.), translated by William Archer and others, edited by William Archer.   1906–12.
A Doll's House; The Wild Duck; The Lady from the Sea, translated by R. Farquharson-Sharp and Eleanor Marx-Aveling.   1910.
"Ghosts" and Two Other Plays (includes *The Warriors at Helgeland*; *An Enemy of the People*), translated by R. Farquharson-Sharp.   1911.
The Pretenders; Pillars of Society; Rosmersholm, translated by R. Farquharson-Sharp.   1913.
Lady Inger of Ostraat; Love's Comedy; The League of Youth, translated by R. Farquharson-Sharp.   1915.
Early Plays (includes *Cataline; The Warrior's Barrow; Olaf Liljekrans*), translated by Anders Orbeck.   1921.
Samlede verker [Collected Works] (21 vols.; includes letters), edited by Francis Bull, Halvdan Koht, and Didrik Arup Seip.   1928–58.
Three Plays (includes *The Pillars of Society; The Wild Duck; Hedda Gabler*), translated by Una Ellis-Fermor.   1950; as *"Hedda Gabler" and Other Plays*, 1963.
"The Master Builder" and Other Plays (includes

Henrik Ibsen

Rosmersholm; Little Eyolf; John Gabriel Borkman), translated by Una Ellis-Fermor.   1958.
The Oxford Ibsen (8 vols.; includes notes and variants), translated by James Walter McFarlane and others, edited by James Walter McFarlane.   1960–77:
   1. *Cataline; The Burial Mound; Norma; or, A Politician's Love; St. John's Night; Lady Inger; The Feast at Solhaug; Olaf Liljekrans.*
   2. *The Vikings at Helgeland; Love's Comedy; The Pretenders.*
   3. *Brand; Peer Gynt.*
   4. *The League of Youth; Emperor and Galilean.*
   5.–8. The 12 plays of contemporary life.
Ghosts; A Public Enemy; When We Dead Awake, translated by Peter Watts.   1964.

The League of Youth; A Doll's House; The Lady from the Sea, translated by Peter Watts.   1965.
The Complete Major Prose Plays (includes the 12 plays of contemporary life), translated by Rolf Fjelde.   1978.
Samlede verker [Collected Works] (7 vols.).   1978.
Plays (6 vols.; some translations published in earlier versions), translated by Michael Meyer.   Volumes 1–4 (include the 12 plays of contemporary life), 1980; Volume 5 (includes *Brand; Emperor and Galilean*), 1986; Volume 6 (includes *Peer Gynt; The Pretenders*), 1987.

Stage Works

Catalina (produced Nya Teatern, Stockholm, 1882).   1850; translated as *Cataline*, in *Early Plays*, 1921 and in *The Oxford Ibsen 1*, 1970.
Kjæmpehøjen (produced Christiana Theatre, Christiana, 1850).   1902; translated as *The Warrior's Barrow*, in *Early Plays*, 1921; as *The Burial Mound*, in *The Oxford Ibsen 1*, 1970.
Norma; ellar, En politikers Kjaerlighd.   In *Andhrimmer*, 1 and 8 June, 1851; translated as *Norma; or, A Politician's Love*, in *The Oxford Ibsen 1*, 1960.
Sankthansnatten (produced Norske Teater, Bergen, 1853).   1909; translated as *St. John's Night*, in *The Oxford Ibsen 1*, 1960.
Fru Inger til Østråt (produced Norske Teater, Bergen, 1855).   1857; revised edition, 1874; translated as *Lady Inger of Ostraat*, in *Prose Dramas*, 1890; as *Lady Inger,* in *The Oxford Ibsen 1*, 1960.
Gildet pa Solhaug (produced Norske Teater, Bergen, 1856).   1856; translated as *The Feast at Solhaug,* in *Collected Works*, 1908.
Olaf Liljekrans (produced Norske Teater, Bergen, 1857).   1898; translated as *Olaf Liljekrans*, in *Early Plays*, 1921.
Hæmændene på Helgeland (produced Norske Teater, Christiania, 1858).   1857; translated as *The Vikings at Helgeland,* in *Prose Dramas*, 1890, and in *The Oxford Ibsen 2*, 1962.
Kjærlighedens komedie (produced Christiana Theatre, Christiania, 1873). 1862; translated as *Love's Comedy,* 1900: several subsequent translations under same title.
Kongs-Emnerne (produced Christiana Theatre, Christiania, 1864).   1863; translated as *The Pretenders*, in *Prose Dramas*, 1890: several subsequent translations under same title.
Brand (produced in part, Christiania, 1866; complete version produced Nya Teatern, Stockholm, 1885).   1866; translated as *Brand*, 1906: several subsequent translations under same title.
Peer Gynt (produced Christiana Theatre, Christiania, 1876). 1867; translated as *Peer Gynt*, 1892: several subsequent translations under same title.
De unges forbund (produced Christiana Theatre, Christiania, 1869).   1869; translated as *The League of Youth*, in *Prose Dramas*, 1890: several subsequent translations under same title.
Kejser og Galilæer (produced in part, Stadttheater, Leipzig, 1896).   1873; translated as *The Emperor and the Galilean*, 1876; as *Emperor and Galilean*, in *The Oxford Ibsen 4*, 1963, and *Plays 5*, 1986.
Samfundets støtter (produced Möllergaten Theatre, Christiania, 1877).   1877; translated as *The Pillars of Society*, in *"The Pillars of Society" and Other Plays*, 1888: several subsequent translations under same title.
Et dukkehjem (produced Kongelige Teater, Copenhagen,

1879).   1879; translated as *Nora*, 1880; as *A Doll's House*, in *Prose Dramas*, 1890: several subsequent translations under same title.
Gengangere (produced Aurora Turner Hall, Chicago, 1882). 1881; translated as *Ghosts*, in *"The Pillars of Society" and Other Plays*, 1888: several subsequent translations under same title.
En folkefiende (produced Christiana Theatre, Christiania, 1883).   1882; translated as *An Enemy of the People*, in *"The Pillars of Society" and Other Plays*, 1888: several subsequent translations under same title; also translated as *A Public Enemy*, in *Ghosts; A Public Enemy; When We Dead Awake*, 1964.
Vildanden (produced Norske Teater, Bergen, 1885).   1884; translated as *The Wild Duck*, in *Prose Dramas*, 1890: several subsequent translations under same title.
Rosmersholm (produced Norske Teater, Bergen, 1887). 1886; translated as *Rosmersholm*, in *Prose Dramas*, 1891: several subsequent translations under same title.
Fruen fra havet (produced Christiana Theatre, Christiania, and Hoftheater, Weimar, 1889).   1888; translated as *The Lady from the Sea*, in *Prose Dramas*, 1891: several subsequent translations under same title.
Hedda Gabler (produced Hoftheater, Munich, 1891). 1890; translated as *Hedda Gabler*, in *Prose Dramas*, 1891: several subsequent translations under same title.
Bygmester Solness (produced by Petersen's touring company, Trondheim, Norway, 1893).   1892; translated as *The Master Builder*, 1893: several subsequent translations under same title.
Lille Eyolf (produced Deutsches Theater, Berlin, 1895).   1894; translated as *Little Eyolf*, in *Collected Works*, 1907: several subsequent translations under same title.
John Gabriel Borkman (produced Swedish and Finnish Theatres, Helsinki, 1897).   1896; translated as *John Gabriel Borkman*, in *Collected Works*, 1907: several subsequent translations under same title.
Når vi døde vågner (produced 1900).   1899; translated as *When We Dead Awaken*, in *Collected Works*, 1907: several subsequent translations under same title; as *When We Dead Awake*, in *Ghosts; A Public Enemy; When We Dead Awake*, 1964.

Verse

Digte [Verse].   1871; augmented edition, 1875.
Lyrical Poems, translated by R.A. Streatfield.   1902.
On the Heights.   1910.
Lyrics and Poems, translated by F.E. Garrett.   1912.
Terje Viken, translated by M. Michelet and G.R. Vowles.   1918.
Poems, edited by John Northam.   1986.

Memoirs and Letters

Correspondence, edited and translated by Mary Morrison.   1905.
Brevveksling med Christiania Theater 1878–1899 (letters), edited by Øyvind Anker.   1965.
Brev 1845–1905 (letters), edited by Øyvind Anker.   1979.

Other

Episke Brand (fragment), edited by Karl Larsen.   1907.
Speeches and New Letters, edited by Lee M. Hollander.   1911.

Letters and Speeches, edited by Evert Sprinchorn.   1965.

*

Bibliographies

H. Pettersen, *Henrik Ibsen Bedømt af samtid og eftertid*, Oslo, 1928.

Annual bibliography in *Ibsen Årbok* [Ibsen Yearbook], 1952—

I. Telford, *Ibsen Bibliography 1928–1957*, Oslo, 1961.

Criticism

Books:

George Bernard Shaw, *The Quintessence of Ibsenism*, 1891; revised edition, 1913.

H.J. Weigand, *The Modern Ibsen*, New York, 1925.

Theodore Jorgenson, *Henrik Ibsen: A Study in Art and Personality*, Northfield, Minnesota, 1945.

M.C. Bradbrook, *Ibsen the Norwegian*, London, 1946; revised edition, 1966.

Brian W. Downs, *Henrik Ibsen: The Intellectual Background*, London, 1946.

P.F.D. Tennant, *Ibsen's Dramatic Technique*, Cambridge, 1948.

Brian W. Downs, *A Study of Six Plays by Ibsen*, Cambridge, 1950.

John Northam, *Ibsen's Dramatic Method*, London, 1952.

F. Bull, *Ibsen: The Man and the Dramatist*, Oxford, 1954.

J. Walter McFarlane, *Ibsen and the Temper of Norwegian Literature*, London, 1960.

G. Wilson Knight, *Henrik Ibsen*, London, 1962.

F.L. Lucas, *The Drama of Ibsen and Strindberg*, London, 1962.

Rolf Fjelde (ed.), *Henrik Ibsen: A Collection of Critical Essays*, Englewood Cliffs, New Jersey, 1965.

Contemporary Approaches to Ibsen (symposia; continuing series), Oslo, 1966—(6 vols. to date).

Michael Meyer, *Henrik Ibsen* (three-volume biography), London, 1967–71; condensed, single-volume edition, Harmondsworth, 1974.

O.I. Holtan, *Mythic Patterns in Ibsen's Last Plays*, Minneapolis, Minnesota, 1970.

J.W. McFarlane (ed.), *Henrik Ibsen: A Critical Anthology*, Harmondsworth, 1970.

Michael Egan (ed.), *Ibsen: The Critical Heritage*, London, 1972.

J. Hurt, *Cataline's Dream: An Essay on Ibsen's Plays*, Urbana, Illinois, 1972.

Charles R. Lyons, *Henrik Ibsen: The Divided Consciousness*, Carbondale, Illinois, 1972.

John Northam, *Ibsen: A Critical Study*, Cambridge, 1973.

Brian Johnston, *The Ibsen Cycle: The Design of the Plays from "Pillars of Society" to "When We Dead Awaken"*, New York, 1975.

Vincent J. Balice, *Ibsen's Feminine Mystique*, New York, 1975.

Harold Clurman, *Ibsen*, New York, 1977.

Ronald Gray, *Ibsen: A Dissenting View*, Cambridge, 1977.

Edward Beyer, *Ibsen: The Man and His Work* (from the German), New York, 1978.

E. Haugen, *Ibsen's Drama: Author to Audience*, Minneapolis, Minnesota, 1979.

Errol Durbach (ed.), *Ibsen and the Theatre: The Dramatist in Production*, New York, 1980.

Brian Johnston, *To the Third Empire: Ibsen's Early Drama*, Minneapolis, 1980.

J.E. Tammany, *Henrik Ibsen's Aesthetic and Dramatic Art*, New York, 1980.

Richard Hornby, *Patterns in Ibsen's Middle Plays*, Lewisburg, Pennsylvania, 1981.

Errol Durbach, *Ibsen the Romantic*, London, 1982.

John S. Chamberlain, *Ibsen: The Open Vision*, London, 1982.

David Thomas, *Henrik Ibsen*, London, 1983 (Macmillan Modern Dramatists series).

William Archer, *William Archer on Ibsen: The Major Essays, 1889–1919*, edited by Thomas Postlewait, Westport, Connecticut, 1984.

G.B. Bryan, *An Ibsen Companion: A Dictionary Guide to the Life, Works, and Critical Reception of Henrik Ibsen*, Westport, Connecticut, 1984.

Michael Meyer (compiler), *Ibsen on File*, London, 1985.

Yvonne Shafer, *Henrik Ibsen: Life, Work and Criticism*, Fredericton, New Brunswick, 1985.

Charles R. Lyons (ed.), *Critical Essays on Henrik Ibsen*, Boston, 1987.

James McFarlane, *Ibsen's Meaning: Studies, Essays and Prefaces 1953–87*, Norwich, East Anglia, 1987.

Frederick J. Marker and Lise-Lone Marker, *Ibsen's Lively Art: A Performance Study of the Major Plays*, Cambridge, 1989.

Brian Johnston, *Ibsen's Text and Supertext*, University Park, Pennsylvania, 1989.

Robin Young, *Time's Disinherited Children: Childhood, Regression and Sacrifice in the Plays of Henrik Ibsen*, Norwich, 1989.

Naomi Lebowitz, *Ibsen and the Great World*, Baton Rouge, Louisiana, 1990.

Serials:

Ibsen Årbok [Ibsen Yearbook], 1952—

*   *   *

In the first decade of his career as a playwright, the 1850's, Ibsen found most of his themes and characters in Norwegian and Danish myths and ballads as well as in Icelandic sagas. The form of his early dramatic efforts shows the influence of playwrights like Shakespeare, Adam Oehlenschläger, and Eugène Scribe. The most ambitious of his early plays was *Lady Inger of Ostraat*, a tragedy with a rather complex plot based on historical studies. The theatre audience was more favourable to Ibsen's next play, however, *The Feast at Solhaug*, a comedy treating the theme of love in a light folk-ballad style. More remarkable is *The Vikings at Helgeland*, with its focus on the passionate and vindictive mind of the woman from the saga who feels betrayed in her love.

In the 1860's Ibsen was concerned more with moral and philosophical principles than with historical themes and characters. *Love's Comedy* is a drama in verse where a Kierkegaardian idealism colours the character of Falk, the poet who breaks his engagement to Svanhild in order to preserve his love for her, unblemished. In this play Ibsen introduced his great talent for irony in depicting the bourgeois characters around the young couple.

In *The Pretenders* he returned to a fateful moment in Norwegian history, the civil war of 1239–40 between King Håkon and his father-in-law. The plot is somewhat over-complex, a weakness this drama shares with *Lady Inger of Ostraat*, but the psychology of the central characters shows an improved grasp of this kind of dramatic treatment. *The Pretenders* is the most powerful history play in Norwegian literature.

During the events of 1864 (the Dano-Prussian War) Ibsen found in what he considered cowardice among the political leaders a target for dramatic satire, and he put all his moral conviction and spiritual force in the writing of *Brand*. Brand ("fire") is a religious leader who confronts the small fjord community with words and deeds amounting to a superhuman demand of "all or nothing". The catastrophic ending is ambiguous, but the ruthless consistency of Brand's fiery rhetoric and fight against mediocrity makes him aesthetically impressive, even in his moment of failure. This drama was a turning point in Ibsen's career.

Peer Gynt is generally seen as the reverse of *Brand*, and there is a certain contrast in moral terms between the two main characters. While Brand is unflinching, Peer Gynt is evasive, always playing safe, and extremely selfish. Brand is true to himself and faithful to his mission, Peer drifts around in the world trying to enrich himself. In terms of dramatic technique, however, the two poems are rather different. *Brand* is a monumental tragedy, while *Peer Gynt* has both comic and tragic elements. *Brand* can be seen as a parable of Kierkegaardian man trying to imitate Christ, while *Peer Gynt* is more like an allegory of man in his moral frailty, a 19th-century version of *Everyman*. With its abundant use of folklore, literary allusions, animal metaphors, ironic hints at contemporary scholarship, and so on, the text of *Peer Gynt* is extremely complex, and yet thematically coherent. It is Ibsen's profoundest work and his most impressive artistic achievement.

After *Brand* and *Peer Gynt*, neither of which were composed with stage performance in mind, Ibsen abandoned the form of verse drama, although he continued to write poems. The illusion of reality, he must have felt, was more easily created by means of a prose dialogue. This idea did not only apply to the writing of plays in a contemporary setting, like *The League of Youth*, a comedy ridiculing unprincipled politicians; it also directed his choice of form in the world-historical drama *The Emperor and the Galilean*. This drama in two parts is the tragedy of Julian the Apostate, Emperor of Rome, who challenged the Christians of his time in a futile effort to stop the growth of that new religion. Ibsen regarded this drama as his masterpiece. It is based on the idea of a universal antithesis between a pagan idea of beauty and a Christian ideal of martyrdom. In spite of the efforts invested, his one attempt to create dramatic art on a foundation of philosophy of history was not successful, although many of the scenes have a certain potential for the stage.

Ibsen's 12 last plays all have a contemporary setting. The action takes place in an atmosphere which, at the start, seems relatively peaceful, but which, with the evolving plot, is soon shattered, as the central characters gradually acquire a radically new insight regarding the past, their own personal guilt, or their prospects for the days ahead. It is evident that Ibsen, in the late 1870's, felt that he had succeeded in creating a dramatic language suitable for the themes and situations he wanted to explore on the stage. The kind of prose drama attempted in *The Pillars of Society*, and fully developed in *A Doll's House*, turned out to be an appropriate vehicle for his poetry of the theatre, and he continued to use it for the rest of his creative life.

The plays from *A Doll's House* to *When We Dead Awaken* —the latter was designated as the epilogue to this series—can be considered as one corpus of variables and invariables. The basic theme common to them all is the idea of freedom, so important to Romantic drama since Schiller. This theme not only pervades the dialogue; it is also expressed symbolically by means of a spatial system of opposites—a narrow inner world and an open outer world. The inner world is generally represented by the stage, in most cases an interior scene. The main character experiences an increasing feeling of claustrophobia, and a longing for freedom in one sense or another. *A Doll's House* presents the sudden spiritual awakening of a young woman through a series of encounters with visitors from the outside world and serious disappointment with her husband. The logical ending of the drama is the sound of a door being slammed as Nora leaves for the greater world outside. In *Ghosts* the doll's house metaphor is replaced by the conservatory (literally the flower room) of Mrs Alving's mansion at Rosenvold—plant symbolism is used to suggest the conditions for human existence in the Alving society. Mrs Alving, who did not leave her husband, has become an extremely protective mother, but she realizes not only that her efforts to save her son have been futile, but that she is, in part, responsible for the late Chamberlain Alving's fateful debaucheries.

In these plays the focus is not so much on social criticism, although there is a certain element of satire, but rather on the moral substance of the individual facing a changed social condition. In *An Enemy of the People* Dr. Stockmann, an apostle of truth, is taught a lesson as to the townspeople's changeable allegiances; but as a Romantic hero he rises to the occasion, defying the small-town society when he is left alone with his family. The theme of freedom is embodied in his final discovery: his complete political and personal independence makes him the strongest man in the world, since he is totally free to decide for himself.

In *The Wild Duck* there is a contrast between the limited conditions of an artificial and protected existence of the interior, metaphorically represented by the menagerie in the Ekdal family flat, and the free world of the exterior, which is the world of truth, too harsh for some people to cope with. The purging mission of the Brand-like idealist Gregers Werle ends in tragedy. In *Rosmersholm* the utopian ideas developed by Johannes Rosmer in his rather confined family mansion turn out to be unsuitable for the greater world outside. Because of his own sense of guilt and that of his lady friend Rebecca West, his vision of nobility of character cannot be realized except through their collective atonement, which means death in the mill-stream where Mrs Rosmer had died before.

Only two of the plays in this series, *The Lady from the Sea* and *Little Eyolf*, end with a positive solution for the man and woman involved, and the critics have, for this reason, been reluctant to accept the endings at face value. In these two plays the settings are less confined to interior scenes.

Hedda Gabler is a tragedy based on the claustrophobic effect of interior seclusion, however. General Gabler's fêted daughter is trapped in a tedious marriage to the pedant Jørgen Tesman. Trying to inspire her admirer Ejlert Løvborg to live a free and daring life, she becomes involved in his death, is utterly confined in the web of her own making, and can only escape through suicide. There is a demonic aspect in Hedda's destructive will to control the lives of men, just as there is a demonic ability to command the affection of women in the architect Halvard Solness in *The Master Builder*. In this tragedy of *hubris*, as in most of the other late plays, there is a certain retrospective questioning about the life led by the artist or professional man combined with an impossible dream of a new start.

In *John Gabriel Borkman* the distinction between the interior and the exterior world is again essential to the scenography as well as to the action. The former bank manager has lived in voluntary seclusion for eight years, following a term of imprisonment, and is waiting for society to ask for his services again. Literally, he is unfit for life in the cold air of the outer world, while his son breaks away from home realizing the dream of freedom and love. In the epilogue to this series of plays, *When We Dead Awaken*, there is a sense of wasted life and a new, tragically impossible determination to reach for the summit of human happiness.

The historical importance of Ibsen should not be sought in his social criticism, his Romantic individualism bordering on political anarchism, or his involvement in the philosophy of history. His greatest achievement is his contribution to the form of modern drama, his eye for the potential of the setting, in conjunction with his stage directions and a dialogue loaded with meaning, to create a supreme dramatic effect within the relatively limited means of the 19th-century theatre.

—Asbjørn Aarseth

See also *Volume 1* entries on *Brand*; *A Doll's House*; *An Enemy of the People*; *Ghosts*; *Hedda Gabler*; *John Gabriel Borkman*; *The Lady From the Sea*; *The Master Builder*; *Peer Gynt*; *The Pillars of Society*; *Rosmersholm*; *When We Dead Awaken*; *The Wild Duck*.

———

INCHBALD, Elizabeth. Born Elizabeth Simpson in Stanningfield, near Bury St. Edmunds, Suffolk, England, 15 October 1753. Married the actor Joseph Inchbald in 1772 (died 1779). Moved to London, 1772; debut as an actress, playing opposite her husband in *King Lear*, Bristol, 1772; actress with West Digges' company, touring Scotland, 1772–76, and, in England, with Joseph Younger's company, 1776–77, and Tate Wilkinson's company, 1777–78; London debut, as Bellario in *Philaster*, 1780; acted in London and Dublin, 1780–89; first play, *A Mogul Tale*, produced 1784; retired from acting in 1789; contributor, *Edinburgh Review* and the *Artist*, 1807–09. Died in London, 1 August 1821.

Works

Collections

Selected Comedies (*I'll Tell You What*; *Such Things Are*; *Everyone Has His Fault*; *The Wedding Day*; *Wives as They Were and Maids as They Are*). 1987.

Stage Works

A Mogul Tale; or, The Descent of the Balloon (produced Theatre Royal, Haymarket, London, 1784). 1788.
I'll Tell You What (produced Theatre Royal, Haymarket, London, 1785). 1786.
Appearance is Against Them (produced Covent Garden Theatre, London, 1785; as *Mistake Upon Mistake* produced 1804). 1785.
The Widow's Vow, from a play by Joseph Patrat (produced Theatre Royal, Haymarket, London, 1786). 1786.
Such Things Are (produced Covent Garden Theatre, London, 1787). 1788.

The Midnight Hour; or, War of Wits, from a play by Dumaniant (produced 1787). 1787.
All on a Summer's Day (produced Covent Garden Theatre, London, 1787).
Animal Magnetism (produced Covent Garden Theatre, London, 1788). 1788(?).
The Child of Nature, from a play by Comtesse de Genlis (produced Covent Garden Theatre, London, 1788). 1788.
The Married Man, from a play by Philippe Néricault-Destouches (produced Theatre Royal, Haymarket, London, 1789). 1789.
The Hue and Cry, from a play by Dumaniant (produced Theatre Royal, Drury Lane, London, 1791).
Next Door Neighbours, from plays by L.S. Mercier and Philippe Néricault-Destouches (produced Theatre Royal, Haymarket, London, 1791). 1791.
Young Men and Old Women, from a play by Gresset (produced Theatre Royal, Haymarket, London, 1792).
The Massacre. 1792.
Every One Has His Fault (produced Covent Garden Theatre, London, 1793). 1793.
The Wedding Day (produced Theatre Royal, Drury Lane, London, 1794). 1794.
Wives as They Were and Maids as They Are (produced Covent Garden Theatre, London, 1797). 1797.
Lovers' Vows, from a play by Kotzebue (produced Covent Garden Theatre, London, 1798). 1798.
The Wise Man of the East, from a play by Kotzebue (produced Covent Garden Theatre, London, 1799). 1799.
To Marry, or Not to Marry (produced Covent Garden Theatre, London, 1805). 1805.
A Case of Conscience. In *Memoirs of Mrs. Inchbald*, by James Boaden (2 vols.), 1833.

Fiction

A Simple Story. 1791.
Nature and Art. 1796.

Other

Editor, *The British Theatre; or, A Collection of Plays with Biographical and Critical Remarks* (25 vols.). 1808.
Editor, *A Collection of Farces and Other Afterpieces* (7 vols.). 1809.
Editor, *The Modern Theatre* (10 vols.). 1809.

*

Bibliographies

G. Louis Joughin, "An Inchbald Bibliography", in *Texas Studies in Literature and Language*, 14, 1934.

Criticism

Books:
James Boaden, *Memoirs of Inchbald* (2 vols.), London, 1833.
Clara Tobler, *Mrs. Inchbald, eine vergessene englische Bühnendichterin und Romanschriftstellerin des 18. Jahrhunderts*, Berlin, 1910.
S.R. Littlewood, *Elizabeth Inchbald and Her Circle*, London, 1921.
François Moreaux, *Inchbald et la comédie sentimentale anglaise au XVIIIᵉ siècle*, 1971.

François Moreaux, *Elizabeth Inchbald et la revendication feminine au dix-huitième siècle* (includes text of *Wives as They Were . . .*), Paris, 1973.

Roger Manvell, *Elizabeth Inchbald: A Biographical Study*, New York, 1987.

*   *   *

Actress, dramatist, novelist, critic and historian of theatre, Elizabeth Inchbald gained a prominent place in the 18th-century world of letters. Her marriage to a fellow actor helped launch her stage career: initially she played Cordelia to his Lear, Desdemona to his Othello, and Anne Bullen to his Cranmer. Although her speech was marred by a habitual stutter, she played major roles, including Jane Shore, Juliet, Imogen, Lady Anne in *Richard III*, Aspasia in *Tamerlane*, Cleopatra in *All for Love*, and the Tragic Muse in the *Jubilee*. She acted with, and became close friends with, Tate Wilkinson, Sarah Siddons, and John Philip Kemble. Kemble's niece Frances recalls her "singular uprightness and unworldliness, and a childlike directness and simplicity of manner . . . both humorous and witty", while Godwin found her a "piquante mixture between a lady and a milkmaid".

Inchbald wrote 21 plays, some adapted from French and German originals. 12 are farces and light comedies; the others are serious comedies, with the exception of one tragedy, the Jacobin-inspired *The French Massacre*, which was never produced. The components of the farces and light comedies often resemble those of comedy of intrigue: stereotypical characters such as tyrannical fathers and conniving servants, "humours" names (such as the amorous Lady Loveall in *Appearance is Against Them*), mistaken identity, and aggravated misunderstandings which are only resolved in the last scene. Although these works may, today, seem overly contrived and insistent upon tidy endings, such deficiences are redeemed by lively pacing and dialogue.

The eight serious comedies—*Next Door Neighbours*, *Every One Has His Fault*, *The Wise Man of the East*, *Wives as They Were and Maids as They Are*, *The Widow's Vow*, *A Case of Conscience*, *To Marry or Not to Marry*, *Lovers' Vows*, *Such Things Are*—take a satiric look at contemporary social and moral problems: *Next Door Neighbours* contrasts the penniless Harry and Eleanor with their spendthrift neighbours to demonstrate the evils of poverty; *Every One Has His Fault* shows how poverty leads to theft; in *Wives As They Were* an addiction to gambling lands Maria and her friend in debtors' prison; and *Such Things Are* deals with prison reform.

Themes of marital discord or inequity recur in several plays: in *The Widow's Vow* the widow's disappointing first marriage leads her to reject men; in *The Married Man*, Sir John Classick tries to conceal his marriage to a penniless girl; *Lovers' Vows* focuses on the miseries of arranged marriages; and a confirmed bachelor's view of matrimony is set forth in *To Marry or Not To Marry*.

As a critic and editor, Inchbald's tastes were very much those of the late-18th century: she expressed a fondness for spectacular or exotic settings, for moralising or sentimental plays, for genteel and decorous characters, and she placed a high value on "sensibility" and refined behaviour. She condemned Farquhar's *The Beaux' Stratagem* for its immorality, and, along with Dr. Johnson, disliked the ribald aspects of Shakespeare. In her contemporaries' works she valued credibility and a closeness to "Nature": thus she approved the naturalistic characterisation of Goldsmith's *She Stoops to Conquer* and the "refined notions, the enthusiastic, yet natural passion" of the lovers in Sheridan's *The Rivals*. Her practical knowledge as dramatist and actress informed her

critical writing, which not only documented trends in public taste, but also advocated the use of theatre as a means of moral and spiritual education.

—R. Valerie Lucas

INGE, William (Motter).   Born in Independence, Kansas, USA, 3 May 1913. Educated at Montgomery County High School, Independence, graduated 1930; University of Kansas, Lawrence, 1930–35, AB 1935; Peabody Teachers College, Nashville, Tennessee, 1935–36, MA 1938; Yale University, New Haven, Connecticut, 1940. Announcer, KFH Radio, Wichita, Kansas, 1936–37; teacher at Columbus High School, Kansas, 1937–38, Stephens College, Columbia, Missouri, 1938–43, and Washington University, St. Louis, 1946–49; arts critic, St. Louis *Star-Times*, 1943–46; first play, *Farther Off from Heaven*, produced 1947; story consultant, *Bus Stop* television series, 1961–62; lecturer, University of North Carolina, Chapel Hill, 1969, and University of California, Irvine, 1970. Recipient: George Jean Nathan Award, 1951; Pulitzer Prize, 1953; New York Drama Critics Circle award, 1953; Donaldson Award, 1953; Oscar, for screenplay, 1962. Committed suicide in Los Angeles, 10 June 1973.

William Inge

Works

Collections

Four Plays (includes *Come Back, Little Sheba; Picnic; Bus
Stop; The Dark at the Top of the Stairs*).   1958.
"Summer Brave" and Eleven Short Plays (includes *To
Bobolink, For Her Spirit; A Social Event; The Boy in the
Basement; The Tiny Closet; Memory of Summer; The Rainy
Afternoon; The Mall; An Incident at the Standish Arms;
People in the Wind; Bus Riley's Back in Town; The Strains
of Triumph*).   1962.

Stage Works

The Dark at the Top of the Stairs (as *Farther Off from Heaven*,
produced Margo Jones' Theatre 47, Dallas, Texas, 1947;
revised version, as *The Dark at the Top of the Stairs*,
produced Music Box Theatre, New York, 1957).   1958.
Come Back, Little Sheba (produced Booth Theatre, New
York, 1950).   1950.
Picnic: A Summer Romance (produced Music Box Theatre,
New York, 1953).   1953; revised version, as *Summer
Brave* (produced 1962), in *"Summer Brave" and Eleven
Short Plays*, 1962.
Bus Stop (produced Music Box Theatre, New York,
1955).   1955.
Glory in the Flower (produced New York, 1959).   In *24
Favorite One-Act Plays*, edited by Bennett Cerf and Van
H. Cartmell, 1958.
The Tiny Closet (produced Spoleto, Italy, 1959).   In *"Sum-
mer Brave" and Eleven Short Plays*, 1962.
A Loss of Roses (produced Eugene O'Neill Theatre, New
York, 1959), 1960.
Natural Affection (produced Phoenix, Arizona, 1962).
1963.
Summer Brave (produced Equity Library Theatre, New
York, 1973).   In *"Summer Brave" and Eleven Short Plays*,
1962.
To Bobolink, for Her Spirit.   In *"Summer Brave" and
Eleven Short Plays*, 1962.
A Social Event.   In *"Summer Brave" and Eleven Short Plays*.
1962.
The Boy in the Basement.   In *"Summer Brave" and Eleven
Short Plays*, 1962.
Memory of Summer.   In *"Summer Brave" and Eleven Short
Plays*, 1962.
The Rainy Afternoon.   In *"Summer Brave" and Eleven Short
Plays* 1962.
The Mall.   In *"Summer Brave" and Eleven Short Plays*,
1962.
An Incident at the Standish Arms.   In *"Summer Brave" and
Eleven Short Plays*, 1962.
People in the Wind.   In *"Summer Brave" and Eleven Short
Plays*, 1962.
Bus Riley's Back in Town.   In *"Summer Brave" and Eleven
Short Plays*, 1962.
The Strains of Triumph.   In *"Summer Brave" and Eleven
Short Plays*, 1962.
Where's Daddy? (as *Family Things, Etc.*, produced
Falmouth, Massachusetts, 1965; as *Where's Daddy?*, pro-
duced Billy Rose Theatre, New York, 1966).   1966.
The Disposal (as *Don't Go Gentle*, produced Los Angeles,
1968; as *The Last Pad*, produced Phoenix, Arizona, 1972).
In *Best Short Plays of the World Theatre 1958–1967*, edited
by Stanley Richards, 1968; revised version, as *The*

Disposal, music by Anthony Caldarella, lyrics by Judith
Gero (produced New York, 1973).
The Call.   In *Two Short Plays*, 1968.
A Murder.   In *Two Short Plays*, 1968.
Midwestern Manic (produced as part of *The Love Death
Plays*, New York, 1975).   In *Best Short Plays 1969*, edited
by Stanley Richards, 1969.
Overnight (produced University of California, Los Angeles,
1969).
Caesarian Operations (produced Los Angeles, 1972).
Margaret's Bed.   In *Best Short Plays of the World Theatre
1968–1973*, edited by Stanley Richards, 1973.
*Love Death Plays: Dialogue for Two Men; Midwestern
Manic; The Love Death; Venus and Adonis; The Wake;
The Star* (produced Billy Munk Theatre, New York, 1975).

Screenplays

Splendor in the Grass (published 1961), 1961; *All Fall Down*,
1962; *Bus Riley's Back in Town*, 1965.

Television Plays

Out on the Outskirts of Town, 1964.

Fiction

Good Luck, Miss Wyckoff.   1971.
My Son is a Splendid Driver.   1972.

*

Criticism

Books:
R. Baird Shuman, *William Inge*, New York, 1966; revised
edition, 1987.
Arthur F. McClure, *Memories of Splendor: The Midwestern
World of William Inge*, Topeka, Kansas, 1989.
Ralph F. Voss, *The Life of William Inge: The Strains of
Triumph*, Lawrence, Kansas, 1989.

Articles:
Jordan Y. Miller, "William Inge: Last of the Realists?", in
Kansas Quarterly, vol.2 no.2, 1970.
"The Works of William Inge" (various essays), *Kansas
Quarterly* special issue, vol.18 no.4, 1986.

* * *

William Inge is the quintessential mid-20th century
Midwestern American playwright. His reputation rests on
four plays written during the 1950's: *Come Back, Little
Sheba*; *Picnic*; *Bus Stop*; and *The Dark at the Top of the
Stairs*. These dramas were among the most popular and critically acclaimed theatrical works in America during the playwright's lifetime, and they continue to be popular staples in
repertory companies across the United States.

Inge's success lies primarily in his understanding of his
audience. He consciously wrote plays for what is now called
"Middle America", and his Midwest settings and characters
express common perceptions held about that segment of the
American population. He was not interested in dramatic
experimentation or innovation in format or characterization.
Inge's works focus on the narrow interests of an audience
with little knowledge of, or concern for, world affairs: the
world of Inge's audience is the world of a small town.

Inge thus chose characters and themes that his audience
was familiar with, and to which they could relate easily. In
Come Back, Little Sheba, a childless married couple, like

George and Martha in Edward Albee's *Who's Afraid of Virginia Woolf?*, must face the reality of life. In *Picnic* Flo, Madge, Millie, Rosemary, and Helen are affected by the appearance of Hal, a sexually attractive man from outside the community. *Bus Stop* is a romantic comedy about a Montana cowboy and a Kansas City nightclub performer. In *The Dark at the Top of the Stairs*, a family confronts the small-town prejudices that lead to the suicide of the daughter's country-club dance partner, a young Jew. The one common element that runs through Inge's four major plays is his utilization of similar images to depict life in a small Midwestern town—images that reflect the setting itself, the character types, and the characters' thoughts.

Inge commented that *Come Back, Little Sheba*, which is set in "late spring", a time of hope and renewal, "was a fabric of life, in which the two characters (Doc and Lola) were a species of the environment". The inner strength of these two people under stress is demonstrated in actions reflecting their Midwestern American culture and its underlying beliefs and traditions.

Picnic contains many of the same common denominators that grow out of a small, Midwestern town setting. Hal Carter is perceived as a threat to the peaceful balance in the town because of the new ideas and experiences from the outside that he embodies. Ironically, one of Hal's motivations is the desire to establish a family, and the family is one of the most important elements in Midwestern society. It is significant that the action takes place on Labor Day, for holidays are important in the Midwest, and as a celebration of summer's end and the beginning of the harvest season the stereotypical picnic symbolically conveys the image of bourgeois values commonly associated with Midwesterners.

Another Midwestern locale, a restaurant/bus stop in a "small Kansas town", is the setting of *Bus Stop*, and the characters are essentially Midwesterners in their attitudes and backgrounds. Again, the value placed on establishing a family is a major motivating force; Bo and Cherie can overcome Bo's uncivilized past and her unsavory career because of their desire to become a family. And, once more, the action takes place in the spring. As the storm that temporarily isolates those in the restaurant illustrates, this season can be very unsettled, yet ultimately it is a time of hope.

The family in a Midwestern context is the theme of *The Dark at the Top of the Stairs* too. By placing the Flood family's residence "*in a small Oklahoma town close to Oklahoma City*", Inge juxtaposes two disparate cultures to demonstrate the strength of the traditional family. This strength is epitomized when Rubin and Cora reaffirm their love, and familial ties lead Cora's older sister to renew their relationship. Sammy Goldenbaum dies because he has neither family nor Midwestern traditions to sustain or support him.

Inge was the first American dramatist to gain prominence on the basis of his presentation of the people and philosophies of the Midwest. His solid, but conventional, plays are filled with images that reinforce his small-town themes in a positive, affectionate manner, and he was successful in presenting to the world a limited but accurate picture of a specific people in a specific place at a specific time.

—Steven H. Gale

See also *Volume 1* entries on *Come Back, Little Sheba*; *Picnic*.

IONESCO, Eugène. Born in Slatina, Romania, 13 November 1909 (some sources suggest 26 November 1912). Grew up in France, 1911–25; returned to Romania with father after parents' divorce, 1925. Educated at the lycée, Craiova, baccalaureate 1928; University of Bucharest, studying French literature, 1928–33, *capitate* [*agrégation de lettres*], 1934. Married Rodica Burileanu in 1936; one daughter. French teacher in Cernavodà and Bucharest, 1936–1938; contributed to *Viata Românesca* [Romanian Life], 1939; travelled to Paris, 1939; lived in Marseilles during World War II; settled in Paris after its liberation, 1944; proofreader, Éditions Administratives, Paris, c.1945, and subsequently full-time writer; first play, *La Cantatrice chauve*, produced 1950. Also an artist: exhibited artwork in Biarritz and the Galérie Mouf, Paris, 1970. Recipient: Tours Festival Prize, for film, 1959; Prix Italia 1963; Society of Authors theatre prize (France), 1966; Grand Prix National for theatre, 1969; Monaco Grand Prix, 1969; Austrian State Prize for European Literature, 1970; Jerusalem Prize, 1973. Honorary doctorates: New York University, 1971, and the universities of Louvain (France), Warwick (England), and Tel Aviv (Israel). Officier de l'Ordre des Arts et des Lettres, 1961; Chevalier, Légion d'Honneur, 1970. Elected to Académie Française, 1970.

Works

Collections

In French:
Théâtre I (includes *La Cantatrice chauve; La Leçon; Jacques, ou, La Soumission; Les Chaises; Victimes du devoir; Amédée, ou, Comment s'en débarrasser*). 1954.
Théâtre II (includes *L'Impromptu de l'Alma, ou, Le Caméléon du berger; Tueur sans gages; Le Nouveau Locataire; L'Avenir est dans les oeufs, ou, Il faut tout pour faire un monde; Le Maître; La Jeune Fille à marier*). 1958.
Théâtre III (includes *Rhinocéros; Le Piéton de l'air; Délire à deux; Le Tableau; Scène à quatre; Les Salutations; La Colère*). 1963.
Théâtre IV (includes *Le Roi se meurt, La Soif et la faim; La Lacune; Le Salon de l'automobile; L'Oeuf dur; Pour préparer un oeuf dur; Le Jeune Homme à marier; Apprendre à marcher*). 1966.
Théâtre V (includes *Jeux de massacre, Macbett, La Vase, Exercices de conversation et de diction françaises pour étudiants américains*). 1974.
Théâtre VI (includes *L'Homme aux valises; Ce Formidable Bordel*). 1975.
Théâtre VII (includes *Voyages chez les morts: Thèmes et variations*). 1981; translated as *Plays XII* (*Journeys Among the Dead*), 1983.
Oeuvres complètes. 1991.

In English:
Plays I (includes *The Chairs; The Bald Soprano; The Lesson; Jack, or, Obedience*). 1958; as *Four Plays* (US edition: same plays with different translations), 1958.
Plays II (includes *Amedee, or, How to Get Rid of It; The New Tenant; Victims of Duty*). 1958.
Plays III (includes *The Killer; Improvisation, or, The Shepherd's Chameleon; Maid to Marry*). 1960.
Plays IV (includes *Rhinoceros; The Leader; The Future is in Eggs, or, It Takes All Sorts to Make a World*). 1960.
Plays V (includes *Exit the King; The Motor Show; Foursome*). 1963.

Plays VI (includes *A Stroll in the Air; Frenzy for Two*). 1965.
Plays VII (includes *Hunger and Thirst; The Picture; Anger; Salutations*).   1968.
Plays VIII (includes *Here Comes a Chopper; The Oversight; The Foot of the Wall*).   1971.
Plays IX (includes *Macbett, The Mire, Learning to Walk*). 1973.
Plays X (includes *Oh What a Bloody Circus; The Hard-Boiled Egg*).   1976.
Plays XI (includes *The Man with the Luggage; The Duel; Double Act*).   1979.
Plays XII (includes *Journeys Among the Dead*).   1983.

Stage Works

La Cantatrice chauve (produced Théâtre des Noctambules, Paris, 1950).   In *Théâtre I*, 1954; translated as *The Bald Soprano*, in *Plays I*, 1958.
La Leçon (produced Théâtre de Poche, Paris, 1951).   In *Théâtre I*, 1954; translated as *The Lesson*, in *Plays I*, 1958.
Les Chaises (produced 1952).   In *Théâtre I*, 1954; translated as *The Chairs*, in *Plays I*, 1958.
Sept petits sketches (*Les Grandes Chaleurs, Le connaissez-vous?, Le Rhume onirique, La Jeune Fille à marier, Le Maître, La Nièce-Épouse, Le Salon de l'automobile*) (produced Théâtre de la Huchette, Paris, 1953).   *La Jeune Fille à marier* included in *Théâtre II*, 1958, and translated as *Maid to Marry*, in *Plays III*, 1960; *Le Maître* included in *Théâtre II*, 1958, and translated as *The Leader*, in *Plays IV*, 1960; *La Nièce-Épouse* translated as *The Niece-Wife*, in *Ionesco* by Richard N. Coe, 1971; *Le Salon de l'automobile* included in *Théâtre IV*, 1966, and translated as *The Motor Show* in *Plays V*, 1963.
Victimes du devoir (produced Théâtre du Quartier Latin, Paris, 1953).   In *Théâtre I*, 1954; translated as *Victims of Duty*, in *Plays II*, 1958.
Amédée; ou, Comment s'en débarrasser (produced Théâtre de Babylone, Paris, 1954).   In *Théâtre I*, 1954; translated as *Amedee*, in *Plays II*, 1958.
Jacques; ou, La Soumission (produced Théâtre de la Huchette, Paris, 1955).   In *Théâtre I*, 1954; translated as *Jack*, in *Plays I*, 1958.
Le Nouveau Locataire (produced in Swedish, Helsinki; produced in French, Théâtre d'Aujourd'hui, Paris, 1955).   In *Théâtre II*, 1958; translated as *The New Tenant*, in *Plays II*, 1958.
Le Tableau (produced Théâtre de la Huchette, Paris, 1955).   In *Théâtre III*, 1963; translated as *The Picture*, in *Plays VII*, 1968.
L'Impromptu de l'Alma; ou, Le Caméléon du berger (produced Studio des Champs-Élysées, Paris, 1956).   In *Théâtre II*, 1958; translated as *Improvisation; or, The Shepherd's Chameleon*, in *Plays III*, 1960.
L'Avenir est dans les oeufs; ou, Il faut tout pour faire un monde (produced Théâtre de la Cité Universitaire, Paris, 1957).   In *Théâtre II*, 1958; translated as *The Future is in Eggs; or, It Takes All Sorts to Make a World*, in *Plays IV*, 1960.
Impromptu pour la Duchesse de Windsor (produced Paris, 1957).
Tueur sans gages (produced Landestheater, Darmstadt, 1958).   In *Théâtre II*, 1958; translated as *The Killer*, in *Plays III*, 1960.
Rhinocéros (produced as *Das Nashörn*, Schauspielhaus, Düsseldorf; produced in French, Odéon, Paris, 1960).   In

Théâtre III, 1963; translated as *Rhinoceros*, in *Plays IV*, 1960.
Scène à quatre (produced Spoleto Festival, Spoleto, Italy, 1959).   In *Théâtre III*, 1963; translated as *Foursome*, in *Plays V*, 1963.
Apprendre à marcher (ballet scenario; produced Théâtre de L'Étoile, Paris, 1960).   In *Théâtre IV*, 1966; translated as *Learning to Walk*, in *Plays IX*, 1973.
Délire à deux (produced Studio des Champs-Élysées, Paris, 1962).   In *Théâtre III*, 1963; translated as *Frenzy for Two*, in *Plays VI*, 1965.
Le Roi se meurt (produced Théâtre de l'Alliance Française, Paris, 1962).   1963; translated as *Exit the King*, 1963.
Le Piéton de l'air (produced as *Der Fussgänger in der Luft*, Schauspielhaus, Düsseldorf, 1962; produced in French, Odéon, Paris, 1963).   In *Théâtre III*, 1963; as *A Stroll in the Air*, in *Plays VI*, 1965.
Les Salutations (produced London, 1970).   In *Théâtre III*, 1963; translated as *Salutations*, in *Plays VII*, 1968.
La Soif et la faim (produced as *Hunger und Durst*, Schauspielhaus, Düsseldorf, 1964; produced in French, Comédie-Française, Paris, 1966).   In *Théâtre IV*, 1966; translated as *Hunger and Thirst*, in *Plays VII*, 1968.
La Lacune (produced Centre Dramatique du Sud-Est, Paris, 1965).   In *Théâtre IV*, 1966; translated as *The Oversight*, in *Plays VIII*, 1971.
Pour préparer un oeuf dur (produced as part of *Mêlées et démêlées*, Théâtre de La Bruyère, Paris, 1966).   In *Théâtre IV*, 1966.
Leçons de français pour Américains (produced Théâtre de Poche, Paris, 1966).   As *Exercices de conversation et diction françaises pour étudiants américains*, in *Théâtre V*, 1974.
Jeux de massacre (produced as *Das grosse Massakerspiel*, Schauspielhaus, Düsseldorf, 1970; produced in French, Théâtre de Montparnasse, Paris, 1970).   1970; translated as *Here Comes a Chopper*, in *Plays VIII*, 1971; as *Killing Game*, 1974.
The Duel (produced Élysée-Montmartre, Paris, 1971).   In *Plays XI*, 1979.
Double Act (produced Élysée-Montmartre, Paris, 1971).   In *Plays XI*, 1979.
Macbett (produced Théâtre Rive Gauche, Paris, 1972).   1972; translated as *Macbett*, in *Plays IX*, 1973.
Ce Formidable Bordel (produced Théâtre Moderne, Paris, 1973).   1973; translated as *A Hell of a Mess*, 1975; as *Oh What a Bloody Circus*, in *Plays X*, 1976.
La Vase.   In *Théâtre V*, 1974.
L'Homme aux valises (produced Théâtre de l'Atelier, Paris, 1975).   1975; translated as *Man with Bags*, 1977; as *The Man with the Luggage*, in *Plays XI*, 1979.
Voyages chez les morts (as *Voyages Among the Dead*, Guggenheim Museum, New York, 1980; scenes produced as part of *Spectacle Ionesco*, Villeurbanne, Lyons, 1983).   As *Théâtre VII* (*Voyages chez les morts: Thèmes et variations*), 1981; translated as *Plays XII* (*Journeys Among the Dead*), 1983.

Screenplays

"La Colère", episode in *Les Sept Péchés capitaux*, 1962; *Monsieur Tête* (animated film), 1970 (text published 1970).

Television Plays

Ballet scenarios with Fleming Flindt: *La Leçon*, 1963, *Le Jeune Homme à marier*, 1965, *The Triumph of Death*, 1971; *La Vase*, 1970 (published in *Théâtre V*, 1974).

Fiction

La Photo du Colonel. 1962; translated as *The Colonel's Photograph*, 1967.
Le Solitaire. 1973; translated as *The Hermit*, 1974.

Other

Elegiï pentru fiinti mici. 1931.
Nu! 1934; in French, as *Non*, 1986.
Notes et contre-notes. 1962; revised edition, 1966; translated as *Notes and Counter-Notes*, 1964.
Entretiens avec Claude Bonnefoy. 1966; translated as *Conversations with Ionesco*, 1970.
Journal en miettes. 1967; translated as *Fragments of a Journal*, 1968.
Présent passé, passé présent. 1968; translated as *Present Past, Past Present*, 1971.
Conte pour enfants (4 vols.). 1969–75; translated as *Story for Children*, 1968–75.
Découvertes, illustrated by the author. 1969.
Mise en train: Première année de français, with Michael Benamou. 1969.
Discours de réception à l'Académie française. . . . 1971.
Entre la vie et la rêve: Entretiens avec Claude Bonnefoy. 1977.
Antidotes. 1977.
Un Homme en question. 1979.
Le Noir et le blanc. 1980.
Hugoliade. 1982; translated as *Hugoliad; or, The Grotesque and Tragic Life of Victor Hugo*, 1987.
Pourquoi J'écris. 1986.
La Quête intermittente. 1987.

*

Bibliographies:

Griffith R. Hughes and Ruth Bury, *Eugène Ionesco: A Bibliography*, Cardiff, 1974.
Wolfgang Leiner, *Bibliographie et index thématique des études sur Eugène Ionesco*, Fribourg, 1980.

Criticism

Books:
Richard N. Coe, *Eugène Ionesco*, New York, 1961; revised edition London, 1971.
Leonard C. Pronko, *Eugène Ionesco*, New York, 1965.
Simone Benmussa, *Textes et propos de Ionesco, documents de mise en scène, points de vue critiques, témoignages, chronologie, bibliographie*, Paris, 1966.
Claude Bonnefoy, *Entretiens avec Eugène Ionesco*, Paris, 1966.
Jean H. Donnard, *Ionesco dramaturge ou l'artisan et le démon*, Paris, 1966.
Philippe Sénart, *Ionesco* (revised edition), Paris, 1966.
Faust Bradesco, *Le Monde étrange de Ionesco*, Paris, 1967.
Kenneth R. Dutton, *Eugène Ionesco: An Introduction to His Work*, Eastwood, New South Wales, 1967.
Ernst Wendt, *Eugène Ionesco*, Velber, 1967.
Peter Ronge, *Polemik, Parodie und Satire bei Ionesco*, Berlin, 1967.
Josephine Jacobsen and William Randolph Mueller, *Ionesco and Genet*, New York, 1968.
Claude Abastado, *Eugène Ionesco* (with interview), Paris, 1971.
Julian H. Wulbern, *Brecht and Ionesco: Commitment in Context*, Urbana, Illinois, 1971.
Ronald Hayman, *Eugène Ionesco*, London, 1972; revised edition, New York, 1976.
Allan Lewis, *Ionesco*, New York, 1972.
Paul Vernois, *La Dynamique théâtrale d'Eugène Ionesco*, Paris, 1972.
Rosette C. Lamont (ed.), *Ionesco: A Collection of Critical Essays*, Englewood Cliffs, New Jersey, 1973.
R. Laubreaux (ed.), *Les Critiques de notre temps et Ionesco*, Paris, 1973.
François Bondy, *Eugène Ionesco in Selbstzeugnissen und Bilddokumenten*, Reinbek, 1975.
Silvana Cavarra, *Ionesco: De l'Absurde à la quête*, Catania, 1976.
Carol Petersen, *Eugène Ionesco*, Berlin, 1976.
Rosette C. Lamont and M.J. Friedman (eds.), *The Two Faces of Ionesco*, New York, 1978.
Moshe Lazar (ed.), *The Dream and the Play: Ionesco's Theatrical Quest*, Malibu, California, 1982.
Ahmad K. Mask, *Ionesco et son théâtre*, Paris, 1987.
Giovanni Lista, *Ionesco* (with bibliography), Paris, 1989.

* * *

Ionesco's first play was *La Cantatrice chauve* (*The Bald Soprano*), a comic antiplay which its author had assumed to be "a tragedy of language". It was staged by Nicolas Bataille on May 11, 1950, at the Noctambules, where it went unnoticed until some established writers (Jean Anouilh, Raymond Queneau), and the critic of the *Figaro*, Jacques Lemarchand supported it, and embarked upon a campaign to attract an audience. They succeeded beyond anyone's expectation.

The Bald Soprano was quickly followed by *La Leçon* (*The Lesson*). It is a terrifying picture of the erotic aspect of tyrannical power. As in *The Bald Soprano*, language is the protagonist and the hero-villain. The Professor will kill the girl student with a knife, as word and object. The murder is also a rape, and the knife is a phallus. The student's preparation for the "total doctorate" to which she aspires is a grotesque mating dance. The lecture on philology unleashes the Professor's murderous sexuality. The play has been called a parable of destruction.

Ionesco's masterpiece of his first period is *Les Chaises* (*The Chairs*). In it the real and the imaginary coincide in a single semicircle of proliferating chairs, seats brought in for imaginary guests entertained by an aged couple. The play reveals the fundamental mechanism of the imagination. It also suggests absence by means of the empty chairs, and it can be viewed as a dramatic tone poem on the ontological void. Although the Old Man hopes to leave a message following a mock-heroic double suicide with his wife, the Orator, who is to deliver these final words, turns out to be afflicted with aphasia. Perhaps the only reality one can be certain of is that of the tender concern felt by the Old Woman for her spouse. Nor should one discount the importance of an apparition, one invisible for the public but deeply moving for the Old Man: the unannounced visit of the "Emperor". Ionesco reveals that the latter is not an earthly ruler, but "the King of Kings".

A mystico-comical ascension and a liberation from a stultifying marriage are portrayed in *Amédée; ou, Comment s'en débarrasser* (*Amedee; or, How to Get Rid of It*). A mysterious corpse, stretched out on the conjugal bed of Amédée and his wife, Madeleine, is afflicted with a peculiar kind of exponential growth process. As the body's legs begin to protrude into the living room (the only room in which the couple is able to continue to live and work), it is clear that soon this space will also become uninhabitable. We are never told when, how, or why the cadaver got into the couple's apartment; its presence is a phenomenological given. It suggests, however, that something has gone wrong with the marriage, that the couple's intimate life is now stifling, unbearable. Madeleine urges her weak, passive husband (with his feminine sounding name) to "get rid" of the body. As Amédée lowers it out from the window, into the street, the whole apartment shakes as though eviscerated. Amédée runs out of the apartment he has not left in years, and drags the corpse in the direction of the Seine. Suddenly the heavy body grows light and floats up like a balloon, taking Amédée with it. The stage fills with light, fireworks explode, the atmosphere is that of a 14th of July celebration. Never has the euphoria of regained freedom been more eloquently concretized upon the stage, and this is one of the rare happy endings in Ionesco's plays.

A reverse apprehension—that of weightiness and secret guilt—informs *Victimes du devoir* (*Victims of Duty*). Here a powerful Oedipal motif underlies the action as Madeleine (wife/mother), and the Detective (father/analyst/judge/policeman) force the protagonist, Choubert, to question his "unfinished symphony" by plumbing his own inner depths. The gaps in Choubert's memory are to be filled with the crusts of the stale bread he is forced to chew and swallow by the Detective-Executioner. An unexpected guest arrives, the ectoplasmic projection of the wicked parents, Nicolas d'Eu, whose name suggests a royal incognito (Nicolas II). Madeleine is as elated by his presence as was the Old Woman of *The Chairs* at the arrival of the invisible Emperor. She turns into a frantic hostess, balancing a proliferating number of coffee cups. Here, what Antonin Artaud called the "anarchy of humor" borders on the demonic. *Victims of Duty* is the play Ionesco rates most highly out of his own works. It can be said to open a cycle, that of dream stage-images, which finds its full expression with the final crystallizations of a Jungian self-analysis, *Man with Bags*, and *Journeys Among the Dead*.

Ionesco is a libertarian, perhaps even a gentle anarchist. Two plays reveal this aspect of his political philosophy: *Tueur sans gages* (*The Killer*) and *Rhinocéros* (*Rhinoceros*). The first of these presents Ionesco's "hero in spite of himself", Bérenger, a heroic anti-hero and the dramatist's everyman. The name Bérenger recurs repeatedly in Ionesco's later plays, and the character remains true to himself whether he is a bourgeois king, like Bérenger Ier in *Exit the King*, a petty bourgeois, or an artist. Timid, honest, secretly lyrical, deeply committed to the survival of the human race and the humanity of the individual, the Bérenger of *The Killer* wanders by error into an *ersatz* paradise, the "radiant city". This architectural marvel can offer its dwellers no protection against the universal human condition of mortality, symbolized by the destructive will of a *tueur sans gages* (literally, an unpaid killer). Bérenger is aghast when the killer's existence is revealed to him by the Architect, an efficient technocrat who takes the scandal of mortality and the presence of evil for granted. At the end of the play, Ionesco's anti-hero finds himself facing the Killer—actually a puny creature. As Bérenger erects a pyramid of arguments in his vain attempt to fathom the mentality of one who destroys for the sake of annihilation, he finds only arguments for his own demise: to argue with nihilism, or against it, means to enter the void, to embrace nothingness. Although armed, Bérenger seems to accept his fate. Today, Ionesco's apprehension of the inability of the liberal, ethical man to deal with the problem of unmoti-

vated urban violence is even more relevant than when he first wrote this searing play.

The Bérenger of *Rhinoceros* may be outwardly a weak man, even a tippler, and a sentimentalist, but he retains his humanity in the face of a universal metamorphosis of humans into beasts. Rhinoceritis is the disease of conformity. Bérenger seems immune, and yet, tragically, he will remain alone at the end of the play, the last human being among creatures whose thick, green skin and hoarse roar he begins to envy. In conversation Ionesco once said: "There was a time when it seemed to me that everyone had become a fascist, all the members of my family, my colleagues, my closest friends. Suddenly, it was up to me to resist, little me. I was no hero, but I could not renounce my humanity". *Rhinoceros* is the stage image of this resistance.

Ionesco's third profoundly political play is his cartoon version of Shakespeare's *Macbeth*, which he called *Macbett*. In Ionesco's version the central image is that of the double, dreadful twins. It shows the ways in which power corrupts. The play is a caricature of Shakespeare's sombre drama; its grotesque humor is suited to our epoch in which even murders are copycat crimes. This is a *Macbeth* read through a former cartoon of the great classic, Alfred Jarry's *Ubu Roi*.

Death, the process of dying, and trying to search for the meaning of life are some of the great themes of Ionesco's later works. One of his greatest plays may well be *Le Roi se meurt* (*Exit the King*). In this stage poem about the fear of death, and the gradual process of acceptance of one's dissolution, we see Bérenger Ier, the sovereign of a decaying country, himself afflicted with the disease of mortality. Early in the play he is informed by his first wife, Marguerite, that he is to die soon, "at the end of the play". The court physician, also the astrologer and executioner, confirm this prognosis. At first, the king refuses to believe this, despite the signs of his own decrepitude, and of the disintegration of his country, but after a while it becomes impossible to ignore that the end is near. The play echoes the lamentations of Job, and of Shakespeare's Richard II. The final monologue of the shrewish-seeming Marguerite, who slowly reveals herself to be the divinity of death, is based on Plato's account of the end of Socrates, and on *The Tibetan Book of the Dead*, one of Ionesco's "bibles".

Exit the King is a paean to life, as well as a tone poem on the process of dying. One of the most moving scenes is that between the desperate man and his humble maid. The latter, whom he has never questioned before, tells him about the hardships she has to endure in day-to-day living. The King envies her every one of them; he would trade places with her if this were possible. "To have a backache means you have a back!" he exclaims. As to the death of Bérenger Ier, it is not merely that of an individual, or even of a powerful ruler, but the decline of civilization, the eventual end of the planet earth. There is no immortality since the earth will be a dead star, with all the books turned to dust, all the music to silence. And yet, the play is built on a comic rhythm, with the dying man stumbling and tumbling on the stage, tripping all the way to the grave. It is a comic apocalypse.

The play that has become a modern classic is the one Ionesco wrote for performance at the Comédie-Française, *La Soif et la faim* (*Hunger and Thirst*). In this allegorical drama, Jean, the protagonist, deserts his wife and small child in order to set out upon a quest of the ideal. He is mistaken as to the path he chooses, and even as to his desires. His thirst cannot be slaked, nor his hunger sated. Finally, he reaches a dubious inn, run by fake monks. This monastic society smells of the concentration camp. He will be held prisoner for an indeterminate time, and will have to serve at table dressed in monk's habit. Time is fragmented into infernal minutes, their numbers appearing on illuminated screens. In this Purgatory, Jean realizes, at last, the mistake he made when he left his home to look for a happiness that was there all along, in his own garden. There is an unforgettable image in this play, when the back wall of the dark, damp, basement apartment grows transparent, revealing a lovely garden graced by a leafy, magical-looking tree, the Tree of Life. For Jean, the discovery comes too late.

Ionesco's complex confessional plays come at the close of his career as a playwright: *L'Homme aux valises* (*Man with Bags*) and *Thème et variations; ou Voyages chez les morts* (*Journeys Among the Dead*). Both deal with voyages of self-discovery, of a man's search for his identity. The latter, in particular, is built as a series of confrontations and conversations between the protagonist, Jean, and his dead relatives and parents. Ancient guilt, remorse, and monetary and moral debts are brought up to the surface. Ionesco's infernal voyages echo those of Odysseus to the land of the Cimmerians and of Aeneas and Dante. W.H. Auden once said that "art is breaking bread with the dead". Ionesco's last play shows us that the way is always open for the living to make contact with their ancestors, to probe their own inner depths.

—Rosette C. Lamont

See also *Volume 1* entries on *The Bald Prima Donna*; *The Chairs*; *The Lesson*; *Rhinoceros*.

ISHERWOOD, Christopher.   See **AUDEN, W. H.**

ITALLIE, Jean-Claude van.   See **VAN ITALLIE, Jean-Claude**

IVANOV, Vsevolod Vyacheslavovich.   Born in Lebyazhye, Pavlodor region of Siberia, Russia (now in Kazakhstan), 12 February (24 February, New Style) 1895. Left home, aged 15; travelled through Siberia, the Urals, and Kazakhstan undertaking a variety of jobs, including work as a typesetter in print shops in Pavlodor and Kurgon, labourer, seaman, actor, and circus entertainer; fought at first with the White Russian forces under Admiral Kolchak: taken prisoner, and then joined the Red guerillas in Siberia, 1917; went to Petrograd, 1920, and was associated with Gorky during the 1920's; joined the "proletarian" literary group the Cosmists: expelled, 1922, for joining the "bourgeois" Serapion Brotherhood; criticised during the 1920's by the Russian Association of Proletarian Writers; journalist, 1941–45: reported on the Russian ad-

vance on Berlin and the Nuremberg war trials for *Izvestiya*, 1945; little literary output after 1945, but revised many of his works after the death of Stalin. Member of the board, USSR Writers' Union, from 1934. Died in Moscow, 15 August 1963.

Works (selected)

Collections

Sobranie sochineny [Complete Works] (7 vols.).   1928–31.
Pesy [Plays].   1954; revised edition, 1979.
Sobranie sochineny [Complete Works] (8 vols.).   1958–60; revised edition, 1973–78.

Stage Works

Bronepoyezd 14–69, from the novella (produced Moscow Art Theatre, 1927).   1927; translated as *Armoured Train 14–69*, 1933 and 1978.
Blokada [Blockade] (produced Moscow Art Theatre, Moscow, 1929).   1931.
Kompromis Naib-Khana [The Compromise of Naib-Khan] (produced Red Army Theatre Central, Moscow, 1931).   1931; alternative version, 1954.
Pole i doroga [Field and Road].   1934.
Dvenadtsat molodtsev iz tabakerki [Twelve Young Men from a Snuffbox].   1936.
Vdokhnoveniye [Inspiration].   1940.
Lomonosov [Lomonosov].   1953.

Fiction

Partizany [Partisan Stories].   In *Krasnaya nov*, 1921–22.
Bronepoyezd No. 14–29 (novella).   In *Krasnaya nov*, 1922.
Loga [Gullies] (stories).   1922.
Sedmoi bereg (stories).   1922.
Tsvetnye vetra [Coloured Winds].   1922.
Golubye peski [Sky-Blue Sands].   1922.
Vozvrashchenie Buddy [Buddha's Return].   1923.
Severostal [Northsteel].   1925.
Taynoye taynykh [The Mystery of All Mysteries] (stories).   1927.
Pokhozhdeniya fakira.   1935; revised edition, as *My idyom v Indiyu* [We're Going to India], 1960; translated as *The Adventures of a Fakir*, 1935.
Parkhomenko.   1938; translated as *Parkhomenko*, 1959.
Edesskaya Svyatnia.   1965.
Dikie lyudi (stories).   1980.
Uzhinsky Kreml [The Kremlin of Uzhya].   1981.
U.   1982.
Selected Stories, translated by Keith Hammond and others.   1983.
Mednaja lampa (stories and novels).   1984.

Verse

Sonety.   1930.

Other

Pri vzyaty Berlina [The Capture of Berlin].   1946.
Vstrechi s Maksymom Gorkim [Meetings with Maxim Gorky].   1947.

*

Criticism

Books:
Robert Russell, *Russia Drama of the Revolutionary Period*, Totowa, New Jersey, 1988.

* * *

Vsevolod Ivanov was born in Siberia in 1895 of lower-middle-class parents. He had little formal education but a large number of jobs in his youth, from seaman to circus performer. He was only 20 when his first writings were published, and he quickly became known as a follower of Gorky, though in the revolutions of 1917 he seems to have displayed little interest and less commitment. In the early 1920's, he was a member of various literary groups, the most important of which was the Serapion Brotherhood.

His best-known work, *Armoured Train 14–69*, began life as a short story published in 1922 when he was still a member of this group, and was dramatised five years later. The stage version has an important place in Soviet theatre history as the first drama presented by the Moscow Art Theatre which clearly endorsed the Bolshevik revolution. Presented by the Art Theatre on the tenth anniversary of the revolution in 1927, *Armoured Train 14–69* marked a shift in Stanislavsky's attitude which led rapidly to his being embraced by Stalin's regime as the authentic voice of Socialist Realism.

In the play, set in far-eastern Siberia, the armoured train is loaded with fleeing White Russians who, under the direction of Captain Nezelasov, believe they can cross the Red-infested countryside and reach the sanctuary of a seaport which is guarded by American and Japanese anti-Red forces. In fact, the train is waylaid by a group of peasant partisans, led by the sturdy Vershinin. At first, Vershinin can see no sense in any political creed, even though his two children have been incinerated by Japanese marauders. But he soon discovers what the Revolution is all about, and drives the train towards the town where the communist uprising has just begun. The train's arrival turns the tide, and the revolution is successful. The story is packed with incidents such as that when Vershinin's party, which must stop the train but not damage it, decide one of their number will have to lie on the rails: if the White driver has been properly trained, he will stop, and they will be able to overpower it. But if not, there will be horrible death as well as failure to capture the train. All the partisans volunteer to lie on the rails; a Chinese, Sin Bin Yu, is given the honour. The train does stop and all is well. But the use of such a clichéd scene, for all its suspense, is some indication of the limited extent of Ivanov's originality.

The plot of melodramatic action surrounding the train itself is reinforced by the plot of the uprising in the town, led by Peklevanov, a slightly eccentric Bolshevik zealot, who is responsible for Vershinin's conversion, and who starts the uprising even before Vershinin, in the armoured train, has arrived. He is, in fact, killed by a Japanese, but his body is hoisted on to the train as a symbol of the cause, and its very presence inspires the revolutionaries. Though the depiction of Nezelasov, Vershinin, and Peklevanov is well done, so that each of them is an interesting character in his own right, and though the language is often vigorous and theatrically effective, the play as a whole remains rather weak. The outcomes of the various situations are always obvious, and the dramatic structure is shaky, though there is more in this play, perhaps, than in the run of Civil War plays produced in Stalin's Soviet Union.

Ivanov's next play was "Blockade", written in 1929 and also for the Moscow Art Theatre, depicting the 1921 Kronstadt rebellion against the Bolsheviks. Unfortunately, he stripped the rebellion of its actual complex causes, and made no attempt to portray the rights and wrongs of what happened. He preferred to treat the Kronstadt sailors as greedy, anarchistic self-seekers pitting their viciousness against the honest integrity of the upright Bolsheviks, especially their leader, Commisar Artem, who selflessly pursues nothing but the will of the people.

None of the rest of Ivanov's output is much superior to this, and in some ways its chief interest lies in the way he chose often to use distant locations or historical settings wherin the melodramatic action might perhaps be less noticeably silly. Thus, "The Compromise of Naib Khan" is set in Afghanistan, "Field and Road" in an inaccessible rural district, "Twelve Young Men from a Snuffbox" is a history play set in 1801, "Inspiration" goes even further back to the reign of Dmitri the Pretender, who ousted Boris Godunov in the early 17th century, and "Lomonosov" deals with the 18th-century writer who is generally regarded as the "father" of modern Russian literature. Most of these exotic settings fail to disguise the thinness of Ivanov's talent, though some of his stories and his journalism (he worked for *Izvestiya*) are perhaps more successful.

The other problem for a writer such as Ivanov, in the time and place in which he found himself, was the nature of the dictatorship imposed on the Soviet Union, for Stalin wished to control not just people's lives, but their thoughts as well. The degree to which this inhibited writers can probably never be properly ascertained, but that it did affect Ivanov is shown by the fact that the last ten years before his death in 1963 were spent in largely rewriting the works he had produced during Stalin's rule.

—Robert Leach

J

JARRY, Alfred (Henri). Born in Laval, France, 8 September 1873. Educated at a school in Saint-Brieuc, 1879–88; lycée in Rennes, 1888–91; Lycée Henri IV, Paris, 1891–93. Contributor, *L'Art littéraire* in the 1890's; co-founder, with Remy de Goncourt, the art review *L'Ymagier*, 1894, and its co-director, 1894–95; brief military service, June–November 1895 (discharged on health grounds); founder and publisher, the art journal *Perhinderion*, 1896 (journal closed after second issue); assistant to Lugné-Poe, director of the Théâtre de l'Oeuvre, 1896; first-produced play, *Ubu Roi*, staged 1896; columnist, *La Revue blanche*, 1900–03; suffering from malnutrition and the consequences of alcoholism, attempted recuperation at his sister's home in Laval, 1906. Died from "meningeal tuberculosis", in Paris, 1 November 1907.

Works

Collections

Oeuvres poétiques complètes, edited by Henri Parisot.   1945.
Oeuvres complètes (8 vols.), edited by René Masset.   1948.
Tout Ubu (includes all the Ubu plays, fragments, variants, and other Ubu material), edited by Maurice Saillet.   1964.
Selected Works (translations), edited by Roger Shattuck and Simon Watson Taylor.   1965.
The Ubu Plays (includes *Ubu Rex; Ubu Cuckolded; Ubu Enchained*), translated by Cyril Connolly and Simon Watson Taylor.   1968.
Oeuvres complètes (2 vols.), edited by Michel Arrivé.   Volume 1, 1972; Volume 2, 1987.

Alfred Jarry

Ubu: Ubu Roi; Ubu cocu; Ubu enchaîné; Ubu sur la butte, edited by Noël Arnaud and Henri Bordillon.   1978.

Stage Works

Césare Antechrist.   1895; translated as *Caesar-Antichrist*, 1971.
Ubu Roi (produced Théâtre de l'Oeuvre,Paris, 1896).   1896; translated as *Ubu Roi*, 1951; as *King Turd*, 1953; as *King Ubu*, in *Modern French Theatre*, edited by Michael Benedikt and George E. Wellwarth, 1964; as *Ubu Rex*, in *The Ubu Plays*, 1968.
Ubu sur la Butte (condensed marionette version of *Ubu Roi*, with songs; produced Cabaret des Quat-z'arts, Paris, 1901).   1906.
Par la taille (for marionettes).   1906.
Ubu enchaîne (produced Comédie des Champs–Élysées, Paris, 1937).   1900; translated as *Ubu Enslaved*, 1953; as *Ubu Enchained*, in *The Ubu Plays*, 1968.
L'Objet aimé (produced Comédie des Champs-Élysées, Paris, 1937).   1953.
Ubu cocu (produced by amateur group, Rheims, 1946).   1944; translated as *Ubu Cuckolded*, in *Horizon*, 1945; in book form, 1965, and in *The Ubu Plays*, 1968.
Le Moutardier du pape.   1907; as *La Papesse Jeanne*, 1981.
Pantagruel, with Eugène Demolder, music by Claude Terasse.   1911.
Les Silènes, from a play by Grabbe.   Edited by Pascal Pia, 1926.

Fiction

Les Jours et les nuits.   1897; translated as *Days and Nights*, 1989.
L'Amour en visites.   1898.
L'Amour absolu.   1899.
Messaline.   1900; translated as *The Garden of Priapus*, 1936; as *Messalina*, 1985.
Le Surmâle.   1902; translated as *The Supermale*, 1968.
Les Gestes et opinions du docteur Faustroll, Pataphysicien.   1911.
La Dragonne, completed by Charlotte Jarry.   1943.

Verse

La Revanche de la nuit, edited by Maurice Saillet.   1949.

Other

Les Minutes de sable, mémorial (miscellany).   1894.
Spéculations.   1911.
"Le Manoir enchanté" et quatre autres oeuvres inédites, edited by Noël Arnaud.   1974.

Various works have been published in the *Cahiers* and *Dossiers* of the Collège de Pataphysique since 1950.

*

Bibliographies

Claude Rameil, "Alfred Jarry: Essai de bibliographie critique", in *Interferences*, 9, 1979.

Criticism

Books:
Roger Shattuck, *The Banquet Years: The Arts in France 1885–1918*, London, 1959; revised edition, 1968.

Henri Béhar, *Jarry: Le Monstre et la marionnette*, Paris, 1973.
Michel Arrivé, *Les Langages de Jarry: Essai de sémiotique littéraire*, Paris, 1974.
Noël Arnaud, *Jarry: D'Ubu roi au "Docteur Faustroll"*, Paris, 1974.
François Caradec, *À la Recherche d'Alfred Jarry*, Paris, 1974.
Michel Arrivé, *Lire Jarry*, Brussels, 1976.
Maurice Marc LaBelle, *Jarry: Nihilism and the Theatre of the Absurd*, New York, 1980.
Henri Béhar, *Jarry, dramaturge*, Paris, 1980.
Linda K. Stillman, *La Théâtralité dans l'oeuvre d'Alfred Jarry*, York, South Carolina, 1980.
Keith Beaumont, *Alfred Jarry: A Critical and Biographical Study*, Leicester, 1984.
Nigey Lennon, *Alfred Jarry: The Man With the Axe*, Los Angeles, California, 1984.
Henri Béhar and Brunella Eruli (eds.), *Jarry et cie: Communications du Colloque international*, Paris, 1985.
Henri Bordillon (ed.), *Alfred Jarry*, Paris, 1985.
Ilse Pollack, *Pataphysik, Symbolismus und Anarchismus bei Jarry*, Vienna, 1984.
Claude Schumacher, *Alfred Jarry and Guillaume Apollinaire*, London, 1984 (Macmillan Modern Dramatists series).
Henri Bordillon, *Gestes et opinions d'Alfred Jarry, écrivain*, Laval, 1986.
Henri Béhar, *Les Cultures de Jarry*, Paris, 1988.

*   *   *

Ubu, one of the rare modern literary figures to acquire the mythological status of a Hamlet or Don Juan, was the creation of a 15-year-old schoolboy. Based on a despised physics teacher, the character of Ubu began life as a puppet when young Jarry, with some of his friends, put on satirical puppet shows to mock the hated master of their lycée in Rennes. As the youngster studied French and English theatrical literature, Ubu took on mock-Shakespearian and mock-heroic characteristics without losing any of his highly individual and idiosyncratic qualities. Jarry wrote three Ubu plays, but only the first, *Ubu Roi* (*King Ubu* or *Ubu Rex*) was published or performed in his lifetime (first performed on 9 December 1896 by the Théâtre de l'Oeuvre, directed by Lugné-Poe and designed by Bonnard, Vuillard, and Toulouse-Lautrec). *Ubu cocu* (*Ubu Cuckolded*), written at the same time as *Ubu Roi*, and perhaps revised in 1896, was not published until 1944; *Ubu enchaîne* (*Ubu Bound*), the final play of the trilogy, completed in 1899, had to wait until 1937 for its first production. These two plays do not possess the theatrical vitality of the initial work and, with the exception of Peter Brook's *Ubu aux Bouffes* (1977–78), which included scenes from *Ubu Bound*, they have never been satisfactorily performed.

The basic plot of *Ubu Roi*, a farcical and vicious parody of *Macbeth*, is straightforward: Ma Ubu, the wife of Pa Ubu, former King of Aragon, and now the trusted aide-de-camp to Wenceslas, King of an imaginary Poland, urges her husband to kill the King, tempting him with goodies like bangers and umbrellas. After a moment's hesitation, he enrols the help of one Captain Macnure, and kills the King. Ubu's first act as ruler is to exterminate the nobility, the judiciary, and the bankers, before setting off himself through the countryside to collect the taxes and blast to smithereens the taxpayers who object to having to pay two or three times over. The Poles' revolt, led by the Tsar, drives the Ubus away, but the ending sees them sailing off to an anticlimatic exile in France.

In *Ubu Roi* all the basic dramaturgical conventions are deliberately subverted and it is the iconoclastic nature of the play that makes it such an important landmark in contemporary world drama. *Ubu Roi* opens with the notorious French expletive "Merdre!" (adorned with a second "r") and this "Shite!" is hurled at 25 centuries of Aristotelian tradition, stultifying academism, well-meaning humanism, the hypocrisy of "Victorian" values, and many other aspects of the Western tradition.

In an article published shortly before the first night of *Ubu Roi*, entitled "On the Uselessness of Theatre in the Theatre", Jarry put forward a number of far-reaching proposals which called for nothing less than a fundamental transformation of the theatre as a whole. The "useless theatre" is the theatre of mimesis, embodied in illusionistic naturalism. He declared that most features of the traditional stage, particularly the set and the actors, were "disgusting and meaningless". Instead of trying to recapture a corner of the world on a tiny stage, the designer's task, said Jarry, should be to activate the spectator's imagination: "A backdrop without colour can be obtained easily and in a way which is symbolically accurate with an unpainted canvas or the reverse side of a set, each spectator creating the space suggested by his own imagination, or, better still if the playwright has done his job properly, the real set is *exosmosed* on the stage". As for the actor, he should be replaced by the puppet, and Jarry, well before Craig, advocated the introduction of the super-marionette—the perfect, abstract, ideal character made manifest without the ponderous, accidental (and accident-prone) material intrusion of the self-seeking actor. The use of masks, which Jarry wanted for *Ubu Roi* (but did not get), would be the first step towards the desired depersonalization of the performer. He agreed with Maeterlinck that true theatre should be "the theatre of the abstract" and that "a masterpiece is a symbol which never brooks the active presence of man".

Such sentiments seem to be utterly at odds with the sheer physicality of Jarry's chief creation. The hugely fat and gross Ubu is the personification of man's baser instincts and negative qualities—greed, cruelty, stupidity, gluttony, selfishness, cowardice, vulgarity, unfaithfulness—and he "embodies everything that is ugly in this world". The creation of such a character, as the apocalyptic 20th century was dawning, was gruesomely prophetic. Ubu's tyrannical savagery, which was seen by many as the mad creation of a deranged mind, seems tame compared with the massacres and genocides of subsequent generations.

Ubu Roi, Jarry's essays on theatre and his "pataphysics" ("the science of imaginary solution" which posits that all things are equal so that $+ = -$ and $0 = \infty$), inspired the surrealist poets of the 1920's and 1930's, fuelled Artaud's imagination, and exerted the most potent influence on the playwrights of the "New Theatre" which took shape immediately after World War II. The seeds of the so-called "theatre of the absurd", of the works of playwrights like Ionesco, Vian, Albee, Mrożek, and so on, of the happenings of the 1960's, of performance art—these are to be found in Jarry. In the theatre the liberating effect of his work is still a ferment a full century after the monstrous Ubu was conceived by a child's imagination. But in "real life" this grotesque, repulsive, and murderous creature is for ever haunting the nightmares of many of our contemporaries for whom, as Jarry always insisted, the monster is not and cannot be a figure of fun.

—Claude Schumacher

See also *Volume 1* entry on *Ubu Roi*.

JELLICOE, (Patricia) Ann. Born in Middlesbrough, Yorkshire, England, 15 July 1927. Educated at Polam Hall, Darlington, County Durham; Queen Margaret's, Castle Howard, Yorkshire; Central School of Speech and Drama, London (Elsie Fogarty Prize, 1947), 1944–47. Married 1) C.E. Knight-Clarke in 1950 (marriage dissolved 1961); 2) Roger Mayne in 1962, one son and one daughter. Actress, stage manager, and director, in London and the provinces, 1947–51; founding director, Cockpit Theatre Club, London, 1952–54; lecturer and director, Central School of Speech and Drama, London, 1954–56; first original play, *The Sport of My Mad Mother*, produced 1958; literary manager, Royal Court Theatre, London, 1973–75; involved with the development of community theatre as founding director, 1979–85, and President, 1986, Colway Theatre Trust. OBE (Officer, Order of the British Empire), 1984.

Works

Stage Works

Rosmersholm, from the play by Ibsen (produced London, 1952; revised version produced London, 1959). 1960.
The Sport of My Mad Mother (produced Royal Court Theatre, London, 1958). In *The Observer Plays*, 1958; revised version, 1964.
The Lady from the Sea, from a play by Ibsen (produced London, 1961).
The Knack (produced Arts Theatre, Cambridge, 1961).
The Seagull, with Adriadne Nicolaeff, from a play by Chekhov (produced Queen's Theatre, London, 1964).
Der Freischütz, from the libretto by Friedrich Kind, music by Weber (produced London, 1964).
Shelley; or, The Idealist (produced Royal Court Theatre, London, 1965). 1966.
The Rising Generation (produced by the Young People's Theatre Studio, Royal Court Theatre, London, 1967). In *Playbill 2*, edited by Alan Durband, 1969.
The Giveaway (produced Edinburgh, 1968). 1970.
You'll Never Guess (for children; produced London, 1973). Included in *3 Jelliplays*, 1975.
Two Jelliplays: Clever Elsie, Smiling John, Silent Peter, and A Good Thing or a Bad Thing (for children; produced Royal Court Theatre, London, 1974). Included in *3 Jelliplays*, 1975.
Flora and the Bandits (produced Dartington, Devon, 1976).
The Reckoning (produced Lyme Regis, Dorset, 1978).
The Bargain (produced Exeter, 1979).
The Tide (produced Axminster, Devon, 1980).
The Western Women, music by Nick Brace, from a story by Fay Weldon (produced Lyme Regis, Dorset, 1984).

Other

Some Unconscious Influences in the Theatre. 1967.
Devon: A Shell Guide, with Roger Mayne. 1975.
Community Plays: How to Put Them On. 1987.

*   *   *

Ann Jellicoe won a prize with *The Sport of My Mad Mother* in a competition for new plays sponsored by the *Observer* newspaper in 1956. The play is self-consciously theatrical in its highly structured verbal rhythms, in exploiting the impact of physical things on the stage, and in establishing a direct relationship of performers to the audience.

Scene from the London Royal Court Theatre's 1958 production of *The Sport of My Mad Mother* by **Ann Jellicoe**.

Jellicoe's later plays have the same concerns. Some, indeed, seem to be exercises exploring one or another of these three aspects. For example, *The Giveaway* deals with the invasion of an ordinary family by a large number of eight-foot-high cartons containing a ten-year supply of breakfast cereal—as if Ionesco had written a three-act light comedy. Her interests coincide with techniques commonly used in children's theatre, and her *3 Jelliplays* ask the audience for crucial interventions in the action. They also borrow from the presentational style of East-Asian theatre, in the Bunraku-style puppet and handler, and the fight in the dark on a fully lit stage of Peking Opera. Even her stylistically most conventional play, *Shelley; or, The Idealist*, a decidedly un-Romantic and terse historical drama, lists the roles as for a 19th-century acting company, with most of them to be doubled by the Heavy, the Walking Gentleman, the Juvenile Character, and so on—an arrangement of which the text itself gives no hint. The work with community plays, to which she has devoted herself in recent years, can be seen as a logical conclusion to her interest in actor-audience relationships, for in them the community provides the material for the play, many of the performers, and audiences which know both.

The Sport of My Mad Mother is an extraordinary and fascinating play. Jellicoe has said of the characters in one scene, "the words they used were meaningless sounds to release emotions". This purpose remains primary in the finished play; for example, a rhythmic rendering of the instructions for a perm, given as it is administered, covers four pages. An onstage percussionist accompanies the more vigorous parts of the action. Inarticulate gang members hang about

on Guy Fawkes' night, fearful of an attack by a rival gang that does indeed end the play. The Kali-like mad mother, Greta, is their leader; it is her world of destruction and, when she gives birth at the end of the play, creation.

Into this world, full of references to events and figures whose relationships we can only slowly guess at, blunder a retarded adolescent, Dodo, and an American. These two characters are the audience's way into understanding the other characters. Dodo is the image of what they all are emotionally. As she says in a short poem, "We, all unresisting, lie/Gazing passive at the sky". On to her the others can project feelings they would otherwise not openly acknowledge; similarly, when Patty, the gang's girl, is asleep, a gang member can look at her hand and say, "like a shell—cor cat me! Aren't I a goon!—Like a shell, a little cave—it'd be ever so nice to creep in there and to go to sleep. . .". The American is interrogated by the gang and later questions Greta; thus, we learn of the gang members' fears and then see Greta through his eyes, "all flaying claws: ten legs like a lobster".

Speaking of the spirit in which the play was written, Jellicoe said, "most playgoers today are not used to taking anything direct in the theatre. What they do is transform it into words and put it through their brain". Yet in revising this "anti-intellect play" after its initial publication in the *Observer* anthology, she made two kinds of changes that detract from the wildness and intensity of the original version. She made the characters more conventionally realistic by cutting Dodo's poems and such touches as the comment on Patty's hand. Second, she changed the American into a "more conventional liberal/intellectual", and put into his mouth some editorializing speeches on violence as a betrayal of mankind and on our mutual responsibility for each other. Similarly the percussionist now explains how "music communicates, it reaches into people and they can forget their brains, their intellects and the way they've been taught to intellectualize about everything, they can just let music happen, let it happen physically to them". This betrays Jellicoe's aim to, indeed, just let it happen, physically, to the audience.

Her most commercially successful play, *The Knack*, again plays with verbal rhythms, but in a light comedy. The adeptly exploitative Tolen offers lessons in the techniques of seduction to the inexperienced Colin. His advice is more effective as self-display, in Pinter-like pseudo-precise verbalizations:

Intuition is, to some degree, inborn, Colin. One is born with an intuition as to how to get women. But this feeling can be developed with experience and confidence, in certain people, Colin, to some degree. A man can develop the knack. First you must realize that women are not just individuals but types. No, not even types, just women. They want to surrender but they don't want the responsibility of surrendering.

It is Tom, quieter and less self-centred, who is more genuinely helpful to Colin's sexual confidence when a young girl, new to London and lost, wanders into the house they all three share. A film adaptation was directed by Richard Lester with a script by Charles Wood.

Early in her career the Girl Guides commissioned a play for a huge cast for presentation in a sports stadium. They rejected the resulting high-spirited feminist extravaganza, *The Rising Generation*. It led, however, to an invitation to produce a community celebration in Winchester. Funding for this was cancelled, but since the mid-1970's Jellicoe has devoted herself to "community plays", as fundraiser, organiser, and in many cases director. The history and talents of a local community, supported by the shaping of a professional playwright and a professional production team, result in large-scale productions in non-theatre settings which dissolve the usual boundaries between audience and performers. This work is a logical continuation of her interests.

—Anthony Graham-White

See also *Volume 1* entry on *The Knack*.

JERROLD, Douglas William. Born in London, 3 January 1803; moved with his family to Sheerness, Kent, where his father, an actor, had a lease on a theatre, 1807; appeared on stage on several occasions as a child. Educated at Mr. Herbert's school in Sheerness. Midshipman in the Royal Navy, 1813–15. Married Mary Ann Swann in 1824; seven children. Printer's apprentice in London, 1816–19; compositor for Mr. Bigg, printer of the *Sunday Monitor*, 1819, and afterwards contributed to the *Sunday Monitor, Monthly Magazine, Athenaeum*, and other periodicals; first plays produced 1821; play adapter for G.B. Davidge, manager of the Royal Coburg Theatre, 1825–29; resident dramatist, Surrey Theatre, London, 1829; co-manager, with William Hammond, Strand Theatre, London, 1836; primarily a journalist from 1840: contributor to *Punch* (and its prototype, *Punch in*

London), 1841–57, and to *Blackwood's* and *New Monthly* magazines; editor, *Illuminated Magazine*, 1843–45; founding editor, *Douglas Jerrold's Shilling Magazine*, 1845–48; owner and editor, *Douglas Jerrold's Weekly Newspaper*, 1846–48; editor, *Lloyd's Weekly Newspaper*, 1852–57. Died in London, 8 June 1857.

Works

Collections

Works (5 vols.). 1863–64.

Stage Works

More Frightened Than Hurt (produced Sadler's Wells Theatre, London, 1821). 1888.
The Chieftains' Oath; or, The Rival Clans (produced Sadler's Wells Theatre, London, 1821).
The Gipsy of Derncleuch, from the novel *Guy Mannering* by Scott (produced Sadler's Wells Theatre, London, 1821). Nd.
The Island; or, Christian and His Comrades, from the poem by Byron (produced Sadler's Wells Theatre, London, 1823).
Dolly and the Rat; or, The Brisket Family (produced Olympic Theatre, London, 1823). Nd.
The Smoked Miser; or, The Benefit of Hanging (produced Sadler's Wells Theatre, London, 1823). 1823(?).
The Living Skeleton (produced Royal Coburg Theatre, London, 1825).
London Characters: Puff! Puff!! Puff!!! (produced Royal Coburg Theatre, London, 1825).
Popular Felons (produced Royal Coburg Theatre, London, 1825).
Paul Pry, from the play by John Poole (produced Royal Coburg Theatre, London, 1827). Nd.
The Statue Lover (produced Vauxhall Gardens, London, 1828). Nd.
Descart, The French Buccaneer (produced Royal Coburg Theatre, London, 1828). 1830(?).
The Tower of Lochlain; or, The Idiot Son (produced Royal Coburg Theatre, London, 1828). Nd.
Wives by Advertisement; or, Courting in the Newspapers (produced Royal Coburg Theatre, London, 1828). With *Winning a Husband* by George Macfarren, 1888.
Ambrose Gwinett; or, A Sea-Side Story (produced Royal Coburg Theatre, London, 1828). 1885.
Two Eyes Between Two; or, Pay Me for My Eye (produced Royal Coburg Theatre, London, 1828). 1888.
Fifteen Years of a Drunkard's Life! (produced Royal Coburg Theatre, London, 1828). Nd.
Vidocq! The French Police Spy (produced Surrey Theatre, London, 1829). Nd.
Bampfyde Moore Carew (produced Surrey Theatre, London, 1829). Nd.
John Overy the Miser; or, The Southwark Ferry (produced Surrey Theatre, London, 1829). Nd.
Law and Lions! (produced Surrey Theatre, London, 1829). Nd.
Black-Eyed Susan; or, All in the Downs (produced Surrey Theatre, London, 1829). 1829.
The Flying Dutchman (produced Surrey Theatre, London, 1829). 1829(?).
The Lonely Man of Shiraz (produced Surrey Theatre, London, 1829).

Thomas à Becket (produced Surrey Theatre, London, 1829). Nd.

The Witch-Finders (produced Theatre Royal, Drury Lane, London, 1829).

Sally in Our Alley (produced Surrey Theatre, London, 1830). 1888(?).

Gervaise Skinner; or, Penny Wise and Pound Foolish (produced Surrey Theatre, London, 1830).

The Mutiny at the Nore; or, British Sailors in 1797 (produced 1830). Nd.

The Press-Gang; or, Archibald of the Wreck (produced Surrey Theatre, London, 1830).

The Devil's Ducat; or, The Gift of Mammon (produced Adelphi Theatre, London, 1830). Nd.

Martha Willis the Servant Maid; or, Service in London (produced 1831). Nd.

The Bride of Ludgate (produced Theatre Royal, Drury Lane, London, 1831). Nd.

The Lady Killer (produced 1831).

The Broken Heart; or, The Farmer's Daughter of the Severn Side (produced New City Theatre, London, 1832).

The Rent Day (produced Theatre Royal, Drury Lane, London, 1832). 1832.

The Golden Calf (produced Strand Theatre, London, 1832). Nd.

The Factory Girl (produced Theatre Royal, Drury Lane, London, 1832).

Nell Gwynne; or, The Prologue (produced Covent Garden Theatre, London, 1833). 1833.

The Housekeeper; or, The White Rose (produced Theatre Royal, Haymarket, London, 1833). 1833.

Swamp Hall; or, The Friend of the Family (produced Theatre Royal, Haymarket, London, 1833). 1833.

The Wedding Gown (produced Theatre Royal, Drury Lane, London, 1834). 1834.

Beau Nash, The King of Bath (produced Theatre Royal, Haymarket, London, 1834). 1834.

The Schoolfellows (produced Queen's Theatre, London, 1835). 1835.

Birds of Paradise (produced London, 1835).

The Hazard of the Die (produced Theatre Royal, Drury Lane, London, 1835). 1835.

Hearts and Diamonds (produced Olympic Theatre, London, 1835).

The Man's an Ass (produced Olympic Theatre, London, 1835).

Doves in a Cage (produced Adelphi Theatre, London, 1835). Nd.

The Painter of Ghent (produced Strand Theatre, London, 1836). Nd.

The Man for the Ladies (produced Strand Theatre, London, 1836). 1885.

The Bill-Sticker; or, An Old House in the City (produced Strand Theatre, London, 1836).

The Perils of Pippins; or, The Man Who "Couldn't Help It" (produced Strand Theatre, London, 1836). Nd.

A Gallantee Showman; or, Mr. Peppercorn at Home (produced Strand Theatre, London, 1837).

The Mother (produced Theatre Royal, Haymarket, London, 1838).

The White Milliner (produced Covent Garden Theatre, London, 1841). Nd.

Bubbles of the Day (produced Covent Garden Theatre, London, 1842). 1842.

The Prisoner of War (produced Theatre Royal, Drury Lane, London, 1842). 1842.

Gertrude's Cherries; or, Waterloo in 1835 (produced Covent Garden Theatre, London, 1842). 1842.

Time Works Wonders (produced Theatre Royal, Haymarket, London, 1845). 1845.

Mrs. Caudle's Curtain Lecture (produced London, 1845). 1846.

A Honeymoon Scruple (produced Surrey Theatre, London, 1845).

The Spendthrift (produced Olympic Theatre, London, 1850).

The Mother's Dream; or, The Gipsy's Revenge (produced Adelphi Theatre, London, 1850).

The Catspaw (produced Theatre Royal, Haymarket, London, 1850). 1850.

Retired from Business (produced Theatre Royal, Haymarket, London, 1851). 1851.

St. Cupid; or, Dorothy's Fortune (produced Windsor Castle, Windsor, 1853). 1853.

A Heart of Gold (produced Princess's Theatre, London, 1854). 1854.

Fiction

Men of Character. 1838.

The Story of a Feather. 1844.

The Chronicles of Clovernook, with Some Account of the Hermit of Bellyfull. 1846.

A Man Made of Money. 1849.

St. Giles and St. James. In *Writings*, 1852.

Cakes and Ale (tales and essays). In *Writings*, 1852.

Tales, edited by J.L. Robertson. 1891.

Other

Facts and Fancies. 1826.

The Hand-Book of Swindling. 1839.

Heads of the People, illustrated by Kenny Meadows (2 vols.). 1840–41.

Punch's Letters to His Son. 1843.

Punch's Complete Letter Writer. 1845.

Mrs. Caudle's Curtain Lectures. 1846; edited by Walter Jerrold, 1902.

Writings (8 vols.). 1851–54.

The Brownrigg Papers, edited by Blanchard Jerrold. 1860.

Other Times, with Blanchard Jerrold. 1868.

The Barber's Chair and the Hedgehog Letters, edited by Blanchard Jerrold. 1874.

Essays, edited by Walter Jerrold. 1903.

The Best of Mr. Punch: The Humorous Writings, edited by Richard Kelly. 1970.

* * *

A prolific writer of dramas, novels, essays, and famed for his involvement with *Punch* magazine, Douglas Jerrold figured as a wit and social campaigner among his contemporaries. Jerrold used various literary genres to protest against social inequality and institutional corruption, his democratic liberalism being prevalent in all of his written work. Remembered in his obituary (*Times*, 9 June 1857) as "the most popular dramatist of his time", and known as "the Surrey Shakespeare", Jerrold was a key character in the "renaissance" movement of the English drama in the 1830's and 1840's. His plays vary widely in content and form, yet the qualities that have been described as his essential Englishness and his comic vitality are evident in his melodramas, farces, and romantic comedies alike.

Like his contemporaries Bulwer-Lytton, Sheridan Knowles, and Macready, Jerrold sought to diminish the detrimental commercialism of the theatrical scene. Reacting against the influx of French and German adaptations, Jerrold used anglicised, and often colloquial, dialogue to emphasise native humour and local characteristics. Similarly, he exploited stereotypic scenes of rural and urban England in order to sever his work, visually, from foreign influences. Popular demand for theatrical spectacle increasingly became anathema to him, and he therefore concentrated on characterisation and wordplay rather than on plot and extravagant visual effects. Thus, one can argue that although Jerrold's plays are not innovative in terms of psychological depth or dramatic realism, his efforts are representative of a serious endeavour to counteract the further deterioration of the English drama in literary and theatrical terms.

During the first decade of his dramatic career, Jerrold acted as house dramatist at the Coburg Theatre, producing numerous farces and melodramas anonymously. Moving to the Surrey Theatre, he had his first real success with the nautical melodrama, *Black-Eyed Susan; or, All in the Downs*. Transferred to Covent Garden, this play was the one which established Jerrold in the "legitimate" milieu and which proved to be his best-remembered piece of dramatic work. One of several melodramas based on a nautical theme (followed by *The Mutiny at the Nore* and *The Press Gang*), *Black-Eyed Susan* is characterised by broad nautical jargon and "business", giving the character William, the jolly jack tar, numerous opportunities for hornpipes and physical heroics. The sentimentilisation of the common sailor figure, a distinctly English, working-class image, proved massively popular, as both a patriotic and domestic symbol. A mixture of comedy, action, and pathos, the play also exemplifies Jerrold's masterly use of the melodramatic form to convey a serious issue to his audience (in this instance, the arbitrary, class-orientated naval regulations of the time). One of Jerrold's earlier plays, *Fifteen Years of a Drunkard's Life*, although a more laborious play, dealt with the causes and effects of alcoholism, placing the blame upon lack of understanding among the working classes and lack of responsibility among the upper and middle classes.

After the success of *Black-Eyed Susan*, Jerrold used the highly accessible melodramatic form to examine social inequalities in rural and urban settings: absentee landlordism in *The Rent Day*; child labour and poor industrial working conditions in *The Factory Girl*; the corruption of rural innocence by urban vice, and the ineptitude of the legal system in *Martha Willis The Servant Maid*. Ever the champion of the abused or the misrepresented, Jerrold also wrote a two-act play defending the moral character of Nell Gwynne as a professional actress. Although the original themes repeatedly collapse into a series of subterfuges, misunderstandings, and coincidences, the form was ideally suited to Jerrold's unproblematic humanitarian stance. Idealising the domestic and familial themes, Jerrold's melodramas are typical in their adherence to myths of angelic womanhood and the sanctity of the English home.

In contrast to the often indulgent characterisation in his earlier writing, Jerrold's later dramatic output takes on a more satiric tone. Catering predominantly for the theatres in Covent Garden, Drury Lane, and the Haymarket, Jerrold refined both the content and the dialogue of his plays in accordance with the expectations of a better class of audience. Representing middle-class and aristocratic life, his later dramas are mainly romantic comedies, offering him full scope to display his skill at writing witty and compact dialogue. It has been argued that in forfeiting his position as a popular melodramatist and seeking recognition for decidedly "literary" writing, Jerrold overstepped the limits of his dramatic talent and sacrificed his role as social campaigner in the theatre. However, it must be noted that his comedies are actually dense with criticisms of those members of the aristocracy and bourgeoisie whom he depicts. Thus, while the characterisation becomes more deft, individual characters become less sympathetic. *Bubbles of the Day* illustrates political and financial corruption; *The Prisoner of War* satirises extreme patriotism and the incompetence of military and diplomatic leaders; and *Retired from Business* offers a critique of the pretentiousness and egocentricity of social climbers.

Often these comedies are uneven in quality and tone, usually beginning in satirical vein, but digressing from the original motif into clichéd sentiment. Using a similar type of denouement to that used by Bulwer-Lytton in his comedies, the central character is invariably called upon to choose between money or love, and having made the correct choice is suitably rewarded for his/her integrity.

One can see in Jerrold's later writing an inherent conflict between his literary ambitions and his awareness of the need for plot and action, a conflict that did not exist in his more consistent melodramas. It is the simplicity and vigour of Jerrold's plays and his bid to reinstate English drama upon the early Victorian stage which make him an engaging and important figure in the 19th-century theatre.

—Samantha Johnson

See also *Volume 1* entry on *Black-Eyed Susan*.

JOHNSTON, (William) Denis. Born in Dublin, Ireland, 18 June 1901. Educated at St. Andrew's College, Dublin; Merchiston Castle, Edinburgh; Christ's College, Cambridge (president of the Union), 1919–23, BA and LL.B 1923, MA, LL.M 1926; Harvard Law School, Cambridge, Massachusetts (Pugsley scholar), 1923–24; barrister, Inner Temple, London, 1925, and King's Inns, Dublin, 1925. Married 1) Shelah Richards in 1928 (divorced 1945), one son and one daughter; 2) Betty Chancellor in 1945, two sons. Producer, Dublin Drama League, Abbey Theatre, and Dublin Gate Theatre, 1927–36; member of the board, Dublin Gate Theatre, 1931–36; features producer, BBC, Belfast, 1936–38; television producer, BBC, London, 1938–39; BBC correspondent, in the Middle East, Italy, France, and Germany, 1942–45: mentioned in despatches; director of television programmes, BBC, London, 1945–47; staff member, *Theatre Guild of the Air* programme, NBC, New York, 1947–49; visiting director, Kirby Memorial Theatre, Amherst, Massachusetts, 1950; professor of English, Mount Holyoke College, South Hadley, Massachusetts, 1950–60; chairman of the department of theatre and speech, Smith College, Northampton, Massachusetts, 1960–66; visiting professor, Amherst College, Massachusetts, 1966–67, University of Iowa, Iowa City, 1967–68, and University of California, Davis, 1970–71; Berg Professor, New York University, 1971–72; Arnold Professor, Whitman College, Walla Walla, Washington, 1972–73; literary editor, Abbey Theatre, Dublin, 1975. Recipient: Allied Irish Banks award, 1977. Litt.D: University of Ulster, 1979. Vice-president, Irish Academy of Letters, 1981–82. OBE (Order of the British Empire), 1946. Died in Dublin, 8 August 1984.

Works

Collections

"The Golden Cuckoo" and Other Plays (includes The Dreaming Dust; A Fourth for Bridge). 1954.
Collected Plays (2 vols.). 1960.
Dramatic Works (2 vols.). 1977–79.
Selected Plays (includes The Old Lady Says "No!"; The Moon in the Yellow River; The Dreaming Dust; The Scythe and the Sunset), edited by Joseph Ronsley. 1983.

Stage Works

The Old Lady Says "No!" (produced Gate Theatre Studio, Dublin, 1929). With The Moon in the Yellow River, 1932.
The Moon in the Yellow River (produced Abbey Theatre, Dublin, 1931). With The Old Lady Says "No!", 1932.
The Indiscreet Goat (ballet scenario; produced Gate Theatre, Dublin, 1931).
A Bride for the Unicorn (produced Abbey Theatre, Dublin, 1933). With Storm Song, 1935.
Storm Song (produced Gate Theatre, Dublin, 1934). With A Bride for the Unicorn, 1935.
Blind Man's Buff, with Ernst Toller, from a play by Toller (produced Abbey Theatre, Dublin, 1936). With Pastor Hall by Toller, 1938.
The Dreaming Dust (as Weep for Polyphemus, broadcast 1938; revised version, as The Dreaming Dust, produced Gaiety Theatre, Dublin, 1940). In "The Golden Cuckoo" and Other Plays, 1954.
The Golden Cuckoo (produced Dublin, 1939). In "The Golden Cuckoo" and Other Plays, 1954; revised version, 1971.
A Fourth for Bridge (as The Unthinking Lobster, televised 1948). In "The Golden Cuckoo" and Other Plays, 1954.
Six Characters in Search of an Author, from a play by Pirandello (produced South Hadley, Massachusetts, 1950); opera version, music by Hugo Weisgall (produced New York, 1959). 1957.
Strange Occurrence on Ireland's Eye (produced Abbey Theatre, Dublin, 1956). In Collected Plays 2, 1960.
Tain Bo Cuailgne (pageant; produced Dublin, 1956). In Dramatic Works 2, 1979.
The Scythe and the Sunset (produced Poets' Theatre, Cambridge, Massachusetts, 1958). In Collected Plays 1, 1960.
Ulysses in Nighttown, from parts of Ulysses by James Joyce (produced New York, 1958).
Finnegans Wake, from the novel by James Joyce (produced New Haven, Connecticut, 1959).
Nine Rivers from Jordan, music by Hugo Weisgall, from the book by Johnston (produced New York, 1969). 1969.

Screenplays

Guests of the Nation, 1933; River of Unrest, 1937; Ourselves Alone, 1937.

Television Plays

The Last Voyage of Captain Grant, 1938; The Parnell Commission, 1939; Weep for the Cyclops, 1946; The Unthinking Lobster, from the stage play A Fourth for Bridge, 1948; The Call to Arms, 1949; Siege at Killyfaddy, 1960.

Radio Plays

Death at Newtownstewart, 1937; Lillibulero, 1937; Weep for Polyphemus, 1938; Multiple Studio Blues, 1938; Nansen of the "Fram", 1940; The Gorgeous Lady Blessington, 1941; The Autobiography of Mark Twain, 1941; Abraham Lincoln, 1941; In the Train, 1946; Not One Returns to Tell, 1946; Verdict of the Court series, 1960.

Memoirs and Letters

Nine Rivers from Jordan: The Chronicle of a Journey and a Search (wartime autobiography). 1953.

Other

In Search of Swift. 1959.
John Millington Synge. 1965.
The Brazen Horn: A Non-Book for Those Who, in Revolt Today, Could Be in Command Tomorrow. 1968; revised edition, 1976.
Alicorn at Fifty-Five: An Extract from the Diary. 1986.

*

Criticism

Books:
Robert Hogan, After the Irish Renaissance: A Critical History of Irish Drama Since "The Plough and the Stars", Minneapolis, Minnesota, 1967.
Gene A. Barnett, Denis Johnston, Boston, 1978.
Joseph Ronsley (ed.), Denis Johnston: A Retrospective (includes check-list of Johnston's works), Boston, 1981.
Harold Ferrar, Denis Johnston's Irish Theatre, Dublin, 1973.

Articles:
Christine St. Peter, "Denis Johnston, the Abbey and the Spirit of the Age", in Irish University Review, 17, 1987.
John O'Brien, "Expressionism and the Formative Years: Insights from the Diaries of Denis Johnston", in Canadian Journal of Irish Studies, vol.15 no.1, 1989.

* * *

Denis Johnston has been compared to Bernard Shaw in his intellectual approach to theatre. But whereas Shaw's characters express the playwright's arguments in forthright terms, Johnston's characters pose questions which he, himself, cannot fully answer. The forms of his plays, stretching from expressionism to naturalism, together with his restless revision of their texts, are part of a pilgrimage of self-discovery as are his prose writings and his varied career as barrister, playwright, BBC producer of radio and television, war correspondent, and professor of drama in America.

His plays may be divided between the categories of the experimental and the broadly realistic. In the former category is his first and most successful experimental play, The Old Lady Says "No!", its title derived from a rejection slip when it was turned down by the Abbey Theatre (Lady Gregory did not like it). In it, Johnston uses a number of expressionist techniques—a sparse plot, choral speech, disruption of time, and fluidity of staging. The plot is a satire on Ireland's propensity to harp back to its romanticised past. An actor playing the part of the rebel, Robert Emmett, in a 19th-century melodrama, is accidentally knocked unconscious by a rifle butt when he is arrested serenading his love, Sarah Curran. Thereafter he wanders in a dream state through Dublin in search of his lover or, perhaps, himself, meeting characters from the city's past and present, including the statue of Henry Grattan who accuses his foolhardy revolution of bringing about the end of Ireland's independent parliament. An old whore who speaks the lines of Yeats's *Cathleen ni Houlihan* turns out to be Sarah Curran. But beneath the satire is Johnston's life-long affection for this "wilful city of savage dreams, so old, so sick with memories".

His other experiments in dramatic form are not so successful. An attempt to ally Dunne's theory of time in *A Bride for the Unicorn* with surrealist and expressionist techniques is heavy going for the audience. *The Dreaming Dust*, a much-revised play about Dean Swift, loses dramatic impetus in Johnston's concern with his controversial theory of Swift's relationship with Stella. But in this play, set in St Patrick's Cathedral, haunted by the darkening mind of the Dean, Johnston makes a passionate plea for compassion, forgiveness, and acceptance of the Divine Will. (Johnston came from a Protestant North of Ireland family; his father was a High Court judge who transferred his loyalties to the Free State.) In Johnston's plays, as in his life, the Protestant ethic is in search of a compromise with his deep affection for his Southern Irish compatriots.

In his most frequently performed play, *The Moon in the Yellow River*, the theme revolves around the conflict between industrial progress (with distinct echoes of the Free State's 1925 Shannon Scheme) and an Ireland clinging to its rural past. Johnston shifts the scene from the Shannon to a disused fort at the mouth of the Liffey where Dobelle, a retired railway engineer, lives with his neglected young daughter, Blanaid, whom he has never been able to forgive for his wife's death in childbirth. The fort also houses the workshop of two eccentric characters, George and Captain Potts, engaged in making a gun. When a young Republican, Darrell Blake, arrives with his troop proposing to blow up the neighbouring Power House, Herr Tausch, the engineer in charge, summons assistance, and Blake is shot in cold blood by a commandant of the Free State Army. Tausch's teutonic sense of law and order is outraged by this flagrant murder.

Tausch: A little give and take. A few words around the table. We were good enemies, Mr Blake and I, and we would have come to understand each other before long.
Dobelle: You would never have understood Blake. He belonged to a different world that had no chance against yours—a world that must inevitably have been destroyed by you. You remember Li Po? He was trying to embrace the moon in the Yellow River.

Meanwhile George and Potts, finding that four out of their five shells are duds, throw the fifth on to the slag heap where it explodes and blows up the Power House. But the violence of the night's events brings about the reconciliation of Dobelle with his neglected child.

In several of his plays, Johnston makes use of actual events as the springboard for the action. *Strange Occurrence on Ireland's Eye*, one of his three court-room dramas, is based on a well-known murder trial. *The Golden Cuckoo* follows, fairly closely, the trial of a harmless eccentric who, in 1926, broke the windows of the Kilkenny post office as an expression of his sense of the injustice of life. Johnston uses a similar plot to point up the difference between law and justice. The 1916 Easter Rising is the subject of Johnston's last and most intense play, *The Scythe and the Sunset*, the title a counterpart to O'Casey's play on the same subject, *The Plough and the Stars*. In it he presents the conflict between

the idealism of Tetley, the leader of the rebel forces, and the pragmatism of Palliser, an Anglo-Irish officer in the British Army who is wounded and captured by the rebels. Tetley, like the real leader, Patrick Pearse, chooses to surrender, believing that his inevitable execution will provide the inspiration for future struggle. Palliser chooses to die in the burning building in which he is held captive as a personal abnegation of the cycle of vengeance that will ensue.

Comparison of Johnston's play with O'Casey's provokes the question of why *The Plough* is universally popular, when Johnston's far deeper study of the Rising has been seldom seen. The answer lies partly in the greater humanity of O'Casey's characters. Fluther, Bessie Burgess, Uncle Peter, and the Covey belong to the world of eternal theatre; Tetley and Palliser belong to the theatre of intellect. Johnston's characters are seldom lovable. His ironic view of human frailty prevents the emotional involvement of his audience. In *The Scythe and the Sunset*, as in other of his plays, Johnston poses questions of deep human importance which are not readily accessible in a single visit to the theatre.

—Hugh Hunt

JONES, Henry Arthur. Born in Grandborough, Buckinghamshire, England, 20 September 1851. Educated at John Grace's Commercial Academy, Winslow, Buckinghamshire, until age 12; subsequently self-educated. Married Jane Eliza Seeley in 1875 (died 1924); three sons and four daughters. Worked for his uncle, a draper in Ramsgate, Kent, 1864–67, and for another draper in Gravesend, Kent, 1867–69; travelling salesman for drapery firms in London, Bradford, and Exeter, 1870–79; first-produced play, *It's Only Round the Corner* (subsequently retitled *Harmony*), staged 1878; full-time writer from 1879; lived in Exeter, 1875–80, and Hampton Wick, Middlesex, from 1880. MA: Harvard University, Cambridge, Massachusetts, 1907. Died in London, 7 January 1929.

Works

Collections

The Theatre of Ideas: A Burlesque Allegory and Three One-Act Plays: The Goal, Her Tongue, Grace Mary. 1915.
Representative Plays (4 vols.), edited by Clayton Hamilton. 1925.
Plays (includes *The Silver King; The Case of Rebellious Susan; The Liars*), edited by Russell Jackson. 1982.

Stage Works

Harmony (as *It's Only round the Corner*, produced Theatre Royal, Exeter, 1878; as *Harmony Restored*, produced Grand Theatre, Leeds, 1879; as *Harmony*, produced Lyceum Theatre, New York, 1884; as *The Organist*, produced Royalty Theatre, London, 1892). 1883.
Hearts of Oak; or, A Chip off the Old Block (produced Theatre Royal, Exeter, 1879). 1879; as *Honour Bright*, 1879.
Elopement (produced Theatre Royal, Oxford, 1879). 1879.
A Clerical Error (produced Court Theatre, London, 1879). 1879.
A Drive in June. 1879.

An Old Master (produced Princess's Theatre, London, 1880). 1880.

A Garden Party. 1880.

Lady Caprice. 1880.

Humbug. 1881.

Home Again (produced Theatre Royal, Oxford, 1881).

His Wife (produced Sadler's Wells Theatre, London).

A Bed of Roses (produced Globe Theatre, London, 1882). 1882.

The Silver King, with Henry Herman (produced Princess's Theatre, London, 1882). 1907; in *Plays*, 1982.

The Wedding Guest. 1882.

Breaking a Butterfly, with Henry Herman, from *A Doll's House* by Ibsen (produced Princess's Theatre, London, 1884). 1884.

Chatterton, with Henry Herman (produced Princess's Theatre, London, 1884).

Saints and Sinners (produced Prince of Wales Theatre, Greenwich, 1884). 1891.

Hoodman Blind, with Wilson Barrett (produced Princess's Theatre, London, 1885). Nd.

The Lord Harry, with Wilson Barrett (produced Princess's Theatre, London, 1886).

The Noble Vagabond (produced Princess's Theatre, London, 1886).

Hard Hit (produced Theatre Royal, Haymarket, London, 1887).

Heart of Hearts (produced Vaudeville Theatre, London, 1887).

Sweet Will (produced New Club, Covent Garden, London, 1887). 1887.

The Middleman (produced Shaftesbury Theatre, London, 1889). 1907.

Wealth (produced Theatre Royal, Haymarket, London, 1889).

Judah (produced Theatre Royal, Haymarket, London, 1890). 1894.

The Deacon (produced Theatre Royal, Haymarket, London, 1890). 1893.

The Dancing Girl (produced Theatre Royal, Haymarket, London, 1891). 1907.

The Crusaders (produced Avenue Theatre, London, 1891). 1893.

The Bauble Shop (produced Criterion Theatre, London, 1893). 1893.

The Tempter (produced Theatre Royal, Haymarket, London, 1893). 1898.

The Masqueraders (produced St. James's Theatre, London, 1894). 1894.

The Case of Rebellious Susan (produced Criterion Theatre, London, 1894). 1894.

The Triumph of the Philistines (produced St. James's Theatre, London, 1895). 1895.

Michael and His Lost Angel (produced Lyceum Theatre, London, 1896). 1896.

The Rogue's Comedy (produced Garrick Theatre, London, 1896). 1896.

The Physician (produced Criterion Theatre, London, 1897). 1897.

The Liars (produced Criterion Theatre, London, 1897). 1901.

The Goal (produced Chicago, 1907). 1898.

The Manoeuvres of Jane (produced Theatre Royal, Haymarket, London, 1898). 1898.

Grace Mary (produced Playhouse, Liverpool, 1930). 1898.

Carnac Sahib (produced Her Majesty's Theatre, London, 1899). 1899.

The Lackey's Carnival (produced Duke of York's Theatre, London, 1900). 1900.

Mrs. Dane's Defence (produced Wyndham's Theatre, London, 1900). 1900.

James the Fogey. 1900.

The Princess's Nose (produced Duke of York's Theatre, London, 1902). 1902.

Chance, The idol (produced Wyndham's Theatre, London, 1902). 1902.

Whitewashing Julia (produced Garrick Theatre, London, 1903). 1903.

Joseph Entangled (produced Theatre Royal, Haymarket, London, 1904). 1904.

The Chevaleer (produced Garrick Theatre, London, 1904). 1904.

Chrysold. 1904.

The Sword of Gideon. 1905.

The Heroic Stubbs (produced Terry's Theatre, London, 1906). 1906.

The Hypocrites (produced Grand Theatre, Hull, 1906). 1906.

The Victory (as *The Evangelist*, produced Knickerbocker Theatre, New York, 1907; as *The Galilean's Victory*, produced Stockport, Cheshire, 1907). 1907.

Dolly Reforming Herself (produced Theatre Royal, Haymarket, London, 1908). 1908; shortened version, as *Dolly's Little Bills* (produced Hippodrome, London, 1912), 1910.

The Knife (produced Palace Theatre, London, 1909).

Fall In Rookies! (produced Alhambra Theatre, London, 1910). 1910.

We Can't Be As Bad As All That! (produced Nazimova Theatre, New York, 1910). 1910.

The Ogre (produced St. James's Theatre, London, 1911).

Lydia Gilmore (produced Lyceum Theatre, New York, 1912).

Her Tongue (produced Garrick Theatre, London, 1912). In *The Theatre of Ideas*, 1915.

Mary Goes First (produced Playhouse, London, 1913). 1913.

The Divine Gift. 1913.

The Lie (produced Harris Theatre, New York, 1914). 1915.

Cock o' the Walk (produced Cohan Theatre, New York, 1915).

The Pacifists (produced Opera House, Southport, 1917). 1917.

Other

The Renascence of the English Drama: Essays, Lectures, and Fragments Relating to the Modern English Stage 1883–94. 1895.

The Foundations of a National Drama: Lectures, Essays, and Speeches 1896–1912. 1913.

Shakespeare and Germany. 1916.

Patriotism and Popular Education. 1919.

My Dear Wells: A Manual for the Haters of England. 1921.

What is Capital? An Enquiry into the Meaning of the Words Capital and Labour. 1925.

The Shadow of Henry Irving. 1931.

*

Bibliographies

J.P. Wearing, "Henry Arthur Jones: An Annotated Bibliography of Writings About Him", in *English Literature in Transition, 1880–1920*, 22, 1979.

Criticism

Books:
Doris Arthur Jones, *The Life and Letters of Henry Arthur Jones* (with bibliography), London, 1930.
Richard A. Cordell, *Henry Arthur Jones and the Modern Drama*, London and New York, 1932.
F.M. Northend, *Henry Arthur Jones and the Dramatic Renascence in England*, London, 1940.
John Russell Taylor, *The Rise and Fall of the Well-Made Play*, London, 1967.
Victor Emaljanow, *Victorian Popular Dramatists*, Boston, 1987.

Articles:
G.A. Wauchope, "Henry Arthur Jones and the New Social Drama", in *Sewanee Review*, 29, 1921.
F.M. Northend, "Jones and the Development of the Modern English Drama", in *Review of English Studies*, 18, 1942.
Joel H. Kaplan, "Henry Arthur Jones and the Lime-lit Imagination", in *Nineteenth Century Theatre*, 15, 1987.
Judith L. Fisher, "The 'Law of the Father': Sexual Politics in the Plays of Henry Arthur Jones and Arthur Wing Pinero", in *Essays in Literature* (Western Illinois University), 16, 1989.

*   *   *

The continuing decline of English drama in the mid-19th-century, despite Tom Robertson's infusion of liveliness in the 1860's, was publicly lamented by Matthew Arnold. In the *Nineteenth Century* (August 1879) he wrote, "we . . . have no modern drama at all", and went on to urge the revitalisation of the "irresistible" theatre. Henry Arthur Jones, as so many of his generation susceptible to Arnold's influence, sought to meet the challenge, bringing to the task no literary training and no theatrical background, but equipped with formidable qualities of industry and persistence.

His early work was inauspicious. He claimed once to have read his way through Samuel French's catalogue of plays, and it showed. His one-acters, some of which he placed with provincial managers, were broadly farcical or melodramatic, sometimes both, and displayed little promise, apart from some evidence of a dependable ear for common speech. He attracted the attention of Wilson Barrett, then providing a season of melodramas at the Princess's Theatre, and was commissioned to write, with a collaborator, a full-length work, *The Silver King*. An episodic but inventive melodrama, owing much to Taylor's *The Ticket of Leave Man*, the piece was a resounding popular and critical success, drawing warm approval from Matthew Arnold for its restrained and naturalistic dialogue.

Jones's other work for Barrett was unambitious and, apart from providing an historically interesting footnote with an early but ludicrously distorted adaptation of Ibsen's *A Doll's House*, unremarkable. The financial security it provided, however, allowed him to attempt a grander design, and *Saints and Sinners* is evidence of a reformist zeal that provides the first example of the mixture of high drama and comedy to which he was frequently to return. Derivative of Hawthorne, and echoing Dickens and other literary sources in its main elements (a seduced daughter and a public confession), it provided, also, well-observed satirical portraits of dissenting hypocrisy which ensured it a controversial reception and marked Jones out as a "dangerous" playwright.

He was also a cautious playwright, however, and he retreated to the safety of unequivocal melodrama until, in *Wealth*, with Tree in the lead, he attempted a serious study of an obsessed man, in a work unrelieved by humour. His mounting confidence in his own worth is suggested by the unmistakeably Shakespearean parallels in character and incident, but, seeking high passion, Jones found only bluster, and the intended tragic intensity remained melodramatic bathos. Nevertheless, it is apparent that Jones had identified for himself the genre he sought—the serious, vernacular play examining an issue of contemporary significance, akin to what later came to be called the problem play. However, he was also attracted to comedy, and was, increasingly shrewdly, aware of what brought commercial success.

His next works, *The Middleman* and *Judah*, confirmed his reputation as a controversial entertainer. Each shows a firm grasp of theatrical contrivance, although Jones had still not shed much that was old-fashioned; each gives the impression of immediacy with well-calculated reference to current activities and ideas; each handles, with confidence, a range of moods, from low comedy to intense emotionalism; above all, each appears to touch contemporary issues of some importance, to question received morality. In truth, in each the "modernness" is superficial and the outcome is safely conventional. More worrying, the objects of Jones's satire, particularly in *Judah*, suggest an unpleasing reactionarism which questions the liberal quality of the avowed ideas.

From his many articles about the stage and his dramatic theory it is apparent that Jones tried to rationalise the conflicting appeal of high drama and comedy. In *The Dancing Girl* he abandoned, temporarily, drama with a "purpose" and paradoxically achieved some of his most effective work, particularly in Act III, balancing well-managed and acutely observed comic scenes with moments of feverish melodrama to create a romance, the more pleasing because it is unpretentious. He had undeniable flair for the theatrical, and here, released from the tyranny of ideas whose pursuit revealed cruelly his intellectual limitations, he created high kitsch.

After an unsuccessful attempt at social satire in *The Crusaders*, marred by a wildly melodramatic sub-plot, and an improbable Shakespearean verse play, *The Tempter* ("a rum business" wrote Shaw), Jones returned to romance with *The Masqueraders*, described by Shaw as "a fairy tale in. . .a country hotel". Here the note struck in *The Dancing Girl* is sounded more firmly. A uniformity of mood, harmonising the elements of comedy and heightened drama, create an entirely satisfying, at times stirring, if broadly theatrical experience.

Jones's growing control over the comic form becomes clear with *The Case of Rebellious Susan*. Written ostensibly to rebuke the "Mrs Grundyish" British who were beginning to resist the neo-Ibsenite "society" play epitomised by Pinero's *The Second Mrs Tanqueray, Susan*, substantially borrowed from Dumas *fils*, was a comedy about a wife's retaliatory adultery. It is adroitly constructed, and introduces a figure, the *raisonneur*, from Dumas, suavely played by Charles Wyndham, and then frequently to recur in Jones's comic work. The play at its best is well-judged society comedy; at its worst, in its glib satirical dismissal of the young feminist and its final retreat from the implications of its theme, it is damagingly reactionary.

Jones made a major effort to bring off the high dramatic play he still aspired to with *Michael and His Lost Angel*, a notorious failure, theatrically a débâcle, and taken off after ten performances. An anecdote about an erring priest, it mistakes priggishness for heroism, and a kind of diseased sentimentality for passion. Seeking tragedy, Jones created only genteel melodrama.

In *The Liars* he returned to comedy and, omitting sub-plot and satire, he achieved an excellent comedy of manners, keeping control over the complications of the plot and sustaining the comic mood with assurance and a sure ear for brittle and amusing dialogue, faltering only when he allowed a certain solemnity to creep into protestations of true love.

After a run of indifferently received work, Jones had a major success with *Mrs. Dane's Defence*, a rather loosely plotted society melodrama, lifted by its third act, a fine example of the court-room cross-examination. He went on to write more than a dozen plays, although he responded to an increasingly cold reception by placing the bulk of his work in the United States, where his stock remained high.

Effectively, Jones's influence on the drama ended with the century. After 1900, the dramatic reform that he had urged and, in part, practised was sought and achieved by other, abler men; but his contribution to the late-Victorian theatre should not be dismissed too readily. He had qualities of moral courage and aggressiveness, as well as a range of theatrical skills that allowed him to undertake an important task at a time when greater talents were unavailable or unwilling to put themselves at the theatre's disposal. Although his talent was not of the first quality, he used it conscientiously, and never wavered in his belief that drama was an art-form of major importance. It was his achievement to help sweep away a certain kind of fustian from the English stage, to introduce well-observed and convincing dialogue, and to help make the commercial theatre topical and intelligent at a time when it was seriously deficient in ideas.

—Robert Silvester

See also *Volume 1* entry on *The Silver King*.

JONES, LeRoi.   See **BARAKA, (Imamu) Amiri.**

JONSON, Ben(jamin). Born in Westminster, London, probably 11 June 1572. Educated at St. Martin's parish school, London; Westminster School, London, under William Camden. Fought for the Dutch against the Spanish in Flanders. Married Anne Lewis in 1594; at least two children. Bricklayer, c.1589–90; actor, then playwright, from 1595; actor for Philip Henslowe, 1597; imprisoned in 1597 for being actor in, and part author of, the satire *The Isle of Dogs* (now lost); killed a fellow actor in a duel, 1598 (escaped hanging by pleading benefit of clergy, but was branded and lost all his property); joined Roman Catholic church, 1598 (returned to Church of England, 1611); imprisoned for debt, 1599; imprisoned in Tower of London for satirical references to James I in *Eastward Ho!*, 1605 (Chapman also imprisoned); wrote masques for the Court at Whitehall and elsewhere, often performed at Christmas, from 1605: masques were designed by Inigo Jones until 1631, when Jonson and Jones quarrelled; travelled in France as tutor to Sir Walter Raleigh's son, 1612–13; given royal pension (in effect becoming first poet laureate) by James I, 1616; attracted circle of young writers who styled themselves Sons (or Tribe) of Ben; visited Scotland, and William Drummond of Hawthornden, 1618–

Ben Jonson (engraving).

19: elected as a burgess of Edinburgh, 1619; possibly lecturer in rhetoric, Gresham College, London, in the 1620's; elected chronologer of London, 1628; stroke in 1628 left him an invalid. MA: Oxford University, 1619. Died in London, 16(?) August 1637.

Works

Collections

Works (plays and verse).   1616; revised edition (2 vols.), 1640.
Works (11 vols.), edited by C. H. Herford, Percy Simpson, and Evelyn Simpson.   1925–52; revised as *Complete Plays* (4 vols.), edited by G.A. Wilkes, 1981–82.
Three Plays (includes *The Alchemist*; *Volpone*; *Bartholomew Fair*), edited by Michael Jamieson.   1966.
Complete Masques, edited by Stephen Orgel.   1969.
Plays and Masques, edited by Robert Martin Adams.   1979.
Five Plays (includes *Every Man in His Humour; Sejanus; Volpone; The Alchemist; Bartholomew Fair*), edited by G.A. Wilkes.   1981.
Selected Plays 1 (includes *Sejanus His Fall; Volpone; Epicoene*), edited by Johanna Procter.   1989.
Selected Plays 2 (includes *The Alchemist; Bartholemew Fair; The New Inn; A Tale of the Tub*), edited by Martin Butler. 1989.

Stage Works

The Case is Altered (produced London, 1597–98?).   1609.
Every Man in His Humour (produced by the Lord

Chamberlain's Men, London, 1598). 1601; revised version (produced at Court, 1605), in *Works*, 1616.

Every Man Out of His Humour (produced by the Lord Chamberlain's Men, Globe Theatre, London, 1599). 1600.

The Fountain of Self-Love; or, Cynthia's Revels (produced by the Chapel Children, Blackfriars Theatre, London, 1600). 1601.

Poetaster; or, The Arraignment (produced by the Chapel Children, Blackfriars Theatre, London, 1601). 1602.

Sejanus His Fall (produced by the King's Men, Globe Theatre, London, 1603). 1605.

Entertainment of the Queen and Prince at Althorp (produced Althorpe, 1603). 1604.

King James His Royal and Magnificent Entertainment, with Dekker (produced London, 1604). Jonson's part published separately, 1604.

A Private Entertainment of the King and Queen at Highgate (produced house of Sir William Cornwallis, Highgate, 1604). In *Works*, 1616.

Eastward Ho!, with Chapman and Marston (produced by the Children of the Queen's Revels, Blackfriars Theatre, London, 1605). 1605.

Volpone; or, The Fox (produced by the King's Men, Globe Theatre, London, 1606). 1607.

The Masque of Blackness (produced at Court, 1605). In *The Characters of Two Royal Masques*, 1608.

Hymenaei (produced at Court, 1606). 1606.

The Entertainment of the Two Kings of Great Britain and Denmark at Theobalds (produced 1606). In *Works*, 1616.

An Entertainment of King James and Queen Anne at Theobalds (produced 1607). In *Works*, 1616.

The Masque of Beauty (produced at Court, 1608). In *The Characters of Two Royal Masques*, 1608.

The Hue and Cry After Cupid (produced Whitehall Palace, London, 1608). In *Works*, 1616.

The Description of the Masque Celebrating the Marriage of John, Lord Ramsey, Viscount Haddington (produced Whitehall Palace, London, 1608). In *Works*, 1616.

The Masque of Queens (produced Whitehall Palace, London, 1609). 1609.

Epicoene; or, The Silent Woman (produced by the Children of the Queen's Revels, Whitefriars Theatre, London, 1609). In *Works*, 1616.

The Speeches at Prince Henry's Barriers (produced at court, 1610). In *Works*, 1616.

The Alchemist (produced by the King's Men, Globe Theatre, London, 1610). 1612.

Oberon, The Faery Prince (produced Whitehall Palace, London, 1611). In *Works*, 1616.

Love Freed from Ignorance and Folly (produced Whitehall Palace, London, 1611). In *Works*, 1616.

Catiline His Conspiracy (produced by the King's Men, 1611). 1611.

Love Restored (produced Whitehall Palace, London, 1612). In *Works*, 1616.

The Irish Masque (produced Whitehall Palace, London, 1613). In *Works*, 1616.

A Challenge at Tilt (produced at Court, 1613). In *Works*, 1616.

Bartholomew Fair (produced by Lady Elizabeth's Men, Hope Theatre, London, 1614). 1631.

The Golden Age Restored (produced at Court, 1615). In *Works*, 1616.

Mercury Vindicated from the Alchemists (produced Whitehall Palace, London, 1616). In *Works*, 1616.

The Devil is an Ass (produced by the King's Men, Blackfriars Theatre, London, 1616). 1631; edited by M. Hussey, 1967.

Christmas His Masque (produced Whitehall Palace, London, 1616). In *Works*, 1640.

The Bloody Brother; or, Rollo, Duke of Normandy, with Fletcher and Massinger; possibly by Fletcher and Massinger only (produced c.1616). 1639.

The Vision of Delight (produced Whitehall Palace, London, 1617). In *Works*, 1640.

Lovers Made Men (produced House of Lord May, London, 1617). 1617.

Pleasure Reconciled to Virtue (produced Whitehall Palace, London, 1618). In *Works*, 1640; revised version, as *For the Honour of Wales* (produced Whitehall Palace, London, 1618), in *Works*, 1640.

News from the New World Discovered in the Moon (produced Whitehall Palace, London, 1620). In *Works*, 1640.

An Entertainment at the Blackfriars (produced Newcastle House, Blackfriars, London, 1620). In *The Monthly Magazine; or, British Register*, 1816.

Pan's Anniversary; or, The Shepherd's Holiday (produced Whitehall Palace, London, 1620). In *Works*, 1640.

The Gypsies Metamorphosed (produced Burley-on-the-Hill, 1621). In *Works*, 1640.

The Masque of Augurs (produced Whitehall Palace, London, 1622). 1622.

Time Vindicated to Himself and to His Honours (produced Whitehall Palace, London, 1623). 1623.

Neptune's Triumph for the Return of Albion. 1624; revised version, as *The Fortunate Isles and Their Union* (produced at Court, 1625), 1625.

The Masque of Owls (produced by Lady Elizabeth's Men, 1624). In *Works*, 1640.

The Staple of News (produced by the King's Men, Blackfriars Theatre, London, 1626). 1631.

The New Inn; or, The Light Heart (produced by the King's Men, Blackfriars Theatre, London, 1629). 1631.

Love's Triumph Through Callipolis (produced Whitehall Palace, London, 1631). 1631.

Chloridia (produced Whitehall Palace, London, 1631). 1631.

The Magnetic Lady; or, Humours Reconciled (produced by the King's Men, Blackfriars Theatre, London, 1632). In *Works*, 1640.

A Tale of a Tub (produced by Queen Henrietta's Men, Cockpit/Phoenix Theatre, London, 1633). In *Works*, 1640.

The King's Entertainment at Welbeck (produced Welbeck, 1633). In *Works*, 1640.

Love's Welcome at Bolsover (produced Bolsover, 1634). In *Works*, 1640.

The Sad Shepherd; or, A Tale of Robin Hood (incomplete). In *Works*, 1640; edited and completed by Alan Porter, 1944.

Verse

[Poems]. In *Works*, 1616.
The Complete Poems, edited by George Parfitt. 1975.
Poems, edited by Ian Donaldson. 1985.

Other

Timber; or, Discoveries Made upon Men and Matter. In *Works*, 1640.
The English Grammar, in *Works*. 1640.
Leges Conviviales. 1692.

Literary Criticism, edited by J.D. Redwine.   1970.

Translator, *Horace His Art of Poetry*, in *Works*.   1640; edited by E.H. Blakeney, 1928.

*

Bibliographies

S.A. Tannenbaum, *Ben Jonson: A Concise Bibliography*, New York, 1938; supplement, with D.R. Tannenbaum, 1947; further supplement in *Elizabethan Bibliographies Supplements 3*, by G.R. Guffey, London, 1968.

D. Heyward Brock and James M. Welsh, *Ben Jonson: A Quadricentennial Bibliography*, Metuchen, New Jersey, 1974.

Walter D. Lehrman, Dolores J. Sarafinski, and Elizabeth Savage, *The Plays of Ben Jonson: A Reference Guide*, Boston, 1980.

Criticism

Books:

J.L. Palmer, *Ben Jonson* (biography), New York and London, 1934.

Robert G. Noyes, *Ben Jonson on the English Stage*, Cambridge, Massachusetts, 1935.

L.C. Knights, *Drama and Society in the Age of Jonson*, London, 1937.

Helena W. Baum, *The Satiric and the Didactic in Jonson's Comedies*, Chapel Hill, North Carolina, 1947; reprinted, New York, 1971.

Freda L. Townsend, *"Apologie for Bartholomew Fayre": The Art of Jonson's Comedies*, London and New York, 1947.

A.H. Gilbert, *The Symbolic Persons in the Masques of Ben Jonson*, Durham, North Carolina, 1948.

Marchette Chute, *Ben Jonson of Westminster*, New York, 1953.

John J. Enck, *Jonson and the Comic Truth*, Madison, Wisconsin, 1957.

Edward B. Partridge, *The Broken Compass: A Study of the Major Comedies of Ben Jonson*, London and New York, 1958; reprinted, Westport, Connecticut, 1958.

Jonas A. Barish, *Ben Jonson and the Language of Prose Comedy*, Cambridge, Massachusetts, 1960; second edition, 1970.

Jonas A. Barish (ed.), *Jonson: A Collection of Critical Essays*, Englewood Cliffs, New Jersey, 1963.

Calvin G. Thayer, *Ben Jonson: Studies in the Plays*, Norman, Oklahoma, 1963.

Robert E. Knoll, *Ben Jonson's Plays: An Introduction*, Lincoln, Nebraska, 1965.

Stephen Orgel, *The Jonsonian Masque*, Cambridge, Massachusetts, 1965.

J.C. Meagher, *Method and Meaning in Jonson's Masques*, Notre Dame, Indiana, 1965.

Larry S. Champion, *Ben Jonson's "Dotages": A Reconsideration of the Late Plays*, Lexington, Kentucky, 1967.

D.C. Boughner, *The Devil's Disciple: Ben Jonson's Debt to Machiavelli*, New York, 1968.

Gabrielle B. Jackson, *Vision and Judgement in Jonson's Drama*, New Haven, Connecticut, 1968.

Coburn Gum, *The Aristophanic Comedies of Jonson*, The Hague and Paris, 1969.

John B. Bamborough, *Ben Jonson*, London, 1970 (British Council booklet).

Alan C. Dessen, *Jonson's Moral Comedy*, Evanston, Illinois, 1971.

Judd Arnold, *A Grace Peculiar: Jonson's Cavalier Heroes*, University Park, Pennsylvania, 1972.

Franz Fricker, *Ben Jonson's Plays in Performance and the Jacobean Theatre*, Bern, 1972.

Irena Janicka, *The Popular Theatrical Tradition and Ben Jonson*, Lødz, Poland, 1972.

M.C. Williams, *Unity in Ben Jonson's Early Comedies*, Salzburg, 1972.

William A. Blissett and others (eds.), *A Celebration of Ben Jonson*, Toronto, 1973.

Joseph A. Bryant Jr., *The Compassionate Satirist: Ben Jonson and His Imperfect World*, Athens, Georgia, 1973.

A. Drew-Bear, *Rhetoric in Ben Jonson's Middle Plays: A Study of Ethos, Character Portrayal and Persuasion*, Salzburg, 1973.

Ingeborg Sturmberger, *The Comic Elements in Jonson's Drama* (2 vols.), Salzburg, 1975.

R.W. Witt, *Mirror Within a Mirror: Ben Jonson and the Play-Within*, Salzburg, 1975.

George Parfitt, *Ben Jonson, Public Poet and Private Man*, London, 1976.

Peter Hyland, *Disguise and Role-Playing in Ben Jonson's Drama*, Salzburg, 1977.

L.A. Beaurline, *Jonson and Elizabethan Comedy: Essays in Dramatic Rhetoric*, San Marino, California, 1978.

James Hogg (ed.), *Recent Research on Ben Jonson*, Salzburg, 1978.

Douglas Duncan, *Jonson and the Lucianic Tradition*, Cambridge, 1979.

Claude J. Summers and Ted-Larry Pebworth, *Ben Jonson*, 1979.

Mary Chan, *Music in the Theatre of Ben Jonson*, Oxford, 1980.

Alexander Leggatt, *Ben Jonson: His Vision and His Art*, London and New York, 1981.

Stephen Orgel, *The Jonsonian Masque*, New York, 1981.

Claude J. Summers and Ted-Larry Pebworth (eds.), *Classic and Cavalier: Essays on Jonson and the Sons of Ben*, Pittsburgh, Pennsylvania, 1982.

Richard Dutton, *Jonson: To the First Folio*, Cambridge, 1983.

D. Heyward Brock, *A Jonson Companion*, Bloomington, Indiana, 1983.

Anne Barton, *Ben Jonson, Dramatist*, Cambridge, 1984.

Katharine Eisaman Maus, *Ben Jonson and the Roman Frame of Mind*, Princeton, New Jersey, 1984.

Don E. Wayne, *Penshurst: The Semiotics of Place and the Poetics of History*, 1984.

Ejner J. Jensen, *Ben Jonson's Comedies on the Modern Stage*, Ann Arbor, Michigan, 1985.

John Gordon Sweeney III, *Jonson and the Psychology of Public Theatre: The Coin the Spirit, Spend the Soul*, Princeton, New Jersey, 1985.

Annemarie Faber, *Contemporary Life and Manners in Jonson's Comedies*, Salzburg, 1985.

Peter Womack, *Ben Jonson*, Oxford, 1986.

Rosalind Miles, *Ben Jonson: His Life and Work*, London, 1986.

K.A. Preuschen, *Ben Jonson als humanistischer Dramatiker*, Frankfurt, 1989.

Robert N. Watson, *Jonson's Parodic Strategy: Literary Imperialism in the Comedies*, Cambridge, Massachusetts, 1987.

Russ McDonald, *Shakespeare and Jonson, Jonson and Shakespeare*, Brighton, Sussex, 1988.

George E. Rowe, *Distinguishing Jonson: Imitation, Rivalry, and the Direction of a Dramatic Career*, Lincoln, Nebraska, 1988.

Robert C. Evans, *Jonson and the Poetics of Patronage*, Lewisburg, Pennsylvania, 1989.

David Riggs, *Ben Jonson: A Life*, Cambridge, Massachusetts, 1989.

D.H. Craig (ed.), *Ben Jonson: The Critical Heritage*, London, 1990.

Rosalind Miles, *Ben Jonson: His Craft and His Art*, London, 1990.

* * *

Had there not been a Shakespeare, Ben Jonson might have become England's greatest dramatist. His *oeuvre* is extensive, comprising plays, masques, poems, and some prose treatises; he lived through three reigns; and he addressed himself not only to the diversion of popular and court audiences but to his self-imposed task of making his auditors—and he always insisted that what was heard from the stage was more important than what was seen on it—"understanders", a word that occurs with great frequency in the prefatory material to his dramatic texts.

Jonson espoused a political and social ideal that was conservative. In his poem celebrating Sir Philip Sidney, "To Penshurst", he constructs an ideal world, infused by ideals of measure, courtesy, and hospitality, and a life close to a pastoral ideal. The villains of his great satirical comedies, on the other hand—Volpone, Subtle the Alchemist, and the petty villains and cony-catchers who inhabit Bartholomew Fair—are speculators and "projectors", or inhabit an urban underworld, products of the rapid growth in population seen in London during Jonson's lifetime, and stand for values that are the opposite of a pastoral ideal: rapacity, lust, and preditariness. They are successful because the world they inhabit is full of "gulls", fools ripe for exploitation.

Jonson's idealism may explain (if not justify) the savage comic punishments he inflicts upon fools like Sir Politic Would-Be in *Volpone*; but elsewhere idealism is tempered by a moral realism. Justice Adam Overdo's mission to root out the "enormities" of Bartholomew Fair comes to an end when his drunken wife is violently sick at the end of the play. At such a moment comedy seems to be no laughing matter—the opinion of Jonson himself.

As in the comedies of his classical predecessors, Jonson's comedies are set in milieux familiar to his audiences (unlike those of Shakespeare, in which characters migrate to worlds of romance) and his themes are vice and folly (rather than romantic love). Jonson's two great tragedies, *Sejanus* and *Catiline*, were set in ancient Rome and are as concerned with an anatomy of society and power structures as they are with the personalities of their over-reaching heroes.

If there are few of the characters in the great comedies who incarnate values that an audience is encouraged to share, many characters are possessed of a ferocious energy which, in good performances, is likely to captivate spectators. They are theatrical in the sense that they speak with invention, wear their disguises, physical and moral, with panache, and dedicate themselves to the pursuit of wealth or power with a perverted joy and with total commitment. Perhaps the key to Jonson's achievement lies in this tension between a rage to order, that led him to loathe the stage's ability to fashion new guises in personality—to make something out of nothing—, and a fascination with this very protean capacity, producing the possibilities of inventing highly ordered plots and letting highly verbal comedy be subsumed by farce, and enabling players to celebrate the quaint and the energetic.

Character is style, and Jonson's dramatic language is radically different from that of Shakespeare. Shakespeare is notable for his metaphors; Jonson's language is metonymic as well as metaphoric—words are chosen because of the way they are associated with the habits or trades of their speakers. In *Every Man in His Humour*, the play which provided Jonson with his first popular success, Lorenzo Junior, a man of wit, describes rustic cousin Stephano to his face thus:

> . . . a man so graced, gilded, or rather, to use a more fit metaphor, tinfoiled by nature-not that you have a leaden constitution, coz, although perhaps a little inclining to that temper, and so the more apt to melt with pity when you fall into the fire of rage; but for your lustre only, which reflects as bright to the world as an old ale-wife's pewter against a good time.

The amplification of idea by means of a display of technical terms, here metallurgical, is typical of Jonson. There is also an allusion to the psychological theory of humours: the mentalities of Jonson's characters were defined by analogy with the proportions in which the "humours" (blood, phlegm, and black and yellow bile) were supposed to be present in the body. (Jonson went out of his way to deny—in the prologue to *Every Man Out of his Humour*—that an individual's behaviour was *defined* by his bodily "complexion".)

Jonson's plays were popular with Jacobean audiences in both the public (open-air) and private (indoor) playhouses—in the latter, plays like *Poetaster* were performed by boys—and he was graced with invitations to write masques for the court. These masques, spectacular dramatic entertainments performed, in the main, by noble amateurs, featured music and dancing and celebrated courtly ideals, offering to instruct by praising, although they could also be ironic. In 1621 George Villiers, Duke of Buckingham and favourite to King James I, played in *The Gypsies Metamorphosed*, the title of which says something about Buckingham's nature. Masques were examples of conspicuous display, lavishly prepared, and graced with the designs of Inigo Jones who brought to England a thorough acquaintance with, for example, the Palladianism that was driving forward the artistic renaissance on the continent. It was typical of Jonson, however, that the collaboration should end in bitterness, Jonson feeling that, for Jones, the spectacle rather than the words comprised what Jonson, in the preface to *Hymenaei*, termed the "soul" of the masque.

Jonson's robust humour fell out of fashion in the reign of Charles I: there were rival writers of masques and Jonson's last plays proved unpopular. These, which include *The New Inn* and *The Magnetic Lady*, were dismissed later by Dryden, quite unjustly, as Jonson's "dotages". The former, in particular, can be read as a moving tribute to Shakespeare in which Jonson takes a romantic plot, which is preposterous in itself but which suffices as a vehicle for a display of the perils of romanticism, and displays an awkward, but charming, ability to write about love.

—Michael Hattaway

See also *Volume 1* entries on *The Alchemist*; *Bartholomew Fair*; *Eastward Ho!*; *Epicoene*; *Every Man in His Humour*; *Sejanus His Fall*; *Volpone*.

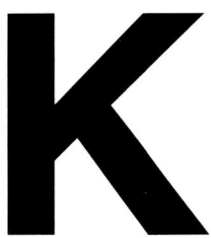

K

KAISER, Georg. Born in Magdeburg, Germany, 25 November 1878. Educated at the school of a Lutheran monastery, 1888–1895. Married Margarete Habenicht in 1908; two sons and one daughter; also had a daughter by Maria von Mühlfeld in 1919. Bookshop assistant in Magdeburg, 1895; apprentice with an import-export business, 1896–1899; sailed to Buenos Aires, Argentina, and began work with the local branch of the Berlin AEG [General Electric Company], 1899; contracted malaria, and returned to Germany, 1901; in sanatorium, following a nervous breakdown, 1902; first-published play, *Die jüdische Witwe*, appeared 1911; first-produced play, *Der Fall des Schülers Vehgesack*, staged 1915; achieved success with the production of *Die Bürger von Calais*, 1917; lost house through financial difficulties, and moved to Munich, 1918; arrested on a charge of embezzlement, because of his selling of rented furniture, and imprisoned in Munich for six months, 1920–21; settled in Berlin after his release, 1921; became Germany's most widely performed dramatist, 1921–33; under the Nazi regime, his works banned from publication or production, from 1933, and his books burnt; continued writing in Berlin, 1934–37; learned of impending investigation by the Gestapo, and fled to Switzerland, via Amsterdam, 1938; lived in various parts of Switzerland, 1939–44. Elected to Prussian Academy of Arts, 1926, and the German Academy, 1930 (membership later withdrawn under Nazi pressure). Honorary president, Association for German Writers in Exile, 1945. Died in Ascona, Switzerland, 4 June 1945.

Works

Collections

Gesammelte Werke (includes 11 plays). 1928–31.
Griechische Dramen (includes *Zweimal Amphitryon; Pygmalion; Bellerophon*). 1948.
Stücke; Erzählungen; Aufsätze; Gedichte, edited by Walther Huder. 1966.
Werke (6 vols.), edited by Walther Huder. 1971–72.
Five Plays (includes *From Morning to Midnight; The Burghers of Calais; The Coral; Gas I; Gas II*), translated by B.J. Kenworthy, Rex Last, and J.M. Ritchie. 1971; reprinted as *Plays 1*, 1985.
Plays 2 (includes *The Flight to Venice; One Day in October; The Raft of the Medusa; David and Goliath; The President*), translated by B.J. Kenworthy, H.F. Garten, and Elizabeth Sprigge. 1981.

Stage Works

Die jüdische Witwe (produced Landestheater, Meiningen, 1921). 1911.

Georg Kaiser

Claudius (produced Neues Theater, Frankfurt, and Städtisches Schauspielhaus, Baden-Baden, 1918). In *Hyperion*, 1911.
Ballade von schönen Mädchen. In *Hyperion*, 1911.
Friedrich und Anna (produced Neues Theater, Frankfurt, and Staatliches Schauspielhaus, Baden-Baden, 1918). In *Hyperion*, 1911.
König Hahnrei (produced Staatliches Schauspielhaus, Berlin, 1931). 1913.
Der Fall des Schülers Vehgesack (produced Neue Bühne, Vienna, 1915). 1914.
Rektor Kleist (produced Neues Schauspielhaus, Königsberg, 1918). 1914.
Grossbürger Möller (produced Schauspielhaus, Düsseldorf,

1915). 1914; revised version, as *David und Goliath* (produced Stadttheater, Minden, 1922), 1920; translated as *David and Goliath*, in *Plays 2*, 1981.

Die Bürger von Calais (produced Neues Theater, Frankfurt, 1917). 1914; translated as *The Burghers of Calais*, in *Five Plays*, 1971.

Europa (produced Grosses Schauspielhaus, Berlin, 1920). 1915.

Der Zentaur (produced Schauspielhaus, Frankfurt, 1917). 1916.

Von morgens bis mitternachts (produced Kammerspiele, Munich, 1917). 1916; translated as *From Morn to Midnight*, in *Poet Lore*, 21, 1920; as *From Morning to Midnight*, in *Five Plays*, 1971.

Die Sorina; oder, Der Kindermord (produced Lessing-Theater, Berlin, 1917). 1917.

Die Versuchung (produced Thalia-Theater, Hamburg, 1917). 1917.

Die Koralle (produced Neues Theater, Frankfurt, 1917). 1917; translated as *The Coral*, 1963, and in *Five Plays*, 1971.

Das Frauenopfer (produced Schauspielhaus, Düsseldorf, 1918). 1918.

Juana (produced Neues Theater, Frankfurt, and Städtisches Schauspielhaus, Baden-Baden, 1918). 1918.

Gas I (produced Neues Theater, Frankfurt, and Schauspielhaus, Düsseldorf, 1918). 1918; translated as *Gas I*, 1925, and in *Five Plays*, 1971.

Der Brand im Opernhaus (produced simultaneously at the Königliches Schauspielhaus, Berlin, Kammerspiele, Hamburg, and Stadttheater, Nuremberg, 1918). 1919; translated as *Fire in the Opera House*, in *Eight European Plays*, 1927.

Hölle Weg Erde (produced simultaneously at the Neues Theater, Frankfurt, Lessing-Theater, Berlin, and Kammerspiele, Munich, 1919). 1919.

Gas II (produced Vereinigtes Deutsches Theater, Brünn [now Brno], Czechoslovakia, 1920). 1920; translated as *Gas II*, 1963, and in *Five Plays*, 1971.

Der gerettete Alkibiades (produced Residenztheater, Munich, 1920). 1920; translated as *Alkibiades Saved*, in *An Anthology of German Expressionist Drama*, edited by Walter H. Sokel, 1963.

Der Protagonist (produced Lobetheater, Breslau, 1922). 1921; translated as *The Protagonist*, in *Tulane Drama Review*, 5, 1960.

Noli me tangere. 1922.

Kanzlist Krehler (produced Kammerspiele, Berlin, 1922). 1922.

Der Geist der Antike. 1923.

Gilles und Jeanne (produced Altes Theater, Leipzig, 1923). 1923.

Die Flucht nach Venedig (produced Intimes Theater, Nuremberg, 1923). 1923; translated as *The Flight to Venice*, in *Plays 2*, 1981.

Nebeneinander (produced Lustspielhaus, Berlin, 1923). 1923.

Kolportage (produced Lessing-Theater, Berlin, 1924). 1924.

Gats (produced Deutsches Volkstheater, Vienna, 1925). 1925.

Der mituge Seefahrer (produced Schauspielhaus, Dresden, 1925). 1926.

Zweimal Oliver (produced simultaneously at the Schauspielhaus, Dresden, and in 7 other cities, 1926). 1926.

Papiermühle (produced Alberttheater, Dresden, 1926). 1927.

Der Zar lässt sich photographieren, music by Kurt Weill (produced Neues Theater, Leipzig, 1928). 1927.

Der Präsident (produced Schauspielhaus, Frankfurt, 1928). 1927; translated as *The President*, in *Plays 2*, 1981.

Oktobertag (produced Kammerspiele, Hamburg, 1928). 1928; translated as *The Phantom Lover*, 1928; as *One Day in October*, in *Plays 2*, 1981.

Die Lederköpfe (produced Neues Theater, Frankfurt, 1928). 1928.

Hellseherei (produced Schauspielhaus, Düsseldorf, 1929). 1929.

Zwei Krawatten (produced Berliner Theater, Berlin, 1929). 1929.

Mississippi (produced Schauspielhaus, Frankfurt, 1930). 1930.

Der Silbersee (produced simultaneously at the Altes Theater, Leipzig, and in 10 other cities, 1933). 1933.

Adrienne Ambrosat (produced Theater in der Josefstadt, Vienna, 1935). 1948(?); translated as *Adrienne Ambrossat*, in *Continental Plays 2*, 1935.

Das Los des Ossian Balvesen (produced Burgtheater, Vienna, 1936). 1947(?).

Der Gärtner von Toulouse (produced Nationaltheater, Mannheim, 1945). 1938.

Der Schuss in die Öffentlichkeit (produced Städtische Bühnen, Magdeburg, 1949). 1939.

Der Soldat Tanaka (produced Schauspielhaus, Zurich, 1940). 1940.

Rosamunde Floris (produced Württembergisches Staatstheater, Stuttgart, 1953). 1940.

Alain und Elise (produced Städtische Bühnen, Frankfurt, 1954). 1940.

Die Spieldose (produced Stadttheater, Basle, 1943). In *Stücke; Erzählungen; Aufsätze; Gedichte*, 1966.

Zweimal Amphitryon (produced Schauspielhaus, Zurich, 1944). In *Griechische Dramen*, 1948.

Das Floss der Medusa (produced Stadttheater, Basle, 1945). 1963; translated as *The Raft of Medusa*, in *First Stage*, 1, 1962, in *Postwar German Theater*, edited by Michael Benedikt and George E. Wellwarth, and in *Plays 2*, 1981.

Agnete (produced Nationaltheater, Mannheim, 1949). 1948(?).

Klawitter (produced Städtische Bühnen, Brandenburg, 1949). 1948(?).

Pygmalion (produced Studio Fink-Kaulbachstrasse, Munich, 1953). In *Griechische Dramen*, 1948.

Bellerophon (produced Stadttheater, Saarbrücken, 1953). In *Griechische Dramen*, 1948.

Napoleon in New Orleans (produced Badisches Staatstheater, Karlsruhe, 1950). In *Stücke; Erzählungen; Aufsätze; Gedichte*, 1966.

Pferdewechsel. 1954(?).

Vincent verkauft ein Bild. 1954(?).

Schellkönig. In *Stücke; Erzählungen; Aufsätze; Gedichte*, 1966.

Das gordische Ei (unfinished). Nd.

Radio Plays

Der englische Sender, 1947 (published c.1947).

Fiction

Es ist genug. 1932.
Villa Aurea. 1940.
Leutnant Welzeck (fragment). In *Stücke; Erzählungen; Aufsätze; Gedichte*, 1966.

Memoirs and Letters

Georg Kaiser in Sachen Georg Kaiser: Briefe 1916–1933, edited by Gesa M. Valk.   1989.

*

Bibliographies

Leroy W. Shaw, "Georg Kaiser (1878–1945): A Bio-Bibliographical Report", in *Texas Studies in Literature and Language*, 3, 1961.

Criticism

Books:
Willibald Omankowski, *Kaiser und seine Bühnenwerke*, Berlin and Leipzig, 1922.
Bernhard Diebold, *Der Denkspieler, Georg Kaiser*, Frankfurt, 1924.
Max Freyhan, *Georg Kaisers Werk*, Berlin, 1926.
Hugo Königsgarten, *Georg Kaiser*, Potsdam, 1928.
Eric A. Fivian, *Georg Kaiser und seine Stellung im Expressionismus*, Munich, 1946.
Brian J. Kenworthy, *Georg Kaiser*, Oxford, 1957.
Wolfgang Paulsen, *Georg Kaiser: Die Perspektiven seines Werkes*, Tübingen, 1960.
Wilhelm Steffens, *Georg Kaiser*, Velber, 1969.
M. Kuxdorf, *Die Suche nach dem Menschen im Drama Georg Kaisers*, Bern, 1971.
Ernst Schürer, *Georg Kaiser und Bertolt Brecht*, Frankfurt, 1971.
Hugo F. Garten, "Georg Kaiser Re-examined", in *Essays in German and Dutch Literature*, edited by W.D. Robson-Scott, London, 1973.
Rudolf Bussmann, *Einzelner und Masse: Zum dramatischen Werk Georg Kaisers*, Kronberg, 1978.
M. Durzak, *Das expressionistische Drama: Carl Sternheim; Georg Kaiser*, Munich, 1978.
A. Arnold (ed.), *Georg Kaiser*, Stuttgart, 1980.
H.A. Pausch and E. Reinhold (eds.), *Georg Kaiser: Ein Aufsatzsammlung*, Berlin and Darmstadt, 1980.
Michael Patterson, *The Revolution in German Theatre 1900–1933*, London, 1981.
Renate Benson, *German Expressionist Drama: Ernst Toller and Georg Kaiser*, London, 1984; German edition, 1987.
Peter K. Tyson, *The Reception of Georg Kaiser 1915–1945: Texts and Analysis* (2 vols.), New York, 1984.
Carol Diethe, *Aspects of Distorted Sexual Attitudes in German Expressionist Drama*, New York, 1988.

Articles:
Paul Davies, "The Political and Social Aspects of Georg Kaiser in the Context of Expressionism", in *Revue Frontenac*, 1, 1983.
R.W. Last, "Symbol and Struggle in Georg Kaiser's *Die Bürger von Calais*", in *German Life and Letters*, 19, 1966.

* * *

Georg Kaiser was not only Germany's most prolific and versatile playwright, but also played a decisive role in the development of German expressionist drama; he is, in fact, best known for that particular period of his career. His early dramas were influenced by naturalism and neo-Romanticism. Of the plays written between 1895 and 1912, only two are noteworthy: *Die jüdische Witwe* (The Jewish Widow), and *König Hahnrei* (King Cuckold). Both are indebted to Frank Wedekind in that they deal predominantly with the erotic nature of man. But the plays display also two main features of Kaiser's dramatic *oeuvre*: his fascination with human psychology, and his penchant for adapting historical facts for the purpose of dramatising contemporary problems and personal concepts. Furthermore, his drama is often so intellectualised that it prompted the critic B. Diebold to classify him as a *Denkspieler* (a manipulator of ideas). Kaiser himself proclaimed that "writing drama means to pursue an idea to the end". His expressionist period reflects this maxim most clearly.

The common theme of his dramas between 1912 and 1923 is man's ethical renewal, which Kaiser probed from various perspectives. In *Von morgens bis mitternachts* (*From Morning to Midnight*), the Cashier, who has stolen a huge amount of money, breaks out from his mindless routine. In his erroneous belief that money can buy him something of value, he moves hectically from one place to another; when he finally realizes that money is the greatest fraud of all, he shoots himself. *Von morgens bis mitternachts* is one of the earliest examples of German *Stationendrama* and contains already, in nucleus, all the features of Kaiser's expressionism.

The Cashier's break away from his past, the search for a renewed existence, and his association with Christ at the close of the play, make him a forerunner of the figure of the "New Man" which Kaiser created in *Die Bürger von Calais* (*The Burghers of Calais*), and which will always be associated with German expressionist drama. While in *Von morgens bis mitternachts* Kaiser probed the power of money as the motivating agent for a renewed existence, he explored the theme of sacrificial death in *Die Bürger von Calais*. According to the historian J. Froissart's account, six noble citizens had to offer their lives to the English King so that he would spare Calais. Typically, Kaiser departed from the historic facts by adding a seventh volunteer, and the play centres on the problem of which one of the seven will escape death. Kaiser, greatly influenced by the Socratic symposium, had Eustache de Saint-Pierre (who—in his wisdom and altruism—is clearly depicted as the New Man) employ its dialetical method of disputation in the process of teaching the other six how to accept their sacrifice freely; he himself commits suicide as an act of moral freedom. *Die Bürger von Calais*, despite its traditional appearance, is also a *Stationendrama* where each of the three acts can be understood as separate stages in the development of the theme of the renewal of man.

In *Der gerettete Alkibiades* (*Alcibiades Saved*), another drama of this period, Kaiser once more rang his own characteristic changes to a familiar story. The play departs from Plato when, with mordant irony, it shows how Socrates' achievements are based on deceit. During a battle, Socrates, who has been incapacitated by a thorn in his sole, rallies the Greeks because of his screams, which are mistaken for shouts of defiance; the Greeks win the battle and Socrates is hailed as a hero. Since he does not rectify this misconception, one lie now entails another. The thorn incident was Kaiser's invention, used as a literal and symbolic device to develop the theme of Socrates' change from a simple artisan into a celebrated philosopher. However, his transformation is accompanied by a constant sting in the flesh, which stands, symbolically, for the exclusive demands of the spirit which Kaiser once called "an incurable wound". Socrates finally welcomes death as a deliverance from his physical pain and mental anguish. This play depicts Socrates—in contrast to Eustache de Saint-Pierre—as a simple human being uninterested in becoming a saviour of mankind.

It is interesting to note that—with the exception of *Hölle, Weg, Erde* (Hell, Way, Earth)—the protagonists of Kaiser's expressionist plays are either killed or commit suicide, demonstrating his inherent pessimism about the possibility of mankind's regeneration. Despite the occasional appearance of a New Man in history (Jesus, Socrates), Kaiser came to feel more and more that human nature was intrinsically corrupt.

The *Gas* plays develop this pessimistic conclusion with relentless logic. *Gas I* demonstrates the futility of the protagonist's efforts to convert the workers from the production of gas to a more humane way of life. However, the play ends with the hope that one day a New Man will fulfil his legacy. The protagonist of *Gas II* is the promised one, but, rejected by the workers, he kills himself and mankind with the ultimate poison-gas and so brings about a universal apocalyptic destruction. *Gas II*, written against the backdrop of the end of World War I and political unrest in Germany, represents the darkest and most misanthropic vision in the expressionist drama.

From 1923 Kaiser turned to comedy because he realised that, in a period of economic and political upheaval, the public preferred lighter fare. He was equally gifted in the comic genre, an integral part of his dramatic output, and he excelled in it primarily because of his sophisticated and witty use of language.

Although Kaiser was never as political a dramatist as Ernst Toller, Walter Hasenclever, or Reinhard Goering, his interest in the political and sociological developments of his time, and his pacifism, are reflected in a number of his later dramas of the 1920's. *Der Silbersee*, for example, written in collaboration with Kurt Weill, satirises Hitler and Nazism. The Leipzig premiere, in early 1933, was interrupted by Nazi stormtroopers, and Kaiser's career began to fade. Similarly, his pacifist play, *Der Soldat Tanaka*, was banned after its 1940 premiere in Switzerland. Of the remaining plays written between 1934–44, five deal with the topic of art and the artist. In his last dramas, the so-called "Greek" plays—*Zweimal Amphitryon*, *Pygmalion*, and *Bellerophon*—Kaiser escaped into a mythical realm where the artist's creation is unchallenged by reality, and where his reward is his apotheosised transformation into a star.

—Renate Benson

See also *Volume 1* entries on *The Gas Trilogy*; *From Morning to Midnight*.

KALIDASA. Born in India, probably in the 5th century. Little known of his life; possibly a poet at the court of King Chandragupta II of Ujjain. Three dramas, two narrative poems, and two lyric poems survive.

Works

Collections

Works, various translators. 1901.
"Shakuntala" and Other Works (includes *Shakuntala; The Cloud Messenger; The Seasons;* and partial translations and summaries of *Urvashi; Malvika and Agnimitra; The*

Dynasty of Raghu; The Birth of the War God), translated by Arthur W. Ryder. 1912.
Works (2 vols.), edited by C.R. Devadhara. 1966-71.
Complete Works. 1976.
Theater of Memory: The Plays of Kalidasa, translated by Barbara Stoler Miller, Edwin Gerow, and David Gitomer. 1984.

Stage Works

Abhijnanasakuntala. 1761; translated as *Shakuntala and the Recovered Ring*, 1789; as *Sakuntalá*, 1853; as *Sakoontalá; or, The Lost Ring*, 1891; as *Shakuntala; or, The Fatal Ring*, 1899: several subsequent translations as *Shakuntala*; as *Sakuntala*, 1920.
Vikramorvasiya. 1830; translated as *Vikramorvasiya*, 1851; by H.H. Wilson as *Vikrama and Urvasi*, in *Select Specimins of the Theatre of the Hindus 1*, 1871; as *Vikramorvasiya*, 1898; as *Vikrama-Urvashi*, in *Works*, 1901; as *Vikramorvasie*, 1911; as *The Hero and the Nymph*, 1911; excerpts translated as *Urvashi*, in *"Shakuntala" and Other Works*, 1912.
Malvikagnimitra. As *Mâlvikâ et Agnimitra*, edited by O.F. Tullberg, 1840; translated as *Malavikagnimitra*, 1896: several subsequent translations under same title; parts translated as *Malvika and Agnimitra*, in *"Shakuntala" and Other Work*, 1912.

Verse

Ritusamhara. 1792; translated as *The Ritusamhâra*, 1886; as *The Ritusanhara*, 1897; as *Ritu-Samhara*, in *Works*, 1901; as *The Seasons*, in *"Shakuntala" and Other Works*, 1912; as *Ritusamhara; or, The Pageant of the Seasons*, 1947; as *The Ritusamhara*, 1970.
Raghuvamsa. Edited by F.A. Stenzler, 1832; translated as *The Raghuvansá*, 1879; as *Raghu-Vamsa*, in *Works*, 1901; as *The Raghuvançá: The Story of Raghu's Line*, 1902; excerpts translated as *The Dynasty of Raghu*, in *"Shakuntala" and Other Works*, 1912, and as *From the Raghuvansa*, 1912; as *The Raghuvamsa*, 1939.
Kumarasambhava. 1838; translated as *The Birth of the War God*, 1853; as *Kumara-Samhavam*, in *Works*, 1901.
Meghaduta. As *Meghaduta et Cringaratilaka*, edited by J. Gildemeister, 1841 (Bonn); translated as *The Megha-Dhuta; or, The Cloud Messenger*, 1813; as *The Messenger Cloud*, 1867; as *The Cloud Messenger*, in *"Shakuntala" and Other Works*, 1912: several subsequent translations under same title; as *The Meghaduta*, 1935; as *The Transport of Love*, 1976.

*

Bibliographies

M. Schuyler, *A Bibliography of the Sanskrit Drama*, New York, 1906.
V. Raghavan, "Bibliography of Translations of Kalidasa's Works", in *Indian Literature*, 11, 1968.
S.P. Narang, *Kalidasa: Bibliography*, New Delhi, 1976.

Criticism

Books:
G. Huth, *Die Daten des Kalidasa*, Berlin, 1890.
A. Hildebrand, *Kalidasa: Ein Versuch zu seiner literarischen Würdigung*, Breslau, 1921; reprinted, 1978.

L. Dhar, *The Birthplace of Kalidasa*, Delhi, 1926.
W. Ruben, *Kalidasa: Die menschliche Bedeutung seiner Werke*, Berlin, 1956; English version, New Delhi, 1984.
S.A. Sabnis, *Kalidasa: His Style and His Times*, Bombay, 1966.
V.V. Mirashi and N.R. Navlekar, *Kalidasa: Date. Life and Works*, Bombay, 1969.
K. Krishnamoorthy, *Kalidasa*, New York, 1972.
M. Mishra, *The Metres of Kalidasa*, Delhi, 1977.
V. Aggarwal, *The Imagery of Kalidasa*, Delhi, 1985.
P.C. Mandel, *Kalidasa as Dramatist*, Dhaka, 1986.

* * *

Kalidasa is generally regarded as the Shakespeare of India—though no two playwrights could have been farther apart in form and spirit—and the most popular, if not the greatest, Sanskrit author. We know even less about Kalidasa's life than about Shakespeare's. There are, however, many legendary accounts of his life. (One most frequently quoted is that he was born in a Brahmin family, was orphaned in infancy, and grew up as an ox-driver and married the Princess of Benaras.)

Most probably Kalidasa lived in the 5th century AD. Tradition has it that he flourished during the reign of Chandragupta II (Vikramaditya), who ruled over the city of Ujjain in west-central India, and who was a great patron of arts and learning. Many talented artists and savants were associated with his Court, the most distinguished of them being the group known as the "nine gems", of which Kalidasa was one. Ujjain thus enjoys the same status in Indian cultural history as does Athens, Rome, and Florence in the European. From references in his own writings, one can gather certain facts concerning Kalidasa's life and personality: he spent some time in the city of Ujjain; he travelled widely in India; he was well-versed in Sanskrit language and literature; he was in full command of the science of grammar, according to the Hindu's "chief of all sciences", as well as of the various systems of orthodox Hindu philosophy from the yoga to Sankhya, from Vaishnavism to Shaivism.

Seven works by Kalidasa have survived: 1) three prose dramas interspersed with lyric poems—*Malavikagnimitra* (*Malavika and Agnimitra*), his first work; *Abhijnanashakuntala* (*The Lost Ring of Shakuntala*), popularly known as *Shakuntala*; and *Vikramorvashiya* (*Urvaçi Conquered by Valor*]; 2) the two narrative poems or *Mahakavyas* (great poems), *Raghuvamsha* (*Dynasty of Raghu*) and *Kumarasambhava* (*Birth of the War God*); 3) the two lyrical poems *Meghaduta* (*Cloud Messenger*) and *Ritusamhara* (*Cycle of the Seasons*). But he seems to have written little more than that which has survived.

In his plays, Kalidasa made little or no attempt to depart from the codes and conventions of Indian dramaturgy, such as the use of the "benediction", addressed either to Vishnu or Shiva, the "prologue" (a form of dialogue between the manager of the play and the female protagonist outlining the subject-matter of the play), the mixture of prose and verse, and the use of dialects or "Prakrits" in juxtaposition with the classical Sanskrit. There is, in Kalidasa's plays, as in classical Indian drama in general, less action but more symbolism, less individuality in the characters but more allegorical richness and poetical depth. As for his poetic diction, as well as prose style, one can praise, as Sri Aurobindo did, its "compact but never abrupt brevity, a soft gravity and smooth majesty, a noble harmony of verse, a strong and lucid beauty of chiselled prose, above all an epic precision of phrase, weighty, sparing and yet full of colour and sweetness"—qualities by virtue of which Kalidasa may be regarded, as Tennyson regarded

Virgil, as a "wielder of the stateliest measure ever moulded by the lips of man".

Malavikagnimitra is a five-act court play in which King Agnimitra falls in love with one of his Queen Dhárini's waiting-maids called Malavika. The Queen puts all sorts of obstacles in the King's way to marrying the maid. But with the help of his friend, Gautama, the King succeeds in surmounting these obstacles and in taking Malvika as a new wife.

Vikramorvashiya, another five-act play, is a fairy-tale of love between a celestial nymph, Urvashi, and the earthly King, Pururavas. The plot is borrowed from an ancient Vedic legend to be found in the *Rig-Veda* and the *Shatapatha-Brahmana*, to which the poet has added new incidents and scenes.

Kalidasa's greatest work, however, which brought him world-wide renown, is the seven-act play *Shakuntala*, based on the story of Shakuntala as narrated in the *Mahabharata*. Here, too, the dramatist enriched the elements he had borrowed through numerous modifications and additions.

During a chariot ride, King Dushyanta encounters Shakuntala at the hermitage of Kanva, falls in love with her, marries her, but is then called home by urgent state business. In her grief-stricken state, Shakuntala shows some discourtesy to an ascetic who then curses her, saying that the King will forget his bride. Later on, the ascetic moderates the curse so that the King's memory can return, provided Shakuntala keeps safe the ring he has given her. But, as fate would have it, while bathing in a river, she loses it. And when, while soon to give birth to the King's child, she goes to the court, she is sent away and finds shelter with the great sage Kashyapa in whose hermitage her son, named Bharata ("the all-tamer") is born. A fisherman finds the ring, the King's memory returns, and while waging war against the demons, he happens to arrive in the neighbourhood of Kashyapa's hermitage where he meets his wife and son, and the happy reunion between them concludes the play.

Shakuntala not only brings into focus Kalidasa's dramatic and inventive powers—for creating suspense, probing into and analysing sentiment, characterization, and devising dramatic situations—but also his lyrical and imaginative powers in dealing with the themes of love, human and external nature, and man's yearning to seek "some higher object" than his everyday life and experience can give him.

—G. Singh

See also *Volume 1* entry on *Shakuntala*.

KANZE Kojirō Nobumitsu.   See *Volume 1* entry on *Benkei in the Boat.*

KANZE Saburō Motokiyo.   See **ZEAMI**.

KARA Jūrō. Born Otsuru Yoshihide in Tokyo, 11 February 1940 (some sources give 1941). Educated at Meiji University, graduated 1962. Married the Korean actress Yi Yong-son, known as Ri Reisen in Japan (divorced 1988). Founder, the Jokyo gekijo (Situation Theatre) company, 1963, which mounted its first production, *Koshimaki Osen* [Petticoat O-Sen], in Shinjuku, 1967: company disbanded, 1988; founder, Kara-gumi (Kara Company), 1988. Also a novelist and songwriter. Recipient: Kishida Prize, 1969; Izumi Kyoka Prize (for fiction), 1978; Akatugawa Prize (for fiction), 1983.

Works

Collections

Kara Jūrō zen sakuhin shu (6 vols.).   1977–80.

Stage Works

Selected titles; publication dates do not necessarily refer to book editions.

Jon Shirubaa.   1966.
Ali Baba.   1966.
Koshimaki Osen.   1966.
Yuhi Shōsetsu.   1968.
Shōjo Kamen.   1969; translated as *The Virgin's Mask*, in *Alternative Japanese Drama*, edited by Robert T. Rolf and John K. Gillespie, 1992.
Shōjo toshi.   1969.
Jon Shirubaa: Ai no kojiki.   1970; translated by David G. Goodman, as *John Silver: The Beggar of Love*, in *Concerned Theatre Japan*, vol. 1 no. 2, 1970, and in book form, 1988.
Kyūketsuki.   1971.
Nito monogatari.   1972.
Tetsu kamen.   1972.
Bengal no tora.   1973.
Mōdōken.   1973.
Umi no kiba.   1973.
Are kara no Jon Shirubaa.   1973
Kara-ban kaze no Matasaburō.   1974.
Yasha kisō.   1974.
Ito hime.   1975.
Kara-ban taki no shiraito.   1975.
Shitamachi no Hoffman.   1975.
Hebi-hime-sama: Waga kokoro no naraja.   1977.
Kappa.   1976.
Futari no onna, from his radio play.   1979; translated as *Two Women*, in *Alternative Japanese Theatre*, edited by Robert T. Rolf and John K. Gillespie, 1992.
Onna Cyrano.   1980.
Shitaya mannenchō monogatari.   1981.
Kuroi tulip.   1983.

Screenplays

Ninkyō gaiden: Genkainada

Radio Play

Futari no onna, 1978.

Other

Sagawa-kun kara no tegami.   1983.

*

Criticism

Articles:
Yamamoto Kiyokazu, "Kara's Vision: The World as Public Toilet", in *Canadian Theatre Review*, 20, 1978.

* * *

Kara was raised in Shitaya Mannen-chō, one of the oldest sections of Tokyo, which was heavily bombed at the end of World War II. Kara remembers vividly growing up among the charred ruins of the city after the War, and his affection for the old city of Tokyo has played an increasingly prominent role in his work in recent years.

Kara became involved in theatre as a child, and worked as a child-actor in the same troupe as Satoh Makoto. He took part in the 1960 demonstrations against the renewal of the US–Japan Mutual Security Treaty, but with less political conviction than many of his generation.

Kara wrote his senior thesis in college on Sartre's *The Respectable Prostitute*, and Sartre's influence is obvious in the name Kara chose for the troupe he founded in 1963, the Situation Theatre (Jokyō gekijō). The conviction that reality is an arbitrary social construction, subject to alteration, is the central tenet of Kara's philosophy of the theatre.

This philosophy governs both Kara's plays and the activities of his troupe. In 1967, he and his troupe performed for the first time in the red tent that has become their emblem. Their aim has been not only to free theatre from the limitations of theatre buildings and the politics that govern them, but also to re-define the social contruction of reality by introducing into it the foreign element of their theatre. Kara has frequently used the technique of opening one side of the tent and co-opting the cityscape as part of his *mise en scène*.

Kara's philosophy is apparent in plays like *John Silver: The Beggar of Love* (*Jon Shirubaa: Ai no kojiki*). The play takes place in a Tokyo public lavatory which the occupants have proclaimed to be the Korean cabaret Pu-shee. One of the central issues in the play is whether the occupants' definition of the place will survive its encounter with the more general social construction. Both definitions of the space are arbitrary, and thus equally valid in Kara's view, but the latter is founded on psychological truth, while the former is backed up by the coercive power of the State.

Kara has been ambivalent, if not utterly antagonistic, in his attitudes to Europe and the United States. In contrast to Terayama Shūji, who performed frequently in Europe and with whom Kara is frequently compared, he has refused to perform in the West. Instead, he and his troupe have performed in Korea (1972), Bangladesh (1973), and in Palestinian refugee camps in Lebanon (1974). The trip to Lebanon was Kara's last such venture abroad, however, for he found in the refugee camps a social construction of reality where psychological truth and political existence were so closely interconnected that the theatre would, he concluded, only be overwhelmed and could not perform its countervailing function.

Subsequently, Kara has devoted himself to more purely literary pursuits. In 1978, he won the Izumi Kyōka Prize for a work of fiction. In 1983 he won the Akutagawa prize for another novel, *Sagawa-kun kara no tegami* (A Letter from Sagawa), which deals with the true story of a Japanese student in Paris who murdered his French girlfriend and then cannibalized her remains.

The Situation Theatre was disbanded in 1988 upon Kara's divorce from his wife, the actress Ri Reisen. The troupe was reorganized as the Kara Company (Kara-gumi).

—David G. Goodman

KARVAŠ, Peter. Born in Banská Bystrica, Czechoslovakia (now Slovakia), 25 April 1920. Educated at Gymnasium, 1930–38; technical college, Prague, 1938–39 (college closed following German invasion), finally graduated 1946; also studied at the University of Bratislava. During World War II held a variety of jobs, including dramaturg at the Komorni [Chamber] Theatre in Martin, central Slovakia, 1943–44; lived for a time with the Slovak partisans in the mountains, and took part in the anti-German uprising, 1944; also worked in radio; first stage play, *Meteor*, produced 1945; dramaturg at the Slovak National Theatre, Bratislava, 1946–49; cultural attaché in Bucharest, Romania, 1949–51; various posts after 1951, including editorship of the periodical *Kulturny tvorba*; began teaching at the Academy, 1956; sided with Dubcek and the Reform Communists, 1968, but following the Soviet invasion lost membership of the Communist Party and his plays of the 1960's were banned from performance; assistant professor of drama at a school of music and dramatic art, 1968–74. Has also written several theoretical works on drama, notably *Zamyšlení nad dramatem* [Reflections on the Drama] and *Zamyšení nad dramaturgií* [Reflections on Dramaturgy].

Works

Collections

Tri slová o vojne [Three Words About War].   1960.
Tri slová o srdci [Three Words About the Heart].   1964.
Sedem hier [Seven Plays].   1987.

Stage Works (selected)

Majak [The Beacon] (produced 1943).
Meteor [Meteor] (produced 1945).   1945.
Spolok piatich "P" [Society of the Paragons "P"] (produced 1946).   1948.
Hra o básnnikovi [A Play About a Poet] (produced 1946).
Basta [The Bastion] (produced 1948).   1948.
Návrat do života [Return to Life] (produced 1946).   1949.
Hanibal pred bránami [Hannibal Before the Gates] (produced 1949).   1949.
L'udia z našej ulice [People from Our Street] (produced 1950).   1951.
Srdce plné radosti [A Heart Full of Joy] (produced 1953).   1954.
Pacient sto trinásť [Patient No. 113] (produced 1955).   1955.
Diplomati [Diplomats] (produced 1958).   1958.
Polnočná omša [Midnight Mass] (produced 1959).   1959.
Zmyrtvychvstanie deduska Kolomana [The Resurrection of Grandfather Kolman] (produced 1960).   1960.

Antigona a tí druhi [Antigone and the Others] (produced 1962).   1961.
Jazva [The Scar] (produced 1963).   1963.
Ve'lká parachňa [The Great Whig] (produced 1965).   1964.
Experiment Damokles [The Damocles Experiment] (produced 1967).   1966.
Absolútny zákaz (produced 1969).   1970.
Nultá hodina [Zero Hour].   In *Sedem hier*, 1987.
Hmlisté ráno [A Foggy Morning].   In *Sedem hier*, 1987.
Súkromná oslava [Private Celebration].   In *Sedem hier*, 1987.
Dvadsiata noc [The Twentieth Night].   In *Sedem hier*, 1987.
Zadný vchod [Back Entrance].   In *Sedem hier*, 1987.
Nebo-peklo [Heaven-Hell].   In *Sedem hier*, 1987.
Nočná návšteva [Night Visit].   In *Sedem hier*, 1987.

Fiction

Most.   1945.
Niet prístavov 1–2.   1946.
Polohlaso.   1947; revised edition, 1966.
Toto pokolenie.   1949.
S nami a protí nám.   1950.
Pokolenie v útoku.   1952.
Dieťa a meč.   1953.
Čert nespí.   1954.
Čertovo kopýtko.   1957.
Leningradské episfoly.   1959.
Výlet na juh.   1960.
Konfety a leporelá.   1961.
Nedokončena pre detský hlas.   1968.
Mal'ovát čerta na stenu.   1970.
Noc v mojom meste.   1979.
V Hniezde.   1981.
Pol'ahčujúca okolnosť.   1991.

Other

Kapitolky o rozhlase [Chapters About the Radio].   1948.
K základným otázkam súčasného slovenského divadla [On Fundamental Questions of Contemporary Slovak Theatre].   1948.
Ùvod do základnych problémov divadla [An Introduction to the Basic Problems of the Theatre].   1948.
K niektorým tvorivým problémom nasej drámy. [On Several Creative Problems of Our Drama].   1956.
Zamyšlení nad dramatem [Reflections on the Drama].   1964.
Zamyšlení nad dramaturgií [Reflections on Dramaturgy].   1969.
Kniha ú l'avy.   1970.
Priestory v divadle a divadlo v priestore 1–2 [Space in the Theatre and the Theatre in Space].   1977.
Humoresky a iné kratochvile (3 vols).   1984–89.
Fascikel S.   1988.

*   *   *

During the late 1950's and 1960's Peter Karvaš became Slovakia's foremost playwright and theatre theoretician. He had begun writing during World War II; his earliest plays were in the genre of socialist realism, at that time obligatory on the Slovak stage, and in many ways appropriate to his way of thinking. His later work, in subject and in structure, was influenced by other trends in European drama. In his theoretical writings he analysed movements in contemporary world theatre, in particular how they related to the theatre in Czechoslovakia.

Karvaš's university education was interrupted by World War II. He was in his second year at technical college in Prague when, in November 1939, the Germans closed the universities, and he unable to graduate until 1946 (in Bratislava). In the meantime he had held a variety of jobs, including a period as dramaturg at the Komorní [Chamber] Theatre in Martin, in central Slovakia. He also lived for a while in the mountains with the Slovak partisans. By this time, Karvaš had already started on a writing career, and his first radio plays were broadcast in the early 1940's. In 1945 his first stage play, *Meteor*, was performed at the theatre in Martin; it was based on the experiences of the partisans during the Slovak Uprising. *Návrat do života* (Return to Life) took as its subject the survivors of the concentration camps, whilst *Basta* (the Bastion) returned to the theme of Slovak resistance, as shown at three different stages of history.

By 1948, when the Communist Party came to power in Czechoslovakia, Karvaš was a leading figure in Slovak cultural life and a dramaturg at the Slovak National Theatre. For the next 20 years he remained a member of the communist establishment. In 1956 he began to teach at the Academy, whilst continuing to write plays. His work during these years included *Pacient sto trinást'* (Patient One-hundred-and-Thirteen) and the comedy *Diplomati* (Diplomats) in which he satirised the world of international intrigue.

His biggest success up to that time came in 1959 with *Polnočná omsa* (Midnight Mass). The play is set in Slovakia during when World War II, when a fascist Slovak regime sided with Hitler's Germany. The action takes place at the time of the Uprising led by the partisans, but, says Karvaš, it is not a play *about* the Uprising. It is, he claims, a study of the negative forces in society which lead to betrayal at both a personal and national level; such betrayal, he implies, could be repeated. *Antigona a tí druhi* (Antigone and the Others) again used a wartime setting, that of a concentration camp. In this it is "the others"—a group of imprisoned resistance fighters—rather than Antigone who are central to his theme. It is they who must show unity by resisting Creon, the camp commandant; and, implicitly, it is their successors who must resist any recurrence of fascism.

Karvaš's analyses of history dealt with more recent events with *Jazva* (The Scar) which opened in Bratislava in 1963. Praised by the critics as an exposure of the "deformations" and "cult of personality" of the 1950's, it actually came closer home than that. The story, about complex relationships between old friends and colleagues, raised moral questions about the abuse of power and individual responsibility, and whether discipline and obedience are automatically in the interests of society. In 1965, *Vel'ka parachňa* (The Great Wig) similarly raised the subject of the purges of the 1950's, this time treated in allegorical form, but one relevant to the contemporary situation. "The Great Wig" is a black comedy about a State in which the bald-heads are held responsible by the hairy-heads for all the mistakes of the past; in the course of the play, the situation is reversed. This allegory, even more than his historical plays, demonstrates his use of characters as emblems of the different sides of a conflict; they are not individuals in their own right, but represent particular arguments.

Karvaš continued during this period to work on his theories of drama, published in *Zamyšlení nad dramatem* (Reflections on the Drama) in 1964 and *Zamyšlení nad dramaturgií* (Reflections on Dramaturgy) in 1969. The first deals with the new possibilities opening in the theatre during the first half of the 1950's, the second with the period up to 1966. In a number of ways Karvaš focused his analysis to prove the necessity of his own kind of drama—the drama of ideas, of philosophical

discussion. In the first "Reflections" he wrote: "Great drama always reveals the central conflict of the time, and brings alongside this conflict an actual conflict involving specific characters". In his commitment to realism he stood apart from the Czech dramatists who inclined towards the theatre of the absurd—Havel, Uhde, Klima, Smoček. At the end of the second "Reflections" he wrote: "If we assume that the basic means of expression in the theatre can be nothing other than the live actor, then the philosophic programme of the theatre of the absurd clashes with the fundamental nature of the art of the theatre".

In 1968, Peter Karvaš took his stand with the reform Communists, and consequently his plays of the 1960's were not performed in Czechoslovakia for over 20 years. However, in the 1970's the conditions for intellectuals in Slovakia were not as harsh as in the Czech lands (Czechoslovakia became a federation in 1969). The Slovak censors took a more pragmatic attitude towards deviant writers, allowing them greater freedom of occupation and publication, so that Bratislava did not produce the community of dissident writers and volumes of *samizdat* [underground] literature that appeared in Prague. Peter Karvaš, whilst not exactly *persona grata*, remained in employment and was able to publish some criticism in specialist papers. He continued to write plays, and a volume of these, written in the years 1972–76, was published in 1987.

—Barbara Day

KATONA, József. Born in Kecskemét, Hungary, 11 November 1791. Educated at schools in Pest, Kecskemét, and Szeged, 1802–07; University of Pest, studying law, 1809–15, diploma in law 1815. Began acting and writing while at university; play translator (particularly of plays by Kotzebue) with the Hungarian Theatre Society in Pest and Buda, 1812–14; practising lawyer, at first in Pest, then in Kecskemét as deputy prosecutor, from 1820, and prosecutor general, from 1826. Died after heart attack, in Kecskemét, 16 April 1830.

Works

Collections

Összes művei [Collected Works] (3 vols.), edited by Lajos Abafi. 1880–81.
Összes művei [Collected Works] (2 vols.), edited by Andor Solt. 1959.

Stage Works

Farsangi utazás (produced 1812).
A Luca széke karácsony éjszakáján (produced 1812). In *Összes müzei*, 1880–81.
István, a magyrok elso királya (produced 1813). In *Összes művei*, 1880–81.
Aubigny Clementia; vagyis, A vallás miatt való zenebona Franciaországban IV. Henrik alatt (produced as *Hédervári Cecilia, a magyar amazon; vagyis, Hédervár ostroma*, 1819). In *Összes művei*, 1880–81.
A borzasztó torony; vagyis, A gonosz talált gyermek (produced 1814). In *Összes művei*, 1880–81.

Gyula E. Kovács in the title-role of *Bánk Bán* [Viceroy Bank] in the Kolozsvár National Theatre's 1892 production of the play by **József Katona**.

Ziska; vagyis, A husziták elso pártütése Csehországban. In *Összes művei,* 1880–81.
Ziska a Calice, a táboriták vezére. In *Összes művei,* 1880–81.
A rózsa; vagyis, A tapasztalatlan légy a pókok között. In *Összes művei,* 2, 1959.
Jeruzsálem pusztulása (produced 1814). In *Összes művei,* 1880–81.
Bánk bán (produced 1833). 1821.
Monostori Veronka; vagy, A harc két ellenkezo ügyért (produced 1825). In *Összes művei,* 1880–81
A Mombelli grófok. In *Összes művei,* 1880–81.

Verse

Verse appears in *Összes művei* 2, 1959.

*

Bibliographies

Anna Fenyvessiné Góhér, *Katona József 1792–1830: Ajánló bibliográfia,* Kecskemét, Hungary, 1957.

* * *

The epithet "founder of the Hungarian national drama" fits József Katona in more than one sense. It generally refers to Katona's intricate tragedy *Bánk bán* (Viceroy Bánk). However, this playwright was also witness to, as well as promoter of, the development of Hungarian theatre in its competition with the German-language drama, which was predominant mostly in the later capital city, Pest, whose burghers were overwhelmingly of foreign ancestry. In the provincial towns (including Katona's birthplace), however, the theatre became instrumental in disseminating Hungarian language and national consciousness, and developed its own country-wide institutions.

While studying law in Pest, Katona actively participated in shaping the Hungarian national theatre. Paradoxically, he also relied heavily on the tradition and themes of the German drama in his original works and translations. His practical knowledge of the stage sets him apart from earlier representatives of the Hungarian drama, such as György Bessenyei (1747–1811), and Mihály Csokonai Vitèz (1773–1805) who wrote exclusively for amateur performances by small circles of friends.

It is no exaggeration to state that the years Katona spent at the Hungarian Theatre in Pest (1812–14) exerted an enormous influence on him. He encountered the great contemporary impulses of world literature, on an intellectual level, and love, ambition and intrigue on a personal one. Like Shakespeare, he too integrated works by less than memorable writers, along with historical or contemporary anecdotes, into his plays—some of which are among the best in Hungarian drama. Yet it is not these casual analogies with long forgotten sources, but the kinship with outstanding European playwrights that any interpretation of Katona's genius must inevitably highlight.

Considering Katona's strong interest in history, the most obvious parallels are to be drawn with Shakespeare and Schiller. The two-part tragedy on the Hussite warlord, Jan Ziska, has been compared to Schiller's *Wallenstein,* inasmuch as the great rebel's motivation is not conviction but ambition and revenge. It is equally persuasive to demonstrate another analogy, between *Bánk bán* and Schiller's *Wilhelm Tell.* In both dramas the hero revolts against a cruel and perverted foreign tyranny whose aim is the destruction of both national identity and individual honour. (The themes of family sanctity and honour also link *Bánk bán* to *Kabale und Liebe,* and to Lessing's *Emilia Galotti.*)

Bánk bán illustrates, however, Katona's clearest conceptual association with Shakespearean themes, such as the conflict between hesitation and determination (as in *Hamlet*) and the systematic cultivation of jealousy in a noble hero (as in *Othello*). Some of these motifs also appear in *Ziska* and *Jeruzsálem pusztulása* (The Destruction of Jerusalem). Other analogies in Katona's tragedies—like those with the classical Greek *hubris* or Corneille's dramatic conflict between duty and passion—also contribute to the interpretation of, but do not dominate, the individual plays; Katona's secret is a fascinating merging of several traditions and themes.

In spite of Katona's general dramatic ability, it is customary to single out *Bánk bán* as his most outstanding tragedy. The plot is drawn from a 13th-century historical event, widely discussed by chroniclers: the uprising of the Hungarian nobility against the despotic rule of King Endre II's German-born wife, Gertrude (a theme also utilized by George Lillo in *Elmerick; or, Justice Triumphant*). The entire tragedy is charged with dramatic tension—between natives and foreigners, assigned and assumed rulers, individual and collective grievances, order and revolt, national and social priorities. A limited cast (some characters are the source of more than one conflict), terse diction, and a precise, calculated use of situations lend a truly dramatic character to the play. As in most post-Romantic plays, characterization is complex: Katona manages to spin the plot in such a way as to assign, equally, innocence and guilt to virtually everybody, thereby skilfully suggesting the moral complexity of human actions.

Bánk bán was not recognized for its qualities by Katona's contemporaries. The question arises whether a work that portrays Germans as enemies and condones the killing of the Queen could have passed imperial censorship at all. The jury of the drama competition to which Katona sent his play did not even acknowledge it. Disappointed, he stopped writing plays, yet managed to publish *Bánk bán* in 1821 and kept writing critical and aesthetic reflections on the theatre. He gained fame posthumously, and even then only gradually. In 1861 Ferenc Erkel composed an opera based on *Bánk bán,* and the play was made into a silent film in 1912.

Besides Katona's perennial achievements and intriguing ambivalence, his statements on his source material were particularly timely. In his introductory notes to *Ziska* and *Bánk bán,* he identifies not only the sources, but also the number of changes he executed in dealing with the historical material. This provocative demonstration of how literature differs from history can be read as a sign of a consciousness which challenged the traditional illusion of artistic reality and recreated history as meta-history with its own frame of reference: the criteria of historical "reality" are no longer valid in historical drama, as this "modern" playwright was eager to assert.

—George Bisztray

KAUFMAN, George S(imon). Born in Pittsburgh, Pennsylvania, USA, 16 November 1889. Educated at Liberty

School, New Castle School, and Central High School, Pittsburgh, graduated 1907; Western University of Pennsylvania Law School (now University of Pittsburgh), 1907. Married 1) Beatrice Bakrow in 1917 (died 1945), one adopted daughter; 2) the actress Leueen MacGrath in 1949 (divorced 1957). Worked as a surveyor, clerk in the Allegheny County Tax Office, and stenographer for the Pittsburgh Coal Company; traveling salesman, Columbia Ribbon Company, Paterson, New Jersey, 1909–12; columnist, Washington *Times*, 1912–13; drama critic, New York *Tribune*, 1914–15; columnist, New York *Evening Mail*, 1915; drama critic, later drama editor, New York *Times*, 1917–30. Writer for the stage from 1918, often in collaboration, notably with Marc Connelly and, later, Moss Hart; first-produced play, *Among Those Present*, staged 1918; stage director from 1928; panelist, *This is Show Business* radio and TV program, 1948–52. Chairman of the Board, Dramatists Guild 1927. Recipient: Megrue Prize, 1931; Pulitzer Prize, 1932, 1937; Tony Award, for directing, 1951. Died in New York, 2 June 1961.

Works

Collections

Six Plays by Kaufman and Hart (includes *Forked Lightning; Once in a Lifetime; Merrily We Roll Along; You Can't Take It with You; The American Way; The Man Who Came to Dinner; George Washington Slept Here*).   1942.
By George: A Kaufman Collection, edited by Donald Oliver. 1979.

Stage Works

Among Those Present, with Larry Evans and Walter C. Percival (produced 1918; as *Someone in the House*, produced 1918).
Jacques Duval, from play by Hans Miller (produced 1919).
Dulcy, with Marc Connelly (produced Frayzee Theatre, New York, 1921).   1921.
To the Ladies!, with Marc Connelly (produced Liberty Theatre, New York, 1922).   1923.
No, Sirree!, with Marc Connelly (produced 49th Street Theatre, New York, 1922).
The 49ers, with Marc Connelly (produced Punch and Judy Theatre, New York, 1922).
West of Pittsburgh, with Marc Connelly (produced 1922; revised version, as *The Deep Tangled Wildwood*, produced, Frayzee Theatre, New York, 1923).
Merton of the Movies, with Marc Connelly, from the story by Harry Leon Wilson (produced Cort Theatre, New York, 1922).   1925.
A Christmas Carol, with Marc Connelly, from the story by Dickens.   In Bookman, December 1922.
Helen of Troy, New York, with Marc Connelly, music and lyrics by Harry Ruby and Bert kalmar (produced Selwyn Theatre, New York, 1923).
Beggar on Horseback, with Marc Connelly, music by Deems Taylor, from a play by Paul Apel (produced Broadhurst Theatre, New York, 1924).   1925.
Sketches in *'Round the Town* (produced 1924).
Be Yourself, with Marc Connelly, music and lyrics by Lewis Genzler and Milton Schwarzwald, additional lyrics by Ira Gershwin (produced Sam H. Harris Theatre, New York, 1924).
Minick, with Edna Ferber, from the story "Old Man Minick" by Ferber (produced Booth Theatre, New York, 1924). In *Old Man Minick: A Short Story . . . Minick: A Play*, 1924.
The Butter and Egg Man (produced Longacre Theatre, New York, 1925).   1926.
The Cocoanuts, music by Irving Berlin (produced Lyric Theatre, New York, 1925).
Business is Business, with Dorothy Parker (produced 1925).
If Men Played Cards Like Women Do.   1926.
The Good Fellow, with Herman J. Mankiewicz (produced Playhouse Theatre, New York, 1926).   1931.
The Royal Family, with Edna Ferber (produced Selwyn Theatre, New York, 1927).   1928; as *Theatre Royal* (produced 1935), 1936.
Animal Crackers, with Morrie Ryskind, music and lyrics by Harry Ruby and Bert Kalmar (produced 44th Street Theatre, New York, 1928).
The Still Alarm (sketch), in *The Little Show* (produced Music Box Theatre, New York, 1929).   1930.
June Moon, with Ring Lardner, from the story "Some Like Them Cold" by Lardner (produced Broadhurst Theatre, New York, 1929).   1930.
The Channel Road, with Alexander Woollcott (produced Plymouth Theatre, New York, 1929).
Strike Up the Band, book by Morrie Ryskind from a libretto by Kaufman, music by George Gershwin, lyrics by Ira Gershwin (produced Times Square Theatre, New York, 1930).
Once in a Lifetime, with Moss Hart (produced Music Box Theatre, New York, 1930).   1930.
The Band Wagon, with Howard Dietz, music by Arthur Schwartz (produced New Amsterdam Theatre, New York, 1931).
Eldorado, with Laurence Stallings (produced Shubert Theatre, New York, 1931).
Of Thee I Sing, with Morrie Ryskind, music by George Gershwin, lyrics by Ira Gershwin (produced Sam H. Harris Theatre, New York, 1931).   1932.
Dinner at Eight, with Edna Ferber (produced Music Box Theatre, New York, 1932).   1932.
Let 'em Eat Cake, with Morrie Ryskind, music by George Gershwin, lyrics by Ira Gershwin (produced Imperial Theatre, New York, 1933).   1933.
The Dark Tower, with Alexander Woollcott (produced Morosco Theatre, New York, 1933).   1934.
Merrily We Roll Along, with Moss Hart (produced Music Box Theatre, New York, 1934).   1934.
Bring on the Girls, with Morrie Ryskind (produced National Theatre, Washington, DC, 1934).
Prom Night.   1934.
Cheating the Kidnappers.   1935.
The Paperhanger, with Moss Hart.   1935(?).
First Lady, with Katharine Dayton (produced Music Box Theatre, New York, 1935).   1935.
Stage Door, with Edna Ferber (produced Music Box Theatre, New York, 1936).   1936.
You Can't Take It with You, with Moss Hart (produced Booth Theatre, New York, 1936).   1937.
I'd Rather Be Right, with Moss Hart, music by Richard Rodgers, lyrics by Lorenz Hart (produced Alvin Theatre, New York, 1937).   1937.
The Fabulous Invalid, with Moss Hart (produced Broadhurst Theatre, New York, 1938).   1938.
The American Way, with Moss Hart, music by Oscar Levant (produced Center Theatre, New York, 1939).   1939.
The Man Who Came to Dinner, with Moss Hart (produced Music Box Theatre, New York, 1939).   1939.

George Washington Slept Here, with Moss Hart (produced Lyceum Theatre, New York, 1940). 1940.

The Land is Bright, with Edna Ferber (produced Music Box Theatre, New York, 1941). 1941.

The Late George Apley, with John P. Marquand, from the novel by Marquand (produced Lyceum Theatre, New York, 1944). 1946.

Local Boy Makes Good, in *The Seven Lively Arts* (produced Ziegfeld Theatre, New York, 1944).

Hollywood Pinafore (produced Alvin Theatre, New York, 1945).

Park Avenue, with Nunnally Johnson, music by Arthur Schwartz, lyrics by Ira Gershwin (produced Shubert Theatre, New York, 1946).

Bravo!, with Edna Ferber (produced Lyceum Theatre, New York, 1948). 1949.

The Small Hours, with Leueen MacGrath (produced National Theatre, New York, 1951). 1951.

Fancy Meeting You Again, with Leueen MacGrath (produced Royale Theatre, New York, 1952). 1952.

The Solid Gold Cadillac, with Howard Teichmann (produced Belasco Theatre, New York, 1953). 1954.

Silk Stockings, with Leueen MacGrath and Abe Burrows, music by Cole Porter, from a work by by Melchior Lengyel (produced Imperial Theatre, New York, 1955). 1955.

Amicable Parting, with Leueen MacGrath (produced Off Broadway Playhouse, Camden, New Jersey, 1957). 1957.

Screenplays

Roman Scandals, with others, 1933; *A Night at the Opera,* with Morrie Ryskind and James Kevin McGuinness, 1935 (published 1972); *Star Spangled Rhythm,* with others, 1942.

*

Criticism

Books:

Howard Teichman, *George Kaufman: An Intimate Portrait,* New York, 1972.

Scott Meredith, *George S. Kaufman and His Friends,* Garden City, New York, 1974; abridged version, as *George Kaufman and the Algonquin Round Table,* 1977.

Malcolm Goldstein, *George S. Kaufman: His Life, His Theater,* New York, 1979.

Rhoda G. Pollack, *George S. Kaufman,* Boston, 1988.

Jeffrey D. Mason, *Wisecreacks: The Farces of George S. Kaufman,* Ann Arbor, Michigan, 1988.

* * *

George Kaufman's simultaneous careers as comic playwright, director and *New York Times* drama editor would today distinguish three separate men or women. Such was the volume of theatre activity in his day that he was not seen as ubiquitous or omnipotent. At least six other playwrights equalled him in hitting the mark with a new play once a season. His skill as a director did not eclipse the talents of George Abbott, Harold Clurman, Herman Shumlin, or any of the Theatre Guild's directors. His position as critical spokesman could be regarded as decisive only if the paper he worked for had then had the power it was to acquire long after Kaufman ceased to practise as a playwright and journalist.

Nevertheless, Kaufman had one attribute that set him apart from the thoroughbred herd: he was, and remains, the master collaborator of American dramatists. He wrote only one original play (*The Butter and Egg Man*) entirely by himself; the other plays and musical libretti were written in collaboration with some dozen authors.

This statistic does not indicate a lack of originality on Kaufman's part. His partners were generally eager to work with him, and he always maintained that collaboration provided a short-cut in the dramaturgical process by offering an immediate audience reaction from the collaborator. Once the authors had tried lines and scenes on each other, so he believed, they had at least some indication of what would work in the theatre. Collaboration with so many others also enabled Kaufman to maintain comic freshness through attempting as many comic forms as were then in vogue. This also meant that he would move more easily with the fashion, directing his satiric punch at a variety of social issues.

With Marc Connelly, his first major collaborator, he concentrated on a series comic types in such plays as *Beggar on Horseback*, *Merton of the Movies*, *Dulcy*, *To the Ladies*, and *Be Yourself*. Written in the early 1920's, these introduced American audiences to indigenously rooted characters, like the pan-handler, the independently-minded housewife, and her counterpart, the henpecked husband. These plays replaced, as one critic said, "the teacups and colonels" of British imports or the "bedroom farces of the French" with immediately topical issues like business, federal taxes, and the general acquisitive streak that was sweeping through the nation's living rooms. If revivals of these plays are rare (and if it becomes difficult, in reading the scripts, to know where the jokes are intended), it may simply point up the fleeting appeal of humour. These plays are important, historically, for anticipating in the American personality an appetite for pointed observation of the contemporary scene.

Kaufman's collaboration with Edna Ferber brought forth another brand of comedy through the marriage of wit with pathos. There is, too, a focus on the theatre itself in *The Royal Family* (about the Barrymores) and in *Stage Door* (about a group of novice actresses eking out an existence in a rooming house while awaiting "the big break").

For the most part, Kaufman tended to collaborate with a particular author on a series of plays before moving on to the next collaborator, as though he was intensely engaged in one comic vein at a time. His partnership with Moss Hart, lasting ten years, has been as seen as the most durable, not only because this was the most critically and commercially successful, but also, perhaps, because with Hart he was able to extend his comic range furthest.

Once in a Lifetime, rewritten from a script Hart presented to Kaufman, satirises Hollywood at the time of the "talkies". (Kaufman himself appeared as the woebegone playwright, forever awaiting assignment by the studio in the studio anteroom.) Though a sensational hit when produced in 1930, the play requires a full exploitation of its harum-scarum crowd scenes in order to hold a present-day audience. *Merrily We Roll Along*, experimentally moving backward in time, is only partly successful in treating material better handled by Philip Barry—a caustic look at Ivy League graduates in the era leading up to the stock market crash.

With their third play, *You Can't Take It with You*, Kaufman and Hart succeeded in creating a style of their own by forging elements of high social satire with refreshing American wise-cracks. The action, pitting a family of happy-go-lucky non-conformists against a respectable couple, provided ample scope for poking fun at American manners, and even succeeded in advancing a formal critique of the business ethic. This theme was later to be mythologised in the work of

William Saroyan. Here it is brought memorably to life through the expert characterisation of a broad range of characters, none of which is allowed to dominate. *You Can't Take It with You* won the Pulitzer Prize for Drama in 1936, and remains the most often revived of any Kaufman play.

The Man Who Came to Dinner presented American drama with a classic Falstaffian portrait, modelled on the figure of the dramatic critic, Alexander Woollcott, and offering recognisably fictionalised cameos of Noël Coward, Harpo Marx and less specific theatrical types in a situation made for comedy: a famous celebrity, on a lecture tour in the Midwest, is forced through accident to convalesce at the home of a quaint and essentially staid American couple, reeking havoc with his outrageous demands and his continuous retinue of eccentric visitors. The theatrical world, explored with Ferber, is brought together with his usual social satire. The play gave Monty Woolley his first and only major role, which he was later to recreate less spectacularly in a series of film parts expressly written for him.

Kaufman's individual contribution to all these plays is most discernible, perhaps, in the element of cynicism that is common to most of them. Whenever a character deflates pomposity or points up absurdity with a well-timed and pithy one-liner, Kaufman's influence is immediately evident. He was to inject the same level of retort into early film scripts for the Marx brothers, in which Groucho is directed to address the camera to deliver whatever barbed observation on the action he wished to share with the audience. Kaufman's ability, in this way, to include his audience in the clever put-down no doubt added to his appeal as a popular satirist. He needed a strong situation, such as he found with Hart or, towards the end of his career, with Howard Teichmann in *The Solid Gold Cadillac*, before the jokes would really hit home. But with the right situation, the Kaufman touch sparked the whole evening.

Small wonder, then, that later wisecracking playwrights like Neil Simon and Herb Gardner fully acknowledged their debt to the mentor. The Kaufman character was, typically, an *idiot savant*, guileless in entering uncharted territory, but sharp enough to retreat from the mayhem eventually to strike a victorious blow for the common mortal. What these characters said was always beyond the wit of their real life counterparts, but they always spoke the words the audiences wished *they* had said. In this way, Kaufman remained a plebeian satirist, even when writing about the *beau monde*.

—James MacDonald

See also *Volume 1* entries on *Once in a Lifetime*; *You Can't Take It with You*.

KAWATAKE Mokuami. See *Volume 1* entry on *Samurai Nao*.

KAZANTZAKIS, Nikos. Born in Heraklion, Crete, 18 February 1883. Educated at French School of Holy Cross, Naxos, 1897–99; Gymnasium, Heraklion, 1899–1902; University of Athens, 1902–06, degree in law; studied in

Nikos Kazantzakis

Paris, Germany, and Italy, 1906–10. Married 1) first wife in 1911 (divorced); 2) Eleni Samios in 1945. Volunteer in the Greek army during the Balkan Wars, 1912–13, but saw no fighting; subsequently pursued career as a writer and traveller; Director General of Ministry of Public Welfare, 1919–20; Cabinet Minister Without Portfolio, 1945, served in Unesco's Department of Translations of the Classics, 1947–48. Recipient: Lenin Peace Prize. Died in Freiburg, West Germany, 26 October 1957.

Works

Collections

Theatro: Tragodies (3 vols.; includes *Promitheas; Kouros; Odhisseas; Melissa; Ioulianos; Nicoferos Fokas; Konstantinos Paleologhos; Kapodistrias; Christoferos Colomvos; Sodoma ke Ghomora; Vudhas*). 1955–56.
Three Plays (includes *Melissa; Kouros; Christopher Columbus*), translated by Athena Gianakas Dallas. 1969.
Two Plays (includes *Sodom and Gomorrah; Comedy*), translated by Kimon Friar. 1982.

Stage Works

Ximeroni [Day is Breaking] (produced Athens, 1907). In *Nea Estia*, 1977.
O Protomastoras [The Master Builder] (produced as operatic

version, music by Manolis Kalomiris, Athens, 1916). In *Panathinea*, 1910.
Nikoforos Fokas [Nicephoros Phokas] (produced by the Regional Theatre of Crete, 1984). 1927.
Christos [Christ]. 1928.
Odhisseas [Odysseus]. 1928.
Melissa (produced in French, Paris, 1960; produced in Greek, National Theatre, Athens, 1962). In *Nea Estia*, 1939; in book form (author's own French translation), with *Thésée*, 1953; translated as *Melissa*, in *Three Plays*, 1969.
Ioulianos o Paravatis [Julian the Apostate] (produced in French, Paris, 1945; produced in Greek, National Theatre, Athens, 1959). 1945.
Kapodhistrias [Capodistria] (produced National Theatre, Athens, 1946). 1946.
Sodhoma ke Ghomora (produced National Theatre, Athens, 1983). In *Nea Estia*, 1949; translated as *Sodom and Gomorrah*, with *Comedy*, 1982.
Konstantinos Paleologhos [Constantine Paleologos] (produced in operatic version, music by Manolis Kalomiris, Athens, 1962; as play, by the American College, Athens, 1965). In *Nea Estia*, 1953.
Kouros, from the radio play (produced by the Spencer Stage Company, New York, 1971; produced in Greek, by the Theatre Company of Crete, 1977). In author's own French translation, as *Thésée*, with *Melissa*, 1953; in Greek, 1955; translated as *Kouros*, in *Three Plays*, 1969.
Promitheas [Prometheus]. In *Theatro*, 1955–56.
Vudhas (produced National Theatre, Athens, 1978). In *Theatro*, 1956; translated as *The Buddha*, 1983.
Christoforos Colomvos (produced by the Greek Popular Theatre, Piraeus, 1975). In *Theatro*, 1955–56; translated as *Christopher Colombus*, in *Three Plays*, 1969.
Comodhia. In *Nea Estia*, 1958; translated as *Comedy*, with *Sodom and Gomorrah*, 1982.
O Othelos Xanayirizi [Othello Returns]. In *Nea Estia*, 1962.
Eos Pote [Until When]. In *Nea Estia*, 1977.
Fasgha [Fasgha]. In *Nea Estia*, 1977.

Radio Plays

Kouros, 1950 (Swedish radio).

Fiction

Ophis ke Krino. 1906; translated as *Serpent and Lily*, 1980.
Toda Raba (written in French). 1934; translated as *Toda Raba*, 1964.
Vios ke Politia tou Alexi Zorba. 1946; translated as *Zorba the Greek*, 1952.
O Kapetan Michalis. 1953; translated as *Freedom or Death*, 1955; as *Freedom and Death*, 1956.
O Christos Xanastavronete. 1954; translated as *The Greek Passion*, 1954; as *Christ Recrucified*, 1954.
O Telefteos Pirasmos. 1955; translated as *The Last Temptation of Christ*, 1960.
O Ftochoulis tou Theou. 1956; translated as *Saint Francis*, 1962; as *God's Pauper*, 1962.
Le Jardin des rochers (written in French). 1959; translated as *The Rock Garden*, 1963.
Aderfofades. 1963; translated as *The Fratricides*, 1964.
Megas Alexandros (for children). 1979; translated as *Alexander the Great*, 1982.
Sta Palatia tes Knossou. 1981; translated and abridged as *At the Palace of Knossos*, 1987.

Verse

Odhissia. 1938; translated as *The Odyssey: A Modern Sequel*, 1958.
Tertsines. 1960.
Symposium. 1971; translated as *Symposium*, 1973.

Memoirs and Letters

Epistoles pros te Galatia. 1958; translated as *The Suffering God: Selected Letters to Galatia and to Papastefanou*, 1979.
Tetrakosia grammata tou Kazantzakis sto Prevelaki (letters). 1965.

Other

O Friderikos Nitse [Friedrich Nietzsche]. 1909.
Salvatores Dei: Askitiki. 1927; revised edition, 1945; as *The Saviors of God: Spiritual Exercises*, 1960.
Taxidevontas (travel). 1927.
Te eida set Rousia (2 vols.). 1928; as *Taxidevontas: Rousia*, 1956; translated as *Russia: A Chronicle of Three Journeys in the Aftermath of the Revolution*, 1989.
Historia tes Rosikes logotechnias (2 vols.). 1930.
Taxidevontas: Ispania. 1937; translated as *Spain*, 1963.
O Morias. 1937; translated as *Journey to the Morea*, 1965; as *Travels in Greece*, 1966.
Taxidevontas II: Iaponia, Kina. 1938; translated as *Japan-China*, 1963; as *Travels in China and Japan*, 1964.
Taxidevontas III: Anglia. 1941; translated as *England*, 1965.
Anafora ston Greco. 1961; translated as *Report to Greco*, 1965.
Journeying: Travels in Italy, Egypt, Sinai, Jerusalem, and Cyprus. 1975.

Translator, *The Divine Comedy* by Dante, *Faust* by Goethe, *Iliad* by Homer, several Platonic dialogues, *The Birth of Tragedy* and *Thus Spake Zarathustra* by Nietzsche, *The Prince* by Machiavelli, *Conversations with Goethe* by Eckermann, *Origin of Species* by Darwin, *On Laughter* by Bergson, and other works, including many books for children.

*

Bibliographies

G.K. Katsimbales, *Kazantzakis bibliografi*, Athens, 1958; supplement, by Peter Bien, in *Mandatoforos*, 5, 1974.
Sandra A. Parker, "Kazantzakis in America; A Bibliography of Translations and Comment", in *Bulletin of Bibliography*, 25, 1968.

Criticism

Books:
Pandelis Prevelakis, *Nikos Kazantzakis and His Odyssey*, 1961.
Helen Kazantkazis, *Kazantzakis: A Biography Based on His Letters*, New York, 1968.
Colette Janiaud-Lust, *Nikos Kazantzakis: Sa Vie, son oeuvre (1883–1957)*, Paris, 1970.
Helen Kazantkazis, *Nikos Kazantkazis*, New York, 1970.
Peter Bien, *Kazantkazis and the Linguistic Revolution in Greek Literature*, Princeton, New Jersey, 1972.

James F. Lea, *Kazantzakis: The Politics of Salvation*, Tuscaloosa, Alabama, 1979.
Morton P. Levitt, *The Cretan Glance: The World and Art of Kazantzakis*, Columbus, Ohio, 1980.
Peter Bien, *Politics of the Spirit*, Princeton, New Jersey, 1990.

Articles:
Peter Bien, "*Buddha*, Kazantzakis' Most Ambitious and Most Neglected Play", in *Comparative Drama*, 11, 1977.
Katerin Angelaki-Rooke, "Kazantzakis's *Buddha*: Phantasmogoria and Struggle", in *Journal of the Hellenic Diaspora*, vol.10 no.4, 1983.
John P. Anton, "Kazantzakis and the Tradition of the Tragic", in *Journal of the Hellenic Diaspora*, vol.10 no.4, 1983.
Aliki Bacopoulou-Halls, *Modern Greek Theatre: Roots and Blossoms*, Athens, 1982.
Peter Bien, "*Christopher Columbus*: Kazantzakis's Final Play", in *Journal of the Hellenic Diaspora*, vol.10 no.4, 1983.
Stratos E. Constantinidis, "The Rebirth of Tragedy: Protest and Evolution in Modern Greek Drama", in *Comparative Drama*, 21, 1987.

*   *   *

Nikos Kazantazakis is one of the most prolific writers of modern Greece and its most Aeschylean of dramatists. A restless man and compulsive traveller, he was married twice but had no children and was known for his ascetic temperament. Faithful to a romantic nationalism which he shared with many other younger writers and artists of his time, he enlisted as a volunteer in the Greek army during the Balkan War of 1912–13 but never saw action in battle.

A similar pattern marked his subsequent life: he tried, more than once (especially in the 1920's when he became a socialist, and in the 1940's) to be a man of social action, as was Tolstoy, only to turn back, disappointed, to his books and thoughtful peregrinations around Europe, the Middle East, and, in his old age, China.

Kazantzakis earned his living and travel expenses by writing school books, translating, and serving as a correspondent for magazines and newspapers. But everything he wrote, whether commissioned by others or not, bears his personal stamp. *Askitiki* (Spiritual Exercises), his philosophical manifesto, reflects the influences of Nietzsche and Bergson, as does the *Odhissia* (*Odyssey*), a long epic of 33,333 17-syllable lines, meant to be a sequel to Homer's *Odyssey*. Although his fame rests mainly on his novels, Kazantzakis was also a playwright.

The major key, in which Kazantzakis wrote his other works, is also evident in his plays, very few of which were staged while he was alive. In fact, disappointed with the world of the theatre early in his career, Kazantzakis turned his back on that world, and every time he wrote or published a new play he claimed he meant it to be read rather than staged: an unnecessary defense, as posthumous productions of his dramas under able directors have brought into relief their inherent dramatic qualities.

The typical protagonist in Kazantzakis's plays is a man with split loyalties and a keen sense of mission, but with no illusions. He is a nihilist who, in most cases, acts with fervour for the sake of action, but who is also courted by a Buddhist kind of resignation (it is significant that Kazantzakis had been writing, off and on, his play *The Buddha*, for 35 years and that he finished it just before he died, which makes it his swan song). Kazantzakis's existential angst, already evident in his early plays, foreshadows (as Karl Kerenyi has noticed) Sartre's and Beckett's "theatre of the absurd". On the other hand, the non-conformism of his characters and their triangular relationships point to Ibsen and the German dramatists of the 19th century. Old-fashioned, too, and Shakespearean, was his habit of writing about figures well known from myth and history. His best play is generally thought to be *Melissa*, in which he dramatized the tragic story of Periander of ancient Corinth, his wife Melissa (whom Periander has murdered), and their two sons.

André Malraux noted that while the French classical theatre is an ordering (*mise en scène*) of the world, Shakespeare and Dostoevsky (in his novels) raise great existential questions. The dramas of Kazantzakis, together with everything else he wrote, belong in this latter category of literary works.

—George Thaniel

————

KEANE, John B(rendan). Born in Listowel, County Kerry, Ireland, 21 July 1928. Educated at Saint Michael's College, Listowel, graduated 1947. Married Mary O'Connor in 1955; three sons and one daughter. Chemist's assistant, 1946–51; street sweeper and furnace operator, Northampton, England, 1952–54; since 1955, pub owner-operator, Listowel; first-produced play, *Sive*, staged 1959, subsequently closely associated with the Southern Theatre Group, Cork, and companies in Dublin. Weekly columnist, Limerick *Leader* and Dublin *Evening Herald*. Since 1973 President, Irish PEN. D.Litt: Trinity College, Dublin, 1977; DFA: Marymount Manhattan College, New York, 1984.

Works

Collections

Values: The Spraying of John O'Dovey; Blackwater; The Pure of Heart.   1973.
Three Plays (includes *Sive; The Field; Big Maggie*).   1990.

Stage Works

Sive (produced Walsh's Ballroom, Listowel, County Kerry, 1959).   1959.
Sharon's Grave (produced Father Mathew Hall, Cork, 1960).   1960.
The Highest House on the Mountain (produced Dublin Theatre Festival, 1961).
Many Young Men of Twenty (produced Father Mathew Hall, Cork, 1961).   1961.
No More in Dust (produced Dublin Theatre Festival, 1962).
Hut 42 (produced Queen's Theatre, Dublin, 1963).   1963.
The Man from Clare (produced Cork, 1963).   1963.
The Year of the Hiker (produced Father Mathew Hall, Cork, 1964).   1964.
The Field (produced Olympia Theatre, Dublin, 1965).   1967.
The Roses of Tralee (produced Opera House, Cork, 1966).
The Rain at the End of the Summer (produced Cork, 1967).   1967.

Faoiseamh (produced Damer Hall, Dublin, 1970).   Nd.
The Change in Mame Fadden (produced Opera House, Cork, 1971).   1973.
Moll (produced Abbey Theatre, Killarney, County Kerry, 1971).   1971.
The One-Way Ticket (produced Plaza Theatre, Listowel, County Kerry, 1972).   1972.
Values: The Spraying of John O'Dovey; Backwater; The Pure of Heart (produced by the Group Theatre, Cork, 1973). 1973.
The Crazy Wall (produced Theatre Royal, Waterford, 1973). 1974.
Matchmaker (produced Dublin, 1975).
The Good Thing (produced City Theatre, Limerick, 1976). 1976.
The Buds of Ballybunion (produced Opera House, Cork, 1979).   1979.
The Chastitute (produced Opera House, Cork, 1980).   1981.

Screenplays

The Field, 1991.

Radio Plays

Barbara Shearing, 1959; *A Clutch of Duckeggs*, 1970; *The War Crime*, 1976 (UK); *The Talk Specific*, 1979; *The Battle of Ballybooley*, 1980.

Fiction

"Death Be Not Proud" and Other Stories.   1976.
More Irish Short Stories.   1981.
The Bodhrán Makers.   1986.
"Love Bites" and Other Stories.   1991.

Verse

"The Street" and Other Poems.   1961.

Other

Strong Tea.   1963.
Self-Portrait.   1964.
Letters of a Successful T.D. [an Irish Parish Priest, an Irish Publican, a Love-Hungry Farmer, a Matchmaker, an Irish Civic Guard, a Country Postman, an Irish Minister of State] (8 vols.).   1967–78.
The Gentle Art of Matchmaking.   1973.
Is the Holy Ghost Really a Kerryman?   1976.
Unlawful Sex and Other Testy Matters.   1978.
Stories from a Kerry Fireside.   1980.
Unusual Irish Careers.   1982.
Man of the Triple Name.   1984.
Owl Sandwiches.   1985.
The Power of Words.   1989.

*

Bibliographies

Kimball King, *Ten Modern Irish Playwrights*, New York, 1979.

Criticism

Books:
Robert Hogan (ed.), *Seven Irish Playwrights 1946–1964*, Minneapolis, 1967.

Robert Hogan, *After the Irish Renaissance*, Minnesota, 1967, London 1968.
Jean M. Pannecoucke, "John Brendan Keane and the New Irish Rural Drama", in *Aspects of the Irish Theatre*, edited by Patrick Rafroidi and others, Lille, 1972.
John M. Feehan (ed.), *Fifty Year Young: A Tribute to John B. Keane*, Cork, 1979.
Michael Etherton, *Contemporary Irish Dramatists*, London, 1989 (Macmillan Modern Dramatists series).

Articles:
Marie H. Kealy, "Spirit of Place: A Context for Social Criticism in John B. Keane's *The Field* and *Big Maggie*", in *Irish University Review*, 19, 1989.
Marie H. Kealy, "The Wall and the Wanderer: Unresolved Domestic Conflict in the Plays of John B. Keane", in *Notes on Modern Irish Literature*, 2, 1990.

*   *   *

Some of the Irish dramatists of the 1950's were closely associated with the amateur movement that was a social and artistic phenomenon in the post-war years in rural Ireland. M.J. Molloy, Bryan MacMahon, and, in an earlier generation, George Shiels were the mainstays of regional theatre. The most popular playwright to emerge from the amateur scene was, however, John B. Keane.

In the annals of amateur drama, 1959 will be remembered as the year in which the Listowel Drama Group's production of *Sive* not only won the national award at the All-Ireland Festival at Athlone, but set a local playwright, John B. Keane, on the high road to success. After the phenomenal success of *Sive*, the Kerry playwright was virtually a playwright-in-residence for the Cork based Southern Theatre Group, and later for Phyllis Ryan's Orion and Gemini companies in Dublin.

Although he wrote mainly in the Abbey theatre tradition, that theatre showed little interest in his work until after the phenomenal success of *Sive*, when the Listowel Drama Group staged a production of the play under the aegis of the Abbey. During the 1980's, *Sive* and other Keane plays were among the most successful in the Abbey repertoire.

In *Sive*, a young orphaned girl named Sive is forced into marriage with a sex-starved doting old man. It is a theme that had been treated in other plays, such as Louis D'Alton's *Lovers Meeting*, but the Keane play succeeds by the introduction of two tinkers or travelling men who, with their satirical songs and music, act as chorus to the action. These characters generate a theatrical excitement of a high order. Keane's racy and authentic dialogue, with a modicum of social satire, also compensates for some contrivance in the plot situations.

Sharon's Grave, staged in 1960 by the Southern Theatre Group, is notable for a startling *coup de théâtre* in which a deformed and evil-minded cripple is carried on the back of his brawny, but simple-minded, brother who is whipped like a beast of burden. It is a folk-play with echoes of George Fitzmaurice's mastery of that genre.

Keane's best play, *The Field*, staged at the Olympia Theatre, Dublin in 1965, with Ray McNally in the leading role of the Bull McCabe, treats the old subject of land hunger in a way that drives men to murder and to the intimidation of a rural community who will not inform to bring violent men to justice. The same theme was handled by George Shiels in *The Rugged Path*, but Keane's treatment is the more effective theatrically.

The Man from Clare deals deftly and, at times, humorously with another rural obsession, sport, in this case Gaelic football. *The Year of the Hiker* is a sensitive handling of a marital situation which drives a man to tramp the roads until imminent death brings reconciliation. *Hut 42*, the only Keane play to have its premiere with the Abbey company, portrays the plight of the Irish navvy in England. It is complementary to his more popular and entertaining ballad-play *Many Young Men of Twenty*, concerning the subject of emigration.

If there is another character in the Keane repertoire who matches his Bull McCabe in *The Field*, it is the eponymous Big Maggie, the bitch-mother of the play of the same name, who rules her orphaned brood with a rod of iron. This Amazon of matriarchy dominates the action to the exclusion of all others.

This prolific writer did not achieve his full potential when he tackled sexual and social subjects, in plays like *The Good Thing* and *The Chastitute*. But even in unpretentious farce he shows a consummate power to relate to an Irish audience and to chronicle the changing mores of provincial life. In 1986 he published a very successful novel, *The Bodhran Makers*, and continues to write humorous pieces, on his favourite subjects, at times in epistolary form.

—Micheal Ó hAodha

KENNEDY, Adrienne (Lita) Born Adrienne Hawkins in Pittsburgh, Pennsylvania, USA, 13 September 1931; grew up in Cleveland, Ohio. Educated in Cleveland public schools; Ohio State University, Columbus, BA in education 1953; Columbia University, New York, 1954–56. Married Joseph C. Kennedy in 1953 (divorced 1966); two sons. Joined Edward Albee's workshop in 1962; first-produced play, *Funnyhouse of a Negro*, staged 1962; lecturer in playwriting, Yale University, New Haven, Connecticut, 1972–74, Princeton University, New Jersey, 1977, and Brown University, Providence, Rhode Island, 1979–80; Chancellor's Distinguished Lecturer, University of California, Berkeley, 1986. Member of the Board of Directors, PEN, 1976–77. Recipient: Obie Award, 1965, and several grants from US cultural foundations.

Works

Collections

Cities in Bezique: 2 One-Act Plays: The Owl Answers and A Beast's Story. 1969.
Adrienne Kennedy in One Act (includes *Funnyhouse of a Negro; The Owl Answers; A Lesson in Dead Language; A Rat's Mass; Sun; A Movie Star Has to Star in Black and White; Electra, Orestes*). 1988.

Stage Works

Funnyhouse of a Negro (produced Circle in the Square Theatre, New York, 1962). 1969.
The Owl Answers (produced White Barn Theatre, Westport, Connecticut, 1963). In *Cities in Bezique*, 1969.
A Beast's Story (produced New York, 1965). In *Cities in Bezique*, 1969.
A Rat's Mass (produced Boston Theatre Company, 1966).

In *New Black Playwrights*, edited by William Couch Jr., 1968.
The Lennon Play: In His Own Write, with John Lennon and Victor Spinetti, from works by John Lennon (produced by the National Theatre, London, 1967; revised version produced London, 1968). 1968.
A Lesson in Dead Language (produced Royal Court Theatre, London, 1968). In *Collision Course*, 1968.
Boats (produced Mark Taper Forum, Los Angeles, 1969).
Sun: A Poem for Malcolm X Inspired by His Murder (produced Royal Court Theatre, London, 1969). In *Scripts 1* (New York), November 1971.
An Evening with Dead Essex (produced American Place Theatre Workshop, New York, 1973).
A Movie Star Has to Star in Black and White (produced Public Theatre Workshop, New York, 1976). In *Wordplays 3*, 1984.
Orestes and Electra (produced Juilliard School of Music, New York, 1980). In *Adrienne Kennedy in One Act*, 1988.
Black Children's Day (produced Brown University, Providence, Rhode Island, 1980).
A Lancashire Lad (for children; produced Empire State Plaza Performing Arts Center, Albany, New York, 1980).
Solo Voyages (includes excerpts from her previous plays; produced Interart Center, New York, 1985).
She Talks. In *Antaeus*, 66, 1991.
Beethoven. In *Anteus*, 66, 1991.

Memoirs and Letters

People Who Led to My Plays (Memoirs). 1987.

Other

Deadly Triplets: A Theatre Mystery and Journal. 1990.

Criticism

Articles:
Herbert Blau, "The American Dream in American Gothic: The Plays of Sam Shepard and Adrienne Kennedy", in *Modern Drama*, 27, 1984.
Adrienne Kennedy and Wolfgang Binder, "A MELUS Interview: Adrienne Kennedy", in *MELUS*, vol.12 no.3, 1985.
Margaret B. Wilkerson, "Diverse Angles of Vision: Two Black Women Playwrights", in *Theatre Annual*, 40, 1985.
Adrienne Kennedy and Elin Diamond, "An Interview with Adrienne Kennedy", in *Studies in American Drama 1945–Present*, 4, 1989.

*   *   *

As black power gathered strength in America in the 1960's, the dramatist Adrienne Kennedy, who is black, was discovering more uses for the word negro. She marks the beginnings of celebratory blackness with *Funnyhouse of a Negro* in which a woman's personal history of miscegenation, rape, and madness inscribes the larger history of black experience in white America, a history that Americans now sanitize and democratize under the rubric "race relations". Kennedy makes no totalizing claims to represent anyone, but the play's motifs resonate sharply in collective history.

In her New York apartment, Kennedy's "Negro-Sarah" enshrines an enormous statue of Queen Victoria and, in the course of the play, splits into a hunchbacked Jesus, the

Duchess of Hapsburg, the African liberation leader Patrice Lumumba, and even Queen Victoria—each denoted as "One of Herselves." This is history and identity in a funnyhouse of distorted mirrors whose reflections are as unthinkable in racist America emerging from the 1950's as Sarah herself, child of a light-skinned black woman supposedly raped by her missionary black husband in Africa. Slowly Sarah's incarnations emerge from darkness to narrate bits of the original trauma—the missionary zeal of the father who "wanted the black man to rise from colonialism", the mother who "didn't want him to save the black race and spent her days combing her hair . . . and would not let him touch her in their wedding bed and called him black", the daughter conceived in violence, who rejects the father but resembles him and watches her mother lapse into madness, then death, the remembered sign for which is hair falling out.

Throughout the play, shining hairless skulls appear in dialogue and enacted fantasy until Sarah tries to stifle her father's (and her race's) claim on her by bludgeoning him with an ebony mask. Yet he returns: "He keeps returning forever, coming back ever and keeps coming back forever". Sarah's white friends whose (Victorian) culture "keep [her] from reflecting too much upon the fact that [she is] a Negro" cannot protect her from this returning and recurring repressed racial memory, signified by the repeated sound of knocking and the obsessively repeated images of fallen hair, kinky and straight, on a white pillow; of yellowness, the sickly white color of Sarah's skin; of swarming ravens and of death's-heads. The expressionistic funnyhouse of Sarah's memory defies linear logic. Her father hangs himself—or does not—in two versions of the story, but the last play image shows Sarah herself hanged, reclaimed by the jungle that engulfs the stage. Sarah's split subjectivity bears the scars of Afro-American history; her identification with her mother and murderous repression of her father's culture engage the discourses of feminism and psychoanalysis, and reveal the desire and exclusion embodied in Kennedy's "Negro".

The Owl Answers brilliantly extends these issues through the laminated identities of Kennedy's protagonist, She who is Clara Passmore who is the Virgin Mary who is the Bastard who is the Owl, whose history generates another violently skewed family romance, this time with a poor black mother and the "Richest White Man in the Town". Gradually a story emerges of a bastard daughter of miscegenous union, adopted by the Reverend Passmore, renamed Clara, but who carries her black mother's color and a passion for her white father's culture, "the England of dear Chaucer, Dickens and dearest Shakespeare", whose works she reads as a child in the Passmore library, and later disseminates as a "plain, pallid" schoolteacher in Savannah, Georgia. The glorious fathers of literary history merge with those of Christian myth as God's white dove (associated with Reverend Passmore's preaching) replaces the jungle father's black ravens in *Funnyhouse*. The adopted Clara identifies with the Virgin Mary, but in a fantasy visit to England the white fathers who have colonized her desire refuse Clara access to St. Paul's where she imagines burying her own white father, and lock her in the Tower of London. Rejected by her father, but unable to bury or repress him, Clara is imprisoned in her own history. In the play's associative logic the Tower is also a New York subway car in which the adult Clara, lost in guilt and rage, picks up a Negro man, introduces herself as Mary, addresses him as God, and tries to stab him.

The surrealistic Tower (dominant white culture) and the High Altar (sacrificial Christianity) are the phallic edifices against which Clara Passmore measures her being. Ultimately she transforms into the screeching Owl, symbol of her black

mother and her criminal origins: "The Owl was [my] beginning". Although her adopted status allows her to "pass more", Clara belongs to the owls as she cannot belong to the world of "Buckingham Palace, . . . the Thames at dusk, and Big Ben" or the "Holy Baptist Church . . . on the top of the Holy Hill". Near the end of the Play, Clara kneels to pray: "I call God and the Owl answers".

This summary conveys nothing of Kennedy's surrealistic spectacle: "There is the noise of the train, the sound of moving steel on the track". "The WHITE BIRD's wings should flutter loudly"—a cacophony that should evoke, says Kennedy, "a sense of exploding imprisonment".

Two shorter works, *A Lesson in Dead Language* and *A Rat's Mass*, add new elements of Kennedy's bestiary. In the first, Western culture in the form of a Latin lesson and a schoolteacher, costumed from waist up as a White Dog, and Christian doctrine in the form of enormous statues of Jesus, Joseph, Mary, two Wise Men, and a shepherd, instruct and overwhelm seven little girls, whose initiation into menstruation marks them (and their white dresses) as guilty. In *A Rat's Mass*, redemptive authority resides in a schoolmate, Rosemary, who refuses to expiate the incestuous crime of Brother and Sister Rat; and the sister goes mad. In this, as in all of Kennedy's beautifully crafted plays, cultural exclusion translates into sexual terror and guilt, the signs of "Negro" womanhood.

Funnyhouse of a Negro won an Obie Award, but Kennedy's work is still rarely discussed or performed in the United States.

—Elin Diamond

See also *Volume 1* entry on *Funnyhouse of a Negro*.

KILROY, Thomas. Born in Callan, County Kilkenny, Ireland, 23 September 1934. Educated at Christian Brothers School, Callan; St. Kieran's College, Kilkenny; University College, Dublin, 1953–59, BA 1956, Higher Diploma in Education 1957, MA in English 1959. Married 1) Patricia Cobey in 1963 (divorced 1980), three sons; 2) Julia Lowell Carlson in 1981. Headmaster, Stratford College, Dublin, 1959–64; Visiting Lecturer in English, University of Notre Dame, Indiana, 1962–63; Visiting Professor of English, Vanderbilt University, Nashville, 1964–65; Assistant Lecturer, Department of Modern English and American Literature, University College, Dublin, 1965–73; first play, *The Death and Resurrection of Mr. Roche*, produced 1968; lecturer, School of Irish Studies, Dublin, 1972–73; visiting professor, Sir George Williams University and McGill University, both Montreal, 1973, University College, Galway, 1975–76 and 1979, Dartmouth College, Hanover, New Hampshire, 1976, University College, Dublin, 1977–78, and Bamberg University, West Germany, 1984; Examiner in Modern English, Trinity College, Dublin, and Thomond College, Limerick, 1983. Has also directed plays with the Irish Field Day Theatre Company. Recipient: Royal Society of Literature Heinemann Award, for fiction, 1972; Irish Academy Prize, 1972. Fellow, Royal Society of Literature, 1972; Member, 1973, and Member of the Council, 1979, Irish Academy of Letters; Member, Aosdana, 1986.

Works

Stage Works

The Death and Resurrection of Mr. Roche (produced Olympia Theatre, Dublin, 1968).
The O'Neill (produced Peacock Theatre, Dublin, 1969).
Tea and Sex and Shakespeare (produced Abbey Theatre, Dublin, 1976).
Talbot's Box (produced Abbey Theatre, Dublin, 1977). 1979.
The Seagull, from a play by Chekhov (produced Royal Court Theatre, London, 1981). 1981
Double Cross (produced by Field Day Theatre Company, Londonderry, 1986). 1986.
Ghosts, from a play by Ibsen (produced Peacock Theatre, Dublin, 1988).
The Madame MacAdam Travelling Theatre (produced Londonderry, 1991). 1991.

Television Plays

Farmers, 1978; *The Black Joker*, 1981.

Radio Plays

The Door, 1967; *That Man, Bracken*, 1986.

Fiction

The Big Chapel. 1971.

Other

Editor, *Sean O'Casey: A Collection of Critical Essays*. 1975.

*

Bibliographies

Kimball King, *Ten Modern Irish Playwrights*, New York, 1979.

Criticism

Books:
D.E.S. Maxwell, *A Critical History of Modern Irish Drama 1891–1980*, Cambridge, 1984.
Anthony Roche, "The Fortunate Fall: Two Plays by Thomas Kilroy" in *The Writer and the City*, Gerard's Cross, Buckinghamshire, 1984.
Frank McGuinness, "The Haunted House: The Theatre of Thomas Kilroy" in *Irish Theatre Today*, Würzburg, 1985.
Nina Witiszek, *The Theatre of Recollection: A Cultural Study of the Modern Dramatic Tradition in Ireland and Poland*, Stockholm, 1988.
Michael Etherton, *Contemporary Irish Dramatists*, London, 1989 (Macmillan Modern Dramatists series).

Articles:
Gerald Dawe, "Thomas Kilroy", in *Theatre Ireland*, 3, 1982.

* * *

Thomas Kilroy's reputation in the contemporary Irish theatre rests primarily on three works, separated from one another by almost a decade: *The Death and Resurrection of Mr. Roche, Talbot's Box*, and his recent play, *Double Cross*. His early historical drama, *The O'Neill* (which deals with material also covered in Brian Friel's *Making History*) is now largely forgotten, and his *Tea and Sex and Shakespeare*, in spite of a 1988 production by Dublin's Rough Magic Theatre Company, is not solidly enough constructed to bear the weight of the philosophical ideas which it attempts to carry.

The Death and Resurrection of Mr. Roche, a naturalistic play set in the Dublin flat of Kelly, a civil servant, was written in a period when the economic expansion of the 1960's was radically altering Irish society. Kelly and his male drinking companions are members of a new, rootless middle class who have emigrated to Dublin from rural Ireland, and the play explores the fragility of their communal sense of identity by contrasting them with the eponymous Mr. Roche. As a homosexual, the enigmatic Mr. Roche is an outsider in the group, and as such his sense of identity derives from an unassailable inner source, which Kilroy imbues with religious overtones in the character's "death" and final triumphant reappearance at the play's conclusion.

The religious connotations of Mr. Roche's "resurrection" are developed in Kilroy's second major play, *Talbot's Box*, which deals with Matt Talbot (1856–1925), a Dublin dock worker who followed a severe daily routine of prayer, fasting and penitence. Since his death there has been a movement for his canonisation, particularly in working-class areas of Dublin. The play, described in its opening lines as "a sorta trial . . . an entertainment . . . a kind of temptation of the saint . . . a sorta quiz-show", takes place in a box which creates the same sense of entrapment as the small flat which forms the sole set of *The Death and Resurrection of Mr. Roche*. Like Mr. Roche, Talbot is taunted, interrogated, tempted, and beaten by the other characters, but retains throughout a private core of belief which is strengthened by continual challenge. "I am fascinated and often appalled", Kilroy wrote of *Talbot's Box*, "by what happens when the intense, concentrated hopes, fears, beliefs of the private person are subjected to the fragmenting, diffusionary effects of public life". Moreover, like the "hopes, fears", and "beliefs" of Mr. Roche, Talbot's faith is ultimately elusive, remaining private, even in the public space of the theatre. When asked by a priest what he sees in his prayer-induced visions, his answer is a brusque "nuthin'".

Kilroy uses the actor/character relationship in *Talbot's Box* to give the opposition between private belief and public pressure a visible, theatrical form. Whereas Matt Talbot is played by the same actor throughout the play, the other four actors assume a variety of roles, in which they repeatedly refer to their own status as actors on a stage, thereby suggesting their mutability, in contrast to Talbot's essential integrity.

Double Cross develops the possible uses of the relationship between actor and character as a means of exploring what Kilroy refers to as "doubleness or doubling, that is, the way things repeat themselves in life or attract their opposites". *Double Cross* reflects this doubleness in its two-act structure: the first act deals with Brendan Bracken, Churchill's Minister of Information during World War II; the second act deals with William Joyce, who broadcast Nazi radio propaganda into England. The stage directions specify that both roles should be played by the same actor (Stephen Rea in the original production), whose transformation from Bracken to Joyce takes place on stage in full view of the audience. The only interaction between the two characters is indirect, as Joyce's voice penetrates Bracken's world through his broadcasts, and as each character appears to the other on a giant video screen suspended above the stage. Nonetheless, the two characters are intimately linked, for both men were originally Irish. Hence, even though the play takes place in London and Berlin, it is essentially concerned with English-Irish relations, and in particular the way in which profound social pressures (such as those of colonialism) are capable of transforming an individual personality into its specular opposite. "This play", writes Kilroy, "attempts to deal with one kind of mobility, one kind of action across the barriers, the restrictive codes which separate countries from one another. It is the kind of action which is usually called treason".

Double Cross was given its premiere by Ireland's Field Day Theatre Company (which Kilroy has called "the most important movement of its kind in Ireland since the beginning of this century"), thereby indicating the respect which Kilroy is accorded in the Irish cultural debate—a respect which has been increased by his astute critical writings and his highly regarded novel *The Big Chapel*. However, with only three plays of any stature to his credit in a career spanning as many decades, his reputation does not measure up to that of his contemporaries Brian Friel and Thomas Murphy, and it is widely felt that Kilroy has yet to realise his full potential.

—Chris Morash

See also *Volume 1* entry on *The Death and Resurrection of Mr Roche*.

KINGSLEY, Sidney. Born Sidney Kirshner in New York City, 22 October 1906. Educated at Townsend Harris Hall, New York, 1920–24; Cornell University, Ithaca, New York (state scholarship), 1924–28, BA 1928. Married the actress Madge Evans in 1939 (died 1981). Actor in the Tremont Stock Company, Bronx, New York, 1928–29; thereafter play-reader and scenario writer for Columbia Pictures; first-produced play, *Men in White*, staged 1933, by the Group Theatre; full-time writer and stage director from 1934 (directed productions of his own plays, except *The Patriots*) served in the US Army, 1941–43: Lieutenant. President, Dramatists Guild, 1961–69; member, New Jersey Motion Picture and TV Authority, and chairman, 1976–80. Recipient: Pulitzer Prize, 1934; New York Theatre Club medal, 1934, 1936, 1943; New York Drama Critics Circle Award, 1943, 1951; Donaldson Award, 1951; American Academy Award of Merit Medal, 1951, Gold Medal, 1986. D.Litt: Monmouth College, West Long Branch, New Jersey, 1978; Ramapo College, Mahwah, New Jersey, 1978.

Works

Stage Works

Men in White (produced Broadhurst Theatre, New York, 1933). 1933.
Dead End (produced Belasco Theatre, New York, 1935). 1936.
Ten Million Ghosts (produced St. James's Theatre, New York, 1936).

The World We Make, from a novel by Millen Brand (produced Guild Theatre, New York, 1939). 1939.
The Patriots (produced National Theatre, New York, 1943). 1943.
Detective Story (produced Hudson Theatre, New York, 1949). 1949.
Darkness at Noon, from the novel by Arthur Koestler (produced Alvin Theatre, New York, 1951). 1951.
Lunatics and Lovers (produced Broadhurst Theatre, New York, 1954). Condensed version in *Theater 1955*, 1955.
Night Life (produced Brooks Atkinson Theatre, New York, 1962). 1966.

Screenplays

Homecoming, with Paul Osborn and Jan Lustig, 1948.

*

Criticism

Books:
Thomas E. Port, *Myth and Modern American Drama* (chapter on *Detective Story*), Detroit, 1969.
S. Smiley, *The Drama of Attack: Didactic Plays of the American Depression*, Columbia, Missouri, 1972.
Jordan Y. Miller and Winifred L. Frazer, *American Drama Between the Wars*, Boston, 1991.

* * *

Certain of Kingsley's plays have probably outlived his reputation. *Dead End*, for example, is likely to evoke recognition among those who are indifferent to the name of its author, largely through its renown on the cinema screen. (Warner Brothers made a series of films after the original adaptation, all of which featured the "Dead End Kids".) But Kingsley, in his time, was acknowledged as "a man of the theatre", one who could be relied on for a solid piece of work with each new play.

It is therefore surprising that his canon is relatively small, compared to the prolific output of his best-known contemporaries. His era, the 1930's, saw only four plays from him, one of which was an adaptation, and another a commercial failure. *Men in White* won for him a Pulitzer Prize at the age of 27, and *Dead End* is commonly cited in accounts of American Depression drama—it ran for 687 performances. But despite his critical and commercial success, he may even be remembered as a "one-play author" by the casual theatregoer.

The "one-play" tag, at least, is erroneous. Both *The Patriots* and *Darkness at Noon*, written in successive decades, were awarded New York Circle of Critics Awards. *Detective Story* was made into an all-celebrity film, which is regularly revived on television. Kingsley always wrote well, if sparingly, and every one of his plays has its distinct architecture. He created whole worlds in his plays, bringing onto sumptuously-detailed sets entire cross-sections from his chosen sphere, frequently in a specific socio-historical context. And if his naturalism stood in the way of experimentation like Elmer Rice's *The Adding Machine*, it was never the gimcrack of later television serials or quasi-pulp fiction.

Kingsley's writing addressed genuine social issues, sometimes much in advance of other dramatists. Even the failure *Ten Million Ghosts* deals with the devastating consequences of large-scale munitions production. American drama had to wait 11 more years before another play, Arthur Miller's *All My Sons*, came anywhere near the seriousness of this theme. Each world of a Kingsley play, too, is as distinct from the others as any one author's could be. *Men in White* features articulate, professional men; the street urchins in *Dead End* use a demotic speech that is hard to decipher on the page; *The Patriots* focuses on the tempestuous relationship between Jefferson and Hamilton; and *Darkness at Noon* (taken from the Arthur Koestler novel) departs from the American scene altogether.

Kingsley was bold enough to address social issues that still feature in today's headlines. *Men in White* and *Detective Story* present abortion almost as a commonplace solution for the disempowered. The random violence in *Dead End* remains a staple of documentaries about juvenile crime. Kingsley's extensive treatment of psycho-analysis in *The World We Make* reveals how superficial its appearance is in the Moss Hart and Kurt Weill musical play, *Lady in the Dark*.

Detractors regularly point out the irksome reliance on familiar plot devices in a Kingsley play. One or two, it is true, come dangerously close to the stock formula of "stranded passengers". One key-turning line ("Didn't you ever make a mistake?") even appears in two of the plays. But the resolutions, finally, cannot be said to be "comfortable", and characterisation is never wholly subservient to a melodramatic conclusion however vulnerable Kingsley may have been to the "problem play" formula. The protagonists of *Dead End* and *Detective Story* are sufficiently rounded never to polarise sympathy absolutely.

The physical defect of the character "Gimpty" in *Dead End* is presented in such a way that its relevance to the theme of urban decay supercedes any possible sentimental interpretation. Gimpty's semi-requited attachment to the mistress of a businessman is convincing precisely because such a defect would adequately define their relationship. It is in the transformation of the character into a clean-limbed but impoverished architect in the film version of *Dead End* that the relationship lacks credibility.

Rarely in Kingsley is the protagonist the play's spokesman. Gimpty betrays boyhood loyalty in his attempt to do right. Macleod's dilemma in *Detective Story* hardly makes him attractive, but it does put into focus the conflicts of an inner-city policeman who resolutely refuses to "look the other way". Jefferson's recourse to traditional political manoeuvring in *The Patriots* points up the limitations in the American political system rather than any venal traits in the personalities of Jefferson, Washington, or Hamilton.

The level of political debate in any Kingsley play is always less extensive than it is in Robert E. Sherwood's plays. Kingsley is far better at identifying a problem than at providing solutions, which restricts his work as "thesis drama". But it is hard to find fault with the careful articulation of issues, and this could occasionally result in positive action outside the theatre. Congressman Robert Wagner initiated a national campaign of slum clearance specifically based on viewing *Dead End*. Less sensationally, other of the plays prefigured reforms in medical care, criminal incarceration, and "head start" education.

An inability to anticipate future social trends may explain the failure of Kingsley's later work. In both *Lunatics and Lovers* and *Night Life* he remained contemporaneous, and the attention to detail is as scrupulous as ever. There is nothing bogus about the characterisation of the gangsters in *Night Life*; it is at least as convincing as Sidney Howard's is in *Lucky Sam McCarver*. Nonetheless, at a time when the Teamsters' boss James Hoffa was under indictment, and his exposure threatened the fabric of the Kennedy administration

(Hoffa's eventual murder was never solved), Kingsley's depiction of racketeering offered nothing new, and was seen, very clearly, as parochial.

By this time his crusading realism had become the province of the more adventurous television detective serials. Kingsley is worthy of remembrance, though, for the enduring quality of his slender output. In percentage terms, he scored higher than any other major American dramatist, though his name was to feature less frequently in both the popular press and in the annals of American drama.

—James MacDonald

See also *Volume 1* entry on *Dead End*.

KINOSHITA Junji.   Born in Tokyo, 2 August 1914. Family moved to Kuamamoto, western Japan, 1921. Educated in Fifth High School, Kuamamoto, to 1936; Tokyo University, specializing in Elizabethan theatre under Nakano Yoshio, 1936–39. Playwright from 1934; created new form of modern play, the *minwageki* [folktale play]; instructor, Hosei University; active in the YMCA, Tokyo, where he lived, 1936–53; co-founder of the *shingeki* [new theatre] group Budo no Kai [Grape Society] after World War II; co-founder, Minwa no Kai [Folktale Society], 1952; travelled throughout Asia and Europe, 1955–56. Also a prolific translator, critic, and theorist of theatre. Recipient: Mainichi Drama Prize, 1949; Kishida Prize, 1954.

Works

Collections

Kinoshita Junji shu (16 vols.; complete plays).   1988–89.

Stage Works

Selected titles; publication dates do not necessarily refer to book editions.

Fūrō [Turbulent Times].   1939; revised edition, 1947.
Omon tota.   1940; translated as *Oman tota*, 1975.
Yūzuru.   1949; translated as *Twilight of a Crane*, 1952; as *Twilight Crane*, in *Playbook: Five Plays from a New Theatre*, 1956.
Yamanami [The Mountain Range].   1949.
Kurai hibana [Dark Spots].   1950.
Kaeru shoten [Ascension of a Frog].   1951.
Onnyoro sisuiki [The Rise and Fall of of Onnyoro].   1957.
Shoko [Proof].   1959.
Okinawa [Okinawa].   1961.
Otto to yobareru nihonjin [A Japanese called Otto].   1963.
Fuyu no jidai [Winter].   1964.
Kami to hito to no aida.   1972; translated as *Between God and Man: A Judgement on War Crimes*, 1979.
Shigosen no matsuri [The Dirge of the Meridian].   1978.

Fiction

Mugen kido [Endless Track].   1966.

Other

Nihon ga Nihon de aru tame no wa (sketches and reminiscences).   1965.
Kinoshita Junji hyoren shu (11 vols.; criticism).   1972–84.

Translator, *Kinoshita Junji sakuhin shu* (8 vols.; Shakespeare's complete works).   1961–71.
Translator of works by Somerset Maugham.

* * *

Kinoshita epitomized modern Japanese drama in the postwar period. He began writing for the theatre while a student. His work falls into two broad categories: realistic historical dramas influenced by, and built upon, the legacy of pre-war realistic dramatists, especially Kubo Sakae; and folk-tale dramas based on traditional Japanese sources. *Fūrō* (Turbulent Times), Kinoshita's first play, completed in 1939 and published in a revised version in 1947, describes in realistic detail the historical situation of Japanese youth in the tumultuous decade following the Meiji Restoration of 1868. *Yūzuru* (Twilight Crane) is representative of the folk-tale dramas Kinoshita began writing during the War.

The bifurcation of Kinoshita's *oeuvre* is evident in his later work as well. *Kami to hito to no aida (Between God and Man)*, for example, consists of two plays, *The Judgment*, a documentary drama of the Tokyo War Crimes Tribunal, and *Summer: A Romance of the South Seas*, which focuses on the shamanistic impulses of the Japanese mind, as it tried to come to terms with the legacy of war.

Kinoshita's historical works are characterized by a Hegelian, tragic dramaturgy that closely identifies dramatic structure with the historical dialectic. As Eric J. Gangloff has noted, "for Kinoshita, drama is inseparable from interpretation of history. The nucleus of his plays is that point where a single character meets with and is defeated by the historical events which surround him".

Ottō to yobareru nihonjin (A Japanese Called Otto), for example, deals with the tragic fate of Ozaki Hotsumi, a Japanese member of the Sorge spy ring, who sold Japanese military secrets to the Soviet Union. Kinoshita describes Ozaki as a man who tried to reverse the tide of history, but who was crushed by it instead.

As Gangloff has noted, however, Kinoshita also "created an entire body of drama as an act of atonement, a symbolic dramatization of his need for antonement before the war dead". *Shōko* (Proof) and *Okinawa*, like *Summer: A Romance of the South Seas*, describe figures who assume burdens of war guilt for crimes they did not commit, in a syncretism of Christ-like suffering and shamanistic communication with the dead.

Kinoshita's experiments with language are also noteworthy. Particularly in his folk-tale dramas, he produced a provincial dialect that drew upon many authentic sources but was identifiable with none. These experiments enriched Japanese stage language but were criticized by purists, notably ethnologist Yanagita Kunio, who called Kinoshita "an enemy of the people" for obscuring what he regarded as the true Japanese tradition.

Kinoshita has been a prolific translator and critic, as well as dramatist. His translations of Shakespeare have been published in an eight-volume collection. His criticism has been published in 11 volumes, and his plays in 16.

—David G. Goodman

———

KIPPHARDT, Heinar. Born Heinrich Mauritius Kipphardt in Heidersdorf, Upper Silesia, Germany, 8 March 1922. Educated at Volksschule, Gnadenfrei, and subsequently at various Gymnasiums: Abitur, 1940; studied medicine in Bonn, Cologne, and Düsseldorf, 1941–42; drafted into the German army: served on the Russian front, 1942–44, and deserted, 1945, to work as doctor in an American hospital; continued medical studies at the Medical Academy, Düsseldorf, 1945–47: awarded title of "doctor", 1950. Married 1) Lore Hannen in 1943 (separated), one daughter and one son; 2) Pia Pavel in 1971 (with whom he had lived since 1963), two sons previous to marriage. Psychiatric assistant, Krefeld and Düsseldorf, 1947–49; emigrated to East Germany, 1949; psychiatric assistant, East Berlin, 1949–50; dramaturg, Deutsches Theater, East Berlin, 1950–59; first-produced play, *Entscheidungen*, produced 1953; emigrated with his family to West Germany, 1959, following the banning of his play *Die Stühle des Herrn Szmil*; bought a mill in Angelsbruck-bei-Erding, Bavaria, 1965; chief dramaturg, Kammerspiele, Munich, 1970–71; visiting artist, Hamburg, 1977. Recipient: National Prize (DDR), 1953; Schiller-Gedächtnispreis, 1962; Gerhart Hauptmann Prize, 1964; Adolf-Grimme Prize, 1964; Prix Italia, 1976; Literature Prize (Bremen), 1977; and several prizes for television work. Member, Deutsche Akademie der darstellenden Künste. Died in Munich, 18 November 1982.

Works

Collections

Stücke (2 vols.).   1973–74.
Theaterstücke (2 vols.).   1978–82.
Theaterstücke: Eine Auswahl (includes *Der Hund des Generals; In der Sache J. Robert Oppenheimer; Joel Brand; Die Soldaten; Die Nacht, in der der Chef geschlachtet wurde; März, Ein Künstlerleben*).   1982.
Gesammelte Werke, with Pia Kipphardt, edited by Uwe Naumann.   1986.

Stage Works

Entscheidungen (produced Deutsches Theater, Berlin, 1952).
Shakespeare dringend gesucht (produced Deutsches Theater, Berlin, 1953).   1954.
Der Aufstieg des Alois Piontek (produced Deutsches Theater, Berlin, 1956).   1956.
Die Stühle des Herrn Szmil (produced Städtische Bühnen, Wuppertal, 1961).   In *Junges deutsches Theater von heute*, 1961; revised version, in *Theaterstücke 1*, 1978.
Der Hund des Generals (produced Kammerspiele, Munich, 1962).   1963.
In der Sache J. Robert Oppenheimer (produced Kammerspiele, Munich, and Freie Volksbühne, Berlin, 1964).   1965; revised version, in *Theaterstücke 1*, 1978; translated as *In the Matter of J. Robert Oppenheimer*, 1967.

Joel Brand: Die Geschichte eines Geschäfts (produced Kammerspiele, Munich, 1965). 1965.
Die Nacht, in der der Chef geschlachtet wurde (produced Württembergisches Staatstheater, Stuttgart, 1967). In *Stücke 2*, 1974.
Die Soldaten, from a play by Lenz (produced Schauspielhaus, Düsseldorf, 1968). 1968.
Sedanfeier: Montage aus Materialien des 70er Krieges (produced Kammerspiele, Munich, 1970). In *Stücke 2*, 1974.
März, ein Kunstlerleben, from his story and television play (produced Schauspielhaus, Düsseldorf, 1980). 1980.
Bruder Eichmann (produced Residenztheater, Munich, 1983). 1983.

Television Plays

Bartleby, from a story by Hermann Melville, 1963; *In der Sache J. Robert Oppenheimer*, 1964 (published 1964); *Der Hund des Generals*, 1964; *Die Geschichte von Joel Brand*, 1964; *Leben des schizophrenen Dichters Alexander März*, 1975 (published 1976); *Die Soldaten*, 1977; *In der Sache J. Robert Oppenheimer* (new version), 1981.

Fiction

Dr Hund des Generals (story). 1957.
Die Ganovenfresse: Zwei Erzählungen. 1966.
März. 1975.
"Der Mann des Tages" und andere Erzählungen (stories). 1977.

Verse

Angelsbrucker Notizen. 1977.

Other

HAP Grieshaber: Engel der Psychiatrie: Farb- und Schwarzweiss-Holzschnitte, text by Kipphardt. 1976.
Traumprotokolle. 1981.

Editor, "Der Zentaur", by Georg Kaiser, in *Neue deutsche Literatur 6*, 1955.
Editor, with Ewald Dede, *Aus Liebe zu Deutschland: Satiren auf Franz Josef Strauss*. 1980.
Editor, with Roman Ritter, *Vom deutschen Herbst zum bleichen deutschen Winter: Ein Lesebuch zum Modell Deutschland*. 1981.

Translator, *Und im Licht mein Herz*, poems by Nazim Hikmet. 1971.

*

Criticism

Books:
Adolf Stock, *Heinar Kipphardt, mit Selbstzeugnissen und Bilddokumenten*, Reinbek, 1987.
W. Karbach, *Mit Vernunft zu rasen: Heinar Kipphardt*, Oberwesel, 1989.
H.L. Arnold, *Heinar Kipphardt*, Munich, 1990.

Articles:
Glenn R. Cuomo, *"Vergangenheitsbewältigung* Through Analogy: Heinar Kipphardt's Last Play *Bruder Eichmann"*, in *Germanic Review*, 64, 1989.

*   *   *

"He drew out of the piece more of the world than it contained", Kipphardt said of a production by the director Erwin Piscator in a commemorative address in 1966. The same words might be applied to his own dramas. The deep sense of conscience in these came from his training as a medical doctor and from his total cynicism towards Nazi propaganda in his youth. This was reinforced by his experiences in East Germany, where he lived from 1949 to 1959, hoping to play his part in the construction of a socialist German state.

His despair at the philistine petty-bourgeois manipulation of socialist ideals emerges in his early plays, the satirical comedy *Shakespeare dringend gesucht* (Shakespeare Urgently Sought) and *Die Stühle des Herrn Szmil* (Mr. Szmil's Chairs), the latter an absurd series of six scenes. The tragicomic farce *Der Aufstieg des Alois Piontek* (The Rise of Alois Piontek) and the bitter satire on war, *Der Hund des Generals* (The General's Dog) also articulate the anger he felt over the obvious signs of a resurgence of fascist ideas in both Germanies. In all of his plays he aimed to use individual characters to portray the typical behaviour of his times and through that their social and political problems. Behind individual passion he hoped to reveal the presence of class warfare. His early works were therefore accounts of individual struggles between authority and those in service, often showing official incompetence being used as a cover-up for personal and political failings.

With *In the Matter of J. Robert Oppenheimer* Kipphardt not only became world-famous, but also marked out his own particular form of documentary drama. His interest in the material lay primarily in the central figure as a "contemporary Faust" (according to a letter of 23 January 1958) and in the whole problem of nuclear power in this one exemplary case. The narrative quality of the earlier plays—fairytale-like in "Mr. Szmil's Chairs", similar to a war diary in "The General's Dog" (which was originally written as a story)—here gives way to the court scene. The sources of dramatic conflict are thus highlighted by the form, and the central figure, as in his later dramas, is ruthlessly cornered. In this approach he was neither trying to explain by psychological analysis, as in Rolf Hochhuth's works, nor trying to provoke anger, as he felt Peter Weiss aimed to do. Kipphardt hoped to present enough of the underlying facts to establish an open mind on the part of the audience as to the central figure's guilt or innocence.

This basic aim to produce a conundrum, not to direct the audience's views, can be seen in his clown plays in the style of Beckett (as in "*Pil and Pal as Servants*", 1966) and in his particular critical understanding of Brecht's aesthetic theories and practice. Above all, he was able to work together with Erwin Piscator on the *Oppenheimer* first production. Piscator's use of varied theatrical techniques clearly played an important part in Kipphardt's choice of material and its presentation in dramatic form. Not least of the effects of the multi-structured, hybrid presentation of documentary evidence is audience awareness of representative significance and of shared responsibility. In *Joel Brand: Die Geschichte eines Geschäfts* (Joel Brand: The Story of a Deal) the different pressures and prejudices operating on a semi-secret organisation of Jews (who are dealing with the Nazi official Adolf Eichmann's bartering of Hungarian Jews for lorries) reveal a whole network of undercover activities. The theatrical effect of such material is largely dependent on one of the less satisfactory aspects of most documentary drama: memories and prejudices on the part of the audience. It also owed much to the publicly screened trial of Eichmann on television in

1961, further exploited by Kipphardt in his final play *Bruder Eichmann* (Brother Eichmann).

Kipphardt's interest in historical events and periods can be seen in his montage of material from the 1870's, *Sedanfeier* (Celebrating Sedan). Here, the *Hurrahpatriotismus* (xenophobia) of the German victors spreads throughout society, and its language must have reminded the German audiences of a hundred years later that Nazi documents, and even some papers of the late 1960's, sounded remarkably similar in tone and style. It was a reminder of the dangers of xenophobia, in protest at the repressive measures against the revolts of the late 1960's.

Equally pointed was his modern adaptation of the "Storm and Stress" writer J.M.R.Lenz's social drama *Die Soldaten* (The Soldiers), which he considered to have been a key work in the development of German drama. Not surprisingly, despite early revulsion for its central character, Kipphardt also tried to rework Kleist's *Prince Friedrich of Homburg* during the early 1970's. In all of these works he highlighted the dialectical relationship between the self-interest of an exploiting class, above all the military, and the struggle for human rights by the majority.

His alignment with revolutionary movements outside Germany can be seen in his "Waiting for the Guerillero?" fragment, written 1972–73. This sympathetic treatment of Uruguayan independence fighters and conditions in the Third World was never finished. He claimed this was because of the taboo subject matter and hysteria about terrorism in West Germany; but in fact it may well have proceeded from his natural reluctance to follow through, realistically, the theme of revolution to its planned theatrical aftermath of collapse and eventual state oppression, in terror. Kipphardt passionately believed that German theatre had become, by the 1970's, a mirror of bourgeois society, with a lack of concern for the pressing problems of two thirds of the world's population.

It is significant that Kipphardt became interested in two sorts of people: those who, in various ways, try to alter the world for the better (that is, revolutionaries), and those who seek to retreat from society (especially the psychically sick). His novel *März*, about the relationship between the psychically disturbed writer Herbrich and the sick society in which he lived, is related in the play version to the "puritanically capitalist society of achievement" in what is perhaps his most outspoken condemnation of our times. Kipphardt's importance lies in the utter sincerity with which he treated contemporary issues, interpreting them as proofs of the failure to learn from the past.

—Brian Keith-Smith

See also *Volume 1* entry on *In the Matter of J. Robert Oppenheimer*.

KISHIDA Kunio. Born in Tokyo, 2 November 1890. Educated at military schools; studied French at the University of Tokyo, 1917–19. Married Murakawa Tokiko in 1927; two daughters. Commissioned as army officer, 1914, but resigned, 1917, and entered university; in France, 1919–23: studied theatre techniques with Jacques Copeau and his Vieux Colombier troupe, 1919–21; returned to Japan, 1923, and appointed lecturer at Hōsei and Chūō universities; associated with the *Bungei Jidai* [Literary History] periodical; co-founder, Tsukijiza [Tsukiji theatre troupe, 1932; founder, *Gekisaku* [Playwriting] magazine to promote Japanese playwriting, 1932; co-founder, Bungakuza [Literary Theatre], 1937, the only theatre troupe allowed to perform during World War II; director of the cultural department of the Taisai Yokus Ankai [Imperial Rule Assistance Association], 1940–42; spent later War years near Tokyo; "purged" by the Allied Occupation forces, 1947. Also novelist and translator of French plays and novels. Elected to Japanese Academy of Arts, 1953. Died 5 March 1954.

Works

Collections

Kishida Kunio zenshū (10 vols.; includes plays and critical writings).   1954.
Five Plays (includes *Paper Balloon; Cloudburst; The Two Daughters of Mr. Sawa; Adoration; Diary of Fallen Leaves*), edited by David G. Goodman.   1989.
Kishida Kunio zenshū (27 vols.; includes plays and critical writings).   1989—

Works

Furio Omocha [Old Toys]. In *Engeki shinchō* [New Currents in Drama], March 1924.
Chiroru no aki. In *Engeki shinchō* [New Currents in Drama], September 1924; translated as *Autumn in the Tyrol*, in *The Reeds*, 11, 1967.
Buranko.   1925; translated as *The Swing*, in *Pilgrimages: Aspects of Japanese Literature and Culture*, by Thomas J. Rimer, 1988.
Kami fūsen (produced 1926). In *Bungei shunjū* [Literary Annals], May 1925; translated as *Paper Balloon*, in *Five Plays*, 1989.
Hazakura (produced by the Shingeki Society, 1927). In *Josei*, [Woman], April 1926.
Okujō teien (produced 1927). In *Engeki shinchō* [New Currents in Drama], November 1926; translated as *Roof Garden*, in *"The Passion" and Three Other Japanese Plays*, translated by Noboru Hidaka, 1933, and in *"The Roof Garden" and Other One-Act Plays*, translated by Kazuo Yamada.
Ashita wa ii tenki.   1926; translated as *It Will Be Fine Tomorrow*, in *Eminent Authors of Contemporary Japan 2*, 1931.
Shūu (produced 1930). In *Bungei shunjū* [Literary Annals], September 1926; translated as *Cloudburst*, in *Five Plays*, 1989.
Mura de ichi ban kuri no ki [The Highest Chestnut in the Village] (produced 1954). In *Josei* [Woman], October 1926.
Ochiba nikki (produced 1965). In *Chūō kōron* [The Central Review], April 1927; translated as *Fallen Leaves: A Diary*, in *The Reeds*, 7, 1961; as *Diary of Fallen Leaves*, in *Five Plays*, 1989.
Ushiyama hoteru [Ushiyama Hotel] (produced 1932). In *Chūō kōron* [The Central Review], January 1929.
Mama sensei to sono otto [Professor Mama and Her Husband] (produced 1932). In *Kaizō* [Reconstruction], October 1930.
Asamayama [Mt. Asama]. In *Kaizō* [Reconstruction], July 1931.
Sawa-shi no futari musume (produced 1951). In *Chūō kōron*

[The Central Review], January 1935; as *The Two Daughters of Mr. Sawa*, in *Five Plays*, 1989.
Shokugyo [Vocation] (produced 1935). In *Chūō kōron* [The Central Review], August 1935.
Saigetsu [Space of Time] (produced 1947). In *Kaizō* [Reconstruction], April 1935.
Fuzoku jihyo [Commentary on Manners]. In *Chūō kōron* [The Central Review], March 1936.
Kaeraji-to [I Shan't Return]. In *Chūō kōron* [The Central Review], June 1943.
Chikara toshite no bunka [Culture as Strength]. 1943.
Hayami onna-juku [Hayamis Girls School]. In *Chūō kōron* [The Central Review], July 1948.
Nyonin katsugō. 1949; translated as *Adoration*, in *Literary Review*, vol. 6 no. 1, 1962, and in *Five Plays*, 1989.
Shinnen kyōsō Kyoku. Translated as *A New Year's Rhapsody*, in *The Reeds*, 12, 1968.

*

Criticism

Books:
Thomas J. Rimer, *Toward a Modern Japanese Theatre: Kishida Kunio*, Princeton, New Jersey, 1974.

Articles:
Thomas J. Rimer, "Kishida Kunio: Europe as Art Object", in his *Pilgrimages: Aspects of Japanese Literature and Culture*, Honolulu, Hawaii, 1988.

*   *   *

Kishida Kunio was the first great modern proponent and practitioner of drama as literature in Japan. He was profoundly influenced by Jacques Copeau, with whom he studied in Paris. After his return to Japan in 1923, Kishida became the leader of those playwrights who felt that modern theatre could only develop in Japan on the basis of high-quality Japanese plays. Strongly influenced by Copeau's ideal of a poetic stage idiom and by his antagonism toward anything "theatrical", Kishida promoted identical ideas in Japan. His plays are consequently delicately nuanced, psychological works with a minimum of action.

Kishida wrote approximately 60 plays during his lifetime. They can be divided into three groups. Half of Kishida's plays were written between 1924 and 1929: these were primarily short, one-act works or sketches. Between 1929 and 1936, he wrote more ambitious full-length works. After a hiatus, during which he wrote mostly fiction, Kishida returned to playwriting in the post-war period.

Kami fūsen (*Paper Balloon*) and *Shūu* (*Cloudburst*) are representative of Kishida's early work. In *Paper Balloon*, Kishida describes with delicate, wry humor a day in the life of Japan's new bourgeoisie. The day is Sunday, and the two characters are a recently wedded couple, at a loss about what to do with their time. Despite its gentle humor, the play depicts the young people in a state of stasis, their relationship slowly deteriorating.

Cloudburst treats a similar disintegrating relationship. Disgusted with her husband, and vowing never to return to him, a newly wedded bride returns alone from her honeymoon. In the course of her conversation with her sister and brother-in-law, it becomes clear that the older couple's relationship is also deteriorating.

Kishida's work of his middle period expands on these

themes. *Sawa-shi no futari musume* (*The Two Daughters of Mr. Sawa*), widely regarded as Kishida's finest play, deals with an ex-diplomat and widower and his relationship with his two grown daughters. Kishida describes the inability of the family members to communicate with one another as their relationships collapse. Like Sartre's *No Exit*, the play gives the strong impression that, in Kishida's work, "Hell is other people".

In the post-war period, Kishida returned to writing short poetic works with a satirical edge. *Adoration* (*Nyonin katsugō*) is representative. Continuing Kishida's fascination with families unable to communicate, *Adoration* portrays an elderly man, estranged from the daughter upon whom he is dependent, who visits a prostitute and confesses his unhappiness to her while she is asleep.

Some scholars regard Kishida's contribution to the development of a rich Japanese stage idiom to be so important that he, in effect, "succeeded singlehandedly in creating a modern theater for Japan". However, the moral ambiguity of Kishida's work has led others to characterize him as a nihilist. Mishima Yukio was probably most accurate when he summed up Kishida's work as "chamber music for the theatre".

Today, Kishida's contribution to the development of modern theatre is commemorated annually with the Kishida Prize for Playwriting, Japan's most coveted award for young playwrights.

—David G. Goodman

KLEIST, (Bernd) Heinrich (Wilhelm) von. Born in Frankfurt an der Oder, Brandenburg (now in Germany), 18 October 1777. Entered the Prussian army, 1792: took part in the siege of Mainz, 1793, was promoted to second lieutenant, 1797, and resigned commission, 1797. Undertook studies with Professor Wünsch, Frankfurt an der Oder, 1799. Travelled throughout Germany, and to Paris and Switzerland, 1800–04; attempted to join the French army, 1803; first-produced play, *Die Familie Schroffenstein*, produced 1804; civil servant, Königsberg, 1805–06; co-founder, with Adam Müller, and editor, *Phöbus*, Dresden, 1808–09, in which several of his writings first appeared; attempted unsuccessfully to publish the newspaper *Germania*, in Prague, 1809; editor, *Berliner Abendblätter*, 1810–11. Suffered many nervous breakdowns. Committed suicide (shot himself) in Wannsee bei Potsdam, 21 November 1811.

Works

Collections

Hinterlassene Schriften, edited by Ludwig Tieck. 1821.
Gesammelte Schriften (3 vols.), edited by Ludwig Tieck. 1826.
Werke (5 vols.), edited by Erich Schmidt and others. 1904–05; revised edition (7 vols.), 1936–38.
Sämtliche Werke und Briefe (2 vols.), edited by Helmut Sembdner. 1961.
Five Plays (includes *Amphitryon*; *The Broken Jug*; *Penthesilea*; *Prince Frederick of Homburg*; *A Fragment of the Tragedy of Robert Guiscard*), translated by Martin Greenberg. 1988.

Fiction

Erzählungen (2 vols.).   1810–11.
"The Marquise of O" and Other Stories (translations).   1960.

Memoirs and Letters

Briefe (2 vols.), edited by Helmut Sembdner.   1964 (from
    1961 *Sämtliche Werke und Briefe*).
An Abyss Deep Enough: Letters of Heinrich von Kleist, with
    essays, translated by Philip B. Miller.   1982.

Other

On a Theatre of Marionettes, translated by G. Wilford.
    1989.

*

Bibliographies

G. Minde-Pouet, "Kleist-Bibliographie", in *Jahrbuch der
    Kleist Gesellschaft*, 1921, 1922, 1923–24, 1929–30, and
    1933–37.
P. Kluckhohn, "Kleist-Forschung 1926–1943", in *Deutsche
    Vierteljahrsschrift für Literaturwissenschaft und Geistes-
    geschichte*, 21, 1943.
E. Rother, "Kleist-Bibliographie 1945–1960", in *Jahrbuch
    der deutschen Schiller-Gesellschaft*, 5, 1961.
H. Sembdner, *Kleist-Bibliographie 1803–1862* (primary litera-
    ture), Stuttgart, 1966.
M. Lefèvre, "Kleist-Forschung 1961–1967", in *Colloquia
    Germanica*, 3, 1969.

Criticism

Books:
E. Kayka, *Kleist und die Romantik: Ein Versuch*, Berlin,
    1906; reprinted, 1977.
H. Meyer-Benfey, *Das Drama Heinrich von Kleists*,
    Göttingen, 1913.
F. Gundolf, *Heinrich von Kleist*, Berlin, 1922.
W. Muschg, *Kleist*, Zurich, 1923.
G. Haupt, *Der Empörer: Das Leben Heinrich von Kleist*,
    Berlin, 1938.
F. Martini, *Heinrich von Kleist und die geschichtliche Welt*,
    Berlin, 1940.
T. Kaiser, *Der Vergleich der Verschiedenen Fassungen von
    Kleists Dramen*, Bern and Leipzig, 1944.
H.M. Wolff, *Heinrich von Kleist: Die Geschichte seines
    Schaffens*, Bern, 1954.
J. Maas, *Kleist: Die Fackel Preussens* (biography), Berne and
    Munich, 1957.
Michael Hamburger, *Reason and Energy*, 1957
F. Koch, *Heinrich von Kleist: Bewusstsein und Wirklichkeit*,
    Stuttgart, 1958.
C. Hohoff (ed.), *Heinrich von Kleist in Selbstzeugnissen und
    Bilddokumenten*, Reinbek, 1958.
Walter Silz, *Heinrich von Kleist: Studies in His Work and
    Literary Character*, Philadelphia, 1961.
E.L. Stahl, *Heinrich von Kleist's Dramas*, Oxford, 1961.
H. Mayer, *Heinrich von Kleist: Der geschichtliche
    Augenblick*, Pfullingen, 1962.
M. Schaub, *Heinrich von Kleist und die Bühne*, Zurich, 1966.
S. Streller, *Das dramatische Werk Heinrich von Kleists*,
    Berlin, 1966.

Heinrich von Kleist (engraving).

Stage Works

Die Familie Schroffenstein (produced Nationaltheater, Graz,
    1804).   1803; translated as *The Feud of the Schroffensteins*,
    1916.
Amphitryon (produced Neues Theater, Berlin, 1899).   1807;
    translated as *Amphitryon*, 1974, and in *Five Plays*, 1988.
Der zerbrochene Krug (produced Weimar, 1808).   1811;
    translated as *The Broken Pitcher*, 1961; as *The Broken Jug*,
    in *Four Continental Plays*, edited by John P. Allen, 1964;
    several subsequent translations under same title.
Penthesilea (produced Königliches Schauspielhaus, Berlin,
    1876).   1808; translated as *Penthesilea*, in *The Classic
    Theatre 2*, edited by Eric Bentley, 1959, and in *Five Plays*,
    1988.
Das Käthchen von Heilbronn; oder, Die Feuerprobe (pro-
    duced Theater an der Wien, Vienna, 1810).   1810; trans-
    lated in *Fiction and Fantasy of German Literature*, by F.E.
    Pierce, 1927.
Prinz Friedrich von Homburg (produced as *Die Schlacht von
    Fehrbellin*, Burgtheater, Vienna, 1821).   In *Hinterlassene
    Schriften*, 1821; translated as *The Prince of Homburg*,
    1956, and in *The Classic Theatre 2*, edited by Eric Bentley,
    1959; as *Prince Friedrich of Homburg*, in *Five Plays*, 1988.
Die Hermannsschlacht (produced Detmolder Hoftheater,
    Bad Pyrmont, 1839).   In *Hinterlassene Schriften*, 1821.
Robert Guiskard (fragment; produced Berliner Theater,
    Berlin, 1901).   In *Gesammelte Schriften*, 1826; translated
    as *A Fragment of the Tragedy of Robert Guiscard*, in *Five
    Plays*, 1988.

John Gearey, *Kleist: A Study in Tragedy and Anxiety*, Philadelphia, 1968.

E. Hoffmeister, *Täuschung und Wirklichkeit bei Heinrich von Kleist*, Bonn, 1968.

H. Reske, *Traum und Wirklichkeit im Werk Heinrich von Kleists*, Stuttgart, 1969.

R. Busch, *Imperialistische und faschistische Kleist-Rezeption 1890-1945*, Frankfurt, 1974.

H. Sembdner, *In Sachen Kleist: Beiträge zur Forschung*, Munich, 1974.

U. Vohland, *Bürgerliche Emanzipation in Heinrich von Kleists Dramen und theoretischen Schriften*, Bern, 1975.

R. Michaelis, *Heinrich von Kleist*, Munich, 1976.

H. Gerlach, *Heinrich von Kleist und sein Schaffen in neuer Sicht*, Dortmund, 1977.

K. Kanzog and H.-J. Kreutzer, *Werke Kleists auf dem modernen Musiktheater*, Berlin, 1977.

K. Birkenhauer, *Kleist* (biography), Tübingen, 1977.

R.M. Loch, *Heinrich von Kleist: Leben und Werk*, Leipzig, 1978.

Ladislaus Löb, *From Lessing to Hauptmann: Studies in German Drama*, 1974.

R.E. Helbling, *The Major Works of Heinrich von Kleist*, New York, 1975.

J.M. Ellis, *Heinrich von Kleist: Studies in the Character and Meaning of His Writings*, Chapel Hill, North Carolina, 1979.

K. Mommsen, *Kleists Kampf mit Goethe*, Frankfurt, 1979 (second edition).

E. Siebert, *Kleist: Leben und Werk im Bild*, Frankfurt, 1980.

Walter Hinderer (ed.), *Kleists Dramen: Neue Interpretationen*, Stuttgart, 1981.

P. Fischer, *Heinrich von Kleist*, Berlin, 1982.

Joachim Maass, *Heinrich von Kleist: A Biography*, London, 1983.

G.M. Wickert, *Das verlorene, heroische Zeitalter: Held und Volk in Heinrich von Kleists Dramen*, Bern, 1983.

D. Harlos, *Die Gestaltung psychischer Konflikte einiger Frauengestalten im Werk Heinrich von Kleists*, Frankfurt, 1984.

E. Irlbeck, *Tragödien der Freiheit: Das Problem der Freiheit im dramatischen Werk Heinrich von Kleists*, Frankfurt, 1986.

Raymond Cooke, *Heinrich von Kleist: A Critical Study*, 1987.

R. Homan, *Selbstreflexion der Literatur: Studien zu Dramen von G.E. Lessing und Heinrich von Kleist*, Munich, 1987.

W. Müller-Seidel (ed.), *Heinrich von Kleist: Aufsätze und Essays*, Darmstadt, 1987 (seventh edition).

J. Pfeiffer, "*Die zerbrochene Bilder*": Gestörte Ordnungen im Werk Heinrich von Kleists", Würzburg, 1989.

H.D. Zimmermann, *Kleist: Die Liebe und der Tod* (biography), Frankfurt, 1989.

F.J. Lamport, *German Classical Drama*, Cambridge, 1990.

* * *

Heinrich von Kleist's dramas are some of the most enigmatic works in German. Not only were they original, unexpected exceptions within the traditions of their time, they also bore witness to the exceedingly complex and often unstable character of their creator; and their form—often like that of a detective novel with the climax closer to the end than in classical drama—was highly expressive.

The first—*Die Familie Schroffenstein* (The Schroffenstein Family)—is imprecise in setting, artificial in characterisation and action, and full of broken fragments in language and gestures. Extreme in its thematic contrasts, and grotesque in its juxtaposition of narrated details, it sets the ravages of suspicion against blind love. It is drama in which malignant fate overcomes order, its originality foreshadowing the violence and variety of some later expressionist works.

Dissatisfied, Kleist tried to combine Shakespearean and classical tragic methods in *Robert Guiskard*. This play he mostly destroyed, despite its obvious high intent, discernible in the few scenes he reworked and published first in his review *Phöbus*. Guiscard, the legendary Norman leader, falls victim to the plague as he reaches Constantinople, still full of titanic plans, notwithstanding the absurdity of his position. Guiscard's defiance was paralleled in Kleist's own situation, when he nearly died from a nervous crisis brought on by writing this play.

Partly as a form of distraction from the increasing pressures on him—having returned to Germany, from France, exhausted—partly competing for a prize, and partly as an analytical enquiry into the machinations of a local tyrant in the figure of Adam, a village judge, Kleist wrote the masterly comedy *Der zerbrochene Krug* (*The Broken Jug*). This outstanding parallel in words to a realist Dutch painting depends, for its effect, on the detailed portraiture of Adam, who attempts to escape detection as a wholly corruptible official, and on Kleist's outstanding use of language, especially repartee. That the action is focused on a broken jug whose symbolic quality is highlighted by Marta, on one level, and whose role as a *corpus delicti* in the Court becomes all important on another, shows Kleist's rare powers of creative imagination to combine comic and potentially tragic aspects in the one object.

In his other comedy, *Amphitryon*, adapted from Molière's version of the story, slapstick is only allowed to support and emphasize the basic tragic handling of an identity crisis, especially in the destruction of confidence in the veracity of instinct and feeling. Alkmene's choice in public of the wrong man from two look-alikes as her "real" husband, and her subsequent correction by the god Jupiter, who has sadistically played with her emotions, is one of the most harrowing moments in German drama.

Equally horrific in its implications is *Penthesilea*, portraying the eponymous Amazon queen's triumphant slaughter of her lover Achilles. Here it is not the act itself, but rather the tearing apart of her inner balance, rendering her incapable of anything but irrational reactions, that dominates the play. This gains immensely from Kleist's use of a double level of language that corresponds to Penthesilea's quest for meaningful images, lost when she realizes her defeat by Achilles, and regained when she sees his corpse. The excesses of this presentation of classical myth point up extreme pressures working on Kleist himself. In both *Amphitryon* and *Penthesilea* divine interference brings ultimate destruction of the humanity of central figures and reduces their behaviour to uncontrolled psychic responses that verge on the bestial.

In *Käthchen von Heilbronn* blind love governs the actions of the central figure. Set in medieval times, it is the least personal of Kleist's dramas, full of obvious theatrical devices, and containing the benign influence of divine forces (especially in the final version where the fairy-tale world is more emphasized and the threat of eventual tragedy downgraded). Kleist's experimental mixed form of verse and prose is, however, only partially successful.

Die Hermannsschlacht (Hermann's Battle) is a laughable piece of propaganda, written to promote Austrian nationalism and the liberation of Germany from France. In the four parallel actions portraying the defeat of the Roman General Varus in 9 AD, in the Teutoburger Wald, deceit is employed as a political weapon even to the point of relishing brutal revenge. The values expressed are confused and pay little attention to ethical codes of behaviour. All the more remarkable, then, are the noble sentiments and balanced motives that mark Kleist's concise and exquisitely formulated final dramatic work, *Prinz Friedrich von Homburg* (*Prince Friedrich of Homburg*).

Kleist's masterpiece is compact and intense, even though a still shorter version was turned into an opera by Hans Werner Henze and Ingeborg Bachmann in 1960. It also interweaves satisfyingly exterior and interior action—the misjudgement, condemnation, and salvation of the Prince, together with his rebelliousness, fear of death, resignation, and awakening to a new life. The key to the character lies in the synthesis of the individual's feelings with the discipline required of him by the State. Friedrich has to learn to overcome his own self, aided by Nathalie and "educated" by his ruler, the Elector, who himself learns from the moral example of Friedrich's progress. By making Friedrich judge himself, the Elector not only assures the continued obedience of his officers, but also finds room for Friedrich to develop within the State's system, without having, finally, to rebel against it. Ideally, self-restraint is willingly put at the service of the State, thus developing it from an autocracy towards a primitive form of democracy.

In the maturing process that brings to the surface, in a self-controlled way, the visions and inspiration of the Prince's subconscious, there is a sign for the Elector that feelings must be given a formative role alongside reasoned disciplinary codes. Friedrich has to accept that he has disobeyed orders, deserves death, and must throw himself on the mercy of the Elector, whose capricious character allows him to play on Friedrich's fears for his life in a serious replay of an earlier party prank. It can be claimed that when, finally, Friedrich is pardoned, despite and because of his acceptance of his fate, the Elector is faced by a superior ethical gesture before which he should bow. Kleist's achievement is to have realized, and perfected, an aesthetically pleasing solution with parallel scenes at the beginning and the end which overshadow the unanswered questions on the moral and political planes: it is, as Friedrich is told in the final scene, "a dream, what else?".

In the last resort, Kleist's dramas must be seen to belong to the Romantic movement, despite their often highly realistic detail, their quest for ethically correct behaviour, and their often closed form. But the emphasis is on subconscious motivations, on cruelty, on the inter-relation of worlds of myth, the divine, the historical, the local, and on the inherent inability of man to distinguish between truth and deception— qualities which give the plays a unique place that defies any ultimate categorization.

—Brian Keith-Smith

See also *Volume 1* entries on *The Broken Jug*; *Penthesilea*; *The Prince of Homburg*.

———————

KOKOSCHKA, Oskar. Born in Pöchlarn, Austria, 1 March 1886. Educated at schools in Vienna; Kunstgewerbeschule [School of Applied Arts], studying under Gustav Klimt, Vienna, 1904–09. First exhibition in Vienna, 1908; first plays produced 1909; lived in Switzerland, 1909–10; visited Berlin, and became associate editor of the expressio-

nist journal *Der Sturm*, 1910; first solo exhibition, in Hagen, 1910; became teacher at the Gewerbeschule, Vienna, 1912; joined the Austrian army, 1914: was wounded and made official war artist, 1915–16; professor at the Art Academy, Dresden, 1919–24; travelled extensively in Europe, then lived in Vienna, 1931–34; his paintings removed from all public galleries in Germany by the Nazi government, 1933; lived in Prague, 1934–38; went into exile in London, 1938–1953: took British citizenship, 1947; founder, "School for Seeing", Salzburg, where he taught, 1953–63; stage designer, Vienna, 1960–61; in later life settled in Villeneuve, Switzerland. Died in Villeneuve, 22 February 1980.

Works

Collections

Dramen und Bilder.   1913.
Vier Dramen.   1919.
Schriften 1907–1955, edited by Hans Maria Wingler.   1956.
Das schriftliche Werk (4 vols.), edited by Heinz Spielmann. 1973–76.

Stage Works

Sphinx und Strohmann (produced Kunstgewerbeschule, Vienna, 1907; revised version produced Dada-Galerie, Zurich, 1917).   In *Dramen und Bilder*, 1913; revised version, in *Schriften*, 1956; revised as *Hiob* (produced Albert-Theater, Dresden, 1917), 1917; revised version of *Hiob*, in *Vier Dramen*, 1919; translated as *Job* in *German Drama Between the Wars*, edited by George E. Wellwarth, 1974, and in *Anthology of German Expressionist Drama*, edited by W.H. Sokel, 1963.
Mörder, Hoffnung der Frauen (produced Gartentheater der Kunstschau, Vienna, 1909).   In *Der Sturm*, 1, 1910; in book form, in *Dramen und Bilder*, 1913; revised version, with *Der brennende Dornbusch*, 1917; translated as *Murderer the Women's Hope*, in *Anthology of German Expressionist Drama*, edited by W.H. Sokel, 1963; as *Murderer Hope of Womankind*, in *Seven Expressionist Plays*, edited by J.M. Ritchie and H.F. Garten, 1968.
Der brennende Dornbusch (produced Albert-Theater, Dresden, 1917).   In *Dramen und Bilder*, 1913; revised version, in *Der jüngste Tag*, 1917.
Orpheus und Euridike (produced Städtisches Schauspielhaus, Frankfurt, 1921).   In *Vier Dramen*, 1919.
Comenius (fragment; produced 1975).   Part published in *Schriften*, 1956; alternative version, in *Das schriftliche Werk 1*, 1973.

Fiction

Der weisse Tiertöter.   1916.
Ann Eliza Reed: Erzahlung.   1952.
Erzählungen (Volume 2 of *Das schriftliche Werk*).   1974.

Verse

Die träumenden Knaben.   1916; as *Der gefesselte Columbus*, 1921.
"Die träumenden Knaben" und andere Dichtungen.   1956.

Dichtungen und Dramen (Volume 1 of *Das schriftliche Werk*). 1973.

Memoirs and Letters

Mein Leben.   1971; translated as *My Life*, 1974.
Briefe (3 vols.), edited by Olda Kokoschka and Heinz Spielmann.   1984–87.

Other

Von der Natur der Gesichte.   1921; translated as *On the Nature of Visions*, 1974.
Der Expressionismus: Edvard Munch.   1953.
Thermopylae: Ein Triptychon, with W. Kern.   1955.
Spur im Treibsand.   1956; translated as *A Sea Ringed with Visions*, 1962.
Word and Vision.   1967.
London Views, British Landscapes.   1972.
Vorträge; Aufsätze; Essays zur Kunst (Volume 3 of *Das schriftliche Werk*).   1975.
Politische Äusserungen (Volume 4 of *Das schriftliche Werk*).   1976.

Illustrator, *Die chinesische Mauer*, by Karl Krauss.   1914.
Illustrator, *Lob des hohen Verstandes*, by Victor Dirsztay.   1917.
Illustrator, *Tubutsch*, by Albert Ehrenstein.   1919.
Illustrator, *Mein Lied 1900–1931*, by Albert Ehrenstein.   1931.
Illustrator, *Irische Legende*, by Werner Egk.   1955.
Illustrator, *Odysee*, by Homer.   1969.
Illustrator, *Saul und David*, by Martin Buber.   1970.
Illustrator, *König Lear*, by Shakespeare.   1971.

*

Criticism

Books:
E. Hoffman, *Oskar Kokoschka: His Life and Art*, Boston, 1947.
Hans M. Winkler, *Oskar Kokoschka: Ein Lebensbild in zeitgenössischen Dokumenten*, Munich, 1956.
B. Bultman, *Oskar Kokoschka*, translated by Michael Bullock, London, 1961.
J.P. Hodin, *Oskar Kokoschka: The Artist and His Time*, New York, 1966.
F. Schmalenback, *Oskar Kokoschka*, translated by V.M. MacDonald, 1967.
R. Brandt, *Figurationen und Kompositionen in den Dramen Oskar Kokoschkas*, Munich, 1968.
G.J. Lischka, *Oskar Kokoschka: Maler und Dichter*, New York, 1972.
Alfred Reisinger, *Kokoschkas Dichtungen nach dem Expressionismus*, Vienna, 1978.
Donald E. Gordon, "Oskar Kokoschka and the Visionary Theatre", in *The Turn of the Century: German Literature and Art 1890–1915*, edited by G. Chapple and H.H. Schulte, Bonn, 1981.
Werner J. Schweiger, *Der junge Kokoschka: Leben und Werk 1904–1914*, Vienna, 1983.
Oskar Kokoschka 1886–1980, London, 1986 (Tate Gallery catalogue).
Frank Whitford, *Oskar Kokoschka: A Life*, London, 1986.

*   *   *

Kokoschka was, in the first instance, a painter of international recognition. Yet he was also a playwright, and his plays, written between 1907 and 1919, were early examples of modernist drama and exercised considerable influence on the expressionist theatre movement, on Dada and surrealism, and have also been regarded as precursors of the "theatre of cruelty", the "theatre of the absurd", and of existentialist drama.

Kokoschkas's plays are, as the critic Alfred Kerr suggested in 1919, nothing but raw material for productions, where Kokoschka, the director and designer, developed his full mastery as a theatre artist. Although the poetic quality of the dialogues is not to be slighted, the highly visual nature of these dramas demands scenic realization in order to be fully appreciated. In the printed versions of the plays, stage directions are often more extensive than the lines to be spoken by the actors. Kokoschka paid great attention to movement, gesture, and mime, and anticipated in his texts complex stage, costume, and lighting designs.

For the dialogues he employed a great variety of forms: prose and verse, choric and solo voices, aria and recitative. The language he uses is not based on logic or conventional usage, but on associative connection. Suggestive expressiveness is more important than clarity of meaning. The imagery employed is highly symbolic, and mythological and biblical allusions are extensive throughout.

According to Kokoschka's early theoretical statements, the artist cannot fathom reality in a rational fashion, but only experience it with his senses and feel its reverberations in his soul. His feelings and visions receive plastic embodiment in his works, and they reveal to the viewer what lies hidden behind the surface of reality. The artist has the mission to communicate these visions to the viewer, to purify his imperfect perceptions, and to activate his desires to ameliorate the deficiencies of the present conditions of the world.

The art work is a medium which communicates with the viewer by way of psychic energies. The viewer reacts to the work of art just like the artists react to the sense-impressions of nature. There is no innate structure or order to these phenomena. The viewer has to learn to see and understand what he perceives. He takes recourse to his other personal experiences and fuses them with his perceptions of nature, so that both become part of the "world's imaginings".

The main theme of Kokoschka's plays is the battle between the sexes, which, in its tragic constellation, assumes cosmic proportion. Kokoschka was an heir to a tradition established by Claudel, Strindberg, and Wedekind; but under the influence of Freud and, in particular, Weininger, his view of the relationship between the sexes took on a new direction. In a letter to Hans Tietze of 1917 he wrote: "I create compositions out of human visions where being battles against being, always in strict opposition, like hatred and love". The figures in his plays are thus representations of elementary forces. The clash between them leads to tragic consequences, and the idea of redemption is extrapolated into an uncertain future.

Kokoschka was no pessimist or fatalist, despite the existentialist and archetypical situations depicted in the plays. He emphasized the potential for positive developments for both man and woman. The main function of his plays is to communicate his vision of the human soul and of the hope to overcome its deficiencies.

Kokoschka's development as an artist and a human being brought about a number of changes in his ideology and artistic theory. As a result of this, he rewrote and altered his plays with each successive edition. It is therefore impossible to rest an interpretation of his plays on one version alone. For a full understanding one also has to take into account his own stage productions, for it is here that the plays found their most complete realizations.

—Günter Berghaus

See also *Volume 1* entry on *Murderer, Hope of Women*.

———————

KONG Shangren.   See *Volume 1* entry on *Peach Blossom Fan*

———————

KOPIT, Arthur (Lee).   Born in New York City, 10 May 1937. Educated at Lawrence High School, New York, graduated 1955; Harvard University, Cambridge, Massachusetts, AB (cum laude) 1959 (Phi Beta Kappa). Married to Leslie Ann Garis; two sons and one daughter. First plays produced at Harvard University, 1957. Playwright-in-residence, Wesleyan University, Middletown, Connecticut, 1975–76; CBS Fellow, 1976–77, and Adjunct Professor of Playwriting, 1977–80, Yale University, New Haven, Connecticut; Adjunct Professor of Playwriting, City College, New York, from 1982. Council member, Dramatists Guild, from 1982. Recipient: Vernon Rice Award, 1962; Outer Circle Award, 1962; American Academy Award, 1971; Italia Prize, for radio play, 1979; Tony Award, 1982.

Works

Collections

"The Day the Whores Came Out to Play Tennis" and Other Plays (includes *The Questioning of Nick; Sing to Me Through Open Windows; Chamber Music; The Conquest of Everest; The Hero*).   1965; as *"Chamber Music" and Other Plays*, 1969.

Stage Works

The Questioning of Nick (produced Harvard University, Cambridge, Massachusetts, 1957). In *"The Day the Whores Came Out to Play Tennis" and Other Plays*, 1965.
Gemini (produced Harvard University, Cambridge, Massachusetts, 1957).
Don Juan in Texas, with Wally Lawrence (produced Harvard University, Cambridge, Massachusetts, 1957).
On the Runway of Life, You Never Know What's Coming Off Next (produced Harvard University, Cambridge, Massachusetts, 1958).
Across the River and into the Jungle (produced Harvard University, Cambridge, Massachusetts, 1958).
To Dwell in a Place of Strangers (produced Harvard University, Cambridge, Massachusetts, 1958). Act I published in *Harvard Advocate*, May 1958.

Aubade (produced Harvard University, Cambridge, Massachusetts, 1959).
Sing to Me Through Open Windows (produced Harvard University, Cambridge, Massachusetts, 1959; revised version, produced Players' Theatre, New York, 1965). In *"The Day the Whores Came Out to Play Tennis" and Other Plays*, 1965.
Oh Dad, Poor Dad, Mamma's Hung You in the Closet and I'm Feelin' So Sad: A Pseudoclassical Tragifarce in a Bastard French Tradition (produced Harvard University, Cambridge, Massachusetts, 1960).   1960.
Mhil'daim (produced New York, 1963).
Asylum; or, What the Gentlemen Are Up To, and As for the Ladies (produced Theatre de Lys, New York, 1963; as *And As for the Ladies*, produced 1964).   As *Chamber Music* (produced Society Hill Playhouse, Philadelphia, 1965), in *"The Day the Whores Came Out to Play Tennis" and Other Plays*, 1965.
The Conquest of Everest (produced New York, 1964). In *"The Day the Whores Came Out to Play Tennis" and Other Plays*, 1965.
The Hero (produced New York, 1964). In *"The Day the Whores Came Out to Play Tennis" and Other Plays*, 1965.
The Day the Whores Came Out to Play Tennis (produced Harvard University, Cambridge, 1964). In *"The Day the Whores Came Out to Play Tennis" and Other Plays*, 1965.
Indians (produced Aldwych Theatre, London, 1968).   1969.
An Incident in the Park. In *Pardon Me, Sir, But is My Eye Hurting Your Elbow?*, edited by Bob Booker and George Foster.   1968.
What's Happened to the Thorne's House (produced Peru, Vermont, 1972).
Louisiana Territory; or, Lewis and Clark—Lost and Found (produced Middletown, Connecticut, 1975).
Secrets of the Rich (produced Eugene O'Neill Theatre, Waterford, Connecticut, 1976).   1978.
Wings (produced Yale Repertory Theatre, New Haven, Connecticut, 1978).   1978.
Nine (libretto), music and lyrics by Maury Yeston, from an adaptation by Mario Fratti of a screenplay by Federico Fellini (produced Eugene O'Neill Theatre, Waterford, Connecticut, 1981).   1983.
Good Help is Hard to Find (produced Ensemble Studio Theatre, New York, 1981).   1982.
Ghosts, from a play by Ibsen (produced Eisenhower Theatre, Washington, DC, 1982).
End of the World (*With a Symposium to Follow*) (produced Music Box Theatre, New York, 1984; as *The Assignment*, produced 1985).   1984.
Bone-the-Fish (produced Actors' Theatre, Louisville, Kentucky, 1989).
The Road to Nirvana (produced New York, 1991).   1991.
Phantom, music and lyrics by Maury Yeston (produced Houston, Texas, 1991).

Television Plays

The Conquest of Television, 1966; *Promontory Point Revisited*, 1969; the mini-series *Hands of a Stranger, Phantom of the Opera*, and *In a Child's Name*.

Radio Plays

Wings, 1977.

*

Bibliographies

Kimball King, *Ten Modern American Playwrights*, New York, 1982.

Philip C. Kolin (ed.), *American Playwrights since 1945: A Guide to Scholarship, Criticism, and Performance*, New York, 1989.

Criticism

Books:

Jürgen Wolter, "Arthur Kopit: Dreams and Nightmares", in *Essays on Contemporary American Theatre*, edited by Hedwig Bock and Albert Wertheim, Munich, 1981.

Doris Auerbach, *Sam Shepard, Arthur Kopit, and the Off-Broadway Theater*, Boston, 1982.

Articles:

Thomas P. Adler, "Public Faces, Private Graces: Apocalypse Postponed in Arthur Kopit's *End of the World*", in *Studies in the Literary Imagination*, 21, 1981.

Margot-Anne Kelly, "Order Within Fragmentation: Postmodernism and the Stroke Victim's World", in *Modern Drama*, vol. 34 no. 3, 1991.

*   *   *

Arthur Kopit's reputation as a dramatist was established with his first successful play, *Oh Dad, Poor Dad, Mamma's Hung You in the Closet and I'm Feelin' So Sad*. Because of the work's title and the absurdist nature of some of its events, Kopit was quickly labelled an "absurdist" by critics and audiences alike. Unfortunately, this is both an unfair and inaccurate assessment of the playwright. One of the most innovative dramatists in the contemporary American theater, Kopit has written several plays that surpass *Oh Dad* in both importance and quality. These include *Sing To Me Through Open Windows*, *Indians*, and *Wings*.

Sensitive to a tension between the dignity of mankind and the absurdity of the human condition, Kopit has utilized a number of experimental formats and techniques. His first play, *The Questioning of Nick*, written while he was a sophomore at Harvard University, is realistic; *Oh Dad* is absurdist; structurally, *Indians* reflects Bertolt Brecht's concept of epic theater; and *Wings* is a surreal, impressionistic, psychologically realistic drama. *Sing to Me*, the best of his early works, shows the influence of Samuel Beckett's *Endgame* and the "theater of the absurd" in a metaphorical depiction of the transitional moment in which a boy moves from childhood into manhood. The absurdist elements of setting, language, the use of pauses, minimal plot, and characterization in this play show up again in the Freudian/Oedipal *Oh Dad*, which is an examination of the relationship between a domineering mother and her timid son, and is thematically related to Sidney Howard's *The Silver Cord*, Harold Pinter's *A Night Out*, and Philip Roth's *Portnoy's Complaint*, and stylistically related to Arthur Miller's *Death of a Salesman* and Joe Orton's *Loot*. While not as absurdist as many critics contend, *Oh Dad* contains a great deal of satire and grotesque humor.

Indians was a quite different play. In this study of the nature of the American character, as illustrated throughout history, and mythic heroes, Kopit utilizes a jumbled chronology to demonstrate that the meaning of the play is applicable across time.

Without a doubt, however, Kopit's finest work is *Wings*. Through a combination of strong emotional expression and intellectual context, Kopit creates an impressionistic representation of the world as perceived by a stroke victim. To replicate this world, as the play moves from fragmentation to integration, the dramatist uses a series of stage effects, such as live and recorded music, colored and flashing lights, a minimal set conveying a sense of limbo, overlapping dialogue, and loudspeakers located throughout the auditorium. As a result of these techniques, which underscore a combination of articulate speech and babble, of logic and nonsense, the audience is presented with an affective portrayal of the protagonist, Emily, as she struggles to restructure her fragmented mind.

Kopit's recent play, which was first performed under the title *Bone-the-Fish* in 1989, and reappeared under the title *The Road to Nirvana* one year later, is a satirical look at the Hollywood film world, somewhat along the lines of David Mamet's *Speed the Plow*. The play dramatizes very imaginatively a world in which clichés are taken literally. As was the case in *Oh Dad*, while interesting, the play is not one of Kopit's best, though it won some critical acclaim as a parody of Mamet's play.

Kopit has demonstrated a diversity of style and range of themes that show great promise far beyond that of his contemporaries. There is no question that his craftsmanship and the significance of his best works make him, potentially, one of the major American playwrights of his generation, with *Indians* being one of the most important American plays of the 1960's and *Wings* being one of the major plays of the 1970's.

—Steven H. Gale

See also *Volume 1* entries on *Indians*; *Oh Dad, Poor Dad, Mamma's Hung You in the Closet and I'm Feeling so Sad*.

———

KOTZEBUE, August von. Born in Weimar (now in Germany), 3 May 1761. Educated at Gymnasium, Weimar; universities of Jena and Duisburg, 1777–79. Married 1) Friedericke von Essen in 1785 (died 1790), four children; 2) Christina von Krusenstern in 1794 (died 1803), three children; 3) Wilhelmina von Krusenstern in 1804. Lawyer in Weimar, 1780; secretary to the Governor General, St. Petersburg, Russia, 1781, where tasks included supervision of the St. Petersburg German theatre; first-produced play, *Demetrius Zar von Moskau*, staged 1782: subsequently an extremely prolific dramatist, whose plays were produced first mainly in Berlin and Vienna; appointed to the Court of the Duchy of Estonia in Reval (now Tallinn): chief justice, 1785–95 (resigned); founded the Lieberhabertheater (amateur theatre) in Reval; following death of first wife, left for Paris, 1790; returned to his estate, Friedenthal, in Estonia, 1791; received a lifelong pension, 1795; director of the Vienna Burgtheater for nine months in 1797; spent a year in Weimar, 1799; returned to Russia, 1800, where he was arrested for suspected political dissent, and imprisoned in Siberia: pardoned after four months and compensated; made director of the German Theatre, St. Petersburg, July 1801; based in Berlin, 1802–06; co-editor of the journal *Der Freimütige*, 1803; travelled to Paris, 1804, Estonia, 1804, Italy, 1805; wrote anti-Napoleonic articles; editor, the quarterly *Die Biene*, 1808–10, *Geist aller Journale*, 1809, *Die Grille*, 1811–

August von Kotzebue (engraving).

12, and *Das russische Volksblatt*, 1813; returned to St. Petersburg; became Consular General, Königsberg, 1813; appointed as State Councillor for Foreign Affairs, St. Petersburg, 1816; personal adviser on German affairs to Tsar Alexander I, from 1817; travelled to Berlin, Weimar, Munich, and Mannheim, where, as editor of *Das literarische Wochenblatt*, 1818–19, he incurred the hostility of German liberals and students. Member of the Prussian Academy. Ennobled by Catherine II of Russia, 1781. Murdered at his lodgings by a theology student, in Mannheim, 23 March 1819.

Works

Collections

Schauspiele (5 vols.).   1797.
Neue Schauspiele (23 vols.).   1798–1819.
Collected Dramas (6 vols.).   1798–99.
Dramatic Works (3 vols.), translated by Charles Smith and Others.   1800.
A Selection of the Best Plays, translated by Anne Plumptre and Henry Neuman.   1800.
Dramatic Works, translated by Benjamin Thompson.   1802.
Almanach dramatischer Spiele (18 vols.).   1803–20.
Theater (54 vols.).   1810–20.
Sämtliche dramatische Werke (64 vols.).   1827–29.
Theater (40 vols.).   1840–41.
Almanach dramatischer Spiele (31 vols.).   1903–33.
Schauspiele, edited by J. Mathes.   1972.

Stage Works

Publication dates with asterisks refer to publication in periodicals or collections/anthologies.   Publication dates without asterisks refer to individual editions.

Demetrius Zar von Moskau (produced St. Petersburg, 1782).
Die Nonne und das Kammermädchen.   1782.*
Der Eremit auf Formentara (produced Nationaltheater, Mannheim, 1788).   1784.
Das Liebhabertheater vor dem Parlament (produced Liebhabertheater, Reval, 1785).   1785.
Adelheid von Wulfingen: Ein Denkmal der Barbarei des XIIIen Jahrhunderts.   1789; translated as *Adelaide of Wulfingen*, 1798.
Die väterliche Erwartung.   1788.
Die Indianer in England (produced Liebhabertheater, Reval, 1789; produced professionally, Königliches Schauspielhaus, Berlin, 1789).   1790; translated as *The East Indian*, 1799.
Menschenhass und Reue (produced Königliches Schauspielhaus, Berlin, 1789).   In book form, 1789; revised version, 1819; adapted as *The Stranger; or, Misanthropy and Repentance*, c.1798: reprinted in *Plays of the Restoration and Eighteenth Century*, edited by D. MacMillan and H.M. Jones, 1938.
Die Corsen (produced Burgtheater, Vienna, 1797).   1790; translated as *The Corsicans*, 1799.
Die Sonnenjungfrau (produced Liebhabertheater, Reval, 1789; produced professionally, Königliches Schauspielhaus, Berlin, 1790).   1791; translated as *The Virgin of the Sun*, 1799.
Doktor Bahrt mit der eisernen Stirn; oder, Die deutsche Union gegen Zimmermann.   1790.
Das Kind der Liebe (produced Liebhabertheater, Reval, 1790; produced professionally, Königliches Schauspielhaus, Berlin, 1791).   1791; translated as *The Natural Son*, 1798; as *Lovers' Vows; or, The Natural Son*, 1800.
Bruder Moritz der Sonderling; oder, Die Kolonie für die Pelew Inseln (produced Königliches Schauspielhaus, Berlin, 1790).   1791.
Der weibliche Jakobinerklub.   1791; translated as *The Female Jacobin-Club*, 1801.
Strassenräuber aus kindlicher Liebe (produced Burgtheater, Vienna, 1791).
Der Papegei; oder, Der Schiffbruch (produced Königliches Schauspielhaus, Berlin, 1791).   1792.
Die edle Lüge.   1792; translated as *The Noble Lie*, 1799.
Der Spiegelritter, music by Walter (produced Nationaltheater, Mannheim, 1793).   1802.
Sultan Wampum; oder, Die Wünsche (produced 1794).   1794.
Armuth und Edelsinn (produced Burgtheater, Vienna, 1794).   1795; translated as *Poverty and Nobleness of Mind*, 1799.
Die Lüge mit der guten Absicht (produced Königliches Schauspielhaus, Berlin, 1794).
Die Spanier in Peru; oder, Rollas Tod (produced Nationaltheater, Mannheim, 1794).   1796; translated as *Rolla; or, The Peruvian Hero*, 1799; as *Pizarro in Peru*, 1800.
Der Mann von vierzig Jahren, from a work by C.-B. Fagan (produced Königliches Schauspielhaus, Berlin, 1795).   1795; translated as *The Man of Forty*, nd.
Graf Benyowsky; oder, Die Verschwörung auf Kamtschatka (produced 1795; translated as *Count Benyowsky*, 1798.
Der Verleumder (produced Königliches Schauspielhaus, Berlin, 1795).   1796; translated as *The Force of Calumny*, 1799.

Die Negersklaven (produced Königliches Schauspielhaus, Berlin, 1796). 1796; translated as *The Negro Slaves*, 1796.

Die Witwe und das Reitpferd (produced Königliches Schauspielhaus, Berlin, 1795). 1796; translated as *The Widow and the Riding Horse*, 1799.

Der Wildfang (produced Königliches Schauspielhaus, Berlin, 1795). 1798; translated as *The Madcap*, 1798; as *The Wild-Goose Chase*, 1800.

Falsche Scham (produced Burgtheater, Vienna, 1796). 1798; translated as *False Shame*, 1799.

La Peyrouse (produced Nationaltheater, Mannheim, 1796). 1798; translated as *La-Peyrouse*, 1799.

Der Opfertod (produced Burgtheater, Vienna, 1797). 1798; translated as *Self-Immolation; or, The Sacrifice in Love*, 1799.

Die Verwandtschaften (produced Burgtheater, Vienna, 1797). 1798; translated as *Kindred*, 1837.

Die Bruderzwist (produced Nationaltheater, Mannheim, 1797). 1798; translated as *The Reconciliation; or, Birthday*, 1799; as *Fraternal Discord*, 1801.

Üble Laune (produced Königliches Schauspielhaus, Berlin, 1797). 1799; translated as *The Peevish Man*, 1799.

Die silberne Hochzeit (produced Königliches Schauspielhaus, Berlin, 1797). 1799; translated as *The Happy Family*, 1799.

Das Dorf im Gebirge (produced 1798). 1798.

Die Unglücklichen. 1798.

Der Schreibepult; oder, Die Gefahren der Jugend (produced Königliches Schauspielhaus, Berlin, 1798). 1800; translated as *The Writing Desk; or, Youth in Danger*, 1799.

Das Epigramm (produced Burgtheater, Vienna, 1798). 1801.

Der Gefangene (produced Burgtheater, Vienna, 1798). 1800.

Lohn der Wahrheit (produced Burgtheater, Vienna, 1798). 1801.

Das rächende Gewissen, from a story by Heinrich Zschokke (produced Burgtheater, Vienna, 1798).

Der Graf von Burgund (produced Burgtheater, Vienna, 1798). 1798; translated as *The Count of Burgundy*, 1798.

Der hyperboräische Esel; oder, Die heutige Bildung. 1799.

Johanna von Montfaucon (produced Burgtheater, Vienna, 1799). 1800; translated as *Johanna of Montfaucon*, 1800.

Die beiden Klingsberg (produced Burgtheater, Vienna, 1799). 1801; translated as *Father and Son; or, Family Frailties*, in *The New British Theatre 3*, edited by John Galt, 1814.

Die kluge Frau vom Walde; oder, Der stumme Ritter (produced Burgtheater, Vienna, 1799). 1801.

Das neue Jahrhundert (produced Königliches Schauspielhaus, Berlin, and Burgtheater, Vienna, 1799). 1801.

Der alte Leibkutscher Peter des Dritten (produced Nationaltheater, Mannheim, 1800). 1799.

Der Taubstumme; oder, Der Abbé de l'Épée, from a play by J.N. Bouilly. 1800; translated as *Deaf and Dumb; or, The Orphan*, 1801.

Gustav Wasa (produced Königliches Schauspielhaus, Berlin, 1800). 1801.

Octavia (produced Burgtheater, Vienna, 1800). 1801.

Bayard, der Ritter ohne Furcht und ohne Tadel (produced Hoftheater, Weimar, 1800). 1801.

Der Besuch; oder, Die Sucht zu glänzen (produced Königliches Schauspielhaus, Berlin, 1800). 1801.

Vituvia. 1801.

Die barmherzigen Brüder. 1801.*

Die Züruckkunft des Vaters. 1801.

Der Wirrwarr; oder, Der Muthwillige (produced Königliches Schauspielhaus, Berlin, 1801). 1803; translated as *The Confusion; or, The Wag*, 1842.

Des Teufels Lustschloss, also known as *Das Zauberschloss*, music by Johann Friedrich Reichardt (produced 1801?). 1801.

Die deutschen Kleinstädter (produced Burgtheater, Vienna, 1802). 1803; translated as *The Good Citizens of Piffelheim*, in *August von Kotzebue: The Comedy, the Man*, by Oscar Mandel, 1990.

Unser Fritz (produced Burgtheater, Vienna, 1802). 1803.

Der Schreiner (produced Nationaltheater, Mannheim, 1802).

Don Raimundo de Colibrados, from a play by Holberg (produced Königliches Schauspielhaus, Berlin, 1802). 1803.

Die Hussiten von Naumburg im Jahr 1432 (produced Königliches Schauspielhaus, Berlin, 1802). 1803; translated as *The Patriot Father*, 1830.

Cleopatra. 1803.

Ariadne auf Naxos. 1804.

Der Schauspieler wider Willen, from a work by Louis A. Dorvigny. 1803.

Die französischen Kleinstädter, from a play by Louis Picard. 1803.

Die Kreuzfahrer. 1803; translated as *Alfred and Emmy*, 1806.

Die schlaue Witwe; oder, Die Temperamente. 1803.

Hugo Grotius (produced Berlin, 1803). 1803.

Der Hahnenschlag (produced Königliches Schauspielhaus, Berlin, 1803). 1803.

Pagenstreiche (produced Königliches Schauspielhaus, Berlin, 1803). 1804.

Der Vater von Ungefähr, from a play by Marie-Joseph Pain and Pierre-Ange Viellard (produced Nationaltheater, Mannheim, 1803). 1804.

Das Urteil des Paris. 1804.*

Der tote Neffe. 1804.

Die Uhr und die Mandeltorte (for children). 1804.

Eduard in Schottland; oder, Die Nacht eines Flüchtlings, from a play by Alexandre Duval. 1804; translated as *The Wanderer; or, The Rights of Hospitality*, 1808.

Incognito. 1804.*

Rübezahl. 1804.

Sultan Bimbam; oder, Der Triumph der Wahrheit. 1804.*

Der Abschied (produced Hoftheater, Vienna, 1804). 1804.

Die Tochter Pharaonis (produced Burgtheater, Vienna, 1804). 1804; translated as *Pharaoh's Daughter*, in *Typical Plays for Secondary Schools*, edited by J.P. Webber and H.H. Webster, 1929.

Die Sparbüchse; oder, Der arme Kandidat (produced Königliches Schauspielhaus, Berlin, 1804). 1805.*

Die Schmuckkästchen; oder, Der Weg zum Herzen (produced Königliches Schauspielhaus, Berlin, 1804). 1806.

Der Gipfel auf der Messe. 1805.*

Der Trunkenboldt, from a play by Holberg. 1805.*

Die hübsche kleine Putzmacherin. 1805.

Die Schule der Frauen, from a play by Molière. 1805.

Fanchon das Leiermädchen, from a play by Jean-Nicolas Bouilly. 1805.

Hygea. 1805.*

Heinrich Reuss von Plauen; oder, Die Belagerung von Marienburg (produced Königliches Schauspielhaus, Berlin, 1805). 1805.

Mädchenfreundschaft; oder, Der türkische Gesandte, from a play by Charles-Guillaume Étienne (produced Königliches Schauspielhaus, Berlin, 1805). 1805.

Die Organe des Schirms (produced Königliches Schauspielhaus, Berlin, 1805). 1806; translated as *The Organs of the Brain*, 1838.

Die Brandschatzung (produced Königliches Schauspielhaus, Berlin, 1805). 1806.*

Carolus Magnus. 1806; revised edition, as *Der Galatag in Krähwinkel*, 1809.

Der Russe in Deutschland. 1806.

Die Beichte. Also known as *Das Geständnis* (produced Königliches Schauspielhaus, Berlin, 1806). 1807.*

Das verlorene Kind (produced Burgtheater, Vienna, 1806). 1806.

Die gefährliche Nachbarschaft, from the ballet by Gaetano Gioia (produced Burgtheater, Vienna, 1806). 1806; translated as *The Party Wall; or, In and Out*, 1842.

Blinde Liebe 1806.

Eulenspiegel (produced Königliches Schauspielhaus, Berlin, 1806). 1807.*

Das Köstlichste. 1807.*

Das liebe Dörflein. 1807.*

Der Kater und der Rosenstock. 1807.

Kaiser Claudius. 1807.*

Das Lustspiel am Fenster (produced Burgtheater, Vienna, 1817). 1807.*

Das Standrecht (produced Königliches Schauspielhaus, Berlin, 1807). 1808.

Der Deserteur (produced Königliches Schauspielhaus, Berlin, 1807). 1808.

Der Leineweber (produced Burgtheater, Vienna, 1807). 1808.

Das Gespens. 1808.

Das Posthaus in Treuenbrietzen. 1808.

Der Graf von Gleichen. 1808.*

Ubaldo. 1808.

Der Stumme. 1808; translated as *The Man Who Couldn't Talk*, in *Poet Lore*, vol. 40 no. 2, 1929.

Die Unvermählte (produced Burgtheater, Vienna, 1808). 1808.

Das Intermezzo; oder, Der Landjunker zum ersten Mal in der Residenz (produced Königliches Schauspielhaus, Berlin, 1808). 1809.

Die Erbschaft (produced Königliches Schauspielhaus, Berlin, 1808). 1808.

Herr Gottlieb Merks, der Egoist und Kritikus. 1810; translated as *Egotist and Pseudo-Critic, Herr Gottlieb Merks*, in *The Drama II*, edited by Alfred Bates, 1903.

Der kleine Deklamator (produced Burgtheater, Vienna, 1810). 1809.*

Die englischen Waren (produced Burgtheater, Vienna, 1810). 1809.*

Die Abendstunde (produced Burgtheater, Vienna, 1811). 1809.*

Der Hagestolz und die Körbe (produced Burgtheater, Vienna, 1816). 1809.*

Das Landhaus an der Heerstrasse (produced Königliches Schauspielhaus, Berlin, 1809). 1809.*

Fedor und Pauline (produced Königliches Schauspielhaus, Berlin, 1809).

Die Seeschlacht und die Meerkatze (produced Königliches Schauspielhaus, Berlin, 1809). 1809.

Die kleine Zigeunerin (produced Königliches Schauspielhaus, Berlin, 1809). 1810.

Der verbannte Amor; oder, Die argwöhnischen Eheleute (produced Königliches Schauspielhaus, Berlin, 1809). 1810.

Die Zerstreuten (produced Königliches Schauspielhaus, Berlin, 1810).*

Des Esels Schatten; oder, Der Prozess in Krähwinkel (produced Königliches Schauspielhaus, Berlin, 1809). 1810.*

Der häusliche Zwist (produced Burgtheater, Vienna, 1809). 1810.*

Der blinde Gärtner; oder, Die blühende Aloe (produced Königliches Schauspielhaus, Berlin, 1813). 1809.

Das arabische Pulver, from a play by Holberg. 1810.

Der Harem. 1810.*

Pandorens Büchse. 1810.*

Deodata (produced Königliches Schauspielhaus, Berlin, 1810).

Sorgen ohne Noth und Noth ohne Sorgen (produced Königliches Schauspielhaus, Berlin, 1810). 1810.

Das zugemachte Fenster (produced Königliches Schauspielhaus, Berlin, 1810). 1811.

Die Glücklichen (produced Königliches Schauspielhaus, Berlin, 1810). 1811.*

Der arme Minnesänger. 1811.*

Die Feuerprobe (produced Königliches Schauspielhaus, Berlin, 1813). 1811.*

Blind geladen (produced Königliches Schauspielhaus, Berlin, 1811). 1811; translated as *How to Die for Love*, 1812.

Die Komödiantin aus Liebe, from a play by Goldoni (produced Königliches Schauspielhaus, Berlin, 1811). 1811.*

Max Helfenstein (produced Königliches Schauspielhaus, Berlin, 1811). 1811.

Pächter Feldkümmel von Teippelskirchen: Ein Fastnachtsspiel. 1811.

Der Brief aus Cadix (produced Königliches Schauspielhaus, Berlin, 1811). 1813.

Die alten Liebschaften (produced Burgtheater, Vienna, 1811). 1812.*

Belas Flucht. 1813.

Das Thal von Almeria. 1812.*

Das unsichtbare Mädchen. 1812.*

Der Lügenfeind. 1812.*

Die Belagerung von Saragossa; oder, Pächter Feldkümmels Hochzeitstag. 1811.*

Die Ruinen von Athen, overture by Beethoven. 1812; translated as *The Ruins of Athens*, 1898.

Pächter Feldkümmel von Tippelskirchen. 1812.*

Ungarns erster Wohlthäter, music by Beethoven. 1812.

Die neue Frauenschule, from a play by Augustin-François Creuz and Joseph-Bernard Rosier (produced Burgtheater, Vienna, 1813). 1811.

Die Quäker (produced Königliches Schauspielhaus, Berlin, 1812). 1812.*

Die deutsche Hausfrau (produced Burgtheater, Vienna, 1812). 1813.

Die Entdeckung im Posthaus (produced Hoftheater, Weimar, 1812). 1812.*

Fedora (produced Königliches Schauspielhaus, Berlin, 1812). 1812.*

Die Rosen des Herrn von Malherbes (produced Königliches Schauspielhaus, Berlin, 1812). 1813.*

Die respektabele Gesellschaft (produced Königliches Schauspielhaus, Berlin, 1812). 1813.*

Zwei Nichten für Eine (produced Burgtheater, Vienna, 1812). 1814.*

Der Flussgott Niemen und Noch-Jemand (produced Reval Theatre, Reval, Estonia, 1813). 1812.

Das getheilte Herz. 1813.*

Die beiden kleinen Auvergnaten (produced 1813). 1813.*

Die Masken (produced Burgtheater, Vienna, 1813). 1813.*

Der arme Poet (produced Burgtheater, Vienna, 1813). 1813.*

Rudolph von Habsburg und König Ottkar von Böhmen (produced Königliches Schauspielhaus, Berlin, 1813). 1816.

Der Kosack und der Freiwillige (produced Königliches Schauspielhaus, Berlin, 1813). 1813.*

Grosse Hofversammlung in Paris: Der Abschied aus Cassel. 1813.

Braut und Bräutigam in einer Person. 1814.*

Der Fluch des Römers. 1814.*

Der Käficht. 1814.*

Die Alpenhütte. 1814.*

Die Nachtmütze des Propheten Elias. 1814.*

Die Prinzessin von Cacambo. 1814.*

Noch-Jemands Reise Abenteuer. 1814.

Pervonte; oder, Die Wünsche. 1814.*

Napoleons Reise-Abenteuer. 1814.

Die seltene Krankheit (produced Hoftheater, Weimar, 1821). 1814.*

Hans Max Giesbrecht von der Humpenberg; oder, Die neue Ritterzeit (produced Burgtheater, Vienna, 1815). 1814.*

Der Rehbock; oder, Die Schuldlosen Schuldbewussten (produced Burgtheater, Vienna, 1814). 1815; translated as *The Roebuck; or, Guilty and Not Guilty*, nd.

Der Schawl (produced Burgtheater, Vienna, 1814). 1815.

Die Rückkehr der Freiwilligen; oder, Das patriotische Gelübde (produced Burgtheater, Vienna, 1814). 1815.*

Der Schutzgeist (produced Burgtheater, Vienna, 1814). 1814.

Bäbbel; oder, Aus zweien Übeln des Kleinste. 1815.*

Der schelmische Freier. 1815.*

Wer weiss wozu das gut ist. 1815.*

Die Grossmama (produced Hoftheater, Weimar, 1816). 1815.*

Der Westindier, from a play by Richard Cumberland (produced Königliches Schauspielhaus, Berlin, 1827). 1815.

Des Hasses und der Liebe Rache (produced Königliches Schauspielhaus, Berlin, 1815). 1816.

Colomanns Rache (produced Burgtheater, Vienna, 1815).

Die Uniform des Feldmarschalls Wellington (produced Königliches Schauspielhaus, Berlin, 1815). 1816.*

Alfred. 1816.*

Der hölzerne Säbel; oder, Die Heerschau. 1816.*

Der Küffhäuser-Berg. 1816.*

Der Verschweigene wider Willen; oder, Die Fahrt von Berlin nach Potsdam. 1816.*

Die Brilleninsel. 1816.*

Drei Väter auf einmal. 1816.*

Der Vielwisser (produced Burgtheater, Vienna, 1816). 1817.

Der Edukationsrath (produced Hoftheater, Weimar, 1816). 1816.*

Die Seelenwanderung; oder, Der Schauspieler wider Willen auf eine andere Manier, from a play by J.-M.-T. Badouin d'Aubigny (produced Königliches Schauspielhaus, Berlin, 1816). 1816.*

Der Rothmantel (produced Königliches Schauspielhaus, Berlin, 1816). 1817.

Der Ruf (produced Burgtheater, Vienna, 1816). 1817.*

Der gerade Weg ist der Beste (produced Königliches Schauspielhaus, Berlin, 1816). 1817.*

Der Kapitän Belronde, from a play by Louis Benoît Picard. 1817.

Der Zitherspieler; oder, Das Gaugericht. 1817.*

Die Bestohlenen. 1817.*

Die Wüste. 1817.*

Der deutsche Mann und die vornehmen Leute (produced Königliches Schauspielhaus, Berlin, 1817). 1818.

Das Taschenbuch (produced Burgtheater, Vienna, 1817). 1818.

Der Freimaurer (produced Königliches Schauspielhaus, Berlin, 1817). 1817.*

U.A.W.G.; oder, Die Einladungskarte (produced Burgtheater, Vienna, 1817). 1818.*

Der Spiegel; oder, Lass das bleiben (produced Burgtheater, Vienna, 1817). 1818.*

Der fürstliche Wildfang; oder, Fehler und Liebe, from a play by Jean Nicolas Bouilly. 1818.*

Marie. 1818.*

Hermann und Thusnelde (produced Königliches Schauspielhaus, Berlin, 1819). 1818.*

Die Verkleidungen (produced Königliches Schauspielhaus, Berlin, 1819). 1818.*

Gisela (produced Hoftheater, Weimar, 1818). 1818.

Die Maschine (produced Königliches Schauspielhaus, Berlin, 1818).

Der Selbstmörder. 1819.*

Die entlarvte Fromme (also known as *Ein Pröbchen vom Zeitgeist*) (unfinished). 1819.*

Pfalzgraf Heinrich (unfinished). 1819.*

Verlegenheit und List, from a work by Pigeault-Lebrun. 1819.*

Die Rosenmädchen (produced Königliches Schauspielhaus, Berlin, 1835). 1819.*

Die eifersüchtige Frau (produced Burgtheater, Vienna, 1819). 1819.*

Die Kreuzfahrer, music by Ludwig Spohr (produced Königliches Schauspielhaus, Berlin, 1845). .

Fiction

Erzählungen. 1781.

Die Leiden der Ortenbergischen Familie (2 vols.). 1785–86; translated as *The Sufferings of the Family of Ortenberg* (2 vols.), 1799.

Zaide; oder, Die Entthronung Muhameds des Vierten. 1786; translated as *Zaida; or, The Dethronement of Muhamed IV,* 1803.

Die Geschichte meines Vaters. 1788; translated as *The History of My Father,* 1798.

Ildegerte, Königin von Norwegen. 1788; translated as *Ildegerte, Queen of Norway* (2 vols.), 1798.

Die gefährliche Wette. 1790.

"The Pastor's Daughter" with Other Romances, translated by Henry Colburn. 1806.

Novellettes (translations). 1807.

Leontine (2 vols.). 1808; translated as *Leontina* (3 vols.), 1809.

Verse

Er und Sie. 1781.

Gedichte (2 vols.). 1818.

Memoirs and Letters

Fliegend Blatt. 1787.

Meine Flucht nach Paris im Winter 1790. 1791.

Die jüngsten Kinder meiner Laune (6 vols.). 1793–97.

Über meinen Aufenthalt in Wien und meine erbetene Dienstentlassung. 1799.

Sketch of the Life and Career of August von Kotzebue, translated by Anne Plumptree. 1800.

Das merkwürdigste Jahr meines Lebens (2 vols.). 1801; translated as *The Most Remarkable Year in the Life of August von Kotzebue,* 1802.

Erinnerungen aus Paris im Jahr 1804. 1804; translated as *Travels from Berlin, through Switzerland, to Paris, in the Year 1804* (3 vols.), 1804.

Erinnerungen von einer Reise aus Liefland nach Rom und

Neapel. 1805; translated as *Travels Through Italy, in the Year 1804 and 1805* (4 vols.). 1806.
Briefwechsel, with Carl August Böttiger, edited by B. Maurach. 1987.

Other

Bibliothek der Journale (2 vols.). 1783.
Kleine gesammelte Schriften (4 vols.). 1787–91.
Vom Adel. 1792.
Fragmente über Recensenten-Unfug. 1797.
Kurze und gelassene Antwort auf eine Schmähschrift des Herrn von Masson. 1802.
Kleine Romane, Erzählungen, Anekdoten und Miscellen (6 vols.). 1805–09; translated as *Historical, Literary, and Political Anecdotes, and Miscellanies* (3 vols.), 1807.
Preussens ältere Geschichte (4 vols.). 1808.
Clios Blumenkörbchen (3 vols.). 1811–12.
Geschichte Kaiser Ludwigs IV. 1812.
Geschichten für meine Söhne. 1812.
Die barmherzigen Brüder. 1812
An die Deutschen und an die deutsche Blätter. 1814.
Politische Flugblätter (2 vols.). 1814–16.
Geschichte des deutschen Reiches (4 vols.). 1814–32.
Opern-Almanach für das Jahr 1815. 1815.
Romanesken. 1816.
Chroniken. 1816.
Opern-Almanach für das Jahr 1817. 1817.
Gottes Gericht (for children). 1817.
Switrigail (historical writings). 1820.
Hinterlassene Papiere, edited by L.J. von Knorring. 1821.
Ausgewählte prosaische Schriften (45 vols.). 1842–43.

Editor, *Nachgelassene Schriften des verstorbenen Professor Musäus.* 1791.
Editor, *Der Freymüthige; oder, Ernst und Scherz: Ein Unterhaltungsblatt* (4 vols.). 1804–07.
Editor, *Taschenbuch auf das Jahr 1807.* 1806.
Editor, *Der russische Kriegsgefangene unter den Franzosen*, by Moritz von Kotzebue. 1816.
Editor, *Erzählung des Kapitän Rikord von seiner Fahrt nach den japanischen Küsten.* 1817.

Translator, *Philosophisches Gemälde der Regierung Ludwig des Vierzehnten*, by Joseph de la Lalee. 1791.
Translator, *Felizens Bild*, by G.W. von Derzchavin. 1792.
Translator, *Gedichte des Herrn Staatsraths von Derschawin.* 1793.
Translator, *Geschichten für meine Tochter*, by Jean Nicolas Bouilly. 1811.
Translator, *Bericht an S.M. den König von Schweden.* 1814.
Translator, *Kurze Übersicht der Manufakturen und Fabriken in Russland.* 1815.
Translator, *Briefe*, by Generalin Bertrand. 1816.
Translator, *Betrachtungen über die Lehre und den Geist der Orthodoxen Kirche.* 1817.

*

Criticism

Books:
Charles Rabany, *Kotzebue, sa vie et son temps, ses oeuvres dramatiques*, Paris, 1893.
W. Sellier, *Kotzebue in England* (in German), Leipzig, 1901.
A.W. Holzmann, *Family Relationships in the Dramas of August von Kotzebue*, Princeton, New Jersey, 1935.

Karl-Heinz Klingenberg, *Iffland und Kotzebue als Dramatiker*, Weimar, 1962.
H.A. Glaser, *Das bürgerliche Rührstück*, Stuttgart, 1969.
Gerhard Giesemann, *Kotzebue in Russland*, Leipzig, 1971.
F. Stock, *Kotzebue im literarischen Leben der Goethezeit: Polemik, Kritik, Publikum*, Düsseldorf, 1971.
A. Denis, *La Fortune littéraire et théâtrale de Kotzebue pendant la révolution* (3 vols.), Paris, 1976.
D. Maurer, *August von Kotzebue: Ursachen seines Erfolgs*, Bonn, 1979.
Peter Kaeding, *August von Kotzebue* (biography), Berlin, 1985.
Oscar Mandel, *August von Kotzebue: The Comedy, the Man* (includes *The Good Citizens of Piffelheim*), University Park, Pennsylvania, 1990.

Articles:
A.P. Coleman, "Kotzebue and Russia", in *Germanic Review*, 5, 1930.
A.P. Coleman, "The Siberian Exile of Kotzebue", in *Germanic Review*, 6, 1931.
R.L. Kahn, "Personality Factors in Kotzebue's Work", in *Philological Quarterly*, 30, 1951.
R.L. Kahn, "Kotzebue's Treatment of Social Problems", in *Studies in Philology*, 49, 1952.
R.L. Kahn, "Kotzebue's *Weltanschauung*", in *Modern Language Forum*, 38, 1953.
D.W. Lindsay, "Kotzebue in Scotland, 1792–1813", in *Publications of the English Goethe Society*, 33, 1963.
Alfred Behrmann, "Kotzebue on the American Stage", in *Arcadia*, 4, 1969.
Jack Zipes, "Dunlap, Kotzebue and the Shaping of American Theater: A Re-Evaluation from a Marxist Perspective", in *Early American Literature*, 8, 1974.
Jenny Broekman de Vries, "August von Kotzebue: His Popularity on the Early American Stage", in *Schatzkammer*, 2, 1976.
Harley U. Taylor Jr., "The Dramas of August von Kotzebue on the New York and Philadelphia Stages from 1798 to 1805", in *West Virginia University Philological Papers*, 23, 1977.

*   *   *

For output and box-office success, Kotzebue was probably unrivalled among playwrights writing in the German language. His creative activity coincided with a period of relative stagnation in much of Europe's theatrical life, and his plays, like those of Schiller, may be said to fill a gap in the development of European drama. Both dramatists represent an important transitional phase between the theatre of the pre-revolutionary period and that of the 19th century. But Kotzebue operates on a lower intellectual and aesthetic plane than his greater German contemporary; despite repeated efforts on his part, his hopes of becoming accepted in the pantheon of German literature were vitiated by deficiencies which, in strictly theatrical terms, may be identified with the very strengths and qualities that made him so popular and famous. He was a middle-brow playwright *par excellence*.

Kotzebue established his reputation with a number of plays which made him the darling of theatrical Europe from 1789, the year of the French Revolution, to the period which followed the fall of Napoleon in 1815. *Menschenhass und Reue* (*Misanthropy and Repentance*, known in Britain as *The Stranger*) took audiences by storm in 1789. It illustrates a recipe which Kotzebue made very much his own. An erring, but sorry and kind-hearted woman, who has retired to the obscurity of a country retreat, is reunited with her withdrawn, embittered, and separated husband through a stratagem which involves their little boy and girl appearing at the very last minute to say "Papa, Mama, we love you!"—at which their parents fall into one another's arms as the curtain falls. Tragedy, neatly averted by ploys associated with comedy, children to tug at the heart-strings, topical references aptly included and contemporary manners unobtrusively observed, and, above all, two roles of considerable theatrical potential in Eulalia and her husband, Count Meinau—these factors, together with uncomplicated language that lends itself readily to translation, ensured international appeal and make the play a notable example of what audiences of the period most enjoyed. Its London premiere, starring Kemble and Mrs Siddons, and produced by Sheridan at Drury Lane in 1798, played to packed houses, inaugurating a tradition of annual revivals there until 1842.

Kotzebue also tried his hand at many other types of drama. *Self-Sacrifice*, in which a bankrupt London merchant attempts to end his life by drowning, in order to liberate his young wife who only married him for his money, shows Kotzebue pioneering what was later to become known as the problem-play. *Die Spanier in Peru; oder, Rolla's Tod* (*Rolla; or, The Spaniards in Peru*) is, in effect, a rediscovery of the potential of baroque heroic drama to provide entertainment of a melodramatic kind for audiences of the Romantic period.

This fertile vein is even better represented by his earlier, and once much admired, drama *Die Sonnenjungfrau* (*The Virgin of the Sun*); here Kotzebue combines an extensive range of motifs to create a stage entertainment which, for a while, put contemporaries in mind of Shakespeare. Rolla, the lonely misunderstood outsider, loves Cora, the chaste yet sensual Inca priestess; affecting scenes of recognition and reunion take place in exotic Peruvian settings where cultures and values clash, and fashionable notions of the noble savage are highlighted in the direst circumstances, as the sensitive hero and heroine struggle to achieve their freedom, their guiding principle being that reason can be reconciled with sentiment to bring about the triumph of humane values. Such ingredients endow the play with a degree of at least historical interest which hardly justifies its present neglect. But perhaps its sheer variety of theme and treatment is too rich in relation to the prose text, which strains after grandeur, occasionally achieves it, but all too often lapses into fustian. When Kotzebue attempted something more controlled and literary, as in his historical verse dramas or *Octavia*, a reworking of the Antony and Cleopatra story, the result tends to oscillate between pretentious neo-Shakespearean or neo-classical grandiloquence and ludicrous bathos.

Kotzebue avoided such perils when he turned his attention to comedy. In this domain his efforts are appealing, if somewhat tame and lacking in rumbustious humour. The most successful of his comedies, and the ones that have held the stage longest, are "The Two Klingsbergs", in which a father and his son engage in amusing amorous rivalry, and especially *Die deutschen Kleinstädter* (The German Small-Town Dwellers, translated as *The Good Citizens of Piffelheim*) an amiable essay in social satire which sends up typical German provincial middle-class foibles with a gentle irony and deft deployment of comic stage techniques. In its mild and unpretentious way, this latter comedy may now be seen as perhaps the best of his many plays, and a worthy product of the golden age of German literature.

—Peter Skrine

———

KRASIŃSKI, Zygmunt. Born into a Polish military family in Paris, 19 February 1812. Grew up on family estate, Opinogóra, Poland. Educated at a lycée; University of Warsaw, until 1829; University of Geneva, c. 1830. Short military service. Married Countess Elzbieta Branicki in 1843. Lived outside Poland after 1829; travelled to St. Petersburg, Russia, with his father, 1832; travelled to Rome; spent 1843–44 in Poland, but returned to Italy on account of illness; also lived in France. Published many of his works anonymously. His two plays, although published in 1835 and 1836, were only produced professionally in the 20th century. Died in Paris, 23 February 1859.

Works

Collections

"The Undivine Comedy" and Other Poems, translated by M.W. Cook. 1875.
Pisma [Works] (8 vols.), edited by Jan Czubek. 1912; edited by L. Piwinski (7 vols.), 1931.
Dziela literacki (literary works) (3 vols.). 1973.

Stage Works

Nieboska komedia (produced Cracow, 1902). 1835; translated as *The Undivine Comedy*, in *"The Undivine Comedy" and Other Poems*, 1875; several subsequent translations under same title.
Irydion (produced Łodz, 1908). 1836; translated as *Iridion*, 1927.

Fiction

Pan trzech pagórków. 1828.
Grób rodziny Reichstalów. 1828.
Sen Elzbiety Pileckiej. 1829.
Wladislaw Herman i dwór jego (3 vols.). 1830.
Agay-Han. 1834.

Verse

Modlitewnik. 1837.
Noc letnia. 1841.
Pokusa. 1841.
Przedswit. 1843.
Psalmy przyszlosci. 1845; augmented edition, 1848.
Ostatni. 1847.
Dzien dzisiejszy. 1847.
Psalm zalu. 1848.
Psalm Dobrej Woli. 1848.
Niedokonczony poemat. 1860.

Memoirs and Letters

Lettres a Montalembert et . . . Lamartine. 1847.
Briefe. 1860.
Briefe (3 vols). 1882–87.

Other volumes of letters: to H. Reeve (2 vols.), 1902; to A. Scheffer, 1909; to S.E. Kozmian, 1912; to A. von Cieszkowski (2 vols.), 1912; to D. Potocka (3 vols.), 1930–38; to his father, 1963; to J. Lubomirski, 1965; to A. Soltan, 1970; to K. Gaszynski, 1971.

Other

Trzy mysli Henryka Ligenzy.   1840.
O stanowisku Polski z Bozych i ludzkich wzgledów (3 vols.).
    1841.

*

Criticism

Books:
J. Kallenbach, *Zygmunt Krasinski* (2 vols.), Lemberg, 1904.
M.M. Gardner, *The Anonymous Poet of Poland: A Life of Zygmunt Krasinski*, Cambridge, 1919.
W. Lendnecki (ed.), *Zygmunt Krasinski: Romantic Universalist: An International Tribute*, New York, 1964.

* * *

Zygmunt Krasiński came from a rich aristocratic family in Poland. His father, Wincenty, was a conservative general in the army of the Congress Kingdom and supported the Tsar and Poland's Russian rulers even during the November Uprising of 1830. Young Zygmunt was sent abroad to finish his higher studies and it was in Geneva that he began writing plays that reflected the major philosophical and social questions of the age. While, to avoid embarrassment for his family, Krasinski first published his works anonymously (as the "Nameless Poet of Poland"), his entire mature life was characterized by a struggle between his conflicting loyalties — whether to side with his father or with the cause of national independence, the fatherland. Krasiński made his home abroad (mostly in Germany), wrote poetry, a vast number of letters and two plays which — though unstaged in his lifetime — belong to the best achievements of Polish Romantic drama.

Although of the plays, *Irydion* (*Iridion*) was conceived first, the final version of *Nieboska komedia* (*The Undivine Comedy*) came to be published first in 1835 in Paris. The latter is a poetic drama in four "parts" (acts) which deals with one of the most crucial issues of the modern age beginning with the French Revolution — the struggle of the "haves" and the "have-nots", that of aristocracy with revolutionary democracy. The background to this historic conflict is provided by the career of Count Henryk. He is first shown to be a failure in private life for he is much more interested in poetry (symbolized by a demonic maiden) than in domestic happiness with his newly wedded wife. In fact, he leaves his wife and is almost killed by the Maiden who wants to lure him to a precipice. At the end of Act I, Henryk's wife dies with the wish that their son Orcio should become a poet — the wish is fulfilled, though Orcio remains incurably blind. The first two acts of the play are very sketchy, but they lead up to the powerful Act III, not unlike Juliusz Slowacki's play *Kordian*.

In one of the scenes of Act II Count Henryk declares: "Farewell, Mother Nature! I leave you, to become a man. I go to fight with my brethren". Abandoning all other myths of Romanticism, Henryk tests the last one: that of progress in society.

The third act takes place some time in the undefined future when the rebellious masses have managed to take over most of the civilized world. Only the Castle of Holy Trinity holds out in a vain attempt to stem the tide. Here all the rich and mighty (aristocrats, bankers, bishops) assemble; down in the valley the vast coalition of the poor and their radical leaders set up their camp to lay siege to the castle. Henryk, at night and in disguise, visits the camp and is appalled by the wrath of the masses and their thirst for revenge. All the same, Krasiński observes and indicates certain latent conflicts between the simple participants of the struggle, their ideologues, and the military "technicians". Henryk's tour of the camp is followed by a return visit by Pankracy, the leader of the revolutionaries, to the castle: his confrontation with Count Henryk (who later is elected Commander-in-Chief by the beleaguered "aristocrats") produces some of the best scenes in the play. The values of both leaders are shown to be flawed: Henryk's concept of "honour" is hopelessly anachronistic, and Pankracy's promise of a radiant future is utopian and clearly unrealizable.

The Undivine Comedy nearly ends with the victory of the revolutionary mobs. Count Henryk prefers to commit suicide at the moment when they take the castle by storm. Nonetheless, the victorious Pankracy is suddenly smitten by a vision of Julian the Apostate: "Galilee vicisti!" (You have won, O Christ!). The message of this unexpected scene is fairly clear: no "godless" revolution can be truly victorious; the new age will not dawn until it finds a way to reconcile democracy with Christianity.

Staged for the first time in our century, *The Undivine Comedy* has been steadily gaining topicality with the rise of (basically anti-Christian) mass totalitarian movements. Mickiewicz, in the middle of the 19th century, regarded it as "the highest achievement of the Slavonic theatre"; Czesław Miłosz called it, more recently, "a truly pioneering work in its treatment of an unusual subject and in its visual elements". Although several English translations exist, the play has been, on the whole, ignored outside Poland, even by directors otherwise interested in the Polish theatre.

Krasiński's other play *Irydion*, published in 1836, takes place in imperial Rome in the 3rd century AD. It is the story of a half-Greek, half-Germanic hero, Iridion ("the son of the rainbow") who is bent on the destruction of corrupt, decadent Rome. To achieve this aim he is ready to sacrifice his sister Elsinoe to the lust of the Emperor Heliogabalus. His plot to subvert and then destroy Rome fails in the end because of the Christians' reluctance to take up arms against their rulers. *Iridion* was written as an indirect response to Mickiewicz's influential poem *Konrad Wallenrod*, a work which advocated revenge against the enemy by any means, including morally reprehensible methods. Krasiński's play is written in an "ornate arhythmical, utterly Romantic prose", as described by Miłosz, partly modelled on Chateaubriand, and while it enjoyed some popularity in the 19th century, it has not been resurrected on the stage in contemporary Poland.

—George Gömöri

See also *Volume 1* entry on *The Undivine Comedy*.

———

KROETZ, Franz Xaver. Born in Munich, Germany, 25 February 1946. Educated at high school, 1956–61; studied acting and direction, in Munich, 1961–63, and with the Max-Reinhardt-Seminar, Vienna, 1964. Has a daughter (born 1974) and a son (born 1975). Worked as acting tutor, and in supermarket, Munich, 1964; first theatrical job, at the Büchner-Theater, Munich, 1965; brief employments as nurse, gardener, truckdriver, and at theatres in Paderborn and Munich, 1966–67; first stage adaptations produced 1968;

director, Ludwig-Thoma-Bühne, Rottach-Egern, 1969; first plays published 1971; joined the DKP (German Communist Party), 1972; first major success, *Stallerhof*, produced 1972; attended "World Congress for Peace", Moscow, 1973; first play production in East Germany (of *Oberösterreich*), 1973; purchased a farm in Kirchberg bei Altenmarkt, 1974; co-founder, Franz-Xaver-Kroetz Dramatik publishing house, 1975; DKP candidate for Bundestag elections, 1976; resumed acting (after a break of eight years) from 1977, often in his own plays; left the DKP, 1980; acted in *Kir Royal* television series, 1987; reported on the Seoul Olympic Games for *Die Welt*, 1987. Has directed many productions of his own plays for stage, television, and radio. Member, Society of German Authors, 1972–83. Recipient: Ludwig-Thoma Medal, 1970; Fontane Prize, 1972; Critics' Prize (West Berlin), 1973; Drama Prize (Hanover), 1974; Wilhelmine-Lübke Prize, 1975; Drama Prize (Mühlheim), 1976; Adolf-Grimme Prize, 1987.

Works

Collections

Drei Stücke (includes *Männersache; Heimarbeit; Hartnäckig*). 1971.
Vier Stücke (includes *Stallerhof; Wunschkonzert; Geisterbahn; Lieber Fritz*). 1972.
Oberösterreich; Dolomitenstadt Lienz; Maria Magdalena; Münchner Kindl. 1974.
Gesammelte Stücke. 1975.
Stücke. 1975 (DDR publication).
Reise ins Glück; Wunschkonzert; Weitere Aussichten . . . 1975.
Weitere Aussichten: Ein Lesebuch (includes some texts of stage, television, and radio plays, with other material) edited by Thomas Thieringer. 1976; as *Weitere Aussichten . . . Neue Texte* (DDR publication), 1976; as *Ein Lesebuch: Stücke; Polemik; Gespräche; Filme; Hörspiele; Analysen*, 1982.
Drei neue Stücke (includes *Mensch Meier; Der stramme Max; Wer durchs Laub geht*). 1979.
Stücke, edited by Jochen Ziller. 1981 (DDR publication).
Nicht Fisch nicht Fleisch; Verfassungsfeinde; Jumbo Track. 1981.
Frühe Stücke, frühe Prosa. 1983.
Stücke (4 vols.). 1989.

Stage Works

Julius Caesar, from the play by Shakespeare (produced Büchner-Theater, Munich, 1968).
Oblomov, from a novel by Ivan Goncharov (produced Büchner-Theater, Munich, 1968).
Hilfe, ich werde geheiratet (produced Ludwig-Thoma-Bühne, Rottach-Egern, 1969). In *Weitere Aussichten . . .*, 1976.
Wildwechsel (produced Städtische Bühnen, Dortmund, 1971). 1973.
Heimarbeit (produced Kammerspiele, Munich, 1971). In *Drei Stücke*, 1971; translated as *Homework*, in *Gambit*, 39–40, 1982.
Michis Blut (produced Pro T., Munich, 1971). In *Neues deutsches Theater*, 1971; translated as *Michi's Blood*, in *"Farmyard" and Four Other Plays*, 1976.
Hartnäckig (produced Kammerspiele, Munich, 1971). In *Drei Stücke*, 1971.
Männersache (produced Landestheater, Darmstadt, 1972).

In *Drei Stücke*, 1971; translated as *Men's Business* in *"Farmyard" and Four Other Plays*, 1976; revised version, as *Ein Mann, ein Wörterbuch* (produced Atelier am Naschmarkt, Vienna, 1977); translated as *A Man, a Dictionary*, in *"Farmyard" and Four Other Plays*, 1976; revised German version, as *Wer durchs Laub geht* (produced Podiumbühne, Marburg, 1981), in *Drei neue Stücke*, 1979; translated as *Through the Leaves*, 1983.
Stallerhof (produced Deutsches Schauspielhaus, Hamburg, 1972). In *Vier Stücke*, 1972; translated as *Farmyard*, in *"Farmyard" and Four Other Plays*, 1976; also translated as *Stallerhof*, with plays by other authors, in *Shakespeare the Sadist (Bauer); Bremer Coffee (Fassbinder); My Foot My Tutor (Handke); Stallerhof (Kroetz)*, 1977.
Geisterbahn (produced Atelier am Naschmarkt, Vienna, 1975). In *Vier Stücke*, 1972.
Lieber Fritz (produced Landestheater, Darmstadt, 1975). In *Vier Stücke*, 1972.
Wunschkonzert (produced Württembergisches Staatstheater, Stuttgart, 1973). In *Vier Stücke*, 1972; translated as *Request Concert*, in *"Farmyard" and Four Other Plays*, 1976.
Dolomitenstadt Lienz (produced Schauspielhaus Kammerspiele, Bochum, 1972). In *Oberösterreich . . .* (collection), 1974.
Globales Interesse (produced Bayerische Staatsschauspiel Studio-Theater, Munich, 1972).
Oberösterreich (produced Städtische Bühnen, Zimmertheater, Heidelberg, 1972). In *Oberösterreich . . .* (collection), 1974.
Maria Magdalena from a play by Hebbel (produced Städtische Bühnen, Heidelberg, 1973). In *Oberösterreich . . .* (collection), 1974.
Münchner Kindl (produced Theater K im Schwabinger Bräu, Munich, 1973). In *Oberösterreich . . .* (collection), 1974.
Sterntaler, with Peter Zwetkoff (produced Staatstheater, Braunschweig, 1977). In *Stücke*, 1975.
Weitere Aussichten (produced Städtisches Theater, Karl-Marx-Stadt, 1975). In *Reise ins Glück . . .* (collection), 1975.
Reise ins Glück (produced Theater am Neumarkt, Zurich, 1976). In *Reise ins Glück . . .* (collection), 1975.
Das Nest (produced Modernes Theater, Munich, 1975). In *Weitere Aussichten . . .*, 1976.
Die Wahl fürs Leben, from the radio play (produced Theater Rechts der Isar, Munich, 1980).
Herzliche Grüsse aus Grado, from the radio play *Inklusive* (produced Schauspielhaus, Düsseldorf, 1976).
Verfassungsfeinde (produced Staatstheater, Dresden, 1977). In *Theater der Zeit*, 12, 1976; in book form, in *Nicht Fisch nicht Fleisch . . .* (collection), 1981.
Agnes Bernauer, from the play by Hebbel (produced Leipziger Theater, Leipzig, 1977). In *Weitere Aussichten . . .*, 1976.
Mensch-Meier (produced in Brazil, 1978; produced in Germany at the Schauspielhaus, Düsseldorf, 1978). In *Mensch Meier . . .* (collection), 1979; translated as *Mensch Meier A Play of Everyday Life*, 1983.
Der stramme Max (produced Ruhrfestspiele, Recklinghausen, 1980). In *Drei neue Stücke*, 1979.
Bilanz, from his radio play (produced Torturmtheater, Sommerhausen am Main, 1980).
Nicht Fisch nicht Fleisch (produced Schauspielhaus, Düsseldorf, 1981). In *Nicht Fisch nicht Fleisch . . .* (collection), 1981.
Jumbo-Track, with Floh de Cologne (libretto; produced Landestheater, Tübingen, 1983). In *Nicht Fisch nicht Fleisch . . .* (collection), 1981.

Gute Besserung, from the radio play (produced Theater K, Munich, 1982).

Als Zeus zum letzten Mal kam; oder, Die Nacht der weissen Segel. In *Frühe Stücke, frühe Prosa* 1983.

In Memorandum Günter Opperman. In *Frühe Stücke, frühe Prosa*, 1983.

Der Soldat. In *Frühe Stücke, frühe Prosa*, 1983.

Furcht und Hoffnung der BRD, with Alexandra Weinert-Purucker (produced Schauspielhaus, Bochum, and Schauspielhaus, Dresden, 1984). 1984.

Der Weihnachtstod. In *Düsseldorfer Debatte*, 4, 1984.

Bauern sterben (produced Kammerspiele, Munich, 1985). 1984.

Beppi im Glück (produced 1985).

Der Nusser (produced Residenztheater, Munich, 1986). In *Theater heute*, 5, 1986.

Screenplays

Wildwechsel, 1973.

Television Plays

Herzliche Grüsse aus Grado, 1972; *Der Mensch Adam Deigl und die Obrigkeit*, from a work by Josef Martin Bauer, 1972; *Maria Magdalena*, 1974; *Weitere Aussichten*, 1975; *Muttertag*, 1975; *Verfassungsfeinde*, 1976; *Das Nest*, 1976 and 1979 (different versions); *Oberösterreich*, 1976; *Heimat*, 1980 (published in *Weitere Aussichten . . .* collection, 1976); *Menschmeier*, 1982.

Radio Plays

Inklusive, 1972 (published in *Weitere Aussichten . . .* collection, 1976); *Bilanz*, 1972 (published in *Stücke*, 1975); *Globales Interesse*, 1972; *Gute Besserung*, 1972 (published in *Stücke*, 1975); *Die Wahl fürs Leben*, 1973 (published in *Weitere Aussichten . . .* collection, 1976); *Oberösterreich*, 1973; *Reise ins Glück*, 1975; *Maria Magdalena*, 1980; *Nicht Fisch nicht Fleisch*, 1982.

Fiction

Der Mondscheinknecht. 1981.

Der Mondscheinknecht: Fortsetzung (sequel). 1983.

Tiroler Elegien. In *Frühe Stücke, frühe Prosa*, 1983.

Koreanische Frühling. In *Frühe Stücke, frühe Prosa*, 1983.

Other

Chiemgauer Geschichten: Bayerische Menschen erzählen. 1977.

Weitere Aussichten: Ein Lesebuch, edited by Thomas Thieringer. 1976; as *Weitere Aussichten . . . Neue Texte*, 1976 (DDR publication); *Ein Lesebuch: Stücke; Polemik; Gespräche; Filme; Hörspiele; Analysen*, 1982.

Fruhe Stücke, frühe Prosa. 1983.

Nicaragua Tagebuch. 1985.

Mythos und Politik: Über die magischen Gesten der Rechten, with Peter Glotz. 1985.

Brasilieren-Peru-Aufzeichnungen. 1991.

*

Bibliographies

Volker Panzer, "Auswahlbibliographie zu Franz Xaver Kroetz", in *Text und Kritik*, 57, 1978.

Michael Töteberg, "Bibliographie Franz Xaver Kroetz", in *Franz Xaver Kroetz*, edited by Otto Riewaldt, Frankfurt, 1985.

Criticism

Books:

Evalouise Panzner, *Franz Xaver Kroetz und seine Rezeption*, Stuttgart, 1976.

Rolf-Peter Carl, *Franz Xaver Kroetz*, Munich, 1978.

Heinz Ludwig Arnold (ed.) *Franz Xaver Kroetz*, Munich, 1978.

Ursula Schregel, *Neue deutsche Stücke im Spielplan: Am Beispiel von Franz Xaver Kroetz*, Berlin, 1980.

Richard W. Blevins, *Franz Xaver Kroetz: The Emergence of a Political Playwright*, New York, 1983.

Denis Calandra, *New German Dramatists*, London, 1983 (Macmillan Modern Dramatists series).

Donna L. Hoffmeister, *The Theater of Confinement: Language and Survival in the Milieu Plays of Marieluise Fleisser and Franz Xaver Kroetz*, Columbia, South Carolina, 1983.

Otto Riewaldt (ed.), *Franz Xaver Kroetz*, Frankfurt, 1985.

Gérard Thériot, *Franz Xaver Kroetz et le nouveau théâtre populaire*, Bern, 1987.

Moray McGowan, "Subject, Politics, Theatre—Reflections on Franz Xaver Kroetz", in *A Radical Stage: Theatre in Germany in the 1970s and 1980s*, edited by W.G. Sebald, Oxford, 1988.

Renate Usmiani, *The Theatre of Frustration: Super Realism in the Dramatic Work of F.X. Kroetz and Michel Tremblay*, New York, 1990.

Ingeborg C. Walther, *The Theater of Franz Xaver Kroetz*, New York, 1990.

Articles:

Dragan Klaic, "The Theatre of Franz Xaver Kroetz", in *Yale/Theatre*, vol.6 no.1, 1974.

Hugh-Rorrison, "Franz Xaver Kroetz Checklist", in *Theatrefacts*, vol.3 no.2, 1976.

Susan L. Cocalis, "*Mitleid* and *Engagement*: Compassion and/or Political Commitment in the Dramatic Works of Franz Xaver Kroetz", in *Colloquia Germanica*, vol. 14 no.3, 1981.

Jeannette R. Malkin, "'Think What You Are Saying': Verbal Politics in the Early Plays of Handke and Kroetz", in *Modern Drama*, 33, 1990.

*   *   *

Franz Xaver Kroetz, one of the most frequently played modern German dramatists, is also one of the most controversial. His earliest work in the 1950's drew heavily on the theatre of Eugène Ionesco and Samuel Beckett, but theatrical collaboration with Rainer Werner Fassbinder opened up for him the folk-theatre traditions of his native Bavaria and of Austria, portraying peasant and working-class life. Kroetz's portrayals, however, have an even harsher socio-critical edge than those of modern precursors like Marieluise Fleisser or Ödön von Horváth. Kroetz is not concerned with depicting a cosy folksiness or a sentimental or satirical "superiority" of ordinary folk to their "betters." As a sometime member of the German Communist Party and an admirer of Bertolt Brecht, Kroetz focuses on the socially conditioned latent violence of the underprivileged. As a result, his writing often seems to sail perilously close to melodramatic sensationalism.

In fact—following Brecht to some extent—he is primarily concerned with the way in which injustices in the system show themselves most seriously in their effects on personal relationships, and very directly in linguistic deprivation. Kroetz's characters do not communicate effectively, not because they consciously or deliberately retreat into themselves, nor simply because they are often illiterate. He shows them as having no grasp of or access to the wider social causes of their misery, and for this reason it is often hard for Kroetz to indicate what those causes actually are. Unlike Georg Büchner for instance, another precursor, Kroetz does not depict direct class oppression, and a number of his plays hover rather uncomfortably between angled social criticism, where characters are seen as victims of socialization processes, and the merely anthropological or pictorial. In this aesthetic problem, as in its everyday proletarian realism, Kroetz's work is reminiscent of Naturalism nearly a century earlier.

Nevertheless, his use of language especially encourages the reader to probe more deeply. He is not in fact attempting a naturalistic phonographic record, and himself states that there is to be just a South German flavour in performance of his dialogue; that is, the realist/illusionist aspect of theatre is present, but very carefully managed and directed. That is evident in his use of setting: there is frequently a pointed contrast between the apparently bucolic or cosily familial context, given in outline, and the action which is violent and crude. Thus Kroetz seems to draw our attention to received notions of the "natural" and "unnatural", showing that what we might deem uncivilized, even bestial, is in another sense paradoxically "normal", because induced in the underprivileged by a society of which they are the helpless victims. It is society that brutalizes, and Kroetz's almost minimalist stage style starkly reveals that what a bourgeois audience might class as the "exceptional" are the bare and inescapable facts of life for the deprived.

A striking example of his work is *Wildwechsel* (Wild Animals), where a 13-year-old girl from an apparently normal working-class home gets pregnant and induces her boyfriend to attempt the murder of her father, who has threatened them with prosecution. What at first may seem a tale of merely pathological brutality is in fact a study of emotional deprivation within a family context ruled by unthinking response to both physical urges and social stereotypes. "Shocking" details, like showing the father urinating on stage, set precisely the level of unreflecting, reactive behaviour typical of the family. They simply accept incongruous external models, whether for their moral sanctions or their sentimental ideals. The text is a powerful study of reliance on cliché at all levels, from buying lotto tickets because otherwise watching the Saturday-night television draw is boring, to defining parent/child relationships. Violence is always close to the surface, as a substitute for the differentiated self-awareness and verbal control not open to these poorly educated, media-dependent characters. The unseen Court, to which the "lovers" are led at the end, is merely an externalization of their total subjection to a depersonalized lifestyle. To such people the fixed norms and rules of society are not a guarantee of freedom, but another form of oppression. If the play has a weakness, it is that the degree to which broader socio-economic underprivilege rather than mere conformism produces this clichéd linguistic prison remains a shade unclear, though there are many hints of a class-typical uncertainty in a fast-changing world, as of the pressures of having only just enough to live "decently".

In later plays Kroetz is more explicitly analytical, particularly where he deals with peasant life. He deconstructs the traditional bourgeois idyllic vision of country life, showing the amputation of personality that results from unremitting hard physical labour. Relative poverty and resultant economic dependence, emotional backwardness and undeveloped social skills, inherited prejudices and crude notions of "normality" defined by lack of education and the central importance of "usefulness": all these are causes of the brutality that derives from the sheer struggle to survive within a social system of "care" that categorizes just as crudely. Such figures can only respond to the mechanics of society with self-mutilation.

Many works continue and adapt these themes, with obvious Brechtian influence as Kroetz became increasingly Marxist in his literary-theoretical views, and this led him away from conventional theatre for a time to work with smaller, often working-class groups. His political views on Germany after the end of the socialist-liberal coalition are powerfully evident in *Furcht und Hoffnung der BRD* (Fear and Hope in the Federal Republic), whose title alone is a tribute to Brecht. He also attacks the emptiness of bourgeois ideology by confronting the 19th-century tradition of *Bürgerliches Trauerspiel* (Bourgeois Tragedy) in plays such as *Maria Magdalena*. Subsequent works have shown him seeking stylistic renewal, experimenting with a mixture of the real and surreal in *Nicht Fisch nicht Fleisch* (Neither Fish Nor Fowl), but his most striking works remain his direct portrayals of lower-class life, into whose effective theatricality some of Kroetz's own experience as an actor has perhaps fed.

—Mary E. Stewart

See also *Volume 1* entry on *Farmyard*.

———

KUAN Han-ch'ing.   See **GUAN Hanqing.**

———

KUBO Sakae. Born in Sapporo, Hokkaidō, Japan, 28 December 1900. Educated at First High School, Tokyo, to 1919; Tokyo University, studying German literature and drama (under Kaoru Osani), 1923–26, degree 1926. Began publishing poetry in *Hototogisu* and *Mizugame* magazines; joined the literary department of the Osani's Tsukiji Shōkegijō [Tsukiji Little Theatre], 1926–28; dramaturg and director for various left-wing troupes, including New Tsukiji Theatre and Sayoku [Left-Wing] Theatre; co-founder, Shinkyō Troupe, 1934: forced by Government to disband, 1940; lecturer, Senshū University, 1939–40; imprisoned for his left-wing views during World War II; began editing his collected works, 1949. Also translated Goethe's *Faust* and about 30 German expressionist plays by Kaiser, Hauptmann, Wedekind, Toller, and others. Committed suicide, 15 March 1958.

Works (selected)

Collections

Kubo Sakae senshū (7 vols.; collected works).   1949–52.
Kubo Sakae zenshū (12 vols.; collected works).   1961–63.

Stage Works

Shinsetsu Kokusenya gassen.   1930.
Yoakemae [Before Dawn] (produced 1934).
Goryōkaku kessho [Blood Petition from Goryōkaku Castle].
    1933.
Kazanbaichi (produced by the Shinkyō Troupe, Tokyo,
    1938).   In *Sincho,* 1937–38; in book form, in *Shōwa bun-
    gakū zenshū,* 1953; translated as *Land of Volcanic Ash,*
    1986.
Ringoen nikki [Apple Orchard Diary].   1947.
Nihon no kishō [The Climate in Japan].   1953.

Fiction

Noborigama.   1952.

Other

Osanai Kaoru (biography).   1947.

* * *

Attracted to the activities of the Tsukiji Little Theatre,
Japan's first theatre devoted to the production of modern
plays, which had been founded in 1924, Kubo entered the
literature department of the troupe in March 1926 and
worked under its principal director, Osanai Kaoru. He subsequently translated more than 30 modern German works,
including plays by Kaiser, Wedekind, and Hauptmann. His
crowning achievement as a translator was his rendition of
Goethe's *Faust.*

After the Tsukiji troupe dissolved, following Osanai's
death in 1928, Kubo emerged as a leading theorist and dramatist of the Marxist contingent. He articulated his philosophy
in his manifesto written in 1934:

> Our realism captures the innermost truths of man and
> society and, cutting through all facades, shows how—
> while antagonistic, contradictory, and interacting in com-
> plex ways—they develop toward a higher stage of unity.
> Without reducing them to stereotypes and without vul-
> garization, we clarify them in terms of the typical form of
> [class] conflict and formulate them with artistry and style.

Kazanbaichi (*Land of Volcanic Ash*) is the monumental
work in which Kubo tried to realize this ideal. The play is
widely regarded as the culmination of the pre-war movement
to establish a realistic theatre in Japan. It strongly influenced
postwar playwrights like Kinoshita Junji. Seven acts long (and
more than 250 pages long in its English translation), the play
takes two nights to perform. Despite its length and complexity, however, the play has been performed repeatedly,
first in 1938 and then in 1948 and 1961.

Land of Volcanic Ash describes in exhaustive detail the life
of a farming community in rural Hokkaido. In it Kubo tried
to achieve "a unification of scientific theory and poetic form".
The main thrust of the story concerns Amamiya Akira, an
agronomist who heads the local agricultural extension station.
In his research, Amamiya discovers that the fertilizer developed and marketed by the local flax mill is inappropriate for
the volcanic soil that predominates in the region. His struggle
to have his discovery recognized reveals the conflicting class-
and personal-interests that comprise local society and the way
in which even the most seemingly insignificant people are
integrated into the system of Japanese militarism and global
capitalism.

Kubo was imprisoned twice during World War II. In the
post-war period he produced a biography of Osanai Kaoru
and two major plays, *Ringoen nikki* (Apple Orchard Diary,
1947) and *Nihon no Kishō* (The Climate in Japan, 1953).

Kubo's work has been widely praised. Critic Yoshimoto
Takaaki has cited it as the only successful attempt at socialist
realism in Japan. Eric J. Gangloff has written that in *Land of
Volcanic Ash,* "we find the first real struggle of a socialist
dramatist to master the art of characterization", and political
scientist Maruyama Masao has emphasized Kubo's importance as one of the few defenders of the critical spirit in the
years immediately prior to the War.

—David G. Goodman

———

KUNDERA, Milan.   Born in Brno, Czechoslovakia, 1 April
1929. Educated at Charles University, Prague; Academy of
Music and Dramatic Arts Film Faculty, Prague, 1956.
Married Věra Hrabánková in 1967. Joined the Communist
Party, 1948, expelled 1950, but re-admitted, 1956. Assistant
professor, teaching world literature, Film School, Academy
of Music and Dramatic Arts, Prague, 1958–69. First play,
Majitelé Klíču [The Owners of the Keys], produced 1962; fell
into official disfavour, and was dismissed from teaching post;
left for France, 1975; professor of comparative literature,
University of Rennes, France, 1975–1980; stripped of Czech
citizenship, 1979, and took French citizenship, 1981;
Professor, École des Hautes Études, Paris, since 1980.
Member of the editorial board, *Literární Noviny,* 1956–59,
1963–68, and *Literární Listy,* 1968–69. Recipient: Writers'
Publishing House Prize, 1961, 1969; Klement Lukeš Prize,
1963; Union of Czechoslovak Writers' Prize, 1968; Médicis
Prize (France), 1973; Mondello Prize (Italy), 1978; Common-
wealth Award (USA), 1981; Europa Prize, 1982; Jerusalem
Prize, 1984; Académie Française Critics Prize, 1987; Nelly
Sachs Prize, 1987; Osterichischeve State Prize, 1987.
Honorary doctorate: University of Michigan, Ann Arbor,
1983. Member, American Academy.

Works

Stage Works

Majitelé klíču [The Owners of the Keys] (produced National
    Theatre, Prague, 1962).   1962.
Dvě uši dvě svatby [Two Ears and Two Weddings] (produced
    as *Ptákovina* [Cock-Up], Theatre on the Balustrade,
    Prague, 1969).   1968.
Jakub a pán (produced Drama Studio of Ústi nad Labem,
    Prague, 1974).   Published in French translation as *Jacques
    et son maître* 1981; translated as *Jacques and His Master,*
    1985.

Screenplays

Nikdo se nebude smát [No Laughing Matter], 1965; *Zert* [The
Joke], from his own novel, with Jaromil Jires, 1968; *Já
Truchlivý Bůh* [I the Sad God], 1969.

Fiction

Směšné lásky [Laughable Loves]; *Druhy sešit směšných lásek*
[A Second Book of Laughable Loves]; *Třeti sešit směšých*

lásek [A Third Book of Laughable Loves] (3 vols.).   1963–69; revised and collected as *Směšné lásek*, 1970; translated as *Laughable Loves*, 1974.

Žert.   1967; translated as *The Joke*, 1969; revised edition, 1992.

La Vie est ailleurs.   1973; translated as *Life is Elsewhere*, 1974; Czech edition, as *Život de jinde* (Toronto), 1979.

La Valse aux adieux.   1976; as *Epilog* ("samizdat" publication), 1976?; translated as *The Farewell Party*, 1976; Czech edition, as *Valčík na rozloučenou* (Toronto), 1979.

Le Livre du rire et de l'oubli.   1979; translated as *The Book of Laughter and Forgetting*, 1980; Czech edition, as *Kniha smíchu a zapomnění (Toronto)*, 1981.

L'Insoutenable Légéreté de l'être.   1984; translated as *The Unbearable Lightness of Being*, 1984; Czech edition, as *Nesnesitelná lehkost bytí* (Toronto), 1985.

L'Immortalité.   1990; translated as *Immortality*, 1991.

Verse

Člověk zahrada širá [Man: A Broad Garden].   1953.

Poslední máj [The Last May].   1955; revised editions, 1961 and 1963.

Monology [Monologues].   1957; revised editions, 1964, 1965, 1967, and 1969.

Other

Umění románu.   1960; translated as *The Art of the Novel*, 1988.

*

Bibliographies

Glen Brand, *Milan Kundera: An Annotated Biography*, New York, 1988.

Criticism

Books:
Paul I. Trensky, *Czech Drama since World War II*, White Plains, New York, 1978.
Robert Porter, *Milan Kundera: A Voice from Central Europe*, Aarhus, 1981.

Articles:
Eva Legrand, "Milan Kundera, auteur de *Jacques le fataliste* . . .", in *Stanford French Review*, 8, 1984.
"Milan Kundera Interviewed by Arthur Holmberg", in *Performing Arts Journal*, 25, 1985.
Ilan Stavans, "*Jacques and His Master*: Kundera and His Precursors", in *Review of Contemporary Fiction*, vol.9 no.2, 1989.

* * *

Milan Kundera's work for the theatre has been overshadowed by his fame as a novelist. After *The Joke*, *The Book of Laughter and Forgetting*, and *The Unbearable Lightness of Being*, he was acknowledged as one of Europe's leading writers; but, inexplicably, his plays are not so well-known. He wrote three: "The Owners of the Keys"; "Cock-Up"; and *Jacques and His Master* (also known as "Jacques the Fatalist"). Each of them was written in different circum-

stances, and reflects a different stage in Kundera's intellectual development.

The late 1950's was a time of political and cultural change in Czechoslovakia; the Soviet Union had signalled a thaw, and daring experiments were taking place in literature, theatre, and film. Kundera came to know Otomar Krejča, at that time Head of the National Theatre, and Krejča, in his search for the new Czech drama, turned not to established playwrights but to poets, amongst them Milan Kundera and Josef Topol. Thus, "The Owners of the Keys" had its premiere in 1962 and was an immediate success.

Initially, the play appears to belong to the popular genre of occupation drama. It takes place in a provincial flat which the middle-aged Krůta and his wife share with their pretty daughter Alena and her husband Jiří. The narrow-minded Krůta family cling to their trivial round of activities and to their material possessions, a preoccupation symbolised by the ownership of the keys to the flat. Jiří, at first bound by his marriage to this petty bourgeois world, is given a chance to rejoin the resistance. In so doing he implicates the Krůta family in a crime of which they are ignorant, but for which they are sure to be executed.

Jiří's dilemma and its resolution belong to the conventions of socialist realist drama: Kundera depicts, on the one hand, the passive evil of the small-minded, self-interested petty-bourgeois; on the other, the flawed hero who redeems himself by returning to the fight. However, instead of structuring the story as a traditional three-act drama, Kundera and Krejča used montage techniques taken from film. The action, which runs without an interval, takes place within the real time of an hour and a half. In Josef Svoboda's setting for the National Theatre production, two trucks represented the rooms of the flat, enabling two conversations to take place simultaneously, whilst on the black-carpeted stage, figures from Jiří's visions expressed the workings of his conscience. Kundera described the play as having two storylines, the first familiar, the second ". . . more like the unfamiliar dramaturgy of the Ionesco type of anti- or pseudo-drama".

"The Owners of the Keys" was written for the well-equipped stage of Prague's National Theatre; Kundera's second play, "Cock-Up," was intended for the avant-garde Theatre on the Balustrade, where it was directed by Václav Hudecek. This stage was too small for Svoboda's elaborate stage machinery, but the bleakness of the setting was appropriate for the satirical intention of the play. "Cock-Up" is set in a world of corrupt banality, where sexual mechanics and ritual humiliation substitute for valid human relationships. A school headmaster plays a practical joke (in the form of a vulgar graffitto) on his prurient staff. But when a schoolboy confesses to the insult, the Headmaster is forced by the sadistic Chairman of the Town Council to cut off the boy's ears, while the boy's teacher, who is also the Headmaster's mistress, is caned on her bottom. The boy is canonised by his revolutionised fellow-pupils, while the Headmaster is driven by his mistress's desire for revenge into seducing the Chairman's fiancée. In spite of his disgust for the fiancée's whorishness, he is blackmailed into a secret and permanent relationship with her. Kundera later wrote: "In every man's life there are moments when man is joking. But then the joke dominates and makes a joke of Man". The theme of the play is moral degradation in a society which has lost sight of its values; its setting is a world which is bizarre, cruel, and yet desperately recognisable.

Kundera's third play, *Jacques and His Master*, was also written for the Theatre on the Balustrade, but, in the "normalised" world of the 1970's, when the best Czech writers were extinguished, one by one, it was never performed there. It was, in fact, produced at the Drama Studio of Ústí nad Labem in 1974, but credited as the work of Denis Diderot or (mysteriously) of the film and theatre director Evald Schorm. Unlike Kundera's first two plays, this used techniques of the cabaret stage, such as direct address to the audience. Until the mid-1980's the production regularly visited the Žižkov Theatre in Prague, drawing large audiences which loudly applauded such lines as: "Forward? That can be in any direction!".

By 1974 Kundera had been dismissed from his post at the Film Faculty, and in 1975 he became guest professor at the University of Rennes in France; after having been stripped of his Czechoslovak citizenship in 1979, he considered himself a permanent resident of France. He never aligned himself with the dissidents in Czechoslovakia (refusing, for example, to support the Charter 77 movement). In the 1980's, whilst feted in the rest of Europe, he found himself under attack in both "official" and "unofficial" publications in Czechoslovakia. For example, when he wrote about the cultural and geographic concept of "central Europe", he was challenged by samizdat critics, who accused him of failing to understand, in exile, what central Europe means to those who remain. Although his name was on the list of banned playwrights whom, in the late-1980's, the theatre reformers were fighting to get reinstated in the repertoire, after the "gentle revolution" the theatres did not immediately rush to put his plays into production. It seemed as though his plays did not rank as highly as those of the heroes of the underground: Václav Havel, Ivan Klíma, and Milan Uhde. Yet his three plays are among the sharpest and most effective written for the Czech theatre, and the cruel yet funny satire of "Cock-Up" is not limited just to Czechoslovakian society.

—Barbara Day

KYD, Thomas. Born in London; baptised 6 November 1558. Educated at Merchant Taylors' School, London, from 1565. Possibly worked as a scrivener; in the service of an unknown lord, 1587–93; shared lodgings with Christopher Marlowe, 1591; arrested on orders of the privy council for inciting riots (then charged with atheism), 1593: released, apparently after implicating Marlowe. Various plays have been ascribed to him, although only *The Spanish Tragedy* and his adaptation of Garnier's *Cornélie* positively. Died in London (?), August 1594.

Works

Collections

Works, edited by F.S. Boas.   1901; revised edition, 1955.

Stage Works

The Spanish Tragedy (produced c.1582–92; first recorded production, by Lord Strange's Men, London, 1592). 1592; with "additions", 1602.
Cornelia, from a play by Robert Garnier.   1594; as *Pompey the Great His Fair Cornelia's Tragedy*, 1595.

Other

The Truth of the Most Wicked and Secret Murdering of John Brewen. 1592.

Translator, *The Householder's Philosophy*, by Tasso.   1588.

*

Bibliographies

S.A. Tannenbaum, *Thomas Kyd: A Concise Bibliography*, 1941; supplement in *Elizabethan Bibliographies 4*, Port Washington, New York, 1967.

Criticism

Books:
F. Carrère, *Le Théâtre de Thomas Kyd*, Toulouse, 1951.
Philip W. Edwards, *Thomas Kyd and Early Elizabethan Tragedy*, London and New York, 1966.
Arthur Freeman, *Thomas Kyd: Facts and Problems*, Oxford, 1967.
Peter B. Murray, *Thomas Kyd*, New York, 1969.
Gordon Braden, *Renaissance Tragedy and the Senecan Tradition*, New Haven, Connecticut, 1985.

*   *   *

It is frustrating how little we know of Kyd's life and work for it is clear that he was an important Elizabethan playwright —"our best for Tragedie", according to Francis Meres' *Palladis Tamia* of 1598—whose contribution to the repertoire and to the establishment of the public playhouse during those vital years of growth between 1586 and 1593 was recognised, long after his death, by figures as diverse as Jonson, Dekker, and Heywood.

Kyd's reputation now rests exclusively on *The Spanish Tragedy*, which was published anonymously in at least 10 editions between 1592 and 1633. Only since 1773, when it was noticed that Kyd had been cited as the author in Heywood's *Apology for Actors*, has his name been added to editions of this play. *Cornelia* (1594), a translation of a tragedy by Robert Garnier, is the only other drama which can be firmly ascribed to him. However, his hand has been detected in *Soliman and Perseda*, *The Troublesome Reign of King John*, *The Contention of York and Lancaster*, *Arden of Feversham*, and *Leire*, but with little critical agreement. He has also been put forward as the author of a lost pre-Shakespearian play on the subject of Hamlet (a play known to have been revived at Henslowe's Rose Theatre on 11th June 1594) and of a putative *Titus and Vespasian*, revised by Shakespeare as *Titus Andronicus*.

It is likely that some of Kyd's theatrical output survives either wrongly attributed, or as anonymous texts, but it is unlikely that any of it will ever be identified conclusively. What is certain is his central position in that formative wave of professional playwrights who created a robust and popular theatre in London. Born six years before Marlowe and Shakespeare, he shares with them much of the credit for its rapid development and for that passionate interest in "personation" which was to become such a vivid and fashionable feature throughout the 1590's. His depiction of Hieronimo in *The Spanish Tragedy* is as definitive in this regard as Marlowe's Tamburlaine or Faustus. The stage persona is larger than life and, as an embodiment of ambiguous emotions, becomes an object for the spectator's contradictory impulses. Hieronimo, as hero, is both victim and murderer. The audience's anxieties are engaged by the energy at play, and the allegorical mode of emblematic staging is animated throughout by a symbolism concerned less with parallels or abstract arguments, and more with ambivalence and resonance. This shift from statement to equivocation is an important development in characterisation on the English stage.

The impact of Kyd's approach to character is evident in the fact that Hieronimo continued to draw large audiences long after the rhetoric seemed old-fashioned and clumsy. It was an approach Shakespeare was quick to use, in his own way, for the figure of Richard III (both in the play of that name and in the earlier *Henry VI, Part Three*)—an approach he was to develop eventually with provoking subtlety, and with reference to Kyd's tragedy, in *Hamlet*.

In its ingenious but full-bloodied exploration of revenge, *The Spanish Tragedy* set the pattern for a distinctive genre in which issues of power and morality could be experienced through a baroque blend of earnestness and play. For the audience, caught up in the machinations of four interlocking schemes of personal vengeance, there is an ironic disjunction between the experienced world of the individual, where com-petitiveness and aggression extends from the battlefield to the court, and the recognition that actions and judgements are made in ignorance of all the facts. Delight in the artifice and symmetries of plotting serves to intensify this disjunction so that the spectator, even more than Hieronimo, becomes "author and actor in this tragedy". This ambivalent theatricality is not alien to the modern stage, where Kyd's conscious and purposeful variety of dramatic styles merits serious attention.

—Leslie du S. Read

See also *Volume 1* entry on *The Spanish Tragedy*.

LABERGE, Marie. Born in Quebec City, Quebec, Canada, 29 November 1950. Educated at the Collège Notre-Dame de Bellevue, and the Collège Saint-Charles-Garnier; Université Laval, Quebec City, 1970–72 (left without graduating); Conservertoire d'Art Dramatique, Montreal, 1972–75. Worked in modern dance with Danse-Partout; also actress, professor of drama, director, and theatre administrator; began playwriting in 1977; member of the Centre d'Essai des Auteurs Dramatiques; administrator, Théâtre du Trident, Quebec City; moved to Montreal, 1981. Recipient: Governor General's Award for Drama, 1977 and 1982.

Works

Stage Works

Profession: Je l'aime (produced Théâtre du Vieux Québec, Quebec City, 1979). 1978.
Éva et Évelyne (produced Théâtre du Vieux Québec, Quebec City, 1979). 1986.
T'sé veux dire (produced Café-Théâtre du Quartier Latin, Montreal, 1980).
On a bien failli d'comprendre (produced Café-Théâtre du Quartier Latin, Montreal, 1980).
Avec l'Hiver qui s'en vient (produced Théâtre du Vieux Québec, Quebec City, 1980). 1981.
Ils étaient venus pour . . . (produced Théâtre du Bois de Coulonge, Quebec City, 1981). 1981.
C'était avant la guerre à l'Anse à Gilles (produced Salle Fred Barry, Montreal, 1981). 1981.
Le Banc (produced Théâtre du Petit Champlain, Quebec City, 1983). 1981.
Jocelyne Trudel trouvée morte dans ses larmes (produced L'Implanthéâtre, Quebec City, 1986). 1983.
Le Bourreau. 1983.
Au bord de la nuit. 1983.
Deux Tangos pour toute une vie (produced Théâtre du Petit Champlain, Quebec City, 1984). 1985.
L'Homme gris (produced Salle Fred Barry, Montreal, 1984). 1986.
Le Night Cap Bar (produced by the Théâtre de la Manufacture, La Licorne, Montreal, 1987). 1987.
Oublier (produced Montreal and Brussels, 1987). 1987.
Aurélie, ma soeur (produced 1988). 1989.

Fiction

Juillet. 1989.

*

Criticism

Books:
André Smith (ed.), *Marie Laberge: Dramaturge*, Montreal, 1989.

Articles:
Marie Laberge and André Dionne, "Marie Laberge, dramaturge: Entrevue", in *Lettres Québécoises*, 25, 1982.
Marie Laberge and André Dionne, "Marie Laberge, dramaturge: Vivre de sa plume au Québec" (interview), in *Lettres québécoises*, 54, 1989.

*   *   *

In the space of a dozen years, Marie Laberge has acquired an international reputation as one of the most talented and original dramatists in the history of French Canada. In her plays, individuals struggle for self-definition in a world concerned only with collective values. Solitude and existential anguish are the price they pay for their refusal to conform; most are vanquished by prevailing laws and mores, but her protagonists' struggles towards personal liberty inspire and edify, as they do in the world of Camus and Sartre.

The emptiness of personal relationships, the ludic illusions of love, the inbred subservience of women in a patriarchal society founded on religious and political conservatism—all are constant themes of her plays. But humour, brilliant dialogue, and superb characterization offer counterpoise, as her alienated individuals explore parameters of the human condition in a theatre that is refreshingly non-didactic.

Far more than most dramatists, Laberge knows theatre from the inside. An actress of note before any of her own plays were produced, she has directed and played in her own works and those of others, has served as administrator for Quebec City's Trident Theatre and, at another extreme, has taught drama at university level. Her practical experience is obvious in the effects achieved onstage, particularly in the astute use of colour, lighting, and symbolic props to suggest different spaces, figurative and real, in which her troubled characters move, physically and mentally. Her preoccupation with the theoretical basis of theatre is also obvious in this constant exploration of spatial and verbal metaphors, and in the reflective, logocentric, and often destructive lucidity her characters bring to bear on their condition. But her major talent is her sure-handed use of dialogue: her conversations, disputes, even monologues are unfailingly convincing in the mouths of characters whose reality seems somehow to transcend our own.

She is the author of some 20 dramatic texts to date. *Éva et Évelyne*, written in 1977, and staged two years later, was the first of these to be published. In it, two ageing, unmarried sisters speak movingly of the solitary lives they have led, deprived of love, and sentenced, as women in Quebec's patriarchal society, to a subservient, marginalized existence. Yet they are neither bitter nor vengeful, but have retained a generous, albeit rueful, sense of humour, a trait that is not characteristic of most of the other female characters in Laberge's drama.

Her second published play, *Avec l'hiver*, is more representative in this respect. Here there is intense confrontation without humour and without resolution. Here, also, the theme of silence is central, with the male protagonist, recently retired, now mute and withdrawn, obsessed by memories of the only true and affective relationship he has had, with an aunt when he was a child. Individual silence, as a reaction to the frustrations of interpersonal relations, is the mark of the female protagonists in *L'Homme gris* and *Jocelyne Trudel* as well.

Less absolutely, the inability to communicate affection is a major handicap for most of Laberge's characters, male and female; and that inability gives rise to the emotional emptiness, the pervasive despair felt by those with whom they interact—the spouses, children, and siblings who long for that affection. This theme is most poignantly expressed in *Oublier*, in which four sisters gather to await their mother's death from Alzheimer's disease—another metaphor for the malaise affecting human relationships in modern society.

C'était avant la guerre à l'Anse à Gilles first brought Laberge to national attention, playing to full houses and enthusiastic reviews in Montreal, Quebec City, and Toronto. With *L'Homme gris* in 1984, staged in Paris (120 performances in its second run in 1986) and Brussels, her international profile was established. Unlike Tremblay's plays, which are performed in *joual*, the homely, popular idiom of urban Quebec even when transported to European stages, *L'Homme gris*, significantly, was "translated" into standard French, for Laberge's exploration of the human condition is not dependent upon any one geographical or cultural location. *Oublier* opened simultaneously in Brussels and Montreal in 1987, to similar admiring reviews, confirming the universality of her themes and her mastery in communicating them.

—Leonard E. Doucette

LABICHE, Eugène (Marin). Born in Paris, 6 May 1815. Educated at the Collège Bourbon, Paris; also studied law. Married Adèle Hubert in 1842. Travelled to Italy and Switzerland, 1834; theatre reviewer, *Revue du théâtre*, until 1838; first plays produced, 1838, and he was subsequently a prolific playwright, 1838–77, usually in collaboration with Marc-Michel, Augustin Lefranc, Édouard Martin, Delacour, and others, chiefly for the boulevard theatres—the Gymnase, the Vaudeville, and the Palais-Royal; unsuccessful candidate for the legislative assembly, 1848; bought château with estate near Souvigny, in the Sologne region, 1853, subsequently dividing his time between Paris and the estate; briefly served as mayor of Souvigny; ceased writing new plays after 1877. Elected to the Académie Française, 1880. Died in Paris, 23 January 1888.

Works

Collections

Théâtre complet (10 vols.; includes about a third of the plays, with a preface by Émile Augier). 1878–79.
Théâtre choisi (includes *La Grammaire: L'Affaire de la rue de Lourcine; La Poudre aux yeux; La Cigale chez les fourmis; Les Deux timides; Embrassons-nous Folleville!*). 1895.
Théâtre (5 vols.). 1949–50.
Nouveau théâtre choisi. 1960.
Théâtre (3 vols.). 1964–71.
Oeuvres complètes (8 vols.). 1966.

Stage Works

Monsieur de Coyllin; ou, L'Homme infiniment poli, with Marc-Michel and Augustin Lefranc (produced Théâtre du Palais-Royal, Paris, 1838). 1838.
L'Avocat Loubet, with Marc-Michel (produced Théâtre du Panthéon, Paris, 1838). 1838.
Le Capitaine d'Arcourt; ou, La Fée du château (produced Théâtre du Luxembourg, Paris, 1838).
La Forge des châtaigniers (produced Théâtre Saint-Michel, Paris, 1839).
La Peine du talion (produced Théâtre du Luxembourg, Paris, 1839).
L'Article 960; ou, La Donation, by Ancelot and "Paul Dandré" (Labiche, Lefranc, and Marc-Michel) (produced Théâtre du Vaudeville, Paris, 1839). 1839.
Le Fin Mot, by "Paul Dandré" (Labiche, Lefranc, and Marc-Michel) (produced Théâtre des Variétés, Paris, 1840). 1840.
Bocquet, père et fils; ou, Le Chemin le plus long, with Laurencin and Marc-Michel (produced Théâtre du Gymnase-Dramatique, Paris, 1840). 1840.
Le Lierre et l'ormeau, with Lefranc and Albert Monnier (produced Théâtre du Palais-Royal, Paris, 1842). 1841.
Le Major Cravachon, with Lefranc and Paul Jessé (produced Théâtre du Palais-Royal, Paris, 1842). 1844.
Les Circonstances atténuantes, with Mélesville and Lefranc (produced Théâtre du Palais-Royal, Paris, 1842). 1842.
L'Homme de paille, with Lefranc (produced Théâtre du Palais-Royal, Paris, 1842). 1843.
Deux Papas très bien; ou, La Grammaire de Chicard, with Lefranc (produced Théâtre du Palais-Royal, Paris, 1843). 1845.
Le Roi des Frontins, with Lefranc (produced Théâtre du Palais-Royal, Paris, 1845). 1845.
L'École buissonnière, with Lefranc (produced Théâtre du Palais-Royal, Paris, 1845). 1845.
L'Enfant de la maison, with Victor Varin and Eugène Nyon (produced Théâtre du Gymnase-Dramatique, Paris, 1845). 1845.
Frisette, with Lefranc (produced Théâtre du Palais-Royal, Paris, 1846). 1846; translated as *John and Jeannette*, 1884.
Mademoiselle ma femme, with Lefranc (produced Théâtre du Palais-Royal, Paris, 1846). 1846.
Rocambole le bateleur, with Lefranc (produced Théâtre des Folies-Dramatiques, Paris, 1846). 1846.
L'Inventeur de la poudre, with Lefranc and Nyon (produced Théâtre du Palais-Royal, Paris, 1846). 1846.
L'Avocat-pédicure, with Lefranc (produced Théâtre du Palais-Royal, Paris, 1846). 1847.
La Chasse aux jobards, with Lefranc. 1847.
Un Homme sanguin, with Lefranc (produced Théâtre du Gymnase-Dramatique, Paris, 1847). 1847.

"Le Théâtre d'**Eugène Labiche**": impressions of several plays (composition by M. Draner)

L'Art de ne pas donner d'étrennes, with Lefranc (produced Théâtre du Gymnase-Dramatique, Paris, 1847).   1847.

Un Jeune Homme pressé, (produced Théâtre de la Montansier, Paris, 1848).   1848.

Le Club champenois, with Lefranc (produced Théâtre de la Montansier, Paris, 1848).   1848.

Oscar XXVIII, with Pierre Decourcelle and Paul Barbier (produced Théâtre des Variétés, Paris, 1848).   1848.

Une Chaîne anglaise, with Saint-Yves (produced Théâtre de la Montansier, Paris, 1848).   1848.

Histoire de rire, with Saint-Yves (produced Théâtre du Gymnase, Paris, 1848).   1848.

Agénor le dangereux, with Decourcelle and Karl (produced Théâtre de la Montansier, Paris, 1848).   1848.

À bas la famille; ou, Les Banquets, with Lefranc (produced Théâtre du Gymnase, Paris, 1848).   1848.

Le Baromètre; ou, La Pluie et le beau temps (produced Théâtre du Vaudeville, Paris, 1848).

À Moitié Chemin (produced Théâtre Beaumarchais, Paris, 1848).

Une Tragédie chez Monsieur Grassot (produced Théâtre du Palais-Royal, Paris, 1848).

Madame Veuve Larifla, with Adolphe Choler (produced Théâtre des Variétés, Paris, 1849).   1849.

Les Manchettes d'un vilain, with Lefranc and Saint-Yves (produced Théâtre de la Montansier, Paris, 1849).   1849.

Une Dent sous Louis XV (monologue), with Lefranc.   1849.

Trompe-la-balle, with Lefranc (produced Théâtre de la Montansier, Paris, 1849).   1849.

Exposition des produits de la République, with Philippe Dumanoir and Louis Clairville (produced Théâtre de la Montansier, Paris, 1849).   1849.

Rue de L'homme-armé, numéro 8 bis, with Nyon (produced Théâtre des Variétés, Paris, 1849).   1849.

Mon Ours (produced Théâtre des Variétés, Paris, 1849).

Traversin et couverture, with Varin (produced Théâtre de la Montansier, Paris, 1850).   1850.

Le Sopha, with Mélesville and Desnoyer (produced Théâtre de la Montansier, Paris, 1850).   1850.

Un Bal en robe de chambre, with Marc-Michel (produced Théâtre de la Montansier, Paris, 1850).   1850.

Embrassons-nous Folleville!, with Lefranc (produced Théâtre de la Montansier, Paris, 1850).   1850.

Un Garçon de chez Véry (produced Théâtre de la Montansier, Paris, 1850).   1850.

La Fille bien gardée, with Marc-Michel (produced Théâtre du Palais-Royal, Paris, 1850).   1850.

Schahabaham XLIV, with Mélesville and Desnoyer (produced Théâtre de la Montansier, Paris, 1850).   1850.

Les Petits Moyens, with Lemoine and Decourcelle (produced Théâtre du Gymnase, Paris, 1850).   1850.

Les Prétendus de Gimblette, by "Paul Dandré" (Labiche) and "Senneif" (Matharel and Fiennes) (produced Théâtre de la Gaîté, Paris, 1850).   1850.

Une clarinette qui passe, with Marc-Michel (produced Théâtre des Variétés, Paris, 1851).   1851.

La Femme qui perd ses jarretières, with Marc-Michel (produced Théâtre de la Montansier, Paris, 1851).   1851.

On demande des culottières, with Marc-Michel (produced Théâtre de la Montansier, Paris, 1851).   1851.

Mamz'elle fait ses dents, with Marc-Michel (produced Théâtre de la Montansier, Paris, 1851).   1851.

En Manches de chemise, with Lefranc and Nyon (produced Théâtre de la Montansier, Paris, 1851).   1851; as an operetta, with music by Villebichot, 1869.

Un Chapeau de paille d'Italie, with Marc-Michel (produced Théâtre de la Montansier, Paris, 1851).   1851; translated as *A Leghorn Hat*, in *Poet Lore*, 28, 1917; as *An Italian Straw Hat*, in *The Modern Theatre 3*, edited by Eric Bentley, 1955; as *The Italian Straw Hat*, with *The Spelling Mistake*, 1967.

Maman Sabouleux, with Marc-Michel (produced Théâtre du Palais-Royal, Paris, 1852).   1852.

Un Monsieur qui prend la mouche, with Marc-Michel (produced Théâtre des Variétés, Paris, 1852).   1852.

Les Suites d'un premier lit, with Marc-Michel (produced Théâtre du Vaudeville, Paris, 1852).   1852.

Soufflez-moi dans l'oeil, with Marc-Michel (produced Théâtre du Palais-Royal, Paris, 1852).   1852.

Canadar père et fils, by "Laurencin" (Labiche) and Marc-Michel (produced Théâtre des Variétés, Paris, 1852).   1852.

Le Misanthrope et l'auvergnat, with Lubize and Paul Siraudin (produced Théâtre du Palais-Royal, Paris, 1852).   1852.

Deux Gouttes d'eau, with Auguste Bourgeois (produced Théâtre des Variétés, Paris, 1852).   1852.

Piccolet, with Lefranc and Montjoie (produced Théâtre du Palais-Royal, Paris, 1852).   1852.

Edgard et sa bonne, with Marc-Michel (produced Théâtre du Palais-Royal, Paris, 1852).   1852.

Le Chevalier des dames, with Marc-Michel (produced Théâtre du Palais-Royal, Paris, 1853).   1853.

Mon Isménie, with Marc-Michel (produced Théâtre du Palais-Royal, Paris, 1853).   1853.

Une Charge de cavalerie, with Moreau and Delacour (produced Théâtre du Palais-Royal, Paris, 1853).   1853.

On dira des bêtises, with Delacour and Deslandes.   1853.

Un Notaire à marier, with Marc-Michel and Arthur de Beauplan (produced Théâtre des Variétés, Paris, 1853).   1853.

Un Ut de poitrine, with Lefranc (produced Théâtre du Palais-Royal, Paris, 1853).   1853.

Un Feu de cheminée, with Beauplan (produced Théâtre du Palais-Royal, Paris, 1853).   1853.

La Chasse aux corbeaux, with Marc-Michel (produced Théâtre du Palais-Royal, Paris, 1853).   1853.

Un Ami acharné, with Alphonse Jolly (produced Théâtre des Variétés, Paris, 1853).   1853.

Deux Profonds Scélérats, with Varin (produced Théâtre du Palais-Royal, Paris, 1854).   1854; translated as *Two Gay Deceivers; or, Black, White and Grey*, 1860.

Un Mari qui prend du ventre, with Marc-Michel.   1854.

Espagnolas et boyardinos, with Marc-Michel (produced 1854).   1854.

Ôtez votre fille s'il vous plaît, with Marc-Michel (produced Théâtre du Palais-Royal, Paris, 1854).   1854.

Les Marquises de la fourchette, with Choler (produced Théâtre du Vaudeville, Paris, 1854).   1854.

La Perle de la Canebière, with Marc-Michel (produced Théâtre du Palais-Royal, Paris, 1855).   1855.

Monsieur votre fille, with Marc-Michel (produced Théâtre du Vaudeville, Paris, 1855).

Les Précieux, with Marc-Michel and Lefranc (produced Théâtre du Palais-Royal, Paris, 1855).   1855.

Si Jamais Je te pince! . . ., with Marc-Michel (produced Théâtre du Palais-Royal, Paris, 1856).   1856.

Un Monsieur qui a brûlé une dame, with Bourgeois (produced Théâtre du Palais-Royal, Paris, 1858).   1856.

Les Cheveux de ma femme, with Battu (produced Théâtre des Variétés, Paris, 1856).   1856.

En Pension chez son groom, with Marc-Michel (produced Théâtre des Variétés, Paris, 1856).   1856.

Monsieur de Saint-Cadenas, with Marc-Michel (produced Théâtre des Variétés, Paris, 1856).   1856.

La Fiancée du bon coin, with Marc-Michel (produced Théâtre des Variétés, Paris, 1856).   1856.

Mesdames de Montenfriche, with Marc-Michel (produced Théâtre des Variétés, Paris, 1856).   1856.

L'Affaire de la rue de Lourcine, with Monnier and Édouard Martin (produced Théâtre du Palais-Royal, Paris, 1857).   1857.

Les Noces de Bouchencoeur, with Monnier and Martin (produced Théâtre du Palais-Royal, Paris, 1857).   1857.

Le Bras d'Ernest, with H. Leroux (produced Théâtre du Palais-Royal, Paris, 1857).   1857.

La Dame aux jambes d'azur, with Marc-Michel (produced Théâtre du Palais-Royal, Paris, 1857).   1857.

Le Secrétaire de Madame, with Marc-Michel (produced Théâtre du Palais-Royal, Paris, 1857).   1857.

Un Gendre en surveillance, with Marc-Michel (produced Théâtre du Gymnase, Paris, 1857).   1858.

Le Clou aux maris, with Eugène Moreau and Mme Réal (produced Théâtre du Palais-Royal, Paris, 1858).   1858.

L'Avare en gants jaunes, with Bourgeois (produced Théâtre du Palais-Royal, Paris, 1858).   1858.

Je croque ma tante, with Marc-Michel (produced Théâtre du Palais-Royal, Paris, 1858).   1858.

Madame est aux eaux, with Vilmar (produced Théâtre du Palais-Royal, Paris, 1858).   1858.

Le Calife de la rue Saint-Bon, with Marc-Michel (produced Théâtre du Palais-Royal, Paris, 1858).   1858.

Deux Merles blancs, with Delacour (produced Théâtre des Variétés, Paris, 1858).

Le Grain de café (produced Théâtre du Palais-Royal, Paris, 1858).

En Avant les Chinois, with Delacour (produced Théâtre du Palais-Royal, Paris, 1858).   1859.

L'Avocat d'un Grec, with Lefranc (produced Théâtre du Palais-Royal, Paris, 1859).   1859.

L'Amour, un fort volume: Prix: 3 fr 50, with Martin (produced Théâtre du Palais-Royal, Paris, 1859).   1859.

L'École des Arthur, with Bourgeois (produced Théâtre des Variétés, Paris, 1859).   1859.

L'Omelette à la Follembuche (comic opera), with Marc-Michel, with music by Delibes (produced Théâtre des Bouffes-Parisiens, Paris, 1859).   1859.

Le Baron de Fourchevif, with Jolly (produced Théâtre du Gymnase, Paris, 1859).   1859.

Les Petites Mains, with Martin (produced Théâtre du Vaudeville, Paris, 1859).   1859.

Le Voyage autour de ma marmite, with Delacour (produced Theatre du Palais-Royal, Paris, 1859).   1860.

Le Rouge-gorge, with Choler (produced Théâtre du Vaudeville, Paris, 1859).   1859.

J'invite le colonel, with Marc-Michel (produced Théâtre du Palais-Royal, Paris, 1859).   1860.

La Sensitive, with Delacour (produced Théâtre du Palais-Royal, Paris, 1859).   1860.

Les Deux timides, with Marc-Michel (produced Théâtre du Gymnase, Paris, 1859).   1860; translated as *A Trumped Suit,* in *Comedies for Amateur Acting,* 1880; as *The Two Cowards,* 1915.

Le Voyage de Monsieur Perrichon, with Martin (produced Théâtre du Gymnase, Paris, 1860).   1860; translated as *The Journey of M. Perrichon,* 1924; as *A Trip Abroad,* in *"Let's Get a Divorce" and Other Plays,* edited by Eric Bentley, 1958; as *Monsieur Perrichon Goes Abroad*; as *Mr. Perrichon's Holiday,* 1965.

Un Gros Mot, with Dumoustier (produced Théâtre du Palais-Royal, Paris, 1860).   1860.

La Famille de l'horloger, with Deslandes (produced Théâtre du Palais-Royal, Paris, 1860).   1860.

Les 37 Sous de Monsieur Montaudoin, with Martin (produced Théâtre du Palais-Royal, Paris, 1860).   1863; translated as *The 37 Sous of Monsieur Montaudoin,* nd.

J'ai compromis ma femme, with Delacour (produced Théâtre du Gymnase, Paris, 1861).   1861.

Les Vivacités du Capitaine Tic, with Martin (produced Théâtre du Vaudeville, Paris, 1861).   1861.

La Poudre aux yeux, with Martin (produced Théâtre du Gymnase, Paris, 1861).   1861; translated as *Throwing Dust in People's Eyes,* 1930; as *Dust in Your Eyes,* with *90° in the Shade,* 1962.

L'Amour en sabots, with Delacour (produced Théâtre des Variétés, Paris, 1861).   1861.

Le Mystère de la rue Rousselet, with Marc-Michel (produced Théâtre du Vaudeville, Paris, 1861).   1861.

La Station Champbaudet, with Marc-Michel (produced Théâtre du Palais-Royal, Paris, 1862).   1862.

Les Petits Oiseaux, with Delacour (produced Théâtre du Vaudeville, Paris, 1862).   1862; translated as *A Pair of Spectacles,* 1899.

Le Premier Pas, with Delacour (produced Théâtre du Gymnase, Paris, 1862).   1862.

Célimare le bien-aimé, with Delacour (produced Théâtre du Palais-Royal, Paris, 1863).   1863; translated as *Célimare the Beloved,* in *"Let's Get a Divorce" and Other Plays,* edited by Eric Bentley, 1958.

La Dame au petit chien, with Demoustier (produced Théâtre du Palais-Royal, Paris, 1863).   1863.

Permettez, Madame!, with Delacour (produced Théâtre du Gymnase, Paris, 1863).   1863.

La Commode de Victorine, with Martin (produced Théâtre du Palais-Royal, Paris, 1863).   1864.

La Cagnotte, with Delacour (produced Théâtre du Palais-Royal, Paris, 1864).   1864 translated as *Pots of Money,* in *The Genius of French Theatre,* edited by Albert Bermel, 1961; as *Three Cheers for Paris,* 1971.

Moi, with Martin (produced Comédie-Française, Paris, 1864).   1864.

Un Mari qui lance sa femme, with Deslandes (produced Théâtre du Gymnase, Paris, 1864).   1864.

Le Point de mire, with Delacour (produced Théâtre Impérial, Compiègne, 1864).   1864.

Premier prix de piano, with Delacour (produced Théâtre du Palais-Royal, Paris, 1865).   1865.

L'Homme qui manque le coche, with Delacour.   1865.

La Bergère de la rue Monthabor, with Delacour (produced Théâtre du Palais-Royal, Paris, 1865).   1865.

Le Voyage en Chine (comic opera), with Delacour, with music by Bazin (produced Opéra-Comique, Paris, 1865).   1865.

Un pied dans le crime, with Choler (produced Théâtre du Palais-Royal, Paris, 1866).   1866.

La Grammaire, with Jolly (produced Théâtre du Palais Royal, Paris, 1867).   1867; translated as *Grammar,* 1915; as *Cabbages and Culture,* 1957

La Main leste, with Martin (produced Théâtre des Bouffes-Parisiens, Paris, 1867).   1867.

Le Fils du brigadier (comic opera), with Delacour, with music by Victor Massé (produced Opéra-Comique, Paris, 1867).   1867.

Le Chemin de fer, with Delacour and Choler (produced Théâtre du Palais-Royal, Paris, 1867).   1867.

Le Papa du prix d'honneur, with Barrière (produced Théâtre du Palais-Royal, Paris, 1868).   1868.

Le Corricolo (comic opera), with Delacour, with music by Ferdinand Poise (produced Opéra-Comique, Paris, 1868).

1868.

Le Petit Voyage (produced Théâtre du Vaudeville, Paris, 1868). 1868.

Le Roi d'Amatibou, with Edmond Cottinet (produced Théâtre du Palais-Royal, Paris, 1868).

En Manches de chemise, music by A. de Villebichot. 1869.

Le Choix d'un gendre, with Delacour (produced Théâtre du Vaudeville, Paris, 1869). 1869.

Le Dossier de Rosafol, with Delacour (produced Théâtre du Palais-Royal, Paris, 1869). 1869.

Le Plus Heureux des trois, with Edmond Gondinet (produced Théâtre du Palais-Royal, Paris, 1870). 1870; translated by Frederick Davies as *The Happiest of the Three*, in *Three French Farces*, 1973.

Le Cachemire X.-B.-T., with Eugène Nus (produced Théâtre du Vaudeville, Paris, 1870). 1870.

Le Livre bleu, with Ernest Blum (produced Théâtre du Palais-Royal, Paris, 1871). 1871.

L'Ennemie, with Delacour (produced Théâtre du Vaudeville, Paris, 1871). 1871.

Il est de la police, with Leroy (produced Théâtre du Palais-Royal, Paris, 1872). 1872.

La Mémoire d'Hortense, with Delacour (produced Théâtre des Variétés, Paris, 1872). 1872.

Doit-On le dire?, with Henri Duru (produced Théâtre du Palais-Royal, Paris, 1872). 1873.

29 Degrés à l'ombre (produced Théâtre du Palais-Royal, Paris, 1873). 1873; translated as *90° in the Shade*, with *Dust in Your Eyes*, 1962.

Garantie dix ans, with Philippe Gille (produced Théâtre des Variétés, Paris, 1874). 1874.

La Pièce de Chambertin, with Dufrenois (produced Théâtre des Variétés, Paris, 1874). 1874.

Madame est trop belle, with Duru (produced Théâtre du Gymnase, Paris, 1874). 1874.

Brûlons Voltaire!, with Leroy (produced Théâtre du Gymnase, Paris, 1874). 1874.

Les Trente Millions de Gladiator, with Gille (produced Théâtre des Variétés, Paris, 1875). 1875.

Les Samedis de Madame, with Duru (produced Théâtre du Palais-Royal, Paris, 1875). 1875.

Un Mouton à l'entresol, with A. Segond (produced Théâtre du Palais-Royal, Paris, 1875).

La Guigne, with Leterrier and Albert Vanloo (produced Théâtre du Palais-Royal, Paris, 1875).

Le Prix Martin, with Émile Augier (produced Théâtre du Palais-Royal, Paris, 1876). 1876.

Le Roi dort (produced Théâtre des Variétés, Paris, 1876).

La Cigale chez les fourmis, with Legouvé (produced Comédie-Française, Paris, 1876). 1876.

La Clé, with Duru (produced Théâtre du Palais-Royal, Paris, 1877). 1877; translated as *Artful Cards*, 1877.

La Lettre chargée. 1877.

L'Amour de l'art. 1877.

Un Coup de rasoir. 1878.

Fiction

Études de moeurs: la clef des champs. 1839.

*

Criticism

Books:

A. Carel, *Eugène Labiche: Histoire anecdotique des contemporains*, np, 1885.

Philippe Soupault, *Eugène Labiche, Sa Vie, son oeuvre*, Paris, 1945; revised edition, 1964.

Jacqueline Autrusseau, *Labiche et son théâtre*, Paris, 1971.

Leonard Pronko, *Eugène Labiche and Georges Feydeau*, London, 1982 (Macmillan Modern Dramatists series).

E. Haymann, *Labiche, ou l'esprit du Second Empire*, Paris, 1988.

*   *   *

France's greatest comic dramatist of the 19th century, Eugène Labiche brought together thematic and structural tendencies of the mid century and polished them into finely crafted comic masterpieces. As heir to the well-made play of Scribe, he brought realism to the pretentious language, reality to the hollow characters, and deep laughter to the empty clichés of the master. With *An Italian Straw Hat*, Labiche set the French farce form known as *vaudeville* on a new path. Keeping the clever little songs, set to well-known tunes, that characterized the form, Labiche complicated the plot, compounded the misunderstandings, set the speed at a frantic pace, and turned everything around a gigantic double pursuit. After *An Italian Straw Hat*, *vaudevilles* based on the chase proliferated, reaching their climax in Feydeau's end-of-the-century masterpieces.

The hectic action and implausible antics of the characters are only one aspect of Labiche's art, but certainly an important one, for it was Labiche who first pushed the situations to such absurd lengths that they seem to prefigure the plays of Ionesco and other absurdists. His gift for fantasy allowed him to show his contemporaries in ways that verge on the nightmarish and remind us of the world let loose from reason's bonds that we find in the surrealists. But Labiche's plays are always based solidly in reality. The author was, after all, a contemporary of Dumas *fils*, Augier, and Flaubert. The characters he depicts live in solid, heavily curtained, middle-class living rooms, spend their time keeping their accounts and trying to hide their humble beginnings as store-keepers or pharmacists. Labiche's central character is invariably the bourgeois, that materialistic, selfish, role-playing Philistine who dominated the 19th century, and who, since he is so recently rich, feels he should adhere to the rules of society and show off his newly acquired wealth and learning. This "Daumier of the theatre", as a contemporary called Labiche, wove endless variations on the bourgeois: "That beast", he said, "offers endless resources to anyone who knows how to look at him. He is inexhaustible, a pearl of stupidity that can be set in any way".

While *An Italian Straw Hat* emphasizes the breathless, foolish activity of this creature, other of Labiche's major plays slow down the tempo and focus on the character portrait—although rarely at the expense of humor and movement. *Le Voyage de Monsieur Perrichon* (*A Trip Abroad*) proved that the master vaudevillist was at the same time a skilled portrayer of manners and characters. The portrait of Perrichon, self-satisfied, vain, pretentious, cowardly, boastful, yet likeably naive and jovial, offers a universal type, yet he is deeply rooted in the reality of Second Empire France, a wealthy carriage-maker who is a monster of ingratitude, a living example of the famous moralist La Rochefoucauld's maxim to the effect that "we can forgive those who are indebted to us, but never those to whom we are indebted". The typical comedic story of two suitors vying for the hand of one daughter is used to reveal Perrichon's character, as he becomes more and more irritated by Armand, who saved his life when he fell into a glacier at Mont Blanc, while he becomes ever more fond of Daniel, who had the foresight to fall into the glacier and allow Perrichon to save *his* life. Daniel, witnessing the ingratitude of Perrichon, comments, "he is even truer than life!". This perhaps is Labiche's greatest secret: his characters and situations are somehow archetypal, reduced not to caricatures, but to simple outlines that stress the faults, underline the grotesqueness, while never abandoning the precise realities of everyday living.

Since Plautus, comedy has been concerned with characters attempting to get married, and Labiche shows the bourgeoisie eager to make good marriages and increase its holdings. As early as his first major success, the one-act *Jeune Homme pressé* (Young Man in a Hurry), he wrote about young men setting their sights on young ladies—and significantly, in this play there are no women, for in reality the young lady had no voice at all in the making of her marriage. Marriage is a major concern of *An Italian Straw Hat* and *Perrichon*, while in *Célimare le bien aimé* (Celimare) Labiche blends the wild pursuit of the former play with the character portraits of the latter, and develops the marriage theme around his major character, an ageing Don Juan who has decided to give up his amours in order to settle down to family life. Unfortunately for Celimare, the uncomprehending husbands of his former mistresses will not leave him alone. Pursued by two husbands who refuse to renounce his friendship, Celimare finally gets rid of them by asking for a large loan. His disabused conclusion is, "ask anything of a friend, take anything from a friend—even his wife—but never touch his purse".

Several times in his career Labiche treated the sacred cows of his era with unforgivable frankness and his plays failed. Most often however, as in *Célimare*, he was able to mask the bitter truth under absurdity of situation and folly of character, so that the spectators were little disposed to identify too closely with the foolishness they saw on stage.

Having set French farce on a new path and having enriched it with more sophisticated character portrayal and manners, with *Le Plus Heureux des trois* (The Happiest of the Three) Labiche renewed the *vaudeville* once more, this time with the theme of the ménage à trois, a subject that was to prosper far beyond anything Labiche could have foreseen. Labiche was equally at home in simple humorous sketches of life which occasionally, for all their fun and skilful craftsmanship, approach the "slice-of-life" picture that was to be the goal of the Naturalists during the last years of the playwright's life. In *29 Degrés à l'ombre* (translated as *90° in the Shade*), one of his later plays and one of the few he wrote without collaboration, we simply witness the events of a lazy Sunday afternoon in the country near Paris. There are, admittedly, a few zany happenings, like the sudden kiss given the lady of the house, Mme Pomadour, by the would-be dapper visitor, Adolphe. But our attention is directed chiefly to the portraits of the pretentious cowardly husband, the ageing Don Juan character, and above all, the somewhat romantic wife who is gradually wakening to love. The wakening is handled so subtly, and the buzzing, country atmosphere of a Sunday is so skilfully created, that the reader or spectator almost feels he is inhabiting an impressionist painting.

Modest almost to a fault, Labiche felt he was merely an entertainer. Today he is recognized as the author who gave style to the well-made play, and infused it with an irrepressible comic spirit and a sense of reality derived from the bourgeois world he knew so intimately. His limitations are doubtless his strengths, for the world he painted belongs to an era long past. And yet, the newfound popularity of Labiche, whose plays are rarely absent from the Paris stage, seems to indicate that we are still ready to see these situations and people who are, in so many ways, like ourselves. Whereas the "serious" authors of the second half of the 19th century now seem sadly dated, Labiche is as fresh today as he was a century ago.

—Leonard C. Pronko

See also *Volume 1* entry on *An Italian Straw Hat*.

———

LAGERKVIST, Pär (Fabian). Born in Växjö, Sweden, 23 May 1891. Educated at the University of Uppsala, 1911–12. Married 1) Karen Dagmar Johanne Sørensen in 1918 (divorced 1925); 2) Elaine Luella Hallberg in 1925. First-published play, *Sista Mänsken* [*The Last Man*], appeared 1917; theatre critic, *Svenska Dagbladet*, Stockholm, 1919; the first of several plays to be produced at the Kungliga Dramatiska Teatern [Royal Dramatic Theatre], or Dramaten, Stockholm, *Den osynlige* [The Invisible One] was staged in 1924; his final play, *Barabbus*, produced 1953. Collaborated with the theatre director Per Lindberg, until the latter's death in 1944. Recipient: Samfundet De Nio Prize, 1928; Bellman Prize, 1945; Saint-Beuve Prize, 1946; Foreign Book Prize (France), 1951; Nobel Prize for Literature, 1951. Honorary degree: University of Gothenburg, 1941. Member, Swedish Academy of Literature, 1940. Died in Stockholm, 11 July 1974.

Works

Collections

Dramatik [Plays]. 1946; revised edition, 1956.
Modern Theatre: Seven Plays and an Essay (includes the essay "Points of View and Attack" and the plays *The Difficult Hour I–III; The Secret of Heaven; The King; The Hangman; The Philosopher's Stone*), translated by Thomas R. Buckman. 1966.

Stage Works

Sista Mänskan. 1917; translated as *The Last Man*, in *Five Early Works*, 1989.
Den svåra stunden (3 one-act plays; produced Schauspielhaus, Dresden, 1918). In *Teater*, 1918; translated as *The Difficult Hour I–III*, in *Modern Theatre*, 1966.
Himlens hemlighet (produced Intima Theatre, Stockholm, 1921). In *Kaos*, 1919; translated as *The Secret of Heaven*, in *Modern Theatre*, 1966.
Den osynlige [The Invisible One] (produced Dramaten, Stockholm, 1924). 1923.
Han som fick leva om sitt liv (produced Dramaten, Stockholm, 1928). 1928; translated as *The Man Who Lived His Life Over*, in *Five Scandinavian Plays*, 1971.
Konungen (produced City Theatre, Malmö, 1950). 1932; translated as *The King*, in *Modern Theatre*, 1966.
Bödeln, from his own novel (produced in Norwegian, Bergen, Norway, 1934; produced in Swedish, Vasa Theatre, 1934). In *Dramatik*, 1946; translated as *The Hangman*, in *Modern Theatre*, 1966.
Mannen utan själ (produced Dramaten, Stockholm, 1938).

Scene from the Stockholm Dramaten's 1938 production of *Mannen utan själ* [*The Man Without a Soul*] by **Pär Lagerkvist**, with (left to right) Olof Widgren, Hilda Borgström, and Märta Ekström.

1936; translated as *The Man Without a Soul*, in *Scandinavian Plays of the Twentieth Century 1*, 1944.

Seger i mörker [Victory in Darkness] (produced Dramaten, Stockholm, 1940). 1939.

Midsommardröm i fattighuset (produced Blanche Theatre, Stockholm, 1941). 1941; translated as *Midsummer Dream in the Workhouse*, 1953.

De vises sten (produced Dramaten, Stockholm, 1948). 1947; translated as *The Philosopher's Stone*, in *Modern Theatre*, 1966.

Låt människan leva (produced City Theatre, Gothenburg, 1949). 1949; translated as *Let Man Live*, in *Scandinavian Plays of the Twentieth Century 3*, 1951.

Barabbas, from his own novel (produced Dramaten, Stockholm, 1953). 1953.

Fiction

Människor [People]. 1912.

Två sagor om livet [Two Tales About Life]. 1913.

Järn och människor. 1915; translated as *Iron and Men*, in *Five Early Works*, 1989.

Det eviga leendet. 1920; translated as *The Eternal Smile*, 1934.

Onda sagor [Evil Tales]. 1924.

Kämpande ande [Struggling Spirit]. 1930; translated in part as *Masquerade of Souls*, 1954.

Bödeln. 1933; translated as *The Hangman*, in *Guest of Reality*, 1936.

I den tiden [In That Time]. 1935.

Dvärgen. 1944; translated as *The Dwarf*, 1945.

Barabbas. 1950; translated as *Barabbas*, 1951.

"The Eternal Smile" and Other Stories. 1954.

"The Marriage Feast" and Other Stories. 1955.

Sibyllan. 1956; translated as *The Sibyl*, 1958.

Pilgrimen. 1966; individual parts:
  Ahasverus' död. 1960; translated as *The Death of Ahasuerus*, 1962.
  Pilgrim på havet. 1962; translated as *Pilgrim at Sea*, 1964.
  Det heliga landet. 1964; translated as *The Holy Land*, 1966.

Mariamne. 1967; translated as *Herod and Mariamne*, 1968.

Verse

Motiv [Motifs]. 1914.

Ångest [Angst]. 1916.

Den lyckliges väg [Happy Road]. 1921.

Hjärtats sänger [Songs of the Heart]. 1926.

Vid lägereld [By the Campfire]. 1932.

Genius. 1937.

Sång och strid [Song and Battle]. 1940.

Dikter [Verse]. 1941; revised edition, 1958, 1974.

Hemmet och stjärnan [The Home and the Stars]. 1942.

Aftonland. 1953; translated as *Evening Land*, 1975.

Valda dikter [Selected Poems]. 1967.

Other

Ordkonst och bildkonst [The Art of Words and the Art of Pictures]. 1913.
Kaos [Chaos]. 1919.
Gäst hös verkligheten. 1925; translated as *Guest of Reality*, in *Guest of Reality* (collection), 1936; also translated, 1989.
Det besegrade livet [The Conquered Life]. 1927.
Skrifter [Writings] (3 vols.). 1932.
Den knutna näven. 1934; translated as *The Clenched Fist*, in *Five Early Works*, 1989.
Guest of Reality (includes *Guest of Reality; The Eternal Smile; The Hangman*). 1936.
Den befriade människan [Liberated Man]. 1939.
Prosa (5 vols.). 1945; revised edition, 1949.
Antecknat [Noted] (diary), edited by Elin Lagerkvist. 1977.
Five Early Works (includes *Iron and Men; The Last Man; The Expectant Guest; The Morning; The Clenched Fist*), translated by Roy Arthur Swanson. 1989.

*

Bibliographies

U. Willers, *Pär Lagerkvists bibliografi*, Stockholm, 1951.
A. Ryberg, *Pär Lagerkvist in Translation: A Bibliography*, Stockholm, 1964.
R. Yrlid, *Pär Lagerkvists kritiker: En recensionsbibliografi*, Stockholm, 1970.

Criticism

Books:
O. Oberholzer, *Pär Lagerkvist: Studien zu seiner Prosa und seinen Dramen*, Heidelberg, 1958.
Irene Scobbie, *Pär Lagerkvist: An Introduction*, 1963.
Irene Scobbie (ed.), "Lagerkvist", in *Essays on Swedish Literature from 1880 to the Present Day*, 1978.
Winston Weathers, *Pär Lagerkvist: A Critical Essay*, 1968.
Robert Spector, *Pär Lagerkvist*, New York, 1973.
Frederick J. and Lise Lone Marker, *The Scandinavian Theatre*, Oxford, 1975.
Leif Sjöberg, *Pär Lagerkvist*, New York, 1976.
Irene Scobbie, "Pär Lagerkvist's play *Den Osynlige*", in *20th-Century Drama in Scandinavia*, edited by Johan Wrede, Helsinki, 1979.
Ray Lewis White, *Pär Lagerkvist in America*, Stockholm, 1979.

Articles:
Lagerkvist Supplement in *Scandinavica*, 1971.
E.M. Ellestad, "Lagerkvist and Cubism: A Study of Theory and Practice", in *Scandinavian Studies*, 45, 1973.

* * *

Pär Lagerkvist is Strindberg's most significant Swedish heir. He first attracted attention with *Ångest* (Angst) a cycle of expressionistic poems, and followed this with his first play, *Sista mänskan* (The Last Man) in which the last remnants of mankind express their anguish as the sun deserts a frozen universe. Unfortunately, the play's theme cannot sustain three acts.

In his 1918 essay "*Synpunkter och angrepp*" (translated as "Points of View and Attack") he attacks naturalism, including Ibsen's "silent pacing on carpets for five long acts with words, words, words", and exhorts dramatists to eschew slavish realism, to be imaginative, and to emulate miracle plays (and above all Strindberg's post-Inferno plays). The essay marks a turning point in Scandinavian theatre. Three one-act plays entitled *Den svåra stunden* (*The Difficult Hour*) were published with it, showing Lagerkvist following his own prescription. All three deal with approaching death, and establish an atmosphere of momentary horror leading to desolation or despair. The first was initially produced by Knut Ström at the Düsseldorf Schauspielhaus under the title *The Tunnel* and still enjoys international success.

In 1919 Lagerkvist completed the one-acter *Himlens hemlighet* (*The Secret of Heaven*), in which a group of helpless, isolated characters endure a seemingly pointless existence in an alien world. A production with sets designed by Yngve Berg caught Lagerkvist's nightmare vision with concentrated and sometimes horrifying effect. There followed the three-act *Den osynlige* (The Invisible One) where, in lyrical language, Lagerkvist explores man's suffering. The Invisible Being is on stage almost throughout, seemingly a combined everyman and *deus ex machina*, until he finally declares himself to be man's spirit, combatting evil, suffering, but unquenchable.

It was Lagerkvist's good fortune that his next play *Han som fick leva om sitt liv* (The Man Who Lived His Life Over) brought about an association with the renowned producer, Per Lindberg. The theme of the play is again: what is reality or the point of existence? but abstract symbols have given way to a concrete framework. Daniel, a cobbler, struggling to make his second life better than the first, encounters convincing representatives of good and evil, and evinces our sympathy as he delivers his anguished protest against an indifferent universe.

Aware of the international situation, Lagerkvist reflected political views in *Konungen* (The King). It is set in ancient Babylon, where, in accordance with religious custom, King Amar-Azu relinquishes the throne for three days in favour of a beggar (Frazer's *Golden Bough* was well-known to Lagerkvist). The beggar unleashes evil forces, bringing about a brutal revolution; but Lagerkvist believed that good can come out of evil. The philosophical Amar-Azu recognises that once the primitive passions have been spent a happier state will emerge.

The political and existentialist elements fused well in *Bödeln* (*The Hangman*). This play is in two parts, the first set in a medieval tavern, the second in a modern restaurant. The Hangman is present throughout, inspiring the awe and respect of the crude, superstitious medieval craftsmen, but the familiarity of the brutal modern degenerates. When the Aryans direct a frenzied attack on negro jazz players, the play captures the horror of unbridled human excesses. The symbolic Hangman's final monologue imparts the metaphysical message: he is the representative that evil man deserves. In Lindberg's production the play was an outstanding success.

International events also inspired *Mannen utan själ* (*The Man Without a Soul*), the eponymous Man being a revolutionary in a police state. He develops from a single-minded terrorist into a man of conscience—in fact, he finds his soul before being executed. In *Seger i mörker* (Victory in Darkness), also a polemic against brutality in a totalitarian state, the democratic Gabriel is deposed by his deformed step-brother; but in defeat Gabriel and his wife have achieved a moral victory.

Tiring of political plays, Lagerkvist then sought to write a play "imbued with music, desire, dreams". The result was *Midsommardröm i fattighuset* (*Midsummer Dream in the Workhouse*), a title rightly suggesting the influence of

Calderón and Strindberg. *Blind-Jonas*, a resident of the workhouse (a symbol of imperfect humanity), achieves through his dream a world of happiness, goodness, and love. It is a lyrical, quintessentially Swedish play.

De vises sten (*The Philosopher's Stone*) has a medieval setting and an alchemist, Albertus at its centre. His daughter is loved by Jacob, a rabbi's son, but she becomes the Prince's mistress. When, in defending her, Jacob kills a guard, he triggers off anti-semitic riots. The play is symbolic, the Prince representing cynical materialism, while Albertus is a Faustus figure, impervious to the suffering of others in his ruthless search for truth. Despite its Lagerkvistian theme, the play, structurally, continues a development discernible from *The King* onwards, a harking-back to the well-made play. Indeed, Albertus resembles an Ibsen figure finally obliged to take stock of his own attitude.

The Philosopher's Stone was Lagerkvist's last-written play play, although he dramatised his novel *Barabbas* in 1952, which portrays the robber released in Christ's place spending the remainder of his life searching for a religion. The novel's existentialist theme and use of inner monologue is essentially unsuited to dramatic form, and the highly successful novel, largely responsible for Lagerkvist being awarded the Nobel Prize in 1951, is thus less successful as a play.

In retrospect, Lagerkvist stands as an expressionistic dramatist whose best works remain the plays up to the early 1930's when, stimulated by Lindberg, he successfully combined a philosophical and a political message couched in an imaginative symbolic form.

—Irene Scobbie

See also *Volume 1* entry on *The Hangman*.

———

LANGER, František. Born in Prague, Bohemia (then in the Austro-Hungarian Empire, now in the Czech Republic), 3 March 1888. Educated at Gymnasium, Prague, to 1907; studied medicine at the Charles University, Prague, degree 1914. Member of the literary group, the Pragmatists; conscripted into the Austro-Hungarian army as a doctor, 1914: captured by the Russians, 1916, but released to serve with the Czech Legion, 1917; travelled to Japan, China, and India; returned to Prague, 1920; dramaturg at the Municipal Theatre of the Vinohrady district (also known as the Vinohrady Theatre), Prague, 1930–38: lost job soon after the Nazi occupation of Czechoslovakia; fled to Poland, then to France, 1939; served as military doctor in France and England during World War II; returned to Czechoslovakia after the War; his work not published again until 1956, and plays not performed under the Communist regime. Made a National Artist, 1948. Died in Prague, 2 August 1965.

Works

Collections

Vybor [Selection].   1957.
Tři hry o spravodlnosti [Three Plays About Justice] (includes *Periferie*; *Andelé mezi námi*; *Dvaasedmdesátka*).   1957.
Tři veselé hry [Three Cheerful Plays] (includes *Velbloud*

uchem jehly; Grandhotel Nevada; Obracení Ferdyse Pistory).   1959.

Stage Works

Svaty Václav [Saint Václav] (produced 1912).   1912.
Milíony [Millions] (produced Plzeň, Bohemia, 1916).   1920.
Vítezové [The Conquerors] (trilogy; produced Šarka Valley, Prague, 1920).   1920.
Noc [Night] (produced Švanda Theatre, Prague-Smíchov, 1922).   1925.
Velbloud uchem jehly (produced Švanda Theatre, Prague, 1923).   1923; translated as *The Camel Through the Needle's Eye*, 1929.
Periferie [The Outskirts] (produced Vinohrady Theatre, Prague, 1925).   1925.
Grandhotel Nevada (produced Vinohrady Theatre, Prague, 1927).   1927.
Obrácení Ferdyše Pištory [The Reversal of Ferdyš Pištora] (produced Vinohrady Theatre, Prague, 1929).   1929.
Andělé mezi námi [Angels in our Midst] (produced Vinohrady Theatre, Prague, 1931).   1931.
Princ Kašpárek a jeho koníček [Prince Kaspárek and His Pony] (puppet play).   1931.
Perníková chaloupka [The Gingerbread House] (puppet play).   1932.
Kašpárek jako detektiv [Kašpárek as Detective] (puppet play).   1932.
O čem král doma nevěděl [What the King Didn't Know at Home] (puppet play).   1932.
Zlá princezna a hodný drak [The Evil Princess and the Lovable Dragon].   1932.
Manželství s.r.o. [Marriage Ltd.] (produced Vinohrady Theatre, Prague, 1935).   1934.
Koníčky [Ponies] (puppet play).   1935.
Jízdní hlídka [Mounted Patrol] (produced privately, 1935).   1935.
Jiskra v popelu [A Spark in the Ashes] (produced National Theatre, Prague, 1948).   1935.
Dvaasedmdesátka [Number 72] (produced Vinohrady Theatre, Prague, 1937).   1937.
Bronzova rapsódie (produced 1970).   1962.

Screenplays

Velbloud uchem jehly, 1937.

Fiction

Zlatá Venuse [Golden Venus] (stories).   1910.
Za cizí mesto [Outside a Foreign Town].   1919.
Železný vlk [Iron Wolf] (stories).   1920.
Pět povídek z vojny [Five Stories from the Days of Military Service].   1920.
Snílci a vrahové [Visionaries and Murderers].   1921.
Pes druhé roty [The Dog of the Second Company] (story).   1923.
Předměstské povídky [Suburban Stories].   1926.
Kratší a delší [Shorter and Longer].   1927.
Zázrak v rodině [A Prodigy in the Family] (2 vols.).   1929.
Mrtví chodí mezi námi [Dead Men Walk Among Us].   1930.
Bratrstvo bílého klíče [Brotherhood of the White Key] (novel for children).   1934.
"The Man Who Sold Dreams" and Other Stories.   1945.
Děti a dýka (novel).   1946; translated as *Children and the Dagger*, 1944.
Pražské legendy [Prague Legends] (stories).   1956.
Filatelistické povídky [Philatelists' Tales] (stories).   1964.
Malířské povídky [Tales of a Painter] (stories).   1966.

Nadšenci a podivíni [Enthusiasts and Eccentrics] (stories). 1987.
Ves [Countryside]. 1986.
Město každý den [A Town Everyday]. 1988.
Prodavač snů [The Man Who Sold Dreams]. 1988.

Memoirs and Letters

Byli a bylo [They Were and It Was] (memoirs). 1963.

Other

Divadelníkkem z vlastní vůle: Výbor z praci o divadle a dramatu (writings on theatre). 1986.

* * *

František Langer grew up in the Vinohrady district of Prague, where at an early age his parents introduced him to the theatre—at first the open-air summer arenas, and later the National Theatre and the Municipal Theatre of Vinohrady. He was still at school when he began to publish short pieces in magazines and, at the age of 24 in 1912, he won success with the production of one of his plays at the National Theatre. *Svatý Václav* (Saint Václav), directed by Jaroslav Kvapil, was a historical drama on the theme of resistance to evil.

By the start of the first World War, having graduated in medicine, Langer was an established editor and writer with a collection of short stories, *Zlatá Venuše* (Golden Venus), to his credit. He and his circle were known as the "Pragmatists", a group including Edmond Konrad and the brothers Karel and Josef Čapek which belonged to the avant-garde of Czech literature, and was sharply critical of contemporary society. Another close friend of Langer was the anarchist Jaroslav Hašek (author of *Švejk*), with whom he wrote and performed cabaret.

With the outbreak of war, Langer was conscripted as a doctor in the Austro-Hungarian army; in 1916 he was captured and interned by the Russians, but the following year released to serve with the Czechoslovak legion. He did not return to Prague until 1920, returning home via Japan, China, and India. On his return he wrote three short plays about the legion, collectively titled *Vítezové* (The Conquerors) which were staged as part of a spectacular open-air event in the Šarka valley in Prague. The same year, the National Theatre presented his play *Milíony* (Millions), completed before the War and already staged in Plzeň in 1916. Written in a realist, neo-classical style, its subject is the tragedy of power and the curse of wealth. In 1922 another of his pre-war plays, *Noc* (Night), had its premiere in the Švanda Theatre in Prague-Smíchov.

However, with the passing of the War years, Czech society had changed, and so had the Pragmatists. They were now living in the Czechoslovak Republic, which their generation had been instrumental in creating, and towards which they felt a new, though critical, loyalty. The role of the avant-garde was assumed by a younger circle, few of whom had been old enough to participate in the War and the struggle for national identity. They saw themselves as internationalists and were attracted by left-wing ideals and the emergence of the USSR. In 1921, under the leadership of Karel Teige, they formed themselves into the iconoclastic Devětsil.

Langer, on the other hand, moved away from his belligerent pre-war themes; Czech culture was no longer embattled, no longer fighting for its existence under a German-speaking regime. He turned to Prague, his native city, and especially the district of Vinohrady for his themes and characters. In *Velbloud uchem jehly* (The Camel Through the Needle's Eye),

Langer took as his heroine Zuzka, an unemployed working-class girl who becomes mistress to the heir of a big business. She confounds his family and social circle by using the money she makes on the stock exchange to start her own dairy and employ her lover as cellarman.

In 1925 the most famous of Langer's plays, *Periferie* (The Outskirts of the City), opened at the Municipal Theatre in Vinohrady, directed by Jaroslav Kvapil. (It is noteworthy that Langer did not release any of his plays to K.H. Hilar, Kvapil's dynamic successor at the National Theatre. Hilar was notorious for his cavalier treatment of an author's work.) The play is set in the the desolate outer reaches of a big city. Josef Čapek's expressionist cyclorama for Kvapil's production shows a bleak, smoky landscape in which tenement blocks stand like tombstones. "The Outskirts of the City" is the story of Franta and his proletarian comrades, especially the poor girl-turned-prostitute, Anna, in whose defence Franta murders an upper-class client. In a series of cinematically juxtaposed scenes we see how the workings of Franta's conscience lead him to redemption through the death of Anna.

By now Langer's success was established; "The Outskirts of the City" was produced the same year at the Josefstadter Theater in Vienna, directed by Max Reinhardt. The following year *The Camel Through the Needle's Eye* was filmed, and in 1927 "Grand Hotel Nevada" opened at the theatre in Vinohrady, directed by Kvapil, and with Karel Čapek's wife, Olga Scheinpflugová, playing the leading role of Lucy. This is a comedy set in the USA, featuring Czech immigrants' experience of American life. It was followed in 1929 by another comedy, *Obrácení Ferdyše Pištory* (The Reversal of Ferdyš Pištora). In 1930 Langer became dramaturg at the Municipal Theatre of Vinohrady, a post he held until 1938.

The 1930's were a time of success for Langer; his new plays were performed successfully at home and abroad, as well as being filmed. Amongst them were *Andělé mezi námi* (Angels), a fantasy dramatising the subject of euthnasia, and *Jízdní hlídka* (Mounted Patrol), based on his experience as a military prisoner during the Russian Revolution. However, the Langers were a Jewish family, and the events that followed the Munich Agreement of 1938 brought about a sharp reversal. In October, František Langer was sacked from the Vinohrady theatre, and the following year he fled to Poland, and from there to France. One of his brothers fled to Palestine; the other committed suicide. In France and in England he served as a military doctor; in the course of time he found opportunities to write, broadcast, and publish. On his return to Prague after the War he was made a National Artist, and a new comedy, *Jiskra v popelu* (A Spark in the Ashes), was produced by the National Theatre company in 1948.

To the new communists' regime, however, František Langer was a remnant of the pre-war "bourgeois" republic. There were no more honours, and it was 1956 before his work began to be republished. His plays remained unperformed from 1938 until the 1960's, and therefore had little influence on the new generations of playwrights. He died in 1965, the last remaining representative of the "Čapek generation".

—Barbara Day

LAO She. See *Volume 1* entry on *Teahouse*.

LAURENTS, Arthur. Born in Brooklyn, New York, 14 July 1918. Educated at Cornell University, Ithaca, New York, BA 1937. Served in the US Army, 1940–45: Sergeant; radio playwright, 1943–45 (Citation, Secretary of War, and *Variety* radio award, 1945). Early plays produced on radio; first-produced stage play, *Home of the Brave*, performed 1945; subsequently wrote the books for several musicals. Also a stage director, and has been involved in several productions of his own work. Director, Dramatists Play Service, New York, 1961–66. Council member, Dramatists Guild, from 1955. Recipient: American Academy Award, 1946; Sidney Howard Memorial Award, 1946; Tony Award, for play, 1967, for directing, 1984; Vernon Rice Award, 1974; Golden Globe Award, 1977; Screenwriters Guild Award, 1978;

Stage Works

Home of the Brave (produced Belasco Theatre, New York, 1945; as *The Way Back*, produced London, 1949).   1946.
Heartsong (produced Shubert Theatre, New Haven, Connecticut, 1947).
The Bird Cage (produced Coronet Theatre, New York, 1950).   1950.
The Time of the Cuckoo (produced Empire Theatre, New York, 1952).   1953.
A Clearing in the Woods (produced Belasco Theatre, New York, 1957).   1957; revised edition, 1960.
West Side Story, music by Leonard Bernstein, lyrics by Stephen Sondheim (produced Winter Garden Theatre, New York, 1957).   1958.
Gypsy, music by Jule Styne, lyrics by Stephen Sondheim, from a book by Gypsy Rose Lee (produced Broadway Theatre, New York, 1959).   1960.
Invitation to a March (produced Music Box Theatre, New York, 1960).   1961.
Anyone Can Whistle, music by Stephen Sondheim (produced Majestic Theatre, New York, 1964).   1965.
Do I Hear a Waltz?, music by Richard Rodgers, lyrics by Stephen Sondheim (produced 46th Street Theatre, New York, 1965).   1966.
Hallelujah, Baby!, music by Jule Styne, Lyrics by Betty Comden and Adolph Green (produced Martin Beck Theatre, New York, 1967).   1967.
The Enclave (produced Theatre Club, Washington, DC, 1973).   1974.
Scream (produced Alley Theatre, Houston, Texas, 1978).
The Madwoman of Central Park West, with Phyllis Newman, music by Peter Allen and others, from the play *My Mother Was a Fortune Teller* by Newman (produced 22 Steps Theatre, New York, 1979).
A Loss of Memory (produced Southampton College, Southampton, New York, 1981).   In *The Best Short Plays*, 1983.

Screenplays

The Snake Pit, with Frank Partos and Millen Brand, 1948; *Rope*, with Hume Cronyn, 1948; *Anna Lucasta*, with Philip Yordan, 1949; *Caught*, 1949; *Anastasia*, 1956; *Bonjour Tristesse*, 1958; *The Way We Were*, 1973; *The Turning Point*, 1977.

Television Plays

The Light Fantastic, 1967.

Radio Plays

Now Playing Tomorrow, 1939 (published in *Short Plays for Stage and Radio*, edited by Carless Jones, 1940); *Hollywood Playhouse, Dr. Christian, The Thin Man, Manhattan at Midnight,* and other series, 1939–40; *Western Electric Communicade*, 1944 (published in *The Best One-Act Plays of 1944*, edited by Margaret Mayorga, 1944), *The Last Day of the War*, 1945 (published in *Radio Drama in Action*, edited by Erik Barnouw, 1945), *The Face*, 1945 (published in *The Best One-Act Plays of 1945*, edited by Margaret Mayorga, 1945), and other plays for *The Man Behind the Gun, Army Service Force Presents,* and *Assignment: Home* series, 1943–45; *This is Your FBI* series, 1945.

Fiction

The Way We Were.   1972.
The Turning Point.   1977.

* * *

Laurents's debut in 1946, with *Home of the Brave*, placed him alongside Tennessee Williams, Arthur Miller and William Inge in the vanguard of post-war American playwrights whose works (including *Mister Roberts, Command Decision, The Teahouse of the August Moon* and *The Caine Mutiny Court Martial*) criticised military conduct and ethics at a cruicially patriotic time. In this study of an enlisted man's strange trauma, Laurents was able to strike at the very heart of the "American dream" by questioning the values underpinning notions of heroism, physical perfection, and the inherent rightness of a given "just cause". The play also assails the myth of inter-racial harmony among first- and second-generation Americans, all fighting on the same side, by exposing the class and racial hatred among a select group of engineering experts assigned to carry out a secret mission against the Japanese. While offering no profound statement of abiding belief, as Williams's and Miller's work does, *Home of the Brave* anticipated much liberal thinking in the United States for the next generation, simply by offering an alternative level of acceptance to the standards epitomised by the Eisenhower Administration.

It is duly perplexing, therefore, that Laurents's subsequent career failed to develop from this auspicious beginning. The plays after *Home of the Brave* were not disappointing so much as disconcerting. Though an interest in psychological delineation of character links a number of the plays, this in itself is insufficient as a basis for a whole theatrical mode. His choice of subjects, too, seems almost arbitrary, and each of the plays after *Home of the Brave* lacks contextual weight. The body of work, finally, is too slight to carry a major dramatic talent. These limitations become clearer when the plays are compared to the work of Laurents's contemporaries.

The Bird Cage is a study of sexual frustration in the case of a vicious night-club owner. The characterisation is acute, the analysis sound, and scenes between the protagonist and his adolescent son are particularly effective. But a similar theme is treated far more substantially in Inge's *Come Back, Little Sheba*, where a whole world is evoked through minute concentration on "ordinary people" beset by drabness. Laurents's play has not a quarter of Inge's grounding in a recognisable social context; he does not even specify time and place. And though there is frequent reference to the economic conditions, these are not drawn into the play.

Social context is more firmly established in *The Time of the Cuckoo*, a comedy about a summer romance between an unmarried woman in her 30's and a married Italian in Venice. Laurents develops his theme about the loss of romantic love through four distinct couples, each one well characterised. There is a great deal, too, about the contrast in values between America and Europe, and a social critique is offered in the thoroughly-wrought notion of "the price of love". This play is, on the whole, successful, though its effectiveness depends on strong acting in the central roles, taken originally by Shirley Booth and Dino Di Luca. And the sudden shift into the comic mode is immediately puzzling, since Laurents does not display a natural talent for it.

He gives fullest treatment to the theme of romantic love in the expressionistic *A Clearing in the Woods*, in which personality is anatomised by having five characters portray different strands and different stages of development in the central character, a woman, whose self-destructive search for "something magic" results in the destruction of all her previous relationships. Though this play has nothing like the force and the sweep of Strindberg's "dream" plays it effectively delineates social values through examination of an individual, and prefigures the later, feminist drama in showing an American woman's disaffection with a dated value system.

Social context and personality are integrated more successfully than in anything since *Home of the Brave* in *Invitation to a March*, in which traditional notions of marriage are satirised against the background of an imminent Long Island marriage. Laurents comes down on the anti-Establishment side by having the bride walk out on the promised "brilliant" marriage in favour of an uncertain match with an assumed social misfit. The production was distinguished by a cast that included such celebrities as the young Jane Fonda, Celeste Holm, and Madeleine Sherwood. The dialogue is peppered with such trenchant observations as, "people may forgive you for what you do for love, but never for what you do for passion", and, "marriage is an institution, and no institution was founded on love". The depiction of non-conformity is altogether more tame than it is in the best work of William Saroyan, largely because Laurents has failed to create any truly memorable characters.

His adherence to conventional realism may provide an important insight into his limitations. His characters, for all their inner turmoil, continue to inhabit only their own world. Individually, they may be every bit as neurotic as are Williams's women, but, except in *Home of The Brave*, they fail to speak for a civilisation, as do Williams's; they signify too little. Sexual frustration in *The Bird Cage* might have been more engaging as a theme if Laurents had managed to evaluate cultural attitudes through it, as both Williams and Inge do. Though ordinary people in extraordinary circumstances, Laurents's characters refuse to speak with a truly representative voice.

His own original work has been supplemented by numerous commissions to write the books for popular musicals, most notably for *West Side Story* and *Gypsy*. These are successful in their own terms; and they even achieve a degree of social commentary untapped in most of his plays. But musicals are a necessarily indirect vehicle for acute social comment, and even if Laurents may be taken as having broken new ground in "legitimising" the musical "book" by addressing serious issues, commercial restraints obviously limit the impact of "the bits in between" the musical numbers. In terms of "shocking" subject matter for a musical, in any case, Laurents's handling of the striptease artist Gypsy Rose Lee was altogether more acceptable to Broadway audiences than was John O'Hara's unsentimental rendering of the night club heel and probable pimp in *Pal Joey*. One possible explanation for Laurents's success as a librettist may be that his

task there has been roughly half what it is in a full-length, straight play—at best he has always been only half successful as a playwright. This fact is particularly dispiriting in one who promised so much with his first, really notable play.

—James MacDonald

LAWLER, Ray(mond Evenor). Born in Footscray, Melbourne, Victoria, Australia, in 1921. Left school at age 13. Married Jacklyn Kelleher; three children. Worked in a foundry, 1934–45; actor, Sid Turnbull's Melbourne Repertory Company, 1946–49; actor and producer, National Theatre Company, Melbourne, 1950–54; director, Union Theatre Repertory Company, Melbourne University, 1954–55; lived in Denmark, England, and mainly in Ireland, early 1960's–1975; director and literary adviser, Melbourne Theatre Company, 1976–86. OBE (Officer, Order of the British Empire), 1981.

Works

Collections

The Doll Trilogy (includes *Kid Stakes; Other Times; Summer of the Seventeenth Doll*). 1978.

Stage Works

Cradle of Thunder (produced Melbourne, 1949).
Summer of the Seventeenth Doll (produced Union Theatre, Melbourne, 1955). 1957.
The Piccadilly Bushman (produced Theatre Royal, Sydney, 1959; Liverpool, 1965). 1961.
The Unshaven Cheek (produced Edinburgh Festival, 1963).
A Breach in the Wall (televised 1967; produced Canterbury, Kent, 1970).
The Man Who Shot the Albatross (produced Princess Theatre, Melbourne, 1972).
Kid Stakes (produced Russell Street Theatre, Melbourne, 1975). In *The Doll Trilogy*, 1978.
Other Times (produced Russell Street Theatre, Melbourne, 1976). In *The Doll Trilogy*, 1978.
Godsend (produced Melbourne, 1982).

Television Plays

A Breach in the Wall, 1967; *Sinister Street* serial, from the novel by Compton Mackenzie, 1968; *Cousin Bette* serial, from the novel by Balzac, 1971; *The Visitors* serial, from the novel by Mary McMinnies, 1972; *Two Women* serial, from a novel by Alberto Moravia, 1972; *Mrs. Palfrey at the Claremont*, from the novel by Elizabeth Taylor, 1973; *After the Party*, from the story by W. Somerset Maugham, 1974; *Seeking the Bubbles* (*The Love School* series), 1975; *True Patriots All*, 1975; *Husband to Mrs. Fitzherbert*, 1975.

*

Criticism

Books:
Leslie Rees, *A History of Australian Drama* (2 vols.), Sydney, 1978.

Articles:

Ray Lawler and Alrene Sykes, "Interview: Ray Lawler Talks to Alrene Sykes", in *Australasian Drama Studies*, vol. 3 no. 2, 1985.

* * *

Ray Lawler's reputation as one of Australia's most distinguished playwrights is still based largely on one extremely successful play, *Summer of the Seventeenth Doll*. The play came at a crucial time, not only for the narrow world of the Australian theatre but for Australian culture generally. The 1950's were a time of national self-consciousness, when former ideas of "Australianness" were being, to a certain extent, reassessed. The *Doll* took the traditional legend of the laconic, hard-bitten Australian bushman, which had been an important part of the national self-image since the 1890's, and dragged it, almost literally, kicking and screaming into the cities to face the realities of post-war urban Australia.

The play's warm portrayal of distinctive bush and city character-types was greeted with delighted recognition by middle-class audiences for whom the original legend had, in fact, only ever been an exotic dream. The two tough cane-cutters, Roo and Barney, who come down from the Queensland cane-fields each year to spend the "lay-off" season whooping it up in Melbourne, represented a vanishing national type with whom the city audiences liked to identify.

The *Doll* shows these two legendary characters failing to deal with the new urban Australia. The romantic dream of the lay-offs—times of innocent loving fun for the men and their barmaid girlfriends—is already beginning to fail as the play opens. Olive, Roo's partner, tries to sustain her vision of a nobler life than that which the "soft city blokes" have to offer, and she clings to it even when it brings personal tragedy for her; but the world of the soft city blokes wins, practically if not emotionally. For contemporary audiences, perhaps, the portrayal of Olive as a foolish woman who refuses to grow up (confirmed in the expanded *The Doll Trilogy*) has dated. There is some justice in her claim to have found a serious alternative to marriage, but after a series of reversals at the end we are left with a final ironic triumph of the legend, as Roo and Barney stagger out to head back north, leaving Olive alone in her grief. *The Doll*'s appeal is based in the solid, old-fashioned virtues of well-made realism: detailed and consistent characterisation, a wonderfully rich use of vernacular, and a complex and carefully plotted action.

The extraordinary success of the *Doll* meant that Lawler's next plays were bound to be received with disappointment. *The Piccadilly Bushman* is a technically competent play which explores the self-image of an Australian expatriate actor who has achieved success as an actor in England and returns to confront what he now sees as his embarrassing "colonial" past. *The Man Who Shot the Albatross* is an historical play about a much-treated subject in Australian drama—the colonial Governor Bligh, struggling to deal with mutinous local bigwigs, and haunted by the memory of the other more famous mutineers on the *Bounty*. The play presents its subject largely in terms of personal conflict between Bligh and the politically astute landowner, John Macarthur—avoiding any wider historical or political exploration. For this reason, perhaps, it seemed rather old-fashioned in 1972. Neither of these two plays has had much impact in the Australian theatre.

Lawler lived abroad during the great upsurge in Australian drama of the early 1970's, but he returned in the mid-1970's to produce two plays which revived his reputation—*Kid Stakes* and *Other Times*. These plays form a trilogy, with the *Doll*, and their action is set prior to that in the *Doll*. They go back to the first and the ninth "lay-offs," introducing the appealing character of Nancy, whose memory so dominates the *Doll*, and generally filling in the background to what had by the mid-1970's become a well-known and well-loved part of the national heritage. *Kid Stakes* is a play of great charm. Its delightful portrait of an innocent young Australian society before World War II shows Lawler at his full strength, lamenting the loss of a simpler world. *Other Times*, set during the War, in winter, is written in a minor key, introducing a note of bitterness which anticipates the tragedy of the *Doll*. The effect of the trilogy, ironically, has been to lessen the impact of the original play. The new plays take so much trouble to plant hints anticipating the action of the *Doll* that the brilliant Ibsenite exposition in the original becomes rather pointless and the story and characters move into a new world of sophisticated soap opera.

In 1982 Lawler produced his first major work since the trilogy, *Godsend*. The "godsend" is the discovery in a small rural church in Kent of the lost tomb of St. Thomas à Becket. Each of the four central characters—a traditionalist Catholic bishop, the Anglican archbishop, an idealistic parson, and his agnostic wife—has a different interest in the holy remains, and through their conflict the play explores the nature of religious faith and the difficulties of sustaining it. Stylistically the play is a departure from the well-made realism of *The Doll Trilogy*, especially in its complex use of direct audience address. It is the work of a mature dramatist with accomplished skills, and has not yet had the impact it deserves.

Lawler's place in the development of Australian drama is still assured by the *Doll*. If he has never repeated that success, it is perhaps partly because his dramatic interests have become less relevant to the issues which now involve Australian audiences, but he remains one of the most technically capable of all Australian dramatists, and one who has contributed some of the best-loved characters in the culture.

—John McCallum

See also *Volume 1* entry on *The Doll Trilogy*.

———

LAWRENCE, D(avid) H(erbert). Born in Eastwood, Nottinghamshire, England, 11 September 1885. Educated at Nottingham High School, 1898–1901; University College, Nottingham (now University of Nottingham), 1906–08, teacher's certificate, 1908. Eloped with Frieda von Richthofen Weekley in 1912, married in 1914. Clerk for a firm of surgical appliance makers, Nottingham, 1901; pupil-teacher in Eastwood and Ilkeston, Nottinghamshire, 1902–06; teacher, Davidson Road School, Croydon, Surrey, 1908–12; full-time writer from 1912; lived in Germany, Italy, and Switzerland, 1912–14, and in England, 1914–19; prosecuted for obscenity (*The Rainbow*), 1915; founder, with Katherine Mansfield and John Middleton Murry, *Signature* magazine, 1916; lived in Florence, Capri, and Sicily, 1919–22; first-produced play, *The Widowing of Mrs. Holroyd*, given a schools performance, 1920; travelled to Ceylon and Australia, 1922; lived in the USA and Mexico, 1922–23, England, France, and Germany, 1924, New Mexico and Mexico, 1924–25, Italy, 1925–28, and France, 1928–30. Several of his plays only published and produced posthumously. Also a painter: one-man show, London, 1929 (closed by the police). Recipient: James Tait Black Memorial Prize, 1921. Died 2 March 1930.

Works

Collections

Plays (includes *The Widowing of Mrs. Holroyd; Touch and Go; David*).   1933.
Complete Plays.   1965.
Three Plays (includes *A Collier's Friday Night; The Daughter-in-Law; The Widowing of Mrs. Holroyd*).   1969.
[*Works*] (Cambridge Edition), edited by James T. Boulton and Warren Roberts.   1980–

Stage Works

The Widowing of Mrs. Holroyd (produced Unitarian Schools, Altrincham, Surrey, 1920). 1914.
Touch and Go (produced Questors Theater Ealing, London, 1973).   1920.
David (produced Regent Theatre, London, 1927).   1926.
Keeping Barbara (produced as *The Fight for Barbara*, Mermaid Theatre, London, 1967). In *Argosy 14*, December 1933; as *The Fight for Barbara*, in Complete Plays, 1965.
A Collier's Friday Night (produced Royal Court Theatre, London, 1965).   1934.
The Daughter-in-Law (produced as *My Son's Son*, Playhouse Theatre, London, 1936; produced as *The Daughter in Law*, Royal Court Theatre, London 1967).   In *Complete Plays*, 1965.
The Merry-Go-Round (produced Royal Court Theatre, London, 1973).   In *Complete Plays*, 1965.
The Married Man.   In *Complete Plays*, 1965.
Altitude.   In *Complete Plays*, 1965.
Noah's Flood.   In *Complete Plays*, 1965.

Fiction

The White Peacock.   1911,
The Trespasser.   1912.
Sons and Lovers.   1913.
The Prussian Officer and Other Stories.   1914.
The Rainbow.   1915.
Women in Love.   1920.
The Lost Girl.   1920.
Aaron's Rod.   1922.
"England My England" and Other Stories.   1922.
The Ladybird; The Fox; The Captain's Doll.   1923; as *The Captain's Doll: Three Novelettes*, 1923.
Kangaroo.   1923.
The Boy in the Bush, with M.L. Skinner.   1924.
St. Mawr, Together with The Princess.   1925.
The Plumed Serpent (*Quetzalcoatl*).   1926.
Sun (story).   1926; unexpurgated edition, 1928.
Glad Ghosts (story).   1926.
Rawdon's Roof (story).   1928.
"The Woman Who Rode Away" and Other Stories.   1928.
Lady Chatterley's Lover.   1928; *The First Lady Chatterley* (first version), 1944; *La Tre Lady Chatterley* (three versions), in Italian, 1954; unexpurgated edition, 1959; *John Thomas and Lady Jane* (second version), 1972.
The Escaped Cock.   1929; as *The Man Who Died*, 1931.
The Virgin and the Gipsy.   1930.

"Love Among the Haystacks" and Other Pieces.   1930.
The Lovely Lady (stories).   1933.
A Modern Lover (stories).   1934.
A Prelude (story).   1949.
"The Princess" and Other Stories, and *"The Mortal Coil" and Other Stories* (2 vols.), edited by Keith Sagar.   1971.
Mr. Noon, edited by Lindeth Vasey.   1984.
Complete Short Novels, edited by Keith Sagar and Melissa Partridge.   1982.
Selected Short Stories, edited by Brian Finney.   1982.

Verse

Love Poems and Others.   1913.
Amores.   1916.
Look! We Have Come Through!   1917.
New Poems.   1918.
Bay.   1919.
Tortoises.   1921.
Birds, Beasts, and Flowers.   1923.
Collected Poems (2 vols.).   1928.
Pansies.   1929.
Nettles.   1930.
The Triumph of the Machine.   1931.
Last Poems, edited by Richard Aldington and Giuseppe Orioli.   1932.
"Fire" and Other Poems.   1940.
Complete Poems, edited by Vivian de Sola Pinto and Warren Roberts (2 vols.).   1964.
Selected Poems, edited by Keith Sagar.   1972; revised edition, as *Poems*, 1986.

Memoirs and Letters

Letters, edited by Aldous Huxley.   1932.
Collected Letters, edited by Harry T. Moore (2 vols.).   1962.
Lawrence in Love: *Letters to Louie Burrows*, edited by James T. Boulton.   1968.
Centaur Letters, edited by Edward D. McDonald.   1970.
Letters to Martin Secker 1911–1930, edited by Martin Secker.   1970.
The Quest for Ranamin: *Letters to S.S. Koteliansky 1914–1930*, edited by G.J. Zytaruk.   1970.
Letters to Thomas and Adele Seltzer: *Letters to His American Publishers*, edited by Gerald M. Lacy.   1976.
Letters, edited by James T. Boulton.   1979—

Other

Twilight in Italy.   1916.
Movements in European History.   1921; revised edition, 1926.
Psychoanalysis and the Unconscious.   1921.
Sea and Sardinia.   1921.
Fantasia of the Unconscious.   1922.
Studies in Classic American Literature.   1923; edited by Armin Arnold, as *The Symbolic Meaning: The Uncollected Versions*, 1962.
"Reflections on the Death of a Porcupine" and Other Essays.   1925.
Mornings in Mexico.   1927.
The Paintings of Lawrence.   1929.
My Skirmish with Jolly Roger (introduction to *Lady Chatterley's Lover*).   1929; as *A Propos of Lady Chatterley's Lover*, 1930.
Pornography and Obscenity.   1929.
Assorted Articles.   1930.

Apocalypse. 1931.
Etruscan Places. 1932.
We Need One Another. 1933.
Phoenix: *The Posthumous Papers*, edited by Edward D. McDonald. 1936.
The Paintings, edited by Mervyn Levy. 1964.
Phoenix II: Uncollected, Unpublished, and Other Prose Works, edited by Warren Roberts and Harry T. Moore. 1968.
A Selection, edited by R.H. Poole and P.J. Shepherd. 1970.
"Study of Thomas Hardy" and Other Essays, edited by Bruce Steele. 1985.
Memoir of Maurice Magnus. 1987.

Translator, with S.S. Koteliansky, *All Things Are Possible*, by Leo Shestov. 1920.
Translator, *Mastro-Don Gesualdo*, by Giovanni Verga. 1923.
Translator, *Little Novels of Sicily*, by Giovanni Verga. 1923.
Translator, *Cavalleria Rusticana and Other Stories*, by Giovanni Verga. 1928.
Translator, *The Story of Doctor Manente*, by A.F. Grazzini. 1929.
Translator, with S.S. Koteliansky, *The Grand Inquisitor*, by Dostoevsky. 1930.

*

Bibliographies

John E. Stoll, *D.H. Lawrence: A Bibliography 1911–1975*, Troy, New York, 1977.
James C. Cowan, *D.H. Lawrence: An Annotated Bibliography of Writings About Him* (2 vols.), 1982–85.

Criticism

Books:
Alastair Niven, *D.H. Lawrence: The Writer and His Work*, London, 1980 (British Council pamphlet).
Sylvia Sklar, *The Plays of D.H. Lawrence*, New York, 1975.
Keith Sagar, *D.H. Lawrence: Life Into Art*, London and New York, 1985.
T.R. Sharma (ed.), *Essays on D.H. Lawrence*, Meerut, India, 1987.
John Worthen, *D.H. Lawrence: The Early Years, 1885–1912*, Cambridge, 1991.

Articles:
Keith Sagar, "D.H. Lawrence: Dramatist", in *D.H. Lawrence Review*, 4, 1971.

* * *

Lawrence was little regarded as a playwright in his own lifetime, and with the exception of two pieces, *The Widowing of Mrs. Holroyd*, a powerful piece of domestic social drama, and *David*, a biblical play, both of which were given restricted performances by the Stage Society, his plays were not produced at all during his lifetime, and indeed some were not even published until after World War II. Criticism, too, neglected the plays, and the full quality and significance of his plays was not really appreciated until the mid to late 1960's. At that time a more sympathetic stage and social climate, along with keen critical interest in his novels, led to a revaluation of Lawrence's plays, particularly after some were produced at the Royal Court Theatre in London between 1965 and 1967. Today, of Lawrence's distinction as a dramatist, there can be little doubt, and in the field of early 20th-century provincial naturalism he has few equals.

Perhaps the most suprisingly original of the Lawrence plays produced at the Royal Court was his first comedy, *A Collier's Friday Night*, written in 1906. It is a remarkably mature piece for a writer still only beginning to find his talent. Other comparable working-class social dramas followed at the Court, and Lawrence's pieces in the comic vein, too, were re-examined. In fact, Lawrence's dramatic output is both larger and much more varied than is generally assumed: he wrote, in addition to those plays already mentioned, *The Daughter-in-Law*, the comedies *The Fight for Barbara* (published first as *Keeping Barbara*) and *The Married Man*, *Touch and Go*, and the dramatic fragments *Altitude*, 1912, and *Noah's Flood*, 1925. Thus, Lawrence attempted work in several quite different dramatic genres, but that in which he most excelled was naturalistic, working-class, domestic drama, reflective of the life of the labouring classes among whom he had grown up. In his own time the English theatre was dominated by more genteel forms of bourgeois naturalism, which admitted little of the plain, touching, amusing, sympathetic and altogether persuasive pictures of ordinary working-class life in which Lawrence, at his best, excelled. His finest dramatic work is, then, perhaps that closest to his earliest novels, *The White Peacock* and *Sons and Lovers*.

It is rather ironic that Lawrence should have attempted epic religious drama in *Noah's Flood* and *David*, a kind of dramatic writing rather fashionable at the time he wrote, and that reflected notions of what constituted seriousness in dramatic subject matter. This form had about it all too many of the marks of that "deadly theatre" that Lawrence shrewdly condemned in the work of many of his contemporaries: the "rather bony, bloodless dramà we get nowadays". (He had in mind the theatrically effective, but emotionally rather insipid or strained drama of writers like Galsworthy and Granville Barker.)

Lawrence is most unusual for the period in which he wrote, in that he instinctively avoided sentimentality in his treatment of the working class. In his best work, like *A Collier's Friday Night*, *The Widowing of Mrs. Holroyd*, and *The Daughter-in-Law*, there is an unpatronising acceptance of the characters and a directness in the way in which they are depicted, not only beyond the capability of Lawrence's contemporaries (even those, like Houghton or Monkhouse, who dealt in provincial naturalism), but from which many modern political dramatists of the Left could well learn. Lawrence created a serious drama of common life in which he explored simple domestic situations and familial relationships, particularly those familiar to him as the son of a Nottinghamshire miner.

Lawrence was an admirer of the plays of Synge and Chekhov, and their influence is to be felt in his own work, and perhaps even more important than his rich stage naturalism was his emotionally and psychologically mature treatment of personal relationships. Lawrence's dialogue, while reflecting appropriate working-class and lower-middle-class idioms, like real speech, yet tighter and more intense, offered, too, a sharp, intelligent, ironic humour rooted in social observation. These qualities help to give the plays a very keen edge.

Lawrence's was a form of naturalism with which the theatre of the day could not cope. That his plays were for so long neglected is testimony to the extent to which theatre before

and between the wars was dominated by the tastes and preoccupations of a social and cultural minority.

—Kenneth Richards

———————

LAWSON, John Howard. Born in New York City, 25
September 1894. Educated at the Halstead School, Yonkers,
New York; Cutler School, New York, graduated 1910;
Williams College, Williamstown, Massachusetts, 1910–14,
BA 1914. Served in the American Ambulance Service in
France and Italy during World War I. Married 1) Kathryn
Drain in 1919 (divorced 1923), one son; 2) Susan Edmond in
1925, one son and one daughter. Cable editor, Reuters Press,
New York, 1914–15; first-produced play, *Servant-Master-
Lover*, staged 1916; lived in Paris for two years after the War;
director, New Playwrights Theatre, New York, 1927–28;
screenwriter in Hollywood, 1928–47. Council member,
Authors League of America, 1930–40; founding President,
1933–34, and member of the Executive Board, 1933–40,
Screen Writers Guild. One of the "Hollywood Ten": served a
one-year sentence for contempt of the House Un-American
Activities Committee, 1950–51. Died in San Francisco, 11
August 1977.

Works

Stage Works

Servant-Master-Lover (produced Los Angeles, 1916).
Standards (produced Syracuse, New York, 1916).
Roger Bloomer (produced 48th Street Theatre, New York,
    1923). 1923.
Processional: A Jazz Symphony of American Life (produced
    Garrick Theatre, New York, 1925). 1925.
Nirvana (produced Greenwich Village Theatre, New York,
    1926).
Loudspeaker (produced 52nd Street Theatre, New York,
    1927). 1927.
The International (produced Cherry Lane Theatre, New
    York, 1928). 1928.
Success Story (produced Maxine Elliot Theatre, New York,
    1932). 1932.
The Pure in Heart (produced Longacre Theatre, New York,
    1934). In *With a Reckless Preface: Two Plays*, 1934.
Gentlewoman (produced Cort Theatre, New York, 1934).
    In *With a Reckless Preface: Two Plays*, 1934.
Marching Song (produced Nora Bayes Theatre, New York,
    1937). 1937.
Parlor Magic (produced 1963).

Screenplays

Dream of Love, with others, 1928; *The Pagan*, with Dorothy
Farnum, 1929; *Dynamite*, with Jeanie Macpherson and
Gladys Unger, 1929; *The Sea Bat*, with others, 1930; *Our
Blushing Brides*, with Bess Meredyth and Helen Mainard,
1930; *The Ship from Shanghai*, 1930; *Bachelor Apartment*,
with J. Walter Rubin, 1931; *Success at Any Price*, with others,
1934; *Blockade*, 1938; *Algiers*, with James M. Cain, 1938
(published in *Foremost Films of 1938*, edited by Frank

Vreeland, 1939); *They Shall Have Music*, with Irmgard Von
Cube, 1939; *Four Sons*, with Milton Sperling, 1940; *Earth-
bound*, with Samuel C. Engel, 1940; *Sahara*, with others,
1943; *Action in the North Atlantic*, with others, 1943;
Counter-Attack (One Against Seven), 1945; *Smash-Up—The
Story of a Woman*, with others, 1947.

Other

Theory and Technique of Playwriting. 1936; revised edition,
    as *Theory and Technique of Playwriting and Screenwriting*,
    1949.
*The Hidden Heritage: A Rediscovery of the Ideas and Forces
    That Link the Thought of Our Time with the Culture of the
    Past.* 1950.
Film in the Battle of Ideas. 1953.
*Film: The Creative Process: The Search for an Audio-Visual
    Language and Structure.* 1964; revised edition, 1967.

*

Criticism

Books:
Karen M. Taylor, *People's Theater in America*, New York,
    1973.
R.C. Reynolds, *Stage Left: The Development of the American
    Social Drama in the Thirties*, Troy, New York, 1986.

Articles:
Kshamanidhi Mishra, "Lawson's *Roger Bloomer* and
    Processional: A Blend of Political Radicalism and
    Theatrical Experimentation", in *PURBA* (Panjab
    University), vol.21 no.1, 1990.

*   *   *

John Howard Lawson's eight major plays markedly reflect
a commitment to social protest and a zest for theatrical
experimentation. Also they exemplify the root concept of
Lawson's dramatic theory expressed in his *Theory and
Technique of Playwriting and Screenwriting*, namely that
dramatic conflict is *social conflict* predicated on the exercise
of the *conscious will*, whereby the protagonist must strive to
understand the world in order to be able consciously to
choose a course of action. Lawson's first two major plays,
Roger Bloomer and *Processional*, focus on an initially naive
or socially unaware central figure who follows a rugged path
from ignorance or indifference to self-discovery and social
awareness.

The young protagonist of *Roger Bloomer* is the naïve son of
a materialistic midwestern businessman who rejects a Yale
education to follow a dissatisfied, home-town, working girl to
New York, where she ultimately commits suicide. Wrongly
accused of responsibility for her death, the title character is
thrown in jail, where, at the drama's climax, he undergoes an
expressionistic dream sequence in which distorted apparitions
from his past and his imagination appear to free him from his
inner turmoil of fears and guilt and prepare him for maturity
at the conclusion. Both the stylized nature of the dream
sequence projecting convoluted aspects of American life,
and, in previous scenes, the mechanical and exaggerated
behavior of characters accenting the influence of empty capitalistic values identify *Roger Bloomer* as an early example of
American expressionism pre-dating Elmer Rice's *The Adding
Machine*. Faulted by self-conscious poetic language, simplis-

tic characters, and sentimentalized romance, the play has flaws, which, from our contemporary perspective, curtail its durability.

Processional eclectically combines elements of expressionism, jazz, and vaudeville to make a sardonic statement about American social problems. Set in a West Virginia coal-mining community divided by a strike, the play presents caricatured figures of capitalistic authority, from businessman and reporter to law officers and the Ku Klux Klan, while also offering a cartoon-like one-dimensionality to working-class characters and such aspects of American life as a strike, a July 4th celebration, the press, the military, vigilantism, and romance.

The hero is the tough, brawling, politically-unaware miner Dynamite Jim Flimmins, who defies, and is relentlessly pursued by, anti-labor authorities until finally caught and blinded. During the pursuit Jim suffers confinement, in a series of hiding places, which generates revelations through such expressionistic devices as "voices", causing his conversion from ignorant brawler to inchoate political anarchist. Along the way he impregnates a town girl whom, at the play's conclusion, the blinded protagonist marries as the strike is unexpectedly settled and a presidential telegram arrives ironically proclaiming that "all men are brothers". The author discloses his social criticism while sardonically presenting the flaws of both sides in the labor struggle. Although dated in its content and approach, *Processional* remains an interesting example of 1920's American protest drama and possesses a lively eclectic style.

Loudspeaker employs farce to examine critically American politics in its essential absurdity. Here the protagonist is the unethical Babbitt, with gubernatorial ambitions which he ultimately realizes, but at the cost of a falsely idealized family life being exposed as a sham. Cartoon-like characters and a cliché-ridden romance detract from the drama's credibility, yet Lawson's observations on politics and political aspirants can find parallels today.

The International extravagantly, if somewhat incoherently, mixes song, dance, choral movement, and vaudevillian and epic-theatre devices to attack an acquisitive society. Set in Tibet, the sprawling plot concerns the rebellion of a businessman's son converted to world revolution by his love for a female Soviet agent, with whom he dies a martyr's death for a noble, but ill-fated, cause. Romance is again treated sentimentally, and the language throughout is more rhetorical than realistic.

In later plays Lawson turned from theatrical experimentation to realism, while maintaining his social criticism. *The Pure in Heart* follows the fortunes of an innocent small-town heroine to the big city, where her determination to be an actress brings her into a backstage world of unprincipled sophisticates and to an ex-convict, with whom she falls in love. A romance develops which ends in death, in a callous world destructive of innocence and humanity.

Success Story chronicles the rise and fall of slum-born and success-driven New Yorker Sol Ginsberg, who betrays his left-wing beliefs and a loving girlfriend for a successful advertising career and his employer's materialistic mistress, whom he marries. His lust for wealth and power ultimately destroy him, demonstrating the author's overstated view that capitalistic values corrupt.

In *Gentlewoman*, its author dramatizes the ineffectual sterility of upper-class society. Into the milieu of the rich and well-educated comes unpolished Rudy Flannigan, a Lawson proletarian hero who finds his strong attraction to the urbane title character, Gwyn Ballentine, reciprocated. A relationship between them is short-lived, for she is too much imprisoned by her ingrained values to live without wealth and to accept Rudy as he is, and he realizes that remaining with Gwyn will compromise his proletarian ideals. The title character is one of Lawson's most successfully drawn.

Marching Song, Lawson's most didactic work, overstates the theme of group solidarity as a requisite for social action in the midst of capitalistic exploitation. The play eschews the stylistic devices of *Processional*, but chooses a similar locale: a company town beset by a labor dispute. Striking workers, portrayed as heroically noble and victimized, suffer cruel reprisals to win a costly victory after seizing a power station.

In overview, Lawson's plays lack contemporaneity and durability. His ideological themes have grown outdated—particularly in the light of recent world events. His theatrical experiments, which do not always mix styles and effects successfully, are now familiar and better-integrated elements of modern drama. Many of his characters lack humanly credible three-dimensionality and are not well-served by stilted or artificial language. Despite these shortcomings, however, Lawson is historically significant as an early innovator of American expressionism and as a major contributor to American social protest drama of the 1920's.

—Christian H. Moe

See also *Volume 1* entry on *Processional*.

———

LEE, Nathaniel. Born in Hatfield, Hertfordshire, England, c.1645–52. Educated at Charterhouse School, London, from 1658; Trinity College, Cambridge, 1665–68, BA 1669. Actor in London, with the Duke's Men and the King's Company, 1672–75; wrote for the Duke's and King's companies, 1674–80, and for the combined United Company, after 1682; confined in Bethlehem Hospital (Bedlam), 1684–88. Died (buried) in London, 6 May 1692.

Works

Collections

Works, edited by Thomas B. Stroup and Arthur L. Cooke (2 vols.). 1954–55.

Stage Works

Nero, Emperor of Rome (produced Theatre Royal, Drury Lane, London, 1674). 1675.
Sophonisba; or, Hannibal's Overthrow (produced Theatre Royal, Drury Lane, London, 1675). 1675.
Gloriana; or, The Court of Augustus Caesar (produced Theatre Royal, Drury Lane, London, 1676). 1676.
The Rival Queens; or, The Death of Alexander the Great (produced Theatre Royal, Drury Lane, London, 1677). 1677.
Oedipus, with Dryden (produced Dorset Garden Theatre, London, 1678). 1679.
Mithridates, King of Pontus (produced Theatre Royal, Drury Lane, London, 1678). 1678.
Caesar Borgia, The Son of Pope Alexander the Sixth (produced Dorset Garden Theatre, London, 1679). 1679.

Lucius Junius Brutus, Father of His Country (produced Dorset Garden Theatre, London, 1680).   1681.

Theodosius; or, The Force of Love (produced Dorset Garden Theatre, London, 1680).   1680.

The Princess of Cleve, from a novel by Mme. de la Fayette (pageant; produced London, c.1680–82).   1689.

The Duke of Guise, with Dryden (produced Theatre Royal, Drury Lane, London, 1682).   1683.

Constantine the Great (produced Theatre Royal, Drury Lane, London, 1683).   1684.

The Massacre of Paris (produced Theatre Royal, Drury Lane, London, 1689).   1689.

Verse

To the Prince and Princess of Orange upon Their Marriage. 1677.

To the Duke on His Return.   1682.

On the Death of Mrs. Behn.   1689.

On Their Majesties' Coronation.   1689.

*

Bibliographies

A.L. McLeod, Bibliography in *Restoration and 18th Century Theatre Research*, 1, 1962.

J.M. Armistead, *Four Restoration Playwrights: A Reference Guide*, Boston, 1984.

Criticism

Books:

Roswell G. Ham, *Thomas Otway and Nathaniel Lee*, New Haven, Connecticut, 1931.

J.M. Armistead, *Nathaniel Lee*, Boston, 1979.

Articles:

Francis Barbour, "The Unconventional Heroic Plays of Nathaniel Lee", in *Studies in English* (University of Texas), 4026, 1940.

*   *   *

"An operatic genius who mistook his medium": Bonamy Dobrée's assessment of Lee has been echoed by numerous other critics who agree that Lee should have been born into an age other than the Restoration, whether it be that of the Artaudian "theatre of cruelty", the Senecan school of the Jacobeans, or the grotesquerie of Gothic melodrama. Nevertheless, Lee's first three plays conform—if uncomfortably—to the structural parameters of the rhymed heroic play, and make more than a token gesture to satisfy the rigid morality of neoclassical drama. However, his selection and distortion of material from classical history (the source of most of his plays) pays relatively little attention to models of heroic virtue, and focuses on hyperactive protagonists who are virtually arbitrary and irrational tyrants, not answerable to any exterior ethical system.

His first and obvious choice was Nero, in *Nero, Emperor of Rome*, who in the first scene disposes of Agrippina, and in the second the "crazy Caterpillar", Seneca. The emperor's lusts are clearly threatening to outstrip his inventiveness, and to rectify this Lee introduces the figure of Petronius Arbiter who, for the rest of the action, functions as the "think tank"

behind the imperial libido; but even Petronius fails to conceive the idea of burning Rome, which comes from a visit by the ghost of Caligula. Any other Restoration dramatist would have kept Seneca on stage for much longer, if only as a yardstick for stoical rectitude or principled rebellion; but Lee fills out the action with murders, mad scenes, and ghosts, and ends it with an epilogue in the style of comedy.

Rather more Roman virtue emerges through the portrait of Scipio in the more successful *Sophonisba*, but the most startling distortion of historical portraiture is that of Augustus in *Gloriana*, where Ovid's (dramatised) influence over Julia is wittily reflected in her dialogue, to the wrath of the emperor who, in the last scene, lurches forward in his nightgown to kill Caesario. The failure of this play no doubt influenced Lee to abandon formal heroic drama in favour of blank verse, a transition which he made ahead of most other Restoration playwrights, and his first work in this mode was also for a long period regarded as his masterpiece—*The Rival Queens*.

A summary of *The Rival Queens* might suggest that this play was simply an extension of the sensationalism which characterised all his work: Alexander the Great, poised to enter Babylon, has been exercising his paranoia by torturing, executing, and insulting his generals, but the account of this is interrupted by the appearance of the ghost of King Philip "shaking a Trunchion". In Babylon, Alexander's problems are intensified by the presence of the two Queens, but he deals with this by getting drunk, and when censured by an old adviser throws apples and—more effectively—a javelin at him. A courtier drinks himself to death at this, but meanwhile the Queens are active elsewhere in a scene with slaves, daggers, and ghosts of the former generation. Such complications concern Alexander only briefly as he drifts through hallucinations about his former military grandeur, and dies. If the plot line remains crude, the play is significant in its development of theatre language, in that Lee's early tendency to jolt through sequences of bizarre images begins to yield to a more modulated rhetoric in which rant persists, but it is at least fluid rant.

Mithridates and *Caesar Borgia* are further studies in escalating political malignancy, and even *Oedipus*, co-written with Dryden, starts with streets full of plague-smitten bodies and has central scenes of necromancy, heavenly visitations, and Oedipus soliloquising while sleepwalking in his shirt (all of which, like the ambition theme, echo *Macbeth*) before there is a vividly indulgent account of his blinding. His onstage death is effected by throwing himself from a window. Lee's continued use of distanced historical material was no doubt influenced by the banning of *The Massacre of Paris*, which occurred, according to Dryden, on the intervention of the French ambassador. It led, however, to the writing of another Roman play which is now belatedly regarded as among his best and which, ironically, was also banned because of its political implications.

This play, *Lucius Junius Brutus*, is of particular interest in both ethical and stylistic terms. Both the title-character and Lucrece provide partial models for stoical behaviour, and the charge that in this play Lee was less interested in Brutus's principles than in his severity to his wayward sons is not substantiated by the distribution of dialogue. Brutus is provided with a pattern for his own conduct in Lucrece's suicide after the rape that starts the play, a suicide characterised by a total absence of feeling towards her family around her. Later, Brutus will show an even more intense apathy in the presence of female passion when he condemns his sons to death. The play has one central sensation scene of human sacrifice, but otherwise its central focus is on the building up of Brutus's character and stature through sophisticated blank verse which expresses consolidation of an ethical position and never dissolves into bombast or rant.

Lee's other late tragedies develop a similarly less diabolical view of character within Christian contexts. In *Theodosius*, this is tempered by a context of cultural syncretism, and *Constantine the Great* has Arius, the heretic who precipitated the Nicaean controversy, in a role similar to Ovid's in *Gloriana*. Arius, however, is active throughout the play and dies in the last scene in a poisoned bath, while Constantine, helping to hold him down, moves rapidly towards medieval Christianity.

In addition to these serious works, Lee, in his last phase, wrote a curious scabrous sex comedy which has sometimes been related to the alcoholism that probably led to his committal to Bedlam and the end of his writing career. Most of his tragedies have comic prose episodes which sometimes include a sexual dimension; even *Lucius Junius Brutus* contains an account of the "slimy joys" of marriage. *The Princess of Cleve*, however, ends with the indefatigable libertine Nemours allowing his passions to accelerate into the future, laying bets that he will "bed" the princess "eighteen months three weeks hence, at half an hour past two in the morning". The management skills he displays in the play give some credence to his boast, but for all that the play does not celebrate his predatory heroics, and its sometimes sordid realism has led most critics to believe Lee's assertion that his purpose was a Juvenalian satire on licentiousness, targeting, some have argued, Rochester.

J.M. Armistead's excellent study of Lee is particularly insightful in terms of the connections that are made in the plays between personality and society, connections which interestingly recall Dobrée's statement of the affinity between Lee and the German expressionists: "Both his plays and those of the Expressionists are plays of life approached from a bewildered intellectual angle. Lee's are an attempt at adjustment in a world of heroic thoughts, Herr Toller's of adjustment in a world of mass emotions, but both try to deal direct with the symbol, and expect life to emerge from it . . .".

—Howard McNaughton

LEIGH, Mike. Born in Salford, Lancashire, England, 20 February 1943. Educated at Salford Grammar School; Royal Academy of Dramatic Art (RADA), London, 1960–62; Camberwell School of Arts and Crafts, London, 1963–64; Central School of Art and Design, London, 1964–68; London Film School, 1965. Married the actress Alison Steadman in 1973; two sons. Founder, with David Halliwell, Dramagraph production company, London, 1965; associate director, Midlands Arts Centre for Young People, Birmingham, 1965–66; first-produced play, *The Box Play*, staged 1965; actor, Victoria Theatre, Stoke-on-Trent, Staffordshire, 1966; assistant director, Royal Shakespeare Company, 1967–68; lecturer, Sedgley Park and De La Salle colleges, Manchester, 1968–69, and London Film School, 1970–73. Has directed all his own plays and films, many of them created through improvisation with the actors. Recipient: Chicago Film Festival and Locarno Film Festival awards, for screenplay, 1972; George Devine Award, 1974; Venice Film Festival Critics Award, 1988; National Society of Film Critics Award (USA), 1991.

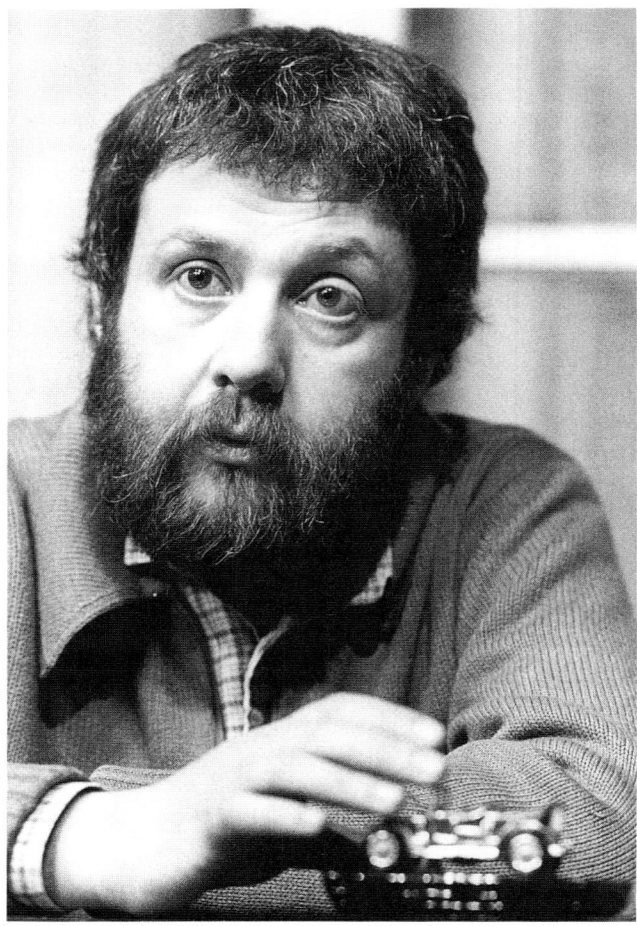

Mike Leigh (1988).

Works

Stage Works

The Box Play (produced Midland Arts Centre, Birmingham, 1965).
My Parents Have Gone to Carlisle (produced Midland Arts Centre, Birmingham, 1966).
The Last Crusade of the Five Little Nuns (produced Midland Arts Centre, Birmingham, 1966).
Waste Paper Guards (produced Midland Arts Centre, Birmingham, 1966).
NENAA (produced RSC Studio Theatre, Stratford-on-Avon, 1967).
Individual Fruit Pies (produced by East 15 Acting School, Loughton, Essex, 1968).
Down Here and Up There (produced Royal Court Theatre Upstairs, London, 1968).
Big Basil (produced Manchester Youth Theatre, Manchester, 1969).
Epilogue (produced Sedgley Park and De La Salle Colleges, Manchester, 1969).
Glum Victoria and the Lad with Specs (produced Manchester Youth Theatre, Manchester, 1969).
Bleak Moments (produced Open Space Theatre, London, 1970).
A Rancid Pong (produced Basement Theatre, London, 1971).

Wholesome Glory (produced Royal Court Theatre Upstairs, London, 1973).

The Jaws of Death (produced Traverse Theatre, Edinburgh, 1973).

Dick Whittington and His Cat (produced Royal Court Theatre Upstairs, London, 1973).

Babies Grow Old (produced The Other Place, Stratford-on-Avon, 1974; revised version produced Institute of Contemporary Arts, London, 1975).

The Silent Majority (produced Bush Theatre, London, 1974).

Abigail's Party (produced Hampstead Theatre, London, 1977). With *Goose-Pimples*, 1983.

Ecstasy (produced Hampstead Theatre, London, 1979). With *Smelling a Rat*, 1989.

Goose-Pimples (produced Hampstead Theatre, London, 1981). With *Abigail's Party*, 1983.

Smelling a Rat (produced Hampstead Theatre, London, 1988). With *Ecstasy*, 1989.

Greek Tragedy (produced Belvoir Street Theatre, Sydney, 1989).

Screenplays

Bleak Moments, 1972; *The Short and Curlies*, 1987; *High Hopes*, 1988; *Life is Sweet*, 1991.

Television Plays

A Mug's Game, 1973; *Hard Labour*, 1973; *The Permissive Society*, 1975; "Five Minute Films": *The Birth of the 2001 FA Cup Final Goalie*, *Old Chums*, *Probation*, *A Light Snack*, and *Afternoon*, all 1975; *Nuts in May*, 1976; *Knock for Knock*, 1976; *The Kiss of Death*, 1977; *Who's Who*, 1979; *Grown-Ups*, 1980; *Home Sweet Home*, 1982; *Meantime*, 1983; *Four Days in July*, 1985.

Radio Plays

Too Much of a Good Thing, 1992.

*

Criticism

Books:

Paul Clements, *The Improvised Play*: *The Work of Mike Leigh*, London, 1983.

*   *   *

"Theatre is the art of the present moment", said Jean-Louis Barrault. Mike Leigh's working methods, honed and refined over the last 25 years, celebrate Barrault's assertion.

For reasons which will become clear, Leigh is notoriously reluctant to publish the scripts of his work. Those in print are prefaced with the phrase "evolved from scratch entirely by rehearsal through improvisation". Leigh does not claim to *write* plays. He prefers to describe his function as the distiller of the collaborative process undertaken by whichever group of actors he works with on a project. Indeed, the commentator is obliged to ask, "when is a play not a play?", for Leigh's approach undermines the whole concept of individual authorship.

Leigh's work also questions fundamental assumptions about the role of the actor. Leaving RADA in 1962, Leigh quickly realised that however large and demanding the part, to be cast in an existing, completed play is to be, at best, an interpreter. Leigh wanted the actor to be creative rather than pro-active. Hence his working methods are based on characters that are chosen by the actors and then developed in tandem with Leigh. The process is characterised by scrupulous attention to research, accurate observation, and objectivity. Actors refer to their character in the third person while rehearsing, in sharp contrast to the empathy normally encouraged and expected. The action of the plays (as we must call them for want of a better word) evolves from the characters, for the relationships which develop determine plot and location, not vice versa. This process argues against those who insist that Leigh's work is director-centred.

Leigh also wished to change the nature of the audience's relationship to the performance. What evolves from his working method substitutes the real in the present moment for the recreated and attendant suspension of disbelief of the traditional play. Given these basic principles, finished scripts are unlikely to capture or accurately represent such a process and product. Indeed, there is something profoundly weird about the popularity of *Abigail's Party*, whose small cast and single set make it a favourite for revivals. How can other actors take on the words and relationships created by the original cast? A revival of a Leigh work is almost a contradiction in terms. Certainly, it undermines the principles discussed above.

The most common criticism of the plays is that, brilliant though the observation may be, what is captured is as trivial as most people's lives. Well, yes, the plays relentlessly capture the vapidity of everyday speech and action. Leigh would not dispute the banality of speech, location, and incident, an effect compounded by the single sets and small time-scales of the plays. Clearly, this is deliberate. The question must be "why?".

This question is connected to the other main criticism: that the finished work is clinically detached and condescends to the characters depicted. Such an attitude is always a danger in the dynamic between observer and subject. The stage directions and props list for *Abigail's Party* read like checklists of status for the aspiring middle classes in the mid 1970's. The characters are surrounded by ornamental fibre lights and room-divider shelf-units, sitting on three-piece real leather suites, playing Donna Summer and José Feliciano on their music-centres, consuming gin and tonic, discussing cars, and displaying (but not reading) embossed editions of Dickens and Shakespeare. Every detail becomes an indicator of the emptiness of the characters' lives.

To condemn the judgements Leigh supposedly makes about his characters is to miss the point (and, quite possibly, to impose upon Leigh the critics' own assumptions about people who don't like olives). For Leigh's pieces raise banality to a mythic level. There is no body of work so full of the everyday eating, drinking, smoking, and the consequent pissing, vomiting, and indiscretion which characterise everyday existence. Despite, or because of, the acutely and minutely observed realism, Leigh distils recognisable life and transforms it into distended caricature. The vicious evening in Beverley and Lawrence's dream home in *Abigail's Party*, the brothel-like design of Vernon's flat in *Goose-Pimples*, the overriding sense of emptiness and dishonesty—all are metaphors for the way we live. To criticise Leigh's work for concentrating on a narrow social band is to confuse story with intention. His is the work of an outraged moralist scourging the values that our society substitutes for decency and compassion with the savage realism of his depiction of how people live. Leigh seeks to liberate actors from the confines of script. He is still waiting for the liberation of society from the false values of the late 20th century, and the constricting effect on people's lives.

—Joss Bennathon

————

LENZ, Jakob Michael Reinhold. Born in Sesswegen, Russian Baltic Province of Livonia, 23 January [12 January, Russian calendar] 1751. Family moved to Dorpat (now Tartu, Estonia), 1759. Educated at University of Königsberg, studying theology, 1768–71. Tutor in Strasbourg, 1771, and entered literary circles, meeting Goethe, Kleist, and others; full-time writer, from 1774, supplementing income with intermittent tuition; first plays and adaptations published, 1774; co-founder, Deutsche Gesellschaft [German Society], Strasbourg, 1775, and contributor to its journal *Der Bürgerfreund*; travelled throughout Germany and Switzerland, 1776–77; suffered first bout of mental illness, 1777; first suicide attempt, 1778; taken by his brother to Riga, 1779; travelled to St. Petersburg, 1780, where attempts to become teacher and soldier failed, and to Moscow, 1781, where he gained employment as tutor at a boarding school; suffered great deterioration in mental health during the 1780's. Died in Moscow, 4 June 1792.

Works

Collections

Lustspiele nach dem Plautus (adaptations from Plautus). 1774.
Dramatischer Nachlass, edited by Karl Weinhold. 1884.
Gesammelte Schriften (5 vols.), edited by Franz Blei. 1909–13.
Werke und Schriften (2 vols.), edited by Britta Titel and Hellmut Haug. 1966–67.
Werke und Schriften, edited by Richard Daunicht. 1970.
Werke und Briefe (3 vols.), edited by Sigrid Damm. 1987.

Stage Works

Der Hofmeister; oder, Die Vorteile der Privaterziehung (produced Hamburg, 1778). 1774; translated as *The Tutor*, with *The Soldiers*, 1972.
Das Väterchen, from a play by Plautus. In *Lustspiele nach dem Plautus*, 1774.
Die Aussteuer, from a play by Plautus. In *Lustspiele nach dem Plautus*, 1774.
Die Entführungen, from a play by Plautus. In *Lustspiele nach dem Plautus*, 1774; early version, as *Truculentus*, in *Dramatischer Nachlass*, 1884.
Die Buhlschwester, from a play by Plautus. In *Lustspiele nach dem Plautus*, 1774; early version, as *Miles Gloriosus*, in *Dramatischer Nachlass*, 1884.
Die Türkensklavin, from a play by Plautus. In *Lustspiele nach dem Plautus*, 1774.
Die beiden Alten, from a play by Plautus. In *Lustspiele nach dem Plautus*, 1774.

Amor vincit omnia, from *Love's Labour's Lost* by Shakespeare. With *Anmerkungen übers Theater*, 1774.
Die neue Menoza; oder, Die Geschichte des cubanischen Prinzen Tandi. 1774.
Die Soldaten (produced in adapted form, Burgtheater, Vienna, 1863). 1776; translated as *The Soldiers*, with *The Tutor*, 1972.
Pandämonium Germanicum. 1776.
Die Freunde machen den Philosophen. 1776.
Der Engländer. 1777.
Die sizilianische Vesper. In *Liefländisches Magazin der Lektüre*, 1782.
Myrsa Polagi. In *Liefländisches Magazin der Lektüre*, 1782.
Tantalus. 1798.
Leopold Wagner, Verfasser eines Schauspiels von den neuen Monaten im Walfischbauch; oder, Eine Matinee. 1828.
Der verwundete Bräutigam, edited by K.L. Blum. 1845.
Catherina von Siena. In *Dramatischer Nachlass*, 1884.
Fragments: *Die Kleinen; Der tugendhafte Taugenichts; Henriette von Waldeck, oder, Die Laube; Cato; Die alte Jungfer; Zum weinen, oder, Weil ihrs so haben wollt; Graf Heinrich; Die Familie der Projektenmacher*. All in *Dramatischer Nachlass*, 1884.
Coriolan, from *Coriolanus* by Shakespeare. In *Gesammelte Schriften*, 1909–13.

Verse

Die Landplagen. 1769.
Der Herr Professor Kant. 1770.
Petrarch. 1776.
Poems collected in *Gedichte und Briefe* (Volume 3 of *Werke und Briefe*). 1987.

Memoirs and Letters

Briefe von und an J.M.R. Lenz (2 vols.), edited by Karl Freye and Wolfgang Stammler. 1918.
Letters collected in *Gedichte und Briefe* (Volume 3 of *Werke und Briefe*). 1987.

Other

Anmerkungen übers Theater. With *Amor vincit omnia*, 1774.
Tagebuch. In *Deutsche Rundschau*, 11, 1877; in book form, in *Werke und Briefe*, 1987.
Aesthetic and theatrical writings collected in *Prosa Dichtungen und Schriften* (Volume 2 of *Werke und Briefe*). 1987.

*

Criticism

Books:
E. Genton, *J.M.R. Lenz et la scène allemande*, Paris, 1966.
R. Girard, *Lenz 1751–1792: Genèse d'une dramaturgie du tragicomique*, Paris, 1968.
R. Ottomar, *J.M.R. Lenz: Moralist und Aufklärer*, Bad Homburg, 1969.
C. Hohoff, *J.M.R. Lenz in Selbstzeugnissen und Bilddokumenten*, Reinbek, 1977.
E.M. Inbar, *Shakespeare in Deutschland: Der Fall Lenz*, Tübingen, 1982.
J.D. Guthrie, *Lenz and Büchner: Studies in Dramatic Form*, Frankfurt and Bern, 1984.

I. Stephan and H.-G. Winter, *"Ein vorübergehender Meteor?" J.M.R. Lenz und seine Rezeption in Deutschland*, Stuttgart, 1989.

H.-G. Schwarz, *Dasein und Realität: Theorie und Praxis des Realismus bei J.M.R. Lenz*, Bonn, 1985.

S. Damm, *Vögel, die verkünden Land: Das Leben des J.M.R. Lenz*, Berlin, Weimar, 1986.

H.-G. Winter, *J.M.R. Lenz*, Stuttgart, 1987.

*   *   *

After Goethe, the major German dramatist to emerge from the "Storm and Stress" movement of the 1770's was Jakob Michael Reinhold Lenz. Unlike Goethe's, Lenz's creative work was confined to this decade. After 1780 he lost contact with literary developments in Germany; thus deprived of the opportunity to develop his talents as a playwright into maturity, his reputation rests, like Büchner's, on two plays of precocious originality, completed before he had reached the age of 25. Because of the unhappy circumstances of his later life and death, and particularly the abrupt and still unexplained ending of his friendship with Goethe in 1776, he has acquired, within the history of German literature, an almost symbolic significance, and has been seen as the source of an alternative tradition of drama, leading through playwrights such as Büchner and Wedekind to Brecht.

At the age of 15, Lenz completed his first play, *Der verwundete Bräutigam* (The Wounded Bridegroom). Although an occasional drama of conventional character, composed for the wedding celebrations of a local aristocrat, it already shows Lenz's interest in the tensions between different classes in society arising from stifled longings and wounded pride. It was not, however, until he left his native Baltic province for the stimulating intellectual environment of Strasbourg in the early 1770's that Lenz began serious reflection on dramatic form. Under the influence of Herder, whose new historicist aesthetics had been instrumental in bringing about a reappraisal of the drama of Shakespeare, Lenz himself wrote an important dramaturgical essay, *Anmerkungen übers Theater* (Notes on the Theatre), in which he joined in the attack on Classical Aristotelian principles and argued against the reliance on Greek and French models of drama.

He began immediately to write plays in the same iconoclastic spirit, most successfully in *Der Hofmeister* (The Tutor) and *Die Soldaten* (The Soldiers). Superficially these two plays have the form of the social-critical *pièce-à-thèse*. *Der Hofmeister* is concerned with the practice of education by private tutor, as favoured by the nobility, and its consequences both for the recipients and for the exploited underclass of the tutor, to which Lenz himself had belonged; a *raisonneur*-figure argues in favour of public education for all classes in schools and universities. *Die Soldaten* argues in the same explicit way against the law which forbade soldiers to marry, drawing attention to the disruptive consequences of this for the lives of honest citizens and their daughters.

Both plays are not without a certain grotesque element: in the former, the tutor resorts to the extreme act of self-castration out of misplaced remorse; while the latter concludes with a proposal for the institution of state brothels, which seems only peripherally related to the kind of problems which the play has brilliantly illustrated. The thesis ostensibly argued in fact provides no more than a basis for Lenz to examine social relationships, especially those which cross the class boundaries or which, as in the family context, involve the questioning of traditional authority from an emancipatory point of view. This is an area which Lenz explores with great subtlety, showing not only the strength of the assertive impulse, but also the doubts which inhibit its free expression, and the dangers which it courts.

Lenz's major contribution to the development of drama, however, lies in the boldness with which he abandoned the traditional conventions. He extended the process of democratisation, which he inherited from domestic tragedy, by reaching out beyond the middle-class family to the wider world of student and garrison life; he rejected the constraints of *bienséance* in a highly provocative way; and he completely ignored the strict generic distinctions between tragedy and comedy. His plays are written in prose, apart from occasionally interpolated songs, with language being used as a significant and subtle instrument of characterisation. While he preserved the five-act structure, it is the *scene*, which tends to be short and self-contained, that is the basic dramaturgical unit, creating a fast-moving, varied montage, in which the plot advances elliptically and unevenly.

Of Lenz's other dramatic works, only *Der neue Menoza* (The New Menoza) has enjoyed any significant exposure on the German stage. The two major plays, like the dramas of Büchner, have become established in the repertoire only in the 20th century. Their dissemination has owed much to adaptation, Brecht having rewritten *Der Hofmeister* for his own production with the Berliner Ensemble, and Heinar Kipphardt having prepared a version of *Die Soldaten* for the modern stage. Both of these modern adaptations are more explicit and, in certain respects, cruder than the originals, whose psychological subtleties and frequently understated humour tend to be lost under the weight of a more narrowly political reading.

—John Osborne

See also *Volume 1* entries on *The Soldiers*; *The Tutor*.

LEONARD, Hugh. Pseudonym for John Keyes Byrne. Born in Dublin, Ireland. 9 November 1926. Educated at Presentation College, Dun Laoghaire, 1941–45. Married Paule Jacquet in 1955; one daughter. Civil servant, Dublin, 1945–59; first play, *The Italian Road*, produced 1954; script editor, Granada Television, Manchester, 1961–63; literary editor, Abbey Theatre, Dublin, 1976–77; programme director, Dublin Theatre Festival, 1978–80. A prolific writer and adaptor for television. Recipient: Italia Prize, for television play, 1967; Writers Guild of Great Britain Award, 1967; Tony Award, 1978; New York Drama Critics Circle Award, 1978; Outer Circle Award, 1978; Vernon Rice Award, 1978. DHL: Rhode Island College, Providence, 1980. D.Litt: Trinity College, Dublin, 1989.

Works

Collections

Da; A Life; Time Was.   1981.
Selected Plays.   1992.

Stage Works

The Italian Road (produced Dagg Hall, Dublin, 1954).
The Big Birthday (produced Abbey Theatre, Dublin, 1956).

A Leap in the Dark (produced Abbey Theatre, Dublin, 1957).

Madigan's Lock (produced Globe Theatre, Dublin, 1958).

A Walk on the Water (produced Eblana Theatre, Dublin, 1960).

The Passion of Peter Ginty, from a play by Ibsen (produced Gate Theatre, Dublin, 1961).

Stephen D, adaptation of the works *A Portrait of the Artist as a Young Man* and *Stephen Hero* by James Joyce (produced Gate Theatre, Dublin, 1962). 1965.

Dublin One, from stories by James Joyce (produced Gate Theatre, Dublin, 1963).

The Poker Session (produced Gate Theatre, Dublin, 1963). 1963.

The Family Way, from a play by Eugène Labiche (produced Gate Theatre, Dublin, 1964).

A View from the Obelisk, from the television play (produced in *Scorpions*, Dublin, 1983).

The Saints Go Cycling In, from the novel *The Dalkey Archives* by Flann O'Brien (produced Dublin Theatre Festival, 1965).

Mick and Mick (produced Dublin Theatre Festival, 1966; as *All the Nice People*, produced Olney Theatre, Olney, Maryland, 1976). 1966.

A Time of Wolves and Tigers, from the television play (produced in *Irishmen*, Olney Theatre, Olney, Maryland, 1975). In *Suburb of Babylon*, 1983.

The Quick, and The Dead (produced Olympia Theatre, Dublin, 1967).

The Au Pair Man (produced Gate Theatre, Dublin, 1968). In *Plays and Players* (London), December 1968; in book form, 1974.

The Barracks, adaptation of the novel by John McGahern (produced Olympia Theatre, Dublin, 1969).

The Patrick Pearse Motel (produced Olympia Theatre, Dublin, 1971). 1972.

Da (produced Olney Theatre, Olney, Maryland, 1973). 1976; revised version, 1978.

Summer (produced Olney Theatre, Olney, Maryland, 1974). 1979.

Suburb of Babylon (includes *A Time of Wolves and Tigers; Nothing Personal; The Last of the Last of the Mohicans*; produced as *Irishmen*, Olney Theatre, Olney, Maryland, 1975). 1983.

Some of My Best Friends Are Husbands, from a play by Eugène Labiche (produced London, 1976).

Liam Liar, from a play by Keith Waterhouse and Willis Hall (produced Dublin, 1976).

Time Was (produced Abbey Theatre, Dublin, 1976). In *Da; A Life; Time Was*, 1981.

A Life (produced Abbey Theatre, Dublin, 1979). 1980.

Kill (produced Dublin Festival, 1982).

Scorpions (includes *A View from the Obelisk, Roman Fever, Pizzazz*; produced Dublin Festival, 1983). *Pizzaz* published, 1986.

The Mask of Moriarty, based on characters by Arthur Conan Doyle (produced Dublin Festival, 1985).

Moving (produced Abbey Theatre, Dublin, 1992).

Screenplays

Great Catherine, 1967; *Interlude*, with Lee Langley, 1967; *Whirligig*, 1970; *Percy*, with Terence Feely, 1970; *Our Miss Fred*, 1972; *Widows' Peak*, 1986; *Da*, 1989.

Television Plays

The Irish Boys (trilogy), 1962; *Saki* series, 1962; *A Kind of Kingdom*, 1963; *Jezebel Ex-UK* series, 1963; *The Second Wall*, 1964; *A Triple Irish*, 1964; *Realm of Error*, 1964; *My One True Love*, 1964; *The Late Arrival of the Incoming Aircraft*, 1964; *Do You Play Requests?*, 1964; *A View from the Obelisk*, 1964; *The Hidden Truth* series, 1964; *Undermind* series, 1964; *I Loved You Last Summer*, 1965; *Great Big Blond*, 1965; *Blackmail* series, 1965; *Public Eye* series, 1965; *Simenon* series: *The Lodger* and *The Judge*, 1966; *Insurrection* (8 parts), 1966; *Second Childhood*, 1966; *The Retreat*, 1966; *Silent Song*, from a story by Frank O'Connor, 1966; *The Liars* series, 1966; *The Informer* series, 1966; *Out of the Unknown* series, 1966–67; *A Time of Wolves and Tigers*, 1967; *Love Life*, 1967; *Great Expectations* (serialization), from the novel by Dickens, 1967; *Wuthering Heights* (serialization), from the novel by Emily Brontë, 1967; *No Such Things as a Vampire*, 1968; *The Corpse Can't Play*, 1968; *A Man and His Mother-in-Law*, 1968; *Assassin*, 1968; *Nicholas Nickleby* (serialization), from the novel by Dickens, 1968; *Conan Doyle* series: *A Study in Scarlet* and *The Hound of the Baskervilles*, 1968; *Hunt the Peacock*, from a novel by H.R.F. Keating, 1969; *Talk of Angels*, 1969; *The Possessed* (serialization), from a novel by Dostoevsky, 1969; *Dombey and Son* (serialization), from the novel by Dickens, 1969; *Somerset Maugham* series: *P & O*, 1969, and *Jane*, 1970; *A Sentimental Education* (serialization), from a novel by Flaubert, 1970; *The Sinners* series, 1970–71; *Me Mammy* series, 1970–71; *White Walls and Olive Green Carpets*, 1971; *The Removal Person*, 1971; *Pandora*, 1971; *The Virgins*, 1972; *The Ghost of Christmas Present*, 1972; *The Truth Game*, 1972; *Tales from the Lazy Acres* series, 1972; *The Moonstone* (serialization), from the novel by Wilkie Collins, 1972; *The Sullen Sisters*, 1972; *The Watercress Girl*, from the story by H.E. Bates, 1972; *The Higgler*, 1973; *High Kampf*, 1973; *Milo O'Shea*, 1973; *Stone Cold Sober*, 1973; *The Bitter Pill*, 1973; *Another Fine Mess*, 1973; *Judgement Day*, 1973; *The Travelling Woman*, 1973; *The Hammer of God, The Actor and the Alibi, The Eye of Apollo, The Forbidden Garden, The Three Tools of Death*, and *The Quick One* (*Father Brown* series), 1974; *London Belongs to Me*, from the novel by Norman Collins, 1977; *Bitter Suite*, 1977; *Teresa, The Fur Coat*, and *Two of a Kind*, from stories by Sean O'Faolain, 1977; *The Last Campaign*, from the novel *The Captains and the Kings* by Jennifer Johnston, 1978; *The Ring and the Rose*, 1978; *Strumpet City*, from the novel by James Plunkett, 1980; *The Little World of Don Camillo*, from a novel by Giovanni Guareschi, 1981; *Good Behaviour*, from a work by Molly Keane, 1983; *O'Neill* series, 1983; *The Irish R.M.* series, 1985; *Hunted Down*, from a story by Dickens, 1985; *Troubles*, 1987; *Parnell and the Englishwoman*, 1991.

Fiction

Parnell and the Englishwoman. 1990.

Memoirs and Letters

Home Before Night: Memoirs of an Irish Time and Place. 1980.

Out After Dark (memoirs). 1989.

Rover and Other Cats (memoirs). 1992.

Other

Leonard's Last Book (essays). 1978.

A Peculiar People and Other Foibles (essays). 1979.

Leonard's Year (journalism). 1985.

*

Bibliographies

Kimball King, *Ten Modern Irish Playwrights*, New York, 1979.

Criticism

Books:

Keith Cushman, "'Stand-Up Poker' in Hugh Leonard's *The Poker Session*", in *Journal of Irish Literature*, vol.8 no.2, 1979.

* * *

Hugh Leonard is arguably one of the two or three best Irish playwrights currently at work, and for the last dozen years or so, he has unquestionably been the most successful commercially. The problem with being an "Irish playwright", he noted back in the 1980's, is that audiences are "conditioned to expect feyness and parochial subject matter". Leonard's "subject matter", of course, is Ireland, but "only to the degree in which I can use it as a microcosm". This qualification calls for themes of a universal nature, "themes which are free of Catholicism and politics, both of which I detest, and which deprive one's work of applicability outside Ireland".

To say that Leonard's work is "free" of religion and politics is, of course, not quite true, for although he now claims to be an agnostic, Catholicism is still present, if only in the background, in his plays. However, Irish politics is, with rare exception (usually in the earlier work), often little more than a minor motif. By the 1980's he had come to find political matters "boring for dramatic reasons", and preferred drama "to be about men, not abstractions". In the best of his recent work for the stage, the drama centres on characters and situations immediately recognizable all over the globe for their human dimensions. "I am an Irish person who writes plays", he wrote in a 1979 note to *Summer*, "not a person who writes Irish plays".

Leonard's range of themes is impressive and remarkably wide: parental love; personal and familial guilt and betrayal; a portrait of the artist as a boy and young man; sexual awakening, sexual fulfilment, and adultery; the price of success and the cost of failure; mortality and the advent of death; the nature of time and the co-existence of the past with the present; the comic clash between traditional and modern Ireland; exile, and sometimes the return, of young Irish; suburbia in an era of prosperity; the comic side of nostalgia crazes; Irish avarice; Ireland's uneasy relationship with England; political unrest in Ireland; and the role of the Church and clergy in Irish society.

The characters who animate Leonard's themes are not the familiar landed Anglo-Irish aristocrats or Irish peasants, or even Dublin tenement dwellers. Most often they are middle-class suburbanites, as upwardly mobile as their counterparts anywhere in the more prosperous parts of the world. Leonard is at his best, however, when he recreates, with affection and objectivity, the characters drawn from autobiographical materials, such as his parents and the people he knew growing up in Dalkey, a suburb of Dublin.

Leonard is very interested in matters of structure and dramatic form. (He is an admirer of certain plays of Lennox Robinson and the comedies of Kaufman and Hart.) *Da*, widely considered his best play and certainly his best-known work for the stage, is (like *The Glass Menagerie*) a "memory play", fluidly cinematic in structure, and free-ranging in time and space via a series of brief, constantly shifting scenes. Two actors in *Da* play the roles of the son, Charley and Young Charley, while in *A Life*, a teenage quartet is the counterpart of the four middle-aged principals, a device which permits an easy shifting and interweaving of time past and present. *Summer*, almost completely realistic in style, includes one sequence (set apart by lighting changes) with interior monologues along the lines of those in O'Neill's *Strange Interlude*.

In tone, as in structure, there is an equally wide range, as the playwright moves from the robust satire and knockabout comedy, borrowed from 19th-century French bedroom farce, in *The Patrick Pearse Motel*, to the psychological realism of *The Poker Session*, the melancholy, poetic ambience of *Summer*, and the symbolic allegory of *The Au Pair Man*.

Leonard's writing has not been entirely in the dramatic form. For years he has written a weekly, diary-like column for the *Sunday Independent*, and some of these have been collected in book form. More importantly, in 1980 he published *Home Before Night*, a charming and very funny memoir in novelistic style that variously covered his life up to 1970, concentrating on his early years and a 14-year-stint as a civil servant in the Land Commission office, with only brief reference to the years in England. It is a fuller account of the materials already drawn on for *Da* and *A Life*. Further volumes of memoirs have since been published.

—Gene A. Barnett

See also *Volume 1* entry on *Da*.

LERMONTOV, Mikhail Yurevich. Born in Moscow, 2–3 October 1814 (Old Style). Educated at School for the Nobility, 1828–30; University of Moscow, faculty of Moral and Political Sciences, 1830–32; Junker [Guards'] School, St. Petersburg, 1832–34. Commissioned as a cavalry coronet in the Regiment of Life Guard Hussars, 1834; first poetry published in 1835; exiled to the Caucasus for his poems on Pushkin's death, 1837–38; exiled again (for duelling) to the Tenginsky Infantry Regiment, near the Black Sea, 1840–41. Died in a duel, Piatigorsk, 15 July 1841 (Old Style).

Works

Collections

Polnoe sobranie sochineny [Complete Collected Works], edited by B. Eichenbaum. 1948.
Sochineniya (6 vols.). 1954–57.
Izbranie sochineny [Selected Works] (4 vols.). 1958–59.
Selected Works. 1976.
Sobranie sochineny [Collected Works] (4 vols.), edited by L. Nauka. 1979.
Sobranie sochineny, edited by I.L. Andronikov. 1983–

Stage Works

Maskarad (produced Maly Theatre, Moscow, 1862). 1842; translated as *Masquerade*, in *Russian Literature Triquarterly*, Winter 1974.

Spany [The Spaniards].   In collected edition, 1880.
Menschen und Leidenschaften [Men and Passions].   In collected edition, 1880; revised version translated as *A Strange One*, in *A Lermontov Reader*, 1965.
Dve Braty.   In collected edition, 1880; translated as *The Two Brothers*, in *Michael Lermontov: Biography and Translation*, by C.E. L'Ami and Alexander Welikonty, 1967.

Fiction

Geroy nashevo vremeni.   1840; translated as *Sketches of Russian Life in the Caucasus*, 1853; as *A Hero of Our Times*, 1854; as *The Heart of a Russian*, 1912; as *A Hero of Our Time*, 1975.
Vadim.   In *Vestnik europy* [The Messenger of Europe], 1873; translated as *Vadim*, 1984.

Verse

Chadzhi Abrek.   1835.
Boyarin Orsha.   1835.
Pesnya pro carya Ivana Vasilyevicha.   1837.
Mtsyri.   1840; translated as *The Caucasian Boy*, 1875.
Demon.   1842; translated as *The Demon*, 1875.
Stikhotvoreniya (collected poetry).   1940.
Major Poetical Works, edited and translated by Anatoly Liberman.   1983.
Narrative Poems by Alexander Pushkin and Michael Lermontov, translated by Charles Johnston.   1983.

*

Criticism

Books:
Janko Lavrin, *Lermontov*, London, 1959.
Laurence Kelly, *Lermontov: Tragedy in the Caucasus* (with bibliography), London, 1977.
John Garrard, *Lermontov*, 1982.

* * *

Remembered primarily for *A Hero of Our Time*, a novel of unusual construction and great psychological interest, and as one of Russia's best-loved lyric poets, Mikhail Lermontov also wrote for the stage. All of his plays involve Romantic passions, strong characters, and deep pathos. His first ideas for a play were shaped by reading Shakespeare and watching brilliant performances by Mochalov on the Moscow stage, particularly of Schiller's *The Robbers*.

After several false starts he wrote his first full-length play at the age of 16, a verse tragedy set in Spain and entitled "The Spaniards". It presents a story of murder and intrigue, stark contrasts, and stormy action. The hero, Fernando, is a rebellious nobleman of great courage whose impassioned monologues penetrate beyond generalised appeals for justice to the realm of overt criticism levelled against cruel government, and obviously transferable to contemporary Russia. In view of this, and the play's immaturity, it is hardly surprising that it had to wait 50 years for publication.

The next two plays, although still those of a youthful talent, are more realistic, written in prose, and partly autobiographical. *Menschen und Leidenschaften* is based upon circumstances surrounding the death of Lermontov's mother, particularly the bitter quarrelling between his grandmother and his father (who was deemed unsuitable for bringing up the two-year-old baby). In *The Strange One*, a not dissimilar quarrel over their son occurs between a mother and father; the action culminates in malediction and violent, tragic death. The elevated ideas and lofty aspirations expressed in these plays owe much to German Romanticism and specific scenes derive directly from Schiller. These plays also remained unpublished for half a century.

Lermontov's most successful play, *Masquerade*, was written after a further five years, though the author was still only 22. This four-act drama is written in verse, using iambic lines discreetly varying in length; the poetry is allowed to flow in natural conversational Russian, which sometimes attains memorable aphoristic sharpness. However, the characters, emotions, and events of the play still verge upon the melodramatic. Taking the Othello theme directly from Shakespeare, Lermontov presents the story of Evgeny Arbenin, a reformed libertine and cynic, who becomes insanely jealous of his young wife, Nina, and poisons her, only to discover too late that her behaviour has been entirely innocent. An important secondary theme of the play is the corruption of high society in St. Petersburg, which is castigated bitterly in a series of impassioned monologues. This criticism was pointed enough to attract the censor's attention; the play was banned for three decades. It has sufficient quality to merit performance still in its own country.

Lermontov's final play, *The Two Brothers* is of little significance, reverting as it does to his earlier preoccupations with Schiller and events from his own life.

Although he was always attracted to the theatre, Lermontov failed to make his mark there, never quite containing the excesses of European Romanticism to which he was temperamentally prone.

—Anthony D.P. Briggs

See also *Volume 1* entry on *Masquerade*.

———

LESAGE, Alain-René.   Born in Sarzeau, Brittany, France, 13 December 1668. Educated by Jesuits in Vannes, Brittany; studied law in Paris. Married Marie-Élizabeth Huyard in 1694; three sons, including the actor Montménil, and one daughter. Possibly a lawyer in Paris; wrote original plays and adaptations/translations from the Spanish for the Comédie-Française, Paris, 1700–09; broke with the Comédie-Française, and subsequently wrote farces, comic operas, *vaudevilles*, and other pieces for the Paris fairs of St. Germain and St. Laurent, often in collaboration with Louis Fuzelier, d'Orneval, and others; lived with one son, the Abbé de Lyonne, in Boulogne, from 1743. Died in Boulogne, 7 November 1747.

Works

Collections

Le Théâtre de la foire; ou, L'Opéra-comique (10 vols.: two of them numbered as 9).   1721–37.
Recueil des pièces mises au Théâtre Français (includes final versions of *Turcaret; Crispin, rival de son maître; La Tontine*).   1738.

Stage Works (adaptations and plays for the legitimate stage)

Le Traître puni, from a play by Rojas Zorilla. In *Théâtre espagnol*, 1700.

Don Félix de Mendoce, from a play by Lope de Vega. In *Théâtre espagnol*, 1700.

Le Point d'honneur, from a play by Rojas Zorilla (produced Comédie-Française, Paris, 1702). 1739.

Don César Ursin, from a play by Calderón (produced Comédie-Française, Paris, 1707). 1739.

Crispin, rival de son maître (produced Comédie-Française, Paris, 1707). 1707; revised version, in *Recueil des pièces au Théâtre Français*, 1739; translated as *Neck or Nothing*, 1766; as *Crispin, Rival of His Master*, 1915; as *The Rival of His Master*, in *Tulane Drama Review*, vol.6 no.4, 1962.

Turcaret (produced Comédie-Française, Paris, 1709). 1709; revised version, in *Recueil des pièces au Théâtre Français*, 1739; translated as *Turcaret*, in *French Comedies of the Eighteenth Century*, edited by Richard Aldington, 1923; also translated, 1989.

La Tontine (produced Comédie-Française, Paris, 1732). In *Recueil des pièces au Théâtre Français*, 1738.

Les Amants jaloux (produced Comédie-Italienne, Paris, 1735). 1736.

Stage Works

Pièces forains produced at Fair of St. Germain; the dates given are those of first production.

Le Retour d'Arlequin à la foire, 1712; *Arlequin Baron Allemand*, 1712; *Arlequin roi de Sérendib*, 1713; *Arlequin colonel*, 1714; *La Ceinture de Vénus*, 1715; *Parodie de l'opéra de Télémaque*, 1715; *Arlequin gentilhomme malgré lui*, with d'Orneval, 1716; *Le Temple d'ennui*, with Louis Fuzelier, 1716; *Le Tableau du mariage*, with Louis Fuzelier, 1716; *L'École des amants*, with Louis Fuzelier, 1716; *L'Ombre de la foire*, with d'Orneval, 1720; *L'Île du Gougou*, with d'Orneval, 1720; *Arlequin roi des ogres; ou, Les Bottes de sept lieues*, with d'Orneval and Fuzelier, 1720; *La Queue de vérité*, with d'Orneval and Fuzelier, 1720; *Magotin*, with d'Orneval, 1721; *Prologue*, with d'Orneval and Fuzelier, 1721; *Arlequin Endymion*, with d'Orneval, 1721; *La Forêt de Dodône*, with d'Orneval, 1721; *L'Ombre du cocher poète*, with d'Orneval and Fuzelier, 1722; *L Rémouleur d'amour*, with d'Orneval and Fuzelier, 1722; *Pierrot Romulus; ou, Le Ravisseur poli*, with d'Orneval and Fuzelier, 1722; *Arlequin barbet, pagode et médicin*, with d'Orneval, 1723; *Les Trois Commères*, with d'Orneval, 1723; *Les Couplets en procès*, with d'Orneval, 1729; *La Reine du Barostan*, with d'Orneval, 1729; *L'Opéra-comique assiégé*, with d'Orneval, 1730.

Stage Works

Pièces forains produced at the Fair of St. Laurent; the dates given are those of first production.

Les Petits-maîtres, 1712; *Arlequin et Mezzetin morts par amour*, 1712; *Arlequin Thétis*, 1713; *Arlequin invisible*, 1713; *La Foire de Guibray*, 1714; *Arlequin Mahomet*, 1714; *Le Tombeau de Nostradamus*, 1714; *Le Temple du destin*, 1715; *Les Eaux de Merlin*, 1715; *Colombine Arlequin; ou, Arlequin Colombine*, 1715; *Arlequin Hulla; ou, La Femme répudiée*, with d'Orneval, 1716; *La Princesse de Charizme*, 1718; *La Querelle des théâtres*, with Joseph de Lafont, 1718; *Le Monde renversé*, with d'Orneval, 1718; *Les Amours de Nanterre*, with d'Orneval and Jacques Autreau, 1718; *Les Funérailles de la*

foire, with d'Orneval and Fuzelier, 1718; *La Statue merveilleuse*, with d'Orneval, 1720; *L'Île des Amazones*, with d'Orneval, 1720; *La Fausse foire*, with d'Orneval and Fuzelier, 1721; *La Boîte de Pandore*, with d'Orneval and Fuzelier, 1721; *La Tête noire*, with d'Orneval and Fuzelier, 1721; *Le Rappel de la foire à la vie*, with d'Orneval and Fuzelier, 1721; *Le Régiment de la Calotte*, with d'Orneval and Fuzelier, 1721; *Le Jeune Vieillard*, with d'Orneval and Fuzelier, 1722; *Le Dieu du hasard*, with d'Orneval and Fuzelier, 1722; *La Force de l'amour*, with d'Orneval and Fuzelier, 1722; *La Foire des fées*, with d'Orneval and Fuzelier, 1722; *Les Captifs d'Alger*, with d'Orneval, 1724; *La Toison d'or*, with d'Orneval, 1724; *L'Oracle muet*, with d'Orneval, 1724; *La Pudeur à la foire*, with d'Orneval, 1724; *La Matrone de Charenton*, with d'Orneval, 1724; *Les Vendages de la foire*, with d'Orneval, 1724; *L'Enchanteur Mirliton*, with d'Orneval and Fuzelier, 1725; *Le Temple du mémoire*, with d'Orneval and Fuzelier, 1725; *Les Enragés; ou, La Rage d'amour*, with d'Orneval and Fuzelier, 1725; *Les Pèlerins de la Mecque*, with d'Orneval, 1726; *Les Comédiens corsaires*, with d'Orneval and Fuzelier, 1726; *L'Obstacle favorable*, with d'Orneval and Fuzelier, 1726; *Les Amoliurs déguisés*, with d'Orneval and Fuzelier, 1726; *Achmet et Almanzine*, with d'Orneval and Fuzelier, 1728; *La Pénélope moderne*, with d'Orneval and Fuzelier, 1728; *Les Amours de Protée*, with d'Orneval and Fuzelier, 1728; *La Princesse de la Chine*, with d'Orneval, 1729; *Les Spectacles malades*, with d'Orneval, 1729; *L'Industrie*, with d'Orneval and Fuzelier, 1730; *Zémine et Almanzor*, with d'Orneval and Fuzelier, 1730; *Les Routes du monde*, with d'Orneval and Fuzelier, 1730; *L'Indifférence*, with d'Orneval and Fuzelier, 1730; *L'Amour marin*, with d'Orneval and Fuzelier, 1730; *L'Espérance*, with d'Orneval and Fuzelier, 1730; *Roger roi de Sicile, surnommé le roi sans chagrin*, with d'Orneval, 1731; *Les Désespérés*, with d'Orneval, 1732; *Sophie et Sigismond*, with d'Orneval, 1732; *La Sauvagesse; ou, La Fille sauvage*, with d'Orneval, 1732; *Le Rival dangereux*, 1734; *Les Deux Frères*, 1734; *La Première Représentation*, 1734; *Les Mariages de Canada*, 1734; *L'Histoire de l'Opéra-Comique; ou, Les Métamorphoses de la foire*, 1736; *Le Mari préféré*, 1736; *Les Vieillards rajeunis*, with Nicolas Fromaget, 1736; *Le Neveu supposé*, 1738.

Fiction

Nouvelles Aventures de l'admirable Dom Quichott de la Manche. 1704.

Le Diable boiteux. 1707; revised editions, 1726 and 1737; translated as *The Devil upon Two Sticks*, 1708: several subsequent translations under same title; as *The Devil upon Crutches*, 1748; as *Asmodeus; or, the Devil upon Two Sticks*, c.1881.

Gil Blas de Santillane (4 vols.). 1715–35; revised edition, 1747; translated as *The History and Adventures of Gil Blas of Santillane* (2 vols.), 1716; as *The Adventures of Gil Blas* (4 vols.), 1749: several subsequent translations under same title.

Roland l'amoureux, from *Orlando inamorato* by Boiardo. 1717.

Histoire de Guzman d'Alfarache, from a romance by Matheo Aleman. 1732; translated as *The Pleasant Adventures of Gusman of Alfarache* (3 vols.), 1812.

Les Aventures de Monsieur Robert Chevalier. 1732; translated as *The Adventures of Robert Chevalier*, 1745.

Histoire d'Estevanille Gonzalez, from a work by Vincention Espinella. 1734.

Une Journée des parques. 1734.

Le Bachelier de Salamanque (6 vols.). 1736–38; translated as *The Batchelor of Salamanca* (2 vols.), 1737–39: several subsequent translations under same title.

La Valise trouvée.   1740.

Other

Mélanges amusant, de saillies d'esprit et de traits historiques des plus frappants.   1743.

*

Criticism

Books:

V. Barbaret, *Lesage et le théâtre de la foire*, Nancy, 1887.

E.F. Lintilhac, *Lesage*, Paris, 1893.

L. Claretie, *Lesage*, Paris, 1894.

V.B. Grannis, *Dramatic Parody in Eighteenth Century France*, New York, 1931.

M. Spaziani, *Il teatro minore de Lesage*, Rome, 1957.

M. Spaziani, *Lesage e il teatro comico al principio del '700*, Rome, 1959.

G. Gouvernet, *Le Type du valet chez Molière et ses successeurs: Regnard, Dufresny, Dancourt et Lesage*, New York, 1985.

W.E. Rex, "Crispin's Inventions", in his *The Attractions of the Contrary*, Cambridge, 1987.

* * *

Lesage's reputation rests chiefly on his achievement as a novelist and his influence was certainly more pronounced in the field of prose fiction than in the theatre. He was the author of some half-dozen novels, the earliest of which, *The Devil on Two Sticks*, inspired by a Spanish work of similar title, became the foundation of his literary career. It tells the story of a young student who, in return for liberating the devil Asmodeus from an astrologer's phial, is carried above the rooftops of Madrid clinging to the devil's cloak and is magically empowered to see what is happening in the privacy of every household. This was followed by the even more successful *Gil Blas de Santillane*, another picaresque romance. Its eponymous hero sets out to study at university in Salamanca, but never reaches it; instead, he meets with all manner of adventures in the highest, as well as the lowest, orders of society, before ultimately settling down in rustic wedded bliss. Although ostensibly set in Spain, both novels take a wider view of the foibles and misdemeanours of mankind and could just as easily be seen as portraits of life in early 18th-century France.

It was just this contemporary realism, an unblinking, dispassionate observation of the social scene, that Lesage was to inject into French comedy. There is no hint of it in his first four dramatic works, all adapted from Spanish originals, and only two of which were staged: *Le Point d'honneur*, from Francisco de Rojas, which enjoyed two performances at the Comédie-Française in 1702, and *Don César Ursin*, from Calderón, which fared little better in 1707. But in the same year he produced *Crispin, Rival of His Master*, his first truly original comedy, with a sting in its tail.

In this play Crispin's master, Valère, has fallen in love with Angélique, daughter of the rich Parisian bourgeois, M. Oronte, who has already promised her to Damis. From the latter's valet, La Branche, Crispin discovers that Damis has got himself married and that La Branche has come to Paris to break off the engagement. Crispin decides to impersonate Damis in order to secure the dowry, which the two valets will then divide before absconding. After several close shaves

their fraud is finally unmasked but, instead of punishment, they are both given business appointments in which they can exercise their initiative less illegally for gain. That their private enterprise almost succeeds is revealing: not only does Crispin seem able, in language and comportment, to counterfeit the master, but he considers himself just as worthy of the prize as Valère, whom he suspects of seeing Angélique's wealth as her principal attraction. At bottom, the piece remains a fast-moving, economically engineered farce, and there is no sign of class subversion—far from it—but it does imply a degree of confusion in the social stratification of the day, and the possibility of upward mobility in a money-orientated society.

Lesage's next two plays were also concerned with financial matters. *La Tontine*, written in 1708, but not performed until 1732, is even more emphatically than its predecessor a one-act farce, in which the mutual insurance scheme of the title is simply a datum of the action, without any sociological overtones; but with *Turcaret* of 1709 the dramatist reached maturity as an ironic commentator on the ethos of the time. *Turcaret* presents us with a whole chain of rapacity and deception, in which there is scarcely a single sympathetic character, and human conduct seems totally subordinated to the profit motive. At its heart is M. Turcaret, a former lackey, but now a powerful, usurious tax-farmer; he lavishes gifts on a young widowed baroness who encourages his attentions, and he is in turn exploited by a knight as a means of paying his gambling debts. Together they conspire to have Frontin, the knight's valet, placed in Turcaret's service, the better to fleece him. Also in the baroness's circle is a drunken spendthrift marquis who is indulged on all sides in expectation of an inheritance which he hopes shortly to be able to dissipate. It is an image of a society steeped in materialism, where greed, self-interest, and dishonesty prevail, and there is no trace of decent feeling. Finally, when Turcaret is seized by creditors and his parasites receive their come-uppance, the only gainer is the unscrupulous opportunist Frontin, whose closing words —"so ends M. Turcaret's reign; mine is about to begin"— supply the play's sardonic coda.

Not surprisingly, *Turcaret's* presentation at the Comédie-Française encountered strenuous resistance in financial circles, and despite healthy box-office takings, it was withdrawn after only seven performances. Thereafter, Lesage transferred his allegiance to the theatre of the Paris fairs, for which he wrote over a hundred pieces, often in collaboration with Louis Fuzelier, d'Orneval, and others, the majority of which were published in his fascinating, nine-volume *Le Théâtre de la foire*. To circumvent a legal prohibition on spoken dialogue his texts had to be written in successive monologues, or on placards carried by the actors, or suspended from the flies, or set to music to constitute so-called "opéra-comique", and liberally sprinkled with mime, dance, and visual business. On the other hand, freedom from the constraints of orthodox dramaturgy, coupled with the availability of changeable scenery and machinery, offered an invitation to fantasy, made for greater animation, and gave unlimited scope to Lesage's satirical and parodic invention. These plays, plus a handful for the Comédie-Italienne, and his continuing output of fiction sustained this resilient professional writer for more than a quarter of a century.

—Donald Roy

See also *Volume 1* entry on *Turcaret*.

LESSING, Gotthold Ephraim. Born in Kamenz, Saxony (then part of the Holy Roman Empire), 23 January 1729. Educated at school of St. Afron, Meissen, 1741–46; studied theology, then medicine, at University of Leipzig, 1746–48; University of Wittenberg, 1748, 1751–52, Master of Arts 1752. Married Eva König in 1776 (died 1778); one son. Writer from 1748 in Berlin; first play, *Der junge Gelehrte*, produced 1748; editor, with Christlob Mylius, *Beiträge zur Historie und Aufnahme des Theaters*, 1750; Editor, *Theatralische Bibliothek*, 1754–58, and *Briefe, die neueste Literatur betreffend (Literaturbriefe)*, 1759; official secretary to General Bogislaw von Tauentzien, Breslau, 1760–65; resident adviser to the National Theatre in Hamburg, 1767–68; librarian to the Duke of Brunswick, Wolfenbüttel, 1770–81. Member, Academy of Mannheim, 1776. Died in Braunschweig, 15 February 1781.

Works

Collections

Schriften (6 vols.).   1753–55; revised edition, 1771.
Lustspiele (2 vols.).   1767.
Trauerspiele.   1772.
Dramatic Works, translated by Ernest Bell.   1878.
Sämtliche Schriften (23 vols.), edited by Karl Lachmann, revised by Franz Muncker.   1886–1924.
Werke (25 vols.), edited by Julius Petersen and Waldemar von Olshausen.   1925; supplement (5 vols.), 1929–35.
Werke (8 vols.), edited by H.G. Göpfert and others.   1970–79.

Stage Works

Der junge Gelehrte, with others (produced by Johann Neuber's company, Leipzig, 1748).   In *Schriften*, 1754.
Die alte Jungfer.   1749.
Samuel Henzi.   In *Schriften*, 1753.
Die Juden (produced by Johann Neuber's company, Leipzig, 1749).   In *Schriften*, 1754.
Der Freygeist (produced Frankfurt, 1767).   In *Schriften*, 1753–55.
Miss Sara Sampson (produced by Ackermann's company, Frankfurt an der Oder, 1755).   In *Schriften*, 1755; translated as *Miss Sara Sampson*, in *World Drama*, edited by Barrett Clark, 1933; also translated, 1977.
Der Misogyn.   In *Schriften*, 1755 (1-act version); revised version (3 acts), in *Lustspiele 1*, 1767.
Der Schatz, from a play by Plautus.   In *Schriften*, 1755.
Faust (fragment).   In *Briefe 1*, 1759.
Philotas (produced by Ludwig Schröder's company, Hamburg, 1780).   1759.
Minna von Barnhelm; oder, Das Soldatenglück (produced Nationaltheater, Hamburg, 1767).   1767; translated as *The Disbanded Officer*, 1786; as *The School for Honor*, 1789; as *Minna von Barnhelm*, 1805; several subsequent translations under same title.
Emilia Galotti (produced Hoftheater, Brunswick, 1772).   In *Trauerspiele*, 1772; translated as *Emilia Galotti*, 1800, in *Five German Tragedies*, 1969, and 1979.
Nathan der Weise (produced by the Döbbelin company, Theater in der Behrenstrasse, Berlin, 1783).   1779; edited by P. Demetz, 1966; translated as *Nathan the Wise*, 1868, and with *Laocoon* and *Minna von Barnhelm*, 1930.

Memoirs and Letters

Briefwechsel über das Trauerspiel, edited by J. Schulte-Sasse.   1972.
Briefe aus Wolfenbüttel, edited by Günter Schulz.   1975.
Meine liebste Madam: Briefwechsel, with Eva König, edited by Günter and Ursula Schulz.   1979.

Other

Fabeln.   1759; revised edition, 1777; translated as *Fables*, 1829.
Laokoon; oder, Über die Grenzen der Malerei und Poesie.   1766; translated as *Laocoon; or, The Limits of Poetry and Painting*, 1853, and subsequently.
Briefe, antiquarischen Inhalts (2 vols.).   1768.
Berengarius Turonensis.   1770.
Zur Geschichte und Literatur [so-called *Wolfenbütteler Beiträge*].   1773–81.
Anti-Goeze, 1–11.   1778.
Ernst und Falk.   1778–81; translated as *Ernst and Falk*, 1854–72; as *Masonic Dialogues*, 1927.
Die Erziehung des Menschengeschlechts.   1780; translated as *The Education of the Human Race*, 1858; also translated in *Lessing's Theological Writings*, 1956.
Theologischer Nachlass, edited by K.G. Lessing.   1784.
Theatralischer Nachlass, edited by K.G. Lessing (2 vols.).   1784–86.
Literarischer Nachlass, edited by K.G. Lessing (3 vols.).   1793–95.
Hamburgische Dramaturgie (1767–69), edited by O. Mann.   1958.
Lessing im Gespräch, edited by Richard Daunicht.   1971.

*

Bibliographies

G. and S. Bauer, *Gotthold Ephraim Lessing*, 1968; revised edition, Darmstadt, 1986.
S. Seifert, *Lessing-Bibliographie*, Berlin and Weimar, 1973.
W. Albrecht, "Lessing-Forschung 1979–1983", in *Weimarer Beiträge*, 31, 1985.
D. Kuhles, *Lessing-Bibliographie 1971–1985*, Berlin, 1988.

Criticism

Books:
J. Clivio, *Lessing und das Problem der Tragödie*, Zurich, 1928.
H. Rempel, *Tragödie und Komödie im dramatischen Schaffen Lessings*, Berlin, 1935; reprinted, 1967.
H.B. Garland, *Lessing, The Founder of Modern German Literature*, Cambridge, 1937; revised edition, London and New York, 1962.
J.G. Robertson, *Lessing's Dramatic Theory*, Cambridge, 1939; reprinted, New York, 1965.
M. Kommerell, *Lessing und Aristoteles: Untersuchungen über die Theorie der Tragödie*, 1940; revised and corrected fifth edition, Frankfurt, 1984.
H. Schneider, *Lessing: Zwölf biographische Studien*, Berlin, 1951.
P. Rilla, *Lessing und sein Zeitalter*, Berlin, 1958; revised edition, 1981.
W. Drews, *Gotthold Ephraim Lessing in Selbstzeugnissen und Bilddokumenten*, Reinbek, 1962; revised edition, 1987.

Gotthold Ephraim Lessing (engraving).

H.J. Schrimpf, *Lessing und Brecht: Von der Aufklärung auf dem Theater*, Pfullingen, 1965.

Henry E. Allison, *Lessing and the Enlightenment*, 1966.

M.M. Metzger, *Lessing and the Language of Comedy*, The Hague, 1966.

W. Ritzel, *Gotthold Ephraim Lessing*, Stuttgart and Berlin, 1966; revised edition, Munich, 1978.

K.S. Guthke and H. Schneider, *Gotthold Ephraim Lessing*, Stuttgart, 1967; third, revised edition, 1979.

A. Brown, *Gotthold Ephraim Lessing* (biography), New York, 1971.

O. Mann and R. Straube-Mann, *Lessing-Kommentar* (2 vols.), Munich, 1971.

J. Schröder, *Gotthold Ephraim Lessing: Sprache und Drama*, Munich, 1972.

W. Barner, *Produktive Rezeption: Lessing und die Tragödien Senecas*, Munich, 1973.

H.C. Seeba, *Die Liebe zur Sache: öffentliches und privates Interesse in Lessings Dramen*, Tübingen, 1973.

M. Gräfin Hoensbroech, *Die List der Kritik: Lessings kritische Schriften und Dramen*, Munich, 1976.

A. Neuhaus-Koch, *Gotthold Ephraim Lessing: Die Sozialstrukturen in seinen Dramen*, Bonn, 1977.

P.H. Neumann, *Der Preis der Mündigkeit: über Lessings Dramen*, Stuttgart, 1977.

V. Nölle, *Subjektivität und Wirklichkeit in Lessings dramatischen und theologischen Werke*, Berlin, 1977.

U. Schulz, *Lessing auf der Bühne: Chronik der Theateraufführungen 1748–1789*, Wiesbaden, 1977.

L.P. Wessell, *Lessing's Theology*, 1977.

D. Hildebrandt, *Lessing: Biographie einer Emanzipation*, Munich and Vienna, 1979.

D. Diederichsen and B. Rudin (eds.), *Lessing im Spiegel der Theaterkritik 1945–1979*, Berlin, 1980.

F.W.O. Röhrs, *Narrative Strukturen in Lessings Dramen*, Heidelberg, 1980.

F.J. Lamport, *Lessing and the Drama*, Oxford, 1981.

A.M. Reh, *Die Rettung der Menschlichkeit: Lessings Dramen in literaturpsychologischer Sicht*, Bern and Munich, 1981.

H. Schnierle, *Gotthold Ephraim Lessing*, Salzburg, 1981.

C. Albert, *Der melancholische Bürger: Ausbildung bürgerlicher Deutungsmuster im Trauerspiel Diderots und Lessings*, Frankfurt, 1983.

W. Rülskamp, *Dramaturgie ohne Publikum: Lessings Dramaturgie*, Cologne and Vienna, 1984.

J. Bark, *Gotthold Ephraim Lessing: Leben und Werk*, Stuttgart, 1986.

J. Jacobs, *Lessing: Eine Einführung*, Munich and Zurich, 1986.

P. Pütz, *Die Leistung der Form: Lessings Dramen*, Frankfurt, 1986.

G. Ter-Nedden, *Lessings Trauerspiele*, Stuttgart, 1986.

W. Barner, *Lessing: Epoche—Werk—Wirkung*, Munich, 1987 (revised fifth edition).

Serials
Lessing Yearbook, 1969—

*   *   *

Lessing spent much of his time while a student in Leipzig (where he had matriculated to read first theology, and then medicine) backstage with the theatre company of Caroline Neuber. From them he learned the practical requirements theatre practitioners make of their authors. The Neuber Company was at the time performing the French-inspired plays of the theatre reformer Gottsched. Lessing's first attempts at writing for the theatre were staged by the Neuber Company, but they are derivative and of little interest.

It was not until 1755 that Lessing broke new ground in the German theatre. Influenced by English novels of the time (in particular Richardson's *Clarissa*), he wrote *Miss Sara Sampson*, in which he introduced bourgeois tragedy to the German stage. Set in England, this lachrymose and excessively wordy play was well received by its first audiences. They responded to its contemporaneity of setting, its bourgeois characters, and its unstilted prose dialogue.

The Seven Years War prevented Lessing from travelling through Europe as he had intended. Instead, he, a Saxon, worked as secretary to a Prussian general. This experience, and his desire to foster a spirit of tolerance after the end of the War, led to the writing of *Minna von Barnhelm* in 1767. Although initially unsuccessful (it was not staged at first for fear of offending the King of Prussia), the play soon established its place in the German theatre repertoire—a place it has maintained for two centuries.

One of the few classic German comedies, *Minna von Barnhelm* shows how a witty and wily Saxon woman can ultimately trick her stiff-necked Prussian officer fiancé into admitting his true feelings of love for her. Minna is arguably the first liberated woman in German comedy. She is not frightened to pursue her lover, neither is she afraid to stand up to the importunate questioning of the landlord. She also acts as a mouthpiece for Lessing in her rejection of French language and manners, in favour of her native German ones.

Lessing's major contribution to theatre criticism, *Die Hamburgische Dramaturgie* (The Hamburg Dramaturgy) was the result of his acting as resident critic to the then newly established National Theatre in Hamburg. It starts as a series of reviews of the ill-fated theatre's productions; but Lessing soon digresses into discussions on the nature and the role of theatre and drama, especially tragedy, and suggestions for the improvement of the German theatre repertoire. In his analysis of catharsis, he rejected the view, current at the time, that tragedy achieves its effect on the audience by way of pity and terror. For terror, he, more correctly, substitutes fear. The audience is to feel pity for the hero in his suffering; the fear is the pity of the audience turned on itself. Lessing, the quintessential bourgeois, largely ignored the admiration which other critics had seen as an essential reaction of an audience towards a tragic hero. Instead, he suggests that our pity is more likely to be excited by the sufferings of our social equals, rather than of a remote nobleman or a mythological figure. In this, and in his insistence that the aim of tragedy, as of all genres of poetry, should be the moral improvement of the audience, he provided the theoretical basis of German domestic tragedy. He rejected the contemporary French adherence to the Aristotelian unities, and suggested that the English drama would prove a better model for the Germans in their attempts to establish a national theatre repertoire. He went so far as to declare that Shakespeare remained truer to the Greeks in breaking the unities than the French writers who attempted strictly to observe them. Shakespeare stayed true to the spirit of Aristotle because his theatre was "characteristic" of its age and people, as the classical Greek theatre, described by Aristotle, was of its own age, whereas the French neo-classical theatre was not.

In 1772 he published a version of the Virginia story, his bourgeois tragedy *Emilia Galotti*, in which the middle-class heroine, the object of a prince's desire, persuades her father to kill her rather than succumb to his advances, after her fiancé has been murdered by the prince's evil adviser. The play had a considerable influence on the writers of the *Sturm und Drang* movement, because of its characterisation and vivid dialogue, but also because of its outspoken social criticism: although set in Italy, the abuses of absolute power highlighted in the play were clearly relevant to the situation in contemporary Germany.

In later life Lessing withdrew into his work as a librarian, while engaging in protracted theological disputes, in which he espoused the cause of tolerance against orthodoxy. The theatrical result of these concerns, and his last play, was the allegorical verse play *Nathan der Weise* (*Nathan the Wise*). Set in Jerusalem at the time of the Crusades, the play portrays three great religions in the persons of a young templar (in love with the adopted daughter of Nathan), Saladin, and Nathan himself. In the retelling of the parable of three rings, Lessing argues for the equal validity of all religions and makes a noble plea for religious tolerance. The play pioneered the use of blank verse in German drama, and, while not performed in his lifetime, has, since its first production by Goethe in Weimar, in 1801, found an important place in the German theatre repertoire. It has been frequently revived, most significantly after the defeat of the Nazis in 1945.

Lessing was too modest in his assessment of his plays, which he hoped would serve as models for subsequent dramatists of greater genius than himself. This they did, and still do, but he was himself a playwright of considerable talent and originality, and the outstanding critic of his age.

—Anthony Meech

See also *Volume 1* entries on *Emilia Galotti*; *Minna von Barnhelm*.

LEWIS, Leopold.   See *Volume 1* entry on *The Bells.*

LI Xingfu.   See *Volume 1* entry on *The Chalk Circle.*

LILLO, George.   Born in Moorfields, London, 3 February 1691. Partner in his father's jewellery business in London. First-produced play, *Silvia; or, The Country Burial*, produced 1730. Died in London, 3 September 1739.

Works

Collections

Works (2 vols.).   1775; edited by Trudi Drucker, 1979.

Stage Works

Silvia; or, The Country Burial (produced Lincoln's Inn Fields Theatre, London, 1730).   1730.
The London Merchant; or, The History of George Barnwell (produced Theatre Royal, Drury Lane, London, 1731).   1731.

The Christian Hero (produced Theatre Royal, Drury Lane, London, 1735).   1735.
Fatal Curiosity (produced Little Theatre, Haymarket, London, 1736; as *Guilt Its Own Punishment*, produced 1736).   1737.
Marina, from the play *Pericles* by Shakespeare (produced Covent Garden Theatre, London, 1738).   1738.
Elmerick; or, Justice Triumphant (produced Theatre Royal, Drury Lane, London, 1740).   1740.
Britannia and Batavia.   1740.
Arden of Faversham, completed by John Hoadly, from the anonymous play (produced Theatre Royal, Drury Lane, London, 1759).   1762.

*

Criticism

Books:
George Wellwarth, *George Lillo and the Finger-Wagging Drama*, Leeds, 1970 (pamphlet).
Bernard Beckerman, "Schemes of Show: A Search for Critical Norms", in *The Stage and the Page*, edited by George Winchester Stone Jr., Berkeley, California, 1981.

Articles:
D.B. Pallette, "Notes for a Biography of Lillo" in *Philological Quarterly*, 19, 1940; supplement, "Further Notes for a Biography of Lillo", by C.B. Burgess, in *Philological Quarterly*, 46, 1967.
Stephen L. Trainor, "Context for a Biography of Lillo" in *Philological Quarterly*, 64, 1985.

* * *

The theatrical record of Lillo's plays shows how hard it was to earn a living from the theatre in the 1730's, a decade when the repertory of the patent theatres only rarely found room for new plays. A playwright received the profits from the third night's performance, and each subsequent third performance, as well as from any sale for publication. Of Lillo's seven plays, three gained him a single night's profits, and two were only performed posthumously.

Lillo's one success, and the only one of his plays to be occasionally revived today, was *The London Merchant*. It is a tragedy in prose about ordinary people, and "the beginning of the first act occasioned a sneer in the audience", the *Weekly Register* reported, "as if 'twas impossible they should receive any delicate pleasure from such an entertainment; but, before the end of it, the case was quite alter'd, and a most profond silence argued the deepest attention, and the sincerest pleasure imaginable". The tragedy was henceforth performed annually at one or other of the London theatres on the major holidays of the year, as edifying entertainment for apprentices, until 1819.

The only others of his works to be revived after their initial performances were his first produced work, the ballad-opera *Silvia*, and *Fatal Curiosity*, his other tragedy of ordinary people. Both are melodramas *avant la lettre*. In *Fatal Curiosity* a young man, tossed on the shore of his native village by a shipwreck, visits first his fiancée, Charlotte, who has waited seven years for him, and then "the hoary, helpless, miserable pair", his parents. Unrecognized, he has the sentimental satisfaction of hearing all of them pour out their feelings for him. But his parents, driven by "necessity, impatience, and despair" to stifle "pity, mercy, or remorse", murder this stranger for the casket of jewels he has brought back from India, in a scene irresistibly and unfortunately reminiscent of Macbeth's murder of Duncan. When they learn the truth, his father kills his wife and then himself.

Lillo intended Sophoclean simplicity but has Charlotte speak of how "frequent instances of others woe/Must give a gen'rous mind a world of pain"; one is too conscious of the inflation of emotions by, among other devices, the ubiquitous trios of emotive phrases. Lillo is also prone to reach beyond the particular for the willed general truth, as when *Silvia*'s heroine proclaims, "the world owes its order, kingdoms their peaceful regular succession, and private families their domestic happiness to marriage".

A newspaper praised *Fatal Curiosity* for "scenes of distress . . . artfully work'd up", but it is precisely the consciousness of this that is likely to make modern readers feel out of sympathy with the tragedies' emotional tone. The contrast between the anonymous Elizabethan *Arden of Faversham* and Lillo's adaptation demonstrates how the vivid specificity of the original evaporates in Lillo's version. The plain speaking of Arden to his wife Alice's lover Mosbie—"But I must have a mandate for my wife;/They say you seek to rob me of her love:/Villain, what makes thou in her company?"—becomes (even her name has been elaborated), "But my just right to false Alicia's heart,/(So dearly purchas'd with a husband's name,/And sacred honour of a gentleman)/I shall assert myself, and thus secure/From further violation". The sordid grittiness of the original—"The next time that I take thee neare my house,/Instead of legs I'll make thee crawl on stumps"—is transformed into the images of the conventional tragedy of his age: ". . . I'll follow thee to the ocean's brink, /Or to the edge of some dread precipice,/Where terror and despair shall stop thy flight,/And force thy trembling hand to guard thy life".

Lillo's *Marina*, taken from the last two acts of Shakespeare's *Pericles*, suffers in the same way. So do his two historical tragedies, *The Christian Hero* and *Elmerick; or, Justice Triumphant*. They may be left in the rhetorical kingdoms of medieval Albania and Hungary in which they are respectively set. In both, the loyalties of love, running across the divisions of faction, conflict with the sexual violence of the villains.

Silvia is delightful nonsense. The plot turns upon the resolve of her wooer, Sir John Freeman, never to marry. Rejected by Silvia, he carries off the very willing village girl, Lettice, whose mother, in a farcical subplot, is buried, but then recovers from an alcoholic stupor. Freeman teeters between the principled libertinism of the Restoration rake that his name suggests and a sentimental remorse quite alien to the Restoration. In an overheated ending he laments the ruin he has brought on so many, though in fact everyone seems happy with events. Rather unnecessarily, since Silvia and Freeman are now matched, her father reveals that because infants were switched at birth—as a birthmark proves—Silvia is the true inheritor of Freeman's estate.

Whatever the differences in taste between Lillo's and our own time, the three plays revived in the 18th century are the three of most interest now. Nevertheless, Lillo's reputation will continue to rest primarily on the innovations of subject matter and style in *The London Merchant*.

—Anthony Graham-White

See also *Volume 1* entry on *The London Merchant*.

LINDSAY, Sir David.   See *Volume 1* entry on *A Satire of the Three Estates*.

LOPE DE VEGA CARPIO.   See **VEGA CARPIO, Lope de.**

LORCA, Federico García.   See **GARĆIA LORCA, Federico.**

LUDLAM, Charles.   Born in Floral Park, New York, USA, 12 April 1943. Educated at Hofstra University, Hampstead, New York, 1961–65, BA in Drama, 1965. Member, John Vaccaro's Play-House of the Ridiculous, New York, 1965–67; founding director, Ridiculous Theatrical Company [RTC], 1967, for which he wrote, acted, and directed until his death; lecturer, University of Massachusetts, Amherst, 1972, University of New London, Connecticut, 1974 and 1975; American University, Washington, DC, 1976; New York University, 1977 and 1979–80; adjunct associate professor, Yale University, New Haven, Connecticut, 1982–83; directed for the Santa Fe Opera Company, 1985–86. Recipient: Obie Award, 1969, 1973, 1975, 1977, 1985, 1987; Drama Desk Award, 1982, 1985; Rosamund Gilder Award, 1986. Died in New York, 28 May 1987.

Works

Collections

Complete Plays.   1989.

Stage Works

All original plays are contained in *Complete Plays*, 1989. Earlier publications given below.

Big Hotel (produced Gate Theatre, New York, 1967).
Conquest of the Universe; or, When Queens Collide (produced as Gate Theatre, New York, 1967).
Turds in Hell, with Bill Vehr (produced Gate Theatre, New York, 1969).   In *Drama Review*, September 1970.
The Grand Tarot (produced Millenium Film Workshop, New York, 1969; revised version produced New York, 1971).
Bluebeard (produced La Mama Experimental Theatre, New York, 1970).   In *More Plays from Off-Broadway*, edited by Michael Smith, 1972; published separately, 1987.
Eunuchs of the Forbidden City (produced Berlin, 1971; first produced in the USA, Theatre for the New City, New York, 1972).   In *Scripts 6*, April 1972.

Corn, music by Virgil Young (produced 13th Street Theatre, New York, 1972).

Camille: A Tear-Jerker, from a play by Dumas *fils* (produced 13th Street Theatre, New York, 1973).

Hot Ice (produced Tamanous Playhouse, Vancouver, British Columbia, 1973).   In *Drama Review*, June 1974.

Stage Blood (produced Evergreen Theatre, New York, 1975).   1979.

Professor Bedlam's Educational Punch and Judy Show (puppet play; produced Evergreen Theatre, New York, 1975).

Caprice (produced Provincetown Playhouse, New York, 1976; revised version, as *Fashion Bound*, produced New London, Connecticut).

Jack and the Beanstalk (for children; produced New York, 1976).

The Adventures of Karagöz (produced Festival Mondial du Théâtre, Nancy, France, 1976).

Der Ring Gott Farblonjet, music by Jack McElwaine (produced Truck and Warehouse Theatre, New York, 1977).

Aphrodisiamania (dance scenario; produced Brooklyn Academy of Music, Brooklyn, New York, 1977).

The Ventriloquist's Wife (produced One Sheridan Square, New York, 1978).

Anti-Galaxie Nebulae, with Bill Vehr and Everett Quinton (puppet play; produced One Sheridan Square, New York, 1978).

Utopia Incorporated (produced One Sheridan Square, New York, 1978).

The Enchanted Pig (produced One Sheridan Square, New York, 1979).   1989.

The Elephant Woman (produced One Sheridan Square, New York, 1979).

A Christmas Carol, from the story by Dickens (produced One Sheridan Square, New York, 1979).

Reverse Psychology (produced One Sheridan Square, New York, 1980).   1989.

The Production of Mysteries, music by Peter Golub (libretto; produced by the City Symphony, Bennington, Vermont, 1980).

Love's Tangled Webb (produced One Sheridan Square, New York, 1981).   1989.

Secret Lives of the Sexists (produced One Sheridan Square, New York, 1982).

Exquisite Torture (produced One Sheridan Square, New York, 1982).

Galas (produced One Sheridan Square, New York, 1983).

Le Bourgeois Avant-Garde (produced One Sheridan Square, New York, 1983).

The Mystery of Irma Vep (produced One Sheridan Square, New York, 1984).   1987.

Salammbó, from the novel by Flaubert (produced One Sheridan Square, New York, 1985).

The Artificial Jungle (produced One Sheridan Square, New York, 1986).   1987.

Die Fledermaus (libretto; produced Santa Fe Opera, Santa Fe, New Mexico, 1986).

Medea.   1988.

Isle of the Hermaphrodites; or, The Murderered Minion.

How Not to Write a Play.

Screenplays

The Sorrows of Dolores; *The Museum of Wax*.

Other

Ridiculous Theatre: Essays and Opinions.   1993.

*

CriticismBooks:
Stefan Brecht, *Nuovo teatro americano 1968–1973*, Rome, 1974.
Steven Samuels, "A Brief Life", in Ludlam's *Complete Plays*, New York, 1989.
Ruby Cohn, *New American Dramatists 1960–1990*, London, 1991 (Macmillan Modern Dramatists series).

Articles:
Martin Andrucki, "'Ah the old questions, the old answers . . .': Postmodernism and Poetic Justice in the Plays of Charles Ludlam", in *Text and Performance Quarterly*, 10, 1990.

*   *   *

Actor, director, designer, and playwright Charles Ludlam, founder of New York's Ridiculous Theatrical Company, employed all his diverse theatrical skills for one overriding purpose—to make people laugh. In his 20-year career—cut short by his untimely death from AIDS—he proved himself a comic master.

Ludlam's playwriting achievements include almost 30 plays, plus a dance scenario, two films, a couple of puppet serials, a frame tale for a cabaret, and two opera librettos. In writing and mounting them, Ludlam adhered to principles that comedy should combine humor and pathos, should dramatize serious themes by means of farce, wit, parody, melodrama, and satire, should concern hypocrisy and moral paradox, and should take risks.

Like Joe Orton, Ludlam often shows himself a strict moralist, even though his standards may differ from the norm. Whereas several Ludlam plays explicitly personify good and bad angels, or devils versus angelic figures, or feature death as a character or force, Ludlam more often indicts the objects of his ridicule for violating his own humanistic standards (as when the lovers in *The Artificial Jungle* live by an amoral "law of the jungle"). Although conservatives might label his obscenity and scatology proof of moral iconoclasm, his work suggests nothing is sacred only in areas such as sex, which have always been the province of satirists and farceurs. But even as he frees our inhibitions, moving spectators quickly from incredulity at his daring to joining him in raucous belly laughs, Ludlam demonstrates outrage at hypocrisy, cruelty, greed, con-games, sycophancy, and other violations of his own moral imperatives.

Ludlam staged his indictments of human folly and Aristophanic celebrations of the free spirit with overtly theatrical, yet traditional methods—what Ludlam called "lost strains in theatre craft"—such as footlights, thunder sheets, wind machines, and outrageous but carefully crafted costumes designed by Ludlam's successor as Artistic Director of the RTC, Everett Quinton.

Ludlam tends to acknowledge, in presentational fashion, that spectators are watching a play rather than observing real life. In *Big Hotel* one character laments, "two deaths in one play", while another complains, "I've lost the thread of the narrative". *The Conquest of the Universe*'s Tamberlaine plans to go to the theatre to see the play in which we're watching him; later Zabina protests: "That was the worst line I've ever had to say in *any* play". In addition, characters discuss the play and/or the playwright in *Hot Ice*, *Stage Blood*, *How Not to Write a Play*, and *The Ventriloquist's Wife*. Rarely does Ludlam's theatricality fail: in one play he invents a hunchback, pinhead, sex maniac who sneaks into a convent disguised as Santa Claus and is met by a nun on roller skates; in another, he creates for a gay actor (originally played by

Ludlam himself) the role of a straight job-applicant, who impersonates a gay physical culture expert, who's pretending to be a heterosexual anti-feminist woman, who's mistaken by a female bedmate for a lesbian!

Of course, Ludlam lifts his plots and gags from all of Western culture, particularly its films, books, plays, and operas. Although partly parodying his originals, Ludlam also reveres them; he sticks so closely to his sources in his classic adaptations that his departures prove all the more hilarious. Ludlam rifles from Chaucer, Shakespeare, and numerous other dramatists, novelists (including the Brontës, Dickens, and Zola), fairy tales (*Cinderella*, *Rumpelstiltskin*, *Beauty and the Beast*, *Bluebeard*, and *Jack and the Beanstalk*), films (*Grand Hotel*, *Sunset Boulevard*, *White Heat*, and *Double Indemnity*), and even Wagner's *Ring* and the American Declaration of Independence.

Each script revels in wordplay—"gownless evening strap", "molten irony", "I'm too Jung to be Freudened", "the plot sickens", "the Enema of the People"—and puns proliferate. Careful attention rewards the listener with verbal gems harder to catch on first hearing. Even the mock-heroic plays, where opportunity presents itself less often, interrupt the bombast with delicious colloquialisms.

Ludlam employs all the other tried-and-true sources of humor, from pie-in-the-face slapstick in *Camille* and *Hot Ice*, to bedroom farce in *Bluebeard*, *Reverse Psychology*, and *Secret Lives of the Sexists*, and cross-dressing in numerous plays. One of his most successful farces, *How to Write a Play*, finds the character of Ludlam at his typewriter, trying to meet a script deadline while mobbed by a suicidal woman, gay seniors, a belly dancer, a balloon folder, and a gorilla; in the midst of all this he's forced to try to raise money for his theatre by impersonating his (fictional) twin sister. Yet Ludlam likewise succeeds with horror farce (*Salammbô*) and black comedy (*The Artificial Jungle*). Ludlam's topical targets of satire include diets high in sugar, fat, and chemical additives; cryogenic freezing of corpses; the fashion industry; psychiatrists and modern art; seeming excesses and pretensions in avant-garde music, dance, and theatre (and their critics); and feminists. And Ludlam builds entire scripts from the self-parody of melodrama. Thus we laugh at the material itself, exaggerated only mildly, in such plays as *Salammbô*, *A Christmas Carol*, *Medea*, *Isle of the Hermaphrodites; or, The Murdered Minion*, *Love's Tangled Web*, and *Exquisite Torture*.

Ludlam mixes ridicule with reverence in his best known works. Thus, when he played Camille, his sincerity moved spectators to tears, even while he carefully revealed the hairy chest beneath the *décolletage*, intentionally undercutting the perfect verisimilitude. Ludlam also travesties, yet pays tribute to, the Victorian penny-dreadful in his *tour de force*, *The Mystery of Irma Vep*. This side-splitting Gothic horror spoof concerns Lord Edgar's marriage to a new wife, Lady Enid, even though the loyalties of the servants, Jane and Nicodemus, still belong to their first mistress, Irma Vep (the name is an anagram of vampire). Joining in the mayhem at the manor are a monster, an Egyptian con-artist, a mummy, and an apparition of Irma Vep. Moreover, in the original production Nicodemus transformed into a werewolf—onstage—as Ludlam simultaneously acted both, plus the role of Lady Enid.

Although he directed his plays, Ludlam did not star in them all. His famous parts included Norma Desmond in *Big Hotel*, the title roles in *Camille* and *Galas*, and the 13-year-old virgin priestess of the moon in *Salammbô* (all in drag), as well as Hamlet in *Stage Blood*, Dr. Silver in *Reverse Psychology*, Dr. Rufus Foufas in *Le Bourgeois Avant-Garde*, Dickens'

Scrooge in *A Christmas Carol*, the Ventriloquist in *The Ventriloquist's Wife*, and the title role in *Bluebeard*. A balding gnome, he became gorgeous in women's roles. Ludlam likewise possessed a beautifully trained and versatile voice, physical exuberance and agility, expert timing, mobile features, and a gift for mimicry.

—Tish Dace

LYLY, John. Born in the Weald of Kent, England, c. 1554. Educated probably at King's School, Canterbury, Kent; Magdalen College, Oxford, 1569–75, BA 1573, MA 1575; incorporated MA, Cambridge University, 1579. Married Beatrice Browne in 1583; several children. In the service of Lord Delawarr, 1575–80, and the Earl of Oxford from 1580; became partner in leasing Blackfriars Theatre, London, c.1584: wrote for the children's acting companies of the Chapel Royal and St. Paul's, London, until their suspension in 1591; Member of Parliament for Hindon, 1589, Appleby, 1593 and 1601, and Aylesbury, 1596; lived mainly in Mexborough, Yorkshire, 1590–95. Died (buried) in London, 30 November 1606.

Works

Collections

Dramatic Works (2 vols.), edited by F.W. Fairholt. 1858–92.
Complete Works (3 vols.), edited by R.W. Bond. 1902.
Plays, edited by Carter A. Daniel. 1989.

Plays

Alexander, Campaspe, and Diogenes (produced by Oxford's Boys, Blackfriars Theatre, London, c.1584). 1584; as *Campaspe*, 1584.
Sappho and Phao (produced by Oxford's Boys, Blackfriars Theatre, London, 1584). 1584.
Galathea (produced by the Children of St. Paul's, London, 1584–85?). 1592.
Mother Bombie (produced by the Children of St. Paul's, London, 1587–90?). 1594.
Endimion, The Man in the Moon (produced by the Children of St. Paul's, Greenwich, London, 1588). 1591.
Midas (produced by the Children of St. Paul's, London, 1589). 1592,
Love's Metamorphosis (produced by the Children of St. Paul's, London, 1589–90?). 1601.
The *Woman in the Moon* (produced London?, 1590–95?). 1597.

Fiction

Euphues: The Anatomy of Wit. 1578; augmented edition, 1579.
Euphues and His England. 1580.
Euphues (both parts). 1617.

Other

Pap with a Hatchet, Alias a Fig for My Godson; or, Crack Me This Nut; or, A Country Cuff, That is, A Sound Box of the Ear, for the Idiot Martin. 1589.

A Whip for an Ape; or, Martin Displayed. 1589; as *Rhythms Against Martin Mar-Prelate*, 1589 (possibly not by Lyly).

*

Bibliographies

S.A. Tannenbaum, *John Lyly: A Concise Bibliography*, New York, 1940; supplement in *Elizabethan Bibliographies 5*, Port Washington, New York, 1967.
R.C. Johnson, *John Lyly 1935–1965*, London, 1968.

Criticism

Books:
J.C. Child, *John Lyly and Euphuism*, Erlangen, 1894.
John Dover Wilson, *John Lyly*, Cambridge, 1905.
V.M. Jeffrey, *John Lyly and the Italian Renaissance*, Paris, 1928.
G.K. Hunter, *John Lyly: The Humanist and Courtier*, Cambridge, Massachusetts, 1962.
Jocelyn Powell, "John Lyly and the Language of Play", in *Elizabethan Theatre*, edited by John Russell Brown and Bernard Harris, London, 1966 (Stratford-upon-Avon Studies).
G.K. Hunter, *John Lyly and George Peele*, London, 1968.
Peter Saccio, *The Court Comedies of Lyly: A Study in Allegorical Dramaturgy*, Princeton, New Jersey, 1969.
Joseph W. Houppert, *John Lyly*, Boston, 1975.
J.B. Altman, *The Tudor Play of Mind: Rhetorical Inquiry and the Development of English Drama*, Berkeley, 1978.

Articles:
G. Wilson Knight, "Lyly", in *Review of English Studies*, 15, 1939.
B.F. Huppe, "Allegory of Love in Lyly's Court Comedies", in *English Literary History*, 1947.
Michael Best, "The Staging and Production of the Plays of John Lyly", in *Theatre Research*, 9, 1968.
Marco Mincoff, "Shakespeare and Lyly", in *Shakespeare Survey*, 14, 1961.

* * *

"Our intent was at this time to move inward delight, not outward lightness, and to breed, if it might be, soft smiling, not loud laughing" (prologue, *Sapho and Phao*). While Lyly's intent, expressed in the neat antitheses characteristic of his prose, was fulfilled in a series of Court comedies, the subsequent neglect of those plays may also stem from the conscious refinement of his art. Lyly's plays are neither revived professionally, nor given great attention by students of the drama. They were carefully shaped to the capacity of his troupe of boy actors, and written for a coterie audience. Deliberately light in subject matter ("we, calling Alexander from his grave, seek only who was his love" notes the prologue to *Campaspe*), meticulously regular in plot, and decorous in wit ("What do you think best for your sighing, to take it away? Yew, Madam. Me? No, madam, yew of the tree. Then I will love yew the better"), the comedies lack the robustness of contemporary Tudor comedy.

Lyly would have been a good dramatist in any age: fashionable, flattering, and adroit, but a minor dramatist nevertheless. Resemblance can be found in sentimental, rather than the more durable laughing comedy. Reality impinges upon the static, self-scrutinising world of his main-plot characters as it does in the plays of Sir Richard Steele, from the viewpoint of the servants (see Lucinda and Phyllis in Steele's *The Conscious Lovers*, Act III, Scene 1), but the glimpse of absurdity is never detrimental to the flourishing of refined feeling. Love, Lyly's main subject, is either appropriately conquered by those who ought, by status, to be above it, or it conquers those it will elevate rather than diminish. Campaspe nervously prefers Apelles the painter to Alexander the Great, who is regally magnanimous; Sapho takes over Cupid from "Immodest Venus"; Gallathea urges the female part of the audience to "yield, ladies, yield to love, ladies".

Lyly's prose (only *The Woman in the Moon* is in verse, and was written for an adult company) varies from a fully Euphuistic high style for his goddesses or monarchs, through a more energetic *pro et contra* disputation, characteristic of his lovers, to the dullard's question and the servant's quick answer of his comic scenes. The rhythm of soliloquy, colloquy, and exhortation tends, in reading, to seem over-regular: Lyly's best dramatic art occurs in scenes where music and spectacle give a wider appeal than the clever, graceful, but ultimately docile, quality of his stage language: Act IV, Scene 2 of *Gallathea*, where Cupid tries to untie the love knots that bind Diana's nymphs, could be realised as a Fragonard painting with sound and motion.

Shakespeare learnt much from Lyly, drawing on, for example: the shimmer of gender in *Gallathea*, where the shepherdesses, disguised by their fathers as boys to escape sacrifice, meet in the woods and fall in love, wooing one another tentatively, each hoping that the other has not told the same lie about herself, each giving out ambiguous declarations; the eavesdropping scene in the same play, where Diana's nymphs, one by one, enter to confess love; and the exploitation of the comic potential of love conflicting with friendship. These elements suggest how close Lyly was to the life of *As You Like It*, *Love's Labour's Lost*, and *Two Gentlemen of Verona*. *Sapho and Phao* has the play apologetically presented as a dream, or, in its epilogue, as a "dance of a fairy in a circle". *Endimion*, alone, features a quarrel about height between two girls (like Helena and Hermia), a burlesque lover who sleeps and wakes alongside the true lover (like Bottom), and a moon-suffused text, all in multiple resemblance to *A Midsummer Night's Dream*.

Nicholas Hilliard sought in his portrait miniatures to record "those lovely graces, wittye smilings, and those stolne glances which sudainly like lightning passe and another countenance taketh place": a Court art which idealised the Court. In intention and execution, Lylian drama is directly comparable, an art very much of its period, but somehow lacking in the challenge normally associated with great art.

—Roy Booth

See also *Volume 1* entry on *Endimion*.

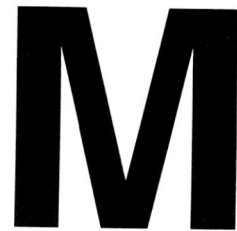

MACARTHUR, Charles. See *Volume 1* entry on *The Front Page.*

MACHIAVELLI, Niccolò (di Bernardo dei). Born in Republic of Florence (now in Italy), 3 May 1469. Married Marietta Corsini in 1501; five children. Probably involved in overthrowing the Savonarolist government, 1498; appointed to head the new government's Second Chancery, 1498, and secretary of an agency concerned with warfare and diplomacy, 1498–1512: some 6000 surviving documents record his unceasing activity, including trips to visit Caterina Sforza, 1499, Cesare Borgia, 1502, Rome, 1503 and 1506, France, 1504 and 1510, and Germany, 1507–08; helped to set up a standing army (which reconquered Pisa, 1509); the Florentine Republic ended with the return to power of the Medici family (under Piero dei Medici), 1512: Machiavelli was jailed and exiled to Sant'Andrea in Percussina where he spent his remaining years in retirement, though he was given a few diplomatic or writing jobs. Died in Florence, 21 June 1527.

Works

Collections

Opere inedite in prosa e in verso. 1763.
The Literary Works (includes the plays *Mandragola* and *Clizia*, and other works), translated by John R. Hale. 1961.
Opere letterarie, edited by Luigi Blasucci. 1964.
The Chief Works and Others (3 vols.; *Mandragola* and *Clizia* in Volume 2), translated by Allan Gilbert. 1965.
Opere (4 vols.; literary works in Volume 4), various editors. 1968–89.
Tutte le opere, edited by Mario Martelli. 1971.
Teatro (includes *Mandragola; Clizia; Andria*), edited by G. Davico Bonino. 1979.
"Mandragola" e "Clizia", edited by R. Raimondi. 1984.
The Comedies (includes *The Woman from Andros; The Mandrake; Clizia*), edited and translated by David Sices and James B. Atkinson. 1985.

Stage Works

La Mandragola (produced at the House of B. di Giordana, Florence, c.1518–20). Published c.1518–24; translated as *Mandragola*, 1927: several subsequent translations under same title; also translated as *The Mandrake*, in *The Comedies*, 1985.
La Clizia (produced at the house of Jacopo di Filippo Falconetti, Florence, 1525). 1532; translated as *Clizia*, in *The Literary Works*, 1961.
Andria, from the play by Terence. In *Opere inedite in prosa e in verso*, 1763; translated as *The Woman from Andros*, in *The Comedies*, 1985.

Fiction

Novella di Belfagor arcidiavolo. 1545; translated as *Belfagor*, in *The Literary Works*, 1961.

Verse

Decennale Primo. 1504(?).
Lust and Liberty, translated by Joseph Tusiani. 1963.

Memoirs and Letters

Letters: A Selection, edited by Allan H. Gilbert. 1961.

Other

Discorso dell'ordinare lo stato di Firenze alle armi. 1507(?).
Dell'arte della guerra. 1521; translated as *The Art of War*, 1562.
Discorsi sulla prima deca di Tito Livio. 1531; translated as the *Discourses on Livy*, 1636, translation edited by Bernard Crick, 1971.
Discorsi. 1531; translated as *Discourses* (2 vols.), 1950.
Il principe. 1532; translated as *The Prince*, 1560: numerous subsequent translations under same title.
Istorie fiorentine. 1532; translated as *Florentine History*, 1595; as *History of Florence and of the Affairs of Italy*, 1960.
Discorso o dialogo intorno a la nostra lingua. Translated as *A Dialogue on Language*, in *The Literary Works*, 1961.
Legazioni, commissarie, scritti di governo, edited by Fredi Chiappelli. 1971–
"The Prince" and Other Political Writings, edited by Bruce Penman. 1981.

*

Bibliographies

S. Bertelli and P. Innocenti, *Bibliografia machiavelliana*, Verona, 1979.

Niccolò Machiavelli (portrait by Santi di Tito; Palazzo Vecchio, Florence).

Criticism

Books:

R. Ridolfi, *Vita di Niccolò Machiavelli*, Rome, 1954; revised edition, 1981; English edition, as *The Life of Machiavelli*, 1963.

R. Ridolfi, *Studi sulle commedie del Machiavelli*, Pisa, 1968.

C.D. Tarleton, *Fortune's Circle: A Biographical Interpretation of Niccolò Machiavelli*, Chicago, 1970.

E. Raimondi, *Politica e commedia*, Bologna, 1972.

G. Ferroni, *"Mutazione" e "riscontro" nel teatro di Machiavelli e altri saggi sulla commedia del Cinquecento*, Rome, 1972.

M. Baratto, *La commedia del Cinquecento*, Vicenza, 1975.

P. Bosisio, *Popolarità nel classicità nel teatro comico del Cinquecento*, Milan, 1975.

S. Ruffo-Fiore, *Niccolò Machiavelli* (in English), Boston, 1982.

Articles:

E. Raimondi, "Il teatro di Machiavelli", in *Studi storici*, vol.10 no.4, 1969.

D. Perocco, "Rassegna di studi sulle opere letterarie di Machiavelli 1969–1986", in *Lettere italiane*, 1987.

* * *

Machiavelli is obviously better known as a political theorist and historian; but it has been traditional to see his comedy *La Mandragola* as the masterpiece of Italian humanist *commedia erudita*, and although that estimate could be subject to reservations, he has an established place in Italian drama history.

La Mandragola (*The Mandrake*) is generally believed to have been staged in a private house in Florence, under the auspices of a kind of literary and social club. (Florence did not have any princely Court, in the true sense, until 1530 or so, and early experiments with classical-style theatre tended to be private initiatives.) The plot is devoted, single-mindedly and with no digressions, to just one piece of deception and sexual intrigue. A desperate young gentleman, Callimaco, is determined to get into bed with Lucrezia, the virtuous wife of a farcically gullible lawyer, named Nicia. Callimaco is aided in his plot by the wily parasite Ligurio, and also by Fra Timoteo, the corrupt friar, with Lucrezia's own mother, Sostrata, lending a hand. The trick is based on Nicia's desperate desire to have a son. Callimaco, posing as a doctor, says that an infusion of mandrake will cure Lucrezia's alleged sterility, but will poison and kill the first person who has intercourse with her. The solution is to pick up some unknown vagabond from the streets (Callimaco again, in disguise), and force him to lie with Lucrezia and thus draw off the poison. Thus an astute lover triumphs over a stupid husband, and lusty youth over impotence, in the best traditions of a novella from Boccaccio's *Decameron*.

Readers and spectators of such a story would know whose side they were supposed to be on, and Nicia is set up as the "deserving" idiot victim with as much zest as one would expect. What complicates the play is that Lucrezia, herself, is also ignorant of the plot, unlike most of Boccaccio's lustful wives, and the deception which is practised against her, as well as against her husband, is actually a kind of rape. This produces a fascinating and possibly insoluble ambiguity, at least for modern practitioners of theatre: is this a bawdy romp, or is it a black comedy of violence against the innocent? When Lucrezia, at the end, predictably, accepts Callimaco as her official lover (with her excited husband still not really aware of what is going on), has she been sexually liberated, as Callimaco himself thinks, or is she accepting an unwanted fate with grim resignation, even in a spirit of revenge?

It is such questions which give the play its interest, together with the colloquial Florentine economy of Machiavelli's dialogue. Because of the author's wider reputation, critics have read a number of other factors into the play as well—not only social satire, in the figure of Fra Timoteo, but everything from political allegory to immensely detailed psychology. It may be worth asking, though, how much of the play's undoubtedly powerful ambiguity is a deliberate dramatic strategy; and how much comes, on the other hand, from a mystery at its centre which could even rank as dramaturgical ineptitude by our standards—Lucrezia, as a character, is given so little to say that we do not know, from the printed text, what she is thinking. It could be that some subtle interpretations may stem more from enthusiastic critics than from Machiavelli himself.

The second comedy of 1525, *La Clizia*, has had a less favourable press, but in many ways is more typical of the new comedy of the early 16th century. The plot is based very heavily on Plautus' *Casina*: an old man has become besotted with his young female ward (whom his son also loves), and is determined to possess her in a shameful manner by marrying her to a complaisant servant and taking over the husband's role on the wedding night. His wife Sofronia, however, restores family honour and brings him to his senses by dressing a page boy as the bride, and thus submits the head of household to a humiliating night of revelation which he recounts at great (and perhaps psychologically implausible) length in Act V. The young son gets the girl when her rich relative turns up to establish her in a suitable match.

The astonishing thing is that this implacable put-down of an old man's amorous aspirations seems to be aimed at the author himself—the protagonist is called Nicomaco (NICcolò MAChiavelli?), and the first performance involved musical interludes by a young female singer with whom Machiavelli, then aged 56, was known to be besotted. The bare plot developments are simple enough only to occupy about half the play—the rest is devoted to dialogues in which various members of the household deploy persuasive or evasive eloquence in situations of conflict and rivalry. They can seem a bit tedious to read, but may have been fascinating in performance to the 1525 audience, unused as they still were to such attempts to depict the verbal diplomacy of public and family life in a dramatic mode that could claim a reasonable dose of realism.

It is often forgotten that Machiavelli was one of the pioneers of modern secular comedy, and thus everything he did was effectively experimental—he was not responding to an existing theatrical tradition, but helping to create one out of nothing. He was one of the first and most influential practitioners of the more "realist" strand of Italian comedy, where characters and themes are made to emerge not from overtly theatrical games, but from dialogue and behaviour which aim to be convincingly mimetic. He put into his plays both his characteristic verbal energy and his observation, as a professional politician, of the language and behaviour of stratagem and conflict. If his dramaturgy also contains some uncertainties (and not all would agree that it does, in *La Mandragola* at least), then at the birth of a new genre this was only to be expected.

—Richard Andrews

See also *Volume 1* entry on *Mandragola*.

MACKAYE, (James Morrison) Steele. Born in Buffalo, New York, 6 June 1842. Studied art, with William Hunt; attended École des Beaux Arts, Paris, 1858–59. Married 1) Jenny Spring in 1862 (divorced); 2) Mary Keith Medbery in 1865, several children including the writer, Percy Mackaye. Joined Union forces during the American Civil War: member of the 7th Regiment, and took part in regimental theatre performances; returned to Paris and studied acting and theatre technique with François Delsarte, 1869; taught Delsarte's system in the USA, from 1871; professional acting debut in his own play, *Monaldi*, 1872; acted Hamlet in London, 1874; opened his "school of expression", New York, 1875; took over the Fifth Avenue Theatre, New York, refitted it with new technology, and re-opened it as the Madison Square Theatre, 1879: manager until he fell out with his financial backers, 1884; built Lyceum Theatre, New York, 1884, and established acting school there (later known as the American Academy of Dramatic Art). Innovator in scenic construction, electrical lighting, elevator staging, and other aspects of theatrical technology. Died in Timpas, Colorado, 25 February 1894.

Works

Collections

"An Arrant Knave" and Other Plays (includes *Rose Michel; Won at Last; In Spite of All*), edited by Percy Mackaye. 1941; reprinted 1963.

Stage Works (selected)

Monaldi, with Francis Durivage, from the novel by Washington Allston (produced New York, 1872).

Marriage, from a play by Octave Feuillet (produced New York, 1872).

Silas Marner, from the novel by George Eliot (produced New York, c. 1873).

Rose Michel, from a play by Ernest Blum (produced New York, 1875). 1928.

Won at Last (produced Wallack's Theatre, New York, 1877). In *"An Arrant Knave" and Other Plays*, 1941.

Money Mad (produced Standard Theatre, New York, 1880).

Hazel Kirke (produced Providence, Rhode Island, 1880; produced as *An Iron Will*, Madison Square Theatre, New York, 1880). 1880.

A Fool's Errand, with Allen W. Tourgee (produced New York, 1881). Edited by Dean H. Keller, 1969.

In Spite of All, from a play by Sardou (produced New York, 1882). In *"An Arrant Knave" and Other Plays*, 1941.

Arkwright's Wife, from a play by Tom Taylor (produced New York, 1883).

Dakolar, from a play by George Ohnet (produced New York, 1885).

The Drama of Civilization (produced Madison Square Theatre, New York, 1887).

Paul Kauvar; or, Anarchy (produced as *Anarchy*, New York, 1887; produced as Paul Kauvar, 1888). In *Representative Plays by American Dramatists 3*, 1921.

Father Ambrose. 1894.

An Arrant Knave. In *"An Arrant Knave" and Other Plays*, 1941.

*

Criticism

Books:
Percy Mackaye, *Epoch: The Life of Steele Mackaye* (2 vols.). 1927.

* * *

No American theatre personality before or after Mackaye has been so versatile or involved in so many aspects of the American theatre. As an actor, though not a major actor, he concentrated on the study of bodily science and introduced the Delsarte system to America in 1871. He also founded the Lyceum Theatre School, New York, in 1884, which later became the American Academy of Dramatic Art. Actor, teacher, playwright, designer, director, and theatre manager during very important years in the development of American theatre, Mackaye was also an inventor and an innovator beyond comparison. For his Madison Square Theatre, which he opened in 1880, he created a huge elevator stage which could replace a scene in two minutes.

His greatest achievement in theatre design was to be a gigantic Spectatorium for the Chicago World's Fair—480 feet long, 380 feet wide and 270 feet high with 25 telescopic stages for the production of a dramatic spectacle depicting Columbus's discovery of America. Unfortunately, financial problems and a storm destroyed his plans, which were eventually realized after his death in a much scaled-down version called *The World Finder*, produced in the smaller Scenitorium. As a man of the theatre, no one matched his magnificent and lofty conceptions nor his genius for creating theatrical wonders.

As a dramatist Mackaye wrote some 30 plays between 1872 and 1894 in which he tried to suit his ideas to the popular tastes of the American audience. Although his work is infrequently associated with the American West, his notebooks and memorabilia at the Dartmouth College Library indicate that the West was on his mind a good deal in unproduced and unpublished playscripts like "Colorado Joe", "Grizzly Jack", and "Reckless". His Madison Square Garden production in 1887, entitled *The Drama of Civilization*, and comparable to the gigantic productions of the currently popular Buffalo Bill Wild West Shows, illustrated his tendency to think on a very large scale, and suggests the vision that he tried to realize in his aborted production at the Chicago Exposition of 1893.

Most of Mackaye's plays, and particularly those that were successful in the theatre, are social or domestic melodramas, always stressing an issue that Mackaye regarded as a serious one in modern society. In the tradition of his time, a number of these plays were adapted from European models, and Mackaye, carefully educated and having the experience of living in France as a young man, was well equipped to translate and adapt French works. *Marriage* was taken from the French of Octave Feuillet's *Julie*. Set in Newport, the play dramatizes the agony of a woman planning to leave her husband and daughter to find happiness with a man she loves. In a letter to the *New York World*, Mackaye explained that he wanted to excite "serious thought on the terrible danger of marriage which was not founded on character, mutual respect and love". *Rose Michel*, based on a new French play by Ernest Blum, is a romantic melodrama dramatizing the lengths to which a mother will go to protect her child. *Won at Last*, an original play, tells of a man who marries for purely cynical reasons and then discovers that he loves his wife. With its interest in realistic character and a well-focused social issue, this play might have become good social comedy had not Mackaye shown that his greater interest was in writing melodrama. With *In Spite of All*, suggested by Sardou's *Andrea*, Mackaye dealt with a wife's determination to keep her husband and save her marriage in spite of all of his indiscretions. As popular plays of this period by Augustin Daly and Bronson Howard reveal, a realistic approach to domestic problems in America was part of the main stream of a developing drama, and Mackaye was appropriately shrewd to write in this genre.

Mackaye's best and most successful play was *Hazel Kirke*, first played under the title of *An Iron Will*. It was extremely successful, playing more than two years in New York before touring for a number of years in America and Europe and making a fortune for its producers. (Unfortunately, it was consistent with Mackaye's careless interest in his financial dealings that he made nothing from this great success in American theatre history.) The story is of Dunstan Kirke, a man indeed of iron will, who had long ago promised his daughter, Hazel, to Rodney when this man had saved him from bankruptcy. Therefore, when Hazel grows up and falls in love with Arthur Carringford, Dunstan's bad temper overcomes him and he curses her: "May my eyes never more behold thee".

Misfortunes follow Hazel as her marriage to Arthur seems illegal, and she returns home to a blind Dunstan who refuses to forgive her. Despondent, she tries to drown herself as Dunstan agonizes helplessly, but she is saved by Arthur, and forgiven by her father. Basically, the play is a sentimental melodrama very carefully crafted and made fresh and truthful by the realistic characters of Hazel and Dunstan. It was this realism that underscored its success on stage. The more psychologically penetrating realism, of the kind written by Ibsen, would have to wait until the 20th century was well underway before it would be acceptable on the American stage.

With his rich and varied career, Steele Mackaye contributed to American theatre on many levels. His realistic melodramas place him among those who brought distinction and world attention to a developing American drama, and his innovations in practical theatre have earned him a permanent place in its history. In everything that he did, he was an intense person, a man who believed in his work and concentrated his efforts without regard to his own financial reward. He was concerned with a realistic approach to social problems and with the ideals of truth, honesty, and justice, his intense interest in the trial of the anarchists after the Harmarket Square riot in Chicago in 1886, and the play he wrote entitled *Paul Kauvar*, epitomize this man whose genius was as often frustrated as it was appreciated.

—Walter J. Meserve

MADÁCH, Imre. Born in Alsóztregova, Nóvgrád region, Hungary (now Dolná Strehová, Slovakia), then part of the Austrian Empire, 21 January 1823. Educated privately, until 1837, then at Piarist Gymnasium, Vác; University of Pest, studying philosophy, then law, from 1837, passed bar examinations 1845. Married Erzsébert Fráter in 1845 (divorced 1854). After university studies, returned to his native district of Nóvgrád as administrator, then deputy clerk, in Balassagyarmat; resigned on health grounds; became district court judge, 1844; contributed satirical pieces to the news-paper *Pesti hirlap* [Pest News], 1844–47; moved to family estate at Csesztve, 1845; elected chief commissioner for Nóvgrád region, 1846: resigned 1847; imprisoned briefly by the ruling Habsburg authorities, 1853, for his part in hiding János Rákóczy, a leading figure in the nationalist revolt of 1848; elected Member of Parliament for Balassagyarmat, March 1861. Elected to the Kisfaludy Society, 1862, and the Hungarian Academy of Sciences, 1863. Died in Alsóztregova, 5 October 1864.

Works

Collections

Összes művei [Collected Works] (3 vols.; plays in vols. 2–3), edited by Pál Gyulai.   1880; revised edition, 1894–95.
Összes művei [Collected Works] (2 vols.), edited by Gábor Halász.   1942.

Stage works

Nápolyi Endre [King Endre of Naples].   In *Összes művei*, 1942.
Férfi és nő [Man and Woman].   In *Összes művei*, 1880.
Csák végapjai [The Last Days of Csák] (produced Kolozsvári Színház, Budapest, 1886).   In *Összes művei*
Mária királynő [Queen Mary].   In *Összes művei*, 1880.
Csak tréfa [Only a Joke].   Parts published in *Összes művei*, 1880.
A civilizátor [The Civilizer].   In *Összes művei*, 1880.
Az ember tragédiája (produced Nemzeti Színház, Budapest, 1883).   In *Drámai koltemény*, 1861; corrected edition, 1863; translated as *The Tragedy of Man*, 1909: several subsequent translations under same title.
Mózes [Moses] (produced Nemzeti Színház, Budapest, 1888).   In *Összes művei*, 1894–95.
Tündérálom [A Fairy Dream] (fragment).   In *Összes művei*. 1880.

Verse

Lant-virágok.   1840.
Lyrai költemények (Volume 1 of *Összes művai*).   1894.

Memoirs and Letters

Összes levelei [Collected Letters], edited by Géza Staud. 1942.

*

Bibliographies

Albert Tezla, *Hungarian Authors: A Bibliographical Handbook*, Cambridge, Massachusetts, 1970.

Criticism

Books:
W. Margendorff, *Imre Madách*, 1943.
Dieter P. Lotze, *Imre Madách* (in English), Boston, 1981.

* * *

In his native country, Madách is regarded as a "philosopher

of the stage". This is a convenient label which, however, diverts attention from the playwright's multi-faceted *oeuvre* and his masterful utilization of dramatic conflict. As author of a dozen plays, he is renowned mostly for his *Az ember tragédiája* (*The Tragedy of Man*), one of the great universal dramas of world theatre. But he wrote in a variety of traditions or dramatic genres. He wrote the mythological allegory, *Férfi és nő* (Man and Woman), and a biblical allegory, *Mózes* (Moses), the historical plays *Nápolyi Endre* (King Endre of Naples) and *Csák végnapjai* (The Last Days of Csák), a fairytale play, *Tündérálom* (A Fairy Dream), social drama in *Csak tréfa* (Only a Joke), and an Aristophanic comedy, *A civilizátor* (The Civilizer). He renewed these conventions by adding original touches—typically, a reckoning with romantic illusions and facing the frustrating realities of a post-revolutionary age. As he pointed out in "The Last Days of Csák", the time of old heroism was over: people cherished everyday existence and security more than ideas, even that of freedom. Drama, especially tragedy, had to renew itself by finding standards other than moral or historical idealism as its moving force.

While Madách read much in his rural seclusion, the two philosophers that his works bring to mind were, ironically, unknown to him. One is Kierkegaard—especially in his idea that religious belief is the highest degree of consciousness and, at the same time, absurd—the other is Oswald Spengler, whose outlook on history was developed more than half a century after Madách's death.

The Tragedy of Man (or, as Hungarians often call it, "*The Tragedy*") illustrates these philosophical aspects. Of its 15 scenes, the first three narrate the Biblical tale of God's work challenged by the Devil after the Creation and the Fall. The next 11 scenes are flash-forwards created by Lucifer, representing stages of history in which Adam and Eve re-emerge, playing various roles, accompanied by the Devil. The historical scenes range from Ancient Egypt to 19th-century London, but Madách also adds three futuristic scenes showing the age of egalitarian communism, space travel, and the end of mankind as a result of environmental destruction. The last scene is a return to Adam and Eve's shack outside Paradise, where Adam, discouraged by witnessing a senseless future, regains his will to live through God's enigmatic closing words: "I told you, Man, to strive and keep your faith". This can be read as a Kierkegaardian ending, leading to modern existentialism with its acceptance of the absurd. On the other hand, the historical sequence showing the progress of human ideals, in a Hegelian series of conflicts, to the height of the French Revolution, then into the pessimistic future perspective, recalls Spengler's view on the decline of the West after having run its circular course for many thousands of years.

Some of the main themes of *The Tragedy* also occur in other interestingly developed, but less complexly structured, plays. Madách's fascination with leadership and the relationship between the great individual and the masses especially, inspired the biblical tragedy "Moses". In this play, the masses are represented as a fundamental power, indispensable for any major historical action though they may follow false advice and be led astray. Madách's personal misfortune in his marriage probably motivated his image of women who, like Eve in *The Tragedy*, appear as both a driving force and constant challenge for the more idealistic, static male protagonists. Women's role in history and their relations with their male partners are other post-Romantic elements in Madách; he foreshadows Strindberg's complex, tortured representation of modern man–woman relationships, as in "Man and Woman".

Unlike most other Hungarian playwrights (such as Katona and Molnár). Madách had no practical affiliation with the theatre except for his playwriting. Even so, the dramatic effects he could create through character and language show that he possessed the vision necessary to create a "theatre of the mind". Some of his ambitious stage directions demand as grandiose a performance style as seen in productions by Max Reinhardt, yet no effect or setting that he imagined was beyond the technical potential of his age.

In spite of this, one of the two biases that long hampered Madách's appreciation and staging was related to the impression that the philosophical structure of his works, notably *The Tragedy*, was not sufficiently dramatic. This play, although its publication brought instant recognition to the author, was first performed only long after Madách's death: it was regarded as a book drama which resisted the basic requirements of a theatrical performance. While later it became one of Hungary's celebrated national plays, it was frequently staged with significant omissions, ostensibly in order to cope with time restrictions.

Another biased opinion that was spread, especially by German critics, was that of epigonism: *The Tragedy* was, so they claimed, inspired by Goethe's *Faust*. One could compile a long list of obvious differences to repudiate this view: for instance, *Faust* is a tragedy of the individual, while Madách's is that of mankind; the function of women in the two plays is diametrically opposite; and so on. The real reason for this bias was the perception and jealousy of Madách's congeniality.

Even for Hungary, however, the sad truth holds that the 19th century did not understand *The Tragedy*. Indeed, Madách is rather a playwright for the 20th century, whose many ideas he anticipated. Regrettably, his work has only been staged (repeatedly) by Hungary's German- and Slavic-speaking neighbours, but not yet discovered by the leading theatre centres of the Western world. In 1922, Bela Lugosi staged it in New York, playing Lucifer himself—but this performance was also in Hungarian.

—George Bisztray

See also *Volume 1* entry on *The Tragedy of Man*.

MAETERLINCK, Maurice. Born Mauritius Polydorus Maria Bernardus Maeterlinck in Ghent, Belgium, 29 August 1862. Educated at Institut Central, Ghent, 1869–73; Jesuit Collège de Sainte-Barbe, 1874–81; studied law at the University of Ghent, 1881–85, Dr. of Law 1885, and registered as barrister 1885. Lived with Georgette Leblanc, 1896–1918; married Renée Dahon in 1919. Practised law in Ghent, 1886–89; first play, *La Princesse Maleine*, published 1889; first-produced play, *L'Intruse*, staged 1891; lived in Paris, 1896–1906, Grasse, 1906–11, Nice, 1911–39, Portugal, 1939–40, USA, 1940–47, and Nice again, after 1947. Recipient: Nobel Prize for Literature, 1911; Medal of the French Language, 1948. Honorary degrees: Glasgow University, 1919; University of Brussels, 1920; Rollins Park College, Florida, 1941. Member, Belgian Royal Academy, 1920. Grand Officier, 1912, and Grand Croix, 1920, Order of Leopold; Order of St. James of the Sword, Portugal, 1939. Created Count of Belgium, 1932. Died in Nice, 6 May 1949.

Maurice Maeterlinck collecting his letters (1915).

Works

Collections

Trois Petits Drames pour marionnettes (includes *Alladine et Palomides; Intérieur; La Mort de Tintagiles*). 1894.
Plays (2 vols.), translated by Richard Hovey. 1894–96:
  1. *Princess Maleine; The Intruder; The Blind; The Seven Princesses.* 1894.
  2. *Alladine and Palomides; Pélléas and Mélisande; Home; The Death of Tintagiles.* 1896.
Alladine and Palomides; Interior; The Death of Tintagiles: Three Little Dramas for Marionnettes, translated by Alfred Sutro and William Archer. 1899; as *Three Plays*, 1909; as *Three Little Dramas*, 1915; as *"The Death of Tintagiles" and Other Plays.* 1924.
Théâtre (3 vols.). 1901–02; reprinted, 1979.
"A Miracle of St. Antony" and Five Other Plays (includes *Pelleas and Melisande; Interior; The Death of Tintagiles; Alladine and Palomides; The Intruder*), various translators. 1917.
Théâtre inédit (includes *L'Abbé Sétubal; Les Trois Justiciers; Le Jugement dernier*). 1959.

Stage Works

La Princesse Maleine. 1889; translated as *The Princess Maleine,* with *The Intruder,* 1892, and in later collections.
Les Aveugles (produced Théâtre de l'Art, Paris, 1891).

1890; translated as *The Blind*, with *The Intruder*, 1891; as *The Sightless*, with *Pelléas and Mélisande*, 1895.
L'Intruse (produced Théâtre de l'Art, Paris, 1891). 1890; translated as *The Intruder*, with *The Blind*, 1891, and in later collections.
Les Sept Princesses (produced Théâtre des Bouffes-Parisiennes, Paris, 1893). 1890; translated as *The Seven Princesses*, in *Plays 1*, 1894.
Pelléas et Mélisande (produced Théâtre des Bouffes-Parisiennes, Paris, 1893). 1892; translated as *Pelléas and Mélisande*, in *Plays 2*, 1896.
Intérieur (produced Théâtre de l'Oeuvre, Paris, 1895). In *Trois Petits Drames . . .*, 1894; translated as *Home*, in *Plays 2*, 1896; as *Interior*, in *Alladine and Palomides; Interior; The Death of Tintagiles*, 1899.
Alladine et Palomides (produced 1896). In *Trois Petits Drames . . .*, 1894; translated as *Alladine and Palomides*, in *Plays 2*, 1896, and in *Alladine and Palomides; Interior; The Death of Tintagiles*, 1899.
La Mort de Tintagiles (produced Théâtre des Mathurins, Paris, 1905). In *Trois Petits Drames . . .*, 1899; translated as *The Death of Tintagiles*, *Plays 2*, 1896, and in *Alladine and Palomides; Interior; The Death of Tintagiles*, 1899.
Annabella: 'Tis Pity She's a Whore, from the play by John Ford (produced 1894). 1895.
Aglavaine et Sélysette (produced 1896). 1896; translated as *Aglavaine and Selysette*, 1897.
Ariane et Barbe-Bleue; ou, La Délivrance inutile, music by Paul Dukas (produced Opéra-Comique, Paris, 1907). In *Théâtre 2*, 1901; translated as *Ariane and Barbe-Bleue*, 1901.
Soeur Béatrice (produced Berlin, 1901). In *Théâtre 2*, 1901; translated as *Sister Beatrice*, 1901.
Monna Vanna (produced Nouveau-Théâtre, Paris, 1902). 1901; translated as *Monna Vanna*, 1903.
Joyzelle (produced Théâtre du Gymnase, Paris, 1903). 1903; translated as *Joyzelle*, 1906.
Le Miracle de Saint-Antoine (produced Geneva, 1903). 1919; translated as *A Miracle of Saint Anthony*, in *"A Miracle of Saint Antony" and Other Plays*, 1917.
L'Oiseau bleu (produced Moscow Art Theatre, 1909; translated as *The Blue Bird*, 1909.
Macbeth, from the play by Shakespeare (produced Abbey of St. Wandrille, Normandy, 1909). 1910.
Marie-Magdeleine (produced Neues Stadttheater, Leipzig, 1910; produced in France, Théâtre du Châtelet, Paris, 1913). 1913; translated as *Mary Magdalene*, 1910.
Le Malheur passe (produced 1916?). 1925; translated as *The Cloud That Lifted*, with *The Power of the Dead*, 1923.
Le Bourgmestre de Stilmonde (produced Buenos Aires, 1918). With *Le Sel de la vie*, 1919; translated as *The Burgomaster of Stilmonde*, 1918.
Les Fiançailles (produced Shubert Theatre, New York, 1918). 1918; translated as *The Betrothal; or, The Blue Bird Chooses*, 1919.
Le Sel de la vie. With *Le Bourgmestre de Stilmonde*, 1919.
Berniquel (produced 1923). 1929.
La Puissance des morts. 1926; translated as *The Power of the Dead*, with *The Cloud That Lifted*, 1923.
Marie-Victoire. 1927.
Juda de Kérioth. 1929.
La Princesse Isabelle (produced Teatro Nacional, Lisbon, Portugal, 1935). 1935.
L'Abbé Sétubal (produced 1941). In *Théâtre inédit*, 1959.
Jeanne d'Arc. 1948.
Les Trois Justiciers. In *Théâtre inédit*, 1959.
Le Judgement dernier. In *Théâtre inédit*, 1959.

Fiction

Deux contes: Le Massacre des innocents; Onirologie.   1918;
first story translated as *The Massacre of the Innocents*,
1918.

Verse

Serres chaudes: Poèmes.   1889; translated as *Poems*, 1915.
Album de douze chansons.   1896; translated as *XII Songs*,
1912.
Serres chaudes, suivi de quinze chansons.   1900.
Serres chaudes, quinze chansons, vers de fin.   1947.
Serres chaudes: Chansons complètes.   1955.
Poésies complètes, edited by Joseph Hanse.   1965.

Other

Le Trésor des humbles.   1896; translated as *The Treasure of
the Humble*, 1897; excerpt, as *The Inner Beauty*, 1910.
La Sagesse et la destinée.   1898; translated as *Wisdom and
Destiny*, 1898.
La Vie des abeilles.   1901; translated as *The Life of the Bee*,
1901; excerpt as *The Swarm*, 1906.
Le Temple enseveli.   1902; translated as *The Buried Temple*,
1902.
Le Double Jardin.   1904; translated as *The Double Garden*,
1904; as *"Old-Fashioned Flowers" and Other Out-of-Door
Studies*, 1905; excerpt as *Our Friend the Dog*, 1904; as *My
Dog*, 1906.
L'Intelligence des fleurs.   1907; translated as *Life and
Flowers*, 1907; as *Intelligence of the Flowers*, 1907; excerpt
as *Measure of the Hours*, 1907.
"Chrysanthemums" and Other Essays (translations).   1907.
La Mort.   1913; translated as *Death*, 1911; revised edition,
as *Our Eternity*, 1913.
Hours of Gladness (translations).   1912; as *"News of Spring"
and Other Nature Studies*, 1913.
"On Emerson" and Other Essays (translations).   1912.
L'Hôte inconnu.   1917; translated as *The Unknown Guest*,
1914.
Les Débris de la guerre.   1916; translated as *The Wrack of
the Storm*, 1916.
Les Sentiers dans la montagne.   1919; translated as *Mountain
Paths*, 1919.
Le Grand Secret.   1921; translated as *The Great Secret*, 1922.
En Égypte: Notes de voyage.   1928; translated as *Ancient
Egypt*, 1925.
En Sicile et en Calabre.   1927.
Le Vie des termites.   1927; translated as *The Life of the White
Ant*, 1927.
La Vie de l'espace.   1928; translated as *The Life of Space*,
1928.
*La Grande Féerie: Immensité de l'univers, notre terre, influ-
ences sidérales.*   1929; translated as *The Magic of the Stars*,
1930.
La Vie des fourmis.   1930; translated as *The Life of the Ant*,
1930.
L'Araignée de verre.   1932; excerpt translated as *Pigeons
and Spiders (The Water Spider)*, 1934.
La Grande Loi.   1933; translated as *The Supreme Law*,
1934.
Avant le grand silence.   1934; translated as *Before the Great
Silence*, 1935.
Le Sablier.   1936; translated as *The Hour-Glass*, 1936.
L'Ombre des ailes.   1936.
Devant Dieu.   1937.

La Grande Porte.   1939.
L'Autre Monde; ou, Le Cadran stellaire.   1942; translated as
The Great Beyond, 1947.
Bulles bleues: Souvenirs heureux.   1948.
Le "Cahier bleu", edited by Joanne Wieland-Burston.   1977.

Translator, *L'Ornement des noces spirituelles*, by Jan van
Ruysbroeck.   1891; translated as *Ruysbroeck and the
Mystics*, 1894.
Translator, *Les Disciples à Saïs*, by Novalis.   1895.

*

Bibliographies

Maurice Lecat, *Bibliographie de Maeterlinck: Litérature,
science, philosophie*, 1939; revised edition, in *Le
Maeterlinckisme*, 2, 1941.
R. Brucher, *L'Oeuvre et son audience: Essai de bibliographie
1883–1960*, Brussels, 1972; supplement in *Annales de la
Fondation Maurice Maeterlinck*, 18–19, 1972–73.

Criticism

Books:
Francoise Dony Cartwright, *Maeterlinck und Amerika*,
Berlin, 1935.
G. Compère, *Le Théâtre de Maurice Maeterlinck*, Brussels,
1955.
J.M. Andrieu, *Maurice Maeterlinck*, Paris, 1962.
R. Bodart, *Maurice Maeterlinck*, Paris, 1962.
Le Centenaire de Maeterlinck, Brussels, 1964.
Vernon Mallinson, *Modern Belgian Literature, 1830–1960*,
New York, 1966.
Marcel Postic, *Maeterlinck et le symbolisme*, Paris, 1970.
Miroslav Hanak, *Maeterlinck's Symbolistic Drama*, Louvain,
1974.
Paul Gorceix, *Les Affinités allemandes de Maeterlinck*, Paris,
1975.
W.D. Halls, *Maeterlinck: A Study of His Life and Thought*,
1975.
Bettina L. Knapp, *Maurice Maeterlinck*, Boston, 1975.
Beatrix Vedder, *Das symbolistische Theater Maurice
Maeterlincks*, Frankfurt, 1978.
Patrick Mahony, *Maurice Maeterlinck, Mystic and Dramatist*
(biography), New York, 1984.
S. Gross, *Maeterlinck: oder, Der symbolistische Sadismus des
Humors*, Frankfurt and Bern, 1985.
Lectures de Maeterlinck, Brussels, 1985.
Katharine Worth, *Maeterlinck's Plays in Performance* (book
and slide set), Cambridge, 1985.
Maryse Deschamps, *Maeterlinck*, Brussels, 1986.
Linn B. Konrad, *Modern Drama as Crisis: The Case of
Maeterlinck*, Frankfurt, 1986.
Carole J. Lambert, *The Empty Cross: Medieval Hopes,
Modern Futility* (includes chapter on Maeterlinck), New
York, 1990.

* * *

"Is a static theatre possible?", asked Maurice Maeterlinck
in an essay of 1897. His attempts to find an answer to that
question initiated a theatrical revolution which resonated
throughout Europe. In his early plays of the 1890's — *The
Intruder* (*L'Intruse*), *The Sightless* (*Les Aveugles*), *Interior*

(*Intérieur*), and the rest—he created a symbolist drama of "total theatre" which made an impact on playwrights as diverse as Strindberg, Oscar Wilde, W.B. Yeats, and John Millington Synge. Stanislavsky was proud to obtain *The Blue Bird* (*L'Oiseau bleu*) for its premiere in Moscow and Debussy to be the composer chosen to set *Pelléas and Mélisande* to music. The use of silence and stillness, light and dark in the plays of Samuel Beckett and Harold Pinter can be seen as a new phase in a tradition deriving from Maeterlinck.

Although his later plays lacked the profound originality of his earlier ones (and for a long time he was out of fashion as a playwright), Maeterlinck has to be seen as one of the great liberating forces in modern theatre. He was a man of contradictions. Coming from the prosperous Belgian bourgeoisie (he had been intended for a lawyer), Maeterlinck, in his youth, was drawn to a theatre of poverty. The mysticism which was a strain in his otherwise pragmatic character (a distinctive Flemish mix) impelled him to explore, on stage, an austere, visionary inner landscape—a world of the "soul" or the unconscious. He was fortunate to discover in the young French actor, Aurelien Lugné-Poe, a director who shared his wish to create a theatre "of all the arts" and had friends among the Nabis group of painters: they contributed their talents to his Théâtre d'Art and its successor, the Théâtre de l'Oeuvre (set up, on a shoe-string budget, in 1893).

Maeterlinck's first published play, the five-act *The Princess Maleine*, won him the embarrassing accolade of "the Belgian Shakespeare". Its violent plot, loaded with Shakespearean echoes, was made remarkable by a "sleep-walking" effect which hinted continually at psychic traumas beyond rational control. In the one-act form more characteristic of his early phase, his first performed play, *The Intruder*, was produced by the Théâtre d'Art in a benefit programme for Verlaine and Gauguin, and was the surprise success of the mixed bill. Lugné-Poe, who played the blind grandfather, devised a scenic method (dim lighting, a gauze drawn between actors and audience) and an acting technique of slow movements and level tones to capture the other-worldly quality of Maeterlinck's dialogue. This "interior" language was first spoken on stage by ordinary, modern characters.

In the play, a Flemish family wait for one of their members to arrive while, behind closed doors at the back of the stage, a young mother lies ill after childbirth. The impalpable moment when death "intrudes" into the room is recognised only by the blind grandfather. Maeterlinck saw him as primitive man, in touch with the unknown in a way sophisticated modern people had ceased to be. He used the image of an old man sitting under the lamplight, "interpreting" the atmosphere around him, in the essay on theatre, "The Tragical in Everyday Life" ("Le Tragique quotidien"), which is one of the key documents of modern dramatic theory. It appeared in *The Treasure of the Humble* (*Le Trésor des humbles*), the work in which he asked his important question about the feasibility of a static drama.

By this time, Lugné-Poe had helped him to show that immobility and inwardness could be made theatrically gripping. *The Sightless* declares itself a static drama from the start with its symbolic tableau of 12 blind people, facing each other symmetrically, hardly distinguishable from the tree stumps on which they sit. Lost in an ancient forest, not even knowing that their guide, the priest, is sitting dead among them, the blind are inhibited, afraid to move. They both dread and long for the future, which looms up at the end of the play in the sound of approaching footsteps. Only the baby, the one sighted person among them, can see what draws near, but its only way of communicating is a cry. The grim joke here, about humanity's inability to comprehend the meaning of existence, anticipates much in Ionesco and the "theatre of the absurd".

Maeterlinck tended to alternate between subjects taken from bourgeois life and fairy tale or legend. Common motifs connect the two worlds. Viewing characters at a distance, through glass, provides an equally strange, disorientating perspective in *The Seven Princesses* (produced with marionettes), where the great window through which the prince gazes at the sleeping girls is part of a romantic, almost Pre-Raphaelite iconography, and in *Interior*, which shows a homely family scene through the window of a commonplace house. An early critic, C.E. Montague, thought the scenic image worked in the theatre as Maeterlinck had intended. Seen in the lighted frame, silently moving about their ordinary business, unaware that they are being watched from their garden by a messenger bringing tidings of death, the characters seemed to inhabit some other dimension. They are "spiritualised", Maeterlinck said, "by the distance, the light and the transparent film of the window-panes".

In *The Death of Tintagiles* and *Pelléas and Mélisande*, imagery of castles and subterranean vaults makes a symbolist backcloth to the strange, dark fairy tale which represented Maeterlinck's idea of human life at that time. Looking back on these plays from his later, more optimistic position, he identified "dread of the unknown" as their keynote. "The problem of existence was answered only by the enigma of annihilation" (*The Buried Temple*). An inscrutable fate was in control (he described one of his collections as "three little plays for marionettes"). Tintagiles is taken from his sister behind an impassable wall (Charles Ricketts represented it as a towering, classically sculpted curtain); Pelléas finds himself staying in in the fatal castle against his conscious intention. Maeterlinck's distinctive technique of stumbling words, unfinished sentences, and sudden silences, delicately communicates the immense difficulty of communication at the level where his characters have their being.

Pelléas and Mélisande attracted actors like Mrs. Patrick Campbell and John Martin-Harvey, and had a success in the fashionable theatre, as did the still more popular *The Blue Bird*. Debussy's opera, however, eventually became better known than the play. Though Maeterlinck extended his range as a playwright (*The Burgomaster of Stilmonde* is an effective piece of naturalism), he lost his audience during the inter-war period. Signs of revival appeared in the 1960's in Belgium and France, where productions by directors such as Henri Ronse, and by the enterprising Rideau de Bruxelles, have stripped off some of the old romantic colouring and allowed freer play to the "absurd" elements. They have helped to confirm Maeterlinck's right to be regarded as a great original and one of the masters of modern drama.

—Katharine Worth

See also *Volume 1* entries on *The Blue Bird*; *Pelléas and Mélisande*.

————————

MAIAKOVSKII, Vladimir.   See **MAYAKOVSKY, Vladmir**.

————————

MAILLET, Antonine. Born in Bouctouche, New Brunswick, Canada, 10 May 1929. Educated at the Collège Notre-Dame d'Acadie, Moncton, BA 1950; University of Moncton, MA, 1959; University of Montreal, Licence ès lettres 1962; Université de Laval, Quebec Ph.D, 1970. Teacher, Collège Notre-Dame d'Acadie, 1954–60, University of Moncton, 1965–67, and Collège des Jésuites, Québec, 1968–69; professor, Université de Laval, Quebec, 1971–74, and University of Montreal, 1974–75; full-time writer after 1975; visiting professor, University of California, Berkeley, 1983; Chancellor, University of Moncton, 1989. Recipient of many literary awards, including: Dominion Drama Festival Prize, 1958; Champlain Prize, 1960; Governor-General's Award, 1972; Volcans Prize (France), 1975; France-Canada Prize, 1975; Goncourt Prize, 1979; Chalmers Prize, 1980. Recipient of honorary degrees from the University of Lyons, 1989, and numerous Canadian and US universities, 1972–90. Member of the Académie Canadienne-Française, Officier, 1976, and Compagnon, 1982, de l'Ordre du Canada; Officier des Palmes Académiques Françaises, 1980; Chevalier de l'Ordre de la Pléiade, Fredericton, New Brunswick; Officier de l'Ordre des Arts et des Lettres (France), 1985; Officier de l'Ordre National du Québec, 1990.

Works

Stage Works

Entr'acte (produced Collège Notre-Dame d'Acadie, Moncton, New Brunswick, 1957).
Poire Acre (produced Collège Notre-Dame d'Acadie, Moncton, New Brunswick, 1959).
Bulles de savon (produced Collège Notre-Dame, Moncton, New Brunswick, 1959).
Les Jeux d'enfants sont faits (produced Dominion Drama Festival, Halifax, Nova Scotia, 1960).
Les Crasseux (produced by the Compagnie Jean Duceppe, Montreal, 1974). 1968; revised version, 1974.
La Sagouine, from the radio series (produced Théâtre du Rideau Vert, Montreal, 1972). 1971; translated as *La Sagouine, 1979.*
Gapi et Sullivan (produced in a revised version, as *Gapi*, Théâtre du Rideau Vert, Montreal, 1977). 1973; translated as *Gapi and Sullivan*, 1987.
La Contrabandière, from her novel *Mariaàgélas* (produced as *Mariaàgélas*, Théâtre du Rideau Vert, Montreal, 1974; produced as *La Contrabandière*, Montreal, 1981). 1981.
La Sagouine II (produced Montreal, 1975).
Évangéline Deusse (produced Théâtre du Rideau Vert, Montreal, 1976). 1975; translated as *Evangeline the Second*, 1987.
La Veuve enragée, from her novel *Les Cordes-de-bois* (produced Théâtre du Rideau Vert, Montreal, 1978). 1977.
Le Bourgeois Gentilhomme, from the play by Molière (produced Théâtre du Rideau Vert, Montreal, 1978). 1978.
Emmanuel à Joseph à Dâvit, from her novel (produced Théâtre du Rideau Vert, Montreal, 1979).
La Joyeuse criée (produced Théâtre du Rideau Vert, Montreal, 1983).
Les Drôlatiques, Horrifiques et Épouvantables Aventures de Panurge, ami de Pantagruel, from Rabelais (produced Théâtre du Rideau Vert, Montreal, 1983). 1983.
Garrochés en Paradis (produced Théâtre du Rideau Vert, Montreal, 1986). 1986.
Margot la folle (produced Théâtre du Rideau Vert, Montreal, 1987). 1987.

Les Fantastiques, from a play by Tom Jones (produced Ottawa, 1988).
Richard III, from the play by Shakespeare (produced Ottawa, 1990). 1989.
William S (produced Montreal, 1991). 1991.

Television Plays

La Sagouine, 1975.

Radio Plays

La Sagouine, 1969–70.

Fiction

Pointe-aux-Coques. 1958.
On a mangé la dune. 1962.
Don l'Original. 1972; translated as *The Tale of Don l'Original*, 1978.
Par Derrière chez mon père. 1972.
Mariaàgélas. 1973; translated as *Mariaàgélas*, 1986.
Emmanuel à Joseph à Dâvit. 1975.
Les Cordes-de-bois. 1977.
Pélagie-la-Charrette. 1979; translated as *Pélagie-la-Charrette*, 1982; as *Pelagie: The Return of a Homeland*, 1982.
Cent Ans dans les bois. 1981.
La Gribouille. 1982.
Crache-à-Pic. 1984; translated as *The Devil is Loose!*, 1986.
Le Huitième Jour. 1986; translated as *On the Eighth Day*, 1989.
L'Oursiade. 1990.

Other

Rabelais et les traditions populaires en Acadie. 1971.
L'Acadie pour quasiment rien: guide touristique. 1973.
Christopher Cartier de la Noisette, dit Nounours (for children). 1981; translated as *Christopher Cartier of Hazelnut, Also Known as Bear*, 1984.

*

Criticism

Books:
Bruno Drolet, *Entre Dune et aboiteaux . . . un peuple: Étude critique des oeuvres d'Antonine Maillet*, Montreal, 1975.
Marjorie A. Fitzpatrick, "Antonine Maillet and the Epic Heroine", in *Traditionalism, Nationalism, and Feminism: Women Writers of Quebec*, edited by Paula Gilbert Lewis, Westport, Connecticut, 1985.
Donald Smith, with others, *Voices of Deliverance: Interviews with Quebec and Acadian Writers* (includes interview with Maillet), Toronto, 1986.
Claude Pelletier (ed.), *Antonine Maillet III: Dossier de presse 1971–1987*, Sherbrooke, Quebec, 1988.

Articles:
Marjorie A. Fitzpatrick, "Antonine Maillet: The Search for a Narrative Voice", in *Journal of Popular Culture*, Winter 1981.
Michèle Lacomb, "Breaking the Silence of Centuries", in *Canadian Theatre Review*, 46, 1986.
Antonine Maillet issue of *Québec Studies*, 4, 1986.

Renate Usmiani, "Recycling an Archetype: The Anti-Evangelines", in *Canadian Theatre Review*, 46, 1986.

Phyllis Wrenn, "Ortho- and Morphographic Transcoding of Acadian 'Franglais'", in *Visible Languages*, vol.21 no.1, 1987.

Janis Pallister, "Antonine Maillet's *Évangéline Deusse*: Historical, Popular and Literary Elements" in *American Review of Canadian Studies*, Summer 1988.

*   *   *

The dominant literary artist and the most eloquent advocate of Acadia, Antonine Maillet has succeeded in attracting international attention to her tenacious people, their colourful idiom and enduring traditions. This is the driving force which infuses her drama and her prose fiction, all of which use, to varying degrees, the archaic dialect of Acadia, the first French colony in North America, long marginalized in the pan-Canadian context.

She has created some of the most memorable characters in Canadian literature, beginning with the dramatic monologue entitled *La Sagouine*, first performed on radio in her home province of New Brunswick in 1969. The effect of this simple piece, in which a 72-year-old Acadian charwoman comments on her life and the status of her tiny francophone community, was immediate and pervasive. Within a few years, it had become one of the best-known and best-loved Canadian dramas, on stage and television, in English and in French. And it is from the extraordinary success of this character—played on stage and screen by the Acadian actress Viola Léger, who has now become identified with the role—that the inspiration for most of Maillet's subsequent theatre has come.

La Sagouine is the prototype also of the dominant, resourceful female characters who populate Maillet's fiction, notably the eponymous heroine of her novel *Pélagie-la-Charrette*, for which she was awarded France's prestigious Prix Goncourt in 1980. Explicit political advocacy of her people's cause is inseparable from virtually all of Maillet's literary activity to date. A strong feminist commitment characterizes her work as well. Thus *Évangéline Deusse*, the play which is ranked second in importance and influence to *La Sagouine*, is a conscious effort to topple the literary heroine who had, for too long, been the symbol of her people—the American poet Longfellow's Evangeline—passive, lachrymose, and barren. Maillet's heroine ("deusse" is "deux", in the Acadian dialect, thus "Evangeline the Second"), by contrast, is the widowed mother of a large family; she is enterprising and irrepressible, despite her 80 years, and quite aware of her literary namesake's unproductive symbolism and determined to depose her. In this play, as elsewhere in Maillet's literary universe, male characters are largely ineffectual, subordinate to the staunch, committed females who goad them and guide them forward.

Today, some 20 years after the creation of *La Sagouine*, a dispassionate reassessment of Maillet's role in the evolution of drama in Canada seems necessary. It is generally felt that her profound and pervasive commitment to the Acadian cause, initially an attraction for audiences and readers because of its exoticism, has sometimes been a hindrance to her theatre's reception outside Atlantic Canada. Critical reaction to her *Le Bourgeois Gentilhomme*, for example, an attempt to adapt Molière's classic comedy to an Acadian setting, has been largely negative. In the plays written since *Évangéline*, readers and spectators familiar with her early works too often encounter predictable messages, predictably quaint diction, and characters moving in the same limited spheres. It is obvious, also, that her remarkable popularity in France was due, at least initially, in a large degree to the exotic flavour of the idiom in which her characters speak (an archaic language accessible, however, to any educated speaker of French). The power, eloquence, and originality of her first plays have not been consistently visible. Since 1975 Maillet has turned mainly to prose fiction. Most of the plays she has written since then are adaptations of her own novels (*La Veuve enragée* from *Les Cordes-de-bois*; *La Contrabandière* from *Maria-agélas*; *Emmanuel à Joseph à Dâvit* from the novel of the same title).

Despite these qualifications, the importance of Antonine Maillet's contribution is undeniable. If she were the author only of *La Sagouine* and *Évangéline Deusse*, her role in the history of modern French-Canadian theatre would be secure. Rarely has a Canadian dramatist achieved the poignant immediacy of effect and the paradoxical universality that pervade Maillet's first few plays. Recently, as well, there has been evidence of a new direction in her dramaturgy, in plays such as *Garrochés en Paradis* and *Margot la folle*.

—Leonard E. Doucette

See also *Volume 1* entry on *La Sagouine*.

MAIRET, Jean (de). Born in Besançon, Province of Franche-Comté, Holy Roman Empire (now in France); baptised 10 May 1604. Married Jeanne de Cardouan, 1647. Entered the service of Henri II, Duc de Montmorency, 1625; first-produced play, *Chryséide et Arimand*, staged at the Hôtel de Bourgogne, Paris, 1625; following execution of Montmorency, entered service of Comte de Belin, 1633; associated with Montdory's company at the Théâtre du Marais during the 1630's; strongly critical of Pierre Corneille during the quarrel over the latter's *Le Cid*, 1637; last play, *Sidonie*, produced 1640; granted a pension by Richelieu; pursued diplomatic career after 1640: representative for Franche-Comté in Paris, 1647, and negotiated treaties of neutrality with France, but was exiled from Paris by Cardinal Mazarin, 1653. Received letters of nobility (enabling him to use "de" in his name), 1668. Died in Besançon, 31 January 1686.

Works

Stage Works

Chryséide et Arimand (produced Théâtre de l'Hôtel de Borgogne, Paris, 1625). 1630.

Sylvie (produced Théâtre de l'Hôtel de Bourgogne, Paris, 1626). 1632.

Sylvanire (produced Théâtre de l'Hôtel de Bourgogne, Paris, 1629–30). 1632.

Les Galanteries du Duc d'Ossonne (produced Théâtre du Marais, Paris, 1632–33). 1636.

Virginie (produced Théâtre du Marais, Paris, 1633). 1635.

Sophonisbe (produced Théâtre du Marais, Paris, 1635). 1635.

Marc Antoine; ou, La Cléopatre (produced Théâtre du Marais, Paris, 1635). 1637.

Le Grand et dernier Solyman; ou, La Mort de Mustapha

(produced Théâtre de l'Hôtel de Bourgogne, Paris, 1637). 1639.

L'Illustre Corsaire (produced Théâtre de l'Hôtel de Bourgogne, Paris, 1637). 1640.

Roland furieux (produced Théâtre de l'Hôtel de Bourgogne, Paris, 1638). 1640.

Athénais (produced Théâtre de l'Hôtel de Bourgogne, Paris, 1638–39). 1642.

Sidonie (produced Théâtre de l'Hôtel de Bourgogne, Paris, 1640). 1640.

Other

Mairet's contributions to the "Querelle du *Cid*" appear in *La Querelle du "Cid"*, by A. Gasté. 1898; reprinted, 1970.

*

Bibliographies

Giovanni Dotoli, *Bibliographie critique de Jean Mairet*, Paris, 1973.

Criticism

Books:
E. Dannheisser, *Studien zu Jean de Mairets Leben und Werke*, Ludwigshafen am Rhein, 1888.
R. Mantero, *Corneille critique et son temps: Ogier, Mairet, Scudéry*, Paris, 1964.
Giovanni Dotoli, *La Datazione del teatro di Jean Mairet*, Bari, 1971.
William A. Bunch, *Jean Mairet*, Boston, 1975.
B. Kay, *The Theatre of Mairet*, The Hague, 1975.
G. Dotoli, *Le Langage dramatique de Mairet*, Paris, 1978.
P. Tomlinson, *Mairet et ses protecteurs*, Paris, 1983.

Articles:
J. Guicharnaud, "Beware of Happiness: Mairet's *Sophonisbe*", in *Yale French Studies*, 38, 1967.
F.K. Dawson, "The Notion of Necessity in Mairet's *Sophonisbe*", in *Nottingham French Studies*, 7, 1968.

* * *

Jean Mairet was the first of the new generation of French playwrights who followed after Alexandre Hardy. Influenced especially by Théophile de Viau, Mairet himself significantly affected the development of classicism in the French theatre. Along with Du Ryer, Rotrou, and Pierre Corneille, Mairet took advantage of the establishment of two permanent theatre companies in Paris in the late 1620's and early 1630's. Following the unparalleled success of his pastoral, *Sylvie*, in 1626, Mairet was the leading Parisian playwright until he was deposed by Corneille in 1637.

Although not as prolific as his rivals Corneille and Rotrou, Mairet wrote at least four plays that were both successful and influential. Beginning with a series of pastorals, he moved on to comedy and then to tragedy. His *Sophonisbe* is generally recognized as the first classical tragedy written for the 17th-century French theatre. Although Mairet has been remembered chiefly as an envious antagonist of Corneille during the quarrel about *Le Cid*, a growing interest in baroque music and drama in recent years has brought him once again to public attention, and his comedy *Les Galanteries du Duc*

d'Ossone (The Amourous Adventures of the Duc d'Ossone) was produced at the Grand Théâtre de Chaillot, Paris, in 1988.

Mairet's first three plays, all dramatic pastorals, reflect the popularity of Honoré d'Urfé's *Astrée*, a vast compilation of pastoral tales and themes that appeared between 1607 and 1628. The most popular of the three was *Sylvie*, reprinted 14 times between 1628 and 1635, and probably the most widely read play in France before 1637. In it, a prince falls in love with a shepherdess; their union is stoutly opposed by parents on both sides. Although Mairet uses fewer romanesque elements than do many pastoral writers of the Baroque, the play comes to a spectacular conclusion when the brave knight Florestan battles his way through evil spirits to break the spell that keeps the lovers apart. *Sylvie* was followed by *Silvanire*, another pastoral, now best known for its preface in which Mairet elucidated for the French some rules for the composition of plays according to the ancient authorities.

Mairet's only comedy, *Les Galanteries du Duc d'Ossonne*, was performed by Montdory's company for carnival in 1633. Perhaps imbued with the carnival spirit, it was for a long time condemned as too licentious to be produced. Based on the exploits of an actual nobleman, a Spanish viceroy and friend of Henri IV, the play follows the amatory adventures of a chain of lovers: the Duke loves Émilie who loves Camille who loves Flavia who loves the Duke. Like the lovers in *A Midsummer Night's Dream*, the four chop and change until, finally evading Émilie's horrible husband, they settle into happily adulterous couples. Perhaps a parody of the traditional comedies of the period, which often ended in a series of marriages, *Les Galanteries* is praised for its gaiety of tone and the cleverness of its intrigue.

The following year, 1634, saw the production by Montdory and his company of *Sophonisbe*, Mairet's first tragedy and the first play to attempt to practise what the neoclassical theorists were preaching. Scudéry, in 1636, listed it among the four greatest tragedies of the time, and it stayed in the active repertory for 30 years. It was first French play in some time to be based on Roman history, and it relates the story of Massinisse, who falls in love with, and marries, Sophonisbe, the wife of his defeated enemy, Syphax. When required to give her up to his Roman allies, Massinisse instead sends her poison, which she takes.

Mairet made several changes in this story, derived from Livy and Appian, to make it conform to classical principles. He had Syphax die in the battle, so that the proprieties would not be outraged by bigamy, and he had Massinisse commit suicide himself so he would not be thought to take Sophonisbe's death lightly. D'Aubignac praised him for substituting the probable (*vraisemblable*) for the true (*vrai*). Mairet also moved the scene of the battle to the outskirts of Massinisse's city in order to make unity of time and place possible.

Most important, however, to the development of the classical ideal was *Sophonisbe*'s emphasis on the psychological struggle in the soul of Massinisse: should he give Sophonisbe up to the Romans? On the other hand, Mairet did not strictly maintain progression of scenes, and critics of the day complained that the proprieties were violated by a kiss and by the language with which Syphax accuses Sophonisbe of infidelity. Finally, the play lacks the deep internal conflicts that were to mark later classical tragedies. Its popularity was, according to Saint-Evremond, derived from the pleasure which the ladies and the courtiers took in Sophonisbe's "romantic soul".

Sophonisbe was Mairet's last great success, although he was to write another six plays. In 1637 Mairet became embroiled in the controversy over Pierre Corneille's *Le Cid*. Apparently a firm convert to classicism, Mairet was both one of the first French writers to enunciate its rules and the author of classicism's "model tragedy". When the controversy arose over Corneille's heroic tragicomedy, Mairet joined the battle with a claim that Corneille had plagiarized entirely a Spanish source. Although his attack on Corneille endeared him to Cardinal Richelieu, who granted him a pension, Mairet then renounced the practice of classicism and, perhaps in imitation of his rival, wrote a series of baroque tragicomedies, which failed however. In 1640 he gave up writing for the theatre.

Mairet is often remembered as an influential transitional playwright, whose theoretical writings, along with his important tragedy, *Sophonisbe*, helped to establish the ascendancy of prescriptive neoclassical theory in the 17th-century French theatre. In fact, it should also be remembered that Mairet wrote in the full range of genres and styles popular between 1625 and 1640, and that his practice was far less classical than his theory—true of many French playwrights during the period. His popularity was brief but well-deserved; he understood how to develop dramatic action and how to create characters with strong motivations and complex psychologies. Although his plays have been out of the active repertory for more than 300 years, the 1988 production in Paris of *Les Galanteries du Duc d'Ossone* suggests that Mairet's work is not necessarily inappropriate for today's theatre.

—Virginia Scott

David Mamet (1984).

MAMET, David (Alan).   Born in Flossmoor, Illinois, USA, 30 November 1947. Educated at Rich Central High School; Francis W. Parker School; Goddard College, Plainfield, Vermont, BA in English 1969; Neighborhood Playhouse School, New York, 1968–69. Married 1) the actress Lindsay Crouse in 1977, one daughter; 2) Rebecca Pidgeon. Actor in summer stock, 1969; stage manager, *The Fantasticks*, New York, 1969–70; lecturer in drama, Marlboro College, Marlboro, Vermont, 1970; artist-in-residence, Goddard College, 1971–73; founder and artistic director, St. Nicholas Company, Plainfield, Vermont, 1972, and St. Nicholas Players, Chicago, 1974–76; faculty member, Illinois Arts Council, 1974; contributing editor, *Oui* magazine, 1975–76; visiting lecturer, University of Chicago, 1975–76 and 1979, and New York University, 1981; teaching fellow, Yale University School of Drama, New Haven, Connecticut, 1976–77; associate artistic director, Goodman Theatre, Chicago, 1978–84; associate director, New Theater Company, Chicago, 1985; associate professor of film, Columbia University, New York, since 1988. Recipient: Joseph Jefferson Award, 1974; Obie Award, 1976, 1983; New York Drama Critics Circle Award, 1977, 1984; Outer Circle award, 1978; Society of West End Theatre Award, 1983; Pulitzer Prize, 1984; Dramatists Guild Hall-Warriner Award, 1984; American Academy Award, 1986; Tony Award, 1987.

Works

Collections

American Buffalo; Sexual Perversity in Chicago; Duck Variations: Three Plays.   1978.

Short Plays and Monologues (includes *All Men Are Whores; The Blue Hour: City Sketches; In Old Vermont; Litko; Prairie du Chien; A Sermon; Shoeshine*).   1981.
Goldberg Street: Short Plays and Monologues.   1985.
Dramatic Sketches and Monologues (includes *Five Unrelated Pieces; The Power Outrage; The Dog; Film Crew; 4 A.M.; Food; Pint's a Pound the World Around; Deer Dogs; Columbus Avenue; Conversations with the Spirit World; Maple Sugaring; Morris and Joe; Steve McQueen; Yes; Dowsing; In the Mall; Cross Patch; Goldberg Street*).
Three Children's Plays (includes *The Poet and the Rent; The Revenge of the Space Pandas; The Frog Prince*).   1986.
Three Jewish Plays (includes *Disappearance of the Jews; Goldberg Street; Luftmensch*).   1987.
Plays 1.   1992.

Stage Works

Lakeboat (produced Marlboro Theatre Workshop, Marlboro, Vermont, 1970; revised version produced Repertory Theatre, Milwaukee, 1980).   1981.
Duck Variations (produced Goddard College, Plainfield, Vermont, 1972).   With *Sexual Perversity in Chicago*, 1978.
Mackinac (for children; produced Chicago, 1972?).
Marranos (produced Chicago, 1972–73?).
Litko (produced Body Politic, Chicago, 1973).   In *Short Plays and Monologues*, 1981.
The Poet and the Rent: A Play for Kids from Seven to 8:15 (produced Chicago, 1974).   In *Three Children's Plays*, 1986.

Squirrels (produced by St. Nicholas Theatre Company, Chicago, 1974).   1982.

Sexual Perversity in Chicago (produced by Organic Theater Company, Chicago, 1974).   With *Duck Variations*, 1978.

American Buffalo (produced Goodman Theatre Stage Two, Chicago, 1975).   1977.

Reunion (produced Actors' Theatre, Louisville, Kentucky, 1976).   With *Dark Pony*, 1979.

The Woods (produced by St. Nicholas Theatre Company, Chicago, 1977).   1979.

All Men Are Whores (produced Yale Cabaret, New Haven, Connecticut, 1977).   In *Short Plays and Monologues*, 1981.

A Life in the Theatre (produced Goodman Theatre Stage Two, Chicago, 1977).   1978.

The Revenge of the Space Pandas; or, Binky Rudich and the Two-Speed Clock (produced by St. Nicholas Theatre Company, Chicago, 1977).   In *Three Children's Plays*, 1986.

Dark Pony (produced Yale Repertory Theatre, New Haven, Connecticut, 1977).   With *Reunion*, 1979.

The Water Engine: An American Fable (produced by St. Nicholas Theatre Company, Chicago, 1977).   With *Mr. Happiness*, 1978.

Mr. Happiness (produced Plymouth Theatre, New York, 1978).   With *The Water Engine*, 1978.

Lone Canoe; or, The Explorer, music and lyrics by Alaric Jans (produced Goodman Theatre, Chicago, 1979).

The Sanctity of Marriage (produced Circle Repertory Theatre, New York, 1979).   With *Reunion and Dark Pony*, 1982.

Shoeshine (produced Ensemble Studio Theatre, New York, 1979).   In *Short Plays and Monologues*, 1981.

A Sermon (produced Ensemble Studio Theatre, New York, 1981).   In *Short Plays and Monologues*, 1981.

Prairie du Chien (broadcast 1978; produced Lincoln Center, New York, 1985).   In *Short Plays and Monologues*, 1981.

City Sketches.   In *Short Plays and Monologues*, 1981.

In Old Vermont.   In *Short Plays and Monologues*, 1981.

Edmond (produced Goodman Theatre, Chicago, 1982).   1983.

The Disappearance of the Jews (produced Goodman Theatre, Chicago, 1983).

Glengarry Glen Ross (produced National Theatre, London, 1983).   1984.

Red River, adaptation of a play by Pierre Laville (produced Goodman Theatre, Chicago, 1983).

Five Unrelated Pieces (includes *Two Conversations; Two Scenes; Yes, But So What*) (produced Ensemble Studio Theatre, New York, 1983).   In *Dramatic Sketches and Monologues*, 1985.

The Dog (produced Jason's Park Royal, New York, 1983).   In *Dramatic Sketches and Monologues*, 1985.

Film Crew (produced Jason's Park Royal, New York, 1983).   In *Dramatic Sketches and Monologues*, 1985.

4 A.M. (produced Jason's Park Royal, New York, 1983).   In *Dramatic Sketches and Monologues*, 1985.

Vermont Sketches (includes *Pint's a Pound the World Around, Deer Dogs, Conversations with the Spirit World, Dowsing*) (produced Ensemble Studio Theatre, New York, 1984).   In *Dramatic Sketches and Monologues*, 1985.

The Frog Prince (produced Actors' Theatre, Louisville, Kentucky, 1984).   In *Three Children's Plays*, 1986.

The Spanish Prisoner (produced Goodman Theatre, Chicago, 1985).

The Shawl (produced Goodman Theatre, Chicago 1985).   With *Prairie du Chien*, 1985.

The Cherry Orchard, from a play by Chekhov (produced Chicago, 1985).   1987.

Cross Patch, from the radio plays (produced Ensemble Studio Theatre, New York, 1990).   In *Dramatic Sketches and Monologues*, 1985.

Goldberg Street, from the radio plays (produced Ensemble Studio Theatre, New York, 1990).   In *Dramatic Sketches and Monologues*, 1985.

The Power Outrage.   In *Dramatic Sketches and Monologues*, 1985.

Food.   In *Dramatic Sketches and Monologues*, 1985.

Columbus Avenue.   In *Dramatic Sketches and Monologues*, 1985.

Maple Sugaring.   In *Dramatic Sketches and Monologues*, 1985.

Morris and Joe.   In *Dramatic Sketches and Monologues*, 1985.

Steve McQueen.   In *Dramatic Sketches and Monologues*, 1985.

Yes.   In *Dramatic Sketches and Monologues*, 1985.

In the Mall.   In *Dramatic Sketches and Monologues*, 1985.

Vint, from a story by Chekhov, in *Orchards* (produced Urbana, Illinois, 1985).   1986.

Luftmensch.   In *Three Jewish Plays*, 1987.

Uncle Vanya, from a play by Chekhov (produced American Repertory Theatre, Cambridge, Massachusetts, 1988).   1989.

Speed-the-Plow (produced Lincoln Center, New York, 1987).   1988.

Where Were You When it Went Down?, music by David Shire, lyrics by Richard Maltby Jr. (produced as part of *Urban Blight*, New York, 1988).

Bobby Gould in Hell (produced as part of *Oh Hell!*, Lincoln Center, New York, 1989).   1989.

Three Sisters, from a play by Chekhov (produced Festival Theatre, Philadelphia, 1990).   1991.

Oleanna (produced Orpheum Theatre, New York, 1992).   1993.

Screenplays

The Postman Always Rings Twice, 1981; *The Verdict*, 1982; *The Untouchables*, 1987; *House of Games*, 1987 (published 1987); *Things Change*, with Shel Silverstein, 1988 (published 1988); *We're No Angels*, 1990 (published 1990); *Homicide*, 1991 (published 1991); *Glengarry Glen Ross*, 1992.

Radio Plays

Prairie du Chien, 1978; *Cross Patch*, 1985, and *Goldberg Street*, 1985 (both published in *Dramatic Sketches and Monologues*, 1985); *Dintenfass*, 1989.

Television Plays

A Waitress in Yellowstone, The Museum of Science and Industry Story, A Wasted Weekend, We Will Take You There, Bradford (all published in *Five Television Plays*, 1990).

Fiction

The Owl (for children), with Lindsay Crouse.   1987.

Verse

The Hero Pony.   1990.

Other

Writing in Restaurants (essays).   1988.
Some Freaks (essays).   1989.
On Directing Film.   1991.

*

Bibliographies

Kimball King, *Ten Modern American Playwrights*, New York, 1982.
J. Madison Davis and John Coleman, "David Mamet: A Classified Bibliography", in *Studies in American Drama 1945-Present*, 1, 1986.
Jürgen C. Wolter, "David Mamet in German-Speaking Countries: A Classified Bibliography", in *Studies in American Drama 1945-Present*, 5, 1990.

Criticism

Books:
C.W.E. Bigsby, *David Mamet*, London, 1985.
C.W.E. Bigsby, *A Critical Introduction to Twentieth-Century American Drama 3: Beyond Broadway* (includes chapter on Mamet), Cambridge, 1985.
Dennis Carroll, *David Mamet*, London and New York, 1987 (Macmillan Modern Dramatists series).
Anne Dean, *David Mamet: Language and Dramatic Action*, Rutherford, New Jersey, 1990.

Articles:
Henry I. Schvey, "The Plays of David Mamet: Games of Manipulation and Power", in *New Theatre Quarterly*, 13, 1988.

*   *   *

From his breakthrough year of 1975 to the present, David Mamet's reputation has steadily escalated. He is currently regarded as one of the most original and idiosyncratic of American playwrights—and this is mostly due to what has been called "Mametspeak", his inimitable reification of Chicago dialogue. Only Shepard has a comparably emphatic signature style—and Shepard's depends less on the audial shape of words and more on an offbeat and surreal use of scenic elements. Mamet is regarded as being one of the most "European" of American playwrights, with an indebtedness to Pinter, Beckett, and the absurdists palpable in the tone of the work and in the downbeat stasis of many of his endings. However, his recent work, including the films he has written and directed, stamp him as a quintessentially American, and specifically a Chicago, playwright. Moreover, his respect for Stanislavskian definitions of acting and action stamp him as firmly in the American realist theatrical tradition.

Mamet is a moralist filled with dismay at the obsolescence and covert predatoriness of certain American myths, especially the "Horatio Alger" and the frontier myths. His most powerful play, *Glengarry Glen Ross*, as well as the earlier *American Buffalo*, deal with the way that nascent friends betray each other for "business" principles that are, in fact, nothing more than moves for material advantage in vicious one-upmanship. In both these plays, possibilities for fulfilling human relationships are scuttled for material gain and/or survival in the competitive rat-race.

In *Glengarry Glen Ross*, set in the environs of an off-color Chicago real estate office, the central character, Levine, is an ageing salesman who is about to be sacked, and who is revealed at the denouement as the culprit in a shabby office robbery. Earlier, we see Levine's pathetic desperation, his need for comradeship, respect, and a decent self-image, but also his resilience and his elation when he believes that he has made a successful sale. Mamet, with no sentimental sign-posting, expresses his moral outrage at the various salesmen's tactics and actions, but also communicates his paradoxical respect for their energy, sleazy resourcefulness, and persistent ability to bounce back. The precise and deadpan surface of the play is a carapace for great complexity and compassion—the play became the *Death of A Salesman* for the 1980's.

In the earlier *American Buffalo*, three small-time crooks, who are planning to steal a coin-collection, evoke the same pieties, hypocrisies, and maxims as might any capitalist businessman in a boardroom. The instigator of the plan attempts to destroy a gentle father-son surrogate relationship between the junkshop owner and his young gofer. Their strategies for the break-in, which swing between the vicious and the hilariously incompetent, ensure that their attempt never gets off the ground.

If these powerful plays show friendship between men destroyed by the competitivness of "business", another group shows nascent love between men and women destroyed by a more complicated array of forces. In *Sexual Perversity in Chicago*, a romance between an inexperienced pair of lovers is soured by pettiness, hesitancy about self-disclosure, the pressure of the downtown office scene, and the cynical ministrations of two older mentor-figures. In *Speed-the-Flow*, an attraction between a tempoary secretary and a jaded film producer is torpedoed by a self-seeking agent who characterises the woman's feeling as being motivated only by her ego in the promotion of a "property". In *The Woods*, Mamet focuses exclusively on two lovers in an isolated cabin, and he reveals the insecurities of the male on the verge of a deeper commitment.

Other plays deal more positively with the possibilities of genuine communion in love or freindship. *A Life in the Theatre* and *Lakeboat* are male rite-of-passage plays and studies of mentor-protegé relationships in which the protegé moves beyond the mentor, or moves out of the mentor's sphere. *Reunion* is a tender meeting between an estranged father and daughter who have not met for 20 years. *The Shawl* builds to an unexpected communion between a "clairvoyant" and a wealthy woman he had earlier planned to cheat out of her fortune. *Edmond* presents a more complex and ironic pattern in which "communion" for the protagonist is only reached on the other side of murder, in jail, in a homosexual bond with a black prisoner.

The most obvious component of Mamet's signature style is his dialogue, which brought him early acclaim, but which has tended to be examined too much apart from its context and purpose. Though based on the Chicago idiom, the dialogue is carefully heightened—the degree of ebullience and rhythmic confidence is almost always in proportion to the extent to which the speaker has been coerced and denatured by his social role. The plays in which the characters have reached a point where they can set aside such roles and risk self-disclosure have a different kind of dialogue—more halting and less rhythmically "effective".

The other salient feature of Mamet's work—which many find has strong European parallels—is his "minimalism". This is very apparent in the printed scripts, in the compact dialogue of some episodes, in the lack of stage directions, and in the taciturn description of action and—most important of all—reaction. It is also evident in the plays in production, especially when staged with emphasis on tableau and spareness of movement and action. Mamet's minimalism is very apparent in the brief experimental pieces gathered in the collection *Goldberg Street*.

The structure of Mamet's plays is more unified than it appears to be, even in the early, more episodic pieces. In the late 1970's Mamet was influenced by the "mythic" or "fabular" definitions of narrative action, as explicated by Campbell and Bettelheim, in which a hero sets out on a voyage of discovery, is transformed in some way, and is finally reintegrated into the community—a pattern also notable in some of the recent screenplays.

Mamet is also an essayist, director, adaptor (notably of Chekhov), and children's theatre playwright. No other playwright of his generation has written so consistently or successfully for the screen. One of the screenplays he has directed himself bears a close relationship to the plays about lovers betrayed by "business" principles. In *House of Games*, a successful woman psychologist becomes a compulsive thief after being duped, financially and sexually, by a gangster and then murdering him in revenge.

By the early 1990's Mamet's international reputation, especially in Europe and England, was second to none, and it is likely that his career will continue to yield important and successful plays.

—Dennis Carroll

See also *Volume 1* entries on *American Buffalo*; *Glengarry Glen Ross*.

MARINETTI, F(ilippo) T(ommaso). Born in Alexandria, Egypt, 22 December 1876. Educated at French Jesuit school, Alexandria, from 1888; lycée, Paris, from 1893; University of Padua; University of Genoa, 1894–99, degree in law 1899. Married Benedetta Cappa; three daughters. Pursued literary career on leaving university; early plays and much verse written in French; founder, the periodical *Poesia* (in which much of his writing subsequently first appeared), 1904; first-produced play, *Le Roi Bombance*, staged in Paris, 1905; involved in car accident, 1908; published the "Foundation and Manifesto of Futurism" in *Le Figaro*, Paris, 20 February 1909, and continued to publish theoretical and polemical articles on futurism until 1921; first *serate* performed 1910; war correspondent in Libya, 1911; travelled to Russia, 1914; arrested after interventionist demonstration in Milan, 1914, and after publishing interventionist manifestos, 1915; volunteered for the Front following Italy's entry into World War I, 1915; during and after the War, increasingly associated with Mussolini and the fascists, supporting their views in print and through political action: arrested with Mussolini and others, 1919; travelled to Argentina and Brazil on a conference tour, 1925; participated in the Italian invasion of Ethiopia, 1937. Elected to the Accademico d'Italia, 1929. Died in Bellagio, 2 December 1944.

Works

Collections

Elettricità sessuale (3 vols.; includes *Simultaneità; Il teatrino dell'amore; Antineutralità; Vengono; Un chiaro di luna; Le*

basi; *Le mani; L'arresto; La camera dell'ufficiale; I vasi comunicanti; Il soldato lontano; Paralleli; I Ghiri; Runio Clacla; L'improvvisata;* and the manifesto "Il teatro futurista sintetico"). 1920.
Teatro (3 vols.; includes plays and manifestos), edited by Giovanni Calendoli. 1960.
Teatro della sorprese, edited by F. Cangiullo. 1968.
"Marinetti's Short Plays" (includes nine playlets), translated by V. Kirby. In *Tulane Drama Review*, vol.17 no.4, 1973.

Stage Works

Le Roi Bombance (produced Théâtre de l'Oeuvre, Paris, 1909). In *Mercure de France*, 1905; Italian version, translated by Decio Cinti, as *Re Baldoria* (produced Rome, 1922), 1910.
Poupées électriques (produced Théâtre de l'Oeuvre, Paris, 1909). 1909; Italian version (produced as *La donne è mobile*, Teatro Alfieri, Turin, 1909; Act II produced as *Elettricità*, Palermo, 1914, as *Elettricità sessuale*, Milan, 1914, and as *Fantocci elettrici*, Teatro degli Indipendenti, Rome, 1925), as *Elettricità sessuale*, in the periodical *Teatro*, January 1926.
Simultaneità (produced by the Berti-Masi company, Ancona, 1915). 1920.
Il tamburo di fuoco (produced Teatro Communale, Pisa, 1922). 1922.
Bianco e rosso (produced Teatro degli Indipendenti, Rome, 1923). In *Teatro 3*, 1960.
Prigioneri (produced as *I prigionieri e l'amore*, Teatro di Villa Ferrari, Rome, 1925). With *Vulcani*, 1927.
Vulcani (produced Teatro d'Arte, Rome, 1926). With *Prigionieri*, 1927; as *Vulcano*, in *Teatro 3*, 1960.
L'oceano del cuore (produced Teatro Argentina, Rome, 1927). In *Comoedia*, March-April, 1928.
Luci veloci (produced Turin, 1929). In *Comoedia*, December 1929-January 1930.
Il suggeritore nudo (produced Teatro degli Indipendenti, Rome, 1929). In *Comoedia*, December 1929-January 1930.
Simultanina (collection of *sintesi*; produced Padua, 1931). In *Teatro 3*, 1960.
Patriottismo insetticida. 1939.
Locomotive. In *Teatro 3*, 1960.
Riconstruire l'Italia con architettura futurista Sant'Elia. In *Teatro 3*, 1960.

Fiction

Mafarka le futuriste. 1910.
L'isola dei baci, with Bruno Corra. 1918.
Un ventre di donna, with Enif Roberts. 1919.
8 anime in una bomba: romanzo esplosivo. 1919.
L'alcova d'acciaio. 1927.
Lo Zar non è morto. 1929.

Verse

La Conquête des étoiles. 1902.
Destruction: Poèmes lyriques. 1904.
La Ville charnelle. 1908.
Le Monoplan du pape. 1912.
La battaglia di Tripoli (26 ottobre 1911). 1912.
Zang Tumb Tumb; Adrianopoli ottobre 1912; Parole in libertà. 1914.
Scelta di poesia; Versi liberi; Parole in libertà. 1919.
Les Mots en liberté futuristes. 1919.

Parole in libertà futuriste tattili-termiche-olfattive, edited by Tullio d'Albisola.   1932.
Poemi simultanei futuristi.   1933.
L'aeropoema del golfo della Spezia.   1935.
Il poema african della Divisione "XXVIII ottobre".   1937.
Il poema del vestito di latte.   1937.
Canto uomini di guerra e dopoguerra mussoliniana, with others.   1942.
L'aeropoema di Cozzarini primo eroe dell'esercito repubblicano.   1944.
Poesie à Beny.   1971.

Memoirs and Letters

Lettere ruggenti, edited by Giovanni Lugaresi.   1969.

Other

Le Futurisme: Théories et mouvement.   1904.
Come si seducono le donne.   1917.
I manifesti del futurismo.   1919.
Democrazia futurista; Dinamismo politico.   1919.
Les Mots en liberté futuristes.   1919.
Come si seducono le donne e si tradiscono gli uomini.   1920.
Lussuria velocità.   1921.
Futurismo e fascismo.   1924.
Scatole d'amore in conserva.   1927.
Primo dizionario aereo italiano, with Fedele Azari.   1929.
Il paesaggio e l'estetica futurista della machina.   1931.
La cucina futurista, with Fillìa.   1931.
Spagna veloce e toro futurista.   1931.
Il club dei simpatici.   1931.
Il fascino dell'Egitto.   1933.
L'originalità napoletana del poeta Salvatore di Giacomo.   1936.
Umberto Notari, scrittore nuovo.   1937.
Il poema di Torre Viscosa.   1938.
Il poema non umano dei tecnicismi.   1940.
Il teatro futurista sintetico, with others.   1941.
Teoria e invenzione futurista, edited by Luciano De Maria.   1968.
Selected Writings, translated by R.W. Flint (with A. Cappotelli).   1972.
La grande Milano tradizionale e futurista, edited by Luciano De Maria.   1969.
Scritti francese 1, edited by Pasquale A. Jannini.   1983.

Translator, *Versi e prose di S. Mallarmé*.   1916.

*

Bibliographies

Brunella Eruli, "Bibliografia delle opere di F.T. Marinetti (1898–1909)", in *Rassegna dalla letteratura italiana*, 72, 1968.

Criticism

Books:
Sandro Biosi, *Marinetti*, Florence, 1929.
V. Schilirò, *Marinetti e il futurismo*, 1929.
W. Vaccari, *Vita e tumulti di F.T. Marinetti*, Milan, 1959.

Michael Kirby and Victoria Nes Kirby, *Futurist Performance*, New York, 1971.
Giovanni Lista, *Marinetti*, Paris, 1976.
Giovanni Lista, *Le Théâtre futuriste italien* (2 vols.), Lausanne, 1976.
Giovanni Lista, *Marinetti et le futurisme*, Lausanne, 1978.
Giovanni Lista, "Marinetti: Auteur dramatique", in *Marinetti*, edited by Gérard G. Lamaire, Paris, 1984.
Antonio Saccone, *Marinetti e il futurismo*, Naples, 1984.
Guisis Baldissone, *Filippo Tommaso Marinetti*, Milan, 1986.
Claudia Salaris, *Filippo Tommaso Marinetti*, Scandicci, 1988.

Articles:
Donald Marinelli, "Marinetti's *Lulu*", in *Theater Three*, 2, 1987.

* * *

Marinetti, Italian poet, playwright, journalist, and novelist, was the dynamic leader and guiding spirit of the Italian futurist movement which he founded in 1909. In this capacity he introduced daring ideas which had a profound impact on modern literature and theatre. While he wrote a number of full-length plays throughout his career, it is with the new futurist dramatic forms—the manifestos, *parole in liberta*, *serate*, and *sintesi*—that he left his mark on the theatre.

Marinetti made his literary debut in 1898 when his poem "L'Échanson" appeared in the bilingual Milanese journal *Anthologie-Revue*. His collaboration on numerous literary journals brought him frequently to Paris where he eased himself into French literary circles. His early work as a poet— "La Conquête des étoiles", "La Momie sanglante", "Destruction", "La Ville charnelle"—shows the influence of Mallarmé, Baudelaire, Maeterlinck, Verhaeren, and of the turn-of-the-century decadent–symbolist school. In 1904 he founded the journal *Poesia* in order to introduce the symbolist aesthetic to Italy; Italian literature was, according to Marinetti, mired in classicism and the past.

By 1909 there was a significant change in Marinetti's writing. While an anarchistic defiance of the cosmos still inspired him, his earlier images of dynamic communion with the ocean were replaced by images of the intoxicating sensations of speed; and images of the vitality of liquid elements by those of the vitality of technology. Marinetti's relationship with the machine was not always an easy one. He was not interested in the social progress that the technological revolution would bring, but in the inebriating effect of speed and the sometimes frightening experience of the power of the machine.

Marinetti wrote two full-length plays before founding the futurist movement. *Le Roi Bombance*, inspired by Jarry's *Père Ubu*, but in no way comparable, uses a gastronomical metaphor to explore the relationship between the ruling elite and starving, rebellious subjects. It was inspired by the failure of the 1904 general strike in Milan, which showed, according to Marinetti, "the tragic and fatal victory of idealist individualism over the brutal masses". Heavy-handed in its symbolism, the play presents a pessimistic view of the human condition; it shows Marinetti's obsession with the powerful influence exercised by the past on the present. This obsession played an important role in the development of his futurist philosophy. In the play, the Vampire savant exclaims, "The future, that's the only religion! . . . When you regret something . . . that's already a germ of death you're carrying around with you".

The plot of *Poupées électriques* stems from the bourgeois theatre, but introduces robot characters who live with a married couple, Marie and Jean, and who are the "alogical synthesis" of deadening forces that are part of their lives. The theme of the play is again (but on an intimate level this time) the difficulty of escaping from the past.

On 20 February 1909, *Le Figaro* published Marinetti's "Foundation and Manifesto of Futurism", in which he proclaimed his revolutionary aim of abolishing the past and its established institutions. He and his futurist followers, who were artists of all kinds, were to publish hundreds more manifestos in subsequent years. This movement, which continued into the 1940's, influenced music, painting, sculpture, dance, cinema, as well as the theatrical arts in Italy, Europe, and Russia. In the theatre it had two major poles: the futurist *serate*, or evenings; and the futurist *sintesi*, or theatre of synthesis.

The first futurist *serata* was at the Politeama Rossetti, Trieste, on 12 January 1910, and Marinetti and his followers subsequently travelled to many cities throughout Italy holding these *serate*. They consisted of a mixture of politics and art and prefigured the "happening": paintings were exhibited, speeches made, films showed, manifestos declaimed, music played. The evenings often intentionally provoked the audience to violence: it was part of Marinetti's futurist program to abolish the traditional performer-audience relationship and to provoke the audience out of its comfortable ways.

In his manifesto of 21 November 1913, "The Variety Theatre", Marinetti drew on nightclubs, circuses, and music hall as inspiration for futurist theatre. He extolled their various qualities: the speed, invention, simultaneity, and dynamism; the short numbers; the non-psychological, non-literary, primitive approach to entertainment; the elements of surprise, improvisation, and spectacle, and the free-floating actor-audience relationship. In line with his idealization of war, danger, and violence, he praised the variety theatre for encouraging acts of heroism and feats of strength.

During these years, Marinetti developed the concept of *parole in libertà*, which carried the symbolist poet Lucini's ideas of free verse one step farther by eliminating any rules regarding versification, spelling, syntax, spatial distribution of words on a page, and typology. These *parole in libertà* were presented as theatricalized performances. Marinetti's *Zang-Tumb-Tumb* describes the siege of Adrianapole during the Balkan War. These performances began in 1914 at the Sprovieri Cabarets in Rome and Naples, continuing the tradition of the symbolist cabarets. These were different from the *serate* in that costumes, sets, sound, music were used to dramatic effect and multiple performers were often involved. At times Marinetti called them "dynamic and synoptic declamations".

Marinetti also left an impression on the theatre with his futurist *sintesi*, a concept inspired by Rosso di San Secondo who published seven of them in 1911. Marinetti's aim with the *sintesi* was brevity of expression—for instance, transmitting the essentials of a five-act play with a few scenes—simultaneity, and a breakdown of the fourth wall. During 1915–16, acting companies, among them Ettore Petrolini's, toured Italy presenting a program of these short pieces. Marinetti's are among the best. *Vengono* may have had a direct influence on Ionesco's *The Chairs*. His *Simultaneità* is a good example of Marinetti's idea of simultaneity in the theatre. It comprises two different scenes that co-penetrate. A bourgeois family spends an evening quietly around a table. Meanwhile, in their midst, but unseen by them, a beautiful call-girl does her toilette and receives several visitors. She then breaks the invisible wall, walks to the table, and tells the family to go to bed. Marinetti explained that the call-girl is "a synthesis of the feelings of luxury, disorder, adventure, and waste, experienced as anguish, desire, or regret in the nerves

of those in the peaceful family setting". In *I Vasi Comunicanti* Marinetti again explores the idea of simultaneity with three sets and a group of soldiers who break through the separating walls.

The full-length plays that belong to Marinetti's later period, such as *Il tamburo di fuoco*, *Prigionieri*, and *Vulcani* are lively and inventive. They show, however, more of a stylistic resemblance to expressionism and symbolism and are infused with few of the experimental aspects of futurism. *Tamburo*, set in an unidentified place and time, tells the mysterious story of a Black prophet who meets defeat and betrayal when he tries to save his people. In *Vulcani* a competition takes place between a poet, a pyrotechnist, the moon, and Mount Etna.

Marinetti had an often contradictory and fluctuating relationship with the Fascist party. Despite his devotion to the anarchic revolutionary principles of futurism, he was able—whether out of nationalistic feeling or because of traumatic childhood experiences—to justify his participation in Mussolini's repressive totalitarian regime. This paradoxical tie should not, however, lead us to deny either the originality of his work or the enormous influence it had on the development of the theatre.

—Jane House

MARIVAUX, Pierre Carlet de Chamblain de.   Born Pierre Carlet, in Paris, 4 February 1688. Studied law in Paris, 1710–13, graduated 1721. Married Colomb Bollogne in 1717 (died 1723), one daughter; lived with Mlle. Angélique Anquetin de la Chapelle de Saint-Jean, from 1744. Began using name Carlet de Marivaux, c.1616; contributor, *Le Nouveau Mercure*, from 1717–21; lost much of his fortune, 1720, and subsequently earned living as a professional writer; wrote primarily for the Italian players, the Comédie-Italienne, Paris, from 1720; founder and publisher, *Le Spectateur français*, 1721–24, and *L'Indigent Philosophe*, 1726–27; also wrote plays for the Comédie-Française, especially 1724–30. Elected to the Académie Française, 1742: Chancellor, 1750, and Director, 1759. Died in Paris, 12 February 1763.

Works

Collections

Oeuvres de théâtre (5 vols).   1758.
Oeuvres complètes (12 vols.).   1781.
Théâtre complet (2 vols.), edited by Frédéric Deloffre. 1968.
Seven Comedies (includes *Robin, Bachelor of Love; Double Infidelity; Money Makes the World Go Round; The Game of Love and Chance; The Wiles of Love; Sylvia Hears a Secret; The Test*), translated by Oscar Mandel.   1968.
Plays (includes *The Double Inconstancy; The False Servant; The Game of Love and Chance; Careless Vows; The Feigned Inconstancy; Harlequin's Lesson in Love; Slave Island; The Will; A Matter of Dispute; The Constant Players*), various translators, introduced by Claude Schumacher.   1988.

Stage Works

Le Père prudent et équitable; ou, Crispin l'heureux fourbe (produced by amateur group, Limoges, 1712).   1712.

L'Amour et la vérité, with Chevalier Rustaing de Saint-Jory (produced Comédie-Italienne, Paris, 1720). In *Théâtre complet*, 1968.

Arlequin poli par l'amour (produced Comédie-Italienne, Paris, 1720). 1723; translated as *Robin, Bachelor of Love*, in *Seven Comedies*, 1968.

Annibal (produced Comédie-Française, Paris, 1720). 1727.

La Surprise de l'amour (produced Comédie-Italienne, Paris, 1722). 1723.

La Double Inconstance (produced Comédie-Italienne, Paris, 1723). 1723; translated as *Double Infidelity*, in *Seven Comedies*, 1968; as *Infidelities*, in *The Game of Love and Chance; Infidelities; Up from the Country*, 1980; as *The Double Inconstancy*, in *Plays*, 1988.

Le Prince travesti; ou, L'Illustre Aventurier (produced Comédie-Italienne, Paris, 1724). 1727.

La Fausse Suivante; ou, Le Fourbe puni (produced Comédie-Italienne, Paris, 1724). 1729; translated as *The False Servant*, in *Plays*, 1988.

Le Dénouement imprévu (produced Comédie-Française, Paris, 1724). 1727.

L'Île des esclaves (produced Comédie-Italienne, Paris, 1725). 1725; translated as *Slave Island*, in *Plays*, 1988.

L'Héritier du village (produced Comédie-Italienne, Paris, 1725). 1729.

L'Île de la raison; ou, Les Petits Hommes (produced Comédie-Française, Paris, 1727). 1727.

La (Seconde) Surprise de l'amour (produced Comédie-Française, Paris, 1727). 1728.

Le Triomphe de Plutus (produced Comédie-Italienne, Paris, 1728). 1739; translated as *Money Makes the World Go Round*, in *Seven Comedies*, 1968.

La Colonie (as *La Nouvelle Colonie*, produced Comédie-Italienne, Paris, 1729; revised version, produced 1750). In *Théâtre complet*, 1968.

Le Jeu de l'amour et du hasard (produced Comédie-Italienne, Paris, 1730). 1730; translated as *Love in Livery*, 1907; as *The Game of Love and Chance*, in *French Comedies of the 18th Century*, 1923, and in later collections.

La Réunion des amours (produced Comédie-Française, Paris, 1731). 1732.

Le Triomphe de l'amour (produced Comédie-Italienne, Paris, 1732). 1732.

Les Serments indiscrets (produced Comédie-Française, Paris, 1732). 1732; translated as *Careless Vows*, in *Plays*, 1988.

L'École des mères (produced Comédie-Italienne, Paris, 1732). 1732.

L'Heureux Strategème (produced Comédie-Italienne, Paris, 1733). 1733; translated as *The Agreeable Surprise*, in *Poetical Blossoms*, translated by John Rule, 1766; as *The Wiles of Love*, in *Seven Comedies*, 1968; as *The Feigned Inconstancy*, in *Plays*, 1988.

La Méprise (produced Comédie-Italienne, Paris, 1734). 1739.

Le Petit-Maître corrigé (produced Comédie-Française, Paris, 1734). 1739.

La Mère confidante (produced Comédie-Italienne, Paris, 1735). 1735.

Le Legs (produced Comédie-Italienne, Paris, 1736). 1736; translated as *The Legacy*, 1915; as *The Will*, in *Plays*, 1988.

Les Fausses Confidences (produced as *La Fausse Confidence*, Comédie-Italienne, Paris, 1737; produced as *Les Fausses Confidences*, 1738). 1738; translated as *The False Confessions*, in *The Classic Theatre 4*, edited by Eric Bentley, 1961; as *Sylvia Hears a Secret*, in *Seven Comedies*, 1968.

La Joie imprévue (produced Comédie-Italienne, Paris, 1738). 1738.

Les Sincères (produced Comédie-Italienne, Paris, 1739). 1739.

L'Épreuve (produced Comédie-Italienne, Paris, 1740). 1740; translated as *The Test*, in *Poet Lore*, 35, 1924, and in *Seven Comedies*, 1968.

La Commère (produced Comédie-Française, Paris, 1967). In *Théâtre complet*, 1968.

La Dispute (produced Comédie-Française, Paris, 1744). 1747; translated as *A Matter of Dispute*, in *Plays*, 1988.

Le Préjugé vaincu (produced Comédie-Française, Paris, 1746). 1747.

La Femme fidèle (produced Théâtre de Société de Berny, 1755). In *Théâtre complet*, 1968.

Félicie (produced 1957). In *Le Mercure*, March 1757.

Les Acteurs de bonne foi (produced 1947). Published anonymously in *Le Conservateur*, November 1757; translated as *The Constant Players*, in *Plays*, 1988.

La Provinciale (produced by the amateur troupe of the Comte de Clermont, 1761). Published anonymously in *Le Mercure*, 1761.

Fiction

Les Aventures de***; ou, Les Effets surprenants de la sympathie (5 vols.). 1713–14.

La Voiture embourbée. 1714.

La Vie de Marianne; ou, Les Aventures de Mme. la comtesse de*** (11 vols.). 1731–41; translated as *The Life of Marianne*, 1736–42; as *The Virtuous Orphan*, 1743; as *The Life and Adventures of Indiana*, 1746; as *The Hand of Destiny*, 1889.

Le Paysan parvenu; ou, Les Mémoires de M.*** (5 vols.). 1734–35; translated as *The Fortunate Villager*, 1765; as *The Upstart Peasant*, 1974; as *Up from the Country*, in *The Game of Love and Chance; Infidelities; Up from the Country*, 1980.

Le Télémaque travesti. 1736.

Pharsamon; ou, Les Nouvelles Folies romanesques. 1737; translated as *Pharsamond; or, The New Knight-Errant* (2 vols.), 1750; as *Pharsamond*, 1950.

Romans. 1949.

Verse

L'Homère travesti; ou, L'Iliade en vers burlesques (2 vols.). 1716.

Other

Le Spectateur français (2 vols.). 1723–24; augmented edition, 1725.

L'Indigent Philosophe; ou, L'Homme sans souci. 1727.

Le Cabinet du philosophe. 1734.

Le Miroir. 1755.

Journaux et oeuvres diverses, edited by Frédéric Deloffre and Michel Gilot. 1969.

Oeuvres de jeunesse, edited by Frédéric Deloffre and Claude Rigault. 1972.

*

Bibliographies

Ch. Miething, *Marivaux*, Darmstadt, 1979.

Criticism

Books:

Frédéric Deloffre, *Une Préciosité nouvelle: Marivaux et le marivaudage*, Paris, 1955; revised edition, 1971.

Kenneth N. McKee, *The Theatre of Marivaux*, New York, 1958.

J.B. Ratermanis, *Étude sur le comique dans le théâtre de Marivaux*, Ghent and Paris, 1961.

E.J.H. Greene, *Marivaux*, Toronto and London, 1965.

Valenti Papadapoulou Brady, *Love in the Theatre of Marivaux*, Ghent, 1970.

S. Mühlemann, *Ombres et lumières dans l'oeuvre de Marivaux*, Bern, 1970.

M. Descotes, *Les Grands Rôles du théâtre de Marivaux*, Paris, 1972.

L. Desvignes-Parent, *Marivaux et l'Angleterre*, Paris, 1970.

Oscar A. Haac, *Marivaux*, Boston, 1973.

Henri Coulet and Michel Gilot, *Marivaux: Un Humanisme expérimental*, 1973.

N. Bonhôte, *Marivaux ou les machines de l'opéra*, Lausanne, 1974.

J.C. Lacant, *Marivaux en Allemagne*, Paris, 1975.

Ch. Miething, *Marivauxs Theater: Identitätsprobleme in der Komödie*, Munich, 1975.

R. Tomlinson, *La Fête galante: Watteau et Marivaux*, Ghent, 1981.

M. Deguy, *La Machine matrimoniale chez Marivaux*, Paris, 1981; revised edition, 1986.

Patrice Pavis, *Marivaux à l'épreuve de la scène*, Paris, 1986.

C. Poe, *The Rococo and Eighteenth-Century France: A Study Through Marivaux's Theater*, New York, 1987.

J.K. Sanaker, *Le Discours mal apprivoisé: Essai sur le dialogue de Marivaux*, Paris, 1987.

J. Terrasse, *Le Sens et les signes: Étude sur le théâtre de Marivaux*, Sherbrooke, Quebec, 1987.

W.H. Trapnell, *Eavesdropping in Marivaux*, Ghent, 1987.

Henri Coulet and Jean Ehrard (eds.), *Marivaux hier, Marivaux d'aujourd' hui*, Lyons, 1991.

* * *

Marivaux is perhaps the most original French dramatist of the 18th century. He stands apart from his contemporaries in his creation of a comedy that eschewed the classical conventions of verse and a five-act structure, and avoided the extremes of satirical cynicism or sentimental moralising which were features of "comic" theatre in the first half of the century. He wrote many of his plays for the *Italiens*, who were establishing themselves as an important theatrical presence in Paris after their return to France in 1716, and was to find much inspiration in the *commedia dell'arte*, with its use of mime and improvised dialogue, its simple plots and stock characters, from Arlequin, the great clown, to Silvia, the beautiful *ingénue*.

Unlike French comic writers before him—with the possible exception of Corneille—Marivaux placed love at the centre of many of his plays. This love is neither intellectualised nor brutishly physical, but blends a discreet sensuality with the capacity for critical self-observation. His interest lay not in the characters as individuals but in the relationships between them, and he created comic effects from the (often imaginary) obstacles, confusions, jealousies, and finally pleasures which accompany the birth of love. Extremes of emotion are carefully avoided, and the audience is kept detached from the action, encouraged to view with a sympathetic irony the slow but inevitable disintegration of pretence and self-deception; truth is finally recognised by the lover and avowed in words, both to the self and to the other.

Particularly striking is the economy of Marivaux's theatrical effects. Plots are often quite simple, and he could distill and suggest all the difficulties of expression, knowledge and self-knowledge into the meeting of two lovers; in such scenes, speech becomes action. The secret of the dramatist's success lies in the unique nature of his language. It is a language that seeks to recreate the natural rhythms of speech, to suggest an element of the improvised and the spontaneous. Words do not have the function simply of expressing clearly understood and firmly defined feelings, but they serve rather to trace the tortuous path towards articulation and certainty. The delicate gradations of feeling revealed and explored through this subtly refined language were not always appreciated by his contemporaries, and the term *marivaudage*, coined to describe both the style and subject matter of these comedies, was often used to denote excessive, even precious, sensitivity.

To characterize Marivaux's work in this way, though, is to suggest a uniformity of approach belied by the plays themselves: the dramatist himself would have argued that nothing is as infinitely varied and variable as the human heart, and no two plays, like no two lovers, reveal quite the same problems and aspects of feeling. In addition, the dramatist changed his settings from play to play, from the purely fantastical to the contemporary, thereby varying the dosage of psychological, social, or financial preoccupations which disturb and complicate the course of love.

Furthermore, such comedies of love constitute only a part of the dramatist's output; other plays are more allegorical or philosophical in their themes and conception. Several take as their setting an island whose different conditions throw into relief the nature of European customs and attitudes, or imagine "natural" man untouched by "civilisation".

L'Île des esclaves is an allegory set on an island where servants rule: on arrival a master and mistress are made to exchange roles with their servants and are slowly cured of their feelings of superiority. Marivaux explores with great subtlety the nature of this cure; it is not brought about by physical suffering or ridicule, but, more interestingly, by confronting the superiors with the extent of their dependence on their servants for their very identity as masters.

Similarly, in *La Colonie*, the dramatist imagined what might happen if man had to establish, from scratch, the machinery of self-government. Men are seen to claim dominance, but the women of all classes articulately expose the social, rather than natural forces which determine their own traditionally subordinate role. By the end, though, social identity emerges as a more powerful force than sexual identity, and the dream of female solidarity cannot subdue the self-interest engrained in distinctions of class. Such plays offer probing insights into man's assumptions and behaviour, but they are not merely abstract philosophical dialogue. Marivaux exploits the comic potential of confrontation between conflicting groups, and creates a theatrical entertainment in which fantasy interacts with, and sharpens, the portrayal of human nature.

Other plays again suggest different areas of interest and experiment. *La Mère confidente* anticipates by some 20 years certain aspects of the *drame*, notably in the play's sensitive exploration of a mother's relationship with her daughter; *Le Petit-Maître corrigé* moves into the realm of social satire with its ridicule of the over-confident fop; and the dramatist's last play, *Les Acteurs de bonne foi*, takes the form of a play-within-a-play and evokes the potentially painful misunderstandings which arise when characters are unable to distinguish between pretence and reality.

Marivaux's *oeuvre* clearly has many different aspects, but all reveal similar theatrical qualities: innovation and imagination in different forms of comedy; a keen sense of comic situation; shrewd insight into human relationships; and, finally, a concern for the audience which ensures their participation and pleasure in the delicate analysis of feelings, manners, and values.

—G. Jonathon Mallinson

See also *Volume 1* entries on *The Double Inconstancy*; *The Game of Love and Chance*.

MARLOWE, Christopher. Born in Canterbury, Kent, England, 6 February 1564. Educated at King's School, Canterbury, 1579; Benet College (now Corpus Christi College), Oxford (Archbishop Parker scholar), 1581–84, BA 1584, MA 1587. Apparently a government agent in Rheims, spying on expatriate English Roman Catholics, 1586; lived in London from 1587, and wrote plays for the Lord Admiral's Company and Lord Strange's Company; arrested and charged with murder, 1589, but released; shared lodgings with Thomas Kyd, 1591; deported from the Netherlands for attempting to issue counterfeit coins, 1592; charged by the Privy Council with heresy and blasphemy, 1593: fatally stabbed at a meeting in Deptford before the charge was considered (Kyd later testified against him). Died 30 May 1593.

Works

Collections

Works, edited by R.H. Case and others (6 vols.).   1930–33.
Complete Plays, edited by J.B. Steane.   1969.

Woodcut from a 1636 edition of *The Tragical History of Doctor Faustus* by **Christopher Marlowe**: Mephistophilis appears to Faustus who is safely enclosed within his magic circle.

Plays, edited by Roma Gill. 1971.
Complete Works, edited by Fredson Bowers (2 vols.). 1973; revised edition (2 vols.), 1981.
Complete Plays and Poems, edited by E.D. Pendry. 1976.
Complete Works, edited by Roma Gill. 1987—

Stage Works

Dido, Queen of Carthage (produced c.1585–91). 1594.
Tamburlaine the Great (2 parts; produced by the Admiral's Men, Rose Theatre, London, c.1587–88). 1590.
Doctor Faustus (produced 1588?; earliest known production, by the Admiral's Men, Rose Theatre, London, 1594). Published in two differing texts: "A" text, 1604; "B" text, 1616.
The Rich Jew of Malta (produced London, 1589?). 1633; later editions as *The Jew of Malta*.
Edward II (produced probably by Pembroke's Men, London, 1592?). 1594.
The Massacre at Paris (produced by Lord Strange's Men, London, 1593). 1594(?).

Verse

Epigrams and Elegies of Ovid, with John Davies. 1595(?); as *All Ovid's Elegies: 3 Books, with Epigrams by John Davies*, after 1602.
Hero and Leander, completed by George Chapman. 1598.
Lucan's First Book Translated Line for Line. 1600.
Poems, edited by Millar MacLure. 1968.

*

Bibliographies

S.A. Tannenbaum, *Christopher Marlowe: A Concise Bibliography*, New York, 1937; supplement, 1947; supplement by R.C. Johnson, 1967.
Lois Mai Chan, *Marlowe Criticism: A Bibliography*, Boston, 1978.
Kenneth Friedenreich, *Christopher Marlowe: An Annotated Bibliography of Criticism Since 1950*, Metuchen, New Jersey, 1979.

Criticism

Books:
J.L. Hotson, *The Death of Christopher Marlowe*, London, 1925.
Una Ellis-Fermor, *Christopher Marlowe*, London, 1927.
M.B. Smith, *Christopher Marlowe's Imagery and the Marlowe Canon*, Philadelphia, 1940.
John E. Bakeless, *The Tragical History of Christopher Marlowe* (2 vols.), Cambridge, Massachusetts, 1942.
M. Poirier, *Marlowe*, London, 1951.
Harry Levin, *The Overreacher: A Study of Marlowe*, Cambridge, Massachusetts, 1952.
F.P. Wilson, *Marlowe and the Early Shakespeare*, Cambridge, 1953.
D. Cole, *Suffering and Evil in the Plays of Marlowe*, Princeton, New Jersey, 1962.
Paul H. Kocher, *Christopher Marlowe: A Study of His Thought, Learning, and Character*, New York, 1962.
E.M. Waith, *The Herculean Hero in Marlowe, Chapman, Shakespeare and Dryden*, London, 1962.

Clifford Leech (ed.), *Marlowe: A Collection of Critical Essays*, Englewood Cliffs, New Jersey, 1964.
J.B. Steane, *Marlowe: A Critical Study*, Cambridge, 1964.
A.D. Wraight and V.F. Stern, *In Search of Marlowe: A Pictorial Biography*, London, 1965.
Brain Morris (ed.), *Christopher Marlowe*, London, 1968.
W. Sanders, *The Dramatist and the Received Idea: Studies in the Plays of Marlowe and Shakespeare*, London, 1968.
R.E. Knoll, *Christopher Marlowe*, New York, 1969.
J. O'Neill (ed.), *Critics on Marlowe*, London, 1969.
C.G. Masinton, *Christopher Marlowe's Tragic Vision*, Athens, Ohio, 1972.
J.P. Cutts, *The Left Hand of God: A Critical Interpretation of the Plays of Christopher Marlowe*, Haddonfield, New Jersey, 1973.
Claude J. Summers, *Marlowe and the Politics of Power*, Salzburg, 1973.
V.M. Meehan, *Christopher Marlowe: Poet and Playwright*, The Hague, 1974.
L.M. Benaquist, *The Tripartite Structure of Marlowe's Tamburlaine Plays and "Edward II"*, Salzburg, 1975.
Gerald Pinciss, *Marlowe*, New York, 1975.
James Robinson Howe, *Marlowe, Tamburlaine, and Magic*, Athens, Ohio, 1976.
Judith Weil, *Christopher Marlowe: Merlin's Prophet*, Cambridge, 1977.
Mary Elizabeth Smith, *"Love Kindling Fire": A Study of Marlowe's "The Tragedy of Dido, Queen of Carthage"*, Salzburg, 1977.
Della Hilton, *Who Was Kit Marlowe? The Story of the Poet and Playwright*, London, 1977.
F. Bosonnet, *The Function of Stage Properties in Christopher Marlowe's Plays*, Bern, 1978.
Millar MacLure (ed.), *Marlowe: The Critical Heritage 1588–1896*, London, 1979.
F.B. Asibong, *Comic Sensibility in the Plays of Marlowe*, Ilfracombe, 1979.
Constance B. Kuriyama, *Hammer or Anvil: Psychological Patterns in Marlowe's Plays*, Brunswick, New Jersey, 1980.
Malcolm Kelsall, *Marlowe*, Leiden, 1981.
R.M. Cornelius, *Christopher Marlowe's Use of the Bible*, New York, 1984.
B.E. Brandt, *Christopher Marlowe and the Metaphysical Problem Play*, Salzburg, 1985.
Clifford Leech and Anne Lancashire (eds.), *Christopher Marlowe: Poet for the Stage*, New York, 1986.
Simon Shepherd, *Marlowe and the Politics of Elizabethan Theatre*, Brighton, Sussex, 1986.
William Empson, *Faustus and the Censor: The English Faust-Book and Marlowe's Doctor Faustus*, edited by John Henry Jones, Oxford, 1987.
Kenneth Friedenreich, Roma Gill, and Constance B. Kuriyama (eds.), *A Poet and a Filthy Play-Maker: New Essays on Marlowe*, 1988.
William Urry, *Marlowe and Canterbury*, edited by Andrew Butcher, London, 1988.
William M. Tydeman, *Christopher Marlowe: A Guide Through the Critical Maze*, Bristol, 1989.

*   *   *

There has been much speculation about the private life of Christopher Marlowe. He has been vilified as spy, homosexual, atheist, and blasphemer, but reliable biographical information is extremely scant. He probably worked for the secret service set up by Francis Walsingham, Queen Elizabeth I's notorious minister, and his death, following a tavern brawl, may have been connected in some way with his espionage activities. Nonetheless, wild theories about his life abound, one of the more ludicrous being that his death was faked and he continued writing plays under Shakespeare's name.

Marlowe graduated from Cambridge and was associated with a group of writers known collectively as the "University wits". Despite the ubiquitous evidence of classical knowledge in his plays, he was not as academic a writer as this label might imply. Admittedly, *Dido, Queen of Carthage*, written for the Children of the Chapel Royal, translations of Ovid's *Amores* and Lucan's *Pharsalia*, and the unfinished epic poem *Hero and Leander* are all illustrative of the work of Marlowe the scholar-poet. But in the plays which he wrote in his short career he also displayed an extraordinary stylistic versatility and a shrewd awareness of the demands of the popular theatre. Several of his plays became an established part of the repertoire of the Lord Admiral's Men, one of the leading London companies, with the famous actor Edward Alleyn performing the central roles.

Alleyn became renowned for his performances as Tamburlaine in Marlowe's first play for the public stage, *Tamburlaine the Great*. As the title-page of the first printed edition informs us, the play shows how Tamburlaine "from a Scythian shepherd, by his rare and wonderful conquests became a most puissant and mighty monarch". The play is emblematic, progressing through a series of tableaux depicting Tamburlaine's inevitable ascendancy. Ironically, his invincibility and concomitant brutality are matched by a magnificent eloquence in speech, revealing how language can be manipulated to gloss over the most barbarous acts of tyranny. Hyperbole, rhetoric, and visual splendour are all part of Tamburlaine's armoury of terrorism. Though the issues raised in this play were likely to lead Marlowe into trouble with the authorities (Tamburlaine's ascendancy is a direct challenge to the notion of the Divine Right of kings), the play was a success, and a sequel, *Tamburlaine the Great, Part II*, was written soon after.

Barabas in *The Jew of Malta* is another of the so-called Marlovian "overreachers". From his first entrance in this grotesque satire he establishes himself as both a parody of the stereotypical Jew and a direct commentator on the action for the audience. Delighting in his acts of villainy, he reveals a world of pervasive exploitation and corruption in which the only way to survive is to live by "Machiavellian" principles. Behind the farcical humour lurks a damning critique of Christianity, with Ferneze, the Christian governor of Malta, emerging as the arch-manipulator in the play.

In *Edward II* Marlowe used the popular Elizabethan form of the chronicle history play. Edward's cavalier approach to the responsibilities of kingship is shockingly revealed by his uncontrollable need for the company of Gaveston, his homosexual lover. The Machiavellian Mortimer's challenge to Edward's authority raises the issue of rebellion and its legitimacy. Tensions between personal desire and public duty are played out against a background of feudal power-struggles. Marlowe neither takes sides nor neatly resolves the problems that he raises. We are invited to share the perspectives of the four central characters, King Edward, Gaveston, Queen Isabella, and Mortimer, but none of them emerges as a mouthpiece for the author. The play's episodic style and shifting viewpoints were much admired by Bertolt Brecht and were influential in his development of "epic" theatre.

The Massacre at Paris deals with historical events in France, including the barbarous St Bartholomew's Day massacre of Protestants in 1572. The role of the Duke of Guise, a Catholic villain to be hissed at by English Protestants in the audience, seems to demand a sardonic style of performance

similar to that of Barabas in *The Jew of Malta*. Critics have commented on the "mangled" form of the text that has survived, but incompleteness in the form can be seen as a challenge to the providentialist view of history, with its moral certainties and coherent sense of nation. Marlowe showed his contemporary world to be disordered and open to manipulation by ruthless power seekers.

Dr Faustus is thought by many critics to be Marlowe's last play, though there is no conclusive evidence for this. Two unsatisfactory texts of the play survive, and it is often suggested that several of the farcical scenes are the work of other authors. However, this mixture of styles is characteristic of Elizabethan popular theatre. The orthodox reading of the play is to view it as an advanced morality drama, with Faustus as yet another example of a Marlovian overreacher who provokes fate. A more radical interpretation might stress the conflict between the aspirations of Faustus as Renaissance man and the limitations placed upon him by his lowly status as scholar. God's supremacy and restriction of legitimate knowledge might be understood as an oblique reference to the censoring authority of the Elizabethan Establishment.

—Andy Piasecki

See also *Volume 1* entries on *Doctor Faustus*; *Edward II*; *The Jew of Malta*; *Tamburlaine the Great, Parts One and Two*.

MARQUÉS, René. Born in Arecibo, Puerto Rico, 4 October 1919. Educated at College of Agriculture and Mechanics, San Juan, degree in agronomy 1942; University of Madrid, studying literature, 1946; Columbia University, New York, studying drama in Piscator's workshop, 1949. Married Serena Velasco in 1942 (divorced); one daughter and two sons. Agronomist, Department of Agriculture, Puerto Rico, 1943–46; contributor, *Alma latina*; manager of department store, 1946–49; founder, the theatre group Pro Arte de Arecibo, 1947; contributor, *El Mundo*, *Puerto Rico Ilustrado*, *Asomante*, *Artes y Letras*, and other periodicals, from the late 1940's; journalist, *Diario de Puerto Rico*, 1949–50; writer, 1950, and editorial director, 1953–69, for the Puerto Rican Department of Education; co-founder, with José Lacomba, Nuestro Teatro, 1950; Secretary of the Puerto Rican Ateneo [Atheneum], San Juan, 1951; co-founder, with Lacomba, and director, the Ateneo's Teatro Experimental, 1951–54: left board of the Ateneo following controversy over his *La carreta*, 1953; co-founder, Club del Libro de Puerto Rico [Book Club of Puerto Rico], 1959. Recipient of many awards, including: Ateneo awards, 1949, 1958 and 1962; Casa de Las Americas Honourable Mention, 1962; Diplo Trophy, 1970; Diploma of Honour (Puerto Rican Institute of Culture), 1979. Died in San Juan, 22 March 1979.

Works

Collections

Teatro (includes *Los soles truncos*; *Un niño azul para esa sombra*; *La muerte no entrará en palacio*).   1959.
Teatro (3 vols.).   1970–71.
Dos dramas de poder, amor y desamor (includes *Tito y Berenice*; *David y Jonatán*).   1970.

Stage Works

El hombre y sus sueños.   In *Asomante*, vol.4 no.2, 1948; in book form, in *Teatro 2*, 1971.

Palm Sunday (produced San Juan, 1956).   1949.

El sol y los MacDonald (produced Teatro de la Universidad de San Juan, 1950).   In *Asomante*, vol.13 no.1, 1957; in book form, in *Teatro 2*, 1971.

La carreta (produced New York, 1953; produced San Juan, 1954).   In *Asomante*, vol.7 no.4, 1951; in book form, 1961; translated as *The Oxcart*, 1969.

Los inocentes y la huida a Egipto.   1956?

Juan Bobo y la dama del occidente (ballet scenario).   1956.

Los soles truncos (produced Festival de Teatro, San Juan, 1958).   In *Tecetro* and *Teatro puertorriqueño: Primer festival*, both 1959; translated as *The Fanlights*, in *The Modern Stage in Latin America: Six Plays*, edited by George Woodyard, 1971.

Un niño azul para esa sombra (produced Festival de Teatro, San Juan, 1960).   In *Teatro*, 1959.

La muerte no entrará en palacio.   In *Teatro*, 1959.

La casa sin reloj.   1962.

El apartamiento (produced Festival de Teatro, San Juan, 1964).   In *Teatro puertorriqueño: Séptimo festival*, 1965; single edition, 1971.

Mariana; o, El alba (produced Festival de Teatro, San Juan, 1965).   1966.

Sacrificio en el Monte Moriah.   1969.

David y Jonatán.   In *Dos dramas de poder, amor y desamor*, 1970.

Tito y Berenice.   In *Dos dramas de poder, amor y desamor*, 1970.

Carnaval afuera, carnaval adento.   1971.

Fiction

La metrópoli.   1952.

Otro día nuestro (stories).   1955.

La vispera del hombre.   1959.

En una ciudad llamada San Juan (stories).   1960.

Purificación en la calle del Cristo (story).   With *Los soles truncos*, 1963.

Verse

Peregrinación.   1944.

Other

Ensayos 1953–1966.   1966; as *"El puertorriqueño dócil" y otras ensayos*, 1971; revised and augmented edition, as *Ensayos 1953–1971.*

Via crucis del hombre puertorriqueño ("oratorio").   1971.

Editor, *Cuentos puertorriqueños de hoy*.   1959.

*

Bibliographies

Amilcar Tirado and Nélida Pérez, *René Marqués 1919–1979*, New York, 1986.

Criticism

Books:
Jordan B. Phillips, *Thirty Years of Puerto Rican Drama 1938–1968*, Madrid, 1971; as *Contemporary Puerto Rican Drama*, New York, 1972.

Tamara Holzapfel, "The Theater of René Marqués: In Search of Identity and Form", in *Dramatists in Revolt*, edited by George Woodyard and Leon F. Lyday, Austin, Texas, 1976.

Eleanor J. Martin, *René Marqués*, Boston, 1979.

Bonnie H. Reynolds, "The Multiples of Reality in René Marqués' *El apartamiento*", in *Selected Proceedings of the Mid-America Conference on Hispanic Literature*, Lincoln, Nebraska, 1986.

Ileana Diéguez Caballero, *Lo trágico en el teatro de René Marqués*, Havana, Cuba, 1985.

Bonnie H. Reynolds, *Space, Time and Crisis: The Theatre of René Marqués*, York, South Carolina, 1988.

Articles:
Frank N. Dousler, "The Theater of Rosé Marqués", in *Symposium*, vol. 18 no.1, 1964.

Donald L. Shaw, "René Marqués' *La muerte no entrará en palacio*: An Analysis", in *Latin American Theatre Review*, 2, 1968.

Angel M. Aguirre, "René Marqués and the Struggle of the Puerto Rican Theatre", in *Revista/Review interamericana*, 2, 1973.

William L. Siemens, "Assault on the Schizoid Wasteland: René Marqués' *El apartamiento*", in *Latin American Theatre Review*, 7, 1974.

Timothy Murad, "René Marqués' *Juan Bobo y la dama de occidente*: Folklore as Pantomime and the Art of Cultural Affirmation", in *Revista Chicano-Riqueña*, vol.7 no.4, 1979.

Julia O. Griffin, "The Puerto Rican Woman in René Marqués' Drama", in *Revista chicano-requeña*, 2, 1983.

Bonnie H. Reynolds, "Cotaneity: A Sign of Crisis in *Un niño azul para esa sombra*" in *Latin American Theatre Review*, 17, 1983.

Bonnie H. Reynolds, "*La carreta*: Virtual Space and Broken Rhythm", in *Critica hispánica*, 7, 1985.

*   *   *

A prolific writer, René Marqués is most recognized for his contributions to the theatre in his native Puerto Rico. He was responsible for introducing to Puerto Rico the newest authors and theatrical innovations of his time from both Europe and the United States: he was especially interested in Pirandello, Chekhov, Proust, Kafka, O'Neill, and Tennessee Williams, in the existential philosophies of Camus, Sartre, and Heidegger, and in the writings of Miguel de Unamuno. At the same time, he expressed political ideas in his own plays that sparked antagonism on the one hand, and a dedicated following on the other.

Marqués was associated with the "Generation of the Forties" (his own phrase) in Puerto Rico's literary history. The authors of this generation continued the impulse of the writers of the 1930's who had attempted the revalorization of Puerto Rican identity in the face of the traditional literary dependence on Spain and the encroaching presence of the United States in Puerto Rico's culture, economy, and politics. Marqués was particularly concerned about what he believed to be the erosion of Puerto Rican cultural values as a result of

US influence and his countrymen's reluctance, or failure, to defend their cultural identity (his concept of the "docile Puerto Rican"). He was also critical of the lack of freedom both of Puerto Rico as a nation, and of Puerto Ricans as individuals—the results, Marqués believed, of Puerto Rico becoming an *estado libre asociado* (free associated state) of the United States in 1953.

Marqués' insistence on the freedom—both political and personal—of the Puerto Rican people is overtly expressed in the majority of his plays. Almost all of his characters suffer crises in which their way of life is threatened by some more powerful force, resulting in their struggle to maintain, find, or acknowledge their national and individual identity within a culture under stress. That threat is associated directly or indirectly with the United States' presence in Puerto Rican life. The resolutions of these dramatic crises show the injustice of the system and the individual's complicity in maintaining it by virtue of inaction, which always leads to disaster.

Marqués combines the elements of real stage space—the set, lights, colors, sounds, props—to create a virtual space whose architectural ambience is at the heart of the crisis dramatized. Each play's created space is a form of family living quarters, reflecting the conscious or subconscious states of mind of the principal characters, which offers protection from outside threats; they are thus escapist worlds that symbolize the self-condemnation of the indiviudals confined to them.

Time serves to heighten the urgency of the major conflicts, occasionally becoming a powerful antagonistic element. The longer the characters procrastinate, the more relentlessly time passes until it is transformed into an uncontrollable, life-destroying force. Time manifests itself in various ways: Marqués often toys with his spectator through the use of the cinematic flashback or the creation of a temporal universality in which past, present, and future co-exist. In addition, history, manifested as actual or fictionalized events, always influences the present of the characters.

Marqués', characters usually face a struggle between the fear of losing personal security and the desire for the freedom of dignity and self-respect. In *Un niño azul para esa sombre* (A Blue Boy for That Shadow) and *Los soles truncos* (The Fanlights) past, present and future coexist—in the former, in the innermost consciousness of the child protagonist, Michelin, and in the second, within the family home and the interpersonal relationships of the three Burkhart sisters. In these two plays, a final forced confrontation with the limits of space and time results in the characters' suicide. However, the acts of suicide are themselves to be seen as neutral, and the choice made less important than the fact of having taken a stand.

The crises arising in *La carreta (The Oxcart)* and *Carnaval afuera, carnaval adento* (Carnival Outside, Carnival Inside) are signposted by the use of rhythm. The first play begins with the slow, peaceful life of the country, represented by the sound of the oxcart, and develops into the fragmented, non-rhythmic noise of city life, represented by a jackhammer, corresponding to the ultimate breakdown of the protagonist's family. The rhythm of "Carnaval Outside, Carnival Inside" reflects the chaos of carnival superimposed upon the tranquility that the artist's name, Angel, suggests. This rhythmic conflict is mirrored in the characters' speeches and actions and in the stage set, a colonial house whose features are covered, but not totally hidden, by trite, contemporary decor. The title indicates that the conflict is also spatial, with the "outside" being the actual carnival in which participants are masked, and the "inside" being the individual's disguising of his/her hypocritical motivations.

The historical space of the past plays a key role in *La muerte no entrará en palacio* (Death Will Not Enter the Palace) and *Mariana; o, El alba* (Mariana or the Dawn). The first dramatizes Governor Muñoz Marin's 1953 signing of the Commonwealth agreement with the USA, surrounding that occasion with an aura of myth and immortality. The well-known events are fictionalized, as the famous and popular governor is murdered by his own daughter before he is able to sign the agreement. The palace, where the play takes place—in fact, the official residence of the governor of Puerto Rico—is transformed into a figurative prison, and the assassination in this famous space leaves the spectator to cope with Marqués' rewriting of history.

In "Mariana or the Dawn" the history recreated is faithful in detail, but the historical space and events are unfamiliar to the audience (or were at the time of the play's writing). The play emphasizes the experience of time through waiting: the characters wait for the unsuccessful revolution and Mariana's stillborn child; at play's end, the audience finds itself uncomfortably charged with initiating the unfulfilled revolution. Thus, past, present, and future are again fused in Marqués' stage world.

Marqués' characters, always held accountable for their own actions, play out their dramas within their living quarters, from which they may not or will not leave. In *El apartamiento* (The Apartment) and *La casa sin reloj* (The House Without a Clock), the characters are trapped because of their own fear of exposing themselves to the unknown. In each case, the result of this fear is either the fragmentation, but co-existence, of past, present, and future within the space that the characters inhabit, as in "The Apartment", or the futile attempt to suppress time, as in "The House Without a Clock". In both, the characters' ways of resolving their dilemma imply the necessity of making choices and expressing one's true feelings in today's world rather than opting for self-repression and greater security.

Sacrificio en el Monte Moriah (Sacrifice on Mount Moriah) and the unperformed twin plays, *David y Jonatán* (David and Jonathan), and *Tito y Berenice* (Tito and Berenice), treat space and time quite differently, but the crises themselves follow a pattern comparable to that of the other plays. The times and spaces dramatized are from a remote biblical past, and only the stories themselves are familiar. Abraham, the protagonist of "Sacrifice on Mount Moriah", epitomizes the "docility" of which Marqués accuses his own countrymen. Abraham's thirst for material comforts and security result in the victimization of Sara and Isaac. As the scenes shift between one stage space and another, almost cinematically, Marqués makes explicit the message that submitting to the materialistic values of a more powerful society leads to the violent destruction of humanistic values.

Events in the twin plays are presented in short, impressionistic scenes, with very few details, and flashbacks reveal the characters' motives that led to earlier scenes. In all three plays there are structural parallels between the dramatized events and Puerto Rico's political and economic relationship to the United States.

While he has received much praise and many awards from his countrymen, as well as from critics in the United States and other countries, Marqués has also been the object of a controversy that continues to influence Puerto Rico's writers and critics of the present, revolving around his portrayal of the "docile" Puerto Rican. Many writers and critics, especially those who support US statehood for the island, resent such ideas, resulting in the polarization of Puerto Rican theatre professionals and critics. Despite, or perhaps because of, this conflict, Marqués' work continues to influence Puerto

Rico's intellectual circles; he created a body of plays that has helped to define dramaturgy in Puerto Rico as well as in other parts of the Hispanic world, including the Hispanic community in the country he saw as one of his principal antagonists—the USA.

—Bonnie Hildebrand Reynolds

See also *Volume 1* entry on *Los soles truncos*.

MARSTON, John. Born in Wardlington, Oxfordshire, England; baptized 7 October 1576. Educated at Brasenose College, Oxford, 1592–94, BA 1594; member of the Middle Temple, London, 1592–1608. Married Mary Wilkes in 1605; one son. Wrote plays for Children of St. Paul's company, 1600–01, then for Children of the Queen's Revels at Blackfriars; manager, Queen's Revels company, after 1604; imprisoned in Newgate for unknown reasons, 1608; studied for the priesthood at St. Mary's College, Oxford, 1609: ordained, 1609; curate, Barford St. Martin, Wiltshire, 1610; rector of Christchurch, Hampshire, 1616–31 (resigned); thereafter lived in London. Died in London, 25 June 1634.

Works

Collections

Works. 1633; as *Tragedies and Comedies*, 1633.
Works, edited by A.H. Bullen (3 vols.). 1887.
Plays, edited by H. Harvey Wood (3 vols.). 1934–39.
Selected Plays (*Antonio and Mellida; Antonio's Revenge; The Malcontent; The Dutch Courtesan; Sophonisba*), edited by MacDonald P. Jackson and Michael Neill. 1986.

Stage Works

Histriomastix; or, The Player Whipped, possibly not by Marston, from an anonymous play (produced by the Children of St Paul's, London, 1599). 1610.
Antonio and Mellida, part 1 (produced by the Children of St Paul's, London, 1600). 1602.
Antonio's Revenge (part 2 of *Antonio and Mellida*; produced by the Children of St Paul's, London, 1600). 1602.
Jack Drum's Entertainment; or, The Comedy of Pasquill and Katherine (produced by the Children of St Paul's, London, 1600). 1601.
What You Will (produced by the Children of St Paul's, London, 1601?). 1607.
Satiromastix, with Thomas Dekker, or by Dekker alone (produced by the Children of St Paul's, London, c.1600). 1602.
The Malcontent (produced by the Children of the Queen's Revels, Blackfriars Theatre, London, 1602–03?). 1604.
The Dutch Courtesan (produced by the Children of the Queen's Revels, Blackfriars Theatre, London, 1604–05?). 1605,
Parasitaster; or, The Fawn (produced by the Children of the Queen's Revels, Blackfriars Theatre, London, 1604–05?). 1606,
Eastward Ho, with Chapman and Jonson (produced by the Children of the Queen's Revels, Blackfriars Theatre, London, 1605). 1605.
The Wonder of Women; or, The Tragedy of Sophonisba (produced by the Children of the Queen's Revels, Blackfriars Theatre, London, 1606). 1606.
The Honorable Lord and Lady of Huntingdon's Entertainment at Ashby (produced Ashby, Derbyshire, 1607). In *Works*, 1887.
The Insatiate Countess, completed by William Barksted (produced Whitefriars Theatre, London, 1610?). 1613.

Verse

The Metamorphosis of Pygmalion's Image, and Certain Satires. 1598.
The Scourge of Villainy: Three Books of Satires. 1598; revised edition, 1599.
Poems, edited by Arnold Davenport. 1961.

*

Bibliographies

S.A. Tannenbaum, *John Marston: A Concise Bibliography*, New York, 1940; supplement in *Elizabethan Bibliographies 4*, by C.A. Pennel and W.P. Williams, 1968.
Kenneth Tucker, *John Marston: A Reference Guide*, Boston, 1985.

Criticism

Books:
A.J. Axelrod, *Un Malcontent élizabéthain: John Marston*, Paris, 1955.
E. Egli, *John Marstons Dramen*, Winterthur, 1956.
Anthony Caputi, *John Marston, Satirist*, Ithaca, New York, 1961.
Brian Gibbons, *Jacobean City Comedy*, Cambridge, 1968.
P.J. Finkelpearl, *John Marston of the Middle Temple: An Elizabethan Dramatist in His Social Setting*, Cambridge, Massachusetts, 1969.
John Scott Colley, *John Marston's Theatrical Drama*, Salzburg, 1974.
R.W. Ingram, *John Marston*, Boston, 1978.
Michael Scott, *John Marston's Plays: Theme, Structure, and Performance*, London, 1978.
Ejner J. Jensen, *John Marston, Dramatist: Themes and Imagery*, Salzburg, 1979.
George L. Geckle, *John Marston's Drama: Themes, Images, Sources*, Rutherford, New Jersey, 1980.

* * *

Even if no biographical information had survived, we would probably be able to deduce from his texts alone that John Marston wrote to serve the tastes of a theatrical coterie at a very particular period—Marston's theatrical career spanned only about seven years. The plays often begin with inductions that make explicit the conventions of the action that is to follow so that, by implication, they "deconstruct" the art that had produced the great heroic plays of the English Renaissance, as in *Antonio and Mellida*:

    Alberto: Whom do you personate?
    Piero: Piero, Duke of Venice.
    Alberto: O, ho; then thus frame your exterior shape
               To haughty form of elate majesty
               As if you held the palsy-shaking head
               Of reeling Chance under your fortune's belt
               In strictest vassalage; grow big in thought
               As swoll'n with glory of successful arms.

The diction is mannered, often Latinate, proclaiming its allegiance to the epic dramas written by Kyd and Marlowe a few years before; the players—here boys, the Children of Paul's—are creating a kind of theatrical response that disinvites the suspension of disbelief, and which is not dissimilar from the conventions of a modern pantomime. The aim of those writing in the Italianate Senecan tradition was to evoke admiration or wonder in the audience: wonder, in Marston, is always punctuated with wit, and the author might have been exploiting the discrepancy between the stature of the boy actors and the status of the parts they played. (The theatrical nature of the entertainments in these playhouses were brought out further by the habit of playing music between the acts.)

Perhaps the style is a house-style: Marston, writing for the Paul's company, and Jonson, writing for the Children of the Chapel, satirized each other on stage during what Dekker called the "poetomachia", the so-called "War of the Theatres". (Marston pilloried Jonson as Brabant Senior in *Jack Drum's Entertainment* and as Lampatho Doria in *What You Will*, and Marston was probably the original for Hedon, a "light voluptuous reveller", in Jonson's *Cynthia's Revels*.) The playhouses were small, the audiences drawn from a narrow band in the social spectrum, their members presumably well known to each other. Sometimes the texts tilt towards parody; more often (as in the quotation from Antonio and Mellida), conventional styles are deliberately defamiliarized in order that the strange may be revealed as the true. Spectators may have come largely from the Inns of Court that were situated near the playhouse. The plays, like those of so many of Marston's contemporaries, tend to centre on Court intrigue, and it was to the Court, increasingly the centre of power, that these young lawyers were professionally drawn, even if they knew that it was at the Court that political corruption and social vice tended to thrive. The plays, therefore, open on to "life" as well as "art", and this particular combination of parody and satire (Marston also wrote rough and snarling satirical poems) may be thought of as a species of pastiche, the reinvigorating of an outworn convention deployed in the investigation of new fashions of behaviour.

Marston's plays were, despite their fustian language and infusions of grotesquerie, always criticisms of life. *Histriomastix*, his first play, which was written for the Christmas revels of the Middle Temple, is in form an old-fashioned morality play with each of the six acts being presided over by an allegorical genius: Peace, Plenty, Pride, Envy, War, and Poverty. It also claims for the poet a noble mission to bring truth to light. Later, in *What You Will*, we hear speeches ringing out from the play against extravagance in apparel and the deceptiveness of appearances that seem to derive from an almost Augustinian view of the vanity of this world and the fallen nature of man.

Marston's masterpiece, *The Malcontent*, first performed by the boys' company at the Blackfriars Theatre (to which Marston had transferred his allegiance) and later played by the adults of the King's Men, is a prime example of this kind of pastiche, taking its theme of court corruption and revenge from Shakespeare's *Hamlet*. It has a dispossessed ruler, Altofronto, who returns to his court physically disguised as a kind of court jester or railer, Malevole: ". . . In night all creatures sleep;/Only the malcontent, that 'gainst his fate/Repines and quarrels—alas, he's goodman tell-clock". (Marston uses the device of the disguised ruler commenting on the corruption of his kingdom again in a later play, *The Fawn*.)

Malevole's style is witty and scabrous, and he is obviously as at home among the bawds and Machiavels of the new regime as among the "nobles". He seems to have adopted a mask for disguise, but, as in the celebrated mime of Marcel Marceau, in which the artist tries to remove an imagined comic mask which seems to have become stuck, the role takes over the personality, the grimace becomes fixed. The play deals therefore, like *Hamlet* and like Jonson's *Every Man Out of His Humour*, with contradictions in behaviour that point to divisions in personality. Structurally the play is a kind of tragicomedy, but it stands out as being as important for its texture as its structure, a feast of language in a mannerist mode that yet has something to say about psychological realities.

The women in Marston's plays, more than usually in the period, seem to cater for an undergraduate male sensibility. They are triumphant in their constancy (see, for example, Sophonisba, the heroine of Marston's tragedy of that name) or they are arrant whores, their virtues depending entirely upon their sexuality. *The Dutch Courtesan* parades such prejudices and offers a gallery of Italianate sexual *roués* and degenerates that threatens to overwhelm the romantic plot which attempts some serious debate between, for example, Freevill, a libertine, and Malheureux, who stands for orthodox morality.

—Michael Hattaway

See also *Volume 1* entries on *Eastward Ho!*; *The Malcontent*.

MARTYN, Edward (Joseph). Born at Tulira, in Ardrahan, County Galway, Ireland, 30 January 1859. Educated at Beaumont College, London, 1870–77; Christ Church, Oxford, 1877–79. Lived at his family home, Tulira, County Galway, in the 1880's; co-founder, with Lady Gregory, George Moore, and William Butler Yeats, Irish Literary Theatre, 1897: resigned after quarrel with Yeats, 1902; first-produced play, *The Heather Field*, staged 1899; founder, Palestrina Society, Dublin, 1901; president, Sinn Fein (Irish republican political movement), 1904–08; helped organize the Theatre of Ireland, 1906; founded the Irish Theatre, to present plays in Gaelic, 1914. Died in Tulira, 5 December 1923.

Works

Stage Works

The Heather Field (produced Ancient Concert Rooms, Dublin, 1899). With *Maeve*, 1899.
Maeve (produced Gaiety Theatre, Dublin, 1900). With *The Heather Field*, 1899.
An Enchanted Sea (produced Ancient Concert Rooms, Dublin, 1904). With *The Tale of a Town*, 1902.
The Tale of a Town (produced Molesworth Hall, Dublin, 1905). With *An Enchanted Sea*, 1902.
The Place-Hunters. In *Leader*, 26 July 1902.
Romulus and Remus. In *Irish People*, 21 December 1907.
Grangecolman (produced Abbey Theatre, Dublin, 1912). 1912.
The Dream Physician (produced Dublin, 1914). 1914.
Privilege of Place (produced Hardwick Street Hall, Dublin, 1915).
Regina Eyre (produced Irish Theatre, Dublin, 1919).

Fiction

Morgante the Lesser: His Notorious Life and Wonderful Deeds. 1890.

*

Criticism

Books:
Denis Gwynn, *Edward Martyn and the Irish Revival*, London, 1930.
Marie-Therese Courtney, *Edward Martyn and the Irish Theatre*, New York, 1956.
Jan Setterquist, *Ibsen and the Beginnings of Anglo-Irish Drama 2*, New York, 1960.
Wayne E. Hall, *Shadowy Heroes: Irish Literature of the 1890s*, Syracuse, New York, 1980.

* * *

"He is like Ireland, the country he came from; sometimes a muddling fog; sometimes a delicious mist with a ray of light striking through", wrote George Moore in his slightly malicious satire of "dear Edward" in *Hail and Farewell*.

Martyn was a paradoxical character, descended from the Norman invaders under Strongbow, his ancestors being among the few Catholic landowners exempted from the confiscation of their estates. Educated by the Jesuits in Ireland, and at Christchurch, Oxford, he remained an ardent Catholic in the European tradition throughout his life. He was a misogynist and a gourmet, a supporter of the Gaelic League and the Sinn Fein movement, of which he became the first president; at the same time he was a member of the almost exclusively Protestant Kildare Street Club. He made a major contribution to the birth of the Irish dramatic movement by founding the Irish Literary Theatre together with Yeats, Lady Gregory and George Moore in 1899.

Martyn travelled widely in Europe and developed a deep interest in Russian and Scandinavian theatre, especially the plays of Ibsen. It was the Norwegian playwright's influence that coloured his whole approach to drama. Unfortunately his attempts to infuse the spirit of Ibsen into his plays was not matched by his own dramatic ability. His plays, like his life, show a mass of conflicting tendencies. The action is static, the endings melodramatic, the dialogue stilted, the characters too often stereotypes of his personal obsessions and prejudices. Yet for all his shortcomings, Martyn showed the possibilities of a new kind of drama, a drama both Irish and cosmopolitan which was never fully understood by Yeats and effectively rejected by Lady Gregory and Synge. Among his many contributions to Ireland he should be remembered as the first person to call for a national theatre and a state-aided school of acting.

His best plays are *The Heather Field* and *Maeve*. *The Heather Field* was produced in combination with Yeats's play *The Countess Cathleen* in the first season of the Irish Literary Theatre in 1899. It was generally held to be the better play of the two, through some critics considered its reflexion of Irish life was not convincing. The central theme is the clash between dream and reality.

Carden Tyrrell, a west of Ireland landlord, is obsessed with the dream of restoring the heather field of his barren mountain to fertility. For him it is a symbol of the regeneration of Ireland's rural prosperity to which he is determined to dedicate his life and fortune, despite his wife's efforts to have him certified as insane. His efforts to drain the mountainside result in flooding, provoking the anger of his tenants. They threaten to shoot him when he refuses their demand for a reduction of their rents. Carden, whose whole life depends upon his communication with nature, finds himself a prisoner in his own house. His reason begins to desert him when his debtors close in on him. For a brief moment he believes his task has succeeded and the heather field is conquered; but reality breaks in when his young son arrives with a bunch of heather buds, culled on the mountain. Carden is plunged into insanity. He has returned to his childhood happiness on the heather-covered mountain. It is a powerful theme and Martyn's best play. Its strength lies in the poetic intensity of Carden Tyrrell's belief in his mission to which, like Brand in Ibsen's play of that name, he is prepared to sacrifice wife and child.

Maeve, an adaptation of a novel by Martyn, is subtitled "a psychological drama". Once again, the scene is the west of Ireland, where an impoverished landlord seeks to restore his fortunes by marrying off his daughter, Maeve, to a wealthy Englishman. But Maeve has lost her heart to a mysterious lover from the legendary past who appears in her dreams. Seduced by the tales of her old nurse, she spends the night in search of Queen Maeve and her Court. Seated at her window looking out at the beauty of the frosty moonlit night, she falls into a trance in which she sees the Queen and her fairy retinue accompanied by her ghostly lover on their way to the Land of Youth. Maeve's spirit goes out to meet them and on the morning of her wedding day she is found lifeless at the open window.

Martyn's choice of subject might suggest he was more influenced by the mystic paintings of George Russell (Æ) or the early poetry of Yeats. In fact, the play follows closely the later symbolic dramas of Ibsen; of little Eyolf drawn magnetically to his death by the Rat Wife, or Brand haunted by Gerd and the Ice Church. Martyn's real strength lies in this strange union of reality and the supernatural, which he makes further use of in *An Enchanted Sea*. But in his attempts to follow in the Norwegian master's footsteps as a social playwright, notably in *Grangecolman* and his disastrous play, *The Tale of a Town*, which Moore rewrote under the title *The Bending of the Bough*, Martyn exposes his real weakness as a dramatist—his failure to achieve Ibsen's insight into character. As a result, his dialogue is impersonal—it expresses his own ideals and prejudices rather than those of real men and women.

It was the rejection of *The Tale of a Town* by Yeats and Moore that severed Martyn's connection with the new theatre movement inaugurated by the Literary Theatre (which was to blossom later into the Abbey Theatre). It could be said that had he remained as a leading light, his influence might have acted as a valuable corrective to the prevalent doctrine of folk drama and enlarged the whole scope of Irish theatre.

—Hugh Hunt

MASON, Bruce (Edward George). Born in Wellington, New Zealand, 28 September 1921. Educated at Takapuna Grammar School, Auckland; Wellington Boys' College; Victoria University College (now Victoria University of Wellington), BA 1945. Served in the New Zealand Army, 1941–43, Royal New Zealand Naval Volunteer Reserve,

1943–45: sub-lieutenant. Married Diana Manby Shaw in 1945; one son and two daughters. Research assistant, War History Branch, Wellington 1946–48; assistant curator of manuscripts. Alexander Turnbull Library, Wellington, 1948–49; travelled in Europe, 1949–51; public relations officer, New Zealand Forest Service, Wellington, 1951–57; radio critic, 1955–61, record critic, 1961–62, and music critic, 1964–69, *New Zealand Listener*, Wellington; senior journalist, Tourist and Publicity, Wellington, 1957–58; drama critic, *Dominion*, Wellington, 1958–60; editor, *Te Ao Hou* (Maori Affairs), Wellington, 1960–61; editor, *Act*, Wellington, 1967–70; senior copywriter, Wood and Mitchell Advertising, Wellington. 1969–71. President, secretary and committee member, Unity Theatre, Wellington, 1948–60; first plays produced 1953; New Zealand delegate, International Drama Conference, Edinburgh, 1963. Full-time actor, producer, and director: directed first productions of most of his own plays, operas for the New Zealand Opera Company, and revues for the Unity Theatre and Downstage, Wellington. Recipient: British Drama League Prize, five times; Auckland Festival Prize, 1958. D.Litt: Victoria University of Wellington, 1977. CBE (Commander, Order of the British Empire), 1980. Died 31 December 1982.

Works

Collections

Bruce Mason Solo (includes *The End of the Golden Weather; To Russia, With Love; Not Christmas, But Guy Fawkes; Courting Blackbird*). 1981.
The Healing Arch (includes *Hongi; The Pohutukawa Tree; The Hand on the Rail; Swan Song; Awatea*). 1987.

Stage Works

The Bonds of Love (produced Unity Theatre, Wellington, 1953).
The Evening Paper (produced Unity Theatre, Wellington, 1953).
The Light Enlarging (produced Unity Theatre, Wellington, 1953).
The Licensed Victualler, music by Mason (produced Unity Theatre, Wellington, 1954).
The Verdict (produced Unity Theatre, Wellington, 1955).
Wit's End (revue; produced Unity Theatre, Wellington, 1956).
A Case in Point (produced Unity Theatre, Wellington, 1957).
The Pohutukawa Tree (produced New Zealand Players' Theatre Workshop, Wellington, 1957). 1960; revised version, 1985.
Birds in the Wilderness (produced Auckland, 1958).
The End of the Golden Weather (produced Wellington, 1959). 1962.
We Don't Want Your Sort Here, music by Mason (cabaret; produced Wellington, 1961). 1963.
The Counsels of the Wood (produced Downstage Theatre, Wellington, 1965).
The Hand on the Rail (produced Wellington, 1965). In *The Healing Arch*, 1987.
Swan Song (produced Wellington, 1965). In *The Healing Arch*, 1987.
The Waters of Silence, from a work by Vercors (produced Wellington, 1965).
To Russia with Love (produced Wellington, 1965). In *Bruce Mason Solo*, 1981.

Awatea, from the radio play (produced 1968). 1969; revised version, 1978.
Hongi, from the radio play (produced 1971). In *Contemporary New Zealand Plays*, edited by Howard McNaughton, 1974.
Zero Inn (produced Christchurch, 1970). 1970.
Not Christmas, But Guy Fawkes (produced Rotorua, New Zealand, 1976). In *Bruce Mason Solo*, 1981.
Courting Blackbird (produced Christchurch, 1976). In *Bruce Mason Solo*, 1981.
Blood of the Lamb; or, Cosi fan Poche: A Three-Part Invention in Homage to W.A. Mozart and G.B. Shaw (produced Court Theatre, Christchurch, 1980). 1981.

Television Plays

The Garlick and Thrust, 1983; *Daphne and Chloe*, 1983; *Do Not Go Gentle*, 1983.

Radio Plays

The Cherry Orchard, from a play by Chekhov, 1960; *Awatea*, 1965; *Hongi*, 1968.

Other

Theatre in Danger: A Correspondence with John Pocock. 1957.
New Zealand Drama: A Parade of Forms and a History. 1973.
Every Kind of Weather, edited by David Dowling. 1986.

*

Criticism

Books:
Howard McNaughton, *Bruce Mason*, Wellington, 1976.
David Dowling, *Introducing Bruce Mason*, Auckland, 1982.
J. Thomson, *New Zealand Drama 1930–1980*, Auckland, 1984.

*   *   *

Bruce Mason was enormously influential in New Zealand, possibly less for his plays themselves than because he was the first New Zealand professional writer for whom playwriting was the preferred genre. He crusaded for the role of drama (and his own plays in particular) and against philistinism in all its forms, in a society he saw as still defining its own identity. He was a vulnerable writer, full of the joy of creativity, but impelled to demand the recognition and praise he was afraid might not otherwise be forthcoming.

The plays do command respect in their own right, however, despite flaws, for Mason had a fine ear for the idiosyncrasies of New Zealand speech, a wickedly satirical bent (in the service of a deep belief in the value of cultural expression), and a concern for relations between Maori and pakeha (non-Maori, European) that provided major thematic challenges. He also brought, as a gifted solo performer, an experience of live theatre to even the smallest New Zealand towns and communities.

Mason was already known as a short-story writer when he started writing realist one-act plays for British Drama League festivals in New Zealand in the early 1950's, and for Wellington's Unity Theatre. (Unity was based on the left-wing Unity Theatre in London, which Mason had visited on leave during World War II. He also managed during this period to discuss his writing ambitions with both J.B. Priestley and Bertolt Brecht.) These early plays of "social significance" combine cruel satire with a pessimistic, and even sordid, portrayal of grey, ordinary lives, and resulted in some hostile criticism of a dramatist who dared to portray "God's Own Country" in such an unflattering light. The reaction when *The Evening Paper* was broadcast on New Zealand television in 1965, more than ten years after its first stage presentation, was even more virulent: he had "besmirched the name of this fair land", wrote one correspondent, and apparently, had insulted New Zealand womanhood.

Mason's full-length plays, particularly *The Pohutukawa Tree* and *Awatea*, adopted a similarly critical stance, but now turned to the bi-racial nature of New Zealand society. Mason found in Maori culture a rhetorical richness and ritual that appealed to the musician and opera-lover in him. (The central role in *Awatea* was written for the great Maori bass Inia Te Wiata.) While the still-very-British-Pakeha society could be realistically or satirically portrayed as inarticulate, dull, and uncultured, his Maori characters were given magnificent speeches in both English and Maori, as well as ritual songs and chants. His treatment of the Maori issues seems slightly condescending now, tinged as it is by myths of the "noble savage" and colonial "fatal impact"; and even at the time he was criticized for lack of authenticity. Mason was the first dramatist, however, to tackle Maori-Pakeha relations in a serious way, and to write central roles for Maori actors. With a grand, rather old-fashioned romantic dramaturgy, the tragedies of his protagonists in these two plays (both Maori elders who have, ironically, embraced pakeha values) are sufficiently complex and vital to avoid any charge of easy stereotyping. Furthermore, the plays have an immense power in the theatre.

This concern with Maori themes continued in a series of plays first conceived for radio. (Most were subsequently rewritten for the stage as well.) Radio writing was one of the few avenues open after the collapse, in 1960, of New Zealand's only professional theatre company. Solo performance was another alternative for a playwright in a society with no professional theatre. Mason had seen Emlyn Williams' readings of Dickens, and used them as a model. In *The End of the Golden Weather*, he created a 12-year-old boy viewing the adult world through the last vestiges of childhood innocence during the summer Christmas holiday at the beach. Mason's acting skill, rich rhetoric, and gift for mimicry made this a surprisingly theatrical performance. He gave voices to over 40 characters, and avoided sentimentality by adding the ironic persona of an adult narrator who described the Mason-like boy in the third person. Even here, however, in a fundamentally warm and often comic nostalgia, the recurrent themes are evident: the casual destruction of sensitivity, aspiration, and individuality by bland mediocrity and ignorant conformism.

Throughout the 1960's and 1970's, at the same time that he was writing and touring various solo works (nearly 2,000 performances in all), he was also actively engaged in editing and journalism. Particularly important was his role as drama critic in Wellington, a role he performed with pugnacious and grandiloquent pleasure. He championed the work of new New Zealand playwrights with great generosity (if seldom with equivalent modesty about his own role), and worked energetically to support the development of Wellington's new professional theatre. He also founded and edited an important theatre magazine.

When facial cancer ended his solo performances in the late 1970's, he returned once more to writing for the now firmly established professional theatres, with *Blood of the Lamb*. This play (written like virtually all the others with specific production circumstances in mind—in this case, three actresses and a tiny studio theatre) is about two lesbian women bringing up a daughter who now demands to know the truth about her parentage. Again, the structure is operatic (it is subtitled, "Cosi Fan Poche: A Three Part Invention in Homage to W.A. Mozart and G.B. Shaw"), and the themes are those of intolerance (particularly male, but including Maori; the "noble savage" is specifically disowned), materialism (including some gruesome images of the bloodletting on which New Zealand's agricultural prosperity is based), and the joys of learning and high culture.

Bruce Mason's final writing was for television. Three dramas were broadcast after his death, and revealed a dramatist developing new skills and insights even as he was dying.

—David Carnegie

See also *Volume 1* entry on *The Pohutukawa Tree*.

MASSINGER, Philip. Born in Salisbury, Wiltshire, England; baptized 24 November 1583. Educated at St. Alban Hall, Oxford, 1602–06, but did not take degree. Moved to London, 1606; collaborated as playwright with Nathan Field, Tourneur, Dekker, and regularly with Fletcher, 1613–25; imprisoned for debt, c.1613; wrote for the King's Men, 1613–23, and Christopher Beeston's companies at the Phoenix (or Cockpit) Theatre, Drury Lane, 1623–25; after Fletcher's death in 1625 rejoined the King's Men at the Blackfriars and Globe theatres as their chief writer. Probably wrote over 50 plays. Died (buried) in London, 18 March 1640.

Works

Collections

Three New Plays (includes *The Guardian; A Very Woman; The Bashful Lover*).   1633.
Comedies and Tragedies, by Beaumont and Fletcher (includes collaborative works).   1647.
The Dramatic Works in the Beaumont and Fletcher Canon (includes collaborative works), edited by Fredson Bowers.   1966–
Plays and Poems (5 vols.; excludes plays written in collaboration with Beaumont and Fletcher, except for *A Very Woman*), edited by Philip Edwards and Colin Gibson.   1976.
Selected Plays (includes *The Duke of Milan; The Roman Actor; A New Way to Pay Old Debts; The City Madam*), edited by Colin Gibson.   1978.

Stage Works

The Bloody Brother; or, Rollo, Duke of Normandy, with Fletcher, possibly also with Jonson (produced by the King's Men, London, c.1616).   1639.
The Queen of Corinth, Massinger's contribution uncertain;

Philip Massinger (engraving)

with Fletcher and possibly with Nathan Field (produced by the King's Men, Blackfriars Theatre, London, c.1616–18). In *Comedies and Tragedies* by Beaumont and Fletcher, 1647.

The Knight of Malta, with Fletcher and Nathan Field (produced by the King's Men, Blackfriars Theatre, London, c. 1616–19). In *Comedies and Tragedies* by Beaumont and Fletcher, 1647.

The Fatal Dowry, with Nathan Field (produced by the King's Men, London, 1617–19). 1632.

Sir John van Olden Barnavelt, with Fletcher (produced by the King's Men, London, 1619). Edited by A.H. Bullen, in *A Collection of Old English Plays 2*, 1883.

The Custom of the Country, with Fletcher (produced by the King's Men, Blackfriars Theatre, London, 1619–20?). In *Comedies and Tragedies* by Beaumont and Fletcher, 1647.

The Little French Lawyer, with Fletcher (produced by the King's Men, London, 1619–23). In *Comedies and Tragedies*, by Beaumont and Fletcher, 1647.

The False One, with Fletcher (produced by the King's Men, Blackfriars Theatre, London, 1619–23). In *Comedies and Tragedies* by Beaumont and Fletcher, 1647.

The Double Marriage, with Fletcher (produced by the King's Men, Blackfriars Theatre, London, 1619–23). In *Comedies and Tragedies* by Beaumont and Fletcher, 1647.

The Virgin Martyr, with Dekker (produced by the Red Bull Company, Red Bull Theatre, London, 1620). 1622.

Thierry, King of France, and His Brother Theodoret, with Beaumont and Fletcher (produced ?). 1621.

The Maid of Honour (produced by the Red Bull Company, Red Bull Theatre, London, 1621?). 1632.

The Duke of Milan (produced by the King's Men, Blackfriars Theatre, London, 1621–22). 1623.

The Spanish Curate, with Fletcher (produced by the King's Men, Blackfriars Theatre, London, 1622). In *Comedies and Tragedies* by Beaumont and Fletcher, 1647.

The Prophetess, with Fletcher (produced by the King's Men, Blackfriars Theatre, London, 1622). In *Comedies and Tragedies* by Beaumont and Fletcher, 1647.

The Sea Voyage, with Fletcher (produced by the King's Men, London, 1622). In *Comedies and Tragedies* by Beaumont and Fletcher, 1647.

The Beggars' Bush, with Fletcher (produced by the King's Men, 1622). In *Comedies and Tragedies* by Beaumont and Fletcher, 1647.

The Bondman: An Ancient Story (produced by Lady Elizabeth's Men, Cockpit/Phoenix Theatre, London, 1623). 1624.

The Parliament of Love (produced by Lady Elizabeth's Men, Cockpit/Phoenix Theatre, London, 1624). Edited by William Gifford, 1805.

The Renegado (produced by Lady Elizabeth's Men, Cockpit/Phoenix Theatre, London, 1624). 1630.

The Unnatural Combat (produced by the King's Men, London, 1624–25). 1639.

A New Way to Pay Old Debts (produced by Queen Henrietta's Men?, 1625?). 1633.

The Elder Brother, with Fletcher (produced by the King's Men, Blackfriars Theatre, London, 1625?). 1637.

The Fair Maid of the Inn, with Fletcher and others (produced by the King's Men, 1626). In *Comedies and Tragedies* by Beaumont and Fletcher, 1647.

The Roman Actor (produced by the King's Men, Blackfriars Theatre, London, 1626). 1629.

The Great Duke of Florence (produced by Queen Henrietta's Men, Cockpit/Phoenix Theatre, London, 1627). 1636.

The Picture (produced by the King's Men, Blackfriars Theatre?, London, 1629). 1630.

The Emperor of the East (produced by the King's Men, London, 1631). 1632.

Believe As You List (produced by the King's Men, London, 1631). Edited by T.C. Croaker, 1849.

The City Madam (produced by the King's Men, Blackfriars Theatre, London, 1632). 1658.

The Guardian (produced by the King's Men, Blackfriars Theatre, London, 1633). In *Three New Plays*, 1655.

Cleander, revised version of *The Lovers' Progress* by Fletcher (produced by the King's Men, London, 1634). As *The Lovers' Progress*, in *Comedies and Tragedies* by Beaumont and Fletcher, 1647.

A Very Woman; or, The Prince of Tarent, with Fletcher (produced in a revised version, by the King's Men, London, 1634). In *Three New Plays*, 1655.

The Bashful Lover (produced by the King's Men, Blackfriars Theatre, London, 1636). In *Three New Plays*, 1655.

Love's Cure, by Beaumont and Fletcher, revised by Massinger (produced ?). In *Comedies and Tragedies*, 1647 by Beaumont and Fletcher.

*

Bibliographies

S.A. and Dorothy R. Tannenbaum, *Philip Massinger: A Concise Bibliography*, New York, 1938; supplement in

Elizabethan Bibliographies Supplements 8, by C.A. Pennell and W.P. Williams, 1968.

Criticism

Books:
Alfred H. Cruickshank, *Philip Massinger*, Oxford, 1920.
Maurice Chelli, *Le Drame de Massinger*, 1923.
T.A. Dunn, *Philip Massinger, The Man and the Playwright*, London, 1957.
Donald S. Lawless, *Philip Massinger and His Associates*, Muncie, Indiana, 1967.
F.D. Evenhuis, *Philip Massinger's Imagery*, Salzburg, 1973.
Bertha Hensman, *The Shares of Fletcher, Field, and Massinger in Twelve Plays of the Beaumont and Fletcher Canon* (2 vols.), Salzburg, 1974.
Martin Garrett, *A Diamond, Though Set in Horn: Philip Massinger's Attitude to Spectacle*, Salzburg, 1984.
Douglas Howard, *Philip Massinger: A Critical Reassessment*, Cambridge, 1985.
Martin Garrett (ed.), *Philip Massinger: The Critical Heritage*, London, 1990.

* * *

Although there have been recent revivals of his fine city comedy *The City Madam* and the tragedy *The Roman Actor*, Massinger is now known to the modern English and American theatre chiefly as the author of *A New Way to Pay Old Debts*, the comedy which has held the stage since its revival by Garrick in 1748, and has been given more performances than any but the most famous of Shakespeare's and Jonson's works.

These plays are the survivors from a prolific output, for Massinger's career as a dramatist lasted some 30 years, rising to a peak of success about 1634. Massinger began writing in collaboration before 1613, working particularly with John Fletcher, but also with with Daborne, Field, Dekker, and others to supply plays for the London manager Philip Henslowe and the King's Men as well as Christopher Beeston's companies at the Phoenix (or Cockpit) Theatre. In the 1620's he succeeded in establishing himself as an independent writer; in 1625 he replaced Fletcher as the chief dramatist for the King's Men, writing at least 18 plays for them during the next 14 years. It is now impossible to establish exactly how many plays he wrote, co-wrote, or revised, but it is certain that he became an unusually experienced and fully professional dramatist, and from 1625 until near his death in 1640 was the chief writer for the principal Caroline theatrical company.

As a team-writer, Massinger excelled in the exposition and conclusion of a multi-layered plot, occasionally writing up himself one of the narrative lines, but in general leaving his partners to develop the emotional implications and story complications of the material laid down in the first act. Although the majority of his surviving collaborations are with Fletcher, in plays like *The Little French Lawyer* or *The Elder Brother* there are obvious signs of different artistic temperaments somewhat uneasily yoked together. Fletcher's delight in dramatic artifice and his predilection for witty and roguish characters caught in the feather-weight complications of romance are answered by Massinger's more reflective interest in moral dilemmas of real gravity and painfulness, and in characters whose emotions often have a violent, primitive force, and whose apparent virtues and vices are subjected to strenuous testing both by accident and human design. Moral scrutiny is the crucial activity of Massinger's drama, as moral complexity rising out of natural human strength and weakness is the characterising mark of his vision of human life.

Both the history play and the masque lay outside his interests and imaginative range, but Massinger practised his art in the other major dramatic forms of his time—comedy (both romantic and city comedy), tragedy, and tragicomedy. For the independent plays and the collaborative works he drew plot material from his wide reading in classical and modern history, the ethical dilemmas proposed and debated in the Roman rhetorician Seneca's *controversiae*, Italian and Spanish fiction, and the plays of his English contemporaries, especially Shakespeare, Jonson, Marston, and Middleton. Despite the variety of imaginative contexts these source works provided (Ancient Rome, modern London, Renaissance Italy, France, Hungary, or the Algerian coast), like most artists Massinger worked out the potential of certain key story configurations and human situations through a number of plays, sometimes in similar language and with similar thematic concerns.

The corruption of political power through the weakness or tyranny of a ruler, the insidious influence of flatterers and favourites, the neglect of government and the defence of the realm; the threat to an established social order posed by unscrupulous ambition backed by wealth and commercial power; the disastrous effects of obsessive and unbalanced passion (shown equally in male and female lustfulness, uxoriousness, pride, and vengefulness); the sudden collapse of trust and integrity in the face of temptation or the triumph of long-suffering love and honour: these are some of Massinger's major thematic preoccupations. In his finest plays, what gives the dramatisation of such subjects, not uncommon in Jacobean and Caroline drama, a special forcefulness is the tension between the framework of traditional religious, moral, and humanist values that the plays presume, and the complex, ambivalent, and often ironic presentation of the realities of human behaviour. *The Roman Actor* argues the loftiest view of Massinger's own art as educational and corrective, but its plot demonstrates an equal power to corrupt and a radical failure to reform vice.

Massinger's achievement as a theatre poet has given rise to strikingly different opinions, reflected in his contemporaries' comments as well as in the evaluations of later poets like Coleridge, who praised it as "the nearest approach to the language of real life compatible with a fixed metre", and T.S. Eliot, who damned it as showing "the highest degree of verbal excellence compatible with the most rudimentary development of the senses". Massinger has been granted the colder rhetorical virtues of stateliness and eloquence, without sharing in the general modern admiration for the poetic language of the greatest Elizabethan and Stuart dramatists.

However, it is agreed that the Massingerian style is distinctive and distinguishable from that of his collaborators. Without attempting to recreate the dense figurative textures of his predecessors, he worked for the mutual reinforcement of verbal and stage images and their close co-operation in the representation of character, carefully deploying vocabulary, imagery, and scenic action to give powerful expression to the controlling ideas of each play. Harmony, dignity, and sententiousness are key elements in this dramatist's linguistic strategy, brought to a height in that austere tragedy *The Roman Actor*, but in both comedy and tragicomedy he aimed at extracting maximum theatrical effect from flexible language contrasts and variation. In a play such as *The City Madam*, Massinger brilliantly adjusted stylistic levels to discriminate between different social ranks and to differentiate modes of feeling and thought. As a result, the mode of speech of a Luke, an Overreach, a Sophia, or an Antiochus becomes highly individualised and memorable, like the voice of their sober and thoughtful creator.

—Colin Gibson

See also *Volume 1* entry on *A New Way to Pay Old Debts*.

————

MAUGHAM, W(illiam) Somerset. Born in Paris, of English parents, 25 January 1874. Educated at King's School, Canterbury, Kent, 1885–89; University of Heidelberg, 1891–92; studied medicine at St. Thomas's Hospital, London, 1892–97: intern in Lambeth, London; qualified as surgeon, LRCP, MRCS, 1897. Married the interior designer Syrie Barnardo Wellcome in 1917 (divorced 1927); one daughter. Accountant, briefly, 1892; writer from 1896; lived mainly in Paris, 1897–1907; first-produced play, *Marriages Are Made in Heaven*, produced in German, 1902; during World War I, served in a Red Cross ambulance unit in Flanders, 1914–15, and in the British Intelligence Corps, 1916–17; travelled widely from 1916: visited the South Seas, China, Malaya, and Mexico; lived at Villa Mauresque, Cap Ferrat, France, from 1928; lived in the USA during World War II; instituted annual prize for most promising young British writer, 1947. D.Litt: Oxford University, 1952; University of Toulouse. Fellow, and Companion of Literature, 1961, Royal Society of Literature. Commander, Legion of Honour; honorary senator, University of Heidelberg; honorary fellow, Library of Congress, Washington, DC; honorary member, American Academy of Arts and Letters. Companion of Honour, 1954. Died in Nice, France, 16 December 1965.

Works

Collections

Dramatic Works (6 vols.). 1931–34; as *Collected Plays* (3 vols.), 1952.
Six Comedies (includes *The Unattainable; Home and Beauty; The Circle; Our Betters; The Constant Wife; The Breadwinner*). 1937.

Stage Works

Marriages Are Made in Heaven (as *Schiffbrüchig*, produced Schall und Rauch, Berlin, 1902). In *The Venture Annual*, edited by Maugham and Laurence Housman, 1903.
A Man of Honour (produced Imperial Theatre, London, 1903). 1903.
Mademoiselle Zampa (produced Avenue Theatre, London, 1904).
Lady Frederick (produced Royal Court Theatre, London, 1907). 1911.
Jack Straw (produced Vaudeville Theatre, London, 1908). 1911.
Mrs. Dot (produced Comedy Theatre, London, 1908). 1912.
The Explorer: A Melodrama (produced Lyric Threatre, London, 1908; revised version produced 1909). 1912.
Penelope (produced Comedy Theatre, London, 1909). 1912.

The Noble Spaniard, from a work by Ernest Grenet-Dancourt (produced Royalty Theatre, London, 1909). 1953.
Smith (produced Comedy Theatre, London, 1909). 1913.
The Tenth Man: A Tragic Comedy (produced Globe Theatre, London, 1910). 1913.
Landed Gentry (as *Grace*, produced Duke of York's Theatre, London, 1910). 1913.
Loaves and Fishes (produced Duke of York's Theatre, London, 1911). 1924.
A Trip to Brighton, from a play by Abel Tarride (produced New Theatre, London, 1911).
The Perfect Gentleman, from a play by Molière (produced His Majesty's Theatre, London, 1913). In *Theatre Arts*, November 1955.
The Land of Promise (produced Hyperion Theatre, New Haven, Connecticut, 1913). 1913.
The Unattainable (as *Caroline*, produced New Theatre, London, 1916). 1923.
Our Betters (produced Nixon Theatre, Atlantic City, New Jersey, 1917). 1923.
Love in a Cottage (produced Globe Theatre, London, 1918).
Caesar's Wife (produced Royalty Theatre, London, 1919). 1922.
Home and Beauty (produced Booth Theatre, New York, 1919; as *Too Many Husbands*, produced Globe Theatre, Atlantic City, New Jersey, 1919). 1923.
The Unknown (produced Aldwych Theatre, London, 1920). 1920.
The Circle (produced Theatre Royal, Haymarket, London, 1921). 1921.
East of Suez (produced His Majesty's Theatre, London, 1922). 1922.
The Camel's Back (produced Worcester Theatre, Worcester, Massachusetts, 1923).
The Constant Wife (produced Ohio Theatre, Cleveland, Ohio, 1926). 1927.
The Letter, from his own story (produced Playhouse, London, 1927). 1927.
The Sacred Flame (produced Belasco Theatre, New York, 1928). 1928.
The Bread-Winner (produced Vaudeville Theatre, London, 1930). 1930.
For Services Rendered (produced Globe Theatre, London, 1932). 1932.
The Mask and the Face, from a play by Luigi Chiarelli (produced Colonial Theatre, Boston, Massachusetts, 1933).
Sheppey (produced Wyndham's Theatre, London, 1933). 1933.

Screenplays

The Verger, 1950 (published in *Trio*, with works by R.C. Sheriff and Noel Langley, 1950).

Fiction

Liza of Lambeth. 1897; revised edition, 1904.
The Making of a Saint. 1898.
Orientations (stories). 1899.
The Hero. 1901.
Mrs. Craddock. 1902.
The Merry-Go-Round. 1904.
The Bishop's Apron: A Study in the Origins of a Great Family. 1906.
The Explorer. 1907.
The Magician. 1908; with *A Fragment of Autobiography*, 1956.

Of Human Bondage.   1915.
The Moon and Sixpence.   1919.
The Trembling of the Leaf: Little Stories of the South Sea Islands.   1921; as *"Sadie Thompson" and Other Stories of the South Seas*, 1928; as *"Rain" and Other Stories*, 1933.
The Painted Veil.   1925.
The Casuarina Tree: Six Stories.   1926; as *The Letter: Stories of Crime*, 1930.
Ashenden; or, The British Agent.   1928.
Cakes and Ale; or, The Skeleton in the Cupboard.   1930.
Six Stories Written in the First Person Singular.   1931.
The Book-Bag.   1932.
The Narrow Corner.   1932.
Ah King: Six Stories.   1933.
The Judgement Seat (story).   1934.
East and West: Collected Short Stories.   1934; as *Altogether*, 1934.
Cosmopolitans (stories).   1936.
Favorite Short Stories.   1937.
Theatre.   1937.
Christmas Holiday.   1939.
The Mixture as Before: Short Stories.   1940 as *Great Stories of Love and Intrigue*, 1947.
Up at the Villa.   1941.
The Hour Before the Dawn.   1942.
The Unconquered (story).   1944.
The Razor's Edge.   1944.
Then and Now.   1946.
Creatures of Circumstance: Short Stories.   1947.
Catalina: A Romance.   1948.
East of Suez: Great Stories of the Tropics.   1948.
Here and There (stories).   1948.
Complete Short Stories (3 vols.).   1951.
The World Over: Stories of Manifold Places and People.   1952.
Selected Novels (3 vols.).   1953.
Best Short Stories, edited by John Beecroft.   1957.
A Maugham Twelve: Stories, edited by Angust Wilson.   1966; with *Cakes and Ale*, 1967.
Malaysian Stories, edited by Anthony Burgess.   1969.
Seventeen Lost Stories, edited by Craig V. Showalter.   1969.

Memoirs and Letters

Letters to Lady Juliet Duff, edited by Loren D. Rothschild.   1982.

Other

The Land of the Blessed Virgin: Sketches and Impressions of Andalusia.   1905.
On a Chinese Screen.   1922.
The Gentleman in the Parlour: A Record of a Journey from Rangoon to Haiphong.   1930.
The Non-Dramatic Works (28 vols.).   1934–69.
Don Fernando; or, Variations on Some Spanish Themes.   1935.
My South Sea Island.   1936.
The Summing Up.   1938.
Books and You.   1940.
France at War.   1940.
Strictly Personal.   1941.
The Maugham Sampler, edited by Jerome Weidman.   1943; as *The Maugham Pocket Book*, 1944.
Of Human Bondage, with a Digression on the Art of Fiction (address).   1946.
Great Novelists and Their Novels: Essays on the Ten Greatest Novels of the World and the Men and Women Who Wrote Them.   1948; revised edition, as *Ten Novels and Their Authors*, 1954; as *The Art of Fiction*, 1955.
A Writer's Notebook.   1949.
A Maugham Reader, edited by Glenway Wescott.   1950.
The Writer's Point of View (lecture).   1951.
The Vagrant Mood: Six Essays.   1952.
Mr. Maugham Himself, edited by John Beecroft.   1954.
The Partial View (includes *The Summing Up* and *A Writer's Notebook*).   1954.
Points of View.   1958; as *Points of View: Five Essays*, 1959.
Purely for My Pleasure.   1962.
Selected Prefaces and Introductions.   1963.
Wit and Wisdom, edited by Cecil Hewetson.   1966.
Essays on Literature.   1967.
A Traveller in Romance: Uncollected Writings 1901–1964, edited by John Whitehead.   1984.

Editor, with Laurence Housman, *The Venture Annual of Art and Literature* (2 vols.).   1903–04.
Editor, *The Truth at Last*, by Charles Hawtrey.   1924.
Editor, *The Travellers' Library.*   1933; as *Fifty Modern English Writers*, 1933.
Editor, *Tellers of Tales: 100 Short Stories from the United States, England, France, Russia, and Germany.*   1939; as *The Greatest Stories of All Times*, 1943.
Editor, *A Choice of Kipling's Prose.*   1952; as *Maugham's Choice of Kipling's Best: Sixteen Stories*, 1953.

*

Bibliographies

K.W. Jones, *A Bibliography of the Writings of W. Somerset Maugham*, Folcroft, Pennsylvania, 1950; revised edition, 1969.
Raymond Toole Scott, *A Bibliography of the Works of W. Somerset Maugham*, London, 1956, revised edition, London, 1973.
E.H. Mikhail, "Somerset Maugham and the Theater: A Selected Bibliography", in *Bulletin of Bibliography*, 27, 1970.
Charles Saunders, *Maugham: An Annotated Bibliography of Writings About Him*, DeKalb, Illinois, 1970; supplemented in *English Literature in Transition*, 15, 1972.

Criticism

Books:
P. Dottin, *Le Théâtre de William Somerset Maugham*, Paris, 1937.
R.H. Ward, *W. Somerset Maugham*, London, 1937.
Gertrud Savini, *Das Weltbild in William Somerset Maughams Dramen*, Erlangen, 1939.
J. Brophy, *W. Somerset Maugham*, London, 1952, revised edition, 1958.
K.W. Jonas (ed.), *The Maugham Enigma*, New York, 1954.
Raymond Mander and Joe Mitchenson, *Theatrical Companion to W. Somerset Maugham: A Pictorial Record of the First Performance of the Plays of Maugham*, New York, 1955.
K.W. Jonas (ed.), *The World of W. Somerset Maugham*, New York, 1959.
K.G. Pfeiffer, *W. Somerset Maugham: A Candid Portrait.* 1959.

Richard A. Cordell, *Somerset Maugham: A Biographical and Critical Study*, London, 1961; revised edition, Bloomington, Indiana, 1969.

Laurence Brander, *Somerset Maugham: A Guide*, Edinburgh and London, 1963.

Wilmon Menard, *The Two Worlds of Maugham*, New York, 1965.

Garson Kanin, *Remembering Mr. Maugham*, London and New York, 1966.

Robin Maugham, *Somerset and All the Maughams*, 1966.

M.K. Naik, *W. Somerset Maugham*, Norman, Oklahoma, 1966.

Beverley Nichols, *A Case of Human Bondage*, 1966.

Ronald E. Barnes, *The Lramatic Comedy of William Somerset Maugham*, The Hague, 1968.

Ivor Brown, *Maugham*, London, 1970.

Robert L. Calder, *W. Somerset Maugham and the Quest for Freedom*, London, 1972.

Anthony Curtis, *The Pattern of Maugham: A Critical Portrait*, London, 1974.

Anthony Curtis, *Somerset Maugham*, New York, 1977.

Frederic Raphael, *W. Somerset Maugham and His World*, London, 1976, revised edition, 1989.

Robin Maugham, *Conversations with William: Recollections of Somerset Maugham*, London, 1978.

Ted Morgan, *Somerset Maugham*, London, 1980.

Anthony Curtis and John Whitehead (eds.), *W. Somerset Maugham: The Critical Heritage*, London, 1987.

Archie K. Loss, *W. Somerset Maugham*, New York, 1987.

John Whitehead, *Maugham: A Critical Reappraisal*, London, 1987.

Robert L. Calder, *Willie: The Life of Somerset Maugham*, London, 1989.

Articles:

Christopher Innes, "Somerset Maugham: A Test Case for Popular Comedy", in *Modern Drama*, 30, 1987.

*   *   *

Maugham's success with his novel *Liza of Lambeth* confirmed him in his intention to pursue a literary career, rather than the one in medicine for which he had been trained. Possessed of a fluent pen, a brilliant sense of narrative, and a keen appreciation of how to engage the interest of readers, he quickly won a reputation as an engaging story-teller. But it was his work for the theatre that was to provide him with financial independence. After a rather tentative beginning with pieces like *Schiffbrüchig*, done in German in Berlin in 1902, and *A Man of Honour*, performed in London in 1903, he achieved great success with a social comedy, *Lady Frederick*, and within a year had not only that play, but three others, *Jack Straw*, *Mrs Dot*, and *The Explorer*, all running in London.

In part these pieces rode on the success of *Lady Frederick*, but, from the first, Maugham had begun to develop in drama the qualities that mark his novels and short stories: a tight, plain, economical prose style, an ability to characterise persuasively, and an engagingly witty and cynical manner. All three of these plays, like *Lady Frederick* itself, show, too, that Maugham had mastered the business of play construction, could turn effective dialogue, and was attuned to the taste of the London theatre-going public.

Maugham attempted many dramatic forms, from farce to melodrama; his early forte, however, and the dramatic form with which he triumphed on the London stage, was comedy of social manners. His best work in this vein stands firmly in that long English tradition running from Restoration comedy, through Goldsmith and Sheridan, to Wilde; it is a comedy that treats human follies, especially amatory confusions and entanglements, with cynical detachment, and with an indulgent, amused, slightly superior tone. Maugham's work in this line is certainly not of the first rank, most of his plays being superficial society dramas trading in elegant conversation, but containing a satiric tone of mild edge and easy wit. These are fashionable drawing-room dramas, calculated to appeal to largely undemanding bourgeois audiences who delighted in the polite entertainment they offered in the pert, witty dialogue, the "daring" subject matter of amorous intrigues and shady pasts, and the elegant stage settings and rich costumings.

After *Lady Frederick*, throughout the 1920's and 1930's, Maugham produced a regular stream of highly successful commercial pieces, all eminently stageable and excellent vehicles for the leading players of the day: pieces like *East of Suez*, *The Sacred Flame*, or *The Letter*, his only thriller. Maugham was more than a mere purveyor of stage *grande dame* chatter and intrigue. His work was rooted in observation of human conduct. He was adept at crafting witty, mildly cynical studies of the idealistic convictions entertained by the young caught in the power of love, and was a master, too, at depicting the clashes and contrasts between male and female, young and old.

It was probably not, however, until the production of his serious domestic comedy, *Our Betters*, in 1917, that Maugham came to be recognised as more than a mere *boulevardier*. Dealing with the fortunes of socially aspirant Americans in London society, this bitter, cynical comedy is more astringently scathing and analytical than the customary Maugham comedy-of-manners fare.

No less impressive in adding a further dimension to Maugham's familiar range were *The Circle*, a witty domestic comedy, and *The Constant Wife*, one of the poised comedies on which, today, his reputation largely rests. Pieces of this kind remain eminently performable, as does perhaps his finest serious drama, *For Services Rendered*, a persuasive, if somewhat sentimental, treatment of the effects wrought by war on a typical English middle-class family.

The qualities most marked in Maugham's writing were a sharp dramatic sense, technical mastery of the stage, and ability to turn witty, colloquial dialogue. His comedy was light and brittle, and his mildly mocking satirical depictions of English upper-class society were rarely corrosive, and never subversive: like a lot of satirical manners comedy, it covertly admired the attitudes it purported to criticise.

But Maugham was willing, too, to work occasionally with new ideas, and that he had aspirations to write a serious drama engaged with more than high-society small-talk, and dealing in more than the amatory entanglements of the *haute bourgeoisie*, is clear from the importance he gave to his last play, *Sheppey*. The failure of this curious experimental and gently moving piece led Maugham to give up writing for the London stage.

—Kenneth Richards

See also *Volume 1* entry on *For Services Rendered*.

MAYAKOVSKY, Vladimir (Vladimirovich). Born in Bagdadi (now Mayakovsky), Georgia (then part of the

Russian Empire), 7 July (19 July, New Style) 1893. Educated at Gymnasium, Kutais, 1902–06; school in Moscow, 1906–08; Stroganov School of Industrial Arts, Moscow, 1908–09; Moscow Institute of Painting and Sculpture and Architecture, 1911–14. Political activities led to his being jailed, 1909–10; in futurist circles after 1912; first major play, *Vladimir Mayakovsky: A Tragedy*, produced 1913; editor, "Seized" and "New Satyricon", Petrograd; served in the army, 1917; reader at Poets Cafe, Moscow, 1918; editor, "Futurist Gazette", 1918; began collaborating on theatre productions with the director Meyerhold and the designer Malevich, from 1918; associated with the magazine "Art of the Commune", 1918–19, and "Art", Petrograd; designed posters and wrote short propaganda playlets and texts for Russian Telegraph Agency (Rosta), Moscow, 1919–21; co-founder, with Osip Brik, *Lef*, 1923–25, and *Novy Lef*, 1927–28. Also writer and actor for films. Committed suicide in Moscow, 14 April 1930.

Works

Collections

Sobranie sochineny [Collected Works] (4 vols.). 1925.
Polnoe sobranie sochineny [Complete Collected Works] (13 vols.), edited by V.A. Katanyan. 1955–61.
Complete Plays, translated by Guy Daniels. 1968.
Selected Works (3 vols.), various translators. 1985–87:
  1. *Poetry*. 1985.
  2. *Longer Poems*. 1986.
  3. *Plays; Articles; Essays*. 1987.

Stage Works (excluding the propaganda playlets)

Vladimir Mayakovsky (produced Luna Park Theatre, St. Petersburg, 1913). 1914; translated as *Vladimir Mayakovsky: A Tragedy*, in *Complete Plays*, 1968.
Misteriya-Buff (produced Conservatoire, Petrograd, 1918). 1918; revised version (produced RSFSR 1 Theatre [Sohn Theatre], Moscow, 1921). 1921; translated as *Mystery-Bouffe*, in *Masterpieces of the Russian Drama 2*, edited by G.R. Noyes, 1933, and in *Complete Plays*, 1968.
Klop (produced Meyerhold Theatre, Moscow, 1929). 1929; translated as *The Bedbug*, in *"The Bedbug" and Selected Poetry*, 1960, and in *Complete Plays*, 1968.
Banya (produced Meyerhold Theatre, Moscow, 1930). 1930; translated as *The Bathhouse*, in *Complete Plays*, 1968.

Verse

Oblako v shtamakh. 1915; revised edition, 1918; translated as *Cloud in Pants*, in *Selected Works 2*, 1986; as *A Cloud in Trousers*, in *Mayakovsky*, 1965, and with *How Are Verses Made?*, 1990.
Fleyta pozvonochnik [The Backbone Flute]. 1916.
Prostnoe Kak mychanie [Simple as Mooing]. 1916.
Voyna i mir. 1916; translated as *War and the World*, in *Selected Works 2*, 1986.
Vse sochinennoye Vladimirom Mayakovskim [Everything Written by Vladimir Mayakovsky]. 1919.
150,000,000. 1921.
Pro eto [About This]. 1923; translated as *It*, in *Selected Works 2*, 1986.
Lirika [Lyrics]. 1923.
Vladimir Ilyich Lenin. 1924; translated as *Vladimir Ilyich Lenin*, in *Selected Works 2*, 1986.

Khorosho!. 1927; translated as *Fine!*, in *Selected Works 2*, 1986.
Mayakovsky and His Poetry, edited by Herbert Marshall. 1942; revised edition, 1945.
Mayakovsky (selection), translated by Herbert Marshall. 1965.
Wi the Haill Voice (Scottish version), translated by Edwin Morgan. 1972.
Poems (selection), translated by Dorian Rottenburg. 1972.
Listen! Early Poems 1913–1918, translated by Maria Enzensberger. 1987.

Memoirs and Letters

Pisma [Letters], edited by Lili Brik. 1956.
Love is the Heart of Everything: Correspondence Between Vladimir Mayakovsky and Lili Brik 1915–1930. 1986.

Other

Ya: Futur-almanakh vselensky samosti [Me: Futuro-Miscellany of Universal Selfhood]. 1913.
Moye otkrytiye Ameriki [My Discovery of America]. 1926.
Kino. 1937.
"The Bedbug" and Selected Poetry, edited by P. Blake. 1960.
How Are Verses Made? 1970.
Essays on Paris. 1975.
"How Are Verses Made?" with "A Cloud in Trousers" and "To Sergey Esenin", translated by G.M. Hyde. 1990.

*

Bibliographies

G. Darring, "Mayakovsky: A Bibliography of Criticism (1912–1930)", in *Russian Literature Triquarterly*, 2, 1972; reprinted in *10 Bibliographies of 20th Century Russian Literature*, edited by F. Moody, Ann Arbor, Michigan, 1977.
Nick Worrall, "Theatre Checklist No. 13: Vladimir Mayakovsky", in *Theatre Facts*, 13, 1977.

Criticism

Books:
A.M. Ripellino, *Mayakovski e il teatro russo d'avanguardia*, Turin, 1959; translated into German, Cologne, 1964.
Lawrence Leo Stahlberger, *The Symbolic System of Mayakovskij*, The Hague, 1964.
V.H. Huppert, *Vladimir Majakovskij in Selbstzeugnissen und Bilddokumenten*, Reinbek, 1965.
Wiktor Woroszylski, *The Life of Mayakovsky* (from the Polish), New York, 1970.
Viktor Shklovsky, *Mayakovsky and His Circle*, 1972.
Edward J. Brown, *Mayakovsky, A Poet in the Revolution*, Princeton, New Jersey, 1973.
B. Jangfeldt, *Mayakovsky and Futurism 1917–1921*, Stockholm, 1976.
A.D.P. Briggs, *Vladimir Mayakovsky: A Tragedy*, Oxford, 1979.
Ann and Samuel Charters, *I Love: The Story of Mayakovsky and Lili Brik*, London, 1979.
Harold B. Segel, *Twentieth-Century Russian Drama*, New York, 1979.

Vladimir Mayakovsky

V. Terras, *Vladimir Mayakovski*, Boston, 1983.
J. Stapanian, *Mayakovsky's Cubo-Futurist Vision*, Houston, Texas, 1986.
Robert Russell, *Russian Drama of the Revolutionary Period*, Totowa, New Jersey, 1988.

Articles:
Frantisek Déak, "The Agit Prop and Circus Plays of Vladimir Mayakovsky", in *Tulane Drama Review*, vol.17 no.1, 1973.
Robert Leach, "A Good Beginning: *Victory over the Sun* and *Vladimir Mayakovsky: A Tragedy* Reassessed", in *Russian Literature*, 13, 1983.

* * *

Mayakovsky's was a prodigious poetic talent, but only a fraction of that talent expressed itself in work for the theatre. Apart from a handful of plays, he also wrote agit-prop sketches and a number of film scenarios, as well as acting both on stage and on screen, co-directing his own plays and, on one occasion, designing his own settings and costumes (for *Mystery-Bouffe*). His connection with the Russian Futurist movement was sustained throughout his career, his first two dramas exploiting a futurist verse-style, and his two satires, written during the late 1920's, involving imaginative projections into future time.

His first, short, two-act play, *Vladimir Mayakovsky: A Tragedy*, is a celebration of the poet's ego. Set in a city with its "spider web of streets", it portrays Mayakovsky as the poet of the city, accompanied by his very tall girl friend (over 13 feet high), and encountering images of human pain, whose burden he takes upon himself. These include a thousand-year-old man with scrawny black cats, a man with one eye and one leg, and three women with tears of different sizes. The talk is of dancing chimney pots, of streets with their sleeves rolled up for action, of God, of machines for cutting up chops and traps for bedbugs. The old man suggests stroking the cats to generate electricity and, in an allegory of revolution, the world of things rebels in the face of Time while the poet seeks to discover new words with which to describe reality. Finally, clad in a toga and crowned with a wreath of laurel, Mayakovsky packs the tears of the world into his suitcase and sets out for the North accompanied, according to accounts of the performance given at the Luna Park Theatre (1913), by the laughter and jeers of the audience.

As the title of his next futurist work, *Mystery-Bouffe*, suggests, the play owes a debt to the religious mysteries as well as to the comic tradition of the "buffo". Mayakovsky took the story of Noah's Ark and adapted it to make it a celebration of world-inundation by the waters of proletarian revolution. In the poet's naive, quasi-religious reconstruction of the myth, the meek (in the shape of the "unclean" workers of the world) inherit the earth from the "clean" (ruling class and bourgeoisie) who, like the rich, are sent away, empty. The production was staged hurriedly, on the first anniversary of the Revolution, with a cast of enthusiastic amateurs. Stage designs were by the "suprematist" artist, Kasimir Malevich, and Mayakovsky distinguished himself in the role of Simply Man, who makes his entrance, like Christ, walking on water but, in this instance, by seeming to hang in mid-air leaning out from behind the proscenium from a leather belt attached to an invisible ladder.

A revised version of the play, staged in 1921, included political figures of the day and a scene in the "Land of Fragments", to suggest the havoc caused by Civil War and foreign intervention. Lunacharsky described it as one of the best productions of the season but thought the play contained "hooligan" elements as, for example, when the Man of the Future (formerly Simply Man) echoes Christ's words with: "Come unto me all ye/ Who can plunge a knife calmly into the body of the enemy/ And go on your way with a song". He also objected to the introduction of music from *Il Trovatore* and *The Gollywog's Cakewalk*.

The Bedbug was solicited from Mayakovsky by the director Meyerhold, who had been responsible for both productions of *Mystery-Bouffe*. The original material was contained in a film scenario which Mayakovsky had written at the end of 1927 for Kozintsev and Trauberg, but which was never used. The ostensible subject of the play is the resurgence of bourgeois philistinism consequent to Lenin's introduction of the New Economic Policy in 1921, which gave rise to the so-called "NEP people". Mayakovsky was closely involved with rehearsals. Shostakovich wrote the music, while the "Kukriniksy" group of artists and Alexander Rodchenko designed the "present" and "future" halves of the play respectively.

Meyerhold compared the importance of the play to Griboyedov's *Woe from Wit*, stating that Mayakovsky wished to show the deep roots of a social sickness. In this sense, the play can be seen as a comment on the persistence of the past in the present, the fact of revolution having constituted no final surgical cure for a cancer whose signs can recur. The play, as such, becomes a parable about democracy and totalitarianism, as well as dealing with the vulgarisation and philistine accommodation of ideals. What Mayakovsky finally presents, in the second half of the play, is a society whose "perfection" has not been democratically created but imposed as an aspect of paternalistic protectionism. This then renders such an artificially created society vulnerable to sickness, because it has no organically created anti-bodies. Critics complained that the production appeared to suggest that depersonalisation and mechanisation were characteristic of socialist society; others thought the play a satire on petty-bourgeois visions of socialism; while some considered the mechanised and automatised depiction of people to be "anti-Soviet slander".

A "Drama in Six Scenes with a Circus and Fireworks", *The Bathhouse* is similar in theme to many poems which Mayakovsky wrote for newspapers and journals between 1926 and 1929 on the subject of bureaucracy. The Leningrad premiere in January 1930 was a disaster and Meyerhold's Moscow production, in March, was received equally coldly. A play which its director said bore comparison with Molière, and which was designed to be intelligible at a popular level, was judged by critics to be incomprehensible. The "circus", in Act III, where simplistic communist slogans and stereotypes are guyed and "proletarian" ballets mocked, was completely misunderstood. The production was a flop and was subsequently subjected to the most hostile reviews, with the Association of Proletarian Writers leading the assault.

The Bathhouse is a deeply felt cry of anguish, as well as a warning about the future of the Soviet Union. The play also expresses an equally heartfelt faith in the powers of ordinary people. The future needs to be believed in, Mayakovsky would seem to be saying, despite its inevitable imperfections, which are a consequence of an inevitable continuity with the past—bureaucratic warts and all. The "March of Time", which accompanies those who believe in the future and enter the "time machine" to be transported forward to the year 2030, gains pathos, less in the face of the unknown, than in the face of what is known and can be anticipated about that future. The "Phosphorescent Woman", for all that she represents of that glorious future, remains something of an insensitive bureaucrat, who reminds one of inventor Chudakov's warning about a "disaster" on the path to that future, which can now be read, simply, as Stalinism. The accepted imperfections are seen for what they are, but a ratifying humanity is focused in the most ordinary characters —the typist and the workers—who carry the thematic burden of naive optimism. It is against the values that these people represent, Mayakovsky seems to suggest, that any future communist society should seek to judge itself, in terms which need to take their ordinary humanity into account.

—Nick Worrall

See also *Volume 1* entries on *The Bedbug*; *Mystery-Bouffe*.

McGEE, Greg(ory William). Born in Oamaru, New Zealand, 22 October 1950. Educated at Waitaki Boys High School; University of Otago, Dunedin, LL.B 1973. Married Mary Davy; one daughter. First play, *Foreskin's Lament*, produced 1980; subsequently a full-time writer; literary fellow, University of Auckland, 1982.

Works

Stage Works

Foreskin's Lament (produced Theatre Corporate, Auckland, 1980; revised version produced His Majesty's Theatre, Auckland, 1986).   1981.
Tooth and Claw (produced Downstage Theatre, Wellington, 1983).   1984.
Out in the Cold (produced Depot, Wellington, 1983).   1984.
Whitemen (produced Auckland, 1986).

Television Plays

Free Enterprise, 1982; *Mortimer's Patch* series, 1984; *Roche* series, 1985.

*

Criticism

Articles:
Sebastian Black, "Playboys of the South Pacific: The Plays of Greg McGee", in *Australasian Drama Studies*, 17, 1990.

*   *   *

Greg McGee's reputation rests on an output of only four plays: *Foreskin's Lament*, his first and most important play, in which rugby becomes a metaphor for New Zealand's troubled nationhood; *Tooth and Claw*, in which the legal profession is similarly used; *Out in the Cold*, a short naturalistic piece set in a freezing works; and *Whitemen*, a grotesque farce about the Rugby Union committee deliberating on whether to send an All Black team to South Africa.

McGee evokes the powerful bonds of everyday work and male popular culture as if from within. He may be fiercely critical and mockingly satirical of the unthinking, selfish, and intolerant smugness of his "ordinary blokes", but he never

patronizes them. He celebrates the myths of consensus New Zealand, in sport and in work. His settings are indicative: a rugby changing shed (in a society where, at the time, virtually every male had played rugby); the cool-store of an abattoir (where seasonal employment used to make a strange mixture of old hands, students, itinerant workers, and so on); a rugby committee room. The lawyer's office of *Tooth and Claw* is obviously an exception, but not entirely: McGee is drawing on (one might say exorcising) a working world he knew intimately, and the high-rise glass-fronted office was, in the early 1980's, a potent and immediate symbol for the monetarist land-speculation unleashed on a previously tightly regulated New Zealand economy.

Foreskin's Lament, above all, demonstrates McGee's ability to draw on popular culture in both a sophisticated and passionately visceral way. Rugby—New Zealand's national sport, defining myth and, until recently, a quasi-religion—is a game McGee himself played to the highest level. He knows the game and the people. The strength and enormous popularity of the play lies in its ability both to celebrate the joys, legends, and bonding of rugby, and at the same time to reveal the hypocrisy, intolerance, and brutality at its heart. This, he suggests, is the uncomfortable dualism underlying a seemingly placid, homogeneous society.

Social critique is central to all McGee's plays, the impulse behind them. He uses comedy for a fierce didactic purpose. *Tooth and Claw*, like *Foreskin's Lament*, lacerates the hypocrisy of a comfortable closed elite. Lawyers, like rugby players, can afford to ignore the less fortunate; and can also bend the rules when it suits them, behind a facade of dedication and integrity. The less privileged—women, homosexuals, Maoris—are recognized as victims, though not, for the most part, given major roles. Judy, in *Out in the Cold*, is an exception. She has passed herself off as a man (not difficult under the balaclava and heavy clothing required to work at −18° C) in order to get a desperately needed job, and applies a feminist critique to the language, attitudes, and behaviour of the two men she has to work with.

McGee's plays usually start with a lot of comedy—crude language, vulgar jokes, topical one-liners—that relaxes an audience into easy, familiar territory. Then, as the paradoxes start to bite, the humour becomes more bitter. Characters erupt into unexpected tirades which reveal a depth of anger, fear, uncertainty, and self-knowledge. Since all the plays are, in effect, about the national character and social conditions, an audience finds that its earlier complicity with the easy humour has left it the target of the playwright's satire. The dramaturgy in effect evokes a dialectic between how a society reacts and how it would like to have itself seen as reacting.

The liberal protagonists of the plays face the same dilemma. Affection for the world of rugby or of law confounds the critique of its shortcomings. As Foreskin says, "This is my earth. I'm rooted in it, whatever my fine aspirations". Hence his lament. Indeed, all the plays are cries of anguish, in one way or another, at the state of our society. McGee's skill has been to avoid placing himself in a holier-than-thou position, but rather to share his laughter and anguish in an entertaining way.

The disappointing aspect of McGee's career as a playwright has been his failure to sustain the formidable achievement of *Foreskin's Lament*. *Tooth and Claw* is skilfully crafted, and makes interesting use of a surreal recurring nightmare of an assault, but the liberal protagonist is less vital than Foreskin. At the end of the play he simply barricades himself in his office, unable to face the world. *Out in the Cold* (based on an earlier short story) is more successful, but much less ambitious. Basically a long one-act play, its plot revelation that

Judy is a woman leads to amusing but pessimistic debate on the plight of the powerless in society. Only the role-playing of one of the other workers, in a desperate attempt to create an alternative to the mind-numbing routine of work, creates distinctive character interest.

McGee's instant fame from the success of *Foreskin's Lament* in 1980 and 1981 (and its seemingly prophetic explication of the social violence in New Zealand brought about by the 1981 South African Springbok rugby tour) led to offers of writing for television and film, and he gradually abandoned playwriting in the course of the 1980's in favour of, as he put it, reaching a wider, popular audience. This decision may well have been aided by the critical and financial disaster of his final play, *Whitemen*, for which he arranged private financial backing (not common in a country in which most plays are presented by the state-subsidized professional regional theatres). *Whitemen* abandoned the more traditional dramaturgy of the earlier plays in favour of revue-style caricatures, but the undergraduate humour based on energetic bad taste and grotesquerie had neither plot, characters, nor theme to engage an audience.

It remains an open question whether Greg McGee will be remembered for one landmark play, *Foreskin's Lament*, or if he will return to the stage and fulfil the potential he always seemed to promise.

—David Carnegie

See also *Volume 1* entry on *Foreskin's Lament*.

McGRATH, John (Peter). Born in Birkenhead, Cheshire, England, 1 June 1935. Educated at Alun Grammar School, Mold, Wales; St. John's College, Oxford (Open Exhibitioner), 1955–59, Dip.Ed. Married Elizabeth MacLennan in 1962; two sons and one daughter. Farm worker, Neston, Cheshire, 1951; served in the British Army (national service), 1953–55; first plays produced 1958; play reader, Royal Court Theatre, London, and television writer and director, 1959–65. Since 1971 founder and artistic director, 7:84 Theatre Company (divided into Scottish and English companies, 1973); Judith E. Wilson Fellow, Cambridge University, 1979; since 1983 founding director, Freeway Films; director, Channel Four television, since 1989. Has also directed many productions of his work.

Works

Stage Works

A Man Has Two Fathers (produced Oxford University, 1958).
The Invasion, with Barbara Cannings, from a play by Arthur Adamov (produced Oxford University, 1958).
The Tent (produced Edinburgh Festival, 1958).
Why the Chicken (produced Cranston Street Hall, Edinburgh, 1959; revised version produced on tour, 1960).
Tell Me Tell Me (produced Institute of Contemporary Arts, London, 1960). In *New Departures* (London), 1960.
Take It (produced Institute of Contemporary Arts, London, 1960).
The Seagull, adaptation of a play by Chekhov (produced Repertory Theatre, Dundee, 1961).
Basement in Bangkok, music and songs by Dudley Moore (produced by students, Bristol, 1963).

Events While Guarding the Bofors Gun (produced Hampstead Theatre, London, 1966). 1966.
Bakke's Night of Fame, adaptation of the novel *A Danish Gambit* by William Butler (produced London, 1968). 1973.
Comrade Jacob, adaptation of the novel by David Caute (produced Falmer, Sussex, 1969).
Random Happenings in the Hebrides; or, The Social Democrat and the Stormy Sea (produced Lyceum Theatre, Edinburgh, 1970). 1972.
Sharpeville Crackers (produced Lyceum Theatre, London, 1970).
Angel of the Morning (produced as part of *Unruly Elements*, Everyman Theatre, Liverpool, 1971). As part of *Plugged-in*, in *Plays and Players*, November 1972.
Plugged-in to History (produced as part of *Unruly Elements*, Everyman Theatre, Liverpool, 1971). As part of *Plugged-in*, in *Plays and Players*, November 1972.
They're Knocking Down the Pie-Shop (produced as part of *Unruly Elements*, Everyman Theatre, Liverpool, 1971). As part of *Plugged-in*, in *Plays and Players*, November 1972.
Hover Through the Fog (produced as part of *Unruly Elements*, Everyman Theatre, Liverpool, 1971).
Out of Sight (produced as part of *Unruly Elements*, Everyman Theatre, Liverpool, 1971).
My First Interview (produced as part of *Unruly Elements*, Everyman Theatre, Liverpool, 1971).
Trees in the Wind (produced Cranston Street Hall, Edinburgh, 1971).
Soft or a Girl (produced Everyman Theatre, Liverpool, 1971; revised version, as *My Pal and Me*, produced Edinburgh, 1975).
The Caucasian Chalk Circle, from a play by Brecht (produced Everyman Theatre, Liverpool, 1972).
Prisoners of the War, from the play by Peter Terson (produced Everyman Theatre, Liverpool, 1972).
Underneath (produced Everyman Theatre, Liverpool, 1972).
Serjeant Musgrave Dances On, from a play by John Arden (produced Macbeth's Castle, Stirling, 1972).
Fish in the Sea, music by Mark Brown (produced Everyman Theatre, Liverpool, 1972; revised version produced Half Moon Theatre, London, 1975). 1977.
The Cheviot, The Stag, and the Black, Black Oil (produced at the "What Kind of Theatre" conference, Edinburgh, 1973). 1973; revised version, 1975; further revised version, 1981.
The Game's a Bogey (produced Aberdeen, 1974). 1975.
Boom (produced Golspie, Sutherland, 1974; revised version produced His Majesty's Theatre, Aberdeen, 1974). In *New Edinburgh Review*, August 1975.
Lay Off (produced University of Lancaster, 1975).
Little Red Hen (produced Lyceum Theatre, Edinburgh, 1975). 1977.
Oranges and Lemons (produced Amsterdam, 1975; produced Birmingham, 1977).
Yobbo Nowt, music by Mark Brown (produced Arts Centre, York, 1975; as *Mum's the Word*, produced Everyman Theatre, Liverpool, 1977; as *Left Out Lady*, produced Labor Theatre, New York, 1981). 1978.
The Rat Trap, music by Mark Brown (produced Mickery Theatre, Amsterdam, 1976).
Out of Our Heads, music by Mark Brown (produced Aberdeen, 1976).
Trembling Giant (English version; produced University of Lancaster, 1977).
Trembling Giant (Scottish version; produced Dundee, 1977).

The Life and Times of Joe of England (produced Basildon, Essex, 1977).
Big Square Fields, music by Mark Brown (produced Bradford, 1979).
Joe's Drum (produced Arts Centre, Aberdeen, 1979).   1979.
Bitter Apples, music by Mark Brown (produced Everyman Theatre, Liverpool, 1979).
If You Want to Know the Time (produced Royal Court Theatre, London, 1979).
Swings and Roundabouts (produced Arts Centre, Aberdeen, 1980).   In *Two Plays for the Eighties*, 1981.
Blood Red Roses (produced Church Hill Theatre, Edinburgh, 1980; revised version produced Everyman Theatre, Liverpool, 1982).   In *Two Plays for the Eighties*, 1981.
Nightclass, music by Rick Lloyd (produced Corby, Northamptonshire, 1981).
The Catch, music by Mark Brown (produced Edinburgh Festival, 1981).
Rejoice!, music by Mark Brown (produced Edinburgh Festival, 1982).
On the Pig's Back, with David MacLennan (produced for the People's March for Jobs, Kilmarnock, Ayrshire, 1983).
The Women of the Dunes (produced in Dutch, Ijmuiden, Netherlands, 1983).
Women in Power; or, Up the Acropolis, music by Thanos Mikroutsikos, from plays by Aristophanes (produced Edinburgh Festival, 1983).
Six Men of Dorset, music by John Tams, from a play by Miles Malleson and Harry Brooks (produced Crucible Theatre, Sheffield, 1984).
The Baby and the Bathwater: The Imperial Policeman (produced Cumbernauld, Dunbartonshire, 1984; revised version produced Edinburgh Festival, 1985).
The Albannach, music by Eddie McGuire, from the novel by Fionn MacColla (produced Edinburgh, 1985).
Behold the Sun (opera libretto), with Alexander Goehr, music by Goehr (produced Oper-am-Rhein, Duisburg, West Germany, 1985).
All the Fun of the Fair, with others (produced London, 1986).
Border Warfare (produced Transport Museum, Glasgow, 1989).
John Brown's Body (produced Transport Museum, Glasgow, 1990).
Watching for Dolphins (produced London, 1991).

Screenplays

Billion Dollar Brain, 1967; *The Bofors Gun*, 1968; *The Virgin Soldiers*, with John Hopkins and Ian La Fresnais, 1969; *The Reckoning*, 1970. *The Dressmaker*, 1989.

Television Plays

Scripts for *Bookstand* series, 1961; *People's Property* (*Z Cars* series), 1962; scripts for *Tempo* series, 1963; *Diary of a Young Man* series, with Troy Kennedy Martin, 1964; *The Entertainers* (documentary), 1964; *The Day of Ragnarok*, 1965; *Mo* (documentary), 1965; *Shotgun*, with Christopher Williams, 1966; *Diary of a Nobody*, with Ken Russell, from the novel by George and Weedon Grossmith, 1966; *Orkney*, from stories by George Mackay Brown, 1971; *Bouncing Boy*, 1972; *Once upon a Union*, 1977; *The Adventures of Frank*, from his play *The Life and Times of Joe of England*, 1979; *Sweetwater Memories* (documentary), 1984; *Blood Red Roses*, 1986; *There is a Happy Land*, 1987.

Radio Plays

The Game's a Bogey, 1979.

Other

A Good Night Out: Popular Theatre: Audience, Class and Form.   1981.
The Bone Won't Break: On Theatre and Hope in Hard Times.   1990.

Translator, with Maureen Teitelbaum, *The Rules of the Games* (screenplay), by Jean Renoir.   1970.

*

Bibliographies

Malcolm Page, "John McGrath" (checklist and bibliography), in *New Theatre Quarterly*, vol.1 no.4, 1985.

Criticism

Books:
Peter Ansorge, *Disrupting the Spectacle*, London, 1975.
Ronald Hayman, *British Theatre since 1955*, London and New York, 1979.
Sandy Craig (ed.), *Dreams and Deconstructions*, Derbyshire, 1980.
Catherine Itzin, *Stages in the Revolution*, London, 1980.
Christian W. Thomsen, "Three Socialist Playwrights" in *Contemporary English Drama*, London and New York, 1981.
Alan Bold, *Modern Scottish Literature*, London, 1983.
John McGrath, "7:84 Theatre Company Scotland", in *Kreativität und Dialog: Theaterversuche der 70er Jahre in Westeuropa*, edited by Joachim Fiebach and Helmer Schramm, Berlin, 1983.
Andreas Jäger, *John McGrath und die 7:84 Company Scotland: Politik, Popularität und Regionalismus im Theater der siebziger Jahre in Schottland*, Amsterdam, 1986.

Articles:
Bernd Schliephake, "Politisches Theater in Schottland: John McGrath und die Gruppe 7:84", in *Englisch-Amerikanische Studien*, 2, 1980.
Christopher Bigsby, "The Politics of Anxiety" in *Modern Drama*, 24, 1981.

*   *   *

Since his first play in 1958, McGrath has produced a wide range of work for the stage, television, and film. While he is best known for his work as a socialist playwright with the Scottish 7:84 Theatre Company, he began writing in a different context, reversing the direction taken by other political dramatists who left the fringe to accept opportunities to work in the subsidized establishment. Although he had written and directed scripts for productions at Oxford University, the Royal Court Theatre, BBC Television, and the American film industry, McGrath stated in a 1975 interview, when asked what he would do if Peter Hall (then Director of the National Theatre) were to commission a play from him, "I would run 25 miles. . . . I'd rather have a bad night in Bootle".

McGrath's work in theatre and other media before 1970 differs in style from the more overtly socialist plays which followed. While the concern with class conflict is evident in this period, he eventually broke away from the naturalistic treatment of time and character in early plays such as *Events While Guarding the Bofors Gun* and the documentary realism of the television police series *Z Cars*. *Random Happenings in the Hebrides* marks a turning point in McGrath's writing. The play covers a longer time-span and explores issues which became the focus of his work with 7:84 in Scotland, namely, the factors affecting rural life in the Hebrides and Highlands, and industrial labour politics.

In his plays for the Liverpool Everyman Theatre in 1971–72, McGrath turned his attention to community theatre and writing for working-class audiences. He began to experiment with popular forms of entertainment, introducing songs and comedy into plays dealing with Liverpool life (*Soft or a Girl* and *Fish in the Sea*). It was also at this time that McGrath founded the left-wing touring group, the 7:84 Theatre Company (the name was based on a 1988 statistic which revealed that 7% of the population controlled 84% of the nation's wealth). His first 7:84 plays included *Trees in the Wind*, *Plugged-in to History* (renamed from *Unruly Elements*), *Out of Sight*, *Underneath*, and *Serjeant Musgrave Dances On* (an updated version of John Arden's play). Of the work produced between 1971–72, the Liverpool plays, in terms of style and context, were perhaps more indicative of the direction McGrath was to take in subsequent years.

In 1973, 7:84 split into two companies: an English company, for which McGrath continued to write plays, and a Scottish company which he formed along with Elizabeth and David MacLennan. The company came together as a collective with the aim of producing plays which addressed issues affecting the lives of Scottish people and touring them to small, outlying communities as well as urban centres.

Given the various roles McGrath was to assume within 7:84 (Scotland)—artistic director, writer, director—and the group's collective approach to researching, developing, and producing plays, it becomes increasingly difficult to separate his work from that of the company. It is equally problematic to discuss the "plays" as dramatic "texts". Even the published scripts cannot be treated as definitive texts since they have likely undergone revisions in the course of touring. At most, they offer an idea of the structure and concerns of a given production.

The company's first and most important production, *The Cheviot, the Stag and the Black, Black Oil*, represents a significant achievement in formal innovation in British theatre in this period. In the form of a ceilidh, which has a long tradition as a form of entertainment in the Highlands, the play combines songs (in English and Gaelic), sketches, and direct statements from historical accounts of the events. *The Cheviot* traces the effects of "the savage process of capitalism" on the Highland people from the time of the Clearances in 1745 to the takeover by multi-national companies in the 1970's, establishing the connections between driving people off the land to make room for sheep and accommodating the demands of a booming oil industry. The production (also filmed for television) was a huge success and broke new ground in the context of contemporary Scottish theatre.

Many of the issues concerning ownership of land and imperialist powers, as well as caricatures of aristocrats, politicians, and foreign investors, are reworked in subsequent plays produced specifically for tours in the Highlands and Islands. *Boom* deals with the impact of the oil industry, while *The Catch* explores the effects of NATO military presence and nuclear waste on fishing communities. McGrath's Highland productions in the 1980's, such as *The Albannach* (adapted from the novel by Fion MacColla), *There is a Happy Land*, and *Mairi Mhor—The Woman from Skye*, take a more celebratory approach to aspects of Highland music and history.

At the same time, the company toured different plays to the central and industrial centres in Scotland. McGrath wrote *The Game's a Bogey*, *Little Red Hen*, *Out of Our Heads*, *Joe's Drum*, and *Blood Red Roses*, as well as *Lay Off* and *Yobbo Nowt* for 7:84 England, for urban audiences and the plays examine aspects of Scottish working-class life and labour history from a Marxist perspective. For the forms of these shows, McGrath drew on techniques used in club entertainment, stand-up comedy, and rock music.

McGrath outlined the basis for his approach to form in a series of lectures for Cambridge University, published as *A Good Night Out*. Although a great deal of controversy has surrounded McGrath's theatre practices since the 1970's, the book remains an important attempt to explore the ways in which cultural forms are socially determined, making distinctions between working class and bourgeois forms of entertainment. He resigned as artistic director of 7:84 in 1988, but his recent book, *The Bone Won't Break*, examines the history of the company in the Thatcher years and builds on issues raised in the first book. Along with producing a large body of plays, McGrath has contributed to the debates surrounding political theatre practices and the state of arts funding in a significant way.

The recent plays, written after leaving 7:84, *Border Warfare* and *John Brown's Body*, were staged as promenade productions in the Glasgow Transport Museum, and mark a new direction in the form and scale of McGrath's ongoing work.

—Maria Dicenzo

See also *Volume 1* entry on *The Cheviot, the Stag, and the Black, Black Oil*.

MEDWALL, Henry.   See *Volume 1* entry on *Fulgens and Lucrece*.

MENANDER.   Born into an Athenian family, c.342–41 BC. Studied with the philosopher Theophrastus, and was associated with Demetrius of Pahleron, ruler of Athens, 317–07 BC. First-produced play, *Orge* [Anger], staged 321 BC; won eight dramatic prizes; titles of more than 100 of his plays are known (some possibly alternative titles). Existing texts and fragments only discovered and published in the 20th century. Died in Athens c.293–289 BC.

Works

Collections

Reliquae selectae [Selected Texts], edited by F.H. Sandbach. 1972; revised editions, 1972 and 1990.

Menander (statue in the Museo Vaticano, Rome).

Menander 1 (with translations), edited by W.G. Arnott. 1979 (Loeb Classical Library).
Plays and Fragments, translated by Philip Vellacott. 1967.
Plays, translated by Lionel Casson.   1971.
Plays and Fragments, translated by Norma Miller. 1987.

Stage Works (Greek texts in *Reliquae selectae*)

Dyscolos (produced Leneaen Festival, Athens, c.316 BC). Translated as *The Dyskolos*, 1960 and 1977; as *The Bad-Tempered Old Man*, 1960; as *The Cross Old Devil*, translated by H.C. Fay, in *Three Classical Comedies*, 1967; as *The Grouch*, in *Plays*, 1971; as *Feast of Pan*, 1977; as *Old Cantankerous*, in *Plays and Fragments*, 1987.
Samia (produced Athens, c.315–09 BC). Translated as *Samia*, 1951; as *The Woman from Samos*, in *Plays*, 1971; as *The Girl from Samos*, 1972, and in *Plays and Fragments*, 1987.
Epitrepontes (fragmentary text; produced ?).   Translated as *The Arbitration*, 1945: several subsequent translations under same title.
Perikeiromene (fragmentary text; produced ?).   Translated as *The Rape of the Locks*, 1942, and in *Plays and Fragments*, 1987; as *She Who Was Shorn*, in *Plays*, 1971.
Aspis (fragmentary text; produced ?).   Translated as *The Shield*, in *Plays*, 1971, and *Plays and Fragments*, 1987.
Sikyonius (fragmentary text).   Translated as *The Sikyonian*, in *Plays and Fragments*, 1987.

Translations of smaller fragments appear in *Plays and Fragments*, 1987 (see Collections).

*

Criticism

Books:
T.B.L. Webster, *Studies in Menander*, Manchester 1950; revised edition, 1960.
Eric W. Handley, *Menander and Plautus: A Study in Comparison*, 1968.
E.G. Turner, *Ménandre*, Ghent, 1970.
A.W. Gomme and F.H. Sandbach, *Menander: A Commentary*, Oxford, 1973.
N. Holzberg, *Menander: Untersuchungen zur dramatischen Technik*, Nuremberg, 1974.
T.B.L. Webster, *An Introduction to Menander*, Manchester, 1974.
A.G. Katsouris, *Linguistic and Stylistic Characterization: Tragedy and Menander*, Ioannina, Greece, 1975.
W.G. Arnott, *Menander, Plautus and Terence*, Oxford, 1975.
F.H. Sandbach, *The Comic Theatre of Greece and Rome*, London, 1977.
John Blundell, *Menander and the Monologue*, Göttingen, 1980.
Sander M. Goldberg, *The Making of Menander's Comedy*, London, 1980.
R.L. Hunter, *The New Comedy of Greece and Rome*, Cambridge, 1985.
K.B. Frost, *Exits and Entrances in Menander*, Oxford, 1988.
David Wiles, *The Masks of Menander*, Cambridge, 1991.

*   *   *

Menander is probably the most important of all the Greek poets whose work was not preserved for the modern world through the normal manuscript tradition. Although much-revered in antiquity as the greatest composer of New Comedy, until this century no substantial portion of his work was discovered (although there were many fragments), and in its absence it was very difficult to evaluate properly his qualities and importance. Menander could only be assessed on the basis of piecemeal quotations taken out of context, and the indirect and unreliable evidence of later Roman works thought to have been directly influenced by him. Now, however, with the gradual discovery and publication first of more significant fragments, and then, in 1959, a complete play, the *Dyscolus* (*The Bad-Tempered Old Man*), followed by the nearly complete *Samia* (*Woman of Samis*), and a large portion of the *Aspis* (*The Shield*), together with substantial portions of three other works, scholars are able to make some better-informed judgements.
   The ancients admired Menander most of all for what was described as his exact representation of life, his comic vigour, and the humane good sense expressed by his plays through refined and eloquent language. On the whole, Menander, if he has not yet entirely justified his ancient reputation, continues to grow in critical estimation as a fuller picture emerges with the recovery and careful examination of the new material. His characterisation, relying on the use of standard figures, is occasionally somewhat superficial, the wit restrained (certainly less impressive to our contemporary taste than the achievements of Plautus), and his language sometimes lacks (at least to the modern ear) the subtlety that

ancient accounts had led us to expect. But there is also much to admire.

So far as it is possible to extrapolate from what survives, Menander composed fairly short plays of about 1000 lines, which were divided into five acts, and normally preceded by a prologue, sometimes, but not invariably, delivered by a god. Between the acts there was some sort of musical diversion, but little within the play itself. The stories are presented in a direct and clear-cut fashion with none of the complications or interruptions commonly found in the adaptations by Plautus. The plots, which were always set in Greece, and frequently in Athens, are essentially mild-mannered, sober, and urbane intrigues, and they followed a broadly similar pattern of action. A young man is infatuated with a girl who, initially, is unattainable. After some not-too-unseemly adventures in which he overcomes the problems facing him, while gaining a few edifying lessons, he discovers that she is, in fact, a fit choice for marriage. There is invariably an element of love-interest motivating the plot, although the actual subject may centre on some other problem of morals or character. (In the *Dyscolus*, for example, the ethical subject at the heart of the drama is misanthropy.)

Although relying upon mistaken identity, reversal, and the discovery of long-lost relatives, the plots are generally plausible and the characters, although exaggerated for comic effect, and subject to errors of judgement, sympathetic. These characters have little interest in the wider world beyond their immediate domestic circumstances. They are never presented as vicious or entirely reprehensible. Menander handles them with good-natured tolerance, tempered by irony. The language is refined, sensible, and decorous. Although the characters found in the surviving works are rarely entirely "stock" (in the *Perikeiromene*, for example, the soldier Polemon has none of the traditional qualities of the vainglorious military man), Menander was credited by ancient commentators as having, at least at times, relied upon a recurrent set of them. Ovid asserts that, "so long as the deceiving slave, the strict father, the villainous pimp, and the deceitful courtesan survive, so long will Menander live" (in *Amores*). The Menandrian originals subsequently recycled by Plautus in his adaptations were undoubtedly simplified and more coarsely drawn.

Despite the repetition of somewhat similar characters and devices in the plots, Menander invariably introduces a good deal of variety and dramatic interest into his plays. The stories are skilfully constructed and full of surprises. The characters are often very sympathetically drawn, with enough attention to individual traits of personality to hold the interest of an audience and appeal to its powers of empathy, particularly at those moments in which characters, alone on the stage, engage in extensive direct address, explaining themselves and their most intimate concerns. Although difficult to render in translation, he made the most skilful use of his verse both to highlight individual characters' traits with appropriate language, and to underscore the meaning and emotion of their expressions by changes in rhythm and patterns of sound.

Menander draws his *dramatis personae* from all walks of life and social strata and, far from caricaturing them, provides just enough detail to allow the audience to "flesh out" and interpret the characters. In both the *Samia* and the *Dyscolus*, for example, Menander creates highly effective contrasts between his characters through their use of language and particular traits and attitudes. It is perhaps these factors, above all else, that gained for Menander his reputation for being true to life, and simultaneously made his plays so successful as works for the theatre. As literature they may be perceived as somewhat "thin"; unfolding on the stage however, and in the hands of skilful actors, they were carefully crafted to gain and hold the attention of sophisticated spectators and sustain their interest, while not distracting them with superfluous detail, boring them with tedious slapstick, or offending them with vulgarity. His lessons are never heavy-handed, or achieved at the expense of theatrical effectiveness, but they are clearly, unobtrusively there, and the lightness of touch with which Menander delivered them may also have won favour with his urbane audience.

—Richard C. Beacham

See also *Volume 1* entry on *The Bad-Tempered Old Man*.

MERCER, David. Born in Wakefield, Yorkshire, England, 27 June 1928. Educated at King's College, Newcastle upon Tyne, BA (honours) in fine art (Durham University) 1953. Married twice; one daughter. Laboratory technician, 1942–45; served as a laboratory technician in the Royal Navy, 1945–48; lived in Paris, 1953–54; supply teacher, 1955–59; teacher, Barrett Street Technical College, 1959–61; first plays produced on television in the early 1960's; first stage play, *The Buried Man*, produced 1962. Recipient: Writers Guild Award, for television play, 1962, 1967, 1968; BAFTA Award, 1966; French Film Academy César Award, 1977; Emmy Award, 1980. Died in Haifa, Israel, 8 August 1980.

Works

Collections.

The Generations: A Trilogy of Plays (includes *Where the Difference Begins; A Climate of Fear; The Birth of a Private Man*). 1964; as *Collected TV Plays 1*, 1981.
Three TV Comedies (includes *A Suitable Case for Treatment; For Tea on Sunday; And Did Those Feet*). 1966.
"The Parachute" with Two More TV Plays: Let's Murder Vivaldi; In Two Minds. 1967.
"On the Eve of Publication" and Other Plays (television plays; includes *The Cellar and the Almond Tree* and *Emma's Time*). 1970.
"The Bankrupt" and Other Plays (includes *You and Me and Him; An Afternoon at the Festival; Find Me*). 1974.
"Huggy Bear" and Other Plays (includes *The Arcata Promise* and *A Superstition*). 1977.
Collected TV Plays 1–2 (2 vols.; includes *Where the Difference Begins; A Climate of Fear; The Birth of a Private Man; A Suitable Case for Treatment; For Tea on Sunday; And Did Those Feet; The Parachute; Let's Murder Vivaldi; In Two Minds*). 1981.
Plays 1 (includes *Where the Difference Begins; The Governor's Lady; A Suitable Case for Treatment; On the Eve of Publication; The Cellar and the Almond Tree; Emma's Time; After Haggerty*). 1990.

Stage Works

The Buried Man (produced Manchester, 1962).
The Governor's Lady, from the radio play (produced Aldwych Theatre, London, 1965). 1968.

Ride a Cock Horse (produced Playhouse, Nottingham, 1965). 1966.

Belcher's Luck (produced Aldwych Theatre, London, 1966). 1967.

White Poem (produced Institute of Contemporary Arts, London, 1970).

Flint (produced Playhouse, Oxford, 1970).   1970.

After Haggerty (produced Aldwych Theatre London, 1970), 1970.

Blood on the Table (produced London, 1971).

Let's Murder Vivaldi, from the television play (produced London, 1972).   In *The Best Short Plays 1974*, edited by Stanley Richards, 1974.

In Two Minds, from the television play (produced Bush Theatre, London, 1973).

Duck Song (produced Aldwych Theatre, London, 1974). 1974.

The Arcata Promise, from the television play (produced New York, 1982).

Cousin Vladimir (produced Aldwych Theatre, London, 1978).   With *Shooting the Chandelier*, 1978.

Then and Now (produced Hampstead Theatre, London, 1979).   With *The Monster of Karlovy Vary*, 1979.

The Monster of Karlovy Vary.   With *Then and Now*, 1979.

No Limits to Love (produced Warehouse Theatre, London, 1980).   1981.

Screenplays

90 Degrees in the Shade (English dialogue), 1965; *Morgan! A Suitable Case for Treatment*, 1966; *Family Life* (*Wednesday's Child*), 1972; *A Doll's House*, with Michael Meyer, 1973; *Providence*, 1978.

Television Plays

Where the Difference Begins (broadcast 1961).   In *The Generations*, 1964.

A Climate of Fear (broadcast 1962).   In *The Generations*, 1964.

A Suitable Case for Treatment (broadcast 1962).   In *Three TV Comedies*, 1966.

The Birth of a Private Man (broadcast 1963).   In *The Generations*, 1964.

A Buried Man, from the stage play (broadcast 1963).

For Tea on Sunday (broadcast 1963).   In *Three TV Comedies*, 1966.

A Way of Living (broadcast 1963).

And Did Those Feet (broadcast 1965).   In *Three TV Comedies*, 1965.

In Two Minds (broadcast 1967).   In "*The Parachute*" . . . (collection), 1967.

The Parachute (broadcast 1968).   In "*The Parachute*" . . . (collection), 1967.

Let's Murder Vivaldi (broadcast 1968).   In "*The Parachute*" . . . (collection), 1967.

Robert Kelvin trilogy: *On the Eve of Publication* (broadcast 1968); *The Cellar and the Almond Tree* (broadcast 1970); *Emma's Time* (broadcast 1970).   All in "*On the Eve of Publication*" *and Other Plays*, 1970.

The Bankrupt (broadcast 1972).   In "*The Bankrupt*" *and Other Plays*, 1974.

You and Me and Him (broadcast 1973).   In "*The Bankrupt*" *and Other Plays*, 1974.

An Afternoon at the Festival (broadcast 1973).   In "*The Bankrupt*" *and Other Plays*, 1974.

Barbara of the House of Grebe, from a story by Thomas Hardy (broadcast 1973).

Find Me (broadcast 1974).   In "*The Bankrupt*" *and Other Plays*, 1974.

The Arcata Promise (broadcast 1974).   In "*Huggy Bear*" *and Other Plays*, 1977.

Huggy Bear (broadcast 1976).   In "*Huggy Bear*" *and Other Plays*, 1977.

A Superstition (broadcast 1977).

Shooting the Chandelier (broadcast 1977).   With *Cousin Vladimir*, 1978.

The Ragazza (broadcast 1978).

A Rod of Iron (broadcast 1980).

A Dinner of Herbs (broadcast 1988).

Radio Plays

The Governor's Lady (published in *Stand*, Spring 1962), 1960; *Folie à Deux*, 1974.

*

Bibliographies

Francis Jarman, John Noyce, and Malcolm Page, *The Quality of Mercer: A Bibliography of Writings by and About David Mercer*, Brighton, Sussex, 1974.

Criticism

Books:
Paul Madden (ed.), *David Mercer: Where the Difference Begins*, London, 1981.
John Russell Taylor, *The Second Wave: British Drama for the Seventies*, New York, 1971.
Klaus P. Steiger, *Das englische Drama nach 1945*, Darmstadt, 1983.
Don Taylor, *Days of Vision: Working with David Mercer*, 1990.

Articles:
"Birth of a Playwriting Man" (interview and list of works), in *Theatre Quarterly*, 9, 1973.

*   *   *

The tensions between utopia and defeat in David Mercer's major plays can be regarded as a triangle whose points are North, South, and East. Heroes of Yorkshire or Midlands working-class origin struggle to reconcile their fame among the London literati with their commitment to a socialism that may have been born in the Marxist East. Their guilt at growing away from their inarticulate origins is underscored by the sceptical or indifferent women with whom they live or whom they divorce.

Children, in some form or another, are an obsessive presence, although Mercer never creates a conventional nuclear family. Peter, a successful Yorkshire novelist, shuttles between three women in *Ride A Cock Horse*. His wife, Nan, a doctor, cannot have children; his actress girlfriend, Myra, is past the menopause; he impregnates his other girlfriend, Fanny, but she aborts the child, which is what Peter really wanted. Bernard Link's flat, in *After Haggerty*, is invaded by an aggressive American, Claire, with an infant, Raskolnikov, who is never seen but who, like his absent father, Haggerty, comes increasingly to dominate the household. Ossian Flint, a 70-year old communist vicar, motorcycles off to Rome and

Greece with 19-year-old Dixie, pregnant by Arthur the anarchist, in *Flint*. Lucy, the serving-girl, is pregnant by Belcher, the handyman, from start to finish in *Belcher's Luck* (1966), but Belcher has only contempt for his living son, Victor, who has been adopted and cossetted by the asexual lord of the manor, Catesby.

Such an emphasis on birth and children is unusual for a Marxist writer; it can be read as a further intensification, at the domestic level, of Mercer's contradictory emotions towards radicalism in the political sphere. The exchange between Nan and Peter in Act II, Scene 1 of *Ride A Cock Horse* dramatically freezes the opposing impulses of female and male:

Nan: . . . . Well. I want to go back up there—
Peter: I shall go abroad. I shall go to Warsaw.

Earlier Peter has tried to resolve his stasis by appropriating the language of birth for males and for adults only: "I am the proud father of a lovely, bouncing wife", he shouts at his passive wife. He follows up with, "Clever people know that the hip thing is to give birth to adults". Peter's attempts at self-birthing fail. Both his mistresses finish up at Nan's hospital, and Peter is reduced, at the end of the play, to a sobbing wreck, clinging like a child to his father who has come down from his Yorkshire pit to try and save the marriage.

The play reads like *Look Back in Anger* with an extra female character. Nan is accused of the same passivity as Alison, and Peter's fantasy and vituperation descend from Jimmy Porter. Rooms trap and offer solace to both Peter and Jimmy. But Peter has an outlet, the East, that Osborne does not give Jimmy. The description of the death of Jimmy's father is an occasion for harrowing pathos, and his allegiance to the International Brigade gets much less emphasis.

Parents in Mercer's plays are alive and are perceived as great boulders across the highway to internationalist self-fulfilment. Bernard Link, in *After Haggerty*, cannot get past the opening lines of his lectures in Paris, Prague, or Havana —key cities for the international Left of the 1960's—before lapsing into mental dialogues of love and hate with his parents in Yorkshire. Peter, at moments of acute crisis, addresses interior letters to his parents. Victor Belcher, to evade his father's contemptuous presence, invents imaginary conversations with Kant, Hegel, and Marx.

Only *Flint* combines paternity with freedom, but the child is not his, and he himself is a caricature of an English stereotype, the Red Dean. His bid for liberty takes him, not to Moscow, but to the centres of classical culture, Rome and Athens, and he dies a futile death, in the flames of the tanker into which his motorcycle crashes. He has been an arsonist anyway in his life, pursuing a politics as gestural as Peter's firing of his own flat to try to cut through the contradictions of desire, fatherhood, and artistry.

When Link Senior visits his son's ménage, he sits there like a pillar of common-sense refuting the flighty radicalism of Claire and Bernard. When Bernard says, "The question of the father will have to be gone into at some time", he is speaking about Raskolnikov, but implicitly also circling around the central question of Mercer's work—what does an artist father?

On the Eve of Publication, *The Cellar and the Almond Tree*, and *Emma's Time*, a trilogy of plays for television, concentrates on this issue with great dramatic bravura and foreshadows the next radical question for the 1970's—what does a woman mother? The trilogy traces the slow death of Robert Kelvin, a quarrelsome and distinguished Marxist novelist, through an alternation of narratives set in publishing London, in a central European country after communist tak-

eover and, less extensively, in Nottingham and Paris. Stock film footage from Wajda's *Ashes and Diamonds*, the unemployed in the 1930's, and Lenin's funeral points up the political dimension in Kelvin's work, but its "realism" is designed to emphasise the fragility of Kelvin's writing. We know now how profoundly the East failed to deliver socialism. Kelvin is as sardonic about the possibility of its success as his Czech friend, Sladek, who is tortured by Nazi and Stalinist alike, and humiliated by an aristocratic Countess. But it is still a possibility, the dull, battered apex to Mercer's triangle.

Working slowly beneath this history, however, and barely surfacing at the end of the trilogy, is an alternative radicalism for the future, that of women. Obsessed as he is with plots and metaphors of birth and inheritance, Mercer gives considerable space to women in his plays. Even in their misery they are articulate. "I co-operate in my own humiliation", says Myra. "There's no limit to what men can do to me, because I'd sooner be tortured than ignored". And Fanny is clear about her situation: "I—feel meaningless without a man. And I resent it. I feel humiliatingly feminine".

By 1970 Claire is cussing Bernard in the opening lines of *After Haggerty* and she has something of the *hauteur* of Helen Rawston in *Belcher's Luck*. But American heiresses and English upper-class bitches have dominatrix histories long pre-dating feminism. Much more interesting is Emma in the trilogy. She is a middle-class Cambridge graduate, aged 24, and is constant companion to the 64-year-old Kelvin. She services him in every way and has no interest in politics, indeed no interests of her own. She appears to everyone as a passive, beautiful receptacle. She has the language to estimate her own failings: "My sort of . . . sensitive, erudite . . . inertia of self-pity . . . the refuge of feeling masochistic, of only being an object". But she lacks even the self-dramatization that supports Myra in her suicide attempt. Mercer gives her the same kind of coolness and assurance without depth that Maitland inveighs against in Osborne's *Inadmissible Evidence*.

Sladek tracks her down at the end, silent in her bare, white room. He wants them, together, to write up his memoirs and dedicate them to Robert. Emma's role, we can imagine, will be that of amanuensis and typist to another Marxist hero. Yet the last play is entitled *Emma's Time*. Mercer is right. It will be Emma's time. She sums up, with sensitive prescience, everything that the feminists will theorize and fight against. But she is of exactly the class and education from which those feminists will derive. When Emma says to Sladek, just before she agrees to the memoirs, "I'm—blank", she signifies both the nadir of female self-abasement, and a nothingness which will be fruitful, a space to be inscribed with dozens of configurations of new female selves in the years to come. Emma is not pregnant. She is a "zero" waiting to be politicised. If men cannot father themselves, women will mother themselves. David Mercer's work is as apposite to the 1990's as it was to the 1960's.

—Tony Dunn

See also *Volume 1* entry on *After Haggerty*.

MICKIEWICZ, Adam.   See *Volume 1* entry on *Forefathers' Eve*

MIDDLETON, Thomas. Born in London; baptised 18 April 1580. Educated at Queen's College, Oxford, 1598–1601. Married Magdalen Marbeck in 1602; one son. Playwright for Philip Henslowe by 1602; several plays written in collaboration, notably with William Rowley; city chronologer of London, 1620–27. Died (buried) in Newington Butts, Surrey, 4 July 1627.

Works

Collections

Works (5 vols.), edited by Alexander Dyce. 1840.
Works, edited by A.H. Bullen (8 vols.). 1885–86.
Thomas Middleton (2 vols. containing 10 plays), edited by A.C. Swinburne and Havelock Ellis. 1887–90.
Three Plays (includes A Chaste Maid in Cheapside; Women Beware Women; The Changeling), edited by Kenneth Muir. 1975.
Selected Plays (includes The Changeling; Women Beware Women; A Chaste Maid in Cheapside; A Mad World, My Masters), edited by David L. Frost. 1978.
Five Plays (includes A Trick to Catch the Old One; The Revenger's Tragedy; A Chaste Maid in Cheapside; Women Beware Women; The Changeling), edited by Bryan Loughrey and Neil Taylor. 1988.

Stage Works

The Phoenix (produced by the Children of St. Paul's, London, 1603–04). 1607.
The Honest Whore, part 1, with Dekker (produced by Prince Henry's Men, 1604). 1604; as The Converted Courtesan, 1604.
A Mad World, My Masters (produced by the Children of St. Paul's, London, 1604–06). 1608.
A Trick to Catch the Old One (produced by the Children of St. Paul's, London, 1604–06). 1608.
Michaelmas Term (produced by the Children of St. Paul's, London, 1604–06?). 1607.
The Family of Love (produced by the Children of St. Paul's, London, 1604–07). 1608.
The Revenger's Tragedy, possibly by Tourneur (produced by the King's Men, Globe Theatre, London, c.1606–07). 1607.
Your Five Gallants (produced 1607). 1608(?).
Sir Robert Sedley, His Royal Entertainment (produced 1609?). 1609.
The Roaring Girl; or, Moll Cut-Purse, with Dekker (produced by Prince Henry's Men, Fortune Theatre, London, 1611). 1611.
No Wit, No Help Like a Woman's (produced c.1611). Revised version published 1657.
Chryso-Thriambos (pageant; produced London, 1611). 1611.
A Chaste Maid in Cheapside (produced by Lady Elizabeth's Men, Swan Theatre, London, c.1611). 1630.
The Triumphs of Truth: A Solemnity (pageant; produced London, 1613). 1613.
The New River Entertainment (produced 1613). 1613.
The Witch (produced by the King's Men, Blackfriars Theatre, London, 1613–16). 1778.
More Dissemblers Besides Women (produced by the King's Men, London, 1615?). In Two New Plays, 1657.
The Nice Valour; or, The Passionate Madman, with Fletcher (produced c.1615–16). In Comedies and Tragedies, by Beaumont and Fletcher, 1647.

A Fair Quarrel, with William Rowley (produced by Prince Charles' Men, London, 1615–17). 1617.
Hengist, King of Kent; or, The Mayor of Quinborough (produced 1615–20?). 1661.
Civitatis Amor, the City's Love: An Entertainment by Water (produced 1616). 1616.
The Widow (produced by the King's Men, Blackfriars Theatre, London, c.1616). 1652.
The Triumphs of Honour and Industry (pageant; produced London, 1617). 1617.
The Old Law; or, A New Way to Please You, with William Rowley (produced 1618?). 1656.
The Inner Temple Masque; or, Masque of Heroes (produced Inner Temple, London, 1619). 1619.
The Triumphs of Love and Antiquity: An Honourable Solemnity (pageant; produced London, 1619). 1619.
The World Tossed at Tennis, with William Rowley (produced 1619–20). 1620.
Wit at Several Weapons, with William Rowley, from a play by Fletcher (produced before 1620). In Comedies and Tragedies, by Beaumont and Fletcher, 1647.
Honourable Entertainments (contains ten short "entertainments"; produced 1620–21?). 1621.
Anything for a Quiet Life, with Webster (produced by the King's Men, Blackfriars Theatre, London, 1620–21). 1621.
The Sun in Aries: A Noble Solemnity (pageant; produced London, 1621). 1621.
An Invention for the Service of Edward Barkham, Lord Mayor of London (produced London, 1622). In Works, 1885–86.
The Triumphs of Honour and Virtue (pageant; produced London, 1622).
The Changeling, with William Rowley (produced by Lady Elizabeth's Men, Cockpit/Phoenix Theatre, London, 1622). 1653.
The Triumphs of Integrity (pageant; produced London, 1623). 1623.
A Game at Chess (produced by the King's Men, Globe Theatre, London, 1624). 1625.
Women Beware Women (produced London, c.1625–27). 1653.
The Triumphs of Health and Prosperity: A Noble Solemnity (pageant; produced London, 1626). 1626.

Verse

The Wisdom of Solomon Paraphrased. 1597.
Microcynicon: Six Snarling Satires. 1599.
The Ghost of Lucrece. 1600.

Other

The Ant and the Nightingale; or, Father Hubbard's Tales. 1604; revised edition, as Father Hubbard's Tales, 1604.
The Black Book. 1604.
The Marriage of the Old and New Testament. 1609.

*

Bibliographies

S.A. Tannenbaum, Thomas Middleton: A Concise Bibliography, New York, 1940; supplement in Elizabethan Bibliographies Supplements 1, by Dennis G. Donovan, London, 1967.

Sara J. Steen, *Thomas Middleton: A Reference Guide*, Boston, 1984.

Dorothy Wolff, *Thomas Middleton: An Annotated Bibliography*, New York and London, 1985.

Criticism

Books:

W.D. Dunkel, *The Dramatic Technique of Thomas Middleton in His Comedies of London Life*, Chicago, 1925.

M.G. Christian, *Non-Dramatic Sources for the Rogues in Middleton's Plays*, Chicago, 1936.

B. Johansson, *Religion and Superstition in the Plays of Ben Jonson and Thomas Middleton*, Uppsala, Sweden, and Cambridge, Massachsetts, 1950.

Samuel Schoenbaum, *Thomas Middleton's Tragedies*, New York, 1955.

Richard H. Barker, *Thomas Middleton*, London and New York, 1958.

David M. Holmes, *The Art of Thomas Middleton: A Critical Study*, Oxford, 1970.

John F. MacElroy, *Parody and Burlesque in the Tragicomedies of Middleton*, Salzburg, 1972.

Norman A. Brittin, *Thomas Middleton*, New York, 1972.

Barbara J. Baines, *The Lust Motif in the Plays of Thomas Middleton*, Salzburg, 1973.

Caroline L. Cherry, *The Most Unvaluedst Purchase: Women in the Plays of Thomas Middleton*, Salzburg, 1973.

Anthony Covatta, *Middleton's City Comedies*, Lewsiburg, Pennsylvania, 1973.

Dorothy M. Farr, *Middleton and the Drama of Realism*, Edinburgh and London, 1973.

Carolyn Asp, *A Study of Thomas Middleton's Tragicomedies*, Salzburg, 1974.

David J. Lake, *The Canon of Middleton's Plays*, London, 1975.

Charles A. Hallett, *Middleton's Cynics*, Salzburg, 1975.

Bruno Nauer, *Thomas Middleton: A Study of the Narrative Structures*, Zurich, 1977.

MacDonald P. Jackson, *Studies in Attribution: Middleton and Shakespeare*, Salzburg, 1979.

George E. Rowe, *Thomas Middleton and the New Comedy Tradition*, Lincoln, Nebraska, 1979.

J.R. Mulryne, *Thomas Middleton*, Harlow, Essex, 1979.

Margot Heinemann, *Puritanism and Theatre: Thomas Middleton and Opposition Drama under the Early Stuarts*, Cambridge, 1980.

Kenneth Friedenreich (ed.), *Accompaninge the Players: Essays Celebrating Thomas Middleton 1580–1980*, New York, 1983.

A.L. Kistner and M.K. Kistner, *Middleton's Tragic Themes*, New York, 1984.

* * *

Like Dekker, Jonson, and Heywood, Middleton was a prolific writer of plays, producing works during the reigns of Elizabeth, James, and Charles. The authorship of many plays to which his name is or has become attached, however, is a matter for scholarly dispute. Middleton certainly collaborated with Dekker, Drayton, Munday, Rowley, and Webster, and, possibly, Shakespeare (on *Timon of Athens*). He began his career, like so many of his contemporaries, by writing verse as well as prose satires, then moved on to write plays for both the adult and boys' companies.

From 1604–1611 he produced, for the boy players, a string of city comedies which satirized those who sacrificed everything to the accumulation of wealth; from 1613–1618 his output centred on tragicomedies, and from 1618 on tragedies which were, in the main, performed by the King's Men. From 1607 he also produced masques and pageants for the City, and always maintained an important connection with City interests and with parliamentary Puritans. Towards the end of his career his allegorical play *A Game at Chess* mercilessly satirized the pro-Catholic and pro-Spanish politics of the court in 1624. This play, in particular, seems to have been designed to appeal to a City and puritan audience.

In his life-time, however, he was not highly regarded: Ben Jonson, whose *oeuvre*, like that of Middleton, is devoted to the indictment of affluence and materialism, sought his patronage from the Court, and wrote the "oppositional" Middleton off as a "base fellow". It is only in this century that the value of his texts has been recognized.

It was T.S. Eliot who laid down a challenge for all who seek to put Middleton into a critical perspective: "Middleton is solicitous to please his audience with what they expect; but there is underneath the same steady impersonal passionless observation of human nature . . . He has no message; he is merely a great recorder . . . Middleton is the greatest 'realist' in Jacobean comedy" (in his *Selected Essays*). Yes, many London place-names appear in the plays, as sometimes do contemporary personalities (for example Mary Frith, the central character in *The Roaring Girl*) and incidents. These serve, however, merely to a constitute a "reality effect" and Middleton is no mere transcriber of city life: like Jonson, his work is informed by a stern morality, a desire to make his audience understand the ethos of the unbridled pursuit of wealth — and its human costs.

His realism is social and not mimetic — and may derive from a religious view of life which saw clearly the nature of earthly corruption. In his comedy *A Trick to Catch the Old One*, for example, some (minor) characters bear ordinary names (Joyce, George), others bear names that suggest their moral natures (Witgood, Hoard), and a third category (Host, and importantly, the Courtesan) have names which indicate how their personality has been subordinated to their trade. The opening sequence, in which Witgood demonizes the Courtesan, blaming her for consuming his wealth which derives from a country estate, is a masterful portrait of self-deception in which the language deliberately sets a "natural" and human order against the false values of city rapacity.

At the moral centre of the play lies the grotesque and allegorical figure of Dampit ("damn pit"), a usurer and, as Middleton calls him, a "famous, infamous trampler of time" who holds the "fooliaminy and coxcombry of the country" in his clutches. Middleton's "Puritanism" centres on his elevation of industriousness over idleness as well as in his indictment of depravity. During the denouement, the Courtesan, who has redeemed herself from poverty by marriage, attempts to redeem herself in the eyes of the audience by a confession in rhyming couplets. It is difficult to establish the tone here, and perhaps the original boy actor was able to suggest that only the economically secure can lead a moral life — such may be the nature of Middleton's "realism".

Romantic comedy makes its appearance in works *No Wit, No Help Like a Woman's*, where a wily son is set against a father who serves to frustrate happiness, but the play also satirizes a gallery of worldlings, the hero is a melancholic on the brink of suicide, the action is as much concerned with property as with passion, and the complications of the plot may be an index of the inscrutable workings of God's "secret powers".

The characters of Middleton's late tragedies are not only

interesting for their psychology but also for their social roles. He may well have written *A Yorkshire Tragedy* in which, as in *A Trick*, characters are named by their relationships with one another (Husband, First Son, etc.) in a play that demonstrates how a husband's prodigality generates brutality in his family. In a prefatory verse to *Women Beware Women*, Nathaniel Richards speaks of how ". . . Drabs of state, vexed,/Have plots, poisons, mischiefs that seldom miss,/To murder virtue with a venom kiss": it is a tale of intrigue at court where marriages are made for money and undone by lust. In a subplot, the Ward boasts repulsively and tediously of his virility: no comic relief this, for it indicates that, as Richards implies, women are made drabs by men. The celebrated comic subplot of madmen in *The Changeling* is also part of the play's moral structure: the imbecility of the court is no different from that of the madhouse. (The same point is implied at the conclusion of *The Honest Whore* (Part One), which Middleton wrote with Dekker, when the Duke of Milan goes at the end of the play to visit the local asylum or "bedlam".)

As in comedy, Middleton's tragic endings are theatrical. *Women Beware Women* ends with a masque in which the bad are made to bleed in quaint ways that match the nature of their crimes. Justice in the world, however, is unlikely to match that imposed by the playwright—as the author's theatrical tone implies. Moreover, Middleton's demonstration of the consequences of rampant masculine desire make an audience conclude that the play might be better titled "Women Beware Men".

—Michael Hattaway

See also *Volume 1* entries on *The Changeling*; *A Chaste Maid in Cheapside*; *The Revenger's Tragedy*; *Women Beware Women*.

MILLER, Arthur. Born in New York City, 17 October 1915. Educated at Abraham Lincoln High School, New York, graduated 1932; University of Michigan, Ann Arbor (Hopwood Award, 1936, 1937), 1934–38, AB 1938. Married 1) Mary Slattery in 1940 (divorced 1956), one son and one daughter; 2) the actress Marilyn Monroe in 1956 (divorced 1961); 3) Ingeborg Morath in 1962, one daughter. Worked in automobile supply warehouse, 1932–34; member of the Federal Theatre Project, 1938; writer for CBS and NBC Radio Workshops; first professionally produced play, *The Man Who Had All the Luck*, staged 1944; Associate Professor of Drama, University of Michigan, 1973–74. International President, PEN, London and New York, 1965–69. Recipient: Theatre Guild Award, 1938; New York Drama Critics Circle Award, 1947, 1949; Tony Award, 1947, 1949, 1953; Pulitzer Prize, 1949; American Academy Gold Medal, 1959; Peabody Award, for television play, 1981; Bobst Award, 1983; Commonwealth Award, 1992; National Arts Club Award, 1992. DHL.: University of Michigan, 1956; Litt.DL: University of East Anglia, Norwich, 1984. Member, American Academy, 1981.

Works

Collections

Collected Plays (includes *All My Sons; Death of a Salesman; The Crucible; A Memory of Two Mondays; A View from the Bridge*). 1957.
Collected Plays 2 (includes *The Misfits; After the Fall; Incident at Vichy; The Price; The Creation of the World and Other Business; Playing for Time*). 1981.
Plays (3 vols.; Volumes 1 and 2 as *Collected Plays* 1 and 2; Volume 3 includes *The American Clock; The Archbishop's Ceiling; Two-Way Mirror*). 1990.

Stage Works

Honors at Dawn (produced University of Michigan, Ann Arbor, 1936).
No Villains (*They Too Arise*) (produced University of Michigan, Ann Arbor, 1937).
The Man Who Had All the Luck (produced Forrest Theatre, New York, 1944). In *Cross-Section 1944*, edited by Edwin Seaver, 1944.
That They May Win (produced Brooklyn, New York, 1944). In *Best One-Act Plays of 1944*, edited by Margaret Mayorga, 1945.
All My Sons (produced Coronet Theatre, New York, 1947). 1947.
Death of a Salesman: Certain Private Conversations in Two Acts and a Requiem (produced Morosco Theatre, New York, 1949). 1949.
An Enemy of the People, from a play by Ibsen (produced Broadhurst Theatre, New York, 1950). 1951.
The Crucible (produced Martin Beck Theatre, New York, 1953). 1953.
A View from the Bridge (produced Coronet Theatre, New York, 1955). With *A Memory of Two Mondays*, 1955; revised version in two acts (produced Comedy Theatre, London, 1956), 1957.
A Memory of Two Mondays (produced Coronet Theatre, New York, 1955). With *A View from the Bridge*, 1955.
After the Fall (produced by ANTA, Washington Square Theatre, New York, 1964). 1964.
Incident at Vichy (produced by ANTA, Washington Square Theatre, New York, 1964). 1965.
The Price (produced Morosco Theatre, New York, 1968). 1968.
Fame (produced Off-Broadway, New York, 1970). In *Yale Literary Magazine*, March 1971.
The Reason Why (produced Off-Broadway, New York, 1970).
The Creation of the World and Other Business (produced Shubert Theatre, New York, 1972). 1973; revised version, as *Up from Paradise*, music by Stanley Silverman (produced Power Center, Ann Arbor, Michigan, 1974).
The Archbishop's Ceiling (produced Kennedy Center, Washington, DC, 1977; revised version produced Cleveland, Ohio, 1984). 1984.
The American Clock, from a work by Studs Terkel (produced Harold Clurman Theatre, New York, 1980). 1980.
Elegy for a Lady (produced Yale Repertory Theatre, New Haven, Connecticut, 1982). 1982; also in *Two-Way Mirror*, 1984; revised version in *Plays 3*, 1990.
Some Kind of Love Story (produced Yale Repertory Theatre, New Haven, Connecticut, 1982). 1983; also in *Two-Way Mirror*, 1984; revised version in *Plays 3*, 1990.

Arthur Miller

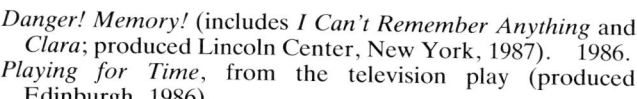

Danger! Memory! (includes *I Can't Remember Anything* and *Clara*; produced Lincoln Center, New York, 1987).   1986.
Playing for Time, from the television play (produced Edinburgh, 1986).
Speech to the Neighborhood Watch Committee, music by David Shire, lyrics by Richard Maltby Jr. (produced as part of *Urban Blight*, Manhattan Theatre, New York, 1988).
The Ride Down Mount Morgan (produced Wyndham's Theatre, London, 1991).   1992.
The Last Yankee (produced Ensemble Studio Theatre, New York, 1991).   1993.

Screenplays

The Story of G.I. Joe (uncredited), 1945; *The Witches of Salem*, 1958; *The Misfits*, 1961 (published in *Collected Plays 2*, 1981); *Everybody Wins*, 1990 (published 1990).

Television Plays

Playing for Time, 1980 (published in *Collected Plays 2*, 1981).

Radio Plays

The Pussycat and the Expert Plumber Who Was a Man, and *William Ireland's Confession* (both published in *100 Non-Royalty Radio Plays*, edited by William Kozlenko, 1941); *Grandpa and the Statue* (published in *Radio Drama in Action*, edited by Erik Barnouw, 1945); *The Story of Gus* (published in *Radio's Best Plays*, edited by Joseph Liss, 1947); *The Guardsman*, from a play by Molnár, and *Three Men on a Horse*, from the play by George Abbott and John Cecil Holm (published in *Theatre Guild on the Air*, edited by William Fitelson, 1947); *The Golden Years*, 1987 (published with *The Man Who Had All the Luck*).

Fiction

Focus.   1945.
The Misfits (novelisation of screenplay).   1961.
I Don't Need You Any More: Stories.   1967.

Memoirs and Letters

Timebends (autobiography).   1987.

Other

Situation Normal.   1944.
Jane's Blanket (for children).   1963.
In Russia, photographs by Inge Morath.   1969.
The Portable Arthur Miller, edited by Harold Clurman.   1971.
In the Country, photographs by Inge Morath.   1977.
The Theatre Essays of Arthur Miller, edited by Robert A. Martin.   1978.
Chinese Encounters, photographs by Inge Morath.   1979.
"Salesman" in Beijing.   1984.

*

Bibliographies

Tetsumaro Hayashi, "Arthur Miller: The Dimension of His Art: A Checklist of His Published Works" in *Serif*, June 1967.

Tetsumaro Hayashi, *Arthur Miller Criticism (1930–1967)*, New Jersey, 1969; revised as *An Index to Arthur Miller Criticism*, 1976.
George H. Jensen, *Arthur Miller: A Bibliographical Checklist*, Columbia, South Carolina, 1976.
John H. Ferres, *Arthur Miller: A Reference Guide*, Boston, 1979.

Criticism

Dennis Welland, *Arthur Miller*, Edinburgh and New York, 1961.
Robert Hogan, *Arthur Miller*, Minneapolis, 1964.
Sheila Huftel, *Arthur Miller: The Burning Glass*, New York and London, 1965.
Leonard Moss, *Arthur Miller*, New York, 1967; revised edition, 1980.
Edward Murray, *Arthur Miller, Dramatist*, New York, 1967.
Robert W. Corrigan (ed.), *Arthur Miller: A Collection of Critical Essays*, Englewood Cliffs, New Jersey, 1969.
Richard I. Evans, *Psychology and Arthur Miller*, New York, 1969.
Sidney H. White, *The Merrill Guide to Arthur Miller*, Columbus, 1970.
Benjamin Nelson, *Arthur Miller: Portrait of a Playwright*, New York and London, 1970.
Ronald Hayman, *Arthur Miller*, London, 1970.
James J. Martine (ed.), *Critical Essays on Arthur Miller: New Perspectives*, Englewood Cliffs, New Jersey, 1979.
Dennis Welland, *Miller: A Study of His Plays*, London, 1979; revised as *Miller the Playwright*, 1983; further revised edition, 1985.
Neil Carson, *Arthur Miller*, London and New York, 1982 (Macmillan Modern Dramatists series).
N. Bhaskara Panikkar, *Individual Morality and Social Happiness in Arthur Miller*, Atlantic Heights, New Jersey, 1982.
Santosh K. Bhatia, *Arthur Miller: Social Drama as Tragedy*, New Delhi, 1985.
Harold Bloom (ed.), *Arthur Miller: Modern Critical Views*, New York, 1987.
Matthew C. Roudané (ed.), *Conversations with Arthur Miller*, Jackson, Mississippi, 1987.
C.W.E. Bigsby (compiler), *File on Miller*, London, 1988.
Atma Ram (ed.), *Perspectives on Arthur Miller*, New Delhi, 1988.
Martina Wächter, *Darstellung und Deutung der Vergangenheit in den Dramen Arthur Millers*, Frankfurt, 1989.
Christopher Bigsby (ed.), *Arthur Miller and Company* (interviews and commentary), London, 1990.

*   *   *

To categorise Miller purely as a dramatist has long been misleading. He has also written a novel (*Focus*), short stories, a film script (*The Misfits*), several television scripts including *Playing for Time*, a large number of theatre essays, and the monumental autobiography, *Timebends*.

Well-known as an outspoken liberal since his courageous resistance in the 1950's to the notorious House Un-American Activities Committee's witch-hunting fervour, he has become a familiar, intelligent, and relaxed television interviewee on an increasing range of subjects in addition to drama, while the soundness of his grasp of all aspects of the craft of the theatre has combined with the attractive shrewdness of his personality so that his collaboration is eagerly sought by actors, directors, and designers (Elia Kazan and Jo Mielziner were early examples). He also continues to hold the respect of critics, academics, and journalists. In his 70's his creativity is undiminished and his achievements have made him unquestionably the doyen of 20th-century dramatists, not merely in the USA, but internationally too, as the success of the Chinese version of *Death of a Salesman* in Beijing proved in 1983.

That degree of recognition, however, was not quickly won, especially in his native America: indeed, for many years he was much more widely esteemed in Europe than at home. The controversial topicality of his earlier plays in particular, and their frank criticism of the American way of life, is only a partial explanation of this. His own distinction between Britain and the USA—"You have a theatre. We have shows" —also applies.

What is impressive is the extent to which the passage of time has illuminated the universality of Miller's themes and his presentation of them. The further the 1950's recede the easier it is to see *The Crucible* less as an oblique attack on McCarthyism than as a profound commentary on the dangers of any fanaticism as well as a thoughtful, vividly realised re-creation of 17th-century New England. It has also become increasingly possible to separate *After the Fall* from the tragic death of Miller's wife, Marilyn Monroe (a connection which led originally to hostile suggestions of tastelessly opportunistic sensationalism), and to revalue its painful but incisive insights into the inextricable interaction between public and private responsibilities and interests.

Miller's beginnings in Ibsenite realism in *All My Sons* and his lively adaptation of *An Enemy of the People*, as well as his abiding preoccupation with the effects of the Depression of the 1930's and with the Nazi Holocaust, led to a facile pigeon-holing of him as a social dramatist, so that *Death of a Salesman* was initially interpreted, sometimes in narrowly political and ideological terms, rather as a critique of American capitalism than as a poignantly balanced study of a man who had "the wrong dreams. All, all wrong". Essentially the dramatist of ordinary people, Miller is always concerned with the likes of Willy Loman, who "is not the finest character who ever lived", but is "a human being" to whom "attention must be finally paid". The dramatic attention Miller has paid to such characters and the depth of his understanding of them raises more than one of his plays to the level of tragedy. Guilt, integrity, and loyalty within the family are his themes; but they gain an added dimension from the vision he defined thus: "The way I see life is that there are no public issues: they are all private issues. We have gotten divided. We are political men or private men. I can't see the separation".

Miller has become important, too, in a way not foreseeable 40 years ago, for his timely insistence, both in theory and practice, on the primacy of language in the theatre. To his belief that "language is the most subtle thing we've got, the most subtle form of expression", actors have responded with a gratifying enthusiasm. When O'Neill dominated the American stage it was axiomatic that American dramatic dialogue was flat and clumsy, but Miller's contemporary British playwrights could usefully learn from him. His language, one British actor observes, "looks so ordinary, and yet you realise that it has its own kind of unobtrusive eloquence". A comparison of *The Crucible* with *A View from the Bridge* exemplifies the range and subtlety of that eloquence clearly.

Miller's dramatic range, thematically and structurally, is equally remarkable. Themes and situations (particularly the familial ones) recur, but not in an exclusively American context, and he never repeats himself. At one end of his structural range are the near-expressionist memory plays; yet contrasting *Death of a Salesman* with *After the Fall* demonstrates that, far from being formless in their time-shifts, both are rigorously ordered, although in quite different ways. At the other end of this spectrum is *The Price*, surely of all modern plays the one which adheres most strictly, most purposefully, and with the greatest stagecraft to the Aristotelian unities.

Somewhat neglected since its appearance in 1968, *The Price* has, at last, begun to earn well-deserved respect not only for its consummate structuring but also for the depth of its characterisation and dialogue. The secondhand furniture dealer, Gregory Solomon, has become recognised as one of Miller's most complex creations—at once an amusing exploitation of an unsuspected vein of comedy in Miller, and an embodiment of the virtues of tolerant wisdom, patience with the inexperience of others (both springing from his receptivity to the lessons of his own life), and an unending fascination with the unpredictability of human behaviour—qualities that characterise all Miller's work. Similarly the deceptively every-day dialogue envelops such a complexity of meaning and interpretation of past events that "whoever speaks last seems to command the truth", and the action is no more reducible to one irrefutably "true" interpretation than is human life itself, nor can blame be judicially and indisputably apportioned.

More recently Miller has developed this ambivalence of vision interestingly in double bills, containing two contrasting one-acters with an over-arching unity of theme, and he seems capable of still further experimentation.

—Dennis Welland

See also *Volume 1* entries on *After the Fall*; *All My Sons*; *The Crucible*; *Death of a Salesman*; *A View From the Bridge*.

MITCHELL, Langdon (Elwyn). Born in Philadelphia, Pennsylvania, USA, 17 February 1862; son of the writer S. Weir Mitchell. Educated at St. Paul's School, Concord, New Hampshire; studied for three years in Dresden and Paris, then studied law at Harvard Law School, Cambridge, Massachusetts, and Columbia University, New York; admitted to New York bar, 1886, but did not practise. Married the actress Marion Lea in 1892; one son and two daughters. Playwright and author from mid-1880's; first-produced play, *George Cameron*, staged 1891; lecturer in English, George Washington University, Washington, DC, 1918–20; professor of playwriting, University of Pennsylvania, Philadelphia, 1928–30. Member, American Academy. Died in Philadelphia, 21 October 1935.

Works

Stage Works

Sylvian. In *Sylvian: A Tragedy, and Poems*, 1885.
George Cameron (produced Steinway Hall, London, 1891).
In the Season (produced Strand Theatre, London, 1892). 1898.
Ruth Underwood (produced Strand Theatre, London, 1892).
Don Pedro (produced Strand Theatre, London, 1892).
Deborah (produced Avenue Theatre, London, 1892; as *The Slave Girl*, produced Princess's Theatre, Bristol, 1893).

Becky Sharp, from a novel by Thackeray (produced Fifth Avenue Theatre, New York, 1899). Edited by J.B. Russak, in *"Monte Cristo" and Other Plays*, 1941.
The Adventures of Françoise, from a novel by S. Weir Mitchell (produced Park Theatre, Philadelphia, 1900).
The Kreutzer Sonata, from a work by Jacob Gordin based on a novel by Tolstoy (produced Lyric Theatre, New York, 1906). 1907.
The New York Idea (produced Lyric Theatre, New York, 1906). 1908.
The New Marriage (produced Empire Theatre, Syracuse, New York, 1911).
Major Pendennis, from the novel by Thackeray (produced Criterion Theatre, New York, 1916).

Fiction

Love in the Backwoods (stories). 1897.

Verse

Sylvian: A Tragedy, and Poems. 1885.
Poems. 1894.

Other

Understanding America. 1927.

*

Criticism

Books:
Arthur Hobson Quinn, *A History of American Drama from the Civil War to the Present Day 2*, New York, 1927.

* * *

At the time of his death in 1935, Langdon Mitchell was hailed as the "dean of American playwrights". In a long career in the theatre, he had achieved this fame by writing numerous plays, though with only one memorable blockbuster, *The New York Idea*. The son of the celebrated physician and novelist S.Weir Mitchell, he grew up in a milieu which heightened his realization of social distinctions, and was surrounded by affluence and privilege. He attended leading schools and colleges, and he travelled, lived, and studied in Europe. Much of the brilliant dialogue of his plays suggests that he had a fine ear for the rhythms of speech of cultivated people.

His first attempt at playwriting was a closet drama, *Sylvian*, written in 1885 in blank verse and prose. This work, published under the pseudonym John Philip Varley, was never played on the stage. He wanted to write plays with plots of revenge, unfaithful loves, and violence. He finally shifted from this romantic viewpoint by the time that he presented his first stage production, *In the Season*, at the St. James's Theatre, London, 1892. He successfully dramatized Thackeray's *Vanity Fair* as *Becky Sharp*, with the leading actress Minnie Maddern Fiske in the title role. Mrs. Fiske's reputation and acting skills helped this drama to have a long Broadway run and to be revived several times in the next 30 years.

Having written one successful adaptation, Mitchell wrote a less well-received dramatization, this time of his father's novel, *The Adventures of Françoise*. Mrs. Fiske then suggested that he write a light comedy about divorce which she would bring to the stage. The result was *The New York Idea*, which has held the attention of the theatre public ever since it appeared during the season of 1906–07. He followed that success with another play for Mrs. Fiske, *The New Marriage*, which closed after three performances. Mitchell retreated again to adaptations, with *Major Pendennis*, based on Thackeray's *Pendennis*, which was a moderate success somewhat due to the fame of its leading actor, John Drew.

At this point, Mitchell ceased being an active playwright with works produced on the stage. He continued to write, but never again were any of his plays produced: he attempted to dramatize the problems of divorce in two works left in manuscript, "Before Dawn" and "The Second Generation". His high standards made him very self-critical, keeping him from finishing his works.

He was a realist in his acceptance of dramatic principles, for as an adaptor of novels he respected the novelist at the same time that he recognized the needs of the theatre. For example, he did not hesitate to introduce new plot material into *Becky Sharp*, his adaptation of *Vanity Fair*. (His best roles were written for women. His colorful female roles were packed with intelligence and vitality.)

Langdon Mitchell is thus remembered largely for *The New York Idea*. Since 1900 the American theatre had been somewhat humdrum, but this play, a mixture of merry comedy and satire on divorce, struck a chord within the national consciousness, for divorce and the ease with which it was achieved was under much discussion in America. What might be termed only a slight comedy became a problem drama, exposing frivolous attitudes toward love and marriage. The comedy derived from fast-moving situations and the lightness and liveliness of the play sprung from deft and sparkling dialogue. With penetrating and perceptive satire, the eccentricities of smart society succeeded in amusing, baffling, surprising, and stimulating audiences. Sometimes the ploys of farce were substituted for the intellectuality of high comedy. Occasionally, the vivid personalities of the main characters pushed into the background the problems of divorced couples. Critics writing from 1906 through 1977 have been fulsome with praise, declaring it to be a true American comedy of manners, full of marvelous roles and sophisticated humors with an Edwardian flavor.

With a perspective of over 80 years distance, *The New York Idea* emerges as the best American social comedy produced in the early 20th century, comparing favorably with the works of Henry Arthur Jones, Arthur Wing Pinero, and George Bernard Shaw. It has been translated and played in German, Danish, Swedish, and Hungarian, quite frequently revived, and reprinted in many anthologies of outstanding dramas. Eric Bentley, in choosing five plays for his modern drama series, chose it from thousands to represent the American spirit, and Arthur Hobson Quinn, in his *History of the American Drama From the Civil War to the Present*, described it as an important part of the "advance guard of the new drama" of the 20th century.

—Charles L. Leavitt

See also *Volume 1* entry on *The New York Idea*.

MOLIÈRE. Born Jean-Baptiste Poquelin in Paris, 15 January 1622. Educated at Collège de Clermont, to 1641;

Louis XIV (seated, right) demonstrating his support of **Molière** (seated, left) by dining with him before assembled courtiers at Versailles (painting by Ingres, 1857).

probably attended University of Orléans, studying law, law degree 1642. Married Armande Béjart in 1662; two sons (died in infancy) and one daughter. Inherited father's post as Tapissier du Roi [Royal Upholsterer], and accompanied Court to Narbonne, 1642–43; co-founder, with the Béjart family and others, the Illustre Théâtre, Paris, 1643; adopted the stage name Molière, 1643; Théâtre Illustre disbanded, 1645; member, 1645–58, and director, from c.1650, Dufresne's touring theatre troupe: troupe returned to Paris, 1658, and, under patronage of Louis XIV's brother, Duc d'Orléans, 1658–65, and under that of Louis himself, from 1665 (when it became the Troupe du Roi), it was based at the Théâtre du Petit-Bourbon, 1658–60, then at the Palais Royal, from 1660; considerable controversy over supposed immorality in his work, from the mid-1660's: *Dom Juan* not revived after 1665, and a revised version of *Tartuffe* banned on its first performance, 1667 (ban rescinded 1669). Molière frequently acted the leading roles in his plays, several of which received their first performances before Louis XIV at Versailles, Chambord, or Saint Germain, prior to their public productions. Died in Paris, 17 February 1673.

Works

Collections

Oeuvres (2 vols.).   1663, and later editions, 1664 and 1666.
Oeuvres (7 vols.).   1673.

Oeuvres (8 vols.; includes *Oeuvres posthumes*), edited by C. de la Grange and Vinot.   1682.
Oeuvres complètes (14 vols.), edited by E. Despois and P. Mesnard.   1873–1900.
Plays (bilingual edition; 8 vols.), edited and translated by A.R. Waller.   1926.
Oeuvres complètes (Bibliothèque de la Pléaide edition; 2 vols.).   1933; revised editions, 1959 and 1971.
Five Plays (includes *The Would-Be Gentleman; That Scoundrel Scapin; The Miser; Love's the Best Doctor; Don Juan*), translated by John Wood.   1953; retitled as *"The Miser" and Other Plays*, 1960.
Six Prose Comedies (includes *The Burgher in Purple: Scapin the Scamp; Don Juan; Forced to Be a Doctor; The Miser; Coxcombs in Petticoats*), translated by George Gravely. 1956.
Oeuvres complètes (2 vols.), edited by Maurice Rat.   1956; revised by Georges Coutin, 1971.
Eight Plays (includes *The Precious Damsels; The School for Wives; The Critique of the School for Wives; The Versailles Impromptu; The Would-Be Gentleman; Tartuffe; The Misanthrope; The Physician in Spite of Himself*), translated by Morris Bishop.   1957.
"The Misanthrope" and Other Plays (includes *The Misanthrope; The Sicilian; Tartuffe; A Doctor in Spite of Himself; The Imaginary Invalid*), translated by John Wood.   1959.
One-Act Comedies, translated by Albert Bermel.   1964.
"Tartuffe" and Other Plays (includes *The School for*

Husbands; The School for Wives; Don Juan; Tartuffe; The Critique of the School for Wives; The Ridiculous Précieuses; The Versailles Impromptu), translated by Donald Frame. 1967.

Four Short Farces (includes The School for Husbands; The Flying Doctor; The Uneasy Husband; Love is the Best Remedy), translated and adapted by Allan Clayson. 1969.

Five Plays (includes The Misanthrope; Tartuffe; The School for Wives; The Miser; The Hypochondriac), translated by Richard Wilbur and Alan Drury. 1981.

Stage Works

Le Médecin volant (attributed to Molière; produced on tour before 1655). 1819; translated as The Flying Doctor, in Four Short Farces, 1969.

La Jalousie du barbouillé (attributed to Molière; produced on tour before 1655). 1819.

L'Étourdi; ou, Les Contre-temps (produced 1655?). 1663; translated as The Blunderers, 1762.

Le Dépit amoureux (produced Béziers, 1656). 1663; translated as The Amorous Quarrel, 1762; as Lovers' Quarrels, in Plays 2, 1926; as The Love Tiff, 1930.

Les Précieuses ridicules (produced Théâtre du Petit-Bourbon, Paris, 1659). 1660; translated as The Conceited Young Ladies, 1762; as The Affected Young Ladies, 1915; as The Precious Damsels, in Eight Plays, 1957; as The Pretentious Young Ladies, 1959; as The Ridiculous Précieuses, in "Tartuffe" and Other Plays, 1967.

Sganarelle; ou, Le Cocu imaginaire (produced Théâtre du Petit-Bourbon, Paris, 1660). 1660; translated as The Picture, 1745; as Sganarelle, in Plays 2, 1926.

Don Garcie de Navarre; ou, Le Prince jaloux (produced Théâtre du Palais-Royal, Paris, 1661). In Oeuvres posthumes, 1684; translated as Don Garcie de Navarre, in Plays 2, 1926.

L'École des maris (produced Théâtre du Palais-Royal, Paris, 1661). 1661; translated as The School for Husbands, in Plays 2, 1926, and in "Tartuffe" and Other Plays, 1967.

Les Facheux (produced House of Superintendent Fouquet, Vicomte-le-Vaux, 1661). 1662; translated as The Impertinents, 1732; as The Boors, in Plays 2, 1926.

L'École des femmes (produced Théâtre du Palais-Royal, Paris, 1662). 1663; translated as The School for Wives, in Plays 2, 1926: several subsequent translations under same title.

La Critique de L'École des femmes (produced Théâtre du Palais-Royal, Paris, 1663). 1663; translated as The Critique of the School for Wives, in Eight Plays, 1957, and "Tartuffe" and Other Plays, 1967.

L'Impromptu de Versailles (produced Théâtre du Palais-Royal, Paris, 1663). In Oeuvres posthumes, 1684; translated as The Versailles Impromptu, in Eight Plays, 1957, and "Tartuffe" and Other Plays, 1967.

Le Mariage forcé (produced Louvre, Paris, 1664). 1664; translated as The Forced Marriage, 1762, and in Tulane Drama Review, vol. 8 no. 2, 1963.

La Princesse d'Élide (produced Versailles, 1664). 1674.

Tartuffe; ou, L'Imposteur (three-act version produced Versailles, 1664; revised version, in five acts, produced Théâtre du Palais-Royal, Paris, 1667). 1669 (five-act version); translated as Tartuffe, 1670: several subsequent translations under same title.

Les Plaisirs de l'île enchantée (produced Raincy, 1664). 1664.

Dom Juan; ou, Le Festin de Pierre (produced Théâtre du Palais-Royal, Paris, 1665). 1683; translated as Don Juan, in Plays 4, 1926: several subsequent translations under some title.

L'Amour médecin (produced Versailles, 1665). 1666; translated as The Quacks, 1705; as Doctor Love, 1915; as Love is the Best Remedy, in Four Short Farces, 1969.

Le Misanthrope (produced Théâtre du Palais-Royal, Paris, 1666). 1667; translated as The Misanthrope, 1762: several subsequent translations under same title; also translated as The Man-Hater, 1770.

Le Médecin malgré lui (produced Théâtre du Palais-Royal, Paris, 1666). 1667; translated as The Dumb Lady, 1672; as Love's Contrivance, 1703; as The Mock Doctor, 1732; as The Doctor in Spite of Himself, 1914; as The Physician in Spite of Himself, in Plays, 1924; as The Unwilling Doctor, 1962.

Mélicerte (produced Saint-Germain-en-Laye, 1666). In Oeuvres posthumes, 1684; translated as Mélicerte, in Plays 5, 1926.

La Pastorale comique, music by Lully (produced Saint-Germain-en-Laye, 1666). In Théâtre, 1888–93.

Le Sicilien; ou, L'Amour peintre (produced Saint-Germain-en-Laye, 1667). 1668; translated as The Sicilian, 1732, and in "The Misanthrope" and Other Plays, 1959.

Amphitryon (produced Théâtre du Palais-Royal, Paris, 1668). 1668; translated as Amphitryon, 1690.

George Dandin; ou, Le Mari confondu (produced Versailles, 1668). 1669; translated as George Dandin; or, The Husband Defeated, 1732.

L'Avare (produced Théâtre du Palais-Royal, Paris, 1668). 1669; translated as The Miser, 1672: several subsequent translations under same title.

Monsieur de Pourceaugnac (produced Château de Chambord, 1669). 1670; translated as The Cornish Squire, 1734; as Monsieur de Pourceaugnac, in Plays 6, 1926.

Les Amants magnifiques (produced Saint-Germain-en-Laye, 1670). In Oeuvres posthumes, 1684; translated as The Courtly Lovers, in Plays 7, 1926.

Le Bourgeois Gentilhomme (produced Château de Chambord, 1670). 1670; translated as The Citizen Turned Gentleman, 1672; as The Merchant Gentleman, 1915; as The Prodigious Snob, 1952; as The Would-Be Gentleman, in Five Plays, 1953; as The Self-Made Gentleman, in Six Prose Comedies, 1956; as The Middle-Class Gentleman, 1957; as The Proper Gent, 1966; as The Bourgeois Gentleman, with The Doctor in Spite of Himself, 1987.

Psyché, with Corneille and Philippe Quinault, music by Lully (produced Tuileries, Paris, 1671). 1671.

Les Fourberies de Scapin (produced Théâtre du Palais-Royal, Paris, 1671). 1671; translated as The Cheats of Scapin, 1677; as Scapin the Scamp, in Six Prose Comedies, 1956; as That Scoundrel Scapin, in Five Plays, 1953; as The Rogueries of Scapin, 1968.

La Comtesse d'Escarbagnas (produced Saint-Germain-en-Laye, 1671). In Oeuvres posthumes, 1684; translated as The Countess of Escarbagnas, in Plays 8, 1926.

Les Femmes savantes (produced Théâtre du Palais-Royal, Paris, 1672). 1673; translated as The Female Virtuosos, 1693; as Blue Stockings, 1884; as The Learned Ladies, in Molière, 1908: several subsequent translations under same title; as The Learned Women, in "The Misanthrope" and Other Plays, 1968.

La Malade imaginaire (produced 1673). 1673–74; translated as Doctor Last in His Chariot, 1769; as The Imaginary Invalid, 1925: several subsequent translations under same title; as The Would-Be Invalid, 1950; as The

Hypochondriac, in *Three Great French Plays*, 1961, and *Five Plays*, 1982.

*

Bibliographies

R. Saintonge and R. Wilson Christ, *Fifty Years of Molière Studies: A Bibliography*, London, 1942; supplement, "Thirty Years of Molière Studies: A Bibliography 1942–1971", in *Molière and the Commonwealth of Letters*, edited by R. Johnson and others, Jackson, Mississippi, 1975.

M. Jurgens and M. Maxfield-Miller, *Cent Ans de recherches sur Molière*, Paris, 1963.

W. Leiner, "Contributions américaines aux études molièresques 1959–1972", in *Romance Notes*, 15, 1973–74.

Criticism

Books:

H.C. Chatfield-Taylor, *Molière: A Biography*, New York, 1905.

E. Faguet, *Rousseau contre Molière*, Paris, 1912.

W.G. Moore, *Molière: A New Criticism*, 1949; revised edition, 1968.

Jacques Audiberti, *Molière dramaturge*, Paris, 1954.

René Bray, *Molière, Homme du théâtre* (biography), Paris, 1954.

L. Emelina, *Les Valets et servantes dans le théâtre de Molière*, Aix-en-Provence, 1958.

Ramon Fernandez, *Molière: The Man Through His Plays*, New York, 1958.

D.B. Wyndham Lewis, *Molière: The Comic Mask*, New York, 1959.

M. Descotes, *Les Grands Rôles de théâtre de Molière*, Paris, 1960.

Judd Hubert, *Molière and the Comedy of Intellect*, Berkeley, California, 1962.

Lionel Gossman, *Men and Masks: A Study of Moliere*, Baltimore, Maryland, 1963.

J. Guicharnaud, *Molière: Une Aventure théâtrale*, Paris, 1963; revised edition, 1984.

J. Mayer, *Molière* (biography), Paris, 1963.

Jacques Guicharnaud, *Molière: A Collection of Critical Essays*, Englewood Cliffs, New Jersey, 1963.

Percy Addison Chapman, *The Spirit of Molière*, edited by J.A. Bede, New York, 1965.

M. Gutwirth, *Molière ou l'invention comique*, Paris, 1966.

G.A. Warner, *Le Monologue chez Molière*, Caen, 1966.

G. Bordonove, *Molière, génial et familier*, Paris, 1967.

H. Charden (ed.), *Nouveaux Documents sur les comédiens de campagne et la vie de Molière* (2 vols.), Paris, 1968.

F.L. Lawrence, *Molière: The Comedy of Unreason*, New Orleans, 1968.

B. Master, *Molière: Students' Guide*, London, 1970.

Hallam Walker, *Molière*, New York, 1971.

F. Chevalley (ed.), *Molière et son temps*, Ghent, 1973.

Alvin Eustis, *Moliere as Ironic Comtemplator*, Paris, 1973.

W.D. Howarth and M. Thomas (eds.), *Molière: Stage and Study*, Oxford, 1973.

Harold C. Knutson, *Molière: An Archetypal Approach*, Toronto, 1976.

P. Gaxotte, *Molière*, Paris, 1977.

Robert McBride, *The Sceptical Vision of Molière*, London, 1977.

G. Defaux, *Molière ou les métamorphoses du comique*, Lexington, Kentucky, 1980.

Roger W. Herzel, *Original Castings of Molière's Plays*, Ann Arbor, Michigan, 1981.

Nathan Gross, *From Gesture to Idea: Esthetics and Ethics in Molière's Comedy*, New York, 1982.

W.D. Howarth, *Moliere: A Playwright and His Audience*, Cambridge, 1982.

G. Conesa, *Le Dialogue molièresque*, Paris, 1983.

C. Abraham, *On the Structure of Molière's "Comédies-ballets"*, Paris, 1984.

S. Chevalley, *Molière, sa vie, son oeuvre*, Paris, 1984.

J.F. Gaines, *Social Structure in Molière's Theater*, Columbus, Ohio, 1984.

Hugh Gaston Hall, *Comedy in Context: Essays on Molière*, Jackson, Mississippi, 1984.

N. Corvin, *Molière et ses metteurs en scène aujourd'hui*, Paris, 1985.

A. Szogyi, *Molière abstrait*, Paris, 1985.

J. Truchet (ed.), *Thématique de Molière*, Paris, 1985.

F. Mallet, *Molière*, Paris, 1986.

T.M. Malachy, *Molière: Les Métamorphoses du carnaval*, Paris, 1987.

A. Simon, *Molière: Une Vie*, Lyon, 1987.

Harold C. Knutson, *The Triumph of Wit: Molière and Restoration Comedy*, Columbus, Ohio, 1988.

Albert Bermel, *Moliere's Theatrical Bounty: A New View of The Plays*, 1989.

* * *

Jean-Baptiste Poquelin, under his assumed name Molière (for which no certain source has ever been discovered) achieved, in an astonishingly brief career—he was to die when just 51—recognition by his contemporaries as an outstanding man of the theatre, and was soon acknowledged by posterity as the greatest comic writer of all time.

Brought up in comfortable bourgeois circumstances, Molière studied law, and would, in the normal course of things, have succeeded his father in his hereditary office as Court upholsterer. But the theatre captured his imagination from an early age: we are told that his maternal grandfather used to take him as a youngster to see the celebrated trio of farce players at the Hôtel de Bourgogne theatre; and in 1643 he scandalised his respectable family by joining the Illustre Théâtre, a company whose nucleus was the Béjart family. He became the lover of Madeleine Béjart, a talented actress with whom he was to have a long professional association, and had soon taken over the direction of the company which, beset by debts, left Paris in 1645 for the itinerant life of a provincial troupe.

Intermittent traces of Molière's journeyings can be seen, especially in the south and west of France, during the next 13 years; but in 1658 he and his colleagues felt sufficiently confident to try their fortunes in Paris once more. They brought with them the customary repertory of tragedies, full-length comedies, and short comic curtain-raisers; and it was with one of Molière's own one-act comedies, *Les Précieuses ridicules*, that the company first attracted enthusiastic acclaim: although this was a farce in plot and structure, it made a sharp satirical comment on a topical subject—the social and literary phenomenon of preciosity—and this struck a novel note.

As an actor, Molière had ambitions to shine in tragedy as well as in comedy, but contemporary comment is unanimous in indicating that this was not where his talent lay: not only was he lampooned by spokesmen for the rival company, established at the Hôtel de Bourgogne, but it is clear from more objective sources that his manner as a tragic actor was not sufficiently stylised and declamatory to suit the prevailing taste.

In comedy, it was a different matter. Molière began by sharing a theatre with the Italian players, and it is often suggested that he developed his gifts as a comic actor by modelling himself on Scaramouche (Tiberio Fiorillo), with whom he enjoyed an excellent relationship. The registers kept by Molière's colleague La Grange, from soon after the company's return to Paris through to Molière's death and beyond, show a progressive reduction in the proportion of tragedies performed, as well as of comedies by other authors; and towards the end of his career Molière's company had become primarily a vehicle for his own plays, written to cater for the talents of his colleagues, and in particular for his own comic skills.

Molière had begun by specialising in the Italianate role of Mascarille, an extrovert, scheming, and resourceful valet; but in 1660 this character-type was permanently replaced (with very few exceptions, such as the Scapin of *Les Fourberies de Scapin*), by a role owing much more to sources in native French farce, as well as to Molière's observation of his fellow-men. Sganarelle, a more passive, introspective character, easily duped by others and prone to self-delusion even when he is not the victim of others' wiles, was much richer in potential for development; and as well as appearing under his own name in half-a-dozen plays, this type can be seen as the basis for a series of distinctive comic figures appearing throughout Molière's mature plays. It has been said that the whole of Molière's comedy is characterised by the interplay between two kinds of imagination: whereas the Mascarille/Scapin type represents the imaginative artistry of the consummate trickster, the derivatives of Sganarelle are characters who try to impose a subjective fantasy of their own imagining on those around them. Of this character-type, the best-known examples are no doubt Arnolphe in *L'École des femmes* (*The School for Wives*), Orgon in *Tartuffe*, Alceste in *Le Misanthrope*, Harpagon in *L'Avare* (*The Miser*), Monsieur Jourdain in *Le Bourgeois Gentilhomme* (*The Would-Be Gentleman*), and Argan in *Le Malade imaginaire* (*The Imaginary Invalid*).

Molière's success was not achieved without making enemies among rival actors and playwrights (a particularly scurrilous campaign alleged that his wife, Armande, whom he married in 1662, was not the younger sister of Madeleine Béjart but her—and therefore probably Molière's—daughter); and several of his plays, especially *Tartuffe* and *Dom Juan*, were subjected to fierce opposition from the Church authorities, the former play being banned from 1664 until public performance was finally authorised in 1669. Throughout these years, however, Molière was able to count on the King's protection; and his company was in regular demand for performances at court or at one of the great princely houses.

As a result of the King's patronage, Molière developed quite early, alongside the series of plays written for his town theatre (the Palais-Royal, which his company occupied from 1660 onwards), a genre specifically conceived in response to the requirements of court entertainment. This new art-form, the *comédie-ballet*, bore some relation to the court ballet (and the English court masque) popular in previous reigns, but its originality was the integration of the interludes of music and dance into the narrative framework of comic drama. The Italian musician Lully collaborated with Molière in a number of such works, of which *Le Bourgeois Gentilhomme* is the undoubted masterpiece, while Molière's last play, *Le Malade imaginaire*, was a *comédie-ballet* created in collaboration with Charpentier.

If the development of this mixed genre shows Molière's ability to exploit the tastes of Louis XIV and his courtiers to positive artistic effect, he was no less able, at the same time, to exert a decisive influence on the evolution of mainstream comic drama to mould the taste of Paris audiences, and to impose on them an equally original conception of comedy—and all this in spite of the active opposition of jealous rivals, and of the pedants, the *précieuses*, and the prudes whom he satirised in his brilliant conversation-piece *La Critique de l'École des femmes*.

Before Molière's day, comic drama had been polarised into the literary, mimetic comedy of manners developed by Corneille in the 1630's, and the extra-(or sub-) literary genre of popular farce. Molière's originality lay in incorporating the aesthetic principle of farce (depending on exaggeration and extravagant invention) into the literary form of a five-act play, often in verse, which mirrored recognisably the ordinary and the everyday, and was capable of providing a vehicle for serious social comment. A case in point is *Tartuffe*. From one point of view, the exposure of the religious hypocrite could not be more serious; but side by side with the formal arguments of the reasonable Cléante are scenes of farce, such as that in which Orgon hides under the table to watch the hypocrite try to seduce his wife, or those involving Mme. Pernelle, Orgon's mother, who was originally played by a man in the manner of a pantomime dame.

This marriage of the mimetic and the ludic, explicitly defended by Molière in the *Critique* (and by an anonymous supporter in the "Letter on Tartuffe"), was to establish him as the unrivalled master of modern comic drama, played with undiminished success in France and throughout the Western world for over three centuries. It was a dramatic formula which emerged from the author's own gifts as a comic actor and the range of talents available in the company for which he was responsible. Never has there been such a remarkable example of a major playwright who was also an outstanding actor-manager; and that this triumphant success was achieved in the brief spell of less than 15 years is little short of miraculous.

Plautus and Terence; Rabelais, Cervantes, Corneille; the Italian *commedia* and the native French farce: all of these, and many another identifiable source, provided Molière with material, for he was well educated and eclectic in his reading. But as has been wisely said, the truly original writer is not one whose sources cannot be identified, but one who cannot be imitated; and despite the attempts of many later dramatists, Molière has remained literally inimitable.

Temperamentally, Molière is known to have been thoughtful and introspective rather than extrovert. His marriage was not a happy one, but he inspired loyalty and affection in his colleagues, and friendship in a wide range of men with a similar taste for independent thought and a dislike for the pedantry and affectation that he lampoons in a number of plays, particularly in *Les Femmes savantes* (*The Learned Ladies*). Several plays ridicule representatives of the medical profession, notably *L'Amour médecin* (*Love is the Best Remedy*) and *Le Malade imaginaire*. It is sadly ironic that, after years of ill-health, he should have been struck down, dying almost on stage, while playing the hypochondriac, Argan, in the latter play.

—William D. Howarth

See also *Volume 1* entries on *Don Juan*; *The Imaginary Invalid*; *The Learned Ladies*; *The Misanthrope*; *The Miser*; *The Pretentious Young Ladies*; *The School for Wives*; *Tartuffe*; *The Would-Be Gentleman*.

MOLNÁR, Ferenc. Born Ferenc Neumann in Budapest, Hungary, 12 January 1878. Educated at Református Gymnázium, Budapest, 1887–95; studied law in Budapest and Geneva, 1895. Married 1) Margit Vészi in 1906 (divorced 1910), one daughter; 2) the actress Sári Fedák in 1922 (divorced 1924); 3) the actress Lili Darvas in 1926 (separated c.1932). Journalist with *A Hét, Uj Idok*, and *Pesti Hírlap* [Pest News]; changed name to Molnár, 1896; first play, *A doktor úr* [The Lawyer], produced at the Budapest Vigszinház [Comedy Theatre], 1902; correspondent, *Budapesti Napló* [Budapest Diary], from 1906; war correspondent in Galicia, 1914–15; first trip to the USA, 1927; travelled in Europe, 1932, and with his companion Wanda Bartha, 1934–36; left Budapest for final time, 1937, travelled to France and Switzerland, and settled in the USA, 1940; resided at the Plaza Hotel, New York, from 1940 until his death; suffered heart attack, 1943; took US citizenship, 1947. Recipient: Voinits Prize (Hungary), 1916. Elected to Petöfi Society, 1908, and the Kisfaludy Society, 1911. Order of Franz Josef, 1916; Légion d'honneur (France), 1927. Died in New York, 1 April 1952.

Works

Collections

Molnár Ferenc művei (collected works in 20 vols.; Volumes 15–20 contain the plays published to 1928). 1928.
Plays (includes *Liliom; Husbands and Lovers; Fashions for Men; The Swan*), translated by Benjamin F. Glazer. 1927.
Plays of Molnár (includes *The Lawyer; The Devil; Liliom; The Guardsman; The Tale of the Wolf; The White Cloud; Carnival; Fashions for Men; The Swan; A Prologue to "King Lear"; Marshal; The Violet; Heavenly and Earthly Love; Mima; The Glass Slipper; Riviera; Still Life; The Play's the Thing; The Witch; Olympia*), edited by by Louis Rittenberg. 1929; retitled as *All the Plays of Molnár*, 1937.
Romantic Comedies (includes *Actor from Vienna; President; Waxworks; Arthur; Blue Danube; The Good Fairy; Anniversity Dinner; Game of Hearts*). 1952.
Színház (selected works). 1961.

Stage Works

A doktor úr (produced Vigszinház, Budapest, 1902). 1902; translated as *The Lawyer*, in *Plays of Molnár*, 1929.
Józsi [Jozsi] (produced Vigszinház, Budapest, 1904). 1902.
Az ördög (produced Vigszinház, Budapest, 1907). 1907; translated as *The Devil*, 1908, and in *Plays of Molnár*, 1929.
A vacsora (produced Vigszinház, Budapest, 1915). 1909; translated as *Dinner*, in *Smart Set*, 67, 1922; as *The Host*, in *One-Act Plays for Stage and Study*, 1925; as *Anniversary Dinner*, in *Romantic Comedies*, 1952.
Liliom (produced Vigszinház, Budapest, 1909). 1909; translated as *Liliom*, 1921: several subsequent translations under same title.
A testőr (produced Vigszinház, Budapest, 1910). 1910; translated as *The Guardsman*, 1910: several subsequent translations under same title.
A farkas (produced Magyar Színház, Budapest, 1912). 1912; translated as *The Tale of the Wolf*, in *Plays of Molnár*, 1929; as *The Wolf*, 1975.
A fehér felho (produced Nemzeti Színház, 1916). 1916; translated as *The White Cloud*, in *Plays of Molnár*, 1929.
Farsang (produced Vigszinház, Budapest, 1916). 1917; translated as *Carnival*, in *Plays of Molnár*, 1929.

Úridivat (produced Nemzeti Színház, Budapest, 1917). 1917; translated as *Fashions for Men*, 1922, and in *Plays of Molnár*, 1929.
A hattyú (produced Vigszinház, Budapest, 1920). 1921; translated as *The Swan*, 1923, and in *Plays of Molnár*, 1929.
Színház [Theatre] (one act plays; produced Magyar Színház, Budapest, 1921). 1923; individual titles:
   1. *Elojáték Lear királyhoz*. Translated as *Prologue to "King Lear"*, in *Plays of Molnár*, 1929.
   2. *Marsall*. Translated as *Marshal*, in *Plays of Molnár*, 1929; as *Actor from Vienna*, in *Romantic Comedies*, 1929.
   3. *Az ibolya*. Translated as *The Violet*, in *Plays of Molnár*, 1929.
Égi és földi szerelem (produced Magyar Színház, Budapest, 1923). 1922; translated as *Heavenly and Earthly Love*, in *Plays of Molnár*, 1929.
A vörös malom [The Red Mill] (produced Magyar Színház, Budapest, 1922). 1923; translated as *Mima*, in *Plays of Molnár*, 1929.
Az üvegcipő (produced Vigszinház, Budapest, 1924). 1924; translated as *The Glass Slipper*, in *Plays of Molnár*, 1929.
Riviera (produced Theater in der Josefstadt, Vienna, 1925). 1926; translated as *Riviera*, in *Plays of Molnár*, 1929.
Csendelet (produced Vigszinház, Budapest, 1925). In translation as *Still Life*, in *Plays of Molnár*, 1929; Hungarian version, in *Színhaz*, 1963.
Játék a kastélyban (produced Magyar Színház, Budapest, 1926). 1926; translated as *The Play's the Thing*, 1927, and in *Plays of Molnár*, 1929; adapted as *Rough Crossing*, 1985.
A boszorkany (produced Andrássy-uti Színház, Budapest, 1927). Translated as *The Witch*, in *Plays of Molnár*, 1929.
Olimpia (produced Magyar Színház, Budapest, 1928). 1928; translated as *Olympia*, 1928, and in *Plays of Molnár*, 1929.
Egy, kettő, három [One, Two, Three] (produced Vigszinház, Budapest, 1929). 1929; translated as *President*, in *Romantic Comedies*, 1952.
A jó tündér (produced Vigszinház, Budapest, 1930). 1930; translated as *The Good Fairy*, 1932, and in *Romantic Comedies*, 1952.
Valaki [Somebody] (produced Belvárosi Színház, Budapest, 1932). 1932; translated as *Arthur*, in *Romantic Comedies*, 1952.
Harmónia [Harmony] (produced Magyar Színház, Budapest, 1932). 1932.
Csoda a hegyek közt [Miracle in the Mountains] (produced Vigszinház, Budapest, 1936). 1933.
Menyegző [Wedding Day] (produced Andrássy-uti Színház, Budapest, 1935). 1933.
Az ismeretlen lány [The Unknown Girl] (produced Vigszinház, Budapest, 1934). 1934.
A cukrászné (produced Andrássy-uti Színház, Budapest, 1935). 1934; translated as *Delicate Story*, 1941.
Nagy szerelem [Great Love] (produced Vigszinház, Budapest, 1935). 1935.
Delila (produced Pesti Színház, Budapest, 1937). 1937; translated as *Delilah*, 1947; as *Blue Danube*, in *Romantic Comedies*, 1952.
Panoptikum, from the play *Merciless Mrs. Roy* (produced Akademietheater, Vienna, 1948). 1941; translated as *Waxworks*, in *Romantic Comedies*, 1952.
The King's Maid (produced Bass Rocks Theater, Gloucester, Massachusetts, 1941).
A császár [The Emperor] (produced Vigszinház, Budapest, 1946).
Pit-a-Pat (produced as *Das Spiel des Herzen*, Theater in der

Josefstadt, Vienna, 1971). In translation as *Game of Hearts*, in *Romantic Comedies*, 1952.

Fiction

"Magdolna" és egyéb elbeszélések ["Magdalena" and Other Stories]. 1898.
"A csókok éjszakája" és egyéb elbeszélések ["The Kiss at Night" and Other Stories]. 1899.
Az éhes város [The Hungry City]. 1901.
Egy gazdátlam csónok története. 1901; translated as *The Derelict Boat*, with *Eva*, 1924.
Eva. 1903; translated as *Eva*, with *The Derelict Boat*, 1924.
Egy pesti leány története [A Budapest Girl's Story]. 1905.
A Pál-utcai fiúk. 1907; translated as *The Paul Street Boys*, 1907.
Rabok. 1908; translated as *Prisoners*, 1924.
Muzsika [Music] (stories). 1908.
"Báro Márczius" és egyéb elbeszélések ["Márczius Báro" and Other Stories]. 1913.
Kis hármaskönyv [Three in One] (stories). 1914.
"Az óriás" és egyéb elbeszélések ["The Giant" and Other Stories]. 1917.
Széntolvajok. 1918.
Andor [Andor]. 1918.
A gőzoszlop [The Steam Chimney]. 1926.
"A csók" és egyéb elbeszélések ["The Kiss" and Other Stories]. 1927.
A zenélő angyal. 1933; translated as *Angel Making Music*, 1935.
A zöld huszár [The Green Hussar]. 1937.
Őszi utazás [Autumn Journey]. 1939.
A kékszemu (stories). In translation, as *The Blue Eyed Lady*, 1942; Hungarian edition, 1958.
Isten veled szivem. In translation, as *Farewell My Heart*, 1945; Hungarian edition, 1947.

Memoirs and Letters

Utitárs a számúzetésben. In translation, as *Companion in Exile: Notes for an Autobiography*, 1950; Hungarian edition, 1958.

Other

"Józsi" és egyéb kis komédiák ["Józsi" and Other Small Comedies]. 1902.
Gyerekek [Children]. 1905.
Ketten beszélnek (sketches). 1909; translated as *Stories for Two*, 1950.
Pesti erkölcsök [Metropolitan Morals]. 1909.
Hétágú síp [Pipes of Pan]. 1911.
"Az aruvimi erdő titka" es egyéb szatirák ["The Secret of the Aruwim Forest" and Other Satires]. 1916.
Egy haditudósító emlékei [A War Correspondent's Diary]. 1916.
Ismerosök [Acquaintances]. 1917.
Ma, tegnap, tegnapelőtt [Today, Yesterday, Tomorrow] (journalism). 1912.
"Vacsor" és egyéb jelenetek. 1917.
Toll [Pen]. 1928.
Szülőfalum, Pest (miscellany). 1962.

*

Bibliographies

Albert Tezla, *Hungarian Authors: A Bibliographical Handbook*, Cambridge, Massachusetts, 1970.
Elizabeth M. Rajec, *Ferenc Molnár: A Bibliography* (2 vols.), Vienna, 1986.

Criticism

Books:
Emro J. Gergely, *Hungarian Drama in New York*, New York, 1947.
Delfino Tinelli, *Molnár*, Brescia, Italy, 1967.
Clara Györgyey, *Ferenc Molnár* (in English), Boston, 1980.
Georg Kóváry, *Der Dramatiker Ferenc Molnár*, Innsbruck, 1984.

Articles:
Elizabeth M. Rajec, "Names of Characters in Plays by Molnár", in *Literary Onomastics Studies*, 12, 1985.

*   *   *

Decades after his death, Ferenc Molnár is still regarded as Hungary's internationally best-known playwright. Literary connoisseurs bemoan this lack of attention to Hungarian drama, overlooking two crucial points. One is the difficulty that the unique Hungarian language generally poses for wider recognition of its literary tradition. Breaking out of such isolation is no mean feat. The other circumstance is the goodwill service Molnár did for Hungary abroad, making this country appear as one centre of European theatrical life whose inhabitants were lovable and artistic—if slightly cynical—hedonists.

One secret of Molnár's success was his eclecticism. He offered a recognizable segment of life for everybody—something familiar to tingle his spectators' fantasy. While some of his greatest successes, including *A hattyú* (*The Swan*), *Játék a kastélyban* (*The Play's the Thing*), and *Olympia* carry us into the world of the upper classes, others (among them *Liliom*) do just the opposite, representing the life of lower-class urbanites. In addition, his indebtedness to past traditions and contemporary trends gives the audience a sweet sense of *déjà-vu*.

While often labelled a cosmopolitan by conservative Hungarian critics, Molnár fits into the country's dramatic tradition in more than one way. Like Károly Kisfaludy (1788–1830), the "father of the Hungarian comedy", Molnár also created a middle-class tradition in the lighter vein, shedding the overwhelming rural mannerisms of Hungarian drama. His work was similar to the "folksy" comedies of Ede Szigligeti (1817–79) as well as the more ironic, urbane humour of Gergely Csiky (1842–91). His international success, however, can be attributed rather to his European models. As an ardent theatregoer and a much-travelled writer with no concern for economic stringencies, Molnár sampled and integrated the most talked-about literary styles of the 19th and early 20th centuries.

French theatre held an especial interest for Molnár, notably Scribe's *pièce bien faite* and its melodramatic (in Sardou and Dumas *fils*) and pedestrianized (boulevard play) versions. Technique and virtuosity became essential characteristics of his plays. Naturalism was not alien to him either, but it never dominated any of his work, and neither did the numerous other, seemingly disparate, trends that appear carefully distributed in his *oeuvre*. These include the Austrian popular comedy, Oscar Wilde's decadent frivolousness (Molnár imitated Wilde in his appearance), Shaw's exhaustive, reflective stage directions, or Maeterlinck's and Hauptmann's fairy-tale symbolism (especially evident in *Liliom*). Probably Molnár's most innovative facet was a form of relativism, allying him with Schnitzler (who was more cynical) and Pirandello (who was more philosophical, although Molnár's one-act play *Elöjáték Lear királyhoz* (*Prologue to "King Lear"*) and *The Play's the Thing* approximate Pirandello's intellectual virtuosity).

Relativism was, of course, a catchword of the time. The *Zeitgeist* of Molnár's plays' ambiance, an immorality hiding behind chastity, characterized a world that was swept away by World War I. The writer reflected his own situation in these plays, featuring either himself or some ironic *alter ego* as one of his characters. In addition, the central role of women in Molnár's plays is partly due to their function as protagonists of relativism and illusion.

Women also frequently turn these plays into *drames à clef*: the plays can be seen as parables of the playwright's attraction to, and conquests or failures with, the belles of Budapest. Contemporary spectators believed they could recognize many other sarcastic allusions to the social world of the time in his plays (such as an assumed parallel between the marriage of the last Habsburg king and the plot of *The Swan*). Genre parody was also in Molnár's vein: in *A farkas* (*The Wolf*), the heroine dreams of a love affair with her butler, a clear reference to Strindberg's *Miss Julie*. Generally, there is a balance between illusion and reality, sophistication and vulgarity, truth and affected sentiment, genuineness and kitsch.

International success followed Molnár's third play, *Az ördög* (*The Devil*). After its Budapest premiere it was staged in Turin, then in Berlin and other European capitals. In a year it reached Broadway and made Molnár a life-long favourite with American theatregoers. But the international reception of his plays was uneven. For example, *Liliom*, now considered Molnár's most memorable play, flopped at its Budapest (1909) and London (1920) premieres, but was an instant success in Vienna (1913) and New York (1921). *Liliom* also served as the basis for the Rodgers and Hammerstein musical *Carousel*, and other Molnár plays became cinematic successes (*The Swan* has had three film versions).

Molnár's influence was wide ranging and considerable. A writer of novels, short stories, journalistic prose and war reports, Molnár nevertheless excelled on the stage. Many of Molnár's plays remain among the popular evergreens of world drama and, occasionally, they even provide interesting philosophical and psychological insights.

—George Bisztray

See also *Volume 1* entry on *Liliom*.

———

MOLINA, Tirso de.   See **TIRSO DE MOLINA**

———

MONTHERLANT, Henry (Millon) de. Born in Neuilly-sur-Seine, suburb of Paris, 21 April 1896. Educated at

Henry de Montherlant (portrait by Jacques Émile Blanche, 1923; Musée des Beaux-Arts, Rouen).

the Lycée Janson-de-Sailly; Institution Saint-Pierre, Paris, 1907–10; École Sainte-Croix, Neuilly, 1911–12; Institut Catholique, studying law: failed examinations, 1913. Enlisted with French army, 1916: wounded in 1918, and became interpreter for US army, 1919; travelled widely in Spain, Italy, and the Mediterranean countries, 1925–30; in North Africa (mainly Algeria), 1930–32; returned to Paris, 1932; contributed to various opposition newspapers and magazines during the 1930's, including *Candide*, *Le Figaro*, *Vendredi*, *Commune*, *Ce Soir*, and *Revue des deux mondes*; began his literary career with essays and novels; first-produced play, *Pasiphaé*, staged 1938; lost sight of one eye, 1968. Recipient: Grand Prix de Littérature de l'Académie Française, 1934; Northcliffe-Heineman Prize, 1934. Elected to Académie Française, 1960. Committed suicide in Paris, 21 September 1972.

Works

Collections

"The Master of Santiago" and Other Plays (includes *Queen After Death*; *No Man's Son*; *Malatesta*; *Tomorrow the Dawn*), translated by Jonathon Griffin.   1951.
Théâtre complet (2 vols.).   1950–51.
Théâtre (Bibliothèque de la Pléiade edition).   1958.

Stage Works

L'Exil (one scene produced 1934).   1929.
Pasiphaé (produced Théâtre Pigalle, Paris, 1938).   1936.

La Reine morte; ou Comment on tue les femmes (produced Comédie-Française, Paris, 1942). 1942; translated as *Queen After Death*, in *"The Master of Santiago" and Four Other Plays*, 1951.

Fils de personne; ou, Plus que le sang (produced Théâtre Saint Georges, Paris, 1943). 1944; translated as *No Man's Son*, in *"The Master of Santiago" and Four Other Plays*, 1951.

Un Incompris (produced Théâtre Saint Georges, Paris, 1944). 1944.

Malatesta (produced Théâtre Marigny, Paris, 1948). 1946; translated as *Malatesta*, in *"The Master of Santiago" and Four Other Plays*, 1951.

Le Maître de Santiago (produced Théâtre Hébertot, Paris, 1948). 1947; translated as *The Master of Santiago*, in *"The Master of Santiago" and Four Other Plays*, 1951.

Demain il fera jour (produced Théâtre Hébertot, Paris, 1948). 1949; translated as *Tomorrow the Dawn*, in *"The Master of Santiago" and Four Other Plays*, 1951.

Celles qu'on prend dans ses bras (produced Théâtre de la Madeleine, Paris, 1950). 1950.

La Ville dont le prince est un enfant (produced Théâtre Michel, Paris, 1967). 1951.

Port-Royal (produced Comédie-Française, Paris, 1954). 1954.

Brocéliande (produced Comédie-Française, Paris, 1956). 1956.

Don Juan (produced Théâtre de l'Athénée, Paris, 1958). 1958.

Le Cardinal d'Espagne (produced Comédie-Française, Paris, 1960). 1960.

La Guerre civile. 1965?; translated as *Civil War*, in *Theatre at War*, edited by Robert Baldick, 1967.

Fiction

Le Songe. 1922; translated as *The Dream*, 1963.
Les Bestiaires. 1926; translated as *The Bullfighters*, 1927; as *The Matador*, 1957.
La Petite Infante de Castille. 1929.
Les Célibataires. 1934; translated as *Lament for the Death of an Upper Class*, 1935; as *Perish in Their Pride*, 1936; as *The Bachelors*, 1960.
Les Jeunes Filles (4 vols). Translated as *The Girls*, 1966–68; individual volumes:
   Les Jeunes Filles. 1936; translated as *Young Girls*, with *Pity for Women*, 1937.
   Pitié pour les femmes. 1936; translated as *Pity for Women*, with *Young Girls*, 1937.
   Le Démon du bien. 1937; translated as *Demon of Good*, 1940; translated as *Costals and the Hippogriff*, 1940.
   Les Lépreuses. 1939; translated as *The Lepers*, 1940.
L'Histoire d'amour de "La Rose de sable". 1954; translated as *Desert Love*, 1957.
Romans (2 vols). 1959 and 1982.
Le Chaos et la nuit. 1963; translated as *Chaos and Night*, 1964.
La Rose de sable. 1968.
Les Garçons. 1969.
Un Assassin est mon maître. 1971.

Verse

Encore un instant de bonheur. 1934.

Memoirs and letters

Correspondance: Henry de Montherlant, Roger Peyrefitte. 1983.
Lettres à Michel de Saint Pierre. 1987.

Other

La Relève du matin, 1920.
Chant funèbre pour les morts de Verdun. 1924.
Les Olympiques (2 vols.). 1924.
Aux Fontaines du désir. 1927.
Mors et vita. 1932.
Service inutile. 1935.
L'Équinoxe de septembre. 1938.
Le Solstice de juin. 1941.
Un Voyageur solitaire est un diable. 1945.
Textes sous une occupation. 1953.
Carnets 1930–1944. 1947–56.
Selected Essays, edited by Peter Quennell. 1961.
Essais. 1963.
Va Jouer avec cette poussière (*Carnets 1958–1964*). 1966.
La Tragédie sans masque: Notes de théâtre. 1972.
La Marée du soir (*Carnets 1968–1971*). 1972.

*

Bibliographies

Daniel E. Neville, *Henry de Montherlant and His Critics*, Isabella, Michigan, 1967.
Georges G. Place, *Henry de Montherlant 1896–1972: Bibliographie de l'oeuvre*, Paris, 1974.

Criticism

Books:
J. Cruikshank, *Montherlant*, 1964.
André Marissel, *Henry de Montherlant* (biography), Paris, 1966.
J. Batchelor, *Existence and Imagination: The Theatre of Henry Montherlant*, St. Lucia, Queensland, 1967.
André Blanc, *Montherlant: Un pessimisme heureux*, Paris, 1968.
Robert B. Johnson, *Henry de Montherlant*, New York, 1968.
Auréliu Weiss, *Héroïnes du théâtre de Montherlant*, Paris, 1968.
Jean M. Gautier, *Le Théâtre d'Henry de Montherlant*, Paris, 1969.
H. Perruchot, *Montherlant* (biography), Paris, 1969.
Philippe de Saint-Robert, *Montherlant le séparé*, Paris, 1969.
Lucille Becker, *Henry de Montherlant: A Critical Biography*, Carbondale, Illinois, 1970.
Sylvie Chevally and Jacques de Laprade (eds.), *Henry de Montherlant: Homme du théâtre*, Paris, 1970.
Ferdinando Banchini, *Le Théâtre de Montherlant*, Rome, 1971.
Marcel Lobet, *Montherlant et le sacré*, Brussels, 1972.
Paul d'Arx, *La Femme dans le théâtre de Henry de Montherlant*, Paris, 1973.
André Blanc (ed.), *Les Critiques de notre temps et Montherlant*, Paris, 1973.
Paul Ginestier, *Montherlant: Textes de Montherlant, points de vue critiques, témoignages, chronologie, bibliographie, illustrations*, Paris, 1973.
Jacques Robichez, *Le Théâtre de Montherlant*, Paris, 1973.
Pierre Sipriot, *Montherlant sans masques* (2 vols.), Paris 1982–90.

P. Durosin, *Montherlant et l'antiquité*, Paris, 1987.

Jean P. Krémer, *Le Désir dans l'oeuvre de Montherlant*, Paris, 1987.

Richard J. Golsan, *Service inutile: A Study of the Tragedic in the Theatre of Montherlant*, University of Mississippi, 1988.

Peter Norrish, *New Tragedy and Comedy in France 1945–70*, London, 1988.

Articles:

Jonathon R. Price, "Montherlant: The Jansenist Libertine", in *Renascence*, 19, 1967.

Angela Belli, "The Rugged Individualists of Henry de Montherlant", in *Modern Drama*, 13, 1970.

* * *

Henry de Montherlant came to the theatre relatively late in life, with his reputation clearly made as a novelist and his stance as an aristocrat disillusioned with the modern world well fixed in the public's mind. He was 46 when *La Reine morte* (*The Queen After Death*) was produced at the State-subsidised Comédie-Française in 1942 and became one of the great successes marking the renaissance of the French theatre during the World War II German Occupation. The contempt which he had not hesitated to express for his fellow countrymen at the time of the catastrophic defeat of June 1940 comes through in the play's self-conscious evocation of nobler, more aristocratic times.

Although ostentatiously unmarried, and given to using his novels to express scorn and distaste for women, he concentrated his next play, *Fils de personne* (*No Man's Son*), on the moral worthlessness of French youth. The play was less successful than *La Reine morte*, which was still playing to full houses at the Comédie-Française when the former was taken off to make way for another exercise in aristocratic and religious nostalgia, Paul Claudel's *Le Soulier de satin* (*The Satin Slipper*).

However, the success in 1948 of *Le Maître de Santigo* (*The Master of Santiago*) at the Théâtre Hébertot proved that the end of the War had not diminished the French public's enthusiasm for aristocratic escapism. A Spanish 16th-century aristocrat, Don Alvaro Dabo, rejects the urgent and eloquent invitations of his friends to play the part befitting his rank in the establishment of the Spanish empire in the New World. It is, as he rightly points out, an enterprise rendered totally corrupt by the greed for gold inspiring most of those taking part in it. Any argument that the conquest is a crusade justified by the salvation which it brings to the Indians is, in his view, totally unacceptable. The Christian values which had earlier inspired the reconquest of Spain from the Moors in the 15th century are completely dead. All that a man of honour can do is to reject the modern world completely, and this Don Alvaro proceeds to do. Accompanied by his only daughter, Maria, whom he wraps in the enormous white cloak which is the uniform of the chivalric order of which he is the head, he shuts himself away in his castle to await death. Maria, happy to be the Iphigenia to his proud and self-defeating Agamemnon, sacrifices her life to keep him company.

The great success of *Le Maître de Santiago*, like that of *La Reine morte*, stemmed primarily from the elegance, precision, and nobility of Montherlant's language. It is a characteristic of the traditional French theatre that the audience listens in order to hear why the characters are behaving as they are. The result of their actions is either announced in advance or is so predictable as to remove any curiosity as to the outcome. What matters is the reasons given and arguments presented.

Montherlant satisfied French taste in this respect, while at the same time providing an alternative to the politically committed theatre of Jean-Paul Sartre. While Sartre urged his contemporaries to involve themselves closely with the political issues of the time, the Montherlant of *La Reine morte* and *Le Maître de Santiago* recommended an attitude of aristocratic, slightly Jansenist, detachment. It was a view which the failure of the Fourth Republic to give reality to the hopes of the resistance movement made peculiarly attractive, especially to members of the social class to which Montherlant belonged by birth and preference. Aristocratic values, he told his audience, could flourish only in periods distant and different from our own.

In 1950, his evocation of the world of the Italian renaissance in *Malatesta* reinforced this impression, with Jean-Louis Barrault even more predictably himself than usual in the title role in his own production at his own theatre, the Marigny. The recreation of the atmosphere of Montherlant's more mysogynistic novels in *Celles qu'on prend dans ses bras* (The Ones You Take in Your Arms), also produced in 1950 (but at the Théâtre de la Madeleine) was less successful, and it was not until 1954, with the production at the Comédie-Française of his *Port Royal* that Montherlant once again became one of the most admired authors of the French Catholic Right. Although the pagan attitudes informing some of his other works cast a certain doubt on the authenticity of his own religious faith, his evocation of the intensely spiritual world of the Jansenist movement in *Port Royal* was extremely successful.

In his original conception, *Port Royal* was to have been the third play in a "Catholic Trilogy" of which *Le Maître de Santiago* was the first part, and *La Ville dont le prince est un enfant* the second. However, although *La Ville* was accorded the apparently unique honour of being accepted for production at the Comédie-Française by a unanimous decision of the selection committee at its very first reading, it was never performed in a commercial theatre in Montherlant's lifetime. His respect for the established authorities of the Catholic Church led him to delay permission for this study of intense emotional friendship in a residential Catholic boys' school to be put on stage until a general change in public attitudes made the performance of such a play more acceptable. This happened in 1967, when it was produced with great success at the Théâtre Michel.

—Philip Thody

See also *Volume 1* entry on *Queen After Death*.

———

MOODY, William Vaughn. Born in Spencer, Indiana, USA, 8 July 1869. Educated at New Albany High School, Indiana, graduated 1885; Riverview Academy, Poughkeepsie, New York, 1887–89; Harvard University, Cambridge, Massachusetts (editor, *Harvard Monthly*), 1889–94, AB 1893, AM 1894. Married Harriet Tilden Brainard in 1909. High school teacher, Corydon Pike, 1886, and Spencer, 1886–89, both Indiana; instructor in English, Harvard University and Radcliffe College, Cambridge, Massachusetts, 1894–95; instructor in English and Rhetoric, 1895–99, and non-teaching assistant professor of English, 1901–08, University of Chicago; first play, *The Masque of Judgement*, published 1900; first-produced play, *The Great Divide*, staged 1906; full-time writer after 1908. Litt.D: Yale University, New Haven, Connecticut, 1908. Member, American Academy, 1908. Died in Colorado Springs, Colorado, 17 October 1910.

Works

Collections

Poems and Plays (2 vols.), edited by John M. Manly.   1912.

Stage Works

The Masque of Judgment: A Masque-Drama.   1900.
The Fire-Bringer.   1904.
The Great Divide (as *A Sabine Woman*, produced Garrick Theatre, Chicago, 1906; revised version, as *The Great Divide*, produced Princess Theatre, New York, 1906). 1909.
The Faith Healer.   1909; revised version (produced Savoy Theatre, New York, 1910).
The Death of Eve (incomplete).   In *Poems and Plays*, 1912.

Verse

Poems.   1901; as *"Gloucester Moors" and Other Poems*, 1909.
Selected Poems, edited by Robert Morss Lovett.   1931.

Memoirs and Letters

Some Letters, edited by Daniel Gregory Mason.   1913.
Letters to Harriet, edited by Percy MacKaye.   1935.

Other

A History of English Literature, with Robert Morss Lovett. 1902, revised edition, 1918; simplified edition, as *A First View of English Literature*, 1905; as *A First View of English and American Literature*, 1909.

Editor, *The Pilgrim's Progress*, by Bunyan.   1897.
Editor, *"The Rime of the Ancient Mariner" by Coleridge and "The Vision of Sir Launfal" by Lowell*.   1898.
Editor, *The Lady of the Lake*, by Scott.   1899.
Editor, with Wilfred Wesley Cressy, *The Iliad of Homer*, books 1, 6, 22, 24, translated by Alexander Pope.   1899.
Editor, *The Complete Poetical Works of Milton*.   1899.
Editor, with George Cabot Lodge and John Ellerton Lodge, *The Poems of Trumbull Stickney*.   1905.
Editor, *Selections from De Quincey*.   1909.

*

Bibliographies

Maurice F. Brown, "William Vaughn Moody", in *Bulletin of Bibliography*, 28, 1971.
Maurice F. Brown, "William Vaughn Moody (1868–1910)" (research review), in *American Literary Realism*, 6, 1973.

Criticism

Books:
David D. Henry, *William Vaughn Moody: A Study*, Boston, 1934.

A.H. Quinn, *American Drama from the Civil War to the Present Day 2*, New York, 1936.
Martin Halpern, *William Vaughn Moody*, New York, 1964.
Maurice F. Brown, *Estranging Dawn: The Life and Works of William Vaughn Moody*, Carbondale, Illinois, 1973.

Articles:
Jerry V. Pickering, "William Vaughn Moody: The Dramatist as Social Philosopher", in *Modern Drama*, 14, 1971.

* * *

Blank verse drama has, since the Elizabethans, proved a will-o'-the-wisp that has lured many writers of varying calibre into the backwaters of dramatic creation, among them William Vaughn Moody. An almost exact contemporary of Stephen Phillips in Britain, he enjoyed, like him, a high reputation in his lifetime as a poet; his verse plays, unlike those of Phillips, being dramatic poems rather than poetic dramas, were never staged, though there is evidence that they were conceived with the theatre in mind. Indeed, as a dramatist Moody might have sunk into a posthumous obscurity even more complete than Phillips's had it not been for a total change of direction in one influential play.

By inclination and profession an academic, he edited works by several English and American poets (mostly Romantics) but was also friendly with many leading men of letters of his time. He abandoned teaching in his early 30's to concentrate on writing poetry, painting, and travelling. The dramatic trilogy, *The Fire-Bringer*, *The Masque of Judgment*, and the incomplete *The Death of Eve*, though not written or published in that sequence, exhibits his Romantic affinities, his idealism, and a Hellenistic aestheticism influenced by Walter Pater, as well as an eclectic verse style echoing the Pre-Raphaelites and others. An ambitious but uneasy amalgam of the pagan and the Christian (a Shelleyan Prometheus in the first drama, a galaxy of Miltonic angels in the second, and the post-lapsarian heroine of the third), the trilogy attempts a celebration of a life force and of creativity human, divine, and anthropomorphic. Religion and sensuality co-exist uneasily throughout: a theme predominantly but not exclusively Christian is presented in a style faintly Swinburnian. His undistinguished blank verse reflects the facility to be expected from one who once described it as "easier to write than prose".

The Great Divide, though also uneven, enjoyed successful stage runs in New York and London after opening in Chicago as *A Sabine Woman*. That too seems to have been originally conceived as a blank-verse play, though Moody would have had even more difficulty there in reconciling the medium with the plot. This was based on an actual occurrence of which he had heard, and he was also fired by a personal enthusiasm for Colorado. Despite its western setting and theme, the divide of the title is moral and cultural rather than topographical, the divide between the established affluent society of the eastern seaboard and the more earthy primitivism of the frontier. This is symbolised in the yoking together, by violence of circumstance, of the civilised New England woman and the rough and ready pioneer of the West.

A potentially melodramatic first act sees the heroine, accidentally left alone in a remote western cabin, confronted by three drunken miners who threaten her with—the phrase is appropriate to the tone of the play—a fate worse than death. She is rescued from this by the intervention of one of them, to whom, in return, she promises to devote the rest of her life. In Act II Ghent has made good, become prosperous, and grown genuinely fond of his wife, but they are divided by his imperfect sensitivity, Ruth's agonised struggle to regain her self-respect, and the intervention of her family who encourage her to return to Massachusetts with them. Act III resorts to the familiar device of the faithful, but abandoned, husband becoming the unknown benefactor who saves Ruth's family from bankruptcy; this, and her pregnancy, bring about a final reconciliation.

Summarised thus it sounds stereotypical, sentimental, and theatrical in the worst sense, and it is not helped by the obliqueness with which convention constrains Moody's treatment of the crucial latent sexuality. What redeems it is the freshness of the approach to the East/West theme, and his judicious balancing of the strengths and weaknesses of the couple's differing backgrounds. What must have struck his contemporaries as the dialogue's racy realism (even though it now seems dated), the topicality of the theme, and the twists in the plot, explain its popularity in its day. Ruth, the would-be emancipated, vivacious woman, forced to reconcile the wilder side of her nature with the restricting code of her latter-day Puritan upbringing, is Moody's most successfully realised character.

Ruth embodies the concept of woman as a reconciling agent between man and God, a concept which underlies *The Death of Eve*, unfinished as that work is. His other prose play, *The Faith Healer*, is, by comparison, disappointing despite the labour he devoted to it. The heroine, Rhoda, is in the same mould as Ruth, but less fully drawn, less lively. The action turns on her love for the eponymous hero, but the sexual transgression implied in her past is allowed to loom too large in temporarily inhibiting her restoration to the healer of his wavering faith in his mission; similarly, his intense attraction to her, to which this wavering is attributed, comes across merely as a rather unconvincing infatuation. The play is certainly not the challenge to sexual repression that *The Great Divide* seemed to promise. In both pieces, too, Moody tends to introduce a larger cast-list than is strictly necessary and he lacks the dramatic ability to establish most of them as characters in their own right. Both, however, have value as dramas characteristic of their place and time without encouraging excessive evaluations of Moody's potential as a dramatist had he lived longer.

—Dennis Welland

See also *Volume 1* entry on *The Great Divide*.

MORATÍN, Leandro Fernández de. See **FERNÁNDEZ DE MORATÍN, Leandro.**

MORTIMER, John (Clifford). Born in Hampstead, London, 21 April 1923. Educated at Harrow School, Middlesex, 1937–40; Brasenose College, Oxford, 1940–42, BA 1947; called to the bar, 1948. Served with the Crown Film Units as scriptwriter during World War II. Married 1) Penelope Dimont (i.e., the writer Penelope Mortimer) in 1949 (divorced 1971), one son and one daughter; 2) Penelope Gollop in 1972, two daughters. Barrister and writer; first-produced plays, *The Dock Brief* and *What Shall We Tell Caroline?*, staged 1958; drama critic, *New Statesman, Evening Standard*, and *Observer*, 1972, all London. Member of the National Theatre Board, 1968–88; Master of the Bench, Inner Temple, 1975; president, Berkshire, Buckinghamshire, and Oxfordshire Naturalists' Trust, from 1984; chairman, League of Dramatists; chairman of the council, Royal Society of Literature, from 1989; chairman, Royal Court Theatre, from 1990; president, Howard League for Penal Reform, 1992. Recipient: Italia Prize, for radio play, 1958; Screenwriters Guild Award, for television play, 1970; BAFTA Award, for television play, 1980. D. Litt: Susquehanna University, Selinsgrove, Pennsylvania, 1985; University of St. Andrews, Fife, 1987; University of Nottingham, 1989; LL. D: Exeter University, 1986. CBE (Commander, Order of the British Empire), 1986.

Works

Collections

Three Plays (includes *The Dock Brief; I Spy; What Shall We Tell Caroline?*). 1958.
"Lunch Hour" and Other Plays (includes *Collect Your Hand Baggage; David and Broccoli; Call Me a Liar*). 1960.
Five Plays (includes *The Dock Brief; What Shall We Tell Caroline?; I Spy; Lunch Hour; Collect Your Hand Baggage*). 1970.
Three Boulevard Farces (adaptations of plays by Feydeau; includes *A Little Hotel on the Side; A Flea in Her Ear; The Lady from Maxim's*). 1984.
Plays (includes *Voyage Round My Father; The Judge; Collaborators; The Dock Brief; Two Stars for Comfort*). 1989.

Stage Works

The Dock Brief (broadcast 1957; produced Lyric Theatre, Hammersmith, London, 1958). In *Three Plays*, 1958.
What Shall We Tell Caroline? (produced Lyric Theatre, Hammersmith, London, 1958). In *Three Plays*, 1958.
I Spy (broadcast 1957; produced Playhouse, Salisbury, Wiltshire, 1959). In *Three Plays*, 1958.
Sketches in *One to Another* (produced 1959). 1960.
The Wrong Side of the Park (produced Cambridge Theatre, London, 1960). 1960.
Lunch Hour (broadcast 1960; produced Playhouse, Salisbury, Wiltshire, 1960). In *"Lunch Hour" and Other Plays*, 1960.
Call Me a Liar, from the television play (produced 1968). In *"Lunch Hour" and Other Plays*, 1960.
Collect Your Hand Baggage (produced London Academy of Music and Dramatic Art, 1961). In *"Lunch Hour" and Other Plays*, 1960.
Sketches in *One over the Eight* (produced London, 1961).
Two Stars for Comfort (produced Garrick Theatre, London, 1962). 1962.
Sketches in *Changing Gear* (produced London, 1965).
A Flea in Her Ear, from a play by Feydeau (produced by the National Theatre, Old Vic, London, 1966). 1967.
The Judge (produced Cambridge Theatre, London, 1967). 1967.
Home (ballet scenario; produced 1968).
Cat Among the Pigeons, from a play by Feydeau (produced Prince of Wales Theatre, London, 1969). 1970.

Come As You Are: Four Short Plays (includes *Mill Hill;
Bermondsey; Gloucester Road; Marble Arch*; produced
New Theatre, London, 1970). 1971.
A Voyage Round My Father, from the radio play (produced
Greenwich Theatre, London, 1970). 1971.
The Captain of Köpenick, from a play by Carl Zuckmayer
(produced by the National Theatre, Old Vic, London,
1971). 1971.
Conflicts, with others (produced London, 1971).
I, Claudius, from novels by Robert Graves (produced
Queen's Theatre, London, 1972).
Collaborators (produced Duchess Theatre, London, 1973).
1973.
The Fear of Heaven (as *Mr. Luby's Fear of Heaven*, broadcast
1976; as *The Fear of Heaven*, produced with *The Prince of
Darkness* as *Heaven and Hell*, Greenwich Theatre,
London, 1976). 1978.
The Bells of Hell (as *The Prince of Darkness*, produced with
The Fear of Heaven as *Heaven and Hell*, Greenwich
Theatre, London, 1976; as *The Bells of Hell*, produced
Richmond, Surrey, 1977). 1978.
The Lady from Maxim's from a play by Feydeau (produced
National Theatre, London, 1977). 1977.
When That I Was (produced Arts Centre, Ottowa, Ontario,
1982).
A Little Hotel on the Side, from a play by Feydeau and
Maurice Desvalliers (produced National Theatre, London,
1984). In *Three Boulevard Farces*, 1985.
Die Fledermaus, music by Johann Strauss, from the libretto
by Henri Meilhac and Ludovic Halévy (produced London,
1989). 1989.

Screenplays

Ferry to Hong Kong, with Lewis Gilbert and Vernon Harris,
1959; *The Innocents*, with Truman Capote and William
Archibald, 1961; *Guns of Darkness*, 1962; *I Thank a Fool*,
with others, 1962; *Lunch Hour*, 1962; *The Running Man*,
1963; *Bunny Lake is Missing*, with Penelope Mortimer, 1964;
A Flea in Her Ear, 1967; *John and Mary*, 1969.

Television Plays

The Dock Brief, 1957; *I Spy*, 1958; *Call Me a Liar*, 1958
(published in *"Lunch Hour" and Other Plays*, 1960); *David
and Broccoli*, 1960 (published in *"Lunch Hour" and Other
Plays*, 1960); *A Choice of Kings*, 1966 (published in *Playbill
3*, edited by Alan Durband, 1969); *The Exploding Azalea*,
1966; *The Head Waiter*, 1966; *Hughie*, 1967; *The Other Side*,
1967; *Desmond*, 1968 (published in *The Best Short Plays
1971*, edited by Stanley Richards); *Infidelity Took Place*,
1968; *Married Alive*, 1970; *Swiss Cottage*, 1972; *Knightsbridge*, 1972 (published 1973); *Rumpole of the Bailey*, 1975,
and series, 1978, 1979, 1987, 1988; *A Little Place off the
Edgware Road, The Blue Film, The Destructors, The Case for
the Defence, Chagrin in Three Parts, The Invisible Japanese
Gentlemen, Special Duties*, and *Mortmain*, all from stories by
Graham Greene, 1975–76; *Will Shakespeare*, 1978; *Rum-
pole's Return*, 1980; *Unity*, from the book by David Pryce-
Jones, 1981; *Brideshead Revisited*, from the novel by Evelyn
Waugh, 1981; *The Ebony Tower*, from the story by John
Fowles, 1984; *Paradise Postponed*, from his own novel, 1986;
Summer's Lease, from his own novel, 1989; *The Waiting
Room*, 1989; *Titmuss Regained*, 1991.

Radio Plays

Like Men Betrayed, 1955; *No Hero*, 1955; *The Dock Brief*,
1957; *I Spy*, 1957; *Three Winters*, 1958; *Lunch Hour*, 1960;
The Encyclopedist, 1961; *A Voyage Round My Father*, 1963;
Personality Split, 1964; *Education of an Englishman*, 1964; *A
Rare Device*, 1965; *Mr. Luby's Fear of Heaven*, 1976; Edwin,
1982 (published in *"Edwin" and Other Plays*, 1984);
Rumpole, from his own stories, 1988; *Glasnost*, 1988.

Fiction

Charade. 1947.
Rumming Park. 1948.
Answer Yes or No. 1950; as *The Silver Hook*, 1950.
Like Men Betrayed. 1953.
The Narrowing Stream. 1954.
Three Winters. 1956.
Will Shakespeare: The Untold Story. 1977.
Rumpole. 1980; includes:
  Rumpole of the Bailey. 1978.
  The Trials of Rumpole. 1979.
Regina v. Rumpole. 1981; includes:
  Rumpole's Return. 1980.
  Rumpole for the Defence. 1982.
Rumpole and the Golden Thread. 1983.
The First Rumpole Omnibus (includes *Rumpole of the Bailey:
The Trials of Rumpole; Rumpole's Return*). 1983.
Paradise Postponed. 1985.
The Second Rumpole Omnibus (includes *Rumpole for the
Defence; Rumpole and the Golden Thread; Rumpole's Last
Case*). 1987.
Summer's Lease. 1988.
Rumpole and the Age of Miracles. 1988.
Titmuss Regained. 1990.
Rumpole à la Carte. 1990.

Memoirs and Letters

Clinging to the Wreckage: A Part of Life. 1982.

Other

No Moaning of the Bar. 1957.
With Love and Lizards (travel), with Penelope Mortimer.
1957.
In Character (interviews). 1983.
The Liberty of the Citizen (lecture), with Franklin Thomas
and Lord Hunt of Tanworth. 1983.
Character Parts (interviews). 1986.

Editor, *Famous Trials*, edited by Harry Hodge and James H.
Hodge. 1984.
Editor, *Great Law and Order Stories*. 1990.
Editor, *The Oxford Book of Villains*. 1992.

*

Criticism

Books:
John Russell Taylor, *Anger and After*, London, 1962; revised
edition, 1969; US edition as *The Angry Theatre*, New York,
1962.

* * *

In several respects it is difficult to categorise John Mortimer's writing for the theatre with the work of his playwriting contemporaries in post-war Britain. During the late 1950's and 1960's, at a time when an "angry" generation of writers (John Osborne, Ann Jellicoe, John Arden, Arnold Wesker, Shelagh Delaney, and so on) was exploring the theatre's potential to address social and political tensions at breaking point as a new youth became estranged from dominant cultural values, Mortimer charted the less turbulent waters of the affairs of the middle-classes, and very much followed mainstream theatrical traditions.

Perhaps Mortimer's cultural background—he was a barrister's son and the quintessentially English product of a public school and Oxford University education—made this difference of interest inevitable. At a time when duffle-coated young writers sat in clouds of smoke around Soho café tables, Mortimer was keeping one foot in the establishment camp by following in his father's profession as a lawyer. Both father and son spent a great deal of their time in the London law courts acting as counsel for any number of unhappy couples petitioning for divorces. Perhaps as a consequence, not only do judges, lawyers, and court clerks feature prominently in his plays, but adulterous relationships, eternal love triangles, and menopausal middle-aged males sowing long-tamed oats with younger women frequently provide the substance of his dramatic impulses.

More prolific and perhaps successful with the one-act structure than the full-length play, Mortimer has demonstrated a consistent interest in exploiting the comic potential of domestic situations and sexual relationships. Sometimes this is manifest in a very physical way (as with, for example, the farce *Marble Arch* as well as his Feydeau adaptations), and also in the intricate and skilled construction of dialogue, often with three characters engaged in argument and sexual rivalry, thematically reminiscent of several of Harold Pinter's plays such as *A Slight Ache*, *Old Times*, and *Betrayal*.

But where Pinter intensifies jealousies, creating menacing layers of unverifiable meaning, John Mortimer frequently inverts expected responses, with comic intention. For example, in *Edwin*, Sir Fennimore's ostentatious, quasi-judicial inquiry into the parentage of his supposed son points the finger at his rival Marjoriebanks, only for his wife to hint, at the end of the play, about an illicit liaison with Cattermole, the gardener, all those summers ago.

Similarly, in the early double-bill *The Dock Brief* and *What Shall We Tell Caroline?* Mortimer arouses certain expectations, ripe for inversion, in setting up two situations, a barrister counselling a domestic murderer, and an 18th-birthday party for the daughter of an irascible provincial prep-school headmaster, Morgenhall, suspicious of his wife's involvement with a "debonair" assistant teacher. The hopeless Morgenhall proves to be in a far worse state than the self-confessed murderer, whose release is eventually secured on the grounds of his barrister's incompetence. Caroline's birthday silence triggers the temporary dissolution of the Headmaster's imaginary *ménage-à-trois*, much to his disappointment. Her mother's admission of her own enjoyment of this illusory infidelity and the Headmaster's mock jealous rages prompt Caroline's departure for an independent metropolitan life.

30 years on, Mortimer's characters, at their worst, can resound with hollowness, stereotypically drawn from a stock repertoire not of life observed, but of *stage* life observed. Seeming to inhabit a distant world, Mortimer's stage men are Colonel Cardews and Sir Fennimore Truscotts who find themselves in tweed coats and flannel trousers discussing extra-marital sex and the public indiscretion of naked bathing. His stage women make tea, prune roses, are beautiful (indeed, enter beauty competitions), and leave for their sisters in Ruislip when it all gets too much. Yet while these plays fail to travel well into the 1990's, from a sociological and historical perspective many of them provide valuable insights into the rigidity of the English class system, presenting highly conventional images of women as wives, mothers, and, if they are lucky, lovers.

With one notable exception, Mortimer's well-made plays are written with the proscenium-arch theatre in mind, with stage settings furnished to create the illusion of the missing fourth wall. *A Voyage Round My Father*, his best and probably most famous play because of its later adaptation for television, successfully managed to abandon this convention, providing an autobiographical account of the playwright's relationship with his once-sighted, idiosyncratic father. The play requires a fluidity of action, moving from the breakfast table to school hall, film-set to barristers' chambers. The easy transitions are assisted by the character of the Son, who acts, at first, as narrator for the audience, then neatly steps fully into role in a kind of theatrical tag when his younger counterpart's prep-school days are over. Scenes are kept short to provide an economical, chronological collage of key moments of experience, often liberally sprinkled with Mortimer's brand of humour, and generally managing to steer clear of sentimentality.

Yet Mortimer's plays are not without a kind of pre-war nostalgia and fondness for characterising English foibles and eccentricities. The narrowness of his range, and gentle comic treatments inspired by the myriad life-sustaining illusions of the middle-classes, are, in their way, much more celebratory than finger-waggingly polemical. Finding fun in the values and practice of bourgeois domesticity paradoxically reinforces Mortimer's notion of their indestructible nature. Ronald Bryden once commented, in *The Observer*, that among the playwrights of his generation, John Mortimer had "the clearest eye for how Britain actually looked, talked and comported itself in the fifties and sixties". With hindsight, it is pleasing to know there was light at the end of the tunnel.

—Chris Banfield

————

MOWATT, Anna Cora. Born Anna Ogden in Bordeaux, France, 5 March 1819, to American parents. Lived in or near Bordeaux as a child; moved with her family to New York City, 1826. Educated at Mrs. Okill's School, New York, 1826–28, and at a school in New Rochelle, New York, 1828–31. Married 1) James Mowatt in 1834 (died 1851), three adopted children; 2) William Foushee Ritchie in 1854. Travelled abroad for her health, 1837–38; returned to New York and began writing for the stage, 1839; appeared in recitals of poetry, New York and Boston, 1841–42, and thereafter wrote under the pseudonym Helen Berkley for *Godey's Lady's Book, Graham's*, and other magazines, and compiled books on cooking, etiquette, etc., for various publishers; made debut as actress, New York, 1845, and appeared, with E.L. Davenport as leading man, in New York and other American cities, London, and Dublin, 1846 until she retired in 1854; full-time writer from 1854; lived abroad after 1861, mainly in Florence. Active in the campaign to preserve Mount Vernon: Vice-Regent, Mount Vernon Ladies

Association of the Union, 1858–66. Died in Twickenham, Middlesex, England, 21 July 1870.

Works

Stage Works

Gulzara; or, The Persian Slave (produced New York, 1840).
   In *The New World*, 1840.
Fashion; or Life in New York (produced Park Theatre, New
   York, 1845).   1849.
Armand; or, The Peer and the Peasant (produced Park
   Theatre, New York, 1847).   1849.

Fiction

*The Fortune Hunter; or, The Adventures of a Man about
   Town: A Novel of New York Society.*   1842.
Evelyn; or, A Heart Unmasked.   1845.
Mimic Life; or, Before and Behind the Curtain
   (stories).   1856.
Twin Roses.   1857.
Fairy Fingers.   1865.
The Mute Singer.   1866.
"The Clergyman's Wife" and Other Sketches.   1867.

Verse

Pelayo; or, The Cavern of Covadonga.   1836.
Reviewers Reviewed: A Satire.   1837.

Memoirs and Letters

*Autobiography of an Actress; or Eight Years on the
   Stage.*   1853.

Other

Life of Goethe.   1844.
Etiquette of Courtship and Marriage.   1844.
The Management of the Sick Room.   1844.
The Memoirs of Madame d'Arblay.   1844.
Italian Life and Legends.   1870.

*

Criticism

Books:
Marius Blesi, *Life and Letters*, 1952.
Eric Wollencott Barnes, *Anna Cora: The Life and Theatre of
   Mowatt*, London, 1954; as *The Lady of Fashion*, 1955.

* * *

Anna Cora Mowatt's life is more unusual than any of her writings, and Edgar Allen Poe praised her for having "undoubtedly wrought a deeper impression on the public than anyone of her sex in America". The claim is even more remarkable since the sphere of her influence was the theatre, in which American ladies in the 1840's were not expected to shine. However, Poe rather undermines the praise by focusing it on the mere fact that she *is* a woman, and thus doing less than justice to the full range of her talents; about some of

these he is decidedly more equivocal than about her physical appearance.

Mrs. Mowatt might never have needed to seek a livelihood had it not been for a reversal in her husband's fortunes. Determining to turn to financial advantage a long interest in amateur theatricals, she began with poetry readings on the Chatauqua lecture circuit so popular in America then, and weathered the scandalised criticism that it provoked in genteel ladies' magazines. In her own time she achieved prominence as an actress; today she is noteworthy as the author of one play — *Fashion*.

That the United States, independent for over half a century, should still be so dependent for its culture and its literature on Britain was a matter of growing concern, especially to American writers. One journalist in 1845, having read the script of *Fashion*, hailed it as the answer to two topical questions: "Are there materials in American society for constructing a successful comedy? And is there a writer capable of adapting these materials?".

In *Fashion*, a *nouveau riche* New York socialite, Mrs. Tiffany, allows her dedication to fashion to force her husband into speculation in order to support her extravagance, while she tries to marry off her daughter, Seraphina, to a French gallant, Count Jolimaitre. He, however, turns out to be a masquerading valet, already betrothed to Seraphina's French maid. Comic relief is provided by Mr. T. Tennyson Twinkle, a pompous poetaster, Mr. Fogg, a bored young man-about-town, and Zeke, an inept black footman. (Zeke's role in the plot, though, is a more serious one than was usually assigned to a black character.) Mr. Tiffany is being blackmailed by his clerk, but is rescued from this and from the consequences of his dishonesty by the generosity of the upright American farmer, Adam Trueman, and the blackmailer is exposed. A sub-plot deals with the love affair between Seraphina's genteel but impoverished companion, Gertrude, and an American colonel. This culminates, in true sentimental manner, in the disclosure that she is Trueman's long-lost granddaughter, and all ends happily.

Novelty, an element of spectacle, and a star cast combined to make the play an immediate stage success, which was all the author hoped for from her work. The social satire is good-natured rather than penetrating, moralistic rather than witty. Fashion is epitomised, rather platitudinously, by Trueman as:

> An agreement between certain persons to live without
> using their souls! To substitute etiquette for virtue —
> decorum for purity — manners for morals! To affect a
> shame for the works of their Creator! And expend all
> their rapture upon the works of their tailors and
> dressmakers!

Humour in the dialogue takes familiar forms such as the malapropisms of Zeke and the gaffes of Mrs. Tiffany's pronunciation of the French words with which she seeks to impress. The play's Americanness is expressed chauvinistically, as in Trueman's attack on liveries: "To make men wear the badge of servitude in a land of liberty — that's the fashion, is it? Hurrah for republican simplicity!"; or his dismissal of the exposed French count: "I belong to a land in which I rejoice to find that you are a foreigner". Nevertheless, *Fashion* suited, and to some extent created, the taste of its age. It is not surprising that a New York revival of it in 1924 achieved a run of 235 performances by making fun of the crudeness of characterisation, dialogue, and sentiment that had so delighted its original audience.

Mowatt's other principal excursion into play–writing was quite different from *Fashion. Armand* was set in 18th-century France and was a derivative romantic drama, largely in blank verse, and with Mrs. Mowatt herself playing the heroine. Here the republicanism of Trueman makes an unexpected appearance in the court of Louis XV, but Mowatt candidly admitted that "the plot is not strictly historical". Again, it suited the America of its day, but its political sentiments had to be toned down for presentation on her generally successful tour of Great Britain. They were, however, very popular when restored for performances in Dublin.

Her other main contributions to the history of the theatre were her *Autobiography* and the semi–fictitious stories in *Mimic Life; or, Before and Behind the Curtain*.

—Dennis Welland

See also *Volume 1* entry on *Fashion*.

MROŻEK, Sławomir. Born in Borzęcin, Poland, 29 June 1930. Studied painting and architecture at the Academy of Fine Arts, Cracow. Married 1) Maria Obremba in 1959 (died 1969); remarried in 1987. Journalist, cartoonist, and critic with local newspapers, from 1950; associated with the student theatre Rim-Rom; visited the USSR and Western Europe, 1956; first play, *Policja* [*The Policeman*], staged 1958; moved to Warsaw, 1959; left Poland for Italy, 1963; moved to France, 1968; his works banned in Poland, 1968–73, following his opposition to the Warsaw Pact invasion of Czechoslovakia in 1968; settled in France, 1968; travelled in North and South America in the early 1970's; visited Poland, 1978; moved to Mexico (his second wife's home), 1988. Recipient: Black Humour Prize (France), 1964; Austrian State Prize for European Literature, 1972.

Works

Collections

Utwory sceniczne [Stage Plays] (2 vols.). 1963–73.
Six Plays (includes *The Policeman; The Martyrdom of Piotr Ohey; Out at Sea; Charlie; The Party; The Enchanted Night*), translated by Nicholas Bethell. 1967.
Three Plays (includes *Striptease; Repeat Performance; The Prophets*). 1972.
Utwory sceniczne nowe [New Stage Plays]. 1973.
Wybor dramatów i oppowiadán [Selected Dramas and Short Stories]. 1975.
Amor (includes the television play, *Amor*, and the stage plays *Krawiec; Polowanie na lisa; Serenada; Lis filozof; Lis aspirant*). 1979.
Wybór dramatów [Selected Dramas]. 1987.

Stage Works

Policja (produced Teatr Dramatyczny, Warsaw, 1958). In *Dialog*, 6, 1958; in book form, in *Utwory sceniczne*, 1963; translated as *The Policeman*, in *Six Plays*, 1967.
Professor [The Professor] (produced 1958). 1968?
Męczenstwo Piotra Oheya (produced Teatr Groteska, Cracow, 1959). In *Dialog*, 6, 1959; in book form, in *Utwory sceniczne*, 1963; translated as *The Martyrdom of Piotr Ohey*, in *Six Plays*, 1967.

Indyk [The Turkey] (produced Teatr Stary, Cracow, 1961). In *Dialog*, 10, 1960; in book form, in *Utwory sceniczne*, 1963.
Na pełnym morzu (produced Teatr Modrzejewska, Zakopane, 1961). In *Dialog*, 2, 1961; in book form, in *Utwory sceniczne*, 1963; translated as *Out at Sea*, in *Six Plays*, 1967.
Karol (produced Teatr Modrzejewska, Zakopane, 1961). In *Dialog*, 3, 1961; in book form, in *Utwory sceniczne*, 1963; translated as *Charlie*, in *Six Plays*, 1967.
Striptease (produced Teatr Modrzejewska, Zakopane, 1961). In *Dialog*, 6, 1961; in book form, in *Utwory sceniczne*, 1963; translated as *Striptease*, in *Six Plays*, 1967.
Zabawa (produced Teatr Dramatyczny, Wrocław, 1963). In *Dialog*, 10, 1962; in book form, in *Utwory sceniczne*, 1963; translated as *The Party*, in *Six Plays*, 1967.
Kynolog w rozterce [Dog Fancier in a Dilemma] (produced Teatr Muzyczny, Cracow, 1967). In *Dialog*, 11, 1962; in book form, in *Utwory sceniczne*, 1963.
Czarowna noc (produced Teatr Groteska, Cracow, 1963). In *Utwory sceniczne*, 1963; translated as *The Enchanted Night*, in *Six Plays*, 1967.
Smierć porucznika [Death of a Lieutenant] (produced Teatr Dramatyczny Theatre, Warsaw, 1963). In *Dialog*, 5, 1963; in book form, in *Utwory sceniczne*, 1963.
Tango (produced Teatr Wspolczesny, Warsaw, 1964). In *Dialog*, 11, 1964; in book form, in *Utwory sceniczne*, 1973; translated as *Tango*, 1968.
Poczwórka [The Foursome] (produced Teatr Wybrzeze, Gdansk, 1967). In *Dialog*, 1, 1967.
Dom na granicy [Home on the Border] (produced Teatr Groteska Lalka i Maski, Cracow, 1968). In *Dialog*, 5, 1967; in book form, in *Utwory sceniczne*, 1973.
Testarium (produced West Germany, 1968; produced in Poland, 1982). In *Dialog*, 11, 1967; in book form, in *Utwory sceniczne*, 1973; translated as *The Prophets*, in *Three Plays*, 1972.
Drugie danie (produced in West Germany, 1968; produced in Poland, Teatr Nowy, Łodz, 1977. In *Dialog*, 5, 1968; in book form, in *Utwory sceniczne*, 1973; translated as *Repeat Performance*, in *Three Plays*, 1972.
Vatzlav (produced in English, Festival Theatre, Stratford, Ontario, 1970; produced in Poland, 1979). In translation, as *Vatslav*, 1970 (New York); Polish edition, 1982 (Paris).
Szczesliwe wydarzenie [Blessed Event] (produced West Germany, 1971; produced in Poland, Teatr Wyspolczesny, Warsaw, 1973). 1971 (Paris); published in Poland, in *Dialog*, 4, 1973.
Rzeznia [The Slaughterhouse] (produced Teatr Dramatyczny, Warsaw, 1975). In *Dialog*, 9, 1973.
Emigranci (produced Paris, 1974; produced in Poland, Teatr Wspolczesny, Warsaw, 1975). In *Dialog*, 8, 1974; in book form, in *Utwory sceniczne nowe*, 1975; translated as *The Emigrants*, 1984.
Garbus [The Hunchback] (produced Teatr Stary, Cracow, 1975). In *Dialog*, 9, 1975.
Serenada [Serenade] (produced Teatr Nowy, Zabrze, 1977). In *Dialog*, 2, 1977. in book form, in *Amor*, 1979.
Lis filozof [Philosopher Fox] (produced Teatr Nowy, Zabrze, 1977). In *Dialog*, 3, 1977; in book form, in *Amor*, 1979.
Polowanie na lisa [Foxhunt] (produced Teatr Nowy, Zabrze, 1977). In *Dialog*, 5, 1977; in book form, in *Amor*, 1979.
Krawiec [The Tailor] (produced Teatr Wspolczesny, Szczecin, 1978). In *Dialog*, 11, 1977; in book form, in *Amor*, 1979.
Lis aspirant [Aspiring Fox] (produced 1979). In *Dialog*, 7, 1978; in book form, in *Amor*, 1979.

Pieszo [On Foot] (produced 1980).
Ambasador [The Ambassador] (produced 1981). With *Vatzlav*, 1982.
Letni dzień [A Summer's Day] (produced as *A Summer's Day*, London, 1985).
Alfa [Alpha] (produced New York, 1984; produced in Poland, 1989). 1984 (Paris).
Kontrakt [The Contract] (produced 1986).
Portret [The Portrait] (produced 1987).

Television Plays

Amor (published in *Amor* collection, 1979).

Fiction

Opowiadania z Trzmielowej Góry [Stories from Bumble Bee Hill]. 1953.
Połańcerze praktyczne [Practical Half-Armours] 1953.
Maleńkie lato [The Small Summer]. 1956.
Słoń. 1957; translated as *The Elephant*, 1962.
Wesele w Atomicach [A Wedding in Atomtown]. 1959.
Ucieczka na południe [Escape Southward]. 1961.
Deszcz [Rain]. 1962.
Opowiadania [Stories] (3 vols.). 1964–81.
The Ugupu Bird (selection). 1968.
Dwa listy i inne opowiadania [Two Letters and Other Stories]. 1970 (Paris).
Parabellum. 1979.
Moniza Clavier. 1983.
Wybór opowiadań, 1982–1985 [Selected Stories 1982–1985]. 1985 ("samizdat" edition).
Opowiadania [Stories]. 1985.
Wybor Opowiadán. 1987.

Other

Polska w obrazach [Poland in Pictures] (cartoons). 1957.
Postęowiec [The Progressive] (cartoons). 1960.
Przez okulary [Through Sławomir Mrożek's Glasses] (cartoons). 1968.
Małe listy [Little Letters]. 1982.
Rysunki [Drawings]. 1982.
Donosy [Denunciations]. 1983.

*

Criticism

Books:
Alek Pohl, *Strukturanalysen zu Sławomir Mrożek*, Berlin, 1972.
Jan Klossowicz, *Mrozek*, Warsaw, 1980 (in English).
Marketa Goetz-Stankiewicz, "Sławomir Mrożek: The Moulding of a Polish Playwright", in *The Tradition of Polish Ideals*, edited by W.J. Stankiewicz, London, 1981.
Edward J. Czerwiński, *Contemporary Polish Theater and Drama (1956–1984)*, Westport, Connecticut, 1984.
Mary K. Dahl, "*The Prophets*: Catharsis Complete", in her *Political Violence in Drama*, Ann Arbor, Michigan, 1987.

Articles:
Mrożek issue of *Drama at Calgary*, vol.3 no.3, 1969.
Edward J. Czerwiński, "Sławomir Mrożek: Jester in Search of an Absolute", in *Canadian Slavic Studies*, vol.3 no.4, 1969.
Barbara Kejna-Sharratt, "Sławomir Mrożek and the Polish Tradition of the Absurd", in *New Zealand Slavonic Journal*, 1, 1974.
Manabendra Bandyopadhyay, "Three Men in a Raft with All Provisions Gone: An Introduction to Mrożek's Theatre", in *Jadavpur Journal of Contemporary Literature*, 13, 1975.
Anthony M. Bednarczyk, "Mrożek and the Form Theory Revised", in *Polish Review*, vol.23 no.1, 1978.
Regina Grol-Prokopczyk, "Sławomir Mrożek's Theatre of the Absurd", in *Polish Review*, vol.14 no.3, 1979.
Daniel Gerould, "Contexts for *Vatzlav*: Mrożek and the Eighteenth Century", in *Modern Drama*, vol.27 no.1, 1984.
Halina Stephan, "Sławomir Mrożek: From Satire to National Drama", in *Polish Review*, vol.34 no.1, 1989.

* * *

For 30 years—from the late 1950's to the collapse of communism—Sławomir Mrożek has been the most widely performed author in his native Poland and the pre-eminent dramatist of eastern Europe, even though he has lived abroad in the West since 1963. Distance has only sharpened his satirical vision and provided a broad perspective from which to castigate the follies of an oppressive system that he has left, but never forgotten.

Mrożek owes his commanding position in the former Eastern Bloc to the diagnostic power of his *oeuvre* and the therapeutic value of the laughter that sudden, deft unmasking always provokes. More incisively than any other playwright, he has dissected the power game, showing how human beings terrorize themselves and one another. His witty and sardonic analyses of the various manifestations of totalitarianism have had great resonance—political and moral—for audiences in eastern Europe during the three decades and more when public discussion of these issues was possible only in the theatre.

Portret (The Portrait), Mrożek's final play of the 1980's, is a work dealing with the legacy of Stalinism and the human costs of its liquidation. A fitting obituary to the Cold War, the drama demythologizies all the rationalizations used to justify submission to historical necessity. The title refers specifically to a picture of the Soviet dictator, but more figuratively the playwright paints the portrait of an entire generation crippled by fanaticism in the cause of utopian abstractions.

In a short autobiography (written in 1988 as the author was leaving Europe for Mexico) Mrożek undertakes a reckoning with the past, acknowledging his own deluded enthusiasm for Stalin from 1950 to 1953, and detailing his painfully acquired understanding of the pitfalls of ideology. Although, as an author, he avoids confession and direct revelation of personal feelings, his entire body of work—stories, cartoons, films, and plays—gives the collective self-portrait of an age scarred by war and communism. The story is not that of Poland alone, but of all the nations of eastern Europe, and of the Soviet Union.

While at first glance they are most strikingly applicable to the victims of dialectical materialism, Mrożek's studies of tyranny will scarcely lose their significance for eastern European audiences even after the old communist regimes are dismantled—unless, of course, humanity can finally escape from history and eliminate the mechanisms of dominance and subjection. Like all effective parables, his plays are cast in universal forms that leave the determination of particular meanings to the spectator. For this reason, readers and viewers in the West, responding on the basis of a quite different historical experience, are likely to discover in his dramas a more personal and psychological dimension.

A successful cartoonist and writer of fables before turning to playwriting, Mrożek conceives of drama not as a direct imitation of reality, but rather as the construction of model situations revealing cultural, social, and historical processes. His early plays, concerned with the operation of power in a monolithic regime, start from absurd premises and suddenly imposed dilemmas, which are then developed to their logical consequences. In *Policja* (*The Police*), the last political prisoner finally abandons his opposition to the regime, forcing the police to recruit from their own ranks a freedom-loving revolutionary and then to imprison him in order to ensure their continued existence. In ingeniously schematic one-act plays, such as *Out at Sea* and *Striptease*, victims are defined by arbitrary situations which compel them to invent reasons for their own victimization. The structure of these tragi-farces is neatly symmetrical, and the dialogue rich in circular reasoning, rhetorical self-deception, and logical quibbles. The dramatic rhythm accelerates as the human puppets—drawn with a few bold, cartoon-like strokes—succumb to inscrutable forces that rob them of their clothes, their dignity, and ultimately their lives. Within closed systems set in confined spaces, no change or escape seems possible; self-perpetuation is the only ruling principle, allowing new power-wielders to replace old.

In *Tango*, the culmination of Mrożek's first period of work, the microcosmic world, or scale model, is a family drama, played out among three generations, which is made to chart the course of European social, cultural, and intellectual history from turn-of-the-century liberalism through inter-war avant-garde experimentation to the triumph of totalitarianism. By the use of parody and allusion (citations come from Shakespeare and the Polish Romantic and modernist traditions), Mrożek creates a many-layered work which serves as a prism for viewing the relation of culture to power. At the end of the play, order is restored and the circle closed when old Europe is forced to dance the tango with brute strength.

Written after Mrożek took political asylum in France, *Vatzlav* is a transitional work presenting a more open dramatic universe in which moral choices are made, no matter how risky their outcome. A pastiche of 18th-century French philosophical tales like Voltaire's *Candide* and Sade's *Justine*, the play takes the episodic form of a series of picaresque adventures in which an ex-slave, caught between worlds, embarks on a perilous emigration in quest of elusive freedom.

The scope and variety of Mrożek's work continued to grow as the playwright tempered the paradigmatic with concreteness of experience and detailed interplay among human characters. *Emigrants* depicts a further stage in the travels of the exiled. A haughty intellectual and primitive boor—opposite halves of a composite national type—share a grimy basement apartment in a large Western city, sustained in the vacuum of lonely and alienated lives abroad by a symbiotic relationship of mutual antagonism. The emigrés have created a surrogate family to satisfy longings for an absent homeland. Captives of illusory freedom, the former playthings of the state are now trapped in a self-made prison.

In his dramas of the 1970's and 1980's, Mrożek intensified his quest for moral truth and intellectual lucidity in a world of growing chaos. Dramatic theorems based on the antithetical terms of nature and nurture, barbarism and civilization, *Rzeźnia* (The Slaughterhouse) and *Krawiec* (The Tailor) explore, in an openly theatricalist manner, the relations of art to civilization and its basis in violence. Located in real time and space, *Pieszo* (On Foot) presents an apocalyptic historical panorama of the vast displacements and collapse of values that took place in Poland during the last years of World War II, when the Nazis were replaced by the communists as the imposers of a new order. Cast in the mould of a *fin-de-siècle* comedy of manners, *The Hunchback* is an enigmatic drama predicting social unrest and a breakdown of identities in times of conspiracy and paranoiac fear of terrorism.

Mrożek's animal fables in the manner of Lafontaine, such as *Polowanie na lisa* (Foxhunt) and *Lis filozof* (Philosopher Fox), are witty variations on serious themes—the seductions of power, the struggle for existence, man's place in the scheme of things. A direct response to the suppression of the Solidarity movement in 1981, *Alfa* (Alpha) attempts to deal with contemporary history by exploding the myth of the hero; interned during the imposition of martial law, the great national leader is erected into a mummified symbol to be manipulated by all parties. A virtuoso two-character drama of verbal innuendo and sinister subtext, *Kontrakt* (The Contract) pits a dying representative of old European values, world-weary and guilt-ridden, against a young Polish adventurer playing games of masked identity as a revolutionary terrorist.

Over the years Mrożek has acquired great mastery of dramatic form, without committing himself to any single style. He plays with conventions, modes, and traditions; through pastiche and parody he avails himself of an entire cultural heritage but refuses to be enrolled under any fashionable banner, whether it be black humor, the grotesque, or the absurd. He goes against the current of late-20th-century stage practice in asserting the primacy of the word in the theatre and allowing little freedom of invention for the director.

A rationalist and moralist, Mrożek defends the individual against the State and takes satirical aim at social norms and cultural stereotypes. Rejecting the notion of total theatre or theatre of cruelty as subjugation by paroxysm, he has created a drama addressed to the mind, which enables spectators to draw conclusions and make decisions themselves.

—Daniel Gerould

See also *Volume 1* entry on *Tango*.

MÜLLER, Heiner. Born in Eppendorf, Saxony, Germany, 9 January 1929. Educated at an Oberschule, Abitur 1945. Married to Inge Müller (died 1966). Military service during later stages of World War II: taken prisoner by American forces, then returned to Soviet zone (subsequently East Germany); worked in a bookshop, and began writing journalism, after c.1946; worked with the Schriftstellerverband [Union of Writers], and editor, *Junge Kunst*, in the mid-1950's; first-produced play, *Zehn Tage, die die Welt erschütterten*, produced 1957; staff-member, Maxim-Gorki-Theater, East Berlin, 1958–60; expelled from the Union of Writers following controversy over his *Die Bauern*, 1961: subsequently several of his plays not produced or published in East Germany; dramaturg, Berliner Ensemble, 1970–76; visited the USA, 1975; dramaturg, Volksbühne, East Berlin, from 1976. Recipient: Heinrich Mann Prize, 1959; Erich Weinert Medal, 1964; BZ Critics Prize, 1970, 1976; Lessing Prize, 1975; Büchner Prize, 1985.

Works

Collections

Texte (11 vols.).   1974–89; contains the following collections:
1) *Geschichten aus der Produktion 1.*   1974.
2) *Geschichten aus der Produktion 2.*   1974.
3) *Die Umsiedlerin; oder, Das Leben auf dem Lande.* 1975.
4) *Theater-Arbeit.*   1975.
5) *Germania Tod in Berlin.*   1977.
6) *Mauser.*   1978.
7) *Herzstück.*   1983.
8) *Shakespeare Factory 1.*   1985.
9) *Shakespeare Factory 2.*   1989.
10) *Kopien 1.*   1989.
11) *Kopien 2*, with Ginka Tscholakowa.   1989.

Stücke (includes *Der Lohndrücker; Die Bauern; Der Bau; Herakles 5; Philoktet; Der Horatier; Weiberkomödie; Macbeth; Zement*).   1975.
Kopien: 3 Versuche Shakespeare zu töten.   1977.
Die Schlacht; Traktor; Leben Gundlings Friedrich von Preussen Lessings Schlaf Traum Schrei.   1977.
Shakespeare Factory 2.   1980.
Der Auftrag; Der Bau; Herakles 5.   1981.
"Hamletmachine" and Other Texts for the Stage (includes *The Correction; Gundlings Life Frederick of Prussia Lessing's Sleep Dream Scream; The Task; Quartet; Heartpiece; Despoiled Shore Medeamaterial Landscape with Argonauts*), translated by Carl Weber.   1984.
Stücke, edited by Joachim Fiebach.   1988.
Revolutionsstücke, edited by Uwe Wittstock.   1988.
Stücke: Texte über Deutschland (1957–1979), edited by Frank Hörnigk.   1989.
Wolokolamsker Chaussee 1–5.   1989.
The Battle: Plays, Prose, Poems, translated by Carl Weber.   1989.

Stage Works

Zehn Tage, die die Welt erschütterten, with Hagen Müller-Stahl, from a work by John Reed (produced Volksbühne, Berlin, 1957).   1958.
Der Lohndrücker, with Inge Müller (produced Städtisches Theater, Leipzig, 1958).   1958.
Die Korrektur, with Inge Müller (produced Maxim-Gorki-Theater, Berlin, 1958).   1959.
Die Umsiedlerin (produced Studentbühne, Hochschule für Ökonomie, Karlshorst, 1961).   In *Die Umsiedlerin; oder, Das Leben auf dem Lande* (*Texte 3*), 1975; revised version, as *Die Bauern* (produced Volksbühne, Berlin, 1976), in *Stücke*, 1975.
Herakles 5 (produced Schiller-Theater, Berlin, 1974).   With *Philoktet*, 1966.
Philoktet (produced Residenztheater, Munich, 1968).   With *Herakles 5*, 1966; translated as *Philoctetes*, 1981.
Ödipus Tyrann, from the work by Hölderlin (produced Deutsches Theater, Berlin, 1967).   1968.
Prometheus (produced Schauspielhaus, Zurich, 1969).   In *Spectaculum*, 11, 1968, and in *Geschichten aus der Produktion 2* (*Texte 2*), 1974.
Die Aristokraten, with Benno Besson, from a play by Molière (produced Deutsches Theater, Berlin, 1968).
Wie es euch gefällt, from *As You Like It* by Shakespeare (produced Residenztheater, Munich, 1968).   In *Kopien*, 1977.
Drachenoper, from the opera *Lancelot* by Paul Dessau (pro-

duced Deutsche Staatsoper, Berlin, 1969).   In *Theater-Arbeit* (*Texte 4*), 1975.
Horizonte, from a work by Gerhart Winterlich (produced Volksbühne, Berlin, 1969).   In *Theater-Arbeit*, 1975; as *Waldstück*, in *Shakespeare Factory 1* (*Texte 8*), 1985.
Weiberkomödie, from a radio play by Inge Müller (produced Städtisches Theater, Magdeburg, 1970).   Included in *Theater-Arbeit*, 1975.
Arzt wider Willen, with Benno Besson, from a play by Molière (produced Volksbühne, Berlin, 1970).
Die Möwe, with Ginka Tscholakowa, from a play by Chekhov (produced Volksbühne, Berlin, 1972).   In *Kopien 2* (*Texte 11*), 1989.
Macbeth, from the play by Shakespeare (produced Theater des Stadt, Brandenburg, 1972).   In *Theater der Zeit*, 4, 1972; in book form, in *Stücke*, 1975.
Tarelkins Tod, with Ginka Tscholakowa, from a play by Alexander Sukhovo-Kubylin (produced Theater der Stadt, Brandenburg, 1972).   In *Kopien 2* (*Texte 11*), 1989.
Der Horatier (produced Schiller-Theater, Berlin, 1973).   In *Stücke*, 1975; translated as *The Horatian*, in *Minnesota Review*, 6, 1976.
Zement, from a work by Fyodor Gladkov (produced Berliner Ensemble, Berlin, 1973).   In *Geschichten aus der Produktion 2* (*Stücke 2*), 1974; translated as *Cement*, in *New German Critique 16*, Winter 1979.
Traktor (produced Friedrich-Wolf-Theater, Neustrelitz, 1975).   In *Geschichten aus der Produktion 2* (*Texte 2*) 1974.
Der Bau (produced Volksbühne, Berlin, 1980).   In *Geschichten aus der Producktion 1* (*Texte 1*), 1974.
Die Schlacht (produced Volksbühne, Berlin, 1975).   1977.
Mauser, from a novel by Sholokhov (produced by the Austin Theatre Group, Austin, Texas, 1975; produced in German, Schauspielhaus, Cologne, 1980).   Published in translation, as *Mauser*, in *New German Critique*, 8, 1976; in German, in *Mauser* (*Texte 6*), 1978.
Glücksgott, from a play by Brecht.   In *Theater-Arbeit* (*Texte 4*), 1975.
Leben Gundlings Friedrich von Preussen Lessings Schlaf Traum Schrei (produced Schauspielhaus, Frankfurt, 1979).   With *Die Schlacht* and *Traktor*, 1977; translated as *Gundling's Life Frederick of Prussia Lessing's Sleep Dream Scream*, in *Hamletmachine . . .* (collection), 1984.
Hamlet, with Matthias Langhoff, from the play by Shakespeare (produced Volksbühne, Berlin, 1977).   In *Shakespeare Factory 2*, 1980.
Germania Tod in Berlin (produced Kammerspiele, Munich, 1978).   1977.
Untergang des Egoisten Fatzer, from fragments by Brecht (produced Deutsches Schauspielhaus, Hamburg, 1978).
Herzstück (produced Frankfurt, 1979).   In *Herzstück* (*Texte 7*), 1983; translated as *Heartpiece*, in *Hamletmachine . . .* (collection), 1984.
Die Hamletmaschine (produced Théâtre Gérard-Philippe, Paris, 1979; first produced in Germany, Kammerspiele, Munich, 1977).   In *Mauser* (*Texte 6*), 1978; translated as *Hamletmachine*, in *Hamletmachine . . .* (collection), 1984.
Der Auftrag (produced Volksbühne, Berlin, 1980).   With *Der Bau* and *Herakles 5*, 1981; translated as *The Mission*, in *Gambit*, 39–40, 1982; as *The Assignment*, 1984; as *The Task*, in *Hamletmachine . . .* (collection), 1984.
Quartett, from a novel by Choderlos de Laclos (produced Schauspielhaus, Bochum, 1982).   1981; translated as *Quartet*, in *Hamletmachine . . .* (collection), 1984; also translated in the *GDR Monitor* Literature in Translation Series, 1984.

Verkommenes Ufer Medeamaterial Landschaft mit Argonauten (produced Schauspielhaus, Bochum, 1983). 1982; translated as *Despoiled Shore Medeamaterial Landscape with Argonauts*, in *Hamletmachine . . .* (collection), 1984.

Wladimir Majakowski Tragödie, with Ginka Tscholakowa, from a play by Mayakovsky (produced Schiller-Theater Werkstatt, Berlin, 1983). 1985.

The CIVIL warS. a tree is best measured when it is down, with Robert Wilson (produced Schauspielhaus, Cologne, 1984). 1985.

Bildbeschreibung (produced by Vereinigte Bühnen, Graz, 1985). 1985.

Anatomie Titus Fall of Rome (produced Schauspielhaus, Bochum, 1985). In *Theater heute*, 3, 1985; in book form, in *Shakespeare Factory 2* (*Texte 9*), 1989.

Wallenstein, from the trilogy by Schiller (produced Schiller-Theater, Berlin, 1985).

Wolokolamsker Chaussee I: Russische Eröffnung (produced Deutsches Theater, Berlin, 1985). In *Shakespeare Factory 1* (*Texte 8*), 1985.

Quai West, from a work by Bernard-Marie-Koltès (produced Schauspielhaus, Bochum, 1986). 1986.

Wolokolamsker Chaussee II: Wald bei Moskau, from a work by Alexander Bek (produced Hans-Otto-Theater, Potsdam, 1986). In *Theater der Zeit*, 41, 1986; in book form, in *Shakespeare Factory 2* (*Texte 9*), 1989.

Wolokolamsker Chaussee III: Das Duell, from a work by Anna Seghers (produced Hans-Otto-Theater, Potsdam, 1987). In *Shakespeare Factory 2* (*Texte 9*), 1989.

Wolokolamsker Chaussee IV: Kenaturen. In *Shakespeare Factory 2* (*Texte 9*), 1989.

Wolokolamsker Chaussee V: Der Findling, from a play by Kleist. In *Shakespeare Factory 2* (*Texte 9*), 1989.

Radio Plays

Klettwitzer Bericht (published in *Junge Kunst*, 8, 1958); *Der Horatier*, 1973; *Die Korrektur* (published in *Geschichte aus der Produktion 1*, 1974); *Die Befreiung der Prometheus*, 1986.

Other

Gesammelte Irrtümer: Interviews und Gespräche (2 vols.). 1986–90.

Sprach-Spiel-Spass: . . . manchmal in Fraktur. 1988.

"Explosion of a Memory" and Other Writings, translated by Carl Weber. 1989.

The Battle: Plays. Prose, Poems, translated by Carl Weber. 1989.

Heiner Müller "zur Lage der Nation" (interview), with Frank M. Raddatz. 1990.

Ein Gespenst verlässt Europa, photographs by Sibylle Bergemann. 1990.

*

Criticism

Books:
Genia Schulz, *Heiner Müller*, Stuttgart, 1980.
Marc Silberman, *Heiner Müller*, Amsterdam, 1980.
Theo Girshausen, *Realismus und Utopie; Die frühen Stücke Heiner Müllers*, Cologne, 1981.
Georg Wieghaus, *Heiner Müller*, Munich, 1981.
Heinz Ludwig Arnold (ed.) *Müller*, Munich, 1982.

Denis Calandra, *New German Dramatists*, London, 1983.
Arrigo Subiotto, "Heiner Müller", in *The Writer and Society in the GDR*, edited by Ian Wallace, Tayport, Fife, 1984.
Georg Wieghaus, *Zwischen Auftrag und Verrat: Werk und Ästhetik Heiner Müllers*, Frankfurt, 1984.
Arlene A. Teroaka, *The Silence of Entropy or Universal Discourse: The Postmodernist Poetics of Heiner Müller*, New York, 1985.
Klaus Teichmann, *Der verwundete Körper: Zu Texten Heiner Müllers*, Freiburg, 1986.
Reinhard Tschapke, *Studentblätter Heiner Müller*, Stuttgart, 1986.
Pasquale Gallo, *Il teatro dialettico di Heiner Müller*, Lecce, 1987.
Carlotta von Maltzan, *Zur Bedeutung von Geschichte, Sexualität und Tod im Werk Heiner Müllers*, Frankfurt, 1988.
J.H. Reid, "Homburg-Machine: Heiner Müller in the Shadow of Nuclear War", in *A Radical Stage: Theatre in Germany in the 1970s and 1980s*, edited by W.G. Sebald, Oxford, 1988.
Norbert O. Eke, *Heiner Müller: Apokalypse und Utopie*, Paderborn, 1989.
Joachim Fiebach, *Inseln der Unordnung: Fünf Versuche zu Heiner Müllers Theatertexten*, Berlin, 1990.

Articles:
Helen Fehervarey, "Enlightenment or Entanglement: History and Aesthetics in Bertolt Brecht and Heiner Müller", in *New German Critique*, 8, 1976.
Joel Schlechter, "Heiner Müller and Other East German Dramaturgs", in *Yale/Theatre*, vol. 8 nos. 2–3, 1977.
Carl Weber, "A Landscape on the Other Side of Death: Writing against Interpretation", in *Theater Three*, 3, 1987.
Max Harris, "Müller's *Cement*: Fragments of a Heroic Myth", in *Modern Drama*, 31, 1988.
Nicholas Zurbrugg, "Post-Modernism and the Multi-media Sensibility: Heiner Müller's *Hamletmachine* and the Art of Robert Wilson", in *Modern Drama*, 31, 1988.

*   *   *

Heiner Müller established himself in the 1970's and 1980's as the leading dramatist in East Germany (the German Democratic Republic), equalled in output, quality, and production figures in the German-speaking world only, in his very different style, by Botho Strauss in the Federal Republic.

Müller has always been an awkward Marxist. The picture of the DDR in his early plays was so frank and devoid of cosmetic touches that they were banned by the authorities in 1961 and Müller was expelled from the Writers' Union. He was rehabilitated in the 1970's, and by the mid-1980's had been awarded the State Prize for Literature. He also won the prestigious Büchner Prize in the BRD.

Such recognition in both Germanys could only be the result of a prodigious balancing act. He lived and worked in the DDR but was only partly published and performed there, while his more radical dramatic excursions into German history, like *Germania Tod in Berlin* (Germania Death in Berlin), his more salacious work, like *Quartett* (*Quartet*), and his inscrutable fragmentary pieces, like *Hamletmaschine*, were only published and performed in the West. Müller commuted freely from DDR to BRD, aware that this was a rare privilege. He cultivated a sybilline mode of response in his many interviews, balancing skilfully and wittily on the Wall, disrespectfully critical of both houses.

Müller's chronology is complicated by censorship, long lead times to production, and the author's working methods. For example, "Resettling a Peasant's Widow or Life on the Land" was written between 1956 and 1961 and revised in 1964 as *Die Bauern* (The Peasants). The first version was banned after a student production in 1961, and the second was only premiered at the Berlin Volksbühne in 1975. It deals with the collectivisation of agriculture and, conforming broadly to the prescriptions of German socialist realism, can be grouped with *Der Bau* (The Building Trade) and *Der Lohndrucker* (*The Scab*) which also show life at the workplace under socialism.

Der Lohndrucker dramatizes the case of Hans Garbe, the first Hero of Labour in the DDR. Garbe had repaired a kiln without waiting for it to cool properly and had raised the work-norms for his fellow workers. Müller showed the tensions and resentments among the workforce and the absence of a socialist work ethic in an interlocking sequence of terse Brechtian scenes. It ends with a pragmatic compromise: the Scab and his main opponent bury their differences and agree to build socialism together. When he came to direct a revival of the play in 1988, Müller discovered that his text had captured many of the ills that were by then killing the GDR. With the reconciliation removed and the contradictions highlighted, *Der Lohndrucker* toured the European festival circuit as a theatrical plea for *glasnost* which antedated any real movement on the East German political front.

In the 1960's Müller adopted the classic German strategy to outwit the censors: he produced a series of classical translations and adaptations, *Ödipus*, *Philoktet* (*Philoctetes*), *Prometheus*, and *Der Horatier* (*The Horatian*). These plays are written in supple, muscular verse, and the ancient stories are informed by Müller's worldview and critical concerns. The cryptic theme of *Der Horatier* is the sanctity of history which must not be manipulated for political purposes. *Philoktet* shows the triumph of the pragmatist over the idealist in promoting the national cause. The cynicism of Odysseus, who outmanoeuvres the callow Neoptolemos, is the cynicism of Stalin, who also, as it happens, tampered with history books.

Shakespeare, too, provided cover for Müller, though his radical reworking of *Macbeth*, to which he added the peasantry whom Shakespeare had ignored, making them as vile and bloodthirsty as the nobility, attracted the charge of historical pessimism, a dire misdemeanour in the GDR. In 1977 it was Shakespeare who provided Müller with a poetic vehicle when his morale was low. In *Hamletmachine* Müller reduces *Hamlet* to a background of allusion, while in the foreground he articulates the barriers that personal experience and historical necessity have erected between him and the play, which he sees as a prophetic, if optimistic picture of 20th-century politics. The piece is structured in Müller's later, enigmatic mode, a dense, bleak, allusive prose poem which combines the anguish of a Marxist intellectual and the predicament of Shakespeare's Hamlet.

The 1970's saw the staging of Müller's three plays on German history, *Die Schlacht* (*Slaughter*), *Germania Tod in Berlin* (Germania Death in Berlin), and *Leben Gundlings . . .* (*Gundling's Life Frederick of Prussia Lessing's Dream Sleep Scream*). *Die Schlacht* presents the brutality of German to German, between 1933 and 1945, in five laconic verse scenes. *Germania* is an epic revue of the history of the DDR to 1956, in which each scene about the DDR is preceded by an episode from earlier history. The very condensed episodes range in style from outrageous cabaret (the founding of the BRD is treated as a Nativity parody) to the naturalism of the final scene in which the Old Communist is allowed to die with

his illusions intact. In a similar mode, *Gundling's Life* debunks the achievements of the German Enlightenment.

From 1979 Müller was keeping abreast of the avant-garde in the West with enigmatic pieces like *Hamletmachine* and *Der Auftrag* (*The Mission*) which he subtitled "Memory of a Revolution". He was, by this time, being produced regularly by Claus Peymann at Bochum, and he was collaborating with Robert Wilson. The disconnected structure and clashing stylistic elements in his plays were beginning to be called postmodern. His recent work however, *Wolokolamsker Chaussee* (Volokolamsk Highway), although in verse with five acts which are only thematically connected, constitutes a return to coherent dramatic statement.

Müller is now emerging as a director of note. His *Der Lohndrucker* at the Deutsches Theater, into which he inserted *Der Horatier*, *Kenaturen* (The Centaur—Act IV of *Volokolamsker Chaussee*), and a couple of clips of silent film, was a riveting critique of the DDR in its dying fall. In 1990 Müller directed a marathon *Hamlet/Hamletmaschine* at the Deutsches Theater which was, in part, a reckoning with his own role in the DDR.

—Hugh Rorrison

MUNK, Kaj (Harald Leininger). Born Harold Leininger Peterson in Maribo, Lolland, Denmark, 31 January 1898. Lost parents early in life, and took name of Munk after his adoptive father, 1916. Educated at a Gymnasium; studied theology in Copenhagen from 1917, degree in divinity 1924. Vicar in Vedersø, West Jutland, from 1924; first-produced play, *En Idealist* [An Idealist], produced 1928; subsequent plays mostly produced at the Kongelige Teater [Royal Theatre], Copenhagen; became Denmark's most prominent playwright during the 1930's; strong supporter of Hitler and Mussolini in the 1930's, his sympathy declining during the German occupation of Denmark from 1940; arrested by the Gestapo, 1944. Murdered by the Gestapo, in Silkeborg, 4 January 1944.

Works

Collections

Mindeudgave (collected works; 9 vols.), edited by Niels Nøjgaard and Knud Bruun-Rasmussen. 1948–49:
1. *"Cant" og andre Skuespil* (includes *Cant; De Udvalgte; Sejren; Døden; Diktatorinden*). 1948.
2. *"Pilatus" og andre Skuespil* (includes *Pilatus; Samson; Operationen; En Idealist*). 1948.
3. *"Eglykke" og andre Skuespil* (includes *Han sidder ved Smeltediglen; Puslespil; Egelykke; Atterdag; Niels Ebbesen; Kongen; De Herrer Dommere; Før Cannae; Ewalds Død*). 1949.
4. *"Kærlighed" og andre Skuespil* (includes *Ordet; Kærlighed; I Brændingen; Fø Tidehvervet; Kardinalen og Kongen*). 1948.
5. *"En Digters Vej" og andre Artikler (1916–1937)*. 1948.
6. *"Dagen er inde" og andre Artikler (1938–1943)*. 1949.
7. *Prædikener (1919–1943)*. 1948.
8. *Digte*. 1949.

9. *Foraaret saa sagte kommer*.   1949.
Five Plays (translations; includes *Herod the King; He Sits at the Melting Pot; The Word; Before Cannae; Cant*), edited by R.O. Keigwin.   1953.

Stage Works

En Idealist (produced Kongelige Teater, Copenhagen, 1928). 1928; translated as *Herod the King*, in *Five Plays*, 1953.
I Brændigen (produced by the Betty Nansen Teatret, 1937). 1929.
Cant (produced Kongelige Teater, Copenhagen, 1931). 1931; translated as *Cant*, in *Five Plays*, 1953.
Ordet (produced as *I Begyndelsen var Ordet*, by the Betty Nansen Teatret, 1937).   1932; translated as *The Word*, in *Five Plays*, 1953.
De Udvalgte [The Elect] (produced Kongelige Teater, Copenhagen, 1933).   1933.
Kærlighed [Love] (produced Kongelige Teater, Copenhagen, 1935).   In *"Kærlighed" og andre Skuespil*, 1948.
Sejren [Victory] (produced Norske Teatret, Oslo, 1936). 1936.
10 Oxford-Snapshots (produced Kulturelle Teater, Copenhagen, 1936).   1936.
Pilatus [Pilate] (produced Sorø Theatre Academy, 1941; produced professionally, Kongelige Teater, Copenhagen, 1947).   1937.
Han sidder ved Smeltedligen (produced Norske Teatret, Oslo, 1938).   1938; translated as *He Sits at the Melting Pot*, in *Five Plays*, 1953.
Diktatorinden [The Dictator] (produced Kongelige Teater, Copenhagen, 1938).   In *"Cant" og andre Skuespil*, 1948.
Fugl Fønix [Bird Phoenix] (produced Midnatsforestilling i Studenterforeningen, Copenhagen, 1938).   1939.
Puslespil [Puzzle] (produced by the Folketeatret, 1939).   In *"Egelykke" og andre Skuespil*, 1949.
Egylykke (produced Kongelige Teater, Copenhagen, 1940). 1940.
Præsten i Vejlby, from a novel by St. Blicher (produced by the Folketeatret, 1942).
Niels Ebbesen [Niels Ebbeson] (produced Svenske Dramatikers Studio, Gothenburg, Sweden, 1943).   1942.
Før Cannae (produced Kongelige Teater, Copenhagen, 1945).   1943; translated as *Before Cannae*, in *Five Plays*, 1953.
Ewalds Død (produced Kongelige Teater, Copenhagen, 1943).   1943.
Døden [The Dead].   In *"Cant" og andre Skuespil*, 1948.
Kardinalen og Kongen (produced Palaeet, Copenhagen, 1945).   In *"Kærlighed" og andre Skuespil*, 1948.
Alverdens-Urostifterne.   1947.
Samson [Samson].   In *"Pilatus" og andre Skuespil*, 1949.
Operationen [Operations].   In *"Pilatus" og andre Skuespil*, 1949.
Atterdag [Another Day].   In *"Egylykke" og andre Skuespil*, 1949.
Kongen [The King].   In *"Egylykke" og andre Skuespil*, 1949.
De Herrer Dommere. [These Noble Lords].   In *"Egylykke" og andre Skuespil*, 1949.

Screenplays

Det gyldne Smil, 1935; *Filmen om Christiern den Anden*, 1934 (published 1938).

Verse

Os baerer den himmelske Glaede.   1934.
Knaldperler.   1936.
Tempelvers.   1939.
Navigare necesse.   1940.
Sværg det Drenge.   1941.
Det unge Nord.   1942.
Den Skæbne ej til os.   1943.
Den blaa Anemone.   1943.
Vers.   1943.
8 nye Digte.   1944.
Saml dig, Norden.   1945.
Et norsk digt om Norge.   1946.
Digte [Poems] (Volume 8 of *Mindeudgave*).   1949.

Memoirs and Letters

Foraaret saa sagte kommer: Erindringer.   1942.

Other

Vedersø-Jerusalem retur (travel writing).   1934.
Liv og glad Dage (essays).   1936.
Himmel og Jord (articles).   1938.
Dett Dødsens Legeme (essays).   1938.
Danske Prædikener (3 vols.)   1941–46:
  Ved Babylons Floder.   1941.
   Med Ordets Svaerd.   1942.
   I Guds Bismer.   1946.
Med Sol og megen Glaede.   1942.
Smaabyens Sjæl (poem and article).   1943.
Danmark.   1943.
Tre Prædikener.   1943.
Jesus' Historier.   1943.
Apostlenes Gerninger, from the Bible.   1944.
Saa fast en Borg.   1946.
Ansigter.   1947.
Landlige interiører i lollandsk bondemäl.   1948.

*

Criticism

Books:
Melville Harcourt, *Portraits of Destiny* (includes biography), New York, 1966.
Alfred O. Schwede, *Verankert im Unsichtbaren: Das Leben Kaj Munks*, Berlin, 1971.
Alda Castagnoli Manghi, "Il teatro di Kaj Munk", in *Teatro danese de Novecento*, edited by Karen Ascani and others, Rome, 1983.
Marc Auchet, "Un Ecrivain 'inspiré': Le Dramaturge danois Kaj Munk", in *L'Homme et l'autre de Suzo à Peter Handke*, edited by Jean M. Paul, Nancy, 1990.

* * *

Kaj Munk is one of the most significant and controversial playwrights of 20th-century Denmark. His dramatic work can be seen as a continuous and never fully resolved discussion for and against the anti-democratic ideas of the 1930's and 1940's, expressing an unusual combination of Christian humanism, political elitism, and national romanticism.
   Munk's dramatic work was highly topical, highly successful, and very much debated in the Scandinavia of the 1930's

and 1940's. Munk's attitude to Fascism and Nazism was dominated by admiration in the 1930's, but changed into rejection and resistance in the 1940's. He became one of the leading voices of Danish resistance to the Nazi occupation and was, tragically, murdered by the Nazis in January 1944.

It was Kaj Munk's ambition to re-create the great symbolic drama of ideas. It was his aim to establish an alternative to the naturalistic drama of social and psychological problems of the tradition of Ibsen and Bjørnson. Drama was seen as a cult by Munk: it should appeal to the collective emotions of the audience rather than show them what they already know (as was the case—Munk claimed—in the naturalistic drama). The result was a number of powerful plays written between 1917 and 1943.

A Munk melodrama typically portrays a passionate and single-minded personality pursuing a calling. It measures the actions of the protagonists against the ideal claims of Christianity. Munk's plays share an ambivalent attraction to the strong, single-minded leader figure; but they also share a belief in the power of a personal God.

Munk's plays fall into two groups. The first consists of political plays, often set in historic and international surroundings. *En Idealist* (translated as *Herod the King*) was the first Munk play to be published and performed. In 1928 it was a fiasco, but ten years later it became a clear success. The principal character is Herod the Great, King of Judaea, whose lust for power is confronted by Christian values. The play comes out in favour of the Christian values, although not unambiguously. In the 1930's, Munk's political plays expressed considerable sympathy with the ambitions of the dictators. This sympathy culminated in *Sejren* (Victory), which is a clear vote of confidence in Mussolini and his desire to conquer Abyssinia. Towards the end of the 1930's, however, with Munk's sympathy with the dictatorships fading (he was incensed by the racial ideology of the Nazis and by the persecution of the Jews), he wrote *Han sidder ved Smeltediglen* (*He Sits at the Melting Pot*), an exposure of anti-Semitism. In his last drama, the one-act play *Fær Cannae* (*Before Cannae*), Munk juxtaposes the Roman commander and statesman Fabius Maximus, "the delayer", and his Carthaginian counterpart, Hannibal. In this play Munk definitively dissociates himself from a positive view of military aggression, represented by Hannibal.

In the second group of plays Munk focused his attention on the Danish people and their religious endeavours. In this category the masterpiece is *Ordet* (*The Word*), which was first performed in 1932, and immediately became a resounding success. It is set in the Jutland countryside and culminates with the insane Johannes performing a miracle and bringing a dead woman back to life through the power of his belief. The play is an allegorical tribute to the great personality who can awaken the Danish people from its spiritual sleep. *Ordet* was filmed twice, by the Swedish director Gustaf Molander in 1943, and by the Danish director Carl Dreyer in 1954.

The expressive power of Kaj Munk's plays, his personal charisma, and his martyrdom have all contributed to this playwright's fame.

—Bjarne T. Thomsen

MURPHY, Tom [Thomas] (Bernard). Born in Tuam, County Galway, Ireland, 23 February 1935. Educated at Vocational School, Tuam; Vocational Teachers' Training College, Dublin. Married Mary Hippisley; three children. Apprentice fitter and welder, Tuam, 1953–55; engineering teacher, Vocational School, Mountbellow, County Galway, 1957–62. Actor and director, 1951–62; first-produced play, *On the Outside*, staged 1961; moved to London, 1962; returned to Ireland, 1970; member of the Board of Directors, 1972–83, and since 1986 writer-in-association, Irish National Theatre (Abbey Theatre), Dublin; founding member, Moli Productions, Dublin, 1974; Regents Lecturer, University of California, Santa Barbara, 1981; writer-in-association, Druid Theatre, Galway, 1983–85. Recipient: Irish Academy of Letters Award, 1972; Independent Newspapers Award, 1983; Harvey's Award, 1983, 1986. Member, Irish Academy of Letters, 1982, and Aosdána, 1984.

Works

Collections

After Tragedy (includes *The Gigli Concert; Conversations on a Homecoming; Bailegangaire*). 1988.
"*A Whistle in the Dark*" *and Other Plays* (includes *A Crucial Week in the Life of a Grocer's Assistant; On the Outside; On the Inside*). 1989.
Plays 1 (includes *Famine; The Patriot Game; The Blue Macushla*). 1992.
Plays 2 (includes *Bailegangáire; Conversations on a Homecoming; A Thief of a Christmas*). 1993.

Stage Works

On the Outside, with Noel O'Donoghue (produced Cork, 1961). With *On the Inside*, 1976.
A Whistle in the Dark (produced Theatre Royal, Stratford East, London, 1961). 1971.
Famine (produced Peacock Theatre, Dublin, 1966). 1977.
The Orphans (produced Peacock Theatre, Dublin, 1968). 1974.
A Crucial Week in the Life of a Grocer's Assistant, from the television play (produced as *The Fooleen*, Abbey Theatre, Dublin, 1969). 1970.
The Morning After Optimism (produced Abbey Theatre, Dublin, 1971). 1973.
The White House (produced Abbey Theatre, Dublin, 1972).
On the Inside (produced Project Arts Centre, Dublin, 1974). With *On the Outside*, 1976.
The Vicar of Wakefield, from the novel by Goldsmith (produced Abbey Theatre, Dublin, 1974).
The Sanctuary Lamp (produced Abbey Theatre, Dublin, 1975). 1976; revised version, 1984.
The J. Arthur Maginnis Story (produced by the Irish Theatre Company, Dublin, 1976).
Epitaph under Ether, from works by Synge (produced Abbey Theatre, Dublin, 1979).
The Blue Macushla (produced Abbey Theatre, Dublin, 1980). In *Plays 1*, 1992.
The Informer, from the novel by Liam O'Flaherty (produced Olympia Theatre, Dublin, 1981).
She Stoops to Conquer, from the play by Oliver Goldsmith (produced Abbey Theatre, Dublin, 1982).
The Gigli Concert (produced Abbey Theatre, Dublin, 1983). 1984.
Bailegangáire (produced Druid Theatre, Galway, 1985) 1986.
A Thief of a Christmas (produced Abbey Theatre, Dublin, 1985).

Conversations on a Homecoming, from the television play (produced Druid Theatre, Galway, 1985).   1986.
Too Late for Logic (produced Abbey Theatre, Dublin, 1989). 1990.
The Patriot Game.   In *Plays 1*, 1992.

Television Plays

The Fly Sham, 1963; *Veronica*, 1963; *A Crucial Week in the Life of a Grocer's Assistant*, 1967; *Snakes and Reptiles*, 1968; *Young Man in Trouble*, 1970; *The Moral Force, The Policy, Relief* (trilogy), 1973; *Conversations on a Homecoming*, 1976; *Speeches of Farewell*, 1976; *Bridgit*, 1981; *Fatalism*, 1981.

Radio Plays

On the Outside, with Noel O'Donoghue, 1962.

*

Bibliographies

Kimball King, *Ten Modern Irish Playwrights*, New York, 1979.

Criticism

Books:
Hans G. Stalder, *Anglo-Irish Peasant Drama: The Motifs of Land and Emigration*, Bern, 1978.
D.E.S. Maxwell, *A Critical History of Modern Irish Drama 1891–1980*, Cambridge, 1984.
Michael Etherton, *Contemporary Irish Dramatists*, London, 1989 (Macmillan Modern Dramatists series).

Articles:
Richard Kearney, "Tom Murphy's Long Night's Journey into Night", in *Studies*, 72, 1983.
Christopher Murray (ed.), "Thomas Murphy Issue" of *Irish University Review* (includes 13 essays), 17, 1987.
Shaun Richards, "Refiguring Lost Narratives—Prefiguring New Ones: The Theatre of Tom Murphy", in *Canadian Journal of Irish Studies*, vol.15 no.1, 1989.
John Hargaden, "The Stage Irishman in Modern Irish Drama", in *Studies*, 313, 1990.
Desmond Maxwell, "New Lamps for Old: The Theatre of Tom Murphy", in *Theatre Research International*, 15, 1990.
Harry White, "Brian Friel, Thomas Murphy and the Use of Music in Contemporary Irish Drama", in *Modern Drama*, 33, 1990.

*   *   *

Tom Murphy has created a body of work suspended between two competing interpretations, both of which suggest the uneasiness which his plays are capable of evoking in audiences. When his first play, *A Whistle in the Dark*, opened in London in 1962, the critic Kenneth Tynan described it as "the most uninhibited display of brutality that the London theatre has ever witnessed". Indeed, a simmering violence, not unlike that which exists in the work of Tennessee Williams, whom Murphy cites as a "liberating influence", has continued to be one of the defining characteristics of his work, up to, and including, *Too Late for Logic* (1989). In recent years, however, the Irish critic Fintan O'Toole has

stressed the admirable formal control and elements of transcendence in Murphy's best work, arguing that it constitutes a form of modern tragedy which has come into being "after tragedy".

Any understanding of Murphy's challenging theatrical vision must take into account his continued engagement with the past and the present of his native Ireland. His earliest plays, *On the Outside*, *A Whistle in the Dark*, and *A Crucial Week in the Life of A Grocer's Assistant* (published in the USA as *The Fooleen*) draw directly upon his experience of growing up in a small town in the west of Ireland. *Famine* deals with one of the most horrific periods in Irish history, the Great Famine of the late 1840's. Comparable in many ways to Bertolt Brecht's *Mother Courage*, the play employs the fragmented structure of Brechtian epic theatre to represent the situation of the leader of a starving peasant community, John O'Connor, who wants to "do what is right" at a time when the harsh contingencies of existence have made "right" and "wrong" relative concepts. Murphy's later works, including *Too Late for Logic*, continue his exploration of this moral relativism in the changing society of contemporary Ireland.

Related to the perception of shifting values and beliefs is a recurrent sense of loss. From *A Whistle in the Dark*, through *The Sanctuary Lamp*, *The Gigli Concert*, *Conversations on a Homecoming*, *Bailegangáire*, and *Too Late for Logic*, many of his plays centre upon absent characters. Such characters may be simply referred to, like Olga in *Sanctuary Lamp* and J.J. Kilkelly in *Conversations on a Homecoming*; or they may communicate with the characters on the stage only by telephone, as in *The Gigli Concert* or *Too Late for Logic*. In both cases the audience is made aware of an absence in the lives of Murphy's characters. In the Irish context of the plays, this recognition of absence marks out such characters as representatives of a transitional society, denied access to the assumption of an organic community which informs the theatre of Yeats and Synge earlier in the century. In a wider context, however, Murphy's work constitutes a prolonged meditation on the nature of the theatrical experience itself, in which the stage is understood, to use Peter Brook's phrase, as "a place where the invisible can appear".

In *The Sanctuary Lamp*, written shortly after Murphy had spent two years on the commission to translate the Catholic liturgy into English, the dialectic of absence and presence is written into the play's physical space. Set in an empty church, dominated by the glow of a sanctuary lamp—an institutionalised symbol of eternal presence—the play's three main characters argue, fight, drink the sacristy wine, and sleep in an overturned confessional, in a struggle to imbue what are seen as dead religious images with new meanings. Ultimately, the transformation of the eponymous sanctuary lamp from a religious icon to a theatrical icon, in which the characters find a form of secular salvation, suggests the redemptive nature of the stage as a place of transformation.

This understanding of art as a force capable of conferring a necessary illusion of wholeness is central to Murphy's theatrical vision, and finds one of its clearest expressions in *The Gigli Concert*, in which a successful builder finds himself incapacitated by an irrational desire to sing like an operatic tenor, Beniamino Gigli. Employing a device reminiscent of Peter Shaffer's *Equus*, the builder (identified only as "Irish Man") transfers his obsession to a quack psychologist, J.W.P. King, who, in the play's final scene, magically sings like Gigli in a moment which transcends the bounds of realism. Hence, in *The Gigli Concert*, art is represented as a force capable of both disrupting and healing wounded lives, and the artist is understood to be a combination of scapegoat, confidence man, and saviour.

In *Bailegangáire*, it is the art of the story-teller which gives the play its central metaphor, as Mommo, an old woman, narrates the story of how the town of Bailegangaire, "the town without laughter", came by its name. Mommo's tale progresses fitfully, stopping, repeating itself, and starting again, while its past-tense nature contrasts with the presence on the stage of her two granddaughters, Dolly and Mary, as they struggle with their lives, Mommo, and each other. As *Bailegangáire* develops, however, it becomes apparent that the story Mommo is telling is the story of how Dolly and Mary's brother, Tom, was killed in childhood. Hence, when the play closes with Mary finally completing her grandmother's story, the formal closure of the narrative creates a structure in which past and present find reconciliation in a moment of aesthetic completion.

In spite of the considerable achievement of plays such as *The Sanctuary Lamp*, *The Gigli Concert*, and *Bailegangáire*, Murphy's reputation outside of his native Ireland has never returned to the levels which it reached in the early 1960's with *A Whistle in the Dark*, when he was compared to John Osborne and Harold Pinter (who has acknowledged *A Whistle in the Dark* as one of the sources for his play of 1965, *The Homecoming*). This relative neglect can be attributed in part to Murphy's subtle use of colloquial dialogue, and his relentless interrogation of his own society, both of which make his theatre more readily accessible to an Irish audience than to those unfamiliar with its context. And yet, in the sheer theatricality of his vision, Murphy's work extends beyond the specific context from which it arises to demonstrate the potential of the stage as a place of revelation.

—Christopher Morash

MURRAY, T(homas) C(ornelius). Born in Macroom, County Cork, Ireland, 17 January 1873. Educated at St. Patrick's Teachers Training College, Drumcondra, 1891–93. Teacher in Cork schools; co-founder, Cork Dramatic Society, 1908; first-produced play, *Birthright*, staged by the Abbey Theatre, 1910; contributor, *New Ireland Review*, *Dublin Magazine*, and *The Bell*; headmaster, Inchicore Model Schools, Dublin, 1915–1932 (retired); Director, Authors' Guild of Ireland. Founding member, later Vice-President, Irish Academy. Member, Film Censorship Appeal Board. D.Litt (Honorary): National University of Ireland, 1949. Died in Ballsbridge, Dublin, 7 March 1959.

Works

Collections

"Spring" and Other Plays (includes *Sovereign Love; The Briery Gap*). 1917.

Stage Works

Sovereign Love (produced as *The Wheel of Fortune*, Cork, 1909; revised version, as *Sovereign Love*, produced Abbey Theatre, Dublin, 1913). In *"Spring" and Other Plays*, 1917.
Birthright (produced Abbey Theatre, Dublin, 1910). 1911.

Maurice Harte (produced Court Theatre, London, 1912). 1912.
Spring (produced Abbey Theatre, Dublin, 1918). In *"Spring" and Other Plays*, 1917.
The Briery Gap (produced Peacock Theatre, Dublin, 1948). In *"Spring" and Other Plays*, 1917.
Aftermath (produced Abbey Theatre, Dublin, 1922). 1922.
Autumn Fire (produced Abbey Theatre, Dublin, 1924). 1925.
The Pipe in the Fields (produced Abbey Theatre, Dublin, 1927). With *Birthright*, 1927.
The Blind Wolf (produced Abbey Theatre, Dublin, 1928).
A Flutter of Wings (produced Gate Theatre, Dublin, 1929).
Michaelmas Eve (produced Abbey Theatre, Dublin, 1932). 1932.
A Stage at Bay (produced Abbey Theatre, Dublin, 1934). With *Maurice Harte*, 1934.
A Spot in the Sun (produced Abbey Theatre, Dublin, 1938).
Illumination (produced Abbey Theatre, Dublin, 1939).

Fiction

Spring Horizon. 1937.

*

Criticism

Books:
N. Sahhal, *Sixty Years of Realistic Irish Drama*, Bombay, 1971.

Articles:
Dorothy Macardle, "The Dramatic Art of T.C. Murray", in *Dublin Magazine*, 2, January 1925.
Micheál Ó hAodha, "T.C. Murray and Some Critics", in *Studies*, 47, 1958.
T. Gerald FitzGibbon, "The Elements of Conflict in the Plays of T.C. Murray", in *Studies*, 64, 1975.

* * *

Murray was a 37-year-old Cork schoolteacher when his first important play, *Birthright*, was staged at the Abbey Theatre in 1910. It was included in the repertory when the Abbey Company made its first momentous tour of the USA in the following year. This stark two-act tragedy of jealousy between two brothers over the inheritance of a small farm ends in fratricide. It made a powerful impression on the young Eugene O'Neill and influenced his treatment of a similar situation in his first full-length play, *Beyond the Horizon*. After the production of Murray's second play at the Abbey in 1912, W.B. Yeats wrote: "If Mr. Murray can give us more plays equal in intensity to *Maurice Harte* then we shall deserve, perhaps, as much attention as any contemporary theatre".

After this brilliant but rather late start as a dramatist, Murray wrote 13 more plays, but whether his contribution to the theatre won the attention that Yeats suggested remains an open question. *Maurice Harte* is the story of a spoiled priest in a West Cork setting, a daring subject for a rural schoolmaster in those days. An archetypal Irish mother's relentless ambition to make her son become a priest ends in tragedy for both. Seldom before was a religious situation handled with such sincerity and restraint.

A classical theme, the marriage of an old widower to a

spirited young bride, is the subject of *Autumn Fire*, staged at the Abbey Theatre in 1924, a year which also saw the first production of Eugene O'Neill's play on the same subject, *Desire Under the Elms*. Critics like Joseph Wood Krutch and Allardyce Nicoll noticed the coincidence, drawing attention to the tighter construction and more evocative dialogue in Murray's version.

Murray was the first realistic playwright to write tragedies of Irish rural life from the his own experience. Restraint is the keynote; the characters in his best plays are neither flamboyantly romantic nor luridly brutal, and the more sensitive among them, in Thoreau's phrase, lead lives of quiet desperation. The themes are elemental: exile, the loveless marriage, the slavery of the hired man, the bleak years of the old, the endless vigil of mothers. Some of the shorter pieces, like *Spring* and *The Briery Gap*, show a concern with social problems; but his characters, in the main, show little interest in ideologies or politics, caring little for what goes on beyond the stone walls of their little mountain farms.

The most serious fault in Murray's work, is, perhaps, a defect stemming from his being a peasant playwright. Writing from within the world of his characters, being so much of his people, he seemed to share, at times, some of the inhibitions and prejudices of the environment he depicted. In the mid-1920's, when he was at the height of his powers, he turned away from the milieu and characters he knew best, to write of middle-class problems, or to contrast the freedom of the city with the narrowness of country life. Most of these experiments lacked inner conviction.

A strong case can be made for the inclusion of one of his last plays, *Michaelmas Eve*, as worthy of attention as a major work. In spite of the rather contrived poisoning scene which ends the play, it has much of Murray's old mastery; there is a poetic surge in the dialogue with its suggestion of a more full-blooded life outside the boundary ditch of the farm—the life of Moll Garvey's tinker clan who are always wanting the stars. But Hugh, the servant-boy who loves Moll, is tied, like his masters, to the acre of good earth and closes his ears to the call of the road.

In at least six of his published plays, Murray left an authentic expression of a way of life which has almost vanished in a changing Ireland. Nowadays his work is seldom staged professionally, but even a reading of the texts shows a sense of literature and a serious approach in the handling of elemental themes.

—Micheál Ó hAodha

MURRELL, John. Born in Lubbock, Texas, USA, 15 October 1945. Educated at schools in Alberta, Canada; Southwestern University, Georgetown, Texas, BFA 1966; University of Calgary, Alberta, B.Ed. 1969. Married with one daughter. Schoolteacher for five years; playwright-in-residence, Alberta Theatre Projects, Calgary, 1975; associate director, Stratford Festival, Stratford, Ontario, 1977–78; director, Banff Centre School of Fine Arts Playwrights Colony, 1986; head of theatre section, Canada Council, 1988. Recipient: Clifford E. Lee Award, 1975; Chalmers Award, 1986.

Stage Works

Metamorphosis.   1970.
Haydn's Head (produced Edmonton, 1973).

Power in the Blood (produced Edmonton, 1975).
Arena (produced by Alberta Theatre Projects, Calgary, 1975).
Teaser, with Kenneth Dyba (produced by Alberta Theatre Projects, Calgary, 1975).
A Great Noise, A Great Light (produced by Alberta Theatre Projects, Calgary, 1976).
Waiting for the Parade: Faces of Women in War (produced by Alberta Theatre Projects, Calgary, 1977).   1980.
Memoir (produced Spring Festival, Guelph, Ontario, 1977; revised version produced Calgary, 1981).   1978.
Uncle Vanya: Scenes from Rural Life, adaptation of a play by Chekhov (produced Stratford Festival, Stratford, Ontario, 1978).
Mandragola, from the play by Machiavelli (produced Theatre Calgary, Calgary, 1978).
Bajazet, from the play by Racine (produced Tarragon Theatre, Toronto, 1979).
The Seagull, from a play by Chekhov (produced Stratford Festival, Stratford, Ontario, 1980).
Farther West (produced Theatre Calgary, Calgary, 1982). With *New World*, 1985.
Divorçons, from the play by Sardou (produced Theatre Calgary, Calgary, 1983).
Bygmester Solness, from a play by Ibsen (produced Tarragon Theatre, Toronto, 1983).
New World (produced Ottawa, 1984).   With *Farther West*, 1985.
Oedipus the King, from the play by Sophocles (produced Stratford Festival, Stratford, Ontario, 1988).
October (produced Tarragon Theatre, Toronto, 1988).

*

Criticism

Books:
Eugene Benson and L.W. Conolly, *English-Canadian Theatre*, Oxford, 1987.

*   *   *

Murrell's enduring interest in recreating the past is evidenced in his first play of note, *A Great Noise, A Great Light*. This play recreates the 1937 political world of Premier William Aberhart of Alberta and his Social Credit party.

Waiting for the Parade, one of the most popular plays in the modern Canadian repertoire, subtitled *Faces of Women in War*, is an impressionistic series of 24 vignettes or cameos portraying the lives of five Calgary women during World War II. A "photo album of staged nostalgia", as it has been called, the play's episodic action is given coherence through song, music, and radio broadcasts (brass bands, canteen dances, battles in Europe). The women's roles are sketched rather than fully drawn, but so sympathetic and sensitive is Murrell's art that the general effect is satisfying and theatrical. Particularly affecting among the women is Catherine, who, forgetting what her soldier-husband (missing at Dieppe) looks like, has entered into an affair with an older man. The role of Marta, originally born in Germany and burdened with a father who remembers the fatherland with nostalgia and not with the hatred the times demand, offers the most depth.

First performed in 1977, *Memoir* has been performed in some 25 countries, and has been translated into 15 languages. It dramatizes a day in the last summer of Sarah Bernhardt's life as she works on her memoirs on her island home off the coast of Brittany in 1922. As foil to Bernhardt is her middle-aged, pedantic, and devoted secretary, Pitou, who is forced by her to play certain roles in order to jog her memory, thus creating a series of cameo two-handers, the most beautiful of which is an 1890's meeting at St. Tropez between Bernhardt and Oscar Wilde. Sarah's speech, beginning, "We are the last ones, Oscar Wilde", is a virtuoso piece of writing evoking at once pathos, nostalgia, and a faded *fin-de-siècle* elegance.

Much of the play's strength derives from Bernhardt's fame and colorful life, and Murrell, drawing skilfully and economically on the actress's 60-year career, focuses on key people, events, and theatrical roles—her mother; memories of Rostand, Coquelin, and Ellen Terry among a multitude of actors; her American tours ("weariness, dust, dollars"); Queen Victoria and the Tsar Nicholas; her most famous death scene as Marguerite Gauthier in *The Lady of the Camelias*; and past, dead lovers. Throughout the play the sun, setting and rising, is a symbol of immortality, and a burning reminder of Sarah's imminent death. At the play's Guelph Spring Festival premiere in Canada the distinguished Irish actress Siobhan McKenna played Sarah, and the Irish-Canadian actor Gerald Parkes played Pitou. Translated into French by George Wilson as *Sarah et le cri de langouste* (1982), this one-act adaption of the original two-act play ran for three years in Paris with Wilson as Pitou and Delphine Seyrig as Sarah.

Farther West represents a radical departure from the introspective, elegiac mood of the two previous plays; here Murrell traces the westward journey, from eastern Canada to the Pacific coast, of a prostitute, May Buchanan, in the years between 1886 and 1892. The play takes its origins from an adaption of John Ford's *'Tis Pity She's a Whore*, which Murrell began for Canada's Stratford Festival; if Ford deals with the pathology of honour and love, Murrell deals in his play with the pathology of sexuality and erotic obsession. May is pursued by two men across a continent; they cannot understand that her journey westward is symbolic of her wish to flee the conventions that bind women in the name of love and marriage. May is destroyed at the play's close, as are the men, unable to cope with the emotional and sexual freedom sought by May at the edge of accepted mores. The development of this theme in the play is marked by scenes of sexual degradation and brutal violence—the final murder scene was thought by some critics to be gratuitously offensive.

New World, a comedy of family reunion set on Vancouver Island, draws upon Chekhov and Shakespeare, and especially on *The Tempest* with its hopes of new beginnings. Two brothers and a sister, from England, meet on the western shore of Canada where in the course of a simple day they take stock of the past and regroup to face, fearfully, the future. The blue glass float of a fishing net found on shore, so delicate yet able to bear the pressure of the ocean, is a symbol of the fragility of their lives and the fragility of any hope offered these people. *New World* is the most elegantly contoured play Murrell has written, with haunting resonances evoked through constant allusions to Puccini's *Girl of the Golden West* and Shakespeare's *Tempest*.

In *October* Murrell turned once again to theatrical figures of the past, but this dramatization of a meeting between actress Eleonora Duse and dancer Isadora Duncan has not enjoyed the success of *Memoir*.

—Eugene Benson

See also *Volume 1* entry on *Waiting for the Parade*.

MUSSET, (Louis-Charles-) Alfred de. Born in Paris, 11 December 1810. Educated at the Collège Henri IV, Paris, until the age of 16; briefly studied law and medicine. Entered Parisian literary circles in the late 1820's; clerical worker for a heating company, 1829–30; first-produced play, *La Nuit vénitienne*, staged 1830, and then he wrote plays intended just for reading until c.1847, when he began writing for the stage again; contributor, *Revue des deux mondes* (in which many of his works first appeared), from 1832; travelled to Italy with the writer George Sand, his lover at the time, 1834; librarian, Ministry of the Interior, Paris, 1838–48, and the Ministry of Education, from 1853. Elected to the Académie Française, 1852. Died in Paris, 2 May 1857.

Works

Collections

Un Spectacle dans un fauteuil (verse and plays). 1833; second series (2 vols.), 1834.
Comédies et proverbes. 1840; augmented and revised edition (2 vols.), 1853.
Oeuvres complètes (10 vols.), edited by Paul de Musset. 1865–66.
Oeuvres posthumes (2 vols.). 1878.
Comedies, translated by S.S. Gwyn. 1890.
Complete Writings (10 vols.). 1905; Volumes 3 and 5 reprinted as *Ten Plays* (includes *A Venetian Night; André del Sarto; The Follies of Marianne; Fantasio; No Trifling with Love; Barbarine; A Caprice; The Door Must Be Either Open or Shut; Louison; One Cannot Think of Everything*), 1987.
Oeuvres complètes (9 vols.). 1907–08.
Oeuvres complètes illustrées (10 vols.). 1927–29.
Oeuvres complètes en prose; Théâtre complet; Poésies complètes (3 vols.), edited by Maurice Allem. 1951–58.
Seven Plays (includes *Marianne; Fantasio; Camille and Perdican; The Candlestick; A Diversion; A Door Must Be Kept Open or Shut; Journey to Gotha*), translated by Peter Meyer. 1962.
Oeuvres complètes, edited by Philippe Tieghem. 1963.
Théâtre (2 vols.), edited by Maurice Rat. 1964.

Stage Works

La Nuit vénitienne (produced Théâtre de l'Odéon, Paris, 1830). In *Un Spectacle dans un fauteuil*, 1834; translated as *A Venetian Night*, in *Complete Writings*, 1905.
André del Sarto (produced Comédie-Française, Paris, 1848). In *Un Spectacle dans un fauteuil*, 1834; revised version (produced 1848), 1851; translated as *André del Sarto*, in *Complete Writings*, 1905.
Les Caprices de Marianne (produced Comédie-Française, Paris, 1851). In *Un Spectacle dans un fauteuil*, 1834; revised version (produced 1851), 1851; translated as *A Good Little Wife*, nd (1847?); as *The Follies of Marianne*, in *Complete Writings*, 1905.
On ne badine pas avec l'amour (produced Comédie-Française, Paris, 1861). In *Un Spectacle dans un fauteuil*, 1834; translated as *No Trifling with Love*, in *Comedies*, 1890; as *Love is Not to Be Trifled With*, 1957; as *Camille and Perdicon*, 1961.
Fantasio (produced Comédie-Française, Paris, 1866). In *Un Spectacle dans un fauteuil*, 1834; translated as *Fantasio*, in *Comedies*, 1890: several subsequent translations under same title.

Alfred de Musset with the actress Rachel (lithograph by Talin; Musée Carnavalet, Paris).

Lorenzaccio (produced Théâtre de la Renaissance, Paris, 1896). In *Un Spectacle dans un fauteuil*, 1834; translated as *Lorenzaccio*, 1907; several subsequent translations under same title.
Le Chandelier (produced in a revised version, Théâtre Historique, Paris, 1848). In *Comédies et proverbes*, 1840; revised version, 1848; translated as *The Candlestick*, in *Seven Plays*, 1962.
Il ne faut jurer de rien (produced Comédie-Française, Paris, 1848). In *Comédies et proverbes*, 1840.
Un Caprice (produced St. Petersburg, Russia, 1837; first produced in French, St. Petersburg, 1843). In *Comédies et proverbes*, 1840; translated as *A Caprice*, in *Poet Lore*, 33, 1922: several subsequent translations under same title; as *A Diversion*, in *Seven Plays*, 1962.
La Quenouille de Barberine. In *Comédies et proverbes*, 1840; revised version, as *Barberine* (produced 1882), in *Comédies et proverbes*, 1853; translated as *Barberine*, in *Comedies*, 1890, and in *Complete Writings*, 1905.
Il faut qu'une porte soit ouverte ou fermée (produced Comédie-Française, Paris, 1848). 1848; translated as *A Door Must Be Either Open or Shut*, in *Comedies*, 1890, and in *Complete Writings*, 1905.
L'Habit vert, with Émile Augier (produced Comédie-Française, Paris, 1849). 1849; translated as *The Green Coat*, 1914.
Louison (produced Comédie-Française, Paris, 1849). 1849; translated as *Louison*, in *Complete Writings*, 1905.
On ne saurait penser à tout (produced Salle Pleyel, Paris, 1849). In *Comédies et proverbes*, 1853; translated as *One Cannot Think of Everything*, in *Complete Writings*, 1905.
Bettine (produced Théâtre du Gymnase, Paris, 1851). 1851.
Carmosine (produced Théâtre de l'Odéon, Paris, 1865). In *Comédies et proverbes*, 1853; translated as *Carmosine*, nd (1865?).
L'Âne et le ruisseau (produced Conservatoire National de Musique, Paris, 1876). In *Oeuvres posthumes*, 1860; translated as *All is Fair in Love and War*, 1868.
La Quittance du diable (produced 1938). 1896.

Fiction

La Confession d'un enfant du siècle (2 vols.). 1836; translated as *The Confession of a Child of the Century*, 1892.
Nouvelles. 1848; translated as *Tales from Musset*, 1888, and *The Two Mistresses, etc.*, 1900.
Contes. 1854.
Two Fables. 1925.
Contes d'Espage et d'Italie, edited by Margaret Rees. 1973.

Verse

Les Contes d'Espagne et d'Italie. 1830.
Poésies complètes. 1840.
Premières poésies; Poésies nouvelles (2 vols.). 1852.
Poésies complètes (2 vols.). 1854.

Memoirs and Letters

Correspondance, edited by Léon Séché. 1907.
Lettres d'amour à Aimée d'Alton, edited by Léon Séché. 1910.
Oeuvres complémentaires, edited by Maurice Allem. 1911.
George Sand et Musset: Correspondance . . ., edited by Louis Évrard. 1956.

Other

Mélanges de littérature et de critique (essays and criticism). 1867.

Translator, *L'Anglais Mangeur d'opium*, by Thomas de Quincey. 1828.

*

Bibliographies

Patricia Joan Seigel, *Alfred de Musset: A Reference Guide*, Boston, 1982.

Criticism

Books:
J. Lafoscade, *Le Théâtre de Musset*, Paris, 1901; revised edition, 1966.
L. Séché, *Alfred de Musset* (biography; 2 vols.), Paris, 1907.
W.A. Geyer, *Alfred de Musset in seinem dramatischen Werk*, Giessen, 1923.
P. Gastinel, *Le Romantisme d'Alfred de Musset*, Paris, 1933.
Philippe van Tieghen, *Musset: L'Homme et l'oeuvre*, Paris, 1944; revised edition, 1967.
J. Pommier, *Variétés sur Alfred de Musset et son théâtre*, Paris, 1947.
H. Lefebvre, *Alfred de Musset: Dramaturge*, Paris, 1955; revised edition, 1970.
J. Pommier, *Alfred de Musset*, Oxford, 1957.
Philippe Soupault, *Alfred de Musset*, Paris, 1957.
Charlotte Haldane, *Alfred: The Passionate Life of Musset*, 1960.
A. Lebois, *Vues sur le théâtre de Musset*, Avignon, 1966.
Herbert S. Gochberg, *Stage of Dreams: The Dramatic Art of Musset*, Ghent, 1967.
G. Kobow, *Absurdes Lebensgefühl und szenische Struktur im dramatischen Frühwerk (1833–1834)*, Berlin, 1967.
F. Tonge, *L'Art du dialogue dans les comédies en prose d'Alfred de Musset*, Paris, 1967.
S. Jeune, *Musset et sa fortune littéraire*, Paris, 1970.
Margaret A. Rees, *Alfred de Musset*, New York, 1971.
Charles Affron, *A Stage for Poets: Studies in the Theatre of Hugo and Musset*, Princeton, New Jersey, 1971.
G. Guillemin, *La Liaison Musset-Sand* (biography), Paris, 1972.
B. Guthmüller, *Die Rezeption Mussets im Second Empire*, Frankfurt, 1973.
E.L. Gans, *Musset et le "drama tragique"*, Paris, 1974.
David Sices, *Theatre of Solitude: The Drama of Musset*, Hannover, New Hampshire, 1974.
E. de Domenico, *Musset et l'Italie*, Turin, 1976.
P.-G. Castex, *Études sur le théâtre de Musset* (2 vols.), Paris, 1978–79.
C. Malthus, *Musset et Shakespeare*, New York, 1988.

* * *

The youngest among the prominent figures of French Romanticism, Musset was welcomed as a prodigy into the *cénacle* of Victor Hugo in 1828, at the age of 18. His temperament was ill-suited to the grandiose ambitions of the movement, however, and in his poems and prose he established himself as something of a free, inconsistent spirit, driven chiefly by the impulses of his own sensibility; paradoxically, he came thereby to express perhaps the fundamental nature of Romanticism.

At the end of 1830 his first play to be produced, *La Nuit vénitienne* (*The Venetian Night*), was very badly received, and he resolved never again to have dealings with the stage. Nonetheless, he continued to write plays as the mood took him, with a lack of concern for the practical exigencies of the theatre which allowed free rein to his fertile imagination. He published a first collection of such works under a title he was to re-use subsequently, and which established a genre: *Un Spectacle dans un fauteuil* (Theatre in an Armchair). Thereafter his output included a regular flow of dramatic works conceived in the same vein.

In 1837 a Russian translation of *Un Caprice* (*A Caprice*) was played in St. Petersburg, prompting a visiting French actress, Mme Allan-Despréaux, to stage the French version there in 1843. On her return to Paris she insisted on seeing it staged at the Comédie-Française, where she played the lead role in a hugely successful production in 1847. Henceforth Musset's plays were to feature regularly in the repertoire, though on the occasions when he tried to write directly for the stage he continued to founder. By the late 1840's, however, Musset was sliding into a decline brought on by illness and subsequently hastened by the self-destructive abuse of alcohol in reaction to a series of tormented love-affairs.

Musset's plays present a kaleidoscope of time, place, and mood. The scenes switch fluidly between chateaux, woods, streets, fountains; the era varies from the Renaissance to the 18th century; the locations are Bavaria, Hungary, Bohemia, Italy—or "wherever one likes". Essentially, all takes place in a dream world, in which the action reflects a state of mind or a personal vision. But if, on the surface, these works are governed by fantasy, they are nevertheless anchored in the emotional reality of the author's own sensibility. This sensibility is as much of the 18th as of the early 19th century: in Musset the passion of Romanticism is subjected to the analytical mentality that was a legacy of the enlightenment. Like Marivaux, Musset combines preciosity with spontaneity; he can be sentimental and mocking by turns; he is an heir of Greuze and Fragonard.

From the 18th century he also took and made his own the form of the "proverb", the *jeu de salon*, developing a witty dialogue around an everyday moral precept. On this slight foundation he built from *Il faut qu'une porte soit ouverte ou fermée* (*A Door Must be Either Open or Closed*) and *Il ne faut jurer de rien* (Do Not Swear to Anything), to *On ne badine pas avec l'amour* (*No Trifling with Love*), one of his finest achievements.

In Musset's works the impulses to debauchery and violent emotion conflict with spiritual aspirations: the libertine debates with the idealist. He is not subject to romantic illusions, though he may, briefly, evoke them the better to demonstrate his detachment; his aptitude for inner dialogue finds a kind of fulfilment in the the dramatic form and the ebb and flow of contrasting moods. Heine said of Musset that the muse of comedy had kissed him on the lips and the muse of tragedy had kissed him on the heart. Attempts have been made to classify his plays along these lines: *André del Sarto*, *Les Caprices de Marianne*, and *Lorenzaccio* present intense tragic action, while *Fantasio*, *Un Caprice*, and *Le Chandelier* are comedies. But he is at his best when he sets the burlesque or light-hearted alongside the emotional.

Musset had a particular gift for the comic puppet used as a secondary character to highlight the drama of his heroes and heroines: the old judge Claudio in *Les Caprices de Marianne*; the prince of Mantua in *Fantasio*; and most memorable of all, Blazius, Bridaine, Dame Pluche, and the Baron—the gallery of grotesques which underpins the action in *On ne badine pas avec l'amour*.

Musset's male protagonists are, without exception, facets of the author in varying moods and states of mind: Fantasio, frivolous and melancholy, debauched and disabused, but driven on by the possibility of reviving true love; Perdican (in *On ne badine pas avec l'amour*), torn between his pride and his emotions; and Lorenzaccio, Musset's most profound creation, who tests the very notion of identity through his assumption of a false personality, and stumbles upon upon a void at the centre of his being. Often the author's own duality is reflected in pairings of male characters, as when Octave, the worldly libertine, assists his timid friend Celio to woo the haughty Marianne (in *Les Caprices de Marianne*); or when the avuncular Van Buck remonstrates with Valentin the roué (in *Il ne faut jurer de rien*).

Musset created compelling female figures embodying the charm and cruelty of those for whom he had suffered: Mariane, proud, headstrong, who on the death of one suitor offers to console his grieving friend who had acted as intermediary; Camille, determined to refuse male blandishments in order to avoid suffering, but snared by the urgings of her pride when she discovers Perdican may turn to another. Most remarkable of all, Lorenzaccio seeks to avenge the debauched town of Florence (and by implication, downtrodden feminity) by taking the place of a woman for an assignation in the bedchamber which he has fixed on as the place to assassinate the tyrannical duke. In his analysis of emotions and subconscious impulses, Musset demonstrates that a sense of psychology is stronger in him than in any other Romantic. Indeed, if it were not for his plays, the theatre would arguably not have gained anything enduring from French Romanticism.

—David H. Walker

See also *Volume 1* entry on *Lorenzaccio*.

N

NESTROY, Johann Nepomuk. Born in Vienna, Austria, 7 December 1801. Educated at a Gymnasium, 1811–16; University of Vienna, studying law, 1817–21 (did not take degree). Married Wilhelmine von Nespiesni, 1823 (separated 1827, divorced 1845), one son; lived with the singer Marie Weiler from 1827, one son and one daughter. Stage debut, as an operatic bass, singing the role of Sarastro in Mozart's *The Magic Flute*, Vienna, 1822; actor and singer with the German Theatre of Amsterdam, 1823–25, Nationaltheater in Brünn (now Brno, Czechoslovakia), 1825–26, and the theatres in Graz and Pressburg, 1826–28; first-produced play, *Der Zettelträger Papp*, staged 1827; returned to Vienna, 1829; guest singer at Theater in der Josefstadt and Kärtnertortheater, 1829–31; with Marie Weiler joined Karl Carl's theatre company, based at the Theater an der Wien (from 1845 at the Theater in der Leopoldstadt, renamed the Carltheater, 1847), as comic actor and writer, 1831–54, director and manager, 1854–60: dominated Vienna's commercial stage as its leading comic actor, appearing in his own plays; undertook guest seasons in various parts of Germany and central Europe during the 1840's and 1850's; his satirical play, *Die Freiheit in Krähwinkel* banned during political turbulence, 1848; retired to his house in Graz, 1860, subsequently appearing for occasional performances. Died in Graz, 25 May 1862.

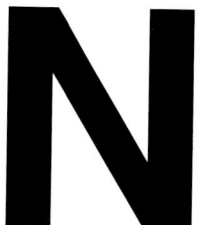

Johann Nestroy (right) and the manager Karl Carl (centre) in a scene from Nestroy's *Der böse Geist Lumpazivagabundus* at the Theater an der Wien, Vienna, 1833.

Works

Collections

Gesammelte Werke (12 vols.), edited by Vincenzo Chiavacci and Ludwig Ganghofer. 1890–91.
Sämtliche Werke (15 vols.), edited by Fritz Brukner and Otto Rommel. 1924–30.
Gesammelte Werke (6 vols.), edited by Otto Rommel. 1948–49.
Unbekannter Nestroy (includes *Zwölf Mädchen in Uniform; Ein gebildeter Hausknecht; Friedrich, Prinz von Korsika*). 1953.
Three Comedies (includes *A Man Full of Nothing; The Talisman; Love Affairs and Wedding Bells*), translated and adapted by Max Knight and Joseph Fabry. 1967.
Komödien, edited by F.H. Mautner. 1970.
Sämtliche Werke (continuing series), edited by Jürgen Hein and Johann Hüttner. 1977—
Three Viennese Comedies (includes *The Talisman; Judith and Holofernes; The House of Humors*), translated by Robert Harrison and Katharina Wilson.

Stage Works

Zwölf Mädchen in Uniform (produced Graz, 1827). With *Ein gebildeter Hausknecht*, 1943.
Der Zettelträger Papp, from a play by Hermann Herzenskron (produced Graz, 1927). In *Sämtliche Werke 9*, 1927.
Die Verbannung aus dem Zauberreiche; oder, Dreissig Jahre aus dem Leben eines Lumpen (produced Graz, 1828). In *Sämtliche Werke 1*, 1924.
Der Einsilbige; oder, Ein Hummer Diener seines serrn (produced Theater in der Josefstadt, Vienna, 1829).
Der Tod am Hochzeitstage; oder, Mann, Frau, Kind (produced Theater in der Josefstadt, Vienna, 1829). In *Sämtliche Werke 1*, 1924.
Der unzusammenhängende Zusammenhang (produced Graz, 1830).
Magische Eilwagenreise durch die Komödienwelt (produced Pressburg, 1830). In *Sämtliche Werke 9*, 1927.
Zwei Schüsseln voll Faschingskrapfen (produced Pressburg, 1831).
Der gefühlvolle Kerkermeister; oder, Adelheid, die verfolgte Wittib (produced Theater an der Wien, Vienna, 1832). In *Gesammelte Werke*, 1890–91.
Nagerl und Handschuh; oder, Die Schicksale der Familie Maxenpfutsch, from a libretto by C.-G. Étienne (produced Theater an der Wien, Vienna, 1832). In *Gesammelte Werke*, 1890–91.
Humoristische Eilwagenreise durch die Theaterwelt (produced Theater an der Wien, Vienna, 1832). In *Sämtliche Werke 9*, 1927.
Zampa der Tagdieb; oder, Die Braut von Gips (produced Theater an der Wien, Vienna, 1832). In *Gesammelte Werke*, 1890–91.
Der konfuse Zauberer; oder, Treue und Flatterhaftigkeit (produced Theater an der Wien, Vienna, 1832). In *Gesammelte Werke*, 1890–91.
Die Zauberreise in die Ritterzeit; oder, Die Übermütigen (produced Theater an der Wien, Vienna, 1832). In *Gesammelte Werke*, 1890–91.
Der Zauberer Februar; oder, Die Überraschungen (produced Theater an der Wien, Vienna, 1833). In *Samtliche Werke 1*, 1924.
Der böse Geist Lumpazivagabundus; oder, Das liederliche Kleeblatt (produced Theater an der Wien, Vienna, 1833). 1835.
Robert der Teuxel (produced Theater an der Wien, 1833). In *Gesammelte Werke*, 1890–91.
Der Tritschtratsch (produced Theater an der Wien, Vienna, 1833). In *Gesammelte Werke*, 1890–91.
Der Zauberer Sulphurelektrimagnetikophosphoratus und die Fee Walpurgiblocksbergiseptemtrionalis . . . (produced Theater an der Wien, 1834). In *Gesammelte Werke*, 1890–91.
Müller, Kohlenbrenner und Sesselträger; oder, Die Träume von Schale und Kern (produced Theater an der Wien, Vienna, 1834). In *Gesammelte Werke*, 1890–91.
Die Gleichheit der Jahre (produced Theater an der Wien, Vienna, 1834). In *Gesammelte Werke*, 1890–91.
Die Familien Zwirn, Knieriem und Leim; oder, Der Welt-Untergangs-Tag (produced Theater an der Wien, Vienna, 1834). In *Gesammelte Werke*, 1890–91.
Die Fahrt mit dem Dampfwagen (produced Theater an der Wien, Vienna, 1834). In *Gesammelte Werke*, 1890–91.
Weder Lorbeerbaum noch Bettelstab (produced Theater an der Wien, Vienna, 1835). In *Gesammelte Werke*, 1890–91.
Eulenspiegel; oder, Schabernack über Schabernack (produced Theater an der Wien, Vienna, 1835). 1839.
Zu ebener Erde und erster Stock; oder, Die Launen des Glückes, from a play by C.-D. Dupeuty and Frédéric de Courcy (produced Theater an der Wien, Vienna, 1835). 1838.
Der Treulose; oder, Saat und Ernte (produced Theater an der Wien, Vienna, 1836). In *Gesammelte Werke*, 1890–91.
Die beiden Nachtwandler; oder, Das Notwendige und das Überflüssige (produced Theater an der Wien, Vienna, 1836). In *Gesammelte Werke*, 1890–91.
Der Affe und der Bräutigam (produced Theater an der Wien, Vienna, 1836). In *Gesammelte Werke*, 1890–91.
Eine Wohnung ist zu vermieten in der Stadt . . . (produced Theater an der Wien, Vienna, 1837). In *Gesammelte Werke*, 1890–91.
Moppels Abenteuer im Viertel unter Wiener Wald, in Neu-Seeland und Marokko (produced Theater an der Wien, Vienna, 1837). In *Gesammelte Werke*, 1890–91.
Das Haus der Temperamente (produced Theater an der Wien, Vienna, 1837). In *Gesammelte Werke*, 1890–91; translated as *The House of Humors*, in *Three Viennese Comedies*, 1986.
Glück, Missbrauch und Rückkehr; oder, Das Geheimnis des grauen Hauses, from a novel by Paul de Kock (produced Theater an der Wien, Vienna, 1838). 1845.
Der Kobold; oder, Staberl im Feendienst (produced Theater an der Wien, Vienna, 1838). In *Gesammelte Werke*, 1890–91.
Gegen Torheit gibt es keine Mittel (produced Theater an der Wien, Vienna, 1838). In *Gesammelte Werke*, 1890–91.
Die verhängnisvolle Faschingsnacht, from a play by Holtei (produced Theater an der Wien, Vienna, 1839). 1842.
Der Färber und sein Zwillingsbruder, from a libretto by Adolphe de Leuven and Léon Lhérie (produced Theater an der Wien, Vienna, 1840). In *Gesammelte Werke*, 1890–91.
Der Erbschleicher (produced Theater an der Wien, Vienna, 1840). In *Gesammelte Werke*, 1890–91.
Die zusammengestoppelte Komödie (produced Theater an der Wien, Vienna, 1840).
Der Talisman (produced Theater an der Wien, Vienna, 1840). 1843; translated as *The Talisman*, in *Three Comedies*, 1967, and in *Three Viennese Comedies*, 1986.

Das Mädl aus der Vorstadt; oder, Ehrlich währt am längsten (produced Theater an der Wien, Vienna, 1841).   1845.

Friedrich, Prinz von Korsika (produced Theater an der Wien, Vienna, 1841).   In *Unbekannter Nestroy*, 1953.

Einen Jux will er sich machen, from a play by John Oxenford (produced Theater an der Wien, Vienna, 1842).   1844; translated and adapted as *The Merchant of Yonkers*, 1939; as *The Matchmaker*, 1954; as *On the Razzle*, 1981.

Die Ereignisse im Gasthofe (produced Theater an der Wien, Vienna, 1842).

Die Papiere des Teufels; oder, Der Zufall (produced Theater an der Wien, Vienna, 1842).   In *Gesammelte Werke*, 1890–91.

Liebesgeschichten und Heiratssachen (produced Theater an der Wien, Vienna, 1843).   In *Gesammelte Werke*, 1890–91; translated as *Love Affairs and Wedding Bells*, in *Three Comedies*, 1967.

Das Quodlibet verschiedener Jahrhunderte (produced Theater an der Wien, Vienna, 1843).   In *Sämtliche Werke 9*, 1927.

Nur Ruhe! (produced Theater an der Wien, Vienna, 1843).   In *Gesammelte Werke*, 1890–91.

Eisenbahnheiraten; oder, Wien, Neustadt, Brünn (produced Theater an der Wien, Vienna, 1844), from a play by J.-F.-A. Bayard and Victor Varin.   In *Gesammelte Werke*, 1890–91.

Hinüber-Herüber (produced Theater an der Wien, Vienna, 1844).   1852.

Der Zerrissene (produced Theater an der Wien, Vienna, 1844).   1845; translated as *A Man Full of Nothing*, in *Three Comedies*, 1967.

Die beiden Herren Söhne (produced Theater an der Wien, Vienna, 1845).   In *Gesammelte Werke*, 1890–91.

Das Gewürzkrämerkleeblatt; oder, Die unschuldige Schuldigen, from a play by J.-P. Lockroy and Auguste Anicet-Bourgeois (produced Theater an der Wien, Vienna, 1845).   In *Gesammelte Werke*, 1890–91.

Unverhofft, from a play by J.-F.-A. Bayard and Phillipe Dumanoir (produced Theater an der Wien, Vienna, 1845).   1848.

Der Unbedeutende (produced Theater in der Leopoldstadt, Vienna, 1846).   1849.

Zwei ewige Juden für einen (produced Theater in der Leopoldstadt, Vienna, 1846).   As *Zwei ewige Juden und keiner*, in *Gesammelte Werke*, 1890–91.

Der Schützling (produced Theater in der Leopoldstadt, Vienna, 1847).   In *Gesammelte Werke*, 1890–91.

Die schlimmen Buben in der Schule, from a play by J.-P. Lockroy and Auguste Anicet-Bourgeois (produced Carltheater, Vienna, 1847).   In *Gesammelte Werke*, 1890–91.

Martha; oder, Die Mischmonder Markt-Mägde-Mietung, from a libretto by W.F. Riese and Saint-Georges (produced Carltheater, Vienna, 1848).   In *Gesammelte Werke*, 1890–91.

Die Anverwandten, from a novel by Dickens (produced Carltheater, Vienna, 1848).

Freiheit in Krähwinkel (produced Carltheater, Vienna, 1848).   1849; translated as *Liberty Comes to Krähwinkel*, 1961.

Lady und Schneider (produced Carltheater, Vienna, 1849).   In *Gesammelte Werke*, 1890–91.

Judith und Holofernes, from a play by Hebbel (produced Carltheater, Vienna, 1849).   In *Gesammelte Werke*, 1890–91; translated as *Judith and Holofernes*, in *Three Viennese Comedies*, 1986.

Höllenangst, from a play by J.-B. d'Épagny and J.-H. Dupin (produced Carltheater, Vienna, 1849).   In *Gesammelte Werke*, 1890–91.

Sie sollen ihn nicht; oder, Der holländische Bauer (produced Carltheater, Vienna, 1850).   In *Gesammelte Werke*, 1890–91.

Karikaturen-Charivari (produced Carltheater, Vienna, 1850).   In *Gesammelte Werke*, 1890–91.

Alles will den Propheten sehen (produced Carltheater, Vienna, 1850).   In *Gesammelte Werke*, 1890–91.

Verwickelte Geschichte (produced Carltheater, Vienna, 1850).   In *Gesammelte Werke*, 1890–91.

Mein Freund (produced Carltheater, Vienna, 1851).   1851.

Der gutmütige Teufel; oder, Die Geschichte vom Bauer und der Bäuerin (produced Carltheater, Vienna, 1851).   As *Der gemütliche Teufel*, in *Gesammelte Werke*, 1890–91.

Kampl; oder, Das Mädchen mit den Millionen und die Näherin (produced Carltheater, Vienna, 1852).   1852.

Heimliches Geld, heimliche Liebe (produced Carltheater, Vienna, 1853).   In *Gesammelte Werke*, 1890–91.

Theaterg'schichten durch Liebe, Intrige, Geld und Dummheit (produced Carltheater, Vienna, 1854).   1854.

Umsonst (produced Carltheater, Vienna, 1857).

Tannhäuser, from the libretto by Richard Wagner (produced Carltheater, Vienna, 1857).   1857.

Lohengrin, from the libretto by Richard Wagner (produced Carltheater, Vienna, 1859).   In *Gesammelte Werke*, 1890–91.

Frühere Verhältnisse (produced Quai-Theater, Vienna, 1962).   In *Gesammelte Werke*, 1890–91.

Zeitvertreib (produced 1862).   In *Gesammelte Werke*, 1890–91.

Häuptling Abendwind; oder, Das greuliche Festmahl, from an operetta by Jacques Offenbach (produced Quai-Theater, Vienna, 1862).   In *Sämtliche Werke 14*, 1930.

Der alte Mann mit der jungen Frau (produced in revised version, as *Der Flüchtling*, Deutsches Volkstheater, Prague, 1890; original version produced Theater in der Josefstadt, Vienna, 1948).   In *Gesammelte Werke*, 1890–91.

Genius, Schuster und Marqueur; oder, Die Pyramiden der Verzauberung.   In *Sämtliche Werke 1*, 1924.

Der Feenball; oder Tischler, Schneider und Schlosser.   In *Sämtliche Werke 1*, 1924.

"Nur keck!" (produced Burghtheater, Vienna, 1943).   In *Sämtliche Werke 14*, 1930.

Ein gebildeter Hausknecht.   With *Zwölf Mädchen in Uniform*, 1943.

Memoirs and Letters

Gesammelte Briefe und Revolutionsdokumente (1831–1862), edited by Fritz Brukner.   1938.

Briefe, edited by Walter Obermaier.   1977.

*

Bibliographies

Jürgen Hein, Bibliography of criticism in *Das wiener Volkstheater*, 1978.

G. Conrad, *Johann Nepomuk Nestroy: Bibliographie zur Nestroy-Forschung und -Rezeption*, Berlin, 1980.

Criticism

Books:

K. Kraus, *Nestroy und die Nachwelt*, Vienna, 1912; revised edition, 1987.

F.H. Mautner, *Johann Nestroy und seine Kunst*, Vienna, 1937.

O. Forst-Battaglia, *Johann Nestroy: Abschätzer der Menschheit, Magier des Wortes*, Munich, 1962.

Otto Basil, *Johann Nestroy in Selbstzeugnissen und Bilddokumenten*, Reinbek, 1967.

S. Brill, *Die Komödie der Sprache: Untersuchungen zum Werke Nestroys*, Nuremberg, 1967.

A. Hillach, *Die Dramatisierung des komischen Dialogs: Figur und Rolle bei Nestroy*, Munich, 1967.

H. Weigel, *Johann Nestroy*, Velber, 1967.

Rio Preisner, *Johann Nepomuk Nestroy: Der Schöpfer der tragischen Posse*, Munich, 1968.

L. Tönz, *Die künstlerische Eigenständigkeit und Eigenart Nestroys*, Vienna, 1969.

Jürgen Hein, *Spiel und Satire in der Komödie Johann Nestroys*, Bad Homburg, 1970.

Kurt Kahl, *Johann Nestroy oder der wienerische Shakespeare*, Vienna, 1970.

R. Koth, *Nestroys dramatische Technik*, Berlin, 1972.

W.E. Yates, *Nestroy: Satire and Parody in Viennese Popular Comedy*, Cambridge, 1972.

Laurence V. Harding, *The Dramatic Art of Ferdinand Raimund and Johann Nestroy*, The Hague, 1974.

Franz H. Mautner, *Nestroy*, Heidelberg, 1974.

B. Hannemann, *Johann Nestroy: Nihilistisches Welttheater und verflixter Kerl*, Bonn, 1977.

H. Schwarz, *Johann Nestroy im Bild: Eine Ikonographie*, Graz, 1977.

Jürgen Hein, *Das wiener Volkstheater: Raimund und Nestroy*, Darmstadt, 1978.

H. Ahrens, *"Bis zum Lorbeer versteig ich mich nicht": Johann Nestroy—ein Leben*, Frankfurt, 1982.

W.E. Yates and John R.P. McKenzie (eds.), *Viennese Popular Theatre: A Symposium*, 1985.

Jürgen Hein, *Johann Nestroy*, Stuttgart, 1990.

Serials:

Nestroyana, 1979—

* * *

Nestroy had an unusual background for a writer of dialect comedies: his father, like the father of his contemporary Grillparzer, was a lawyer in the wealthy centre of Vienna. Nestroy himself combined an earthy humour with sophisticated wit and wide reading. The greatest of the actor-dramatists in the Viennese commercial theatre, he was a phenomenally hard-working and charismatic performer, and the author of over 80 plays. He used the generic designation *Posse mit Gesang* ("farce with music"), but contemporary reviewers were often uneasily aware that the term "farce" did not do justice to the depth and satirical force of his comedy.

His plays were written for the specific actors at his disposal. He usually borrowed the bare bones of the plot, most often from contemporary French plays. Writing wholly new dialogue, he transferred the action to Vienna, refashioned the plot around roles for himself and his main partner, Wenzel Scholz, who functioned as a rotund foil to the aggressive style of the tall and angular Nestroy. The action was interspersed with solo scenes for the central comic figures (often just for the character played by Nestroy himself, a satirical *raisonneur*). In these scenes—precursors of the commentary characteristic of 20th-century "epic theatre"—the fiction is suspended in monologue and satirical song, in which the vocabulary of the character's craft or trade is exploited in metaphorical wordplay, shifting the focus onto the world outside the dramatic action and so suggesting the wider satirical implications of the play. Nestroy had a good bass voice, and his solo scenes were eagerly awaited high points in every performance.

Nestroy's voice was also put to good use in long parodic medleys, assembled by his composer (most frequently Adolf Müller, with whom he worked very closely). These medleys, many of which have survived in Müller's autograph scores, are based largely on melodies from the most popular operas of the day. The parodic element is strong in Nestroy's work: as well as collaborating on parodies of operas by composers ranging from Meyerbeer to Wagner, he also parodied serious dramas of the time, including Hebbel's *Judith*. The object of his attack was always pretentiousness and artifice, confronting the falsity of the originals with standards of naturalness represented in Viennese life.

Nestroy began by satirising the old allegorical plays-with-magic, associated with Raimund; from the mid-1830's his work was consistently set in what is recognisably Vienna, though until the brief spell of freedom from censorship during the 1848 revolution the setting is rarely specified. He also steadily reduced the amount of incidental music, concentrating on using the musical element to support the satirical effect. The sharpness of his comic formula met with resistance from conservative critics who preferred the rather sentimental humour of Raimund and found Nestroy's comedy negative. Their demands for edifying didactic plays were met by another fertile dramatist, Friedrich Kaiser, in whose plays Nestroy regularly played the main role; their close association did not stop Nestroy from ridiculing Kaiser's "sad farce" in *Der Talisman*.

Nestroy's dialogue is extremely rich in wordplay, often involving extravagant flights of comic imagery and frequent literary allusion, and he made much use of contrasting registers of language, from stagey pseudo-literary German to broad dialect (itself often stylised). These distinctive linguistic effects have made his work notoriously difficult to translate, but his satire of language has won him distinguished admirers, including Wittgenstein and Karl Kraus, who perceived in him "the most uncompromising satirical thinker" in the German language.

Direct reference to particular incidents and individuals was always impossible in Metternich's Austria; the pettiness of the restrictions is documented in the numerous manuscripts that have survived with the censor's deletions marked. When censorship was briefly lifted in 1848 Nestroy promptly provided, in *Freiheit in Krähwinkel*, a play that amounts to a satirical documentary of the revolution itself. In the main body of his *oeuvre—Der Talisman* is the classic example—he presented a cumulative picture of a society of arbitrary privilege, in which human conduct is governed by self-interest and materialism, and tainted with pretentiousness, and which is upheld by a world-order that is providentially unjust.

In Nestroy's comedies, the constraints of everyday life are lifted in the open improbabilities of farce, and his characters escape the privations of daily existence by intrigue or adventure, or through sudden access to wealth. One example may be seen in the exploits of *Einen Jux will er sich machen* (the spirit of the title is excellently caught by Tom Stoppard's free rendering, *On the Razzle*): at the end, the artifice of the conventional happy ending is openly commented on—Nestroy's characters are often disconcertingly aware of their own fictional status—to bring out the improbability of happy endings in real life in a society where wealth, distributed in a way that bears no relation to talent or deserts, is the only route to social standing, the only "talisman" that counts.

—W. E. Yates

NGUGI wa Thiong'o. Formerly wrote as James T. Ngugi. Born in Kamiriithu, near Limuru, Kiambu District, Kenya, 5 January 1938. Educated at Kamaandūra School, Limuru; Karing'a School, Maanguū; Alliance High School, Kikuyu; University College, Kampala, Uganda (editor, *Penpoint*), 1959–63, BA 1963; Leeds University, Yorkshire, England, 1964–67, BA 1964. Married Nyambura in 1961; two sons and three daughters. Columnist ("As I See It"), in early 1960's, and reporter, 1964, Nairobi *Daily Nation*; first-produced play, *The Black Hermit*, staged 1962; editor, *Zuka*, Nairobi, 1965–70; lecturer in English, University College, Nairobi, 1967–69; Fellow in Creative Writing, Makerere University, Kampala, 1969–70; visiting lecturer, Northwestern University, Evanston, Illinois, 1970–71; senior lecturer, associate professor, and chairman of the Department of Literature, University of Nairobi, 1972–77. Imprisoned under Public Security Act, 1977–78, and has lived abroad, mainly in England, since 1982. Recipient: East African Literature Bureau Award, 1964.

Works

Collections

This Time Tomorrow (includes *This Time Tomorrow; The Rebels; The Wound in the Heart*).   1970.

Stage Works

The Black Hermit (produced National Theatre, Kampala, Uganda, 1962).   1968.
The Rebels. In *This Time Tomorrow* (collection), 1970.
The Wound in the Heart. In *This Time Tomorrow* (collection), 1970.
The Trial of Dedan Kimathi, with Micere Mugo (produced 77 Festac, Lagos, Nigeria, 1977).   1976.
Ngaahika Ndeenda (in Kikuyu), with Ngugi wa Mirii (produced Kamiriithu Community Educational and Cultural Centre, Limuru, Kenya, 1977).   1980; as *I Will Marry When I Want*, 1982.
Maitu Njurig [Mother, Sing to Me], with others (produced University of Nairobi, Kenya).

Radio Plays

This Time Tomorrow, 1967 (published in *This Time Tomorrow* (collection), 1970).

Fiction

Weep Not, Child.   1964.
The River Between.   1965.
A Grain of Wheat.   1967.
"Secret Lives" and Other Stories.   1975.
Petals of Blood.   1977.
Caitaani Mutharaba-ini (in Kikuyu).   1980; as *Devil on the Cross*, 1982.
Marigari ma Ngirūūngi (in Kikuyu).   1986.

Other

Homecoming: Essays on African and Caribbean Literature, Culture, and Politics.   1972.
The Independence of Africa and Cultural Decolonisation, with *The Poverty of African Historiography*, by A.E. Afigbo.   1977.
Writers in Politics: Essays.   1981.
Detained: A Writer's Prison Diary.   1981.
Education for a National Culture.   1981.
Barrel of a Pen: Resistance to Repression in Neo-Colonial Kenya.   1983.
Decolonising the Mind: The Politics of Language in African Literature.   1986.
Njamba Nene and the Cruel Chief (for children).   1986.
Njamba Nene's Pistol (for children).   1986.
Writing Against Neocolonialism.   1986.
Walter Rodney's Influence on the African Continent.   1987.

*

Criticism

Books:
Clifford Robunsin, *Ngugi wa Thiong'o*, London, 1979.
G.D. Killam, *An Introduction to the Writings of Ngugi*, London, 1980.
David Cook and Michael Okenimkpe, *Ngugi wa Thiong'o: An Exploration of His Writings*, London, 1983.

*   *   *

Ngugi wa Thiong'o's plays are the minor works of a major novelist. Indeed, one book on his work tacitly ignores the plays. Nevertheless, his first play remains important for its historical priority and in his later work he offers an aesthetic —and, indeed, moral—example of how dramatists may serve a popular audience. For several years after its production in 1962, Ngugi's *The Black Hermit* was the only full-length play in English from East Africa. Written just before Kenya achieved independence, the play is a pessimistic look at the rival claims of traditional and modern ways of life, traditional and modern religions, public service and private fulfilment. Unfortunately, the claims of nation, ideology, family, and love are only touched upon, not explored. The shuffling of the different issues—now one, now another held before us—produces melodrama. The author himself has called the play "very confused".

Remi, the first of his tribe to go to college, loved Thoni, who married his brother while he was away. On the death of his brother, Remi's father urged him to follow tradition and marry his brother's wife. This he did, though he felt that he could never love one who was another's. He fled from her, and from the expectations of the tribe that he would be their political leader, to the city and the love of a white girl. The play opens with the efforts of his mother and wife to get him to return. The pastor will visit Remi on their behalf. Meanwhile, the elders also send emissaries, bearing "medicine". Weighing the Bible in one hand, the "medicine" in the other, Remi is moved by these "pieces of superstition" and returns home. He holds a successful political rally, against tribalism, but while he discusses future plans a woman enters with a letter from:

> She who was kind.
> She who was true.
> A tender sapling growing straight.
> Though surrounded by weed.

His wife had loved him, and deep down he had loved her, but she had heard him say that he had been wrong to follow custom in marrying her, and so committed suicide, leaving the letter to state that she has always loved him. The play ends with Remi kneeling beside her body and declaring "I came to break Tribe and Custom, Instead, I've broken you and me".

More interesting is a short radio play, *This Time Tomorrow*. A slum, ironically named Uhuru (Freedom) Market, is to be bulldozed because "tourists from America, Britain and West Germany are disgusted with the dirt that is slowly creeping into a city that used to be the pearl of Africa". In the slum live Njango, wife of a freedom fighter, and her dreaming daughter Wanjiro. During the play, Wanjiro's lover persuades her to move into his house, and Njango attends a protest meeting, led by the Stranger, a former freedom fighter who is arrested. A bulldozer razes the hut as Njango ends the play: "If only we had stood up against them! If only we could stand together!". Against the actualities of the situation, caught in a soliloquy of Wanjiro's—"How often have I leaned against this very post, and watched the city awake. Just now, noise is dead in the city. It is so dark outside—the crawling maggots in the drains are hidden"—are set the bland phrases of the journalist, with which the play opens—"the filthy mushrooms—inhabited by human beings—besieging our capital city, came tumbling down yesterday".

As an epigraph to his collection of essays *Writers in Politics*, Ngugi quotes Karl Marx: "The profound hypocrisy and inherent barbarism of bourgeois civilization lies unveiled before our eyes, turning from its home, where it assumes respectable forms, to the colonies, where it goes naked . . .". The struggle against colonialism is dramatized in *The Trial of Dedan Kinwthi*, while *I Will Marry When I Want* attacks the new black bourgeois exploiters. Both plays convey his views insistently and even stridently.

Kimathi was a leader of the Mau Mau rebellion who was captured and shot by the British. In Ngugi's play Kimathi's brief arraignment and trial frame four "trials" of his resolution in his cell, reminiscent of the visits of the tempters to Eliot's Becket. The last of these is followed by a flashback to a trial over which Kimathi presided, to judge traitors in the guerrilla ranks. Woven between are scenes which focus on a boy and a girl whom a female colleague of Kimathi's recruits for a rescue attempt. These scenes allow Ngugi to describe the life of the most destitute, stress women's contribution to the liberation struggle, and show the spirit of revolt passed to the next generation. The complexity of the play's structure saves it from being too pietistic or too obviously didactic.

There are flashbacks to the independence struggle in *I Will Marry When I Want*, but they seem to serve more as excuses for the songs and dances that befit a popular piece rather than to have a dramatic purpose. The play has a narrower focus than *The Trial of Dedan Kimathi*, showing the destruction of a simple bourgeois family, whose members are both hypocritically Christian and the black tools of foreign capitalism. The didactic message is spelled out by a neighbor *raisonneur*.

All Ngugi's plays contrast tradition with the exploitation of (neo-)colonialists and their agents. Disgust at official and religious cant is sharpened by a sense that Uhuru has brought nothing to the common people. A believer in the collectivization of economic resources and the "release of a people's creative spirit [through] the active work of destroying an inhibitive social structure and building a new one" (*Homecoming*), Ngugi developed *I Will Marry When I Want* in his home village as "a community product". Its performance led to his being jailed for a year amid charges that he was subverting national unity by promoting the Kikuyu language in which it was written. His last attempt to develop a drama of the people was *Maitu Njuriga* (Mother, Sing for Me), with

songs in five of Kenya's languages. Its official performance was not allowed, but many people saw a series of "rehearsals".

—Anthony Graham-White

NICHOLS, Peter (Richard). Born in Bristol, England, 31 July 1927. Educated at Bristol Grammar School, 1936–44; Bristol Old Vic Theatre School, 1948–50; Trent Park Teachers' Training College, Hertfordshire, 1955–57. Served in the Royal Air Force, 1945–48. Married Thelma Reed in 1959; three daughters and one son. Actor, in repertory, television, and films, 1950–55; teacher in primary and secondary schools, 1957–59; has also worked as a park keeper, English language teacher in Italy, cinema commissionaire, and clerk. Visiting playwright, Guthrie Theatre, Minneapolis, 1977. Governor, Greenwich Theatre, London, 1970–76; member, Arts Council Drama Panel, 1972–75. Recipient: several *Evening Standard* awards; John Whiting Award, 1968; Society of West End Theatre Award, 1978, 1982; Tony Award, 1985. Fellow, Royal Society of Literature, 1983.

Works

Collections

Plays 1 (includes *Forget-Me-Not Lane; Hearts and Flowers; Neither Up nor Down; Chez Nous; The Common*, revised version; *Privates on Parade*).
Plays 1 (revised edition; includes *A Day in the Death of Joe Egg; The National Health; Forget-Me-Not Lane; Hearts and Flowers; The Freeway*). 1991.
Plays 2 (includes *Chez Nous; Privates on Parade; Born in the Gardens; Passion Play; Poppy*). 1991.

Stage Works

The Hooded Terror (televised 1963; produced Bristol Old Vic, 1964).
A Day in the Death of Joe Egg (produced Glasgow Citizens Theatre, Glasgow, 1967). 1967; as *Joe Egg* (New York), 1967.
The National Health; or, Nurse Norton's Affair (produced by the National Theatre, Old Vic, London, 1969). 1970.
Forget-Me-Not Lane (produced Greenwich Theatre, London, 1971). 1971.
Neither Up Nor Down (produced Almost Free Theatre, London, 1972). In *Plays 1*, 1987.
Chez Nous (produced Globe Theatre, London, 1974). 1974.
The Freeway (produced by the National Theatre, Old Vic, London, 1974). 1975.
Harding's Luck, from the novel by E. Nesbit (produced Greenwich Theatre, London, 1974).
Privates on Parade (produced Aldwych Theatre, London, 1977). 1977.
Born in the Gardens (produced Theatre Royal, Bristol, 1979). 1980.
Passion Play (produced Aldwych Theatre, London, 1981). 1981; as *Passion* (produced New York, 1983), 1983.

Poppy, music by Monty Norman (produced Barbican Theatre, London, 1982).   1982.
A Piece of My Mind (produced Nuffield Theatre, Southampton, 1987).
About Turner.   1991.

Screenplays

Catch Us if You Can (Having a Wild Weekend), 1965; *Georgy Girl*, with Margaret Forster, 1966; *A Day in the Death of Joe Egg*, 1972; *The National Health*, 1973; *Privates on Parade*, 1983 (published 1983); *Changing Places*, 1984.

Television Plays

Walk on the Grass, 1959; *After All*, with Bernie Cooper, 1959; *Promenade*, 1959 (published in *Six Granada Plays*, 1960); *Ben Spray*, 1961 (published in *New Granada Plays*, 1961); *The Big Boys*, 1961; *The Reception*, 1961; *The Heart of the Country*, 1962; *Ben Again*, 1963; *The Hooded Terror*, 1963; *The Continuity Man*, 1963; *The Brick Umbrella*, 1964; *When the Wind Blows*, 1965; *The Gorge*, 1968 (published in *The Television Dramatist*, edited by Robert Muller, 1973); *Majesty*, from a story by F. Scott Fitzgerald, 1968; *Winner Takes All*, from a story by Evelyn Waugh, 1968; *Daddy Kiss it Better*, 1968; *Hearts and Flowers*, 1970 (published in *Plays 1*, 1987); *The Common*, 1973 (published in revised form in *Plays 1*, 1987).

Memoirs and Letters

Feeling You're Behind: An Autobiography.   1984.

*

Criticism

Books:
John Russell Taylor, *The Second Wave*, London and New York, 1971.
Oleg Kerensky, *The New British Drama*, London, 1979.
George W. Brandt (ed.), *British Television Drama*, London, 1981.
Susan Risinko, *British Drama 1950 to the Present: A Critical History*, Boston, 1989.

Articles:
Richard Foulkes, "'The Cure is Removal of Guilt': Faith, Fidelity and Fertility in the Plays of Peter Nichols", in *Modern Drama*, 29, 1986.
William B. Worthen, "Deciphering the British Pantomime: *Poppy* and the Rhetoric of Political Theater", in *Genre*, 19, 1986.
Peter Nichols and William Demastes, "Peter Nichols on His Art, Politics, and Peers: An Interview", in *Journal of Dramatic Theory and Criticism*, vol.3 no.1, 1988.

* * *

Peter Nichols has always camouflaged his artistry by the extreme unpretentiousness with which he presents himself in interview, describing his developing plays from his diaries, learning his craft from army revues, using ready-made sketches to expand full-length plays, writing more than a dozen television scripts to make a living before his first stage success, and even confessing to a daily writing routine that he

has compared with Trollope's. He has called his playwriting "efforts to find out how worthwhile an idea is", and perhaps his deepest insight into his art has been in scrutinising his efforts to keep audiences in a state of "comic alarm". His career has resembled Osborne's in that his success has gradually declined, to the extent that in the 1980's he commanded little of the critical attention he received in the late 1960's, and in 1983 announced his retirement from playwriting, albeit prematurely.

Yet Nichols' stature remains high, not only in terms of cultural history, but also in the idiosyncracies of his dramaturgy, and in his strategies of confronting taboos and educating audiences into a more expansive acknowledgement of the society to which they belong. This latter feature is most obvious in *A Day in the Death of Joe Egg*, which questions not only societal attitudes to the handicapped, but also the validity of using comedy as a survival technique in the face of an impossible reality. Like most of the later plays, it draws laughter that is rich, complex, and subtle, but each laugh raises a new threshold of appropriateness; this may not seem remarkable for a play first produced at the Glasgow Citizens Theatre, but it certainly became so when it found success in London's West End and even had a brief run on Broadway.

Similarly, *Privates on Parade* announces in its title a dimension of innuendo which is only marginally more profound than that of his autobiography, *Feeling You're Behind*, and this seems to be extended through the music-hall routines and melodramatic peripheral action of the play's depiction of an army concert party in Malaya. Yet even this play also shifts its audience through many attitudinal adjustments towards the homosexual subculture of most of the characters. Just as spastics like Joe Egg had been a playground target for schoolchildren's ridicule, so had the "pansies" of the concert party been a victimised minority in adult society of the 1960's. Nichols regenerates an element of this victimisation through the swaggering butchness of his first scene, but then sets about an elaborate scheme of audience compromise as characters briefly display their vulnerability before dissolving back into pure theatre. Unsurprisingly, the play was both attacked and applauded by gay liberation groups.

The title of Nichols' prefatory essay to *Plays 1*, "Casting the Audience", aptly pinpoints his idiosyncratic theatricality. Many of his techniques initially seem Brechtian, but his application of them is in quite another direction, away from ideology and judgement. The interpreter figure who recurs throughout most of the stage plays at first seems to be a mediator, facilitating the audience's access to the world of the stage. But the interpreter's credibility never lasts long. In the rape scene in *Privates on Parade* characters evaluate the performance from the auditorium as if it were a striptease; in *The National Health* Barnet, the orderly, speaks to the audience with the same dark wit as Joe Egg's father, culminating in a speech praising the Great Reaper's "Grand Design" in producing a double bus-crash where the 60 killed or injured were all either pensioners or mongols. This portrayal of the Reaper is a clear variant on the much-quoted image of God in *Joe Egg* as a manic depressive rugby-footballer, but *Forget-Me-Not Lane*, a wryly amusing dramatic reverie, renames the Reaper "old butter-fingers up there", who is thrown the responsibility for mismanaging all departments of the downstage interpreter's earlier life. Even *The Freeway*, a futuristic dystopia which Nichols felt the need to tell us is *not* "an Orwellian nightmare", has ironically out-of-touch media reports on the huge traffic jam that represents the absurd archaism of British society pretending to live in the late-20th century.

Although Nichols considered it his best play, *The Freeway*

was a commercial failure and was widely seen as an unsuccessful search for a new direction. However, as the critic Helen Dawson noted (in *Plays and Players*), the play amplified only slightly the degree of symbolism latent in plays like *The National Health*, and if nothing else it did alert critics to the possibility of reading much of Nichols as a microcosmic vision of contemporary society. The freeway of the title is little more than the very conventional metaphor of the road that has been used by Bunyan, Strindberg, and Tennessee Williams, except that here movement has stopped, because all the travellers are exercising their freedom in the same direction. The car is a symbol of affluence, and motoring has become a metaphor for existence; as Nichols said in his preface, the villain is the widely-held belief that the car is "liberty incarnate, the great surviving champion of the free-for-all life-style". A similar metaphorical strategy operates in the musical *Poppy*, where contemporary social issues are transposed to the Victorian period and partially cushioned in the genre of pantomime, used like the revue element in *Privates on Parade*.

Dawson also pointed out that *The Freeway* lacked passion, an observation that could be made about most of Nichols's plays—although none of them could be called dispassionate. As if to correct this, he entitled his major play of the 1980's *Passion Play*, and surprised audiences by locating it in an ordinary domestic interior. He had, in fact, used such settings —with the motif of marital comedy—earlier in television plays and in *Chez Nous*; but *Passion Play* seemed, initially, to celebrate adultery in the mainstream style of bourgeois prurience. Rather—like *Chez Nous*—it examined the male drive towards polygamy by the use of alter-ego figures who, with an effect like that of O'Neill's *Strange Interlude*, express secret thoughts and propensities. His earlier stage plays, like *Joe Egg* and *National Health*, had been related to the Shavian reading of Ibsen as "problem plays", but the "domestic" plays more accurately address Ibsen's principle of the "life-lie", the notion that people's tolerance for truth about their inner proclivities is severely limited.

—Howard McNaughton

See also *Volume 1* entry on *A Day in the Death of Joe Egg*.

NORÉN, Lars. Born in Stockholm, Sweden, 9 April 1944. Married with two children. First poetry collection, *Syrener, snö* [Lilacs, Snow], published 1963; first-produced play, *Fursteslickaren* [The Prince's Bootlicker], staged 1973; has subsequently become Sweden's foremost contemporary dramatist.

Works

Collections

Tre skådespel (includes *Modet att dåda; Akt utan nåd; Orestes*). 1980.
Två skådespel (includes *Natten är dagens mor; Kaos är granne med Gud*). 1983.

Stage Works

Fursteslickaren [The Prince's Bootlicker] (produced National Theatre, Stockholm, 1973).

Orestes [Orestes] (produced Dramaten, Stockholm, 1979). In *Tre skådespel*, 1980.
Underjordens leende [The Smiles of the Underworld] (produced Kongelige Teater, Copenhagen, 1980).
Akt utan nåd [Act Without Mercy]. In *Tre skådespel*, 1980.
En fruktansvärd lycka [A Terrible Happiness] (produced Stadsteater, Stockholm, 1981).
Natten är dagens mor [Night is Mother to the Day] (produced Stadsteater, Malmö, Sweden, 1982). With *Kaos är dagens med Gud*, 1983.
Kaos år dagens med Gud [Chaos is God's Neighbour] (produced Stadsteater, Gothenburg, Sweden, 1983). With *Natten är dagens mor*, 1983.
Demoner [Demons] (produced Stadsteater, Stockholm, 1984).
Nattvarden [Holy Communion] (produced National Theatre, Stockholm, 1984).
Stillheten [Stillness] (produced National Theatre, Stockholm, 1984). 1984.
Modet att döda, from the television play (produced as *The Courage to Kill*, Theatre Clwyd, Mold, Wales, 1984).
München—Athen [Munich—Athens], from the television play (produced as *Munich—Athens*, Soho Poly Theatre, London, 1987).
Endagsvarelser [Dragonflies] (produced Staatstheater, Kassel, West Germany, 1989). 1990.
Hebriana (produced The Hague, Netherlands, 1989).
Autumn and Winter (produced Caféteatern, Copenhagen, 1989).
Och ge oss skuggorna [And Grant Us the Shadows] (produced in Norwegian, Oslo, 1991; produced in Swedish, Stockholm, 1991).

Television Plays

Kingsdom Hotell [Kingdom Hotel], 1968; *En hungersaga* [A Hunger Story], 1970; *Amalia, Kamala*, 1971; *Modet att döda* [Courage to Kill], 1978 (published in *Tre skådespel*, 1980); *München-Athen*, 1982; *Komedianter* [Strolling Players], 1987.

Radio Plays

Box ett [Box One] (published 1972); *Röster* [Voices], 1973; *Akt utan nåd* [Act Without Mercy], 1978; *När dom brände fjärilar på Lilla Scenen* [When They Burnt Butterflies on the Small Stage], 1980.

Verse

Syrener, snö [Lilacs, Snow]. 1963.
De verbala resterna av en bildprakt som förgår [The Verbal Remains of a Vanishing Pictorial Splendor]. 1964.
Inledning n:r 2 till Schizz [Introduction No. 2 to Schizz(ophrenia)]. 1965.
Encyklopedi: Mémoires sur la fermentation 1–3 [Encyclopedia]. 1966.
Stupor: Nobody Knows You When You're Down and Out. 1968.
Revolver. 1969.
Solitära dikter [Solitary Poems]. 1972.
Viltspeglar [Mirror of the Wild]. 1972.
Kung Mej, och andra dikter [King Mej, and Other Poems]. 1973.
Dagliga och nattliga dikter [Daily and Nightly Poems]. 1974.
Dagbok augusti-oktober 1975 [Diary August–October 1975]. 1976.
Nattarbete: Del 2 [Night Work: Part 2]. 1976.

Hans Bellmer: bilder från åren 1934–1950 [Hans Bellmer: Pictures from the Years 1934–1950], with prose by Ragner von Holten.   1978.
Order [The Command].   1978.
Murlod [Wall Plumbing].   1979.
Den ofullbordade stjärnan [The Incomplete Star]. 1979.
Hjärta i hjärta [Heart to Heart].   1980.

Fiction

Salome—Sfinxerna [Salome—The Sphinxes].   1968.
Biskötarna [The Beekeepers].   1970.
I den underjordiska himlen [In the Underground Sky].   1972.

*

Criticism

Books:
Suzanne Osten, "Lars Norén: A Working Process for the Director", in *Not Only Strindberg*, edited by Egil Törnqvist, Amsterdam, 1985.

Articles:
Lotta Neuhauser, "Theatre with the Intoxication of Insight: Notes on Lars Norén", in *Yale/Theatre*, vol. 22 no. 1, 1991.
Egil Törnqvist, "Strindberg, O'Neill, Norén: A Swedish-American Triangle", in *Eugene O'Neill Review*, 1991.

* * *

Since the early 1980's, Lars Norén has held the position of the most frequently performed living Swedish playwright, while at the same time he has established himself internationally. Coming to drama from poetry, he was not immediately successful as a playwright. His first performed stage play, *Fursteslickaren* (The Prince's Bootlicker) received mixed reviews, ranging from praise to outright rejection when it first opened in 1973. Sorely bruised, Lars Norén withdrew, not to return with his next play, *Orestes*, until 1979. This time, the reception was unreservedly favourable. This play was soon followed by others, to similar critical acclaim—*En fruktansvärd lycka* (A Terrible Happiness) and *Underjordens leende* (Smiles of the Underworld), establishing Lars Norén as Sweden's leading playwright.

Best known to Swedish theatre audiences of his early work are *Natten är dagens mor* (Night is Mother to the Day) and its sequel, *Kaos är granne med Gud* (Chaos is God's Neighbour). The titles of both plays are taken from a poem by Swedish poet Erik Johan Stagnelius. Although written prior to both of these plays, *Modet att döda* (Courage to Kill) constitutes the last part of what the playwright himself views as a trilogy.

The trilogy deals with relationships between the different members of a nuclear family. Drawing on his own adolescence and early manhood in southern Sweden, in *Natten* Norén gives us a family running a small provincial hotel in Skåne, struggling to make ends meet. As always, he masterfully captures the mood of an era, here the 1950's: in Copenhagen, Stan Getz is playing in concert, and Caryl Chessman's long campaign for a reprieve from the electric chair has met with failure in the USA. Equally masterful is the portrayal of the interpersonal relationships among the members of the family, in the sibling rivalry between the older and the younger brother (Lars Norén's *alter ego*), the furtively alcoholic father, and the "stoop-to-conquer" yet domineering mother.

In *Kaos*, the mother's illness has been diagnosed as cancer. She returns home, on a last visit from hospital, to meet the family, including the younger son, himself released temporarily from hospital following a nervous breakdown. While, in the final scene, we witness the death of the mother, in *Modet att döda* we take part in the events leading to the death of the father, this death even more brutally portrayed since it is by the hand of the younger son.

All three plays bear the hallmarks of Lars Norén's dramatic output—the keen perception of interpersonal relationships, the lightness of touch in dialogue, and the all-pervasive atmospheric mood of the period.

Having documented his early years, also portrayed in *Stillheten* (Stillness), Norén's later plays have tended to focus on the now middle-ageing, often financially successful children of the 1960's. Among early plays in this category are *En fruktansvärd lycka* (A Terrible Happiness), *Underjordens leende* (Smiles of the Underworld), and *Demoner* (Demons). More recent plays on this theme include *Nattvarden* (Holy Communion), *München—Athen*, and *Komedianter* (Strolling Players). As always, the focus of interest is personal relationships, but the setting is now the 1980's. The outwardly successful members of the Swedish middle classes confront each other and their own lives, their waning idealism having been dealt a death blow by the assassination of the Prime Minister, Olaf Palme.

A keen observer of human behaviour, Lars Norén points squarely to the discrepancy between verbal behaviour and physical actions, between apparent happiness and manifest inability to experience emotions, not least recognizable in these representatives of the newly affluent society, steeped in the neurosis of (rapid) achievement. When *München—Athen* was performed at the Soho Poly Theatre in London, as "Munich—Athens" in 1987, the magazine *City Limits* referred to Sarah and David, the two protagonists, as "a modern, recognisable urban couple". The theme gained a further dimension in *Komedianter*, when directed by Björn Melander for Swedish television, with the focus of interest now shifted to the child, the pawn in the parental struggle for power.

This last play, like all of Lars Norén's work, is several hours long, perhaps the reason why he has remained less well known in the commercial theatre world outside the subsidised theatres. His plays are moods and atmospheres out of which a dramatic structure emerges, easily lost in translation or in the hands of a less-than-sensitive director. Early attempts to stage his plays in the USA were less than successful, and even though "Munich—Athens" was hailed as "a compulsively watchable play", it has usually been in the more closely related, linguistically as well as culturally, language areas on the Continent and in northern Europe that Lars Norén's work has most readily been admired for the contribution it makes to contemporary drama.

1989, however, saw the world premieres of *Hebriana* in The Hague, *Endagsvarelser* (Dragonflies) in Kassel, and *Autumn and Winter* in Copenhagen, a clear indication that Lars Norén was becoming firmly established internationally. His content and style are also becoming more easily accessible. Although in *Autumn and Winter* we return to the familiar territory of the nuclear family, locked in the grip of never-ending domestic combat, the tone is now less relentless, almost conciliatory. It also runs for a "mere" three hours, requiring less than the usual amount of directorial intervention.

Och ge oss skuggorna [And Grant Us the Shadows], produced in 1991, is a play about Eugene O'Neill, the American playwright. This time it is the sealed cell of a playwright's domestic destruction that is the object of Lars Norén's dissection, a territory which he documents with the same precision and perception as Strindberg did before him. What Norén tells us about the human condition may not be altogether new, but he says it with a voice that deserves to be heard across linguistic and cultural boundaries.

—Gunilla Anderman

NORMAN, Marsha. Born Marsha Williams in Louisville, Kentucky, USA, 21 September 1947. Educated at Durrett High School, Louisville; Agnes Scott College, Decatur, Georgia, BA in philosophy 1969; University of Louisville, 1969–71, MA 1971. Married 1) Michael Norman in 1969 (divorced 1974); 2) Dann C. Byck Jr. in 1978 (divorced 1986); 3) Tim Dykman in 1987. Worked with disturbed children at Kentucky Central State Hospital, 1969–71; teacher, Brown School, Louisville, from 1973; book reviewer and editor of children's supplement (*Jelly Bean Journal*), Louisville *Times*, mid-1970's; playwright-in-residence, Actors' Theatre, Louisville, 1977–78, and Mark Taper Forum, Los Angeles, 1979. Treasurer, Dramatists' Guild, since 1988. Recipient: American Theatre Critics Association Prize, 1978; Oppenheimer Award, 1979; Susan Smith Blackburn Prize, 1983; Pulitzer Prize, 1983; American Academy Award, 1986; Tony Award, 1991.

Works

Collections

Four Plays (includes *Getting Out*; *Third and Oak*; *The Holdup*; *Traveler in the Dark*). 1988.

Stage Works

Getting Out (produced Actors' Theatre, Louisville, Kentucky, 1977). 1980.
Third and Oak: The Laundromat (produced Actors' Theatre, Louisville, Kentucky, 1978). 1980.
Third and Oak: The Pool Hall (produced Actors' Theatre, Louisville, Kentucky, 1978). 1985.
Circus Valentine (produced Actors' Theatre, Louisville, Kentucky, 1979).
Merry Christmas, in *Holidays* (produced Actors' Theatre, Louisville, Kentucky, 1979).
'night, Mother (produced American Repertory Theatre, Cambridge, Massachusetts, 1982). 1983.
The Holdup (produced American Conservatory Theatre, San Francisco, 1983). 1987.
Traveler in the Dark (produced American Repertory Theatre, Cambridge, Massachusetts, 1984; revised version produced Los Angeles, 1985). In *Four Plays*, 1988.
Sarah and Abraham (produced Actors' Theatre, Louisville, Kentucky, 1988).
The Secret Garden, music by Lucy Simon, from the novel by Frances Hodgson Burnett (produced Virginia State Theatre, Norfolk, 1990).
D. Boone (produced Actors' Theatre, Louisville, Kentucky, 1988).

Television Plays

It's the Willingness (*Visions* series), 1978; *In Trouble at Fifteen* (*Skag* series), 1980.

Fiction

The Fortune Teller.   1987.

*

Bibliographies

Philip C. Kolin, *American Playwrights since 1945: A Guide to Scholarship, Criticism, and Performance*, New York, 1989.

Criticism

Books:
Esther Harriott, *American Voices: Five Contemporary Playwrights in Essays and Interviews*, Jefferson, North Carolina, 1988.
Sally Browder, "'I Thought You Were Mine': Marsha Norman's 'night Mother", in *Mother Puzzles: Daughters and Mothers in Contemporary American Literature*, edited by Mickey Pearlman, Westport, Connecticut, 1989.
Jenny S. Spencer, "Marsha Norman's She-Tragedies", in *Making a Spectacle: Feminist Essays on Contemporary Women's Theatre*, edited by Lynda Hart, Ann Arbor, Michigan, 1989.
Katharine H. Burkman, "The Demeter Myth and Doubling in Marsha Norman's 'night Mother", in *Modern American Drama: The Female Canon*, edited by June Shlueter, Rutherford, New Jersey, 1990.
Janet Brown, *Taking Center Stage: Feminism in Contemporary US Drama*, Metuchen, New Jersey, 1991.
Richard G. Scharine, *From Class to Caste in American Drama* (includes section on *Getting Out*), New York, 1991.

Articles:
Marsha Norman and Robert Brustein, "Conversations with . . . Marsha Norman", in *Dramatists Guild Quarterly*, vol.21 no.3, 1984.
Madonne Miner, "'What's these bars doin' here?': The Impossibility of *Getting Out*", in *Theatre Annual*, 40, 1985.
Lynda Hart, "Doing Time: Hunger for Power in Marsha Norman's Plays", in *Southern Quarterly*, vol.25 no.3, 1987.
Lisa J. McDonnell, "Diverse Similitude: Beth Henley and Marsha Norman", in *Southern Quarterly*, vol.25 no.3, 1987.
Jenny S. Spencer, "Norman's 'night, Mother: Psycho-Drama of Female Identity", in *Modern Drama*, 30, 1987.
Patricia R. Schroeder, "Locked Behind the Proscenium: Feminist Strategies in *Getting Out* and [Kesselman's] *My Sister in This House*", in *Modern Drama*, 32, 1989.
Richard Wattenberg, "Feminizing the Frontier Myth: Marsha Norman's *The Holdup*", in *Modern Drama*, 33, 1990.

* * *

When *Performing Arts Journal* printed a symposium on "The 'Woman' Playwright Issue" in 1983, the opening contributor began with a broadside on Marsha Norman, then a recent recipient of a Pulitzer Prize: "For all intents and purposes, *'night, Mother* was written in 1949 by Arthur

Miller. . . . By canonizing these works, effectively suppressing alternative visions, we are . . . crippling an art form . . .". The critic, Colette Brooks, went on to invoke the spirit of Hrotsvitha, who would be "appalled at our current state of confusion".

If Norman has not exactly been ostracised by feminist scholarship, she has certainly been neglected in many analyses of women playwrights, left to fend for herself in the male theatre world where she has, accidentally, found success. Ironically, it is only in *Traveler in the Dark*, her major work since *'night, Mother*, that she begins to converge on the tradition of patriarchal saga that has been staked out as the territory of Miller and O'Neill. Even this play, though, is anything but masculinist in its study of the transmission of values, such as gentleness and spirituality, through three generations between polarities of individuality.

The social consciousness that permeates most of Norman's work from *Getting Out* to *The Holdup* is a reflection of her early career, but is not contained by gender boundaries. Certainly, the victim-protagonist of the first play can only be female, and the suffering she endures in her first 24 hours of parole (essentially the play's whole action) places her as the target of male power and exploitation. Arlene's landlord, pimp, father, and prison guard all appear as real or memory figures to construct a pattern of entrapment that is just as strong outside the prison as within, leaving her the product of conditioning forces that almost defy resistance. That Arlene has some capacity to survive such pressures, in a way that Willy Loman in Miller's *Death of a Salesman* cannot, shows Norman's assertion of the power of female individuality. The play's weakness lies not in any traditional value-structure but in its dramaturgy, which pivots on the theatrical cliché of representing the protagonist by two actors, showing two facets of identity. Though this appears as a clumsy device, not uncommon in a first play, it does establish Norman's interest in psychological dissection on stage, which she would perfect in *'night, Mother*.

Not all of Arlene's oppressors, however, are males, and the most keenly-felt rejection is by her mother, who some would see as perpetrating patriarchal domesticity. Similarly, Thelma, the mother of Jessie in *'night, Mother*, is sustaining a structure of dependence, but this play is remarkable in that the concluding behaviour (Jessie's suicide) is in no way predicated on the information flow between mother and daughter that has occupied most of the play: the play is structured in defiance of Aristotle as much as of Arthur Miller, and its crisis is totally devoid of any hint of anagnorisis in Jessie. Also, whereas for Sophocles, Ibsen, Pinero, or Miller, suicide is a simplifying gesture, freeing society of someone who has violated fundamental taboos, the central action of *'night, Mother* is placid, organising, and structured, but the suicide is an action raising problems, suddenly making the mother's world very complex indeed; this is much more than a mere dilemma, and is more intense in production than the end of *Ghosts* because there is no simple choice left.

For Jessie, self-knowledge is a state rather than an event. In the last year she has "gained control of her mind and body", and this includes her physical debility (epilepsy), the fragmented relationships that surround her, and her attitude to her parents. Though Norman does not causally relate it to the suicide, Jessie has an acute curiosity about what she looks like during her fits, to see herself as "other", just as she sees her own baby photographs as representing "somebody else, not me"; here, the playwright addresses the problem of treating alterity in drama which she dealt with clumsily in *Getting Out*.

As with Hedda Gabler, it is important to Jessie that she kills herself with her father's gun, and especially in this respect the play invites a neo-Freudian reading: both women use their fathers' guns to annihilate themselves as women and as daughters at the point that they are stepping outside of the passivity that is their place in the symbolic. They have asked questions, they have disturbed the nature of things under patriarchy, and because patriarchy only offers women absence, it seems appropriate that it is a phallic symbol that blows Jessie away.

Not all would subscribe to such a reading, and perhaps least of all Hrotsvitha, the 10th-century religious writer invoked by Colette Brooks. But there is a fascinating similarity between Jessie's undeviating course towards death and the constancy of Hrotsvitha's female martyrs in the face of the highly inventive oppression of the pagan male emperors of her plays. Neither they nor Jessie seem to have any awareness of a theatre of "confusion".

—Howard McNaughton

NORTON, Thomas. See *Volume 1* entry on *Gorboduc*

NOWRA, Louis. Born in Melbourne, Victoria, Australia, in 1950. Educated at La Trobe University, Bundoora, Victoria. Married Sarah de Jong in 1974. Writer-in-residence, University of Queensland, Brisbane, 1979, Lighthouse Company, Adelaide, 1982, Playbox Theatre, Melbourne, 1985, and Capricornia Institute, 1987; associate artistic director, Sydney Theatre Company, 1980, and Lighthouse Company, 1983.

Stage Works

Kiss the One-Eyed Priest (produced Melbourne, 1973).
Albert Names Edward, from the radio play (produced Melbourne, 1976). With *Inner Voices*, 1983.
Inner Voices (produced Nimrod Theatre, Sydney, 1977). 1978.
Visions (produced Paris Theatre, Sydney, 1978). 1979.
The Lady of the Camellias, from a play by Dumas *fils* (produced by Sydney Theatre Company, 1979).
Inside the Island (produced Nimrod Theatre, Sydney, 1980). With *The Precious Woman*, Sydney, 1981.
The Precious Woman (produced by the Sydney Theatre Company, Sydney, 1980). With *Inside the Island*, Sydney, 1981.
Cyrano de Bergerac, adaptation of the play by Rostand (produced by the Sydney Theatre Company, Sydney, 1980).
The Song Room, from his radio play. Stage version in *Seven One-Act Plays*, edited by Rodney Fisher, 1983.
Death of Joe Orton (produced Adelaide, 1980).
Beauty and the Beast (produced by the Sydney Theatre Company, Sydney, 1980).
Lulu, from a play by Frank Wedekind (produced by the State Theatre of South Australia, Adelaide, 1981).

Spellbound (produced Lighthouse Theatre, Adelaide, 1982).
Royal Show (produced Lighthouse Theatre, Adelaide, 1982).
The Prince of Homburg, from a play by Heinrich von Kleist (also director: produced Lighthouse Theatre, Adelaide, 1982).
Sunrise (produced Lighthouse Theatre, Adelaide, 1983).   1983.
The Golden Age (produced Studio Theatre, Melbourne, 1985).   1985; revised edition, 1989.
Ghosts, from a play by Ibsen (produced Sydney, 1988).
Whitsunday, music by Brian Howard (produced Sydney, 1988).
Capricornia, from the novel by Xavier Herbert (produced Belvoir Street Theatre, Sydney, 1988).   1988; revised edition, 1992.
Byzantine Flowers (produced Sydney, 1989).
The Watchtower (produced Sydney, 1990).
Summer of the Aliens, from the radio play (produced Melbourne, 1992).   1992.
Cosi (produced Belvoir Street Theatre, Sydney, 1992).   1992.

Television Plays

Displaced Persons, 1985; *Hunger*, 1986; *The Lizard King*, 1987; *The Last Resort* (series), 1988.

Radio Plays

Albert Names Edward, 1975 (published in *Five Plays for Radio*, edited by Alrene Sykes, 1976); *The Song Room*, 1980; *The Widows*, 1986; *The Summer of the Aliens*, 1989.

Fiction

The Misery of Beauty: The Loves of Frogman.   1976.
Palu.   1987.

Other

Editor, *The Cheated* (journalism).   1979.

*

Criticism

Books:
Veronica Kelly (ed.), *Louis Nowra*, Amsterdam, 1987.
Leslie Rees, *Australian Drama 1970–1985*, North Ryde, 1987.

Articles:
Louis Nowra, "Translating for the Australian Stage: A Personal Viewpoint", in *Australian Literary Studies*, vol. 10 no. 3, 1982.
Gareth Griffiths, "Australian Subjects and Australian Style: The Plays of Louis Nowra", in *Commonwealth Essays and Studies*, 6, 1984.
Louis Nowra, "At the Crossroads", in *Australasian Drama Studies*, vol. 2 no. 2, 1984.
Veronica Kelly, "A Mirror for Australia: Louis Nowra's Emblematic Theatre", in *Against the Stream: Melbourne New Theatre 1936–1986*, edited by Angela Hillel, Clifton Hill, 1986.

* * *

Louis Nowra is one of the most important writers of the "Second Wave" of Australian playwrights who emerged in the mid-1970's. His early plays, *Inner Voices* and *Visions*, use an expressionistic, visual dramaturgy with discrete scenes, abrupt tonal shifts between lyricism, farce, or horror, and a blurring of the boundaries between inner and outer action. In these plays and their successors, *The Precious Woman* and *Inside the Island*, which also chart the destinies of entire countries, he developed a quasi-Brechtian epic, or open, structure. This allusive and multi-stranded dramaturgy persists in his recent plays *Sunrise*, *The Golden Age*, *Capricornia*, and *Byzantine Flowers*, which have strong central romantic narratives and allusions to Greek myth and folklore motifs.

He has an interest in, and knowledge of, European theatre, particularly the German and French repertoire, and has translated Wedekind and Kleist. His early plays show the influence of this highly imagistic and visual style, as well as the themes of the outsider or exile, the fragility of perception and the power of eroticism.

Nowra's theatre shows the influence of non-naturalistic and popular theatrical forms such as the musical, with a strong input of gothic motifs such as violence, physical impairment, and the grotesque. His working-class, disabled, or otherwise marginalised figures are characterised with respect, and dominate their plays thematically. He has an almost painterly preference for composing what he calls "figures in a landscape": human action is placed in the sometimes overwhelming context of a physical environment—be it outback, jungle, swamp, or rainforest. Strong and central roles for women are constants in his theatre—Su Ling (*The Precious Woman*), Lillian Dawson (*Inside the Island*), Madame Lynch (*Visions*), the child Venice (*Sunrise*), Betsheb (*The Golden Age*), and Roma (*Byzantine Flowers*).

Nowra's plays show a profound interest, relevant to Australia's post-colonial situation, in the sometimes calamitous, sometimes creatively syncretic meeting of cultures. A constant theme is the complicit relationship between language and power. Mute characters, such as the boy-king Ivan of *Inner Voices* or the Juana of *Visions*, have their own language brutally denied them by imperial conquest, usurpation, or the imposition of "polite" metropolitan norms. In these situations characters develop private languages, thus displaying their disempowerment by the colonising discourse, or else their bodies bear witness to their inner worlds. The frequent device of the muted or mentally impaired character shows the conflict of dominant and marginalised experiences. The plays explore and dramatise the inner world of dream, vision, and nightmare, and the conflict between these internalised historical expressions and the public turmoil of societies in transition.

In the earlier plays, the mute or visionary characters are unable to survive or surpass the imposed brutalities of their societies; the young soldiers of *Inside the Island*, for example, maddened by ergot-infected flour, run wild in a private nightmare which prefigures the horrors of World War I. However, in recent plays such as *The Golden Age* and *Byzantine Flowers*, and in the opera *Whitsunday*, a hybrid character of mixed or minority racial origin—Betsheb, Roma, or Clara—is able to counter the historical nightmare with her own vision and to effect some measure of regeneration.

Nowra's favourite metaphor is the island—the island Australia, or the island of the individual consciousness with its immense powers for creativity or destruction. His theatre dramatises the volatile energies liberated as these two related entities come into historical conjunction. His first plays were set in foreign or past societies—Russia (*Inner Voices*), Paraguay (*Visions*), or China (*The Precious Woman*), but from *Inside the Island* they are set in Australia, and their functions as national parables are thus clarified. From the outset the plays explore the pervasive influence over the present of past historical traumas, such as Maralinga (*Sunrise*), Gallipoli and Vietnam (*Inside the Island*), fascism and the convict system (*The Golden Age*), and, implicitly or explicitly in all the plays, the settlement of Australia with the subsequent muting of Aboriginal experience.

While most of Nowra's work treats the Aboriginal experience allusively—as in *The Golden Age*, where white convict experience stands, metonymically, for black history—since adapting Xavier Herbert's novel *Capricornia*, with its Asian and Aboriginal characters, Nowra has ventured, in *Whitsunday* and *Byzantine Flowers*, to create specifically Aboriginal and Kanak characters. His work thus contributes to the construction of national discourses of multiculturalism, a trend particularly evident in his television work, where, for example, in *Displaced Persons* the dialogue of non-English-speaking European characters was subtitled into English. His work is both an indictment of colonialism and a radical exploration of its continuing psychic effects on the colonised subject. However this subject is not powerless, and in the conflict of vision against vision the old order may be redeemed (as in *The Golden Age*) or overthrown (as in *Byzantine Flowers*).

Nowra's theatre does not sit comfortably with the naturalistic strand of bourgeois comedy of manners developed most notably by David Williamson; but it can be seen as part of what has been called the "internationalist" strand in recent Australian writing—theatre which can use a non-Australian or a local setting as a metaphoric site for the exploration of Australian reality. Stephen Sewell, Patrick White, Michael Gow, Janis Balodis, David Malouf, and Alma De Groen are writers who, like Nowra, have used non-naturalistic dramaturgy and mythic themes in order to "write back" (in Salman Rushdie's phrase) to the European dramatic heritage of Shakespeare and the Greeks and re-inscribe it with indigenous meanings. Nowra is arguably the most consistent, creative, and prolific dramatist in this endeavour, and his work continues to expand both thematically and dramaturgically.

—Veronica Kelly

See also *Volume 1* entry on *The Golden Age*.

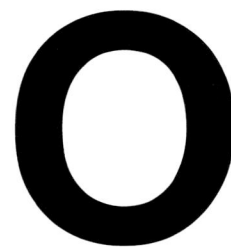

OBALDIA, René de. Born in Hong Kong, 22 October 1918, the son of the Panamanian ambassador to the colony. Grew up in France. Educated in Paris. Held captive in Germany during World War II; playwright since 1949; assistant director, Centre Culturel de Royaumont, 1949–52, during which time his first plays were produced. Recipient: Grand Prix de Paris, 1958; Grand Prix du Théâtre de l'Académie-Française, 1985. Chevalier de l'Ordre de Balboa (Panama).

Works

Collections

Sept impromptus à loisir (includes *L'Azote; Le Défunt; Le Sacrifice du bourreau; Édouard et Agrippine; Les Jumeaux étincelants; Le Grand Vizir; Poivre de Cayenne*). 1961.
Plays (4 vols. of translations). 1965–85:
  1. *Jenusia; Seven Impromptus for Leisure.* 1965.
  2. *The Satyr of La Villette; The Unknown General; Wide Open Spaces.* 1970.
  3. *Two Women for One Ghost; The Baby-Sitter.* 1982.
  4. *Monsieur Klebs and Rozalie; Wind in the Branches of the Sassafras.* 1985.
Théâtre (4 vols.). 1966–68:
  1. *Génousie; Le Satyre de la Villette; Le Général inconnu.* 1966.
  2. *L'Air du large; Du vent dans les branches de sassafras; Le Cosmonaute agricole.* 1966.
  3. *Sept Impromptus à loisir.* 1967.
  4. *Le Damné; Les Larmes de l'aveugle; Urbi et Orbi.* 1968.
  5. *Deux femmes pour un fantôme; Le Baby-Sitter; Classe terminale; Le Banquet des méduses.* 1973.
  6. *. . .Et à la Fin était le bang; Monsieur Klebs et Rosalie.* 1976.
  7. *Grasse matinée; Les Bons bourgeois.* 1981.

Stage Works

Sept impromptus à loisir (includes *L'Azote; Le Défunt; Le Sacrifice du bourreau; Édouard et Agrippine; Les Jumeaux étincelants; Le Grand Vizir; Poivre de Cayenne*; parts produced Cercle International de Culture de Royaumont, 1949–52). 1961; translated as *Seven Impromptus for Leisure*, in *Plays 1*, 1965.
Génousie (produced by the Théâtre National Populaire, Théâtre de la Récamier, Paris, 1960). 1960; translated as *Jenusia*, in *Plays 1*, 1965.
Le Satyre de la Villette (produced Théâtre de l'Atelier, Paris, 1963). In *L'Avant-Scène*, May 1963; in book form, in *Théâtre 1*, 1966; translated as *The Satyr of La Villette*, in *Plays 2*, 1970.

Le Général inconnu (produced Théâtre de Lutèce, Paris, 1964). In *L'Avant-Scène*, 324, 1964; in book form, in *Théâtre 1*, 1966; translated as *The Unknown General*, in *Plays 2*, 1970.
L'Air du large (produced Teatro La Farsa, Buenos Aires, 1965). In *L'Avant-Scène*, 324, 1964; in book form, in *Théâtre 2*, 1966; translated as *Wide Open Spaces*, in *Plays 2*, 1970.
Du Vent dans les branches de sassafras (produced Brussels, 1965). In *Théâtre 2*, 1966; translated as *Wind in the Branches of the Sassafras*, in *Plays 4*, 1985.
Le Cosmonaute agricole (produced Théâtre d'Essai, Musée d'Art Moderne, Paris, 1966). In *Théâtre 2*, 1966.
Et à la Fin était le bang (produced Théâtre des Célestins, Lyons, 1969). In *Théâtre 6*, 1976.
Deux Femmes pour un fantôme (produced produced Théâtre de l'Oeuvre, Paris, 1971). In *Théâtre 5*, 1973; translated as *Two Women for One Ghost*, in *Plays 3*, 1982.
La Baby-sitter (produced Théâtre de l'Oeuvre, Paris, 1971). In *Théâtre 5*, 1973; translated as *The Baby-Sitter*, in *Plays 3*, 1982.
Le Damné, from his radio play (produced with *Classe terminale* as *Underground Etablissement*, Chapelle du Calvaire, Paris, 1973).
Classe terminale (produced with *Le Damné* as *Underground Etablissement*, Chapelle du Calvaire, Paris, 1973). In *Théâtre 5*, 1973.
Monsieur Klebs et Rosalie (produced Théâtre de l'Oeuvre, Paris, 1975). In *Théâtre 6*, 1976; translated as *Monsieur Klebs and Rozalie*, in *Plays 4*, 1985.
Le Banquet de méduses, from the radio play (produced Théâtre Montansier, Versailles, 1979).
Les Bons bourgeois (produced Théâtre Hébertot, Paris, 1980). In *Théâtre 7*, 1981.

Screenplays

La Difficulté d'être infidèle, from *La Bonne Anna* by Marc Camoletti, 1964.

Television Plays

Fugue à Waterloo, 1976.

Radio Plays

Génousie, 1957; *Le Damné*, 1962 (published in *Théâtre 4*, 1968); *Les Larmes de l'aveugle*, 1964 (in *Théâtre 4*, 1968); *Urbi et Orbi*, 1967 (in *Théâtre 4*, 1968); *Le Banquet des méduses*, 1971 (in *Théâtre 5*, 1973); *Grasse matinée*, 1981 (in *Théâtre matinée*, 1981).

Verse

Les Richesses naturelles.   1952.
Innocentines.   1969.

Fiction

Midi.   1949.
Tamerlan des coeurs.   1955.
"Fugue à Waterloo" suivi de "Le Graf Zeppelin; ou, La Passion d'Émile".   1956.
Le Centenaire.   1959; translated as *The Centenarian*, 1970.

*

Criticism

Books:
Gérard D. Farcy, *Encyclobaldia: Petite Encyclopédie portative du théâtre de Obaldia*, Paris, 1981.

Articles:
Anne C. Murch, "Réflexions sur le théâtre de René de Obaldia", in *Études françaises*, 7, 1971.
Jean Onimus, "Obaldia ou le langage en fête", in *Travaux de linguistique et de littérature*, vol.20 no.3, 1982.

*   *   *

The theatre of René de Obaldia, overtly comic, parallels the developments of the French avant-garde. The imaginative, dark comedy of Obaldia is not ground-breaking or revolutionary in form, but nonetheless contains an anarchic spirit. Obaldia combats the claustrophobic, pressing anxieties of the modern world with a derisive humor that is in striking contrast to the sober, empty worlds of many of his contemporaries. While vehemently protesting the advances of super technology and the deterioration of interpersonal communication, Obaldia instils an element of hope for the rescue of our society through illumination and changes in the attitudes of men and women.

Obaldia introduces disparate and unpredictable elements into commonplace situations, thereby creating juxtapositions that are inherently funny. In *La Baby-sitter* (*The Baby Sitter*), subtitled "A Psychosomatic Comedy", Sister Thorn invades the urban apartment of Elvira and Franklin, mundane parents frustrated by their 14 years of marriage. Sister Thorn enlivens the tense environment, as the couple awaits the arrival of the sitter, with her ecstatic, almost possessed, fountain of pious clichés. The rupture that her appearance creates brings about a series of realizations on the part of both Elvira and Franklin, resulting in a melodramatic rebirth of their forgotten passion.

Similarly, in *Édouard et Agrippine*, one of Obaldia's early "impromptus", a teenage thief, Leather Jacket, bursts into the depressing boudoir of long-married Agrippina and Edward, interrupting Agrippina's nagging and Edward's pedantic and satirical responses. Shocked with fright, Agrippina has a heart attack and dies. Edward, in turn, thanks Leather Jacket, and with pedestrian calm, offers him a drink.

Obaldia strives to make the most incredible and impossible situations believable and playable for the theatre. His plays offer a realistic setting where an unreal event transpires. Dream and reverie are frequently utilized to illustrate the passage out of reality. In *Génousie* (*Jenusia*), Christian and Irène are shown as lovers in a dream sequence before their extra-marital affair develops into a reality. Caroline, the middle-aged wife of the old and eccentric John Emery Rockefeller in *Du Vent dans les branches de Sassafras* (*Wind in the Branches of the Sassafras*), can see the future and the past in her crystal ball. In this capacity to drift from one world to another, Obaldia's comic drama draws inspiration from the plays of Luigi Pirandello and from the free and flexible genres of the cinema. *Wind in the Branches of the Sassafras* is essentially an elaborate and inventive parody of an American Western movie.

The precision of Obaldia's preposterous characterizations is complemented by his unique poetic language. He has been compared to Jacques Audiberti for his ability to incite great verbal showers. Obaldia plays with the absurdity of language, even through the invention of his own language, "génousien", for the 1960 production of *Jenusia*, directed by Jean Vilar. There is a connection in his use of words and language with the verbal experiments of Eugène Ionesco. Like many of his contemporary dramatists, René de Obaldia was born outside of France—in Hong Kong in fact—and may have benefited from a multi-lingual environment through his Panamanian father. Much of his comedy is focused upon language: the deliberate use of clichés, the insertion of English words and phrases, and an extensive employment of argot. The plays are also reliant upon exaggerated physicality and rhythmic gesture, so that the satire is grounded equally in the visuals and in the text.

There is an acceptable naiveté in Obaldia's comic drama that assumes an element of play like that of children. The plays are not childish, but rather *child-like*. They maintain a spirited freedom while dealing with serious themes as vast as the exploration of space or the explosion and development of nuclear bombs. Obaldia believed that the public was better served by tension-releasing laughter than by laborious "intellectual exercises". His particular style of macabre humor and tragic farce is a testament to the ability of comic drama to serve a social function and work for a positive change in the lives of individuals.

Very little is required to make Obaldia's theatre come to life: he relied upon the strengths of actors to make his plays succeed. He kept close contact with the productions of his plays, reflecting upon the role that that the theatre had played in Elizabethan culture. He wished to emulate the Elizabethan theatre in his own work, and maintain a close contact between his drama and everyday life. He wanted to appeal to a large and varied audience, as well. In his attempt to make this possible, Obaldia often contrasted the world of the peasant and the urban dweller. His plays of the 1960's and 1970's reflect the movement away from the fabricated world of the city toward a simpler lifestyle in the country, where man may renew a healthy contact with the rhythms of nature.

—Ron Popenhagen

———

OBEY, André.   Born in Douai, France, 8 May 1892. Began dramatic career in 1921; met Jacques Copeau and joined his theatre company, Les Copiaus, 1929; resident dramatist with Michel Saint-Denis's Compagnie des Quinze, 1931–33; director of the Comédie-Française, Paris, 1946–47. Recipient: Prix Théophraste-Renaudot; Prix Eugène Brieux, 1931. Died in Montsoreau, 14 April 1975.

Works

Collections

Théâtre 1 (includes *Noé; Le Viol de Lucrèce; La Bataille de la Marne; Vénus et Adonis*).   1948.
Théâtre antique, with others (includes *Agamemnon; Les Choéphores; Les Euménides*, and Greek classics translated by others).   1956.

Stage Works (selected)

La Souriante Mme. Beudet, with Denys Amiel (produced 1921).   1922.
La Carcasse, with Denys Amiel (produced 1926).
Noé (produced Théâtre du Vieux-Colombier, Paris, 1931)   1931. translated as *Noah*, 1935.
Le Viol de Lucrèce (produced Théâtre du Vieux-Colombier, Paris, 1931).   1931; translated as *Lucrece*, 1933.
La Bataille de la Marne (produced Théâtre du Vieux-Colombier, Paris, 1932).   In *Théâtre 1*, 1948.
Richard III, from the play by Shakespeare (produced Théâtre d'Atelier, Paris, 1933).   1933.
Loire.   1933.
Le Trompeur de Séville (produced 1937; revised version, as *L'Homme de cendres*, produced Comédie-Française, Paris, 1949).   1950?.
800 Mètres (produced Stade Roland Garros, Paris, 1940).
Vénus et Adonis.   In *Théâtre 1*, 1948; translated as *Venus and Adonis*, in *From the Modern Repertoire 2*, edited by Eric Bentley, 1952.
Lazare (produced 1952?).
Les Geueux aux Paradis, from the work by Gaston Marie Martens.   1953; translated as *The Hopeful Travellers*, 1953.
Une Fille pour le vent (produced 1953).   Edited by J.R. van der Linden, 1954.
L'Orestie: Agamemnon; Les Choéphores; Les Euménides, from the trilogy by Aeschylus (produced by the Renaud-Barrault company, 1955).   In *Théâtre antique*, 1956.
La Chatte sur un toit brûlant, from a play by Tennessee Williams (produced 1956).   With *Un Tramway nommé Desir*, by Williams, 1963.
Plus de Miracles pour Noël (produced c.1957).
Douze Hommes en colère, from a work by Reginal Rose.   1958.
Les Trois Coups de minuit (produced 1958).   1959; translated as *Frost at Midnight*, 1960.

Fiction

Le Joueur de triangle.   1954.

Other

Les Objets égyptiens et égyptisants du mobilier funéraire carthaginois, with Gaston Marie Martens.   1945.

*

Criticism

Books:
Claus Clüver, *Thornton Wilder und André Obey: Untersuchungen zum modernen epischen Theater*, Bonn, 1978.
André Obey: Homme du théâtre (exhibition catologue), Douai, 1985.

* * *

The career of André Obey in the French theatre is fundamentally linked with the theory and practice of Jacques Copeau. It is highly possible that Obey would not have succeeded as a playwright without the encouragement and guidance that Copeau offered. Copeau was in search of a poet who could work as a dramatist with the actors he had trained at the Vieux-Colombier. Obey responded to the challenge by observing the actors at work and then writing, initially, for Copeau's group—Les Copiaus. Three important plays, *Noé* (*Noah*), *Le Viol de Lucrèce* (The Rape of Lucretia), and *La Bataille de la Marne* (The Battle of the Marne) were eventually produced by La Compagnie des Quinze, a company comprised of Copeau-trained actors. These plays, highly dependent upon mimed action and a physical acting style, directly reflect Copeau's emphasis upon a theatre of movement and diction to be performed upon a "*tréteau nu*". It was a theatre where the actor existed in a simplified but expansive space. Obey was able to match this style in the writing of his texts.

These early plays (the first was performed in 1931), have often been criticized as drama because of the extreme importance laid upon the images and action. Their success was largely due to the brilliant *mise en scène* of Michel Saint-Denis, and to the professional skill of the ensemble acting. Certainly the plays merit attention; the mime element does not reduce their importance. The attention given to choral text and movement, unusual for this era, does not in any way detract from the beauty of the language. Nor does the intermingling of poetic passages with those utilizing argot create any major stylistic conflict. To be understood, these plays must be read as scripts for actors.

Obey's plays are precisely what Copeau wanted them to be—the point of departure for a performance. Obey approached the writing of these plays with images from the mystery plays (for *Noé*), from the Elizabethan theatre (for *Le Viol de Lucrèce*), and from the Greek tragedies (for *La Bataille de la Marne*). All three plays demonstrate his ability to write texts with a grand dimension.

While experimental in form, Obey's dramas have taken the classical theatre as a model; therefore, they are neo-classical in tone, and they reflect very little other movements towards a realistic drama. Obey acknowledged only the playwrights Jean Cocteau and Paul Claudel as influences. He worked throughout his life with adaptations of Greek drama, including a treatment of the Iphigenia legend based upon Euripides. Obey's play, entitled *Une Fille pour le vent* (One for the Wind), alters Euripides' concept slightly by making Ulysses clearly the protagonist of the play. Obey also adapted the *Oresteia* for a 1955 *mise en scène* by Jean-Louis Barrault.

In Obey's rewriting of myths, legends, and Biblical themes, he humanized the characters, showing them as real men and women, often with insurmountable problems. Noah, a farmer who accepts God's authority, is hampered by domestic problems. There are eventual power struggles with his sons, and his wife becomes insane once the ark has regained the earth. Noah is caught between the everyday and the divine. His most sympathetic companions are the animals which accompany the family on the ark. They speak as real animals in a refreshing *coup de théâtre*.

Obey wrote three versions of the Don Juan story, between 1934 and the early 1970's. Again the protagonist is humanized and presented as a character who is a victim of contemporary political and social forces beyond his control. In the final version, *L'Homme de cendres* (The Phoenix) Don Juan is a warm and sincere man who desires the companionship of a woman, but cannot accept the possibility of being possessed by someone. He has violent outbursts throughout the play, and anticipates, even awaits his own death. Obey makes the character very complex and multi-faceted, and his Don Juan voluntarily moves towards his own unraveling and elimination with an inexplicably appealing innocence.

The Obey plays have a popular appeal. It is for this reason that they have often been revived by directors who wish to broaden their audience base. Jean Dasté, a member of the original Compagnie des Quinze, revived *Noé* in the 1945–46 season, as part of his campaign for a national popular theatre. Jean-Louis Barrault, attracted by the mime elements in the text, directed *Le Viol de Lucrèce* in 1961. There is a universal and lasting quality to Obey's plays, attractive not only to adult audiences, but to children too. There is an element of storytelling in the plays, as with the two narrators who recount the story, to the actions of the characters, in *Le Viol de Lucrèce*, and the messenger-type speeches that tell of the battles in *La Bataille de la Marne*.

There are flashes of Jean Giraudoux in the more poetic sequences of Obey's plays, but Obey avoids the extreme sentimental quality of many of Giraudoux's works. The relationship between Jacques Copeau, Les Copiaus, La Compagnie des Quinze, and Obey was the model for the playwright/director rapport that developed between Jean Giraudoux and Louis Jouvet. Obey's working relationship with actors remains a noteworthy model for both young playwrights and developing theatre companies. It is this unique experience in the early 1930's that is the root of Obey's legacy, and its impact was felt beyond the boundaries of France, especially in the British and American theatre. (Obey's writing for the neutral stage had a direct impact upon Thornton Wilder's conception of *Our Town*).

—Ron Popenhagen

O'CASEY, Sean. Born John Casey in Dublin, Ireland, 30 March 1880. Educated at schools in Dublin; lived in extreme poverty as a child. Married Eileen Carey Reynolds in 1927; two sons and one daughter. Worked in the stockroom of a hardware company from age 14; intermittently employed in clerical jobs; manual worker, Great Northern Railway, Ireland, 1901–11 (dismissed for union activities); wrote for nationalist and labour journals from 1907; member, Gaelic League, then Irish Republican Brotherhood, in the early 1900's; involved in the Dublin transport strike, 1913; resigned from the Irish Republican Brotherhood when they failed to support locked-out workers, and helped form the Irish Citizen Army, 1913–14 (primarily supported socialist, rather than nationalist, goals); first-produced play, *The Shadow of a Gunman*, staged 1923; associated with the Abbey Theatre, Dublin, 1923–28; moved to England, 1926; drama critic, *Time and Tide*, London, in the 1930's. Recipient: Hawthornden Prize, 1926. Died in Torquay, Devon, 18 September 1964.

Works

Collections

Five Irish Plays (includes *Juno and the Paycock; The Shadow of a Gunman; The Plough and the Stars; The End of the Beginning; A Pound on Demand*). 1935.
Collected Plays (4 vols.). 1949–51; augmented edition, as *The Complete Plays* (5 vols.), 1984.

Selected Plays. 1954.
Three Plays (includes *Juno and the Paycock; The Shadow of a Gunman; The Plough and the Stars*). 1957.
Behind the Green Curtains; Figuro in the Night; The Moon Shines on Kylenamoe: Three Plays. 1961.
Three More Plays. 1965.
The Sean O'Casey Reader, edited by Brooks Atkinson. 1968.
Seven Plays, edited by Ronald Ayling. 1985.

Stage Works

The Shadow of a Gunman (produced Abbey Theatre, Dublin, 1923). In *Two Plays*, 1925.
Cathleen Listens In: A Phantasy (produced Abbey Theatre, Dublin, 1923). In *Feathers from the Green Crow*, 1962.
Juno and the Paycock (produced Abbey Theatre, Dublin, 1924). In *Two Plays*, 1925.
Nannie's Night Out (produced Abbey Theatre, Dublin, 1924). In *Feathers from the Green Crow*, 1962.
The Plough and the Stars (produced Abbey Theatre, Dublin, 1926). 1926.
The Silver Tassie (produced Apollo Theatre, London, 1929). 1928.
Within the Gates (produced Royalty Theatre, London, 1934). 1933; revised version in *Collected Plays 2*, 1949.
The End of the Beginning (produced Abbey Theatre, Dublin, 1937). In *Windfalls*, 1934.
A Pound on Demand (produced Q Theatre, London, 1939). In *Windfalls*, 1934.
The Star Turns Red (produced Unity Theatre, London, 1943). 1940.
Purple Dust: A Wayward Comedy (produced People's Theatre, Newcastle-upon-Tyne, 1943). 1940.
Red Roses for Me (produced Olympia Theatre, Dublin, 1943). 1942.
Oak Leaves and Lavender; or, A World on Wallpaper (produced Stadteater, Helsingborg, Sweden, 1947). 1946.
Cock-a-Doodle Dandy (produced People's Theatre, Newcastle-upon-Tyne, 1949). 1949.
Bedtime Story: An Anatole Burlesque (produced Yugoslav-American Hall, New York, 1952). In *Collected Plays 4*, 1951.
Hall of Healing: A Sincerious Farce (produced Yugoslav-American Hall, New York, 1952). In *Collected Plays 3*, 1951.
Time to Go: A Morality Comedy (produced Yugoslav-American Hall, New York, 1952). In *Collected Plays 4*, 1951.
The Bishop's Bonfire (produced Gaiety Theatre, Dublin, 1955). 1955.
The Drums of Father Ned: A Mickrocosm of Ireland (produced Little Theatre, Lafayette, Indiana, 1959). 1960.
The Moon Shines on Kylenamoe (produced Theatre de Lys, New York, 1962). In *Behind the Green Curtains . . .*, 1961.
Behind the Green Curtains (produced University of Rochester, Rochester, New York, 1962). In *Behind the Green Curtains . . .*, 1961.
Figuro in the Night (produced Hofstra University Playhouse, New York, 1962). In *Behind the Green Curtains . . .*, 1961.
The Harvest Festival. 1979.

Screenplays

Juno and the Paycock (*The Shame of Mary Boyle*), with Alma Reville and Alfred Hitchcock, 1929.

Sean O'Casey

Verse

Songs of the Wren (2 vols.).   1918.
More Wren Songs.   1918.

Memoirs and Letters

Mirror in My House: The Autobiographies (2 vols.).   1956;
    as *Autobiographies* (2 vols.), 1963. Individual volumes:
  1. *I Knock at the Door: Swift Glances Back at Things That
     Made Me*.   1939.
  2. *Pictures in the Hallway*.   1942.
  3. *Drums under the Windows*.   1945.
  4. *Inishfallen, Fare Thee Well*.   1949.
  5. *Rose and Crown*.   1952.
  6. *Sunset and Evening Star*.   1954.
Letters, edited by David Krause.   1975 —

Other

The Story of Thomas Ashe.   1917(?).
The Sacrifice of Thomas Ashe.   1918.
The Story of the Irish Citizen Army.   1919.
Windfalls: Stories, Poems, and Plays.   1934.
The Flying Wasp (on theatre).   1937.
The Green Crow (essays and stories).   1956.
Feathers from the Green Crow 1905–1915 (miscellany), edited
    by Robert Hogan.   1962.
*Under a Colored Cap: Articles Merry and Mournful with
    Comments and a Song*.   1963.

Blasts and Benedictions: Articles and Stories, edited by
    Ronald Ayling.   1967.
The Sting and the Twinkle: Conversations with O'Casey,
    edited by E. H. Mikhail and John O'Riordan.   1974.

*

Bibliographies

E.H. Mikhail, *Sean O'Casey: A Bibliography of Criticism*,
    Seattle, Washington, 1972.
Ronald Ayling and Michael J. Durkan, *Sean O'Casey: A
    Bibliography*, London, 1978; supplement in *O'Casey
    Annual*, 2, 1983.
E.H. Mikhail, *Sean O'Casey and His Critics: An Annotated
    Bibliography 1916–1982*, Metuchen, New Jersey, 1985.

Criticism

Books:
Jules Koslow, *The Green and the Red: O'Casey, The Man and
    His Plays*, 1950, revised edition, New York, 1966.
Robert Hogan, *The Experiments of O'Casey*, New York,
    1960.
David Krause, *Sean O'Casey: The Man and His Work*,
    London and New York, 1960; revised edition, 1975.
David Krause, *O'Casey and His World*, 1976.
David Krause (ed.), *A Self-Portrait of the Artist as a Young
    Man: O'Casey's Letters*, Dublin and London, 1968.
Saros Cowasjee, *O'Casey: The Man Behind the Plays*,
    London 1963.
Gabriel Fallon, *O'Casey: The Man I Knew*, London, 1965.
Sean McCann, *The World of O'Casey*, London, 1966.
William A. Armstrong, *Sean O'Casey*, London, 1967 (British
    Council pamphlet).
Klaus Völker, *Irisches Theater II: Sean O'Casey*, Velber,
    1968.
Ronald Ayling (ed.), *O'Casey: Modern Judgements*, London,
    1969.
Maureen Malone, *The Plays of Sean O'Casey*, Carbondale,
    Illinois, 1969.
Martin B. Margulies, *The Early Life of Sean O'Casey*,
    Dublin, 1970.
Bernard Benstock, *O'Casey*, 1970.
Eileen O'Casey, *Sean*, edited by J.C. Trewin, London, 1971.
Herbert Goldstone, *In Search of Community: The
    Achievement of Sean O'Casey*, Cork, 1972.
Thomas Kilroy (ed.), *O'Casey: A Collection of Critical
    Essays*, Englewood Cliffs, New Jersey, 1975.
Ronald Ayling, *Continuity and Innovation in O'Casey's
    Drama*, Salzburg, 1976.
Bernard Benstock, *Paycocks and Others: Sean O'Casey's
    World*, Dublin, 1976.
John P. Frayne, *Sean O'Casey*, New York, 1976.
Doris Da Rin, *Sean O'Casey*, New York, 1976.
Donald D. Wilson, *Sean O'Casey's Tragi-Comic Vision*, New
    York, 1976.
James R. Scrimgeour, *Sean O'Casey*, Boston, 1978.
B.L. Smith, *O'Casey's Satiric Vision*, Kent, 1978.
Ronald G. Rollins, *O'Casey's Drama: Verisimilitude and
    Vision*, University of Alabama, 1979.
C. Desmond Greaves, *Sean O'Casey: Politics and Art*,
    Atlantic Highlands, New Jersey, 1980.
Hugh Hunt, *Sean O'Casey* (biography), Dublin, 1980.
David Krause and Robert G. Lowery (eds.), *O'Casey:*

Centenary Essays, Gerrard's Cross, Buckinghamshire, 1980.

Jack Mitchell, *The Essential O'Casey: A Study of the Twelve Major Plays*, New York, 1980.

Micheál Ó hAodha (ed.), *The O'Casey Enigma*, Dublin, 1980.

Robert G. Lowery (ed.), *Essays on Sean O'Casey's Auto-biographies*, London, 1981.

Robert G. Lowery, *O'Casey's Autobiographies: An Annotated Index*, Westport, Connecticut, 1983.

Brooks Atkinson, edited by Robert G. Lowery, *O'Casey: From Times Past*, London, 1982.

Carol Kleiman, *O'Casey's Bridge of Vision: Four Essays on Structure and Perspective*, Toronto, 1982.

James Simmons, *Sean O'Casey*, London, 1983.

John O'Riordan, *A Guide to O'Casey's Plays*, London, 1984.

Ronald Ayling (ed.), *Sean O'Casey: The Dublin Trilogy: A Casebook*, London, 1985.

Heinz Kosok, *O'Casey the Dramatist*, Gerrards Cross, 1985.

Nesta Jones, *File on O'Casey*, London, 1986.

Harold Bloom (ed.), *Sean O'Casey: Modern Critical Views*, New York, 1987.

Jacqueline Genet and Wynne Hellegouac'h (eds.), *Studies on O'Casey*, Caen, France, 1987.

Nesta Jones, *O'Casey and Expressionism* (book and slide set), Cambridge, 1988.

Garry O'Connor, *Sean O'Casey: A Life*, London, 1988.

Nicole Vigouroux-Frey, *Sean O'Casey: La Trilogie dublinoise*, Tours, 1988.

Serials

Sean O'Casey Review, 1975–81; as *O'Casey Annual*, 1982—

*   *   *

In the course of his long career, the Irish playwright Sean O'Casey wrote a large number of plays characterized by a remarkably all-embracing range of techniques. A typical O'Casey play combines in varying proportions vaudeville turns, melodramatic discoveries, sentimental song, strange noises, tired clichés, poetic speeches, angry polemics, romantic encounters, circling dancers, flamboyant costumes and miraculous transformations.

This "inclusiveness" is in part the result of O'Casey's delight in creating hybrid dramatic forms and styles. For example, in the "Dublin Trilogy" (*The Shadow of a Gunman, Juno and the Paycock*, and *The Plough and the Stars*), O'Casey successfully mixed tragedy and comedy to create a theater of bittersweet ironies, not exactly comic and not precisely tragic, but a union of the two that has overwhelming dramatic force. In *The Silver Tassie*, elements of naturalism and expressionism co-exist and amplify the perspectives from which the horrors of World War I assault the audience. And in late works like *Cock-a-Doodle Dandy* and *The Drums of Father Ned*, O'Casey blends realism and fantasy to create a world of promise and wonder in which all things are possible, even an enchanted bird whose anarchic sexual power can release the rebelliousness of the young and thereby threaten and subvert the repressive forces of an authoritarian Church and a conservative State.

O'Casey's use of language is another source of variety. O'Casey's characters share a malleable speech that ranges from the cadences of the King James Bible to the coarseness of the local "snug". The colloquial Hiberno-English that flows effortlessly from the lips of many characters is so enriched with colorful imagery, persistent alliteration, unexpec-

ted turns of phrase, and quotations from Shakespeare, Milton, Pope, and Shelley, that it is often described as "Elizabethan".

Some characters use highly individualized idioms and verbal idiosyncrasies: no one else in an O'Casey play sounds like either Fluther Good in *The Plough and the Stars*, with his repeated comic assurances that he does not mean anything "derogatory", or like Joxer Daly in *Juno and the Paycock*, with his grab-bag of tag endings and clichés. Such peculiarities of speech are more than just verbal decorations. Specialized vocabularies such as Donal Davoran's heightened poetic constructions (in *The Shadow of a Gunman*), O'Dempsey's insistent references to Celtic mythology, (in *Purple Dust*), Mrs. Gogan's habitual elaborations on the details of death (in *The Plough and the Stars*) and the Croucher's ironic reversals of Ezekial (in *The Silver Tassie*) delineate character and advance plot.

Variety also characterizes O'Casey's manipulation of all the other resources of the theater. For example, O'Casey used lighting in his stage directions to suggest a world of multiple and fluctuating realities. By literally blotting out and obliterating the foolishness of the characters, the sudden darkness that engulfs the stage towards the end of *Purple Dust* severs the dead past from the emergent future. In Act III of *Red Roses for Me*, the mauve and bronze lighting that gradually drenches the stage reveals the previously concealed beauties of the disinherited.

O'Casey used directions for sets in the same dynamic way as he used lighting. Walls crumble (in *Purple Dust*), houses are transformed into factories (in *Oak Leaves and Lavender*), furniture is added and subtracted (in *Juno and the Paycock*), characters appear and disappear through windows (in *Juno and the Paycock*), doors (in *The Plough and the Stars*) and ceilings (in *Purple Dust*). In plays like *The Plough and the Stars, Oak Leaves and Lavender, Purple Dust, Cock-a-Doodle Dandy*, and *The Drums of Father Ned*, O'Casey manipulated stage space so that noises, shouts, songs and speeches from the outside blend insistently with the action going on indoors. Through this layering effect, O'Casey demonstrated that his stage reality is embedded in a more comprehensive external reality.

O'Casey's all-embracing theatre expressed his profound sense of the palpable richness of life. At the same time, his plays recognize that social and political conditions (often conveyed by the intrusive world outside) frequently prevent that richness from being realized. They also explore the ways by which society may be transformed and humanized to accommodate the expansive needs of the human spirit, and the reasons why such social change is often frustrated. O'Casey's plays do not, however, offer characters and audiences the easy fatalism of defeat by immutable forces. Inherent in the life of his impoverished but resilient characters is the possibility for revolutionary change, and he judged the characters by their ability to respond positively to this political challenge.

O'Casey's dramatic techniques and political preoccupations reflected his socialist perspective. Although the early plays (*The Shadow of a Gunman, Juno and the Paycock, The Plough and the Stars, The Silver Tassie*, and *Within the Gates*) are frequently viewed as being hostile to politics *per se*, O'Casey was, in fact, only critical of those political activities that ignored the reality of poverty, in which most of his characters live out their lives. He was also critical of the anti-political attitudes of many of his characters, particularly those of such otherwise admirable women as Juno (in *Juno and the Paycock*) and Nora (in *The Plough and the Stars*): their devotion to irrelevant and unachievable private strategies of salvation in a time of political and economic collapse is understandable, yet evidently completely inappropriate. O'Casey judged both political and private activities to be failures because they did not address what were, for him, the destructive manifestations of poverty—tuberculosis, unemployment, chronic drunkenness, and premature death.

In the plays of the middle period (*The Star Turns Red*, *Purple Dust*, *Red Roses for Me*, and *Oak Leaves and Lavender*), sometimes referred to as the "coloured plays", O'Casey dramatized more explicitly than elsewhere the challenge to entrenched power by radical change. *The Star Turns Red*, for example, unashamedly presents the red star (communism) supplanting the Star of Bethlehem. In the late plays (*Cock-a-Doodle Dandy*, *The Bishop's Bonfire*, *The Drums of Father Ned*, *Behind the Green Curtains*, *Figuro in the Night*), O'Casey attacked the dominant ideology of Ireland for what he regarded as its stultifying combination of political conservatism, clerical domination, and sexual and artistic repression. At the same time, and often with great comic abandon, he dramatized the power of unrestrained sexuality to challenge the repressive authority of the Establishment.

O'Casey's plays, particularly the "Dublin Trilogy", continue to be performed throughout the world.

—Bernice Schrank

See also *Volume 1* entries on *Cock-a-Doodle Dandy*; *Juno and the Paycock*; *The Plough and the Stars*; *The Silver Tassie*.

ODETS, Clifford. Born in Philadelphia, Pennysylvania, USA, 18 July 1906; grew up in the Bronx, New York. Educated at Morris High School, New York, 1921–23. Married 1) the actress Luise Rainer in 1937 (divorced 1941); 2) Bette Grayson in 1943 (divorced 1951), one son and one daughter. Actor on radio and on Broadway, 1923–28, and with Theatre Guild Productions, New York, 1928–30; wrote for the stage, particularly for the Group Theatre, from 1933; joined Communist Party, 1934 (resigned 1934); first-produced play, *Waiting for Lefty*, staged 1935; first screenplay produced 1936. Recipient: New Theatre League Prize, 1935; Yale Drama Prize, 1935; American Academy Award of Merit Medal, 1961. Died in Los Angeles, 14 August 1963.

Works

Collections

Three Plays (includes *Waiting for Lefty*; *Awake and Sing!*; *Till the Day I Die*).   1935.
Six Plays (includes *Waiting for Lefty*; *Awake and Sing*; *Till the Day I Die*; *Paradise Lost*; *Golden Boy*; *Rocket to the Moon*).   1939.

Stage Works

Waiting for Lefty (produced Civic Repertory Theatre, New York, 1935).   In *Three Plays*, 1935.
Awake and Sing! (produced Belasco Theatre, New York, 1935).   In *Three Plays*, 1935.
Till the Day I Die (produced Longacre Theatre, New York, 1935).   In *Three Plays*, 1935.

I Can't Sleep: A Monologue (produced Mecca Auditorium, New York, 1935).   In *New Theatre 3*, 1936.
Paradise Lost (produced Longacre Theatre, New York, 1935).   1936.
Golden Boy (produced Belasco Theatre, New York, 1937).   1937.
Rocket to the Moon (produced Belasco Theatre, New York, 1938).   1939.
Night Music (produced Broadhurst Theatre, New York, 1940).   1940.
Clash by Night (produced Belasco Theatre, New York, 1941).   1942.
The Russian People, from a play by Konstantin Simonov (produced Guild Theatre, New York, 1942).   In *Seven Soviet Plays*, edited by H.W.L. Dana, 1946.
The Big Knife (produced National Theatre, New York, 1949).   1949.
The Country Girl (produced Lyceum Theatre, New York, 1950).   1951; revised version, as *Winter Journey* (produced Greenwich Mews Theatre, New York, 1952), 1955.
The Flowering Peach (produced Belasco Theatre, New York, 1954).   1954.
The Silent Partner (produced Actors' Studio, New York, 1972).

Screenplays

The General Died at Dawn, 1936; *Black Sea Fighters*, 1943; *None But the Lonely Heart*, 1944 (published in *Best Film Plays 1945*, edited by John Gassner and Dudley Nichols, 1946); *Deadline at Dawn*, 1946; *Humoresque* with Zachary Gold, 1946; *Sweet Smell of Success*, with Ernest Lehman, 1957; *The Story on Page One*, 1960; *Wild in the Country*, 1961.

Television Plays

Big Mitch, 1963, and *The Mafia Man*, 1964 (both for *The Richard Boone Show*).

Other

Rifle Rule in Cuba, with Carleton Beals.   1935.
The Time is Ripe: The 1940 Journal of Clifford Odets.   1988.

*

Bibliographies

Robert Cooperman, *Clifford Odets: An Annotated Bibliography 1935–1989*, Westport, Connecticut, 1990.

Criticism

Books:
Edward Murray, *Clifford Odets: The Thirties and After*, New York, 1968.
Michael J. Mendelsohn, *Clifford Odets: Humane Dramatist*, Deland, Florida, 1969.
Harold Cantor, *Clifford Odets: Playwright-Poet*, Metuchen, New Jersey, 1978.
Gerald Weales, *Clifford Odets: Playwright*, New York, 1971; revised edition, 1985.
Margaret Brenman-Gibson, *Clifford Odets, American Playwright: The Years from 1906 to 1940*, New York, 1981.

Jürgen Gross, *Protest und Prophetis: Die frühen Dramen von Clifford*, Frankfurt, 1985.

Gabriel Miller, *Clifford Odets*, New York, 1989.

William W. Demastes, *Clifford Odets: A Research and Production Sourcebook*, New York, 1991.

Gabriel Miller (ed.), *Critical Essays on Clifford Odets*, Boston, 1991.

*   *   *

When Odets told the House Un-American Activities Committee that he had written his first play to be staged, *Waiting for Lefty*, entirely from his imagination, and that he had never been involved in a strike, he was widely thought to be lying in self-defence. Certainly, the play reflected—and in audience terms extended—the violent 40-day strike by 40,000 New York taxi drivers in 1934, and its production by the Group Theatre obviously endorsed the left-wing values of the strikers. But, as John Gassner said of that play, Odets may also be seen to be "playing Pindar to a working class to which he belonged only by bohemian adoption". If that view is accepted, then the elements of Hollywood sentimentality and Broadway realism in his subsequent output may be construed not as a betrayal of his first ideology, but as a regression to his more basic propensity.

The theatrical significance of *Waiting for Lefty* was enormous. Almost immediately it was being produced internationally from gestetnered scripts circulated by the Communist Party before the published text was available. It continued to be central to the canon of "Unity" and "Workers" theatres in the 1950's, and it became a model for much other left-wing agit-prop drama. Predictably, the play was pirated and reshaped into localised versions, and—a dimension often forgotten—Odets' use of the vernacular valorised a relatively new theatre language. But, ideology aside, few playwrights would want to commit their careers to the 40-minute form that was effectively the limit of agit-prop, and Odets had already completed more conventional full-length work when *Waiting for Lefty* was first performed.

Six other plays were done for the Group Theatre, and although none of them is as uncompromisingly propagandist as *Waiting for Lefty*, most do have an embedded argument that addresses issues of social significance, and the one-act *Till the Day I Die* is an overt anti-Nazi polemic. *Awake and Sing!*, the most famous of his full-length plays, presents its characters as products and victims of the Depression, and has dimensions of subtext and social realism that are much subtler than in most of the other Group plays. Much of the play's irony and pessimism is generated by the Jewish characters' search for a promised land in the face of hopeless adversity, and in *Paradise Lost*, the other early full-length play, a middle-class family—also from the Bronx, but this time not explicitly Jewish—goes through an odyssey of disaster in the face of capitalism. This play has more obvious symbolic elements, and most of the male characters are debilitated in some way, ranging from an impotent businessman to a former sports hero who now has a weak heart; the latter is the prototype of several of Odets' later characters, and may also be seen as an ironic glimpse of the American Dream as Albee would develop it in the 1960's.

Odets' move from the Group Theatre to Hollywood was planned as a short-term money-making venture to support stage production, but the models of success he encountered there influenced both his ambitions and his style. *The Silent Partner*, not produced until after his death, is in the vein of *Paradise Lost*, and Harold Clurman's demand for a rewrite because the theme seemed *passé* fundamentally affected Odets' relationship with the Group; shortly before his death, he told a *Theatre Arts* interviewer that it was "the best labor play that was ever written in the United States". He went on to say that "in the development of my work it was very necessary, and I should have insisted that the play be produced. It's the kind of writing that I have not done since, and I don't think I'm capable of now . . . if I had continued writing from there on . . . something extraordinary might have come out".

Odets' first screenplay, *The General Died at Dawn*, deals with a Chinese peasants' revolt, but its obvious socialist elements are crudely sensationalised, and his next major stage-play, *Golden Boy*, was first subtitled "A Modern Allegory", which clearly increased its acceptability to the Group. For all that, the play's commercial success (which Odets was consciously aiming at) was predictable, in that it does not compel audiences to go beneath the strata of sentimentality and melodramatic devices that reviewers widely labelled "cinematic". As a narrative of the spectacular rise and eventual suicide of a sporting hero, it had an unashamedly popular theme which instantly reached the mass imagination, but it also further developed the American Dream motif through the boxer's success story and subjected it to criticism through the many other conflicts in the competitive society that elevates fighting to such status.

Odets' last two Group plays, *Rocket to the Moon* and *Night Music*, are even softer in their audience manipulation, though their treatment of personal relationships introduces factors such as alcoholism and media-constructed identity which would be developed in the post-war plays. *Clash by Night* deals with marital conflict in terms which occasionally evoke the Strindbergian sex war and marked his final dissociation from the (nearly defunct) Group, although its cast, led by Tallulah Bankhead and Lee J. Cobb, was directed by Lee Strasberg.

Apart from *The Flowering Peach*, which remobilises elements of the allegory, poetry, and judaism of the plays of the 1930's, Odets' later plays have been seen as the work of a man fatigued and conditioned by years of screenwriting. Some of his screenplays—notably *None But the Lonely Heart*—had been recognised as distinguished, but his sense of achievement was eroded by recurrent official accusations from 1947 until 1952 of being "active in Communist work in film colony". Most importantly though, the last stage-plays were written with an awareness that the audience of the 1930's no longer existed, and that Group members were now dominating the Actors' Studio and achieving major successes with the plays of Miller and Williams. *The Big Knife* and *The Country Girl* are both studies of actors as products of an industry, and alcoholism is presented in an unglamorised—if not exactly sordid—manner. These plays were taken by moralistic critics as pivoting on "weakness of character", augmented by shallowness of characterisation; however, their lasting effectiveness has more to do with their vision of people degenerating as the victims of a falsely-constructed public identity.

—Howard McNaughton

See also *Volume 1* entries on *Awake and Sing!*; *Waiting for Lefty*.

O'KEEFFE, John. Born in Dublin, Ireland, 24 June 1747. Educated at a Jesuit school in Saul's Court, Dublin; possibly studied art in London, 1762–63. Married the actress Mary Heaphy in 1774 (separated 1781); two sons and two daughters. Actor on tours throughout Ireland, 1764–77, and in England, 1777–79; first plays produced 1767; moved to London, 1781, and wrote for the Haymarket and Covent Garden theatres; blind from mid-1780's; retired from play-writing, 1798; received an annuity from Covent Garden, 1803, and treasury pensions, 1808, 1826. Died in Southampton, 4 February 1833.

Works

Collections

Dramatic Works (4 vols.).   1798.

Stage Works

The She Gallant; or, Square-Toes Outwitted (produced Smock Alley Theatre, Dublin, 1767).   1767; revised version, as *The Positive Man,* music by Samuel Arnold and Michael Arne (produced Covent Garden Theatre, London, 1782), in *Dramatic Works,* 1798.

Harlequin in Waterford; or, The Dutchman Outwitted (produced 1767; as *Harlequin in Derry,* produced 1770).

Colin's Welcome (produced Belfast Theatre, Belfast, 1770).

The India Ship (produced Cork, c.1770).

Tony Lumpkin's Ramble Through Cork (produced Cork, 1773).

Tony Lumpkin in Town (produced Theatre Royal, Haymarket, London, 1774).   1780.

The Comical Duel; or, The Good Boy (produced Cork, 1775).

The Poor Soldier (as *The Shamrock, or, St.Patrick's Day,* produced Crow Street Theatre, Dublin, 1777; revised version, as *The Poor Soldier,* music by William Shield, produced Covent Garden Theatre, London, 1783).   1784.

The Son-in-Law, music by Samuel Arnold (produced Theatre Royal, Haymarket, London, 1779).   1783.

The Dead Alive, music by Samuel Arnold (produced Theatre Royal, Haymarket, London, 1781).   1783.

The Agreeable Surprise, music by Samuel Arnold (produced Theatre Royal, Haymarket, London, 1781).   1783.

The Banditti; or, Love's Labyrinth, music by Samuel Arnold (produced Covent Garden Theatre, London, 1781). Songs published 1781; revised version, as *The Castle of Andalusia* (produced Covent Garden Theatre, London, 1782), 1783; revised version (produced 1788).

Harlequin Teague; or, The Giant's Causeway, with George Colman the Elder, music by Samuel Arnold (produced Theatre Royal, Haymarket, London, 1782).   Songs published 1782.

Lord Mayor's Day; or, A Flight from Lapland, music by William Shield (produced Covent Garden Theatre, London, 1782).   Songs published 1782.

The Maid the Mistress, from a play by G.A. Federico (produced Covent Garden Theatre, London, 1783). Songs published 1783.

The Young Quaker (produced Theatre Royal, Haymarket, 1783).   1784.

The Birthday; or, The Prince of Arragon, music by Samuel Arnold, from a play by Saint-Foix (produced Theatre Royal, Haymarket London, 1783).   1783.

Gretna Green (lyrics only), play by Charles Stuart, music by Samuel Arnold (produced Theatre Royal, Haymarket London, 1783).   1783.

Friar Bacon; or, Harlequin's Adventures in Lilliput, Brobdignag etc. (lyrics only), play by Charles Bonner, music by William Shield (produced Covent Garden Theatre, London, 1783; as *Harlequin Rambler,* produced 1784).   Songs published 1783.

Peeping Tom of Coventry, music by Samuel Arnold (produced Theatre Royal, Haymarket, London, 1784).   1785.

Fontainebleau; or, Our Way in France, music by William Shield (produced Covent Garden Theatre, London, 1784). 1785.

The Blacksmith of Antwerp (produced Covent Garden Theatre, London, 1785).   In *Dramatic Works,* 1798.

A Beggar on Horseback, music by Samuel Arnold (produced Theatre Royal, Haymarket, London, 1785).   In *Dramatic Works,* 1798.

Omai; or, A Trip round the World, music by William Shield (produced Covent Garden Theatre, London, 1785). Songs published 1785.

Love in a Camp; or, Patrick in Prussia, music by William Shield (produced Covent Garden Theatre, London, 1786). 1786.

The Siege of Curzola, music by Samuel Arnold (produced Theatre Royal, Haymarket, London, 1786).   Songs published 1786.

The Man Milliner (produced Covent Garden Theatre, London, 1787).   In *Dramatic Works,* 1798.

Love and War, from a play by Robert Jephson (produced Covent Garden Theatre, London, 1787).

The Generous Tar (produced Covent Garden Theatre, London, 1787).

The Farmer, music by William Shield (produced Covent Garden Theatre, London, 1787).   1788.

Tantara-Rara, Rogues All, from a play by A.J. Bourlin (produced Covent Garden Theatre, London, 1788).   In *Dramatic Works,* 1798.

The Prisoner at Large (produced Theatre Royal, Haymarket, London, 1788).   1788.

The Highland Reel, music by William Shield (produced Covent Garden Theatre, London, 1788).   1789.

Aladdin; or, The Wonderful Lamp, music by William Shield (produced Covent Garden Theatre, London, 1788). Songs published 1788.

The Lie of the Day (as *The Toy,* produced Covent Garden Theatre, London, 1789; revised version, as *The Lie of the Day,* produced Covent Garden Theatre, London, 1796). In *Dramatic Works,* 1798.

The Faro Table, from a play by Susanna Centlivre (produced Covent Garden Theatre, London, 1789).

The Little Hunch-Back; or, A Frolic in Bagdad (produced Covent Garden Theatre, London, 1789).   1789.

St. George's Day; or, Britons Rejoice (produced 1789).

The Czar Peter, music by William Shield (as *The Czar,* produced Covent Garden Theatre, London, 1790; as *The Fugitive,* produced Covent Garden Theatre, London, 1790).   In *Dramatic Works,* 1798.

The Basket-Maker, music by Samuel Arnold (produced Theatre Royal, Haymarket, London, 1790).   In *Dramatic Works,* 1798.

Modern Antiques; or, The Merry Mourners (produced Covent Garden Theatre, London, 1791).   1792.

Wild Oats; or, The Strolling Gentleman (produced Covent Garden Theatre, London, 1791).   1791.

Sprigs of Laurel, music by William Shield (produced Covent Garden Theatre, London, 1793).   1793; revised version, as *The Rival Soldiers* (produced Covent Garden Theatre, London, 1797).

The London Hermit; or, Rambles in Dorsetshire (produced Theatre Royal, Haymarket, London, 1793).   1793.

The World in a Village (produced Covent Garden Theatre, London, 1793).   1793.

Life's Vagaries (produced Covent Garden Theatre, London, 1795).   1795.

The Irish Mimic; or, Blunders at Brighton, music by William Shield (produced Covent Garden Theatre, London, 1795). 1795.

Merry Sherwood; or, Harlequin Forester (lyrics only), play by Mark Lonsdale and William Pearce, music by William Reeve (produced Covent Garden Theatre, London, 1795). Songs published 1795.

The Lad of the Hills; or, The Wicklow Gold Mine, music by William Shield (produced Covent Garden Theatre, London, 1796).   1814; revised version, as *The Wicklow Mountains* (produced Covent Garden Theatre, London, 1796), 1797.

The Doldrum; or, 1803 (produced Covent Garden Theatre, London, 1796).   In *Dramatic Works*, 1798.

Alfred; or, The Magic Banner (produced Theatre Royal, Haymarket, London, 1796).   1796.

Olympus in an Uproar; or, The Descent of the Deities, from a play by Kane O'Hara (produced Covent Garden Theatre, London, 1796).   Songs published 1796.

Britain's Brave Tars; or, All for St. Paul's, music by Thomas Attwood (produced Covent Garden Theatre, London, 1797).

She's Eloped (produced Theatre Royal, Drury Lane, London, 1798).

The Eleventh of June; or, The Daggerwoods at Dunstable (produced Theatre Royal, Drury Lane, London, 1798).

A Nosegay of Weeds; or, Old Servants in New Places (produced Theatre Royal, Drury Lane, London, 1798).

Verse

Oatlands; or, The Transfer of the Laurel.   1795.
O'Keeffe's Legacy to His Daughter, Being the Poetical Works, edited by Adelaide O'Keeffe.   1834.

Memoirs and Letters

Recollections of the Life of O'Keeffe, Written by Himself (2 vols.).   1826.

*

Bibliographies

Frederick M. Link, *John O'Keeffe: A Bibliography*, Lincoln, Nebraska, 1983.

Criticism

Books:
Frederick M. Link, Introduction in *Plays* (see Collections).

* * *

Before John O'Keeffe came to London he had already served a long apprenticeship in the art of pleasing the paying public in Ireland. He was recognized as an accomplished comic actor, with an especial bent for farce, and he could sing well too. Not content with just performing, he had also begun to write for the stage. In one sense, he may be seen as putting all this experience to good use on his arrival in London where

the many plays and adaptations that he wrote at a remarkable speed and with seemingly indefatigable facility made him the natural heir to the tradition of Isaac Bickerstaffe.

An alternative view would be that O'Keeffe was all too ready to bow to the necessity of satisfying an undemanding public which asked for nothing original in its drama apart from a little passing topically and a couple more catchy new songs. To O'Keeffe's credit stand three-score plays of one sort and another and, notwithstanding the lack of any really outstanding triumph, a record of considerable if not uninterrupted success in his own day. He deserves respect for achieving this. Posterity, however, has judged O'Keeffe, like most of his contemporaries, harshly, with regard both to individual works and the theatrical tradition of which they, all too obviously, form part. *Wild Oats* has been revived in recent times, but the production of this five-act comedy, which does not in fact represent the form in which O'Keeffe mainly worked, cannot be said to have inspired further explorations of his plays.

Comic opera is the name generally given to the dramatic form with which O'Keeffe made and sustained his reputation, but it might be more accurate to think in terms of light comedy with opportunities for song. One weakness, at least for modern critics, is that the lyrics are for the most part no more than adequate, and that no great ingenuity is shown in making them a genuine, integral part of the dramatic experience. Problems for modern directors lie not only in the difficulty of assembling a cast who can sing well enough to satisfy modern demands, but also in deciding on the correct style both for the actor who sings and, even more difficult, for the others who have to stand by and listen to two or three stanzas to the same tune. The more elaborate finales too are not particularly well motivated, so that what might well be a climax is, in fact, not very much more than a conventional conclusion to the entertainment.

It can, of course, be argued that hearing the musical element in its correct place would make all the difference, but Dr. Samuel Arnold and William Shield, O'Keeffe's most frequent associates, for instance, were not composers of any marked originality or personality. True, the songs are tuneful and the act-finales, like the overtures, have that somewhat predictable 18th-century gracefulness, without much harmonic inventiveness, which is found attractive by many today, just as it was when the plays were first offered to the public. What is missing is the heightening of emotion and dramatic tension that comes in comic opera when words and music form a genuine unified whole.

O'Keeffe also took little pains over his plots, which were not infrequently adaptations of those used by earlier dramatists. His expositions have the merit of clarity, though the devices employed are generally of the simplest description, and after that the aim is rather to provide a sequence of opportunities for songs, farcical routines, and meetings between the characters, than to construct a significant chain of events. The conclusions are satisfying only in the sense that everything works out well in the end. O'Keeffe appears to have been interested less in plot than in situations, and he did not baulk at a high degree of contrivance to bring together as many as possible. The result can, at its best, be lively and quite hilarious; on the other hand, there is, for want of development, some trivialization which dimishes the value of the plays.

For his characters, frequently devised to suit the style of particular actors, O'Keeffe turned to the stereotypes of the comic stage in his period. How much observation there is in his jolly Jack-Tars, his Quakers, and his solid Old English gentlemen is hard to say; but the types, which he juxtaposes with a verve that may well indicate his realization that something had to be done to breathe new life into them, serve their comic purposes well enough. Foreigners, too, make their way on to O'Keeffe's stage, sometimes with ludicrous accents, and generally with characteristics that play up to the chauvinistic tendencies of the London audience of the day.

The range of material covered is large, ranging from spectacular fairy pantomimes (*Aladdin*) adapted from sources that had already become traditional, to occasional pieces (*Lord Mayor's Day*), comedies that got some fun out of the characteristics of different parts of England, Ireland, and Scotland (such as *The Highland Reel*, which the author declared owed something to the journey to the Hebrides made by Boswell and Johnson), and plays that, to some extent, reflected current affairs (such as *Le Grenadier*, which became controversial as a comment on the French Revolution).

It is, of course, essential to appreciate that many of O'Keeffe's plays were intended to be—or, in some cases, were adapted to be—afterpieces. In other words, they were not the main dramatic entertainment offered in an evening, but served as light relief to something more serious that had gone before, providing the peformers with the opportunity of showing their paces in a different style. Even the five-act comedies, of which *Wild Oats* is now the best-known example, are, however, somewhat underdeveloped, rather lightweight, with the familiar ingredients stretched out to a greater length. O'Keeffe's importance in the theatrical life of his time is undeniable, but it is doubtful whether in the future we shall see productions of many of his plays, apart from the odd revival of *Wild Oats*.

—Christopher Smith

See also *Volume* 1 entry on *Wild Oats*.

———

O'NEILL, Eugene (Gladstone).   Born in New York City, 16 October 1888; son of the actor James O'Neill. Toured with his father as a child, and educated at Catholic boarding schools, and at Betts Academy, Stamford, Connecticut; attended Princeton University, New Jersey, 1906–07, and George Pierce Baker's "47 Workshop" at Harvard University, Cambridge, Massachusetts, 1914–15. Married 1) Kathleen Jenkins in 1909 (divorced 1912), one son; 2) Agnes Boulton in 1918 (divorced 1929), one son and one daughter; 3) the actress Carlotta Monterey in 1929. Worked for New York-Chicago Supply Company mail order firm, New York, 1907–08; gold prospector in Honduras, 1909; seaman on a Norwegian freighter to Buenos Aires, and advance agent and box-office man for his father's company, 1910–11; reporter, New London *Telegraph*, Connecticut, 1912; patient in a tuberculosis sanitarium, 1912–13; full-time writer from 1914; first plays produced 1914; writer and actor with the Provincetown Players, based in Provincetown, Massachusetts, and, from 1916, at the Playwrights' Theatre (also known as the Provincetown Playhouse), New York, 1916–20; co-director, with Kenneth Macgowan and the designer Robert Edmond Jones, of the reconstituted Provincetown Players, now based at the Provincetown and Greenwich Village theatres, New York, 1923–27; wrote several plays for the Theatre Guild; a founding editor, *American Spectator*, 1934; in ill-health from 1934: in later years suffered from a degenerative brain disease. Recipient: Pulitzer Prize, 1920, 1922, 1928, 1957; American Academy of Arts and Letters Gold Medal, 1922; Nobel Prize for Literature, 1936; New York Drama Critics Circle award, 1957. Litt.D: Yale University, New Haven, Connecticut, 1926. Member, American Academy, 1923, and Irish Academy of Letters. Died in Bolton, 27 November 1953.

Works

Collections

"Thirst" and Other One Act Plays (includes *The Web; Warnings; Fog; Recklessness*).   1914.
"The Moon of the Caribbees" and Six Other Plays of the Sea. (includes *In the Zone; The Long Voyage Home; Ile; The Rope; Where the Cross is Made*).   1919.
S.S. Glencairn: Four Plays of the Sea (includes *Bound East for Cardiff; In the Zone; The Long Voyage Home; The Moon of the Caribbees*).   1926.
Complete Works (2 vols.).   1924.
Lost Plays (includes *Abortion; The Movie Man; The Sniper; Servitude; A Wife for a Life*), edited by Lawrence Gellert.   1950.
Ten "Lost" Plays.   1964.
Children of the Sea and Three Other Unpublished Plays (includes *Bread and Butter; Now I Ask You; Shell Shock*), edited by Jennifer McCabe Atkinson.   1972.
Complete Plays (3 vols.), edited by Travis Bogard.   1988.

Stage Works

Thirst (produced Wharf Theatre, Provincetown, Massachusetts, 1916).   In *"Thirst" and Other Plays*, 1914.
Fog (produced Provinceton Playhouse, New York, 1917). In *"Thirst" and Other Plays*, 1914.
Recklessness.   In *"Thirst" and Other Plays*, 1914.
The Web.   In *"Thirst" and Other Plays*, 1914.
Warnings.   In *"Thirst" and Other Plays*, 1914.
Bound East for Cardiff (produced Wharf Theatre, Provincetown, Massachusetts, 1916).   In *The Moon of the Caribbees . . .*, 1919.
Before Breakfast (produced Provinceton Playhouse, New York, 1916).   1916.
The Sniper (produced Provincetown Playhouse, New York, 1917).   In *Lost Plays*, 1950.
In the Zone (produced Comedy Theatre, New York, 1917). In *The Moon of the Caribbees. . .*, 1919.
The Long Voyage Home (produced Provincetown Playhouse, New York, 1917).   In *The Moon of the Caribbees . . .*, 1919.
Ile (produced Provincetown Playhouse, New York, 1917). In *The Moon of the Caribbees . . .*, 1919.
The Rope (produced Provincetown Playhouse, New York, 1918).   In *The Moon of the Caribbees, . . .*, 1919.
Where the Cross is Made (produced Provincetown Playhouse, New York, 1918).   In *The Moon of the Caribbees . . .*, 1919.
The Moon of the Caribbees (produced Provincetown Playhouse, New York, 1918).   In *The Moon of the Caribbees . . .*, 1919.
The Dreamy Kid (produced Provincetown Playhouse, New York, 1919).   In *Complete Works 2*, 1924.
Beyond the Horizon (produced Morosco Theatre, New York, 1920).   1920.
Anna Christie (as *Chris*, produced Atlantic City, New Jersey,

1920; revised version, as *Anna Christie*, (produced Vanderbilt Theatre, New York, 1921). With *The Hairy Ape, The First Man*, 1922; original version, as *Chris Christophersen*, 1982.

Exorcism (produced Provincetown Playhouse, New York, 1920).

The Emperor Jones (produced Provincetown Playhouse, New York, 1920). With *Diff'rent, The Straw*, 1921.

Diff'rent (produced Provincetown Playhouse, New York, 1920). With *The Emperor Jones, The Straw*, 1921.

The Straw (produced Greenwich Village Theatre, New York, 1921). With *The Emperor Jones, Diff'rent*, 1921.

Gold (produced Frazee Theatre, New York, 1921). 1921.

The First Man (produced Neighborhood Playhouse, New York, 1922). With *The Hairy Ape, Anna Christie*, 1922.

The Hairy Ape (produced Provincetown Playhouse, New York, 1922). With *The First Man, Anna Christie*, 1922.

Welded (produced 39th Street Theatre, New York, 1924). With *All God's Chillun Got Wings*, 1924.

The Ancient Mariner: A Dramatic Arrangement of Coleridge's Poem (produced Provincetown Playhouse, New York, 1924).

All God's Chillun Got Wings (produced Provincetown Playhouse, New York, 1924). With *Welded*, 1924.

Desire under the Elms (produced Greenwich Village Theatre, New York, 1924). In *Complete Works 2*, 1924.

The Fountain (produced Greenwich Village Theatre, New York, 1925). With *The Great God Brown, The Moon of the Caribbees*, 1926.

The Great God Brown (produced Greenwich Village Theatre, New York, 1926). With *The Fountain, The Moon of the Caribbees*, 1926.

Marco's Millions (produced Guild Theatre, New York, 1928). 1927.

Lazarus Laughed (produced Community Playhouse, Pasadena, California, 1928). 1927.

Strange Interlude (produced John Golden Theatre, New York, 1928). 1928.

Dynamo (produced Martin Beck Theatre, New York, 1929). 1929.

Mourning Becomes Electra: A Trilogy (produced Guild Theatre, New York, 1931). 1931.

Ah, Wilderness! (produced Nixon Theatre, Pittsburgh, Pennsylvania, 1933). 1933.

Days Without End (produced Henry Miller's Theatre, New York, 1934). 1934.

The Iceman Cometh (produced Martin Beck Theatre, New York, 1946). 1946.

A Moon for the Misbegotten (produced Hartman Theatre, Columbus, Ohio, 1947). 1952.

Abortion. In *Lost Plays*, 1950.

The Movie Man. In *Lost Plays*, 1950.

Servitude (produced International Airport, New York, 1960). In *Lost Plays*, 1950.

A Wife for a Life. In *Lost Plays*, 1950.

Long Day's Journey into Night (produced Royal Dramatic Theatre, Stockholm, 1956; produced in the USA, Helen Hayes Theatre, New York, 1956). 1956.

A Touch of the Poet (produced Royal Dramatic Theatre, Stockholm, 1957; produced in the USA, Helen Hayes Theatre, New York, 1957). 1957.

Hughie (produced Royal Dramatic Theatre, Stockholm, 1958; produced in the USA, Royale Theatre, New York, 1964). 1959.

More Stately Mansions (produced Royal Dramatic Theatre, Stockholm, 1962; produced in the USA, Broadhurst Theatre, New York, 1967). 1964.

Children of the Sea. In *"Children of the Sea" and Three Other Unpublished Plays*, 1972.

Bread and Butter. In *"Children of the Sea" and Three Other Unpublished Plays*, 1972.

Now I Ask You. In *"Children of the Sea" and Three Other Unpublished Plays*, 1972.

Shell Shock. In *"Children of the Sea" and Three Other Unpublished Plays*, 1972.

The Calms of Capricorn scenario by O'Neill, completed by Donald Gallup. 1982.

The Personal Equation. In *The Unknown O'Neill*, 1988.

The Reckoning. In *The Unknown O'Neill*, 1988.

The Guilty One. In *The Unknown O'Neill*, 1988.

Verse

Poems 1912–1944, edited by Donald Gallup. 1980.

Memoirs and Letters

Inscriptions: O'Neill to Carlotta Monterey O'Neill, edited by Donald Gallup. 1960.

O'Neill at Work: Newly Released Ideas for Plays, edited by Virginia Floyd. 1981.

The Theatre We Worked For: The Letters of O'Neill to Kenneth Macgowan, edited by Jackson R. Bryer. 1982.

As Ever, Gene: The Letters of Eugene O'Neill to George Jean Nathan, edited by Nancy L. and Arthur W. Roberts. 1987.

Selected Letters, edited by Travis Bogard and Jackson Bryer. 1988.

Other

The Unknown O'Neill: Unpublished or Unfamiliar Writings, edited by Travis Bogard. 1988.

The Unfinished Plays (notes and drafts), edited by Virginia Floyd. 1988.

*

Bibliographies

Jennifer M. Atkinson, *Eugene O'Neill: A Descriptive Bibliography*, Pittsburgh, 1974.

Jordan Y. Miller, *Eugene O'Neill and the American Critic: A Bibliographical Checklist* (second edition), Hamden, Connecticut, 1973.

Madeleine Smith and Richard Eaton, *Eugene O'Neill: An Annotated Bibliography*, New York, 1988.

Criticism

Books:

Edwin A. Engel, *The Haunted Heroes of Eugene O'Neill*, Cambridge, Massachusetts, 1953.

Doris V. Falk, *Eugene O'Neill and the Tragic Tension* (second edition), 1958; revised edition, New York, 1982.

Oscar Cargill and others (eds.), *Eugene O'Neill and His Plays: Four Decades of Criticism*, London, 1961.

Doris Alexander, *The Tempering of Eugene O'Neill*, New York, 1962.

Arthur and Barbara Gelb, *O'Neill*, New York, 1962; revised edition, New York, 1974.

Frederick I. Carpenter, *Eugene O'Neill*, Boston, 1963; revised edition, Boston, 1979.

Eugene O'Neill

John Gassner (ed.), *A Collection of Critical Essays*, Englewood Cliffs, New Jersey, 1964.

Jordan Y. Miller, *Playwright's Progress: O'Neill and the American Critic*, London, 1965.

Olivia E. Coolidge, *Eugene O'Neill*, New York, 1966.

Louis Shaeffer, *O'Neill, Son and Playwright* (biography), Boston, 1968; as *O'Neill, Son and Artist*, 1973.

Timo Tiusanen, *O'Neill's Scenic Images*, Princeton, New Jersey, 1968.

Egil Törnqvist, *A Drama of Souls: Studies in O'Neill's Super-Naturalistic Technique*, New Haven, Connecticut, 1969.

Rolf Scheibler, *The Late Plays of O'Neill*, Bern, 1970.

François du Chaxel, *Eugene O'Neill: Textes, points de vue critiques, témoignages, chronologie, bibliographie, illustrations*, Paris, 1971.

Horst Frenz, *Eugene O'Neill*, New York, 1971.

Travis Bogard, *Contour in Time: The Plays of Eugene O'Neill*, New York, 1972; revised edition, 1988.

Bhagwat S. Goyal, *The Strategy of Survival: Human Significance of O'Neill's Plays*, Ghaziabad, India, 1975.

Leonard Chabrowe, *Ritual and Pathos: The Theater of O'Neill*, Lewsiburg, Pennsylvania, 1976.

Harry Cronin, *Eugene O'Neill, Irish and American: A Study in Cultural Context*, New York, 1976.

Ernest G. Griffin (ed.), *Eugene O'Neill: A Collection of Criticism*, New York, 1976.

Jean Chothia, *Forging a Language: A Study of the Plays of Eugene O'Neill*, Cambridge, 1979.

Virginia Floyd (ed.), *Eugene O'Neill: A World View*, New York, 1979.

Normand Berlin, *Eugene O'Neill*, London, 1982.

Michael Mannheim, *Eugene O'Neill's New Language of Kinship*, Syracuse, New York, 1982.

John Orlandello, *O'Neill on Film*, Rutherford, New Jersey, 1982.

James A. Robinson, *Eugene O'Neill and Oriental Thought*, Carbondale, Illinois, 1982.

Chaman Ahuja, *Tragedy, Modern Temper, and O'Neill*, Delhi, 1984.

Horst Frenz and Susan Tuck (eds.), *Eugene O'Neill's Critics: Voices from Abroad*, Carbondale, Illinois, 1984.

James J. Martine (ed.), *Critical Essays on Eugene O'Neill*, Boston, 1984.

Margaret L. Ranald, *The Eugene O'Neill Companion*, Westport, Connecticut, 1984.

Judith E. Barlow, *Final Acts: The Creation of Three Late O'Neill Plays*, Athens, Georgia, 1985.

Foster Hirsch, *Eugene O'Neill: Life, Work, and Criticism*, Fredericton, New Brunswick, 1986.

Harold Bloom (ed.), *Eugene O'Neill: Modern Critical Views*, New York, 1987.

Virginia Floyd, *The Plays of Eugene O'Neill: A New Assessment*, New York, 1987.

Hari M. Prasad, *The Dramatic Art of Eugene O'Neill*, New Delhi, 1987.

Shyamal Bagchee (ed.), *Perspectives on O'Neill: New Essays*, Victoria, 1988.

Laurin R. Porter, *The Banished Prince: Time, Memory, and Ritual in the Late Plays of Eugene O'Neill*, Ann Arbor, Michigan, 1988.

Edward L. Shaughnessy, *Eugene O'Neill in Ireland: The Critical Reception*, Westport, Connecticut, 1988.

John H. Stroupe (ed.), *Critical Approaches to O'Neill*, New York, 1988.

Ronald H. Wainscott, *Staging O'Neill: The Experimental Years 1920–1934*, New Haven, Connecticut, 1988.

Normand Berlin (ed.), *Eugene O'Neill: Three Plays: A Collection of Critical Essays*, London, 1989.

Mark Kobernick, *Semiotics of the Drama and the Style of Eugene O'Neill*, Philadelphia, 1989.

Edwin J. McDonough, *Quintero Directs O'Neill . . . 1956–1981*, Ann Arbor, Michigan, 1989.

Marc Maufort (ed.), *Eugene O'Neill and the Emergence of American Drama*, Amsterdam, 1989.

Carol Olin (ed.), *Eugene O'Neill Centennial Colloquium*, Pueblo, Colorado, 1989.

Mark W. Estrin (ed.), *Conversation with O'Neill*, Jackson, Mississippi, 1990.

Richard F. Moorton (ed.), *Eugene O'Neill's Century: Centennial Views on America's Foremost Tragic Dramatist*, New York, 1991.

Serials

Eugene O'Neill Newsletter, 1977–88; as *Eugene O'Neill Review*, 1989—

* * *

The author of over 60 completed and partly written plays, Eugene O'Neill brought high seriousness to the American drama. From the beginning of his career, he reacted against the escapist theatre of his actor-father, epitomized by James O'Neill Sr.'s financially successful role as Edmond Dantès in *The Count of Monte Cristo*.

From the earliest plays (produced at the Provincetown Playhouse, Massachusetts, and its New York City theatre) O'Neill presented the perennial cosmic theme, humanity's powerlessness before fate. This is shown in enslavement to the sea in the S.S. Glencairn plays, *Ile*, and *Anna Christie*. But equally as important, O'Neill continually insisted on the need of an artist to honor and use his gift. Throughout the O'Neill canon, denial of one's talent causes destruction of the individual, from Robert Mayo in *Beyond the Horizon*, O'Neill's first Broadway success, to Simon Harford in *A Touch of the Poet*. This theme is also the basis of other plays in that proposed saga of American acquisitiveness, "A Tale of Possessors, Self-Dispossessed".

Another important O'Neill theme is that of "belonging", and this shades into nostalgia for a pre-mechanistic past—the days of sail, for instance. He excoriates the depersonalization of the individual in modern society, particularly in the expressionistic drama *The Hairy Ape*, in which Yank, the servant and apostle of the machine, is psychologically castrated by a female member of the ruling class in a mere seven words: "Take me away! Oh! The filthy beast!". This play is the only one in which the politics of class struggle are fully relevant, though two other works, *The Personal Equation* and *The Reckoning* (published 1988) are concerned with aspects of trade unionism.

O'Neill was a pioneer in theatrical race relations. His very early one-act play *Thirst* had a West-Indian mulatto sailor, played by O'Neill himself, as one of the three characters on a life raft, while a second one-acter, *The Dreamy Kid*, concerned a small-time black gangster. This was the first occasion on which a white company hired an entire company of black actors to play black roles. *The Emperor Jones* went further by making use of integrated casting. Charles Gilpin, a black actor, created the central role in this Jungian-influenced expressionistic monologue portraying African-American history in reverse. Gilpin's success led to a partial opening of the doors to professional theatre for African-American actors.

Even more controversial was *All God's Chillun Got Wings*, recounting the marriage of the white girl, Ella Downey, to the

African-American Jim Harris. Though this play caused a furore of prejudice on its original production, race relations are not its true theme, which, once again, is that of the artist-figure, here the ambitious law student, Jim Harris, who is thwarted and destroyed by his wife's possessiveness and lack of understanding.

Ever the experimenter, O'Neill now turned to masks, and with *The Great God Brown* he offered his first fully masked play. He had already used an African mask in *All God's Chillun* as a means of showing the threat offered to the white, effete Ella Downey by Jim's alien and elemental world. In *The Hairy Ape* he had employed masks in the Fifth Avenue expressionistic scene, at the suggestion of Blanche Hays, the costume designer; but in *The Great God Brown* he wished to develop "a drama of souls" to gain "insight into the inner forces motivating the actions and reactions of men and women". As O'Neill himself put it, "one's outer life passes in a solitude haunted by the masks of others; one's inner life passes in a solitude haunted by the masks of oneself" (in his "Memoranda on Masks").

With *Lazarus Laughed*, a "play for an imaginative theatre", in four acts, eight scenes, and over 420 roles, O'Neill used masks for all characters except Lazarus, who celebrates life, having no fear of death. In this play, which goes beyond the economic limits of the professional theatre, and has, at the time of writing, yet to achieve a fully professional performance, he tried to recreate ritual theatre, analogous to that which grew out of the ancient worship of Dionysus, which could serve again as "practical interpretation and celebration of life". Later, in *Days Without End*, he returned to the use of masks to distinguish the protagonist John from his antagonist *alter ego*, Loving.

O'Neill tested his theories of drama in the further experimental plays *The Fountain* and *Marco Millions*. With the sympathetic co-operation of Kenneth Macgowan as director, and Robert Edmond Jones as scene designer, he aimed at presenting total theatre, or plastic theatre, pressing on the limits of the stage, and applying imaginative techniques to dramatic form, theme, and scenic design. Ambitiously, he now wished to educate his audience in philosophy through a comprehensive theatrical experience. These plays, along with *Lazarus Laughed*, are all intellectually and speculatively important, but are only stageable in the theatre of the mind, even though O'Neill showed in them some of his best writing and deepest poetic thought, in attempting a synthesis of history, satire, religion, reconciliation, and love.

His next technical experiment was the nine-act drama *Strange Interlude*, which dealt openly with the taboo subjects of abortion and adultery. Here, O'Neill later wished he had used masks, but instead employed interior monologue to convey the secret thoughts of the protagonists. Thus, the double action portrays outward reality contrasted with inward contemplation and evaluation of that reality. Conflicts, then, are both overt and psychic as O'Neill also played with time, projecting the final act 17 years beyond the date of the play's original production. The true theme is the psychological life of woman in the three manifestations imaged by O'Neill—mother, wife, mistress-whore—within a dramatic structure of gestation and the eternal return.

O'Neill's tragic vision, with its solid grounding in the resonances of myth, naturally led him to attempt the creation of a new, original mythology to reflect the concerns of the 20th century, a task that occupied him for the remainder of his life. Two plays, *Desire Under the Elms* and *Dynamo*, demonstrate O'Neill as an excellent *myth user*, but less successful as *myth maker*. Consequently, it is something of a tragedy for American drama that he spent so much of his productive life endeavoring to produce the ultimate myth of acquisitive American civilization in his proposed 11-play cycle "A Tale of Possessors, Self-Dispossessed".

In *Mourning Becomes Electra*, his next experiment in mythology, O'Neill recreated the classical trilogy format in its three full-length plays, *The Homecoming*, *The Hunted*, and *The Haunted*. Here, as with his larger experiments in total theatre, *The Fountain* and *Lazarus Laughed*, O'Neill appealed to the theatre of the mind, rather than the limitations of the professional stage. In this work, his most creative employment and amalgamation of diverse myths, he used the fate of the House of Atreus as a basis, deliberately adapting the myth to an archetypal American time and place, fashioning "a modern drama in which the Greek fates are replaced by forces which are more comprehensible in an age without religion and without commitment to gods".

O'Neill then turned to myth-making. After the completion of *Marco Millions* he began to think in terms of a trilogy to be called "Myth-Plays for the God-Forsaken". Here he hoped to reforge a modern belief independent of established religions, and suitable for a world that had lost its spiritual way. He set out to reveal the sickness of materialistic American society as he attacked "repressive organized religion with its fear of human sexuality and physicality". In the first of these plays, *Dynamo*, O'Neill seized on the suggestion of Henry Adams in "The Dynamo and the Virgin" that for the 20th century the force and energy of the dynamo are analogous to the medieval cultural and constructive creativity generated by worship of the Virgin. O'Neill portrayed the fate of young Reuben Light who worships the dynamo as his anthropomorphic earth mother/goddess and is destroyed by it, perhaps because he is unworthy. After the unsuccessful *Days Without End*, the second play of this abortive trilogy, O'Neill abandoned the project.

However, *Days Without End* represents a development that led to the last cycle, "A Tale of Possessors, Self-Dispossessed", which "planned to use the saga of one family to illustrate the central theme of the corrupting influence of possessions upon their owners" (see *The Eugene O'Neill Companion*); and more than coincidentally, it emphasizes a series of marriages and family dramas in much the same way as O'Neill finally used his own family to create a new mythology of human relationships.

Familial relationships are, in fact, a central thematic strand of much of O'Neill's work, from *Bread and Butter* and *Servitude*; in the latter a major theme is "Servitude in love! Love in servitude!". This is taken up in *Welded*, *The First Man*, by Elsa Loving in *Days Without End*, and by both Nora and Sara Melody in *A Touch of the Poet*, though later, in *More Stately Mansions*, Sara displays the acquisitive, sensual side of her personality. But O'Neill's family members are almost invariably at each other's throats—except in *Ah, Wilderness!*, a traditionally sentimental, comedic exercise in wish-fulfilled remembrance.

Even *The Iceman Cometh* is a kind of familial drama, because the denizens of the "Last Chance Bar" form a community which is temporarily shattered by the intrusion of Theodore Hickman, who brings death and disruption to those who are bonded by their withdrawal from life. Conversely, *Hughie*, a self-contained monologue, features, in "Erie" Smith, a character who is trying to reach out, "to belong", one who, like the characters of *The Iceman Cometh* and Cornelius Melody in *A Touch of the Poet*, takes refuge in the Ibsenesque "saving lie" to continue living. In effect, all "these last plays continue the theme of the mask which hides the psychic identity of the individual . . . while the action shows characters being stripped of pretense" (see *The Eugene*

O'Neill Companion).

With his Pulitzer Prize-winning *Long Day's Journey Into Night* and *A Moon for the Misbegotten*, O'Neill developed his personal, psychological myth-making into high art, paradoxically by returning to realistic techniques. With selective memory, he whitewashed himself by omitting his first marriage, and made peace with his father and brother, paying tribute to their idiosyncrasies, while sympathizing with their weaknesses. However, he never forgave his mother. She remains unhistorically unsalvable, just as the portrait of James O'Neill as irremediable alcoholic and miser is untrue. Indeed, O'Neill seems never to have appreciated the struggle Ella O'Neill underwent in overcoming her addiction to morphine. But then again, his attitude towards women throughout the plays is flawed. For him, woman is virgin/mother/whore, one who must serve man: Josie Hogan in *A Moon for the Misbegotten* is her earth-mother epitome as she cradles Jamie's head in her lap in a Pietà.

Ironically, by the end of his working life, O'Neill had become disenchanted with the theatre—*Hughie* was the only completed play of another projected series, entitled "By Way of Obit". Each of the proposed eight monologue-plays was meant to consist of one scene, with one character and one life-size marionette, the Good Listener. The reactions of this listener, if one can take *Hughie* as representative, are almost entirely non-verbal, and clues to his reactions are in the stage directions, rather than in the dialogue.

"Eclectic to a fault" (as one critic, Christopher Bigsby, has described O'Neill) and permanently experimental, O'Neill's distinguishing characteristics include high seriousness, contrived mass effects, heavy use of irony, melodramatic situations, sardonic humour, imaginative intellectual exploration, and genuine dramatic talent. In his synthesis of myth, past and present, he was pre-eminently successful in giving to the American theatre a unique sense of the tragic human condition.

—Margaret Loftus Ranald

See also *Volume 1* entires on *Desire Under the Elms*; *The Emperor Jones*; *The Great God Brown*; *The Hairy Ape*; *The Iceman Cometh*; *Long Day's Journey Into Night*; *Mourning Becomes Electra*.

ÖRKÉNY, István. Born in Budapest, Hungary, 5 April 1912. Educated at Piarist Gymnasium, Budapest, to 1930; also trained as a chemical engineer and pharmacist. Contributed articles to various literary magazines during the 1930's; drafted into a forced-labour unit during World War II; captured, 1943, and held prisoner in the Soviet Union until 1947; on return to Hungary, became dramaturg at the Ifjúsági Színház [Youth Theatre], 1949–51, and at the Hungarian People's Army Theatre, 1951–53; his support for the liberalisation made him fall into disfavour after 1956; employed in a chemical works in the 1960's, and could not publish any writings, 1958–66; rehabilitated in the late 1960's; first-produced play, *Tóték* [The Tót Family], staged 1967. Recipient: Attila József Prize, 1967; Kossuth Prize, 1973. Died in Budapest, 24 June 1979.

Works

Collections

Időrendben: Szinművek [Plays in Chronological Order] (includes the plays *Voronyezs; Tóték; Sötet galamb; Macskajáték; Pisti a vérzivatarban*). 1972.
Élőszóval: Drámák (includes all his original plays). 1978.
Művei [Works] (9 vols.). 1980–86; plays, screenplays, and television plays in Volumes 1–3 (*Drámák*), 1982.

Stage Works

Tóték [The Tót Family], from his story (produced Thália Szinház, Budapest, 1967). In *Időrendben: Szinművek*, 1972.
Voronyezs (televised 1969). 1969.
Sötét galamb [Dark Dove] (produced Nemzeti Színház, Budapest, 1970). In *Időrendben: Szinművek*, 1972.
Macskajáték, from his story (produced Szigligeti Színház, 1971). In *Időrendben: Szinművek*, 1972; translated as *Catsplay*, 1976.
Pisti a vérzivatarban [Stevie in the Bloodstorm] (produced Pesti Színház, Budapest, 1979). In *Időrendben: Szinművek*, 1972.
A holtak hallgatása [The Deadly Silence] (produced Pesti Színház, Budapest, 1973). In *Élőszával: Drámák*, 1978.
Vérrokonok [Blood Relatives] (produced Pesti Színház, Budapest, 1974). In *Élőszóval Drámák*, 1978.
Kulcskeresők [Keysearchers] (produced Szigligeti Színház, 1975; Nemzeti Színház, Budapest, 1977). In *Előszóval: Drámák*, 1978.
A falu rossza, from a play by Ede Tóth. In *Drámák 3*, 1982.
Zsugori uram, from a play by Molière. In *Drámák 3*, 1982.

Screenplays

Isten hozta, örnagy úr!, 1969; *Macskajáték* [Catsplay], 1974; *Forgatókönyv* [Screenplay] (published 1979); *Babik* (published in *Drámák 3*, 1982).

Television Plays

Voronyezs, 1969; *A Hanákné-ügy* and *Egy szakmai siker modellje* (both published in *Drámák 3*, 1982).

Fiction

Budai bojt (stories). 1948.
Koránkelő emberek. 1952.
Jerusalem Hercegnoje. 1966.
Nászutasok a Légypapiron. 1967.
A flocsek bukása. 1968.
Egyperces novellák. 1968; translated as *Minuten Novellen/One Minute Stories* (bilingual German and English edition), 1979.
Időrendben: Novellák [Stories in Chronological Order]. 1971.
Időrendben: Archépek, korképek. 1973.
Időrendben: Regények [Novellas in Chronological Order] (includes *Glória; Macskajáték; Tóték*). 1974.
Rózsakiállítás. 1977.
Az utolsó vonat (includes stories and novellas). 1977.

Fiction collected in Volumes 1–2 and 4–8 of *Művei*, 1980–86.

Other

Négyeskönyv (miscellany).   1987.

*

Criticism

Articles:
Anna B. Katona, "Ideological Implications of Absurd Drama", in *Theatre Annual*, 42, 1987.

* * *

István Örkény was a pharmacist and a chemical engineer who began writing short stories in the late 1930's. His writing talent blossomed during five years as a prisoner of war in Russia, and he published several volumes shortly after his return in 1946. However, despite considering himself a communist, he was regularly rebuked by the Party's cultural authorities. Consequently, he became a leading proponent of change during the "thaw" after 1953, culminating in open opposition to the Party and active encouragement of the 1956 Revolution. He was silenced from 1958, and although he continued writing, he did not publish again until 1966.

Beginning in 1957, he dramatized several of his novels, becoming the earliest Hungarian playwright to work in the absurdist tradition (labelled "grotesque" in Hungary). The first of these plays to be staged—and extremely successfully—was *Tóték* (The Tót Family), which deals with the value of insanity as an escape from the relative sanity of blind obedience. In it, a family opens its home to the Major, their son's commander, who is on leave from the front on account of his nervous exhaustion. In order to assure the welfare of their son (unbeknownst to them, he is already dead), they do everything in their power to please the visitor. But instead of restful leisure in the health-inducing mountain air, the Major needs and demands "order", represented by feverish makework activity, keeping the family awake all night, and not tolerating yawns. Meanwhile he hears insults which, in fact, are never uttered. When no longer able to tolerate the imposed "sane" order, Mr. Tót abruptly, and brutally, puts an end to it and the Major.

During this time Örkény began publishing his "one minute short-stories", also marked by a poignant grotesque tone. Produced in 1969, *Sötét galamb* (Dark Dove) did not match the first play's success. On the other hand, *Macskajáték* (Catsplay), a tale of two sisters separated by countries (and regimes) as well as by their personalities, told in a series of dramatized letters, proved to be more popular both at home and abroad than *Tóték*. Meanwhile film versions of both these plays were made: *Isten hozta, örnagy úr!* (Welcome, Major!) in 1969, and *Macskajáték* (Catsplay), in 1974.

Örkény's next play, *Vérrokonok* (Blood Relatives), dealt with a bitter family feud that contained unmistakeable allusions to the national trauma under the Kádár regime. Although written earlier, *Pisti a vérzivatarban* (Stevie in the Bloodstorm) was not deemed appropriate for performance by the authorities for years, yet stirred a great deal of public debate on the basis of widespread private reading in MS form. Production of this semi-autobiographical World War II odyssey, which blends epic and absurd traditions, was finally realized only months before the author's death of cancer.

—Robert K. Sarlós

ORTON, Joe. Born John Kingsley Orton in Leicester, England, 1 January 1933. Educated at Clark's College, Leicester, 1945–47; Royal Academy of Dramatic Art, London (Leicester Educational Committee grant), 1951–53, diploma 1953. Lived with Kenneth Halliwell, from 1953. Amateur actor, Leicester and London, 1949–51; assistant stage manager, Ipswich Repertory Company, Suffolk, 1953; worked part-time in Cadbury's chocolate factory, London, 1957–59; served six-month prison term with Halliwell (for theft of and malicious damage to library books), Wormwood Scrubs Prison, London, and Eastchurch Prison, Sheerness, Kent, 1962; first stage play, *Entertaining Mr. Sloane*, produced 1964; travelled with Halliwell to Morocco, 1967. Murdered by Halliwell at their home in London, 9 August 1967.

Works

Collections

The Complete Plays.   1976.

Stage Works

Entertaining Mr. Sloane (produced New Arts Theatre, London, 1964).
Loot (produced Arts Theatre, Cambridge, 1965; revised version produced Jeanetta Cochrane Theatre, London, 1966).   1967.
The Ruffian on the Stair, from the radio play (produced as part of *Crimes of Passion*, Royal Court Theatre, London, 1967).   In *Crimes of Passion*, 1967.
The Erpingham Camp, from the television play (produced as part of *Crimes of Passion*, Royal Court Theatre, London, 1967).   In *Crimes of Passion*, 1967.
What the Butler Saw (produced Queen's Theatre, London, 1969).   1969.
Until She Screams (sketch), in *Oh! Calcutta!* (produced The Roundhouse, London 1970).   In *Evergreen Review*, May 1970.

Screenplays

Up Against It: A Screenplay for the Beatles (published 1979).

Television Plays

The Erpingham Camp, 1966; *The Good and Faithful Servant*, 1967, and *Funeral Games*, 1968 (published together, 1970).

Radio Plays

The Ruffian on the Stair, 1964.

Fiction

Head to Toe.   1971.

Memoirs and Letters

The Diaries, edited by John Lahr.   1986.

*

Criticism

Books:
John Lahr, *Prick Up Your Ears: The Biography of Joe Orton*, London and New York, 1978.

Joe Orton in front of the collage-poster created by Kenneth Halliwell (1966).

C.W.E. Bigsby, *Joe Orton*, London, 1982.

Maurice Charney, *Joe Orton*, London and New York, 1984 (Macmillan Modern Dramatists series).

Peter Walcot, "An Acquired Taste: Joe Orton and the Greeks", in *Legacy of Thespis*, edited by Karelisa V. Hartigan, Lanham, Maryland, 1984.

Simon Shepherd, *Because We're Queers: The Life and Crimes of Kenneth Halliwell and Joe Orton*, London, 1988.

Leslie Smith, *Modern British Farce*, Totowa, New Jersey, 1989.

*   *   *

As a consequence of journalists' insistence on viewing his life and work as an emblem of the anarchic spirit of the "Swinging Sixties", Joe Orton's brief but meteoric career as a comic playwright is still the subject of serious misinterpretation. Voyeuristic interest in the more exotic details of his homosexual exploits has coloured critical responses to his plays, leading critics to treat them as the mischievous clowning of an egocentric immoralist. This persona was, in fact, assiduously cultivated by Orton himself as an ironic rejoinder to the puritanical outcries which his unsparing exposure of middle-class prejudice and hypocrisy habitually provoked.

A heavily biographical interpretation of the plays not only runs counter to Orton's overt statements of satiric intent, but also ignores the social criticism which motivates the structure of every play from *Entertaining Mr. Sloane* to *What the Butler Saw*. The truth is that, as with most satirical writers, Orton's work is the product of a kind of righteous anger at personal

and social hypocrisy, revealing him as something of a moralist, albeit an unconventional one. As a homosexual man, he was inevitably forced to confront the homophobia and misogyny produced by a patriarchal culture, and was not content merely to dramatise the spectacle of an absurd universe in an apparent state of entropy. The shocking counterpoint of witty speech and violent action in the plays constitutes a calculated and often savage attack on the false moralisms of post-war British society. Although the style of the plays may encourage critics to treat them as examples of "camp", in fact they represent a consistent comic strategy aimed at exposing the contradictions inherent in Western capitalist societies.

Orton was quite conscious of what he was doing: "To be destructive, words must be irrefutable. Print was less effective than the spoken word because the blast was greater. . . . But if you could lock the enemy into a room somewhere, and fire the sentence at them you could get a sort of seismic disturbance" (from "The Vision of Gombold Proval", published posthumously as *Head to Toe*). These words almost constitute a programme for his work as a commercial playwright creating subversive comedies for middle-brow audiences.

While many plays of the early 1960's—the so-called "angry young men"—were following John Osborne's in launching direct rhetorical broadsides against the class inequalities and hypocrisies of a Britain struggling to find a post-colonial role in world affairs, Orton's first two plays, *The Ruffian on the Stair* (written for radio) and *Entertaining Mr. Sloane* revealed him as a disciple of Harold Pinter. The detailed naturalistic evocation of a shabby middle-class milieu in each play, and the blend of menace and comedy characteristic of the stage thriller, inevitably remind one of Pinter's early plays.

But it is characteristic of Orton that, even when most obviously influenced by the already established Pinter, a certain tendency towards conscious parody manifests itself. Here the traditions of witty writing absorbed through Orton's close reading of Wilde and the camp satirical novelist, Ronald Firbank, are noticeable. By choosing to engineer a comic collision between the working-class, or lower-middle-class, style and milieu of early Pinter, and the upper-class comedy-of-manners idiom, Orton invented his own entirely original comic form. The manner in which his "wide boy" characters rationalise their louche behaviour in the epigrammatic style of Welfare State dandies produces explosive comedy; likewise, the banal pseudo-morality of his respectable middle-aged, middle-class hypocrites and megalomaniac authority figures is funny because their idiom—the debased language of the tabloid press—is revealed to be morally bankrupt and in a perpetual state of self-contradiction. The more energetically these characters attempt to repress or conceal their real motives through pseudo-Wildean witticisms, the more nakedly is their cupidity and lust exposed for what it is. These middle-aged hypocrites are 1960's versions of Wilde's Lady Bracknell, jealously devoting themselves to censuring in others the ruthless egotism they cultivate in themselves.

In his second play, *Entertaining Mr. Sloane* (his first stage play), Orton developed this technique of subverting the stylistic expectations evoked by the opening milieu to create a parody of middle-brow entertainment (well-made West End thriller), which so closely approximates to the real thing that the subversion of middle-class values is often either perceived as genuinely immoral or, alternatively, as a light-hearted pastiche. The proprieties of middle-class commercial theatre are maintained throughout the play in respect of the naturalistic setting and stage business. But from the opening conversation between the landlady, Kath, and her prospective lodger, Sloane, which plays with the relationship between social politeness and sexual flirtation ("The bedroom was perfect", remarks Sloane), the dialogue teases the audience into a comic recognition of the gulf separating the characters' true motives from their reflexes of social behaviour.

By the end of the play, everything in this lower-middle-class world is the opposite of what it had appeared to be: the innocent young lodger is a callous murderer and bisexual prostitute; the kind and matronly landlady is his mistress, prepared to use blackmail to retain his sexual favours; her brother, the apparently respectable and macho businessman, Ed, is revealed as homosexual and totally without scruple in concealing Sloane's murder of his father from the police; even the seemingly pathetic old father, Kemp, is shown to be malicious and potentially violent. The ending, in which Kath and Ed unceremoniously agree to share Sloane, is a calculated affront to the sentimental expectation that in the real world such criminal immorality would be discovered and punished.

With *Loot*, *The Erpingham Camp* (made for television), and *What the Butler Saw*, Orton made a distinctive contribution to modern British drama by fusing his unique linguistic style with the structure of farce. Characters and situation combine in each of the plays to generate action which serves as a wild kinetic and visual accompaniment to the explosive effects of the dialogue.

Loot makes the drab milieu of shabby lower-middle-class gentility the scene of a black farce whose dynamic arises from the contradiction between the surface respectability of the McLeavy household and the anarchic stage business which works as so many permutations of the basic gag, involving the substitution of the stolen cash for the corpse of Mrs. McLeavy in the coffin. While replacing the well-made-play/comedy-of-manners formula of *Entertaining Mr. Sloane* with a farce plot, Orton's master-stroke is the introduction of an actual representative of institutional authority in the person of Inspector Truscott. Unlike Ed, in that he is a member of the CID, and therefore *does* represent the repressive force of social order, Truscott is as arbitrary as Ed in employing the mask of authority to hide his own corrupt motives. Farce conventions allow Orton the possibility of elaborating the contradictions within each character so that the action assumes the surrealistic playfulness of *The Importance of Being Earnest* while maintaining a wholly naturalistic anchor in the banal clichés of the lower-middle-class suburban scene.

The highly original holiday camp setting of *The Erpingham Camp* permits the development of the *Loot* formula in an even more anarchic manner: in running his camp, Erpingham aims to control the way every holidaymaker achieves pleasure. Society's tendency towards rampant authoritarianism extends to include every aspect of social life. The absurd and degrading attempts of the camp officers to entertain the campers become pointless strategies for social control, the officers collaborating to reinforce Erpingham's megalomaniacal vision of himself as a peculiarly British tyrant. The terrible, though more-or-less unintentional, revenge wrought on the camp authorities by the campers constitutes a hilarious parody of Euripides' *The Bacchae*. The camper's anarchic individualism is expressed through a mask of self-righteous moralism, just as the puritanical desire of the institutional authority to discipline and punish is presented as respect for a civilised order.

Orton's experiment with a epic form prepared him for *What the Butler Saw*, which is generally regarded as his masterpiece. His last play is a summation of all he had previously achieved—an end-of-the-pier peepshow version of *The Importance of Being Earnest*. The farce formula is here explicitly indicated by the insane-asylum setting, the doors of which function brilliantly to enhance the accelerating con-

fusion that alludes to the type of plot-complication associated with a classic Feydeau farce. The choice of setting is also clearly emblematic of the madness that Orton presents as a function of institutional authority. Motifs used in previous plays are multiplied. One authority figure, the corrupt and psychologically unstable psychiatrist, Dr. Prentice, is set up to be replaced by another psychiatrist, Dr. Rance—who turns out to be an insane megalomaniac who has pretended to be investigating Dr. Prentice as a pretext for gaining scandalous material for a best-seller he is writing!

The exposure of authority figures is reduced to its most primitive slapstick roots by the treatment of the traditional figure of popular entertainment, the policeman, as a ludicrous fall guy. Sergeant Match's complete incompetence is signalled by the loss of his trousers, which causes him, at the end of the play, to have to lead the characters—drugged and weary and bearing aloft the missing parts of a statue of Sir Winston Churchill—out of the locked asylum through a skylight, attired in a leopard-skin dress in a parody of a Dionysian ritual of liberation. By the end of the play, conventional gender categories have been shown to conceal the complexities of sexual identity, just as the normal distinction between sanity and madness has been revealed as totally unreliable. The implication of the ending is highly ambiguous: if Orton is savage in his satirical attack on the structures of society, he is also as sceptical as Euripides with regard to the liberating effects of orgy.

By the age of 34 Orton had achieved wide-ranging re-interpretations of the forms and values of West End theatre. It is tantalising to speculate on how his dramaturgy may have developed had he lived longer than he did.

—Robert Gordon

See also *Volume 1* entries on *Entertaining Mr. Sloane*; *What the Butler Saw*.

OSBORNE, John (James). Born in London, 12 December 1929. Educated at Belmont College, Devon. Married 1) Pamela Lane in 1951 (marriage dissolved 1957); 2) the actress Mary Ure in 1957 (marriage dissolved 1963); 3) the writer Penelope Gilliatt in 1963 (marriage dissolved 1968), one daughter; 4) the actress Jill Bennett in 1968 (marriage dissolved 1977); 5) Helen Dawson in 1978. Journalist, 1947–48; toured as an actor, 1948–49; first-produced play, *The Devil Inside Him*, produced 1950; actor-manager, Ilfracombe Repertory, 1951; also in repertory, as actor and stage manager, in Leicester, Derby, Bridgewater, and London; co-director, Woodfall Films, from 1958; director, Oscar Lewenstein Plays Ltd., London, from 1960. Member of the Council, English Stage Company, based at the Royal Court Theatre, London, 1960–82. Recipient: New York Drama Critics Circle Award, 1958, 1965; Tony Award, 1963; Oscar, for screenplay, 1964. Honorary Doctor, Royal College of Art, London, 1970. Member, Royal Society of Arts.

Works

Collections

Four Plays: West of Suez; A Patriot for Me; Time Present; The Hotel in Amsterdam. 1973.

Stage Works

The Devil Inside Him, with Stella Linden (produced Theatre Royal, Huddersfield, Yorkshire, 1950).
Personal Enemy, with Anthony Creighton (produced Grand Opera House, Harrogate, Yorkshire, 1955).
Look Back in Anger (produced Royal Court Theatre, London, 1956). 1957.
The Entertainer, music by John Addison (produced Royal Court Theatre, London, 1957). 1957.
Epitaph for George Dillon, with Anthony Creighton (produced Royal Court Theatre, London, 1958). 1958.
The World of Paul Slickey, music by Christopher Whelen (produced Pavilion, Brighton, 1959). 1959.
Luther (produced Royal Court Theatre, London, 1961). 1961.
Plays for England: The Blood of the Bambergs and *Under Plain Cover* (produced Royal Court Theatre, London, 1962). 1963.
Inadmissible Evidence (produced Royal Court Theatre, London, 1964). 1965.
A Patriot for Me (produced Royal Court Theatre, London, 1965). 1966.
A Bond Honoured, from a play by Lope de Vega (produced by the National Theatre, Old Vic, London, 1966). 1966.
The Hotel in Amsterdam (produced Royal Court Theatre, London, 1968). With *Time Present*, 1968.
Time Present (produced Royal Court Theatre, London, 1968). With *The Hotel in Amsterdam*, 1968.
Very Like a Whale (televised 1980). 1971.
West of Suez (produced Royal Court Theatre, London, 1971). 1971.
Hedda Gabler, from the play by Ibsen (produced Royal Court Theatre, London, 1972). 1972.
A Sense of Detachment (produced Royal Court Theatre, London, 1972). 1973.
A Place Calling Itself Rome, from *Coriolanus* by Shakespeare. 1973.
The Picture of Dorian Gray: A Moral Entertainment, from the novel by Oscar Wilde (produced Greenwich Theatre, London, 1975). 1973.
Jill and Jack (as *Ms.; or, Jill and Jack*, televised 1974). With *The End of Me Old Cigar*, 1975.
The End of Me Old Cigar (produced Greenwich Theatre, London, 1975). With *Jill and Jack*, 1975.
Watch it Come Down (produced by the National Theatre, Old Vic, London, 1976). 1975.
The Father, from a play by Strindberg (produced National Theatre, London, 1988). With *Hedda Gabler*, 1989.
Déjà Vu (produced Thorndike Theatre, Leatherhead, 1992). 1990.

Screenplays

Look Back in Anger, with Nigel Kneale, 1959; *The Entertainer*, with Nigel Kneale, 1960; *Tom Jones*, 1963 (published 1964); *Inadmissible Evidence*, 1968; *The Charge of the Light Brigade*, with Charles Wood, 1968.

Television Plays

Billy Bunter, 1952, and *Robin Hood*, 1953 (*For the Children* series); *A Matter of Scandal and Concern*, 1960; *The Right Prospectus*, 1970 (published 1970); *The Gift of Friendship*, 1972 (published 1972); *Ms.; or, Jill and Jack*, 1974; *Almost a Vision*, 1976; *You're Not Watching Me Mummy*, 1980 (published with *Try a Little Tenderness*, 1978); *Very Like a Whale*,

1980; *A Better Class of Person*, and *God Rot Tunbridge Wells*, 1985 (published together, 1985).

Memoirs and Letters

A Better Class of Person: An Autobiography 1929–1956. 1981.
Almost a Gentleman (volume 2 of his autobiography). 1991.

*

Bibliographies

Cameron Northouse and Thomas P. Walsh, *John Osborne: A Reference Guide*, Boston, 1974.

Criticism

Books:
John Russell Taylor, *Anger and After*, London, 1962; as *The Angry Theatre* (US edition), 1962; revised edition 1969.
Ronald Hayman, *John Osborne*, London, 1968.
Martin Banham, *John Osborne*, Edinburgh, 1969.
Simon Trussler, *The Plays of John Osborne: An Assessment*, London, 1969.
Simon Trussler, *John Osborne*, London, 1969.
Alan Carter, *John Osborne*, Edinburgh, 1969.
John Russell Brown, *Theatre Language: A Study of Arden, Osborne, and Pinter, and Wesker*, London and New York, 1972.
Harold Ferrar, *John Osborne*, New York, 1973.
Michael Anderson, *Anger and Detachment: A Study of Arden, Osborne, and Pinter*, London, 1976.
Herbert Goldstone, *Coping with Vulnerability: The Achievement of John Osborne*, Washington, DC, 1982.
Malcolm Page (ed.), *File on Osborne*, London, 1988.
Arnold P. Hinchcliffe, *John Osborne*, Boston, 1984.

* * *

Although John Osborne has an unassailable place in theatrical history, the critical view of his work remains uncertain. He is the most directly confrontational English dramatist of the century, offending the audience in his declared determination to make people *feel*, and resisting assimilation to the polite complacency of middle-class society.

The first of his plays to be performed, *Look Back in Anger*, was the harbinger of the most abundant and vigorous development of new play writing in the English theatre since the 17th century. It was a clear sign of the effect of the post-war reorganisation of the theatre with government support, administered by the Arts Council, and the corresponding vision of George Devine, founder of the English Stage Company, to nurture a new, native drama at the Royal Court Theatre. The play came at a time when British political life seemed to be in the doldrums, with little perceptible difference between the political parties: as a result the hub of radical change was located in a theatre in Sloane Square. The impact of the play on its audiences led to the broadcasting of an excerpt on television, and the subsequent effect at the box office turned the financial tide in the theatre's favour; and the existence of a new, enormously wide audience for visual drama had to be recognised.

Osborne had recorded social changes which had hardly penetrated the general consciousness and had certainly not been reflected in the theatre before, and his play, in turn, became an instrument of change. It showed how out of touch with contemporary life was the current repertoire of the West End theatres, the extent to which observation had faded into convention, and the very limited area of British society which was represented on the stage; it forced into existence a new school of actors whose working-class origins and regional accents were valued, not to be buried under Kensington or classical stage speech and manners; and for society at large it made articulate the hooligan protest threatening its break-up, but did not condemn it.

Osborne continued to bring an element of shock and danger into the theatre. *The World of Paul Slickey*, a play about journalism, aroused such fury from the press, intent on defending its own, that the production—unprotected by the Royal Court umbrella and the stubbornness of George Devine—was brought to a premature close. Missiles were thrown at the actors in *A Sense of Detachment. Watch it Come Down*, commissioned by the National Theatre, provoked individual members of the audience to shout at the stage or walk out ostentatiously, as *Look Back in Anger* had done. Although not all his plays have aroused hostility, he has remained unpredictable and a forceful conductor of the current of violence in society, even through the barrier of the small screen, as in the ironically titled *Try a Little Tenderness*. (Osborne's television plays are as seriously to be reckoned with as his stage plays.) Not surprisingly, the Lord Chamberlain's blue pencil was active on Osborne's scripts, and they formed a test case in the campaign which eventually brought theatre censorship in Britain to an end in 1968.

However sardonically adopted, the general title, *Plays for England*, given to *The Blood of the Bambergs* and *Under Plain Cover*, proclaims Osborne's recognition of the public nature of theatre. In *The Entertainer*, he set up his own versions of Brechtian distancing and distortion to expose the tawdriness of a contemporary Britain embarked on a belated imperialist conflict over the Suez Canal: the Royal Court stage was transformed by the trappings of a run-down music-hall, and Archie Rice's patter and parodic songs cast the Sloane Square audience in the role of an ignorant public with media-fabricated attitudes to their country and the Welfare State. By the time of *Watch it Come Down* his image of England took the form of a dismantled railway station adapted for living in by a motley crew; and *West of Suez* depicts the doom of the colonial mentality in another distortion of naturalism.

Bernard Shaw's *Heartbreak House* is the most obvious precedent for Osborne's technique of symbolic naturalism, as Shaw's self-appointment as conscience to the nation anticipated Osborne's functioning as troubler of the public. No-one since Shaw had dared make the long monologue a main feature of his plays, though it must be said that Osborne's monologues carry an emotional weight rare in Shaw. Reviewers generally associated *Luther* with Brecht's use of history in *Galileo*; but Osborne's technique in this play is closer to Shaw's in *Saint Joan* than to Brecht's, as is his interpretation of the central figure. However, *The World of Paul Slickey*, criticised by some for an inappropriate use of the middle-class form of the musical, in fact renewed a tradition from the Brecht-Weill *Threepenny Opera*, and its Auden-Isherwood derivatives, and pioneered an explosion of "alternative" versions of the form.

Osborne has revealed that it was the image of an army ball in drag (the scene which provoked a ban on public performance of the play) which dominated his shaping of *A Patriot for Me*, an audacious parody of a society fixed in the uniform of authoritarian repression as a society in fancy dress, at once

flaunting and denying its secrets. The mocking transformation becomes ambivalent, as the transvestite ball also suggests a celebration of the ultimate dissidence of being human. Sexual ambivalence is not unusual in his work, and has been a main source of critical perplexity. *The Hotel in Amsterdam*, in which Osborne keeps his usual dominant character off-stage and presents only the ensemble of those he dominates, has been under-realised when the corrosive acid within the blandness is not released.

Kenneth Tynan, the influential critic who championed Osborne's *Luther* and *A Patriot for Me* against a savage assault by the American Mary McCarthy, responded to a revival of *Look Back in Anger* by deciding that Osborne had never been a political revolutionary, but was chiefly concerned with intimate emotional relationships—most evident in *Inadmissible Evidence*—and nostalgia for the manners and values of Edwardian England. This revised view has been widely accepted. Certainly Osborne is not a dramatist of political ideas. The power of his plays derives more from an intuitive dissidence and a willingness to write more out of the pain and rage of being alive than from ideology, logical argument, or mastery of form (obviously flawed in many of his plays). The guilt and self-hatred of the dissident figure, a Jimmy Porter, Archie Rice, Bill Maitland in *Inadmissible Evidence*, George Holyoake in *A Matter of Scandal and Concern*, or the archetypal dissident, Luther, are inseparable, in Osborne's plays, from the contempt and satiric rancour most of them turn on society.

His plays have provided many rewarding roles for leading actors: playing Archie Rice gave a new direction to Olivier's career; Bill Maitland made a star of Nicol Williamson; Albert Finney (as Luther), Richard Burton (as Holyoake), and a series of talented actors from Kenneth Haigh to Kenneth Branagh who have played Jimmy Porter have enhanced their reputations through Osborne's roles, while the female equivalent of Jimmy Porter, Pamela in *Time Present*, was one of a number of parts Osborne wrote for his then wife, Jill Bennett.

—Margery Morgan

See also *Volume 1* entries on *The Entertainer*; *Look Back in Anger*.

OSTROVSKY, Alexander Nikolayevich. Born in Moscow, 31 March 1823 (Old Style). Educated at the First Moscow Gymnasium, 1835–40; University of Moscow, studying law, 1840–43 (did not take degree). Married 1) Agafya Ivanovna (surname unknown) in 1849 (died 1865); 2) the actress Maria Vasileva in 1869. Entered the civil service, 1843: clerk in commercial court, Moscow, 1843–51 (lost post on account of police surveillance, following his satirical playwriting); thereafter professional playwright; first play, *Bankrut* [*The Bankrupt*], published 1847; editor and critic, *Moskvityanin* [The Muscovite], 1850–51, and several of his early plays published in this journal; first-produced play, *Ne v svoi sani ne sadis!* [Keep to Your Own Sledge!], produced 1853; published many plays for the first time in the periodicals *Sovremennik* [The Contemporary], 1856–66, and *Otechestvennye zapiski* [Annals of the Fatherland], 1868–84; undertook expedition to the sources of the Volga, recording his observations for the Marine Ministry, 1856–57; travelled in

Scene from Vsevolod Meyerhold's 1924 production of *Les* [*The Forest*] by **Alexander Ostrovsky**.

Western Europe, 1862; co-founder, Moscow Arts Circle, 1865; founder and director, the Association of Russian Playwrights and Composers, 1870, and worked for the Imperial Commission on the Theatre; finally granted a state pension by Alexander III, 1884; appointed director of the Moscow Imperial theatres, 1886. Recipient: Uvanov Prize, 1860 and 1863. Died In Shchelykoo [now Ostrovskoe Raion], Kostroma Oblast, 2 June 1886 (Old Style).

Works

Collections

Sochineniya [Works] (2 vols.).   1859.
Sobranie sochineny [Collected Works] (10 vols.).   1874–84.
Polnoe sobranie sochineny [Complete Collected Works], edited by Modest Pisarev.   1904–05.
Plays (includes *It's a Family Affair—We'll Settle it Ourselves; Poverty is No Crime; The Storm; Even the Wise Can Err; More Sinned Against Than Sinning*), translated by G.R. Noyes.   1917.
"Easy Money" and Two Other Plays (includes *Even a Wise Man Stumbles; Wolves and Sheep*), translated by David Magarshack.   1944.
Polnoe sobranie sochineny [Complete Works] (16 vols.), edited by A.I. Reviakin and others.   1949–53.

Stikhotvornye dramy [Verse Plays] (second edition), edited by Lidya Mikhailovna.   1961.
Five Plays (includes *The Scoundrel; It's a Family Affair—We'll Settle it Ourselves; The Forest; The Poor Bride; The Storm*), translated by E.K. Bristow.   1969.
Polnoe sobranie sochineny [Complete Collected Works] (12 vols.).   1973–80.
Plays (includes *Poverty is No Crime; The Storm; Even the Wise Can Err; More Sinned Against Than Sinning*), edited by Margaret Wettlin.   1974.

Stage Works

Publication dates given below are not for single editions: almost all the plays were published first in journals—*Moskvityanin* [The Muscovite] in the early 1850's, *Sovremennik* [The Contemporary], 1856–66, and *Otechestvennye zapiski* [Annals of the Fatherland], 1868–84.

Bankrut [The Bankrupt].   In *Moskovsky gorodskoy listok*, 1847; revised version, as *Svoi lyudi-sochtemsya!* (produced Theatre of the Cadet Corps, Voronezh, 1860).   1850; revised version translated as *It's a Family Affair—We'll Settle it Ourselves*, in *Plays*, 1917.
Semeynaya kartina (produced Alexandrinsky Theatre, St. Petersburg, 1855).   In "Moscow Municipal Bulletin",

March 1847; translated as *A Domestic Picture*, in *A Treasury of Classic Russian Literature*, edited by J. Cournos, 1961.

Neozhidanny sluchay [An Unexpected Event] (produced Alexandrinsky Theatre, St. Petersburg, 1902).   1851.

Ne v svoi sani ne sadis! [Keep to Your Own Sledge!] (produced Maly Theatre, Moscow, 1853).   1853.

Bednaya nevesta (produced Maly Theatre, Moscow, 1853). 1854; translated as *The Poor Bride*, in *Masterpieces of the Russian Drama 1*, edited by G.R. Noyes, 1933; also in *Five Plays*, 1969.

Bednost ne porok (produced Maly Theatre, Moscow, 1854). 1854; translated as *Poverty's No Vice*, in *Plays*, 1917; as *Poverty is No Crime*, in *Plays*, 1974.

Ne tak zhivi, kak khochetsya (produced Maly Theatre, Moscow, 1854).   1854; translated as *You Can't Just Live as You Please*, in *Poet Lore*, 49, 1943.

V chuzhom piru pokhmelye [Hangover from Someone Else's Party] (produced Alexandrinsky Theatre, St. Petersburg, 1863).   1857.

Dokhodnoye mesto [A Profitable Position] (produced Alexandrinsky Theatre, St. Petersburg, 1863).   1857.

Prazdichny son—do obeda [Holiday Dream—Before Dinner] (produced Alexandrinsky Theatre, St. Petersburg, 1857). 1857.

Ne soshlis kharakterami (produced Alexandrinsky Theatre, St. Petersburg, 1858).   1858; translated as *Incompatibility of Temper*, in *The Humour of Russia*, by E. Voynich, 1895.

Vospitannitsa (produced privately, St. Petersburg, 1859; produced publicly, Maly Theatre, Moscow, 1859).   1860; translated as *A Protégée of the Mistress*, in *Plays*, 1917.

Groza (produced Maly Theatre, Moscow, 1859).   In *Biblioteka dlya chteniya* [Readers' Library], January, 1860; translated as *The Thunderstorm*, 1927, and in *World Drama 2*, edited by G.R. Noyes and B.H. Clarke, 1956; as *The Storm*, in *"The Storm" and Other Russian Plays*, translated by David Magarshack, 1960; as *Thunder*, in *Four Russian Plays*, translated by Joshua Cooper, 1972.

Stary drug luchshe novykh dvukh [An Old Friend is Better Than Two New Ones] (produced privately, Krasnovorotsky Theatre, Moscow, 1860; produced publicly, Alexandrinsky Theatre, St. Petersburg, 1860).   1860.

Svoi sobaki gryzutsya, chuzhaya ne pristavay [When Your Dogs Fight, Other Dogs Should Keep Out] (produced Maly Theatre, Moscow, 1861).   1861.

Za chem poydesh, to i naydesh (Zhenitba Balzaminova) [What You Seek You'll Find—Zhenitba's Wedding] (produced Alexandrinsky Theatre, St. Petersburg, 1863). 1861.

Kozma Zacharich Minin, Sukhoruk [From the One-Armed Zakharich Minin] (produced Alexandrinsky Theatre, St. Petersburg, 1866).   1862.

Grekh da beda na kogo ne zhivyot (produced Maly Theatre, Moscow, 1863).   1863; translated as *Sin and Sorrow Are Common To All*, in *Plays*, 1917.

Tyazhelye dni [Hard Times] (produced Maly Theatre, Moscow, 1863).   1863.

Shutniki [Jokers] (produced Alexandrinsky Theatre, St. Petersburg, 1864).   1864.

Voevoda: Son na Volge [Dream on the Volga] (produced Alexandrinsky Theatre, St. Petersburg, 1865).   1865; revised version (produced Maly Theatre, Moscow, 1886). 1890.

Na boykom meste (produced Maly Theatre, Moscow, 1865). 1865; translated as *At the Jolly Spot*, in *Poet Lore*, 36, 1925.

Puchina [Abyss] (produced Maly Theatre, Moscow, 1866). 1866.

Dmitry Samozvanets i Vasily Shuysky [The False Dimitry and Vasily Shuysky] (produced Maly Theatre, Moscow, 1867). 1867.

Tushino [Tushino] (produced Maly Theatre, Moscow, 1867). 1867.

Vasilisa Malentyeva [Vasilisa Malentyeva], with Stepan Gedeonov (produced Maly Theatre, Moscow, 1868). 1868.

Na vsyakogo dovolno prostoty (produced Alexandrinsky Theatre, St. Petersburg, 1868).   1868; translated as *Enough Stupidity in Every Wise Man*, in *Moscow Art Theatre Series of Russian Plays 2*, edited by O.M. Sayler, 1923; as *Even a Wise Man Stumbles*, in *Easy Money* (collection), 1944; as *Diary of a Scoundrel*, 1948 (retitled as *Too Clever by Half*, 1988); as *The Scoundrel*, in *Five Plays*, 1969; as *Even the Wise Can Err*, in *Plays*, 1974.

Goryachee serdtse [The Ardent Heart] (produced Maly Theatre, Moscow, 1869).   1868.

Besheny dengi (produced Alexandrinsky Theatre, St. Petersburg, 1870).   1870; translated as *Fairy Gold*, in *Poet Lore*, 40, 1929; as *Easy Money*, in *Easy Money* (collection), 1944.

Les [The Forest] (produced Alexandrinsky Theatre, St. Petersburg, 1871).   1871; translated as *The Forest*, 1926; several subsequent translations under same title.

Ne vse kot maslenitsa (produced Maly Theatre, Moscow, 1871).   1871; translated as *A Cat Has Not Always Carnival* in *Poet Lore*, 36, 1925.

Ne bylo ni grosha, da vdrug sltyn [Not a Kopeck, Then Suddenly a Rouble] (produced Alexandrinsky Theatre, St. Petersburg, 1872).   1871.

Komik XVII stoletiya [A Comedian of the 17th Century] (produced Maly Theatre, Moscow, 1872).   1873; translated as *The King of Comedy*, 1937.

Snegurochka [The Snow Maiden] (produced Bolshoi Theatre, Moscow, 1873).   1873.

Pozdnyaya lyubov [Late Love] (produced Maly Theatre, Moscow, 1873).   1873.

Trudovoy khleb [Hard-Earned Bread] (produced Maly Theatre, Moscow, 1874).   1874.

Volki i ovtsy (produced Alexandrinsky Theatre, St. Petersburg, 1875).   1875; translated as *Wolves and Sheep*, in *Poet Lore*, 37, 1926, and in *Easy Money* (collection), 1944.

Bogatye nevesty [Rich Brides] (produced Alexandrinsky Theatre, St. Petersburg, 1875).   1876.

Pravda khorosho, a schastye luchshe [The Truth is Good, But Happiness is Better] (produced Maly Theatre, Moscow, 1876).   1877.

Schastlivy den [The Lucky Day], with Nikolai Solovyev (produced Maly Theatre, Moscow, 1877).   1877.

Poslednyaya zhertva (produced Maly Theatre, Moscow, 1877).   1878; translated as *The Last Sacrifice*, in *Poet Lore*, 39, 1928.

Zhenitba Belugina [Belugin's Wedding] (produced Maly Theatre, Moscow, 1877).   1878.

Bespridannitsa [The Girl Without a Dowry] (produced Maly Theatre, Moscow, 1878).   1879.

Dikarka [A Wild Woman], with Nikolai Solovyev (produced Maly Theatre, Moscow, 1879).   1880.

Serdtse ne kamen [The Heart is Not Made of Stone] (produced Alexandrinsky Theatre, St. Petersburg, 1879). 1880.

Svetit, da ne greyet [It Lights Up, But Doesn't Heat] (produced Maly Theatre, Moscow, 1880).   1881.

Nevolnitsy (produced Maly Theatre, Moscow, 1880).   1880; translated as *Bondwoman*, in *Poet Lore*, 36, 1925.

Blazh [A Whim], with Pyotr Nevezhin (produced Maly Theatre, Moscow, 1880. 1881.

Staroye po-novomu [The Old in a New Manner] (produced Maly Theatre, Moscow, 1882). 1881.

Talanty i poklonniki (produced Maly Theatre, Moscow, 1881). 1882; translated as *Artists and Admirers*, 1970.

Krasavets-muzhchina [A Good-Looking Man] (produced Maly Theatre, Moscow, 1882). 1883.

Bezvinny vinovatye (produced Maly Theatre, Moscow, 1884). 1884; translated as *More Sinned Against Than Sinning*, in *Plays*, 1974.

Ne ot mira sego [Not of This World] (produced Alexandrinsky Theatre, St. Petersburg, 1885). 1885.

*

Bibliographies

K. Muratova, *Bibliografiya literatury ob Alexander Nikolaevich Ostrovsky 1847–1917*, Leningrad, 1974.

Criticism

Books:
J. Patouillet, *Ostrovsky et son théâtre des moeurs russes*, Paris, 1912.
M. L. Hoover, *Alexander Ostrovsky*, Boston, 1981.

* * *

A prolific playwright and champion of rights for the theatrical profession, Ostrovsky was essentially the founder of Russian national drama, which was later to flower with Stanislavsky and the Moscow Art Theatre. Although he was preceded by greater playwrights—Griboyedov, Pushkin, Gogol—their output was small and their subject matter diverse, and there is little distinctively Russian about them. By the time of his death Ostrovsky had written nearly 50 plays—comedies, tragedies, historical dramas, contemporary and realistic dramatizations, and fairy tales—and had played a leading role in achieving certain far-reaching reforms in the theatre—increases in fees for actors, playwrights, and composers, extension of copyright, attempts at attaining equal rights for women in the theatre, and the establishment of an Actors' Club which, besides its social functions, provided training for aspiring actors and actresses where ensemble playing took preference over a star system.

Born into a comfortably-off family where his lawyer father earned his living by representing clients from the increasingly influential middle classes, he was brought up in the commercial district of Moscow, "over the river" from the Kremlin. Most of his earlier plays portray the uncultured, grasping, narrow lives of the tradespeople, merchants, and minor civil servants, some of whom had only recently escaped from serfdom—people he knew personally. Although other Russian playwrights had toyed with this environment briefly, Ostrovsky was the first to deal seriously with this inward-looking, crude, and uncivilized milieu, which he compared to the *Arabian Nights* in its magical atmosphere and fantastical characters—a world of crooks, financial speculators, domestic tyrants, oppressed civil servants, and the like.

The themes he treats, in this environment where the acquisition of money and its dubious, if not illegal, uses are the only goals in life, concentrate on what he saw as the results of incipient capitalism—fictitious bankruptcies, fraud, blackmail, bribery, and corruption, not only in the business and legal worlds, but in the family, too, where the old unbending, un-Westernized, patriarchal ways were as strongly felt as ever. The pictures he paints are not attractive and the negative aspects of life almost invariably triumph in the end. The majority of the plays of this period are somewhat loosely plotted and constructed and Ostrovsky rarely states his own point of view—he points to the problems, but offers no solutions. His attitudes and his writing style are both rather prosaic, even though his language is faithful to the world in which his plays are set—strong, expressive, and idiomatic, which makes for difficulties in translation.

The particularly Russian world—so different from that of Turgenev, Tolstoy, and Chekhov—coupled with the colloquial speech go some way to explaining why Ostrovsky is so popular in the country of his birth yet relatively little-known outside it, although *The Storm* is revived from time to time in England and America (albeit in France as *L'Orage* it fares better) and *Enough Stupidity in Every Wise Man* was produced to great acclaim as *Too Clever by Half* at the Old Vic in London in 1988.

The most characteristic of Ostrovsky's plays were all written in the period leading up to the emancipation of the serfs in 1861. The first, *Bankrut* (The Bankrupt), was a striking debut; there is not a single positive character in it, something which Ostrovsky had learnt from Gogol's *The Government Inspector*; but, unlike Gogol, he does not allow virtue to win in the end. It is realistic and there is no hint of caricature; the plot is minimal and all the action stems from the characters, who are all from the business world. In it, an old merchant declares himself bankrupt for profit, and is then deserted by his son-in-law and an accomplice, and is left to be sent to the debtors' prison. These are specific people, not universal types.

The Poor Bride, set among minor officials, does have one positive character, but the heroine is let down by her shallow admirer and agrees to marry a rich but uncivilized man, who saves her mother from financial ruin: with Ostrovsky, even the good and admirable are forced to submit to the circumstances of their lives. This pattern is repeated in *A Protogée of the Mistress* where the unbearable power of a selfish, wealthy, older woman stifles the life of all those under her control. This character is the representative of what Ostrovsky called the *samodur*. Her most terrifying portrayal occurs in undoubtedly the best play of this period, *The Storm*, in the figure of Kabanova, who, by her behaviour, drives the heroine, Katerina, to suicide.

After 1861 Ostrovsky changed both his subject matter and his style: he all but deserted the world of the merchants and became rather more traditional in his techniques. The plots become longer and his characters become more universal than the specific Russian types of the earlier plays. Although professional critics tend to value them less than his earlier plays, many of them proved even more popular with the theatre-going public. The best of these are *Enough Stupidity in Every Wise Man* (or *The Scoundrel*), *Wolves and Sheep*, and the first of his plays about actors, *The Forest*, which has equal claims with *The Storm* as the best of all his plays. Although *The Forest* possesses its share of selfish, mean-spirited, and generally negative characters, it is perhaps the only play of Ostrovsky's to celebrate the essential nobility of man.

At his death, Ostrovsky was the dominant figure of the Russian stage, not only because of the large number of plays with their excellent parts which he bequeathed to the Russian repertoire, but also for all he had done to improve the theatrical profession. He was succeeded by imitators and minor, largely untalented, playwrights and producers until the appearance of Stanislavsky, Nemirovich-Danchenko, and the Moscow Art Theatre towards the end of the century—and Chekhov. It is fitting that Moscow's Maly Theatre, which saw the majority of his triumphs, should still be known as "The House of Ostrovsky".

—A.V. Knowles

See also *Volume 1* entries on *The Forest*; *The Storm*.

———

OTWAY, Thomas. Born in Milland, Sussex, England, 3 March 1652. Educated at Winchester College, Hampshire, 1668; Christ Church, Oxford, 1669–71. Actor in London, 1671–75; first-produced play, *Alcibiades*, staged 1675; wrote for the Duke's Company at the Dorset Garden Theatre, 1675–82; served in the Duke of Monmouth's regiment in Flanders, 1678–79: lieutenant; tutor to Charles Beauclerk, Nell Gwyn's son by Charles II, late 1670's. MA, Cambridge University, 1680. Died in London, 14 April 1685.

Works

Collections

Works, edited by J.C. Ghosh (2 vols.). 1932.

Stage Works

Alcibiades (produced Dorset Garden Theatre, London, 1675). 1675.
Don Carlos, Prince of Spain (produced Dorset Garden Theatre, London, 1676). 1676.
Titus and Berenice, from a play by Racine (produced Dorset Garden Theatre, London, 1676). 1677.
The Cheats of Scapin, from a play by Molière (produced Dorset Garden Theatre, London, 1676). In *Titus and Berenice*, 1677.
Friendship in Fashion (produced Dorset Garden Theatre, London, 1678). 1678.
The History and Fall of Caius Marius (produced Dorset Garden Theatre, London, 1679). 1680.
The Orphan; or, The Unhappy Marriage (produced Dorset Garden Theatre, London, 1680). 1680.
The Soldier's Fortune (produced Dorset Garden Theatre, London, 1680). 1681.
Venice Preserved; or, A Plot Discovered (produced Dorset Garden Theatre, London, 1682). 1682.
The Atheist; or, The Second Part of the Soldier's Fortune (produced Dorset Garden Theatre, London, 1683). 1684.

Verse

The Poet's Complaint of His Muse; or, A Satire Against Libels. 1680.
Windsor Castle in a Monument to Our Late Sovereign Charles II. 1685.

Memoirs and Letters

Familiar Letters (by Rochester, Otway, and Katherine Philips), edited by Tom Brown and Charles Gildon (2 vols.). 1697.

Translator, *The History of the Triumvirates*, by Samuel de Broe. 1686.

*

Bibliographies

J.M. Armistead, *Four Restoration Playwrights: A Reference Guide*, Boston, 1984.

Criticism

Books:
Roswell G. Ham, *Thomas Otway and Nathaniel Lee*, New Haven, Connecticut, 1931.
Aline M. Taylor, *Next to Shakespeare: Otway's "Venice Preserved" and "The Orphan" and Their History on the London Stage*, Durham, North Carolina, 1950.
Kerstin Warner, *Thomas Otway*, 1982.

* * *

Otway's first play, *Alcibiades*, was in the short-lived Restoration genre of heroic tragedy. The earliest heroic plays, by Davenant and Orrery, had stressed man's social qualities, exalting obligation and friendship above personal desire, but Dryden had modified the genre, emphasizing the inevitable persistence of disruptive impulses both in State and individual character. Otway followed Dryden's lead, portraying a dislocated, problematic hero, exiled from his homeland for sacrilege, and siding with the enemy, heroically punctilious in loyalty—but loyal to the wrong side. Such dislocation is, in Otway, a universal human condition, for families and States are gatherings of strangers, offering no community or stability. Alcibiades' friend Patroclus becomes estranged from his evil father, and at the end of the play discovers that his beloved Draxilla has wandered untraceably into exile. Such is the consistency of Otway's tragic vision that the same structure of dislocation opens his last tragedy, *Venice Preserved*, where a father disowns his daughter, and she and her husband lose their home.

In *Don Carlos*, Otway blended the heroic play with Shakespeare, drawing both on *Othello* and Dryden's *Aureng-Zebe*. Political and familial order is again frail: King Philip marries the fiancée of Carlos, his son, causing Carlos to feel like a displaced person ("a naked wanderer") and to contemplate rebellion. The King's growing jealousy resembles Othello's, but he is an Othello with much to be jealous about, for chaotic sexual forces constantly threaten Carlos's duty as son and subject. An Iago, the disruptive outsider in *Othello*, is here unnecessary, for there is a destructive alien within each individual, and the would-be Iago, Rui-Gomez, cannot keep pace with the characters' own self-destructiveness: when he poisons Carlos's bath, Carlos promptly climbs in and slits his own veins.

In his next two tragedies Otway continued to work according to pre-existing models. *Titus and Berenice*, from Racine's *Bérénice*, portrays a corrupting surrender of personal desire to public duty; and loss of the personal also dominates *The History and Fall of Caius Marius*, which transfers the story of Romeo and Juliet to the Rome of Marius and Sulla. Exile is again a prominent theme, and life lacks any significant social context, for loyalty to the State is meaningless where indistinguishable factions battle with indistinguishable slogans for domination. Nor can individuals create private patterns of order: the hero expresses his love in the same terminology of bondage that permeates the political rhetoric, and the lovers' deaths lack individual stature, being swallowed in the mass carnage of a political purge. The play coincided with the political crisis caused by the Popish Plot scare and the consequent attempt to exclude the future James II from the succession, and reveals the deep political pessimism that co-existed with Otway's support for James.

In *The Orphan* and *Venice Preserved*, Otway turned from the alienation of the socially exalted to that of private characters, resentful of their own insignificance, and in both plays he created powerful images of inner isolation, portraying characters whose minds withdraw from the shared social setting into the solitude of imaginary wildernesses.

The Orphan depicts another disintegrating family. Polydore furtively supplants his brother in the heroine's bedroom, unaware that she is not his brother's mistress but his wife. In the dark, silent copulation, Polydore exchanges the complexities of language and social identity for the simple, inarticulate instincts of the wilderness; but the exchange cannot last, and he is destroyed by the discovery of his unwitting incest: man is too much a creature of the wilderness to inhabit society, but too much a creature of society to inhabit the wilderness.

The same paradox dominates *Venice Preserved*, where rebels aspire to the primal freedoms of the wilderness, but succumb to an insurmountable instinct for slavery. The hero, Jaffeir, vacillates between insurrection and masochistic subjugation to his wife, and the intertwined impulses to power and subjection are most plainly portrayed in the two scenes in which a senator (a figure of power) pays a prostitute to dominate him.

Otway's first comedy, the farce *The Cheats of Scapin*, was another adaptation (from Molière), performed as a double-bill with *Titus and Berenice*. His three original comedies are far weightier, and reflect the darkening of Restoration sex-comedy in reaction to Etherege's *The Man of Mode*, with its detached analysis of the predatory rake. *Friendship in Fashion* presents the rake as a vain unpopular drunk and, as its title indicates, depicts the collapse of social bonds, culmi-

nating in yet another image of dislocation, the dissolution of a household.

Such images intensify in the two later comedies. In *The Soldier's Fortune*, two gentleman have become virtual vagabonds, and, in a gloriously absurd image of personal and social dislocation, one of them dangles helplessly in a basket outside his mistress's window, singing a song of praise to Charles II. In *The Atheist*, characters actually believe that they have been transported to an enchanted world whose time is not that of England.

The constant physical dislocation reflects the disorientation of accepted social categories. The most socially exalted character in *The Soldier's Fortune*, Sir Jolly Jumble, is voyeur and pimp as well as knight, and his pimping constitutes the prime form of social bonding: it even unites the hero and heroine, under whose bed he aspires to lie. Women, in particular, lack a fitting and natural role. Two heroines of *The Atheist*, Lucretia and Porcia, are named after classical heroines who immolated themselves for their husbands, so that an oppressive masculine culture is recorded in the very names that seem to individuate them. Conversely, two tyrannical men, Theodoret and Gratian, represent an enduring male monopoly in language and authority, being named after a church historian and a canon lawyer. The tyrants are defeated, but the prospects for the women are uncertain, and Lucretia's problems are left completely unresolved. Otway's *oeuvre* begins with a rootless ancient hero; it ends with a rootless modern woman, cursed with an ancient, heroic name.

—Derek Hughes

See also *Volume 1* entry on *Venice Preserved*.

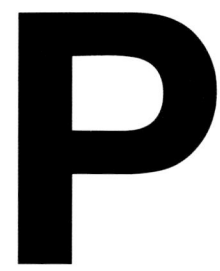

PARKER, (James) Stewart. Born in Belfast, Northern Ireland, 20 October 1941. Educated at Queen's University, Belfast, BA 1963, MA 1965. Married Kate Ireland in 1964. Instructor in English, Hamilton College, Clinton, New York, 1964–67, and Cornell University, Ithaca, New York, 1967–69. Recipient: *Evening Standard* Award, 1977; Christopher Ewart-Biggs Memorial Prize, 1979; Banff International Television Festival prize, 1985. Died in London, 2 November 1988.

Works

Stage Works

Spokesong, music by Jimmy Kennedy (produced Dublin Theatre Festival, 1975). 1980.
The Actress and the Bishop (produced King's Head Theatre, London, 1976).
Catchpenny Twist (televised 1977; produced Abbey Theatre, Dublin, 1977). 1980.
Kingdom Come, music by Shaun Davey (produced King's Head Theatre, London, 1978).
Tall Girls Have Everything (produced Actors' Theatre, Louisville, Kentucky, 1980).
Nightshade (produced Abbey Theatre, Dublin, 1980). 1980.
Pratt's Fall (produced Glasgow Theatre Club, Glasgow, 1983).
Northern Star (produced Lyric Theatre, Belfast, 1984).
Heavenly Bodies (produced Birmingham Repertory Theatre, 1986).
Pentecost (produced Guildhall, Londonderry, 1987).

Television Plays

Catchpenny Twist, 1977; *I'm a Dreamer, Montreal*, 1979; *The Kamikaze Ground Staff Reunion Dinner*, 1981; *Iris in the Traffic, Ruby in the Rain*, 1981; *Joyce in June*, 1982; *Blue Money*, 1984; *Radio Pictures*, 1985; *Lost Belongings*, 1987.

Radio Plays

Speaking of Red Indians, 1967; *Minnie and Maisie and Lily Freed*, 1970; *Requiem*, 1973; *The Iceberg*, 1974 (published in *Honest Ulsterman*, 1975); *I'm a Dreamer, Montreal*, 1976; *The Kamikaze Ground Staff Reunion Dinner*, 1979 (published in *Best Radio Plays of 1980*, 1981); *The Traveller*, 1985.

Verse

The Casualty's Meditation. 1967.
Maw. 1968.

Other

Editor, *Over the Bridge*, by Sam Thompson.   1970.

*

Criticism

Books:
Andrew Parkin, "Metaphor as Dramatic Structure in Plays by Stewart Parker", in *Irish Writers and the Theatre*, edited by Masaru Sekine, Gerrards Cross, Buckinghamshire, 1986.
Elmer Andrews, "The Will to Freedom: Politics and Play in the Theatre of Stewart Parker", in *Irish Writers and Politics*, edited by Okifumi Komesu and Masaru Sekine, Savage, Maryland, 1990.

*   *   *

With its witty alertness to the unconscious felicities and incongruities of everyday speech, Stewart Parker's dialogue embodies that resilience and energy in the midst of routine and deadness which is the chief concern of his plays. Form and stagecraft reinforce this impression, for Parker typically establishes and develops his themes less by soberly discursive means than by a constant play of allusion, symbol, and metatheatrical reference operating within a fast-moving, eventful narrative. (Music and song frequently enhance the charm and energy of the action.) Parker's is a virtuoso stagecraft, joyfully unafraid of self-display.

This is a comic writer at home with serious subjects. The Troubles are, not unnaturally for a Northern Irish playwright, ominously present either within or behind most of Parker's work. He saw himself as preoccupied "with the challenge of forging a unifying dramatic metaphor for the Northern Irish human condition". His interest is in cultural and psychological consequences, rather than political causes or solutions: the pressures of circumstances created by sectarian violence and a military presence are shown, in such pieces as *I'm a Dreamer, Montreal* and the "Caribbean-Irish Musical Comedy" *Kingdom Come* (which, like the radio play *The Iceberg*, allegorizes the situation), to stifle the energy of the individual.

Parker's best-known piece, *Spokesong*, was intended as "a play about violence which would ambush the audience with pleasure". It is typical of his work in its (oblique) treatment of the Troubles and in its clever stagecraft. Frank's attempt to woo Daisy (in competition with his "implacably bitter" brother Julian) and to preserve the family bicycle-shop in Belfast from the ravages of urban "development" and terrorist bombs is presented concurrently with his grandparents' courtship and his grandfather's service in World War I. The "bicycle-philosophy" of Frank's family is shown to represent physical energy, freedom, health and beneficial social change amidst the chaos and constriction of the "diseased", car-dominated city. Frank is driven almost to despair by the surrounding pressures, but Daisy steps in to save the shop and stand with him. Their united resolve promotes an affirmation not so much of the eccentric bicycle-philosophy, as of human energy and independence *per se*.

By remaining in Belfast, Frank and Daisy acknowledge and confront the historical past and its consequences. But the catchpenny songwriters of *Catchpenny Twist* find themselves with little choice in the same matter. When their exuberance gets them the sack from their teaching jobs, Ray and Martyn are forced to leave Belfast because of terrorist death-threats. The threats pursue them, through growing emotional turmoil (caused largely by their singer, Monagh), first to Dublin, and then to London. The "twist" comes when, having missed their chance of a break in a European song-contest, they are blown up by a parcel-bomb at a foreign airport. Their Republican "friend" considers their endeavour puerile because of its lack of connection with the serious business of their country's political past; yet the final effect of the play's wit and the energy of its songs is to question the moral adequacy of a seriousness that inhibits feeling and destroys life.

It would be misleading to suggest that Parker's work is concerned exclusively with Northern Ireland and its problems. For example, both *Nightshade*, a vivid, whirling piece about the need to confront the reality of death, and *Pratt's Fall*, a poignant late comedy which opposes the truths of reason and science with those of imagination and belief, meditate entertainingly on the necessity for art and the artist, and in doing so handle characteristic themes outside the characteristic Troubles-context. Nevertheless it was to the North of Ireland and its cultural past that Parker turned for what was to be his final project, a "triptych" of history plays, "dealing roughly with the struggle between the individual will and the forces of the Age in which it operates". These plays present (in the author's own words), "three self-contained groups of figures, from the eighteenth, nineteenth and twentieth centuries respectively, hinged together in a continuing comedy of terrors".

The dramatic format of the first two plays of the triptych is that of a man near or at the point of death reviewing his life and actions in a series of key flashbacks which counterpoint or parody various dramatic styles or scenes. The central figure of the first, *Northern Star*, is the great Protestant United Irishman, Henry Joy McCracken. After the "stillborn" attempt of the 1798 rising to create a united Irish nation, McCracken is on the run and being sheltered by his toughly commonsensical mistress, Mary Bodle, in a semi-ruined farm labourer's cottage outside Belfast. The time is "the continuous past", with "deliberate anachronisms and historical shifts". "McCracken's Night Thoughts" (the play's original subtitle) are presented by him, in modern idiom, in a sequence of dramatic scenes which chart the course through Seven (ironic) Ages of his attempt to forge a united Ireland. Each "Age" is a pastiche of the style of a famous Irish playwright: Innocence (Sheridan); Idealism (Boucicault); Cleverness (Wilde); Dialectic (Shaw); Heroism (Synge); Compromise (O'Casey); Shame (Behan)—and a terminal monologue after Beckett. The ambition is Joycean—nothing less than an attempt to transform an individual's history, through a virtuoso theatrical digest, into a nation's, and thus to suggest how an escape from the dungeon of history might be effected by way of moral and creative, rather than physical, force.

In the less interesting second play of the triptych, *Heavenly Bodies*, the Victorian Irish playwright Dion Boucicault has been metamorphosed from object of pastiche to central character. He is put on trial for his afterlife and found guilty of a self-serving opportunism that has led him to exploit his suffering fellow-countrymen for the sake of showbusiness and a glittering career ("You *are* the Age", he is told). The trial is conducted by Boucicault's "Mephistophelean sparring partner", the Irish singing clown Johnny Patterson, who was murdered by his audience. He is the most impressive of Parker's many artist-performers. His belief in the "commingling of the Orange and the Green", and his fatal efforts to bring it about, place him alongside McCracken as a symbol of the possibility of creative reconciliation.

The "climactic piece" of the triptych, *Pentecost*, is Parker's last play, and his best. The time is 1974 and the setting Belfast—specifically a "*respectable working class 'parlour' house*", described as "slap bang in the firing line", and "eloquent with the history of this city". When Marian, a Catholic, moves into the house in an attempt to take refuge from life, she is (literally) haunted by the ghost of the only previous tenant, Lily Matthews, whose life the house and its hoarded contents plainly embody ("she never threw anything away"). As the "lingering tribal suicide" of the Loyalist workers' protest strike takes its course on the streets outside, Marian discovers evidence of the life-denying price of Lily's Protestant "godliness": an abandoned illegitimate child which, together with Marian's own dead baby, Christopher ("he was a kind of Christ to me"), comes to symbolize not just loss of personal hope, but the absence of a cultural future. Yet "the ways of life" are finally affirmed when Marian and her "holy family" of fellow refugees—her childhood friend Ruth, her "free-spirited" estranged husband Lenny, and his friend Peter (the names are significant)—gather in a passionate impromptu wake for the province. As Pentecost Sunday dawns, a visionary and prophetic flame lights on story, recitation, song, and confession, prompting a painful celebration of the human love and self-delight that is being corrupted by a barren culture.

—Paul Lawley

PAVLOVSKY, Eduardo. Born in Buenos Aires, Argentina, 1933. Studied medicine at the Faculty of Medicine, Buenos Aires, to 1957; studied psycho-drama in New York, 1963. Playwright and actor: founder, the theatre company Grupo Experimental Latinoamericano, 1968. Also psychologist and psychotherapist: co-founder, Movimentio Psicodramático en la Argentina; head of the Asociación Argentina de Psicología y Psicoterapia de Grupo and the International Association of Group Psychotherapy; visiting professor, University of Gothenburg, Sweden; director, Asociación Psicoanalítica Argentina, until 1971; founder, dissident group Plataforma, 1971. Recipient: Premio Molière, 1967; Premio Pepino, 1988.

Works

Collections

Teatro de la vanguardia (includes *Somos; La espera trágica; Un acto rápido; El robot; Alguien*).   1966.

Teatro de la vanguardia 2 (includes *Último match* and *La cacería*), with Juan Carlos Hermes. 1967.
La mueca; El señor Galíndez; Telerañas. 1981.
El señor Galindez; Pablo. 1986.
La mueca; Cerca. 1988.

Stage Works

Somos (produced 1961). In *Teatro de la vanguardia*, 1966.
La espera trágica (produced 1964). c.1962.
Un acto rápido. In *Teatro de la vanguardia*, 1966.
El robot. In *Teatro de la vanguardia*, 1966.
Alguien In *Teatro de la vanguardia*.
Último match, with Juan Carlos Hermes (produced 1970). In *Teatro de la vanguardia 2*, 1967.
La cacería. In *Teatro de la vanguardia 2*, 1967.
La mueca. In *Tres obras de teatro* (with plays by other authors), 1970; single edition, 1971.
El señor Galíndez (produced 1973). In *Primer acto*, 179–181, 1975; in book form, 1976.
Telarañas (produced 1976). 1976.
Cámaralenta (produced 1982). 1979.
El señor Laforgue (produced 1982). 1982.
Cerca (produced 1983). With *La mueca*, 1988.
Potestad (produced 1985). 1987.
Pablo (produced 1986). With *El señor Galíndez*, 1986.
Voces (produced 1989). 1989.
Paso de dos (produced 1990).

*

Criticism

Books:
Severino Joao Albuquerque, *Violent Acts: A Study of Contemporary Latin American Theatre*, Detroit, 1991.

Articles:
Marguerite Feitlowitz, "A Dance of Death: Eduardo Pavlovsky's *Paso de dos*", in *The Drama Review*, vol.35 no.2, 1991.

*   *   *

Eduardo Pavlovsky is one of Argentina's most aesthetically innovative and psychologically insightful playwrights. Pavlovsky's particular strength comes, in part, from his dual career: he is a professional psychotherapist specializing in psychodrama and an award winner actor and dramatist. Pavlovsky's psychoanalytic work affects both the content and the form of his plays. From his first major play, *La mueca* (The Grimace), to *Voces* (Voices), he has focused on perverted, criminal minds struggling to justify or survive their aberrant actions. Structurally, moreover, his later plays, *Potestad* (Impunity) and *Voces* resemble psychoanalytic encounters; there are two characters, one engages in a devastating monologue while the other listens. Pavlovsky stresses the spontaneous, interactive nature of these works by specifying that in some cases the performance preceded the script. The published script of *Potestad*, for example, comes from a tape-recording of his monologue in the leading role. Thus, Pavlovsky is not, strictly speaking, a "playwright" in the conventional sense.

Pavlovsky's development as a dramatist is instructive for those unfamiliar with Latin American theatre. His early pieces, such as *Somos* (We Are), *La espera trágica* (The Tragic Wait), *Un acto rápido* (A Fast Act), *El robot* (The Robot), and *Alguien* (Someone), are reminiscent of works by European dramatists such as Beckett, Ionesco, Dürrenmatt, and Sartre. Like the so-called absurdists, Pavlovsky's early works accentuate the breakdown of language, communication, and identity, but leave the socio-political tensions precipitating the existential crisis unexplored.

However, it would be misleading to group the Argentine playwright with these Europeans. What makes Pavlovsky a major dramatist lies in the qualities that differentiate him from his models. The excruciating intensity which has come to characterize Pavlovsky's theatre becomes apparent only when he applies the absurdists' fragmentary and bizarre techniques to the examination of Argentina's increasingly grotesque political violence. Rather than perpetuate the absurdist vision, expressed by writers and commentators from Albert Camus to Martin Esslin, that life has lost all meaning ("in a universe that is suddenly deprived of illusions and of light, man feels a stranger"), Pavlovsky encourages us to ask questions as to who is responsible for the creation of the moral vacuum, and who profits from killing illusion and extinguishing the light.

Pavlovsky's theatre of the late 1960's and 1970's, notably his award-winning plays *Último match* (Last Match, written in collaboration with Juan Carlos Hermes), *La cacería* (The Hunt), and *La mueca*, focuses on violence—violence for pleasure, violence for profit, violence as a spectator sport. Masterful and fascinating as these works are, few plays anywhere can compete with the urgency and power of Pavlovsky's most terrifying depictions of torture and torturers, *El señor Galíndez* (Mr. Galindez), *El señor Laforgue* (Mr. Laforgue), *Potestad*, and *Voces*. In these plays, as in the early absurdist pieces, the dialogue is broken, repetitive, and incoherent. The characters, especially the EL (He) and ELLA (She) of the latest plays, have little or no identity. *El señor Laforgue*, too, portrays a man who is given rebirth by his new mother, the military; he acquires a new name, a new face, a modified body. His memory is being erased and new memories are pumped into his seemingly empty head. At this point in his dramaturgy, Pavlovsky was depicting Argentina's dirty politics in the "Dirty War" (1976–1983), a period during which the military waged undeclared war on its civilian population, exterminating or "disappearing" an estimated 15,000 people.

Mr. Laforgue, like many actual military officers had done, has piloted one of the planes which took the disappeared (referred to in Argentina as "future corpses") over the sea to be dumped alive into the water below. With the Dirty War over, the officials are trying to clean up their crimes, and they transform the pilot into an "innocent" civilian who teaches body-building in Philadelphia. But the buried will not stay buried. Not only do corpses wash ashore (as they actually did in Argentina), but Laforgue's memory will not stay repressed. He suffers from nightmares, and when the time comes for him to leave for his new career abroad, he cannot board the airplane that is to take him to Philadelphia.

In *Potestad*, EL tells of the time when two men walked into his house one Saturday afternoon and took away his only daughter, a young girl named Adriana, while he and his wife were unable to stop them. Much as in psychodrama, the character, initially alone onstage, obsessively re-enacts the movements of the family on that Saturday afternoon: "I'm sitting over here (*he points to the chair on the right*). Ana María my wife, is sitting here . . . (*he points to the chair on the left*). About four feet, four feet two inches from the angle of the left foot of the armchair sits my daughter Adriana (*he points to the place where Adriana is sitting with his right* foot)". The only way he can approach or contemplate the tragedy that has befallen them, he tells us, is by taking everything apart, detail by detail: "It seems incredible that in life, when we study every little gesture, the arbitrary, daily gestures of living, everything seems funny. If we divide things up . . . everything can seem funny. The problem is to unite things, to totalize, that's where tragedy appears . . . human tragedy in all its dimensions".

Unlike Peter Shaffer's *Equus*, *Potestad* does not introduce psychodramatic techniques to make the past accessible, but to render it controllable. During the final part of this one-act play, a woman (ELLA) enters, and EL continues his narration to her, while she keeps her distance as if she were an analyst. As EL relates the misery of his present existence, we, as audience, come to realize that in fact *he*, as a physician during the Dirty War, was the one who kidnapped Adriana in the first place. One afternoon, a Sunday afternoon, he had been called to sign a death certificate for a young couple shot to death by the military. After he wipes out their crime by attributing the deaths to natural causes, the gunmen leave. Only then does he hear the sound of a very young child crying in the next room: "Don't ask any questions", he instructs his wife after he takes the little child home, "*I* earned her. This little girl is ours, *I* earned her! *Me!*".

Voces, like *Potestad*, echoes the psychoanalytic situation as EL entreats ELLA to communicate with him, answer him, name him. Again, the use of the psychoanalytic discourse calls attention to the fact that this very concept of the individual underlying psychoanalysis is missing. EL, who, it turns out, tortured ELLA during the Dirty War, has to reconstitute his identity vis-à-vis her, having attempted to destroy her identity. With a tone and urgency suggestive of the questions a torturer asks his victim, he demands, he threatens, he begs that she name him, that she denounce him, that she scream out what he did to her. She turns the torturers' tactics back on him, however, by refusing to name him. Just as he, like Argentina's other torturers, had denied his victim's humanity, identity, and name (see Jacobo Timerman's testimony, *Prisoner Without a Name, Cell Without a Number*, concerning the same period), she denies his: "I won't name you". She tells him:

> You'd prefer that I denounce you . . . I know that would make you feel better, proud that everyone will know that you touched me . . . you want to be a hero like all the rest of them, proud again of everything you did . . . proud that you're free, defiant, on the look-out . . . heroes again . . . I'm not going to name you, you're going to have to keep on waiting, and keep on waiting, that will be your little torment.

Memory, for the tortured as for the torturers, has to be tricked, forced, and controlled in order for them to go on living.

Pavlovsky's theatre from the late 1960's onwards examines the effects and scars of socio-political violence played out on the human body. The torturers remake and reshape the body through the infliction of pain, but in so doing they are unmaking themselves. In the end they, like their victims, stand in need of new names, new faces.

—Diana Taylor

PEELE, George. Born in London, 25(?) July 1556. Educated at Christ's Hospital, London, from 1562;

Broadgates Hall (later Pembroke College), Oxford, 1571–74, and Christ Church, Oxford, matriculated 1574, BA 1577, MA 1579. Married 1) Ann Christian in 1580 (died c.1587); 2) possibly married Mary Yates c.1591. Moved to London, 1581; wrote several of the lord mayor's pageants for the City of London. Died (buried) in London, 9 November 1596.

Works

Collections

Life and Works (3 vols.), edited by C.T. Prouty. 1952–70.
[Selections], edited by Sally Purcell. 1972.

Stage Works

The Arraignment of Paris: A Pastoral (produced by the Children of the Chapel, at Court, London, c.1581–1584). 1584.
The Device of the Pageant Borne Before Wolstan Dixie, Lord Mayor of London (pageant; produced London, 1585).
The Hunting of Cupid (produced London?, 1582–91). Fragments edited by W. W. Greg, 1911.
The Old Wives Tale (produced by the Queen's Men, 1588–94). 1595.
The Battle of Alcazar (produced London?, 1589?). 1594.
Descensus Astraeae: The Device of a Pageant Borne Before William Webb, Lord Mayor of London (pageant; produced London, 1591). 1591.
King Edward the First, Surnamed Edward Longshanks (produced London?, 1592–93). 1593.
The Love of King David and Fair Bethsabe (produced London?, 1594?). 1599.

Verse

Pareus (in Latin). 1585.
An Eclogue Gratulatory to Robert, Earl of Essex for His Welcome into England from Portugal. 1589.
A Farewell to Sir John Norris and Sir Francis Drake; A Tale of Troy. 1589; revised edition of *The Tale of Troy*, 1604.
Polyhymnia, Describing the Honourable Triumph at Tilt Before Her Majesty. 1590
The Honour of the Carter. 1593.
Anglorum Feriae: England's Holidays, edited by R. Fitch. 1830(?).

Others

Life and Minor Works of Peele, by D. H. Horne. 1952.
George Peele (selections), edited by Sally Purcell. 1972.

*

Bibliographies

S.A. Tannenbaum, *George Peele: A Concise Bibliography*, New York, 1940.
R.C. Johnson, *George Peele 1939–1965*, London, 1968.

Criticism

Books:
P.H. Cheffaud, *George Peele* (in French), Paris, 1913.
O.H. Horne, *The Life and Minor Works of George Peele*, New Haven, Connecticut, 1952.

Leonard R.N. Ashley, *Authorship and Evidence: A Study of Attribution and the Renaissance Drama Illustrated By the Case of George Peele, 1556–1596*, Geneva, 1968.

G.K. Hunter, *John Lyly and George Peele*, London, 1968.

Leonard R.N. Ashley, *George Peele*, New York, 1970.

Werner Senn, *Studies in the Dramatic Construction of Robert Greene and Peele*, Berne, 1973.

Inga-Stina Eubank, "'What Words, What Looks, What Wonders?': Language and Spectacle in the Theatre of George Peele", in *Elizabethan Theatre 5*, 1975.

A.R. Braunmuller, *George Peele*, Boston, 1983.

* * *

In the ten years from 1584 to 1594 a group of "University wits" was transforming English drama. Lyly, Kyd, Greene, Marlowe, and Peele achieved the characteristics that we think of as Elizabethan, in the handling both of dramatic structure and of the verse line. Peele was unusual in that he brought to his plays a strong interest in pageantry, derived from his father's work as a designer of pageants. George Peele was involved in producing occasional entertainments at Christ Church, Oxford, even after graduation, and wrote Lord Mayor's pageants, two of which survive. His plays can be seen as different attempts to match spectacle and poetry to dramatic action.

The dates of all Peele's plays are uncertain, especially since the search for any clues in textual references is bedeviled by probable revisions. The quarto of *The Battle of Alcazar* is presumed to be a version abridged for a small acting company. *The Old Wives Tale* has traditionally been seen similarly, though recently it has been argued that it is intentionally brief because intended for private performance, perhaps as a marriage entertainment.

His earliest play, *The Arraignment of Paris*, was, like a pageant, an occasional piece, written for Court performance. Paris's dilemma of whether to award the prize for beauty to Juno, Venus, or Diana, a pretext for a *débat* on the nature of beauty, is finally turned into a compliment to Elizabeth, when the goddesses give the apple to this "phoenix of our age".

The Battle of Alcazar dramatizes a military expedition into North Africa by the King of Portugal, which led to the loss of his life and kingdom. The rival Moorish factions and their claims are so complex that Peele offers three separate expositions. So, neither the King, nor Captain Stukeley, a renegade but popular Briton who joined his expedition, appears until the end of Act II. Perhaps the complexity accounts for Peele's unique experiment of having a Presenter appear before each act and, with the help of dumbshows which include Nemesis, "Fame like an Angel", and fireworks, explain the action to come. Or perhaps this variant on the Senecan chorus was to strengthen the sense of fate.

Peele took a different tack, however, in *Edward I*, where he sought to impose dramatic structure on the King's repeated wars against the Welsh and Scots by personalizing motivations, and inventing various love relationships that cross the Welsh/English divide. Formal pageantry uneasily co-exists with the Welsh leader Llewelyn as a "Robin Hood of the great mountain", complete with a comical Friar Tuck, and with a Queen Elinor whom revisions have left schizophrenic —in some scenes Edward's hearty Nell, in others a haughty Spaniard so spiteful the earth swallows her and vomits her up again.

David and Bethsabe better integrates military and romantic actions. Peele may have been interested in a generic counterpoint: *The Love of David and Faire Bersabe, with the Tragedie of Absalon* is the quarto's title. This play is the culmination of Peele's concern with the power of visual appeal. At the play's opening David watches Bethsabe as she bathes and sings:

Hot sun, cool fire, tempered with sweet air,
Black shade, fair nurse, shadow my white hair.
Shine sun, burn fire, breathe air, and ease me,
Black shade, fair nurse, shroud me and please me.
Shadow (my sweet nurse) keep me from burning,
Make not my glad cause, cause of mourning.
Let not my beauties fire
Enflame unstayed desire,
Nor pierce any bright eye,
That wandreth lightly.

But David already finds "my longings tangled in her hair", an image which, besides its immediacy of feeling, carries a proleptic irony, for the longings of David's son Absolom will lead to his death with his hair tangled between Heaven and earth.

Some critics consider *David and Bethsabe* Peele's finest play, but *The Old Wives Tale* is the most anthologized and has an obvious appeal on the stage. In the folk motifs, around which the play is built, Peele found a way to integrate the visual and the dramatic, for in folk tales the visual is often both symbolic and climactic. We are led into the action by three pages, Antic, Frolic, and Fantastic, whose names already invite us to wander away from the everyday world. They seek the hospitality of Madge, who starts to tell them the stories we see enacted as briefly as in a dream.

Within this frame we meet a variety of characters seemingly in as muddled a fashion as Madge's storytelling. But, as the action proceeds, they converge into a satisfying pattern. Two brothers wish to find their lost princess sister while Lampriscus wishes to lose his two daughters, one "foul" in appearance, one shrewishly "curst", by marrying them off. Each line of action focuses upon a magical setpiece: a buried lamp which, so long as it stays alight, maintains the magician Sacrapant, who has kidnapped the princess, as a young man rather than the old man he truly is; and a magic well from which a head rises to address each sister:

Gently dip, but not too deep,
For fear you make the golden head to weep.
Fair maiden, white and red,
Stroke me smooth, and comb my head,
And thou shalt have some cockle-bread [a love charm].

The "foul" sister gets a blind, and the "curst" a deaf, husband. And the princess gives her hand to the wandering knight, Eumenides, who rescues her.

The Old Wives Tale is the only one of Peele's plays where he is not wrestling with often intractable source material. The folk-tale material is, for his audience's amusement, tricked out with classical touches, as when the braggart soldier Huanebango declares himself of the family of Polimackeroeplacidus, and the audience is left to choose whether to be charmed by the material, or laugh at it as Madge's country tales, or respond both ways by turns.

—Anthony Graham-White

See also *Volume 1* entry on *The Old Wives Tale*.

———

PETRUSHEVSKAYA, Lyudmila (Stefanova). Born in Moscow, 26 May 1938. Grew up in an orphanage in Ufa, in the Urals. Educated at Moscow University, Faculty of Journalism. Has worked as nurse and journalist; prolific writer of short stories in the 1960's: first of them published in *Avrora*, 1972; editor with Soviet television, 1972; member of Alexei Arbuzov's playwrights' workshop in the 1970's; achieved reputation in the unofficial theatre in the mid-1970's, and plays produced more widely in the Soviet Union from 1985.

Works

Collections

Pesy [Plays]. 1983.
Four (includes *Love; Come Into the Kitchen; Nets and Traps; The Violin*). 1984.
Pesni XX veka [Songs of the 20th Century] (includes *Urokoi muzyka; Kvartina Kolombiny; Monologi;* the cycle *Temnaya komnata*). 1988.
Cinzano: Eleven Plays (includes *Cinzano; Smirnova's Birthday; Music Lessons; Three Girls in Blue; The Stairwell; Love; Nets and Snares; The Execution; The Meeting; A Glass of Water; Isolation Box*), translated by Stephen Mulrine. 1991.

Stage Works

Seti i lovushki. In *Avrora*, 4, 1974; translated as *Nets and Traps*, in *Four*, 1984; as *Nets and Snares*, in *Cinzano: Eleven Plays*, 1991.
Dva okoshka [Two Windows]. 1975.
Bystro khorosho ne byvaet; ili, Chemodan chepukhi [Things Don't Get Better Quickly; or, The Suitcase of Nonsense]. In *Odnoaktnye pesy*, 1978.
Prokhodite v kukhniu. In *Odnoaktnye pesy*, 1979; translated as *Come Into the Kitchen*, in *Four*, 1984.
Vse ne kak u lyudei [Different from People]. In *Odnoaktnye komedy*, 1979.
Liubov (produced Taganka Theatre, Moscow, 1981). In *Teatr*, 3, 1979; translated as *Love*, in *Four*, 1979, and in *Cinzano*, 1991.
Ozelenenie [Making it Green]. In *Odnoaktnye pesy*, 2, 1980.
Tri devshki v golubom (produced 1986). In *Sovremennaya dramaturgiya*, 3, 1983; translated as *Three Girls in Blue*, in *Cinzano: Eleven Plays*, 1991.
Uroki muzyki (produced Moscow, 1983). In *Pesy*, 1983; translated as *Music Lessons*, in *Cinzano: Eleven Plays*, 1991.
Stakan vody (produced Moscow, 1983). As part of *Temnaya komnata*, in *Pesni XX veka*, 1988; translated as *A Glass of Water*, in *Cinzano: Eleven Plays*, 1991.
Lestnichnaya kletka [The Staircase]. In *Pesy*, 1983; translated as *The Stairwell*, in *Cinzano: Eleven Plays*, 1991.
Chinzano (produced 1987). In translation as *Cinzano*, in *Cinzano: Eleven Plays*, 1991.
Ia za shvetsyu. Translated as *I'm for Sweden*, 1988.
Andante [Andante]. 1988.
Kvartira Kolumbiny [Columbine's Apartment] (produced Sovremennik Theatre, Moscow, 1985). In *Pesni XX veka*, 1988.
Monologi [Monologues]. In *Pesni XX veka*, 1988.
Temnaya komnata [The Dark Room] (short plays). In *Pesni XX veka*, 1988; parts translated as *The Meeting, The Execution, A Glass of Water,* and *Isolation Box*, in *Cinzano*, 1991.

Novye Robinzony: Khronika XX veka [The New Robinsons: Chronicle of the 20th Century]. In *Novy mir*, 8, 1989.
Krokhmal E Razmyshlenya u razbitogo koryta . . . . In *Grani* (Frankfurt), 157, 1990.
Krokhmal E Chernaya koshka v "temnoi komnate". In *Grani* (Frankfurt), 158, 1990.
Smirnova's Birthday. In *Cinzano: Eleven Plays*, 1991.

Fiction

Bessmertnaya lyubov [Undying Love]. 1988.
Svoi krug. 1990.

*

Criticism

Books:
M.T. Smith, "in *Cinzano* veritas: The Plays of Liudmila Petrushevskaia", in *Recent Polish and Soviet Theatre and Drama*, edited by J.A. Phillips, Stony Brook, New York, 1985.

Articles:
Victoria Vainer, "About Brother and Sisters, Fathers and Sons", in *Soviet Theatre*, 2, 1988.
Lyudmilla Petrushevskaya and Victoria Vainer, interview in *Yale/Theatre*, vol. 20 no.3, 1989.

* * *

Petrushevskaya is the most original and provocative talent of the Russian "new-wave" or "post-Vampilov" drama. The comparison with Vampilov is inevitable, as she herself has said that he was her "guiding star". Her plays are far starker and coarser-textured than the Siberian dramatist's, however, and lack his release into poetry and symbolism. Petrushevskaya's basic subject matter is Soviet life *in extremis*, especially for women. She pulls absolutely no punches, and to read or watch her plays in Russian is a draining, rather than cathartic, experience, with more than a hint of Dostoevsky. It was her raw realism, of course, that prevented her plays being publicly performed in the 1970's. During this period, the elder dramatist Arbuzov said of her that she "scared him out of his wits". Even in 1988 the editors of the Russian Union of Theatre Workers were reluctant, at first, to publish her cycle *Temnaya komnata* (The Dark Room), which includes two plays dealing with the periods before and after an execution, and one set in a hospital terminal ward.

The usual background of Petrushevskaya's plays is the interminable search in the USSR for living space, edible food, effective medical care, and a viable wage (which may have to come from prostitution). The action of *Three Girls in Blue*, probably Petrushevskaya's most popular play, revolves around the question of which of the three single mothers, with their children and an elderly relative, is to have which room in the ramshackle dacha they have rented for the summer. One room has no lavatory to it, but gives onto an occupiable verandah; another has a lavatory, but also a hole in the roof that necessitates them all moving around the house when it rains; the third is the landlady's. These issues, the question of the rent, and the illness and fighting of their three male children drag the girls down to the depths of bitchiness. Nevertheless, when the heroine, Ira, returns to the dacha (after following her worthless Party lover on holiday) to find that the others have occupied her room, the situation is resolved amicably, and to another character's line, "All men are brothers", she replies ("*joyfully*"), "Not all—some are sisters!".

Petrushevskaya has given a devastatingly truthful picture of the destruction of Russian manhood in the Soviet period. Nearly all the male characters in her plays are idle, devoid of self-respect, completely faithless; they are fornicators, drunkards, and cowards. As Yura in *The Stairwell* puts it, "the family no longer exists. There is just the female tribe with their young ones, and lone males". Petrushevskaya undoubtedly shows that it is the women who have the sheer biological will to survive beyond despair, but her theatre is hardly a feminist one: what often pulls them through is their love for their usually *male* children and their inextinguishable longing for a really loving heterosexual partner. Indeed, one of the few rays of hope in Petrushevskaya's world is the relative maturity and forgiving nature of some of the boy characters (as in *I'm For Sweden*).

The ending of *Three Girls in Blue* highlights one of the problems of Petrushevskaya's writing so far. The inalienably Russian logic of her dialogues and the authentic irrationality and sudden reverses of action in her plays suggest, as Victoria Vainer has pointed out, that her "plots are not man-made; they have been invented by [Russian] life itself". But this aspect tends to make the plays' conclusions appear just as more scenes of peripeteia. To avoid this effect, Petrushevskaya has tried "lifting" endings, but this attempt has tended to leave contrived impressions, at variance with the realism of the greater parts of the plays. Almost the only feature of *Three Girls in Blue* that qualifies it for its sub-title "Comedy" is the ending: Ira suddenly returns, she is glad to see everyone, she suddenly does not mind the others using her room. But to this conclusion are added the facts that she smiles, for the first time in the play, and that the symbolic lost kitten, referred to somewhat heavy-handedly throughout the play, is suddenly found and brought onstage. The final effect is curiously trivialising.

Similarly, Petrushevskaya's strongest full-length play, *Music Lessons*, is a brilliantly alive and realistic account of a Soviet "proletarian" family's values; but the ending consists of two of the heroines suddenly appearing on swings above the stage, delivering surreal lines to the other characters, and being lowered to dive-bomb them. It seems that Petrushevskaya's problems with endings derive from her reluctance, or inability (by contrast with Vampilov), to move towards even the mildest ethical focus in her work.

Basically, Petrushevskaya sees the life which she transfers to the stage almost entirely from the inside. Her plays are acts of near-religious empathy with the most broken victims of Soviet life. Apparently she writes sporadically but very quickly (*Three Girls in Blue* was written in four days). It seems there is an element of "automatic writing", then, which prevents her from attempting a more conscious art because that would seem "a lie" to the life she is unburdening herself of. This aspect emerges most clearly in her tendency to use monologue. Understandably, in the Soviet context any true and spontaneous "confession" by a character who is lonely or obsessed by terrible experiences is likely to be interesting, if not powerful. In her full-length plays, however, such monologues tend to sound spurious.

The context of Russian national degeneration has not proved difficult to transfer to the English stage, as seen in productions of *Three Girls in Blue* and *Cinzano*. A much greater difficulty facing her plays on the English-language stage is their language. Although containing few obscenities, their vocabulary and intonation are stunningly alive and accurate; but without four-letter words it is hardly possible in contemporary English drama to convey the same grittiness. It is still early days for Petrushevskaya in English, however, and in any case one has the distinct impression that her best work is still to come.

—Patrick Miles

PIÑERA, Virgilio (Llera). Born in Cárdenas, Matanzas region, Cuba, 4 August 1912. Family moved to Camagüey, 1925. Educated at the University of Havana, c.1932–37 (studies interrupted during Machado era), BA; University of Havana, Faculty of Philosophy and Letters, 1937–41, doctorate. Founding editor, *Poeta*, 1942; lived in Buenos Aires, Argentina, 1946–58, working as clerk in the Cuban Consulate, examiner, and translator for the publishing firm Argos; first play, *Electra Garrigó*, produced 1948; co-founder and secretary, the literary periodical *Ciclón*, 1955; after the Cuban revolution (1959), contributor to *Revolución* and numerous other Latin American periodicals; director, the publishing company Ediciones Erre, 1960–64; arrested on grounds of his homosexuality, 1961. Recipient: Casa de las Américas Prize, 1968. Died in Havana, 19 October 1979.

Works

Collections

Teatro completo (includes *Electra Garrigó; Jésus; Aire frío; Falsa alarma; La boda; El flaco y el gordo; El filántropo*). 1960.

Stage Works

Electra Garrigó (produced 1948).   In *Teatro completo*, 1960.
Jésus.   In *Prometeo*, vol.3 no.26, 1951; in book form, in *Teatro*, 1960.
Aire frío.   1959; translated as *Cold Air*, 1985.
Falsa alarma.   In *Teatro completo*, 1960.
La boda.   In *Teatro completo*, 1960.
El flaco y el gordo.   In *Teatro completo*, 1960.
El filántropo.   In *Teatro completo*, 1960.
Dos viejos pánicos.   1968.
Estudio en blanco y negro.   In *Teatro breve hispanoamericano contemporáneo*, edited by Carlos Solórzano, 1970.
Una caja de zapatos vacía, edited by Luis F. González-Cruz. 1986.

Fiction

Le carne de René.   1953.
Cuentos fríos (stories).   1956.
Pequeñas maniobras.   1963.
Cuentos.   1964.
Presiones y diamantes.   1967.
El que vino a salvarme (stories).   1970.
Cuentos.   1983.
Un fogonazo (stories).   1987.

Verse

Las furias.   1941.
La isla en peso.   1943.

Other

Poesia y prosa.   1944.

Editor, *Teatro del absurdo* (anthology).   1967.
Editor, *Teatro de la crueldad.*   1967.
Editor, *Antonin Artaud: El teatro y su doble.*   1969.

Translator, *Mineral negro: Poemas,* by René Dépestre, 1962, *Así habló el tío,* by Jean Price Mars, 1968, *Jean Azul,* by Jean Giono, and *Tribálicas,* by Henri Lopes.

*

Criticism

Books:
Matías Montes Huidobro, *Persona, vida y máscara en el teatro cubano,* Miami, Florida, 1973.

Articles:
Ainslee A. McLees, "Elements of Sartrian Philosophy in *Electra Garrigó*", in *Latin American Theater Review*, 7, 1973.
Eleanor J. Martin, *"Dos viejos pánicos*: A Political Interpretation of the Cuban Theater of the Absurd", in *Revista/Review Interamericana*, 9, 1979.

*   *   *

By any standard Virgilio Piñera must be considered one of the major Cuban writers of the 20th century. Through his writing he invested heavily in the fight against fear and oppression in the struggle for decency for the common person. In Cuba he lived under the regimes of various dictators, culminating with the corrupt Batista who fell from power when Fidel Castro entered Havana triumphantly on 1 January 1959. In spite of Piñera's dreams for a better society at the time he published his *Teatro completo* in 1960, he was to see a continuation of the repression, with rule by fear, during the final years of his life.

Piñera was primarily, but by no means exclusively, a playwright. His writings include several volumes of poetry and short stories plus at least three novels, in addition to various works that were still unpublished at the time of his death. In the theatre his life was marked both by success and frustration. It was difficult to stage his plays, and years would elapse between their times of composition and their premieres, when the productions might run a single night. With little reinforcement from public or critics, he wrote only seven plays in a period of 20 years. Only ten plays exist in published form, although there may be as many as four others extant.

Piñera pursued relentlessly a goal of capturing the spirit of his beloved Cuban people. Although he considered himself to be a member of the "middle class", his literate and professional family suffered great indignities and deprivation. His theatre reflects his insights into the customs, the values, and the psyche of his island nation. Piñera has often been considered by the critics as an "existentialist" or "absurdist" writer, appellations that he himself declined to confirm because the plays which evoked the terms anticipated, by several years, the great French writers with whom they are associated. If his plays contained elements of the absurd, he said that was because they were an accurate reflection of the Cuban society and not because he had read Ionesco. He depended on humor, as did the Cuban people, to bridge the absurdity of life and he loved to tell an anecdote about Ionesco who turned back when approaching the island because he realized he had nothing to offer.

Piñera's first work, *Electra Garrigó*, depends on metatheatrical techniques and distancing in order to establish the Greek myth as an internal structure. In more recent years, after its 1948 staging, this is the play that critics have alleged anticipated the absurd in its language and technical effects. The classical figures of Electra and Orestes, functioning within a Cuban ambiance in which Blacks and Caribbean music set the tone, question their projects of human destiny and the role of power—an early indication of Piñera's political posture. *Jesús* continued the sense of political frustration with the search for a savior. Jesús García, the barber who appears to work small miracles, declines to accept the role of the Messiah imposed on him by the people, and as a result is sacrificed uselessly. Although the play has no overt political reference, it reveals a deep-seated nostalgia for paradise, a metaphor for an improved political situation between Grau and Prío in 1948.

Falsa alarma (False Alarm) and *La boda* (The Wedding) illustrate exaggerated situations. The first consists mostly of a dialogue between a judge and a widow in the presence of the murderer of the woman's husband. In this Kafka-like system of corrupt justice, the prisoner is left with his conscience to decide his own fate. *La boda,* accused of being sensationalistic or even pornographic in its time, deals with a broken romance brought about by a strange intrigue in which a friend reveals to the suitor that his fiancée has sagging breasts. *El flaco y el gordo* (Thin Man and Fat Man) suggests an endless cycle of eating and being eaten—that is, a metaphor of power that corrupts.

One of Piñera's best efforts is *Aire frío* (A Cold Draft), a realistic and partially autobiographical piece written on the eve of the Revolution, and indicative of the economic and moral stagnation of Cuba at the time. The need for an electric fan binds this family together across time (1940–58) and serves as the principal motif in the absence of a central conflict or a unified plot. The family's frustrations and disappointments are played out on a minor scale that reinforces the painfulness of everyday decisions and interactions. A play absolutely without pretensions, it communicates with feeling the anguish of the times.

Piñera was arrested for homosexual activity in 1961 and was thereafter out of favor with the government; but he managed to write at least three more plays: *Dos viejos pánicos* (Two Old Persons in Panic), *Estudio en blanco y negro* (Study in Black and White) and *Una caja de zapatos vacía* (An Empty Shoebox). All continue the absurdist language and situations that had characterized some earlier plays, but with a greater sense of urgency and desperation. In *Dos viejos pánicos,* two old folk engage in role-playing, twisted games, and other rituals in order to exorcise both their fear of death and the greater fear that haunts their daily existence. *Estudio en blanco y negro* engages two men in a discussion of their preference as to black or white, which culminates in the absurd intervention of another who prefers yellow. *Una caja de zapatos vacía,* a play known only since Piñera's death, continues the use of games and rituals in dealing with torture, with the same intention of preparing the participant to deal with any eventuality.

When Fidel Castro gave his famous speech "Words to the Intellectuals", admonishing them that only pro-revolutionary writing was acceptable (and therefore nothing was neutral; if works were not pro-revolutionary they were automatically anti-revolutionary), Piñera is reported to have stood and said, "I am afraid; I am very afraid". His early concerns were clearly justified in light of his truncated career subsequently. Nevertheless, Piñera has taken his place as one of the most important Cuban writers of the 20th century.

—George Woodyard

PINERO, (Sir) Arthur Wing. Born in Islington, London, 24 May 1855. Educated at Exmouth Street School, London, 1860–65, and in evening classes at Birkbeck Literary and Scientific Institution, London, 1870–74. Married Myra Emily Hamilton (née Moore, the actress Myra Holme) in 1883 (died 1919); one stepdaughter. Worked and studied in his father's law office, London, 1865–70; solicitor's clerk, Lincoln's Inn Fields, London, 1870–74; actor with the Theatre Royal, Edinburgh, 1874–75, the Royal Alexandra Theatre, Liverpool, 1875–76, and in London, 1876; actor with Henry Irving's Lyceum Company, 1876–81, and the Haymarket Theatre Company, London, 1881–82, 1884–85; first-produced play, *£200 a Year*, staged 1877; retired from acting to become full-time playwright, 1885. Member, Garrick Club, 1887; Vice-President, College Council, 1899–1921; Council member, Royal Academy of Dramatic Art, London, 1906–26; first President, Dramatists' Club, 1909. Fellow, Royal Society of Literature, 1910. Knighted, 1909. Chairman, United Artists' Rifles during World War I. Died in London, 23 November 1934.

Works

Collections

Social Plays (4 vols.), edited by Clayton Hamilton. 1917–22.
Three Plays (includes *The Magistrate; The Second Mrs. Tanqueray; Trelawny of the "Wells"*), edited by Stephen Wyatt. 1985.
Plays (includes *The Schoolmistress; The Second Mrs. Tanqueray; Trelawny of the "Wells"; The Thunderbolt*), edited by George Rowell. 1986.

Stage Works

£200 a Year (produced Globe Theatre, London, 1877).
La Comète; or, Two Hearts (produced Theatre Royal, Croydon, 1878). Nd.
Two Can Play at That Game (produced Lyceum Theatre, London, 1878).
Daisy's Escape (produced Lyceum Theatre, London, 1879).
Hester's Mystery (produced Folly Theatre, London, 1880). 1893.
Bygones (produced Lyceum Theatre, London, 1880).
The Money Spinner (produced Prince's Theatre, Manchester, 1881). 1900.
Imprudence (produced Folly Theatre, London, 1881).
The Squire (produced St. James's Theatre, London, 1881). 1905.
Girls and Boys: A Nursery Tale (produced Toole's Theatre, London, 1882).
The Rector: The Story of Four Friends (produced Court Theatre, London, 1883).

Lords and Commons (produced Theatre Royal, Haymarket, London, 1883).
The Rocket (produced Prince of Wales's Theatre, Liverpool, 1883). 1905.
Low Water (produced Globe Theatre, London, 1884).
The Iron-Master from Georges Ohnet (produced St. James's Theatre, London, 1884).
In Chancery (produced Lyceum Theatre, Edinburgh, 1884). 1905.
Mayfair, from a play by Sardou (produced St. James's Theatre, London, 1885).
The Magistrate (produced Court Theatre, London, 1885). 1892.
The Schoolmistress (produced Court Theatre, London, 1886). 1894.
The Hobby-Horse (produced St. James's Theatre, London, 1886). 1892.
Dandy Dick (produced Court Theatre, London, 1887). 1893.
Sweet Lavender (produced Terry's Theatre, London, 1888). 1893.
The Weaker Sex (produced Theatre Royal, Manchester, 1888; revised version produced 1889). 1894.
The Profligate (produced Garrick Theatre, London, 1889). 1891.
The Cabinet Minister (produced Court Theatre, London, 1890). 1892.
Lady Bountiful: A Story of Years (produced Garrick Theatre, London, 1891). 1891.
The Times (produced Terry's Theatre, London, 1891). 1891.
The Amazons (produced Court Theatre, London, 1893). 1894.
The Second Mrs. Tanqueray (produced St. James's Theatre, London, 1893). 1895.
The Notorious Mrs. Ebbsmith (produced Garrick Theatre, London, 1895). 1895.
The Benefit of the Doubt (produced Comedy Theatre, London, 1895). 1895.
The Princess and the Butterfly; or, The Fantastics (produced St. James's Theatre, London, 1897). 1898.
Trelawny of the "Wells" (produced Court Theatre, London, 1898). 1899.
The Beauty Stone, with J. Comyns Carr, music by Arthur Sullivan (produced Savoy Theatre, London, 1898). 1898.
The Gay Lord Quex (produced Globe Theatre, London, 1899). 1900.
Iris (produced Garrick Theatre, London, 1901). 1902.
Letty (produced Duke of York's Theatre, London, 1903). 1904.
A Wife Without a Smile: A Comedy in Disguise (produced Wyndham's Theatre, London, 1904). 1905.
His House in Order (produced St. James's Theatre, London, 1906). 1906.
The Thunderbolt (produced St. James's Theatre, London, 1908). 1909.
Mid-Channel (produced St. James's Theatre, London, 1909). 1911.
Preserving Mr. Panmure (produced Comedy Theatre, London, 1911). 1912.
The "Mind the Paint" Girl (produced Duke of York's Theatre, London, 1912). 1913.
The Widow of Wasdale Head: A Fantasy (produced Duke of York's Theatre, London, 1912). In *Representative Plays*, edited by Barrett H. Clark, 1921.
Playgoers (produced St. James's Theatre, London, 1913). 1913.

Arthur Wing Pinero (left) and George Bernard Shaw (caricature by Max Beerbohm).

The Bulkeley Peerage. In *Pearson's Magazine*, Christmas 1914.

The Big Drum (produced St. James's Theatre, London, 1915). 1915.

Mr. Livermore's Dream (produced Coliseum, London, 1917).

The Freaks: An Idyll of Suburbia (produced New Theatre, London, 1918). 1922.

Monica's Blue Boy, music by Frederic Cowen (produced New Theatre, London, 1918).

Quick Work (produced Springfield, Massachusetts, 1919).

A Seat in the Park (produced Winter Garden Theatre, London, 1922). 1922.

The Enchanted Cottage (produced Duke of York's Theatre, London, 1922). 1922.

A Private Room (produced Little Theatre, London, 1928). 1928.

Dr. Harmer's Holidays (produced Shubert Theatre, Washington, DC, 1931). In *Two Plays*, 1930.

Child Man. With *Dr. Harmer's Holidays*, 1930.

A Cold June (produced Duchess Theatre, New York, 1932). 1932.

Memoirs and Letters

Collected Letters, edited by J.P. Wearing. 1974.

Other

Robert Louis Stevenson the Dramatist. 1903; edited by C. Hamilton, 1914.

*

Bibliographies:

J.W. Weaver and E.J. Wilcox, "Pinero: An Annotated Bibliography of Writings About Him", in *English Literature in Translation*, 23, 1981.

Criticism

Books:
H. Hamilton Fyfe, *Arthur Wing Pinero's Plays and Players*, London, 1930.

Wilbur Dwight Dunkel, *Arthur Wing Pinero: A Critical Biography with Letters*, Chicago, 1941.

Walter Lazenby, *Arthur Wing Pinero*, New York, 1972.

Jeffrey H. Hubermann, *Late Victorian Farce*, Ann Arbor, Michigan, 1986.

C. Clarke, *Edwardian Drama*, London, 1989.

Leslie Smith, *Modern British Farce: A Selective Study of British Farce from Pinero to the Present*, London and New York, 1989.

Penny Griffin, *Arthur Wing Pinero and Henry Arthur Jones*, London, 1991 (Macmillan Modern Dramatists series).

Articles:
J.P. Wearing, "Pinero the Actor" and "Pinero's Professional Dramatic Roles 1874–1884", in *Theatre Notebook*, Vol. 26 no.4, 1972.

*   *   *

Rather like Tom Taylor before him, Pinero was seen to be more important in his own times than in the perspective of history. In the 1890's he dominated the London stage, producing "serious" social dramas and comedies, ranging from *The Notorious Mrs Ebbsmith* to *The Gay Lord Quex*, and a string of brilliant farces. Among the former *The Second Mrs Tanqueray* has a special significance. It confirmed Pinero's leading role in the British theatre of the time and established the reputation of the actress Mrs. Patrick Campbell. It has remained in the repertoire of the British theatre to the present day.

Both *Ebbsmith* and *Tanqueray* deal with women who, in the eyes of society, have transgressed, who have either quietly pursued their sexual independence or have been "used" by men and compromised as a result. Both—Mrs Ebbsmith particularly—show dignity and strong will-power, though neither can finally be brought to anything so vulgar as to assert her right as a woman to live life on her own terms. Agnes Ebbsmith comes closest to it: in a final *cri* she exclaims, "*I—I* was to lead women! *I* was to show them . . .how men and women may live independent and noble lives without rule, or guidance, or sacrement". But in the end Pinero subjects her to a sentimental retreat. Paula Tanqueray, outmanoeuvred by the selfishness and hypocrisy of others, is brought to suicide. In both cases Pinero backs away from an unconventional resolution, and offers only theatrical cliché.

Both of these plays were produced in 1895, and their "daring" has to be put into the context of Ibsen's much more dynamic treatment of controversial themes as early as 1879, in *A Doll's House*, and 1881, in *Ghosts*—works not unknown on the British stage by the 1890's. But, by way of illustration, though Shaw's independent women were on the stage in the 1890's, the truly controversial Mrs. Warren had to wait until 1902.

In his farces Pinero rivalled, and in many ways bettered, those of the French stage. Plays such as *The Magistrate*, *The Schoolmistress*, and *Dandy Dick* remain brilliant examples of their craft and entirely sustainable in the contemporary theatre. At the centre, they are all powered by plots of splendid English dottiness, which gives them a style and eccentric verve that distinguishes them from the farces of Feydeau, Sardou, and the French school (with their manic sexual adventures).

In *The Magistrate* we have a flirtatious young man brought up to believe by his mother that he is only 14 (in order to "adjust" her own age). His precocity leads everyone into riotous affairs which culminate in the magistrate having to sentence his wife to prison for undignified transgressions in which he, himself, was involved.

In *The Schoolmistress*, the heroine leads a double life, being, by day, principal of Volumnia College for the Daughters of Gentlemen and, by night, Miss Constance Delaporte, artiste at the Comic Opera! In *Dandy Dick* the Rural Dean finds himself implicated in nobbling a racehorse in aid of Parish Funds. Pinero crafts his farces with consummate skill, maintaining pace of wit and incident and elaborating the action by the introduction of masterfully conceived scenes and characters—for instance, Mr. Goff, the fireman, in *The Schoolmistress*, whose function it is to calm the ladies in the midst of conflagration by retelling interesting anecdotes from his career.

That the same skill shown in the farces cannot usually be seen in the many of Pinero's other comedies and social dramas (which now have a historical rather than a social bite to them) should not persuade us to diminish their impact at the time of composition. The best of his comedies have a delicate charm. His failures were, perhaps, those of discretion and understatement—a wish not to be too shocking—and a vulnerable sentimentality. But the theatrical craftsmanship in all areas of his work was never less than competent (refining the worst excesses of melodrama into highly charged dramas), and at its best (as in the farces), unrivalled.

Trelawny of the "Wells" stands on its own as one of the most effective pieces of theatrical nostalgia on the British stage—a tribute to Tom Robertson. In a sense, this play symbolises Pinero's role as a writer of, and for, the 19th century. His playwriting in the 20th century contained a number of plays of note—*His House in Order* and *The Thunderbolt* among them—but, like too many English cricket teams, the tail was rather long, and his writing into the 1930's failed to maintain the considerable strengths of the 1890's and the early years of this century.

—Martin Banham

See also *Volume 1* entries on *The Magistrate*; *The Second Mrs. Tanqueray*.

PINGET, Robert. Born in Geneva, Switzerland, 19 July 1919. Educated at Collège de Genève; school of law, law degree; École des Beaux-Arts, Paris. Practised law, 1944–46; moved to France, 1946, and worked as painter; also briefly a journalist; secondary-school teacher of drawing and French, near London, 1950; freelance writer from 1951: mainly a novelist during the 1950's; first-produced play, *Lettre morte*, staged 1960; exhibited his paintings in Paris, 1964. Recipient: Prix des Critiques, 1960; Prix Femina, 1965. Grand Prix National des Lettres, 1987; Grand Prix de la Société.

Works

Collections

"Ici ou ailleurs" suivi de "Architruc" et de "L'Hypothèse". 1961.
Plays 1 (includes *The Old Tune; Clope; Dead Letter*), translated by Samuel Beckett and Barbara Bray. 1963; as *Three Plays* (US edition), 1966.
Plays 2 (includes *Architruc; About Mortin; The Hypothesis*), translated by Barbara Bray. 1967; as *Three Plays* (US edition), 1968.
Paralchimie; Architruc; L'Hypohthèse; Nuit. 1973.
Un Testament bizarre; Mortin pas mort; Dictée; Sophisme et sadisme; Le Chrysanthème; Lubie. 1986.

Stage Works

Lettre morte, from the novel *Le Fiston* (produced Théâtre Récamier, Paris, 1960). 1959; translated as *Dead Letter*, in *Plays 1*, 1963.
Ici ou ailleurs, from the novel *Clope au dossier* (produced in German, Schauspielhaus, Zurich, 1961). In *Ici ou ailleurs . . .* (collection), 1961; translated as *Clope*, in *Plays 1*, 1963.
Architruc, from the novel *Baga* (produced Comédie de Paris, 1962). In *Ici ou ailleurs . . .* (collection), 1961; translated as *Architruc*, in *Plays 2*, 1967.
L'Hypothèse (produced Musée d'Art Moderne, Paris,

1965). In *Ici ou ailleurs . . .* (collection), 1961; translated as *The Hypothesis*, in *Plays 2*, 1967.
La Manivelle, from the radio play (produced Théâtre de Lutèce, Paris, 1961).
Identité (produced Petit Odéon, Paris, 1972). With *Abel et Bela*, 1971.
Abel et Bela (produced L'Absidiole, Paris, 1971). With *Identité*, 1971.
Paralchimie (produced Petit Odéon, Paris, 1977). In *Paralchimie . . .* (collection), 1973.
Autour de Mortin (produced Théâtre Essaïon, Paris, 1979).
Nuit. In *Paralchimie . . .* (collection), 1973.
Un Testament bizarre. In *Un Testament bizarre . . .* (collection), 1986; translated as *A Bizarre Will*, 1987.
Mortin pas mort. In *Un Testament bizarre . . .* (collection), 1986.
Dictée. In *Un Testament bizarre . . .* (collection), 1986.
Sophisme et sadisme. In *Un Testament bizarre . . .* (collection), 1986.
Le Chrysanthème. In *Un Testament bizarre . . .* (collection), 1986.
Cette Chose, with Jean Deyrolle. 1990.

Radio Plays

Tous ceux qui tombent, from a radio play by Beckett (published 1957); *La Manivelle* (published, with English translation as *The Old Tune*, 1960); *Autour de Mortin* (published 1965; translated as *About Mortin*, in *Plays 2*, 1967); *Le Réscapé*, 1974; *Le Bourreau*, 1975 (as *Wer spricht?*), 1978 (as *Le Bourreau*); *Lubie* (published in book form, 1986).

Fiction

Entre Fantoine et Agapa (stories). 1951; translated as *Between Fantoine and Agapa*, 1983.
Mahu; ou, Le matériau. 1952; translated as *Mahu; or, The Material*, 1966.
Le Renard et la boussole. 1953.
Graal Flibuste. 1956; revised edition, 1966.
Baga. 1958; translated as *Baga*, 1967.
Le Fiston. 1959; translated as *No Answer*, 1961; as *Monsieur Levert*, 1961.
Clope au dossier. 1961.
L'Inquisitoire. 1962; translated as *The Inquisitory*, 1966.
Quelqu'un. 1965; translated as *Someone*, 1984.
Le Libéra. 1968; translated as *The Libera Me Domine*, 1972.
Passacaille. 1969; translated as *Recurrent Melody*, 1975; as *Passacaglia*, 1978.
Fable. 1971; translated as *Fable*, 1980.
Cette voix. 1975; translated as *That Voice*, 1982.
L'Apocryphe. 1980; translated as *The Apocrypha*, 1987.
Monsieur Songe. 1982; translated as *Monsieur Songe*, 1989.
Le Harnais. 1984.
Charrue. 1985.
L'Ennemi. 1987.
Du Nerf. 1990.
Théo ou le temps neuf. 1991.

*

Criticism

Articles:
Robert M. Henkels, "Rats, Cats and Bats: Character, Plot and Language in Roger Pinget's Plays", in *Review of Contemporary Fiction*, vol.3 no.2, 1983.

* * *

Robert Pinget's dramatic writings are original, challenging, and often cruelly funny. They are also largely devoid of the traditional theatrical attributes. Indeed, *Autour de Mortin*—arguably the most developed of his dramatic works—is habitually identified not as a play, but as a series of 'dialogues' (although it includes at least one monologue). Both it and *La Manivelle* (1960) were written for radio. Since he writes to be heard, this is a medium in which—like his friend and translator Samuel Beckett—Pinget excels.

Pinget is widely known as a *nouveau romancier* (though it is a label that he himself shuns) and several of his writings for the stage are closely related to the novels that preceded them. Thus, for example, *Architruc, Lettre Morte (Dead Letter)*, and *Ici ou Ailleurs (Clope)* are based respectively on the novels *Baga, Le Fiston*, and *Clope au dossier*. In his plays Pinget works, with seemingly quixotic determination, against the grain of theatrical convention—even, one might argue, against the theatrical medium itself. It would be churlish to suggest that this is simply because he is a better novelist than playwright. In fact, he has a clear and individualistic conception of his theatrical aims, and pursues them consistently. He seems largely uninterested in the physical possibilities of the stage. His work contains no Beckettian experimentation with movement in space. He eschews psychology and the development of character, makes minimal use of physical action, and has no use for plot. Instead, for both dramatic and comic effect, he relies largely on linguistic means. The chief structural feature of his plays is repetition, and he derives dramatic tension principally from contradiction. Pinget's sources of humour include malapropism, misunderstanding, and—above all—biting verbal irony. His ear for the spoken language is second to none, and his ability to write for spoken delivery is masterly. He is equally at home with monologue and dialogue. Habitually, his characters speak a French that is non-literary, even *encanaillé*. But Pinget is capable of writing in a range of styles, varying from the terse, spare, almost stichomythic exchanges of *Architruc*, to the pedantic circumlocutions of *Un Testament bizarre (A Bizarre Will)*.

Pinget's scorn of convention is both formally and thematically manifest in his work. In *Abel et Bela* he satirizes the worst excesses of French boulevard theatre by depicting two actors in the process of writing a play, which starts out as a comedy of manners set in English high society between the wars, evolves into a scenario for an orgy, and then somehow becomes a dance of death. Each genre is as derivative as the last. The whole is interspersed with Abel's and Bela's reflections on the nature of theatre. Abel duly concludes that its essence lies in the examination of the self. Sadly he is also forced to recognize that there is little in the human soul worthy of prolonged scrutiny. The play's less-than-definitive ending is provided by Bela's plaintive remark, "je descends en moi-même et je trouve quoi? (*Un temps*) Je trouve quoi?". The emptiness and unoriginality of human existence are recurrent themes for Pinget, just as inconclusiveness is a formal hallmark of his dramas. Characteristically these end with the three *points de suspension*. In a world as inconsequential as that depicted by Pinget, no meaningful conclusion can possibly be drawn.

As one might expect of a playwright with such a bleak vision, décor is scant and frequently non-existent. Where physical setting is exploited, it is normally non-realistic. *Ici ou ailleurs* deals with the futility of our attempts to change our lives by physical displacement. Here Pinget's protagonist inhabits a hut covered in leaves, bizarrely located in the entrance hall of a railway station, a setting which encapsulates the ambivalence of his attitude to travel. Having spent the whole of the play dissuading others from going on the journeys they want to undertake, he himself finally packs up and departs. In other works too, Pinget uses décor to comment ironically on the aspirations of his characters. In *Architruc*, a distinctly unimposing king is discovered in what looks like a kind of squalid royal bedsitter: "*une chambre pauvre meublée avec prétention*". As the play opens, his minister, Baga, who addresses him impertinently throughout as "tu", is audibly answering the call of nature behind a screen. The play consists largely of overtly bogus routines acted out by Baga for his master, possibly a representation of the power of words to create imaginary scenes. (In French, "le bagou" means volubility, glibness, the gift of the gab. Baga may simply be an embodiment of language itself.) The play's title suggests both creation (an "architecte" designs buildings) and falsehood ("truquer" = to fake). By implication, the play questions the claim of the writer of fiction to be an authoritative voice in human matters. The inherent contradictions of his situation are evoked precisely by the discordant décor in which Pinget places him.

Pinget's attitude to character is uncompromisingly dismissive. Frequently, his speakers are either identified simply by their initials or left in anonymity. Where characters do have names, these are often either clichéd, grotesque, or absurd. Thus Clope (Cigarette Butt) and Flan (Waffle), the two main characters of *Ici ou ailleurs*, have names which evoke only worthlessness. The protagonist of *Lettre morte*, the mythomaniac M. Levert, bears a surname notable only for its banality. Pinget's characters can lay claim to no core of self. They exist without essence. Their reality—scarcely a stable or unproblematical one—is to be found nowhere but in the words they speak, or in those that are spoken about them. Even the writer, Mortin, who may be Pinget's *alter ego*, is someone we glimpse only through the circumstantial and conflicting testimony of others.

Language is thus central to Pinget's theatre. In all the plays, language is both Pinget's material of construction and his chief subject matter. He explores—in the light of his convictions—a range of fundamental notions associated with its use. As well as authorship, authority, and identity, these include authenticity, value, and truth. On a thematic level, Pinget's findings are pessimistic: concepts normally taken for granted evaporate under the glare of his scrutiny, and not a single one of his characters seems capable even of originality, let alone of the other qualities customarily ascribed to language. Formally, however, what he has to offer is more encouraging, for proof that it is possible to speak in a fresh voice can be found in his originality as playwright itself. Pinget's idiosyncrasy as a dramatist is no accident: it is his highest achievement.

—Tim Lewis

PINTER, Harold. Born in Hackney, London, 10 October 1930. Educated at Hackney Downs Grammar School, 1943–47; Royal Academy of Dramatic Art, London, 1948. Married 1) the actress Vivien Merchant in 1956 (divorced 1980), one son; 2) the writer Lady Antonia Fraser in 1980. Professional actor, 1949–60, and occasionally since then; first-produced play, *The Room*, staged 1957; Associate Director, National

Theatre, London, 1973–83; director, United British Artists, 1983; editor and publisher, Greville Press, Warwick, from 1988; member of the editorial board, *Cricket World*, from 1989. Also stage director. Recipient: Italia prize, for television play, 1962; Berlin Film Festival Silver Bear, 1963; Screenwriters Guild Award, for television play, 1963, for screenplay, 1963; New York Film Critics Award, 1964; BAFTA award, 1965, 1971; Tony Award, 1967; Whitbread Award, 1967; New York Drama Critics Circle Award, 1967, 1980; Writers Guild Award, 1971; Cannes Film Festival Golden Palm, 1971; Austrian State Prize, 1973; Pirandello Prize, 1980; Donatello Prize, 1982; Giles Cooper Award, 1982; Bobst Award, 1984. D.Litt: universities of Reading, 1970, Birmingham, 1971, Glasgow, 1974, East Anglia, Norwich, 1974, Stirling, 1979, Hull, 1986, Sussex, 1990, Brown University, Providence, Rhode Island, 1982. Fellow, Royal Society of Literature. Honorary fellow, Modern Language Association (US), 1970. CBE (Commander, Order of the British Empire), 1966.

Works

Collections

"The Birthday Party" and Other Plays (includes *The Dumb Waiter* and *The Room*).   1960.
"A Slight Ache" and Other Plays (includes *The Dwarfs; A Night Out*; and sketches).   1961.
"The Collection" and "The Lover" (includes the prose piece *The Examination*).   1963.
"The Dwarfs" and Eight Revue Sketches (includes *Trouble in the Works; The Black and White; Request Stop; Last to Go; Applicant; Interview; That's All; That's Your Trouble*). 1965.
"Tea Party" and Other Plays.   1967.
Early Plays: A Night Out; Night School; Revue Sketches.   1968.
"Landscape" and "Silence" (includes *Night*). 1969.
Five Screenplays (includes *The Caretaker; The Servant, The Pumpkin Eater; Accident; The Quiller Memorandum*). 1971; modified version, omitting *The Caretaker* and including *The Go-Between*, 1971.
Plays (4 vols.).   1975–81; as *Complete Works* (US edition; 4 vols.), 1977–81.
"The French Lieutenant's Woman" and Other Screenplays (includes *Langrishe; Go Down; The Last Tycoon*).   1982.
Other Places (includes *Family Voices; Victoria Station; A Kind of Alaska*).   1982.
"The Comfort of Strangers" and Other Screenplays (includes *Reunion; Turtle Diary; Victory*).   1990.

Stage Works

The Room (produced Bristol University, Bristol, 1957).   In *"The Birthday Party" and Other Plays*, 1960.
The Birthday Party (produced Arts Theatre, Cambridge, 1958).   1959; revised version, 1965.

Harold Pinter (right, playing Mick) with actor Donald Pleasance (playing Davies) during rehearsals of Pinter's *The Caretaker* at the Duchess Theatre, London, 1961.

Sketches in *One to Another* (produced Lyric Theatre, Hammersmith, London, 1959). 1960.

Sketches in *Pieces of Eight* (produced Apollo Theatre, London, 1959). In *"A Slight Ache" and Other Plays*, 1961.

A Slight Ache (broadcast 1959; produced Arts Theatre, London, 1961). In *"A Slight Ache" and Other Plays*, 1961.

The Dumb Waiter (produced in German, Frankfurt, 1959; produced, in English, Hampstead Theatre, London, 1960). In *"The Birthday Party" and Other Plays*, 1960.

The Dwarfs (broadcast 1960; produced Arts Theatre, London, 1963; revised version produced 1966). In *"A Slight Ache" and Other Plays*, 1961.

The Caretaker (produced Arts Theatre, London, 1960). 1960.

A Night Out (produced Comedy Theatre, London, 1961). In *"A Slight Ache" and Other Plays*, 1961.

The Collection (produced Aldwych Theatre, London, 1962). 1962.

The Lover (produced Arts Theatre, London, 1963). With *The Collection*, 1963.

Tea Party (televised 1965; produced Eastside Playhouse, New York, 1968). 1965; revised version, 1968.

The Homecoming (produced New Theatre, Cardiff, 1965). 1965; revised version, 1968.

Sketches: *That's Your Trouble; That's All; Applicant; Interview*. In *"The Dwarfs" and Eight Revue Sketches*, 1965.

The Basement (televised 1967; produced Eastside Playhouse, New York, 1968). In *"Tea Party" and Other Plays*, 1967.

Landscape (broadcast 1968; produced Aldwych Theatre, London, 1969). 1968.

Silence (produced Aldwych Theatre, London, 1969). With *Landscape* and *Night*, 1969.

Night. In *Mixed Doubles* (produced Hampstead Theatre, London, 1969). With *Landscape* and *Silence*, 1969.

Old Times (produced Aldwych Theatre, London, 1971). 1971.

No Man's Land (produced by the National Theatre, Old Vic, London, 1975). 1975.

Betrayal (produced National Theatre, London, 1978). 1978.

The Hothouse (produced Hampstead Theatre, London, 1980). 1980; revised version (produced 1982), 1982.

Family Voices, from the radio play (produced National Theatre, London, 1981). 1981.

Victoria Station (produced as part of *Other Voices*, London, 1982). In *Other Voices*, 1982.

A Kind of Alaska (produced as part of *Other Voices*, London, 1982). In *Other Voices*, 1982.

Precisely (sketch), in *The Big One* (produced London, 1983).

One for the Road (produced Lyric Theatre, Hammersmith, London, 1984). 1984; revised version, 1985.

Mountain Language (produced National Theatre, London, 1988). 1988.

Party Time (produced Almeida Theatre, London, 1991). With *Mountain Language*, 1991.

The New World Order (produced Royal Court Theatre, London, 1991).

Screenplays

The Compartment. In *Project 1*, with Samuel Beckett and Eugène Ionesco. 1963.

The Servant (released 1963). In *Five Screenplays*, 1971.

The Guest (The Caretaker) (released 1964). In *Five Screenplays*, 1971.

The Pumpkin Eater (released 1964). In *Five Screenplays*, 1971.

The Quiller Memorandum (released 1964). In *Five Screenplays*, 1971.

Accident (released 1967). In *Five Screenplays*, 1971.

The Birthday Party (released 1968).

The Go-Between (released 1971). In *Five Screenplays* (revised edition), 1971.

The Homecoming (released 1976).

The Last Tycoon (released 1976). In *"The French Lieutenant's Woman" and Other Screenplays*, 1982.

The Proust Screenplay: A la Recherche du temps perdu. 1977.

The French Lieutenant's Woman (released 1981). 1981.

Betrayal (released 1983).

Turtle Diary (released 1985). In *"The Comfort of Strangers" and Other Screenplays*, 1990.

The Trial (released 1989).

The Handmaid's Tale (released 1990).

Reunion (released 1990). In *"The Comfort of Strangers" and Other Screenplays*, 1991.

The Comfort of Strangers (released 1991). In *"The Comfort of Strangers" and Other Screenplays*.

Victory. In *"The Comfort of Strangers" and Other Screenplays*, 1991.

Television Plays
(most published in stage versions: see Stage Works)

Night School, 1960 (published in *Plays 2*, 1979); *A Night Out*, 1960; *The Collection*, 1961, revised version, 1978; *The Lover*, 1963; *Tea Party*, 1965 (published 1965); *The Basement*, 1967 (published with *Tea Party*, 1967); *Monologue*, 1973 (published 1973); *No Man's Land*, 1978; *Langrishe, Go Down*, from the novel by Aidan Higgins, 1978 (published in *"The French Lieutenant's Woman" and Other Screenplays*, 1982); *A Kind of Alaska*, 1984; *One for the Road*, 1985; *Mountain Language*, 1988; *The Heat of the Day*, from the novel by Elizabeth Bowen, 1989 (published 1989); *Party Time*, 1992.

Radio Plays
(most published in stage versions: see Stage Works)

A Slight Ache, 1959; *The Dwarfs*, 1960 (published in *"A Slight Ache" and Other Plays*, 1961); *A Night Out*, 1960; Sketches: *That's Your Trouble; That's All; Applicant; Interview*, 1964; *Dialogue for Three*, 1984 (published in *Stand*, 6, 1963; in book form, in *Plays 3*, 1978); *Landscape*, 1968; *Family Voices*, 1981 (published 1981); *Players*, 1985.

Fiction

The Dwarfs. 1990.

Verse

Poems, edited by Alan Clodd. 1968; revised edition, 1971.
I Know the Place. 1979.

Other

Mac (on Anew McMaster). 1968.
Poems and Prose 1949–1977. 1978; revised edition, as *Collected Poems and Prose*, 1986.

Editor, with John Fuller and Peter Redgrove, *New Poems 1967: A PEN Anthology*. 1968.

Editor, with Geoffrey Godbert and Anthony Astbury, *100 Poems by 100 Poets*. 1986.

*

Bibliographies:

Rudiger Imhof, *Pinter: A Bibliography: His Works and Occasional Writings with a Comprehensive Checklist of Criticism and Reviews of the London Productions*, London, 1975.
Steven H. Gale, *Harold Pinter: An Annotated Bibliography*, Boston and London, 1978.

Criticism

Books:
Arnold P. Hinchcliffe, *Harold Pinter*, New York, 1967; revised edition, 1981.
Walter Kerr, *Harold Pinter*, New York, 1967.
Ronald Hayman, *Harold Pinter*, London, 1968; revised edition, 1980.
John Russell Taylor, *Harold Pinter*, London, 1969.
Lois Gordon, *Stratagems to Uncover Nakedness: The Dramas of Harold Pinter*, Columbia, Missouri, 1969.
James H. Hollis, *Harold Pinter: The Poetics of Silence*, Carbondale, Illinois, 1970.
Alrene Sykes, *Harold Pinter*, St Lucia (Queensland) and New York, 1970.
Martin Esslin, *The Peopled Wound: The Plays of Harold Pinter*, London and New York, 1970; revised edition, as *Pinter: A Study of His Plays*, London, 1973; with further revisions, 1977; further revised edition, as *Pinter: The Playwright*, London, 1982.
Katherine H. Burkman, *The Dramatic World of Harold Pinter: Its Basis in Ritual*, Columbus, Missouri, 1971.
Herman T. Schroll, *Harold Pinter: A Study of His Reputation (1958–69) and a Checklist*, Metuchen, New Jersey, 1971.
Arthur Ganz (ed.), *Harold Pinter: A Collection of Critical Essays*, Englewood Cliffs, New Jersey, 1972.
Simon Trussler, *The Plays of Harold Pinter: An Assessment*, London, 1973.
Arnold P. Hinchcliffe, *Harold Pinter*, New York, 1975.
Austin E. Quigley, *The Pinter Problem*, Princeton, New Jersey, 1975.
Lucina Paquet Gabbard, *The Dream Structure of Pinter's Plays: A Psychoanalytic Approach*, Rutherford, New Jersey, 1976.
Bernard F. Dukore, *Where the Laughter Stops: Pinter's Tragi-Comedy*, Columbia, Missouri, 1976.
Steven H. Gale, *Butter's Going Up: A Critical Analysis of Harold Pinter's Work*, Durham, North Carolina, 1977.
Surendra Sahai, *Harold Pinter: A Critical Evaluation*, Salzburg, 1981.
Bernard F. Dukore, *Harold Pinter*, London and New York, 1982.
Kristin Morrison, *Canters and Chronicles: The Use of Narrative in the Plays of Samuel Beckett and Harold Pinter*, Chicago, 1983.
Guido Almansi and Simon Henderson, *Harold Pinter*, London, 1983.
David T. Thompson, *Pinter: The Player's Playwright*, London and New York, 1985.
Elin Diamond, *Pinter's Comic Play*, Lewisburg, Pennsylvania, 1985.

Alan Bond (ed.), *Harold Pinter: You Never Heard Such Silence*, London and New York, 1985.
Joanne Klein, *Making Pictures: The Pinter Screenplays*, Columbus, Ohio, 1985.
Steven H. Gale (ed.), *Harold Pinter: Critical Approaches*, New Jersey, 1986.
Michael Scott (ed.), *Harold Pinter: The Birthday Party; The Caretaker; The Homecoming: A Casebook*, London, 1986.
Elizabeth Sakellaridou, *Pinter's Female Portraits: A Study of Female Characters in the Plays of Harold Pinter*, London, 1988.
Bernard F. Dukore, *Harold Pinter* (second edition), London, 1988.
Volker Strunk, *Harold Pinter: Towards a Poetics of His Plays*, New York, 1989.
Susan H. Merritt, *Pinter in Play: Critical Strategies and the Plays of Harold Pinter*, Durham, North Carolina, 1990.

* * *

Harold Pinter is widely considered the best, most important, and most influential British dramatist of the second half of the 20th century; some critics would even consider him the most important English playwright of the entire century.

At the beginning of his career Pinter was considered an obscurist, even a member of the "theatre of the absurd", both of which are erroneous assessments. Part of the problem that the popular audience and critics alike had with Pinter's early plays was that the dramas are not traditional in either style or theme. However, as audiences have learned to approach Pinter without any preconceived notions about the nature of what his drama *should* be, they have also come to understand it better.

A Pinter play is very much like life; if one gets on a bus and sits behind two people already engaged in conversation, there is no expectation that those two people will explain who or what they are discussing. If either the listener or those conversing leave the bus before the discussion is completed, the listener must make sense of the conversation on the basis of the short portion that has been heard. So it is with a Pinter play.

Pinter's ability to reproduce ordinary speech with such accuracy that his dialogue has been labeled "tape-recorder-dialogue" was especially frustrating to audiences at the beginning of his career because the realistic conversation contrasted so vividly with the seemingly illogical events that transpired on the stage. A careful analysis of the plays, though, shows that these actions are in fact very logical and that the entire structure of the plays themselves is quite logical.

Pinter's first three plays, *The Room*, *The Birthday Party*, and *The Dumb Waiter*, became known as "comedies of menace". In many ways they established the stylistic and thematic directions that Pinter has developed throughout his career. In *The Room* Mrs. Hud, the protagonist, seeks sanctuary from the outside world in her room, but a visitor enters and his presence leads to her breakdown. In Pinter's early plays a sense of menace is omnipresent. While the room may serve as a sanctuary, anything outside the door may represent a threat to those within. This creates a need for verification— that is, a need to determine whether the person on the other side of the door is a friend or an enemy. In order to make this determination, however, communication is required, and those within are unwilling to communicate fully with those outside because, if they do so, they may reveal some vulnerability which will allow the intruder to destroy them. A vicious circle is thus created. In *The Birthday Party* the protagonist tries to run away from danger, but is pursued and captured. In *The Dumb Waiter* the menacers, two hired killers, are themselves threatened.

Pinter then turned to an examination of the nature of menace in his next series of plays, *A Slight Ache*, *The Caretaker*, *The Collection*, *The Lover*, and *The Homecoming* showing it to be more internal than external. It also differs from person to person, but is based on psychological needs which are unfulfilled, and which therefore cause the characters to do almost anything in a desperate attempt to fulfill these needs.

Beginning with *Landscape*, Pinter turned his attention to the workings of the human mind—a natural, organic thematic development. In *Silence* and *Night*, Pinter illustrates how "real" imaginary events can be and how important memory is in creating the world in which we live. In a sense, memory transcends time because frequently we can remember events that took place ten or twenty years ago more clearly than those which took place last week or even yesterday. The culmination of this group of plays is *Old Times*, in which one of the characters observes that, "There are some things one remembers even though they may never have happened. There are things I remember which may never have happened but as I recall them so they take place". In this play two characters are in conflict for the affections of a third person. In order to make themselves more attractive to the third person, and simultaneously to denigrate their opponent, both create stories about their pasts which place them in a good light and their opponent in a bad light. *No Man's Land* and *Betrayal* are Pinter's last two major plays to have been performed, and they are both in this category of "memory plays".

More recently Pinter has written a number of short pieces which are very political in nature, clearly signalling another change of direction in the themes that he is exploring.

What makes Pinter unique is that he examines a problem in a series of plays, he brings together all of his thoughts about that subject, and then moves to another set of plays which is a logical extension of the previous set. In addition, the themes of Pinter's plays—the nature of reality, human interaction, the workings of the human mind—are of universal concern.

A final element of Pinter's dramaturgy that sets him above his contemporaries is his craftsmanship. As a former repertory actor (who still acts on occasion) and director, Pinter is well aware of the elements that are required for a successful stage production. He has written numerous highly acclaimed film scripts, too, and his experience in the cinema is evident in the structures of some of his stage plays. All of this comes together impressively when his stylistics are examined in comparison with his thematic development. It is obvious that at each stage of his development Pinter has utilized a style that is particularly appropriate for the thematic cluster that he is exploring. Thus, the early stage plays are full of harsh, sharp imagery and dialogue, whereas the later plays are much more lyrical and poetic in nature, a reflection of the movement from a concern with the physical world to concern with abstract subject matter.

The number of playwrights worldwide who admit to having been influenced by Pinter is, in itself, significant and an indication of his importance in the history of world theater. His imaginative and masterful approach to the dramatic expression of consequential themes is the characteristic that has made Harold Pinter one of England's most important playwrights.

—Steven H. Gale

See also *Volume 1* entries on *The Birthday Party*; *The Caretaker*; *The Homecoming*; *No Man's Land*; *Old Times*.

PIRANDELLO, Luigi. Born in Agrigento, Sicily, 28 June 1867. Educated at schools in Agrigento, to 1882, and Palermo, to 1886; University of Palermo, 1886–87; studied law at the University of Rome, 1887–89; studied philology at the University of Bonn, 1889–91, received doctorate. Married Antonietta Portulano in 1894 (committed to a mental clinic from 1919); two sons and one daughter. Writer in Rome from 1891; teacher, Regio Istituto Superiore di Magistero Femminile, 1897–1922; co-editor, *Ariel*, 1898; financial disaster in 1903 forced him to increase his income by tutoring and working as travelling examination commissioner; first-produced play, *L'epilogo*, staged (as *La Morsa*) 1910; became involved more in the theatre during World War I; director, with Nino Martoglio, Teatro Mediterraneo troupe, Rome, 1919; co-founder, Teatro d'Arte di Roma, 1925–28; joined Fascist Party, 1924, but his relations with it were strained; lived outside Italy, mainly in Berlin and Paris, 1928–33. Recipient: Nobel Prize for Literature, 1934. Member, Italian Academy. Légion d'Honneur (France). Died in Rome, 10 December 1936.

Luigi Pirandello in his garden in Rome.

Works

Collections

Three Plays (includes *Six Characters in Search of an Author; Right You Are (If You Think You Are); Henry IV*), translated by A. Livingston and E. Storer. 1922.
"Each in His Own Way" and Two Other Plays (includes *The Pleasure of Honesty* and *Naked*). 1923.
The One-Act Plays (includes *The Vise; Sicilian Limes; The Doctor's Duty; The Jar; By Judgement of the Court; Chee-Chee; The Imbecile; At the Gate; The House with the Column; The Man with the Flower in His Mouth; Our Lord of the Ship*), translated by E. Abbott, A. Livingston, and B.V. Mitchell. 1928.
Naked Masks (includes *Six Characters in Search of an Author; Henry IV; It Is So (If You Think So); Each in His Own Way*), edited by Eric Bentley. 1952.
Opere (6 vols.). 1956–60.
"The Mountain Giants" and Other Plays (includes *The New Colony; When Someone is Somebody*), translated by Marta Abba. 1958.
Three Plays (includes *The Rules of the Game; Henry IV; Right You Are (If You Think You Are)*), translated by F. May and R. Rietty. 1969.
Collected Plays, various translators, edited by Robert Rietty. 1985—:
　1. *Henry IV; The Man with the Flower in His Mouth; Right You Are (If You Think You Are); Lazarus*. 1985.
　2. *Six Characters in Search of an Author; All for the Best; Clothe the Naked; Limes from Sicily*. 1988.
　3. *The Rules of the Game; Each in His Own Way; Grafted; The Other Son*. 1992.

Stage Works

L'epilogo. 1898; as *La morsa* (produced Teatro Metastasio, Rome, 1910), 1926; translated as *The Vise*, in *One-Act Plays*, 1928.
Scamandro (produced Teatro dell'Accademia dei Fidenti, Florence, 1928). 1909.
Lumie di Sicilia (produced 1910). 1911; translated as *Sicilian Limes*, in *One-Act Plays*, 1928; as *Limes from Sicily*, in *Collected Plays 2*, 1988.
Il dovere di medico (produced Sala Umberto I, Rome, 1913). 1912; translated as *The Doctor's Duty*, in *One-Act Plays*, 1928.
Se non così (produced Teatro Manzoni, Milan, 1915). 1915; revised version, as *La ragione degli altri*, 1921.
L'aria del continente, with Nino Martoglio (produced 1916).
Pensaci Giacomino! (produced Teatro Nazionale, Rome, 1916). 1917.
La giara (produced Teatro Nazionale, Rome, 1916). 1925; translated as *The Jar*, in *One-Act Plays*, 1928.
Il berretto a sonagli (produced Teatro Nazionale, Rome, 1916). 1918.
Liolá (produced Teatro Argentina, Rome, 1916). 1917; translated as *Liola*, in *Naked Masks*, 1952; revised version, music by Giuseppe Mule (produced 1935).
'A vilanza, with Nino Martoglio (produced Teatro Argentina, Rome, 1917).
Così è (si vi pare) (produced Teatro Olimpico, Milan, 1917). 1918; translated as *Right You Are (If You Think So)*, in *Three Plays*, 1922; as *It is So (If You Think So)*, in *Naked Masks*, 1952; as *Right You Are (If You Think You Are)*, in *Collected Plays 1*.
Il piacere dell'onesta (produced Teatro Carignano, Turin,

1918). 1918; translated as *The Pleasure of Honesty*, in *"Each in His Own Way" and Two Other Plays*, 1923.
Il giuoco delle parti (produced Teatro Quirino, Rome, 1918). 1919; translated as *The Rules of the Game*, in *Three Plays*, 1959; several subsequent translations under same title.
Ma non è una cosa seria (produced Teatro Rossini, Livorno, 1918). 1919.
La patente (produced Teatro Argentina, Rome, 1919). 1918; translated as *By Judgement of the Court*, in *One-Act Plays*, 1928.
L'uomo, la bestia, e la virtù (produced Teatro Olimpico, Milan, 1919). 1922; translated as *Man, Beast and Virtue*, 1989.
'U ciclopu, from *Cyclops* by Euripides (produced Teatro Argentina, Rome, 1919). 1967.
L'innesto (produced Teatro Manzoni, Milan, 1919). 1921; translated as *Grafted*, in *Collected Plays 3*, 1992.
Come prima, meglio di prima (produced Teatro Goldoni, Venice, 1920). 1921.
Tutto per bene (produced 1920). 1920; translated as *All for the Best*, 1960, and in *Collected Plays 2*, 1988.
La signora Morli, una e due (produced Teatro Argentina, Rome, 1920). 1922.
Cecè (produced Teatro del Gran Casino, San Pellegrino, 1920). 1926; translated as *Chee-Chee*, in *One-Act Plays*, 1928.
Sei personaggi in cerca d'autore (produced Teatro Valle, Rome, 1921). 1921; translated as *Six Characters in Search of an Author*, in *Three Plays*, 1922: several subsequent translations under same title.
Vestire gl'ignudi (produced Teatro Quirino, Rome, 1922). 1923; translated as *Naked*, in *"Each in His Own Way" and Two Other Plays*, 1923; as *To Clothe the Naked*, 1962; as *Clothe the Naked*, in *Collected Plays 2*, 1988.
Enrico IV (produced Teatro Manzoni, Milan, 1922). 1922; translated as *Henry IV*, in *Three Plays*, 1922: several subsequent translations under same title.
L'imbecille (produced Teatro Quirino, Rome, 1922). 1926; translated as *The Imbecile*, in *One-Act Plays*, 1928.
All'uscita (produced Teatro Quirino, Rome, 1922). 1926; translated as *At the Gate*, in *One-Act Plays*, 1928.
Cappiddazzu paga tuttu, with N. Martoglio. In *Teatro dialecto siciliano 7*, by Martiglio, 1922.
La vita che ti diedi (produced Teatro Quirino, Rome, 1923). 1924; translated as *The Life I Gave You*, in *Three Plays*, 1959.
L'altro figlio (produced Teatro Nazionale, Rome, 1923). 1925; translated as *The House with the Column*, in *One-Act Plays*, 1928; as *The Other Son*, in *Collected Plays 3*, 1992.
L'uomo dal fiore in bocca (produced Teatro degli Indipendenti, Rome, 1923). 1926; translated as *The Man with the Flower in His Mouth*, in *One-Act Plays*, 1928; and in *Collected Plays 1*, 1985.
Ciascuno a suo modo (produced Teatro dei Filodrammatici, Milan, 1924). 1924; translated as *Each in His Own Way*, 1923; and in *Collected Plays 3*, 1992.
La sagra del signore della nave (produced Teatro Odesealchi, Rome, 1925). 1925; translated as *Our Lord of the Ship*, in *One-Act Plays*, 1928.
Diana e la Tuda (produced Schauspielhaus, Zurich, 1926). 1927; translated as *Diana and Tuda*, 1950.
L'amica delle mogli (produced Teatro Argentina, Rome, 1927). 1927; translated as *The Wives' Friend*, 1960.
La nuova colonia (produced Teatro Argentina, Rome, 1928). 1928; translated as *The New Colony*, in *"The Mountain Giants" and Other Plays*, 1958.
Lazzaro (produced as *Though One Rose*, Theatre Royal,

Huddersfield, Yorkshire, 1928). 1929; translated as *Lazarus*, 1952, and in *Collected Plays 1*, 1985.
Bellavita (produced Teatro Eden, Milan, 1927). 1937.
La salamandra, music by Massimo Bontempelli (produced Teatro della Pantomima Futuristica, Turin, 1928).
O di uno o di nessuno (produced Teatro di Torino, Turin, 1929?). 1929.
Questa sera si recita a soggetto (produced Neues Schauspielhaus, Königsberg, 1930). 1930; translated as *Tonight We Improvise*, 1932.
Come tu mi vuoi (produced Teatro dei Filodrammatici, Milan, 1930). 1930; translated as *As You Desire Me*, 1931.
Sogno (ma forse no) (produced Teatro Nacional, Lisbon, 1931). 1936.
Trovarsi (produced Teatro dei Fiorenti, Naples, 1932). 1932; translated as *To Find Oneself*, 1960.
Quando si e qualcuno (produced Teatro Odeón, Buenos Aires, Argentina, 1933). 1933; translated as *When Someone is Somebody*, in *"The Mountain Giants" and Other Plays*, 1958.
La favola del figlio cambiato, music by Malpiero (produced Landestheater, Braunschweig, 1934). 1938.
Non si sa come (produced National Theatre, Prague, 1934). 1935; translated as *No One Knows How*, 1963.
I giganti della montagna (unfinished; produced Boboli Gardens, Florence, 1937). 1938; translated as *The Mountain Giants*, in *"The Mountain Giants" and Other Plays*, 1958.

Screenplays

Pantera nera, with Arnaldo Frateili, 1920; *Acciaio*, with Stefano Landi, 1933; *Pensaci Giacomino!*, with others, 1935.

Fiction

Amori senza amore. 1894.
L'esclusa. 1901; translated as *The Outcast*, 1925.
Beffe della morte e della vita (2 vols.). 1902–03.
Quand'ero matto. . . . 1902.
Il turno. 1902.
Il fu Mattia Pascal. 1904; revised edition, 1921; translated as *The Late Mattia Pascal*, 1923.
Bianche e nere. 1904.
Erma bifronte. 1906.
La vita nuda. 1910; translated as *The Naked Truth*, 1934.
Suo marito. 1911; translated as *Giustino Roncella nato Boggiolo*, 1953.
Terzetti. 1912.
I vecchi e i giovani (2 vols.). 1913; translated as *The Old and the Young* (2 vols.), 1928.
Le due maschere. 1914; translated as *Tu Ridi*, 1920.
La trappola. 1915.
Erba del nostro orto. 1915.
Si gira. . . . 1916; translated as *Quaderni di Serafino Gubbio, operatore*, 1925; as *Shoot!*, 1926; as *The Notebooks of Serafino Gubbio, or Shoot!*, 1990.
E domani, lunedi. 1917.
Un cavallo nella luna. 1918; translated as *The Horse in the Moon*, 1932.
Berecche e la guerra. 1919.
Il carnevale dei morti. 1919.
Novelle per un anno (15 vols.). 1922–37(?).
Uno, nessuno, e centomila. 1926; translated as *One, None and a Hundred Thousand*, 1933.
Better Think Twice About It. 1933.
A Character in Distress. 1938.

Four Tales. 1939; translated as *"Limes from Sicily" and Other Stories*, 1942.
Short Stories, edited by Frederick May. 1965.
Tales of Suicide, translated by Giovanni R. Bussino. 1988.

Verse

Mal giocondo. 1889.
Pasqua di Gea. 1891.
Pier Gudrò. 1894.
Elegie renane. 1895.
Zampogna. 1901.
Fuori di chiave. 1912.

Other

Laute und Lautentwicklung der Mundart von Girgenti. 1891.
Arte e Scienza. 1908.
L'umorismo. 1908; translated as *On Humor*, 1974.

Translator, *La filologia romanza*, by Fed. Neumann. 1893.
Translator, *Elegie romane*, by Goethe. 1896.

*

Bibliographies

Manlio Lo Vecchio-Musti, *Bibliografia di Pirandello*, Milan, 1952.
Alfredo Barbina, *Bibliografia della critica pirandelliana 1889–1961*, Florence, 1967.
Corrado Donati, *Bibliografia della critica pirandelliana 1962–1981*, Florence, 1986.

Criticism

Books:
V.F. Nardelli, *L'Uomo segreto: Vita e croce di Luigi Pirandello*, Verona, 1932; fourth edition, 1986.
D. Vittorini, *The Drama of Pirandello*, Philadelphia, 1935.
S. D'Amico, *Luigi Pirandello*, Milan, 1937.
Walter Starkie, *Pirandello 1867–1936*, London, 1937; fourth edition, 1967.
A. Janner, *Luigi Pirandello* (biography), Florence, 1948.
Lander McClintock, *The Age of Pirandello*, Bloomington, Indiana, 1951.
L. Sciasia, *Pirandello e il pirandellismo*, Palermo, 1953.
C. Guasco, *Ragione e mito nell'arte di Luigi Pirandello*, Rome, 1954.
G.B. Angioletti, *Luigi Pirandello: Narratore e drammaturgo*, Florence, 1958.
L. Ferrante, *Luigi Pirandello*, Milan, 1958.
F. Puglisi, *L'arte di Luigi Pirandello*, Messina and Florence, 1958.
G. Calendoli, *Luigi Pirandello*, Rome, 1962.
V. Pandolfi, *Racconto e dramma in Pirandello*, Turin, 1962.
F. Puglisi, *Pirandello e sua lingua*, Bologna, 1962.
A. Vallone, *Profilo di Pirandello*, Rome, 1962.
N. Ciarletta, *Temi di Pirandello*, Urbino, 1963.
F.L. Lucas, *The Drama of Chekhov, Synge, Yeats and Pirandello*, London, 1965.
Thomas Bishop, *Pirandello and the French Theatre*, New York, 1960.
Oscar Büdel, *Pirandello*, London, 1966.

G. Giacolone, *Luigi Pirandello*, Brescia, 1966.

Mario Pomilio, *La formazione critico-estetica di Pirandello*, Naples, 1966.

Glauco Cambon (ed.), *Pirandello: A Collection of Critical Essays*, Englewood Cliffs, New Jersey, 1967.

Aldo Borlenghi, *Pirandello o dell'ambiguità*, Padua, 1968.

Gaetano Munafo, *Conoscere Pirandello*, Florence, 1968; revised edition, 1984.

Nicole Blanc, *I rapporti difficili del teatro di Pirandello*, Agrigento, 1969.

Luigi Ferrante, *Pirandello e la riforma teatrale*, Parma, 1969.

Arminio Janner, *Luigi Pirandello*, Florence, 1969.

Gianfranco Morra, *Il teatro di orandello*, Udine, 1969.

Paolo Sacripanti, *Luigi Pirandello*, Catania, 1969.

Gérard Genot, *Pirandello: Textes de Pirandello, points de vue critiques, témoignages, chronologie, bibliographie*, Paris, 1970.

Lucio Lugnani, *Pirandello: Letteratura e teatro*, Florence, 1970.

Filippo Puglisi, *Pirandello e sua opera innovatrice*, Catania, 1970.

C. Vicentini, *L'estetica di Pirandello*, Milan, 1970.

A. Navarria, *Pirandello, prima e dopo*, Milan, 1971.

Roberto Alonge, *Pirandello tra realismo e mistificazione*, Naples, 1972.

Mariapia Bonanate, *Luigi Pirandello*, Turin, 1972.

Leonardo Bragaglia, *Interpreto pirandelliani, 1910–1969* (second edition), Rome, 1973.

Renate Mattei, *Luigi Pirandello* (in English), New York, 1973.

F.T. Roffarè, *L'essenzialità problematica e dialettica dal teatro di Pirandello*, Florence, 1973.

Victor Carrabino, *Pirandello and Picasso: A Pragmatic View of Reality*, Parma, 1974.

Silvana Monti, *Pirandello*, Palermo, 1974.

Anne Paolucci, *Pirandello's Theater: The Recovery of the Modern Stage for Dramatic Art*, Carbondale, Illinois, 1974.

Vincenzo Di Maria, *Il teatro di Pirandello: Dal paradosso al mito poetico*, np, 1974.

Ettore Mazzali, *Luigi Pirandello*, Florence, 1974.

Fernando Balestra, *Pirandello e il teatro dei problemi*, Rome, 1975.

Gaspare Giudici, *Pirandello: A Biography*, London, 1975 (from 1963 Italian edition).

Ferdinando Virdia, *Invito alla lettura di Luigi Pirandello*, Milan, 1975.

Antonietta Gaglio, *Pirandello nel suo caos*, Palermo, 1976.

Antonio Illiano, *Introduzione alla critica pirandelliana*, Verona, 1976.

G. Romanato, *Pirandello e il suo teatro*, Rovigo, 1976.

Simona Costa, *Luigi Pirandello*, Florence, 1978.

Paolo Puppa, *Fantasmi contro giganti: Scena e immaginario in Pirandello*, Bologna, 1978; revised edition, 1984.

Douglas Radcliffe-Umstead, *The Mirror of Our Anguish: A Study of Pirandello's Narrative Writings*, Rutherford (New Jersey), and London, 1978.

Giovanni R. Bussino, *Alle forti di Pirandello*, Florence, 1979.

Graziella Corsinovi, *Pirandello e l'espressionismo*, Genoa, 1979.

Alfred Merkli, *La ricerca dell'oggetto nell'opera di Pirandello*, Zurich, 1979.

Roger W. Oliver, *Dreams of Passion: The Theater of Luigi Pirandello*, New York, 1979.

Corrado Donati, *La solitudione allo specchio: Luigi Pirandello*, Rome, 1980.

Olga Ragusa, *Luigi Pirandello: An Approach to His Theatre*, Edinburgh, 1980.

Massimo Castri, *Pirandello ottanta*, Milan, 1981.

Giovanni Macchia, *Pirandello o la stanza di tortura*, Milan, 1981.

Gian Franco Venè, *Pirandello fascista: La conscienza borghese tra ribellione e rivoluzione*, Venice, 1981.

A. Richard Sogliuzzo, *Luigi Pirandello, Director: The Playwright in the Theatre*, Metuchen (New Jersey) and London, 1982.

Susan Basnett-McGuire, *Luigi Pirandello*, London, 1983 (Macmillan Modern Dramatists series).

Graziella Corsinovi, *Pirandello: Tradizione e tragressione*, Genoa, 1983.

Stefano Milioto (ed.), *Pirandello e il teatro del suo tempo*, Agrigento, 1983.

Stefano Milioto and Enzo Scrivano (eds.), *Pirandello e la cultura del suo tempo*, Milan, 1984.

Dorothea Stewens, *Pirandello, scrittura e scena*, 1983.

Gabriel Marcel, *Il problema pirandelliano*, Padua, 1984.

Eric Bentley, *The Pirandello Commentaries*, Lincoln, Nebraska, 1985.

Enzo Scrivano (ed.), *Pirandello e la drammaturgia tra le due guerre*, Agrigento, 1985.

Renato Barilli, *Pirandello: Una rivoluzione culturale*, Milan, 1986.

Giovanni Cappello, *Quando Pirandello cambia titolo: occasionalità o strategia?*, Milan, 1986.

Sarah E. Enzo Zappulla, *Pirandello e il teatro siciliano*, Catania, 1986.

Paolo Puppa, *Dalle parti di Pirandello*, Rome, 1987.

A. Alessio and others (eds.), *L'enigma Pirandello: Atti del congresso internazionale, Ottawa . . . 1986*, Ottawa, 1988.

Anthony Francis Caputi, *Pirandello and the Crisis of Modern Consciousness*, Urbana, Illinois, 1988.

Mario B. Mignone (ed.), *Pirandello in America: Atti del simposio internazionale 1986*, Rome, 1988.

Stefano Milioti (ed.), *La donna in Pirandello*, Agrigento, 1988.

Susan Basnett (compiler), *File on Pirandello*, London, 1989.

Madeleine Strong Cincotta, *Luigi Pirandello: The Humourous Existentialist*, North Wollongong, 1989.

Jennifer Stone, *Pirandello's Naked Prompt*, Ravenna, 1989.

Felicity Firth, *Pirandello in Performance* (book and slide set), Cambridge, 1990.

Mario Valentini, *Shakespeare e Pirandello*, Rome, 1990.

John Louis DiGaetani (ed.), *A Companion to Pirandello Studies*, New York and London, 1991.

Articles

Antonio Illiano, "Pirandello Criticism in England and the United States: A Chronological List of Criticism", in *Bulletin of the New York Public Library*, 71, 1967.

Serials

Quaderni dell'Instituto di Studi Pirandelliani (Rome), 1973—
Revista di studi pirandelliani, 1978—
Yearbook of the British Pirandello Society (Bristol), 1981—

* * *

Luigi Pirandello was a prolific playwright whose fame surprisingly rests on very few plays, principally on *Six Characters in Search of an Author, Henry IV, Right You Are* and *The Rules of the Game*, all of which date from the early period of his dramatic writing. Pirandello was well-established in the Italian literary world before he started to write plays, and in fact had expressed scepticism and even contempt for theatre prior to becoming involved in promoting the cause of Sicilian dialect theatre. He was fortunate in being able to work with some very good theatre professionals, notably Nino Martoglio and the great actors Ruggero Ruggeri and Lamberto Picasso. By 1925, when he set up his own company, he was totally committed to theatre and saw his role as one of improving the poor quality of work in the Italian theatre of the day. In his theatre practice, he was heavily influenced by Russian directors and writers such as Stanislavsky and Evreinov.

Pirandello has frequently been described as a "cerebral" or "intellectual" playwright, because many of his plays, like his prose work (and a lot of the plays are reworkings of short stories) involve complex games about identity, the relativity of truth, the boundaries of madness, and the absurdity of the human condition. In many respects Pirandello's work prefigured the absurdist playwrights and the writing of Samuel Beckett, and his theory of humour, established in his seminal *Essay on Humour*, places him in the mainstream of modernist thought. But it is a mistake to focus too closely on Pirandello as an intellectual, since a large part of his life's work was spent endeavouring to deconstruct intellectualism, and a consideration of his work in the theatre shows the importance he gave to practical work and to the craftmanship of theatremaking.

The short-lived Art Theatre Project is extremely significant, because it demonstrates the extent of Pirandello's commitment to theatre. In setting up the company he took on board the difficulties of fund-raising, of creating a new performance space, of forming a company that would exemplify his views on what good acting ought to be. He believed that the extant Italian repertoire was derelict, that many of his contemporaries (such as D'Annunzio) were inadequate playwrights, that Italian acting was of poor quality. He was particularly indignant about the old tradition of the "star's company", where a famous actor, whose name could attract audiences, would form a company of inferior players (or even of good actors who were not allowed to show their skills) and tour plays that provided the star with a vehicle to show off his or her talents. Pirandello's company was established on a different principle and the actors had to undergo rigorous training sessions. Unfortunately, the short life of the Art Theatre meant that his dream of a permanent actor-training school could not be realized either.

Through his encounter with the practicalities of theatre, Pirandello's writing style changed, and although the plays written around the time of *Six Characters* tend to be conventionally structured, the plays after 1923, the year of Pitoëff's staging of *Six Characters*, become more experimental. Once he began to work with Ruggeri, and then with Marta Abba, he wrote expressly for these actors (along with others) and began trying out new forms.

Six Characters is the first of three plays known as the "theatre-in-the theatre trilogy", the other two being *Each in His Own Way* and *Tonight We Improvise*. For the opening of the Art Theatre in 1925 he created a one-act pageant play for a huge cast, and thereafter his plays fall into roughly two categories: rather bitter tragi-comedies which use the form of the well-made play but distort it in significant ways (such as *Finding Oneself*, *When One is Somebody*), and what he called "mythical" plays, with large casts, which are closer to the surreal (*The New Colony*, *The Mountain Giants*). It is ironic that at the point when he began to learn how to experiment with theatre form in several different ways, Pirandello's work declined in popularity, and the later plays have never had much impact either in Italy or overseas.

The basic material of much of Pirandello's drama is a tragic domestic situation—a love triangle, an unwanted child, doubtful paternity, excessive jealousy, bereavement. His characters are always ordinary people, usually lower-middle-class, and occasionally, in the dialect plays, peasants, who find themselves trapped in situations that cause a great deal of pain but from which they can see no way of escape.

The archetypal Pirandello plot is the story-line of *Right You Are, If You Think So*, where a group of petty-bourgeois townspeople try to discover the "truth" about a married couple who have come to live nearby with the wife's mother who is not allowed to visit their house. The quest for certainty leads nowhere, as characters accuse one another of being mad, and the play ends in deadlock. In this, as in many of the early plays, there is one character who has the role of ironic commentator, and it has often been suggested that this character is Pirandello's alter-ego personified.

The vision of the world that emerges from Pirandello's plays (and from all his other writing) is a pessimistic one. He depicts humanity as constantly involved in a fruitless search for certainty, security, and fixity, but because he sees life as movement, it is necessarily unfixed, insecure, and uncertain. This dichotomy lies at the heart of the existential predicament, which he dramatized in various ways, most successfully by using theatre itself as a metaphor. He repeated, in many of his plays, the Shakespearean notion that all the world is a stage, and used the image of the mask to exemplify this view. The mask, he suggested over and again in his plays, is not hiding a truth, it is hiding nothing. Once the mask is stripped away, his characters lose everything they have—the protagonist of *The Rules of the Game* wins the game but destroys any chance of happiness he may have had, while the protagonist of *To Clothe the Naked* loses the "clothing" that has been provided by lies she has told, and is left naked, with death as the only option open to her.

In one of his last great speeches on theatre, the Address to the Volta Conference on Dramatic Theatre in 1934, Pirandello made a passionate defence of drama, pointing out that every period of human history has handed down its own theatre. "The play", he reminded his listeners, "is what remains . . . the theatre is the form that contains and mirrors most intimately all moral values". In this vision, at least, he transcended even his own pessimism.

—Susan Bassnett

See also *Volume 1* entries on *Henry IV*; *Right You Are (If You Think You Are)*; *Six Characters in Search of an Author*.

PIXÉRÉCOURT, René-Charles Guilbert de. Born in Nancy, France, 22 January 1773. Studied law in Paris: studies interrupted by the French Revolution. Married; one child. His aristocratic background forced him to seek refuge in Koblenz during the Revolution, 1791; returned to Paris, living secretively; painted fans and began writing for the theatre in the early 1790's; civil servant until 1835, initially at the War Office, later as Directeur des Domaines; first-produced play, *Les Petits Auvergnats*, staged 1797; his first melodrama, *Victor; ou, L'Enfant de la forêt*, staged 1798; subsequently a prolific playwright, sometimes in collaboration, until 1835; a director, Théâtre de la Gaîté, Paris, 1825–35, at which many of his plays were produced: lost much of his earnings when the theatre burnt down, 1835; also a director of the Opéra-Comique, Paris; retired to Nancy, 1835. Died in Nancy, 27 July 1844.

Works

Collections

Bibliothèque de M. Guilbert de Pixérécourt.   1838.
Théâtre choisi (4 vols.).   1841–43.

Stage Works

Sélico.   1793.
Claudine.   1793.
Le Jacobin en mission.   1799.
Les Petits Auvergnats (produced Théâtre de l'Ambigu-Comique, Paris, 1797).   1798.
La Forêt de Sicilie.   1798.
Victor; ou, L'Enfant de la forêt, from the novel by François Ducray-Duminil (produced Théâtre Favart, Paris, 1798).   1798.
Le Château des Apennins (produced Théâtre de l'Ambigu-Comique, Paris, 1798).   1799.
Zozo; ou, Le Mal-avisé (produced Théâtre de Montansier, Paris, 1799).   1800.
Rosa; ou, L'Hermitage du Torrent.   1800.
La Soirée des Champs-Élysées.   1800.
Le Petit Page; ou, La Prison d'état, music by Rudolph Kreutzer (produced Théâtre Feydeau, Paris, 1800).   1800.
Coelina; ou, L'Enfant du mystère, from a story by François Ducray-Duminil (produced Théâtre de l'Ambigu-Comique, Paris, 1800).   1800; revised edition, 1841; translated as *Coelina; or, A Tale of Mystery,* 1802.
Le Chansonnier de la paix (produced Théâtre Feydeau, Paris, 1802).
Flaminius à Corinthe with L.T. Lambert, music by Rudolph Kreutzer and Nicolò Isouard (produced Théâtre des Arts, Paris, 1801).   1801.
Le Pèlerin blanc (produced Théâtre de l'Ambigu-Comique, Paris, 1801).   1802; translated and adapted as *The Wandering Boys; or, The Castle of Olival,* 1850.
L'Homme à trois visages; ou, Le Proscrit (produced Théâtre de l'Ambigu-Comique, Paris, 1801).   1801; translated and adapted as *The Venetian Outlaw, His Country's Friend,* 1805.
Le Vieux Major, with François Léger (produced Théâtre de Montansier, Paris, 1801).   1801.
La Peau de l'ours, with L.T. Lambert (produced Théâtre Montansier, Paris, 1802).   1802.
Raymond de Toulouse; ou, Le Retour de la Terre-Sainte, music by Jacques and François Foignet (produced Théâtre de la Rue Bondy, Paris, 1802).   1802.
Pizarre; ou, La Conquête de Pérou (produced Théâtre de la Porte-Saint-Martin, Paris, 1802).   1802.
La Femme à deux maris (produced Théâtre de l'Ambigu-Comique, Paris, 1802).   1802; translated as *The Wife of Two Husbands,* 1803; as *The Wife with Two Husbands,* 1803.
Les Deux Valets (produced Théâtre de la Porte-Saint-Martin, Paris, 1803).   1803.
Les Mines de Pologne (produced Théâtre de l'Ambigu-Comique, Paris, 1803).   1803.
Téléki; ou, La Siège de Mongatz (produced Théâtre de l'Ambigu-Comique, Paris, 1803).   1804.
Les Maures d'Espagne; ou, Le Pouvoir de l'enfance (produced Théâtre de l'Ambigu-Comique, Paris, 1804).   1804.
Avis aux Femmes; ou, Le Mari en colère, music by Pierre Gaveaux (produced Opéra-Comique, Paris, 1804).   1804.
Le Grand Chasseur; ou, L'Île des palmiers, with Joseph-Marie Loaisel de Tréogate (produced Théâtre de l'Ambigu-Comique, Paris, 1804).   1804.

La Forteresse de Danube (produced Théâtre de la Porte-Saint-Martin, Paris, 1805).   1805.
Robinson Crusoé, music by Alexandre Piccini and Gerardin Lacour (produced Théâtre de la Porte-Saint-Martin, Paris, 1805).   1805.
La Solitaire de la Roche Noire, music by Alexandre Piccini (produced Théâtre de la Porte-Saint-Martin, Paris, 1806).   1806.
Les Fausses Déclarations; ou, La Veuve (produced Théâtre des Jeunes Artistes, Paris, 1806).
Koulouf; ou, Les Chinois, music by Nicolas Dalayrac (produced Opéra-Comique, Paris, 1806).   1807.
L'Ange tutélaire; ou, Le Démon femelle, music by Alexandre Piccini (produced Théâtre de la Gaîté, Paris, 1808).   1808.
La Rose blanche et la rose rouge, music by Pierre Gaveaux (produced Opéra-Comique, Paris, 1809).   1809.
La Citerne (produced Théâtre de la Gaîté, Paris, 1809).   1809.
Marguerite d'Anjou, music by Gérardin Lacour (produced Théâtre de la Gaîté, Paris, 1810).   1810.
Les Trois Moulins, with Jean-Baptiste Dubois (produced Théâtre de la Gaîté, Paris, 1810).   1810.
Les Ruines de Babylone; ou, Giafar et Zaïda (produced Théâtre de la Gaîté, Paris, 1810).   1810.
Le Précipe; ou, Les Forges de Norvège (produced Théâtre de la Gaîté, Paris, 1811).   1811.
Le Fanal de Messine (produced Théâtre de la Gaîté, Paris, 1812).   1812.
Le Petit Carillonneur; ou, La Tour ténébreuse (produced Théâtre de la Gaîté, Paris, 1812).   1812.
L'Ennemi des modes; ou, La Maison de Choisy (produced Théâtre de l'Odéon, Paris, 1813).   1814.
Le Chien de Montargis; ou, La Forêt de Bondy (produced Théâtre de la Gaîté, Paris, 1814).   1814; translated as *The Forest of Bondy; or, The Dog of Montargis,* 1820.
Charles le Téméraire; ou, Le Siège de Nancy (produced Théâtre de la Gaîté, Paris, 1814).   1814.
Christophe Colomb; ou, La Découverte du Nouveau Monde (produced Théâtre de la Gaîté, Paris, 1815).   1815.
Le Suicide; ou, Le Vieux Sergent (produced Théâtre de la Gaîté, Paris, 1816).   1816.
Le Monastère abandonné; ou, La Malédiction paternelle (produced Théâtre de la Gaîté, Paris, 1816).   1816.
La Chapelle des bois; ou, Le Témoin invisible, with Michel Balisson de Rougemont (produced Théâtre de la Gaîté, Paris, 1818).   1818.
Le Belvédère; ou, La Vallée de l'Etna (produced Théâtre de l'Ambigu-Comique, Paris, 1818).   1819.
La Fille de l'exilé; ou, Huit mois en deux heures (produced Théâtre de la Gaîté, Paris, 1819).   1819.
Les Chefs écossais (produced Théâtre de la Porte-Saint-Martin, Paris, 1819).   1819.
Bouton de Rose (produced Théâtre de la Gaîté, Paris, 1819).   1819.
Le Mont Sauvage; ou, Le Solitaire (produced Théâtre de la Porte-Saint-Martin, Paris, 1821).   1821.
Valentine; ou, La Séduction (produced Théâtre de la Gaîté, Paris, 1821).   1821.
Le Pavillon des fleurs; ou, Les Pêcheurs de Grenade, music by Nicolas Dalayrac (produced Opéra-Comique, Paris, 1822).   1822.
Ali Baba; ou, Les Quarante Voleurs (produced Théâtre de la Gaîté, Paris, 1822).   1822.
Le Château de Loch-levon; ou, Le Captivité de Marie Stuart (produced Théâtre de la Gaîté, Paris, 1822).   1822.
La Place du palais (produced Théâtre de la Gaîté, Paris, 1824).   1824.

Le Baril d'olives, with Nicolas Brazier and Mélesville (produced Théâtre des Variétés, Paris, 1825).   1825.
Le Moulin des étangs (produced Théâtre de la Gaîté?, Paris 1826).
Les Natchez; ou, La Tribu des Serpents (produced Théâtre de la Gaîté, Paris, 1827).
La Tête de mort; ou, Les Ruines de Pompeia, music by Alexandre Piccini (produced Théâtre de la Gaîté, Paris, 1827).   1828.
La Muette de la forêt, with Benjamin Antier (produced Théâtre de la Gaîté, Paris, 1828).   1828.
La Peste de Marseille (produced Théâtre de la Gaîté, Paris, 1828).   1828.
Polter; ou, Le Bourreau d'Amsterdam, with Victor Ducange (produced Théâtre de la Gaîté, Paris, 1828).   1840.
Guillaume Tell, from a play by Schiller (produced Théâtre de la Gaîté, Paris, 1829).   1828.
L'Aigle des Pyrénées, with Mélesville (produced Théâtre de la Gaîté, Paris, 1829).   1829.
Olivier; ou, Les Compagnons du chêne (produced Paris, 1829).
Alice; ou, Les Fossoyeurs écossais (produced Paris, 1829).
Ondine; ou, La Nymphe des eaux, music by Alexandre Piccini (produced Théâtre de la Gaîté, Paris, 1830).   1830.
Le Jésuite, with Victor Ducange (produced as *Judacin; ou, Les Filles de la veuve*, Théâtre de la Gaîté, Paris, 1830). 1840.
Le Lettre de cachet, with Pigeault-Lebrun (produced Paris, 1831).
L'Abbaye au bois; ou, La Femme de chambre, with B.L.H. Martin (produced Théâtre de la Gaîté, Paris, 1832).   1832.
Le Petit Homme rouge, with Nicolas Brazier and Pierre Carmouche, music by Alexandre Piccini (produced Théâtre de la Gaîté, Paris, 1832).   1832.
Six Florins; ou, La Brodeuse et la dame (produced Paris 1832).
L'Allée des veuves; ou, La Justice en 1773, music by Alexandre Piccini (produced Théâtre de la Gaîté, Paris, 1833).   1833.
Les Quatre Éléments, with Nicolas Brazier and Théophile Dumersam (produced Théâtre de la Gaîté, Paris, 1833). 1833.
Valentine; ou, Le Château et la ferme, with Francis Cornu (produced Théâtre de la Gaîté, Paris, 1834).   1834.
Latude; ou, Trent-cinq ans de captivité, with Anicet Bourgeois (produced Théâtre de la Gaîté, Paris, 1834). 1834.
Le Berceau (produced Cirque Olympique, Paris, 1838). 1839.
Bijou; ou, L'Enfant de Paris, with Nicolas Brazier and Félix-Auguste Duvert (produced Cirque Olympique, Paris, 1838).   1839.

Other

Observations sur les théâtres et la Révolution.   1735.
Vie de Dalayrac.   1810.
Guerre au mélodrame.   1818.
Le Mélodrame.   1832.
Dernières réflexions sur le mélodrame.   1843.

*

Criticism

Books:
A. Virely, *René-Charles Guilbert de Pixérécourt (1773–1884)*, Paris, 1909.

P. Ginisty, *Le Mélodrame*, Paris, 1913.
W.J. Hartog, *Guilbert de Pixérécourt: Sa Vie, sa technique et son influence*, Paris, 1913.
J.M. Thomasseau, *Le Mélodrame*, Paris, 1984.

Articles:
Oscar G. Brockett, "The Function of Dance in the Melodramas of Pixérécourt", in *Modern Philology*, 56, 1958–59.

*   *   *

René-Charles Guilbert de Pixérécourt, known as "le Corneille des boulevards" by his admiring contemporaries, was a prolific author of comedies, *vaudevilles*, *opéras-comiques*, and, above all, *mélodrames*—a type of play then new which he popularized in the *théâtres du boulevard*. Over 100 of his plays (often adapted from novels of the day) were produced in the years between 1798 and 1835, of which more than 59 were melodramas.

Pixérécourt was not melodrama's sole exponent—other celebrated contributors to the genre included Caigniez and Ducange—but more than any other he established, codified, and illustrated the form, and his *Coelina* is considered by many to be the first true melodrama. Neither can Pixérécourt be said to have invented melodrama, which some critics have considered a product of the decadence of tragedy. In fact, it probably evolved from the popular boulevard genre of heroic pantomime in the years following the abolition of the Comédie-Française's monopoly on spoken drama in 1791, hence the importance of the role played by mime, music, and spectacle.

In fact, if melodrama can be said to have been "total theatre", Pixérécourt was a true "man of the theatre", acting at once as producer, author, director, stage manager, and designer. His works exploit all the resources of theatrical illusion, and feature sensational plots centring on the conflict between innocence and evil, illustrated by episodes of music and dancing, and elaborate and frequently spectacular stage settings and special effects. These were employed particularly for the denouements, in which, often by a sudden, astonishing reversal of fortune, virtue is rewarded and vice graphically punished.

Melodrama had no rival as a popular art-form in the first 20 years of the 19th century. It was described by the critic Charles Nodier in Pixérécourt's *Théâtre choisi* as "a new genre . . . at once the true depiction of the world which society has created for us and the only popular tragedy fitting for the period in which we live". In these years of political and social upheaval, melodrama corresponded exactly to the demands of a theatre public that was, for the most part, ignorant, uneducated, greedy for sensation, action, movement, and spectacle, and in which the events of the Revolution had created, according to one commentator in 1811, a demand for "strong emotions, violent shocks, no matter how and at whatever price". It is a mistake, however, to overestimate the ignorance of Pixérécourt's audience, for even if he himself said, "I write for those who cannot read", his melodramas were equally as popular with the bourgeois and the critics in the audience as they were with the common people who crowded the galleries of the boulevard theatres.

As can be seen from the socially mixed nature of its audience, and as might be expected given the nature of its origins, melodrama was essentially a democratic art-form. This can be seen, too, in the fact that, despite the nostalgically feudal nature of the majority of the social structures represented (the plays generally feature members of the landed gentry or bourgeoisie surrounded by their faithful retainers), villains are most often depicted as tyrants and oppressors, whereas their ultimately triumphant victims, whatever their class origin, believe in merit rather than privilege and the existence of a fraternity of the good.

French society of this time has been described as a "post-sacred universe", and in this secular world Pixérécourt apparently intended to imbue his work with a degree of social utility by having it serve as a morally instructive interpretation of the universe. In the words of his biographer, Virely, "for him, the theatre was always a platform from which to denounce injustice . . . condemning vice with implacable rigour". Nodier goes further, writing of Pixérécourt's plays, "I have seen them, in the absence of religious worship, take the place of the silent pulpit . . . in this difficult period, when the people could begin anew its religious education only at the theatre". It would be a mistake, however, to attach too much importance to such noble claims, and there is little doubt that the greater part of Pixérécourt's audience sought, in his works, a source of entertainment rather than enlightenment.

It is a critical commonplace to say that Pixérécourt's melodrama had a profound influence on the development of the Romantic drama. Indeed, Nodier went so far as to say that, "tragedy and drama of the new school are scarcely other than melodramas relieved of the artificial pomp of lyricism". Clearly, similarities exist between the two genres, not least in the tastes for the Gothic and the arousal of violent emotion. What is more, the innovations in stage design introduced with melodrama did much to sweep away those classical conventions so derided by the Romantics. Nevertheless, Norma Perry, in her edition of *Coelina*, sees only a very tenuous link between the works of Victor Hugo or Dumas *père* and those of Pixérécourt.

Even so, the plays of Pixérécourt are still deserving of attention in that they admirably illustrate the technical capabilities of the contemporary stage, as well as providing us with a fascinating insight into the tastes and values of theatre audiences in those troubled times.

—Janet Clarke

See also *Volume 1* entry on *Coelina*.

PLANCHÉ, James Robinson. Born in London, 27 February 1796. Educated at Rev. Farrer's school, 1804–08, and Monsieur de Court's school, 1809–10, both London; articled to a bookseller, 1810. Married Elizabeth St. George in 1821 (died 1846); two daughters. Amateur actor at various private theatres in London, and began writing for the theatre, 1818; resident writer, Adelphi Theatre, 1820–21, Covent Garden Theatre, 1822–28, and Theatre Royal, Drury Lane, from 1828; wrote first opera, 1822; designed costumes and supervised the production of the revival of Shakespeare's *King John* at Covent Garden, 1823; concert manager, Vauxhall Gardens, summers 1826–27; manager, Adelphi Theatre, 1830; as resident writer and director of costumes worked in partnership with the actress/manager Madame Vestris, first at the Olympic Theatre, later at Covent Garden, the Lyceum, Theatre Royal, Drury Lane, and Theatre Royal, Haymarket, 1831–56; continued to write for other managements until 1872; lived in Kent, 1852–53, and in London from

1854. Also an antiquary and scholar of heraldry and costume: Rouge Croix Pursuivant of Arms at the College of Heralds, 1854–66; Somerset Herald, 1866–80. Fellow, Society of Antiquaries, 1829; founding member, Garrick Club, 1831, and British Archaeological Association, 1843. Granted Civil List pension, 1871. Died in London, 30 May 1880.

Works

Collections

Extravaganzas 1825–1871, edited by T.F. Dillon Croker and Stephen Tucker (5 vols.). 1879.
Plays (includes *The Vampire; The Garrick Fever; Beauty and the Beast; Fortunio and His Seven Gifted Servants; The Golden Fleece; The Camp at the Olympic; The Discreet Princess*), edited by Donald Roy. 1986.

Stage Works

Amoroso, King of Little Britain, music by Tom Cooke (produced Theatre Royal, Drury Lane, London, 1818). 1818.
Rodolph the Wolf; or, Columbine Red Riding-Hood (produced Olympic Theatre, London, 1818). 1819.
The Troubadours; or, Jealousy Out-Witted (produced Olympic Theatre, London, 1819).
Abudah; or, The Talisman of Oromanes, music by Michael Kelly (produced Theatre Royal, Drury Lane, London, 1819).
The Czar; or, A Day in the Dockyards, from a French play (produced Sadler's Wells Theatre, London, 1819).
The Caliph and the Cadi; or, Rambles in Bagdad (produced Sadler's Wells Theatre, London, 1819).
Fancy's Sketch; or, Look Before You Leap (produced Adelphi Theatre, London, 1819).
Odds and Ends; or, Which is the Manager? (produced Adelphi Theatre, London, 1819).
The Vampyre; or, The Bride of the Isles, from a French play (produced English Opera House, London, 1820). 1820; as *The Vampire*, in *Plays*, 1986.
A Burletta of Errors; or, Jupiter and Alcmena (produced Adelphi Theatre, London, 1820). Songs published 1820.
Who's to Father Her? or, What's Bred in the Bone Won't Come Out of the Flesh (produced Adelphi Theatre, London, 1820).
The Deuce Is in Her! or, Two Nights in Madrid (produced Adelphi Theatre, London, 1820).
Zamoski; or, The Fortress and the Mine (produced Adelphi Theatre, London, 1820).
Dr. Syntax; or, Harlequin in London (produced Adelphi Theatre, London, 1820).
Giovanni the Vampire; or, How Shall We Get Rid of Him? (produced Adelphi Theatre, London, 1821).
Kenilworth Castle; or, The Days of Queen Bess, from a novel by Scott (produced Adelphi Theatre, London, 1821).
Lodgings to Let (produced Adelphi Theatre, London, 1821).
Half an Hour's Courtship; or, La Chambre à Coucher (produced Adelphi Theatre, London, 1821).
Sherwood Forest; or, The Merry Archers (produced Adelphi Theatre, London, 1821).
The Mountain Hut; or, The Tinker's Son (produced Sadler's Wells Theatre, London, 1821).
Peter and Paul; or, Love in the Vineyards (produced Theatre Royal, Haymarket, 1821). 1887.
The Witch of Derncleuch, music by William Reeve, from a

James Robinson Planché

novel by Scott (produced English Opera House, London, 1821).

Capers at Canterbury (produced Adelphi Theatre, London, 1821).

The Corsair's Bride; or, The Valley of Mount Etna (produced Adelphi Theatre, London, 1821).

Love's Alarum (produced Adelphi Theatre, London, 1821).

Le Solitaire; or, The Unknown of the Mountain (produced Olympic Theatre, London, 1821).

Marplot in Spain, music by William Reeve, from the play by Susanna Centlivre (produced 1821; as *Too Curious by Half*, produced English Opera House, London, 1823).

The Pirate, from the novel by Scott (produced Olympic Theatre, London, 1822).   1822.

All in the Dark; or The Banks of the Elbe, music by Barham Livius, from a play by H.J.B.D. Victor (produced Lyceum Theatre, London, 1822).   1822.

The Fair Gabrielle, music by Barham Livius (as *Henri Quatre and the Fair Gabrielle*, produced English Opera House, London, 1822; as *The Fair Gabrielle*, produced 1822).   1822.

Ali Pacha; or, The Signet-Ring, from a play by John Howard Payne (produced Covent Garden Theatre, London, 1822).   1822.

Maid Marian; or, The Huntress of Arlingford, music by Henry Bishop, from the novel by Peacock (produced Covent Garden Theatre, London, 1822).   1822.

Clari; or, The Maid of Milan (songs only), play by John Howard Payne, music by Henry Bishop (produced Covent Garden Theatre, London, 1823).   1823.

I Will Have a Wife!, music by William Reeve (produced English Opera House, London, 1823).

Cortez; or, The Conquest of Mexico, music by Henry Bishop (produced Covent Garden Theatre, London, 1823).   1823.

St. Ronan's Well, from the novel by Scott (produced Adelphi Theatre, London, 1824).

Military Tactics, music by William Reeve, from a French play (produced English Opera House, London, 1824).

The Frozen Lake, music by William Reeve, from a play by Scribe (produced English Opera House, London, 1824). Songs published 1824.

Der Freischütz; or, The Black Huntsman of Bohemia, music by Barham Livius, from the opera by J.F. Kind, music by Weber (produced Covent Garden Theatre, London, 1824).   1825.

A Woman Never Vext; or, The Widow of Cornhill, from a play by William Rowley (produced Covent Garden Theatre, London, 1824).   1824.

The Coronation of Charles X of France (produced Covent Garden Theatre, London, 1825).

Lilla (produced Covent Garden Theatre, London, 1825).

Jocko; or, The Brazilian Monkey (produced Covent Garden Theatre, London, 1825).

Success; or, A Hit if You Like It (produced Adelphi Theatre, London, 1825).   In *Extravaganzas 1*, 1879.

Oberon; or, The Elf-King's Oath, from a poem by Wieland, music by Weber (produced Covent Garden Theatre, London, 1826).   1826.

Returned Killed, from a French play (produced Covent Garden Theatre, London, 1826).   1826.

All's Right; or, The Old School-Fellow (produced Theatre Royal, Haymarket, London, 1827).

Pay to My Order; or, A Chaste Salute (produced Vauxhall Gardens, London, 1827; as *The Chaste Salute*, produced Sadler's Wells Theatre, London, 1831).

The Rencontre; or, Love Will Find Out the Way, music by Henry Bishop (produced Theatre Royal, Haymarket, London, 1827).

You Must Be Buried, from a play by Scribe (produced Theatre Royal, Haymarket, London, 1827).

Paris and London; or, A Trip Across the Herring Pond (produced Adelphi Theatre, London, 1828).   1829.

The Merchant's Wedding; or, London Frolics in 1638, from plays by Jasper Mayne and by William Rowley (produced Covent Garden Theatre, London, 1828).   1828.

Carron Side; or, The Fête Champêtre, music by Giovanni Liverati (produced Covent Garden Theatre, London, 1828).

My Daughter, Sir; or, A Daughter to Marry, from a play by Scribe (as *A Daughter to Marry*, produced Theatre Royal, Haymarket, London, 1828; as *My Daughter, Sir!*, produced Olympic Theatre, London, 1832).   1830(?).

The Green-Eyed Monster, from a French play (produced Theatre Royal, Haymarket, London, 1828).   1830(?).

The Mason of Buda, from a play by Scribe, music by Auber, arranged George Rodwell (produced Adelphi Theatre, London, 1828).   1828.

Charles XII; or, The Siege of Stralsund (produced Theatre Royal, Drury Lane, London, 1828).   1830(?)

Thierna-na-Oge; or, The Prince of the Lakes, music by Tom Cooke (produced Theatre Royal, Drury Lane, London, 1829).

The Partisans; or, The War of Paris in 1649, from a French play (produced Theatre Royal, Drury Lane, London, 1829).

Manoeuvring, from a play by Scribe (produced Theatre Royal, Haymarket, London, 1829).   1829.

Der Vampyr, music by Heinrich Marschner arranged by William Hawes, from a libretto by W. A. Wohlbrück (produced English Opera House, London, 1829).

The Brigand Chief, music by Tom Cooke (produced Theatre Royal, Drury Lane, London, 1829).   1830(?).

Hofer; or, The Tell of the Tyrol, music by Rossini, arranged by Henry Bishop, from an opera by Jouy, Bis, and Marrast (produced Theatre Royal, Drury Lane, London, 1830). 1830.

The National Guard; or Bride and No Bride, from an opera by Scribe, music by Auber (produced Theatre Royal, Drury Lane, London, 1830).   Songs published 1830.

The Dragon's Gift; or, The Scarf of Flight and the Mirror of Light, music by Tom Cooke (produced Theatre Royal, Drury Lane, London, 1830).

The Jenkinses; or, Boarded and Done For (produced Theatre Royal, Drury Lane, London, 1830).   1853.

Olympic Revels; or, Prometheus and Pandora, with Charles Dance (produced Olympic Theatre, London, 1831). 1834.

The Romance of a Day, music by Henry Bishop (produced Covent Garden Theatre, London, 1831).   1831.

My Great Aunt; or, Where There's a Will (produced Olympic Theatre, London, 1831).   1846.

The Legion of Honour, from a French play (produced Theatre Royal, Drury Lane, London, 1831).

A Friend at Court (produced Theatre Royal, Haymarket, London, 1831).

The Army of the North; or, The Spaniard's Secret (produced Covent Garden Theatre, London, 1831).

The Love Charm; or, The Village Coquette, music by Auber, arranged by Henry Bishop, from an opera by Scribe (produced Theatre Royal, Drury Lane, London, 1831).

Olympic Devils; or, Orpheus and Eurydice, with Charles Dance (produced Olympic Theatre, London, 1831). 1831.

The Compact (produced Theatre Royal, Drury Lane, London, 1832).

His First Campaign (produced Covent Garden Theatre, London, 1832).

The Paphian Bower; or, Venus and Adonis, with Charles Dance (produced Olympic Theatre, London, 1832). In *Extravaganzas 1*, 1879.

Little Red Riding-Hood; or, The Fairy of the Silver Lake (produced 1832).

Promotion; or, A Morning at Versailles in 1750 (produced Olympic Theatre, London, 1833).   1852.

Reputation; or, The Court Secret (produced Covent Garden Theatre, London, 1833).   1833.

The Students of Jena; or, The Family Concert, from a French opera, music by Hippolyte Chelard (produced Theatre Royal, Drury Lane, London, 1833).

The Court Masque; or, Richmond in the Olden Time, music by William Hawes, from an opera by F. A. F. de Planard, music by Hérold (produced Adelphi Theatre, London, 1833).

High, Low, Jack, and the Game; or, The Card Party, with Charles Dance (produced Olympic Theatre, London, 1833).   1833.

Gustavus III; or, The Masked Ball, music by Tom Cooke, from an opera by Scribe, music by Auber (produced Covent Garden Theatre, London, 1833).   1833.

The Deep Deep Sea; or, Perseus and Andromeda, with Charles Dance (produced Olympic Theatre, London, 1833).   1834.

The Challenge (songs only), libretto by H. M. Milner, music by Hérold, arranged by Tom Cooke, from a French play (produced Covent Garden Theatre, London, 1834).

Secret Service, from a play by Mélesville and Duveyrier (produced Theatre Royal, Drury Lane, London, 1834).   1834.

The Loan of a Lover (produced Olympic Theatre, London, 1834).   1834; revised version, as *Peter Spyk* (produced 1870).

My Friend the Governor (produced Olympic Theatre, London, 1834).   1834.

The Regent, from a play by Scribe and Mélesville (produced Theatre Royal, Drury Lane, London, 1834).   1834.

The Red Mask; or, The Council of Three, music by Tom Cooke from an opera by A. Berrettoni, music by Marliani (produced Theatre Royal, Drury Lane, London, 1834). Songs published 1834.

Telemachus; or, The Island of Calypso, with Charles Dance (produced Olympic Theatre, London, 1834). In *Extravaganzas 1*, 1879.

The Court Beauties (produced Olympic Theatre, London, 1835).   1835.

The Travelling Carriage (produced Theatre Royal, Drury Lane, London, 1835).

The Jewess, music by Halévy, arranged by Tom Cooke, from a libretto by Scribe (produced Theatre Royal, Drury Lane, London, 1835).   1835.

Chevy Chase, music by George Macfarren (produced Theatre Royal, Drury Lane, London, 1836).   Songs published 1836.

Court Favour; or, Private and Confidential (produced Olympic Theatre, London, 1836).   1838.

The Siege of Corinth, music by Tom Cooke, from an opera by C. della Valle, music by Rossini (produced Theatre Royal, Drury Lane, London, 1836).   Songs published 1836.

The Two Figaros, from a French play (produced Olympic Theatre, London, 1836).   1837.

Riquet with the Tuft, with Charles Dance, from a French play (produced Olympic Theatre, London, 1836).   1837.

A Peculiar Position, from a play by Scribe (produced Olympic Theatre, London, 1837).   1837(?).

Norma, from a libretto by F. Romani (produced Theatre Royal, Drury Lane, London, 1837).   1848.

The New Servant (produced Olympic Theatre, London, 1837).

The Child of the Wreck, music by Tom Cooke (produced Theatre Royal, Drury Lane, London, 1837).   1859.

Caractacus, music by Michael Balfe, from a play by Fletcher (produced Theatre Royal, Drury Lane, London, 1837).

Puss in Boots, with Charles Dance (produced Olympic Theatre, London, 1837).   1837.

The Magic Flute, music by Mozart, arranged by Tom Cooke, from an opera by Emanuel Schikaneder (produced Theatre Royal, Drury Lane, London, 1838).   Songs published 1838.

The Drama's Levée; or, A Peep at the Past (produced Olympic Theatre, London, 1838). In *Extravaganzas 2*, 1879.

The Printer's Devil (produced Olympic Theatre, London, 1838).   1838(?).

The Queen's Horse; or, The Brewer of Preston, with M.B. Honan (produced Olympic Theatre, London, 1838). 1839.

Blue Beard, with Charles Dance (produced Olympic Theatre, London, 1839).   1839.

Faint Heart Ne'er Won Fair Lady (produced Olympic

Theatre, London, 1839).   Nd.

The Garrick Fever (produced Olympic Theatre, London, 1839).   1855.

The Fortunate Isles; or, The Triumphs of Britannia, music by Henry Bishop (produced Covent Garden Theatre, London, 1840).   1840.

The Sleeping Beauty in the Wood (produced Covent Garden Theatre, London, 1840).   1840.

The Spanish Curate, from the play by Fletcher and Massinger (produced Covent Garden Theatre, London, 1840). 1887.

Harlequin and the Giant Helmet; or, The Castle of Otranto, from a novel by Horace Walpole (produced Covent Garden Theatre, London, 1840).

The Captain of the Watch, from a play by Lockroy (produced Covent Garden Theatre, London, 1841).   1841.

The Embassy (produced Covent Garden Theatre, London, 1841).

Beauty and the Beast (produced Covent Garden Theatre, London, 1841).   1841.

The Marriage of Figaro, from an opera by Lorenzo da Ponte, music by Mozart (produced Covent Garden Theatre, London, 1842).   Songs published 1842.

The White Cat, music by J.H. Tully (produced Covent Garden Theatre, London, 1842).   1842.

The Follies of a Night, music by Tom Cooke, from a French play (produced Theatre Royal, Drury Lane, London, 1842).   1842.

The Way of the World, from the play by Congreve (produced Theatre Royal, Haymarket, London, 1842).

Fortunio and His Seven Gifted Servants (produced Theatre Royal, Drury Lane, London, 1843).   1843.

Who's Your Friend? or, The Queensberry Fête, from a French play (produced Theatre Royal, Haymarket, London, 1843).   1843.

The Fair One with the Golden Locks (produced Theatre Royal, Haymarket, London, 1843).   1844.

Grist to the Mill, from a French play (produced Theatre Royal, Haymarket, London, 1844).   1844.

The Drama at Home; or, An Evening with Puff (produced Theatre Royal, Haymarket, London, 1844).   1844.

Somebody Else (produced Theatre Royal, Haymarket, London, 1844).   1845.

Graciosa and Percinet (produced Theatre Royal, Haymarket, London, 1844).   1845.

The Golden Fleece; or, Jason in Colchis and Medea in Corinth (produced Theatre Royal, Haymarket, London, 1845). 1845.

A Cabinet Question (produced Theatre Royal, Haymarket, London, 1845).   1845.

The Bee and the Orange Tree; or, The Four Wishes (produced Theatre Royal, Haymarket, London, 1845).   1846.

The Irish Post (produced Theatre Royal, Haymarket, London, 1846).   1846.

The Birds of Aristophanes (produced Theatre Royal, Haymarket, London, 1846).   1846.

Queen Mary's Bower, from a French play (produced Theatre Royal, Haymarket, London, 1846).   1847.

Spring Gardens (produced Theatre Royal, Haymarket, London, 1846).   1846.

Story-Telling; or, Novel Effects (produced Theatre Royal, Haymarket, London, 1846).

The Invisible Prince; or, The Island of Tranquil Delights (produced Theatre Royal, Haymarket, London, 1846). 1846.

The New Planet; or, Harlequin Out of Place (produced Theatre Royal, Haymarket, London, 1847).   1847.

The Jacobite (produced Theatre Royal, Haymarket, London, 1847).   1847.

The Pride of the Market (produced Lyceum Theatre, London, 1847).   1847.

The Golden Branch (produced Lyceum Theatre, London, 1847).   1848.

Not a Bad Judge (produced Lyceum Theatre, London, 1848). 1848.

Thesus and Ariadne; or, The Marriage of Bacchus (produced Lyceum Theatre, London, 1848).   1848.

The King of the Peacocks (produced Lyceum Theatre, London, 1848).   1849.

A Romantic Idea (produced Lyceum Theatre, London, 1849).   1849.

Hold Your Tongue (produced Lyceum Theatre, London, 1849).   1849.

The Seven Champions of Christendom, from a work by Richard Johnson (produced Lyceum Theatre, London, 1849).   1849.

A Lady in Difficulties (produced Lyceum Theatre, London, 1849).   1849.

The Island of Jewels (produced Lyceum Theatre, London, 1849).   1850.

Fiesco; or, The Revolt of Genoa, from a play by Schiller (produced Theatre Royal, Drury Lane, London, 1850).

Cymon and Iphigenia, from a play by Garrick (produced Lyceum Theatre, London, 1850).   1850.

My Heart's Idol; or, A Desperate Remedy (produced Lyceum Theatre, London, 1850).

The White Hood (produced Lyceum Theatre, London, 1850).

A Day of Reckoning (produced Lyceum Theatre, London, 1850).   1852.

King Charming; or, The Blue Bird of Paradise (produced Lyceum Theatre, London, 1850).   In *Extravaganzas 4*, 1879.

The Queen of the Frogs (produced Lyceum Theatre, London, 1851).   In *Extravaganzas 4*, 1879.

The Prince of Happy Land; or, The Fawn in the Forest (produced Lyceum Theatre, London, 1851).   1851.

The Mysterious Lady (produced Lyceum Theatre, London, 1852).   1853.

The Good Woman in the Wood (produced Lyceum Theatre, London, 1852).   In *Extravaganzas 4*, 1879.

Mr. Buckstone's Ascent of Mount Parnassus (produced Theatre Royal, Haymarket, London, 1853).   1853(?); in *Extravaganzas 4*, 1879.

The Camp at the Olympic (produced Olympic Theatre, London, 1853).   1854.

Harlequin King Nutcracker (produced Strand Theatre, London, 1853).   1853.

Once upon a Time There Were Two Kings (produced Lyceum Theatre, London, 1853).   1853.

Mr. Buckstone's Voyage Round the Globe (in Leicester Square) (produced Theatre Royal, Haymarket, London, 1854).   In *Extravaganzas 5*, 1879.

The Knights of the Round Table (produced Theatre Royal, Haymarket, London 1854).   Nd.

The Yellow Dwarf and the King of the Gold Mines (produced Olympic Theatre, London, 1854).   In *Extravaganzas 5*, 1879.

The New Haymarket Spring Meeting (produced Theatre Royal, Haymarket, London, 1855).   In *Extravaganzas 5*, 1879.

The Discreet Princess; or, The Three Glass Distaffs (produced Olympic Theatre, London, 1855).   In *Extravaganzas 5*, 1879.

Young and Handsome (produced Olympic Theatre, London,

1856).   In *Extravaganzas 5*, 1879.
An Old Offender (produced Adelphi Theatre, London, 1859).
Love and Fortune (produced Princess's Theatre, London, 1859).   In *Extravaganzas 5*, 1879.
My Lord and My Lady; or, It Might Have Been Worse, from a play by Dumas *père* (produced Theatre Royal, Haymarket, London 1861).   1862.
Love's Triumph, music by Vincent Wallace (produced Royal Opera House, Covent Garden, London, 1862).   1862.
Orpheus in the Haymarket, from an opera by H. Crémieux and L. Halévy, music by Offenbach (produced Theatre Royal, Haymarket, London, 1865).   In *Extravaganzas 5*, 1879.
Queen Lucidora, the Fair One with the Golden Locks, and Harlequin Prince Graceful; or, The Carp, the Crow, and the Owl (produced Sadler's Wells Theatre, London, 1868).
Pieces of Pleasantry for Private Performance During the Christmas Holidays.   1868.
King Christmas (produced Royal Gallery of Illustration, London, 1871).   In *Extravaganzas 5*, 1879.
Babil and Bijou; or, The Lost Regalia (songs only), play by Dion Boucicault (produced Royal Opera House, Covent Garden, London, 1872).

Verse

Shere Afkun, The First Husband of Nourmahal: A Legend of Hindoostan. (2 vols.).   1823.
William with the Ring: A Romance in Rhyme.   1873.
Songs and Poems from 1819 to 1879.   1881.

Memoirs and Letters

Recollections and Reflections: A Professional Autobiography (2 vols.).   1872; revised edition, 1901.

Other

Costumes of Shakespeare's King John (and other plays) (5 vols.).   1823–25.
Lays and Legends of the Rhine (2 vols.).   1827; as *The Rhenisch Keepsake*, 1837.
Descent of the Danube from Ratisbon to Vienna During the Autumn of 1827.   1828; as *The Danube from Ulm to Vienna*, 1836.
History of British Costume.   1834.
Regal Records; or, A Chronicle of the Coronation of the Queens Regnant of England.   1838.
The Pursuivant of Arms; or, Heraldry Founded upon Facts.   1852; revised edition, 1858.
A Corner of Kent; or, Some Account of the Parish of Ash-Next-Sandwich.   1864.
The Conqueror and His Companions (2 vols.).   1874.
A Cyclopaedia of Costume; or, Dictionary of Dress (2 vols.).   1876–79.
Suggestions for Establishing an English Art Theatre.   1879.

Editor, A *Complete View of the Dress and Habits of the People of England*, by Joseph Strutt.   1842.
Editor, *The Regal and Ecclesiastical Antiquities of England*, by Joseph Strutt.   1842.

Translator, *King Nut-Cracker: A Fairy Tale.*   1853.
Translator, *Fairy Tales*, by Mme. de Aulnoy.   1855.
Translator, *Four and Twenty Fairy Tales.*   1858.

*

Criticism

Books:
Harley Granville-Barker, "Exit Planché—Enter Gilbert" in *The Eighteen-Sixties*, edited by John Drinkwater, 1932.
Eric Walter White, *The Rise of English Opera*, London, 1951.
V.C. Clinton-Baddeley, *The Burlesque Tradition in English Theatre after 1660*, London, 1952.
Michael R. Booth, *Prefaces to English Nineteenth Century Theatre*, Manchester, 1980.
Michael R. Booth, *Victorian Spectacular Theatre 1850–1910*, London and Boston, 1981.
Russell Jackson (ed.), *Victorian Theatre*, London, 1989.

Articles:
Dugald MacMillan, "Planché's Early Classical Burlesques" in *Studies in Philology*, 25, 1928.
Dugald MacMillan, "Some Burlesques with a Purpose 1830–1870" in *Philological Quarterly*, 8, 1929.
Dugald MacMillan, "Planché's Fairy Extravaganzas" in *Studies in Philology*, 28, 1931.
Stanley Wells, "Shakespeare in Planché's Extravaganzas" in *Shakespeare Survey*, 16, 1963.
Paul Reinhardt, "The Costume Designs of Planché" in *Educational Theatre Journal*, 20, 1968.
P.T. Dircks, "Planché and the English Burletta Tradition" in *Theatre Survey*, 17, 1976.

*   *   *

Irrespective of posterity's judgement on his work as a playwright, Planché will always command a place in the history of the 19th-century stage by virtue of the sheer range of his activities and interests. Inside the theatre proper, he was engaged at one time or another as stock author, costume or scenic designer, stage manager, house manager, and campaigner for sundry theatrical causes; outside, but at a fruitful tangent to the theatre, he was also a poet, a travel writer, a translator of French and German fairy-tales, an antiquary, an authority on historical dress, armour, and heraldry, and, ultimately, a member of the College of Arms performing ceremonial duties as Rouge Croix Pursuivant and later as Somerset Herald. As a dramatist his output was prodigious—some 180 pieces produced at a dozen different theatres, covering every conceivable permutation of genre from grand opera to extravaganza.

Much of the most interesting, as well as the most workaday, of this *oeuvre* was written for particular managers or actor-managers and their accredited companies. As a professional playwright without other sources of income, Planché had no option but to work within the existing theatrical establishment and he seems to have been able not only to accommodate himself to its constant pressures and demands but also to find in them a source of inspiration and impetus for his own ideas. It was, for instance, while he was engaged by Charles Kemble at Covent Garden between 1822 and 1828 that he persuaded the manager to depart from conventional practice by mounting a production of *King John* in painstakingly researched, historically accurate costume, an experiment that proved so successful that it was repeated by Kemble with other plays in subsequent seasons, preparing the ground for the Shakespearian productions of Macready, Phelps, and, most remarkably, Charles Kean. This same engagement gave him opportunities to develop a skill that he was to exercise throughout his career, that of writing words to music. It was here, and during several engagements at Drury Lane between 1828 and 1836, that he wrote his celebrated libretto for Weber's *Oberon* and collaborated with other composers, notably Henry Bishop, on a whole series of operas, melodramas, and historical dramas with music (variants between which 19th-century practice made no clear-cut distinction).

It was, however, his long association with Madame Vestris and her husband, Charles James Mathews, that provided the stimulus for his most original work. He wrote *Olympic Revels* to inaugurate the former's management of the Olympic Theatre in 1831, and maintained his creative partnership with the couple for more than 20 years, throughout their tenancies of Covent Garden and the Lyceum and their acting engagements with Macready at Drury Lane, and with Benjamin Webster at the Haymarket. One of Planché's perennial strengths was his ability to write for individual actors, and the interplay between this gift and the particular talents and personalities of Vestris and Mathews, and those of other leading performers, helped to produce some accomplished examples of high comedy, and, above all, a corpus of 44 extravaganzas which formed the cornerstone of his reputation in his lifetime.

These latter works fall into three main categories: the "Classical" extravaganzas, which parody Greek myths and the conventions of Greek drama in a manner that contrives to be at once scholarly and entertaining; the "revues", whose purpose Planché described as offering "a running commentary on recent metropolitan events" (the London theatrical scene in particular), thus providing a mine of information for theatre historians; and, most imaginatively of all, the "fairy" extravaganzas, a type suggested to Planché initially by the French *féerie*, but which he rapidly naturalized to English taste and fashioned into a confection of great charm and wit.

There is abundant inventiveness as well as intertextuality in their travesties of traditional songs, drawing-room ballads, arias and choruses from fashionable opera, and, above all, Shakespeare. There is much satirical reference, occasionally trenchant, more often benign, to life in contemporary England, which serves to counterpoint and, as it were, to domesticate the fairy world. Yet, at the same time, there is visual enchantment of a high order, thanks in no small measure to Planché's being entrusted by the Vestris-Mathews management with overall responsibility for stage decoration and his collaboration during the Lyceum years with an inspired designer-machinist in William Beverley. The result was stage spectacle of sophistication and beauty which enhanced the fairy-tale atmosphere of his text, and eventually, to Planché's dismay, began to swamp it, just as his earlier crusade for historical authenticity in costume led to an excess of antiquarianism in stage presentation which he bitterly regretted.

Nonetheless, and even without benefit of performance, there is much to admire in his fairy extravaganzas, as they show his characteristic talents at their best: versifying skill, an absurd sense of fun and ability to create unforgettable eccentrics, an eye for the possibilities of scenic imagery, and, before all else, a delicacy of touch which allows comedy to go hand-in-hand with pathos and even with a strain of seriousness. In all these pieces the narrative and moral thrust of the original fairy-tale are never lost sight of, betokening an underlying respect for the marvellous which has an almost child-like quality. Small wonder that they were so phenomenally successful and came to exercise a strong influence on the development of English pantomime, particularly in the growing importance attached to the "transformation scene" and the emergence of the "principal boy", who owes much to the comely, blue-blooded breeches-roles that Planché devised for Eliza Vestris and her successors. Similarly, his distinctive

idiom in extravaganza was widely imitated and had much to do with the inordinate popularity of burlesque in the second half of the century, though he deplored its grosser manifestations, and recognized a true heir only in W.S. Gilbert, whose elegant and urbane humour was to outstrip his own.

Ironically, then, Planché's very achievements contributed to the decline and discredit into which his dramatic work so quickly fell. It also has to be admitted that the earnestness with which he saw his vocation as a playwright, the self-righteous claim that he had never intentionally sacrificed his principles "at the shrine of popularity", is not always reflected in the plays themselves, and helps to explain why they have not been staged in the present century. Even so, some of them—several farces, unorthodox self-referential comedies like *The Two Figaros* and *A Romantic Idea*, his melodrama *The Vampire*, and many of the extravaganzas—undeniably deserve a full-scale revival: only then will a proper reappraisal of his stature be possible.

—Donald Roy

PLAUTUS, Titus Maccius (possibly a pseudonym or nickname). Born in Sarsina, Umbria (now in Italy), c.254 BC. Playwright c.200–184 BC; associated with the actor and impresario T. Publius Phellio on the plays *Stichus* and *Epidichus*. Of the 130 plays listed under his name, 21 survive (probably the same works that the Roman scholar Verro listed as being genuine), all based on Greek New Comedy sources. Died c.184 BC.

Works

Collections

Comoediae (2 vols.), edited by F. Leo.   1895–96.
Comoediae (2 vols.), edited by Wallace M. Lindsay.   1903–05 (Oxford Classical Texts).
Plautus: Five of His Plays (includes *The Pot of Gold; The Captives; The Twin Brothers; The Tempest; Amphitryon*), translated by Sir Robert Allison.   1914.
Plautus (parallel texts; 5 vols.), translated by Paul Nixon. 1916–38 (Loeb Classical Library).
Three Plays (includes *The Slip Knot; The Crock of Gold; The Trickster*), translated by F.A. Wright and Lionel Rogers. 1925.
Complete Roman Drama (2 vols,; includes translations of all the plays), edited by George Duckworth.   1942.
Six Plays (*Amphitryon; The Pot of Gold; Casina; The Menaechmus Twins; Pseudolos; The Rope*), translated by Lionel Casson.   1960.
"The Rope" and Other Plays (includes *The Ghost; A Three-Dollar Day; Amphitryo*), translated by E.F. Watling. 1964.
"The Pot of Gold" and Other Plays (includes *The Prisoners; The Brothers Menaechmus; The Swaggering Soldier*), translated by E.F. Watling.   1965.
Three Comedies (includes *The Braggart Soldier; The Brothers Menaechmus; The Haunted House*), translated by Erich Segal.   1969.
Rudens; Curculio; Casina, translated by Christopher Stace. 1981.

The Darker Comedies (includes *Bacchides; Casina; Truculentus*), translated by James Tatum. 1983.

Three Plays (includes *Miles Gloriosus; Amphitryon; The Prisoners*), translated by Paul Roche. 1984.

Three Comedies (includes *Miles Gloriosus; Pseudolos; Rudens*), translated by Peter L. Smith. 1991.

Stage Works

In addition to translations mentioned below, the plays appear also in *Complete Roman Drama* (see collections).

Amphitryo. Translated as *Amphitryon*, with *Epidicus and Rudens*, 1694: several subsequent translations under same title; as *Amphitruo*, 1746; as *Amphitryo*, in *"The Rope" and Other Plays*, 1964.

Asinaria. Translated by E.H. Sugden as *Asinaria*, in his *Plautus: Comedies*, 1893: several subsequent translations under same title; as *The Comedy of Asses*, in *Plautus 1* (Loeb edition).

Aulalaria. Translated by G.S. Cotter, as *Aulalaria*, in his *Comoediae septem selectae*, 1827: several subsequent translations under same title; as *The Pot of Gold*, in *Plautus: Five of His Plays*, 1914, and in *"The Pot of Gold" and Other Plays*, 1965; as *The Crock of Gold*, in *Three Plays*. 1925.

Bacchides. Translated by E.H. Sugden, as *Bacchides*, in his *Plautus: Comedies*, 1893: several subsequent translations under same title; as *The Two Bacchises*, in *Plautus 1* (Loeb edition).

Captivi. Translated as *Captivi*, 1888, and *The Captives*, in *Plautus: Five of His Plays*, 1914: several subsequent translations under both titles; as *The Prisoners*, in *"The Pot of Gold" and Other Plays*, 1965, and *Three Plays*, 1984.

Casina. Translated as *Casina*, in *Plautus* (Loeb edition): several subsequent translations under same title.

Cistellaria. Translated as *The Casket Comedy*, in *Plautus 2* (Loeb edition).

Curculio. Translated as *The Weevil*, 1968; as *Curculio*, in *Plautus 2* (Loeb edition) and *Rudens; Curculio; Casina*, 1981.

Epidicus. Translated as *Epidicus*, with *Amphitryo and Rudens*, 1694: several subsequent translations under same title.

Menaechmi. Translated by G.S. Cotter as *Menaechmi*, in his *Comoediae septem selectae*, 1827: several subsequent translations under same title; as *The Twin Brothers*, in *Plautus: Five of His Plays*, 1914; as *The Two Menaechmuses*, in *Plautus 2* (Loeb edition); as *The Menaechmus Twins*, in *Six Plays*, 1960; as *The Menaechmi Twins*, in *Roman Drama*, edited by Samuel Lieberman, 1964; as *The Brothers Menaechmus*, in *"The Pot of Gold" and Other Plays*, 1965, and *Three Comedies*, 1969.

Mercator. Translated by G.S. Cotter as *Mercator*, in his *Comoediae septem reliquae*, 1827: several subsequent translations under same title as *The Merchant*, in *Plautus 2* (Loeb edition).

Miles Gloriosus. Translated as *The Braggart Warrior*, in *Plautus 2* (Loeb edition); as *The Braggart Soldier*, 1963; as *The Swaggering Soldier*, in *"The Pot of Gold" and Other Plays*, 1965; as *Miles Gloriosus*, in *Three Plays*, 1984, and *Three Comedies*, 1991.

Mostellaria. Translated as *The Haunted House* (parallel text), 1890: several subsequent translations under same title; as *The Ghost*, in *"The Rope" and Other Plays*, 1964; as *Mostellaria*, 1972.

Persa. Translated as *The Persian*, in *Plautus* (Loeb edition).

Poenulus. Translated as *The Little Carthaginian*, in *Plautus 4* (Loeb edition).

Pseudolus. Translated by G.S. Cotter as *Pseudolus*, in his *Comoediae septem selectae*, 1827: several subsequent translations under same title; as *The Trickster*, in *Three Plays*, 1925.

Rudens. Translated as *Rudens*, with *Amphitryo* and *Epidicus*, 1694: several subsequent translations under same title; as *The Slip Knot*, in *Three Plays*, 1925; as *The Rope*, 1956: several subsequent translations under same title.

Stichus. Translated as *The Tempest*, in *Plautus: Five of His Plays* 1914; as *Stichus*, in *Plautus 5* (Loeb edition).

Trinummus. Translated by G.S. Cotter as *Trinummus*, in his *Comoediae septem selectae*, 1827; as *Trinummus, or Three Bob Day*, in *Plautus 5* (Loeb edition) as *A Three-Dollar Day*, in *"The Rope" and Other Plays*, 1964.

Truculentus. Translated as *Truculentus*, in *Plautus 5* (Loeb edition) and *The Darker Comedies*, 1983.

Vidularia (fragment). Translated as *Vidularia*, in *Plautus 5* (Loeb edition).

Fragments. Translated in *Plautus 5* (Loeb edition).

*

Bibiographies

J. David Hughes, *A Bibliography of Scholarship on Plautus*, Amsterdam, 1975.

Erich Segal, "Scholarship on Plautus 1965–76", in *Classical World*, vol. 74 no. 7, 1981.

Criticism

Books:

Charles H. Buck, *A Chronology of the Plays of Plautus*, 1940.

George Duckworth, *The Nature of Roman Comedy*, Princeton, New Jersey, 1952.

G. Norwood, *Plautus and Terence*, New York, 1963.

Erich Segal, *Roman Laughter: The Comedy of Plautus*, New York, 1968.

Eric W. Handley, *Menander, and Plautus: A Study in Comparison*, London, 1968.

John H. Wright, *Dancing in Chains: The Stylistic Unity of the Comoedia Palliata*, 1974.

W.G. Arnott, *Menander, Plautus, and Terence*, Oxford, 1975.

Kenneth McLeish, *Roman Comedy*, Basingstoke, 1976.

Netta Zagagi, *Tradition and Originality in Plautus*, 1980.

David Konstan, *Roman Comedy*, Ithaca (New York) and London, 1983.

F.H. Sandbach, *The Comic Theatre of Greece and Rome*, London, 1985.

Niall W. Slater, *Plautus in Performance*, Princeton, New Jersey, 1985.

Richard C. Beacham, *The Roman Theatre and Its Audience*, London, 1991.

* * *

Plautus, the earliest Latin author whose works are preserved, is the father of farce, and his influence upon later playwrights, who freely borrowed his characters, plots, and jokes, has been immense. His plays, of which 21 survive wholly or in part, are all believed to have been based on earlier Greek New Comedy texts by writers such as

Menander, Diphilus, and Philemon. But instead of translating them directly into Latin, Plautus, as he freely admitted, "transformed" them into his "barbarian" versions, in adaptations that were conditioned by his own abilities and preferences, which, in turn, undoubtedly reflected directly the taste and pressure of his Roman public.

Plautus took the rather urbane and decorous Greek comedies and injected them with a great deal of vitality, comic fun, and vulgarity. Their generally high-minded and thoughtful characters are, in his hands, more vigorously drawn and cynically motivated. The language of his own laughable and sometimes grotesque characters is cruder, more ribald and playful, but also much richer in complex, and sometimes fantastical, imagery. Their intrigues tend to be less plausible than those found in the New Comedy models, but they are more ingeniously and energetically pursued. For the delectation of his Roman holiday audience Plautus increased greatly the amount of song and dance, adding, too, many references to Roman customs, and often breaking the dramatic illusion entirely to allow his performers to speak directly to the audience about their own functions as actors, or about the play itself. A fine example is Mercury in the Prologue to *Amphitruo*, who constantly moves in and out of the world of the play, shifting as he does so from speaking as an actor, to portraying the character. Plautus was fond, too, of such devices as soliloquies and overheard conversations.

His plots abound in trickery and, serving as their mischievous agents (and foils), he greatly increased the role of slaves, such as Palaestrio in the *Miles Gloriosus (The Braggard Soldier)*, or Pseudolus in *Pseudolus*, as its title indicates, literally his own play. These slaves are threatened with extreme violence. But pain, beatings, threats of torture are not only a source of fun; they become important motivations of plot and action. There is also a great deal of verbal violence. Both are evident in the opening scene of the *Casina*, in which two rival slaves threaten one another with the direst torture, while engaging in elaborately abusive insults. Violence was not prevalent in earlier comedy; Plautus deliberately increased it, perhaps to cater to a taste for violent slapstick in an audience accustomed to earlier unscripted knock-about entertainments.

In addition to displaying this violent streak, Plautus' plays are inclined also towards coarse and sometimes indecent humor, and exhibit a fondness for disguise and crude deception, slapstick, a preference for fooling over the development of emotional interest or the advancement of the plot, and a festive conclusion. Less frequently, as in the case of the *Rudens (The Rope)* or the *Captivi (The Captives)*, the play is informed by more ethical and philosophical concerns, while still achieving a happy conclusion.

Another likely legacy of earlier forms of popular drama taken up and developed by Plautus may be discerned in his use of music and mastery of a great variety of metrical forms. Plautus strives to create mood and enhance the emotional impact of characters' lauguage through close attention to sound: alliteration, rhyme, assonance, and word play are all abundant, and these are presented in a great variety of both spoken and lyric meters. Passages, which in his Hellenistic models were prose, are transformed into song, and in performance would probably have been accompanied by heightened gesticulation and dance. In the course of his career this metrical richness and dexterity, unmatched by any other Latin author, increased, until his later plays might best be characterised as something akin to modern musical comedy, written in verse. Over a third of his last play, the *Casina*, is in lyric meters.

One of the recurrent elements of Plautine drama is that the characters appear to make up the comedy as they go along: they contrive the very plot in which they take a part. Probably this directly reflects the legacy of a more tentative dramatic fare: improvised, non-literary entertainments long favoured by his audience, which the actors are thought to have assembled on the basis of stock characters and situations, some well-worn but ever-popular bits of comic business, and the barest outline of a scenario. We trace the influence of such performances in Plautus' deliberate choice to "make believe" that his own plays are unscripted, taking shape in the presence of an audience which, in turn, assists in their formation.

The chief agent of this dramaturgical self-consciousness is usually the "clever slave" who fashions the play around himself to become simultaneously its author and hero. He fills this role by virtue of his wit and intelligence, triumphing over adversity and the social facts of life in a way which no actual Roman slave could ever do. Masters are tricked, freedom is won, and the clever slave enjoys impunity. In the surviving plays nothing dire ever actually happens to him, despite circumstances of ever-present danger. Indeed, Plautus' protagonists make a point of positively disdaining and mocking the fates which, but for their success in fashioning unlikely, anti-realist plots, would tumble down upon them.

This is one key to his enduring popularity. The audience enjoys the pretense of the *actors'* theatrical improvisation, while in the process, admiring and experiencing a mildly subversive "saturnalian" pleasure in the *characters'* ability to salvage something redemptive from their dramatic situation and get away with it. Moreover, compounding the pleasure and release of tension and moral restraint is the awareness that all the plots and characters are notionally set safely and unthreateningly in Greece: in the time-honoured tradition of ethnic and minority humour, a Plautine play is one extended "Greek joke".

Although the changes and innovations which Plautus wrought on his models must surely have helped ensure the success of his plays in performance, they did little to endear him to generations of critical classicists who, too often, considered him to be at best a hack translator and adaptor of what (in their absence) were believed to be the sublime comedies of the Greek New Comedy playwrights. Many scholars appeared to be far more concerned with what Plautus might have read than with what he actually wrote, which they dismissed as sub-literary bufoonery. Only recently has a fresh approach begun to recognise him for what he was: a superbly gifted comic craftsman who mastered and employed every theatrical skill for the benefit and appreciation of an audience that had already acquired an impressive degree of experience, and some sophistication, in responding to dramaturgical technique. His plays will reward further research, and deserve more frequent performance.

—Richard C. Beacham

See also *Volume 1* entries on *The Braggart Soldier*; *The Brothers Menaechmus*; *The Rope*.

POLIAKOFF, Stephen. Born in London, 14 December 1952. Educated at Westminster School, London; King's College, Cambridge, 1972–73. Married Sandy Welch in 1983; one daughter. First-produced play, *Granny*, staged 1969;

writer-in-residence, National Theatre, London, 1976–77. Recipient: BAFTA Award, 1980; Venice Film Festival Prize, 1989.

Works

Collections

Plays 1 (includes *Clever Soldiers; Hitting Town; City Sugar; Shout Across the River; American Days; Strawberry Fields*). 1989.

Stage Works

Granny (produced London, 1969).
Bambi Ramm (produced Abbey Community Centre, London, 1970).
A Day with My Sister (produced Traverse Theatre, Edinburgh, 1971).
Lay-By, with others (produced Traverse Theatre, Edinburgh, 1971). 1972.
Pretty Boy (produced Royal Court Theatre, London, 1972).
Theatre Outside (produced London, 1973).
Berlin Days (produced London, 1973).
The Carnation Gang (produced Bush Theatre, London, 1974).
Clever Soldiers (produced Hampstead Theatre, London, 1974). In *Plays 1*, 1989.
Heroes (produced Royal Court Theatre Upstairs, London, 1975).
Hitting Town (produced Bush Theatre, London, 1975). With *City Sugar*, 1976.
City Sugar (produced Comedy Theatre, London, 1975). With *Hitting Town*, 1976.
Strawberry Fields (produced National Theatre, London 1977). 1977.
Shout Across the River (produced The Warehouse, London, 1978). 1979.
American Days (produced Institute of Contemporary Arts, London, 1979). 1979.
The Summer Party (produced Crucible Theatre, Sheffield, 1980). 1980.
Favourite Nights (produced Lyric Theatre, Hammersmith, London, 1981). With the television play *Caught on a Train*, 1982.
Breaking the Silence (produced National Theatre, London, 1984). 1984.
Coming in to Land (produced National Theatre, London, 1987). 1987.
Playing with Trains (produced The Pit, Barbican Centre, London, 1989). 1990.
Sienna Red (produced Richmond Theatre, Richmond, 1992). 1992.

Screenplays

Runners, 1983 (published with the television play *Soft Targets*); *Hidden City*, 1988, and *She's Been Away*, 1989 (published together, 1989); *Close My Eyes*, 1991 (published 1992).

Television Plays

Stronger Than the Sun, 1977; *Bloody Kids*, 1980; *Caught on a Train*, 1980 (published with the stage play *Favourite Nights*, 1982); *Soft Targets*, 1982 (published with the screenplay *Runners*, 1984).

*

Criticism

Articles:
D. Keith Peacock, "The Fascination of Fascism: The Plays of Stephen Poliakoff", in *Modern Drama*, 27, 1984.

* * *

Stephen Poliakoff first achieved recognition with the two related plays *Hitting Town* and *City Sugar* in 1975. The plays attacked a series of readily identifiable targets—the tackiness and squalor of new inner-city developments, the alienating effects of fast-food shops and discos, and the banality of pop radio disc-jockeys. But here, as so often subsequently, the rather crude political context is less the real subject of the drama than a convenient back-drop against which a series of strangely vulnerable, odd-ball characters rehearse their particular desperation. Poliakoff's is a theatre of individual gesture rather than generalised political analysis. Although his plays appear to offer a series of thematically related attacks on contemporary society in loosely political terms, it is the emotional sub-text that is most important.

So, in *Hitting Town*, it is the awkward movement of a lonely woman and her waywardly embittered younger brother through a desolate provincial night on the town, and towards an incestuous bed, that creates most of the dramatic tension; just as in the more recent screenplay for *Runners* it is the tentative efforts of the father to achieve some kind of relationship with his young runaway daughter that holds the attention, rather than the more general theme of hopelessness in the face of mass youth unemployment that the film presents as its primary concern. And indeed, the daughter is not presented as a passive victim of circumstances. Like so many of Poliakoff's protagonists, she is a survivor, shell-shocked, but still in possession of a tentative resilience; surviving in a half-glimpsed London world of the dispossessed by distributing advertising literature.

Poliakoff returns continually to city night-life. It is when his characters can be displayed at their loneliest—a situation that brings about the very existence of the all-night radio phone-in which provides the structural continuity of *City Sugar*. And it is this pervading sense of isolation in supposedly crowded locations that gives his plays their peculiar clarity. For Poliakoff's stage city is a curiously unpopulated one. In *Hitting Town* the sister and brother first visit a Wimpy Bar in which the only other person present is a waitress who will again be the sole witness to their dialogue in the shopping precinct. Whether other people are assumed to be present (and thus a further cause of the sister's worry at her brother's deliberately provocative behaviour) is deliberately left unclear; but no such ambiguity exists by the time the three of them arrive at a disco in which the only direct evidence of the presence of others comes from the voice of the unseen disc jockey.

Again, in *Favourite Nights*, Catherine, language teacher by day, and escort by night, takes her German businessman student and her sister to a casino in which we otherwise see only a croupier, an American punter, and Alan, an official of the club. The absence of characters who must be understood to be present in night spots such as discos and casinos intensifies the way in which Poliakoff's characters see themselves as part of, and yet separate from, the contemporary world. Catherine's manic attempts to beat the bank yet again, in order to avoid the sexual compromise potentially involved in letting her client pay for their evening out, is seen as if in a filmic close-up from which all the extras are excluded; and the attempts to communicate with her lover, Alan, in a locale in which contact between staff and punters is banned, is given a curious intensity by the presence of spy cameras, yet with the absence of other members of the casino management.

It is not surprising, given all this, that the medium of film has come to seem increasingly attractive to Poliakoff. In *Hidden City*, the first film to be directed by him, the fascination with the city as secret world is still evident. A bored mathematical psychologist meets up with a strange young women who reveals a literal underworld of tunnels and hidden chambers in pursuit of officially-dead newsreel film footage, stumbling by accident on evidence of a long-since buried nuclear scandal. But afterwards it is the image of the "hidden city" rather than the thematic concern with the hidden scandal that remains in the mind.

Even when Poliakoff moves out of a city environment, as in *Strawberry Fields*, he takes his characters from London and up the motorway vertebrae of England, in and out of service stations and lay-bys which are as unpopulated as his all-night bars and casinos. Kevin and Charlotte set off to meet other members of the fascist group to which they belong at pre-arranged points. In this instance, the lack of contact with other characters—with the exception of a police constable and a hitch-hiker, who are shot dead at the ends of the first and second acts respectively—stresses their lack of contact with any reality, other than Kevin's half-remembered images of the 1960's, to support their ideology. They see themselves, increasingly, as a latter-day Bonnie and Clyde, but the paranoia of persecution and pursuit, on which their stance is built, is undercut by the non-appearance of the police who are supposedly chasing them.

This thematic use of the journey is another manifestation of the characters as socially and politically rootless and unconnected to the details of everyday life. In his 1980 television play, *Caught on a Train*, Poliakoff uses a railway journey across Europe, in which a series of characters—from a collection of anarchically politicised football hooligans to a young American thoroughly disenchanted with Europe—meet in transit without ever properly communicating, as an informing metaphor for an account of the contemporary malaise. This film marked a major development in his work and, interestingly, he was to return to the central motif of the train journey in what has been his most impressive stage play to date—*Breaking the Silence*—and in the later *Playing with Trains*.

For the first time since his earliest work, Poliakoff moved the action into the past for *Breaking the Silence*—Russia in the immediate aftermath of the Revolution. Nikolai, a wealthy Jewish aristocrat, based loosely on the playwright's own Russian grandfather, is turned out of his spacious accommodation, and is made Telephone Surveyor of the Northern Railway. To this end he is given a train to patrol a region where telephone poles have yet to be erected, all the time working single-mindedly towards his life's ambition of producing the first synchronised talking pictures. He is to be thwarted, finishing the play preparing for exile in England, his pictures as silent as the Northern region's telephone system. It is again a journey of isolation, in which all attempts at communication are literally, and metaphorically, denied; but it is also again a story of a survivor. Poliakoff, for the first time, properly united the individual concerns of the narrative with a larger thematic structure.

His concern with the links between the political worlds of the East and West, and thus with his own sense of cultural duality, was continued in *Coming in to Land*, which opened at the National Theatre in 1987.

—John Bull

POLLOCK, Sharon. Born Sharon Chalmers in Fredericton, New Brunswick, Canada, 19 April 1936. Educated at the University of New Brunswick, Fredericton, 2 years. Married Ross Pollock in 1954; six children. Actress in New Brunswick, and with touring group, Prairie Players, Calgary; head of the playwriting division, Department of Drama, University of Alberta, Edmonton, 1976–77; director of the Playwrights' Colony, Banff School of Fine Arts, Alberta, 1977–81; playwright-in-residence, Alberta Theatre Projects, Calgary, 1977–79, National Arts Centre, Ottawa, 1981, 1982, and Regina Public Library, Saskatchewan, 1986–87; dramaturg, 1982–83, associate artistic director, 1983–84, and artistic director, 1984, Theatre Calgary; artistic director, Theatre New Brunswick, 1988. Member, 1979–80, and Chairman, 1980–81, Canada Council Advisory Arts Panel; Vice-Chairman, Playwrights Canada National Executive, 1981–83. Recipient: Dominion Drama Festival Award, for acting, 1966; Nellie Award, for radio play, 1981; Governor-General's Award, 1981, 1986; Alberta Award of Excellence, 1983; Chalmers Award, 1984; Alberta Writers Guild Award, 1986; Alberta Literary Foundation Award, 1987. Honorary Doctorate: University of New Brunswick, 1986.

Works

Collections

"Blood Relations" and Other Plays (includes *One Tiger to a Hill; Generations*). 1981.

Stage Works

A Compulsory Option. 1970; revised version (produced New Play Centre, Vancouver, 1972; as *No! No! No!*, produced Toronto, 1977), 1972.
Walsh (produced Theatre Calgary, Calgary, Alberta, 1973). 1972; revised version (produced Stratford Festival, Stratford, Ontario, 1974), 1974.
New Canadians (for children; produced Playhouse Holiday, Vancouver, 1973).
Superstition Throu' the Ages (for children; produced Playhouse Holiday, Vancouver, 1973).
Wudjesay? (for children; produced Playhouse Holiday, Vancouver, 1974).
A Lesson in Swizzlery (for children; produced by Caravan Theatre, New Westminster, British Columbia, 1974).
The Rose and the Nightingale (for children), from the story by Oscar Wilde (produced Playhouse Theatre School, Vancouver, 1974).
The Star-child (for children), from the story by Oscar Wilde (produced Playhouse Theatre School, Vancouver, 1974).
The Happy Prince (for children), from the story by Oscar Wilde (produced Playhouse Theatre School, Vancouver, 1974).

And Out Goes You? (produced Playhouse, Vancouver, 1975).

The Komagata Maru Incident (produced Vancouver East Cultural Centre, Vancouver, 1976). 1978.

Blood Relations (as *My Name is Lisbeth*, produced Douglas College, New Westminster, British Columbia, 1976; revised version, as *Blood Relations*, produced Theatre Three, Edmonton, Alberta, 1980). In *"Blood Relations" and Other Plays*, 1981.

Tracings: The Fraser Story (collective work), with others (produced by Theatre Network, Edmonton, Alberta, 1977).

The Wreck of the National Line Car (for children; produced by Alberta Theatre Projects, Calgary, Alberta, 1978).

Mail vs. Female (produced by Lunchbox Theatre, Calgary, Alberta, 1979).

Chautauqua Spelt E-N-E-R-G-Y (for children; produced by Alberta Theatre Projects, Calgary, Alberta, 1979).

One Tiger to a Hill (produced Citadel Theatre, Edmonton, Alberta, 1980; revised version produced Festival Lennoxville, Lennoxville, Quebec, 1981). In *"Blood Relations" and Other Plays*, 1981.

Generations, from her radio play (produced by Alberta Theatre Projects, Canmore Opera House, Calgary, Alberta, 1980). In *"Blood Relations" and Other Plays*, 1981.

Whiskey Six (produced Theatre Calgary, Calgary, Alberta, 1983).

Doc (produced Theatre Calgary, Calgary, Alberta, 1984; revised version produced Free Theatre, Toronto, 1984; alternative version, as *Family Trappings*, produced Theatre New Brunswick, Fredericton, New Brunswick, 1986). 1986.

Television Plays

Portrait of a Pig, 1973; *The Larsens*, 1976; *Ransom*, 1976; *Free Our Sisters, Free Ourselves*; *The Person's Case, Country Joy* (6 episodes), with others, 1979–80.

Radio Plays

Split Seconds in the Death of, 1971; *31 for 2*, 1971; *We to the Gods*, 1971; *Waiting*; *The Triple B Plan*; *In Memory Of*; *Walsh*, 1974; *Generation*, 1978; *Sweet Land of Liberty*, 1979; *Intensive Care*, 1983; *Whiskey Six Cadenza*, 1983; *Mary Beth Goes to Calgary*; *Mrs. Yale and Jennifer* (8 episodes); *In the Beginning Was*; *One Tiger to a Hill*, 1985.

*

Criticism

Books:

Diane Bessai, "Sharon Pollock's Women: A Study in Dramatic Process", in *A Mazing Space: Writing Canadian Women Writing*, edited by Shirley Neumann and Smaro Kamboureli, Edmonton, Alberta, 1986.

Sharon Pollock, "Interview" in *Fair Play: 12 Women Speak: Conversations with Canadian Playwrights*, edited by Judith Rudakoff and Rita Much, Toronto, 1990.

Articles:

Malcolm Page, "Sharon Pollock: Committed Dramatist", in *Canadian Drama*, 5, 1979.

Robert C. Nunn, "Sharon Pollock's Plays: A Review Article", in *Theatre History in Canada*, 5, 1984.

*   *   *

Since 1974, when *Walsh* brought her to national attention, Sharon Pollock has explored consistent themes in a characteristic dramatic design, while becoming more intimate and more feminist in focus. Her concern has moved from large issues of racial and class domination to the politics of family and the position of individuals—and individual women—within the family structure. Her early style was overtly documentary (as was much Canadian theatre of the 1970's); her more recent plays still present personal histories in a loosely documentary style, but place more importance on the narrative and staging, and less on the explication of documents. Even the early plays, however, employ a highly selective and interpretive record, calling on the audience to assess historical scenes which are highly coloured for emotional impact, and to judge rather than simply to receive information. Indeed, Pollock reports that her research for *Walsh* taught her how subjective historical information really is, "how relative truth is".

Walsh is the story of Major John Walsh, a Royal Canadian Mounted Police officer who found himself in the unenviable position of restraining Chief Sitting Bull and the Sioux Nation at the border after they entered Canada from the USA, and who negotiated their return to America. His is the plight of the middle-manager, trapped between a growing sympathy for the Indian philosophy and his responsibility to the Force. Clarence, a naive young recruit who comes to understand the mysteries of the "Sacred Hoop" and to question his own role as an agent of white civilization, becomes a foil against whom Walsh, increasingly insincerely, argues. Chief Sitting Bull is drawn as a shaman, yet also as the victim of circumstances over which he has no control. Pollock uses this triangle of men to show power to be essentially meaningless and apparent helplessness to contain the only hope for moral victory: such a theme is typical of the early Pollock. In a powerful scene, Walsh capitulates to the police authority in order to save his career, and then, spiritually bankrupt, stages a fake Indian attack on a trainload of eastern politicians and reporters, giving them the wild-west myth they want to see, rather than the sad truth of the expulsion of the Sioux to certain genocide. This cynical comment on the falsity of political force becomes the central thrust of the play; a prologue shows a ruined Walsh after his fall, and the narrative unfolds to the sham attack, framing the central action with its ethical consequences. It also makes the design of the play itself a metaphor for its comment—a dramaturgical approach which can be seen increasingly in Pollock's work.

The Komagata Maru Incident continues Pollock's investigation of the politics of domination and her exposure of historical evils. It also shows a development in her control of theatrical design: the narrative is controlled by a ringmaster, moving back and forth from a shipload of refugees trapped in the Vancouver harbour to other locales. Secondary characters are interesting in themselves and the protagonist is more fully drawn than Walsh, though his dilemma is similar.

In *Blood Relations*, Pollock further focuses her concern, exploring the domination of a female protagonist, the American folk villain, Lizzie Borden. Although Pollock denies that her argument is feminist, pointing out that the issues which confront a female hero necessarily involve her being a woman, other critics have countered that it is inconceivable that this play could be written by a man, and that the subjugation of Miss Lizzie within the 19th-century family structure suggests larger issues of the control of women by society. Pollock employs an original documentary design: the play opens in 1902 with the friendship of Lizzie and an actress, and then moves in simultaneous action back to 1892 when the axe murder is alleged to have been committed. The Actress becomes a surrogate Lizzie, directed and prompted to a final epiphany by the real Lizzie posing on the edge of the action as the Maid. This "game" grows from the question which permeates the play: "Did you [commit the murders], Lizzie, did you?", a question the narrative appears to answer, but which the dramaturgy renders complex.

As the events in 1892 display Lizzie's frustration, entrapment, and sexual repression, the summer heat fuels the family tension, leading to a bloody climax. The dramatic design allows for highly poetic dream interludes in which Lizzie's inner passions are powerfully presented within a series of rigorously maintained image patterns of birds, domesticated animals, and tomboy bruises. These scabs on the young girl's knees, which real "ladies" never suffer, link with images of blood in various aspects: the blood of family, which Lizzie fights to protect from an avaricious stepmother; the blood of her pet pigeons butchered by her furious father; mother's blood spilt at Lizzie's birth; female blood in the abstract; and the blood-letting with which Lizzie frees herself through murder. Driven by guilt for her mother's death and her own failure to live up to social standards of femininity, Lizzie finally experiences "one moment of absolute clarity": she sees her own life as worthwhile and moves to protect it.

The narrative strongly suggests that she *did* commit the crime, but on stage it is the Actress who lifts the axe. The dramaturgy permits Lizzie's highly suggestive final response, "I didn't. You did", and allows an enigmatic ending in which Pollock suggests the crime may have been committed by Lizzie, by the Actress as actor in a social drama, by other family forces, or even by the audience to whom the remark is actually addressed: as participants in the folk tradition maintaining her guilt, the spectators are part of an historiography which condemns Lizzie, despite her acquittal.

In *Doc*, Pollock moves further into the female psyche in a semi-autobiographical return home. Again, complicated staging allows simultaneous action and the meeting of the protagonist with herself as a memory-child. Dead and missing family members share the stage with "real" figures, allowing the threads of memory to interweave in a static resolution which is barely hopeful. The play shows both Pollock's growing use of metadramatic technique and a movement inward, and at the same time her continued concern for those crushed (or frozen) by external forces, whether political or familial. It also shows the growing skill which has given Pollock a justified place in the top ranks of Canadian writers for the stage.

—S. Reid Gilbert

See also *Volume 1* entry on *Blood Relations*.

PREVELAKIS, Pandelis. Born in Rethymnon, Crete, 13 February 1909. Studied literature and art at the University of Athens, University of Paris, licence ès lettres; Paris Institute for Art and Architecture, diploma; University of Thessalonika, Ph.D 1933. Director of Fine Arts, Greek Ministry of Education, 1937–40; professor of Art History, School of Fine Arts, Athens, 1939–74. Recipient: Greek State Prize for Theatre, 1961; Academy of Vienna Herder Prize, 1975; Prize for Excellence, Greek Academy. Honorary

doctorates from the universities of Athens, 1982, and Crete, 1984. Elected to the Greek Academy, 1978. Died in Ekali, Greece, 15 March 1986.

Stage Works

O Mimos [The Mime].   In periodical form, 1928.
I Arostia tou Eona [The Sickness of the Century] (trilogy):
  1. *O Thanatos tou Medhikou* [The Death of the Medici]. 1939; revised version, as *To Iero Sfayo* [The Sacrificial Victim] (produced National Theatre, Athens, 1966), 1952; translated as *The Last Testament*, in *Introduction to Greek Literature: An Anthology of Fiction, Drama and Poetry*, edited by Mary P. Gianos, 1969.
  2. *Ta Heria tou Zontanou Theou* [The Hands of the Living God] (produced National Theatre, Athens, 1955). 1957.
  3. *Lazaros* [Lazarus] (produced National Theatre, Athens, 1975). 1957.
To Ifestio [The Volcano] (produced National Theatre, Athens, 1966).   1962.
Mousafirei sto Stepanchikovo [Guests at Stepanchikova] (produced National Theatre, Athens, 1973).   1972.
Monaxia [Solitude].   1981.
To Heri tou Skotomenu (produced National Theatre, Athens, 1979).   1971; translated as *The Hand of the Slain*, in *The Charioteer*, 16–17, 1974–75.
I Dhefteri Endoli [The Second Command].   With *To Trelo Ema*, 1974.
To Trelo Ema [The Crazy Blood].   With *I Dhefteri Endoli*, 1974.

Fiction

To hroniko mias politias.   1938.; translated as *The Tale of a Town*, 1976.
Pandermi Kriti [Desolate Crete].   1945.
O Kritikos [The Cretan] (trilogy).   1948–50:
    To Dentro [The Tree].   1948.
    I Proti Eleftheria. [The First Freedom].   1949.
    I Politeia [The Town].   1950.
I Dromi tis Dimiourgias [The Roads of Creation] (trilogy).   1952–63:
    O Artos ton Angelon [The Bread of the Angels].   1952.
    O Ilios tou Thanatou.   1959; translated as *The Sun of Death*, 1964.
    I Kefali tis Medhousas [The Medusa's Head].   1963.

Verse

Stratiotes [Soldiers].   1928.
I yimni piisi [Naked Poetry].   1939.
I pio yimni piisi [Most Naked Poetry].   1941.

Other

Domenikos Theotokopoulos.   1930.
Theotokopoulos: Ta biografika [The Biography of Theotokopoulos].   1942.
Greco in Roma [Greco in Rome].   1941.
O piitis ke to piima tis "Odhyssias" [The Poet and the Poem of the Odyssey].   1958; translated as *Nikos Kazantzakis and His "Odyssey"*, 1961.

Translator, *Medea* and *Bacchae* by Euripides, plays by Macchiavelli, Calderón, Molière, Jacinto Benavente, Paul Claudel, Henry de Montherlant, poetry by Paul Valéry and Luis Cernuda, and Cassio's study of El Greco.

* * *

As an art historian Prevelakis dealt particularly with El Greco and the art of the Renaissance; but he is best known for his literary work, above all for his novels (which belong in the class of the *Bildungsroman*, like Goethe's *Wilhelm Meister*) and his plays, which reflect his existential anxieties and his sensitivity to ethical questions and the right conduct in life.

Prevelakis wrote ten plays, some of which were staged while he was alive. The one-act *O Mimos* (The Mime), published in 1928, and the full-length *Monaxia* (Solitude), accepted by the Greek National Theatre but never produced (and published only in 1981), foreshadow themes which he elaborated in his mature dramas of the early 1950's: man's alienation from his natural and spiritual environment, the individual's acute awareness of such alienation, and the need for the one to sacrifice himself in order to redeem the many.

In his dramatic trilogy under the general title *I Arostia tou Eona* (The Sickness of the Century) Prevelakis drew inspiration from tradition and history, as well as from previous literature. *To Iero Sfayio* (The Holy Victim) dramatizes a novelette which Prevelakis had written earlier. The hero is a characteristic Renaissance man, Juliano dei Medici, who willingly accepts his death at the hands of conspirators because he yearns for "total freedom". *Ta Heria tou Zondanou Theou* (The Hands of the Living God) developed from a narrative in Dostoevsky's *Brothers Karamazov*. Though twice a murderer, the hero, an officer in the Russian army, is finally tried and purged not by others, but by his own living god, his conscience. In *Lazaros* (Lazarus), the biblical hero returns from the grave not to disclose the secrets of Hades to the curious but to preach the real meaning of life and submit to a second and final death in a preview of Christ's passion. This closing part of the trilogy is structured like an ancient tragedy, with a chorus, and written in a poetic language that is reminiscent of dramas by other Greek writers like Sikelianos and Kazantzakis.

Mousafirei sto Stepanchikovo (Guests at Stepanchikovo), Prevelakis's only comedy of manners, was finished in 1961, but was produced by the Greek National Theatre in 1973–74. The title reflects the source of inspiration—a little known novella, "The Village Stepanchikovo", by Dostoyevsky. The themes are again man's metaphysical impasse, "dead time", and the conflict of good and evil.

The four remaining plays deal with the history and social structure of Crete, but have broader human interest. *To Ifestio* (The Volcano) was performed by the Greek National Theatre in 1966, the centennial of an historic event—the 1866 self-immolation, at the monastery of Arkadi in Crete, of many Cretans fighting for freedom, besieged by a Turkish army. It is a conventional but powerful drama whose immediate source was a chapter in Prevelakis's own novel *Pandermi Kriti* (Desolate Crete). *To Heri tou Skotomenou* (The Hand of the Slain) was staged by the Greek National Theatre in 1979 and by other theatrical groups at other times. It treats the age-old custom of the blood feud, or *vendetta*, which Crete shares with Sicily. The protagonist, a female this time, faces a tragic dilemma: she has to exact revenge for the death of her husband by killing the man she loves. *I Dhefteri Endoli* (The Second Command) and *To Trelo Ema* (The Crazy Blood) portray, again, simple characters, set off in triangles, governed by dark forces, but also responsive to the moral law rooted deeply in their souls.

Prevelakis's plays are well crafted and, like most of his other works, poetic in atmosphere, but never nebulous or dreamy. Clarity and seriousness of purpose are their main features. As a service to Greek theatre Prevelakis also translated ten plays, two ancient tragedies, *Medea* and *Bacchae* by Euripides, and several European classical plays, by Machiavelli, Calderón, Molière, Claudel, Montherlant, and others.

—George Thaniel

PRIESTLEY, J(ohn) B(oynton). Born in Bradford, Yorkshire, England, 13 September 1894. Educated at Belle Vue Grammar School, Bradford, to age 16; Trinity Hall, Cambridge, 1919–21, BA in history 1921, MA. Married 1) Patricia Tempest (died 1925), two daughters; 2) Mary Wyndham Lewis in 1926 (divorced 1952), two daughters and one son; 3) the writer and archaeologist Jacquetta Hawkes in 1953. Employee, Clerk, Helm & Co., wool firm, Bradford, 1911–14; served in the Duke of Wellington's and Devon regiments, 1914–19; freelance journalist and reviewer, and reader for Bodley Head publishers, London, 1922–29; first-produced play, *The Good Companions*, staged 1931; director, Mask Theatre, London, 1938–39; radio lecturer on BBC programme "Postscripts", 1940; regular contributor, *New Statesman*, London. President, PEN, London, 1936–37; United Kingdom delegate, and chairman, Unesco International Theatre Conference, Paris, 1947, and Prague, 1948; chairman, British Theatre Conference, 1948; president, International Theatre Institute, 1949; member, National Theatre Board, London, 1966–67. Recipient: James Tait Black Memorial Prize, 1930; Ellen Terry Award, 1948. LL.D: University of St. Andrews, Fife; D.Litt: University of Birmingham; University of Bradford. Honorary freeman, City of Bradford, 1973; honorary student, Trinity Hall, Cambridge, 1978. Order of Merit, 1977. Died in Stratford-on-Avon, 14 August 1984.

Works

Collections

Three Plays and a Preface (includes *Dangerous Corner; Eden End; Cornelius*). 1935.
Two Time Plays (includes *Time and the Conways* and *I Have Been Here Before*). 1937.
Three Plays (includes *Music at Night; The Long Mirror; They Came to a City*). 1943.
Four Plays (includes *Music at Night; The Long Mirror; They Came to a City; Desert Highway*). 1944.
Three Comedies (includes *Good Night Children; The Golden Fleece; How Are They at Home?*). 1945.
Three Time Plays (includes *Dangerous Corner; Time and the Conways; I Have Been Here Before*). 1947.
Plays (3 vols.). 1948–50; Volume 1 as *Seven Plays*, 1950.

Stage Works

The Good Companions (book only), with Edward Knoblock, lyrics by Harry Graham and Frank Eyton, music by Richard Addinsell, from the novel by Priestley (produced His Majesty's Theatre, London, 1931). 1935.
Dangerous Corner (produced Lyric Theatre, London, 1932). 1932.

"Good Companionship": impressions of **J.B. Priestley** (by Fernando Autori, in *The Graphic*, 24 January 1931).

The Roundabout (produced Playhouse, Liverpool, 1932). 1933.

Laburnum Grove: An Immoral Comedy (produced Duchess Theatre, London, 1933). 1934.

Eden End (produced Duchess Theatre, London, 1934). 1934.

Cornelius: A Business Affair in Three Transactions (produced Theatre Royal, Birmingham, 1935). 1935.

Duet in Floodlight (produced Playhouse, Liverpool, 1935). 1935.

Bees on the Boat Deck: A Farcical Tragedy (produced Lyric Theatre, London, 1936). 1936.

Spring Tide, with George Billam (produced Duchess Theatre, London, 1936). 1936.

The Bad Samaritan (produced Playhouse, Liverpool, 1937).

Time and the Conways (produced Duchess Theatre, London, 1937). 1937.

I Have Been Here Before (produced Royalty Theatre, London, 1937). 1937.

People at Sea (as *I Am a Stranger Here*, produced 1937; as *People at Sea*, produced Apollo Theatre, London, 1937). 1937.

Mystery of Greenfingers: A Comedy of Detection (produced Fortune Theatre, London, 1938). 1937.

The Rebels (produced Civic Playhouse, Bradford, 1938).

When We Are Married: A Yorkshire Farcical Comedy (produced St. Martin's Theatre, London, 1938). 1938.

Music at Night (produced Festival Theatre, Malvern, Worcestershire, 1938). In *Three Plays*, 1943.

Johnson over Jordan (produced New Theatre, London, 1939). Published as *Johnson over Jordan: The Play, and All About It (An Essay)*, 1939.

The Long Mirror (produced Playhouse, Oxford, 1940). In *Three Plays*, 1943.

Good Night Children: A Comedy of Broadcasting (produced New Theatre, London, 1942). In *Three Comedies*, 1945.

Desert Highway (produced Playhouse Theatre, London, 1943). 1944.

They Came to a City (produced Globe Theatre, London, 1943). In *Three Plays*, 1943.

How Are They at Home? A Topical Comedy (produced Apollo Theatre, London, 1944). In *Three Comedies*, 1945.

The Golden Fleece (as *The Bull Market*, produced Civic Theatre, Bradford, 1944). In *Three Comedies*, 1945.

An Inspector Calls (produced Opera House, Manchester, 1945). 1947.

Jenny Villiers (produced Theatre Royal, Bristol, 1946).

Ever Since Paradise: An Entertainment, Chiefly Referring to Love and Marriage (produced Lyceum Theatre, Sheffield, 1946). 1949.

The Linden Tree (produced Lyceum Theatre, Sheffield, 1947). 1948.

Home is Tomorrow (produced Cambridge Theatre, London, 1948). 1949.

The High Toby: A Play for the Toy Theatre. 1948.

Summer Day's Dream (produced St. Martin's Theatre, London, 1949). In *Plays 3*, 1950.

The Olympians, music by Arthur Bliss (produced Royal Opera House, Covent Gorden, London, 1949). 1949.

Bright Shadow: A Play of Detection (produced Coliseum, Oldham, 1950). 1950.

Treasure on Pelican (as *Treasure on Pelican Island*, televised 1951; as *Treasure on Pelican*, produced King's Theatre, Hammersmith, London, 1952). 1953.

Dragon's Mouth: A Dramatic Quartet, with Jacquetta Hawkes (produced Winter Garden Theatre, London,

1952). 1952.

Private Rooms: A One-Act Comedy in the Viennese Style. 1953.

Mother's Day. 1953.

Try it Again (produced London, 1965). 1953.

A Glass of Bitter. 1954.

The White Countess, with Jacquetta Hawkes (produced Gaiety Theatre, Dublin, 1954).

The Scandalous Affair of Mr. Kettle and Mrs. Moon (produced Duchess Theatre, London, 1955). 1956.

Take the Fool Away (produced Burgtheater, Vienna, 1955; produced in English, Playhouse, Nottingham, 1959).

These Our Actors (produced Citizens' Theatre, Glasgow, 1956).

The Glass Cage (produced Piccadilly Theatre, London, 1957). 1958.

The Thirty-First of June (produced Crest Theatre, Toronto, Canada, 1957).

A Pavilion of Masks (produced Nordmark Landestheater, Schleswig, 1962; produced in English, Theatre Royal, Bristol, 1963). 1958.

The Rack (produced as *Die Tortur*, Staatstheater, Karlsruhe, 1959).

A Severed Head, with Iris Murdoch, from the novel by Murdoch (produced Theatre Royal, Bristol, 1963). 1964.

Screenplays

Sing as We Go, with Gordon Wellesley, 1934; *Look Up and Laugh*, with Gordon Wellesley, 1935; *We Live in Two Worlds*, 1937; *Jamaica Inn*, with Sidney Gilliat and Joan Harrison, 1939; *Britain at Bay*, 1940; *Our Russian Allies*, 1941; *The Foreman Went to France (Somewhere in France)*, with others, 1942; *Last Holiday*, 1950.

Television Plays

The Rose and Crown, 1946 (published 1947); *Whitehall Wonders*, 1949; *Treasure on Pelican Island*, 1951; *You Know What People Are*, 1953; *The Stone Faces*, 1957; *Now Let Him Go*, 1957; *Lost City* (documentary), 1958; *The Rack*, 1958; *Doomsday for Dyson*, 1958; *The Fortrose Incident*, from his play *Home is Tomorrow*, 1959; *Level Seven*, from the novel by Mordecai Roshwald, 1966; *The Lost Peace* series, 1966; *Anyone for Tennis*, 1968; *Linda at Pulteney's*, 1969.

Radio Plays

The Return of Jess Oakroyd, 1941; *The Golden Entry*, 1955; *End Game at the Dolphin*, 1956; *An Arabian Night in Park Lane*, 1965.

Fiction

Adam in Moonshine. 1927.

Benighted. 1927; as *The Old Dark House*, 1928.

Farthing Hall, with Hugh Walpole. 1929.

The Good Companions. 1929.

The Town Major of Miraucourt (story). 1930.

Angel Pavement. 1930.

Faraway. 1932.

Albert Goes Through (story). 1933.

I'll Tell You Everything, with Gerald Bullett. 1933.

Wonder Hero. 1933.

They Walk in the City: The Lovers in the Stone Forest. 1936.

The Doomsday Men. 1938.

Let the People Sing. 1939.

Black-Out in Gretley: A Story of—and for—Wartime. 1942.
Daylight on Saturday: A Novel About an Aircraft Factory. 1943.
Three Men in New Suits. 1945.
Bright Day. 1946.
Jenny Villiers: A Story of the Theatre. 1947.
Going Up: Stories and Sketches. 1950.
Festival at Farbridge. 1951; as *Festival*, 1951.
The Other Place and Other Stories of the Same Sort. 1953.
The Magicians. 1954.
Low Notes on a High Level: A Frolic. 1954.
Saturn over the Water. 1961.
The Thirty-First of June. 1961.
The Shapes of Sleep: A Topical Tale. 1962.
Sir Michael and Sir George. 1964.
Lost Empires. 1965.
Salt is Leaving. 1966.
It's an Old Country. 1967.
The Image Men: Out of Town and *London End* (2 vols.). 1968.
"The Carfitt Crisis" and Two Other Stories. 1975.
Found, Lost, Found; or, The English Way of Life. 1976.

Verse

The Chapman of Rhymes (juvenilia). 1918.

Other

Brief Diversions, Being Tales, Travesties, and Epigrams. 1922.
Papers from Lilliput. 1922.
I for One. 1923.
Figures in Modern Literature. 1924.
The English Comic Characters. 1925.
George Meredith. 1926.
Talking. 1926.
(Essays). 1926.
Open House: A Book of Essays. 1927.
Thomas Love Peacock. 1927.
The English Novel. 1927; revised edition, 1935.
Apes and Angels: A Book of Essays. 1928; as *Too Many People and Other Reflections*, 1928.
The Balconinny and Other Essays. 1929.
English Humour. 1929.
Self-Selected Essays. 1932.
Four-in-Hand (miscellany). 1934.
English Journey, Being a Rambling But Truthful Account of What One Man Saw and Heard and Felt and Thought During a Journey Through England During the Autumn of the Year 1933. 1934.
Midnight on the Desert: A Chapter of Autobiography. 1937.
Rain upon Godshill: A Further Chapter of Autobiography. 1939.
Britain Speaks (radio talks). 1940.
Postscripts (radio talks). 1940; as *All England Listened*, 1968.
Out of the People. 1941.
Britain at War. 1942.
British Women Go to War. 1943.
Manpower: The Story of Britain's Mobilisation for War. 1944.
Here Are Your Answers. 1944.
Letter to a Returning Serviceman. 1945.

The Secret Dream: An Essay on Britain, America, and Russia. 1946.
Russian Journey. 1946.
The New Citizen (address). 1946.
Theatre Outlook. 1947.
The Arts under Socialism (lecture). 1947.
Delight. 1949.
The Priestley Companion: A Selection from the Writings. 1951.
Journey down a Rainbow (travel), with Jacquetta Hawkes. 1955.
All about Ourselves and Other Essays, edited by Eric Gillett. 1956.
The Writer in a Changing Society (lecture). 1956.
Thoughts in the Wilderness (essays). 1957.
The Art of the Dramatist: A Lecture Together with Appendices and Discursive Notes. 1957.
Topside; or, The Future of England: A Dialogue. 1958.
The Story of Theatre (for children). 1959; as *The Wonderful World of the Theatre*, 1959.
Literature and Western Man. 1960.
William Hazlitt. 1960.
Charles Dickens: A Pictorial Biography. 1961; as *Charles Dickens and His World*, 1969.
Margin Released: A Writer's Reminiscences and Reflections. 1962.
Man and Time. 1964.
The Moments and Other Pieces. 1966.
The World of Priestley, edited by Donald G. MacRae. 1967.
Essays of Five Decades, edited by Susan Cooper. 1968.
Trumpets over the Sea, Being a Rambling and Egotistical Account of the London Symphony Orchestra's Engagement at Daytona Beach, Florida, in July–August 1967. 1968.
The Prince of Pleasure and His Regency 1811–1820. 1969.
The Edwardians. 1970.
Anton Chekhov. 1970.
Snoggle (for children). 1971.
Victoria's Heyday. 1972.
Over the Long High Wall: Some Reflections and Speculations on Life, Death, and Time. 1972.
The English. 1973.
Outcries and Asides. 1974.
A Visit to New Zealand. 1974.
Particular Pleasures, Being a Personal Record of Some Varied Arts and Many Different Artists. 1975.
The Happy Dream: An Essay. 1976.
English Humour (not the same as 1929 book). 1976.
Instead of the Trees: A Final Chapter of Autobiography. 1977.
Seeing Stratford. 1982.
Musical Delights. 1984.

Editor, *Essayists Past and Present: A Selection of English Essays.* 1925.
Editor, *Fools and Philosophers: A Gallery of Comic Figures from English Literature.* 1925.
Editor, *Tom Moore's Diary: A Selection.* 1925.
Editor, *The Book of Bodley Head Verse.* 1926.
Editor, *Our Nation's Heritage.* 1939.
Editor, *Scenes from London Life, from Sketches by Boz*, by Dickens. 1947.
Editor, *The Best of Leacock.* 1957; as *The Bodley Head Leacock*, 1957.
Editor, with Josephine Spear, *Adventures in English Literature.* 1963.

*

Bibliographies

Alan E. Day, *J.B. Priestley: An Annotated Bibliography*, New York, 1980.

Criticism

Books:
Susan Cooper, *J.B. Priestley: Portrait of an Author*, London, 1970.
John Atkins, *J.B. Priestley*, New York, 1978.
A.A. DeVitis and Albert E. Kalson, *J.B. Priestley*, Boston, 1980.
John Atkins, *J.B. Priestley: The Last of the Sages*, London, 1981.

* * *

Priestley was a writer of remarkably wide talents, being dramatist, novelist, travel writer, literary critic, essayist, political commentator, and journalist. It was the dramatisation of his own highly successful novel *The Good Companions*, in 1931, that first took him into the theatre, and he soon became a proficient playwright, able to supply the British theatre throughout the 1930's and 1940's with nearly a play a year.

His work in drama is as various as his general writing, and included domestic comedy, social problem plays, psychological and philosophical drama, melodrama, and plays of detection. Perhaps inevitably, with so varied an output, his writing is very uneven, and many of the weaknesses of his first independent pieces, like *The Roundabout* and *Cornelius*, including crude characterisation and run-of-the-mill plotting, recur even in late work, But he had an instinctive theatrical sense and a good feel for stage dialogue. He was unwilling, too, to settle just for commercial success, as he might easily have done following the popularity of his plays of the early 1930's, like *Dangerous Corner* and *Eden End*: having won a reputation, he proceeded to attempt more demanding subject matter and to explore more experimental dramatic forms.

His early successes show something of his versatility: the first, *Dangerous Corner*, was a psychological melodrama; this he followed with something wholly different, a popular comedy of lower-middle-class, suburban, domestic life, *Laburnum Grove*, which nonetheless managed to achieve a wide social appeal, and is still revived today; third, and likewise still holding the stage, was *Eden End*, an effective attempt to dramatise the kind of material Priestley had handled in his late-1920's novel, *The Good Companions*, in that it is set in the drab world of theatre before World War I and admirably recreates the sleazy atmosphere of the provincial stage, its practitioners and "stage-struck" aspirants, and their families.

But Priestley was content neither to settle just for commercial success, nor to be a mere observer and chronicler; he had serious artistic aspirations, and saw himself, too, as a social and political commentator of moderately radical inclination. Unlike many of his contemporaries he took the business of writing for the theatre seriously, and even in light-entertainment pieces, like *Bees on the Boatdeck*, a mixture of fantasy, comedy, and topical comment, he introduced an element of reflection on, and mild criticism of, the prevailing social order.

More manifestly reaching for a serious dimension were the "time and space" plays, like *Time and the Conways*, *I Have Been Here Before*, and *I'm a Stranger Here*. In these, Priestley was much influenced, indeed rather too obviously so, by the contemporary populatisers of scientific ideas, like Dunne and Ouspensky. The plays, actually have little philosophical depth, and perhaps too much has been made of them as plays of "ideas"; rather, the idea functions simply as a *donné* on which the dramatist builds the real substance of his play, the fortunes of individuals living out their lives in a particular time and place, with specific interests and aspirations, and subject to recognisable human and social pressures. If Priestley is now considered to be one of the very few British dramatists of significance to write between the wars, this is less, one suspects, for the intellectual substance of his best work, than for his ability to craft plays which, when realised by actors, retain their felt humanity and persuade as truthful, credible reflections of life. This in part accounts for the fact that although the "philosophical" and "experimental" plays are the ones critics feel they ought, perhaps, to admire most, those they prefer are mainly those endorsed by audiences and still found on the contemporary stage—not "ideas" pieces like the quasi-expressionistic *Johnson over Jordan* or the socially polemical *They Came to a City*, but the plays rooted in recognisable worlds, treating recognisable characters and situations, like *Laburnum Grove*, *The Linden Tree*, and *When We are Married* (hence, too, the fact that the most enduring of Priestley's "time" plays on the stage is *An Inspector Calls*).

Priestley was not a major dramatist, but he became a very fine craftsman (as Iris Murdoch found when she collaborated with him on the stage adaptation of her novel *The Severed Head*), able to engage the interest of mainstream London theatre audiences in plays of human and social concern—no mean feat in an inter-war-years' theatre that had seemingly relegated anything looking remotely like serious drama to the "little theatre" fringe. Artistically he was not radically innovative, nor indeed was he conspicuously radical in his social and political concerns. His stance was that of the socially aware, liberal-humanist reformer. His strategy in the theatre was to vary his more serious drama with solid, often run-of-the-mill, pieces carpentered for commercial stage managements, although, as said, some of these last, like *When We Are Married*, a Yorkshire domestic farce, must be ranked among his most stage-worthy pieces. He was a writer in whom the boundary between the creative artist and the workaday journalist was thin, and it is easy to complain that his output is more conspicuous for quantity than quality; but he was a fine story-teller, could fashion a character, had a keen theatrical sense, and was not afraid to spice a play with argument and polemic.

Today his work is perhaps more frequently seen on the television screen than in the theatre; television has exploited his skill at crafting character and plot line, his ability to create a sense of period and, more particularly, his intimate knowledge of the early 20th-century theatre and its social ambience, most recently in the 1980's television dramatisations of his novels *Lost Empires* and *The Good Companions*.

25 years after he ceased to write for the theatre, and 40 years or more after his theatrical heyday, at least four or five of his plays remain securely in the performed repertory. That cannot be said of many dramatists in the English theatre—or any other for that matter.

—Kenneth Richards

See also *Volume 1* entry on *An Inspector Calls*.

PRZYBYSZEWSKA, Stanisława. Born in Cracow, Poland, 1 October 1901, daughter of the impressionist painter Aniela Pajak and the writer Stanisław Przybyszewski. Lived with mother and mother's relatives in France, Austria, Switzerland, 1907–16, then returned to Poland. Name officially changed to Przybyszewska, 1914. Educated at the Teachers' College, Cracow, 1916–20; University of Poznan, c.1920–21. Married Jan Panienski in 1923 (died 1925). Post office clerk, Poznan, 1920; moved to Warsaw, 1922; salesgirl, communist bookshop: arrested for supposed radical activity and imprisoned for one week; moved to the free city of Danzig (now Gdansk) with her husband, 1923; lived in isolation and poverty after death of husband, 1925, giving occasional language lessons; only play produced in her lifetime, *Sprawa Dantona* [*The Danton Case*], staged 1931. Also wrote under the pseudonym Andrée Lynne. Died of malnutrition and ill health after longstanding morphine addiction, 14 or 15 August 1935.

Works

Collections

Dramaty [Dramas] (2 vols.).   1975.
The Danton Case; Thermidor, translated by Boleslaw Taborski.   1989.

Stage Works

Sprawa Dantona (produced Teatr Wielki, Lwow, 1931). Published in part, 1929; in full, in *Dramaty*, 1975; translated as *The Danton Case*, with *Thermidor*, 1989.
Dziewiecdziesiaty trzeci [Ninety-Three] (produced Wrocław TV Theatre, 1969). In *Dramaty*, 1975.
Thermidor (produced Teatr Polski, Wrocław, 1971). In *Dramaty*, 1975; translated as *Thermidor*, with *The Danton Case*, 1989.

Fiction

Ostatni noce Ventôse'a [The Last Night of Ventose].   1958(?).

Memoirs and Letters

Listy [Letters] (3 vols.).   1978–85.

*

Criticism

Books:
Jadwiga Kosicka and Daniel Gerould, *A Life of Solitude: Stanisława Przybyszewska*, London, 1986.
Daniel Gerould, "Stanisława Przybyszewska and the Mechanism of Revolution," in *The Danton Case; Thermidor*, 1989.

* * *

Although Stanisława Przybyszewska wrote three plays in all, she has earned her place in the history of Polish and European theatre for *The Danton Case*, a "historical chronicle" in five acts and 20 scenes. A penetrating, tough-minded study of the mechanism of revolution, *The Danton Case* is a

major contribution to dramatic literature about the French Revolution. Conceived as a response to Büchner's *Danton's Death*, Przybyszewska's play rehabilitates Robespierre and redresses the balance between the two heroes. Whereas Büchner's drama is a static and loosely constructed meditation on death from the viewpoint of a world-weary, nihilistic Danton, *The Danton Case* presents a tense, concentrated duel between equally matched political adversaries who are brought to life in rich physical and psychological detail. The extensive stage directions in *The Danton Case* establish an almost cinematographic gestural language, focusing attention on facial expression and subtle play of features and hands. Details define the essence of character, as in Robespierre's constant fixing of his cuffs and brushing of crumbs from his clothes. The playwright, imaginatively, identified so strongly with the people of 1789 that she began to date her letters according to the revolutionary calendar and to regard Robespierre and Danton as her contemporaries.

Przybyszewska's anatomy of the workings of political power is cast in a traditional dramatic mold, but informed by a modern sensibility that explores the bitter paradox of a noble struggle for freedom quickly transformed into self-destructive tyranny. The action of the play is limited to the last eight days of Danton's life, concerning his arrest, trial for corruption, condemnation, and execution. Within these highly theatrical confines that focus on intense confrontations in the tribunal, courtroom, and prison, the author presents a broad and dynamic canvas of the Revolution at the most critical moment in its history, showing the mob's fluctuations. The heart of the drama is the battle for power at the top, seen in the opposition between the corrupt, unscrupulous, but humanly vital Danton, and Robespierre, the icy, highly principled genius of the Revolution, who knows that by institutionalizing the Terror so that the government may survive, he is bringing about his own downfall and sowing the seeds of dictatorship that will be reaped by Bonaparte. For Przybyszewska, as for her master Bernard Shaw, history is made by great men.

Although documentary in spirit and based on extensive research into sources, particularly new revisionist interpretations of the French Revolution that rehabilitated Robespierre (such as Albert Mathiez's Marxist approach), the play is anything but a costume drama or attempted historical reconstruction; rather, it offers a contemporary reading of the past, based on the parallel that the author perceived between the events in France at the end of the 18th century and those taking place in Russia in the 20th century (Stalin's elimination of rivals). The drama's verbal anachronisms and Soviet-style acronyms emphasize the continuity between 1789 and 1917. *The Danton Case* is a study of the mechanisms of power and the inevitable drift of revolution towards totalitarianism by a writer sympathetic to the cause of radical social change, but without any illusions as to the outcome. Przybyszewska's goal was to treat "revolution on a universal plan" with maximum fidelity to the historical record. Striving for clarity, precision, and detachment, the playwright pursued a creative path akin to the *Neue Sachlichkeit* of the later 1920's in Germany, the "new matter-of-factness" that reacted against the subjective excesses of expressionism in favor of documentation and reporting.

The text of *The Danton Case* underwent three complete revisions. Przybyszewska worked painstakingly on the musical structure of the play and paid close attention to the rhythm of contrasted scenes, alternating stormy public gatherings with introspective private tableaux. She was well aware that to be successful, a historical drama of such dimensions would require a large company of extraordinary actors and a superb director like the leftist Leon Schiller, who, because of the oppressive political climate, could not undertake such a risky project. *The Danton Case* was staged twice in the author's lifetime—in 1931 and 1933—but these productions of truncated versions did not serve the play well.

In 1967 Jerzy Krasowski revived *The Danton Case* successfully in Wrocław. But the play found its most original interpreter in Andrzej Wajda, who admired the psychologically complex characters, the moral and intellectual truth, and the scope and richness of interpretive possibilities, as well as the forceful evocation of the "pressure of history", to which Poles have always been remarkably sensitive. His austere, unadorned staging of *The Danton Case* in Warsaw in 1975 made the audience into a dramatic character; Robespierre and Saint-Just spoke directly from the podium to the spectators who became both the jury at the Revolutionary Tribunal and the deputies at the Convention. In 1980 Wajda directed a joint French-Polish film version, *Danton*, in which the play's text was freely rewritten in favor of Danton (Gerard Dépardieu), the man of natural appetites and political concession, and at the expense of Robespierre (Wojciech Pszoniak), the ideological maximalist.

Przybyszewska's two other plays are of far less importance. The earlier *Thermidor* (written in German, and surviving only in an incomplete form) takes place two days before the end of the Terror at a meeting of the Committee of Public Safety, where a desperate endgame is played out between Robespierre and his former allies. *Ninety-Three* is a one-act drama of passion and revenge, set on the day of Marat's funeral, but with an entirely non-historical cast of characters. In her letters, the author describes her creative struggles and ceaseless battle for material survival; she also gives detailed analyses of her plays and discusses her attitudes towards the French Revolution and its heroes.

Przybyszewska's special accomplishment is to have rendered human and credible, if not necessarily likable, the usually reviled scapegoat of the Terror. In her plays, Robespierre is the pure, ascetic, intellectual absolutist, pitted against the sensual and cynical pragmatic compromiser, Danton. The argument between these two archetypal political beings has never been resolved. So subtle and even-handed is the author of *The Danton Case* in maintaining the balance of sympathies that audiences must make up their own minds.

—Daniel Gerould

PUSHKIN, Alexander (Sergeyevich). Born in Moscow, 26 May 1799 (Old Style). Educated at home and at Imperial lycée in Tsarskoye Selo, near St. Petersburg, 1812–17, where he joined the Arzamas and Green Lamp literary groups. Married Natalya Goncharova in 1831. Civil servant, St. Petersburg, 1817–20; exiled to southern Russia, 1820–26; returned to St. Petersburg, 1826; fought with Russian army against the Turks, in Transcaucasia, 1829; wrote his "little tragedies" in 1830; editor, *Sovremennik* [The Contemporary], 1836–37. Died of wounds received in a duel, St. Petersburg, 29 January 1837 (Old Style).

Works

Collections

Works, edited by Avrahm Yarmolinsky. 1939.
Polnoe sobranie sochineny [Complete Collected Works] (10 vols.), edited by B.V. Tomachevskim. 1977–79.
Selected Works, translated by Irina Zheleznova and others. 1974.
Mozart and Salieri: The Little Tragedies (includes *Mozart and Salieri; The Miserly Knight; The Stone Guest; The Feast During the Plague*), translated by Antony Wood. 1983; revised edition, 1987.

Stage Works

Boris Godunov (produced Maryinsky Theatre, St. Petersburg, 1870). 1831; translated as *Boris Godunov*, in *Translations from Pushkin*, 1899: single edition, 1918, and several subsequent translations under same title.
Mozart i Salieri (produced Bolshoi Theatre, St. Petersburg, 1832). 1831; translated as *Mozart and Salieri*, in *Translations from Pushkin*, 1899: several subsequent translations under same title.
Pir vo vremya chumy (produced Alexandrinsky Theatre, St. Petersburg, 1899). 1832; translated as *The Feast During the Plague*, in *The Little Tragedies*, 1946, and in *Mozart and Salieri: The Little Tragedies*, 1983.
Skupoy rytsar (produced Alexandrinsky Theatre, St. Petersburg, 1832). 1836; translated as *The Covetous Knight*, in *Works*, 1939; as *The Miserly Knight*, in *Mozart and Salieri: The Little Tragedies*, 1983.
Stseny iz rytsarskikh vryemen [Scenes from the Age of Chivalry] (produced Bolshoi Dramatic Theatre, Leningrad, 1937). In *Sovremennik*, 1837.
Rusalka [Rusalka] (unfinished; produced Alexandrinsky Theatre, St. Petersburg, 1838). 1837.
Kamenny gost (produced Alexandrinsky Theatre, St. Petersburg, 1847). 1839; translated as *The Statue Guest*, in *Translations from Pushkin*, 1899; as *The Stone Guest*, in *Works*, 1939, and in *Mozart and Salieri: The Little Tragedies*, 1983.

Fiction

Povesti pokoynovo I.P. Belkina. 1830; translated as *Tales of P. Bielkin*, 1947; as *The Tales of Belkin, and The History of Goryukhino*, 1983.
Pikovaya dama. 1834; translated as *The Queen of Spades*, with *The Captain's Daughter*, 1858.
Kapitanskaya dochka. 1836; translated as *The Captain's Daughter*, 1846; as *Marie: A Story of Russian Love*, 1877.
Dubrovsky (fragment). 1841.
Prose Tales, translated by T. Keane. 1894.
Russian Romances. 1875.
Complete Prose Tales, translated by Gillon R. Aitken. 1966.
Russian Tales, translated by Peter Tempest, Avril Pyman, Louis Zellikov. 1990.

Verse

Stikhotvoreniya. 1826; revised edition (4 vols.), 1829–35, and later editions.
Evgeny Onegin. 1833; translated as *Eugene Onegin*, 1881: several subsequent translations under same title.
Selections from the Poems, edited by Ivan Panin. 1888; translated as *Poems*, 1888.

Pushkin Threefold: Narrative, Lyric, Polemic, and Ribald Verse, translated by W. Arndt.   1972.
The Bronze Horseman: Selected Poems, translated by D.M. Thomas.   1982.
Narrative Poems by Pushkin and Lermontov, translated by Charles Johnston.   1983.
Collected Poetry, translated by Walter Arndt.   1983.

Memoirs and Letters

Letters (3 vols.), translated by J. Thomas Shaw.   1963.
Letters.   1964.

Other

Puteshestviye v Arzrum [The Journey to Arzrum].   1836.
Critical Prose, edited by Carl R. Proffer.   1969.
Pushkin in Literature, edited by Tatiana Wolff.   1971.

*

Criticism

Books:
David Magarshack, *Alexander Pushkin: A Biography*, 1967.
Henri Troyat, *Alexander Pushkin*, 1974.
Antony D.P. Briggs, *Alexander Pushkin*, London, Canberra, and Totowa (New Jersey), 1983.

* * *

The founder of the modern Russian literary language, widely acknowledged as Russia's foremost poet and the creator of masterpieces in many different literary genres, Alexander Pushkin is an important figure in the development of the Russian theatre.

Captivated by the theatre from childhood onwards, Pushkin became "a fierce legislator of the theatre, an inconstant worshipper of charming actresses and an honorary citizen of behind the scenes" (words used to describe Eugene Onegin). More significantly, in his maturity he wrote widely about the theatre, and for it. His theoretical writings are based on close familiarity with both Classical and European drama, of which his knowledge was encyclopaedic. Disgusted with the current state of Russian playwriting, which he saw as outdated and imitative, he proposed a quite new approach. His method was to draw attention to the great gulf which he saw as separating his revered Shakespeare from the giants of the 17th-century French theatre. Shakespeare he described as a "genuine romantic", much superior to Molière, Corneille, and Racine. In a notable juxtaposition, Pushkin compared Harpagon with Shylock and concluded that, "Molière's miser is miserly—and that's it; Shakespeare's Shylock is miserly, resourceful, vindictive, a fond father, witty". Pushkin asserted the need for a realism grounded not on exactitude of historical detail but on psychological truth. This led him also to attack the unities as a basis for good theatre. Unity of action he found essential for effective drama, but the unities of place and time he dismissed as capricious, constraining, and ludicrously at variance with common sense. The French classical theatre, for all its great virtues, was ultimately aristocratic and artificial. As for the Russians, he proclaimed that they were perpetuating these disadvantages without the redeeming virtues.

Pushkin made a great effort to put these principles into practice when he wrote his historical tragedy, *Boris Godunov*, in 1825. Selecting a theme not unknown to Shakespeare, that of usurpation during a dynastic upheaval, Pushkin dealt with the period of Russian history known as the "Time of Troubles" (roughly 1595–1605). The Regent of Russia, Boris Godunov, is threatened by Dmitri, a false pretender to the throne. The victory goes to Dmitri, but by then Boris has, in any case, died from a stroke. Pushkin wrote in blank verse, producing a wide range of well-authenticated characters, interpolating scenes in prose, and in other identifiable respects following his English master. In two matters of form he asserted his independence: his iambic pentameter is of the French type (with a caesura after the second foot) and his 23 scenes are deliberately not divided into acts, even though the play does appear to have a five-act underlying structure.

The poetry of this play is one of the great glories of Russian literature, but the work has generally been considered unstageable in view of the large number of scene changes and "once-on" characters. Political controversy also prevented performance for several decades; thus, the intended impact on the Russian theatre did not materialise.

Pushkin's second serious attempt to establish himself as a playwright, in 1830, produced a series of dramatic sketches after the manner of Barry Cornwall, the "Little Tragedies". There are four of them: *The Covetous Knight*, *Mozart and Salieri*, *The Stone Guest* (Pushkin's version of the Don Juan story), and *The Feast During the Plague* (the last-named being more of a translation and adaptation of a scene from John Wilson). Many critics take these miniatures to be among Pushkin's finest masterpieces. It is true that they contain superb poetry and a fascinating depiction of monomaniacal passion, but as pieces for the theatre they are unsuccessful. Ironically, they are brought down by the very faults of oversimplified characterisation and unreal, even melodramatic, action which Pushkin, himself, had elsewhere castigated.

—Anthony D.P. Briggs

See also *Volume 1* entry on *Boris Godunov*.

Q

QUINAULT, Philippe. Born in Paris, 3 June 1635. Married a widow in 1660. Valet to Tristan L'Hermite, from whom he received some education; playwright for the companies at the Hôtel de Bourgogne and the Théâtre du Marais, Paris, 1653–71; from 1671 wrote only libretti, notably his 11 *tragédies lyriques* with composer Jean-Baptiste Lully, 1673–77 and 1680–86, which were produced by the recently formed Académie Royale du Musique, at its Théâtre de l'Opéra, Paris (the Palais-Royal), and at Saint-Germain-en-Laye and Versailles; granted a royal pension; held posts as "avocat au parlement" and "valet du Roi". Elected to the Académie Française, 1670, and to the Académie des Inscriptions, Médailles et Belles-Lettres (Petite Académie), 1674. Died in Paris, 26 November 1688.

Works

Collections

Théâtre. 1715.
Théâtre choisi. 1882.

Stage Works

Les Rivales (produced Théâtre de l'Hôtel de Bourgogne, Paris, 1653). 1661.
La Généreuse Ingratitude (produced Théâtre de l'Hôtel de Bourgogne, Paris, 1654). 1656.
L'Amant indiscret; ou, Le Maître étourdi (produced Théâtre de l'Hôtel de Bourgogne, Paris, c.1654). 1656.
Les Coups de l'amour et de la fortune (produced Théâtre de l'Hôtel de Bourgogne, Paris, 1655). 1655.
La Comédie sans comédie (produced Théâtre du Marais, Paris, 1655). 1657.
Le Fantôme amoureux (produced Théâtre de l'Hôtel de Bourgogne, Paris, 1656). 1658.
Amalasonte (produced Théâtre de l'Hôtel de Bourgogne, Paris, 1657). 1660.
Le Feint Alcibiade (produced Théâtre de l'Hôtel de Bourgogne, Paris, 1658). 1658.
Le Mariage de Cambyse (produced Théâtre de l'Hôtel de Bourgogne, Paris, 1658). 1659.
La Mort de Cyrus (produced Théâtre de l'Hôtel de Bourgogne, Paris, c. 1659). 1659.
Stratonice (produced Théâtre de l'Hôtel de Bourgogne, Paris, 1660). 1660.
Agrippa; ou, Le Faux Tibérinus (produced Théâtre de l'Hôtel de Bourgogne, Paris, 1662). 1660; translated as *Agrippa, King of Alba; or, The False Tiberinus*, 1675.
Astrate, Roi de Tyr (produced Théâtre de l'Hôtel de Bourgogne, Paris, c.1664). 1665.

La Mère coquette (produced Théâtre de l'Hôtel de Bourgogne, Paris, 1665). 1666.
Pausanias (produced Théâtre de l'Hôtel de Bourgogne, Paris, 1668). 1669.
La Grotte de Versailles: Églogue en musique, music by Lully (produced Versailles, 1668). As *L'Églogue de Versailles*, in *Recueil général des opéra 3*, 1703; as *La Grotte de Versailles*, 1768.
Bellérophon (produced Théâtre de l'Hôtel de Bourgogne, Paris, 1670). 1671.
Psyché, with Pierre Corneille and Molière (comédie-ballet; produced Tuileries, Paris, 1671). 1671.
Les Fêtes de l'amour et de Bacchus, from plays by Molière, music by Lully (produced Théâtre de l'Opéra, Paris, 1672). 1672.
Cadmus et Hermione, music by Lully (produced Théâtre de l'Opéra, Paris, 1673). 1673.
Alceste; ou, Le Triomphe d'Alcide, music by Lully (produced Théâtre de l'Opéra, Paris, 1674). 1674.
Thésée, music by Lully (produced Saint-Germain-en-Laye, 1675). 1675.
Atys, music by Lully (produced Saint-Germain-en-Laye, 1676). 1676.
Isis, music by Lully (produced Saint-Germain-en-Laye, 1677). 1677.
Proserpine, music by Lully (produced Saint-Germain-en-Laye, 1680). 1680.
Le Triomphe d'amour, music by Lully (ballet scenario; produced Saint-Germain-en-Laye, 1681). 1681.
Persée, music by Lully (produced Théâtre de l'Opéra, Paris, 1682). 1682.
Phaéton, music by Lully (produced Versailles, 1683). 1683.
Amadis, music by Lully (produced Théâtre de l'Opéra, Paris, 1684). 1684.
Roland, music by Lully (produced Versailles, 1685). 1685.
Le Temple de la Paix, music by Lully (comédie-ballet scenario; produced Fontainebleu, 1686). 1685.
Armide, music by Lully (produced Théâtre de l'Opéra, Paris, 1686). 1686; translated as *Armida* with new music by Gluck, 1906.

Verse

Au Roy. 1672.
Deux Poèmes à la louange du Roy. 1674.
Sceaux. 1813.

* * *

Philippe Quinault was a reasonably successful playwright who began his career in 1653 with a comedy, *Les Rivales*, a revised version of Rotrou's *Les Deux Pucelles* (The Two

Philippe Quinault (bust by Jean Jacques Caffieri; Bibliothèque Sainte-Geneviève, Paris).

Virgins). Between 1653 and 1671, Quinault wrote 17 plays for the Hôtel de Bourgogne and the Théâtre du Marais. After 1671, he was exclusively occupied as a librettist, and his *tragédies lyriques*, written with composer Jean-Baptiste Lully, make up the founding repertory of the French Académie du Musique. Never very popular with critics, Quinault's success was as much a result of his political skills as of his talents. Born the son of a baker, he moved steadily up the social and economic ladder, marrying into money, frequenting salons, and buying a post in the *chambre des comptes*. Quinault became a member of both the Académie Française and the Académie des Inscriptions, Médailles, et Belles-Lettres, or Petite Académie. He was included on the royal pension list for an annual 2,000 livres.

Quinault wrote the usual heterogeneous mix of plays for the commercial theatres of the third quarter of the 17th century. Beginning with comedies, he moved on to tragicomedies and historical romances, finally to tragedies. His best-known play, first produced at the Marais c.1655, is *La Comédie sans comédie* (The Play Without Comedy), a metatheatrical pastiche. The frame employs the members of the troupe as themselves, eager to demonstrate the value of their profession to the father of two young women beloved by the actors La Roque and Hauteroche. Acts II through V demonstrate the various genres of the theatrical repertory: pastoral, farce, tragedy, and tragicomedy. The play lacks the baroque metaphysics of such forerunners as Pierre Corneille's *L'Illusion comique* (*The Theatrical Illusion*) and Rotrou's *Le Véritable Saint Genest*; it is a more straightforward defense of the profession of acting and justification of the theatre as a place of moral edification.

In 1671 Quinault was part of the team, with Molière and Pierre Corneille, responsible for the text of *Psyché*, a machine play first performed at the Tuileries in one of the most expensive productions of the period. His Majesty Louis XIV spent nearly 254,000 livres on his evening's pleasure. Quinault wrote the verses which were sung to music composed by Lully. Presumably, this was the first occasion for the alliance which was to be the foundation of French opera.

When Lully was awarded the patent for the Académie de Musique and invited Quinault to be his collaborator, the two men set out to devise a new genre, the *tragédie lyrique*, different both musically and textually from Italian opera. It is a dramatic as well as a musical genre, with plays constructed according to thematic and structural formulae. Each play presents the entwined themes of love and glory. The central character, a prince, god, or legendary hero, performs great deeds from the noblest of motives. If he falls victim to passion, he proves himself unworthy and falls from grace. If he maintains the ideals of chivalry, he is rewarded with perfect love. Structurally, the *tragédie lyrique* follows some of the neoclassical rules. *Liaison des scenes*, for instance, is observed, musically with the continuo as well as dramatically, as are the rules governing the proprieties. The unities, on the other hand, are not honored, and the marvelous is given full play in the elaborate spectacle which was as important to the success of the new entertainment as text and music.

At the heart of the idea of *tragédie lyrique* was the royal policy of using art to serve the glorification and idealization of the monarchy. The Académie des Inscriptions, or Petite Académie, was the institution charged with approving symbolic representations of the King and the State. Thus, it seems logical that the Petite Académie was given the power to oversee the texts of the *tragédies lyriques*. In 1673 the Petite Académie consisted of Chapelain, Tallement *le jeune*, Charpentier, and Perrault. In 1674 Quinault himself replaced Chapelain; other members during the years in question were La Chapelle, Racine, and Boileau.

The process of creating the annual *tragédie lyrique* began when Quinault submitted a list of several subjects to the King. Once the subject was chosen, the Petite Académie helped to decide on the structure of acts and scenes and the placement of the *divertissements*. As the libretto took form, it was seen, periodically, both by the King and by the academicians. Later, Lully himself became part of the process of revision. Given these circumstances, the libretti cannot be taken as the sole products of Quinault's imagination. Quinault's distinction was his ability to collaborate, not only with the composer, but with a whole range of special interests. It is hardly surprising that "charming" is one of the words most frequently used to describe his work.

Discounting their first collaboration, a pastiche selected from earlier works by Lully and Molière, Quinault and Lully were responsible for 11 *tragédies lyriques* between 1673 and 1686. The first eight were based on classical sources, most usually Ovid, and include *Atys*, *Isis*, *Perseus*, and *Phaéton*, selected at least in part for their opportunities for spectacle. The final three, *Amadis*, *Roland*, and *Armide*, were taken from European romances. Most have a detached prologue proclaiming the glory of Louis XIV.

Quinault's critical reputation, never substantial, suffered from the decline of interest in Lully. In recent years, however, a growing fondness for baroque music has led devotees to the works of the long ignored Florentine composer. A splendid production of *Atys* by Les Arts Florissants, in cooperation with the Paris Opéra, had its premiere in 1987, and was seen in New York in 1989. Magnificently dressed and mounted, and beautifully sung, *Atys* was missing only the multiple settings and mechanical effects of the original embellishments not affordable in a world without the patronage of a Sun King. One New York critic, who found the production an "important step toward making music of the past a meaningful music of the present", characterized the libretto, however, as "snotty, sexist, reactionary, and patronizing", and condemned the original production style as designed to please the "baroque love of loony stage machinery, fancy painted sets, and garish costumes" (Mark Swed in *7 Days*).

Quinault and Lully and their third collaborator, the designer Carlo Vigarani, would have found it hard to understand this critical distinction between music, text, and spectacle. *Tragédie lyrique* was devised as an integrated genre—story and words, music and spectacle, all combining to delight the senses and divert the mind. Quinault's contribution to the development of this new genre was significant and should not be overlooked.

—Virginia Scott

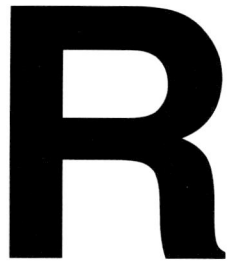

RABE, David (William). Born in Dubuque, Iowa, USA, 10 March 1940. Educated at Loras College, Dubuque, BA in English 1962; Villanova University, Pennsylvania, 1963–64, 1967–68, MA 1968. Served in the United States Army, 1965–67. Married 1) Elizabeth Pan in 1969, one son; 2) the actress Jill Clayburgh in 1979. Feature writer, New Haven *Register*, Connecticut, 1969–70. Assistant professor, 1970–72, and from 1972 consultant, Villanova University. Recipient: Associated Press Award, for journalism, 1970; Obie Award, 1971; Tony Award, 1972; Outer Circle Award, 1972; New York Drama Critics Circle Award, 1976; Dramatists Guild Hull-Warriner Award, 1972; American Academy Award, 1974.

Works

Stage Works

Sticks and Bones (produced Villanova University, Villanova, Pennsylvania, 1969). With *The Basic Training of Pavlo Hummel*, 1973.
The Basic Training of Pavlo Hummel (produced Estelle R. Newman Theatre, New York, 1971). With *Sticks and Bones*, 1973.
The Orphan (produced Florence Sutro Anspacher Theatre, New York, 1973). 1975.
In the Boom Boom Room (as *Boom Boom Room*, produced Lincoln Center, New York, 1973; revised version, as *In the Boom Boom Room*, produced Florence Sutro Anspacher Theatre, New York, 1974). 1975; revised version (produced New York, 1986), 1986.
Burning (produced Martinson Hall, New York, 1974).
Streamers (produced Long Wharf Theatre, New Haven, Connecticut, 1976). 1977.
Goose and Tomtom (produced Shakespeare Festival Public Theatre, New York, 1982). 1986.
Hurlyburly (produced Goodman Theatre, Chicago, 1984). 1985; revised version (produced Los Angeles, 1988), 1990.
Those the River Keeps (produced McCarter Theatre, Princeton, New Jersey, 1991). 1991.

Screenplays

I'm Dancing as Fast as I Can, 1982; *Streamers*, 1983; *Casualties of War*, 1989.

*

Bibliographies

Philip C. Kolin, *David Rabe: A Stage History and a Primary and Secondary Bibliography*, New York, 1988.

Criticism

Books:
N. Bradley Christie, "David Rabe's Theater of War and Remembering", in *Search and Clear: Critical Responses to Selected Literature and Films of the Vietnam War*, edited by William J. Searle, Bowling Green, Ohio, 1988.
Philip D. Beidler, *Re-Writing America: Vietnam Authors in Their Generation*, Athens, Georgia, 1991.

*   *   *

David Rabe's deeper concerns as a playwright have been obscured by his early categorization as the first playwright to deal powerfully, and from first-hand experience, with the impact of the Vietnam War on Americans. The success of *The Basic Training of Pavlo Hummel* and *Sticks and Bones* created critical expectations which were difficult to transcend. In the mid 1970's, a move to wider subject matter in *The Orphan* and *In the Boom Boom Room* created a less positive response. He returned to Vietnam-related subject matter in *Streamers*. However, with the two plays of the 1980's set outside Vietnam, *Hurlyburly* and *Goose and Tom Tom*, certain underlying themes common to all the plays, whatever their milieux, have been apparent.

A recurring concern is the way that a family or its surrogate, often a social institution, fails to provide an infrastructure to nurture, rather than limit, the individual: in *Sticks and Bones*, the estranged middle-class family of the returning veteran; in *Pavlo Hummel* and *Streamers*, the army; in *Hurlyburly*, a substitute "family" of divorced male roommates hustling to get ahead in the film industry; in *Goose and Tomtom*, a cadre of nervously ruthless jewel thieves. In every case, the search for identity and fulfilment is fruitless, and religion or metaphysical belief-systems afford no consolation. And in the late Rabe plays, the sense of a hostile fate overcoming his characters becomes increasingly strong.

Of the two early Vietnam plays which made Rabe's reputation, it now seems that *The Basic Training of Pavlo Hummel* is the major work and the one that has worn its years best. It is not an "anti-war" play, as Rabe himself has stressed; and it chronicles movingly the fate of an eager individual who becomes more and more lost as he comes to let himself be more and more shaped and co-opted by the army. The surreal, and at times simultaneous scenic structure, and the complex, shifting function of the black "alter ego" character, Ardell, give the play fascination, if not always a clear focus. The stature of the play was confirmed in a 1977 revival on Broadway with Al Pacino in the title role.

Sticks and Bones, with its cartoon archetypes and its more programmatic ritualized action, now seems a much more unsophisticated play, and more thoroughly dependent on the "social mask" techniques of the alternative theatre of the time. *In the Boom Boom Room*, especially in its revised version, has a similar structure and impact to *Pavlo Hummel*, and also deals with the destruction of an "innocent". Here, the forces of co-option include the legion of go-go dancers who surround the heroine, a predatory, lesbian troupe-leader, and a series of selfish or loutish males who are bent on dominating or denaturing the heroine.

Rabe's two more structurally and stylistically experimental plays, *The Orphan* and *Goose and Tomtom*, are separated from each other by several years, and involve some of the same patterning, but include more pervasive metaphysical concerns. *The Orphan*, however, is thematically semaphoric in its melding of motifs from Aeschylus' *Oresteia* and contemporary history (including Vietnam and the Manson killings), and its dialogue ineffectively juxtaposes an archaic portentousness with colloquial, "hip" modernisms. *Goose and Tomtom*, on the other hand, juxtaposes intriguingly the helplessness of its human characters with the teeming immensity of the astral and natural world lying just beyond their material and domestic conflicts.

Perhaps *Streamers* and *Hurlyburly* present Rabe's pessimistic indictment of modern social institutional structures most tellingly. *Streamers* is set in a quonset hut for new army recruits in 1965 and focuses on the way societal restriction limits and perverts individuality, identity and male sexuality. At its climax the conflicts explode beyond their racial and sexual motivations to form a composite image of violence, which spreads of its own momentum. *Hurlyburly* deals with men disoriented from failed marriages and by the demands of high-pressure careers, and of how a central friendship between two of them is not strong enough to prevent one of them killing himself.

Rabe's plays all suggesting utilize vivid scenic metaphors suggesting the forces allied with those systems that limit the individual. They often incorporate a raised stage area, the "inner above" Elizabethan thrust adaptation of Joseph Papp's New York Shakespeare Theatre, where the early plays were first staged professionally. For example, in *The Basic Training of Pavlo Hummel*, the metaphor is the military control tower which will take over Pavlo, the inchoate, insecure young recruit; in *In The Boom Boom Room*, it is the raised go-go dancers' cages which are not only the insignia of their profession but also the environments which degrade and imprison them; in *Hurlyburly*, it is the jungle plants which can be seen encroaching on the house through the windows. And in all of the plays, the space demarcates no clear boundaries between the public and the private, so we are aware that these families and substitute families deny the protagonists the right and the solace of a "private" space in which their individuality might grow.

Rabe's use of language was marked, early on, by a dichotomy between the received language of some institution—often the army—and a kind of fractured and instinctively poetic language used, at least before their institutional co-option, by the protagonists. The two kinds of language come closer together in the plays of the 1980's; in them, the major characters consciously exploit the societal language of their milieux to defend themselves against personal disclosure to those they do not trust.

In both style and structural strategies, Rabe appears to have been influenced by the international trend of a return to a more apparently conservative realism in the late 1970's; he abandoned the fractured, episodic surrealism of *The Basic Training of Pavlo Hummel* and *Sticks and Bones*, not to mention the convoluted mythic citation and polymorphous chronology of *The Orphan*. But even in *Streamers* and *Hurlyburly*, many scenes are structurally redundant or over-extended by "well-made" standards. The long verbal "arias" sometimes function as narrative metaphors for central themes, and sometimes as seismographs of the consciousness of the major characters. They are often the determining factors in the structure and rhythm of the plays and give them their idiosyncratic shapes.

—Dennis Carroll

See also *Volume 1* entry on *The Basic Training of Pavlo Hummel*.

RACINE, Jean. Born in La Ferté-Milon, near Soissons, France, 22 December 1639. Educated by Jansenists at the Convent of Port Royal, Paris; Collège d'Harcourt, Paris, 1658–59; studied theology under his uncle at Uzès, Languedoc, 1661–63. Married Catherine de Romanet in 1677; five daughters and two sons. First two plays, *La Thébaïde* and *Alexandre le Grand*, produced by Molière's troupe at the Palais Royal, Paris, 1664; broke with Molière, and his plays to 1677 produced at the Hôtel de Bourgogne, Paris; appointed royal historiographer (with Boileau) by Louis XIV, 1677; wrote no plays, 1677–89; his final two plays written for the Institut de Saint-Cyr, the girls' school patronized by Madame de Maintenon. Elected to the Académie Française, 1673. Died in Paris, 21 April 1699.

Works

Collections

Oeuvres (2 vols.). 1675–76.
Oeuvres (2 vols.). 1687.
Oeuvres (4 vols.). 1697.
Oeuvres: Nouvelle Édition (3 vols.). 1755–60.
Oeuvres complètes (revised edition; 10 vols.), edited by P. Mesnard. 1885.
The Best Plays of Racine (includes *Andromaque; Britannicus; Phèdre; Athalie*), translated by Lacy Lockert. 1936; as *Racine's Mid-Career Tragedies*, 1958.
Oeuvres complètes (2 vols.), edited by Raymond Picard. 1950–52.
Five Plays (includes *Andromaque; Britannicus; Bérénice; Phèdre; Athalie*), translated by Kenneth Muir. 1960.
Three Plays (includes *Andromache; Britannicus; Phaedra*), translated by George Dillon. 1961.
Iphigenia; Phaedra; Athaliah, translated by John Cairncross. 1963.
Complete Plays (2 vols.), translated by Samuel Solomon. 1967.
Andromaque; Britannicus; Bérénice, translated by John Cairncross. 1967.
Oeuvres complètes, edited by Jacques Morel and Alain Viala. 1980.
Four Greek Plays (includes *Andromache; Iphigenia; Phaedra; Athaliah*), translated by R. C. Knight. 1982.
Britannicus; Phaedra; Athaliah, translated by C. H. Sisson. 1987.

Stage Works

La Thébaïde; ou, Les Frères ennemis (produced Théâtre du Palais-Royal, Paris, 1664). 1664; translated as *The Fatal*

Jean Racine reading *Esther* to the young ladies of Mme. de Maintenon's school at Saint Cyr (engraving after J. Boily, 1820–30).

Legacy, 1723; as *The Theban Brothers*, in *Complete Plays 1*, 1967.

Alexandre le Grand (produced Théâtre du Palais-Royal, Paris, 1665). 1666; translated as *Alexander the Great*, 1714, and in *Complete Plays 1*, 1967.

Andromaque (produced Théâtre de l'Hôtel de Bourgogne, Paris, 1667). 1668; translated as *Andromache*, 1675, and *Andromaque*, in *The Best Plays of Racine*, 1936: several subsequent transactions under both titles; as *The Distresst Mother*, 1712.

Les Plaideurs (produced Théâtre de l'Hôtel de Bourgogne, Paris, 1668). 1669; translated as *The Litigants*, 1715, and in *Complete Plays 1*, 1967; as *The Suitors*, 1862.

Britannicus (produced Théâtre de l'Hôtel de Bourgogne, Paris, 1669). 1670; translated as *Britannicus*, 1714: several subsequent translations under same title.

Bérénice (produced Théâtre de l'Hôtel de Bourgogne, Paris, 1670). 1671; translated as *Titus and Berenice*, 1701; several subsequent translations as *Berenice* or *Bérénice*.

Bajazet (produced Théâtre de l'Hôtel de Bourgogne, Paris, 1672). 1672; translated as *The Sultaness*, 1717; as *Bajazet*, 1964.

Mithridate (produced Théâtre de l'Hôtel de Bourgogne, Paris, 1673). 1673; translated as *Mithridates*, 1926.

Iphigénie (produced Versailles, 1674). 1675; translated as *Achilles; or, Iphigenia in Aulis*, 1700; as *The Victim*, 1714;

as *Iphigenia*, 1861: several subsequent translations under same title.

Phèdre (produced Théâtre de l'Hôtel de Bourgogne, Paris, 1677). As *Phèdre et Hippolyte*, 1677; translated as *Phaedre and Hippolytus*, 1756; as *Phedra*, 1776; as *Phèdre*, 1885, and *Phaedra*, 1914: several subsequent translations under both titles.

L'Idylle de la paix, music by Lully (produced Académie Royale de Musique, Paris, 1685). 1685.

Esther (produced École de Saint-Cyr, 1689). 1689; translated as *Esther; or, Faith Triumphant*, 1715: several subsequent translations as *Esther*.

Athalie (produced Versailles, 1691). 1691; translated as *Athaliah*, 1722; as *Athalie*, 1880, and as *Athalia*, with *Esther*, 1803: several subsequent translations under both titles.

Verse

La Nymphe de la Seine. 1660.
Ode sur la convalescence du Roi. 1663.
Cantiques spirituels. 1694.
Campagne de Louis XIV, with Boileau. 1730; as *Éloge historique du Roi, Louis XIV*, 1784.
Poésies sacrées. 1914.
Poésies, edited by Gonzague Truc. 1936.

Poésies religieuses inconnues. 1954; translated as *Confessions: Unpublished Sonnets.* 1956.

Other

Abrégé de l'historie de Port Royal. 1742.

*

Bibliographies

L. Goldmann, *Situation de la critique racinienne*, Paris, 1971.
W. Thiele, *Die Racine-Kritik bis 1800*, Munich, 1974.

Criticism

Books:
Thierry Maulnier, *Racine*, Paris, 1935.
R. Moreau, *Racine: L'Homme et l'oeuvre*, Paris, 1943.
Martin Turnell, *The Classical Moment*, London, 1947.
G. May, *Tragédie cornélienne, tragédie racinienne*, Urbana, Illinois, 1948.
Jean Giraudoux, *Racine*, Paris, 1950.
R.C. Knight, *Racine et la Grèce*, Paris, 1950.
R.C. Knight, *Racine: Convention and Classicism*, Swansea, 1952.
Jean Pommier, *Aspects de Racine*, Paris, 1978.
John C. Lapp, *Aspects of Racinian Tragedy*, Toronto, 1955; revised edition, 1964.
M. Descotes, *Les Grands Rôles du théâtre de Racine*, Paris, 1957.
J.D. Hubert, *Les Secrets témoins: Essai d'exégèse racinienne*, Paris, 1958.
R. Jasinski, *Vers le vrai Racine* (2 vols.), Paris, 1958.
Philip Butler, *Classicisme et baroque dans l'oeuvre de Racine*, Paris, 1959.
Bernard Weinberg, *The Art of Jean Racine*, Chicago and London, 1963.
Peter France, *Racine's Rhetoric*, Oxford, 1965.
J. Mercanton, *Racine*, Paris, 1966.
Odette de Mourgues, *Autonomie de Racine*, Paris, 1967.
M. Descotes, *Racine*, Bordeaux, 1969.
R. Elliot, *Mythe et légende dans le théâtre de Racine*, Paris, 1969.
R.C. Knight (ed.), *Racine: Modern Judgements*, London, 1969.
A. Bonzon, *La Nouvelle Critique et Racine*, Paris, 1970.
M. Delcroix, *Le Sacré dans les tragédies profanes de Racine*, Paris, 1970.
Bettina Knapp, *Racine: Myths and Renewal in Modern Theatre*, University of Alabama, 1971.
J.-J. Roubine, *Lectures de Racine*, Paris, 1971.
M. Edwards, *La Tragédie racinienne*, Paris, 1972.
Martin Turnell, *Jean Racine: Dramatist*, London and New York, 1972.
Gordon Pocock, *Corneille and Racine: Problems of Tragic Form*, Cambridge, 1973.
Lucien Goldmann, *Racine*, London, 1973.
Clément Borgal, *Racine*, Paris, 1974.
Philip Butler, *Racine: A Study*, London, 1974.
A. Niderst, *Les Tragédies de Racine*, Paris, 1975.
Emy Batache-Watt, *Profils des héroïnes raciniennes*, Paris, 1976.
C. Abraham, *Jean Racine*, Boston, 1977.
W.J. Cloonan, *Racine's Theatre*, University of Mississippi, 1977.
A. Niderst, *Racine et la tragédie classique*, Paris, 1978.
Philip John Yarrow, *Racine*, Oxford, 1978.
Jean-Louis Backès, *Racine*, Paris, 1981.
Jean Prophète, *Les Para-Personnages dans les tragédies de Racine*, Paris, 1981.
Constant Venesoen, *Jean Racine et le procès de la culpabilité*, Paris, 1981.
H.T. Barnwell, *The Tragic Drama of Corneille and Racine: An Old Parallel Revisited*, Oxford, 1982.
Jacques Scherer, *Racine et/ou la cérémonie*, Paris, 1982.
Eugène Vinaver, *Entretiens sur Racine*, Paris, 1984.
Ingrid Heyndells, *Le Conflit racinien: Esquisse d'une système tragique*, Brussels, 1985.
Marie-Florine Bruneau, *Racine: Le Jansénisme et la modernité*, Paris, 1986.
Nina Ekstein, *Dramatic Narrative: Racine's Recits*, New York, 1986.
Catherine Spencer, *La Tragédie du prince*, Paris, 1987.
R.I. Burnett (ed.), *Rélectures raciniennes*, Paris, 1988.
Alain Viala, *Racine: La Stratégie du caméléon*, Paris, 1990.
David Maskell, *Racine: A Theatrical Reading*, Oxford, 1991.
Henry Phillips, *Racine: Appraisal and Reappraisal*, Bristol, 1991.
Christine M. Hill (ed.), *Racine: Théâtre et poésie: Actes du troisième Colloque Vinaver*, Leeds, 1991.
Michael Hawcroft, *Word as Action: Racine, Rhetoric and Theatrical Language*, Oxford, 1992.

Serials:
Cahiers raciniens, 1957—

* * *

Racine is considered one of the two greatest French tragic playwrights and France's most intense dramatic poet, His output included nine tragedies staged between 1664 and 1677: five on Greek subjects—*La Thébaïde (The Theban Brothers)*, *Alexandre le Grand* (part of a now neglected magnification of Louis XIV through parallels with Alexander the Great), *Andromaque, Iphigénie*, and *Phèdre*—, three Roman tragedies, if *Mithridate* is counted with *Britannicus* and *Bérénice* as a Roman subject, and *Bajazet* (Racine's darkest tragedy), based on diplomatic despatches from Ottoman Turkey concerning a relatively recent imperial fratricide.

Racinian tragedy is often contrasted with the heroic tragedy of his senior contemporary and main rival, Pierre Corneille, and with Shakespeare. Racine was seen as the poet of persons as they are, Corneille, as they ought to be. Later, Houdar de La Motte made Racine the more pure and Corneille the more sublime. In *Racine and Shakespeare* (1827) Stendhal developed a Romantic contrast between the infinite variety of Shakespearian drama and the regularity of French neoclassical traditions associated with Racine. Elsewhere Stendhal observed that if Corneille is sublime, Racine is the "poète de l'anxiété"—the poet of anguish. Racine's inspiration from the Greeks (especially Aristotle, for tragic theory, and Euripides), from Latin classics (especially the works of Seneca, Virgil, and Ovid) and from somewhat senior French dramatic poets (including Racan, Tristan L'Hermite, Scudéry, and Desmarets) is well documented.

No other French dramatist exemplifies so well the energy obtainable in psychological drama from an exact observance of the neoclassical unities of time (limited to a notional 24 hours), place (imaginary space co-extensive with the playing place), action (a unified plot in which every event is related), and tone (the radical separation of genres). In Racinian tragedy all is concentration and elevation. Its structure minimizes sub-plots, admits no digressions, clowns, or comic scenes. Its style excludes trivial and colloquial language and even graphic visual imagery. At the linguistic surface, often ironically contrasted with a violent passion, physical realities are subordinated to psychological tensions arising from exacerbated sexuality, sexual jealousy, ambition, shame and/or guilt. Probably no other European dramatist has used such a restricted conventional vocabulary (under 2000 words in the tragedies) with such thematic accuracy and intensity. At the same time, no contemporary French playwright dramatizing mythological subjects succeeded so well in imbuing the tragic atmosphere with what might be called mythological "local colour" by naming—in imitation of Ovid's *Metamorphoses*—a host of specific mythological places and people as Racine does in *Phèdre*.

Though adapted in part from Rotrou's *Antigone*, Racine's first tragedy, *La Thébaïde*, produced by Molière's troupe, seems to invert the major themes of Corneille's *Rodogune*. Racine's Roman tragedy *Britannicus*, with its famous portrait of the Emperor Nero as a monster in the making, takes as its point of departure a contrast with the final self-mastery of the emperor Augustus as depicted in Corneille's *Cinna*.

The heroine of *Phèdre*, poisoned with adulterous and incestuous passion for her son-in-law, Hippolyte, and with guilt which she seems powerless to control, exemplifies the Aristotelian idea of the flawed hero, neither altogether good nor altogether evil. She is sometimes said to embody the neo-Augustinian or Jansenist notion of an unwilling sinner to whom grace is denied, but the idea of a protagonist unable to reject passions and behaviour which she herself deplores is already well developed in Euripides and echoed in Ovid.

Andromaque is based on a concatenation of unreciprocated love reminiscent of dramatic pastoral (Oreste loves Hermione, who loves Pyrrhus, who is in love with the captive widow Andromaque), except that Andromaque's pious commitment to Hector and to their son Astyanax (an absent character through whom Pyrrhus attempts to coerce Andromaque, notable as the legendary ancestor of the kings of France, protected providentially) both prevents a happy double-marriage denouement and redeems Andromaque (who ultimately survives as queen of Epirus) from the disintegration of the other characters.

The elegiac *Bérénice* is notable both as a play invented from a single sentence in Suetonius and as a tragedy without bloodshed in which a Virgilian sense of the "tears of things" (Racine's "*tristesse majestueuse*") greatly expands the compassion of Aristotelian tragic theory at the expense of terror.

In 1689–91 Racine returned to tragic drama with, in effect, two Old Testament oratorios: *Esther* and *Athalie*, written for the select girls' school at St-Cyr, with choruses in imitation of Greek tragedy and music by J.-B. Moreau. Neither of these tragedies were performed by professional actors until 1716 (*Athalie*). Translations of *Esther* and *Athalie* reset to the music of Handel initiated the English sacred oratorio.

Racine also wrote a witty satirical comedy, *Les Plaideurs* (*The Litigants*), adapted from *The Wasps* of Aristophanes. At the Comédie-Française it came fourth in the entire repertory in frequency of performances and was much the most successful of Racine's plays on stage from 1680 to 1900, overtaken only in the 20th century by *Andromaque* and *Phèdre*. Racine's other writings include lyric poetry, personal and polemical letters, official histories, and *A Short History of Port-Royal*, the controversial Cistercian abbey near Paris where the orphaned infant Racine was educated by Jansenist

dissidents (especially Pierre Nicole), against whose oppressive cultural attitudes Racine rebelled in the early 1660's, although he later repented.

—H. Gaston Hall

See also *Volume 1* entries on *Andromache*; *Berenice*; *Britannicus*; *Phaedra*.

————

RAIMUND, Ferdinand. Born Ferdinand Reimann in Vienna, Austria, 1 June, 1790. Educated at St. Anna's school, Vienna, 1800–04. Married Luise Gleich in 1820 (divorced 1822), one daughter (died in infancy); lived with the actress Antonie Wagner from 1830. Baker's assistant and sweet vendor, 1804–05; failed acting auditions at Viennese theatres owing to speech impediment, and joined travelling troupe, 1808, performing in Austria and Bohemia; joined the company of Christoph Kuntz, 1810; returned to Vienna, 1814, and joined the company at the Theater in der Josefstadt: achieved first acting success in the role of Kratzerl in Gleich's *Musikanten auf dem Hohenmarkt*, 1815, and was made director of the company, 1816; joined the company at the Theater in der Leopoldstadt, Vienna, 1817, and signed

Ferdinand Raimund as Aschenmann in his *Das Mädchen aus der Feenwelt*, 1826 (lithograph after a drawing by M. von Schwind).

long-term contract with it, 1821; first-produced play, *Das Barometer auf der Zauberinsel*, staged 1823; subsequently plays produced in Vienna, 1823–34; appointed artistic director at the Theater in der Leopoldstadt, following its change of ownership, 1828: resigned 1830, after disagreements with the new owner; subsequently a successful guest actor, performing in Germany and Austria. Shot himself, fearing he had contracted rabies, and died in Pottenstein, Lower Austria, 5 September 1836.

Works

Collections

Sämtliche Werke, edited by Johann Nepomuk Vogl.   1837.
Sämtliche Werke, edited by Carl Glossy and August Sauer.   1881.
Sämtliche Werke, edited by Eduard Castle.   1903.
Sämtliche Werke (3 vols.), edited by Otto Rommel.   1908–12.
Sämtliche Werke: Historisch-kritische Säkularausgabe (critical edition; 6 vols.), edited by Fritz Bruckner and Eduard Castle.   1925–34.
Dramatische Werke (2 vols.), edited by Gustav Pichler.   1960.
Werke (2 vols.), edited by Franz Hadamowsky.   1984.

Stage Works

Der Barometermacher auf der Zauberinsel (produced Theater in der Leopoldstadt, Vienna, 1823).   In *Sämtliche Werke*, 1837.
Der Diamant des Geisterkönigs (produced Theater in der Leopoldstadt, Vienna, 1824).   In *Sämtliche Werke*, 1837.
Das Mädchen aus der Feenwelt; oder, Der Bauer als Millionär (produced Theater in der Leopoldstadt, Vienna, 1826).   In *Sämtliche Werke*, 1837.
Mosaisurs Zauberfluch (produced Theater an der Wien, Vienna, 1827).   In *Sämtliche Werke*, 1837.
Die gefesselte Phantasie (produced Theater in der Leopoldstadt, Vienna, 1828).   In *Sämtliche Werke*, 1837.
Der Alpenkönig und der Menschenfeind (produced Theater in der Leopoldstadt, Vienna, 1828).   In *Sämtliche Werke*, 1837; translated and adapted as *The King of the Alps*, 1852.
Die unheilbringende Krone (produced Theater in der Leopoldstadt, Vienna, 1829).   In *Sämtliche Werke*, 1837.
Der Verschwender (produced Theater in der Josefstadt, Vienna, 1834).   In *Sämtliche Werke*, 1837; translated as *The Spendthrift*, 1949.

Memoirs and Letters

Briefe.   In *Sämtliche Werke: Historisch-kritische Säkularausgabe*, 1925–34.

Other

Der unbekannte Raimund: Gedichte, Tagebuchblätter, Szenen, und Briefe, edited by Gustav Pichler.   1962.

*

Criticism

Books:
R. Smekal, *Ferdinand Raimund*, Vienna, 1920.
Franz Hadamowsky, *Ferdinand Raimund als Schauspieler*, Vienna, 1925.

O. Rauscher, *Ferdinand Raimund*, Leipzig, 1936.
H. Kindermann, *Ferdinand Raimund*, Vienna, 1943.
Otto Rommel, *Ferdinand Raimund und die Vollendung des Alt-Wiener Zauberstückes*, Vienna, 1947.
Otto Rommel, *Die Alt-Wiener Volkskomödie*, Vienna, 1952.
Kurt Kahl, *Raimund*, Velber, 1967.
John Michalski, *Ferdinand Raimund*, New York, 1968.
Jürgen Hein, *Ferdinand Raimund*, Stuttgart, 1970.
Dorothy Prohaska, *Raimund and Vienna*, Cambridge, 1970.
Frank Schaumann, *Gestalt und Funktion des Mythos in Ferdinand Raimunds Bühnenwerken*, Vienna, 1970.
Gunther Wiltschko, *Raimunds Dramaturgie*, Munich, 1973.
Norbert Glas, *Ferdinand Raimund: Sein Leben und sein Schicksal*, Stuttgart, 1974.
Laurence V. Harding, *The Dramatic Art of Ferdinand Raimund and Johann Nestroy*, The Hague, 1974.
Jürgen Hein, *Das Wiener Volkstheater: Raimund und Nestroy*, Darmstadt, 1978.
R. Wimmer, *Ferdinand Raimunds Zauberspiele*, Munich, 1984.
Renate Wagner, *Ferdinand Raimund: Eine Biographie*, Vienna, 1985.

Serials:

Raimund-Almanach, 1936—(intermittently).

*   *   *

If English-speaking audiences are at all familiar with the works of the old Viennese popular theatre, it is probably through Mozart's operas, *Die Entführung aus dem Serail* (*The Abduction from the Seraglio*, 1782) and *Die Zauberflöte* (*The Magic Flute*, 1791). These two works are, however, an inadequate representation of a theatrical tradition that enjoyed almost two centuries of vigorous activity, from the improvised performances of Johann Stranitsky early in the 18th century to the ingenious, witty comedies of Nestroy in the mid-19th century. The work of Ferdinand Raimund epitomizes much that is original in this uncommonly attractive phase of theatre history.

After some years touring in the Habsburg provinces, Raimund first made his mark on the Viennese theatre as an actor in the Theater in der Josefstadt, where he became celebrated for his skilful comic representations of stock character-types familiar to the stages of the city's suburban theatres. He was especially adept at transforming himself entirely into the character he played and for introducing a wistfully melancholic tone into a theatre that usually presented unabashedly cheerful comedy. Consequently, he found the dramatic fare offered by the journeyman playwrights of this theatre unsuited to his talents, and when one of them, Karl Meisl, failed to complete a play specifically written for one of his benefit performances, Raimund turned to playwriting himself.

While his first two plays, *Der Barometermacher auf der Zauberinsel* and *Der Diamant des Geisterkönigs*, were successful primarily because they provided roles congenial to the playwright–actor, they are also characteristic of the *Zauberspiel* (magic play) that was so popular in Vienna during the late 18th and early 19th centuries. In it, the planes of ordinary Viennese life, presented in a sentimentally idealised fashion, and of a generally benign metaphysical world denizened by fantastic fairy creations, become closely associated. The central character, played by Raimund, was understood to personify the average Viennese citizen. As the barometer-maker Bartholomäus Quecksilber or, in *Diamant*, as the servant

Florian Waschblau, this figure becomes involved in fantastic adventures and quests in the realm of the spirits, only at the end to return to the genial world of Vienna, reconciled to his human limitations, and with a newly fortified love for his native city. The plays required elaborate stage-machinery through which the most spectacular and often bizarre scenic transformations could be effected, a common feature of all *Zauberspiele* of this time. The action is frequently punctuated by songs and more elaborate musical ensembles in which issues raised in the course of the action are wittily encapsulated. Several of these songs, which might be performed with some stanzas improvised, would contain good-humoured satire on contemporary Viennese life. In fact, one can only come to a full understanding of the action and appreciation of the comedy if one has a close acquaintance with the life and customs of the Vienna of Raimund's day. This means that these plays have been rarely performed outside their native city.

Like several notable comic performers, Raimund wished to extend his range to include work of a tragic dimension. However, the theatre for which he wrote was singularly incapable of satisfying this ambition, for it was devoted mainly to providing entertainment on a commercial basis for the various classes of the city. Furthermore, the censorship imposed by the government of Metternich did not allow the stage to challenge the status quo or cast any doubt upon fundamental religious beliefs. As a result, the philosophy of plays staged in the Viennese suburban theatres was overwhelmingly optimistic, and Raimund's attempts to introduce more serious, darker themes onto the stage were not entirely successful. *Die gefesselte Phantasie*, an interesting allegory on the creative imagination, was rejected by the Viennese public as it did not fulfil their expectations of what a Viennese comedy should be, though it was successful elsewhere in the German-speaking world. *Mosaisurs Zauberfluch*, a fable set in mythical India, is noted for its unmediated representation of the forces of evil, which again unsettled Raimund's audiences; so too did the commentary on modern militarism in *Die unheilbringende Krone*. But the comparative failure of these works cannot be attributed solely to external conditions. As a playwright, Raimund was clearly more skilled at comedy than tragedy; his serious characters are often too abstract and purely symbolic for successful stage representation, while the poetry of the non-comic sequences tends to be turgid and stilted. The most successful passages are those involving the comic roles that Raimund, ever attentive to the demands of the box-office, continued to write for himself. Despite some notable modern revivals it is difficult to see in these generically indeterminate works the Viennese equivalent of the tragicomedies of Shakespeare or Calderón.

In the realm of pure comedy, however, Raimund's achievements can properly be compared with those of the greatest dramatists. His three masterpieces, *Der Bauer als Millionär*, *Der Alpenkönig und der Menschenfeind*, and *Der Verschwender*, might, if they ever receive adequate translation, be recognised as lasting contributions to world drama. The prime reason for the plays' appeal, both in their own day and later, lies in the resourcefulness and ingenuity by which the final conclusion, the happy acceptance of modest limits to one's wealth and to one's emotional life, is achieved. In this regard, the outstanding play, which is still regularly revived throughout the German-speaking world, is *Der Alpenkönig und der Menschenfeind*. The way in which an appalling misanthrope is converted to love of humanity by, literally, seeing his double, represented by the benignly daemonic King of the Alps, provides scenes of the very richest comedy through which the happy ending appears to be entirely necessary. The play is also noted for its resourceful use of Romantic scenery —at one point a coach and four is swallowed whole in a mountain face—and an ingratiating score by Wenzel Müller.

The inventiveness and lack of strain in Raimund's dramaturgy, the felicity of his imagery, and the absence of constant close allusion to the life of his city and time suggest that Raimund's three masterpieces have the potential to appeal to a far wider audience than the Viennese alone. They also greatly enriched the popular theatre of Vienna and provided a welcome depth and complexity of feeling in a dramatic tradition that was always in danger of limiting itself through triviality.

Despite the immense success of these three plays and his great popularity as an actor, not only in Vienna but in major German cities such as Berlin, Hamburg, and Munich, the melancholic traits of Raimund's character predominated. He died some days after shooting himself, ostensibly out of fear that he had contracted rabies from a dog-bite. However, biographers have suggested that his suicide may have been caused by a growing awareness that public taste for the theatre for which he wrote was dying. In 1833, three years before Raimund's death, Johann Nestroy achieved his first great hit with his comedy *Lumpazivagabundus*, in which the satire of Viennese life was unusually bitter, even vituperative, and the happy ending, as it represented no easy outcome of the action, was clearly ironic. Nestroy was a playwright who would find his apogee in the revolution of 1848; Raimund was essentially a product of Biedermeier Vienna.

—Simon Williams

RASTELL, John. Born in London c.1475. Trained as a lawyer at the Inns of Court, London: in the Middle Temple, 1502. Married Elizabeth More, sister of Thomas More; one son. City coroner, Coventry, 1506; presided over Court of Statute Merchant (mercantile law), 1506–09; printer in London, mainly of legal books (including first dictionary of legal terms), 1510–31; in service of Sir Edward Belknap, a privy councillor to Henry VIII, by 1512: responsible for the transport of artillery to France in 1512–14 war; invested in unsuccessful trading venture to the New World, 1517; designed royal pageants and entertainments, 1520, 1522, 1527; lawyer in Chancery, 1529; member of Parliament for Dunheved, Cornwall, 1529–36; imprisoned for opposition to a royal proclamation, 1535–36. Died June 1536.

Works

Collections

Three Rastell Plays (includes *The Nature of the Four Elements; Calisto and Melebea; Gentleness and Nobility*), edited by Richard Axton.   1979.

Stage Works

The Nature of the Four Elements (produced c.1516–c.1518).   1525–30(?).
Terence in English, from *Andria* by Terence, possibly not by Rastell.   1516–30(?).

Gentleness and Nobility, probably by John Heywood (produced c.1527–30). 1527–30(?).
Calisto and Melebea, from the *Celestina* by Rojas (produced c.1527–30). 1527–30(?).

Other

The Pastime of People. 1529; edited by Albert J. Geritz, with *A New Book of Purgatory*, 1985.
A New Book of Purgatory. 1530; edited by Albert J. Geritz, with *The Pastime of People*, 1985.

Editor and Translator, *The Exposition of the Terms of the Laws of England.* 1526 (and later versions in English and French).
Editor and Translator, *The Statutes.* 1527 (and later versions in English and French).

*

Criticism

Books:
A.W. Reed, *Early Tudor Drama*, London, 1926.

*   *   *

The authorship of one entire play only, *The Nature of the Four Elements*, can be positively assigned to John Rastell. His profession as a lawyer and printer, however, and the circles in which he moved, involves him more in early 16th-century English theatre than this output might suggest. Rastell was educated at the Inns of Court, and married Elizabeth, sister of Sir Thomas More, who was himself a keen theatrical according to Roper's *Life*. Rastell, therefore, developed connections through the court and the law which placed him at the heart of London's humanist circle in the early 16th century, a circle in which the theatre both as vehicle for ideas and as entertainment played a central part.

The Nature of the Four Elements employs the procedures of the medieval morality play in constructing a drama, the major preoccupations of which are typically English humanist—the secular education of the audience, the fashionable physical sciences, and the adequacy of the English language as a vehicle for conveying learned material. What is more, Rastell's work demonstrates how the "moral interlude", the established English dramatic form of the previous century, could be adapted from teaching men about the world of the spirit to fulfil the humanist mission of offering instruction about the observable cosmos.

The play is, more specifically, a mouthpiece for Rastell's own knowledge of, and interest in, the New World. It does not have one direct source but appears to draw eclectically on popular encyclopaedic materials ranging from *The Travels of Sir John Mandeville* and Bartholomaeus Anglicanus' *De Proprietatibus Rerum*, to Caxton's *Mirrour of the World*, Amerigo Vespucci's *Quattuor navigationes*, and contemporaries such as John Schöner and John Stobnicza, all of which were the object of the author's study for a quite different purpose. Rastell himself was, in 1517, engaged in an abortive venture to the New World which, because of the perfidy of seamen (who are attacked in a brief and embittered digression in the play), got no further than Ireland. Of his two sons, the elder, William, turned to the law and printing, while John, the younger, made it to Labrador.

Through the framework of the morality play, with its prosopopeic characters—unstable protagonist, vices and virtues—and its classic plot-pattern of fall and redemption, Rastell conveys information ranging from the natural properties of the world, to the nature of the indigenous American population, naked, savage, and godless. The overall effect is of a play whose form has been massaged to contain a geography lesson, a curious mixture owing something to the travelogue, to *Mankind*, and to the parable of the prodigal son. The logic of the allegorical frame cannot always sustain the dramatist's determination to convey blocks of barely digestible factual information, as, notoriously, at one point, while the fallen protagonist, Humanity, is at sport with Sensual Appetite, his Studious Desire is engaged in a long and earnest debate about the properties of the world with the chief educator, Experience. This debate is focused on the centrepiece which Rastell devised for the play, a *figura*, presumably a mechanical model of the cosmos, which Studious Desire carries on at his first entrance.

The play is a testimonial to its author as adventurer, but also as theatrical impresario, for it demonstrates Rastell's experience and judgement as theatrical practitioner in a particular milieu. The prefatory notes to *The Nature of the Four Elements* show the playwright at work, thinking of likely settings and audiences for his play, and, despite much of its apparently doctrinaire content, giving precedence to the exigencies of performance. Before the names of the players and a synopsis of the "*dyvers matters whiche be in this interlude conteynyd*", there is the celebrated authorial note:

A NEW INTERLUDE AND A MERY, OF THE NATURE OF THE FOUR ELEMENTS, declarynge many propyr poyntys of phylosophy naturall, and of dyvers straunge landys, and of dyvers straunge effectis and causis; which intelude, yf the hole matter by playde, wyl conteyne the space of an hour and a halfe; but yf ye lyst ye may leve out muche of the sad mater, as the messengers parte, and some of Naturys parte and some of Experyens parte, and yet the matter wyl depend convenyently, and than it wyll not be paste thre quarters of an hour of length.

Although Rastell may have been a failed adventurer, the only complete play which survives from his hand shows him to have been a practised theatrical and one urbanely prepared to sacrifice the ideas contained in his play to its success as entertainment and diversion for a given audience, possibly between courses at a banquet. His other suggestion, characteristic of the interlude genre, that, "*Also yf ye lyst ye may brynge in a dysgysynge*", dispels all suspicion that he was a playwright who saw the theatre solely or chiefly as a medium for the tract.

Other aspects of Rastell's activities substantiate the evidence of his play that he was deeply engaged in many aspects of theatrical activity in the capital. He was engaged to devise scenic machinery for various public shows, assisted in the design of the Field of Cloth of Gold, and is known to have constructed a stage in the grounds of his own house at Finsbury Fields. Above all, however, it is through his printing activities that Rastell's major contribution to English drama was made. He printed Henry Medwall's *Fulgens and Lucrece*, *Gentleness and Nobility* by John Heywood (who married his daughter), and John Skelton's *Magnificence*. The anonymous *Calisto and Melebea*, also from his press, is a considerably trimmed and anodyne dramatic adaptation of Fernando de Rojas's Spanish dialogue-novel of the same name, commonly known after its most memorable character as *La Celestina*. The attraction of this play to Rastell supports a view of him as having been on the very cusp between the old and new in

Tudor theatre: it owes as much to the crude wooing farces, *Dame Sirith* and *Interludum de Clerico et Puella*, as it does to the revival of Terentian comedy which was one of the major currents of the coming age. The torrid Spanish tale is turned to something which naturally anticipates its English epilogue, possibly added by Rastell himself, and certainly characteristic of him in its sentiments:

> And ye faders, moders, and other which be
> Rulers of yong folkis, your charge is dowtles
> To bryng them up verteously and to see
> Them occupied styll in some good bysynes,
> Not in idell pastyme or unthryftynes,
> But to teche them some art, craft ot lernyng,
> Whereby to be able to get theyr lyffyng.

Rastell's work shows clear evidence of latent Protestantism, and indeed in later life he became a political ally of Thomas Cromwell and was in the vanguard of the Reformation, dying in prison in 1536.

—Pamela M. King

* * *

RATTIGAN, (Sir) Terence (Mervyn). Born in Kensington, London, 10 June 1911. Educated at Sandroyd School, Cobham, Surrey, 1920–24; Harrow School, Middlesex (scholar), 1925–30; Trinity College, Oxford (history scholar), 1930–33, BA 1933. Served in the Coastal Command of the Royal Air Force, 1939–45: flight lieutenant. First play, *First Episode*, in collaboration with Philip Heimann, produced 1933. Recipient: Ellen Terry Award, 1947, 1948; New York Drama Critics Circle Award, 1948. CBE (Commander, Order of the British Empire), 1958. Knighted, 1971. Died in Hamilton, Bermuda, 30 November 1977.

Works

Collections

Collected Plays (4 vols.).   1953–78.
Plays (2 vols.).   1981:
  1. *French Without Tears; The Winslow Boy; The Browning Version; Harlequinade.*
  2. *The Deep Blue Sea; Separate Tables; In Praise of Love.*

Stage Works

First Episode, with Philip Heimann (produced Q Theatre, London, 1933).
French Without Tears (produced Criterion Theatre, London, 1936).   1937; revised version, music by Robert Stolz, lyrics by Paul Dehn, as *Joie de Vivre* (produced Queen's Theatre, London, 1960).
After the Dance (produced St. James's Theatre, London, 1939).   1939.
Follow My Leader, with Anthony Maurice (produced Apollo Theatre, London, 1940).
Grey Farm, with Hector Bolitho (produced Hudson Theatre, New York, 1940).
Flare Path (produced Apollo Theatre, London, 1942).   1942.
While the Sun Shines (produced Globe Theatre, London, 1943).   1944.

Love in Idleness (produced Lyric Theatre, London, 1944). 1945; as *O Mistress Mine* (produced 1946), 1949.
The Winslow Boy (produced Lyric Theatre, London, 1946). 1946.
The Browning Version (produced Phoenix Theatre, London, 1948).   With *Harlequinade* as *Playbill*, 1949.
Harlequinade (produced Phoenix Theatre, London, 1948). With *The Browning Version* as *Playbill*, 1949.
Adventure Story (produced St. James's Theatre, London, 1949).   1950.
Who is Sylvia? (produced Criterion Theatre, London, 1950). 1951.
The Deep Blue Sea (produced Duchess Theatre, London, 1952).   1952.
The Sleeping Prince (produced Phoenix Theatre, London, 1953).   1954.
Separate Tables (includes *Table by the Window* and *Table Number Seven*; produced St. James's Theatre, London, 1954).   1955.
Variation on a Theme (produced Globe Theatre, London, 1958).   1958.
Ross: A Dramatic Portrait (produced Theatre Royal, Haymarket, London, 1960).   1960.
Man and Boy (produced Queen's Theatre, London, 1963). 1963.
A Bequest to the Nation, from the television play *Nelson* (produced Theatre Royal, Haymarket, London, 1970). 1970.
All on Her Own, from the television play (produced Kingston-on-Thames, 1974; as *Duologue*, produced King's Head Theatre, London, 1976).   In *The Best Short Plays 1970*, edited by Stanley Richards, 1970.
In Praise of Love: Before Dawn, and *After Lydia* (produced Duchess Theatre, London, 1973).   1973; revised version of *After Lydia* (as *In Praise of Love*, produced Morosco Theatre, New York, 1974), 1975.
Cause Célèbre (broadcast 1975; produced Her Majesty's Theatre, London, 1977).   1978.

Screenplays

The Belles of St. Clement's, 1936; *Gypsy*, with Brock Williams, 1937; *French Without Tears*, with Anatole de Grunwald and Ian Dalrymple, 1939; *Quiet Wedding*, with Anatole de Grunwald, 1941; *The Day Will Dawn (The Avengers)*, with Anatole de Grunwald and Patrick Kirwan, 1942; *Uncensored*, with Rodney Ackland and Wolfgang Wilhelm, 1942; *English Without Tears (Her Man Gilbey)*, with Anatole de Grunwald, 1944; *The Way to the Stars (Johnny in the Clouds)*, with Anatole de Grunwald, 1945; *Journey Together*, with John Boulting, 1945; *Brighton Rock (Young Scarface)*, with Graham Greene, 1947; *While the Sun Shines*, with Anatole de Grunwald, 1947; *The Winslow Boy*, with Anatole de Grunwald, and Anthony Asquith, 1948; *Bond Street*, with Rodney Ackland and Anatole de Grunwald, 1948; *The Browning Version*, 1951; *The Sound Barrier (Breaking the Sound Barrier)*, 1952; *The Final Test*, 1953; *The Deep Blue Sea*, 1955; *The Man Who Loved Redheads*, 1955; *The Prince and the Showgirl*, 1957 (published 1957); *Separate Tables*, with John Gay, 1958; *The VIPs*, 1963; *The Yellow Rolls-Royce*, 1964; *Goodbye Mr. Chips*, 1969; *A Bequest to the Nation (The Nelson Affair)*, 1973.

Television Plays

The Final Test, 1951; *Heart to Heart*, 1962 (published in *Collected Plays 3*, 1964); *Ninety Years On*, 1964; *Nelson*,

Terence Rattigan (left) with actors Zoë Caldwell and Ian Holm during rehearsal period for his *A Bequest to the Nation*, 1970.

1966; *All on Her Own*, 1968; *High Summer*, 1972 (published in *The Best Short Plays 1973*, edited by Stanley Richards, 1973).

Radio Plays

A Tale of Two Cities, with John Gielgud, from the novel by Dickens, 1950; *Cause Célèbre*, 1975.

Criticism

Books:
J.C. Trewin, *Dramatists of Today*, Harlow, Essex, 1953.
Michael Darlow and Gillian Hodson, *Terence Rattigan: The Man and His Work*, London, 1979.
Susan Ruskino, *Terence Rattigan*, Boston, 1983.
B.A. Young, *The Rattigan Version: Sir Terence Rattigan and the Theatre of Character*, London, 1986.

Articles:
Robert F. Gross, "'Coming Down in the World': Motifs of Benign Descent in Three Plays by Terence Rattigan", in *Modern Drama*, 33, 1990.

*   *   *

The fortunes of Terence Rattigan fluctuated during his lengthy career from his youthful West End debut in 1936 with *French Without Tears* through his war-time successes (*Flare Path* and *While the Sun Shines*) to his post-war heyday (*The Winslow Boy*, *Playbill*, and *The Deep Blue Sea*), his eclipse in the wake of Royal Court "kitchen-sink" drama, and finally, his eventual rehabilitation towards the end of his life (with *In Praise of Love* and *Cause Célèbre*). Despite these vicissitudes (due both to changes in public taste and the variable quality of his work) Rattigan displayed a remarkable continuity in technical skill and theme.

In his preface to the second volume of his *Collected Plays* in 1953, Rattigan confessed that the plays "are all . . . 'well-made', which means that they have a beginning, a middle and an end". Although the virtues of such craftsmanship were generally acknowledged during the first two decades of Rattigan's career, they were later disparaged as what Rattigan himself termed "French Window Drama". In his own defence Rattigan asserted that "Ibsen had French windows", and even Kenneth Tynan, an uncompromising critic of Rattigan's plays, conceded that "whatever his short-comings as a theorist, nobody can deny Rattigan's supreme agility as a craftsman. His mastery of exposition is complete: give one of his characters a telephone, and within a minute, imperceptibly, the essentials of the situation will have been clearly sketched in".

Rattigan's dependence upon these modern props was evident when he ventured beyond contemporary subjects, as in *Adventure Story* (about Alexander the Great), in which he essayed a looser (more epic) form, but without real success. A similar structural experiment in *Ross* (about T. E. Lawrence) also failed, and it was not until his last play, *Cause Célèbre* (revised from a radio script), that he showed mastery of a freer form.

Tynan's strictures on Rattigan's "shortcomings as a theor-ist" would hardly have troubled the dramatist, who in a controversial article entitled "Concerning the Plays of Ideas" in *The New Statesman* (4 March 1950) wrote: "I believe that the best plays are about people, and not about things . . . from Aeschylus to Tennessee Williams the only theatre that

has ever mattered is the theatre of character and narrative". Much of Rattigan's best work was derived from personal experience. *French Without Tears* dramatises his visit, as an Oxford undergraduate, to an intensive study course in France; *Flare Path* incorporates his own war-time experience in the R.A.F; *The Browning Version* is based on an incident during his school days at Harrow; the opening scene (with the apparently gassed Hester Collyer) of *The Deep Blue Sea* recalls the suicide of his friend Kenneth Morgan; *Separate Tables* evokes the Kensington hotel in which his mother lived; *Variation on a Theme* explores aspects of actress Margaret Leighton's relationship with Laurence Harvey; and *After Lydia* is based on Rex Harrison's experience with his ter-minally ill wife Kay Kendall. The relative failure of Rattigan's historical plays (*A Bequest to the Nation*, about Nelson and Lady Hamilton, as well as *Adventure Story* and *Ross*) under-lines the importance of personal experience to his inspiration.

Although Rattigan proclaimed his rejection of the "play of ideas", there is in fact a thematic consistency running through his *oeuvre*. As Rattigan's biographers Michael Darlow and Gillian Hodson pointed out, "the conflict between emotion and reason which is a motif in all Rattigan's plays surfaces repeatedly in *French Without Tears*". In play after play, Rattigan explored the triangular situation of a character torn between the rival claims of potential lovers. Of the rival lovers, one invariably embodies the "higher love" (rational; socially and intellectually compatible), such as Sir William Collyer, Hester's husband and a judge in *The Deep Blue Sea*; the other (e.g. Freddie Page in the same play) embodies irrational attraction based on sexual gratification and little else.

Except for *Variation on a Theme*, in which Ron has forsaken his male partner for Rose, these relationships are heterosexual, or at least apparently so. However it is gener-ally accepted that often Rattigan was, as one critic put it "depicting homosexual characters or relationships . . . in the guise of heterosexual ones". Rattigan's own relationships ranged from that with the infamous Chips Channon (*The Winslow Boy* is dedicated to his son Paul, in later life a Minister for the Arts) to the young actor Kenneth Morgan, whose suicide provided the seed for *The Deep Blue Sea*. It has been suggested that Hester Collyer in that play should be portrayed as a male character, but the evidence of *Separate Tables* (in *Table Number Seven*) shows that such a transfer-ence is not straightforward. In his draft, Rattigan made Major Pollock's offence homosexual (as Mr. Miller's had originally been in *The Deep Blue Sea*), but he changed it to importuning a woman in the cinema. When the play was staged in the more liberal sexual climate of New York it was intended to revert to the earlier version, but in practice this did not work and the revision was retained.

Rattigan's diffidence was based partly on personal discre-tion and the pre-Wolfenden Report (1957) laws, but it was also in deference to the archetypal theatre-goer whom Rattigan created in his preface to Volume Two of his *Complete Plays* (p.xi)—Aunt Edna, "a nice respectable, middle-class, middle-aged maiden lady . . . She is universal and immortal, and she has lived for two thousand years". Rattigan's detractors accused him of deferring too much to Aunt Edna, not only in his treatment of sexual themes, but in his willingness to compromise in the endings to his plays. The professional and matrimonial uncertainty of Crocker Harris's fate in *The Browning Version* is tenable (Rattigan had con-sidered dispatching him with a heart attack), but many critics felt that he should not have forestalled Hester Collyer (in *The Deep Blue Sea*) from the suicide to which the play seemed to be inexorably moving. In *After Lydia* (by which time Aunt

Edna was effectively pensioned off) Rattigan had the courage to deny his audiences a sentimental ending.

Rattigan himself avowed that there was no incompatibility between popular success and quality: "I am not in the least tempted to believe that the failure of a play with an audience means that it must therefore possess some special artistic merit". Tynan was not convinced, concluding his dialogue review of *Separate Tables* with the following exchange between Aunt Edna and the Young Perfectionist:

Aunt Edna: Clearly, there is something here for both of us.
Young Perfectionist: Yes. But not quite enough for either of us.

Posterity will deliver its verdict on Rattigan, but in the years since his death, enough of his plays (ranging from *French Without Tears* to—pre-eminently—*The Browning Version*) have received successful (both critically and commercially) revivals to indicate that his place in the living canon of 20th-century drama is assured.

—Richard Foulkes

See also *Volume I* entries on *The Browning Version*; *Separate Tables*.

RAVENSCROFT, Edward. Born in England c.1643. Admitted to the Middle Temple, London, c.1659. Married Frances Stock. Wrote for the Duke's Company at the Dorset Garden Theatre, 1672–76 and 1681, the King's Company at the Theatre Royal, Drury Lane, 1677–79, the United Company, 1683–94, and Thomas Betterton's company at Lincoln's Inn Fields, 1696–97. Date and place of death unknown.

Works

Collections

The Careless Lovers; The Canterbury Guests, edited by Edmund S. Henry. 1987.

Stage Works

The Citizen Turned Gentleman, from a play by Molière (produced Dorset Garden Theatre, London, 1672). 1673; as *Mamamouchi*, 1675.
The Careless Lovers (produced Dorset Garden Theatre, London, 1673). 1673.
The Wrangling Lovers; or, The Invisible Mistress (produced Dorset Garden Theatre, London, 1676). 1677.
Scaramouche a Philosopher, Harlequin a School-Boy, Bravo, Merchant and Magician (produced Theatre Royal, Drury Lane, 1677). 1678.
The English Lawyer, from a Latin play by George Ruggle (produced Theatre Royal, Drury Lane, London, 1677). 1678.
King Edgar and Alfreda (produced Theatre Royal, Drury Lane, London, 1677). 1677.
Titus Andronicus; or The Rape of Lavinia, from the play by

Shakespeare (produced Theatre Royal, Drury Lane, London, 1679). 1687.
The London Cuckolds (produced Dorset Garden Theatre, London, 1681). 1682.
Dame Dobson; or, The Cunning Woman, from a play by Thomas Corneille (produced Dorset Garden Theatre, London, 1683). 1684.
The Canterbury Guests; or, A Bargain Broken (produced Theatre Royal, Drury Lane, London, 1694). 1695.
The Anatomist; or, The Sham Doctor (produced Lincoln Inn's Fields Theatre, London, 1696). 1697.
The Italian Husband (produced Lincoln Inn's Fields Theatre, London, 1697). 1698.

* * *

It is quite clear from Ravenscroft's first play, *The Citizen Turned Gentleman*, that he aimed at entertainment rather than edification. His plays were never acceptable to the critical establishment, although the best of them were enormously popular with the audiences of his day. Ravenscroft was roundly criticized for indecency, plagiarism, and absurdity. This negative assessment of his work persists. John Wilcox remarks of *The Citizen Turned Gentleman* that "Molière furnished the striking situations, the theatrical effectiveness of the details, and whatever originality remains in the characters. In this play Ravenscroft started a long career of totally uninspired adaptation of others' plays" (*The Relation of Molière to Restoration Comedy*). Even Wilcox confesses, however, that Ravenscroft had an excellent sense of what was theatrically effective.

The Citizen Turned Gentleman is an extremely diverting play. Recognizing that the English stage demanded a multiplicity of actions, Ravenscroft effectively combined elements of two plays by Molière, *Le Bourgeois Gentilhomme* and *Monsieur de Pourceaugnac*, successfully transposing them into an English setting, and pulled off a spectacular final act. "I must admit", Robert Hume comments, "that if I wanted an evening's fun, I would far rather see a spirited production of *The Citizen Turned Gentleman* than any performance imaginable of Wycherley's *Gentleman Dancing Master* (1672). Not surprisingly, this was the verdict of the Carolean audience too".

Although he professed in the Prologue to *The Careless Lovers* that "all that's in it is extempore wit", Ravenscroft's second play, like his first, derives in part from Molière. Two couples are contrasted, the normative "Platonic" lovers, Lovell and Jacinta, and the libertine "gay couple", Careless and Hillaria, who are closely related to Dryden's Celadon and Florimell in *Secret Love*. Like them they engage in a battle of wits, and are given a proviso scene which prefigures that between Mirabell and Millamant in Congreve's *The Way of the World*.

The Wrangling Lovers, an undistinguished Spanish intrigue play set in Toledo, was followed by the far more innovative *Scaramouche a Philosopher* in which Ravenscroft exploited the craze for commedia dell 'arte, fostered by the visits of Tiberio Fiorilli and his Italian troupe to London in the mid-1670's. The play was based on Molière's *Les Fourberies de Scapin*, and Ravenscroft complained bitterly about the long delays in production which resulted in Otway's *The Cheats of Scapin* anticipating his own play by several months. The two plays, as Sutherland points out, started a minor theatrical fashion: Harlequin and Scaramouche appeared in subsequent productions by Aphra Behn and William Mountfort at the Dorset Garden Theatre.

In the tragicomedy *King Edgar and Alfreda*, Ravenscroft

added to his central plot two additional love interests: Alfreda's brother Aldernald woos Princess Matilda, and Durzo, a "blunt sea captain", pursues Hillaria, a court lady. This play was followed in the same year by *The English Lawyer*, an adaptation of George Ruggle's Latin comedy *Ignoramus* (1615). In 1679, Ravenscroft presented, again at Drury Lane, his adaptation of Shakespeare's *Titus Andronicus*.

Ravenscroft returned to Dorset Garden with *The London Cuckolds* in 1681. Here, in arguably his most successful play, Ravenscroft was particularly well served by his actors. The three aldermen, Doodle, Wiseacres, and Dashwell (the cuckolds in question) were played by three consummate comedians—James Nokes, Cave Underhill, and Antony Leigh. Each believes that his wife has qualities that will keep her faithful: Dashwell thinks his wife pious, Doodle that his wife is a wit, and Wiseacres, like Pinchwife in Wycherley's *The Country Wife*, has married an innocent country girl. The wives are preyed upon by Townley, his less fortunate companion Ramble, and a young merchant, Mr. Loveday. The play is indecent and frenetic: in a characteristic incident Ramble, trapped in a cellar window, has a chamber pot emptied on his head and is blackened and robbed by two passing chimney sweeps. Although it met with critical disapproval—in 1709 Steele referred to it in *The Tatler* as "that heap of vice and absurdity"—Ravenscroft's wild farce was so popular that it was regularly performed on Lord Mayor's day until Garrick put an end to the custom in 1751.

Contemporary objections to the indecency of *The London Cuckolds* may account for the relative restraint of *Dame Dobson; or, The Cunning Woman*, an adaptation of Thomas Corneille's *La Devineresse*, which Ravenscroft ironically called his "recantation play". The critic Hume says of it that Ravenscroft "has some trouble juggling the large number of characters", a problem that he attributes to the general tendency to employ large casts after the theatre companies combined to form the United Company in 1682.

In *The Canterbury Guests*, Ravenscroft plagiarized himself. The characters Lovell, Jacinta, Careless, and Hillaria are taken from *The Careless Lovers*. Durzo, the sea captain, comes directly from *King Edgar and Alfreda*, but the play itself is poorly constructed in comparison with *The Careless Lovers*. *The Anatomist*, Ravenscroft's last venture into farce, is far more successful, and it benefited enormously from being performed with Motteux's masque *The Loves of Mars and Venus* as an afterpiece. In a cut-down version it enjoyed a long career as an afterpiece.

Ravenscroft's final play, *The Italian Husband*, performed by the breakaway company at Lincoln's Inn Fields, is quite different from anything that he had written before. Designed, as he said, "to bring a guilty person to be pity'd in her circumstances", it deals with the Duke Frederico's assassination of his wife, Alouisa, after he has first had her lover killed. It is, in its brutal simplicity, extremely effective.

From 1672 until almost the close of the century Ravenscroft was one of the most popular British playwrights, producing in 1677 plays, and continuing to have original plays performed even during the arid 1680's when very little new work was produced. Blatantly derivative, he was able, nevertheless, to exploit current trends and to produce effective entertainments, the best of which are still capable of captivating a modern audience.

—Colin Wills Visser

READE, Charles. Born in Ipsden, Oxfordshire, England, 8 June 1814. Educated by Mr. Slatter at Rose Hill, near Iffley, 1822–27; at the school of Rev. Hearn in Staines, Middlesex, 1827–29; Magdalen College, Oxford, 1831–35, BA 1835, MA 1838, DCL 1847; entered Lincoln's Inn, London, 1836: called to the bar, 1843; studied medicine in Edinburgh, 1846. Lived with the actress Laura Seymour from 1854 (died 1879). Probationary fellow, 1835–41, Vinerian fellow from 1842, bursar, 1844 (re-elected 1849), Dean of Arts, 1845, and Vice-President, 1851, all at Magdalen College; violin dealer, Birkenhead, 1847, and in Europe, 1848; first-produced play, *The Ladies' Battle* (an adaptation), staged 1851; theatre manager and playwright in London from 1852: manager, Strand Theatre, 1852; joint manager, St. James's Theatre, 1854–55, and Adelphi Theatre, 1870. Died in London, 11 April 1884.

Works

Collections

Works. 17 vols., 1895.
Plays (includes *Masks and Faces; The Courier of Lyons; It's Never Too Late to Mend*), edited by Michael Hammet. 1986.

Stage Works

The Ladies' Battle; or, Un Duel en Amour, from a play by Scribe and Legouvé (produced Olympic Theatre, London, 1851). 1851.
Peregrine Pickle, from the novel by Smollett (produced St. James's Theatre, London, 1854). 1851.
Angelo, from the play by Victor Hugo (produced Olympic Theatre, London, 1851). 1851.
Rachel the Reaper, from a work by George Sand (as *A Village Tale*, produced Strand Theatre, London, 1852; revised version, as *Rachel the Reaper*, produced Queen's Theatre, London, 1874). 1871.
The Lost Husband, from a play by A. Bourgeois (produced Strand Theatre, London, 1852). 1852.
Masks and Faces; or, Before and Behind the Curtain, with Tom Taylor (produced Theatre Royal, Haymarket, London, 1852). 1854.
Gold! (produced Theatre Royal, Drury Lane, London, 1853). 1853.
The Courier of Lyons; or, The Attack upon the Mail, from a work by Moreau, Siraudin, and Delacour (produced Princess Theatre, London, 1854). 1854; as *The Lyons Mail* (produced Lyceum Theatre, London, 1877), 1895.
The King's Rival, with Tom Taylor (produced St. James's Theatre, London, 1854). 1854.
Honour Before Titles; or, Nobs and Snobs (produced St. James's Theatre, London, 1854).
Two Loves and a Life with Tom Taylor (produced Adelphi Theatre, London, 1854). 1854.
Nance Oldfield, from a play by Fournier (as *Art*, produced St. James's Theatre, London, 1855; revised version, as *An Actress by Daylight*, produced St. James's Theatre, London, 1871; as *Nance Oldfield*, produced Olympic Theatre, London, 1883). 1883.
Poverty and Pride from a play by Édouard Brisebarre and Eugène Nus. 1856.
The First Printer, with Tom Taylor (produced Princess Theatre, London, 1856).
The Hypochondriac, from a play by Molière (produced 1858;

as *The Robust Invalid*, produced Adelphi Theatre, London, 1870).   1857.
Le Faubourg Saint-Germain (in French).   1859.
It's Never Too Late to Mend, from his own novel (produced Leeds, 1864).   1865.
The Prurient Prude.   1866.
Dora, from a poem by Tennyson (produced Adelphi Theatre, London, 1867).   1867.
Kate Peyton; or, Jealousy, from his novel *Griffith Gaunt* (as *Griffith Gaunt*, produced 1867; as *Kate Peyton's Lovers*, produced Queen's Theatre, London, 1873).   1872.
The Double Marriage, from a play by August Maquet (produced Queen's Theatre, London, 1867).   1867; revised version (produced Prince of Wales's Theatre, London, 1868).
Foul Play, with Dion Boucicault, from their novel (produced Holborn Theatre, London, 1868).   1871(?); revised by Reade, 1883; revised version, as *Our Seamen* (produced 1874); as *The Scuttled Ship* (produced Olympic Theatre, London, 1877).
The Well-Born Workman; or, A Man of the Day, from his novel *Put Yourself in His Place* (as *Put Yourself in His Place*, produced Leeds, 1870; as *Free Labour*, produced Adelphi Theatre, London, 1870).   1878.
Shilly Shally, from a novel by Anthony Trollope (produced Gaiety Theatre, London, 1872).
The Wandering Heir, from his own novel (produced Amphitheatre, Liverpool, 1873).
Joan, from the novel *That Lass o' Lowrie's* by Frances Hodgson Burnett (produced Amphitheatre, Liverpool, 1878).
The Countess and the Dancer, from a play by Sardou (as *Jealousy*, produced Olympic Theatre, London, 1878; revised version, as *The Countess and the Dancer*, produced Olympic Theatre, London, 1886).   1883.
Drink, from a play by Zola, Busnach, and Gastineau (produced Princess Theatre, London, 1879).
Love and Money, with Henry Pettitt (produced Adelphi Theatre, London, 1882).   1883.
Singleheart and Doubleface, from his novel (produced Princess Theatre, Edinburgh, 1882; as *Double Faces*, produced Olympic Theatre, London, 1883).

Fiction

Peg Woffington.   1853.
Christie Johnstone.   1853.
Clouds and Sunshine; Art: A Dramatic Tale.   1855.
It is Never Too Late to Mend: A Matter of Fact Romance.   1856.
The Course of True Love Never Did Run Smooth (stories).   1857.
Propria Quae Maribus: A Jeu d'Esprit, and The Box Tunnel: A Fact.   1857.
White Lies.   1857; as *Double Marriage; or, White Lies*, 1868.
Cream (stories).   1858.
"A Good Fight" and Other Tales.   1859.
Love Me Little, Love Me Long.   1859.
The Cloister and the Hearth.   1861.
Hard Cash.   1863.
Griffith Gaunt; or, Jealousy.   1866.
Foul Play, with Dion Boucicault.   1868.
Put Yourself in His Place.   1870.
A Terrible Temptation.   1871.
The Wandering Heir.   1872.
A Simpleton.   1873.
The Jilt.   1877.

A Woman-Hater.   1877.
Golden Crowns: Sunday Stories.   1877.
Singleheart and Doubleface.   1882.
"Good Stories of Man" and Other Animals.   1884.
"The Jilt" and Other Stories.   1884.
A Perilous Secret.   1884.
The Picture.   1884.

Other

It is Never Too Late to Mend: Proofs of Its Prison Revelations.   1859.
Monopoly Versus Property.   1860.
The Eighth Commandment.   1860.
To the Editor of the Daily Globe, Toronto: A Reply to Criticism.   1871.
The Legal Vocabulary.   1872.
Cremona Violins.   1873.
A Hero and a Martyr: A True and Accurate Account of the Heroic Feats and Sad Calamity of James Lambert.   1874.
Trade Malice: A Personal Narrative, and The Wandering Heir.   1875.
The Coming Man (letters).   1878.
Dora; or, The History of a Play.   1878.
Readiana: Comments on Current Events.   1883.
Bible Characters.   1888.

*

Bibliographies

M.L. Parrish, *Wilkie Collins and Charles Reade: First Editions*, London, 1940.
Francesco Cordasco and Kenneth Scott, *Collins and Reade: A Bibliography of Critical Notices and Studies*, 1949.

Criticism

Books:
Charles L. Reade and Compton Reade, *Charles Reade: Dramatist, Novelist, Journalist: A Memoir* (2 vols.), London, 1887.
J. Coleman, *Charles Reade as I Knew Him*, London, 1903.
Malcolm Elwin, *Charles Reade: A Biography*, London, 1931.
Elton E. Smith, *Charles Reade*, Boston, 1976.

Articles:
S.M. Smith, "Realism in the Drama of Charles Reade", in *English*, 12, 1958.

*   *   *

Charles Reade is remembered mainly for his novel, *The Cloister and the Hearth*, but in his day he was a prolific and successful dramatist. He thought of himself as a dramatist first and foremost, but his novels survive whereas many of his plays do not. Many were not published in his lifetime, though a few were privately printed: most are lost. Many of his works appeared in both narrative and dramatic versions, which, as previous commentators have noted, makes for bibliographical difficulties.

In 1851 he met the playwright Tom Taylor, who was already established, and they agreed to collaborate. The first play written by Reade and Taylor together was *Masks and Faces*, about the actress Peg Woffington, who rejects the advances of Sir Charles Pomander to accept an invitation from a Mr Vane, unaware that he is married. In revenge, Sir Charles plots the early return of Vane's innocent wife, Mabel, when her husband is entertaining a troupe of actors, who are passed off as gentlefolk. Eventually Mabel discovers, through the agency of Mr Triplet, playwright and portrait painter, that she has been deceived. Mabel is held up for admiration as an angel in the house. The rakish actress is, however, far more appealing than the "good" woman. Peg, having proved herself generous with money (having commissioned Triplet to paint her portrait), proves kind to her lover's wife, telling her, "such as you are the diamonds of the world!!!", and the two women swear eternal sisterhood.

Later Reade took it upon himself to publish a novelisation of the play, which both he and Taylor had worked on, under his own name as *Peg Woffington*.

Reade was perpetually fascinated by the prospect of a sentimental alliance between two women, rivals for the love of the same man. Rivalry is the mainspring of *Two Loves and a Life*, set in the 1745 rebellion. One of the girls persuades the Duke of Cumberland not to execute the object of their rivalry. The plot also reflects Reade's other preoccupation — the priest barred from marriage, with a history of illicit passion.

Like *Peg Woffington, The King's Rival* (also written with Tom Taylor) hinges on sexual intrigue and prurience combined with sanctimonious uplift. Its cast includes Charles II, Nell Gwynne, and that "prince of newsmongers, Sam Pepys". The noble Frances Stewart and Nell Gwynne embrace, Stewart imploring her, "Oh lay that honest heart to mine!", to which Nelly, whose accomplishments include a readiness to quote Milton, replies "I love you . . . I would die to serve you . . .". The King says, "See how empty, how desolate, is this heart of mine. In its better moments it yearns for something to believe in and look up to", while Nelly announces "private friendship must give way to public morality".

Although Reade and Taylor worked together on later plays, the collaboration was not happy: the two angrily rewrote each other's work and quarrelled over denouements. Reade was impervious to advice.

In 1853 he produced a drama, *Gold*, at Drury Lane. In accordance with his usual practice, he converted it into the novel with a purpose, *It's Never too Late to Mend*. The success of the book led to a new play based on the novel, and the play *It's Never Too Late To Mend* was a favourite with dramatic companies until World War I. It is an attack on the inhumanity of the prison system, and the inhumanity of the rich towards the poor, which leads to eviction from cottages, and prison sentences for starving people who steal a few potatoes. Reade anticipated George Bernard Shaw in seeing the theatre as a means of instruction reflecting social problems.

The story is based on a scandal occurring in a Birmingham jail in 1853, where a 15-year-old boy was driven to suicide. The Governor was tried and condemned for abuses. Fry, the prison warder, says "The SYSTEM is a grand SYSTEM, a beautiful SYSTEM, dissolves the carmints into tears, and grinds 'em into bible texts and bone dust; but somehow they do hang themselves SYSTEMATIC, to get out of the SYSTEM . . .". This sub-Dickensian rhetoric is Reade at his best.

Reade's most popular work in his lifetime reflected his social conscience, though even there his passion for social justice was tempered with romantic respect for the squirearchy to which he belonged: his heroes, even when unfortunately circumstanced, tend to be gentlemen born. His greatest commercial success was his last work, an adaptation

of Zola's *L'Assommoir*, under the title *Drink*, performed in 1879. Reade's dialogue rarely rose above the sentimental clichés of melodrama, his plays have much business, but little real action and no character development.

—Valerie Grosvenor Myer

REANEY, James (Crerar). Born in South Easthope, Ontario, Canada, 1 September 1926. Educated at Elmhurst Public School, Easthope Township, Perth County; Central Collegiate Vocational Institute, Stratford, Ontario, 1939–44; University College, Toronto (Epstein award, 1948), BA 1948, MA 1949, graduate study, 1956–58, Ph.D in English 1958. Married Colleen Thibaudeau in 1951; two sons and one daughter. Member of the English Department, University of Manitoba, Winnipeg, 1949–56; professor of English, Middlesex College, University of Western Ontario, London, from 1960; first plays produced 1960; founding editor, *Alphabet* magazine, London, 1960–71; active in little theatre groups in Winnipeg and London: founder, Listeners Workshop, London, 1966; collaborated with Keith Turnbull and the NDWT Theatre Company, Toronto, 1972–82. Recipient: Governor-General's Award, for poetry, 1950, 1959, 1963, for drama, 1963; University of Western Ontario President's Medal, 1955, 1958; Massey Award, 1960; Chalmers Award, 1975, 1976. D.Litt: Carleton University, Ottawa, 1975. Officer, Order of Canada, 1975; Fellow, Royal Society of Canada, 1978.

Works

Collections

"The Killdeer" and Other Plays (includes *The Sun and the Moon; One-Man Masque; Night-Blooming Cereus*). 1962.
Masks of Childhood (includes *The Easter Egg; Three Desks*; revised version of *The Killdeer*), edited by Brian Parker. 1972.
"Apple Butter" and Other Plays for Children (includes *Apple Butter; Names and Nicknames; Ignoramus; Geography Match*). 1973.
The Donnellys: A Trilogy (includes *Sticks and Stones; The St. Nicholas Hotel; Handcuffs*). 1983.

Stage Plays

Night-Blooming Cereus, music by John Beckwith (broadcast 1959; produced Hart House Theatre, Toronto, 1960). In *"The Killdeer" and Other Plays*, 1962.
One-Man Masque (produced Hart House Theatre, Toronto, 1960). In *"The Killdeer" and Other Plays*, 1962.
The Killdeer (produced Coach House Theatre, Toronto, 1960). In *"The Killdeer" and Other Plays*, 1962; revised version (produced Stage Campus '70, Vancouver, 1970), in *Masks of Childhood*, 1972.
The Easter Egg (produced Coach House Theatre, Toronto, 1962). In *Masks of Childhood*, 1972.
The Sun and the Moon (produced Oasis Restaurant Theatre, London, Ontario, 1965). In *"The Killdeer" and Other Plays*, 1962.

Developmental workshop at the University of Western Ontario for *Wacousta!* by **James Reaney** (1980–81).

Names and Nicknames (for children; produced Manitoba Theatre Centre, Winnipeg, 1963). 1969.
Aladdin and the Magic Lamp; Apple Butter; Little Red Riding Hood (puppet plays; produced Western Fall Fair, 1965). *Apple Butter* in *"Apple Butter" and Other Plays*, 1973.
Let's Make a Carol (for children), music by Alfred Kunz. 1965.
Ignoramus (for children; produced London, Ontario, 1966). In *Apple Butter and Other Plays*, 1973.
Listen to the Wind (produced Althouse College, London, Ontario, 1966). 1972.
The Canada Tree (produced Morrison Island, Ontario, 1967).
Colours in the Dark (for children; produced Avon Theatre, Stratford, Ontario, 1967). 1970.
Geography Match (for children; produced by school students, London, Ontario, 1967). In *Apple Butter and Other Plays*, 1973.
Three Desks (produced Grand Theatre, London, Ontario, 1967). In *Masks of Childhood*, 1972.

Don't Sell Mr. Aesop (produced London, Ontario, 1968).
Genesis (produced London, Ontario, 1968).
Masque, with Ron Cameron (produced Toronto, 1972). 1974.
All the Bees and All the Keys, music by John Beckwith (for children; produced Toronto, 1972). 1976.
Sticks and Stones (produced Tarragon Theatre, Toronto, 1973). 1975.
The St. Nicholas Hotel (produced Tarragon Theatre, Toronto, 1974). 1976.
Handcuffs (produced Tarragon Theatre, Toronto, 1975). 1977.
Baldoon, with C.H. Gervais (produced Bathurst Street Theatre, Toronto, 1976). 1976.
The Dismissal; or, Twisted Beards and Tangled Whiskers (produced Hart House Theatre, Toronto, 1977). 1979.
The Death and Execution of Frank Halloway; or, The First Act of John Richardson's Wacousta (produced Calgary, Alberta, 1977). In *Jubilee 4*, 1978; complete version, as

Wacousta! (produced General Amherst High School, Amherstburg, 1978), 1979.
At the Big Carwash (puppet play; produced Armstrong, British Columbia, 1979).
King Whistle! (produced Avon Theatre, Stratford, 1979). In *Brick 8*, Winter 1980.
Antler River (produced Grand Theatre, London, Ontario, 1980).
Gyroscope (produced Tarragon Theatre, Toronto, 1981). 1983.
The Shivaree (opera), music by John Beckwith (produced St. Lawrence Centre, Toronto, 1982).
I, the Parade (produced Humanities Theatre, Waterloo, Ontario, 1982).
The Canadian Brothers, from a novel by John Richardson (produced Reeve Theatre, Calgary, Alberta, 1983). In *Major Plays of the Canadian Theatre 1934–1984*, edited by Richard Perkyns, 1984.
Take the Big Picture (for children; produced 1986).
Crazy to Kill, music by John Beckwith (produced Guelph Spring Festival, Guelph, Ontario, 1989).
Serinette, music by Harry Somers (produced 1990).

Radio Plays

Night-Blooming Cereus, 1959; *Wednesday's Child*, 1962; *Canada Dash, Canada Dot* (3 parts), music by John Beckwith, 1965–67.

Verse

The Red Heart.   1949.
A Suit of Nettles.   1958.
Twelve Letters to a Small Town.   1962.
The Dance of Death at London, Ontario.   1963.
Poems, edited by Germaine Warkentin.   1972.
Selected Shorter [and *Longer*] *Poems* (2 vols.), edited by Germaine Warkentin.   1975–76.
Imprecations: The Art of Swearing.   1984.
Performance.   1990.

Other

The Boy with an "R" in His Hand (for children).   1965.
14 Barrels from Sea to Sea (journal of theatre tour).   1977.
Take the Big Picture (for children).   1986.

*

Criticism

Books:
Alvin A. Lee, *James Reaney*, New York, 1968.
Ross G. Woodman, *James Reaney*, Toronto, 1971.
Mavor Moore, *4 Canadian Playwrights*, Toronto, 1973.
J. Stewart Reaney, *James Reaney*, Toronto, 1977.
Stan Dragland (ed.), *Approaches to the Work of James Reaney*, Downsview, Ontario, 1983.
Gerald D. Parker, *How to Play: The Theatre of James Reaney*, Toronto, 1991.

Articles:
Louis Dudek, "The Problem of Meaning: The Plays of James Reaney", in *Canadian Literature*, 59, 1974.
Mary Barr, "James Reaney and the Tradition of Poetic Drama", in *Canadian Drama*, 2, 1976.

James Reaney special issue of *Essays on Canadian Writing*, 24–25, 1982–83.

*   *   *

Before turning to playwriting in the 1960's Reaney had already won two Governor General's Awards for two volumes of poetry, *The Red Heart* and *A Suit of Nettles*. All his plays are marked by a sense of poetic fancy and an imaginative use of words. Indeed, in his first play, *One-Man Masque*, he took eight of his own poems which dealt with childhood, adolescence and sex, old age, death, apocalypse, Armageddon, and childhood rediscovered, and combined them with (in his own words) "a series of comic and macabre monologues to be performed in between the poems". The result is a striking piece of theatre. But *The Killdeer, The Easter Egg, The Sun and the Moon*, and *Listen to the Wind* are marred by melodramatic plots and far-fetched situations. In *The Killdeer*, for example, a female prisoner, accused of murder, is made pregnant by the hero to save her from the gallows; Madame Fay is unmasked in a final courtroom scene; Dr. Ballard is a *deus ex machina* who resolves the play's mysteries.

Colours in the Dark continues, in terms of theme and technique, and on a more complex scale, what Reaney had dealt with in *One-Man Masque*. *Colours* dispenses almost entirely with conventional structure and with traditional plot and characterization. A "playbox" of impressions, the play is given structure by the letters of the alphabet, the books of the Bible, and the seasons, which elements are used to develop the play's theme—a Fall and possible redemption. Another key structural element linking the play's multiple incidents and the rapid switches from mood to mood is the poetry, Reaney's own published poems, which are deployed throughout the play and which are themselves given coherence by the central "Existence" poem. First produced at Canada's Stratford Festival in 1967, *Colours in the Dark* is Reaney's finest play.

Reaney is best known for his Donnelly trilogy—*Sticks and Stones, The St. Nicholas Hotel*, and *Handcuffs*—about the 1880 murder of members of a notorious south-western Ontario family. What is striking about the trilogy is the way in which Reaney combines folktales, history, myth, multiple role-playing, dancing, mime, and a wide variety of ingenious theatrical devices and technique. When he is at his best Reaney is able to dramatize large symbolic patterns of life and death while presenting a documentary-type panorama of rural Canadian life; however, because the trilogy deals with so many incidents and covers a 36-year period, the action sometimes becomes too diffuse, the styles too various, and the characterization too one-dimensional.

Reaney's work in the theatre since the Donnelly trilogy has been marked by the same concern to dramatize Ontarian and Canadian subject matter, although none of these plays has gained popular or critical success. *Baldoon*, for example, tells of the attempt of a witch-finder to account for ghostly apparitions in the 1830's Ontario settlement of Baldoon; *Wacousta!* and *The Canadian Brothers* dramatize two melodramatic 19th-century novels by Major John Richardson.

Reaney's many plays for children reveal also that he is a profound believer in art as collaboration, since many of the plays grew out of workshops conducted with children.

Reaney's influence on Canadian theatre has been considerable. He has taken great risk in developing an unconventional dramaturgy that seeks to relate the arcane and the popular; he has championed the virtues of regionalism as opposed to "international" art; and, influenced by Northrop Frye, he has explored archetypal patterns of birth and death, of innocence and experience, with courage and great intelligence.

—Eugene Benson

See also *Volume 1* entry on *The Donnelly Plays*.

RÉGIO, José. Born José Maria dos Reis Pereira, in Vila do Conde, Portugal, 17 September 1901. Educated at Oporto Grammar School; studied Romance languages at Coimbra University, 1919–25. First volume of poetry published, 1925; co-founder, with B. da Fonseca and J.G. Somoes, and managing editor, the influential literary periodical *Presença*, 1927–40; spent most of his life in Portalegre, teaching at the local grammar school. Died in Vila do Conde, 22 December 1969.

Works

Collections

Primereo Volume de Teatro (includes *Jacob e o ango; Três Máscaras; Postfacio*).   1940.
Três Peças em um Acto (includes *Três Máscaras; O Meu Caso; Mário ou Eu Próprio, o Outro*).   1957.
Obras Completas.   1964–69; revised edition, 1971.

Stage Works

Jacob e o Anjo (produced Studio des Champs-Élysées, Paris, 1952; produced in Portugal, 1968). In *Revista de Portugal*, edited by Vitorino Nemésio, 1937; in book form, in *Primeiro Volume de Teatro*, 1940.
Três Máscaras.   In *Primeiro Volume de Teatro*, 1940; revised version, in *Três Peças em um Acto*, 1957.
Postfácio.   In *Primeiro Volume de Teatro*, 1940.
Benilde; ou, A Virgem-Mãe (produced Teatro Naçional, Lisbon, 1947).   1947.
El-rei Sebastião.   1949.
A Salvação do Mundo (produced Teatro São Luis, Lisbon, 1971).   1954.
O Meu Caso.   In *Três Peças em um Acto*, 1957.
Mário; ou, Eu-próprio, o Actro.   In *Três Peças em um Acto*, 1957.

Fiction

Jogo de Cabra Cega.   1934.
Davam Grandes Passeis aos Domingos.   1941.
O Principe Com Orelas de Burro.   1942.
A Velha Casa (5 vols.).   1945–66:
Uma Gota de Sangue.   1945.
As Raízes do Futuro.   1947.
Os Avisos do Destino.   1953.
As Monstruosidades Vulgares.   1960.
Vidas São Vidas.   1966.
Histórias de Mulheres.   1946.
Há Mais Mundos (stories).   1962.
"O Vestido Cor de Fogo" e Outras Histórias.   1972?

Verse

Poemas de Deus e do Diablo.   1925.
Biografia. 1929; revised edition, 1939.

As Encruzilhadas de Deus.   1935/36.
Fado.   1941.
Mas Deus é Grande.   1945.
Filho do Homem.   1961.

Other

Críticos e Criticados.   1936.
António Botto e o Amor.   1937/38.
Em Torno da Expressao Artística.   1940.
Peguena História da Moderna Poesia Portuguesa.   1941.
Introduction a Texeira de Pascoães.   1953.
Estética Presencista, with João Gaspa Simoes.   Nd.

Editor, *As Mais Belas Líricas Portuguesas.*   1944.
Editor, *Luís de Camões.*   1944.
Editor, with Alberto de Serpa, *Poesia de Amor.*   1945.
Editor, with Alberto de Serpa, *Alma Minha Gentil.*   1957.
Editor, with Alberto de Serpa, *Na Mao de Deus.*   1958.

*

Criticism

Books:
Luciana Stegagno Picchio, *História do Teatro Português*, Lisbon, 1968.
Alvaro Ribeiro, *A Literatura de José Régio*, Lisbon, 1969.
In Memoiriam de José Régio, Oporto, 1970.
Eugénio Lisboa, *José Régio: A Obra e o Homem*, Lisbon, 1976.
Duarte Faria, *Metamorfoses do Fantástico na Obra de José Régio*, Paris, 1977.
Jorge de Sena, *Régio, Casais, a "Presença" e Outros Afins*, Oporto, 1977.
Eugénio Lisboa, *José Régio: Um Literatura Viva*, Lisbon, 1978.
Eugénio Lisboa, *José Régio ou a Confissão relutante*, Lisbon, 1988.

* * *

Although better known for his poetry and fiction, Régio himself considered that it was as a dramatist that he produced his most original work. He began writing for the stage in 1934, with the one-act play *Três Máscaras* (Three Masks) a "dramatic fantasy", published first in *Presença*. It appeared in a revised version in 1957 together with two other one-act plays—*O Meu Caso* (My Case), the only farce he wrote, and *Mário; ou, Eu-próprio o Outro* (Mário; or My-Self the Other), a "tragic-comic episode" dramatising the suicide of the poet Mário de Sá-Carneiro. "Three Masks", introduces the theme of the mask, as a means of liberation from reality. Though they are unable to communicate directly with each other, through their rôle playing the three characters reveal their true identities.

Although José Régio is probably the best Portuguese playwright of his time his plays have been very little performed. *Jacob e o Anjo* (Jacob and the Angel) was not staged in Portugal until 1968, 30 years after it had been written. Previously it had been produced in Paris in 1952 in the Champs-Élysées studio. *Benilde; ou, A Virgem-Mãe* (Benilde; or, The Virgin-Mother) was performed in Lisbon by the National Theatre in 1947 and in the Graça Theatre in 1990. *A Salvação do Mundo* (The Salvation of the World) was staged in Lisbon in 1971 at the St. Luis Theatre. During Salazar's dictatorship (1932–68) the only plays which were allowed to be staged were either sentimental or naturalistic melodramas, burlesque or musical productions.

Régio's theatre is regarded as being outside the mainstream of Portuguese drama. His principal artistic debt is to the theatre of Claudel and Pirandello as well as to the German expressionist theatre. *Jacob e o Anjo*, categorised by the author as a mystery in three acts with prologue and epilogue, appeared first in 1937 in *Revista de Portugal*, edited by Vitorino Nemésio. Régio's play dramatizes the history of King Afonso VI who reigned in Portugal from 1656–67, was mentally unstable, and made a disastrous marriage in 1666 to the Duchess of Nemours. Soon the Queen started a liaison with Pedro, Afonso's brother, and began conspiring with him against her husband. The marriage was annulled by the Pope and in 1668 the Cortes deposed Afonso. The Queen married Pedro and Afonso was exiled at first to the Azores and, after an attempted uprising to install him as King again, he was imprisoned in a palace in Sintra where he died suddenly in 1693. This plot-material had already been used by D. João da Câmara in 1890, for his five-act historical play in verse, *Afonso VI*.

Régio, however, is not concerned with historical truth. *Jacob e o Anjo* is an allegorical story of a King who is robbed of the throne and of his wife and who is abandoned by all, including his trusted minister. The play opens as the King is wrestling with the Angel, which recalls Genesis, Chapter 33, verse 24: "And Jacob was left alone; and there wrestled a man with him until the breaking of the day". The Angel is personified in the figure of a court jester. Like Pirandello's Henry IV, King Afonso is considered mad, but he seems at times to be more lucid and clairvoyant than those who conspire against him. He is surrounded by traitors who try to excuse and rationalise their treason, but he sees clearly through them. He is a tortured man, fighting his demons, humiliated by wife, brother and courtiers. He, himself, humiliates and cruelly mistreats those who have loved and trusted him. His quest is a search for an absolute, for grace. According to Régio, grace is only attained through great pain and it is through the mortification of body and soul that the King finds peace. He both fears and loves the Angel, but it is only through him that he finally reaches a state of grace. The King's conflict is an inner conflict—the Angel tells him that all human tragedy stems from the fact "that no human being can belong to or possess another human being".

Like *Jacob*, *Benilde* is also a mystical play. It is a three-act drama telling the story of a young girl convinced that she is a new Virgin Mary. The plot is very simple. Benilde becomes pregnant and believes that it happened because of divine intervention. She is the daughter of a mystic mad woman. She has been educated by her father in a mansion, almost in complete seclusion. Sometimes, at night, she would go into the garden, in a somnambulist state, attracted by the howls of a fool. Her pregnancy may, therefore, be explained in a natural way and both her doctor and her aunt Etelvina, mother of her fiancé Eduardo, believe in a natural explanation. However the priest believes in Benilde's sincerity, and so eventually does Eduardo, who asks her to marry him. Benilde refuses, because she feels that she belongs to God. Benilde is mad according to our world, but is shown to be spiritually pure and to have achieved a state of grace. As in all Régio's plays the themes here concern the duality of good and evil, spirit and matter, and are related to man's quest for God. Oscar Lopes compares the language of *Benilde* for its natural dignity and beauty with that of Garrett's *Frei Luis de Sousa*. *Jacob e o Anjo* and *Benilde* are Régio's finest plays and have rightly been considered by Jorge de Sena as two masterpieces of modern Portuguese theatre.

El-rei Sebastião (King Sebastian), a "spectacular poem" in three acts, uses a subject often treated in Portuguese literature—the myth of Sebastianism, or messianism. Régio portrays a visionary king, searching for an absolute which can only be found in death. Sebastian believes that he can redeem himself through a crusade against the Moors. His mother, Queen Catarina, and his councillors speak for common sense and advise against it. The King leads his people against the Moors in pursuit of a mad dream of glory, but dies in the battle, destroying also the country's independence. Nevertheless Sebastian survives in spirit to become a symbol for the Portuguese people, the new Messiah, who will one day save Portugal.

A Salvação do Mundo (The World's Salvation), a tragicomedy in three acts, dramatises the story of the prince with donkey's ears, the message of which is that the world does not wish to be saved.

Régio's plays demand a poetic response from the reader or audience to an essentially lyrical expression of the characters' fantasies, fears, and hopes. There is a poignancy about his principal characters, who are locked within themselves, living their mad dreams and struggling in their quest for an absolute. Régio makes use of music, ballet, and pantomine, and even though some of his plays are perhaps rhetorical, they are nonetheless powerful dramatic creations.

—Maria Guterres

REGNARD, Jean-François. Born in Paris; baptised 8 February 1655. Travelled to Italy, and possibly Constantinople, 1674–75; captured by pirates, 1678, and imprisoned in Algiers until ransomed for 12,000 livres, 1679; travelled to Flanders, Holland, Denmark, Sweden, and Lappland, 1681–82; became Treasurer of France, 1683; involved in the theatre, c.1688–1709: wrote plays initially for the Comédie-Italienne, Paris, 1690–95, and for the Comédie-Française, Paris, from 1695; purchased the Château and estate of Grillon, near Dourdan, Seine-et-Oise, 1699; held posts as "Grand Bailli" of the province of Hurepoix and "Lieutenant des eaux et des chasses" (regulating hunting and fishing) for the Forest of Dourdan, 1700. Died at the Château of Grillon, 4 September 1709.

Works

Collections

Oeuvres (2 vols.).   1708; augmented edition (5 vols.), 1731.
Oeuvres complètes (2 vols.), edited by M. Beuchot.   1854.
Oeuvres complètes, edited by E. Fournier.   1875.
Le Joueur; Le Distrait; Les Folies amoureuses; Les Ménechmes; Le Légataire universel.   1904.
Théâtre choisi, edited by G. Roth   1913.
Comédies du théâtre italien de Regnard, edited by A. Calame.   1981.

Stage Works

Le Divorce (produced Comédie-Italienne, Paris, 1688).   In *Théâtre italien*, 1694.

Arlequin, Homme à bonne fortune (produced Comédie-Italienne, Paris, 1690). In *Théâtre italien*, 1694.

Les Filles errantes (produced Comédie-Italienne, Paris, 1690). In *Théâtre italien 3*, 1700.

La Coquette; ou, L'Académie des dames (produced Comédie-Italienne, Paris, 1691). In *Théâtre italien 3*, 1700.

Les Chinois, with Charles Dufresny (produced Comédie-Italienne, Paris, 1693). Third act, as *La Baguette de Vulcain*, in *Théâtre italien*, Paris, 1694; complete, in *Théâtre italien 4*, 1700.

Attendez-moi sous l'orme (produced Comédie-Française, Paris, 1693). 1694.

Le Bourgeois de Falaise. 1694.

La Naissance d'Amadis (produced Comédie-Italienne, Paris, 1694). In *Théâtre italien 5*, 1694.

La Sérénade (produced Comédie-Française, Paris, 1694). 1695.

La Foire Saint-Germain, with Charles Dufresny (produced Comédie-Italienne, Paris, 1695). In *Théâtre italien 6*, 1700.

Les Momies d'Égypte, with Charles Dufresny (produced Comédie-Italienne, Paris, 1696). In *Théâtre italien 6*, 1700.

Mezzetin aux Enfers (produced Comédie-Italienne, Paris, 1696). In *Théâtre italien*, 1700.

Le Bal (produced Comédie-Française, Paris, 1696).

Le Joueur (produced Comédie-Française, Paris, 1696). 1697.

Le Distrait (produced Comédie-Française, Paris, 1697). 1698.

Le Carnaval de Venise, music by André Campra (ballet scenario; produced Théâtre de l'Opéra, Paris, 1699). 1699.

Démocrite (produced Comédie-Française, Paris, 1700). 1700.

Le Retour imprévu (produced Comédie-Française, Paris, 1700). 1700.

Les Folies amoureuses (produced Comédie-Française, Paris, 1704). 1704.

Les Ménechmes (produced Comédie-Française, Paris, 1705). 1706.

Le Légataire universel (produced Comédie-Française, Paris, 1708). 1708.

La Critique du Légataire (produced Comédie-Française, Paris, 1708). 1708.

Les Vendages; ou, Le Bailli d'Asnières. In *Oeuvres*, 1731.

Les Souhaits. In *Ouevres*, 1731.

Sapor. In *Ouevres*, 1731.

Other

La Satire contre les maris. 1694.

Voyages. 1731.

Voyage de Regnard en Flandre, en Hollande, en Danemark et en Suède, edited by A. de Marsy. 1874

Voyage de Laponie, edited by A. Lepage. 1875.

Voyage de Normandie, edited by G. Bourbon. 1883.

La Provençale. With *La Satire contre les maris*, edited by E. Pilon, 1920.

*

Bibliographies

Compaignon de Marcheville, *Bibliographie et iconographie des oeuvres de Jean-François Regnard*, Paris, 1877.

Criticism

Books:

F. Guyot, *Le Poète Jean-François Regnard en son Château de Grillon*, Paris, 1907.

André Halleys, *Regnard*, Paris, 1929.

G. Jamati, *La Querelle du "Joueur": Regnard et Dufresny*, Paris, 1936.

A. Calame, *Regnard, sa vie et son oeuvre*, Paris, 1960.

D.-M. Medlin, *The Verbal Art of Jean-François Regnard*, New Orleans, 1966.

* * *

Dramatic historians no longer automatically cite Jean-François Regnard as France's second greatest comic dramatist, and it is remarkable to note how spectacularly his standing has plummeted in the present century, to a point where it is sometimes alleged that his theatre, though exhibiting wit and verve, lacks both dramatic craftsmanship and the social comment or depth of character-study that distinguish major comedy.

Regnard began his dramatic career by writing for the Italian actors who performed in Paris in the late-17th century. Although his plays—some written in collaboration with Charles Dufresny—were in French, they were pretexts for the inclusion of large amounts of the kind of comedy for which the Italians were best known, the prime features of which were exaggerated gestures and other visual devices, mimicry, parody, stock characters, and above all improvisation. Rational continuity of plot or characterization was scarcely important. Later, Regnard transferred his allegiance to the rival company of French actors, and it is upon his work for them that his reputation rests. His previous experience had a telling influence on his style and dramatic technique, and the success of his short plays is explained principally by their Italianate vivacity. His longer plays—many of them in verse, a medium which other comic dramatists had by Regnard's time virtually abandoned—also display the other aspects of his varied achievement.

For subject matter, he often sought material of immediate contemporary significance. *Le Légataire universel* (The Sole Heir) illustrates the financial greed and corruption of the early years of the 18th century. *Le Joueur* (The Gambler), written when Paris society was in the grip of gambling fever, portrays the efforts of the wastrel Valère to obtain money to pay for his vice. After an acrimonious interview with his father, who urges him to marry and pay off his debts, Valère is reconciled with Angélique, and promptly pawns for its valuable frame the portrait she gives him as a token of her love. The action is enlivened by Valère's cynical valet, Hector, and by a false marquis who courts Angélique's sister, the Countess, but is rejected when he is unmasked as a commoner. The dull but upright Dorante wins Angélique when she renounces Valère, who, none too heartbroken, decides to console himself by gambling. The countess's attempts to make herself look young and the exaggerated behaviour of the transparently fraudulent marquis provide visual humour, as do Crispin's disguises in *Le Légataire universel*.

In these plays, as in others such as *Démocrite* and *Les Ménechmes* (The Menechme Twins), the dialogue, much of it lively repartee, is laced with puns, absurdly extended metaphors, and verbal parody. The abundant visual and verbal humour of Regnard's theatre creates an air of fantasy and absurdity which extends to the characters and their relationships with each other. This atmosphere is often so overwhelming that, despite the contemporary subject matter, realism appears less important than the inducement of laughter by whatever means the playwright's vivid and imaginative inspiration could devise, and it is in turn sustained by the momentum of its own dotty logic. Thus, in *Le Légataire universel*, having accepted Crispin's ability to fool Géronte by means of various improbable disguises, one is not dismayed when a further disguise solves the problem which confronts the conspirators when Géronte appears to die intestate. Moreover, so unlikely are the situations that Regnard frequently creates additional comedy by having characters point out absurdities, yet still ignore the evidence of their senses. Géronte knows he is being deceived but, carried along by the crazy logic of the situation, eventually assists in his own defeat.

Regnard considered himself a writer of comedy of character in the tradition of Molière, but his achievement cannot fairly be said to lie in that quarter. In *Le Distrait* (The Absent-Minded Lover) it is not the absent-mindedness of Léandre which affords the greatest interest, but the wit of the dialogue, the absurdity of the situations, and the acuteness of the social comment. In *Le Joueur*, Valère feels no sense of guilt or shame, and is never seen trying to reconcile his conflicting passions. When Angélique rejects him, it is not finally because of his gambling but because of his untrustworthiness as a lover. In *Le Légataire universel*, the role of Éraste has the makings of a character study, for Éraste's apparently unscrupulous determination to become his uncle's heir is at first tinged by the genuine feeling he has for the old man. All this is swept away, however, by Crispin's machinations, which constitute the major interest of the play. Éraste, in the last analysis, proves yet again that Regnard's characters are not so much psychological studies as pretexts for social comment and for the improbable intrigue and witty use of language that were his hallmarks.

Nonetheless, Regnard possessed more than the talent to depict his age, and his lightness of touch should not be mistaken for lack of depth. His social comment is perspicacious and often biting. The foppish Chevalier in *Le Distrait* provides a pointed example of a particular phenomenon frequently satirized by Regnard—the young wastrels and parasites whose presence in Paris society was an embarrassment to all, not least to their own families. Valère, another from the same mould, also embodies a sharp satire on gambling mania. Moreover, however exaggerated and farcical the portrayal of the boasting but cowardly marquis may be, the abuse of titles was endemic and the authorities frequently sought to suppress it, not least because of the tax privileges claimed by the nobility. These and other examples make Regnard the foremost exponent, in a general sense, of *comédie de moeurs* (social comedy), even though, as it happens, he was not responsible for the greatest masterpiece of the genre, the *Turcaret* of Alain-René Lesage. At the same time, his irrepressible gaiety and feeling for the absurd and the fantastic render him less the heir of Molière than of Paul Scarron, Raymond Poisson, and Philippe Quinault, whose influence he himself acknowledged.

—William Brooks

RICE, Elmer. Born Elmer Leopold Reizenstein in New York City, 28 September 1892. Educated at a high school in

Elmer Rice

New York to age 14; earned high school diploma and studied law in night school, LL.B (cum laude), New York Law School, 1912; admitted to New York bar, 1913. Married 1) Hazel Levy in 1915 (divorced 1942), one son and one daughter; 2) the actress Betty Field in 1942 (divorced 1956), two sons and one daughter; 3) Barbara A. Marshall in 1966. Claims clerk, Samstag and Hilder Brothers, New York, 1907; law clerk, 1908–14; began writing and producing for the theatre, 1914; first play, *On Trial*, produced 1914; dramatic director, University Settlement, 1915–16, and Chairman, Inter-Settlement Dramatic Society, New York; scenarist, Samuel Goldwyn Pictures Corporation, Hollywood, 1918–20; freelance writer for Famous Players, the Lasky Corporation, and Real Art Films, Hollywood, 1920; lived in Paris, 1928–30; returned to New York and organized the Morningside Players, with Hatcher Hughes; purchased and operated the Belasco Theatre, New York, 1934–37; regional director, Federal Theatre Project (Works Progress Administration), New York, 1935–36; founder, with Robert E. Sherwood, Maxwell Anderson, S.N. Behrman, Sidney Howard, and John F. Wharton, Playwrights Company, 1938; lecturer in English, University of Michigan, Ann Arbor, 1954; adjunct professor of English, New York University, 1957–58. President, Dramatists Guild, 1939–43, and Authors League of America, 1945–46; International Vice-President, and Vice-President of the New York Center, PEN, 1945–46. Recipient: Pulitzer Prize, 1929. Litt. D: University of Michigan, 1961. Member, American Academy. Died in Southampton, England, 8 May 1967.

Works

Collections

Three Plays Without Words (includes *Landscape with Figures; Rus in Urbe; Exterior*). 1934.
Seven Plays (includes *On Trial; The Adding Machine; Street Scene; Counsellor-at-Law; Judgement Day; Two on an Island; Dream Girl*). 1950.

Stage Works

On Trial (produced Candler Theatre, New York, 1914). 1919.
The Iron Cross (produced Comedy Theatre, New York, 1917). 1965.
The Home of the Free (produced Comedy Theatre, New York, 1917). 1934.
For the Defense (produced Playhouse Theatre, New York, (1919).
Wake Up, Jonathan, with Hatcher Hughes (produced Henry Miller's Theatre, New York, 1921). 1928.
It is the Law, from a novel by Hayden Talbot (produced Ritz Theatre, New York, 1922).
The Adding Machine (produced Garrick Theatre, New York, 1923). 1923.
The Mongrel, from a play by Hermann Bahr (produced Longacre Theatre, New York, 1924).
Close Harmony; or, The Lady Next Door, with Dorothy Parker (produced Gaiety Theatre, New York, 1924). 1929.
Is He Guilty?, from a play by Rudolph Lothar (produced Boston, 1927).
Cock Robin, with Philip Barry (produced 48th Street Theatre, New York, 1928). 1929.
Street Scene (produced Playhouse Theatre, New York, 1929). 1929; revised version, music by Kurt Weill, lyrics by Langston Hughes (produced Adelphi Theatre, New York, 1947), 1948.
The Subway (produced Cherry Lane Theatre, New York, 1929). 1929.
A Diadem of Snow. In *One-Act plays for Stage and Study 5*, edited by Rice, 1929.
See Naples and Die (produced Vanderbilt Theatre, New York, 1929). 1930.
The Left Bank (produced Little Theatre, New York, 1931). 1931.
Counsellor-at-Law (produced Plymouth Theatre, New York, 1931). 1931.
The House in Blind Alley. 1932.
Black Sheep (produced Morosco Theatre, New York, 1932). 1938.
We, The People (produced Empire Theatre, New York, 1933). 1933.
The Gay White Way. In *One-Act Plays for Stage and Study 8*, 1934.
Judgement Day (produced Belasco Theatre, New York, 1934). 1934.
The Passing of Chow-Chow (produced 1934). 1934(?).
Landscape. In *Three Plays Without Words*, 1934.
Rus in Urbe. In *Three Plays Without Words*, 1934.
Exterior. In *Three Plays Without Words*, 1934.
Between Two Worlds (produced Belasco Theatre, New York, 1934). In *Two Plays*, 1935.
Not for Children (produced Fortune Theatre, London, 1935; as *Life is Real*, produced 1937). In *Two Plays*, 1935;

revised version (produced Coronet Theatre, New York, 1951), 1951.
American Landscape (produced Cort Theatre, New York, 1938). 1939.
Two On an Island (produced Broadhurst Theatre, New York, 1940). 1940.
Flight to the West (produced Guild Theatre, New York, 1940). 1941.
A New Life (produced Royale Theatre, New York, 1943). 1944.
Dream Girl (produced Coronet Theatre, New York, 1945). 1946.
The Grand Tour (produced Martin Beck Theatre, New York, 1951). 1952.
The Winner (produced The Playhouse, New York, 1954). 1954.
Cue for Passion (produced Henry Miller's Theatre, New York, 1958). 1959.
Love Among the Ruins (produced University of Rochester, Rochester, New York, 1963). 1963.
Court of Last Resort. 1985.

Screenplays

Help Yourself, with others, 1920; *Rent Free*, with Izola Forrester and Mann Page, 1922; *Doubling for Romeo*, with Bernard McConville, 1922; *Street Scene*, 1931; *Counsellor-at-Law*, 1933; *Holiday Inn*, with Claude Binyon and Irving Berlin, 1942.

Fiction

A Voyage to Purilia. 1930.
Imperial City. 1937.
The Show Must Go On. 1949.

Other

The Supreme Freedom. 1949.
The Living Theatre. 1959.
Minority Report: An Autobiography. 1963.

Editor, *One-Act Plays for Stage and Study 5*. 1929.

*

Criticism

Books:
G. Rablein, *Drama and Commitment*, Bloomington, Indiana, 1964.
R. Hogan, *The Independence of Elmer Rice*, Carbondale, Illinois, 1965.
Frank Durham, *Elmer Rice*, New York, 1970.
Malcolm Goldstein, *The Political Stage*, New York, 1974.
Anthony F.R. Palmieri, *Elmer Rice: A Playwright's Vision of America*, Rutherford (New Jersey) and London, 1980.

Articles:
R.L. Collins, "The Playwright and the Press: Elmer Rice and His Critics", in *Theatre Annual*, 7, 1949.
R. Hogan, "Elmer Rice: The Public Life of a Playwright" (with primary bibliography), in *Modern Drama*, 8, 1966.

* * *

"This concept of man as a social mechanism helplessly

caught in the toils of forces beyond his understanding was to find its way, in one form or another, into many postwar American plays". Rice's observation in *The Living Theatre* is as valid a generalisation about his own extensive dramatic output as it is about the broader American context that he was analysing. It also establishes a set of values which vindicate him in the face of his most recurrent criticism—that whatever his dramatic mode, he failed to create characters in much depth. In a letter to David Sievers, Rice explained that in *The Adding Machine*, his most famous early work, he was depicting "the slave psychology": "the one thing that the slave hates and fears beyond all other things is liberty. For the slave senses unconsciously that authority means not only exemption from thought, but security. The power which enslaves him protects him as well". The trajectories of this Adlerian slave psychology through society are visible in almost all of Rice's work, whether brutally stylised socio-expressionism or realistic Shavian polemics against modern society.

The Adding Machine, more than any other play, established continental expressionism on the New York stage, making it receptive to the more idiosyncratic kinds of stylisation that O'Neill would develop in the 1920's. Its leading theme   is the threatened inferiority of man to the machine, and this is asserted by a severe depersonalisation of the characters, including the main one, indicatively named Mr. Zero. For many of the critics of the 1920's, however, it was difficult to acknowledge depersonalisation as a valid dramatic technique, and there was an insistence that Rice's characters were not mindless robots as in the Čapeks' *R.U.R.*; one critic, in defence of Rice's apparent limitation, went to absurd lengths, arguing that he gives his characters "the breath of life in a dialogue that is homely, sharp, at once American, and with an emotional dimension".

Another machine drama written in the same year, but not produced until 1929, did develop personality as one of the victims of mechanisation: *The Subway* follows the collapse of Sophie Smith in the face of an automated social environment expressed, as in the earlier play, in office terms but also more prominently through the subway itself. Her final suicide under the train is submission to this insuperable antagonist, but the play also amply explores psychological recesses, including her claustrophobia, her masochism, her puritanical guilt, and her erotic flights of fantasy and reality. That the subway may well represent her subconscious is suggested in the second scene, when she steps off the train and is surrounded by men wearing hideous animal masks, closing in on her.

Even before World War I, Rice had produced work that was seen as innovative. *On Trial* is regarded as the first American play to use extensively the flashback technique that would become a commonplace with the cinema, and its production-demands achieved a minor revolution in Broadway stagecraft. A more strident social and political awareness came through the anti-war *The Iron Cross* and the indictment of child labour in (the unproduced) *The House in Blind Alley*, both of which used realism to express issues of immediate social relevance in a manner that would become the dominant style of Rice's maturity.

Street Scene, his most famous work in this mode, deploys a very large cast to achieve something of the "street corner objectivity" that Shaw had prescribed for the new drama in the first decade of the century. Objectivity, however, exists only within the terms of Rice's reformist perspective: American capitalism and its whole economic system are implicitly indicted in numerous ways, such as the presentation

of a "charity" worker. *We, the People* also offers a huge social panorama, with 56 characters and a large number of settings, to illustrate the effects of economic privation. Such a play reflects a belief that the cogency of an argument is dependent on the quantity of supporting data, and this recurs in *Judgement Day*, questioning the justice system, and *Between Two Worlds*, where totalitarianism is attacked in an action set on a transatlantic liner with another very large cast representing many strata of (mainly American) society. *American Landscape* shows a slight change in mood, in that it is patriotic almost to a simplistic degree, but it has some technical interest in the way it mobilises ghosts of the American past to give support to the living. *Flight to the West* is more obviously a war-time work where another transatlantic trip gives the context for dialogue generally against Nazism; this play may with some validity be compared with Shaw's *Heartbreak House*, a parallel which was less plausibly argued in the case of *Between Two Worlds*.

Throughout this period, Rice was also developing a less polemical drama which would later merge with his attempts at commercialism. Sometimes satirically, *The Left Bank* examines the position of American expatriates in Europe, and *Black Sheep* has a similar tone in its presentation of the problems facing the creative writer in America. *Two On an Island* has affinities with *Street Scene*, but is much less intense in its elements of social dissection, and thus reflects Rice's best-known "commercial" play, *See Naples and Die*, a light comedy with an occasional satirical edge but which mainly seems to emulate the repartee of Van Druten or Coward at its most vapid.

There were, however, commercial successes in which Rice did not compromise himself so thoroughly. *Counsellor-at-Law* takes place in a law office in a New York skyscraper, and with a cast of only 28 encapsulates many of the features of his other drama—a broad social panorama, the mechanisation of an office environment, and what Rice termed "the enslavement of a man of good will by careerism and sexual infatuation". Though most of the characters may be seen as expressions of the lawyer's energy, the play is realistic rather than expressionistic and was popular in part because of the well-developed central character. *Dream Girl*, the major success of his last phase, also uses realism to accommodate elements that he would earlier have shaped into pure expressionism in the fantasy life of a "perfectly healthy, normal person". The recurrent critical comparison with Walter Mitty does Rice a disservice; the title character here is highly adventurous in her fantasies, which reflect the world around her.

—Howard McNaughton

See also *Volume 1* entries on *The Adding Machine*; *Street Scene*.

———

RICHARDSON, Jack (Carter). Born in New York City, 18 February 1935. Educated at Columbia University, New York, 1954–57, BA (summa cum laude) in philosophy 1957 (Phi Beta Kappa); University of Munich (Adenauer Fellow), 1958. Served in the US Army, in France and Germany, 1951–54. Married Anne Grail Roth in 1957; one daughter. First-produced play, *The Prodigal*, staged 1960; wrote mainly for the stage before 1965; theatre critic, *Commentary*, from 1966, and for other publications.

Works

Stage Works

The Prodigal (produced Downtown Theatre, New York, 1960). 1960.
Gallows Humor (produced Gramercy Arts Theatre, New York, 1961). 1961.
Lorenzo (produced Plymouth Theatre, New York, 1963).
Xmas in Las Vegas (produced Ethel Barrymore Theatre, New York, 1965). 1966.
As Happy as Kings (produced New Theatre Workshop, New York, 1968).
Juan Feldman. In *Pardon Me, Sir, But is My Eye Hurting Your Elbow?*, edited by Bob Booker and George Foster, 1968.

Fiction

The Prison Life of Harris Filmore. 1961.

Other

Memoir of a Gambler. 1979.

*

Criticism

Books:
Gerald Weales, *The Jumping-Off Place: American Drama in the 1960's*, New York, 1969.

Articles:
Gilbert Debusscher, "Jack Richardson: Dramaturge américain", in *Revue des langues vivantes*, 37, 1971.

*   *   *

At the outset of the 1960's four young playwrights, Edward Albee, Jack Richardson, Arthur Kopit, and Jack Gelber, held the attention of the American theatre as its best prospects for the future since the post-war emergence of Tennessee Williams and Arthur Miller. The four became acquainted, and in the season of 1962–63 they were simultaneously active in the Playwrights' Unit of the Actors' Studio in New York. Jack Richardson's particular position in this rather brilliant quartet was achieved by the success of two splendid plays produced off-Broadway, *The Prodigal*, his retelling in his own contemporary idiom of the Orestes story, and *Gallows Humor*, two linked tragicomic plays in a modern setting. In these plays Richardson stands apart from his three immediate contemporaries for certain defining characteristics unmistakably his own, characteristics that also mark his subsequent and somewhat parallel pair of Broadway plays, *Lorenzo* and *Xmas in Las Vegas*.

The plays, all vividly theatrical, are notable for being intentionally intellectual in the French tradition—somewhat unusual in American drama, although less so perhaps for a graduate in philosophy from Columbia University—and for their almost neo-classical emphasis upon verbal precision and formal control. At the same time, the plays share a conscious concern for previous dramatic materials and conventions—Classical, medieval, Renaissance—and are unified by Richardson's persistent and strongly held view of the human predicament as man's forced participation in a destructive conflict between fundamental opposites: life, individuality, imaginative illusion, but chaos on the one hand; and death, conformity, reality, and order on the other.

The first pair of plays, *The Prodigal* and *Gallows Humor*, are written with an exhilarating wit and a Shavian exuberance hard to find the equivalent of in recent drama in English, and they are contrasting but complementary in method, with the Classically inspired play modern by implication, and the modern by medieval allusion universal or timeless in intent. In the former play Richardson personifies his characteristic and paradoxically grouped opposites in the figures of Aegisthus and Agamemnon. In their conflicting views of man as either lesser or greater than he is, Richardson also reflects Aristotle's definitions of comedy and tragedy. Orestes, the perfect tragicomic hero, succeeds for a time in avoiding either view and the destructive oppositions Aegisthus and Agamemnon represent. He seeks instead to "walk along the shore" and adopts the detachment of "laughter". But this modern stance, interestingly prophetic of the disillusion of youth in the later 1960's, proves a precarious stasis which cannot hold, and the murder of his father compels Orestes' participation in the battle of extremes he sought to avoid. The seeming inevitability of his decision is doubly reinforced in the play by the revenge theme of the myth itself and by the return motif of the biblical reference to the prodigal son, and at the play's close Orestes identifies his own decision with the general fate of man:

> The sea will always roar with Electra's cry: the waters will always rush toward Agamemnon's vengeance. It will cleanse or wash away the earth entirely, but it will never change . . . I can resist these forces no longer. I will go back, murder, and say it's for a better world.

In *Gallows Humor* its two component plays are linked by their common theme and by the fact that each play exactly reverses the central characters, condemned and executioner, and their points of view, and the effect of reversal is heightened by the appearance of the actors in the first play as their counterpart selves in the second. Walter, the condemned murderer, has a surprising passion for order and conformity, strives to keep his cell immaculate, and to go to his death with his "number patch" in place. But in the last hours, at the imminence of death, he is seduced back toward a celebration of life, illusion, and chaos by the prison prostitute Lucy. In the second play, Phillip the executioner, properly "dressed in the trousers, shirt, and tie of his official uniform", has an irresistible attraction toward revolt and wishes, for the coming solemnities, "to dress up like a headsman from the Middle Ages" in "a black hood". But his cold and practical wife Martha reasons him back toward conformity and order. The hood, Lucy's face, like a "carnival mask", the essential brutality of the execution itself, and the appearance of Death from the old morality plays to deliver the prologue, give the play its comparative time metaphor. Although modern appearances are confusing, and Death complains that it is now difficult for him to "tell the hangman from the hanged", Richardson's essential oppositions, life or death, order or disorder, conformity or individuality, illusion or reality, and hangman or hanged, are reasserted as Walter and Phillip, do end up playing their destined roles.

To an extent *Lorenzo* is a Renaissance variation of *The Prodigal*, but with a special emphasis upon illusion and reality, and the gambling metaphor in *Xmas in Las Vegas*, with its insistence upon the either/or of winner and loser, repeats the executioner-condemned contraries of *Gallows Humour* in a zany world and manner reminiscent of Kaufman and Hart and *You Can't Take It with You*. Lorenzo, "director of the theatrical troupe 'Theatre of the First Dove'", is caught up in the midst of a "small war of the Renaissance" in Italy, and like Orestes he tries vainly not to become involved in the destructive conflict of opposites, polarized here in the impractical Duke, Filippo, and his general, the realist Van Miessen. In *Xmas in Las Vegas* Wellspot is the inveterate gambler condemned to lose, and Olympus, the casino owner, is the financial executioner. Olympus, with his evocation of the gods, gambling as fate or destiny, and the sacrificial connotations of Christmas, all enlarge the dimension of this modern parable.

Although there are important contemporary influences and parallels in his work—Anouilh's wryly detached sense of humor, for example, Genet's concern with illusion, and especially Genet's and Beckett's preoccupation with opposites—Richardson's plays (and it is their limiting strength) insist upon his own almost geometrically precise view of the human condition where everything is energized as it is drawn toward its opposite and toward its destruction. It is this underlying and rather formulaic purity which initiates a sense of tragic inevitability beneath the comic facades of his plays.

More recently in other forms of writing, in periodical essays and in a splendid and revealing book *Memoir of a Gambler*, Richardson has continued to develop, with his accustomed precision, the preoccupations of his plays. But although this non-dramatic writing has been deservedly successful and represents a high level of accomplishment, one hopes that he will once more be lured back to that special, indeed incurable kind of gambling, theatre, in which he has in the past so skilfully played his hand.

—Gaynor F. Bradish

RINGWOOD, Gwen(dolyn Margaret) Pharis. Born in Washington, DC, 13 August 1910. Family moved to Lethbridge, Alberta, Canada, 1913. Educated at the University of Montana; University of Alberta, Edmonton, graduated 1934; University of North Carolina, Chapel Hill, 1937–39, MA 1939. Married J.B. Ringwood in 1939; four children. Registrar, Banff School of Fine Arts, Banff, Alberta, 1935; first-produced play, *The Dragons of Kent*, produced 1935; wrote radio plays for the "New Lamps for Old" series, University of Alberta Radio, 1936–37; collaborated with the Carolina Playmakers, Chapel Hill, 1937–39; director of drama, University of Alberta, Edmonton, from 1939, and taught acting and playwriting at the Banff School of Fine Arts; wrote plays for the Alberta Folklore and History Project, 1944–46; moved to Williams Lake, northern British Columbia, 1953: the town theatre named the Gwen Ringwood Theatre in her honour, 1968. Recipient: Governor General's Medal, 1941. Honorary doctorates: University of Victoria, 1981; University of Lethbridge, 1982. Died in Williams Lake, 24 May 1984.

Works

Collections

Collected Plays (includes *One Man's House; Chris Axelson, Blacksmith; Still Stands the House; Pasque Flower; Dark Harvest; Red Flag at Evening; The Days May Be Long; Saturday Night: The Courting of Marie Jenvrin; The Rainmaker; Stampede; A Fine Coloured Easter Egg; Widger's Way; Lament for Harmonica; The Deep Has Many Voices; Wail, Wind, Wail; Compensation Will Be Paid; The Stranger; A Remembrance of Miracles; The Lodge; Mirage; Garage Sale; The Furies*), edited by Enid D. Rutland. 1982.

Stage Works

Still Stands the House (produced University of North Carolina, Chapel Hill, 1938). 1931.
The Dragons of Kent (produced Banff School of Fine Arts, Banff, Alberta, 1935).
One Man's House (produced University of North Carolina, Chapel Hill, 1937). In *Collected Plays*, 1982.
Chris Axelson, Blacksmith (produced University of North Carolina, Chapel Hill, 1938). In *The Carolina Playbook*, 1939; in *Collected Plays*, 1982.
Pasque Flower (produced University of North Carolina, Chapel Hill, 1939). In *Collected Plays*, 1982.
Red Flag at Evening (produced Youth Training Schools, Edmonton, Alberta, 1939). In *Collected Plays*, 1982.
The Courting of Marie Jenvrin (produced Banff School of Fine Arts, Banff, Alberta, 1941). 1951.
The Jack and the Joker (produced Banff School of Fine Arts, Banff, Alberta, 1944). 1943.
Dark Harvest (produced University of Manitoba, Winnipeg, 1945). 1945; revised version, in *Canadian Theatre Review*, 5, 1975.
The Rainmaker (produced Banff School of Fine Arts, Banff, Alberta, 1945). 1975.
Stampede (produced University of Alberta, Edmonton, 1946). In *Collected Plays*, 1982.
A Fine Coloured Easter Egg (produced Banff School of Fine Arts, Banff, Alberta, 1946). In *Collected Plays*, 1982.
Widger's Way (produced University of Alberta, Edmonton, 1952). 1976.
Lament for Harmonica (produced as *Maya*, Little Theatre, Ottawa, 1959). In *Ten Canadian Short Plays*, 1975; in *Collected Plays*, 1982.
Look Behind You Neighbour, music by Chet Lambertson (produced Edson High School, Edson, Alberta, 1961).
The Sleeping Beauty (for children; produced Cariboo Indian School, Williams Lake, British Columbia, 1965). With *The Golden Goose*, 1979.
The Three Wishes (produced Williams Lake, British Columbia, 1965).
The Road Runs North, music by Art Rosoman (produced Junior High School, Williams Lake, British Columbia, 1967).
Jana (produced Gwen Ringwood Theatre, Williams Lake, British Columbia, 1971).
The Deep Has Many Voices, from the television play (produced Gwen Ringwood Theatre, Williams Lake, British Columbia, 1971). In *Collected Plays*, 1982.
The Magic Carpets of Antonio Angelini (produced Multicultural Festival, Winnipeg, Manitoba, 1976). In *Kids' Plays: Six Canadian Plays for Children*, with others, 1980.
The Lodge (produced Little Theatre, West Vancouver, 1977). In *Collected Plays*, 1982.
The Golden Goose (for children). With *The Sleeping Beauty*, 1979.
Mirage, music by Gary Walsh and Alvin Cairns (produced University of Saskatchewan, Saskatoon, 1979). In *Collected Plays*, 1982.
Garage Sale (produced New Play Centre, Vancouver, 1981).

The Stranger (produced as part of *Drum Song*, University of Victoria, British Columbia, 1982). In *Canadian Drama*, vol. 5 no. 2, 1979; in book form, in *Collected Plays*, 1982.
The Furies (produced as part of *Drum Song*, University of Victoria, British Columbia, 1982). In *Collected Plays*, 1982.
Wail, Wind, Wail. In *Collected Plays*, 1982.
Saturday Night. In *Collected Plays*, 1982.
The Days May Be Long. In *Collected Plays*, 1982.
Compensation Will Be Paid. In *Collected Plays*, 1982.

Television Plays

Lament for Harmonica, 1960; *The Deep Has Many Voices*, 1967.

Radio Plays

Beethoven, The Man Who Freed Music, Christopher Columbus, Florence Nightingale, Galileo—Father of Science, Henry the Navigator, Nansen of the North, Oliver Cromwell, Socrates—Citizen of Athens, Threat to Planet Earth, Valley of Ignorance, all in the series *New Lamps for Old*, 1936–37; *The Fight Against the Invisible*, 1945; *Niobe House*, 1945; *Frontier to Farmland*, 1952; *The Bells of England*, 1953; *A Fine Coloured Easter Egg*, 1953; *Still Stands the House*, 1953; *The Wall*, music by Bruce Haak, 1954; *So Gracious the Time*, 1955; *Restez, Michelle, Don't Go!*, 1977; *Lament for Harmonica*, 1979; *A Remembrance of Miracles*, 1979 (published in *Collected Plays*, 1982); *Garage Sale*, 1981.

Fiction

Younger Brother.   1959.

*

Criticism

Books:
Gwen Pharis Ringwood, interview in *Stage Voices: 12 Canadian Playwrights Talk About Their Lives and Work*, edited by Geraldine Anthony, Toronto, 1978.
Geraldine Anthony, *Gwen Pharis Ringwood*, Boston, 1981.
Ann Saddlemyer, "At Home in the Theatre: Ireland's Lady Gregory and Canada's Gwen Pharis Ringwood", in *Literary Interrelations: Ireland, England, and the World 2*, edited by Wolfgang Zach and Heinz Kosok, Tübingen, 1987.

Articles:
Anton Wagner, "Gwen Pharis Ringwood Rediscovered", in *Canadian Theatre Review*, 5, 1975.
L.W. Connolly, "The Collected Plays of Gwen Pharis Ringwood: A Review Essay", in *Canadian Drama*, 9, 1983.
Denyse Lynde, "The Dowser Character in the Plays of Gwen Pharis Ringwood", in *Ariel*, vol.18 no.1, 1987.

* * *

A key influence on Ringwood when she was studying playwriting at the University of North Carolina was Professor Frederick Koch who, in his teaching, extolled the virtue of folk drama with its emphasis on peasant or working-class themes, its strong sense of regionalism, and its use of colloquial speech. Ringwood was immediately attracted to these

ideas because between 1933 and 1937 she had travelled throughout Alberta as assistant to Elsie Park Gowan who, under a Carnegie Foundation grant, was appointed to develop community theatre—what Ringwood called "Prairie Theatre"—throughout the province. Four of the five plays she wrote at the University of North Carolina were produced by the University's Carolina Playmakers—*Chris Axelson, Blacksmith, Still Stands the House, Pasque Flower*, and *One Man's House*, all one-act plays. The fifth, *Dark Harvest* (a three-act, revised version of *Pasque Flower*), was first performed in 1945.

Still Stands the House, perhaps the most frequently performed one-act play in the Canadian dramatic repertoire, presents a grim metaphor of Canadian prairie life in the Depression years. Winter blizzards and summer droughts are Ringwood's images of disorder in Nature which reflect the disorder of the Warren household. The play's action is developed with stark economy. A real estate salesman comes to the Warren's prairie farm offering the young wife, Ruth, a new home, with water and flowers, close to a city, if the Warrens will sell the farm. Hester Warren, sister to Ruth's husband, Bruce, is a pioneer figure, sexually repressed, bound to the land and to a house as sterile as her own life. The opposition of Ruth and Hester is subtly reinforced by a sparse, functional symbolic pattern in which images of spring and flowers and birth (Ruth is pregnant) are juxtaposed with images of storm, repression of the sexual instinct, and death. As the outcome of the tragic clash between the two women, Ruth and her husband die in a blizzard while Hester, succumbing to madness, barricades herself inside the storm-lashed house. *Still Stands the House* has the direct and raw tragedy that Ringwood so admired in J.M. Synge's *Riders to the Sea*.

In *Dark Harvest*, subtitled "A Tragedy of the Prairies", obsession with the land is represented by Garth Hansen, an Albertan farmer. The key theme of the play is the relationship between Hansen and his God, whom he sees as a malevolent force fighting him for control of the land. Complementing this theme is the relationship between Garth and his wife and brother who are in love. At the play's close Garth sacrifices himself to save his brother, thus suggesting that he has found a higher purpose. Although *Dark Harvest* has a powerful and tragic theatricality, the relationship between the brother and Garth's wife is not handled convincingly, seeming to lack passion.

Among Ringwood's comedies are *The Courting of Marie Jenvrin*, a slight play about a young woman's wish to have a cow transported to Yellowknife, in Canada's Northwest Territories, and the men who want to marry her, and the more substantial *The Jack and the Joker*. This is a witty exposé of bigotry in a small prairie town, in which a newspaper editor reveals a politician's part in fraudulent land dealing. *The Rainmaker* is notable for its gallery of interesting characters and the warmth with which Ringwood portrays them. *Widger's Way*, arguably Ringwood's best comedy, is sparkling and inventive, mixing comedy, farce, and melodrama with absolute assurance. Widger, the farmer who is accosted one night by a stranger and finds himself caught up in an intrigue involving gold and murder, with himself as the prime suspect, is a comic creation of rare appeal.

Ringwood's interest in furthering community theatre led her to write such historical musicals as *Look Behind You, Neighbour* and *The Road Runs North* which celebrate an Alberta community and a British Columbia community respectively.

Ringwood's close contact with the Indian tribes of British Columbia reinforced her strong feeling for the marginalized, making her the first major English-Canadian dramatist to present the problems facing Canada's native peoples in a white society. Her "Indian" trilogy—*Lament for Harmonica* (or *Maya*), *The Stranger*, and *The Furies*—represents a searing dramatization of those problems. In *Lament for Harmonica* Maya kills an Indian who loves her to save the white man who is the father of her child. *The Stranger* is a Canadian *Medea*. Jana, a chief's daughter, has been wronged by her white common-law husband and father of her child. When the white woman, Barbara, gelds Jana's stallion and steals her husband, Jana poisons Barbara and kills herself and her child. In *The Furies* four young Indian girls, seduced by a white man, hang themselves and so drive him to madness; this plot is balanced against another in which the rape and murder of a young Indian girl is avenged by three old Indian women (the Furies) who castrate the murderer. In this trilogy Ringwood experiments with chanting, music, and choruses, while attempting, successfully, to find a new poetic speech.

Ringwood has been an important figure in Canadian drama, especially in western Canada. At a time where there was very little indigenous professional theatre in Canada and very few indigenous Canadian plays being written, she showed how it was possible, with little professional means, to find native themes that could be articulated in a distinctive Canadian theatrical voice.

—Eugene Benson

T. W. Robertson

ROBERTSON, T(homas) W(illiam). Born in Newark-on-Trent, Nottinghamshire, England, 9 January 1829; son of professional actors. Educated at Henry Young's Academy, Spalding, Lincolnshire, 1836–41; Moore's School, Whittlesey, Cambridgeshire, 1841–43. Married 1) the actress Elizabeth Burton in 1856 (died 1865), one son and two daughters; 2) Rosetta Feist in 1867, one daughter. Child actor, 1834–36; stagehand, prompter, songwriter, and subsequently actor for his father's company in Lincoln, 1843–48; on break-up of the company moved to London, 1848; usher at a school in Utrecht for a few weeks in 1848, then returned to London; freelance writer and journalist, also stage manager, prompter, and later actor in the smaller London theatres and in the provinces, 1848–60, touring with his wife, 1856–59; retired as an actor, 1859; editor, drama critic, *Illustrated Times*, and translator for the publisher Lacy, 1859–64, then full-time writer. Died in London, 3 February 1871.

Works

Collections

Principal Dramatic Works (2 vols.). 1889.
Plays (includes *Society; Ours; Caste; School*), edited by William M. Tydeman. 1982.

Stage Works

The Battle of Life, from the story by Dickens (produced Boston, Lincolnshire, 1843–47?).
The Haunted Man, from the story by Dickens (produced Boston, Lincolnshire, 1843–48?).

The Chevalier de St. George, from a play by Duveyrier and Roger de Beauvoir (produced Princess Theatre, London, 1845). 1870.
Noémie, from a play by A. Dennery and Clément (as *Ernestine*, produced Princess Theatre, London, 1846; as *Clarisse*, produced 1855; as *The Foster Sisters*, produced 1855). 1855.
A Night's Adventure; or, Highways and Byways, from a novel by Bulwer-Lytton (produced Olympic Theatre, London, 1851).
Castles in the Air (produced City of London Theatre, 1854).
My Wife's Diary, from a play by A. Dennery and Clairville (as *A Wife's Journal*, produced Olympic Theatre, London, 1854). 1855.
The Star of the North, from a play by Scribe (as *The Northern Star*, produced Sadler's Wells Theatre, London, 1855). 1871.
The Clockmaker's Hat (produced Adelphi Theatre, London, 1855; as *Betty Martin*, produced St. James's Theatre, London, 1865). 1855(?).
Peace at Any Price (produced Strand Theatre, London, 1856). 1872.
The Muleteer of Toledo (produced Grecian Saloon, Hoxton, London, 1856).
The Half-Caste; or, The Poisoned Pearl (produced Surrey Theatre, London, 1856). 1872.
Two Gay Deceivers; or, Black, White, and Grey, with T.H. Lacy, from a play by Labiche (produced 1858). Nd.

Our Private Theatricals. In *An Evening's Entertainment*, 1860.

Robinson Crusoe. In *An Evening's Entertainment*, 1860.

The Cantab (produced Strand Theatre, London, 1861). In *An Evening's Entertainment*, 1860.

Jocrisse the Juggler, from a play by A. Dennery and Jules Brésil (as *Magloire the Prestigitator*, produced Adelphi Theatre, London, 1861). 1861.

David Garrick, from a play by Duveyrier (produced Prince of Wales's Theatre, Birmingham, 1864). 1864; as *Sullivan* (produced 1873), 1873.

Constance, music by Frederick Clay (produced Opera House, Covent Garden, London, 1865).

Society (produced Prince of Wales Theatre, Liverpool, 1865). 1866.

Ours (produced Prince of Wales Theatre, Liverpool, 1866). 1866(?).

Shadow-Tree Shaft (produced Princess Theatre, London, 1867).

A Rapid Thaw, from a play by Sardou (produced St. James's Theatre, London, 1867).

A Dream in Venice (produced Royal Gallery of Illustration, London, 1867).

Caste, from his story "The Poor-Rate Unfolds a Tale" (produced Prince of Wales Theatre, London, 1867). 1868.

The Ladies' Battle, from a play by Scribe and Legouvé. 1867.

For Love (produced Holborn Theatre, London, 1867).

The Sea of Ice; or, The Prayer of the Wrecked (produced Colosseum, Glasgow, 1867?).

Play (produced Prince of Wales's Theatre, London, 1868). 1868(?).

Passion Flowers, from a work by Alfred de Musset (produced Theatre Royal, Hull, 1868).

Home, from a play by G.V.E. Augier (produced Theatre Royal, Haymarket, London, 1869). 1869.

School, from a play by Roderick Benedix (produced Prince of Wales. Theatre, London, 1869). 1879.

Dreams (as *My Lady Clara*, produced Alexandra Theatre, Liverpool, 1869; as *Dreams*, produced Gaiety Theatre, London, 1869). 1879.

A Breach of Promise (produced Globe Theatre, London, 1869). 1888.

Dublin Bay (produced Manchester, 1869).

Progress, from a play by Sardou (produced Globe Theatre, London, 1869). 1891.

The Nightingale (produced Adelphi Theatre, London, 1870). In *Principal Dramatic Works*, 1889.

M.P. (produced Prince of Wales's Theatre, London, 1870). In *Principal Dramatic Works*, 1889.

Birth (produced Bristol, 1870). In *Principal Dramatic Works*, 1889.

War (produced St. James's Theatre, London, 1871). 1871.

Policy (produced Glasgow, 1871).

Not at All Jealous (produced Court Theatre, London, 1871). 1872.

Birds of Prey; or, A Duel in the Dark. 1872.

Which is It? (produced Theatre Royal, Drury Lane, London, 1881).

Other Days (produced Theatre Royal?, Hull, 1883).

A Row in the House (produced Toole's Theatre, London, 1883). 1888.

Cinderella (produced Theatre Royal?, Newcastle, 1892).

Over the Way (produced Court Theatre, London, 1893).

Fiction

David Garrick. 1865.

Other

Editor, with E.P. Hingston, *Artemus Ward's Panorama*. 1869.

*

Criticism

Books:

T. Edgar Pemberton, *The Life and Writings of T.W. Robertson*, London, 1893.

Maymard Savin, *T.W. Robertson: His Plays and Stagecraft*, Providence, Rhode Island, 1950.

George Rowell, *The Victorian Theatre*, London, 1956; revised edition, 1978.

* * *

Tom Robertson's reputation as a dramatist rests mainly, in the late-20th century, on a single play, *Caste*. This is, however, only the most remarkable of a series of plays by Robertson that were produced at the Prince of Wales's Theatre, London, during the last few years of his short life— *Society*, *Ours*, *Play*, *School*, and *M.P.* All of these are comedies, all received popular and critical acclaim, and as a group they are generally regarded as a transitional step towards the "new drama" of Pinero, Jones, Shaw, and Galsworthy, later in the century. At the same time, they betray their origins in those dramatic and theatrical forms (farce, melodrama, and English adaptations of French "well made" plays) which were most popular during Robertson's lifetime, and which provided him with material for his own very large dramatic output of more than 50 plays.

Robertson's plays cannot be discussed usefully outside the context of his stage experience. Born into a theatrical family, Robertson gained an extensive, practical knowledge of all aspects of stage production, and working in the declining years of the provincial "circuit" theatres, he had of necessity to learn how to please a paying audience. Despite this, a strong sense of artistic professionalism led him to revolt against many of the current practices of theatrical companies- —hasty rehearsals; flimsy, inadequate and non-functional sets and properties; the lack of any concept of "ensemble" playing or overall direction; inattention to detail; a reliance on type-casting which encouraged laziness in actors and inhibited subtlety and sophistication in characterization. As a playwright, too, he became interested in ways to make drama both more "natural" and more reflective of contemporary realities and social issues (though he never challenged the social system itself).

These aims resulted in Robertson's first play in the new mode, *Society*, which, after several rejections, had its first success in Liverpool before being brought to London by the popular actress Marie Wilton and her husband Squire Bancroft, owners of the newly refurbished Prince of Wales Theatre (where Robertson was to direct all the plays he wrote for the company). *Society* concerns the attempts of the rich (but not well born) Chodd family to buy their way into a high society that is willing to assist the family's political and marital ambitions for the sake of their money. They are opposed by a poor young lawyer with literary interests and strong principles. At the centre of the plot is Maud, the lawyer Sidney Daryl's sweetheart, whom her aunt Lady Ptarmigant is prepared to marry to John, the Chodd family heir. After Sidney has bitterly attacked Lady Ptarmigant's mercenary attitudes, thereby exposing the hypocrisy of society's values, he enters a parliamentary election in opposition to John and wins both the seat and, after some misunderstandings have been resolved, Maud. To cap his success, he becomes the recipient of a legacy.

Like *Society*, Robertson's next play, *Ours*, was also an immediate critical and financial success. The title refers to a regiment of British soldiers about to depart for the war in the Crimea, leaving their women at home. Robertson demonstrated his growing dramatic assurance by keeping three romantic stories going at the same time, eventually bringing them to resolution in the final act when the women visit the men at their winter encampment in the Crimea. *Ours* is probably the least likely of Robertson's plays to be well received in a modern revival, given its uncritical patriotism and its admiration of military heroism; yet the critics of 1866 found its dialogue, characterization and detailed stage effects highly realistic, and were not disturbed that the horrors of the war had been treated so lightly.

Caste has sometimes been discussed as the earliest of Victorian "problem plays". A story of marriage between people of different social classes, it is technically a comedy but seems consistently to flirt with the possibilities of disaster, even of tragedy. Esther Eccles, daughter of the drunken, non-working workingman Eccles, marries the Honorable George D'Alroy, an army officer and son of the haughty Marquise de St. Maur. George is sent to India soon after the wedding; Esther gives birth to a son; George is reported killed in action; Esther refuses financial help from the Marquise, and since her father has gained control of the money that George left for her, she is reduced to poverty. George's friend Hawtree returns from India and helps her. Then (with no hint having been given to the audience by Robertson), George returns "from the dead" and all is happiness again. Meanwhile, Esther's sister Polly, an actress, has married the ambitious tradesman Sam Gerridge, who has bought up a plumbing business.

Robertson's answer to the question of whether the classes can live happily together, with a free interchange between them, and without a social revolution, is clearly affirmative. But he avoids having to tackle the problem of whether Esther could have survived in Victorian society if George actually had been killed. Robertson's followers in the drama, particularly Pinero, were more sceptical. William Archer tells us that the problem in *The Second Mrs. Tanqueray* is implicit in *Caste*, that is, in Robertson's comedy marriage between the classes produces happiness, but in Pinero's drama the social ostracism that such a couple have to endure wrecks the marriage.

Play, set in a German gambling resort, was Robertson's least successful comedy for the Bancrofts, but in *School* his talent for combining light but realistic dialogue, vivid character drawing, and credible plot structure makes this modern Cinderella story into one of his most charming pieces of comic romanticism. With his two characters, the school teachers Bella and Naomi, he perfected a device he had used before: playing off a lively, pert young woman against a more traditionally restrained, yet romantic, friend. *M.P.* takes up again the themes of class, money, and politics, and is for that reason reminiscent of *Society*; but it was written in the last few months of Robertson's life, and though it is an interesting play it is not surprising that it lacks the vigour and control of the earlier work.

—John D. Hurrell

See also *Volume 1* entry on *Caste*.

ROBINSON, (Esmé Stuart) Lennox. Born in Douglas, County Cork, Ireland, 4 October 1886. Educated at Bandon Grammar School, 1900–04. Served in the Irish Volunteers, 1914–18. Married Dorothy Travers Smith in 1931. First-produced play, *The Clancy Name*, staged 1908; manager and producer, 1909–14 (resigned after unprofitable US tour), play director and producer, 1923–35, and member of the Board of Directors, 1923–58, Abbey Theatre, Dublin: also a founder of the Peacock Theatre (the Abbey's experimental stage), 1925, and the Abbey School of Acting, 1926; file clerk, Teachers Pension Fund, 1915; organizing librarian, Carnegie Trust, 1915–24; sponsor, Drama League, 1919–28; drama critic, *Observer*, London, 1924–25; lecturer and guest producer in USA, 1929, 1930, 1931; visiting professor, Bowling Green State University, Ohio, 1947–48; columnist ("I Sometimes Think"), *Irish Press*, 1953–56. Chairman, PEN Irish Centre, 1956. D.Litt: Trinity College, Dublin, 1948. Founding member, Irish Academy of Letters, 1932. Died in Monkstown, County Dublin, 14 October 1958.

Works

Collections

Plays. 1928.
"Killycreggs in Twilight" and Other Plays (includes *Bird's Nest* and *Is Life Worth Living?*). 1939.
Selected Plays, edited by Christopher Murray. 1982.

Stage Plays

The Clancy Name (produced Abbey Theatre, Dublin, 1908; revised version produced 1909). With *Harvest*, 1911.
The Cross-Roads (produced Abbey Theatre, Dublin, 1909). 1909.
The Lesson of His Life (produced Cork, 1909).
Harvest (produced Abbey Theatre, Dublin, 1910). With *The Clancy Name*, 1911.
Patriots (produced Abbey Theatre, Dublin, 1912). 1912.
The Dreamers (produced Abbey Theatre, Dublin, 1915). 1915.
The Whiteheaded Boy (produced Abbey Theatre, Dublin, 1916). 1920.
The Lost Leader (produced Abbey Theatre, Dublin, 1918). 1918.
The Round Table (produced Abbey Theatre, Dublin, 1922). 1924; revised version (produced 1927), 1928.
Crabbed Youth and Age (produced Abbey Theatre, Dublin, 1922). 1924.
Never the Time and the Place (produced Abbey Theatre, Dublin, 1924). 1953.
Portrait (produced Abbey Theatre, Dublin, 1925). With *The White Blackbird*, 1926.
The White Blackbird (produced Abbey Theatre, Dublin, 1925). With *Portrait*, 1926.
The Big House (produced Abbey Theatre, Dublin, 1926). 1928.
The Far-Off Hills (produced Abbey Theatre, Dublin, 1928). 1931.
Give a Dog — (produced Strand Theatre, London, 1929). 1928.
Ever the Twain (produced Abbey Theatre, Dublin, 1929). 1930.
The Critic, from the play by Richard Brinsley Sherindan (produced Abbey Theatre, Dublin, 1931).
All's Over, Then? (produced Abbey Theatre, Dublin, 1932). In *More Plays*, 1935.

Drama at Inish (produced Abbey Theatre, Dublin, 1933). 1933; as *Is Life Worth Living?* (produced 1933), 1933.
Church Street (produced Abbey Theatre, Dublin, 1934).   In *More Plays*, 1935.
When Lovely Women (produced Abbey Theatre, Dublin, 1936).
Killycreggs in Twilight (produced Abbey Theatre, Dublin, 1937).   In *"Killycreggs in Twilight" and Other Plays*, 1939.
Bird's Nest (produced Abbey Theatre, Dublin, 1938).   In *"Killycreggs in Twilight" and Other Plays*, 1939.
Roly Poly, from a story by Maupassant (produced Abbey Theatre, Dublin, 1940).
Forget Me Not (produced Abbey Theatre, Dublin, 1941).
Pictures in a Theatre.   1947.
The Lucky Finger (produced Abbey Theatre, Dublin, 1948; revised version produced 1948).   1949.
The Demon Lover (produced Dublin?, 1954).

Radio Plays

Let Well Alone, 1940 (published in *The Bell*, January 1941).

Fiction

A Young Man from the South.   1917.
Eight Short Stories.   1920.

Memoirs and Letters

Three Homes (autobiography), with Tom Robinson and Nora Doman.   1938.
Curtain Up: An Autobiography.   1942.

Other

Dark Days (political sketches).   1918.
Bryan Cooper (biography).   1931.
Towards an Appreciation of the Theatre.   1945.
Palette and Plough (biography of Dermod O Brien).   1948.
Ireland's Abbey Theatre: A History 1899–1951.   1951.
I Sometimes Think (essays).   1956.

Editor, *Further Letters of John B. Yeats*.   1920.
Editor, *A Golden Treasury of Irish Verse*.   1925.
Editor, *Poems*, by Thomas Parnell.   1927.
Editor, *A Little Anthology of Modern Irish Verse*.   1928.
Editor, *The Irish Theatre* (lectures).   1939.
Editor, *Lady Gregory's Journals 1916–1930*.   1946.
Editor, with Donagh MacDonagh, *The Oxford Book of Irish Verse*. 1958.

*

Criticism

Books:
Michael J. O'Neill, *Lennox Robinson*, New York, 1934.
Hans G. Stalder, *Anglo-Irish Peasant Drama*, Bern, 1978.
Sean Dorman, *Limelight over the Liffey*, Fowey, Cornwall, 1983.

Articles:
Ida G. Everson, "Young Lennox Robinson and the Abbey Theatre's First American Tour (1911–1912)", in *Modern Drama*, 9, 1966.
Christopher Murray, "Lennox Robinson: The Abbey's Anti-

Hero", in *Irish Writers and the Theatre*, edited by Masaru Sekine, Gerrard's Cross, Buckinghamshire, 1986.

*   *   *

In her *Journals* Lady Gregory wrote that Lennox Robinson "waded through blood to write, at last, *The Whiteheaded Boy*". Throughout his life Robinson was afflicted with moods of pessimism and self-depreciation; but, having at last found his true genius as a sympathetic, whimsical, and witty observer of provincial society, he wrote comedies unsurpassed by any dramatist of the Irish theatre. He began writing plays at a crucial stage in the development of the Irish dramatic movement. The death of Synge in 1909 signalled the end of the theatre of poetic myth and folk drama. It was replaced by plays concerned with a harsh and realistic presentation of life to which Robinson's early plays made a major contribution. For nearly 50 years he was associated with the Abbey Theatre as play director, manager and member of its Board of Directors. Of his plays, 22 were written for, or presented by, the Abbey; inevitably he became largely influential in establishing what may be broadly called "the Abbey play".

Brought up in a strictly Protestant and Unionist family—his father was Rector of a country parish in West Cork—he claimed to have been converted to the cause of Irish independence after seeing, at the age of 20, Yeats's *Kathleen ni Houlihan* and Lady Gregory's *The Rising of the Moon* performed by the Abbey players at the Cork Opera House. But whilst his sympathy for Irish nationalism never waned, he was unable to free himself completely from his Anglo-Irish background. Torn between two ways of life, he failed to find a positive philosophy that would have enabled him to become emotionally involved in his characters. As a result his excursions into tragedy often fail to resolve through the characterisation and Robinson is forced to resort to imposed or melodramatic endings. His early plays are starkly realistic. *The Clancy Name*, written in 1908, presents a hard-working, thrifty mother who has fought to keep her farm together for the sake of her son and to preserve the good name of her family, only to find that her son has committed a murder. The play ends with the son taking the secret of his crime to the grave when he is killed trying to rescue a child from a runaway horse.

In 1909, at the age of 24, he was appointed to the Abbey as play director and manager. Here he came under Yeats's powerful influence—an influence that tended to make him dependent on Yeats's good opinion, emphasising the element of self-depreciation in his character and preventing him from fully realising his own unique talent. His political plays, *The Dreamers*, *Patriots* and *The Lost Leader*, reflect Yeats's romantic view of Ireland's national heroes—Robert Emmett, John O'Leary, Charles Stuart Parnell. *The Lost Leader*, however, written in 1918 when Robinson had left the Abbey to become an organising librarian for the Carnegie Trust, shows a marked improvement in his creative writing. The plot is based on the hypothesis that Parnell did not die in 1891 but is living in the disguise of an old part-time hotel-keeper in a remote part of Ireland. His accidental death, resulting from a riot caused by his denunciation of the squabbling politicians and the greed of the "gombeen men", leaves the question of his identity unproven.

Robinson's political plays display a less pessimistic tone in his writing and are softened by greater sympathy for his characters. His travels throughout Ireland in his work for the Carnegie Trust gave him the opportunity to obtain a wider observation of Irish characters, and freedom from the anxieties of theatre management for which he was ill-suited led to a

series of comedies of which *The Whiteheaded Boy* is his masterpiece. In it he displays for the first time gaiety and wit combined with good-humoured irony in this portrait of a doting mother's favouritism for her youngest son at the expense of the marriage prospects and careers of the rest of her family. The play became a mainstay of the Abbey's repertoire during the bleak years of the struggle for independence and the Civil War. It ran for a year in London and was translated into many languages, including Chinese.

In 1919 Robinson returned to the Abbey where he remained until 1935 as play director. No longer content with the parochial realism of the conventional Abbey play he sought to widen his and his fellow dramatists' horizons by promoting the Dublin Drama League offering, like the London Stage Society, occasional performances of the avant-garde plays of Europe and America. Robinson, himself, wrote a series of plays between 1925 and 1934 in which he abandoned his familiar coutry town world for plays with a vaguely metropolitan or unspecified background, introducing techniques borrowed from Pirandello, O'Neill, Strindberg, and contemporary Spanish playwrights. His only real success was a one-act play, *Church Street*. In this work, a young playwright returns from London to his home in Ireland, disillusioned by his failure to write plays that deal with a life that is alien to him. Guided by a perceptive old aunt he looks afresh at his fellow countrymen in the form of the guests at a party given by his mother to celebrate his return. Using Pirandello's technique in *Six Characters in Search of an Author* he reveals, in a number of short scenes, their problems and tragedies, discovering in the process that abundant material for drama lies at his doorstep.

Church Street has obvious autobiographical implications, and marks the end of Robinson's search for new forms. But even during the ten years of experimentation he never lost sight of his attachment to what he called "this strange Irish Thing". In 1926 he treated the subject of the decline and fall of an Anglo-Irish family in *The Big House*, a theme he repeated ten years later in *Killicreggs in Twilight*. Neither play is entirely successful, owing to Robinson's hesitancy to commit himself to a positive philosophy in his treatment of tragic subjects. In *The Far-Off Hills*, however, written in 1928, he revealed once again his instinctive flair for comedy in one of his most delightful plays set in a small country town and among a family similar to *The Whiteheaded Boy*. In 1933 he celebrated his final release from alien forms in the hilarious *Drama at Inish*, known overseas as *Is Life Worth Living?*. Its plot concerns the arrival of a theatrical touring company in a seaside resort, intent on presenting productions of the deepest Strindbergian gloom with devastating effect on the life-style and morals of the inhabitants. Normal life is restored by the timely arrival of a circus. Inish became the home of four of his last comedies, but his final plays lack the ironic wit of his best work.

Even in his less successful plays Robinson showed himself a master craftsman both in his portrayal of character and in his succinct and true-to-life dialogue. His three great comedies—*The Whiteheaded Boy*, *The Far-Off Hills*, and *Drama at Inish*—will always hold their place in the repertoire of Irish drama.

—Hugh Hunt

RODRIGUES, Nélson. Born in Recife, Pernambuco, Brazil, 23 August 1912. Moved to Rio de Janeiro, 1916.

Wrote articles on crime for his father's newspaper *A Mañha*, from the age of 13, and continued working as a journalist thereafter; first-produced play, *Vestido de Noiva*, staged 1943. Also wrote fiction under the pseudonym Suzana Flag. Died in Rio de Janeiro, 22 December 1980.

Works

Collections

Anjo Negro; Vestido de noiva; A Mulher sem Pecado.   1948.
Teatro (2 vols.).   1959–60.
Teatro Quase Completo (4 vols.; includes all plays except *O Anti-Nélson Rodrigues* and *A Serpente*).   1965–66; revised edition (includes all plays), as *Teatro completo* (4 vols.), edited by S. Magaldi, 1981–84.

Stage Works

Vestido de Noiva (produced 1943).   In *Anjo Negro . . .* (collection); revised version, in *Teatro*, 1959–60; translated as *Wedding Dress*, 1980.
A mulher sem Pecado (produced Rio de Janeiro, 1945).   In *Anjo Negro . . .* (collection), 1948.
Anjo Negro.   In *Anjo Negro . . .* (collection), 1948.
Album de Família.   In *Teatro*, 1959–60.
Senhora dos Afogados (produced 1945).   In *Teatro*, 1959–60.
Dorotéia (produced 1949).   In *Teatro*, 1959–60.
A Valsa n. 6 (produced 1950).   In *Teatro*, 1959–60.
A Falecida (produced 1953).   In *Teatro*, 1959–60.
Perdoa-me por Me Traíres (produced 1957).   In *Teatro*, 1959–60.
Viúva, Porém Honesta (produced 1957?).   In *Teatro*, 1959–60.
Os Sete Gatinhos (produced 1959).   In *Teatro*, 1959–60.
Boca de Ouro (produced 1960).   In *Teatro*, 1959–60.
O Beijo no Asfalto (produced 1960).   1961.
Toda Nudez Será Castigada.   In *Teatro Quase Completo*, 1965–66.
Bonitinha, Mas Ordinariá.   In *Teatro Quase Completo*, 1965–66.
O Anti-Nélson Rodrigues (produced 1974?).   In *Teatro Completo*, 1980–84.
A Serpente.   1980.

Fiction

100 Contos Escolhidos; A Vida Como Ela é (stories).   1961. Also published several novels pseudonymously, including *Meu Destino é Pecar.*

Memoirs and Letters

O Reacionário (memoirs).   Nd.

Other

O Obvio Ululante (journalism).   1968.

*

Criticism

Books:
Maria F. Susskind, *Nélson Rodrigues e o Fundo Falso*, Brazilia, 1977.

Ronaldo L. Lins, *O Teatro de Nélson Rodrigues: Uma Realidade em Agonia*, Rio de Janeiro, 1979.

Marina Spinu, *Das dramatische Werk des Brasilianers Nelson Rodrigues*, Frankfurt, 1986.

Stella Rodrigues, *Nélson Rodrigues, Meu Irmão*, Rio de Janeiro, 1986.

José M. Sábato Rodríguez, *Nelson Rodrigues: Dramaturgia e Encenações*, São Paulo, 1987.

* * *

Nélson Rodrigues wrote 17 plays that gained him a reputation as the most powerful Brazilian playwright ever. Today he is the most admired dramatist in Brazil and his plays are among the most often translated into other languages. On the cover of the first volume of Rodrigues' *Teatro Quase Completo* (Almost Complete Works), Prudente de Morais Neto compares the playwright's artistic contribution to the Brazilian theatre to that of Hector Villa-Lobos in music, Cândido Portinari in painting, Carlos Drummond de Andrade in poetry, and Oscar Niemeyer in architecture. His plays were classified thematically by a Brazilian critic, Sábato Magaldi, as "psychological", "mythical", and "*tragédias cariocas*" (tragedies from Rio de Janeiro).

Rodrigues also wrote four novels, a volume of short stories and numerous articles for newspapers. His experience as a journalist (he began to work as a reporter for a crime column at the age of 13) had an impact on his approach to theatre. His "journalistic style", consisting of short, often abrupt dialogues, use of colloquialisms and slang expressions, as well as his predilection for "street-wise" types as characters, is evident in the later plays, known as "*tragédias cariocas*". Even though these plays were not intended as, and cannot be perceived as, realistic, the characters and situations used in the "*tragédias cariocas*" are modelled on those from Rio's poor neighborhoods of Zona Norte, which Rodrigues became familiar with when working as a reporter.

As for style, the author himself wrote in his memoirs *O Reacionário* (The Reactionary): "Plays can be divided into 'interesting' and 'vital'. Giraudoux wrote 'interesting' texts. The melody of his prose is a glamorous disguise for his creative impotence. All 'vital' plays belong to 'unpleasant theatre'". Rodrigues perceived his own plays as "vital" and the term "unpleasant theatre" was one most often used by the critics to comment on Rodrigues' work.

The term "unpleasant theatre" was coined a few years after the successful staging of *Vestido de Noiva* (Wedding Dress), and referred mainly to three plays that Magaldi calls "mythical": *Album de Família* (Family Album), *Anjo Negro* (The Black Angel), and *Senhora de Afogados* (Our Lady of the Drowning). Rodrigues' "revolutionary" approach to archetypes and primitive unconsciousness in these texts, the introduction of such themes as incest, homicide, and madness, caused an immediate reaction from the censors; *Album de Família* was banned from the Brazilian stages until 1965. The other two plays were also forbidden, even though for a much shorter period of time.

A mulher sem pecado (A Woman Without Sin) and *Vestido de Noiva*, classified by Magaldi as "psychological", were enthusiastically received by the critics. With these two works Rodrigues gained his reputation as an innovator of the Brazilian stage. In both works he abandoned the "exterior" world in order to explore the secrets of the mind and, equally importantly, he found an adequate stage language to express these concerns.

In his "mythical" tragedies, Rodrigues explored the most obscure aspects of the human mind. In spite of the negative reception from the critics and the audience, these were also his favorite plays and he felt more accomplished artistically writing them than any other of his earlier or later works. Each of these purposely disturbing and highly symbolic dramas—where the graphic reality presented is only a pretext to explore, in a poetic manner, more universal truths about the absurdity of human existence—are regarded by some critics as similar in mode to the theatre of Eugene O'Neill. These are also the plays in which Rodrigues, like O'Neill, uses masks. In *Doroteia* (Dorothy), his last play from the "mythical cycle", Rodrigues uses the mask as a device to tell the ultimate truth about the characters.

The playwright's fondness for the "mythical plays", which belong to the "unpleasant theatre", can be explained in the context of his remarks in *O Reacionário* about Glauber Rocha's film *A Terra em Transe* (The Earth in Trance): "*Terra em Transe* is Brazil. All these guys dancing their hideous dances represent us. We wanted to see tables covered with nice tablecloths, with plates and silverware in the right places, like in a commercial ad. in *Manchete*. Instead, Glauber Rocha offered us triumphal vomit. *Os Sertões* (The Back Country) by Euclides da Cunha was also a vomited Brazil. Any work of art in order to have meaning in Brazil needs to be hideous". As for the condition of the true artist, Rodrigues wrote about Glauber Rocha in the same book of memoirs: "There are many things that I like about Glauber Rocha, including the following: he is a neurotic; he is on the verge of madness, and this vicinity, in my opinion, is vital for the work of art".

After several years of silence, caused by the negative reception of his "mythical plays", Rodrigues wrote *A Falecida* (The Deceased), a play which opened a new phase in his writing, called by Magaldi "*tragédias cariocas*". The last play from this cycle, *A Serpente* (The Snake), was also the last play written by Rodrigues. Even though most of the eight tragedies in this group synthesize some of the disturbing themes from the "mythical" and "psychological" plays, they introduce an additional social dimension, as they deal with everyday life in Rio de Janeiro. The social problems, however, are not introduced in a direct, realistic manner, nor is the author's intention ideological. The author opted for more common types and situations, with which the audience could identify, in order to proceed with his exploration of the subconscious. Some of the motifs that appear in these plays are unnatural death caused by either homicide or suicide, incest, madness, physical disability, machismo, and homosexuality.

In most of Rodrigues' plays, the climate of fatalism, the irrationality of the characters' situation, and the characters' tendency towards self-destruction suggest some parallels with the expressionist theatre. As in plays by Kaiser the characters in Rodrigues' "mythical" plays and in his "*tragédias cariocas*" are possessed by dangerous forces, over which they do not have any control. It is doubtful that Rodrigues had read or seen the plays of the German expressionists. He was able, however, to read the works of O'Neill and become familiar with the expressionistic cinema of the 1920's.

Cinema had probably the greatest influence on Rodrigues' artistic formation, and psychoanalysis was another phenomenon that influenced Rodrigues in the structuring of the dramatic discourse. Both phenomena suggested to Rodrigues a possibility of breaking away from a one-dimensional, linear type of theatrical narrative. In most of his works, without repeating the same pattern, the narrative is used to project on stage the inner worlds of the characters. This projection is carried out through visual as well as verbal means. Cinematic flashbacks are among his most used devices; they allow the characters to move freely from one plane to another, from the present to the past, from the real to the subconscious, and so on. The influence of cinema in Rodrigues' theatre can also be found in the author's rejection of the decorativeness and literariness ascribed for centuries to dramatic dialogue, as well as in his denial of dialogue's theatrical supremacy.

—Elzbieta Szoka

See also *Volume 1* entry on *Wedding Dress*.

ROJAS, Fernández de.   See *Volume 1* entry on *Celestina*

ROMERIL, John.   Born in Melbourne, Victoria, Australia 26 October 1945. Educated at Brighton Technical School and Brighton High School, South Australia; Monash University, Clayton, Victoria, 1966–71, BA (honours) in English 1970. First plays produced 1968; writer-in-residence, Australian Performing Group, Melbourne, 1974, Western Australian Institute of Technology, Bentley, 1977, University of Newcastle, New South Wales, 1978, Jigsaw Theatre Company, Canberra, 1980, Troupe, Adelaide, 1981, Flinders University, Bedford Park, South Australia, 1984, Magpie, Adelaide, 1985, National University of Singapore, 1986–87; Mathew J. Cody Artist-in-Residence, Victorian Arts Centre, Melbourne, 1985. Also a director and actor. Recipient: Canada-Australia Prize, 1976.

Stage Works

A Nameless Concern (produced Melbourne, 1968).
The Kitchen Table (produced Melbourne, 1968).   With *Brudder Humphrey*, 1971.
Scene One, with John Minter (produced Melbourne, 1969).
The Man from Chicago (produced Melbourne, 1969).
The American Independence Hour (produced Melbourne, 1969).
Mr. Big, The Big, Big Pig (produced Melbourne, 1969).
In a Place Somewhere Else (produced Melbourne, 1969).
I Don't Know Who to Feel Sorry For (produced Melbourne, 1969).
Chicago Chicago (produced Melbourne, 1970).   In *Plays*, 1970.
Marvellous Melbourne, with Jack Hibberd (produced Melbourne, 1970).   In *Theatre Australia*, July–September 1977.
Dr. Karl's Kure (produced Melbourne, 1970).
200 Years (produced Melbourne, 1970).
The Magnetic Martian (produced Melbourne, 1971).
Whatever Happened to Realism (produced Melbourne, 1971).
Mrs. Thally F (produced Melbourne, 1971).   In *Seven One-Act Plays*, edited by Rodney Fisher, 1983.
Rearguard Action (produced Melbourne, 1971).
Brudder Humphrey.   With *The Kitchen Table*, 1971.
A Night in Rio and Other Bummerz with Tim Robertson (produced Melbourne, 1972).

Hackett Gets Ahead, with Bill and Lorna Hannan (produced Melbourne, 1972).
He Can Swagger Sitting Down (produced Melbourne, 1972).
Bastardy (produced Melbourne, 1972).   1982.
The Earth, Air, Fire, and Water Show (produced Melbourne, 1975).
Waltzing Matilda: A National Pantomime with Tomato Sauce, with Tim Robertson (produced Melbourne, 1974).   1984.
The Floating World (produced Melbourne, 1974).   1975; revised version,1982.
The Golden Holden Show (produced Melbourne, 1975).
Dudders, with John Timlin (produced Melbourne, 1976).
The Radio-Active Horror Show (produced Melbourne, 1977).
The Accidental Poke (produced Melbourne, 1977).   In *Popular Short Plays for the Australian Stage*, edited by Ron Blair, 1985.
Mickey's Moomba (produced Melbourne, 1979).
Carboni (produced Melbourne, 1980).
700,000 (produced Canberra, 1980).
Samizdat (produced Adelaide, 1981).
Centenary Dance (produced Adelaide, 1984).
The Kelly Dance (produced Adelaide, 1984).
Definitely Not the Last (produced Adelaide, 1985).
Jonah, music by Alan John, from the novel by Louis Stone (produced Sydney, 1985).
Legends, with Jennifer Hill and Chris Anastassiades (produced Melbourne, 1985).   1986.
Koori Radio (produced by the Salamanca Theatre Company, Hobart, Tasmania, 1987).
The Imposter, from a play by Sha Yexin (produced Melbourne, 1987).
History of Australia (produced Melbourne, 1988).
Top End with Tim Robertson and Don Watson (produced Melbourne, 1989).
Lost Weekend (produced Adelaide, 1989).
Black Cargo. from a story by John Morrison (produced Melbourne, 1991).
Reading Boy (produced Adelaide, 1991).
Working Out (produced Melbourne, 1991).

Television Plays

Bonjour Balwyn, 1969; *The Best of Mates*, 1972; *Charley the Chequer Cab Kid*, 1973; *The Great McCarthy*, from a novel by Barry Oakley, 1975; *6 of the Best* series, 1981–82; *Mr. Steam and Dry*, 1986.

Other

6 of the Best: An Introduction to the Television Drama Series. 1984.

*

Criticism

Articles:
John Romeril, interview in *Meanjin*, 3, 1978.
John Romeril and Leah Mercer, "A Fairly Hybrid Talent" (interview), in *Australasian Drama Studies*, 17, 1990.

* * *

Since the late 1960's John Romeril has been the most prolific playwright in Australia, and yet much of his work remains unpublished and has had little critical attention.

Many of his plays are occasional pieces, written in conjunction with regional, community-based theatre companies, theatre-in-education teams, or groups who have come together for single projects. This is part of a considered "industrial" ethics, wherein Romeril sees himself as a "public servant of the pen", taking his material from the community in which he is working, processing it according to his specific industrial skills, and giving it back to the community.

Like other playwrights of the "New Wave" of Australian playwriting, such as David Williamson, Alexander Buzo, and Jack Hibberd, Romeril first came to prominence as a young "alternative" writer in the late 1960's. His theatre was the Australian Performing Group (APG) in Melbourne, a self-consciously radical company, working as a co-operative, using "consensus creativity" to strive for a distinctively populist Australian way of presenting political material. The company's work was a curious mixture: it was heavily influenced by the radical American theatre of the 1960's as well as by various modernist dramatic movements such as absurdism, which had hitherto had little influence on Australian playwriting. In its early years, at the small La Mama theatre in Melbourne, the restrictions of a tiny performance-space led to an intimate style which the company called (after O'Neill) "supernaturalism". Later, in the larger, rowdier space of the Pram Factory, the company developed a more overtly theatrical, presentational mode of performance, drawing on the traditions of vaudeville and melodrama.

Of the many writers who cut their theatrical teeth with the APG, Romeril remained the most faithful to the theatre's original spirit. For ten years he worked with them, ignoring the attractions of the growing professional theatrical establishment to which many of his fellow writers drifted. When the APG finally closed in 1981 Romeril moved on to work on the series of political and community projects which has ensured him a low profile in the academic histories.

Romeril's unpublished plays make up an impressive body of work. Many of them show the marks of their origins, as pieces written for a specific group or political situation. The writing is often rushed and unrefined, but it has an energy and a theatrical exuberance that are very appealing. Romeril likes to speak of the "10% innovation" whereby the audience is given 90% of the material in a familiar genre or style and 10% new, challenging matter. Many of the occasional pieces are written in established conventions: vaudeville musicals, children's plays, or soap opera, for example, with an injection of original material, often with a political point.

Romeril has also produced a few plays, bearing the marks of a more individual impulse, which have become minor classics of the Australian drama of the 1970's. Undoubtedly the most important is *The Floating World*, a comic but finally gruelling study of Australian xenophobia and some of the very real historical events and political considerations which have created it. Major aspects of Australia's involvement in two World Wars are seen through the eyes of an old soldier who goes quietly mad reliving his experience as a prisoner of war on the notorious Burma-Thailand railway while on a "Woman's Weekly Cherry Blossom Cruise" to Japan. This central character, Les Harding, is first presented to us as a typically vulgar Australian male, an "ocker" of the sort which became a common theatrical stereotype in the 1970's. The play sets up, in the first half, a series of comic images of Australian aggressive self-assertion. As the cruise ship nears its destination, however, Les's past begins to consume him and we are led into the depths of the frightened insecurity which underlies the stereotyped social mask he has created for himself. The play succeeds particularly well in showing the personal feeling which lies behind the public mask of the cliched Australian male. It ends with a neat irony, as Les finds himself at last able to describe his personal crisis in the War, a moment when after all the pain of his imprisonment he became physically "well again". As he says it we watch him, strait-jacketed, finally and irrevocably insane.

I Don't Know Who to Feel Sorry For is an earlier work which also examines the individual feeling behind the social masks which the characters use, vainly, in an attempt to control their lives. In this case the central characters, Celia and Lenny, play out their relationship in a series of cannibalistic games which reveal a Strindbergian paranoia with regard to the possibilities of male-female relationships. *Chicago Chicago* is a rather unwieldy but at times powerful picture of those violent and amoral aspects of American society which, after the Chicago demonstrations of 1968, most terrified radical Australians, especially in the context of the Australian commitment to the war in Vietnam. The play employs a number of expressionist dislocating effects which make it, even now, one of the most formally adventurous of Australian plays of the New Wave. *Bastardy* is a bleak, unrelentingly naturalistic study of the "lower depths" of society. It presents the emotional (and physical) violence which its characters exhibit towards one another as being systematic and socially determined.

These plays, and others unpublished, reveal a dimension to Romeril's writing which seems to belie his modest claim to be a "public servant of the pen", as do the sudden flashes of originality in his formulaic writing for theatre-in-education and community companies, and, more recently, for television. More than any other Australian writer, including his intellectual and artistic confrère Stephen Sewell, Romeril has addressed the problem of politically radical writing which aims to make social and political, as well as artistic, statements in a manner that is accessible to audiences who are not part of the normal theatre-going public.

—John McCallum

See also *Volume 1* entry on *The Floating World*.

ROSTAND, Edmond (-Eugène). Born in Marseilles, France, 1 April 1868. Educated at Thedanat School, Marseilles; lycée, Marseilles, 1878–1884; Collège Stanislas, Paris, 1884–86. Married Rosemonde Gérard in 1890; several children. Early writings appeared in the literary periodical *Mireille*, 1884; first play, *Le Gant rouge*, produced 1888; poet and playwright, based in Paris, from the late 1880's: his dramatic roles interpreted by the leading actors, notably Coquelin and Sarah Bernhardt; retired to Cambo-les-Bains, in the Basque country, 1900, because of ill health. Elected to the Académie Française, 1901. Chevalier, Légion d'Honneur, 1900. Died in Paris, 2 December 1918.

Works

Collections

Oeuvres complètes (5 vols.). 1910–11; supplementary volume, 1925.
Plays (2 vols.), translated by Henderson Daingerfield Norman. 1921:

1. *The Romantics; The Princess Far Away; The Woman of Sumaria; Cyrano de Bergerac.*
2. *The Eaglet; Chantecleer.*

Stage Works

Le Gant rouge with Henry Lee (produced Théâtre de Cluny, Paris, 1888).
Les Deux Pierrots. 1891.
Les Romanesques (produced Comédie-Française, Paris, 1894). 1894; translated as *The Romancers*, 1899: several subsequent translations under same title; as *The Fantasticks*, 1900; as *The Romantics*, in *Plays 1*, 1921.
La Princesse lointaine (produced Théâtre de la Renaissance, Paris, 1895). 1895; translated as *The Princess Far Away*, 1899: several subsequent translations under same title; as *The Far Princess*, 1925.
La Samaritaine (produced Théâtre de la Renaissance, Paris, 1897). 1897; translated as *The Woman of Sumaria*, in *Plays 1*, 1921.
Cyrano de Bergerac (produced Théâtre de la Porte-Saint-Martin, Paris, 1897). 1898; translated as *Cyrano de Bergerac*, 1898: several subsequent translations under same title.
L'Aiglon (produced Théâtre Sarah-Bernhardt, Paris, 1900). 1900; translated as *The Eaglet*, in *Plays 2*, 1921; as *L'Aiglon*, 1927.
Le Bois sacré (pantomime; produced Théâtre Sarah-Bernhardt, Paris, 1910). 1908.
Chantecler (produced Théâtre de la Porte-Saint-Martin, Paris, 1910). 1910; translated as *Chantecler*, 1910; as *Chantecleer*, in *Plays 2*, 1921.
La Dernière Nuit de Don Juan (produced Théâtre de la Porte-Saint-Martin, Paris, 1922). 1921; translated as *The Last Night of Don Juan*, in *Poetic Drama*, edited by Alfred Kreymborg, 1941.

Verse

Les Musardises. 1890; revised edition, as *Les Musardises 1887–1893*, 1911.
Un Soir à Hernani. 1902.
Le Vol de la Marseillaise. 1919.
Le Cantique de l'aile. 1922.
Choix de poésies. 1925.

Other

Discours de réception à l'Académie Française. 1903.

*

Criticism

Books:
G. Haraszti, *Edmond Rostand*, Paris, 1913.
J. Suberville, *Le Théâtre d'Edmond Rostand: Étude critique*, Paris, 1919.
A. Lautier and F. Keller, *Edmond Rostand: Son Oeuvre*, Paris, 1924.
J. W. Grieve, *L'Oeuvre dramatique d'Edmond Rostand*, Paris, 1931.
E. Katz, *L'Esprit français dans le théâtre d'Edmond Rostand*, Toulouse, 1934.
Émile Ripert, *Edmond Rostand: Sa Vie et son oeuvre*, Paris, 1968.

Enrico Pappacena, *Edmond Rostand (1868–1918): Saggi*, Palo del Colle, 1972.
Marcel Migeo, *Les Rostand*, Paris, 1973.
Alba Amoia, *Edmond Rostand*, Boston, 1978.
Marc Andry, *Edmond Rostand: Le Panache et la gloire*, Paris, 1986.

* * *

There is little in the origins of Edmond Rostand to suggest that he would become the author of the most successful, and one of the most distinguished, French plays of the 19th century. A southerner, born at Marseilles into a cultured family, he completed his schooling in Paris, and began to write for the theatre while still a law-student. His first play, *Les Romanesques*, was performed at the Comédie-Française in 1894, and was followed by two plays written for Sarah Bernhardt at her Théâtre de la Renaissance—*La Princesse lointaine* (*The Faraway Princess*) and *La Samaritaine*. In the first of these, a dramatisation of a medieval legend, the central character of Mélissinde was judged too enigmatic, while in the latter, based on the biblical account of the encounter between Christ and the Samaritan woman, critical opinion found that Rostand had not entirely solved the problems inherent in showing Christ on stage. Although all three plays aroused serious critical interest, Rostand was classed as a somewhat lightweight talent, with a pleasing gift for rhyming, but whose ability was best seen in the construction of single scenes or tableaux rather than on the level of a full-scale work. This was a respectable debut for a minor playwright, but one which gave little indication of the impact *Cyrano de Bergerac* was to have in December 1987.

Cyrano was written in response to an offer from Constant Coquelin, probably the greatest actor of the day, who was so impressed by *La Princesse lointaine* that he sent a message to Rostand: "Write me a part and I'll play it whenever and wherever you like"; and the Porte-Saint-Martin theatre was chosen because the Comédie-Française was not immediately available. Author and cast were apprehensive before the first night: the bizarre character of the central figure, the length of the play, the exuberance of the spectacle, and competition with other works currently playing in Paris, all militated against the likelihood of success. Critical notices were unanimously enthusiastic, however, many quite extravagantly so, and *Cyrano* was soon being hailed as the most outstanding success since that of Corneille's *Le Cid* in 1637—all the more remarkable since, as Joseph Bédier was to write, "this was the success of *Le Cid* without the controversy surrounding *Le Cid*, the success of *Hernani* without the battle of *Hernani*". The initial impact in the theatre owed much to Coquelin—as director as well as actor—and also, no doubt, to contemporary audiences' subconscious need for a boost to national morale. But the play's success was far from ephemeral, and *Cyrano de Bergerac* continues to be revived frequently, both in France and abroad in translation.

Moving, amusing, entertaining, *Cyrano* owes its success above all to the author's verbal virtuosity: his dazzling wordplay, together with an audacious use of the Alexandrine verseform and especially of rhyme—perfectly suited to the chosen vehicle, the swashbuckling soldier-poet whose dexterity with words matches his physical prowess and his idealistic panache. This is literary drama at its best, and it was allied in the theatre to a succession of spectacular visual effects. Virtually contemporary with *Ubu Roi*, Jarry's provocatively avant-garde play of 1896, *Cyrano de Bergerac* is unashamedly traditional in its form and style. It is, in fact, the ultimate vindication of Victor Hugo's formula for lively, colourful, historical drama in verse, and one would like to think that if Hugo had still been

Edmond Rostand discussing his *Chantecler* with a member of the cast, 1910.

alive he would have been generous enough to welcome Rostand's achievement.

Rostand's second masterpiece, indeed his only other play to register an unqualified success, was *L'Aiglon* (*The Eaglet*). This was written for the Théâtre Sarah-Bernhardt, where Bernhardt herself played the part of the young Duc de Reichstadt, son of Napoleon Bonaparte, on whom, for a time, hopes for a Napoleonic revival had centred. The play is set in the last two years of the young Prince's life—he died in 1832—at the Imperial court in Vienna. While the historical atmosphere is authentic enough, the central figure himself owes a good deal to poetic licence: Rostand's imaginative manipulation of history shows the hero's attitude to his father's memory to be an ambivalent one. When his bid to restore the Bonapartist fortunes has ended in failure, he is presented as willing to accept his own death as expiation of his father's crimes against humanity, and the appalling loss of life which had been the price of his military victories—an interesting interpretation, but one for which there exists no historical warrant. The writing has something of the verve Rostand had shown in *Cyrano*, but although the play achieved considerable success it did not have—and did not deserve—the outstanding triumph of the earlier play, nor has it had *Cyrano de Bergerac*'s lasting appeal for later audiences.

Chantecler was less successful, and although it had its warm supporters, the medium chosen here by Rostand—a fable in which, as he wrote, "I have used animals to evoke and relate the sentiments, passions and dreams of men"—was bound to make it, in spite of its striking allegorical and satirical qualities, a piece for the connoisseur rather than for the general public. His last play, *La Dernière Nuit de Don Juan* (*The Last Night of Don Juan*), performed posthumously in 1922, was a complete failure.

Rostand published several volumes of poetry, but his reputation rested almost entirely on his work for the theatre. He was elected to the French Academy in 1901, the youngest writer ever to be so honoured; but the last 20 years of his life were overshadowed by constant ill-health.

—William D. Howarth

See also *Volume 1* entry on *Cyrano de Bergerac*.

ROSWITHA.   See HROTSVITHA.

ROTIMI, (Emmanuel Gladstone) Ola(wale). Born in Sapele, Nigeria, 13 April 1938. Educated at Methodist Boys' High School, Lagos, 1952–56; Boston University (President, African Students Union, 1962–63), 1959–63, BFA 1963; Yale University School of Drama, New Haven, Connecticut (Rockefeller scholar, 1963–66; Student Drama prize, 1966), 1963–66, MFA 1966. Married Hazel Mae Gaudreau in 1965; three sons and one daughter. Executive director and artistic director, University of Ife Theatre, Ife, Nigeria, 1973–77; since 1977 director of the University theatre, Dean of Student Affairs, 1979–80, Dean of the Faculty of Humanities, 1982–84, and since 1982 Head of the Department of Creative Arts, all University of Port Harcourt, Nigeria. Has directed productions of all his own plays and works by others. Recipient: *African Arts* Prize, 1969; Oxford University Press Prize, 1970; Nigerian National Festival of the Arts Prize, 1974.

Works

Stage Works

Our Husband Has Gone Mad Again (produced Yale University, New Haven, Connecticut, 1966). 1977.
The Gods Are Not to Blame (produced University of Ife, 1968; London, 1978). 1971.
Kurunmi: An Historical Tragedy (produced Ife Festival, 1969). 1971.
The Prodigal (dance play; produced Ife Festival, 1969).
Holding Talks (produced University of Ife, 1970).
Ovonramwen Nogbaisi (produced Ife Festival, 1971).
Initiation into Madness, from a play by Adegoke Duro-jaiye (produced University of Ife, 1973).
Grip Am (produced University of Ife, 1973).
Akassa Youmi (produced Port Harcourt, 1977).
If: A Tragedy of the Ruled (produced University of Port Harcourt, 1979). 1983.
Hopes of the Living-Dead (produced University of Port Harcourt, 1985). 1988.

Radio Plays

Everyone His/Her Own Problem, 1987.

*

Bibliographies

O. Lalude, bibliography in *Bibliographic Series 1*, Port Harcourt, 1984.

Criticism

Books:
Martin Banham and Clive Wake, *African Theatre Today*, London, 1976.
Dapo Adelugba, "Three Dramatists in Search of a Language" in *Theatre in Africa*, Ibadan, 1978.
Akanju Nasiru, "Ola Rotimi's Search for Technique" in *New West African Literature*, edited by Kolawole Ogungbesan, London, 1979.
Biodun Jeyifo, "The Search for a Popular Theatre" in *Drama and Theatre in Nigeria*, Lagos, 1981.
Femi Osofisan, *Beyond Translation: Tragic Paradigms and the Dramaturgy of Ola Rotimi and Wole Soyinka*, Ife, 1985.

Articles:
Ola Rotimi and Onura O. Enekwe, "Interview with Ola Rotimi", in *Okike*, 25–26, 1984.
Kalu Okpi, "Ola Rotimi: A Popular Nigerian Dramatist and Man of the Theatre", in *Literary Criterion*, vol. 23 nos. 1–3, 1988.
Martin Banham, "Ola Rotimi: 'Humanity as My Tribesman'", in *Modern Drama*, 33, 1990.

Chinyere G. Okafor, "Ola Rotimi: The Man, the Playwright, and the Producer on the Nigerian Theater Scene", in *World Literature Today*, 64, 1990.

* * *

Ola Rotimi was born of Yoruba and Ijo parents, a significant cross-cultural relationship in Nigerian terms, and one that gives added dynamic to his committed stance against the destructive elements of tribalism. In his work he has developed a trans-Nigerian theatrical idiom, bringing together performance traditions from various cultural groups and experimenting successfully with ways of making from the many languages of Nigeria a mutually comprehensible tongue.

Rotimi's early work was satirical comedy, specifically *Our Husband Has Gone Mad Again*, which was produced first at Yale University in 1966, though not published until 1977. On his return to teach at the University of Ife in Nigeria in 1966, and through a commission for the first Ife Festival of the Arts in 1968, he began to write on a larger scale, experimenting with creative adaptation (*The Gods Are Not to Blame* is a version of Sophocles' *Oedipus Rex*) and with themes from Nigerian history (*Kurunmi*, which is placed in the Yoruba (Ijaiye) wars of the 19th century, and *Ovonramwen Nogbaisi*, which takes its title from the king of the kingdom of Benin, sacked by a British punitive expedition in 1897). All three plays, however, could be seen to comment on contemporary affairs in post-independence Nigeria. All are, in some part, political plays, dealing with the havoc and misery caused by factional conflict. For Nigerian audiences their targets and comments were not difficult to locate.

At the same time Rotimi was developing and refining his theatrical craftsmanship, creating work on an epic scale, incorporating dance, music, and spectacle. He was particularly attracted to the informal (and traditional) actor/audience relationship of the round, expressed for him in—literally—concrete terms by the creation of open-air courtyard theatres for his productions. His play *If*, first performed at the University of Port Harcourt Theatre in 1979, is a powerful political allegory set in a typical multi-tenanted compound which replicates the courtyard form. Though the physical size of the play is less then the preceding works, the imaginative scope is vast. The compound accommodates characters of different class, occupation, and linguistic background. It is a microcosm of Nigerian society, and the play, which makes its political statement directly, concerns the exploitation of the people by the powerful elites. In *If* Rotimi shows that though the diversity of tongues among Nigerians may be used by the politically devious to divide and corrupt, by determined effort and commitment people can break through these barriers. This is no empty sloganising: in the play Rotimi uses English, pidgin English, and indigenous languages and devises a process of translation that is one of the most effective features of the play.

This experiment was carried on into *Hopes of the Living-Dead* (first produced at the University of Port Harcourt Theatre in 1985) which, like *If*, is overtly political in tone and function. Rotimi returns to a theme from contemporary history, the life of Ikoli Harcourt Whyte (1905–77), a man famed for his work as a composer of choral music, but also a leper. Harcourt Whyte led a protest of leprosy patients when, in 1924, attempts were made by the authorities to close down their hospital and send the patients back to their communities. The play chronicles the protest and the eventual triumph of the lepers who were able to form the self-help community of the Uzuakoli Leper Settlement. However, the

play is about more than this. It shows, once again, how people of various backgrounds and languages, oppressed by authority, can fight back by finding the means and the will to unite. 15 languages are used in the play, where the simultaneous translation woven into the action gives the work an extraordinary dynamic.

Ola Rotimi is an accomplished director who has directed the first productions of all his plays in Nigeria. His work is widely accessible, theatrically inventive, and politically engaged, and he must be seen as one of the leading playwrights of Africa.

—Martin Banham

ROTROU, Jean (de). Born in Dreux, Normandy, France; baptised 21 August 1609. Studied in Paris, from c.1620. Married Marguerite Camus de Mantes in 1640; six children. Officially contracted playwright, probably succeeding Alexandre Hardy, for the Comédiens du Roi at the Hôtel de Bourgogne, Paris, c.1629–36, and continued to write for the Hôtel thereafter; associate of the influential dramatic theoretician, Jean Chapelain; member, with Pierre Corneille and others, of the "Cinq Auteurs" group, assembled to write plays for Cardinal Richelieu, 1635–37; awarded pension by Richelieu; bought the civil post of "lieutenant particulier au baillage" in Dreux, 1639; remained in Dreux to fulfil his civic office during an epidemic, eventually succumbing to it. Died (buried) in Dreux, 28 June 1650.

Works

Collections

Autres Oeuvres poétiques. 1631.
Autres Oeuvres. 1635.
Oeuvres (5 vols.), edited by E.-E. Viollet-le-Duc. 1820; reprinted, 1967.
Théâtre choisi (2 vols.; includes *Hercule mourant; Antigone; Saint Genest; Dom Cernard de Cabrère; Venceslas; Cosroès*), edited by L. de Ronchaud. 1882.
Théâtre choisi (includes *Les Sosies; Laure persécutée; La Soeur; Saint Genest; Dom Bernard de Cabrère; Venceslas; Cosroès*), edited by Félix Hémon. 1883; reprinted 1925.
"Saint Genest" and "Venceslas", edited by Thomas F. Crane. 1907.
The Chief Rivals of Corneille and Racine (includes Rotrou's *Chosroes* and *Wenceslaus*), translated by Lacy Lockert. 1956.
Théâtre du XVIIe siècle (includes *La Bague de l'oubli; La Belle Alphrède; Laure persécutée; Saint Genest; Venceslas; Cosroès*), edited by Jacques Scherer. 1975.

Stage Works

L'Hypochondriaque; ou, Le Mort amoureux (produced Théâtre de l'Hôtel de Bourgogne, Paris, 1628). 1631.
La Bague de l'oubli, from a play by Lope de Vega (produced Théâtre de l'Hôtel de Bourgogne, Paris, 1629?). 1635.
Les Ménechmes, from a play by Plautus (produced Théâtre de l'Hôtel de Bourgogne, Paris, 1630–31). 1636.

La Céliane (produced Théâtre de l'Hôtel de Bourgogne, Paris, 1631–32).   1637; as *La Belle Céliane*, 1642.

La Diane, from a play by Lope de Vega (produced Théâtre de l'Hôtel de Bourgogne, Paris, 1632–33).   1635.

La Pélerine amoureuse, from a play by Girolamo Bargaglia (produced Théâtre de l'Hôtel de Bourgogne, Paris, 1633?).   1637; as *Angélique; ou, la Pélerine amoureuse*, 1637.

La Filandre (produced Théâtre de l'Hôtel de Bourgogne, Paris, 1633).   1637.

Les Occasions perdues, from a play by Lope de Vega (produced Théâtre de l'Hôtel de Bourgogne, Paris, 1633).   1635.

La Célimène (produced Théâtre de l'Hôtel de Bourgogne, Paris, 1633).   1636.

L'Heureuse Constance, from plays by Lope de Vega (produced Théâtre de l'Hôtel de Bourgogne, Paris, c.1633).   1636.

Amélie (produced Théâtre de l'Hôtel de Bourgogne, Paris, 1633?).   1638.

Cléagénor et Doristée, from a novel by Charles Sorel (produced Théâtre de l'Hôtel de Bourgogne, Paris, 1634).   As *La Doristée*, 1635; as *Cléagénor et Doristée*, 1635.

Hercule mourant, from a play by Seneca (produced Théâtre de l'Hôtel de Bourgogne, Paris, 1634).   1636.

L'Heureux Naufrage (produced Théâtre de l'Hôtel de Bourgogne, Paris, 1634/35?).   1637; as *Cléandre, ou, L'Heureux Naufrage*, 1637.

L'Innocente Infidélité (produced Théâtre de l'Hôtel de Bourgogne, Paris, 1634/35).   1637.

Crisante (produced Théâtre de l'Hôtel de Bourgogne, Paris, 1635?).   1640.

La Florimonde (produced Théâtre de l'Hôtel de Bourgogne, Paris, 1635–36?).   1655.

Clorinde (produced Théâtre de l'Hôtel de Bourgogne, Paris, 1635).   1637.

La Comédie des Tuileries, with Pierre Corneille and others (produced Théâtre du Marais, Paris, 1635–36).   1638.

La Belle Alphrède (produced Théâtre de l'Hôtel de Bourgogne, Paris, 1636?).   1639.

Agésilan de Colchos, from the romance *Amadis de Gaule* (produced Théâtre de l'Hôtel de Bourgogne, Paris, 1636).   1637.

Les Deux Pucelles, from a play by Cervantes (produced Théâtre de l'Hôtel de Bourgogne, Paris, 1636?).   1639.

Les Sosies, from a play by Plautus (produced Théâtre de l'Hôtel de Bourgogne, Paris, 1636–37).   1638.

Antigone (produced Théâtre de l'Hôtel de Bourgogne, Paris, 1636–37?).   1639.

L'Aveugle de Smyrne, with Pierre Corneille and others (produced Palais Cardinal, Paris, 1637).   1638.

Laure persécutée, from a play by Lope de Vega (produced Théâtre de l'Hôtel de Bourgogne, Paris, 1637?).   1639.

Les Captifs, from a play by Plautus (produced Théâtre de l'Hôtel de Bourgogne, Paris, 1638?).   1640.

Iphigénie, from a play by Euripides (produced Théâtre de l'Hôtel de Bourgogne, Paris, 1640?).   1641; as *Le Sacrifice d'Iphigénie*, 1642.

Clarice; ou, L'Amour constant, from a work by Sforza Oddi (produced Théâtre de l'Hôtel de Bourgogne, Paris, 1641).   1643.

Bélisaire, from a play by Antonio Mira de Amescua (produced Théâtre de l'Hôtel de Bourgogne, Paris, 1642–43?).   1644.

Célie (produced Théâtre de l'Hôtel de Bourgogne, Paris, 1644–45?).   As *Célie, ou, Le Vice-roy de Naples*, 1646.

La Soeur, from a play by Giambattista Della Porta (produced Théâtre de l'Hôtel de Bourgogne, Paris, 1645).   1647.

Le Véritable Saint Genest, from a play by Lope de Vega (produced Théâtre de l'Hôtel de Bourgogne, Paris, 1647?).   1647.

Dom Bernard de Cabrère (produced Théâtre de l'Hôtel de Bourgogne, Paris, 1646?).   1647.

Venceslas, from a work by Francisco de Rojas Zorilla (produced Théâtre de l'Hôtel de Bourgogne, Paris, 1647).   1648; translated as *Wenceslaus*, in *The Chief Rivals of Corneille and Racine*, 1956.

Cosroès (produced Théâtre de l'Hôtel de Bourgogne, Paris, 1647).   1649; translated as *Chosroes*, in *The Chief Rivals of Corneille and Racine*, 1956.

Dom Lope de Cardone, from the play by Lope de Vega (produced Théâtre de l'Hôtel de Bourgogne, Paris, 1651).   1652.

L'Illustre Amazone, possibly not by Rotrou.   In *Oeuvres 5*, 1820.

Verse

Ode à M le Cardinal Duc de Richelieu.   1634.
Amarillis.   1653.

*

Criticism

Books:

Saint-René Taillandier, *Rotrou, sa vie et ses oeuvres*, Paris, 1865.

H. Chardon, *La vie de Rotrou mieux connue*, Paris, 1884.

J. van Baelen, *Rotrou: Le Héros tragique et la révolte*, Paris, 1965.

H.C. Knutson, *The Ironic Game: A Study of Rotrou's Comic Theater*, Berkeley, California, 1966.

J. Morel, *Jean Rotrou, dramaturge de l'ambiguité*, Paris, 1968.

R.J. Nelson, *Immanence and Transcendence: The Theater of Jean Rotrou*, Columbus, Ohio, 1969.

J. Morel, *Jean de Rotrou*, Boston, 1980.

D.A. Watts, "Rotrou's Problematical Tragedies", in *Form and Meaning*, edited by W.D. Howarth and others, Amersham, 1982.

Articles:

H. Wood, "The Language of Love in Rotrou's Comedies", in *Romanic Review*, 75, 1984.

* * *

Jean Rotrou, a leading member of the second generation of 17th-century French playwrights, which included Mairet, Du Ryer, Pierre Corneille, and others, was a prolific professional. More than 30 of his plays have survived, produced between 1628 and 1651. His first comedy, *L'Hypocondriaque*, was produced when he was only 19; his first great success, *La Bague de l'oubli* (The Ring of Forgetfulness), opened the following year. By 1632 he was the official playwright of the company which occupied the Hôtel de Bourgogne, and between 1633 and 1636, 18 of his plays were performed by the troupe. Awarded a pension by Cardinal Richelieu, Rotrou was also one of the five playwrights selected by the Cardinal to write plays by committee. None of the three plays thus generated was successful. After 1639, Rotrou lived in his native city of Dreux and, away from the pressures of Paris, wrote his best plays, notably *Venceslas* and *Le Véritable Saint Genest*.

According to his title pages, Rotrou's output consisted of tragedies, tragicomedies, and comedies, but since Rotrou had a baroque rather than a classical sensibility, his plays rarely fit the rigid categories established by the neoclassical critics. Rotrou was also especially attracted to Spanish plays as sources, and is among those responsible for introducing the imitation of Lope de Vega and others into the French theatre. He borrowed from the Italians, as well, and even wrote three plays in imitation of Plautus.

The *Hypocondriaque* is a flamboyant, baroque tragicomedy full of deceit and disguise, death, and madness, ending in a dance of the risen dead accompanied by music and pistol shots. *La Bague de l'oubli*, a somewhat pastoral comedy based on Lope de Vega's *Sortija del Olvido*, is much the same sort of thing. It features a ring which affects the mental state and memory of its wearer. The plot follows the ring and the characters who wear it through the consequences of actions they do not remember taking. These journeyman plays, though not of special interest to literary historians, are first-class examples of popular theatrical fare at that point of transition in Paris when farces and touring companies gave way to established theatres. Rotrou continued to write in the tragicomic, pastoral mode until the fashion for pastorals died out in the mid-1630's.

Rotrou's best-known comedies are *Les Sosies* (The Doubles), an adaptation of Plautus's *Amphitryon*, which was a great popular success in 1636, and *La Soeur* (The Sister), based on Giambattista Della Porta's *La Sorella*, produced in 1645. The latter play, a cleverly constructed comedy of intrigue, is also probably the source of the *deus-ex-machina* ending of Molière's *L'Avare* (The Miser), as in it an Italian gentleman named Anselme has lost his wife and daughter to Turkish pirates.

Probably Rotrou's most popular play, performed well into the 19th century, was *Venceslas*, produced first at the Hôtel de Bourgogne in 1647 and later reprised by Molière's troupe at the Petit-Bourbon and kept in the repertory. Although Rotrou is usually characterized as a baroque playwright, *Venceslas* is often admired for its relative conformity to neoclassical norms. Based rather loosely on Francisco de Rojas's *No hay ser padre siendo rey*, Rotrou's play omits the comic characters from the original, reduces the physical action, and gives the central character an inner moral struggle. Nonetheless, the play's plot is centered on a love rivalry between two brothers which leads to fratricide and concludes when the murderous brother succeeds to the crown and is thus, by Spanish custom, placed above the law. The woman in question, although shocked by the turn of events, implies that she will in time accept his suit, an ending with a clear similarity to that of Pierre Corneille's *Le Cid*. Thus, though the structure of the play follows the unities and the action is simplified, the moral universe of the play is still that of the Spanish baroque.

An even more clear example of baroque dramaturgy is *Le Véritable Saint Genest*, a tragi-comedy first produced c.1645 at the Hôtel de Bourgogne, rediscovered by the Odéon in the middle of the 19th century, and recently produced by the Comédie-Française in 1988. Generally considered by modern critics to be Rotrou's most interesting play, *Le Véritable Saint Genest* combines multiple levels of reality, metatheatricality, and the marvelous with a somewhat forced adherence to the unities and the proprieties of neoclassicism.

The central action of the play concerns the Roman actor Genest, or Genesius, who undergoes conversion to Christianity while performing a play for the emperors Dioclétien and Maximin about the conversion and martyrdom of the Roman soldier Adrian. This central action, with its interplay of reality and illusion, is framed by a love story between Maximin and Dioclétien's daughter, Valérie, which gives rise to the occasion for the Court entertainment. The play follows two theatrical traditions of the 1630's and 1640's—the religious play or Christian tragedy, best exemplified by Pierre Corneille's *Polyeucte*, and the metatheatrical comedy, such as Scudéry's *La Comédie des comédiens* (The Actors' Comedy) and Pierre Corneille's *L'Illusion Comique* (The Theatrical Illusion). Rotrou's play is usually classified as a tragicomedy because of the ambiguity of its ending. On the one hand, Genest is tortured and put to death, although from a Christian point of view martyrdom is not tragic; on the other, the play ends with the wedding characteristic of comedy.

Even more in the spirit of the baroque is the play's use of theatre as metaphor. Not only does Rotrou employ the common baroque theme of "all the world's a stage", but he also explores the psychology of the actor and the relationship of actor to character. Genest "becomes" Adrian, and in this act of *metempsychose*, or transmigration of the soul, ceases to be the actor Genest and becomes the Christian Genest. This ability to "change souls" is at the heart of the actor's mystery, and may go a long way to explain the Church's exaggerated fear of and contempt for the theatrical profession. When Genest reveals his conversion, he "raises the mask", regrets having "scandalized the laws of the Christian God", and renounces "this perishable world, and its frivolous glory, a play in which I was ignorant of my role".

Although many of Rotrou's plays, especially those written during his tenure as playwright-in-residence at the Hôtel de Bourgogne, are of little interest, his major plays—and especially *Le Véritable Saint Genest*—are quite remarkable examples of French baroque dramaturgy, once overshadowed by literary classicism but now once again revealed as the products of a rich theatrical imagination.

—Virginia Scott

ROWE, Nicholas. Born in Little Barford, Bedfordshire, England; baptised 30 June 1674. Educated at a school in Highgate, London; Westminster School, London (King's scholar), 1688–91; Middle Temple, London, from 1691, called to the bar, 1696. Married 1) Antonia Parsons in 1693 (died 1712), seven children; 2) Anne Devenish in 1716, one daughter. First-produced play, *The Ambitious Step-Mother*, staged 1700; under-secretary to James Douglas, Duke of Queensberry and secretary of state for Scotland, 1709–11; clerk, council of the Prince of Wales (later George II), 1714; land surveyor of customs, London, 1716; clerk of presentations to the Lord Chancellor, 1718. First modern editor of Shakespeare, 1709. Poet laureate, 1715–18. Died in London, 6 December 1718.

Works

Collections

Tragedies (2 vols.). 1714.
Plays, edited by Anne Devenish (2 vols.). 1747.
Three Plays (includes *Tamerlane; The Fair Penitent; Jane Shore*), edited by James R. Sutherland. 1929.

Stage Works

The Ambitious Step-Mother (produced Lincoln's Inn Fields
    Theatre, London, 1700). 1701.
Tamerlane (produced Lincoln's Inn Fields Theatre, London,
    1701). 1702.
The Fair Penitent, from a play by Massinger and Nathan Field
    (produced Lincoln's Inn Fields Theatre, London,
    1703). 1703.
The Biter (produced Lincoln's Inn Fields Theatre, London,
    1704). 1705.
Ulysses (produced Queen's Theatre, Haymarket, London,
    1705). 1706.
The Royal Convert (produced Queen's Theatre, Haymarket,
    London, 1707). 1708; as *Ethelinda* (produced 1776).
Jane Shore (produced Theatre Royal, Drury Lane, London,
    1714). 1714.
Lady Jane Gray (produced Theatre Royal, Drury Lane,
    London, 1715). 1715.

Verse

*A Poem upon the Late Glorious Successes of Her Majesty's
    Arms.* 1707.
Poems on Several Occasions. 1714.
Poetical Works. 1715.
Ode for the New Year 1716. 1716.
Ode for the Year 1717. 1717.
Ode to the Thames for the Year 1719. 1719.

Other

Editor, *Poetical Miscellanies 5–6*, by Dryden and others (2
    vols.). 1703–09.
Editor, *Works of Shakespeare* (6 vols.). 1709.

Translator, *The Life of Pythagoras* (verse only). 1706.
Translator, with others, *Callipaedia*, by Claudius Quillet.
    1712.
Translator, with others, *Ovid's Metamorphoses.* 1717.
Translator, *Lucan's Pharsalia.* 1719.

*

Criticism

Books:
Landon C. Burns, *Pity and Tears: The Tragedies of Nicholas
    Rowe*, Salzburg, 1974.
Douglas Canfield, *Nicholas Rowe and Christian Tragedy*,
    Gainesville, Florida, 1977.
Annibel Jenkins, *Nicholas Rowe*, Boston, 1977.

Articles
A. Jackson, "Rowe's Historical Tragedies", in *Anglia*, 54,
    1930.

* * *

The acceptance of his first play, *The Ambitious Step-Mother*,
by the breakaway theatre company at Lincoln's Inn Fields
initiated a long-standing collaboration between Nicholas
Rowe and the distinguished actors Elizabeth Barry, Anne
Bracegirdle; and Thomas Betterton. Barry and Bracegirdle

created a series of matched female roles, devised to suit their
particular skills: Artemisa and Amestris (*The Ambitious
Step-Mother*), Arpasia and Selima (*Tamerlane*), Calista and
Lavinia (*The Fair Penitent*), and Penelope and Semanthe
(*Ulysses*).

It seems likely that Rowe's initial commitment to a company of
older actors who had made their reputations in the plays of
illustrious predecessors such as Dryden and Otway led him to
imitate a dramatic form that they would have found congenial,
but which was already outmoded. *The Ambitious Step-Mother* is
a heroic play in the style of Dryden and Lee. The setting is exotic
and spectacular, the figures public, the preoccupation is with
affairs of State. The play also marks a departure from the earlier
heroic plays—although this, too, is anticipated by Dryden—in
that Rowe introduces an element of pathos that was to be more
fully explored in his later works.

The goal of tragedy, Rowe professed in the dedication of
The Ambitious Step-Mother, is pity and terror, but the
audience, he continued, should always "go away with pity, a
sort of regret proceeding from good-nature, which, though an
uneasiness, is not altogether disagreeable to the person who
feels it". It was to achieve this objective that he was prepared
to allow the relationship between the virtuous pair,
Artaxerxes and Amestris, to end unfortunately, in spite of the
claims of poetic justice.

Typical of the earlier heroic plays in general had been a
preoccupation with succession, a question that was particularly relevant during the reign of the Charles I, who had no
legitimate issue. Succession is also a concern in *The
Ambitious Step-Mother*: William and Mary, who were then on
the throne, were childless. *Tamerlane*, which succeeded
Rowe's first play in 1701, is primarily a political work, referring as it does to William III in the figure of Tamerlane, and
Louis XIV in that of Bajazet. The political references are so
overt that *Tamerlane* was performed every year until 1815, on
November 4th, William's birthday, or on the following day,
the anniversary of his first landing in England.

"Long has the fate of kings and empires been/ The common
business of the tragic scene", Rowe declared in the prologue
to *The Fair Penitent*. His theme would now be "a melancholy
tale of private woes". Central to the play is the doomed figure
of the beautiful but errant Calista. The role was perfectly
suited to Elizabeth Barry, who had created Otway's beautiful
but doomed heroines. The difference from Otway is immediately apparent, however. Rowe's object is not to indulge
emotions but to achieve moral instruction. *The Fair Penitent*
addresses moral issues which would immediately engage his
audience, and Rowe creates a central figure whose indictment
of male oppression speaks directly to the women who were
now so important a part of his audience.

Rowe's only attempt at comedy, *The Biter*, although not the
complete failure that it is sometimes said to be, never
achieved the lasting success of the best of his tragedies. In his
following two plays Rowe reverted to heroic drama with its
strong political concerns. *Ulysses* was written for the tried
team of Betterton, Barry, and Bracegirdle. Penelope (Barry),
as one would expect, exemplifies marital fidelity, and is a
flattering reference to the virtues of Queen Anne; the concern
with succession in the apparent absence of Ulysses is typical of
the period and of the heroic play. In *The Royal Convert* the
political issues are even more overt. Set in Kent after the first
Saxon invasions, the play opposes the King, Hengist, who is in
love with Ethelinda, with his brother, Aribert, to whom
Ethelinda is, in fact, secretly married. Ethelinda, the
daughter of a British chieftain, is a Christian and converts
Aribert to Christianity. Juxtaposed with her is Rodogune,
played by Elizabeth Barry. After various vicissitudes and

spectacular scenes, Hengist is killed, Rodogune thwarted, and the union of Aribert and Ethelinda is, in effect, also that of Saxon and Briton. The preoccupation with union picks up the contemporary concern with the Union of England and Scotland, and the unequivocal support of Christianity and the Church was also calculated to appeal to Queen Anne as head of both Church and State.

Jane Shore, the first of Rowe's plays to be acted at Drury Lane, is also his masterpiece. In it he returns to the domestic tragedy of *The Fair Penitent*, although it is set in a context of State affairs. *Jane Shore*, Rowe declared on the title page, is "written in imitation of Shakespeare's style". It is typical of the 18th-century attitude to Shakespeare that in the prologue to his play Rowe should declare that Shakespeare wrote, "By no quaint rules, nor hampering critics taught,/ With rough, majestic force he moved the heart,/ And strength, and nature made amends for art".

Jane Shore draws on Rowe's earlier achievements: the concerns of public life had been broached in the earlier heroic plays; domestic tragedy and private issues seen from a female perspective had characterized *The Fair Penitent*; Hastings is a more complex version of Lothario in the earlier play; and the juxtaposition of two contrasting female roles, had distinguished Rowe's work from the beginning, is present in the contrasting figures of Jane and Alicia. What sets *Jane Shore* apart is greater psychological depth, a more profound analysis of the issues of sin and redemption, and a greater simplicity and directness in dramatic structure and language.

In contrast, Rowe's final play, *The Tragedy of Lady Jane Gray*, is disappointing. Its preoccupation with the political issues of succession and its vigorous defence of Protestantism link it to the earlier heroic plays. These concerns detract, however, from the central figure of Lady Jane Gray, who is one-dimensional and lacks the internal contradictions that enliven the character of Jane Shore.

—Colin Wills Visser

See also *Volume 1* entry on *The Fair Penitent*.

ROWLEY, William. See *Volume 1* entries on *The Changeling* and *The Witch of Edmonton* .

RÓŻEWICZ, Tadeusz. Born in Radomsko, Poland, 9 October 1921. Secondary education interrupted by the German invasion of Poland, 1939. Had various jobs as messenger, clerk, and carpenter's apprentice; from 1942 attended secret military training and became an active member of the resistance movement, the Home Army; also published poetry and prose, and edited an underground magazine. Resumed secondary education in Czestochowa after the War; studied art history at the Jagelonian University, Cracow, 1948–53. Married in 1949; two sons. Moved to Gliwice, 1950; first-produced play, *Kartoteka* [*The Card Index*], staged 1960; moved to Wrocław, 1968; visited the USA, 1975 and 1987.

Recipient: State Prize, 1955 and 1966; Cracow Prize, 1959; Minister of Culture's Prize, 1962; Wrocław Prize, 1972; Austrian State Prize, 1982. Member, Bavarian Academy of Fine Arts.

Works

Collections

Utwory dramatyczne [Dramatic Works] (includes *Kartoteka; Grupa Laokoona; Smieszny staruszek; Spaghetti i miecz; Wyszedl z domu; Akt przerywany*).   1966.
"*The Card Index*" *and Other Plays* (includes *Gone Out; The Interrupted Act*), translated by Adam Czerniawski.   1969.
"*The Witnesses*" *and Other Plays* (includes *The Funny Old Man* and *The Old Woman Broods*), translated by Adam Czerniawski.   1970.
Sztuki teatralne [Theatrical Plays].   1972.
"*Biale malżeństwo*" *i inne utwory sceniczne* (includes *Biale malżeństwo; Dzidzibobo . . .; Sobowtor; Dramat rozbiezny; Czego pyrzbywa czego ubywa*).   1975.
Teatr niekonsekwencji [Theatre of Inconsistencies] (see Stage Works for contents).   1979.
"*Mariage Blanc*" *and* "*The Hunger Artist Departs*", translated by Adam Czerniawski.   1983.
Teatr (2 vols.).   1988.

Stage Works

Kartoteka (produced Teatr Dramatyczny, Warsaw, 1960). 1961; translated as *The Card Index*, in "*The Card Index*" *and Other Plays*, 1969.
Grupa Laokoona [Laocoon Group] (produced Teatr Dramatyczny, 1961).   In *Nic w plaszczu Prospera*, 1962.
Świadkwie; albo, Nasza mala stabilizacja (produced Schiller-Theater, Berlin, 1963; produced Teatr Ludowy, Warsaw, 1964).   In *Nic w plaszczu Prospera*, 1962; translated as *The Witnesses*, in "*The Witnesses*" *and Other Plays*, 1970.
Akt przerywany (produced Ulmer Theater, Ulm-Donau, West Germany, 1964; produced in Polish, Teatr im Osterwy, Lublin, 1970).   In *Utwory dramatyczne*, 1966; translated as *The Interrupted Act*, in "*The Card Index*" *and Other Plays*, 1969.
Śmieszny staruszek (produced Teatr Ateneum, Warsaw, 1965).   In *Utwory dramatyczne*, 1966; translated as *The Funny Old Man*, in "*The Witnesses*" *and Other Plays*, 1970.
Spaghetti i miecz [Spaghetti and the Sword] (produced Teatr Dramatyczny, Warsaw, 1967).   In *Utwory dramatyczne*, 1966.
Wyszedl z domu (produced Teatr Stary, Cracow, 1965).   In *Utwory dramatyczne*, 1966; translated as *Gone Out*, in "*The Card Index*" *and Other Plays*, 1969.
Przyrost naturalny (produced Teatr Wspólczesny, Wrocław, 1979).   In *Dialog*, April 1968; translated as *Birth-Rate*, in *20th-Century Polish Avant-Garde Plays*, edited by Daniel Gerould, 1977.
Stara kobieta wysiaduje (produced Teatr Wspólczesny, Wrocław, 1968).   In *Dialog*, 8, 1968; in book form, with *Smieszny staruszek*, 1970; translated as *The Old Woman Broods*, in "*The Witnesses*" *and Other Plays*, 1970.
Pogrzeb naturalny [A Funeral, Polish Style] (produced Teatr Polski, Wrocław, 1971).   In *Dialog?*, 1972.
Na czworakach [On All Fours] (produced Teatr Dramatyczny, Warsaw, 1972).   In *Dialog*, 9, 1971.
Biale malżeństwo (produced Teatr Maly, Warsaw, 1975). In *Biale malżeństwo. . .* (collection), 1975; translated as *Mariage Blanc*, with *The Hunger Artist Departs*, 1983.

Dzidzibobo; czyli, miłość romantyczna czeka już pod drzwiami [Boobsi Tootsie; or, Romantic Love is Already Waiting at the Door]. In *Biale małżeństwo. . .* collection), 1975.
Dramat rosbiezny [A Discordant Drama]. In *Biale małżeństwo. . .* (collection), 1975.
Sobowtór [The Double]. In *Biale małżeństwo. . .* (collection), 1975.
Czego pyrsbywa czego ubywa [What Comes, What Goes]. In *Biale malzenstow. . .* (collection), 1975.
Odejście głodomora (produced Teatr Wspólczesny, Wrocław, 1977). In *Dialog*, September 1976; translated as *The Hunger Artist Departs*, with *Mariage Blanc*, 1983.
Teatr niekonsekwencji [Theatre of Inconsistencies] (short plays; includes *Straż porządkowa* [The Guard]; *Rajski ogródek* [The Little Garden of Eden]; *Metamorozy* [Metamorphoses]; *Co tu maci* [What Have You Got]; *Wielkości* [Greats]; *Zacieranie rąk* [Hand-Rubbing]; *Dramat postaw moralnych* [A Drama of Moral Attitudes]; all produced 1979). 1979.
Do piachu [To the Boneyard] (produced Teatr na Woli, Warsaw, 1979). In *Dialog*, February 1979.
Pułapka (produced Norway, 1983; produced in Poland, 1984). In *Dialog*, June 1982; translated as *The Trap*, 1984.

Fiction

Opadly liście z drzew [The Leaves Have Fallen from the Trees]. 1955.
Przerwany egzamin [The Interrupted Examination]. 1960.
Wycieczka do muzeum [An Excursion to a Museum]. 1966.
Opowiadania wybrane [Selected Stories]. 1968.
Śmierć w starych dekoracjach [Death amid Old Stage Props]. 1970.
Opowiadania traumatyczne [Traumatic Stories]. 1979.
Tarcza z pajeczyny. 1980.

Verse

Niepokój [Anxiety]. 1947.
Czerwona rekawiczka [The Red Glove]. 1948.
Czas który idzie [The Time Which Goes By]. 1951.
Wiersze i obrazy [Poems and Images]. 1952.
Równina [The Plain]. 1954.
Uśmiechy [Smiles]. 1955.
Srebrny klos [Silver Grain]. 1955.
Poemat otwarty [An Open Room]. 1956.
Poezje zebrane [Selected Poems]. 1957.
Formy [Forms]. 1958.
Rozmowa z ksieciem [Conversation with a Prince]. 1960.
Glos anonima [The Anonymous Voice]. 1961.
Zielona róza [Green Rose]. With *Kartoteka*, 1961; translated as *Green Rose*, 1982.
Nic w plaszczu Prospera [Nothing in Prospero's Cloak] (includes the plays *Świadkowie* and *Grupa Laokoona*). 1962.
Niepokój: Wybór wierszy 1945–1961 (selection). 1963.
Twarz [The Face]. 1964.
Twarz trzecia [The Third Face]. 1968.
Regio [That Area]. 1969.
Faces of Anxiety, translated by Adam Czerniawski. 1969.
Wiersze [Poems]. 1974.
"The Survivor" and Other Poems, translated by Magnus I. Krynski and Robert A. Maguire. 1976.
Selected Poems, translated by Adam Czerniawski. 1976.
Poezje zebrane. 1976.

Unease. 1980.
"Conversation with the Prince" and Other Poems, translated by Adam Czerniawski. 1982; revised edition, as *They Came to See a Poet*, 1991.
Na powierzchni poematu i w środku: nowy wybór wierszy. 1983.
Poezje [Poems]. 1987.
Poezja [Poetry] (2 vols.). 1988.
Paskorzeżba. 1991.

Other

Kartki z Wegier [Notes from Hungary]. 1953.
Przygotowanie do wieczoru autorskiego [Preparations for a Poetry Reading]. 1971.
Proza [Prose]. 1973.
Duszyczka [A Little Soul]. 1977.
Próba rekonstrukcji [A Trial of Reconstruction]. 1979.
Echa leśne. 1985.

*

Criticism

Books:
Henryk Volger, *Rozewicz* (in English), Warsaw, 1976.
Halina Filipowicz, *A Laboratory of Impure Forms: The Plays of Tadeusz Różewicz*, New York, 1991.

Articles:
Mieczyslaw Orski, "Różewicz Abroad", in *Polish Perspectives*, 18, 1975.
Rochelle Stone, "The Use of Happenings in Tadeusz Różewicz's Drama", in *Pacific Coast Philology*, 11, 1976.
Halina Filipowicz, "Tadeusz Różewicz's Postmodern Trilogy", in *Polish Review*, vol. 36 no.1, 1991.

* * *

The most provocative and controversial of Polish playwrights in the post-war period, Różewicz is also the most original. For violating moral and social taboos and challenging preconceptions about the mission of drama, he has been attacked by the Catholic Church, the patriotic defenders of Poland's honor, and almost the entire critical establishment. His work, subject to frequent censorship, has often left audiences baffled, although several plays gained popularity in the 1970's and 1980's. Outstanding Polish directors have sought to realize his work in production, despite inherent tensions between the author's radically innovative propositions and the nature of theatre itself.

With his first play Różewicz (already a major poet) introduced a new theatrical language of fragmented structure and imagistic montage which, at first, seemed disorienting but eventually came to be accepted as the expression of post-war sensibility. Europe's experience of wholesale death and destruction had rendered obsolete beauty, ideals, and noble words; the new aesthetic had to take Auschwitz as its basic premise. Repudiating ideologies, moral judgments, and intellectual speculations as empty abstractions, the writer clung to the bare facts of human life as the only truths and values.

Of Polish playwrights since 1945, Różewicz has been the most restless experimenter with form. In a number of plays he undertakes an ontological analysis of theatre that questions the very assumptions making drama possible. Recognizing that reality will not submit to the artistic conventions of the past, he strives to go beyond the limits of the genre. In rejecting hierarchical notions of high and low, foreground and background, beginning, middle, and end, Różewicz posits a drama starting at point zero with an undifferentiated aleatory mass of sights and sounds, and existing as pure duration.

Różewicz's accomplishment has been to create a drama that is truly realistic and at the same time poetic. His work is realistic in the sense of being totally immersed in existence in all its corporeality; the ordinary, the banal, and the bodily are the playwright's materials which he refuses to imbue with any transcendent meaning. But it is an unorthodox "realism" unencumbered by illusionistic conventions. Externals of plot and cause-and-effect sequentiality are eliminated in favor of interior action that reveals life as it is experienced in the depths of stillness. The method of composition is poetic counterpoint producing a polyphonic form capable of accommodating a rich mixture of styles ranging from the colloquial, racy, and obscene to ingenious parody and pastiche of different literary traditions.

The Card Index gave Polish literature an anti-hero emblematic of the entire post-war generation of survivors. Crushed by the traumas of recent history, the anonymous protagonist—a contemporary Everyman of indefinite age, profession, and outlook—lies passively in bed and contemplates the little toe on his left foot, attempting to remain impervious to society's demands. His room is a crossroads of time and space where past recollections and present realities flow disconnectedly, as friends, relatives, lovers, and strangers drop by and try to rouse the dozing Hero to action. The world theatre of public events intersect with his subjective monodrama, but cannot elicit any response. Interrogated about his political beliefs, love of mankind, and desire for world peace, the hero remains silent. A memory- or dream-play of startling discontinuities, *The Card Index* mixes the farcically grotesque and the lyrical; it is a montage of shreds and fragments, citations from classics, advertisements, news items, and nursery rhymes, and even includes a Chorus of Elders who complain about the absence of action in the play—only to be killed by the Hero.

Subsequent dramas deal directly with the creative process and the precarious position of the artist in the modern world. The satirical repetition of clichés in *Grupa Laokoona* (Laocoon Group) represents the inauthenticity of art in an age of mechanical reproduction, proliferating copies, and the bureaucratization of culture for the masses. Unable to write anything more (even with the aid of a poodle named Mephisto), the great "poet laureate" in *Na czworakach* (On All Fours) spends his days crawling on the floor accompanied by his admirers, interpreters, and biographers.

Faced with the increasing difficulty of writing plays, Różewicz has produced a new kind of script (half treatise and polemic with his predecessors) in which extended stage directions serve as commentary to interrupt the action and disintegrate the dramatic form. The playwright has created drama out of his dissatisfaction with existing techniques, including those of modernism and the avant-garde which he tests and discards. *The Interrupted Act* (coitus, artistic creation, the division of a drama) cannot be completed; the conflict is between the idea of the play and the impossibility of its realization on stage.

An open score for the theatre inviting the collaboration of a director, *The Old Woman Broods* (first produced by Jerzy Jarocki) portrays the end of the world as the growing rubbish heap of civilization where, after the apocalypse, life goes on much the same as before. Amidst the constantly accumulating trash and cultural waste, people sun themselves, copulate, wage war, and go shopping. Called by the author "the biography of a play", *Birth Rate* is a conceptual piece about the author's inability to write a play on the population explosion since biological proliferation will not fit into any theatrical mold. The unwritten drama was staged ten years later by Kazimierz Braun.

Mariage Blanc, Różewicz's most successful work for the theatre, is also a biological drama, but of a more private nature, dealing with the sexual coming of age of two adolescent girls at the turn of the century, presented within a narrative framework. Because of its erotic daring, ribald language, and earthy humor, this compassionate probing of gender and identity aroused a storm of criticism.

Even more virulent attacks greeted *Do piachu* [To the Boneyard], a powerful naturalistic tragedy about a young partisan in the anti-communist Home Army executed by his own unit for rape and robbery. The primitive hero is a contemporary Woyzeck, unaware of himself, his destiny, and the moral values he has been accused of violating. Begun early in the poet's career, the play could not be shown for many years because of censorship and then proved too uncompromising for the public.

Kafka, who, along with Chekhov and Beckett, serves as a model for Różewicz's concept of inner drama, directly inspired two of the author's last works. *The Hunger Artist Departs* is a highly personal adaptation of Kafka's tale. Based loosely on the diaries and letters of the Czech author, but not a biographical play, *The Trap* dramatizes the anxieties and nightmares of the artist as he himself experiences them in relation to his father, fiancée, and other existential and social threats of confinement. A worthy companion piece to his early masterpiece, *The Card Index*, this play is more realistic in having a particularized hero named Franz, but equally poetic in its fluid handling of his story in time. An image that incoporates all of the playwright's obsessions, the "trap" is not only biology but also history. The future already exists in the present. The Nazis are waiting behind the scenes throughout the play. As the actors playing Kafka and his family take their bows, the Executioner-Guards come out from behind the black wall which opens at the back of the stage and brutally push them off to the trains leaving for the death camps. The wall closes and only desperate fingers and palms of hands can be seen.

Różewicz's probing of the boundaries traditionally imposed on theatre have put him in the forefront of artistic innovators along with Tadeusz Kantor and Jerzy Grotowski.

—Daniel Gerould

See also *Volume 1* entry on *Mariage Blanc*.

RUDKIN, (James) David. Born in London, 29 June 1936. Educated at King Edward's School, Birmingham, 1947–55; St. Catherine's College, Oxford, 1957–61, MA 1961. Served in the Royal Corps of Signals, 1955–57. Married Alexandra Thompson in 1967; two sons and two daughters. Assistant master of Latin, Greek, and music, County High School, Bromsgrove, Worcestershire, 1961–64; first-produced play, *Afore Night Come*, staged 1960. Recipient: John Whiting Award, 1974; Obie Award, 1977; New York Film Festival Gold Medal, 1987; European Festival Special Jury Award, 1990.

David Rudkin

Stage Works

Afore Night Come (produced Oxford, 1960). In *New English Dramatists* 7, 1963; published separately, 1966.

Moses and Aaron, translation of the libretto, music by Schoenberg (produced Royal Opera House, Covent Garden, London, 1965). 1965.

The Grace of Todd, music by Gordon Crosse (produced Aldeburgh Festival, Aldeburgh, Suffolk, 1969). 1970.

Sun into Darkness (ballet scenario; produced by Western Theatre Ballet, 1966).

Burglars (for children; produced Oval Theatre, Kensington, London, 1970). In *Prompt Two*, edited by Alan Durband, 1976.

The Filth Hunt (produced Almost Free Theatre, London, 1972).

Cries from Casement as His Bones Are Brought to Dublin (broadcast 1973; produced Place Theatre, London, 1973). 1974.

Ashes (produced Hamburg, 1973; Open Space Theatre, London, 1974). 1978.

No Title (produced Birmingham Repertory Theatre, 1974).

The Sons of Light (produced by the Tyneside Theatre Company, Newcastle-upon-Tyne, 1976). 1981.

Sovereignty under Elizabeth (produced Almost Free Theatre, London, 1977).

Hippolytus, from the play by Euripides (produced The Other Place, Stratford-on-Avon, 1978). 1980.

Hansel and Gretel (produced The Other Place, Stratford-on-Avon, 1980).

The Triumph of Death (produced Birmingham Repertory Theatre, 1981). 1981.

Peer Gynt, from the play by Ibsen (produced The Other Place, Stratford-on-Avon, 1982). 1983.

Space Invaders (produced The Other Place, Stratford-on-Avon, 1984).

Will's Way (produced The Other Place, Stratford-on-Avon, 1985).

The Saxon Shore (produced Almeida Theatre, London, 1986). 1986.

Deathwatch, from a play by Genet (produced The Pit, Barbican Centre, London, 1987).

The Maids, from a play by Genet (produced The Pit, Barbican Centre, London, 1987).

When We Dead Awake, from a play by Ibsen (produced Almeida Theatre, London, 1990). 1990.

Screenplays

Additional dialogue for *Fahrenheit 451*, 1966, and *Mademoiselle*, 1966; *Testimony*, 1988; *December Bride*, 1989.

Television Plays

The Stone Dance, 1963; *Children Playing*, 1967; *House of Character*, 1968; *Blodwen, Home from Rachel's Marriage*, 1969; *Bypass*, 1972; *Atrocity*, 1973; *Penda's Fen*, 1974 (published 1974); *Pritan* and *The Coming of the Cross* (Churchill's *People* series), 1975; *The Ash Tree*, from the story by M.R. James, 1975; *The Living Grave* (*Leap in the Dark* series), 1981; *Artemis 81*, 1981; *Across the Water*, 1983; *White Lady*, 1987; *Gawain and the Green Knight*, 1990.

Radio Plays

No Accounting for Taste, 1960; *The Persians*, from the play by Aeschylus, 1965; *Gear Change*, 1967; *Cries from Casement as His Bones Are Brought to Dublin*, 1973; *Hecuba*, from the play by Euripides, 1975; *Romersholm*, from the play by Ibsen, 1990.

*   *   *

This troubling and most darkly romantic of contemporary dramatists works through complex poetic language and stage directions to create moral landscapes that uniquely externalise inner turmoil. Rudkin explores what constitutes human identity and the terms of its manifestation in social crisis, with characteristic references to imperialism, religion, the animal savagery of instinct, and the darkest recesses of sexuality. His nightmarish fables often depict the needs to survive and to transmit knowledge to the future in collision with the dictates of the collective, tribal ideal.

Rudkin's television play *Penda's Fen* opens with the protagonist, teenage schoolboy Stephen, saying, "Oh my country . . . I *am* one of your sons, it is true. Yet how shall I show my love?". This question is crucial to many Rudkin dramas. The answer might be "only on your own terms". Many Rudkin characters refuse incorporation into any social fiction that does not acknowledge their self-invented uniqueness—hence the lack of meeting grounds for many characters, who are, rather, involved in constructing separate realities. In *The Sons of Light*, the inscrutable hero John triggers a "surrection" of underground workers, demanding response on individual terms: there is no paternalistic attempt to prepare the masses for interpretation of their experience in some ratified, utopian way.

Rudkin's heroes are often Promethean figures, frustrated by the rigidities of orthodoxy, and therefore determined to break interpretative restrictions and so radically transform the designated norm, accepting the penalties of isolation, excommunication, scorn, and destruction that this may involve.

The theme of self-mythologisation is also central. In *Cries from Casement*, Roger Casement wrestles with various notions of national and sexual identity. In *Penda's Fen*, Stephen likewise confronts the legion voices in his self and reads into/out of them a parable for the education of self and others, through a visionary connection to a metaphorical dimension of being which has little to do with conventional identifications of history. In *The Saxon Shore*, social determinism issues in the Gothic infestation of the protagonist, who both resists and capitulates to the pressure of joining his community, through becoming a werewolf.

Rudkin's drama frequently extols the liberation of some "primal genie of the earth" through a demonic reinvestment of social ritual. The objective is an exposure of life-enhancing chaos, an essential human ungovernableness. Rudkin's work testifies to the hope that resides in the imaginative abilities of each individual to recreate myth in their own individual terms.

This most profoundly challenging, anarchic, and existential of Anglo-Irish dramatists has suffered gross misprision from the English and Irish critical and theatrical establishments in the 1980's. Whilst recently moving towards a simpler, sparer style, Rudkin's work remains deliberately opposed to a rationalist, populist intellectual/cultural climate such as held sway during that decade (significantly predicted in Rudkin's bleakest work, *The Triumph of Death*). During this time, his imagination has been accordingly restricted to screenplay adaptations and translations. A reappraisal, and resurgence, of his own original work for the stage is overdue, and might find a more conducive ambience in a decade imaginatively less retrenched.

—David Ian Rabey

RUIZ DE ALARCÓN (Y MENDOZA), Juan. Born in Mexico City, Mexico (then the Vice-Royalty of New Spain), c.1581. Studied Canon Law at the Royal and Pontifical University of Mexico, Mexico City, 1596–1600, *licenciado* 1609; studied Canon and Civil law at the University of Salamanca, Spain, 1600–05, degrees in both subjects. Lived in Seville, 1606–08; advocate, court of Seville, 1607; lawyer and judge in Mexico, 1609–14; returned to Spain, 1614, and settled in Madrid; probably wrote his plays before 1626; temporary court reporter, from 1626, and permanent court reporter, from 1633, Royal Council for the Indies. Died in Madrid, 4 August 1639.

Works

Collections

Parte primera de las comedias, edited by Juan González. 1626.
Parte segunda de las comedias, edited by Sebastián Cormellas. 1634.

Comedias, edited by Juan Eugenio Hartzenbusch.   1852.
Teatro (2 vols.), edited by García-Ramon.   1884.
Teatro completo, edited by Ermilio Abreu Gómez.   1951.
Obras completas (3 vols.), edited by Agustín Millares Carlo. 1957–68.
Obras completas (2 vols.), edited by Alva Ebersole.   1966.

Stage Works

El semejante a sí mismo (produced Madrid, 1614?).   In *Parte primera de las comedias*, 1628.
Las peredes oyen (produced Madrid, 1617).   In *Parte primera de las comedias*, 1628.
La manganilla de Melilla (produced 1617?).   In *Parte segunda de las comedias*, 1634.
Los favores del mundo (produced before 1618).   In *Parte primera de las comedias*, 1628.
Ganar amigos (produced 1618?; produced before Queen Isobel de Bourbón, 1621).   In *Parte veinte y cuatro de las comedias del Fénix de España Lope de Vega Carpio*, 1633.
El desdichado en fingir (produced before 1622).   In *Parte primera de las comedias*, 1628.
La industria y la suerte.   In *Parte primera de las comedias*, 1628.
Todo es ventura (produced before 1622).   In *Parte primera de las comedias*, 1628.
Mudarse por mejorarse (produced before 1622).   In *Parte primera de las comedias*, 1628.
El Antichristo (produced by the Company of Manuel Vallejo, Madrid, 1623).   In *Parte segunda de las comedias*, 1634.
La crueldad por el honor (produced by the company of Juan Jerónimo Velenciano, at Court, 1623).   In *Parte segunda de las comedias*, 1634.
Siempre ayuda la verdad, attributed; (produced Teatro del Palacio Real, Madrid, 1623).   In *Parte segunda de las comedias del Maestro Tirso de Molina*, 1635.
El tejador de Segovia II (produced before 1624).   In *Parte segunda de las comedias*, 1634.
Los pechos privilegiados (produced 1625?).   In *Parte segunda de las comedias*, 1634.
La verdad sospechosa.   In *Parte veinte y dos de las comedias del Fénix de Espaça Lope de Vega Carpio*, 1630; translated as *The Truth Suspect*, in *Poet Lore*, 38, 1927, and in *Spanish Drama*, translated by Robert C. Ryan, 1962.
El examen de maridos.   In *Parte XXIV de las comedias del Fénix de España Lope de Vega Carpio*, 1633.
Los empeños de un engaño.   In *Parte segunda de las comedias*, 1634.
La prueba de las promesas.   In *Parte segunda de las comedias*, 1634.
El dueño de las estrellas.   In *Parte segunda de las comedias*, 1634.
La amistad castigada.   In *Parte segunda de las comedias*, 1634.
La culpa busca la pena y el agravio la venganza   In *Comedias de diferentes autores 41*, 1646.
No hay mal que por bien no venga.   In *Laurel de comedias: Quarta parte de diferentes autores*, 1653.
El tejador de Segovia I.   1771.
Quien mal anda en mal acaba.   Nd.

*

Bibliographies:

E. Abreu Gómez, *Ruiz de Alarcón: Bibliografía crítica*, Mexico City, 1939.

Walter Poesse, *Ensayo de una bibliografia de Juan Ruiz de Alarcón y Mendoza*, Valencia, 1964.

Criticism

Books:
Julio Jiménez Rueda, *Juan Ruiz de Alarcón y su tiempo*, Mexico City, 1939.
E.E. Hamilton, *The Structure of the Alarconian Comedia*, Austin, Texas, 1940.
Antonio Castro Leal, *Juan Ruiz de Alarcón: Su vida y su obra*, Mexico City, 1943.
Juana Granados, *Juan Ruiz de Alarcón e il suo teatro*, 1954.
Antonio Alatorre, *Brief History of a Problem: The "Mexicanidad" of Ruiz de Alarcón*, 1956.
Alva V. Ebersole, *El ambiente español visto por Juan Ruiz de Alarcón*, Valencia, 1959.
Carmen Olga Brenes, *El sentimiento democrático en el teatro de Juan Ruiz de Alarcón*, Valencia, 1960.
Ellen Claydon, *Juan Ruiz de Alarcón: Baroque Dramatist*, Chapel Hill, North Carolina, 1970.
Augusta Espantoso Foley, *Occult Arts and Doctrine in the Theatre of Juan Ruiz de Alarcón*, Geneva, 1972.
James A. Parr (ed.) *Critical Essays on the Life and Work of Juan Ruiz de Alarcón*, Madrid, 1972.
Walter Poesse, *Juan Ruiz de Alarcón*, New York, 1972.

Articles:
D. Schons, "The Mexican Background of Alarcón", in *Bulletin hispanique*, 43, 1941.
A. Paulin, "The Religious Motive in Alarcón", in *Hispanic Review*, 29, 1961.

* * *

By general consent, Alarcón ranks today after Lope de Vega, Tirso de Molina, and Calderón as the fourth major dramatist of the Spanish theatre in its Golden Age (1580–1650). Like the others, he wrote *comedias*, verse dramas in three acts after the formula laid down by the doyen of the Golden-Age *comedia*, Lope de Vega. Unlike Lope and the others, he was lionised neither by the public nor the theatrical pundits of the day; but with regard to his posthumous reputation in the history of world theatre, he shares the fate of his friend and exact contemporary, Tirso de Molina (creator of the Don Juan figure in European theatre): both men were destined to be better known outside Spain for an adaptation of one of their plays than for any of their original plays in their own right. While Molière adapted Tirso's *El Burlador de Sevilla* in order to write his *Dom Juan*, Corneille's most famous comedy, *Le Menteur*, is a skilful adaptation of Alarcón's most celebrated play, *La verdad sospechosa*. Corneille describes the plot as "si spirituel et si bien tourné" and the play overall as "ingénieuse". Brief though it is, this near contemporary opinion gives an accurate, albeit incomplete, impression of the virtues of Alarcón's theatre.

Alarcón's career as a writer for the stage was far shorter than that of the other three great *comediantes* and he was far less prolific. This has led critics to view him as a careful craftsman, each of whose creations was a closely meditated work of art, carefully polished over a long period of time. This is probably true only in part. Like the others he certainly wrote for money and consequently with some speed. Once he had secured a regular income in the law he wrote no more. The peculiar characteristics of his theatre probably owe more

to his temperament and personal view of the world. That he is, at his best, an author of well-constructed plays there is no doubt. His best plays are further enhanced by a soberly and wrily humorous view of contemporary mores and the human frailties that abound within them.

La verdad sospechosa has always been Alarcón's most admired and most edited play. This is due partly to its excellence and partly to the extent to which it exhibits the peculiar qualities and characteristics of his output as a whole. It is indeed well constructed. The action is simplicity itself: a wealthy young gentleman, lately arrived at Court, loses the girl he loves because he mistakes her for her best friend and because of his compulsive mendacity. The entire plot depends upon this central action (the lack of secondary plot in almost all Alarcón's plays is a trait that has been attributed to his training in law). The plot then revolves around the central figure of Don García, the young liar. *La verdad sospechosa* offers a chief protagonist who is an engaging anti-hero because of the vice which blights his life.

In *Las paredes oyen* we are presented with another young suitor whose enterprise comes to nought because of an equally noxious vice: he is a slanderer. Both this play and *La verdad sospechosa* offer striking dramatic illustrations of an all-consuming vice so that Alarcón's reputation was, for a long time, that of playwright with a moralising mission. In fact, in this respect, these two plays are exceptional in his output as a whole. If Alarcón is the moralist among the great playwrights of the Golden Age, then his mission should be seen in a more diffused and subtle light.

In *Examen de maridos* Doña Inés seeks a husband. Like Portia in Shakespeare's *The Merchant of Venice* she decides to put each of her suitors to the test. To one of them she is far more partial than to the rest. The course of true love does not run smoothly due to the intervention of Blanca, a jealous former love of the favourite suitor. A whole gamut of vices and failings, including mendacity and slander, are on display in this delightfully wrought comedy, before justice is done at the close.

In *La prueba de las promesas* Don Illán de Toledo wants his daughter to marry Don Enrique, member of a family with whom the Toledos have feuded for many years, and with whom he seeks reconciliation. His daughter loves Don Juan de Ribera. Versed in the magic arts, Don Illán decides to test the constancy of Don Juan, weaving a spell which suspends all sense of passing time and creating in Juan the illusion of a vertiginous material and social success until he finds himself a marquis and president of the Council of Castile. He now holds both father and daughter in contempt and reneges on his promise to the latter, whereupon Don Illán breaks the spell and Juan retires, shamed and humiliated. The daughter now accepts the more constant Enrique.

Thus it can be seen that Alarcón's treatment of the major themes of the *comedia* is unusual. As is well known, honour is the overriding theme of many *comedias* of the Spanish Baroque drama, and when it is not, honour usually underpins the thematics of the play. In Alarcón's theatre this characteristic is less evident, as one can see from the plots described above. The theme of honour and the accompanying ones of jealousy and vengeance are intermittent and muted, with one or two notable exceptions, the most powerful of which is *El tejedor de Segovia*, one of Alarcón's few plays with a medieval setting. A sense of honour is present in almost all his plays but rarely does he write dramas of honour in which the *pundonor* (point of honour) lies at the centre of the plot. In *La verdad sospechosa* Don García loses his honour and dishonours his father by his antics, but the main points of the play's ending are his discomfiture and his defeat and loss in the game of love. The honour theme in Alarcón is subordinated to a sense of moral rectitude and of fairness and justice in human affairs.

More important than honour is the role of reason in society. The action of *La verdad sospechosa* emphasises Don Garcia's inability or unwillingness to apply his reason and consequently to moderate his conduct. In a number of plays Alarcón shows a need for reason to triumph in society. Loyalty, constancy, and the value of friendship are also themes frequently expressed in his plays, and are forcefully treated in *El semejante a sí mismo* and *Ganar amigos*. As for love, it is an obvious motivation for action but is rarely portrayed as an authentic passion lying at the heart of the drama.

Many attempts have been made to set Alarcón apart from the other dramatists of the Golden Age. His tempered and apparently detached view of Spanish society is often explained autobiographically. In an obvious sense he was an outsider. As a Mexican, he had to struggle hard for acceptance in Spain. We have documentary evidence that he was ridiculed by his literary enemies because of his physical deformity: he was a hunchback. From this, it is a short step to exaggerating the differences between Alarcón and his contemporaries among writers. Alarcón's achievement was to have created a handful of sophisticated and amusing comedies containing characters, major as well as minor, who come vividly to life on the stage. Not the least of the remarkable features of his most famous play is the relationship between Don García and his servant Tristán. The *gracioso*, or amusing servant/confidant, was a feature of the Golden Age *comedia* which undoubtedly impressed both Corneille and Molière. Tristán, and Beltrán in *Las paredes oyen*, are such figures—urbane, wise, sententious, droll, and more than a match for their masters—and are engaging characters in their own right.

What Alarcón offers us today is an acutely observed dramatisation of middle- and upper-class Madrid society of the early years of the 17th century by means of a series of ingenious plots, lively and humane characterisations, and witty dialogue. As a dramatist whose humour is thought-provoking he has been called "the Spanish Terence". Certainly, instead of accepting the moral code of the day, Alarcón meditated upon it, adding his own modifying commentary, while he took a decidedly sceptical view of romantic love. Today he is viewed, not without cause, as a father of the modern comedy of character.

—R.J. Oakley

RUZ(Z)ANTE. Born Angelo Beolco in Padua, territory of Venice (now Italy), c.1495/96, the illegitimate son of a nobleman. Trained in law. Married Giustina Palatino, c.1526. Began acting, c.1515–18: actor, assuming the stage name Ruzante (or Ruzzante), in carnival plays in Venice and Padua, from c.1520; in the service of Alvise Cornaro, from 1525; received modest inheritance following his father's death, 1526, and later received power-of-attorney for his half-brothers' shares in their father's estate, dividing it in 1540; banished to Ferrara, 1539. Died in Padua, c.17 March 1542.

Works

Collections

Il Ruzzante: Angelo Beolco, edited by G.A. Cibotto.   1958.
Commedie del Cinquecento 2 (includes *La pastorale; Moschetta; Fiorina*), edited by Aldo Borlenghi.   1959.
Teatro, edited by Ludovico Zorzi.   1967.
La pastorale; La prima oratione; Una lettera giacosa, edited by Giorgio Padoan.   1978.
I dialoghi; La seconda oratione; I prologhi alla Moschetta, edited by Giorgio Padoan.   1981.

Stage Works

Parlamento de Ruzante che iera vegnú de campo (produced Padua, c.1515?).   In *Due dialoghi di Ruzante in lingua rustica*, 1551; translated as *Ruzzante Returns from the Wars*, in *The Classic Theatre 1*, edited by Eric Bentley, 1958.
La pastorale (produced Padua, 1517?).   1951.
La Betía (produced carnival, Venice, 1523?).   Fragment in *Antichi testi di letteratura pavana*, edited by E. Lovarini, 1894; complete in *Teatro*, 1967.
Dialogo facetissimo (produced carnival, Venice, 1525?; produced Alvise Cornaro's Hunting Lodge, Fosson, 1529). 1554.
La fiorina (produced 1531–32?).   1548.
La moscheta (produced Padua or Ferrara, c.1532).   1551.
La piovana (produced Ferrara, 1532).   1548.
La vaccaria, from a play by Plautus (produced Palazzo Cornaro, Padua, 1533).   After 1548.
L'anconitana.   Nd. (after 1548).
Bilora.   In *Due dialoghi di Ruzante in lingua rustica*, 1551; translated as *Bilora*, in *World Drama*, edited by Barrett H. Clark, 1933, and in *Masterworks of World Drama 3*, edited by Anthony Caputi, 1968.

*

Bibliographies

Emilio Lippi, "Vent'anni di critica ruzantesca (1966–1985)", in *Quaderni veneti*, 2 and 3, 1985–86.

Criticism

Books:
G. Baldrin, *Angelo Beolco detto il Ruzzante*, Padua, 1924.
A. Cataldo, *Il Ruzzante*, Milan, 1933.
Carlo Grabher, *Ruzzante*, Milan, 1953.
E. Lovarini, *Studi sul Ruzzante e la letteratura pavana*, Padua, 1965.
M. Baratto, *Tre studi sul teatro: Ruzzante, Aretino, Goldoni*, Vicenza, 1966.
Mario Prosperi, *Angelo Beolco nominato Ruzante*, Padova, 1970.
Nancuyt Dershofi, *Arcadia and the Stage*, Madrid, 1978.
G. Padoan, *La commedia rinascimentale veneta*, Vicenza, 1982.
Linda L. Carroll, *Language and Dialect in Ruzzante and Goldoni*, Ravenna, 1981.
E. Lovarini, *Ruzzante*, Padua, 1988.
Linda L. Carroll, *Angelo Beolco (Il Ruzzante)*, Boston, 1990.

Articles:
Franco Fido, "An Introduction to the Theater of Angelo
    Beolco", in *Renaissance Drama*, 6, 1973.

*   *   *

Illegitimate son of a Dean of Medicine in Padua, Beolco
received legal training and entered the service of a powerful
and idiosyncratic local landowner, Alvise Cornaro. Although
his official functions in the household were varied, he became
increasingly known as a writer, performer, and organizer of
stage entertainments, and effectively came as close to being a
professional theatre practitioner as was possible in his time
without losing his already shaky gentlemanly status. His surviving theatrical texts from the 1520's and 1530's were mostly
published in the 1550's, but some of the earliest and most
innovative only reached a printer in modern times. However,
his reputation seems to have grown steadily after his death in
the 16th century, and he is now seen as a unique dramatist for
his era. His stage name, Ruzante (or Ruzzante), was the
name of the vulgar peasant mask which he generally played in
his own compositions; and not least among his recognized
achievements is that of having forced Italian Renaissance
audiences, who were usually quite unsympathetic to the countryside, to take some account of peasant values and peasant
language. The peasant is both a figure of fun and, paradoxically, a source of natural wisdom, offering a unique example
in Renaissance Italy of the "fool literature" which is, by
contrast, so common in England and northern Europe.

Beolco's earliest compositions, perhaps mounted in the
metropolis of Venice itself, are his most individual and owe
almost nothing to classical models. *La pastorale* is memorable
for the eruption of the coarse Ruzante figure in the midst of a
sentimental "pastoral" plot of wimpish literary shepherds:
academic courtly clichés (in literary Italian) are confronted
and subverted by the stark vulgarity of the peasant survival
ethic (in Paduan country dialect), with a comic doctor and
something like a braggart soldier thrown in for good measure.
Then, in the two versions of *La Betía*, Beolco drew extensively and originally on a local form of drama, the *mariazo*, in
which peasant betrothal and wedding rituals were caricatured
on stage by students. Ruzante's version, in five acts of verse
and entirely in dialect, ranges through leisurely disputes,
satirizing refined neoplatonic love doctrines, to a peasant
plot, involving the most vulgar *double-entendres* and lewd
gestures. Zilio (probably Beolco's Ruzante mask) is the
booby peasant version of a melting, inadequate lover, derided by his Betía, and on the way to being cuckolded by his
helpful go-between friend. A series of set-piece scenes include a ritual abduction, a fight on stage, a formal betrothal, a
mock death, and a speech allegedly from Hell—many of these
undoubtedly based on folk mumming plays, on street theatre
routines, or on the patter monologues of Court entertainers.

However, there were a couple of moments which shocked
polite Venetian society, and Beolco's dramatic efforts seem
to have been banished for a while to the protective family
estate of his master Alvise Cornaro. Here he mounted, in his
master's hunting lodge in January 1529, the *Dialogo
facetissimo*—an occasional piece of great variety, mixing
Paduan peasant characters and bullies with a symbolic forest
magician and the offstage spirit of a dead friend. Cornaro's
personal ethic, and the solidarity of the assembled household,
are celebrated and mocked in the grim contemporary context
of a disastrous famine.

Also in 1529 are placed Beolco's two one-act *dialoghi*, first
published in 1551, his most astonishing and unconventional
pieces. In the *Parlamento*, Ruzante is a conscripted peasant
returning destitute from the war, finding that his wife, Gnua,
has been stolen by a local thug, who beats up Ruzante. *Bilora*
is named after its Paduan peasant protagonist whose wife has
been abducted by a rich Venetian merchant; after increasingly frustrating exchanges in front of the merchant's house
with a friend, Pittaro, with the wife, Dina, and with the
merchant Andronico himself, Bilora gets drunk, ambushes
Andronico, and kills him with a dagger. Neither play relates
at all to the five-act structure of current *commedia erudita*,
nor to the sophisticated entertainment and mockery which
such comedy contains. The *Parlamento* has the tone of knockabout farce, but still leaves a stark picture of the effects of war
on the poorest classes. *Bilora* has much less laughter to offer,
and seems more, in its poise between realism and melodrama,
like a sketch for a late 19th-century opera. The linking themes
are the impotent exasperation of a peasant protagonist with
the powerful figures who control and ruin his life, and the
resigned cynicism, not unmixed with compassion, of wives
who have to put their personal need to eat and survive before
their allegiance to their husbands.

In the same year, perhaps, Beolco used a similar cast of
characters—inadequate husband, elusive wife, bully, and
treacherous friend—to produce a more classical five-act play
in *La moscheta* (the title could be translated as "Talking
Posh"). The menu of dialogues, tricks, and scenes in a wide
range of dialects is served up with great virtuosity and stage
craftsmanship, but the comedy sees the beginning of Beolco's
acceptance of (some might say surrender to) the demands of
current theatrical convention. *La fiorina*, *La piovana*, *La
vaccaria*, and *L'anconitana* (all from the 1530's, all published
between 1548 and 1552) retain various elements of Beolco's
individuality, especially in the use of different dialects and
linguistic registers; but all respond to the preference of
patrons and audiences for a greater degree of humanist conformity. *La piovana*, indeed, is an eccentric rewrite of
Plautus' *Rudens*, with contributions from other Roman comedies. They all attracted attention and respect from
Renaissance readers and publishers—it is hard now to know
whether modern preferences for Beolco's earlier subversive
work involves reading some things into it which the author
did not realize were there.

—Richard Andrews

RYGA, George. Born in Deep Creek, Alberta, Canada, 27
July 1932. Educated at local schools to age 12, and by correspondence courses; attended Banff School of Fine Arts,
Alberta, summers 1949–50. Married to Norma Lois
Campbell; five children (three adopted). Farm and construc-
tion worker; copywriter and producer (*Reverie* programme)
for CFRN radio station in Edmonton, 1950–54; lived in
Europe, mainly in Scotland, 1955–56; advertising copywriter,
Edmonton, 1956; worked at various jobs, 1957–62, then full-
time writer; first-produced stage play, *Nothing But a Man*,
performed 1966; taught playwriting at University of British
Columbia, Fredericton, Simon Fraser University, Burnaby,
British Columbia, and Banff School of Fine Arts, Banff,
1970's; writer-in-residence, University of Ottawa, 1980.
Recipient: Edinburgh Festival award, 1973; Academy of
Performing Arts Award (Frankford), 1980. Died in
Summerland, British Columbia, 18 November 1987.

Works

Collections

"The Ecstasy of Rita Joe" and Other Plays (includes *Indian* and *Grass and Wild Strawberries*), edited by Brian Parker. 1971.
Country and Western (includes *A Portrait of Angelica; Ploughmen of the Glacier; Seven Hours to Sundown*). 1976.

Stage Works

Indian, from his television play (produced Winnipeg, 1974). In *"The Ecstasy of Rita Joe" and Other Plays*, 1971.
Nothing But a Man (produced Walterdale Playhouse, Edmonton, 1966). Nd.
The Ecstasy of Rita Joe (produced Vancouver Playhouse, Vancouver, 1967). 1970.
Just an Ordinary Person (produced Metro Theatre, Vancouver, 1968).
Grass and Wild Strawberries (produced Vancouver Playhouse, Vancouver, 1969). In *"The Ecstasy of Rita Joe" and Other Plays*, 1971.
Captives of a Faceless Drummer, music and lyrics by Ryga (produced Vancouver Art Gallery, Vancouver, 1971). 1971.
Sunrise on Sarah, music by Ryga (produced Banff School of Fine Arts, Banff, 1972). 1973.
Portrait of Angelica (produced Banff School of Fine Arts, Banff, 1973). In *Country and Western*, 1976.
A Feast of Thunder, music by Morris Surdin (produced Massey Hall, Toronto, 1973).
Paracelsus and the Hero (produced Vancouver Playhouse, Vancouver, 1986) In *Canadian Theatre Review*, Autumn 1974; in book form, as *Paracelsus*, with *Prometheus Bound*, 1982.
Twelve Ravens for the Sun, music by Mikis Theodorakis (produced 1975?).
Ploughmen of the Glacier (produced by Western Canada Theatre Company, Kamloops, British Columbia, 1976). In *Country and Western*, 1976.
Seven Hours to Sundown (produced University of Alberta, Edmonton, 1976). In *Country and Western*, 1976.
Last of the Gladiators, from his novel *Night Desk* (produced by Giant's Head Theatre Company, Summerland, British Columbia, 1976).
Jeremiah's Place (for children; produced Victoria, British Columbia, 1978).
Laddie Boy (produced Thunder Bay, Ontario, 1981). In *Transactions 1*, edited by Edward Peck, 1978.
Prometheus Bound, from a play by Aeschylus. In *Prism International*, 1981; in book form, with *Paracelsus*, 1982.
A Letter to My Son (produced Kam Theatre, Thunder Bay, Ontario, 1981). With *Portrait of Angelica*, 1984.

Television Plays

The Storm, 1962; *Indian*, 1963; *Bitter Grass*, 1963; *For Want of Something Better to Do*, 1963; *The Tulip Garden*, 1963; *Two Soldiers*, 1963; *The Pear Tree*, 1963; *Man Alive*, 1965; *The Kamloops Incident*, 1965; *A Carpenter by Trade* (documentary), 1967; *The Manipulators* series (2 scripts), 1968; *The Name of the Game* series (1 script), 1969; *Ninth Summer*, 1972; *The Mountains* (documentary), 1973; *The Ballad of Iwan Lepa* (documentary), 1976.

Radio Plays

A Touch of Cruelty, 1961; *Half-Caste*, 1962; *Masks and Shadows*, 1963; *Bread Route*, 1963; *Departures*, 1963; *Ballad for Bill*, 1963; *The Stone Angel*, from the novel by Margaret Laurence, 1965; *Miners, Gentlemen, and Other Hard Cases* series, 1974–75; *Seasons of a Summer Day*, 1975; *Advocates of Danger* series, 1976; *One Sad Song for Henry Doyle Matkevitch*, 1981.

Fiction

Hungry Hills. 1963.
Ballad of a Stone-Picker. 1966; revised edition, 1976.
Night Desk. 1976.
In the Shadow of the Vulture. 1985.

Other

Beyond the Crimson Morning: Reflections from a Journey Through Contemporary China. 1979.
Brief to the Federal Cultural Policy Review Committee. 1981.

*

Criticism

Books:
Brian R. Parker, "The Ballad-Plays of Ryga", in Ryga's *"The Ecstasy of Rita Joe" and Other Plays*, Toronto, 1971.
Mavor Moore, *4 Canadian Playwrights*, Toronto, 1973.
G. McCaughey, *George Ryga*, Agincourt, Ontario, 1977.

Articles:
Christopher D. Innes, "The Many Faces of Rita Joe: The Anatomy of a Playwright's Development", in *Canadian Drama*, 10, 1984.
Bonnie Worthington, "Ryga's Women" in *Canadian Drama*, 5, 1979.

*   *   *

The art of George Ryga confronts us with a multitude of fascinating contradictions. His career as a playwright as well as a writer of novels, short stories, radio and television plays, poems, songs and ballads, and even polemical essays and travel books, frustrates critical scrutiny with its sheer multifariousness. In addition, his work displays a welter of ideologies, styles, and influences, and is complicated further by the unfamiliarity of its cultural and social determinants. His Ukrainian background, his childhood on a marginal Alberta farm, the poverty that deprived him of a normal education, and his intimate association with the local Indians, all figure in the making of Ryga as an artist.

Unlike most writers among whose influences are the works of other writers, Ryga, because of his unusual education, was relatively untouched by literature. The two main influences on his imagination were his boyhood experience with poverty and social injustice, and his artistic apprenticeship writing drama for radio. The former gave his work a left-wing, Marxist sympathy which persisted even after his disaffection with the Communist Party over the Hungarian uprising of 1956. The latter bequeathed him a theatrical style in which realism and a kind of lyrical expressionism are mingled in various proportions.

Ryga's leftism was always more emotionally than systematically Marxist because a strain of romanticism persistently undermined his socialist aims so that he was never able to see characters only as social entities, but always perceived the social situation in terms of character. His protagonists are outsiders, underdogs, misfits, Indians, the poor and dispossessed, or the aged. Ryga saw them being ground under by the instruments of the *status quo*, and by the general tyranny of established political systems and conventional moral attitudes, including institutionalized benevolence. But instead of extracting ideological clichés from this material, Ryga's penchant for seeing individual pain and suffering took over, saving him from simple-minded polemicism, but only too frequently also undermining every position with qualifications. Thus, in the play *Indian*, the protagonist is lazy, drunken, unreliable, and a murderer, yet is nobler and more dignified than any of the "respectable" characters. While this qualifying technique works very well in this play, it shows up as ambivalence in *The Ecstasy of Rita Joe*, where Rita Joe has the same mixture of characteristics as Indian, but makes decisions which emphasize the negative side of her character and in doing so cloud the central meaning of the play.

While Marxism was the primary influence on Ryga's choice of dramatic themes, his early practical experience with radio had the greatest impact on his style. His first creative works were 12 short stories and two plays written for radio in 1961–62, followed by four more radio plays in 1963. Although written specifically for television, *Indian* illustrates all the qualities of Ryga's radio experience in its honed down situations, minimal action, psychologically simple characters, limited number of voices contrasted by speech differences, and simple but striking sound effects. While these factors always remained central to his work, gradually the visual dimension of the stage allowed Ryga to enrich his largely realistic radio plays with the techniques of expressionist theatre. Fantasies, flashbacks of memory, reveries, dreams, and premonitions coalesced to reveal the inner sufferings and anxieties of his characters. In *Sunrise on Sarah*, the eponymous heroine is confined to her bedroom, which the stage directions describe as her "*private cell*", and which an early draft even set in a structure formed surrealistically like the inside of her head. The other 13 characters in the play exist in Sarah's memory or as extensions of her fantasy life. Time is nullified by the free association of Sarah's reveries, and this temporal fluidity is paralleled by the equally free use of space. Ramps running above, below, or circling off the conventional stage provide constantly changing areas with lighting used to create emotional space rather than illuminate specific locations.

In his stage directions Ryga even suggests blocking that not only supports but encapsulates the meaning of a play. In one example of his finest work, *The Ecstasy of Rita Joe*, the actors move down ramps in ever smaller circles as the protagonist's options narrow. At the centre of this vortex is a monumental judge's chair, symbolic of the intransigence of white justice. The prison room in *Captives of a Faceless Drummer* symbolizes the claustrophobia of the prisoners' emotional and social inhibitions, whereas the featureless plain in *Indian* does the opposite by creating a sense of insignificance and helplessness in an enormous and impersonal landscape.

Ryga's expressionism can be seen at its most extreme and most inventive in *Grass and Wild Strawberries*, though it also loses touch with realism to disadvantage. The movement of the play is jerky with each scene an entity in itself; comic book characters such as Captain Nevada and White Rabbit are juxtaposed jarringly with realistic figures like Uncle Ted; and film collages are not only projected onto the stage but also swung out directly towards the spectators, apparently with the object of propelling them into active emotional participation. Similarly, the 15 songs which the play contains operate as a descant on the text and serve to involve the audience, particularly at the end when the spectators are encouraged to join the actors on the stage for a final dance and song.

There is no straight line of development in Ryga's work. He was temperamentally both courageous and experimental, seeking ever more demanding forms in order to present the themes he considered significant. He wrote his best works for the theatre because this was the art form which allowed him to explore the permanant and frightening forces behind society as well as the limitations, dangers, and excitements of personal, subjective experience.

—Dorothy Parker

See also *Volume 1* entry on *The Ecstasy of Rita Joe*.

———

S

SACKVILLE, Thomas.   See *Volume 1* entry on *Gorboduc.*

———————

SALACROU, Armand.   Born in Rouen, France, 9 August 1899. Educated at Lycée du Havre; studied law, medicine, and philosophy at the Sorbonne, Paris, from 1918. Married Jeanne Jeandet in 1922; two daughters. Published first short story, 1916; joined the French Socialist Party, 1920; drama critic, socialist newspaper *L'Humanité*; journalist for the communist *Internationale*, 1921–22; first-produced play, *Tour à terre*, staged 1925; worked in the film industry, 1925–27; secretary to Charles Dullin at the Théâtre de l'Atelier, Paris, 1929–32; began marketing his father's pharmaceuticals, from 1929, and subsequently made a considerable fortune in advertising before World War II; drafted into the French forces, 1940: captured by German forces, June 1940, but immediately escaped to the Vichy sector, and settled in Lyons; joined the left-wing Front National and worked with the underground press; returned to Paris, 1943, and subsequently concentrated on his career as playwright; refused the directorship of the Comédie-Française, 1947. Several plays staged in collaboration with the director Charles Dullin. President, Unesco International Institute of the Theatre; Member, Académie Goncourt, 1949–83; President, Cannes Film Festival, 1963; President, Society of French Dramatists, from 1965. Recipient: Palmes Académiques. Grand Officier, Légion d'Honneur. Died in Le Havre, 23 November 1989.

Works

Collections

Théâtre (8 vols.).   1943–66; revised edition, 1977–
Three Plays (includes *Marguerite; The World is Round; When the Music Stops*).   1967.

Stage Works

Magasin d'accessoires.   In *Sélection* (Antwerp), vol. 4 no. 10, 1925.
Les Trente Tombes de Judas.   In *Sélection* (Antwerp), vol. 5 no. 9, 1926; in book form, in *Théâtre 1* (revised edition), 1977.
La Boule de verre.   In *Intentions*, vol. 3 nos. 28–30, 1924; in book form, 1958.
Le Casseur d'assiettes (produced Leids Studenten Toneel, Leiden, Netherlands, 1954).   1924.

Tour à terre (produced Théâtre de l'Oeuvre, Paris, 1925). With *Le Pont de l'Europe*, 1929.
Le Pont de l'Europe (produced Théâtre de l'Odéon, Paris, 1927).   With *Tour à terre*, 1929.
Patchouli (produced Théâtre de l'Atelier, Paris, 1930).   1930.
Atlas-Hôtel (produced Théâtre de l'Atelier, Paris, 1931). 1931.
La Vie en rose (produced Théâtre du Vieux-Colombier, Paris, 1931).   1936.
Les Frénétiques (produced Théâtre Daunou, Paris, 1934).   1935.
Une Femme libre (produced Théâtre de l'Oeuvre, Paris, 1934).   With *Atlas-Hôtel*, 1934.
L'Inconnue d'Arras (produced Comédie des Champs-Élysées, Paris, 1935).   1936.
Un Homme comme les autres (produced Théâtre de l'Oeuvre, Paris, 1936).   1937.
La Terre est ronde (produced Théâtre de l'Atelier, Paris, 1938).   With *Un Homme comme les autres*, 1938; translated as *The World is Round*, in *Three Plays*, 1967.
Histoire de rire (produced Théâtre de la Madeleine, Paris, 1939).   1940; translated as *When the Music Stops*, in *Three Plays*, 1967.
La Marguerite (produced Théâtre Pigalle, Paris, 1944).   With *Histore de rire* and *Le Casseur d'assiettes*, 1941; translated as *Marguerite*, 1967.
Les Fiancés du Havre (produced Comédie-Française, Paris, 1944).   1944.
Le Soldat et la sorcière (produced Théâtre Sarah-Bernhardt, Paris, 1945).   1946.
Les Nuits de la colère (produced Théâtre Marigny, Paris, 1946).   1946.
L'Archipel Lenoir (produced Théâtre Montparnasse, Paris, 1947).   1948.
Pourquoi pas moi? (produced Palais des Beaux-Arts, Brussels, 1948).   With *Poof*, 1948.
Poof (produced Paris, 1950).   With *Pourquoi pas moi?*, 1948.
Dieu le savait (produced Théâtre Saint-Georges, Paris, 1951). With *Pourquoi pas moi?*, 1951.
Sens interdit (produced Théâtre du Quartier Latin, Paris, 1953).   1952.
Les Invités du Bon Dieu (produced Théâtre du Parc, Brussels, 1953).   1953.
Le Miroir (produced Théâtre des Ambassadeurs, Paris, 1956).   In *Theatre 7*, 1956.
Une Femme trop honnête; ou, Tout est dans la façon de le dire (produced Théâtre Édouard-VII, Paris, 1956).   1956.
Histoire de cirque.   1960.
Boulevard Durand (produced Centre Dramatique du Nord, Le Havre, 1961).   1960.

Comme les chardons (produced Comédie-Française, Paris, 1964). 1964.
La Rue noire. 1967.

Screenplays

Histoire de rire, with Georges Neveux, 1941; *La Beauté du diable*, with René Clair, 1950 (published in *Comédies*, by Clair, 1959).

Radio Plays

Le Casseur d'assiettes, 1941.

Other

Les Idées de la nuit. 1960.
Impromptu délibéré: Entretiens avec Paul-Louis Mignon. 1966.
Dans la salle des pas perdus (2 vols.). 1974–76.

*

Criticism

Books:
J. van der Esch, *Armand Salacrou: Dramaturge de l'angoisse*, Paris, 1947.
P.-H. Simon, *Théâtre et destin: L'Athéisme anxieux d'Armand Salacrou*, Paris, 1959.
Paul-Louis Mignon, *Salacrou*, Paris, 1960.
Jacques Guicharnand, *Modern French Theatre*, New Haven, Connecticut, 1961; revised edition, 1967.
Dorothy Knowles, *French Drama of the Inter-War Years*, London, 1967.
Juris Silenieks, *Themes and Dramatic Forms in the Plays of Armand Salacrou*, Lincoln, Nebraska, 1967.
Fiorenzo Di Franco, *Le Théâtre de Salacrou*, Paris, 1970.
Anne Ubersfeld, *Armand Salacrou: Textes de Salacrou, points de vue critiques, témoignages, chronologie, bibliographie, illustrations*, Paris, 1970.
Philippe Bébon, *Salacrou*, Paris, 1971.
Colin B. Radford, *A Dramatist in Search of His Public*, Belfast, 1977.
Harold Hobson, *French Theatre Since 1830*, London, 1978.
David Loosely, *A Search for Commitment: The Theatre of Armand Salacrou*, Exeter, 1985.

* * *

Armand Salacrou was one of the outstanding playwrights of 20th-century French theatre. His long career as a dramatist spanned almost 50 years, interrupted only by World War II when, as a mark of respect for his Jewish friends, he refused to allow any of his plays to be performed. From his early, fanciful, and almost surrealist one-acters in the 1920's to his last play, *La Rue noire* (written in the 1960's but never performed because, Salacrou said, the actress for whom a leading role was created was not available), he wrote some 30 plays which, by their varied subject matter and great technical skill, entertained Parisian audiences, and which, by the constancy of their central themes, enabled Salacrou to explore his own philosophical and metaphysical preoccupations.

The drama of Armand Salacrou is intensely personal. In spite of his justifiable complaint that some critics adopt an excessively biographical approach, it is difficult not to see, in his plays, reflections of, and references to, his own immensely varied and dynamic career, to a point where one critic has described Salacrou's theatre as the story of one man's life and evolution.

The most overtly aubiographical works are the early plays, like *Histoire de cirque* (published 1960), *Magasin d'accessoires*, and, *Casseur d'assiettes*, which are set in a theatre or music hall and deal with a young bewildered hero attempting to give meaning and direction to his life; and the style of these short pieces from the 1920's is clearly influenced by the surrealism of the young artists and writers then among his Parisian friends. Thereafter, it is possible to relate the choice of subject in all his plays to various stages of his own life, with rare excursions into the realm of history such as *La Terre est ronde*, which centres on the life of Girolamo Savonarola in 15th-century Florence, and *Le Soldat et la sorcière* (written in 1943), whose hero is the tyrannical Maurice de Saxe; so that, even in these two works, the public was able to find allusions to fascism and the political state of contemporary Europe.

There were more obviously personal associations in *Atlas Hôtel* and *Les Frénétiques*, which were based on his recent experiences in North Africa and the film industry, the latter providing a very clear example of Salacrou's technical originality by the invention of the "flash-back", subsequently popularised by the cinema. Two plays deal with the traumatic wars which scarred his life and modern French history: World War I in *L'Inconnue d'Arras*, where the alternation between reality and illusion is reminiscent of Pirandello; and World War II in *Les Nuits de la colère*, which deals with the French underground movement (and which was, incidentally, one of the surprisingly few plays by Salacrou to be performed in London). His highly successful commercial career is reflected in *Poof*, a comedy-ballet about advertising, first performed in 1950, and in *La Rue noire*, which describes a bitter conflict to dominate the international market in cosmetics.

Regularly throughout his career, Salacrou returned to his native Normandy in his plays, as in *Les Fiancés du Havre*, produced at the Comédie-Française immediately after the liberation of Paris in 1944, and *Boulevard Durand*, a play about a trade unionist wrongly condemned to death for a murder on the docks of Le Havre. For political reasons the production of *Boulevard Durand* was delayed, with the result that the first performance in 1961 took place not in Paris, but in Le Havre—a happy coincidence since Salacrou had been attempting, since the 1930's, to encourage a decentralisation of theatrical activity in France.

Taken together, these two plays alone provide a good illustration of Salacrou's range of interests, his technical skill, and the diversity of his talents. *Les Fiancés du Havre* is an example, like *Histoire de rire* and *Les Invités du bon Dieu*, of Salacrou in *boulevard* mood: it is an intricate comedy (at least, superficially) with sparkling dialogue and immense verve; invariably, however, there is a serious undertow. As one critic has observed, Salacrou's farces might have been written by a Noël Coward who had studied Pirandello or even Strindberg. *Boulevard Durand* is a sombre chronicle of an event that occurred virtually in the next street when the dramatist was 11 years old, and the play is a moving condemnation of human injustice and suffering. The two plays reveal more than their author's technical virtuosity: they demonstrate two sides of a complex personality, striving constantly and imaginatively to find an appropriate response to the human predicament in what Salacrou, even before Albert Camus, saw as an absurd world. Some critics have placed excessive stress upon Salacrou's concern with the problem of evil, with his denial of human liberty (rendered all the more unfashionable at a time when Sartre's existentialism was in vogue), and what is interpreted as a radically pessimistic outlook. Conversely, there emerges from Salacrou's drama a positive ethic based on a re-affirmation of traditional values: courage, pity, charity, and purity.

—Colin Radford

SANTARENO, Bernardo. Born António Martinho do Rosário in Santarém, Portugal, 19 November 1920. Studied medicine at the University of Coimbra, graduated 1950. Doctor on a fishing vessel, Newfoundland, Canada, for two seasons; psychiatrist in Lisbon; first plays published 1957; first-produced play, *A Promessa*, staged 1958; his plays of the early 1960's banned from performance; co-founder, Movement of Intellectual Workers (MUTI); a militant member of the left-wing political party MDP CDE. Member, Portuguese Society of Authors, 1965, and from 1980 (Society shut down by the authorities in intervening years). Died in Lisbon, 30 August 1980.

Works

Collections

Obras (4 vols.), edited by Luiz Francisco Rebello.   1984–87.

Stage Works

A Promessa (produced Teatro Experimental, Oporto, 1958).
    In *Teatro*, 1957; translated as *The Promise*, 1981.
O Bailarino.   In *Teatro*, 1957.
A Excomungado.   In *Teatro*, 1957.
O Lugre (produced Teatro Naçional, Lisbon, 1959).   1959.
O Crime de Aldeia Velha (produced Teatro Experimental,
    Oporto, 1959).   1959.
António Marinheiro (produced Teatro Municipal, São Luis,
    1967).   1960.
Irma Natividade.   With *O Pecado de Joao Agonia*, 1961.
O Pecado de João Agonia (produced by the company of the
    Teatro Naçional, Teatro Capitólio, Lisbon, 1969).   1961.
Os Anjos e o Sangue.   1961.
O Duelo (produced by the company of the Teatro Naçional,
    Teatro da Trindade, Lisbon, 1971).   1961.
Anunciacão.   1962.
O Judeo (produced Teatro Naçional de D. Maria II, Lisbon,
    1981).   1966.
O Inferno.   1967.
A Traição do Padre Martinho (produced Sala El Sótano,
    Havana, Cuba, 1970; produced in Portugal, Teatro Maria
    Matos, Lisbon, 1974).
*Os Vendedores de Esperança; A Guerra Santa; O Milagre das
    Lágrimas* (produced as part of *Pira Trás Mija a Burra*).   In
    Obras 4, 1987.
Monsanto (produced as *Na Berma do Caminho*, by the Grupo
    A. Barraca, 1977).   In *Os Marginais e a Revolução*, 1979.
Restos (produced by the Seiva Truppe, 1979).   In *Os
    Marginais e a Revolução*, 1979.
A Confissão (produced by the Seiva Truppe, 1980).   In *Os
    Marginais e a Revolução*, 1979.
Vida Breve em 3 Fotografias.   In *Os Marginais e a
    Revolução*, 1979.
O Punho.   In *Obras 4*, 1987.

Fiction

Nos Mares do Fin do Mundo.   1959.

Verse

A Morte na Raiz.   1954.

*

Criticism

Books:
José Oliveira Barata, *Para uma Leitura de "O Judeu" de
    Bernardo Santareno*, Oporto, 1981.
M.A. Ribeiro, *A Milogénese no Teatro de Bernardo
    Santareno*, Rio de Janeiro, 1981.

Articles:
David J. Viera, "The Jew in Modern Portuguese Theatre", in
    Journal of the American Portuguese Society, 13, 1979.
Gloria F. Waldman, "Character and Space in Two Tragedies
    by Bernardo Santareno", in *Gestos*, 6, 1988.

* * *

Bernardo Santerno's work falls into two categories. The plays written up to 1965 owe a great deal to neorealism, the classical tragedy, existentialism, and Lorca's theatre. From 1966 the main influence is that of Brecht and epic theatre. He follows in the footsteps of Sttau Monteiro's "Fortunately the Moon is Shining" (1961) and Cardoso Pires's, "Relieving the Heroes" (1965) in their Brechtian techniques of alienation and in the use of the past in order to illuminate the present. From 1957 to 1979 Santareno wrote nearly 20 plays, but very few were performed in his lifetime by the main theatres. The Experimental Theatre of Oporto, under the direction of António Pedro, was the first theatre to stage some of his plays—*A Promessa* (*The Promise*) in 1957 (it was banned after ten days by the police and performed again in 1967 in the Monumental Theatre in Lisbon), and *O Crime de Aldeia Velha* (The Crime of the Old Village) in 1959. From 1960 to 1962 Santareno wrote seven plays, but owing to Salazar's censorship, none was performed.

The major themes in Santareno's plays are fate, sexual repression, superstition, social injustice, and religious doubt. Santareno was a committed left-wing writer and his theatre stems from his politics. He wrote at a time when there was no freedom in his country, and in his plays he tried to portray the social conditions of the common people and to show how they were exploited by society because of their ignorance. His first cycle of plays focuses on the life of peasants, fishermen, and workers, on their religious superstitions, their sexual repression, and their violence when they are confronted with an affront to their honour. Fate plays an important role in his drama, paticularly in *A Promessa*, *O Lugre* (The Lugger), *O Crime de Aldeia Velha*, and *António Marinheiro* (*Alfama Oedipus*). He uses the stage to show man in conflict with himself and with society at large. He portrays the traditional conventions of Portuguese society of his time and presents man as a victim of political, social, and religious repression.

A characteristic concern of his plays is with man as he is crushed by authority, be it that of the Church or the State. *A Promessa* encapsulates Santareno's themes, imagery, and dramatic techniques. The play is set in a small fishing village, whose people eke a poor living out of the sea. The central event of the play is the religious promise made by a young man and accepted by his future wife. If God spares his father and he returns safe from the sea after a tempest, they will marry but practise chastity. It is an unnatural situation and, as time passes, the couple show signs of their sexual frustration. When the wife is courted by a man, who was saved from the sea and an outsider, the husband, thinking wrongly that he has been dishonoured, castrates and kills the stranger. The play ends with the consummation of the marriage followed by the imprisonment of the husband. All the issues important to Santareno are represented here: religious superstition, the ignorance of the common people, the submission of women, sexual violence, and the destructive power of fate. But at the end nature overcomes religious superstition and in a certain respect, this is a victory. Santareno uses Freudian imagery to portray the couple's sexual frustration. His taste is for melodrama and he uses the genre boldly, though not always entirely successfully. It can sometimes obscure the significant moral exploration of the play.

The second cycle is best represented by *O Judeo* (The Jew), a dramatic narrative in three acts, portraying the life of the 18th-century playwright António José da Silva (1705–39), who was burned at the stake by the Portuguese Inquisition. António José da Silva was a "new-Christian"—his Jewish parents had converted to Christianity. He was also a very successful and popular playwright. The King and court attended performances of his plays, mainly satires of the court and Lisbon society or comedies after the fashion of Plautus. The narrator in *O Judeo* is the writer Cavaleiro de Oliveira (1702–83), who was an "estrangeirado". He lived most of his life in exile in Vienna, and in Amsterdam and London where he converted to Protestantism and died. He was considered a heretic by the Inquisition and was burnt in effigy in 1761 at an *auto-da-fé* in Lisbon. Cavaleiro de Oliveira is the author's mouthpiece. He advises the Jew to go into exile while there is still time, contrasts the life of the King with that of his people, and comments on the hypocrisy and bigotry of the court and Church. He also addresses the spectators, comparing the persecution of the Jews in Portugal to the atrocities of the Nazis, stressing at the same time, but in an ironic way, that what was happening in the 18th century could not happen in the 20th century.

Santareno portrays António José da Silva convincingly, showing his courage during his torture, his fears, and his hopes. He knew he was innocent of heresy and he had faith in the King and the common people who admired his plays, but both failed him. The King would not oppose the Inquisition and, after the Jew's sentence, attended his *auto-da-fé*, surrounded by the people of Lisbon, seemingly enjoying the grim spectacle. Santareno's portrayal of 18th-century Portugal is very accurate and the historical facts are correct. The play ends with a cry from Cavaleiro da Oliveira about the "enlightened people of Portugal". That was the author's aim: the present is seen through the eyes of the past. *O Judeo* was not allowed to be performed until after the Revolution of 25 April 1974, which ended 40 years of fascism in Portugal. It is a very long play which would take nearly five hours to perform in its entirety. So the only time the work was staged it was done so in shortened form.

In conclusion one can say that Santareno wrote too much, too quickly, and therefore sometimes repeated himself, but he was undoubtedly a powerful and successful dramatist.

—Maria Guterres

SARDOU, Victorien. Born in Paris, 7 September 1831. Studied medicine. Married 1) the actress Mlle. de Brécourt in 1859 (died 1866); 2) Anne Soulié in 1872, three children. Freelance journalist, 1850–60; first-produced play, *La Taverne des étudiants*, staged 1854, and subsequently a prolific playwright: hired to write for the actress Pauline Déjazet at her Paris theatre, from 1859, and wrote several plays for Sarah Bernhardt, from 1876; lived mainly at his château in Marly-le-Roi after 1871, becoming mayor of the town; in later years took out lawsuit for plagiarism of his *Tosca* against the writers Giacosa and Illica for their operatic version, eventually winning in 1908. Elected to the Académie Française, 1878. Died in Marly-le-Roi, 8 November 1908.

Works

Collections

Théâtre complet (15 vols.). 1934–61.

Stage Works

La Taverne des étudiants (produced Théâtre de l'Odéon, Paris, 1854). 1854.
Les Premières Armes de Figaro, with E. Vanderburch (produced Théâtre Déjazet, Paris, 1859). 1860.
Les Gens nerveux, with Th. Barrière (produced Théâtre du Palais-Royal, Paris, 1859). 1859.
Candide. 1860.
Monsieur Garat (produced Théâtre Déjazet, Paris, 1859). 1860.
Les Pattes de mouche (produced Théâtre du Gymnase, Paris, 1860). 1860; translated and adapted as *A Scrap of Paper*, nd.
Les Femmes fortes (produced Théâtre du Vaudeville, Paris, 1860). 1861.
L'Écureuil (produced Théâtre du Vaudeville, Paris, 1861). 1861.
Piccolino (produced Théâtre du Gymnase, Paris, 1861). 1861; musical version, music by Ernest Giraud (produced Théâtre des Variétés, Paris, 1876), 1876.
Nos intimes (produced Théâtre du Vaudeville, Paris, 1861). 1862; translated and adapted as *Friends or Foes?*, nd; as *Our Friends*, 1879.
La Papillonne (produced Comédie-Française, Paris, 1862). 1862.
La Perle noire (produced Théâtre du Gymnase, Paris, 1862). 1862; translated as *The Black Pearl*, 1915.
Les Prés Saint-Gervais (produced Théâtre Déjazet, Paris, 1862). 1862; musical version (produced Théâtre des Variétés, Paris, 1874); translated as *The Meadows of St. Gervais*, 1871.
Les Ganaches (produced Théâtre des Gymnase, Paris, 1862). 1862; translated and adapted as *Progress*. 1893.
Bataille d'amour (libretto; produced Opéra-Comique, Paris, 1863). 1863.
Les Diables noirs (produced Paris, 1863). 1864.
Le Dégel (produced Théâtre Déjazet, Paris, 1984). 1864.
Don Quichotte (produced Théâtre du Gymnase, Paris, 1864). 1864.
Les Pommes du voisin (produced Théâtre du Palais-Royal, Paris, 1864). 1864.
Le Capitaine Henriot (libretto; produced Opéra-Comique, Paris, 1864).
La Famille Benoîton (produced Théâtre du Vaudeville, Paris, 1865). 1865.

Victorian Sardou at his writing table.

Les Vieux Garçons (produced Théâtre du Gymnase, Paris, 1865). 1865.

Nos Bons villageois (produced Théâtre du Gymnase, 1866). 1866.

Maison neuve (produced Théâtre du Vaudeville, Paris, 1866). 1867.

Séraphine (produced Théâtre du Gymnase, Paris, 1868). 1879.

Patrie! (produced Théâtre de la Porte-Saint-Martin, Paris, 1869; musical version produced Théâtre de l'Opéra, Paris, 1886). 1869; translated as *Patrie!*, 1915; as *Native Land!*, in *Plays for the College Theater*, edited by G.H. Leverton, 1934.

Fernande (produced Théâtre du Gymnase, Paris, 1870). 1870; translated and adapted as *Fernande*, 1883.

Rabegas (produced Théâtre du Vaudeville, Paris, 1872). 1872.

Le Roi Carotte (libretto; produced Théâtre de la Gaîté, Paris, 1872). 1872.

Les Merveilleuses (produced Théâtre des Variétés, Paris, 1873). 1873; translated and adapted as *The Women Dandies*, 1906.

Le Magot (produced Théâtre du Palais-Royal, Paris, 1874). 1873.

Andréa (produced Théâtre du Gymnase, Paris, 1873). 1875.

Ferréol (produced Théâtre du Gymnase, Paris, 1875). 1873; translated as *Ferreol*, 1876.

L'Oncle Sam (produced Théâtre du Vaudeville, Paris, 1873). 1875.

L'Hôtel Godelot (produced Théâtre du Gymnase, Paris, 1876).

Les Exilés (produced Boston Theatre, New York, 1877).

Dora (produced Théâtre du Vaudeville, Paris, 1877). 1877; translated as *Dora*, 1877.

L'Heure du spectacle. 1878.

Les Bourgeois de Pont-Arcy (produced Théâtre du Vaudeville, Paris, 1878). 1878; translated as *The Inhabitants of Pontarcy*, 1878.

André Fortier (produced Boston Theatre, New York, 1879).

Daniel Rochat (produced Comedie-Française, Paris, 1880). 1880.

Divorçons! (produced Théâtre du Palais-Royal, Paris, 1880). 1883; translated as *Let Us Be Divorced!*, 1881; as *Let's Get a Divorce!*, in *"Let's Get a Divorce!" and Other Plays*.

Odette (produced Théâtre du Vaudeville, Paris, 1881). 1881.

Fédora (produced Théâtre du Vaudeville, Paris, 1882). 1882; translated and adapted as *Fedora*, 1883.

Théodora (produced Théâtre de la Porte-Saint-Martin, Paris, 1884). 1884; translated as *Theodora*, 1885.

Georgette (produced Théâtre du Vaudeville, Paris, 1885).   1885; translated as *Georgette*, 1886.
Le Crocodile (produced Théâtre de la Porte-Saint-Martin, Paris, 1886).   1886.
La Tosca (produced Théâtre de la Porte-Saint-Martin, Paris, 1887).   1887.
Marquise (produced Théâtre du Vaudeville, Paris, 1889).   1889.
Belle Maman (produced Théâtre du Gymnase, Paris, 1889).   1889.
Cléopatre (produced Théâtre de la Porte-Saint-Martin, Paris, 1890).   1890.
Thermidor (produced Comédie-Française, Paris, 1890).   1891.
Robespierre (produced Lyceum Theatre, London, 1899).   1899.
A Woman's Silence (produced Lyceum Theatre, New York, 1892).
Gismonda (produced Théâtre de la Renaissance, Paris, 1894).
Marcelle (produced Théâtre du Gymnase, Paris, 1895).
Paméla, marchande de frivolité (produced Théâtre du Vaudeville, Paris, 1898).
Spiritisme (produced Théâtre de la Renaissance, Paris, 1897).   1898.
La Fille de Tabarin (produced Opéra-Comique, Paris, 1901).   1901.
Les Barbares, with Pierre Gheusi, music by Saint-Saëns (produced Théâtre de l'Opera, Paris, 1901).   1901.
Danté (produced Theatre Royal, Drury Lane, London, 1903).
Par Instinct.   1904.
La Sorcière (produced Théâtre Sarah-Bernhardt, Paris, 1903).   1904.
Tel chante le vieux coq!.   1904.
Fiorella. with Pierre Gheusi (produced Waldorf Theatre, London, 1905).   1905.
La Piste (produced Théâtre des Variétés, Paris, 1906).   1906.
Madame Sans-Gêne, with Émile Moreau (produced Théâtre du Vaudeville, Paris, 1893).   1907.
L'Affaire des poisons (produced Théâtre de la Porte-Saint-Martin, Paris, 1907).   1908.
La Haine (produced Théâtre de la Gaîté, Paris, 1874).   1875.

Fiction

La Perle noire.   1862.
Carlin.   1932.

Other

Mes Plagiats.   1883.
Notes et croquis.   1885.
Les Papiers de Victorien Sardou: Notes et souvenirs, edited by Georges Mouly.   1934.

*

Criticism

Books:
L. Lacour, *Trois théâtres*, Paris, 1880.
H. Rebell, *Victorien Sardou: Le Théâtre et l'époque*, Paris, 1903.

J.A. Hart, *Sardou and the Sardou Plays*, Philadelphia, 1913.
G. Mouly, *La Vie prodigieuse de Victorien Sardou*, Paris, 1931.
Louis J. Colvet and Jean C. Klein, *Faut-il brûler Sardou?*, Paris, 1978.
F. Sardo, *Les Sardou de père en fils: Souvenirs*, Paris, 1982.
Anne Steinmetz, *Scribe, Sardou, Feydeau: Untersuchungen zur französischen Unterhaltungskomödie im 19. Jahrhundert*, Frankfurt, 1984.
Sigrid Mahsberg, *Theatergeschichte und Theatersemiotik: Die Bedeutung Victorien Sardous für die Entwicklung des modernen Regietheaters*, Frankfurt, 1990.

Articles:
George Rowell, "Sardou on the English Stage", in *Theatre Research International*, 2, 1976.
Mark Eccles, "*Measure for Measure*, Montmorency, and Sardou's *La Tosca*", in *Comparative Drama*, 14, 1980.

*   *   *

Sardou's name will always carry the dual handicap of his dependence on his mentor Scribe and his critical annihilation at the hands of Shaw in the essay "Sardoodledom". Invaluably provocative as Shaw's attack was, it offered a view of that playwright almost as unbalanced as his canonificatory *Quintessence of Ibsenism*. And in appropriating the structural methods of Scribe, Sardou was doing little more than the commonplace 19th-century practice of valuing other playwrights' proven formulas over any bid for creative originality. In fact, Sardou's dramaturgy shows a greater flexibility than Scribe's, in the sense that it does not defer to the accepted decorum of genre, and hybridises the dramatic forms of the first half of the century under the general methods of the *pièce bien faite*.

Sardou's first real success, *Les Pattes de mouche* (*A Scrap of Paper*), illustrates the complexity and ingenuity—often called implausibility—of the well-made play. Even the title, which literally means "fly tracks", probably alludes to the minute meanderings of the central action, and the play contains a lot of insect imagery that suggests a self-contained microcosmic drama. The dynamics of the play lie not in issues of motivation—if they did, the common accusation of psychological shallowness might have some significance—but in the curious career of the letter which gives the English version its title. As always in the well-made play and melodrama, the dynamics of the action are not a matter of motivation but of causation, through what happens to and through inert objects which have some bearing on the lives of the characters. In this case—as commonly—it is a compromising letter between former lovers, and the communication or non-communication of its contents will obviously engineer the play's resolution. The suspense-generating potential of a device like this is enormous: such a letter can lie in a mailbox for half an hour of stage time, it can fall into the wrong hands, there can be uncertainty about whether it has been lost or destroyed, or—as in this play—it can rest forgotten in a public place for three years until someone remembers its damaging potential. Such dramatic mechanics Shaw found absurdly contrived, but they are essentially no different from the use of the telephone in today's television drama as a device to inject vital information at a dramaturgically convenient moment.

A number of successful *pièces bien faites* and farces followed, including *Divorçons* (*Let's Get a Divorce!*) which bases its premise on wrong information about new divorce legislation. In 1882, however, Sardou found an association which was to determine the best of his later work: he began writing for Sarah Bernhardt with *Fédora*, a script in which was embedded what would become writing and acting specialities for each of them. In a loosely historical context, the title character plans revenge for the murder of her fiancé; she miscalculates, finds new evidence about the murder, and finally commits suicide. Bernhardt's artistry found its pinnacle in female suicide scenes—giving rise to the phrase *faire sa Sarah*—and Sardou would supply them generously, but the play also abounded in blood, sex, suspense, and passion, as well as requiring the spectacular and extravagant production that the technology of the late 19th-century theatre could generate amply. These features would recur in numerous plays with a historical or quasi-historical setting, including *Théodora*, *La Tosca*, *Cléopâtre*, and *Gismonda*, all of which involve the well-made morality of a fallen woman finding she has no right to exist. The technique became formulaic, to the extent that William Archer would eventually draw up "a little tabular statement of the amours and homicides in which Sardou has made himself her [Bernhardt's] accomplice". The listing, in spread-sheet fashion, gave a special field to the instruments: Letters, Hairpin, Bread-knife, and Hatchet.

Nor was the suspense value of fallible communications devices overlooked in these plays, and Shaw actually focused on this aspect of *Fédora*:

> The postal arrangements, the telegraphic arrangements, the police arrangements, the names and addresses, the hours and seasons, the tables of consanguinity, the railway and shipping time-tables, the arrivals and departures, the whole welter of Bradshaw and Baedeker, Court Guide and Post Office Directory, whirling round one incredible little stage murder and finally vanishing in a gulp of impossible stage poison, made up an entertainment too Bedlamite for any man with settled wits to preconceive.

Shaw's stylistic flourishes found ready acceptance with an intellectual public that was beginning to acknowledge the behavioural implications of naturalism and embryonic psychology, but it is ironic that in another two decades German expressionism would create figures lost in a mechanistic universe not unlike Shaw's account of *Fédora*.

Not all of Sardou's later work was dependent on Bernhardt's performance. The Byzantine lavishness of *Théodora* extended to a very large cast and a costume budget that was colossal even for that period, but even that was surpassed by the Lyceum premiere of *Robespierre*, which had 69 speaking parts and over 250 supernumeraries and other performers, largely used for a finale in the hall of the Convention. This play adhered closer to history than any of its precedents, possibly because Sardou was not writing for the virtuosity of a particular actor: though the title part was prepared for Henry Irving, it was done during his convalescence from a serious onslaught of pleurisy. Also, as if the carnage of the French Revolution did not provide enough sensational detail, Sardou built in a scene in which Robespierre is haunted by the ghosts of his victims.

Sardou's later work included historical comedy (*Madame Sans-Gêne*) and historical thriller (*L'Affaire des poisons*), as well as several plays which reverted to the lightweight fictional style of *Les Pattes de mouche*. However, the leaning towards the occult foreshadowed in *Robespierre* became more prominent in some plays such as *Spiritisme*, *La Sorcière* (his last for Bernhardt), and *Dante*. The last play, written for the aging Irving, had a cast of 49, including the spirits of Beatrice, Vergil, Cain, Charon, and two cardinals, and had scenes at the Door of Hell, the Fiery Graves, and the Circle of Ice before it returned for a final act at the papal palace,

Avignon. *La Sorcière* was more modest in its scope but more spectacular in its effects: its portrayal of Catholic priests caused riots in Montreal.

—Howard McNaughton

SAROYAN, William. Born in Fresno, California, USA, 31 August 1908. Educated at public schools in Fresno to age 15. Served in the US Army, 1942–45. Married Carol Marcus in 1943 (divorced 1949; remarried 1951; divorced 1952); one son (the writer Aram Saroyan) and one daughter. Worked as grocery clerk, vineyard worker, post office employee; clerk, telegraph operator, then office manager, Postal Telegraph Company, San Francisco, 1926–28; co-founder, Conference Press, Los Angeles, 1936; first-produced plays staged 1939; founder and director, Saroyan Theatre, New York, 1942; writer-in-residence, Purdue University, Lafayette, Indiana, 1961. Recipient: New York Drama Critics Circle Award, 1940; Pulitzer Prize, 1940 (refused); Oscar, for screenplay, 1944. Member, American Academy, 1943. Died in Fresno, 18 May 1981.

Works

Collections

Three Plays: My Heart's in the Highlands; The Time of Your Life; Love's Old Sweet Song. 1940.
Three Plays: The Beautiful People; Sweeney in the Trees; Across the Board on Tomorrow Morning. 1941.
Razzle Dazzle; or, The Human Opera, Ballet, and Circus; or, There's Something I Got to Tell You: Being Many Kinds of Short Plays As Well As the Story of the Writing of Them (includes *Hello, Out There; Coming Through the Rye; Talking to You; The Great American Goof; The Poetic Situation in America; Opera, Opera; Bad Men in the West; The Agony of Little Nations; A Special Announcement; Radio Play; The People with Light Coming Out of Them; There's Something I Got to Tell You; The Hungerers; Elmer and Lily; Subway Circus; The Ping Pong Players*). 1942; abridged edition, 1945.
Don't Go Away Mad and Two Other Plays: Sam Ego's House; A Decent Birth, A Happy Funeral. 1949.
Four Plays: The Playwright and the Public; The Handshakers; The Doctor and the Patient; This I Believe. In *Atlantic*, April 1963.
"The Time of Your Life" and Other Plays. 1967.
"The Dogs; or, The Paris Comedy" and Two Other Plays: Chris Sick; or, Happy New Year Anyway, Making Money, and Nineteen Other Very Short Plays. 1969.

Stage Works

The Man with the Heart in the Highlands. In *Contemporary One-Act Plays*, edited by William Kozlenko, 1938; revised version, as *My Heart's in the Highlands* (produced Guild Theatre, New York, 1939), 1939.
The Time of Your Life (produced Booth Theatre, New York, 1939). In *The Time of Your Life* (miscellany), 1939.
The Hungerers (produced Provincetown Playhouse, New York, 1945). 1939.

Love's Old Sweet Song (produced Plymouth Theatre, New York, 1940). In *Three Plays*, 1940.

Subway Circus. 1940.

Something About a Soldier (produced in stock, 1940).

Hero of the World (produced in stock, 1940).

The Great American Goof (ballet scenario; produced New York, 1940). In *Razzle Dazzle*, 1942.

The Ping-Pong Game (produced Provincetown Playhouse, New York, 1945). 1940; as *The Ping-Pong Players*, in *Razzle Dazzle*, 1942.

Sweeney in the Trees (produced in stock, 1940). In *Three Plays*, 1941.

The Beautiful People (produced Lyceum Theatre, New York, 1941). In *Three Plays*, 1941.

Across the Board on Tomorrow Morning (produced Pasadena Community Playhouse, California, 1941). In *Three Plays*, 1941.

Hello, Out There, music by Jack Beeson (produced Lobero Theatre, Santa Barbara, California, 1941). In *Razzle Dazzle*, 1942.

Jim Dandy (produced Pasadena Community Playhouse, California, 1941). 1941; as *Jim Dandy: Fat Man in a Famine*, 1947.

Talking to You (produced Belasco Theatre, New York, 1942). In *Razzle Dazzle*, 1942.

Coming Through the Rye. In *Razzle Dazzle*, 1942.

The Poetic Situation in America. In *Razzle Dazzle*, 1942.

Elmer and Lily. In *Razzle Dazzle*, 1942.

The Agony of Little Nations. In *Razzle Dazzle*, 1942.

The People with Light Coming Out of Them. In *Razzle Dazzle*, 1942.

There's Something I Got to Tell You. In *Razzle Dazzle*, 1942.

Opera, Opera (produced Amato Theatre, New York, 1955). In *Razzle Dazzle*, 1942.

Bad Men in the West (produced Stanford University, Stanford, California, 1971). In *Razzle Dazzle*, 1942.

Get Away Old Man (produced Cort Theatre, New York, 1943). 1944.

Sam Ego's House (produced Circle Theatre, Los Angeles, California, 1947). In *"Don't Go Away Mad" and Two Other Plays*, 1949.

Don't Go Away Mad (produced Master Institute Theatre, New York, 1949). In *"Don't Go Away Mad" and Two Other Plays*, 1949.

A Happy Funeral. In *"Don't Go Away Mad" and Two Other Plays*, 1949.

The Son (produced Circle Theatre, Los Angeles, California, 1950).

A Lost Child's Fireflies (produced Round-Up Theatre, Dallas, Texas, 1954).

Once Around the Block (produced Master Institute Theatre, New York, 1956). 1959.

The Cave Dwellers (produced Bijou Theatre, New York, 1957). 1958.

Ever Been in Love with a Midget (produced Congress Hall, Berlin, 1957).

The Slaughter of the Innocents (produced The Hague, The Netherlands, 1957). 1958.

Cat, Mouse, Man, Woman. In *Contact 1*, 1958.

The Accident. In *Contact 1*, 1958.

The Dogs; or, The Paris Comedy (as *The Paris Comedy; or The Secret of Lily*, produced Vienna, 1960; as *Lily Dafon*, produced Berlin, 1960). In *"The Dogs; or, The Paris Comedy" and Two Other Plays*, 1969.

Settled Out of Court, with Henry Cecil, from the novel by Cecil (produced Strand Theatre, London, 1960). 1962.

Sam, The Highest Jumper of Them All; or, The London Comedy (produced Theatre Royal, Stratford East, London, 1960). 1961.

High Time along the Wabash (produced Purdue University, Lafayette, Indiana, 1961).

Ah Man, music by Peter Fricker (produced Aldeburgh Festival, Suffolk, England, 1962).

The Playwright and the Public. In *Atlantic*, April 1963.

The Handshakers. In *Atlantic*, April 1963.

The Doctor and the Patient. In *Atlantic*, April 1963.

This I Believe. In *Atlantic*, April 1963.

Dentist and Patient. In *The Best Short Plays 1968*, edited by Stanley Richards, 1968.

Husband and Wife. In *The Best Short Plays 1968*, edited by Stanley Richards, 1968.

Chris Sick; or, Happy New Year Anyway. In *The Dogs . . .* (collection), 1969.

Making Money. In *The Dogs . . .* (collection), 1969.

"Nineteen Short Plays". In *The Dogs . . .* (collections)

The New Play. In *The Best Short Plays 1970*, edited by Stanley Richards, 1970.

People's Lives (produced Manhattan Theatre Club, New York, 1974).

Armenians (produced New York, 1974).

The Rebirth Celebration of the Human Race at Artie Zabala's Off-Broadway Theatre (produced Shirtsleeve Theatre, New York, 1975).

Assassinations. In *Two Short Paris Summertime Plays of 1974*, 1979.

Jim, Sam, and Anna. In *Two Short Paris Summertime Plays of 1974*, 1979.

Screenplays

The Good Job (documentary), 1942; *The Human Comedy*, with Howard Estabrook, 1943.

Television Plays

The Oyster and the Pearl, 1953 (published in *Perspectives USA*, Summer 1953); *Ah Sweet Mystery of Mrs. Murphy*, 1959; *The Unstoppable Gray Fox*, 1962; *"Making Money" and Thirteen Other Very Short Plays* (published 1970).

Radio Plays

Radio Play, 1940 (published in *Razzle Dazzle*, 1942); *A Special Announcement*, 1940 (published 1940); *There's Something I Got to Tell You*, 1941 (published in *Razzle Dazzle*, 1942); *The People with Light Coming Out of Them*, 1941 (published in *The Free Company Presents*, 1941).

Fiction

The Daring Young Man on the Flying Trapeze and Other Stories. 1934.

Inhale and Exhale (stories). 1936.

Three Times Three (stories). 1936.

Little Children (stories). 1937.

The Gay and Melancholy Flux: Short Stories. 1937.

Love, Here is My Hat (stories). 1938.

A Native American (stories). 1938.

The Trouble with Tigers (stories). 1938.

Peace, it's Wonderful (stories). 1939.

3 Fragments and a Story. 1939.

My Name is Aram (stories). 1940.

Saroyan's Fables. 1941.

"The Insurance Salesman" and Other Stories.   1941.
48 Saroyan Stories.   1942.
Best Stories.   1942.
Thirty-One Selected Stories.   1943.
Some Day I'll Be a Millionaire: 34 More Great Stories.   1943.
The Human Comedy.   1943.
Dear Baby (stories).   1944.
The Adventures of Wesley Jackson.   1946.
The Saroyan Special: Selected Short Stories.   1948.
The Fiscal Hoboes (stories).   1949.
*The Twin Adventures: The Adventures of Saroyan: A Diary;
    The Adventures of Wesley Jackson: A Novel.*   1950.
The Assyrian and Other Stories.   1950.
Rock Wagram.   1951.
Tracy's Tiger.   1951.
The Laughing Matter.   1953; as *A Secret Story*, 1954.
The Whole Voyald and Other Stories.   1956.
Mama I Love You.   1956.
Papa You're Crazy.   1957.
Love (stories).   1959.
Boys and Girls Together.   1963.
One Day in the Afternoon of the World. 1964.
*After Thirty Years: The Daring Young Man on the Flying
    Trapeze* (includes essays).   1964.
Best Stories of Saroyan.   1964.
My Kind of Crazy Wonderful People: 17 Stories and a Play.
    1966.
An Act or Two of Foolish Kindness: Two Stories.   1977.
Madness in the Family, edited by L. Hamalian.   1988.
*"The Man with the Heart in the Highlands" and Other Early
    Stories.*   1989.

Verse

A Christmas Psalm.   1935.
Christmas 1939.   1939.

Memoirs and Letters

The Bicycle Rider in Beverly Hills (autobiography).   1952.
Here Comes, There Goes, You Know Who (autobiography).
    1962.
Not Dying (autobiography).   1963.
Short Drive, Sweet Chariot (autobiography).   1966.
Famous Faces and Other Friends: A Personal Memoir.
    1976.
Sons Come and Go, Mothers Hang in Forever (memoirs).
    1976.

Other

Those Who Write Them and Those Who Collect Them.
    1936.
The Time of Your Life (miscellany).   1939.
Harlem as Seen by Hirschfeld.   1941.
Hilltop Russians in San Francisco.   1941.
Why Abstract?, with Henry Miller and Hilaire Hiler.   1945.
The Saroyan Reader.   1958.
A Note on Hilaire Hiler.   1962.
Me (for children).   1963.
*Look at Us: Let's See: Here We Are: Look Hard: Speak Soft:
    I See, You See, We all See; Stop, Look, Listen; Beholder's
    Eye; Don't Look Now But Isn't That You? (us? U.S.).*
    1967.
Horsey Gorsey and the Frog (for children).   1968.
*I Used to Believe I Had Forever; Now I'm Not So
    Sure.*   1968.

Letters from 74 rue Taitbout.   1969; as *Don't Go But If You
    Must Say Hello to Everybody*, 1970.
Days of Life and Death and Escape to the Moon.   1970.
Places Where I've Done Time.   1972.
The Tooth and My Father (for children).   1974.
Morris Hirshfield.   1976.
Chance Meetings.   1978.
Obituaries.   1979.
Births.   1983.
My Name is Saroyan (miscellany), edited by James H. Tas.
    1983.

Editor, *Hairenik 1934–1939: An Anthology of Short Stories
    and Poems.*   1939.

*

Bibliographies

Elisabeth C. Foard, *William Saroyan: A Reference Guide*,
    Boston, 1989.

Criticism

Books:
Howard R. Floan, *William Saroyan*, New York, 1966.
Aram Saroyan, *Last Rites: The Death of William Saroyan*,
    New York, 1982.
Aram Saroyan, *William Saroyan*, San Diego, California,
    1983.
Lawrence Lee and Barry Gifford, *Saroyan: A Biography*,
    New York, 1984.
Leo Hamalian (ed.), *William Saroyan: The Man and the
    Writer Remembered*, Rutherford, New Jersey, 1987.

Articles:
Thelma J. Shinn, "William Saroyan: Romantic Existential-
    ist", in *Modern Drama*, 15, 1972.

* * *

It has become almost mandatory to dismiss Saroyan as a one-play writer, whose enormous output of drama and fiction has never matched the promise of *The Time of Your Life*, the only one of his works to have had extensive professional revival. Critics have patronised him as sentimental, naive, innocent, optimistic, and childlike, and his plays as formless, loose, and melodramatic. Certainly, in his own writing about his plays there is an intellectual slackness that does not encourage close reading of his work. One critic even observed that "if Saroyan would only keep his big mouth shut about the speed with which he writes, he would be regarded by his critics with considerably more sobriety". George Jean Nathan in 1942 wrote a 13-page essay addressing the question, "Is Saroyan crazy?". Yet the playwright himself also stated that the plays of Ionesco "bewilder, delight, annoy, astonish, amaze and amuse me the most", and that "I cherish every cockeyed moment of *Waiting for Godot*". Nor was his appreciation on a level with Bert Lahr's fondness for such plays, which he took essentially as vaudeville; Saroyan could articulate the value of these writers, and then go on to assess their limits, arguing that "they lack size and rage".

The unpretentiousness of Saroyan does not mean triteness. Post-modernist readings in the 1980's of Sam Shepard's use of the Old West in plays like *Geography of a Horse Dreamer* draw attention to the way that in 1939 Saroyan had done precisely the same thing by bringing Kit Carson into the world of *The Time of Your Life*, and thus based the play's premise not on naturalistic issues in the characters' backgrounds but on the sometimes foolish dreams, goals, and ideals they live by. At the same time, in that play he delineated an alcoholic microcosm that has often been compared with O'Neill's (later) *The Iceman Cometh* and a man-versus-machine drama that recalls Rice's *The Adding Machine*.

Before *The Time of Your Life*, Saroyan had written numerous one-acters characterised by a dreamlike atmosphere and an infantilised perspective in which some critics would find the embryo of what they would term his surrealism. *My Heart's in the Highlands*, the most famous of these, was produced as an "experimental" piece by The Group Theatre, Clurman explaining that he had argued against Kazan that it had "freedom, simplicity, hobo charm, delicate sentiment, and humor". The play gradually transmutes the oppressive atmosphere of 1914 into general optimism about humanity through the agency of a Scottish immigrant to California who bolsters up an assortment of waifs with his bravado, tall stories, songs, and playing the title tune on his bugle.

A similar atmosphere and philosophy pervade *Love's Old Sweet Song* and *The Beautiful People*, although the former has a satirical dimension which would be developed to major proportions in *Get Away Old Man*, taking Hollywood as its target. The play is more clearly plotted than any of his others, but its failure on Broadway after only 13 performances led him back to more than a decade of stylised, sometimes defiantly uncommercial dramatic writing. Symbolism, surrealism, insanity, dada, and self-parodying psychoanalysis merge in many of these plays, and though they tend to end happily there is often a pervasive tone of bitterness. *Sweeney in the Trees* chides at capitalism, *Sam Ego's House* is an asylum inhabited by the Urges, and *Jim Dandy* presents a library in the midst of ruins perceived through an eggshell. The situation anticipates that of *The Cave Dwellers* in its clustering of heterogeneous characters in an unlikely refuge, and in the way that the race is poised between collapse (represented on stage by an apeman hybrid) and redemption (through the curiously opportune arrival of materials for a Eucharist).

The Cave Dwellers was Saroyan's first new play on Broadway in 15 years. Written before the notion of "metatheatre" had been legitimised as critical currency, the play is based on an audacious extension of cultural "ready-mades" into a new microcosmic theatrical context, a technique which had been foreshadowed in *The Time of Your Life*. In the new play, a group of down-and-out former entertainers are revealed living underground beneath a New York theatre, while off-stage explosions indicate chaos outside. A process of regression to a neolithic—if not animal—state is occurring, but the characters have taken the names of their former roles: a stage Queen, a clown King, and a boxer Duke. Their apparent degeneration is arrested by the arrival of various other figures including a terrified girl, a man and a pregnant woman, and a trained bear. The bear and new-born baby give some stimulus to the resurgence of the human spirit, and towards the end of the play the King observes: "What are we doing in a cave? We're angels."

A similar dramaturgy lies beneath another play produced in the same year, *The Slaughter of the Innocents*. It is set in the characteristic Saroyan bar, but the alcoholic subculture transmutes into a courtroom where a perverse justice is being administered. The play may be read as a futuristic dystopia or as an alcoholic reverie which turns into nightmare, but again a buoyant faith reasserts itself when the barman slugs the judge and announces freedom for all and drinks on the house. For all that, the central action has an unnerving depiction of the arbitrariness of totalitarian government, and a passionate commitment to socio-political issues that is surprising in Saroyan.

Was Saroyan crazy? Eric Bentley once provocatively put him beside J.B. Priestley to argue that they "are the two prime instances in the dramatic world of highbrows trying to be lowbrows without losing caste. Hence their exaggerated hominess, their forced simplicity, their patriotism and insistent local color, their chronic fear of the esoteric". To which Saroyan indirectly replied, commenting on one of his plays, "I got the idea from alley cats, whom I had watched carefully".

—Howard McNaughton

See also *Volume 1* entry on *The Time of Your Life*.

———

SARRAUTE, Nathalie (née Tcherniak). Born in Ivanovo, Russia, 18 July 1900 (New Style). Moved, following parents' divorce, to Paris, 1902–1906, St. Petersburg, Russia, 1906–08, returning to Paris, 1908, to live with her father. Educated at Lycée Fénelon, Paris, from 1914; the Sorbonne, Paris, *licence* in English 1920; studied history at the University of Oxford, 1920–21, and sociology at the University of Berlin, 1921–22; École de Droit, Paris, 1922–25, law degree 1925. Married Raymond Sarraute in 1925; three daughters. Member of the French Bar, 1926–41; full-time writer since 1941, although the German occupation of France delayed publication of much work; first-produced play, *Le Silence*, broadcast on radio, 1964, and staged (with *Le Mensonge*), 1967. Recipient: Formentor Prize, 1964. Honorary doctorates: Trinity College, Dublin, 1976; University of Kent, Canterbury, 1980; University of Oxford, 1991.

Works

Collections

Théâtre (includes *Elle est là; C'est beau; Isma; Le Mensonge; Le Silence*) 1978.
Collected Plays (includes *It is There, It's Beautiful; Izzuma; The Lie; Silence*). 1980.

Stage Works

Le Silence, from the radio play (produced Petit-Odéon, Paris, 1967). With *Le Mensonge*, 1967; translated as *The Silence*, with *The Lie*, 1969.
Le Mensonge, from the radio play (produced Petit-Odéon, Paris, 1967). With *Le Silence*, 1967; translated as *The Lie*, with *The Silence*, 1967.
Isma (produced Espace Cardin, Paris, 1973). With *Le Silence* and *Le Mensonge*, 1970; translated as *Izzuma*, in *Collected Plays*, 1980.
C'est beau (produced Petit d'Orsay, Paris, 1975). In *Cahiers Renaud-Barrault*, 83, 1973; in book form, in *Théâtre*, 1978; translated as *It's Beautiful*, in *Collected Plays*, 1980.
Elle est là (produced Centre Georges Pompidou, Paris,

1978).   In *Théâtre*, 1978; as *It is There*, in *Collected Plays*, 1980.
Pour Un Oui ou pour un non (produced Petit-Théâtre du Rond-Pont, Paris, 1986).   1982.
Enfance, from her autobiography (produced Théàtre du Rond-Point, Paris, 1984).

Radio Plays

Le Silence, 1964; *Le Mensonge*, 1965; *Isma*, 1970.

Fiction

Tropismes.   1939; revised edition, 1957; translated as *Tropisms*, with *The Age of Suspicion*, 1963; published separately, 1967.
Portrait d'un inconnu.   1948; translated as *Portrait of a Man Unknown*, 1958.
Martereau.   1953; translated as *Martereau*, 1959.
Le Planétarium.   1959; translated as *The Planetarium*, 1960.
Les Fruits d'or.   1963; translated as *The Golden Fruits*, 1964.
Entre la Vie et la mort.   1968; translated as *Between Life and Death*, 1969.
Vous les entendez?   1972; translated as *Do You Hear Them?*, 1973.
"disent les imbéciles".   1976; translated as *"fools say"*, 1977.
L'Usage de la parole.   1980; translated as *The Use of Speech*, 1980.
Tu ne t'aimes pas.   1989; translated as *You Don't Love Yourself*, 1990.

Memoirs and Letters

Enfance (autobiography).   1983; translated as *Childhood*, 1984.

Other

L'Ère du soupçon.   1956; translated as *The Age of Suspicion*, 1963; with *Tropisms*, 1963.
Paul Valéry et l'enfant d'éléphant; Flaubert le précurseur (two essays).   1986.
Nathalie Sarraute, qui êtes-vous?: Conversations avec Simone Benmussa.   1987.

*

Bibliographies

Sheila M. Bell, *Nathalie Sarraute: A Bibliography*, London, 1982.

Criticism

Books:
Ruth Z. Temple, *Nathalie Sarraute*, New York, 1968.
Steen Jansen, *Analyse de la forme dramatique du "Mensonge" de Nathalie Sarraute*, Copenhagen, 1976.
Gretchen Rous Besser, *Nathalie Sarraute*, Boston, 1979.
Arnaud Rykner, *Théâtres du nouveau roman*, Paris, 1988.

Articles:
Denise Goitein, "Nathalie Sarraute as Dramatist", in *Yale French Studies*, 46, 1971.
Bettine L. Knapp, "Nathalie Sarraute: A Theatre of Tropisms", in *Performing Arts Journal*, vol. 1 no. 3, 1977.

Judith G. Miller, "Nathalie Sarraute: How to Do Mean Things with Words", in *Modern Drama*, vol. 34 no. 1, 1990.

*   *   *

Nathalie Sarraute is best known both in France and abroad as a novelist of the *nouvelle vague*, her work including *Portrait of a Man Unknown*, *The Planetarium*, *Martereau*, and *Between Life and Death*. Her plays have received comparatively little exposure in stage performance either in France or elsewhere, although they have been quite widely broadcast in Europe in radio productions. Like her novels, Sarraute's plays present of sensations, subtle feelings which rise to the surface in apparently trivial, even rather commonplace conversations. Hers is a minimalist art in the sense that it deals with small movements, what she called *tropisms*, subtle shifts of language, and nuances of style and expression. In some respects her literary strategy invites stage exploration for, concerned as she is with a very precise use of language in order to suggest elusive feelings and surface appearances, the movement, gesture, and vocal inflection required of performance serve to enrich and refine expression by expanding the language through which these can be conveyed.

Perhaps the best known of her plays are *Le Silence* (*Silence*) and *Le Mensonge* (*The Lie*). The former was first produced in German by Süddeutscher Radiofunk, on 1 April 1964, and has subsequently been produced on Belgian, Swedish, Danish, Norwegian, Swiss, and Finnish radio. *The Lie* was first performed on 2 March 1966, when it was given on both French and German radio, and has since been done on Swedish radio. Stage performances of these plays have been less frequent, but they were first given as a double bill at the smaller stage of the Odéon Theatre de France, 14 January 1967, in an adaptation by Jean-Louis Barrault, which he himself directed and in which his wife, Madeleine Renault, played the part of Woman I in *Silence*.

In *The Lie* five women and four men discuss an acquaintance, a certain Madelaine Styvers, their feelings finding gradual but elliptical expression in complex, indirect ways. *Silence* consists of an essentially casual, but nonetheless serious discussion between a man and a woman, with interjections by others, male and female. The characters reminisce about their past lives, loves, and friendships, about people they have known and places they have been to. As they talk, feelings edge to the surface, ambivalent attitudes emerge, a close mesh of emotional inter-relationships appears to be exposed. Sarraute's approach lends itself particularly to monologue and highly discursive dialogue. At times the influence of Samuel Beckett seems present in her work, although this impression can be deceptive, for Sarraute is undoubtedly a very distinctive and individual writer. If echoes of her style and approach are to be felt in English drama, they are perhaps evident in some of the later work of a writer like Harold Pinter.

—Francesca Richards

———————

SARTRE, Jean-Paul (-Charles-Aymard).   Born in Paris, 21 June 1905. Educated at Lycée Montaigne and Lycée Henri-IV, Paris; École Normale Supérieure, Paris, *agrégation* in

Jean-Paul Sartre (c.1950).

philosophy 1929. Began lifelong relationship with the writer Simone de Beauvoir in 1929; had one adopted daughter. Served in the French Army, 1929–31; professor: Lycée du Havre, 1931–32 and 1934–36, Lycée de Laon, 1936–37, Lycée Pasteur, Paris, 1937–39; mobilized in 1939, but captured, 1940, and imprisoned in Staleg XIID, near Trier, where his play *Bariona* was produced: escaped, 1941; professor, Lycée Condorcet, Paris, 1941–44; first professionally produced play, *Les Mouches*, staged 1943; founding editor, with de Beauvoir, *Les Temps modernes*, 1945; visited the USA as journalist for *Combat*, the former Resistance newspaper, and *Le Figaro*; lectured in the USA, 1945, and in Italy and Switzerland, 1946; member, Rassemblement Démocratique Revolutionnaire (RDR), 1948–49; travelled and lectured extensively during the 1950's and 1960's; signed the "Manifeste des 121", supporting Algerian independence, with other prominent French cultural figures, 1960, and supported numerous left-wing causes; member of Bertrand Russell's International War Crimes Tribunal, 1966; editor, *La Cause du Peuple*, from 1970, *Tout*, 1970–74, *Révolution*, 1971–74, and *Libération*, 1973–74; founder, with Maurice Clavel, Liberation news service, 1971; suffered declining health throughout the 1970's. Recipient: New York Drama Critics Circle Award, 1947; Grand Novel Prize, 1950; Omegna Prize (Italy), 1960; Nobel Prize for Literature, 1964 (refused). Foreign Member, American Academy of Arts and Sciences. Died in Paris, 15 April 1980.

Works

Collections

Théâtre 1 (includes *Les Mouches; Huis clos; Morts sans sépulture; La Putain respecteuse*).   1947.
Three Plays (UK edition; includes *Men Without Shadows; The Respectable Prostitute; Crime Passionel*).   1949; US edition, with alternative titles (*The Victors; The Respectful Prostitute; Dirty Hands*), 1949.
"The Devil and the Good Lord" and Two Other Plays (includes *Kean* and *Nekrassov*), various translators.   1960.
Altona; Men Without Shadows; The Flies, various translators.   1962.

Stage Works

Bariona; ou, Le Fils du tonnerre (produced during captivity, 1940).   1962; translated as *Bariona; or, The Son of Thunder*, in *The Writings 2*, 1974.
Les Mouches (produced Théâtre de la Cité, Paris, 1943).   1943; translated as *The Flies*, with *In Camera*, 1946.
Huis clos (produced Théâtre du Vieux-Colombier, Paris, 1944).   1945; translated as *In Camera*, with *The Flies*, 1946; as *No Exit*, with *The Flies*, 1947.
Morts sans sépulture (produced Théâtre Antoine, Paris, 1946).   1946; translated as *Men Without Shadows*, in *Three Plays* (UK), 1949; as *The Victors*, in *Three Plays* (USA), 1949.
La Putain respectueuse (produced Théâtre Antoine, Paris, 1946).   1946; translated as *The Respectable Prostitute*, in *Three Plays* (UK), 1949; as *The Respectful Prostitute*, in *Three Plays* (USA), 1949.
Les Mains sales (produced Théâtre Antoine, Paris, 1948).   1948; translated as *Crime Passionnel*, in *Three Plays* (UK), 1949; as *Dirty Hands*, in *Three Plays* (USA), 1949.
Le Diable et le bon Dieu (produced Theatre Antoine, Paris, 1951).   1951; translated as *Lucifer and the Lord*, 1953; as *The Devil and the Good Lord*, in *"The Devil and the Good Lord" and Two Other Plays*, 1960.
Kean, from the play by Dumas *père* (produced Théâtre Sarah-Bernhardt, Paris, 1953).   1954; translated as *Kean*, 1954.
Nekrassov (produced Théâtre Antoine, Paris, 1955).   1956; translated as *Nekrassov*, 1956.
Les Séquestrés d'Altona (produced Théâtre de la Renaissance, Paris, 1959).   1960; translated as *Loser Wins*, 1960; as *The Condemned of Altona*, 1961.
Les Troyennes, from a play by Euripides (produced Théâtre du Palais de Chaillot, Paris, 1965).   1965; translated as *The Trojan Women*, 1967.

Screenplays

Les Jeux sont faits (released 1947; released in English as *The Chips Are Down*).   Published 1947; translated as *The Chips Are Down*, 1948.
L'Engrenage (released 1948).   Published 1948; translated as *In the Mesh*, 1954.
Sorcières de Salem (released 1957; released in English as *Witches of Salem*).
Le Scénario Freud.   Published 1984; translated as *The Freud Scenario*, 1985.

Fiction

La Nausée. 1938; translated as *The Diary of Antoine Roquentin*, 1949; as *Nausea*, 1949.

Le Mur. 1939; translated as *"The Wall" and Other Stories*, 1949; as *"Intimacy" and Other Stories*, 1949.

L'Âge de raison. 1945; translated as *The Age of Reason*, 1947.

Le Sursis. 1945; translated as *The Reprieve*, 1947.

La Mort dans l'âme. 1949; translated as *Iron in the Soul*, 1950; as *Troubled Sleep*, 1951.

Oeuvres romanesques, edited by Michel Contat and Michel Rybalka. 1981.

Memoirs and Letters

Les Mots (autobiography). 1963; translated as *Words*, 1964; as *The Words*, 1964.

Les Carnets de la drôle de guerre: Novembre 1939–Mars 1940. 1983; translated as *War Diaries: Notebooks from a Phoney War: November 1939–March 1940*, 1984; as *The War Diaries of Jean-Paul Sartre: November 1939–March 1940* (US edition), 1985.

Lettres au Castor et à quelques autres, edited by Simone de Beauvoir. 1983.

Thoughtful Passions: Intimate Letters to Simone de Beauvoir. 1987.

Other

L'Imagination. 1936; translated as *Imagination: A Psychological Critique*, 1962.

Esquisse d'une théorie des émotions. 1939; translated as *The Emotions: Outline of a Theory*, 1948; as *Sketch for a Theory of the Emotions*, 1962.

L'Imaginaire: Psychologie phénoménologique de l'imagination. 1940; translated as *Psychology of the Imagination*, 1949.

L'Être et le néant: Essai d'ontologie phénoménologique. 1943; translated as *Being and Nothingness*, 1956.

L'Existentialisme est un humanisme. 1946; translated as *Existentialism*, 1947; as *Existentialism and Humanism*, 1948.

Explication de "L'Étranger." 1946.

Réflexions sur la question juive. 1947; translated as *Anti-Semite and Jew*, 1948; as *Portrait of an Anti-Semite*, 1948.

Baudelaire. 1947; translated as *Baudelaire*, 1949.

Situations 1–10 (10 vols.). 1947–76; selections translated as: *What is Literature?*, 1949; *Literary and Philosophical Essays*, 1955; *Situations*, 1965; *The Communists and Peace*, 1965; *The Ghost of Stalin*, 1968 (as *The Spectre of Stalin*, 1969); *Between Existentialism and Marxism*, 1974; *Life/ Situations*, 1977; *Sartre in the Seventies*, 1978.

Entretiens sur la politique, with others. 1949.

Saint Genet, comédien et martyr. 1952; translated as *Saint Genet, Actor and Martyr*, 1963.

L'Affaire Henri Martin, with others. 1953.

The Transcendence of the Ego: An Existentialist Theory of Consciousness. 1957.

Critique de la raison dialectique: Théorie des ensembles pratiques. 1960; translated as *Critique of Dialectical Reason: Theory of Practical Ensembles*, 1976.

On Cuba. 1961.

Essays in Aesthetics, edited by Wade Baskin. 1963.

Que peut la littérature? with others. 1965.

The Philosophy of Sartre, edited by Robert Denoon Cumming. 1966.

Of Human Freedom, edited by Wade Baskin. 1967.

Essays in Existentialism, edited by Wade Baskin. 1967.

On Genocide. 1968.

Les Commununistes ont peur de la révolution. 1969.

L'Idiot de la famille: Gustave Flaubert de 1821 à 1857 (3 vols.). 1971–72; translated as *The Family Idiot: Gustave Flaubert 1821–1857*, 1981–82.

War Crimes in Vietnam, with others. 1971.

Un Théâtre de situations, edited by Michel Contat and Michel Rybalka. 1973; translated as *Sartre on as Theatre*, 1976.

Politics and Literature. 1973.

The Writings 2: Selected Prose, edited by Michel Contat and Michel Rybalka. 1974.

On a raison de se révolter, with others. 1974.

Cahiers pour un morale. 1983.

Mallarmé; or, The Poet of Nothingness. 1987.

*

Bibliographies

Michel Contat and Michel Rybalka, *Les Écrits de Sartre: Chronologie, bibliographie commentée*, Paris, 1970.

Robert Wilcocks, *Jean-Paul Sartre: A Bibliography of International Criticism*, Edmonton, Alberta, 1975.

Françoise and Claire Lapointe, *Jean-Paul Sartre and His Critics: An International Bibliography 1938–1988*, Bowling Green, Ohio, 1981.

Criticism

Books:

Iris Murdoch, *Sartre, Romantic Rationalist*, London, 1953.

Philip Thody, *Sartre: A Literary and Political Study*, London, 1960.

Henry Peyre, *Jean-Paul Sartre*, New York, 1968.

George H. Bauer, *Sartre and the Artist*, Chicago, 1969.

Dorothy McCall, *The Theatre of Jean-Paul Sartre*, New York, 1969.

Philip Thody, *Sartre: A Biographical Introduction*, London, 1971.

Mary Warnock (ed.), *Sartre: A Collection of Critical Essays*, Garden City, New York, 1971.

Philip Thody, *Sartre: A Biographical Introduction*, London, 1971.

Pierre Vestraeten, *Violence et éthique*, Paris, 1972.

Jacques Lecarme, *Les critiques de notre temps et Sartre*, Paris, 1973.

Robert Lorris, *Sartre dramaturge*, Paris, 1975.

Peter Caws, *Sartre*, London, 1979.

Luciano Verona, *Le Théâtre de Jean-Paul Sartre*, Milan, 1979.

Robert Champigny, *Sartre and Drama*, Birmingham, Alabama, 1982.

Michael Issacharoff and Jean C. Vilquin (eds.), *Sartre et la mise en signe*, Paris, 1982.

Annie Cohen-Salal, *Sartre 1905–1980*, Paris, 1985.

Ingrid Galster, *Le Théâtre de Jean-Paul Sartre devant ses premiers critiques*, Tübingen, 1986.

Ronald Hayman, *Sartre: A Life*, New York, 1987.

Christina Howells, *Sartre: The Necessity of Freedom*, Cambridge, 1988.

Robert Wilcocks (ed.), *Critical Essays on Jean-Paul Sartre*, Boston, 1988.

Liliane Siegel, *In the Shadow of Sartre*, 1990.

Philip R. Wood, *Understanding J P Sartre*, 1990.

Articles:
Keith O. Gore, "The Theatre of Sartre: 1940–65", in *Books Abroad*, 41, 1967.
Lucien Goldmann, "The Theatre of Sartre", in *Tulane Drama Review*, vol. 15 no.1, 1970.
Judith Zivanovic, "Sartre's Drama: Key to Understanding His Concept of Freedom", in *Modern Drama*, 14, 1971.

* * *

Like Sartre's novels, essays, short, stories and formal philosophy, his plays are shot through with a series of contradictions which make him one of the most intriguing of writers to analyse as well as one of the most challenging to discuss. He intensely disliked the bourgeoisie, and yet found his keenest admirers among the middle class. His ideal would have been to write plays for a working-class audience, but his reception was most enthusiastic in the theatres of the right rather than of the left bank in Paris. He despised conventional literature and yet gave his best play, *Les Mains sales* (*Crime Passionnel*) the form of a thriller with a twist in its tail that would have done credit to Agatha Christie. He wanted to write committed literature in favour of the left, but provided in *Les Mains sales* one of the most telling indictments available on stage of left-wing opportunism and realpolitik. As a man of the Left, he believed passionately in human freedom and the possibility of bringing about a better, more humane society. But his best known play, *Huis Clos* (*No Exit*) is devised to prove the thesis that "Hell is other people". Only perhaps in his 1959 play *Les Séquestrés d'Altona* (*The Condemned of Altona*), with its attack on French colonial policy in Algeria, is there a successful attempt to bring together his left-wing ideals and his practice as a playwright.

Huis Clos was originally written to provide a vehicle for three actors to remain on stage throughout the whole of the action. None of the three, the child-murderess Estelle, the coward Garcin, and the lesbian Ines, ever runs the risk of leaving the stage and allowing the others the chance of saying the best lines. It is only gradually that the truth about them is revealed and that both they and the audience realise that their punsishment, throughout eternity, will be to torment one another. The same theme of imprisonment and sequestration recurs in *Les Mains sales*, when the revolutionary leader Hoederer, his supposed secretary Hugo, and Hugo's vapid wife, Jessica, are all in a villa where Hugo has to perform his chosen task of killing Hoederer in order to prevent him from changing the party line. Hugo eventually succeeds, only to discover that the change which Hoederer had wanted to implement has become the new orthodoxy. *Les Séquestrés d'Altona*, as its name implies, is also about the impossibility of escape, this time from the past. A German officer, Franz von Gerlach, has tried to deny that the defeat of Germany in World War II which he had used all means, including torture, to avoid, was the best thing that could happen to his country. When forced to admit the truth, he commits suicide, and the message that the best thing that could happen to France in 1959 was to lose the Algerian war disappears in yet another demonstration of man's inability to escape from his past and in a neo-Wagnerian Götterdämmerung which emphasised how large an inheritance Sartre's existentialism had received from the aberration known as Romanticism.

Sartre's more optimistic plays are much more open in their dramatic structure and much less satisfying as theatre. His first play to be produced in Paris, *Les Mouches* (*The Flies*) uses the classical legend of Orestes, Clytemnestra, and Aigisthos to demonstrate to the French, by allegory, that even the most terrible crimes can be justified if liberty is their objective. When Orestes avenges the murder of his father, Agamemnon, by killing not only the usurper Aigisthos but also his own mother, Clytemnestra, who had collaborated in the crime, the political message is clear: do not be held back from killing not only Germans but also French collaborators if this is the only way of bringing about the liberation of France. And *Le Diable et le bon Dieu* (*Lucifer and the Lord*) uses a peasants' revolt in 16th-century Germany to drive home the same message. The revolutionary leader Goetz stabs a peasant who refuses to obey orders, thus illustrating the thesis that the revolution can triumph only by using violence to impose the strictest of discipline, even on those whom it tries to serve. Neither play has proved particularly successful in the theatre, and only Sartre's 1955 adaptation of Alexandre Dumas's *Kean* has been as popular with audiences as his more sombre and introverted works. *Kean* deals with the paradox of the actor who can achieve authenticity only by pretending to be what he is not, and sacrificing his own personality to the series of imaginary heroes whom he incarnates for one evening before letting them die. The need to become what one is by perfoming a role is a central theme in Sartre's philosophy, and the role of Kean gave Pierre Brasseur, an actor who liked to ham his parts, one of the best roles of his career.

—Philip Thody

See also *Volume 1* entry on *The Flies*; *No Exit*.

———

SASTRE, Alfonso. Born in Madrid, Spain, 20 February 1926. Educated at the Instituto Cardenal Cisneros, Madrid, from 1936; studied philosophy and literature at the universities of Madrid and Murcia, 1947–53. Married Eva Forest in 1955; two sons and one daughter. Co-founder, Arte Nuevo theatre group, 1945: disbanded 1948; his first plays produced by Arte Nuevo in 1946; collaborated with the Teatro Universitario de Ensayo (TUDE), Madrid, 1948; theatre editor, *La Hora*, 1948–50; published the manifesto "Teatro de Agitación Social", written with José María de Quinto, 1950; briefly imprisoned for political reasons, 1956; co-founder, with de Quinto, Grupo de Teatro Realista, 1960: group's work frequently censored by the Franco regime; joined the secret Communist Party of Spain, 1962; imprisoned again, 1962; travelled to Portugal and Cuba, 1964; imprisoned for non-payment of fine after involvement in anti-government protest, 1966; travelled to Colombia, 1969, Chile and Sweden, 1971, Cuba, 1972, Venezuela, 1973; many works published and performed abroad in the 1970's; his wife arrested for alleged involvement with Basque terrorists, 1974; left Communist Party, 1974; imprisoned again, 1974–75: released after international protests; moved to France with his daughter, 1975: returned by French police to the Spanish authorities; his wife released from prison, 1977, and they moved to Fuenterrabia, in the Basque region; visiting professor, University of California, San Diego, 1987–88. Member, editorial board of the theatre journal *Gestos*, from

1986. Recipient: Viareggio-Versilia Prize (Italy), 1976; Reseña Prize, 1978; National Theatre Prize, 1985.

Works

Collections

Teatro de vanguardia (includes *Uranio 235*; *Cargamento de sueños*; and, with Medardo Fraile, *Ha sonado de muerte* and *Comedia sonámbula*). 1949.
Teatro (includes *Escuadra hacia la muerte*; *Tiera roja*; *Ana Kleiber*; *Muerte en el barrio*; *Guillermo Tell tiene los ojos tristes*; *El cuervo*). 1960.
Cuatro dramas de la revolución. 1963.
Cargamento de sueños; *Prólogo patético*; *Asalto nocturno*. 1964.
Teatro selecto. 1966.
Obras completas (plays). 1967.
El escenario diabólico: El cuervo, Ejercicios de terror, Las cintas magnéticas. 1973.
Teatro político (includes *Askatasuna!*; *El camarada oscuro*; *Análisis espectral de un Comando al servicio de la Revolución Proletaria*). 1979.

Stage Works

Uranio 235 (produced Teatro Beatriz, Madrid, 1946). In *Teatro de vanguardia*, 1949.
Ha sonado la muerte, with Medardo Fraile (produced Teatro Beatriz, Madrid, 1946). In *Teatro de vanguardia*, 1949.
Cargamento de sueños (produced Teatro Ramiro de Maeztu, Madrid, 1948). In *Teatro de vanguardia*, 1949.
Comedia sonámbula, with Medardo Fraile. In *Teatro de vanguardia*, 1949.
Escuadra hacia la muerte (produced Teatro María Guerrero, Madrid, 1953). In *Teatro*, 1960; translated as *The Condemned Squad*, in *The Modern Spanish Stage*, edited by Marion P. Holt, 1970.
La mordaza (produced Teatro Reina Victoria, Madrid, 1954). 1965; edited by Farris Anderson, with *Escuadra hacia la muerte*, 1975.
La sangre de Dios (produced Teatro Serrano, Valencia, 1955). 1959.
Ana Kleiber (produced Athens, 1960). 1957; translated as *Anna Kleiber*, in *The New Theatre of Europe*, edited by Robert W. Corrigan, 1962.
El pan de todos (produced Teatro Windsor, Barcelona, 1957). 1960.
El cuervo (produced Teatro María Guerrero, Madrid, 1957). 1960.
Medea (produced Teatro Griego, Montjuich, 1958). 1963.
Muerte en el barrio (produced Colegio Mayor Francisco, Madrid, 1959). In *Teatro*, 1960.
La cornada (produced Teatro Lara, Madrid, 1960). 1965; translated as *Death Thrust*, in *Masterpieces of the Modern Spanish Theatre*, edited by Robert W. Corrigan, 1967.
Tierra roja (produced Montevideo). In *Teatro*, 1960.
Guillermo Tell tiene los ojos tristes (produced by Grupo Bululú, Madrid, 1965). In *Teatro*, 1960; translated as *Sad Are the Eyes of William Tell*, in *The New Wave Spanish Drama*, edited by George E. Wellwarth, 1970.
En la red (produced Teatro Recoletos, Madrid, 1961). 1961.
Los acreedores, from a play by Strindberg (produced Teatro Valle Inclán, Madrid, 1962).
Mulato, from a play by Langston Hughes (produced Madrid, 1963).

Asalto nocturno (produced Teatro Club Iber, Barcelona, 1965). With *Cargamento de sueños*, 1964.
Prólogo patético. With *Cargamento de sueños*, 1964; translated as *Pathetic Prologue*, in *Modern International Drama*, March 1968.
M.S.V.; o, La sangre y la ceniza (produced by Colectivo El Búho, Barcelona, 1976). In Italian, as *Il sangue e la cenere*, 1967; in Spanish, with *Crónicas romanas*, 1979.
Oficio de tinieblas (produced Teatro de la Comedia, Madrid, 1967). 1967.
El circulito de tiza (produced in part, Alicante, 1969). In *Obras completas*, 1967.
Marat-Sade, from the play by Peter Weiss (produced Barcelona, 1968).
La . . . respetuosa and *A puerta cerrada*, from plays by Sartre (produced Madrid, 1968).
Rosas rojas para mí, from a play by O'Casey (produced Madrid, 1969).
Crónicas romanas (produced Avignon Festival, France, 1982). In Italian, as *Cronache romane*, 1970; in Spanish, with *M.S.V.*, 1979.
Las moscas, from a play by Sartre (produced Madrid, 1970).
Los secuestrados de Altona, from a play by Sartre (produced Madrid, 1972).
Ejercicios de terror (produced in part, by the Compañia Julián Romea, Murcia, 1981). In *El escenario diabólico*, 1973.
Las cintas magnéticas (produced Lyons, France, 1973). In *El escenario diabólico*, 1973.
El camarada oscuro. In *Teatro politico*, 1979.
Ahola no es de leil (produced Madrid, 1979). 1980.
Tragedia fantástica de la gitana Celestina (produced Rome, 1979). In *Primer acto*, 192, January–February 1982.
El hijo único de Guillermo Tell. In *Estreno 9*, Spring 1983.
La taberna fantástica, edited by Mariano de Paco (produced Madrid, 1985). 1983.
Jenofa Juncal. In *Gestos*, 1, 1986; translated as *The Red Gipsy*, 1990.
El viaje infinito de Sancho Panza. 1987.
Los hombres y sus hombres: Terrores y miserias del IV Reich. 1988.
Asalto a una ciudad, from a play by Lope de Vega. 1988.
Los últimos dias de Emmanuel Kant contados por Ernesto Teodoro Amadeo (produced Madrid, 1990). 1989.

Television Plays

Askatasuna!, 1974 (published in *Teatro político*, 1979).

Fiction

Las noches lúgubres. 1964.
El paralelo 38. 1965.
Flores rojas para Miguel Servet. 1967.
Lumpen, marginacion, y jerigonca. 1980.
El lugar del crimen—Unheimlich. 1982.
Historia de una muñeca abandonada. 1989.

Verse

"Balada de Carabanchel" y otros poemas celulares. 1976.
El español al alcance de todos. 1978.
TBO. 1978.

Other

Drama y sociedad. 1956.
Anatomía del realismo. 1965; revised edition, 1974.

Flores rojas para Miguel Servet.   1967.
La revolución y la crítica de la cultura.   1970.
Crítica de la imaginación.   1978.
Escrito en Euskadi.   1982.

Translator, *El retrato de Dorian Gray*, by Oscar Wilde. 1988.
Translator, *Novelas y cuentos; Teatro; Poemas en prosa; Ensayos; Cartas y otros escritos*, with José Sastre, from works by Oscar Wilde.   1988.

*

Bibliographies

Marsha Forys, *Antonio Buero Vallejo and Alfonso Sastre: An Annotated Bibliography*, Metuchen, New Jersey, 1988.

Criticism

Books:
Farris Anderson, *Alfonso Sastre*, New York, 1971.
Francis Donahue, *Alfonso Sastre: Dramaturgo y preceptista*, Buenos Aires, 1973.
Anje C. van der Naald, *Sastre, dramaturgo de la revolución*, New York, 1973.
Magda Ruggeri Marchetti, *Il teatro di Alfonso Sastre*, Rome, 1975.
Marion Peter Holt, *The Contemporary Spanish Theatre (1949–1972)*, Boston, 1975.
Gwynne Edwards, *Dramatists in Perspective: Spanish Theatre in the Twentieth Century*, Cardiff, 1985.
Felicia Hardison Londré, "The Theatrical Gap Between Sastre's Criticism and His Later Plays", in *The Contemporary Spanish Theater*, edited by Martha T. Halsey and Phyllis Zatlin, Lanham (Maryland) and New York, 1988.

Articles:
Anthony M. Pasquariello, "Alfonso Sastre: Dramatist in Search of a Stage", in *Theater Annual*, 22, 1965–66.
Kessel Schwartz, "Tragedy and the Criticism of Alfonso Sastre", in *Symposium*, 21, 1967.
John A. Moore, "Sastre, Dramatist and Critic", in *South Atlantic Bulletin*, vol. 35 no. 2, 1970.
Lynette H. Seator, "Alfonso Sastre, Committed Dramatist", in *Papers on Language and Literature*, 15, 1979.

*   *   *

Alfonso Sastre began his playwriting career in the 1940's within the experimental Arte Nuevo theatre group. His early works, emphasizing the anguish and frustration of the individual, utilize the dreamlike techniques associated with surrealism and expressionism. More significant are the socially committed plays, dating from the early 1950's. The dramas written in this second style are distinguished by their greater realism and their espousal of personal and political action.

Sastre's first major work, *Escuadra hacia la muerte* (*The Condemned Squad*), was first produced in 1953 and established his reputation nationally and internationally even though it was closed by the censor for its anti-militarism after only three performances. The action takes place during an imaginary Third World War; the characters are a corporal and five soldiers, stationed at a remote outpost as punishment for past offenses. In essence theirs is a suicide mission, for

they expect to die when the enemy assault begins. In their closed world, tensions mount and four of the soldiers unite to kill the corporal, whose rigid, indeed obsessive, discipline has become intolerable. The enemy troops never come, but now the squad will face execution for their crime.

Escuadra hacia la muerte is an overtly existentialist work, with Sartrean overtones. The several soldiers, of varying backgrounds and temperaments, reveal their life experiences to one another and explore philosophical questions relating to individual and social responsibility, the absurdity of life, and the inevitability of death. The text readily falls within Sastre's explanation, in *Drama y sociedad* (Drama and Society), of the metaphysical dimension of tragedy. Consistent with his own definition, his characters, who are condemned to death, find themselves existing within a closed situation; their desire for happiness and their struggle cannot overcome their destiny or their guilt. The one hope within this bleak view of the human condition is the innocent Luis, who is willing to assume responsibility with the others for their collective action but will nevertheless be saved.

Other dramas of this second period similarly deal with issues of social responsibility and personal rebellion. In *La mordaza* (The Gag), Luisa overcomes the fear that has silenced her and her family in order to denounce her tyrannical father-in-law for a murder she had seen him commit. At the time of its writing, the drama lent itself well to a metaphorical reading in which the repressive patriarch could be equated with Franco. *La cornada* (*Death Thrust*), which superficially centers on the world of the bullfight, is open to a range of metaphorical interpretations. Overcome by fear and unable to choose between his authentic self and materialistic ambition, Alba allows his manipulative manager to force him into the arena and certain death. On an ideological level, *La cornada* reveals capitalistic exploitation; in a money-making sport, the individual is sacrificed to greed. Through the presence of secondary figures, including one ex-bullfighter who has given up his dream of fame and fortune and another whose life has been destroyed, the audience is made to share a sense of responsibility and compassion for society's victims. Along these same lines, *Muerte en el barrio* (Death in the Neighborhood) focuses on the righteous anger of the poor, who rise up and kill a public-health doctor when his flagrant neglect has resulted in the death of a neighborhood child.

At times Sastre's theatre goes beyond personal rebellion to treat political revolution. The protagonist of *Guillermo Tell tiene los ojos tristes* (*Sad Are the Eyes of William Tell*), like the historical figure on which he is based, liberates his country from tyranny. In this existentialist modernization, however, the hero must assume the responsibility for his act which, in Sastre's ironic inversion, includes the death of Tell's son. *En la red* (In the Net) is one of several works that center on the revolutionary process and the moral ambiguity of terrorism and violence.

By the late 1950's and early 1960's, Sastre set aside the Aristotelian concepts of tragedy that underpinned many of his early works and moved to a Brechtian, epic theatre. One of his first plays to highlight the influence of Brecht and one of his most frequently performed plays internationally is *Historia de una muñeca abandonada* (Story of an Abandoned Doll), a charming reworking as children's theatre of *The Caucasian Chalk Circle*.

Dating from the mid-1960's are post-Brechtian works that Sastre has labeled "complex tragedies"; they tend to combine elements of classic tragedy with Brechtian techniques and a use of the grotesque reminiscent of Valle-Inclán. These include the historical epic plays *Crónicas romanas* (Roman Chronicles), dealing with the siege and destruction of

Numancia, and *M. S. V.; o, La sangre y la ceniza* (Blood and Ashes), focusing on the life and execution of Miguel Servet. Although these have both been produced successfully outside Spain, Sastre's long-awaited integration into mainstream Spanish theatre was not to come until 1985, and then through *La taberna fantástica* (The Fantastic Tavern), a complex tragedy of contemporary setting.

The reality that Sastre chose to portray in *La taberna fantástica*, written in 1966, was that of the *quinquilleros*, the shanty-dwelling nomadic street-vendors and handymen who were viewed during the Franco years as undesirables and social outcasts. Gerardo Malla's staging of the prize-winning play was both hyper-realistic (the tavernkeeper fried real eggs on a real grill) and theatricalist (the author-character directly addressed the audience). The protagonist, Rogelio, fits Sastre's own definition of a "laughable hero". His story, which culminates in his senseless death in a knife fight after successfully eluding the police, is told in comic and grotesque tones until the final tragic moment.

Throughout the Franco era, Sastre's theatre was more frequently staged outside Spain than in his native land, where many of his works were prohibited by the censor. For a decade following the dictator's death in 1975, his plays were still relegated to experimental and university groups. The enthusiastic acceptance of *La taberna fantástica* has led, however, to other major productions, including, in 1990, the premiere by the national drama centre of *Los ultimos dias de Emmanuel Kant contados por Ernesto Teodoro Amadeo Hoffmann* (The Last Days of Emmanuel Kant as Told by Ernst Theodor Amadeus Hoffmann). This recent work is a complex layering of historical epic with metatheatre, somewhat in the mould of Weiss's *Marat/Sade*. By choosing as protagonist the dying senile Kant, Sastre has demythologized the German philosopher; by choosing to filter the episodes through the imaginary pen of E. T. A. Hoffmann, he has also cast the historical reality in the fantastic mode. The dual focus apparently signals a new direction for Sastre's concept of complex tragedy.

—Phyllis Zatlin

SATOH Makoto. Born in Tokyo, 23 August 1943. Educated at Christian schools; attended night classes at Waseda University, studying Western philosophy, but left before graduating; Actors' Theatre school, Tokyo, graduated 1965. Took part in demonstrations against the US-Japanese Mutual Security Treaty, 1960; principal playwright and director of the Black Tent Theatre, 1968–71. Also a director of opera.

Works

Collections

Atashi no biitoruzu.   1970.
Nezumi Kozō Jirokichi.   1971.
Kigeki Shōwa no sekai (3 vols.).   1976–79.
Yoru to yoru no yoru.   1981.

Stage Works (selected titles, with published translations)

Hikaeshitsu.
Ismene.   Translated as *Ismene*, in *Alternative Japanese*

Drama, edited by Robert T. Rolfe and John K. Gillespie, 1992.
Chikatetsu [The Subway] (produced 1967).
Atashi no Beatles (produced 1969).   Translated as *My Beatles*, in *Concerned Theatre Japan*, vol. 2 nos. 3–4, 1973, and in *Japanese Drama and Culture in the 1960's*, edited by David G. Goodman, 1988.
Onna-goroshi abura no jigoku.
Nezumi Kozō Jirokichi.   Translated as *The Rat*, in *Concerned Theatre Japan*, vol. 1 no. 1, 1970; as *Nezumi Kozō: The Rat*, in *After Apocalypse: Four Plays of Hiroshima and Nagasaki*, edited and translated by David G. Goodman, 1986.
Ukiyo konyoku Nezumi Kozō Jirokichi.
Inga ehon Nezumi Kozō Jirokichi.
Tsubasa o moyasu tenshi-tachi no butō, with others. Translated as *The Dance of Angels Who Burn Their Own Wings*, in *Concerned Theatre Japan*, vol.1 no.4, 1971, and in *Japanese Drama and Culture in the 1960's*, edited by David G. Goodman, 1988.
Koi-koi karuta Nezumi Kozo Kirokichi.
Aa Nezumi Kozo Jirokichi.
Nigatsu to kinema.
Abe Sada no inu.
Buranki-goroshi, Shanhai no haru.
Yoru to yoru no yoru.
Titanic chinbotsu.

Other

Gankyū shaburi.   1979.

*   *   *

There were three major influences on Satoh Makoto during his youth. The first was the legacy of Japanese nationalism: Satoh's mother had been raised by her uncle Anami Korechika, the ultra-nationalist army minister who committed suicide on the day of Japan's World War II surrender. Coming to terms with Japanese nationalism and the emperor system, as both a personal and historical theme, has been one of Satoh's central preoccupations.

The second influence was Christianity. Although he rebelled and refused to continue his early education in missionary schools, Satoh was fascinated by Western philosophy, especially by St. Augustine and Søren Kerkegaard, whose complete works he read as a high school student. Notions of a transcendent, omnipotent God, an "end of days", and of human redemption appear in his earliest work and have played an important role throughout his career.

The third influence was left-wing politics. Satoh's participation as a high school student in the 1960 demonstrations against the renewal of the US-Japan Mutual Security Treaty was perhaps the single most important event in his life. Disillusioned with the Old Left, and its approach to both politics and art, he went on to become a leader of the New Left movement in theatre. Maturing in the late 1960's, he became part of the international revolt that rocked the arts at that time.

Satoh's basic formulation has been that fanaticism and self-destructiveness are an integral part of Japanese and human nature. Satoh believes that there is a goal to history when the revolution/redemption of humanity will take place and when humanity can be saved from its own self-destructiveness, but for him that goal does not lie at the end of a linear historical process conceived in neat Hegelian or Marxist terms. His dramaturgy thus differs fundamentally from that of his predecessors, especially Kinoshita Junji, who identified dramaturgy with the Hegelian dialectic and produced modern tragedies.

Satoh's non-tragic dramaturgy is evident in his earliest works. *My Beatles* (*Atashi no Beatles*), for example, demonstrates how the mechanism of tragedy is counter-productive in dealing with the legacy of Japanese imperialism in Korea. In *Nezumi Kozō: The Rat* (*Nezumi Kozō Jirokichi*), Satoh argues that the Japanese wished the bombing of Hiroshima upon themselves, thus depicting it as the most recent and terrible attempt by humanity to destroy itself. In the same play, Satoh posits the possibility of redemption/revolution, not as the end of a linear historical process, but as a potential immanent in every moment of time.

The three plays that comprise Satoh's "The World of Shōwa: A Comedy" (*Kigeki Shōwa no sekai*) are a brilliant recapitulation of the history of Japan in the Shōwa period (1926–89). In terms of their scale of vision, there is nothing to match them in modern Japanese drama.

—David G. Goodman

SAUNDERS, James (A.). Born in Islington, London, 8 January 1925. Educated at Wembley County School; University of Southampton. Married Audrey Cross in 1951; one son and two daughters. English teacher in London; since 1962 full-time writer for theatre, television, and radio, undertaking many adaptations as well as his own original work. Recipient: Writers Guild Award, 1966.

Works

Collections

"Neighbours" and Other Plays (includes *Trio; Alas, Poor Fred; Return to a City; A Slight Accident; The Pedagogue*). 1968.
"Savoury Meringue" and Other Plays. (includes *Who Was Hilary Maconochie?; Poor Old Simon; Play for Yesterday; Birdsong*) 1980.
"Bye Bye Blues" and Other Plays (includes *The Island* and *Random Moments in a May Garden*). 1980.

Stage Works

Cinderella Comes of Age (produced London, 1949).
Moonshine (produced by Inter-Action London, 1955).
Dog Accident (broadcast 1958; revised version produced by Inter-Action, London, 1969). In *Ten of the Best*, edited by Ed Berman, 1979.
Barnstable (broadcast 1959; produced Dublin, 1960). 1965.
Alas, Poor Fred: A Duologue in the Style of Ionesco (produced Stephen Joseph Theatre-in-the-Round, Scarborough, 1959) 1960.
The Ark, music by Geoffrey Wright (produced Westminster Theatre, London, 1959).
Committal (produced in *Ends and Echoes*, London, 1960).
Return to a City (produced in *Ends and Echoes*, London, 1960). In *"Neighbours" and Other Plays*, 1968.
A Slight Accident (produced Playhouse, Nottingham, 1961). In *"Neighbours" and Other Plays*, 1968.

Double, Double (produced Questors Theatre, Ealing, London, 1962). 1964.
Opus (produced Schauspielhaus, Hamburg, 1962).
Next Time I'll Sing to You (produced Questors Theatre, Ealing, London, 1962; revised version produced New Arts Theatre, London, 1963). 1963.
Who Was Hilary Maconochie? (produced Questors Theatre, Ealing, London, 1963). In *"Savoury Meringue" and Other Plays*, 1980.
The Pedagogue (produced Questors Theatre, Ealing, London, 1963). In *"Neighbours" and Other Plays*, 1968.
Neighbours (produced Questors Theatre, Ealing, London, 1964. In *"Neighbours" and Other Plays*, 1968.
A Scent of Flowers (produced Duke of York's Theatre, London, 1964). 1965.
Triangle, with others (produced Close Theatre, Glasgow, 1965).
Trio (produced Traverse Theatre, Edinburgh, 1967). In *"Neighbours" and Other Plays*, 1968.
The Italian Girl, with Iris Murdoch, from the novel by Murdoch (produced Bristol, 1967). 1969.
Haven, later called *A Man's Best Friend*, in *We Who Are About to . . .*, later called *Mixed Doubles* (produced Hampstead Theatre, London, 1969). 1970.
The Travails of Sancho Panza, based on *Don Quixote* by Cervantes (produced National Theatre, London, 1969). 1970.
The Borage Pigeon Affair (produced Questors Theatre, Ealing, London, 1969). 1970.
Savoury Meringue (produced Almost Free Theatre, London, 1971). In *"Savoury Meringue" and Other Plays*, 1980.
After Liverpool (broadcast 1971; produced Edinburgh, 1971). 1973.
Games (produced Edinburgh, 1971). 1973.
Hans Kohlhaas, from the story by Heinrich von Kleist (produced Questors Theatre, Ealing, London, 1972; as *Michael Kohlhaas*, produced London, 1987).
Bye Bye Blues (produced Orange Tree Theatre, Richmond, Surrey, 1973). In *"Bye Bye Blues" and Other Plays*, 1980.
Poor Old Simon (in *Mixed Blessings*, produced Capitol Theatre, Horsham, Sussex, 1973). In *"Savoury Meringue" and Other Plays*, 1980.
A Journey to London, completion of the play by Vanbrugh (produced Greenwich Theatre, London, 1975).
Play for Yesterday (produced Orange Tree Theatre, Richmond, Surrey, 1975; London, 1983). In *"Savoury Meringue" and Other Plays*, 1980.
The Island (produced Questors Theatre, Ealing, London, 1975). In *"Bye Bye Blues" and Other Plays*, 1980.
Squat (produced Orange Tree Theatre, Richmond, Surrey, 1976).
Mrs. Scour and the Future of Western Civilisation (produced Orange Tree Theatre, Richmond, Surrey, 1976).
Bodies (produced Orange Tree Theatre, Richmond, Surrey, 1977). 1979.
Over the Wall (produced Orange Tree Theatre, Richmond, Surrey, 1977). In *Play Ten*, edited by Robin Rook, 1977.
What Theatre Really Is. In *Play Ten*, edited by Robin Rook. 1977.
Random Moments in a May Garden, from the radio play (produced Questors Theatre, Ealing, London, 1977). In *"Bye Bye Blues and" Other Plays*, 1980.
Player Piano, adaptation of the novel by Kurt Vonnegut (produced by Inter-Action, Almost Free Theatre, London, 1978).
The Caucasian Chalk Circle, from a play by Brecht (produced Orange Tree Theatre, Richmond, Surrey, 1979).

Birdsong (produced Orange Tree Theatre, Richmond, Surrey, 1979. In *"Savoury Meringue" and Other Plays*, 1980.

The Girl in Melaine Klein, from the novel by Ronald Harwood (produced Questors Theatre, Ealing, London, 1980).

Fall (produced Orange Tree Theatre, Richmond, Surrey, 1981). 1985.

Nothing to Declare (broadcast 1982; produced Orange Tree Theatre, Richmond, Surrey, 1983).

Redevelopment, from a play by Václav Havel (produced Orange Tree Theatre, Richmond, Surrey, 1990). 1990.

Making it Better (produced Hampstead Theatre, London, 1992). 1992.

Television Plays

Just You Wait (version of *Double, Double*), 1963; *Watch Me I'm a Bird*, 1964; *The White Stocking, New Eve and Old Adam, Tickets Please, Monkey Nuts, Two Blue Birds, In Love*, and *The Blue Moccasins*, all from works by D.H. Lawrence, 1966–67; *The Beast in the Jungle*, from the story by Henry James, 1969; *Plastic People*, 1970; *The Unconquered*, 1970; *Craven Arms*, from a story by A.E. Coppard, 1972; *The Mill*, 1972; *The Black Dog*, 1972; *Blind Love*, from the story by V.S. Pritchett, 1977; *The Healing Nightmare*, 1977; *People Like Us*, with Susan Pieat and Ian Curteis, from the novel by R.F. Delderfield, 1978; *Bloomers* series, 1979; *The Sailor's Return*, from the novel by David Garnett, 1980; *The Captain's Doll*, from the story by D.H. Lawrence, 1983; *The Magic Bathroom*, 1987.

Radio Plays

Love and a Limousine, 1952; *The Drop Too Much*, 1952; *Nimrod's Oak*, 1953; *Women Are So Unreasonable*, 1957; *Dog Accident*, 1958; *Barnstable*, 1959; *Gimlet* (version of *Double, Double*), 1963; *It's Not the Game it Was*, 1964; *Pay As You Go*, 1965; *After Liverpool*, 1971; *Random Moments in a May Garden*, 1974; *The Last Black and White Midnight Movie*, 1979; *Nothing to Declare*, 1982; *The Flower Case*, 1982; *A Suspension of Mercy* (*Murder for Pleasure* series), from the novel by Patricia Highsmith, 1983; *Menocchio* 1985 (published in *Best Radio Plays of 1985*, 1986); *The Confidential Agent*, from the novel by Graham Greene, 1987; *Headlong Hall*, from the novel by Thomas Love Peacock, 1988; *Making it Better*, 1991.

*

Criticism

Articles:
Kathy J. Gentile, "A Hermit Dramatized", in *Modern Drama*, 28, 1985.
Neil Sammells, "Giggling at the Arts: Tom Stoppard and James Saunders", in *Critical Quarterly*, vol.28 no.4, 1986.

*   *   *

James Saunders' work is notable for its diversity and consistency, the author for his eclecticism and iconoclasm. The author of comparatively few full-length plays (of which *Next Time I'll Sing To You* and *Bodies* are the best sustained and searching), but of a substantial number of sketches and one-act dramas (notably *Random Moments in a May Garden* and *Bye Bye Blues*), Saunders has employed, without respect to

chronology or artistic "development", a range of modes from the naturalistic to the metatheatrical to articulate what Elizabeth Haddon has termed the "excommunicated proximity" within which people live their lives.

"If there is any theme that runs through all my work", Saunders has commented, "it's the absurdity of finding logic in anything at all", and much of the drama explores the manner in which isolated individuals (Zoe in *A Scent of Flowers*, the Actor in *Triangle*), tenuous pairs and couples (in *Bodies, A Man's Best Friend, Double Double*), unstable families and groups (in *Next Time I'll Sing To You, Fall, Trio, Poor Old Simon*) alternately search for and evade the meanings, and thereby responsibilities, with which existence is capable of being invested. Freedom is both a privacy and a privation, communication an imperiling commitment to community. Saunders' best work succeeds in developing dramatic possibilities for the staging of choices, of alternative lives, and life stories. Theatre as "playspace", as Saunders has termed it, and as a "rebellion against the tyranny of life as a mechanical operation" can reveal what has hitherto been concealed but, as for example in *Birdsong* and *The Island*, show this as but a further strategy of concealment.

The range of Saunders' dramatic modes is considerable, although the foray into a Strindbergian drama of expressionist and ritualistic forms in *A Scent of Flowers* is uncharacteristic and not wholly compelling. Though much the same might be opined of the Brechtian imperatives (via Arden and D'Arcy) informing the more socially and politically motivated *The Borage Pigeon Affair, Verfremdungseffekt* is, to largely existential ends (though see *Games*), a crucial aspect of Saunders's dramatic sensibility. Indeed, with the powerful exception of *Neighbours* (*Fall*, for example, is much inferior to Friel's *Aristocrats* and Hare's *The Secret Rapture*, plays with which it bears comparison), his more naturalistic work can, in the absence of a sufficiently resourceful dramatic circumstance, best be imagined on radio, a medium within which some of Saunders' work has also found a voice. The middle ground between the naturalistic and the overtly metatheatrical, occupied for example by *Alas, Poor Fred* and *A Slight Accident*, is the absurdist, often domestic, drama familiar from Ionesco and N.F. Simpson and, shorn of some of its extravagance, in Pinter, to whose work Saunders's *Bye Bye Blues* and *Random Moments in a May Garden* ought to enjoy a comparable standing.

It should be observed that Saunders' work is highly verbal and that his most beleaguered characters (Rudge and Dust in *Next Time I'll Sing To You*, Merwyn in *Bodies*, Hessian in *Savoury Meringue*) are wonderfully adroit at articulating, with energy and wit, their anger and puzzlement. In the absence of a compelling dramatic circumstance, however, as in that akin to allegory in *Birdsong*, verbal rumination is in danger of becoming arch garrulity. In *Bodies*, by contrast, Merwyn's verbal pyrotechnics (fuelled by alcohol) are precisely staged with reference on the one hand to David and Helen's tranquil dissociation of sensibility, and on the other to Merwyn's suicidal student, the silent body brought to mind throughout the drama; in *Next Time I'll Sing To You*, the grief brought to life in the staging of the hermit's life story is most evident outside the play's verbal gamesmanship, in "the silence after a joke", in "loneliness where there is no escape" except in the routines and rituals within which grief hides. "Theatre is non-verbal", Saunders has remarked. "[It] tries to get . . . underneath the words . . . it *uses* words". The "suite of pieces" entitled *After Liverpool* explores precisely such uses and abuses when, as one member of the couple remarks, "we are talking to ourselves". Communication becomes a taut display of privacies.

Bye Bye Blues and *Random Moments in a May Garden* explore more dramatically and pictorially (albeit through retrospection—the remembered instance and the photograph) the parallel and competing possibilities that both bind and blind individual lives. *Games*, developing the more compacted material in *What Theatre Really Is*, foregrounds through metatheatre the power-structures that language and the space of drama, in its production and reception, throw up. It is a process which implicates both actors (as in *Trio*) and audience (as in *The Pedagogue*) and finds perhaps its fullest treatment in *Next Time I'll Sing to You*. The debt to Pirandello and Beckett should obscure neither Stoppard's confessed debt to Saunders' play in the formation of *Rosencrantz and Guildenstern Are Dead*, nor the successful compacting of a variety of dramatic modes into the staging of an enterprise which Rudge, the play producer, concedes is not so much a discussion of "the man nor even the reason for the man but the reason for the discussion of the reason for the man". For Saunders, problems of purpose and identity are problems of art: the "tyranny of life" can be broken down in the making up of theatre as it reveals the possibilities and represents the choices tyranny suppresses and obscures. In his best work, the seriousness of verbal play and the ingenuity of dramatic metaphor can do just that.

—James Hansford

See also *Volume 1* entry on *Next Time I'll Sing to You*.

SCHILLER, (Johnann Christoph) Friedrich von. Born in Marbach am Neckar, Duchy of Württemberg, 10 November 1759. Educated at village school in Lorch; Latin school, Ludwigsburg, 1766–72. Married Charlotte von Lengefeld in 1790; two sons and two daughters. Conscripted in 1773, and studied law, later medicine, in military academy of Duke Karl August of Württemberg: regimental surgeon, 1780; his writing displeased the Duke, so he fled Württemberg, 1782, and sought refuge in the Palatinate, where he received contract to write for the Nationaltheater, Mannheim, until 1784; first-produced play, *Die Räuber*, staged 1782; editor, *Rheinische Thalia*, 1785–93; joined the Körner circle, in Leipzig, then in Dresden; in Weimar, 1787: through Goethe's help, obtained professorship of history at University of Jena, 1789–91 (resigned because of illness); refused professorship in Tübingen, 1795; lived in Weimar after 1799, and several plays produced under Goethe's direction at the Hoftheater. Raised to nobility by Emperor Franz II, 1802. Died in Weimar, 9 May 1805.

Works

Collections

Works (Bohn Standard Library edition; 4 vols.).   1846–49.
Sämtliche Werke: Säkularausgabe (16 vols.), edited by Eduard von der Hellen.   1904–05.
Sämtliche Werke (20 vols.), edited by Otto Güntter and Gerhard Witkowski.   1910–11.
Werke [Nationalausgabe], edited by Julius Petersen and Gerhard Fricke.   1943–

DRUCK UND VERLAG VON VOIGT & GUENTHER

Friedrich von Schiller

Sämtliche Werke (5 vols.), edited by Gerhard Fricke, H.G. Göpfert, and H. Stubenrauch. 1958–59.
The Robbers; Wallenstein, translated by F.J. Lamport. 1979.
Plays (includes Intrigue and Love; Don Carlos; Letters on Don Carlos), translated by Walter Hinderer. 1983.

Stage Works

Die Räuber (produced Nationaltheater, Mannheim, 1782). 1781; translated as The Robbers, 1792, and with Wallenstein, 1979; adapted as The Red Cross Knights, 1799, and Lorenzo, 1823.
Die Verschwörung des Fiesko zu Genua (produced by Grossmann's Schauspieler-Gesellschaft, Bonn, 1784). 1783; translated as Fiesco; or, The Genoese Conspiracy, 1796.
Kabale und Liebe (produced by Grossmann's Schauspieler-Gesellschaft, Frankfurt, 1784). 1784; translated as Cabal and Love, 1795; as The Minister, 1798; as The Harper's Daughter, 1813; adapted as Ravenna; or, Italian Love, 1824; as Power and Principle, 1850; as Intrigue and Love, in Plays, 1983.
Don Carlos (produced Nationaltheater, Hamburg, 1787). 1787; translated as Don Carlos, 1798: several subsequent translations under same title.
Egmont, from the play by Goethe (produced Hoftheater, Weimar, 1796). 1857.
Wallenstein (trilogy; includes Wallensteins Lager, Die Piccolomini and Wallensteins Tod; parts produced individually, Hoftheater, Weimar, 1798–99; trilogy produced Hoftheater, Weimer, 1799). 1800; trilogy translated as Wallenstein (includes Wallenstein's Camp; The Piccolomini; Wallenstein's Death), 1800: several subsequent translations of the trilogy and its individual parts under same titles.
Maria Stuart (produced Hoftheater, Weimar, 1800). 1801; translated as Mary Stuart, 1801: several subsequent translations under same title; as Maria Stuart, with Joan of Arc, 1987.
Macbeth from the play by Shakespeare (produced Hoftheater, Weimar, 1800). 1801.
Nathan der Weise, from the play by Lessing (produced Hoftheater, Weimar, 1801).
Die Jungfrau von Orleans (produced Leipzig 1801). 1801; translated as The Maid of Orleans, 1835; as Joan of Arc, with Mary Stuart, 1987.
Turandot, from the play by Gozzi (produced Hoftheater, Weimar, 1802). 1802.
Der Neffe als Onkel, from a play by Louis-Benoit Picard (produced Hoftheater, Weimar, 1803). 1842; translated as The Nephew as Uncle, 1856.
Der Parasit, from a play by Louis-Benoit Picard (produced Hoftheater, Weimar, 1803). 1806; translated as The Parasite, 1856.
Die Braut von Messina (produced Hoftheater, Weimar, 1803). 1803; translated as The Bride of Messina, 1837.
Wilhelm Tell (produced Hoftheater, Weimar, 1804). 1804; translated as William Tell, 1825; several subsequent translations under same title.
Die Huldigung der Künste (produced Hoftheater, Weimar, 1804). 1805.
Phädra, from the play by Racine (produced Hoftheater, Weimar, 1805). 1805.
Iphigenie in Aulis, from the play by Euripides. 1807.
Demetrius (fragment). As Szenen aus Demetrius, in Morgenblatt, nos. 258–259, 1815; edited by G. Kettner, 1894.

Fiction

Der Verbrecher aus Infamie. In Thalia, vol. 1 no. 2, 1786; as Der Verbrecher aus verlorener Ehre, in Kleine prosaische Schriften 1, 1792; translated as The Dishonoured Irreclaimable, 1826.
Der Geisterseher (fragment). 1789; translated as The Ghost Seer, or Apparitionist, 1795; as The Armenian, 1800.
Spiel des Schicksals. 1789.

Verse

Anthologie auf das Jahr 1782. 1782.
Gedichte (2 vols.). 1800–03.
The Poems and Ballads, translated by Sir Edward Bulwer Lytton. 1844.
The Poems of Schiller Complete, translated by E.A. Bowring. 1851.

Memoirs and Letters

Briefwechsel, with Wilhelm von Humboldt. 1830.
Briefwechsel, with Cotta, edited by W. Vollmer. 1876.
Briefwechsel, with Goethe, edited by F. Muncker (4 vols.). 1892.
Briefe, edited by Fritz Jonas (7 vols.). 1892–96.
Briefwechsel, with Körner, edited by L. Gaiger (4 vols.). 1893.
Briefe 1776–1789, edited by Karl Pörnbacher. 1969.

Other

Die Geschichte des Abfalls der vereinigten Niederlande von der spanischen Regierung. 1788; translated as History of the Rise and Progress of the Belgian Republic, 1807.
Über die tragische Kunst. In Neue Thalia, nos. 1–2, 1792; in book form, in Kleinere prosaische Schriften 4, 1802.
Kleinere prosaische Schriften (4 vols). 1792–1802.
Geschichte des dreissigjährigen Krieges (3 vols.). 1793; translated as The History of the Thirty Years' War in Germany, 1799.
Über naive und sentimentalische Dichtung. In Die Hören, 1795–96; in book form, in Kleinere prosaische Schriften 2, 1800; translated as On Simple and Sentimental Poetry, in Essays Aesthetical and Philosophical, 1884; as On the Naive and Sentimental in Literature, 1981.
Briefe über die ästhetische Erziehung des Menschen. In Die Hören, 1795; in book form, in Kleinere prosaische Schriften 3, 1801; translated as Upon the Aesthetic Culture of Man, in Philosophical and Aesthetic Letters and Essays, 1845; as On the Aesthetic Education of Man, 1954.

*

Bibliographies

W. Vulpius, Schiller-Bibliographie 1893–1958, Weimar, 1959; supplemented in Jahrbuch der deutschen Schiller-Gesellschaft 1962, 1966, 1970, and regularly thereafter.

Criticism

Books:
W. Spengler, Das Drama Schillers: Seine Genesis, Leipzig, 1932.

G. Storz, *Das Drama Friedrich Schillers*, Frankfurt, 1938.

K. May, *Friedrich Schiller: Idee und Wirlichkeit im Drama*, Göttingen, 1948.

E.L. Stahl, *Schiller's Drama: Theory and Practice*, Oxford, 1954.

Stanley S. Kerry, *Schiller's Writings on Aesthetics*, Manchester, 1961.

Ronald D. Miller, *The Drama of Schiller*, Harrogate, Yorkshire, 1963.

Bernt von Heiseler, *Friedrich Schiller* (in English), London, 1962.

Walter M. Simon, *Schiller, The Poet as Historian*, Keele, Yorkshire, 1966.

E. Staiger, *Friedrich Schiller*, Zurich, 1967.

H.B. Garland, *Schiller 1759–1805: The Dramatic Writer*, Oxford, 1969.

B. Lecke, *Friedrich Schiller* (2 vols.), Munich, 1969.

H. Rischbieter, *Friedrich Schiller* (2 vols.), Velber, 1969.

G. Sautermeister, *Idyllik und Dramatik im Werk Friedrich Schillers*, Stuttgart, 1971.

K.L. Berghahn and R. Grimm, *Schiller zur Theorie und Praxis seiner Dramen*, Darmstadt, 1972.

D. Borchmeyer, *Tragödie und Öffentlichkeit*, Munich, 1973.

John E. Prudhoe, *The Theatre of Goethe and Schiller*, Oxford, 1973.

Ilsa Graham, *Schiller's Dramas: Talent and Integrity*, London, 1974.

Ilsa Graham, *Schiller: A Master of the Tragic Form*, Pittsburgh, Pennsylvania, 1975.

Charles E. Passage, *Friedrich Schiller*, New York, 1975.

A. Siekmann, *Drama und sentimentalisches Bewusstsein: Zur klassischen Dramatik Schillers*, Frankfurt, 1980.

P. Lahnstein, *Schillers Leben*, Munich, 1981.

John D. Simons, *Schiller*, Boston, Massachusetts, 1981.

Walter Hinderer (ed.), *Schillers Dramen: Neue Interpretationen*, Stuttgart, 1983.

Julie D. Prandi, *Spirited Women Heroes: Major Female Characters in the Dramas of Goethe, Schiller and Kleist*, New York, 1983.

H.-D, Mück and others, *Schau-Bühne: Schillers Dramen 1945–1984*, Marbach, 1984.

Ronald D. Miller, *Interpreting Schiller: A Study of Four Plays*, Harrogate, 1986.

Marie-Luise Waldeck, *The Theme of Freedom in Schiller's Plays*, Stuttgart, 1986.

H. Mayer, *Versuche über Schiller*, Frankfurt, 1987.

H. Koopmann, *Schiller: Eine Einführung*, Munich and Zurich, 1988.

Alexej Ugrinsky, *Friedrich von Schiller and the Drama of Human Existence*, New York, 1988.

Lesley Sharpe, *Schiller and the Historical Character*, Oxford, 1982.

T.J. Reed, *Friedrich Schiller*, Oxford, 1991.

Lesley Sharpe, *Friedrich Schiller: Drama, Thought and Politics*, Cambridge, 1991.

Serials:
Jahrbuch der deutschen Schiller-Gesellschaft, 1957—

*   *   *

Schiller is generally regarded as the major classic dramatist of the German-speaking countries. If he had not existed, the course of German drama during the last two centuries would have been very different. This is because Schiller set a model of excellence against which many leading dramatists have reacted (including Hauptmann, Wedekind, Brecht), but which also stimulated notable achievements such as the historical plays of Grillparzer and Hebbel.

Schiller's stature in German eyes is easily explained. In him occurred an extraordinary coincidence of intellectual power and creative exuberance which made his example irresistibly appealing to a society which attaches as much importance to the intellectual demands as it does to the entertainment value of plays. Both the actor and the academic scholar find gratification in what Schiller has to offer in his nine completed dramas. These range widely in style, mood, and subject-matter from the turbulence and passion of *Die Räuber* (*The Robbers*) to the mature composure of *Wilhelm Tell* (*William Tell*), and from the brooding complexities of his neo-Jacobean trilogy *Wallenstein* to the romantic heroism of *Die Jungfrau von Orleans* (*The Maid of Orleans*) or the dignified, almost statuesque neo-classicism of *Die Braut von Messina* (*The Bride of Messina*).

In Germany itself, Schiller's example satisfied national pride, for here was a playwright who used his flair for the stage to create a dramatic *oeuvre* that fulfilled the aesthetic needs of a nation politically fragmented but united by its sense of a common culture. His concept of the stage as the ally of law and religion was set out in a published lecture, "The Theatre as a Moral Institution" (1785). Taking up ideas already put forward by Lessing, he effectively argued that the theatre is capable of moulding the moral consciousness of society through its ability to expose folly and vice to promote wisdom and understanding; Schiller's community of purpose with later German dramatists (such as Brecht) is clear despite sometimes enormous differences of style and approach.

No dramatist working in the German language has equalled Schiller for verve and pathos, or for sheer delight in the sound of words; none has provided audiences with so many memorable moments in the theatre, or gripped the imagination of the spectators and held them breathless with that particular blend of suspense and admiration which, underpinned by a remarkable command of stage technique and timing, is one of the greatest strengths of his dramatic genius. This quality is demonstrated most memorably in incidents such as the famous apple-shooting scene in *William Tell* or in the remarkable uses of teichoscopy in the final battle scene in *The Maid of Orleans* and in *Maria Stuart* (*Mary Stuart*) when the Earl of Leicester, alone on stage, listens to the heroine's execution off-stage and communicates its mounting horror to the audience. Schiller was adept at handling scenes of pomp and pageantry, such as the coronation of the Dauphin in *The Maid of Orleans*, and responded to the challenge of a *scène à faire*, most notably in the central act of *Mary Stuart*, where he deliberately departed from history for the sake of dramatic truth, and provided his audience with what is probably the most famous scene in the German classical repertoire. The exciting encounter between Mary and Elizabeth in the grounds of Fotheringhay Castle also impels the dramatic action forward, since in it Mary scores a moral victory over her rival for which she finally forfeits her life. The ability to make a theatrically satisfying episode serve the less obvious underlying purpose of a drama as a whole is another of Schiller's strengths.

Almost all of Schiller's nine dramas proved to be box-office successes from the start (and fertile inspiration for opera composers too, including Verdi, Donizetti, and Tchaikovsky). The great Schiller roles rival Shakespeare's in the annals of German stage history—Karl and Franz Moor, the two sharply contrasted brothers in his first play, *The Robbers*, King Philip II of Spain and his enigmatic favourite the Marquis of Posa in his first verse tragedy *Don Carlos*, the rival queens in *Mary Stuart*, and the hero and the two young lovers, Max and Thekla, in *Wallenstein*. But these roles require stage presence and ringing voices, just as the plays in which they occur need producers with a sense of movement and colour to do full justice to Schiller's texts, which may appear excessively expansive and rhetorical by some modern standards. This is Schiller's liability in the contemporay theatre, just as it is his strength in the context of German dramatic poetry.

As a professional historian Schiller set new standards in the dramatization of famous historical events and personalities. But there was another side to him, as is demonstrated by his one foray into the genre of domestic tragedy, *Kabale und Liebe* (*Intrigue and Love*). Here the aspirations of a pair of young lovers are thwarted by the vested interests of privilege and the cynical manipulation of the conventions of a cruel and amoral social system. This almost realistic prose tragedy, written five years before the French Revolution, brought Schiller to prominence as a castigator of a corrupt society heartless in its treatment of innocent human beings. For the remainder of his career Schiller was to return repeatedly to his instinctive championship of human rights; his impulse was to unmask political corruption and flawed moral standards and to expose the reality beneath appearances. Paradoxically, perhaps, Germany's most famous dramatist could be at one and the same time a masterly creator of stage illusion and costume drama and an upholder of timeless values. As an idealist he identified such values as valid goals for human society as well as with the vulnerable, isolated individuals who tragically succumb in many of his plays. He never tried his hand at comedy.

Until recently Schiller has not fared well on the English-speaking stage, perhaps on account of his superficial similarities to Shakespeare, whom he greatly admired (he made a fine translation of *Macbeth*). But his plays, though mainly in blank verse, inhabit a different world from Shakespeare's and should rather be seen as a forward-looking and masterly fusion of romantic and neoclassical impulses designed to rouse and reinforce the moral and political awareness of a predominantly middle-class audience. He saw to it, however, that his plays did not forfeit critical respect because of their popularity by writing also a series of deeply considered essays on related topics including "On the Sublime", 1801, and "On the Use of the Chorus in Tragedy", 1803. These reveal other sides of his creative personality, such as his intellectual response to the philosophy of Kant, his indebtedness to the French example set by Pierre Corneille, and his familiarity with the tragedians and theorists of ancient Greece. His last play, *Demetrius*, left incomplete at his death, may be seen as a modern re-exploration of the Oedipus situation in terms of a crisis of identity undergone by the successful pretender to the Russian throne. This fascinating dramatic "torso" gives clear indiction that Schiller had a long creative life ahead of him when he died prematurely in 1805, five months after Napoleon's coronation and shortly before the defeat of Austria and Prussia by France. To the theatre-goer outside the German cultural tradition, it may seen amazing that this contemporary of far-reaching political and military upheaval was also, with Goethe, one of the chief embodiments of the classical ideal associated with their place of residence, the small town of Weimar, which in their lifetime became known as a new Athens. It was for the Weimar Court Theatre, managed by Goethe, that the majority of Schiller's plays were written.

—Peter Skrine

See also *Volume 1* entries on *Mary Stuart*; *The Robbers*; *Wallenstein*.

SCHNITZLER, Arthur. Born in Vienna, Austria, 15 May 1862. Educated at the Akademisches Gymnasium, Vienna, 1871–79; studied medicine at the University of Vienna, 1879–85, MD 1885. Married Olga Gussmann in 1903 (separated 1921); one son and one daughter. Assistant doctor in a general hospital and a clinic, 1885; psychiatric assistant, 1886, and assisted his father (the director of the Vienna Poliklinik) in the late 1880's; co-editor of his father's journal, *Internationale klinische Rundschau*, from 1887, and began publishing his own medical research, 1889; first-produced play, *Das Abenteuer seines Lebens* [The Adventure of His Life], staged 1891; opened private medical practice, 1893; Viennese premiere of *Reigen* closed by police, and Berlin premiere resulted in court case, 1921; first major meeting with Sigmund Freud, 1922. Recipient: Bauernfeld Prize, 1899; Grillparzer Prize, 1908; Raimund Prize, 1914. Died in Vienna, 21 October 1931.

Works

Collections

Gesammelte Werke (7 vols.). 1912; augmented edition (9 vols.), 1922.
Gesammelte Werke (5 vols.), edited by Robert O. Weiss. 1961–67.
"The Green Cockatoo" and Other Plays (includes *Paracelsus* and *The Mate*), translated by Horace B. Samuel. 1910.
Three Plays (includes *The Lonely Way; Intermezzo; Countess Mizzi*), translated by Edward Björkman. 1915.
Plays and Stories (includes *La Ronde* and *Countess Mitzi*, with several stories), translated by Egon Schwarz. 1982.
"The Round Dance" and Other Plays (includes *Anatol* and *Love Games*), translated by Charles Osborne. 1982.

Stage Works

Das Abenteuer seines Lebens (produced Theater in der Josefstadt, Vienna, 1891). 1888.
Das Märchen (produced Deutsches Volkstheater, Vienna, 1893). 1891(stage script); book version, 1894.
Anatol: series of one-act plays; includes *Die Frage nach dem Schicksal* (produced Carola-Theater, Leipzig, 1896); *Weihnachtseinkäufe* (produced Sofien-Säle, Vienna, 1898); *Episode* (produced Ibsen-Theater, Leipzig, 1898); *Denksteine* (produced Volksbildungshaus der Urania, Vienna, 1916); *Abschiedssouper* (produced Stadttheater, Bad Ischl, 1893); *Agonie*; *Anatols Hochzeit* (produced Langenbeck-Haus, Berlin, 1901). 1892; cycle translated as *Anatol : A Sequence of Dialogues*, 1911; as *The Affairs of Anatol*, 1933; as *Anatol*, in "The Round Dance" and Other Plays, and separately, 1982.
Liebelei (produced Burgtheater, Vienna, 1895). 1896; translated as *Light-o'-Love*, 1912; as *Playing with Love*, 1914; as *Love Games*, in "The Round Dance" and Other Plays, 1982; as *Dalliance*, with *Undiscovered Country*, 1986.

Freiwild (produced Prague, 1897). 1898; translated as *Free Game*, 1913.
Das Vermächtnis (produced Deutsches Theater, Berlin, 1898). 1899; translated as *The Legacy*, in *Poet Lore*, July-August 1911.
Paracelsus (produced Burgtheater, Vienna, 1899). In *Der grüne Kakadu . . .* (collection), 1899; translated as *Paracelsus*, in *"The Green Cockatoo" and Other Plays*, 1913.
Die Gefährtin (produced Burgtheater, Vienna, 1899). In *Der grüne Kakadu . . .* (collection), 1899; translated as *The Mate*, in *"The Green Cockatoo" and Other Plays*, 1913.
Der grüne Kakadu (produced Burgtheater, Vienna, 1899). In *Der grüne Kakadu . . .* (collection), 1899; translated as *The Duke and the Actress*, 1910; as *The Green Cockatoo*, in *"The Green Cockatoo" and Other Plays*, 1913.
Der Schleier von Beatrice (produced Lobe-Theater, Breslau, 1900). 1901.
Reigen (produced in part by the Akademisch-Dramatischer Verein, Studententheater, Munich, 1903; produced complete, Kleines Schauspielhaus, Berlin, 1920). 1900 (private printing); 1903 (official publication); translated as *Hands Around*, 1920; as *Couples*, 1927; as *Merry-Go-Round*, 1953; as *La Ronde*, 1959: several subsequent translations under same title; as *The Round Dance*, in *"The Round Dance" and Other Plays*, 1982.
Lebendige Stunden (includes the one-act plays *Die Frau mit dem Dolche*; *Die letzten Masken*; *Literatur*; produced Deutsches Theater, Berlin, 1902). 1902; translated as *Living Hours* (individual titles: *The Lady with the Dagger*; *Last Masks*; *Literature*), 1913.
Der Puppenspieler (produced Deutsches Theater, Berlin, 1903). In *Marionetten*, 1906.
Der einsame Weg (produced Deutsches Theater, Berlin, 1904). 1904; translated as *The Lonely Way*, 1904; as *The Lonely Road*, 1985.
Der tapfere Cassian (produced Kleines Theater, Berlin, 1904). In *Marionetten*, 1906; revised version, music by Oscar Strauss (produced Neues Stadttheater, Leipzig, 1909), 1909; translated as *Gallant Cassian*, 1914.
Zwischenspiel (produced Burgtheater, Vienna, 1905). 1906; translated as *Intermezzo*, in *Three Plays*, 1915.
Der Ruf des Lebens (produced Lessing-Theater, Berlin, 1906). 1906.
Zum grossen Wurstel (produced Lustspiel-Theater, Vienna, 1906). In *Marionetten*, 1906.
Komtesse Mizzi; oder, Der Familientag (produced Deutsches Volkstheater, Vienna, 1909). 1909; translated as *Countess Mizzie*, 1907; as *Countess Mitzi; or, The Family Reunion*, in *Plays and Stories*, 1982.
Der Schleier der Pierette (pantomime), music by Ernst von Dohnányi (produced Königliches Opernhaus, Dresden, 1910). 1910.
Der junge Medardus (produced Burgtheater, Vienna, 1910). 1910.
Das weite Land (produced Lessing-Theater, Berlin, 1911). 1911; translated as *Undiscovered Country*, 1980.
Professor Bernhardi (produced Kleines Theater, Berlin, 1912). 1912; translated as *Professor Bernhardi*, 1913.
Komödie der Worte (includes the one-act plays *Stunde des Erkennens; Grosse Szene; Das Bacchusfest*; produced simultaneously at the Neues Theater, Frankfurt, and the Hoftheater, Darmstadt, 1915). 1915; translated as *Comedies of Words* (individual titles: *The Hour of Recognition; The Big Scene; The Festival of Bacchus*), in *"Comedies of Words" and Other Plays*, 1917.

Fink und Fliederbusch (produced Deutsches Volkstheater, Vienna, 1917). 1917.
Die Schwestern; oder, Casanova in Spa (produced Burgtheater, Vienna, 1920). 1919.
Komödie der Verführung (produced Burgtheater, Vienna, 1924). 1924.
Der Gang zum Weiher (produced Burgtheater, Vienna, 1931). 1926.
Im Spiel der Sommerlüfte (produced Volkstheater, Vienna, 1929). 1930; translated as *Summer Breeze*, 1989.
Zug der Schatten, edited by Françoise Derre. 1970.

Fiction

Sterben. 1895.
Die Frau des Weisen: Novelletten. 1898.
Leutnant Gustl. 1901; translated as *None But the Brave*, 1926.
Frau Bertha Garlan. 1901; translated as *Bertha Garlan*, 1913.
Die griechische Tänzerin: Novellen. 1905.
Dämmerseelen: Novellen. 1907.
Der Weg ins Freie. 1908; translated as *The Road to the Open*, 1923.
Die Hirtenflöte. 1912.
Masken und Wunder: Novellen. 1912.
Frau Beate und ihr Sohn. 1913; translated as *Beatrice*, 1926.
Viennese Idylls. 1913.
Doktor Gräsler, Badearzt. 1917; translated as *Dr. Graesler*, 1923.
Casanovas Heimfahrt. 1918; translated as *Casanova's Homecoming*, 1921.
Der Mörder. 1922.
"The Shepherd's Pipe" and Other Stories. 1922.
Fräulein Else. 1924; translated as *Fräulein Else*, 1925.
Die dreifache Warning: Novellen. 1924.
Die Frau des Richters. 1925.
Traumnovelle. 1926; translated as *Rhapsody: A Dream Novel*, 1927.
"Beatrice" and Other Stories. 1926.
Spiel im Morgengrauen. 1927; translated as *Daybreak*, 1927.
Therese: Chronik eines Frauenlebens. 1928; translated as *Theresa: The Chronicle of a Woman's Life*, 1928.
Gesammelte Schriften (6 vols.). 1928.
Little Novels. 1929.
Flucht in die Finsternis. 1931; translated as *Flight into Darkness*, 1931.
Viennese Novelettes. 1931.
Abenteuernovelle. 1937.
Vienna 1900: Games with Love and Death. 1973.

Memoirs and Letters

Breifwechsel, with Otto Brahm, edited by Oskar Seidlin. 1953; revised edition, 1964.
Briefwechsel, with Georg Brandes, edited by Kurt Bergel. 1956.
Briefwechsel, with Hugo von Hofmannsthal, edited by Therese Nickl and Heinrich Schnitzler. 1964.
Jugend in Wien: Eine Autobiographie, edited by Therese Nickl and Heinrich Schnitzler. 1968; translated as *My Youth in Vienna*, 1971.
Liebe, die starb vor der Zeit: Ein Briefwechsel, with Olga Waissnix, edited by Therese Nickl and Heinrich Schnitzler. 1970.
Briefwechsel, with Max Reinhardt, edited by Renate Wagner. 1971.

Correspondence, with Raoul Auernheimer, edited by David
G. Daviau and Jorun B. Johns.   1972.
Briefe 1875–1912, edited by Therese Nickl and Heinrich
Schnitzler.   1981.
Tagebuch 1909–1912, edited by Peter M. Braunworth and
others.   1981; further volumes: *1913–1916*, 1983; *1917–1919*, 1985; *1879–1892*, 1987.

Other

*Buch der Sprüche und Bedenken: Aphorismen und
Fragmente*.   1927.
Der Geist im Wort und der Geist in der Tat.   1927.
Über Krieg und Frieden.   1939.

*

Bibliographies

Richard H. Allen, *An Annotated Arthur Schnitzler
Bibliography*, Chapel Hill, North Carolina, 1966.
Jeffrey A. Berlin, *An Annotated Arthur Schnitzler
Bibliography 1965–1977*, Munich, 1978.

Criticism

Books:
R. Specht, *Arthur Schnitzler: Der Dichter und sein Werk*,
Berlin, 1922.
H.W. Reichart and Herman Salinger, *Studies in Schnitzler*,
Chapel Hill, North Carolina, 1963.
Françoise Derré, *L'Oeuvre d'Arthur Schnitzler*, Paris, 1966.
Christa Melchinger, *Illusion und Wirklichkeit im drama-
tischen Werk Arthur Schnitzlers*, Heidelberg, 1968.
Marie P. Alter, *The Concept of the Physician in the Writings
of Hans Carossa and Arthur Schnitzler*, Bern, 1971.
Martin Swales, *Arthur Schnitzler: A Critical Study*, Oxford,
1971.
Renate Wagner and Brigitte Vacha, *Wiener Schnitzler-
Aufführungen 1891–1970*, Munich, 1971.
Reinhard Urbach, *Arthur Schnitzler* (from the German),
New York, 1973.
Klaus Killian, *Die Komödien Arthur Schnitzlers*, Düsseldorf,
1972.
Ernst L. Offermanns, *Arthur Schnitzler: Das Komödienwerk
als Kritik des Impressionismus*, Munich, 1973.
Heinz Rieder, *Arthur Schnitzler: Das dramatische Werk*,
Velber, 1973.
Alfred Fritsche, *Dekadenz im Werk Arthur Schnitzlers*, Bern,
1974.
Jürg Scheuzger, *Das Spiel mit Typen und
Typenkonstellationen in den Dramen Arthur Schnitzlers*,
Zurich, 1975.
Günter Selling, *Die Einakter und Einakterzyklen Arthur
Schnitzlers*, Amsterdam, 1975.
Hartmut Scheible, *Arthur Schnitzler in Selbstzeugnissen und
Bilddokumenten*, Hamburg, 1976.
Renate Wagner, *Arthur Schnitzler: Eine Biographie*, Velber,
1981.
Elisabeth Heresch, *Schnitzler und Russland: Aufnahme,
Wirkung, Kritik*, Vienna, 1982.
Hans U. Lindken (ed.), *Arthur Schnitzler: Aspekte und
Akzente*, Frankfurt, 1984.
Petrus W. Tax and Richard H. Lawson (eds.), *Arthur
Schnitzler and His Age*, Bonn, 1984.

Giuseppe Farese (ed.), *Akten des Internationalen
Symposiums: Arthur Schnitzler und seine Zeit*, Bern, 1985.
Michael A. Perlmann, *Arthur Schnitzler*, Stuttgart, 1987.
Michael A. Perlmann, *Der Traum in der literarischen
Moderne: Untersuchungen zum Werk Arthur Schnitzlers*,
Munich, 1987.
Adrian C. Roberts, *Arthur Schnitzler and Politics*, Riverside,
California, 1989.
Peter N. Skrine, *Hauptmann, Wedekind and Schnitzler*,
London, 1989 (Macmillan Modern Dramatists series).
Brenda Keiser, *Deadly Dishonor: The Duel and the Honor
Code in the Works of Arthur Schnitzler*, New York, 1990.
Bruce Thompson, *Schnitzler's Vienna: Image of a Society*,
London, 1990.

Articles:
Rena A. Schein, "Arthur Schnitzler: Author-Scientist", in
Modern Austrian Literature, vol. 1 no. 2, 1968.
Robert O. Weiss, "The Human Element in Arthur
Schnitzler's Social Criticism", in *Modern Austrian
Literature*, vol. 9 no. 2, 1976.
Joanne C. Ellis, "Schnitzler in the Popular Press, 1904–33",
in *University of Dayton Review*, vol. 20 no. 3, 1990.

* * *

Arthur Schnitzler embodies Vienna. His finest plays capture the atmosphere of Austria's capital as it is, or at least it
was at the turn of the century, and convey its *joie de vivre*,
often tinged with sadness, its nostalgia for a grander past, and
its apprehension about the future. Vienna was for him the
mirror of the world.

Schnitzler arrived as a playwright in 1895, when his play
Liebelei (or *Dalliance*, as Tom Stoppard's version is called)
opened at the Vienna Burgtheater and aroused such interest
that it was taken up at the Deutsches Theater in Berlin. Over
40 plays followed; the exact number is hard to calculate
because several consist of almost independent components.
In Austria, and to a lesser extent in the rest of the German-
speaking world, the Schnitzler canon includes plays whose
resonance is greater at home than abroad. Not all his plays
travel well: the full-length *Der einsame Weg* (*The Lonely
Way*) and *Das weite Land* (*Undiscovered Country*) are obvious examples. His output also includes works which are
seldom performed today but command respect as literature:
Paracelsus and *Der Schleier der Beatrice* are poetic dramas in
the grand manner, while *Der junge Medardus* treats subject
matter from the Napoleonic period seen through Austrian
eyes. The content of these plays, and their particular type of
theatricality, stand in the way of modern international acceptance. This is certainly not the case with the ironic, bitter-
sweet Viennese plays with which his name is most closely
associated: *Anatol*, *Liebelei* (*Love Games*), and *Reigen*.
These three masterpieces contain virtually all the themes and
features that make up his portrayal of *fin-de-siècle* Vienna.

Anatol is a cycle of one-act playlets which centre on the
figure of Anatol, a Viennese man-about-town. Each presents
the final moments of one of his affairs with a succession of
well-differentiated but equally attractive women. The lightness of touch, the wit, and the apparent superficiality are
deceptive; the playlets are more thoughtful than at first sight
they appear, and the frivolous tone belies the underlying
seriousness. Schnitzler's penetrating psychological insights
are a reminder that he was a contemporary of the pioneering
Viennese psychoanalyst Freud. His plays often show an
uncomfortable awareness of the cruelty of emotional truth,
while the fact that their actions reveal the supreme import-

ance of the fleeting moment endows every scene and episode with a compellingly authentic immediacy, enabling a sense of underlying unity to be created despite the diversity of situation and character and the constantly shifting mood. In *Anatol* Schnitzler demonstrated what were always to be his strongest qualities. *Liebelei*, a shortish three-acter, illustrates them in a more closely-knit context, which owes much to the German tradition of domestic drama but is also a masterly condensation of contemporary Viennese preoccupations: the dramatized episode, a love affair, is slight, yet its implications are rich in resonance.

A notable story writer, Schnitzler was at his best when his writing was taut and circumscribed. *Reigen* (often known as *La Ronde*) develops the style inaugurated by *Anatol*, though the presentation is more naturalistic and the approach closer to expressionism. Dialogue here becomes the expression of the mindless verbal exchanges prefacing and following the sex act. Structurally, this play without a moral is a sequence of elegantly interlinked encounters, one partner in each reappearing in the next: in it, a wide cross-section of Viennese society passes before the spectators' gaze, from the soldier and the prostitute to the poet, the actress, and the aristocrat, via the middle classes, and ranging, too, from youth to maturity and beyond. Its harshness is muted in the mellower griefs and smiles of *Komtesse Mitzi* (*Countess Mitzi*), a conversation piece for a quartet of voices that points the way to *Das weite Land*, where Schnitzler blends his own formulae with techniques and motifs drawn from Ibsen and Hauptmann to produce a rich and complex fabric well worthy of the best drama of its period.

Professor Bernhardi, one of the best-known Schnitzler plays, turns on anti-semitic prejudice in a Vienna hospital, and reveals Schnitzler as the master of a tautly constructed type of drama very different from the concept of theatre which had made his name. So, too, though in a very different mode, does his costume drama *Der grüne Kakadu* (*The Green Cockatoo*), set in Paris at the outbreak of the French Revolution. This is a *tour-de-force* of construction which blends realism, melodrama, farce, and pathos to create a disturbing piece of theatre that works on many different levels and demonstrates, in contrasting ways, the illusion of reality and the reality of illusion. His later works, written after World War I, did not achieve the distinction of his early masterpieces.

—Peter Skrine

See also *Volume 1* entry on *La Ronde*.

SCRIBE, (Augustin) Eugène. Born in Paris, 24 December 1791. Educated at the Collège de Sainte-Barbe and Lycée Napoléon, both Paris; briefly studied law. Playwright from 1810: first-produced play, *Le Prétendu sans le savoir; ou, L'Occasion fait le larron*, staged 1810; in a commercially successful career, went on to write more than 330 (and possibly as many as 400) works for the stage, including plays and *comédies-vaudevilles* for the Parisian boulevard theatres (especially the Gymnase, for which he was resident dramatist, 1821–31, and the Vaudeville) and later for the Comédie-Française, and libretti for operas, *opéras-comiques*, and ballets for the Paris Opéra and Opéra-Comique. His principal dramatic collaborators included Germain Delavigne, Henri Dupin, Mélesville, and E.-W. Legouvé, and he wrote libretti to the music of leading composers, including Auber, Donizetti, Boïeldieu, Gounod, Meyerbeer, Rossini, and Verdi. Elected to the Académie Française, 1834. Died in Paris, 20 February 1861.

Works

Collections

Oevres complètes (5 vols.). 1840–42.
Oeuvres complètes (16 vols.). 1853.
Oeuvres illustrées (2 vols.). 1853.
Théâtre. (10 vols.). 1856–59.
Oeuvres complètes (76 vols.). 1874–85; includes five series:
  1. *Comédies-drames* (9 vols.).
  2. *Comédies-vaudevilles* (33 vols.).
  3. *Opéras; Ballets* (6 vols.).
  4. *Opéras-comiques* (20 vols.).
  5. *Proverbes; Nouvelles; Romans* (8 vols.).

Stage Works (selected)

The list below includes those plays and libretti, out of his canon of over 330, that have been translated into English. Non-musical collaborators are not listed (sources differ over attribution for particular titles). See the Scribe entries of the *McGraw-Hill Encyclopedia of World Drama* (revised edition), 1982 (which follows the arrangement and scope of the 76-volume *Oeuvres complètes* of 1874–85), and Anthony Levi's *Guide to French Literature 2*, 1992 (which follows chronological order of publication), for more extensive listings.

Le Gastronome sans argent (produced Théâtre du Gymnase, Paris, 1821). 1821; translated as *A Race for Dinner*, 1829.
Le Somnambule (produced Théâtre du Vaudeville, Paris, 1819). 1821; translated as *The Somnambulist*, 1850.
Michel et Christine (produced Théâtre du Gymnase, Paris, 1821). 1821; translated as *Love in Humble Life*, 1850.
Le Vieux Garçon et la petite fille (produced Théâtre du Gymnase, Paris, 1822). 1822; translated as *The Popular Farce Called Young and Old*, 1822.
Le Menteur véridique (produced Théâtre du Gymnase, Paris, 1823). 1823; translated as *He Lies Like Truth*, 1850.
Léocadie, music by Daniel Auber (produced Opéra-Comique, Paris, 1824). 1824; translated as *Léocadia*, 1835.
La Chatte métamorphosée (produced Théâtre de Madame, Paris, 1827). 1827; translated as *The Woman That Was a Cat*, 1840.
Le Comte Ory, music by Rossini (produced Théâtre de l'Opéra, Paris, 1828). 1828; translated as *The Count Ory*, 1829.
La Muette de Portici, music by Daniel Auber (produced Théâtre de l'Opéra, Paris, 1828). 1828; translated as *Mansaniello; or, The Dumb Girl of Portici*, 1850.
Robert-le-Diable, music by Giacomo Meyerbeer (produced Théâtre de l'Opéra, Paris, 1831). 1831; translated as *Robert le Diable*, 1832.
Gustave III; ou, Le Bal masqué, music by Daniel Auber (produced Théâtre de l'Opéra, Paris, 1833). 1833; translated as *Gustavus the Third; or, The Masked Ball*, 1833.
Salvoisy; ou, L'Amoureux de la reine (produced Théâtre du Gymnase, Paris, 1834). 1834; translated as *The Queen's Champion*, 1886.

La Frontière de Savoie (produced Théâtre du Gymnase, Paris, 1834). 1834; translated as *A Peculiar Position*, 1837, and in *"Camille" and Other Plays*, edited by Stephen Sadler Stanton, 1957.

La Juive, music by Jacques Halévy (produced Théâtre de l'Opéra, Paris, 1835). 1835; translated as *The Jewess*, 1835 and 1854.

Le Cheval de bronze, music by Daniel Auber (produced Opéra-Comique, Paris, 1835). 1835; translated as *Opera of the Bronze Horse*, 1836.

Les Huguenots, music by Giacomo Meyerbeer (produced Théâtre de l'Opéra, Paris, 1836). 1836; translated as *The Huguenots*, nd.

Fra Diavolo; ou, L'Hôtellerie de Terracine, music by Daniel Auber (produced Opéra-Comique, Paris, 1836). 1836; translated as *Fra Diavolo: A Comic Opera*, 1854.

Le Domino noir, music by Daniel Auber (produced Opéra-Comique, Paris, 1837). 1837; translated as *The Black Domino; or, A Night's Adventure*, 1837.

César; ou, Le Chien du château (produced Théâtre du Gymnase, Paris, 1837). 1837; translated as *Caesar: The Watchdog of the Castle*, 1886.

La Reine d'un jour, music by Adolphe Adam (produced Opéra-Comique, Paris, 1839). 1839; translated as *Opera of a Queen for a Day*, 1841.

Les Martyrs, music by Gaetano Donizetti (produced Théâtre de l'Opéra, Paris, 1842). 1852; translated as *The Martyres*, 1852.

Le Verre d'eau; ou, Les Effets et les causes (produced Comédie-Française, Paris, 1840). 1840; translated as *A Glass of Water*, 1850: several subsequent translations under same title.

Les Diamants de la couronne, music by Daniel Auber (produced Opéra-Comique, Paris, 1841). 1841; translated as *The Crown Diamonds*, 1844.

Une Chaîne (produced Comédie-Française, Paris, 1841). 1841; translated as *In Honour Bound*, 1885.

Dom Sébastien, roi de Portugal, music by Gaetano Donizetti (produced Théâtre de l'Opéra, Paris, 1843). 1843; translated as *Don Sebastiano: A Tragic Opera*, 1860.

La Part du diable, music by Daniel Auber (produced Opéra-Comique, Paris, 1843). 1843; translated as *Asmodeus, the Little Demon*, 1850.

La Sirène, music by Daniel Auber (produced Opéra-Comique, Paris, 1844). 1844; translated as *The Syren*, 1849.

Haydée; ou, Le Secret, music by Daniel Auber (produced Opéra-Comique, Paris, 1847). 1848; translated as *Haydee; or, The Secret*, 1848.

Le Prophète, music by Giacomo Meyerbeer (produced Théâtre de l'Opéra, Paris, 1849). 1849; translated as *The Opera of The Prophet*, 1850.

Adrienne Lecouvreur (produced Comédie-Française, Paris, 1849). 1849; translated as *Adrienne Lecouvreur*, 1883.

L'Enfant prodigue, music by Daniel Auber (produced Théâtre de l'Opéra, Paris, 1830). 1850; translated as *The Prodigal*, 1851.

Giralda; ou, La Nouvelle Psyché, music by Adolphe Adam (produced Opéra-Comique, Paris, 1850). 1850; translated as *Giralda; or, Which is My Husband?*, 1850; as *Giralda; or, The Invisible Husband*, 1850.

La Dame de pique, music by Jacques Halévy (produced Opéra-Comique, Paris, 1851). 1851; translated as *The Queen of Spades*, nd.

Bataille des dames (produced Comédie-Française, Paris, 1851). 1851; translated as *The Ladies' Battle*, 1850.

Zerline; ou, La Corbeille d'oranges, music by Daniel Auber (produced Théâtre de l'Opéra, Paris, 1851). 1851; translated as *Zerlina*, 1851.

Marco Spada, music by Daniel Auber (produced Opéra-Comique, Paris, 1852). 1851; translated as *Marco Spada*, 1850.

L'Étoile du nord, music by Giacomo Meyerbeer (produced Opéra-Comique, Paris, 1854). 1854; translated as *The Star of the North*, 1855.

Les Doigts de fée (produced Comédie-Française, Paris, 1858). 1858; translated as *The World of Fashion*, 1860; as *Fairy Fingers*, in *Easy French Plays*, edited by C.W. Benton, 1901.

L'Africaine, music by Giacomo Meyerbeer (produced Théâtre de l'Opéra, Paris, 1851). 1865; translated as *L'Africaine*, 1866.

Fiction

La Maîtresse anonyme. 1840.
Maurice. 1845.
Piquillo Alliaga; ou, Les Maures sous Philippe III (2 vols.). 1847; translated as *The Victim of the Jesuits; or, Piquillo Alliaga* (3 vols.), 1848.
Le Filleul d'Amadis; ou, Les Amours d'une fée (3 vols.). 1858.
Les Yeux de ma tante (6 vols.). 1859.
Fleurette la bouquetière (6 vols.). 1861; translated as *Fleurette*, 1886.
Noélie (4 vols.). 1862.

Other

Proverbes et nouvelles. 1840.
Nouvelles. 1856.
Historiettes et nouvelles. 1856.

*

Criticism

Books:
E. de Mirécourt, *Scribe*, Paris, 1854.
E. Legouvé, *Eugène Scribe*, Paris, 1912.
N. Cole Arvin, *Eugène Scribe and the French Theatre 1815–1860*, Cambridge, Massachusetts, 1924.
K. Pendle, *Scribe and the French Opera of the Nineteenth Century*, Ann Arbor, Michigan, 1979.
H. Koop and R. Switzer, *Eugène Scribe*, Boston, 1979.

Articles:
D. Cardwell, "The Role of Stage Properties in the Plays of Scribe", in *Nineteenth-Century French Studies*, 16, 1987–88.

* * *

Although he is generally regarded as the progenitor of the "well-made play" (*pièce bien faite*), Scribe's enormous output includes substantial contributions to six precisely defined genres: *vaudeville, comédie-vaudeville,* comedy of intrigue, historical drama, opera, and ballet-opera. That none of these plays has attained classic status in the 20th-century theatre is perhaps less important than the fact that his work permeated the 19th-century Western stage, directly influencing many dozens of other playwrights, including—most notably—Ibsen. It was Ibsen's gradual rejection of Scribean dramaturgy in favour of the "discussion" mode of his maturity that

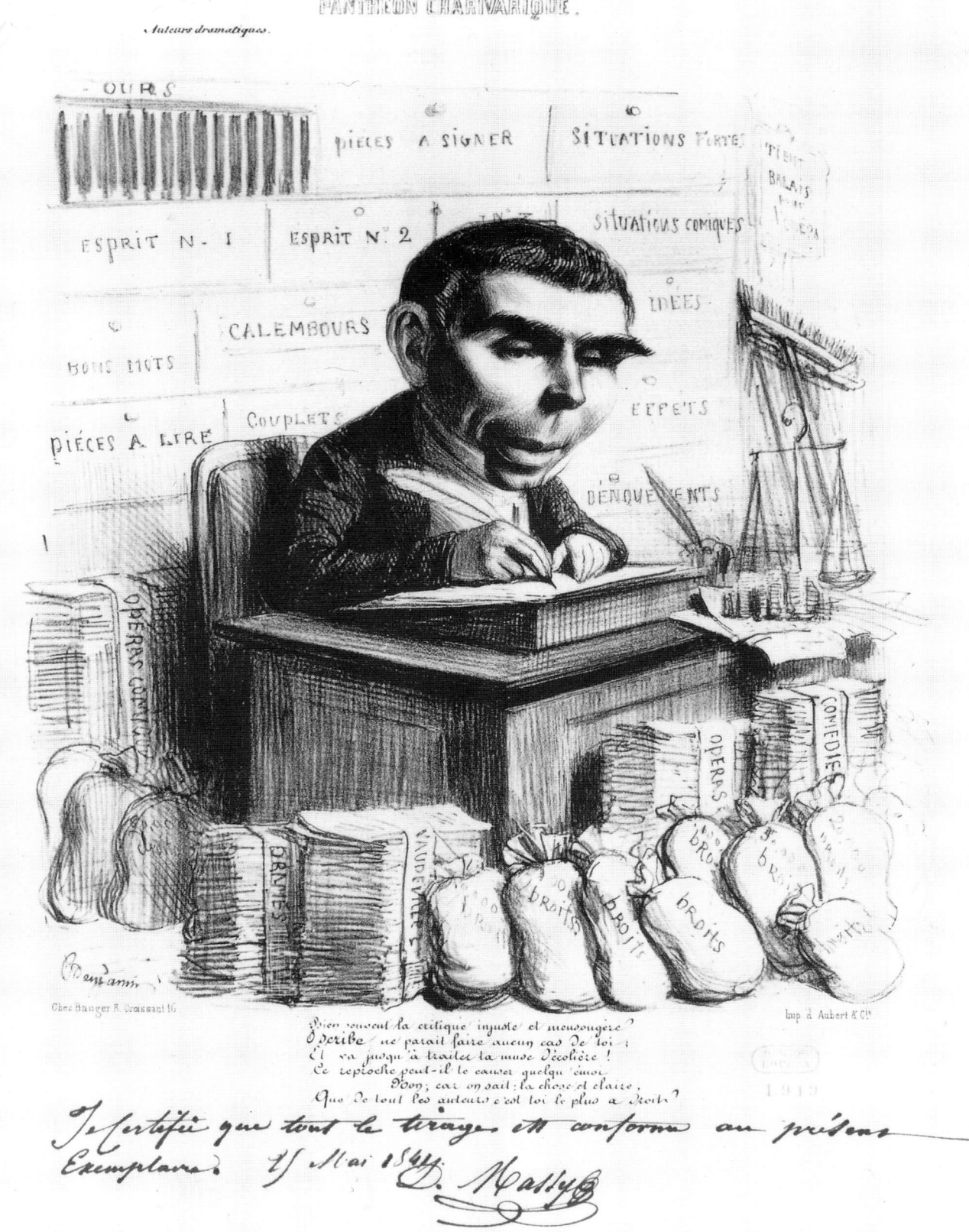

Eugène Scribe (caricature by Benjamin, from the journal *Le Charivari*, 1841).

quickly led, in the 1890's, to a critical rejection of Scribe as epitomising an artificiality that was out of touch with the new values of realism. The vehemence of this rejection by London critics such as William Archer and Shaw, more than 30 years after Scribe's death, is itself remarkable evidence of the influence of a playwright who had viewed much of his work as necessarily ephemeral and who, by working largely in collaboration with other writers, created a presence as a European playwright which haunted the theatre long after it had ceased to delight it.

The production history of a late work written jointly with Ernest Legouvé, *Adrienne Lecouvreur*, called by some a tragedy, illustrates the vicissitudes of Scribe's reception. The play is loosely based on the story of the historical title character, an actress, who killed herself in 1730 by inhaling some poisoned flowers she had sent to her thoroughly unfaithful lover. Historically, her death was probably suicide, but Scribe reconstructs it so that a sequence of accidents and misunderstandings relays the bouquet through unsympathetic hands, and its return is wrongly construed as rejection; she loses the ennobling status of suicide and retains, at most, the poignancy of the "well-made" ethic that a woman with a past has no right to a future as well. As such, the play was one of the most famous vehicles for the mid-century *tragédienne* Rachel Félix, for whom it was tailored to the extent that, at one point, Adrienne quotes from *Phèdre*, one of Rachel's other celebrated roles. However, when the play was revived in London in 1893, William Archer lavishly praised Janet Achurch's "thrilling" death but dismissed the play as sensationalism, "which ought to be kept under a glass case in a historical museum". But Shaw, after commenting on the "unparalleled blastedness of the play", went on to illustrate that "Janet was transcendently bad". Even Sarah Bernhardt, who had first done the part in London in 1880 and in 1905 stretched the play out to six acts with her own writing, found it "prolix and rambling".

The *vaudeville* of Scribe's earliest theatre has no direct connection with the American variety programme of the same name, but refers to a farce filled out with popular songs. A major early success in this mode was *L'Ours et le pacha* (The Bear and the Pasha), which develops as a stratagem to circumvent the legendary ruler's fury on the death of his pet bear. The coincidental death of various other local bears, and the availability and resourcefulness of some itinerant bear trainers, leads to an elaborate deferral ruse, and the imminent decapitation of both bearskin-clad trainers is avoided only by a mood-swing in the Pasha, who pardons them.

Character development was scarcely a high priority in *vaudeville*, or in the structurally more complex form of the *comédie-vaudeville*, where a more ingenious intrigue pattern comes closer to what became known as the *pièce bien faite*. *Le Menteur véridique* (The Honest Liar) revolves around a marriage/dowry stratagem, in a manner that illustrates the ultimate dependence of the genre on the Latin New Comedy of Terence and its neoclassical French derivatives. It is in *Le Verre d'eau* (A Glass of Water), however, that Scribe's well-made dramaturgy found its most famous illustration, at least on the English stage, and it was the peculiarities of this type of play which descended most obviously to the style of his most famous disciple, Sardou. As with a lot of his work, the play is a heavily fictionalised piece of distorted history. The pivot of the action is the vital—but totally impersonal—instrument announced in the title, which signals the collapse of a complex pattern of subterfuge, jealousy, and deceit, centering on Bolingbroke and Marlborough.

The polarisation of Scribe and Ibsen has allowed a common inference that everything that manifested itself in Ibsen was absent in Scribe. Though it would be absurd to claim depth of characterisation or of social insight in Scribe's plays, it must also be remembered that notions of what constitutes realism develop considerably from decade to decade. Scribe's contemporary audiences certainly valued symmetries and mechanistic completeness, but that did not mean that for them his plays were out of touch with actuality, especially as photography had not yet redefined the notion of mimesis. Many of his plays, in fact, have a substantial dimension of satire. A play as early as *Encore une nuit de la Garde Nationale* (Another Night with the National Guard) satirises military decorum, and *Le Mariage d'argent* (The Marriage of Money) has a view of marriage that is soberingly unsentimental beside the 18th-century tradition. *La Camaraderie* (The Faction) is a highly cynical attack on electioneering.

There can be no doubt that such plays touched a nerve of realism; indeed, the unpopularity of some of them was for precisely this reason, an indication that their author was not solely concerned to gratify a market demand. Yet even in such satirical plays Scribe cushioned his attack with a well-made *scène à faire* (show-down scene) so that the final curtain presented a consoling reassertion of audience norms which the central action had threatened.

—Howard McNaughton

See also *Volume 1* entry on *The Glass of Water*.

SCUDÉRY, Georges de. Born in Le Havre, France; baptised 12 August 1601. Parents died in 1613. Married the writer Marie-Madeleine de Montcal de Martinvast in 1654; one son. Pursued military career, c.1623–29: served in the Piedmont campaign under the Duc de Longueville and Prince de Carignan, and was involved in the retreat at the Pas de Suze, 1629; playwright from c.1629: first-produced play, *Lygdamon et Lidias; ou, La Ressemblance*, staged 1630; wrote for the Théâtre du Marais, 1630–36, and for the Hôtel de Bourgogne, after 1637; initiated the attack on Corneille's *Le Cid* (the "Querelle du *Cid*") with his *Observations sur "Le Cid"*, 1637; settled in the Marais district of Paris with his sister, the writer Madeleine de Scudéry (whose fiction he contributed to), 1637; governor, fort of Notre-Dame-de-la-Garde, Marseilles, 1644–c.1661, although continued to live in Paris for much of this period. Elected to the Académie Française, 1650. Died in Paris, 14 May 1667.

Stage Works

Lygdamon et Lidias; ou, La Rassemblance (produced Théâtre du Marias?, Paris, 1630). 1631.
Le Trompeur puni; ou, L'Histoire septentrionale (produced Théâtre du Marias, Paris, 1631). 1633.
Le Vassal généreux (produced Théâtre du Marais, Paris, 1632). 1636.
Orante (produced Théâtre du Marais, Paris, 1633). 1635.
La Comédie des comédiens (produced Théâtre du Marais, Paris, 1634). 1635.
Le Fils supposé (produced Théâtre du Marais, Paris, 1634). 1636.
Le Prince déguisé (produced Théâtre du Marais, Paris, 1634). 1636.

La Mort de César (produced Théâtre du Marais, Paris, 1635). 1636.

Didon (produced Théâtre du Marais, Paris, 1635–36). 1637.

L'Amant libéral (produced Théâtre du Marais, Paris, 1636–37). 1638.

L'Amour tyrannique (produced Théâtre de l'Hôtel de Bourgogne, Paris, 1638). 1639.

Andromire (produced Théâtre de l'Hôtel de Bourgogne, Paris, 1640) 1641.

Ibrahim; ou, L'Illustre Bassa, from the romance written with Madeleine de Scudéry (produced Théâtre de l'Hôtel de Bourgogne, Paris, 1641–42). 1643.

Axiane (produced Théâtre de l'Hôtel de Bourgogne, Paris, 1642–43). 1644.

Arminius; ou, Les Frères ennemis (produced Théâtre de l'Hôtel de Bourgogne, Paris, 1643). 1644.

Fiction

Ibrahim; ou, L'Illustre Bassa (4 vols,), with Madeleine de Scudéry. 1641; translated as *Ibrahim; or, The Illustrious Bassa*, 1652.

Artamène; ou, Le Grand Cyrus (10 vols.), with Madeleine de Scudéry. 1649–53; translated as *Artamenes; or, The Grand Cyrus*, 1653–55.

Clélie (10 vols.), with Madeleine de Scudéry. 1654–60; translated as *Clelie*, 1655–61.

Almahide; ou, L'Esclave reine (8 vols.). 1660–63.

Verse

Élégie sur l'arrest de Théophile. 1623.

La Temple. 1633.

Discours de la France à Mgr. le cardinal Duc de Richelieu après son retour de Nancy. 1635.

Epitaphe sur le Roi Louis XIII. 1643.

L'Ombre du grand Armand. 1643.

Le Cabinet de M. de Scudéry. 1646.

Le Grand Exemple. 1647.

Poésies diverses. 1649.

Salomon instruisant le Roi. 1651.

Alaric; ou, Rome vaincue. 1654.

Ode sur le retour de M. le Prince. 1660.

Poésies nouvelles. 1661.

Other

Observations sur "Le Cid". 1637.

La Preuve des passages alléguées dans Les Observations sur Le Cid. 1637.

L'Apologie du théâtre. 1639.

Les Femmes illustres; ou, Les Harangues héroïques (2 vols.). 1642–44; translated as *Les Femmes Illustres; or, The Heroick Haranguers of the Illustrious Women*, 1681; as *The Female Orators; or, The Courage and Constancy of Divers Famous Queens and Illustrious Women*, 1714.

Discours politiques des rois. 1647; translated as *Curia Politiae; or, The Apologies of Severall Princes*, 1654.

*

Criticism

Books:

A. Batereau, *Georges de Scudéry als Dramatiker*, Leipzig, 1902.

Charles Clerc, *Un Matamore des lettres: La Vie tragi-comique de Georges de Scudéry*, Paris, 1929.

D. Guichemerre, *La Comédie en France avant Molière*, Paris, 1972.

Eveline Dutertre, *Georges de Scudéry, dramaturge*, Geneva, 1988.

Eveline Dutertre, *Georges de Scudéry: Théoricien du classicisme*, Paris, 1991.

*   *   *

If Georges de Scudéry has not been granted the place he deserves in the panoply of French dramatists, this is chiefly because he is so easily portrayed as the villain in the quarrel over Pierre Corneille's play *Le Cid*, which he attacked with gusto. He also had the misfortune to be overshadowed as a creative writer by his undoubtedly more gifted sister, the novelist Madeleine de Scudéry, and as a playwright not only by Corneille himself, but also by other exact contemporaries such as Jean Mairet and Jean Rotrou. Moreover, on first acquaintance, his plays appear both archaic in tone and chaotic in construction. Instant judgements in histories of literature, largely based on these well-grounded perceptions, have doubtless contributed to critical neglect.

Several of his early plays are disorganized and full of unlikely situations. *Le Trompeur puni* (The Deceiver Punished), in which two actions are juxtaposed, has a structure which lacks the justification that underlies *La Comédie des comédiens* (The Actors' Comedy), wherein one action introduces another in the form of a play within the play. The latter, moreover, doubtless helped to inspire Corneille's use of the stratagem in *L'Illusion comique* (The Theatrical Illusion). Never an imaginative writer, Scudéry habitually borrowed material from contemporary novels, troubling only to versify it. *Axiane*, in prose, is almost a word-for-word copy of part of a novel by his sister. His plays are repetitive, in that certain scenes, twists of plot, even passages of text, recur frequently both within plays and from play to play, and they are often formally unprogressive.

While Mairet and others experimented with what came to be called "the rules", Scudéry resisted, declaring in the preface to *Lygdamon et Lidias* that he found them too limiting and preferred to ignore them. His plays feature spectacle and surprise, movement, physical action, change, pomp and solemnity, set pieces of eloquence; and he readily included immoral behaviour and scabrous language. His characters frequently travel great distances; alternatively, separate actions involve two sets of characters at a distance, coming together only in a final episode. Given the constantly shifting scenes, the numerous characters, and the endless whirl of events, it is surprisingly paradoxical to note how much he simplified his source material, even though he often did so by removing what little interior action there was: spectacle replaces dramatic action, and everything contributes to the creation of spectacle.

His dramatic career lay in the period dominated by Richelieu, and his *Observations sur "Le Cid"* betoken the Cardinal's influence. It is indicative of his opportunism that this erstwhile scourge of "the rules" and apologist for the licentious was so quick to condemn the heroine, Chimène, as shameless and to attack Corneille's dramatic structure. Afterwards, he tried to keep to his newly-learned precepts, but his greatest box-office success, *L'Amour tyrannique* (The Tyrant in Love), betrays his hankering after a freer code.

He is certainly noteworthy for his enormous variety, from the vitality and excitement of the chaotic early examples to the sober merit and almost classical simplicity of *La Mort de*

César (The Death of Caesar), his only serious attempt to work within "the rules". By his choice of subject matter, Scudéry helped to establish Roman history as an appropriate choice for serious drama, and to pave the way for Corneille's great Roman tragedies. In this particular play, he also introduced for the first time in his own work a political dimension, here advocating an ideal of kingship that Richelieu doubtless approved. Seriousness of tone is one of its strengths, but the pathetic cry "Ah! treacherous Casca", uttered by Caesar as the first conspirator stabs him, exemplifies Scudéry at his most chaotic, for he has suppressed Casca from the story, and the blow is struck by Cassius. Worse, while the best lines advocating monarchy on the Richelieu model are given to Brutus (the main character), Scudéry's Brutus, scarcely "the noblest Roman of them all", is a contemptible, double-dealing rascal whose actions, inconsistent with the majesty and force of his language, are emphatically discredited.

After *La Mort de César* Scudéry, though never again aspiring to such simplicity, showed greater rigour in selecting and arranging material. Well-observed psychological action and the serious exploration of a moral conflict distinguish *Ibrahim*, and dignity of style graces *Arminius*.

L'Amour tyrannique, written as a pendant to the *Observations* and as a lesson to Corneille, provided the critic J.-F. Sarasin with a pretext for the *Discours de la tragédie* which prefaced it. It is dominated by a really black villain, Tiridate, who is untroubled by self-doubt, and it contains such serious themes as an examination of love and fate, as well as that of kingship. It explores the rights and duties of kings, and reaffirms the sacred nature of monarchy. However, its subject is not historical, and its language is exceptionally subtle, so that it remains an example of the romanesque and the precious. Despite this, the nobility of tone and the seriousness of its subject matter lift it above the common run of tragi-comedies of the time. Indeed, as it does not mix the genres, Sarasin was reluctant to account it a tragi-comedy, and felt it deserved classification as a tragedy.

That Pierre Corneille eclipses Scudéry is a truism. None the less, it remains undeniable that, as a writer of comedy, tragi-comedy, and tragedy, Scudéry provides a good, if by no means unique, example of a talented and successful exponent of the exuberant baroque theatre that was swept away all too definitively by the triumph of the organized genius of Corneille, against whom so few early contemporaries sought to compete after 1642–43.

—William Brooks

SENECA, Lucius Annaeus. Born in Corduba (now Cordoba, Spain), c.4 BC; son of the writer and teacher of rhetoric Lucius Annaeus Seneca the elder. Studied philosophy in Rome. Married Pompeia Paulina; one son. Spent some time in Egypt for his health; returned to Rome, c.31; elected quaestor in 30's; exiled to Corsica by Caligula, 41–49; tutor to Nero, and designated praetor, 50; with Burrus, adviser and minister to Nero, 54–62: consul, 56; on Burrus's death in 62, was asked to retire, and did so. Forced to commit suicide for supposed participation in Pisonian conspiracy, 65 AD.

Works

Collections

Seneca: His Tenne Tragedies, various translators. 1581; reprinted 1927 and 1966.
Opera, edited by F. Haase. 1852.
Opera (3 vols.), edited by E. Hermes and others. 1898–1907.
Opera, edited by R. Peiper and G Richter. 1902.
The Ten Tragedies, translated by Walter Bradshaw. 1902.
Tragedies, translated by Ella I. Harris. 1904.
The Tragedies (2 vols.; parallel texts), translated by Frank Justus Miller. 1917–18 (Loeb Classical Library).
Complete Roman Drama (translations; 2 vols.), edited by George Duckworth. 1942.
Tragoediae (2 vols.), edited by G.C. Giardina. 1966.
Four Tragedies and "Octavia" (includes *Thyestes; Phaedra; The Trojan Women; Oedipus*), translated by E.F. Watling. 1966.
Tragoediae, edited by Otto Zwierlein. 1986.
Three Tragedies (includes *Trojan Women; Medea; Phaedra*), translated by Frederick Ahl. 1986.
Tragedies 1 (includes *Trojan Women; Thyestes; Medea; Agamemnon*), translated by David R. Slavitt. 1992.

Stage Works (first published in collected editions in the 1470's)

Hercules Furens. Translated as *Hercules Furens*, in *Tenne Tragedies*, 1581: several subsequent translations under same title.
Troades. Translated as *Troas*, 1559; as *Troades*, 1660, and *Trojan Women*, in *Four Tragedies and "Octavia"*, 1966: several subsequent translations under both titles; as *The Daughters of Troy*, in *Two Tragedies of Seneca*, 1898.
Phoenissae. Translated as *Thebais*, in *Tenne Tragedies*, 1581.
Medea. Translated as *Medea*, in *Tenne Tragedies*: several subsequent translations under same title.
Phaedra (also known as *Hippolytus*). Translated as *Hippolitus*, 1561; as *Hippolytus*, 1581; modern translations as *Phaedra*.
Oedipus. Translated as *Oedipus*, 1563: several subsequent translations under same title.
Agamemnon. Translated as *Agamemnon*, 1566: several subsequent translations under same title.
Thyestes. Translated as *Thyestes*, 1560: several subsequent translations under same title.
Octavia, now thought not to be by Seneca. Translated as *Octavia*, 1566: several subsequent translations under same title.
Hercules Oetaeus, probably not by Seneca. Translated as *Hercules Oetaeus*, in *Tenne Tragedies*, 1581, and in *Ten Tragedies*, 1902.

Verse

Apocolocyntosis divi Claudii. Translated as *Apocolocyntosis; or, A Mockery upon the Death and Deification of Claudius Caesar*, 1664: several subsequent translations as *Apocolocyntosis*; as *The Satire of Seneca on the Apotheosis of Claudius*, 1902.

Other

De Remediis Fortuitorum. Translated as *De Remediis Fortuitorum*, 1547.

De Beneficius. Translated as *Concerning Benefyting*, 1578; as *On Benefits*, 1887 and 1889.

De Consolatione. Translated as *Consolation to Marcia*, 1635.

De Clementia. Translated as *Clemency*, 1653.

De Providentia. Translated as *Why Good Men Suffer Misfortunes, Seeing There is a Divine Providence*, 1648.

De Brevitate Vitae. Translated as *The Shortness of Life*, 1663.

Ad Lucilium Epistulae Morales. 1917–25 (3 vols., parallel texts; Loeb Classical Library); edited by L.D. Reynolds (2 vols.), 1965; translated as *The Epistles*, 1786; as *Select Letters of Seneca*, by W.C. Summers, 1910; by E.P. Barker as *Seneca's Letters to Lucilius* (2 vols.), 1932; by Robin Campbell as *Letters from a Stoic*, 1969.

Moral Essays (3 vols.; parallel texts). 1928–35 (Loeb Classical Library).

Naturales Quaestiones. 1522; translated as *Physical Science in the Time of Nero*, 1910; as *Natural Questions* (2 vols., parallel texts; Loeb Classical Library), 1971.

*

Bibliographies

Anna L. Motto, *Seneca: A Critical Bibliography 1900–1980: Scholarship on His Life, Thought, Prose and Influence*, Amsterdam, 1989.

Criticism

Books:

F.L. Lucas, *Seneca and Elizabethan Tragedy*, London, 1922.

W. Cornwallis, *Discourses upon Seneca the Tragedian*, Gainesville, Florida, 1952.

Anna L. Motto, *Seneca Sourcebook*, Amsterdam, 1971.

Ronald W. Tobin, *Racine and Seneca*, Chapel Hill, North Carolina, 1971.

Anna L. Motto, *Seneca*, New York, 1973.

C.D.N. Costa (ed.), *Seneca*, London, 1974.

Miriam Tamara Griffin, *Seneca: A Philosopher in Politics*, Oxford, 1976.

Norman T. Pratt, *Seneca's Drama*, Chapel Hill (North Carolina) and London, 1983.

Villy Sørensen, *Seneca: The Humanist at the Court of Nero*, Edinburgh, 1984.

J. David Bishop, *Seneca's Daggered Stylus: Political Code in the Tragedies*, Königstein, 1985.

Denis Henry, *The Mask of Power: Seneca's Tragedies and Imperial Rome*, Warminster, Wiltshire, 1985.

Dana F. Sutton, *Seneca on the Stage*, Leiden, 1986.

Anna L. Motto, *Senecan Tragedy*, Amsterdam, 1988.

Thomas G. Rosenmeyer, *Senecan Drama and Stoic Cosmology*, Berkeley (California) and London, 1989.

Robert S. Miola, *Shakespeare and Classical Tragedy: The Influence of Seneca*, Oxford, 1992.

Articles:

C.J. Herington, "Senecan Tragedy", in *Arion*, 5, 1966.

R.J. Tarrant, "Senecan Drama and its Antecedents", in *Harvard Studies in Classical Philology*, 82, 1978.

*   *   *

The politician, philosopher, and playwright Seneca was the heir to a rich dramatic tradition: his primary source was Greek tragedy of the 5th-century BC, especially Euripidean

Seneca (engraving, c.1584).

drama, but a considerable debt also was owed to Roman predecessors. The influence of the latter is reflected in a penchant for exalted language and horrific themes; to these Seneca added an element special to himself, the teachings of Stoic philosophy. Seneca's distance from his Greek models can be seen if we compare Euripides' and his own versions of the *Trojan Women* or Sophocles' and Seneca's treatments of the Oedipus story. One third of the Roman *Trojan Women* is devoted to a debate in which Andromache attempts to save her infant son from Ulysses, an episode which seems to be Seneca's personal contribution and typical of his fondness for rhetorical display. To Sophocles' *Oedipus Rex* Seneca has added two scenes of divination and necromancy, in the first of which, with total lack of restraint, Manto reports to the blind Tiresias a horrendously perverted sacrifice, while in the second Creon describes how he conjured up from the shades the ghost of the murdered Laius.

Were Seneca's tragedies intended for the stage, possibly for the emperor Nero's private theatre? Does their heavily rhetoric content imply declamation rather than performance? Is Seneca far too vague when it comes to signalling entrances and exits, and was it possible to stage an incident like Theseus' effort in the *Phaedra* to put together the pieces of Hippolytus' mangled body without the effect appearing totally absurd? Certainly Seneca has been staged often enough since antiquity, and plays like Shakespeare's *Titus Andronicus* or Webster's *The Duchess of Malfi* pose no fewer problems. At the same time characters who speak all "with the same voice, and at the top of it" and the uneven pace of action, when linked, furthermore, to an aristocratic prejudice against the theatre, make it extremely doubtful that Seneca wrote with the intention of a public as opposed to a private production.

Seneca's tragedies represent melodrama rather than drama. Their author was obsessed with destructive passions. Whereas Euripides saw the whole person from whom passions arise, as in the instance of the Greek Medea, passion for Seneca seems to have a vitality of its own, largely divorced from the character projecting that passion. As a result characters, for Seneca, tend to be wholly black or, less frequently, wholly white. Take the case of Phaedra in Seneca's play of that name: she makes no attempt to conquer her passion for her step-son, but approaches Hippolytus herself; and she does not commit suicide when repulsed but personally accuses him of rape to Theseus, his father. On the other hand, Phaedra's Nurse strikes a remarkably moral note at first, but, of course, she has a mistress who needs to be restrained and certainly not encouraged. Yet when Phaedra has been spurned, it is the Nurse who screams "rape", undergoing a change of character that ignores consistency in order to advance the plot. But no one is quite such an embodiment of evil as Atreus in the *Thyestes*: read the messenger's account of the slaughter of Thyestes' sons and, even worse, the account of Atreus's preparation of the bodies to provide a banquet for their parent. A monster of depravity, Atreus is later to regret not serving Thyestes with blood from his sons' living bodies or having Thyestes roast his own children.

Judged simply as song, their opulence of language and imagery makes Senecan choruses a joy to read; but in dramatic terms they are less satisfactory, for often they are not obviously relevant to the action of the play. An exception is offered by the second choral ode from the *Thyestes* which describes the "true" king, the man of clear conscience who is willing to endure whatever fate ordains, greeting death as a friend and wanting nothing, for at the beginning of the third act Thyestes rejects temporal power, finding a kingdom unlimited in having no kingdom at all. The acceptance of fate as much as the rejection of power represents a Stoic tenet, and philosophizing of this kind certainly imparts a special quality to the tragedies of Seneca. But we are wrong, however, to make too much of the Stoic influence, even if two plays feature Hercules, the Stoic hero, and there is a preoccupation with death as a release from the horrors of this world, or a use of fire imagery redolent of Stoic physics.

The theory that individual tragedies exemplify particular Stoic ideas—in *Trojan Women* the problems of life, death, and destiny, in *Phaedra* the problem of sexual passion, in *Oedipus* the problems of free choice, sin, and retribution—is grotesque. Seneca was writing drama but often was led astray by both too desperate a desire to innovate, as when, with an irony that is quite macabre, he had the living son Astyanax concealed in the tomb of the dead father Hector in his *Trojan Women*, and by an inability to resist bombast, though some of his bombast—for example, Jocasta's last speech in *Oedipus*—can be absolutely superb. The influence of Seneca, both in the original Latin and in translation, on Renaissance drama must never be forgotten, and what appealed in the 15th and 16th centuries was Seneca's sense of the horrific, the theatrical, the supernatural, and the moral—and here he undoubtedly excelled.

—Peter Walcot

See also *Volume 1* entries on *Oedipus*; *Phaedra*.

SEWELL, Stephen. Born in Sydney, Australia, 1953. Educated at the University of Sydney, BS 1975. Writer-in-residence, Nimrod Theatre, Sydney, 1981–82. Recipient: Australian Writers Guild Award, 1982; New South Wales Premier's Award, 1985.

Works

Stage Works

The Father We Loved on a Beach by the Sea (produced La Boîte Theatre, Brisbane, 1978).   1976.
Traitors (produced Pram Factory, Melbourne, 1979).   1983.
Welcome the Bright World (produced Nimrod Theatre, Sydney, 1982).   1983.
The Blind Giant is Dancing (produced Adelaide, 1983).   1983; revised version, 1985.
Burn Victim, with others (produced Sydney, 1983).
Dreams in an Empty City (produced Adelaide Festival, 1986).   1986.
Hate (produced Belvoir Street Theatre, Sydney, 1988).
Miranda (produced La Boîte Theatre, Brisbane, 1989).
Sisters (produced Playbox Theatre, Melbourne, 1991).
King Golgrutha (produced by the South Australian Theatre Company, 1991).
In the City of Grand-Daughters (produced Playbox Theatre, Melbourne, 1993).

Screenplays

Isabelle Eberhardt, 1993.

*

Criticism

Articles:
John McCallum, "The World Outside: Cosmopolitanism in the Plays of Nowra and Sewell", in *Meanjin*, 43, 1984.
Four articles on Sewell in special issue of *Australian Drama Studies*, 14, 1989.

*   *   *

The first production of *Traitors* in 1979 established Stephen Sewell as one of the most exciting and challenging of the new generation of Australian playwrights. His work is distinctive for the power and complexity of its political vision, and in this sense is more appropriately compared with recent left-wing British theatre than with the mostly comic, mostly celebratory style of satire which has dominated Australian stages over the last two decades. Recent plays, like *The Blind Giant is Dancing*, *Dreams in an Empty City*, and *Hate*, share some of the concerns of that tradition, in the ways they present patterns of social interaction which offer distinctive images of contemporary Australian culture. As a sceptical Marxist, though, Sewell grounds the analysis of interpersonal politics always in the context of structures of power that exist beyond the individual, and beyond the bounds of the particular society.

Sewell's first play, *The Father We Loved on a Beach by the Sea*, reflects in its structure the dual concerns of the public and seemingly private worlds, but presents them in juxtaposition rather than analytical reconciliation. Its two time-frames (remembrance of things past as experienced by Joe, as quintessential Aussie "battler", and a hypothetical revolutionary future focused on Dan, Joe's activist son) entail an ambitious mixture of playing-styles which anticipates the complexity of the later plays set in a contemporary Australia; here perhaps the absence of a point of present vantage between warmly stereotypical past and coldly apocalyptic future indicates a little uncertainty of focus behind the power of the play.

Its immediate successors, *Traitors* and *Welcome the Bright World*, were greeted as distinguished instances of a "new internationalism" opposed to the very self-consciously Australian "New Wave" of the 1970's. Their settings—respectively Stalinist Russia between the wars and Germany through the 1970's—certainly seemed to represent a conspicuous refusal to be parochial. But the relevance of a concept like "internationalism" to Sewell's work can be sought more profitably in the nature of his political analysis and the theatrical company he (metaphorically) keeps than in matters of literal placement.

The very concentrated action of *Traitors* explores the efforts of individuals to find some place for love and some sense of personal purpose in a society where betrayal and oppression appear to pre-empt such things. *Welcome the Bright World*, with its much more obvious ambitions of scope, shared those concerns, and placed them in an even more esoteric context; the intricacies of Soviet factionalism make *Traitors* a demanding play intellectually as well as emotionally, but the incorporation of the insights of contemporary speculative physics in *Welcome the Bright World* (as a subject for debate within the play, an analogy for its vision of the dynamic of human relationships, and a structural principle) firmly established Sewell's reputation as a writer who will not make theatrical compromises in his mission to address audiences intelligently. The largeness of the play, in every sense, becomes effectively an aspect of its power.

The Blind Giant is Dancing and *Dreams in an Empty City* are set in a very recognizable Australia. Their subjects—political corruption and financial disintegration—are examined in terms of the consciences of individuals under intense moral pressure, but also warrant the panoramic scale on which they are staged. The vastness and seeming disparateness of the action are contained in both cases not only by a coherent political analysis and by the interconnections of the plots, but also by the invocation of a myth central to Western culture: Sewell is quite unembarrassed in his application of the Faust story to the corrosiveness of compromise in the political progress of Allen Fitzgerald, and in the overt references to the life and crucifixion of Christ which inform the struggle of Chris, in *Dreams*, to defy the apparent logic of despair.

The force which in *The Blind Giant* threatens to undermine all positions of integrity is cynicism, seeming to blight all political stances in the play. In *Dreams*, that force is given a spiritual dimension, which reflects the intensity of Sewell's own religious thinking in its exploitation of symbols drawn from his lapsed Catholicism. Even the most venal of the predators in the latter play appeals at some point to a perception of the world as irredeemably fallen in order to mask his/her opportunism with moral repugnance. *Dreams* ends, like *The Blind Giant* and *The Father*, on a note of apocalyptic fantasy—in this case, nothing less than the collapse of international capitalism. The passion of the presentation ensures that, perhaps improbably, it works powerfully.

The five-hander *Hate* and the three-hander *Miranda*—the single-set plays which have followed these giants—may well reflect a decision on the playwright's part that economies are necessary. If that is the case, it is a pity; though *Hate*,

especially, has all the characteristic emotional intensity, and even some of the density of mythic reference, of its predecessors, Sewell's imagination and his perception of the relation of the personal to the political seem to call for a bigger arena. Certainly it is this vision, and a distinctive understanding of what the stage can and should do, that, in the past decade, has enlarged the scope of Australian theatre.

—Peter Fitzpatrick

SHADWELL, Thomas. Born in Broomhill, Norfolk, England, 24 March 1640 or 1641. Educated at King Edward VI Grammar School, Bury St. Edmunds, Suffolk, 1654–56; Gonville and Caius College, Cambridge, 1656–58; Middle Temple, London, from 1658. Married the actress Anne Gibbs, c.1665. Travelled in Europe, early 1660's, then returned to London and began writing for the stage; his plays produced from 1668 by the Duke's Men, and after 1682 by the United Company; involved in a feud with Dryden from 1682. Poet laureate and historiographer royal, 1689–92. Died in London, 19 November 1692.

Thomas Shadwell (engraving by A. Duncan).

Works

Collections

Complete Works (5 vols.), edited by Montague Summers. 1927.

Stage Works

The Sullen Lovers; or, *The Impertinents*, from a play by Molière (produced Lincoln's Inn Fields Theatre, London, 1668). 1668.
The Royal Shepherdess, from a play by John Fountain (produced Lincoln's Inn Fields Theatre, London, 1669). 1669.
The Humorists (produced Lincoln's Inn Fields Theatre, London, 1670). 1671.
Epsom Wells (produced Dorset Garden Theatre, London, 1672). 1673.
The Miser, from a play by Molière (produced Theatre Royal, Bath Street, London, 1672). 1672.
The Tempest; or, *The Enchanted Island*, from the play by Shakespeare (produced Dorset Garden Theatre, London, 1674). 1674.
The Triumphant Widow; or, *The Medley of Humours*, with William Cavendish (produced Dorset Garden Theatre, London, 1674). 1677.
Psyche, music by Matthew Locke (produced Dorset Garden Theatre, London, 1675). 1675.
The Libertine (produced Dorset Garden Theatre, London, 1675). 1676.
The Virtuoso (produced Dorset Garden Theatre, London, 1676). 1676.
A True Widow (produced Dorset Garden Theatre, London, 1678). 1679.
Timon of Athens, The Man-Hater, from the play by Shakespeare (produced Dorset Garden Theatre, London, 1678). 1678.
The Woman-Captain (produced Dorset Garden Theatre, London, 1679). 1680.
The Lancashire Witches and Tegue o Divelly the Irish Priest (produced Dorset Garden Theatre, London, 1681). 1682.
The Squire of Alsatia (produced Dorset Garden Theatre, London, 1688). 1688.
Bury Fair (produced Dorset Garden Theatre, London, 1689). 1689.
The Amorous Bigot, with the Second Part of Tegue o Divelly (produced Theatre Royal, Drury Lane, London, 1691). 1691.
The Scourers (produced Theatre Royal, Drury Lane, London, 1690). 1691.
The Volunteers; or, *The Stock Jobbers* (produced Theatre Royal, Drury Lane, London, 1692). 1693.

Verse

The Medal of John Bayes: A Satire Against Folly and Knavery. 1682.
A Lenten Prologue. 1683.
The Tenth Satire of Juvenal. 1687.
A Congratulatory Poem on His Highness the Prince of Orange His Coming into England. 1689.
A Congratulatory Poem to the Most Illustrious Queen Mary upon Her Arrival in England. 1689.
Ode on the Anniversary of the King's Birth. 1690.
Ode to the King, on His Return from Ireland. 1690(?).
Votum Perenne: A Poem to the King on New Year's Day. 1692.
Ode on the King's Birthday. 1692.

Other

Notes and Observations on The Empress of Morocco by Settle, with Dryden and John Crowne. 1674.
Some Reflections upon the Pretended Parallel in the Play "The Duke of Guise". 1683.

*

Bibliographies

J.M. Armistead and W. Bies, *Four Restoration Playwrights: A Reference Guide*, Boston, 1984.

Criticism

Books:
Albert S. Borgman, *Thomas Shadwell: His Life and Comedies*, New York, 1928.
Michael W. Alssid, *Thomas Shadwell*, New York, 1967.
Don Kinz, *The Drama of Thomas Shadwell*, Salzburg, 1972.
August Steiger, *Thomas Shadwell "Libertine": A Complementary Study to the Don-Juan Literature*, Hildesheim, 1975.
M.F. McBride, *Folklore of Dryden's England: Gleanings from the Plays of MacFlecknoe*, Washington, DC, 1982.
Brian Corman, "Thomas Shadwell and the Jonsonian Comedy of the Restoration", in *From Renaissance to Restoration: Metamorphoses of the Drama*, edited by Robert Markley and Laurie Finke, Cleveland, Ohio, 1984.

* * *

Next to Etherege, Wycherley, and perhaps Dryden, Thomas Shadwell was the most important writer of English stage comedy in the first generation after the 1660 Restoration. Between 1668 and 1692, 19 of his plays were produced, 15 of them comedies. His sustained level of productivity was unrivaled by his contemporaries. Almost all of his plays had at least respectable first runs, and nine remained in the repertory, with varying degrees of success, into the 18th century.

Shadwell was the most self-conscious follower of Ben Jonson after the Restoration. His early comedies are supported by polemical prefaces, prologues, and epilogues, calling for the recognition of Jonsonian "humours" comedy as the central and most valuable tradition in English comedy. In his first play, *The Sullen Lovers*, Shadwell followed in his master's footsteps by concentrating on fashionable London follies. Its initial success was due largely to the caricature of Sir Robert Howard as Sir Positive At-All. Sir Positive is but one of the many fools who dominated Shadwell's early plays. Like the early Jonson, Shadwell here subordinated the larger concerns of plot to the display of humours. But Shadwell differed significantly from Jonson in his conception of humours comedy. Jonson presented his humours characters in order to purge them of their vices and follies. For Shadwell, the stage was a mirror in which the audience was to recognize its vices and follies in order to correct them. There was no longer a need to correct the characters on stage, a change that modified the Jonsonian humour, at least in theory, almost beyond recognition.

It was with *Epsom Wells* (1672), his sixth play, that Shadwell reached maturity as a dramatist. Again, like Jonson, he entered a middle period when his obsession with humours was mitigated by closer attention to the other elements of drama, particularly plot construction and the representation of non-humours characters. He also came to terms with the kind of comedy increasingly preferred by Restoration audiences, a comedy that included love intrigues and considerable attention to sex. In 1671, Shadwell claimed that Etherege's *She Would if She Could* (1668) was "the best comedy that has been written since the restoration of the stage". Shadwell then followed Etherege's lead in using traditional comic plot elements to contain and structure his presentation of humours. The balance does not duplicate Etherege's, as Shadwell's first interest—and greatest skill—remained with his humours. But Shadwell's version provided him with a flexible formula that made him a successful comic playwright.

In *Epsom Wells*, Shadwell included not only two pairs of witty lovers on their way to matrimony, but also an early and sceptical view of what happens after marriage. His interest in marital discord signalled the darker side of his comedy, one that would recur frequently in the 1670's, and one that led naturally to his experiments in tragedy. *The Libertine* and *Timon of Athens* extended the satiric examination of human vice and folly that began with the early humours beyond the realm of comedy. Don John, the protagonist in *The Libertine* (Shadwell's version of Molière's *Dom Juan*), is the Restoration rake taken to his extreme but logical conclusion, a rapist and murderer whose demonic energies are so far out of control that he is beyond reform or redemption. Timon (in Shadwell's adaptation of Shakespeare's play) is a less violent character than John, but he too allows his personal instincts, ultimately misanthropic, to dominate him so thoroughly that he cannot maintain his place in society. Both of these tragic figures share many of the attractive features of the comic heroes of the Restoration stage. Like the Jonson of *Sejanus*, Shadwell showed that there was nothing inherently good in the qualities so often favored in the comedy of the period.

The Virtuoso (1676), the middle play in the Shadwell canon, is usually considered his finest. Like *Epsom Wells*, it mixes love intrigue and humours comedy with a liberal sprinkling of sex and farce. Sir Nicholas Gimcrack, the title character, is an ardent practitioner of speculative pseudo-science as well as the guardian of the two young women of the marriage plot. Their lovers disguise themselves as fellow virtuosi in order to gain access to the household and fend off the challenge of their rival suitors, two more vintage Shadwell humours—an orator and a witwoud. Shadwell also includes Sir Nicholas's uncle, an old man who longs for the better days of his youth, the whores for both uncle and nephew, the lustful Lady Gimcrack, and her gigolo, in an effective display of Shadwellian comedy at its best.

Other noteworthy plays of Shadwell's middle period include: *A True Widow*, with its interesting treatment of a highly successful female rogue, a play that has impressed recent critics far more than its original audience; *The Woman-Captain*, with a title character who resorts to cross-dressing to gain freedom and power—it is generally considered a potboiler, though it pleased its original audience and was performed in London as late as 1744; and *The Lancashire Witches*, which was heavily censored because of its partisan Whig politics, but, despite severe cutting, was one of Shadwell's longest running plays—it seemed to have provoked a seven-year period of absence from the stage, ended only by the Revolution of 1688.

Shadwell's final five plays form a third unit; again, like Jonson, he ended his career with mellower, more experimental plays. *The Squire of Alsatia* was the greatest success of Shadwell's career and the play that remained the longest in the repertory. Shadwell's adaptation of Terence's *Adelphi* explores alternative models for educating the young, as a young man who has known harsh treatment in the country is contrasted with his brother, who has enjoyed a liberal, urban upbringing. To no one's surprise, the harsh methods inflicted on the country son are repudiated; what makes the play challenging is that the methods applied to the second son do not go unquestioned. Shadwell was rewarded with the laureateship soon after, and lived to write four more plays, most notably *Bury Fair*, as well as the required laureate verse that he added to his earlier, largely satirical, occasional poems.

—Brian Corman

See also *Volume 1* entry on *The Virtuoso*.

————

SHAFFER, Peter (Levin). Born in Liverpool, Lancashire, England, 15 May 1926; twin brother of the playwright Anthony Shaffer. Educated at a preparatory school in Liverpool; Hall School, London; St. Paul's School, London; Trinity College, Cambridge (co-editor, *Granta*), 1947–50, BA in history 1950. Conscript coalminer, Chislet colliery, Kent, 1944–47; worked in Doubleday bookstore, an airline terminal, at Grand Central Station, Lord and Taylors department store, and in the acquisition department, New York Public Library, all New York, 1951–54; staff member, Boosey and Hawkes, music publishers, London, 1954–55; literary critic, *Truth*, London, 1956–57; first-produced play, *Five Finger Exercise*, staged 1958; music critic, *Time and Tide*, London, 1961–62. Recipient: New York Drama Critics Circle Award, 1960, 1975; Tony Award, 1975, 1981; Outer Critics Circle Award, 1981; Vernon Rice Award, 1981; Oscar, for screenplay, 1985. CBE (Commander, Order of the British Empire), 1987.

Works

Collections

The Collected Plays (revised texts; includes *Five Finger Exercise; The Private Ear; The Public Eye; The Royal Hunt of the Sun; White Liars; Black Comedy; Equus; Shrivings; Amadeus*). 1982.

Stage Works

Five Finger Exercise (produced Comedy Theatre, London, 1958). 1958.
The Private Ear, and The Public Eye (produced Globe Theatre, London, 1962). 1962.
The Merry Roosters' Panto, music and lyrics by Stanley Myers and Steven Vinaver (produced Wyndham's Theatre, London, 1963; as *It's About Cinderella*, produced London, 1969).
Sketch in *The Establishment* (produced New York, 1963).
The Royal Hunt of the Sun: A Play Concerning the Conquest of Peru (produced Festival Theatre, Chichester, 1964). 1965.
Black Comedy (produced Festival Theatre, Chichester, 1965). In *"Black Comedy", Including "White Lies"*, 1967.

White Lies (produced Ethel Barrymore Theatre, New York, 1967). In *"Black Comedy", Including "White Lies"*, 1967; as *White Liars* (produced Lyric Theatre, Hammersmith, London, 1968), 1967; revised version (produced Shaw Theatre, London, 1976), 1976.

Shrivings (as *The Battle of Shrivings*, produced Lyric Theatre, Hammersmith, London, 1970; revised version, as *Shrivings*, produced New York, 1975). 1974.

Equus (produced by the National Theatre, Old Vic, London, 1973). 1973.

Amadeus (produced National Theatre, London, 1979). 1980; revised version (produced Broadhurst Theatre, New York, 1980), 1981.

Black Mischief (produced Bristol, 1983).

Yonadab (produced National Theatre, London, 1985). Revised version, with *Lettice and Lovage*, 1989.

Lettice and Lovage (produced Theatre Royal, Haymarket, London, 1987; revised version produced Globe Theatre, London, 1988). 1988; revised version, with *Yonadab*, 1989.

The Gift of the Gorgon (produced The Pit, Barbican Centre, London, 1992). 1993.

Screenplays

Lord of the Flies, with Peter Brook, 1963; *The Public Eye* (*Follow Me!*), 1972; *Equus*, 1977; *Amadeus*, 1984.

Television Plays

The Salt Land, 1955; *Balance of Terror*, 1957.

Radio Plays

Alexander the Corrector, 1946; *The Prodigal Father*, 1957; *Whom Do I Have the Honour of Addressing?*, 1989 (published 1990).

Fiction

The Woman in the Wardrobe. 1951.
How Doth the Little Crocodile? with Anthony Shaffer. 1952.
Withered Murder, with Anthony Shaffer. 1955.
Whom Do I Have the Honour of Addressing? 1990.

*

Bibliographies

Dennis A. Klein, *Peter and Anthony Shaffer: A Reference Guide*, Boston, 1982.
Thomas Eberle, *Peter Shaffer: An Annotated Bibliography*, New York, 1991.

Criticism

Books:
John Russell Taylor, *Peter Shaffer*, London, 1974.
Dennis A. Klein, *Peter Shaffer*, Boston, 1979.
Virginia Cooke and Malcolm Page (compilers), *File on Shaffer*, London, 1987.
Gene A. Plunka, *Peter Shaffer: Roles, Rites and Rituals in the Theater*, Rutherford, New Jersey, 1988.
Petra Iking, *Strukturen gestörter Kommunikation in den Dramen Peter Shaffers*, Essen, 1989.

C.J. Gianakaris (ed.), *Peter Shaffer: A Casebook*, New York, 1991.

* * *

Peter Shaffer is an anomaly in today's theatre world: he writes dramas that probe metaphysical issues of the grandest intellectual order, at the same time fashioning them into theatrically rich spectacles which become smash hits on commercial stages around the world. Moreover, he has successfully staged plays written in a wide range of theatrical styles, from meticulous naturalism to epic stylisation and slapstick farce. He is one of the few dramatists now writing whose each new play becomes a theatre event.

One source of Shaffer's broad-based popularity is the duality of his themes. He shrewdly combines concerns for man as social creature and man the spiritual seeker. Shaffer's earlier pieces are set in contemporary times and centre on domestic issues. *Five Finger Exercise*, his first work, in some ways resembles other dramas of social realism by Osborne, Wesker, and Miller then dominating world stages. Like those plays, *Five Finger Exercise* displays a timely topic conveyed through well-rounded, well-motivated characters. Yet, audiences sense more in Shaffer's work than polemics to set right social evils. Psychological probes into each of the five characters, which reveal people searching for their true selves within personal and social morality, add philosophical resonance to his plays. And with Shaffer, morality always is a factor of deific order. Latent here is an attempt to locate and define the logic of a god-driven cosmos.

The early one-act comedies examine the joys and pitfalls of love, often concluding on a bittersweet note. Although witty and full of laughs, the one-acters *The Private Ear* and *White Lies* end with characters sceptically contemplating a nonbenevolent world at best. There exists a lighter side in Shaffer's humour. *The Public Eye* is resolved merrily in the traditional comic fashion with love reavowed in a marriage context. *Black Comedy* is peopled with numerous zany characters to produce Shaffer's fine all-out farce. After 25 years of writing more serious dramas, Shaffer recently returned to his comedy lodestone with *Lettice and Lovage*, an elegantly written, highly articulate, and effectively funny work. With it, Shaffer reasserted his genuine ability with comedy.

Yet, except occasionally in some of the comedies, Peter Shaffer's dramatic parables inevitably conclude on a sceptical note echoing the existential ethos of the times. His favourite theme long has involved a search for answers to metaphysical puzzles: is there a deity to lend order to a seemingly unjust universe, and if so, what should our relationship be to him? And if no God exists, how does man intuit an order—call it morality—through which to lead a satisfying life? Time and again his protagonists nearly catch the elusive God sought in each play, but are stymied when no firm evidence arises to confirm God's existence. Walter Langer's idealism in *Five Finger Exercise* is shown to be misguided; Pizarro's momentary display of faith leads instead to profound disillusionment in *Royal Hunt*; Sir Petrie's unshakable faith in *Shrivings* is shattered by Mark's raw evil; Dysart ultimately conspires with society to cut off Alan's personal horse-god in *Equus*; Salieri is double-crossed in *Amadeus* by his more cunning godly adversary; Yonadab futilely tries to construct his own godhead among mortals. Shaffer's searching hero is not Voltaire's innocent Candide but Camus's existential Meursault.

With such thematic moorings, it is logical that Shaffer will be best remembered for his serious dramas. Even before *Five*

Finger Exercise reached the stage, he had a draft written of what would become *The Royal Hunt of the Sun*. *Royal Hunt* was a pivotal work in Shaffer's career, because it codified so many of the themes and techniques he was anxious to try on stage. His view of the metaphysical conundrums facing humankind was hinted at in *Five Finger Exercise*, but did not unfold in full complexity until *Royal Hunt*. *The Battle of Shrivings*—Shaffer's only unmitigated disaster in the theatre—centred on the same problem, but failed theatrically because of unrelatable characters and stifled rhetoric. *Equus*, however, succeeded mightily because its story allowed for metaphysical queries to be manifested effectively in a contemporary fable. An intriguing plot, coupled with ingenuity of theatrical devices, promise *Equus* will remain a modern classic.

Amadeus generally is considered Shaffer's finest work to date, and perhaps one of the greatest theatrical achievements of our time. All of the ingredients for an engrossing stage work are here. Beginning with the well-publicized rivalry between Mozart and another musician in Emperor Joseph II's Viennese court, one Antonio Salieri, Shaffer contrives an ingenious tale of 18th-century intrigue. Appropriate theatrical technique is essential for this drama to work—a need adroitly answered by the playwright. The events in *Amadeus* all are seen through the eyes of Salieri, a factor facilitated by having Salieri both an active participant in the plot *and* the narrator who steps outside the story to address the audience directly. Structured as a giant detective story, Shaffer's drama has mesmerized and pleased audiences both in its stage version and as an eight-Oscar-winning film. *Yonadab* again focuses on a God-seeking protagonist, and the play proved modestly successful. *Lettice and Lovage*, though a comedy and less adventuresome than the dramas, confirms the playwright's mastery of theatre, serious and humourous.

Paradoxically, Shaffer elicits passionate dislike from some intellectuals who resent that his intelligent play-scripts which concern thought-provoking themes can possibly gain enormous popularity with audiences. Yet the seeming anomaly is explained by Shaffer's powerful stage techniques. He produces possibly the most articulate dialogue written today for the theatre. Additionally, he eagerly seeks fresh, daring staging techniques suggestive of Brecht, Wilder, and Artaud. The result, as critic Simon Trussler notes, is that Shaffer "remains one of our very few dramatists able to command with assurance *all* the resources of the stage, with an almost Elizabethan feeling for the impact . . . of the visual dimension of theatre".

—C.J. Gianakaris

See also *Volume 1* entries on *Equus*; *The Royal Hunt of the Sun*.

SHAKESPEARE, William. Born in Stratford-on-Avon, Warwickshire, England; baptized 26 April 1564. Educated probably at King's New School, Stratford, 1571–77. Married Anne Hathaway in 1582; two daughters and one son. Possibly taught at a school in or near Stratford; moved to London c. 1588; well-known as an actor and had begun to write for the stage by 1592; shareholder in the Lord Chamberlain's Men (after James I's accession in 1603, called the King's Men) by 1594, and co-owner of their playhouse from 1598: company

Title-page of the 1623 First Folio of works by **William Shakespeare**.

performed at the Globe Theatre from 1599, and also at the Blackfriars Theatre after 1608; bought New Place in Stratford, 1597, and acquired land in Stratford; retired to Stratford c.1611–13. Texts (not all considered authoritative) of his plays collected for the first time in *Comedies, Histories, and Tragedies* (the First Folio), 1623. Died in Stratford-on-Avon, 23 April 1616.

Works

Collections (the First Folio and major modern editions)

Comedies, Histories, and Tragedies (First Folio), edited by John Heming and Henry Condell. 1623.
Works (multi-volume New Variorum Edition), edited by H. H. Furness and others. 1871—
Works (New Shakespeare edition), edited by J. Dover Wilson and Arthur Quiller-Couch. 1921–66.

The New Arden Shakespeare (multi-volume series), edited by Una Ellis-Fermor and others. 1951—
Complete Works, edited by Peter Alexander. 1951.
Complete Works, edited by C. J. Sisson. 1954.
The New Penguin Shakespeare, edited by T.J.B. Spencer. 1967—
Complete Works (Pelican Shakespeare), edited by Alfred Harbage. 1969.
The Riverside Shakespeare, edited by G. Blakemore Evans and others. 1974.
New Cambridge Shakespeare (newly edited versions based on the New Shakespeare edition), various editors. 1984—
Complete Works (Oxford Shakespeare; contains two versions of *King Lear*), edited by Stanley Wells and Gary Taylor (general editors). 1986; *Original-Spelling Edition*, 1986; *A Textual Companion*, 1987; some plays have appeared in single editions, with textual and critical apparatus, from 1982.

Stage Works

Plays after c.1594 produced by Lord Chamberlain's Men (King's Men after 1603), probably mainly at their Globe Theatre, London.

Henry VI, part 1 (produced 1589–91?). In First Folio, 1623.
Henry VI, part 2 (produced 1590–92?). 1594 ("bad" quarto).
Henry VI, part 3 (produced 1590–92?). 1595 ("bad" quarto).
Romeo and Juliet (produced 1591–96?). 1597 ("bad" quarto); "good" quarto, 1599.
The Comedy of Errors (produced 1591–94?). In First Folio, 1623.
Richard III (produced 1592?). 1597.
The Two Gentlemen of Verona (produced 1592–98?). In First Folio, 1623.
Titus Andronicus (produced 1592–94?). 1594.
The Taming of the Shrew (produced before 1592?). As *The Taming of a Shrew*, 1594; without Christopher Sly episodes, in First Folio, 1623.
King John (produced 1594–96?). In First Folio, 1623.
Love's Labour's Lost (produced 1594?). 1598.
Richard II (produced 1595?). 1597.
A Midsummer Night's Dream (produced 1596?). 1600.
Henry IV, part 1 (produced 1596–98?). 1598.
The Merchant of Venice (produced 1596–97?). 1600.
Henry IV, part 2 (produced 1597–98?). 1600.
The Merry Wives of Windsor (produced 1598–99?). 1602 ("bad" quarto).
Much Ado About Nothing (produced 1598–99?). 1600.
Henry V (produced 1598–99). 1600 ("bad" quarto).
Julius Caesar (produced 1599). In First Folio, 1623.
As You Like It (produced 1599?). In First Folio, 1623.
Hamlet (produced 1599–1601?). 1603 ("bad" quarto); "good" quarto, 1604.
Twelfth Night; or, What You Will (produced 1601–02?). In First Folio, 1623.
Troilus and Cressida (produced 1602–03?). 1609.
All's Well That Ends Well (produced 1602?). In First Folio, 1623.
Othello (produced 1602–03?). 1622.
Macbeth (produced 1602–06?). In First Folio, 1623.
Measure for Measure (produced 1603–04?). In First Folio, 1623.
King Lear (produced 1605). 1608 ("bad" quarto).

Antony and Cleopatra (produced 1606?). In First Folio, 1623.
Coriolanus (produced 1607–10?). In First Folio, 1623.
Timon of Athens (produced 1607?). In First Folio, 1623.
Pericles, possibly with George Wilkins (produced 1608?). 1609.
Cymbeline (produced 1610?). In First Folio, 1623.
The Tempest (produced 1610–11?). In First Folio, 1623.
The Winter's Tale (produced 1611?). In First Folio, 1623.
Henry VIII, with Fletcher (produced 1612?; definitely produced 1613). In First Folio, 1623.
The Two Noble Kinsmen, with Fletcher (produced 1613?). 1634.
Sir Thomas More, with Munday and others (produced 1954). Edited by Alexander Dyce, 1844, and by Vittorio Gabrieli and Giorgio Melchiori, 1990.

Verse (early editions)

Venus and Adonis. 1593.
Lucrece. 1594; as *The Rape of Lucrece*, 1616.
Sonnets. 1609.
Poems. 1640.

*

Bibliographies

Walther Ebisch and Levin L. Shucking, *A Shakespeare Bibliography*, Oxford, 1931; supplement, 1937.
Gordon Ross Smith, *A Classified Shakespeare Bibliography 1936–1958*, University Park, Pennyslvania, 1963.
J.W. Velz, *Shakespeare and the Classical Tradition: A Critical Guide to the Commentary 1660–1960*, Minneapolis, 1968.
E.G. Quinn, J. Ruoff, and J. Grennen, *The Major Shakespearian Tragedies: A Critical Bibliography*, New York, 1973.
Stanley Wells (ed.), *Shakespeare: Select Bibliographical Guide*, London, 1973; revised and augmented edition, Oxford, 1990.
David Bevington, *Shakespeare*, Arlington Heights, Illinois, 1978 (Goldentree Bibliographies).
Larry S. Champion, *The Essential Shakespeare: An Annotated Bibliography of Major Modern Studies*, Boston, 1986.
David M. Bergeron and Geraldo U. de Sousa, *Shakespeare: A Study and Research Guide*, Lawrence, Kansas, 1987.
Philip C. Kolin, *Shakespeare and Feminist Criticism: An Annotated Bibliography and Commentary*, New York and London, 1991.

See also the annual bibliography in *Shakespeare Quarterly*, 1950—

Criticism

Books:
William Hazlitt, *Characters of Shakespeare's Plays*, London, 1817.
A.C. Bradley, *Shakespearean Tragedy*, London, 1904.
M.W. MacCallum, *Shakespeare's Roman Plays and Their Background*, London, 1910.
E.K. Chambers, *Shakespeare: A Survey*, London, 1925.
Harley Granville Barker, *Prefaces to Shakespeare* (5 vols.), London, 1927–48; revised edition (2 vols.), 1946–47; edited by Muriel St. Clare Byrne (4 vols.), 1963.

John Dover Wilson, *Six Tragedies of Shakespeare: An Introduction for the Plain Man*, London, 1929.

T.M. Raysor (ed.), *Coleridge's Shakespearean Criticism* (2 vols.), London, 1930.

Lily B. Campbell, *Shakespeare's Tragic Heroes: Slaves of Passion*, Cambridge, 1930.

E.K. Chambers, *Shakespeare: A Study of Facts and Problems* (2 vols.), London, 1930.

G. Wilson Knight, *The Wheel of Fire: Essays in Interpretation of Shakespeare's Sombre Tragedies*, London, 1930; revised edition, 1949.

G. Wilson Knight, *The Imperial Theme: Further Interpretations of Shakespeare's Tragedies, Including the Roman Plays*, London, 1931.

William Witherle Lawrence, *Shakespeare's Problem Comedies*, New York, 1931.

Caroline Spurgeon, *Shakespeare's Imagery and What it Tells Us*, Cambridge, 1935.

Derek A. Traversi, *An Approach to Shakespeare*, London and Glasgow, 1938; revised edition, 1956; third edition (2 vols.), 1968–69.

Alfred Harbage, *Shakespeare's Audience*, New York, 1941.

Theodore Spencer, *Shakespeare and the Nature of Man*, Cambridge, 1943.

S.L. Bethell, *Shakespeare and the Popular Dramatic Tradition*, Westminster, 1944.

G. Wilson Knight, *The Olive and the Sword: A Study of England's Shakespeare*, London, 1944.

E.M.W. Tillyard, *Shakespeare's History Plays*, London, 1944.

J.L. Palmer, *Political Characters in Shakespeare*, London, 1945.

J.L. Palmer, *Comic Characters in Shakespeare*, London, 1946.

Lily B. Campbell, *Shakespeare's "Histories"*, San Marino, California, 1947.

Eric Partridge, *Shakespeare's Bawdy*, London, 1947; revised edition, 1969.

G. Wilson Knight, *The Crown of Life: Essays in Interpretation of Shakespeare's Final Plays*, London, 1947.

J.I.M. Stewart, *Character and Motive in Shakespeare: Some Recent Appraisals Examined*, London, 1949.

Willard Farnham, *Shakespeare's Tragic Frontier: The World of His Final Tragedies*, Berkeley (California) and Los Angeles, 1950.

E.M.W. Tillyard, *Shakespeare's Problem Plays*, London, 1950.

Wolfgang Clemen, *The Development of Shakespeare's Imagery*, London, 1951.

H.C. Goddard, *The Meaning of Shakespeare*, Chicago, 1951.

Arthur Sewell, *Character and Society in Shakespeare*, Oxford, 1951.

W.W. Greg, *The Editorial Problems in Shakespeare: A Survey of the Foundations of the Text*, Oxford, 1954.

John Russell Brown, *Shakespeare and His Comedies*, London, 1957.

Geoffrey Bullough (ed.), *Narrative and Dramatic Sources of Shakespeare* (8 vols.), London and New York, 1957–75.

M.M. Mahood, *Shakespeare's Wordplay*, London, 1957.

Irving Ribner, *The English History Plays in the Age of Shakespeare*, Princeton, New Jersey, 1957.

Kenneth Muir, *Shakespeare and the Tragic Pattern*, 1958

Bernard Spivack, *Shakespeare and the Allegory of Evil*, London and New York, 1958.

C.L. Barber, *Shakespeare's Festive Comedy: A Study of Dramatic Form and its Relation to Social Custom*, Princeton, New Jersey, 1959.

Bertrand Evans, *Shakespeare's Comedies*, Oxford, 1960.

Irving Ribner, *Patterns in Shakespeare's Tragedy*, London, 1960.

John Holloway, *The Story of the Night: Studies in Shakespeare's Major Tragedies*, 1961.

Kenneth Muir, *Shakespeare's Sources* (2 vols.), London, 1961.

Kenneth Muir and Una Ellis Fermor, *Shakespeare the Dramatist*, London, 1961.

Robert Ornstein (ed.), *Discussions of Shakespeare's Problem Comedies*, Boston, 1961.

M.M. Reese, *The Cease of Majesty: A Study of Shakespeare's History Plays*, London, 1961.

John Russell Taylor and Bernard Harris (ed.), *Early Shakespeare*, London, 1961.

Bernard Beckerman, *Shakespeare at the Globe 1599–1609*, New York, 1962.

Anne Righter, *Shakespeare and the Idea of the Play*, London, 1962.

John Dover Wilson, *Shakespeare's Happy Comedies*, London, 1962.

Charlton Hinman, *The Printing and Proof-Reading of the First Folio of Shakespeare* (2 vols.), Oxford, 1963.

Roland M. Frye, *Shakespeare and Christian Doctrine*, Princeton (New Jersey) and London, 1963.

Alfred Harbage, *Shakespeare: A Reader's Guide*, 1963.

Frank Kermode, *William Shakespeare: The Final Plays*, London, 1963.

T.J.B. Spencer, *William Shakespeare: The Roman Plays*, London, 1963.

Nevill Coghill, *Shakespeare's Professional Skills*, Cambridge, 1964.

Jan Kott, *Shakespeare, Our Contemporary*, London, 1964.

Maurice Charney (ed.), *Discussions of Shakespeare's Roman Plays*, Boston, 1964.

Northrop Frye, *A Natural Perspective: The Development of Shakespearean Comedy and Romance*, New York and London, 1965.

Robert G. Hunter, *Shakespeare and the Comedy of Forgiveness*, New York and London, 1965.

Frank Kermode (ed.), *Four Centuries of Shakespearian Criticism*, New York, 1965.

Kenneth Muir (ed.), *Shakespeare: The Comedies: A Collection of Critical Essays*, Englewood Cliffs, New Jersey, 1965.

Gordon Ross Smith (ed.), *Essays on Shakespeare*, University Park, Pennsylvania, 1965.

E.M. Waith (ed.), *Shakespeare: The Histories: A Collection of Critical Essays*, Englewood Cliffs, New Jersey, 1965.

O.J. Campbell and Edward G. Quinn (eds.), *The Reader's Encyclopedia of Shakespeare*, 1966.

John Russell Brown, *Shakespeare's Plays in Performance*, London, 1966.

Northrop Frye, *Fools of Time: Studies in Shakespearean Tragedy*, Toronto and London, 1967.

D.G. James, *The Dream of Prospero*, Oxford, 1967.

G. Wilson Knight, *Shakespeare and Religion: Essays of Forty Years*, London, 1967.

L. Lernber, *Shakespeare's Comedies: An Anthology of Modern Criticism*, Harmondsworth, 1967.

Arthur Sherbo (ed.), *Johnson on Shakespeare* (2 vols.), 1968.

L.S. Champion, *The Evolution of Shakespeare's Comedy*, Cambridge, Massachusetts, 1970.

Andrew Gurr, *The Shakespearean Stage*, Cambridge, 1970; revised edition, 1980; further revised edition, 1991.

Francis Fergusson, *Shakespeare: The Pattern in His Carpet*, New York, 1970.

Samuel Schoenbaum, *Shakespeare's Lives*, Oxford, 1970; revised edition, 1991.

R.A. Foakes, *Shakespeare: The Dark Comedies to the Last Plays*, London, 1971.

Kenneth Muir and Samuel Schoenbaum (eds.), *A New Companion to Shakespeare Studies*, London, 1971.

H. Felperin, *Shakespeare and Romance*, Princeton, New Jersey, 1972.

Leslie Fiedler, *The Stranger in Shakespeare*, New York, 1972.

Joan Hartwig, *Shakespeare's Tragicomic Vision*, Baton Rouge, Louisianna, 1972.

Kenneth Muir, *Shakespeare's Tragic Sequence*, London and Liverpool, 1972.

Robert Ornstein, *A Kingdom for a Stage: The Achievement of Shakespeare's History Plays*, Cambridge, Massachusetts, 1972.

H. Smith, *Shakespeare's Romances*, San Marino, California, 1972.

David P. Young, *The Heart's Forest: A Study of Shakespeare's Pastoral Plays*, New Haven (Connecticut) and London, 1972.

Maynard Mack Jr., *Killing the King: Three Studies in Shakespeare's Tragic Structure*, New Haven (Connecticut) and London, 1973.

Bernard McElroy, *Shakespeare's Mature Tragedies*, Princeton, New Jersey, 1973.

Kenneth Muir, *Shakespeare the Professional and Related Studies*, London, 1973.

D.L. Peterson, *Time, Tide, and Tempest: A Study of Shakespeare's Romances*, San Marino, California, 1973.

M.E. Prior, *The Drama of Power: Studies in Shakespeare's History Plays*, Evanston, Illinois, 1973.

J.L. Simmons, *Shakespeare's Pagan World: The Roman Tragedies*, Charlottesville, Virginia, 1973.

Robert Speaight, *Shakespeare on the Stage: An Illustrated History of Shakespearean Performance*, London, 1973.

Alexander Leggatt, *Shakeapeare's Comedy of Love*, London, 1974.

Leo Salingar, *Shakespeare and the Traditions of Comedy*, London, 1974.

Robert Y. Turner, *Shakespeare's Apprenticeship*, Chicago and London, 1974.

Brian Vickers (ed.), *Shakespeare: The Critical Heritage 1623–1801* (6 vols.), London, 1974–81.

Marjorie B. Garber, *Dream in Shakespeare: From Metaphor to Metamorphosis*, New Haven (Connecticut) and London, 1974.

E.J. Berry, *Patterns of Decay: Shakespeare's Early Histories*, Charlottesville, Virginia, 1975.

Samuel Schoenbaum, *William Shakespeare: A Documentary Life*, Oxford, 1975.

M.C. Bradbrook, *The Living Monument: Shakespeare and the Theatre of His Time*, Cambridge, 1976.

E.A.J. Honigmann, *Shakespeare: Seven Tragedies: The Dramatist's Manipulation of Response*, London, 1976.

Robert G. Hunter, *Shakespeare and the Majesty of God's Judgement*, Athens, Georgia, 1976.

Harry Levin (ed.), *Shakespeare and the Revolution of the Times: Perspectives and Commentaries*, New York, 1976.

Giorgio Melchiori, *Shakespeare's Dramatic Meditations: An Experiment in Criticism*, London, 1976.

Barbara Mowat, *The Dramaturgy of Shakespeare's Romances*, Athens, Georgia, 1976.

Paul A. Cantor, *Shakespeare's Rome: Republic and Empire*, Ithaca (New York) and London, 1976.

Peter Saccio, *Shakespeare's English Kings: History, Chronicle, and Drama*, London, 1977.

Robert Speaight, *Shakespeare: The Man and His Achievement*, London, 1977.

John Wilders, *The Lost Garden: A View of Shakespeare's English and Roman History Plays*, London, 1978.

Bertrand Evans, *Shakespeare's Tragic Practice*, Oxford, 1979.

L.C. Knights, *Hamlet and Other Shakespearean Essays*, Cambridge, 1979.

Kenneth Muir, *Shakespeare's Comic Sequence*, Liverpool, 1979.

Samuel Schoenbaum, *Shakespeare: The Globe and the World*, New York and Oxford, 1979.

Susan Snyder, *The Comic Matrix of Shakespeare's Tragedies*, Princeton (New Jersey) and Guildford, Surrey, 1979.

Ruth Nevo, *Comic Transformations in Shakespeare*, London, 1980.

Norman Rabkin, *Shakespeare and the Problem of Meaning*, Chicago and London, 1980.

M.M. Reese, *Shakespeare: His World and His Work* (revised edition), London, 1980.

Murray M. Schwartz and Coppelia Kahn (eds.), *Representing Shakespeare*, Baltimore (Maryland) and London, 1980.

John Bayley, *Shakespeare and Tragedy*, London, 1981.

Ralph Berry, *Changing Styles in Shakespeare*, London, 1981.

G.R. Hibbard, *The Making of Shakespeare's Dramatic Poetry*, Toronto, 1981.

Samuel Schoenbaum, *William Shakespeare: Records and Images*, London, 1981.

R.P. Wheeler, *Shakespeare's Development and the Problem Comedies*, Berkeley, California, 1981.

E.A.J. Honigmann, *Shakespeare's Impact on His Contemporaries*, London, 1982.

Northrop Frye, *The Myth of Deliverance: Reflections on Shakespeare's Problem Comedies*, Brighton, Sussex, 1983.

R.S. Miola, *Shakespeare's Rome*, Cambridge, 1983.

David Sundelson, *Shakespeare's Restoration of the Father*, New Brunswick, New Jersey, 1983.

M. Bradbury and D. Palmer (eds.), *Shakespearean Tragedy*, London, 1984.

Jonathon Dollimore, *Radical Tragedy*, Chicago, 1984.

Keir Elam, *Shakespeare's Universe of Discourse*, Cambridge, 1984.

L.L. Harris, M.W. Scott, and others, *Shakespearian Criticism*, Detroit, 1984– (annual anthologies).

R.B. Heilman (ed.), *Shakespeare: The Tragedies: New Perspectives*, Englewood Cliffs, New Jersey, 1984.

W.C. Carroll, *The Metamorphoses of Shakespearean Comedy*, Princeton, New Jersey, 1985.

Jonathon Dollimore and Alan Sinfield (eds.), *Political Shakespeare*, Manchester, 1985.

John Drakakis (ed.), *Alternative Shakespeares*, London and New York, 1985.

Peter Erickson, *Patriarchal Structures in Shakespeare's Drama*, Berkeley (California) and London, 1985.

M. Goldman, *Acting and Action in Shakespearean Tragedy*, Princeton, New Jersey, 1985.

Graham Holderness, *Shakespeare's History*, Dublin and New York, 1985.

E.A.J. Honigmann, *Shakespeare: The Lost Years*, Manchester, 1985.

K. Newman, *Shakespeare's Rhetoric of Comic Character*, New York and London, 1985.

Kenneth Muir, *Shakespeare: Contrasts and Controversies*, Brighton, Sussex, 1985.

Samuel Schoenbaum, *Shakespeare and Others*, Washington (DC) and London, 1985.

Gary Taylor, *Moment by Moment by Shakespeare*, London, 1985.

A. Brennan, *Shakespeare's Dramatic Structures*, London, 1986.

Alan C. Dessen, *Shakespeare and the Late Moral Plays*, Lincoln, Nebraska, 1986.

William Empson, *Essays on Shakespeare*, edited by David B. Pirie, Cambridge, 1986.

M. Evans, *Signifying Nothing*, Brighton, Sussex, 1986.

Terry Eagleton, *William Shakespeare*, Oxford, 1986.

Northrop Frye, *On Shakespeare*, edited by R. Sandler, New Haven, Connecticut, 1986.

Robert Ornstein, *Shakespeare's Comedies: From Roman Farce to Romantic Mystery*, Newark, New Jersey, 1986.

Leo Salingar, *Dramatic Form in Shakespeare and the Jacobeans*, Cambridge, 1986.

L. Tennenhouse, *Power on Display: The Politics of Shakespeare's Genres*, New York and London, 1986.

Stanley Wells (ed.), *The Cambridge Companion to Shakespeare Studies*, Cambridge, 1986.

G. Bradshaw, *Shakespeare's Scepticism*, Brighton, Sussex, 1987.

Andrew Gurr, *Playgoing in Shakespeare's London*, Cambridge, 1987.

Ruth Nevo, *Shakespeare's Other Language*, London, 1987.

V. Thomas, *The Moral Universe of Shakespeare's Problem Plays*, London, 1987.

Graham Holderness (ed.), *The Shakespeare Myth*, Manchester, 1988.

Alexander Leggatt, *Shakespeare's Political Drama: The History Plays and the Roman Plays*, London, 1988.

Philip Brockbank, *On Shakespeare*, Oxford, 1989.

J.D. Cox, *Shakespeare and the Dramaturgy of Power*, Princeton, New Jersey, 1989.

E.A.J. Honigmann, *Myriad-Minded Shakespeare*, Basingstoke and London, 1989.

M. and R. Thompson, *Shakespeare and the Sense of Performance*, Newark, New Jersey, 1989.

Charles Boyce, *Shakespeare A-Z*, Oxford and New York, 1990.

C. Pye, *The Regal Phantasm: Shakespeare and the Politics of Spectacle*, London, 1990.

D. Young, *The Action to the Word: Structure and Style in Shakespearean Tragedy*, New Haven, Connecticut, 1990.

Serials:
Shakespeare Survey (annual), 1948—
Shakespeare Quarterly, 1950—
Shakespeare Studies, 1965—

* * *

The greatness of William Shakespeare as a playwright lies beyond dispute. The publication of the Folio of his works in 1623, with its glowing prefatory tributes from actors and playwrights, serves as testimony to his contemporary reputation. Even Ben Jonson, a grudging admirer, characterised his work as "not of an age but for all time". The financial success that allowed Shakespeare to return to Stratford-on-Avon as a leading citizen derived more, probably, from his business success as a sharer in the Lord Chamberlain's Company, later the King's Men, than from the rewards of acting or writing. Yet his career in theatre, from early association with such companies as Strange's or Pembroke's to the relative prominence of his place as major dramatist of the King's Men, with that company's association with Court performance and Court ceremonial, certifies the upward mobility of his professional achievements. Shakespeare's plays were performed in his lifetime in many kinds of theatrical space, from college halls and inns of court to specially built theatres, fit-up spaces on tour, and even on shipboard; from 1599 they were regularly seen at The Globe, on the south bank of the Thames, and from 1608 also at the newly adapted indoor theatre, the Blackfriars. His play-texts were modified to suit varying locations and playing companies; the so-called "bad" quarto of *Hamlet*, published in 1601, looks like a report from memory of a reduced version of the play suitable for performance on tour, while two widely-differing texts of *King Lear*, published in 1608 and 1623, can plausibly be seen as the dramatist's first and revised versions of his greatest tragedy.

For purposes of summary, it is possible to see Shakespeare's writing career as falling into a number of phases. The earliest work is that of the jobbing playwright looking for employment wherever he can get it. The three parts of *King Henry VI*, written around 1590, draw on the theatrical techniques and profit from the stage success of Thomas Kyd and Christopher Marlowe, as well as exploiting a current interest in England's contentious history. *Richard III*, a year or so later, develops that interest by blending historical material with the stage methods and the psychological concerns of tragedy; Shakespeare's earliest essay in that genre, *Titus Andronicus*, had been both lurid and sophisticated, drawing together Elizabethan pleasure in the tragedy of blood and a Renaissance reading of classical literature, especially Ovid. The earliest comedies, *The Taming of the Shrew*, *The Comedy of Errors*, *Love's Labour's Lost*, and *The Two Gentlemen of Verona*, also blend elements from the native English tradition with sophisticated comic structures deriving from Plautus, Terence, and writers of the Italian Renaissance.

These plays of the earlier 1590's established Shakespeare's reputation, and led on through a mixed group of tragedy, history, and comedy—*Romeo and Juliet*, *A Midsummer Night's Dream*, *Richard II*, *The Merchant of Venice*, and perhaps *King John*—towards the core of Shakespeare's playwriting career as a leading dramatist. The plays show an increasingly flexible use of dramatic language, as the inventive brilliance of the earlier comedies makes way for stage-writing that, while still attracted by opportunities for the flamboyant set piece, is more disciplined by character and action. With the *Henry IV* plays, *Henry V*, *As You Like It*, and *Twelfth Night*, all written at the end of the 1590's or the turn of the century, Shakespeare's writing achieved the mature correlation of eloquence and incident, actor's role and stage action, to which his earlier work pointed.

The period of the great tragedies, *Hamlet*, *Othello*, *King Lear*, *Macbeth*, *Antony and Cleopatra*, followed between about 1601 and 1607, providing powerful stage-roles for the company's leading actor Richard Burbage and providing demanding opportunities too for the apprentices, boys or young adults, who played the major women's parts. Interspersed with the tragic writing came mixed-mode plays, neither comic nor tragic, such as *Troilus and Cressida*, *All's Well That Ends Well*, and *Measure for Measure*, experimental pieces, wryly humorous or satiric, depending to a considerable extent on how they are played. Shakespeare's reading of Roman history, especially Plutarch's, had already led, around the turn of the century, to *Julius Caesar*, and about 1607 to *Antony and Cleopatra*, where the texture of the dramatic writing is profoundly influenced by the historian's interests and methods; it now led to *Coriolanus*, and in a somewhat different vein to *Timon of Athens*, a play of trenchantly condensed writing which some critics think an unfinished sketch.

The last segment of Shakespeare's career takes in such plays as *Pericles*, *Cymbeline*, *The Winter's Tale*, *The Tempest*, and *Henry VIII*, the first and last of which are collaborations, *Henry VIII*, probably with John Fletcher, co-author also with Shakespeare of *The Two Noble Kinsmen*, and by this date established as the company's successor to Shakespeare as leading dramatist. Each play shows an interest in spectacular stage action, for example in Jupiter's descent on a property swan in *Cymbeline*, or the masque of Juno and Ceres in *The Tempest*, deriving from new audience tastes, the influence of court patronage, and improved stage technology (including artificial lighting) associated with the use of the indoor Blackfriars as principal playing-space after 1608.

"Shakespeare" means the career described above, but also takes in the performance history of the plays from the 16th century on. In the playwright's lifetime, revivals and command performances at Court provided opportunities for new interpretations, owing to changes in company personnel and changes in audience. Each new era has remade Shakespeare's work in its own idiom, responsive to cultural, architectural, and technical change. Germany, France, and latterly the eastern European countries have created their own "Shakespeares"; in this century distinctively Russian, Japanese, and Chinese "Shakespeares" have emerged; a long tradition of playing Shakespeare in the USA has produced a characteristic American "Shakespeare". "Shakespeare", like all significant terms, is subject to ideological interpretation. As a consequence, his work has been victim and beneficiary of much cultural re-making, testifying to the central place he holds in the national and trans-national imagination.

—J. R. Mulryne

See also *Volume 1* entries on *All's Well That Ends Well*; *Antony and Cleopatra*; *As You Like It*; *The Comedy of Errors*; *Coriolanus*; *Cymbeline*; *Hamlet*; *Henry IV, Parts One and Two*; *Henry V*; *Henry VI, Parts One and Two*; *Henry VIII*; *Julius Caesar*; *King John*; *King Lear*; *Love's Labour's Lost*; *Macbeth*; *Measure for Measure*; *The Merchant of Venice*; *The Merry Wives of Windsor*; *A Midsummer Night's Dream*; *Much Ado About Nothing*; *Othello*; *Pericles*; *Richard II*; *Richard III*; *Romeo and Juliet*; *The Taming of the Shrew*; *The Tempest*; *Timon of Athens*; *Titus Andronicus*; *Troilus and Cressida*; *Twelfth Night*; *The Two Gentlemen of Verona*; *The Two Noble Kinsmen*; *The Winter's Tale*.

SHANGE, Ntozake. Born Paulette Williams in Trenton, New Jersey, USA, 18 October 1948; took name Ntozake Shange in 1971. Educated at schools in St. Louis and New Jersey; Barnard College, New York, 1966–70, BA (cum laude) in American studies 1970; University of Southern California, Los Angeles, 1971–73, MA in American studies 1973. Married David Murray in 1977 (2nd marriage); one daughter. Faculty member, Sonoma State College, Rohnert Park, California, 1973–75, Mills College, Oakland, California, 1975, City College, New York, 1975, Douglass College, New Brunswick, New Jersey, 1978, and University of Houston, from 1983. Artist-in-residence, Equinox Theatre, Houston, from 1981. Recipient: New York Drama Critics Circle Award, 1977; Obie Award, 1977, 1980; New York State Council of the Arts Award, 1981.

Works

Collections

Three Pieces: spell #7; A Photograph: Lovers-in-Motion; Boogie Woogie Landscapes. 1981.
Plays 1 (includes *For Colored Girls Who Have Considered Suicide/When the Rainbow is Enuf; spell #7; I Heard Eric Dolphy in His Eyes; The Love Space Demands: A Continuing Saga*). 1992.

Stage Works

For Colored Girls Who Have Considered Suicide/When the Rainbow is Enuf (produced Bacchanal women's bar, Berkeley, California, 1974). 1976; revised version, 1977.
A Photograph: Lovers-in-Motion (as *A Photograph: A Still Life with Shadows, A Photograph: A Study of Cruelty* produced Shakespeare Festival Public Theatre, New York, 1977; revised version, as *A Photograph: Lovers-in-Motion*, produced Houston, Texas, 1979). 1981.
Where the Mississippi Meets the Amazon, with Thulani Nkabinda and Jessica Hagedorn (produced Shakespeare Festival Public Theatre Cabaret, New York, 1977).
spell #7 (produced Shakespeare Festival Public Theatre, New York, 1979). In *Three Pieces*, 1981; published separately, 1985.
Black and White Two-Dimensional Planes (produced Sounds in Motion Studio Works, New York, 1979).
Boogie Woogie Landscapes (produced New York Writers' Workshop, 1979). In *Three Pieces*, 1981.
Mother Courage and Her Children, from a play by Brecht (produced Shakespeare Festival Public Theatre, New York, 1980).
From Okra to Greens: A Different Kinda Love Story (as *Mouths*, produced Barnard College, New York, 1981; as *From Okra to Greens*, in *Three for a Full Moon*, produced Mark Taper Forum Laboratory, Los Angeles, 1982). 1983.
Three for a Full Moon (produced Mark Taper Forum Laboratory, Los Angeles, 1982).
Bocas (produced Mark Taper Forum Laboratory, Los Angeles, 1982).
Educating Rita, from the play by Willy Russell (produced Mark Taper Forum Laboratory, Alliance Theatre Studio, Atlanta, 1983).
Betsey Brown, from her novel (produced Shakespeare Festival Public Theatre, New York, 1986).
Three Views of Mount Fuji (produced [reading] by New Dramatists, New York, 1987).
The Love Space Demands: A Continuing Saga (produced London, 1992).

Fiction

Sassafrass: A Novella. 1977.
Sassafrass, Cypress and Indigo. 1982.
Betsey Brown. 1985.

Verse

Melissa and Smith. 1976.
Natural Disasters and Other Festive Occasions. 1977.
Nappy Edges. 1978
A Daughter's Geography. 1983.
From Okra to Greens: Poems. 1984.
Ridin' the Moon in Texas: Word Paintings. 1987.

Other

See No Evil: Prefaces, Essays, and Accounts 1976–1983. 1984.

*

Criticism

Books:
Interview with Shange in *In the Memory of Frances, Zora, and Lorraine: Essays and Interviews on Black Women and Writing*, edited by Juliette Bowles, Washington, 1979.

Articles:
Interviews with Shange in: *Massachusetts Review*, 28, 1987; *Black American Literature Forum*, 24, 1990; *Studies in American Drama 1945–Present*, 5, 1990; *Journal of Dramatic Theory and Criticism*, vol. 6 no. 1, 1991.

* * *

Ntozake Shange is best known as the creator of the choreo-poem form for the stage. The choreopoem, a uniquely African-American form of performance, is a collection of related poems combined with song and dance. Shange's famous choreopoem, *For Colored Girls Who Have Considered Suicide/When the Rainbow is Enuf*, allowed the seven women performers, each dressed in a color of the rainbow, to express their emotional experiences in dance, song, and poetry written in African-American dialect. When Shange played the part of the Lady in Orange in the Broadway production, she created a uniquely African-American grammar of gestures and strides to accompany the dialect. Shange has created an innovative, distinctive style of oral and visual presence for the African-American performer.

Shange has also pioneered a sucessful rebellion against the hegemony of the well-made play through creating innovative narrative strategies and through parodying racist representations. In *spell #7*, a giant minstrel mask, suggesting both the horrific minstrel shows performed by whites in black-face and a black African mask, hangs over the stage. The plot of the play consists of struggling actors and actresses taking up the position of narrator as the remaining cast enact the story, so that the actors do not retain fixed identities, but are portrayed as fluid constructions, subjects-in-process. The performers dress up and play racist stereotypes such as "picaninnies", the stereotype of African-Americans as happy farmers. Lou, dressed as the traditional interlocuter of the minstrel show, intervenes between the audience's complicity in accepting the black performers as minstrels by citing black history, confronting them with the implications of racism. In this play, all are under the spell of the black minstrel mask, the sceptre of white culture's appropriation and degradation of African-American art forms, and yet African-American men and women can dis-spell the spell through black magic. This black magic consists of coding "whiteness" as an ethnic category in a reversed minstrel show, as the black cast put on white face and perform "white experience".

In *A Photograph: Lovers in Motion*, Sean's camera functions as the technological equivalent of the minstrel mask in *spell #7*. Sean, a photographer, tries to take control of the means of representation. Shange reveals the camera as a tool that can record the unrepresented, freeing them from domination, at the the same time as the camera itself is a tool of objectification and oppression. In the play, Sean objectifies the female Michael, and his desire to photograph her becomes a means of possessing and dominating her. The play suggests that the camera, which can produce images in black-and-white or color, still can photograph only in black and white; African-Americans cannot merely appropriate the means of representation without subjecting the structure of representation, whether it be the well-made play or photography, to reconsideration.

Boogie Woogie Landscapes dramatizes a woman's dreams, memories, and experiences in a stream-of-consciousness style. As in *spell #7*, Layla and the other six characters are night-life performers who sing, dance, and narrate their emotional experiences in a powerful, lyrical form. As Layla sleeps, the other characters present scenes of her life and dramatize her thoughts. With this formal innovation, Shange again provides an alternative to the notion of character as a stable identity performed by only one performer.

In the American theatre, any one image of an African-American character can become representative of the entire race of African-Americans. To subvert the white liberal assumption that one fictional story of an African-American facilitates an understanding of the African-American experience, Shange's characters tell many different stories within each choreopoem, all imaginative constructions of the devastating effects of racism and sexism. None of these stories can be subsumed beneath one hegemonic notion of what it means to be an African-American. Similarly, in *For Colored Girls Who Have Considered Suicide/When The Rainbow is Enuf*, seven women tell their own stories. The play does not amount to one narrative but is composed of conflicting stories which do not give rise to a mythic notion of the African-American woman. The spectator leaves the theatre with a plurality of women's voices ringing in her ear. Shange herself stresses: "I feel that as an artist my job is to appreciate the differences among my women characters . . . what is fascinating is the multiplicity of individual responses to this kind of oppression [racism]". Instead of producing myths, stereotypes, or positive images of African-Americans, Shange's plays examine how the representations of African-Americans both determine and obfuscate their real existence.

In her foreward to *Three Pieces*, Shange reveals that she has been influenced by Frantz Fanon's theory of "combat breath", the lived struggle of the colonized subject contending with foreign occupation and surveillance. She admits that Fanon's descriptions of a colonized existence made her conscious of her own status as a victim of American colonization: "although Fanon was referring to francophone colonies, the schema he draws is sadly familiar". All of Shange's work reflects her astute consciousness that the means of representation, including the English language and the theatrical stage, are mechanisms of colonialism bearing traces of a violent history.

In her plays, Shange writes a different history, a history of resistance, which requires linguistic and formal innovations. Her use of lower-case letters, contractions, transcriptions of oral speech, and slashes reflect her desire to "attack deform and maim the language that i waz taught to hate myself in". She speaks of deconstructing language: "i haveta fix my tool to my needs/ i have to take it apart to the bone/so that the malignancies/fall away/leaving us space to literally create our own image". Shange writes with the consciousness that she is at war with the symbolic order, with the pre-constituted, colonizing representations which inform African-American experience.

Sandra L. Richards notes that Shange's style is rooted in the spiritual African perspective, in which the world is conceived "as animated by the interplay of energy fields or forces

. . .". The language, music, dance, props, and costumes function as *mojos*, spiritual fields of energy which allow the subject to experience cosmic wholeness. For Richards, Shange's plays are extraordinary because they portray a dialectic between social oppression and spiritual resistance and transcendence. "In Shange's drawing upon this black aesthetic lies the will to divinity, an impulse which her characters experience as an opposition to combat breath".

—Karen Cronacher

See also *Volume 1* entry on *For Colored Girls Who Have Considered Suicide/When the Rainbow is Enuf.*

SHAW, George Bernard.   Born in Dublin, Ireland, 26 July 1856. Educated at Wesleyan Connexional School, 1867–68, Central Model Boys' School, 1868, and English Scientific and Commercial Day School, 1869, all Dublin. Married Charlotte Payne-Townshend in 1898 (died 1943). Office boy and cashier, Charles Townshend estate agents, Dublin, 1871–76; moved to London, 1876; ghosted music criticism, 1876–77, 1881; staff member, Edison Telephone Company, 1879–80; wrote novels for serialization and literary and art criticism for various magazines (especially *Pall Mall Gazette*) and newspapers, 1879–83; became a socialist, 1882; public speaker and lecturer from 1883; joined the Fabian Society, 1884: member of the executive committee, 1885–1911 (Fabians helped launch the Labour Party, 1893); reviewer, *Pall Mall Gazette*, 1885–88; music critic, *Dramatic Review*, 1886; art critic, 1886–89, and music critic, 1890–94, the *World*; first-produced play, *Widowers' Houses*, staged 1892; music critic (as "Corno di Bassetto"), the *Star*, 1888–90; drama critic, *Saturday Review*, 1895–98; with Sidney and Beatrice Webb helped establish the London School of Economics, 1895, and with the Webbs founded the *New Statesman*, 1913; vestryman and councillor, Borough of St. Pancras, London, 1897–1903; lived mainly at his country home in Ayot Saint Lawrence, Hertfordshire, from 1906; member, British Interplanetary Society, 1950. Lifelong advocate of spelling reform and a phonetic alphabet. Recipient: Nobel Prize for Literature, 1926; Irish Academy of Letters medal, 1934; Oscar, for screenplay, 1939. Freeman, City of London, 1935, and City of Dublin, 1946. Died in Ayot Saint Lawrence, 2 November 1950.

Works

Collections

Plays Pleasant and Unpleasant (2 vols.; includes *Arms and the Man; Candida; The Man of Destiny; Widowers' Houses; Mrs. Warren's Profession; The Philanderer*).   1898.
Three Plays for Puritans (includes *The Devil's Disciple; Captain Brassbound's Conversion; Caesar and Cleopatra*).   1901.
John Bull's Other Island; Major Barbara; How He Lied to Her Husband.   1907.
The Doctor's Dilemma; Getting Married; The Shewing-Up of Blanco Posnet.   1911.
Misalliance; The Dark Lady of the Sonnets; Fanny's First Play.   1914.

Androcles and the Lion; Overruled; Pygmalion.   1916.
Heartbreak House; Great Catherine; Playlets of the War.   1919.
Translations and Tomfooleries.   1926.
Complete Plays.   1931; revised edition, 1934, 1938, 1950, 1952, 1965.
Works (Standard Edition; 37 vols.).   1931–50.
Too True to Be Good; Village Wooing; On the Rocks.   1934.
The Simpleton; The Six of Calais; The Millionairess.   1936.
Geneva; Cymbeline Refinished; In Good King Charles's Golden Days.   1946.
Buoyant Billions; Farfetched Fables; Shake Versus Shav.   1951.
Ten Short Plays.   1960.
Collected Plays and Their Prefaces (Bodley Head Shaw; 7 vols.), edited by Dan H. Laurence.   1970–74.
The Portable Shaw, edited by Stanley Weintraub.   1977.
Collected Screenplays (includes all the screenplays), edited by Bernard F. Dukore.   1980.

Stage Works

Publication dates refer to first English-language editions, although some plays appeared earlier in German versions.

Widowers' Houses: A Didactic Realistic Play (produced by the Independent Theatre Society, Royalty Theatre, London, 1892). 1893; revised version, in *Plays Unpleasant*, 1898.
Arms and the Man (produced Avenue Theatre, London, 1894). In *Plays Pleasant*, 1898.
Candida (produced Her Majesty's Theatre, Aberdeen, 1897). In *Plays Pleasant*, 1898.
The Devil's Disciple (produced Bijou Theatre, London, 1897). In *Three Plays for Puritans*, 1901.
The Man of Destiny (produced Grand Theatre, Croydon, 1897). In *Plays Pleasant*, 1898.
The Gadfly; or, The Son of the Cardinal, from the novel by Ethel Voynich (produced Bijou Theatre, London, 1898). In *Bodley Head Shaw 7*, 1974.
You Never Can Tell (produced by the Stage Society, Royalty Theatre, London, 1899). In *Plays Pleasant*, 1898.
Mrs. Warren's Profession (produced by the Stage Society, New Lyric Club, London, 1902). In *Plays Unpleasant*, 1898.
The Philanderer (produced Cripplegate Institute, London, 1905). In *Plays Unpleasant*, 1898.
Captain Brassbound's Conversion (produced by the Stage Society, Strand Theatre, London, 1900). In *Three Plays for Puritans*, 1901.
Caesar and Cleopatra (produced in German, Neues Theater, Berlin, 1906; produced in English, New Amsterdam, New York, 1906). In *Three Plays for Puritans*, 1901.
The Admirable Bashville; or, Constancy Rewarded, from his novel *Cashel Byron's Profession* (produced in amateur performance, Pharos Club, Covent Garden, 1902; produced professionally, by the Stage Society, Imperial Theatre, London, 1902). In *Cashel Byron's Profession*, 1901.
Man and Superman: A Comedy and a Philosophy (produced without Act III, Court Theatre, London, 1905; complete text produced Lyceum Theatre, Edinburgh, 1915).   1903.
How He Lied to Her Husband (produced Berkeley Lyceum, New York, 1904). With *John Bull's Other Island; Major Barbara*, 1907.
John Bull's Other Island (produced Court Theatre, London, 1904). With *How He Lied to Her Husband* and *Major Barbara*, 1907.

George Bernard Shaw (1930's).

Passion, Poison, and Petrification; or, The Fatal Gazogene (produced Regent's Park, London, 1905). In *Translations and Tomfooleries*, 1926.
Major Barbara (produced Court Theatre, London, 1905). With *How He Lied to Her Husband* and *John Bull's Other Island*, 1907.
The Doctor's Dilemma (produced Court Theatre, London, 1906). With *Getting Married* and *The Shewing-Up of Blanco Posnet*, 1911.
The Interlude at the Playhouse (produced Playhouse Theatre, London, 1907). In *Behind the Scenes with Cyril Maude*, 1927.
Getting Married (produced Theatre Royal, Haymarket, London, 1908). With *The Doctor's Dilemma* and *The Shewing-Up of Blanco Posnet*, 1911.
The Shewing-Up of Blanco Posnet (produced Abbey Theatre, Dublin, 1909). 1909.
Press Cuttings (produced Court Theatre, London, 1909). 1909.
Misalliance (produced Duke of York's Theatre, London, 1910). With *The Dark Lady of the Sonnets* and *Fanny's First Play*, 1914.
The Dark Lady of the Sonnets (produced Theatre Royal, Haymarket, London, 1910). With *Misalliance* and *Fanny's First Play*, 1914.
Fanny's First Play (produced Little Theatre, London, 1911). With *Misalliance* and *The Dark Lady of the Sonnets*, 1914.
Overruled (produced Duke of York's Theatre, London, 1912). With *Androcles and the Lion* and *Pygmalion*, 1916.
Androcles and the Lion (produced in German, Kleines Theater, Berlin, 1912; produced in English, St. James's Theatre, London, 1913). With *Overruled* and *Pygmalion*, 1916.
Great Catherine (produced Vaudeville Theatre, London, 1913). 1914.
Pygmalion (produced in German, Hofburg Theater, Vienna, 1913; produced in English, His Majesty's Theatre, London, 1914). With *Overruled* and *Androcles and the Lion*, 1916.
The Music-Cure (produced 1914). In *Translations and Tomfooleries*, 1926.
The Inca of Perusalem (produced Birmingham Repertory Theatre, 1916). In *Great Catherine; Heartbreak House; Playlets of the War*, 1919.
Augustus Does His Bit (produced by the Stage Society, Court Theatre, London, 1917). In *Great Catherine; Heartbreak House; Playlets of the War*, 1919.
O'Flaherty, V.C. (produced by the Royal Flying Corps, Belgium, 1917; produced professionally, 39th Street Theatre, New York, 1920). In *Great Catherine; Heartbreak House; Playlets of the War*, 1919.
Annajanska, the Bolshevik Empress (produced Coliseum, London, 1918). In *Great Catherine; Heartbreak House; Playlets of the War*, 1919.
Heartbreak House (produced Garrick Theatre, New York, 1920). In *Great Catherine; Playlets of the War*, 1919.
Back to Methuselah (produced Garrick Theatre, New York, 1922). 1921.
Jitta's Atonement, from a work by Siegfried Trebitsch (produced Shubert Theatre, Washington, DC, 1923). In *Translations and Tomfooleries*, 1926.
Saint Joan (produced Garrick Theatre, New York, 1923). 1924.
The Glimpse of Reality (produced Fellowship Hall, Glasgow, 1927). In *Translations and Tomfooleries*, 1926.
The Fascinating Foundling (produced Arts Theatre, London, 1928). In *Translations and Tomfooleries*, 1926.

The Apple Cart (produced in Polish, Teatr Polski, Warsaw, 1929; produced in English, Malvern Festival, Worcestershire, 1929). 1930.
Too True to Be Good (produced National Theatre, Boston, Massachusetts, 1932). With *Village Wooing* and *On the Rocks*, 1934.
On the Rocks (produced Winter Garden Theatre, London, 1933). With *Village Wooing* and *Too True to Be Good*, 1934.
Village Wooing (produced Little Theatre, Dallas, Texas, 1934). With *Too True to Be Good* and *On the Rocks*, 1934.
The Six of Calais (produced Open Air Theatre, Regent's Park, London, 1934). With *The Simpleton of the Unexpected Isles* and *The Millionairess*, 1936.
The Simpleton of the Unexpected Isles (produced Guild Theatre, New York, 1935). With *The Six of Calais* and *The Millionairess*, 1936.
The Millionairess (produced in German, Akademietheater, Vienna, 1936; produced in English, King's Theatre, Melbourne, Australia, 1936.). With *The Six of Calais* and *The Simpleton of the Unexpected Isles*, 1936.
Cymbeline Refinished (produced Embassy Theatre, Swiss Cottage, London, 1937). With *Geneva* (revised version) and *In Good King Charles's Golden Days*, 1946.
Geneva (produced Malvern Festival, Worcestershire, 1938). 1939; revised version, 1940.
In Good King Charles's Golden Days (produced Malvern Festival, Worcestershire, 1939). 1939.
Buoyant Billions (produced in German, Schauspielhaus, Zurich, 1948; produced in English, Malvern Festival, Worcestershire, 1949). 1949.
Shakes Versus Shav: A Puppet Play (produced Malvern Festival, Worcestershire, 1949). With *Buoyant Billions; Farfetched Fables*, 1951.
Farfetched Fables (produced Watergate Theatre, London, 1950). With *Buoyant Billions; Shakes Versus Shav*, 1951.
Why She Would Not (produced Grolier Club, New York, 1957). In *Ten Short Plays*, 1960.
Passion Play: A Dramatic Fragment, 1878, edited by Jerald E. Bringle. 1971.

Screenplays

How He Lied to Her Husband (dialogue), 1931; *Arms and the Man*, 1932 (published in *Collected Screenplays*, 1980); *Pygmalion*, with others, 1938 (published 1941); *Major Barbara*, with Anatole de Grunwald, 1941 (published 1946); *Caesar and Cleopatra*, with Marjorie Deans and W.P. Lipscomb, 1946 (published in *Collected Screenplays*, 1980).

Fiction

Cashel Byron's Profession. 1886; revised edition, 1889, 1901.
An Unsocial Socialist. 1887.
Love among the Artists. 1900.
The Irrational Knot. 1905.
Immaturity, in *Works*. 1930.
The Adventures of the Black Girl in Her Search for God. 1932.
My Dear Dorothea: A Practical Guide of Moral Education for Females, edited by Stephen Winsten. 1956.
An Unfinished Novel, edited by Stanley Weintraub. 1958.

Memoirs and Letters

Letters to Miss Alma Murray.   1927; *More Letters*, 1932.
Ellen Terry and Shaw: A Correspondence, edited by Christopher Saint-John.   1931.
Shaw Gives Himself Away: An Autobiographical Miscellany. 1939.
Florence Farr, Shaw, and W.B. Yeats: Letters, edited by Clifford Bax.   1941.
The Voice: An Autobiographical Explanation.   1952.
Shaw and Mrs. Patrick Campbell: Their Correspondence, edited by Alan Dent.   1952.
Letters to Harley Granville Barker, edited by C.B. Purdom. 1957.
To a Young Actress: Letters to Molly Tompkins, edited by Peter Tompkins.   1960.
Collected Letters (4 vols.), edited by Dan H. Laurence.   1965–88.
An Autobiography (2 vols.) edited by Stanley Weintraub. 1969–70.
Shaw and Alfred Douglas: A Correspondence, edited by Mary Hyde.   1982.
The Playwright and the Pirate: Shaw and Frank Harris: A Correspondence 1898–1930, edited by Stanley Weintraub. 1982.
Letters to Siegfried Trebitsch, edited by Samuel A. Weiss. 1986.
The Diaries 1885–1897, with Early Autobiographical Notebooks and Diaries, and an Abortive 1917 Diary (2 vols.), edited by Stanley Weintraub.   1986.

Other

The Quintessence of Ibsenism.   1891; revised edition, 1913.
The Fabian Society: What it Has Done, and How it Has Done It.   1892.
The Irresponsibilities of Anarchism. 1893.
Manifesto of English Socialists, with William Morris and H.M. Hyndman.   1893.
A Plan of Campaign for Labour.   1894.
Report on Fabian Policy and Resolutions.   1896.
The Perfect Wagnerite: A Commentary on the Ring of the Niblungs.   1898.
Socialism for Millionaires.   1901.
The Author's Apology to Mrs. Warren's Profession. 1902.
The Common Sense of Municipal Trading.   1904.
Fabianism and the Fiscal Question.   1904.
Is Free Trade Alive or Dead? 1906.
Dramatic Opinions and Essays (2 vols.)   1906.
The Sanity of Art.   1908.
Socialism and Superior Brains.   1909.
Common Sense About the War.   1914.
How to Settle the Irish Question.   1917.
Peace Conference Hints.   1919.
Irish Nationalism and Labour Internationalism.   1920.
Ruskin's Politics.   1921.
A Discarded Defence of Roger Casement.   1922.
Table-Talk of G.B.S.: Conversations Between Shaw and His Biographer, with Archibald Henderson.   1925; revised edition, 1925.
Shaw and Fascism.   1927.
Do We Agree? A Debate, with G.K. Chesterton.   1928.
The Intelligent Woman's Guide to Socialism and Capitalism. 1928; revised edition, 1937.
The League of Nations.   1929.
Socialism: Principles and Outlook, and Fabianism.   1930.
What I Really Wrote About the War.   1930.

What Shaw Told the Americans About Russia!   1932.
Nine Answers.   1932.
The Future of Political Science in America.   1933; as *The Political Madhouse in America and Nearer Home*, 1933.
Are We Heading for War?   1934.
What I Said in New Zealand.   1934.
Prefaces.   1934; revised editions, 1938, 1965.
William Morris as I Knew Him.   1936.
Everybody's Political What's What?   1944.
Shaw on Vivisection, edited by G.H. Bowker.   1949.
Rhyming Picture Guide to Ayot Saint Lawrence.   1950.
Plays and Players: Theatre Essays, edited by A.C. Ward. 1952.
Advice to a Young Critic and Other Letters: Letters to Golding Bright, edited by E.J. West.   1958.
Shaw on Theatre: Sixty Years of Letters, Speeches, and Articles, edited by E.J. West.   1958.
Shaw on Shakespeare, edited by Edwin Wilson.   1961.
How to Become a Musical Critic, edited by Dan H. Laurence. 1961.
Platform and Pulpit, edited by Dan H. Laurence.   1962.
The Matter with Ireland, edited by Dan H. Laurence and David H. Green.   1962.
Shaw on Language, edited by Abraham Tauber.   1963.
The Religious Speeches, edited by W.S. Smith.   1963.
The Rationalization of Russia, edited by Harry M. Geduld. 1964.
Shaw on Religion, edited by W.S. Smith.   1967.
The Road to Equality: Ten Unpublished Lectures and Essays 1884–1918, edited by Louis Crompton.   1971.
Non-Dramatic Literary Criticism, edited by Stanley Weintraub.   1972.
Practical Politics: Twentieth-Century Views on Politics and Economics, edited by Lloyd J. Hubenka.   1976.
Flyleaves, edited by Dan H. Laurence and Daniel J. Leary. 1977.
The Great Composers: Reviews and Bombardments, edited by Louis Crompton.   1978.
Shaw and Ibsen: The Quintessence of Ibsenism and Related Writings, edited by J.W. Wisenthal.   1979.
Shaw's Music: The Complete Musical Criticism (3 vols.), edited by Dan H. Laurence.   1981.
Shaw on Dickens, edited by Dan H. Laurence and Martin Quinn.   1984.
Agitations: Letters to the Press 1875–1950, edited by Dan H. Laurence and James Rambeau.   1985.
Shaw on Photography: Essays and Photographs, edited by Bill Jay and Margaret Moore.   1989.
Shaw on the London Art Scene 1885–1950, edited by Stanley Weintraub.   1990.

Editor, *Fabian Essays on Socialism*.   1889; revised edition, 1908; revised edition, as *Fabian Essays Forty Years Later*, 1931.
Editor, *The Co-Operative Commonwealth*, by L. Gronlund. 1892.
Editor, *Fabianism and Empire: A Manifesto*.   1900.

*

Bibliographies

G.H. Wells, *Bibliography of George Bernard Shaw*, Boston, 1979.
Dan H. Laurence, *Bernard Shaw: A Bibliography* (2 vols.), Oxford, 1983.

J.P. Wearing and Donald Haberman (eds.), *George Bernard Shaw: An Annotated Bibliography of Writing About Him* (2 vols.), DeKalb, Illinois, 1986–87.

F.P. McDowell, "A Bernard Shaw Bibliography", in *Philological Quarterly*, 66, 1987.

Criticism

Books:

H.L. Mencken, *George Bernard Shaw: His Plays*, London, 1905.

G.K. Chesterton, *George Bernard Shaw*, New York and London, 1909; revised edition, 1935.

Frank Harris, *On Shaw: An Unauthorized Biography*, London, 1931.

Archibald Henderson, *Shaw: Playboy and Prophet*, London, 1932.

Hesketh Pearson, *Shaw: His Life and Personality*, London, 1942; revised edition, 1951; as *Bernard Shaw: A Biography*, London, 1975.

Stephen Winsten (ed.), *G.B.S. 90: Aspects of Shaw's Life and Works*, London, 1946.

Eric Bentley, *Bernard Shaw: A Reconsideration*, Norfolk, Connecticut, 1947; revised edition, as *Shaw*, 1957.

Alick West, *A Good Man Fallen among Fabians*, London, 1950; revised edition, 1974.

Desmond McCarthy, *Shaw*, London, 1951; as *Shaw's Plays in Review*, New York, 1951.

Louis Kronenberger (ed.), *George Bernard Shaw: A Critical Survey*, Cleveland (Ohio) and New York, 1953.

Raymond Mander and Joe Michenson, *A Theatrical Companion to Bernard Shaw*, London, 1954.

St. John Ervine, *Bernard Shaw: His Life, Work, and Friends*, London, 1956.

Archibald Henderson, *George Bernard Shaw: Man of the Century*, London, 1956.

Donald P. Costello, *The Serpent's Eye: Shaw and the Cinema*, Notre Dame, Indiana, 1960.

Richard M. Ohmann, *Shaw: The Style and the Man*, Middletown, Connecticut, 1962.

Martin Meisel, *Shaw and the Nineteenth-Century Theater*, Princeton (New Jersey) and London, 1963.

H.E. Woodbridge, *Shaw: Creative Artist*, 1963.

Barbara Bellow Watson, *A Shavian Guide to the Intelligent Woman*, London, 1964.

R.J. Kaufmann (ed.), *George Bernard Shaw: A Collection of Critical Essays*, Englewood Cliffs, New Jersey, 1965.

John O'Donovan, *Shaw and the Charlatan Genius*, Dublin, 1965.

J. Percy Smith, *The Unrepentant Pilgrim: A Study of the Development of Shaw*, Boston, 1965.

Harold Fromm, *Shaw and the Theater in the Nineties: A Study of Shaw's Dramatic Criticism*, Lawrence, Kansas, 1967.

Charles A. Carpenter, *Shaw and the Art of Destroying Ideals: The Early Plays*, Madison, Wisconsin, 1969.

Allan Carpenter, *Shaw: The Chucker-Out*, 1969.

Louis Crompton, *Shaw the Dramatist*, Lincoln, Nebraska, 1969.

Anthony M. Gibbs, *Shaw*, Edinburgh, 1969.

John A. Mills, *Language and Laughter: Comic Dialogue in The Plays of Shaw*, Tucson, Arizona, 1969.

Stanley Weintraub, *Shaw: An Autobiography 1856–1898*, 1969.

Colin Wilson, *Bernard Shaw: A Reassessment*, London, 1969.

Stanley Weintraub, *Journey to Heartbreak: The Crucible Years of Shaw 1914–1918*, New York, 1971.

Norman Rosenblood (ed.), *Shaw: Seven Critical Essays*, 1971.

Bernard F. Dukore, *Bernard Shaw, Director*, London, 1971.

Elsie B. Adams, *Bernard Shaw and the Aesthetes*, Columbus, Ohio, 1971.

Margery Morgan, *The Shavian Playground: An Exploration of the Art of George Bernard Shaw*, London, 1972.

Alan P. Barr, *Victorian Stage Pulpiteer: Shaw's Crusade*, 1973.

Charles A. Berst, *Bernard Shaw and the Art of Drama*, Urbana, Illinois, 1973.

Maurice Valency, *The Cart and the Trumpet: The Plays of George Bernard Shaw*, New York, 1973.

Bernard F. Dukore, *Shaw, Playwright*, Columbia, Missouri, 1973.

Paul A. Hummert, *Bernard Shaw's Marxian Romance*, Lincoln, Nebraska, 1973.

J.L. Wisenthal, *The Marriage of Contraries: Shaw's Middle Plays*, Cambridge, Massachusetts, 1974.

Daniel Dervin, *Bernard Shaw: A Psychological Study*, Lewisburg, Pennsylvania, 1975.

Phyllis Hartnoll, *Who's Who in Shaw*, London, 1975.

T.F. Evans (ed.), *Shaw: The Critical Heritage*, London, 1976.

Alfred Turco, *Shaw's Moral Vision: The Self and Salvation*, 1976.

Rodelle Weintraub (ed.), *Fabian Feminist: Shaw and Women*, University Park (Pennsylvania) and London, 1977.

Robert F. Whitman, *Shaw and the Play of Ideas*, Ithaca (New York) and London, 1977.

Benny Green, *Shaw's Champions: G.B.S. and Prizefighting from Cashel Byron to Gene Tunney*, London, 1978.

Eldon C. Hill, *George Bernard Shaw*, Boston, 1978.

Michael Holroyd (ed.), *The Genius of Shaw*, London, 1979.

Margot Peters, *Bernard Shaw and the Actresses*, New York, 1980.

Charles A. Berst (ed.), *Shaw and Religion*, University Park, Pennsylvania, 1981.

Samuel A. Yorks, *The Evolution of Shaw*, Washington, DC, 1981.

W.S. Smith, *Bishop of Everywhere: Bernard Shaw and the Life Force*, University Park, Pennsylvania, 1982.

Arnold Silver, *Shaw: The Darker Side*, Stanford, California, 1982.

Stanley Weintraub, *The Unexpected Shaw: Biographical Approaches to G.B.S. and His Work*, New York, 1982.

Arthur Ganz, *George Bernard Shaw*, London, 1983.

Anthony M. Gibbs, *The Art and Mind of Shaw: Essays in Criticism*, London, 1983.

John O'Donovan, *George Bernard Shaw*, Dublin, 1983.

Nicholas Grene, *George Bernard Shaw: A Critical View*, London, 1984.

Keith May, *Ibsen and Shaw*, London, 1985.

Harold Bloom (ed.), *George Bernard Shaw: Modern Critical Perspectives*, New York, 1987.

Michael Holroyd, *Shaw: The Search for Love, The Pursuit of Power, The Lure of Fantasy* (biography; 3 vols.), London, 1988–91.

J.L. Wisenthal, *Shaw's Sense of History*, Oxford, 1988.

Margery Morgan (compiler), *File on Shaw*, London, 1989.

Harry Morrison, *The Socialism of Bernard Shaw*, London, 1989.

D.J. Gordon, *Bernard Shaw and the Comic Sublime*, New York, 1990.

John A. Bertolini, *The Playwriting of Bernard Shaw*, Carbondale, Illinois, 1991.

* * *

Shaw remains the best-known British playwright of the 20th century throughout the world, and the theatrical potential of his plays is still being discovered (such as *The Simpleton of the Unexpected Isles*, produced at Canada's annual Shaw festival in 1983). When his first play was produced by a Sunday-night play-producing society in 1892, English drama seemed to be a phenomenon of the past, something which had flourished in the late 16th and early 17th centuries, resurfacing as a more limited art in the Restoration period, and virtually dying out in the 18th century. "Modern drama" consisted mainly of successful French "well-made" plays, adapted for English commercial theatres operating on the principle of giving audiences "what the public wants" when that public had no experience of anything better. Then there was Ibsen, whose way to the English stage was blocked by theatrical censorship, circumvented by the foundation of private theatre societies, particularly the Independent and the Stage Society, which formed the nursery for Shaw's early plays. Shaw had already established a reputation as a journalist; in his bid for a place in the theatre, he took on a fight against bardolatry (a worship of the glory of Shakespeare which seemed to imply that the dramatic genius of the race had been exhausted in a single sunburst), and so arose the legend of Shaw "better than Shakespeare" ("better a live dog than a dead lion" is the Brechtian version).

The little societies, supported by intellectuals and men of letters, were not Shaw's idea of theatre, which was distinctly populist, with roots in the unpretentious forms of entertainment mounted in huge theatre buildings for the pleasure of the masses in 19th-century industrial towns. Shaw's upbringing, and perhaps his temperament, caused him to reject some forms of vulgarity and to relish most the "innocent" fun and thrills provided by farce, fantasy, and melodrama, circus acts or comic monologues. In addition he had a great love of music, particularly opera, acquired in his often unsatisfactory boyhood home in Dublin, which made him an outstanding professional music critic before he became a playwright. All these tastes he brought to the writing of drama in which his powerful, unconventional, and energetic mind could express itself freely on any subject that interested him. His mother's charismatic music teacher had a theory of training the singing voice which helped focus Shaw's attention on the importance of vocal flexibility and expressiveness to the art of acting, an attitude he shared with William Poel, the eccentric pioneer of the open-stage presentation of Elizabethan plays.

The theatre societies involved Shaw in advising on the production of his work, even when he did not undertake the entire direction (which he always referred to traditionally as "stage management"). The habit stayed with him: though another name might appear on the programme as "producer", a major part in the direction of the first English productions of his plays was taken by Shaw himself until near the end of his life. Reverting to the earlier 19th-century practice of "stock" companies, he liked to cast according to type, and attended particularly to vocal quality, associating the main roles in a play with soprano, tenor, alto, and bass voices. He required such a breadth of acting style as the large, old-fashioned theatres had necessitated, and paid as much attention to the vocal delivery of speeches as if he had been rehearsing opera singers. A Shavian tirade is, in fact, the equivalent of an aria. His letters to Mrs. Patrick Campbell, for whom he wrote the part of Eliza in *Pygmalion*, include detailed illustrations of how he advised actors, with a mixture of bullying and persuasion. They leave the reader, as they must have left Mrs. Campbell, uncertain as to whether his chief concern was with the woman or the role she was to play.

Most people seem to meet Shaw's plays first in published

form. He started issuing them in print in 1898 (except for *Widowers' Houses* in 1893) as a result of his general failure to persuade managers to put them on in the public theatres. To make them more easily readable by those accustomed to read novels, but not plays, he added the commentaries which came to be called rather inaccurately "stage directions", together with a prefatory essay for good measure. In this form they were widely enjoyed, though the verdict of A.B. Walkley, theatre critic of *The Times*, that they were "not plays", gained currency. It took the efforts of a small group of campaigners for a National Theatre to demonstrate their stage-worthiness. Granville Barker, with J.E. Vedrenne as his business manager, took over the (Royal) Court Theatre in Sloane Square in 1904 to present a repertory of new plays, which included 11 by Shaw over the next three years. It also included a number of verse translations of Euripides by a young professor of Greek, Gilbert Murray (the original for Cusins in *Major Barbara*, which Shaw dedicated to him). Friendship with Murray deepened Shaw's interest in, and knowledge of, ancient Greek drama and the philosophy of Plato, with important consequences for his own later plays.

His early drama, the plays categorised as "Unpleasant" in his first collection (*Widowers' Houses*, *The Philanderer*, and *Mrs. Warren's Profession*), reflect the attitudes and interests of the generally left-wing London intelligentsia Shaw was associating with. The first and last were sometimes called "bluebook plays" by critics, since, like parliamentary reports, they exposed public evils to be legislated against. Although there is a measure of truth in this summation, the plays are more complex than the term implies. There is an unusual quality of savage comedy in *Widowers' Houses*, extended into the ironic farce of *The Philanderer*, while *Mrs. Warren's Profession* is a tragicomedy requiring considerable range of emotion and psychological depth in the playing of the leading roles. Structurally, these plays follow the lines of Ibsen's social drama and carry audiences through to the discovery of a more truthful view of society and of themselves as implicated in its corruption. With *Arms and the Man*, Shaw began to introduce fantasy, as an aspect of the unreality of the Ruritanian type of play he chose as his model. This play, which has remained one of his best-liked, shares with *You Never Can Tell*, from the same collection of "Pleasant" plays, the capacity to treat not only serious themes but serious emotions with a beguiling lightness of touch. There is nothing in human experience that Shaw could not bring within the range of some kind of comic vision, distanced or distorted. Challenged to write a tragedy, he came up with *The Doctor's Dilemma*, which takes a tragic idea, includes a death to illustrate it, and debates it with the aid of a chorus of satirically drawn doctors. Occasionally, the divorce of Shaw's abstract thinking from any immediacy of feeling is a shocking element in his work; but a passionate concern with social morality is never far away, however indirectly implied.

The problem of combining relaxed enjoyment with philosophical distancing is solved in a number of the plays by variations on parody: so *The Devil's Disciple* and *Androcles and the Lion* employ and transform the conventions of romantic melodrama. Historical costume drama is similarly treated in a number of plays, ranging from *The Man of Destiny* to *Saint Joan*, among which *Caesar and Cleopatra* stands out as conducting a form of dialogue on values with Shakespeare's *Antony and Cleopatra*, a play from which Shaw also took his loose, episodic structure. In *Pygmalion*, an analytical critique of social and sexual inequality is in tension with the archetypal Cinderella story, and the conflict between them remains, happily, incompletely resolved.

Shaw created a gallery of star roles for actresses. He did not always share his full view of a character with the actress he wanted to play it. To Ellen Terry he described Candida in glowing terms as the ideal "virgin mother", and Sybil Thorndike's success in the part came from playing it that way, with no hint of the author's ambivalence. His ironic strategy was to include Candida's father, Burgess, in the play—a comic villain apparently irrelevant to the plot. A similarly subversive irony is easier to detect in *Man and Superman*, and it is closely connected with Shaw's sustained attack on the hypocrisy of English society as a bulwark against reform, all the more effective for working through ignorance and self-complacency. Shaw accepts human nature as it is, and so his plays (as distinct from individual characters) never express righteous indignation. Thus the self-complacent "villain", Broadbent, in *John Bull's Other Island*, is a more genial character than his partner, Larry Doyle, in whom the bitterness of self-knowledge is concentrated. There seems to be no end to the irony of Undershaft, the armaments manufacturer in *Major Barbara*, and it may even be benevolent.

Man and Superman (Act III in particular), *Major Barbara*, and the post-war five-play cycle *Back to Methuselah* are most obviously the work of a philosophical dramatist. He declared his intention of creating "a pit of philosophers" at the Court Theatre and offered his plays as a training ground for thinking on the subjects he proposed. He admired the dramatic quality of the Dialogues of Plato and came closest to them in sections of *Major Barbara* and in *Getting Married*, in which a large cast of characters, identified with a plethora of views, is organised after the manner of Greek comedy. Writing for uninterrupted performance in a single setting, Shaw called this "the Greek form", and he returned to it in *Misalliance*, where the farcical action arises from a kind of travesty of *The Bacchae* of Euripides. The surreal quality of *Misalliance* was further developed in *Heartbreak House*, where it seems particularly appropriate to the consciousness of civilisation collapsing, during World War I.

The political dimension of Shaw's drama underwent a major change with *Major Barbara*. Although the satiric presentation, in *Candida* and in *Man and Superman* of Morell and Tanner as socialists intoxicated on their own words is echoed later in the absurd behaviour of the Cabinet in *The Apple Cart* and the Prime Minister in *On the Rocks*, in which compulsive talking in meaningless clichés is mistaken for thought, the probing of the question of power in relation to morality in *Major Barbara* initiates a more radical concern with the State. *Back to Methuselah* and most of the late plays look hypothetically into the future, using imaginative speculation as a means towards the wisdom which might make democratic government work.

—Margery Morgan

See also *Volume 1* entries on *Back to Methuselah*; *Candida*; *Heartbreak House*; *Major Barbara*; *Man and Superman*; *Misalliance*; *Mrs. Warren's Profession*; *Pygmalion*; *Saint Joan*; *Too True to Be Good*.

SHEPARD, Sam. Born Samuel Shepard Rogers in Fort Sheridan, Illinois, USA, 5 November 1943. Educated at Duarte High School, California, graduated 1960; Mount San Antonio Junior College, Walnut, California, 1960–61. Married O-Lan Johnson in 1969 (divorced), one son; one daughter by the actress Jessica Lange. Worked as: hot walker at the Santa Anita Race Track, stable hand at the Connolly Arabian Horse Ranch, Duarte, herdsman at the Huff Sheep Ranch, Chino, orange picker in Duarte, and sheep shearer in Pomona, all in California; actor with Bishop's Company Repertory Players, Burbank, California, and on US tour, 1962; car wrecker, Charlemont, Massachusetts; bus boy, Village Gate, 1963–64, waiter, Marie's Crisis Café, 1965, and musician with the Holy Modal Rounders, 1968, all in New York; first plays produced 1964; lived in England, 1971–74, and in California since 1974; co-founder, with Murray Mednick, John Steppling, and others, Padua Hills Playwrights Workshop and Festival, Los Angeles, 1978. Director of many of his own plays; film actor: roles in *Brand X*, 1970, *Days of Heaven*, 1978, *Resurrection*, 1981, *Raggedy Man*, 1981, *Frances*, 1982, *The Right Stuff*, 1983, *Country*, 1984, and *Fool for Love*, 1985. Recipient: Obie Award, 1967, 1970, 1973, 1975, 1978 (twice), 1980, 1984; Pulitzer Prize, 1979.

Works

Collections

Five Plays. 1967; as *"Chicago" and Other Plays* (includes *Icarus's Mother*; *Fourteen Hundred Thousand*; *Red Cross*; *Melodrama Play*), 1982.
"The Unseen Hand" and Other Plays (includes *The Rock Garden*; *4-H Club*; *Forensic and the Navigators*; *The Holy Ghostly*; *Shaved Splits*; *Back Bog Beast Bait*). 1971.
"Mad Dog Blues" and Other Plays (includes *Cowboys #2*; *Cowboy Mouth*). 1971.
"Angel City" and Other Plays (includes *Killer's Head*; *Curse of the Starving Class*; *Action*. 1976.
"Buried Child" and Other Plays. 1979; as *Buried Child*; *Seduced*; *Suicide in B Flat*, 1980.
Four Two-Act Plays (includes La Turista; The Tooth of Crime; Geography of a Horse Dreamer; Operation Sidewinder). 1980.
Seven Plays (includes Buried Child; Curse of the Starving Class; The Tooth of Crime; La Turista; True West; Tongues; Savage/Love). 1981.
"Fool for Love" and Other Plays. 1984.

Stage Works

Cowboys (produced St. Mark's Church, New York, 1964).
The Rock Garden (produced St. Mark's Church, New York, 1964; excerpt produced in *Oh! Calcutta!*, Eden Theatre, New York, 1969). In *"The Unseen Hand" and Other Plays*, 1971.
Up to Thursday (produced Cherry Lane Theatre, New York, 1965).
Dog (produced La Mama Experimental Theatre, New York, 1965).
Rocking Chair (produced New York, 1965).
Chicago (produced St. Mark's Church, New York, 1965). In *Five Plays*, 1967.
Icarus's Mother (produced Caffe Cino, New York, 1965). In *Five Plays*, 1967.
4-H Club (produced Cherry Lane Theatre, New York, 1965). In *"The Unseen Hand" and Other Plays*, 1971.

Fourteen Hundred Thousand (produced Firehouse Theatre, Minneapolis, Minnesota, 1966). In *Five Plays*, 1967.

Red Cross (produced Judson Poets Theatre, New York, 1966). In *Five Plays*, 1967.

La Turista (produced American Place Theatre, New York, 1967). 1968.

Melodrama Play (produced Martinique Theatre, New York, 1967). In *Five Plays*, 1967.

Cowboys #2 (produced by Old Reliable, New York, 1967). In *"Mad Dog Blues" and Other Plays*, 1971.

Forensic and the Navigators (produced St. Mark's Church, New York, 1967). In *"The Unseen Hand" and Other Plays*, 1971.

The Holy Ghostly (produced on tour, 1969). In *"The Unseen Hand" and Other Plays*, 1971.

The Unseen Hand (produced La Mama Experimental Theatre, New York, 1969). In *"The Unseen Hand" and Other Plays*, 1971.

Operation Sidewinder (produced Vivian Beaumont Theatre, Lincoln Center, New York, 1970). 1970.

Shaved Splits (produced La Mama Experimental Theatre, New York, 1970). In *"The Unseen Hand" and Other Plays*, 1971.

Mad Dog Blues (produced by Theatre Genesis, St. Mark's Church, New York, 1971). In *"Mad Dog Blues" and Other Plays*, 1971.

Cowboy Mouth, with Patti Smith (produced Traverse Theatre, Edinburgh, 1971). In *"Mad Dog Blues" and Other Plays*, 1971.

Back Bog Beast Bait (produced American Place Theatre, New York, 1971). In *"The Unseen Hand" and Other Plays*, 1971.

The Tooth of Crime (produced McCarter Theatre, Princeton, New Jersey, 1972). With *Geography of a Horse Dreamer*, 1974.

Blue Bitch (televised 1972; produced Theatre Genesis, New York, 1973).

Nightwalk, with Megan Terry and Jean-Claude van Itallie (produced St. Clement's Church, New York, 1973). In *Tyre Works by the Open Theatre*, 1974.

Little Ocean (produced Hampstead Theatre, London, 1974).

Geography of a Horse Dreamer (produced Royal Court Theatre Upstairs, London, 1974). With *The Tooth of Crime*, 1974.

Action (produced Royal Court Theatre Upstairs, London, 1974). With *The Unseen Hand*, 1975.

Killer's Head (produced American Place Theatre, New York, 1975). In *"Angel City" and Other Plays*, 1976.

Angel City (produced Magic Theatre, San Francisco, 1976). In *"Angel City" and Other Plays*, 1976.

Suicide in B Flat (produced Yale Repertory Theatre, New Haven, Connecticut, 1976). In *"Buried Child" and Other Plays*, 1979.

The Sad Lament of Pecos Bill on the Eve of Killing His Wife (produced Legion of Honor Theatre, San Francisco, 1976). With *Fool for Love* 1983.

Curse of the Starving Class (produced Shakespeare Festival Public Theatre, New York, 1977). In *"Angel City" and Other Plays*, 1976.

Inacoma (produced Magic Theatre, San Francisco, 1977).

Buried Child (produced Theatre of the New City, New York, 1978). In *"Buried Child" and Other Plays*, 1979.

Seduced (produced American Place Theatre, New York, 1978). In *"Buried Child" and Other Plays*, 1979.

Tongues, with Joseph Chaikin, music by Shepard, Skip LaPlante, and Harry Mann (produced Eureka Theatre Festival, San Francisco, 1978). In *Seven Plays*, 1981.

Savage/Love, with Joseph Chaikin, music by Shepard, Skip LaPlante, and Harry Mann (produced Eureka Theatre Festival, San Francisco, 1979). In *Seven Plays*, 1981.

True West (produced Magic Theatre, San Francisco, 1980). 1981.

Jackson's Dance, with Jacques Levy (produced New Haven, Connecticut, 1980).

Superstitions (produced Intersection Theatre, San Francisco, 1981).

Fool for Love (produced Magic Theatre, San Francisco, 1983). 1984.

A Lie of the Mind (produced Promenade Theatre, New York, 1985). 1987.

Hawk Moon (produced Gate Theatre, London, 1989).

States of Shock (produced American Place Theatre, New York, 1991).

Screenplays

Me and My Brother, with Robert Frank, 1969; *Zabriskie Point*, with others, 1970; *Ringaleevio*, 1971; *Paris, Texas*, with Wim Wenders, 1984 (published 1984); *Fool for Love*, 1985.

Television Plays

Blue Bitch, 1972.

Radio Plays

The War in Heaven, with Joe Chaikin, 1985.

Other

Hawk Moon: A Book of Short Stories, Poems, and Monologues. 1973.

Rolling Thunder Logbook. 1977.

Motel Chronicles. 1982.

Joseph Chaikin and Sam Shepard: Letters and Texts 1972–1984, edited by Barry V. Daniels. 1989.

*

Bibliographies

Luther S. Luedtke, "Sam Shepard: A Bibliographical Guide", in *New Essays on American Drama*, edited by Gilbert Debusscher and Henry I. Schvey, Amsterdam, 1989.

Criticism

Books:

Bonnie Marranca (ed.), *American Dreams: The Imagination of Sam Shephard*, New York, 1981.

Doris Auerbach, *Sam Shephard, Arthur Kopit and the Off Broadway Theatre*, Boston, 1982.

Ron Mottram, *Inner Landscapes: The Theater of Sam Shephard*, Columbia, Missouri, 1984.

Vivian M. Patraka and Mark Siegel, *Sam Shepard*, Boise, Idaho, 1985.

Don Shewey, *Sam Shepard: The Life, the Loves, Behind the Legend of a True American Original*, New York, 1985.

Michael Krekel, *Von Cowboys bis True West: Shepards Drama*, Frankfurt, 1986.

Ellen Oumano, *Sam Shepard: The Life and Work of an American Dreamer*, New York, 1986.

Lynda Hart, *Sam Shephard's Metaphorical Stages*, Connecticut, 1987.

John Dugdale (compiler), *File on Shepard*, London, 1989.

Kimball King (compiler), *Sam Shepard: A Casebook*, New York, 1988.

Ulrich Adolfs, *Die Tyrannei der Bilder: Shepards Dramen* (with English summary), Frankfurt, 1990.

* * *

Sam Shepard is almost certainly the most distinctive and important of the playwrights launched during the Off-Off-Broadway movement of the mid-1960's. Many other playwrights of his generation have won a Pulitzer Prize, but only a few have an equally voluminous output; and none, with the possible exception of David Mamet, has the sharply distinctive signature of his plays, even though this has eroded a little in *Fool for Love* and *A Lie of the Mind*. This style also marks his collaborations with Joseph Chaikin and his screenplays.

The distinctiveness of a Shepard play has been aptly summed up by director Robert Woodruff as an "incredible journey opening up in the pieces". The embedded verbal inscapes of his characters' "arias" fracture the narrative "journey", and two disparate tracks of images are often projected simultaneously, the one in the words, the other in the scenography. These images are extraordinary and often quintessentially American; they fuse or surreally juxtapose elements of the past and present, and they are geographically located in the southern-California landscape, where the "mod-cons" and slick mythologies of 20th-century American civilization are threatened by icons of the 19th-century Western frontier, the ritual totems of dispossessed Indians, or the hallucinatory topography of the primeval desert landscape. And sluicing through this fractured and surreal world is the music-making of much of the plays, which has the feel of jazz and the impact of rock, especially in *Melodrama Play, Cowboy Mouth*, and *Suicide in B Flat*.

Shepard's career so far can be seen as falling into three phases. As the Off-Off-Broadway iconoclast, he established his reputation with a series of short plays which are still undervalued by some critics and, arguably, consist of his most powerful work. *Cowboys #2* can serve as illustration and prototype. Against an abstract and sparse open area, sawhorse, and blinking yellow light, two buddies play what seems to be a game of cowboys and indians, re-enacting key episodes from Western mythology—episodes which lead to decay, stasis, and the apparent death of one of them. These two men are counterpointed with two others, who briefly talk of mundanities such as rents and social welfare, and at the end are seen dressed for what seems to be an audition, reading the opening lines of the play from scripts. Apparently, Western myth, if played for real, can lead to collapse; if played for profit, it is innocuous and sanitized. But the play does not spell out its meanings, and is one of several written in this period, including *Chicago, Icarus's Mother*, and *Red Cross*, which juxtapose poetic freedom of the imagination with threatening, or merely innocuous, outer worlds with equal memorability.

In the late 1960's and 1970's Shepard extended his grasp to produce full-length works employing the same kind of surreal individuality. The prototype here is *The Tooth of Crime*, in which two rock-stars of different generations battle for territorial domination of an empire; metaphoric references to science fiction, the Old West, and music are mesmerically fused, and the mythic duel to the death is not a gun-battle, but a rap session where the duelling instruments are verbal incantations which seek to pierce the mask and unseat the confidence of the opponent. Leading up to this play, Shepard wrote *La Turista* and *Operation Sidewinder*, in which the structure is not as clearly patterned and in which the different metaphorical modes do not overlay each other or dovetail as effectively. Later plays from this phase include the fascinating but opaque *Suicide in B Flat*, about the "disappearance" of a star musician, apparently fleeing from his own fame, and *Seduced*, which is thematically related to the former in that it explores the way in which a seductive legend about an individual can supersede and destroy his living reality. *Action* is a vision of nuclear holocaust and the dysfunction of an extended family.

In the following year Shepard began to write a series of plays focusing more on the nuclear family and somewhat more representational in style. The first of these was *Curse of the Starving Class*, followed by *Buried Child*, for which he received a Pulitzer Prize in 1979. The modified, somewhat more realistic, style of this new phase of Shepard's writing was even more marked in the three plays that followed. But Shepard retained both the verbal and the scenographic vividness of his earlier manner, as well as devices of a disturbing and imaginative surrealism, such as the 24 stolen toasters in *True West*, or the absent-but-present father, to the side in a chair in a separate area but able to confer, preternaturally, with the son and daughter who have conjured him up in *Fool for Love*.

The fractured "unity in pieces" of the style often breaks up into ambiguity at the very end in much the same way that certain thematic premises are set up and then questioned or exploded. For example, a certain mythology seems affirmed in a play's early stages, then is exposed as misguided, outmoded, or debased; health often turns to putrefaction or decay through the oft-repeated metaphor of breakfast food going rotten, or decaying, or simply being abused. Families at a play's beginning seem precariously stable, but then can neither stay intact nor nurture their members; the domestic is suddenly blown apart by violence and disorder (as in *Curse of the Starving Class, Buried Child*, and *True West*). Apparent male bonding (often between father and son) flares up instead into fatally destructive competitiveness. And in so many of the plays the "unity in pieces" is fragile throughout, with intimations of apocalypse just around the corner.

But it is the stylistic motif of the disparate "tracking" of images that expresses one of Shepard's strongest thematic concerns. This is the characters' compulsion to escape, set against the prosaic pull of circularity or stasis. Most often the desire to escape is articulated in the construction of alternative worlds of the verbal "arias"; but sometimes it is expressed by scenography as well, as in the memorable closing image of *La Turista*, in which the hero leaves a hole in the back wall as he, literally, crashes through it to "freedom". A second major theme is the need to act oneself out, to establish new masks and identities that can be shifted at will; but a mask identity ends up as less flexible than its inventor supposes and can stick with the awful finality of myth, as it does in *Seduced* and *Suicide in B Flat*. And against the impulse to set new identities is the contrary impulse to hold onto one that is constant, based on heredity and family. This second theme is embodied less in the simultaneous "tracking" than it is in the full working out of the "unity in pieces" of the plays' action.

—Denis Carroll

See also *Volume 1* entries on *Fool For Love*; *The Tooth of Crime*; *True West*.

———————

SHERIDAN, Richard Brinsley (Butler). Born in Dublin, Ireland, in September or October 1751. Educated at Samuel Whyte's Grammar School, Dublin, 1757; Harrow School, Middlesex, 1762–68; Middle Temple, London, 1773. Married 1) Elizabeth Ann Linley in 1773 (died 1792), one son and one daughter; 2) Hester Jane Ogle in 1795, one son. Lived in London, 1768–69; staff member of his father's Academy of Oratory, Bath, 1770–71; eloped with Elizabeth Linley to Europe, wounded in a duel, and sent to Farm Hill, near Waltham Abbey, 1772; first-produced play, *The Rivals*, staged 1775; part-owner and director, Theatre Royal, Drury Lane, London, 1776–78, sole proprietor from 1779: theatre demolished and rebuilt, 1792, theatre funds impounded, 1802, theatre burned down, and company re-established at the Lyceum, 1809; Member of Parliament for Stafford, 1780–1806, Westminster, 1806–07, and Ilchester, 1807–12: Under-Secretary of State for foreign affairs (Northern Department), in Rockingham administration, 1782; Secretary of the Treasury in the coalition ministry of Charles James Fox and Lord North, 1783; manager of the trial of Warren Hastings by Parliament, 1788–94; bought Polesden Lacey estate, 1796; Receiver-General of the Duchy of Cornwall, 1804; treasurer of the Navy, 1806; imprisoned for debt, 1813. Member of Samuel Johnson's literary club, 1777. Died in London, 7 July 1816.

Works

Collections

Works, edited by F. Stainworth.   1874.
Plays, edited by Lewis Gibbs.   1906.
Plays and Poems (3 vols.), edited by R. Crompton Rhodes.   1928.
Dramatic Works (2 vols.), edited by Cecil Price.   1973.

Stage Works

The Rivals (produced Covent Garden Theatre, London, 1775).   1775.
St. Patrick's Day; or The Scheming Lieutenant (produced Covent Garden Theatre, London, 1775).   1788.
The Duenna, music by Thomas Linley and others (produced Covent Garden Theatre, London, 1775).   1794.
A Trip to Scarborough, from a play by Vanbrugh (produced Theatre Royal, Drury Lane, London, 1777).   1781.
The School for Scandal (produced Theatre Royal, Drury Lane, London, 1777).   1780.
The Camp, music by Thomas Linley (produced Theatre Royal, Drury Lane, London, 1778).   1795.
The Critic; or, A Tragedy Rehearsed (produced Theatre Royal, Drury Lane, London, 1779).   1781.

Richard Brinsley Sheridan (engraving, after a portrait by Sir Joshua Reynolds).

The Storming and Taking of Fort Omoa (interlude in *Harlequin Fortunatus* by Henry Woodward; produced Theatre Royal, Drury Lane, London, 1780).
Robinson Crusoe; or, Harlequin Friday, music by Thomas Linley (produced Theatre Royal, Drury Lane, London, 1781).   Songs published 1781.
The Glorious First of June, with James Cobb (benefit entertainment; produced Theatre Royal, Drury Lane, London, 1794).   Songs published 1794; revised version, as *Cape St. Vincent* (produced Theatre Royal, Drury Lane, London, 1797), songs published 1797.
The Stranger, from a translation by Benjamin Thompson of a play by Kotzebue (produced Theatre Royal, Drury Lane, London, 1798).
Pizarro, from a play by Kotzebue (produced Theatre Royal, Drury Lane, London, 1799).   1799.

Verse

The Ridotto of Bath: A Panegyric.   1771.
The Love Epistle of Aristaenetus, with Nathaniel Halhed.   1771.
The Rival Beauties, with Miles Peter Andrews(?).   1772.
Verses to the Memory of Garrick.   1779; as *The Tears of Genius*, 1780.

Memoirs and Letters

Letters, edited by Cecil Price (3 vols.).   1966.

Other

*A Familiar Epistle to the Author of the Epistle to William
   Chambers.*   1774.
Speeches (5 vols.).   1816.

*

Bibliographies

Bibliography in *Plays and Poems*, Oxford, 1928.
Jack D. Durant, *Richard Brinsley Sheridan: A Reference
   Guide*, Boston, 1981.

Criticism

Books:
Walter S. Sichel, *Sheridan* (2 vols.), London, 1909.
M.T.H. Sadler, *The Political Career of Richard Brinsley
   Sheridan*, Oxford, 1912.
R. Compton Rhodes, *Harlequin Sheridan: The Man and the
   Legends*, Oxford, 1933.
Alice Glasgow, *Sheridan of Drury Lane*, New York, 1940.
Lewis Gibbs, *Sheridan*, London, 1947.
G. Sinko, *Sheridan and Kotzebue: A Comparative Essay*,
   Wrocław, 1949.
Madeleine Bingham, *Sheridan: The Track of a Comet*,
   London, 1972.
Jack D. Durant, *Richard Brinsley Sheridan*, Boston, 1975.
John Loftis, *Sheridan and the Drama of Georgian England*,
   Oxford, 1976.
Mark S. Auburn, *Sheridan's Comedies: Their Contexts and
   Achievements*, Lincoln, Nebraska, 1977.
Marlies K. Danziger, *Oliver Goldsmith and Richard Brinsley
   Sheridan*, New York, 1978.
Stanley Ayling, *A Portrait of Sheridan*, London, 1985.
James Morwood, *The Life and Works of Richard Brinsley
   Sheridan*, Edinburgh, 1985.
Peter Davison (ed.), *Sheridan: Comedies: A Casebook*,
   London, 1986.
E. H. Mikhail (ed.), *Sheridan: Interviews and Recollections*,
   Basingstoke and London, 1989.
Shashi Shekhar Sinha, *The Mind and Art of Richard Brinsley
   Sheridan*, Delhi, 1989.

* * *

Sheridan had the Irish genius for writing close to the personal events of life and turning them into high comedy. His stylised art derived from classical tradition but he fused plots and types inherited from Shakespeare, Restoration comedy, or *commedia dell'arte* with situations he had experienced, often far from comic when they occurred. The duel he fought with an importunate rival over the young singer Elizabeth Linley (who became his wife) was serious in actuality but in *The Rivals* was transformed into an absurd event: a duel that is never fought, and a rival who does not really exist. Sheridan merrily endorsed the connection by setting his play in Bath, which many of his original audience would recognise as the scene of his real-life romance (the exaggerated newspaper rumours that circulated about it were a source of inspiration for *The School for Scandal*). His last major comedy, *The Critic*, was in a familiar tradition of theatre burlesque (Buckingham's *The Rehearsal* was one recent model), but again Sheridan gave it his personal stamp by weaving in with the invented drama (itself in double layers of illusion, with its preposterous inner play) mischievous references to the real theatre, Drury Lane, which was also the scene of the inset "Spanish Armada" play. The real Tom King, playing imaginary Mr. Puff, was called on to heap extravagant praise on himself as an actor in Mr. Puff's play. Sheridan struck metatheatrical notes here which made his comedy seem an appropriate choice for a recent production by Britain's National Theatre in a double bill with Stoppard's *The Real Inspector Hound*.

Sheridan's career as a writer of comedy was short: his major plays were all written within four years. He became manager of Drury Lane on Garrick's invitation in 1776 and retained that position even after turning to politics in 1780. There were some links between his life in politics and in the theatre. He attracted huge audiences, like an actor, for his brilliant speeches in the trials of Warren Hastings. His emphasis on the value of family piety in these speeches, and his aversion to what he saw as tyranny, figure also in *Pizarro*, the one major piece of writing for the stage that Sheridan undertook after entering the Commons. It was not an original work, but an adaptation of Kotzebue's romantic semi-operatic historical melodrama *Die Spanier in Peru*. It expressed some of Sheridan's real sentiments but it has always been seen as a great irony that so much of the play—with its inflated rhetoric and dominating scenic effects—was just what he had mocked so wittily 20 years before, in *The Critic*.

Sheridan had an easy entry into the theatre, being invited to write a play for Covent Garden when he was only 23 and theatrically inexperienced, despite being the son of Thomas Sheridan, the Irish actor-manager, and Frances, the novelist and playwright (from whom he took ideas). He showed his talent for writing at speed (much needed, as he was a notorious procrastinator) when he revised *The Rivals* for "tenth night" performance after the audience had rejected the first version. It had been found too long (like Puff, Sheridan was inclined to be "over luxuriant") and there were objections to the coarse characterisation of the Irish fire-eater, Sir Lucius O'Trigger. Sheridan toned him down, a process he repeated on a larger scale in 1777 when he adapted Vanbrugh's *The Relapse* (as *A Trip to Scarborough*) to the squeamish taste of his genteel audience, cutting out the freer sexual witticisms and keeping the adulteries intended rather than realised.

Witty improvisations are a feature of Sheridan's comedy, linking it with the theatrical world of Harlequin, a popular figure on the 18th-century stage, and with comic opera to which he was drawn by his own taste (his dialogue has strongly marked, quasi-musical rhythms and repetitions) and by his connection with the talented Linleys. They wrote the music for *The Duenna*, the comic opera set in Spain (its opening scene curiously anticipates *Don Giovanni*) which was the triumphant climax of his first year. It was his most popular theatre work: Byron ranked it higher than *The Beggar's Opera*. Like the one-act farce, *St Patrick's Day; or, The Scheming Lieutenant* which preceded it (and like *The Rivals*), *The Duenna* presents young lovers outwitting curmudgeonly parents and guardians by adroit deceits and tricks in a tradition that stretches back to antiquity. Jack Absolute, in *The Rivals*, creates an alter-ego to suit Lydia Languish's romantic humour and deceive the "dragon", Mrs Malaprop, another familiar type to which Sheridan gave new life by inspired misapplications of language; the "Scheming Lieutenant" dons actual disguises (music master, doctor) to hoodwink his girl's father; and Louisa escapes from parental tyranny, masked and costumed as her (eponymous) duenna, leaving that plain penniless person to deceive the avaricious suitor, Isaac

Mendoza, into taking her for the young heiress. Inventive love-cheats by mercurial Harlequin-like adventurers are a mainspring of Sheridan's comedy.

Sheridan enjoyed many jokes at the expense of the sentimental comedy fashionable in his day. He mocks false sentiment in *The Rivals*, lightly in Lydia Languish, more seriously in the absurdly self-tormenting Faulkland. Sheridan has his own sentiment and morality, however. He laughs at "humours" characters like Bob Acres or the irascible Sir Anthony Absolute but allows them sympathy too. Warm hearts prevailing against cold ones is the rule. Sheridan's masterpiece *The School for Scandal* dazzles by its wit and the malicious sparkle of its scandal-mongering scenes but also by his ability to touch softer notes and indicate psychological depths through brilliantly comic situations. Charles Surface redeems himself by sentimentally retaining "old Noll's" portrait in the witty picture auction. And the tender feeling that Sir Peter Teazle reveals for his skittish young wife during the wickedly funny screen scene introduces a new, poignant interest into that favourite situation of Restoration comedy, the old bachelor married to the young country girl. Sheridan probed into his own complicated personality (so his father maintained) to create the most intriguing character-relationship in his plays, that between Joseph and Charles Surface—a relationship of opposites with Wildean overtones.

Sheridan's scene darkened in his last years. He saw through a major rebuilding of Drury Lane when it was converted in 1809 to the new size demanded by plays like *Pizarro*. He also saw the theatre burn down, watching it from a chair opposite and reacting with the aplomb of an Absolute or a Surface: "May not a man take a drink by his own fireside?". Plagued by drink and debts, he died indigent, but his comedies immediately began the glittering after-life, which drew a famous tribute from Charles Lamb: "Among the mortifying circumstances attendant upon growing old, it is something to have seen *The School for Scandal* in its glory".

—Katharine Worth

See also *Volume 1* entries on *The Critics*; *The Rivals*; *The School For Scandal*.

SHERMAN, Martin. Born in Philadelphia, Pennsylvania, USA, 22 December 1938. Educated at Boston University, 1956–60, BFA 1960. First-produced play, *A Solitary Thing*, staged 1963; playwright-in-residence, Playwrights Horizons, New York, 1976–77. Recipient: Dramatists Guild Hull-Warriner Award, 1980.

Stage Works

A Solitary Thing, music by Stanley Silverman (produced Mills College, Oakland, California, 1963).
Fat Tuesday (produced Actors' Studio, New York, 1966).
Next Year in Jerusalem (produced Herbert Berghof Playwrights Foundation, New York, 1968).
The Night Before Paris (produced Actors' Studio, New York, 1969).
Things Went Badly in Westphalia (produced University of Connecticut, Storrs, 1971). In *The Best Short Plays 1970*, edited by Stanley Richards, 1970.

Passing By (produced Playwrights' Horizons, New York, 1974; London, 1975). In *Gay Plays 1*, edited by Michael Wilcox, 1984.
Soaps (produced Playwrights' Horizons, New York, 1975).
Cracks (produced Eugene O'Neill Theatre, Waterford, Connecticut, 1975). In *Gay Plays 2*, edited by Michael Wilcox, 1986.
Rio Grande (produced Playwrights' Horizons, New York, 1976).
Blackout (produced New York, 1978).
Bent (produced Eugene O'Neill Theatre, Waterford, Connecticut, 1978). 1979.
Messiah (produced Hampstead Theatre, London, 1982). 1982.
When She Danced (produced Guildford, Surrey, 1985).
A Madhouse in Goa (produced Lyric Theatre, Hammersmith, London, 1989). 1989.

Television Plays

The Clothes in the Wardrobe, from Alice Thomas Ellis's *The Summerhouse Trilogy*, 1992.

*   *   *

An East Coast American of European immigrant stock, Martin Sherman is unusual in the canon of American playwrights of his generation. Unlike Mamet, Shepard, or Lanford Wilson, he has moved away from an exploration of the myths and debased realities of contemporary US society into more socio-political subjects in historical European settings. Often in a strongly satirical vein—less usual for American playwrights—Sherman's rich humour leavens the most painful of situations, investing character with warmth and ironic wit, which frequently leaves audiences with a sense of an affirmation of human strength and resilience. Yet for many Sherman characters, survival is touch and go; often on the very brink of despair, disaster and/or death, most survive, though not all, and none unscathed. For Sherman, it seems that affirmation is not synonymous with facile optimism: the survivor's humour is tinged with pain.

Though his work is strikingly diverse in both subject matter and style, it is this particular blend of laughter and tears which is Sherman's hallmark. In *Passing By*, a charming early piece concerning two gay men in New York who meet, make love, fall ill, and convalesce together before parting as friends, the tears are muted. It is a warmly funny two-hander, and the banter of the pair as they bicker and console each other wins sympathy; yet beneath the wit is a thread of the loneliness of outsiders whom society will not freely embrace, and about whom society frowns in disapproval when they embrace one another.

Later, more complex, plays such as *Bent, Messiah, When She Danced*, and *A Madhouse In Goa* develop the emotional ambivalences further. In these plays, Sherman's concern with language is traceable, for its felicities, its purposes, its successes/failures. In *Bent*, Sherman's most famous play which concerns the fate of a decadent homosexual, Max, in the maelstrom of a Nazi Germany apparently as virulently homophobic as it is anti-Semitic, language is both theme and a major component of stagecraft. Whereas in earlier satirical works such as *Soaps* and *Cracks*—satires upon genres, audiences, and the society which generates both—language is predominantly a source of humourous wit, in *Bent* language establishes mood, character, and situation. The deliberately parodic camp of the opening scenes, reminiscent of Isherwood and Mart Crowley's *The Boys In The Band*, renders Max and his lover, Rudy, particularly vulnerable to the Nazi brutalities. Whereas in Act I characters talk freely and often outrageously, in Act II communication of any kind is forbidden and potentially lethal; it is a transition marked by two key scenes: one in which Max and his Uncle Freddy discuss the necessity of cloaking their sexuality under a tissue of lies and evasions, and a second in which Max must deny both his sexuality and any knowledge of Rudy to save his own skin. *Bent*'s most celebrated scene depends upon language — the simultaneous orgasm achieved by Max and Horst under the noses of their Dachau guards, portrayed through descriptive language and the receptor's imagination.

The fallibility, but also the capacity for honesty, invested in language is perhaps most winningly dramatised in the character Rachel, heroine of *Messiah*. Set in a 17th-century Poland ravaged by Cossacks, the play details the rise and fall of the false prophet Sabbatai Sevi through his impact upon a peasant woman, her family, and her community. As usual with Sherman's characters, Rachel is socially disadvantaged; not, as with Max, by an alternative sexuality, but by her physical ugliness and her — it is felt — unwarranted choosiness in the matter of a husband. The play's strongest thread is Rachel's relationship with her God, dramatised through a series of chatty prayer-monologues which chart, wittily and movingly, both her sexual liberation and her growing despair. For Rachel comes to understand God's humour, an almost absurdist understanding.

Language in *When She Danced*, a study of Isadora Duncan in decline in Paris in 1923, repeatedly fails to fulfil its basic function of communication. This skilfully crafted play both mocks and celebrates the legendary Duncan whose inspirational dancing many characters try — and fail — to describe. But one, a translator, thrillingly describes the effect upon her of seeing Duncan dance. Immediately, Sherman undercuts this impression with an onstage imitation of the Duncan style by a clod-hopping teenage Swedish acolyte. The set-piece of the play is a dinner party at which all speak their own language and properly understand no other, giving rise to confusions and mistakes.

A Madhouse In Goa develops this theme in an altogether darker vein. Structurally, the play is a diptych of one-act pieces; the first, *A Table for A King*, set on Corfu in 1966, around the time of the Greek junta, deals with a gauche homosexual, a Mississippi widow, and the betrayals and compromises that enmesh them both. Reminiscent of Tennessee Williams or Somerset Maugham, the piece is deliberately lightweight. The second play, *Keeps Rainin' All the Time*, delivers the punch: one year in the future on the volcanic island of Santorini, the young homosexual reappears as an aphasic older man, a writer whose "famous novel" was the story we have seen dramatised in *Table*. This aphasia — the loss of language — seems almost retributive for his trimming and evasiveness in constructing the earlier story, eschewing all political significance — a retribution to be compounded further by the bowdlerisation of his novel as a Hollywood musical by a born-again producer.

Apocalyptic in tone, character, and situation — acid rain falls ceaselessly upon Santorini following a Chernobyl-like nuclear accident and every person is either terminally ill or morally and culturally incapacitated — this difficult play seems to engage head-on with the responsibility of the writer to be truthful: the disasters wreaked upon the characters, which reach their climax in a destructive volcanic eruption, seem to be a metaphorical working-out of Nemesis for a betrayal of that (seemingly) sacred duty. It is the most ambitious, pessimistic, and challenging work to date from Sherman. Now an expatriate living in England amid the complex shifts of European cultural evolution, Sherman produces work that continually offers intriguing assessments from an outsider's perspective.

—Val Taylor

SHERRIFF, R.C. See *Volume 1* entry on *Journey's End*.

SHERWOOD, Robert E(mmet). Born in New Rochelle, New York, USA, 4 April 1896. Educated at Milton Academy, Massachusetts, 1909–14; Harvard University, Cambridge, Massachusetts (editor, *Harvard Lampoon*), 1914–17, AB 1918. Served in the Canadian Black Watch, 1917–19: wounded in action, 1918. Married 1) Mary Brandon in 1922 (divorced 1934), one daughter; 2) Madeline Hurlock Connelly in 1935. First plays produced while student, 1916; drama editor, *Vanity Fair*, New York, 1919–20; founder, with Robert Benchley, Dorothy Parker, and others, Algonquin Hotel Round Table, 1920; film reviewer and associate editor, 1920–24, and editor, 1924–28, *Life* magazine, New York; literary editor, *Scribner's*, New York, 1928–30; first screenplay filmed, 1924; full-time playwright from 1930; founder, with Elmer Rice, Sidney Howard, Maxwell Anderson, S.N. Behrman, and John F. Wharton, Playwrights Company, 1938; served as special assistant to the Secretary of War, Washington, DC, 1939–42; director, Overseas Branch, Office of War Information, 1942–44; special assistant to the Secretary of the Navy, Washington, DC, 1945. Secretary, 1935, and President, 1937–40, Dramatists Guild; President, American National Theatre and Academy, 1940. Recipient: Megrue Prize, 1932; Pulitzer Prize, 1936, 1939, 1941, and, for biography, 1949; American Academy Gold Medal, 1941; Oscar, for screenplay, 1946; Bancroft Prize, for history, 1949; Gutenberg Award, 1949. D. Litt: Dartmouth College, Hanover, New Hampshire, 1940; Yale University, New Haven, Connecticut, 1941; Harvard University, 1949; DCL: Bishop's University, Lennoxville, Quebec, 1950. Died in New York, 14 November 1955.

Stage Works

A White Elephant (produced Harvard University, Cambridge, Massachusetts, 1916).
Barnum Was Right (produced Harvard University, Cambridge, Massachusetts, 1918).
The Road to Rome (produced Playhouse, New York, 1927). 1927.
The Love Nest, from the story by Ring Lardner (produced Comedy Theatre, New York, 1927).
The Queen's Husband (produced Playhouse, New York, 1928). 1928.
Waterloo Bridge (produced Fulton Theatre, New York, 1930). 1930.
This is New York (produced Plymouth Theatre, New York, 1930). 1931.

Reunion in Vienna (produced Martin Beck Theatre, New York, 1931). 1932.
Acropolis (produced Lyric Theatre, London, 1933).
The Petrified Forest (produced Broadhurst Theatre, New York, 1935). 1935.
Idiot's Delight (produced Shubert Theatre, New York, 1936). 1936.
Tovarich, from a play by Jacques Deval (produced Plymouth Theatre, New York, 1936). 1937.
Abe Lincoln in Illinois (produced Plymouth Theatre, New York, 1938). 1939.
There Shall Be No Night (produced Alvin Theatre, New York, 1940). 1940.
The Rugged Path (produced Plymouth Theatre, New York, 1945). Shortened version in *The Best Plays of 1945–46*, edited by Burns Mantle, 1946.
Miss Liberty, music by Irving Berlin (produced Imperial Theatre, New York, 1949). 1949.
Second Threshold, completion of a play by Philip Barry (produced Morosco Theatre, New York, 1951). 1951.
Small War on Murray Hill (produced Ethel Barrymore Theatre, New York, 1957). 1957.

Screenplays

The Hunchback of Notre Dame, with others, 1924; *The Lucky Lady*, with James T. O'Donohoe and Bertram Bloch, 1926; *The Age for Love*, 1931; *Around the World in Eighty Minutes with Douglas Fairbanks*, 1931; *Cock of the Air*, with Charles Lederer, 1932; *Roman Scandals*, with others, 1933; *The Scarlet Pimpernel*, with others, 1935; *The Ghost Goes West*, with Geoffrey Kerr, 1936 (published in *Successful Film Writing*, by Seton Margrave, 1936); *Over the Moon*, with others, 1937; *Thunder in the City*, with others, 1937; *The Adventures of Marco Polo*, 1938 (published in *How to Write and Sell Film Stories*, by Frances Marion, 1937); *The Divorce of Lady X*, with Lajos Biro, 1938; *Idiot's Delight*, 1939; *Abe Lincoln in Illinois*, 1940; *Rebecca* with others, 1940 (published in *Twenty Best Film Plays*, edited by John Gassner and Dudley Nichols, 1943); *The Best Years of Our Lives*, 1946; *The Bishop's Wife*, with Leonardo Bercovici, 1947; *Man on a Tightrope*, 1953; *Main Street to Broadway*, with Samson Raphaelson, 1953.

Television Plays

The Backbone of America, 1954.

Radio Plays

An American Crusader, 1941 (published in *The Free Company Presents*, edited by James Boyd, 1941).

Fiction

The Virtuous Knight. 1931; as *Unending Crusade*, 1932.

Other

Roosevelt and Hopkins: An Intimate History. 1948; revised edition, 1950; as *The White House Papers of Harry L. Hopkins* (2 vols.). 1948–49.

Editor, *The Best Moving Pictures of 1922–23, Also Who's Who in the Movies and the Yearbook of the American Screen*. 1923.

*

Criticism

Books:
John M. Brown, *The Worlds of Robert E. Sherwood*, New York, 1965.
John M. Brown, *The Ordeal of a Playwright: Robert E. Sherwood and the Challenge of War*, New York, 1970.
Walter J. Meserve, *Robert E. Sherwood: Reluctant Moralist*, New York, 1970.
N. S. Sahu, *Theatre of Protest and Anger: Studies in the Dramatic Works of Maxwell Anderson and Robert E. Sherwood*, Delhi, 1988.

Articles:
R. Baird Shuman, "The Shifting Pacifism of Robert E. Sherwood", in *South Atlantic Quarterly*, 65, 1966.

* * *

Playwriting was a major part of Sherwood's life, but not all of it. In 1938 he was one of five playwrights who founded the Playwrights Company in order to have their plays more effectively produced in New York. He wrote an excellent historical biography entitled *Roosevelt and Hopkins* for which he received his fourth Pulitzer Prize. He was a movie critic of exceptional quality during the 1920's when little movie criticism was being written; he was a cinema writer, writing the screenplay for *Idiot's Delight*, for example, and a television writer. He was also an effective ghost writer for Franklin D. Roosevelt as well as Director of the Overseas branch of the Office of War Information during World War II. His skills as a playwright were important to him in all of these endeavors, and it was the career for which he prepared from his Harvard College days onward.

Sherwood's place in American drama is as a part of that group of people—including Maxwell Anderson, Elmer Rice, S. N. Behrman, Philip Barry, Sidney Howard, Paul Green, and George S. Kaufman—who brought American drama to the attention of the world during the period between the two World Wars. In the brilliance of particular plays, some of which have dated rapidly, he distinguished himself for his craftsmanship and his idealistic beliefs. He did not present penetrating ideas, create unforgettable characters, or tell memorable stories, but he did deal honestly, if superficially, with emotions that Americans wanted to feel: belief in God, freedom, peace, and truth. If he asked his audiences to think, it was only for a moment. Yet within a 13-year period he produced six plays which must be considered major successes in the American theatre.

It all started with *The Road to Rome*, ostensibly a potent anti-war play stemming from Sherwood's wartime service and subsequent hatred of war. Concerned with the "human equation", more beautiful than war, according to Sherwood, it addressed the question "why didn't Hannibal destroy Rome when he had the opportunity?". It was not an anti-war argument which deterred Hannibal, however, but a beautiful woman, and herein lies a problem which characterized Sherwood throughout his playwriting career. He always started his plays, he confessed, with a "big message and ended up with nothing but good entertainment". With *Reunion in Vienna*, he thought he had satirized modern science in the guise of a (presumably) intellectual psychiatrist who is cuckolded, but audiences failed to see the conflict of humanity versus science and, instead, thoroughly enjoyed the rollicking, bed-rolling farce written for two exceptional actors, Alfred Lunt and Lynn Fontanne. In *The Petrified Forest*, he tried to express the despair of the vanishing intellectual, "Homo-Semi-Americanus—a speciman of the in-between age", but again produced first-rate theatrical entertainment in a romantic melodrama that linked the gunman and the poet.

Sherwood's anti-war seriousness appeared again in *Idiot's Delight*, which takes place in an Italian resort hotel where a song-and-dance troupe and various guests are stranded as war breaks out. The horror of war is expressed with considerable power as the German scientist rages against the "obscene maniacs" whom he must join, while the little Frenchman attacks the "League of Death"—the munition makers of the world. Yet the romantic plotline again dominated Sherwood's interest in democracy and Christianity as bombs fall to create a theatrically brilliant climax at the final curtain. Not until *Abe Lincoln in Illinois* did Sherwood manage to avoid hokum. Here he dramatized seriously a period of decision in Lincoln's life as he accepted the nomination for the presidency and was elected. 1861 was a terrible time to be President, and 1938 was also a time of anguish for Sherwood who was struggling with contradictory virtues—peace and right. A man of peace filled with compassion for suffering humanity, Sherwood was still unwilling to yield to the disaster of tyranny that he saw in Hitlerism. Finally, in *There Shall Be No Night*, he spoke out in an emotional editorial which demanded that people "stand up and fight for their freedom against forces of atavistic despotism". The play was a brilliant stage success, and for the student of theatre as a propaganda force it showed clearly why Roosevelt did well to select Sherwood as his speech writer. Unfortunately, when the War was over, Sherwood was never again to write successfully for the theatre.

Throughout his career as a dramatist Sherwood believed that the theatre had two essentially equal functions: to entertain and to bring stern realties to the audience. As a moralist and an idealist, he tried to accomplish both and inevitably failed in his own eyes because critics did not understand the serious purpose within the slight framework of plays he so carefully embellished with humor. He never seemed to be able to reach the Horacian ideal because he always succumbed to an evident need to undercut his seriousness with comedy. In only one play did he try to express his thoughts unadorned by any glittering wit. For *Acropolis*, he chose the 5th century BC as his scene and pitted practical men of war against thoughtful men concerned with life and beauty. The play was not successful on stage, however, and Sherwood was never able to write a satisfactory revision. It would seem that Sherwood's message in this play was in Socrates' confession that he is "beginning to believe reluctantly that there are no final answers". But there is a strange light on top of the Parthenon at the close of the play, vaguely suggesting that Socrates' belief in pessimism as a final optimism was not a sufficient answer.

Emotionally and intellectually incapable of resting finally upon paradox or ambiguity, Sherwood found *Acropolis* a constant frustration and kept trying in later plays to dramatize that "human equation" that he delighted in discussing as part of his "Road to Rome". He needed a simple and direct motivation, and the War eventually provided that. An honest man, he did what he felt was demanded by life and by the theatre. His three Pulitzer Prize awards for drama indicate his success with that fickle theatre-going public, and for that brief period between the two World Wars he was a major contributor to popular American theatre.

—Walter J. Meserve

See also *Volume 1* entry on *The Petrified Forest*.

———

SHIELS, George. Born in Ballymoney, County Antrim, Ireland, 24 June 1886. After school, emigrated to Canada; was paralysed as a consequence of a railway accident; returned to Ballymoney and wrote articles and fiction for newspapers; first-produced play, *Away from the Moss*, staged 1918, and early plays appeared under the pseudonym "George Morshiel"; plays from 1921 produced at the Abbey Theatre, Dublin. Throughout his career, his paralysis made him unable to see productions of his work. Died in Ballymoney, 19 September 1949.

Works

Collections

Three Plays (includes *Professor Tim; Paul Twyning; The New Gossoon*).   1945.

Stage Works

Except where otherwise noted, all produced at the Abbey Theatre, Dublin.

Away from the Moss (produced Opera House, Belfast, 1918).
Felix Reid and Bob (produced Opera House, Belfast, 1919).
Bedmates (produced 1921).   1922.
Insurance Money (produced 1921).
Paul Twyning (produced 1922).   In *Three Plays*, 1945.
First Aid (produced 1923).
The Retrievers (produced 1924).
Professor Tim (produced 1925).   In *Three Plays*, 1945.
Cartney and Kevney (produced 1927; revised version produced 1937).   With *Mountain Dew*, 1930.
Mountain Dew (produced 1929).   With *Cartney and Kevney*, 1930.
The New Gossoon (produced 1930).   In *Three Plays*, 1945.
Grogan and the Ferret (produced 1933).   1947.
The Passing Day (produced 1936; Gaelic version, as *Ay Baint lae as*, produced 1952).   With *The Jailbird*, 1937.
The Jailbird (produced 1936).   With *The Passing Day*, 1937.
Quin's Secret (produced 1937).   1947.
Neal Maquade (produced 1938).
Give Him a House (produced 1939).   1947.
The Rugged Path (produced 1940).   With *The Summit*, 1942.
The Summit (produced 1941).   With *The Rugged Path*, 1942.
The Fort Field (produced 1942).   1947.
The New Regime (produced 1944).
Tenants at Will (produced 1945).   1947.
The Old Broom (produced 1946).   1948.
The Caretakers (produced 1948).   1948.

*

Criticism

Books:
N. Sahal, *Sixty Years of Realistic Irish Drama (1900–1960)*, Bombay, 1971.

Articles:
David Kennedy, "George Shiels: A Playwright at Work", in *Threshold*, 25, 1974.
Daniel J. Casey, "George Shiels: The Enigmatic Playwright", in *Threshold*, 33, 1983.

* * *

George Shiels was one of the most popular Abbey Theatre dramatists between the years 1921 and 1948, as well as one of the most prolific. Nearly all of his plays were first produced at the Abbey though he, himself, like his contemporaries, St. John Ervine and Joseph Tomelty, was a native of Northern Ireland. The popularity of his seemingly undemanding comedies provided one of the mainstays of the theatre's box-office during the difficult years following the partition of the country and the Civil War. It must also be said that the frequent revivals of his popular comedies alienated many of the theatre's serious patrons. But, whilst individual examples of his comedies were regarded as little more than light entertainment at the time, his total contribution to Irish theatre demands a higher status. Behind the melodramatic plots and easy laughs is a bitter criticism of human behaviour that reaches beyond his time and the limitations of his technique.

Paralysed as a result of a railway accident whilst working in Canada, Shiels returned to his native County Antrim to be confined for life to a wheel-chair. (Only once did he see one of his plays on the stage when I drove him to Belfast to watch from the wings of the Opera House one of his plays performed by the Abbey Company on tour.) This isolation from live theatre limited the form of his plays. A typical Shiels comedy follows a conventional formula—linear development of plot, clear-cut division into acts, melodramatic situations spiced with laugh-lines, and endings that are contrived and sentimentalised.

Shiels' physical disability also confined his view of society to his immediate surroundings. His comedies are firmly set among the village folk, farmers, and small-town merchants of his native county. His early plays revolve around crafty, but benign, rogues in the manner of Boucicault's Irish melodramas. The eponymous hero of *Paul Twyning*, a vagrant plasterer, engineers the marriage of the timid Dan and Rose against the wishes of their respective parents, but has no scruples about stealing £600 in the process. In one of Shiels' most popular comedies, *Professor Tim*, a bogus professor is the catalyst of the action. In *The New Gossoon* Luke, the son of a hard-working farming family, sees nothing wrong in stealing sheep, money, and eggs to obtain petrol for his motor-bike in order to gamble on greyhounds. In these early comedies Shiels showed a reluctance to make moral judgements for fear of displeasing his audience, leading Yeats to declare in 1927 that *Cartney and Kevney* "displayed a series of base actions without anything to show its author disapproved or expected us to do so".

In Shiels' more mature plays the rogues become mean or vicious and the underlying tone is both critical and grim. *The Passing Day* is his only play that does not follow a linear plot development. The scene is a hospital where John Fibbs, a miserly merchant, is dying, surrounded by his avaricious wife, his nephew and nephew's girl friend, and a nurse; each one is scheming to benefit from his will. The action moves in flash-backs to his boyhood where his parents are seen as being as miserly as himself, and to his last day in his general store where he shows no mercy to his creditors, provoking a grave-digger to hope that Fibbs will "pay the balance afore night . . . that I may dig a hole for ye within three days". *The Passing Day* profoundly shocked the traditional Shiels audience when it was first performed. Later it came to be recognised as one of his most powerful plays. But his best plays were still to come.

In 1940 *The Rugged Path* broke Abbey records for the length of its run. The play takes place in the border country where the Dolis Clan claim to have pursued their lawless lives for 1,000 years. They live by terrorising the neighbouring farms with their knives and guns, burning their ricks, killing their dogs, stealing their sheep, secure in the knowledge that the shame of being denounced as an "informer" will prevent witnesses to their crimes appearing in court. The scattered police force can do nothing to control them and juries will not convict for fear of reprisals. The message Shiels gives is that terrorists can only be defeated when a united front of Irishmen is prepared to stand up against them.

Shiels' only historical play, *Tenants at Will*, can hardly be considered a comedy. It is set in 1844, a year before the potato blight and famine of 1845, among a peasant community where tenants, burdened by rates, crippling rents, and tithes paid to an alien Church, are denied rights of tenure; where bailiffs and landlords' agents dispossess them of their miserable small-holdings, and charity is dispensed by "moral agents" of the Big House. The climax of the play is the murder of the landlord and his son by Patrick, a skilled platelayer, who has worked in France and picked up the rhetoric and activism of revolution. Patrick is reprieved, and the evictions and rent arrears are forgiven, but this contrived "happy ending" does not conceal the fact that the evil of landlordism remained.

In these plays Shiels entered the world where comedy wears a grim mask and laughter is dulled by a deeper truth. It is by his last plays that he earns a place among the foremost playwrights of his time.

—Hugh Hunt

————————

SHIRLEY, James. Born in Walbrook, London; baptised 7 September 1596. Educated at Merchant Taylors' School, London, 1608–12; possibly St. John's College, Oxford, 1612; St. Catherine's Hall, Cambridge, 1615–17, BA 1617. Married Elizabeth Gilmet in 1618; three sons and two daughters. Ordained in Church of England: parish priest in Wheathampstead, Hertfordshire, c.1618–21; headmaster, Edward VI Grammar School, St. Albans, Hertfordshire, 1621–24; moved to London, 1624, and had joined Roman Catholic Church by this time; wrote for Queen Henrietta's Men at the Cockpit Theatre (also known as Phoenix Theatre), 1625–36; gentleman in the Queen's household, 1634; wrote for John Ogilby's St. Werbergh Street theatre in Dublin, after plague closed London theatres, 1636–40; returned to London, as chief dramatist for the King's Men, until Parliament closed the theatres, 1642; fought for the royalists during the English Civil War, under his patron the Earl of Newcastle, 1642–44; schoolteacher in London from 1644. Died (buried) in London, 29 October 1666.

Works

Collections

Six New Plays (includes *The Doubtful Heir; The Imposture; The Brothers; The Cardinal; The Court Secret; The Sisters*). 1653.
Dramatic Works and Poems, edited by William Gifford and Alexander Dyce (6 vols.). 1833.
Plays (includes *The Witty Fair One; Hyde Park; The Triumph of Peace*), edited by Edmund Gosse. 1888.

Stage Works

The School of Compliment or, Love Tricks (produced by Lady Elizabeth's Men, Cockpit/Phoenix Theatre, London, 1625). 1631; as *Love Tricks*, 1667.
The Wedding (produced by Lady Elizabeth's Men, Cockpit/Phoenix Theatre, London, 1626?). 1629.
The Maid's Revenge (produced by Queen Henrietta's Men, Cockpit/Phoenix Theatre, London, 1626). 1639.
The Witty Fair One (produced by Queen Henrietta's Men, Cockpit/Phoenix Theatre, London, 1628). 1633.
The Grateful Servant (produced by Queen Henrietta's Men, Cockpit/Phoenix Theatre, London, 1629). 1630.
The Traitor (produced by Queen Henrietta's Men, Cockpit/Phoenix Theatre, London, 1631). 1635.
Love's Cruelty (produced by Queen Henrietta's Men, Cockpit/Phoenix Theatre, London, 1631). 1640.
The Humorous Courtier (as *The Duke*, produced by Queen Henrietta's Men, Cockpit/Phoenix Theatre, London, 1631). 1640.
Changes; or, Love in a Maze. 1632.
The Ball (produced by Queen Henrietta's Men, Cockpit/Phoenix Theatre, London, 1632). 1639.
Hyde Park (produced by Queen Henrietta's Men, Cockpit/Phoenix Theatre, London, 1632). 1637.
The Bird in a Cage; or, The Beauties (produced by Queen Henrietta's Men, Cockpit/Phoenix Theatre, London, 1632–33?). 1633.
A Contention for Honour and Riches. 1633; revised version, as *Honoria and Mammon*, 1658.
The Gamester (produced by Queen Henrietta's Men, Cockpit/Phoenix Theatre, London, 1633). 1637.
The Young Admiral (produced by Queen Henrietta's Men, Cockpit/Phoenix Theatre, London, 1633). 1637.
The Example (produced by Queen Henrietta's Men, Cockpit/Phoenix Theatre, London, 1634). 1637.
The Triumph of Peace (masque; produced at Court, Whitehall Palace, London, 1634). 1634.
The Opportunity (produced by Queen Henrietta's Men, Cockpit/Phoenix Theatre, London, 1634). 1640.
The Night-Walker; or, The Little Thief, from a play by Fletcher (produced by Queen Henrietta's Men, Cockpit/Phoenix Theatre, London, 1634). 1661.
The Lady of Pleasure (produced by Queen Henrietta's Men, Cockpit/Phoenix Theatre, London, 1635). 1637.
The Coronation (produced by Queen Henrietta's Men, Cockpit/Phoenix Theatre, London, 1635). 1640.
Chabot, Admiral of France, from the play by Chapman (produced by Queen Henrietta's Men, Cockpit/Phoenix Theatre, London, 1635). 1639.
The Arcadia, from the work by Sidney (produced by Queen Henrietta's Men, Cockpit/Phoenix Theatre, London, before 1636). 1640.
The Duke's Mistress (produced by Queen Henrietta's Men, Cockpit/Phoenix Theatre, London, 1636). 1638.
The Constant Maid; or, Love Will Find Out the Way (produced by Ogilby's Men, Dublin?, 1636–40?). 1640; as *Love Will Find Out the Way*, 1661.
The Royal Master (produced by Ogilby's Men, Dublin, 1637). 1638.
The Doubtful Heir; or, Rosania (produced by Ogilby's Men, Dublin, 1638?). In *Six New Plays*, 1653.
The Country Captain, with William Cavendish (produced by the King's Men, Blackfriars Theatre, London, 1639?). With *The Variety*, 1649; as *Captain Underwit*, in *Old English Plays 2*, edited by A. H. Bullen, 1883.
St. Patrick for Ireland, part 1 (produced by Ogilby's Men, Dublin, 1639?). 1640.
The Politician (produced by Ogilby's Men, Dublin, 1639?). 1655.
The Gentleman of Venice (produced by Ogilby's Men, Dublin, 1639?; or possibly produced by Queen Henrietta's Men, London, 1639). 1655.
The Imposture (produced by the King's Men, Blackfriars Theatre, 1640). In *Six New Plays*, 1653.
The Brothers; or, The Politic Father (produced by the King's Men, Blackfriars Theatre, London, 1641?). In *Six New Plays*, 1653.
The Cardinal (produced by the King's Men, Blackfriars Theatre, 1641). In *Six New Plays*, 1653; edited by E.M. Yearling, 1986.
The Court Secret. In *Six New Plays*, 1653.
The Sisters (produced by the King's Men, Blackfriars Theatre, 1642). In *Six New Plays*, 1653.
The Contention of Ajax and Ulysses for the Armour of Achilles (produced 1645–58?). With *Honoria and Mammon*, 1658.
The Triumph of Beauty. In *Poems*. 1646.
Cupid and Death, music by Matthew Locke (masque; produced London?, 1653). 1653.

Verse

Poems. 1646.
The Rudiments of Grammar: The Rules Composed in Verse for the Greater Benefit and Delight of Young Beginners. 1656; revised edition, as *Manductio*, 1660.
Dramatic Works and Poems (see Collections).

Other

Via ad Latinam Linguam Complanata, The Way Made Plain to the Latin Tongue. 1649; as *Grammatica Anglo-Latina*, 1651.
The True Impartial History and Wars of the Kingdom of Ireland. 1693.

*

Bibliographies

R.K. Zimmer, *James Shirley: A Reference Guide*, Boston, 1980.

Criticism

Books:
R.S. Forsythe, *The Relations of Shirley's Plays to the Elizabethan Drama*, New York, 1914.
Hanson T. Parlin, *A Study of Shirley's Comedies of London Life*, 1914.

A.H. Nason, *James Shirley, Dramatist: A Biographical and Critical Study*, New York, 1915.

S.J. Radtke, *James Shirley: His Catholic Philosophy of Life*, Washington, DC, 1929.

Alfred Harbage, *Cavalier Drama*, London, 1938.

Margot Heinemann, *Puritanism and Theatre*, Cambridge, 1980.

Ben Lucow, *James Shirley*, Boston, 1981.

Martin Butler, *Theatre and Crisis, 1632–1642*, Cambridge, 1984.

Sandra A. Burner, *James Shirley: A Study of Literary Coteries and Patronage in Seventeenth-Century England*, Lanham, Maryland, 1988.

Articles:

R. Morton, "Deception and Social Distinction: An Aspect of James Shirley's Drama", in *Renaissance Drama*, 9, 1966.

D. Stevens, "The Stagecraft of James Shirley", in *Educational Theatre Journal*, 29, 1977.

* * *

James Shirley was a prolific and able dramatist who in the Caroline period developed a long-standing relationship with the second most prestigious London company, the Queen's Men, and who ended his playwriting career as Philip Massinger's successor as principal playwright to the King's Men. At the outset of his career, his inventive, easy-going and elegant manner readily filled a gap which had been left at the death of John Fletcher, and his plays quickly became a staple of the Caroline repertoire. Although he was adept as a writer of fluent tragicomedy, and particularly well-versed in the arts of the intricate plot, the teasingly contrived situation and the character poised between laughter and tears, Shirley's real talent lay in the direction of comedy of manners. A series of brilliant successes in this form—*The Wedding, The Witty Fair One, Hyde Park, The Ball,* and *The Lady of Pleasure*—established him as easily the most skillful depictor of the emerging world of fashion. He also scored a decisive success in 1634 with *The Triumph of Peace*, a masque presented at Whitehall by gentlemen of the Inns of Court which was paraded in advance through the city streets as one of the most remarkable public spectacles of Charles's reign. His career took an unexpected direction in 1636 when, with the London playhouses closed because of plague, he went to Ireland, probably in the train of Lord Deputy Wentworth. These middle-period plays, and the prologues which introduced them, evinced considerable uncertainty about what would take with his Irish audience. On return to London in 1640, Shirley substantially abandoned his earlier comic bent, and re-established himself as a specialist in tragicomedy and tragedy of a Websterian flavour.

Shirley was entirely a dramatist of the fashionable audiences of gentrified London. Many of his friendships seem to have been centred on the Inns of Court, and he had little regard for the traditions of drama associated with the popular playhouses of his day. The smooth tragicomedy *The Young Admiral* was so admired by the Master of the Revels as an example of what decent drama ought to be like that he entered its name in his office book "for direction to my successor, and for example to all poets", and the comedy *The Gamester* was written by Shirley specifically to a plot given him by the King himself. The height of social success came in 1634 when, as a reward for the success of *The Triumph of Peace*, he achieved direct patronage from the Queen. Yet Shirley was never entirely a creature of the Court. In a minor war of the theatres that erupted around 1629–30, Shirley

came out on the side of Massinger, Randolph, and Habington, all writers of an independent frame of mind, and opposed to Davenant and Carew who were more determined courtly careerists. He ran into trouble over *The Ball* for its too overtly satirical representations of court personalities, and *The Triumph of Peace* complimented the King, but also warned him seriously about the abuse of power. Shirley's politics were paternalistic but not slavishly obsequious: gentlemen in his comedies have a way of putting aristocrats right on matters of principle.

Shirley's enduring achievements are his comedies of manners which focus intensely on a narrow, leisured society straddling the boundary between gentility and nobility, and perambulating a characteristic territory of drawing-room, bedroom, and park. These plays were crucibles of genteel conduct. Resonant with the speaking-tones of a gentry class moving up to London, and featuring grand social events at which the interactions of poised and ceremonious people of fashion are studied, Shirley's comedies of manners were both reflecting a new kind of social self-consciousness and helping to bring it into being. In the best example, *The Lady of Pleasure*, Shirley tested the practices of mannered society by pitting witty behaviour against worthy behaviour. On the one hand there is the prodigal lady of pleasure, Aretina, who fritters her husband's estate away on the vanities of the town; on the other hand there is the decent lady Celestina, who indulges in the delights of society but keeps a firm eye on the monetary and moral limits of her freedoms. The argument is further ramified by the presence of Lord A., who supposes that Celestina's openness indicates a promiscuity which he may exploit. In the play's culminating event, Celestina disciplines the renegade lord in the proper understanding of his honour. Similar testing and reforming scenes recur over and again in *Hyde Park, The Ball,* and *The Example*: Shirley's drama was defining and policing the norms of a society aware that it was passing through a process of change. The lessons are made lively by the vigorous congeries of wits and fools, stewards and secretaries, servants, maids, pages, barbers, and jockeys, amongst which they take place.

After the closing of the playhouses, Shirley returned to schoolmastering but continued his writing with a number of masques for amateur or schoolboy performance; these possess considerable charm. His comedies were frequently revived in the early years of the Restoration, though they did not constitute a powerful link between the drama before and after the Civil War. Though they were important as transition pieces between Jacobean and Restoration comedy, they were rather too moralistic and old-fashioned for Restoration taste, and were, early on, dislodged by the plays of more current writers.

—Martin Butler

See also *Volume 1* entry on *Hyde Park*.

———

SHVARTS, Evgeny (Lvovich). Born in Kazan, Russia, 9 October (21 October, New Style) 1896. Studied law at Moscow University, but abandoned studies in 1915. Married 1) actress from the Rostov theatre troupe (divorced); 2) Yekaterina Ivanovna. Moved to Rostov-on-Don after university, and there joined P.K. Veysbrem's experimental theatre company as actor, 1919: moved with the company to Petrograd, 1921, but after two seasons mostly gave up acting and turned to writing humorous articles and sketches for the "House of Arts" writers' club; moved to Bakhmut, in the Donbass region, and joined staff of a newspaper, 1923–24; returned to Leningrad (previously Petrograd), and worked on Samuil Marsak's magazines *Yozh* [The Hedgehog] and *Chizh* [The Finch] for the childrens' department of Gosizdat, the State publishing house; first-produced play, *Undervud* [Underwood], staged 1929; during World War II, remained in Leningrad during its siege as a defence warden, leaving only in 1942; his plays suffered from censorship during Stalinist period; in later years, lived outside Leningrad in the Komarovo artists' community. Died in Leningrad, 15 January 1958.

Works

Collections

"Ten" i drugie pesy ["The Shadow" and Other Plays] (includes *Dva klyona; Snezhnaya Koroleva; Ten; Odna noch; Obyknovennoe chudo; Zolushka*).   1956.
Pesy [Plays] (includes *Dva klyona; Snezhnaya Koroleva; Ten; Obyknovennoe chudo; Zolushka; Klad; Goly korol; Drakon; Povest o molodykh; Don Kikhot*).   1960.
Pesy i kinostsenary [Plays and Screenplays].   1962.
Skazki; Povesti; Pesy [Fairy Tales; Stories; Plays].   1969.
Pesy [Plays].   1972 (contents as 1960 edition, excepting *Goly korol*, but adding *Krasnaya Shapochka*).   1972.
Goly Korol; Ten; Drakon, edited by Avril Peyman.   1972 (Oxford).
The Naked King; The Shadow; The Dragon, translated by Elisaveta Fen.   1976.

Stage Works

Undervud [Underwood] (produced Children's Theatre, Leningrad, 1929).   1930.
Pustaky [Trifles] (puppet play) (produced Demenni Theatre, Leningrad, 1932).   1932.
Klad [The Treasure] (produced Children's Theatre, Leningrad, 1933).   In *Pesy*, 1960.
Priklyucheniya Gogenshtaufen [The Adventures of Hohenstaufen] (produced Moscow Central Children's Theatre, 1988).   In *Zvezda*, 1934.
Brat i sestra [Brother and Sister] (produced Children's Theatre, Leningrad, 1936).   1936.
Krasnaya Shapochka [Little Red Riding Hood] (produced Children's Theatre, Leningrad, 1937).   1936?; in book form, in *Pesy*, 1972.
Snezhnaya Koroleva [The Snow Queen] (produced New Children's Theatre, Leningrad, 1939).   In *"Ten" i drugie pesy*, 1956.
Kukolny gorod [Puppet City] (puppet play; produced Demmeni Theatre, Leningrad, 1939).   In *Kukolny gorod: Pesy dlya teatra kukol*, 1959.
Nashe gosteprymstvo [Our Hospitality].   1939.
Skazka o poteryannom vremeni [A Tale of Stolen Time] (puppet play; produced Demmeni Theatre, Leningrad, 1940).   1948?
Ten (produced Comedy Theatre, Leningrad, 1940).   In *Literaturny sovremennik*, 1940; in book form, in *"Ten" i drugie pesy*, 1956; translated as *The Shadow*, in *An Anthology of Russian Plays 2*, edited by F.D. Reeve, 1963, and in *The Naked King . . .* (collection), 1976.

Odna noch [One Night].   In *"Ten" i drugie pesy*, 1956.
Pod lipami Berlina [Under the Berlin Lindens] (produced Comedy Theatre, Leningrad, 1942).
Drakon (produced by the Leningrad Comedy Theatre, Dushanbe, 1944).   1944; translated as *The Dragon*, 1963; several subsequent translations under same title.
Daloky kray [Distant Land].   1950.
Dva klyona (produced Children's Theatre, Leningrad, 1954).   In *"Ten" i drugie pesy*, 1960; translated as *The Two Maples*, in *Russian Plays for Young Audiences*, edited by M. Morton, 1979.
Obyknovennoe chudo [An Ordinary Miracle] (produced Comedy Theatre, Leningrad, 1956).   In *"Ten" i drugie pesy*, 1960.
Povest o molodykh suprugakh [Story of the Newlyweds] (produced Comedy Theatre, Leningrad, 1957).   In *Pesy*, 1960.
Goly Korol (produced Sovremennik Theatre, Moscow, 1960).   In *Pesy*, 1960; translated as *The Naked King*, in *Contemporary Russian Drama*, translated by F.D. Reeve, 1968, and in *The Naked King . . .* (collection), 1979.
Zolushka [Cinderella].   In *"Ten" i drugie pesy*, 1956.

Screenplays

Zolushka [Cinderella]; 1947, *Snezhnaya Koroleva* [The Snow Queen], 1950; *Don Quixote*, from Bulgakov's adaptation, 1957 (published in *Pesy*, 1960); *Tsar Vodokrut* (published in *Pesy i kinostsenary*, 1962); *Kain XVIII* [Cain XVIII], completed by Nikolai Erdman, 1963.

Fiction

Rasskaz staroy balalyki (story).   1925.

Memoirs and Letters

Memuary (autobiography).   1982.

*

Criticism

Books:
Lionel R. Simard, "Evgenij Svarc: Dramatist, Satirist, Wizard", in *Symbolae in honorem Georgii Y Shevelov*, edited by William E. Harkins and others, Munich, 1971.
L. Debüser (ed.), *Evgenii Swarz, Mensch und Schatten*, Berlin, 1972.
Amanda J. Metcalf, *Evgenii Shvarts and His Fairy-Tales for Adults*, Birmingham, 1979.
Harold B. Segel, *Twentieth-Century Russian Drama*, New York, 1979.

Articles:
J. Douglas Clayton, "The Theatre of E.L. Shvarts: An Introduction", in *Études slaves et est-européennes*, 19, 1974.
Irina H. Corten, "Evgeny Lvovich Shvarts: A Biographical Sketch", in *Russina Literature Triquarterly*, 16, 1979.
Felicia H. Londré, "Evgeny Shvarts and the Uses of Fantasy in the Soviet Theatre", in *Research Studies* (Washington State University), 47, 1979.

* * *

Evgeny Shvarts (also transliterated as Schwarz) in spite of his German-sounding name and the fact that his father, a doctor, was of Jewish background, was wholly Russian. He came from a cultivated family, but in 1915 abandoned his law studies at Moscow University and moved to Rostov-on-Don, where in 1919 he joined an experimental theatre group, becoming a competent comic character actor. In 1921 the troupe moved to Petrograd, where experimental theatre was being encouraged in the early years of Soviet rule, but did not survive there more than two seasons.

Shvarts now gave up acting almost completely and became a popular member of the "House of Arts", a Petrograd writers' club, for which he wrote humorous skits. Towards the end of 1923 he moved south to the town of Bakhmut (now Artemovsk) in the Donbass where he joined the staff of a local newspaper, organising and contributing to a literary supplement. In 1925, back in Petrograd, which had now become Leningrad, he became writer for and part editor of two children's magazines, working for the children's division of the State publishing house, Gosizdat, which at the time was headed by the outstanding Soviet writer for children, Samuil Marshak, to whom Shvarts later acknowledged his heavy debt.

Shvarts's career as a playwright officially began in 1929, the year of his first play *Undervud* ("Underwood", or "The Typewriter") about a witch who steals a typewriter and is eventually caught by a little girl, member of the Young Pioneers' Organisation. This was successfully staged at the Leningrad Theatre for Young Viewers (ie. Children's Theatre), but the fantasy element did not find favour with those militant right-wing self-styled "pedologists", influential at a time when Stalin was beginning to assert his authority over the arts, who believed that children should not be encouraged by fairy tales to use their imaginations. After an unsuccessful puppet play called *Pustyaki* (Trifles), in 1934 Shvarts wrote three plays: *Klad* (The Treasure), about young Soviets prospecting for copper in the Caucasus, *Priklyucheniya Gogenshtaufena* (The Adventures of Hohenstaufen), realistically set in a business office, but turning into fantasy (not performed until 1988), and his first significant play, derived from Hans Christian Andersen, *Goly Korol* (The Naked King), not staged until 1960.

In 1937 he wrote *Krasnaya Shapochka* (a lively version of the Little Red Riding Hood tale) and in 1938 *Snezhnaya Koroleva* (The Snow Queen), also after Andersen, made into a film in 1950. By this time Shvarts was also writing puppet plays and film scripts, as he continued to do for the rest of his life.

In 1940, the first of his best known plays, *Ten* (The Shadow), based on Andersen's story about the man who lost his shadow, was produced at the Leningrad Comedy Theatre. This was the first play by Shvarts specifically aimed at an adult audience. Set in an imaginary kingdom, it mercilessly satirises the self-seeking, the greedy, the hypocritical, the sycophantic. The Shadow of the title is a kind of dark spectre of mediocrity, haunting even the good characters, chief among whom is the Scholar. With the German invasion of the Soviet Union in 1941 the Comedy Theatre closed. Even after the War, in the period 1945–53, Stalin's oppressive regime ensured that Shvarts's play was not revived, as its relevance to Soviet society was all too clear. At that time Soviet writers were compelled to depict the Soviet Union in generally positive colours. *The Shadow* was given a new production in 1960. After being temporarily dropped from the repertory of the Comedy Theatre it was revived in December, 1984, and it now holds a popular place in the Soviet repertory. It was filmed in 1952.

During World War II Shvarts lived in Leningrad at the worst time of the German blockade, leaving the city only in

1942. Having written two unsuccessful realistic patriotic plays, he turned again to fantasy and began work on what became his acknowledged masterpiece, *Drakon* (The Dragon). In 1944 this was performed by the company of the Leningrad Comedy Theatre. It was banned after the first performance, and the director, Nikolai Akimov, was to recall later that a "super-alert high-up" saw something in the play that wasn't there. It was presented for a season in 1960, but, although repeatedly staged abroad, it remained for the most part out of the Soviet theatre until Gorbachev ushered in the *glasnost* period in 1985.

Like *The Shadow*, *The Dragon* is a fairy-tale for adults. Its basis is the legend of St. George, but Shvarts's hero, typically, is the mild unassuming Lancelot who arrives in town and duly slays the dragon (whose first appearance is in human form) that has held the people in fear for many years. But the unscrupulous Mayor, aided and abetted by his ambitious son, takes the opportunity to increase his authority, so becoming a "dragon" in his own right. Shvarts was emphasising that human beings are only too apt to submit to those in power, and if one "dragon" is slain, they may well create another in its place. In 1944 this message was seen as applying to Hitler's Germany, but its relevance to Soviet Russia before and after Stalin's death helps to explain why it was, for so long, under a ban.

It was inevitable, in view of Shvarts's detestation of tyranny, that under Stalin in the post-war period he wrote comparatively little for the stage, although he did publish a number of children's stories. In the last years of his life, with Stalin out of the way, Shvarts lived quietly in the country near Leningrad in a kind of artists' colony, finally able to enjoy a reasonably comfortable existence. In 1956 his last major play *Obyknovennoe chudo* (An Ordinary Miracle) was premiered in Moscow and Leningrad. This was filmed in 1964. Reflecting Shvarts's happier frame of mind, it is an optimistic fairy-tale comedy about the wonder-working power of love, lacking the darker shades and underlying bitterness of *The Dragon* and *The Shadow*. After this, Shvarts's principal work was the writing of a film scenario for *Don Quixote*. Directed by Grigory Kozintsev, this achieved worldwide success.

Shvarts's contribution to the theatre was comparatively small, but in his "fairy-tales for adults" he achieved a delightful blend of fantasy, humour, wit, and satire, presented in lively and colourful theatrical style. By using fairy tales he was able to focus on basic human characteristics so that a play like *The Dragon* is relevant, not only to Hitler's Germany or Stalin's Russia, but to any society anywhere. All his plays end positively, showing that Shvarts, whose career was by no means an easy one, never lost his optimistic view of life. He deserves to be better known than he is.

—John Goodliffe

See also *Volume 1* entry on *The Dragon*.

———————

SILVA, António José da. Born into a Jewish family, Rio de Janeiro, Brazil, 8 May 1705. Family ordered back to Portugal by the Inquisition, 1712. Studied law at the University of Coimbra, 1726: studies interrupted by period of imprisonment and torture. Married his cousin, Leonor Maria de Carvalho, in 1734 or 1735; one daughter. Returned briefly to

Rio de Janeiro, 1726; arrested, tortured, and eventually released after renouncing his Jewish faith; settled in Lisbon and opened law practice; first-produced play, *Vida do Grand D. Quixote de la Mancha e do Gordo Sancho Panza*, staged 1733; was denounced for reverting to the Jewish faith and, with his wife and mother, arrested, 1737: imprisoned 1737–39. Executed in an *auto-da-fé* in Lisbon, 18 October 1739.

Works

Collections

Theatro Cómico Portuguez (2 vols.), edited by Francisco Luís Ameno. 1744.
Óperas Portuguesas. 1746.
Teatro (2 vols.), edited by João Ribeiro. 1911.
Obras Completas (4 vols.), edited by João Pereira Tavares. 1957–58.

Stage Works

Vida do Grande D. Quixote de la Mancha e do Gordo Sancho Pança (produced Teatro do Bairro Alto, Lisbon, 1733). In *Theatro Cómico Portuguez*, 1744.
Esopaida; ou, Vida Esopo (produced Teatro do Bairro Alto, Lisbon, 1734). In *Theatro Cómico Portuguez*, 1744.
Encantos de Medea (produced Teatro do Bairro Alto, Lisbon, 1735). In *Theatro Cómico Portuguez*, 1744.
Anfitrião; ou, Júpiter e Alcmena (produced Teatro do Bairro Alto, Lisbon, 1736). In *Theatro Cómico Portuguez*, 1744.
O Laberinto de Creta (produced Teatro do Bairro Alto, Lisbon, 1736). Edited by António Isidoro da Fonseca, 1736.
Guerras do Alecrim e Mangerona (produced Teatro do Bairro Alto, Lisbon, 1737). Edited by A.I. da Fonseca, 1737.
Variedades de Proteu (produced Teatro do Bairro Alto, Lisbon, 1737). Edited by António Isodoro da Fonseca, 1737.
Precipócio de Faetonte (produced Teatro do Bairro Alto, Lisbon, 1738). In *Theatro Cómico Portuguez*, 1744.

Fiction

Obras do Diabinho da Mão Furadat (novella), edited by João Ribeiro. 1911.
El Prodigio de Amarante (attributed), edited by Claude-Henri Frèches. 1967.

*

Criticism

Books:
C. Jucá Filho, *António José, o Judeu*, Rio de Janeiro, 1940.
Luciana Stegagno Picchio, *Storia del teatro portoghese*, Rome, 1964.
L.F. Rebello, *História do Teatro Português*, Lisbon, 1967.
Cl.-H. Frèches, *António José da Silva et l'Inquisition*, Paris, 1982.

Articles
Cl.-H. Frèches, "Introduction au théâtre du 'Judeu' (António José da Silva)", in *Bulletin d'histoire du théâtre portugais*, 1, 1950.
P. Furter, "La Structure de l'univers dramatique de A.J. da Silva, 'o Judeu'", in *Bulletin des études portugaises et de l'Institut Français au Portugal* (new series), 25, 1964.

*   *   *

António José da Silva, known "o Judeu" (the Jew), is the playwright who stands out in Portugal's otherwise dramatically weak 18th century. His eight plays, called *operas*, are comedies in prose, interspersed with recitations of sonnets and arias, the music for which was composed by António Teixeira, who had studied in Italy. Influences on Silva include the Spanish cloak-and-sword plays and the picaresque; the native Vicentine tradition, and its breakdown into the *entremeses*, or dramatic sketches, mostly spectacle and of little dramatic value; Italian opera, which had become fashionable and popular at the Court of D. João IV; and the increasing influence of French theatre, replacing the longstanding dominance of Castilian culture.

Performed exclusively by puppets, Silva's plays were all produced at the Theatre of the Bairro Alto in Lisbon. The audience was drawn from the common people and the petty bourgeoisie, though it is possible that some of the nobility frequented the Theatre. The divergence between two kinds of theatre and their venues, begun during the Spanish Occupation of 1580–1640 (Castilian plays and Jesuit neo-classical drama being performed at Court, while the Vicentine *auto* continued to be performed for the common people in open-air venues, or *pátios*) developed into a clear division in the 18th century.

Silva's characters, deriving ultimately from Roman comedy and the picaresque, are principally on two levels: the nobles, often impoverished yet clinging to outmoded ideals and beliefs, and the sharp-witted servants, frank and realistic in their words and deeds. Other stock figures are the newly-rich bourgeois with pretensions to nobility, the elderly female go-betweens, and the marriageable girls jealously guarded by father or uncle. All but three of the plays are based on mythological characters and themes.

The plots revolve ostensibly around courtship and marriage, the *gracioso* playing the key role in furthering the amorous aims of his master; but this plotting is merely a springboard for Silva's satiric view of Portuguese society. The comedy of manners and of situation is carried along by the witty language in short scenes that do not necessarily advance the dramatic action. Farcical situations and confusions of identity and purpose are conveyed by a range of linguistic registers, from puns, racy jokes, and *double entendre*, popular neologisms, and proverbs, to Gongoric declarations of love, macaronic Latin, and arias. The staging of the plays required fantastic effects and machinery, creating a world of illusions and magical transformations. The set and props for *D. Quixote*, for example, included a lion in a wheeled cage; horses; Mount Parnassus complete with Muses, Apollo, and Pegasus; a boat; a flying horse; a cloud; and a pig.

The immediate appeal of these plays lies in their comedy, linking characters and events by language open to ambiguity. The confusions arising from such ambiguity also lead to mistaken comprehension and feelings. In *Encantos de Medea*, *Anfitrião*, and *O Laberinto de Creta*, the labyrinth of love is applied to a dramatic universe where appearance takes precedence over reality. Jealousy, arising from the mistaking of the one for the other, not only serves a comic purpose but also acts to complicate further the dramatic action. The early plays, *D. Quixote* and *Esopaida*, aim to demonstrate a "truth" that is evident from the start and which is not dependent on a progression in the action. The later plays, such as *Guerras*, are more successful in dove-tailing the many scenes to the demands of the plot.

The purpose behind the play between appearance and reality is to enlighten. The practical sense of the *gracioso* contrasts with the fantasy vision of the nobility. By mocking the outmoded and idealised sentiments declared by their masters, the servants not only satirise the false language of love but also criticise the society that those masters direct. As agents of the action, the servants ridicule institutions that they cannot attack in practice. By parody and caricature of the representatives of power—kings, princes, judges—Silva subverts the values of Portuguese society. No longer are the morals and behaviour of the aristocracy those to be aspired to. The implication is that a more realistic and open spirit is needed if Portugal is to survive.

Although it is generally held that Silva was arrested by the Inquisition for his relapse into Judaism, it is possible that his incisive satires on the establishment contributed to his fate. In *D. Quixote*, the scene in which Sancho Pança, as Governor of the Island of Lizards, dispenses justice, is a bitter but veiled attack on the fatuous and arbitrary nature of the judiciary. In *Labirinto de Creta*, the old unjust order represented by King Minos is brought to an end. This is one of the most complex of Silva's plays: not only is there the literal and allegorical labyrinth of the myth, but also the structural labyrinth of the plot and the psychological one of the three sets of lovers (Theseus, Ariadne, and Phaedra, with their respective suitors) and the servants. Exchange of identities and the deceptions and jealousies arising therefrom are directed by the servants. Implicit in the play is the notion that it is they, as agents of the action, who cause the change in the situation and psychology whereby a new, just order is brought into being.

Silva's most popular and often-performed play, *Guerras do Alecrim e Mangerona*, centres on the wooing of two wealthy young girls of *arriviste* origin by two impoverished and dim-witted noblemen, against the background of Lisbon at carnival time. Like the carnival, the play has a serio-comic purpose. The satire is aimed not just at the ridiculously partisan nature of the rival groups who take herbs or flowers as their emblems (hence the "Wars"), but at the social structure that permits or supports such folly. The comedy exploits the absurd stratagems resorted to by the servants to further their masters' and mistresses' love matches. The various social types are well drawn (the pretentious D. Tibúrcio, cousin and unwelcome suitor of the girls, has many affinities with Molière's Monsieur Jourdan in *Le Bourgeois Gentilhomme*), the language is richly inventive and witty, and the breakneck speed at which confusion follows upon confusion makes this one of the most accessible of the plays to a modern audience.

Silva's life has been the subject of a novel, *O Judeu* (The Jew), by the 19th-century writer Camilo Castelo Branco; the play *O Judeu*, by Bernardo Santareno, focuses on Silva's imprisonment and trial; and the final scene of José Saramago's 1982 novel, *Memorial do Convento* (translated as *Baltasar and Blimunda*), takes place at the *auto-da-fé* when Silva was put to death.

—Juliet Perkins

SILVA LEITÃO DE ALMEIDA GARRETT, João Baptista da. See GARRETT, João . . .

SIMON, (Marvin) Neil. Born in the Bronx, New York, 4 July 1927. Educated at De Witt Clinton High School, New York, graduated 1943; New York University, 1944–45; University of Denver, 1945–46. Served in the United States Army Air Force, 1945–46: Corporal. Married 1) Joan Baim in 1953 (died 1973), two daughters; 2) the actress Marsha Mason in 1973 (divorced 1983); 3) Diane Lander in 1987. Radio and television writer, 1948–60; writer of screenplays, from 1966. Recipient: Emmy Award, for television writing, 1957, 1959; Tony Award, 1965, 1970, 1985, 1991; Shubert Award, 1968; Writers Guild of America West Award, for screenplay, 1969, 1971, 1976; PEN Los Angeles Center Award, 1982; New York Drama Critics Circle Award, 1983; Outer Circle Award, 1983, 1985; New York State Governor's Award, 1986; Pulitzer Prize, 1991. LHD: Hofstra University, Hempstead, New York, 1981; Williams College, Williamstown, Massachusetts, 1984.

Works

Collections

The Comedy of Neil Simon (includes *Come Blow Your Horn; Barefoot in the Park; The Odd Couple; The Star-Spangled Girl; Plaza Suite; Promises, Promises; Last of the Red Hot Lovers*).   1972.
Collected Plays 2 (includes *The Sunshine Boys; Little Me; The Gingerbread Lady; The Prisoner of Second Avenue; The*

Neil Simon (1990).

Good Doctor; God's Favorite; California Suite; Chapter Two). 1979.

Collected Plays 3 (includes *Sweet Charity; They're Playing Our Song; I Ought to Be in Pictures; Fools; The Odd Couple* (women's version); *Brighton Beach Memoirs; Biloxi Blues; Broadway Bound*). 1992.

Stage Works

Sketches (produced Tamiment, Pennsylvania, 1952, 1953).

Sketches, with Danny Simon, in *Catch a Star!* (produced Plymouth Theatre, New York, 1955).

Sketches, with Danny Simon, in *New Faces of 1956* (produced Ethel Barrymore Theatre, New York, 1956).

Adventures of Marco Polo: A Musical Fantasy, with William Friedberg, music by Clay Warnick and Mel Pahl.

Heidi, with William Friedberg, music by Clay Warnick, the novel by Johanna Spyri. 1959.

Come Blow Your Horn (produced Bucks County Playhouse, New Hope, Pennsylvania, 1960).

Little Me, music by Cy Coleman, lyrics by Carolyn Leigh, from the novel by Patrick Dennis (produced Lunt-Fontanne Theatre, New York, 1962; revised version produced New York, 1982). In *Collected Plays 2*, 1979.

Barefoot in the Park (as *Nobody Loves Me*, produced Bucks County Playhouse, New Hope, Pennysylvania, 1962; as *Barefoot in the Park*, produced Biltmore Theatre, New York, 1963). 1964.

The Odd Couple (produced Plymouth Theatre, New York, 1965; revised [women's] version produced Ahmanson Theatre, Los Angeles, 1985). 1966.

Sweet Charity, music by Cy Coleman, lyrics by Dorothy Fields, based on a screenplay by Federico Fellini and others (produced Palace Theatre, New York, 1966). 1966.

The Star-Spangled Girl (produced Plymouth Theatre, New York, 1966). 1967.

Plaza Suite (includes *Visitors from Mamaroneck; Visitor from Hollywood; Visitor from Forest Hills*; produced Plymouth Theatre, New York, 1968). 1969.

Promises, Promises, music and lyrics by Burt Bacharach and Hal David, based on a screenplay by Billy Wilder and I.A.L. Diamond (produced Shubert Theatre, New York, 1968). 1969.

Last of the Red Hot Lovers (produced Eugene O'Neill Theatre, New York, 1969). 1970.

The Gingerbread Lady (produced Plymouth Theatre, New York, 1970).

The Prisoner of Second Avenue (produced Eugene O'Neill Theatre, New York, 1971). 1972.

The Sunshine Boys (produced Broadhurst Theatre, New York, 1972). 1973.

The Good Doctor, music by Peter Link, lyrics by Simon, adaptation of stories by Chekhov (produced Eugene O'Neill Theatre, New York, 1973). 1974.

God's Favorite (produced Eugene O'Neill Theatre, New York, 1974). 1975.

California Suite (includes *Visitor from New York; Visitor from Philadelphia; Visitor from London; Visitor from Chicago*; (produced Los Angeles, 1976; Eugene O'Neill Theatre, New York, 1976). 1977.

Chapter Two (produced Los Angeles, 1977; Imperial Theatre, New York, 1977). 1979.

They're Playing Our Song, music by Marvin Hamlisch, lyrics by Carol Bayer Sager (produced Los Angeles, 1978; Imperial Theatre, New York, 1979). 1980.

I Ought to Be in Pictures (produced Los Angeles, 1980; Eugene O'Neill Theatre, New York, 1980). 1981.

Fools (produced Eugene O'Neill Theatre, New York, 1981). 1982.

Brighton Beach Memoirs (produced Ahmanson Theatre, Los Angeles, 1982). 1984.

Actors and Actresses (produced Hartman Theatre, Stamford, Connecticut, 1983).

Biloxi Blues (produced Ahmanson Theatre, Los Angeles, 1984). 1986.

Broadway Bound (produced Broadhurst Theatre, New York, 1986). 1987.

Rumors (produced Old Globe Theatre, San Diego, California, 1988; revised version produced Chichester Festival Theatre, 1990). 1990.

Jake's Women (produced Old Globe Theatre, San Diego, California, 1990).

Lost in Yonkers (produced Richard Rodgers Theatre, New York, 1991). 1992.

Screenplays

After the Fox, with Cesare Zavattini, 1966; *Barefoot in the Park*, 1967; *The Odd Couple*, 1968; *The Out-of-Towners*, 1970; *Plaza Suite*, 1971; *The Heartbreak Kid*, 1972; *The Last of the Red Hot Lovers*, 1972; *The Prisoner of Second Avenue*, 1975; *The Sunshine Boys*, 1975; *Murder by Death*, 1976; *The Goodbye Girl*, 1977; *The Cheap Detective*, 1978; *California Suite*, 1978; *Chapter Two*, 1979; *Seems Like Old Times*, 1980; *Only When I Laugh*, 1982; *I Ought to Be in Pictures*, 1982; *Max Dugan Returns*, 1983; *Lonely Guy*, 1984; *The Slugger's Wife*, 1985; *Brighton Beach Memoirs*, 1987; *Biloxi Blues*, 1988; *The Marrying Man*, 1991.

Television Plays

Phil Silvers Show, 1948; *Tallulah Bankhead Show*, 1951; *Your Show of Shows*, 1956; *Sid Caesar Show*, 1956–57; *Jerry Lewis Show*; *Jacky Gleason Show*; *Red Buttons Show*; *Sergeant Bilko* series, 1958–59; *Garry Moore Show*, 1959–60; *The Trouble with People*, 1972; *Happy Endings*, with others, 1975; *Broadway Bound*, 1992.

Radio Plays

Scripts for Robert Q. Lewis Show.

*

Bibliographies

Kimball King, *Ten Modern American Playwrights*, New York, 1982

Criticism

Books:
Edythe M. McGovern, *Neil Simon: A Critical Study*, New York, 1979.
Robert K. Johnson, *Neil Simon*, Boston, 1983.

Articles:
Helen McMahon, "A Rhetoric of American Popular Drama: The Comedies of Neil Simon", in *Players*, 51, 1975.
Ayako Sato, "Neil Simon's Comic Vision and its Significance", in *Sophia English Studies*, 7, 1982.

* * *

Literary criticism is not without its prejudices. Analyses of meaning, judgments of quality, and even inclusion in the accepted canon are based on assumptions about what constitutes real art, which don't always hold up under close scrutiny. One type of writer that academic critics seem simply incapable of dealing with is the skilled craftsman, the artisan who has limited ambitions but achieves them with consistency and perhaps some flair. And thus Neil Simon is accorded very little respect (if he is considered at all), even though he does what he does better than anyone else.

Neil Simon is, commercially, probably the most successful playwright in history. Since *Come Blow Your Horn* there has been hardly a Broadway season without at least one Simon play, and sometimes several, running. He is a master (as comparison to other writers of the genre will show) of a particular type of entertainment: the uncomplicated, unpretentious, unthreatening comedy, guaranteed to supply an evening's worth of laughter. With a couple of isolated exceptions, his plays do not try to explore the human condition, illuminate universal truths, or make more than the simplest of moral comments. They are funny. That's all they set out to be. And with machine-like efficiency and regularity, they generally succeed.

Simon is primarily a joke writer. His plays are built on verbal and visual gags, artfully constructed with the form, rhythm, and frequency that will produce the greatest number of laughs. If his characters sometimes sound the same (a frequent criticism), it is because he puts the joke where it is needed, regardless of who is talking at the moment. If his plots seem slim (another recurring complaint), it is because each twist comes only when it is dictated by the need for a laugh. That may sound "unartistic" as a way of creating a play, but it is not easy to do, and there *is* an art to it.

This sort of thing does not lend itself to analysis; one can only point out examples. Consider the central running gag in *Barefoot in the Park*, the fact that the main characters live in a fifth-floor walk-up flat, so that everyone comes onstage in a state of near-collapse. The joke is a slim one to begin with, and should grow old quickly, but Simon works new variants on breathless exhaustion each time, so that the audience continues to look forward to the next entrance. Consider, also, the skill with which he uses and reuses ancient joke structures: the "don't tell me" joke ("I don't even want to hear his name"—"Who? Felix?"—"I told you not to mention his name"); the straight man's set-up ("We really wouldn't have to worry about money if you would let me do what I suggested"—"What's that?"—"Selling you to a medical school"); the reversal ("You won't believe me"—"I'll believe you. . . Where are your clothes?"—"I don't know"—"I don't believe you"); the repetition ("I once got a call where this psycho actually described vile and indecent acts for over fifteen minutes"—"FIFTEEN MINUTES!").

Virtually every Simon play has one character with a short temper, who can be relied on to explode comically at regular intervals (such as Oscar Madison in *The Odd Couple*); virtually every play has an innocent who will be slow to grasp what's going on or ask the wrong question at the wrong time (such as Vinnie in the same play). Simon skilfully builds laughs on name-dropping: he knows when it is funnier to say "Oh, God, what I'd give for a good Compazine spansule" than " . . . antacid". And he is attuned to just when a familiar social type has become automatically funny: the playboy of *Come Blow Your Horn*, the hippie of *Last of the Red-Hot Lovers*, the swinging singles of *Chapter Two*, the aging yuppies of *Rumors*.

If the lines quoted above don't seem particularly funny in print, it is because Simon's jokes are written to be heard. (Try reading them aloud, with the proper tone of tension or exasperation.) Indeed, part of their power comes from Simon's mastery of the rhythm of joke construction, which makes some weaker gags work just because they *sound* like jokes. (Read some of those jokes aloud, converting the words into nonsense syllables; they will still recognizably be jokes.)

A few plays stand out from the others in ways that might attract the notice even of literary critics. Almost alone among his comedies, *The Odd Couple* is based on a real psychological and social insight (that is also inherently comic): that two divorced men living together will create a kind of marriage, with each playing exactly the same exasperating role that drove his wife crazy, and each being driven crazy just like the wife he replaced. And although Simon's infrequent earlier attempts to insert a serious note into his plays were all maudlin or simply wooden (as in *The Gingerbread Lady*), the autobiographical trilogy of *Brighton Beach Memoirs*, *Biloxi Blues*, and *Broadway Bound* somehow freed him to create recognizably human characters who were not just joke machines, and to touch sensitively and realistically on some of the darker and more painful aspects of family relationships.

—Gerald M. Berkowitz

See also *Volume 1* entry on *Brighton Beach Memoirs*; *The Odd Couple*.

SIMPSON, N(orman) F(rederick). Born in London, 29 January 1919. Educated at Emanuel School, London, 1930–37; Birkbeck College, University of London, 1950–54, BA (honours) 1954. Served in the Royal Artillery, 1941–43, and the Intelligence Corps, 1943–46. Married Joyce Bartlett in 1944; one daughter. Staff member, Westminster Bank, London, 1937–39; teacher, College of St. Mark and St. John, London, 1939–41, and City of Westminster College, London, and extra-mural lecturer, 1946–62; first-produced play, *A Resounding Tinkle*, staged 1957; literary manager, Royal Court Theatre, London, 1976–78.

Works

Collections

"The Hole" and Other Plays and Sketches (includes shortened version of *A Resounding Tinkle*, and *The Form; Gladly Otherwise; Oh; One Blast and Have Done*).   1964.
Some Tall Tinkles: Television Plays (includes *We're Due in Eastbourne in Ten Minutes; The Best I Can Do by Way of a Gate-Leg Table is a Hundredweight of Coal; At Least it's a Precaution Against Fire*).   1968.

Stage Works

A Resounding Tinkle (produced Royal Court Theatre, London, 1957). In *The Observer Plays*, 1958; shortened version (produced Royal Court Theatre, London, 1958) in *"The Hole" and Other Plays and Sketches*, 1964.
The Hole (produced Royal Court Theatre, London, 1958). 1958.
One Way Pendulum (produced Royal Court Theatre, London, 1959). 1960.

Sketches in *One to Another* (produced Lyric Theatre, Hammersmith, London, 1959). 1960.

Sketches in *You, Me and the Gatepost* (produced Playhouse, Nottingham, 1960).

Sketches in *On the Avenue* (produced Globe Theatre, London, 1961).

Sketches in *One over the Eight* (produced Duke of York's Theatre, London, 1961).

The Form (produced Arts Theatre, London, 1961). 1961.

Oh (produced 1961). In *"The Hole" and Other Plays and Sketches*, 1964.

The Cresta Run (produced Royal Court Theatre, London, 1965). 1966.

We're Due in Eastbourne in Ten Minutes, from his television play (produced, London, 1971). In *Some Tall Tinkles*, 1968.

Playback 625, with Leopoldo Maler (produced Royal Court Theatre, London, 1970).

Was He Anyone? (produced Royal Court Theatre Upstairs, London, 1972). 1973.

In Reasonable Shape (produced London, 1977). In *Play Ten*, edited by Robin Rook, 1977.

Anyone's Gums Can Listen to Reason. In *Play Ten*, edited by Robin Rook. 1977.

Inner Voices, from a play by Eduardo De Filippo (produced National Theatre, London, 1983). 1983.

The Other Side of London (produced with earlier sketches as *How Are Your Handles?*, Green Banana Restaurant, London, 1970).

Napoli Milionaria, from a play by Eduardo de Filippo (produced National Theatre, London, 1991).

Screenplays

One Way Pendulum, 1964; *Diamonds for Breakfast*, with Pierre Rouve and Ronald Harwood, 1968.

Television plays

Make a Man, 1966; *Three Rousing Tinkles* series: *The Father by Adoption of One of the Former Marquis of Rangoon's Natural Granddaughters, If Those Are Mr. Heckmondwick's Own Personal Pipes They've Been Lagged Once Already*, and *The Best I Can Do by Way of a Gate-Leg Table is a Hundredweight of Coal*, 1966 (published in *Some Tall Tinkles*, 1968); *Four Tall Tinkles* series: *We're Due in Eastbourne in Ten Minutes* (published in *Some Tall Tinkles*, 1968), *In a Punt with Friends Under a Haystack on the River Mersey, A Row of Potted Plants*, and *At Least it's a Precaution Against Fire*, 1967 (published in *Some Tall Tinkles*, 1968); *World in Ferment* series, 1969; *Charley's Grants* series, 1970; *Thank You Very Much*, 1971; *Elementary, My Dear Watson*, 1973; *Silver Wedding*, 1974; *An Upward Fall* (*Crown Court* series), 1977; *Wainwrights' Law* series, 1980.

Radio Plays

Something Rather Effective, 1972; *Sketches for Radio*, 1974.

Fiction

Harry Bleachbaker. 1976; as *Man Overboard: A Testimonial to the High Art of Incompetence*, 1976.

Criticism

Books:

Martin Esslin, *The Theatre of the Absurd*, New York, 1961, and later editions.

Kenneth Tynan, *Curtains*, London and New York, 1961.

Nigel Dennis, *Dramatic Essays*, London, 1962.

Articles:

C.Z. Fothergill, "Echoes of *A Resounding Tinkle*: N.F. Simpson Reconsidered", in *Modern Drama*, 16, 1973.

* * *

N.F. Simpson's most active period as a dramatist falls mainly within the decade 1955–65, when nearly all of his best known plays were written and staged. After 1966 he wrote mostly one-acters and television plays, except for the full-length drama *Was He Anyone?*. He owes his fame not so much to the prize he got at *The Observer* play competition (1956), as to the fact that he soon became known as one of the Royal Court "new" playwrights. In fact his most significant plays—*A Resounding Tinkle, The Hole*, and *One Way Pendulum*—were all produced by the English Stage Company and directed by William Gaskill, after which he was to become attached to the Royal Court, where he would later hold the post of literary manager. From his very first productions —*A Resounding Tinkle* in its full-length version (1957) and in its shorter one-act version that made up a double bill together with *The Hole* (1958)—he was labelled as a writer of "absurd" or nonsense drama, which led some critics to hail him as a British Ionesco, while others tried to trace his *non-sequiturs* back to the native tradition of Edward Lear and Lewis Carroll.

His drama, though original and, in a sense, unique—his plays have proved to defy classification by critics—has some significant features in common with other Royal Court plays of the late 1950's—a simplified setting, usually consisting of a room that can be turned into different locations by means of lighting effects; social satire embedded in humorous situations; lack of communication as a major problem in contemporary life; a constant attack on middle-class moral standards; and a veiled moral purpose behind every nonsensical situation. Like the work of most Royal Court playwrights, excepting perhaps such well-known names as John Osborne, Arnold Wesker, and Harold Pinter, Simpson's plays have always appealed to minority rather than to large audiences, except for *One Way Pendulum*, which was undoubtedly a great success in London and elsewhere in 1959, and was again revived in 1988 (London and Toronto).

Simpson's main achievement, and his most important devices, involve language, as his dramas on the whole tend to be rather static and devoid of action. In most cases characters are unable to communicate since they exchange little information, their utterances consisting of monologues by means of which they show their *idées fixes* and obsessions: for example Aunt Mildred, in *One Way Pendulum*, keeps talking about her trip around the Outer Hebrides, although she is in fact a cripple and can only move around the room in her wheel-chair. Simpson's middle-class characters tend to employ everyday clichés and routine expressions in the most striking situations, and this is probably one of his major sources of humour; thus in *Was He Anyone?*, members of the "National Help-You-Out Year Week" try to argue why a man should be playing the piano shortly before he drowns in the sea. Religious and legal formulae are also the butt of the playwright's ironic attacks. In *A Resounding Tinkle* and in

The Hole, characters utter long absurd prayers. In the latter play Soma delivers a long sermon in praise of electricity which predictably ends with the formula "In the name of Volta, Ampere and Galvani". Similarly, in Act II of *One Way Pendulum*, characters parody the legal jargon of British court-rooms.

A favourite device with Simpson is a long series of *non sequiturs* in the course of a cross-examination or interview, such as the ones in *The Form*, *Was He Anyone?*, and especially in *One Way Pendulum*. Sometimes interviewer and interviewee change places and a mysterious sense of guilt pervades the whole dialogue. In this sense Simpson's plays have some affinities with those of Pinter. Language often becomes repetitive and mechanical as characters seem to be far more keen on form than on content: in *One Way Pendulum* machines can speak and sing, whereas Kirby—a man—can only eat after hearing the bell of a cash register as he has trained himself by the Pavlov method; in *A Resounding Tinkle*, Middie cannot find a new topic for their talk and she suggests that they should "have a nice long conversation about the conversation we had at the Wordsworths'". In this same play, the speakers on the radio and the listeners employ identical sentences.

Simpson sets his dramas in a middle-class environment—hence the significant part living-rooms play in them—but he turns all the everyday conventions upside down. In *The Hole*, a character gets claustrophobia whenever he is out in the open air; in *A Resounding Tinkle* Uncle Ted is, in fact, a woman and when it comes to drinking a toast he and the other characters cut out passages from books which, after saying "cheers", they all read "looking up abstractedly"; in *One Way Pendulum* a skull on the mantelpiece is supposed to be a *memento mori*, but it does not seem to work as such, whereas other characters pretend it is simply a clock.

Apart from a certain obscure symbolism always present in his works, a very negative and pessimistic message seems to come across in Simpson's plays, namely that present-day life is void of direction and purpose owing to the gradual loss of moral, religious, and political values. Although one or two of his dramas are likely to appeal to future generations, most of his output does seem to be firmly rooted in the anxieties and worries of the late 1950's and therefore may seem somewhat outdated to a contemporary audience.

—Juan Carlos Hidalgo and Rafael Portillo

SOLOGUB, Fyodor. Born Fyodor Kuzmich Teternikov in St. Petersburg, 17 February (1 March, New Style) 1863. Educated at Teachers' Institute, St. Petersburg. Married Anastasiya Chebotarevskaya in 1908 (committed suicide 1921). Teacher of mathematics, then district schools inspector, in the Russian provinces, to 1892; teacher and administrator, St. Petersburg, 1892–1907: gave up career in education to concentrate on writing; co-founder of symbolist group, 1906; first-produced play, *Poberta smerti* [*The Triumph of Death*], staged 1907; had difficulty getting works published after 1923 because of his apolitical stance during the Revolution, and earned his income from translating French novels. Chairman, Leningrad Union of Writers, to 1927. Died in Leningrad, 5 December 1927.

Works

Collections

Sobranie sochineny [Collected Works] (12 vols.; plays in Volume 8). 1909–12.
Sobranie sochineny [Collected Works] (20 vols. intended: not all published). 1913–14.

Stage Works

Liturgiya nme [A Liturgy for Myself]. 1907.
Dar mudrykh pchyol [The Gift of The Wise Bees]. In *Zolotoe runo*, 2–3, 1907; in book form, 1918.
Lyubvi [Loves]. In *Pereval*, 8–9, 1907; in book form, in *Sobranie sochineny 10*, 1910.
Pobeda smerti (produced Kommissarzhevskaya's Theatre, St. Petersburg, 1907). In *Fakely*, 3, 1908; translated as *The Victory of Death*, 1916; as *The Triumph of Death*, in *The Russian Symbolist Theatre*, edited and translated by Michael Green, 1986.
Vanka klyuchnik i pazh Zhean (produced Vera Kommissarzhevskaya's Theatre, St. Petersburg, 1909). 1909; translated as *Vanka the Steward and Jehan the Page*, in *The Unknown Russian Theatre*, edited by Michael Green and Jerome Katsell, 1991.
Noch nye plyaski [Nocturnal Dances] (produced Evreinov's Happy Theatre for Adult Children, St. Petersburg, 1909). In *Sobranie sochineny 10*, 1910.
Melky bes [The Petty Demon] from the novel (produced Nezlobin Theatre, Moscow, 1910). 1909.
Zalozhniki zhizni [The Hostages of Life] (produced Alexandrinsky Theatre, St. Petersburg, 1913). In *Literaturnochudozhestvenny almanach*, 18, 1912; in book form, in *Sobranie sochineniy 8*, 1913.
Lyubov nad bezdnami [Love over an Abyss]. 1914.
Provody. In *Teatr i iskusstvo*, 1914.
Kamen, broshenny v vodu. In *Teatr i iskusstvo*, 1915.
Lyubov i vernost. In *Russkaya mysl*, 5–6, 1917.
Strazh velikogo tsarya [The Guard of the Great Tsar]. In *Sochtennye dni* (see Fiction), 1921.

Fiction

Teni [Shadows] (stories). 1896.
Tyazhyolye sny. 1896; translated as *Bad Dreams*, 1978.
Zhalo smerti [The Sting of Death]. 1904.
Istlevayushchie lichiny [Decaying Masks] (stories). 1907.
Melky bes. 1907; translated as *The Little Demon*, 1916; as *The Petty Demon*, 1962.
Tvorimaya legenda. In journals, 1908–12; revised in book form (3 vols.), 1914; translated as *The Created Legend*, 1916; as *A Legend in Creation*, 1979.
Kniga ocharovany [A Book of Charms] (stories). 1909.
Alchushchy zhazhdushchy. 1910.
Malenkiy chelovek; K zvezdam; Snegutochka (tales). 1911.
Ostrok Lin; Pretvorivshaya vodu v vino; Alchushchy i zhazhdushchy; Elkich; Dva Gotika (stories). 1911.
Slashche yada (2 vols.). 1913.
"The Sweet-Scented Name" and Fairy Tales, Fables, and Stories, translated by Stephen Graham. 1915.
Jary god. 1916.
"The Old House" and Other Stories, translated by John Cournos. 1916.
Little Tales, translated by John Cournos. 1917.
Alaja lenta; Krasnogubaya gostya; Krasota (stories). 1917.
Pomnish, ne zabudesh. 1918.

Slepaya babochka. 1918.
Opechalennaya nevesta; Smert po ob-yavleniyu; V plenu (stories). 1920.
Carica poceluev. 1921.
Sochtennye dni. 1921.
Baryshnya Liza. 1923.
"The Kiss of the Unborn" and Other Stories, translated by Murl. G. Barker, 1977.
Rasskazy [Stories], edited by E. Bristol. 1979.

Verse

Stikhi [Poems]. 1896.
Sobranie stichov 1897–1903 [Collected Poems 1897–1903]. 1904.
Rodine [To the Homeland]. 1906.
Zmy [Serpent]. 1907.
Pol Verlen [Paul Verlaine] 1908.
Plammenny Krug [The Circle of Fire]. 1908.
Voyna. 1915.
Zemlya rodnaya: Vybrannye stikhi. 1916.
Aly mak: Kniga stichov. 1917.
Fimiamy. 1921.
Nebo goluboe. 1921.
Odna lyubov. 1921.
Soborny blagovest. 1921.
Charodeynaya chasha. 1922.
Koster dorozhny. 1922.
Svirel. 1922.
Veliky blagovest. 1923.
Stikhi [Poems]. 1923.
Stikhotvoreniya. 1939.

Other

Teni: Rasskazy i stichi [Shadows: Tales and Poems]. 1896.
Kniga skazok. 1905.
Politicheskie skazochki. 1906.
"The Theatre of the Will" (essay), in *The Russian Symbolist Theatre*, edited and translated by Michael Green. 1986.

*

Criticism

Articles:
Daniel C. Gerould, "Sologub and the Theatre", in *The Drama Review*, vol. 21 no. 4, 1977.

* * *

Fyodor Kuzmich Sologub (real name Teternikov) was a Russian symbolist. Like many symbolists, he was a school-master by trade, but he had fought his way into literature from an exceptionally unhappy working-class background. His work is characterized by great unevenness—sometimes intended to shock—although he consistently followed Oscar Wilde's idea of art as "a beautiful way of lying". His greatest achievements were in lyrical poetry, particularly the reinter-pretation of the Don Quixote story, and his best known work is the novel *Melky bes* (*The Petty Demon*). Between 1906 and 1912, however, much of his output was drama, and, although few have been translated, and none performed on the Western stage, Sologub's "decadent" or "symbolist" plays are of more than historical interest.

In 1906 Sologub helped to found a group of symbolist poets who intended, with the active co-operation of the direc-tor Meyerhold and sympathetic actors such as Vera Kommissarzhevskaya, to create a non-realist theatre in Russian that would match the theatre of Maeterlinck in the West and counteract the influence of the post-Chekhovian realist theatre of Gorky's school. Sologub, like other Russian symbolists such as Innokenti Annensky or Alexander Blok, showed a sense of split personality in his lyrical poetry that naturally led to dramatic form; like Annensky and Western symbolists such as Mallarmé he was drawn to the ritual drama of classical Greece. One of Sologub's first dramatic efforts was the pseudo-Greek tragedy "The Gift of the Wise Bees", in which he adapted the Orphic legend of Laodamia redeem-ing her dead husband Protesilas from Hades, and dying when Hades reclaims him. The theme of love triumphant over death, of the other ideal world being the only tolerable alternative to the cruelties and injustices of this world, is merely a transposition of the obsessions of Sologub's lyrics and narrative prose. Even Meyerhold, however, was unable to stage this half-Wagnerian, half-Sophoclean ritual, and in-stead another play by Sologub was staged in Vera Kommissarzhevskaya's theatre.

This next play, *The Triumph of Death*, again adapts a legend to reinterpret Sologub's own symbolist cult of ideal and absolute love, but the legend is derived from the Dark Ages story of the parentage of Charlemagne. Charlemagne's mother, the ugly Berta, is replaced in the King's bed by her servant girl, Algista, who comes to love and influence the King to the good. When her action is discovered, she is executed; her ghost calls the King to follow her to a better world, but the King, unlike Laodamia, refuses to follow his love into Hades and is literally petrified.

Real acclaim was given to Sologub's most adventurous and entertaining play, *Vanka the Steward and Jehan the Page*, where the scenes alternate between medieval Russia and medieval France, telling a similar story of a servant who seduces the lord's wife. The Russian scenes retell a notorious folk poem about an unfortunate tragedy in the house of Prince Volkonsky, but Sologub softened the ending by spar-ing the adulterous butler from the gallows. While Sologub was here still dealing with his contrasts of sacred and profane love, the play was treated by the public as a satirical comment on male and female sexuality and on the contrasts of East and West. The innovation of semi-nudity and of suggested sexual intercourse took the Russian theatre further than it had ever gone—or would ever go.

Sologub was less successful in his attempts to deal with contemporary life. He dramatized his novel *The Petty Demon* in 1909, two years after the novel had been published in full; probably because the novel had been so effectively narrated, with irony and profound sadness, critics reacted against the play. The central character Peredonov is a paranoid school-teacher, tormented by a poltergeist only he can see, the fiery *nedotykomka*, until he slaughters a colleague. The climax of both play and novel synchronizes this murder with a grotes-que town fancy-dress ball at which the boy pupil, whom Peredonov had been persecuting, is stripped of his woman's kimono. There is no doubt about Sologub's skilful crescendo to the horrific finale, but, without the ironic narrator, the central character becomes almost sympathetic in his illness, and the detachment of the novel is lost.

Sologub had perhaps finally lost his audiences with a short play of 1907, "Loves" (or "To love", the Russian *Lyubvi* is ambiguous), which shocked even liberal Russian critics. A widower sailor comes home to his daughter to find her en-gaged to a mediocrity. He convinces her his love is stronger, tells the fiancé that she is not really his legitimate daughter, and apparently persuades her into incest. Sologub was enlarging themes found in contemporary German prose of Munich and Vienna, the theme of hidden incestuous paternity in Dostoevsky, but his explicit approval aroused indignation and mockery. The play was suppressed and has only recently been republished (Munich, 1984).

—Donald Rayfield

SOLÓRZANO, Carlos. Born in San Marcos, Guatemala, 1 May 1922. Moved to Mexico, 1939. Studied literature and architecture at the Universidad Nacional Autónoma de México [UNAM], Mexico City, from 1939, MA 1944, Doctor en Letras [Ph.D], 1946; studied drama in France on Rockefeller grant, 1948–50. Married Beatrice Caso in 1946; one son and one daughter. Artistic director, UNAM's Teatro Universitario, Mexico City, 1952–62; professor of dramatic art, UNAM, 1960–85; executive director, reorganization of the Teatro de la Nación [Mexican National Theatre], for the Department of Social Security, 1976–85; emeritus professor, since 1985. Visiting professor, University of Southern California, Los Angeles, and University of Kansas, Lawrence. Also a novelist and writer of dramatic criticism and history.

Works

Collections

Tres actos (includes *Cruce de viás; Los fantoches; El crucificado*). 1959.
Teatro (includes *Los fantoches; El crucificado; Las manos de Dios; El sueño del ángel*). 1972.
Teatro breve (includes *El zapato; Cruce de viás; El sueño del ángel; Mea culpa; El crucificado; Los fantoches*), edited by Joaqin Mortiz. 1977.

Stage Works

La muerte hizo la luz. In *Epoca*, 1, 1951.
Doña Beatriz, la sin ventura (produced 1952). In *Cuadernos americanos*, 59, 1951; in book form, 1954.
El hechicero (produced 1954). 1955.
Las manos de Dios (produced Teatro del Seguro Social, Mexico City, 1956). 1957; translated as *The Hands of God*, 1968.
Mea culpa (produced 1956). In *Epoca*, 43, 1967; in book form, in *Teatro breve*, 1977.
El crucificado (produced 1958). With *El lépro*, by Carlos Prieto, 1957; in *Tres actos*, 1959; translated as *The Crucifixion*, in *The Orgy: Modern One-Act Plays from Latin America*, edited by Gerardo Luzuriaga and Robert S. Rudder, 1974.
Los fantoches (produced 1958). In *Tres actos*, 1959.
Cruce de viás (produced 1959). In *Tres actos*, 1959; translated as *Crossroads*, in *Selected Latin American One Act Plays*, edited by Francesca Colecchia and Julio Matas, 1973.
El sueño del ángel (produced 1960). In *Tercera antologia de obras en un acto* (with plays by others), 1960; in *Teatro*, 1972.

El zapato (produced 1966). In *Cosmos*, 2, 1966; in book form, in *Teatro breve*, 1977.
El visitante (produced 1966).

Fiction

Los falsos demonios, from his own play. 1966.
Las celdas. 1971.

Other

Del sentimiento de lo plástico en la obra de Unamuno. 1944.
Espejo de novelas. 1945.
Unamuno y el existencialismo. 1946.
Novelas de Unamuno. 1948.
Teatro latinoamericano del siglo XX. 1961; revised edition, 1963.
Testimonios teatrales de México. 1973.

Editor, *Teatro guatemateco contemporáneo.* 1964.
Editor, *El teatro hispanoamericano contemporáneo* (2 vols.). 1964.
Editor, *Teatro breve hispanoamericano contemporáneo.* 1970.
Editor, *El teatro actual latinoamericano.* 1972.

*

Bibliographies

Pedro F. de Andrea, "Carlos Solórzano: Bibliografía", in *Comunidad latinoamericana de escritores: Bulletin*, 7, 1970 (also issued separately).

Criticism

Books:
Esteban Rivas, *Carlos Solórzano y el teatro hispanoamericano*, Mexico City, 1970.

Articles:
Frank N. Dawster, "The Drama of Carlos Solórzano", in *Modern Drama*, 7, 1964.
D. Radcliff-Umstead, "Solórzano's Tormented Puppets", in *Latin America Theatre Review*, vol. 4 no. 2, 1971.
Wilma Feliciano, "Myth and Theatricality in Three Plays By Carlos Solórzano", in *Latin American Theatre Review*, vol.25 no.1, 1991.

* * *

Carlos Solórzano is widely known and greatly respected throughout the theatre-world of Latin America for his work as a playwright as well as for his work as a critic and editor. Born in San Marcos, Guatemala, he moved to Mexico in 1939 to pursue studies in architecture and literature. In 1948 he earned the degree Doctor en Letras from the National Autonomous University of Mexico (UNAM) and then continued with specialized studies in dramatic art in France under the auspices of a Rockefeller grant. During the many years in which he served as director of the Teatro Universitario in Mexico, and later as professor of dramatic art in the University of Mexico, he actively and passionately promoted the theatre through histories, anthologies, articles, lectures, and festivals.

Solórzano's theatre is a reflection of his existentialist approach to contemporary situations. His anguished characters strive to establish meaningful communication and relationships within a world of alienation. Steeped in the works of Michel de Ghelderode and Albert Camus during his years in Paris, Solórzano established close relationships with the two writers and admits having inherited from them a predilection for a symbolic and philosophical theatre.

The freedom to be oneself is perhaps the basic tenet of all Solórzano's theatre. "Men are born free. It's other men who make them prisoners afterwards", says the Devil in *Las manos de Dios* (*The Hands of God*). For Solórzano freedom is a complex, multi-faceted concept; individuals should have freedom of election in their political, social, moral, and religious structures. His plays underscore in theme and technique the processes that accompany an existentialist view of freedom of choice.

His career as a playwright was launched in 1952 with the premiere of *Doña Beatriz, la sin ventura* ("The Unfortunate"), wife of Pedro de Alvarado who was sent by Hernán Cortés to conquer Guatemala. Doña Beatriz suffers the indignities of the New World where she is a creature out of time and space. Bound by traditions and the Church, her loyalties remain with Spain as she struggles to maintain her identity. The structural oppositions between Beatriz and Pedro's *mestiza* daughter Leonor, as well as between Don Pedro and Beatriz's brother Rodrigo, emphasize the conflicts and the struggle for power in this hostile environment. The psychological anguish apparent throughout the play is, in the end, exacerbated by the forces of nature when Beatriz, long estranged from her profligate and ambitious husband, admits defeat and surrenders to the flood that carries her away. Beatriz's death and Leonor's survival can be seen as symbols of the end of an old world-order and the beginning of a new society.

In 1954 Solórzano, in his second play *El hechicero* (*The Sorcerer*), continued his fascination with earlier times and other places to dramatize his concept of freedom. Set in "these Middle Ages which have not yet ended", the play presents the struggle of Merlin the magician to find the secret of the philosopher's stone in order to change lead into gold. This discovery will enable him to purchase the freedom of his townspeople from the Duke, whose troops occupy the village and will not be withdrawn until each of the inhabitants pays the tribute demanded. The conflict involves Merlin's daughter Beatriz and his wife, who plots to kill him, steal the secret, and marry her husband's brother. This configuration allows Solórzano the artistic licence to explore issues of economic freedom, physical freedom from incarceration, and freedom from irrational action without a sense of responsibility.

Solórzano's masterwork is *Las manos de Dios* which became an instant success when it opened in 1956. In a tightly-knit conflict, the young protagonist, Beatriz, is challenged to steal jewels from the Church in order to bribe the jailer to free her brother. The forces in conflict are expressed dramatically by the Devil, who provokes Beatriz, and by the authoritarian figures of the Church, who represent traditional values. The townspeople waver symbolically, like a Greek chorus, between the opposing forces. While attacking both Church and State for keeping people enslaved in a state of ignorance, Solórzano dramatizes the plight of the individual who must make decisions that are critical for his or her own self-realization. In attempting to secure the freedom of her brother (who represents mankind), Beatriz achieves the freedom that comes from commitment without regret (existential choice). Her death at the end is inconsequential in proportion to her existential victory. The play provides a superb integration of theme and technique and is considered one of the classics of the contemporary theatre.

In addition to these three major plays, Solórzano is the author of six one-act plays, most of which continue similar preoccupations. In *Los fantoches* (The Puppets), a play built around the use of Mexican fireworks in religious celebrations, the Big-Head determines the fate of the other puppets by random selection. The central figure functions metaphorically as a god disposing human lives without love or compassion. In *El crucificado* (*The Crucifixion*) a drunken Mexican peasant is crucified to re-enact the Passion of Christ and predictably those who participate later deny responsibility for their actions. *El sueño del ángel* (The Angel's Dream) pairs a woman with her Guardian Angel who insists she must expiate her sin, an act of adultery committed years before. *Mea culpa* is a weaker play also dealing with fear and guilt produced by religious imbalance. *Cruce de vías* (Railroad Crossing) epitomizes hopelessness through a missed encounter: a man and a woman search for each other in a scene with touches of a silent movie while the switchman serves as a foil to their existentialist game. The other very short play, *El zapato* (The Shoe), takes the metaphor of an old shoe, which hurts the young boy's foot to explore not only a sinister and perhaps incestuous relationship with his mother but also the guilt and recrimination that he experiences before his father, a god-like figure who insists on subjugation, guilt, and repentance.

Carlos Solórzano has made extraordinary contributions not only to the Latin American theatre, but also to critical study of the theatre: he is the author of books that provided the first panoramic views of Latin American theatre as an entity.

—George Woodyard

See also *Volume* 1 entry on *The Hands of God*.

SOPHOCLES. Born in Colonus, near Athens, c.496 BC. Married Nicostrate, one son; also had a son by his concubine Theoris. Won his first playwriting prize in 468; served as imperial treasurer, 443–42; elected general twice, the first time in 440 when he was a colleague with Pericles in suppressing the Samian revolt; advisory commissioner for recovery after defeat at Syracuse, 413. Also served as priest of the hero Halon(?), a cult associated with that of Asclepius, and founded a literary club. 122 titles (some possibly subtitles) of plays known, and he won a total of 18 victories at the Great (City) Dionysia, and six at the Lenea festivals. Also an actor in his early plays. Died late 406 BC.

Works

Collections

The Tragedies (2 vols.), translated by G. Adams.   1729.
The Plays and Fragments (Greek and English; 7 vols.), edited and translated by Richard Jebb.   1883–96; second edition, 1887–98.
Sophocles (parallel texts; 2 vols.), edited and translated by F. Storr.   1912–13 (Loeb Classical Library).
Fabulae, edited by A.C. Pearson.   1924.
The Theban Plays, translated by E.F. Watling.   1947.

Sophocles (bust in the Museo Capitolano, Rome).

"Electra" and Other Plays (includes *Ajax; Philoctetes; Women of Trachis*), translated by E.F. Watling. 1953.
Sophocles (2 vols.), various translators. 1954–57 (Complete Greek Tragedies series).
Three Theban Plays, translated by Theodore Howard Banks. 1956.
The Oedipus Plays, translated by Paul Roche. 1958.
Three Tragedies (includes *Antigone; Oedipus the King; Electra*), translated by H.D.F. Kitto. 1962.
Four Plays (includes *Ajax; Electra; Philoctetes; Women of Trachis*), translated by Theodore Howard Banks. 1966.
Tragediae (2 vols.), edited by R.D. Dawe. 1975–79.
Electra; Antigone; Philoctetes, translated by Kenneth McLeish. 1979.
The Three Theban Plays, translated by Robert Fagles. 1982.
The Theban Plays, translated by Don Taylor. 1986.
The Three Theban Plays, translated by C.A. Trypanis. 1986.
Fabulae, edited by Hugh Lloyd-Jones and N.G. Wilson. 1990.
Plays 2 (includes *Ajax; Women of Trachis; Electra; Philoctetes*), various translators, edited by J. Michael Walton. 1990.

Stage Works

Ajax (produced Athens, c.441 BC?). Translated as *Ajax*, 1714: numerous subsequent translations under same title.
Antigone (produced Athens, c.441 BC). Translated as *Antigone*, in *The Tragedies*, 1729: numerous subsequent translations under same title.
Oedipus Tyrannus (produced Athens, after 430 BC). Translated as *Oedipus, King of Thebes*, 1715, and as *Oedipus Tyrannus*, 1759: numerous subsequent translations under both titles; as *Oedipus the King*, 1919: several subsequent translations under same title; as *King Oedipus* in *The Theban Plays*, translated by E.F. Watling, 1947, and in *The Three Theban Plays*, translated by C.A. Trypanis, 1986; as *Oedipus Rex*, 1949.
Trachiniae (produced Athens, c.430–420 BC). Translated as *Trachiniae*, in *The Tragedies*, 1729: several subsequent translations under same title; as *The Trachinian Maidens*, 1909; as *The Wife of Hercules*, 1948, as *Women of Trachis*, in *"Electra" and Other Plays*, 1953: several subsequent translations under same title.
Electra (produced ?). Translated as *Electra*, 1649: numerous subsequent translations under same title.
Philoctetes (produced Athens, 409 BC). Translated as *Philoctetes*, in *The Tragedies*, 1729: numerous subsequent translations under same title.
Oedipus Coloneus (produced Athens, 401 BC). Translated as *Oedipus Coloneus*, in *The Tragedies*, 1729, and as *Oedipus at Colonus*, 1841: several susbequent translations under both titles.
Ichneutae (fragment of satyr play). Translated as *Ichneutae*, 1919; as *The Searching Satyrs*, in *Two Satyr Plays*, translated by Roger Lancelyn Green, 1957.
Fragments. In *Plays and Fragments*, edited and translated by Richard Jebb, 1883–96.

*

Criticism

Books:
T.B.L. Webster, *An Introduction to Sophocles*, Oxford, 1936.
C.M. Bowra, *Sophoclean Tragedy*, Oxford, 1944.
F.R. Earp, *The Style of Sophocoles*, Cambridge, 1944.
A.J.A. Waldcock, *Sophocoles the Dramatist*, Cambridge, 1951.
C.H. Whitman, *Sophocles: A Study of Heroic Humanism*, Cambridge, Massachusetts, 1951.
J.C. Opstelton, *Sophocles and Greek Pessimism*, translated by J. Ross, Amsterdam, 1952.
V. Ehrenberg, *Sophocles and Pericles*, Oxford, 1954.
S.M. Adams, *Sophocles the Playwright*, Toronto, 1957.
G.M. Kirkwood, *A Study of Sophoclean Drama*, Ithaca, New York, 1958.
H.D.F. Kitto, *Sophocles, Dramatist and Philosopher*, London, 1958.
M.H. Shackford, *Shakespeare, Sophocles: Dramatic Themes and Modes*, New Haven, Connecticut, 1960.
J.T. Sheppard, *Aeschylus and Sophocles: Their Work and Influence*, New York, 1963.
B.M.W. Knox, *The Heroic Temper: Studies in Sophoclean Tragedy*, Berkeley, California, 1964.
H.D.F. Kitto, *Poiesis: Structure and Thought*, Berkeley, California, 1966.
T.M. Woodard (ed.), *Sophocles: A Collection of Critical Essays*, Englewood Cliffs, New Jersey, 1966.
W. Walter, *The Plays of Sophocles*, New York, 1966.
H. Musurillo, *The Light and the Darkness: Studies in the Dramatic Poetry of Sophocles*, Leiden, 1967.
A.A. Long, *Language and Thought in Sophocles*, New York, 1968.

G. Ronnet, *Sophocle: Poète tragique*, Paris, 1969.

G.H. Gellie, *Sophocles: A Reading*, Carleton, Australia, 1972.

S. Melchinger, *Sophocles* (from the German), New York, 1974.

K. Reinhardt, *Sophocles*, Oxford, 1979.

R.W.B. Burton, *The Chorus in Sophocles' Tragedies*, 1980.

R.P. Winnington-Ingram, *Sophocles: An Interpretation*, Cambridge, 1980.

V. Leinieks, *The Plays of Sophocles*, Amsterdam, 1982.

Charles Segal, *Tragedy and Civilization: An Interpretation of Sophocles*, Cambridge, Massachusetts, 1981.

Charles Rillig, *Sophocles* (biography), Salzburg, 1982.

D. Seale, *Vision and Stagecraft in Sophocles*, Chicago, 1982.

G.P. Gardiner, *The Sophoclean Chorus: A Study of Character and Function*, Iowa City, Iowa, 1987.

Mary Whitlock Blundell, *Helping Friends and Harming Enemies: A Study of Sophocles in Greek Ethics*, Cambridge, 1989.

*   *   *

The seven surviving works of Sophocles go far towards supporting the belief, widely held in antiquity, that he was the greatest of the Greek tragic writers. Aristotle, who used him as the model, and frequently the source of illustrations, for the aesthetic principles laid out in the *Poetics*, credited him with introducing the third actor into the drama, and if true, it helps to explain a number of Sophocles' most characteristic and powerful qualities as a playwright. By virtue of this innovation (whether his own or another's) he was able both to increase the complexity of plots, and to create more subtle development and exposition of the individuality of characters and their relationships. In his hands, the drama is less monumental, more intimate, and the style of tragic diction becomes far more flexible than any examples known to us from his predecessor, Aeschylus. The situations in which he portrayed his characters, and the confrontations that take place between them demanded that they express themselves in a more varied, vivid, and idiosyncratic manner. In place of the great heroes of Aeschylean tragedy we are presented with characters who are more recognisably human, faced with situations that may have a divine dimension and cosmic implications, yet must, at the same time, provoke our emotional response because they function on a more immediate level of ordinary human suffering. A particularly effective example is *Philoctetes*, whose "hero" is wretched with physical pain and whose character poignantly illustrates the degradation and brutalisation wrought by suffering and injustice. Sophocles examines the cause and course of such suffering in moving and closely observed detail and in ways which come across in their theatrical enactment as being far more realistic and nuanced than earlier tragedy.

Sophocles was particularly adept at creating psychologically believable and sympathetic characters, and at placing these characters in situations where their attitudes and circumstances must inevitably lead them into conflict and catastrophe. This conflict, arising as it does from the nature and desires of the individual characters, in turn supports the underlying structure and motivation of the dramatic action; indeed, the use of plot to explore and explicate ethical and psychological conflict as embodied in the individual characters and their deeds is one of the greatest achievements of Sophocles. Characters and action are inextricably fused, just as they are in the ordinary experience of life, whose meanings Sophocles seeks to discern through the situations, attitudes, actions, and personalities he depicts. The existence of a third actor was crucial to this development in that it allowed for the presence of an intermediary charged with judging between the rigid and opposing views represented by two characters in conflict—one whose presence, in turn, encouraged a critical attitude in the audience itself. We can see all of these elements put to effective use in *Antigone*, in which the fundamental confrontation between Antigone and Creon is subjected to the sceptical scrutiny of such characters as Antigone's sister Ismene, Creon's son Haemon, and the prophet Teiresias.

The third actor also allowed Sophocles to use the chorus as a less actively engaged element in the drama than had been possible when the burden of the dramatic enactment was shared with only two actors. In Sophocles' works the chorus sometimes tends to become a more lyrical element, relatively detached from the action of the play, while providing comment and observation which conditions audience response and articulates the emotional essence of a scene. At other moments, however, Sophocles gives it a more "activist" role; it has its own "voice" and attitude and energetically espouses the cause of a particular character, or urges a course of action so that its own role approaches that of an individual character in the drama. Its insights are by no means infallible and its point of view often subsequently demonstrated to be wrong; indeed Sophocles uses this as a highly effective means for creating, within his drama, greater tension as well as a pervasive irony as the chorus repeatedly misinterprets the meaning of a scene or incorrectly anticipates a particular outcome. The use of the chorus in this way is strikingly evident in the *Oedipus Tyrannus*, where it reinforces the "wishful thinking" of the characters.

The increased flexibility of his dramatic medium enabled Sophocles to present and investigate complex moral and philosophical questions with great subtlety. Over a very long life, which came close to spanning the whole of the extraordinary 5th century, he had witnessed enormous development and change at Athens, which had been accompanied by profound intellectual crisis as traditional values and beliefs were tested and transformed. Although there is little of the deep scepticism and iconoclastic expression that pervades the work of Euripides, Sophocles constantly probes and questions at the deepest level the meaning of man's life, and of his relations with other men, the nature of human society and its government, and, above all, the role of the gods. The exploration of these subjects is centred on a number of recurrent themes: the nature of fate, the role of oracles, the conflict between human and divine law, the capacity and limits of human reason and understanding, and the meaning of justice. He selected and manipulated his mythic material (for example the story of Oedipus) and fashioned his characters to highlight and examine these most profound and basic subjects —the questions that lie at the centre of human existence— and he did so with consummate dramatic skill, extraordinary intelligence and understanding, and through the medium of some of the most exquisite poetry ever written.

—Richard C. Beacham

See also *Volume 1* entries on *Ajax*; *Antigone*; *Electra*; *Oedipus at Colonus*; *Oedipus the King*; *Philoctetes*; *The Women of Trachis*.

SORGE, Reinhard (Johannes). Born in Rixdorf, Germany, 29 January 1892. Moved to Jena after his father's death, 1909. Educated at Gymnasium, Jena, 1909–10. Married Susanne Hendewerk in 1913; two sons. Writer from 1911; actor in Berlin, 1911; first play, *Der Bettler*, published 1912 and produced posthumously in 1917; converted with his wife to Catholicism, 1913: took the name "Johannes" and began writing in a more religious vein; studied philosophy at the Kollegienhaus von Maria Hilf, with the aim of becoming a priest; following the outbreak of World War I, was drafted into the German Army, May 1915. Recipient: Kleist Prize, 1912. Died from wounds received in battle, Ablaincourt, France, 20 July 1916.

Works

Collections

Der Jüngling (includes *Der Jüngling*; *Odysseus*; *Guntwar*; *Zarathustra*; *Prometheus*; *Antichrist*), edited by Susanne Songe. 1925.
Werke (3 vols.), edited by Gerd Rötzer. 1962–67.

Stage Works

Der Bettler (produced Deutsches Theater, Berlin, 1917). 1912; translated as *The Beggar*, in *Anthology of German Expressionist Drama*, edited by W.H. Sokel, 1963.
Guntwar, Die Schule eines Propheten. 1914.
Metanoeite. 1915.
König David. 1916.
Gericht über Zarathustra. 1921.
Der Sieg des Christos. 1925.
Der Jüngling. In *Der Jüngling* (collection), 1925.
Odysseus. In *Der Jüngling* (collection), 1925.
Zarathustra. In *Der Jüngling* (collection), 1925.
Prometheus. In *Der Jüngling* (collection), 1925.
Antichrist. In *Der Jüngling* (collection), 1925.
Das Unbekannte. In *Werke*, 1962–67.
Spartacus, from the fragment by Lessing. In *Werke*, 1962–67.

Verse

Mutter der Himmel. 1917.
Mystische Zwiesprache. 1922.
Preis der Unbefleckten. 1924.
Der Jüngling: Dei frühe Dichtungen. 1925.
Nachgelassene Gedichte. 1925.

*

Criticism

Books:
Michel Becker, *Reinhard Johannes Sorge*, Würzburg, 1924.
Franz Kohnen, *Der deutsche Expressionismus und Reinhard Johannes Sorge*, Rio de Janeiro, 1963.

Articles:
Ward B. Lewis, "The Early Dramas of Reinhard Johannes Sorge: A Poet's Search for the Inner Light", in *Modern Drama*, 14, 1972.
Allan J. McIntyre, "Drama as Rite: R.J. Sorge's *Odysseus*", in *German Quarterly*, 50, 1977.

* * *

Sorge's first extant drama, *Das Unbekannte* (The Unknown, written 1908), deals with a twofold problem: first the protagonist's marriage is based on deceit—she has borne a child that is not her husband's—and although she wishes desperately to reveal her guilty past, she cannot do so since she does not want to risk her family's happiness. Sorge, who earlier had defended self-sacrifice for the sake of the happiness of others, stated quite clearly in *Das Unbekannte* that this constitutes a betrayal of one's self. The protagonist's escape into the world of art produces a second dilemma, namely, how to combine harmoniously the unconditional demands of the creative mind with societal conventions. Sorge chose an easy solution—the protagonist destroys her sculpture ("The Temptation of Christ") when it is rejected by the clergy, and then commits suicide.

In 1910 Sorge turned to the philosophy of Nietzsche. Influenced especially by *Zarathustra*, he now saw the artist as a prophet proclaiming his own ecstatic visions to be universal law, with the aim of creating an ultimate harmony between man and the world. Sorge was not a philosopher; he took from Nietzsche only what fitted his own philanthropic *Weltbild*, ignoring completely Nietzsche's scepticism and sarcasm. A number of works, especially *Odysseus*, *Prometheus*, *Zarathustra*, and *Antichrist*, all written in 1911, show clear evidence of his preoccupation with Nietzsche. Odysseus is the bringer of a new dawn; Prometheus, celebrated as the giver of light, creates the Superman; *Antichrist* depicts Christ and Nietzsche as spiritual brothers. The sun, the light, cosmic relations, and natural mysticism play a major role in these early dramatic attempts. Sorge's aim was to dramatize the process of man's regeneration; typically, another one-act drama, *Guntwar*, is subtitled *Ein Werden* (A Becoming). Sorge's language, however, is rife with romantic pathos, ecstatic screams and stammer, and his symbolic language is often hollow. Yet because Sorge had begun to develop his personal conception of the artist in these early works, they can be considered preparatory stages for his major and most original achievement, *Der Bettler*, the first German expressionist drama.

Although outwardly structured in the traditional form of the five-act play, *Der Bettler* established the key features of the new drama. The characters are nameless types, and the juxtaposition of realistic and dream episodes reveals a *Stationendrama* dealing with the transformation theme on several levels. Like the Wanderer in Strinderg's *To Damascus*, the Poet progresses from one stage to another in his attempt to free himself from his past—his romantic beginnings as an artist, his domineering father, his friends and critics—in order to gain a transcendental experience that will enable him to "renew mankind through the spirit". Sorge saw each of the play's five acts as circles, each offering a higher level of awareness to the Poet, whose role is dramatized in typical ecstatic, expressionist fashion bordering on a naive *hubris* in that his "holy" vision is presented as the only acceptable one, and his power as saviour absolute. The Poet's call in the play to his public expresses Sorge's own conception of his role:

Look, I rush to you brandishing the red torch.
Receive me!
Crowd around me! I am filled with blessing! . . .
I will take the world upon my shoulders
And carry it to the sun with praise.

However, the drama remains open-ended. The Poet's pilgrimage towards the sun continues; he does not find the new symbolic language which would enable him to express the unspeakable and the eternal which he perceives as the essence of art.

In February 1912, on the island of Norderney, Sorge experienced a religious revelation of such power and depth that—like Paul Claudel—he decided to "make Christ's style his pen—until death". This experience influenced greatly his next drama, *Guntwar*, which Sorge considered a sequel to *Der Bettler*, providing the answer to all those questions which had remained unanswered in that play.

In *Guntwar* the Poet's message in *Der Bettler* is replaced with God's message. The drama is in five acts, with a prologue and epilogue reminiscent of Goethe's *Faust*, and three scenic interludes. The plot depicts the relentless drive of the play's various characters and forces, including a Guardian Angel, to convince the protagonist Peter of the truth and beauty of the Catholic faith. Guntwar, clearly Sorge himself, acts as God's messenger with a religious zeal bordering on the fanaticism sometimes seen in new converts. In the interludes, Sorge attacked the decadence of society, and any form of art that does not put itself "at the service of God". Despite the obvious autobiographical aspects of *Guntwar*, it is very rich in its formal aspects. The dramatic action is developed in a quasi-naturalist dialogue, while Sorge employed a wide variety of poetic forms ranging from a child's prayer to baroque religious hymns to a Dante-inspired damnation of the wicked and godless.

Sorge's remaining works were written almost exclusively to praise and promote Catholicism. The three mysteries, *Metanoeite*—including "Mary's Conception", "The Nativity", and "Christ's Teaching in the Temple"—are among the best examples of the liturgical drama Sorge had begun to develop in *Guntwar*; furthermore, they display his growing interest in biblical topics. The text of *König David* often draws verbatim on the Bible. The play is such an intimate and firm statement of Sorge's religious conviction and feelings that it has justifiably been called a "non-drama".

Sorge's last dramatic "vision", *Der Sieg des Christos*, is divided into two parts: *Franziskus, der heilige Bettler* (Francis, the Holy Beggar) and *Martin Luther, der ohne Reichtum* (The One without Riches). Although Sorge thought of these as his most important achievements, they represent merely further dramatized testimony to his religious ardour, which, unfortunately, culminated in an uncompromising self-righteousness, narrowing Sorge's importance as a writer, and allowing appreciation of his later works only to kindred spirits.

—Renate Benson

See also *Volume 1* entry on *The Beggar*.

SOUTHERNE, Thomas. Born in Oxmantown, near Dublin, Ireland, 12 February 1660. Educated at Trinity College, Dublin (pensioner), 1676–78; entered the Middle Temple, London, 1680. Served as an ensign in Princess Anne's Regiment, and rose to the command of a company, 1685–88. Married Agnes Atkyns c.1696; one daughter. First-produced play, *The Loyal Brother*, staged 1682. Protégé and friend of Dryden. MA: Trinity College, 1696. Died in London, 26 May 1746.

Works

Collections

Works (2 vols.), edited by Robert Jordan and Harold Love. 1988.

Stage Works

The Loyal Brother; or, The Persian Prince (produced Theatre Royal, Drury Lane, London, 1682). 1682.
The Disappointment; or, The Mother in Fashion (produced Theatre Royal, Drury Lane, London, 1684). 1684.
Sir Anthony Love; or, The Rambling Lady (produced Theatre Royal, Drury Lane, London, 1690). 1691.
The Wives' Excuse; or, Cuckolds Make Themselves (produced Theatre Royal, Drury Lane, London, 1691). 1692.
Cleomenes, The Spartan Hero, by Dryden, completed by Southerne (produced Theatre Royal, Drury Lane, London, 1692). 1692.
The Maid's Last Prayer; or, Any, Rather Than Fail (produced Theatre Royal, Drury Lane, London, 1693). 1693.
The Fatal Marriage; or, The Innocent Adultery, from a novel by Aphra Behn (produced Theatre Royal, Drury Lane, London, 1694). 1694.
Oroonoko, from the novel by Aphra Behn (produced Theatre Royal, Drury Lane, London, 1695). 1696.
The Fate of Capua (produced Lincoln's Inn Fields Theatre, 1700). 1700.
The Spartan Dame (produced Theatre Royal, Drury Lane, London, 1719). 1719.
Money the Mistress (produced Lincoln's Inn Fields Theatre, 1726). 1726.

*

Bibliographies

J.M. Armistead, "Thomas Southerne: Three Centuries of Criticism", in *Bulletin of Bibliography*, 41, 1984.

Criticism

Books:
John W. Dobbs, *Thomas Southerne, Dramatist*, New Haven, Connecticut, 1933.
Kenneth Muir, *The Comedy of Manners*, London, 1970.
Robert L. Root Jr., *Thomas Southerne*, Boston, 1981.

* * *

Thomas Southerne is the very model of a successful Restoration playwright, with a highly developed skill in tailoring his works to the taste of a fashionable audience, so that he was one of the few playwrights of his age to die a rich man.

His second play, *The Disappointment*, reveals his skills in embryo. Some critics have claimed an innovatory role for it as an early domestic drama and a precursor of sentimentalism, but set against other Spanish-style romantic tragicomedies of the time, and seen in the light of Thomas Otway's *The Orphan* and *Venice Preserved* (produced a few years earlier) its novelty is not particularly noticeable. In the character of Erminia, however, it provides an early example of what was to become one of Southerne's specialities, the distressed heroine or hero, a model of virtue who becomes the innocent victim of mistake, mischance, or malice. The character is essentially passive, and the appeal lies in watching his or her responses to suffering, which usually take the form of bravura set speeches, charged with emotion and rich in pathos.

The Disappointment appears to have been only a mild success, and it was a decade or so before Southerne was to capture the public imagination with two splendidly successful tragedies in this pathetic mode, *The Fatal Marriage* and *Oroonoko*. Isabella, in the former play, who innocently stumbles into bigamy and descends from thence into madness and death, is the most passionately distressed of all his heroines, and Oroonoko is, effectively, the male equivalent of the type—innocent, noble, loving, the long-suffering victim of serial treachery. Male values, of course, require that he should be a brave warrior and so, at suitable intervals, he is roused to action, but for much of the time he is immobile, paralysed by honor, trustfulness, or love, with a stoic dignity to replace Isabella's "feminine" proneness to hysteria, and with an alien cultural background to assist in keeping audience scepticism at bay.

The Fatal Marriage and *Oroonoko* became the cornerstones of Southerne's subsequent reputation, completely eclipsing his other works and becoming two of the most frequently produced plays of the 18th century. As such they are significant documents in the study of that age's sensibility, though for us *Oroonoko* has more immediate interest as a seminal work on black/white relations, and *The Fatal Marriage* as a study in the plight of women. These considerations, however, have not yet brought either play firmly back into the repertoire, though occasional productions of *Oroonoko* have been received with mild interest.

Curiously enough it was a period in which Southerne's feeling for his audience seemed to have deserted him completely, and in which he tried a quite radical departure from the standard fare of his time, that produced the two plays of greatest interest to critics now, and the plays perhaps most deserving of revival. In 1690 Southerne tried his hand at comedy, and achieved a brilliant if short-lived success with *Sir Anthony Love*, in which he took the highly popular woman-in-breeches motif to new heights of extravagance and impropriety. Two more comedies promptly followed, *The Wives' Excuse* and *The Maid's Last Prayer*, but instead of clinging to the light-hearted formula of *Sir Anthony Love*, Southerne here made a sharp turn into mordant social satire. Both plays were dismal failures, and disappeared from view for over 200 years. First noticed again in the late 1940's, they are now sometimes put on a level with the works of Wycherley and Vanbrugh.

These two plays take the whole of polite society as their target. Both are structured around a series of public occasions —raffles, balls, music-meetings—and while, in each play, one relationship is given some degree of prominence, both of them involve a multiplicity of intrigues, so that attention is spread across a wide range of characters. This dispersal of attention is nowhere more obvious than in the crowd scenes, which employ the technique of rapidly shifting the focus of attention from one small group to another, in an interwoven set of private conversations conducted as asides from the main group.

This sounds like the recipe for a formless, shapeless play, but *The Wives' Excuse*, in particular, develops a powerful dramatic rhythm out of its alternation of large-scale scenes of public entertainment with the chill and intimate interludes in which the private consequences of these gatherings are explored. For behind all the glittering social whirl the society is revealed as heartless, cynical, and predatory. It is also, of course, dominated by a male value-system. The women are there for the sexual gratification of the men and are pursued remorselessly. In the face of this value system Mrs. Friendall, of *The Wives' Excuse*, who wishes to preserve her virtue, must do so not through a ringing assertion of the moral verities, but through an embarrassed apology for her odd behaviour, while her would-be seducer is left not only amazed and resentful, but also unchastened and disbelieving.

To survive in this society it is crucial to control or suppress any tender feelings. *The Maid's Last Prayer* shows a whole group of women whose capacity for this enables it to gain the ascendency over its men, despite the prevailing ethos. Mrs. Friendall, in contrast, is made so vulnerable because she cannot achieve this self-control. She is Southerne's distressed heroine figure adapted to the everyday world, and plaintive rather than impassioned in her distress. Her acquaintance, Mrs. Sightly, manages things much more effectively, freely enjoying the pleasures of society but always aloof and self-contained. Such a world has as little room for friendship as for selfless love. For all the conviviality these characters are very much alone, existing in a world of superficial agreeableness which barely masks the selfishness beneath, and which accords readily with a self-protective detachment.

What gives these plays their ultimate power to disturb, however, is that the author seems to share in the emotional detachment and self-concealment of his characters. For all the baseness that he depicts, there is no display of moral outrage, nor any voice raised in judgment. There is not even the satisfaction of a firm conclusion, for both plays end in ambiguity, or with problems unresolved. Southerne's world continues unreformed, and its author gives away nothing.

—Robert Jordan

See also *Volume 1* entry on *Oroonoko*.

———————

SOYINKA, Wole. Born Akinwande Oluwole Soyinka in Abeokuta, Nigeria, 13 July 1934. Educated at St. Peter's School, Ake, Abeokuta, 1938–43; Abeokuta Grammar School, 1944–45; Government College, Ibadan, 1946–50; University College, Ibadan (now University of Ibadan), 1952–54; University of Leeds, Yorkshire, England, 1954–57, BA (honours) in English. Married; has several children. Play reader, Royal Court Theatre, London, 1957–59; founding director, Masks Theatre, 1960, and Orisun Theatre, 1964, Lagos and Ibadan; co-editor, *Black Orpheus*, 1961–64; Rockefeller research fellow in drama, University of Ibadan, 1961–62; lecturer in English, University of Ife, 1963–64; senior lecturer in English, University of Lagos, 1965–67; tried and acquitted of armed robbery, 1965; political prisoner, detained by the Federal Military Government, Lagos and Kaduna, 1967–69; head of the Department of Theatre Arts, University of Ibadan, 1969–72 (appointment made in 1967); visiting professor, Churchill College, Cambridge, 1973–74, University of Ghana, Legon, 1973–74, University of Sheffield, 1974; professor of comparative literature, and head of the Department of Dramatic Arts, University of Ife, 1975–85; editor, *Transition* (later *Ch'indaba*) magazine, Accra, Ghana, 1975–77; founding director, Unife Guerilla Theatre, Ife, 1978; visiting professor, Yale University, New Haven, Connecticut, 1979–80, and Cornell University, Ithaca, New York, 1986; Goldwin Smith Professor of Africana Studies and

Wole Soyinka on the steps of his residence in Ibadan, shortly after release from detention (1969).

Theatre, Cornell University, from 1988. Secretary-general, Union of Writers of the African Peoples, 1975. Recipient: Dakar Festival Award, 1966; John Whiting Award, 1967; Nobel Prize for Literature, 1986; AGIP-Mattei Award, 1986; Benson Medal, 1990; Premio Letterario Internazionale Mondello, 1990. D.Litt: University of Leeds, 1973; Yale University, 1981; Paul Valéry University, Montpellier, France, 1984; University of Lagos; Morehouse College, Atlanta, 1988; University of Bayreuth, Germany, 1989. Fellow, Royal Society of Literature; Member, American Academy, and Academy of Arts and Letters of the German Democratic Republic (DDR). Commander, Federal Republic of Nigeria, 1986, Légion d'Honneur (France), 1989, and Order of the Republic of Italy, 1990; Akogun of Isara, 1989; Akinlatun of Egbaland, 1990.

Works

Collections

Three Plays (includes *The Swamp Dwellers; The Trials of Brother Jero; The Strong Breed*). 1963; as *Three Short Plays*, 1969.
Five Plays: A Dance of the Forests; The Lion and the Jewel; The Swamp Dwellers; The Trials of Brother Jero; The Strong Breed. 1964.

Collected Plays:

1. *A Dance of the Forests; The Swamp Dwellers; The Strong Breed; The Road; The Bacchae.* 1973.
2. *The Lion and the Jewel; Kongi's Harvest; The Trials of Brother Jero; Jero's Metamorphosis; Madmen and Specialists.* 1974.

Six Plays (includes *The Trials of Brother Jero; Jero's Metamorphosis; Camwood on the Leaves; Death and the King's Horseman; Madmen and Specialists; Opera Wonyosi*). 1984.

Stage Works

The Swamp Dwellers (produced London University Drama Festival, 1958). In *Three Plays*, 1963.
The Lion and the Jewel (produced Arts Theatre, University of Ibadan, 1959). 1963.
The Invention (produced Royal Court Theatre, London, 1959).
A Dance of the Forests (produced by 1960 Masks, Independence Celebrations, Lagos, 1960). 1963.
The Trials of Brother Jero (produced Arts Theatre, University of Ibadan, 1960). In *Three Plays*, 1963.
The Republican and *The New Republican* (satirical revues; produced 1963).
The Strong Breed (produced Arts Theatre, University of Ibadan, 1964). In *Three Plays*, 1963.
Kongi's Harvest (produced Federal Palace Hotel, Lagos, 1965). 1967.
Before the Blackout (revue; includes *Childe International;*

produced Arts Theatre, University of Ibadan, 1965). 1971.

The Road (produced Theatre Royal, Stratford East, London, 1965). 1965.

Rites of the Harmattan Solstice (produced Lagos, 1966).

Madmen and Specialists (produced Eugene O'Neill Theatre, Waterford, Connecticut, 1970; revised version produced University of Ibadan, 1971). 1971.

Jero's Metamorphosis (produced Bristol University, 1974). In *The Jero Plays*, 1973.

The Bacchae: A Communion Rite, from the play by Euripides (produced by the National Theatre, Old Vic, London, 1973). 1973.

Death and the King's Horseman (produced Ife, 1976). 1975.

Opera Wonyosi, from *The Threepenny Opera* by Brecht (produced University of Ife, 1977). 1981.

Golden Accord (produced Actors' Theatre, Louisville, Kentucky, 1980).

Camwood on the Leaves, from the radio play (produced National Theatre, Lagos, 1982).

Priority Projects (revue; produced on tour, Nigeria, 1983).

Requiem for a Futurologist (produced on tour, Nigeria, 1983). 1985.

A Play of Giants (produced Yale University, New Haven, Connecticut, 1984). 1984.

From Zia, with Love. With *A Scourge of Hyacinths*, 1991.

Screenplays

Kongi's Harvest, 1970.

Television Plays (documentaries)

Joshua: A Nigerian Portrait, 1962; *Culture in Transition*, 1963.

Radio Plays

Camwood on the Leaves, 1960 (published with *Before the Blackout*), 1974; *The Detainee*, 1965; *Die Still, Dr. Godspeak*, 1981; *A Scourge of Hyacinths*, 1990 (published with *From Zia, with Love*, 1991).

Fiction

The Interpreters. 1965.
Season of Anomy. 1973.

Verse

"*Idanre*" *and Other Poems*. 1967.
Poems from Prison. 1969.
A Shuttle in the Crypt. 1972.
Ogun Abibimañ. 1976.
"*Mandela's Earth*" *and Other Poems*. 1988.

Memoirs and Letters.

Aké: The Years of Childhood (autobiography). 1981.

Other

The Man Died: Prison Notes. 1972.
In Person: Achebe, Awoonor, and Soyinka at the University of Washington. 1975.
Myth, Literature, and the African World. 1976.
The Critic and Society (essay). 1981.

The Past Must Address Its Present (lecture). 1986; as *This Past Must Address Its Present*, 1988.

Art, Dialogue and Outrage: Essays on Literature and Culture. 1988.

Isara: A Voyage Around "Essay". 1989.

Continuity and Amnesia. 1991.

The Essential Soyinka: A Reader, edited by Henry Louis Gates Jr. 1991.

Editor, *Poems of Black Africa*. 1975.

Translator, *The Forest of a Thousand Daemons: A Hunter's Saga*, by D.O. Fagunwa. 1968.

*

Bibliographies

B.M. Okpu, *Wole Soyinka: A Bibliography*, Lagos, 1984.

James Gibbs, Ketu H. Katrak, and Henry L. Gates, *Wole Soyinka: A Bibliography of Primary and Secondary Sources*, Westport, Connecticut, 1986.

Criticism

Books:

Gerald Moore, *Wole Soyinka*, London and New York, 1971; revised edition, 1978.

Eldred D. Jones, *The Writing of Wole Soyinka*, London, 1973; revised edition, 1983; further revised edition, 1989.

Oyin Ogunba, *The Movement of Transition: A Study of the Plays of Wole Soyinka*, Ibadan, 1975.

Rita Bottcher-Wobcke, *Komik, Ironie, und Satire im Dramatischen Werk von Wole Soyinka*, Hamburg, 1976.

Jonathan Peters, *A Dance of Masks: Senghor, Achebe, Soyinka*, Washington, DC, 1978.

E.M. Parsons (ed.), *Notes on Wole Soyinka's The Jero Plays*, London, 1979.

James Gibbs (ed.), *Critical Perspectives on Wole Soyinka*, Washington, DC, 1980.

Martin Banham, *The Lion and the Jewel: A Critical View*, London, 1981.

Alain Ricard, *Theatre and Nationalism: Wole Soyinka and LeRoi Jones*, Ife, 1983.

Stephan Larsen, *A Writer and His Gods: A Study of the Importance of Yoruba Myths and Religious Ideas in the Writing of Wole Soyinka*, Stockholm, 1983.

Femi Osofisan, *Beyond Translation: Tragic Paradigms and the Dramaturgy of Ola Rotimi and Wole Soyinka*, Ife, 1985.

James Gibbs, *Wole Soyinka*, London and New York, 1986.

Obi Maduakor, *Wole Soyinka: An Introduction to His Writing*, New York, 1986.

Wole Soyinka, *Soyinka as Director* (interview), Ife, 1986.

Ketu E. Katrak (ed.), *Wole Soyinka and Modern Tragedy: A Study of Dramatic Theory and Practice*, New York, 1986.

Dapo Adelugba (ed.), *Before Our Very Eyes: Tribute to Wole Soyinka*, Ibadan, 1987.

Alain Ricard, *Wole Soyinka, ou l'ambition démocratique*, Paris, 1988.

* * *

The award of the Nobel Prize for Literature to Wole Soyinka in 1986 was seen to be not only a recognition of Soyinka's own work but also a tribute to the literature of contemporary Africa. It was in these terms that Soyinka received the prize, but his stature amongst his fellow African writers is unchallenged. His has been the major and most prolific talent of the period since the late 1950's, which has seen the development of a vigorous and varied literature from Africa in English, French, and indigenous languages. Although Soyinka is usually seen as a dramatist, his novels, autobiographical works, poetry, and criticism are of equal importance. Many of the incidents that form the plots of his plays may be seen to be exercised elsewhere in his work. The prison diary *The Man Died*, for instance, is closely paralleled by the play *Madmen and Specialists*. His poetry has a dramatic and a theatrical dimension to it which demands to be spoken aloud and responds (as in the case of the Royal Shakespeare Company's version of *Ogun Abibiman*) to dramatisation. Our concentration here on his plays should be seen in this context.

Soyinka's early writing for the theatre was predominantly humorous and satirical. From *The Lion and the Jewel* to *Kongi's Harvest* we see Soyinka observing the absurdities of his society with an eye that was initially tolerant and affectionate, but which became fiercer and more specific as, in the world about him, the aspirations of independence turned sour. The vast early work, *A Dance of the Forests*, which may be seen to some extent as a source for a number of his later plays, warned of this very possibility. *The Swamp Dwellers*, which with *The Lion and the Jewel* was first drafted during Soyinka's student days in Britain, sounds the first note of pessimism in Soyinka's writing, telling a story of betrayal and dislocation in a rural community. His writing has always engaged with the political realities of the time. Younger critics have sometimes accused him of a lack of commitment but this impatient view is starkly countered by the personal suffering that Soyinka has experienced not only as a result of his outspoken writing but also because of his belief that the artist must express his concerns as much by action as by words. Plays such as *Kongi's Harvest*, *Opera Wonyosi*, and *A Play of Giants* present identifiable villains on the stage—the politicians who, in Soyinka's terms, have failed their people. In other plays—*The Strong Breed*, *The Road*, *The Swamp Dwellers*—more metaphysical themes are explored that are concerned with the spiritual vitality of the community.

These qualities are brought powerfully together in *Madmen and Specialists* and *Death and the King's Horseman*, two plays Soyinka wrote after his release from detention during the Nigerian Civil War. The first is a bitter allegory on cannabalism, the second a study of the failure of spiritual and political will. Many of Soyinka's later plays have, as an underlying theme, the exploration of the moment of transition between the present day world and the world of the ancestors—collectively the past and the future. In *The Road*, for instance, the main character, a crazed "Professor", obsessively seeks, through the carnage of road accidents, to find the route of death. In *Death and the King's Horseman*, the Elesin—chief minister to the dead King—is seen to be frustrated by both personal and external forces in his act of ritual suicide. His failure has profound and destructive implications for the community, throwing the delicate and fundamental relationship between the worlds past, present, and future into chaos.

A graphic theatrical illustration of this sense of the co-existence of time can be seen in the dance of the half-child, an incident towards the end of *A Dance of the Forests*, where spirits and humans dispute the future of the half-born child. The rite of passage in a community context is also treated in, for instance, the lyrical battle of wills between the old and the young in *The Lion and the Jewel* and in the more sombre play *The Strong Breed*, where the hero takes on himself the role of

the "carrier" who will take away from a community the ills of the past year in order to cleanse the new year. (We may also be tempted, in this play, to see Soyinka offering the idea of the artist's responsibility within society to be one of the "strong breed" and to use his or her gifts unselfishly in the service of the community.)

All of Soyinka's writing is in English, with the exception of Yoruba words or phrases introduced for specific effect and passages of pidgin. African artists concern themselves deeply with the matter of language, seeing English and French and other European languages as the tongue of the colonial power, the tool and stigma of imperialism. The Kenyan Ngugi wa Thiongo has taken one stance on this matter by reverting to writing in his own language and relying on translation to make his works available in English. Soyinka, on the other hand, whilst acknowledging the ideological point, uses English because of its *national* as well as international function as a vehicle of communication in a multilingual country such as Nigeria. The richly poetic and sometimes complex language he employs may be seen to reflect the subtlety and range of Yoruba, a tonal language that, in use, works through allusion and verbal wit and decoration. The translation of these elements into English gives Soyinka's writing a quality found rarely in contemporary writing in English. Visual and aural images complement the poetic in a way that makes much European theatre, by contrast, look positively anaemic. Soyinka has established himself as one of the major writers in English for the contemporary stage.

—Martin Banham

See also *Volume 1* entry on *Death and the King's Horseman*; *Madmen and Specialists*; *The Road*.

STALLINGS, Laurence.   See *Volume 1* entry on *Winterset*.

SPERR, Martin. Born in Steinburg, Lower Bavaria, Germany, 14 September 1944. Educated at schools in Wendelskirchen, Algasing, and Munich, to 1961; briefly took an industrial apprenticeship, 1961; studied acting: in Munich, from 1961, and at the Max-Reinhardt-Seminar, Vienna, 1962–64. Married to 1) Monika Sperr, 1967–68; 2) the actress Silvia Sperr from 1971; one daughter. Acting debut at Theater 44, Munich, 1962; actor with the Schauspielhaus, Bremen, 1965–66; writer from 1966: first-produced play, *Jagdszenen aus Niederbayern*, staged 1966; career interrupted by a severe stroke, 1972–74; company member, Volkstheater, Munich, 1983–88, and subsequently guest actor at various Munich theatres. Recipient: Hauptmann Prize, 1965; Ernst Hoferichter Prize, 1977; Mulheim Drama Prize, 1978.

Works

Collections

Bayrische Trilogie (includes *Jagdszenen aus Niederbayern*; *Landshuter Erzählungen*; *Münchner Freiheit*).   1972.

Stage Works

Jagdszenen aus Niederbayern (produced Bühnen der Freie Hansestadt, Bremen, 1966). In *Theater heute*, 7, 1966; in book form, in *Bayrische Trilogie*, 1972.

Landshuter Erzählungen (produced Kammerspiele, Munich, 1967). In *Theater heute*, special issue, 1967; in book form, in *Bayrische Trilogie*, 1972; translated as *Tales from Landshut*, 1969.

Gerettet, from a play by Edward Bond (produced Munich, 1967).

Mass für Mass, from *Measure for Measure* by Shakespeare (produced Bremen Theater, 1967).

Koralle Meier (produced Württembergisches Staatstheater, Stuttgart, 1970). 1970 (stage version).

Die Kunst der Zähmung, from *The Taming of the Shrew* by Shakespeare (produced Bremen Theater, 1971). 1981.

Münchner Freiheit (produced Schauspielhaus, Düsseldorf, 1971). In *Theater heute*, 12, 1971; in book form, in *Bayrische Trilogie*, 1972.

Die Spitzeder, from the television play *Adele Spitzeder* (produced Theater der Stadt, Bonn, 1977). 1980.

Television Plays

Kneissl, 1971 (published as *Der Räuber Mathias Kneissl*, 1971); *Adele Spitzeder*, 1972.

Radio Plays

Lemsond, with Dieter Kühn, 1974; *Babb ma derf net sei!*, from a play by Karl Otto Mühl, 1977; Adele Spitzeder, 1979.

Other

Willst du Giraffen ohreigen, musst du ihr Niveau haben: Eine Legende, Prose, Gedichte, Zeichnungen. 1979.

*

Criticism

Books:
H. Karasek, *Die Erneuerung des Volksstücks*, Kronberg, 1977.
G. Müller, *Das Volksstück von Raimund bis Kroetz*, Munich, 1979.
Eva Kormann, "Martin Sperr: *Jagdszenen* und anderes", in her "*Der täppische Prankenschlag eines einzelgangerischen Urviechs . . .*": *Das neue kritische Volksstück*, Tübingen, 1990.

Articles:
W.G. Marigold, "Martin Sperr and Franz Xaver Kroetz: New Directions for Left-Wing Playwrights", in *Perspectives on Contemporary Literature*, 2, 1976.

*   *   *

The plays of Martin Sperr represent meticulously detailed, critical investigations of the social behaviour in the villages, towns, and state-capital of Bavaria; they are firmly rooted in a realistic tradition that goes back to Ödön von Horváth and especially to the work of Marielouise Fleisser (1901–74); the latter referred to Sperr as to Sperr's contemporaries Rainer Maria Fassbinder and Franz Xaver Kroetz, as "her boys". His *Bayrische Trilogie* (*Bavarian Trilogy*) begins with *Jagdszenen*

aus Niederbayern (Hunting Scenes from Lower Bavaria): shortly after World War II in 1948, an (homosexual) outsider in a village is stigmatized and intimidated by the community until he is pushed into murdering a girl, only to be hunted down as a "perverted criminal". The fable creates models of popular attitudes, particularly an ignorance which detests and tends to exterminate the "other" of whatever kind. The second part, *Landshuter Erzählungen* (*Tales from Landshut*), depicts a brutal struggle between two building contractors in 1958, the time of the West German "economic miracle". The fight is decided by the killing of one family's father by his son, who then marries the daughter of the other contractor family, merging their companies to gain the monopoly in a town where Bavarian joviality poorly hides the ruthless backstabbing, perjury, and anti-semitism which are rampant. Finally, in *Münchner Freiheit* (Munich Freedom)—the title refers to Münchner Freiheit, a square in Munich's Schwabing quarter —Sperr turns even more melodramatic in his unmasking of the business methods by which architects, contractors, and politicians exploit the re-zoning of a city quarter for their personal profit in 1968, a time when the city prepared itself for the Olympic Games of 1972.

While in his "Bavarian Trilogy" Sperr portrayed the social and ethical attitudes in his home state as they played themselves out in post-war history, pinpointing a different social group each time in ten-year intervals from 1948 to 1968, he went a decade back to Hitler's Third Reich, in the late 1930's, in his "play with music", *Koralle Meier* (Coral Meyer), the story of a prostitute who, in a small Bavarian town, tries to quit her profession and open a grocery store. She fails tragically, owing to the prejudices, envies, and latent fears of the community. Seemingly "normal" lower-middle-class sentiments and beliefs are revealed as the seedbed of fascism—a recurrent theme in Sperr's work.

Another dark yet comic view of Bavarian—and German— society and its traditions is presented in *Adele Spitzeder*, a play based on the life of a mid-19th century entrepreneur. She, the owner of a bank, invents a savings scheme to attract the accounts of small-time depositors, only to finance her own luxurious way of life; she maintains that her pyramid game is intended to help the common people of the mainly rural background. (In 1978, Martin Sperr himself performed the title role in a production at Munich's Studio Theater.)

Sperr also adapted several plays from English. His Munich-jargon version of Edward Bond's *Saved* was Peter Stein's directing debut and a resounding success. He also adapted *Measure for Measure* and *The Taming of the Shrew* for the Bremen Theatre. For television, he scripted two films. *The Kneissl* retold the life of a notorious criminal who was eventually arrested and executed for armed robbery and murder in 1902 (Kneissl became a legendary character among Bavarian countryfolk and was revered in a Robin Hood fashion). Sperr did not glorify his protagonist, yet showed precisely the environment of rural poverty and a repressive state that pushed Kneissl into a life of crime. The second film was *Adele Spitzeder*, which he later adapted for the stage.

Sperr's works are limited in scope and number, mainly owing to his severe illness in 1972. Together with Kroetz and, to a lesser degree, Fassbinder, he revived the genre of the *Volksstück*, a popular play of serious intention, which had been ignored by the German theatre since Fleisser's work and Brecht's *Puntila*. The influence of Fleisser and Brecht is clearly evident in Sperr's dramaturgy, as well as in the poetically heightened Bavarian dialect employed in his dialogue. The plays provide us with a harsh but precise portrayal of South German society during Nazism and the early years of the West German republic; they expose the poisoned roots this society had grown from, however much the establishment of the period tried to ignore or hide this. With the exception of Kroetz, there has not been another playwright since World War II who has so consistently and sharply dissected social and economic trends and their impact on the people of the South-German Länder.

Sperr belongs to that remarkable generation of German playwrights that suddenly burst on the scene in the late 1960's and left its indelible mark. What will remain of their work is still to be decided. Of Sperr's plays, only "Hunting Scenes from Lower Bavaria" has had a continuing life in the German repertoire, and it has received many productions abroad, for instance in London and New York. It may well be the one work that will survive, thanks to its powerful fable, its fascinating and rich characters, and its capacity to stand as a profound document of its time.

—Carl Weber

Act III, Scene 4 of *The Conscious Lovers* by **Sir Richard Steele**, showing Mrs. Abington as Phillis in the 1776 Drury Lane production.

STEELE, Sir Richard.   Born in Dublin; baptized 12 March 1672. Educated at Charterhouse, London, where he met Joseph Addison, 1684–89; Christ Church, Oxford, 1690; Merton College, Oxford (scholar), 1691–94. Married 1) Margaret Ford Stretch in 1705 (died 1706); 2) Mary Scurlock in 1707 (died 1718), two sons and two daughters; also had one illegitimate daughter. Served in the Life Guards, 1692–95: probably served in Flanders, 1692–93; served in the Coldstream Guards, 1695–97: captain; confidential secretary to Lord Cutts, 1696–97; stationed at the Tower of London by 1700, and in Lord Lucas's regiment at Landguard Fort, Suffolk, 1702–05; first-produced play, *The Funeral*, staged 1701; gentleman-waiter to Queen Anne's husband, Prince George of Denmark, 1706–08; gazetteer (manager of the *Gazette*, the official government publication), 1707–10; commissioner of stamps, 1710–13; founding editor, the *Tatler* (first English periodical with regular theatre reviews), to which Joseph Addison was a major contributor, 1709–11; founder, and editor with Addison, the *Spectator*, 1711–12; founding editor, the *Guardian*, 1713; Member of Parliament for Stockbridge, Hampshire, 1713–14: expelled for anti-Government views expressed in *The Crisis*; founding editor, the *Englishman*, 1713–14, the *Lover*, 1714, and the *Reader*, 1714; on accession of George I, 1714, appointed justice of the peace, Deputy Lieutenant for Middlesex, Surveyor of the royal stables at Hampton Court, and Governor of the Theatre Royal, Drury Lane; granted life patent of Drury Lane, 1715 (patent revoked, 1718); Member of Parliament for Boroughbridge, Yorkshire, 1715; founding editor, *Town Talk*, 1715–16, the *Tea-Table*, 1716, and *Chit-Chat*, 1716; appointed commissioner for forfeited estates in Scotland, 1716; founding editor, the *Plebeian*, 1719, and the *Theatre*, 1720; Member of Parliament for Wendover, Buckinghamshire, 1722; retired to Carmarthen, Wales, 1724. Died in Camarthen, 1 September 1729.

Works

Collections

Dramatic Works, edited by George A. Aitken.   1894.
Plays, edited by Shirley Strum Kenny.   1971.

Stage Works

The Funeral; or, Grief a-la-Mode (produced Theatre Royal, Drury Lane, London, 1701).   1702.
The Lying Lover; or, The Ladies' Friendship (produced Theatre Royal, Drury Lane, London, 1703).   1704.
The Tender Husband; or, the Accomplished Fools (produced Theatre Royal, Drury Lane, London, 1705).   1705.
The Conscious Lovers (produced Theatre Royal, Drury Lane, London, 1722).   1722.

Verse

The Procession: A Poem on Her Majesty's Funeral.   1695.
Occasional Verse, edited by Rae Blanchard.   1952.

Memoirs and Letters

Mr. Steele's Apology for Himself and His Writings.   1714.
Correspondence, edited by Rae Blanchard.   1941; revised
    edition, 1968.

Other

*The Christian Hero, An Argument Proving That No Principles
    But Those of Religion Are Sufficient to Make a Great Man*.
    1701.
The Tatler, with Addison (4 vols.).   1710–11.
The Spectator, with Addison (8 vols.).   1712–15.
*An Englishman's Thanks to the Duke of Marl-
    borough*.   1712.
A Letter to Sir M. W[arton] Concerning Occasional Peers.
    1713.
The Importance of Dunkirk.   1713.
The Guardian, with others (2 vols.).   1714.
The Englishman (2 series, and an epistle; 3 vols.).   1714–16.
*The Crisis, with Some Seasonable Remarks on the Danger of a
    Popish Successor*.   1714.
*The French Faith Represented in the Present State of
    Dunkirk*.   1714.
*A Letter Concerning the Bill for Preventing the Growth of
    Schism*.   1714.
A Letter from the Earl of Mar to the King.   1715.
A Letter Concerning the Condemned Lords.   1716.
Account of Mr. Desagulier's New-Invented Chimneys.   1716.
An Account of the Fish Pool, with Joseph Gillmore.   1718.
*The Joint and Humble Address to the Tories and Whigs
    Concerning the Intended Bill of Peerage*.   1719.
A Letter to the Earl of O—d Concerning the Bill of Peerage.
    1719.
The Plebeian.   1719.
The Spinster, in Defence of the Woolen Manufactures.   1719.
The Crisis of Property, 1720.
*A Nation a Family; or, A Plan for the Improvement of the
    South-Sea Proposal*.   1720.
*The State of the Case Between the Lord Chamberlain and the
    Governor of the Royal Company of Comedians*.   1720.
The Theatre.   1720.
Tracts and Pamphlets, edited by Rae Blanchard.   1944.
*Periodical Journalism 1714–1716: The Lover, The Reader,
    Town Talk, Chit-Chat*, edited by Rae Blanchard.   1959.

Editor, *The Ladies Library* (3 vols.).   1714.
Editor, *Poetical Miscellanies*.   1714.

*

Criticism

Books:
George A. Aitken, *The Life of Richard Steele* (2 vols.),
    London, 1889.
Willard Connely, *Sir Richard Steele*, London and New York,
    1934.
John Loftis, *Steele at Drury Lane*, Berkeley, California, 1952.
Calhoun Winton, *Captain Steele: The Early Career*, and *The
    Later Career* (2 vols.), Baltimore, Maryland, 1964–70.
Edward A. Bloom and Lillian D. Bloom (eds.) *Addison and
    Steele: The Critical Heritage*, London, 1980.

* * *

As a playwright, Richard Steele is best remembered today

for his comedy *The Conscious Lovers*. One of the most
influential plays of the 18th century, it broke box-office records, went through 48 editions by the end of the century, and
was translated into French, German, and Italian. It is for us
the purest example of "sentimental" comedy. Of crucial importance to Steele's dramatic work was the appearance of
Jeremy Collier's *A Short View of the Immorality and
Profaneness of the English Stage* (1698). Steele sympathized
with Collier, and set out to moralize the stage.

His first comedy, *The Funeral*, is the only one of his plays not to
depend on foreign sources. The plot is Steele's invention and his
satire on undertakers in the first act is wholly original. The rest of
the play depends on well-established comic formulae. Two pairs
of lovers are thwarted by the machinations of a "blocking figure",
Lady Brumpton. The couples are carefully balanced: the conventional Lord Hardy and Sharlot are set against Campley and
Harriot, who are more capricious but, unlike their Restoration
predecessors, perfectly decorous.

The central situation concerns Lord Brumpton, who is
believed to be dead, and who is persuaded by his servant
Trusty to continue the misunderstanding in order to observe
the perfidy of his wife, Lady Brumpton. In the final act, the
nature of the play changes completely and the action becomes
melodramatic. The vicious wife is exposed, Lord Brumpton,
in an emotional scene, is reconciled to his son, Lord Hardy,
and the play collapses into sententious blank verse.

In *The Lying Lover*, taken in large measure from Pierre
Corneille's *Le Menteur*, Steele fell into the same errors as he
did in his first play. Here again his technique was to create a
traditionally comic first four acts involving disguises, discoveries, and transformations. Latine and Young Bookwit,
newly down from Oxford, cast lots to see who will pose as the
servant of the other, a device that George Farquhar would
later adopt in *The Beaux' Stratagem*. The play changes direction at the close of the fourth act. Bookwit challenges his
apparent rival, Lovemore, to a duel and believes he has killed
him. The duel is utterly alien to the comedy as it has been
developed up to this point, but furnishes occasion for sententious comments on a topic that was always close to Steele's
heart. Bookwit is thrown into prison, Latine is prepared to
sacrifice himself for his friend, and Lovemore is persuaded by
Bookwit's repentance from anger to forgiveness. As in *The
Funeral* the close is excessively moralistic and emotional.

Perhaps in reaction to the sentimental excesses of *The Lying
Lover*, *The Tender Husband*, which followed later that same
year, avoids sentiment almost entirely. Often ignored as uncharacteristic of Steele, it is now increasingly considered to be his
comic masterpiece. The play depends in part on Molière's *Le
Sicilien* and *Les Précieuses ridicules*. From the latter he derived
the figure of Biddy Tipkin, who is infatuated with romances and
deplores her impending marriage to the country bumpkin,
Humphrey Gubbin. Biddy Tipkin is swept off her feet by Captain
Clerimont, who affects a romantic disposition to achieve the
conquest of both Biddy and her fortune. This is all straightforward and accomplished comedy. Where the play becomes far
more problematic is in the action concerning Clerimont Senior,
the "tender husband" of the title, and his feckless wife.
Clerimont persuades his mistress, Lucy, to disguise herself as a
young man, Faithlove, in order to seduce and thus expose his
wife, Mrs. Clerimont. Mrs. Clerimont is surprised with
Faithlove. Although she has little intention of surrendering her
virtue to him, she is overcome with remorse, Clerimont kindly
forgives her, and Lucy is married off to Humphrey Gubbin.
Although Steele professed to be writing a moral play,
Clerimont's treatment of both his wife and mistress is
disconcerting.

Although 17 years elapsed between the first performance of

The Tender Husband and that of *The Conscious Lovers*, Steele may have begun his last play as early as 1707. He continued to work on it until it finally appeared in 1722. Here Steele brought to fruition his earlier attempts to create an "innocent" didactic comedy. Whereas he had previously failed because he insisted on bringing a comic action to a melodramatic conclusion, he now solved the problem by confining the exemplary element to the main plot, and restricting the wit and humour to the secondary characters.

The main plot of *The Conscious Lovers* is taken from Terence's *Andria*. Bevil Junior and Indiana, whom Bevil rescues and who is later found to be the wealthy merchant Sealand's lost daughter, are both irreproachable in their morals. Steele allowed secondary characters to be aberrant, and Myrtle, Bevil's friend, is excessively jealous, a condition he manages to overcome.

Set against the melodramatic central plot, the witty servants, Tom and Phillis—introduced, it is said, at the suggestion of Colley Cibber—afford some light relief. They translate the conventions of the gay couple of Restoration comedy into a lower-class decorum. Wit, like outmoded clothing, is handed down to the servants. Mrs. Sealand and Cimberton, whom she proposes as a rival to Myrtle, are both treated satirically, and we do not sympathize with them and they do not repent.

Although it is less amusing than *The Tender Husband*, Steele managed in *The Conscious Lovers* to combine diverse elements more successfully than he had managed to do in his earlier plays.

—Colin Wills Visser

See also *Volume 1* entry on *The Conscious Lovers*.

STERNHEIM, Carl. Born in Leipzig, Germany, 1 April 1878. Educated at Gymnasium, Berlin; studied literature, history, philosophy at the universities of Munich, Leipzig, Göttingen, and Berlin, 1897–1902. Married 1) Eugenie Hauth in 1900 (divorced 1906), one son; 2) Thea Bauer in 1907 (divorced 1927), one daughter (born 1905) and one son; 3) the actress Pamela Wedekind (daughter of Frank Wedekind) in 1930 (divorced 1934). Converted to Protestantism, 1897; over next ten years suffered increasingly from nervous illnesses: in a sanatorium in Freiburg, 1906; following second marriage, moved into the "Bellemaison" mansion, near Munich, 1907; co-founder, with Franz Blei, the literary periodical *Hyperion*, 1908: resigned from it, 1912; wrote the plays that make up the *Aus dem bürgerlichen Heldenleben* group, 1911–14; moved to Brussels, 1912; began writing fiction, 1912; was turned down for military service, 1914; suffered further nervous problems, and travelled to Switzerland, Dresden, and London in the 1920's; in a sanatorium after complete nervous breakdown, 1928; returned to Brussels with his third wife, 1930; his plays banned from production or publication by the Nazi regime, 1933; travelled to London hoping to interest British publishers and directors in his plays, 1934; last years spent in isolation in Brussels, protected from the occupying German authorities through the intervention of the Italian embassy. Died in Brussels, 3 November 1942.

Works

Collections

Das Dramatische Werk (2 vols.).   1948.
Gesammelte Werke (6 vols.), edited by Fritz Hofmann.   1963–68.
Gesamtwerk (11 vols.), edited by Wilhelm Emrich and Manfred Linke.   1963–76.
Aus dem bürgerlichen Heldenleben (2 vols.), edited by Friedrich Eisenlohr.   1947.
Das dramatische Werk (2 vols.: *Lustspiele* and *Historische Schauspiele*).   1948.
Aus dem bürgerlichen Heldenleben: Sechs Dramen.   1969.
Aus dem bürgerlichen Heldenleben: Stücke (Reclam edition).   1969.
Plays (includes *Paul Schippel Esq.*; *The Bloomers*; *The Snob*; *1913*; *The Fossil*), various translators.   1970.

Stage Works

Der Heiland.   1898.
Judas Ischarioth.   1901.
Auf Krugdorf.   1902.
Vom König und der Königin (produced as *Die Königin*, 1929).   1905.
Ulrich und Brigitte (produced by the Freie Literarisch-Künstlerische Gesellschaft, Darmstadt, 1916). 1907.
Don Juan.   1909.
Die Hose (produced as *Der Reise*, Kammerspiele, Deutsches Theater, Berlin, 1911).   1911; translated as *A Pair of Drawers*, in *Translation* (Paris), 6–9, 1927; as *The Underpants*, in *The Modern Theatre 6*, edited by Eric Bentley, 1960; as *The Bloomers*, in *Plays*, 1970.
Die Kassette (produced Kammerspiele, Deutsches Theater, Berlin, 1911).   1912; translated as *The Strong Box*, in *Anthology of German Expressionist Drama*, edited by Walter Sokel, 1963; as *The Money Box*, in *Plays*, 1970.
Bürger Schippel (produced Kammerspiele, Deutsches Theater, Berlin, 1913).   1913; operatic version, as *Tenor*, music by Ernst von Dohnányi (produced Deutscher Opernhaus, Berlin, 1928); translated as *Paul Schippel Esq.*, in *Plays*, 1970.
Der Snob (produced Kammerspiele, Deutsches Theater, Berlin, 1914).   1914; translated as *A Place in the World*, in *Eight European Plays*, edited by W. Katzin, 1927; as *The Snob*, in *From the Modern Repertoire 1*, edited by Eric Bentley, 1949, and in *Plays*, 1970.
Der Kandidat (produced Volksbühne, Vienna, 1915).   1914.
1913 (produced Schauspielhaus, Frankfurt, 1919).   1915; translated as *1913*, in *Plays*, 1970.
Das leidende Weib, from a work by Friedrich Maximilian Klinger (produced privately, Kammerspiele, Deutsches Theater, Berlin, 1916).   1915.
Der Scharmante, from a story by Maupassant (produced Kammerspiele, Deutsches Theater, Berlin, 1915).   1915.
Der Geizige, from a play by Molière (produced Deutsches Theater, Berlin, 1917).   1916.
Tabula rasa (produced Kleines Theater, Berlin, 1919).   1916.
Perleberg (produced Schauspielhaus, Frankfurt, 1917).   1917.
Die Marquise von Arcis, from a play by Diderot (produced Schauspielhaus, Frankfurt, 1919).   1918; translated as *The Mask of Virtue*, 1935.
Die entfesselte Zeitgenosse (produced Hessisches Landestheater, Darmstadt, 1921).   1920.

Manon Lescaut, from the novel by Prévost (produced Theater in der Königgrätzer Strasse, Berlin, 1921).   1921.

Der Abenteurer.   1922.

Der Nebbich (produced Hessisches Landestheater, Darmtstadt, 1922).   1922.

Das Fossil (produced Kammerspiele, Hamburg, 1923).   1925; translated as *The Fossil*, in *Plays*, 1970.

Oskar Wilde (produced Deutsches Theater, Berlin, 1925).   1925.

Die Schule von Uznach; oder, Neue Sachlichkeit (produced simultaneously in Hamburg, Cologne, and Mannheim, 1926).   1926.

Maske (produced Theater in der Behrenstrasse, Berlin, 1928).

John Pierpont Morgan.   1930.

Die Vater; oder, Knock Out.   In *Gesamtwerk 10*, 1976.

Aut Caesar aut Nihil   In *Gesamtwerk 10*, 1976..

Fiction

Die drei Erzählungen.   1916.

Posinsky.   1917.

Mädchen.   1917; revised edition, 1926.

Chronik von des zwangzigsten Jahrhunderts Beginn (2 vols.).   1918; individual parts published in book form:
  Napoleon.   1927.
  Busekow.   1928.

Vier Novellen.   1918.

Europa (2 vols.).   1919–20.

Fairfax.   1921; translated as *Fairfax*, 1923.

Libussa, des Kaisers Leibross.   1922.

Verse

"Fanale!".   1901.

Memoirs and Letters

Vorkriegseuropa im Gleichnis meines Lebens (autobiography).   1936.

Briefe, edited by Wolfgang Wendler.   1988.

Other

Prosa.   1918.

Die deutsche Revolution.   1919.

Berlin; oder, Juste Milieu (essays).   1920.

Tasso; oder, Kunst des Juste Milieu: Ein Wink für die Jugend (essays).   1921.

Gaugin und Van Gogh.   1924.

Lutetia (travel essays).   1926.

Kleine Katechismus für das Jahr 1930/31.   1930.

*

Bibliographies

Rudolf Billetta, *Sternheim-Kompendium: Carl Sternheim: Werk, Weg, Wirkung: Bibliographie und Bericht*, Wiesbaden, 1975.

Rudolf Billetta, "Auswahlbibliographie", in *Text und Kritik*, 87 (Sternheim issue), 1985.

Criticism

Books:

Franz Blei, *Über Wedekind, Sternheim und das Theater*, Munich, 1951.

Hellmuth Karasek, *Carl Sternheim*, Velber, 1965.

Wolfgang Wendler, *Carl Sternheim: Weltvorstellung und Kunstprinzipien*, Frankfurt, 1966.

Winfried G. Sebald, *Carl Sternheim: Kritiker und Opfer der wilhelminischen Ära*, Stuttgart, 1969.

Jürgen Sang, *Ideologiekritik und dichterische Form bei Wedekind, Sternheim, Kaiser*, Tokyo, 1972.

Jörg Schönert (ed.), *Carl Sternheims Dramen: Zur Textanalyse, Ideologiekritik und Rezeptionsgeschichte*, Heidelberg, 1975.

Winifried Freund, *Die Bürgerkomödien Carl Sternheims*, Munich, 1976.

Karl Deiritz, *Geschichtbewusstsein, Satire, Zensur: Eine Studie zu Carl Sternheim*, Königstein, 1979.

Manfred Linke, *Carl Sternheim in Selbstzeugnissen und Bilddokumenten*, Reinbek, 1979.

Eckehard Czucka, *Idion der Entstellung: Auffaltung des Satirischen in Carl Sternheims "Aus dem bürgerlichen Heldenleben"*, Aschendorff Münster, 1982.

Manfred Durzak (ed.) *Zu Carl Sternheim*, Stuttgart, 1982.

Articles:

David Myers, "Carl Sternheim: Satirist or Creator of Modern Heroes?", in *Monatshefte*, 65, 1973.

Wolfgang Wendler (ed.), *Carl Sternheim: Materialienbuch*, Darmstadt, 1980.

*   *   *

Carl Sternheim's dramas, especially his comedies, have been among the most successful in Germany from 1911 to 1925, when he was regarded as a German Molière, and since 1960 alongside those of Gerhart Hauptmann and Bertolt Brecht. Yet they are hard to interpret, for their style suggests either satirical intent or an attempt to portray anarchic alternatives to traditional social behaviour. The social values Sternheim portrayed and, at times, held up to ridicule were not only applicable to Wilhelmine Germany, but also to any group of people where struggling for social recognition and conforming to social standards dominate life. One of their attractions lies in the uncertainty of Sternheim's intentions: are his central figures objects of ridicule or "heroes"? Sternheim's own thoroughly upper-middle-class way of life gave him an unfailingly keen eye for the petty details and the human foibles of bourgeois life.

After early experiments in search of his individual style, he started his most famous series of comedies *Scenes from the Heroic Life* with *Die Hose* (*The Bloomers*). In the three generations of the Maske family shown here, and in *Der Snob* (*The Snob*) and *1913*, the parvenu rules supreme. Callousness, cynicism, and icy arrogance triumph over genuine feelings and claim their victims in this take-off of Wilhelmine society just before the World War I, as it became aware of its imminent fall. The success of such "heroes" (or are they monsters?) depends on their ruthlessness, but also on the gullibility of the minor characters, especially the women who mainly worship the male chauvinists. Only Sofie, the eldest daughter in *1913*, manages to seize power when her businessman father falls ill and irresponsibly carries out his plans to their logical and fatal conclusion.

Taken as a series, these plays show the rise to power of a family dynasty and its descent, through degeneracy, towards apparently inevitable doom—the portrayal, then, of German society, perhaps of bourgeois society as a whole, at its apparent zenith before its collapse. The plays fascinate because they highlight the validity of everyday decisions and attack the artificiality of the ideal. The ideal—either a bourgeois way of life with taboos and polite formulae bolstered up by self-confidence yet riddled with irrational fears, or an attempt to act out life in a sentimentalized, romantic way—is shown to be false. Only self-knowledge, clear-headed vision, or self-control succeed. Yet, Sternheim's characters are portrayed as learners from life and are never completely outsiders. Precisely the problem of lack of communication, because of society's taboos, and Sternheim's use of stylized language enables Theobald, Christian, and Schippel (in *Paul Schippel Esq.*) to speak directly and act out their thoughts almost naively. Because others hardly dare to oppose them, they can articulate in their behaviour, and with stenographic style, truths that in real life no bourgeois would ever dare to mouth. The audience is thus presented with a logical, often grotesque extension of those features of bourgeois society it cannot bring itself to express. The supreme self-confidence of the central figures allows them to triumph, yet Theobald confesses, "my featurelessness is a camouflage behind which I can indulge my whims and my innermost nature without hindrance". Christian, the social-climber, ironically becomes the victim of his success when he comes to believe in the bourgeois way of life he has originally so much despised. Schippel, in confronting the demands of society when he becomes the missing member of a singing group, despite his humble origins, learns more than he could have done at a distance.

"If you can't beat them, join them" becomes the Maske family principle. The result is a process of double unmasking: that of showing up social behaviour, and that of revealing the individual's own potentials and limitations despite, and yet within, society. That such parvenus are aware of the collapse about to befall the society they have joined adds to the fascination of these plays.

Sternheim contributed to the tension by lacing his dramas with sudden surprises, so that they are deliberately inconsistent in their form, yet logical when seen in retrospect. The charaters thus seem to lead a charmed life as if they are figures out of a fairy-tale world. Their antics are sometimes close to farce, and their behaviour strikes the audience often as melodrama of a vulgar kind. Such effects can, however, be seen instantly as part of Sternheim's method of criticism and re-evaluation.

Faced with the opportunities and challenges life offers, often unexpectedly, Sternheim's central figures develop the courage to be themselves and to adapt, sometimes hypocritically, to new situations. This can lead, for instance in *Die Marquise von Arcis* (*The Mask of Virtue*), to a spiritual rebirth that provokes other characters to equal triumphs over "immorality". Sternheim's adaptation of Diderot's story and his play *Oscar Wilde* reveal his increasing sense of personal isolation and his insistence on the moral integrity of many outsider figures. They are individualists, youthful and passionate lovers—characters notably lacking in the poseurs of the earlier works. Sternheim's references back to cultural sources in these dramas, and in others such as *Manon Lescaut* and the travel book based on Heine, *Lutetia*, reflected his awareness that the post-war world had totally changed social values. In *Die Schule von Uznach* (*Uznach School*), set in a ladies' finishing school where total female emancipation subjects the individual to an educational programme and sexuality is mechanized, old-fashioned seduction and romantic dreaming reassert their power.

Throughout his works, Sternheim seems to have supported those who showed the strength of character to make out of

life the most it can offer. Situational ethics became for him the answer to the false gentilities of over-civilisation.

—Brian Keith-Smith

See also *Volume 1* entry on *Scenes From the Heroic Life of the Middle Classes*.

STOPPARD, Tom. Born Tom Straussler in Zlin, Czechoslovakia, 3 July 1937. Family moved to Singapore, 1939, Darjeeling, India, 1942, and England, 1946. Educated at Dolphin School, Nottinghamshire, 1946–48; Pocklington School, Yorkshire, 1948–54. Married 1) Jose Ingle in 1965 (marriage dissolved 1971), two sons; 2) Miriam Moore-Robinson (the writer and broadcaster Miriam Stoppard) in 1972, two sons. Journalist, *Western Daily Press*, Bristol, 1954–58, and Bristol *Evening World*, 1958–60, then freelance journalist and writer; drama critic, *Scene*, London, 1962–63; first plays produced and broadcast 1964; member of the board, Royal National Theatre, London, from 1989. Recipient: John Whiting Award, 1967; *Evening Standard* Award, 1967, 1973, 1975, 1979, 1983; Italia Prize, for radio play, 1968; Tony Award, 1968, 1976, 1984; New York Drama Critics Circle Award, 1968, 1976, 1984; Shakespeare Prize (Hamburg), 1979; Outer Circle Award, 1984; Drama Desk Award, 1984. M. Lit: University of Bristol, 1976; Brunel University, Uxbridge, Middlesex, 1979; University of Sussex, Brighton, 1980; honorary degrees: Leeds University, 1980; University of London, 1982; Kenyon College, Gambier, Ohio, 1984; York University, 1984. Fellow, Royal Society of Literature. CBE (Commander, Order of the British Empire), 1978.

Works

Collections

"*Albert's Bridge*" and Other Plays (includes *Artist Descending a Staircase; If You're Glad I'll Be Frank; A Separate Peace; Where Are They Now?*).   1977.
"*The Dog it Was That Died*" and Other Plays (includes *The Dissolution of Dominic Boot; "M" is for Moon Among Other Things; Teeth; Another Moon Called Earth; Neutral Ground; A Separate Peace*)   1983.
Four Plays for Radio (includes *Artist Descending a Staircase; Where Are They Now?; If You're Glad I'll Be Frank; Albert's Bridge*).   1984.
The Radio Plays 1964–1983.   1990.

Stage Works

A Walk on the Water, from his television play (produced Hamburg, 1964; as *Enter a Free Man* produced St. Martin's Theatre, London, 1968).   As *Enter A Free Man*, 1968.
The Gamblers (produced University of Bristol, 1965).
Tango, from a play by Sławomir Mrożek, translated by Nicholas Bethell (produced Aldwych Theatre, London, 1966).   1968.
Rosencrantz and Guildenstern Are Dead (produced Cranston Street Hall, Edinburgh, 1966; revised version produced by the National Theatre, Old Vic, London, 1967).   1967.
The Real Inspector Hound (produced Criterion Theatre, London, 1968).   1968.
If You're Glad I'll Be Frank, from his radio play (produced

Tom Stoppard (1978).

St. Mary's Hall, Edinburgh, 1969). With *Albert's Bridge*, 1969; revised version, published separately, 1978.
After Magritte (produced Green Banana Restaurant, London, 1970). 1971.
Dogg's Our Pet (produced Almost Free Theatre, London, 1971). In *Ten of the Best*, edited by Ed Berman, 1979.
Jumpers (produced by the National Theatre, Old Vic, London, 1972). 1972; revised versions, 1973 and 1986.
The House of Bernarda Alba, from a play by García Lorca (produced Greenwich Theatre, London, 1973).
Travesties (produced Aldwych Theatre, London, 1974). 1975.
Dirty Linen, and New-found-land (produced Almost Free Theatre, London, 1976). 1976.
The Fifteen Minute Hamlet (as *The [Fifteen Minute] Dogg's Troupe Hamlet*, produced London, 1976). 1978.
Every Good Boy Deserves Favour: A Play for Actors and Orchestra, music by André Previn (produced Royal Festival Hall, London, 1977). With *Professional Foul*, 1978.
Night and Day (produced Phoenix Theatre, London, 1978). 1978; revised version, 1979.
Albert's Bridge Extended (produced Edinburgh Festival, 1978).
Undiscovered Country, from a play by Schnitzler (produced National Theatre, London, 1979). 1980.
Dogg's Hamlet, Cahoot's Macbeth (produced University of Warwick, 1979). 1980.

On the Razzle, from a play by Nestroy (produced National Theatre, London, 1981). 1981.
The Real Thing (produced Strand Theatre, London, 1982). 1982; revised version (produced Strand Theatre, London, 1984), 1984.
The Love for Three Oranges, from the opera by Prokofiev (produced by Glyndebourne Touring Opera, 1983).
Rough Crossing, from a play by Ferenc Molnár (produced National Theatre, London, 1984; revised version produced New York, 1989). 1985.
Dalliance, from a play by Schnitzler (produced National Theatre, London, 1986). With *Undiscovered Country*, 1986.
Largo Desolato, from the play by Václav Havel (produced Old Vic, Bristol, 1986). 1987.
Hapgood (produced Aldwych Theatre, London, 1988). 1988.
Arcadia (produced National Theatre, London, 1993). 1993.

Screen Plays

The Romantic Englishwoman, with Thomas Wiseman, 1975; *Despair*, 1978; *The Human Factor*, 1980; *Brazil*, with Terry Gilliam and Charles McKeown, 1985 (published in *The Battle of Brazil*, by Jack Mathews, 1987); *Empire of the Sun*, 1988; *Rosencrantz and Guildenstern Are Dead*, 1990.

Television Plays

A Walk on the Water (broadcast 1963; revised version, as *The Preservation of George Riley*, broadcast 1964).
A Separate Peace (broadcast 1966). 1977.
Teeth (broadcast 1967). In *"The Dog it Was That Died" and Other Plays*, 1983.
Another Moon Called Earth (broadcast 1967). In *"The Dog it Was That Died" and Other Plays*, 1983.
Neutral Ground (broadcast 1968). In *"The Dog it Was That Died" and Other Plays*, 1983.
The Engagement, from his radio play *The Dissolution of Dominic Boot* (broadcast 1970).
One Pair of Eyes (documentary; broadcast 1972).
The Boundary (*Eleventh Hour* series), with Clive Exton (broadcast 1975).
Three Men in a Boat, from the novel by Jerome K. Jerome (broadcast 1975).
Professional Foul (broadcast 1977). With *Every Good Boy Deserves Favour*, 1978.
Squaring the Circle: Poland 1980–81 (broadcast 1984). With *Every Good Boy Deserves Favour* and *Professional Foul*, 1984.

Radio Plays

The Dissolution of Dominic Boot (broadcast 1964). In *"The Dog it Was That Died"* and Other Plays, 1983.
"M" is for Moon Among Other Things (broadcast 1964). In *"The Dog it Was That Died" and Other Plays*, 1983.
If You're Glad I'll Be Frank (broadcast 1966). With *Albert's Bridge*, 1969.
Albert's Bridge (broadcast 1967). With *If You're Glad I'll Be Frank*, 1969.
Where Are They Now? (broadcast 1970). With *Artist Descending a Staircase*, 1973.
Artist Descending a Staircase (broadcast 1972). With *Where Are They Now?*, 1973.
The Dog it Was That Died (broadcast 1982). In *"The Dog it Was That Died" and Other Plays*, 1983.
In the Native State (broadcast 1991).

Fiction

Lord Malquist and Mr. Moon.   1966.

*

Bibliographies

David Bratt, *Tom Stoppard: A Reference Guide*, Boston, 1982.

Criticism

Books:
C.W.E. Bigsby, *Tom Stoppard*, London, 1976; revised, 1979.
Ronald Hayman, *Tom Stoppard*, London and Totowa, New Jersey, 1977; fourth edition, 1982.
Victor L. Cahn, *Beyond Absurdity: The Plays of Tom Stoppard*, New Jersey, 1979.
Felicia Hardison Londré, *Tom Stoppard*, New York, 1981.
Joan Fitzpatrick, *Tom Stoppard: Comedy as a Moral Matrix*, Columbia, 1981.
Lucina Paquet Gabbard, *The Stoppard Plays*, New York, 1982.
Jim Hunter, *Tom Stoppard's Plays*, London and New York, 1982.
Thomas R. Whitaker, *Tom Stoppard*, London and New York, 1983.
Richard Corballis, *Stoppard: The Mystery and the Clockwork*, New York, 1984, Oxford, 1985.
Tim Brassell, *Tom Stoppard: An Assessment*, London and New York, 1985.
Malcolm Page (ed.), *File on Stoppard*, London, 1986.
Susan Rusinko, *Tom Stoppard*, Boston, 1986.
Michael Billington, *Stoppard the Playwright*, London, 1987.
Anthony Jenkins, *The Theatre of Tom Stoppard*, London and New York, 1987; second edition, 1989.
Neil Sammells, *Tom Stoppard: The Artist as Critic*, London, 1988.
John Harty III (ed.), *Tom Stoppard: A Casebook*, New York, 1988.
Stephen Hu, *Stoppard's Stagecraft*, New York, 1989.
Anthony Jenkins, *The Theatre of Tom Stoppard*, Cambridge, 1987; revised edition, 1989.
Anthony Jenkins (ed.), *Critical Essays on Tom Stoppard*, Boston, 1990.
T. Bareham (ed.), *Tom Stoppard: Rosencrantz and Guildenstern Are Dead; Jumpers; Travesties: A Casebook*, Macmillan, 1990.
Paul Delaney, *Tom Stoppard: The Moral Vision of the Major Plays*, London, 1990.
Robert Gordon, *Rosencrantz and Guildenstern Are Dead; Jumpers; The Real Thing*, London, 1991 (Text and Performance series).
Katherine Kelly, *Tom Stoppard and the Craft of Comedy*, Ann Arbor, Michigan, 1991.

* * *

It is by now a cliché of Stoppard criticism that his work underwent a radical change in 1977. Before that, the argument goes, he produced a series of brilliant but superficial entertainments—especially *Travesties* ("a triple-decker bus that isn't going anywhere", in Kenneth Tynan's memorable phrase), *After Magritte* (an elaborate pun on the word "after") and *The Real Inspector Hound* (a sort of meta-whodunit).

On the other side of the watershed, it is suggested, lie two categories of deeper drama. First there are the political plays: *Every Good Boy Deserves Favour, Professional Foul, Cahoot's Macbeth*, and *Squaring the Circle*—all of them attacks on the oppressive old regimes of Eastern Europe. His translation of Vaclav Hável's *Largo Desolato* in effect belongs with this group.

Largo Desolato and *Professional Foul* overlap with the second category, which comprises plays in which character is investigated to an extent unprecedented (except for the derivative *Enter a Free Man*) in his early work. In this category belong *Night and Day*, his two translations from Schnitzler, *Undiscovered Country* and *Dalliance* (both of which actually sell Schnitzler's characters rather short), and the quasi-autobiographical play, *The Real Thing*. *Hapgood* should probably be added to this list, although many critics, dazzled by the preoccupation with quantum physics, have relegated it to the company of the early entertainments.

One thing that certainly changed after 1977 was Stoppard's approach to interviews. In his early years he was tricksy and evasive, frequently baffling his interrogators with carefully rehearsed aphorisms like "I should have the courage of my lack of convictions". Since 1977 his responses have been franker. What this new openness often reveals, however, is that (to quote a 1978 interview) he "was always morally, if not politically, involved"—in other words, that from first to last his plays have been consistent in *theme*. *Jumpers*, with its acrobats, its trapeze, its giant television screen, its trick doors, and its dermatograph, certainly has a higher-tech surface than *The Real Thing* (and is therefore suitable only for well-heeled companies like London's National Theatre, for which it was written), but at a deeper level the two plays are alike: George Moore (in *Jumpers*) and Henry (in *The Real Thing*) both battle their way towards what Henry calls "self-knowledge through pain", while all about them are content to trust in glib formulae.

Like *Jumpers*, *Rosencrantz and Guildenstern Are Dead* presents a dazzling surface littered with ingenious and irreverent responses to the text of *Hamlet*. But beneath that surface we find again two bewildered individuals battling hopelessly (and with an ever-increasing recognition of their plight—a characteristic which distinguishes them from Beckett's Vladimir and Estragon, whom they resemble in most other respects) against a pre-ordained plot, over which the inscrutable and sinister Tragedians preside. And at the other end of the Stoppard canon the inhuman world of espionage continually frustrates Elizabeth Hapgood's search for love.

There is nothing particularly remarkable about this formula of a deep, developing character set against a group of shallow and less engaging types. Indeed, without the word-play and the imaginative choice of setting, *Professional Foul* would be a run-of-the-mill play about a rather precious middle-aged character who finds a new lease of life. Much the same could be said of *The Real Thing*—and in this case the central character's development is slightly fudged as well, since his wife loses interest in the other men in her life before he has really begun to face up to her infidelity. It is probably because they are his most conventional plays that these two are often cited as Stoppard's best.

Two factors, however, generally combine to lift Stoppard out of the ruck of conventional dramaturgy. The first is the way he boldy overstates the basic dialectic of each play. His plots often amount to little more than juxtapositions. ("Firstly, A. Secondly, minus A", as he put it in an early interview.) And the antagonist (the "minus A") tends to be absorbed into an impersonal collective of some kind—a play-within-the-play in *Rosencrantz and Guildenstern Are Dead, The Real Inspector Hound, Travesties, Dogg's Hamlet Cahoot's Macbeth* and *The Real*

Thing, an orchestra-within-the-play in *Every Good Boy Deserves Favour*, and other highly codified systems such as the secret service (in *Neutral Ground*, *The Dog it Was That Died*, and *Hapgood*) and academic philosophy (in *Albert's Bridge*, *Jumpers*, and *Professional Foul*). These artificial backgrounds act as foils which highlight the fragile humanity of the various protagonists. The simplified framework of the plays gives Stoppard a very sturdy peg on which to hang the dazzling inventions of his wit. His habit of providing an abstract of the framework in a brief prologue (the first library scene in *Travesties*, the party in *Jumpers*, the coin-spinning in *Rosencrantz and Guildenstern Are Dead*, Guthrie's dream in *Night and Day*) makes the peg even sturdier, though the dazzling surface—most of all, perhaps, in *Travesties*—can still blind audiences to the structure beneath.

It is, of course, the dazzling wit that constitutes the second distinctive feature of Stoppard's art. His exuberant way with words has propelled him often in the direction of farce, with mixed results: *Dirty Linen* works well enough, but *Rough Crossing* is generally reckoned a failure, and even *On the Razzle* (his acknowledged masterpiece in this genre) does not always succeed in fusing luxuriant language with manic action. In his more serious plays the outright wit is generally lavished on the antagonists (the Player in *Rosencrantz and Guildenstern Are Dead*, Archie in *Jumpers*, Joyce in *Travesties*), while the protagonists are blunderers who evoke sympathetic laughter by their maladroit responses to others' initiatives. In a way, wit is thus thrown into disrepute, and Stoppard almost seems to be intent on discrediting his own most obvious asset. But in a different way, each play as a whole—*Jumpers*, *Rosencrantz and Guildenstern Are Dead*, and so on, as well as the farces—is a triumph of wit. Stoppard's startling experiments with dialogue (for example, the "time-slips" and extended monologues of *Travesties*), with characterization (such as the betrayal of the dumb blonde stereotype in *Dirty Linen*), with stagecraft (such as the on-stage jeep and helicopter in *Night and Day*), with the conventions of dramatized documentary (the counterpoint between the Narrator and the Witness in *Squaring the Circle*), and with other aspects of his craft mark him out as one of the most consistently inventive dramatists of his generation.

Stoppard's assiduous attention to detail is also remarkable. Like Shakespeare and Wilde, he has sometimes been portrayed as a careless genius, warbling his native wood-notes wild and tossing off epigrams with reckless abandon. The exquisitely devised time-frame of *Artist Descending a Staircase* and the prismatic construction of *The Real Thing*, where each successive living-room puts the nature of love into a new perspective, give the lie to this portrait. To his natural genius is wedded a meticulous sense of craftsmanship, of which even Ben Jonson would surely have been proud.

—Richard Corballis

See also *Volume 1* entries on *Jumpers*; *The Real Thing*; *Rosencrantz and Guildenstern Are Dead*; *Travesties*.

STOREY, David (Malcolm). Born in Wakefield, Yorkshire, 13 July 1933. Educated at Queen Elizabeth Grammar School, Wakefield, 1943–51; Wakefield College of Art, 1951–53; Slade School of Fine Art, London, 1953–56, diploma in fine arts 1956.

Married Barbara Rudd Hamilton in 1956; two sons and two daughters. Played professionally for the Leeds Rugby League Club, 1952–56; first-produced play, *The Restoration of Arnold Middleton*, staged 1966; associate artistic director, Royal Court Theatre, London, 1972–74. Has collaborated with director Lindsay Anderson on several premieres of his plays. Fellow, University College, London, 1974. Recipient: Rhys Memorial Award, for fiction, 1961; Maugham Award, for fiction, 1963; New York Drama Critics Circle Award, 1971, 1973, 1974; Obie Award, 1974; Booker Prize, for fiction, 1976.

Works

Collections

Early Days; Sisters; Life Class.   1980.
Plays 1 (includes *The Contractor; Home; Stages; Caring*). 1992.

Stage Works

The Restoration of Arnold Middleton (produced Edinburgh, 1966).   1967.
In Celebration (produced Royal Court Theatre, London, 1969). 1969.
The Contractor (produced Royal Court Theatre, London, 1969).   1970.
Home (produced Royal Court Theatre, London, 1970). 1970.
The Changing Room (produced Royal Court Theatre, London, 1971).   1972.
The Farm (produced Royal Court Theatre, London, 1973). 1973.
Cromwell (produced Royal Court Theatre, London, 1973). 1973.
Life Class (produced Royal Court Theatre, London, 1974). 1975.
Mother's Day (produced Royal Court Theatre, London, 1976).   1977.
Sisters (produced Royal Exchange Theatre, Manchester, 1978).   In *Early Days; Sisters; Life Class*, 1980.
Early Days (produced National Theatre, London, 1980).   In *Early Days, Sisters, Life Class*, 1980.
Phoenix (produced Questors Theatre, Ealing, London, 1984).
The March on Russia (produced National Theatre, London, 1989).   1990.
Stages (produced National Theatre, London, 1992).   In *Plays 1*, 1992.

Screenplays

This Sporting Life, 1963; *In Celebration*, 1976.

Television Plays

Grace, from the story by James Joyce, 1974.

Fiction

This Sporting Life.   1960.
Flight into Camden.   1960.
Radcliffe.   1963.
Pasmore.   1972.
A Temporary Life.   1973.
Saville.   1976.

STOREY 923

A Prodigal Child. 1982.
Present Times. 1984.

Verse

Storey's Lives: Poems 1951–1991. 1992.

Other

Writers on Themselves, with others. 1964.
Edward, drawings by Donald Parker. 1973.

*

Criticism

Books:
John Russell Taylor, *The Second Wave,* London and New York, 1971.
John Russell Taylor, *David Storey,* London, 1974.
William Hutchings, *The Plays of David Storey: A Thematic Study,* Carbondale, Illinois, 1988.
Susan Rusinko, *British Drama 1950 to the Present,* Boston, 1989.

Articles:
Mike Bygrave, "David Storey: Novelist or Playwright?" in *Theatre Quarterly,* 1, 1971.
William J. Free, "The Ironic Anger of David Storey", in *Modern Drama,* 16, 1973.
Austin E. Quigley, "The Emblematic Structure and Setting of David Storey's Plays", in *Modern Drama,* 22, 1979.
Janelle Reinelt, "The Central Event in David Storey's Plays", in *Theatre Journal,* 31, 1979.

* * *

Along with Edward Bond, David Storey was the principal dramatist of the "second wave" of new writers whose work was presented by the English Stage Company at the Royal Court Theatre in London. The first of these plays, *The Restoration of Arnold Middleton,* was directed by Robert Kidd, but Lindsay Anderson had already directed the film based on Storey's novel, *This Sporting Life,* and Anderson and David Storey have comprised perhaps the most remarkable of the Royal Court's playwright-director pairings, in that the director's methods and preferences have actually influenced the way Storey wrote some of his best plays.

David Storey is remarkable in that he is both novelist and dramatist to a roughly equal degree and standard of achievement. More of his time has been occupied in novel-writing, and he has commented on the swiftness with which he has been able to write his plays, almost as a relief from the novels. Much of the relatively small amount of critical discussion of his work has been employed, not too illuminatingly, in identifying relationships between plays and novels in the use of the same material. The general valid point has been made that he is the kind of writer who returns over and over to the same areas of experience, exploring their significance through diverse approaches. This lends probability to the suggestion that the plays have emerged so quickly because of the extent to which their material had already been processed, emotionally and imaginatively, at some level of consciousness. He has talked of starting with a blank page and no preconceived plan, writing to see what what would come out.

This improvisatory method as a strategy for artistic creation is sometimes employed by expressionist painters, and there

may be no better way in to some of David Storey's plays, and indeed some of his novels, than to keep in mind that he was trained as a painter at one of England's most prestigious art schools, the Slade. The fact that neither narrative nor argument is an obvious field for painting, where the values of composition and colour predominate, linked up with Lindsay Anderson's repudiation of a conceptual approach to direction: avoiding analysis of motives and discussion of meaning, he preferred to build up the production through precise, practical attention to detail, out of which such generalities as form, rhythm, and meaning (whatever that is) would emerge.

As a writer of northern working-class origins, Storey has not surprisingly been influenced by D.H. Lawrence, particularly the Lawrence of *Sons and Lovers,* and this is a meeting-point between his plays and novels (some of which, or sections of which, are written to a large extent in a spare, dialogue form). *In Celebration* was the first-produced of a group of family-centred plays which explore the tensions, the generally unspoken pain, within the closest family ties—the source from which the individual's emotional life flows, and the reality to which most of us are reluctant to return. The late 1950's movement—associated with Beckett and Pinter—away from fully articulated prose discourse towards a pared-down dialogue in which individual words have more weight, as in a poem, accompanies an extreme of naturalism in Storey's plays that is comparable with Chekhov's struggle to exclude the last traces of artificial plotting in order to let the simple truth of human experience come through. (The ironically titled *The March on Russia,* a later and less bitter family play, may awake echoes of Chekhov's three sisters' dream of visiting Moscow.) Yet Storey goes further than Chekhov in revealing the family as an isolating unit, without healthy, living connections to a wider society, and within which the individual is peculiarly lonely.

Another group of plays—the chief and most distinctive fruit of his collaboration with Anderson—identifies and adopts a given framework from the social rituals of work and endeavour that bring men together. In *The Contractor,* the aim and final achievement of the men's work appears on stage as a tent, erected and made beautiful for a wedding reception—a symbol for the work of art, which has the ephemerality of the collaborative onstage creation of the performed play. *The Changing Room* has echoes of the heroics on the field, only to focus on the process whereby disparate individuals change into a team of footballers, a group with its own codes and language, its own power and identity, dynamics of unity and conflict, until, the match over, the temporary social structure fragments, comradeship dissolves, and differences once more prevail.

The desire of critics and audiences, as well as some actors, to keep a grip on conventional certainties persuaded David Storey to agree that he had set *Home* in a lunatic asylum without at first realising it. Arguably, the force and universality of the play are increased by keeping it unlocalised with any particularity (as, indeed, *Cromwell* is unlocalised). It shows the kindly accommodations the merest acquaintances make for each other's solitude, allowing identity and dignity to be established and preserved. The contrast between the male and female couples seems to mark a class difference, as there is certainly a difference between spontaneity and self-consciousness; but this obvious patterning merely sets off the amorphous life of feeling against the forms of inhibition, personal and social. The classic first production of this play (also recorded on film), with John Gielgud and Ralph Richardson, realised fully what Storey's more and less realistic plays share—the quality of inviting a rich collaboration from performers, as every line has an emotional subtext to be discovered and interpreted.

Although there is a gravity within all Storey's plays, they are far from humourless. In approaching his eccentrics sympathetically, he does not deny them their comedy, as in *Early Days* (centred on another Ralph Richardson role), and he even has passages of farcical action in *The Restoration of Arnold Middleton*, which portrays a character at the end of his tether struggling back to some degree of wholeness and social communication, and the much less liked *Mother's Day*.

The closest David Storey comes to any overt statement about his art within the plays, is, not unexpectedly, in *Life Class*, set in the art studio of a polytechnic and precisely set in period. The student revolt of the 1960's in Britain started in the art schools, where it had the immediate objective of overthrowing an outmoded academicism in the syllabus. The lively, bantering, and needling relationship between Storey's students and their self-doubting lecturer is weighted with the artistic speculations and theories of the time, and culminates dramatically in a "happening", that new art form focusing on questions of the relationship of art to life, which provided the main sensation of one Edinburgh Festival.

—Margery Morgan

See also *Volume 1* entries on *The Contractor*; *Home*.

STRAUSS, Botho. Born in Naumburg, Saale, Germany, 2 December 1944. Educated at schools in the Ruhr and Hesse; studied German, theatre history, and sociology in Cologne and Munich. Co-editor and critic with the prominent periodical *Theater heute*, 1967–70; dramaturg for the Schaubühne am Halleschen Ufer, Berlin, under its artistic director Peter Stein, from 1970; first-produced original play, *Die Hypochonder* [The Hypochondriacs], staged 1972. Recipient: Hanover Drama Prize, 1974; Baden-Württemberg Förder Prize, 1977; Bavarian Academy Literature Prize, 1981.

Works

Collections

Besucher: Drei Stücke (includes *Besucher; Die Zeit und das Zimmer; Sieben Türen*). 1988.
Theaterstücke (2 vols.). 1991.

Stage Works

Peer Gynt, from the play by Ibsen (produced Schaubühne am Halleschen Ufer, Berlin, 1971). In *Programmheft* accompanying premiere, 1971.
Prinz Friedrich von Homburg, with Peter Stein, from the play by Kleist (produced Schaubühne am Halleschen Ufer, Berlin, 1972). In *Programmheft* accompanying premiere, 1971.
Die Hyperchonder (produced Schauspielhaus, Hamburg, 1972). In *Spielplatz 1: Jahrbuch für Theater 71/72*, 1972; with *Bekannte Gesichter, gemischte Gefühle*, 1979.
Das Sparschwein, from a play by Labiche (produced Schaubühne am Halleschen Ufer, Berlin, 1973). 1981.
Sommergäste, with Peter Stein, from a play by Gorky (produced Schaubühne am Halleschen Ufer, Berlin, 1974). In

Programmheft accompanying premiere, 1974; in book form, in *Theaterstücke 1*, 1991.
Bekannte Gesichter, gemischte Gefühle (produced Württembergisches Staatstheater, Stuttgart, 1975). In *Theater heute: Jahressonderheft*, 1974; in book form, in *Spectaculum* (anthology), 1977.
Trilogie des Wiedersehens (produced Deutsches Schauspielhaus, Hamburg, 1977). 1976; translated as *Three Acts of Recognition*, 1981.
Gross und klein (produced Schaubühne am Halleschen Ufer, Berlin, 1978). 1978; translated as *Big and Little*, 1979.
Kalldewey Farce (produced Deutsches Schauspielhaus, Hamburg, 1982). 1981.
Der Park (produced Stadttheater, Freiburg, 1984). 1983; translated as *The Park*, 1988.
Die Fremdenführerin (produced Schaubühne am Lehniner Platz, Berlin, 1985). 1986; translated as *The Tourist Guide*, in *Plays International*, May 1987.
Besucher. In *Besucher . . .* (collection), 1988.
Die Zeit und das Zimmer. In *Besucher . . .* (collection), 1988.
Sieben Türen. In *Besucher . . .* (collection), 1988.
Schlusschor. In *Theaterstücke 2*, 1991.
Angelas Kleider. In *Theaterstücke 2*, 1991.

Television Plays

Trilogie des Wiedersehens, 1979; *Gross und klein*, 1980.

Fiction

Schützenehre. 1974.
Marlenes Schwester: Zwei Erzählungen (also includes *Theorie der Drohung*). 1975.
Die Widmung. 1977; translated as *Devotion*, 1979.
Rumor. 1980; translated as *Tumult*, 1984.
Paare Passanten. 1981.
Der junge Mann. 1984.
Kongress. 1989.

Other

Niemand anderes. 1987.
Fragmente der Undeutlichkeit. 1989.

*

Bibliographies

Hans Wolfschütz, "Bibliographie zu Botho Strauss", in *Text und Kritik*, 81, 1984.

Criticism

Books:
Gerhard vom Hofe and Pater Pfaf, *Das Elend des Polyphien: Zum Thema der Subjektivität Thomas Bernhard, Peter Handke, Wolfgang Koeppen und Botho Strauss*, Königstein, 1980.
Denis Calandra, *New German Dramatists*, London, 1983.
Siegfried Steinmann, *Sprache, Handlung, Wirklichkeit im deutschen Gegenwartsdrama: Studien zu Thomas Bernhard, Botho Strauss und Bodo Kirchhoff*, Frankfurt, 1985.
Monika Sandhack, *Jenseits des Rätsels: Versuch einer*

Spurensicherung im dramatischen Werk von Botho Strauss, Frankfurt, 1986.

Ursula Kapitza, *Bewusstseinsspiele: Drama und Dramaturgie bei Botho Strauss*, Frankfurt, 1987.

Verena Plümer, *Zur Entwicklung und Dramaturgie der Dramen von Botho Strauss*, Frankfurt, 1987.

Michael Radix, *Strauss lesen*, Munich, 1987.

Katrin Kazubko, *Spielformen des Dramas bei Botho Strauss*, Hildesheim, 1990.

* * *

Botho Strauss is a West German of the generation whose ideals peaked and foundered with the student protest movement of the late 1960's. As a staff critic on *Theater heute* from 1967 to 1970, he noted that documentary theatre, which was then in vogue, had shackled creative imagination in the theatre, and he singled out Samuel Beckett, Thomas Bernhard, and Peter Handke as dramatists to emulate. Strauss then learnt the craft of theatre by working as dramaturg, adapting scripts for Peter Stein at the Berlin Schaubühne.

His early pieces derive partly from his script work: Stein's *Peer Gynt* was followed by *Die Hyperchonder* (The Hypochondriacs), in which six enigmatic figures live out opaque private dramas of crime and sexuality in an icily stylish Amsterdam hotel in 1901, and the Strauss/Stein reading of Kleist's *Prince Friedrich von Homburg* as a dream of reality was followed by the dreamlike *Bekannte Gesichter, gemischte Gefühle* (Known Faces, Mixed Feelings), with its time-shifts and apparitions as a couple and their friends prepare in a hotel for the West German ballroom-dancing championships. This last play, with its tawdry aspirations and stunted communication, can already be read as a metaphor for the Federal Republic as perceived through the collapsing ideals of the post-Adenauer generation. These exercises in style are rarely revived.

Strauss's breakthrough came with *Trilogie des Wiedersehens* (*Three Acts of Recognition*). At the Schaubühne he had removed the scene-breaks and turned Gorky's *Summerfolk* into a panorama of a doomed society. *Three Acts of Recognition* applied the same fluid pattern of interlocking conversations to a provincial arts society which is preparing an exhibition of "Capitalist Realism". The bickering dialogue flickers from group to group, focusing intermittently on the gallery director and his neurotic partner, Susanne, in full, mutual mid-life crisis. "These people are us", said cast member Otto Sander of the Schaubühne production, and Peter Stein anticipates that Strauss will be a valuable source for future social historians. *Gross und Klein* (*Big and Little*) too offers a cross-section of German society (and a plum part for an actress), as its heroine seeks in vain, from package-holiday Algeria to north German Sylt, for a vestige of real human contact in a world where self-obsession rules. Strauss, with his fine ear for contemporary idiom, is like an urban anthropologist, avidly collecting specimens of the contemporary emotional and intellectual climate wherever people brush against one another.

Kalldewey Farce, with its lesbians and feminists, its echoes of the *Bacchae* of Euripides (an offending husband's severed head rotates in a washing machine), and above all with the bawdy, Puckish figure of Kalldewey, marked a shift from comedy of manners to satirical farce, and Strauss's exploration of new forms continued with *Der Park* (*The Park*), a transposition of *A Midsummer Night's Dream* to a sordid urban park, where Oberon and Titania are reduced to the roles of flashers in a vain attempt to revive true lust in the night people. Germans abroad fare little better: in *The Tourist Guide*, a two-hander, a teacher on sabbatical leave attempts, abortively, under the liberating Greek sun, to play Pan to a young tourist-guide's nymph.

In 1988 Strauss published three plays in one volume. *Besucher* (Visitors), the most substantial of them, is a play about the theatre. A vain and hammy veteran (some of the lines derive from Will Quadflieg's autobiography) spars in rehearsal with an angular young realist who has recently defected from the German Democratic Republic. They are in the provinces rehearsing a play about a gene-technologist who has (possibly) engineered a giant toad. The female lead is taken by an actress who is an ecology and animal welfare freak. Not content with this, the plot plunges into the surreal. With *Die Zeit und das Zimmer* (Time and the Room) Strauss totally abandons plot. The room in which the brief encounters of Marie Steuber take place provides continuity, while the scenes are so unconnected that they seem to belong to different lives, though the girl remains the same. The precise variations on a role—Marie Steuber the wrathful wife defending Medea's need for grand passion, Marie Steuber the boss interviewing three men for jobs—offer a challenging psychological quick-change part for a versatile comic actress. *Sieben Türen* (*Seven Doors*) consists of 10 unrelated "bagatelles", witty, clever but slight contemporary sketches.

Strauss subtitled *Schlusschor* (Final Chorus), his first play after German reunification, "Three Acts", but it is actually three one-acters deceptively disguised as a play. In Act I, a group posing for a photo makes the bungling photographer self-destruct; in Act II, an architect surprises his client in the nude, but the cool latter-day Bathsheba drives her besotted admirer to suicide; in Act III, two East Germans confront the clientèle of a West Berlin café on the night the Berlin Wall came down. It ends with a conservative aristocrat mating, Leda-style, with an eagle (the German eagle?). The flow of suave, enigmatic, pessimistic comedies, with surreal twists and mythological allusions, continues.

—Hugh Rorrison

STRINDBERG, August. Born in Stockholm, Sweden, 22 January 1849. Educated at Uppsala University, 1867, 1870–72, no degree. Married 1) Baroness Siri von Essen in 1877 (divorced 1891), three children; 2) Frida Uhl in 1893 (divorced 1897), one daughter; 3) the actress Harriet Bosse in 1901 (divorced 1904), one daughter. Teacher, tutor, actor, journalist; first-produced play, *I Rom* [In Rome], staged 1870; trained as telegraph-clerk, 1873; assistant librarian, Royal Library, Stockholm, 1874–79; centre of a group of radical writers in 1880's; tried for blasphemy, but acquitted, 1884; lived in France, Switzerland, Bavaria and Denmark, 1883–87; opened an experimental theatre in Copenhagen, 1889: closed the same year; lived in Berlin, 1892–94, Paris, 1894–96, Lund, 1896–99, and Stockholm after 1899; suffered his "Inferno" crisis, 1894–97: stayed at a mental clinic in Ystad, Sweden, 1895 and 1896; founder, Intima Teater [Intimate Theatre], Stockholm, 1907, for which a number of his plays were written: theatre closed in 1910; received a State gift of 50,000 kronor, 1912. Also a painter. Died in Stockholm, 14 May 1912.

Scene from the Stockholm Intima Teater's 1909 production of *Brott och brott* [*There Are Crimes and Crimes*] by **August Strindberg**.

Works

Collections

Samlade skrifter [Collected Writings] (55 vols.), edited by John Landquist. 1912–20; supplemented with *Samlade otryckta skrifter* (2 vols.), 1918–19.

Plays (4 vols.), translated by Edwin Björkman. 1912–16.

Skrifter [Writings] (14 vols.), edited by Gunnar Brandell. 1945–46.

Eight Famous Plays (includes *The Link; The Father; Miss Julie; The Stronger; There are Crimes and Crimes; Gustavus Vasa; The Dance of Death; The Spook Sonata*), translated by Edwin Björkman and N. Erichson. 1949; as *Eight Best Plays*, 1979.

The Washington Strindberg, translated by Walter Johnson. 1955—:
1. *Queen Christina; Charles XII; Gustav III.* 1955.
2. *The Last of the Knights; The Regent; Earl Birger of Bjälbo.* 1956.
3. *Gustav Adolf.* 1957.
4. *Open Letters to the Intimate Theater.* 1959.
5. *The Saga of the Folkungs; Engelbrekt.* 1959.
6. *The Vasa Trilogy: Master Olof; Gustav Vasa; Erik XIV.* 1959.
7. *Pre-Inferno Plays* (includes *The Father; Lady Julie; Creditors; The Stronger; The Bond*). 1970.
8. *"A Dream Play" and Four Chamber Plays* (includes

Stormy Weather; The House that Burned; The Ghost Sonata; The Pelican). 1973.
9. *Dramas of Testimony* (includes *The Dance of Death; Advent; Easter; There are Crimes and Crimes*). 1976.
10. *Plays of Confession and Therapy* (includes *To Damaskus I–III*). 1979.
11. *Apologia and Two Folk Plays* (includes *The Great Highway; The Crownbride; Swanwhite*). 1981.
12. *Plays from the Cynical Life* (includes *Playing with Fire; Debit and Credit; Mother Love; The First Warning; Facing Death; Pariah; Simoon*). 1983.

Six Plays (includes *The Father; Miss Julie; The Stronger; Easter; A Dream Play; The Ghost Sonata*), translated by Elizabeth Sprigge. 1955.

Three Plays (includes *The Father; Miss Julia; Easter*), translated by Peter Watts. 1958.

Five Plays (*Creditors; Crime and Crime; The Dance of Death; Swanwhite; The Great Highway*), translated by Elizabeth Sprigge. 1960.

Seven Plays (includes *The Father; Miss Julie; Comrades; The Stronger; The Bond; Crimes and Crimes; Easter*), translated by Arvid Paulson. 1960.

The Chamber Plays (includes *Storm Weather; The Burned House; The Ghost Sonata; The Pelican*), translated by Evert Sprinchorn and others. 1962.

Dramer [Dramas] (3 vols.), edited by C.R. Smedmark. 1962—

Twelve Plays (compilation of *Six Plays*, 1955, *Five Plays*,

1960, with *The Bond*), translated by Elizabeth Sprigge. 1963.

Eight Expressionist Plays (includes *Lucky Per's Journey; The Keys to Heaven; To Damascus I–III; A Dream Play; The Great Highway; The Ghost Sonata*), translated by Arvid Paulson. 1965.

Strindberg's One-Act Plays, translated by Arvid Paulson. 1969.

World Historical Plays (includes *The Nightingale of Wittenberg; Through Deserts to Ancestral Lands; Hellas; The Lamba and the Beast*), translated by Arvid Paulson. 1970.

Plays (2 vols.; includes *The Father; Miss Julie; Creditors; The Stronger; Playing with Fire; Erik the Fourteenth; Storm; The Ghost Sonata; To Damascus; Easter; Dance of Death; The Virgin Bride; A Dream Play*), translated by Michael Meyer.   1964–75; US edition (1 vol.), 1973; selected plays reissued as *Plays* (3 vols. to date; Volume 3 adds *Master Olof*), 1976—

Samlade verk [Collected Works], edited by Lars Dahlbäck and others.   1980—

Stage Works

I Rom [In Rome] (produced Dramaten, Stockholm, 1870). 1870.

Hermione [Hermione].   1870.

Den fredlöse (produced Dramaten, Stockholm, 1871).   1881; translated as *The Outlaw*, in *Plays*, 1912.

Mäster Olof (prose version; produced Nya Teater, Stockholm, 1881).   1881; revised version, in verse (produced Dramaten, Stockholm, 1890).   1878; translated as *Master Olof*, 1915: several subsequent translations under same title.

Gillets hemlighet [The Secret of the Guild] (produced Dramaten, Stockholm, 1880).   1880.

Anno fyrtioåtta [Anno Forty-Eight].   1881.

Lycko-Pers resa (produced Nya Teater, Stockholm, 1883). 1882; translated as *Lucky Pehr*, 1912; as *Lucky Peter's Travels*, 1930; as *Lucky Per's Journey*, in *Eight Expressionist Plays*, 1965.

Herr Bengts hustru [Sir Bengt's Wife] (produced Nya Teater, Stockholm, 1882).   1882.

Kamraterna (produced Lustspieltheater, Vienna, 1905). 1886; translated as *Comrades*, in *Plays*, 1913.

Fadren (produced Casino Theatre, Copenhagen, 1887). 1887; translated as *The Father*, 1889: several subsequent translations under same title.

Fröken Julie (produced by the Students' Association, University of Copenhagen, 1889).   1888; translated as *Countess Julie*, 1912; as *Miss Julie*, in *Plays*, 1913: several subsequent translations under same title; as *Lady Julie*, in *"Lucky Peter's Travels" and Other Plays*, 1931; as *Miss Julia*, in *Three Plays*, 1958.

Paria (produced Dagmar Theatre, Copenhagen, 1889). 1890; translated as *Pariah*, 1913, and in *The Washington Strindberg 12*, 1983.

Den starkare (produced Dagmar Theatre, Copenhagen, 1889).   1890; translated as *The Stronger*, in *Plays*, 1912; several subsequent translations under same title.

Fordringsägare (produced Dagmar Theatre, Copenhagen, 1889).   1890; translated as *The Creditors*, 1909: several subsequent translations under same title.

Samum (produced Svenska Teater, Stockholm, 1890). 1890; translated as *Simoon*, in *Plays*, 1913, and in *The Washington Strindberg 12*, 1983.

Hemsöborna [The Natives of Hemsö], from the novel (produced Djurgårdsteater, Stockholm, 1889).

Bandet (produced Kleines Theater, Berlin, 1902; produced in Swedish, Intima Teater, Stockholm, 1908).   1892; translated as *The Link*, in *Plays*, 1912, and as *The Bond*, 1930: several subsequent translations under both titles.

Leka med elden (produced Lessing-Theater, Berlin, 1893; produced in Swedish, Stockholm, 1907).   1892; translated as *Playing with Fire*, 1930: several subsequent translations under same title.

Debet och kredit (produced Kleines Theater, Berlin, 1893; produced in Swedish, Intima Teater, Stockholm, 1908). 1892; translated as *Debit and Credit*, in *Plays*, 1913.

Moderskärlek (produced Berlin, 1894).   1892; translated as *Motherlove*, 1910, and in *The Washington Strindberg 12*, 1983.

Första varningen (produced Residenztheater, Munich, 1893). 1892; translated as *The First Warning*, in *Plays*, 1916, and in *The Washington Strindberg 12*, 1983.

Inför döden (produced Residenztheater, Berlin, 1893; produced in Swedish, Intima Teater, Stockholm, 1910). 1892; translated as *Facing Death*, 1915, and in *The Washington Strindberg 12*, 1983.

Advent (produced Kammerspiele, Munich, 1915; produced in Swedish, Dramaten, Stockholm, 1926).   1898; translated as *Advent*, in *Plays*, 1913; several subsequent translations under same title.

Till Damaskus (trilogy): *Till Damaskus I* (produced Dramaten, Stockholm, 1900); *Till Damaskus II* (produced Lorensbergsteater, Gothenburg, 1924); *Till Damaskus III* (produced Lorensbergsteatern, Gothenburg, 1922).   Parts I and II published together, 1900; Part III published 1904; translated as *To Damascus*, 1913: several subsequent translations under same title.

Folkungasagen (produced Svenska Teater, Stockholm, 1901). 1899;   translated as *The Saga of the Folkungs*, in *"Master Olof" and Other Plays*, 1931, and with *Engelbrekt*, 1959 (*The Washington Strindberg*).

Gustav Vasa (produced Svenska Teater, Stockholm, 1899). 1899; translated as *Gustavus Vasa*, in *Plays*, 1916; as *Gustav Vasa*, in *The Vasa Trilogy*, 1959 (*The Washington Strindberg*).

Erik XIV (produced Svenska Teater, Stockholm, 1899). 1899; translated as *Erik XIV*, in *"Master Olof" and Other Plays*, 1931, and in *The Vasa Trilogy*, 1959 (*The Washington Strindberg*).

Brott och brott (produced Dramaten, Stockholm, 1900). 1899, translated as *There Are Crimes and Crimes*, 1912: several subsequent translations under same title; as *Crimes and Crimes*, in *Seven Plays*, 1960.

Påsk (produced Schauspielhaus, Frankfurt, 1901; produced in Swedish, Dramaten, Stockholm, 1901).   1900; translated as *Easter*, in *"Easter" and Stories*, 1912: several subsequent translations under same title.

Gustav Adolf (produced Berliner Theater, Berlin, 1903; produced in Swedish, Cirkus, Stockholm, 1912).   1900; translated as *Gustav Adolf*, in *Plays*, 1912, and 1957 (*The Washington Strindberg*).

Svanevit (produced Swedish Theatre, Helsinki, 1908).   1901; translated as *Swanwhite*, 1909: several subsequent translations under same title.

Karl XII (produced Dramaten, Stockholm, 1905).   1901; translated as *Charles XII*, in *The Washington Strindberg 1*, 1955.

Dödsadansen I-II (produced Residenztheater, Cologne, 1905; produced in Swedish, Intima Teater, Stockholm, 1909).   1901; translated as *The Dance of Death*, in *Plays*, 1912: several subsequent translations under same title.

Engelbrekt (produced Svenske Teater, Stockholm, 1901).

1901; translated as *Engelbrekt*, 1955, and with *The Saga of the Folkungs* (*The Washington Strindberg*), 1959.

Modsommar (produced Svenska Teater, Stockholm, 1901). 1901.

Kronbruden (produced Swedish Theatre, Helsinki, 1906). 1902; translated as *The Bridal Crown*, in *Plays*, 1912; as *The Virgin Bride*, in *Plays*, 1975; as *The Crownbride*, in *Apologia and Two Folk Plays* (*The Washington Strindberg*), 1981.

Gustav III (produced Nya Intima Teater , Stockholm, 1916). 1902; translated as *Gustav III*, in *The Washington Strindberg 1*, 1955.

Ett drömspel (produced Svenske Teater, Stockholm, 1907). 1902; translated as *The Dream Play*, in *Plays*, 1912; several subsequent translations under same title or as *A Dream Play*.

Näktergalen i Wittenberg (produced Deutsches Künstlertheater, Berlin, 1914; produced in Swedish, Svenske Teater, Stockholm, 1917). 1903; translated as *The Nightingale of Wittenberg*, in *World Historical Plays*, 1970.

Himmelrikets nycklar. In *Samlade dramatiska arbeten*, 1903–04; translated as *The Keys of Heaven*, in *Eight Expressionist Plays*, 1965.

Kristina (produced Intima Teater, Stockholm, 1908). 1904; translated as *Queen Christina*, in *The Washington Strindberg 1*, 1955.

Spöksonaten (produced Intima Teater, Stockholm, 1908). 1907; translated as *The Spook Sonata*, in *Plays*, 1916; as *The Ghost Sonata*, in *"Easter" and Other Plays*, 1929: several subsequent translations under both titles.

Oväder (produced Intima Teater, Stockholm, 1907). 1907; translated as *The Storm*, in *Plays*, 1912; as *Storm Weather*, in *The Chamber Plays*, 1962; as *Stormy Weather*, in *"A Dream Play" and Four Chamber Plays* (*The Washington Strindberg*), 1973.

Brända tomten (produced Intima Teater, Stockholm, 1907). 1907; translated as *After the Fire*, in *Plays*, 1913; as *The Burned House*, 1962; as *The House That Burned*, in *"A Dream Play" and Four Chamber Plays* (*The Washington Strindberg*), 1973.

Pelikanen (produced Intima Teater, Stockholm, 1907). 1907; translated as *The Pelican*, in *Plays*, 1916: several subsequent translations under same title.

Abu Casems tofflor [Abu Casem's Slippers] (produced Gåvle, Sweden, 1908). 1908.

Siste riddaren (produced Dramaten, Stockholm, 1908). 1908; translated as *The Last of the Knights*, in *The Washington Strindberg 2*, 1956.

Riksföreståndaren (produced Dramaten, Stockholm, 1911). 1908; translated as *The Regent*, in *The Washington Strindberg 2*, 1956.

Bjälbo-Jarlen (produced Svenska Teater, Stockholm, 1909). 1908; translated as *Earl Birger of Bjälbo*, in *The Washington Strindberg 2*, 1956.

Svarta handksen (produced Intima Teater, Stockholm, 1909). 1909; translated as *The Black Glove*, in *Plays*, 1916.

Stora landsvägen (produced Intima Teater, Stockholm, 1910). 1909; translated as *The Great Highway*, 1945: several subsequent translations under same title.

Genom öknar till arvland; eller, Moses (produced Stadttheater, Hanover, 1922). In *Samlade otryckta skrifter*, 1918–19; translated as *Moses*, in *Plays*, 1916; as *Through Deserts to Ancestral Lands*, in *World Historical Plays*, 1970.

Toten-Insel. In *Samlade skrifter*, 1918; translated as *Isle of the Dead*, in *Modern Drama*, 3, 1962.

Hellas; eller, Sokrates (produced Stadttheater, Hanover, 1922; produced in Swedish, Stockholm, 1942). In *Samlade otryckta skrifter*, 1918–19; translated as *Hellas*, in *World Historical Plays*, 1970.

Lammet och vilddjuret; eller, Kristus (produced Stadttheater, Hanover, 1922). In *Samlade otryckta skrifter*, 1918–19; translated as *The Lamb and the Beast*, in *World Historical Plays*, 1970.

Fiction

Röda rummet.   1879; translated as *The Red Room*, 1913, and 1967.

Sverska öden och äventyr [Swedish Fates and Adventures]. 1882–91 and 1904.

Giftas.   1884–85; translated as *Married*, 1913; complete version, as *Getting Married*, 1972.

Hemsöborna.   1887; translated as *The Natives of Hemsö*, 1959.

Skärkarlsliv [Life in the Skerries].   1888.

Tschandala (in Danish).   1889.

I havsbandet.   1890; translated as *By the Open Sea*, 1913.

Fagervik och Skamsund.   1902; translated as *Fair Haven and Foul Strand*, 1913.

Sagor.   1903; translated as *Tales*, 1930.

Götiska rummen [The Gothic Rooms].   1903.

Historiska miniatyrer.   1905; translated as *Historical Miniatures*, 1913.

Svarta fanor [Black Banners].   1907.

Taklagsöl [Topping Out].   1907.

Syndabocken.   1907; translated as *The Scapegoat*, 1967.

Klostret.   1966; translated as *The Cloister*, 1969.

Verse

Dikter [Poems].   1883.

Memoirs and Letters

Brev till Harriet Bosse [Letters to Harriet Bosse].   1923.

Brev, edited by Torsten Eklund.   1948—

Letters to Harriet Bosse, edited by Arvid Paulson.   1959.

Brev till min dotter Kerstin, edited by Karin Boye and Åke Thulstrup.   1961.

Other

Svenska folket [The Swedish People] (2 vols.).   1880–82.

Det nya riket [The New Kingdom].   1882.

Utopier i verkligheten [Utopias in Reality].   1884.

Tjästekvinnans son (4 vols.).   1886–87; translated in part as *The Son of a Servant*, 1913 and 1967.

Blomster malningar och djurstycken [Flower Pictures and Animal Pieces].   1888.

Le Plaidoyer d'un fou.   1895; as *En dåres försvarstal*, 1914; translated as *The Confessions of a Fool*, 1912; as *A Madman's Defense*, 1967.

Inferno.   1897; translated as *Inferno*. 1967.

Legender [Legends].   1898.

Ensam.   1903; translated as *Alone*, 1968.

Hövdingaminnen [Memories of Leaders].   1906.

En blå bok (4 vols.).   1907–12; translated in part as *Zones of the Spirit*, 1913.

Öppna brev till Intima Teatern.   1908; translated as *Letters to the Intimate Theatre*, edited by Walter Johnson, 1967.

Tal till svenska nationen [Speeches to the Swedish Nation]. 1910.

"Easter" and Stories (miscellany).   1912.
Likt och olikt [This and That] (2 vols.).   1913.
Vivisektioner (essays), edited by Torsten Eklund.   1958.
Ur ockulta dagboken, edited by Torsten Eklund.   1963; complete version, 1977; translated in part as *From an Occult Diary*, 1965.

*

Bibliographies

Esther H. Rapp, "Strindberg's Reception in England and America", in *Scandinavian Studies*, 23, 1951; supplemented by Jackson R. Bryer in *Modern Drama*, 5, 1962, and Birgitta Steene in *Structures of Influence: A Comparative Approach to Strindberg*, edited by Marilyn John, Blackwell, 1981.
Paul Fritz, *August Strindberg*, Stuttgart, 1979.

Criticism

Books:

Brita Mortensen and Brian W. Downs, *Strindberg: An Introduction to His Life and Work*, Cambridge, 1949.
Elizabeth Sprigge, *The Strange Life of August Strindberg*, London, 1949.
B.G. Madsen, *Strindberg's Naturalistic Theatre*, Copenhagen, 1962.
Walter Johnson, *Strindberg and the Historical Drama*, Seattle, Washington, 1963.
Carl R. Smedmark (ed.), *Essays on Strindberg*, Stockholm, 1966.
Walter Johnson, *August Strindberg*, Boston, 1976.
Martin Lamm, *August Strindberg* (from the Swedish), New York, 1971.
Otto Reinert (ed.), *Strindberg: A Collection of Critical Essays*, Englewood Cliffs, New Jersey, 1971.
Anthony Swerling, *Strindberg's Impact in France*, Cambridge, 1971.
Birgitta Steene, *The Greatest Fire: A Study of August Strindberg*, Carbondale, Illinois, 1973; revised edition, as *August Strindberg: An Introduction to His Major Works*, Stockholm, 1982.
Gunnar Brandell, *Strindberg in Inferno*, Cambridge, Massachusetts, 1974.
Strindberg and Modern Theatre, Stockholm, 1975 (no author).
John Ward, *The Social and Religious Plays of August Strindberg*, London, 1979.
Harry G. Carlson, *Strindberg and the Poetry of Myth*, Berkeley, California, 1982.
Egil Tornqvist, *Strindbergian Drama*, Stockholm, 1982.
Evert Sprinchorn, *Strindberg as Dramatist*, New Haven, Connecticut, 1982.
Olof Lagercrantz, *August Strindberg*, London, 1983.
Donald K. Weaver (ed.), *Strindberg on Stage* (symposium), Stockholm, 1983.
Michael Meyer, *August Strindberg: A Biography*, London, 1985.
Margery Morgan, *August Strindberg*, London, 1985 (Macmillan Modern Dramatists series).
Michael Meyer (compiler), *File on Strindberg*, London, 1986.
Michael Robinson, *Strindberg and Autobiography*, Norwich, 1986.
Göran Stockenström, *Strindberg's Dramaturgy*, Minneapolis, 1988.

* * *

August Strindberg's contribution to world drama is twofold, consisting in the naturalistic plays of the late 1880's and early 1890's and the expressionist works dating from 1898 onwards. The naturalistic plays combine a scrupulous attention to the Aristotelian unities with the exploitation of heredity, milieu, and immediate circumstances as the bases for complex modern characters. The expressionist plays, by contrast, take us inside individual characters as their minds unfold on stage, frequently in terms of powerful visual imagery. Paralleling and enlarging many of the discoveries made around the same time in the fields of psychology and psychoanalysis, these latter plays depend not on the classical unities, but on the individual, subjective mind for their overall shape, with the erratic structures of dreams playing a prominent part.

A prolific author, Strindberg wrote more than 60 plays in four decades while being no less productive in a range of other genres. His extensive theoretical writings on drama show him to have been acutely aware of his role as an innovator. Thus, his naturalistic plays were a reaction against the standard French intrigue-drama with its elaborate plot and fixed characters: wanting to create a drama that was true to life, Strindberg advocated focusing on decisive psychological conflicts and giving scope to character subjectivity. His emphasis on subjectivity brings out the connection between his naturalism and his expressionism; and as a result of recent research, the demarcation line between these two phases of Strindberg's playwriting is becoming less distinct.

Mäster Olof, Strindberg's first major play, is a historical drama, but it characteristically subverts the genre—the most prestigious of its day—by drawing on Shakespeare and clearing away a host of dead theatrical practices. The play was rejected by the Dramatiska Teatern in Stockholm and rewritten several times, but the original version has subsequently come to be regarded as the superior one. Strindberg returned to historical drama at several junctures in his career, and plays such as *Gustav Vasa* and *Erik XIV* belong to his major works for the theatre.

Fadren (*The Father*) marks the breakthrough of Strindberg's naturalistic drama. The spouses' battle for control of their daughter is fought at the psychological level, yet unfolds with the inevitability of a Greek tragedy and assumes archetypal proportions. In *Fröken Julie* (*Miss Julie*), the gender conflict is combined with a conflict of class, the play being about a noblewoman who is seduced by her father's valet and commits suicide as a result; it draws on the characters' mutual powers of psychological suggestion. The play's famous preface, designed to cement the links between *Miss Julie* and naturalism as defined by Émile Zola and André Antoine, highlights the extent to which the characters are fragmented "agglomerations" of old and new. It also underlines the role of formal innovations in enabling the playwright to retain his grip on the spectators: *Miss Julie* is written in a single act, with only a short silent scene and a "ballet" indicating the tripartite structure.

When Strindberg wrote *Fröken Julie* he had not only Antoine's Parisian Théâtre Libre in mind, but also the new Scandinavian Experimental Theatre which he had helped to set up in Copenhagen. For this latter theatre he subsequently wrote a number of one-act naturalistic plays, several of them according to the pattern of the Théâtre Libre's famous *quart d'heures*. Using few characters and simple sets, these plays explore intense psychological power struggles, often with marital dimensions.

Till Damaskus (*To Damascus*), which followed after the

mental and religious crisis of the mid-1890's which Strindberg has depicted in the prose work entitled *Inferno*, marked a radically new departure. The psychological battles of the earlier plays are here located within the individual character The Stranger, struggling with the issues of guilt, atonement, and identity. A world beyond that of humankind was emerging, but with an anonymous "Eternal One" or "The Invisible" in command rather than the conventional Christian God. A drama of pilgrimage, *To Damascus* is structured around a series of visually precise yet evocative scenes, their repetition indicative of a Schopenhauerian view of the role of suffering and atonement in human life.

Dödsdansen (*The Dance of Death*), which at first sight may look like a return to naturalism with its single setting, few characters, and renewed attention to marital conflict, strikingly reinforces the expressionist pattern: the characters turn out to have grotesque dimensions, and the isolated fortress which the spouses inhabit underscores the notion of marriage as Hell on earth, escapable only when death parts husband and wife. *Ett drömspel* (*A Dream Play*) relates the marital nightmare to a wider context. The boldly innovatory form projects the action on the stage as the dream of the spectator and involves sudden, fluid transformations sustained by sharply realistic detail. Here the Daughter of the god Indra tries out the cycle of human life only to return to her father, overwhelmed by the sufferings of human beings. "Humankind is to be pitied" is the refrain bringing out the bleakly metaphysical perspective of this play.

Posing exceptional problems for the producer, *A Dream Play* was successfully staged at the Intimate Theatre in Stockholm which Strindberg had helped to found in 1907. For this theatre he wrote the series of five "Chamber Plays", describing them as attempts to translate the idea of chamber music into dramatic form. Mood and atmosphere are more important than any conventional plot as states of mind are projected on the stage. In *Spöksonaten* (*The Ghost Sonata*), as in several of these plays, a building is the focal point, the respectable façade contrasting with the truths about the characters inhabiting the rooms. Evil pervades this world, the only glimmer of light consisting in the fact that the truth is revealed before death comes.

Enjoying only limited success in Sweden during Strindberg's life-time, both his naturalistic and his expressionist plays were quickly appreciated abroad, especially in Germany. Strindberg's expressionist works, in particular, have had an immeasurable significance for the development of 20th-century drama and theatre production.

—Helena Forsås-Scott

See also *Volume 1* entries on *The Dance of Death, Parts One and Two*; *A Dream Play*; *The Father*; *The Ghost Sonata*; *Miss Julie*; *To Damascus*.

SUDERMANN, Hermann. Born in Matziken, East Prussia, 30 November 1857. Attended Realgymnasium in Elbning; studied history and philosophy at the Universities of Königsberg, 1875–77, and Berlin, from 1877. Married the writer Klara Lauckner in 1891. Journalist, then editor, with *Deutsche Reichsblatt*, 1881–82; then private tutor until he became a full-time writer; first-produced play, *Die Ehre*, staged 1889. Died in Berlin, 22 November 1928.

Works

Collections

Dramatische Werke (6 vols.).   1923.
Die Reise nach Tilsit: Prosa und Dramen.   1971.

Stage Works

Die Ehre (produced Lessing-Theater, Berlin, 1889).   1890.
Sodoms Ende (produced Lessing-Theater, Berlin, 1890). 1891.
Heimat (produced Lessing-Theater, Berlin, 1893).   1893; translated as *Magda*, 1899.
Die Schmetterlingsschlacht (produced Lessing-Theater, Berlin, and Burgtheater, Vienna, 1894).   1895.
Das Glück im Winkel (produced Burgtheater, Vienna, 1895). 1896.
Morituri (trilogy; includes *Teja; Fritzchen; Das ewig Männliche*; produced Burghtheater, Vienna, 1896).   1897; translated as *Morituri: Three One-Act Plays*, 1912.
Johannes (produced Deutsches Theater, Berlin, and Königliches Hoftheater, Dresden, 1898).   1898; translated as *John the Baptist*, 1909.
Die drei Reiherfedern (produced Deutsches Theater, Berlin, and in Dresden and Stuttgart, 1899).   1899.
Johannisfeuer (produced Lessing-Theater, Berlin, 1900). 1900.
Es lebe das Leben (produced Deutsches Theater, Berlin, 1902).   1902; translated as *The Joy of Living*, 1903.
Der Sturmgeselle des Sokrates (produced Lessing-Theater, Berlin, 1903).   1903.
Die Sturmgesellen (produced Lessing-Theater, Berlin, 1903). 1903(?).
Stein unter Steinen (produced Lessing-Theater, Berlin, 1905). 1905.
Das Blumenboot (produced Alexandrinsky Theatre, St. Petersburg, Russia, 1906; produced in Germany, Lessing-Theater, Berlin, 1906).   1905.
Rosen (includes *Lichtbänder; Margot; Der letzte Besuch; Die ferne Prinzessin*; produced Burgtheater, Vienna, 1907). 1907; translated as *Roses: Four One-Act Plays*, 1912.
Strandkinder (produced Königliches Schauspielhaus, Berlin, 1909).   1909.
Der Bettler von Syrakus (produced Königliches Schauspielhaus, Berlin, 1911).   1911.
Der gute Ruf (produced Deutsches Theater, Berlin, and Königliches Hoftheater, Munich, 1913).   1913.
Die Lobgesänge des Claudian (produced Deutsches Schauspielhaus, Hamburg, 1914).   1914.
Die entgötterte Welt: Szenische Bilder aus einer kranken Zeit (trilogy; includes *Die Freundin; Die gutgeschnittene Ecke; Das höhere Leben*; produced Lessing-Theater, Berlin, and Schauspielhaus, Munich, 1916).   1915.
Regina, from his novel *Der Katzensteg* (produced Theater an der Königgrätzersstrasse, Berlin, 1919).   1916.
Die Raschhoffs (produced Neues Schauspielhaus, 1919). 1919.
Das deutsche Schicksal (trilogy; includes *Notruf; Heilige Zeit; Opfer*).   1920–21.
Wie die Träumenden.   1922; as *Die Entscheidung der Lissa Hart*, 1932.
Der Hasenfellhändler.   1927.

Fiction

Im Zwielicht.   1886.
Frau Sorge.   1887; translated as *Dame Care*, 1891.

Der Katzensteg.   1888; translated as *Regine*, 1894; as *Regina; or The Sins of the Fathers*, 1898.
Geschwister.   1888.
Jolanthes Hochzeit.   1892; translated as *Iolanthe's Wedding*, 1918.
Es war.   1893; translated as *The Undying Past*, 1906.
Drei Reden.   1900.
Das hohe Lied.   1908; translated as *The Song of Songs*, 1913.
Die indische Lilie.   1911; translated in *"The Indian Lily" and Other Stories*, 1911.
Litauische Geschichten.   1917.
Der verwandelte Fächer.   1918.
Romane und Novellen (6 vols.).   1919.
Jons und Erdme.   1921.
Zwischen den Wäldern.   With *Auf eigener Scholle*, 1924.
Auf eigener Scholle.   With *Zwischen den Wäldern*, 1924.
Der tolle Professor.   1926; translated as *The Mad Professor*, 1929.
Die Frau des Steffen Tromholt.   1927.
Purzelchen. 1928.
Romane und Novellen (10 vols.).   1928.
"Miks Bumbullis" und andere Geschichten.   1958.

Memoirs and Letters

Das Bilderbuch meiner Jugend.   1922; translated as *The Book of My Youth*, 1923.
Briefe an seine Frau, edited by Irmgard Leux.   1932.

Other

Verrohung in der Theaterkritik.   1902.

*

Criticism

Books:
K. Knortz, *Sudermanns Dramen*, Halle, 1908.
K. Busse, *Hermann Sudermann: Sein Werk und sein Wesen*, Stuttgart, 1927.
T. Duglor (ed.), *Hermann Sudermann*, Troisdorf, 1958.
Walter T. Rix (ed.), *Hermann Sudermann: Werk und Wirkung*, Würzburg, 1980.

Articles:
Raleigh Whitinger, "Self-Consciousness in *Die Ehre*: A Revised View of Hermann Sudermann's First Drama", in *Journal of English and Germanic Philology*, 89, 1990.

*   *   *

The autumn of the year 1889 saw the breakthrough of naturalism in the German theatre. Hard on the heels of the stormy premiere of Gerhart Hauptmann's *Vor Sonnenaufgang (Before Dawn)*, there followed the premiere of Sudermann's first drama *Die Ehre* (Honour). Unlike Hauptmann, whose play was put on in a private performance for the members of the Berlin Free Theatre, Sudermann made his debut in the commercial theatre. His play was an immediate success with the public, and its author was acclaimed as the Schiller of the new literary movement. After a slight setback with his second play, *Sodoms Ende*, Sudermann consolidated his position as the most popular and commercially successful dramatist of the day with *Heimat* (translated as *Magda*).
Such rapid success rested on a remarkable ability to com-

bine the topical material and the problems of Naturalist literature with the form and structure of boulevard theatre. These early dramas exploit the conventions of the problem play in a domestic, usually middle-class, interior with a theatricality that owes more to Dumas *fils*, Sardou, and Scribe than to the psychologically more penetrating and intellectually more challenging dramas of Ibsen. The characteristic situation of a Sudermann drama is that of a hero or heroine uprooted from his or her social environment, but not yet fully absorbed into another socially superior, but morally ambivalent, milieu.
The construction of the plot around a character placed between two contrasting worlds proved a highly effective way of emphasising the social determinism that is such a central pillar of Naturalist theory. This technique was skilfully supported by careful attention to detail in the depiction of milieu, be it the squalid proletarian quarters of the Heinecke family, their unkempt appearance, and their Berlin dialect, in *Die Ehre*, or the formality, respectability, and patriarchal values of the household of a retired Prussian officer and his social circle in the provincial setting of *Heimat*. At the same time, the stark contrasts which the dramatist created contribute significantly to the process of the unmasking of false values which constituted Sudermann's central theme.
The problem is dealt with most paradigmatically in *Die Ehre*, where two families, one wealthy, one poor, are shown alongside each other in a relationship governed by social, economic, and sexual factors. The symmetry is disturbed by the different concepts of honour that operate on the different levels of society: the poor Robert Heinecke renounces the wealthy Lenore Mühlingk for the "honourable" reason of his inferior socio-economic status; whereas the wealthy Mühlingks simply buy off the Heineckes, who take the cash rather than support Robert as he seeks to defend the "honour" of his sister, seduced by Lenore's brother, Kurt.
The weakness of Sudermann as a dramatist, and the point at which he parts company from his more serious contemporaries, lies in his evident reluctance to adopt a form in which the questions he handles with such telling dramatic effect are left open in such a way as to confront his audiences with a genuine social, political, or moral challenge. His conventional sense of theatre always required strong dramatic, not to say melodramatic, closure: in *Die Ehre*, the hero is rescued from his predicament by the intervention of a wealthy friend whose generosity conveniently puts all to rights; in *Sodoms Ende* the artist-hero, who finally recognises his own corruption by Berlin high society, suddenly dies of a stroke, as does the heroine's father in *Heimat* before he can carry out his threat to shoot his daughter.
After the demise of Naturalism, Sudermann continued to write prolifically, but without repeating his early successes. In the one-act play *Fritzchen*, on the subject of duelling, and in *Stein unter Steinen*, a play concerned with the rehabilitation of a man who has served a prison sentence, he persevered with social themes and the realist mode, but without overcoming his weakness for the melodramatic. In general, however, the eclecticism of his later work, in which he tried his hand at symbolism (*Die drei Reiherfedern*), biblical drama (*Johannes*), and verse drama (*Der Bettler von Syrakus*), confirms the judgement of the most perceptive of his early critics, Otto Brahm, Franz Mehring and, above all, Alfred Kerr, who saw in him a technically skilful, but essentially opportunist, exponent of the literary and theatrical resources of his day. His attempts to counter-attack with polemical essays of his own (*Verrohung in der Theaterkritik*) proved rather clumsy and, despite the continued popularity

of certain of his earlier works, his reputation as a serious dramatist did not survive.

—John Osborne

See also *Volume 1* entry on *Magda*.

SUDRAKA, King. See *Volume 1* entry on *The Little Clay Cart*.

SUKHOVO-KOBYLIN, Alexander Vasilievich. Born into the nobility, in Voskresensky, Russia, 17 September 1817 (Old Style). Educated at the University of Moscow, 1834–38; universities of Heidelberg and Berlin, 1838–42. Married 1) Baroness Marie de Bouglon in 1859 (died 1860); 2) Emily Smith in 1867 (died 1868). Travelled widely in the years after 1838; suspected of the murder of his former French mistress, Louise Simon-Dimanche, and subjected to imprisonment and court hearings, 1850–57: eventually acquitted of the crime, 1857; the first play of a trilogy, *Svadba Krechinskogo* [*Krechinsky's Wedding*], written in prison, 1854, and produced 1855; emigrated to France, 1858; in later life devoted to himself to metaphysics and the study of Hegelian philosophy; his home and library destroyed by fire during the 1890's; his trilogy produced on successive evenings by a touring company, Moscow, 1901. Elected honarary member of the Russian Academy of Sciences, 1902. Died in Beaulieu, France, 11 March 1903.

Works

Collections

Trilogia [The Trilogy], edited by L.P. Grossman. 1927; later editions: edited by I.D. Glikman, 1959, and by K. Rudnitsky, 1966.
The Trilogy, translated by Harold B. Segel. 1969.

Stage Works

Svadba Krechinskogo (produced Maly Theatre, Moscow, 1855). In *Kartiny proshedshego* [Scenes of the Past], 1869; translated as *Krechinsky's Wedding*, 1961, and in *The Trilogy*, 1969.
Delo (produced as *Ozhitoye vremya* [Past Times], Maly Theatre, Moscow, 1882; produced as *Delo*, Russian Theatre, Moscow, 1882). In *Kartiny proshedshego* [Scenes of the Past], 1869; translated as *The Case*, in *The Trilogy*, 1969.
Smert Tarelkina (produced as *Vesyolye Rasplyuyevskiye* [Rasplyuev's Merry Days], Suvorin's Literary-Artistic Theatre, St. Petersburg, 1900). In *Kartiny proshedshego* [Scenes of the Past], 1869; translated as *The Death of Tarelkin*, in *The Trilogy*, 1969.

*

Criticism

Books:
Harold B. Segel, "Introduction", in *The Trilogy*, New York, 1969.
R. Fortune, *Alexander Sukhovo Kobylin*, Boston, 1982.

Articles:
N. Brodyanska, "Sukhovo-Kobylin", in *Slavonic Review*, 1947.
Erik Egeberg, "Wenn der Antichrist die Welt regiert: Zur Deutung des Dramas *Delo* von. A.V. Sukhovo-Kobylin", in *Scando-Slavica*, 16, 1970.

*   *   *

Sukhovo-Kobylin's life as a rich aristocrat was completely disrupted when he was accused of the murder of his French mistress in Moscow in 1850. The investigations continued for nearly seven years, and though he was finally exonerated in 1857, he was not really free of suspicion for the rest of his life. It has never been conclusively established whether Sukhovo-Kobylin or the dead woman's servants were responsible for the crime, though the servants' guilt seems by far the most probable. The remarkable plays that comprise his long-neglected, but now justly acclaimed, trilogy grew directly out of this traumatic experience. The comedy *Svadba Krechinskogo* (*Krechinsky's Wedding*) was mostly written while Sukhovo-Kobylin was imprisoned in 1854. The bitterly satirical *Delo* (*The Case*) and *Smert Tarelkina* (*The Death of Tarelkin*) were completed in 1861 and 1869 respectively, and remain unsurpassed as indictments of the Russian bureaucracy, legal system, and police. The trilogy was published in 1869, under the title *Kartiny proshedshego* (Scenes of the Past), but only *Krechinsky's Wedding* was regularly performed in the author's lifetime. The other plays were banned by the censor, with the result that Sukhovo-Kobylin abandoned writing for the theatre and devoted himself to Hegelian philosophy. In a letter of 1892, he aptly summed up the anguished frustrations of his career as a dramatist: "Fancy living for 75 years and not managing to get three plays on the stage. How terrible to muzzle for life a man with the ability to speak! And what for? Because his satire of vice makes people shudder rather than laugh".

Krechinsky's Wedding is a three-act comedy, influenced by the French "well-made play" (*pièce bien faite*). Its amusing scenes, witty and colloquial dialogue, and memorably negative characters have ensured it a popular place in the repertoire since its successful premiere of 1855. Krechinsky, a charming but worthless gambler of high birth, seeks to resolve his desperate financial problems by a cynical and predatory marriage to Lidochka, the naive daughter of a provincial landowner, Muromsky. Aided by Rasplyuev, a stupid and vulgar scoundrel, Krechinsky attempts to swindle a pawnbroker, using a diamond pin borrowed from Lidochka. When he is finally exposed, the Muromsky family is humiliated but the lovelorn Lidochka saves Krechinsky from arrest. Though the play satirizes the false glitter of Moscow society and the corrupting power of money and greed, and suggests that goodness is relatively powerless in the face of evil, it is more light-hearted in tone that the two later plays, from which it stands somewhat apart, but to whose nightmarish and bleak world it serves as an introduction.

The Case, a five-act drama, is Sukhovo-Kobylin's artistic revenge for his own sufferings—a powerful and uncompromising denunciation of the judicial system, which is condemned from top to bottom as ludicrous and corrupt. Lidochka has been unjustly implicated in Krechinsky's fraud as his alleged accomplice and mistress, and for six years Muromsky has struggled to clear her name, while refusing to bribe officials, in the naive belief that the innocent should not have to purchase justice. Eventually his resistance crumbles when Varravin, the head of the Department, orders a reinvestigation of the case and threatens to subject the now devout Lidochka to an intimate examination to prove her liaison with Krechinsky. Muromsky sells everything to raise the necessary money, but is tricked by Varravin who pockets most of the cash, but then denounces Muromsky for attempted bribery. At this Muromsky collapses and subsequently dies. The play ends with Tarelkin, an official in the same department, pleading in vain with Varravin for his share of the spoils.

Sukhovo-Kobylin's vision in *The Case* is deeply pessimistic. Truth and morality are scorned with impunity, and good is at the mercy of evil. Though all know that the case is based on nothing, Muromsky is inevitably doomed, caught in a Kafka-esque web from which there is no escape. Sinister officials use the law to oppress rather than protect the innocent; bribery and extortion are endemic; and the individual is crushed by the power of the State, whose representatives are shamelessly hypocritical and ruthlessly dishonest. Though the play has comic and farcical aspects, its didactic savagery is rivalled in Russian literature only by some of the works of Saltykov-Shchedrin.

The Death of Tarelkin, the finest and most original play of the trilogy, is a three-act black farce and absurdist exposé of bureaucratic and police depravity, in which Tarelkin steals compromising letters from Varravin, fakes his own death, takes on the identity of a dead neighbour, and attempts to get his hands on Muromsky's bribe-money by blackmail. Rasplyuev, Krechinsky's former henchman, reappears as a bullying and credulous policeman, who is duped by Varravin into arresting and torturing Tarelkin. Tarelkin confesses to being a blood-sucking vampire and conspirator, and Rasplyuev gloats at the thought of arresting "the whole of Russia". Sukhovo-Kobylin makes skilful use of absurd and grotesque elements to suggest that the corrupt bureaucracy, backed by a brutal police force, feeds on the very life-blood of Russia. Virtue is totally absent, the foul Varravin again triumphs, and the play, though funny and entertaining, is the author's darkest comment on humanity.

Sukhovo-Kobylin's trilogy, his sole contribution to the theatre, deserves to be much more widely known and performed. The plays are linked in plot, themes, and characters, but contrast sharply in genre, mood, and style. They are remarkable for their stagecraft and caricatured portraits of evil characters, while their uniquely pungent satire of oppression ensures their continuing relevance. It is little wonder they attracted the attention of director Vsevolod Meyerhold, who staged all three plays in 1917, followed by further productions of *The Death of Tarelkin* and *Krechinsky's Wedding* in 1922 and 1933 respectively.

—Peter Doyle

SUTHERLAND, Efua. Born in Cape Coast, Ghana, 27 June 1924. Educated at St. Monica's School and Training College, Cape Coast; Homerton College, Cambridge, BA; School of Oriental and African Studies, University of London. Married William Sutherland in 1954; three children. Schoolteacher in Ghana, 1951–54; devised plays for Ghana Radio's "The Singing Net" series; founding director, Experimental Theatre Players, 1958, and Ghana Drama Studio since 1961 (incorporated into the University of Ghana, 1962), both in Accra; has pursued theatrical research in the

Institute of African Studies, University of Ghana. Founder, Ghana Society of Writers (subsequently the University of Ghana Writers' Workshop) and Kusum Agoromba children's theatre group, Legon. Co-founder, *Okyeame* magazine, Accra. Has written and devised plays both in English and the Ghanaian dialect of Twi, but little of her work has been published.

Works

Stage Works (most also broadcast in radio versions)

Odasani, from the medieval play *Everyman* (produced Drama Studio, Accra, 1960).
Foriwa, (produced Drama Studio, Accra, 1962).   1967.
Edufa, from a play by Euripides (produced Drama Studio, Accra, 1962).   1967.
Anansegoro: *You Swore an Oath*, (produced Drama Studio, Accra, 1963?).   In *Présence africaine* (in English), 22, 1964.
Vulture! Vulture!.   In *Two Rhythm Plays*, 1968.
Tahinta.   In *Two Rhythm Plays*, 1968.
Ananse and the Dwarf Brigade (for children; produced Cleveland, Ohio, 1971).
The Marriage of Anansewa: *A Storytelling Drama*, from the radio play (produced Accra, 1971).

Other Plays

The Proposal, from a play by Chekhov; *The Pineapple Child*; *Nyamekye*; *Tweedledum and Tweedledee*, from *Alice in Wonderland* by Lewis Carroll.

Verse

Playtime in Africa (for children), photographs by Willis E. Bell.   1960.

Other

The Roadmakers (for children), photographs by Willis E. Bell.   1961.
The Original Bob: The Story of Bob Johnson, Ghana's Ace Comedian, illustrated by Willis E. Bell.   1970.
The Voice in the Forest: A Tale from Ghana.   1983.

*

Criticism

Books:
Martin Owusu, "*Edufa*", in his *Drama of the Gods: A Study of Seven African Plays*, Roxbury, Massachusetts, 1983.
Adetokunbo Pearce, "The Didactic Essence of Efua Sutherland's Plays", in *Women in African Literature Today*, edited by Eldred D. Jones and Estace Palmer, London, 1987.

Articles:
E.J. Asgill, "African Adaptations of Greek Tragedies", in *African Literature Today*, 11, 1980.
Chinyere Okafor, "Parallelism Versus Influence in African Literature: The Case of Efua Sutherland's *Edufa*", in *Kiabàrà*, vol.3 no.1, 1980.
John C. Hagan, "The Influence of Folklore on *The Marriage of Anansewa*", in *Okike*, 27–28, 1988.

* * *

Efua Sutherland brought playwriting and theatrical production together in Ghana. The few plays that predate Ghanaian independence in 1957 and the founding of her Experimental Theatre Group in 1958 were essentially closet dramas. Moreover, from the start she was concerned to bring drama to the people. She was, thus, also concerned with bringing drama to children and encouraging their participation in drama, by drawing upon local folk stories, lyrics and dances, and by performing in Twi as well as English. Her work attracted American support from the Rockefeller Foundation and the Fund for Tomorrow. With their funding, and government support, the first professional theatre, the Ghana Drama Studio, was built and opened in 1961. In 1962 the Drama Studio became a part of the newly established School of Music and Drama at the University of Ghana. Continuing her concern with reaching the ordinary person, Sutherland designed a courtyard theatre derived from traditional performance areas. From the Studio she sent out a company to tour schools and colleges performing, in Twi and English, original works and her own adaptations of *Everyman* and *Alice in Wonderland*.

The example and influence of Sutherland's production work is likely to prove to be of greater significance than her plays. Indeed, one wonders how concerned she is for publication; of all her work for children, for example, she has published only the extremely brief *Vulture! Vulture! Two Rhythm Plays*. The skilful dramatization of a traditional tale of a deer-woman, *Anansegoro: You Swore an Oath*, appeared without her advance knowledge. Of her three full-length plays the first, *Edufa*, is an adaptation of Euripides' *Alcestis* —or, rather, since the values given to many of the characters are reversed, a counter-argument to *Alcestis*. While there are various critical interpretations of Euripides' play, to see it as a celebration of hospitality makes sense of the play as a whole. It is because of his reputation for hospitality that Admetus is allowed to let someone else die for him—his wife, Alcestis— and that even in the midst of his grief for Alcestis he plays host to the visiting Heracles, who then pursues Death and wrestles Alcestis away from him and returns her to Admetus. The play was presented not as a tragedy but in place of a satyr play. *Edufa*, however, is a tragedy, with the Alcestis-figure's death ending the play. Moreover, with heavy irony, the action is set against an annual ceremony in which funeral songs are sung as evil is expelled from the town. The evil is in Edufa, Sutherland's Admetus-figure, a selfish member of the new class of privileged *nouveaux riches*, who, behind his facade of a man emancipated from traditional beliefs by his education, secretly resorts to diviners in terror at the coming of death. Similarly, the Heracles character is a seedy intellectual. In contrast the father, a self-centered hypocrite in Euripides' play, becomes a representative of the dignity and wisdom of the older generation. The focus, as the title suggests, is on the educated modern man and the loss of moral orientation in his alienation from traditional values.

Foriwa is more didactic. Labaran, a university graduate, has come to transform a provincial town. He tells the audience:

> I am keeping vigil here, placing my faith in some daybreak after this long night when the townsmen shall wake and shake my soul with vibrant talk . . . I was impatient at the beginning: in haste. Seeing the raggedness of my people's homes, I was ashamed, even angry. I heard it screamed: Progress! Development! I wanted it far and everywhere.

From this straightforward statement of the theme, we expect —quite correctly—that the play will end with his triumph.

Yet the play is distinctively original. First, Sutherland eschews the conflicts between generations, tradition and modernization, on which many African plays about social change are based. Labaran's ally is the retired postmaster, the Queen-Mother is herself a reformer, and the climax is her use of a traditional ceremony to win endorsement for change. Second, the tone of the play is set not by the struggle for social change, but by the joyous youthfulness and self-discovery of the title character, the Queen-Mother's daughter. She and Labaran take the length of the play to fall in love. Since he is a Hausa from the distant north, this is yet another symbol of unity for progress.

The Marriage of Anansewa is a divertissement on the theme of the rascally father who encourages various wealthy suitors to woo his daughter. When the juggling of visitors becomes too complicated, the only way to end the solicitations is for Anansewa to "die" and, after a final round of generous gifts to the "dead" girl from the other suitors, to be miraculously revived by the messenger of the Chief-Who-is-Chief. Since the wooing is all by messenger, and since Anansewa is silent while she is "dead", Sutherland can keep her untainted by her father's mercenary schemes. By keeping her uninvolved, however, Sutherland also leaves her character undeveloped. The effect is rather as if Jonson, in his *Volpone*, had given Celia to Mosca to hustle for instead of to Volpone.

Sutherland's interest is, one suspects, in the traditional story-telling manner of presentation of this play rather than the subject. Each of her plays experiments with the involvement of the spectators. *Edufa* keeps the chorus from *Alcestis* and was intended for presentation in the Ghana Drama Studio's courtyard theatre, with spectators and actors entering through the same gate. *Foriwa* was written for performance "in a street in any of many small Ghanaian towns" and the hero explains his intentions directly to the audience. Most ambitiously, *The Marriage of Anansewa* attempts to recapture the atmosphere of traditional story-telling sessions by keeping the performers onstage throughout as an onstage audience with whom Sutherland hopes the real audience will "feel as one."

—Anthony Graham-White

SYNGE, (Edmund) J(ohn) M(illington). Born in Newtown Villas, Rathfarnham, near Dublin, Ireland, 16 April 1871. Educated at private schools until 1885; with a private tutor, 1885–88; Trinity College, Dublin, 1888–92, BA 1892; studied piano and violin at the Royal Irish Academy of Music, Dublin, 1889–92; studied music and travelled in Germany, 1893, France, 1894, and Italy, 1895; settled in Paris and studied intermittently at the Sorbonne, 1895–97. Met Yeats, who encouraged him to write, 1896; visited Ireland, 1897, and summers 1898–1902, living part of the time in the Aran Islands; involved in the initial planning of the Irish Literary Theatre, 1899, which became the Irish National Theatre Society at the Abbey Theatre, Dublin, 1904: director of the Abbey Theatre, 1904–09; public anger at his play *The Playboy of the Western World* resulted in "the *Playboy* riots" at the Abbey Theatre, 1907. Suffered from Hodgkin's disease from 1897. Died in Dublin, 24 March 1909.

John Millington Synge

Works

Collections

Plays and Poems, edited by T. R. Henn.   1963; plays republished as *Complete Plays*, 1981.
Plays (2 vols.) edited by Ann Saddlemyer.   1968.

Stage Works

In the Shadow of the Glen (produced Molesworth Hall, Dublin, 1903).   1904.
Riders to the Sea (produced Molesworth Hall, Dublin, 1904). With *In the Shadow of the Glen*, 1905.
The Well of the Saints (produced Abbey Theatre, Dublin, 1905).   1905.
The Playboy of the Western World (produced Abbey Theatre, Dublin, 1907).   1907; edited by Malcolm Kelsall, 1975.
The Tinker's Wedding (produced His Majesty's Theatre, London, 1909).   1907.
Deirdre of the Sorrows (produced Abbey Theatre, Dublin, 1910).   1910.
When the Moon Has Set, edited by Mary King.   In *Long Room*, Spring-Autumn 1982.

Verse

Poems and Translations.   1909.
Poems, edited by Robin Skelton.   1962.

Memoirs and Letters

A Few Personal Recollections.   1915.
Some Unpublished Letters and Documents.   1959.
The Autobiography, Constructed from the Manuscripts, edited by Alan Price.   1965.
Theatre Business: The Correspondence of the First Abbey Theatre Directors: William Butler Yeats, Lady Gregory, and Synge, edited by Ann Saddlemyer.   1982.
Collected Letters (2 vols.), edited by Ann Saddlemyer.   1983–84.

Other

The Aran Islands.   1907.
In Wicklow, West Kerry, and Connemara.   1911; revised edition, 1912.
Prose, edited by Alan Price.   1966.
My Wallet of Photographs: The Collected Photographs, edited by Lilo M. Stephens.   1971.

*

Bibliographies

E. H. Mikhail, *John Millington Synge: A Bibliography of Criticism*, Totowa, New Jersey, 1975.
Edward A. Kopper Jr., *John Millington Synge: A Reference Guide*, Boston, 1979.

Criticism

Books:

F.L. Bickley, *J.M. Synge and the Irish Dramatic Movement*, London, 1912.
John Masefield, *John Millington Synge: A Few Personal Recollections*, London, 1915.
Daniel Corkey, *Synge and Anglo-Irish Literature*, Dublin and Cork, 1931.
L.A.G. Strong, *John Millington Synge*, New York, 1941.
David H. Greene and Edward M. Stephens, *J.M. Synge*, 1959; revised edition, 1989.
Alan Price, *J.M. Synge and Anglo-Irish Drama*, London, 1961.
Elizabeth Coxhead, *J.M. Synge and Lady Gregory*, London, 1962.
Denis Johnston, *John Millington Synge*, New York, 1965.
Donna L. Gerstenberger, *John Millington Synge*, New York, 1965; revised edition, Boston, 1990.
Ann Saddlemyer, *John Millington Synge and Modern Comedy*, Dublin, 1968.
Robin Skelton, *The Writings of J.M. Synge*, London, 1971.
Robin Skelton, *J.M. Synge and His World*, New York, 1971.
Robin Skelton, *J.M. Synge*, Lewisburg, Pennsylvania, 1972.
Maurice Harmon (ed.), *J.M. Synge Centenary Papers*, Dublin, 1972.
J.B. Bushrui (ed.), *Sunshine and the Moon's Delight: A Centenary Tribute to John Millington Synge*, New York, 1972.
Nicholas Grene, *John Millington Synge: A Critical Study of the Plays*, London, 1975.
E.H. Mikhail (ed.), *J.M. Synge: Interviews and Recollections*, London, 1977.
Weldon Thornton, *J.M. Synge and the Western Mind*, Gerrard's Cross, Buckinghamshire, 1979.

Declan Kiberd, *J.M. Synge and the Irish Language*, London, 1979.

Eugene Benson, *J.M. Synge*, London, 1982.

Toni O'Brien Johnson, *Synge: The Medieval and the Grotesque*, Gerrard's Cross, Buckinghamshire, 1982.

Mary C. King, *The Drama of J.M. Synge*, London, 1985.

P.C. David, *The Tragic View in the Plays of J.M. Synge*, Bareilly, 1988.

Edward A. Kopper, Jr. (ed), *A J.M. Synge Literary Companion*, Westport, Connecticut, 1988.

Edward A. Kopper, *Synge: A Review of the Criticism*, Lyndora, Pennsylvania, 1989.

*   *   *

The most important influence on Synge's art was undoubtedly that exercised by his visits to the Aran Islands. The primitiveness of this island life, with its violence and death, rescued him from the literary decadence that had infected such early writings as "Vita Vecchia", a suite of poems, or "Étude Morbide", a prose work, while the islanders' Gaelic peasant speech helped Synge discover his own unique voice.

The action of *Riders to the Sea* takes place on the Aran Islands. The central character is the mother, Maurya, an old woman who has lost her husband, her father-in-law, and five sons to the sea. As she waits, hoping that the body of her son Michael will be washed ashore, her sixth son, Bartley, her last and youngest, prepares for a journey to the mainland. In this extremely short one-act play Synge, with extraordinary command of artistic form, reveals that Michael has indeed been drowned at sea even as Bartley is thrown from his horse, himself drowned in the sea, and returned home for burial. The final third of the play is an extended threnody in which Maurya and her two daughters preside over the burial rites for Bartley; as Maurya chants the names of all those in her family who have drowned at sea, the enactment of Bartley's death becomes symbolic of every man's death just as the sea becomes a symbol of an implacable mortality that renders existence meaningless and Christian belief (as represented by the play's young priest) irrelevant.

The Shadow of the Glen, based on a story Synge heard on the Aran Islands, is about an old husband who feigns death to discover whether his young wife is unfaithful. While the play, on one level, is a study of a sexually repressed woman, intensely aware of the passing of time and the imminence of death, Synge introduces into his play a strain of mordant humour totally lacking in the Aran Island tale. The wife's final leaving of her husband to go off with another man (the Tramp) evoked outrage on the part of some Dublin critics.

The Tinker's Wedding is a slight piece in which Synge dramatized the comic predicament of a tinker woman, Sarah Casey, who wants to regularize, through marriage, her relationship with a man by whom she has had many children. But Synge, who in all his work reveals a profound distrust of established religion, seeks too patently to show the superiority of the tinkers' "natural" religion to that represented by the priest. The best feature of the play is the portrait of Sarah who, in her beauty and violence, anticipates *The Playboy*'s Pegeen Mike.

The Well of the Saints, a black comedy about two blind married beggars, Martin and Mary Doul, tells how their sight is restored by the Saint, how the two quarrel, drift apart, become blind again, and reject the chance of being "cured" again, thus abandoning the gross world of reality for a consciously chosen world of illusion. The play is notable for its brutality (which Synge thought essential for art), and for its views on the nature and relationship of illusion and reality.

The Playboy of the Western World is Synge's masterpiece, a masterpiece in its extravagant and provocative recreation of the Oedipal theme, in its dramatization of the clash between the world of dream and illusion (the Playboy's world) and the world of prosaic reality unredeemed by the imagination (the peasants' world), and in its rich use of colloquial West Ireland speech.

Interpretations of *The Playboy* are many: it has been viewed as an allegory of Synge's own growth as an artist; as a parody of Christ's ministry and Crucifixion; as an allegory of Ireland's subjection to the Church (Pegeen Mike will marry Shawn in accordance with the dispensation from Rome); as a successful translation (by Christy Mahon the Playboy) of dream into reality.

Contemporary Dublin audiences rioted when *The Playboy* was first presented by the Abbey Theatre, and it has been widely accepted that they did so outraged by Christy's image of Mayo girls naked under their shifts. But in fact audiences were offended by *The Playboy*'s deliberate glorification of parricide and its portrayal of degeneracy, violence, and betrayal.

It might seem that the epic story of Deirdre's tragic love for Naisi (they both know that she is destined to bring about the death of Naisi and his brothers) should have lain outside the scope of Synge's dramatic genius which, in his previous plays, had been concerned with Ireland's peasantry. But Synge characteristically demythologized his characters in order to make them more human in his *Deirdre of the Sorrows*. He recapitulates on a grand scale the themes and motifs that characterize Synge's *oeuvre*. Central to his work is the struggle between those forces that restrict human liberty and those energies that enhance it, and there is in all his work a deep sense of mortality linked to a pathetic reaching-out, by all his characters, for a finer destiny which seems always to be denied them.

—Eugene Benson

See also *Volume 1* entries on *Playboy of the Western World*; *Riders to the Sea*.

T

TAGORE, (Sir) Rabindranath. Born in Calcutta, India, 6 May 1861; son of Maharshi Tagore, grandson of Prince Tagore. Educated privately, and at University College, University of London, 1878–80. Married Mrinalinidebi in 1884; one son and one daughter. Began producing his own plays privately in Calcutta, in the 1880's. Managed family estates at Shileida from 1885; founder, 1889, and editor, 1894, *Sādhanā*; editor, *Bhārati*, 1898; founded the Santiniketan, a school to blend Eastern and Western philosophical/ educational systems (at which he directed students in productions of his plays in Bengali), Bolpur, Bengal, 1901, which later developed into the international institution Visva-Bharti; editor, *Bāngadarsham*, 1901–06; visited England, 1912; contributed regularly to the *Visvabharati Quarterly*; Hibbert lecturer, Oxford University, 1930. Painter from 1929: exhibitions in Moscow, Berlin, Munich, Paris, and New York. Recipient: Nobel Prize for Literature, 1913. D.Lit: University of Calcutta; Hindu University, Benares; University of Dacca; Osmania University, Hyderabad; D.Litt: Oxford University. Knighted, 1915: resigned knighthood in 1919 as protest against British policies in the Punjab. Wrote in Bengali and translated many of his own works into English. Died in Calcutta, August 1941.

Works (published/produced in English)

Collections

"Sacrifice" and Other Plays (includes *Malini; Sanyas, or, The Ascetic; The King and the Queen*). 1917.
Collected Poems and Plays (includes *"Sacrifice" and Other Plays*). 1936.
Three Plays (includes *Muktadhara; Natir Puja; Candalika*), translated by Marjorie Sykes. 1950.

Stage Works

The Post Office, from the Bengali *Daghar* (produced Abbey Theatre, Dublin, 1913). 1914.
Chitra, from the Bengali *Citrangada* (produced Prince of Wales Theatre, London, 1920). 1914.
The King of the Dark Chamber, from the Bengali *Raja*. 1914.
Malini (produced by the Indian Dramatic Society, Grafton Galleries, London, 1915). In *"Sacrifice" and Other Plays*, 1915.
The Cycle of Spring. 1917.
Sanyasi; or, The Ascetic, from the Bengali *Prakrtir Parisodh*. In *"Sacrifice" and Other Plays*, 1917.
The King and the Queen, from the Bengali *Raja o Rani* (produced by the Indian Dramatic Society, Comedy Theatre, London, 1919). In *"Sacrifice" and Other Plays*, 1917.
Sacrifice, from the Bengali *Visarjana* (produced King George's Hall, London, 1918). In *"Sacrifice" and Other Plays*, 1917.
The Fugitive. 1918.
The Mother's Prayer (produced Wigmore Hall, London, 1920). 1919.
Autumn Festival, from the Bengali *Saradotsava* (produced Wigmore Hall, London, 1920). 1920.
The Farewell Curse, from the Bengali *Viday-abhisap* (produced Wigmore Hall, London, 1920).
The Deserted Mother (produced Wigmore Hall, London, 1920).
The Sinner (produced Wigmore Hall, London, 1920).
Suttee (produced Wigmore Hall, London, 1920).
Trial by Luck (produced Wigmore Hall, London, 1921).
The Farewell (produced Devonshire Park Theatre, Eastbourne, Sussex, 1924).
Red Oleanders, from the Bengali *Raktu-Karabi*. 1925.
Worship of the Dancing Girl (produced Santiniketan School, Bolpur, 1925).
Karna and Kunti. In *Collected Poems and Plays*, 1936.
Muktadhara. In *Three Plays*, 1950.
Natir Puja. In *Three Plays*, 1950.
Canadalika. In *Three Plays*, 1950.
The Housewarming, from his Bengali story *Sesher Ratri*. In *"The Housewarming" and Other Selected Writings*, 1965.
Consequences, from his Bengali story *Karmaphal*. In *"The Housewarming" and Other Selected Writings*, 1965.

Fiction

Glimpses of Bengal Life (stories). 1913.
The Hungry Stones and Other Stories, translated by C.F. Andrews and others. 1916.
Mashi and Other Stories. 1918.
The Parrot's Training. 1918.
The Home and The World, translated by Surendranath Tagore. 1919.
The Wreck. 1921.
Gora. 1924.
Broken Ties and Other Stories. 1925.
Two Sisters, translated by Krishna Kripalani. 1943.
Farewell My Friend, with The Garden, translated by Krishna Kripalani. 1946.
Four Chapters, translated by Surendranath Tagore. 1950.
More Stories from Tagore. 1951.
Binodini, translated by Krishna Kripalani. 1959.
"The Runaway" and Other Stories, edited by Somnath Maitra. 1959.
Caturanga, translated by Asok Mitra. 1963.

Lipika, translated by Indu Dutt. 1969; translated by Aurobindo Bose, 1977.
The Broken Nest, translated by Mary Lago and Supriya Sen. 1971.

Verse

Gitanjali. 1912.
The Gardener. 1913.
The Crescent Moon: Child-Poems. 1913.
Fruit-Gathering. 1916.
Lover's Gift, and Crossing. 1918.
Poems. 1922.
The Curse at Farewell, translated by Edward Thompson. 1924.
Fireflies. 1928.
Fifteen Poems. 1928.
Sheaves: Poems and Songs, edited and translated by Nagendranath Gupta. 1929.
The Child. 1931.
The Golden Boat, translated by Chabani Bhattacharya. 1932.
Poems, edited by Krishna Kripalani. 1942.
A Flight of Swans, translated by Aurobindo Bose. 1955.
Syamali, translated by Sheila Chatterjee. 1955.
The Herald of Spring, translated by Aurobindo Bose. 1957.
Wings of Death: The Last Poems, translated by Aurobindo Bose. 1960.
Devouring Love, translated by Shakuntala Sastri. 1961.
A Bunch of Poems, translated by Monika Varma. 1966.
One Hundred and One. 1967.
Last Poems, translated by Shyamasree Devi and P. Lal. 1972.
Later Poems, translated by Aurobindo Bose. 1974.
Selected Poems, translated by William Radice. 1985.

Memoirs and Letters

My Reminiscences, translated by Surendranath Tagore. 1917.
Letters. 1917.
Letters from Abroad, edited by C.F. Andrews. 1924; revised edition, as *Letters to a Friend*, 1928.
My Boyhood Days. 1940.
Letters from Russia, translated by Sasadhar Sinha. 1960.

Other

Sadhana: The Realisation of Life. 1913.
Stray Birds (aphorisms). 1916.
Nationalism. 1917.
Personality: Lectures Delivered in America. 1917.
Greater India (lectures). 1921.
Thought Relics. 1921.
Creative Unity. 1922.
The Visvabharati, with C.F. Andrews. 1923.
Talks in China. 1925.
Lectures and Addresses, edited by Anthony X. Soares. 1928.
City and Village. 1928.
The Religion of Man. 1932.
Man (lectures). 1937.
Eighty Years, and Selections. 1941.
A Tagore Testament. 1953.
Our Universe, translated by Indu Dutt. 1958.
Tagore, Pioneer in Education: Essays and Exchanges Between Tagore and L.K. Elmhirst. 1961.

A Visit to Japan, translated by Shakuntala Shastri. 1961.
Towards Universal Man. 1961.
On Art and Aesthetics. 1961.
A Tagore Reader, edited by Amiya Chakravarty. 1961.
The Diary of Westward Voyage, translated by Indu Dutt. 1962.
On Rural Reconstruction. 1962.
The Cooperative Principle. 1963.
Boundless Sky (miscellany). 1964.
"The Housewarming" and Other Selected Writings, edited by Amiya Chakravarty. 1965.
Collected Essays, edited by Mary Lago and Ronald Warwick. 1989.

*

Bibliographies

Katherine Henn, *Rabindranath Tagore: A Bibliography*, Metuchen, New Jersey, 1985.
M. Kämpchen, *Rabindranath Tagore and Germany: A Bibliography*, Calcutta, 1991.

Criticism

Books:
E. Thompson, *Rabindranath Tagore: Poet and Dramatist*, London, 1926; revised edition, 1948.
A. Aronson, *Rabindranath Through Western Eyes*, Allahabad, 1943; revised edition, 1978.
Krishna Kripalani, *Rabindranath Tagore: A Biography*, London and New York, 1962; revised edition, Calcutta, 1980.
G.D. Khanolkar, *The Lute and the Plough: A Life of Rabindranath Tagore*, Bombay, 1963.
K.R. Srinivasa Iyengar, *Rabindranath Tagore: A Critical Introduction*, New Delhi, 1965; revised edition, 1986.
Sati Ghosh, *Rabindranath*, Calcutta, 1966.
Mulk Raj Anand, *The Volanco: Some Comments on the Development of Tagore's Aesthetic Theories*, 1968.
S.N. Hay, *Asian Ideas of East and West: Tagore and His Critics in Japan, China and India*, Cambridge, Massachusetts, 1970.
Birenda C. Chakravorty, *Rabindranath Tagore: His Mind and Art*, New Delhi, 1971.
S.K. Chatterjee, *World Literature and Tagore*, Santiniketan, 1971.
P.K. Mukherji, *Life of Rabindranath Tagore*, New Delhi, 1975.
Mary M. Lago, *Rabindranath Tagore*, Boston, 1976.
O.P. Mathur, "'Love's Lotus': A Study of the Protagonist in Tagore's Major Plays", in *Indo-English Literature: A Collection of Critical Essays*, edited by K.K. Sharma, Ghaziabad, 1977.
M.K. Naik and S. Mokashi-Punekar, *Perspectives on Indian Drama in English*, Madras, 1977.
Renuka Biwas (ed.), *On Tagore*, New York, 1984.
T.R. Sharma (ed.), *Perspective on Rabindranath Tagore*, Ghaziabad, 1986.
Sisirkumar Ghose, *Rabindranath Tagore*, New Delhi, 1986.
S. Krishna Bhatta, *Indian English Drama: A Critical Study*, London, 1987.
Andrew Robinson, *The Art of Rabindranath Tagore*, Calcutta, 1989.
Mary Lago and Ronald Warwick (eds.), *Tagore: Perspective in Time*, Basingstoke, 1989.

K.K. Sharma, *Rabindranath Tagore's Aesthetic Theories*, New Delhi, nd.

Articles:

Satyendranath Ghoshal, "Rabindranath Tagore and His Dramatic Genius", in *Patna University Journal*, vol. 22 no. 1, 1967.

Mohan L. Sharma, "Rabindranath Tagore as a Playwright", in *Modern Drama*, 13, 1970.

Sombhu Mitra, "Building from Tagore", in *Tulane Drama Review*, vol. 15 no. 2, 1971.

M.N. Sundararaman, "The Theme of Martyrdom in Three Plays of Tagore", in *Scholar Critic*, vol. 1 no. 1, 1981.

Yeong Yoo, "On Tagore's drama", in *Inmun Kwahāk: The Journal of Humanities*, vol. 48, 1982.

* * *

Although associated with the Bengal theatre, Tagore represents a broader Indian theatre for the Western world. As playwright, novelist, poet, actor, composer, singer, teacher, and theatre director—and most of all as an idealistic philosopher whose faith in the basic goodness of man guided his life—Tagore's work became a powerful inspiration for people everywhere who did not wish to have their mental horizons limited by lesser visions of temporal confinement. Governed by a supreme idealism, Tagore worked within the practical sphere, starting, in 1901 at Santiniketan, a school called the Institute for Rural Reconstruction, where he taught self expression of a transcendental character. Later, in 1927, he flouted the Hindu/Moslem prejudice against women appearing on stage by casting the female students from his university in his own play *Worship of the Dancing Girl*, and training them himself. Nowhere does Tagore argue more effectively the power of imaginative idealism over the limitations of practical traditions in the theatre than in an essay entitled "The Stage", written about 1905 and published in *The Drama* (November 1920). Rather than a contributive and co-operative art, the true poem, he explained—dramatic or otherwise—is completely independent and needs "none other than the understanding mind".

Best remembered for his poetic plays—most of them written in blank verse—Tagore showed the influence of the works of Kalidasa and the writings from the *Upanishads* in plays that revealed his own reactions to contemporary society. *The Genius of Valmiki*, based on the legend of the first epic poet of India, was his first musical drama. He himself acted the role of Valmiki. *Nature's Revenge*, sometimes called *Sanyasi; or, The Ascetic*, tells of an ascetic who shuts himself in a cave, proclaiming his mastery over self, and condemning worldly attitudes such as love and pity because of their human qualities. When an Untouchable girl clings to him, he runs away, afraid to become human, and on return finds her dead. He then realizes the concept of the great in the small, the infinite in the finite and the "eternal freedom of the soul in love". *Sacrifice* is both an indictment of the traditional Hindu ritual of animal sacrifice to please Kali, the goddess of death, and a veiled anti-war play. In *The King and the Queen*, Tagore presented a traditional theme known well in both Eastern and Western worlds: the conflict between love and duty.

In a number of his plays Tagore found his themes in stories from the great Indian epic, the *Mahabharata*, or from Buddhist legend. *Chitra*, a lyrical drama in blank verse which is considered by some to be Tagore's finest play, was taken in part from the *Mahabharata*, and it attracted particular attention in Tagore's production with its concentration on colored lights rather than painted scenery. *The Curse at Farewell*, also taken from the *Mahabharata*, dramatized once again the conflict of knowledge and duty versus love. In *Malini*, Tagore confronted the forces of Hindu orthodoxy with the challenge of compassion and universal love in the teachings of Buddha. Both *Worship of the Dancing Girl* and "The Untouchable Girl" (1933) were based on Buddhist legends.

In his later plays Tagore wrote in a more determined manner against oppression, stupidity, and violence. Institutions and political parties offered little hope for him, although he never lost his faith in the individual. "The Immovable" (1911) satirized Hindu society and mocked its absurd orthodoxies. "The Waterfall" (1922) was basically a tribute to Ghandi and his campaign of non-violence, but it also depicted the diabolical use of technology, symbolized by the Machine, to exploit colonial societies. *Red Oleanders* carries this concept further by dramatizing the fundamental issue of the free spirit of life opposed to the machine of an organized and highly industrialized society which turns men into robots and reduces them to numbers rather than names. But this oppressive society, which Tagore challenged in his plays, did not overshadow his balanced spirit. *Autumn Festival* has been described as a "hymn to the joy of living", and *The Cycle of Spring* is a delightful fantasy in which a King, finding a few grey hairs on his head, fears death and seeks comfort from the Court jester—originally played by Tagore—who diverts the King with a play about Old Man Winter who, pursued by a group of small boys who pull off his outer garments, is discovered to be none other than Spring.

One play by Tagore that has impressed a great number of Western writers is *The Post Office*, the story of a sick child, Amal. Custom demands that the sick boy avoid life, but Amal wants to learn from life—from the Dairyman who comes past his window and tells Amal that he has taught him "to be happy selling curds"; from the Watchman who tells him about the post office of the King who sends letters to little boys. Amal desperately wants a letter but is mocked by the Headman, an unpleasant authority figure. From a flower girl who makes Amal think of "some late star in the morning", Amal senses beauty; he finds joy in watching a group of boys playing, and gives them his toys as he prepares for sleep. Confined to his bed in Act II, Amal hears stories of the Parrot Isle where men are unimportant compared to nature. He now knows the route of the King's postman and feels his coming nearer as he wants to become the postman, the messenger who will wander "far and wide, delivering his message from door to door". Sleep finally comes to Amal; and the flower girl returns as she had promised. "When will he awake?", she asks; "directly the King comes and calls him", replies the physician, and the events of the play can be seen as an allegory for man seeking deliverance.

A startling simplicity underscores the beauty and depth of thought in Tagore's plays—a quality which greatly impressed the Irish poet-dramatist, W. B. Yeats and awakened the West to Tagore's genius. Although playwrights from the major areas of India are active today in creating largely socially realistic dramas, which speak to the temporal needs of a troubled society, no single Indian dramatist has appeared to continue Tagore's contribution to world theatre in a comparably sublime fashion.

—Walter J. Meserve

See also *Volume 1* entry on *The Post Office*.

TANG Xianzu. Courtesy name, Yireng; cognomen Ruoshi; old-age cognomen, Jianweng; studio name, Yu-ming-tang [Jade Tea Hall]. Born in Linchuan, Jiangxi province, China, 24 September 1550. Educated at the National University, Nanjing, 1576; obtained *jinshi* doctorate in imperial law exams, 1583. Was named Erudite of the Imperial Southern Grand Constancy Office, Nanjing, 1584; after criticism of government, demoted to post of local magistrate in Guangdong, 1591; promoted to magistrate in Zhejiang, 1593; returned to Linchuan, and thereby contrived his own dismissal, 1598; all his titles taken away, 1600. Died in Linchuan, 29 July 1616.

Works

Collections

Yu-ming-tang chuan-qi [Complete Collection].   1612.
Yu-ming-tang-ji [Collection].   1621.
Yu-ming-tang zhi meng-qu [Dream-Plays].   17th or 18th century (Qing Dynasty).
Tang Xianzu ji [Collected Works].   1961.
Tang Xianzu xiqu ji [Collected Plays].   1982.

Stage Works

Zi-xiao ji [Scarlet Flute].   1577–79.
Zi-chai ji [Scarlet Hairpin].   1587.
Mu-dan ting.   1598; translated as *Peony Pavilion*, 1980.
Nan-ke ji [Southern Axe-Handle].   1600.
Han-dan ji [Handan].   1601.

Verse

Hong-quan yi-cao [Red Spring Free Spirit Draft].   1575.
Yong-zao [Graceful Algae].   1576.
Wen-ji you cao [Question Briar Mail-Halt Draft].   1579.

Other

Yu-ming-tang wen-ji [Collected Prose].   Before 1616.

*

Criticism

Books:
C.T. Hsia, "Time and the Human Condition in the Plays of T'ang Hsien-t'su", in *Self and Society in Ming Thought*, edited by W.T. de Bary, New York, 1970.
C. Birch, "Some Concerns and Methods of the Ming 'ch'uan ch'i' Drama", in *Studies in Chinese Literary Genres*, edited by W.T. de Bary, Berkeley, California, 1974.

* * *

Nearly contemporaneous with Shakespeare, Tang Xianzu came from a noted scholarly family and was acquainted with many of the main intellects of his age. He took the triennial imperial civil service exams for the *jinshi* "doctorate" in Peking, but failed each of the four times he tried, having fallen foul of the Principal Grand Counsellor, Zhang Juzheng (1525–82). It wasn't until after Zhang's death that he was successful in the exams and became a mandarin. He was closely associated with the literatus opposition to the established imperial government to such an extent that his first play, *Zi-xiao ji* (Scarlet Flute), was suspected of being anti-government, and banned. Revising the play, he gave it the new title of *Zi-chai ji* (Scarlet Hairpin). When he openly memorialised the throne with devastating criticisms of the late Zhang Juzheng and the current premier, Shen Shixing (1535–1614), he was banished to be a mere county police magistrate and jail warden, at the lowest mandarin rank.

Later appointed magistrate of Sichang in present Zhejiang province, Tang Xianzu held the post for five years, running a kindly administration, but, faced with the imminent visit of rapacious tax officials, returned to Linchuan, thus contriving his dismissal. His principled opposition to corrupt administration well matches the love of human freedom and individual liberty so evident in his writings.

All Tang Xianzu's plays are marked by a scintillating lyrical style, great wit, and poetry of rich intricacy and finesse. Often we see the impulsive generosity of attitude that we know to have been a large part of his own nature. He lived in a merry disordered condition among books and friends, finding much serenity in leisurely barding. The dreams depicted in his four plays, three ultimately based on novellas of the Tang dynasty (618–907) and another on a later short-story, allowed great scope for his unbounded imagination.

"Scarlet Flute" survives as 34 acts, perhaps about half of the intended plot. A love story with supernatural aspects, even its dialogue was written in an elaborate, euphuistic prose style. All the same, as the episodes were completed they were eagerly seized by first-rate actors and performed to huge audiences, "as many as ten thousand people", with great success. The revision, "Scarlet Hairpin", ran to 53 acts and created a much more complex and lively development of the plot.

In *Mu-dan ting (Peony Pavilion)*, in 55 acts, and one of the most celebrated of all Chinese plays, the heroine dreams of her lover and pines away. In real life, he, a stranger, falls in love with her portrait, not knowing who she is. Her spirit returns from the Underworld, makes love to him, and is then restored to her body and mortal life. They marry, and after many vicissitudes achieve family acceptance and happiness. The play is an outpouring of subtle and exquisite emotions, interspersed with much sparkling and frolicsome humour, plenty of action, and much incomparable poetry. Parts of the play were attractively performed in Britain by a Kunju troupe in 1987, and Cyril Birch produced a superb complete translation in 1980, a first-ever achievement as regards satisfactory renderings of the longer Chinese dramas into English.

The 30-act *Han-dan ji* (Handan) and 44-act *Nan-ke ji* (Southern Axe-Handle), both about enlightening dreams, and dealing respectively with Taoist and Buddhist rejections of the mundane human career world, chime in with Tang's championing of emotion over reasoning, and with his increasing interest in philosophies of withdrawal during his later years.

Tang Xianzu's contemporary and subsequent fame has been very great. Certain dramatists who followed aspects of his style in those times were, with limited accuracy, termed the Linchuan School or Jade Tea Hall School. Another creative giant, Shen Jing (1553–1610), criticised his plays for their supposed musical shortcomings, failing to recognise the worth of deliberate innovations. Shen Defu (1578–1642) said that *Peony Pavilion* was recited from house to house, almost surpassing China's most famous play of all times, *Xi-xiang ji* (*West Wing*), by the 13th-century Wang Shifu, in its popularity, and talked of Tang's "plentiful immortal genius". Lü Tiancheng (fl. c.1573–1619) called Tang "the greatest genius of all time" and "the master song-craftsman of this thousand years". And indeed, his influence on the literature of later ages was strong.

—William Dolby

TARDIEU, Jean. Born in Saint-Germain-de-Joux, France, 1 November 1903. Raised in Paris from 1905. Educated at Lycée Condorcet and the Sorbonne, both Paris. Married Marie-Laure Blot in 1932; one daughter. First poetry published in *Nouvelle Revue Française*, 1927; editor, Hachette publishers, 1939; drafted into the French forces, 1939–40; involved with the underground press during the German occupation of France, 1941–44; head of drama, 1944–45, director of Club d'Essai experimental drama studio, 1945–60, programme director ("France Musique"), 1954–64, and council member, 1964–74, all for Radiodiffusion-Télévision Française (RTF); first-produced play, *Qui est là?*, staged 1949. Recipient: Grand Prix de Poésie de l'Académie-Française, 1972; Prix de la Critique, 1976; Grand Prix de Théâtre (Society of Playwrights), 1979; Grand Prix de Poésie de la Ville de Paris, 1981; Grand Prix de la Société des Gens de Lettres, 1983 and 1986; SACEM Grand Prix, 1989. Officier, Légion d'Honneur. Commandeur de l'Ordre des Arts et des Lettres.

Works

Collections

Théâtre de chambre. 1955; augmented edition (includes *Qui est là; La Politesse inutile; Le Sacre de la nuit; Le Meuble; La Serrure; Le Guichet; Monsieur Moi; Faust et Yorick; La Sonate et les trois messieurs; La Société Apollon; Oswald et Zénaïde; Ce que parler veut dire; Il y avait foule au manoir; Eux seuls le savent; Un Mot pour un autre; Un Geste pour un autre; Conversation-sinfonietta*), 1966.
Théâtre 2: Poèmes à jouer. 1960; augmented edition (includes *L'A.B.C. de notre vie; Rythme à trois temps; Une Voix sans personne; Les Temps du verbe; Les Amants du métro; Tonnerre sans orage; Des Arbres et des hommes; Trois Personnes entrées dans des tableaux; Malédictions d'une Furie*), 1969.
"The Underground Lovers" and Other Experimental Plays (includes *Who Goes There?; Courtesy Doesn't Pay; The Contraption; The Enquiry Office; Mr. Me; Faust and Yorick; The Sonata and the Three Gentlemen; The Apollo Society; The Crowd Up at the Manor; They Alone Knew; Conversation-Sinfonietta*). 1968.
Théâtre 3: Une Soirée en Provence (includes *Une Soirée en Provence* and other radio plays; *Un Clavier pour un autre; Souper; Le Club Archimède*). 1975.
Théâtre 4: "La Cité sans sommeil" et autres pièces (includes *Le Rite du premier soir, ou, Le Petit Voleur; Pénombre et chuchotements; L'Épouvantail; De Quoi s'agit-il?, ou, La Méprise; La Galerie, ou, Comment parler peinture; Un Film d'art et d'aventures, ou, L'Art à la portée de tous*). 1984.

Stage works

Qui est là? (produced by Théâtre du Foyer, Antwerp, 1949). In *Théâtre de chambre*, 1966; translated as *Who Goes There?*, in *The Underground Lovers* (collection), 1968.

Jean Tardieu (1954).

La Politesse inutile (produced Brussels, 1950). In *Théâtre de chambre*, 1966; translated as *Courtesy Doesn't Pay*, in *The Underground Lovers* (collection), 1968.
Un Mot pour un autre (produced Théâtre Agnès-Capri, Paris, 1950). In *Théâtre de chambre*, 1966.
Faust et Yorick (as *Mi-figure, mi-raisin*, produced by Compagnie Michel de Ré, Paris, 1951). In *Théâtre de chambre*, 1966; translated as *Faust and Yorick*, in *The Underground Lovers* (collection), 1968.
Oswald et Zénaïde (produced by Compagnie Michel de Ré, Paris, 1951). In *Théâtre de chambre*, 1966.
Ce que parler veut dire (produced by Compagnie Michel de Ré, Paris, 1951). In *Théâtre de chambre*, 1966.
Il y avait foule au manoir (produced by Compagnie Michel de

Ré, Paris, 1951). In *Théâtre de chambre*, 1966; translated as *The Crowd up at the Manor*, in *The Underground Lovers* (collection), 1968.

Un Geste pour un autre (produced by Compagnie Michel de Ré, Paris, 1951). In *Théâtre de chambre*, 1966.

Conversation-sinfonietta (produced by Compagnie Michel de Ré, Paris, 1951). In *Théâtre de chambre*, 1966; translated as *Conversation-Sinfionietta*, in *The Underground Lovers* (collection), 1968.

Eux seuls le savent (produced by Compagnie Michel de Ré, Paris, 1952). In *Théâtre de chambre*, 1966; translated as *They Alone Knew*, in *The Underground Lovers* (collection), 1968.

Les Amants du métro (produced Théâtre Lancry, Paris, 1952). In *Théâtre 2*, 1969; translated as *The Underground Lovers*, in *The Underground Lovers* (collection), 1968.

Le Meuble (produced by Compagnie Jean Ber, Bienne, 1954). In *Théâtre de chambre*, 1966; translated as *The Contraption*, in *The Underground Lovers* (collection), 1968.

La Serrure (produced Théâtre de la Huchette, Paris, 1955). In *Théâtre de chambre*, 1966.

Le Guichet (produced Théâtre de la Huchette, Paris, 1955). In *Théâtre de chambre*, 1966; translated as *The Enquiry Office*, in *The Underground Lovers* (collection), 1968.

La Sonate et les trois messieurs (produced Théâtre de la Huchette, Paris, 1955). In *Théâtre de chambre*, 1966; translated as *The Sonata and the Three Gentlemen*, in *The Underground Lovers* (collection), 1968.

La Société Apollon (produced Théâtre de la Huchette, Paris, 1955). In *Théâtre de chambre*, 1966; translated as *The Apollo Society*, in *The Underground Lovers* (collection), 1968.

Une Voix sans personne (produced Théâtre de la Huchette, Paris, 1956). In *Théâtre 2*, 1969.

Les Temps du verbe (produced Théâtre de la Huchette, Paris, 1956). In *Théâtre 2*, 1969.

Rythme à trois temps (produced Paris, 1969).

L'A.B.C. de notre vie (produced Théâtre d'Alliance Française, Paris, 1959). In *Théâtre 2*, 1969.

Monsieur Moi (produced in English, as *Mr. Me*, London, 1972). In *Théâtre de Chambre*, 1966; translated as *Mr. Me*, in *The Underground Lovers . . .* (collection), 1968.

Tonnere sans orage. In *Théâtre 2*, 1969.

Des arbres et des hommes. In *Théâtre 2*, 1969.

Trois Personnes entrées dans des tableaux. In *Théâtre 2*, 1969.

Malédictions d'une Furie. In *Théâtre 2*, 1969.

Joyeux retour, music by Marius Constant (produced as *Le Souper*, Festival de Besançon, Arc-et-Senans, 1969). In *Théâtre 3*, 1975.

Un Clavier pour un autre, music by Claude Arrieu (produced Opéra d'Avignon, 1971). In *Théâtre 3*, 1975.

Le Club d'Arthur (libretto). In *Théâtre 3*, 1975.

La Cité sans sommeil (produced as *The Sleepless City*, La Mama Experimental Theatre, New York, 1987). In *Théâtre 4*, 1984; translated as *The Sleepless City*, in *The Paris Stage: Recent Plays*, 1988.

Le Rite du premier soir; ou, Le Petit Voleur. In *Théâtre 4*, 1984.

Pénombre et chuchotements. In *Théâtre 4*, 1984.

L'Épouvantail. In *Théâtre 4*, 1984.

De Quoi s'agit-il?; ou, La Méprise. In *Théâtre 4*, 1984.

La Galerie; ou, Comment parler peinture. In *Théâtre 4*, 1984.

Un Film d'art et d'aventures; ou, L'Art à portée de tous. In *Théâtre 4*, 1984.

La Comédie de la comédie. With *La Comédie des arts*, 1990.

La Comédie des arts. With *La Comédie de la comédie*, 1990.

L'Archipel sans nom. 1991.

Radio Plays

Candide, from the story by Voltaire, 1944 (published in *Théâtre 3*, 1975); *Une Soirée en Provence, Une Consultation, Les Mots inutiles, L'Île des lents et l'île des vifs, Le Style enfantin, Les Oreilles de Midas* (all published in *Théâtre 3*, 1975).

Verse

Le Fleuve caché   1933.

Accents.   1939.

Le Témoin invisible.   1943.

Poèmes.   1944.

Les Dieux étouffés.   1946.

Le Démon de l'irréalité.   1946.

Jours pétrifiés.   1948.

Monsieur monsieur.   1951.

Une Voix sans personne (includes prose).   1954.

L'Espace et la flûte, illustrated by Picasso.   1958.

Histoires obscures.   1961.

Choix de poèmes (1924–1954).   1961.

Le Fleuve caché (Poésies 1938–1961).   1968.

Formeries.   1976; translated as *Formeries*, 1983.

Comme ceci, comme cela.   1979.

L'Accent grave et l'accent aigu: Poèmes 1976–1983.   1986.

Margeries: Poèmes inédits 1940–1985.   1986.

The River Underground: Selected Poems and Prose, translated by David Kelley.   1991.

Other

Figures.   1944.

Bazaine, Estève, Lapicque, with André Frénaud and Jean Lescure.   1945.

Il était une fois, deux fois, trois fois.   1947.

La Première Personne du singulier.   1952.

Farouche à quatre feuilles, with others.   1954.

De La Peinture abstraite.   1960.

Hollande.   1963.

Pages d'écriture.   1967.

Les Portes de toile.   1969.

Grandeurs et faibleses de la radio.   1969.

La Part de l'ombre.   1972.

Obscurité du jour.   1974.

Bazaine, with Jean-Claude Schneider and Viveca Bosson.   1975.

"Les Tours de Trébizonde" et autres textes.   1983.

Causeries devant la fenêtre (interviews), with Jean-Pierre Vallotton.   1988.

La Prononciation de l'anglais.   1989.

On vient chercher Monsieur Jean.   1990.

*

Criticism

Books:

Martin Esslin, *The Theatre of the Absurd*, London, 1962; revised editions, 1968 and 1980.

Leonard C. Pronko, *The Experimental Theatre in France*, Berkeley, California, 1962.

George E. Wellwarth, *The Theatre of Protest and Paradox*, New York, 1964.

E. Noulet, *Jean Tardieu*, Paris, 1964; revised edition, 1978.

Sidney L. Pellissier, "Avant-Garde Theater and Musical Forms: Jean Tardieu's Attempt at Fusion of the Arts", in *French Literature and the Arts*, edited by Phillip Grant, Columbia, South Carolina. 1978.

Edmond Kinds, *Jean Tardieu; ou, l'énigme d'exister*, Brussels, 1973.

Sylvie D. Henning, "The Theater of Jean Tardieu: Experiments in the Grotesque", in *Savage Comedy: Structures of Humor*, edited by Kenneth S. White, Amsterdam, 1978.

Eugène Schwarz, *Musikananaloge Idee und Struktur im französischen Theater: Untersuchungen zu Jean Tardieu und Eugène Ionesco*, Munich, 1981.

Paul Vernois, *La Dramaturgie poétique de Jean Tardieu*, Paris, 1984.

Jean Onimus, *Jean Tardieu: Un Rire inquiet*, Seyssel, 1985.

J.-Y. Debreuille (ed.), *Lire Tardieu*, Lyons, 1988.

Articles:

C. Evans, "The New Dramatists, 6: Temporal Aesthetics and the Dramaturgy of Jean Tardieu", in *Drama Survey*, vol.2 no.3, 1963.

Sylvie D. Henning, "Jean Tardieu and the Structure of the Grotesque", in *Romance Notes*, 19, 1978.

Nancy Lane, "Surrealism and the Theater of Jean Tardieu", in *South Atlantic Review*, November 1987.

Marilyn Sparks Severson, "An Introduction to the Theatre of Jean Tardieu", in *European Studies Journal*, vol.5 no.1, 1988.

* * *

Jean Tardieu's first "dramatic poems" were published in *L'arbalète* in 1946. *Qui est là?* and *La Politesse inutile* mark the beginnings of his quest for a new dramaturgical style. *Qui est là?* was performed in Anvers, and *Un Mot pour un autre* in Paris in 1949. Although he has been called an absurdist, Tardieu never joined any movement or school. He was not associated with the surrealists, nor does he consider himself to be part of what Martin Esslin calls the "theatre of the absurd". He is the predecessor of Eugène Ionesco in the investigation of what he calls "la comédie du langage" and "la comédie de la comédie". Despite the emphasis on the word "comedy", Tardieu's work reveals a fundamentally anguished apprehension. As he states in his 1924 poem, "L'écran-langage", language is a tool to scrutinize language. A screen may hide or protect, but it is also used to project images, to reflect. As Tardieu writes in the same poem, "my language looks to make sure that language is looking at language". In his foreword to *Margeries*, the "marginal" poems written throughout his lifetime, Tardieu explains that "a soft, secret voice, which spoke to me throughout my life, commanded that I seek to 'translate' the unknown language that this confusing world allows us to hear without yielding its key".

The "absolute precursor" of this new theatre is Tardieu's ironic hypostasis, Professor Froeppel, "who carried out his research between 1944 and 1947". Pretending to be the editor of his posthumous *oeuvre*, Tardieu explains that Froeppel has kept clear of all the linguistic and philosophic movements of his time, devoting himself to the exploration of the "infinitely small", such as stammering, interjections, exclamations, onomatopoetic inventions, childish babbling, erotic twittering, "the conjugal and concubinal" lexicon, as well as gestural language, particularly that of a subconscious nature. These infra-signs constitute a parallel language to the one we associate with communication, constituting "a semiotics of failed acts", of unexpressed desires and longings, a language close to that of dumb animals or even plants. Tardieu's Froeppel is a biologist, a zoologist, and an anthropologist rolled into one. He is the author of several "posthumously" published plays: *Un Mot pour un autre*, *Les Mots inutiles*, *Finissez Vos Phrases*, and *De Quoi s'agit-il?*. Froeppel/Tardieu's plays are characterized by the fact that the only *dramatis persona* is language itself. The first play is written in an invented tongue, words distorted in such a way that one is able to substitute for each one a familiar term. "Every poet", Tardieu says, "wishes to substitute a word for another". Words, he claims, take us towards unexpected places, invite us to dream.

In *Finissez Vos Phrases* there are no substitutions, but every line remains suspended, unfinished. Yet Monsieur A and Madame B understand one another perfectly; they are able to complete in their minds what their interlocutor is saying. Moreover, when they sit down at the *terrasse* of a café, their waiter adopts at once their form of expression. The less the couple resorts to traditional forms of communication, the closer they get. The play culminates in ecstatic babble, the language of love which is beyond language.

Tardieu's early work was collected in *Théâtre de chambre I*, to be followed by *Théâtre II: Poèmes à jouer*. Interspersed among the light-hearted comedies of the first volume, there are three particularly sombre tragicomedies: *Le Meuble* (*The Contraption*), *La Serrure*, and *Le Guichet* (*The Enquiry Office*).

Le Meuble consists of a monologue by the inventor of an invisible (off-stage) piece of furniture addressed to an equally invisible potential buyer. Tardieu specifies in his stage directions that the buyer can also be introduced on the stage, but must remain silent, looking intently across the stage in the direction of the object. The latter can be all things to all men. Its creator, who states that he has spent 25 years building and perfecting it, lists its numerous features: it can produce a dozen oysters, a musical composition, the solution of an algebraic problem, a stereoscopic landscape, a spray of perfume, legal advice, even a feather-duster. In fact, following the pressing of some buttons that spell out the desired article, a mechanical arm emerges from behind the half-closed curtain proffering this modest household tool. An ironic contrast is established between the loud clanging and rasping of the invisible machine, and the ordinariness of what it produces. Long before the proliferation of computers Tardieu was satirizing our technological achievements. A give-away to Tardieu's point can be found in the inventor's statement that this piece of furniture can be traced back to the 18th century, the optimistic Age of Enlightenment and Reason. Very quickly into this short sketch, the audience is made to realize that the machine is not working correctly. Its jumbled recitation of a poem suggests Molière's Monsieur Jourdain's letter to his "belle marquise". The inventor is horrified, blaming the malfunction on the fact that he has overworked his machine. Furious, he rushes behind the curtain, allowing us still to see part of his back as he pummels and kicks his *oeuvre* (Tardieu is also poking fun at all creators, including poets and playwrights). Emerging from this battle, the master-creator promises something wondrous. He urges the "client" to close his eyes. Once again an arm emerges from behind the curtain; this time it is armed with a revolver. A shot is heard. If the client is on the stage, he is seen dropping dead. The sketch ends, as it began, with the old-fashioned sound of an organ-grinder. So much for technological wonders. This capsule of a playlet asks fundamental questions about so-called progress and its lethal effect upon humanity.

The next playlet, *La Serrure*, is informed by the infernal

vision of Baudelaire, that reflected in "Une Charogne". There are only two characters in this brief sketch—the madame of a very special house of prostitution (the French call it "une maison de rendez-vous") and a client. The latter has come to catch a glimpse through a large keyhole of the woman he adores. The audience never sees the man's "lady love". It simply hears his fervent, then horrified description as he bends down to peer through the hole. The madame, who later discreetly disappears, expresses herself in terms of coarse innuendoes. The "lover" speaks the impassioned language of a knight or a troubadour. He does not aspire to possessing the lady of his dreams; he merely wishes to see her denude herself. At the promised hour of six, a tiny alarm tinkles through the closed double door. The client approaches the keyhole and is at first filled with awe and delight. The lady takes off her garments one by one. The lover trembles with delight, erotic bliss. Then something peculiar begins to happen: the lady not content with stripping goes further, and begins to peel off her flesh, baring her skeleton. The lover watches with mounting horror the allegorical figure of Death moving in the direction of the door, closer to him. As he shouts "Je viens!", he falls down in a swoon, or dead. This is the supreme *Liebestod*.

The third and final sketch of *La Triple Mort du client*, *Le Guichet*, is the most terrifying. Again there are only two characters—a clerk in an information office and a "client". The latter has come to seek some relevant information about trains he might take "to embrace for the last time his aged uncle in Aix-en-Provence" or his dying cousin in Brest. He finds that his query is not being answered; in fact he has come under questioning. The *locus* of the office is uncertain. At first it seems to be a train station (we hear a loudspeaker announcing departures), then it appears to be a marriage bureau. As the investigation takes its course, we are introduced to every banal detail of this man's existence. Filled with "metaphysical anguish", he compares himself to Dostoevsky's "underground man". These philosophical speculations lead to the ultimate question: "When am I going to die?". The clerk answers: "As soon as you exit". The question and the answer render all the previous questions and answers irrelevant. The client departs, and we hear a car horn, the screeching of brakes, and a cry of pain, but these sounds become drowned by a popular song over the radio. The clerk resumes rummaging through his papers.

Had Tardieu written nothing else, this brief trilogy would suffice to establish him as one of the leading practitioners of the metaphysical farce.

If the actors needed in the three playlets that constitute *La Triple Mort du client* are few (one for the first, two for the others), an ultimate reduction characterizes *Une Voix sans personne*. Staged at the tiny Left-Bank theatre of La Huchette, this play shows the empty living-room of an abandoned country house. Two voices can be heard—that of a man standing at one side of the stage, out of the lights' range, looking at the room (his voice is to be depersonalized since it has been pre-recorded), and that of a woman, who could be one of many women (a mother, a sister, a sweetheart, a wife), laughing, calling, occasionally humming. The décor is an interior, somewhat like those of the painter Vuillard, which reminds us that Tardieu's father was an Impressionist painter. The shadowy presence might be that of a son who has returned to the empty house to people it with his memories, or who is, perhaps, in some other space, dreaming, recalling. The carefully orchestrated text, a Mallarméan stage poem about absence and death, is as eloquent as the mute sofas and armchairs placed in a circle. Included later in *Théâtre II: Poèmes à jouer*, *Une Voix sans personne* serves as the perfect

transition between the poetry of Tardieu and his radio plays collected in *Théâtre III: Une Soirée en Provence*.

Une Soirée en Provence, a radio play "in four movements", has, once again, two characters, or interlocutors, A and B. A is proud of his quasi-Buddhist detachment, whereas B is passionately connected to everyday life. However, both agree that they are "imaginary beings", nameless voices to be heard over the air waves. The radio plays are, indeed, essentially musical.

Loss, death, and the language—spoken and gestural—in which to convey them may the principal subjects of Tardieu, but he is also a troubadour, the bard of love. His lovers struggle to remain joined in the midst of a cruel, indifferent society. Such is the fate of Elle and Lui, the protagonists of *Les Amants du métro* (*The Underground Lovers*), "a comic ballet without dance or music".

The ballet is divided into two "tableaux", composed of numerous vignettes. Seven actors interpret the roles of 23 anonymous subway passengers who come and go, jostle each other, but try to avoid bodily contact. Tardieu specifies that "the total impression is that of a kind of ballet in which reality is conveyed by pure rhythmic patterns". The two lovers, the only individualized characters, are caught in this faceless crowd. Separated in the tightly packed subway car, they must pass the "obstacles" of various people—the newspaper reader, the offended lady, the understanding working man, the movie star, a mannequin, and finally the individual melting in the crowd: these are veritable rites of passage. Finally reunited, the lovers exit from the car and waltz away in perfect unison.

This touching couple reappears in Tardieu's recent play, *La Cité sans sommeil* (*The Sleepless City*). This full-length drama in three acts (Tardieu calls them "tableaux") is an abstractly political dream play. It presents a society ruled by a dictator who has decreed that no one in his city should sleep; people will work around the clock. Anyone caught falling asleep will be put to death. Here the two young lovers will finally save the city by the power of their love.

The cruel state of sleeplessness unleashes all the monsters of the subconscious. The city is suddenly surrounded and slowly invaded by all manner of grotesque, menacing creatures. While this is taking place, Paola (the female half of the couple) finds that she is unable to keep her eyes open; she is constantly falling asleep. Mario, her lover, tries to keep her awake by moving her through graceful dance steps, but most of the time he is carrying an unconscious body. Suddenly, at the very moment when the couple is surrounded by armed guards, it is reported that the monsters are drawing back. Clearly, Paola's deep sleep, and the profound love between the two young people have saved the people. The dictator and his wife are arrested; the inhumane system will be replaced by an order based on the acceptance of nature and the reign of love.

The world premiere of *The Sleepless City* took place in New York in 1987. Jean Tardieu composed this play, his crowning work, when he was in his 80's. To this writer he said, "as a playwright, I am *un écrivain maudit*". He feels, with complete justification, that he has not yet been discovered by his countrymen, that he has remained a peripheral writer. The time will come, however, when he will be recognized as the creator of the metaphysical farce, and as one of the great writers of our century. If he is seen as marginal, he has made of the margin the very *locus* of imaginative life.

—Rosette C. Lamont

TASSO, Torquato. Born in Sorrento, territory of Naples, 11 March 1544. Son of the poet Bernardo Tasso. Educated at a Jesuit school in Naples; at Court of Urbino by his father, 1557–60; studied law at University of Padua, 1560–62, and in Bologna, 1562–64; joined Accademia degli Eterei (under Scipione Gonzaga), Padua, 1564–65. In household of Cardinal Luigi d'Este, Ferrara, 1565–70, and Paris, 1570–71; in Duke Alfonso d'Este's household, 1572–78; his play *Aminta* produced in the garden of Belvedere Palace, on an island in the Po river near Ferrara, 1573; fearful of persecution, fled to Sorrento, 1577, and on to Rome, Mantua, Padua, and Venice, returning to Ferrara for medical treatment, 1579; confined as insane in the hospital of Sant'Anna, 1579–86: released into care of the Duke of Mantua, and spent remaining years wandering through Italy, to Naples, Rome, Florence, and Mantua; granted pension by Pope Clement VIII, 1595. Died in Rome, 25 April 1595.

Works

Collections

Opere. 1722–36.

Stage Works

Aminta (produced Belvedere Palace, Belvedere Island in the River Po, 1573). 1581; translated in *The Countess of Pembroke's Ivychurch*, 1591; as *Aminta*, 1628; as *Amyntas*, 1900.
Il Re Torrismondo. 1586.
Intrighi d'amore (produced 1598). 1604.

Verse

Rinaldo. 1562; translated as *Rinaldo*, 1792.
Gerusalemme liberata. 1580 (as *Il Goffredo*); complete version, 1581; revised edition, 1581; translated by Edward Fairfax as *Godfrey of Bouillon: The Recovery of Jerusalem*, 1600, and by Joseph Tusiani as *Jerusalem Delivered*, 1970.
Gerusalemme conquistata. 1593.
Le sette giornate del mondo creato. 1607; translated as *Creation of the World*, 1982.
Tasso's Sonnets, translated by Charles Chorley. 1867.
Later Work of Torquato Tasso, translated by Henry Cloriston. 1907.
Opere minori in versi, edited by Angelo Solerti (3 vols.). 1891–95.
Rime, edited by Angelo Solerti (3 vols.). 1898–1902.

Memoirs and Letters

Lettere, edited by Cesare Guasti (5 vols.). 1852–55.

Other

Rime e prose. 1581.
Discorsi dell'arte poetica (lecture). 1587; revised version, as *Discorsi del poema eroico*, 1594; translated as *Discourses on the Heroic Poem*, 1973.
Prose diverse, edited by Cesare Guasti (2 vols.). 1875.
Tales from Tasso, translated by G. Grinnell Milne. 1909.
Dialoghi, edited by Ezio Raimondi. (3 vols.). 1958; as *Tasso's Dialogues: A Selection, with Discourse on the Art of the Dialogue*, edited by Carnes Lord and Dain A. Trafton, 1983.

*

Bibliographies

A. Tortoreto and J.G. Fucilla, *Bibliografia analitica tassiana*, Milan, 1935; supplements: A Tortoreto, "Nuovi studii su Torquato Tasso: Bibliografia analitica 1931–1945", in *Aevum*, 20, 1946; updated bibliographies in *Studii tassiani* from 1952.
B. Basile, "Rassegna di studii tassiani 1970–1980", in *Lettere italiane*, July–September 1981.

Criticism

Books:
William Boulting, *Tasso and His Times*, London, 1907.
G. Getto, *Interpretazione del Tasso*, Naples, 1951; revised edition, 1967.
B.T Sozzi, *Studi sul Tasso*, Pisa, 1954.
L. Caretti, *Ariosto e Tasso*, Turin, 1961; second edition, 1973.
B.T. Sozzi, *Nuovi studi sul Tasso*, Bergamo, 1963.
C.P. Brand, *Torquato Tasso: A Study of the Poet and of His Contribution to English Literature*, Cambridge, 1965.
F. Ulivi, *Il manirismo del Tasso e altri studi*, Florence, 1966.
F. Bruni, *Prospettive sul Tasso*, Naples, 1969.
A. Moretti, *Torquato Tasso*, Bari, 1973.
C. Varese, *Torquato Tasso*: *Epos, parola, scena*, Messina, 1976.
G. Baldassarri, *Tasso*, Turin, 1979.
F. Pittorru, *Torquato Tasso: L'uomo, il poeta, il cortigiano*, Milan, 1982.

Serials:
Studi tassiani, 1951—

*   *   *

If Tasso had not written his masterpiece, the long and influential poem, *Gerusalemme liberata*, he would still be remembered for his pastoral play *Aminta*, the most famous work of its kind, which has frequently been translated into several languages, and the first English translation of which goes back to 1591. Though he also wrote another play *Il Re Torrismondo*, a tragedy, and is supposed to have written *Intrighi d'amore*, a comedy, it is largely by virtue of *Aminta* that Tasso claims his place as a playwright.

Aminta is a pastoral play in five acts. It was performed in the same year as it was composed, in the Island of Belvedere on the Po river, near Ferrara. Through a masterly blend of the idyllic and the sensuous, the pastoral and the courtly, Tasso brings out the best that pastoral literature could achieve. The plot is fairly simple and straightforward. Aminta, the shepherd, falls in love with Silvia, who is primarily interested in hunting and, in spite of goadings from her friend, Dafne, doesn't entertain Aminta's advances of love. But one day when Nerina, a hunting companion of Silvia, tells Aminta that she has seen wolves hovering upon Silvia's blood-stained garments, he concludes she has died, and in a moment of despair throws himself from a precipice. When Silvia, who was, in fact, alive, comes to know about this, she bursts into tears, confesses her love for Aminta and throws herself upon his dead body. But, as luck would have it, Aminta wasn't really dead; he was only wounded. This means that the two can now love one another and get married, which is how the story ends.

Though cast in a dramatic mould, *Aminta*, with imitations of or echoes from Theocrites, Moschus, and Anacreonte, as well as Virgil, Ovid, and Propertius, is both an idealization of courtly life and a lyric celebration of pastoral love in the context of idyllic nature—a celebration conditioned neither by the exigencies of time or place, nor by those of everyday reality. In this respect it embodies and gives vent to Tasso's nostalgia as well as that of his century for the Golden Age. It can therefore be considered, as Sapegno considers it, "a form of literary autobiography". However, the play is not only lacking in dramatic action, but also in moral and psychological tension, though it makes up for it through a pervasively mystical, as well as impassioned, tone and a musical effusiveness—the result of what Carducci was to call the "harmony between inspiration and expression". Leigh Hunt, who translated *Aminta* into English, prefaced his translation, which he dedicated to Keats, with a perceptive and enthusiastic introduction in which he praised the play's "brief and touching simplicity": "the action is simple, the incidents necessary and happily interwoven; the images—all rural and proper; the events at once new, unexpected and natural".

Il Re Torrismondo, on the other hand, is a classical tragedy in five acts, the plot of which is based on Sophocles's *Oedipus Rex*. In 1573 Tasso had written the first draft of this tragedy, consisting of the first complete and the second incomplete act, and it was called *Galealto Re di Norvegia*. In 1583, when he completed the work, he entitled it *Il Re Torrismondo*. Instead of the zest, spontaneity, and happiness of innocent and youthful love, we have here the frustration, disillusionment, and bitterness of mature love. The King of the Goths, being aware of the prophecy that his daughter, Alvida, will bring about the ruin of his kingdom and the death of her own brother, Torrismondo, sends her away from his house and substitutes for her Rosmunda, Alvida's wet nurse's daughter. After many vicissitudes, Alvida comes to be adopted by the King of Norway, and ends up by marrying Torrismondo. It is Rosmunda who reveals to Torrismondo her own identity and that of Alvida, so that he realizes that the woman he has married is his own sister. But Alvida, who is too much in love with Torrismondo and who refuses to believe all this, commits suicide; and Torrismondo, suffering from the guilt of incest, does likewise.

The play deals with those aspects of love that were quite congenial to Tasso—conflict between the passion of love and the sense of sin; frustration in love which, by its very nature, cannot be wholly realized; the quandary and moral and existential solitude in which a protagonist finds himself, and from which there is no escape except through death.

The last and the least important of Tasso's plays, if in fact he wrote it at all, is *Intrighi d'amore*, which also deals with the theme of incest, but, unlike *Torrismondo*, has a happy ending.

—G. Singh

See also *Volume 1* entry on *Aminta*.

TATE, Nahum. Born Nahum Teate in Dublin, Ireland, c.1652. Educated at Trinity College, Dublin, 1668–72, BA 1672. Moved to London c.1672; first poetry published 1677; first play, *Brutus of Alba*, produced 1678; editor and translator of works by several writers; co-editor, the *Monitor*, 1713. Poet laureate, 1692–1715; historiographer royal from 1702. Died in London, 30 July 1715.

Works

Stage Works

Brutus of Alba; *or, the Enchanted Lovers* (produced Dorset Garden Theatre, London, 1678).   1678.
The Loyal General (produced Dorset Garden Theatre, London, 1679).   1680.
King Richard the Second, from the play by Shakespeare. 1681; as *The Sicilian Usurper* (produced Theatre Royal, Drury Lane, London, 1680), 1691; as *The Tyrant of Sicily* (produced Theatre Royal, Drury Lane, London, 1681).
King Lear, from the play by Shakespeare (produced Dorset Garden Theatre, London, 1681).   1681.
The Ingratitude of a Commonwealth; *or, The Fall of Caius Martius Coriolanus*, from *Coriolanus* by Shakespeare (produced Theatre Royal, Drury Lane, London, 1681). 1682.
A Duke and No Duke, from a play by Aston Cokayne (produced Theatre Royal, Drury Lane, London, 1684).   1685.
Cuckold's Haven; *or, An Alderman No Conjuror*, from the play *Eastward Ho!* by Jonson, Chapman, and Marston (produced Dorset Garden Theatre, London, 1685).   1685.
The Island Princess, from the play by Fletcher (produced Theatre Royal, Drury Lane, London, 1687).   1687.
Dido and Aeneas, music by Henry Purcell (produced Josias Priest's Boarding School, Chelsey, 1689).   1690.
Injured Love; *or, The Cruel Husband*.   1707.

Verse

Poems.   1677; revised edition, 1684.
The Second Part of Absalom and Achitophel, with Dryden. 1682; edited by James Kinsley and Ellen Kinsley, 1961.
On the Sacred Memory of Our Late Sovereign.   1685.
A Pastoral in Memory of the Duke of Ormond.   1688.
A Poem Occasioned by His Majesty's Voyage to Holland. 1691.
A Poem Occasioned by the Late Discontents.   1691.
Characters of Virtue and Vice, Attempted in Verse from a Treatise of Joseph Hall.   1691.
An Ode upon Her Majesty's Birthday.   1693.
A Present for the Ladies.   1693.
A Poem upon the Late Promotion of Several Eminent Persons.   1694.
In Memory of Joseph Washington: An Elegy.   1694.
An Ode upon the University of Dublin's Foundation.   1694.
Mausolaeum: A Funeral Poem on Our Late Queen.   1695.
An Elegy on the Late Archbishop of Canterbury.   1695.
The Anniversary Ode for His Majesty's Birthday.   1698.
A Consolatory Poem to Lord Cutts.   1698.
Elegies.   1699.
An Essay of a Character of Sir George Treby.   1700.
Funeral Poems.   1700.
Panacea: A Poem upon Tea.   1700; as *A Poem upon Tea*, 1702.
An Elegy in Memory of Ralph Marshall.   1700.
A Congratulatory Poem on the New Parliament.   1701.
The Kentish Worthies.   1701.
A Monumental Poem in Memory of Sir George Treby.   1702.
Portrait-Royal: A Poem upon Her Majesty's Picture.   1703.
The Song for New Year's Day.   1703.
The Triumph: A Poem on the Glorious Successes of the Last Year.   1705.
Britannia's Prayer for the Queen.   1706.
The Triumph of Union.   1707.

A *Congratulatory Poem to Prince George of Denmark*.   1708.
The Muse's Memorial to the Earl of Oxford.   1712.
The Muse's Bower.   1713.
The Triumph of Peace.   1713.
A Poem Sacred to the Memory of Queen Anne.   1714.

Other

An Essay for Promoting of Psalmody.   1710.

Editor, *Poems by Several Hands*.   1685.
Editor, *A Memorial for the Learned*, by J.D.   1686.
Editor, *The Life of Alexander the Great*, by Quintus Curtius Rufius.   1690.
Editor, *The Political Anatomy of Ireland*, by Sir William Petty.   1691.
Editor, *Guzman*, by Roger Boyle.   1693.
Editor, *The Four Epistles of A.G. Bushbequius*.   1694.
Editor, *Miscellanea Sacra; or, Poems on Divine and Moral Subjects*.   1696; revised edition, 1698.
Editor, *An Essay on Poetry*, by John Sheffield, Duke of Buckingham.   1697.
Editor, *The Original of the Soul* (Nosce Teipsum), by Sir John Davies.   1697.
Editor, *The Innocent Epicure; or, The Art of Angling*, by J.S.   1697.

Translator, with others, *Ovid's Epistles*.   1680.
Translator, *Syphilus: A Poetical History of the French Disease*, by Fracastoro.   1686.
Translator, with "a person of quality", *The Aethiopian History*, by Heliodorus.   1686; as *The Triumphs of Love and Constancy*, 1687.
Translator, with others, *Cowley's Six Books of Plants*.   1689.
Translator, *The Life of Louis of Bourbon, Late Prince of Condé* (2 vols.).   1693.
Translator, with others, *The Satires of Juvenal*, with *The Satires of Persius*, translated by Dryden and others.   1693.
Translator, with Nicholas Brady, *A New Version of the Psalms of David*.   1696; revised edition, 1696; *Supplement*, 1700.
Translator, *Majestas Imperii Britannici, The Glories of Great Britain*, by Mr. Maidwell.   1706.
Translator, with Aaron Hill, *The Celebrated Speeches of Ajax and Ulysses*, by Ovid.   1708.
Translator, with others, *The Works of Lucian* (4 vols.).   1710–11.
Translator, with others, *Ovid's Art of Love and His Remedy of Love*.   1712.

*

Criticism

Books:

Hazelton Spencer, *Shakespeare Improved*, Cambridge, Massachusetts, 1927.
Christopher Spencer, *Nahum Tate*, New York, 1972.
Dorothy E. Nameri, *Three Versions of the Story of King Lear Studied in Relation to One Another*, 1976.
Ruth McGugan, *Nahum Tate and the Coriolanus Tradition in English Drama, with a Critical Edition of Tate's "The Ingratitude of a Commonwealth"*, New York and London, 1987.
Peter Holland, "Nahum Tate's Defence of Farce", in *Farce*,

edited by James Redmond, Cambridge, 1988 (*Themes in Drama* series).

*   *   *

In the course of a 39-year career, Nahum Tate established himself as one of the more important journeyman writers of the late 17th century. Like a number of other politically acceptable journeymen, he was appointed poet laureate (succeeding Shadwell), a post he held for 23 years. Tate had early success as a poet (most notably with Dryden in the sequel to *Absalom and Achitophel*), a translator, and a playwright, the areas that would continue to attract most of his literary energies. He seemed to recognize that invention was not his strength as a writer, and focused his efforts on various kinds of translations and adaptations. His versions of Ovid and Juvenal won him considerable respect, and his metrical version (with Nicholas Brady) of the Psalms of David is still used in many hymnals.

Tate's first two plays were his most original; but neither was successful. *Brutus of Alba* is a reworking of Virgil's account of the story of Dido and Aeneas, a typically derivative first play, representative of the transition between the heroic play and the affective blank-verse tragedy that was replacing it in the late 1670's, strongly influenced by Dryden's *All for Love*. Tate's other original play, *The Loyal General*, contains a similar mix of heroic and affective elements, and of virtuous lovers who fall victim to egotistical villains. It has little to recommend it aside from a fine Dryden prologue. Its failure encouraged Tate to follow the lead of Dryden, Otway, and Lee in adapting Renaissance plays that required revision to please Restoration audiences. The foremost writer of these plays was Shakespeare.

Tate's next three plays were all adaptations from Shakespeare. The first-written was *King Lear*, his greatest hit as a playwright and the basis for his subsequent critical reputation. In his preface, Tate explains why he chose to alter a work he greatly admired. His principles remain constant throughout his career as an adapter: (1) he wished to make the play more acceptable morally by bringing it in line with the demand for poetic justice; (2) he regularized the language to meet the more refined norms of the Restoration stage; (3) he clarified the motivations of the characters; (4) he purified the plot by eliminating extraneous and indecorous elements (such as Lear's Fool). These were Tate's stated goals; to them he added several others which also remain consistent in his later endeavors: (1) special attention was given to enhancing women's roles to take advantage of the change from the boys who performed them on Shakespeare's stage to the women of Tate's; (2) the political themes were updated for the world of Restoration politics and redirected in line with Tate's own royalist views; (3) affective elements and effects were maximized; (4) the play was shortened.

The result was Tate's notorious *Lear* with its happy ending, including the marriage of Edgar and Cordelia, a version that pleased its audience far more than Shakespeare's. (*The History of) King Lear* is merely a representative, competent, reworking by an inferior hand of a masterpiece. What is unusual about it is its extraordinary stage history—it kept Shakespeare's *Lear* off the stage for 150 years. This fact continues to outrage bardolators, who coined the word "Tatification" to describe the efforts of those who tinker with Shakespearean texts. But while Tate's *Lear* has had attention (both favorable and unfavorable) beyond its merits, both *(The History of) King Richard the Second* and *The Ingratitude of a Commonwealth* were soon all but forgotten. Tate's version of *Richard II* perhaps deserved a better fate: it was banned in December 1680 (and again, after cosmetic revision, a month later) for political reasons—it was the wrong story to tell during the Exclusion Crisis—and never revived, though it shares the strengths and weaknesses of Tate's *Lear*. *The Ingratitude*, Tate's *Coriolanus*, on the other hand, is an inferior play most notably because it diffuses the tragedy with widespread violence, death, and pathos in a rewritten fifth act (the first four remain close to the original), which turns the title character into just another victim of the forces inevitably unleashed by commonwealths.

In his next two adaptations, Tate moved from tragedy to farce. *A Duke and No Duke* is the result of a similar process of simplifying, clarifying, and cutting, this time of *Trappolin Supposed a Prince* (1633) by the minor Caroline writer Sir Aston Cockain. Tate's "Preface Concerning Farce" is an impressive early English defense of farce (heavily dependent though it is on Agesilao Mariscotti's 1610 treatise); Tate's arguments have rarely been improved by later critics. The play was, except for *Lear*, Tate's most successful, remaining in the repertory well into the 19th century. *A Duke and No Duke* maintains an important place in theatre history as an early example of farce in English. Tate attempted to repeat his success with *Cuckold's Haven*, an adaptation of Ben Jonson, George Chapman, and John Marston's city comedy *Eastward Ho!*. The choice was not a promising one since so much of the original depended on literary and topical allusions no longer current in 1685. The play failed, closing Tate's career as a comic writer. In his final two adaptations, Tate returned to serious drama, first with a version of Beaumont and Fletcher's *The Island Princess*, another failure, and finally (at least 15 years later) *Injured Love*, a version of John Webster's *The White Devil*. It was never staged.

Though Tate's contribution is not often noticed, his best-known work today next to *King Lear* is his libretto for Henry Purcell's *Dido and Aeneas*. Purcell scholars credit Tate for an exemplary libretto, with lines ideally suited for musical setting and for singing. On the evidence of *Dido and Aeneas* and the Psalms, it is arguable that Tate's greatest literary talent was as a writer of lyrical texts to be set to music. Tate was a modest man of modest gifts, a competent writer-translator-adapter whose minor contributions earned him his small place in the history of the English theatre.

—Brian Corman

TAWFIQ AL-HAKIM. Born Husay Tawfiq Ismail Ahmad al-Hakim in Alexandria, Egypt, 9 October 1898. Educated at Damanhur infant school; Muhammad Ali Secondary School, Cairo to 1921; law school at University of Cairo, 1921–25; the Sorbonne, Paris, 1925–28. Married in 1944 (wife died 1977); one son and one daughter. Apprentice public prosecutor, in Alexandria, 1928–29, then public prosecutor in small towns, 1929–34; Director of Investigation Bureau, Ministry of Education, 1934–39; Director of Social Guidance, Ministry of Social Affairs, 1939–43; then full-time writer: associated with the newspapers *Akhbar al-Yawm* and *Al-Ahram*; Director general of Egyptian National Library, 1951–56; Member of the Egyptian Higher Council of Arts, Literature, and Social Sciences, 1956–59, 1960 onwards. Egyptian representative, Unesco, Paris, 1959–60. President, Nadi al-Qissa, 1974. Recipient: State Literature Prize, 1961. Awarded Cordon of

the Republic, 1958. Member, Academy of the Arabic Language, 1954. Died in Cairo, 26 July 1987.

Works

Collections

Masrahiyat [Plays] (2 vols.). 1937.
Masrah al-Mujtama [The Theatre of Society]. 1950.
Al-Masrah al-Munawwa [The Diverse Theatre]. 1956.
Al-Hubb [Love]. 1973.
"Fate of a Cockroach" and Other Plays (includes *The Song of Death; The Sultan's Dilemma; Not a Thing Out of Place*). 1973.
Plays, Prefaces, and Postscripts (2 vols.; includes *Shahrazad; The Wisdom of Solomon; King Oedipus; Tender Hands; Voyage to Tomorrow; Food for the Millions; Princess Sunshine*). 1981–84.
'Imarat al-Mu'allim Kanduz [The Building of Master Kandux]. 1981.

Stage Works

Ahl al-Kahf. 1933; translated as *The People of the Cave*, 1989.
Shahrazad. 1934; translated as *Shahrazad*, in *Plays, Prefaces, and Postscripts*, 1981.
Muhammad. 1936; translated as *Muhammed*, 1964.
Nahr al-Junun. In *Masrahiyat* [Plays], 1937; translated as *The River of Madness*, in *Islamic Literature*, 1963.
Praxagora. 1939.
Nashid al-Anshad [The Song of Songs]. 1940.
Pygmalion. 1942.
Sulayman al-Hakim. 1941; translated as *The Wisdom of Solomon*, in *Plays, Prefaces, and Postscripts*, 1981.
Shajarat al-Hukm [The Rulership Tree]. 1945.
Al-Malik Udib. 1949; translated as *King Oedipus*, in *Plays, Prefaces, and Postscripts*, 1981.
Masrah al-Mujtama [The Theatre of Society] (collection). 1950.
Al-Aydi al-Na'ima. 1954; translated as *Tender Hands*, in *Plays, Prefaces, and Postscripts*, 1981.
Isis. 1955; translated as Isis, 1975.
Al-Masrah al-Munawwa' [The Diverse Theatre] (collection). 1956.
As-Safqa [The Deal]. 1956.
Rihla ila al-Ghad [Voyage to Tomorrow]. 1957; as *Al-'Alam al-Majhul* [The Unknown World], 1973; translated as *Voyage to Tomorrow*, in *Plays, Prefaces, and Postscripts*, 1981.
La'bat al-Mawt [Death Game]. 1957.
Ashwak as-Salam [The Thorns of Peace]. 1957.
Al-Sultan al-Ha'ir. 1960; translated as *The Sultan's Dilemma*, in *"Fate of a Cockroach" and Other Plays*, 1973.
Ya Tali' al-Shajara. 1962; translated as *The Tree Climber*, 1966.
Al-Ta'am li-Kull Fam. 1963; as *Samira wa Hamdi*, 1973; translated as *Food for the Millions*, in *Plays, Prefaces, and Postscripts*, 1981.
Rihlat ar-Rabi' wa-l-Kharif [Spring and Autumn Journeys] (includes verse). 1964; as *Ma'a az-Zaman* [Over the Years], 1973.
Shams an-Nahar. 1965; as *Shams wa Qamar*, 1973; translated as *Princess Sunshine*, in *Plays Prefaces, and Postscripts*, 1981.
Al-Warta. 1966; translated as *Incrimination*, in *Plays, Prefaces, and Postscripts*, 1981.

Bank al-Qalaq [Anxiety Bank]. 1966.
Masir Sarsar. 1966; translated as *Fate of a Cockroach*, in
  "Fate of a Cockroach" and Other Plays, 1973.
Majlis al-'Adl [Council of Justice]. 1972.
Al-Hubb [Love] (collection). 1973.
Ad-Dunya Riwaya Hazaliya. 1974; translated as *The World
  is a Comedy*, with *A Conversation with the Planet Earth*,
  1985.
Al-Hamir [Donkeys]. 1975.
Ashad as-Sa'ada az-Zawjiya [Happily Married] (collection).
  1981.
Imsik Harami [Catch a Thief]. 1981.
Ah . . . Law 'Arafa ash-Shabab [Oh . . . If Only Youth
  Knew]. 1981.
'Imar Mu'allim Kanduz [The Building of Master Kanduz]
  (collection). 1981.

Fiction

Awdat al-Ruh [Return of the Spirit]. 1933.
Ahl al-Fann [Artistes]. 1934.
Al-Qasr al-Mashur [The Enchanted Castle], with Taha
  Husayn. 1936.
Yawmyyat Na'ib fi al-Aryaf. 1937; translated as *The Maze
  of Justice*, 1947.
Tarikh Hayat Ma'ida [Biography of a Stomach]. 1938; as
  Malik at-Tufayliyin [King of the Moochers], 1946; as
  Ash'ab, Amir at-Tufayliyin [Ash'ab, Prince of Moochers],
  1963.
'Usfur min ash-Sharq. 1938; translated as *Bird of the East*,
  1966.
'Ahd ash-Shaytan [Pact with Satan]. 1938; as *Madrasat ash-
  Shaytan* [Satan's School], 1955.
Raqisat al-Ma'bad [The Temple Dancer]. 1939.
Ar-Ribat al-Muqaddas [The Sacred Bond]. 1944.
Qisas [Stories] (2 vols.). 1949.
'Adala wa Fann [Justice and Art]. 1953; as *Ana wa'l-Qanun
  wal'Fann* [The Law, Art, and I], 1973.
Arini Allah [Show Me God]. 1953.
Min Dhikrayat al-Fann wa'l-Qada' [Memories of Art and
  Justice]. 1953.
Madrasa al-Mughaffalin [School for Fools]. 1953.
Laylat az-Zifaf [Wedding Night]. 1966.
Al-Amira al-Bayda aw Bayad an-Nahar [Snow
  White]. 1978.

Other

Tahta Shams al-Fikr [By the Light of the Sun of Thought].
  1938.
Himar al-Hakim [Al-Hakim's Ass]. 1940.
Sultan az-Zalam [The Reign of Darkness]. 1941.
Taht al-Misbah al-Akhdar [By the Light of the Green Lamp].
  1941.
Min al-Burj al-'Aji [From the Ivory Tower]. 1941.
Zahrat al-'Umr [The Flower of Life]. 1943.
Himari Qala li [My Donkey Told Me]. 1945.
Fann al-Adab [The Art of Literature]. 1952.
'Asa al-Hakim [Al-Hakim's Staff]. 1954.
Ta'ammulat fi as-Siyasa [Reflections on Politics]. 1954.
At-Ta'aduliya [The Art of Balance]. 1955.
Adab al-Hayat [The Literature of Life]. 1959.
Sijn al-'Umr [The Prison of Life]. 1964.
Qalibuna al-Masrahi [Our Theatrical Form]. 1967.
Qult . . . dhat Yawm [I Said . . . One Day]. 1970.
Tawfiq al-Hakim yatahaddath [Tawfiq al-Hakim
  Discusses]. 1971.

Thawrat ash-Shabab [Revolt of the Young]. 1971.
Ahadith ma'a Tawfiq al-Hakim min sana 1951–1971 [Conver-
  sations with Tawfiq al-Hakim], edited by Salah
  Tahir. 1971.
Rahib bayna Nisa' [A Monk Among Women]. 1972.
Rihla bayna 'Asrayn [Journey Between Two Ages]. 1972.
Himari wa'Asaya wa'l-Akharun [My Donkey and Stick and
  the Others]. 1972.
Hadith ma'a al-Kawtab. 1974; translated as *A Conversation
  with the Planet Earth*, with *The World is a Comedy*, 1985.
'Awdat al-Wa'y. 1974; translated as *The Return of Con-
  sciousness*, 1985.
*Safahat min at-Tarikh al-Adabi min Waqi' Rasa'il wa-
  Watha'iq* [Pages from Literary History: Selected Letters
  and Documents]. 1975.
Bayn al-Fikr wa'l-Fann [Between Thought and Art]. 1976.
Ta'am al-Fann wa'r-Ruh wa'l-Aql [Food for Art, Spirit, and
  Intellect]. 1977.
Malamih Dakhiliya [Inner Features]. 1982.
Equilibrium and Islam. 1983.

Criticism

Books:
Gilbert Tutunji, *Tawfiq al-Hakim and the West*,
  Bloomington, Indiana, 1966.
J. Fontaine, *Mort—résurrection: Une Lecture de Tawfiq al-
  Hakîm*, Tunis, 1978.
Richard Long, *Tawfiq al Hakim: Playwright of Egypt*,
  London, 1979.
Paul Starkey, *From the Ivory Tower: A Critical Study of
  Tawfiq al-Hakim*, London, 1987.
M.M. Badawi, *Modern Arabic Drama in Egypt*, Cambridge,
  1988.

Articles:
Nada Tomiche, "Un Dramaturge égyptien: Tawfiq al-Hakîm
  et l'"avant-garde"", in *Revu de littérature comparée*, 45,
  1971.
Paul Starkey, "Philosophical Themes in Tawfiq al-Hakim's
  Drama", in *Journal of Arabic Literature*, 8, 1977.
P. Cachia, "Idealism and Ideology: The Case of Tawfiq al-
  Hakim", in *Journal of the American Oriental Society*, 100,
  1980.
Mahmoud al-Shetawi, "The Treatment of Greek Drama by
  Tawfiq al-Hakim", in *World Literature Today*, 63, 1989.
Paul Starkey, "Tawfiq al-Hakim (1898–1987): Leading Play-
  wright of the Arab World", in *Theater Three*, 6, 1989.

*   *   *

Tawfiq al-Hakim is widely regarded both as the founder of
the modern Egyptian theatre, and as a major contributor to
the development of the modern Arabic novel.

Though he had already written some plays in colloquial
Arabic for the popular theatre while studying in Cairo, it was
al-Hakim's stay in France between 1925 and 1928 which
played the major role in determining the course of his future
literary career. In Paris, he fell under the spell of avant-garde
authors such as Shaw, Maeterlinck, and Pirandello, and it is
these writers' influence that is apparent in the "intellectual"
plays for which al-Hakim is best known.

The first of these dramas, *Ahl al-Kahf* (*The People of the
Cave*), related the Koranic story of the sleepers of Ephesus to
the contemporary situation of Egypt, as the country woke
from a long period of stagnation to face the challenges of the

20th century. The Pirandellian confusion between fantasy and reality apparent here was carried further in *Shahrazad*, in which the heroine of the *Thousand and One Nights* is presented as the embodiment of a "mysterious woman", whose nature is interpreted by the other main characters each according to his own disposition, but whose true nature remains elusive to the end of the play. Meanwhile, al-Hakim had already produced his first novel, *Awdat al-Ruh*, a work set at the time of the 1919 uprising against British rule. This work, characterised by a vision of the Egyptian peasant as the direct descendant of his Pharaonic forebears, marked the beginning of a new realistic trend in the Arabic novel, and was much admired by, among others, Nasser.

The series of "intellectual" dramas begun with *Ahl al-Kahf* and *Shahrazad* was continued with *Pygmalion*—partly inspired by Shaw's play of the same title—and *Al-Malik Udib* (*King Oedipus*), an attempt, according to the author, to rework the legend of Oedipus in accordance with Islamic beliefs, eliminating the concept of fate. Though these plays have apparently little direct relevance to contemporary Egyptian society, elsewhere al-Hakim's treatment of his themes is clearly intended to relate to the Egypt of the day. *Sulayman al-Hakim* (*The Wisdom of Solomon*), for example, discusses the relationship between wisdom and power, using stories from the Qur'an and the *Thousand and One Nights*; *Isis* takes as its main theme the question of whether the end justifies the means; and in *Al-Sultan al-Ha'ir* (*The Sultan's Dilemma*)—a play set in Mamluke Egypt—al-Hakim discusses a question which he regarded as crucial for the world, and the Egypt, of the 1960's: should the country seek to resolve its problems by the application of law, or by force?

In addition to these "intellectual" plays, al-Hakim composed, between 1945 and 1950, a series of short plays on Egyptian social themes—of widely varying quality—which were later collected and published in book form.

Unlike most Egyptian writers of his generation, al-Hakim had not allowed himself to become identified with any particular political party in the inter-war years. This attitude of detachment stood him in good stead with the new regime which came to power in 1952, and in the following years he received a number of honours and official appointments. His attitude towards the new regime was expressed in the play *Al-Aydi al-Na'imah* (*Tender Hands*), the main theme of which is the need for reconciliation between the various classes of Egyptian society. Meanwhile, he had continued to produce a stream of essays and articles in the Egyptian press, in addition to three more major novels, including *Yawmiyyat Na'ib fi al-Aryaf* (*The Maze of Justice*), the work regarded by some as his masterpiece. This work, in diary form, and based on al-Hakim's own experiences as a rural prosecutor, presents a damning picture of corruption in Egyptian rural society, highlighting the gulf between the mentality of the Egyptian *fellah* and that of the European-style legal system imposed on him.

Two main trends can be seen in al-Hakim's work during the post-1952 period. Firstly, his major works are for the most part all plays; secondly, his work shows a new enthusiasm for technical experiment, largely, though not exclusively, inspired by developments in contemporary Western theatre. The first, and most successful, of these experimental plays— *Ya Tali 'al-Shajara*—(*The Tree Climber*) shows the influence of the "theatre of absurd", with which al-Hakim had become acquainted on a recent visit to Paris; while *Al-Ta'am li-Kull Fam* (*Food for the Millions*), for example, seems to have been influenced by Brecht.

By the end of his life, al-Hakim had become almost a national institution in his native Egypt. The range of themes

and influences evident in his work, however, makes an overall evaluation difficult; and his work is further marked by an inconsistency both of quality and of outlook. On the one hand, his use of language is characterised by an admirable simplicity of style; on the other, much of his work is marred by a tendency to quasi-philosophical rambling at the expense of artistic unity. Many of his plays lack dramatic qualities, and were—on his own admission—intended to be read rather than acted. The best of them, however, have an appeal far beyond the Arab world, and assure him of a lasting place in the history of modern Arabic literature.

—Paul Starkey

TAYLOR, Tom. Born in Bishop Wearmouth, Sunderland, 19 October 1817. Educated at the Grange School, Sunderland; University of Glasgow (gold medallist three times); Trinity College, Cambridge, matriculated 1837, BA (first-class honours) 1840, fellow 1842, MA 1843; entered the Middle Temple, London: called to the Bar, 1846. Married Laura Barker in 1855. Tutor at Cambridge, 1843–44; moved to London, 1844, and was immediately successful as a playwright and occasional actor: associated with the Olympic Theatre, 1853–60, and the Theatre Royal, Haymarket, London, 1857–70; also journalist: became leader writer for the *Morning Chronicle* and *Daily News*, began life-long association with *Punch*; art critic of the *Times* and *Graphic* for many years; professor of English literature and language, University of London, 1845–47; lawyer on the northern circuit, 1847–50; assistant secretary, Board of Health, London, 1850–54, and secretary, 1854–71 (the Board of Health was absorbed in the Local Government Board, and his post became that of secretary to the Sanitary Department); editor, *Punch*, 1874–80. Died 12 July 1880.

Works

Collections

Three Dramas (*Masks and Faces; The King's Rival; Two Loves and a Life*), with Charles Reade.   1854.
Historical Dramas (includes *The Fool's Revenge; Joan of Arc; 'Twixt Axe and Crown; Lady Clancarty; Anne Boleyn; Plot and Passion; Arkwright's Wife*).   1877.
Plays (includes *Still Waters Run Deep; The Contested Election; The Overland Route; The Ticket-of-Leave Man*), edited by Martin Banham.   1985.

Stage Works

A Trip to Kissingen (produced Lyceum Theatre, London, 1844).   With *The Garrick Fever*, by Planché, 1881.
Valentine and Orson, with Albert R. Smith and James Kenny (produced Lyceum Theatre, London, 1844).   1844(?).
Cinderella, with Albert R. Smith and James Kenny (produced Lyceum Theatre, London, 1845).
Friends at Court (produced Lyceum Theatre, London, 1845).
The Enchanted Horse (produced Lyceum Theatre, London, 1845).
To Parents and Guardians (produced Lyceum Theatre, London, 1846).   Nd.
Wanted a Hermit (produced Lyceum Theatre, London, 1847).
Diogenes and His Lantern; or, The Hue and Cry After Honesty (produced Strand Theatre, London, 1849).
The Vicar of Wakefield; or, The Pastor's Fireside (produced Olympic Theatre, London, 1850).   1851.

The Philosopher's Stone (produced Strand Theatre, London, 1850). 1850(?).

Novelty Fair; or, Hints for 1851, with Albert R. Smith (produced Lyceum Theatre, London, 1850). Nd.

Prince Dorus; or, The Romance of the Nose (produced Olympic Theatre, London, 1850). 1850.

Sir Roger de Coverley; or, The Widow and Her Wooers (produced Olympic Theatre, London, 1851). 1851.

Little Red Riding Hood (produced Adelphi Theatre, London, 1851).

Our Clerks; or, No. 3, Fig Tree Court, Temple (produced Princess's Theatre, London, 1852). Nd.

Wittikind and His Brothers; or, The Seven Swan Princes and the Fair Melusine (produced Princess's Theatre, London, 1852). Nd.

Masks and Faces; or, Before and Behind the Curtain, with Charles Reade (produced Theatre Royal, Haymarket, London, 1852). 1854.

Slave Life; or, Uncle Tom's Cabin, with Mark Lemon (produced Adelphi Theatre, London, 1852). 1852.

Plot and Passion, with John Lang (produced Olympic Theatre, London, 1853). 1869.

A Nice Firm (produced Lyceum Theatre, London, 1853). Nd.

Harlequin Columbus; or, The Old World and the New (produced Olympic Theatre, London, 1853).

To Oblige Benson (produced Olympic Theatre, London, 1854). Nd.

Barefaced Imposters (produced Theatre Royal, Canterbury, 1854). 1854.

The King's Rival, with Charles Reade (produced St. James's Theatre, London, 1854). 1854.

A Blighted Being (produced Olympic Theatre, London, 1854). 1857(?).

Two Loves and a Life, with Charles Reade (produced Adelphi Theatre, London, 1854). 1854.

Guy Fawkes; or, A Match for a King, with others (produced Olympic Theatre, London, 1855). 1855.

Still Waters Run Deep (produced Olympic Theatre, London, 1855). 1856(?).

Helping Hands (produced Adelphi Theatre, London, 1855). Nd.

The First Printer, with Charles Reade (produced Princess's Theatre, London, 1856).

Retribution (produced Olympic Theatre, London, 1856). 1856(?).

William Tell, with others (produced Lyceum Theatre, London, 1856).

A Sheep in Wolf's Clothing (produced Olympic Theatre, London, 1857). 1870(?).

Victims (produced Theatre Royal, Haymarket, London, 1857). 1860(?).

An Unequal Match (produced Theatre Royal, Haymarket, London, 1857). 1874.

Going to the Bad (produced Olympic Theatre, London, 1858). Nd.

Our American Cousin (produced Laura Keene's Theatre, New York, 1858). 1869.

Nine Points of the Law (produced Olympic Theatre, London, 1859). Nd.

The House or the Home? (produced Adelphi Theatre, London, 1859). Nd.

The Contested Election (produced Theatre Royal, Haymarket, London, 1859). 1868.

Payable on Demand (produced Olympic Theatre, London, 1859). Nd.

Garibaldi (produced Astley's Amphitheatre, London, 1859).

The Fool's Revenge, from a play by Hugo (produced Sadler's Wells Theatre, London, 1859). 1877.

The Late Lamented (produced Theatre Royal, Haymarket, London, 1859).

A Tale of Two Cities (produced Lyceum Theatre, London, 1860). 1868.

The Overland Route (produced Theatre Royal, Haymarket, London, 1860). 1866.

The Seasons (produced The Standard Theatre, London, 1860).

A Christmas Dinner (produced Olympic Theatre, London, 1860).

A Lesson for Life (produced Lyceum Theatre, London, 1860 (amateur performance); produced professionally, Theatre Royal, Haymarket, London, 1866). 1867.

The Brigand and His Banker (produced Lyceum Theatre, London, 1860).

Up at the Hills (produced St. James's Theatre, London, 1860). Nd.

The Babes in the Wood (produced Theatre Royal, Haymarket, London, 1860; also produced as *Eloped*). Nd.

A Duke in Difficulties (produced Theatre Royal, Haymarket, London, 1861).

Court and Cottage, music by Fred Clay (produced Royal Opera House, Covent Garden, 1861).

The Ticket-of-Leave Man (produced Olympic Theatre, London, 1863). 1863.

An Awful Rise in Spirits (produced Olympic Theatre, London, 1863).

Sense and Sensation; or, The Seven Saints of Thule (produced Olympic Theatre, London, 1864). Nd.

The Hidden Hand, from a play by J. Dennery and C. Edmond (produced Olympic Theatre, London, 1864). 1870(?).

Settling Day (produced Olympic Theatre, London, 1865). Nd.

Hearts and Hands (produced Manchester, 1865).

The Serf; or, Love Levels All (produced Olympic Theatre, London, 1865). Nd.

Henry Dunbar; or, A Daughter's Trial (produced Olympic Theatre, London, 1865). Nd.

The White Boy (produced Olympic Theatre, London, 1866).

A Sister's Penance, with Augustus W. Dubourg (produced Adelphi Theatre, London, 1866). Nd.

The Antipodes; or, The Ups and Downs of Life (produced Holborn Theatre, London, 1867).

Narcisse (produced Lyceum Theatre, London, 1868).

Won by a Head; or, Forewarned is Forearmed (produced Queen's Theatre, London, 1869).

Mary Warner; or, Tried in the Fire (produced Theatre Royal, Haymarket, London, 1869).

New Men and Old Acres; or, A Managing Mama, with Augustus W. Dubourg (produced Theatre Royal, Manchester, 1869).

'Twixt Axe and Crown; or, The Lady Elizabeth (produced Queen's Theatre, London, 1870; revised version, produced 1889). 1877.

Handsome is That Handsome Does: A Story of the Lake Country (produced Olympic Theatre, London, 1870).

Joan of Arc (produced Queen's Theatre, London, 1871). 1877.

Dead or Alive (produced Queen's Theatre, London, 1871). 1877.

Arkwright's Wife, with John Saunders (produced Globe Theatre, London, 1873). 1877.

Lady Clancarty; or, Wedded and Wooed (produced Olympic Theatre, London, 1874). Nd.

The White Cockade (produced Croydon, 1874).
Abel Drake, with John Saunders (produced Princess's Theatre, London, 1874).
Anne Boleyn (produced Theatre Royal, Haymarket, London, 1876). 1877.
Such is the Law, with Paul Merritt (produced St. James's Theatre, London, 1878).
Love and Life, with Paul Merritt (produced Olympic Theatre, London, 1878).

Verse

Storm at Midnight and Other Poems, edited by J.H. Burn. 1893.

Other

Birket Foster's Pictures of English Landscape, with Pictures in Words by Taylor. 1853.
Handbook of the Pictures in the International Exhibition of 1862. 1862.
The Railway Station, Painted by W.P. Frith, Described. 1862.
A Marriage Memorial: Verse and Prose, Commemorative of the Wedding of the Prince and Princess of Wales. 1863.
Life and Times of Sir Joshua Reynolds, by C.R. Leslie, completed by Taylor (2 vols.). 1865.
English Painters of the Present Day: Essays, with J.B. Atkinson. 1871.
The Theatre in England: Some of Its Shortcomings and Possibilities. 1871.
Leicester Square: Its Associations and Its Worthies, with *A Sketch of Hunters' Scientific Character and Works*, by Richard Owen. 1874.

Editor, *Life of B.R. Haydon*. 1853.
Editor, *Autobiographical Recollections*, by C.R. Leslie (2 vols.). 1860.
Editor, *Pen Sketches by a Vanished Hand*, by Mortimer Collins (2 vols.). 1879.

Translator, *Ballads and Songs of Brittany*, by Vicomte Hersart de la Villemarqué. 1865.

*

Criticism

Books:
Winton Tolles, *Tom Taylor and the Victorian Drama*, New York, 1940.
George Rowell, *The Victorian Theatre 1792–1914*, Cambridge, 1956; revised edition, 1978.

* * *

For 30 years, from the 1840's to the 1870's, Tom Taylor supplied the theatre with a range of burlesques, farces, comediettas, comedies, historical plays, and dramas that made him one of the most famous of British Victorian dramatists, and for significant periods the "house" dramatist to such important London theatres as the Olympic and the Haymarket. It is remarkable that one of the most popular playwrights of his day should be relatively forgotten 100 years later. But Taylor himself certainly did not write with an eye to posterity: his work was practical, income-producing crafts-

manship, written to serve immediate purposes and markets. In this approach, he was typical of his contemporaries, contributing to a period of English drama that, without being greatly distinguished in itself, served to prepare the ground for the more substantial work of the playwrights of the end of the century. It also hugely entertained large and enthusiastic audiences.

Taylor's plays were often adapted from other sources, either novels or short stories or dramas, very often French. Such adaptation was common practice: the theatre of the time was eager for new material and theatres changed their programmes day by day thereby increasing the demand for "new" material. Charges of plagiarism were commonplace for writers such as Taylor. He himself made a nice distinction between those of his plays that he regarded as "new"—such as an adaptation from the French, "new" in English—and his "new and original" plays, that is, plays that were entirely his own creation. Controversies concerning authorship exercised critics in contemporary newspapers and journals, but did nothing to destroy Taylor's popularity with the audiences he entertained or the actors and actresses with whom he worked.

Although Taylor had a special affection for his historical dramas, his most successful work lay elsewhere. He has a certain morbid reputation as the author of *Our American Cousin*, the play President Abraham Lincoln was watching when he was assassinated by John Wilkes Booth. It is not, in fact, a particularly good play, but it became a vehicle for a famous piece of acting by E.H. Sothern, who turned the minor role of Lord Dundreary into a starring part through his eccentric interpretation.

Taylor's best play, and certainly the only one of his plays to have stayed in the repertoire of the British theatre to the present day, is *The Ticket-of-Leave Man*. It combines melodrama, sentiment, social observation, and humour. It creates two substantial characters, that of the ticket-of-leave man himself, Bob Brierly, "a Lancashire lad", and the detective Hawkshaw. The actor Henry Neville created his reputation playing the role of Brierly, and Horace Wigan as Hawkshaw established the tradition of the stage detective who was to fascinate and delight audiences throughout the 19th century. The play's social comment concerns the difficulties experienced by ex-convicts in rehabilitating themselves into decent society, but also touches upon other concerns of the day, including the upsurge in violence on the streets and the methods of policing evolved to deal with it. The play offered a range of roles that exploited the talents of the Victorian theatre, including various male and female comedians, villains, sentimental heroines, and a breeches role.

Other Taylor plays of note include *The Overland Route*, a sophisticated and witty comedy set on board a P&O liner returning to England shortly after the Indian Mutiny, *Still Waters Run Deep*, a domestic melodrama, which had an extra lease of life in the early years of the 20th century as a silent film with Lady Tree in the starring role, the fine sentimental comedy *Masks and Faces* (written with Charles Reade), the election comedy *The Contested Election*, and the historical fantasy *Arkwright's Wife*, concerning the man described as the founder of the modern factory system—another of Taylor's northern heroes.

—Martin Banham

See also *Volume 1* entry on *The Ticket-of-Leave Man*.

TCHEKHOV, Anton.   See **CHEKHOV, Anton.**

TÉLLEZ, Fray Gabriel.   See **TIRSO DE MOLINA**.

TERAYAMA Shūji.   Born in Aomori Prefecture, Japan, 10 December 1935. Educated at Waseda University, but withdrew before graduating. Initially a poet, but playwright and director from 1955; founder, Tenjō Sajiki [Upper Balcony] theatre troupe, 1967, which later performed widely in Europe. Also a scenarist and maker of documentary and feature films, writing scripts for directors Shinoda Masahiro, Hani Susumu, and others. Died 4 May 1983.

Works (selection)

Collections

Terayama Shūji no gikyoku (5 vols.).   1969–72.

Stage Works (publication dates do not necessarily refer to single book editions)

Chi wa tatta mama nemutte iru.   1960.
Aomori no semushi otoko.   1967.
Kegawa no Mari.   1967.
Sho o suteyo machi ni deyō.   1968.
Inugami.   1969.
Garigari hakase no hanzai.   1969.
Jinriki hikoki soromon.   1970.
Jashūmon.   1971.
Ahen sensō.   1972.
Knock.   1975; translated as *Knock: Street Theater*, in *Alternative Japanese Drama*, edited by Robert T. Rolf and John K. Gillespie, 1992.
Nuhikun.   1978.
Lemming.   1979.
Hyakunen no kodoku.   1981.

Verse

Den'en ni shisu [To Die in the Country].   1965.

Other

Iede no susume.   1963.

* * *

Terayama Shūji first attracted attention in 1954 as a writer of 31-syllable *tanka* poetry, which he continued to compose throughout his life. His first play, *Chi wa tatta mama nemutte iru* (Blood Sleeps Standing Up), was completed in 1957 and later performed in 1960 by the Shiki Troupe, which specialized, at the time, in producing the work of French playwrights like Anouilh and Giraudoux.

Influenced by writers like Lautréamont and André Breton, and inspired by surrealism, Dadaism, and expressionism, Terayama may be regarded as an authentically avant-garde artist in the European mould. Like his European counterparts, his work was characterized by contempt for all established standards of taste and by a fascination with the arbitrary and random.

Terayama combined this European-style avant-gardism with a set of symbols and images derived from his lonely youth in north-eastern Japan, a bleak, backward region known for its superstitions and shamanistic religion. His general method was to shock his Japanese audience with images and symbols that were taboo or anathema to them. The image of rape in a paddy field by a militarist, which appears in his autobiographical, Fellini-esque film *Den'en ni shisu* (Cache Cache Pastoral, 1975), was typical. Images of pederasty, transvestitism, and paedophilia, and the use of physical deformity (obesity and dwarfism) were Terayama's stock in trade.

The presentation of Japanese exotica in a recognizable avant-garde framework made Terayama and his troupe, Tenjō Sajiki, the darling of European theatre festivals, where they performed almost annually in the 1970's.

The logical culmination of Terayama's avant-gardism came in works like *Knock*. The work was "performed" over a period of 30 hours in 27 locations throughout Tokyo. Members of the audience were given maps that led them from one event to another in random sequence, so in theory no two spectators would see the same play.

In *Jashūmon* (Heretics' Gate), first performed at the Nancy Festival in France in 1971, Terayama combined the forms of kabuki, rock musical, and shamanistic ritual with physical assaults on the audience to evoke an experience of primal terror. In *Nuhikun* (Directions for Servants) Terayama adapted Jonathan Swift's classic tract to the stage.

Terayama died prematurely at the age of 47 from the kidney disease that had plagued him since 1955. He left a legacy of fearless iconoclasm, which continues to inspire artists today.

—David G. Goodman

TERENCE [Publius Terentius Afer].   Born c.194, 190, or 186–85 BC. Had a daughter. Possibly a freed slave in household of Terentius Lucanus, Rome; his plays produced in the 160's. Died 159 BC.

Works

Collections

Comediaru Liber Incipit feliciter.   1470.
Terence in English: Fabulae (Latin and English).   1598.
Terence's Comedies Made into English, translated by Lawrence Echard.   1694; re-edited, by Robert Graves, as *The Comedies of Terence*, 1962.
Comedies (in Latin), edited by S.G. Ashmore.   1908.
Terence (2 vols.; parallel texts), translated by John Sargeaunt.   1912 (Loeb Classical Library)
Comoediae, edited by Robert Kauer and Wallace M. Lindsay.   1926; revised by O. Skutsch, 1956.

Frontispiece from the illuminated *Terence des Ducs* (c.1400) showing a play by **Terence** being read and mimed (Bibliothèque de l'Arsenal, Paris).

Plays, translated by William Ritchie.   1927.
Complete Roman Drama (translations; 2 vols.), edited by George Duckworth.   1942.
Complete Comedies, various translators, edited by Palmer Bovie.   1974.
Comedies, translated by Betty Radice. 1976 (translations originally in *"The Brothers" and Other Plays*, 1965, and *"Phormio" and Other Plays*, 1967).

Stage Works (first published in 1470—see Collections)

Andria (produced Megalensian Games, Rome, 166 BC). Translated as *Andria*, c.1520: numerous subsequent translations under same title; as *The Andrian*, 1777 and 1814; as *The Lady of Andros*, in *Terence*, 1912 (Loeb edition); as *The Girl from Andros*, in *Plays*, 1976.
Hecyra (produced Megalensian Games, Rome, 165 BC). Translated as *Hecyra*, in *Terence in English: Fabulae*, 1598, and as *The Mother-in-Law*, in *Terence*, 1912: several subsequent translations under both titles.
Heauton Timorumenos (produced Megalensian Games, Rome, 163 BC).   Translated as *Heauton Timoroumenos*, in *Terence in English: Fabulae*, 1598, and *The Self-Tormentor*, in *Terence*, 1912: several subsequent translations under both titles.
Eunuchus (produced Megalensian Games, Rome, 161 BC). Translated as *Eunuchus*, in *Terence in English: Fabulae*, 1598 and *The Eunuch*, 1627: several subsequent translations under both titles.
Phormio (produced Roman Games, 161 BC).   Translated as *Phormio*, in *Terence in English: Fabulae*, 1598: numerous subsequent translations under same title.
Adelphoe [also known as *Adelphi*] (produced Funeral Games for L. Aemilius Paullus, Rome, 160 BC).   Translated as *Adelphoe*, in *Terence in English: Fabulae*, 1598, as *Adelphi*, 1777, as *The Brothers*, 1777: several subsequent translations under all titles.

*

Bibliographies

Sander M. Goldberg, "Scholarship on Terence and the Fragments of Roman Comedy 1959–1980", in *Classical World*, 75, 1981.
G. Cupaiolo, *Bibliografia terenziana (1470–1983)*, Naples, 1984.

Criticism

Books:
G. Norwood, *The Art of Terence*, Oxford, 1923.
E. Reitzenstein, *Terenz als Dichter*, Amsterdam, 1940.
A. Barbieri, *La vis comica in Terenzio*, Milan, 1951.
George Duckworth, *The Nature of Roman Comedy*, Princeton, New Jersey, 1952.
J. Strauss, *Terenz und Menander*, Zurich, 1955.
G. Norwood, *Plautus and Terence*, New York, 1965.
W.G. Arnott, *Menander, Plautus, and Terence*, Oxford, 1968.
B.A. Taladoise, *Térence: Un Théâtre de la jeunesse*, Paris, 1972.
L. Perelli, *Il teatro di Terenzio*, Florence, 1973.
K. Büchner, *Das Theater des Terenz*, Heidelberg, 1974.
Kenneth McLeish, *Roman Comedy*, Bristol, 1976.

David Konstan, *Roman Comedy*, Ithaca, New York, 1983.
W.E. Forehand, *Terence*, Boston, 1985.
F.H. Sandbach, *The Comic Theatre of Greece and Rome*, London, 1985.
Sander M. Goldberg, *Understanding Terence*, Princeton, New Jersey, 1986.
J.N. Grant, *Studies in the Textual Tradition of Terence*, Toronto and London, 1986.
Richard C. Beacham, *The Roman Theatre and Its Audience*, London, 1991.

* * *

If we can believe Suetonius' sources (there is ample pretext not to), the most celebrated of all Latin poets next to Virgil was also the most unlikely: he was neither Greek nor Roman, but a native of Rome's arch-enemy, Carthage, his first language a dialect of Phoenician, and he rose from slavery to the highest circles of the Roman literary aristocracy; he wrote six mould-breaking plays in fewer years, with results ranging from overwhelming popular success to legendary theatrical disaster; and, at the age of 24, he vanished so softly and suddenly off the face of the earth that nobody ever discovered what happened to him.

Terence was the last and strangest master of the *fabula palliata*, Roman adaptations of the (lost) plays of Menander and his contemporaries. Less translations than free dramatic reworkings for a radically different performance idiom and audience, these versions from the Greek rewrote the text, cut the chorus, set large chunks of the dialogue to music, and radically abridged, expanded, deleted, or inserted whole dialogue passages, scenes, characters, and even subplots—often with a systematic re-emphasis of tone, theme, or roles. Terence felt no more reverence for the sanctity of the original Greek text than Plautus had before him; but where Plautus had radically subverted the central elements of Menandrean plot, character, style, world, and meaning to meet the quite different demands of Roman taste, Terence tried to recreate, or even improve, Menandrean comedy for a Roman public. He returned the dramatic centre of gravity, hijacked in Plautus by the slaves and *demi-monde*, to the citizen characters and the family; he checked the slapstick, gag routines, punchline jokes, and verbal fireworks in favour of a far closer concentration on subtleties of psychology and plot; and he displaced the broad fantasy and exuberance of Plautine performance with a deft naturalism previously unknown on the Roman stage. The titles are left in Greek, rather than translated into Latin or discarded for new ones; the operatic Plautine lyrics virtually disappear; and the Menandrean-Plautine prologue is split functionally and structurally into two, with the expository part handled entirely by inter-character dialogue, and the direct address to the audience shifted to a wholly extra-dramatic prologue of astounding disingenuousness in the poet's or producer's own voice.

It was a controversial programme, and not always a successful one. His first play, the *Andria*, ran into criticism for "polluting" the Menandrean original with mysterious additional material from Menander's *Perinthia* and a subplot possibly of Terence's own invention. His second, the *Hecyra* (*The Mother in Law*), never completed a performance until a third attempt at the very end of his career; and his probable next play, the *Heauton Timoroumenos* (*The Self Tormentor*), went further than either in its baffling convolutions of intrigue and misapprehension. The turning point came with the extraordinary *Eunuch*, which, in a blatant compromise with audience taste, took an already uncharacteristically rumbustious source and grafted in extra comic characters and scenes from a second play previously translated by Plautus himself. Despite accusations of plagiarism, the *Eunuch* was a massive success, rewarded with the highest fee ever paid for a comedy; and the two subsequent plays, *Phormio* and *Adelphoe* (*The Brothers*), ingeniously apply the crowd-pleasing lessons of the *Eunuch* with judicious use of farce and Plautine comic types, while reverting to the uncompromisingly complex and thoughtful family comedy of his early work.

Terence's plays are the most densely-plotted of all classical drama, with a particular fascination for symmetrical patterns of situation and relationships that borders on obsession. One trademark is the so-called "double plot", consisting of a pair of contrasting young men with different kinds of problem love affair, which turn out, in the event, to solve one another. In the *Andria*, at least, this second strand is Terence's outright addition; and in the last plays the complementary strands extend to a second generation, with a counterplot involving the young men's contrasting fathers. (A different bilateral structure governs the *Hecyra*, built around a lone couple's relations with two sets of in-laws.) As in Menander, these complex ironic patterns are mapped out spatially in the movements of characters between the family houses represented on- (and sometimes off-) stage. But Terence has, additionally, a fondness for abstraction, for plots that take place largely in the characters' heads, placing unprecedented demands on the audience's ability to follow multiple misapprehensions and counter-bluffs on the part of the different characters. And often, in stark difference to the cavalier plot-cuts of Plautus, Terence can be caught in the act of complicating the Greek original still further, by bringing on stage scenes merely reported in the Greek, or, crucially, inserting a fourth speaking character beyond the maximum of three permitted in Greek New Comedy.

Like Menander (but not Plautus, or apparently Menander's major rivals), Terence's main preoccupations are love, liberality, and the family. Attracted by Menander's philosophy of human politics, which stresses the virtues of tolerance, generosity, and a readiness to admit weakness rather than judge others, Terence attempts to reconcile this vision of *humanitas* (the traditional term is unfortunate, as its source, the *Heauton Timoroumenos* uses it ironically) with the more austere Roman ideology of civic and family obligation. The tensions between these Greek and Roman ideals are a prime source

of complexity in the plays—last and most critically in the *Adelphoe*, where the strange parallels between the relationships in the play and the adoptive Aemiliani who sponsored the production seem to have forced a radical and paradoxical reinterpretation of the original Menandrean conclusion.

There has not, as yet, been the paradigm shunt in Terentian studies that the last 20 years have seen for Plautus. Terence remains a phenomenally complex, technically virtuosic, writer elusively suspended between Hellenistic and Roman sensibilities, whose dazzling contributions to the art of comic plotting and cross-cut dialogue-writing are matched by a deep ironic intelligence and an exquisite sense of the language that has never found an adequate translator. For most of the history of European drama, Terence has been its most influential single figure. It would be a neat joke if, as his ancient biographers claimed, he was not a European at all.

—N. J. Lowe

See also *Volume 1* entries on *The Brothers*; *Phormio*.

TERRY, Megan. Born Marguerite Duffy in Seattle, Washington, USA, 22 July 1932. Educated at Banff School of Fine Arts, Alberta, Canada, summers 1950–53, 1956; University of Washington, Seattle, 1950, 1953–56, B.Ed. 1956; University of Alberta, Edmonton, 1951–53. Drama teacher and director of the Cornish Players, Cornish School of Allied Arts, Seattle, 1954–56; founding member, 1963, and director of the playwrights workshop, 1963–68, Open Theatre, New York; writer-in-residence, Yale University School of Drama, New Haven, Connecticut, 1966–67; founding member, Women's Theatre Council, 1971; founding member and treasurer, New York Theatre Strategy, 1971; since 1971 resident playwright and literary manager, Omaha Magic Theatre, Omaha, Nebraska, which has produced and published many of her works; Bingham Professor of Humanities, University of Louisville, Kentucky, 1981; Hill Professor of Fine Arts, University of Minnesota, Duluth, 1983; visiting artist, University of Iowa, Iowa City, 1992. Recipient: Obie Award, 1970; Dramatists Guild Award, 1983.

Works

Collections

Four Plays (includes *Keep Tightly Closed in a Cool Dry Place; Comings and Goings; The Gloaming, Oh My Darling; Viet Rock*). 1967.
Three One-Act Plays (includes *Sanibel and Captiva; One More Little Drinkie; The Magic Realists*). 1972.
High Energy Musicals from the Omaha Magic Theatre, with Jo Ann Schmidman (includes *American King's English for Queens; Babes in the Bighouse; Running Gag*). 1983.
Two by Terry Plus One (includes *The Pioneer; Pro Game*). 1984.

Stage Works

Beach Grass (produced Cornish Players Theatre, Seattle, 1955).
Seascape (produced Cornish Players Theatre, Seattle, 1955).
Go Out and Move the Car (produced Cornish Players Theatre, Seattle, 1955).
New York Comedy: Two (produced Saratoga, New York, 1961).
Ex-Miss Copper Queen on a Set of Pills (produced Cherry Lane Theatre, New York, 1963). With *The People vs. Ranchman*, 1968.
When My Girlhood Was Still All Flowers (produced Open Theatre, New York, 1963).
Eat at Joe's (produced Open Theatre, New York, 1964).
Calm Down Mother (produced Open Theatre, New York, 1965). In *Eight Plays from Off-Broadway*, edited by Smith and Orzel, 1966; single edition, 1970.
Keep Tightly Closed in a Cool Dry Place (produced Open Theatre New York, 1965). In *Four Plays*, 1967.
The Magic Realists (produced Open Theatre, New York, 1966). In *Three One-Act Plays*, 1972.
Comings and Goings (produced New York, 1966). In *Four Plays*, 1967.
The Gloaming, Oh My Darling (produced Firehouse Theatre, Minneapolis, 1966). In *Four Plays*, 1967.
Viet Rock: A Folk War Movie (produced Open Theatre, New York, 1966). In *Four Plays*, 1967.
The Key is on the Bottom (produced Mark Taper Forum, Los Angeles, 1967).
The People vs. Ranchman (produced Firehouse Theatre,

Minneapolis, 1967).   With *Ex-Miss Copper Queen on a Set of Pills*, 1968.

Home; or, Future Soap (televised 1968; revised version, as *Future Soap*, produced Omaha Magic Theatre, Omaha, Nebraska, 1987).   1972.

Jack-Jack (produced Firehouse Theatre, Minneapolis, 1968).

Massachusetts Trust (produced Brandeis University, Waltham, Massachusetts, 1968). In *The Off-Off-Broadway Book*, edited by Albert Poland and Bruce Mailman, 1972.

Changes, with Tom O'Horgan (produced La Mama Experimental Theatre, New York, 1968).

Approaching Simone (produced Boston University, Boston, 1970).   1973.

The Tommy Allen Show (produced College of the Immaculate Heart, Los Angeles, and New York, 1970).   In *Scripts 2* (New York), December 1971.

Grooving (produced Brooklyn Academy of Music, New York, 1972).

Choose a Spot on the Floor, with Jo Ann Schmidman (produced Omaha Magic Theatre, Omaha, 1972).

Couplings and Groupings (monologues and sketches). 1973.

Susan Peretz at the Manhattan Theatre Club (produced Manhattan Theatre Club, New York, 1973).

Thoughts (lyrics only), book by Lamar Alford (produced Theatre de Lys, New York, 1973).

Nightwalk, with Sam Shepard and Jean-Claude van Itallie (produced St. Clement's Church, New York, 1973).   In *Open Theater*, 1975.

St. Hydro Clemency; or, A Funhouse of the Lord: An Energizing Event (produced St. Clement's Church, New York, 1973).

The Pioneer, and *Pro-Game* (produced Omaha Magic Theatre, Omaha, 1973).   1975.

Hothouse (produced Circle Theatre, New York, 1974).   1975.

Babes in the Bighouse (produced Omaha Magic Theatre, Omaha, 1974).   1979.

All Them Women, with others (produced Westbeth Playwrights' Feminist Co-Operative, New York, 1974).

We Can Feed Everybody Here (produced Westbeth Playwrights' Feminist Co-Operative, New York, 1974).

Hospital Play.   1974.

Henna for Endurance.   1974.

The Narco Linguini Bust (produced Omaha Magic Theatre, Omaha, 1974).

100, 001 Horror Stories of the Plains (produced Omaha Magic Theatre, Omaha, 1976).   1979.

Sleazing Towards Athens.   1977; revised version (produced Omaha Magic Theatre, Omaha, 1986), 1986.

Willie-Willa-Bill's Dope Garden.   1977.

Brazil Fado (produced Omaha Magic Theatre, Omaha, 1977).   1977; revised version (produced Santa Fe, 1978), 1979.

Lady Rose's Brazil Hide Out (produced Omaha Magic Theatre, Omaha, 1977).

American King's English for Queens (produced Omaha Magic Theatre, Omaha, 1978).   1978.

Goona Goona (produced Omaha Magic Theatre, Omaha, 1979).   1985.

Attempted Rescue on Avenue B: A Beat Fifties Comic Opera (produced Chicago, 1979).   1979.

Fireworks, in *Holidays* (produced Actors' Theatre, Louisville, Kentucky, 1979).   1987.

Running Gag (lyrics only), book by Jo Ann Schmidman (produced Omaha Magic Theatre, Omaha, 1979).   1981.

Objective Love I (produced Omaha Magic Theatre, Omaha, 1980).   1985.

Scenes from Maps (produced Omaha Magic Theatre, Omaha, 1980).   1980.

Advances (produced Omaha Magic Theatre, Omaha, 1980). 1980.

Flat in Afghanistan (produced Omaha Magic Theatre, Omaha, 1981).   1981.

Objective Love II (produced Omaha Magic Theatre, Omaha, 1981).   1985.

The Trees Blew Down (produced Los Angeles, 1981).   1981.

Winners (produced Santa Barbara, California, 1981).

Kegger (produced Omaha Magic Theatre, Omaha, 1982).

Fifteen Million Fifteen-Year-Olds (produced Omaha Magic Theatre, Omaha, 1983).

Mollie Bailey's Traveling Family Circus, Featuring Scenes from the Life of Mother Jones, music by Jo Anne Metcalf. 1983.

The Pioneer.   In *Two by Terry Plus One*, 1984.

Pro Game.   In *Two by Terry Plus One*, 1984.

X-rayed-iate (produced Omaha Magic Theatre, Omaha, 1984).

Katmandu.   In *Open Spaces* (Columbia, Missouri), 1985.

Retro (produced Omaha Magic Theatre, Omaha, 1988). 1985.

Family Talk (produced Omaha Magic Theatre, Omaha, 1986).

Sea of Forms (collaborative work), text and lyrics with Jo Ann Schmidman (produced Omaha Magic Theatre, Omaha, 1986).   1987.

Walking Through Walls (collaborative work), text and lyrics with Jo Ann Schmidman (produced Omaha Magic Theatre, Omaha, 1987).   1987.

Dinner's in the Blender (produced Omaha Magic Theatre, Omaha, 1987).   1987.

Amtrak (produced Omaha Magic Theatre, Omaha, 1988).   1990.

Headlights (produced Little Rock, Arkansas, 1988).   1989.

Do You See What I'm Saying? (produced Chicago, 1990). 1991.

Breakfast Serial (produced Omaha Magic Theatre, Omaha, 1991).   1991.

Body Leaks, with Jo Ann Schmidman and Sora Kimberlain (produced Omaha Magic Theatre, Omaha, 1991).   1992.

Sound Fields (produced Omaha Magic Theatre, Omaha, 1992).

Television Plays

The Dirt Boat, 1955; *Home; or, Future Soap*, 1968; *One More Little Drinkie*, 1969 (published in *Three One-Act Plays*, 1972).

Radio Plays

Sanibel and Captiva, 1968 (published in *Three One-Act Plays*, 1972); *American Wedding Ritual Monitored/Transmitted by the Planet Jupiter*, 1972.

Other

Right Brain Vacation Photos: Omaha Magic Theatre Production Photographs 1972–1992.   1992.

*

Bibliographies

Philip C. Kolin (ed.), *American Playwrights since 1945: A Guide to Scholarship, Criticism, and Performance*, New York, 1989.

Criticism

Books:
Jan Breslauer and Helene Keyssar, "Making Magic Public: Megan Terry's Travelling Family Circus", in *Making a Spectacle: Feminist Essays on Contemporary Women's Theatre*, edited by Lynda Hart, Ann Arbor, Michigan, 1989.

Articles:
Kathleen G. Klein, "Language and Meaning in Megan Terry's 1970s 'Musicals'", in *Modern Drama*, 27, 1984.
June Schlueter, "Keep Tightly Closed in a Cool Dry Place: Megan Terry's Transformational Drama and the Possibilities of Self", in *Studies in American Drama 1945–Present*, 2, 1987.
Judith Babnich, "Megan Terry's *100,001 Horror Stories of the Plains*: Tall Tales and Stories from the People of the Midwest", in *Mississippi Folklore Register*, 22, 1988.
Megan Terry, "Anybody is as Their Land and Air Is", in *Studies in American Drama 1945–Present*, 4, 1989.
Megan Terry and Felicia Londré, "An Interview with Megan Terry", in *Studies in American Drama 1945–Present*, 4, 1989.

* * *

A prolific author with over 60 plays to her credit, Megan Terry has consistently experimented with different styles, allowing the content of each project to dictate the form of the piece. She has written in a traditional, realistic format, most notably in *Hothouse*, a play about three generations of women in a single family during the 1950's, and in *Home; or, Future Soap*, which carefully creates a futuristic world based on the assumption of over-population. More frequently, however, Terry's plays are episodic and presentational, emphasizing the importance of the performance event rather than the complete representation of a fictional world. She is probably best known for her innovative use of "transformation" in which character, time, and place shift rapidly in full view of the audience. *Comings and Goings*, subtitled "a theatre game", is a series of seemingly unrelated scenes designed to engage performers and audience in a spirited imaginative exercise. In *Calm Down Mother*, three actresses explore various aspects of women's roles through a series of different characters. *Keep Tightly Closed in a Cool Dry Place* is set initially in a prison, but the three male performers, in addition to assuming traditional character identities as inmates, play out scenes derived from history, the movies, and their own real or imagined pasts.

These transformation-plays from the 1960's were developed while Terry was associated with the Open Theatre (1963–68) in New York and reflect that company's experimentation with techniques to circumvent typecasting and psychological realism. *Viet Rock*, perhaps Terry's most famous play, and one of the first rock musicals, was developed in workshop with Open Theatre actors, and combined the use of changing realities with political comment as it explored the effects of the war in Vietnam. Terry has con-

tinued to incorporate music in plays that address serious issues and has remained committed to developing scripts in collaboration with other theatre artists. Since she joined the Omaha Magic Theatre as playwright-in-residence, Terry has worked closely with visual artists to create vibrant, often humorous, performances. Trained as a designer, Terry typically relies heavily on visual images to convey emotional and intellectual content, a characteristic accentuated in her collaborative work. Some of these Magic Theatre productions, such as *Sea of Forms* and *Walking Through Walls*, have completely converted the performance space into a new, abstract environment for audience and performers.

Terry's willingness to experiment with theatrical form has allowed her to tackle a wide variety of subject matter. In 1983 she was recognized by the Dramatists Guild as a "writer of conscience and controversy", emphasizing the fact that she has dealt with large social, political, and ethical issues perhaps more than any other contemporary playwright in the USA. Along with the US involvement in Vietnam, her early work addressed such topics as the single-minded pursuit of monetary gain (*The Magic Realists*), political assassination (*The Massachusetts Trust*), and the sensationalism of a rape trial (*The People Versus Ranchman*). At the Magic Theatre she and her colleagues have continued this commitment to socially aware theatre, often working closely with their audiences and using the tools of research and interview to develop meaningful scripts of particular topical concern. *Kegger*, for example, deals with teenage use and abuse of alcohol; *Goona Goona* is concerned with domestic violence, *Dinner's in the Blender* with family communication, and *Headlights* with the national problem of illiteracy.

Terry is recognized by critics as a pioneer in feminist theatre, frequently putting women and gender-related problems at the center of her plays. *Approaching Simone*, which won the Obie Award for best play in 1970, explores the life of philosopher Simone Weil through a series of scenes demonstrating her strength of spirit and determination to learn and serve, in spite of the limitations placed upon her by society. *Mollie Bailey's Traveling Family Circus, Featuring Scenes from the Life of Mother Jones* juxtaposes the lives of the 19th-century mother-and-show-business-entrepreneur with that of the more well-known labor activist to create a portrait of two strong, maternal, but otherwise very different historical figures. In examining the stark reality of the lives of women in prison, *Babes in the Bighouse* utilized the same actors to play both guards and inmates and both men and women to play female characters in order to emphasize the adopted characteristics of social roles.

Recurring themes in Terry's work include the relationship of the individual to larger social units (family, peer groups, government) and to the natural environment, power relationships (domination and submission), and the interplay of reason and intellectual control with the more primitive, biological self. She often addresses the world of people who are outside the power structures of the capitalist society—battered women, teenagers, children, prisoners, the illiterate, the elderly—and the content of her plays is intimately connected with the professional choices she has made. Terry has consistently worked outside of the established system of commercial theatre in the USA. The Magic Theatre tours frequently to prisons, schools, and other communities in an attempt to reach the widest audience possible. When her work suggests a course of action, it tends to be an awakening of conscience and consciousness, or a rejection of victimization and discovery of individual strength. *Body Leaks*, Terry's recent collaboration with Schmidman and Sora Kim which deals with insecurity and self-censorship, encapsulates this strain of Terry's work with its refrain of "Take a risk, darling!".

Because of the commitment to a type of theatre in which the text is only one element in the total production experience, Terry's printed plays may be difficult to read and visualize. They range from complex works, in which the layering of image and dialogue repay careful and intense study, to the straightforward presentation of message. In much of her work, Terry challenges the notion that "serious" drama must, of necessity, end pessimistically; in doing so she serves as a voice of hope in the American theatre.

—Kathy Fletcher

TIECK, Ludwig. Born in Berlin, Prussia (now in Germany), 31 May 1773. Educated at Gymnasium, Berlin, 1782–92; studied theology, philosophy, and English literature at the universities of Halle and Göttingen, 1792–93. Married Amalie Alberti in 1798; two daughters. Travelled to Franconia, 1793; began work with the Berlin publisher Christoph Friedrich Nicolai, 1794; contributor to the literary magazine *Die Straussfedern* 1795–98; became associated with the artistic group the Jena Romanticists, which included the Schlegels and the philosopher Fichte; broke with Nicolai's publishing house, c.1797; began suffering from rheumatoid arthritis in the 1790's; travelled to Hamburg, Berlin, and Dresden seeking employment, 1800–02; lived in Ziebungen, near Frankfurt-an-der-Oder, 1802–10; travelled to Prague, Baden-Baden, and Berlin, 1811–17; visited England (where he met the poet Coleridge), 1817; moved to Dresden, 1819, and was appointed dramaturg at the Dresden Theatre; subsequently worked in Prussian theatres: dramaturg in Berlin, from 1841. Died in Berlin, 28 April 1853.

Works

Collections

Schriften (28 vols.).   1828–54.
Werke (3 vols.), edited by Gotthold Ludwig Klee.   1892.
Ausgewählte Werke (4 vols.), edited by Georg Wittkowski.   1903.
Werke (6 parts), edited by Eduard Berend.   1908.
Werke (4 vols.; plays in Volume 2), edited by Marianne Thalmann.   1963–66.
Schriften, edited by Manfred Frank.   1935—

Stage Works

Ritter Blaubart.   In *Volksmärchen 2* and a single edition, 1797.
Karl von Berneck.   In *Volksmärchen 3*, 1797.
Der gestiefelte Kater (produced Berlin, 1844).   In *Volksmärchen 2* and a single edition, 1797; augmented edition in *Schriften 5* (see Collections); translated as *Puss in Boots*, in *German Classics of the Nineteenth and Twentieth Centuries 4*, edited by Kuno Francke and W.G. Howard, 1914.
Die verkehrte Welt.   In *Bambocciaden 2*, attributed mostly to F.A. Bernhardi, 1799; augmented edition, in *Phantasus 2*, 1814; translated as *The Land of Upside Down*, 1978.

Prinz Zerbino; oder, Die Reise nach dem guten Geschmack.   1799.
Leben und Tod der heiligen Genoveva.   In *Romantische Dichtungen 1*, 1799; revised version, in *Schriften 2* (see Collections).
Fortunat.   In *Phantasus 3*, 1816; also in *Schriften 5* (see Collections).
Kaiser Oktavianus.   1804.

Fiction (selected)

Ryno.   As *Die eiserne Maske*, 1792; as *Ryno*, in *Nachgelassene Schriften*, 1855.
Abdallah.   1795.
Die Geschichte des herrn William Lovell (3 vols).   1795–96; as *Berlin und Leipzig*, 1795–96.
Peter Leberecht, eine Geschichte ohne Abenteuerlichkeiten.   1795.
Die sieben Weiber des Blaubart.   1797.
Franz Sternbalds Wanderungen (2 vols.).   1798.
Das Ungeheuer und der verzauberte Wald (story).   1800.
Die Gemälde.   1823; translated as *The Pictures*, with *The Betrothal*, 1825; as *The Legacy*, 1883.
Die Verlobung.   1823; translated as *The Betrothal*, with *The Pictures*, 1825.
Der Geheimnisvolle (novelle).   1823.
Novellen (7 vols.).   1823–28.
Der Aufruhr in den Cevennen.   1826; translated as *The Rebellion in the Cevennes*, 1845.
Der Alte vom Berge, und Die Gesellschaft auf dem Lande: Zwei Novellen.   1828.   1828; *Der Alte vom Berge* translated as *The Old Man of the Mountain*, 1831.
Der junge Tischlermeister.   1836.
Vittoria Accrombona.   1840; translated as *The Roman Matron; or, Vittoria Accrombona* (3 vols.), 1845.
The Faithful Eckart; The Mysterious Cup; The Runenberg, translated by F.H.C. de la Motte Fouqué.   1843.
Tales from the "Phantasus", translated by J.C. Hale.   1845.
Gesammelte Novellen (vols. 21–28 of *Schriften*).   1852–54.
The Fair-Haired Eckbert; The Trusty Eckart; The Runenberg; The Elves; The Goblet, translated by Thomas Carlyle.   1858.

Verse

Gedichte (3 vols.).   1821–23.

Memoirs and Letters

Aus Tiecks Novellenzeit: Briefwechsel zwishen Ludwig Tieck und F.A. Brockhaus.   1928.
Tieck and Solger: The Complete Correspondence, edited by Percy Matenko.   1933.
Ludwig Tieck und Ida von Lüttichau in ihren Briefen, edited by Otto Fiebiger.   1937.
Letters of Ludwig Tieck Hitherto Unpublished, 1792–1853, edited by Edwin H. Zeydel and others.   1937.
Letters to and from Ludwig Tieck and His Circle, edited by Edwin H. Zeydel and others.   1967.
Ludwig Tieck und die Brüder Schlegel: Briefe, edited by Edgar Löhner.   1972.

Other

Volksmärchen herausgegeben von Peter Leberecht (stories, plays, and other works; 3 vols.).   1797.
Phantasien über die Kunst, with material by Wilhelm

Heinrich Wackenroder (essays). 1799; translated as "Fantasies on Art for Friends of Arts", in *Confessions and Fantasies*, translated by Mary Hurst Shubert, 1971.

Phantasus (stories, plays, and other works; 3 vols.). 1812–16.

Dramaturgische Blätter (3 vols.). 1825–52.

Kritische Schriften (4 vols.). 1848–52.

Nachgelassene Schriften, edited by Rudolf Köpke (2 vols.). 1855.

Editor, *Minnelieder aus dem schwäbischen Zeitalter*. 1803.

Editor, *Alt-englisches Theater; oder, Supplemente zum Shakspeare* (2 vols.). 1811.

Editor, *Frauendienst; oder, Geschichte und Liebe des Ritters und Sängers Ulrich von Lichtenstein*. 1812.

Editor, *Deutsches Theater* (anthology of works by Hans Sachs, A. Gryphius and others). 1817.

Editor, *Hinterlassene Schriften* (4 vols.), by Heinrich von Kleist. 1821–26.

Editor, *Shakespeare's Vorschule* (2 vols). 1823–29.

Editor, *Gesammelte Schriften*, by J.M.R. Lenz. 1825.

Editor, *Sämtliche Schriften*, by F.A. Schulze. 1843.

Editor, *Evremont*, by Sophie Bernhardi (his sister). 1836.

Editor, with E. von Bülow, *Gesammelte Schriften*, by Novalis. 1837–46.

Editor, *Gesammelte Novellen*, by F. Berthold. 1842.

Editor, *Gedichte*, by K. Förster. 1843.

Editor, *Altestes Liederbuch*, by Goethe. 1844.

Translator, *Der Sturm*, by Shakespeare. 1796.

Translator, *Don Quixote von La Mancha*, by Cervantes. 1800.

Translator, *Dramatische Werke*, by Shakespeare. 1826–32.

Translator, *Leben unde Begebenheiten des Escudero Marcus Obregon; oder, Autobiographie des spanischen Dichters Vicente Espinel*. 1827.

Translator, *Vier Schauspiele*, by Shakespeare. 1836.

Translator, *Mucedorus: Ein englisches Drama aus Shakespeares Zeit*. 1893.

*

Bibliographies

M. Thalmann, "Hundert Jahre Tieck-Forschung", in *Monatshefte*, 45, 1953.

Criticism

Books:

J.-J. Bertrand, *Ludwig Tieck et le théâtre espagnol*, Paris, 1914; revised edition, 1970.

K. Brodnitz, *Die vier Märchen-Komödien von Ludwig Tieck*, Erlangen, 1912.

E. Görke, *Der junge Tieck und die Aufklärung*, Berlin, 1926.

A.E. Lasky, *Tieck's Romantic Irony*, Chapel Hill, North Carolina, 1932.

Edwin H. Zeydel, *Ludwig Tieck: The German Romanticist: A Critical Study* (second edition), Princeton, New Jersey, 1933.

Percy C. Matenko, *Ludwig Tieck and America*, 1954.

M. Thalmann, *Ludwig Tieck, der romantische Weltmann aus Berlin*, Bern and Munich, 1955.

James Trainer, *Ludwig Tieck, from Gothic to Romantic*, The Hague, 1964.

Wulf Segebrecht (ed.), *Ludwig Tieck: Wege der Forschung*, Darmstadt, 1976.

J.P. Kern, *Ludwig Tieck: Dichter einer Krise*, Heidelberg, 1977.

Klaus Günzel, *König der Romantik: Das Leben des Dichters Ludwig Tieck in Briefen, Selbstzeugnissen, und Berichten*, Tübingen, 1981.

Roger Paulin, *Ludwig Tieck: A Literary Biography*, Oxford, 1985.

*   *   *

Ludwig Tieck was one of the most prolific literary men of his day. A leading exponent of German Romanticism, he wrote in almost every literary genre and contributed to the German Romantic canon three major works: a statement on the importance of art and its connection to other forms of cultural expression, published under the title *Herzensergiessungen eines kunstliebenden Klosterbruders* (*Outpourings from the Heart of an Art-Loving Monk*) and the two short stories *Der blonde Eckbert* (*Blond Eckbert*) and *Der Runenberg* (*Rune Mountain*). Long after the day of Romanticism was past, however, Tieck remained influential as dramatic adviser to the theatre at Dresden, and as an editor of Hans Sachs, Opitz, Gryphius, and Lohenstein and—more importantly—of Kleist and Lenz. His commentaries on Shakespeare and his collaboration with Schlegel in the major German edition of Shakespeare's plays helped to give the English playwright his unique status in Germany and represented a major contribution to international Shakespeare scholarship.

In spite of Tieck's remarkable fecundity as a playwright, he was destined to remain one of the "great unproduced" of the German dramatic tradition. It is doubtful if he wrote with a view to actual production on the stage and certainly none of his plays ever established itself as part of the repertoire of the German theatre. The Germans have a long tradition of the *Buch-* or *Lesedrama*, of course, but even as plays intended to be read, Tieck's dramas have not worn well. Behind the apparent simplicity of the subject matter, his comedies, especially, are highly intellectual products that invite the reader simultaneously to enjoy literature and reflect on its nature; yet the constant use of Romantic irony, the playful creation and destruction of illusion and mood, delightful as it may be on first acquaintance, readily becomes tedious if repeated, and the satire of contemporary literary figures and conventions all too frequently is merely boring for generations who can only understand the references with the aid of footnotes. In his serious dramas, a love of allegory, a predilection for a plethora of different verse forms, and a certain sentimental and twee quality all pose considerable difficulties for the modern reader. This is not to say, however, that Tieck does not have unique historical importance as the embodiment of German Romantic drama and for his anticipation of many future developments.

His earliest works, *Der Abschied* (The Farewell) and *Karl von Berneck* introduced the tragedy of fate, with its array of sinister objects, guilt-laden inheritances, and sinful ghosts into German drama. But both plays avoid the rather fatuous mechanistic quality that was to characterise the work of lesser practitioners and are remarkable for their evocation of a spooky doom-laden atmosphere in which dark forebodings and darker deeds are matched by a *décor sympathique*.

Like most Romantics, Tieck had a deep interest in older German literature and used it as a basis for characteristic dramas: *Leben und Tod der heiligen Genoveva* (Life and Death of the Saintly Genoveva), *Kaiser Oktavianus*

(Emperor Octavianus) and *Fortunat* (Fortunatus). Of these, *Genoveva* is probably the most satisfying. The tale of the maligned and outcast Countess Palatine, who is wrongly accused of adultery and rejected by her husband, is an attempt, not to create a psychologically convincing action in a traditional dramatic sense, but to embrace the totality of the world in a spirit reminiscent of the medieval mystery play.

Tieck's comedies, equally, are based on popular literature —Perrault's *Contes de ma mère, l'oie* (1697)—but again he seeks to do more than merely cast fairy tales into dramatic form. *Der gestiefelte Kater* (*Puss in Boots*) dramatises a production of a play about Puss in Boots and effectively exploits the conceit of the play-within-the-play in order to launch an ironic attack on the narrow pedantry and rationalism of the Enlightenment and assert the rights of the imagination against the claims of the intellect. To this end, Tieck breaks with the realist tradition and blurs the distinction between reality and illusion. The "spectators" are drawn into the action and their bewilderment and negative reactions become part of the drama. Errors of production are "written in" in order to alienate as well as amuse the "real" audience: the curtain rises too soon and the embarrassed author has to explain to the stage audience that this is a mistake, and so on. For a modern audience brought up on the techniques of Brecht, such devices are unremarkable; but, historically, they nonetheless represented a startling innovation. The treatment of the Bluebeard story (*Ritter Blaubart*) and the "continuation" of *Der gestiefelte Kater* in *Prinz Zerbino; oder, Die Reise nach dem guten Geschmack* (Prince Zerbino; or, The Voyage in Search of Good Taste) are less appealing. The former, particularly, suffers from an unsuccessful attempt to emulate Shakespearean humour, and the interest of these plays is largely historical and antiquarian.

—W.A. Coupe

See also *Volume 1* entry on *Puss in Boots*.

TIRSO DE MOLINA. Born Fray Gabriel Téllez in Madrid, 1580 or 1581. Educated at the universities of Alcalá and Guadalajara. Entered the order of Mercy (also known as the Mercedarian Order) as novitiate, 1601; friar, probably in Toledo, 1605–15, and Santo Domingo, Hispaniola (now Dominican Republic, West Indies), 1616–18; based in Madrid, 1621–25; following opposition to his playwriting from the Council of Castile, was forbidden to write further secular plays and was banished to the remote friary at Trujillo, where he was Prior, 1626–29; became official chronicler of the Order, c.1632; in Barcelona, Madrid, and Toledo, during the 1630's; banished again, 1640, to Soria, where he became Prior, 1645–47. The majority of his plays written before 1625: possibly the author of as many as 300–400. Died in Almazán, 1648.

Works

Collections

Comedias (5 vols.), edited by Francisco de Ávila.   1627–36.
Comedias escogidas.   1826–34.

Teatro escogido (includes 36 *comedias*).   1848.
Comedias (2 vols.; includes 45 *comedias*), edited by E. Cotarelo y Mori.   1906–07.
Obras dramaticas completas (3 vols.), edited by Blanca de los Rios.   1946–58; revised edition (4 vols.), 1989.

Stage Works

Attribution of some works is uncertain. All plays in the following list are included in *Obras dramaticas completas* (1989). Plays first published 1627–36 appeared in the original five volumes of *Comedias*; other publication dates do not necessarily refer to single book editions.

La niña del cielo, condesa bandolera, y obligaciones de honor (produced 1613).
La Santa Juana II (produced Duke of Lerma's orchard, 1614).   1636.
La villana de Vallecas (produced 1620).   1626.
Le elección por la virtud (produced 1622).   1634.
Siempre ayuda la verdad (produced 1623).   1635.
Palabras y plumas.   1623.
El celoso prudente.   1624.
Cómo han de ser los amigos.   1624.
Le vergonzoso en palacio.   1624.
Amar por razón de estado.   1626.
El mayor desengaño.   1626.
El pretendiente al revés.   1626.
El arbol del mejor fruto.   1627.
El castigo del penséque.   1627; translated as *The Opportunity*, 1640.
El celosa de si misma.   1627.
La gallega Mari-Hernández.   1627.
El melancólico.   1627.
Quien calla ortorga; O, El castigo del penséque II.   1627.
Tanto es lo de más como lo de menos.   1627.
El burlador de Sevilla.   In *Doce comedias nuevas de Lope de vega y otros autores*, 1630; translated as *The Love Rogue*, 1923; as *The Trickster of Seville and the Guest of Stone*, in *Masterpieces of the Golden Age*, edited by Angel Flores, 1957; as *The Trickster of Seville*, in *The Classic Theatre*, edited by Eric Bentley, 1959; as *The Rogue of Seville*, in *Spanish Drama*, edited by Angel Flores, 1962; as *The Playboy of Seville*, in *The Theatre of Don Juan*, edited by Oscar Mandel, 1963, and *Eight Spanish Plays of the Golden Age*, edited by Walter Starkie, 1964; as *The Joker of Seville*, 1979.
El rey Don Pedro en Madrid; o, El infanzón de Illescas.   1633.
El amor y la amistad.   1634.
Averíguelo Vargas.   1634.
Del enemigo, el primer consejo.   1634.
La fingida Arcadia.   1634.
La huerta de Juan Fernández.   1634.
El mejor espigadera.   1634.
No hay peor sordo.   1634.
La prudencia en la mujer.   1634; translated as *Prudence in Women*, in *The Genius of the Spanish Theatre*, edited by Robert O'Brien, 1964.
La venganza de Tamar.   1634; translated as *Tamar's Vengeance*, 1988.
Ventura te dé Dios, hijo.   1634.
La villana de la Sagra.   1634.
Adversa fortuna de Don Álvaro de Luna, a Próspera fortuna de Don Álvaro de Luna II.   1635.
Los amantes de Teruel.   1635.
Amar por arte mayor.   1635.

Amazonas de las Indias: Las hazañas de Pizarros II.   1635.
El amor, médico.   1635.
Amor y celos hacen discretos.   1635.
Antona García.   1635.
Cautela contra cautela.   1635
Celos con celos se curan.   1635.
El condenado por desconfiado.   1635; translated as *Damned for Despair* (parallel text), 1986.
La dama del olivar.   1635.
Don Gil de las calzas verdes. 1635; translated as *Don Gil of the Green Breeches*, 1991.
Doña Beatriz de Silva.   1635.
Esto sí que es negociar.   1635.
La lealtad contra la envidia: Las hazañas de Plos Pizarros III. 1635.
Marta la piadosa. 1635.
La mujer por fuerza. 1635.
La mujer que manda en casa; o, Jezabel. 1635.
La pena de Francia.   1635.
Por el sótano y el torno. 1635.
Privar contra su gusto.   1635.
Próspera fortuna de Don Álvaro y adversa fortuna de ruy López Davales.   1635.
Quien habló, pagó.   1635.
La reina de los reyes.   1635.
Santo y sastre.   1635.
Todo es dar en una cosa: Trilogía de los Pizarros.   1635.
Los balcones de Madrid.   1636.
Escarmientos para el cuerdo.   1636.
Los lagos de San Vicente.   1636.
Quien no cae, no se levanta.   1636.
La república al revés.   1636.
La Santa Juana.   1636.
La vida y muerte de Herodes.   1636.
El aquilés.   1638.
Bellaco sois (produced Madrid, 1643).   In *Obras 3*, 1958.
La firmeza en la hermosura.   1646.
Desde Toledo a Madrid.   1666.
Amar por señas.   1667.
La ventura con el nombre.   1667.
El caballero de gracia.   1669.
La romera de Santiago.   1670.
En Madrid y en una casa.   1671.
El cobarde más valiente.   In *Comedias*, 1906–07.
Las quinas de Portugal.   In *Comedias*, 1906–07.
La Santa Juana III.   In *Comedias*, 1906–07.
Habladme en entrando.   In *Obras dramaticas completas*, 1989.
El honroso atrevimiento.   In *Obras dramaticas completas*, 1989.
La joya de las montañas, y Verdadera historia de Santa Orosia.   In *Obras dramaticas completas*, 1989.
Quien da luego, da dos veces.   In *Obras dramaticas completas*, 1989.

The following *autos* are included in *Obras dramaticas completas*, 1989: *El colmenero divino; Los hermanos parecidos; El laberinto de Creta; La madrina del cielo; La ninfa del cielo; No le arriendo la ganancia.*

Fiction

El bandolero, edited by Luis Carlos Viada y Lluch.   1915.

Verse

Acto de contricion.   1630.
Poesías líricas, edited by Ernesto Jareño.   1969.

Other

Cigarrales de Toledo (miscellany).   1621; translated in part as *Three Husbands Hoaxed*, 1955.
Deleitar aprovechando.   1635.
Una obra inédita (La vida de la santa Madre doña Maria de Cervellón), edited by M. Menéndez y Pelayo.   1908.
Historia general de la Orden de Nuestra Señora de las Mercedes (2 vols.), edited by Manuel Penedo Rey.   1974.

*

Bibliographies

Vern G. Williamsen and Walter Poesse, *An Annotated Analytical Bibliography of Tirso de Molina Studies 1627–1977*, Columbia (Missouri) and London, 1979.

Criticism

Books:
Ivy L. McClelland, *Tirso de Molina: Studies in Dramatic Realism*, Liverpool, 1948.
G. Mancini and others (eds.), *Studii tirsiani*, Milan, 1958.
K. Vossler, *Lecciones sobre Tirso de Molina*, Madrid, 1965.
Ion T. Agheana, *The Situational Drama of Tirso de Molina*, New York, 1972.
Ruth Lee Kennedy, *Studies in Tirso: The Dramatist and His Contemporaries 1620–26*, Chapel Hill, North Carolina, 1974.
Henry W. Sullivan, *Tirso and the Drama of the Counter Reformation*, Amsterdam, 1976.
M. Wilson, *Tirso de Molina*, Boston, 1977.
A.N. Hughes, *Religious Imagery in the Theatre of Tirso de Molina*, Macon, 1984.
María Santomauro, *El gracioso en el teatro de Tirso de Molina*, Madrid, 1984.
J.M. Solá-Solé (ed.), *Tirso de Molina, vida y obra: Actas del I Simposio Internacional sobre Tirso, Washington 1984*, Madrid, 1987.
Tirso de Molina: Immagine e rappresentazione: Segundo coloquio international, Salerno 1989, Naples, 1991.
Xavier A. Fernández, *Las comedias de Tirso de Molina: Estudios y métodos de crítica textual* (3 vols.), Kassel, 1991.

*   *   *

Tirso's fame and reputation as a dramatist of international standing rest heavily on his dramatization of the Don Juan theme—the first in world literature—in *El burlador de Sevilla*. *El burlador* (*The Trickster of Seville*) is doubtless Tirso's most famous play, but his dramatic production ranges widely and his importance cannot be limited to the influence of this work, however great.

The majority of Tirso's dramatic works follow the normative patterns established for the Spanish stage by Lope de Vega. However, Tirso introduced several significant modifications and adapted the Lopean formula in a variety of ways. In general, the intrigues in Tirso's plays are more tightly constructed and more intense than those in Lope's plays. Often, they focus on the psychological manipulations of jealous lovers in their attempts to deceive or gain superiority over one another. In the best of these plays, such as *Don Gil de las calzas verdes*, the result is an engaging drama; in the worst of instances, the intrigues become too thick to follow or to appreciate. In addition, Tirso developed characterizations in greater depth than is common in Lope's plays. His characters require this greater depth in part because the motives involved in their various strategies of jealousy and deception are often at issue. But Tirso seems also to have had a keener sensibility for the effects of human passion, or seems, in any event, better able to display the effects of those passions in dramatic terms than Lope, for whom the most important of motives seem always to be social and historical ones.

Besides these innovations, Tirso developed a "situational" form of drama in which characters are created and in which incidents evolve as a function of engagements with surroundings, which inevitably include other characters. In this respect, Tirso followed the example of the late-medieval Spanish dialogue *La Celestina* more closely than many other dramatists of the Spanish Golden Age. Whereas it would be true to say that in the plays of Lope de Vega or Calderón de la Barca the characters are identified by their language, and that the language creates the theatrical scenery and many of the effects necessary for the unfolding of the drama, Tirso allows his characters and their dramatic sense to emerge as a function of their involvement with their contexts. Accordingly, Tirso's characterization is contextual and the movement of dialogue is of enormous importance in his works. Although Tirso continued to include long poetic monologues, many of which were composed in a baroque style, and although these often have a structural importance in the overall scheme of his works, the action in Tirso's plays proceeds largely through situational encounters and dialogue.

Tirso's characters, like Don Juan, tend to be more flexible and supple than the characters typically found in the works of Lope or Calderón. Oftentimes, they define themselves solely in negative terms, or identify themselves only provisionally, through the use of constantly shifting disguises. In extreme cases, the constant use of disguise, coupled with strategies of deceit, tends to cancel the underlying identity of the character in question. For example, Don Juan Tenorio identifies himself at the beginning of *El burlador de Sevilla* as a "man with no name" ("un hombre sin nombre"). As the action of the play unfolds, we witness a character who is subjected to a process of gradual self-erasure as the various disguises assume priority over the self's identity. It is this process of self-erasure that requires an equivalent effort of self-assertion at the conclusion of the work, as Don Juan agrees to meet the "stone guest" at a banquet in Hell.

While many of Tirso's works are overtly moral in nature, and while many have a theological undercurrent not unusual for works of the Counter-Reformation in Spain, Tirso's plays can also be understood apart from these moral and theological contexts, as reflections of an aristocratic society in decline or decay. The deceived nobility in Tirso's plays are no more to be exonerated than those who do the deceiving, themselves often also of the nobility. At their most pointed, Tirso's plays call into question the alliance between the theological structure of belief in Spain and the existing order of social ranks. They represent a questioning of social hierarchies and demonstrate the power of desires to exert a levelling effect on inherited structures and beliefs. To this extent, Tirso's work can be compared to Thomas Hobbes's later analyses of the passions. And yet, unlike Hobbes, Tirso is concerned to contain human desire within a framework of moral and theological order. Thus, in spite of the fact that some critics, beginning with members of the Generation of 1898 in Spain, have attempted to read plays like *El burlador de Sevilla* in tragic terms, raising, in this case, Don Juan's sheer willpower to heroic proportions, Tirso's plays in fact conform to the pattern of comedy. Because the comic structure of these plays allows the damages suffered by society to be repaired, they tend to reinforce and to be reinforced by the structure of society as it stands.

—Anthony J. Cascardi

See also *Volume 1* entry on *The Trickster of Seville*.

TOLLER, Ernst. Born Samotschin, Germany (now Szamocin, Poland), 1 December 1893. Educated at Realgymnasium, Bromberg, from 1906; studied law at the University of Grenoble, France, 1914; University of Munich, 1916–17; University of Heidelburg, 1917–18. Married the actress Christiane Grautoff in 1934 (separated 1938). Joined a Bavarian regiment at the outbreak of World War I: at the Western Front, 1916, but soon invalided out on account of mental breakdown; supported striking munitions workers in Munich, 1918, and arrested and imprisoned for three months on a charge of treason; involved in the revolutionary events in Munich and Bavaria, 1918–19: chairman, USPD (socialist party), 1919, and section-leader of the Red Army (later resigned); on the revolution's collapse, was arrested and imprisoned, 1919–23, during which time he wrote most of his plays; first-produced play, *Die Wandlung* [*Transformation*], staged 1919; lectured and lobbied widely, in Europe, the Soviet Union, and the USA in the 1920's and 1930's, espousing various artistic, social, and political (especially anti-fascist) causes; while in Yugoslavia, his German citizenship withdrawn by the Nazi regime, 1933, and his works banned and burned; lived mainly in England and Switzerland, 1933–35; travelled to Portugal and Spain, 1936; settled in Santa Monica, California, 1936; screenwriter for Metro-Goldwyn-Mayer, 1936–38; travelled to Mexico, 1937; activist for pro-Republican intervention in the Spanish Civil War, lobbying in the USA, France, England, and Sweden, 1938. Committed suicide (hanged himself) in a hotel room, New York, 22 May 1939.

Works

Collections

Seven Plays (includes *Transfiguration; Masses and Man; The Machine Wreckers; Hinkemann; Hoppla, Such is Life!; Mary Baker Eddy; The Blind Goddess*), various translators. 1935.
Prosa; Briefe; Dramen; Gedichte. 1961.
Gesammelte Werke (5 vols.; plays in Volumes 2 and 3), edited by John M. Spalek and Wolfgang Frühwald.   1978.

Stage Works

Die Wandlung (produced Die Tribüne, Berlin, 1919).   1919; translated as *Transfiguration*, in *Seven Plays*, 1935.
Masse-Mensch (produced Stadttheater, Nuremberg, 1920). 1921; translated as *Masses and Man*, 1923, and in *Seven Plays*, 1935; as *Man and the Masses*, 1924.
Die Maschinenstürmer (produced Grosses Schauspielhaus, Berlin, 1922). 1922; translated as *The Machine Wreckers*, 1923, and in *Seven Plays*, 1935.

Ernst Toller (c.1924)

Hinkemann (produced Altes Theater, Leipzig, 1923). 1923; translated as *Brokenbrow*, 1926; as *Hinkemann*, in *Seven Plays*, 1935.

Der entfesselte Wotan (produced in Russian, Bolshoi Dramatic Theatre, Moscow, 1924; produced in German, Deutsches Theater, Prague, 1925). 1923.

Hoppla, wir leben! (produced Kammerspiele, Hamburg, 1927; revised version produced Theater am Nollendorfplatz, Berlin, 1927). 1927; translated as *Hoppla!*, 1928; as *Hoppla, Such is Life!*, in *Seven Plays*, 1935.

Bourgeois bleibt Bourgeois, with Hasenclever, from a play by Molière (produced Lessingtheater, Berlin, 1929).

Feuer aus den Kesseln (produced Theater am Schiffbauerdamm, Berlin, 1930). 1930; translated as *Draw the Fires!*, 1934.

Wunder in Amerika. 1931 (acting version); translated as *Mary Baker Eddy*, in *Seven Plays*, 1935.

Die blinde Göttin (produced Raimund-Theater, Vienna, 1932). 1933; translated as *The Blind Goddess*, 1934, and in *Seven Plays*, 1935; as *Blind Man's Buff*, 1938.

Nun wieder Fricke, music by Hanns Eisler (produced in English, Gate Theatre, London, 1936). In English, as *No More Peace*, 1937; in German, in *Gesammelte Werke*, 1978.

Pastor Hall (produced Deutsches Theater, Berlin, 1947). In English, as *Pastor Hall*, 1939; in German (stage version), in *Stücke gegen den Faschismus*, edited by Karl Heinz Schmidt, 1970; revised version, in *Gesammelte Werke*, 1978.

Radio Plays

Berlin—letzte Ausgabe! (published in *Frühe sozialistische Hörspiele*, edited by S.B. Würffel, 1982).

Verse

Der Tag des Proletariats. 1920.
Gedichte der Gefangenen. 1921.
Vormorgen. 1924; parts translated in *Letters from Prison*, 1936.

Other

Das Schwalbenbuch. 1924; translated as *The Swallow Book*, 1924.
Justiz: Erlebnisse. 1927.
Quer durch: Reisebilder und Reden. 1930; part translated as *Which World? Which Way?*, 1931.
Nationalsozialismus (interview). 1930.
Eine Jugend in Deutschland. 1933; translated as *I Was a German*, 1934.
Briefe aus dem Gefängnis. 1935; translated as *Letters from Prison* (including poems), 1936; as *Look Through the Bars*, 1937.
Kritische Schriften; *Reden*; *Reportagen* (Volume 1 of *Gesammelte Werke*). 1978.

*

Bibliographies

John M Spalek, *Ernst Toller and His Critics*, Charlottesville, Virginia, 1968.

Criticism

Books:
F. Droop. *Ernst Toller und seine Bühnenwerke*, Berlin, 1922.
P. Singer, *Ernst Toller*, 1924.
William A. Willibrand, *Ernst Toller, Product of Two Revolutions*, Norman, Oklahoma, 1941.
William A. Willibrand, *Ernst Toller and His Ideology*, Iowa City, 1945.
Thomas Bütow, *Der Konflikt zwischen Revolution und Pazifismus im Werk Ernst Tollers*, Hamburg, 1975.
Carel ter Haar, *Ernst Toller: Appell oder Resignation?*, Munich, 1977.
Wolfgang Frühwald and John M Spalek (eds.), *Der Fall Toller: Kommentar und Materialien*, Munich, 1979.
Malcolm Pittock, *Ernst Toller*, Boston, 1979.
René Eichenlaub, *Ernst Toller et l'expressionisme politique*, Paris, 1980.
Michael Ossar, *Anarchism in the Dramas of Ernst Toller: The Realm of Necessity and the Realm of Freedom*, New York, 1980.
Jost Hermand (ed.), *Zu Ernst Toller: Drama und Engagement*, Stuttgart, 1981.
Wolfgang Rothe, *Ernst Toller in Selbstzeugnissen und Bilddokumenten*, Reinbek, 1983.
Renate Benson, *German Expressionist Drama: Ernst Toller and Georg Kaiser*, London, 1984.
Richard Dove, *Revolutionary Socialism in the Work of Ernst Toller*, New York, 1986.
Andreas Lixl, *Ernst Toller und die Weimarer Republik 1918–1933*, Heidelberg, 1986.
Martin Kane, *Weimar Germany and the Limits of Political Art: A Study of the Work of George Grosz and Ernst Toller*, Tayport, Fife (Scotland), 1987.
Sigurd Rothstein, *Der Traum von der Gemeinschaft: Kontinuität und Innovation in Ernst Tollers Dramen*, Frankfurt and New York, 1987.
Klaus Bebendorf, *Tollers expressionistische Revolution*, Frankfurt, 1990.
Richard Dove, *He Was a German: A Biography of Ernst Toller*, London, 1990.

Articles:
Nicholas Hern, "The Theatre of Ernst Toller", in *Theatre Quarterly*, vol.5, 1972.
Harald H. Ohlendorf, "W. H. Auden: 'In Memory of Ernst Toller'", in *Comparative Criticism: A Yearbook*, 1979.
Ralph Ley, "The Revolutionist as Poet: The Prison Plays of Ernst Toller", *University of Dayton Review*, vol.17 no.3, 1985–86.
Richard Dove, "The British Connection: Aspects of the Biography of Ernst Toller", in *German Life and Letters*, 40, 1987.

* * *

Ernst Toller ranks alongside Georg Kaiser as the leading dramatists of German expressionism, but Toller's plays, like Kaiser's, are rarely performed, even in Germany, and then only by students or experimental groups. His involvement in the turbulent birth of the Weimar Republic makes his life of more enduring interest, since he was, if only briefly, a poet-politician. Tankred Dorst's 1968 play *Toller* documented this episode in his life.

Toller was born in Samotschin near Poznan in what is now Poland, but he later saw himself in a wider context when he said, "a Jewish mother bore me, Germany nurtured me, my homeland is the earth, and the world is my fatherland". In 1914, however, his fatherland was still Germany, and he dashed back from Grenoble to enlist. Neither his patriotic fervour nor his health survived the trenches, and he was invalided out of the army in 1917. Now a pacifist, he became a left-wing student activist.

His first play, *Die Wandlung* (*Transfiguration*), which gave Berlin its first taste of full-blooded expressionism when it was staged at the Tribüne in 1919, dramatised the hero Friedrich's development from patriot to pacifist in seven stations. Set on a black stage with crudely painted plywood cut-outs representing shell-bursts or houses, it was a strident plea for mankind to unite in brotherhood. Partly on the strength of *Transfiguration*, Toller found himself chairman of the Munich Soviet and narrowly escaped summary execution when it was brutally suppressed by military units despatched from Berlin. He was sentenced to five years in prison where he wrote four plays.

Masse Mensch (*Masses and Man*) is a schematic distillation of his Munich experiences in which Toller's own humanitarian socialism, represented by Sonia Irene L., confronts and exposes the inhumanity of what we would now call Marxism-Leninism, represented by the Nameless One. The characters are types and represent classes (Worker), professions (Priest), or predicaments (Prisoner, Husband). Scenes tracing the involvement of a female bourgeois socialist in an abortive revolution alternate with scenes that externalize the conflicts in the woman's conscience. The real and the symbolic scenes are all written in compressed verse with fractured syntax and extreme pathos.

Die Maschinenstürmer (*The Machine-Wreckers*), for which Toller studied Marx and Engels, is based on the Luddite movement in England in 1815. The basic conflict mirrors that in *Masses and Man*: Jimmy Cobbet is an educated idealist who preaches the socialization of the machine which must be used rationally to serve mankind. He is opposed by John Wible, the voice of the masses, who demands the destruction of the machines that are taking away the workers' livelihoods. Cobbet is killed by the workers, but his utopian message survives. The play has a cast of 35 plus extras, not counting the Lord Chancellor, Byron, and Castlereagh who appear in the prologue.

Hinkemann tells the story of a soldier who comes back from the War, castrated by shrapnel, and tries to save his marriage and eke out an existence biting off the heads of small birds and animals in a fairground booth. Büchner's *Woyzeck* is the model for this grotesque study in degradation which Franz Xaver Kroetz has tried to modernize.

The last of Toller's prison plays, *Wotan Unbound*, features W.D. Wotan, a barber and con-man, who leads a nationalist rising against the Weimar Republic and ends up in prison where he writes his memoirs. It is a comedy which satirizes political demagogy, anti-semitism, Hitler, nationalism, and the more overblown features of expressionism.

Toller's lyrical expressionism was regarded as soft-centred by the more radical Brecht and Piscator, but his *Hoppla, wir leben!* (*Hoppla, Such is Life!*) was nonetheless the first production at the Piscatorbühne in 1927. This complicated play shows a communist, who has been committed to an asylum in 1919, trying to adapt, when released, to the changed Berlin of 1927. Toller prescribed a film prologue, in part assembled from newsreel clips, which summarized the social and political events of the detainee's lost years. In *Hoppla* expressionism gives way to *Neue Sachlichkeit* (New Objectivity), and telegraphese to normal speech, but the play's comprehensive gallery of figures and attitudes from 1927, for all its historical interest, has no dramatic life today.

Though he wrote several more plays, Toller's day was past. His 1937 anti-Nazi melodrama *Pastor Hall* was filmed in England and first performed at the Deutsches Theater in East Berlin in 1947. In 1933 Toller emigrated to the USA, via Switzerland, France, and Spain, and gave readings and worked for political charities. In 1939, suffering from insomnia and plagued by a sense of political impotence, he hanged himself in a New York hotel.

—Hugh Rorrison

See also *Volume 1* entries on *Hoppla!*; *Masses and Man*.

———

TOLSTOY, Alexei Konstantinovich. Born in St. Petersburg, Russia, 5 September (Old Style) 1817. A distant relative of Leo Tolstoy. Grew up with his uncle in the Ukraine. Educated at Moscow University. Married Sofya Andreyevna Miller in 1865. Joined the civil service, working for the Moscow Archives at the Foreign Ministry; diplomat, Russian Embassy, Frankfurt, 1836; returned to Russia, and worked in the Imperial Chancery, 1840; wrote short stories from c.1841; published satirical verse and theatrical pastiches, co-written with his relatives, the Zhemchuznikovs, under the pseudonym of civil-service clerk "Kosma Prutkov", 1853–63; undertook military service in the Crimean War, 1855, where he contracted typhus; subsequently inherited his uncle's estate, Krasny Rog, near Chernigov, Ukraine; first-produced play, *Smert Ioanna grotznogo* [*The Death of Ivan the Terrible*], staged 1867. Member, Russian Academy of Science, 1873. Died in Krasny Rog, 10 October 1875

Works

Collections

Dramatiskaya trilogiya. 1876.
Polnoe sobranie sochineny [Complete Collected Works] (4 vols.), edited by D.N. Certelev. 1882–83.
Polnoe sobranie sochineny [Complete Collected Works] (4 vols.). 1907.
Polnoe sobranie sochineny [Complete Collected Works] (3 vols.). 1921–22.

Stage Works

Smert Ioanna grotznogo (produced Alexandrinsky Theatre, St. Petersburg, 1867). 1866; translated as *The Death of Ivan the Terrible*, 1869 and 1926; as *The Terrible Czar*, 1904.
Tsar Fyodor Ioannovich (produced Suvorin's Theatre, St. Petersburg, 1898). 1868; translated as *Tsar Fyodor Ivanovitch*, 1923; as *Czar Feodor Ionannovitch*, 1924.
Tsar Boris [Tsar Boris]. 1870.

Fiction

Knyats Serebryany. 1862; translated as *Prince of Outlaws— Prince Serébryany*, 1927.
Upyr (stories). 1841.

Verse

Polnoe sobranie stikhotvoreny [Complete Collected Verse], edited by E.I. Prochorov.   1984.

Other

Byliny, ballady, pesny [Epics; Ballads; Plays].   1948.
O literature i iskusstve [On Literature and Art], edited by I. Yampolsky.   1984.

*

Criticism

Books:
M. Dalton, *A.K. Tolstoy*, Boston, 1972.

*   *   *

Alexei Tolstoy began his career as a writer of light verse and theatrical parodies before turning to historical subjects which were fashionable during the 1860's. He concentrated his attention on one period: that of Ivan the Terrible and his successors. His first historical work was the novel *Prince Serebryany*. For this he drew much of his material from Karamzin's *History of the Russian State*. However, he took considerable liberties with chronology in order to make dramatic points. His literary models were Shakespeare, as transmitted by Pushkin, and Schiller, whose work and method of shaping historical events for dramatic purposes he knew well. Piotr Gnedich, who directed the first production of *Tsar Fyodor*, suggested Edward Bulwer-Lytton as another influence, and this suggests the degree of romance contained in the works. In his own comments, Tolstoy compared the difference between the history play and the chronicle play to that between the portrait and the photograph. His interest was in the psychology of the protagonists. he had quite definite ideas on the way his plays should be produced, and wrote extensive notes on staging and characterization for both *The Death of Ivan the Terrible* and *Tsar Fyodor*.

The Death of Ivan the Terrible was first presented in St. Petersburg at the Alexandrinsky Theatre in 1867; but despite considerable efforts to make the staging both spectacular and authentic, it did not establish a firm place in the repertoire. The problem lay in the miscasting of a comic actor in the title role, for which Tolstoy himself was responsible. Bad casting was also responsible for the play's lack of success the following year at the Maly Theatre in Moscow. After its initial run, it received only a handful of performances in 1869, then disappeared from the repertoire until 1874, when it was given four performances.

Tsar Fyodor Ivanovitch was banned by the censor, like so many other works which touched on subjects, either historical or contemporary, which were considered politically sensitive. Like all Russian literature of the period, the trilogy was a coded message, and Tolstoy's contemporaries were easily able to identify the political figures, both domestic and foreign, who were represented by the characters.

In 1898 Stanislavski and Nemirovich-Danchenko decided to open the new Moscow Art Theatre with the latter play. Stanislavski felt that it provided the opportunity for a spectacular production, which would impress audiences. A rival production was planned at the same time at Suvorin's Theatre, in St. Petersburg. However, the play was not released by the censor until the late summer, and then with considerable cuts which, Stanislavski maintained, made nonsense of the verse. The play opened on 12 October 1898 in St. Petersburg and on 14 October in Moscow. Stanislavski's production was acclaimed both for its historical accuracy, originality of design, and psychological depth, and remained in the repertoire for many years. The central character, meek, ill, full of good intentions and kindness, is Tolstoy's psychologically most interesting creation. He has been compared to Prince Mishkin in Dostoevsky's *The Idiot*, which appeared in the same year, and also to the King in Schiller's *Maid of Orleans*. He was played by the young Ivan Moskvin, who was given the part in competition with Vsevolod Meyerhold. Stanislavski maintained that the real hero of the play was the Russian people and slanted his production accordingly, filling out the action with crowd scenes.

The Death of Ivan the Terrible was revived by the Art Theatre to open the 1899 season, but was only moderately successful. A weaker play than *Tsar Fyodor*, its chances of success were not helped by the fact that Stanislavski, who was playing the leading role, was ill on the first night, and also by the fact that Stanislavsky had overdirected it, burdening a slight text with a wealth of detail. Over the year it received only 50 performances, as distinct from *Tsar Fyodor* which received 666.

Tsar Boris was accounted the weakest of the trilogy and has been rarely performed.

Contemporary critics were aware of the trilogy's shortcomings—the failure of the love interest in *Tsar Fyodor* and the tedium of the opening scenes in *Tsar Boris*. They were forced to admit, however, that these were the only historical plays of any merit after Pushkin's *Boris Godunov*. In modern times it is the memory of the historic Art Theatre production of *Tsar Fyodor* and Moskvin's masterly performance in the title role that has kept Tolstoy's reputation alive. The play was revived in March 1973 at the Maly Theatre, with Innokenti Smoktunovski as Fyodor.

—Jean Benedetti

TOLSTOY, Leo (Count).   Born Lev Nikolayevich Tolstoy at Yasnaya Polyana, near Tula, Russia, 28 August (Old Style) 1828. Educated at home, in Moscow 1837–41, and in Kazan 1841–44; Kazan University, 1844–47. Married Sofya Andreyevna Behrs in 1862; 13 children; also had one illegitimate son. Landowner on his inherited estate, 1847–48; in Moscow, 1848–51; visited his brother's military unit in Caucasus, and joined artillery battery as non-commissioned officer, 1851–54, then transferred to a unit near Bucharest, 1854, and, as sub-lieutenant, in Sevastopol, 1854–55: resigned as lieutenant, 1855; travelled to France, Switzerland, and Germany. A conscientious landowner on his Yasnaya Polyana estate: set up school, and edited the school journal *Yasnaya Polyana*, 1862–63 (and was member of local educational committee, 1870's); disseminated his social and religious views widely in last decades of his life: his religious views excluded him from the Orthodox Church, 1901. Because of censorship, many works first published abroad. Died in Astapovo, 7 November (Old Style)1910 .

Works

Collections

Plays (includes *The Power of Darkness; The First Distiller: The Fruits of Culture*), translated by Louise and Aylmer Maude. 1903; augmented edition (adding *The Live Corpse; The Cause of it All; The Light Shines in Darkness*), 1915.

Complete Works (24 vols.), edited by Leo Wiener. 1904–05.

The Dramatic Works (includes *The Power of Darkness; The First Distiller; The Fruits of Enlightenment; The Live Corpse; The Light Shines in the Darkness; The Root of All Evil; The Wisdom of Children*), translated by N. Dole. 1923.

Stories and Dramas (includes the fragment *Dramatic Scenes About the Pen Who Became a Beggar* and *Peter the Publican*, the plays *The Nihilist* and *The Contaminated Family*, and stories), various translators. 1926.

Polnoe sobranie sochineny [Complete Collected Works] (90 vols.). 1928–58.

Works (Centenary Edition; 21 vols.), translated by Aylmer Maude. 1929–37.

Stage Works

Zarazhennoye semeystvo. In *Polnoe sobranie sochineny*, 1928; translated as *The Contaminated Family*, in *Stories and Dramas*, 1926.

Nigilist (produced on Tolstoy's estate, Yasnaya Polyana, 1863). In *Polnoe sobranie sochineny*, 1928; translated as *The Nihilist*, in *Stories and Dramas*, 1926, and in *Literary Fragments, Letters and Reminiscences Not Previously Published*, 1931.

Pervy vinokur; ili, Kak chertyonok krayushku zasluzhil (produced Porcelain Factory Marionette Theatre, St. Petersburg, 1886). 1886?; translated as *The First Distiller*, in *Plays*, 1903, and in *Dramatic Works*, 1923.

Vlast Tmy; ili, "Kogotok uvyaz, vsey ptishke propast" (produced in French, Théâtre Libre, Paris, 1888; produced in Russian, Alexandrinsky Theatre, St. Petersburg, 1895). 1887; translated as *The Dominion of Darkness*, 1887; as *The Power of Darkness*, in *Plays*, 1903: several subsequent translations under same title.

Plody prosvescheniya (produced on Tolstoy's estate, Yasnaya Polyana, 1889; produced professionally, Alexandrinsky Theatre, St. Petersburg, 1891). 1891; translated as *The Fruits of Culture*, 1891, and in *Plays*, 1905; as *The Fruits of Enlightenment*, 1891: several subsequent translations under same title.

Zhivoy trup (produced Moscow Art Theatre, 1911). 1911?; translated as *The Living Corpse*, 1912; as *The Live Corpse*, in *Plays*, 1915, and *Dramatic Works*, 1923.

I svet vo tme svetit. 1911?; translated as *The Light Shines in Darkness*, in *Plays*, 1915, and *Dramatic Works*, 1923.

Ot ney vse kachestva. 1913?; translated as *The Cause of it All*, in *Plays*, 1915.

Fiction

Sevastopolskiye rasskazy. 1855–56; translated as *Sebastopol*, 1887; as *The Sebastopol Sketches*, 1986.

Semeynoye schaste. 1859; translated as *Katia*, 1887; as *Family Happiness*, 1888; as *My Husband and I*, 1888; as *The Romance of Marriage*, 1890.

Kazaki. 1863; translated as *The Cossacks*, 1878: several subsequent translations under same title.

Voyna i mir. 1863–69; translated as *War and Peace*, 1886: several subsequent translations under same title.

Anna Karenina. 1875–77; translated as *Anna Karenina*, 1886: several subsequent translations under same title.

Kreytserova sonata. 1891; translated as *The Kreutzer Sonata*, 1890: several subsequent translations under same title.

Khozyain i rabotnik. 1895; translated as *Master and Man*, 1895: several subsequent translations under same title.

Voskreseniye. 1899; translated as *Resurrection*, 1899.

The stories have appeared in several volumes of translations, including: *"A Russian Proprietor" and Other Stories*, 1887, *"The Invaders" and Other Stories*, 1889, and *"The Long Exile" and Other Stories*, 1889, all translated by N.H. Dole; *"Life is Worth Living" and Other Stories*, translated by Count Nairrakow, 1892; *More Tales from Tolstoi*, translated by R.N. Bain, 1902; *"Esarhaddon" and Other Stories*, 1903, *"In the Days of Serfdom" and Other Stories*, 1911, *"The Cossacks" and Other Tales of the Caucasus*, 1917, *Nine Stories*, 1934, all translated by Louise and Aylmer Maude; *"King Assarhadon" and Other Stories*, translated by V. Tchertkoff and I.F. Mayo, 1903(?); *"The Death of Ivan Ilyitch" and Other Stories*, translated by Constance Garnett, 1915; *Tales*, translated by Louis Segal, 1935; *"Notes of a Madman" and Other Stories*, translated by S.S. Koteliansky, 1943; *"The Empty Drum" and Other Stories*, translated by E.C. Parnwell, 1955; *Tales of Sevastopol; The Cossacks*, 1983; *Varya and Her Greenfinch: Little Stories*, 1986; *Stories for My Children*, translated by James Riordan, 1988; *Tolstoy's Short Fiction: Revised Translations, Backgrounds and Sources, Criticism*, translated by Michael R. Katz, 1991.

Memoirs and Letters

On the Personal Christian Life (letters). [1914.

The Diaries of Leo Tolstoy 1847–1852, translated by C.J. Hogarth and A. Sirnis. 1917.

The Journals of Leo Tolstoy 1895–1899, translated by Rose Stransky. 1917.

Love Letters, translated by S.S. Koteliansky and Virginia Woolf. 1923.

The Private Diary of Leo Tolstoy, 1853–1857, translated by Louise and Aylmer Maude. 1927.

Letters, edited by R.F. Christian (2 vols.). 1978.

The Letters of Tolstoy and His Cousin Countess Alexandra Tolstoy 1837–1903, translated by Leo Islavin. Nd.

Diaries, translated by R.F. Christian. 1985.

Other

Detstvo, Otrochestvo, Yunost'(3 vols.). 1852–57; translated as *Childhood, Boyhood, Youth*, 1886; as *Childhood, Adolescence, Youth*, 1981.

Azbuka [An ABC Book]. 1872; revised edition, 1875.

Ispoved. 1884; translated as *A Confession*, 1885.

V chom moya vera? 1884; translated as *My Religion*, 1885; as *What I Believe*, 1885.

In Pursuit of Happiness (essays), translated by Mrs. A. Detano. 1887.

Tak chtozhe nam dela'? 1902; translated as *What to Do*, 1887; uncensored edition, 1888.

O zhizni. 1888; uncensored edition, 1891; translated as *Life*, 1888; as *On Life*, 1902.

The Physiology of War. 1889.

Gospel Stories. 1890.

Kritika dogmaticheskovo bogosloviya [An Examination of Dogmatic Theology]. 1891.

Soyedineniye i perevod chetyryokh evangely (3 vols.). 1892–94; translated as *The Four Gospels Harmonized and Translated*, 1895–96; shortened version, 1890; as *The Gospel in Brief*, 1896.

Tsarstvo Bozhye vnutri vas (2 vols.). [1893–94; translated as *The Kingdom of God is Within You* 2 vols. 1894.

Pisma o Genre Dzhorzhe [Letters on Henry George]. 1897.

Kristianskoye ucheniye. 1898; translated as *The Christian Teaching*, 1898.

Chto takoye iskusstvo? 1898; translated as *What is Art?*, 1898.

Rabstvo nashevo vremeni. 1990; translated as *The Slavery of Our Times*, 1900.

Essays and Letters, translated by Aylmer Maude. 1903.

Christianity and Patriotism. 1905.

End of the Age; The Crisis in Russia. 1906.

The Russian Revolution, translated by Aylmer Maude and others. 1907.

The Hanging Czar, translated by Louise and Aylmer Maude. 1908.

Social Evils and Their Remedy. 1915.

A Confession; What I Believe. 1921; with *The Gospel in Brief*, 1940.

Tolstoy on Art, translated by Aylmer Maude. 1924.

"On Life" and Essays on Religion, translated by Aylmer Maude. 1934.

"The Kingdom of God" and Peace Essays, translated by Aylmer Maude. 1936.

Recollections and Essays, translated by Aylmer Maude. 1937.

The Way to Peace and Greetings to Conscientious Objectors. 1940.

Essays from Tula, translated by Evgeny Lampert. 1948.

Tolstoy on Education, translated by Leo Wiener. 1967.

Tolstoy's Writings on Civil Disobedience and Non-Violence. 1968.

Tolstoy on Education, edited by Alan Pinch and Michael Armstrong. 1982.

"A Confession" and Other Religious Writings, translated by Jane Kentish. 1987.

The Lion and the Honeycomb: The Religious Writings of Tolstoy, translated by Robert Chandler. 1987.

*

Bibliographies

Garth M. Terry, "Tolstoy Studies in Great Britain: A Bibliograhical Survey", in *New Essays on Tolstoy*, by Malcolm Jones, 1978.

David R. Egan, *Lev Tolstoy: An Annotated Bibliography of English-Language Sources to 1978*, Metuchen (New Jersey) and London, 1978.

Criticism

Books:

Aylmer Maude, *Leo Tolstoy*, London, 1918.

G. Abraham, *Tolstoy*, London, 1935.

E. Simmons, *Leo Tolstoy*, Boston, 1946.

Henri Troyat, *Leo Tolstoy: A Biography*, Garden City, New York, 1967.

E. Simmons, *Introduction to Tolstoy's Writings*, Chicago and London, 1968.

R.F. Christian, *Tolstoy: A Critical Introduction*, London, 1969.

R.E. Matlaw (ed.), *Leo Tolstoy: A Collection of Critical Essays*, Englewood Cliffs, New Jersey, 1967.

Henry Gifford (ed.), *Leo Tolstoy: A Critical Anthology*, Harmondsworth, 1971.

Logan Spiers, *Tolstoy and Chekhov*, London, 1971.

E.B. Greenwood, *Tolstoy: The Comprehensive Vision*, London, 1975.

Leo Hecht, *Tolstoy the Rebel*, New York, 1976.

T.G.S. Cain, *Tolstoy*, London, 1977.

Malcolm Jones, *New Essays on Tolstoy*, Cambridge, 1978.

Henry Gifford, *Tolstoy*, Oxford, 1982.

Alexander Fodor, *Tolstoy and the Russians: Reflections on a Relationship*, Ann Arbor, Michigan, 1984.

Harold Bloom (ed.), *Leo Tolstoy*, New York, 1986.

William W. Rowe, *Leo Tolstoy*, Boston, 1986.

Andrew Donskov, *Essays on L.N. Tolstoj's Dramatic Art*, Wiesbaden, 1988.

A.N. Wilson, *Tolstoy: A Biography*, London, 1988.

* * *

The author of *War and Peace* and *Anna Karenina* is not nearly so widely known as a playwright, but the neglect is only partly justified. Tolstoy is himself responsible: in his later writings, notably "What is Art?" and "On Shakespeare and Drama", he virtually rejected all drama—classical, Romantic, and contemporary—as artificial, inflated, barbaric, nonsensical, and immoral. His denunciations of Shakespeare are especially virulent (George Orwell mocked them in his essay "Tolstoy, Lear and the Fool"):

Not only did I get no enjoyment [from Shakespeare's plays], but I felt an ineluctable revulsion, boredom and bewilderment: was I mad to think these works contemptible, outright bad, when they are thought to be the height of perfection by the entire educated world, or was the significance attached by this educated world to Shakespeare's works mad?

Tolstoy attributed the reputation of Shakespearean and all modern drama to a conspiracy of critics and the gullibility of popular opinion: he called for a complete purge:

The sooner people are freed from false praise of Shakespeare, the better—firstly because when people are freed of this lie they will have to understand that any drama which does not have a religious element at its core is . . . the most vile and despicable business . . . Shakespeare's and his imitators' contemptible and immoral works, which aim only to distract and amuse spectators, can in no way be life teachers, and until we have real religious drama, we have to seek a teaching for life from other sources.

Tolstoy exonerated no secular drama, except for a few ethnic dramatic rituals, from his condemnation: even Pushkin, otherwise sacrosanct, was belittled for writing *Boris Godunov* under Shakespearian influence, while the Greek classics were dismissed as aliens. The people, he insisted, were in danger of corruption from the "erotomania" of a dramatic culture forced on them by their corrupt betters. Thus, although it may seem as surprising that Tolstoy should write plays as that a teetotaller should open a chain of breweries, his own dramatic work was meant to provide a moral counterblast to the existing repertoire.

Tolstoy had, in fact, toyed with dramatic form when he first began to write in the 1850's, exploring very similar moral and social themes as in his first short stories. His first completed play, *An Infected Family*, was a polemical comedy attacking both revolutionary youth and serf-owning reactionaries: wisely, it was not then published or performed. In the 1870's, writing *Anna Karenina*, it might be said that Tolstoy succeeded in re-creating classical tragedy within the framework of the modern novel and no longer needed to envisage stage forms.

In 1886, however, after his "spiritual crisis" in which he forswore literature as entertainment, Tolstoy completed his first successful play, *The Power of Darkness*, and, when it was eventually staged in 1895, it turned the Russian theatre in a new direction. Medieval in its morality and modern in its brutality, it shows, in terms not then seen on the stage before, a progression from adultery to child-murder. Tsar Alexander III showed critical perspicacity when he wrote, banning it from theatres and bookstalls, "this drama cannot be staged: it is too real and too horrible in its topic".

Tolstoy's comedy, also of the mid 1880's, *The Fruits of Enlightenment*, likewise combines archaic features (the devices of Molière's comedies) with radically modern topics and patriarchal Christian morality, but was written for an amateur troupe. Both plays show a total disregard for practicalities of staging, for acting techniques, for the autonomy of the theatre: the results on stage disconcerted Tolstoy. When the audience laughed at his comedy, he reacted, "my peasants' speeches constantly express complaint, sometimes an attempt at protest. Their words ought in my opinion to arouse compassion for their hopeless situation, certainly not laughter". The tragic horror of *The Power of Darkness* and the wit of *The Fruits of Enlightenment* are triumphs of Tolstoy the unconscious artist over Tolstoy the conscious moraliser and political axe-grinder, and have kept them on the periphery of the world's repertoire despite their sermonising, inherent improbabilities, and novel-sized casting and scene-setting.

Tolstoy's greatest play, however, is probably his *The Living Corpse*; while it proved to be impressive cinema in the early 1960's, it has not, however, established itself in repertory outside Russia. For late Tolstoy it is an extraordinarily open-minded "problem" play with many Ibsenesque, even Chekhovian overtones. At times it almost seems a revision of *Anna Karenina*—in fact the surname Karenin is re-used for the secondary hero. It is a play about bigamy in which the unreformable husband, Fedya Protasov, feigns suicide—becoming "a living corpse"—so that his wife, Liza, can marry the family friend Victor Karenin. The ruse is discovered, Liza and Victor are threatened with disgrace, even internal exile in Siberia, but are saved by Fedya's final suicide. The impossible situation and the living corpse's obsession with a gypsy girl are dramatised with a power equal to that of Tolstoy the novelist at his greatest. What is new is the moral tolerance, the implication that human beings have a right to marital happiness, which not only makes the play far more accessible to the unconverted, but seems to contradict the intransigent views of the author. The play, in fact, closely follows a real predicament told to Tolstoy by the son of the original characters. Out of consideration for the feelings of his living models, Tolstoy did not publish the play in his lifetime and withheld his usual moral verdict. It was performed in 1911, a year after Tolstoy's death, by Meyerhold's expressionist theatre, which proved to be the right vehicle for Tolstoy's dramatic form, so saturated with characters, tableaux, and social critique. The play's viability was proven by 9,000 performances in ten months of 1912.

Tolstoy's other late plays mostly reverted to a more medieval pattern of simple morality plays addressed to the peasantry. Only his five-act drama *The Light Shines in the Darkness* stands out as a personal work, whose rebellious

hero, Nikolai Saryntsev, summarises Tolstoy's own religious revolt against his own background; but its dramatic impact is blunted by this partisan autobiographical thread and by its cast of over 50.

There are other reasons why a playwright of Tolstoy's stature should have such a marginal status in the world's theatre. Apart from his Christian morality that sometimes appears Islamic in its stringency, much of his power is lost in translation. The awe of *The Power of Darkness* and the pithiness of *The Fruits of Enlightenment* owe much to Tolstoy's ear for peasant speech, for proverbs, for rhythmic phrasing and echoes of liturgy and gospels that are unique to the peasantry he knew; *The Living Corpse* is saturated with the music and the alien phrases of Russian gypsies. The Russian idiolect of Tolstoy's dramas becomes bland in translation, whereas the characters of his novels speak a literary, international Russian that survives translation. Finally, the structure and apparatus of the plays are so heavily loaded that they require the resources of a Stanislavski or a Meyerhold to mobilise and balance them.

—Donald Rayfield

See also *Volume 1* entries on *The Fruits of Enlightenment*; *The Power of Darkness*.

———————

TOPOL, Josef. Born near Benešov, Czechoslovakia, 1 April 1935. Studied at the Academy of Performing Arts, Prague, 1954–59. Appointed librarian and archivist in Emil František Burian's theatre, Prague, 1953; his first play, *Půlnoční vítr* [Midnight Wind], produced 1955; worked with Otomar Krejča at the Narodni Divadlo [National Theatre], Prague, c.1959, and at the Theatre Beyond the Gate, Prague, from 1965 until its closure (by the government) in 1972; subsequently made a living by translating and editing, but his plays not produced 1968–89; after signing the Charter 77 for human rights, 1977, was forced to abandon writing altogether, and worked as stonemason; with the collapse of the Czech communist regime, 1989, his plays were being performed again.

Works

Stage Works

Půlnoční vítr [Midnight Wind] (produced Army Theatre, Prague, 1955). 1956.

Jejich den [Their Day] (produced National Theatre, Prague, 1959). 1962.

Konec masopustu [The End of the Carnival] (produced National Theatre, Prague, 1964). 1963.

Kočka na kolejích [Cat on the Rails] (produced Theatre Beyond the Gate, Prague, 1965). In *Divadlo*, October–December 1968.

Slavík na večeři [Nightingale for Supper] (produced Theatre Beyond the Gate, Prague, 1967). In *Divadlo*, March 1967.

Hodina lásky [An Hour of Love] (produced Theatre Beyond

the Gate, Prague, 1968).   In *Divadlo*, October-November 1968.

Sbohem Sokrate [Goodbye, Socrates].   In German, as *Auf Wiedersehen, Sokrates*, 1971.

Dvě noci s dívkou [Two Nights with a Girl].   In German, as *Zwei Nächte mit einem Mädchen; oder, Wie man Diebe bestiehlt*, 1972.

Hlasy ptáků [The Voices of Birds] (produced Vinohrady Theatre, Prague, 1989).

*   *   *

Josef Topol's approach to the theatre is that of a poet; not one who writes poetry for actors to recite, but one who works with images that can still revive the collective memory of the audience. His work belongs to the tradition of Czech theatre that, so often suppressed in its ability to speak openly, has developed a subtle sense of allusion and allegory. Topol learnt much from E.F. Burian, whose work before World War II had exemplified that tradition. During the early 1950's Burian's political commitment forced him, in his theatrical work, to adopt socialist realism; through his collaboration on Topol's first play, *Půlnoční vítr* (Midnight Wind), Burian broke with socialist realism and, in the last years of his life, returned to the poetic theatre.

"Midnight Wind", a historical drama inspired by Shakespeare, is in many ways a young man's conventional first play; but it is unconventional in its refusal to conform to the prevailing standards of socialist realism. It is about the idealism of youth in conflict with the jealousy of the established leaders of society. The production was seen by Otomar Krejča, who, in 1956, became head of the drama company at the National Theatre. His aim was to build up a repertoire of contemporary drama (Krejča's dramaturg, Karel Kraus, was Topol's tutor at the Academy of Performing Arts). In Krejča's "workshop", Topol wrote *Jejich den* (Their Day), which, like "Midnight Wind", contrasted the idealism of youth with the apathy of middle age. This time, however, the setting was contemporary—a provincial town similar to Topol's own birthplace.

Topol continued to collaborate with Krejča and Kraus. These were the early years of the Prague Spring, when the ice of communism seemed to be thawing, and anything might be possible. His next play, *Konec masopustu* (The End of the Carnival), is probably the most original and theatrically imaginative to emerge from the Czech theatre of the 1960's. The situation—the collectivisation of the land—could have been taken from the village drama of the 1950's. But essentially the play is a treatment of the responsibilities of the individual towards the community and towards his own inner self. The story of Král (or King), the passionately independent farmer, is interwoven with that of his daughter's lover, Rafael. Both of them possess the individual determination not to be coerced into a collective society. The fluid structure of the play enabled Topol to incorporate elements of folk traditions and superstitions, the members of the collective farm sometimes being depicted as their own petty selves, and sometimes as the grotesque and terrifying figures of carnival. "The End of the Carnival" is a play without heroes, a play which recognises the frailty of human ideals and the ambiguities of human motivation.

"The End of the Carnival" was, and remains, the most ambitious and complicated of Topol's plays. When Krejča and Kraus left the National Theatre to found the Theatre Beyond the Gate, Topol went with them and his next three plays were written for that more intimate environment. *Kočka na kolejích* (Cat on the Rails) in a double-bill with

Michel de Ghelderode's *Les Masques ostendais*, was the theatre's opening production in 1965. Virtually a two-hander for Krejča's leading actors, Marie Tomášová and Jan Tříska, the play took as its theme the relationship between a pair of lovers, who find themselves waiting for a train at a lonely railway halt. Vena is restless and searching, while Evi longs for the fulfilment brought by a peaceful and loving life together. There can be no resolution: the two lines run parallel into eternity. Topol was writing not only about the relationship between two individuals, but about irreconcilable conflicts within the single soul. Later that year, Krejča wrote: "Topol is convinced that the protagonist of the contemporary drama is one who does not swim with the tide, who is full of doubt and uncertainty, who is always seeking. The protagonists of our theatres should be just as dissatisfied, searching personalities".

Topol followed "Cat on the Rails" with *Slavík na večeři* (Nightingale for Supper) and *Hodina lásky* (An Hour of Love). "Nightingale for Supper" takes place in a world which, as in our nightmares, resembles real life. The cruel image of the title—a fragile songbird served at a banquet—metamorphoses first into a banal joke—Mr. Nightingale has been invited for an evening meal—and then into grotesque realisation: the natural beauty of the world is indeed going to be devoured by vulgar apathy. The play was a sad metaphor for the decade to come. "An Hour of Love" is another two-hander: El and Ela play the game of love as though they were to part in an hour's time; the intensity thus provoked virtually exhausts their love.

The poetic structure of Topol's plays was undoubtedly influenced by his translations from Shakespeare, two of which (*Romeo and Juliet* and *Love's Labour's Lost*) were produced by Krejča. However, in the early 1970's this collaboration was forcibly ended when the authorities closed down the Theatre Beyond the Gate, and Topol had to earn his living by routine translating and editing. After he signed Charter 77, even these activities were forbidden, and he worked as a stone mason until an injury forced him to retire. The only play he was known to have written during this period was *Sbohem Sokrate* (Goodbye, Socrates), a play full of complex and convoluted metaphors, constantly reflecting and recalling its own imagery.

Towards the end of the 1980's there began to be signs of cultural change, particularly in the theatre, foreshadowing the events of the "Velvet Revolution". Theatre workers, who later became revolutionaries, pressed for the rehabilitation of forbidden playwrights, and Josef Topol was the first. In January 1989, after 20 years' absence from the stage, "The End of the Carnival" was revived in the provinicial town of Cheb. Six months later, a new play, *Hlasy Ptáků* (The Voices of Birds) opened on the stage of the prestigious Vinohrady Theatre in Prague. The Vinohrady Theatre, with its reputation for powerful and spectacular productions, was probably the wrong setting for this subtle and poetic play. "The Voices of Birds" is an examination of the continuity of a man's life and of the legacy of his work; the chief character is the Master, a flamboyant and egocentric actor. In his old age the Master comes face to face with those who, in their different ways, have loved him, and who now question the value, even the existence, of that love. His mistress, agent, sons, former wife, and brash new wife come and go; in the shadows are his housekeeper and his unacknowledged son. The ending conveys Chekhovian resignation, but it takes place in a madhouse; as in Topol's earlier plays, there is no solution to the necessity of existence.

Topol is a poet whose dramatic talents were shaped by Burian, Krejča, and Kraus; his development as a playwright was ended by a bureaucrat's rubber stamp. It remains to be seen whether, in the Czech Republic's new world, the opportunities of the lost 20 years can be repeated.

—Barbara Day

TOURNEUR, Cyril. Born, possibly in Essex, England, c.1575–80. Served the Cecils, the Veres, and the Earl of Essex at various times during his career, much of which was spent in military or diplomatic service; possibly in first Cadiz expedition, led by Essex and Francis Drake, 1596; government courier in 1613; campaign soldier, probably in the Low Countries, 1614; brought before the privy council and briefly imprisoned, 1617; appointed secretary to the council of war and secretary to the marshal's court by Sir Edward Cecil, Lord Marshal of the fleet: accompanied Cecil on second Cadiz expedition, 1625–26. Died from illness incurred during the Cadiz expedition, in Kinsale, Ireland, 28 February 1626.

Works

Collections

Works, edited by Allardyce Nicoll.   1930.
Plays, edited by George Parfitt.   1978.

Plays

The Revenger's Tragedy, possibly by Middleton (produced by the King's Men, London, 1606–07?).   1607.
The Atheist's Tragedy; or, *The Honest Man's Revenge* (produced 1607–11?).   1611.

Verse

The Transformed Metamorphosis.   1600.
A Funeral Poem upon the Death of Sir Francis Vere, Knight. 1609.
A Grief on the Death of Prince Henry.   In *Three Elegies*, 1613.

*

Bibliographies

S.A. Tannenbaum and D.R. Tannenbaum, *Cyril Tourneur: A Bibliography*, New York, 1947.
Kenneth Tucker, *A Bibliography of Writings by and About John Ford and Cyril Tourneur*, Boston, 1977.

Criticism

Books:
Peter B. Murray, *A Study of Cyril Tourneur*, Philadelphia, 1964.
Samuel Schuman, *Cyril Tourneur*, Boston, 1977.

*   *   *

The known facts about the life of Cyril Tourneur are extremely scant. It is thought that he was born sometime during the 1570's and he seems to have had close connections throughout his life with two renowned aristocratic families, the Veres and the Cecils. His attempts to establish a literary career appear to be confined to the first decade of the 17th century, when Tourneur was probably in his mid-20's to 30's. By 1613, he was working in government service as an emissary. In 1617 he was briefly imprisoned, for some unknown misdemeanour, before going into service with the Cecils. In 1625 he accompanied an unsuccessful naval expedition to Cadiz under Sir Edward Cecil. On the journey home the ship docked at Kinsale in Ireland. Tourneur, who had fallen ill, was put ashore along with other sick and wounded, and died there in February 1626.

His first published work, in 1600, is a rather impenetrable allegorical and satirical poem called *The Transformed Metamorphosis*. Four other poems, which would appear to be aristocratic commissions, are known to have been written by him. These include *A Funeral Poem upon the Death of Sir Francis Vere*, entered in the Stationers' Register in 1609, and the funeral elegy *A Grief on the Death of Prince Henry*, printed in 1613. Tourneur's survival as a literary name is a consequence of a widely held view that he was the author of *The Revenger's Tragedy*, published anonymously in 1607, which provides us today with an exemplary illustration of the then popular revenge-play genre. However, the play's true authorship is a matter of controversy and critics have suggested that the real author might be Thomas Middleton, John Marston, or John Webster. The problem with the Tourneur attribution is that there is only one other play of his available with which to compare *The Revenger's Tragedy*. This is *The Atheist's Tragedy* (subtitled *The Honest Man's Revenge*), published in 1609, an experimental work, which is sometimes said to mark the end of the full-blooded revenge-play genre (a dubious argument since dramatic techniques of revenge plays were used by later dramatists, notably Webster, and many plays of the period are now lost, so it is difficult to define the beginnings and endings of such genres with absolute certainty). Tourneur is known to have written a third play, *The Nobleman*, which was performed in 1612 by the King's Men, the leading theatre company at that time. He seems also to have had a hand in a play, written around 1613, called *Ye Arraignment of London* or possibly *The Bellman of London*.

The Revenger's Tragedy uses the context of Italian court life to portray, through sensationally violent iconography, a world of grotesque corruption, which might well be interpreted as a carefully distanced reflection on the lifestyle of members of the Jacobean aristocracy. The play is clearly influenced by medieval thought and imagery in its depiction of a macabre dance of death, in which nearly all the characters are hurtled headlong to Hell by their uncontrollable lusts. Vindice, whose betrothed has been poisoned by the Duke for refusing his advances, determines on revenge and arranges a secret meeting between the Duke and "a country lady", who turns out to be the disguised and poisoned skull of Vindice's betrothed. The Duke's embrace with the skull proves fatal, and in his death agony he is forced to witness another secret liaison, this time between his wife and Spurio, his bastard son. Vindice then engineers the destruction of the rest of the Duke's family, who are locked in their own treacherous power struggle, and the play ends in a grand masque of death. Vindice's glee in the magnificent theatricality of his own revenge-schemes reveals the extent of his own personal corruption and provides an ironic comment on the role of the dramatist. As a moral lesson, Vindice is put to death at the end of the play.

The critic Muriel Bradbrook has described *The Atheist's Tragedy* as a "*drame à thèse*", since it tests, through action, the philosophical belief of its central character D'Amville. As such, it is very different from the medieval world-view of *The Revenger's Tragedy*, and looks forward to the dramatic approach of the later 17th-century French dramatist Pierre Corneille. Certainly the play does not have the same intensity of pace, of gleeful violence and corruption, as *The Revenger's Tragedy*. The action is often slow, if not ponderous. In the first scene we are given a lengthy explanation by D'Amville, the atheist, of his personal creed that pleasure and profit are the only worthwhile pursuits in life. Unlike the characters in *The Revenger's Tragedy*, who are reduced, as it were, to bestiality by their own lusts and passions, D'Amville quite consciously argues for a "natural" affinity between man and beast, with the essential difference being that man has the power to increase his pleasure and profit before being reduced to dust. Rationality, based upon "false" premises (since there is no place in this scheme for the existence of God), is the key to his character and, as such, provides a satire upon the emergent scientific thinking of the age. D'Amville uses his theoretical position to justify disinheritance, murder, and incestuous rape. Unfortunately for him, his schemes do not go to plan. The most bizarre piece of bad fortune befalls him at the end of the play when he is about to execute the innocent lovers Charlemont and Castabella, but accidently bashes in his own brains with the axe. This sudden reversal of fortune leads to his last-minute abandoning of his atheistical beliefs and accepting of the existence of a power above nature.

One of the difficulties of the play, in terms of dramatic action, is that D'Amville's chief adversary, the disinherited Charlemont, whose father is murdered at the instigation of D'Amville, is a passive, God-fearing, and rather lacklustre character who exemplifies the maxim that "patience is the honest man's revenge". His stoical acceptance of his fate means that there is no counter-force to move the action forward with any sense of urgency. Despite this lack of tension, there is an interesting mix of several dramatic styles, and the boldest illustration of this is a graveyard scene, where satirical and bawdy farce is juxtaposed with moments of great pathos and melodrama.

—Andy Piasecki

See also *Volume 1* entries on *The Atheist's Tragedy*; *The Revenger's Tragedy*

TRAVERS, Ben(jamin). Born in Hendon, Middlesex, England, 12 November 1886. Educated at the Abbey School, Beckenham, Kent; Charterhouse, Godalming, Surrey, until 1904; studied in Dresden, 1904. Married Violet Mouncey in 1916 (died 1951); one daughter and two sons. Worked in the family wholesale grocery business, John Travers and Sons, in London, 1904 and 1909–11, and in Singapore and Malacca, 1905–08; staff member, Bodley Head, publishers, London, 1911–14; served in the Royal Naval Air Service, 1914–17: squadron commander; transferred to the Royal Flying Corps as major, 1918: Air Force Cross, 1920; full-time writer from 1919: first-produced play, *The Dippers*, staged 1922, and he wrote nine "Aldwych farces", 1925–33, most of which had

their London runs at the Aldwych Theatre; joined the Royal Air Force, 1939: squadron leader, attached to Ministry of Information, 1940. Prime warden, Fishmongers Company, London, 1946; president, Dramatists Club, 1956–60. CBE (Commander, Order of the British Empire), 1976. Died in London, 18 December 1980.

Works

Collections

Five Plays (includes *A Cuckoo in the Nest; Rookery Nook; Thark; Plunder; The Bed Before Yesterday*).   1977.

Stage Works

The Dippers, from his novel (produced Court Theatre, Liverpool, 1922).
The Three Graces, from the play by Carl Lombardi and A.M. Willner, music by Franz Lehar (produced Empire Theatre, London, 1924).
A Cuckoo in the Nest, from his novel (produced Court Theatre, Liverpool, 1925).   1938.
Rookery Nook, from his novel (produced King's Theatre, Southsea, 1926).   1930.
Thark (produced King's Theatre, Southsea, 1927).   1932.
Plunder (produced King's Theatre, Southsea, 1928).   1931.
Mischief, from his novel (produced King's Theatre, Southsea, 1928).
A Cup of Kindness (produced King's Theatre, Southsea, 1929).   1934.
A Night Like This (produced Aldwych Theatre, London, 1930).
Turkey Time (produced Aldwych Theatre, London, 1931).   1934.
Dirty Work (produced Aldwych Theatre, London, 1932).
A Bit of a Test (produced Aldwych Theatre, London, 1933).
Chastity, My Brother (produced Embassy Theatre, London, 1936).
Nun's Veiling (as *O Mistress Mine*, produced St. James's Theatre, London, 1936; revised version, as *Nun's Veiling*, produced Bromley, Kent, 1953).   1956.
Banana Ridge (produced Strand Theatre, London, 1938).   1939.
Spotted Dick (produced Strand Theatre, London, 1939).
She Follows Me About (produced Garrick Theatre, London, 1943).   1945.
Outrageous Fortune (produced Winter Garden Theatre, London, 1947).   1948.
Runaway Victory (produced Brighton, 1949).
Wild Horses (produced Manchester, 1952).   1953.
Corker's End (produced Yvonne Arnaud Theatre, Guildford, Surrey, 1968).
The Bed Before Yesterday (produced Lyric Theatre, London, 1975).   In *Five Plays*, 1977.
After You with the Milk.   1985.

Screenplays

A Little Bit of Fluff (Skirts), with Ralph Spence and Wheeler Dryden, 1928; *Rookery Nook (One Embarrassing Night)*, with W.P. Lipscomb, 1930; *Thark*, 1932; *A Night Like This*, 1932; *Just My Luck*, 1933; *Turkey Time*, 1933; *A Cuckoo in the Nest*, with A.R. Rawlinson, 1933; *Up to the Neck*, 1933; *Dirty Work*, 1934; *Lady in Danger*, 1934; *A Cup of Kindness*, 1934; *Fighting Stock*, 1935; *Stormy Weather*, 1935; *Foreign*

Ben Travers with Polly Adams (left) and Winifred Shotter during rehearsals for the 1976 National Theatre revival of Travers' *Plunder*: Winifred Shotter played Joan Hewlett in the 1928 Aldwych Theatre production, and Polly Adams acted the role in the revival.

Affaires, 1935; *Pot Luck*, 1936; *Dishonour Bright*, 1936; *For Valour*, 1937; *Second Best Bed*, 1938; *Old Iron*, 1938; *So This is London*, with others, 1939; *Banana Ridge*, with Walter C. Mycroft and Lesley Storm, 1941; *Uncle Silas (The Inheritance)*, 1947; *Fast and Loose*, with A.R. Rawlinson, 1954.

Television Plays

Potter, 1948; *Picture Page*, 1949.

Fiction

The Dippers. 1920.
A Cuckoo in the Nest. 1922.
Rookery Nook. 1923.
Mischief. 1925.
The Collection Today (stories). [1929.
The Dippers, Together with Game and Rubber and The Dunkum Jane. 1932.
Hyde Side Up. 1933.

Memoirs and Letters

Vale of Laughter (autobiography). 1957.
A-Sitting on a Gate (autobiography). 1978.

Other

94 Declared: Cricket Reminiscences. 1981.

Editor, *The Leacock Book*. 1930.
Editor, *Pretty Pictures, Being a Selection of the Best American Pictorial Humour*. 1932.

*

Criticism

Books:
Leslie Smith, *Modern British Farce*, London, 1989.

* * *

In a remarkably long career as a prolific dramatist, screenwriter, and novelist, Ben Travers enjoyed two distinct periods of fame and popularity. From 1925 to 1933 his series of nine farces delighted audiences at London's Aldwych Theatre. 50 years later, much to his own amazement, Travers was "rediscovered". In 1976 his highly successful new comedy *The Bed Before Yesterday* was running simultaneously in London with two farce revivals, *Plunder* and *Banana Ridge*. In the last six years of his life Travers became a much-feted theatrical personality, celebrated for his longevity and sprightliness and once more in favour with producers and audiences who, tired of social-realist plays, embraced the survivor of an earlier popular-theatre tradition. Ironically, the "rediscovery" had been launched by the Royal Court Theatre which had, uncharacteristically, revived *A Cuckoo in the Nest* in 1964; but in reality, many of the early farces had maintained their position in the repertoires of provincial and amateur theatres, and something akin to a folk-memory had formed around the Aldwych farces. Bearing scant relation to the political and social conditions of their time of writing they existed, like P.G. Wodehouse's novels with which they have much in common, in a timeless comic world.

Travers' theatrical roots reached back to Pinero, whose farces Travers studied for their construction, and to the acting styles of Seymour Hicks, Charles Hawtrey, and Gerald du Maurier. Travers stated his farce formula simply: "Act II—the sympathetic and guileless hero is landed in the thick of some grievous dilemma or adversity. Act I—he gets into it. Act III—he gets out of it". The best of his farces—*A Cuckoo in the Nest*, *Rookery Nook*, *Thark*, *Plunder*, and *A Night Like This*—are more loosely plotted and less urgent than Feydeau's, and rely on wordplay, nonsense, insults, set routines and eccentrically named characters who muddle through in peculiarly English fashion.

Almost invariably the plots feature a sympathetically raffish hero and his naive, flapping friend who press-gang a grotesquely hen-pecked husband into helping them out of a scrape involving an often scantily clad young woman in difficulties. Although nothing improper ever occurs, the men are panicked by the presence of sweet but suspicious fiancées and wives, or by middle-aged termagants in the shape of mothers-in-law, cleaning ladies, or hotelkeepers who patrol the plays sniffing out improprieties. Despite gross male incompetence, these mountainous guardians of respectability are ultimately trounced, the situation retrieved, and morality upheld.

Formulaic he may have been, but Travers was superbly served by the Aldwych company headed by Tom Walls and Ralph Lynn. Walls produced, and alternated portraying irascible old buffers with an eye for a trim ankle with younger racy men-about-town, while monocled Lynn exercised precise vocal and physical comic timing as the silly-ass friends. A *Times* review of *Turkey Time* singled out Lynn's trick of "dropping verbal bricks and retrieving them an inch from the ground". The central male trio was completed by Robertson Hare as the gormless hen-pecked, put-upon friend, ruthlessly bullied by his co-conspirators. Among others in the regular team were Mary Brough, specialist in formidable matrons with a touch of vulgarity, and Winifred Shotter, who supplied the love interest in many of the farces. Something of their ensemble quality can be glimpsed in the filmed versions of these farces, despite their wooden direction.

So successful was Travers' formula that he rarely departed from it. One measure of the popularity of the Aldwych series is Travers' convention of having the principals speak their opening lines off-stage, allowing audiences their moment of recognition and applause without holding up the action. As the sequence progressed, audiences carried expectation and goodwill from one play to the next. Travers was in no position to deny them their favourite sequences: the two heroes acting incompetently in concert or warily in competition for the girl; the inveigling of the Hare character into some dubious escapade; the rehearsed excuses which founder disastrously when deployed. Playful language, which encompasses cross-talk, running gags, silly puns, comic vocal mannerisms and broken-backed insults, may look leaden on the page, but proved eminently performable. Modern revivals, however, have sometimes struggled to capture Travers' idiom, substituting

over-elaborate business for the honed skills of the original players and the unscripted rapport they enjoyed with their audiences.

The sexual content of the farces is now so tame as to be almost non-existent. Bedroom scenes demonstrate the hero's discomfort rather than sexual prowess, and provide opportunities for extended comic routines. In *Cuckoo*, Wykeham (originally played by Lynn) attempts to snuggle down on the floor of a cramped bedroom of an inn, while his untroubled lady companion luxuriates in the bed, in a scene reminiscent of W.C. Fields' vaudeville sketch "A Night on the Porch". In *Thark* the two heroes uneasily share a bed in a haunted room. A bedroom becomes the scene of a fumbled jewel robbery in *Plunder*, while in the remaining farces, as *Rookery Nook*'s cleaning lady Mrs. Leverett says, "the other bedrooms is elsewhere". None of the early farces poses any real threat to conventional morality, with the exception of *Plunder*, a suspenseful mix of farce and thriller, described by Travers as "a nice study in ethics". It has the two leads murder one of the characters, and subversively proposes that all property is theft, a challenge muffled by Travers' manipulation of audience sympathy and his adoption of the gentleman crook format. *Plunder* alone anticipates later reworkings of the genre, notably Orton's *Loot*. Nevertheless, in Travers' farces, beneath the froth one can detect a muted plea for guilt-free sexual enjoyment which he finally voiced in his 90th year in *The Bed Before Yesterday*.

This comic and unexpectedly touching portrayal of the sexual awakening of a middle-aged woman reverses the conventions of his farces, which depict such women as unpleasured and unpleasurable and allow the men all the running; but the play carries a plot old-fashioned even for its 1930's setting. The later *After You with the Milk* entertainingly distinguishes between married love and sexual pleasure, but failed to gain comparable success. *Malacca Linda* remains unproduced. Travers' reputation seems certain to rest on his first, rather than last, flowering of talent.

—Ronald W. Strang

TREMBLAY, Michel. Born in Montreal, Quebec, Canada, 25 June 1942. Educated at École Saint-Stanislas, Montreal, 1955–59. Linotypist, costume department of Radio-Canada television, 1963–66; first plays staged 1965; full-time writer since 1967. Recipient of many awards, including: Chalmers award, 1972, 1973, 1974, 1975, 1978, 1986, 1989; Prix Victor Morin, 1974; Canadian Film Festival Award, 1975; Ontario Lieutenant-Governor's Medal, 1976 (twice); Prix France-Quebec, 1981, 1985; Festival du Théâtre des Amériques Award, 1985; 1990; Grand Prix du Public, 1990; Jacques-Cartier Lyon Prize, 1991. Honorary doctorates: Concordia University, 1990; McGill University, 1991. Chevalier, 1984, and Officier, 1991, l'Ordre des Arts et des Lettres (France).

Works

Collections

"La Duchesse de Langeais" and Other Plays (includes *La Duchesse de Langeais*; *Berthe*; *Johnny Mangano and His*

Astonishing Dogs; Gloria Star; Surprise! Surprise!).
[1976.
Théâtre I (includes 10 plays).   1991.
"The Guid Sisters" and Other Plays (includes *Manon/Sandra; Albertine in Five Times*), various translators.   1991.

Stage Works

Le Train (broadcast on radio, 1964; produced Montreal, 1965).   1990.
Messe noir, from the stories in *Contes pour buveurs attardés* (produced Théâtre du Gésu, Montreal, 1965).
En Pièces détachées (produced as *Cinq*, Théâtre de Quat'Sous, Montreal, 1966; revised version, as *En Pièces détachées*, produced Théâtre de Quat'Sous, Montreal, 1969).   With *La Duchesse de Langeais*, 1970; translated as *Like Death Warmed Over*, 1973; as *En Pièces détachées*, 1975.
Les Belles-Soeurs (produced Théâtre du Rideau Vert, Montreal, 1968).   1968; translated as *Les Belles Soeurs (The Sisters-in-Law)*, 1974; as *The Guid Sisters*, in *"The Guid Sisters" and Other Plays*, 1991.
Lysistrata, with André Brassard, from the play by Aristophanes (produced National Arts Centre, Ottawa, 1969).   1969.
La Duchesse de Langeais (produced by Les Insolents de Val d'Or, Quebec, 1969).   With *En Pièces détachées*, 1970; translated in *"La Duchesse de Langeais" and Other Plays*, 1976.
Les Paons (produced National Arts Centre, Ottawa, 1971).   1969.
L'Effet des rayons gamma sur les vieux-garçons, from a play by Paul Zindel (produced Théâtre de Quat' Sous, Montreal, 1970).   1970.
Et Mademoiselle Roberge boit un peu, from a play by Paul Zindel (produced Montreal, 1972).   1971.
Le Pays du dragon, from four one-act plays by Tennessee Williams (produced Montreal, 1971).
À Toi, pour toujours, ta Marie-Lou (produced Théâtre de Quat'Sous, Montreal, 1971).   1971; translated as *Forever Yours, Marie-Lou*, 1975.
Demain Matin, Montréal m'attend, music by François Dompierre (produced Jardin des Étoiles, La Ronde, Montreal, 1970).   1972.
Hosanna (produced Théâtre de Quat'Sous, Montreal, 1973).   With *La Duchesse de Langeais*, 1973; translated as *Hosanna*, 1974.
Mistero buffo, from the play by Dario Fo (produced Théâtre du Nouveau Monde, Montreal, 1973).
Bonjour, là, bonjour (produced National Arts Centre, Ottawa, 1974).   1974; translated as *Bonjour, là, bonjour*, 1975.
Mademoiselle Marguerite, from a play by Roberto Athayde (produced National Arts Centre, Ottawa, 1976).   1975.
Les Héros de mon enfance (produced Théâtre de la Marjolaine, Eastman, Quebec, 1975).   1976.
Surprise! Surprise! (produced Théâtre du Nouveau Monde, Montreal, 1975).   With *Damnée Manon, sacrée Sandra*, 1977; translated as *Surprise! Surprise!* in *"La Duchesse de Langeais" and Other Plays*, 1976.
Sainte-Carmen de la Main (produced by Compagnie Jean-Duceppe, Montreal, 1976).   1976; translated as *Saint Carmen of the Main*, 1981.
Damnée Manon, sacrée Sandra (produced Théâtre du Quat' Sous, Montreal, 1977).   With *Surprise! Surprise!* 1977; translated as *Damnée Manon, sacrée Sandra*, 1981; as

Manon/Sandra, in *"The Guid Sisters" and Other Plays*, 1991.
L'Impromptu d'Outremont (produced Théâtre du Nouveau Monde, Montreal, 1980).   1980; translated as *The Impromptu of Outremont*, 1981.
Les Grandes Vacances (produced by Théâtre de l'Oeil, Salle Fred Barry, Montreal, 1981).
Les Anciennes Odeurs (produced Théâtre du Quat'Sous, Montreal, 1981).   1981; translated as *Remember Me*, 1984.
Oncle Vania with Kim Yaroshevskaya, from a play by Anton Chekhov (produced National Arts Centre, Ottawa, 1984).   1983.
Albertine en cinq temps (produced National Arts Centre, Ottawa, 1984).   1984; translated as *Albertine in Five Times*, 1987, and in *"The Guid Sisters" and Other Plays*, 1991.
Le Gars de Québec, from a play by Gogol (produced by Compagnie Jean-Duceppe, Théâtre Port Royal de la Place des Arts, Montreal, 1985).   1985.
Six Heures au plus tard, from the play by Marc Perrier.   1986.
Le Vrai Monde? (produced National Arts Centre, Ottawa, and Théâtre du Rideau Vert, Montreal, 1987).   1987; translated as *The Real World*, 1988.
Nelligan, music by André Gagnon (produced Théâtre Maisonneuve, Montreal, 1990).   1990.
La Maison suspendue (produced by Compagnie Jean-Duceppe, Montreal, 1990).   1990; translated as *La Maison suspendue*, 1991.

Screenplays

Françoise Durocher, Waitress, with André Brassard, 1972; *Il était une fois dans l'est*, with André Brassard, 1973; *Parlez-vous d'amour*, 1976; *Le Soleil se lève en retard*, 1977; *Le Coeur découvert*, 1986; *Le Grand Jour*, 1988; *Six Heures plus tard*, 1988; *Le Vrai Monde?*, 1991.

Television Plays

Trois petit tours (includes the sketches *Berthe*; *Johnny Mangano and His Astonishing Dogs*; *Gloria Star*), 1969 (published 1971); *En Pièces détachées*, 1971; *Bonheur d'occasion*, from the novel by Gabrielle Roy, 1977.

Radio Plays

Le Train, 1964; *Saint Carmen of the Main*, 1987.

Fiction

Contes pour buveurs attardés.   1966; translated as *Stories for Late Night Drinkers*, 1977.
La Cité dans l'oeuf.   1969.
C't'à ton tour, Laura Cadieux.   1973.
La Grosse Femme d'à côté est enceinte.   1978; translated as *The Fat Woman Next Door is Pregnant*, 1981.
Thérèse et Pierrette à l'école des Saints-Anges.   1980; translated as *Therese and Pierrette and the Little Hanging Angel*, 1984.
La Duchesse et le roturier.   1982.
Des Nouvelles d'Édouard.   1984.
Le Coeur découvert: Roman d'amours.   1986; translated as *The Heart Laid Bare*, 1989; as *Making Room*, 1990.
Le Premier Quartier de la lune.   1989.
Les Vues animées.   1990.

Other

Québec, trois siècles d'architecture, with Claude Paulette and Luc Noppen.   1979.

*

Bibliographies

P. Lavoie, "Bibliographie", in *Voix et images*, Winter 1982.

Criticism

Books:
Michel Bélair, *Michel Tremblay*, Montreal, 1972.
Geraldine Anthony (ed.), *Stage Voices: Twelve Canadian Playwrights Talk About Their Lives and Work*, New York, 1978.
Renate Usmiani, *Michel Tremblay: A Critical Study*, Vancouver, Douglas, and McIntyre, 1982.
Ruth B. Antosh, "Michel Tremblay and the Fantastic of Violence", in *Aspects of Fantasy*, edited by William Coyle, Westport, Connecticut, 1986.
Claude Pelletier (ed.), *Michel Tremblay II: Dossier de presse 1968–1986*, Sherbrooke, Quebec, 1986.

Articles:
Catherine McQuaid, "Michel Tremblay's Seduction of the 'Other Solitude'", in *Canadian Drama*, 2, 1976.
Bruce Serafin, "Five Short Plays by Tremblay", in *Essays on Canadian Writing*, 11, 1978.
Renate Usmiani, "Where to Begin the Accusation" (interview) and "The Tremblay Opus: Unity in Diversity," in *Canadian Theatre Review*, 24, 1979.
John Ripley, "From Alienation to Transcendence: The Quest for Selfhood in Michel Tremblay's Plays", in *Canadian Literature*, 85, 1980.
Pierre Gobin, "Michel Tremblay: An Interweave of Prose and Drama", in *Yale French Studies*, 65, 1983.
Eugene Benson (ed.), "*Saint Carmen of the Main* and the Plays of Michel Tremblay: A Panel Discussion", in *Canadian Drama*, 14, 1988.

*   *   *

The major Quebec playwright of the past 25 years, Michel Tremblay is now recognized as well as one of the great innovators of modern drama. Few works have ever represented such a universally recognized turning point in the evolution of a national stage as did his *Les Belles-Soeurs* in 1968: it is now normal to refer to theatre before that date as "French-Canadian", afterwards, and as "Québécois".

Initially the furore aroused by the language of this play obscured its innate merits. Many of the established critics in Montreal were scandalized by the use of undiluted *joual*, the disjointed, anglicized French of the semi-literate urban Québécois, hitherto considered too ugly for public exposition. For generations Quebec audiences had accepted a neutral, international French as standard in the theatre, except in popular entertainments such as burlesque. Tremblay, himself a product of working-class Montreal, rejected this tradition, seeing in it both the very essence of French-Canadians' feelings of alienation and cultural inferiority and a basic reason why theatre had never become popular in his country, except, significantly, for burlesque and revue. Within a few months the controversy had subsided, and even the most grudging critics were forced to admit that *Les Belles-Soeurs* was the most powerful and most original play per-

formed in Quebec to that date. The decades since then have only confirmed that judgement. The play could only have been written in *joual*: the language itself is at the same time the most striking symptom of Québécois alienation, and the most effective means of expressing it—the medium *is* most of the message.

For the next decade Tremblay's theatre dealt with the same shabby settings, the same lives of quiet and not-so-quiet despair as in *Les Belles-Soeurs*, with many of the same characters re-appearing from one work to the next. These plays, especially *À Toi pour toujours, ta Marie-Lou (Forever Yours, Marie-Lou)*, *Sainte Carmen de la Main*, and the last in the series, *Damnée Manon, sacrée Sandra (Manon/Sandra)*, represent a sort of aesthetic exorcism by the author of the personal demons inherited from his past. And, as with *Les Belles-Soeurs*, that exorcism is achieved through complex effects of lighting and decor, with stylized choruses, lyric monologues, flashbacks and other anti-realistic devices, in intensely theatrical productions directed by Tremblay's close adviser and collaborator, André Brassard. Nothing like these had been seen before in Quebec; and these productions have influenced, directly or indirectly, virtually every play written in the province since 1968.

Michel Tremblay's strong political commitment (he favours separate nationhood for his native province) underlay all the writing of his first, "angry", period up to 1976, the year when the separatist Parti Québécois came to power. As has happened with many other intellectuals in Quebec, he has tended to distance himself from overt political statement or action since then, turning instead to more universal concerns. And, as with Marcel Dubé, one observes, in the evolution of Tremblay's theatre since 1977, a movement away from working-class characters and situations towards middle-class settings and preoccupations, particularly evident in *L'Impromptu d'Outremont* and *Les Grandes Vacances*. Since that time also, Tremblay has turned more frequently to prose fiction rather than to drama, establishing himself as one of the most important Quebec novelists of the 1980's. In drama, he has turned his hand more frequently to adaptations of foreign works and, recently, to opera, in his highly successful *Nelligan*, with music by André Gagnon, produced at the Montreal Opera in February 1990. This opera in two acts focuses on the best-known tragic Quebec poet Émile Nelligan, in whose personal tragedy (he died in an insane asylum) Tremblay sees a parable for French-Canadians of his time. The most convincing proof that his dramaturgical talent is undiminished since 1976, however, is *Albertine, en cinq temps (Albertine in Five Acts)*, a poignant, masterful depiction of five stages in the life of one ageing woman, all five in constant dialogue with each other, in that relentless pursuit of self-knowledge and self-possession which characterizes his best work. *Albertine* is considered by many critics to be his best play to date; by some, it is judged the most powerful play in Quebec's entire repertory. With the increasing political and cultural independence of Quebec, it is expected that Tremblay's skill will henceforth continue to be directed towards universal human topics as evident in *Albertine*, and that his initial obsession with personal and national identification, essential to his own maturing as a playwright, will now diminish.

—Leonard E. Doucette

See also *Volume 1* entry on *The Sisters-in-Law*.

TRETYAKOV, Sergei (Mikhailovich). Born in Goldingen, Kurland, Russian Empire (now Kuldiga, Latvia), 8 June (21 June, New Style) 1892. Educated at Gymnasium, Riga; studied law at Moscow University, graduated 1916. Married Olga Viktorovna Gomolitskaya in 1920; one daughter (adopted). Cultural administrator, writer, and journalist, in Siberia and the Soviet Far East, 1917–22; involved with the futurist Creation movement, 1919–22, and edited the artistic journal *Tvorchestvo* [Creative Work]; taught Russian in China, at Beijing University, 1924–25; returned to Moscow and collaborated on plays with the directors Sergei Eisenstein (at the Proletkult Theatre) and Vsevolod Meyerhold, 1922–27; first plays produced 1923; wrote for the journals *Lef*, 1923–25, and *Novy Lef*, 1927–28 (the last issues of which he edited, following Mayakovsky's suicide); editor, *International Literature*; travelled to Germany, Austria, and Denmark, 1930–31; met Bertolt Brecht and Erwin Piscator, 1931, and subsequently translated three of Brecht's plays; fell into official disfavour, and was arrested on an accusation of spying, 16 July 1937. Executed 10 September 1937 (some sources give 1939).

Works

Collections

Slyshish, Moskva?!; Protivagazy; Rychi Kitai! [Are You Listening, Moscow?!; Gas Masks; Roar China!]. 1966.

Stage Works

Na vsyakogo mudretsa dovolno prostoty [Even A Wise Man Stumbles], from a play by Ostrovsky (produced Proletkult Theatre, Moscow, 1923).
Neporochnoye zachatiye [Immaculate Conception] (produced 1923).
Slyshish, Moskva?! [Are You Listening, Moscow?!] (produced Proletkult Theatre, Moscow, 1923). 1924.
Zemlya dybom, from a play by Marcel Martinet (produced Sohn Theatre, Moscow, 1923). 1924?; translated as *Earth Rampant*, in *Early Soviet Drama*, 1991.
Protivogazy [Gas Masks] (produced in a factory hall, Moscow, 1924). 1924.
Rychi Kitai! (produced Meyerhold Theatre, Moscow, 1926). 1926; translated as *Roar China!*, 1931.
Khochu rebenka [I Want a Baby] (produced Meyerhold Theatre, Moscow, 1929).
Epicheskiye dramy [Epic Plays] (translations of *Die Mutter*, *Die Massnahme*, and *Heilige Johann der Schlachthöfe*, from plays by Brecht. 1934.

Screenplays

Eliso, 1928; *Sol svanety*, 1930; *Chabarda*, 1931.

Sergei Tretyakov (seated, right of centre), Vladimir Mayakovsky (seated, right), with other members of the *Lef* group and Boris Pasternak.

Fiction

Den Shi-Hua. 1930; translated as *Chinese Testament: The Autobiography of Tan Shih-hua*, 1934.

Verse

Zheleznaya pauza. 1919.
Yasnich. 1919.
Itogo. 1924.
Rechevik. 1929.

Other

Chzhungo [Jong-guo] (essays on China). 1927.
Mesyats v derevne [A Month in the Country] (essays). 1931.
Vyzov [The Challenge] (essays on collectivisation). 1933.
Tysyacha i odin trudoden [1001 Workdays]. 1934.
Lyudi odnogo kostra [People of a Single Bonfire] (essays). 1936.
Strana-perekrestok [A Country at a Crossroads] (essays on Czechoslovakia). 1937.
Den Shi-khua; Lyudi odnogo kostra; Strana perekrestok, edited by V. Pertsov. 1962.

*

Criticism

Books:
Fritz Mierau, *Erfindung und Korrektur: Tret' jakows Ästhetik der Operativität*, Berlin, 1976.

Articles:
Fritz Mierau, "Tatsache und Tendenz: Der Schriftsteller Sergej Tretjakow", in *Weimarer Beiträge*, 3, 1972.
Fritz Mierau, "Sergej Tret' jakow und Bertolt Brecht: Das Produktionsstück *Xocu rebenka*", in *Zeitschrift für Slawistik*, 20, 1975.
Walter J. and R.I. Meserve, "The Stage History of *Roar China*", in *Theatre Survey*, May 1980.

* * *

Tretyakov began his career as a futurist poet, turning to the more public form of drama only after the Revolution. Yet the fact that Bertolt Brecht called him "my teacher" indicates that his plays form a fascinating and important *oeuvre*. His first full length dramas were adaptations: *Earth Rampant* from Martinet's *Night* and "A Wise Man" from Ostrovsky's *Even a Wise Man Stumbles*. These paved the way for his "agit" plays, "Are You Listening, Moscow?!" and "Gas Masks" as well as his "epic" dramas, *Roar, China!* and "I Want a Baby".

Tretyakov wrote from a position of enthusiastic, perhaps idealistic, support for the Revolution because he believed it gave society the chance to review and renew every area of life. The playwright had the duty "to lift the playgoer out of his equilibrium, so that he will not leave [the theatre] serene but ready for action". This meant, first, creating plays which scrutinized not only overtly political actions, but also less obviously political topics such as safety at work (Gas Masks), or human sexuality (I Want a Baby). And second, it involved the kind of methods already pioneered by Vsevolod Meyerhold who directed *Earth Rampant*—projected captions, constructivist settings, an "open" ending, and, most

importantly, an episodic structure. Indeed, Tretyakov described *Earth Rampant* as a "montage" of the text of Martinet's original, by which he meant a concentration on moments of action, "poster-like turning-points", which interrupted one another rather than flowing smoothly to a conventional climax.

His next work after *Earth Rampant*, "A Wise Man", was characterized by its director, Sergei Eisenstein, as "a montage of attractions", defining an "attraction" as "any aggressive moment in theatre" which produces "emotional shocks in the spectator". In "A Wise Man", the attractions were spectacular and flamboyant, especially the circus tricks like the tightrope walk over the audience's heads, and clown antics such as the water fight near the end.

This "circusization" of theatre certainly produced "emotional shocks" in its audiences, but failed to focus the issues so that the spectators were made "ready for action". In "Are You Listening, Moscow?!" and "Gas Masks", both also directed by Eisenstein, Tretyakov worked hard to keep a stimulating level of theatricality (though not, perhaps, circusization), which would yet retain the capacity to make the audience rethink particular issues. How he did this may be illustrated from "Gas Masks". A scene of skullduggery between foreman and director is interrupted by a comic chase when a worker is pursued by women with ikons, and a Punch-and-Judy-like combat ensues. The director is perched precariously up a ladder during this episode ("attraction"), which is actually like traditional anti-religious farce. When they go, the director craftily takes out a bottle and gives the foreman a swig. But they are interrupted again, this time by a group of Komsomol youths, who enter "*leaping gymnastically over the benches*". They are seeking to buy equipment with funds from the factory. Each episode is, first, intense, funny, gripping, whatever, but complete in itself; and second each interacts reverberatively with the others to direct attention to the problems of factory organization and finance, as well as to the responsibilities of director, foreman, workers, cleaners, and others in the work place.

Of Tretyakov's last two plays, *Roar, China!* was his most performed work (it was even staged in Shanghai after the communists took over in 1949), while "I Want a Baby" was banned when in rehearsal at the Meyerhold Theatre in 1927. *Roar, China!* raises comparatively predictable questions about imperialism and colonial freedom, but "I Want a Baby" addresses an altogether thornier subject, though one which was of enormous importance for both futurists and Bolsheviks—the begetting of future generations.

The play deals on one level with a typical triangle, consisting of Milda, the commissar who wants to breed a genetically sound proletarian child, Yakov, a building worker whom she chooses for the father, and Lipa, his girlfriend, who wants nothing so much as to settle down and have a family. But this apparently conventional framework is constantly interrupted by scenes dealing with other characters who want babies: Varvara, for instance, who is besotted with Filirinov, a drug addicted poet; Ksenichka, the doll-like object of Andryusha's schoolboy lust, who is raped in one of the most brutal scenes of Soviet drama; Kitty, the would-be actress, seduced by the cynical theatre manager, Saxoulsky; the woman whose pelvis is too narrow to give birth; and other girls and men who love, lust, dote, and delight. The effect is kaleidoscopic, and the action set within a fierce battle which bears directly on the social context within which the babies will grow up: the ultrakeen Communist Volunteer Social Organizers in confrontation with the truculent and loutish hooligans, one sort of proletarian against another, in the brand-new proletarian State.

The play dares us to ask what is right, or wrong, for this society, and why? This is unmistakable in the final scene, set in 1930, that is, three years "hence". By showing the not-so-distant future, which may become reality if certain current policies are continued, Tretyakov makes the present appear like history, and thereby become amenable to the kinds of judgement we use in historical assessment.

After the play was banned, Tretyakov rewrote it, removing the galaxy of sex-oriented characters, as well as the Voluntary Organisers and the hooligans, and set it on a collective farm, where child conception is juxtaposed with pig and rabbit breeding and selecting strains of wheat. The loss of the urban context, however, though it distances the action, also manages to attenuate the urgency. Nevertheless, even this muti-lated version retains Tretyakov's unorthodox dramaturgy, which taught so much to Brecht, Mayakovsky, and others, though after Tretyakov's arrest this influence could not be admitted. Earlier, in 1934, Brecht was able to assert that Tretyakov was virtually the only dramatist in Europe "work-ing along the right lines"; he had, said Brecht, "found quite new means of expression". It is a judgment with which it is hard to disagree.

—Robert Leach

TRIANA, José. Born in Camagüey, Cuba, 4 January 1931. Educated at Escuela Bautista, Bayamo, to 1950; Faculty of Humanities, Instituto de Manzanillo, Oriente, degree 1952; Universidad de Madrid, Spain, 1955 (studies not completed); studied theatre under José Franco, Circulo de Bellas Artes, Madrid, 1956. Married Chantel Dumaine in 1968. Lived in Spain, 1955–59: actor with the troupe Grupo Didi, 1956–57, and scenic artist with Teatro Ensayo, 1958; travelled to France, Belgium, Italy and England, 1958–59; returned to Cuba at the time of the Revolution, 1959; employee, Cuban telephone company; first plays produced 1960; actor and adviser, Sala Prometeo; literary adviser, Editora Nacional de Cuba and Instituto Cubano del Libro, during 1960's; con-tributor to numerous Cuban periodicals, including *Ciclón*, and *Revolución*, and the French *Lettres nouvelles* and *Cahiers Renaud-Barreault*; attended the Théâtre des Nations festival, Paris, 1967; following increasing government restriction on his writing, defected to France, 1980; visiting professor, Dartmouth College, Hanover, New Hampshire, 1981–82. Recipient: Casa de las Americas Prize, 1965; Gallo de La Habana, 1966.

Works

Collections

El parque de la fraternidad (includes *Medea en el espejo; El mayor general; El parque de la fraternidad*). 1962.

Stage Works

La visita del ángel (produced Sala Arelquín, Havana, 1960).
El mayor general hablará de teogonía (produced Sala Arlequín, Havana, 1960). In *El parque . . .* (collection), 1962.

Medea en el espejo (produced 1960). In *El parque . . .* (collection), 1962.
Edipo rey, from a play by Sophocles (produced Cuba, 1961).
La casa ardiendo (produced Cuba, 1962). 1962.
El parque de la fraternidad (produced Cuba, 1962). In *El parque . . .* (collection), 1962.
La muerte del ñeque (produced Cuba, 1963). 1964.
La tía de Carlos, from a work by Brandon Thomas (produced Cuba, 1964).
La noche de los asesinos (produced Sixth Festival of Latin American Theatre, Havana, 1966). 1965; translated as *The Criminals*, in *The Modern Stage in Latin America: Six Plays*, edited by George Woodyard, 1971.
Palabras comunes (produced as *World's Apart*, The Other Place (Royal Shakespeare Company), Stratford-on-Avon, 1986). As *Worlds Apart*, 1986; Spanish edition, 1987.
Ceremonial de guerra. 1990.

Verse

De la madera de los sueños. 1958.
Coloquio de sombras. 1981.
Cuaderno de familia. 1990.

Other

Editor, *La generación del 98*. 1965.
Editor, *Teatro*, by Jean Giraudoux. 1965.
Editor, *Teatro español actual*. 1970.

*

Criticism

Books:

Matias Montes Huidobro, *Persona, vida y máscara en el teatro cubano*, Miami, Florida, 1973.
Frank N. Dauster, "The Game of Chance: The Theater of José Triana", in *Dramatists in Revolt: The New Latin American Theatre*, edited by Leon F. Lyday and George Woodyard, Austin, Texas, 1976.
Román V. de la Campa, *José Triana: Ritualización de la sociedad Cuba*, Minneapolis, 1979.
Diana Taylor (ed.), *Ensayos críticos sobre Griselda Gambaro y José Triana*, Ottawa, 1989.
Diana Taylor, "Theatre and Revolution: José Triana", in *Theatre of Crisis: Drama and Politics in Latin America*, Lexington, Kentucky, 1991.

Articles:

Anne C. Murch, "Genet—Triana—Kopit: Ritual as 'Danse Macabre'", in *Modern Drama*, 15, 1973.
Diana Taylor, "Framing the Revolution: Triana's *La noche de los asesinos*, and *Ceremonial de guerra*", in *Latin American Theatre Review*, vol. 24, 1990.

* * *

José Triana is perhaps the best-known and most widely acclaimed contemporary Latin American playwright, due primarily to the enthusiastic critical and audience response to *La noche de los asesinos* (*The Criminals*), which was first produced in Cuba in 1966. The year before it had received the prestigious Premio Casa de las Américas award for play-writing, and in subsequent years it has been, and continues to be, staged throughout Europe, the USA, and Latin America.

In *La noche de los asesinos*, Triana tells the tale of two sisters and a brother who play-act the murder of their parents. Reminiscent of Jean Genet's *The Maids*, Triana's play is notable for its ambiguity and rich symbolic texture. These children of indeterminate age retreat to the attic (or the basement) of their house, where they engage in an elaborate ritual of rebellion against parental authority and tyranny. Their ritual appears to be a two-act rehearsal for the real show to come, as the actors prepare by exchanging roles and by establishing the limits of their text. On the other hand, their games may be only a self-indulgence that allows them to feign rebellion while never having to commit themselves wholly to action. Triana's text is open-ended, for it does not make absolutely clear against whom and what the characters are rebelling, and whether they are to be seen as noble rebels, common criminals, or just spoiled and confused children. Some readings of the play see it in existential terms, as a commentary on human bondage and rebellion in general; others consider it a veiled allusion to political repression and resistance in Cuba before and/or during the Castro Revolution. Whatever the interpretation, *La noche de los asesinos* has had a felicitous stage life precisely because of these ambiguities and the almost hallucinatory world it depicts.

Although none of Triana's plays prior to, or after, *La noche de los asesinos* has been as successful, they all share with it certain themes and motifs. Primary among these are family relations, violence, repressed sexuality, and the past as a reiteration of the present. In *El mayor general hablará de teogonía* (The Major General Will Speak of Theogony), two sisters, Eliseria and Petronilia, live in the General's house along with Petronilia's husband. They are obssessed with the past and with the baby that Petronilia miscarried when she suffered an accident 25 years earlier. They are also under the spell of the General, whom they plan to murder because of his power over them. Absent for most of the play, the General hardly turns out to be the terrible and fearsome tyrant the other characters make him out to be; instead, he is just a tired old man. His would-be killers, like the siblings in *La noche de los asesinos*, never manage their rebellion against this father/Christ figure; the family here is impotent and worn out from guilt or existential exhaustion.

The family in *Medea en el espejo* (Medea in the Mirror) takes on a more clearly Cuban identity, although the plot closely follows Euripides' tragedy *Medea*. In his version, Triana has the characters live in an Havana tenement and speak a Spanish heavily influenced by the Yoruba of Cuba's black population. Indeed, race is a major force in the play, just it has been in Cuban history; Triana's María/Medea is a mulatto, whereas her lover is not only white but also blond, making for an explosive attraction between the races. *La muerte del ñeque* (The Death of the Boogieman) also echoes the tragic paradigm, in the depiction of Hilario, a corrupt mulatto policeman whose fall from power and murder is executed by three thugs, modern-day Cuban Furies who are not perchance a black man, a white man and a mulatto.

The connection between race, violence, and sexuality is quite explicit in Triana's *Palabras comunes*, which was first performed by the Royal Shakespeare Company in 1986 under the English title *Worlds Apart*. This ambitious play, with some 60 scenes and 20 characters, takes place between 1894 and 1914, a turbulent period in Cuba's history, marking the island's independence from Spain and the beginning of its dependence on the USA. *Palabras comunes* traces the progressive decay during these years of a once-wealthy family, obsessed with social status, propriety, and racial purity. The young girl, Victoria, is the victim of her social class as well as

the prisoner of Cuban "machismo". She ultimately "explodes", giving free reign to a burning sexuality that was first awakened by a black man, the forbidden fruit denied to "decent" white girls. Victoria's rebellion is short-lived, as she once again conforms to the rigid codes of her social class, although the world of her family is dying of corruption, alcohol abuse, and venereal disease.

This image of family rot in *Palabras comunes* is clearly tied to the fall of an entire way of life in Cuba. However, there is here the sense that the new society will mimic much of the old in its dependency on a foreign power and corruptability. The history of 20th-century Cuba confirms this view, with its legacy of political decadence and vicious dictatorships, its colonial status, and its reputation as a playground for mobsters and hedonistic tourists. The Castro Revolution meant to change all that, but once again, the cycle seems to have repeated itself, albeit with different players.

This sense of the past infiltrating the present, of parents repeating themselves in their children, is also palpable in *La noche de los asesinos*, where the siblings emulate their elders' behavior even while trying to defy it; and in *Ceremonial de guerra* (Ceremony of War), the action again takes place in 1895 and the conflicts between abstract revolutionary principles and individual beliefs, between the common good and personal gain, are, by implication, the same ones that have confronted Cubans throughout their history. These are the very same conflicts that led to Triana's decision to leave Cuba in 1980, just as they will almost certainly continue to define his work as being unmistakably Cuban, despite his many years as a writer far from home.

—Kirsten F. Nigro

See also *Volume 1* entry on *The Criminals*.

TSAO Yu.   See **CAO Yu**.

TSURYA Nanboku IV.   See *Volume 1* entry on *The Scarlet Princess of Edo*.

TURGENEV, Ivan (Sergeyevich).   Born in Orel, Russia, 28 October (Old Style) 1818. Educated at home; briefly at Armenian Institute and Weidenhammer's boarding school in Moscow; University of Moscow, 1833–34; University of St. Petersburg, 1834–37; University of Berlin, 1838–41; completed master's exam in St. Petersburg, 1842. Civil servant in Ministry of the Interior, 1843–45; then mainly interested in country pursuits, especially hunting; went to France with the singer Pauline Viardot and her husband, 1845–46, and again

1847–50; first-produced play, *Kholostyak* [*The Bachelor*], staged 1849; exiled to his country estate for a "faulty" obituary of Gogol, 1852–53; in Western Europe again for long spells after 1856, often in Baden-Baden after 1863, and in Paris with the Viardots, 1871–83. Corresponding Member, Imperial Academy of Sciences, 1860. Dr. of Civil Laws, Oxford University, 1879. Died in Bougival, near Paris, 3 September 1883.

Works

Collections

Sobranie sochineny [Collected Works] (5 vols.). 1860–61, and later editions.
Polnoe sobranie sochineny [Complete Collected Works]. 1915.
Plays (includes *Where it's Thin, There it Tears; The Bachelor; A Conversation on the Highway; The Provincial Lady; A Month in the Country; The Family Charge; An Evening in Sorrento*), translated by M.S. Mandell.   1924.
Three Famous Plays (includes *A Month in the Country; A Poor Gentleman; A Provincial Lady*), translated by Constance Garnett.   1934.
Polnoe sobranie sochineny i pisem [Complete Collected Works and Letters] (28 vols.).   1960–68.

Stage Works

Neostorozhnost [Indiscretion].   In *Otechestvenye zapiski* [Notes of the Fatherland], 1843.
Bezdenezhe (produced Alexandrinsky Theatre, St Petersburg, 1852).   1846; translated as *A Poor Gentleman*, in *Three Famous Plays*, 1934.
Gde tonko, tam i rvetsya (produced Alexandrinsky Theatre, St. Petersburg, 1851).   1848; translated as *One May Spin a Thread Too Finely*, in *Fortnightly Review*, 85, 1909; as *Where it's Thin, There it Tears*, in *Plays*, 1924.
Zavtrak upredvoditelya [Lunch with the Marshal of the Nobility] (produced Alexandrinsky Theatre, St. Peterburg, 1849).   1856.
Kholostyak (produced Alexandrinsky Theatre, St. Peterburg, 1849).   1849; translated as *The Bachelor*, in *Plays*, 1924.
Razgovor na bolshoi doroge (produced 1850).   1851; translated as *A Conversation on the Highway*, in *Plays*, 1924.
Provintsialka (produced Maly Theatre, Moscow, 1851).   1851; translated as *The Provincial Lady*, in *Plays*, 1924; as *A Provincial Lady*, in *Three Famous Plays*, 1934.
Mesyats v derevne (produced Maly Theatre, Moscow, 1872).   In *Sovremennik* [The Contemporary], 1855; in book form, in *Sobranie sochineny* [Collected Works], 1869; translated as *A Month in the Country*, in *Plays*, 1924: several subsequent translations under same title.
Nakhlebnik [The Parasite] (produced Bolshoi Dramatic Theatre, Moscow, 1862).   As *Chuzhoy Khleb* [Alien Bread], 1857; translated as *The Family Charge*, in *Plays*, 1924.
Vecher v Sorrente (produced St. Petersburg, 1882).   1891; translated as *An Evening in Sorrento*, in *Plays*, 1924.

Fiction

Zapiski okhotnika.   1852; translated as *Russian Life in the Interior*, 1855; as *Annals of a Sportsman*, 1885; as *A Sportsman's Sketches*, 1932; as *Sketches from a Hunter's Album*, 1967 (complete edition, 1990); as *A Sportsman's Notebook*, 1992.

Povesti i rasskazy [Tales and Stories].   1856.
Rudin.   1856; translated as *Dimitri Roudine*, 1873.
Asya.   1858; translated as *Annouchka*, 1884.
Dvoryanskoye gnezdo.   1859; translated as *A Nest of Gentlefolk*, 1869; as *Lisa*, 1872; as *Home of the Gentry*, 1970.
Pervaya lyubov.   1860; translated as *First Love*, 1884.
Nakanune   1860; translated as *On the Eve*, 1871.
Ottsy i dety.   1862; translated as *Fathers and Sons*, 1867: several subsequent translations under same title; as *Fathers and Children*, 1928.
Dym.   1867; translated as *Smoke; or, Life at Baden*, 1868.
Neschastnaya.   1869; translated as *An Unfortunate Woman*, 1886.
Stepnoy Korol Lir.   1870; translated as *A Lear of the Steppe*, with *Spring Floods*, 1874.
Veshniye vody.   1872; translated as *Spring Floods*, with *A Lear of the Steppe*, 1874.
Nov.   1877; translated as *Virgin Soil*, 1877.
Klara Milich.   1883.
Novels, translated by Constance Garnett (15 vols.).   1894–99.
Novel and Stories (13 vols.), translated by Elizabeth F. Hapgood.   1903–04.
"The Brigadier" and Other Stories, translated by Moura Budberg.   1962.
Youth and Age (includes *Bunin and Baburin; The Inn; The Watch*), translated by Marion Mainwaring.   1968.
The Two Friends.   1936.
The Song of Triumphant Love.   1990.

Verse

Parasha.   1843.
Razgovor [The Conversation].   1845.
Andrey.   1846.
Pomeshchik [The Landowner].   1846.
Senilia.   1878; as *Stikhotvoreniya v proze*, 1882; translated as *Poems in Prose*, 1883; as *Senilia: Poems in Prose*, 1890; bilingual edition, 1951.

Memoirs and Letters

Literaturnye i zhiteyskiye vospominaniya.   1874; revised edition, 1880; translated as *Literary Reminiscences and Autobiographical Fragments*, 1958.
Tourgéneff and His French Circle (letters), translated by Ethel M. Arnold.   1898.
Letters (selection), translated by Edgar H. Lehrman.   1961.
Nouvelle correspondance inédite (2 vols.), edited by A. Zviguilsky.   1971–72.
Lettres inédites à Pauline Viardot et à sa famille, edited by A. Zviguilsky.   1972.
Letters (selection), edited by A.V. Knowles.   1983.
Letters (selection; 2 vols.) edited by David Lowe.   1983.
Flaubert and Turgenev: A Friendship in Letters, translated by Barbara Beaumont.   1985.

Other

Hamlet and Don Quixote (lecture).   1907.

*

Bibliographies

Rissa Yachnin and David H. Stam, *Turgenev in English: A Checklist of Works by and About Him*, New York, 1962.

Nicholas G. Zekulin, *Turgenev: A Bibliography of Books 1843–1982 by and About Ivan Turgenev*, Calgary, 1985.

Criticism

Books:
A. Yarmolinsky, *Turgenev: The Man, His Art, and His Age*, New York and London, 1926; second edition, 1959.
David Magarshack, *Turgenev: A Life*, London, 1954.
Eva Kagan-Kans, *Hamlet and Don Quixote: Turgenev's Ambivalent Vision*, Paris and The Hague, 1975.
V.S. Pritchett, *The Gentle Barbarian: The Life and Works of Turgenev*, London, 1977.
Leonard Schapiro, *Turgenev: His Life and Times*, London, 1978.
Patrick Waddington, *Turgenev and England*, London, 1980.
Nick Worrall, *Nikolai Gogol and Ivan Turgenev*, London, 1982 (Macmillan Modern Dramatists series).
Walter Koschmal, *Das poetische System der Dramen I.S. Turgenevs: Studien zu einer pragmatischen Dramenanalyse*, Munich, 1983.
Hildegard Kottmann, *Ivan Turgenevs Bühnenwerk*, Frankfurt, 1984.
Henri Troyat, *Turgenev: A Biography* (from the French), New York, 1988.
D. Lowe, *Critical Essays on Ivan Turgenev*, Boston, 1989.

Serials:
Cahiers I. Tourguéniev (Paris), 1977—

* * *

Like his elder contemporary, Gogol, Turgenev is known to the world primarily as a writer of fiction, his dramatic reputation resting on a single play, his "Comedy in Five Acts" *A Month in the Country*. The standard editions of Turgenev's dramatic works usually include a total of ten plays, tending not to take account of the early Romantic drama in verse (influenced by Byron's *Manfred*), "Steno", or the unfinished extravaganza, "The Temptation of St. Antony". Of the ten, *A Month in the Country* is the only play in five acts. *Kholostyak* (*The Bachelor*) describes itself as "A Comedy in Three Acts", *Nakhlebnik* (The Parasite, translated as *The Family Charge*) as "A Comedy in Two Acts". All the others are comedies in one act.

There is little doubt that Turgenev wished to make his mark as a dramatist, rather than as a novelist. Most of his work between 1843 and 1852 is in dramatic form. His decision to turn to the novel and the short story was one prompted, less by a sense of failure, than by the unsatisfactory nature of performance conditions in the theatre of his day (despite the excellent actor Shchepkin) and by constant brushes with the Tsarist censorship, which either seriously hampered Turgenev's attempts to get his plays staged, or frustrated them altogether. Like Gogol, whom he admired, Turgenev also sought to be a reformer of the Russian stage. He attacked the kind of melodramatic, high-minded, historico-patriotic plays which were popular during the 1840's, targeting in particular the work of Gedeonov and Kukolnik. At the same time, he praised Gogol's *The Government Inspector* as an example to be followed. Turgenev also took issue with the abstract idealism which he noted in the plays of Schiller and Goethe, whom he otherwise admired, and praised the realism which he saw in the early plays of his compatriot, Alexander Ostrovsky. It was this "realistic" direction in Russian theatre that he sought to pursue in his own dramatic work. One manifestation of this intention was his incorporation within the play-text of precise stage directions, including the positions of doors and windows, which often amounted to a complete plan of the stage.

In Turgenev's later fiction one finds little evidence of the influence of Gogol. What makes his plays interesting, and differentiates them sharply from his fiction, is the extent to which the debt to Gogol is obvious. *Bezdenezhe* (*A Poor Gentleman*) belongs to the tradition of Russian vaudeville and has a central character, the penniless nobleman Zhazikov, who is second-cousin to Gogol's Khlestakov. His servant, Matvey, is likewise a direct descendant of Osip in *The Government Inspector*. The play itself, like *The Government Inspector*, makes much of the contrast between life in St. Petersburg and life in the provinces. Here the irony is at the expense of the Khlestakov figure, who lives in straitened circumstances in a top-floor Petersburg apartment, constantly dunned by his creditors and berated by his long-suffering servant. He meanwhile praises a Petersburg highlife, which he cannot afford, to an acquaintance from the despised countryside who is rapidly buying up the superannuated estates owned by a profligate aristocracy personified by Zhazikov.

Gde tonko, tam i rvetsya (*Where it's Thin, There It Tears*) can be described as a version of Gogol's *Marriage* when, at one point, the hero, Gorsky, threatened with marriage declares that he will escape this fate by leaving through the door into the garden rather than by jumping out of the window, like Podkolesin in Gogol's play. "The Parasite" also has indirect connections with Gogol. In this instance the parasite in question, Kuzovkin, makes claims for his own importance which are described as "mad" by the group of unattractive aristocrats that surrounds him; the claim can be seen to have unhappy associations with Poprishchin's belief, in Gogol's *Diary of a Madman*, that he is the King of Spain. Similarly, *The Bachelor* is a Gogolian grotesque tragicomedy in which the central character, Moshkin, a childless bachelor who has been a minor official all his life, suddenly seizes on a chance to live life more fully and, in the process, imposes his own emotional imperatives on the life of an orphaned girl under his guardianship, to whom he proposes marriage in a scene at the end of a play of semi-hysterical pathos. *Zavtrak s predvoditelya* (Lunch with the Marshal of the Nobility), like *A Poor Gentleman*, owes a debt to the vaudeville and to Gogol's short plays. It also anticipates Chekhov's one-act "jokes"—the quarrel between brother and sister over land rights being an almost exact precursor of a similar quarrel, in Chekhov's *The Proposal*, between Lomov and his prospective fiancée.

Turgenev's last major play before *A Month in the Country*, *Provintsialka* (*A Provincial Lady*) also highlights a major theme in his plays, which might be described as sympathy for woman's plight. An early play, *Neostorozhnost* (Indiscretion) deals with the vulnerability of woman, in the person of one Donna Dolores, who is made to suffer the indignity of a loveless marriage to an older man as well as having to endure unsolicited courtship from a calculating and self-regarding seducer before being murdered at the hands of her proprietorial husband. The theme of the suffering and exploited woman resurfaces—in "The Parasite", in the person of the parasite's illegitimate daughter, Olga; in *The Bachelor*, in the plight of the pathetic orphan, Masha; and even in "Lunch with the Marshal of the Nobility", where Turgenev appears to have some sympathy for the stubbornly litigious widowed sister of the quarrelsome Bespandin. *A Provincial Lady* reveals a sympathetic woman who is married to an inadequate official, and who is courted by an absurdly self-satisfied aristocrat who had previously ignored her. In this case, the central question is one of a woman's thwarted sexual energy, and her charity in face of a male world the inadequacy of which she tolerates with good humour. The play is conceived as a puppet-show, played out in the mind of the powerful female protagonist, and as if projected on stage. In what might be described as the provincial lady's "theatre of the mind" the men appear to assume the characteristics of marionettes.

Women, of course, played an important part in Turgenev's own life. His permanent bachelordom can, in part, be attributed to the formative influence of a despotic mother, while his lifelong devotion to another's wife, Pauline Viardot, was, in all probability, an entirely platonic relationship. A similar platonic relationship, between Rakitin and Natalya Petrovna, dominates his final play, *A Month in the Country*, where, again, the contrast is between passionate, frustrated women and ineffectual or inadequate men. As in many of Turgenev's novels, love is viewed as a kind of bacillus, which spreads in the blood like a raging infection. The "month in the country" is, in this sense, an incubatory period during which the love virus, introduced by the tutor, Belyaev, spreads among a group of aristocratic estate dwellers. Its most powerful effects are felt by the women—Natalya Petrovna, her ward Vera, and, in parodied form, by her mother's female companion, Lizaveta Bogdanovna. As the play is a comedy, the effects are not tragic, unlike in the novels where the infection of love often leads to the deaths of the heroes.

—Nick Worrall

See also *Volume 1* entry on *A Month in the Country*.

———

TYL, Josef Kajetán. Born in Kutná Hora, Bohemia (then in the Austrian Empire, now in the Czech Republic), 4 February 1808. Educated at Gymnasium, Hrad Králové; studied philosophy in Prague to 1829. Editor of the Czech-language periodical *Květy*, from 1833; directed his own theatre company, U Kajetanů, to 1837; appointed director of Czech performances at the Theatre of the Estates, Prague, 1846; member of political delegation seeking more autonomy for Bohemia, 1848; appointed director of the open-air Arena Theatre, Pstroska, 1849: resigned, 1851, and returned to acting. Died in Plzeň, 11 July 1856.

Works

Collections (Modern)

Spisy [Works] (20 vols).   1952–89; plays are in vols. 17–20:
  17. *První dramata* [First Plays].   1957.
  18. *Dramatické obrazy ze života* [Dramatic Portraits from Life].   1954.
  19. *Dramatické báchorky* [Fairy-Tale Plays].   1953.
  20. *Historická dramata* [Historical Dramas].   1954.

Stage Works

Publication information refers to individual volumes of the modern collected edition *Spisy* (see above).

Výhoň Dub [Vyhon Dub] (produced 1832).

Fidlovačka [Filovacka Fair] (produced 1834).   In *První dramata*, 1957.
Čestmír [Čestmir] (produced 1835).   In *První dramata*, 1957.
Slepý mládenec [Blind Young Man] (produced 1836).   In *První dramata*, 1957.
Brunsvik [Brunswick] (produced 1843).   In *První dramata*, 1957.
Pani Marjánka, matka pluku [Mrs. Marjanka, Mother of the Regiment] (produced 1845).   In *Dramatické obrazy ze života*, 1954.
Pražský flamendr [The Boozer of Prague] (produced 1846?).   In *Dramatické obrazy ze života*, 1954.
Paličova dcera [The Incendiary's Daughter] (produced 1847).   In *Dramatické obrazy ze života*, 1954.
Strakonický Dudák [Švanda the Bagpiper] (produced 1847).   In *Dramatické báchorky*, 1953.
Bankrotář [The Bankrupt] (produced 1848).   In *Dramatické obrazy ze života*, 1954.
Chudý kejklíř [The Impoverished Mountebank] (produced 1848).   In *Dramatické obrazy ze života*, 1954.
Kutnohorští havíři [The Miners of Kutná Hora] (produced 1848).   In *Historická dramata*, 1954.
Jan Hus [Jan Hus] (produced 1848).   In *Historická dramata*, 1954.
Krvavé křtiny [The Blood-Stained Christening Party] (produced 1849).   In *Historická dramata*, 1954.
Žižka z Trocnova [Žižka Troconov] (produced 1849).   In *Historická dramata*, 1954.
Tvrdohlavá žena [The Pig-Headed Woman] (produced 1849).   In *Dramatické báchorky*, 1953.
Jiříkovo vidění [St. Patrick's Purgatory] (produced 1849).   In *Dramatické báchorky*, 1953.
Čert na zemi [Devil on Earth] (produced 1850).   In *Dramatické báchorky*, 1953.
Lesní panna [The Dryad] (produced 1850).   In *Dramatické báchorky*, 1953.
Mestané a studenti [Burghers and Students] (produced 1850).   In *Historická dramata*, 1954.
Staré mesto a malá strana [The Old Town and the Lesser Town].   In *Historická dramata*, 1954.
Jeden za všecky [One for All].   In *První dramata*, 1957.
Brěněk Švihovský [Brěněk Svihovský].   In *První dramata*, 1957.

Fiction (modern editions)

Historické povídky [Historical Tales] (vols. 7–10 of *Spisy*). 1955–64.
Novely a arabesky [Novellas and Arabesques] (vols. 3–6 of *Spisy*).   1958–77.

Other

Miscellaneous writings collected in volumes 1–2 and 11–15 of *Spisy*; principal observations on theatre in volume 15: *Divadelní referáty a stati* [Theatre Reviews and Essays], 1960.

*   *   *

Josef Kajetán Tyl was an energetic theatre director, playwright, and actor, whom legend turned into a national hero. In Bohemia and Moravia, the early 19th century was the period of the National Revival. A handful of enthusiasts were fighting to restore the dignity of the Czech language, and few weapons were more effective than the theatre. In the cities, the upper classes still spoke German, while Czech was considered to be the language of servants and tradespeople. Nationalists were keen to propagate Czech as a language

Scene from the Prague National Theatre's 1943 production of *Strakonický Dudák* [Svanda the Bagpiper of Stratonice] by **Josef Tyl**.

capable of expressing man's highest ideals and aspirations. Language and national identity were inextricably linked; it was believed that on hearing profound thoughts uttered in their native tongue, audiences would reflect on the destiny of their nation. One of the early landmarks of the National Revival was Karel Ignác Thám's translation into Czech of Shakespeare's *Macbeth* (1786), for Shakespeare, until then, was known only in the original or in German adaptations.

The nationalists, aware that theatre was the most direct way of capturing public interest, struggled to secure the German theatres for occasional performances in the Czech language. It was at first a problem to find original drama, and most performances were of translations and adaptations. One successful playwright, Jan Nepomuk Štěpánek, was also a director of the Theatre of the Estates; another was the more original writer, Václav Kliment Klicpera, a teacher in Hradec Králové, whose work for the theatre ranged from poetic drama to parody. Devotees of Klicpera's dramas complained that Štěpánek neglected his rival's plays in favour of his own, inferior, work. Among them was one of Klicpera's former pupils, Josef Kajetán Tyl, from 1833 the editor of a weekly Czech-language journal, *Květy*, in which he wrote: "What harm could it do if the Director—be it only in jest—agreed to show us a mere half or even a *third* of *original* Czech plays . . . ? What could not be achieved out of love for our mother tongue and for a good cause?".

By 1834 Tyl had already spent several years as a semi-professional actor, and to prove his point about Štěpánek's

neglect of Klicpera's drama, he formed his own theatre group —largely composed of contributors to *Květy*—which performed in the refectory of the monastery *U Kajetánů* in the Malá Strana district of Prague. There were only 28 performances in the theatre's three-year existence, but with these Tyl set new standards of production for Czech-language theatre. Far more careful attention was given to rehearsal and preparation than was the case in Štěpánek's company, and most of the work was original, including plays by both Klicpera and Tyl. In 1834 Tyl produced his own comedy, *Fidlovačka*, based on his own observation of local life. (*Fidlovačka* was the name of a spring fair held in the Nusle valley of Prague.) One of the songs written for the play, "Where is My Homeland?" ("Kde domov můj?") was later to become the first part of the Czechoslovak national anthem. In 1835, the production of *Čestmír* showed Tyl as a Romantic dramatist; the hero was modelled in some ways on his own character, depicting a rebel fighting the idealistic battle of youth against established society. Nevertheless, the play ends on a note of reconciliation, an acknowledgement that the freedom of the individual is circumscribed by the interests of the community. It can be seen as a negative tendency, the inability of a subject nation to face maturity, or more positively, as the deliberate policy of nationalist writers to encourage co-operation and trust. It also had the practical advantage of making the play acceptable to the censorship authorities.

In 1846 Tyl became director of the Czech performances of the Theatre of the Estates. The following year two of his most popular plays were given their premieres: *Paličova dcera* (The Incendiary's Daughter), a drama set partly in Prague and partly in the Bohemian countryside, in which Rozarka suffers for her father's crimes but is saved by other bonds of family and friends; and the domestic fairy-tale, *Strakonický Dudák* (Švanda the Bagpiper). Švanda, son of a villager and a forest fairy, sets out to seek his fortune in the wide world. After many adventures, the wanderer is happy to return to his village and his own people. Both plays were praised for their depiction of original Czech characters. In the same year, his historical play *Kutnohorští havíri* (The Miners of Kutná Hora) was banned by the Austrian censors: the subject of the 15th-century uprising was deemed too close to contemporary unrest.

In the revolutionary year 1848, Tyl was named a member of the delegation that was prepared to establish a provisional government for Bohemia under federal Austria—an ambition suppressed by the absolutist government which regained power in Vienna. A more strongly political member of that delegation was the writer and editor Karel Havlíček Borovský. Havlíček was a sharp critic of Tyl's theatre policies, seeing him as a compromiser who weakened the Czech position by his willingness to co-operate with the authorities.

Later that year, Tyl wrote one of his most openly political plays, *Jan Hus*, which had its premiere in December to an audience which crowded the theatre an hour before the start in an effort to gain seats. Tyl portrayed the historic preacher and martyr as a fighter for democratic rights and free speech, a leader who saw language and not force as the weapon that the Czech people must learn to use. In 1850, performances of *Jan Hus* were forbidden by the censor's office.

In 1849 Tyl accepted the directorship of the Arena in Pštroska, a cheaply built open-air theatre for the Czech public, condemned by Havlíček as a pitiful wooden hut. In Tyl's eyes, it was at last an opportunity to establish the basis of a permanent professional Czech-language company. But Tyl's ideas about nationalist drama and his plays glorifying Czech history were now considered by the Prague critics to be old-fashioned and inappropriate. In 1851 he was forced to resign, becoming once again an itinerant actor, and he died five years later. His place was taken by his long-time rival, Josef Jiří Kolár, who had started his career as an actor with Tyl's theatre company *U Kajetánů*; in 1873 Kolár became the head of the Provisional Theatre—the forerunner of the Czech National Theatre.

—Barbara Day

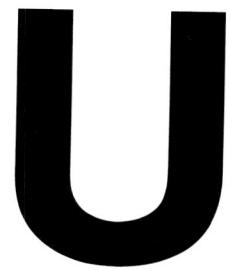

UDALL, Nicholas. Born in Southampton, Hampshire, in December 1504. Educated at Winchester College, Hampshire (scholar), 1517–20; Corpus Christi College, Oxford, admitted a scholar 1520, BA 1524, probationer-fellow 1524, full fellow 1526, MA 1534. Tutor in logic and Greek, Corpus Christi College, 1524–29; headmaster, Eton College, Berkshire, 1534–41; vicar of Braintree, Essex, 1537–44; prebendary of Windsor, 1552; rector of Calbourne, Isle of Wight, 1553; appointed playwriter to Queen Mary, 1554; headmaster, Westminster School, London, 1555–56. Died (buried) 23 December 1556.

Works

Stage Works

Ralph Roister Doister (produced Windsor?, 1552?). 1556(?).
Respublica (produced London, 1553). Edited by J.P. Collier, in *Illustrations of English Literature*, 1866.
Jack Juggler (produced ?), possibly not by Udall. 1563.
Jacob and Esau (produced ?), possibly not by Udall. 1568.

Other

Flowers for Latin Speaking, from Terence. 1533.
Apothegms, from Erasmus. 1542.
The Paraphrase of Erasmus upon the New Testament. 1548.
A Discourse Concerning the Lord's Supper, from Peter Martyr Vermigli. 1550(?).

Translator, *Compendiosa Totius Anatomie Delineatio* (in English), by Thomas Geminus. 1553; revised edition, 1559.

Bibliographies

D.J. White, *Early English Drama: "Everyman" to 1580*, Boston, 1986.

Criticism

Books:
F.S. Boas, *University Drama in the Tudor Age*, Oxford, 1914.
William L. Edgerton, *Nicholas Udall*, New York, 1966.

David M. Bevington, *Tudor Drama and Politics*, Cambridge, Massachusetts, 1968.
F.P. Wilson, edited by G.K. Hunter, *The English Drama 1485–1585*, Oxford, 1968.
R.F. Wilson Jr., *"Their Form Comfounded": Studies in the Burlesque Play from Udall to Sheridan*, Paris, 1975.

*   *   *

Nicholas Udall is the known author of only one extant play, *Ralph Roister Doister*, and of one lost one, *Ezechias* (acted 1564, but possibly Henrician in date and polemical in matter). He has been credited with *Thersites*, *Jack Juggler*, *Respublica*, and *Jacob and Esau*; of these the last three are more likely to be his than the first, both for their Terentian structure and for their versification and diction (especially the last two). Writing for boy actors, he reflected the new interest in classical comedy (he published a Terentian Latin-English phrase-book, *Flowers for Latin Speaking*) as studied in schools. The models of *Ralph Roister Doister*, Terence's *Eunuchus* and *Miles Gloriosus*, gave Udall his comic duo of braggart lover and flattering parasite, here called Ralph Roister Doister and Matthew Merrygreek (nearly all the names alliterate). The braggart's wooing proceeds from one disaster to another: his love-tokens are refused, his commissioned love-letter ruined by his own mispunctuation, his assault on his intended wife's house repulsed by her and her servants with kitchen armaments—to the barely concealed enjoyment of Merrygreek, who, at one point, reads a mock requiem over his despairing patron. After a brief misunderstanding between the lady and her accepted suitor, the latter is convinced that Roister Doister's courtship was without her encouragement, and a general feast ends the play.

Respublica (which survives in a manuscript stating that it was played by boys before Mary I) is a political morality in Terentian technique, showing how Avarice and his subordinate vices Insolence, Oppression, and Adulation take false names in order to exploit Respublica and oppress her rustic servant People under the guise of reforming their estate, until Nemesis (identified with the Queen) exposes them. *Jacob and Esau* treats the biblical story in the manner of the humanist religious drama, equipping the main characters with neighbours and with household servants who would be at home in *Ralph Roister Doister*.

All three plays are divided into acts and scenes, introduce their characters by Terentian techniques, and develop the action systematically to a crisis and catastrophe. They are written in freely rhythmical couplets and all contain songs. The dialogue is idiomatic and there is plenty of English local colour, even in the biblical play. This last point also applies to *Jack Juggler*, but its plot is from Plautus (his *Amphitryon*), not from Terence, it is undivided into acts and scenes, and it contains no songs. (*Thersites*, loosely based on a neo-classical dialogue, is closer akin to the style of earlier than middle 16th-century drama.)

—T.W. Craik

See also *Volume 1* entry on *Ralph Roister Doister*.

USIGLI, Rodolfo. Born in Mexico City, Mexico, 17 November 1905. Educated at Escuela Popular Nocturna de Musica y Declamación, Mexico City, from 1923; studied dramaturgy on a Rockefeller Fellowship at Yale University, New Haven, Connecticut, 1935–36. Teacher of history and drama, Universidad Nacional Autónoma de México, Mexico City, from 1931, and later at Escuela de Verano; director of Teatro Radiofónico, Mexico City, 1933; director and translator of plays by US authors for Teatro de Orientación, Mexico City, from 1938; head of Mexican President's press office, 1938; head of theatre section of the Ministry of Education, 1938–39; founder and director, Teatro de Media Noche, Mexico City, 1940; Mexican cultural attaché, Paris, 1944–46; minister plenipotentiary, Beirut, Lebanon, 1957–60; Mexican ambassador, Oslo, Norway, 1960–72. Recipient: National Prize for Literature (Mexico), 1972. Died in Mexico City, 18 June, 1979.

Works

Collections

Teatro completo (3 vols.).   1963–79.
Tres comedias inéditas (includes *Un navío cargado de . . .; El testamento y el viudo; El encuentro*).   1966.
Corona de sombra; Corona de fuego; Corona de luz.   1973.

Stage Works

El apóstol.   In *Resumen*, January-February 1931; in book form, in *Teatro completo 1*, 1963.
Estado de secreto (produced Teatro Degollado, Guadalajara, 1936).   In *Teatro completo 1*, 1963.
Medio tono (produced Palacio de Bellas Artes, Mexico City, 1937).   1938; translated as *The Great Middle Class*, in *Poet Lore*, Summer 1968.
La mujer no hace milagros (produced Teatro Ideal, Mexico City, 1939).   1949.
La crítica de "La mujer no hace milagros".   In *Letras de México*, 15 January 1940; in book form, in *Teatro completo 1*, 1963.
Vacaciones 1 (produced Teatro Rex, Mexico City, 1940).   In *América*, June 1948.
La familia cena en casa (produced Teatro Ideal, Mexico City, 1942).   1942.
El gesticulador (produced Palacio de Bellas Artes, Mexico City, 1947).   1944.
Otra primavera (produced Teatro Virginia Fábregas, Mexico City, 1945).   1947; translated as *Another Springtime*, 1961.
Corona de sombra (produced Teatro Arbeu, Mexico City, 1947).   1947; translated as *Crown of Shadows*, 1946; part translated in *Spanish-American Literature in Translation 2*, 1966.

Mientras amemos (produced 1956).   1948.
La última puerta.   In *Hoy*, March-April 1948; in book form, in *Teatro completo 1*, 1963.
El niño y la niebla (produced Teatro del Caracol, Mexico City, 1951).   1951.
Noche de estío (produced Teatro Ideal, Mexico City, 1950). In *Teatro completo 1*, 1963.
Los fugitivos (produced Teatro Arbeu, Mexico City, 1950). In *México en la cultura*, 1951.
La función de despedida (produced Teatro Ideal, Mexico City, 1953).   1952.
Aguas estancadas (produced Teatro Colón, Mexico City, 1952).   In *México en la cultura*, April-May, 1952; in book form, in *Teatro completo 1*, 1963.
Jano es una muchacha (produced Teatro Colón, Mexico City, 1952).   1952.
Un día de éstos . . . (produced Teatro Esperanza Iris, Mexico City, 1954).   1957; translated as *One of These Days . . .*, with *Crown of Light*, 1971.
Vacaciones 2.   In *México en la cultura*, February 1956; in book form, in *12 Obras en un acto*, edited by Wilberto L. Cantón, 1967.
La exposición.   1960.
Corona de fuego (produced Teatro Xola, Mexico City, 1961). In *Teatro completo 2*, 1966.
4 Chemins 4.   In *Teatro completo 1*, 1963.
Falso drama.   In *Teatro completo 1*, 1963.
El presidente y el ideal.   In *Teatro completo 1*, 1963.
Alcestes.   In *Teatro completo 1*, 1963.
Tres comedias impóliticas.   In *Teatro completo 1*, 1963.
Corona de luz (produced Teatro Hidalgo, Mexico City, 1969).   1965; translated as *Crown of Light*, with *One of These Days . . .*, 1971.
Dios, Batidillo y la mujer.   In *Teatro completo 2*, 1966.
Las madres y los hijos.   In *Teatro completo 2*, 1966.
La diadema.   In *Teatro completo 2*, 1966.
El encuentro.   In *Tres comedias*, 1967.
Un navío cargado de . . .   In *Tres comedias*, 1967.
El testamento y el viudo.   In *Tres comedias*, 1967.
Carta de amor: Monologo heterodoxo.   In *Revista de la Universidad de México*, June 1968.
El gran circo del mundo.   In *Cuadernos americanos*, January-April 1969.
El caso Flores.   In *Cuadernos americanos*, 1971; in book form, in *Teatro completo 3*, 1979.
Los viejos.   In *Letras vivas*, by Rojas GarciduEñas and others, 1972.
Buenos días, señor Presidente!.   1972.

Radio Plays

Sueño de día, 1939 (published 1949).

Fiction

Ensayo de un crimen.   1944.

Verse

Conversación desperada.   1938.

Memoirs and Letters

Conversaciones y encuentros.   1974.

Other

México en el teatro.   1932; translated as *Mexico in the Theater*, 1976.

Caminos del teatro en México.   1933.
"Itinerario del autor dramático" y otros ensayos.   1940.
Homenaje a Alfredo Gómez de la Vega, with Mauricio Magdaleno.   1959.
Antonio Ruiz de Alarcón et l'arí dangereux de la peinture. 1960.
Ghent.   1966.
Anatomía del teatro.   1967.
Antonio Ruiz de Alarcón en el tiempo.   1967.
Voces: Diario de trabajo.   1967.
Obliteración.   1973.
Imagen y prisma de México: Presencia de Jauréz en el teatro universal.   1976.

Translator, *Walt Whitman, constructor para América,* by Babette Deutsch.   1942.
Translator, *Historia de Vasco,* by Georges Schehadé.   1959.

*

Bibliographies

Wilder P. Scott, "Toward an Usigli Bibliography", in *Latin American Theatre Review,* vol. 11 no. 2, 1972.

Criticism

Books:
J. Karkin Wyatt, *La obra dramática de Rodolfo Usigli,* Mexico City, 1950.
Peter R. Beardsell, "Usigli and the Search for Tragedy: *Corona de fuego*", in *Hispanic Studies in Honour of Frank Pierce,* edited by John England, Sheffield, 1980.

Articles:
Ellis E. Williams, "Abnormal Psychology in Some of Usigli's Works", in *Specialia,* 1, 1969.
Wilder P. Scott, "Rodolfo Usigli and Contemporary Dramatic Theory", in *Romance Notes,* 11, 1970.
Solomon T. Tilles, "Rodolfo Usigli's Concept of Dramatic Art", in *Latin American Theatre Review,* vol. 3 no. 2, 1970.
Vance R. Savage, "Rodolfo Usigli's Idea of Mexican Theater", in *Latin American Theatre Review,* vol. 4 no. 2, 1971.
Wilder P. Scott, "The Genesis and Development of a Female Character in Two Plays of Rodolfo Usigli", in *South Atlantic Bulletin,* vol. 39 no. 4, 1974.
Wilder P. Scott, "Rodolfo Usigli's *4 Chemin 4*: The Quest for a Title", in *Language Quarterly,* vol. 12 nos. 3–4, 1974.
Peter R. Beardsell, "Insanity and Poetic Justice in Usigli's *Corona de sombra*", in *Latin American Theatre Review,* 10, 1976.
"Entretien avec Rodolfo Usigli", in *Langues Néo-Latines,* vol. 73 no. 4, 1979.
Mark E. Finch, "Rodolfo Usigli's *Corona de sombra, Corona de fuego, Corona de luz*: The Mytheopoesis of Antihistory", in *Romance Notes,* 1981.
Ramón Layera, "Rodolfo Usigli (1905–1979)", in *Latin American Writers 3,* 1989.

*   *   *

In common with most members of the artistic and intellectual community who lived through the Mexican Revolution and shared in its populist and nationalistic ideals, Usigli was imbued with its reformist spirit; like others, he dedicated his life and considerable talent to a project of cultural and artistic renovation which concentrated almost exclusively on the dramatic arts. Labelled as the "apostle of Mexican drama" for his unswerving dedication to the establishment of an authentic national theatre in a country with a tradition for slavish imitation of Peninsular Spanish models, Usigli did everything possible to modernize and professionalize the craft. Apart from reading all the classics from ancient and European drama, he created his own repertory company and wrote newspaper theatre-reviews and articles, histories of Mexican drama, and a manual of dramatic theory and composition. He translated plays for the radio and for the stage, and he helped establish Mexico's first school of drama, where he taught dramaturgy to the next generation of playwrights. Above all, he wrote some of Mexico's most representative and best-known drama classics. In fact, his *El gesticulador* (The Imposter) is credited with signalling the beginning of modern Mexican drama.

Most of Usigli's plays reflect the more conventional aspects of dramatic realism in their systematic use of recognizably Mexican historical realities and everyday experiences and social types. But his brand of realism, which has been termed a "poetry of selective realism", benefits from a good measure of discernment and imagination. In his *Corona* (Crown) trilogy he formulates a far-ranging interpretive vision of Mexican history and cultural myths, while in "The Imposter" and several of his comedies he concentrates on the depiction of the more idiosyncratically characteristic features of Mexican life and society. Crediting Hegel, Schopenhauer, and Goethe for his ideas of the importance of myth for the interpretation and understanding of history, like his post-revolutionary fellow artists he regarded the systematic recovery and the critical re-examination of Mexico's past and national myths as a prerequisite for the development of a new national identity. His historical dramas—*Corona de fuego* (Crown of Fire), about the clash and ultimate fusion of the indigenous and the European, *Corona de luz* (Crown of Light), about the spiritual conquest of the native population, and *Corona de sombra* (Crown of Shadows), about the political emancipation of the Mexican republic—effectively subsume the central myths and basic components of Mexico's cultural identity. Similarly, the thematic base of his social and political satires, following Shavian aesthetic methods, provides a rich compendium of Mexican mores and institutions. Like the work of his Anglo-Irish model, Usigli's pioneering and polemic incorporation of the nascent middle class on the Mexican stage, with all its insecure and self-conscious pretentiousness, met equally with spectacular approval and rejection.

An accomplished essayist, novelist, and poet, Usigli was tireless as a teacher and theatre historian, and his efforts were instrumental in the establishment of a credible national theatre movement in Mexico. Because of the accurate portrayal of the Mexican people and their social institutions and the probing examination of their history, no other post-revolutionary artist, with the exception of a number of novelists and muralists, was able to project as authentic and comprehensive an artistic vision of modern Mexico as Usigli.

—Ramón Layera

See also *Volume 1* entry on *El gesticulador.*

VALLE-INCLÁN, Ramón (María) del. Born Ramón José Simón Valle y Peña in Villanueva, Galicia, Spain, 28 October 1866. Studied law at University of Santiago de Compostela, 1887–90, no degree. Married actress Josefina Blanco in 1907 (divorced 1932); six children. Journalist in Madrid, 1890, and in Mexico and Cuba, 1892–93; returned to Galicia, 1893; settled in Madrid, 1895, and frequented artistic circles; stage debut as actor, 1898; his left arm amputated after a fight, 1899; first-produced play, *Cenizas*, staged 1899; regular contributor to the periodical *El imparcial*; toured Spain and South America with his wife's acting company, 1910; unsuccessful political candidacy, 1910; visited Western Front as war correspondent, 1916; visited Mexico, Cuba, and New York, 1921; suffered illness and underwent convalescence in a sanatorium, 1923–24; imprisoned for two weeks under the dictatorship of Primo de Rivera; was unsuccessful Republican candidate for parliament, 1931; appointed director of the Spanish Academy of Fine Arts, Rome, 1934: resigned, 1935; entered a clinic in Santiago de Compostela. Elected President of the Madrid Ateneo, 1932. Died in Santiago de Compostela, 5 January 1936.

Works

Collections

Retablo de la avaricia, la lijuria y la muerte (includes *Ligazón; La rosa de papel; El embrujado; La cabeza del Bautista; Sacrilegio*). 1927.
Martes de carnaval (includes *Las galas del difunto; Los cuernos de don Friolera; La hija del capitán*). 1930.
Obras completas (2 vols.). 1954.
Plays 1 (includes *Divine Words; Bohemian Lights; Silver Face*), translated by Maria Delgado. 1993.

Stage Works

Cenizas (produced Teatro de Lara, Madrid, 1899). 1899; revised version, as *El yermo de las almas*, 1908.
Aguila de blasón (produced Teatro Español, Madrid, 1960). 1907.
El marqués de Bradomín (produced Teatro de la Princesa, Madrid, 1906). 1907.
Romance de lobos (produced Teatro Español, Madrid, 1960). 1908; translated as *Wolves! Wolves!*, 1957.
Cuento de abril (produced Teatro de la Comedia, Madrid, 1910). 1910.
Farsa de la cabeza del dragón (produced Teatro de la Comedia, Madrid, 1910). 1914; translated as *The Dragon's Head*, in *Poet Lore*, 29, 1918; in book form, in *Poet Lore Plays 2*, 1919.

Voces de gesta (produced by the Guerrero-Mendoza Company, Barcelona, 1911). 1911.
La Marquesa Rosalinda (produced Teatro de la Princesa, Madrid, 1912). 1913.
El embrujado (produced Teatro Muñoz Seca, Madrid, 1931) 1914.
Divinas palabras (produced Teatro Español, Madrid, 1920). 1920; translated as *Divine Words*, 1977, and in *Plays 1*, 1993.
Luces de Bohemia (produced in French, by Théâtre National Populaire, International Theatre Festival, Paris, 1963). In *España*, July-October 1920; revised version, in *Opera omnia 19*, 1924; translated as *Bohemian Lights*, in *Modern International Drama*, vol. 2 no. 2, 1968, and in *Plays 1*, 1993; as *Lights of Bohemia*, in *Luces de Bohemia* (parallel text), 1976.
Farsa y licencia de la reina castiza (produced Teatro Muñoz Seca, Madrid, 1922). 1922.
Cara de plata (produced Teatro Español, Madrid, 1960). 1923; translated as *Silver Face*, in *Plays 1*, 1993.
La rosa de papel (produced Teatro del Centro, Madrid, 1924). With *La cabeza del bautista*, 1924.
La cabeza del bautista (produced Teatro del Centro, Madrid, 1924). With *La rosa de papel*, 1924.
Los cuernos de don Friolera (produced Teatro de Zarzuela, Madrid, 1925). 1925.
Las galas del difunto. 1926.
Ligazón (produced Teatro el Mirlo Blanco, Madrid, 1926). In *Retablo de la avaricia . . .* (collection), 1927.
La hija del capitán. 1927.
Sacrilegio. In *Retablo de la avaricia . . .* (collection), 1927.

Fiction

Femeninas (stories). 1895.
Epitalamio. 1897.
Sonata de otoño. 1902; translated in *The Pleasant Memoirs of The Marquis de Bradomin*, 1924.
Jardin umbrío (stories and dialogues). 1903; augmented edition, 1914.
Corte de amor (stories). 1903.
Sonata de estío. 1903; translated in *The Pleasant Memoirs of the Marquis de Bradomin*, 1924.
Sonata de primavera. 1904; translated in *The Pleasant Memoirs of the Marquis de Bradomin*, 1924.
Flor de santidad. 1904.
Sonata de invierno. 1905; translated in *The Pleasant Memoirs of the Marquis de Bradomin*, 1924.
Jardin novelesco (stories). 1905.
Historias pervesas (stories). 1907.
Los cruzados de la causa. 1908.
El resplandor de la hoquera 1909.

Gerifaltes de antaño.   1909.
Cofres de sándalo (stories).   1909.
Mi hermana Antonia (stories).   1918.
Tirano Banderas.   1926; translated as *The Tyrant*, 1929.
La corte de los milagros.   1927.
Viva mi dueño.   1928.
Baza de espadas.   1958.

Verse

Aromas de leyenda.   1907.
La pipa de kif.   1919.
El pasajero.   1920.
Claves líricas.   1930.

Other

La lámpara marvillosa.   1916; translated as *The Lamp of Marvels*, 1986.
La media noche.   1917.
Cuentos, estética y poemas.   1919.

*

Bibliographies

J. Rubia Barcia, *A Bibliography and Iconography of Valle-Inclán*, Berkeley, California, 1960.
Robert Lima, *An Annotated Bibliography of Ramón del Valle-Inclán*, University Park, Pennsylvania, 1972.

Criticism

Books:
José Gómez Marín, *La idea de la sociedad en Valle-Inclán*, Madrid, 1967.
Ramón M del Valle-Inclán, 1866–1966: Estudios reunidos en conmemoración del centenario, La Plata, 1967.
Emili González López, *El arte dramático de Valle-Inclán: del Decadentismo al expresionismo*, New York, 1967.
Ricardo Gullón, (ed.), *Valle-Inclán Centennial Studies*, Austin, Texas, 1968.
Francisco Umbral, *Valle-Inclán*, Madrid, 1968.
Anthony N. Zahareas (ed.), *Ramón del Valle-Inclán: An Appraisal of His Life and Works*, New York, 1968.
Francisco Pina, *El Valle-Inclán que yo conocí y otros ensayos*, Mexico, 1969.
Francisco Ynduráin, *Valle-Inclán: Tres estudios*, Isla de los Ratones, 1969.
Rodolfo Cardona and Anthony N. Zahareas, *Visión del esperpento: Teoría y prática en los esperpentos de Valle-Inclán*, Castalia, 1970.
Manuel Bermejo Marcos, *Valle-Inclán: Introduccíon a su obra*. Salamanca, 1971.
Sumner M. Greenfield, *Valle-Inclán: Anatomía de un teatro problemático*, Madrid, 1972.
Robert Lima, *Ramón del Valle-Inclán*, New York, 1972.
Mariano Tudela, *Valle-Inclán: Vida y milagros*, Madrid, 1972.
José Esteban (ed.), *Valle-Inclán visto por . . .*, Madrid, 1973.
Juan A. Hormigón, *Ramón del Valle-Inclán: La política, la cultura, el realismo y el pueblo*, Madrid, 1973.
Verity Smith, *Ramón del Valle-Inclán*, New York, 1973.
Emma S. Speratti-Piñero, *El ocultismo en Valle-Inclán*, London, 1974.

Eva Llorens, *Valle-Inclán y la plástica: Estudios literarios*, Madrid, 1975.
Joaquina Canoa Galiana, *Semiología de las "comedias bárbaras"*, Madrid, 1977.
María E. Pérez, *Valle-Inclán: Su ambigüedad modernista*, Madrid, 1977.
Antonio Risco, *El demiurgo y su mundo: Hacia un nuevo enfoque de la obra de Valle-Inclán*, Madrid, 1977.
Obdulia Guerrero, *Valle-Inclán y el ovecientos: Apuntes para un estudio biográfico-literario*, Madrid, 1977.
Hebe N. Capanella, *Valle-Inclán: Materia y forma del esperpento*, Buenos Aires, 1980.
Ciriaco Ruiz Fernández, *El léxico del teatro de Valle-Inclán*, Salamanca, 1981.
Valentín Paz-Andrade, *La anunciación de Valle-Inclán*, Madrid, 1981.
José Servera Baño, *Ramon del Valle-Inclán*, Madrid, 1983.
Dru Dougherty, *Un Valle-Inclán olvidado: Entrevistas y conferencias*, Madrid, 1983.
Obdulia Guerrero, *América en Valle-Inclán*, Madrid, 1984.
John Lyon, *The Theatre of Valle-Inclán*, Cambridge, 1984.
Gwynne Edwards, *Dramatists in Perspective: Spanish Theatre in the Twentieth Century*, Cardiff, 1985.
Dru Dougherty, *Valle-Inclán y la Segunda República*, Valencia, 1986.
Claire Paolini, *Valle-Inclán's Modernism: Use and Abuse of Religious and Mystical Symbolism*, Valencia, 1986.
Juan Carlos Esturo Velarde, *La crueldad y el horror en el teatro de Valle-Inclán*, Sada, 1986.
Claire Paolini (ed.), *Genio y virtuosismo de Valle-Inclán*, Madrid, 1987.
Clara Luisa Barbeito (ed.), *Valle-Inclán: Nueva valoración de su obra: Estudios críticos en el cincuentenario de su muerte*, Barcelona, 1988.
Robert Lima, *Valle-Inclán: The Theatre of His Life*, Columbia, Missouri, 1988.
Carlos Jerez Farrán, *El expresionismo en Valle-Inclán*, Sada, 1989.
Sumner M. Greenfield, *Valle-Inclán: Anatomía de un teatro problemático*, Madrid, 1990.

Articles:
Anthony N Zahareas, "The Esperpento and Aesthetics of Commitment", in *Modern Language Notes*, 1966.
Anthony N. Zahareas and Gerald Gillespie, "Ramón Maria del Valle-Inclán: The Theatre of Esperpentos", in *Drama Survey*, 6, 1967.
J. E. Lyon, "Valle-Inclán and the Art of the Theatre", in *Bulletin of Hispanic Studies*, 46, 1969.
Gywnne Edwards, "The *Comedias bárbaras*: Valle-Inclán and the Symbolist Theatre", in *Bulletin of Hispanic Studies*, 60, 1983.
Gwynne Edwards, "Valle-Inclán and the New Art of the Theatre", in *Neophilologus*, 68, 1984.

*   *   *

The literary and theatrical fortunes of the iconoclastic Valle-Inclán have grown considerably over the half-century since his death. A multi-faceted writer who worked in all genres, he is a major figure in Spanish narrative and aesthetic theory. His career is noteworthy for the evolution from the sensual, neo-romantic Hispanic modernism of his youth to the bitingly satirical vein of the work of his maturity. Although initially his most innovative plays, the expressionistic, cinematographic *esperpentos* (grotesque tragicomedies), were thought to be unstageable, they have since been successfully performed internationally. It is largely because of them that their author now ranks with Federico García Lorca as Spain's greatest dramatists of the 20th century, and his works have been compared to Artaud, Brecht, and the writers of the theatre of the absurd.

Despite his extensive work in other genres, Valle-Inclán's strong commitment to the stage is apparent not only in his plays but also in the dramatic structure of his narratives and in his direct involvement in the theatre world, including acting and directing. Through these personal contacts, several of his plays were performed during his lifetime by important companies, notably those headed by María Guerrero and Margarita Xirgu. Among his masterworks, however, are attacks on the military and on traditional morality which, even after the question of their stageability was resolved, continued to be prohibited by the Franco-era censorship, and hence were first performed abroad.

Of the plays from Valle-Inclán's earlier periods several are still of interest today. Staged with greatest frequency is the popular children's farce *La cabeza del dragón* (The Dragon's Head), which Valle later grouped with his "puppet plays for the education of princes"—underlying the comic action is a political and social satire aimed at an adult audience. *La Marquesa Rosalinda*, a "sentimental, grotesque farce", is written in verse and set in the 18th century, and it juxtaposes an acting company, with its stock characters from the *commedia dell'arte*, and the stylized world of the aristocracy, represented by the young Marquise and her jealous old husband. In its use of parody and its criticism of the Spanish code of honor, *La Marquesa Rosalinda* also foreshadows the *esperpento*.

Different in tone from these farces is *Romance de lobos* (Ballad of Wolves), the best known of three *comedias bárbaras* (barbaric comedies). Set in 19th-century Galicia, the trilogy revolves around Don Juan Manuel Montenegro, a patriarchal figure whose carnal excesses are offset by his generosity and nobility of spirit, and his sons, whose degeneracy marks the end of the feudal order. The episodic action of *Romance de lobos* begins with a tempestuous scene in which the drunken old nobleman is beset by witches and ghosts announcing his wife's death, and ends with his own death at the hands of his sons when he storms his ancestral home at the head of a band of beggars. The intertextual references to Shakespeare's King Lear are obvious, as are the aspects of Valle-Inclán's drama that were to influence the grotesque films of Luis Buñuel.

In 1920 Valle-Inclán wrote the two plays that have received the greatest international acclaim: *Divinas palabras* (Divine Words) and *Luces de bohemia* (Bohemian Lights). Like the "barbaric comedies", *Divine Words* portrays the subculture of Galician beggars. In this case, two sisters-in-law fight for the privilege of displaying their hydrocephalic nephew at village fairs. In addition to its corrosive satire of religious superstition and hypocrisy and its introduction of the theme of incest, the text daringly calls for the appearance on stage of a nude actress. When Mari-Gaila, the sexton's adulterous wife, is caught *in flagrante* by the villagers, they bring her naked to the church for her punishment. Only by saying Christ's words in Latin is the cuckolded husband able to prevent them from stoning his wife.

Bohemian Lights is the first of Valle's plays to bear the subtitle *esperpento*, a term defined within the text as a systematic deformation of Spanish reality, as if reflected in concave mirrors. Elsewhere Valle-Inclán clarified the term: in the *esperpento* the perspective of author and spectator on the characters will be from above, not from below as in classic tragedy, or from directly across as in realistic drama. With this aesthetic, the classic heroes of tragedy become, in the *esperpento*, parodic anti-heroes, that is, grotesque puppets.

Bohemian Lights, an epic treatment of a blind poet's descent into the Madrilenian Hell and his eventual death, was followed by three more grotesque tragicomedies, grouped as *Martes de carnaval* (Carnival Tuesday): *Los cuernos de don Friolera* (Don Friolera's Horns), *Las galas del difunto* (The Dead Man's Duds), and *La hija del capitán* (The Captain's Daughter). The latter alluded to actual events, and all three overtly satirize the military. Unlike *Bohemian Lights*, where at least some of the characters escape the process of deformation to gain spectators' sympathies as real human beings, virtually all the characters in these other plays are dehumanized. The best of them, *Los cuernos de don Friolera*, is also a parody of Calderónian honor. This story of a military man, whose wife is allegedly unfaithful, is recounted in three versions—as a puppet play in the prologue, as the "real" action, and as a blind man's ballad in an epilogue. In the central story, the pathetic Friolera is forced by his fellow officers to cleanse his honor by killing his wife; however, he accidentally shoots his daughter instead. The play is generally performed in masks and with human actors, whose grotesque images are silhouetted as they assume the mechanical gestures of puppets.

Aesthetically related to the *esperpentos* are several short plays, published collectively as the *Retablo de la avaricia, la lujuria y la muerte* (Picture of Greed, Lust, and Death). Variously subtitled "melodramas for puppets" and "miracle plays for silhouettes", they are marked by their violent macabre action and their emphasis on sacrilege and superstition. The most performed of these, in Spain and abroad, are *La Rosa de papel* (The Paper Rose) and *Ligazón* (Blood Pact).

—Phyllis Zatlin

See also *Volume 1* entry on *Lights of Bohemia*.

VAMPILOV, Alexander. Born in Kutulik, Siberia, USSR, 19 August 1937. Studied philology at Irkutsk University, graduated 1960. Married; one daughter. Sketch-writer, then editor, newspaper in Irkutsk, 1960–64; moved to Moscow; attended the Gorky Institute of Literature; first-produced play, *Proschaniye v iyune* [*Farewell in June*], staged 1966, bringing him great popularity in provincial theatres. Member, Writers Union, 1965. Died in a boating accident on Lake Baikal, Siberia, 17 August 1972.

Works

Collections

Izbrannoe [Selected Works].   1975; revised edition, 1984.
Ia s vami lyudi [I Am with You, People].   1988.

Stage Works

Schaste Kati Kozlovy [Katya Kozlova's Happiness].   In *Odnoaktnye pesy*, 1959.
Tikhaya zavod [Tichaia Factory].   In *Volzhsky almanakh*, 13, 1960.
Dom oknami v pole (produced 1974).   In *Teatr*, 11, 1964; in book form, 1966; translated as *The House with a View on the Field*, in *Soviet Literature*, 3, 1980.
Proshchaniye v iyune (produced in the Russian provinces,

1966).   In *Teatr*, 8, 1966; translated as *Farewell in June*, 1983.

Predmeste [The Suburb].   In *Angara*, 2, 1968; revised version, as *Starshy syn* (produced Dramatic Theatre, Irkutsk, 1969).   1970; translated as *The Elder Son*, 1983.

Utinaya okhota (produced A. Upit State Academy Theatre of Latvia, Riga, 1976).   In *Angara*, 6, 1970; translated as *Duck Hunting*, 1980.

Dvadtsat minut s "angelom" (produced Bolshoi Dramatic Theatre, Leningrad, 1972).   In *Anagara*, 4, 1970; in book form, in *Provintsialnye anekdoty* [Provincial Anecdotes], 1971; translated as *Twenty Minutes with an "Angel"*, 1979.

Istoriya s metranpazhem (produced Bolshoi Dramatic Theatre, Leningrad, 1972).   In *Provintsialnye anekdoty*, 1971; translated as *Incident with a Paginator*, 1979.

Nesravnenny Nakonechnikov [The Incomparable Nakonechnikov] (unfinished).   1972.

Proshlym letom v Chulimske (produced Bolshoi Dramatic Theatre, Leningrad, 1973).   In *Sibir*, 3, 1973; in book form, 1974; translated as *Last Summer in Chulimsk*, in *Nine Modern Soviet Plays*, 1977.

Voronya roshcha [The Rooky Wood] (produced 1987).   In *Sovremennaya dramaturgiya*, 1, 1986.

Uspekh.   In *Sovremennaya dramaturgiya*, 1, 1986.

Fiction

Stechinie obstoyatelstv [A Chain of Being] (stories), under the pseudonym A. Sanin.   1961.

Other

Belye goroda (stories and journalism).   1979.

*

Criticism

Books:
Harold B Segel, *Twientieth Century Russian Drama from Gorky to the Present*, New York, 1979.
Angelika Germ-Wilkiewicz, *Ethik des Alltags: Die Mehrakter Aleksandr Wampilovs*, Mainz, 1986.

Articles:
A. Demidow, "Zur Dramatik Alexander Wampilows", in *Kunst und Literatur: Sowjetwissenschaft*, 23, 1975.
K Rudnizki, "Zur Dramatik Alexander Wampilows", in *Kunst und Literatur: Sowjetwissenschaft*, vol. 25, 1977.
Gudrun Düwel, "Alexandr Vampilov und Traditionen der russischen vorrevolutionären und sowjetischen Dramatik", in *Wissenschaftliche Zeitschrift der Friedrich-Schiller Universität*, vol. 29 no. 1, 1980.
Milli Martinelli, "Il teatro russo: Aleksandr Vampilov: Una voce della Siberia", in *Lingua e Letteratura*, 1, 1983.

* * *

Vampilov is widely regarded as the finest Russian dramatist of the past 50 years.

At the core of each of his plays is a moral issue of urgent relevance to Russians in the Soviet period, but undoubtedly of universal interest also. In *Farewell in June* the entrepreneur Zolotuev is obsessed with the idea that any person can be bought for a price; this is evaluated through the lives of the other characters, who are mainly students about to graduate. *The Elder Son* examines compulsive deception and whether it can ultimately prevail over love and moral purity. Vampilov combined his two one-acters *Twenty Minutes with an "Angel"* and *Incident with a Paginator* into an almost surreal portrayal of moral degradation entitled "Provincial Anecdotes". In the first, a range of Soviet citizens simply cannot believe the altruism of the "angel's" action, and end by interrogating and torturing him. In the second, the compulsive abusiveness and lying of an ill-tempered Soviet citizen are shown to be motivated by his own terror of authority. All of these themes, together with that of sexual infidelity, are present in Vampilov's masterpiece *Duck Hunting*, which is regarded by many as the classic case-study of *Homo sovieticus*. It is highly contentious whether the hero's unsuccessful suicide attempt at the end of this play definitively burns him out or leads to his regeneration. In his last finished play, *Last Summer in Chulimsk*, Vampilov moved into fresh areas by relating themes as diverse as the past, conscience, rape, and innocence, with the poetry of the Siberian forest and its native peoples.

Basic human ethics are all-pervasive in Vampilov, but unlike the bulk of contemporary Soviet drama his plays are completely unmoralising and untendentious. He was a moralist of the existential type: with total theatrical conviction, his characters *live* their dilemmas of honesty, deceit, fidelity, betrayal, conscience, "pure" love, and so on, hardly ever discussing them abstractly or religiously, but relating them to their fundamental desire to "discover their true selves", "to live as one should", or simply to "be happy". In fact, Vampilov's moral concerns were so *large* as to have eluded many directors and critics. Similarly, Vampilov's plays evoke with uncanny accuracy the texture of Brezhnev's Russia, with its chronic drunkenness, bribery, and sexual promiscuity; the author has been called the theatre poet of Soviet provincial Siberia, but his appeal as a playwright far transcends such limits.

Vampilov had the born dramatist's nose for events in everyday human existence that are about to explode with change. He excelled at orchestrating the rapid realignments of relationships that such changes bring and frequently took them to the pitch of life-or-death "boundary" situations. In *The House with a View in the Field*, *Farewell in June*, and *The Elder Son*, people about to leave established "families" of one kind or another unleash emotional and spiritual chaos. For the wife of Zilov, the hero of *Duck Hunting*, moving into their own, yearned-for flat is meant to be the start of a new married life, but it precipitates total estrangement from him and his own moral and physical collapse. Completely chance encounters also trigger disastrous chain reactions. The confluence of characters, issues, and events in a single, apparently ordinary, day at an ordinary café in the *taiga* (*Last Summer in Chulimsk*) develops with a Racine-like intensity.

It must be stressed that Vampilov's unpredictable, paradoxical development of situations is often extremely funny. His first three plays are each sub-titled "Comedy" and his one-acters are utterly hilarious in the best Gogol and Chekhov traditions. Clearly, though, the farces are "tragic" farces and the comedies very mixed. The theatrical language is also mixed: Vampilov's stage directions read almost naturalistically, but every item, from descriptions of windows and telephones to duck-shooting and silver birches, turns out to be capable of symbolic, indeed poetic, resonance. His use of stage time and space, lighting, and musical accompaniment is highly inventive.

The status of Vampilov's plays in present-day Russia is, at the time of writing, complex. He was a perfectionist who wrote under ruthless censorship, and his plays exist in many versions. Moreover the popularity of *Farewell in June* (uncensored title: "The Market") and *The Elder Son* was the result of directors wilfully adapting them to look like Soviet light drama. As Efremov, director of the Moscow Art Theatre, put it: "It was our own cliché-ridden brains that prevented Vampilov's plays from being heard". The result of these various forms of censorship is that at present the plays tend to be regarded as part of the "compromised past" and are relatively neglected.

Vampilov's work failed to take root in the West during the Brezhnev years because his plays did not seem radical or sensational enough compared with overtly dissident drama. When an outstanding production by Bill Pryde of *Last Summer in Chulimsk* toured England in 1987, critics were puzzled: was it sub-Chekhov or a Soviet soap opera (something akin to British television's *Crossroads*)? It will be some time before Vampilov can be dissociated from Chekhov in Western audiences' minds and before translators do justice to Vampilov's beautifully spare and expressive dialogue.

—Patrick Miles

See also *Volume 1* entry on *Duck Hunting*.

VAN DRUTEN, John (William).   Born in London, 1 June 1901. Educated at University College School, London, 1911–17; worked in a law office and studied law: LL.B, University of London, 1922; qualified as solicitor, 1923. Special Lecturer in English Law and Legal History, University College of Wales, Aberystwyth, 1923–26; first-produced play, *The Return Half*, staged 1924; full-time writer from 1926; moved to the USA, 1926: took US citizenship, 1944. Also stage director: directed *The King and I*, New York, 1951, and several of his own plays. Recipient: American Academy Award of Merit Medal, 1946; New York Drama Critics Circle Award, 1952. Member, American Academy, 1951. Died in Indio, California, 19 December 1957.

Stage Works

The Return Half (produced Royal Academy of Dramatic Art, London, 1924).
Young Woodley (produced Belmont Theatre, New York, 1925). 1926.
Chance Acquaintance (produced Criterion Theatre, London, 1927).
Diversion (produced 49th Street Theatre, New York, 1928). 1928.
The Return of the Soldier, from the novel by Rebecca West (produced Playhouse Theatre, London, 1928). 1928.
After All (produced Apollo Theatre, London, 1929; revised version, produced Arts Theatre, London, 1930). 1929.
London Wall (produced Duke of York's Theatre, London, 1931). 1931.

John Van Druten (seated, right) with members of the cast of his *The Voice of the Turtle*, 1943.

Sea Fever, with Auriol Lee, from a play by Marcel Pagnol (produced New Theatre, London, 1931).

There's Always Juliet (produced Apollo Theatre, London, 1931). 1931.

Hollywood Holiday, with Benn Levy (produced New Theatre, London, 1931). 1931.

Somebody Knows (produced St. Martin's Theatre, London, 1932). 1932.

Behold, We Live (produced St. James's Theatre, London, 1932). 1932.

The Distaff Side (produced Apollo Theatre, London, 1933). 1933.

Flowers of the Forest (produced Whitehall Theatre, London, 1934). 1934.

Most of the Game (produced Cort Theatre, New York, 1935). 1936.

Gertie Maude (produced St. Martin's Theatre, London, 1937). 1937.

Leave Her to Heaven (produced Longacre Theatre, New York, 1940). 1941.

Old Acquaintance (produced Morosco Theatre, New York, 1940). 1941.

Solitaire, from the novel by Edwin Corle (produced Plymouth Theatre, New York, 1942).

The Damask Cheek, with Lloyd R. Morris (produced Playhouse Theatre, New York, 1942). 1943.

The Voice of the Turtle (produced Morosco Theatre, New York, 1943). 1944.

I Remember Mama, from stories by Kathryn Forbes (produced Music Box Theatre, New York, 1944). 1945.

The Mermaids Singing (produced Empire Theatre, New York, 1945). 1946.

The Druid Circle (produced Morosco Theatre, New York, 1947). 1948.

Make Way for Lucia, from novels by E.F. Benson (produced Cort Theatre, New York, 1948). 1949.

Bell, Book, and Candle (produced Ethel Barrymore Theatre, New York, 1950). 1951.

I Am a Camera, from stories by Christopher Isherwood (produced Empire Theatre, New York, 1951). 1952

I've Got Sixpence (produced Ethel Barrymore Theatre, New York, 1952). 1953.

Dancing in the Chequered Shade (produced 1955).

Screenplays

Young Woodley, with Victor Kendall, 1930; *I Loved a Soldier*, 1936; *Parnell*, with S.N. Behrman, 1937; *Night Must Fall*, 1937; *The Citadel*, with others, 1938; *Raffles*, with Sidney Howard, 1940; *Lucky Partners*, with Allan Scott, 1940; *My Life with Caroline*, with Arnold Belgard, 1941; *Johnny Come Lately (Johnny Vagabond)*, 1943; *Old Acquaintance*, with Lenore Coffee, 1943; *Forever and a Day*, with others, 1944; *Gaslight*, with Walter Reisch and John L. Balderston, 1944; *The Voice of the Turtle*, 1948.

Fiction

Young Woodley. 1929.
A Woman on Her Way. 1930.
And Then You Wish. 1936.
The Vicarious Years. 1955.

Memoirs and Letters

The Way to the Present: A Personal Record. 1938.
Playwright at Work. 1953.
The Widening Circle (autobiography). 1957.

*   *   *

No playwright since Dion Boucicault in the mid-19th century enjoyed the kind of success in both England and America that John Van Druten enjoyed. Both authors wrote plays specifically addressing the two cultures, and Van Druten did so more legitimately. Boucicault would often re-write existing plays for the American market, whereas Van Druten wrote his from whole cloth. For some 25 years, first in London, then in the USA after moving there, Van Druten earned his reputation for expert craftsmanship with a series of mainly comedies of manners and of character.

Van Druten's early work, however, was in the "problem play" tradition, and it was the reaction of the English censors that first drove him to New York. His second play, *Young Woodley*, much more a problem play than a comedy of manners, was refused a licence by the Lord Chamberlain until it had been performed in the USA in 1925. The play, to do with a public schoolboy's attachment to a master's wife, was banned in England on the ground that it was too frank an exposé of institutional English respectability. A later English play, *Somebody Knows*, had something of the same élan about it through its daring portrayal of a prostitute who refuses to accept benevolent middle-class encouragement to reform. Once again, middle-class values are questioned in a challenging way, for although the play ends with the do-gooding hero acquitted of a prostitute's murder, the mud is intended to stick, as it does in J.B. Priestley's *An Inspector Calls*, not so much for the actual crime as for the creation of the circumstances leading up to it. Van Druten was again critical of British middle-class values in *After All*, in which various members of a respectable English family go to seed because they are too weak to survive threats to their economic and social status.

Thereafter, Van Druten moved less contentiously toward the material for which he is best remembered. *There's Always Juliet*, *The Distaff Side*, and *Old Acquaintance* all display, at their best, his most enduring skills. The tone is more wry than it is openly comic, and machinations of plot surrender effortlessly to permutations in characterisation, most interestingly of strong-willed women in situations that reveal their individual strengths more than they expose their social limitations. The Chekhovian echoes are conscious in *The Distaff Side*, where sisters trade places, each discovering for the first time facts about the other which their common origin failed to illuminate. This is almost a "what if?" reply to *Three Sisters*. *Old Acquaintance* examines the choices for women by contrasting the paths of a woman who pursues a successful writing career and a woman who settles for marriage. Though the polarisation may be false, the portrayals are real enough, with neither woman enjoying the best of the debate.

In *The Damask Cheek* (co-written with Lloyd Morris), Van Druten self-reflectively addresses transatlantic differences through the adventures of a single English girl in America. In sharp contrast to Henry James as well as to numerous other portrayals of the reverse experience, in which the American girl travelling in Britain is seen as free and frank, Van Druten's heroine challenges New England notions of virtue by appearing "a libertine" in her acceptance of such things as sex outside marriage. Van Druten was to return to the theme more pointedly (albeit in an adaptation of a Christopher Isherwood novel) in his portrayal of Sally Bowles in *I Am a Camera*. And sex-and-the-single-woman was perhaps treated best in the long-running *The Voice of the Turtle*, in which reputation is treated very much as a matter of personal attitude and of temperament, not of nose-thumbing at convention. It is, again, through recognisable characterisation that Van Druten distinguishes shifting social attitudes.

His preoccupation with play technique, perhaps in an effort

to master plotting, led Van Druten to "experiment" with comic potboilers in *Bell, Book, and Candle* and *The Druid Circle*, both about witchcraft. These offer little more than an exhibition of technique, and each play is a staple of amateur dramatic companies, tapping the popular, casual taste for the occult. Van Druten was ever a student of playwriting, and his "textbook" on the subject, *Playwright at Work*, is more valuable as a practitioner's analysis of plays than as a manual for writing successful ones. Generous in his praise of others, Van Druten reveals aspects of plays of his own time altogether missing from the few histories of the period. His comments may not be persuasive enough to stimulate revival, but they are sufficiently painstaking to excite wonder at the belief that the British theatre between the wars was mainly dross.

—James McNaughton

See also *Volume 1* entry on *The Voice of the Turtle*.

VAN ITALLIE, Jean-Claude. Born in Brussels, Belgium, 25 May 1936. Moved to the USA, 1940: took US citizenship, 1952. Educated at Great Neck High School, New York; Deerfield Academy, Massachusetts; Harvard University, Cambridge, Massachusetts, AB 1958; New York University, 1959; studied acting at the Neighborhood Playhouse, New York. Editor, *Transatlantic Review*, New York, 1960–63; playwright-in-residence, Open Theatre, New York, 1963–68; freelance writer on public affairs for NBC and CBS television, New York, 1963–67; first plays produced 1963; taught playwriting at the New School for Social Research, New York, 1967–68, 1972, Yale University School of Drama, New Haven, Connecticut, 1969, 1978, 1984–85, and Naropa Institute, Boulder, Colorado, 1976–83; lecturer, Princeton University, New Jersey, 1973–86, New York University, 1982–86 and 1992, University of Colorado, Boulder, 1985 and 1987–91, and Columbia University, New York, Spring 1986; visiting Mellon Professor, Amherst College, Massachusetts, Autumn 1976, Middlebury College, Middlebury, Vermont, 1990. Recipient: Vernon Rice Award, 1967; Outer Circle Award, 1967; Obie Award, 1968. Ph.D: Kent State University, Kent, Ohio, 1977.

Works

Collections

America Hurrah (includes *Interview*; *TV*; *Motel*). 1967; British edition, with *War* and *Almost Like Being*, as *America Hurrah: Five Short Plays*, 1967.
"War" and Four Other Plays (includes *Almost Like Being*; *I'm Really Here*; *The Hunter and the Bird*; *Where is de Queen?*). 1967.
Seven Short and Very Short Plays (includes *Photographs*; *Eat Cake*; *The Girl and the Soldier*; *Take a Deep Breath*; *Rosary*; *Harold*; *Thoughts on the Instant of Greeting a Friend on the Street*). 1975.
"America Hurrah" and Other Plays (includes *The Serpent*; *A Fable*; *The Hunter and the Bird*; *Almost Like Being*). 1978.

Stage Works

War (produced Vandam Theatre, New York, 1963). In *"War" and Four Other Plays*, 1967; in *American Hurrah: Five Short Plays*, 1967.

From an Odets Kitchen (produced Sheridan Square Playhouse, New York, 1963).
The Murdered Woman (produced Martinique Theatre, New York, 1964).
Almost Like Being (produced Vandam Theatre, New York, 1964). In *"War" and Four Other Plays*, 1967; in *America Hurrah: Five Short Plays*, 1967.
I'm Really Here (produced Vandam Theatre, New York, 1964). In *"War" and Four Other Plays*, 1967.
The Hunter and the Bird (produced Sheridan Square Playhouse, New York, 1964). In *"War" and Four Other Plays*, 1967.
Interview (as *Pavane*, produced Academy Theatre, Atlanta, 1965; revised version, as *Interview*, produced Pocket Theatre, New York, 1966). In *America Hurrah*, 1967.
Where is de Queen? (as *Dream*, produced La Mama Experimental Theatre, New York, 1965; revised version, as *Where is de Queen?*, produced Firehouse Theatre, Mineapolis, 1965). In *"War" and Four Other Plays*, 1967.
Motel (as *America Hurrah*, produced La Mama Experimental Theatre, New York, 1965; revised version, as *Motel*, produced Pocket Theatre, New York, 1966). In *America Hurrah*, 1967.
TV (produced Pocket Theatre, New York, 1966). In *American Hurrah*, 1967.
The Girl and the Soldier (produced Mark Taper Forum, Los Angeles, 1967). In *Seven Short and Very Short Plays*, 1975.
Thoughts on the Instant of Greeting a Friend on the Street, with Sharon Thie (produced Mark Taper Forum, Los Angeles, 1967; in *Collision Course*, produced Café au Go-Go, New York, 1968). In *Seven Short and Very Short Plays*, 1975.
The Serpent: A Ceremony, with the Open Theatre (produced Teatro degli Arte, Rome, 1968). 1969.
Take a Deep Breath (produced in *DMZ*, Village Vanguard, New York, 1968). In *Seven Short and Very Short Plays*, 1975.
Photographs: Mary and Howard (produced Mark Taper Forum, Los Angeles, 1969). In *Seven Short and Very Short Plays*, 1975.
Eat Cake (produced Changing Scene, Denver, Colorado, 1971). In *Seven Short and Very Short Plays*, 1975.
Mystery Play (produced Cherry Lane Theatre, New York, 1973). 1973; revised version, as *The King of the United States*, music by Richard Peaslee (produced Theatre for the New City, New York, 1973), 1975.
Nightwalk, with Megan Terry and Sam Shepard (produced St. Clement's Church, New York, 1973). In *Open Theater* 1975.
The Sea Gull, from a play by Chekhov (produced McCarter Theatre, Princeton, New Jersey, 1973. 1977.
A Fable, music by Richard Peaslee (produced Lenox Arts Center, Lenox, Massachusetts, 1975). 1976.
Rosary. In *Seven Short and Very Short Plays*, 1975.
Harold. In *Seven Short and Very Short Plays*, 1975.
The Cherry Orchard, adaptation of a play by Chekhov (produced Lincoln Center, New York, 1977). 1977.
Medea, the play by Euripides (produced Kent State University, Kent, Ohio, 1979).
Three Sisters (produced Bard College Center, Anandale-on-Hudson, New York, 1979). 1979.
Bag Lady (produced Theatre for the New City, New York, 1979). 1980.
Uncle Vanya, from a play by Chekhov (produced La Mama Experimental Theatre, New York, 1983). 1980.
Naropa, music by Steve Gorn (produced La Mama

Experimental Theatre, New York, 1982).   In *Wordplays 1*, 1980.

Early Warnings (includes *Bag Lady; Sunset Freeway; Final Orders*; produced New York, 1983).   1983.

The Tibetan Book of the Dead; or, How Not to Do it Again, music by Steve Gorn (produced New York, 1983).   1983.

Pride, in *The Show of the Seven Deadly Sins*, with Albee, Durang, Guare, and others (produced McCarter Theatre, Princeton, New Jersey, 1985).

The Balcony, from a play by Jean Genet (produced Cambridge, Massachusetts, 1986).

The Traveler (produced Mark Taper Forum, Los Angeles, 1987).

Struck Dumb (produced Los Angeles, 1989).   In *Best One-Act Plays 1990–91*, 1991.

Ancient Boys (produced Boulder, Colorado, 1990).

Screenplays

The Box is Empty, 1965; *Three Lives for Mississippi*, 1971; *Follies*, 1978.

Television Plays

Scripts for *Look Up* and *Live* series, 1963–65; *Hobbies; or, Things Are All Right with the Forbushers*, 1967; *Take a Deep Breath*, 1969; *Picasso: A Painter's Diary*, 1980.

Other

Calcutta (journal).   1987.

*

Bibliographies

Philip C Kolin (ed.), *American Playwrights Since 1945: A Guide to Scholarship, Criticism, and Performance*, New York, 1989.

Criticism

Books:
Robert Brustein, "Three Views of America", in *Third Theatre*, New York, 1969.
John Lahr, *Up Against the Fourth Wall*, New York, 1970.

Articles:
P.-J Wagner, "Jean-Claude van Itallie: Political Playwright", in *Serif*, vol.9 no.4, 1972.
Jean-Claude van Itallie and Alexis Greene, "An Interview with Jean-Claude van Itallie", in *Studies in American Drama 1945–Present*, 3, 1988.

* * *

Jean-Claude van Itallie first attracted attention with *America Hurrah*, an evening of three one-act plays each offering a metaphor for the emptiness and ugliness van Itallie saw in contemporary American life. In *Interview*, the demeaning rituals of a job interview are the starting point for a phantasmagoria of chaotic city life, with an emphasis on the failure of society's institutions—politics, religion, medicine—to deal effectively with urban horrors or their effect on the individual psyche. *TV* juxtaposes the deadness of office work with the banalities of a range of television programs, and shows the fictions proving stronger than reality, moving outside the frame of the onstage television screen to take over the playing area and affect the behavior of the "real" characters. In *Motel* van Itallie attacks both the emptiness of American culture and its destructive effect on American behavior, by having a motel owner complacently catalogue and extol the tasteless furnishings of a room, not noticing that her guests are viciously vandalizing and destroying it. (The dehumanization and grotesquery in *Motel* is emphasized by having the actors encased in larger-than-lifesize papier-maché puppets.)

The structure of both *Interview* and *TV* is built on an acting exercise called transformation, in which performers instantly and repeatedly switch characterizations and settings, allowing a small cast to fill the stage with characters, and a play to move seamlessly between unrelated episodes. This device was part of the performance style of the Open Theatre, an experimental acting company with which van Itallie was associated, and in fact parts of both plays grew out of actor improvisations. Van Itallie's next major play, *The Serpent*, was also an Open Theatre project, with the company working on improvisations on the theme of the Creation for several months before van Itallie was brought in to transcribe and organize their work, adding material of his own, to produce a final text. (Both van Itallie and Open Theatre director Joseph Chaikin stress, in prefaces to the printed text, that although the play was built on improvisations, its text and staging, like those of other Open Theatre productions, were eventually frozen into a final version not then subject to actors' improvisations in performance.)

The Serpent is a series of scenes and performance pieces dramatizing, responding to, or related through a stream-of-consciousness flow to the story of Adam and Eve. Scenes of the Temptation and Fall, and of the murder of Abel, are accompanied by symbolic stagings of the assassination of President Kennedy, the "begat" genealogies of the Bible, and the emptiness and despair in modern life. The Open Theatre performance style involved extensive use of mime, choreography, chanting, evocations of ritual, and general writhing-around; and these aspects are incorporated into the text. The assassination is precisely choreographed as a slow-motion "film", which is repeated and run backwards to underline its imagery. Eden is populated by actors transforming themselves into animals, with the serpent played by five actors writhing and speaking together; and the genealogy is accompanied by the group miming of intercourse and birth.

It is in the nature of this sort of theatre piece for it not to have a simple, linear "message", but to be built on a series of impressions and epiphanies. (There is a deliberately religious element in the performance style—van Itallie labels the play "a ceremony"—and audiences are supposed to be drawn by its ritualistic qualities to unverbalized insights.) The underlying pattern is of innocence shattered by knowledge, of characters (and thus, implicitly, humanity) taking enormous steps forward or backward in total ignorance, and then having to puzzle out the implications of their actions after the fact. The need for God is, at its root, a need for explanations, an extension of the same search for meaning that motivates the compulsive running and re-running of the "film" of the Kennedy assassination.

None of van Itallie's original work after *The Serpent* has attracted much critical attention. His most significant dramatic contributions have been in a more traditional form of theatre, in a series of translations and adaptations, particularly of Chekhov, which have generally been praised for their idiomatic language and theatrical power.

—Gerald M. Berkowitz

VANBRUGH, Sir John. Born in London; baptised 24 January 1664. Educated possibly at King's School, Chester, to age 19; studied in France, 1683–85. Commissioned ensign in the 13th foot regiment of Lord Huntingdon, 1686; arrested in Calais for spying, and imprisoned in Calais, Vincennes, and Paris, 1688–92; captain in Lord Berkeley's marine regiment, 1695, and Lord Huntingdon's regiment, 1702. Married Henrietta Maria Yarburgh in 1719; one son. Employed by the duchy of Lancaster, 1693–95; first-produced play, *The Relapse*, staged 1696; Comptroller of the Royal Works, 1702–13 and 1715–19; manager, with Congreve, Queen's Theatre, Haymarket, London, 1705–06; surveyor of Greenwich Hospital, 1715; surveyor of gardens and waters, 1715. Also an important architect: works—Castle Howard, Yorkshire, 1700–12 (additions, 1715, 1718, 1725–26); Vanbrugh House, Whitehall, London, 1701; Queen's Theatre (later Opera House), London, 1704–05; Blenheim Palace, Oxfordshire, 1705–16; Kimbolton Castle, Huntingdon, 1707–10; Audley End, Essex, 1708; Chargate, Surrey, 1709–10; King's Weston, Avon, c.1710–14; Claremont, Surrey, 1715–20; Great Kitchen, St. James's Palace, London, 1716–17; Vanbrugh Castle, Greenwich, 1718–c.21; Eastbury, Dorset, 1718–26; Stowe, Buckinghamshire, c.1719–24; Vanbrugh Fields Estate, Greenwich, 1719–25; Seaton Delaval, Northumberland, 1720–28; Lumley Castle, Durham, 1721–22; Somersby Hall, Lincolnshire, 1722; Grimsthorpe Castle, Lincolnshire, 1722–26; Newcastle Pew, Esher Old Church, Surrey, 1723–25. Member, College of Heralds: Carlisle Herald, 1703; Clarenceux King-at-Arms, 1704–25. Knighted, 1714. Died in London, 26 March 1726.

Works

Collections

Plays (2 vols.). 1719.
Complete Works (4 vols.), edited by Bonamy Dobrée and Geoffrey Webb. 1927–28.
Four Comedies (includes *The Relapse*; *The Provoked Wife*; *The Confederacy*; *A Journey to London*), edited by Michael Cordner. 1989.

Stage Works

The Relapse; or, Virtue in Danger (produced Theatre Royal, Drury Lane, London, 1696). 1697.
Aesop, 2 parts, from play by Boursault (produced Theatre Royal, Drury Lane, London, 1696–97). 1976.
The Provoked Wife (produced Lincoln's Inn Fields Theatre, London, 1697). 1697.
The Country House, from a play by Florent Dancourt (produced Theatre Royal, Drury Lane, London, 1698). 1715.
The Pilgrim, from the play by Fletcher (produced Theatre Royal, Drury Lane, London, 1700). 1700.

The False Friend, from a play by Lesage (produced Theatre Royal, Drury Lane, London, 1702). 1702.
Squire Trelooby, with Congreve and William Walsh, from a play by Molière (produced Lincoln's Inn Fields Theatre, London, 1704). Revised version by James Ralph published as *The Cornish Squire*, 1734.
The Confederacy, from a play by Florent Dancourt (produced Queen's Theatre, Haymarket, 1705; also produced as *The City Wives' Confederacy*). 1705,
The Mistake, from a play by Molière (produced Queen's Theatre, Haymarket, 1705). 1706.
The Cuckold in Conceit (produced Queen's Theatre, Haymarket, 1707).
The Provoked Husband; or, A Journey to London, completed by Cibber (produced Theatre Royal, Drury Lane, 1728). 1728.

Other

A Short Vindication of "The Relapse" and "The Provoked Wife" from Immorality and Profaneness. 1698.
Vanbrugh's Justification of What He Deposed in the Duchess of Marlborough's Late Trial. 1718.

*

Criticism

Books:
C. Barman, *Sir John Vanbrugh*, London, 1924.
Laurence Whistler, *Sir John Vanbrugh, Architect and Dramatist 1664–1726*, London, 1938; revised edition, London, and Hillwood, New York, 1978.
Laurence Whistler, *The Imagination of Vanbrugh and His Fellow Artists*, London, 1954.
Bernard A. Harris, *Sir John Vanbrugh*, London, 1967.
Madeleine Bingham, *Masques and Facades: Sir John Vanbrugh, The Man in His Setting*, London, 1974.
Arthur R. Huseboe, *Sir John Vanbrugh*, Boston, 1976.
John Anthony, *Vanbrugh: An Illustrated Life of Sir John Vanbrugh 1664–1726*, Aylesbury, 1977.
Kerry Downes, *Sir John Vanbrugh*, London, 1977.
Gerald M. Berkovitz, *Vanbrugh and the End of Restoration Comedy*, Amsterdam, 1981.
Geoffrey Beard, *The Work of John Vanbrugh*, London, 1986.
Kerry Downes, *John Vanbrugh: A Biography*, London and New York, 1987.

Articles:
Paul Mueschke and Jeannette Fleisher, "A Re-Evaluation of Vanbrugh", in *Publications of the Modern Language Association* [*PMLA*], 49, 1934.

*   *   *

Sir John Vanbrugh's reputation as a major comic dramatist rests on two plays produced within six months of each other at the end of the 17th century, *The Relapse* and *The Provoked Wife*. Like Etherege and Wycherley, the two finest comic playwrights of the previous generation, Vanbrugh was not a professional writer and devoted only a fairly short period of his life to the theatre, so that his output, like theirs, is relatively small. Indeed he is at least as renowned for his architecture, especially Castle Howard and Blenheim Palace, as for his plays. Belonging to the generation of dramatists that includes Congreve, Farquhar, Steele, and Colley Cibber,

Vanbrugh was writing after the Glorious Revolution of 1688 when the theatre was again coming under moralistic attacks because of its alleged licentiousness and obscenity. Vanbrugh himself was criticized in the most influential of these, Jeremy Collier's comprehensive *A Short View of the Immorality and Profaneness of the English Stage* (1698), and published a reply in the same year, *A Short Vindication*, in which he defends *The Relapse* and *The Provoked Wife* against Collier's strictures. At a time when comic drama was beginning to undergo the transformation that led to the homiletic "exemplary" or "sentimental" comedy of the 18th century—which concentrated on providing models of virtue and examples of moral reformation to be emulated rather than on comedy's traditional function of ridiculing vice, folly, and affectation—Vanbrugh was intent on keeping alive the satirical mainstream of 17th-century comedy descending from Ben Jonson. Like Congreve, he was greatly indebted to the dramatists of Charles II's reign who developed the so-called "wit" or "manners" comedy of the Restoration, but because of his originality in handling its conventions he made a distinctive contribution to this kind of comedy. This is partly because of his essentially serious preoccupation with the subject of marriage, especially the tensions between husband and wife in ill-matched and unhappy relationships, and partly because of the robust energy of his plays, which manifests itself in his rich characterization and his inventiveness in creating comic situations. Vanbrugh does in fact cross Shadwell's comedy of "humours" with Etherege's and Congreve's comedy of "wit". Although less caustically satirical than Wycherley, less stylistically refined than Congreve, and less genial than Farquhar, he is undoubtedly one of the wittiest of Restoration writers and for sheer vitality he has few equals among his contemporaries and 18th-century successors.

Vanbrugh wrote *The Relapse*, his first play to be staged, in response to Cibber's *Love's Last Shift* (1696), in which Amanda employs subterfuge and deception, including seduction, to win back her rakish husband Loveless who has deserted her. Cibber presents Amanda's reprehensible conduct as admirable, and Loveless, overwhelmed by her display of wifely love, is instantly reconciled to her and morally reformed. Vanbrugh clearly found this sentimental and sententious denouement facile, dishonest, and unconvincing, and in *The Relapse* wrote a sequel that is also a reply to *Love's Last Shift*. *The Relapse* does, however, stand as a completely independent work that can be appreciated without reference to Cibber's considerably inferior play. Vanbrugh's main plot continues the story of Amanda and Loveless after the penitent's apparent rehabilitation and shows how temporary such reformations usually are. Loveless soon reverts to his promiscuous ways when temptation arrives in the form of Amanda's widowed cousin Berinthia, whereas the virtuous Amanda resists Worthy's offer of adulterous love. At the end of the play Vanbrugh presents no solution to the problem of Amanda and Loveless's marriage, which is left unresolved. Interesting and unusual as this part of the play is, it almost takes second place to the sub-plot concerning Lord Foppington. Vanbrugh again draws on *Love's Last Shift*, since Lord Foppington is Cibber's Sir Novelty Fashion elevated to the peerage, but Vanbrugh also transforms Cibber's amusing portrait of a fop into not only the most rounded presentation of a fashionable beau in contemporary drama but one of the great comic characters of the English stage. Almost as unforgettable is Sir Tunbelly Clumsey, Vanbrugh's version of another stereotype of Restoration comedy, the boorish country knight. Structurally *The Relapse* may be faulty, and Vanbrugh, a fundamentally moral writer, is unable to eschew completely the sentimentality that mars

Cibber's play so badly, but its sustained comic brilliance more than compensates for its defects.

The Provoked Wife, a better organized play than its predecessor, also contains one of the best comic characters of the period, Sir John Brute, the most memorable of the numerous husbands in Restoration comedy who are heartily sick of marriage and their wives and who try, not very successfully, to devote themselves to a life of debauchery. The surly, rude, and stubborn Sir John has ruined his marriage, and Vanbrugh explores sympathetically the predicament of Lady Brute, who is maltreated by her husband but who is too virtuous to give herself to her admirer Constant. Vanbrugh deals with the issue of marital incompatibility, at a time when divorce was virtually impossible, in a sensitive and humane way, not in the flippant and jokey manner typical of contemporary comedy, and is too realistic to offer an easy theatrical solution producing a happy ending for Lady Brute. As in *The Relapse*, there is no tidy resolution of the main plot.

Apart from the unfinished *A Journey to London*, which reached the stage in 1728 in a version revised, completed, and sentimentalized by Colley Cibber entitled *The Provoked Husband*, Vanbrugh's other dramatic works are either adaptations or translations of earlier plays. His one attempt to revamp an English play, a prose version of Fletcher's *The Pilgrim*, impoverishes rather than enriches the original, but the opposite occurs in the case of some of his translations. As a translator of recent French plays, including some of Molière's, Vanbrugh was far from slavish and felt free to alter and add to his sources, the result being that he imbued them with some of his typical vigour and broad humour. The outstanding example is *The Confederacy*, a superb adaptation of Dancourt's *Les Bourgeoises à la mode*, itself a lively and witty comedy that Vanbrugh, by transferring the action from Paris to London, nevertheless succeeds in enhancing from beginning to end. Also worthy of note is *Aesop*, based on Boursault's *Les Fables d'Ésope*, in which Vanbrugh characteristically tones down the sentiment of the original in favour of comic action. Vanbrugh's two masterpieces still hold the stage and *The Confederacy* has been revived in recent years, but the plays are not produced as frequently as they deserve.

—Peter Lewis

See also *Volume 1* entries on *The Provoked Wife*; *The Relapse*.

VEGA Carpio, Lope (Félix) de.   Born in Madrid, Spain, 25 November 1562. Educated at Jesuit Imperial College, 1574–75; Universidad Complutense, 1577. Married 1) Isabel de Urbina in 1588 (died 1595); 2) Juana de Guarda c.1602 (died), several children; also had children by Micaela de Luján and Marta de Nevares, and another illegitimate son. Went to Madrid after leaving university: writer and traveller; patronized by Marqués de Las Navas, 1583–87, and Marqués de Malpica; love affair with Elena Osorio led to accusations of libel, jail, and exile from Castille; joined the Spanish Armada against England in 1588; then lived in Valencia and Toledo; secretary to the Duke of Alba, 1590–95; in household of Marqués de Sarría, 1598–1600; secretary and counsellor to the Duke of Sessa from 1605; also "familiar of the Inquisition", 1608, and prosecutor of Apostolic Chamber;

lived in Madrid after 1610; ordained priest, 1614. Order of Malta, 1627. Claimed to have written 1500 plays, but currently 314–20 of those attributed to him thought to be genuine. Died in Madrid, 27 August 1635.

Works

Collections

Las Comedias (29 vols.).   1604–45(?).
Fiestas des Santíssimo Sacramento   1644.
Colección de las obras sueltas así en prosa, come en verso (21 vols.), edited by F. Cerdá y Rico.   1776–79.
Obras (15 vols.), edited by M. Menédez y Pelayo.   1890–1913; revised edition (13 vols.), edited by E. Cotarelo y Mori, 1916–30.
Four Plays (includes *A Certainty for a Doubt; The King, the Greatest Alcalde; The Gardener's Dog; Fuente Ovejuna*), translated by John Garrett Underhill. 1936.
Obras escogidas (3 vols.), edited by F.C. Sainz de Robles. 1946–55.
Five Plays (includes *Fuente Ovejuna; Justice Without Revenge; The Dog in the Manger; Peribáñez; The Knight of Olmedo*), translated by Jill Booty, edited by R.D.F. Pring-Mill.   1961.

Stage Works (selected)

The following alphabetical list includes those titles that have appeared as modern editions, together with their English translations (where they exist).

El acero de madrid.
Las almenas de toro.
Amar sin saber a quién.
El amor desatinado.
El amor enamorado.
Arminda celosa.
Barlaán y Josafat
Las bizarrías de Belisa.
El Brasil restituido.
Las burlas de amor.
Las burlas veras.
El caballero de Olmedo. Translated as *The Knight from Olmedo*, in *Five Plays*, edited by R.D.F. Pring-Mill, 1961; as *The Gentleman of Olmedo*, with *The Great Pretenders*, 1992.
El cardenal de Belén.
Carlos V en Francia.
Castelviness y Monteses.   Adapted as *Romeo and Juliet*, 1770.
El castigo del discreto.
El castigo sin venganza. Translated as *Justice Without Revenge*, in *Five Plays*, edited by R.D.F. Pring-Mill, 1961, and 1991; as *Lost in a Mirror*, with *Fuente Ovejuna*, 1989.
La corona de Hungría.
La corona merecida.
El cuerdo loco.
La dama boba.   Translated as *The Lady Nit-Wit*, 1958.
El desdén vengado.
La desdichada Estefania.
Dineros son calidad.
El doctor simple.   Translated as *Doctors All*, 1937.
El duque de Viseo.
Los embustes de Celauro.
La estrella de Sevilla.   Translated as *The Star of Castille*, 1950.

Las ferias de Madrid.
La fianza satisfecha.   Translated as *A Bond Honoured*, 1966.
Fuenteovejuna. Translated as *Fuente Ovejuna*, in *Four Plays*, 1936: several subsequent translations under same title; as *All Citizens Are Soldiers*, 1969.
El galán de la membrilla.
Lo que hay que fiar del mundo.
El Marqués de las Navas.
El mayordomo de la duquesa de Amalfi.
El mejor alcalde, el rey.   Translated as *The King, the Greatest Alcalde*, in *Four Plays*, 1936.
El mejor mozo de España.
Los melindres de Belisa.
La moza de cántaro.
La noche de San Juan.
La nueva victoria de don Gonzalo de Córdoba.
El nuevo mundo descubierto por Cristóbal Colón. Translated as *The Discovery of the New World by Christopher Columbus*, 1950.
Las paces de los reyes y judía de Toledo.
El padre engañado.   Translated as *The Father Outwitted*, 1805.
El palacio confuso.
Pedro Carbonero.
Peribáñez y el Comendador de Ocana. Translated as *Peribanez*, 1938; as *The Commander of Ocaña*, 1958; as *Peribáñez and the Comendador de Ocaña*, in *Eight Spanish Plays of the Golden Age*, translated by Walter Starkie, 1964.
El perro del hortelano.   Translated as *The Gardener's Dog*, in *Four Plays*, 1936; as *The Dog in the Manger*, in *Five Plays*, edited by R.D.F. Pring-Mill, 1961.
Il piadoso aragonés.
El príncipe despeñado.
La prueba de los amigos.
Los Ramírez de Arellano.
El remedio en la desdicha.
Santiago el Verde.
El secretario de sí mismo.
El sembar en buena tierra.
Servir a señor discreto.
La siega.
El sufrimiento premiado.
El villano en su rincón.   Translated as *The King and the Farmer*, 1948.
La victoria de la honra.
Ya anda la de Mazagatos.

Fiction

La Arcadia: Prosas y verso.   1598;
El peregrino en su patria. 1604; as *The Pilgrim; or, The Stranger in His Own Country*, 1738.
Pastores de Belén: Prosas y versos divinos.   1612.
La Dorotea: Accion en prosa.   1632.

Verse

La Dragontea.   1598.
Isidro: Poema castellano.   1599.
La hermosura de Angélica, con otras diversas rimas.   1602.
Rimas.   1604.
La Jerusalém conquistada.   1609.
Arte nuevo de hacer comedias en este tiempo.   1609.
Rimas sacras.   1614.
Triunfo de la fee en los reynos del Japón.   1618.
La Filomena con otras diversas rimas, prosas, y versos.   1621.

Lope de Vega Carpio (engraving).

"La Circe" con otras rimas y prosas.   1624.
Romancero espiritual.   1624.
"Triunfos divinos" con otras rimas sacras.   1625.
Corona trágica: Vida y muerte de la Seteníssima Reyna de Escocia María Estuarda.   1627.
Laurel de Apolo, con otras rimas.   1630.
Amarilis: Égloga.   1633.
Rimas humanas y divinas.   1634.
La Gatomaquia.   1807.
Ultimos amores.   1876.
Poemas, edited by L. Guarner.   1935.
Sonetas, edited by Manuel Arce.   1960.

Memoirs and Letters

Epistolario (4 vols.), edited by Agustín González de Amezúa.   1935–43.

Other

Fiesta de Denia al Rey Cathólico Felipe III.   1599.
Iusta poética y alabanzas iustas.   1620.
Cartas completas (2 vols.) edited by Ángel Rosenblatt.   1948.

Translator, *Soliloquios amorosos de un alma a Dios.*   1626.

*

Bibliographies

I. Simon Díaz and J. de José Prades, *Ensayo de una bibliografía de las obras y artículos sobre la vida y escritos de Lope de Vega Carpio,* Madrid, 1955; supplement: *Lope de Vega: Nuevos estudios,* Madrid, 1961.
Robert B. Brown, *Bibliografía de las comedias historicas de Lope de Vega,* Mexico City, 1958.
Jack H. Parker and Arthur M. Fox, *Lope de Vega Studies 1937–1962,* Toronto, 1964.
Maria Cruz Perez y Perez, *Bibliografía del teatro de Lope de Vega,* Madrid, 1973.

Criticism

Books:
R. Schevill, *The Dramatic Art of Lope de Vega,* Berkeley, California, 1918.
H. Renneret and A. Castro, *Vida de Lope de Vega,* Madrid, 1919.
R. Menéndez, *De Cervantes a Lope de Vega,* Madrid, 1935.
M. Romera Navarro, *La preceptiva literaria de Lope de Vega,* Madrid, 1935.
K. Vossler, *Lope de Vega y su tiempo,* Madrid, 1940.
J. de Entrambasaguas, *Estudios sobre Lope de Vega,* Madrid, 1946.
J. de Entrambasaguas, *Vivir y crear de Lope de Vega,* Madrid, 1947.
S. Griswold Morley and Courtney Bruerton, *The Chronology of the Lope de Vega Comedias,* 1940; addenda in *Hispanic Review,* 15, 1947.
Jerome Aaron Moore, *The "Romancero" in the Chronicle-Legend Plays of Lope de Vega,* 1940.
M. Menéndez Pelayo, *Estudios sobre el teatro de Lope de Vega* (6 vols.), Santander, 1949.

Walter Poesse, *The Internal Line-Structure of Thirty Autograph Plays of Lope de Vega,* Bloomington, Indiana, 1949.
J.F. Montesinos, *Estudios sobre Lope de Vega,* Mexico City, 1951.
D. Marín, *La intriga secundaria en el teatro de Lope de Vega,* Mexico City, 1958.
Ruth Lundelius, *Physical Aspects of the Spanish Stage in the Time of Lope de Vega,* Philadelphia, 1961.
L.C. Pérez and F. Sànchez Escribano, *Afirmaciones de Lope de Vega sobre preceptiva dramática,* Madrid, 1961.
J.F. Gatti (ed.), *El teatro de Lope de Vega: Artículos y estudios,* Buenos Aires, 1962.
Francis C. Hayes, *Lope de Vega,* New York, 1967.
A. Castro, *Vida de Lope de Vega,* Madrid, 1968.
Frances Exum, *The Metamorphosis of Lope de Vega's King Pedro,* Madrid, 1974.
José María del Rey Caballero, *La mujer sevillana en la obra de Lope de Vega,* Seville, 1975.
Gustavo Umpierre, *Songs in the Plays of Lope de Vega: A Study of Their Dramatic Function,* London, 1975.
Juan Manuel Rozas, *Significada y doctrina del Arte nuevo de Lope de Vega,* Madrid, 1976.
Eduardo Forastieri Braschi, *Aproximación estructural al teatro de Lope de Vega,* Madrid, 1976.
Donald R. Larson, *The Honor Plays of Lope de Vega,* Cambridge (Massachusetts) and London, 1977.
Simon Anselmus Vosters, *Lope de Vega y la tradición occidental* (2 vols.), Madrid, 1977.
José María Díez Barque, *Sociedad y teatro en la España de Lope de Vega,* Barcelona, 1978.
Lope de Vega y los irígenes del teatro español: Actas del I Congresso Internacional sobre Lope de Vega, Madrid, 1981.
Francisco J. Díez de Revenga, *Teatro de Lope de Vega y lírica tradicional,* Murcia, 1983.
Alix Zuckerman-Ingbor, *"El bien más alto": A Reconsideration of Lope de Vega's Honor Plays,* Gainesville, Florida, 1984.
Nancy D'Antuono, *Boccaccio's Novelle in the Theater of Lope de Vega,* Madrid, 1984.
Melveena McKendrick, *Theatre in Spain 1490–1700,* Cambridge, 1989.
Margaret R. Hicks, *Honor Conflicts and the Role of the Imagination in Selected Plays by John Fletcher and Lope de Vega,* New York and London, 1990.
Elvezio Canónica de Rochemonteiz, *El poliglotismo en el teatro de Lope de Vega,* Kassel, 1991.

* * *

Lope de Vega is Spain's first great dramatist and the most important playwright of the Spanish Golden Age. His dramatic production was both enormous and highly influential. Contemporary sources credit him with more than 1800 works, of which 500 have survived. More important than the quantity of his production is the fact that Lope's dramatic style set the norm for subsequent dramatists in the Golden Age. As Lope explained in a verse epistle written for a group of literary academics in Madrid (*Arte nuevo de hacer comedias*), this style emphasizes a three-act structure using a variety of poetic meters, in which the dramatic events range widely over space and time and often mix serious plots with comic ones. In these ways, Lope flouts the classical dramatic unities of such concern to Renaissance and neoclassical authors. Lope's dramatic style combines learned poetry with popular verse, and makes use of forms derived from the traditional Spanish ballads as well as of more cultivated poetic styles. Whatever the particular form in question, Lope's plays are consistently marked by rich patterns of imagery, which often follow the basic contours of the plot and reinforce its symbolic structure and meaning.

Lope's dramatic production includes almost every kind of play conceivable during the period: honor plays, cloak-and-dagger plays, pastoral plays, domestic comedies, mythological plays, chivalric dramas, plays based on legendary sources, and history plays based on topics ranging from the Bible to contemporary Spanish events. Of these, Lope himself claimed that honor plays were the most important, because these were most certain to engage the public's preoccupation with reaffirming honor through "cleanliness of blood". By witnessing potentially mortal, but nonetheless vicarious, threats to their honor, and by seeing those threats successfully resolved, Lope's honor plays served as vehicles of collective affirmation for a public increasingly uncertain of its own value and status.

Although Lope's history plays span all periods, his favored period of Spanish history was the end of the Middle Ages. As plays like *Fuenteovejuna* and *El caballero de Olmedo* demonstrate best, Lope was nostalgic for the years of the Reconquest, when a collective purpose could be imputed to historical events, and when it was still possible to imagine heroic actions as having a place in the world. Although Lope saw the loss of this period of collective value as potentially tragic, he also glorified the Spain of his own day.

Thus, many of Lope's plays have the formal structure of comedy or romance, in which the emphasis is on the recuperation of losses suffered earlier in the play. In a romance-like work such as *Fuenteovejuna*, the plot centers upon the conflict between a demonic figure (the Comendador) and the idealized village dwellers. This conflict draws the pastoral world into conflict with present history, which Lope saw as somewhat degraded, and in need of redemption by the actions of a hero. In some instances, this hero is a member of the village; in *Fuenteovejuna* it is the village as a collective body. But in all these cases, virtuous actions lead to a more idealized vision of the relationship between the common people and the Crown.

Lope de Vega's works are of crucial importance to the literary history of Spain. On the one hand, Lope carried forward a number of the forms and structures inherited from the late Middle Ages, including the ballad verse (*verso de romance*), the topics of the chronicles, and chivalric themes. At the same time Lope adapted these forms in such a way as to make them the common inheritance of subsequent playwrights and poets of the Golden Age.

Not unexpectedly, Lope de Vega's sources range widely. In many instances he reworked traditional material passed down through the chronicle and ballad traditions. In other instances, he had recourse to the Italian *novelle* of writers such as Bandello. Studies in recent years have shown that Lope was also influenced by the Valencian dramatists during a period of exile he spent in that city. Yet it must be noted that Lope had only a scanty national dramatic tradition on which to draw. The medieval Spanish dramatic tradition consisted largely of liturgical and celebratory works, which have some bearing on the *autos sacramentales* of the Golden Age (of which Lope wrote several), but have little direct relevance to the secular drama written in the Lopean style.

Lope was, in addition, the author of the extended prose dialogue *La Dorotea*. Although not intended for dramatic representation, this work is highly dramatic and is considered important for a number of reasons. *La Dorotea* is principally autobiographical in nature, and shows the literary transformation of various stages in Lope's personal love affairs. In it, Lope drew heavily on the late-medieval work by Fernando de Rojas, *La Celestina*, but introduced a number of lyrical verse forms that give the work a much more refined and cultured tone. Although all of Lope's plays contain fine examples of lyric poetry, *La Dorotea* includes some of Lope's most famous verse, much of it known independently of the work.

—Anthony J. Cascardi

See also *Volume 1* entries on *Fuenteovejuna*; *Justice Without Revenge*; *Peribáñez and the Comendador of Ocaña*.

VIAN, Boris. Born in Ville-d'Avray, France, 1920. Educated at Lycée Hoche, Versailles, 1933–36; Lycée Condorcet, Paris, 1936–39; École Centrale, Paris, from 1939. Married Michelle Léglise in 1941 (divorced 1952), one son and one daughter; 2) Ursula Kübler in 1954. After learning the trumpet, became member of the Claude Abadie jazz orchestra, 1942; engineer for the Association Française de Normalisation, 1941–46; regular contributor, *Jazz-Hot* magazine, 1946–58; published the first of several thrillers, *J'irai cracher sur vos tombes*, under the pseudonym Vernon Sullivan, 1946: the presence of a copy at a real murder provoked its ban and a fine, 1950; stage adaptation of *J'irai cracher* produced 1984; joined the artistic group Collège de "Pataphysique", 1952, and contributed to its publications, 1953–59; undertook music tour, 1954, and recorded many of his songs, 1955; artist and repertoire director, jazz section, Philips Recording Company, 1955–58, and Barclay Recording Company, 1959; health deteriorated, owing to a weak heart, from 1956. Died in Paris, 23 June 1959.

Works

Collections

Théâtre complet. 1965.
Théâtre (2 vols.). 1965–71.
Théâtre inédit. 1971.
Petits Spectacles (see Stage Works for contents), edited by Noël Arnaud. 1977.
Opéras, edited by Noël Arnaud. 1982.

Stage Works

J'irai cracher sur vos tombes, from his novel (produced Paris, 1948).
L'Équarrissage pour tous (produced Théâtre des Noctambules, Paris, 1950). 1950; translated as *Knackery for All*, in *Plays for a New Theatre: Playbook 2*, 1966; as *The Knacker's ABC*, 1968.
Le Dernier des métiers (produced Café-Théâtre de la Grande Séverine, Paris, 1964). 1950.
Mademoiselle Julie, from a play by Strindberg. 1952.
Le Chevalier de neige, music by Georges Delerue (produced Normandy Festival, Caen, 1953; revised version produced Grand Théâtre de Nancy, 1956). Edited by Noël Arnaud, 1974.
Fiesta, music by Darius Milhaud (produced Opernhaus, Berlin, 1958; produced in France, Opéra de Nice, 1972). 1958.
Erik XIV, from a play by Strindberg. 1958.
Les Bâtisseurs d'Empire (produced Théâtre Recamier, Paris, 1959). 1959; translated as *The Empire Builders*, 1967.

Le Goûter des généraux (produced in German, Staatstheater, Braunschweig, 1964; produced in French, Théâtre de la Gaîté-Montparnasse, Paris, 1965). 1962; translated as *The General's Tea Party*, 1962, and in *Theatre of War*, edited by Robert Baldick, 1967.

Lily Strada, music by Éric Bishoff (produced Café-Théâtre de la Grande Séverine, Paris, 1964). In *Opéras*, 1982.

Tête de Méduse. In *Théâtre 2*, 1971.

Série blême. In *Théâtre 2*, 1971.

Le Chasseur français. In *Théâtre 2*, 1971.

Petits Spectacles: Adam, Éve, et le troisième sexe; À Chacun son serpent; Ça vient, ça vient; Paris varie, ou, Fluctuat nec mergitur; Les Yeux croisés; Cinémassacre; Dernière Heure; Les Voitures; Salvador vend des disques. Edited by Noël Arnaud, 1977.

Le Mercenaire (libretto). In *Opéras*, 1982.

Radio Plays

Une Regrettable Histoire, music by Georges Delerue (published as *Arne Saknussem*, in *Opéras*, 1982).

Fiction

Trouble dans les Andains. 1943.

J'irai cracher sur vos tombes (as Vernon Sullivan). 1946; translated as *I Shall Spit on Your Graves*, 1948.

Les Morts ont tous la même peau (as Vernon Sullivan). 1947.

Vercoquin et le plancton. 1947.

L'Écume des jours. 1947; translated as *Froth on the Daydream*, 1967; as *Mood Indigo*, 1969.

L'Automne à Pékin. 1947.

Et on tuera tous les affreux (as Vernon Sullivan). 1948.

Elles se rendent pas compte (as Vernon Sullivan). 1948.

Les Fourmis (stories). 1949.

L'Herbe rouge. 1950.

L'Arrache-coeur. 1953; translated as *The Heartsnatcher*, 1968.

Surprise-partie chez Léobille (story). 1965.

Le Loup-garou. 1970.

Verse

Barnum's Digest. 1948.

Cantilène en gelée. 1950.

Je voudrais pas crever. 1962.

Recordings

Chansons possibles et impossibles, 1955; *Boris Vian*, 1965; *Boris Vian: Intégrales 1*, 1965; *Pas avec le dos de la Q.I.R*, 1965; *Marie-José Casanova et Jacques Higelin chantent Boris Vian*.

Other

Manuel de Saint-Germain-des-Prés. 1951.

En avant la zizique . . . et par ici les gros sous. 1958.

Textes et chansons. 1966.

Chronique de Jazz-Hot. 1967.

Round About Close to Midnight (jazz writings), translated by Mike Zwerin. 1988.

Translator, *Le Grand Horloger*, by Kenneth Fearing. 1947.

Translator, *La Dame du lac*, by Raymond Chandler. 1948.

Translator, *Le Grand Sommeil*, by Raymond Chandler. 1948.

Translator, *Les Femmes s'en balancent*, by Peter Cheney. 1949.

Translator, *Le Jeune Homme à la trompette*, by Dorothy Baker. 1951.

Translator, *Le Bluffer*, by James M. Cain. 1951.

Translator, *Histoire d'un soldat*, by Omar Bradley. 1952.

Translator, *Le Monde des A*, by A.E. Van Vogt. 1953.

Translator, *L'Homme au bras d'or*, by Nelson Algren. 1956.

Translator, *Les Aventures des A*, by A.E. Van Vogt. 1957.

Translator, *Les Trois Visages d'Ève*, by Corbett H. Thigpen and Hervey M. Checkley. 1958.

Translator, *Le Client du matin*, by Brendan Behan. 1959.

*

Criticism

Books:

Henri Baudin, *Boris Vian: La Poursuite de la vie totale*, Paris, 1966.

Jacques Duchateau, *Boris Vian*, Paris, 1969.

Michel Rybalka, *Boris Vian: Essai d'interprétation et de documentation*, Paris, 1969.

Noël Arnaud (ed.), *Les Vies parallèles de Boris Vian: Textes et documents inédits, études et témoignages*, Paris, 1970.

Henri Baudin, *Boris Vian, Humoriste*, Grenoble, 1973.

Alfred Cismaru, *Boris Vian* (in English), New York, 1974.

Michel Fauré, *Les Vies posthumes de Boris Vian*, Paris, 1975.

Jacques Bens, *Boris Vian* (in English), Paris, 1976.

Noël Arnaud and Henri Baudin (eds.), *Boris Vian: Colloque de Cérisy* (2 vols.), Paris, 1977.

Geneviève Beauvarlet, *Boris Vian (1920–1959): Portrait d'un bricoleur*, Paris, 1982.

Jacques Duchateau, *Boris Vian; ou, Les Facéties du destin*, Paris, 1982.

Gilbert Pestureau, *Dictionnaire des personnages de Vian*, Paris, 1985.

Articles:

Charles J. Stivale, "Of Schmürz and Men: Boris Vian's *Les Bâtisseurs d'empire*", in *Romance Studies*, 7, 1988.

*   *   *

As the title of Noël Arnaud's personal account, *Les Vies parallèles de Boris Vian*, suggests, there is more than one Boris Vian. Jazz musician, critic, record-company executive, engineer, novelist, short-story writer, playwright, translator of American hard-boiled detective fiction, science fiction, and American popular music, general *enfant terrible* of post-World-War-II bohemian life of Paris's left bank and the "Zazou movement", Boris Vian possessed a versatility and spontaneity—the very essence of his creativity—that finally undercut his literary reputation, as his habit of writing under a variety of *noms de plume*: Baron Visi, Vernon Sullivan, Hugo Hachebuisson, and the name he would use for the zombie-like whipping-boy of his play, *Les Bâtisseurs d'Empire* (*The Empire Builders*), Adolph Schmürz, among others.

Despite a number of artistic successes, his public image was one of notoriety rather than of fame. In the midst of France's Indo-Chinese and Algerian crises in the mid-1950's, Vian's anti-militarism came to national prominence with a song he composed in 1953, which was recorded by Marcel Mouloudji, son of an Algerian laborer. "Le Déserteur" was a pacifist appeal which encouraged young Frenchmen to refuse the draft. Banned by the French government, "Le Déserteur" was subsequently revived by the American musical group Peter, Paul and Mary to protest about the Vietnam War, and it became a hit after Vian's death even in France, and subsequently spurred the staging of his plays in France and the publication of his plays in the United States. Vian's greatest literary success was *J'irai cracher sur vos tombes* (*I Shall Spit on Your Graves*). With its explicit and varied sexuality, the novel, which he wrote under the name Vernon Sullivan in two weeks to win a bet, was an immediate best-seller. When a copy of the book, however, opened to the page where the hero kills his mistress, was found beside a murder victim in a small Montparnasse hotel, the conservative French government took punitive action, and in the summer of 1950 Vian was fined heavily for an affront to public morals and his book was banned.

Vian began writing plays as early as 1942 when, in collaboration with his first wife, Michelle, he wrote *Notre terre, ici-bas* (Here on Earth), which was neither staged nor published. Although in his shortened career he wrote seven plays, three operas, and some twenty-eight film scripts, Vian's theatrical reputation rests with four plays, only the first of which was produced in his lifetime. In 1946 Vian wrote "a paramilitary vaudeville in one long act", *L'Équarrissage pour tous* (*The Knacker's ABC*), an attack on the "concept of fighting war by means of war". After sitting with producers for nearly three years, the play-script was finally seen by André Reybaz and staged by his Companie du Myrmidon in two weeks (April 1950) at the Théâtre des Noctambules, where shortly thereafter Eugène Ionesco and Arthur Adamov would have plays staged as well. Vian's satire of the Normandy invasion was one of the earliest examples of what critic Martin Esslin would dub the "theatre of the absurd". Attacked by the official press, the play was nonetheless praised by Jean Cocteau and several members of the College of Pataphysicians, a group of avant-garde writers in the anarchic spirit of Alfred Jarry and the surrealists who were dedicated to the denigration of such French institutions as the Académie Française. Vian joined this irreverent group in 1952, and it published his next two plays, *Les Bâtisseurs d'Empire* (*The Empire Builders*), which was staged six months after Vian's death, and his fourth play, *Le Goûter des généraux* (*The General's Tea Party*). Written along with *L'Équarrissage pour tous*, but rejected by the Théâtre des Noctambules because of its profanity, *Le Dernier des métiers* was finally produced by Maurice Girodias at his notorious St. Séverine nightclub in 1964, where Girodias was also staging excerpts from the works of the Marquis de Sade.

All three of Vian's plays translated into English display his characteristic attacks on the sacred institutions of the bourgeoisie, particularly the clergy and the military. Moreover, Vian's nagging suspicion that communication is finally not possible, because words themselves do not signify specific, concrete, discrete objects, emotions or ideas in a stable physical world allies him with his fellow Pataphysician Eugène Ionesco. In the Dada and surrealist tradition, much of Vian's theatre is designed to shock, but as the immediate post-World-War-II era faded, so did the power of Vian's work. Revived in the late 1960's and early 1970's as part of the anti-militarism associated with the Vietnam War protests, Vian's work had again slipped into obscurity with the passing of the 1970's, and while the American edition of *The Knacker's*

ABC in 1968 announced the publication of three of Vian's novels, only *Mood Indigo* subsequently appeared.

—S.E. Gontarski

See also *Volume 1* entry on *The Empire Builders*.

VICENTE, Gil. Born possibly in the province of Beira or the town of Guimaraes, Portugal, c.1465. Married 1) Branca Bezerra c.1484–86 (died 1514), two sons; 2) Melicia Rodrigues, one son and two daughters. Probably a goldsmith by trade, in the service of D. Leonor (widow of D. João II) and her brother D. Manuel I; wrote and recited first dramatic work, 1502: wrote and acted for the Portuguese Court until 1536; worked on the manufacture of the Belém monstrance, 1503–06; goldsmith to D. Leonor, by 1509; appointed inspector and contractor for gold at three important religious houses, 1509; elected goldsmiths' company representative for the Guild of Twenty-Four, 1512; elected as one of four guildsmen on the city council, Lisbon; appointed *mastre de balança* at the royal mint, 1513: sold office, 1517; defended New Christians of Santarém from violence following the Lisbon earthquake, 1531. Died, probably in Évora, c.1536.

Works

Collections

Copilaçam de Todalas Obras, edited by Luis and Paula Vicente. 1562.
Obras (3 vols.), edited by Mendes dos Remedios. 1907–14.
Four Plays (includes *The Soul's Journey; Exhortation to War; The Carriers; Pastoral Tragicomedy of the Serra da Estrella*), translated by Aubrey F.G. Bell. 1920.
Obras completas (6 vols.), edited by Marques Braga. 1942–44.
Obras completas, edited by Álvaro Júlio de Costa Pimpão. 1956; revised editions, 1962 and 1979.
Obras dramáticas castellanas, edited by Thomas R. Hart. 1962.
Obras completas (3 vols.), edited by Reis Brasil. 1966–70.
Early Spanish Plays (includes *The Sailor's Wife; Cassandra the Sibyl; Three Wise Men; The Widower's Comedy; The Serenade*), edited by Robert O'Brien. 1964.
Farces and Festival Plays, edited by Thomas R. Hart. 1972

Stage Works

The publication date 1562 refers to the posthumous collection *Copilaçam de Todales Obras*. Production dates refer to performances at the Portuguese Court.

Auto da Visitação, also known as *Monólogo do Vaqueiro* [Play of the Visitation, or Monologue of the Cowherd] (produced 1502). 1562.
Auto Pastoril Castelhano [Castilian Nativity Play] (produced 1502). 1562.
Auto dos Reis Magos [Play of the Three Magi] (produced 1503). 1562; translated as *Three Wise Men*, in *Early Spanish Plays*, edited by Robert O'Brien, 1964.
Auto de S. Martinho [St. Martin's Play] (produced 1504). 1562.

Auto da Índia [Play of India] (produced 1509). 1562; translated as *The Sailor's Wife*, in *Early Spanish Plays*, edited by Robert O'Brien, 1964.

Quem Tem Farelos? [Begging for Bran] (produced 1508? or 1511?). 1562; translated as *The Serenade*, in *Early Spanish Plays*, edited by Robert O'Brien, 1964.

Auto da Fé [Play of Faith] (produced 1510). 1562.

Auto das Fadas [Play of Witches and Fairies] (produced 1511). 1562.

Auto dos Quatro Tempos [Play of the Four Seasons] (produced 1511?). 1562.

Auto dos Físicos [The Physicians' Farce] (produced 1512?). 1562.

O Velho da Horta [Farce of the Old Man and the Garden] (produced 1512). 1562.

Exortação da Guerra [Exhortation to War] (produced 1513? or 1514? or 1525?). 1562; translated as *Exhortation to War*, in *Four Plays*, 1920.

Auto da Sibila Cassandra [Sibyl Cassandra's Play] (produced 1513). 1562; translated as *Cassandra the Sibyl*, in *Early Spanish Plays*, edited by Robert O'Brien, 1964.

Comédia do Viúvo [The Widower's Comedy] (produced 1514? or 1521?). 1562; translated as *The Widower's Comedy*, in *Early Spanish Plays*, edited by Robert O'Brien, 1964.

Auto da Fama [Play of Fame] (produced 1515?). 1562.

Auto da Festa [Festival Play] (produced 1515? or 1527?). 1906.

Auto da Barca do Inferno or *Auto das Barcas* [The Ship of Hell, or the Play of the Ships] (produced 1517). 1518; translated as *The Ship of Hell*, 1929.

Auto da Alma [Play of the Soul] (produced 1518). 1562; translated as *The Soul's Journey*, in *Four Plays*, 1920.

Auto da Barca do Purgatório [The Ship of Purgatory] (produced 1518). 1562.

Auto da Barca da Glória [The Ship of Heaven] (produced 1519). 1562.

Comédia de Rubena [Rubena's Comedy] (produced 1521). 1562.

Cortes de Júpiter [Jupiter's Parliament] (produced 1521). 1562.

Auto das Ciganas [Gypsies' Play] (produced 1521? or 1525?). 1562.

Dom Duardos [Don Duardos] (produced 1522? or 1525?). 1562; translated as *Dom Duardos*, 1979.

Farsa de Inês Pereira [Farce of Inês Pereira] (produced 1523). Before 1562?

Auto (em) Pastoril Português [Portuguese Nativity Play] (produced 1523). 1562.

Frágoa de Amor [Forge of Love] (produced 1524). 1562.

Farsa do Juiz da Beira [Farce of the Judge from Beira] (produced 1525? or 1526?). 1562.

Templo de Apolo [Apollo's Temple] (produced 1526). 1562.

Nau de Amores [Ship of Love] (produced 1527). 1562.

Comédia sobre a Divisa da Cidade de Coimbra [Comedy on the Device of the City of Coimbra] (produced 1527). 1562.

Farsa dos Almocreves [Farce of the Muleteers] (produced 1527). 1562; translated as *The Carriers*, in *Four Plays*, 1920.

Serra da Estrela [Estrela Mountains Farce] (produced 1527). 1562; translated as *Pastoral Tragicomedy of the Serra da Estrella*, in *Four Plays*, 1920.

Breve Sumário da História de Deus [A Brief Summary of the Story of God] (produced 1526–28?). 1562.

Diálogo sobre a Ressurreição [Dialogue on the Resurrection] (produced 1526–28?). 1562.

Auto da Feira [Play of the Fair] (produced 1527–28?). 1562.

Triunfo do Inverno [Triumph of Winter] (produced 1529). 1562.

O Clérigo da Beira [The Clergyman from Beira] (produced 1529–30?). 1562.

Auto da Lusitânia [Play of Lusitania] (produced 1532). 1562.

Romagem de Agravados [Pilgrimage of the Discontented] (produced 1533). 1562.

Amadis de Gaula [Amadis of Gaul] (produced 1533?). 1562.

Auto da Cananeia [Play of the Woman of Canaan] (produced 1534). 1562.

Auto de Mofina Mendes [Play of Mofina Mendes] (produced 1534?). 1562.

Floresta de Enganos [Forest of Deceit] (produced 1536). 1562.

Obra da Geração Humana, possibly not by Vicente. With *Padre e Justiça e Misericórdia*, edited by I.S. Révah, 1948.

Padre e Justiça e Misericórdia, possibly not by Vicente. With *Obra da Geração Humana*, edited by I.S. Révah, 1948.

*

Bibliographies

Luisa Maria de Castro e Azevedo, *Bibliografia Vicentina*, Lisbon, 1942.

Constantine C. Stathatos, *A Gil Vicente Bibliography (1940–1975)*, London, 1980; supplement, 1982.

Criticism

Books:

T. Braga, *Gil Vicente e as Origens do Theatro nacional*, Oporto, 1898.

T. Braga, *Vida de Gil Vicente e sua Eschola*, Oporto, 1898.

Aubrey F.G. Bell, *Gil Vicente*, Oxford, 1921.

Oscar de Pratt, *Gil Vicente: Notas e Comentários*, Lisbon, 1931.

A. Broamcamp Freire, *Vida e obras de Gil Vicente*, Oporto, 1921; revised edition, 1944.

Joaquim de Carvalho, *Os Sermoes de Gil Vicente e a Arte de Pregar*, Lisbon, 1948.

Carolina Michaëlis de Vasconcelos, *Notas Vicentinas* (second edition), 1959.

P. Teyssier, *La Langue de Gil Vicente*, Paris, 1959.

Laurence Keates, *The Court Theatre of Gil Vicente*, Lisbon, 1962.

A.S. Saraiva, *Gil Vicente e o Fim do Teatro Medieval* (second edition), 1965; third edition, 1981.

Armindo Martins Janeiro, *O Teatro de Gil Vicente e o Teatro Clássico Japonês*, Lisbon, 1967.

Jack Horace Parker, *Gil Vicente*, New York, 1967.

Neil Miller, *O Elemento Pastoril no Teatro de Gil Vicente*, Oporto, 1970.

Sebastiao Pestana, *Estudos Gil-Vicentinos*, Sá da Bandeira, 1972.

José Hermano Saraiva, *Testamunho social e condenaçao de Gil Vicente*, Lisbon, 1975.

Hope Hamilton-Faria, *The Farces of Gil Vicente: A Study in the Stylistics of Satire*, Madrid, 1976.

Celso Lafar, *Gil Vicente e Camões: Dois Estudos sobre a Cultura Portuguesa do Século XVI*, Sao Paolo, 1978.

Thomas R. Hart, *Gil Vicente: Cassandra and Don Duardos*, London, 1981.

René Pedro Garay, *Gil Vicente and the Developement of the Comedia*, Chapel Hill, North Carolina, 1988.

Dalila L. Pereira da Costa, *Gil Vicente e sua época*, Lisbon, 1989.

* * *

Gil Vicente, Portugal's first and most important dramatist, and a lyric poet of distinction, began his literary career with a dramatic monologue in Spanish, welcoming the newborn heir to the throne. Over 40 more plays followed, as well as such compositions as sermons, comic monologues, letters, and ballads. 17 of the plays are wholly in Portuguese, 11 in Spanish, and the rest use both languages, or even a dialect, according to the nationality of the characters.

His theatre falls into three broad categories: religious moralities and devotional plays; farces; romantic, chivalric, and allegorical comedies and fantasies. Attempts to subdivide or classify the plays more rigidly founder on the variety of their content, structure, and purpose, and on the overlapping of genres. They were written as entertainments to mark royal anniversaries, births, betrothals, feast days, entries into cities and other celebrations. Not only was Gil Vicente the author but also stage manager, director and, at times, actor. Invariably they were devised, written, and staged at great speed, which partly explains the frequent repetition of format and situation. The uncertain chronology of many of the plays makes it unwise to draw conclusions about a linear evolution in Gil Vicente's work. There is, however, a preponderance of religious plays during the patronage of D. Leonor, and of secular plays under that of D. Manuel I and D. João III.

As founder of the Portuguese theatre, Gil Vicente had little in the way of dramatic tradition upon which to build—the eclogues of Encina and Lucas Fernández; liturgical drama, religious processions and religious parodies; and the court *momos* (mummeries), rich and splendid allegorical spectacles marking a royal entry or an embassy.

After the earliest pastoral plays depicting simple, good-hearted shepherds, Gil Vicente's distinctive intermingling of allegory, symbolism, and social realism soon appears: in the *Auto da Fé*, two shepherds are lectured on the Incarnation by the allegorical personage Faith; in the *Auto da Sibila Cassandra* (*Cassandra the Sibyl*), a presumptuous young shepherdess allows herself to think she is the virgin who will bear the Messiah, until an assembled company of pagan sibyls and Old Testament prophets disabuse her of this notion. Allegory features strongly in the *Auto dos Quatro Tempos*, another Nativity play, but one in which the unusual combination of angels, the four seasons, and Jupiter offer Jesus the gifts of Nature—stars, mountains, forests—and King David pays him homage.

The culmination of the religious drama is reached with the three *Barca* plays and the *Auto da Alma* (*The Soul's Journey*). The former present a cross-section of society for judgement at the moment of death. In the *Barca do Inferno* (*The Ship of Hell*) the nobleman, usurer, cobbler, friar, procuress, Jew, magistrate, attorney, and hanged man each learn to their surprise and dismay that they are bound for Hell. Only the simpleton and the knights who died overseas defending Christianity are saved. The rural characters in the *Barca do Purgatório* fare a little better: farmer, vegetable-seller, shepherd, and shepherdess are sent to Purgatory, the card-sharper to Hell; an innocent child alone goes straight to Heaven. Not confirmed sinners, as in the first play, they represent the common ruck of humanity, sometimes honest, sometimes not. The most weighty of the three plays, *Barca da Glória*, deals with eight of the highest mortals, from a count to a

pope. Only the intervention of Christ himself can save such sinners from damnation. The masterpiece of liturgical allegory, the *Auto da Alma*, charts the uncertain progress of Soul along the way to the inn, Mother Church, alternately urged onwards by the Angel and falling prey to the blandishments of the Devil. She finally succeeds in repulsing the latter long enough to reach the inn. The second part of the play concerns the supper (Holy Communion) partaken of there by Soul who, now in a state of contrition, is purified of earthly trappings and prepared by the Church Fathers to receive the dishes in the form of the Instruments of the Passion. This stately and serene morality juxtaposes humour and understanding of human nature with theological erudition and Church ritual.

Other religious plays show a Gil Vicente fiercely critical of his age: the *Auto da Feira* is a scathing satire, sparing neither the gullible believers in astrology, nor the overweening clergy, nor the abuses of a sacked Rome, torn apart by territorial and religious strife. In the *Auto de Mofina Mendes*, a Nativity play of devotion to the Virgin Mary, the foolish and flighty Mofina (poles apart from the humble Virgin), her shepherd colleagues (too sleepy to stir themselves to visit the manger), the indifferent Bethlehem townsfolk (turning a blind eye and a deaf ear to Joseph's request to give a light for the candle to illumine the birth of Christ), and the venal clergy are all censured.

Gil Vicente was the first writer in the Iberian Peninsula to construct a well-developed farce of intrigue. The best examples have swift, economical action and strong characterization. The errant wife of the sailor who goes East, in the *Auto da Índia*, juggles her Spanish and Portuguese lovers with skill until her husband returns, disillusioned with war and hardship, and no wealthier than when he set off. In *O Velho da Horta* the folly of the old man, who persists in wooing a young girl even though she gives him the cold shoulder, ends in his destitution, the victim of a rapacious go-between. The eponymous heroine of *Inês Pereira*, indolent and opinionated, makes a disastrous choice of husband. When she is unexpectedly widowed, she accepts the proposal of the simple but rich farmer she had turned down before, and sets about cuckolding him right under his nose: one of Gil Vicente's most successful plays, it shows acute perception of the tension between courtly love, where the man serves the woman, and marriage, where the woman is obedient to the man. In *Quem Tem Farelos?* (*The Serenade*)the butt of humour is the threadbare minor nobility, angling to marry into money however low on the social scale. Also mocked here are the worn-out language and debased conceits of courtly love that were the hallmark of many poets of the *Cancioneiro Geral*.

Gil Vicente is thought to have left the service of the devout D. Leonor soon after 1518, well before her death, in retirement from court, in 1525. Employment by the fun-loving D. Manuel may, however, have had less to do with his composition of numerous secular plays in which the themes of regeneration, rebirth, and the power of love are dominant, than with his remarriage and the birth of three more children when he was well into middle age. His first romantic comedy, the *Comédia do Viúvo*, predates this change, probably being written about the time of his own bereavement in 1514. A widower grieving for his sweet, obedient wife is offered first the consolation of religion and then a diatribe against women. The mood changes in the next part, in which a prince, in love with the widower's two daughters, disguises himself as a servant in their house. When he rather bumptiously reveals his true identity the romantic tone is let down because he cannot make up his mind which sister he prefers. (The stage directions state that at this point the sisters go to the Prince, D. João—present at the first performance—and ask him to decide which one of them is to be married.) Although the *Comédia de Rubena* tells an ostensibly romantic tale, of the offspring of a liaison between an abbot's daughter and a cleric, brought up as a shepherdess, coming into a fortune and winning the heart of a prince (again in disguise), Gil Vicente's treatment of the scenes of the mother's chaotic labour, the intervention of the midwife, witch and devils, the attempts on the girl's virtue, and of the suitors and their mannerisms verges on farce.

The power of love lies at the heart of *Dom Duardos*, an adaptation of an episode in the Spanish romance of chivalry *Primaleón*. Here, the prince, a knight errant, takes the disguise of a gardener in order to establish whether Princess Flérida loves him for himself or for his rank. Recognizing that love conquers all, Flérida gives herself into the hand of D. Duardos, and together they sail for England. This beautiful and poetic play attributes psychological subtlety, delicacy, and common sense to the lovers, who are offset by a burlesque version of chivalry in the shape of the wild man Camilote and his ugly lady, Maimonda. Gil Vicente's other adaptation of a chivalric episode, *Amadis de Gaula*, does not take the ideal at face value. At every turn he betrays an ironic attitude to the conventions of courtly love. In this play, as in so much of his writing, preciosity of sentiment is undermined by blunt, colloquial comments.

With the allegorical fantasies, Gil Vicente allowed free rein to his imagination. As with his religious drama, these elaborate plays betray their processional ancestry. A series of scenes, often with only tenuous connections, richly staged and interpersed with singing and dancing, develops the allegory. In the delightful *Cortes de Júpiter*, performed at the departure of the young Princess D. Beatriz for Nice to join her new husband, the Duke of Savoy, Jupiter, acting on God's orders, calls together the elements and planets to arrange fair weather for the voyage. All the inhabitants of Lisbon are to be changed into fish to escort the fleet out of harbour, while members of the royal family will ride on litters or triumphal cars borne by sea creatures. In the *Frágoa de Amor*, written to celebrate the betrothal of D. João III, the allegory of a castle (Catarina of Castile) taken by a great king, thanks to Cupid acting as his ambassador at Charles V's court, gives way to a scene in which Venus looks for her lost son. He is found in charge of the Forge of Love, into which go, in turn, three discontents, a negro who wants to be white, an old bent woman (Justice) who wants to be straightened and rejuvenated, and a friar who wants to become a layman. These and other fantasies confound expectations, moving from serious allegory to burlesque and farce, from romance to satire. For all their length and diffuseness, however, they hold the attention and offer a rich documentary record of Portuguese life, manners, folk customs, the speech of all classes and conditions, and abundant poetry.

Gil Vicente's work provides a kaleidoscopic view of his age and country. His observation was sharp, his humour biting when necessary, and compassionate when required. His imagination and a gift for language enabled him to create a theatre full of memorable types and characters, all of whom express themselves in fresh and buoyant verse. Only one play is known to have been published during his lifetime. He died while still in the process of collecting his works together for publication. His son, Luís, must bear the blame for the careless and presumptuous editing of the *Copilaçam* of 1562. The Index of 1551 had banned seven plays, all of which had circulated separately, though posthumously. Three were totally suppressed so that no copy survives, but the other four appear in the *Copilaçam*. A rather ambiguous ruling in the 1561 Index could be taken as sanctioning their publication in the collected works (a luxury edition) but maintaining the prohibition on the easily accessible pamphlet editions. Be that as it may, 20 years later the Inquisition subjected the works to severe censorship, the result being the mutilated *Copilaçam* of 1586.

Gil Vicente's standing as a major European dramatist has not been fully appreciated beyond the circles of Portuguese and Spanish scholarship. While there is a wealth of critical material available to the scholar and student of Hispanic literature, there is little for the general reader, and only a small fraction of the plays have been translated into English. Regrettably, they remain unknown to theatre-goers outside the Portuguese- and Spanish-speaking world.

—Juliet Perkins

VIGNY, Alfred (Victor) de. Born in Loches, France, 27 March 1797. Educated at Institution Hix, 1807–11; Lycée Bonaparte (now Lycée Condorcet), Paris, 1811–14. Married Lydia Bunbury in 1825 (died 1862). Sub-lieutenant, 1st Regiment, Gendarmes du Roi, 1814–15; joined 5th Regiment, Garde Royale, 1816: stationed at Versailles, 1816, Vincennes, 1817–19, Courbevoie, 1820, Orthez, 1823; promoted to captain, 55th Regiment of the Line, 1823; left army, 1827, and settled in Paris; first-produced play, *Le More de Venise* (from Shakespeare's *Othello*), staged 1829; elected commander of a National Guard battalion, 1830; contracted cholera, 1832; involved in the fall from power of Louis-Philippe, 1848: subsequently failed in his political ambitions; retired to his manor, Maine-Giraud, near Angoulême, 1853. Elected to Académie Française, 1845: director, October–December 1849. Chevalier, Légion d'Honneur, 1833. Died in Paris, 17 September 1863.

Works

Collections

Oeuvres complètes (7 vols.).   1837–39.
Oeuvres complètes (5 vols).   1863–64.
Oeuvres complètes, edited by F. Baldensperger (7 vols.). 1914–35.
Oeuvres complètes, edited by F. Baldensperger (2 vols.). 1948.

Stage Works

Le More de Venise, from *Othello* by Shakespeare (produced Comédie-Française, Paris, 1829).   With *Le Marchand de Venise*, 1839.
La Maréchale d'Ancre (produced Théâtre de l'Odéon, Paris, 1831).
Quitte pour la peur (produced Théâtre de l'Opéra, Paris, 1833).
Chatterton (produced Comédie-Française, Paris, 1835).   1835; translated as *Chatterton*, 1847.
Le Marchand de Venise, from *The Merchant of Venice* by Shakespeare.   With *Le More de Venise*, 1839; revised version, as *Shylock* (produced 1905), in *Oeuvres complètes*, 1914–35.

Fiction

Cinq-Mars. 1825; translated as *Cinq-Mars*, 1847; as *The Conspirators*, 1877; as *The Spider and the Fly*, 1925.

Stello; ou, Les Diables bleus.   1832; translated as *Stello; or, A Session with Doctor Noir*, 1963.
Servitude et grandeur militaires (short stories).   1835; translated as *Military Servitude and Grandeur*, 1919; as *The Military Necessity*, 1953; as *The Military Condition*, 1964.
Daphné.   1912.

Verse

Poèmes.   1822.
Eloa; ou, La Soeur des anges.   1824.
Poèmes antiques et modernes.   1826; augmented edition, 1829; revised edition, 1837.
Les Destinées, edited by Louis Ratisbonne.   1864.

Memoirs and Letters

Journal d'un poète, edited by Louis Ratisbonne.   1867.
Correspondance 1816–1863, edited by Emma Sakellaridès. 1905.
Correspondance (2 vols.), edited by Léon Séché.   1913.
Lettres inédites d'Alfred de Vigny au Marquis et à la Marquise de La Grange (1827–1861), edited by Albert de Luppé. 1914.
Mémoires inédites, fragments, et projets, edited by Jean Sangnier.   1958.

*

Criticism

Books:
E. Sakellaridès, *Alfred de Vigny: Auteur dramatique*, Paris, 1902.
E. Dupuy, *Alfred de Vigny: Ses amitiés et son rôle littéraire* (2 vols.), Paris, 1910–12.
E. Dupuy, *Alfred de Vigny: La Vie et l'oevure*, Paris, 1915.
P. Flottes, *Alfred de Vigny*. Paris, 1925.
E. Lauvrière, *Alfred de Vigny: Sa Vie et son oeuvre*, Paris, 1945.
P.G. Castex, *Vigny: L'Homme et l'oeuvre*, Paris, 1952.
F. Germain, *L'Imagination d'Alfred de Vigny*, Paris, 1961.
James Doolittle, *Alfred de Vigny*, 1967.
Nicole Casanova, *Alfred de Vigny: Sous le masque de fer*, Paris, 1990.

* * *

An aristocrat from a family of émigrés, Alfred de Vigny took up a career in the army, and it was during his leaves in Paris that he began to frequent the Cénacles, or groups of Romantic writers, formed around Charles Nodier at the Arsenal Library, and later around Victor Hugo. Resigning his commission at 30, he settled in Paris with his invalid English wife, and devoted himself to literary pursuits. His *Poèmes antiques et modernes* were followed by the historical novel *Cinq-Mars*; and his activity in connection with the theatre began with translations from Shakespeare: *Shylock* (completed 1828), *Roméo et Juliette* (accepted by the Comédie-Française in 1828, but not performed), and *Le More de Venise* (*Othello*, performed at the Comédie-Française in 1829). If Dumas *père* brought to the métier of dramatist the natural gifts of a man of the theatre, and Hugo those of a poet, Vigny's endowments were by contrast those of a scho-

lar. The time was ripe for an attempt to bring the real Shakespeare to audiences at the Comédie-Française, who had hitherto been offered merely the neoclassical adaptations of Ducis; but although Vigny's version of *Othello* was conscientious enough to retain the handkerchief and the pillow (at which previous French adaptors had balked), it was too stiff and lifeless to be successful in the theatre.

Vigny's over-literary, scholarly approach to writing for the theatre is also to be seen in his historical play of 1831, *La Maréchale d'Ancre*, set in the Regency following the death of Henri IV when the Queen Mother was dominated by Italian favourites and the country was at the mercy of warring factions. Vigny claimed that his intention was to present "a page of history on stage": but beyond this scrupulous regard for his sources, he was also concerned to offer a philosophical interpretation of the historical process, by showing the workings of justice and retribution. This play stands out from the other historical dramas of the Romantic period in France by presenting a responsible version of an important series of historical events which neither subordinates these events to the personal tragedy of a single protagonist nor uses them as backcloth to an essentially domestic drama. The historical happenings are neither distorted nor trivialised, but the resultant ambiguity of character and complexity of motive would, perhaps, better have suited a historical novel than the concentrated form of a three-hour play; while, in addition to the lack of a clear-cut sympathetic character with whom the audience might identify, Vigny's dialogue must be judged lacking in theatrical impact.

La Maréchale d'Ancre was moderately successful, with a run of 30 performances. It had been written in prose for the Théâtre de la Porte-Saint-Martin, where Marie Dorval, Vigny's mistress, was currently engaged, though unforeseen circumstances dictated a change of plan, and the play was put on at the Odéon. However, Vigny's next full-length play, *Chatterton*, was written quite openly not only as a vehicle for Dorval (who played Kitty Bell), but also as a means of securing her entry into the Comédie-Française company. Completed in June 1834, it was promptly rejected by that theatre's reading committee: the tendentious subject (a plea for public support for young writers and artists of genius, based on the suicide of the young English poet) may have played a part in this decision, but the rejection was largely inspired by enmity towards the outsider, Dorval, on the part of a coterie led by Mlle Mars. The majority of the actors were in fact hostile, and the play was accepted only after intervention by the royal family. Performance was scheduled for February 1835, and rehearsals began in an atmosphere of recrimination and resentment. As the first night approached, Vigny was most apprehensive; but the play was a triumphant success. As in his historical drama, Vigny here too insisted on the philosophical role of the playwright: the individual example of the poet Chatterton was less important to him than the more abstract issue of the place of the genius in a hostile, materialist society. But whether or not this didactic message was to the taste of an intellectual elite, it is certain that the play owed its success with the public at large to the pathos of the domestic drama that Vigny had chosen as the vehicle for his philosphical message—a pathos convincingly expressed by an actress trained outside the formal conventions of the Comédie-Française. This was to remain one of Dorval's most powerful roles, while *Chatterton*, Vigny's outstanding contribution to the theatre of his day, deserves to be ranked among the three or four undoubted masterpieces created by dramatists of the French Romantic school.

Vigny's liaison with Marie Dorval came to an end in 1835, and at the same time he ceased to write for the theatre. His life was henceforth dominated by devoted care for his ailing wife, and when she died in 1862 he outlived her by only a few months. He was never again actively involved in the mainstream literary life of the capital, and spent an increasing amount of time in retirement at a family property he had inherited near Angoulême (it was this retreat that Sainte-Beuve referred to as Vigny's "ivory tower"). Here, he continued to be absorbed in intellectual and literary pursuits, and though his output was slight, some of his most notable poetry was written during this period. *Les Destinées*, a collection of philosophical poems published posthumously, expressed, by the use of memorable concrete images, the poet's pessimistic but stoical view of the world as a place of suffering and abnegation. In his volume of three tales set in the period of the Napoleonic Wars, *Servitude et grandeur militaires* (*Military Service and Grandeur*) (1835), Vigny had presented the soldier's calling in a similar light.

—William D. Howarth

See also *Volume 1* entry on *Chatterton*.

VILLERS, George, Duke of Buckingham. See *Volume 1* entry on *The Rehearsal*.

———

VINAVER, Michel. Born Michel Grinberg in Paris, 1927. Educated at schools in Paris, Cusset, Annecy, and New York, 1938–43; studied English and American Literature at Wesleyan University, Middletown, Connecticut, from 1945, BA in English. Volunteer, French army, 1944–45; first novel published 1950; administrator, rising to executive, Gillette International, 1953–80; first play, *Les Coréens*, produced 1956; has held post at the Institut d'Études Théâtrales, University of Paris III, since 1983. Recipient: Fénéon Prize, 1952; Ibsen Prize, 1986; Kleist Prize, 1986.

Works

Collections

Théâtre de chambre (includes *Dissident, il va sans dire; Nina, c'est autre chose*).   1978.
Théâtre complet (2 vols.).   1986:
  1. *Les Coréens; Les Huissiers; La Fête du cordonnier;*

Scene from the Paris Théâtre Alliance-Française's 1957 production of *Les Coréens* by **Michel Vinaver**, designed by Jean-Marie Serreau.

Iphigénie Hôtel; Par-dessus bord; La Demande d'emploi.
2. *Dissident, il va sans dire; Nina, c'est autre chose; Les Travaux et les jours; À la Renverse; Le Suicidé; L'Ordinaire; Les Estivants; Les Voisins; Portrait d'une femme.*

Stage Works

Les Coréens (produced as *Aujourd'hui, ou, Les Coréens,* Théâtre de la Comédie, Lyons, 1956; produced as *Les Coréens,* Théâtre Alliance-Française, Paris, 1957).   1956.
Les Huissiers. In *Théâtre populaire,* March 1958; revised version (produced Théâtre Les Ateliers, Lyons, 1980), in *Le Livre des huissiers,* 1981.
La Fête du cordonnier, from a play by Thomas Dekker (produced Théâtre National du Palais de Chaillot, Paris, 1959).
Iphigénie Hôtel, part an adaptation of a novel by Henry Green (produced Théâtre du Centre Georges-Pompidou, Paris, 1977).   1963.
Par-dessus bord (produced by Théâtre National Populaire, Villeurbanne, 1973).   1972.
La Demande d'emploi (produced Théâtre 347, Avignon Festival, 1972).   1973.
Dissident, il va sans dire (produced Théâtre de l'Est Parisien, Paris, 1978). In *Théâtre de chambre,* 1976; translated as *Dissident, it Goes Without Saying,* in *Drama Contemporary: France,* edited by Philippa Wehle, 1986.
Nina, c'est autre chose (produced Théâtre de l'Est Parisien, Paris, 1978). In *Théâtre de chambre,* 1976; translated as *Nina, it's Different,* in *Drama Contemporary: France,* edited by Philippa Wehle, 1986.
Les Travaux et les jours (produced Théâtre du Centre Georges-Pompidou, Paris, 1980).   1979.
À la Renverse (produced Théâtre National de Chaillot, Paris, 1980).   1980.
L'Ordinaire (produced Théâtre National de Chaillot, Paris, 1983).   1982.
Les Estivants, from a play by Gorky (produced Théâtre National de Chaillot, Paris, 1983). In *Théâtre complet 2,* 1986.
Le Suicidé, from a play by Nikolai Erdman (produced Théâtre National de l'Odéon, Paris, 1984). In *Théâtre complet 2,* 1986.
Les Voisins (produced Jardin d'Hiver, Théâtre Ouvert, Paris, 1986). In *Théâtre complet 2,* 1986; translated as *The Neighbors,* in *The Paris Stage: Recent Plays,* 1988.
Portrait d'une femme (read publicly, Lyons, 1985; produced-Paris, 1988). In *Théâtre complet 2,* 1986; translated as *Portrait of a Woman,* in *New French Plays,* edited by David Bradby and Claude Schumacher, 1989.
Le Compte rendu d'Avignon.   1987.
Le Dernier Sursaut.   1990.
L'Emission de télévision (produced Théâtre National de l'Odéon, Paris, 1990).   1990.

Fiction

Lataume; ou, La Vie quotidienne.   1950.
L'Objecteur.   1951.
Les Histoires de Rosalie.   1980.

Other

Écrits sur le théâtre, edited by Michelle Henry.   1982.

Translator, *Amour,* by Henry Green.   1954.

Translator, *Jules César,* by Shakespeare.   1990.

*

Criticism

Books:
David Bradby, *Modern French Drama 1940–1980,* Cambridge, 1984; revised and augmented edition, as *Modern French Drama 1940–1990,* 1991.
David Bradby, "'Entre Le Mythique et la question': Myth in the Theatre of Michel Vinaver", in *Myth and Its Making in the French Theatre,* Cambridge, 1988.
Anne Ubersfeld, *Vinaver dramaturge,* Paris, 1989.
David Bradby, *The Theater of Michel Vinaver,* Ann Arbor, Michigan, 1992.
Kevin Elstob, *The Plays of Michael Vinaver,* New York, 1992.

Articles:
Judith D. Suther, "The Medium is Not the Message: Myth in Vinaver's *Iphigénie Hôtel*", in *French Review,* 45, 1972.
Rosette C. Lamont. "'Des Petits Ébranlements capillaires . . .': The Art of Michel Vinaver", in *Modern Drama,* 31, 1988.
David Bradby, "A Theatre of the Everyday: The Plays of Michel Vinaver", in *New Theatre Quarterly,* 27, 1991.

* * *

Michel Vinaver is the leading playwright associated with the Théâtre du Quotidien (Theatre of the Everyday). This movement, which can be defined as "the new realism", includes writers in German such as Kroetz, Fassbinder, and Achternbush, as well as other French writers, such as Jean-Paul Wenzel, Michel Deutsch, and Georges Michel. The term "quoticien", which was born in the 1970's, may echo the French word for a newspaper, *un quotidien.* The plays of the above writers do not present heroic lives; they deal with ordinary people and their problems, people caught in the fabric of their social and professional situations. It is not political theatre, unless we mean by political a way of relating to the real, above all an awareness that one is not an isolated individual but a social creature.

Vinaver's theatre is characterized by the variety of thematic material: war, work, ambition, the open and secret struggles of business interests, the cannibalistic ingestion of fine independent enterprises by faceless international conglomerates, the actual cannibalism practiced by a group of business tycoons stranded in the Andes as a result of a plane crash, the tragedy of becoming a non-person through forced early retirement, the invasion of privacy by the media.

One of the major influences on the French drama of the 1950's proved to be that of Bertolt Brecht, following the 1954 appearance of the Berliner Ensemble in Paris at the yearly International Theatre Festival. Michel Vinaver was a budding writer, the author of two novels (*Lataume; ou, La Vie quotidienne* and *L'Objecteur*) when he discovered Brecht's theatre. Although he would later distance himself from Brecht, he longed to create a theatre that would act upon the world.

The above point of view is evident from the start of Vinaver's career as a dramatist in 1956. Written in 1955, and staged by Roger Planchon the following year at his tiny Théâtre de la Comédie in Lyons, *Les Coréens,* first entitled *Aujourd'hui,* was received as a fusion of Brechtian dramaturgy with the aesthetic of the avant-garde rooted in Jarry's

Ubu Roi, a turn-of-the-century metaphysico-political stage cartoon admired by Vinaver.

Les Coréens is an anti-war play which does not propagandize. It shows how Korean villagers and white soldiers belonging to a United Nations expeditionary force share a common human fear of maiming and death. One of six French soldiers, Captain Belair (originally played by Planchon), disappears in the depths of the forest, where he encounters a girl in search of her brother. The Frenchman accepts the child's invitation to follow her to her village. There he will find the reality which eluded him all this time, and is restored to wholeness.

Written in the autumn of 1957, then published a year later, Vinaver's second play, *Les Huissiers*, is a political fable (about the Algerian crisis) patterned on Sophocles' *Oedipus at Colonus*. Here, the chorus of Theban elders has become one of ubiquitous civil servants. Dramatic dialogue and chorus passages alternate, as in the ancient Greek model.

The next play, *Iphigénie Hôtel*, is also connected to contemporary political events (the 1958 *putsch* in Algeria, and De Gaulle's coming to power), the overlay for an ancient Greek subtext. The action takes place in a small hotel near the ruins of Mycenae. The former owner, Monsieur Oreste (Orestes) is dying in his room, off-stage. His demise marks the end of an era, when the Greek people owned their culture, and their land. The one who will take over is the chief valet, a Frenchman. Vinaver's ironic representation of an ancillary jockeying for power mocks the political struggle going on in French Algeria, and parodies the deadly struggle of the Atreidae.

One of the aspects of the "real" that Vinaver knows best is the machinery of the business world. This is what he exposes in his seven-hour Aristophanic farce, *Par-dessus bord*. The business portrayed is the manufacturing of toilet paper. Vinaver admits to "an interest in defecation." He states that our culture is saturated by references to sexuality, but that this other function remains secret. It is also the common denominator of the everyday. The form of the play is wide open, polyphonic. The banality of the subject serves to draw attention to the musicality of the highly textured language. Vinaver's understanding of the way relations of power are inscribed in language constitutes his strength as one of the leading political playwrights of our time.

Following *Par-dessus bord*, we find a series of chamber plays—*Dissident, il va sans dire* (*Dissident, it Goes Without Saying*), *Nina, c'est autre chose* (*Nina, it's different*) and *La demande d'emploi*. The last two chamber pieces are examples of incisive social comment encapsulated in minimalist dramaticules. *Dissident* depicts a loving mother-and-son couple. The latter character, however, is a kind of drop-out. The mother fails to see that he has become a junkie, associating with riff-raff. At the end, the police arrive to arrest him. *Nina*, the companion piece, has three characters: two brothers, a factory worker and a hairdresser who live together in mourning for their mother who has just died, and the 24-year-old Nina, whom the younger brother has brought home to live with them. She is willing to share her favors between the two, at least until she leaves with a third man, a young Czech dissident painter, fresh from a slave-labor camp. Nina's departure does not terminate the friendship established under the brothers' roof, for Nina has healed their spirits, terminating their obsessive mourning.

The preceding *La Demande d'emploi* has only four characters: Fage, an unemployed executive, Wallace, a personnel interviewer for a tourist agency, Fage's wife, and his young daughter. The four *dramatis personae* never leave the stage, although they do not occupy the same space. All of them are involved in Fage's life, but the center of the action is the "interrogation" by the interviewer. It is a cat-and-mouse game, insidious and secretly violent. We witness Fage's dismemberment, carried out in various ways by the three other characters. *La Demande d'emploi* is a chamber play, yet it is one without a chamber, without walls, brilliantly orchestrated as an atonal composition.

Following the chamber theater, Vinaver resumed his exploration of the complex world of big business—*Les Travaux et les jours*, *À La Renverse*, *L'Ordinaire*, and *L'Emission de télévision*. Several recent plays are psychological dramas—*Portrait d'une femme* (*Portrait of a Woman*) and *Les Voisins* (*The Neighbors*).

L'Ordinaire stands out as a powerful image of man's insatiable appetites. It shows how "ordinary" people, given dire circumstances, can turn to cannibalism to survive. In French, the word *ordinaire* is also a culinary term, meaning fare. Based on the newspaper story about an Uruguayan football team, it also has a mythical dimension connecting it to the *omophagia* of Euripides' *Bacchae*. *L'Ordinaire* is the supreme crystallization of Vinaver's "theatre of energy" (Anne Ubersfeld's term).

A careful examination of his *Théâtre complet* reveals that the common denominator of his work is the process of ingestion and digestion. Societies are composed of killers and their victims. This sombre view is softened by an all-pervasive sense of humor and a superior kind of understanding and acceptance. Vinaver's "Theatre of the Everyday" is essentially a form of witnessing.

—Rosette C. Lamont

VISHNEVSKY, Vsevolod Vitalyevich. Born in St. Petersburg, Russia, 8 December (21 December, New Style) 1900. Educated at Gymnasium, St. Petersburg, to 1914. Joined the Russian army, 1914, and saw active service during World War I; joined Bolshevik group, 1917; took part in Petrograd (formerly St. Petersburg) insurrection; cavalryman and sailor, serving with the Red forces, during the Civil War; editor, journal *Krasnoflotets*; organised large-scale outdoor production in Novorossiysk of a play about the Kronstadt rebellion, 1921; joined Communist Party, 1937; war correspondent in Leningrad (as Petrograd now renamed), 1941–42; settled in Moscow after 1944, and was appointed editor of the journal *Znamya*; assistant general secretary, Writers' Union of the USSR, from 1946. Recipient: Stalin Prize, 1949. Died in Moscow, 28 February 1951.

Works (selection)

Collections

Sobranie sochineny [Collected Works]. 1954–61.
Izbrannoe (includes *Pervaya konnaya*; *Optimistecheskaya tragediya*; *U sten Leningrada*; *My iz Kronstadta*; *My, russky narod*). 1966.

Stage Works (selected)

Pervaya konnaya [The First Cavalry Army] (produced Central Red Army Theatre, Moscow, 1929).

Posledny resistelny [The Last Decisive Battle] (produced Meyerhold Theatre, Moscow, 1931).
Na zapade boy [Fight in the West] (produced Theatre of the Revolution, Moscow, 1931–32).   1933.
Optimistecheskaya tragediya (produced Kamerny Theatre, Moscow, 1934).   In *Novy mir*, 2, 1933; translated as *An Optimistic Tragedy*, in *Four Soviet Plays*, 1937.
Raskinulos more shiroko [Wide Spreads the Sea], with Alexander Kron and Alexander Azarov (produced 1943).
Nezabyvayemy 1919–y [Unforgettable 1919] (produced 1949).

Screenplays

My iz Kronstadta [We from Kronstadt] (published in *Izbrannoe scenary sovetskogo kino 1*, 1949).

Fiction

Za vlast Sovetov (stories).   1924.

Memoirs and Letters

Dnevniki voennykh let (diaries).   1974.

Other

Stati, dnevniki, pisma o literature i iskurstve.   1961.
Vpered smotryashchy (articles and speeches).   1971.

*

Criticism

Books:
Christine Müller-Scholle, *Wischnewskij: "Optimistische Tragödie"—Das russische Drama*, Düsseldorf, 1986.

*   *   *

Vsevolod Vishnevsky, born in 1900, was a man of some physical as well as moral courage. He left school at the age of 14 to join the Russian Imperial Army and fight in World War I. Three years later, he joined the Bolsheviks, and was active in the insurrection in Petrograd. In the Civil War he served as a cavalryman and a sailor, and these experiences provided the material for most of his plays as well as the popular film, "We from Kronstadt", which he scripted.

By then, the heated polemics about Soviet art, especially in the theatre, were virtually over, and "socialist realism" was triumphant. In the arguments Vishnevsky had opposed the "slice of life" treatment of events, with its inevitable emphasis on the psychological problems of the central characters, and had argued for a monumental and heroic drama instead. "Does not the new theatre demand a new form?" he wrote, and dared in a period of almost paranoic xenophobia in the Soviet Union to suggest that Russian writers should not ignore developments in the West. He advocated studying "all the tendencies of Western art", even (most courageously of all) Joyce's *Ulysses*. Vishnevsky seemed to be looking for a reinvigoration of classical tragedy, perhaps with some kind of Soviet consciousness added. Unfortunately he lacked the literary ability to create much more than effective melodrama.

His first play, "The First Cavalry Army", centres on the career of the young Sysoev, who fights in the Tsarist army against the Germans, and then joins Budyonny's cavalry in the Civil War, fighting with the victorious and heroic Reds. Through these experiences Sysoev matures, learning what communism offers. The character clearly is based on Vishnevsky himself, and the last part is intended as a corrective to the recently published "negative" *Red Cavalry* by Isaac Babel. Consequently, there is more than a touch of romantic wish-fulfilment in the work, though it remains lively and actable through the impressive use of a range of epic devices. These include the use of a narrator, and a prologue and epilogue, which, through a series of letters, carry the story up to 1929, the date of the play's composition. There are captions projected on to a screen, and ticker tape and the sound of messages tapped out on telegraphic machines. The action is broken up into a series of episodes, each more or less self-contained, allowing Vishnevsky to create an impression of epic and heroic action in stirring times. This is reinforced through the use of song, music, and especially drums which roll for forward advances, summary executions, and even to suggest the galloping of the cavalry. The play ends with a rousing chorus of the "Internationale".

Vishnevsky's next play took its title from the chorus of that communist anthem: *Posledny resistelny* (The Last Decisive Battle). Less focused than its predecessor, the play begins with a skit on the Bolshoi's ballet about Soviet sailors, *The Red Poppy*, which is cut short by a group of "real" sailors in the audience who clamber onto the stage and promise to show what life in the Red Navy is really like. Their tale concerns a spree in Odessa, with sailors seeking girls and having a good time. But when the Soviet Union is threatened, they fight to the death defending their socialist fatherland. (The battle was presented in the theatre with terrifying realism, such as machine guns blazing at the audience, caught in the probing searchlights, and artillery firing from the back of the auditorium). The very last member of the detachment crawls towards a screen, as Maurice Chevalier's voice resounds from the radio with some shallow bourgeois trifle, and, mortally wounded, he scrawls with chalk the total population of the Soviet Union, 162,000,000, minus 27, the number in the detachment who have been killed, giving a total of 161,999,973, the number left to carry on the fight. He dies, then stands up and invites everyone who would defend the USSR to stand likewise. In the theatre, all the spectators always did.

This play was brilliantly directed by Meyerhold, with whom, however, Vishnevsky quarrelled violently—he was a man of abrasive temperament. Consequently, his next work, the rather feeble *Na zapade boy* (Fight in the West), was taken from Meyerhold, and the more successful *Optimistecheskaya tragediya* (*An Optimistic Tragedy*) was given to Meyerhold's rival, Tairov. It too was memorably produced, with Tairov's wife Alicia Koonen in the central role of a Red Commissar who is sent to tame an unruly group of sailors in the Civil War. They gradually see the error of their ways, so that when the moment comes for them to fight for the cause, they do so to the last man—or, in this case, woman, since the Commissar goes to parley with the enemy, thereby gaining enough time for reinforcements to arrive before her wounds prove mortal. Based on the real life of Larissa Reisner, the play proved immensely popular, but technically and formally it is considerably less interesting than the two earlier works, although the language still has Vishnevsky's characteristic bite and earthiness.

Nevertheless, *An Optimistic Tragedy* seems to mark the beginning of the end of Vishnevsky's career as an original dramatist. "At the Walls of Lenigrad", based on his experience in the terrible Siege of Leningrad, is disappointingly false, and his last play, *Nezabyvayemy 1919-y* (Unforgettable 1919), is an abject piece of pro-Stalin sychophancy, dramatising the apparently documentary truth of how heavily Lenin relied on Stalin in that year. It won him a Stalin Prize, but may be thought a sad end to what once seemed a potentially major career. Indeed, Meyerhold believed that Vishnevsky might go on to become a second Mayakovsky. It was not to be, and he died in 1951, honoured but perhaps unfulfilled.

—Robert Leach

VOLODIN, Alexander. Born Alexander Moiseyevich Lifshits in Minsk, White Russian Republic (now Belarus), 10 February 1919. Brought up by relatives in Moscow, after his mother's death. Military service during World War II: seriously wounded. Studied at the National Institute of Cinematography, graduated 1949. Teacher in documentary film studio, Leningrad; first publication (short stories), 1954; later turned to plays and screenplays. Member of Communist Party, 1949–90. Recipient: RSFSR State Prize, 1979.

Works

Collections

Dlia teatra i kino [For Theatre and Cinema] (includes *Pyat vecherov; Starshaya sestra; Naznechnenie; Idealistika; Proroysshestyvye kotorogo nikto ne zamatil; Pokhozhdeniya zubnogo vracha; Zagadochny indus; Optimisticheskie zapiski*). 1967.
Portret s dozhdem [Portrait with Rain] (includes *Dultsinea Tobosskaya; S lyubimymi ne rasstavaytes; Osenny marafon; Portret s dozhdem; Dve strehly*). 1980.

Stage Works

Fabrichnaya devchonka [Factory Girl]. In *Teatr*, 9, 1956; in book form, 1957.
Pyat vecherov. In *Teatr*, 7, 1959; translated as *Five Evenings*, 1966.
V gostyakh i doma [At Home and Away]. 1960.
(Moya) starshaya sestra [(My) Older Sister]. 1961.
Idealistka [An Idealistic Lady]. In *Dlia teatra i kino*, 1967.
Naznachenie [The New Boss]. In *Dlia teatra i kino*, 1967.
Attraktsiony [Attractions], from the screenplays *Pokhozhdeniya zubnogo vracha* and *Fokusnik*. 1967.
S lyubimymi ne rasstavaytes [Don't Leave Home Without Him]. In *Avrora*, 1, 1969.
Petruchcho (produced 1972).
Dultsinea Tobosskaya [Dulcinea of Toboso]. In *Portret s dozhdem*, 1980.
Osenny marafon [Jogging in Autumn]. In *Portret s dozhdem*, 1980.
Dve strely [Two Arrows]. In *Portret s dozhdem*, 1980.
Portret s dozhdem [Portrait with Rain]. In *Portret s dozhdem* (collection), 1980.
Iashcheritsa [The Lizard]. In *Sovremennaya dramaturgiya*, 2, 1985.
Grafoman. In *Sovremennaya dramaturgiya*, 2, 1985.
Blondinka [The Blonde]. In *Teatr*, 8, 1984.
Kastruchcha [Kastruchcha]. In *Teatr*, 5, 1988.
Mat Iyususa [The Mother of Jesus]. In *Sovremennaya dramaturgiya*, 1, 1989.
Odnomestny tramway. In *Zvezda*, 1, 1991.

Screenplays (selected)

Zvoniat, otkroyte dver [The Doorbell's Ringing, Open the Door], 1965; *Pokhozhdeniya zubnogo vracha* [The Adventures of a Dentist], 1966 (published in *Dli teatra i kino*, 1967); *Moya starshaya sestra* [My Older Sister], 1967; *Zagadochny indus* [The Mysterious Hindu], 1968 (published in *Dlia teatra i kino*, 1967); *Fokusnik* [The Magician], 1968; *Dultsinea Tobosskaya* [Dulcinea of Toboso], 1971; *Osseny marafon*, 1980 (published 1980).

Fiction

Rasskazy [Tales]. 1954.
Stydno byt neschastlivyn [One Should Be Ashamed Not to Be Happy]. 1971.

*

Criticism

Articles:
Emilie Stichling, "Recent Trends in Russian Drama with Special Reference to Alexander Volodin", in *Canadian Slavonic Papers*, 11, 1969.

*   *   *

Perhaps Volodin is too much a child of his time. With Viktor Rozov and Alexei Arbuzov he belongs to the generation of playwrights who inaugurated the "thaw" in theatre and film after Stalin's death. That is, after decades of plays on collective themes of defending the fatherland and producing cement, Volodin, with a new wave of dramatists, turned to the little man—or indeed the unheroic woman—and to his or her uniquely personal feelings. The heroine of Volodin's first play to reach the stage, *Fabrichnaya devchonka* (Factory Girl), like John Osborne's "angry young men" resents the social order, which determines she spend her days at the textile mill and nights in a workers' dormitory. But to escape boredom and go dancing at night in a discotheque precipitates disaster for Zhenia Shulzhenko when her partner is thrown out for disorderly conduct, and she with him. The censure to which she is subjected under pressure from Party authorities almost destroys her, until the very fellow workers who have been pressured into condemning her confess to flaws in their own conduct and urge Zhenia's rehabilitation. The German Slavist, Wolfgang Kasack, says that in this first play, Volodin "attacked a central problem of all life in the Soviet Union, the contrast between the lie of the social order [as described in official Party doctrine] and the truth of daily living".

Although a decade later Volodin did not include "Factory Girl" in his first collected volume of plays (*Dlia teatra i kino*, or "For Theatre and Cinema"), it was on first appearance widely staged and hotly debated by critics and in lay groups. His next play, *Pyat vecherov* (*Five Evenings*), again caused excitement by raising controversial issues: first, the generation gap—that is, the total lack of understanding between the post-World-War-II adolescents and their elders of Volodin's age—and second, society's worship of the success and prestige of high position. A narrator briefly describes Leningrad streets on a wintry night at the start of *Five Evenings*, but his six lines set a lyric mood rather than denote the "epic" style of drama. This first such prelude refers to the time 17 years earlier when the then 19-year-old Ilin was accompanied, as he marched off to serve in World War II, by his sweetheart Tamara. Since then she has not married, though Ilin has stopped corresponding with her. She has risen to authority in her job and brought up her nephew, Slava, now a top-ranking student at the university. Here Ilin again enters her life. A woman Ilin has known only a few days while on leave in Leningrad has taken him up to her apartment for love-making; at his tale of his first love for the beautiful Tamara she wonders why he doesn't go to see her now. On impulse he jumps up to do just that, though it is midnight.

In Ilin's presence Tamara is caught between her seeming contentment with her successful life and the realization of her loneliness without love. The plot becomes more complicated when the characters are forced to confront their own dishonesty about the supposed success of their lives. Tamara has falsified the picture of Slava as a motivated student with the highest grades, and has indignantly dismissed Katia, his lowly paid but bright and devoted date.

Ilin's dishonesty lies in his pretence that he has realized his gift for science and is now in charge of one of the largest chemical conglomerates in Siberia. Revealing the truth to Tamara later, he asks her to return with him to the distant outpost where he is, in reality, only a senior chauffeur, and she first recoils in disdain for his low position. He flees from her contempt, and then she, on second thoughts, vainly pursues him. Whether love triumphs in the end, as the Hollywood convention would have it, is not wholly clear from Volodin's three versions of his play, the second being a screen version for Nikita Mikhalkov and the third a revised stage version. Certainly the love theme of Tamara's—in the original both Tamara's and Ilin's—song is inherent in *Five Evenings*, which by this token is therefore a lyrical play.

With *Moya starshaya sestra* (My Older Sister) two years later, Volodin again offered two interpretations in only a slightly different emphasis in stage and screen versions, on the line, "I insist you have to smile!". The older sister Nadia wants to assure for her younger sister, Lida, a better life's work than her own of accountant in a plywood office on construction sites. When Lida fails the drama-school audition and Nadia, instead, becomes the great actress, she asks for a smile from Lida, whose happiness remains her only aim. She sends away Kirill, the one man Lida loves, in the name of protecting her from him. Lida submits still with the smile that Nadia demands. But later Lida rebels by carrying on an affair with Kirill, who is now married. When Nadia remonstrates, Lida leaves: Nadia has ruined her sister's life. Volodin intended to show in Nadia's Cinderella success as an actress how capricious the gift of artistic talent can be, but also to argue for each person's right to his or her own pursuit of happiness.

Volodin has concerned himself with middle-aged men as well as with women and young people. *Naznachenie* (The New Boss) dramatizes the plight of an introvert intellectual, full of bright ideas but lacking in executive ability. Again in *Osenny marafon* (Jogging in Autumn) a weak-willed professor at the National Institute of Cinematography reveals himself to his fellow-jogger as a man who can't say no—either to his mistress, his wife, his student, or his neighbor, with all of whom he becomes involved in a tissue of lies and emergencies because he lacks the backbone to hurt or displease them. The title heroine of *Mat Iyususa* (The Mother of Jesus) also cannot take a stand on the amazing events of her son's life. After His death, however, she does refuse the healing miracles which the crowds demand from her, and so she remains alone in an empty house in the end.

Just as "The Mother of Jesus" paints a realistic picture of events some two thousand years ago from an ordinary woman's viewpoint, so Volodin increasingly turned to distant times and mythic situations to view them as might an ordinary person today. He applied this form of estrangement to the discovery of the bow and arrow in pre-historic times in *Iashcheritsa* (The Lizard), and he wrote a mystery or "who-done-it" play of the Stone Age in *Dve strely* (Two Arrows). His *Dultsinea Tobosskaya* (Dulcinea of Tobosso) shows a counterpart of the Don being instructed in the pleasure of sex by Don Quixote's revered lady. Certainly, paradox is a frequent device with Volodin.

The multiplicity of Volodin's themes make him difficult to categorize. Despite his tendency to "debunk" or expose, he is not simply a realist. The influence of his cinema training is obvious in the quick succession of brief episodes which characterizes his plays. The frequent reluctance of his characters to reveal their true selves or the overly direct nature of their laconic speech by no means signifies that their feelings lack depth and complication. One critic sees Volodin as gradually withdrawing from the theatre and increasingly resorting to film, with which, whether in cinemas or on television, this dramatic author of the ordinary has reached millions.

—Marjorie L. Hoover

VOLTAIRE. Born François-Marie Arouet in Paris, 21 November 1694. Educated at the Jesuit Collège Louis-le-Grand, Paris, 1704–11; studied law, 1713. Articled by his father to a lawyer, 1714; began frequenting the Société du Temple, Paris, c.1715; arrested and exiled from Paris for 5 months, 1716, imprisoned in the Bastille for 11 months, 1717–18, and exiled to Châtenay, 1718, for his satirical verses; adopted the pen-name Voltaire, 1718; first-produced play, *Oedipe*, staged 1718; received a royal pension, 1725; imprisoned in the Bastille, April 1726, and exiled to England after quarrelling with the Chevalier de Rohan-Chabot; lived in London, 1727–28; returned to Paris, 1729; lived mainly in Château de Cirey, with Mme. du Châtelet (died 1749), 1734–40; first meeting with Frederick the Great of Prussia, 1740; appointed royal historiographer, 1745–50; chamberlain for Frederick the Great, 1750–53; was refused permission to return to Paris, 1753, and lived in Switzerland, 1755–59; bought an estate in Ferney, France, near the Swiss border, where he lived 1759–78; published his *Dictionnaire philosophique*, 1764; returned to Paris and received triumphant welcome from the Académie and Comédie-Française, 1778. Elected to: Royal Society (London); Royal Society of Edinburgh, 1745; Académie-Française, 1746; Academy of St. Petersburg (Russia), 1746. Died in Paris, 30 May 1778.

Works

Collections

Oeuvres complètes (2 vols.).   1732 (first edition of complete works).
Oeuvres complètes (40 vols.).   1775 (last edition of complete works published during Voltaire's lifetime).
Oeuvres complètes (Kehl edition; 70 vols.).   1784–89.
Oeuvres complètes (Moland edition; 52 vols.).   1877–85.
Works (22 vols.).   1901–03; plays reprinted as *Seven Plays* (includes *Mérope; Olympia; Alzire; Orestes; Oedipus; Zaïre; Caesar*), 1988.

Complete Works (Besterman edition, in French; 135 vols.). 1968—

Stage Works

Oedipe (produced Comédie-Française, Paris, 1718). 1719; translated as *Oedipus*, in *Works*, 1901–03, and in *Seven Plays*, 1988.
Artémire (produced Comédie-Française, Paris, 1720). Fragments in *Oeuvres 1*, 1784.
Mariamne (produced Comédie-Française, Paris, 1724; as *Hérode et Mariamne*, produced 1725). 1725.
L'Indiscret (produced Comédie-Française, Paris, 1725). 1725.
Brutus (produced Comédie-Française, Paris, 1730). With the essay "Discours sur la tragédie", 1731.
Ériphile (produced Comédie-Française, Paris, 1732). 1732.
Zaïre (produced Comédie-Française, Paris, 1732). 1733; translated as *Zara*, 1736; translated as *Zaïre*, 1854: several subsequent translations under same title.
Les Originaux (produced 1732). In *Oeuvres 9*, 1820.
Adélaïde du Guesclin (produced Comédie-Française, Paris, 1734). In *Oeuvres 6*, 1745.
La Mort de César (produced Hôtel de Sassenage, Paris, 1735). 1736; translated as *Caesar*, in *Works*, 1901–03, and in *Seven Plays*, 1988.
Alzire; ou, Les Américains (produced Comédie-Française, Paris, 1736). 1736; translated as *Alzira*, 1736; as *Alzire*, in *Works*, 1901–03, and in *Seven Plays*, 1988.
L'Enfant prodigue (produced 1736). 1738.
L'Échange (produced Cirey, 1736; produced as *Le Comte de Boursoufle*, Anet, 1747; revised version, as *Quand est-ce qu'on me marie?*, produced 1761). 1761; as *Le Comte de Boursoufle*, in *Oeuvres 7*, 1819.
Zulime (produced 1740). 1761.
Mahomet (produced Lille, 1741). 1742; as *Le Fanatisme; ou, Mahomet le prophète*, 1743; translated as *Mohamet the Imposter*, 1744; as *Mahomet the Prophet*, in *The Drama 8*, edited by A. Bates, 1903–04.
Mérope (produced Comédie-Française, Paris, 1743). 1744; translated as *Merope*, 1744, in *Works*, 1901–03, and *Seven Plays*, 1988.
La Princesse de Navarre, music by Rameau (produced Versailles, 1745). 1745.
Le Temple de la Gloire, music by Rameau (produced Versailles, 1745). 1745.
Samson, music by Rameau. 1745.
La Prude; ou, La Gardeuse de cassette, from a play by Wycherley (produced Château de Sceaux, 1747). In *Oeuvres 8*, 1748.
Sémiramis (produced Comédie-Française, Paris, 1748). 1749; translated as *Semiramis*, 1760.
Nanine (produced 1749). 1749; translated as *Nanine*, in *Eighteenth-Century French Plays*, edited by C.D. Brenner and N.A. Goodyear, 1927.
Oreste (produced Comédie-Française, Paris, 1750). 1750; translated as *Orestes*, in *Works*, 1901–03, and in *Seven Plays*, 1988.
Catilina; ou, Rome sauvée (produced Château de Sceaux, 1750). 1752; translated as *Rome Preserved*, 1760.
Le Duc de Foix (produced Comédie-Française?, Paris, 1752). 1752; as *Amélie; ou, Le Duc de Foix*, in *Collection complète des oeuvres 11*, 1756.
L'Orphelin de la Chine (produced Comédie-Française, Paris, 1755). 1755; translated as *The Orphan of China*, 1756.
Saül. 1755; translated as *Saul*, 1820.
La Femme qui a raison (produced Carouge, 1758). 1759.

Socrate. 1759; translated as *Socrates*, 1760, and in *The Drama 8*, edited by A Bates, 1903–04.
Tancrède (produced 1760). 1760; translated as *Almida*, 1771.
L'Écossaise (produced Comédie-Française, Paris, 1760). 1760; translated as *The Coffee House*, 1760; as *The Highland Girl*, 1910.
Le Droit de seigneur (as *L'Écueil du sage*, produced Comédie-Française, Paris, 1762). 1763; as *L'Écueil du sage*. 1764.
Olympie (produced Comédie-Française, Paris, 1764). 1763; translated as *Olympia*, in *Works*, 1901–03, and in *Seven Plays*, 1988.
Octave et le jeune Pompée; ou, Le Triumvirat (produced Comédie-Française, Paris, 1764). 1767.
Les Scythes (produced Comédie-Française, Paris, 1767). 1767.
Charlot; ou, La Comtesse de Givri (produced Ferney, 1767). 1767.
Les Guèbres; ou, La Tolérance. 1769.
Sophonisbe (produced Comédie-Française, Paris, 1774). 1770.
Le Dépositaire (produced 1772). 1772.
Les Lois de Minos; ou, Astérie. 1773.
Dom Pèdre, roi de Castille. 1775.
Agathocle (produced 1777). In *Oeuvres 6*, 1784.
Irène (produced Comédie-Française, Paris, 1778). 1779.
Le Duc d'Alençon; ou, Les Frères ennemis, edited by M.L. Dubois. 1821.
L'Envieux. 1834.

Fiction

Collected stories published in 1764, 1771, and 1775; a six-volume edition was published in 1780.

Memnon. Histoire orientale. 1747; as *Zadig; ou, La Destinée. Histoire orientale*, 1748; translated as *Zadig and Astarte*, 1810: several subsequent translations as *Zadig*.
Micromégas. 1752; translated as *Micromegas*, 1753.
Candide; ou, L'Optimisme. 1759; translated as *Candid*, 1759; numerous subsequent translations as *Candide*.
L'Ingénu. 1767; as *Le Huron; ou, L'Ingénu*, 1767; translated as *The Pupil of Nature*, 1771; translated as *The Sincere Huron*, 1786.
La Princesse de Babylone. 1768; translated as *The Princess of Babylon*, 1927.
L'Homme aux quarante écus. 1768; translated as *The Man of Forty Crowns*, 1768.
Les Lettres d'Amabed. 1769.
Le Taureau blanc. 1774; translated as *The White Bull*, 1774.
Histoire de Jenni; ou, Le Sage et l'athée. 1775; translated as *Young James; or, The Sage and the Atheist*, 1776.
Romances, Tales and Smaller Pieces (2 vols.). 1794.
The Philosophical Tales. 1871.
Short Prose Tales, translated by F.F. Roget. 1894.
"Zadig" and Other Romances. 1923.
"Candide" and Other Tales. 1937.
"Candide", "Zadig", and Selected Stories. 1961.
"Zadig" and Other Stories, edited by Haydn T. Mason. 1971.
Romans et contes (2 vols.), edited by Frédéric Deloffre and Jacques den Heuvel. 1978.

Verse

La Ligue; ou, Henri le Grand: Poème épique. 1723; as *La Henriade*, 1728; translated as *Henriade*, 1732.

Le Temple du Goût. 1733; revised edition, as *Le Temple de l'amitié et le temple du goût*, 1733; translated as *The Temple of Taste*, 1734.

Le Mondain. 1736.

La Pucelle d'Orléans. 1755; augmented edition, 1762, 1780; translated as *La Pucelle; or, The Maid of Orleans* (2 vols.), 1785–86.

Poème sur le désastre de Lisbonne. 1756.

Poème sur la loi naturelle. 1756.

Précis de l'Ecclésiaste en vers. 1759.

La Cantique des cantiques en vers. 1759.

Contes de Guillaume Vadé. 1764.

La Guerre civile de Genève. 1767; translated as *The Civil War of Geneva*, 1769.

Épîtres, satires, contes, odes, et pièces fugitives. 1771.

Poèmes, épîtres, et autres poésies. 1777.

Memoirs and Letters

*Letters Addressed to His Highness the Prince of *****.* 1768.

Letters from M. de Voltaire to Several of His Friends. 1770.

Commentaire historique sur les oeuvres de l'auteur de la Henriade (autobiography). 1776; translated as *Historical Memoirs of the Author of the Henriade*, 1977.

Memoirs of the Life of Voltaire Written by Himself. 1784.

Voltaire in His Letters, translated by S.G. Tallentyre. 1919.

Letters of Voltaire and Frederick the Great, translated by Richard Aldington. 1927.

Love Letters of Voltaire to His Niece, translated by Theodore Besterman. 1958.

Select Letters of Voltaire, translated by Theodore Besterman. 1963.

Correspondence (in French). In *Complete Works*, 1968—

Other

Essai sur les guerres civiles de France. 1729; translated as *Essay upon the Civil Wars in France*, 1727.

Histoire de Charles XII, roi de Suède (2 vols.). 1731.

Lettres écrites de Londres sur les Anglais. 1734; as *Lettres philosophiques*, 1734; translated as *Letters Concerning the English Nation*, 1733; as *Letters on England*, 1980.

Eléments de la philosophie de Newton. 1738; translated as *The Elements of Newton's Philosophy*, 1738.

Histoire de la guerre de mil sept cent quarante et un (2 vols.). 1745; translated as *The History of the War of Seventeen Hundred and Forty One*, 1756.

Le Siècle de Louis XIV (2 vols.). 1751; *Supplément*, 1753; translated as *The Age of Louis XIV*, (2 vols.), 1752; revised edition, 1753.

Annales de l'Empire depuis Charlemagne (2 vols.). 1753; translated as *Annals of the Empire from the Reign of Charlemagne*, 1781.

Essai sur l'histoire générale et sur les moeurs et l'esprit des nations (7 vols.). 1756; revised edition (8 vols.), 1761–63; translated as *The General History and State of Europe*, 1754; as *An Essay on Universal History*, 1759.

Histoire de l'empire de Russie sous Pierre le Grand (2 vols.). 1759–63; translated as *The History of the Russian Empire under Peter the Great*, 1763.

Appel à toutes les nations de l'Europe. 1761.

Traité sur la tolérance. 1763; translated as *A Treatise of Religious Tolerance*, 1764.

Dictionnaire philosophique portatif. 1764; revised edition, 1765 (and later editions): revisions include *La Raison par Alphabet* (2 vols.), 1769, and *Questions sur l'Encyclopédie* (9 vols.), 1770–72; translated as *The Philosophical Dictionary for the Pocket*, 1765.

La Philosophie de l'histoire. 1765.

Collection des lettres sur les miracles. 1765; 20 letters also published separately, 1765.

Le Philosophe ignorant. 1766; translated as *The Ignorant Philosopher*, 1767.

Commentaire sur le livre "Des Délits et des peines". 1766.

Les Honnêtetés littéraires. 1767.

Examen important de milord Bolingbroke. 1767.

Lettres sur Rabelais. 1767.

Homélies prononcées à Londres en 1765. 1767; *Cinquième homélie*, 1769.

Le Dîner du comte de Boulainvilliers. 1767.

Les Singularités de la nature. 1768.

L'ABC. 1768.

Histoire du Parlement de Paris (2 vols.). 1769.

Collections d'anciens évangiles; ou, Monument du premier siècle du christianisme. 1769.

Dieu et les hommes: Oeuvre théologique, mais raisonnable. 1769.

Tout en Dieu. 1769.

Les Adorateurs. 1769.

Précis du siècle de Louis XV (2 vols.). 1769; translated as *The Age of Louis XV* (2 vols.), 1774.

Fragments sur l'Inde. 1773; augmented edition, with *Fragments sur l'histoire générale, et sur la France*, 1774; translated as *Fragments Relating to the Late Revolutions in India*, 1774; as *Fragments on India*, 1937.

Le Bible enfin expliquée (2 vols.). 1776.

Dialogue d'Evhémère. 1777.

Commentaire sur l'Esprit des Lois de Montesquieu. 1778.

Prix de la justice et de l'humanité. 1778.

Traité de métaphysique. 1784.

Oeuvres historiques, edited by René Pomeau. 1957.

The Portable Voltaire, edited by Ben Ray Redman. 1968.

Notebooks, edited by Theodore Besterman, in *Complete Works 81–82*. 1968.

Editor, *Anti-Machiavel; ou, Essais critiques sur Le Prince de Machiavel*, by Frederick II. 1740.

Editor, *Testament de Jean Meslier*. 1762.

Editor, *Théâtre de Pierre Corneille avec des commentaires* (12 vols.). 1764; *Commentaires* edited by D. Williams, in *Complete Works 53–55*, 1974–75.

Editor, *Journal de la cour de Louis XIV*, by the Marquis de Dangeau. 1769.

Editor, *Les Souvenirs de Mme. de Caylus*. 1770.

Editor, *Éloge et pensées de Pascal*. 1778.

Translator, *Jules César*, by Shakespeare. In *Théâtre de Pierre Corneille 2*, 1764.

Translator, *L'Héraclius espagnol; ou, Dans cette vie tout est verité et tout mensonge*, by Calderón. In *Théâtre de Pierre Corneille 5*, 1764.

*

Bibliographies

Georges Bengesco, *Voltaire: Bibliographie de ses oeuvres*, Paris, 1882–90 (4 vols.); indexed by Jean Malcolm, 1953.

Mary Margaret Barr, *A Century of Voltaire Study: Bibliography of Writings on Voltaire 1825–1926*, 1929; supplements in *Modern Language Notes*, 48 (1933) and 56 (1941).

Continuing bibliography in *Studies on Voltaire and the Eighteenth Century*, 1955—

Criticism

Books:

H. Lion, *Les Tragédies et les théories dramatiques de Voltaire*, Paris, 1895.

Jean-Jacques Olivier, *Voltaire et les comédiens interprètes de son théâtre*, Paris, 1900.

Haydn Mason, *Voltaire*, London, 1975.

Haydn Mason, *Voltaire: A Biography*, Baltimore, Maryland, 1981.

A.O. Aldridge, *Voltaire and the Century of Light*, Princeton (New Jersey) and London, 1975.

Lillian Willens, *Voltaire's Comic Theatre: Composition, Conflict and Critics*, Banbury, 1975.

Theodore Besterman, *Voltaire*, Oxford, 1976.

Christine Merraud, *Voltaire et Frédéric II: Une Dramaturgie des lumières 1736–1778*, Oxford, 1985.

Eva Jacobs, *Voltaire and Tragedy*, Cambridge, 1987.

Marie A. Wellington, *The Art of Voltaire's Theatre: An Exploration of Possibility*, New York, 1988.

Serials:

Studies on Voltaire and the Eighteenth Century, 1955—

*   *   *

Voltaire, although he is now best known for his philosophical *contes* or crusades against injustice, was, in his own time, a highly regarded and prolific dramatist, who in different ways would have wished to see himself as the continuator of the tradition of Corneille and Racine. He wrote more than 50 plays in a wide variety of styles over a period of 60 years from his first, *Oedipe*, to *Irène*, produced in the year of his death.

He remained very classical in certain respects—he adhered to the Alexandrine and accepted the conventions of the unities—and yet he sought also to innovate and renew. He set out, for instance, to increase the spectacular dimension of tragedy, and to move away from what he saw as too static and verbal a form. He initiated a sequence of more varied settings for the tragic action, no longer confining himself to Ancient Greece and Rome, but bringing onto the stage medieval Syracuse (*Tancrède*), Peru (*Alzire*), Africa (*Zulime*), Jerusalem (*Zaïre*), Mecca (*Mahomet*), and China (*L'Orphelin de la Chine*). Such settings, though, do not reflect a desire for historical authenticity—indeed, details are often as imaginary as they are accurate—but they are there, rather, to create an exotic atmosphere. Similarly he was quite adventurous in his ideas for stage decoration and costume, moving from a mausoleum and hanging gardens in *Sémiramis* to crowds of knights, priests, and a funeral pyre in *Les Scythes*, *Tancrède*, and *Olympie*. Influenced to some extent by the example of Shakespeare, he set out to *show* more and to *describe* less, and to put on stage actions or characters which, in French classical tragedy of the previous century, would certainly have been confined to *récits*: ghosts, marriage ceremonies, gatherings of the Senate, and even, in *Mahomet*, the scene of a son killing his father. In *Adélaïde du Guesclin*, the firing of a cannon is used as a death signal, and thunder is heard in *Sémiramis* and other tragedies.

He was also different from the French classical writers in his greater fondness for effects of pathos, frequently achieved at the expense of *vraisemblance*. Tragic errors or moving recognitions abound in his plays, but these are often made possible only by the most improbable silences, misunderstandings, or coincidences. His goal, though, was not the form of psychological tragedy perfected by Racine; he situated the tragic not so much within individuals, carefully evoked or analysed, as outside them, in their dealings with each other, in their struggles with fate, or in the clash of contrasting principles, extending even to the conflict of civilisations—for example, Peruvian against Spaniard (*Alzire*), Scythian against Persian (*Les Scythes*). And yet, at the same time, his innovations were limited in scope by the force of public taste which he feared to disappoint or offend. In spite of the view, expressed in some of his prefaces, that love was inappropriate as a major component of tragic action, some of his most popular plays contain such elements. In *Oedipe*, a startling success which effectively launched his literary career, he introduced the superfluous but immensely popular invention of Philoctète, a former lover of Jocaste; and in *Zaïre*, the doomed love of the heroine and Orosmane is at the centre of the play.

What characterises Voltaire's tragedies particularly, though, is their dimension of political and philosophical comment. Already in *Oedipe*, he introduced a series of reflections on kingship and the status of priests, and such observations are often built into the very thematic structure of the plays. In *Zaïre* there is a bold juxtaposition of Muslim and Christian, which underpins speculation on the importance of upbringing in determining religion, on the value of Muslim virtue, and on the fruitlessness of Christian sacrifice; in *Alzire* he attacked a conception of Christianity that foresakes humanity and forgiveness; in *Ériphile* there are numerous criticisms of the Court and courtiers; and in *Mahomet*, perhaps his most outspoken tragedy, he launched a fierce attack against crimes committed in the name of religion, religious charlatanism, and fanaticism. In most cases, though, this particular form of expression, fixed as it is by the aesthetic and moral values of a previous age, is a less effective vehicle for such radical questioning than his more modern philosophical *conte*.

Voltaire's output, however, contains plays other than tragedies. His comedies are characteristic of the period in their contemporary plots, familiarity of tone, clear moral intention, and the attempt to merge the comic with the serious. They are often written in varied and quite accomplished metres, and there is a clear attempt to produce plays with some kind of social engagement on familiar issues like equality, tolerance, and the evils of prejudice. They are largely unsuccessful, though. They often have awkward plots, wooden characterisation, and little sense of comic movement; too often they are also heavily moralising. His most successful were *L'Enfant prodigue* and *Nanine*, both of which were essentially sentimental comedies and demonstrate the influence of Samuel Richardson on French drama at this time. His play *L'Écossaise*, a one-act comedy in prose, has a clear satirical purpose to vilify his enemy Freron, portrayed as a starving journalist and cowardly calumniator; but it contains also elements of the *drame* and is typical of the dramatist's desire to experiment.

Although his plays are little read and performed now, Voltaire is an important figure in the development of French theatre. He extended the life of classical tragedy considerably beyond its natural span through a mixture of imaginative innovation and boundless productivity; but he also prepared the way, in his taste for spectacle and pathos, historical evocation and topical comment, for the theatrical vision of the Romantics.

—G. Jonathan Mallinson

See also *Volume 1* entry on *Zaïre*.

———

VON KOTZEBUE, August.   See **KOTZEBUE, August von**.

———

W

WAKEFIELD MASTER, The. See *Volume 1* entry on *The Townley Plays*.

WALCOTT, Derek (Alton). Born in Castries, St. Lucia, West Indies, 23 January 1930. Educated at St. Mary's College, Castries, St. Lucia, 1941–47; University College of the West Indies, Mona, Jamaica, 1950–54, BA 1953. Married 1) Fay Moyston in 1954 (divorced 1959), one son; 2) Margaret Ruth Maillard in 1962 (divorced), two daughters; 3) Norline Metivier in 1982. Teacher, St. Mary's College, Castries, 1947–50 and 1954, Grenada Boys Secondary School, St. George's, 1953–54, and Jamaica College, Kingston, 1955; co-founder, with his brother Roderick, St. Lucia Arts Guild, 1950, and Basement Theatre, Port-of-Spain; first plays produced 1950; feature writer, *Public Opinion*, Kingston, 1956–57; studied theatre in the USA, on a Rockefeller fellowship, 1958–59; founding director, Little Carib Theatre Workshop (later Trinidad Theatre Workshop), 1959–76; feature writer, 1960–62, and drama critic, 1963–68, *Trinidad Guardian*, Port-of-Spain; assistant professor of creative writing, 1981, and from 1985 visiting professor, Boston University; visiting professor, Columbia University, New York, 1981, and Harvard University, Cambridge, Massachusetts, 1982, 1987. Recipient: Royal Society of Literature Heinemann Award, 1966, 1983; Cholmondeley Award, 1969; Gold Hummingbird Medal (Trinidad), 1969; Obie Award, 1971; Guggenheim Award, 1977; Welsh Arts Council International Writers Prize, 1980; Queen's Gold Medal for Poetry, 1988; Nobel Prize for Literature, 1992. D. Litt: University of the West Indies, Mona, 1973. Fellow, Royal Society of Literature, 1966; honorary member, American Academy, 1979. OBE (Officer, Order of the British Empire), 1972.

Derek Walcott

Works

Collections

"*Dream on Monkey Mountain*" *and Other Plays* (includes *Ti-Jean and His Brothers*; *Malcochon*; *The Sea at Dauphin*; and the essay "What the Twilight Says"). 1970.
Three Plays (includes *The Last Carnival*; *Beef, No Chicken*; *A Branch of the Blue Nile*). 1986.

Stage Works

Cry for a Leader (produced St. Lucia, 1950).
Senza Alcun Sospetto (broadcast 1950; as *Paolo and Francesca*, produced St. Joseph's Convent, St. Lucia, 1951?).
Henri Christophe: A Chronicle (produced St. Joseph's Convent, St. Lucia, 1950). 1950.
Robin and Andrea. In *Bim*, December 1950.
Three Assassins (produced St. Lucia, 1951?).
The Price of Mercy (produced St. Lucia, 1951?).
Harry Dernier (as *Dernier*, broadcast 1952; as *Harry Dernier*, produced University of the West Indies, Mona, Jamaica, 1952). 1952.
The Sea at Dauphin (produced by Whitehall Players Theatre, Port-of-Spain, Trinidad 1954). 1954.
Crossroads (produced Jamaica, 1954).
The Charlatan (produced University of the West Indies,

Mona, Jamaica, 1954?; revised version, music by Fred Hope and Rupert Dennison, produced Port-of-Spain, Trinidad, 1973; revised version, music by Galt MacDermot, produced Mark Taper Forum, Los Angeles, 1974; revised version produced Port-of-Spain, Trinidad, 1977).

The Wine of the Country (produced University of the West Indies, Mona, Jamaica, 1956).

The Golden Lions (produced University of the West Indies, Mona, Jamaica, 1956).

Ione: A Play with Music (produced by Word Theatre, Kingston, Jamaica, 1957). 1957.

Ti-Jean and His Brothers (produced Roman Catholic Boys School, Castries, St. Lucia, 1957; revised version produced 1958). In *"Dream on Monkey Mountain" and Other Plays*, 1970.

Drums and Colours (produced Port-of-Spain, Trinidad, 1958). In *Caribbean Quarterly*, vol. 7 nos. 1–2, 1961.

Malcochon; or, The Six in the Rain (produced Port-of-Spain, Trinidad, 1959; as *The Six in the Rain*, produced Royal Court Theatre, London, 1960; as *Malcochon*, produced New York, 1969). In *"Dream on Monkey Mountain" and Other Plays*, 1970.

Jourmard; or, A Comedy Till the Last Minute (produced St. Lucia, 1959).

Batai (carnival show; produced Port-of-Spain, Trinidad, 1965).

Dream on Monkey Mountain (produced Central Library Theatre, Toronto, 1967). In *"Dream on Monkey Mountain" and Other Plays*, 1970.

Franklin: A Tale of the Islands (produced Georgetown, Guyana, 1969; revised version produced Port-of-Spain, Trinidad, 1973).

In a Fine Castle (produced Little Carib Theatre, Port-of-Spain, Trinidad, 1970). Excerpt, as *Conscience of a Revolutionary*, in Port-of-Spain *Express*, 24 October 1971.

The Joker of Seville, music by Galt MacDermot, from a play by Tirso de Molina (produced Little Carib Theatre, Port-of-Spain, Trinidad, 1974). With *O Babylon!*, 1978.

O Babylon!, music by Galt MacDermot (produced Little Carib Theatre, Port-of-Spain, Trinidad, 1976). With *The Joker of Seville*, 1978.

Remembrance (produced Dorsch Centre, St. Croix, US Virgin Islands, 1977). With *Pantomime*, 1980.

Pantomime (produced Little Carib Theatre, Port-of-Spain, Trinidad, 1978). With *Remembrance*, 1980.

Marie Laveau, music by Galt MacDermot (produced St. Thomas, US Virgin Islands, 1979). Excerpts published in *Trinidad and Tobago Review*, Christmas 1979.

The Isle is Full of Noises (produced Hartford Stage, Hartford, Connecticut, 1982).

Beef, No Chicken (produced Little Carib Theatre, Port-of-Spain, Trinidad, 1981). In *Three Plays*, 1986.

Haitian Air (produced in the open air, St. Lucia, 1984).

The Last Carnival (produced by the Group Theatre Company, Seattle, Washington, 1983). In *Three Plays*, 1986.

A Branch of the Blue Nile (produced Stage One, Bridgetown, Barbados, 1983). In *Three Plays*, 1986.

To Die for Grenada (produced Cleveland, Ohio, 1986).

Steel (produced America Repertory Theatre, Cambridge, Massachusetts, 1991).

The Odyssey, from the epic by Homer (produced The Other Place, Stratford-on-Avon, 1992).

Radio Plays

Senza Alcun Sospetto, 1950; *Dernier*, 1952; *Pantomime*, 1979.

Television Plays

The Snow Queen (part published in *People*, April 1977).

Verse

25 Poems. 1948.
Epitaph for the Young: XII Cantos. 1949.
Poems. 1951.
In a Green Night: Poems 1948–1960. 1962.
Selected Poems. 1964.
The Castaway and Other Poems. 1965.
"The Gulf" and Other Poems. 1969; as *The Gulf*, 1970.
Another Life. 1973.
Sea Grapes. 1976.
The Star-Apple Kingdom. 1979.
Selected Poetry, edited by Wayne Brown. 1981.
The Fortunate Traveller. 1981.
The Caribbean Poetry of Walcott and the Art of Romare Bearden. 1983.
Midsummer. 1984.
Collected Poems 1948–1984. 1986.
The Arkansas Testament. 1987.
Omeros. 1989.

Other

The Poet in the Theatre. 1990.

*

Bibliographies

Derek Walcott and Other Caribbean Writers: A Selected Annotated Bibliography, Mold, Clywd, Wales, 1980.
Robert D. Hamner, "Derek Walcott: His Works and His Critics: An Annotated Bibliography, 1947–1980", in *Journal of Commonwealth Literature*, vol. 16 no. 1, 1981.
Irma E. Goldstraw, *Derek Walcott: An Annotated Bibliography of His Works*, New York, 1984.

Criticism

Books:
Edward Baugh, *Derek Walcott: Memory as Vision*, London, 1978.
Robert D. Hammer, *Derek Walcott*, Boston, 1981.
Stewart Brown (ed.), *The Art of Derek Walcott*, Bridgend, 1991.

Articles:
Patricia Ismond, "Walcott's Later Drama: From *Joker* to *Remembrance*", in *Ariel: A Review of International English Literature*, vol. 16 no. 3, 1985.
Erskine Peters, "The Theme of Madness in the Plays of Derek Walcott", in *College Language Association Journal*, 22, 1988.

* * *

Walcott is the major poet, dramatist, and theatre director of the West Indies. He transformed the verse drama movement of the modernists into contemporary national post-colonial theatre rooted in local culture and in the European tradition. Over the years Walcott has integrated European dramatic form with local subject matter (especially of St. Lucia), themes and music (especially Calypso). He trained actors to use their natural body movements and to see the dramatic possibilities of West Indian speech, with its wide range from patois and dialect to British English. He has tried to form actors with a similar expressive range, which would allow them to play everything from Shakespeare to dialect comedy.

While still at school, Walcott began writing verse drama and started a theatre group in St. Lucia. The first influence was Shakespeare's historical plays. *Henri Christophe*, a verse drama about the Haitian revolution, was regarded as cultural and political assertion by the middle-class brown professionals who had agitated for a West Indian Federation independent of England. In *The Sea at Dauphin* Walcott takes Synge and the Irish Renaissance as a model both in creating a drama concerning peasants and in the blend of Jacobean, biblical, and dialect English. Already, his symbols and attitudes are present, including the updating of the romantic-Melvillean image of the sea as a destructive unformed terror expressive of a harsh, godless universe at the core of which is a void that man must confront. Although he lost his faith he retains a strong religious consciousness. *Drums and Colours*, an historical pageant, was performed in Trinidad as part of the celebrations marking what turned out to be the short-lived West Indian Federation of 1958–62. There is a clever, complex use of folktale in *Ti-Jean and His Brothers*, with its cultural and racial affirmations, and in *Malcochon*, a Caribbean folk version of Kurosawa's film *Rashomon*, and a play which also shows Walcott's awareness of Brecht.

In 1959 Walcott started the Trinidad Theatre Workshop in Port of Spain where he tried to train beginners, after their office hours, into an ensemble. They practised improvisations and did not appear before the public for seven years until 1966 when, with Walcott as director, they performed Edward Albee's *The Zoo Story*, Genet's *The Blacks*, Wole Soyinka's *The Road*, Walcott's *The Sea at Dauphin*, and Trinidadian Eric Roach's *Belle Canto*. By the next year they started touring the Caribbean, Canada, and the United States. The major work of this period is *Dream on Monkey Mountain*. As in the earlier *Ti-Jean* Walcott is here concerned with the need to know oneself rather than simply relying on political and racial slogans.

After almost two decades of working with folk material, Walcott's energies began to take other directions. *The Joker of Seville* is an adaptation of Tirso de Molina's famous Don Juan play, *El Burlador de Sevilla*. In Walcott's powerful version, which is set in both the new and old worlds, Don Juan is suggestive of how amoral energies offer the possibility of liberation from social and sexual repression. If he brings the dangers of ostracism, punishment, and death, they are opposed by the positive benefits of love and living fully. Juan argues that he represents "freedom" and "nature", the liberation of women from loveless and stale marriages. He is an existentialist pagan hero living a brief intense life. *O Babylon!* is set in Jamaica; the scene moves between a Rastafarian beach community and a new luxury hotel. Its portrayal of how corrupt Babylon refuses to leave the Rastafarians alone in their pastoral holy life is resolved on a note of being true to one's self. The play is notable for Walcott's ability to transpose both Jamaican and Rastafarian speech into a more widely understandable stage English.

After the earlier exuberance, colour, and theatricality, *Remembrance* seems almost introverted, as Walcott examines the cultural and racial complications of the West Indies in the post-colonial period. Using smaller casts than in previous works, Walcott's later plays explore ideas through personal relations. The interest of the plays is more in their probing, questioning, and revealing of the relationship of the colonial past to the Caribbean present, and the difficulty of coming to terms with what has become a dominant tradition of black consciousness, than in the resolution of such themes. In *Remembrance*, Albert Perez Jordan, whose name recalls the mixed cultural heritage of the islands, represents the well-educated brown school-teachers whom Walcott has often praised as having made possible West Indian poetry and the leadership for independence by giving their students a first-class education. Jordan is also the father, paradoxically, of the new consciousness, which he rejects, represented by his son who died during the black-power rebellion of 1970, and who is now regarded as a hero of the people. *Pantomime* plays on various uses of its title, ranging from British musical hall to silent comedy, in examining the changing yet continuing relationship between England and black West Indians. While there is again a revealing of the past during the play (analogous to Walcott's increasing use of memory and autobiography in his poetry), the focus is more on conflict and dominance in the relations between Harry, a retired English actor who owns a guest-house in Tobago, and Jackson, his all-purpose aid. Harry acted in the British musical hall and Jackson was a Calypso singer. As the plot concerns a Robinson Crusoe show, which Harry wants to be performed for the entertainment of the hotel guests, there are analogies between the personal, the political, and the cultural (especially theatre). The issues revolve around who is to play Crusoe and who Friday and the significance of the Crusoe story.

Walcott's exploration and celebration of colonial history, and of the role of various groups that comprise the Caribbean heritage, continues in *The Last Carnival*, a radical rewriting of his earlier *In a Fine Castle*. The de la Fontaine family represents the European cultural heritage—Victor is a painter in the French tradition—which is ignored after independence. Agatha Willet represents the British political heritage of Trinidad. An English governess of working-class socialist background, she has taught the black maids and local children to demand their parliamentary rights. Contrasted with the de la Fontaine family, which has lost its power, is a black-power political movement which, alluding to actual events in Trinidad in 1970, has failed to set off a national revolt (against the black government). *The Last Carnival* criticizes inverted racism in multicultural Trinidad.

Some of the tensions in creating a Trinidadian theatre that includes white-black relationships are the subject of *A Branch of the Blue Nile*, the plot of which concerns the rehearsing of Shakespeare's *Antony and Cleopatra* by a fledgling West Indian theatre company. Besides a conflict between the white director and a black West Indian actor who has returned from New York, the play deals with the use and misuse of talent, especially in the arts where personal involvement is necessary. The rehearsal for the play is metaphoric of the life of a poet, and is applicable to West Indian society. *A Branch of the Blue Nile* also examines the applicability of European art and ambitions to West Indian society. The actors rehearse a comic play in dialect about which there are divided opinions. One actor argues that the director's attempt to make them into a better company by playing Shakespeare will lead to self-contempt.

Although the relationship of Caribbean popular culture to elite culture is often a theme of his work, Walcott's only published farce is *Beef, No Chicken*. While it is necessary to learn from, and meet, international standards, the sources of creativity are personal and local experience. A nostalgia for the past, for a simpler, less monied, still rural Caribbean society is the basis of *Beef, No Chicken*. Modernization americanizes and brings an increase of economic and spiritual corruption along with new wealth. The Caribbean is changing rapidly and the colonial culture, in which Walcott was raised, is disappearing and now needs to rediscover rather than scorn its past.

—Bruce King

See also *Volume 1* entry on *Dream on Monkey Mountain*.

WALKER, George F(rederick).   Born in Toronto, Ontario, Canada, 23 August 1947. Educated at Riverdale Collegiate, Toronto, to 1965. Married Susan Purdy in 1980; two daughters. Playwright-in-residence, 1971–74, and artistic director, 1978–79, Factory Theatre Lab, Toronto; resident playwright, New York Shakespeare Festival, 1981, and Cornell University, Ithaca, New York, 1982. Recipient of several awards including: Chalmers Award, 3 times; Governor-General's Award, 1984 and 1986.

Works

Collections

Three Plays (includes *Bagdad Saloon; Beyond Mozambique; Ramona and the White Slaves*).   1978.
The Power Plays (includes *Gossip; Filthy Rich; The Art of War*).   1984.
East End Plays (includes *Criminals in Love; Better Living; Beautiful City*).   1987.

Stage Works

The Prince of Naples (produced Factory Theatre Lab, Toronto, 1971).
Ambush at Tether's End (produced Factory Theatre Lab, Toronto, 1971).
Sacktown Rag (produced Factory Theatre Lab, Toronto, 1972).
Bagdad Saloon (produced Factory Theatre Lab, Toronto, 1973).
Demerit (produced Factory Theatre Lab, Toronto, 1974).
Beyond Mozambique (produced Factory Theatre Lab, Toronto, 1974).
Ramona and the White Slaves (produced Factory Theatre Lab, Toronto, 1976).   In *Three Plays*, 1978.
Gossip (produced Toronto Free Theatre, 1977).
Zastrozzi, the Master of Discipline (produced Toronto Free Theatre, 1977).   1977.
Filthy Rich (produced Toronto Free Theatre, 1979).   1981.
Rumours of Our Death, music by John Roby, lyrics by Walker and Roby (produced Factory Theatre Lab, Toronto, 1980).   In *Canadian Theatre Review*, Winter 1980.
Theatre of the Film Noir (produced Factory Theatre Lab, Toronto, 1981).   1981.
Science and Madness (produced Tarragon Theatre, Toronto, 1982).

The Art of War: An Adventure (produced Factory Theatre Lab, Toronto, 1983).
Criminals in Love (produced Factory Theatre Lab, Toronto, 1984).   1985.
Better Living (produced CentreStage, Toronto, 1986).   In *East End Plays*, 1987.
Beautiful City (produced Factory Theatre Lab, Toronto, 1987).   In *East End Plays*, 1987.
Nothing Sacred, from a novel by Turgenev (produced CentreStage, Toronto, 1988).
Love and Anger (produced Factory Theatre Lab, Toronto, 1989).
Escape from Happiness (produced Factory Theatre Lab, Toronto, 1992).
Tough! (produced Vancouver, British Columbia, 1993).

*

Television Plays

Sam, Grace, Doug, and the Dog, 1976; *Microdrama*, 1976; *Strike*, 1976; *Overlap*, 1977; *Capital Punishment*, 1977.

Radio Plays

The Private Man, 1973.

*

Criticism

Books:
Connie Brissenden (ed.), *Factory Lab Anthology*, Vancouver, 1974.

Articles:
Richard Horenblas, "Playnotes", in *Scene Changed*, Toronto, October 1975.
Denis W. Johnston, "George F. Walker: Liberal Idealism and the 'Power Plays'", in *Canadian Drama/L'Art dramatique canadien*, 10, 1984.
Chris Johnson, "George F. Walker directs George F. Walker", in *Theatre History in Canada/Histoire du théâtre au Canada*, 9, 1988.
George F. Walker, "Looking for the light: A Conversation with George F. Walker", in *Canadian Drama/L'Art dramatique canadien*, 14, 1988.
Stephen Haff, "'The Hell with Syntax': George F. Walker's *Love and Anger*", in *Theater Three*, 9, 1990.
Stephen Haff, "Slashing the Pleasantly Vague: George F. Walker and the Word", in *Yale/Theatre*, 1991.

* * *

George F. Walker is generally acknowledged as Canada's foremost author of stage comedy. His dark comedies defy easy classification, and he has been described as a "playwright-in-progress"; but for the most part, his work is non-linear, electronic in sensibility, and features larger-than-life characters given to hilarious pseudo-philosophical observations. Many of his plays take as their starting point a popular art form (the B-movie, the detective novel/movie, film-noir, popular romantic comedy) and through sophisticated, self-referring parody extend the range of the popular form to make possible discussion of Walker's obsessions — power politics, the nature of evil, impending chaos, the restorative power of laughter, obsession itself. All the plays are, to use Walker's term, "wonky", rapidly alternating between high and low comedy, and frenetic in their vigour, anxious pace, and rapid shifts in direction. Walker has been compared to Tom Stoppard for his acrobatic dialogue, and to Sam Shepard for his use of the pop-art icon. The playwright Walker most admires is Edward Bond, and the Canadian playwright's usual stand is anti-establishment, although Walker's political views cannot be neatly contained within the precepts of the traditional Left: his is a more pragmatic, working-class perspective.

Born in 1947 to working-class parents in a working-class neighbourhood, Toronto's East End, Walker left high-school before graduation, married at 18, and worked at various odd jobs while writing as yet unpublished poems and short stories, before turning to playwriting. His one-act play, *The Prince of Naples*, was produced by the Factory Theatre in 1971, the beginning of a long association with that theatre, one of four extremely influential "alternative" theatres established in Toronto in the early 1970's. He served here for some years as playwright-in-residence, and the theatre has premiered most of his plays. Walker's apprentice plays, *The Prince of Naples, Ambush at Tether's End, Sacktown Rag, Bagdad Saloon*, and the unpublished *Demerit* have all been described as derivative of the theatre of the absurd, but *Sacktown Rag*, a garish depiction of an East End childhood subtitled "a cartoon", and *Bagdad Saloon*, with its chaotic melange of figures from American high and low culture, myth, and history, can be seen as the beginning of Walker's artistic exploitation of 20th-century mass entertainment and of the development of a Canadian point of view, seldom concerned with Canadian subject matter, but Canadian in its peculiar stance, intimate with, but peripheral to, American centres of political and cultural power.

Beyond Mozambique shows Walker achieving firmer control of the theatrical medium, and speaking in his own, distinctively quirky voice. A mad Nazi scientist, his deformed assistant, his wife, who thinks she is Olga in Chekhov's *The Three Sisters*, a defrocked priest, an ex-RCMP corporal, and a porn-movie star play out their pop-art fantasies, oblivious to each other and to the surrounding jungle which finally and horrifically overwhelms them—a B-movie-jungle that brings grotesquely to the surface the imperialist and racist assumptions underlying those movies.

Critical response to Walker's early work was often hostile, and in 1975, discouraged, he left Toronto for a year, travelling and writing a naturalistic novel he did not like. His return to the Toronto theatre, *Ramona and the White Slaves*, a darkly compelling revelation of a Medea-like devouring mother/whore, again confused critics and audiences, and it was not until his two next plays, *Gossip* and *Zastrozzi, the Master of Discipline*, that Walker reached a broader audience, began to develop his reputation as a significant Canadian playwright.

Gossip introduces the reporter, Tyrone Power, whose investigation of a society murder uncovers a web of corruption and decadence so comically complex that the original question gets lost. In the other Power plays, *Filthy Rich* and *The Art of War*, the extent of corruption is extended ultimately to the level of federal governments and the international arms trade: Power's futile anger at the misuse of political power and his consequent isolation grow, demonstrating the small-"l" liberal's ultimate dilemma—his inability to resort to violent action against his violent enemies.

Zastrozzi is a loose adaptation of Percy Bysshe Shelley's novella, a swashbuckling gothic melodrama in which the eponym stalks an *artiste* ostensibly for personal revenge, but really because the master criminal hates Verezzi's smile and

what it stands for: amateurism, vagueness, beauty, the dawn of small-"l" liberalism. Victor, a pragmatic everyman with whom we are encouraged to identify, attempts to protect Verezzi, as Walker manipulates empathy in a sequence of moral ambushes, making Zastrozzi engaging one moment, terrifyingly cruel the next: "If you laugh at Zastrozzi's jokes, you can't dissociate yourself from his actions", says Walker. *Zastrozzi* has proven one of Walker's most popular plays, with productions across Canada and the United States, Australia, and Germany.

Other plays from the early 1980's were not as successful, although the pseudo-Ruritanian political fable *Rumours of Our Death* reached a new, young audience in a punk rock production at the Factory, and *Theatre of the Film Noir*, a mystery exposing the collapse of moral boundaries and identities in Paris immediately after its liberation, achieved something of a *succès de scandale* in the Toronto International Theatre Festival. Walker himself feels he repeats himself in *Science and Madness*, a reworking of the Frankenstein story.

Walker's career was reinvigorated by the "East End Plays" —*Criminals in Love* (1984, winner of that year's Governor General's ward); *Better Living* (first produced 1986, but actually begun in 1982 when Walker was playwright-in-residence at Cornell University), and *Beautiful City*. All three plays return to the recognizable and apparently more accessible locale of the East End, although they are all characterized by an increasing tendency to mix dramatic styles and conventions, with the "wonky" elements intruding surprisingly and mysteriously into the mundane world of Toronto kitchens and streets; all three end rather more optimistically than do Walker's earlier plays, offering not "hope", a tone Walker dislikes as false and overly sentimental, but the "possibility" for something better in the characters' lives, always qualified. All three continue the exploration of force, and of the question of morally justifiable force. All concern themselves with the politics of the family, a preoccupation increasingly evident as Walker's three children proceed through the stages of childhood, move towards the inheritance of a world for whose future Walker fears.

Criminals in Love places the fate/freewill debate in the context of high farce. Junior and his girlfriend try to avoid his "destiny", a life of crime arguably "determined" by the socio-economics of his East End background and the "inherited" proclivities of his petty-criminal father. They are assisted by William, a philosophical bum also obsessed by the implication of the "hanging shadow", but an absurd fate in the form of Wineva, Junior's bourgeois revolutionary aunt, takes the "young lovers doomed" through a series of progressively more illegal acts to the inevitable confrontation with the law. Junior and Gail also appear in *Better Living*, a study of a feminine family invaded by the masculine force of a man who may or may not be the father who deserted them years before, and who attempts to assert or reassert control by isolating his family through imposing a regime of survivalism and "consumer socialism", a strange inversion of the "romantic stranger" movie, darkened by strains of child abuse and incest. *Better Living* is evidently the play which most fascinates Walker, as he has returned to revise it, sometimes substantially, at least five times. *Beautiful City* puts three families in conflict—a mother-son team of unscrupulous real-estate developers; a witch/healer, who works in Bargain Harold's, and her petty-criminal in-laws; and two architect brothers. At stake is the architect's soul, and the concept of "community". The playwright's anger is unusually close to the surface of this play, as Walker pillories those he holds responsible for the creeping destruction of his home city, Toronto.

Nothing Sacred is a marked departure, an adaptation of Turgenev's novel, *Fathers and Sons*, commissioned for production at CentreStage, a large, mainstream theatre quite unlike the more alternative venues in which most of Walker's plays have premiered. The reasons for Walker's being attracted to the novel's central character, the nihilist Bazarov, are clear, and the adaptation emphasizes the novel's political dimension by placing off-stage peasants on stage: it is the peasants, not Turgenev's eternal reconciliation and life without end, that are given the last words. They are the ones who are left to try to make sense of Bazarov's enigmatic and interrupted death-bed prophecy, since, in perhaps the most radical and significant departure from the novel, Bazarov dies not from an accidental infection, but somewhat accidentally, and foolishly, in the duel with a much dandified Pavel.

Walker returns to the East End in *Love and Anger*. A corporate lawyer turns renegade after suffering a stroke, sets up a new practice in a run-down neighbourhood, and does battle on behalf of the underdogs—a black woman and a wildly inventive schizophrenic—against the civic powers, represented by his former law partner and the publisher of a right-wing tabloid newspaper (a thinly disguised *Toronto Sun*). While not included in the anthology *East End Plays*, *Love and Anger* resembles the earlier plays in the issues it raises, in its mixture of styles and scale, and, through the establishment of a new family of former strangers, in the focus on family.

Walker's recent play, *Escape from Happiness*, is evidently another East End play, incorporating characters previously seen in *Better Living* and *Beautiful City* and addressing, among other topics, the issue of police corruption; Walker says it concerns "an emotionally complex family and its ongoing struggle with an evasive, hostile, and complex world".

—Christopher Johnson

WALKER, John. See *Volume 1* entry on *The Factory Lad*.

WALSER, Martin. Born in Wasserburg, Germany, 24 March 1927. Educated at Gymnasium, Lindau, 1938–44; Philosophisch-Theologische Hochschule, Regensburg, 1946–48; University of Tübingen, 1948–51, Ph.D 1951. Served in the Deutsche Wehrmacht, 1944–45: captured by American forces. Married Käthe Jehle in 1950; four daughters. Radio and television director, Süddeutscher Rundfunk, Stuttgart, 1949–57; first-produced play, the musical *Kantaten auf der Kellertreppe*, staged 1953; Visiting Professor or Fellow, Middlebury College, Vermont, and University of Texas, Austin, 1973, Warwick University, Coventry, 1975, University of West Virginia, Morgantown, 1976, Dartmouth College, Hanover, New Hampshire, 1979, Princeton University, New Jersey, 1981, and University of California, Berkeley, 1983. Founder, with Rolf Hochhuth, Meersburg summer theatre festival. Recipient: Gruppe 47 Prize, 1955; Hesse Prize, 1957; Hauptmann Prize, 1962; Schiller Prize,

1965; Bodensee Prize, 1967; Schiller Prize, 1980; Heine Medal, 1981; Büchner Prize, 1981; Grand Federal Cross of Merit, 1987; Bavarian Academy Prize, 1990. Honorary doctorate: University of Constance, 1983.

Works

Collections

Gesammelte Stücke (includes *Der Abstecher; Eiche und Angora; Überlebensgross Herr Krott; Der schwarze Schwan; Die Zimmerschlacht; Wir werden schon noch handeln; Ein Kinderspiel*). 1971.
Stücke. 1987.

Stage Works

Kantaten auf der Kellertreppe, music by Otto Erich Schilling (produced Württembergisches Staatstheater, Stuttgart, 1953).
Der Abstecher (produced Kammerspiele, Munich, 1961). 1961; translated as *The Detour*, with *The Rabbit Race*, 1963.
Eiche und Angora: Eine deutsche Chronik (produced Schiller-Theater, Berlin, 1962). 1962; translated as *The Rabbit Race*, with *The Detour*, 1963.
Überlebensgross Herr Krott: Requiem für einen Unsterblichen (produced Württembergisches Staatstheater, Stuttgart, 1963). 1964.
Der schwarze Schwan (produced Württembergisches Staatstheater, Stuttgart, 1964). 1964.
Die Zimmerschlacht (produced Kammerspiele, Munich, 1967). 1967; translated as *Home Front*, in *The Contemporary German Theatre*, 1972.
Wir werden schon noch handeln (as *Der schwarze Flügel*, produced Akademie der Künste, Berlin, 1968). 1968.
Ein Kinderspiel (produced Württembergisches Staatstheater, Stuttgart, 1972). 1970.
Aus dem Wortschatz unserer Kämpfe (as *Ein reizender Abend*, produced Kasemattentheater, Luxembourg, 1972). 1971.
Der Menschenfreund, from a play by Christopher Hampton (produced Berlin, 1971). In *Theater Heute*, February 1971.
Die Wilden, from a play by Christopher Hampton (produced Schauspielhaus, Bochum, 1974). In *Theater Heute*, February 1974.
Das Sauspiel: Szenen aus dem 16. Jahrhundert (produced Deutsches Schauspielhaus, Hamburg, 1975). 1975.
In Goethes Hand: Szenen aus dem 19. Jahrhundert (produced Burgtheater, Vienna, 1982). 1982.
Die Ohrfeige (produced Staatstheater, Darmstadt, 1986). 1986.
Nero lässt grüssen; oder, Selbstportrait des Künstlers als Kaiser (produced Hämmerle-Fabrik, Meersburg, 1989). With *Alexander und Annette*, 1989.
Alexander und Annette. With *Nero lässt grüssen*, 1989.
Antigone, with Edgar Selge, from the play by Sophocles. 1989.

Radio Plays

Die Dummen, music by Otto-Erich Schilling, 1952; *Kantaten auf der Kellertreppe*, music by Otto-Erich Schilling, 1953; *Draussen*, 1953; *Ein grenzenloser Nachmittag*, 1955 (published in *Hörspielbuch*, 1955); *Der kleine Krieg*, 1956; *Angriff*

auf Perduz, 1956; *Aus dem Wortschatz unserer Kämpfe*, 1969; *Welche Farbe hat das Morgenrot*, 1969; *In Goethe's Hand*, 1982; *Ein fliehendes Pferd*. 1986; *Nero lässt grüssen*, 1986; *Säntis* (published 1986); *Die Verteidigung von Friedrichshafen* (published 1991); *Lindauer Pietà* (published 1991); *Das Gespenst von Gattnau*, 1988 (published 1991); *Hilfe kommt aus Bregenz*, 1988 (published 1991); *Zorn einer Göttin*, 1989 (published 1991).

Fiction

"Ein Flugzeug über dem Haus" und andere Geschichten. 1955.
Ehen in Philippsburg. 1957; translated as *The Gadarene Club*, 1960; as *Marriage in Philippsburg*, 1961.
Halbzeit. 1960.
Lügengeschichten 1964.
Das Einhorn. 1966; translated as *The Unicorn*, 1971.
Fiction. 1970.
Die Gallistl'sche Krankheit. 1972.
Der Sturz. 1973.
Jenseits der Liebe. 1976; translated as *Beyond All Love*, 1982.
Ein fliehendes Pferd. 1978; translated as *Runaway Horse*, 1980.
Seelenarbeit. 1979; translated as *The Inner Man*, 1985.
Das Schwanenhaus. 1980; translated as *The Swan Villa*, 1982.
Selected Stories. 1982.
Brief an Lord Liszt. 1982; translated as *Letter to Lord Liszt*, 1985.
Gesammelte Geschichten. 1983.
Brandung. 1985; translated as *Breakers*, 1987.
Dorle und Wolf. 1987; as *No Man's Land*, 1989.
Jagd. 1988.
Armer Nanosh, with Asta Scheib. 1989.
Die Verteidigung der Kindheit. 1991.

Verse

Der Grund zur Freude; 99 Sprüche zur Erbauung des Bewusstseins. 1978.

Other

Lese-Erfahrungen mit Proust. 1960.
Hölderlin auf dem Dachboden. 1960.
Beschreibung einer Form: Versuch über Franz Kafka. 1961.
Mitwirkung bei meinem Ende. 1962.
Erfahrungen und Lese-Erfahrungen. 1965.
Theater, Theater: Ein Bilderbuch des Theaters, with Karl Chargesheimer. 1967.
Heimatkunde. 1968.
Hölderlin zu entsprechen (address). 1970.
Wie und wovon handelt Literatur: Aufsätze und Reden. 1973.
Was zu bezweifeln war: Aufsätze und Reden 1958–1975, edited by Klaus Schuhmann. 1976.
Wer ist ein Schriftsteller? Aufsätze und Reden. 1978.
Heimatlob: Ein Bodensee-Buch, with André Ficus. 1978.
Die Würde am Werktag. 1980.
Heines Tränen: Essay. 1981.
Selbstbewusstsein und Ironie: Frankfurter Vorlesungen. 1981.
Versuch, ein Gefühl zu verstehen, und andere Versuche. 1982.
Liebeserklärungen. 1983.

Goethes Anziehungskraft. 1983.
Variationen eines Würgegriffs: Bericht über Trinidad und Tobago. 1985.
Messmers Gedanken. 1985.
Die Amerikareise: Versuch, ein Gefühl zu verstehen, with André Ficus. 1986.
Geständnis auf Raten. 1986.
Grimmige Märchen, with Ilse Aichinger, edited by Wolfgang Mieder. 1986.
Heilige Brocken: Aufsätze, Prosa, Gedichte. 1986.

Editor, *Die Alternative; oder, Brauchen wir eine neue Regierung?* 1961.
Editor, *Vorzeichen II: Neun neue deutsche Autoren*. 1963.
Editor, *Er: Prosa*, by Kafka. 1963.
Editor, *Die Würde am Werktag: Literatur der Arbeiter und Angestellten*. 1980.

*

Bibliographies

Heinz Saueressig and Thomas Beckermann, *Walser Bibliographie 1952–1970*, Düsseldorf, 1970.
Heinz Saueressig and Thomas Beckermann, "Bibliographie zu Martin Walser", in *Text and Kritik*, 1974.

Criticism

Books:
Thomas Beckermann (ed.), *Über Martin Walser*, Frankfurt, 1970.
Klaus Pezold, *Martin Walser: Seine schriftstellerische Entwicklung*, Berlin, 1971.
Joachim W. Preuss, *Martin Walser*, Berlin, 1972.
Heinz Ludwig Arnold (ed.), *Martin Walser*, Munich, 1974; revised edition, 1983.
Werner Brändle, *Die dramatische Stücke Martin Walsers: Variationen über das Elend des bürgerlichen Subjekts*, Stuttgart, 1978.
Anthony Waine, *Martin Walser: The Development as Dramatist 1950–1970*, Bonn, 1978.
Anthony Waine, *Martin Walser*, Munich, 1980.
Jurgen E. Schlunk and Armand E. Singer (eds.), *Martin Walser: International Perspectives*, New York, 1987.

Articles
K. S. Parkes, "Crisis and New Ways: The Recent Development of Martin Walser", in *New German Studies*, 1, 1973.
Gertrud B. Pickar, "Symbols as Structural Elements in the Dramatic Works of Martin Walser", in *Modern Languages*, 54, 1973.

* * *

Although he is primarily known as a prolific writer of prose fiction and has not published a play for almost a decade, Martin Walser's achievements as a playwright should not be overlooked. The conflict between his love for the stage and his interest in prose writing manifested itself early. Even, while he was writing a thesis on Kafka, he was most actively involved in the Tübingen student theatre.

Walser considers his literary work as a contribution to the change in society towards more democracy. By this he means that the chasm between society's promise and the reality of everyday life must be shown in art, with the expectation that, slowly, the gap may be bridged. However, he is either not naive enough or simply too honest to prescribe solutions. Literature, in his view, can only affect change by demonstrating the negative aspects of human existence under current conditions. His political engagement first developed as a reaction to various problems and provocations in the social and political reality of post-war West Germany. But Walser differs from other "engaged" writers of the intellectual scene by being fiercely independent in his opinions. This independence is illustrated by his short and stormy association with the Gruppe 47, but even more so by the political stances he has taken over the years. Walser has never hidden his sympathy for socialism and has been described as being positioned politically somewhere between the German Communist Party, the DKP (in 1971 he read a declaration at a Communist Party rally), and the social-democratic party, the SPD. Nevertheless he has refused to abide by any kind of conformism. In 1989 he gave his unequivocal endorsement to German unification, a stance which brought the wrath of the intellectual Left upon him.

Walser's activity as a dramatic writer began in the 1950's with radio plays. It was a time during which many German intellectuals, who had considered the collapse of Nazi Germany as a chance for a new beginning, saw the signs of a restoration of old social and economic structures. Consequently, Walser's early radio plays were existentialist parables and naturalistic social tragedies. When Walser finally moved to the stage he found a curious split in the West European theatre scene. Plays either followed the Brechtian, politically committed position *or* they emulated themes of the fashionable "theatre of the absurd" in the style of Beckett and Ionesco. While adopting some of Brecht's theatrical concepts and being influenced by absurd theatre, Walser quickly developed his own style. In the plays of the 1960's Walser dealt with two main topics: a kind of *Vergangenheitsbewältigung* (coming to terms with history) in his demonstration of the relationship between the German past and present, and interpersonal problems, exemplified within the institution of marriage. Both, of course, are topics which are prominent also in his novels. His "German chronicle", *Eiche und Angora* (*The Rabbit Race*) and *Der schwarze Schwan*, shows the emergence of former Nazis in the Federal Republic and demonstrates that patterns of behaviour and social structures have survived intact. The former Nazi functionary and his Schweik-like subordinate carry on in the same master-servant relationship as before. In the second play the son of a former concentration camp doctor realizes, in a confrontation in a mental asylum belonging to a former colleague of his father, that, under similar circumstances, he might have acted just like his father's generation did, a conclusion that drives him to suicide. *Überlebensgross Herr Krott*, finally, portrays the triumph of a type of capitalism in which Brechtian class-confrontation no longer provokes dramatic conflict. Walser seems resigned to this fact and his parable proves, as Anthony Waine has described, "the fallacy for Western society of two of Brecht's most cherished beliefs: the inexorable rise of the 'little man' and the imminent collapse of capitalist bourgeois society".

Private conflicts dominate in *Der Abstecher* (*The Detour*) and in *Zimmerschlacht* (*Home Front*), his most successful play. In *Das Sauspiel* Walser tries to capture the political situation after the 1968 student revolt by transferring the ensuing power play between conservative and progressive forces to the Nuremberg of the period following the failed peasant insurrection of 1526. The true theme of the play is the role of the intellectual who has no economic base and is forced to come to an accommodation with the powers of the day in order to survive. *In Goethes Hand* focuses on the relationship between the literary giant and Eckermann, his faithful secretary. Against this historical background Walser investigates the relationship between German classicism and German history, by confronting Goethe, the *Stabilitätsnarr* (stability freak), with the progressive ideas of Freiligrath and others. Since these last two plays are historical, it should be noted that Walser is not attempting to give an accurate account of historic events. Rather, by confronting the past with a modern point of view, he strives to further a better understanding of both the past and the present.

When Walser started writing for the stage in 1962 there existed practically no German drama that dealt with contemporary issues. By expanding on some of Brecht's concepts and by shifting the emphasis gradually away from society as the dominant force towards his protagonists, he made social forces appear to be less obtrusive but all the more insidious (as Waine has also commented). Thus, Walser created a new, more realistic theatre which demonstrated the interrelationship of society and the individual.

—Manfred K. Kremer

See also *Volume 1* entry on *Home Front*.

WAN Jiabao.   See **CAO Yu**.

WAN Chia-pao.   See **CAO Yu**.

WEBSTER, John.   Born, probably in London, in 1579 or 1580. Educated probably at Merchant Taylors' School, London, from c.1587; possibly entered the Middle Temple, London, 1598. Married Sarah Peniall c.1605; several children. Member, Merchant Taylors' Company; clerk of the parish of St. Andrews, Holborn; writer for Philip Henslowe, 1602. Died in or before 1634.

Works

Collections

Works (4 vols.), edited by F.L. Lucas.   1927; revised edition, 1966.
Three Plays (includes *The Duchess of Malfi; The White Devil; The Devil's Law Case*), edited by D.C. Gunby. 1972.
Selected Plays (includes *The White Devil; The Duchess of*

Malfi; The Devil's Law Case), edited by Jonathan Dollimore and Alan Sinfield. 1983.

Stage Works

Sir Thomas Wyatt, with Dekker and Thomas Heywood (produced by the Earl of Worcester's Men/Queen Anne's Men, Red Bull Theatre, London, 1602–07?). 1607.

Westward Ho, with Dekker (produced by the Children of St. Paul's, London, 1604). 1607.

Northward Ho, with Dekker (produced by the Children of St. Paul's, London, 1605). 1607.

The Devil's Law-Case (produced by Queen Anne's Men, Red Bull Theatre, London, 1610?). 1623

The White Devil (produced by Queen Anne's Men, Red Bull Theatre, London, 1612?). 1612.

The Duchess of Malfi (produced by the King's Men, Blackfriars Theatre, London, 1613?). 1623.

Anything for a Quiet Life, with Middleton (produced by the King's Men, Blackfriars Theatre, London, 1620–21). 1621.

Monuments of Honour (pageant; produced London, 1624). 1624

Appius and Virginia (produced 1624–34?). 1654.

A Cure for Cuckolds, with William Rowley (produced 1624–25?). 1661.

Verse

A Monumental Column, in *Three Elegies on the Most Lamented Death of Prince Henry*. 1613.

*

Bibliographies

William E. Manhaney, *John Webster: A Classified Bibliography*, Salzburg, 1973.

Samuel Schuman, *John Webster: A Reference Guide*, Boston, 1985.

Criticism

Books:

E.E. Stoll, *John Webster*, Boston, 1905.

F.E. Pierce, *The Collaboration of Webster and Dekker*, New York, 1919.

Rupert Brooke, *John Webster and the Elizabethan Drama*, New York, 1916.

Clifford Leech, *John Webster: A Critical Study*, London, 1951.

Travis Bogard, *The Tragic Satire of Webster*, Berkeley (California) and Los Angeles, 1955.

Robert W. Dent, *John Webster's Borrowing*, Berkeley, California, 1960.

Ian Scott Kilvert, *John Webster*, London, 1964.

Don D. Moore, *John Webster and His Critics 1617–1964*, Baton Rouge, Louisiana, 1966.

G.K. and S.K. Hunter, *John Webster: A Critical Anthology*, Harmondsworth, 1969.

Peter B. Murray, *A Study of Webster*, The Hague, 1969.

Brian Morris (ed.), *John Webster*, London, 1970.

Ralph Berry, *The Art of John Webster*, Oxford, 1972.

Richard Bodtke, *Tragedy and the Jacobean Temper: The Major Plays of John Webster*, Salzburg, 1972.

Robert P. Griffin, *John Webster: Politics and Tragedy*, Salzburg, 1972.

Sanford Sternlicht, *John Webster's Imagery and the Webster Canon*, Salzburg, 1972.

R.V. Holdsworth (ed.), *"The White Devil" and "The Duchess of Malfi": A Casebook*, London, 1975.

Floyd Lowell Goodwyn, *Image Pattern and Moral Vision in John Webster*, Salzburg, 1977.

Susan H. McLeod, *Dramatic Imagery in the Plays of John Webster*, Salzburg, 1977.

M.C. Bradbrook, *John Webster: Citizen and Dramatist*, London, 1980.

Jacqueline Pearson, *Tragedy and Tragicomedy in the Plays of John Webster*, Manchester, 1980.

Anthony E. Courtade, *The Structure of Webster's Plays*, Salzburg, 1980.

Don D. Moore (ed.), *John Webster: The Critical Heritage*, London, 1981.

Samuel Schuman, *"The Theatre of Fine Devices": The Visual Drama of John Webster*, Salzburg, 1982.

Lee Bliss, *The World's Perspective: John Webster and the Jacobean Drama*, Brighton, Sussex, 1983.

K.H. Ansari, *Imagery of John Webster's Plays*, Delhi, 1985.

Charles R. Forker, *Skull Beneath the Skin: The Achievement of John Webster*, Carbondale, Illinois, 1986.

Christina Luckyj, *A Winter's Snake: Dramatic Form in the Tragedies of John Webster*, Athens (Georgia) and London, 1989.

Margaret Loftus Ranald, *John Webster*, New York, 1989.

* * *

The position of John Webster as one of a tiny handful of English Renaissance dramatists who stand second only to Shakespeare is generally acknowledged; but the precise nature of his claim has been much disputed. His mannerist combinations of psychological naturalism yoked to ritualized convention have provoked controversy. Critics are divided on whether the horrors of the tragedies depict a moral void in which bleak existential courage is the only virtue, or the elaborate and elliptical structures imply moral norms that may be beyond the comprehension of the characters, yet are consistently affirmed for the audience. What is not in doubt, despite these ambiguities of response, is Webster's ability to reach to the tragic centre of human oppression and suffering.

The son of a prosperous City coach-building family (hence the hostile jibe by a contemporary at "crabbed Websterio, the playwright-cartwright"), Webster may have attended the Middle Temple, where he would have found the material for his frequent trial scenes and dramatic satire on lawyers, and come into contact with other young wits such as Marston and Ford.

He admired, among his contemporaries, not chiefly those who could achieve easy effects, but rather "the full and heightened style of Master Chapman, the laboured and understanding works of Master Jonson". Webster borrowed very widely from other writers, and polished and adapted small phrases and incidents until the finish of his plays resembles a tightly-packed mosaic. The verse is often irregular, sometimes reflecting violently abrupt psychology, elsewhere achieving sudden unexpected harmony. Few other writers present such startling or haunting thoughts or images embedded where least anticipated. And he adapted and re-used images in successive works. He also inserted "sentences" in the classical style, moral tags that imply a playwright's view alongside those of the characters who speak the lines. It was a slow and laborious method, as he confessed (and evident also in his prose and non-dramatic verse), and one wonders how he managed to collaborate as successfully as he evidently did with such prolific writers as Heywood, Dekker, Middleton, and Ford.

Most of his early and late work was in collaboration—the most usual working arrangement in the theatre of the time— and much of that was in comedy and tragicomedy. His reputation, however, now rests principally upon the unaided work of his middle period—the two great tragedies *The White Devil* and *The Duchess of Malfi*, and to a lesser extent the tragicomedy, *The Devil's Law-Case*. The profound pessimism of the two great tragedies is most clearly exemplified in the typical Websterian malcontent villains, Flamineo and Bosola. Both are blunt moralists, exposing the self-seeking hypocrisy and corruption of the high and powerful members of the court whose evil permeates the entire society. Both, however, are cynically engaged in the very evil they despise. In *The White Devil*, only by pimping for his sister, Vittoria, can Flamineo hope to achieve the preferment that might release him from his abject servility; and only by spying on and eventually murdering the Duchess is Bosola, in *The Duchess of Malfi*, awakened to the demands of justice, however ill-fated.

Victims and revengers alike die "in a mist", as uncertain of what follows death as they have been of the values by which to live. The major exception to this pattern is the Duchess, whose death on her knees is truly Christian. Both *The White Devil* and *The Duchess of Malfi* present powerful women whose defiance of social codes is heroic and whose deaths are tragic. But they are very different characters. Vittoria really is guilty, having instigated the murder of both her own husband and her lover's wife, but her magnificent spirit, especially in the great trial scene, wins our admiration and sympathy despite our moral judgement. The Duchess, on the other hand, is warm and vulnerable; her secret marriage seems risky rather than evil, and she grows in moral stature as her brothers' oppression intensifies. Despite his reputation for morbidity, reinforced by T.S. Eliot's view of him ("Webster was much possessed by death/And saw the skull beneath the skin"), Webster also displayed a lively humour that is more evident on the stage than the page. There is, for instance, the fierce sardonic wit of the central malcontent figures—but also the gentle domestic comedy of the Duchess wooing her steward, or teasing him before bed; the sexual sparring of Bosola with a bold courtesan; the satiric liveliness of the *Ho* plays; and the low comedy of Passarello in Webster's additions to Marston's *The Malcontent*.

All these varieties of comedy are found in his best-known tragicomedy, *The Devil's Law-Case*. Its elaborate plot of self-conscious artifice is replete with misdirected love, disguise, near-fatal duels, miraculous cures, and one of the finest comic trial-scenes in English drama. Webster acknowledged in a preface to the published play that "a great part of the grace" of such a play "lay in the action", for despite his literary stance, he was both knowledgeable about and well disposed to the theatre. Although he blamed the ignorance of the audience of the Red Bull playhouse for the failure of *The White Devil*, his praise of Richard Perkins is the first such tribute to an actor appended to a printed play; and the published text of *The Duchess of Malfi* includes the first-ever cast list, identifying the roles played by Burbage and the other actors of the King's Men at the Blackfriars and the Globe.

Furthermore, Webster's use of stage effects is both spectacular and structurally dynamic. The dumbshows, for instance in both the major tragedies (double murders in *The White Devil*, the banishment of the Duchess in *The Duchess of Malfi*), convey essential information in striking *coups de théâtre*. This is not mere showmanship, nor old-fashioned

dramaturgy, for the impact of the spectacle ensures a point of reference to which the rest of the play can constantly refer. Webster never loses sight of the moral pattern implied by the horrific events he portrays.

Webster's greatness (not always evident on the stage, if directors and designers have seized on simply the morbid, the grotesque, or the melodramatic) lies in a dramaturgy that uses both words and stage-images to present audiences with a shocking series of moral implications and perspectives. The intellectual pessimism of a stern moralist is combined with a densely packed imagery that can hook the imagination at the most unexpected moments, and with a deep emotional identification with the torments and despair of victims in a corrupt society. He has also, in Vittoria and the Duchess, written two of the finest roles for women in English drama.

—David Carnegie

See also *Volume 1* entries on *The Duchess of Malfi*; The White Devil.

———

WEDEKIND, (Benjamin) Frank(lin). Born in Hanover, Germany, 24 July 1864. Educated at Gemeindeknabenschule and Bezirksschule, Lenzburg; Kantonsschule, Aarau; universities of Lausanne, 1884, Munich, 1884–85, and Zurich, 1888. Married the actress Tilly Newes (died 1917); two daughters. Journalist and actor: performed in several of his own plays; first-produced play, *Kinder und Narren*, staged 1891; visited Paris, London, Zurich, Berlin; lived mainly in Munich. Died in Munich, 9 March 1918.

Works

Collections

Gesammelte Werke (9 vols.). 1912–21.
Tragedies of Sex (includes *Spring's Awakening; Earth-Spirit; Pandora's Box; Damnation!*), translated by S.A. Eliot. 1923.
Ausgewählte Werke, edited by Fritz Strich (5 vols.). 1924.
Five Tragedies of Sex (includes *Spring's Awakening; Earth Spirit; Pandora's Box; Death and the Devil*), translated by F. Fawcett and S. Spender. 1952.
Prosa, Dramen, Verse, edited by Hans-Georg Maier (2 vols.). 1954–60.
Werke, edited by Manfred Hahn (3 vols.). 1969.
Plays 1 (includes *Spring Awakening; Lulu*), translated by Edward Bond. 1993.

Stage Works

Der Schnellmaler (produced Kammerspiele, Munich, 1916). 1889.
Kinder und Narren. 1891; revised version, as *Die junge Welt* (produced Schauspielhaus, Munich, 1908), 1897.
Frühlings Erwachen (produced Kammerspiele des Deutschen Theater, Berlin, 1906). 1891; translated as *The Awakening of Spring*, 1909; as *Spring's Awakening*, in *Tragedies of Sex*, 1923; as *Spring Awakening*, 1980.
Lulu. 1913; original version, as *Die Büchse der Pandora*,

1988; translated as *The Lulu Plays*, 1967; as *Lulu*, 1971; individual plays:

Der Erdgeist (produced Theatersaal der Krystall-Palast, Leipzig, 1898). 1895; translated as *Earth Spirit*, 1914.

Die Büchse der Pandora (produced Intimes Theater, Nuremberg, 1904). In *Die Insel*, vol. 3 no. 2, 1902; revised versions, 1904, 1906, 1911; translated as *Pandora's Box*, 1914.

Der Kammersänger (produced Neues Theater, Berlin, 1899). 1899; translated as *Heart of a Tenor*, 1913; as *The Tenor*, 1927.

Der Liebestrank (produced Intimes Theater, Nuremberg, 1900). 1899.

Der Marquis von Keith (produced Residenztheater, Berlin, 1901). 1901; translated as *The Marquis of Keith*, in *From the Modern Repertoire 2*, edited by Eric Bentley, 1952: several subsequent translations under same title.

So ist das Leben (produced Schauspielhaus, Munich, 1902). 1902; as *König Nicolo* (produced Schauspielhaus, Leipzig, 1919), 1911; translated as *King Nicolo; or, Such is Life*, 1912.

Die Kaiserin von Neufundland (pantomime; produced by Elf Scharfrichter, Munich, 1902). In English, as *The Empress of Newfoundland*, in *Comparative Criticism Yearbook*, 1982.

Hidalla; oder, Sein und Haben (produced Schauspielhaus, Munich, 1905). 1904; as *Karl Hetmann, der Zwergriese*, in *Gesammelte Werke*, 1913.

Totentanz (produced Intimes Theater, Nuremberg, 1906).

1906; as *Tod und Teufel*, 1909; translated as *Death and Devil*, 1952.

Musik (produced Intimes Theater, Nuremberg, 1908). 1908.

Die Zensur (produced Schauspielhaus, Munich, 1909). 1908.

Oaha (produced Lustspielhaus, Munich, 1911). 1908; as *Till Eulenspiegel*, 1916.

Der Stein der Weisen (produced Die Kleine Bühne, Vienna, 1911). 1909.

In allen Sätteln gerecht. 1910.

Mit allen Hunden gehetzt. 1910.

In allen Wassern gewaschen. 1910.

Schloss Wetterstein (produced Pfauentheater, Zurich, 1917). 1912; translated as *Castle Wetterstein*, 1952.

Franziska (produced Kammerspiele, Munich, 1912). 1912.

Simson; oder, Scham und Eifersucht (produced Lessing-Theater, Berlin, 1914). 1914.

Bismarck (produced Deutsches Nationaltheater, Weimar, 1926). 1916.

Überfürchtenichts (produced Phantastisches Theater, Berlin, 1919). 1917.

Herakles (produced Prinz-Regenten-Theater, Munich, 1919). 1917.

Das Sonnenspektrum (produced Tribüne, Berlin, 1922). As *The Solar Spectrum*, in *Tulane Drama Review*, 4, 1959.

Ein Genussmensch, edited by Fritz Strich. 1924.

Fiction

Die Fürstin Russalka. 1897.

Mine-Haha; oder, Über die körperliche Erziehung der jungen Mädchen. 1901.

Feuerwerk. 1905.

Verse

Lautenlieder. 1920.

Ich hab meine Tante geschlachtet: Lautenlieder und "Simplizissimus"-Gedichte, edited by Manfred Hahn. 1967.

Memoirs and Letters

Gesammelte Briefe (2 vols.), edited by Fritz Strich. 1924.

Selbstdarstellung, edited by Willi Reich. 1954.

Der vermummte Herr: Briefe 1881–1917, edited by Wolfdietrich Rasch. 1967.

Die Tagebücher: Ein erotisches Leben, edited by Gerhard Hay. 1986; translated as *Diary of an Erotic Life*, 1990.

Other

Schauspielkunst: Ein Glossarium. 1910.

*

Frank Wedekind

Bibliographies

A. Kutscher, *Frank Wedekind* (3 vols.), Munich, 1922–31.

Criticism

Books:

P. Fechter, *Frank Wedekind*, Berlin, 1920.

M. Elster, *Frank Wedekind und seine besten Bühnenwerke*, Leipzig, 1922.

Gunter Seehaus, *Frank Wedekind und das Theater*, Munich, 1964.

Karl Ude, *Frank Wedekind*, Mühlacker, 1966.

Frederich Rothe, *Frank Wedekinds Dramen: Jugendstil und Lebensphilosophie*, Stuttgart, 1968.

Sol Gittleman, *Frank Wedekind*, New York, 1969.

Jütgen Sang, *Ideologiekritik und dichterische Form bei Wedekind, Sternheim, Kaiser*, Tokyo, 1972.

Gunter Seehaus, *Wedekind in Selbstzeugnissen und Bilddokumenten*, Reinbek, 1974.

Alan Best, *Frank Wedekind*, London, 1975.

Jürgen Friedmann, *Frank Wedekinds Dramen nach 1900: eine Untersuchung zur Erkenntnisfunktion seiner Dramen*, Stuttgart, 1975.

Hans J. Irmer, *Der Theaterdichter Frank Wedekind: Werk und Wirkung*, Berlin, 1975.

Josephine Schröder-Zebralla, *Frank Wedekinds religiöser Sensualismus: Die Vereinigung von Kirche und Freudenhaus?*, Frankfurt, 1985.

Hans Wagener, *Frank Wedekind*, Berlin, 1979.

Alfons Höger, *Hetärismus und bürgerliche Gesellschaft im Frühwerk Frank Wedekinds*, Copenhagen, 1981.

Thomas Medicus, *"Die grosse Liebe": Ökonomie und Konstruktion der Körper im Werk von Frank Wedekind*, Marburg, 1982.

Michael Meyer, *Theaterzensur in München 1900–1918: Geschichte und Entwicklung der polizeilichen Zensur und des Theaterzensurberates unter besonderer Berücksichtigung Frank Wedekinds*, Munich, 1982.

Mark Muylaert, *L'Image de la femme dans l'oeuvre de Frank Wedekind*, Stuttgart, 1985.

Elizabeth Boa, *The Sexual Circus: Wedekind's Theatre of Subversion*, Oxford, 1987.

Hartmut Vinçon, *Frank Wedekind*, Stuttgart, 1987.

Elke Austermühl and others (eds.), *Frank Wedekind: Texte, Interviews, Studien*, Darmstadt, 1989.

Peter N. Skrine, *Hauptmann, Wedekind and Schnitzler*, London, 1989 (Macmillan Modern Dramatists series).

Articles:

Hector Maclean, "Polarity and Synthesis of the Sexes in Frank Wedekind's Work", in *Australasian Universities Language and Literature Association: Proceedings and Papers of the [annual] Congress*, 1970.

Robert A. Jones, "Frank Wedekind: A German Dramatist of the Absurd", in *Comparative Drama*, 4, 1970–71.

Robert A. Burns, "Wedekind's Concept of Morality: An Extension of the Argument", in *New German Studies*, 3, 1975.

John L. Hibberd, "Frank Wedekind and the First World War", in *Modern Language Review*, 82, 1987.

*   *   *

Frank Wedekind owes his reputation to the fact that he wrote plays about sex. But he also used the stage for the specific purpose of making people think, and devised a whole range of theatrical and acting techniques in order to expose the conventional hypocrisies of pre-1914 society and show the tragicomic consequences of the images people project of themselves or which the world seeks to impose on them.

Frühlings Erwachen (*Spring Awakening*) was his first major creative work and made him notorious as a provocative and controversial playwright, especially when Max Reinhardt produced it at his newly opened experimental theatre in Berlin in 1906. It set the tone for Wedekind's mature drama, and aroused expectations which the playwright fulfilled in the two Lulu plays, *Erdgeist* (*Earth Spirit*) and *Die Büchse der Pandora* (*Pandora's Box*). The stage history of these plays is complicated by the problems concerning theatre censorship which they aroused in Germany and Austria (and elsewhere), but they have come to be widely recognized as among the most ambitious and innovatory masterpieces of early 20th-century theatre. On the printed page Wedekind's plays may look dull and flat, and their quality can be inconsistent. But productions have often demonstrated that a Wedekind text represents a blueprint for stage realization; only in competent, well rehearsed performance, with close attention to timing, lighting, and intonation, can a Wedekind play provide the full theatrical experience its author intended. This is especially true of the Lulu plays, which remain fascinatingly open to reinterpretation, and call for meticulous adherence to their performance style, a concept by which Wedekind set the greatest store. Drama such as his may be experimental, but it is expertly calculated for the professional stage, not intended for amateurs.

More engaging, and certainly less strenuous and depressing, is *Der Marquis von Keith*, a play which deserves its reputation as one of the finest comedies in the German language. Here Wedekind successfully revived the ancient comic *topos* of the braggart confidence-trickster in a manner that, and with results which, may remind English-speaking audiences of Shaw. Equally entertaining is the blend of slapstick and dire humour which makes *Der Kammersänger* (*The Tenor*) one of the most accessible of his socio-satirical plays: its portrayal of a harassed performing artist brings home the gulf between true creative genius and the ability to recreate art without necessarily sharing its aesthetic purpose.

With *Hidalla* (subtitled "The Stunted Giant"), Wedekind entered more thought-provoking ground by having as his protagonist an eccentric individual with a self-imposed mission to improve mankind by promoting the breeding of perfect human beings. Humorous utopianism bordering on satirical caricature is offset by increasingly disturbing, indeed prophetic, glimpses of a reality which was far distant in 1905, the year of its first performance in Munich, a city closely connected with Wedekind's career. It is significant that he was fond of acting, and liked to take the lead role in this remarkable piece of theatre.

The deceptions which society, people, and life itself play on the unsuspecting human being, whether on stage or in the audience, are equally present in *Musik*, a work which the author described as a "portrayal of contemporary manners" and which exposes the paradoxical nature of moral values, the inconsistency of human behaviour, and the double standards which prevail in the world as Wedekind knew it and never tired of presenting it.

Wedekind's work for the theatre may not always achieve the high quality that characterizes his unqualified masterpieces; the plays of his later period tend to lack the distinctive touch and biting edge of his earlier work. At its best, his unique juxtaposition of fantasy and realism, and his ability to combine the serious social and didactic concerns of problem drama and the anxieties of modern people with the extrovert theatricality of farce and burlesque suggest to lovers of the German stage that he is the true link between Büchner and Brecht, whereas to theatre-goers outside the German tradition his novel fusion of tragic and comic impulses brings him close to the best early cinema and places him in the front rank of early 20th-century theatrical pioneers.

—Peter Skrine

See also *Volume 1* entries on *The Lulu Plays*; *Spring's Awakening*.

———

WEISS, Peter (Ulrich). Born in Nowawes (now Neubabelsberg), near Berlin, Germany, 8 November 1916. Educated at Volksschule and Gymnasium, Bremen-Horn; private art lessons, 1932; Rackow-Handelsschule, Berlin, 1933; Polytechnic School of Photography, London, 1935; Kunstakademie, Prague, 1937–38; guest student, Art Academy, Stockholm, 1942. Married 1) Carlotta Dethorey in 1949, one son; 2) the artist and designer Gunilla Palmstierna in 1964; one son (adopted) and one daughter. Began career as writer and painter, later concentrating on his writing. Moved with his family to London, then to Czechoslovakia, sometimes working with his father while studying, 1935–38; first art exhibition, London, 1936; lived in Sweden, from 1939; draftsman and designer, for his father's textile business, 1939–42; exhibited his art at several exhibitions in Sweden, 1941–46; Berlin correspondent, *Stockholms-Tidningen*, 1947; first-produced play, *Der Turm*, staged 1950; joined the Swedish Experimental Film Studio, 1952; travelled to North Vietnam, 1968; travelled to writers' congress, Moscow, 1974; retrospective art exhibition toured Europe, 1976. Wrote in both Swedish and German. Recipient: Charles-Veillon Prize (with Italo Calvi), 1963; Lessing Prize, 1965; Heinrich Mann Prize, 1966; Carl Albert Anderson Prize (Stockholm), 1967; Thomas Dehler Prize, 1978; Cologne Literature Prize, 1981; Büchner Prize, 1982; Bremen Literature Prize, 1982; Swedish Theatre Critics Prize, 1982; De Nios Prize, 1982. Honorary doctorates: Wilhelm Peck University, Rostock, 1982; Philips University, Marburg, 1982. Died in Stockholm, 10 May 1982.

Works

Collections

Dramen (2 vols.).   1968.
Stücke (2 vols.).   1976–77.

Stage Works

Der Turm (broadcast, 1949; produced Studiobühne, Stockholm, 1950).   In *Dramen 1*, 1968; translated as *The Tower*, 1966.
Die Versicherung (produced Städtische Bühnen, Essen, 1971).   1952.
Ein Traumspiel, from a play by Strindberg.   1963.
Nacht mit Gästen (produced Schiller-Theater, Berlin, 1963).   1963; translated as *Night with Guests*, 1968.
Die Verfolgung und Ermordung Jean Paul Marats, dargestellt durch die Schauspielgruppe des Hospizes zu Charenton unter Anleitung des Herrn de Sade (produced Schiller-Theater, Berlin, 1964). 1964; translated as *The Persecution and Assassination of Jean-Paul Marat as Performed by the Inmates of the Asylum of Charenton*

under the Direction of the Marquis de Sade, 1965; play usually known by its abbreviated title, *Marat/Sade*, in both English and German.
Wie dem Herrn Mockinpott das Leiden ausgetrieben wird (produced Landestheater, Hanover, 1968).   In *Dramen 1*, 1968; translated as *How Mr. Mockinpott Was Cured of His Sufferings*, 1971.
Die Ermittlung: Oratorium in elf Gesängen (produced simultaneously, Freie Volksbühne, Berlin, and 15 other theatres, 1965).   1965; translated as *The Investigation: Oratorio in Eleven Cantos*, 1966.
Gesang vom lusitanischen Popanz (produced Scala Theatre, Stockholm, 1967; produced in German, Schaubühne am Halleschen Ufer, Berlin, 1967).   1968; translated as *Song of the Lusitanian Bogey*, in *Two Plays*, 1970.
Diskurs über die Vorgeschichte und den Verlauf des lang andauernden Befreiungskrieges in Viet Nam als Beispiel für die Notwendigkeit des bewaffneten Kampfes der Unterdrückten gegen ihre Unterdrücker, sowie über die Versuche der Vereinigten Staaten von Amerika die Grundlagen der Revolution zu vernichten (produced Städtische Bühnen, Frankfurt, 1968).   1967; translated as *Discourse on the Progress of the Prolonged War of Liberation in Viet Nam*, in *Two Plays*, 1970.
Trotzki im Exil (produced Schauspielhaus, Düsseldorf, 1970).   1970; translated as *Trotsky in Exile*, 1971.
Hölderlin (produced Württembergisches Staatstheater, Stuttgart, 1971).   1971.
Der Prozess, from the novel by Kafka (produced Bremen Theater, Bremen, 1975; revised version produced Volkstheater, Rostock, 1975).
Der neue Prozess (produced Dramaten, Stockholm, 1982).
Der Vater, from a play by Strindberg.   In *August Strindberg: Drei Stücke*, 1981.
Fräulein Julie, from a play by Strindberg.   In *August Strindberg: Drei Stücke*, 1981.

Radio Plays

Der Türm, 1949 (published in *Spectaculum: Texte Moderner Hörspiele*, 1963).

Fiction

Duellen (in Swedish).   1953.
Der Schatten des Körpers des Kutschers.   1960; translated as *The Shadow of the Coachman's Body*, in *Bodies and Shadows*, 1970.
Abschied von den Eltern.   1961; translated as *The Leavetaking*, 1962.
Fluchtpunkt.   1962; translated as *Vanishing Point*, 1966.
Das Gespräch der drei Gehenden.   1963; translated as *Conversations of the Three Wayfarers*, in *Bodies and Shadows*, 1970.
Exile (includes *The Leavetaking* and *Vanishing Point*).   1968.
Die Ästhetik des Widerstands (3 vols.).   1975–81.

Verse

Frän ö till ö [From Island to Island] (in Swedish).   1947.
De besegrade [The Vanquished] (in Swedish).   1948.

Other

Dokument I.   1949.
Avantgardefilm.   1956.

10 Arbeitspunkte eines Autors in der geteilten Welt.   1965.
*Notizen zum kulturellen Leben der Demokratischen Republik
    Viet Nam.*   1968; translated as *Notes on the Cultural Life
    of the Democratic Republic of Vietnam*, 1970.
*Das Material und die Modelle: Notizen zum dokumentaris-
    chen Theater.*   1968.
Rapporte (2 vols.).   1968–71.
*Aufsätze, Journale, Arbeitspunkte: Schriften zu Kunst und
    Literatur*, edited by Manfred Haiduk.   1979.
Der Maler Peter Weiss: Bilder, Zeichnungen, Collagen, Filme.
    1980.
Notizbücher 1971–1980 (2 vols).   1981.

*

Bibliographies

Thomas B. Schumann, "Bibliographie zu Peter Weiss", in
    Text und Kritik, 37, 1973.

Criticism

Books:
Henning Rischbieter, *Peter Weiss*, Velber, 1967.
Volker Canaris (ed.), *Über Peter Weiss*, Frankfurt, 1970.
Ian Hilton, *Peter Weiss: A Search for Affinities*, London,
    1970.
Reinhard Meier, *Peter Weiss: Von der Exilsituation zum poli-
    tischen Engagement*, Zurich, 1971.
Fred Müller, *Peter Weiss: Drei Dramen: Interpretationen* (on
    Marat/Sade; Die Ermittlung; Der Gesang . . .), Oldenburg,
    1973.
Gerd Weinreich, *Peter Weiss*, Frankfurt, 1974.
Wolfgang Kehn, *Von Dante zu Hölderlin: Traditionswahl und
    Engagement im Werk von Peter Weiss*, Cologne, 1975.
Otto F. Best, *Peter Weiss* (from the German), New York,
    1976.
Manfred Haiduk, *Der Dramatiker Peter Weiss* (second edi-
    tion), Berlin, 1977.
Christopher D. Innes, *Modern German Drama*, Cambridge,
    1979.
Ingeborg Schmitz, *Dokumentartheater bei Peter Weiss*,
    Frankfurt, 1981.
Heinrich Vormweg, *Peter Weiss*, Munich, 1981.
Rainer Gerlach, *Peter Weiss*, Frankfurt, 1984.
Roger Ellis, *Peter Weiss in Exile: A Critical Study of His
    Works*, Ann Arbor, Michigan, 1986.
Rainer Gerlach and Matthias Richter (eds.), *Peter Weiss im
    Gespräch*, Frankfurt, 1986.
Jochen Vogt, *Peter Weiss, mit Selbstzeugnissen und
    Bilddokumenten*, Reinbek, 1987.
Jürgen Garbers and others (eds.), *Ästhetik, Revolte,
    Widerstand: Zum literarischen Werk von Peter Weiss*, Jena,
    1990.
Åsa Eldh, *The Mother in the Work and Life of Peter Weiss*,
    New York, 1990.

*   *   *

Behind the plays of Peter Weiss lie early experiences of a
sense of homelessness and isolation. As a child he suffered
from what he saw as repressive but fragile bourgeois norms,
from which he could not liberate himself, and as a half-Jew,
he had to flee Germany for Sweden in 1934. Early autobiographical works reflect these problems, as do his early plays,
especially *Die Versicherung* (The Insurance Policy), which
uses images of violence and chaos to mock grotesquely the
bourgeois desire for security, and which ends with an anarchic
call for revolution. Other early works apply popular dramatic
forms, like the fairground or puppet-show, to reflect a nightmarish sense of insecurity.

If these works suggest Weiss's alienation, then later works
charted his search for some spiritual "home", and in *Marat/
Sade*, the work that established his international reputation,
he played out two possible responses to his sense that the
world was a madhouse: individualistic aristocratic disdain, or
social engagement. Weiss used the fiction of de Sade writing
and producing a play in 1808, in the lunatic asylum at
Charenton, about the assassination of Marat in 1793. The
play also involves a scripted discussion between Marat and de
Sade on the relative importance of self-liberation and social
liberation, and although the script is de Sade's, this discussion
remains inconclusive. However, Marat's position appears
weakened as he seems blind to irrational, instinctual forces,
something which leaves him exposed to assassination, and the
actual murder is committed with evident irrational sexual
gratification.

The style of *Marat/Sade* combines sensual experience and
intellectual stimulation to reflect this conflict, together with
heterogenous theatrical elements (singers and compere,
dance, pantomime, monologue, frequent violence and acts of
eroticism, etc), and also a demanding discussion on the
effects of the French Revolution and the value of social
engagement. Both inner play and discussion are frequently
interrupted by Coulmier, the warden of the asylum, who
praises the humanity of the post-Revolutionary period. The
work ends as the inmates, roused to a frenzy, call for revolution, Napoleon, and copulation, and Coulmier's brutal reaction reveals his true oppressive nature. Although this
discussion reflects Weiss's personal indecision, the real argument is directed against Coulmier, the representative of authority in 1808 and, by extension, in post-war Germany, who
abhors *any* form of liberation, whether de Sade's or Marat's
kind.

The argument is finely balanced. However, in 1965 Weiss
finally embraced socialism as his new "home" and altered the
play in favour of Marat's viewpoint. Subsequently, his next
three plays, written in as many years, reflected this new
security and they apply a theatrical discipline that subordinates means to political ends. Following the interest in documentary theatre of the early 1960's, *Die Ermittlung* (The
Investigation) presents a concentrated version of the
Frankfurt Auschwitz trials of 1963–65. It confronts witnesses
and guards in a stylised court-room, and arranges the material
into an "oratorio with 11 cantos", following the progress of
the inmates from arrival to crematorium. In theoretical
works, Weiss argued that such a montage of authentic material produces an exemplary model indicating general historical developments. In *Die Ermittlung*, he interpreted
Auschwitz as an extreme form of capitalism and suggested
that fascism continued in post-war Germany. His next two
plays, *Gesang vom lusitanischen Popanz* (*Song of the
Lusitanian Bogey*) and (in its abbreviated title) *Vietnam-
Diskurs* (Vietnam-Discourse) attempt even more direct political effect, using elements from agitprop and the political
revue to present the history of the Portuguese African colonies and of Vietnam. Both works parade a deliberate dramatic
unsubtlety and rely on ritual movement, pantomime, dance,
and acrobatics to compensate for the reduction of complicated historical developments to the essentially banal configuration of "oppressors versus oppressed".

The invasion of Czechoslovakia in 1968 and the collapse of

the German student movement shook Weiss's faith in revolutionary socialism, and his last two significant plays, *Hölderlin* and *Trotzki im Exil* (*Trotsky in Exile*), reflected his new scepticism. Like other plays from this period (especially Dorst's *Toller* and Salvatore's *Büchners Tod*) they use historical figures to present reflections on the failure of revolution. Weiss's two figures, an idealistic visionary and a practical revolutionary, fall victim to post–revolutionary developments. Hölderlin is destroyed by the disharmony between ideal and reality, between his dream of the French Revolution and its ultimate reality; Trotsky dies as a result of the distortions of revolutionary socialism under Stalin.

Both plays use dramatic devices from *Marat/Sade*. In *Hölderlin*, there is a "singer", a play within a play, and a chorus; but above all Weiss uses the same combination of diverse elements, with scenes of gratuitous violence and sexuality interrupting the on-going debate between Hölderlin and his caricatured establishment contemporaries. Hölderlin's own vision of revolutionary activity is presented in Empedokles, whom Weiss reinterprets fashionably as a Che Guevara-type guerilla. *Trotzki im Exil* is more subdued, and presents Trotsky's review of his life just before his murder. Weiss reduces theatrical effects here to the minimum necessary to present this (auto)biography, but as in *Marat/Sade* everything is relativised, since stage events reflect only Trotsky's viewpoint, and the resultant positive image remains open to question.

Like *Marat/Sade*, both plays view the results of revolution sceptically, but the individualist alternative proposed by de Sade is not resurrected, and instead Weiss emphasises new, hopeful perspectives for the future: Karl Marx praises Hölderlin for preserving revolutionary ideals and accepts his artistic contribution as valid; Trotsky's concluding "Testament" suggests (again fashionably) that students will bring about the victory of true socialism, which has failed so far only through human weakness. The conflict between mutually exclusive alternatives is replaced by the possibility of new harmonious developments, and even Trotsky's murder leaves this optimism intact.

Weiss's next play, *Der Prozess* (The Trial), was an unsuccessful adaptation of Kafka's novel, reworked with more success as *Der neue Prozess* (The New Trial). Effectively, however, after 1973 Weiss withdrew from playwriting and, until his unexpected death, devoted himself mainly to prose works, the novel *Ästhetik des Widerstands* (Aesthetics of Resistance) and his *Notizbücher 1960–1971* and *Notizbücher 1971–1980* (Notebooks 1960–1971 and 1971–1980).

—John P. Wieczoreck

See also *Volume 1* entries on *The Investigation*; *Marat/Sade*.

WERTENBAKER, (Lael Louisiana) Timberlake. Birth date uncertain. Educated at schools near St. Jean-de-Luz, France; attended university. Journalist in London and New York; teacher of French in Greece, 1 year. Resident writer, Shared Experience, 1983, and Royal Court Theatre, 1984–85, both London. Recipient: Olivier Award, 1989; John Whiting Award, 1989; London Theatre Critics Circle Award, 1991; Writers Guild Award, 1992.

Stage Works

This is No Place for Tallulah Bankhead (produced King's Head Theatre, London, 1978).
The Third (produced King's Head Theatre, London, 1980).
Second Sentence (produced Brighton, 1980).
Case to Answer (produced Soho Poly Theatre, London, 1980).
Breaking Through (produced by the Women's Theatre Group, London, 1980).
New Anatomies (produced Institute of Contemporary Arts, London, 1981). In *Plays Introduction*, 1984.
Inside Out (produced by RAT Theatre, Stoke-on-Trent, 1982).
Home Leave (produced Wolsey Theatre, Ipswich, Suffolk, 1982).
False Admissions, from a play by Marivaux (produced by Shared Experience, London, 1983).
Successful Strategies, from a play by Marivaux (produced by Shared Experience, London, 1983).
Abel's Sister, material by Yolande Bourcier (produced Royal Court Theatre Upstairs, London, 1984).
The Grace of Mary Traverse (produced Royal Court Theatre, London, 1985). 1985.
Mephisto, adaptation of the play by Ariane Mnouchkine, from a novel by Klaus Mann (produced Barbican Theatre, London, 1986).
Our Country's Good, from a novel by Thomas Keneally (produced Royal Court Theatre, London, 1988). 1988; revised edition, 1989.
The Love of the Nightingale (produced The Other Place, Stratford-on-Avon, 1988). 1989.
Pelleas and Melisande, from a play by Maeterlinck (produced London, 1989).
Three Birds Alighting on a Field (produced Royal Court Theatre, London, 1991). 1991.
The Thebans, from plays by Sophocles (produced Swan Theatre, Stratford-on-Avon, 1991). 1992.

Screenplays

The Children, from a novel by Edith Wharton.

Television Plays

Do Not Disturb, 1991.

Radio Plays

Léocadia, 1985 (published in *Five Plays*, by Anouilh, 1987); *La Dispute*, from the play by Marivaux, 1987; *Pelléas and Mélisande*, from a play by Maeterlinck.

*

Criticism

Articles:
David Ian Rabey, "Defining Difference: Timberlake Wertenbaker's Drama of Language, Dispossession and Discovery", in *Modern Drama*, 33, 1990.
Dominica Borg, "New Wave on a Fatal Shore: Timberlake Wertenbaker's *Our Country's Good*", in *Theater Three*, 9, 1990.
Ann Wilson, "*Our Country's Good*: Theatre, Colony and Nation in Wertenbaker's Adaptation of *The Playmaker*", in *Modern Drama*, 34, 1991.

* * *

Timberlake Wertenbaker's plays range from the domestic to the mythic within the duration of each single drama. In their social expositions, these plays identify dispossession and restriction of human potential. Moreover, they demonstrate how these phenomena are the deliberate and intrinsic effects of linguistic systems and terms of reference which define the rights of the individual in exclusively patriarchal terms. But the plays also depict how public experience, and individual communication of that experience, challenge these prescribed definitions. Wertenbaker identifies language as a means not simply of communicating, but of constituting knowledge, both of the self and of the world.

Wertenbaker characteristically locates the seeds of crisis in patriarchal-imperial impositions of definition. Her plays strive towards the discovery of respect for human variety. Her protagonists are in conflict with an authoritarianism specifically paternalistic in nature: it pretends provident fostering care whilst seeking to erode systematically any belief in a possible separateness and difference of individual interests. In Wertenbaker's plays, the ultimate threat of this governing system is to dispossess the individual of speech, and of the right to expression of selfhood. But hope resides in the defiant reactions of her marginalised protagonists.

Wertenbaker's early plays Case to Answer and Abel's Sister identify blind spots in self-righteous characters who find convenient relief in not deigning to translate their abstract social idealisms into practical dealings with individuals; indeed, they seem to feel their ideological postures permit them a degree of separation, aloof from human untidiness.

In New Anatomies, the protagonist Isabelle is dislocated from her childhood idyll with brother Antoine, and she travels through turn-of-the-century Europe and Algeria seeking to elude imposed definitions. Isabelle's intoxicated appetite for life and her naive tendency to see things in terms of inappropriate mythological parallels anticipate the heroine of The Grace of Mary Traverse. Mary's hunger for personal knowledge offends her father's sense of her social utility; so begins her odyssey of inquisitive transgression, in search of "grace", in individually reformulated definitions.

Wertenbaker's Our Country's Good, based on Thomas Keneally's 1987 novel The Playmaker, follows the fortunes of 18th-century convicts deported to Australia. The penal colony governors argue as to whether the convicts are capable of speaking literary language in order to perform a play; Wertenbaker celebrates their discovery of resources through this language. Her most complex play, The Love of the Nightingale, is a version of the Philomel myth, enquiring as to the essences of myth and love, through highlighting the activity of questioning. This drama seems the culmination of Wertenbaker's own questionings of the terms and conditions of using language, making moral judgements, and being human—all demonstrated to be irrevocably linked. Its exhortations of metaphorical insight and moral revaluation distinguish Wertenbaker as one of the most promising dramatists to emerge in the 1980's.

—David Ian Rabey

———

WESKER, Arnold. Born in Stepney, London, 24 May 1932. Educated at Upton House Technical School, Hackney, London, 1943–48; London School of Film Technique, 1955–56. Married Doreen Bicker in 1958; two sons and one daughter. Furniture-maker's apprentice and carpenter's mate, 1948; bookseller's assistant, 1949 and 1952; served in the Royal Air Force, 1950–52; plumber's mate, 1952; seed sorter on farm, 1953; kitchen porter, 1953–54; pastry cook, London and Paris, 1954–58; first-produced play, Chicken Soup with Barley, staged 1958; founder and director, Centre 42, 1961–70. Chairman of the British Centre, 1978–83, and president of the Playwrights Permanent Committee, 1981–83, International Theatre Institute. Recipient: Marzotto Prize, 1964; Best Foreign Play Award (Spain), 1979. Fellow, Royal Society of Literature, 1985. Litt.D: University of East Anglia, Norwich, 1989.

Works

Collections

The Wesker Trilogy (includes Chicken Soup with Barley; Roots; I'm Talking About Jerusalem).   1960.
The Plays of Arnold Wesker:
1. The Kitchen; Chips with Everything; The Wesker Trilogy. 1976; revised as The Wesker Trilogy (includes Chicken Soup with Barley; Roots; I'm Talking About Jerusalem), 1979.
2. The Four Seasons; Their Very Own and Golden City; Menace, The Friends; The Old Ones.   1977; revised as "The Kitchen" and Other Plays (includes revised version of The Four Seasons; The Kitchen; Their Very Own and Golden City), 1990.
3. Chips with Everything; The Friends; The Old Ones; Love Letters on Blue Paper.   1980; revised as "Chips with Everything" and Other Plays, 1990.
4. The Journalists; The Wedding Feast; The Merchant.   1980; revised as "Shylock" and Other Plays (includes The Journalists; The Wedding Feast; The Merchant as Shylock), 1990.
5. One Woman Plays (includes Yardsale; Whatever Happened to Betty Lemon?; Four Portraits of Mothers; The Mistress; Annie Wobbler).   1989.
6. "Lady Othello" and Other Plays (includes One More Ride on the Merry-Go-Round; Caritas; When God Wanted a Son; Bluey).   1990.

Stage Works

Chicken Soup with Barley (produced Belgrade Theatre, Coventry, 1958).   In New English Dramatists 1, 1959.
Roots (produced Belgrade Theatre, Coventry, 1959).   1959.
The Kitchen (produced Royal Court Theatre, London, 1959). In New English Dramatists 2, 1960; expanded version (produced Royal Court Theatre, London, 1961), 1961.
I'm Talking About Jerusalem (produced Belgrade Theatre, Coventry, 1960; revised version produced Royal Court Theatre, London, 1960).   1960.
Chips with Everything (produced Royal Court Theatre, London, 1962).   1962.
The Nottingham Captain: A Moral for Narrator, Voices and Orchestra, music by Wilfred Josephs and Dave Lee (produced Centre 42, Wellingborough, Northamptonshire, 1962).   In Six Sundays in January, 1971.
Their Very Own and Golden City (produced National Theatre of Belgium, Brussels, 1965; revised version produced Royal Court Theatre, London, 1966).   1966; further revised version (produced Aarhus, Denmark, 1974), in The Plays 2, 1977.

The Four Seasons (produced Belgrade Theatre, Coventry, 1965). 1966.
The Friends (produced Stadsteater, Stockholm, Sweden, 1970; produced in English, The Roundhouse, London, 1970). 1970.
The Old Ones (produced Royal Court Theatre, London, 1972). 1973; revised version, edited by Michael Marland, 1974.
The Wedding Feast, from a story by Dostoevsky (produced Stadsteater, Stockholm, Sweden, 1974; revised version produced Playhouse, Leeds, 1980). In *Plays and Players*, April–May 1977; in book form, in *The Journalists; The Wedding Feast; The Merchant*, 1980.
The Journalists (produced Criterion Theatre, Coventry, 1977). Polish version, in *Dialog*, 1974; English edition, 1975.
Love Letters on Blue Paper, from his story (televised 1976; produced Syracuse Stage, Syracuse, New York, 1977). 1978; revised version in *Plays 3*, 1980.
The Merchant (produced Dramaten, Stockholm, Sweden, 1976; revised version produced Plymouth Theatre, New York, 1977). German edition, 1977; in *The Journalists; The Wedding Feast; The Merchant*, 1980; revised version published separately, 1983; revised version, as *Shylock*, in *"Shylock" and Other Plays*, 1990.
Caritas (produced National Theatre, London, 1981). 1981.
Four Portraits—of Mothers (produced Mitzukoshi Theatre, Tokyo, Japan, 1982). In *One-Woman Plays*, 1989.
Annie Wobbler (as *Annie, Anna, Annabella*, broadcast 1983; as *Annie Wobbler*, produced Birmingham Repertory Theatre Studio, 1983). In *One-Woman Plays*, 1989.
Sullied Hand (produced Edinburgh Festival, 1984).
Yardsale (broadcast 1984; produced Edinburgh Festival, 1985). In *One-Woman Plays*, 1989.
One More Ride on the Merry-Go-Round (produced Phoenix Theatre, Leicester, 1985). In *"Lady Othello" and Other Plays*, 1990.
Whatever Happened to Betty Lemon (produced Paris, 1986). In *One-Woman Plays*, 1989.
Little Old Lady (for children; produced Sigtuna, Sweden, 1988). In *New Plays 1*, edited by Peter Terson, 1988.
Beorhtel's Hill (produced Basildon, Essex, 1989).
Shoeshine (for children). In *New Plays 3*, edited by Peter Terson, 1989.
The Mistress (produced Arezzo, Italy, 1991). In *One-Woman Plays*, 1989.
When God Wanted a Son (produced Jackson's Lane Theatre, London, 1989). In *"Lady Othello" and Other Plays*, 1990
Lady Othello. In *"Lady Othello" and Other Plays*, 1990.
Three Woman Talking (produced Evanston, Illinois, 1992).
Letter to a Daughter (produced Seoul, South Korea, 1992).

Screenplays

The Kitchen, 1961.

Television Plays

Menace, 1963 (published in *Six Sundays in January*, 1971); *Love Letters on Blue Paper*, from his story, 1976; *Diary of Jane Somers*, from a novel by Doris Lessing, 1989; *Letter to a Daughter*, 1992.

Radio Plays

Annie, Anna, Annabella, 1983; *Yardsale*, 1984; *Bluey*, 1985 (published in *"Lady Othello" and Other Plays*, 1990).

Fiction

Love Letters on Blue Paper. 1974.
Said the Old Man to the Young Man: Three Stories. 1978.
"Love Letters on Blue Paper" and Other Stories. 1980; revised edition, 1990.

Other

Labour and the Arts II; or, What, Then, is to Be Done? 1960.
The Modern Playwright; or, O Mother, is it Worth It? 1961.
Fears of Fragmentation (essays). 1970.
Six Sundays in January (miscellany). 1971.
Say Goodbye—You May Never See Them Again: Scenes from Two East-End Backgrounds, paintings by John Allin. 1974.
Words as Definitions of Experience. 1976.
Journey into Journalism. 1977.
Fatlips (for children). 1978.
The Journalists: A Triptych (includes the play *The Journalists*; *A Journal of the Writing of The Journalists*; and *Journey into Journalism*). 1979.
Distinctions (lectures, essays, journalism). 1985.

*

Criticism

Books:
Harold U. Ribalow, *Arnold Wesker*, New York, 1966.
Michael Marland (ed.), *Arnold Wesker*, London, 1970.
Ronald Hayman, *Arnold Wesker*, London, 1970; revised edition, New York, 1979.
Glenda Leeming and Simon Trussler, *The Plays of Arnold Wesker: An Assessment*, London, 1971.
Glenda Leeming, *Arnold Wesker*, London, 1972.
Glenda Leeming, *Wesker the Playwright*, London, 1983.
Glenda Leeming (compiler), *File on Wesker*, London, 1985.
Klaus and Valeska Lindemann, *Arnold Wesker*, Munich, 1985.
Robert Wilcher, *Understanding Arnold Wesker*, Columbia, South Carolina, 1991.

*   *   *

Arnold Wesker was one of the leading working-class playwrights to emerge in the 1950's through a state-subsidised theatre dedicated to the encouragement of new work. Although his writing was first seen and recommended to the Royal Court Theatre by Lindsay Anderson, and his pairing with John Dexter was to be one of the famous author-director combinations set up there, the management never seemed quite at ease with his drama. A certain reluctance to accept his work in Sloane Square marked the early stage history of *Chicken Soup with Barley, Roots*, and *Chips with Everything*, which were to prove his most popular plays. Corresponding to this (and possibly anticipated) was the virulent onslaught made by a section of the press on what it called "kitchen sink drama" (a term which also covered John Osborne's *Look Back in Anger*), which actually—and probably deliberately—threatened the whole enterprise. There has been some natural fading of the popularity of *Chips with Everything* as audiences with experience of conscript service in the armed forces have dwindled in the course of time, but the Wesker Trilogy (*Chicken Soup, Roots* and *I'm Talking about*

Jerusalem) has become ever more widely known and respected, transcending the limitations of the London-based middle- and upper-class intelligentsia.

Yet most of the later, various, and exciting plays of this dramatist have had little or no showing in London and, with the consequent absence of successful publicity, have suffered more from neglect throughout Britain than in Europe or the USA. Handled gingerly, as dangerous properties, *Love Letters on Blue Paper* and *Caritas* were briefly included in the repertoire of the National Theatre's small auditorium. Financial pressures on serious theatre in the 1980's were reflected in Wesker's concentration on the cheapest kind of play to produce, the one-character play. That these characters are women maintains a continuity with much of his earlier work in its provision of fine roles for actresses and viewing of society through a woman's eyes, free from the trammels of the propagandist piece.

The ideal of true community—Jerusalem, the Golden City—haunts his work. In *Chicken Soup with Barley* it appears as a child's-eye view of a heroic day when the East End Jewish population of London stopped Oswald Mosley's Blackshirts from marching through their part of London. The negative inverse appears in *The Journalists*, where the image of society is the degraded one of a mechanical process of production associated with distortions of humanity. Outside the theatre, Wesker's lecture entitled "O Mother is it Worth It?" (included in *Fears of Fragmentation*) led on to his involvement with the organisation known as Centre 42, set up to make the arts more generally accessible to all classes throughout the country, with the backing of the trade union movement. The most this directly achieved, before its slow death, was six festivals in working-class towns in 1962. Judged both presumptuous and ingenuous, he was attacked from both the political right and the left, especially in the person of John McGrath (whose fringe-style theatre company, 7:84, was to be exiled by the Arts Council from England to Scotland in the 1980's). McGrath accused him of adopting "the bourgeois concept of culture" and regarding it as "a product to be sold". With a mischievous irony, Wesker responded by presenting those festivals, in *The Friends*, under the guise of a chain of six trendy shops, offering beautiful, high quality goods.

The failure of a grand design is the theme of *Their Very Own and Golden City*, in which architecture provides the symbolism, and of *The Friends*. Yet as early as *Chicken Soup* and *I'm Talking about Jerusalem* the line of the plays' development was through human betrayal of ideals, failure, and disillusionment to the necessity of a persistence in faith. Even the strongly up-beat ending of *Roots* represents a struggle to recover from desolation. The halting celebration of the Jewish festival of Succoth by unbelievers, in *The Old Ones*, is a form of affirmation which corresponds to the playwright's detachment from offical creeds, political or mystical—a pledge of mutual caring among a group of human beings. A sense of the importance of ritual to human life makes its way into the dramatic form of the plays, modifying the naturalism which, in *Chicken Soup*, shows its affinity with O'Casey's tenement plays. In *Chips with Everything*, the imposed ritual of army discipline is converted into another kind of comradeship in the coal-stealing scene. Inspired by a Romanian dance of death, and reminiscent, in the published script, of the Shakespearian robing of Cleopatra, the corpse of the dead Esther is ritually decked out and "resurrected" at the end of *The Friends*, in one of Wesker's remarkable audacities. The use of Christian liturgy, in *Caritas*, is a major element, part of a complex of rituals which brings this play structurally closer to Eliot's *Murder in the Cathedral* than to anything else in modern English drama. They are comparable thematically, too.

The 14th-century setting of *Caritas* at first cloaks the way in which this play, written in 1980, engages with the first two plays of the Wesker Trilogy. It also marks the contrast between British society at the time when Wesker first emerged as a dramatist and Britain in the Thatcher decade. An episodic secular action, which traces the banding together of the peasants against feudal oppression to create a new society and the subsequent brutal suppression of their revolt, intersects with the spiritual tragedy of Christine, who longs to become a channel for divine love by living out her life as an anchoress; and then, when she petitions to be allowed back into the world, she is imprisoned until death by the feudal institution of the Church. Like Beatie Bryant, but in a century when religious mysticism was the only medium through which women's voices were publicly heard, Christine is seeking a finer quality of life; but whereas Beatie is liberated into thinking for herself, finding her own voice, Christine's clear voice is muffled, her spirit shut away, useless to the world of her day—though not to a modern audience.

The other play Wesker based on considerable historical research was *The Merchant*, a re-writing of *The Merchant of Venice* which frees it of conventional 16th-century anti-semitism. It conducts a close commentary on Shakespeare's play, but also stands on its own as a positive expression of Wesker's own values.

—Margery Morgan

See also *Volume 1* entries on *Caritas*; *The Wesker Trilogy*.

————

WHITE, Patrick (Victor Martindale). Born in London, 28 May 1912; taken to Australia, 1912. Educated at Tudor House, Moss Vale, and other schools in Australia, 1919–25; Cheltenham College, England, 1925–29; King's College, Cambridge, 1932–35, BA in modern languages 1935. Worked on sheep stations in New South Wales, 1929–32; lived in London and travelled in Europe, 1935–38; first plays produced 1935; travelled in the USA, 1939–40; served in the Royal Air Force, in Sudan and Egypt, 1940–45: intelligence officer; after 1945 lived with Manoly Lascaris in Castle Hill, New South Wales, and later Sydney. Recipient: Australian Literature Society Gold Medal, 1939; Miles Franklin Award, 1958, 1962; Nobel Prize for Literature, 1973. AC (Companion, Order of Australia), 1975 (returned 1976). Died in Sydney, 30 September 1990.

Works

Collections

Four Plays (includes *The Ham Funeral*; *The Season at Sarsaparilla*; *A Cheery Soul*; *Night on Bald Mountain*). 1965; as *Collected Plays 1*, 1985.

Stage Works

Bread and Butter Women (produced Bryant's Playhouse, Sydney, 1935).

Patrick White (1964).

The School for Friends (produced Bryant's Playhouse, Sydney, 1935).
Return to Abyssinia (produced Bolton Theatre, London, 1947).
The Ham Funeral (produced by University Theatre Guild, Adelaide, 1961). In *Four Plays*, 1965.
The Season at Sarsaparilla (produced Union Theatre, University of Adelaide, 1962). In *Four Plays*, 1965.
A Cheery Soul, from his own story (produced Union Theatre, University of Melbourne, 1963). In *Four Plays*, 1965.
Night on Bald Mountain (produced by University Theatre Guild, Adelaide, 1964). In *Four Plays*, 1965.
Big Toys (produced Parade Theatre, Sydney, 1977). 1978.
Signal Driver: A Morality Play for the Times (produced Playhouse, Adelaide, 1982). 1983.
Netherwood (produced Playhouse, Adelaide, 1983). 1983.
Shepherd on the Rocks (produced Playhouse, Adelaide, 1987).

Screenplays

The Night the Prowler, 1979 (published 1977).

Fiction

Happy Valley. 1939.
The Living and the Dead. 1941.
The Aunt's Story. 1948.
The Tree of Man. 1955.

Voss. 1957.
Riders in the Chariot. 1961.
The Burnt Ones (stories). 1964.
The Solid Mandala. 1966.
The Vivisector. 1970.
The Eye of the Storm. 1973.
The Cockatoos: Shorter Novels and Stories. 1974.
A Fringe of Leaves. 1976.
The Twyborn Affair. 1979.
"A Cheery Soul" and Other Stories. 1983.
Memoirs of Many in One. 1986.
Three Uneasy Pieces. 1988.

Verse

Thirteen Poems. 1930(?).
"The Ploughman" and Other Poems. 1935.
Habitable Places: Poems New and Selected. 1988.

Memoirs and Letters

Flaws in the Glass: A Self-Portrait. 1981.

Other

White Speaks. 1989.

*

Criticism

Books:
John A. Weigel, *Patrick White*, Boston, 1983.
May B. Akerholt, *Patrick White*, Amsterdam, 1988.
John Colmer, *Patrick White*, London, 1984.
Peter Wolfe (ed.), *Critical Essays on Patrick White*, Boston, 1990.

Articles:
May B. Akerholt, "Female Figures in the Plays of Dorothy Hewett and Patrick White", in *Westerly*, vol.29 no.1, 1984.
J. Barbour, "Cheery Souls and Lost Souls: The Outsiders in Patrick White's Plays", in *Southerly*. vol.42 no.2, 1982.

* * *

Patrick White's important contributions to Australian drama are overshadowed by his position as Australia's greatest living novelist and winner of the Nobel Prize. But he was a pioneering playwright in successfully using in Australian drama non-realist devices derived from symbolism, expression and surrealism. Earlier playwrights had made such experiments, but the plays were either short, unproduced, or ineffective, never reaching sizeable audiences. White's breakthrough in the 1960's was perversely aided by philistine objections to his style and subject-matter —most notably in the instance of *The Ham Funeral* being denied an official staging at the 1960 Adelaide Festival because of a minority reader's report which found it "unappetizing fare". It also came at an opportune time, when Australian drama was still relying with diminishing returns on the naturalistic techniques of the 1950's, best exemplified by Ray Lawler's *Summer of the Seventeenth Doll*. Critics at the time noted White's contributions, especially in the direction of a more stylized language removed from the vernacular; but it was only when two of the first plays were restaged in the late

1970's by director Jim Sharman that the effectiveness of White's theatrical stylization beyond mere "heightened language" was proved.

The Ham Funeral is an allegory of maturation set in a London boarding house in the early years of the century. The symbolist stylization is anchored in the spatial organization of the stage—basement kitchen of earthy practicality, upper bedrooms representing introverted aestheticism, and a no-man's land of staircases connecting them. At the beginning, the nascent artist, known only as the Young Man, lives in the realms of imagination, idealism, and non-engagement. The earthy landlady Alma Lusty, after the sudden death of her husband, provides the catalyst for his maturity and his engagement with everyday experience. The play is given distinction by several telling theatrical devices, such as the mirror-movement in the upper rooms whereby an imagined female tenant serves as the Young Man's *anima*, the powerful import of several objects as symbols, and the careful calibration of the levels of language and theatrical style according to the subject matter of different scenes; White heightens these to near-expressionism and lowers them to naturalism where appropriate.

In *The Season at Sarsaparilla*—the mythical Sydney suburb which is an analogue for Castle Hill, in which the author lived for some years—the locale and observation become specifically Australian and the style keyed more to expressionism. The spatial segmentation is, this time, horizontal rather than vertical: three identical box-townhouse kitchens are observed from the rear, inhabited by three contrasting families exemplifying different social strata. Once again there is a young male "artist figure" undergoing a "rite of passage" looking for a way out, but this time less sympathetically than in *The Ham Funeral*, and he also provides commentary which serves as linkage between the three households. The predominant expressionism, at least initially, is defined through the space, but reiterated through other devices—the chorus-device, the use of unified and divided inner soliloquy, and a strobe effect, the "razzle-dazzle of time", which accompanies speeded-up motion. All these elements serve to emphasize the cartoon-like nature of most of the characters early on, but later White changes his strategy, seemingly in spite of himself and, finding sympathy for the characters, rounds them out. This is especially true of the central Alma Lusty-like Nola Boyle—she cuckolds her husband with his visiting "mate" from World-War-II days, but regrets it, and is reconciled with him in a general movement of the play towards reconciliation. There is an underlining of a belief that: "Kindness. Affection. That's all that really matters".

The most stylistically adventurous of the first group of plays is *A Cheery Soul*, which was regarded as a failure after its first production in a theatre ill-equipped to realize its spatial and stylistic demands. Here White evolved his form, which plunges deeply into subjective surrealism, in his leading character Miss Docker, a domineering but pitiable spinster. She fails, with her hectoring literal aggression, to conquer the world of a loving couple she first boards with, a world stylistically characterized by near-naturalism; and she fails to break the solidarity of ladies in the Old Peoples' Home, characterized by symbolist scrims and choruses and gently lit memory-tableaux. But the world of the doubting Reverend Wakeman and his apathetic congregation is more destructively invaded by Miss Docker's mind and will, and becomes splintered by pools of blackness, disembodied voices, and visions of frightening apocalypse. This surreal vision has a threatening malignancy which, once she has set it in motion, seems to proliferate independent of her personality. At the end, Wakeman catatonically collapses in front of his congregation,

and Docker returns to the Old People's Home, a pathetic exemplar of the "destructive power of good".

The later group of plays (as well as the screenplay *The Night the Prowler*), which White wrote in the wake of Jim Sharman's successful revival of *The Season at Sarsaparilla* in 1976, do not have the same historical importance to Australian drama, or quite the same vitality, as these earlier three. White has a tendency to indicate their meanings too obviously. *Big Toys* is a cautionary fable about the mis-uses of privilege in Australia; it deals with the corruption of a working-class Union leader by a homosexual lawyer and his ex-model *arriviste* wife, using the "big toys" of materialism of the title. In *Signal Driver*, a couple is seen drawing closer over a 50-year period as they wait in a trambus shed. The near-naturalism of these encounters is spiked with the music-hall expressionism of two commentators, "super-deros" unseen by the couple, who place their failure to "catch the bus" in the larger picture, linking it to the natural cycles of life and connecting it to their loyalty to each other, and its obverse side—a banal refusal to change and develop. *Netherwood* is set in an experimental "halfway house" for the mentally disturbed, and the two leading characters are their caretakers, sublimating their sexuality into idealistic do-goodism. *Netherwood* unveils an exciting array of non-realist devices new to White, and more characteristic of the "alternative" theatre of the early 1970's, including extensive use of the auditorium space, of voice-over, and of fantasy-scenes and cross-gender "transformations" to reveal the caretakers' inner frustrations and yearnings. But in *Netherwood* there is again the clash between allegorical point-making and naturalistic believability that disfigures *Night on Bald Mountain*, the final play of the first group, especially in the strained "shoot-out" that ends the play in an apocalyptic bloodbath. In all these last plays, White seemed to reverse his earlier, more hopeful, thematic movement towards accommodation and reconciliation.

—Dennis Carroll

See also *Volume 1* entry on *The Season at Sarsaparilla*.

WHITING, John (Robert). Born in Salisbury, Wiltshire, England, 15 November 1917. Educated at Taunton School, Somerset, 1930–34; Royal Academy of Dramatic Art, London, 1935–37. Married Asthore Lloyd Mawson in 1940; two sons and two daughters. Actor in repertory, and in London, 1936–38, 1944–52; served in the Royal Artillery, 1939–44: lieutenant; first radio play produced 1946; first-produced stage play, *A Penny for a Song*, performed 1951; drama critic, *London Magazine*, 1961–62. Member, Arts Council Drama Panel, 1955–63. Recipient: Festival of Britain Award, 1951. John Whiting Award for promising young playwrights established, 1965. Died in London, 16 June 1963.

Works

Collections

Plays (includes *Saint's Day; A Penny for a Song; Marching Song*). 1957.
Collected Plays (2 vols.), edited by Ronald Hayman.   1969.

Stage Works

A Penny for a Song (produced Theatre Royal, Haymarket, London, 1951). In *Plays*, 1957; revised version (produced Aldwych Theatre, London, 1962), 1964.
Saint's Day (produced Arts Theatre, London, 1951). In *Plays*, 1957.
Marching Song (produced St. Martin's Theatre, London, 1954). 1954.
Sacrifice to the Wind, from a play by André Obey (televised 1954; produced Arts Theatre, London, 1955). In *Plays for Radio and Television*, edited by Nigel Samuels, 1959.
The Gates of Summer (produced New Theatre, Oxford, 1956). In *Collected Plays 2*, 1969.
Madame de . . ., from a play by Anouilh (produced Arts Theatre, London, 1959). With *Traveller Without Luggage*, 1959.
Traveller Without Luggage, from a play by Anouilh (produced Arts Theatre, London, 1959). With *Madame de . . .*, 1959.
The Devils, from an account by Aldous Huxley (produced Aldwych Theatre, London, 1961). 1961.
No Why (produced Aldwych Theatre, London, 1964). 1961.
Conditions of Agreement (as *The Conditions of Agreement*, produced Old Vic Theatre, Bristol, 1965). In *Collected Plays 1*, 1969.
The Nomads (produced London, 1965). In *Collected Plays 2*, 1969.
Paul Southman from the radio play (produced London, 1965).
No More A-Roving (broadcast 1979; produced Orange Tree Theatre, Richmond, Surrey, 1987). 1975.

Screenplays

The Ship That Died of Shame, with Michael Relph and Basil Dearden, 1955; *The Good Companions*, with T.J. Morrison and J.L. Hodgson, 1957; *The Captain's Table*, with Bryan Forbes and Nicholas Phipps, 1959; *Young Cassidy*, 1965.

Television Plays

Sacrifice to the Wind, 1954 (published in *Plays for Radio and Television*, edited by Nigel Samuels, 1959); *A Walk in the Desert*, 1960 (published in *Collected Plays 2*, 1969).

Radio Plays

Paul Southman, 1946; *Eye Witness*, 1949; *The Stairway*, 1949; *Love's Old Sweet Song*, 1950; *No More A-Roving*, 1979.

Other

John Whiting on Theatre. 1966.
"The Art of the Dramatist" and Other Pieces, edited by Ronald Hayman. 1970.

*

Criticism

Books:
Ronald Hayman, *John Whiting*, London 1969.
Simon Trussler, *The Plays of John Whiting: An Assessment*, London 1972.
Eric Salmon, *The Dark Journey: John Whiting as Dramatist*, London 1979.

Gabrielle Robinson, *A Private Mythology: The Manuscripts and Plays of John Whiting*, Lewisburg, Pennsylvania, 1989.

* * *

Although a writer whose talents as a dramatist and theatre critic were admired in the 1950's and 1960's, John Whiting and his work receive little attention today, and even the best of his plays are now infrequently performed. Yet his current neglect cannot be accounted for solely in terms of critical and theatrical fashion, for he was, and remains, something of a maverick figure. From the first, his plays ran against both the mainstream and avant-garde tastes of his time. Although they were seen by many in the early and mid-1950's to presage the resurgence of a drama more serious in philosophical and social import, and more technically demanding and innovative than the prevailing quasi-poetic verse and bourgeois drawing-room drama, Whiting's work never managed to establish itself any more firmly when a concerted reaction against the theatrical *status quo* occurred after the Royal Court production of John Osborne's *Look Back in Anger* in 1956.

The most successful with reviewers and theatre audiences alike was his play *The Devils*, an intelligent adaptation, in a somewhat Brechtian manner, of Aldous Huxley's *The Devils of Loudun*. Commissioned by Peter Hall for the Royal Shakespeare Company, it concerns personal corruption, political manoeuvring, and self-destruction against a historical background illustrating the effects of demonic possession in a 17th-century French nunnery. But it is an earlier piece, *Marching Song*, completed in 1952 and first performed and published in 1954, that is now considered his best play, although it was widely thought at the time to break the cardinal rule that a work so public must "communicate". The questions it raises today, however, are less to do with accessibility than with the extent of its verbal and thematic adequacy, and the persuasiveness of its action and characters. Whiting appears to have sought an austerity of form and language by eliminating all suggestion of melodrama, and by stripping dialogue of verbal exuberance and the casual "fillers" characteristic of idiomatic speech. This economy and eschewing of the expected—Whiting himself characterised *Marching Song* as "an anti-theatrical play"—unfortunately results in a loss of dramatic excitement, and a reduction of much of the dialogue to overly portentous generalisations about life, love, solitude, destruction, and the nature of the military man. If he was reacting against the English stage-drawing-room world of what the critic Kenneth Tynan dubbed "Loamshire", Whiting came dangerously close to retreating into that favourite post-war setting for reflective, quasi-philosophical Continental drama (like that of, say, Ugo Betti)—Centraleuropia.

Rupert Foster, a former army general released after seven years of imprisonment, returns to the house of his wealthy former mistress in the hills above an unspecified European city, and there meets up with an odd collection of characters, which includes a faded, bouncy American film director (Harry Lancaster), and a local girl (Dido Morgen), a drifter picked up by Lancaster in a bar on the promise that he put her into his next film. He finds, too, that the democratic government now in power has released him only as a prelude to his standing trial as a scapegoat for past national military defeat. After flirting with defiance under the influence of the life-affirming Dido, he opts for suicide, philosophically embracing his own disposition to self-destruction. Rather too much in this situation lacks persuasion and seems overly contrived: the characters are more ciphers than credible stage figures, their juxtaposition often seems rather forced, with exits and entrances too obviously orchestrated to set up discussion, and the "war crime" committed by Forster sounds more like fiction than real life. The conclusion, with Forster's mistress persuading Dido to stay with her in the house and teach her resignation, is sentimental and overly neat. Notwithstanding its commendable ambitiousness of subject and approach, the play leaves one with the impression of a writer reaching for significant issues, but failing to dramatise them adequately.

Disintegration and destruction, and the sudden arbitrary incursion of violence into lives, are also features of the earlier, and highly controversial, *Saint's Day*, which first brought Whiting to national notice. Awarded the first prize in an Arts Council competition, held in conjunction with the 1951 Festival of Britain, it bewildered most critics and audiences, its seemingly wilful obscurities fuelling a hostility already aroused by the very notion of the Council setting itself up—albeit through a panel of judges (Alec Clunes, Christopher Fry, and Peter Ustinov)—as an arbiter of theatrical excellence. In fact, the judges were not so very misguided. Completed in 1947, and later revised for the Festival competition, it is a young man's play—loose, wordy, and ill-focused—yet for all that has a stage energy and verbal buoyancy wanting in *Marching Song*, and it still comes across as a powerful study of a disintegrating way of life. It is set in the house of a highly respected octogenarian writer, Paul Southman, a still much-admired grand old man of letters who has long been marginalised by the publishing industry for daring to publish a pamphlet entitled "The Abolition of Print". The play provides a sprawling elusive image of the condition of things, more particularly perhaps of Britain, embracing by implication the whole state of culture—not just of the arts, but of political, social, and personal relations. Southman lives in a retirement that is a kind of exile, along with his grand-daughter, Stella, who dreams of the family's financial, and her grandfather's artistic, resurrection. Sharing this retreat with them are Stella's rather feckless husband, Charles, an artist whose work has lost direction, and an independent-minded and oddly threatening house-servant, John Winter. At the play's opening, the family is awaiting the arrival of a young poet, Robert Procathren, calling in order to take the old writer to a London literary dinner, and Winter is despatched to get food from the local villagers. The villagers are hostile to Southman's household, partly for its inability to settle its bills, partly because it represents something different and non-conformist. Southman seems to revel in this hostility, ever disposed to thrive on embattlement, whether with publishers, the literary world, or the local community. When renegade soldiers threaten the village he sides with them, and the violence that eventually erupts leads to the accidental death of his grand-daughter, and the destruction of the village and its church. The young poet, Robert, takes over, and Southman and Charles are condemned to death.

Saint's Day, for all the surface familiarity of its setting and character depiction, is essentially non-naturalistic, and critics have rightly seen in it presages of the later work of Pinter, and even Bond. It is a wordy piece, as loose and rambling in its language as in its structure. But although the dialogue is rarely direct and idiomatic, it has a fluency and naturalness which make it engaging and, much more than *Marching Song*, the play establishes a firm relationship between character and speech. What never adequately cohere, however, are the complex social, political, and spiritual themes. Critics have frequently remarked on Whiting's indebtedness to the verse plays of T.S. Eliot and Christopher Fry, but where their engagement with social and spiritual issues was rooted in their Christian commitment, Whiting's ideological positioning

here, as in his other plays, is far from clear. In fact, much of Whiting's work, and notably *Marching Song*, is perhaps even more firmly embedded in the drama of the 1940's and early 1950's than the Eliot–Fry analogy alone suggests, for behind it there is, too, something of the post-war French drama then popular on London stages, particularly that of Sartre and Anouilh (whose *Le Voyageur sans bagage* Whiting translated in 1959 for a London production). Unfortunately, Whiting lacked the intellectual bite, philosophical depth, and gift for the striking phrase and image of the former writer, and the deftness in play construction and sharp sense of stage effectiveness of the latter.

Whiting wrote several other plays, all of considerable interest, from the early *Conditions of Agreement*, through the comedies of the 1950's, *Penny for a Song* and *The Gates of Summer*, to a comedy found among his papers and published in 1975, *No More a-Roving*. Since his early death, academic critical commentary has given some attention to these, and this has been more sympathetic than were the plays' first reviews. That attention is well merited, even if occasionally tending to allow explication to shade into speculative elaboration, and to pay more attention to the issues the plays sought to engage with rather than to their effectiveness as theatrical works on their own. Some of the reasons for their continuing failure to find a wider theatre public are perhaps indirectly evident in Whiting's theatre criticism, which often seems to lament the failure of the drama under review to observe the concerns and artistic high seriousness of the minority intellectual drama, English and Continental, of the 1930's and 1940's. This tends to suggest the extent to which Whiting, as a dramatist, was a transitional figure, engaged with 1950's concerns, but rooted artistically and intellectually in the austere, even patrician, values of an earlier age. Ultimately one must agree with the general critical view that his work remained forever on the level of the promising; it must be thought significant less for its own intrinsic merits, considerable as they are, than for the example it set a younger generation of British playwrights, who saw a dramatist striving bravely and imaginatively—if ultimately only with partial success—to explore new possibilities for the English stage.

—Kenneth Richards

See also *Volume 1* entry on *The Devils*.

————————

WILDE, Oscar (Fingal O'Flahertie Wills). Born in Dublin, Ireland, 16 October 1854. Educated at Portora Royal School, Enniskillen, County Fermanagh, 1864–71; Trinity College, Dublin, 1871–74; Magdalen College, Oxford (classical demyship; Newdigate prize, for poetry), 1874–78, BA (honours) in classical moderations 1878. Married Constance Lloyd in 1884 (separated 1893; died 1898); two sons. Moved to London, 1878; art reviewer, 1881; engaged by Richard D'Oyly Carte to lecture in the USA and Canada on the aesthetic movement, 1882; lived in Paris, 1883; first-produced play, *Vera; or, The Nihilists*, staged in New York, 1883; gave lecture tour of Britain, 1883–84; regular reviewer, *Pall Mall Gazette*, mid-1880's; editor, *Woman's World*, London, 1887–89; sued the Marquess of Queensberry for slander, 1895, but revelations at the trial about his relations with Queensberry's son, Lord Alfred Douglas (whom Wilde met in 1891), caused him to be prosecuted for offences to minors; tried twice: first trial ended with hung jury, second trial with guilty verdict: sentenced to two years hard labour in Wandsworth prison, London, then Reading Gaol, 1895–97; after release lived in Berneval, near Dieppe, and then in Paris; joined Roman Catholic Church, 1900. Died in Paris, 30 November 1900.

Works

Collections

Works (15 vols.), edited by R. Ross.   1908–22.
Complete Works, edited by G.F. Maine.   1948.
Salomé; A Woman of No Importance; An Ideal Husband.   1948; augmented edition (with *The Importance of Being Earnest* and *Lady Windermere's Fan*), as *Plays*, 1954.
Complete Plays.   1988.

Stage Works

Vera; or, The Nihilists (produced Union Square Theatre, New York, 1883).   1880.
The Duchess of Padua: A Tragedy of the XVI Century (as *Guido Ferranti*, produced Broadway Theatre, New York, 1891).   1883.
Lady Windermere's Fan: A Play About a Good Woman (produced St. James's Theatre, London, 1892).   1893.
A Woman of No Importance (produced Theatre Royal, Haymarket, London, 1893).   1894.
Salomé (in French; produced Théâtre de l'Oeuvre, Paris, 1896).   1893; translated by Alfred Douglas as *Salome* (produced Bijou Theatre, London, 1905), 1894.
An Ideal Husband (produced Theatre Royal, Haymarket, London, 1895).   1899.
The Importance of Being Earnest: A Trivial Comedy for Serious People (produced St. James's Theatre, London, 1895).   1899; 4-act version, edited by Sarah Augusta Dickson, 1956 (2 vols.), and edited by Ruth Berggren, 1987.
A Florentine Tragedy, one scene by T. Sturge Moore (produced King's Hall, Covent Garden, London, 1906).   In *Works 6* (Ross Edition), 1908.
For Love of the King: A Burmese Masque.   1922.

Fiction

"The Happy Prince" and Other Tales.   1888.
The Picture of Dorian Gray.   1891.
"Lord Arthur Savile's Crime" and Other Stories.   1891.
A House of Pomegranates.   1891.
The Portrait of Mr. W.H.   1901.
Complete Shorter Fiction, edited by Isobel Murray.   1979.

Verse

Ravenna.   1878.
Poems.   1881.
The Sphinx.   1894.
The Ballad of Reading Gaol.   1898.
Poems, edited by Denys Thompson.   1972.

Memoirs and Letters

Letters, edited by Rupert Hart-Davis.   1962; *Selected Letters*, 1979; *More Letters*, 1985.

Other

Intentions.   1891.
Oscariana: Epigrams.   1895; revised edition, 1910.
The Soul of Man.   1895; as *The Soul of Man under Socialism*, 1912.
Sebastian Melmoth (miscellany).   1904.
De Profundis.   Expurgated version, edited by Robert Ross, 1905; revised edition, 1909; *Suppressed Portion*, 1913; *The Complete Text*, edited by Vyvyan Holland, 1949; complete version, in *Letters*, 1962.
Decorative Art in America, Together with Letters, Reviews, and Interviews, edited by R.B. Glaenzer.   1906.
Impressions of America, edited by Stuart Mason.   1906.
A Critic in Pall Mall, Being Extracts from Reviews and Miscellanies.   1919.
To M.B.J., edited by Stuart Mason.   1920.
The Portable Wilde, edited by Richard Aldington.   1946; as *Selected Works*, 1946; revised edition, edited by Stanley Weintraub, 1981.
Essays, edited by Hesketh Pearson.   1950.
Selected Essays and Poems.   1954; as *"De Profundis" and Other Writings*, 1973.
Literary Criticism, edited by Stanley Weintraub.   1968.
The Artist as Critic: Critical Writings, edited by Richard Ellmann.   1969.
"The Picture of Dorian Gray" and Other Writings, edited by Richard Ellmann.   1982.
The Annotated Oscar Wilde, edited by H. Montgomery Hyde.   1982.
(Selections), edited by Isobel Murray.   1989.
Sayings, edited by Henry Russell.   1989.
Oxford Notebooks: A Portrait of Mind in the Making, edited by Philip E. Smith II and Michael S. Helfand.   1989.
The Fireworks of Wilde, edited by Owen Dudley Edwards.   1989.
"The Soul of Man" and Prison Writings, edited by Isobel Murray.   1990.

*

Bibliographies

"Stuart Mason" [ie C.S. Millard], *Bibliography of Oscar Wilde*, London, 1908; reprinted, 1967.
E.H. Mikhail, *Oscar Wilde: An Annotated Bibliography of Criticism*, Metuchen, New Jersey, 1978.

Criticism

Books:
Frank Harris, *Oscar Wilde: His Life and Confessions* (2 vols.), London, 1916.
A. Symons, *A Study of Oscar Wilde*, London, 1930.
A. Douglas, *Oscar Wilde: A Summing Up*, London, 1940.
Hesketh Pearson, *The Life of Oscar Wilde*, London, 1946.
Edouard Roditi, *Oscar Wilde*, Norfolk, Connecticut, 1947; revised edition, 1986.
George Woodcock, *The Paradox of Oscar Wilde*, London, 1947; as *Oscar Wilde: The Double Image*, 1989.
H. Montgomery Hyde (ed.), *The Trials of Oscar Wilde*, 1948.
St. John Ervine, *Oscar Wilde: A Present Time Appraisal*, London, 1951.
Vivien Mercer, *The Fate of Oscar Wilde*, 1955.
Vyvyan Holland, *Oscar Wilde: A Pictorial Biography*, London, 1960.

Oscar Wilde in the USA (1882).

Epifanio San Juan, *The Art of Oscar Wilde*, Princeton, New Jersey, 1967.

Richard Ellmann (ed.), *Oscar Wilde: A Collection of Critical Essays*, Englewood Cliffs, New Jersey, 1969.

Karl Beckson, *Oscar Wilde: The Critical Heritage*, London, 1970.

G.A. Cevasco, *Oscar Wilde*, 1972.

Martin Frido, *Oscar Wilde: An Illustrated Biography*, New York, 1973.

Christopher S. Nassaar, *Into the Demon Universe: A Literary Exploration of Oscar Wilde*, New Haven (Connecticut) and London, 1974.

H. Montgomery Hyde, *Oscar Wilde* (biography), New York and London, 1975.

Louis Kronenberger, *Oscar Wilde*, Boston, 1976.

Sheridan Morley, *Oscar Wilde*, New York, 1976.

Alan Bird, *The Plays of Oscar Wilde*, London, 1977.

R. Shewan, *Oscar Wilde: Art and Egotism*, London, 1977.

E.H. Mikhail (ed.), *Oscar Wilde: Interviews and Recollections* (2 vols.), London, 1979.

Robert Keith Miller, *Oscar Wilde*, New York, 1982.

Richard Pine, *Oscar Wilde*, Dublin, 1983.

Katharine Worth, *Oscar Wilde*, London, 1983.

Robert Merle, *Oscar Wilde*, Paris, 1984.

Harold Bloom, (ed.), *Oscar Wilde: Modern Critical Views*, New York, 1985.

Regenia Gagnier, *Idylls of the Marketplace: Oscar Wilde and the Victorian Public*, Stanford, California, 1986.

Jacques de Langlade, *Oscar Wilde; ou, La Vérité des masques*, Paris.

Richard Ellmann, *Oscar Wilde* (biography), New York, 1988.

Jonathan Goodman, *The Oscar Wilde File*, London, 1988.

Peter Raby, *Oscar Wilde*, Cambridge, 1988.

Norbert Kohl, *Oscar Wilde: Works of a Conformist Rebel* (from the German), Cambridge, 1989.

Walter J. Nelson, *Oscar Wilde and the Dramatic Critics: A Study in Victorian Theatre*, Lund, 1989.

Horst Schroeder, *Additions and Corrections to Richard Ellmann's Oscar Wilde*, Braunschweig, 1989.

Margery Morgan (compiler), *File on Wilde*, London, 1990.

Kerry Powell, *Oscar Wilde and the Theatre of the 1890's*, Cambridge, 1990.

Norman Page, *An Oscar Wilde Chronology*, London, 1991.

Patricia Flanagan Behrendt, *Oscar Wilde: Eros and Aesthetics*, London, 1991.

* * *

Wilde brought his Irish wit to play on the themes and conventions of 19th-century drama with devastating effect, skilfully subverting them in the act of raising them to their highest power. He gave irresistible theatrical shape to deep psychic drives. *Salomé* in tragedy and *The Importance of Being Earnest* in farce at once became icons, and have continued to speak for later times with superb assurance.

A melodrama about a Russian nihilist who ends by sacrificing herself for her country might seem an unlikely dramatic debut for Wilde. But *Vera; or, The Nihilists*, with its paradoxical emphasis on self-expression and self-sacrifice, anticipated much in his comedies. Mrs Erlynne (in *Lady Windermere's Fan*) sacrifices herself for her daughter, and Mrs Arbuthnot frees herself from the conventional thinking which has soured her life, taking revenge for a lifetime of enforced good works when she dismisses Lord Illingworth as "a man of no importance", a curtain line neatly reversing his sneer (which provides the title, *A Woman of No Importance*). Wilde was revolutionary in his social sympathies as in his dramatic technique. He attributed the cancellation of the London production of *Vera* to its "avowedly republican sentiments" (it became an uncomfortably topical play when Alexander II was assassinated in 1881). The "Titan cry of the peoples for liberty" was its inspiration, though individual lives, he said, not abstract ideas, were his subject. This was typical, as was his inclusion among the nihilists of their "opposite", the sceptical Prince Paul (some of whose epigrams were economically recycled in *Lady Windermere's Fan* and elsewhere).

Wilde's aesthetic philosophy, already celebrated before he wrote for the theatre, found spectacular expression in *Salomé*, a totally symbolist play which has haunted the European imagination and inspired remarkable adaptations, from Richard Strauss's opera to Lindsay Kemp's transvestite ballet. The play was "total theatre" long before the term came into use. Wilde envisaged it, according to Charles Ricketts, as a symphony in yellow, with Salomé in green "like a curious, poisonous lizard". The dance at its centre was to express the inexpressible, the language, heavily rhythmical, was close to music. Everything about the scenic arrangement was symbolic, from the underground cistern, with its aura of the supernatural, to the moon which turns from virginal white to blood-red when Salomé dances, and to black when she cradles the severed head, exulting "I have kissed thy mouth, Jokanaan". Written in French ("I wanted once to touch this new instrument") and owing much to French artists— Flaubert, Massenet, Moreau (as to Maeterlinck's *La Princesse Maleine*)—*Salomé* is entirely individual in its treatment of its equivocal heroine. Not simply the *femme fatale* of *fin de siècle* mythology, she was, for Wilde, a "tragic daughter of passion", doomed to desire her opposite, who is also her like.

Wilde audaciously counterpointed with these two fanatics the ironic and self-divided Herod, a character who expressed much of Wilde's own nature. Herod and the down-to-earth Herodias bring into the play whiffs of the humour that prevails in *Lady Windermere's Fan*, written in the same year. The "play of modern life" beat *Salomé* to the stage when the latter was banned by the Lord Chamberlain as offensive to the Bible. Wilde was not to hear Sarah Bernhardt, who had already begun rehearsing, lend her golden voice to his heroine, though reports of her performing the part in Paris consoled him when he was in prison. The censor did not spot the subversive elements in *Lady Windermere's Fan*, nor, on the whole, did the fashionable audiences at the St. James's Theatre. It was novel but socially acceptable, as they would have expected from their favourite actor-manager, George Alexander (who, sadly, confirmed his social reliability by removing Wilde's name from the posters for *The Importance of Being Earnest* when the author became a pariah).

Though Wilde's wit was the source of his triumphs, there was a tendency to underestimate its force and originality. Shaw said mockingly that he seemed to be the only critic in London who could not "sit down and write an Oscar Wilde play at will". The wit was in the power of the "fable" and in the underlying dramatic relevance of the intellectual firew-

orks, not just in their isolated brilliance. Lady Bracknell's indignant refusal to let Gwendolen "marry into a cloak-room and form an alliance with a parcel", Jack's melodramatic assurance to an affronted Miss Prism, "Mother, I forgive you", reduce a whole world of Victorian morality to absurdity. Wilde's dandies are not just mouthpieces for repartee. They are differentiated and humanised. In *An Ideal Husband*, Lord Goring may madden his father with provocative sallies—"I love talking about nothing. It's the only thing I know anything about"—but they are a defence against unreal earnestness (seen in the play as a potentially tragic source of corruption). When he replies to his father's charge that he is heartless, with the comment "I hope not, father", he really means it. His private affairs make a little oasis of good feeling in the desert that threatens the self-deceiving Sir Robert and Lady Chiltern.

Wilde's aim was to subvert "monotony of type, slavery of custom, tyranny of habit". He undermined the rigid sexual morality of the boulevard drama, with its obsessive interest in the sexual behaviour of the "woman with a past", challenging stereotyped notions of what constituted a "good woman" in *Lady Windermere's Fan* and *A Woman of No Importance*, and using his witty dandies (including the more unscrupulous ones) to puncture conventional notions. He slyly indicated the gap between dictum and practice. Everything Lord Illingworth says is "excessively immoral"—and "most interesting"—to the discreet conformists in Lady Hunstanton's circle. Wilde diverged from conventional form as well as ideas in that play, devoting the whole of his long first act to conversation: "Absolutely no action at all", he told a journalist, "a perfect act".

Wilde surely found this divergence a relief, because most of the time he was driving two violently incompatible horses: sophisticated, often nihilistic wit, and passionately moral melodrama. Only in *The Importance of Being Earnest* did he arrive at a totally unified style, at once perfectly serious and perfectly absurd. The play was too heartless for Shaw, usually an admirer. Farce's freedom from "heart", however, was what Wilde needed to create his most anarchic, self-revealing work, with its divided young men leading their complicated double lives, and its young women ruthlessly forcing them to wear the mask of "Ernest", a character who does not exist. Jack's comically desperate question to Lady Bracknell, "would you kindly inform me who I am?", has an inescapable existential resonance for modern audiences, tuned as they are to the intellectual possibilities of farce by Eliot, Orton, Stoppard, and the many more who have come under the spell of *The Importance of Being Earnest*. It is the supreme apotheosis of the form.

—Katharine Worth

See also *Volume 1* entries on *The Importance of Being Earnest*; *Lady Windemere's Fan*; *Salomé*.

WILDER, Thornton (Niven). Born in Madison, Wisconsin, USA, 17 April 1897. Educated at Thacher School, Ojai, California, 1912–13; Berkeley High School, California, graduated 1915; Oberlin College, Ohio, 1915–17; Yale University, New Haven, Connecticut, 1917, 1919–20, AB 1920; American Academy in Rome, 1920–21; Princeton

University, New Jersey, 1925–26, AM 1926. Served in the US Coast Artillery Corps, 1918. French teacher, 1921–25, and house master, 1927–28, Lawrenceville School, New Jersey; first-produced play, *The Trumpet Shall Sound*, staged 1926; part-time lecturer in comparative literature, University of Chicago, 1930–36; visiting professor, University of Hawaii, Honolulu, 1935; served in the US Army Air Intelligence, rising to the rank of Lieutenant-Colonel, 1942–45: honorary MBE (Member, Order of the British Empire), 1945; Charles Eliot Norton Professor of Poetry, Harvard University, Cambridge, Massachusetts, 1950–51. US Delegate: Institut de Coopération Intellectuelle, Paris, 1937, International PEN Club Congress, England, 1941, Unesco Conference of the Arts, Venice, 1952. Recipient: Pulitzer Prize, for fiction, 1928, for drama, 1938, 1943; American Academy Gold Medal, 1952; Freedom Prize (Frankfurt), 1957; MacDowell Medal, 1960; Presidential Medal of Freedom, 1963; National Medal for Literature, 1965; National Book Award, for fiction, 1968. D. Litt: New York University, 1930; Yale University, 1947; Kenyon College, Gambier, Ohio, 1948; College of Wooster, Ohio, 1950; Northeastern University, Boston, 1951; Oberlin College, 1952; University of New Hampshire, Durham, 1953; Goethe University, Frankfurt, 1957; University of Zurich, 1961; LL.D: Harvard University, 1951. Chevalier, Légion d'Honneur (France), 1951; member, Order of Merit (Peru); Order of Merit (Germany), 1957; honorary member, Bavarian Academy of Fine Arts; Mainz Academy of Science and Literature; member, American Academy. Died in Hamden, Connecticut, 7 December 1975.

Works

Collections

"The Angel That Troubled the Waters" and Other Plays (includes *Nascuntur Poetae; Proserpina and the Devil; Fanny Otcott; Brother Fire; The Penny That Beauty Spent; The Angel on the Ship; The Message and Jehanne; Childe Roland to the Dark Tower Came; Centaurs; Leviathan; And the Sea Shall Give Up Its Dead; Now Thy Servant's Name Was Malchus; Mozart and the Gray Steward; Hast Thou Considered My Servant Job?; The Flight into Egypt*). 1928.
"The Long Christmas Dinner" and Other Plays in One Act (includes *Queens of France; Pullman Car Hiawatha; Love and How to Cure It; Such Things Only Happen in Books; The Happy Journey to Trenton and Camden*). 1931.
Three Plays (includes *Our Town; The Skin of Our Teeth; The Matchmaker*). 1957.

Stage Works

St. Francis Lake. In *Oberlin Literary Magazine*, December 1915.
Flamingo Red. In *Oberlin Literary Magazine*, January 1916.
Brother Fire. In *Oberlin Literary Magazine*, May 1916.
A Christmas Interlude. In *Oberlin Literary Magazine*, December 1916.
The Walled City. In *Yale Literary Magazine*. April 1918.
In Praise of Guynemer. In *Yale Literary Magazine*, December 1918.
The Trumpet Shall Sound (produced American Laboratory Theatre, New York, 1926). In *Yale Literary Magazine*, October-December 1919, January 1920.
"The Angel That Troubled the Waters" and Other Plays (includes *Nascuntur Poetae; Proserpina and the Devil; Fanny Otcott; Brother Fire; The Penny That Beauty Spent; The*

Thornton Wilder (pencil sketch by Dolbin).

Angel on the Ship; The Message and Jehanne; Childe Roland to the Dark Tower Came; Centaurs; Leviathan; And the Sea Shall Give Up Its Dead; Now the Servant's Name Was Malchus; Mozart and the Gray Steward; Hast Thou Considered My Servant Job?; The Flight into Egypt). 1928.
The Long Christmas Dinner (produced Yale University, New Haven, Connecticut, 1931). In *"The Long Christmas Dinner" and Other Plays*, 1931; libretto for opera version, as *Das Lange Weihnachtsmahl*, music by Paul Hindemith (produced Mannheim, West Germany, 1961), libretto published, 1961.
The Happy Journey to Trenton and Camden (produced Yale University, New Haven, Connecticut, 1931). In *"The Long Christmas Dinner" and Other Plays*, 1931; revised version, as *The Happy Journey*, 1934.
Such Things Only Happen in Books (produced Yale University, New Haven, Connecticut, 1931). In *"The Long Christmas Dinner" and Other Plays*, 1931.
Love and How to Cure It (produced Yale University, New Haven, Connecticut, 1931). In *"The Long Christmas Dinner" and Other Plays*, 1931.
Queens of France (produced Chicago, 1932). In *"The Long Christmas Dinner" and Other Plays*, 1931.
Pullman Car Hiawatha (produced Circle in the Square Theatre, New York, 1962). In *"The Long Christmas Dinner" and Other Plays*, 1931.
Lucrèce, from a play by André Obey (produced Belasco Theatre, New York, 1932). 1933.

A Doll's House, from a play by Ibsen (produced Morosco Theatre, 1937).

Our Town (produced McCarter Theatre, Princeton, New Jersey, 1938). 1938.

The Merchant of Yonkers, from a play by Johann Nestroy, based on *A Well-Spent Day* by John Oxenford (produced Guild Theatre, New York, 1938). 1939; revised version, as *The Matchmaker* (produced Royal Lyceum Theatre, Edinburgh, 1954), in *Three Plays*, 1957.

The Skin of Our Teeth (produced Plymouth Theatre, New York, 1942). 1942.

Our Century (produced by Century Association, New York, 1947). 1947.

The Victors, from a play by Sartre (produced New York, 1949).

Die Alkestiade (as *A Life in the Sun*, produced Assembly Hall, Edinburgh, 1955; as *Die Alkestiade*, music by Louise Talma, produced Städtische Bühnen, Frankfurt, 1962). 1960; as *The Alcestiad; or, A Life in the Sun*, with *The Drunken Sisters: A Satyr Play*, 1977.

Bernice (produced Congresshalle-Theater, Berlin, 1957).

The Wreck of the 5:25 (produced Congresshalle-Theater, Berlin, 1957).

The Drunken Sisters (produced Spencer Memorial Church, Brooklyn Heights, New York, 1970). 1957.

Infancy (produced in *Plays for Bleecker Street*, Circle in the Square Theatre, New York, 1962). 1960.

Childhood (produced in *Plays for Bleecker Street*, Circle in the Square Theatre, New York, 1962). 1961.

Someone from Assissi (produced in *Plays for Bleecker Street*, Circle in the Square Theatre, New York, 1962). 1961.

The Emperor (unfinished). In *The Journals 1939–1961*, 1985.

Screenplays

We Live Again, with others, 1934; *Our Town*, with Frank Craven and Harry Chandlee, 1940; *Shadow of a Doubt*, with others, 1943.

Fiction

The Cabala. 1926.
The Bridge of San Luis Rey. 1927.
The Woman of Andros. 1930.
Heaven's My Destination 1934.
The Ides of March. 1948.
The Eighth Day. 1967.
Theophilus North 1973.

Other

The Intent of the Artist, with others. 1941.
James Joyce 1882–1941. 1944.
Kultur in einer Demokratie. 1957.
Goethe und die Weltliteratur. 1958.
"American Characteristics" and Other Essays, edited by Donald Gallup. 1979.
The Journals 1939–1961 (includes unfinished play *The Emporium*), edited by Donald Gallup. 1985.

*

Criticism

Books:
Gilbert A. Harrison, *The Enthusiast: A Life of Thornton Wilder*, New Haven, Connecticut, 1983.

David Castronovo, *Thornton Wilder*, New York, 1986.
Holger Naatz, *Thornton Wilder als Dramatiker: Analyse der deutschsprachigen Literaturkritik zwischen 1970–82*, Cologne, 1986.

Articles:
Martin Blank, "Thornton Wilder: Broadway Production History", in *Theatre History Studies*, 5, 1985.
Hans J, Lang, "Wilder in Germany: The Political Story after 1945", in *Yearbook of Comparative and General Literature*, 36, 1987.
Joanna Narkiewicz-Jodko, "The Influence of the Oriental Drama on Wilder's Playwriting", in *Acta Universitatis Wratislaviensis*, 1161, 1991.

* * *

In a decade dominated by realistic domestic melodrama, Thornton Wilder was one of the very few significant playwrights to resist the pull of verisimilitude, the pretense of portraying real life on stage, in favor of the exploration of the theatre's potential for universality and magic. From the openly experimental one-act plays of the 1931 volume *The Long Christmas Dinner* through his masterpieces *Our Town* and *The Skin of Our Teeth*, he exploited the drama's plasticity of time and space, making full use of the ability of a stage scene to represent any place, and for time to pass with the speed of an onstage announcement or a programme note. And in a decade during which both writers and audiences could be excused for lapsing into pessimism and doubt, he affirmed, in commercially successful and entertaining plays, a faith in the goodness of life and the value of humanity.

The one-act plays function almost as sketches for the longer works. In *The Long Christmas Dinner*, Wilder manipulates time by condensing 90 years into the table talk of a single meal, showing that an audience can be guided to believe what it is told more than what it sees. *The Happy Journey to Trenton and Camden* and *Pullman Car Hiawatha* prove that a bare stage can appear filled with scenery if the audience is led by the dialogue to provide through imagination what is missing, and that the most ordinary events can be made to seem dramatically interesting if they are presented as such.

In *Our Town*, Wilder celebrates the intrinsic holiness of ordinary life by presenting a simple story of love, marriage, and death in totally unadorned fashion. As is well known (the play, a staple of the amateur and student repertories, is perhaps the most widely known of great American plays), it is played on an almost bare stage, with minimal furniture and the actors' mime replacing realistic sets. The fictional small town of Grover's Corners, New Hampshire, is described by a narrating Stage Manager who leads us through the growing up, falling in love, and marriage of the very ordinary George Gibbs and Emily Webb. The Stage Manager plays secondary parts, fills in narrative gaps, and controls the sequence of events to limit our focus to the bare essentials of the story and characters. All three devices—the absence of scenery, the deliberately uneventful plot, and the narrative manipulation—make what is shown seem important simply because it is all that *is* shown. Combined with Wilder's open and unembarrassed appeals to the emotions, most powerfully in the scenes after Emily's death, when she is allowed to revisit earth and realize the beauty she had overlooked while alive, these technical devices guide the audience to accept the play's assertion that the most mundane elements of everyday life are almost too precious and significant to be appreciated.

If *Our Town* disarms though the illusion of simplicity, *The Skin of Our Teeth* is meant to dazzle through the illusion of extraordinary complexity; but in fact the plays are technically similar in manipulating time and space to focus the audience's attention on universals. Mr. and Mrs. Antrobus are simultaneously an ordinary suburban couple and also Adam and Eve, Noah and his wife, and the spirits of man- and womankind personified. By happily juggling these several levels (having Mr. Antrobus come home from a hard day at the office where he's been inventing the alphabet, for example, or setting Noah's Flood during a Lodge convention in Atlantic City), and while carefully keeping the thread of the narrative clear, Wilder dramatizes the continuity of the human experience, reminding us that the greatest accomplishments of myth and history were the products of people not unlike ourselves. And thus he can reassure us that, like our ancestors, we have the innate human capacity to survive any challenge, if only (as the title suggests) just barely.

Even the lesser comedy *The Merchant of Yonkers* (later revised as *The Matchmaker*, and even later the basis for the musical *Hello, Dolly!*) toys with stage realism through the pointed use of 19th-century conventions such as direct audience address and plot complications based on accident and coincidence. Its conclusion, that every life should contain a little adventure, but ultimately homely pleasures are best, reaffirms Wilder's celebration of the ordinary.

There is no "school of Wilder" among later American dramatists; the American stage was dominated by domestic realism for another 20 years or more before some playwrights of the 1960's rediscovered the pleasures of violating the conventions of realism through self-conscious theatricality, and their inspiration was more likely Brecht and Beckett than Wilder. His importance lies in the plays themselves, affirmations of both theatrical imagination and faith in humanity in accessible and effective popular art.

—Gerald Berkowitz

See also *Volume 1* entries on *Our Town*; *The Skin of Our Teeth*.

WILLEMS, Paul. Born on the family estate of Missembourg, Edegem (near Antwerp), Belgium, 4 April 1912. Educated at the Lycée d'Anvers, from 1924; Université Libre, Brussels, 1930–36, doctorate in law 1936. Married Elza de Groodt in 1942; one son and one daughter. Military attachment to the Belgian army (artillery), 1937–40: mobilised 1940; lawyer, Antwerp, 1937–40; director of maritime fishing, Ministry of Rationing, Brussels, 1941–46; Secretary General, then Director General and delegated administrator, Palais des Beaux-Arts, Brussels, 1947–84; first-produced play, *Le Bon Vin de Monsieur Nuche*, staged 1949; founder, with the Baron de Voghel, bi-annual Europalia festival, 1969; retired to Missembourg, 1984. Secretary General, Fédération Internationale des Jeunesses Musicales. Recipient: Prix Triennal de l'État, 1963 and 1970; Marzotto Prize, 1966; Prix Quinquenal de l'État, 1980. Member, Académie Royale (Belgium). CBE (Commander, Order of the British Empire), 1969; Officier, Orde van Oranje-Nassau (Netherlands), 1973; Grand-Officier de l'Ordre de Léopold (Belgium), 1975; Grosses Verdienstkreuz (Federal Republic of Germany), 1979.

Works

Stage Works

Le Bon Vin de Monsieur Nuche (produced Rideau de Bruxelles, Brussels, 1949).   In *Audace*, 3, 1954; in *Cahiers du Rideau*, 16, 1983.
Lamentable Julie (produced Rideau de Bruxelles, Brussels, 1949).
Peau d'ours (produced Théâtre National, Brussels, 1951). 1958.
Off et la lune (produced Théâtre National, Brussels, 1955). Published in German, as *Bärenhäuter*, 1952.
Il pleut dans ma maison, music by Ralph Darbo (produced in German, Kleines Theater der Josefstadt, Vienna, and Bühnen der Stadt, Cologne, 1958; produced in French, Rideau de Bruxelles, Brussels, 1962).   1962.
La Plage aux anguilles (produced Rideau de Bruxelles, Brussels, 1959).   In *Théâtre de Belgique*, 19, 1963–64.
Warna (produced Rideau de Bruxelles, Brussels, 1962). 1963; revised version, as *Warna; ou, Le Poids de la neige* (produced Rideau de Bruxelles, Brussels, 1964). 1963.
Le Marché des petites heures, music by Eugen Thomas (produced in German, Europa Studio, Salzburg, 1964; produced in French, Rideau de Bruxelles, Brussels, 1966).   In *Textes pour Didascalies*, 6, 1983.
La Ville à voile (produced Théâtre National, Brussels, 1967). 1967.
Le Soleil sur la mer (produced Rideau de Bruxelles, Brussels, 1970).   Published in German, as *Die Sonne über dem Meer*, 1973.
Les Miroirs d'Ostende (produced Rideau de Bruxelles, Brussels, 1974).   1974.
Nuit avec ombres en couleurs (produced Théâtre National, Brussels, 1983).   In *Textes pour Didascalies*, 6, 1983.
Elle disait dormir pour mourir (produced Rideau de Bruxelles, Brussels, 1983).   In *Cahiers du Rideau*, 16, 1983.
La Vita breve (produced Nouveau Théâtre de Belgique, Spa, 1991).   With *La Ville à voile*, 1989.

Television Plays

L'Écho, 1963.

Radio Plays

Plus de danger pour Berto, 1966.

Fiction

Tout est réel ici.   1941.
Blessures.   1945.
La Chronique du cygne.   1949.
La Cathédrale de brume.   1983.
Le Pays noyé.   1990.

Verse

Douze Couplets et un poème pour les treize mois de l'année. 1953.

Other

L'Herbe qui tremble.   1942.
Le Monde de Paul Willems (includes texts, interviews, and

critical studies on Willems), edited by Paul Emond, Henri Ronse, and Fabrice van de Kerckhove.   1984.

Un Arrière-pays.   1989.

*

Criticism

Articles:

Donald F. Friedman, "Spaces of Dream, Protection, and Imprisonment in the Theater of Paul Willems", in *World Literature Today*, vol. 65 no.1, 1991.

* * *

Due to changing cultural politics, Paul Willems is the last representative of a peculiarly Belgian phenomenon—the Flemish playwright writing in French. Thus his work combines the characteristic Flemish blend of earthiness and mysticism with a French linguistic flair. Willems also shares with his predecessors Maeterlinck, Crommelynck, and Ghelderode a penchant for allegory. One may discern in Willems' *oeuvre* affinities with symbolism and surrealism, yet Willems refuses to affiliate himself with any literary movement, considering freedom of thought man's most precious gift.

Willems' plays live on the borders of memory, dream, and fantasy—and those borders are permeable. By weaving a spell of language, the poet seeks to open a passage to a paradise lost, a recurring theme in his work. His characters suffer from nostalgia for an idealized past; their attempts to recapture lost innocence lead them to take shelter in an imaginary world—a world in which time stands still. Cruelly, they sacrifice the living on the altar they erect to their dead memory.

Thus, for instance, in *Warna; ou, Le Poids de la neige* (The Weight of the Snow), the Countess Warna creates a myth glorifying her 25-year-long romance with the knight Ernevelde. In a medieval post-apocalyptic world, the characters seek refuge from anarchy in Warna's castle, but the fortress becomes their prison. Stifled by Warna's myth, Ernevelde abandons her for another woman; Warna waits for his return. When Ernevelde does return, only to throw in Warna's face the truth that he never loved her, the Countess has him shot—then settles down to wait again for the return of her ever-faithful lover Ernevelde.

Critics note the recurrence of doubles and mirrors in Willems' plays. In *La Ville à voile* (The Sailing City), Josty—old, dying, but rich—returns to Antwerp to buy happiness. He attempts to recreate his lost youth by marrying Anne-Marie, the exact replica of the shop-window mannequin that young Josty had fantasized about as his future wife. Mirroring Josty's relationship with Anne-Marie is that between the half-wit servant, Agréable, and the mannequin. Unable to touch the real Anne-Marie, Agréable acts out his fantasy with the mannequin, caressing it and slapping it in jealous rage. The image of woman as mannequin, a blank screen for the projection of male desires, haunts the play.

The image reappears in Willems' recent work, *La Vita breve* (The Brief Life). The former lovers of the Italian courtesan Hamalissa gather on board a ship eight years after her murder. Having fought over her favors, they now fight over a "sailor's doll", a life-sized replica of Hamalissa, leading to the violation of the doll and another jealous murder. Beneath a Maeterlinckian fairy-tale surface, Willems' dramatic worlds evoke a Bosch-like Hell of human passions—adultery, incest, murder, and war. The search for lost innocence is doomed in a world where lovers prefer an image of the beloved to the beloved herself.

Yet it is through doubles and reflections in *Il pleut dans ma maison* (It's Raining in My House) that lovers are reunited and a lost paradise regained. This comic fantasy, a perennial favorite in Belgium, has been revived eight times since its premiere and has toured throughout Europe. With its tree growing in the living room, the old house Grand'Rosière conveys an image of Eden onstage. But this is a fallen world. 50 years ago, Georges and Aunt Madeleine quarrelled, resulting in Georges's death. The split between Georges and Aunt Madeleine represents the "fall" and sets up a tension between opposites: man and woman, city and country, old and young, the living and the dead.

As the play opens, young Madeleine, the double of Aunt Madeleine, has inherited the house and plans to sell it to buy a condominium in town. The reflection of a lovers' quarrel evokes the ghost of Georges, determined to experience everything he missed by his untimely death—including womanly "warmth". Georges pursues young Madeleine, but in the fallen world, language echoes the Tower of Babel, and the opposites speak different languages (producing a failure of communication to which Willems, living in dual-language Belgium, is acutely sensitive). A surrealistic ritual returns the fragmented world to wholeness. To the accompaniment of mystical sitar chords, the ghosts Georges and Aunt Madeleine act out the anniversary dinner they never had, thus creating an imagined reality in which they have lived, loved, and grown old together. This resolution of their aborted love frees them to move on to the "Other Side". The healing on the archetypal level of the original male/female split is reflected on the mundane level, with the reconciliation of all the opposites. The play ends with Bulle's ode to the ephemeral, the ever-changing cycles of life, love, and death—and the reflections that allow us to see ourselves, and thus to grow. Willems' allegory blends elements of Eastern mysticism and Jungian psychology into a myth for our time.

Willems' plays are musical in structure and rhythm. Author of Belgium's first musical comedy, *Le Marché des petites heures* (The Wee Hours Market), Willems often incorporates music into the texture of a play: the shimmering tinkle of falling rain in *Il pleut dans ma maison*, or the tattered player's piano tunes in *La Ville à voile* which stumble into "holes", just as Josty stumbles into moments of paralysis as he faces his approaching death.

Like music, language plays its role in weaving Willems' dreamworlds. Repetition, rhyme, puns, and neologisms abound, as characters play at being poets to conjure their fantasies into existence. Willems' delight in wordplay extends to character names that evoke allegorical associations: the spokesman for the ephemeral in *Il pleut dans ma maison* is named Bulle (Bubble); the feline narrator of *Nuit avec ombres en couleurs* (Night with Colored Shadows) is aptly called "Le Chat Astrophe" (Cat Astrophe). Willems' hypnotic language functions as incantation, coaxing the audience into a world of imagination which illuminates our everyday world. Yet Willems' vision remains essentially pessimistic. "Let us dream", writes Willems. "Our fates are fixed. Dreams and reflections are our only freedom".

—Suzanne Burgoyne

WILLIAMS, Emlyn. See *Volume 1* entry on *The Corn is Green*.

WILLIAMS, Tennessee. Born Thomas Lanier Williams in Columbus, Mississippi, USA, 26 March 1911. Educated at the University of Missouri, Columbia, 1929–31; Washington University, St. Louis, 1936; University of Iowa, Iowa City, 1938, AB 1938. First-produced play, *Beauty is the Word*, staged at university, 1930; clerical worker and manual labourer, International Shoe Company, St. Louis, 1934–35; held various jobs, including waiter and elevator operator, New Orleans, 1939; teletype operator, Jacksonville, Florida, 1940; worked at odd jobs, New York, 1942, and as screenwriter for MGM, Hollywood, 1943; full-time writer from 1944; Distinguished Writer-in-Residence, University of British Columbia, Vancouver, 1980. Recipient: American Academy Gold Medal, 1969; New York Drama Critics Circle Award, 1945, 1948, 1955, 1962; Sidney Howard Award, 1945; Donaldson Award, 1945, 1948; Pulitzer Prize, 1948, 1955; Medal of Freedom, 1980. LHD: Harvard University, Cambridge, Massachusetts, 1982. Member, American Academy, 1976. Died in New York, 25 February 1983.

Works

Collections

"27 Wagons Full of Cotton" and Other One-Act Plays (includes *The Purification; The Lady of Larkspur Lotion; The Last of My Solid Gold Watches; Portrait of a Madonna; Auto-da-Fé; Lord Byron's Love Letter; The Strangest Kind of Romance; The Long Goodbye; Hello from Bertha; This Property is Condemned*). 1946; augmented edition (also includes *Talk to Me Like the Rain and Let Me Listen; Something Unspoken*), 1953.

American Blues: Five Short Plays (includes *Moony's Kid Don't Cry; The Dark Room; The Case of the Crushed Petunias; The Long Stay Cut Short, or, The Unsatisfactory Supper; Ten Blocks on the Camino Real*). 1948.

Dragon Country: A Book of Plays (includes *In the Bar of a Tokyo Hotel; I Rise in Flame, Cried the Phoenix; The Mutilated; I Can't Imagine Tomorrow; Confessional; The Frosted Glass Coffin; The Gnädiges Fräulein; A Perfect Analysis Given by a Parrot*). 1970.

The Theatre of Tennessee Williams:

1. *Battle of Angels; A Streetcar Named Desire; The Glass Menagerie*. 1972.
2. *The Eccentricities of a Nightingale; Summer and Smoke; The Rose Tattoo; Camino Real*. 1972.
3. *Cat on a Hot Tin Roof; Orpheus Descending; Suddenly Last Summer*. 1972.
4. *Sweet Bird of Youth; Period of Adjustment; Night of the Iguana*. 1972.
5. *The Milk Train Doesn't Stop Here Anymore; Kingdom of Earth;* revised version*; Small Craft Warnings; The Two-Character Play*, revised version. 1976.
6. *"27 Wagons Full of Cotton" and Other One Act Plays* (includes *The Unsatisfactory Supper; Steps Must Be Gentle; The Demolition Downtown: Count Ten in Arabic*). 1981.
7. *Dragon Country; Lifeboat Drill; Now the Cats with Jewelled Claws; Now the Peaceable Kingdom*. 1981.

"Stopped Rocking" and Other Screenplays (includes *All Gaul is Divided; The Loss of a Teardrop Diamond; One Arm*). 1984.

Stage Works

Beauty is the Word (produced University of Missouri, Columbia, 1930). In *Missouri Review*, 7, 1984.

Cairo, Shanghai, Bombay!, with Doris Shapiro (produced Memphis Garden Players, Memphis, Tennessee, 1935).

The Magic Tower (produced St. Louis?, 1936).

Headlines (produced Wednesday Club Auditorium, St. Louis, Missouri, 1936).

Candles to the Sun (produced Wednesday Club Auditorium, St. Louis, Missouri, 1937).

Fugitive Kind (produced Wednesday Club Auditorium, St. Louis, Missouri, 1937).

Spring Song (produced University of Iowa, Iowa City, 1938).

The Long Goodbye (produced New School for Social Research, New York, 1940). In *27 Wagons Full of Cotton*, 1946.

Battle of Angels (produced Wilbur Theatre, Boston, 1940). 1945; revised version, as *Orpheus Descending* (produced Martin Beck Theatre, New York, 1957), with *Battle of Angels*, 1958; further revised version, 1976.

At Liberty (produced Quaigh Theatre, New York, 1978). In *American Scenes*, edited by William Kozlenko, 1941.

This Property is Condemned (produced Hudson Park Theatre, New York, 1942). In *27 Wagons Full of Cotton*, 1946.

You Touched Me!, with Donald Windham, from the story by D.H. Lawrence (produced Cleveland, Ohio, 1943). 1947.

The Glass Menagerie (produced Civic Theatre, Chicago, 1944). 1945; revised version, 1970.

The Unsatisfactory Supper (produced Lucille Lortel Theatre, New York, 1986). In *Best One Act Plays of 1945*, 1945.

Portrait of a Madonna (produced Las Palmas Theatre, Los Angeles, 1946). In *27 Wagons Full of Cotton*, 1946.

The Last of My Solid Gold Watches (produced Actors' Laboratory Theatre, Los Angeles, 1947). In *27 Wagons Full of Cotton*, 1946.

Lord Byron's Love Letter (produced New York?, 1947). In *27 Wagons Full of Cotton*, 1946; revised version, music by Raffaello de Banfield (produced Tulane University, New Orleans, 1955), 1955.

Auto-da-Fé (produced Lucille Lortel Theatre, New York, 1986). In *27 Wagons Full of Cotton*, 1946.

The Lady of Larkspur Lotion (produced New York, 1947). In *27 Wagons Full of Cotton*, 1946.

The Purification (produced Dallas, Texas, 1954). In *27 Wagons Full of Cotton*, 1946.

27 Wagons Full of Cotton (produced Tulane University, New Orleans, 1955). In *27 Wagons Full of Cotton*, 1946.

Hello from Bertha (produced Bromley, Kent, 1961). In *27 Wagons Full of Cotton*, 1946.

The Strangest Kind of Romance (produced London, 1969; Lucille Lortel Theatre, New York, 1986). In *27 Wagons Full of Cotton*, 1946.

Moony's Kid Don't Cry (produced Actors' Laboratory Theatre, Los Angeles, 1946). In *American Blues*, 1948.

Stairs to the Roof (produced Playbox Theatre, Pasadena, California, 1947).

A Streetcar Named Desire (produced Ethel Barrymore Theatre, New York, 1947). 1947.

Summer and Smoke (produced Theatre '47, Dallas, Texas,

Tennessee Williams on a trip to Morocco.

1947). 1948; revised version, as *The Eccentricities of a Nightingale* (produced Tappan Zee Playhouse, Nyack, New York, 1964), with *Summer and Smoke*, 1965; further revised version (produced Studio Arena Theatre, Buffalo, New York, 1976).

Ten Blocks on the Camino Real. In *American Blues*, 1948; revised version, as *Camino Real* (produced Martin Beck Theatre, New York, 1953), 1953.

The Case of the Crushed Petunias (produced Shelterhouse Theatre, Cincinnati, Ohio, 1973). In *American Blues*, 1948.

The Dark Room (produced London, 1966). In *American Blues*, 1948.

The Rose Tattoo (produced Martin Beck Theatre, New York, 1951). 1951.

I Rise in Flame, Cried the Phoenix: A Play About D.H. Lawrence (produced Theatre de Lys, New York, 1959). 1951.

Something Unspoken (produced York Playhouse, New York, 1955). In *27 Wagons Full of Cotton*, 1953.

Talk to Me Like the Rain and Let Me Listen (produced White Barn Theatre, Westport, Connecticut, 1958). In *27 Wagons Full of Cotton*, 1953.

Cat on a Hot Tin Roof (produced Morosco Theatre, New York, 1955). 1955; revised version (produced ANTA Theatre, New York, 1973), 1975.

Three Players of a Summer Game (produced White Barn Theatre, Westport, Connecticut, 1955).

Sweet Bird of Youth (produced Studio M Playhouse, Coral Gables, Florida, 1956). 1959.

Period of Adjustment: High Point over a Cavern: A Serious Comedy (produced Coconut Grove Playhouse, Miami, Florida, 1958). 1960.

A Perfect Analysis Given by a Parrot (produced Waterfront Playhouse, Key West, Florida, 1976). 1958.

The Enemy: Time. In *Theatre*, March 1959.

The Night of the Iguana (produced Spoleto, Italy, 1959; revised version, produced Royale Theatre, New York, 1961). 1962.

To Heaven in a Golden Coach (produced Bromley, Kent, 1961).

The Milk Train Doesn't Stop Here Anymore (produced Spoleto, Italy, 1962; revised versions, produced Abington, West Virginia, 1963, New York, 1964, London, 1968). 1964.

The Mutilated (produced Longacre Theatre, New York, 1966). In *Esquire*, August 1965.

The Gnädiges Fräulein (produced Longacre Theatre, New York, 1966). In *Esquire*, August 1965; revised version, as *The Latter Days of a Celebrated Soubrette* (produced Central Arts Theatre, New York, 1974).

Kingdom of Earth. In *Esquire*, February 1967; revised version, as *The Seven Descents of Myrtle* (produced Ethel Barrymore Theatre, New York, 1968), published as *Kingdom of Earth (The Seven Descents of Myrtle)*, 1968; further revised version, in *Theatre 5*, 1976.

The Two-Character Play (produced Hampstead Theatre Club, London, 1967; revised version, produced 1969). 1969; revised version, as *Out Cry* (produced Ivanhoe Theatre, Chicago, 1971), 1973; further revised version (produced New York, 1974).

In the Bar of a Tokyo Hotel (produced Eastside Playhouse, New York, 1969). 1969.

I Can't Imagine Tomorrow (televised 1970; produced London, 1976; Lucille Lortel Theatre, New York, 1986). In *Dragon Country*, 1970.

Confessional (produced Maine Theatre Arts Festival, Bar Harbour, 1970). In *Dragon Country*, 1970; revised version, as *Small Craft Warnings* (produced Truck and Warehouse Theatre, New York, 1972), 1972.

The Frosted Glass Coffin (produced Waterfront Playhouse, Key West, Florida, 1970). In *Dragon Country*, 1970.

The Red Devil Battery Sign (produced Shubert Theatre, Boston, 1975; revised version, produced English Theatre, Vienna, 1976). 1988.

Demolition Downtown: Count Ten in Arabic—Then Run (produced Carnaby Street Theatre, London, 1976). In *Theatre*, 6, 1981.

This is an Entertainment (produced American Conservatory Theatre, San Francisco, 1976).

Vieux Carré (produced St. James Theatre, New York, 1977). 1979.

Tiger Tail (produced Alliance Theatre, Atlanta, Georgia, 1978). With *Baby Doll* (screenplay), 1991.

A Lovely Sunday for Creve Coeur (as *Creve Coeur*, produced Dock Street Theatre, Charleston, South Carolina, 1978; as *A Lovely Sunday for Creve Coeur*, produced Hudson Guild Theatre, New York, 1979). 1980.

Lifeboat Drill (produced Ensemble Studio Theatre, New York 1979). In *Theatre*, 7, 1981.

Some Problems for the Moose Lodge (produced Goodman Theatre, Chicago, 1980; revised versions, as *A House Not Meant to Stand*, produced Goodman Theatre, Chicago, 1981 and 1982).

Steps Must Be Gentle: A Dramatic Reading (produced University of Michigan, Ann Arbor, 1983). 1980.

Kirche, Küchen, und Kinder (produced Jean Cocteau Repertory Theatre, New York, 1980). 1981.

Clothes for a Summer Hotel (produced Kennedy Center, Washington, DC, 1980). 1983.

Will Mr. Merriwether Return from Memphis? (produced Florida Keys Community College, Key West, Florida, 1980).

Something Cloudy, Something Clear (produced Bouwerie Lane Theatre, New York, 1981).

The Notebook of Trigorin, from a play by Chekhov (produced Playhouse Theatre, Vancouver, British Columbia, 1981).

The Remarkable Rooming-House of Mme. Le Monde. 1984.

Screenplays

Senso (*The Wanton Countess*; English dialogue, with Paul Bowles), 1949 (published in *Two Screenplays*, by Luigi Visconti, 1970); *The Glass Menagerie*, with Peter Berneis, 1950; *A Streetcar Named Desire*, with Oscar Saul, 1951 (published in *Film Scripts 1*, edited by Georg Garrett and others, 1971); *The Rose Tattoo*, with Hal Kanter, 1955; *Baby Doll*, 1956 (published 1956); *Suddenly Last Summer*, with Gore Vidal, 1959; *The Fugitive Kind*, with Meade Roberts, 1960 (published 1958); *Boom*, 1968; *All Gaul is Divided, The Loss of a Teardrop Diamond, One Arm* (all published in "*Stopped Rocking*" *and Other Screenplays*, 1984).

Television Plays

Lord Byron's Love Letter, 1953; *I Can't Imagine Tomorrow*, 1970; *Stopped Rocking*, 1975 (published in "*Stopped Rocking*" *and Other Screenplays*, 1984).

Fiction:

"*One Arm*" *and Other Stories.* 1948.
The Roman Spring of Mrs. Stone. 1950.

Hard Candy: A Book of Stories. 1954.
"Three Players of a Summer Game" and Other Stories. 1960.
Grand (stories). 1964.
The Knightly Quest: A Novella and Four Short Stories. 1967; augmented edition, as *The Knightly Quest: A Novella and Twelve Short Stories*, 1968.
Eight Mortal Ladies Possessed: A Book of Stories. 1974.
Moise and the World of Reason. 1975.
"It Happened the Day the Sun Rose" and Other Stories. 1982.
Collected Stories. 1985.

Verse

Five Young American Poets, with others. 1944.
In the Winter of Cities. 1956.
Androgyne, Mon Amour. 1977.

Memoirs and Letters

Memoirs. 1975.
Letters to Donald Windham 1940–1965, edited by Windham. 1976.
Five O'Clock Angel: Letters to Maria St. Just, edited by Maria St. Just and Kit Harvey. 1990.

Other

Where I Live: Selected Essays, edited by Christine R. Day and Bob Woods. 1978.
Conversations with Williams (interviews), edited by Albert J. Devlin. 1986.

*

Bibliographies

John S. McCann, *The Critical Reputation of Tennessee Williams: A Reference Guide*, Boston, 1983.
Drewey Wayne Gunn, *Tennessee Williams: A Bibliography* (second edition), Metuchen, New Jersey, 1991.

Criticism

Books:
Signi Falk, *Tennessee Williams* (second edition), Boston, 1961; revised edition
Benjamin Nelson, *Tennessee Williams: The Man and His Work*, New York, 1961.
Francis Donahue, *The Dramatic World of Tennessee Williams*, New York, 1964.
Esther Jackson, *The Broken Worlds of Tennessee Williams*, Minneapolis, 1965.
Gilbert Maxwell, *Tennessee Williams and Friends*, New York, 1965.
Gerald Weales, *Tennessee Williams*, Minneapolis, 1965.
Norman J. Fedder, *The Influence of D.H. Lawrence on Tennessee Williams*, The Hague, 1966.
Christian M. Jauslin, *Tennessee Williams*, Velber, 1969.
Mike Steen, *A Look at Tennessee Williams*, New York, 1969.
Nancy M. Tischler, *Tennessee Williams*, Austin, Texas, 1969.
Jeanne Fayard, *Tennessee Williams: Textes de Williams, points de vue critiques, témoignages, chronologie, bibliographie, illustrations*, Paris, 1972.
Franz, H. Link, *Tennessee Williams' Dramen: Einsamkeit und Liebe*, Darmstadt, 1974.

Carol Petersen, *Tennessee Williams*, Berlin, 1975.
Ingrid Rogers, *Tennessee Williams: A Moralist's Answers to the Perils of Life*, Frankfurt, 1976.
Maurice Yacowar, *Tennessee Williams and Film*, New York, 1977.
Stephen S. Stanton (ed), *Tennessee Williams: A Collection of Critical Essays*, Englewood Cliffs, New Jersey, 1977.
Jac Tharpe (ed.), *Tennessee Williams: A Tribute*, Jackson, Mississippi, 1977.
Emmanuel B. Asibong, *Tennessee Williams: The Tragic Tension*, Ilfracombe, 1978.
Mohamed Choukri, *Tennessee Williams in Tangier*, Santa Barbara, California, 1979.
Foster Hirsch, *A Portrait of the Artist: The Plays of Tennessee Williams*, Port Washington, New York, 1979.
Felicia H. Londré, *Tennessee Williams*, New York, 1979.
Gene D. Phillips, *The Films of Tennessee Williams*, Philadelphia, 1980.
Dakin Williams and Shepherd Mead, *Tennessee Williams: An Intimate Biography*, New York, 1983.
Margaret A.Van Antwerp, Sally Johns (eds.) *Tennessee Williams: An Illustrated Chronicle*, Detroit, Michigan, 1984.
Catherine Arnott (compiler), *Tennessee Williams on File*, London, 1985.
Dotson Rader, *Tennessee, Cry of the Heart*, New York, 1985.
Donald Spoto, *The Kindness of Strangers: The Life of Tennessee Williams*, London, 1985.
Albert J. Devlin, *Conversations with Tennessee Williams*, Jackson, Mississippi, 1986.
Dotson Rader, *Tennessee Williams: An Intimate Memoir*, 1986.
Harry Rasky, *Tennessee Williams: A Portrait in Laughter and Lamentation*, New York, 1986.
Harold Bloom (ed.), *Tennessee Williams: Modern Critical Views*, New York, 1987.
Roger Boxill, *Tennessee Williams*, London, 1987.
Irene Shaland, *Tennessee Williams on the Soviet Stage*, Lanham, Maryland, 1987.
Donald Windham, *Lost Friendships: A Memoir of Truman Capote, Tennessee Williams, and Others*, New York, 1987.
Judith Thompson, *Tennessee Williams' Plays: Memory, Myth and Symbol*, New York, 1987.
Felicia Londré, *Tennessee Williams: Life, Work, Criticism*, Fredericton, New Brunswick, 1989.
Timothy D. Murray, *Evolving Texts: The Writing of Tennessee Williams*, Newark, Delaware, 1988.
Bruce Smith, *Costly Performances: Tennessee Williams: The Last Stage*, New York, 1990.

* * *

The revitalisation of American drama begun by Eugene O'Neill was ably, if unevenly, continued by Tennessee Williams. The territory changed from O'Neill's New England and New York to the Deep South, but the theme of people tearing themselves and each other apart by the intensity of their passions survived.

Williams's work is best approached through his three most successful plays, *The Glass Menagerie*, *A Streetcar Named Desire* and *Cat on a Hot Tin Roof*. The first has a lyrical, sad gentleness that separates it from the savage cruelty of much of his later work. Its focus on the withdrawn, immature Laura, crippled emotionally as much as physically, shows the playwright's sympathetic insight into female psychology which, despite occasional sentimentalisation, is distinctive of Williams's dramas. Similarly, the use of the eponymous collection of fragile animal-models in the play establishes the delight in symbolism that in later plays is often overworked. The play is non-realistic in its sectionalised house-and-exterior set, in its use of lighting and music, and in the choric use of one character to stress that it is a "memory play".

A Streetcar Named Desire, grimmer altogether, resumes the theme of a woman's self-destructive urge for sexual fulfilment (again in a squalid urban environment suggested by a sectionalised house-and-street set), but this time the heroine is more ambivalently presented as partly the architect of her own destruction. Like Laura, Blanche DuBois has her fantasy world, which is symbolically suggested by her references to Belle Reve (beautiful dream), the old family plantation home. Unlike Laura, she has a sexual appetite which can be predatory and cruel—yet her vulnerable sensitivity is indisputable, and she too is the victim of others. Living dangerously near to the edge of sanity and dependent on "the kindness of strangers", Blanche is the first of a line of characters to protect themselves by "mendacity", a key word in *Cat on a Hot Tin Roof*.

Before this play, however, came three less successful works. In *Summer and Smoke*, Williams's debt to D.H. Lawrence is plain. Less frequently remarked upon is the similarity between many of Williams's characters and the "grotesques" who populate Sherwood Anderson's *Winesburg, Ohio* of 1919. *Summer and Smoke*, like Anderson's short stories, has problems in engaging our complete sympathy for, and comprehension of, these small-town misfits. *The Rose Tattoo*, a turbulently melodramatic celebration of the sexual vigour of Sicilian immigrants, has at least the dramatic robustness to give it a theatrical vitality which, like other Williams plays, transferred effectively to the cinema screen. *Camino Real* sustained his reputation for imaginatively exploring the possibilities of different dramatic idioms, but its expressionism, its laboured symbolism, its lack of realism, and its romanticisation of loneliness ended up bewildering or alienating its audiences.

Cat on a Hot Tin Roof is dedicated to Elia Kazan, who admired its "freedom and flexibility of form" but whose much-discussed influence on it (he directed it) was crucial. As Williams's most vivid excursion into the tensions of family life, it is tightly and more conventionally constructed, displaying a lively, if bitter, sense of humour and a powerful vitality. It balances skilfully the self-destructive stubborn inertia of Brick, the loner, against the sexual energy of his wife Maggie, the cat who stays on the hot tin roof by virtue of her indestructible tenacity. Her will to survive is as dynamic as that of her father-in-law, Big Daddy, who is fighting against terminal cancer and the internecine warfare and malice of his divided, larger-than-life family. Brick is Williams's first full-scale exploration of the homosexuality that was to figure increasingly in the later plays and in his own life. His readiness to rework his plays is exemplified by the alternative versions of the last act—his own and the Kazan-inspired one—however each is evaluated.

After *Cat on a Hot Tin Roof*, Williams concentrated more on the loners than on the family, and the Gothic element of Southern decadence that earned *Streetcar* its initial notoriety became more sensationally sinister. Sexual and other forms of perversity, including cannibalism in *Suddenly Last Summer* and castration in *Sweet Bird of Youth*, figured prominently, and what he once identified as "the passion for declivity" in human nature became paramount. Yet the obsession with cruelty, loneliness, depravity, desperation, and death in these plays is often Jacobean in intensity, feeling, and dramatic energy.

A compulsive writer, Williams also published poetry, short stories, and two novels (*The Roman Spring of Mrs. Stone* and *Moise and the World of Reason*), as well as a volume of *Memoirs* from which his personality emerges as more ebullient than the blackness of his plays might lead one to expect. Some of the fiction he subsequently dramatised, and a study of the non-dramatic work, can often illuminate the dramatist's personality, aims, and achievements. So, too, can the forewords and afterwords which abound. (*Camino Real* has one of each, which reward detailed comparison.) He also had an interesting habit of digressing, in his stage directions, into asides on his intentions.

Comparisons and contrasts with the work of Arthur Miller, whose career coincides with and in many ways complements Williams's, are inevitable. Setting *The Glass Menagerie* so squarely in the Depression of the 1930's seemed to prefigure the emphasis on social context more characteristic of Miller, but this area was not developed further. The afterword to *Camino Real* tries to explain the play's failure by a resentful distinction between "thinking playwrights" and "us who are only permitted to feel": the self-deprecatory emphasis on feeling did the play no good and also did the playwright a disservice, yet his work would have benefitted in many places from a tighter rein on emotionalism and a more rigorous self-discipline. The Williams canon, though larger than Miller's, lacks Miller's abiding urge to explore new subjects and new dramatic forms, showing instead a preference for re-examining a limited range of themes and styles. At his best, however, Williams achieved unforgettably powerful, resonant, and moving theatre.

—Dennis Welland

See also *Volume 1* entries on *Cat on a Hot Tin Roof*; *The Glass Menagerie*; *The Night of the Iguana*; *A Streetcar Named Desire*.

WILLIAMSON, David (Keith). Born in Melbourne, Victoria, Australia, 24 February 1942. Educated at Monash University, Clayton, Victoria, BE in mechanical engineering 1964; Melbourne University. Married 1) Carol Anne Cranby in 1965 (divorced 1972), two children; 2) Kristin Ingrid Lofvén in 1974, two foster children. Design engineer, General Motors-Holden's, Melbourne, 1965; lecturer, Swinburne College of Technology, Melbourne, 1966–72; first-produced plays staged 1970; visiting professor, University of Aarhus, Denmark, 1978. Commissioner, Australian Broadcasting Corporation, 1978–79; Chairman, Australian National Playwrights Conference, 1979–80; President, Australian Writers Guild, 1979–86. Recipient: George Devine Award, 1971; Australian Writers Guild Award, 1972, 1973, 1977, 1979, 1980; Australian Film Institute Award, 1975, 1977. Officer, Order of Australia, 1983.

Works

Collections

The Coming of Stork; Jugglers Three; What If You Died Tomorrow. 1974.

Collected Plays I (includes *The Coming of Stork; The Removalists; Don's Party; Jugglers Three; What If You Died Tomorrow*). 1986.

Stage Works

The Indecent Exposure of Anthony East (produced Union Theatre, University of Melbourne, 1970; revised version produced Australian Theatre, Sydney, 1973).
The Coming of Stork (produced Café La Mama, Melbourne, 1970). In *The Coming of Stork; Jugglers Three; What If You Died Tomorrow*, 1974.
The Removalists (produced Café La Mama, Melbourne, 1971). 1972.
Don's Party (produced Pram Factory, Melbourne, 1971; revised version produced Jane Street Theatre, Sydney, 1971). 1973.
Jugglers Three (produced Russell Street Theatre, Melbourne, 1972). In *The Coming of Stork; Jugglers Three; What If You Died Tomorrow*, 1974.
What If You Died Tomorrow (produced Opera House Drama Theatre, Sydney, 1973). In *The Coming of Stork; Jugglers Three; What If You Died Tomorrow*, 1974.
The Department (produced Playhouse, Adelaide, 1974). 1975.
A Handful of Friends (produced Playhouse, Adelaide, 1976). 1976.
The Club (produced Russell Street Theatre, Melbourne, 1977; as *Players*, produced New York, 1978; as *The Team*, produced Toronto, 1981). 1978.
Travelling North (produced Nimrod Theatre, Sydney, 1979). 1980.
Celluloid Heroes (produced Nimrod Theatre, Sydney, 1980).
The Perfectionist (produced Opera House Drama Theatre, Sydney, 1982) 1983.
Sons of Cain (produced Russell Street Theatre, Melbourne, 1985). 1985.
Emerald City (produced Opera House Drama Theatre, Sydney, 1987). 1987.
Top Silk. 1989.
Siren (produced Melbourne and Sydney, 1992). 1991.
Money and Friends (produced Los Angeles, 1992). 1991.

Screenplays

Stork, 1971; *The Family Man* (episode in *Libido*), 1972; *Petersen*, 1974; *The Removalists*, 1975; *Don's Party*, 1976; *Mrs. Eliza Fraser*, 1976; *The Club*, 1980; *Gallipoli*, 1981 (published in *The Story of Gallipoli*, by Bill Gammage, 1981); *The Year of Living Dangerously*, with Peter Weir and C.J. Koch, 1983; *Phar Lap*, 1983; *Travelling North*, 1988; *Top Silk*, 1989 (published 1989).

Television Plays

The Perfectionist, 1985; *The Four Day Revolution* (series), 1988; *The Four Minute Mile*, 1988; *Emerald City*, 1988.

Other

Counterpointforum: The Australian Image, with Geoffrey Bolton. 1981.

*

Criticism

Books:
Brian Kiernan, "The Games People Play: The Development of David Williamson", in *Contemporary Australian Drama*, 1981.
Ortrun Zuber-Skerritt (ed.), *David Williamson* (includes bibliography), Amsterdam, 1988.
Brian Kiernan, *David Williamson: A Writer's Career*, Port Melbourne, 1990.

Articles:
Margaret Williams, "Mask and Cage: Stereotype in Recent Drama", in *Meanjin*, September 1972.
Alrene Sykes, "Australian Bards and British Reviewers", in *Australian Literary Studies*, May 1975.
David Williamson, "After the *Perfectionist*: An Interview with David Williamson", in *London Magazine*, 23, 1983.
Brian Kiernan, "David Williamson's Plays Since *The Department*", in *Southerly*, March 1986.
John McCallum, "A New Map for Australia: The Plays of David Williamson", in *Australian Literary Studies*, May 1984.
David Williamson, Paul Kavanagh, and Peter Kuch, "Interview", in *Southerly*, June 1986.

*   *   *

David Williamson is Australia's best-known and most popular writer for stage and cinema. The Williamson name is as close to a guarantee of an enthusiastic audience response as anything in Australian theatre could be; the Williamson style, with its blend of acutely observed naturalism and caricature, and its shifting combination of the impulses toward satiric exposure and celebration of the culture, came to define the "New Wave" in Australian theatre of the 1970's which very rapidly became the mainstream. But while no-one would dispute that knowledge of his audience which is part of what the playwright has called a "symbiotic relationship", there is much more to Williamson's achievement as a dramatist than unrivalled success at the box office and an assured sense of what will work on the stage.

From his earliest work with the La Mama Company and the Australian Performing Group at the end of the 1960's, Williamson has been a writer who has consistently shown that serious purposes are not incompatible with a mode of theatre that is much of the time very funny. The first of his plays to make the transition from the alternative theatre to the mainstream was *The Removalists*, in which the satirical treatment of aspects of Australian culture produced a style of tough comedy which had not been seen or heard on Australian stages before. But the play also offered a startling vision, and a shrewd analysis, of violence in Australian society, and remains among the most disturbing works written for the Australian theatre.

Not all Williamson's plays have confronted their audiences as directly as did *The Removalists*, but all of them have involved a challenge that lurks underneath the entertaining surface. One aspect of the challenge, of course, lies in the acuteness of the satirical observation. *Don's Party*, which followed *The Removalists* into the establishment theatres in 1972, was the first of a number of comic exposures of the disillusionments and self-mockery of an educated, affluent bourgeoisie, which bore an uncanny resemblance to the audiences that watched them in the mainstream theatre.

Don's Party defined, in a number of ways, the boundaries which characterized the first decade of Williamson's writing for the theatre. Its speakers were articulate and sophisticated people, but their social dealings gleefully exploited new theatrical freedoms of language and action. This was the world of the "ocker", whose very calculated vulgarity was effective both as a disconcerting strategy and as a clown-mask which disguised his real insecurities. Whether there was really a sensitive soul under all his boorish bravado was beyond the business of the plays; Williamson's fascination with patterns of social manipulation, with the ways in which power is asserted and conceded and the things which people do to deceive themselves and others, leaves one inclined to see in his plays all behaviour as tactical, and all individuals as no more than the sum of the roles they play.

The conversational agenda in the "ocker" plays was distinctly a male preserve. Just as the old mates of *Don's Party* very self-consciously carry all the responsibility for the entertainment, so the men of *Jugglers Three* and *A Handful of Friends* devote much of their time to a self-protective verbal swagger. In the plays concerned directly with institutional infighting, like *The Department* and *The Club*, the male power-games are unadulterated; only one of the nine academics at the meeting in the former, and none of the six conspirators in the latter, is female. The relatively marginal status of women in Wiliamson's plays has been a source of frequent criticism, which the playwright has conspicuously sought to redress in his plays of the 1980's. In his very clever study of marital roles, *The Perfectionist*, Barbara becomes the raisonneur of the piece; significantly, though, most of the comic energy remains with her husband Stuart.

The challenge beneath the ingratiating surface has recently become more exactingly concerned with ethical issues—*Sons of Cain* and *Top Silk* both draw on recognizable contemporary political matters as a focus for the moral dilemmas which they posed for their audiences. These plays, and his recent popular successes *Emerald City* and *Siren*, indicate the playwright's readiness to challenge himself as well—the developing experiments with monologue represent another approach to the analysis of forms of manipulation. In these plays the clearer moral standpoint has been accompanied by a greater emphasis on the mechanics of plot, and a subordination of the impulses to satiric exposure and mythologizing of aspects of Australian society.

Williamson's plays have constructed a very intricate and sophisticated suburban mythology, and many of their images have had an influence well beyond the theatre. *The Club* provided the definitive theatrical treatment of the phenomenon of football as religion, while there will never be an Australian election-night party which does not live, to some extent, in the shadow of Don's. Williamson's screenplays for the cinema, like *Gallipoli* and *Phar Lap*, have been concerned with cultural myths which have been longer established. But all his work has presented audiences, in different degrees, with a mixture of two rich and potent lines of approach: one, the celebration of the culture, is marked by a spirit of understanding and compassion, which has produced, in *Travelling North*, perhaps the finest comedy of reconciliation in Australian theatre; the other has offered a critique of contemporary middle-class life which prizes most the quality it most represents, an intelligent and sceptical self-awareness.

—Peter Fitzpatrick

See also *Volume 1* entries on *The Removalists*; *Travelling North*.

WILSON, August. Born in Pittsburgh, Pennsylvania, USA, 27 April 1945. Educated at Gladstone High School, Pittsburgh, 1960–61. Married Judy Oliver in 1981; one daughter. Founder, Black Horizons Theatre Company, Pittsburgh, 1968; first-produced play, *Black Bart and the Sacred Hills*, staged 1981; since 1980 associate playwright, Playwrights Center, Minneapolis; since 1982 member, New Dramatists, New York. Recipient: New York Drama Critics Circle Award, 1985, 1987, 1988; Whiting Foundation Award, 1986; American Theatre Critics Award, 1986, 1989, 1991; Outer Circle Award, 1987; Drama Desk Award, 1987; John Gassner Award, 1987; Tony Award, 1987; Helen Hayer Award, 1988; Pulitzer Prize, 1987, 1990. Member, American Academy.

Works

Collections

Three Plays (includes *Ma Rainey's Black Bottom*; *Fences*; *Joe Turner's Come and Gone*).   1991.

Stage Works

Black Bart and the Sacred Hills (produced Penumbra Theatre, St. Paul, Minnesota, 1981).
Jitney (produced by Black Horizons Theatre, Pittsburgh, 1982).
The Mill Hand's Lunch Bucket (produced New York, 1983).
Ma Rainey's Black Bottom (produced Yale Repertory Theatre, New Haven, Connecticut, 1984).   1985.
Fences (produced Yale Repertory Theatre, New Haven, Connecticut, 1985).   1986.
Joe Turner's Come and Gone (produced Yale Repertory Theatre, New Haven, Connecticut, 1986).   1988.
The Piano Lesson (produced Yale Repertory Theatre, New Haven, Connecticut, 1987).   1990.
Two Trains Running (produced Yale Repertory Theatre, New Haven, Connecticut, 1990).

*

Bibliographies

Philip C. Kolin (ed.), *American Playwrights Since 1945: A Guide to Scholarship, Criticism, and Performance*, New York, 1989.

Criticism

Articles:
August Wilson, "An Interview with August Wilson", in *Yale/ Theatre*, vol.16 no.1, 1984.
Hilary De Vries, "A Song in Search of Itself: August Wilson as a Chronicler of Black America's Recent Past", in *American Theater*, vol.3 no.10, 1987.
Sandra G. Shannon, "The Long Wait: August Wilson's *Ma Rainey's Black Bottom*", in *Black American Literature Forum*, vol.25 no.1, 1991.

* * *

By the early 1990's, August Wilson has become probably the best known and the most popular African-American play-

August Wilson (left) with director Lloyd Richards on the set of the Yale Repertory Theatre's 1990 production of Wilson's *Two Trains Running*.

wright. His plays have won the major critical awards (including Pulitzer Prizes), and the arrival of his latest play on Broadway is greeted with intense interest and high expectation. He has worked in close, creative collaboration with Lloyd Richards, his plays' premieres have taken place at the Yale School of Drama (Yale Repertory Theater) where Richards was long-time Dean and Artistic Director.

Born in Pittsburgh, Pennsylvania, Wilson first came to the attention of Americans with the appearance of *Ma Rainey's Black Bottom*, produced at Yale and later in New York in 1984. That play, like those which followed it, is a slice of the greater saga of the Afro-American experience in America, which the playwright has dedicated himself to dramatizing. The *whole* story of this experience will be contained in a series of plays set in different decades of the 20th century. Taken together, there is little doubt that this extraordinary project will alter permanently the shape and size of the understanding of black life and history in the United States, and contribute uniquely to the entire body of American knowledge of itself as it is defined through the theatre. "I simply believe", Wilson explains about the ideology which drives his writing, "that blacks have a culture, and that we have our own mythology, our own history, our own social organizations, our own creative motif. That's what I mean when I say cultural nationalism".

Two themes central to Wilson's work are the need to aspire and the search for identity, and his plays define the painful and sometimes violent conflicts which develop when people attempt both to *be* better and to *know* more. Yet his world is

deeply ethical, for his characters, with differing awareness, have a sense of the *moral* territory they are trying to explore and the high odds against their success to make it their own. Within Wilson's world, the white world is the enemy. It uses its economic power or civic authority to crush the Afro-American's aspiration and to deny the sense of selfhood necessary for both wisdom and happiness. At times, the actual humiliation and fear of failure result in a violence which turns on itself, as when in *Ma Rainey* (which is set in the 1920's), the crazed Levee brutally and uselessly murders his fellow jazz musician Toledo after being patronized and swindled by a white music producer.

In *Fences* (first produced in 1985; set in the 1950's), the protagonist Troy Maxon, an illiterate garbage collector, is embittered by the system that has denied him baseball stardom and the pleasure that comes from using and enjoying his natural gifts. He struggles to maintain authority over his family, especially over his son Corey. After Troy's death from a heart attack, his long-suffering, devoted wife Rose describes to their son, who has fled home and joined the Marines, what she came to know about her husband: "You can't be nobody but who you are, Cory. That shadow [of Troy] was nothing but you growing into yourself. You either got to grow into it or cut it down to fit you. But that's all you got to make life with". Thus, says Wilson, we pass on to the next generation our hopes and our deepest fears and, in this play as in the others, beauty and meaning come from the struggle to *articulate* the "voice" within us. *Fences* concludes with Troy's retarded brother Gabriel doing a "*slow, strange dance, eerie and life-giving. A dance of atavistic signature and ritual. He begins to howl in what is an attempt at song, or perhaps a song turning back into itself in an attempt at speech".*

Joe Turner's Come and Gone (first produced in 1986; set in 1911), whose title implies both a visit and a journey, dramatizes the stories of a number of characters who are searching for fulfilment, companionship, and knowledge. Most importantly, it tells the story of Herald Loomis, cruelly imprisoned for seven years by the white authorities (the "Joe Turner" of the title) for an unknown offence, searching for his wife Martha whom he hasn't seen for ten years. ("I been wandering a long time in somebody else's world. When I find my wife that be the making of my own.") His travels with their 11-year-old daughter, Zonia, take him to a Pittsburgh boarding house, where he meets a number of helpful guides on his familial and spiritual journey. In particular, he meets Bynum Walker (a "binding man") and Rutherford Selig (a "finding man") who bring him to his two extraordinary moments of crisis—his reunion with Martha and his discovery of himself. In a final, bloody exorcism, Herald slashes himself with a knife, cutting himself from the ties that bind, and setting himself free for an automomous existence. The last stage direction of the play reads: "*Having found his song, the sound of self-sufficiency, fully resurrected and cleansed and given breath . . . having accepted the responsibility for his own presence in the world, he is free to soar above the environs that weighed and pushed his spirit into terrifying contractions".*

The themes of self-discovery and confrontation with the past, set in an historical environment of racism and economic distress, are also found in *Ma Rainey* and *The Piano Lesson* (first produced in 1987; set in the 1930's), and like *Fences* and *Joe Turner*, they reveal Wilson's deeply poetic sensibility. In their frequent "arias", Wilson's characters attempt to give expression to their deepest feelings, allowing us to hear as well as see Wilson's wide range of theatrical talents, which have been so profoundly influenced by the collision of African and American cultures. "There is no idea in the world that is not contained by black life", he has said. The music and musical instruments he features prominently in his work amplify the dialogue of the plays, and are used to good effect in their poetic prefaces. A paragraph from the note to *Joe Turner* is representative of his relationship to his characters and to the Afro-American experience, and sums up a large part of Wilson's own artistic search: "Foreigners in a strange land, they carry as part and parcel of their baggage a long line of separation and dispersement which informs their sensibilities and marks their conduct as they search for ways to reconnect, to reassemble, to give clear and luminous meaning to the song which is both a wail and a whelp of joy".

—Robert Skloot

See also *Volume 1* entry on *Fences.*

WILSON, Lanford (Eugene). Born in Lebanon, Missouri, USA, 13 April 1937. Educated at Ozark High School, Missouri; Southwest Missouri State College, Springfield, 1955–56; San Diego State College, California, 1956–57; University of Chicago, 1957–58. Various jobs, including work in advertising, Chicago, 1957–62; director, actor, and designer for Caffe Cino and Cafe La Mama (later known as La Mama Experimental Theatre), New York, in the 1960's; since 1969, co-founder and resident playwright, Circle Repertory Company, New York. Has directed several productions of his own plays. Recipient: Vernon Rice Award, 1968; New York Drama Critics Circle Award, 1973, 1980; Obie Award, 1973, 1975, 1983; Outer Circle Award, 1973; American Academy Award, 1974; Pulitzer Prize, 1980; Institute of Arts and Letters Award.

Works

Collections

"*Balm in Gilead*" *and Other Plays* (includes *Home Free!; Ludlow Fair*).   1965.
"*The Rimers of Eldritch*" *and Other Plays* (includes *The Madness of Lady Bright; This is the Rill Speaking; Days Ahead; Wandering: A Turn*).   1967.
"*The Sand Castle*" *and Three Other Plays* (includes *Wandering; Stoop; Sextet (Yes): A Play for Voices*).   1970.
"*The Great Nebula in Orion*" *and Three Other Plays* (includes *Ikke, Ikke, Nye, Nye; The Family Continues; Victory on Mrs. Dandywine's Island*).   1973.
Hall of North American Forests (one act plays; includes *The Bottle of Harp; Say de Kooning; A Betrothal*).   1988.

Stage Works

So Long at the Fair (produced Caffe Cino, New York, 1963).
No Trespassing (produced Caffe Cino, New York, 1964).
Home Free! (produced Caffe Cino, New York, 1964).   In "*Balm in Gilead*" *and Other Plays*, 1965.
Balm in Gilead (produced Cafe La Mama, New York, 1964).   In "*Balm in Gilead*" *and Other Plays*, 1965.
The Madness of Lady Bright (produced Caffe Cino, New York, 1964).   In "*The Rimers of Eldritch*" *and Other Plays*, 1967.
Ludlow Fair (produced Caffe Cino, New York, 1965).   In "*Balm in Gilead*" *and Other Plays*, 1965.
Sex is Between Two People (produced Caffe Cino, New York, 1965).
The Rimers of Eldritch (produced Cafe La Mama, New York, 1965).   In *The Rimers of Eldritch and Other Plays*, 1967.
This is the Rill Speaking (produced Caffe Cino, New York, 1965).   In "*The Rimers of Eldritch*" *and Other Plays*, 1967.
Days Ahead (produced Caffe Cino, New York, 1965).   In "*The Rimers of Eldritch*" *and Other Plays*, 1967.
The Sand Castle (produced Cafe La Mama, New York, 1965).   In "*The Sand Castle*" *and Three Other Plays*, 1970.
Wandering: A Turn (produced Caffe Cino, New York, 1966).   In "*The Rimers of Eldritch*" *and Other Plays*, 1967.
Miss Williams: A Turn (produced Cafe La Mama, New York, 1967).
Untitled Play, music by Al Carmines (produced Judson Poet's Theatre, New York, 1967).
The Gingham Dog (produced Washington Theatre Club, Washington, DC, 1968).   1970.
The Great Nebula in Orion (produced Stables Theatre Club, Manchester, England, 1970).   In "*The Great Nebula in Orion*" *and Three Other Plays*, 1973.
Lemon Sky (produced Studio Arena Theatre, Buffalo, 1970).   1970.
Serenading Louie (produced Washington Theatre Club, Washington, DC, 1970).   1976; revised version (produced New York, 1984), 1985.
Sextet (Yes): A Play for Voices (produced Circle Repertory

Theatre, New York, 1971). In *"The Sand Castle" and Three Other Plays*, 1970.

Summer and Smoke, music by Lee Hoiby, from the play by Tennessee Williams (produced St. Paul, Minnesota, 1971). 1972.

Ikke, Ikke, Nye, Nye, Nye (produced Yale Cabaret, New Haven, Connecticut, 1971). In *"The Great Nebula in Orion" and Three Other Plays*, 1973.

The Family Continues (produced Circle Repertory Theatre, New York, 1972). In *"The Great Nebula in Orion" and Three Other Plays*, 1973.

The Hot l Baltimore (produced Circle Repertory Theatre, New York, 1973). 1973.

The Mound Builders (produced Circle Repertory Theatre, New York, 1975). 1976.

Brontosaurus (produced Circle Repertory Theatre, New York, 1977). 1978.

5th of July (produced Circle Repertory Theatre, New York, 1978). 1979.

Talley's Folly (produced Circle Repertory Theatre, New York, 1979). 1980.

Bar Play, in *Holidays* (produced Actors' Theatre, Louisville, Kentucky, 1979).

Talley and Son (as *A Tale Told*, produced Circle Repertory Theatre, New York, 1981; revised version, as *Talley and Son*, produced New York, 1985). 1986.

Angels Fall (produced Circle Repertory Theatre, New York, 1982). 1983.

Thymus Vulgaris (produced New York, 1982). 1982.

Three Sisters, from a play by Chekhov (produced Hartford Stage, Hartford, Connecticut, 1985).

Say deKooning (produced Southampton, New York, 1985). In *Hall of North American Forests*, 1988.

Sa-Hurt? (produced New York, 1986).

A Betrothal (produced London, 1986). In *Hall of North American Forests*, 1988.

Burn This (produced Mark Taper Forum, Los Angeles and New York, 1987). 1988.

Dying Breed (produced New York, 1987).

A Poster of the Cosmos (produced New York, 1987).

The Bottle of Harp. In *Hall of North American Forests*, 1988.

The Moonshot Tape (produced New York, 1990).

Redwood Curtain (produced Seattle, Washington, 1992).

Screenplays

One Arm, 1970; *Burn This*, 1992; *Tally's Folly*, 1992.

Television Plays

The Migrants, from a story by Tennessee Williams, 1974; *Taxi!*, 1979.

*

Bibliographies

Kimball King, *Ten Modern American Playwrights*, New York, 1982.

Criticism

Books:
Gene A. Barnett, *Lanford Wilson*, Boston, 1987.
Mark Busby, *Lanford Wilson*, Boise, Idaho, 1987.

Articles:
Leslie Kane, "The Agony of Isolation in the Drama of Anton Chekhov and Lanford Wilson", in *West Virginia Philological Papers*, 31, 1985–86.
Martin J. Jacobi, "The Comic Vision of Lanford Wilson", in *Studies in the Literary Imagination*, 21, 1988.
Gary Konas, "Tennessee Williams and Lanford Wilson at the Missouri Crossroads", in *Studies in American Drama 1945 –Present*, 5, 1990.

* * *

Lanford Wilson, inheritor of the mantles of Tennessee Williams, William Inge, and Lillian Hellman, dramatizes philos/aphilos, the mixture of love and hatred which passes for family feeling. When outside the orbit of relatives, Wilson's characters either form surrogate families or endure in lonely isolation.

In offering new American domestic myths, Wilson writes romantically with empathy for his characters' pain, with regret for their loss of love, and with nostalgia for idyllic, supportive familial relationships. Although he often makes us laugh, Wilson has been especially treasured in the United States (and disliked by British critics) for his ability to make us feel. He frequently focuses on the heart-wrenching aspects of our vulnerabilities, our wounds, our anxieties, our insecurities, our loss of love.

Wilson recalls playwright Robert Patrick "saying I'm looking for the perfect family, or at least a workable family. It's obviously a brother hangup. I don't need a father or mother. I need the brothers and sisters." The softer of Wilson's representations of family lack a husband or father figure; the tougher contain such a man who brings others to grief, reflecting Wilson's antipathy to fathers. Siblings appear frequently, and they seem less destructive than characters in other relations to the protagonists. *Lemon Sky*, which the playwright acknowledges as "completely autobiographical", dramatizes Wilson's—or Alan's—reunion at 17 with the father who had left him and his mother when he was five; Douglas, the autocratic father, clashes with Alan, while Alan's half-brothers and stepmother offer support, and his foster sisters exist primarily to further illuminate paternal egocentricity. A somewhat sympathetic character, Douglas nevertheless makes passes at his foster daughters, denies Alan autonomy, and finally throws Alan out of the house because he's not bedding women.

Parent as semi-villain in *Lemon Sky* contrasts with parent as victim in *The Sand Castle*, in which mother Irene and 12-year-old younger son Kenny evoke the most audience sympathy. Like the sand-cliffs which collapse during the play, this family crumbles, its loyalties eroded to the point where Joan seduces her own mother's boyfriend.

In the muted generational conflict between aunt and nephew in *Brontosaurus*, disparity in the characters' views leaves the woman lonely. Other plays which portray the "lonely people" of "Eleanor Rigby" include the fragilely luminous *The Great Nebula in Orion*, in which the married woman feels just as alienated as her single college chum, *The Rimers of Eldritch*, in which stunted, intolerant adults lay waste to the potential of their young people, and the *Hot l Baltimore*, in which the extended family of whores, drifters, the destitute, and the aged inhabit a condemned hotel. This moderately upbeat play, a love song to Americans who are down and out, offers negative images: Millie, the youngest of 14 brothers and sisters, describes familial tensions. The girl explains that her daddy didn't mind her being a hooker as long as she bought his beer. Paul Granger loses interest in providing a home for his grandfather, Jamie abandons her brother, and Mrs. Bellotti regards marriage as an institution which leaves women with invalid husbands but may at least take grown sons off their parents' hands.

When the husband or father appears, domesticity suffers. Marriage is responsible for the bitter, twisted feelings of a couple who have been inflicting dreaful damage on each other in *The Gingham Dog*. Although Wilson moves from disillusion to sadness at the separation by the end of that play, in *The Mound Builders* marriage ends in death for one husband and the loss of professional motivation for another. In *Serenading Louie*, the two couples' middle-American habits mask the pathetic crumbling of illusions, bonds of love, and self-esteem that is symbolized by a cave-in which has killed a three-year-old girl. Wilson's most despairing depiction of family, *Serenading Louie*, culminates in Carl murdering his wife and daughter and taking his own life. Yet the family which survives in a Wilson play may be just as chilling an image as those which disintegrate. *The Family Continues*, for example, demonstrates the perpetuation of destructive patterns that pass from father to son.

Wilson expresses ambivalence towards family in his Talley trilogy, each play beginning on the fourth of July. The last produced, *A Tale Told* (later retitled *Talley and Son*), set in 1944, presents the especially negative side of the household, as this prosperous southern Missouri family bickers, mostly over money. This play presents a finished tale, a summation, a tallying for the Talleys. Its old-fashioned plot, complete with a fainting woman at the end of Act I, resembles Lillian Hellman's *The Little Foxes* in its treatment of a narrow-minded, rapacious family's concern with a profitable textile deal. It depicts endings: of three lives, of many efforts, of false values, of the family business, and of Sally's and Matt's courtship. Sally and Matt, of course, are the characters from *Talley's Folly*, for *A Tale Told* dramatizes the off-stage events which occur while Sally and Matt are down at the boathouse during *Talley's Folly*. We see more clearly why Sally has to get away from her family, and we cheer her on when she enters near the play's end to pack and leave with Matt.

The trilogy's other two parts affirm certain positive possibilities for families. *Talley's Folly* proves to be a frankly romantic play. Its two eccentrics emerge as good, bright, affectionate people who should take a risk and get married. They have suffered from "humpty-dumpty" complexes, that is, from self-protective fears about cracking their shells. They turn out to be perfectly suited to each other because Sally cannot have children and Matt doesn't want any. Significantly, they will make a good family because they will not enlarge it.

The Fifth of July also considers commitment. Wilson describes its protagonist as "willing to sell everything out in order to avoid facing himself". He likewise mocks it as "the best play William Inge ever wrote", but its concern with selling or saving the family estate instead suggests *The Cherry Orchard*. Set in the same house as *A Tale Told*, but in 1977, *The Fifth of July* depicts 65-year-old Sally scattering Matt's ashes over the rose bushes and insisting that Ken Talley and his lover Jed hold on to the house and land—and each other. Although other family relationships in the play appear precarious, those among Sally, Ken, and Jed seem likely to prove workable and enduring.

Burn This likewise dramatizes the fear of risk culminating in a somewhat terrified commitment. The lives of three people afraid of passion are disrupted by the death of a friend and the appearance of his brother Pale, as volatile as they are repressed. Dancer Anna, screenwriter Burton, and ad-writer Larry have been channeling their feelings into creative work.

This nearly asexual surrogate family-unit dissolves, however, when Larry encourages the electrifying attraction between Anna and Pale by writing Pale a note which asks "Why should love always be tragic?" and orders him to "burn this". Priggish Burton advises burning creative work that reveals personal emotions. Instead, Pale's and Anna's elemental feelings and incendiary erotic attraction are what really "burn".

Wilson appreciates the difficulty of living in a family, finds drama in the failed attempts, and creates affecting examples of failures. In his later work, he even portrays successful bonding.

—Tish Dace

See also *Volume 1* entry on *Burn This*.

———

WITKACY.   See **WITIEWICZ, Stanisław Ignacy.**

———

WITKIEWICZ, Stanisław (Ignacy). Born in Warsaw, Poland (Russian sector), 24 February 1885; son of the writer and painter Stanisław Witkiewicz (and used pseudonym "Witkacy" to distinguish himself from his father). Educated at secondary school, Lvov, to 1903; Academy of Fine Arts, Cracow, 1905–06, and in Italy, France, and Germany. Married Jadwiga Unrug in 1923. Served with Tsarist forces in Russia during World War I: wounded, 1915; elected political commissar by his regiment, 1917. Accompanied the anthropologist Bronisław Malinowski on an anthropological expedition to Australia, 1914; painter from 1918; first-produced play, *Pragmatyści* [*The Pragmatists*], staged 1921; founder, Formist Theatre, an amateur group, Zakopane, 1925–27; in later years wrote mainly philosophical works; lived in Zakopane, 1930–39; fled east after the German and Soviet invasions of Poland, 1939. Committed suicide in Jeziory, near Dąbrowica, 18 September 1939.

Works

Collections

Dramaty [Plays] (2 vols.), edited by Konstanty Puzyna. 1962; revised edition, 1972.
"The Madman and the Nun" and Other Plays (includes *The Water Hen; The Crazy Locomotive; The Mother; They; The Shoemakers*), translated by Daniel Gerould and C.S. Durer. 1968.
Tropical Madness: Four Plays (includes *The Pragmatists; Mr. Price; Gyubal Wahazar; Metaphysics of a Two-Headed Calf*), translated by Daniel and Eleanor Gerould. 1972.
Volume 12, Number 1 of the journal *Drama and Theatre* (includes the juvenile plays: *Cockroaches; The Courageous Princess; The Poor Boy; Menagerie; Comedies of Family Life; Princess Magdalena*, translated by Daniel Gerould). 1974.

The Beelzebub Sonata (includes *The Beelzebub Sonata; Dainty Shapes and Hairy Apes; Tumor Brainowicz;* and non-dramatic writings), translated by Daniel Gerould. 1977.

Dzieła wybrane [Selected Works] (5 vols.; includes reprints of the 1972 edition of *Dramaty*). 1985.

Stage Works

Komedie z życia rodzinnego (produced 1983). 1893; translated as *Comedies of Family Life*, in *Drama and Theatre*, vol.12 no.1, 1974.

Pragmatyści (produced Teatr "Elsynor", Warsaw, 1921). In *Zdroj*, 3, 1920; in book form, in *Dramaty*, 1962; translated as *The Pragmatists*, in *Tropical Madness*, 1972.

Tumor Mózgowicz (produced Teatr Słowackiego, Cracow, 1921). 1921; in book form, in *Dramaty*, 1962; translated as *Tumor Brainowicz*, in *The Beelzebub Sonata* (collection).

Kurka wodna (produced Teatr Słowackiego, Cracow, 1922). In *Dramaty*, 1962; translated as *The Water Hen*, in *The Madman and the Nun. . .* (collection), 1968.

W małym dworku [In a Small Country House] (produced Teatr Miejski, Torun, 1923). With *Szewcy*, 1948.

Nowe Wyzwolenie [The New Deliverance] (produced by Teatr Towarzystwo, Zakopane, 1925; produced professionally, Teatr Maly, Warsaw, 1926). In *Zwrotnica*, 3–4, 1922–23; translated as *The New Deliverance*, in *Polish Review*, 1–2, 1973.

Mątwa; czyli, Hyrkaniczny światopogląd (produced Teatr Cricot, Cracow, 1933). In *Zwrotnica*, 5, 1923; in book form, in *Dramaty*, 1962; translated as *The Cuttlefish*, in *Treasury of the Theatre 2*, edited by Bernard F. Dukore and John Gassner, 1969, and in *Twentieth Century Polish Theatre*, edited by Bohdan Drozdowski, 1979.

Wariat i zakonnica; czyli, Nie ma złego, coby na jeszcze gorsze nie wyszło (produced Teatr Miejski, Toruń, 1924). In *Skamander*, 39, 1925; translated as *The Madman and the Nun*, in *The Madman and the Nun. . .* (collection), 1968.

Mister Price; czyli, Bzik tropikalny, with Eugenia Dunin-Borkowska (produced Teatr Nielzależny, Warsaw, 1926). In *Dramaty*, 1962; translated as *Mr. Price; or, Tropical Madness*, in *Tropical Madness*, 1972.

Jan Maciej Karol Wścieklica [Jan Maciej Karol Hellcat] (produced Teatr Fredro, Warsaw, 1925). In *Dramaty*, 1962.

Metafizyka dwugłowego cielęcia (produced Teatr Nowy, Poznan, 1928). In *Dramaty*, 1962; translated as *Metaphysics of a Two-Headed Calf*, in *Tropical Madness*, 1972.

Sonata Belzebuba; czyli, Prawdziwe zdarzenie w Mordowarze (produced Teatr A. Węgierki, Białystok, 1966). In *Ateneum*, 4, 1938; in book form, in *Dramaty*, 1962; translated as *The Beelzebub Sonata*, in *The Beelzebub Sonata* (collection), 1977.

Odważna księżniczka (produced Teatr Marcinek, Poznan, 1970). In *Przekoj*, 106, 1947; translated as *The Courageous Princess*, in *Drama and Theatre*, vol.12 no.1, 1974.

Szewcy (produced Panstwowy Teatr Wybrzeże, Sopot, 1957). With *W malym dworku*, 1948; translated as *The Shoemakers*, in *The Madman and the Nun. . .* (collection), 1968.

Karaluchy (produced by Olawka Theatre Club, Wrocław, 1966). In *Kamena*, 2, 1960; translated as *Cockroaches*, in *Drama and Theatre*, vol.12 no.1, 1974.

Oni [They] (produced Akademicki Teatr, University of Warsaw, 1963). In *Dramaty*, 1962; translated as *They*, in *The Madman and the Nun. . .* (collection), 1968.

Maciej Korbowa i Bellatrix [Maciej Korbowa and Bellatrix]. In *Dramaty*, 1962.

Niepodległość trójkątów [The Independence of Triangles] (produced 1988). In *Dramaty*, 1962.

Gyubal Wahazar; czyli, Na przełęczach absurdu (produced Teatr Polski, Poznan, 1966). In *Dramaty*, 1962; translated as *Gyubal Wahazar; or, Along the Cliffs of the Absurd*, in *Tropical Madness*, 1972.

Bezimienne dzieło (produced Teatr Słowackiego, Cracow, 1967). In *Dramaty*, 1962; translated as *The Anonymous Work*, in *Twentieth-Century Polish Avant-Garde Drama*, edited by Daniel Gerould, 1977.

Nadobnisie i koczkodany; czyli, Zielona pigułka (produced by amateur group, Teatr Studjny, Warsaw, 1967; produced professionally, by Cricot II, Warsaw, 1973). In *Dramaty*, 1962; translated as *Dainty Shapes and Hairy Apes*, in *The Beelzebub Sonata* (collection), 1977.

Szalona lokomotywa (produced Studencki Teatr 38, Cracow, 1965). In *Dramaty*, 1962; translated as *The Crazy Locomotive*, in *The Madman and the Nun. . .* (collection), 1968.

Janulka, córka Fizdejki [Janulka, Daughter of Fizdejko] (produced Teatr Wspolczesny, Wrocław, 1974). In *Dramaty*, 1962.

Matka (produced Teatr Stary, Cracow, 1964). In *Dramaty*, 1962; translated as *The Mother*, in *The Madman and the Nun. . .* (collection), 1968.

Biedny chłopiec (produced Teatr Marcinek, Poznan, 1970). In *Przegladzie humanistycznym*, 1, 1964; translated as *The Poor Boy*, in *Drama and Theatre*, vol.12 no.1, 1974.

Menażeria; cyzli, Wybryk słonia (produced Olawka Theatre Club, Wrocław, 1966). In *Dialog*, 8, 1965; translated as *Menagerie; or, The Elephant's Escapades*, in *Drama and Theatre*, vol.12 no.1, 1974.

Księżniczka Magdalena; czyli, Natrętny książe (produced Olawka Theatre Club, Wrocław, 1966). In *Dialog*, 8, 1965; translated as *Princess Magdalena; or, The Importunate Princess*, in *Drama and Theatre*, vol.12 no.4, 1974.

Panna Tutli-Putli [Miss Tootli-Pootli] (produced Ateneum, Warsaw, 1975). 1974.

Fiction

Pożegnanie jesieni [Farewell to Autumn]. 1927.

Nienasycenie. 1930; translated as *Insatiability*, 1977.

Jedyne wyjście [The Only Way Out], edited by Tomasz Jodelka-Burzecki. 1968.

622 Upadki Burga; czyli, Demoniczna Kobieta [622 Downfalls of Bungo; or, The Demonic Woman]. 1972.

Memoirs and Letters

Listy do Bronisława Malinowskiego [Letters to Bronislaw Malinowski]. 1981.

Other

Nowe formy w malarstwie i wynikające stąd nieporozumienia [New Forms in Painting and the Resulting Misunderstandings]. 1919.

Teatr: Wstęp do teorii czystej formy w teatrze [Theatre: Introduction to the Theory of Pure Form in the Theatre]. 1923; as *Czysta forma w teatrze*, edited by J. Degler, 1977.

Nikotyna, alkohol, kokaina, peyotl, morfina, eter [Nicotine, Alcohol, Cocaine, Peyote, Morphine, Ether]. 1932.

Pojecia i twierdzenia implikowane przez pojecie istnienia [The Concepts and Principles Implied by the Concept of Existence]. 1935.

Pisma filozoficzne i estetyczne [Philosophical and Aesthetic Writings] (4 vols.), edited by J. Leszcynski. 1974–76.

Bez kompromisu: Pisma krytyczne i publicystyczne [No Compromise: Critical and Journalistic Writings], edited by J. Degler. 1976.

Poza rzeczywistoşcia [Outside Reality]. 1977.

Marzenia improducktywne: Dywagacja metafizyczna [Improductive Daydreams: Metaphysical Palaver]. 1977.

Zagadnienie psychofizyczne [A Psychophysical Problem], edited by B. Michalski. 1978.

Niemyte dusze: Studia obyczajowe i społeczne [Unwashed Souls: Studier of Social Manners and Morals]. 1978.

*

Bibliographies

Daniel C. Gerould, "Theatre Checklist No. 6: Stanislaw Ignacy Witkiewicz, in *Theatrefacts*, vol. 2 no. 2, 1975.

Criticism

Books:

Alain van Crugten, *S.I. Witkiewicz: Aux Sources d'un théâtre nouveau*, Lausanne, 1971.

Daniel C. Gerould, *Witkacy: Stanislaw Ignacy Witkiewicz as an Imaginative Writer*, Seattle, Washington, 1981.

Hanna Dziechcinska, (ed.), *Stanislaw Igancy Witkiewicz*, Wrocław, 1986.

Christine Kiebuzinska, *Revolutionaries in the Theatre: Meyerhold, Brecht, and Witkiewicz*, Ann Arbor, Michigan, 1988.

Anna Micinska, *Witkacy: S.I. Witkiewicz: Life and Work* (from the Polish), Warsaw, 1990.

Articles:

Jan Blonski "Witkacy", in *Polish Perspectives*, 11, 1968.

"Witkiewicz Issue" of *Polish Review*, 18, 1973.

Daniel C. Gerould, "The Playwright as a Child: The Witkiewicz childhood Plays", in *Yale/Theatre*, vol. 5 no. 3, 1974.

Lech Sokól, "Witkacy in World Theatre: On European Stages", in *Theatre in Poland*, vol. 16 no. 1, 1974.

Lech Sokól "Witkacy in World Theatre: In America", in *Theatre in Poland*, vol. 16 no. 2, 1974.

Bernard F. Dukore, "Spherical Tragedies and Comedies with Corpses: Witkacian tragicomedy", in *Modern Drama*, 18, 1975.

Jan Kott, "Witkiewicz and Artaud: Where the Analogy Ends", in *Theatre Quarterly*, vol. 18, 1975.

Janusz Degler, "L'Art théâtral dans le système esthétique de Stanislaw Igancy Witkiewicz", in *Cahiers S. I. Witkiewicz/ Witkacy*, 1, 1976.

Janusz Degler, "S.I. Witkiewicza et l'avant-garde polonaise: Thèses générales", in *Acta Universitatis Wratislaviensis*, 462, 1979.

Konstanty Puzyna, "The Genius of Witkacy (Stanislaw Igacy Witkiewicz)", in *Gambit*, vol. 33–34, 1979.

Alain van Crugten (ed.), "Actes du Colloque International 'Witkiewicz' de Bruxelles, Novembre 1981", special issue of *Cahiers S.I. Witkiewicz/Witkacy*, 4, 1982 (includes various articles, in French).

Wladimir Krysinski, "The Pragmatics of Dialogue in the Theatre of St. I. Witkiewicz", in *Modern Drama*, vol. 27, 1984.

Thomas P. Cooke, "The Role of the Actor in the Plays of Witkacy: Genesis of a Polish Acting Style", in *Slavic and East European Arts*, vol. 3 no. 1, 1985.

Janusz Degler, "Witkacy's Theory of Theatre", in *Russian Literature*. vol. 22, 1987.

Christine Kiebuzinska, "Witkacy: The Metaphysical Theater of Pure Form", in *Slavic and East European Arts*, vol. 6 no. 2, 1989.

Anita Dorczak, "S.I. Witkiewicz as an Avant-Garde Writer", in *Australian Slavonic and East European Studies*, vol. 4 nos. 1–3, 1990.

* * *

A marginal writer derided or ignored in his own lifetime, Witkacy is now recognized as Poland's leading theatrical innovator of the inter-war years and is viewed as one of the outstanding creative personalities of the European avant-garde, worthy of a place alongside Jarry, Mayakovsky, and Artaud. As a painter, photographer, novelist, aesthetician, philosopher, cultural critic, and expert on narcotics, this multi-talented artist brought to playwriting an extraordinary breadth of interests and depth of vision.

The distinctive qualities of Witkacy's work are an acute sense of the grotesque and the absurd, a powerful visual imagination that in its obsession with colors and shapes evokes dream states and drug-induced hallucinations, and a deeply felt philosophy of man's tragic isolation in an alien universe, constantly undercut by subversive self-mockery that produces jarring dissonances and unresolved discrepancies in tone.

Artistic practice, the playwright felt, should find its basis in theoretical principles. In philosophy a proponent of biological monadology (derived from Leibniz), Witkacy explored the ontological problem posed by the directly given feeling of the unity of each Individual Being (the "I" or self) as it confronts the plurality of all that lies outside it (the "non-I" or other). These existential premises gave rise to a tragic sense of life, comprised of feelings of extreme loneliness and bewilderment, along with a conciousness of the accidental character of everything, and a recognition of the constant menace of nothingness. The function of art, therefore, was, for Witkacy, to recapture the metaphysical feeling of the mystery of existence, which was in danger of being lost forever in the mechanized "happiness" of the perfect ant-hill society of the future. The theatre's task of reinstating man's sense of primeval wonder could be achieved not by an imitation of reality or the propagation of ideas, but through the purely formal arrangement of component elements, which would directly reflect the structure of the universe.

Witkacy's theory of Pure Form in the theatre was essentially an attack on the psychological-realistic tradition stemming from Stanislavsky. Art for Witkacy meant the creation of form; theatre should be not a means of expression, but a construct in which the actor could function as a pure instrument using words, gesture, and body with mathematical precision rather than pretending to be someone else and faking "living experiences". Witkacy maintained that the wrong people were writing for the stage; children and painters, not professional men of the theatre, should become playwrights. Through the theory and practice of Pure Form, Witkacy hoped to restore to the over-rationalized stage of realism the magical perceptions of childhood, along with the modern painter's sense of color and shape. Theatre would thus become an autonomous art with a scenic language of its own, free of referentiality and literary dominance, which could be fully realized only in performance as created by director, designer, and actor, for whom the playwright provides no more than a scenario.

Acknowledging the impasse brought about by the modern "insatiable craving for form", Witkacy sought renewal through the decomposition of inherited structures. If everything has already been said, the artist may be condemned to the repetitions of a literature of exhaustion, but Witkacy's instinct for parody led him to the creation of new forms by distorting and deforming the established patterns of drama. The structure of his plays relies on dislocation of the normal course of dramatic action by the introduction of surprising discontinuities and starting *coups de théâtre*. A preferred Witkacian device, for example, is the "risen corpse": after committing suicide or being murdered, the dead character nonchalantly comes back to life as if nothing had happened. In *The Madman and the Nun*, when the demented poet Walpurg, who has just hanged himself, returns to confront his own corpse, he is upsetting the *status quo* by suddenly annulling the laws of both nature and drama, thus opening the way for the marvelous.

The *dramatis personae* of Witkacian drama are members of a degenerate band of flamboyant stage characters, playing roles from the modernist repertory—they comprise crazed artist, demonic woman, cosmopolitan playboy, rapacious tycoon, mad scientist, ranting tyrant. Pushed to ultimate extremes, these modern *commedia* types grow self-conciously aware of their own theatricality and literary ancestry, upon which they often comment. They speak a bizarre theatrical metalanguage, based on verbal games, random borrowings and citations, chance associations, and a variety of incompatible "perfomance" styles. There is a postmodern disjunction of action and dialogue. The characters wander off into disquisitions on culture, philosophy, mathematics, and aesthetics, quote the author's own theories of Pure Form and the death of art, and then suddenly make fervid declarations of love or shoot one another. The playwright is not afraid to explore the theatrical values—acoustic and rhythmic—of garrulity and gibberish. The flow of discourse is never linear or informational, but rather emulates the free play of a spiral that circles and mounts ever higher.

In dramaturgical method, Witkacy rejects the old science, the Euclidean geometry and Newtonian mechanics, in favor of the complementarity, uncertainty, and indeterminacy of modern physics. Entropy is a central principle within the Witkacian dramatic universe. Old systems and psyches disintegrate as accelerating disorder moves the universe towards inertia and extinction. In *The Crazy Locomotive* technological society breaks down and sinks back into chaos and darkness. The playwright treats apocalypse and approaching doom with playful, but sinister irony; life goes on after the catastrophe—coffee is drunk, cards are played much as before. In *Janulka, Daughter of Fizdejko*, a post-revolutionary world of endless, meaningless change and experimentation exists within an oppressively static society arrested in boredom and stagnation.

In Witkacy's plays, politics swallow art; personal anguish is inevitably extinguished by the intrusion of totalitarian terror. In *Gyubal Wahazar*, *The Anonymous Work*, and *The Cuttlefish*, lack of authenticity leads to a theatricalized society where histrionic impostors rise to power and manipulate the automated masses by means of rhetoric and ritual. The terrorism unleashed at the end of such plays as *The New Deliverance*, *The Water Hen*, *The Mother*, and *The Shoemakers* signals the triumph of the collective and the tribe.

Witkacy's *oeuvre* is unfailingly resonant in its dramatizations of the individual's role in periods of historical change. By centering "comedies with corpses" like *They* on the response of the intellectual caught in the grinding gears of mass society —his sense of guilt, secret desire for punishment, confession to uncommitted crimes—Witkacy announced what would be a major theme in post-war Eastern European literature.

After the liberalization of 1956, Witkacy became a major influence on the formation of the new Polish theatre. His plays and theory of Pure Form were the perfect antidote to five dreary years of enforced socialist realism, and his sardonic humor and prophetic insights into the workings of history made him, posthumously, a truly subversive and unruly author who attracted many of the most daring directors and designers. The rediscovery of Witkacy—producing a long series of premieres of previously unknown and unproduced plays and frequent clashes with the censor—was one of the most exciting aspects of Polish cultural life from the late 1950's to the 1970's. Starting with his pioneering staging of *The Cuttlefish* in 1956, Tadeusz Kantor devoted Cricot II to Witkacy, using the playwright's texts for all his productions through *The Dead Class* in 1975. Now a classic writer, Witkacy remains the seminal figure in 20th-century Polish drama.

—Daniel Gerould

See also *Volume 1* entry on *The Water Hen*.

WOOD, Charles (Gerald), Born in St. Peter Port, Guernsey, Channel Islands, 6 August 1932. Educated at Chesterfield Grammar School, 1942–45; King Charles I School, Kidderminster, Worcestershire, 1945–48; Birmingham College of Art, 1948–50. Served in the 17/21st Lancers, 1950–55: corporal. Married Valerie Elizabeth Newman in 1954; one son and one daughter. Factory worker, 1955–57; designer, scenic artist, and stage manager, Theatre Workshop, London, 1957–59; staff member, Bristol *Evening Post*, 1959–62. Recipient: Screenwriters Guild Award, 1965; Prix Italia, 1988; BAFTA Award, 1988. Fellow, Royal Society of Literature, 1985.

Stage Works

Cockade (includes *Prisoner and Escort; John Thomas; Spare*) (produced New Arts Theatre, London, 1963). In *New English Dramatists 8*, 1965; published separately, 1967.
Tie Up the Ballcock (produced Bristol University, 1964). In *Second Playbill 3*, edited by Alan Durband, 1973.
Don't Make Me Laugh (produced Aldwych Theatre, London, 1965).
Meals on Wheels (produced Royal Court Theatre, London, 1965; shortened version produced Liverpool, 1971).
Fill the Stage with Happy Hours (produce Playhouse, Nottingham, 1966). In *New English Dramatists 11*, 1967.
Dingo (produced Bristol Arts Centre, 1967). 1969.
Labour (produced Bristol Arts Centre, 1968).
H, Being Monologues at Front of Burning Cities (produced by the National Theatre, Old Vic, London, 1969). 1970.
Colliers Wood (produced Liverpool, 1970).
Veterans; or, Hairs in the Gates of the Hellespont (produced Royal Lyceum Theatre, Edinburgh 1972). 1972.

The Can Opener, from a play by Victor Lanoux (produced
    The Place, London, 1974).
Jingo (produced Aldwych Theatre, London, 1975).
The Script (produced Hampstead Theatre, London, 1976).
Has "Washington" Legs? (produced National Theatre,
    London, 1978; Cambridge, Massachusetts, 1981). With
    Dingo, 1978.
The Garden (produced Sherborne, Dorset, 1982).
Red Star (produced The Pit, Barbican Centre, London,
    1984).
Across from the Garden of Allah (produced Yvonne Arnaud
    Theatre, Guildford, Surrey, 1986).
The Plantagenets, from plays by Shakespeare (produced
    Royal Shakespeare Theatre, Stratford-on-Avon, 1988).
Man, Beast and Virtue, from a play by Pirandello (produced
    National Theatre, London, 1989).
The Mountain Giants, from an unfinished play by Pirandello
    (produced National Theatre, London, 1993).

Screenplays

The Knack, 1965; *Help!*, with Mark Behm, 1965; *Tie Up the
Ballcock*, 1967; *How I Won the War*, 1967; *The Charge of the
Light Brigade*, with John Osborne, 1968; *The Long Day's
Dying*, 1968; *The Bed-Sitting Room*, from the screenplay by
John Antrobus and Spike Milligan, 1969; *Fellini Satyricon*
(English dialogue), 1969; *Cuba*, 1980.

Television Plays

Prisoner and Escort, 1961; *Traitor in a Steel Helmet*, 1961;
Not at All, 1962; *Drill Pig*, 1964; *Drums Along the Avon*,
1967; *A Bit of a Holiday*, 1969; *The Emergence of Anthony
Purdy, Esq.*, 1970; *A Bit of Family Feeling*, 1971; *A Bit of
Vision*, 1972; *Death or Glory Boy*, 1974; *Mützen ab*, 1974; *A
Bit of an Adventure*, 1974; *Love Lies Bleeding*, 1976; *Do as I
Say*, 1977; *Don't Forget to Write!* series, 1977, 1979; *Red
Monarch*, from stories by Yuri Krotkov, 1983; *Wagner*, 1984;
Puccini, 1984; *Dust to Dust* (*Time for Murder* series), 1985;
Company of Adventurers series, 1986 (Canada); *My Family
and Other Animals*, from the book by Gerald Durrell, 1987;
Tumbledown, 1988 (published 1987); *The Setting of the Sun*
(*Inspector Morse* series), 1989; *On the Third Day*, from the
book by Piers Paul Read, 1992.

Radio Plays

Cowhell Jelly, 1962; *Next to Being a Knight*, 1972.

*

Criticism

Books:
    John Russell Taylor, *The Second Wave*, London and New
        York, 1971.
    Katharine J. Worth, *Revolutions in Modern English Drama*,
        London, 1973.
    Ronald Hayman, *British Theatre Since 1955: A Reassessment*,
        London and New York, 1979.

*   *   *

Charles Wood's clearest statement of his view of war and
the army occurs in his most obscure play, *Spare*. The opening
stage direction describes the set as "*a path for encouraging*

*heroes (born) who before it got dangerous used to pass up and
down with the warlike chat meaning to encourage the heroes
(pressed) to go on to join heroes (copped it) . . .*". Faded
regimental flags, such as can be seen in the side-chapels of
churches, hang above tailors' dummies in martial dress. Their
smart appearance is, within a dozen words, set against reality:
"he for instance wet hisself grotesque at Waterloo". What
seems to be a guard-detail turns into roll-call, drill, and the
re-enactment of some past assault in which one of the soldiers
is "killed"; and, with variations, this pattern is repeated, for
in Wood's other-ranks' view, war is the repetition of pointless
and stupidly conducted slaughters. The theatricality of this
war game is emphasized by someone walking back and forth
above the stage, showering the actors with dust. In this, one
of a trio of plays which under the collective title *Cockade*, was
Wood's earliest publication, his other fascination, theatre—
especially in its traditional form of the proscenium-arch stage
—, already appears.

The link between war and theatre for Wood is autobiographical and conceptual. He grew up in a theatrical family, and
he served five years as a regular soldier. In both he sees a
sordid reality sold to the public as glamorous. His most
interesting works—and perhaps, respectively his most and
least successful—are those where the interest in theatre and
war come together—*Dingo* and *H: Being Monologues at
Front of Burning Cities*. *Fill the Stage with Happy Hours* may
be one of the sourest comedies ever written. What we see are
the unhappy hours backstage in the manager's office and
adjoining bar of a tatty repertory company. The characters,
especially Albert the manager and his wife Maggie, whose
acting career has given way to managing the bar, try on
various attitudes as if to see whether they fit the situation—
for example, Albert tries moral indignation at the juvenile
lead's supposed seduction of his son, then later offers his son
a man-to-man chat about seizing career opportunities when
the sexual interest of a visiting *grande dame* of the stage is
evident. Genuine emotion is either no longer possible for
them or can only be shown, ironically, through the adoption
of an appropriate attitude. At the end of the play Maggie tells
Albert what he has refused to recognize: that she is dying of
cancer. The curtain falls slowly as she sings "Smiling through"
and he turns heroic: "By God, I'll do *Ghosts*, I'll show this
bloody town . . . Isn't she marvellous, your mother—that's
what it's about, son—that's how to use it . . . It's given us a
good life, hasn't it Maggie . . .?". Her reply ends the play:
"Shut up, dear—you're not very good at it are you?". In the
original production the actors stopped the fall of the curtain
to bow and blow kisses to the audience, game troupers all.

The sense that we are watching theatrical "turns" is strong
in all of Wood's plays. Since Wood's characters are often
trying out attitudes on each other, particularly in *Veterans*, or
ironically parodying beliefs they do not share, as in *Dingo*,
the audience is made more than usually aware of the transitions from one unit or "beat" to the next. In addition, Wood
brings theatrical performance into the script itself. For
example, almost at the start of *Dingo* we hear the dying
screams of a soldier trapped in a burning tank. His charred
corpse is later treated as a ventriloquist's dummy. There is
also a comedian who attempts to entertain the soldiers stuck
in their desert emplacement, sits on a toilet with Churchill
and Eisenhower glove-puppets arguing about Arnhem, and
acts as master of ceremonies for a climactic POW camp
concert with the men in drag. Wood aims not just to achieve
Brechtian alienation, but to protest against the glamorization
of World War II and to suggest that even the way it was
conducted was affected by how it could be sold to the public.

In *H*, Wood dramatizes the Indian Mutiny in spectacular

Victorian style—set-piece battles, *tableaux vivants*, painted act-drops and front cloths, live actors in the positions of Imperial paintings—subverted by the playwright's mid-20th-century consciousness. The play is in rough and often awkward verse. Extraordinary staging demands are made in the battle scenes—sepoys advance from beneath an elephant, "five men are mutilated in a horrible manner", and a rebel soldier is tied over the mouth of a cannon and blown to bits, raining pieces of flesh in the form of rose petals into the audience. Front-cloths fall as charging officers stagger or slide beneath them. The dramatic interest lies in the different characters of the commanders and officers, and in a Captain's wife who is raped by an Indo-Irish rebel and bears his child at the end of the play. One can admire the play's ambitiousness and ingenuities, but there are too many assaults, and, at the end, too long a death-bed scene.

Wood has twice written plays about making films, *Veterans* and *Has "Washington" Legs?*. The former was inspired by Wood's experience as script-writer for *The Charge of the Light Brigade*. It is bitchy offstage life again, but the tone is nostalgic, even elegiac, set by the ageing stars who are waiting for their call. It is hard to read *Veterans* without hearing the hesitancies and suspended inflections of Gielgud, for whom the principal role was written. In contrast, *Has "Washington" Legs?* deals with the business of making movies, and shows the emptiness not of the performer's assumed or faked emotions but of American corporate happy talk, the manipulative psychobabble of various financial or artistic claimants to a piece of the action who jockey over a lamentably unclear project to film the American Revolution, agreeing only that "in the American Revolution there is something for everybody". Wood's fierceness is undiminished, and his mockery of the mythification of war continues, but his target has changed to the mediators and middle managers of a service-industry society.

—Anthony Graham-White

See also *Volume 1* entry on *Dingo*.

———————

WYCHERLEY, William. Born, probably in Whitchurch, Hampshire, England. March or April 1641. Lived in Angoulême, France, c.1655–60. Attended Queen's College, Oxford (gentleman commoner), 1660; entered the Inner Temple, London, 1660. Married 1) Laetitia-Isabella, Countess of Drogheda in 1679 (died 1685); 2) Elizabeth Jackson in 1715. Spent some time in the household of Sir Richard Fanshawe, ambassador in Madrid, early 1660's; probably took part in naval battle against the Dutch, 1665; captain in Duke of Buckingham's regiment, 1672–74; first-produced play, *Love in a Wood*, staged 1672; suffered a stroke from which he never fully recovered, 1678; given patronage by Charles II until 1680, when the King banished him from Court because of his marriage; imprisoned in Newgate, and possibly Fleet, prison, for debt on his wife's estate, 1682–86: released and given pension by James II, 1686; retired to Clive, near Shrewsbury, Shropshire. Died in London, 31 December 1715.

William Wycherley (engraving by H. Robinson, after the portrait by Sir Peter Lely).

Works

Collections

Complete Works, edited by Montague Summers (4 vols.). 1924.
Complete Plays, edited by Gerald Weales. 1966.
Plays, edited by Arthur Friedman. 1979.

Stage Works

Love in a Wood; or, St. James's Park (produced Theatre Royal, Bridges Street, London, 1671). 1672.
The Gentleman Dancing-Master (produced Dorset Garden Theatre, 1672). 1673.
The Country Wife (produced Theatre Royal, Drury Lane, London, 1675). 1675.
The Plain-Dealer (produced Theatre Royal, Drury Lane, London, 1676). 1677.

Verse

Hero and Leander in Burlesque. 1669.
Epistles to the King and Duke. 1683.
Miscellany Poems. 1704.
The Idleness of Business: A Satire. 1705.
On His Grace the Duke of Marlborough. 1707.

Other

Posthumous Works (2 vols.), edited by Lewis Theobald and
    Alexander Pope. 1728–29.

*

Bibliographies

B. Eugene McCarthy, *William Wycherley: A Reference
    Guide*, Boston, 1986.

Criticism

Books:
John Palmer, *The Comedy of Manners*, London, 1913.
Charles Perromat, *William Wycherley: Sa Vie, son oeuvre*,
    Paris, 1921.
Bonamy Dobrée, *Restoration Comedy 1660–1720*, Oxford,
    1924.
W. Connely, *Brawny Wycherley*, New York and London,
    1930.
Norman D. Holland, *The First Modern Comedies: The
    Significance of Etherege, Wycherley and Congreve*,
    Cambridge, Massachusetts, 1959.
Anne Righter, "William Wycherley", in *Restoration Theatre*,
    edited by John Russell Brown and Bernard Harris,
    London, 1965.
Rose A. Zimbardo, *Wycherley's Drama: A Link in the
    Development of English Satire*, New Haven, Connecticut,
    1965.
P.F. Vernon, *William Wycherley*, London, 1965.
Katharine M. Rogers, *William Wycherley*, New York, 1972.
Ursula Jantz, *Targets of Satire in the Comedies of Etherege,
    Wycherley, and Congreve*, Salzburg, 1978.
Peter Holland, *The Ornament of Action: Text and
    Performance in Restoration Comedy*, Cambridge, 1979.
B. Eugene McCarthy, *William Wycherley: A Biography*,
    Athens, Ohio, 1979.
James Thompson, *Language in Wycherley's Plays:
    Seventeenth-Century Language Theory and Drama*,
    University of Alabama, 1984.
Robert Markley, *Two-Edg'd Weapons: Style and Ideology in
    the Comedies of Etherege, Wycherley, and Congreve*,
    Oxford, 1988.

* * *

Despite a brief five-year career as a playwright, and a total
output of four plays, William Wycherley remains the pre-
eminent writer of comedies of the first generation after the
Restoration. His high reputation in the 20th century is based
on the continuing success enjoyed by *The Country Wife* on
stage (it is probably the most frequently performed play from
the late 17th and early 18th centuries, a favourite of amateur
and professional companies alike), and by *The Country Wife*
and *The Plain-Dealer* in the classroom and study.

Wycherley's first play, *Love in a Wood*, made him an
instant celebrity, as much because of the attention it gained
him from the Duchess of Cleveland as from its great success
in the theatre. It is a typical first play, in that it is a highly
derivative amalgam of elements from earlier plays, a version
of Calderón's *Mañanas de abril y mayo* made English by
translating the action to London and adding a semi-
independent low plot. The result is a work in the tradition of

the three-level, multiple-plot plays popular early in the 17th
century. Wycherley's most interesting formal innovation, the
abandonment of verse in the high plot, points to the tendency
in all his plays to level the characters he portrays—that is, to
write about a single, broadly-based, coherent London society. And his greatest success in the play, its low plot, points
to his greatest strength as a playwright—his brilliant development of Jonsonian humours-comedy in a distinctly
Restoration mode.

Wycherley's other apprentice piece, *The Gentleman
Dancing-Master*, is also based—though more loosely still—on
a Calderón play, *El maestro de danzar*. The action is again
moved to London where the affectation of Spanish and
French manners becomes the principal target of ridicule. The
plot is streamlined and tightly structured (in contrast to *Love
in a Wood*), but *The Gentleman Dancing-Master* is generally
seen as Wycherley's weakest and least effective play, a judgment shared by its original audience. It was Wycherley's only
play not to enter the repertory.

It is with his last two plays that Wycherley reached maturity
as a writer. Again he turned to foreign sources for inspiration,
but continued to depart from his sources in his settings (but
London) and in most other aspects of import. Wycherley
clearly preferred not to invent his own plots, but he chose to
use his sources as rough blueprints only. *The Country Wife* is
based on Molière's *L'École des femmes* and, possibly, on a
number of other French sources including *L'École des maris*.
The result, however, is uniquely Wycherley's. *The Plain-
Dealer* is based more closely (though not exclusively) on
Molière's *Le Misanthrope*, but the differences are again more
important than the similarities. Both plays were—and continue to be—as controversial as they were successful.
Wycherley's first plays dealt with many of the same themes as
these two—the hypocrisy of fashionable society, human
inconstancy, the corruption of love by lust and money, the
evils of arranged marriages, and the social problems resulting
from an increasingly mercenary society. But only in the
second pair of comedies did Wycherley perfect the tone and
style to convey his complex views of his society.

These views were produced by a distinctive moral sensibility, one that anticipated Jonathan Swift's in many important
ways. Wycherley was recognized by his contemporaries as a
stern and fearless social critic, a writer of serious moral satire
for the stage. He was also considered an obscene writer, one
whose language was as nasty as the behaviour he chose to
represent on stage, and one whose satire was unmitigated by
a clearly formulated vision of the way things should be. As
tastes changed in the 18th century, Wycherley (like Swift) was
increasingly seen as a depraved misanthropist; his plays were
damned for their apparent want of redeeming social value. It
is only in the 20th century that this view has once more been
countered by critics and audiences who appreciate
Wycherley's form of satiric comedy.

Wycherley wrote little criticism, seldom reflecting publicly
on his art. He did defend *The Country Wife* from charges of
obscenity in the "china scene" by having the notorious hypocrite Olivia attack it in *The Plain-Dealer*. Her cousin, the
virtuous Eliza, defends it, pointing out that those who are
offended by seeing vicious behaviour revealed on stage are
likely to be those most in need of the satirist's lash.
Wycherley provided *The Plain-Dealer* with a heavily ironic (it
would be called Swiftian today) mock-encomium to Mother
Bennett, a notorious bawd and prostitute, in place of a conventional dedication. He signed his dedication "The Plain-
Dealer", identifying his kind of moral satire with a heavily
ironic style, and compounding the irony by encouraging his
readers to identify the author with the title character.

Wycherley's critics are often distracted by attempts to find Wycherley's voice in Manly or even in Horner (the fact that he was called "Manly Wycherley" as well as "The Plain-Dealer" encourages the confusion). Both characters indeed frequently voice sentiments shared by their author, but trying to force a closer identification produces results similar to trying to equate Lemuel Gulliver with Swift. Like Swift, Wycherley employed changing perspectives on his characters —including his protagonists—to reveal the complexities of social behaviour that engage the thoughtful moralist.

Wycherley's characters are almost all humours-characters inhabiting a world of moral decay and corruption. And since, unlike Ben Jonson, he did not believe that humours could be corrected, and unlike 18th-century writers of humours-comedy, he was unwilling to embrace that which could not be changed, Wycherley could not offer the kinds of affirmation frequently required by audiences and readers. The 18th-century solution to the disagreeable aspects of *The Country Wife* and *The Plain-Dealer* was to produce heavily bowdlerized adaptations (by Garrick and Bickerstaff respectively). Wycherley's contemporary Gerard Langbaine described him (in 1691) as "a Gentleman, whom I may boldly reckon amongst the Poets of the First Rank: no Man that I know, except the Excellent *Johnson* [sic], having outdone him in Comedy". If with "comedy" we add "Jonsonian" or "humours" or "satiric", that judgment still holds true today.

—Brian Corman

See also *Volume 1* entries on *The Country Wife*; *The Plain Dealer*.

WYSPIAŃSKI, Stanisław (Mateusz Ignacy). Born in Cracow, Poland (then part of the Russian Empire) 15 January 1869. Educated at College of St. Anne, Cracow, 1879–87; Academy of Fine Arts and Jagellonian University, Cracow, from 1887, with frequent study-trips in Europe; studied art and architecture on three trips to Paris, 1891–94. Painter and draftsman, from late 1880's; created the stained-glass windows for the Franciscan Church, Cracow, 1895; co-editor, *Życie* [Life], from 1898; first-produced play, *Warszawianka* [Song of Warsaw], staged at Cracow's Teatr Miejski [Municipal Theatre], which staged many of his subsequent plays, 1898; debut as stage designer and director, 1898; physical breakdown, caused by syphilis, 1903; worked on renovation of the royal castle in Cracow, 1904–05; elected alderman of Cracow, 1905; second physical breakdown, 1906: bedridden at his home in Wegrzce, 1906–07. Died in Cracow, 28 November 1907.

Works

Collections

Dzieła [Works] (8 vols.), edited by Adam Chmiel, Tadesuz Sinko, and Léon Ploszewski. 1924–32.
Dzieła zebrane [Collected Works] (16 vols.). 1958–71.

Stage Works

Legenda 1 (produced Teatr Miejski, Lvov, 1905). 1897.
Warszawianka [Song of Warsaw] (produced Teatr Miejski, Cracow, 1898). In *Życie*, 45, 1898; in book form, 1901.
Meleager (produced Teatr Miejski, Cracow, 1908). 1898; translated as *Meleager*, 1933.

Lelewel [Lelewel] (produced Teatr Miejski, Cracow, 1899). 1899.
Klątwa [The Curse] (produced Teatr Miejski, Lodz, 1909). In *Życie*, 15–16, 1899; in book form, 1901.
Protesilas i Laodamia (produced Teatr Miejski, Cracow, 1903). In *Przegląd Polski*, 34, 1899; in book form, 1901; translated as *Protesilaus and Laodamia*, in *Slavonic Review*, 11, 1933.
Legion (produced Teatr Miejski, Cracow, 1911). 1900.
Kazimierz Wielki. In *Czas*, 148–152, 1900; in book form, 1901.
Wesele (produced Teatr Słowackiego, Cracow, 1901). 1901; translated as *The Wedding*, 1904.
Bolesław Śmiały [Boleslaw the Bold] (produced Teatr Miejski, Cracow, 1903). 1902 (first complete edition); revised version, 1903.
Henryk Pobozny. In *Kuryer Warszawski*, 98, 1903; in book form, in *Dzieła 7*, 1932.
Achilleis [Achilles] (produced Teatr Bugusławskiego, Warsaw, 1925). 1903.
Wyzwolenie [Deliverance] (produced Teatr Miejski, Cracow, 1903). 1903.
Noc listopadowa [November Night] (produced Teatr Miejski, Cracow, 1908). 1904.
Legenda II [A Legend II] (produced Teatr Miejski, Lvov, 1905). 1904.
Akropolis [Acropolis] (produced in part, Teatr Miejski, Cracow, 1916; produced in full, Cracow, 1926). 1904.
Hymne Veni Creator. In *Nowa Reforma*, 125, 1906; in book form, in *Dzieła 7*, 1932.
Śmierć Ofelji [The Death of Ophelia] (fragment; produced Teatr Miejski, Cracow, 1909). In *Nowa Reforma*, 114, 1906; in book form, in *Pisma pośmiertne 2*, 1910.
Zaïre, from the play by Voltaire (incomplete). In *Nowa Reforma*, May 1906.
Skałka [The Rock] (produced Teatr Klasyczny, Warsaw, 1957). 1906.
Powrót Odysa (produced Teatr Miejski, Cracow, 1917). 1907; translated as *The Return of Odysseus*, 1966.
Sędziowie (produced Teatr Miejski, Vilnius, Lithuania, 1907). 1907.
Samuel Zborowski [Samuel Zborowski] (fragment). Parts in *Nowa Reforma*, 593 supplement, 1907; all fragments in *Dzieła 6*, 1932.
Cyd, from a play by Pierre Corneille (produced Teatr Miejski, Cracow, 1907). In *Nowa Reforma*, June 1906; in book form, 1907.
Wernyhora (fragments). Parts in *Lamus*, 1, 1908–09; all fragments in *Dzieła 7*, 1932.
Święty Stanislaw. In *Pamietnik literacki*, 1–2, 1908; in book form, in *Dzieła 7*, 1932.
Daniel (produced Teatr Zydowski, Cracow, 1927). In *Pisma pośmiertne 1*, 1908.
Jadwiga [Jadwiga] (fragment; produced Teatr Wielki, Warsaw, 1914). In *Przegląd Powszechny*, February 1908; in book form, in *Pisma pośmiertne 2*, 1910.
Królowa polskiej korony (produced Teatr Miejski, Lvov, 1919). In *Czas*, 61, 1908; in book form, in *Pisma pośmiertne 2*, 1910.
Piastowicze [The Descendants of the Piasts] (fragment). In *Krytyka*, November 1909; in book form, in *Dzieła 6*, 1932.
Batory pod Pskowem [Batory at Pskov] In *Pisma pośmiertne 2*, 1910.
Feakowie [The Phaeacians]. In *Pisma pośmiertne 2*, 1910.
Król Kazimierz Jagiellonczyk [King Casimir the Jagellonian]. In *Pisma pośmiertne 2*, 1910.
Mąż [The Husband]. In *Pisma pośmiertne 2*, 1910.

Juliusz II [Juliusz II] (fragment; produced Teatr Artystyczny, Warsaw, 1911).   In *Dzieła 8*, 1932.

Ajas [Ajax] (fragment).   In *Szutka*, January 1913; in book form, in *Dzieła 6*, 1932.

Zygmunt August [Zygmunt August] (fragments; parts produced Teatr Polski, Warsaw, 1915).   1930 (first edition with all existing scenes).

Rudera [The Ruin] (fragment).   In *Dzieła 6*, 1932.

Weimar (fragment; produced Teatr Słowackiego, Cracow, 1932).   In *Dzieła 6*, 1932.

Verse

Collected poetry in *Dzieła 7*, 1932.

Other

Dzieła 8 (includes writings on theatre, his study of Shakespeare's *Hamlet*, and his *mise en scène* for Mickiewicz's *Dziady*).   1932.

*

Bibliographies

Maria Stokowa, *Monografia bibliograficzna III–IV: Teatr Wyspiańskiego*, Cracow, 1968.

Criticism

Books:

B. Rosenthal, *Heinrich von Kleist und Stanislaw Wyspiański: Ein Vergleich der Tragik in ihren Dramen*, Cracow, 1938.

Claude Backvis, *Le Dramaturge Stanislaw Wyspianski*, Paris, 1952.

Tymon Terlecki, *Stanislaw Wyspianski* (in English), Boston, 1983.

Articles:

S. Srebrny, "Stanislaw Wyspiański", in *Slavonic Review*, 2, 1923.

W. Borowy, "Stanislaw Wyspiański", in *Slavonic Review*, 11, 1933.

Tymon Terlecki, "Stanislaw Wyspiański and the Poetics of Symbolist Drama", in *Polish Review*, vol. 15 no. 4, 1970.

Tymon Terlecki, "The Greatness and Ill Fortune of Stanislaw Wyspiański", in *Antemurale*, 15, 1971.

Nina Taylor, "Stanislaw Wyspiański and Symbolist Drama: The Work of Art as *Dramatis Persona*", in *Slavonic and East European Review*, 66, 1988.

*   *   *

Wyspiański was a great reformer of Polish theatre and in that sense an avant-garde playwright; but he was also a poet of national commitment, with an ambition to preach, prophesy, and command in accordance with the tradition of Polish 19th-century patriotism. A talented painter, close to Gauguin and the Nabis, he broadened the limits of drama as a literary genre by combining poetry and dialogue with a vision of their theatrical embodiment. His work for the Municipal Theatre (Teatr Miejski) in Cracow here offered practical experience. His birthplace, that is, the old city of Cracow, full of history and monuments of art, exerted a powerful influence on his imagination, and, as an admirer of ancient cul-

ture, he blended this with Greek mythology and the Holy Bible. In Wyspiański's plays realistic setting can co-exist with legend, myth, or animated works of art, and his dramatic output forms a specific mixture of mimetic representation and pure literariness, a mixture of the present and the past, and of Poland and mythological or biblical antiquity.

Wyspiański, who was initially interested mainly in painting, became attracted to the theatre when he had an opportunity to see the operas of Richard Wagner in Germany. This "monumental theatre" of many actors and numerous stage-effects paved the way for his idea of a cumulative art. During his four-year sojourn in Paris, Wyspiański increased his knowledge of the theatre by attending the Comédie-Française and the Théâtre Libre, and was particularly fascinated by the production of he saw Sophocles' *Oedipus the King*. Cracow was an ambitious centre of arts, with the newly founded Municipal Theatre soon achieving its pre-eminent status in Poland. Its repertoire included not only leading contemporary European plays, but also Polish Romantic drama, until then regarded as unsuitable for the stage. Wyspiański's vivid interest in the theatrical potential of the latter was reflected in his remarks about the Cracow production of Mickiewicz's *Forefathers' Eve*. His theories of drama and the theatre can be found in the correspondence, and above all in the critical discussion of *Hamlet*, which also contains general remarks about Shakespearean tragedy and modern drama.

Wyspiański was one of the first Polish playwrights to be interested in the theatre *per se*. He made a distinction between literary texts and their theatrical production, and although he believed that the former should determine the character of the latter, he paid much attention to extra-verbal effects, such as scenery, music, dancing, and pantomime. These were described in detail in his ample stage directions. Polish director Leon Schiller claimed later that Wyspiański went even further than Gordon Craig in opposing "that theatre which had been destroyed by literature" and attempting to create a pure and autonomous one, "possessing its own aesthetics and its own craft". Despite a certain element of exaggeration, this opinion rightly indicates Wyspiański's place in the development of modern Polish theatre.

Wyspiański's dramatic output consists of plays diverse in subject matter and form. It includes dramas based on Greek mythology, the history of Cracow and its Wawel Castle, plays about the November Uprising of 1831, and plays about contemporary times. Their dramatic technique displays a variety of inspirations, from ancient tragedy, through Romantic drama, up to contemporary symbolism. It can combine sophisticated theatrical devices with colloquial language and common events.

In his book about *Hamlet*, Wyspiański placed drama within the "theatrum mundi", as a part and symbolic expression of the overall structure of the real world. He also introduced the idea of "intellectual drama", originated by Shakespeare and best exemplified by *The Tempest*. This concept, in his understanding, was at the centre of modern drama and depended on a search for truth by the unmasking of human lies and deceits.

The first important play, *Warszawianka* (The Song of Warsaw), carried out both his artistic and his intellectual quests. Subtitled "The Song of 1831", it reflected the author's views on the November Uprising not only in the structure of events and dialogues, but also in the use of music, pantomime, and visual and acoustic effects. This is his first assault upon a "patriotic theatre" in real life, represented here by young ladies and officers gathered together in a suburban drawing room. Their lofty rhetoric and gestures are contrasted with the simplicity of a silent scene, where the Old

Soldier, straight from the battlefield, hands over a message, salutes, and leaves. While the officers have been revelling in the beauty of heroic death and consequently creating an atmosphere of inescapable tragic fate, the soldier simply performs his duties.

Tragedy as the result of human mystification appears also in *Klątwa* (The Curse), an unusual blend of a Greek-style tragedy and a modern questioning of people's responsibility for their actions. It is set in a contemporary Galician village afflicted by a disastrous drought. Since the locals believe that a drought is God's punishment for the sins of the parish priest, who has had an affair with his housekeeper, they ruthlessly demand an atonement. The hypocritical priest absolves himself from blame and joins the common claim that to appease God his mistress and their two children should be sacrificed by burning, as an offering. The Old Testament story of Abraham's test is carried out to its bitter end, but, instead of repelling ill fate and reconciling the village with the Almighty, it brings about a just punishment in the shape of storm and thunder. The priest and the villagers thus discover the nature of their tragic guilt when subjected to celestial fire and destruction.

Tragedy generated by self-deception finds its best expression in *Wesele* (The Wedding), Wyspiański's most popular drama, which in a semi-realistic and semi-symbolic style portrays the dangers of a national mythology. Its accusation about the deceptive power of art over the Polish mind is continued in *Wyzwolenie* (Deliverance). This unusual work, set on the stage of the Cracow Municipal Theatre, represents theatre-in-the-theatre, and is perhaps the most avant-garde and complex of Wyspiański's plays. Experimentalism has found its best realization in the second act, where the protagonist Konrad's internal struggle is translated into dialogues between him and theatrical masks. As a whole, the play is a sort of poetic drama, without plot, logical order, or consistency in the fabric of its reality. Events apparently "belong" to the theatre, where a play about Poland is being rehearsed, but their transparent structure surpasses these limits and directly refers to the outer world of the real country. Conversely, the status of the protagonist oscillates between that of a real man, a playwright, and a literary symbol, that is, a direct allusion to Mickiewicz's Konrad from *Forefathers' Eve*. Poland, in turn, resembles a great theatre herself, with people wearing "masks" and playing "roles" in political life, to the extent of becoming inauthentic. The theatre thus be-comes a symbol of the country dominated by illusion and false rhetoric.

Acropolis is another experimental drama or dramatic poem, founded on the imaginary animation of the works of art in the Wawel Cathedral in Cracow. During one night, old statues engage in conversation, and human figures step down from tapestries to recreate events there represented, taken from the Bible (the story of Jacob) and the Trojan War. In this device, Wyspiański took advantage of an extraordinary blend of time and space. The Wawel Castle has been identified with Acropolis and Vistula with Scamander, while Polish history intertwined with Biblical and Trojan events express his views on human responses to the outer world and its pressures. The play eventually advocates a union with God, symbolized by the arrival of the Saviour.

Noc listopadowa (November Night) follows the pattern of Polish Romantic drama and consists of loosely connected episodes, set in Warsaw at the very beginning of the November Uprising. The world of Polish events has been extended and universalized by the introduction of the animated statues of Greek gods, standing in the Łazienki Park. They enhance the atmosphere of these events by making them more dignified, and open new possibilities for interpretation. In particular, the Eleusinian myth of eternal revival seems to suggest that even in its partly self-inflicted defeat the insurrection paved the way for future survival. In his Greek dramas, based mostly on the reinterpretation of Homeric epic, like *Achilleis* (Achilles) and *Powrót Odysa* (The Return of Odysseus), the poet also showed his concern with human fate and its moral aspects.

Wyspiański's extraordinary theatre has its admirers and detractors. His influence on Polish modern drama however, is without question great, and followers include Mrożek and Bryll. Andrzej Wajda filmed *The Wedding* (1972) and directed the stage production of "November Night" in Cracow in 1974; it has also been recorded on film, and shown by British television.

—Stanislaw Eile

See also *Volume 1* entry on *The Wedding*.

YACINE, Kateb. Born in Constantine, Algeria, 6 August 1929. Educated at Qur'anic school; transferred to French lycée, Collège de Setif, 1936: involved in anti-French demonstrations, 1945, and arrested and imprisoned for several months; on release, was expelled from lycée. First publication, the poetry collection *Siloloques*, appeared 1946; employed as dock worker; visited France for the first time, 1947; joined Algerian Communist Party and worked as correspondent for its newspaper, *Alger républicain*, 1949–51; travelled to France and worked as labourer, 1950; undertook a variety of jobs in Paris, 1951; began full-time writing, 1952; remained in France during the Algerian War of Independence; early plays banned in France, and first-produced play, *Le Cadavre encerclé*, staged in Belgium, 1958; worked in community theatre, in French and Arabic, with the Théâtre de Mer company, from 1970. Died in Grenoble, France, 28 October 1989.

Works

Collections

Le Cercle des représailles (includes *Le Cadavre encerclé; La Poudre d'intelligence; Les Ancêtres redoublent de férocité*). 1958.

Stage Works

La Femme sauvage. 1954.
Le Cadavre encerclé (produced by Théâtre National Populaire, Brussels, 1964). In *Le Cercle des représailles*, 1958.
Le Poudre d'intelligence. In *La Cercle des représailles*, 1958; translated as *The Intelligence Powder*, 1985.
Les Ancêtres redoublent de férocité (produced by Théâtre National Populaire as *La Femme sauvage*, 1967). In *La Cercle des représailles*, 1958.
L'Homme aux sandales de caoutchouc (produced Théâtre du VIIIe., Lyons, 1971). 1970.
Mohamed, prends ta valise (produced by Théâtre de Mer, Paris, 1972).

Fiction

Nedjma. 1956; translated as *Nedjma*, 1961.
Le Polygone étoile. 1966.

Verse

Soliloques. 1946.
Mélancolie. 1976.
Les Chemins de ma mémoire. 1977.

Other

Abdelkader et l'indépendance algérienne. 1947?
L'Oeuvre en fragments, edited by Jacqueline Arnaud. 1986.

*

Bibliographies

Jean Déjeux, "Kateb Yacine: Romancier, poète et dramaturge algérien", in *Présence francophone*, 15, 1977.
Jean Déjeux, "Kateb Yacine", in *Revue Celfan/Celfan Review*, vol. 5 no. 3, 1986.

Criticism

Books:
Jean Déjeux, *Littérature maghrébine de langue française*, Ottawa, 1973.
Taïeb Sbouaï, *La Femme sauvage de Kateb Yacine: Essai de lecture active suivi d'inédits*, Paris, 1985.

Articles:
Ghali Shoukri, "The Popular Hero in the Arabic play", in *Afro-Asian Writings*, 5, 1970.
Bernard Aresu, "Algerian Theater of the Fifties: Kateb Yacine's *Les Ancêtres redoublent de férocité*, in *San José Studies*, vol. 4 no. 2, 1978.
"Le Théâtre révolutionnaire algérien: Un Entretien de Jacques Alessandra avec Kateb Yacine", in *Travail théâtre*, 32–33, 1979.
Bernard Aresu, "Les Tragédies de Kateb Yacine devant la critique", in *Oeuvres & critiques*, vol. 4 no.2, 1979.

* * *

There are many playwrights whose works form cycles, but few are so tightly interwoven as Kateb Yacine's, bound together by an almost obsessional thematic consistency and by a poetic impatience with the norms of theatrical practice. This has led to a tangled bibliographical situation. For example, *La Femme sauvage* is *Le Cadavre encerclé*, with a prologue and epilogue added. The one play of Kateb's translated into English, *La Poudre d'intelligence*— uncharacteristically a comedy or, at least, a series of satiric sketches—ends with scenes that Kateb describes as there only to form a transition to the tragedy that followed it on initial publication, scenes which he states cannot be there when the comedy is treated as a separate entity. Kateb wrote dramatic sketches using the characters and situations of both these plays—and sometimes the titles—as recently as 1982. An enormous work of the late 1960's that dramatizes world conflicts has had parts published in French, *L'Homme aux sandales de caoutchouc*, and had parts re-worked in Arabic.

"I recognize", Kateb said in 1967, "that I am the writer of a single work. In the beginning it was a poem, then it changed itself into a novel and into plays". Nedjma, the older cousin whom he loved but who married someone else when he was still a teenager, gives her name as the title of the poem (1948) and novel (1956) and is a central character in his first plays. The other traumatic event of his youth was his arrest in 1945, when his involvement in an anti-French demonstration resulted in his being held in jail for three days. These two events are linked in his works. Nedjma, whom Kateb represents as born of a rape and therefore half-French, half-Arab, can stand for Algeria; his sense of loss in childhood, as he moves from the Arabic-speaking world of his mother to the French-speaking world of his father, can stand for the loss of a cultural heritage. One critic (Arnaud) wrote:

> The horror of life, the ecstasy of life: it is between these poles that Kateb is pulled, like Baudelaire before him. . . . One must always return to the point from which one departed, to a childhood fascinating but already menacing, with its absolute needs for pleasure, love, justice, and liberty. . . . The poet refuses the responsibilities of adulthood; rather, he takes an oath to maintain the sense of primary need . . . Kateb makes war on the alibis of mediocrity and reasonableness: he remains, unconquered, a savage, an innocent.

The placing of his family name first, as it appeared on the roster of the French-run school he attended, symbolizes that refusal and Kateb Yacine's sense of alienation. Perhaps, too, his peripatetic exile from Algeria from 1951 to 1970, maintained even after Algeria's independence in 1962, had more to do with his vision of the isolated poet, and his self-styled "Promethean sadness", than with his involvement in the Communist Party and revolutionary struggle.

Kateb once described himself as caught between interior monologue and the needs of the theatre. And indeed, one senses this in his plays on the Algerian struggle, published under the collective title *Le Cercle des représailles*, because the dramatic action lies not in the lengthy speeches, often recounting a vision of the past or future, nor in the exchanges between characters, who often either share a vision in counterpoint or talk past each other, but in the stage directions. These often call for light to pick an image—of death, of faces in a jail cell, of an embrace—out of surrounding shadows. Kateb also calls for projections, notably of the vulture which symbolizes the fierce integrity of his ancestors, and which, in the last of these plays, converses with the now-insane Nedjma. A symbolic level is suggested by the names: Nedjma is "star" in Arabic, and Lakhdar, the central male figure, means "green", with connotations of fruitfulness; a French girl who, in *Le Cadavre encerclé*, becomes involved with the victims, is Marguerite, a name that evokes the destruction of innocence. The plays have a hallucinatory intensity akin to that of the plays of Genet, whose own fascination with the polarities represented by the Algerian struggle produced *The Screens*.

The more recent *L'Homme aux sandales de caoutchouc* is very different. The stage is bare, the speeches mostly brief verse lines, and the stage directions limited to exits and entrances. The man in the sandals cut from rubber tires is Ho Chi Minh and the play is a history of the anti-colonialist struggles of Vietnam, from Louis XIV on, with glances elsewhere. Enormously long and highly episodic, it demands a naïf style of staging, as choruses of sans-culottes, Chinese Communists on the Long March, French workers, Venezuelan guerrillas, and Black Panthers in Harlem, are brought on, sometimes for a single line. There is also a speaking toad that jumps on to someone's face, a boxing-match between Christ and Buddha, and Americans circling the stage with their arms out as bomber pilots. This is crude stuff; for example, the bombing of Hiroshima, "in the name of Jesus Christ", leads to the gift of a skull to Chiang Kai-shek —"A Japanese girl/The way you like them". Madame Nhu reviews the troops in her slip for the sake of a pun on Nhu (French *nu* =nude). In one episode Krushchev and Nixon try to raise the tombstones of communism, only to drop them on their feet; Lyndon Johnson finds Mao's Red Book beneath one. Then he and a military liaison visit two red planets, inhabited by Marx, Engels, Lenin, and Stalin; they plant the American flag but it will not fly. Moreover, despite two visits to Vietnam, Kateb seems patronising to the "simple inhabitants of the Vietnamese earth".

After returning to Algeria, Kateb spent his later career working with a regional theatre company and writing in colloquial Arabic.

—Anthony Graham-White

YEATS, W(illiam) B(utler). Born in Sandymount, County Dublin, Ireland, 13 June 1865; son of the artist John Butler Yeats and older brother of the artist Jack Butler Yeats. Educated at Godolphin School, Hammersmith, London, 1875–80; Erasmus Smith School, Dublin, 1880–83; Metropolitan School of Art, Dublin, 1884–86; Royal Hibernian Academy School, 1886. Married Georgiana Hyde-Lees in 1917; one daughter and one son. Lived mainly in London from 1887, spending part of each year in Ireland, 1890–1921; a founder of the Rhymers' Club, London, 1891, and member of the *Yellow Book* group; helped found Irish Literary Society, London, 1891, and National Literary Society, Dublin, 1892; met Lady Gregory, 1896, and thereafter spent many of his summer holidays at her home in Sligo; first-produced play, *The Countess Kathleen*, staged 1899; co-founder, with Lady Gregory, Edward Martyn, and George Moore, Irish Literary Theatre, 1899, which became the Irish National Theatre Society at the Abbey Theatre, Dublin, 1904: director of the Abbey Theatre, 1905–39; editor, *Beltaine*, 1899–1900, *Samhain*, 1901–08, and the *Arrow*, 1906–09; gave lecture tours of the USA, 1903–04, 1913, 1919–20, 1932; lived in Oxford, 1920–21, and Ireland, mainly Dublin, from 1922; Senator of the Irish Free State, 1922–28. Recipient: Nobel Prize for Literature, 1923. D. Litt: Queen's University, Belfast, 1922; Trinity College, Dublin, 1922; Oxford University, 1931; Cambridge University, 1933. Died in Cap Martin, France, 28 January 1939.

Works

Collections

"The Hour Glass" and Other Plays, Being Volume 2 of Plays for an Irish Theatre (includes *Cathleen ni Houlihan* and *The Pot of Broth*). 1904.

Collected Works (8 vols.; plays in Volumes 2–4).   1908.
Four Plays for Dancers (includes *At the Hawk's Well. The Only Jealousy of Emer; The Dreaming of the Bones; Calvary*).   1921.
Plays in Prose and Verse (*Collected Works 2*).   1922.
Plays and Controversies (*Collected Works 3*).   1923.
Collected Plays.   1934; revised edition, 1952.
Nine One-Act Plays (includes *The Land of Heart's Desire; Cathleen ni Houlihan; The Hour Glass; The Pot of Broth On Baile's Strand; Deirdre; The Green Helmet; The Shadowy Waters; The Words Upon the Window-pane*).   1937.
"The Herne's Egg" and Other Plays (includes *A Full Moon in March* and *The King of the Great Clock Tower*).   1938.
Poems; Prose; Plays; and Criticism (selections), edited by A. Norman Jeffares (4 vols.).   1963–64.
Variorum Edition of the Plays, edited by Russell K. Alspach and Catherine C. Alspach.   1966.
The Cornell Yeats.   1986—

Stage Works

The Countess Kathleen (produced Ancient Concert Rooms, Dublin, 1899).   In *"The Countess Kathleen" and Various Legends and Lyrics*, 1892; revised version, as *The Countess Cathleen*, 1912.
The Land of Heart's Desire (produced Avenue Theatre, London, 1894).   1894.
The Shadowy Waters (produced Molesworth Hall, Dublin, 1904).   1900; revised version, in *Poems*, 1906.
Diarmuid and Grania, with George Moore (produced Dublin, 1901).   1951.
Cathleen ni Houlihan (produced St. Theresa's Hall, Dublin, 1902).   1902.
The Pot of Broth (produced Ancient Concert Rooms, Dublin, 1902).   In *"The Hour Glass" and Other Plays*, 1904.
Where There is Nothing (produced Court Theatre, London, 1904).   1902; revised version, with Lady Gregory, as *The Unicorn from the Stars* (produced Abbey Theatre, Dublin, 1907).   1908.
The Hour Glass: A Morality (produced Molesworth Hall, Dublin, 1903).   1903; revised version (produced Abbey Theatre, Dublin, 1912), in *The Mask*, April 1913.
The King's Threshold (produced Molesworth Hall, Dublin, 1903).   1904; revised version (produced Abbey Theatre, Dublin, 1913), in *Poems*, 1906.
On Baile's Strand (produced Abbey Theatre, Dublin, 1904).   In *Plays for an Irish Theatre 3*, 1904; revised version, in *Poems*, 1906.
Deirdre (produced Abbey Theatre, Dublin, 1906).   In *Plays for an Irish Theatre 5*, 1907.
The Golden Helmet (produced Abbey Theatre, Dublin, 1908).   1908; revised version, as *The Green Helmet* (produced Abbey Theatre, Dublin, 1910), 1910.
The Travelling Man, with Lady Gregory (produced Abbey Theatre, Dublin, 1910).   In *Seven Short Plays* by Lady Gregory, 1909.
At the Hawk's Well; or, Waters of Immortality (produced privately, Lady Cunard's House, Cavendish Square, London, 1916).   In *The Wild Swans at Coole*, 1917.
The Only Jealousy of Emer (produced Amsterdam, c.1926).   In *Two Plays for Dancers*, 1919; prose version, as *Fighting the Waves* (produced Abbey Theatre, Dublin, 1929), in *Wheels and Butterflies*, 1934.
The Dreaming of the Bones (produced Abbey Theatre, Dublin, 1931).   In *Two Plays for Dancers*, 1919.

W.B. Yeats (chalk drawing by Ivan Opffer, 1935?).

The Player Queen (produced King's Hall, London, 1919).   1922.
Calvary.   In *Four Plays for Dancers*, 1921.
The Cat and the Moon (produced Abbey Theatre, Dublin, 1926).   In *"The Cat and the Moon" and Certain Poems*, 1924.
King Oedipus, from the play by Sophocles (produced Abbey Theatre, Dublin, 1926).   1928.
The Resurrection (produced Abbey Theatre, Dublin, 1934).   1927.
Oedipus at Colonus, from a play by Sophocles (produced Abbey Theatre, Dublin, 1927).   In *Collected Plays*, 1934.
Words upon the Window Pane (produced Abbey Theatre, Dublin, 1930).   1934.
The King of the Great Clock Tower (produced Abbey Theatre, Dublin, 1934).   In *"The Herne's Egg" and Other Plays*, 1938.
Purgatory (produced Abbey Theatre, Dublin, 1938).   In *Last Poems and Two Plays*, 1939.
The Herne's Egg (produced by Lord Longford's company, 1939).   1938.
A Full Moon in March.   In *"The Herne's Egg" and Other Plays*, 1938.
The Death of Cuchulain (produced Abbey Theatre, Dublin, 1945).   In *Last Poems and Two Plays*. 1939.

Fiction

John Sherman and Dhoya.   1891.
The Secret Rose (stories).   1897.

The Tables of the Law; The Adoration of the Magi.   1897.
Stories of Red Hanrahan.   1905.
Stories of Red Hanrahan; The Secret Rose; Rosa Alchemica.   1913.

Verse

Mosada: A Dramatic Poem.   1886.
"The Wanderings of Oisin" and Other Poems.   1889.
"The Countess Kathleen" and Various Legends and Lyrics.   1892.
Poems.   1895; revised editions, 1899, 1901, 1904, 1908, 1912, 1913, 1927, 1929.
The Wind Among the Reeds.   1899.
In the Seven Woods, Being Poems Chiefly of the Irish Heroic Age.   1903.
Poems 1899–1905.   1906.
Poetical Works: Lyrical Poems, Dramatical Poems (2 vols.).   1906–07; revised edition, 1912.
Poems, Second Series.   1909.
The Green Helmet and Other Poems.   1910; revised edition, 1912.
A Selection from the Poetry.   1913.
A Selection from the Love Poetry.   1913.
Poems Written in Discouragement 1912–1913.   1913.
Nine Poems.   1914.
Responsibilities: Poems and a Play.   1914.
"Responsibilities" and Other Poems.   1916.
The Wild Swans at Coole, Other Verses, and a Play in Verse.   1917; revised edition, 1919.
Nine Poems.   1918.
Michael Robartes and the Dancer.   1921.
Selected Poems.   1921.
Later Poems (Collected Works 1).   1922.
Seven Poems and a Fragment.   1922.
"The Cat and the Moon" and Certain Poems.   1924.
October Blast.   1927.
The Tower.   1928.
Selected Poems, Lyrical and Narrative.   1929.
The Winding Stair.   1929.
"Words for Music Perhaps" and Other Poems.   1932.
"The Winding Stair" and Other Poems.   1933.
Collected Poems.   1933; revised edition, 1950.
Wheels and Butterflies.   1934.
The King of the Great Clock Tower: Commentaries and Poems.   1934.
A Full Moon in March.   1935.
Poems.   1935.
New Poems.   1938.
Last Poems and Two Plays.   1939.
Selected Poems, edited by A. Holst.   1939.
Last Poems and Plays.   1940.
The Poems (2 vols.).   1949.
Variorum Edition of the Poems, edited by Peter Allt and Russell K. Alspach.   1957; revised edition, 1967.
The Poems, edited by Richard J. Finneran.   1983; revised edition, 1989.
Poems: A New Selection.   1984.
Poems, edited by A. Norman Jeffares.   1989.
Poems, edited by Daniel Albright.   1990.

Memoirs and Letters

Autobiographies (Collected Works 6).   1926.
Estrangement, Being Some Fifty Thoughts from a Diary Kept in 1909.   1926.
The Death of Synge and Other Passages from an Old Diary.   1928.

The Autobiography.   1938; revised edition, as Autobiographies, 1955.
Florence Farr, Bernard Shaw, and W.B. Yeats: Letters, edited by Clifford Bax.   1941.
Letters, edited by Allan Wade.   1954.
Memoirs, edited by Denis Donogue.   1972.
The Correspondence of Robert Bridges and W.B. Yeats, edited by Richard J. Finneran.   1977.
Theatre Business: The Correspondence of the First Abbey Theatre Directors: W.B. Yeats, Lady Gregory, and J.M. Synge, edited by Ann Saddlemyer.   1982.
Collected Letters, edited by John Kelly.   1986—

Other

The Celtic Twilight: Men and Women, Dhouls and Fairies.   1893; revised edition, 1902.
Literary Ideals in Ireland, with George William Russell and John Eglinton.   1899.
Is the Order of R.R. and A.C. to Remain a Magical Order?   1901.
Ideas of Good and Evil.   1903.
Discoveries: A Volume of Essays.   1907.
Poetry and Ireland: Essays, with Lionel Johnson.   1908.
Synge and the Ireland of His Time.   1911.
The Cutting of an Agate.   1912; revised edition, 1919.
Reveries over Childhood and Youth.   1915.
Per Amica Silentia Lunae.   1918.
Four Years.   1921.
The Trembling of the Veil.   1922.
Essays (Collected Works 4).   1924.
A Vision.   1925; revised edition, 1937.
Early Poems and Stories (Collected Works 5).   1925.
A Packet for Ezra Pound.   1929.
Stories of Michael Robartes and His Friends.   1932.
Letters to the New Island, edited by Horace Reynolds.   1934.
Dramatis Personae.   1935.
Dramatis Personae 1896–1902.   1936.
Essays 1931 to 1936.   1937.
On the Boiler (essays; includes verse).   1939.
If I Were Four-and-Twenty.   1940.
Pages from a Diary Written in 1930.   1940.
The Senate Speeches, edited by Donald Pearce.   1960.
Essays and Introductions.   1961.
Explorations.   1962.
Mythologies.   1962.
Reflections, edited by Curtis Bradford.   1970.
Uncollected Prose, edited by John P. Frayne and Colton Johnson (2 vols.).   1970–76.
Yeats and the Theatre, edited by Robert O'Driscoll and Lorna Reynolds.   1975.
Yeats on Yeats: The Last Introductions and the Dublin Edition, edited by Edward Callan.   1981.
The Writing of Sophocles' King Oedipus, edited by David R. Clark and James B. McGuire.   1989.
Prefaces and Introductions: Uncollected Prefaces and Introductions by Yeats to the Works of Other Authors and to Anthologies Edited by Yeats, edited by William H. O'Donnell.   1989.
Vision Papers, edited by Steve L. Adams and others (3 vols.).   1990.

Editor, Fairy and Folk Tales of the Irish Peasantry.   1888; as Irish Fairy and Folk Tales, 1893.
Editor, Representative Irish Tales.   1891.
Editor, Irish Fairy Tales.   1892.

Editor, with E.J. Ellis, *The Works of William Blake* (3 vols.). 1893.

Editor, *The Poems of Blake*.   1893.

Editor, *A Book of Irish Verse*.   1895; revised edition, 1900.

Editor, *Twenty-One Poems*, by Lionel Johnson.   1905.

Editor, *Some Essays and Passages*, by John Eglinton.   1905.

Editor, *Sixteen Poems*, by William Allingham.   1905.

Editor, *Twenty-One Poems*, by Katharine Tynan.   1907.

Editor, with F. Higgins, *Broadsides: A Collection of Old and New Songs* (2 vols.).   1935–37.

Editor, *The Oxford Book of Modern Verse 1892–1935*. 1936.

Editor, and Translator with Shree Purohit Swami, *The Ten Principal Upanishads*.   1937.

*

Bibliographies

Allan Wade, *A Bibliography of the Writings of W.B. Yeats*, London, 1951; revised edition, by Russell K. Alspach, 1968.

K.P.S. Jochum, *W.B. Yeats: A Classified Bibliography of Criticism*, Folkestone, Kent, 1978.

Criticism

Books:

J.M. Hone, *W.B. Yeats*, London, 1942.

Richard Ellmann, *Yeats: The Man and the Masks*, London, 1949; revised edition, 1979.

James W. Hall and Martin Steinmann (eds.), *The Permanence of Yeats: Selected Criticism*, New York, 1950.

Richard Ellmann, *The Identity of Yeats*, London, 1954; revised edition, 1964.

G.S. Fraser, *W.B. Yeats*, London, 1954; revised editions, 1962 and 1965.

George Brandon Saul, *Prolegomena to the Study of Yeats's Plays* (2 vols.), Philadelphia, 1958.

Peter Ure, *Yeats the Playwright: A Commentary on Character and Design in the Major Plays*, New York, 1963.

John Unterecker (ed.), *Yeats: A Collection of Critical Essays*, Englewood Cliffs, New Jersey, 1963.

Helen Vendler, *Yeats's Vision and the Later Plays*, Cambridge, Massachusetts, 1963.

Ann Saddlemyer and Robin Skelton, *The World of Yeats: Essays in Perspective*, Victoria, British Columbia, 1965.

David R. Clark, *Yeats and the Theatre of Desolate Reality*, Dublin, 1965.

S.B. Bushrui, *Yeats's Verse Plays: The Revisions 1900–1910*, Oxford, 1965.

Leonard Nathan, *The Tragic Drama of W.B. Yeats: Figures in a Dance*, Oxford, 1965.

Donald Torchiana, *W.B. Yeats and Georgian Ireland*, Evanston, Illinois, 1966.

Harold Bloom, *W.B. Yeats*, New York, 1970.

Philip L. Marcus, *Yeats and the Beginning of the Irish Renaissance*, Ithaca (New York) and London, 1970.

Denis Donoghue, *W.B. Yeats*, London, 1971.

A. Norman Jeffares, *W.B. Yeats*, London, 1971.

John Rees Moore, *Masks of Love and Death: Yeats as Dramatist*, Ithaca, New York, 1971.

Richard Morton, *An Outline of the Works of Yeats*, 1971

Michael MacLiammoir and Eavan Boland, *W.B. Yeats and His World*, London, 1971.

Daniel Albright, *The Myth Against Myth: A Study of Yeats's Imagination in Old Age*, London, 1972.

Kathleen Raine, *Yeats, The Tarot, and the Golden Dawn*, Dublin, 1972; revised edition, 1976.

George Mills Harper, *Yeats's Golden Dawn*, Wellingborough, 1974.

Philip Edouards, *Nationalist Theatres: Shakespeare and Yeats*, Liverpool, 1976.

James W. Flannery, *W.B. Yeats and the Idea of a Theatre: The Early Abbey Theatre in Theory and Practice*, New Haven (Connecticut) and London, 1976.

A. Norman Jeffares and A.S. Knowland, *A Commentary on the Collected Plays of W.B. Yeats*, London, 1975.

Robert O'Driscoll and Lorna Reynolds (eds.), *Yeats and the Theatre*, New York, 1975.

Richard Taylor, *The Drama of W.B. Yeats: Irish Myth and Japanese No*, New Haven (Connecticut) and London, 1976.

Frank Tuohy, *W.B. Yeats*, London, 1976.

Liam Miller, *The Noble Drama of Yeats*, Dublin, 1977.

Barton R. Friedman, *Adventures in the Deeps of the Mind: The Cuchulain Cycle of Yeats*, Princeton (New Jersey) and Guildford (Surrey), 1977.

A. Norman Jeffares (ed.), *W.B. Yeats: The Critical Heritage*, London, 1977.

E.H. Mikhail (ed.), *Yeats: Interviews and Recollections* (2 vols.), London, 1977.

Stephen Gill, *Six Symbolist Plays of Yeats*, Cornwall, Ontario, 1978.

Andrew Parkin, *The Dramatic Imagination of W.B. Yeats*, Dublin, 1978.

Anthony Bradley, *William Butler Yeats*, New York, 1979.

Mary Helen Thuente, *W.B. Yeats and Irish Folklore*, Dublin, 1980.

Ashley E. Myles, *Theatre of Aristocracy: A Study of Yeats as a Dramatist*, Salzburg, 1981.

Richard F. Peterson, *William Butler Yeats*, Boston, 1982.

Douglas N. Archibald, *W.B. Yeats*, Syracuse, New York, 1983.

Birgit Bramsback, *Folklore and Yeats: The Function of Folklore Elements in Three Early Plays*, Uppsala, Sweden, 1984.

Karen Dorn, *Players and Painted Stage: The Theatre of W.B. Yeats*, Brighton, Sussex, 1984.

Richard Taylor, *A Reader's Guide to the Plays of W.B. Yeats*, London, 1984.

Graham Hough, *The Mystery Religion of Yeats*, Brighton, 1984.

Harold Bloom (ed.), *William Butler Yeats: Modern Critical Views*, New York, 1986.

Heather C. Martin, *W.B. Yeats: Metaphysics as Dramatist*, Gerrard's Cross, Buckinghamshire, 1986.

Kathleen Raine, *Yeats the Initiate: Essays*, Dublin, 1986.

Maeve Good, *Yeats and the Creation of a Tragic Universe*, Basingstoke, 1987.

Ann Saddlemyer, *Wisdom, Magic, Sensation: Yeats in the 1930's*, 1988.

A. Norman Jeffares, *Yeats the European*, Savage, Maryland, 1989.

David Pierce, *Yeats: A Guide Through the Critical Maze*, Bristol, 1989.

Ulick O'Connor, *The Yeats Companion*, London, 1990.

Adrian Frazier, *Behind the Scenes: Yeats, Horniman, and the Struggle for the Abbey Theatre*, Berkeley, California, 1990.

Leonard Orr (ed.), *Yeats and Postmodernism*, Syracuse, New York, 1990.

Masara Sekine and Christopher Murray, *Yeats and the Noh: A Comparative Study*, Gerrards Cross, 1990.

Serials:
Yeats Annual, 1983—

* * *

Yeats's plays are properly overshadowed by his fame as a lyric poet. There are very few moments in the plays where the verse shows his finest inspiration, the famous exception being the song at the beginning of *The Resurrection*, "I saw a staring virgin stand/Where holy Dionysus died", and he includes it among his *Collected Poems*. Nevertheless he started writing plays early in his career and was making corrections to *The Death of Cuchulain* two days before he died. Indeed, his early preoccupation with monologue and dialogue, narrative (in verse and prose), and ballads makes it unsurprising that he should have branched out into drama. Many Romantic poets in English wrote at least one play. Few were men of the theatre.

It is hard to place him in any tradition. He never was obsessed with an English dramatist as he was with Blake and Shelley, despite his father reading Shakespeare aloud and discoursing on his work with great intelligence. Although Yeats later adapted Sophocles he did not come early to Classical drama. His inspiration seems largely negative, a revulsion away from Ibsen and Shaw. He could be interested in Maeterlinck without being enthusiastic. He seemed to go against the most positive energies of modern drama, but just as his lyric verse worked its way out of vapid Romanticism by strange personal paths, including esoteric religion, so he stubbornly, and with amazing persistance, worked to establish a modern poetic drama.

In his talk about Yeats's plays to the Abbey Theatre in 1940, T.S. Eliot said, "The idea of the poetic drama was kept alive when everywhere else it had been driven underground. I do not know where our debt to him as a dramatist ends". But then Eliot's achievement as a dramatist is even less secure than Yeats's.

Yeats's first play was written as part of his courtship of Maude Gonne, and the story of a high born lady who sacrifices her soul to save the Irish poor was a little parable for his beloved, suggesting that her social obsessions were a betrayal of her destiny as a beautiful woman. Few would agree with his moral, although in the context of his life's work one can see its part in his wisdom. *The Countess Cathleen* is based on a folk tale, written in loose blank verse, but more or less realistic in form. He referred to it as a "tapestry". Although the play is obviously written by a poet of considerable intelligence and musical talent, the diction is rootless and a faintly archaic pastiche.

Nearly all Yeats's plays spring from his ambition to create an Irish literature in English, at first using folk material and later the great Irish sagas. He quickly surrounded himself, or was surrounded by, people of similar ambitions. Even writing a play to impress his girlfriend, which might have been esoteric in another writer, was done in the public eye and evoked a good deal of public hostility and admiration. What happened with *The Countess Cathleen* was to happen to Yeats again and again, because his independent and sophisticated mind kept offering material to patriotic Irishmen that they found difficult and often offensive. He had to defend his own plays, and later those of Synge and O'Casey, from audiences, journalists, and clerics who were not prepared to consider

that an Irish woman might sell her soul, or that she might not be sexually virtuous, and so on. When a colony is fighting for independence it requires the arts to back up the freedom-fighters with patriotic propaganda, and Yeats only did this with *Cathleen ni Houlihan* (also starring Maude Gonne) which later caused him some soul searching: "Did that play of mine send out/Certain men the English shot?".

The element of pastiche discolours most of his plays; but his talent and intelligence always present something to admire and think about. Reading the plays now it is hard to believe how often they were printed and performed in the early days. With hindsight we can see that he did not make enough of his Irish subject matter; but at the time his efforts were still part of the patriotic effort, as well as a struggle to fill the vacuum in Irish drama. He himself grew disillusioned with his public role. He had founded a National Theatre and discovered one major talent and offered opportunity to very many playwrights whose final quality has not yet been estimated. At the same time, his role as organiser, witnessed in his contributions to his theatre's magazine, *Samhain*, alerts us to the fact that he was reduced for most of his time to finding positive things to say about a great many very bad plays, pretending he could adjudicate on plays in the Irish language, and indeed pretending to a theatrical authority that for many years he did not have.

He may have made many bad decisions, such as quarrelling with the Fay brothers, who knew a good deal about acting, and turning down O'Casey's fourth play, which had more right to the stage of the Abbey than many subsequent productions, including his own; but his great reputation and his ability as an organiser put him in touch with key figures in modern theatre, like Gordon Craig, Florence Farr, and Ninette de Valois. He was disappointed that his theatre became famous for realistic plays.

What Yeats wrote to Olivia Shakespeare in 1929 about *The Only Jealousy of Emer* suggests what he was after, and what many believe he achieved: "The masks by the Dutchman Krop [were] magnificent and Antheil's music. Everyone here is as convinced as I am that I have discovered a new form by this combination of dance, speech and music". In such mixed forms, the texts do not have final authority but depend on talented co-operation. Done badly they are ridiculous; but there are many ways of doing them. Some have been done by puppets with success.

This approach to drama could also be seen as a serious way of bringing the techniques of symbolist poetry to the stage, in the symbolic nature of the characters, the very compressed plots, the use of colouring, atmosphere, masks, and abstract or symbolic settings. An early symbolist play, *The Shadowy Waters*, is vague and dreamy, like the early poetry; but later plays in this style are brief, taut, and crammed, and often contain fairly close philosophical argument. In *Calvary*, for instance, Yeats is concerned to confront Jesus with characters like Lazarus who suffer from intellectual despair and cannot be saved by one whose ministry is exclusively to those whose "suffering is rooted in death, in poverty, or in sickness, or in sin, in some shape of the common lot". The risible line, "God has not died for the white heron", is repeated in the play, the white heron being symbolic of the melancholy individualist. Yeats presents an undynamic, theological Christ, perhaps unworthy of his great subject, but he knows what he is about.

The early magic realism of *Cathleen ni Houlihan* developed into later plays of considerable strength, like *The Words upon the Window Pane* and *Purgatory*, one in prose, the other in verse. Supernatural events take place in a realistic setting, presented with clear plot, construction, and characters. *The Herne's Egg* might be called surrealistic. *The Green Helmet* is a comedy in rough verse, based on an Irish folk story close to Gawain and The Green Knight. It is robust and amusing in a more developed way than the low characters, the blind man, and the cripple that turn up in several other plays to good effect. Yeats claimed that Lady Gregory wrote all his "low" dialogue for him, though, of course, in such carefully written work the substance of what they say would have been absolutely controlled by Yeats.

A good deal has been written about Yeats's plays, but no critic has made a convincing case for their greatness. On the other hand it is too easy to dismiss them without seeing a good production. Richard Allen Cave, reviewing the Yeats festival at the Abbey Theatre, in 1990, concluded that one cannot produce Yeats properly without "a rigorous lifetime's dedication to pushing body, voice, imagination, and vision to the limits of expressiveness". But all plays are the better for

good actors. It is not certain whether Yeats's are peculiarly worthy of such complete actors or in desperate need of them.

—James Simmons

See also *Volume 1* entries on *At the Hawk's Well*; *The Death of Cuchulain*; *On Baile's Strand*; *Purgatory*.

———

YU-MING-TANG. See **TANG Xianzu.**

———

ZEAMI. Also known as Kanze Saburō or Kanze Zeami Motokiyo. Born Yuzaki Saemon Tayu Motokiyo in Yamada (now Sakurai City, Nara Prefecture), Japan, 1363. Had one daughter and two sons. Received theatrical training from his father, Kannami Kiyotsugu, the originator of Nō drama. Inherited leadership of the Kanze School of Nō from his father; given the name Zeami by his patron, Shogun Ashikaga Yoshimitsu; following death of Yoshimitsu, 1408, his performing career declined; gave over leadership of Kanze theatre to his son, Motomasa, 1422; chief musician to Shogun Ashikaga Yoshimochi, 1424; banished to Sado Island, northern Japan (reasons unknown). Between 79 and 145 Nō plays have been attributed to him. Died on Sado Island, or possibly in Kyoto, c.8 August 1443.

Works

Collections

Tōchū Zeami Nijūsanbushū (includes 23 plays), edited by Kazuma Kawase. 1945.
Nō Plays of Japan (includes *Atsumori; Kagekiyo; Ukai; Aya no Tsuzami; Aoi no Ue; Kantan; Hakurakuten*), translated by Arthur Waley. 1921.
Japanese Noh Drama: Ten Plays (3 vols.; includes *Takasago; Tamura; Sanemori; Kiyotsune; Tōboku; Izutsu; Tadanori; Yuya; Kantan; Aoi no Ue; Kagekiyo; Yamamba*), translated by Nippon Gakujutsu Shinkōkai. 1955–60.
Zeami Jūrokubushū Hyōshaku (includes 16 plays), edited by Asaji Nose. 1962.
Twenty Plays of the Nō Theatre (includes *Komachi at Sekidera; The Brocade Tree; Semimaru; The Deserted Crone; Lady Han; The Reed Cutter*), translated by D. Keene. 1970.
Masterworks of the Nō Theater (includes *Nonomiya; Izutsu; Atsumori; Tadanori; Matsukaze; Higaki; Obasute; Saigyozakura; Nue; Taema; Tōru*), translated by Kenneth Yamada. 1989.
Japanese Nō Dramas (includes *Atsumori; Hanjo; Izutsu; Kinuta; Kureba; Matsukaze; Nonomiya; Saigyo-zakura; Semimaru; Tadanori; Tagasogo; Yamamba; Yashimai;* and plays by other authors), translated by Royall Taylor. 1992.

Stage Works

Selected titles, with published translations, in order of the five play-categories of Nō.

1) Waki/kami Nō (God Plays):
Hakurakuten. Translated as *Hakurakuten*, in *Nō Plays of Japan*, 1921.

Kureba. Translated as *Kureba*, in *Japanese Nō Drama*, 1992.
Oimatsu. Translated as *The Old Pine Tree*, in *"The Old Pine Tree" and other Noh Plays*, 1962.
Takasago. Translated as *Takasogo*, in *Japanese Noh Drama: Ten Plays*, 1955–60, and *Japanese Nō Drama*, 1992.
Yōrō.

2) Shura Nō (Man Plays, or Warrior Plays):
Atsumori. Translated as *Atsumori*, in *Nō Plays of Japan*, 1921: several subsequent translations under same title.
Kiyotsune. Translated as *Kiyotsune*, in *Japanese Noh Drama*, 1955–60.
Sanemori. Translated as *Sanemori*, in *Japanese Noh Drama*, 1955–60.
Tadanori. Translated as *Tadanori*, in *Japanese Noh Drama*, 1955–60: several subsequent translations under same title.
Tamura. Translated as *Tamura*, in *Japanese Noh Drama*, 1955–60.
Tōboku. Translated as *Tōboku*, in *Japanese Noh Drama*, 1955–60.
Yashima. Translated as *The Battle of Yashima*, in *"The Old Pine Tree" and Other Noh Plays*, 1962.
Yorimasa. Translated as *Yashima*, in *Japanese Nō Drama*, 1992.

3) Kazura Nō (Woman Plays, or Wig Plays):
Higaki. Translated as *The Woman Within the Cyprus Fence*, in *"The Old Pine Tree" and Other Noh Plays*, 1962; as *Higaki*, in *Masterworks of the Nō Theater*, 1989.
Izutsu. Translated as *Izutsu (Well-Curb)*, in *The Noh Drama*, 1960, and in *Masterworks of the Nō Theater*, 1989; as *Izutóu: The Well-Cradle*, in *Japanese Nō Drama*, 1992.
Kakitsubata. Translated as *Kakitsubata (The Iris)*, in *Twelve Plays of the Noh and Kyōgen Theaters*, 1988.
Matsukaze. Translated as *Matsukaze*, in *Japanese Noh Drama: Ten Plays*, 1955–60, and *Masterworks of the Nō Theater*, 1989; as *Pining Wind*, in *Japanese Nō Drama*, 1992.
Nonomiya. Translated as *Nonomiya*, in *Masterworks of the Nō Theater*, 1989; as *The Wildwood Shrine*, in *Japanese Nō Drama*, 1992.
Obasute. Translated as *The Deserted Crone*, in *Twenty Plays of the Nō Theatre*, 1970; as *Obasute*, in *Masterworks of the Nō Theater*, 1989.
Saigyō-zakura. Translated as *Saigyō and the Cherry Tree*, in *Twelve Plays of the Noh and Kyōgen Theaters*, 1988; as *Saigyōzakura*, in *Masterworks of the Nō Theater*, 1989; as *Saigyō's Cherry Tree*, in *Japanese Nō Drama*, 1992.
Sekidera Komachi. Translated as *Komachi at Sekidera*, in *Twenty Plays of the Nō Theatre*, 1970, and *Japanese Nō Drama*, 1992.

Unoha. Translated as *Unoha (Cormorant Plumes)*, in *Twelve Plays of the Noh and Kyōgen Theaters*, 1988.
Yura. Translated as *Yuya*, in *Japanese Noh Drama*, 1955–60.

4) Zatsu Nō (Miscellaneous Plays; Madman, Obsession, Present-Life Plays):
Aoi-no-Ue. Translated as *Aoi-no-Ue*, in *Nō Plays of Japan*, 1921, and *Japanese Noh Drama*, 1955–60.
Aya no Tsuzumi. Translated as *Aya no Tsuzumi*, in *Nō Plays of Japan*, 1921.
Ashikari. Translated as *The Reed Cutter*, in *Twenty Plays of the Nō Theatre*, 1970.
Hanjo. Translated as *Lady Han*, in *Twenty Plays of the Nō Theatre*, 1970, and in *Japanese Nō Drama*, 1992.
Hyakuman.
Kagekiyo. Translated as *Kagekiyo*, in *Nō Plays of Japan*, 1921, and *Japanese Noh Drama*, 1955–60.
Kantan. Translated as *Kantan*, in *Nō Plays of Japan*, 1921, and in *Japanese Noh Drama*, 1955–60.
Kayoi Komachi.
Kinuta. Translated as *The Fulling Block*, in *Japanese Nō Drama*, 1992.
Koi no Omoni.
Mitsuyama. Translated as *Jinen the Preacher*, in *"The Old Pine Tree" and Other Noh Plays*, 1962.
Nishikigi. Translated as *The Brocade Tree*, in *Twenty Plays of the Nō Theatre*, 1970.
Semimaru. Translated as *Semimaru*, in *Twenty Plays of the Nō Theatre*, 1970, and *Japanese No Drama*, 1992.
Shunei.

5) Kiri No (Concluding or Demon Plays):
Nomori.
Nue. Translated as *Nue*, in *Masterworks of the Nō Theater*, 1989.
Shoki.
Suma Genji. Translated as *The Tale of Genji*, 1976.
Taema. Translated as *Taema*, in *Monumenta Nipponica*, vol. 25 nos. 3–4, 1970, and in *Masterworks of the Nō Theater*, 1989.
Taizanbukun.
Tōru. Translated as *Tōru*, in *Masterworks of the Nō Theater*, 1989.
Ukai. Translated as *Ukai*, in *Nō Plays of Japan*, 1921.
Yamamba. Translated as *Yamamba*, in *Japanese Noh Drama: Ten Plays*, 1955–60, and *Japanese Nō Drama*, 1992.

Other

On the Art of Nō Drama: The Major Treatises of Zeami, translated by J. Thomas Rimer and Yamazaki Masakazu, 1984.
Sarugaku dangi. Translated as *Zeami's Talks on Sarugaku*, 1986.

*

Criticism

Books:
Nogami Toyoichiro, *Zeami and His Theories on Noh*, Tokyo, 1955.
P.G. O'Neill, *Early Nō Drama: Its Background, Character and Development 1300–1450*, London, 1958.
R. Sieffert, *La Tradition secrète du no*, Paris, 1960.

Donald Keene, *Nō: The Classical Drama of Japan*, Tokyo and Palo Alto, California, 1966.
Masaru Sekine, *Ze-Ami and His Theories of Noh Drama*, Gerrards Cross, Buckinghamshire, 1985.
Thomas Blenman Hare, *Zeami's Style: The Noh Plays of Zeami Motokiyo*, Stanford, California, 1986.
Mae J. Smethurst, *The Artistry of Aeschylus and Zeami: A Comparative Study of Greek Tragedy and Nō*, Princeton (New Jersey) and Guildford (Surrey), 1989.

Articles:
Megumi Sata, "Aristotle's Poetics and Zeami's Teachings on Style", in *Asian Theatre Journal*, vol.6 no.1, 1989.

* * *

The significance of Zeami's contributions to the foundation of the Nō theatre as we know it today is manifold. He was a superb performer who was respected and admired by both aristocrats and the general public.

He wisely realized the enormous advantage of demonstrating his talents as a performer by writing plays for himself, and he proved the validity of his concept through the many masterpieces he wrote.

Beyond these extraordinary contributions as an artist, he was the foremost theorist of Nō theatre and its educator, a fact that was simply demonstrated by the famous 23 treatises he left, some as a secret record of a tradition to be transmitted to his successors and the rest to be left for his colleagues. The remarkable quality of his insight into the art of Nō theatre, as contained in his writings, ranges from how to write an effective play to how to train a professional performer starting at the age of seven years old, and it provides the reader with perceptions as valuable to Nō theatre as Aristotle's *Poetics* was to Greek tragedy, with his subtle discussion of acting as sophisticated as was Stanislavsky's advice to actors.

The first treatise Zeami wrote was *Fūshi Kaden*, commonly known as *Kadensho* (A Book of Transmitting a Flower), dated 1402. This work deals primarily with the innumerable problems a performer faces in obtaining the acknowledgement of the world and in maintaining such fame once he gains it. He analyzes the concept of *hana*, a flower that is the life of art in Nō theatre by which the art itself is illuminated. A flower is something which is capable of charming the audience. *Kadensho* explains how one can make such a flower bloom.

By Zeami's own admission, *Kadensho* was a collection of precepts learned from his father Kannami, who was known as a great master of *monomane* (imitation). He is credited with being a playwright of such plays as *Jinen-koji*, which requires of the main actor an ability to dance several popular dance forms within the play. Zeami's greatness is indicated by the fact that he mastered all the skills required to be a competent performer and saw the importance of entertaining the Shogun Yoshimitsu and his court with ever fresh attractions in Nō, which he provided in order to survive and prosper well into the future.

Zeami saw the enormous potential in the concept of *yūgen* as the aesthetic backbone of his art. The concept was practiced first in religion as something deep and unfathomable, and later in *waka*, the Court poetry in the early 12th-century poetics by Fujiwara Shunzei, as the highest ideal of poetic expression: the feeling which stimulates an image of life's tranquil loneliness as revealed in the truth of nature. The same term was used in the mid-15th century by Shōtetsu, a Zen monk, to mean an infinitely rich and nuanced feeling of grace in ethereal beauty. Shōtetsu posed a rhetorical question, "Could it be possible to explain the style of *yūgen* as the feeling you obtain by seeing four or five finely dressed court ladies who are viewing cherry blossoms in full bloom at the courtyard of the South Wing [of the palace]?". This very same sentiment of *yūgen* is discussed by Zeami in his *Nōsakusho* (Treatise on Playwriting). Thus we may refer to Zeami's *yūgen* as the beauty of elegance. By providing such a refined touch of beauty through a mythical aura, instead of simply relying on the power of imitation, Zeami succeeded in elevating the artistic status of Nō to an entertainment form which satisfied the tastes of the Shogun and his court.

His awareness of the requirements of Nō theatre was well expressed in other works, throughout which he emphasized the significance of "buka nikyoku" (dance and song), two fundamental elements of Nō. In the 600-year span of Nō theatre, there has been no other contributor to rank with Zeami, a genius whose talent was so deeply and widely applied that it covered all aspects of the form. His plays are still performed regularly, and his theories are often consulted in judging the appropriateness of the contemporary practice of Nō theatre.

—Andrew T. Tsubaki

See also *Volume 1* entry on *Well-Curb* (*Izutsu*).

ZOLA, Émile. Born in Paris, 2 April 1840, of Italian father; naturalized French citizen, 1862. Educated at Collège d'Aix; Lycée Bourbon, Aix; Lycée Saint-Louis, Paris, 1858–59. Married Alexandrine-Gabrielle Meley in 1870; also had two children by Jeanne Rozerot. Worked briefly as a clerk in the Excise Office; worked in the dispatch office, then in sales promotion, Hachette publishers, Paris, 1862–66; art critic (as "Claude"), *L'Événement* newspaper, 1866; collaborated with other writers to produce adaptations of his fiction for the stage, from 1867; staff member, *Le Globe* and *L'Événement Illustré*, 1868, and staff member or contributor to other papers until 1900; first instalment of his Rougon-Macquart cycle published 1870; made accusations of false trial during the Dreyfus affair: tried and convicted of libel, 1898: in England, 1898–99. Died in Paris, 29 September 1902.

Works

Collections

Théâtre (includes *Le Bouton de Rose; Les Héritiers Rabourdin; Thérèse Raquin*). 1878.
Trois Pièces (includes *Nana; Pot-Bouille; L'Assommoir* [*L'Assommoir* adaptation not by Zola]). 1885.
Poèmes lyriques (opera libretti; includes *Messidor; L'Ouragan; L'Enfant-Roi; Lazare; Violaine la chevelue; Sylvanire*). 1921.
Oeuvres complètes (50 vols.), edited by Eugène Fasquelle and Maurice Le Blond. 1927–29.
Oeuvres complètes (15 vols.; plays in Volume 15), edited by Henri Mitterand, 1966–69.

Stage Works

Les Mystères de Marseille, with Marius Roux (produced Théâtre du Gymnase, Paris, 1867).

Thérèse Raquin, from his novel (produced Théâtre de la Renaissance, Paris, 1873). 1873; translated as *Thérèse Raquin*, in *From the Modern Repertoire 3*, edited by Eric Bentley, 1956, in *The Seeds of Modern Drama*, 1963, and in a single edition, 1989.
Les Héritiers Rabourdin, from a play by Jonson (produced Théâtre de Cluny, Paris, 1874). 1874; translated as *The Heirs of Rabourdin*, 1893.
Le Bouton de rose (produced Palais-Royal, Paris, 1878). In *Théâtre*, 1878.
Nana, with William Busnach, from the novel by Zola (produced Théâtre de l'Ambigu-Comique, Paris, 1881). In *Trois Pièces*, 1885.
Pot-Bouille, with William Busnach, from the novel by Zola (produced Théâtre de l'Ambigu-Comique, Paris, 1883). In *Trois Pièces*, 1885.
Le Ventre de Paris, with William Busnach, from the novel by Zola (produced Théâtre de Paris, Paris, 1887).
Renée, from his novel *La Curée* (produced Théâtre du Vaudeville, Paris, 1887). 1887.
Germinal, with William Busnach, from the novel by Zola (produced Théâtre du Châtelet, Paris, 1888).
Madeleine (produced Théâtre Libre, Paris, 1889). In *Oeuvres complètes*, 1927–29.
Le Rêve, music by Alfred Bruneau (produced Opéra-Comique, Paris, 1891).
L'Attaque du Moulin, music by Alfred Bruneau (produced Opéra-Comique, Paris, 1893).
Messidor, music by Alfred Bruneau (produced Théâtre de l'Opéra, Paris, 1897). 1897.
L'Ouragan, music by Alfred Bruneau (produced Opéra-Comique, Paris, 1901). 1901.
L'Enfant-roi, music by Alfred Bruneau (produced Opéra-Comique, Paris, 1905). 1905.
Sylvanine; ou, Paris en amour (libretto; produced Paris, 1924). In *Poèmes lyriques*, 1921.
Violaine la chevelue (libretto). In *Poèmes lyriques*, 1921.
Lazarre (libretto). In *Poèmes lyriques*, 1921.

Fiction

Contes à Ninon. 1864; translated as *Stories for Ninon*, 1895.
La Confession de Claude. 1865; translated as *Claude's Confession*, 1888.
Le Voeu d'une morte. 1866; translated as *A Dead Woman's Wish*, 1902.
Les Mystères de Marseille. 1867; translated as *The Mysteries of Marseilles*, 1895.
Thérèse Raquin. 1867; translated as *Thérèse Raquin*, 1887; as *Theresa*, 1952.
Madeleine Férat. 1868; translated as *Madeleine Férat*, 1888; as *Shame*, 1954.
Les Rougon-Macquart (5 vols.), edited by Henri Mitterand. 1960–67; individual titles:
  1. *La Fortune des Rougon*. 1871; translated as *The Fortune of the Rougons*, 1886.
  2. *La Curée*. 1872; translated as *The Rush for the Spoil*, 1886; as *The Kill*, 1895.
  3. *Le Ventre de Paris*. 1873; translated as *La Belle Lisa; or, The Paris Market Girls*, 1882; as *The Fat and the Thin*, 1888; as *Savage Paris*, 1955.
  4. *La Conquête de Plassans*. 1874; translated as *The Conquest of Plassans*, 1887; as *A Priest in the House*, 1957.
  5. *La Faute de l'Abbé Mouret*. 1875; translated as *Abbé Mouret's Transgression*, 1886; as *The Sin of the Abbé Mouret*, 1904.

6. *Son Excellence Eugène Rougon*.   1876; translated as *Clorinda; or, The Rise and Reign of His Excellency Eugène Rougon*, 1880; as *His Excellency Eugène Rougon*, 1886; as *His Excellency*, 1958.

7. *L'Assommoir*.   1877; translated as *L'Assommoir*, 1879; as *Gervaise*, 1879; as *The Dram-Shop*, 1897; as *Drink*, 1903; as *The Gin Palace*, 1952.

8. *Une Page d'amour*.   1878; translated as *Hélène: A Love Episode*, 1878; as *A Page of Love*, 1897; as *A Love Affair*, 1957.

9. *Nana*.   1880; translated as *Nana*, 1884.

10. *Pot-Bouille*.   1882; translated as *Piping Hot!*, 1885; translated as *Pot-Bouille*, 1895; as *Lesson in Love*, 1953; as *Restless House*, 1953.

11. *Au Bonheur des Dames*.   1883; translated as *Shop Girls of Paris*, 1883; as *The Ladies' Paradise*, 1883; as *Ladies' Delight*, 1957.

12. *Le Joie de vivre*.   1884; translated as *How Jolly Life Is!*, 1886; as *The Joy of Life*, 1901; as *Zest for Life*, 1955.

13. *Germinal*.   1885; translated as *Germinal*, 1885.

14. *L'Oeuvre*.   1886; translated as *The Masterpiece*, 1886; as *His Masterpiece*, 1886.

15. *La Terre*.   1887; translated as *The Soil*, 1888; translated as *La Terre*, 1895; as *Earth*, 1954.

16. *Le Rêve*.   1888; translated as *The Dream*, 1893.

17. *La Bête humaine*.   1890; translated as *The Human Beast*, 1891(?); as *The Monomaniac*, 1901; as *The Beast in Man*, 1958.

18. *L'Argent*.   1891; translated as *Money*, 1894.

19. *La Débâcle*.   1892; translated as *The Downfall*, 1892; as *The Debacle*, 1968.

20. *Le Docteur Pascal*.   1893; translated as *Doctor Pascal*, 1893.

Nouveaux contes à Ninon.   1874.
Le Capitaine Burle.   1882.
Naïs Micoulin.   1884.
A Soldier's Honour (short stories).   1888.
The Attack on the Mill (short stories).   1892.
Les Trois Villes:
   Lourdes.   1894; translated as *Lourdes*, 1894.
   Rome.   1896; translated as *Rome*, 1896.
   Paris.   1898; translated as *Paris*, 1898.
Les Quatres Évangiles (incomplete):
   Fécondité.   1899; as *Fruitfulness*, 1900.
   Travail.   1901; as *Labor*, 1901; as *Work*, 1901.
   Vérité.   1903; as *Truth*, 1903.
Madame Sourdis.   1929.
Stories.   1935.

Memoirs and Letters

Letters to J. Van Santen Kolff, edited by Robert J. Niess. 1940.
Lettres inédites à Henry Céard, edited by A.J. Salvan.   1959.
Vingt messages inédits de Zola à Céard, edited by A.J. Salvan. 1961.
Lettres de Paris (articles from *Vestnik Europy*), edited by P.A. Duncan and Vera Erdely.   1963.
Correspondance, edited by B.H. Bakker.   1978—

Other

Mes Haines.   1866; translated as *My Hatreds*, 1991.
Le Roman expérimental.   1880.
Les Romanciers naturalistes.   1881.
Documents littéraires.   1881.

Le Naturalisme au théâtre.   1881.
Nos Auteurs dramatiques.   1881.
Une Campagne.   1882.
The Experimental Novel and Other Essays.   1893.
Nouvelle Campagne.   1897.
La Vérité en marche.   1901.
La République en marche: Chroniques parlementaires (2 vols.), edited by Jacques Kayser.   1956.
Mes Voyages: Lourdes, Rome: Journaux inédits, edited by René Ternois.   1958.
Salons (art criticism), edited by F.W.J. Hemmings and Robert J. Niess.   1959.
L'Atelier de Zola: Textes de journaux 1865–1870, edited by Martin Kanes.   1963.

Writings on theatre are collected in Volumes 10–12 of *Oeuvres complètes*, 1966–69.

*

Bibliographies

Henri Mitterand and Halina Suwala, *Émile Zola, Journaliste: Bibliographie chronologique et analytique* (2 vols.), Paris, 1968–72.
Brian Nelson, *Émile Zola: A Selective Analytical Bibliography*, London, 1982.
David Baguley, *Bibliographie de la critique sur Émile Zola*, Toronto, 1976; supplement, *1971–1980*, 1982.
Brian Nelson, *Émile Zola: A Selective Analytical Bibliography*, London, 1982.

Criticism

Books:
Lawson A. Carter, *Zola and the Theatre*, New Haven (Connecticut) and Paris, 1963.
F.W.J. Hemmings, *Émile Zola*, Oxford, 1966.
Philip D. Walker, *Émile Zola*, London, 1969.
Winston Hewitt, *Through Those Living Pillars: Man and Nature in the Works of Zola*, The Hague and Paris, 1974.
Ronald Daus, *Emile Zola und der französische Naturalismus*, Stuttgart, 1976.
F.W.J. Hemmings, *The Life and Times of Émile Zola*, New York, 1977.
Joanna Richardson, *Emile Zola*, 1978.
Jean-Max Guieu, *Le Théâtre lyrique d'Émile Zola*, Paris, 1983.
Dolores A. Signori and Dorothy E. Spiers, *Émile Zola dans la presse parisienne 1882–1902*, Toronto, 1985.
Philip Walker, *Emile Zola*, London, 1985.
Janice Best, *Expérimentation et adaptation: Essai sur la méthode naturaliste d'Émile Zola*, Paris, 1986.
Henri Mitterand, *Zola et le naturalisme*, Paris, 1986.
Alan Schom, *Émile Zola: A Bourgeois Rebel*, London, 1987.

Articles:
James B. Sanders, "Antoine, Zola et le théâtre", in *Cahiers naturalistes*, 42, 1972.

*   *   *

The quickest and surest way for a budding author to achieve widespread recognition is through a successful play and, as Zola writes in *L'Argent dans la littérature*, the financial rewards in the theatre are far in excess of what a novelist can hope to achieve. Such "bread-and-butter" considerations were as important in Zola's decision to write for the stage as was his genuine passion for the theatre. According to his friend Alexis, he penned his first dramatic texts in his teens. Yet he started his "theatrical" career not as an author, but as a critic in 1865. He was so prolific that in June 1866 he published a collection of essays in book form under the pugilistic title of *Mes Haines*. His critical and journalistic activities continued unabated until 1881–82 (his main essays on theatre were published in *Le Naturalisme au théâtre* and *Nos Auteurs dramatiques*). Indeed, it is as the theorist of naturalist theatre that his action was most powerful and influential: unfortunately where the theorist was radical and forward-looking, the playwright was tame and a respecter of tradition.

Leaving *Thérèse Raquin* aside, Zola wrote five original plays for the theatre: *La Laide* (never performed), *Madeleine* (one well-received performance at the Théâtre Libre, 2 May 1889), *Les Héritiers Rabourdin* (based on Ben Jonson's *Volpone*; 17 performances), *Le Bouton de rose* (seven performances) and *Renée* (adapted from *La Curée*, 38 performances). *Rabourdin* reduces Jonson's biting satire to a meaningless farce and *Le Bouton de rose* is just a second-rate *vaudeville* which failed to raise a laugh. In such plays Zola stuck to the traditional structure of acts and scenes and failed to breathe life into his characters, which are all drawn from convention, but without the skill of the traditionalist playwrights so often attacked by Zola in his critical judgements. Between 1879 and 1888 disappointing adaptations of his novels by Busnach and Gastineau were staged (such as *Nana* and *Germinal*), of which only the first, *L'Assommoir*, was a popular success, but at the price of cheapening and melodramatizing the novel.

In his theoretical writings, Zola called for a modern dramaturgy not dissimilar to Brecht's "epic" construction of the dramatic fable, divided into *tableaux* (as the novel is divided into chapters), based on a precise observation of reality and a panoramic reproduction of contemporary life on stage. This approach has been called *romanisation du drame* (novelization of theatre) in opposition to the mechanical formalism of the well-made play of Scribe, Dumas *fils*, Augier, and Sardou. For Zola, a play was "an action taking place in reality and involving characters experiencing feelings and passions, the analysis of which is the sole purpose of the play, set in a contemporary environment filled with people alive today". The set should determine the action and the behaviour of the characters, and would acquire "in the theatre the importance of the description in our [modern] novel". Beyond its obvious function of presenting the physical reality in which the action takes place, the set should also contribute to the analysis of facts and characters. Zola's bitterest opposition to the theatre of his time was prompted by his perception that the playwrights were pandering to the basest instincts of an idle bourgeois audience, instead of promoting healthy socialist and humanitarian ideals.

An important aspect of Zola's theatrical career concerns his collaboration with the musician Alfred Bruneau, which started with the creation of *Le Rêve* (*drame lyrique* in four acts). As he came to the end of his 20-novel saga of *Les Rougon-Macquart*, Zola was ready to explore new territories, away from the Naturalist doctrine which had guided his literary creation for the previous 25 years. On the threshold of the 1890's, and about to write his idealist and utopian *Les Trois Villes* and *Les Quatre Évangiles*, Zola discovered the power of music and the enchanting world of what he called "*la féerie*". Influenced by Wagner, Zola dreamed of a "total

spectacle", his version of the *Gesamtkunstwerk*, in which "all human artistic endeavour, poetry, music, painting, sculpture, theatrical skills, not forgetting beauty and strength, would join forces and strive to create a wonderful spectacle, a performance which would assault all the senses of the audience and increase their enjoyment tenfold".

Seconded by Bruneau, Zola revolutionized opera by introducing the prose libretto, peopled with "real people delighting in our happiness and suffering our pain". *Le Rêve* (Opéra-Comique, 1891; 93 performances) was a critical as well as a popular success, the first and the most significant in Zola's career as a playwright, and it is ironic that this champion of Naturalism should have succeeded in a genre that is never associated with his name. Nor was it an isolated achievement: his partnership with Bruneau brought forth further successes, like *L'Attaque du moulin* (1893, 53 performances), *Messidor* (1897, 16 performances), *L'Ouragan* (1901, 14 performances). *L'Enfant roi* was performed posthumously in 1905, but *Sylvanire; ou, Paris en amour*, to which Zola was putting the finishing touches when he died, was not performed until 1924.

However Zola's lasting achievement in the theatre, although an indirect one, is linked with Naturalism. André Antoine, founder of the Théâtre Libre (1887–94), who—for better or worse—shaped the theatre of the 20th century by establishing the predominant role of the theatre director, found his inspiration in Zola's theoretical writings and acknowledged his debt to the novelist and critic throughout his career.

—Claude Schumacher

See also *Volume 1* entry on *Thérèse Raquin*.

ZUCKMAYER, Carl. Born in Nackenheim, near Mainz, Germany, 27 December 1896. Educated at Gymnasium, Mainz, 1903–14; universities of Frankfurt and Heidelberg, 1918–20, no degree. Enlisted in the German army, 1914: posted to the Western Front, and later promoted to lieutenant. Married 1) Annemarie Seidel in 1920 (divorced 1920); 2) the actress Alice Frank in 1925, two daughters (one adopted). Contributor, *Das Tribunal*, 1919; moved to Berlin, 1920, and did various jobs; first-produced play, *Kreuzweg*, staged 1920; worked in a Norwegian mine, 1922; dramaturg, Stadttheater, Kiel, 1922–23, and (with Brecht) at Max Reinhardt's Deutsches Theater, Berlin, 1924; his plays banned by the Nazi regime, 1933; settled in Henndorf, near Salzburg, Austria; wrote screenplays for Alexander Korda, travelling intermittently to London, 1933–38; after German annexation of Austria, 1938, travelled to Switzerland, then to the USA via Cuba; briefly screenwriter in Hollywood; lectured with Piscator's Dramatic Workshop, New School of Social Research, New York, 1941; leased a farm in Barnard, Vermont, 1941–46, and obtained American citizenship; returned to Germany as cultural adviser for American military administration, 1946: commuted between homes in Woodstock, Vermont, and Europe, 1951–58; settled in Saas-Fée, Switzerland, 1958; gave up American citizenship. Recipient: Kleist Prize, 1926; Büchner Prize, 1929; Heidelberg Festival Prize, 1929; Goethe Prize (Frankfurt), 1952; Great Order of Merit of the Federal Republic of

Carl Zuckmayer with the actress Christiane Höbiger.

Germany with Star, 1955; Vienna Culture Prize, 1955. Several honorary doctorates. Died in Visp, Switzerland, 18 January 1977.

Works

Collections

Die deutschen Dramen (includes *Schinderhannes; Der Hauptmann von Köpenick; Des Teufels General*).   1947.
Komödie und Volksstück (includes *Der fröhliche Weinberg; Katharina Knie; Der Schelm von Bergen*).   1950.
Gesammelte Werke (4 vols.).   1960.
Meisterdramen (includes *Der fröhliche Weinberg; Schinderhannes; Der Hauptmann von Köpenick; Des Teufels General; Katharina Knie; Der Gesang im Feuerofen*).   1966.

Dramen.   1967.
Werkausgabe (10 vols.).   1976.

Stage Works

Kreuzweg (produced Staatstheater, Berlin, 1920).   1921.
Eunuch, from a play by Terence (produced Stadttheater, Kiel, 1923).
Kiktahan; oder, Die Hinterwälder (produced as *Pankraz erwacht*, Deutsches Theater, Berlin, 1925).   1925; as *Pankraz erwacht*, in *Carl Zuckmayer: Ein Jahrbuch*, 1978.
Der fröhliche Weinberg (produced Theater am Schiffbauerdamm, Berlin, 1925).   1925.
Schinderhannes (produced Lessing-Theater, Berlin, 1927).   1927.
Rivalen, from a play by Maxwell Anderson and Laurence Stallings (produced Theater in der Königgrätzer Strasse, Berlin, 1928).

Katharina Knie (produced Lessing-Theater, Berlin, 1928). 1929.
Kakadu-Kakadu (for children; produced Deutsches Theater, Berlin, 1929). 1930.
Der Hauptmann von Köpenick (produced Deutsches Theater, Berlin, 1931). 1931; translated as *The Captain of Köpenick*, 1932.
Kat, with Heinz Hilpert, from a novel by Ernest Hemingway (produced Deutsches Theater, Berlin, 1931).
Der Schelm von Bergen (produced Burgtheater, Vienna, 1934). 1934.
Ulla Winblad; oder, *Der Musik und Leben des Carl Michael Bellman* (produced as *Bellman*, Schauspielhaus, Zurich, 1938). 1938; revised version (produced Deutsches Theater, Göttingen, 1953), 1953.
Somewhere in France, with Fritz Kortner (produced in English, Guild Theatre, New York, 1941).
Des Teufels General (produced Schauspielhaus, Zurich, 1946). 1946; revised version, 1967; translated as *The Devil's General*, 1953, and in *Masters of Modern Drama*, edited by Haskell M. Block and Robert G. Shedd, 1962.
Barbara Blomberg (produced Deutsches Theater, Constance, 1949). 1949.
Der Gesang im Feuerofen (produced Deutsches Theater, Göttingen, 1950). 1950.
Herbert Engelmann, completion of play by Hauptmann (produced Burgtheater, Vienna, 1952). 1952.
Das kalte Licht (produced Schauspielhaus, Hamburg, 1955). 1955.
Die Uhr schlägt ein (produced Burgtheater, Vienna, 1961). 1961.
Kranichtanz (produced Schauspielhaus, Zurich, 1967). In *Die neue Rundschau*, vol. 74 no. 4., 1961.
Das Leben des Horace A.W. Tabor (produced Schauspielhaus, Zurich, 1964). 1964.
Der Rattenfänger (produced Schauspielhaus, Zurich, 1975). 1975.

Fiction

"Ein Bauer aus dem Taunus" und andere Geschichten. 1927.
Die Affenhochzeit. 1932; translated as *Monkey Wedding*, in *Argosy*, 23, 1938.
Stroller's Fate and the Life of Edmund Kean. 1936.
Salwàre; oder, Die Magdalena von Bozen. 1936; translated as *The Moon in the South*, 1937; as *The Moons Ride Over*, 1937.
Ein Sommer in Österreich. 1937.
Herr über Leben und Tod. 1938.
Der Seelenbräu. 1945.
Die Fastnachtsbeichte. 1959; translated as *Carnival Confession*, 1961.
Geschichten aus vierzig Jahren. 1963.
"Engele von Loewen" und andere Erzählungen. 1965.
Erzählungen. 1965.
Auf einem Weg in Frühling. 1970.

Verse

Der Baum. 1926.
Gedichte 1918–1948. 1948.
Gedichte. 1960.

Memoirs and Letters

Second Wind (autobiography). 1940.
Als wär's ein Stück von mir. 1966; translated as *A Part of Myself*, 1970.

Späte Freundschaft in Briefen. 1977; translated as *A Late Friendship: The Letters of Karl Barth and Carl Zuckmayer*, 1982.

Other

Pro Domo. 1938.
Die Brüder Grimm. 1948.
Die langen Wege. 1952.
Ein Weg zu Schiller. 1959.
Henndorfer Pastorale. 1972.

*

Bibliographies

Arnold J. Jacobius, *Carl Zuckmayer: Eine Bibliographie 1917–1971, ab 1955 fortgeführt und auf den jüngsten Stand gebracht von Harro Kieser*, Frankfurt, 1971.
Barbara Glauert, "Carl Zuckmayer 1971–77: Eine Bibliographie", in *Blätter der Carl-Zuckmayer-Gesellschaft*, 1978.

Criticism

Books:
Rudolf Lange, *Carl Zuckmayer*, Velber, 1969.
Arnold Bauer, *Carl Zuckmayer*, Berlin, 1970.
Arnold J. Jacobius, *Motive und Dramaturgie im Schauspiel Carl Zuckmayers: Versuch einer Deutung im Rahmen des zwischen 1920 und 1955 entstandenen Gesamtwerkes*, Frankfurt, 1971.
Abschied von Carl Zuckmayer: Ehrung, Dank und Freundschaft: eine Dokumentation, Mainz, 1977.
Thomas Ayck, *Carl Zuckmayer in Selbstzeugnissen und Bilddokumenten*, Reinbeck, 1977.
Barbara Glauert (ed.), *Cark Zuckmayer: Das Bühnenwerk im Spiegel der Kritik*, Frankfurt, 1977.
Ausma Balinkin, *The Central Women Figures in Carl Zuckmayer's Dramas*, Bern, 1978.
Siegfried Mews, *Carl Zuckmayer*, Boston, 1981.
Jochen Becker, *Carl Zuckmayer und seine Heimaten: Ein biographischer Essay*, Mainz, 1984.
Harro Kieser (ed.), *Carl Zuckmayer: Materialien zu Leben und Werk*, Frankfurt, 1986.
William Grange, *Partnership in the German Theatre: Zuckmayer and Hilpert, 1925–1961*, New York, 1991.

Articles:
Henry Glade, "Carl Zuckmayer's *The Devil's General* as an Autobiography", in *Modern Drama*, 1966.
Roy C. Cowen, "Type-Casting in Carl Zuckmayer's *The Devil's General*", in *University of Dayton Review*, vol.13 no.1, 1976.

Serials:
Blätter der Carl-Zuckmayer-Gesellschaft, 1975—
Carl Zuckmayer: Ein Jahrbuch, 1978—

* * *

Carl Zuckmayer wrote two of the most successful 20th-century dramas in German—*Der Hauptmann von Köpenick* (*The Captain of Köpenick*) and *Deu Teufels General* (*The Devil's General*)—and many others, now mainly of interest as period pieces. He was a technical master of his craft rather than an innovative, revolutionary force.

Successful period pieces owe much to three features—convincing local setting, powerful characterisation, and mastery of fitting language—often dialect. Zuckmayer became a leading exponent of all three. Even in his earliest, unsuccessful plays—the expressionist *Kreuzweg* (Crossroads), his production of Terence's *Eunuch* in modern garb, and *Pankraz erwacht* (Pancras Awakes)—these features can be seen, but often in isolation. In his breakthrough to fame, *Der fröhliche Weinberg* (The Merry Vineyard), they are inter-related to capture the atmosphere of a Rhineland village in 1921, in an earthy style using dialect playfully to express a home-spun belief in everyday values, an attack on academic abstractions, and a humour that is at times unnecessarily vulgar. A comedy of little consequence, it contains delightful fast-moving interchanges between type-characters and the central figures—Gunderloch, the vineyard owner, and Annemarie Most, the village schemer. Lighthearted flirtatiousness prevents the long drunken inn-scene of Act II and the anti-semitism from burdening the play with serious overtones. It was a fitting piece for the Kleist Prize, and was followed by the portrayal of a Robin Hood-type legendary figure—Bückler in *Schinderhannes*—rebelling against early 19th-century social injustices in Zuckmayer's first successful fusion of dramatic tension and epic reflection, a synthesis that would dominate his later work. In *Katharina Knie* he used a tight-rope walker to emphasize an existence split between the artistic world of her upbringing and the bourgeois world of the man she loves. Her father's long monologues raise the inner action to a more symbolic level, for when he dies she feels bound to replace him as troupe leader and renounce her love.

The Captain of Köpenick, a major German comedy subtitled "a German fairytale", has a serious satirical edge. It is centred on Voigt, a hapless, lonely, pure outcast using, to his advantage, the gullibility of Wilhelmine society when faced with a uniform. Voigt's portrayal is close to that of the traditional hero of a German *Entwicklungsroman* (development novel) and as vulnerable to eventual defeat—thus riveting the audience's attention to both the ridiculous fate of the uniform he wears and to the character's inevitable fall.

Der Schelm von Bergen (The Rogue of Bergen) is remarkable for its short rhythmic patterns of dialect and for its operatic-style conclusion. Monologues in the tradition of some expressionist dramas, helped by the medieval setting and story, transform a love story into a religious fantasy, which dramatises Heinrich Heine's popular legend of the ennobling of a Duchess's dance-partner after a masked ball.

The Devil's General, Zuckmayer's *Faust*, owes its fame to its remarkable evocation of social atmosphere in official Berlin in 1941, and to the much disputed characterisation of its main figure, Air Force General Harras. He overshadows Bückler and Voigt in accepting his guilt as a critic of the Nazi regime while holding high military office. He cannot agree that Oderbruch, his chief engineer, should sabotage the War effort to hasten Germany's defeat, but equally cannot expose the threat stemming from the aircraft factory for which he is responsible. His suicide, taking to the air in a sabotaged aircraft, seems at first an honourable solution. However, Harras is guilty of opportunism and is under Gestapo pressure of ten days' grace to uncover the subversive organisation. In both versions of the play Harras emerges as a daemonic figure—the more Hitler is identified with the devil, the less Harras can be held responsible for his actions. That

Zuckmayer included accusations by the widow of a friend killed piloting a faulty aircraft under Harras's orders, strengthens his credibility as a potentially tragic hero, but weakens his plausibility as a figure who could have existed in real life. Working here within the Faustian tradition, Zuckmayer again fuses vivid evocation of a local setting with literary or legendary tradition.

Zuckmayer's fondness for moments of great human emotion behind historically important figures dominates *Barbara Blomberg*, the story of a former mistress of Holy Roman Emperor Charles V, whose child was taken from her and became Don Juan of Austria. In the most important scene of the play, mother and son meet again, but she renounces her potential position as mother of the newly appointed Governor of the Netherlands, goes to Spain to live with his foster parents and witnesses her son's bier carried towards the Escorial. Court intrigue dominates the musical fantasy *Bellman*, later renamed *Ulla Winblad*. Passive resistance, renunciation, and the hatred of violence in any form are taken a stage further towards a vision of the apocalypse in modern guise in *Der Gesang im Feuerofen* (Song in the Fiery Furnace), where a group of Resistance members celebrate Christmas in a deserted castle, are betrayed to the Germans, and burnt to death. Here the juxtaposition of realistic description, real-life story, and symbolic framework using allegorical figures as commentators, almost turns potentially powerful dramatic material into sentimentality.

Das kalte Licht (The Cold Light) again concentrates on an individual's choice to follow the freedom of his own conscience or accept totalitarian ideology. A nuclear physicist turns traitor, but is eventually won back to a more responsible attitude. The essential theme is almost forgotten however because of the subplots, a weakness that diluted the effect of Zuckmayer's later works. Where he turned from serious examination of contemporary issues, such as the search for authentic living by the children of a rich industrialist who turn to terrorism in *Die Uhr schlägt ein* (The Clock Strikes One), to imaginative reconstructions of distant civilisations, as in *Das Leben des Horace A.W. Tabor* (The Life of Horace A.W. Tabor) a genial and colourful romp through clichés about the Wild West in the 1880's, local colour and characterisation excelled. He was less successful in his modernisations of fictive worlds, as in *Der Rattenfänger* (The Rat Catcher).

Zuckmayer's greatness finally lay in his construction of individually memorable scenes (Voigt's entry for the first time in uniform, or Barbara Blomberg and her son Don Juan, or Harras's moment of truth with Odenbruch). In these he was able to create what he understood by theatre: "space, communication and humanity . . . together with a sense of time or even timelessness" (1961 interview with Horst Bienek). Not surprisingly, many of his plays were made into successful films, where the key components of his success could perhaps be more tightly focused then on the stage.

—Brian Keith-Smith

See also *Volume 1* entry on *The Captain of Köpenick*.

TITLE INDEX

The index is intended to enable the reader to locate the authors in whose entries a particular title appears. It includes (1) all individual titles listed in the Stage Works category and (for non-English language titles) their published English translations, and (2) those screenplays, television plays, and radio plays that have been *published*. Titles, frequently "short" (missing their subtitles or abbreviated) appear first, followed by their authors' names in parentheses. Since titles usually have two or more dates associated with them in the main text, to avoid confusion all dates have been omitted here. Titles of anthologies and collections are not included. The following abbreviations, preceding the authors' names, apply:

r   published radio play
s   published screenplay
t   published television play

A.B.C. de notre vie (Tardieu)
À bas la famille (Labiche)
¡A Belén, pastores! (Casona)
A can che lecca cenere nongli fidar farina (Giacosa)
À Chacun son serpent (Vian)
A Dios por razón de estado (Calderón)
A imagen y semeijanza (Díaz)
A la orilla del mar (Echegaray)
À la Renverse (Vinaver)
A María el corazón (Calderón)
À Moitié Chemin (Labiche)
À Quelle Heure un train partira-t-il pour Paris? (Apollinaire)
À Quelque Chose malheur est bon (Hugo)
A secreto agravio, secreta vengenza (Calderón)
A tavola non si parla d'amore (Fabbri)
À Toi, pour toujours, ta Marie-Lou (Tremblay)
¡A ver qué hace un hombre! (Benavente y Martínez)
'A vilanza (Pirandello)
Aa Nezumi Kozo Jirokichi (Satoh)
A-A-America (Bond)
Abaellino, the Great Bandit (Dunlap)
Abbaye au bois (Pixérécourt)
Abbé Sétubal (Maeterlinck)
Abdelazar (Behn)
Abdicación (Benavente y Martínez)
Abe Lincoln in Illinois (Sherwood)
Abe Sada no inu (Satoh)
Abee de l'Epee (Dunlap)
Abel (Alfieri)
Abel Drake (Taylor)
Abel et Bela (Pinget)
Abele (Alfieri)
Abel's Sister (Wertenbaker)
Abendstunde (Kotzebue)
Abendstunde im Spätherbst (Dürrenmatt)
Abenteuer seines Lebens (Schnitzler)
Abenteurer (Sternheim)
Abenteurer und die Sängerin (Hofmannsthal)
Abhijnanasakuntala (Kalidasa)
Abigail's Party (Leigh)
Abingdon Square (Fornés)

Abito nuovo (De Filippo)
Able's Will (t Hampton)
Abominable Homme des sables (Barbeau)
Abortion (O'Neill)
Abortive (r Churchill)
About Face (Fo)
About Mortin (r Pinget)
About Turner (Nichols)
Above Rubies (Brighouse)
Abracadabra (Holberg)
Abraham (Hrotsvitha)
Abschied (Kotzebue)
Absence of War (Hare)
Absent Friends (Ayckbourn)
Absent Man (Bickerstaff)
Absent-Minded Couple (Harrigan)
Absolute Beginners (t Griffiths)
Absolútny zákaz (Karvaš)
Abstecher (Walser)
Absurd Person Singular (Ayckbourn)
Abu Casems tofflor (Strindberg)
Abudah (Planché)
Abuela y nieta (Benavente y Martínez)
Abuelo y nieto (Benavente y Martínez)
Abundance (Henley)
Acapulco (Berkoff)
Acapulco, los lunes (Carballido)
Acaso y el error (Calderón)
Accident (s Pinter)
Accident (Saroyan)
Accidental Death of an Anarchist (Fo)
Accidental Poke (Romeril)
Ace of Clubs (Coward)
Acero de madrid (Vega)
Aces High (s H. Barker)
Acharnes (Aristophanes)
Acharnians (Aristophanes)
Achilleis (Wyspiański)
Achilles (Gay)
Achilles in Petticoats (Colman the Elder)
Achilles; or, Iphigenia in Aulis (Racine)
Achmet et Almanzine (Lesage)

Achsensprung (t Forte)
Acht Stunden sind kein Tag (t Fassbinder)
Achterloo (Dürrenmatt)
Acid (Edgar)
Acis and Galatea (Gay)
Acquazzoni in montagne (Giacosa)
Acque turbate (Betti)
Acreedores (Sastre)
Acrobats (Horovitz)
Acropolis (Sherwood)
Across from the Garden of Allah (Wood)
Across the Board on Tomorrow Morning (Saroyan)
Across the River and into the Jungle (Kopit)
Act Without Words I–II (Beckett)
Acte sans paroles (Beckett)
Acteurs de bonne foi (Marivaux)
Action (Shepard)
Acto rápido (Pavlovsky)
Actor from Vienna (Molnár)
Actor of All Work (Colman the Younger)
Actors and Actresses (Simon)
Actor's Nightmare (Durang)
Actress and the Bishop (Parker)
Adam and Eve (Bulgakov)
Adam, Ève, et le troisième sexe (Vian)
Adam i Eva (Bulgakov)
Adam Stvořitel (Čapek)
Adam the Creator (Čapek)
Adam und Eva (Hacks)
'Adame Miroir (Genet)
Adding Machine (Rice)
Ad-Dunya Riwaya Hazaliya (Tawfiq al-Hakim)
Adélaïde du Gueslin (Voltaire)
Adelaide of Wulfingen (Kotzebue)
Adelheid von Wulfingen (Kotzebue)
Adelphi (Terence)
Adelphoe (Terence)
Admirable Bashville (Shaw)
Admirable Crichton (Barrie)
Adoración (Benavente y Martínez)
Adoración de los magos (s Carballido)
Adoration (Kishida)
Adored One (Barrie)
Adrian et Jusémina (Ghelderode)
Adrienne Ambrosat (Kaiser)
Adrienne Lecouvreur (Scribe)
Adulatore (Goldoni)
Advances (Terry)
Advantages and Disadvantages of a Name (Calderón)
Advent (Strindberg)
Adventure Story (Rattigan)
Adventures of Françoise (Mitchell)
Adventures of Karagöz (Ludlam)
Adventures of Marco Polo (s Sherwood)
Adventures of Marco Polo (Simon)
Adventures of the Hakata Damsel (Chikamatsu)
Adversa fortuna de Don Álvaro de Luna (Tirso De Molina)
Aeomori no semushi otoko (Terayama)
Aesop I–II (Vanbrugh)
Afectos de odio y amor (Calderón)
Affaire de la rue de Lourcine (Labiche)
Affaire des poisons (Sardou)
Affaire Édouard (Feydeau)
Affairs of Anatol (Schnitzler)
Affari di banca (Giacosa)
Affe und der Bräutigam (Nestroy)
Affected Young Ladies (Molière)

Afore Night Come (Rudkin)
Africa (Arlt)
Africaine (Scribe)
Africans (Colman the Younger)
After All (Van Druten)
After Business Hours (Daly)
After Dark (Boucicault)
After-Dinner Joke (t Churchill)
After Haggerty (Mercer)
After Liverpool (Saunders)
After-Life of Arthur Cravan (De Groen)
After Lydia (Rattigan)
After Magritte (Stoppard)
After Mercer (Hampton)
After Pilkington (t Gray)
After the Assassinations (Bond)
After the Ball (Coward)
After the Dance (Rattigan)
After the Fall (Miller)
After the Fire (Strindberg)
After You with the Milk (Travers)
Aftermath (Murray)
Afternoon at the Festival (t Mercer)
Afternoon Off (t Bennett)
Afuera lleuve (Hernández)
Agamemnon (Aeschylus)
Agamemnon (Alfieri)
Agamemnon (Berkoff)
Agamemnon (Claudel)
Agamemnon (Obey)
Agamemnon (Seneca)
Agamemnons Tod (Hauptmann)
Agamennone (Alfieri)
Agatha et les lectures illimitées (s Duras)
Agathocle (Voltaire)
Age d'or (Feydeau)
Agénor le dangereux (Labiche)
Ages Ago (Gilbert)
Agésilan de Colchos (Rotrou)
Agésilas (P. Corneille)
Agide (Alfieri)
Agis (Alfieri)
Aglavaine et Sélysette (Maeterlinck)
Agnes Bernauer (Hebbel)
Agnes Bernauer (Kroetz)
Agnes Robertson at Home (Boucicault)
Agnete (Kaiser)
Agonía (Hernández)
Agony of Little Nations (Saroyan)
Agradecer y no amar (Calderón)
Agreeable Surprise (Marivaux)
Agreeable Surprise (O'Keeffe)
Agrippa (Quinault)
Aguardiente de caña (Hernández)
Aguas estancadas (Usigli)
Aguila de blasón (Valle-Inclán)
Ägyptische Helena (Hofmannsthal)
Ah . . . Law 'Arafa ash-Shabab (Tawfiq al-Hakim)
Ah Man (Saroyan)
Ah, Wilderness! (O'Neill)
Ahasverus (Heijermans)
Ahen sensō (Terayama)
Ahl al-Kahf (Tawfiq al-Hakim)
Ahnfrau (Grillparzer)
Ahola no es de leil (Sastre)
A-Hunting We Will Go (Feydeau)
Aigle a deux têtes (Cocteau)

Aigle des Pyrénées (Pixérécourt)
Aiglon (Rostand)
Aiguillage (Dubé)
Air du large (Obaldia)
Aire frío (Piñera)
Aiuola bruciata (Betti)
Ajas (Wyspiański)
Ajax (Fassbinder)
Ajax (Sophocles)
Akassa Youmi (Rotimi)
Akropolis (Wyspiański)
Akt przerywany (Różewicz)
Akt utan nåd (Norén)
Al amor hay que mandarlo al colegio (Benavente y
    Martínez)
Al Dio ignoto (Fabbri)
Al fin, mujer (Benavente y Martínez)
Al natural (Benavente y Martínez)
Al pianoforte (Giacosa)
Al servicio de Su Majestad Imperial (Benavente y Martínez)
Alacranes (Díaz)
Aladdin (Byron)
Aladdin (O'Keeffe)
Aladdin and the Magic Lamp (Reaney)
Alain und Elise (Kaiser)
Al-'Alam al-Majhul (Tawfiq al-Hakim)
Alas, Poor Fred (Saunders)
Al-Aydi al-Na'ima (Tawfiq al-Hakim)
Albannach (McGrath)
Albergo sul porto (Betti)
Albert Gates (Brighouse)
Albert Names Edward (Nowra)
Albert Names Edward (r Nowra)
Albertine en cinq temps (Tremblay)
Albertine in Five Times (Tremblay)
Alberto Albertini (Dunlap)
Albert's Bridge (r Stoppard)
Albert's Bridge Extended (Stoppard)
Albion and Albanius (Dryden)
Albovine, King of the Lombards (Davenant)
Album de Família (Rodrigues)
Alcaide de sí mismo (Calderón)
Alcalde de Zalamea (Calderón)
Alcanor (Cumberland)
Alcée (Hardy)
Alceste (Hardy)
Alceste (Quinault)
Alceste secundo (Alfieri)
Alcestes (Usigli)
Alcestiad (Wilder)
Alcestis (Euripides)
Alcestis II (Alfieri)
Alchemist (Barnes)
Alchemist (Jonson)
Alchimiste (Dumas *père*)
Alcibiades (Otway)
Alcméon (Hardy)
Alexander (Dunsany)
Alexander (Grabbe)
Alexander, Campaspe, and Diogenes (Lyly)
Alexander—Die Freunde (Hofmannsthal)
Alexander the Great (Racine)
Alexander und Annette (Walser)
Alexanderzug (Hofmannsthal)
Alexandre le Grand (Racine)
Alfa (Mrożek)
Alfageme de Santarém (Garrett)

Alfiler en la boca (Benavente y Martínez)
Alfilerazos (Benavente y Martínez)
Alfred (Kotzebue)
Alfred (O'Keeffe)
Alfred and Emmy (Kotzebue)
Alfred Dies (Horovitz)
Alfred the Great (Horovitz)
Algiers (s Lawson)
Algo para contar en Navidad (Díaz)
Alguien (Pavlovsky)
Algunas veces aqui (Echegaray)
Algy (Fitch)
Al-Hamir (Tawfiq al-Hakim)
Al-Hubb (Tawfiq al-Hakim)
Ali Baba (Byron)
Ali Baba (Colman the Younger)
Ali Baba (Kara)
Ali Baba (Pixérécourt)
Ali Baba and the Forty Thieves (Byron, Gilbert)
Ali Pacha (Planché)
Alice (Pixérécourt)
Alice Sit-by-the-Fire (Barrie)
Alien Corn (Howard)
Alimentos del hombre (Calderón)
Alison's House (Glaspell)
Alison's Island (Brighouse)
Alixe (Daly)
Alkestiade (Wilder)
Alkestis (Hofmannsthal)
Alkibiades Saved (Kaiser)
All Bleeding (H. Barker)
All Citizens Are Soldiers (Vega)
All Day on the Sands (t Bennett)
All Fall Down (Arden)
All Fools (Chapman)
All for Love (Dryden)
All for the Best (Pirandello)
All Gaul is Divided (s Williams)
All God's Chillun Got Wings (O'Neill)
All Good Men (Griffiths)
All Good Men (t Griffiths)
All Home, Bed, and Church (Fo)
All in the Dark (Planché)
All is Fair in Love and War (Musset)
All Men Are Whores (Mamet)
All My Husband (Feydeau)
All My Sons (Miller)
All on a Summer's Day (Inchbald)
All on Her Own (Rattigan)
All Over (Albee)
All Summer Long (R. Anderson)
All That Fall (Beckett)
All the Bees and All the Keys (Reaney)
All the Fun of the Fair (McGrath)
All the Nice People (Leonard)
All Them Women (Terry)
Alladine et Palomides (Maeterlinck)
Allée des veuves (Pixérécourt)
Allerzielen (Heijermans)
Alles will den Propheten sehen (Nestroy)
Allow Me to Explain (Gilbert)
All's Over, Then? (Robinson)
All's Right (Planché)
All's Well That Ends Well (Shakespeare)
All'uscita (Pirandello)
Alma Mater (Boucicault)
Alma Mater (Green)

Alma triunfante (Benavente y Martínez)
Al-Malik Udib (Tawfiq al-Hakim)
Almanac of Love (Chikamatsu)
Almanaque de Juárez (Carballido)
Almas prisioneras (Benavente y Martínez)
Al-Masrah al-Munawwa' (Tawfiq al-Hakim)
Almenas de toro (Vega)
Almost Like Being (van Itallie)
Alouette (Anouilh)
Alpenhütte (Kotzebue)
Alpenkönig und der Menschenfeind (Raimund)
Alpha Alpha (H. Barker)
Alphabetical Order (Frayn)
Alphée (Hardy)
Alphonsus, King of Aragon (Greene)
Als der Krieg zu Ende war (Frisch)
Als Zeus zum letzten Mal kam (Kroetz)
Al-Sultan al-Ha'ir (Tawfiq al-Hakim)
Al-Ta'am li-Kull Fam (Tawfiq al-Hakim)
Altanima (Audiberti)
Alte Jungfer (Lessing)
Alte Leibkutscher Peter des Dritten (Kotzebue)
Alte Mann mit der jungen Frau (Nestroy)
Alten Liebschaften (Kotzebue)
Altitude (Lawrence)
Altro figlio (Pirandello)
Alverdens-Urostifterne (Munk)
Al-Warta (Tawfiq al-Hakim)
Always Ridiculous (Echegaray)
Alzir (Fonvizin)
Alzire (Voltaire)
Am I Blue? (Henley)
Am Ziel (Bernhard)
Amadan (Boucicault)
Amadeus (Shaffer)
Amadis (Quinault)
Amadis de Gaula (Vicente)
Amado y aborrecido (Calderón)
Amalasonte (Quinault)
Amanha Será Outro Dia (Gomes)
Amant complaisant (Anouilh)
Amant indiscret (Quinault)
Amant libéral (Scudéry)
Amante anglaise (Duras)
Amante di se medesimo (Goldoni)
Amante militare (Goldoni)
Amantes de Teruel (Tirso De Molina)
Amants du métro (Tardieu)
Amants jaloux (Lesage)
Amants magnifiques (Molière)
Amants puérils (Crommelynck)
Amaos los unos sobre los otros (Díaz)
Amar después de la muerta (Calderón)
Amar por arte mayor (Tirso De Molina)
Amar por razón de estado (Tirso De Molina)
Amar por señas (Tirso De Molina)
Amar sin saber a quién (Vega)
Amar y ser amado; divina Filotea (Calderón)
Amazed Evangelist (Bridie)
Amazonas de las Indias (Tirso De Molina)
Amazons (Pinero)
Ambasador (Mrożek)
Amber Empress (Connelly)
Ambiente jurídico (Hernández)
Ambitious Step-Mother (Rowe)
Amboyna (Dryden)
Ambrose Gwinett (Jerrold)

Ambush at Tether's End (Walker)
Amédée (Ionesco)
Ameley, der Biber und der König auf dem Dach (Dorst)
Amelia (Cumberland)
Amélie (Rotrou)
Amélie (Voltaire)
America Hurrah (van Itallie)
Américains chez nous (Brieux)
Americaliente (Díaz)
American (Daly)
American Buffalo (Mamet)
American Clock (Miller)
American Days (Poliakoff)
American Dream (Albee)
American Duchess (Fitch)
American Flag Ritual (Bullins)
American Griot (Bullins)
American Independence House (Romeril)
American King's English for Queens (Terry)
American Lady (Byron)
American Landscape (Rice)
American Way (Kaufman)
American Welcome (Friel)
Amerikanische Soldat (Fassbinder)
Amerikanische Soldat (s Fassbinder)
Amérique à sec (Dubé)
Âmes mortes (Adamov)
Ami acharné (Labiche)
Ami des femmes (Dumas *fils*)
Amica delle mogli (Pirandello)
Amicable Parting (Kaufman)
Amicizia (De Filippo)
Amigo amante y leal (Calderón)
Amigos del hombre (Benavente y Martínez)
Aminta (Tasso)
Amistad castigada (Ruiz de Alarcón)
Amoliurs déguisés (Lesage)
Among Those Present (Kaufman)
Amor (t Mrożek)
Amor asusta (Benavente y Martínez)
Amor de amar (Benavente y Martínez)
Amor de artista (Benavente y Martínez)
Amor de Don Perlimpín con Belisa en su jardin (García
   Lorca)
Amor desatinado (Vega)
Amor em Campo Minado (Gomes)
Amor enamorado (Vega)
Amor, honor y poder (Calderón)
Amor, médico (Tirso De Molina)
Amor muerto (Carballido)
Amor paterno (Goldoni)
Amor und Psyche (Hofmannsthal)
Amor vincit omnia (Lenz)
Amor y celos hacen discretos (Tirso De Molina)
Amor y la amistad (Tirso De Molina)
Amore assottiglia il cervello (Gozzi)
Amore delle tre melarance (Gozzi)
Amori di Alessandro Magno (Goldoni)
Amoroso (Planché)
Amorous Bigot (Shadwell)
Amorous Gallant (T. Corneille)
Amorous Prince (Behn)
Amorous Quarrel (Molière)
Amorus Orontus (T. Corneille)
Amour à la mode (T. Corneille)
Amour de l'art (Labiche)
Amour en sabots (Labiche)

Amour et la vérité (Marivaux)
Amour et piano (Feydeau)
Amour marin (Lesage)
Amour médecin (Molière)
Amour tyrannique (Scudéry)
Amour, un fort volume (Labiche)
Amour victorieux ou vengé (Hardy)
Amours de Nanterre (Lesage)
Amours de Protée (Lesage)
Amours impossibles (Arrabal)
Ampélour (Audiberti)
Amphitryo (Plautus)
Amphitryon (Dryden)
Amphitryon (Hacks)
Amphitryon (Kleist)
Amphitryon (Molière)
Amphitryon (Plautus)
Amphitryon 38 (Behrman)
Amphitryon 38 (Giraudoux)
Amtrak (Terry)
Amusements of Khan Kharuda (Dunsany)
Amy Robsart (Hugo)
An Giall (Behan)
Ananse and the Dwarf Brigade (Sutherland)
Anansegoro (Sutherland)
Anarchie in Bayern (Fassbinder)
Anarchy (Mackaye)
Anatema (Andreyev)
Anathema (Andreyev)
Anatol (Granville-Barker)
Anatol (Schnitzler)
Anatomie Titus Fall of Rome (Müller)
Anatomist (Bridie)
Anatomist (Ravenscroft)
Ancestress (Grillparzer)
Ancêtres redoublent de férocité (Yacine)
Anciennes Odeurs (Tremblay)
Ancient Boys (van Itallie)
Ancient Mariner (O'Neill)
Anconitana (Ruzante)
And As for the Ladies (Kopit)
And Did Those Feet (t Mercer)
And Out Goes You? (Pollock)
And Pippa Dances (Hauptmann)
And the Sea Shall Give Up Its Dead (Wilder)
And They Put Handcuffs on the Flowers (Arrabal)
And What of the Night (Fornés)
Andante (Petrushevskaya)
Andělé mezi námi (Langer)
Andenagora (Esson)
Andorra (Frisch)
Andra upplagan (Bergman)
Andrajos de la púrpura (Benavente y Martínez)
André (Dunlap)
André del Sarto (Musset)
André Fortier (Sardou)
Andréa (Sardou)
Andria (Machiavelli)
Andria (Terence)
Andrian (Terence)
Androcles and the Lion (Shaw)
Andromache (Euripides)
Andromache (Racine)
Andromaque (Racine)
Andrómeda y Perseo (Calderón)
Andromède (P. Corneille)
Andromire (Scudéry)

Andy Blake (Boucicault)
Âne et le ruisseau (Musset)
Anfisa (Andreyev)
Anfitrião (Silva)
Ange tutélaire (Pixérécourt)
Angel City (Shepard)
Angel Comes to Babylon (Dürrenmatt)
Angel of the Morning (McGrath)
Angel on the Ship (Wilder)
Angel That Troubled the Waters (Wilder)
Angelas Kleider (Strauss)
Angèle (Dumas père)
Ángeles ladrones (Díaz)
Angelo (Reade)
Angelo, Tyran de Padoue (Hugo)
Angels Fall (L. Wilson)
Anges du péché (s Giraudoux)
Angst essen Seele auf (s Fassbinder)
Animal Crackers (Kaufman)
Animal Kingdom (Barry)
Animal Magnetism (Inchbald)
Anjo Negro (Rodrigues)
Anjos e o Sangue (Santareno)
Anna Christie (O'Neill)
Anna Kleiber (Sastre)
Annabella (Maeterlinck)
Annajanska, the Bolshevik Empress (Shaw)
Anne Boleyn (Boker)
Anne Boleyn (Taylor)
Anne of the Thousand Days (M. Anderson)
Annibal (Marivaux)
Annibale duca d'Atene (Gozzi)
Annie Wobbler (Wesker)
Anniversary (Chekhov)
Anniversary Dinner (Molnár)
Anno fyrtioåtta (Strindberg)
Annoiati (Giacosa)
Annonce faite à Marie (Claudel)
Annunciation (Fornés)
Año santo en Madrid (Calderón)
Anonymous Work (Witkiewicz)
Another Moon Called Earth (t Stoppard)
Another Part of the Forest (Hellman)
Another Springtime (Usigli)
Another's Nest (Benavente y Martínez)
Anowa (Aidoo)
¡Antes cruzaban rios (Carballido)
Antes que todo es mi drama (Calderón)
Antichrist (Sorge)
Antichristo (Ruiz de Alarcón)
Antidoto (Alfieri)
Anti-Galaxie Nebulae (Ludlam)
Anti-Nélson Rodrigues (Rodrigues)
Antigona a tí druhi (Karvaš)
Antígona Furiosa (Gambaro)
Antigone (Alfieri)
Antigone (Anouilh)
Antigone (Brecht)
Antigone (Cocteau)
Antigone (Hasenclever)
Antigone (Rotrou)
Antigone (Sophocles)
Antigone (Walser)
Antigone des Sophokles (Brecht)
Antigonemodell (Brecht)
Antiochus (T. Corneille)
Antipodes (Brome)

Antipodes (Taylor)
Antler River (Reaney)
Antona García (Tirso De Molina)
Antonio (Barnes)
Antonio and Mellida (Marston)
Antonio e Cleopatra (Alfieri)
António Marinheiro (Santareno)
Antonio's Revenge (Marston)
Antony and Cleopatra (Alfieri)
Antony (Dumas *père*)
Antony and Cleopatra (Shakespeare)
Antropofagio de salón (Díaz)
Ants (r Churchill)
Antwoord (Heijermans)
Anunciacão (Santareno)
Anverwanderten (Nestroy)
Anyone Can Whistle (Laurents)
Anyone's Gums Can Listen to Reason (Simpson)
Anything for a Quiet Life (Middleton, Webster)
Anzuelo de Fenisa (Casona)
Aoi-no-Ue (Zeami)
Aorta (Hibberd)
Apartamiento (Marqués)
Apatista (Goldoni)
Aphrodisiamania (Ludlam)
Apocalypse Sonata (Cook)
Apocrypha (Hernández)
Apokalyptica (Arrabal)
Apollo in New York (Boucicault)
Apollo of Bellac (Giraudoux)
Apollo Society (Tardieu)
Apollon de Bellac (Giraudoux)
Apolo y Climene (Calderón)
Apostasía (Hernández)
Apóstol (Usigli)
Appearance is Against Them (Inchbald)
Appius and Virginia (Webster)
Apple (Gelber)
Apple Cart (Shaw)
Apple Tree (Brighouse)
Apprendre à marcher (Ionesco)
Approaching Simone (Terry)
Apricots (Griffiths)
April Fool (Harrigan)
April Weather (Fitch)
Aquilés (Tirso De Molina)
Arab (Cumberland)
Arabella (Hofmannsthal)
Arabian Night in the Nineteenth Century (Daly)
Arabian Powder (Holberg)
Arabische Pulver (Kotzebue)
Arabiske Pulver (Holberg)
Arbitration (Menander)
Arbitre aux mains vides (Adamov)
Árbol del mejor fruto (Calderón)
Arbol del mejor fruto (Tirso De Molina)
Árboles mueren de pie (Casona)
Arca de Dios cautiva (Calderón)
Arcadia (Shirley)
Arcadia (Stoppard)
Arcangeli non giocano a flipper (Fo)
Arcata Promise (Mercer)
Arcata Promise (t Mercer)
Arc-en-ciel (Ghelderode)
Archangels Don't Play Pinball (Fo)
Archbishop's Ceiling (Miller)
Archers (Dunlap)

Archipel Lenoir (Salacrou)
Archipel sans nom (Tardieu)
Architect and Emperor of Assyria (Hibberd)
Architect and the Emperor of Assyria (Arrabal)
Architecte et l'empereur d'Assyrie (Arrabal)
Architruc (Pinget)
Arcifanfarlo, King of Fools (Auden)
Arden of Feversham (Lillo)
Ardèle (Anouilh)
Are kara no Jon Shirubaa (Kara)
Are You Insured? (Harrigan)
Area fabbricabile (Fabbri)
Arena (Murrell)
Argenis y Poliarco (Calderón)
Argonauts (Grillparzer)
Aria del continente (Pirandello)
Ariadne auf Naxos (Hofmannsthal)
Ariadne auf Naxos (Kotzebue)
Ariadne on Naxos (Hofmannsthal)
Ariadne ravie (Hardy)
Ariane (T. Corneille)
Ariane et Barbe-Bleue (Maeterlinck)
Aristoclée (Hardy)
Aristocrats (Friel)
Aristokraten (Müller)
Aristotle's Bellows (Gregory)
Ark (Saunders)
Arkwright's Wife (Mackaye)
Arkwright's Wife (Taylor)
Arlequin (Regnard)
Arlequin barbet, pagode et médicin (Lesage)
Arlequin Baron Allemand (Lesage)
Arlequin colonel (Lesage)
Arlequin Endymion (Lesage)
Arlequin et Mezzetin morts par amour (Lesage)
Arlequin gentilhomme malgré lui (Lesage)
Arlequin Hulla (Lesage)
Arlequin invisible (Lesage)
Arlequin Mahomet (Lesage)
Arlequin poli par l'amour (Marivaux)
Arlequin roi de Sérendib (Lesage)
Arlequin roi des ogres (Lesage)
Arlequin Thétis (Lesage)
Arm Yrself or Harm Yrself (Baraka)
Armand (Mowatt)
Armas de la hermosura (Calderón)
Armature (Brieux)
Arme Heinrich (Hauptmann)
Arme Minnesänger (Kotzebue)
Arme Poet (Kotzebue)
Arme Vetter (Barlach)
Armenians (Saroyan)
Armer Ritter (Hacks)
Armida (Quinault)
Armide (Quinault)
Arminda celosa (Vega)
Arminius (Scudéry)
Armoire classique (Audiberti)
Armoured Train 14–69 (Ivanov)
Armourer (Cumberland)
Armourer's Escape (J. N. Barker)
Arms and the Man (s Shaw)
Arms and the Man (Shaw)
Armstrong's Last Goodnight (Arden)
Armuth und Edelsinn (Kotzebue)
Army of the North (Planché)
Arne Saknussem (r Vian, Boris)

Arpas blancas, conejos dorados (Hernández)
Arrah-na-Pogue (Boucicault)
Arraignment of Paris (Peele)
Arrant Knave (Mackaye)
Arrest (Anouilh)
Arrestation (Anouilh)
Ars Amandi (Arrabal)
Ars Longa, Vita Brevis (Arden)
Arsacomé (Hardy)
Art (Fornés)
Art de ne pas donner d'étrennes (Labiche)
Art of War (Walker)
Arte della commedia (De Filippo)
Artémire (Voltaire)
Artemisia (Goldoni)
Artful Cards (Labiche)
Artful Widow (Goldoni)
Arthur (Molnár)
Arthur Maxglans (s Bergman)
Article 47 (Daly)
Article 960 (Labiche)
Artifice (Centlivre)
Artificial Jungle (Ludlam)
Artikel 188 (Heijermans)
Artist Descending a Staircase (r Stoppard)
Artist im Moment (Forte)
Artists and Admirers (Ostrovsky)
Artists' Families (Brieux)
Arzt wider Willen (Müller)
Ärztinnen (Hochhuth)
As Happy as Kings (Richardson)
As Husbands Go (Crothers)
As the Leaves (Giacosa)
As We Were (Adamov)
As You Desire Me (Pirandello)
As You Like It (Daly)
As You Like It (Shakespeare)
Asalto a una ciudad (Sastre)
Asalto nocturno (Sastre)
Asamayama (Kishida)
Asanace (Havel)
Ascent of F6 (Auden)
Aschenbrödel (Grabbe)
Ashab as-Sa'ada az-Zawjiya (Tawfiq al-Hakim)
Ashes (Rudkin)
Ashikari (Zeami)
Ashita wa ii tenki (Kishida)
Ashwak as-Salam (Tawfiq al-Hakim)
Así que pasen cinco años (García Lorca)
Asian Oranges (Hibberd)
Asinaria (Plautus)
Askatasuna! (t Sastre)
Asmodeo (Chiarelli)
Asmodeus, the Little Demon (Scribe)
Aspern Papers (Duras)
Aspis (Menander)
As-Safqa (Tawfiq al-Hakim)
Assassinations (Saroyan)
Assemblywomen (Aristophanes)
Assémien Déhylé, roi du Sanwi (Dadié)
Assenti (Fabbri)
Assignation (Dryden)
Assignment (Müller)
Assommoir (Daly)
Astonished Heart (Coward)
Astrate, Roi de Tyr (Quinault)
Astrólogo fingido (Calderón)

Asylum (Kopit)
At Least it's a Precaution Against Fire (t Simpson)
At Liberty (Williams)
At the Big Carwash (Reaney)
At the Bottom (Gorky)
At the Dim'crackr Convention (Baraka)
At the Gate (Pirandello)
At the Hawk's Well (Yeats)
At the Jolly Spot (Ostrovsky)
Atala (Dumas *fils*)
Atashi no Beatles (Satoh)
Athalia (Racine)
Athalie (Racine)
Atheist (Otway)
Atheist's Tragedy (Tourneur)
Athénaïs (Mairet)
Atlanta in Wimbledon (Dunsany)
Atlanterhavet (Grieg)
Atlantique (Ghelderode)
Atlas-Hôtel (Salacrou)
Atmospherics (Dunsany)
Atsumori (Zeami)
Attaque du Moulin (Zola)
Attempted Rescue on Avenue B (Terry)
Attendez-moi sous l'orme (Regnard)
Atterdag (Munk)
Attila, Roi des Huns (P. Corneille)
Attraktsiony (Volodin)
Atys (Quinault)
Au Bord de la nuit (Laberge)
Au Pair Man (Leonard)
Au Retour des oies blanches (Dubé)
Aubade (Kopit)
Aubigny Clementia (Katona)
Auction of Pictures (Foote)
Aucussin und Nicolette (Dorst)
Audaz (Benavente y Martínez)
Audience (Havel)
Auf dem Chimborazo (Dorst)
Auf Krugdorf (Sternheim)
Aufhaltsame Aufstieg des Arturo Ui (Brecht)
Aufstieg (t Forte)
Aufstieg des Alois Piontek (Kipphardt)
Aufstieg und Fall der Stadt Mahagonny (Brecht)
Auftrag (Müller)
Augellin belverde (Gozzi)
Augustus Does His Bit (Shaw)
Aulalaria (Chiarelli)
Aulalaria (Plautus)
Aunt Mahaly's Cabin (Green)
Auntie (Byron)
Aurélia Steiner (s Duras)
Aurélie, ma soeur (Laberge)
Aureng-Zebe (Dryden)
Auristela y Lisidante (Calderón)
Aurora (Fornés)
Aurora en Copacabana (Calderón)
Aurore rouge et noire (Arrabal)
Aus dem Wortschatz unserer Kämpfe (Walser)
Ausnahme und die Regel (Brecht)
Aussi longue absence (s Duras)
Aussteuer (Lenz)
Australia Felix (Esson)
Aut Caesar aut Nihil (Sternheim)
Author (Foote)
Author's Farce (Fielding)
Auto da Alma (Vicente)

Auto da Barca da Glória (Vicente)
Auto da Barca do Inferno (Vicente)
Auto da Barca do Purgatório (Vicente)
Auto da Cananeia (Vicente)
Auto da Fama (Vicente)
Auto da Fé (Vicente)
Auto-da-Fé (Williams)
Auto da Feira (Vicente)
Auto da Festa (Vicente)
Auto da Índia (Vicente)
Auto da Lusitânia (Vicente)
Auto da Sibila Cassandra (Vicente)
Auto da Visitação (Vicente)
Auto das Ciganas (Vicente)
Auto das Fadas (Vicente)
Auto de Gil Vicente (Garrett)
Auto de Mofina Mendes (Vicente)
Auto de S. Martinho (Vicente)
Auto dos Físicos (Vicente)
Auto dos Quatro Tempos (Vicente)
Auto dos Reis Magos (Vicente)
Auto (em) Pastoril Português (Vicente)
Auto Pastoril Castelhano (Vicente)
Automobile Graveyard (Arrabal)
Automóvil (Benavente y Martínez)
Autonomy (Barry)
Autostop (Havel)
Autour de Mortin (r Pinget)
Autre Tartuffe; ou, La Mère coupable (Beaumarchais)
Autumn and Winter (Norén)
Autumn Festival (Tagore)
Autumn Fire (Murray)
Autumn Garden (Hellman)
Autumn in the Tyrol (Kishida)
Autumnal Roses (Benavente y Martínez)
Aux Antipodes (monologue) (Feydeau)
Avant de t'en aller (Dubé)
Avare (Molière)
Avare en gants jaunes (Labiche)
Avare fasteaux (Goldoni)
Avariés (Brieux)
Avaro (Goldoni)
Avec l'Hiver qui s'en vient (Laberge)
Avenir est dans les oeufs (Ionesco)
Aventura en lo gris (Buero Vallejo)
Aventurière (Augier)
Averíguelo Vargas (Tirso De Molina)
Aves (Aristophanes)
Aves y párajaros (Benavente y Martínez)
Aveugle de Smyrne (P. Corneille, Rotrou)
Aveugles (Ghelderode)
Aveugles (Maeterlinck)
Aveva due pistole con gli occhi bianchi e neri (Fo)
Avis aux Femmes (Pixérécourt)
Avocat (Brieux)
Avocat d'un Grec (Labiche)
Avocat Loubet (Labiche)
Avocat-pédicure (Labiche)
Avvenimento (Fabbri)
Avventure della villegiatura (Goldoni)
Avventuriero (Fabbri)
Avventuriero onorato (Goldoni)
Avvocato veneziano (Goldoni)
Awake and Sing! (Odets)
Awakening of Spring (Wedekind)
Awatea (Mason)
Away from the Moss (Shiels)

Awful Rise in Spirits (Taylor)
Axiane (Scudéry)
Axur, King of Ormus (Beaumont)
Aya no Tsuzumi (Zeami)
Azael (Boucicault)
Azote (Obaldia)

Baal (Brecht)
Baal Babylone (Arrabal)
Bäbbel (Kotzebue)
Babes in the Bighouse (Terry)
Babes in the Wood (Bridie)
Babes in the Wood (Taylor)
Babes in the Wood and the Good Little Fairy Birds (Byron)
Babies Grow Old (Leigh)
Babik (s Örkény)
Babil and Bijou (Planché)
Baby and the Bathwater (McGrath)
Baby Doll (s Williams)
Baby Love (Edgar)
Baby-Sitter (Obaldia)
Baby with the Bathwater (Durang)
Bacchae (Euripides)
Bacchae (Soyinka)
Bacchante (Dumas père)
Bacchides (Plautus)
Bacchus (Cocteau)
Bacchusfest (Schnitzler)
Bachelor (Fitch)
Bachelor (Turgenev)
Bachelor Party (s Chayefsky)
Bachelor Party (t Chayefsky)
Back Bog Beast Bait (Shepard)
Back to Adam (Brighouse)
Back to Methuselah (Shaw)
Bad Men in the West (Saroyan)
Bad Samaritan (Priestley)
Bad Seed (M. Anderson)
Bad-Tempered Old Man (Menander)
Badener Lehrstück vom Einverständnis (Brecht)
Bag Lady (van Itallie)
Bagdad Saloon (Walker)
Bagman (r Arden)
Bagrovy ostrov (Bulgakov)
Bague de l'oubli (Rotrou)
Baguette de Vulcain (Regnard)
Baikie Charivari (Bridie)
Bailarino (Santareno)
Bailegangáire (Murphy)
Bain de ménage (Feydeau)
Bai-yue ting (Guan Hanqing)
Bajazet (Murrell)
Bajazet (Racine)
Bakke's Night of Fame (McGrath)
Bal (Regnard)
Bal des voleurs (Anouilh)
Bal en robe de chambre (Labiche)
Bal triste (Dubé)
Balade du grand macabre (Ghelderode)
Balaganchik (Blok)
Balcon (Genet)
Balcones de Madrid (Tirso De Molina)
Balconville (Fennario)
Balcony (Genet)
Balcony (van Itallie)
Baldoon (Reaney)
Ball (Shirley)

Ball Boys (Edgar)
Ballad of Barnaby (Auden)
Ballad of the Brown King (Hughes)
Ballad of the Sad Café (Albee)
Ballade vom schönen Mädchen (Kaiser)
Balloon (Colum)
Ballygombeen Bequest (Arden)
Balm in Gilead (L. Wilson)
Balmoral (Frayn)
Bambi Ramm (Poliakoff)
Bampfyde Moore Carew (Jerrold)
Banana Ridge (Travers)
Banc (Laberge)
Bancarotta (Goldoni)
Band Wagon (Kaufman)
Banda y la flor (Calderón)
Bandet (Strindberg)
bandido Lisandro (Echegaray)
Banditti (O'Keeffe)
Bandolero (Barrie)
Bang (H. Barker)
Banishment of Cicero (Cumberland)
Bank al-Qalaq (Tawfiq al-Hakim)
Bánk bán (Katona)
Bankrotář (Tyl)
Bankrupt (Bjørnson)
Bankrupt (Boker)
Bankrupt (Foote)
Bankrupt (t Mercer)
Bankrut (Ostrovsky)
Baños de Argel (Cervantes)
Banquet de méduses (Obaldia)
Bantam V.C. (Brighouse)
Banya (Mayakovsky)
Baptism (Baraka)
Bar Ber Ous (Harrigan)
Bar Play (L. Wilson)
Barabbas (Ghelderode)
Barabbas (Grieg)
Barabbas (Lagerkvist)
BA-RA-KA (Baraka)
Barbara Blomberg (Zuckmayer)
Barbara Frietchie, the Frederick Girl (Fitch)
Barbara of the House of Grebe (t Mercer)
Barbara's Wedding (Barrie)
Barbares (Sardou)
Barbarians (Gorky)
Barbary Shore (Gelber)
Barberine (Musset)
Barbier de Séville; ou, La Précaution inutile
  (Beaumarchais)
Barby (Hacks)
Barca sin pescador (Casona)
Barefaced Imposters (Taylor)
Barefoot in Athens (M. Anderson)
Barefoot in the Park (Simon)
Bargain (Jellicoe)
Baril d'olives (Pixérécourt)
Bariona (Sartre)
Barlaán y Josafat (Vega)
barmherzigen Brüder (Kotzebue)
Barnes' People I–III (r Barnes)
Barnstable (Saunders)
Barnum Was Right (Sherwood)
Barometermacher auf der Zauberinsel (Raimund)
Baromètre (Labiche)
barón (Fernández de Moratín)

Baron d'Albikrac (T. Corneille)
Baron de Fourchevif (Labiche)
Baron's Will (Bergman)
Barraca de Jipi Japa (Díaz)
Barracks (Leonard)
Barrage (Dubé)
Barrier (Hughes)
Barrière de Clichy (Dumas père)
Barselstuen (Holberg)
Bartholomew Fair (Jonson)
Bartleby (Albee)
Baruffe chiozzote (Goldoni)
Basement (Pinter)
Basement in Bangkok (McGrath)
Basement Window (Buero Vallejo)
Bashful Lover (Massinger)
Basic Training of Pavlo Hummel (Rabe)
Basket-Maker (O'Keeffe)
Basque Imposter (Cervantes)
Bassariden (Auden)
Basset-Table (Centlivre)
Basta (Karvaš)
Basta callar (Calderón)
Basta con i fascisti (Fo)
Bastardy (Romeril)
Bastille (Boucicault)
Batai (Walcott)
Bataille d'amour (Sardou)
Bataille de la Marne (Obey)
Bataille des dames (Scribe)
Bathhouse (Mayakovsky)
Bathilde (Dumas père)
Bâtisseurs d'Empire (Vian)
Batman's Beach-head (Buzo)
Bâton et ruban (r Audiberti)
Batory pod Pskowem (Wyspiański)
Battle of Alcazar (Peele)
Battle of Angels (Williams)
Battle of Hastings (Cumberland)
Battle of Hexham (Colman the Younger)
Battle of Life (Robertson)
Battle of Shrivings (Shaffer)
Battle of Yashima (Zeami)
Battler (Esson)
Battles of Coxinga (Chikamatsu)
Bau (Müller)
Bauble Shop (Jones)
Bauern (Müller)
Bauern sterben (Kroetz)
Bay at Nice (Hare)
Bayard, der Ritter ohne Furcht und ohne Tadel (Kotzebue)
Be Yourself (Connelly, Kaufman)
Beach Grass (Terry)
Bear (Chekhov)
Beast's Story (Kennedy)
Béatrice du Congo (Dadié)
Beau Brummell (Fitch)
Beau Mariage (Augier)
Beau mariage (Benavente y Martínez)
Beau Nash (Jerrold)
Beau's Duel (Centlivre)
Beauté du diable (s Salacrou)
Beautiful City (Walker)
Beautiful Haidée (Byron)
Beautiful Miss Portland (Hewett)
Beautiful People (Saroyan)
Beauty and the Beast (Nowra)

Beauty and the Beast (Planché)
Beauty is Fled (Carroll)
Beauty is the Word (Williams)
Beauty Part (Behrman)
Beauty Stone (Pinero)
Beaux Dimanches (Dubé)
Beaux' Stratagem (Farquhar)
Beaver Coat (Hauptmann)
Becket (Anouilh)
Becky Sharp (Barrie)
Becky Sharp (Brighouse)
Becky Sharp (Mitchell)
Bed Before Yesterday (Travers)
Bed of Roses (Jones)
Bedbug (Mayakovsky)
Bedmates (Shiels)
Bednaya nevesta (Ostrovsky)
Bednost ne porok (Ostrovsky)
Bedroom Farce (Ayckbourn)
Bedside Manners (Behrman)
Bedtime Story (O'Casey)
Bee and the Orange Tree (Planché)
Beeldekens uit het leven van Sint Franciskus van Assisi
    (Ghelderode)
Beelzebub Sonata (Witkiewicz)
Bees on the Boat Deck (Priestley)
Beethoven (Kennedy)
Befehl (Hochwälder)
Before Breakfast (O'Neill)
Before Cannae (Munk)
Before Dawn (Hauptmann)
Before Daybreak (Hauptmann)
Before Sunrise (Hauptmann)
Before the Blackout (Soyinka)
Before We Were So Rudely Interrupted (Feydeau)
Beg (Bulgakov)
Begegnung mit Carlo (Hofmannsthal)
Beggar (Sorge)
Beggar on Horseback (Connelly, Kaufman)
Beggar on Horseback (O'Keeffe)
Beggar or the Dead Dog (Brecht)
Beggars' Bush (Fletcher, Massinger)
Beggar's Opera (Gay)
Beggar's Opera (Havel)
Beggar's Opera Reversed (Colman the Elder)
Behind the Green Curtains (O'Casey)
Behind the Scenes (Harrigan)
Behind the Throne (Brighouse)
Behold the Sun (McGrath)
Behold, We Live (Van Druten)
Beichte (Kotzebue)
Beiden Alten (Lenz)
Beiden Herren Söhne (Nestroy)
Beiden kleinen Auvergnaten (Kotzebue)
Beiden Klingsberg (Kotzebue)
Beiden Nachtwandler (Nestroy)
Beijing Ren (Cao Yu)
Beijo no Asfalto (Rodrigues)
Bekannte Gesichter (Strauss)
Bel Enfant (Audiberti)
Belagerung von Saragosssa (Kotzebue)
Belas Flucht (Kotzebue)
Belcher's Luck (Mercer)
Believe As You List (Massinger)
Bélisaire (Rotrou)
Belisario (Goldoni)
Bell, Book, and Candle (Van Druten)

Bella Ciao (Arrabal)
Bella domenica di settembre (Betti)
Bella Giorgiana (Goldoni)
Bella selvaggia (Goldoni)
Bellaco sois (Tirso De Molina)
Bellavita (Pirandello)
Belle Alphrède (Rotrou)
Belle Égyptienne (Hardy)
Belle et la bête (s Cocteau)
Belle Lamar (Boucicault)
Belle Maman (Sardou)
Belle Vie (t Anouilh)
Bellerophon (T. Corneille)
Bellerophon (Kaiser)
Bellérophon (Quinault)
Belle's Stratagem (Daly)
Belles-Soeurs (Tremblay)
Bellman (Zuckmayer)
Below Ground (Brighouse)
Below the Belt (Hibberd)
Belphegor (Boucicault)
Belshazzar's Feast (Calderón)
Belvédère (Pixérécourt)
Ben Spray (t Nichols)
Ben-Ur (Barbeau)
Bene mio e core mio (De Filippo)
Benefactors (Frayn)
Beneficent Bear (Goldoni)
Benefit of the Doubt (Pinero)
Bengal no tora (Kara)
Benilde (Régio)
Bent (Sherman)
Beorhtel's Hill (Wesker)
Beppi im Glück (Kroetz)
Bequest to the Nation (Rattigan)
Berceau (Brieux)
Berceau (Pixérécourt)
Berço de Herói (Gomes)
Bérénice (T. Corneille)
Bérénice (Racine)
Berg (Bernhard)
Bergbahn (Horváth)
Berger extravagant (T. Corneille)
Bergère de la rue Monthabor (Labiche)
Bergwerk zu Falun (Hofmannsthal)
Beritten hin und zurück (Grass)
Berlin Bertie (Brenton)
Berlin Days (Poliakoff)
Berlin—letzte Ausgabe! (r Toller)
Berliner Antigone (Hochhuth)
Bermondsey (Mortimer)
Bernard Palissy (Brieux)
Bernice (Glaspell)
Bernice (Wilder)
Berniquel (Maeterlinck)
Berretto a sonagli (De Filippo)
Berretto a sonagli (Pirandello)
Berühmten (Bernhard)
Beschuit met muisjes (Heijermans)
Besheny dengi (Ostrovsky)
Bespridannitsa (Ostrovsky)
Besserer Herr (Hasenclever)
Bessmertny (Arbuzov)
Best I Can Do by Way of a Gate-Leg Table (t Simpson)
Bestialité érotique (Arrabal)
Bestohlenen (Kotzebue)
Besuch (Kotzebue)

Besuch der alten Dame (Dürrenmatt)
Besuch der alten Dame (s Dürrenmatt)
Besucher (Strauss)
Bête dans la jungle (Duras)
Bête noire (Audiberti)
Betía (Ruzante)
Betrayal (Colum)
Betrayal (Pinter)
Betrothal (Boker)
Betrothal (Maeterlinck)
Betrothal (L. Wilson)
Betsey Brown (Shange)
Better Class of Person (t Osborne)
Better Dead Than Sorry (Durang)
Better Half (Coward)
Better Late (Feydeau)
Better Living (Walker)
Bettine (Musset)
Bettler (Brecht)
Bettler (Sorge)
Bettler von Syrakus (Sudermann)
Bettleroper (Fassbinder)
Betty's Finish (Fitch)
Between God and Man (Kinoshita)
Between the Battles (Bjørnson)
Between Two Thieves (Fabbri)
Between Two Worlds (Ansky)
Between Two Worlds (Rice)
Beware of Smooth Water (Calderón)
Bewitched (Barnes)
Bewitched (Howard)
Beyond Mozambique (Walker)
Beyond Our Might (Bjørnson)
Beyond Our Power (Bjørnson)
Beyond the Fringe (Bennett)
Beyond the Horizon (O'Neill)
Beyond Therapy (Durang)
Bezdenezhe (Turgenev)
Bezimienne dzieło (Witkiewicz)
Bezvinny vinovatye (Ostrovsky)
Białe małżeństwo (Różewicz)
Bianca contessa di Melfi (Gozzi)
Bianco e rosso (Marinetti)
Biberpelz (Hauptmann)
Bickerstaff's Burying (Centlivre)
Bicyclette du condamné (Arrabal)
Biedermann und die Brandstifter (Frisch)
Biedermann und die Brandstifter (r Frisch)
Biedny chłopiec (Witkiewicz)
Bien vengas, mal si vienes solo (Calderón)
Bienfaiteurs (Brieux)
Big and Little (Strauss)
Big and Little of It (Harrigan)
Big Basil (Leigh)
Big Birthday (Leonard)
Big Bonanza (Daly)
Big Deal (t Chayefsky)
Big Drum (Pinero)
Big Hotel (Ludlam)
Big House (Behan)
Big House (r Behan)
Big House (Griffiths)
Big House (r Griffiths)
Big House (Robinson)
Big Knife (Odets)
Big Maggie (Keane)
Big River (Buzo)

Big Square Fields (McGrath)
Big Toys (White)
Bijou (Pixérécourt)
Bijou de la reine (Dumas *fils*)
Bikoroa Plays (Clark)
Bílá nemoc (Čapek)
Bilan (Dubé)
Bilanz (Kroetz)
Bilanz (r Kroetz)
Bildbeschreibung (Müller)
Billet de Joséphine (Feydeau)
Billet de mille (Feydeau)
Bill-Sticker (Jerrold)
Billy-Club Puppets: Tragicomedy of Don Cristobál and Miss
   Rosita (García Lorca)
Bilora (Ruzante)
Biloxi Blues (Simon)
Bingo (Bond)
Binsen (Hacks)
Biografie (Frisch)
Biography (Behrman)
Biography (Frisch)
Bird Cage (Laurents)
Bird in a Cage (Shirley)
Bird in the Cage (Fitch)
Birds (Aristophanes)
Birds in the Wilderness (Mason)
Bird's Nest (Robinson)
Birds of Aristophanes (Planché)
Birds of Paradise (Jerrold)
Birds of Prey (Robertson)
Birth (Robertson)
Birth of a Private Man (t Mercer)
Birth on a Hard Shoulder (H. Barker)
Birthday (t Frayn)
Birthday (O'Keeffe)
Birthday Party (Pinter)
Birth-Rate (Różewicz)
Birthright (Murray)
Bishop's Bonfire (O'Casey)
Bismarck (Wedekind)
Bit o' Love (Galsworthy)
Bit of a Test (Travers)
Bit of War (Brighouse)
Bite of the Night (H. Barker)
Biter (Rowe)
Bitter Apples (McGrath)
Bitter Tears of Petra von Kant (Fassbinder)
Bitteren Tränen der Petra van Kant (Fassbinder)
Bitter-Sweet (Coward)
Bizarrías de Belisa (Vega)
Bjälbo-Jarlen (Strindberg)
Black and White Two-Dimensional Planes (Shange)
Black Bart and the Sacred Hills (A. Wilson)
Black Cargo (Romeril)
Black Children's Day (Kennedy)
Black Comedy (Shaffer)
Black Commercial No. 2 (Bullins)
Black Domino (Scribe)
Black Eye (Bridie)
Black Glove (Strindberg)
Black Hermit (Ngugi)
Black Maskers (Andreyev)
Black Mass (Baraka)
Black Mass (Bond)
Black Mischief (Shaffer)
Black Nativity (Hughes)

Black Pearl (Sardou)
Black Power Chant (Baraka)
Black Sheep (Rice)
Blackbeard (Green)
Black-Eyed Susan (Jerrold)
Blackout (Sherman)
Blacks (Genet)
Blacksmith of Antwerp (O'Keeffe)
Blanchette (Brieux)
Blancs (Hansberry)
Blancs et les bleus (Dumas *père*)
Blancura de Pierrot (Benavente y Martínez)
Blaubart (Frisch)
Blaubart (t Frisch)
Blaue Boll (Barlach)
Blauw blauw (Claus)
Blazh (Ostrovsky)
Blazhenstwo (Bulgakov)
Bleak Moments (Leigh)
Blechtrommel (s Grass)
Bless Me Father for I Have Sinned (Fo)
Blighted Being (Taylor)
Blind Beggar of Alexandria (Chapman)
Blind (Maeterlinck)
Blind Boy (Dunlap)
Blind geladen (Kotzebue)
Blind Giant is Dancing (Sewell)
Blind Goddess (Toller)
Blind Man's Buff (Johnston)
Blind Man's Buff (Toller)
Blind Men (Ghelderode)
Blind Mice (Friel)
Blind Wolf (Murray)
Blinde (Dürrenmatt)
Blinde Gärtner (Kotzebue)
Blinde Göttin (Toller)
Blinde Liebe (Kotzebue)
Blindeman (Claus)
Blithe Spirit (Coward)
Bloeimaand (Heijermans)
Blokada (Ivanov)
Blondinka (Volodin)
Blood Knot (Fugard)
Blood of a Poet (s Cocteau)
Blood of the Bambergs (Osborne)
Blood of the Lamb (Mason)
Blood on the Neck of the Cat (Fassbinder)
Blood on the Table (Mercer)
Blood Red Roses (McGrath)
Blood Relations (Pollock)
Blood Sports (Edgar)
Blood Wedding (Fornés)
Blood Wedding (García Lorca)
Bloodrites (Baraka)
Bloody Brother (Fletcher, Jonson, Massinger)
Bloody Poetry (Brenton)
Bloody Rosa (Edgar)
Bloomers (Sternheim)
Blow for Blow (Byron)
Blow-in Chorus for Liam Cosgrave (Arden)
Blue and the Gray (Harrigan)
Blue-Apron Statesman (Holberg)
Blue Beard (Byron)
Blue Beard (Colman the Younger)
Blue Beard (Dunlap)
Blue Beard (Planché)
Blue Beard from a New Point of Hue (Byron)

Blue Belle (Boucicault)
Blue Bird (Maeterlinck)
Blue Bitch (Shepard)
Blue Boll (Barlach)
Blue Danube (Molnár)
Blue Devils (Colman the Younger)
Blue Grass (Daly)
Blue-Legged Lady (Gilbert)
Blue Macushla (Murphy)
Blue Mondays (Fennario)
Blue Monster (Gozzi)
Blue Mouse (Fitch)
Blue Ribbon (Harrigan)
Blue Stockings (Molière)
Blue Thunder (Green)
Bluebeard (Ludlam)
Bluey (r Wesker)
Blumenboot (Sudermann)
Blunderers (Molière)
Blurt, Master Constable (Dekker)
Blut am Hals der Katze (Fassbinder)
Boat (Clark)
Boat Without a Fisherman (Casona)
Boats (Kennedy)
Bobby Gould in Hell (Mamet)
Bobolink (Barbeau)
Boca de Ouro (Rodrigues)
Bocas (Shange)
Bocquet, père et fils (Labiche)
Boda (Piñera)
Bodas de sangre (García Lorca)
Bodas trágicas (Echegaray)
Bodega (Carballido)
Bödeln (Lagerkvist)
Bodies (Saunders)
Body Language (Ayckbourn)
Body Leaks (Terry)
Boesman and Lena (Fugard)
Boeuf sur le toit (Cocteau)
Bogatye nevesty (Ostrovsky)
Bogen des Odysseus (Hauptmann)
Bogie Men (Gregory)
Bohemia (Fitch)
Bohemian G'yurl and the Unapproachable Pole (Byron)
Bohemian Lights (Valle-Inclán)
Bohème (Giacosa)
Bois sacré (Rostand)
Boîte de Pandore (Lesage)
Bold Hibernian Boys (Harrigan)
Bold Soprano (Ionesco)
Bold Stroke for a Wife (Centlivre)
Bolesław Śmiały (Wyspiański)
Bon Vin de Monsieur Nuche (Willems)
Bonaparte in England (Dunlap)
Bon-Bons and Roses for Dolly (Hewett)
Bond (Strindberg)
Bond Honoured (Osborne)
Bond Honoured (Vega)
Bondman (Cumberland)
Bondman (Massinger)
Bonds of Interest (Benavente y Martínez)
Bonds of Love (Mason)
Bonduca (Colman the Elder)
Bonduca (Fletcher)
Bondwoman (Ostrovsky)
Bone-the-Fish (Kopit)
Bonitinha, Mas Ordinariá (Rodrigues)

Bonjour, là, bonjour (Tremblay)
Bonnes (Genet)
Bons bourgeois (Obaldia)
Boogie Woogie Landscapes (Shange)
Book of Christopher Columbus (Claudel)
Booker T. Washington at Atlanta (r Hughes)
Boom (McGrath)
Boor Hug (Feydeau)
Boors (Goldoni)
Borage Pigeon Affair (Saunders)
Border Be Damned (Carroll)
Border Warfare (McGrath)
Boris Gudunov (Pushkin)
Born in the Gardens (Nichols)
Borzasztó torony (Katona)
Böse Geist Lumpazivagabundus (Nestroy)
Bösen Köche (Grass)
Bosoms and Neglect (Guare)
Boszorkany (Molnár)
Both Your Houses (M. Anderson)
Botica modelo (Hernández)
Bottega del caffe (Goldoni)
Bottle de sept lieues (Beaumarchais)
Bottle of Harp (L. Wilson)
Bottles and Bones (Coward)
Boucicault in California (Boucicault)
Boulanger, la boulangère, et le petit mitron (Anouilh)
Boule de verre (Salacrou)
Boulevard Durand (Salacrou)
Bound East for Cardiff (O'Neill)
Bourgeois aux champs (Brieux)
Bourgeois Avant-Garde (Ludlam)
Bourgeois bleibt Bourgeois (Hasenclever, Toller)
Bourgeois de Falaise (Regnard)
Bourgeois de Gand (Dumas *père*)
Bourgeois de Pont-Arcy (Sardou)
Bourgeois Gentilhomme (Maillet)
Bourgeois Gentilhomme (Molière)
Bourgeois Gentleman (Molière)
Bourgeon (Feydeau)
Bourgmestre de Stilmonde (Maeterlinck)
Bourreau (Laberge)
Bourru bienfaisant (Goldoni)
Bousille et les justes (Gelinas)
Boutique fermée (Audiberti)
Bouton de rose (Pixérécourt)
Bouton de rose (Zola)
Bow Bells (Byron)
Bow of Ulysses (Hauptmann)
Box and Quotations from Chairman Mao Tse-tung (Albee)
Box ett (r Norén)
Box-Lobby Challenge (Cumberland)
Box Play (Leigh)
Boy and Tarzan Appear in a Clearing (Baraka)
Boy David (Barrie)
Boy in the Basement (Inge)
Boy Meets Girl/Girl Meets Boy (Ayckbourn)
Boy: What Will He Become? (Brighouse)
Boy with a Cart (Fry)
Bradamante (T. Corneille)
Bradford (t Mamet)
Bradys (Harrigan)
Braggart Soldier (Plautus)
Braggart Warrior (Plautus)
Branch of the Blue Nile (Walcott)
Brand (Ibsen)
Brand im Opernhaus (Kaiser)

Brända tomten (Strindberg)
Brandschatzung (Kotzebue)
Brantinghame Hall (Gilbert)
Bras d'Ernest (Labiche)
Brasil restituido (Vega)
Brassneck (Brenton, Hare)
Brat i sestra (Shvarts)
Bratya Lyu (s Erdman)
Braut und Bräutigam in einer Person (Kotzebue)
Braut von Messina (Schiller)
Bravo! (Kaufman)
Brazen Age (Heywood)
Brazil (s Stoppard)
Brazil Fado (Terry)
Breach in the Wall (Lawler)
Breach of Promise (Robertson)
Bread and Butter (O'Neill)
Bread and Butter Come to Supper (Green)
Bread and Butter Women (White)
Bread-Winner (Maugham)
Break of Noon (Claudel)
Breakfast at the Windsor (Hibberd)
Breakfast at Tiffany's (Albee)
Breakfast Serial (Terry)
Breaking a Butterfly (Jones)
Breaking the Silence (Poliakoff)
Breaking Through (Wertenbaker)
Breath (Beckett)
Bremen Coffee (Fassbinder)
Brěněk Svihovský (Tyl)
Brennende Dorf (Fassbinder)
Brennende Dornbusch (Kokoschka)
Breve Sumário da História de Deus (Vicente)
Bréviaire d'amour d'un haltérophile (Arrabal)
Brian Boru (Colum)
Brick-Dust Man (Bickerstaff)
Bridal Crown (Strindberg)
Bridal Tour (Boucicault)
Bride for the Unicorn (Johnston)
Bride of Abydos (Byron)
Bride of Gospel Place (Esson)
Bride of Ludgate (Jerrold)
Bride of Messina (Schiller)
Brief aus Cadix (Kotzebue)
Brief Encounter (s Coward)
Brief in de schemer (Heijermans)
Brief Moment (Behrman)
Briery Gap (Murray)
Brigadier (Fonvizin)
Brigadir (Fonvizin)
Brigand and His Banker (Taylor)
Brigand Chief (Planché)
Brigands (Gilbert)
Brigham Young (Boucicault)
Bright Shadow (Priestley)
Bright Skies (Cao Yu)
Bright Star (Barry)
Brighton Beach Memoirs (Simon)
Brigitta (Audiberti)
Brilleninsel (Kotzebue)
Bring on the Girls (Kaufman)
Britain's Brave Tars (O'Keeffe)
Britannia and Batavia (Lillo)
Britannia Triumphans (Davenant)
Britannia's Honour (Dekker)
Britannicus (Racine)
British Passport (Brighouse)

Brændigen (Munk)
Broadway Bound (Simon)
Brocade Tree (Zeami)
Brocéliande (Montherlant)
Broken Heart (Ford)
Broken Heart (Jerrold)
Broken Hearts (Gilbert)
Broken Jug (Kleist)
Broken Pitcher (Kleist)
Broken Soil (Colum)
Brokenbrow (Toller)
Bronepoyezd 14–69 (Ivanov)
Brontosaurus (L. Wilson)
Bronze Horse (Scribe)
Bronzova rapsódie (Langer)
Brosse (Barbeau)
Brother and Sister (Bolt)
Brother and Sister (Goethe)
Brother Fire (Wilder)
Brother Luiz de Souza (Garrett)
Brothers (Cumberland)
Brothers (Shirley)
Brothers (Terence)
Brothers Menaechmus (Plautus)
Brott och brott (Strindberg)
Browning Version (Rattigan)
Brownsville Raid (Fuller)
Bruce Mason Solo (Mason)
Brudder Humphrey (Romeril)
Bruder Eichmann (Kipphardt)
Bruder Moritz der Sonderling (Kotzebue)
Bruderzwist (Kotzebue)
Bruderzwist in Habsburg (Grillparzer)
Bruid in de morgen (Claus)
Brûlons Voltaire! (Labiche)
Brunsvik (Tyl)
Brute (Chekhov)
Brute Force (Benavente y Martínez)
Bruto primo (Alfieri)
Bruto Secondo (Alfieri)
Brutus (Voltaire)
Brutus of Alba (Tate)
Büchse der Pandora (Wedekind)
Bürger als Edelmann (Dorst)
Bürger als Edelmann (Hofmannsthal)
Bürger Schippel (Sternheim)
Bürger von Calais (Kaiser)
Bürgergeneral (Goethe)
Bubbles of the Day (Jerrold)
Buccaneer (M. Anderson)
Buch der Tanze (Horváth)
Buddha (Kazantzakis)
Budding Lovers (Feydeau)
Buds of Ballybunion (Keane)
Buena boda (Benavente y Martínez)
Buenos días (Usigli)
Buffonata (Dorst)
Bufón de Hamlet (Benavente y Martínez)
Bugiarda (Fabbri)
Bugiardo (Goldoni)
Bugie con le gambe lunghe (De Filippo)
Buhlschweste (Lenz)
Buhos (Benavente y Martínez)
Buikspreker (Heijermans)
Bulkeley Peerage (Pinero)
Bull by the Horns (Byron)
Bull Market (Priestley)

Bulle d'amour (Feydeau)
Bulles de savon (Maillet)
Bulls and Bears (Cibber)
Bundle (Bond)
Bundle of Lies (Daly)
Buon compatriotto (Goldoni)
Buona famiglia (Goldoni)
Buona madre (Goldoni)
Buona moglie (Goldoni)
Buoyant Billions (Shaw)
Buranki-goroshi, Shanhai no haru (Satoh)
Buranko (Kishida)
Bureau de Change (Dunsany)
Bureau des divorces (Brieux)
Bureaucrats (Brighouse)
Buren (Heijermans)
Burglars (Rudkin)
Burgraves (Hugo)
Burgschaft (Hochwälder)
Burial Mound (Ibsen)
Buried Child (Shepard)
Buried Man (t Mercer)
Burlador de Sevilla (Tirso De Molina)
Burlador de Sevilla (Casona)
Burlas de amor (Vega)
Burlas veras (Vega)
Burletta of Errors (Planché)
Burn This (L. Wilson)
Burn Victim (Sewell)
Burned House (Strindberg)
Burning (Rabe)
Burns (Bond)
Burnt Flower-Bed (Betti)
Bury Fair (Shadwell)
Bus Riley's Back in Town (Inge)
Bus Stop (Inge)
Business is Business (Kaufman)
Business of Good Government (Arden)
Bussy D'Ambois (Chapman)
Buster Keaton's Promenade (García Lorca)
Busy Body (Centlivre)
But for Whom Charlie (Behrman)
. . . but the clouds . . . (t Beckett)
Butley (Gray)
Butter and Egg Man (Kaufman)
Butterfly Dream (Guan Hanqing)
Butterfly's Evil Spell (García Lorca)
By Judgement of the Court (Pirandello)
Bye Bye Blues (Saunders)
Bygmester Solness (Ibsen)
Bygmester Solness (Murrell)
Bygones (Pinero)
Bystro khorosho ne byvaet (Petrushevskaya)
Byzantine Flowers (Nowra)

Ça vient, ça vient (Vian)
Cabal and Love (Schiller)
Cabal of Hypocrites (Bulgakov)
Caballero de gracia (Tirso De Molina)
Caballero de las espuelas de oro (Casona)
Caballero de Olmedo (Vega)
Cabbages and Culture (Labiche)
Cabellos de Absalón (Calderón)
Cabeza del Bautista (Valle-Inclán)
Cabinet Minister (Pinero)
Cabinet Question (Planché)
Cabiria (D'Annunzio)

Careless Lovers (Ravenscroft)
Caretaker (Pinter)
Caretakers (Shiels)
Cargamento de sueños (Sastre)
Caridad (Benavente y Martínez)
Carine (Crommelynck)
Caritas (Wesker)
Carless Vows (Marivaux)
Carlos V en Francia (Vega)
Carmelite (Cumberland)
Carmen (Galsworthy)
Carmen (Green)
Carmosine (Musset)
Carnac Sahib (Jones)
Carnation Gang (Poliakoff)
Carnaval afuera, carnaval adento (Marqués)
Carnaval de Venise (Regnard)
Carne bianca (Chiarelli)
Carnival (Molnár)
Carnival Scenes (Caragiale)
Caroline (Maugham)
Carolus Magnus (Kotzebue)
Carreta (Marqués)
Carriers (Vicente)
Carron Side (Planché)
Carta de amor (Usigli)
Carta de una desconocida (Casona)
Cartas boca abajo (Buero Vallejo)
Cartas de amor de una monja portuguesa (Casona)
Cartas de Mozart (Carballido)
Cartney and Kevney (Shiels)
Cas intéressant (Camus)
Casa ardiendo (Triana)
Casa con dos puertas malas es de guardar (Calderón)
Casa de Bernarda Alba (García Lorca)
Casa de la dicha (Benavente y Martínez)
Casa de los celos y selvas de Ardenia (Cervantes)
Casa de los siete balcones (Casona)
Casa nova (Goldoni)
Casa sin reloj (Marqués)
Casa sull'acqua (Betti)
Casanova (Apollinaire)
Casanova (Howard)
Cascando (r Beckett)
Case (Sukhovo-Kobylin)
Case in Point (Mason)
Case is Altered (Jonson)
Case of Conscience (Inchbald)
Case of Rebellious Susan (Jones)
Case of the Crushed Petunias (Williams)
Case of the Workers' Plane (Edgar)
Case to Answer (Wertenbaker)
Casi un cuento de hadas (Buero Vallejo)
Casina (Plautus)
Casket Comedy (Plautus)
Caso Flores (Usigli)
Cassandra the Sibyl (Vicente)
Cassaria (Ariosto)
Casseur d'assiettes (Salacrou)
Castalda (Goldoni)
Caste (Robertson)
Castelviness y Monteses (Vega)
Castigo del discreto (Vega)
Castigo del penséque (Tirso De Molina)
Castigo sin vengenza (Vega)
Castillo de Lindabridis (Calderón)
Castle (H. Barker)

Castle of Andalusia (O'Keeffe)
Castle of Sorrento (Colman the Younger)
Castle Wetterstein (Wedekind)
Castles in the Air (Robertson)
Cat (Bond)
Cat Among Pigeons (Feydeau)
Cat Among the Pigeons (Mortimer)
Cat and the Moon (Yeats)
Cat Changed into a Woman (Boucicault)
Cat Has Not Always Carnival (Ostrovsky)
Cat, Mouse, Man, Woman (Saroyan)
Cat on a Hot Tin Roof (Williams)
Catão (Garrett)
Catastrophe (Beckett)
Catch (Brecht)
Catch (McGrath)
Catch as Catch Can (Anouilh)
Catchpenny Twist (Parker)
Catherina von Siena (Lenz)
Catherine Howard (Dumas *père*)
Cathleen Listens In (O'Casey)
Cathleen ni Houlihan (Yeats)
Catilina (Dumas *père*)
Catilina (Ibsen)
Catilina (Voltaire)
Catiline (Ibsen)
Catiline His Conspiracy (Jonson)
Catspaw (Hewett)
Catspaw (Jerrold)
Catsplay (Örkény)
Caucasian Chalk Circle (Brecht)
Caucasian Chalk Circle (McGrath)
Caucasian Chalk Circle (Saunders)
Caught in the Act! (Feydeau)
Caught Napping (Barrie)
Caught on a Train (t Poliakoff)
Caught Wet (Crothers)
Caught with His Trance Down (Feydeau)
Cause Célèbre (Rattigan)
Cause of it All (L. N. Tolstoy)
Cautela contra cautela (Tirso De Molina)
Cavalcade (Coward)
Cavalier bizarre (Ghelderode)
Cavalier of the Rose (Hofmannsthal)
Cavalier seul (Audiberti)
Cavaliere (Gozzi)
Cavaliere di buon gusto (Goldoni)
Cavaliere di spirito (Goldoni)
Cavaliere e la dama (Goldoni)
Cavaliere giocondo (Goldoni)
Cave Dwellers (Saroyan)
Cave of Salamanca (Cervantes)
Ce formidable bordel (Ionesco)
Ce que parler veut dire (Tardieu)
Cecè (Pirandello)
Cécile (Anouilh)
Cedro del Libano (Fabbri)
Ceinture de Vénus (Lesage)
Ceinture dorée (Augier)
Celebrated Hard Case (Harrigan)
Celebration (Chekhov)
Célèbres (Feydeau)
Celestina (Casona)
Céliane (Rotrou)
Célie (Rotrou)
Célimare le bien-aimé (Labiche)
Célimare the Beloved (Labiche)

Célimène (Rotrou)
Cellar and the Almond Tree (t Mercer)
Celles qu'on prend dans ses bras (Montherlant)
Cellule (t Dubé)
Celluloid Heroes (Williamson)
Celos aún de aire matan (Calderón)
Celos con celos se curan (Tirso De Molina)
Celosa de si misma (Tirso De Molina)
Celoso prudente (Tirso De Molina)
Cement (Müller)
Cena de Baltazar (Calderón)
Cenicienta (Benavente y Martínez)
Cenizas (Valle-Inclán)
Cenodoxus (Forte)
Censo (Carballido)
Censor and the Dramatists (Barrie)
Cent Millions qui tombent (Feydeau)
Centaurs (Wilder)
Centenary Dance (Romeril)
Cepillo de dientes (Díaz)
Cerca (Pavlovsky)
Cerchio magico (Chiarelli)
Cerco de Numancia (Cervantes)
Ceremonia en el tiempo del tigre (Carballido)
Ceremonia ortopédica (Díaz)
Ceremonial de guerra (Triana)
Cérémonie pour un noir assassiné (Arrabal)
Čert na zemi (Tyl)
César Antéchrist (Jarry)
César (Scribe)
Césarée (s Duras)
C'est beau (Sarraute)
C'est une femme du monde! (Feydeau)
Čestmír (Tyl)
C'était avant la guerre à l'Anse à Gilles (Laberge)
C'était le fil de la vie (Dubé)
Cette Chose (Pinget)
Chabot, Admiral of France (Chapman, Shirley)
Chacun pour soi (Crommelynck)
Chagrin d'Hamlet (Ghelderode)
Chaîne (Scribe)
Chaîne anglaise (Labiche)
Chained to the Oar (Byron)
Chains of Dew (Glaspell)
Chains of the Heart (Dunlap)
Chair Endowed (Green)
Chairs (Ionesco)
Chaises (Ionesco)
Challenge at Tilt (Jonson)
Challenge (Planché)
Challenge for Beauty (Heywood)
Challengers (Colum)
Chamber Music (Kopit)
Chambres à louer (Dubé)
Chameleon (Boucicault)
Chamooni III (Boucicault)
Champignol malgré lui (Feydeau)
Chance Acquaintance (Van Druten)
Chance, the Idol (Jones)
Chance Visitor (Arbuzov)
Chances (Fletcher)
Chandelier (Musset)
Change for the Worse (Bridie)
Change in Mame Fadden (Keane)
Changed Bridegroom (Holberg)
Changeling (Middleton)
Changes (Fennario)

Changes (Shirley)
Changes (Terry)
Changing Room (Storey)
Channel Road (Kaufman)
Chansonnier de la paix (Pixérécourt)
Chant du sink (Barbeau)
Chantecler (Rostand)
Chapeau de paille d'Italie (Labiche)
Chapel Perilous (Hewett)
Chapelle des bois (Pixérécourt)
Chapter 17 (Gray)
Chapter Two (Simon)
Charge de cavalerie (Labiche)
Charge de centaures (Arrabal)
Charity (Gilbert)
Charlatan (Walcott)
Charlemagne's Hostage (Hauptmann)
Charles le Téméraire (Pixérécourt)
Charles VII chez ses grands vassaux (Dumas *père*)
Charles XII (Strindberg)
Charles XII (Planché)
Charlie (Fornés)
Charlie (Mrożek)
Charlot (Voltaire)
Charme de la voix (T. Corneille)
Chaser and the Chaste (Feydeau)
Chasse au Chastre (Dumas *père*)
Chasse au roman (Augier)
Chasse aux corbeaux (Labiche)
Chasse aux jobards (Labiche)
Chasse et l'amour (Dumas *père*)
Chasseur français (Vian)
Chaste Maid in Cheapside (Bond)
Chaste Maid in Cheapside (Middleton)
Chastitute (Keane)
Chastity, My Brother (Travers)
Chat en poche (Feydeau)
Château de Bicêtre (P. Corneille)
Château de Loch-Levon (Pixérécourt)
Château des Apennins (Pixérécourt)
Château du diable (Hugo)
Chatsky (Griboyedov)
Chatte metámorphosée (Scribe)
Chatte sur un toit brûlant (Obey)
Chatterton (Jones)
Chatterton (Vigny)
Chaud et froid (Crommelynck)
Chautauqua Spelt E-N-E-R-G-Y (Pollock)
Chayka (Chekhov)
Cheating the Kidnappers (Kaufman)
Cheats of Scapin (Molière)
Cheats of Scapin (Otway)
Chee-Chee (Pirandello)
Cheek (H. Barker)
Cheery Soul (White)
Cheezo (Dunsany)
Chefs écossais (Pixérécourt)
Chemin de Fer (Feydeau)
Chemin de fer (Labiche)
Chemin de Lacroix (Barbeau)
Chen-mu jiao-zi (Guan Hanqing)
Chèvre sur un nuage (Arrabal)
Cher Antoine (Anouilh)
Cher menteur (Cocteau)
Cherry Orchard (Chekhov)
Cherry Orchard (Frayn)
Cherry Orchard (Griffiths)

Cherry Orchard (Mamet)
Cherry Orchard (van Itallie)
Chers Zoizeaux (Anouilh)
Chest (Andreyev)
Cheval de bronze (Scribe)
Chevaleer (Jones)
Chevalier à la lune (Crommelynck)
Chevalier de Maison-Rouge (Dumas *père*)
Chevalier de neige (Vian)
Chevalier de St. George (Robertson)
Chevalier des dames (Labiche)
Chevalier d'Harmental (Dumas *père*)
Chevalier d'Olmedo (Camus)
Chevaliers de la table ronde (Cocteau)
Chevaliers du Lansquenet (Dumas *père*)
Cheveux de ma femme (Labiche)
Cheviot, the Stag, and the Black, Black Oil (McGrath)
Chevy Chase (Planché)
Chez Nous (Nichols)
Chi è cchiù felice 'e me! (De Filippo)
Chi la fa l'aspetta (Goldoni)
Chi lascia la via per la nuova sa quel che lascia (Giacosa)
Chi ruba un piede è fortunato in amore (Fo)
Chi wa tattamama nemutte iru (Terayama)
Chicago (Shepard)
Chicago Chicago (Romeril)
Chicken Soup with Barley (Wesker)
Chidley (De Groen)
Chieftain's Oath (Jerrold)
Chien de Montargis (Pixérécourt)
Chikara toshite no bunka (Kishida)
Chikatetsu (Satoh)
Child Man (Pinero)
Child of Nature (Inchbald)
Child of the Wreck (Planché)
Childe International (Soyinka)
Childe Roland to the Dark Tower Came (Wilder)
Childhood (Wilder)
Children of Heracles (Euripides)
Children of Lir (Colum)
Children of the Sea (O'Neill)
Children of the Sun (Gorky)
Children's Hour (Hellman)
Chimere (Chiarelli)
Chinese Wall (Frisch)
Chinesiche Mauer (Frisch)
Chinois (Regnard)
Chinzano (Petrushevskaya)
Chips Are Down (s Sartre)
Chips with Everything (Wesker)
Chiroru no aki (Kishida)
Chitra (Tagore)
Chloridia (Jonson)
Choéphores (Claudel)
Choéphores (Obey)
Choephoroi (Aeschylus)
Choice of a Tutor (Fonvizin)
Choice of Kings (t Mortimer)
Choix d'un gendre (Labiche)
Choleric Fathers (Holcroft)
Choleric Man (Cumberland)
Choose a Spot on the Floor (Terry)
Choosing a Councilman in Daganzo (Cervantes)
Chopin Playoffs (Horovitz)
Chorus of Disapproval (Ayckbourn)
Chosroes (Rotrou)
Chris Axelson, Blacksmith (Ringwood)

Chris Christophersen (O'Neill)
Chris Sick (Saroyan)
Christian Hero (Lillo)
Christie in Love (Brenton)
Christinas Heimreise (Hofmannsthal)
Christina's Journey Home (Hofmannsthal)
Christina's World (Hewett)
Christine (Dumas *père*)
Christmas Carol (t M. Anderson)
Christmas Carol (Connelly, Kaufman)
Christmas Carol (Horovitz)
Christmas Carol (Ludlam)
Christmas Dinner (Taylor)
Christmas Eve (Hecht)
Christmas His Masque (Jonson)
Christmas Interlude (Wilder)
Christmas Joys and Sorrows (Harrigan)
Christmas Party (Holberg)
Christmas Story (Boucicault)
Christoforos Colomvos (Kazantzakis)
Christoph Columbus (Hasenclever)
Christophe Colomb (Ghelderode)
Christophe Colomb (Pixérécourt)
Christopher Colombus (Kazantzakis)
Christopher Columbus (Ghelderode)
Christopher Columbus (Hasenclever)
Christos (Kazantzakis)
Chronicles of Hell (Ghelderode)
Chrysanthème (Pinget)
Chryséide et Arimand (Mairet)
Chrysold (Jones)
Chryso-Thriambos (Middleton)
Chuckeyhead Story (Carroll)
Chudý kejklíř (Tyl)
Chumingo y el pirata de lata (Díaz)
Church Street (Robinson)
Churchill Play (Brenton)
Chuzhoy Khleb (Turgenev)
Chyba (Havel)
Chyornye maski (Andreyev)
Ci ragione e canto I–III (Fo)
Ciascuno a suo modo (Pirandello)
Cicatrices de la memoria (Díaz)
Ciclo delle noci di cocco (Chiarelli)
Cid (P. Corneille)
Ciel et la merde I–II (Arrabal)
Ciertas cosas (Hernández)
Cigale chez les fourmis (Labiche)
Cigarras hormigas (Benavente y Martínez)
Ciguë (Augier)
Cilindro (De Filippo)
Cimene Pardo (Gozzi)
Cimetière des voitures (Arrabal)
Cinco Fugitivos do Juizo Final (Gomes)
Cinco pasos al cielo (Carballido)
Cinderella (Byron)
Cinderella (Robertson)
Cinderella (Taylor)
Cinderella Comes of Age (Saunders)
Cinémassacre (Vian)
Cinna (P. Corneille)
Cinna's Conspiracy (P. Corneille)
Cinq (Tremblay)
Cintas magnéticas (Sastre)
Cinzano (Petrushevskaya)
Circé (T. Corneille)
Circle (Maugham)

Circonstances atténuantes (Labiche)
Circuit (Feydeau)
Circulito de tiza (Sastre)
Circus Valentine (Norman)
Cisma de Inglaterra. (Calderón)
Cistellaria (Plautus)
Cité sans sommeil (Tardieu)
Citerne (Pixérécourt)
Cities in Bezique (Kennedy)
Citizen Turned Gentleman (Molière)
Citizen Turned Gentleman (Ravenscroft)
Citrouille (Barbeau)
Città morta (D'Annunzio)
City (Claudel)
City (Fitch)
City Heiress (Behn)
City Madam (Massinger)
City Sketches (Mamet)
City Sugar (Poliakoff)
City Wit (Brome)
Ciudad al revés (Díaz)
Ciudad alegre y confiada (Benavente y Martínez)
Ciudad doliente (Benavente y Martínez)
Ciudad que tiene la cara sucia (Díaz)
Civil War (Montherlant)
CIVIL warS. a tree is best measured when it is down
   (Müller)
Civilizátor (Madách)
Civitatis Amor (Middleton)
Clacson, trombette e pernacchi (Fo)
Clancy Name (Robinson)
Clandestine Marriage (Colman the Elder)
Clara ha ragione (Chiarelli)
Clara's Ole Man (Bullins)
Clari (Planché)
Clarice (Rotrou)
Clarinette qui passe (Labiche)
Clarissa Harlowe (Boucicault)
Clash by Night (Odets)
Classe terminale (Obaldia)
Claude's Wife (Dumas *fils*)
Claudine (Pixérécourt)
Claudine von Villa Bella (Goethe)
Claudius (Kaiser)
Claus Peymann kauft sich eine Hose (Bernhard)
Clavier pour un autre (Tardieu)
Clavigo (Goethe)
Claw (H. Barker)
Clé (Labiche)
Cléagénor et Doristée (Rotrou)
Cleander (Massinger)
Cléandre (Rotrou)
Clearing in the Woods (Laurents)
Clemencia (Hernández)
Cleomenes (Southerne)
Cleomenes, the Spartan Hero (Dryden, Southerne)
Cleopatra (Alfieri)
Cleopatra (Kotzebue)
Cléopatre (Sardou)
Clerical Error (Jones)
Clérigo da Beira (Vicente)
Clever Elsie, Smiling John, Silent Peter (Jellicoe)
Clever Soldiers (Poliakoff)
Climate of Fear (t Mercer)
Climbers (Fitch)
Clitandre (P. Corneille)
Clizia (Machiavelli)

Clock Goes Round (Brighouse)
Clockmaker from Cordoba (Carballido)
Clockmaker's Hat (Robertson)
Clockwise (s Frayn)
Clope (Pinget)
Clorinde (Rotrou)
Close Harmony (Rice)
Close My Eyes (s Poliakoff)
Close of Play (Gray)
Close Shave (Feydeau)
Close the Book (Glaspell)
Clothe the Naked (Pirandello)
Clothes for a Summer Hotel (Williams)
Clou aux maris (Labiche)
Cloud Nine (Churchill)
Cloud That Lifted (Maeterlinck)
Cloudburst (Kishida)
Clouds (Aristophanes)
Clouds (Cumberland)
Clouds (Frayn)
Clouds (Gale)
Cloughoughter (Colum)
Club (Williamson)
Club champenois (Labiche)
Club d'Arthur (Tardieu)
Club des menteurs (Ghelderode)
C'mon Back to Heavenly House (Bullins)
Co tu maci (Różewicz)
Coat (Fugard)
Coats (Gregory)
Cobarde más valiente (Tirso De Molina)
Cock o' the Walk (Jones)
Cock Robin (Barry, Rice)
Cockade (Wood)
Cock-a-Doodle Dandy (O'Casey)
Cockroaches (Witkiewicz)
Cocktail Party (Eliot)
Cocoanuts (Kaufman)
Cocu magnifique (Crommelynck)
Coelina (Pixérécourt)
Coeur à cuir (Audiberti)
Coeur de papa (Barbeau)
Coffee House (Goldoni)
Coffee House (Voltaire)
Coffer (Ariosto)
Coggerers (Carroll)
Coi capelli bianchi (De Filippo)
Coincidence (Brighouse)
Cold Air (Fornés)
Cold June (Pinero)
Cold Wind and the Warm (Behrman)
Colin et Colette (Beaumarchais)
Colin's Welcome (O'Keeffe)
Colis (Feydeau)
Collaborators (Mortimer)
Collar de estrellas (Benavente y Martínez)
Colleague Crampton (Hauptmann)
Collect Your Hand Baggage (Mortimer)
Collection (Pinter)
Colleen Bawn (Boucicault)
Colleen Bawn (Byron)
Collier's Friday Night (Lawrence)
Colliers Wood (Wood)
Colmenero divino (Tirso De Molina)
Colomanns Rache (Kotzebue)
Colombe (Anouilh)
Colombine Arlequin (Lesage)

Colonel (Davenant)
Colonel Wotherspoon (Bridie)
Colonie (Marivaux)
Colossal Idea (Gilbert)
Colour the Flesh the Colour of Dust (Cook)
Coloured Baby Show (Harrigan)
Colours in the Dark (Reaney)
Colpa è sempre del diavolo (Fo)
Columbia the Gem of the Ocean (Baraka)
Columbus Avenue (Mamet)
Columbus (Hacks)
Come and Go (Beckett)
Come As You Are (Mortimer)
Come Back, Little Sheba (Inge)
Come Blow Your Horn (Simon)
Come Here (Daly)
Come into the Garden Maud (Coward)
Come into the Kitchen (Petrushevskaya)
Come le foglie (Giacosa)
Come Marching Home (R. Anderson)
Come prima, meglio di prima (Pirandello)
Come tu mi vuoi (Pirandello)
Comeback (Horovitz)
Comédia de Rubena (Vicente)
Comédia do Viúvo (Vicente)
Comedia italiana (Benavente y Martínez)
Comedia nueva (Fernández de Moratín)
Comedia sin desenlace (Echegaray)
Comedia sin titulo (García Lorca)
Comédia sobre a Divisa da Cidade de Coimbra (Vicente, Gil)
Comedia sonambula (Sastre)
Comedians (Griffiths)
Comédie de la Comédie (Tardieu)
Comédie des arts (Tardieu)
Comédie des comédiens (Scudéry)
Comédie des Tuileries (P. Corneille, Rotrou)
Comédie sans comédie (Quinault)
Comédien poète (T. Corneille)
Comédiens corsaires (Lesage)
Comedies of Family Life (Witkiewicz)
Comedies of Words (Schnitzler)
Comedy (Kazantzakis)
Comedy and Tragedy (Gilbert)
Comedy of Asses (Plautus)
Comedy of Errors (Shakespeare)
Comedy, Satire, Irony and Deeper Meaning (Grabbe)
Comenius (Kokoschka)
Comète (Pinero)
Comfort of Strangers (s Pinter)
Comic Artist (Glaspell)
Comic Theatre (Goldoni)
Comical Duel (O'Keeffe)
Comical Lovers (Cibber)
Comical Revenge (Etherege)
Comida de las fieras (Benavente y Martínez)
Coming into Land (Poliakoff)
Coming of Ewn Andzale (Fitzmaurice)
Coming of Mrs. Patrick (Crothers)
Coming of Peace (Hauptmann)
Coming of Stork (Williamson)
Coming Through the Rye (Saroyan)
Comings and Goings (Terry)
Commander of Ocaña (Vega)
Comme les chardons (Salacrou)
Comme Nous avons été (Adamov)
Commedione di Giuseppe Gioacchino Belli (Fabbri)

Commemoration Masque (Hauptmann)
Comment la trouves-tu? (Dumas fils)
Commère (Marivaux)
Commerce of Algiers (Cervantes)
Commissary (Foote)
Commitment (Hibberd)
Committal (Saunders)
Committed for Trial (Gilbert)
Commode de Victorine (Labiche)
Common (t Nichols)
Common Glory (Green)
Common Man (Hecht)
Common Pursuit (Gray)
Communication Cord (Friel)
Communion solennelle (Arrabal)
Cómo empieza y cómo acaba (Echegaray)
Cómo han de ser los amigos (Tirso De Molina)
Comodhia (Kazantzakis)
Compact (Planché)
Compartment (s Pinter)
Compensation Will Be Paid (Ringwood)
Complainte du ridicule (Adamov)
Complainte du pauvr' propriétaire (Feydeau)
Compromise of the King of the Golden Isles (Dunsany)
Compte rendu d'Avignon (Vinaver)
Compulsory Option (Pollock)
Comrade Jacob (McGrath)
Comrades (Strindberg)
Comte de Boursoufle (Voltaire)
Comte de Morcerf (Dumas père)
Comte d'Essex (T. Corneille)
Comte Hermann (Dumas père)
Comte Ory (Scribe)
Comtesse d'Escarbagnas (Molière)
Comtesse d'Orgueil (T. Corneille)
Comtesse Romani (Dumas fils)
Comus (Colman the Elder)
Con quien vengo, vengo. (Calderón)
Conceited Young Ladies (Molière)
Concert at Saint Ovide (Buero Vallejo)
Concert dans un oeuf (Arrabal)
Concierto de San Ovidio (Buero Vallejo)
Conde de Novion (Garrett)
Conde Lotario (Echegaray)
Conde Lucanor (Calderón)
Condemed of Altona (Sartre)
Condemed Squad (Sastre)
Condemned (Dagerman)
Condemned Man's Bicycle (Arrabal)
Condenado por desconfiado (Tirso De Molina)
Conditions of Agreement (Whiting)
Conduct of Life (Fornés)
Confederacy (Boucicault)
Confederacy (Green)
Confederacy (Vanbrugh)
Confession (Cumberland)
Confession at Night (Arbuzov)
Confessional (Williams)
Confidence (Boucicault)
Confidente (Fabbri)
Confidential Clerk (Eliot)
Confissão (Santareno)
Conflagration (Hauptmann)
Conflict (P. Corneille)
Conflicto entre dos deberes (Echegaray)
Conflicts (Mortimer)
Confrarias (Andrade)

Confusion (Kotzebue)
Confusions (Ayckbourn)
Congiura de Pazzi (Alfieri)
Congresswomen (Aristophanes)
Connaissez-vous? (Ionesco)
Connection (Gelber)
Connétable de Bourbon (Dumas *père*)
Conochar (Coulter)
Conquest of Everest (Kopit)
Conquest of Granada I–II (Dryden)
Conquest of the Universe (Ludlam)
Conquête de la toison d'or (P. Corneille)
Conscience (Dumas *père*)
Conscience Money (Byron)
Conscious Lovers (Steele)
Consequencess (Tagore)
Consort of Peace (Cao Yu)
Conspiracy and Tragedy of Charles, Duke of Byron
   (Chapman)
Conspiracy of the Pazzi (Alfieri)
Constance (Robertson)
Constant Couple (Farquhar)
Constant Maid (Shirley)
Constant Players (Marivaux)
Constant Prince (Calderón)
Constant Wife (Maugham)
Constantine the Great (Lee)
Contagion (Augier)
Contaminated Family (L. N. Tolstoy)
Conte de fées (Dumas *père*)
Conte Rosso (Giacosa)
Contemplazione (Fabbri)
Contempt of Court (Boucicault)
Contention for Honour and Riches (Shirley)
Contention of Ajax and Ulysses for the Armour of Achilles
   (Shirley)
Contes de la grand-mère (Crommelynck)
Contestation (Arrabal)
Contested Election (Taylor)
Contrabandière (Maillet)
Contractor (Storey)
Contraption (Tardieu)
Contrattempo (Goldoni)
Contratto (De Filippo)
Control Freaks (Henley)
Conul Leonida faţă cu reacţiunea (Caragiale)
Conversación entre las ruinas (Carballido)
Conversation (Havel)
Conversation Among the Ruins (Carballido)
Conversation at Night with a Despised Character (r
   Dürrenmatt)
Conversation in Paradise (Edgar)
Conversation on the Highway (Turgenev)
Conversation Piece (Coward)
Conversation-sinfonietta (Tardieu)
Conversations in Exile (Brenton)
Conversations on a Homecoming (Murphy)
Conversations with the Spirit World (Mamet)
Conversion of General Gallicanus (Hrotsvitha)
Conversion of the Harlot Thais (Hrotsvitha)
Converts (Brighouse)
Copa encantada (Benavente y Martínez)
Cop-Out (Guare)
Coppia aperta, quasi spalancata (Fo)
Coquette (Regnard)
Coral (Kaiser)
Coralie Lansdowne Says No (Buzo)

Corazón lleno de lluvia (Díaz)
Corbeaux (Becque)
Cordelia's Aspirations (Harrigan)
Cordero de Isaías (Calderón)
Coréens (Vinaver)
Corine (Hardy)
Coriolan (Brecht)
Coriolan (Hardy)
Coriolan (Lenz)
Coriolanus (Brecht)
Coriolanus (Shakespeare)
Corker's End (Travers)
Cormorant Plumes (Zeami)
Corn (Ludlam)
Cornada (Sastre)
Cornelia (Kyd)
Cornélie (Hardy)
Cornelius (Priestley)
Corner (Bullins)
Cornish Squire (Congreve)
Cornish Squire (Molière)
Corona de amor y muerte (Casona)
Corona de fuego (Usigli)
Corona de Hungría (Vega)
Corona de luz (Usigli)
Corona de sombra (Usigli)
Corona merecida (Vega)
Coronation (Shirley)
Coronation of Charles X of France (Planché)
Coronet of the Duchess (Fitch)
Correr en pos de un ideal (Echegaray)
Corricolo (Labiche)
Corruption in the Palace of Justice (Betti)
Corruzione al palazzo di giustizia (Betti)
Corsair's Bride (Planché)
Corsen (Kotzebue)
Corsican Brothers (Boucicault)
Corsican "Bothers" (Byron)
Corsicans (Kotzebue)
Cortes de Júpiter (Vicente)
Cortez (Planché)
Cortigiana (Aretino)
Corvo (Gozzi)
Cosi (Nowra)
Cosi è (si vi pare) (Pirandello)
Cosmonaute agricole (Obaldia)
Cosroès (Rotrou)
Couleur du temps (Apollinaire)
Counsellor-at-Law (Rice)
Counsels of the Wood (Mason)
Count Benyowsky (Kotzebue)
Count Oderland (Frisch)
Count of Burgundy (Kotzebue)
Count Ory (Scribe)
Countdown (Ayckbourn)
Countess and the Dancer (Reade)
Countess Gueki (Daly)
Countess Julie (Strindberg)
Countess Kathleen (Yeats)
Countess Mizzie (Schnitzler)
Countess of Escarbagnas (Molière)
Counting the Ways (Albee)
Country (t Griffiths)
Country Attorney (Cumberland)
Country Captain (Shirley)
Country Dressmaker (Fitzmaurice)
Country Girl (Daly)

Country Girl (Odets)
Country House (Vanbrugh)
Country Wife (Wycherley)
Coup de l'étrier (Dubé)
Coup de rasoir (Labiche)
Coup de tête (monologue) (Feydeau)
Coupe stainless (Barbeau)
Couples (Schnitzler)
Couplets en procès (Lesage)
Couplings and Groupings (Terry)
Coups de l'amour et de la fortune (Quinault)
Courageous One (Gorky)
Courageous Princess (Witkiewicz)
Courier for Hades (Chikamatsu)
Courier for Hell (Chikamatsu)
Courier of Lyons (Reade)
Couronnement (Arrabal)
Court and Cottage (Taylor)
Court Beauties (Planché)
Court Beggar (Brome)
Court Favour (Planché)
Court Gallantry (Cibber)
Court Masque (Planché)
Court of Last Resort (Rice)
Court Secret (Shirley)
Courting Blackbird (Mason)
Courting of Marie Jenvrin (Ringwood)
Courtly Lovers (Molière)
Courtship (Byron)
Cousin Billy (Fitch)
Cousin Vladimir (Mercer)
Couvée (Brieux)
Covent Garden Tragedy (Fielding)
Covetous Knight (Pushkin)
Cowboy and the Lady (Fitch)
Cowboy Mouth (Shepard)
Cowboys (Shepard)
Cowboys #2 (Shepard)
Coxcomb (Beaumont, Fletcher)
Cozeners (Foote)
Crabbed Youth and Age (Robinson)
Cracks (Sherman)
Cradle of Thunder (Lawler)
Crasseux (Maillet)
Crazy Locomotive (Witkiewicz)
Crazy to Kill (Reaney)
Crazy Wall (Keane)
Creation of the World and Other Business (Miller)
Creatures of Impulse (Gilbert)
Credentials of a Sympathizer (H. Barker)
Creditors (Strindberg)
Cresta Run (Simpson)
Creve Coeur (Williams)
Criado de Don Juan (Benavente y Martínez)
Cries from Casement as His Bones Are Brought to Dublin (Rudkin)
Crime de Aldeia Velha (Santareno)
Crime of Louis Riel (Coulter)
Crime Passionnel (Sartre)
Crímen de Lord Arturo (Casona)
Crimes and Crimes (Strindberg)
Crimes in Hot Countries (H. Barker)
Crimes of Passion (Orton)
Crimes of the Heart (Henley)
Criminals (Triana)
Criminals in Love (Walker)
Crimson Island (Bulgakov)

Crisante (Rotrou)
Crisis (Holcroft)
Crispin, rival de son maître (Lesage)
Crispin, Rival of His Master (Lesage)
Criss-Cross (Crothers)
Critic (Daly)
Critic (Robinson)
Critic (Sheridan)
Critic and the Heart (Bolt)
Crítica de "La mujer no hace milagros" (Usigli)
Critical Year (Green)
Crítico incipiente (Echegaray)
Critique de L'École des femmes (Molière)
Critique du Légataire (Regnard)
Critique of the School For Wives (Molière)
Crock of Gold (Plautus)
Crocodile (Sardou)
Cromwell (Hugo)
Cromwell (Storey)
Cromwell et Charles Ier (Dumas *père*)
Crónicas romanas (Sastre)
Cross and Sword (Green)
Cross Old Devil (Menander)
Cross Patch (Mamet)
Cross Purpose (Camus)
Cross-Roads (Robinson)
Crossroads (Solórzano)
Crossroads (Walcott)
Crowd up at the Manor (Tardieu)
Crown Diamonds (Scribe)
Crown of Light (Usigli)
Crown of Shadows (Usigli)
Crown Strike Play (Arden)
Crownbride (Strindberg)
Crows (Becque)
Cruce de viás (Solórzano)
Cruche cassée (Adamov)
Crucial Week in the Life of a Grocer's Assistant (Murphy)
Crucible (Miller)
Crucificado (Solórzano)
Crucifixion (Solórzano)
Cruel Brother (Davenant)
Cruel Games (Arbuzov)
Cruel Gift (Centlivre)
Crueldad por el honor (Ruiz de Alarcón)
Cruelty of the Spaniards in Peru (Davenant)
Crusaders (Jones)
Crushed Actors (Harrigan)
Crusts (Claudel)
Cry for a Leader (Walcott)
Crystal and Fox (Friel)
Csák végapjai (Madách)
Császár (Molnár)
Csendelet (Molnár)
Csoda a hegyek közt (Molnár)
¡Cuál es mayor perfección (Calderón)
Cualquiera lo sabe (Benavente y Martínez)
Cuando los hijos de Eva no son los hijos de Adán (Benavente y Martínez)
4 Chemins 4 (Usigli)
Cuban Thing (Gelber)
Cubo de la Almudena (Calderón)
"Cucarachas" de Yale (Arrabal)
Cuckold in Conceit (Vanbrugh)
Cuckold's Haven (Tate)
Cuckoo in the Nest (Travers)
Cue for Passion (Rice)

Cuento de abril (Valle-Inclán)
Cuento de amor (Benavente y Martínez)
Cuento de Navidad (Carballido)
Cuento de primavera (Benavente y Martínez)
Cuento inmoral (Benavente y Martínez)
Cuentos para armar entre todos (Díaz)
Cuerdo loco (Vega)
Cuernos de don Friolera (Valle-Inclán)
Cuervo (Sastre)
Cuetzalcóatl (Hernández)
Cueva de Salamanca (Cervantes)
Cuishla-Ma-Chree (Boucicault)
Cukrászné (Molnár)
Culotte (Anouilh)
Culpa busca la pena y el agravio la venganza (Ruiz de
    Alarcón)
Culpa es tuya (Benavente y Martínez)
Cuoco della mala cucina (De Filippo)
Cup of Kindness (Travers)
Cupid and Death (Shirley)
Cupid and Psyche (Brighouse)
Cupid's Revenge (Beaumont, Fletcher)
Cura y la enfermedad (Calderón)
Curaggio de nu pumpiere napolitano (De Filippo)
Curculio (Plautus)
Cure for Cuckolds (Webster)
Curiosities of Literature (Boucicault)
Curioso accidente (Goldoni)
Curious Mishap (Goldoni)
Curse of the Langston House (Fornés)
Curse of the Starving Class (Shepard)
Cursi (Benavente y Martínez)
Curtmantle (Fry)
Curve (Dorst)
Custom of the Country (Fletcher, Massinger)
Customs and Excise (Hibberd)
Cut in the Rates (t Ayckbourn)
Cuttlefish (Witkiewicz)
Cycle of Spring (Tagore)
Cyclops (Euripides)
Cyd (Wyspiański)
Cymbeline (Shakespeare)
Cymbeline Refinished (Shaw)
Cymon and Iphigenia (Planché)
Cyrano de Bergerac (Daly)
Cyrano de Bergerac (Fry)
Cyrano de Bergerac (Nowra)
Cyrano de Bergerac (Rostand)
Cyril's Success (Byron)
Czar (Planché)
Czar Feodor Ionannovitch (A. K. Tolstoy)
Czar Peter (O'Keeffe)
Czarowna noc (Mrożek)
Czego pyrsbywa czego ubywa (Różewicz)

D. Boone (Norman)
Da (Leonard)
Dachniki (Gorky)
Daddy (Bullins)
Daddy O'Dowd (Boucicault)
Dad's Tale (Ayckbourn)
Dageraad (Heijermans)
Daglannet (Bjørnson)
Dainty Shapes and Hairy Apes (Witkiewicz)
Daisy Farm (Byron)
Daisy's Escape (Pinero)
Dakolar (Mackaye)

D'ale carnavalului (Caragiale)
Dalliance (Schnitzler)
Dalliance (Stoppard)
Dalmatina (Goldoni)
Dalnyaya doroga (Arbuzov)
Daloky kray (Shvarts)
Dama boba (García Lorca)
Dama Boba (Vega)
Dama del alba (Casona)
Dama duende (Calderón)
Dama prudente (Goldoni)
Damaged Goods (Brieux)
Damask Cheek (Van Druten)
Dame à la licorne (Cocteau)
Dame au petit chien (Labiche)
Dame aux camélias (Dumas *fils*)
Dame aux jambes d'azur (Labiche)
Dame de Challant (Giacosa)
Dame de chez Maxim (Feydeau)
Dame de Monsoreau (Dumas *père*)
Dame de pique (Scribe)
Dame Dobson (Ravenscroft)
Dame Kobold (Hofmannsthal)
Dame of Spades (Boucicault)
Damer's Gold (Gregory)
Dames vengées (T. Corneille)
Damné (Obaldia)
Damned for Despair (Tirso De Molina)
Damnée Manon, sacrée Sandra (Tremblay)
Damoiselle (Brome)
Damon and Phillida (Cibber)
Dan dao hui (Guan Hanqing)
Danae (Hofmannsthal)
Dan-bian duo-shuo (Guan Hanqing)
Dance (Fornés)
Dance of Angels Who Burn Their Own Wings (Satoh)
Dance of Death (Auden)
Dance of Death I–II (Strindberg)
Dance of the Forests (Soyinka)
Dancing at Lughnasa (Friel)
Dancing Bear (Bridie)
Dancing Girl (Jones)
Dancing in the Chequered Shade (Van Druten)
Dandy Dick (Pinero)
Dandy Dolls (Fitzmaurice)
Danger! Memory! (Miller)
Dangerous Corner (Priestley)
Dangerous Liaisons (s Hampton)
Danicheff (Dumas *fils*)
Daniel (Wyspiański)
Daniel Rochat (Sardou)
Dan'l Druce, Blacksmith (Gilbert)
Dan's Tribulations (Harrigan)
Dans van de reiger (Claus)
Danse de mort (Duras)
Dansen (Brecht)
Danske Comoedies Liigbegiaengelse (Holberg)
Dante (Baraka)
Danté (Sardou)
Danton Case (Przybyszewska)
Danton's Death (Brenton)
Danton's Death (Büchner)
Dantons dood (Claus)
Dantons Tod (Büchner)
Danube (Fornés)
Danza del Urogallo múltiple (Hernández)
Daphne and Amintor (Bickerstaff)

Daphne Laureola (Bridie)
Dar la vuelta (Gambaro)
Dar mudrykh pchyol (Sologub)
Dar tiempo al tiempo (Calderón)
Darby's Return (Dunlap)
Darius (T. Corneille)
Dark at the Top of the Stairs (Inge)
Dark City! and Its Bright Side (Daly)
Dark Harvest (Ringwood)
Dark is Light Enough (Fry)
Dark Lady of the Sonnets (Shaw)
Dark Night's Work (Boucicault)
Dark Pony (Mamet)
Dark Room (Williams)
Dark Tower (Kaufman)
Dark Valley (r Auden)
Darkness at Noon (Kingsley)
Darlo todo y no dar nada (Calderón)
Dasspeld (Heijermans)
Daughter of Jorio (D'Annunzio)
Daughter-in-Law (Lawrence)
Daughters of Troy (Seneca)
Dave (Gregory)
David (Lawrence)
David and Broccoli (t Mortimer)
David and Goliath (Kaiser)
David Garrick (Robertson)
David und Goliath (Kaiser)
David y Jonatán (Marqués)
Davor (Grass)
Day for Surprises (Guare)
Day in the Death of Joe Egg (Nichols)
Day of Reckoning (Houghton)
Day of Reckoning (Planché)
Day Out (t Bennett)
Day the Money Stopped (M. Anderson)
Day the Whores Came Out to Play Tennis (Kopit)
Day They Let the Lions Loose (Carballido)
Day We Went West (Harrigan)
Day with My Sister (Poliakoff)
Days Ahead (L. Wilson)
Days Between (R. Anderson)
Days in the Trees (Duras)
Days May Be Long (Ringwood)
Days of the Commune (Brecht)
Days of the Turbins (Bulgakov)
Days of Yore (Cumberland)
Days to Come (Hellman)
Days Without End (O'Neill)
De alivio (Benavente y Martínez)
De cerca (Benavente y Martínez)
De l'Autre Côté du mur (Dubé)
De mala raza (Echegaray)
De muy buena familia (Benavente y Martínez)
De pequeñas causas . . . (Benavente y Martínez)
De Pretore Vincenzo (De Filippo)
De Quoi s'agit-il? (Tardieu)
De un castigo, tres venganzas (Calderón)
De una causa, dos efectos (Calderón)
De vises sten (Lagerkvist)
Deacon (Jones)
Dead Alive (O'Keeffe)
Dead City (D'Annunzio)
Dead End (Kingsley)
Dead Letter (Pinget)
Dead or Alive (Taylor)
Dead Secret (Boucicault)

Dead Timber (Esson)
Deadly Game (r Dürrenmatt)
Deaf and Dumb (Holcroft)
Deaf and Dumb (Kotzebue)
Dealing in Futures (Brighouse)
Dear Antoine (Anouilh)
Dear Brutus (Barrie)
Dear Departed (Houghton)
Dear Departing (Andreyev)
Dearer Than Life (Byron)
Death and Execution of Frank Halloway (Reaney)
Death and Resurrection of Mr. Roche (Kilroy)
Death and the Devil (Wedekind)
Death and the Fool (Hofmannsthal)
Death and the King's Horseman (Soyinka)
Death and Victory of Lord Nelson (Cumberland)
Death Closes All (Carroll)
Death Comes to Us All, Mary Agnes (Durang)
Death List (Bullins)
Death of a Salesman (Miller)
Death of a Traveller (Hibberd)
Death of Bernard the Believer (Horovitz)
Death of Bessie Smith (Albee)
Death of Cuchulain (Yeats)
Death of Doctor Faust (Ghelderode)
Death of Eve (Moody)
Death of Ivan the Terrible (A. K. Tolstoy)
Death of Joe Orton (Nowra)
Death of Malcolm X (Baraka)
Death of Tarelkin (Sukhovo-Kobylin)
Death of the Winged-Tiger General (Guan Hanqing)
Death of Tintagiles (Maeterlinck)
Death Story (Edgar)
Death Thrust (Sastre)
Death Warmed Up (Hibberd)
Deathsheads (Hare)
Deathwatch (Genet)
Deathwatch (Rudkin)
Debauchee (Behn)
Debauchees (Fielding)
Debet och kredit (Strindberg)
Debit and Credit (Strindberg)
Deborah (Fielding)
Deborah (Mitchell)
Deburau (Granville-Barker)
Debutante Ball (Henley)
Decadence (Berkoff)
Decir sí (Gambaro)
Deeds (Brenton)
Deeds (Griffiths)
Deeds (Hare)
Deep Blue Sea (Rattigan)
Deep Deep Sea (Planché)
Deep Has Many Voices (Ringwood)
Deep Tangled Wildwood (Connelly, Kaufman)
Deer Dogs (Mamet)
Defeat (Galsworthy)
Defeat (Grieg)
Definitely Not the Last (Romeril)
Défunt (Obaldia)
Dégel (Sardou)
Deirdre (Yeats)
Deirdre of the Sorrows (r Coulter)
Deirdre of the Sorrows (Synge)
Déjà Vu (Osborne)
Del enemigo (Tirso De Molina)
Del sol naciente (Gambaro)

Dhefteri Endoli (Prevelakis)
Día es un día (Díaz)
Día mayor de los días (Calderón)
Día que se soltaron los leones (Carballido)
Diable à quatre (Gelinas)
Diable et le bon Dieu (Sartre)
Diables noirs (Sardou)
Diablo mundo (Calderón)
Diadem of Snow (Rice)
Diadema (Usigli)
Dialect Determinism (Bullins)
Dialogo facetissimo (Ruzante)
Diálogo secreto (Buero Vallejo)
Diálogo sobre a Ressurreição (Vicente)
Dialogue for Two Men (Inge)
Dialogues (Hernández)
Diamant (Hebbel)
Diamant des Geisterkönigs (Raimund)
Diamants de la couronne (Scribe)
Diana and Tuda (Pirandello)
Diana e la Tuda (Pirandello)
Diane (Augier)
Diane (Rotrou)
Diane de Lys (Dumas *fils*)
Dianora (Hofmannsthal)
Diapason (Feydeau)
Diario di Eva (Fo)
Diarmuid and Grania (Yeats)
Diary of a Scoundrel (Ostrovsky)
Diary of Fallen Leaves (Kishida)
Dicen que la distancia es el olvido (Díaz)
Dicha y desdicha del nombre (Calderón)
Dichterdämmerung (Dürrenmatt)
Dick Deterred (Edgar)
Dick Whittington and His Cat (Leigh)
Dictée (Pinget)
Did You Write My Name in the Snow? (Guare)
Didactic Play of Baden-Baden on Consent (Brecht)
Diderich Menschenskraeck (Holberg)
Diderich the Terrible (Holberg)
Dido (Marlowe)
Dido and Aeneas (Tate)
Didon (Scudéry)
Didon se sacrifiant (Hardy)
Dieu bleu (Cocteau)
Dieu du hasard (Lesage)
Dieu est-il devenu fou? (Arrabal)
Dieu le savait (Salacrou)
Dieu tenté par les mathématiques (Arrabal)
Difficult Hour I–III (Lagerkvist)
Difficult Man (Hofmannsthal)
Diff'rent (O'Neill)
Dikarka (Ostrovsky)
Diktatorinden (Munk)
Dilemma of a Ghost (Aidoo)
Diluvio (Betti)
Diluvio (De Filippo)
Dimboola (Hibberd)
Dimetos (Fugard)
Dindon (Feydeau)
Dineros son calidad (Vega)
Dingo (Wood)
Dinner (Molnár)
Dinner at Eight (Kaufman)
Dinner with the Family (Anouilh)
Dinner's in the Blender (Terry)
Diogenes and His Lantern (Taylor)

Dione (Gay)
Dios, Batidillo y la mujer (Usigli)
Diplomati (Karvaš)
Dippers (Travers)
Directeur de l'Opera (Anouilh)
Director of the Opera (Anouilh)
Diritti dell'anima (Giacosa)
Dirty Hands (Sartre)
Dirty Linen (Stoppard)
Dirty Work (Travers)
Disappearance of the Jews (Mamet)
Disappointment (Southerne)
Disclosure Day (Brighouse)
Discorsi sur terrorismo e la repressione (Fo)
Discourse on the Progress of the Prolonged War (Weiss)
Discovery of the New World by Christopher Columbus (Vega)
Discreet Princess (Planché)
Dish of Chocolate and A Cup of Tea (Foote)
Diskurs über die Vorgeschichte und den Verlauf (Weiss)
Dismissal (Reaney)
Disposal (Inge)
Dispute (Marivaux)
Dissident, il va sans dire (Vinaver)
Dissident, it Goes Without Saying (Vinaver)
Dissolution of Dominic Boot (r Stoppard)
Distaff Side (Van Druten)
Distrait (Regnard)
Distressed Wife (Gay)
Distresst Mother (Racine)
Ditegli sempre di sì (De Filippo)
Dites-le avec des fleurs (Barbeau, Dubé)
Dito nell'occhio (Fo)
Diversion (Musset)
Diversion (Van Druten)
Diversions of the Morning (Foote)
Divertimento (Fabbri)
Divinas palabras (Valle-Inclán)
Divine Gift (Jones)
Divine Philothea (Calderón)
Divine Words (Valle-Inclán)
Divino Jasón (Calderón)
Divino Orfeo (Calderón)
Divorce (Daly)
Divorce (Regnard)
Divorce Court Judge (Cervantes)
Divorcio de almas (Benavente y Martínez)
Divorçons (Murrell)
Divorçons! (Sardou)
Divorzio (Alfieri)
Dmitri (Braun)
Dmitry Samozvanets i Vasily Shuysky (Ostrovsky)
Dnevnik Satany (Andreyev)
Dni nashey zhizni (Andreyev)
Dni Turbinykh (Bulgakov)
Do I Hear a Waltz? (Laurents)
Do piachu (Różewicz)
Do You See What I'm Saying? (Terry)
Do You Turn Somersaults? (Arbuzov)
Doble historia del Doctor Valmy (Buero Vallejo)
Doc (Pollock)
Dock Brief (Mortimer)
Doctor and the Patient (Saroyan)
Dr. Angelus (Bridie)
Doctor Faustus (Marlowe)
Dr. Harmer's Holidays (Pinero)
Dr. Hero (Horovitz)

Doctor Hocus Pocus (Colman the Younger)
Doctor in Spite of Himself (Gregory)
Doctor in Spite of Himself (Molière)
Dr. Karl's Kure (Romeril)
Dr. Kheal (Fornés)
Doctor Knock (Granville-Barker)
Doctor Last in His Chariot (Bickerstaff)
Doctor Last in His Chariot (Molière)
Doctor Love (Molière)
Doctor Simple (Vega)
Dr. Syntax (Planché)
Doctors All (Vega)
Doctor's Dilemma (Shaw)
Doctor's Duty (Pirandello)
Døden (Munk)
Dödens Arlekin (Bergman)
Dödsadansen I–II (Strindberg)
Dödsdömde (Dagerman)
Dodsworth (Howard)
Dog (Mamet)
Dog (Shepard)
Dog Accident (Saunders)
Dog Beneath the Skin (Auden)
Dog Days (Gray)
Dog in the Manger (Vega)
Dog it Was That Died (r Stoppard)
Dogg's Hamlet, Cahoot's Macbeth (Stoppard)
Dogg's Our Pet (Stoppard)
Dogs (Saroyan)
Doigts de fée (Scribe)
Doit-on le dire? (Labiche)
Dokhodnoye mesto (Ostrovsky)
Doktor Bahrt mit der eisernen Stirn (Kotzebue)
Doktor úr (Molnár)
Doldrum (O'Keeffe)
Doll Trilogy (Lawler)
Dollar (Bergman)
Dollars and Sense (Daly)
Doll's House (Hampton)
Doll's House (Ibsen)
Doll's House (Wilder)
Dolly and the Rat (Jerrold)
Dolly Reforming Herself (Jones)
Dolomitenstadt Lienz (Kroetz)
Dolore sotto chiave (De Filippo)
Dom Bernard de Cabrère (Rotrou)
Dom Duardos (Vicente)
Dom Juan (Molière)
Dom Lope de Cardone (Rotrou)
Dom na granicy (Mrożek)
Dom oknami v pole (Vampilov)
Dom Pèdre (Voltaire)
Dom Sébastien, roi de Portugal (Scribe)
Domestic Picture (Ostrovsky)
Domik na okraine (Arbuzov)
Domik v Chernizove (Arbuzov)
Dominion of Darkness (L. N. Tolstoy)
Domino noir (Scribe)
Don Abel Wrote a Tragedy (Granville-Barker)
Don Bertrand de Cigarral (T. Corneille)
Don Caesar de Bazan (Boucicault)
Don Carlos (Dunlap)
Don Carlos (Otway)
Don Carlos (Schiller)
Don César d'Avalos (T. Corneille)
Don César Ursin (Lesage)
Don Félix de Mendoce (Lesage)

Don Garcia (Alfieri)
Don Garcie de Navarre (Molière)
Don Garzia (Alfieri)
Don Gil de las calzas verdes (Tirso De Molina)
Don Gil of the Green Breeches (Tirso De Molina)
Don Giovanni (t Auden)
Don Giovanni Tenorio (Chiarelli)
Don Giovanni Tenorio (Goldoni)
Don Juan (Benavente y Martínez)
Don Juan (Brecht)
Don Juan (Byron)
Don Juan (Chiarelli)
Don Juan (Frisch)
Don Juan (Ghelderode)
Don Juan (Hampton)
Don Juan (Molière)
Don Juan (Montherlant)
Don Juan (Sternheim)
Don Juan Comes Back from the War (Hampton)
Don Juan Comes Back from the War (Horváth)
Don Juan de Marana (Dumas *père*)
Don Juan in Texas (Kopit)
Don Juan kommt aus dem Krieg (Horváth)
Don Juan und Faust (Grabbe)
Don Kikhot (Bulgakov)
Don Magín él de las magias (Benavente y Martínez)
Don Pedro (Cumberland)
Don Pedro (Mitchell)
Don Quichotte (Sardou)
Don Quixote (s Shvarts)
Don Quixote in England (Fielding)
Don Ranudo de Colibrados (Holberg)
Don Rodrigo (Casona)
Don Sanche d'Aragon (P. Corneille)
Don Sebastian, King of Portugal (Dryden)
Don Sebastiano (Scribe)
Donadieu (Hochwälder)
Doncella, el marinero y el estudiante (García Lorca)
Donkeys' Years (Frayn)
Donna bizzarra (Goldoni)
Donna capricciosa (Goldoni)
Donna contraria al consiglio (Gozzi)
Donna di garbo (Goldoni)
Donna di governo (Goldoni)
Donna di testa debole (Goldoni)
Donna forte (Goldoni)
Donna innamorata davvero (Gozzi)
Donna serpente (Gozzi)
Donna sola (Goldoni)
Donna stravagante (Goldoni)
Donna sullo scudo (Betti)
Donna vendicativa (Goldoni)
Donna vendicativa disarmata dall'obbligazione (Gozzi)
Donna volubile (Goldoni)
Donne curiose (Goldoni)
Donne di buonmore (Goldoni)
Donne di casa soa (Goldoni)
Donne gelose (Goldoni)
Donnerstag (Hochwälder)
Dono di Natale (De Filippo)
Doña Beatriz de Silva (Tirso De Molina)
Doña Beatriz, la sin ventura (Solórzano)
Doña Clarines (Granville-Barker)
Doña Rosita la soltera (García Lorca)
Doña Rosita the Spinster (García Lorca)
Donovans (Harrigan)
Don's Party (Williamson)

Don't Go Away Mad (Saroyan)
Don't Go Gentle (Inge)
Don't Make Me Laugh (Wood)
Don't Sell Mr Aesop (Reaney)
Don't Worry About Matilda (Delaney)
Don't You Want to Be Free? (Hughes)
Dood van Ulenspiegel (r Ghelderode)
Door Must Be Either Open or Shut (Musset)
Doorway (Brighouse)
Doppelgänger (r Dürrenmatt)
Dora (Reade)
Dora (Sardou)
Dora Kremer (Heijermans)
Dorf im Gebirge (Kotzebue)
Dorf ohne Männer (Horváth)
Doride (Gozzi)
Dorise (Hardy)
Dormez, je le veux! (Feydeau)
Dorotéia (Rodrigues)
Dorothea Angermann (Hauptmann)
Dorothea Merz (t Dorst)
Dos amantes del cielo (Calderón)
Dos curiosos impertinentes (Echegaray)
Dos fanatismos (Echegaray)
Dos viejos pánicos (Piñera)
Dossier de Rosafol (Labiche)
Dostigaeff and the Others (Gorky)
Dostigayev i drugiye (Gorky)
Dot (Boucicault)
Dou E yuan (Guan Hanqing)
Double Act (Ionesco)
Double Case History of Doctor Valmy (Buero Vallejo)
Double Cross (Kilroy)
Double-Dealer (Congreve)
Double, Double (Saunders)
Double Faces (Reade)
Double Gallant (Cibber)
Double Inconstance (Marivaux)
Double Inconstancy (Marivaux)
Double Infidelity (Marivaux)
Double Marriage (Fletcher, Massinger)
Double Marriage (Reade)
Doubtful Heir (Shirley)
Doubtful Paradise (Friel)
Dr. Getúlio, Sua Vida e Sua Glória (Gomes)
Doutor Ninguém (Gomes)
Douze Hommes en colère (Obey)
Dovere di medico (Pirandello)
Doves in a Cage (Jerrold)
Down Broadway (Harrigan)
Down Here and Up There (Leigh)
Down in Dixie (Harrigan)
Downchild (H. Barker)
Downstairs (Churchill)
Dowsing (Mamet)
Doyle Brothers (Harrigan)
Drachenoper (Müller)
Dragon and the Dove (Bridie)
Dragón de fuego (Benavente y Martínez)
Dragon (Gregory)
Dragon (Shvarts)
Dragonera (Díaz)
Dragon's Gift (Planché)
Dragon's Head (Valle-Inclán)
Dragon's Mouth (Priestley)
Dragons of Kent (Ringwood)
Drakon (Shvarts)

Drama at Home (Planché)
Drama at Inish (Robinson)
Drama of Civilization (Mackaye)
Drama's Levée (Planché)
Dramat post w moralnych (Różewicz)
Dramat rosbiezny (Różewicz)
Dramatists Get What They Want (Barrie)
Draussen vor der Tür (Borchert)
Draw the Fires! (Toller)
Drayman Henschel (Hauptmann)
Dream Girl (Rice)
Dream in Venice (Robertson)
Dream is Life (Grillparzer)
Dream of a Spring Morning (D'Annunzio)
Dream of an Autumn Sunset (D'Annunzio)
Dream on Monkey Mountain (Walcott)
Dream Physician (Martyn)
Dream Play (Strindberg)
Dream Weaver (Buero Vallejo)
Dreamers (Robinson)
Dreaming Dust (Johnston)
Dreaming of the Bones (Yeats)
Dreams (Boucicault)
Dreams (Robertson)
Dreams in an Empty City (Sewell)
Dreams of Leaving (t Hare)
Dreamy Kid (O'Neill)
Drei Reiherfedern (Sudermann)
Drei Väter auf einmal (Kotzebue)
Dreigroschenoper (Brecht)
Drifting Apart (Herne)
Drink (Reade)
Drinking Gourd (Hansberry)
Drive in June (Jones)
Driving Out a Devil (Brecht)
Droghe d'amore (Gozzi)
Droit de seigneur (Voltaire)
Drôlatiques, horrifiques et épouvantables aventures (Maillet)
Drömspel (Strindberg)
Drovers (Esson)
Drowning (Fornés)
Drugie danie (Mrożek)
Druid Circle (Van Druten)
Drum of the Waves of Horikawa (Chikamatsu)
Drumbeats in Georgia (Green)
Drummer (Fugard)
Drums and Colours (Walcott)
Drums Are Out (Coulter)
Drums in the Night (Brecht)
Drums of Father Ned (O'Casey)
Drunken Sisters (Wilder)
Du Vent dans les branches de sassafras (Obaldia)
Dublin Bay (Robertson)
Dublin Boy (Boucicault)
Dublin One (Leonard)
Duc d'Alençon (Voltaire)
Duc de Foix (Voltaire)
Duchess de la Vallière (Bulwer-Lytton)
Duchess of Malfi (Auden)
Duchess of Malfi (Brecht)
Duchess of Malfi (Webster)
Duchess of Padua (Wilde)
Duchesse de Langeais (Tremblay)
Duchesse des Folies-Bergères (Feydeau)
Duck Hunting (Vampilov)
Duck Song (Mercer)

Duck Variations (Mamet)
Duda (Echegaray)
Dudders (Romeril)
Due fratelli nimici (Gozzi)
Due gemelli Veneziani (Goldoni)
Due notti affannose (Gozzi)
Duel (Ionesco)
Duel of Angels (Fry)
Duel of Angels (Giraudoux)
Duelo (Santareno)
Duelos de amor y lealtad (Calderón)
Duendes (Hernández)
Duenna (Sheridan)
Dueño de las estrellas (Ruiz de Alarcón)
Duet in Floodlight (Priestley)
Duke and No Duke (Tate)
Duke and the Actress (Schnitzler)
Duke in Difficulties (Taylor)
Duke of Guise (Dryden, Lee)
Duke of Milan (Cumberland)
Duke of Milan (Massinger)
Duke's Mistress (Shirley)
Dukkehjem (Ibsen)
Dulcamara (Gilbert)
Dulcitius (Hrotsvitha)
Dulcy (Connelly, Kaufman)
Dultsinea Tobosskaya (Volodin)
Dumb Lady (Molière)
Dumb Waiter (Pinter)
D'Un Diable qui prêcha merveilles (Ghelderode)
Dunkirk Spirit (Edgar)
Dunnigan's Daughter (Behrman)
Duplex (Bullins)
Duplicity (Holcroft)
Duque de Viseo (Vega)
Duquesa gitana (Benavente y Martínez)
Dust in Your Eyes (Labiche)
Dutch Courtesan (Marston)
Dutch Lover (Behn)
Dutch Uncle (Gray)
Dutchman (Baraka)
Duvelor (Ghelderode)
Dux (Brighouse)
Dva klyon (Shvarts)
Dva okoshka (Petrushevskaya)
Dvaasedmdesátka (Langer)
Dvadsiata noc (Karvaš)
Dvadtsat minut s "angelom" (Vampilov)
Dve Braty (Lermontov)
Dvě noci s dívkou (Topol)
Dve strely (Volodin)
Dvě uši dvě svatby (Kundera)
Dvenadtsat molodtysev iz tabakerki (Ivanov)
Dvenadtsaty chas (Arbuzov)
Dwarfs (Pinter)
Dwarfs (r Pinter)
Dyadya Vanya (Chekhov)
Dybbuk (Ansky)
Dye-Hard (Brighouse)
Dying Breed (L. Wilson)
Dynamo (O'Neill)
Dynasts (Granville-Barker)
Dyscolos (Menander)
Dzidzibobo (Różewicz)
Dziewiecdziesiaty trzeci (Przybyszewska)

E Chernaya koshka v "temnoi komnate" (Petrushevskaya)

Each in His Own Way (Pirandello)
Eagle Has Landed (Edgar)
Eagle Has Two Heads (Cocteau)
Eaglet (Rostand)
Earl Birger of Bjälbo (Strindberg)
Early Days (Storey)
Early Morning (Bond)
Early Warnings (van Itallie)
Earth, Air, Fire, and Water Show (Romeril)
East (Berkoff)
East Indian (Kotzebue)
East of Suez (Maugham)
Easter (Strindberg)
Easter Egg (Reaney)
Eastward Ho! (Chapman, Jonson, Marston)
Easy Death (Churchill)
Easy Money (Ostrovsky)
Easy Virtue (Coward)
Eat at Joe's (Terry)
Eat Cake (van Itallie)
Eaux de Merlin (Lesage)
Eaux et fôrets (Duras)
Eccentric Lover (Cumberland)
Eccentricities of a Nightingale (Williams)
Ecclesiastes (r Edgar)
Ecclesiazusae (Aristophanes)
Échange (Claudel)
Échange (Voltaire)
Échéance du vendredi (t Dubé)
Échec et Mat (Dumas *père*)
Echten Sedemunds (Barlach)
Éclogue de Versailles (Quinault)
Eco y Narciso (Calderón)
École buissonnière (Labiche)
École des amants (Lesage)
École des Arthur (Labiche)
École des belles-mères (Brieux)
École des bouffons (Ghelderode)
École des femmes (Molière)
École des maris (Molière)
École des mères (Marivaux)
École des princes (Dumas *père*)
Écossaise (Voltaire)
Ecstasy (Leigh)
Ecstasy of Rita Joe (Ryga)
Ecuación (Díaz)
Écueil du sage (Voltaire)
Écureuil (Sardou)
Eden cinéma (Duras)
Eden End (Priestley)
Eden Rose (R. Anderson)
Edgard et sa bonne (Labiche)
Edipo rey (Triana)
Editor (Bjørnson)
Editor's Troubles (Harrigan)
Edle Lüge (Kotzebue)
Edmond (Mamet)
Edmund Kean (Dumas *père*)
Édouard et Agrippine (Obaldia)
Eduard in Schottland (Kotzebue)
Educating Rita (Shange)
Education of Skinny Spew (Brenton)
Edufa (Sutherland)
Edukationsrath (Kotzebue)
Edward II (Brecht)
Edward II (Adamov)
Edward: The Final Days (H. Barker)

Edward IV (Heywood)
Edward II (Marlowe)
Edwin (r Mortimer)
Eén mei (Heijermans)
Effet des rayons gamma sur les vieux-garçons (Tremblay)
Effet Glapion (Audiberti)
Effrontés (Augier)
Égi és földi szerelem (Molnár)
Egmont (Goethe)
Egmont (Schiller)
Ego (Heijermans)
Egotist and Pseudo-Critic, Herr Gottlieb Merks (Kotzebue)
Egotist (Hecht)
Egy, kettő, harom (Molnár)
Egy szakmai siker modellje (t Örkény)
Egylykke (Munk)
Eh Joe (t Beckett)
Ehe des Herrn Mississippi (Dürrenmatt)
Ehe des Herrn Mississippi (s Dürrenmatt)
Ehekomödie (Hasenclever)
Ehen werden im Himmel geschlossen (Hasenclever)
Ehre (Sudermann)
Eiche und Angora (Walser)
Eifersüchtige Frau (Kotzebue)
Eiffel Tower Wedding Party (Cocteau)
1863 (Byron)
Einen Jux will er sich machen (Nestroy)
Einfach kompliziert (Bernhard)
Eingebildete Kranke (Dorst)
Einsame Menschen (Hauptmann)
Einsame Weg (Schnitzler)
Einsilbige (Nestroy)
Eisenbahnheiraten (Nestroy)
Eisenhans (t Dorst)
Eiszeit (Dorst)
Ejercicios de terror (Sastre)
Elder Brother (Fletcher, Massinger)
Elder Son (Vampilov)
Elder Statesman (Eliot)
Eldest Son (Galsworthy)
Eldorado (Kaufman)
Elección de los alcaldes de Daganzo (Cervantes)
Elección por la virtud (Tirso De Molina)
Election (Cumberland)
Election of the Daganzo Aldermen (Cervantes)
Election of the Managers (Colman the Elder)
Electra (Euripides)
Electra (Hofmannsthal)
Electra (Sophocles)
Electra Garrigó (Piñera)
Electre (Giraudoux)
Electronic Nigger (Bullins)
Elefantkalb (Brecht)
Elegy for a Lady (Miller)
Elegy for Young Lovers (Auden)
Elektra (Hauptmann)
Elektra (Hofmannsthal)
Elephant Calf (Brecht)
Elephant Woman (Ludlam)
Elettricità sessuale (Marinetti)
Eleventh of June (O'Keeffe)
Elfie (Boucicault)
Elga (Hauptmann)
Elisabeth II (Bernhard)
Elizabeth (Crothers)
Elizabeth (Fo)
Elizabeth the Queen (M. Anderson)

Elle disait dormir pour mourir (Willems)
Elle est là (Sarraute)
Ellefte Juni (Holberg)
Elmer and Lily (Saroyan)
Elmerick (Lillo)
Elmire (Hardy)
Elojáték Lear királyhoz (Molnár)
Elopement (Jones)
Embargo (J. N. Barker)
Embassy (Planché)
Ember tragédiája (Madách)
Embers (r Beckett)
Embrassons-nous Folleville! (Labiche)
Embrujado (Valle-Inclán)
Embustes de Celauro (Vega)
Emerald City (Williamson)
Emigranci (Mrożek)
Emigrants (Mrożek)
Émile et une nuit (Barbeau)
Emilia Galotti (Lessing)
Emission de télévision (Vinaver)
Emmanuel à Joseph à Dâvit (Maillet)
Emma's Time (t Mercer)
Empeños de un acaso (Calderón)
Empeños de un engaño (Ruiz de Alarcón)
Emperor and the Galilean (Ibsen)
Emperor and the Witch (Hofmannsthal)
Emperor (Wilder)
Emperor Jones (O'Neill)
Emperor of the East (Massinger)
Emperor of the Moon (Behn)
Empire Builders (Vian)
Empress of Newfoundland (Wedekind)
En Attendant Godot (Beckett)
En Avant les Chinois (Labiche)
En el pilar y en la cruz (Echegaray)
En el seno de la muerte (Echegaray)
En esta vida todo es verdad y todo mentira (Calderón)
En este Madrid (Benavente y Martínez)
En la ardiente oscuridad (Buero Vallejo)
En la red (Sastre)
En Manches de chemise (Labiche)
En Pension chez son groom (Labiche)
En Pièces détachées (Tremblay)
Encanto de una hora (Benavente y Martínez)
Encanto sin encanto (Calderón)
Encantos de la culpa (Calderón)
Encantos de Medea (Silva)
Enchanted (Giraudoux)
Enchanted Cottage (Pinero)
Enchanted Horse (Taylor)
Enchanted Land (Fitzmaurice)
Enchanted Maze (Green)
Enchanted Night (Mrożek)
Enchanted Pig (Ludlam)
Enchanted Sea (Martyn)
Enchanted Wood (Byron)
Enchanteur Mirliton (Lesage)
Enclave (Laurents)
Encuentro (Usigli)
End (Edgar)
End of Me Old Cigar (Osborne)
End of Summer (Behrman)
End of the Beginning (O'Casey)
End of the Golden Weather (Mason)
End of the Row (Green)
End of the World (Kopit)

Endagsvarelser (Norén)
Endgame (Beckett)
Endimion (Lyly)
Endormie (Claudel)
Enea come oggi (Chiarelli)
Enemies (Gorky)
Enemies of a Bishop (Auden)
Enemy (Williams)
Enemy of the People (Ibsen)
Enemy of the People (Miller)
Enemy Within (Friel)
Eneo nel Lazi (Goldoni)
Enfance (Sarraute)
Enfant (Brieux)
Enfant de la maison (Labiche)
Enfant prodigue (Scribe)
Enfant prodigue (Voltaire)
Enfant-roi (Zola)
Enfants (Feydeau)
Engaged (Gilbert)
Enfant prodigue (Becque)
Engagements du hasard (T. Corneille)
Engel kommt nach Babylon (Dürrenmatt)
Engelbrekt (Strindberg)
Engländer (Lenz)
England's Ireland (Brenton, Edgar, Hare)
Englische Sender (r Kaiser)
Englischen Waren (Kotzebue)
English Cat (Bond)
English Gentleman (Byron)
English Lawyer (Ravenscroft)
English Merchant (Colman the Elder)
English Moor (Brome)
English Traveller (Heywood)
Englishman Abroad (Bennett)
Englishman Abroad (t Bennett)
Englishman in Paris (Foote)
Englishman Returned from Paris (Foote)
Engrenage (Brieux)
Engrenage (s Sartre)
Enjoy (Bennett)
Enlèvement (Becque)
Nnlutada (Benavente y Martínez)
Ennemi des modes (Pixérécourt)
Ennemie (Labiche)
Ennemis (Adamov)
Enough Stupidity in Every Wise Man (Ostrovsky)
Enquire Within (Boucicault)
Enquiry Office (Tardieu)
Enragés (Lesage)
Enrico VIII (Chiarelli)
Enrico IV (Pirandello)
Enrico, Re di Sicilia (Goldoni)
Entdeckung im Posthaus (Kotzebue)
Entertainer (Osborne)
Entertaining Mr. Sloane (Orton)
Entertaining Strangers (Edgar)
Entertainment at the Blackfriars (Jonson)
Entertainment of King James and Queen Anne at
   Theobalds (Jonson)
Entertainment of the Queen and Prince at Althorp (Jonson)
Entertainment of the Senses (Auden)
Entertainment of the Two Kings of Great Britain and
   Denmark at Theobalds (Jonson)
Entfesselte Wotan (Toller)
Entfesselte Zeitgenosse (Sternheim)
Entführungen (Lenz)

Entgötterte Welt (Sudermann)
Entlarvte Fromme (Kotzebue)
Entr'acte (Maillet)
Entre pícaros (Díaz)
Entremés del mancebo que se casó con mujer brava
   (Casona)
Entretenida (Cervantes)
Entscheidung (Hasenclever)
Entscheidungen (Kipphardt)
Envers d'une conspiration (Dumas père)
Envieux (Voltaire)
Envy (Albee)
Eoghan's Wife (Colum)
Eona (Prevelakis)
Eos Pote (Kazantzakis)
Épée (Hugo)
Ephesian Matron (Bickerstaff)
Epicheskiye dramy (Tretyakov)
Epicoene (Colman the Elder)
Epicoene (Jonson)
Epidicus (Plautus)
Epigramm (Kotzebue)
Epilogo (Pirandello)
Epilogue (Leigh)
Epimenides Erwachen (Goethe)
Épisode de la vie d'un auteur (Anouilh)
Episode in the Life of an Author (Anouilh)
Episode on an Autumn Evening (Dürrenmatt)
Epitaph for George Dillon (Osborne)
Epitaph under Ether (Murphy)
Epitrepontes (Menander)
Épouvantail (Tardieu)
Épreuve (Marivaux)
Epsom Downs (Brenton)
Epsom Wells (Shadwell)
Équarrissage pour tous (Vian)
Équation à deux inconnus (Dubé)
Equites (Aristophanes)
Equus (Shaffer)
Er treibt den Teufel aus (Brecht)
Erasmus Montanus (Holberg)
Erbschaft (Kotzebue)
Erbschleicher (Nestroy)
Erdgeist (Wedekind)
Erede di Shylock (De Filippo)
Erede fortunata (Goldoni)
Ereignisse im Gasthofe (Nestroy)
Eremit auf Formentara (Kotzebue)
Erik XIV (Strindberg)
Erik XIV (Vian)
Ériphile (Voltaire)
Ermesinda (Carballido)
Ermine (Anouilh)
Erminie (Connelly)
Ermittlung (Weiss)
Ernestine (Robertson)
Ernie's Incredible Illucinations (Ayckbourn)
Ernie's Incredible Illucinations (t Ayckbourn)
Eröffnung des indischen Zeitalters (Hacks)
Erpingham Camp (Orton)
Errore necessario (Chiarelli)
Erste (Goering)
Erwin und Elmire (Goethe)
Es Geschah am hellichten Tag (s Dürrenmatt)
Es lebe das Leben (Sudermann)
Es steht geschrieben (Dürrenmatt)
Esami non finiscono mai (De Filippo)

Esca (Hugo)
Escada (Andrade)
Escalinata de un trono (Echegaray)
Escándalo en Puerto Santo (Hernández)
Escape (Brieux)
Escape (Galsworthy)
Escape from Happiness (Walker)
Escapes (Holcroft)
Escapes of Jupiter (Heywood)
Escarmientos para el cuerdo (Tirso De Molina)
Escenas de un grotesco (Arlt)
Escondido y la tapada (Calderón)
Escribo, por ejemplo (Carballido)
Escuadra hacia la muerte (Sastre)
Escuela de las princesas (Benavente y Martínez)
Escuela de maridos (Fernández de Moratín)
Escurial (Ghelderode)
Esels Schatten (Kotzebue)
Esmeralda (Byron)
Esméralda (Hugo)
Esopaida (Silva)
Espagnolas et boyardinos (Labiche)
Espantajo (Díaz)
Espejo de grandes (Benavente y Martínez)
Espera trágica (Pavlovsky)
Espérance (Lesage)
Espigas de Ruth (Calderón)
Esplendor carnal de la ceniza (Díaz)
Esposa del vengador (Echegaray)
Esprits (Camus)
Essere (Chiarelli)
Estado de secreto (Usigli)
Estatua de Prometeo (Calderón)
Estatuas de marfil (Carballido)
Esther (Grillparzer)
Esther (Hasenclever)
Esther (Hochwälder)
Esther (Hughes)
Esther (Racine)
Estigma (Echegaray)
Estivants (Vinaver)
Esto sí que es negociar (Tirso De Molina)
Estrella de Sevilla (Vega)
Estudias o trabajas? (Díaz)
Estudio en blanco y negro (Piñera)
Et à la Fin était le bang (Obaldia)
Et caetera (Barbeau)
Et ils passèrent des menottes aux fleurs (Arrabal)
Et les chiens se taisaient (Césaire)
Et Mademoiselle Roberge boit un peu (Tremblay)
État de siège (Camus)
Été s'appelle Julie (Dubé)
Éternel Retour (s Cocteau)
Étoile du nord (Scribe)
Étourdi (Molière)
Étrangère (Dumas *fils*)
Eugen (Dorst)
Eugénie (Beaumarchais)
Eugénie (Boucicault)
Eulenspiegel (Kotzebue)
Eulenspiegel (Nestroy)
Eumenides (Aeschylus)
Euménides (Claudel)
Euménides (Obey)
Eunuch (Terence)
Eunuch (Zuckmayer)
Eunuchs of the Forbidden City (Ludlam)

Eunuchus (Terence)
Eureka (Harrigan)
Europa (Kaiser)
Europeans (H. Barker)
Eurydice (Anouilh)
Eurydice (Byron)
Eurydice (Fielding)
Eurydice Hissed (Fielding)
Eux seuls le savent (Tardieu)
Éva (Dumas *fils*)
Eva Bonheur (Heijermans)
Éva et Évelyne (Laberge)
Évangéline Deusse (Maillet)
Evangeline the Second (Maillet)
Evangelist (Jones)
Évasion (Brieux)
Eve of Execution (Díaz)
Eve of Retirement (Bernhard)
Eve of St. Mark (M. Anderson)
Evelyn Brown (Fornés)
Even a Wise Man Stumbles (Ostrovsky)
Even Baseless Jealousy Can Kill (Calderón)
Even the Wise Can Err (Ostrovsky)
Evening Clothes (Gale)
Evening in Sorrento (Turgenev)
Evening Lament (Ghelderode)
Evening Light (Arbuzov)
Evening Paper (Mason)
Evening with Dead Essex (Kennedy)
Evening's Love (Dryden)
Events Following the Closure of a Motorcycle Factory
    (Edgar)
Events While Guarding the Bofors Gun (McGrath)
Ever Been in Love with a Midget (Saroyan)
Ever Since Paradise (Priestley)
Ever the Twain (Robinson)
Every Good Boy Deserves Favour (Stoppard)
Every Man in His Humour (Jonson)
Every Man Out of His Humour (Jonson)
Every One Has His Fault (Inchbald)
Everybody Wins (s Miller)
Everyday (Crothers)
Everything in the Garden (Albee)
Everywhere I Roam (Connelly)
Evil Doers of Good (Benavente y Martínez)
Evil Kettle (Dunsany)
Ewalds Død (Munk)
Ewig Männliche (Sudermann)
Exaltación de la cruz (Calderón)
Examen de maridos (Ruiz de Alarcón)
Example (Shirley)
Exception and the Rule (Brecht)
Exchange (Frayn)
Excomungado (Santareno)
Excuses, Excuses (Edgar)
Exécution (Becque)
Execution (Petrushevskaya)
Exercises de conversation et diction françaises pour
    étudiants américains (Ionesco)
Exhibit C (Brighouse)
Exhortation to War (Vicente)
Exil (Montherlant)
Exiled (Galsworthy)
Exiled Princess (Brighouse)
Exilés (Sardou)
Exit the King (Ionesco)
Ex-Miss Copper Queen on a Set of Pills (Terry)

Exorcism (O'Neill)
Exortação da Guerra (Vicente)
Experiment (Bergman)
Experiment Damokles (Karvaš)
Experimental Death Unit #1 (Baraka)
Explorer (Maugham)
Exposición (Usigli)
Exposition des produits de la République (Labiche)
Expressing Willie (Crothers)
Exquisite Torture (Ludlam)
Exterior (Rice)
Extra Dry (Chiarelli)
Extravagant Shepherd (T. Corneille)
Extravagante Réussite de Jésus-Christ (Arrabal)
Eyes and No Eyes (Gilbert)
Eyes on the Harem (Fornés)

Fable (van Itallie)
Fablilla del secreto bien guardado (Casona)
Fabricante de fantasmas (Arlt)
Fabrichnaya devchonka (Volodin)
Fabulazioni della resistenza (Fo)
Fabulazzo osceno (Fo)
Fabulous Invalid (Kaufman)
Fabulous Miss Marie (Bullins)
Face (r Laurents)
Faceache (H. Barker)
Faces of Brass (Augier)
Facheux (Molière)
Facing Death (Strindberg)
Factory Girl (Jerrold)
Fadren (Strindberg)
Fahrt mit dem Dampfwagen (Nestroy)
Faint Heart Ne'er Won Fair Lady (Planché)
Faint Perfume (Gale)
Fair Favourite (Davenant)
Fair Gabrielle (Planché)
Fair Ladies at a Game of Poem-Cards (Chikamatsu)
Fair Maid of the Inn (Fletcher, Massinger)
Fair Maid of the West I–II (Heywood)
Fair One with the Golden Locks (Planché)
Fair Penitent (Rowe)
Fair Quarrel (Middleton)
Fair Slaughter (H. Barker)
Fairy Fingers (Scribe)
Fairy Gold (Ostrovsky)
Fairy Prince (Colman the Elder)
Fairy Star (Boucicault)
Fairy Tale (Colman the Elder)
Fairy's Dilemma (Gilbert)
Faith Healer (Friel)
Faith Healer (Moody)
Faith, Hope and Charity (Hampton)
Faith, Hope and Charity (Horváth)
Faith of Our Fathers (Green)
Faithful Servant of His Master (Grillparzer)
Faithful Shepherdess (Fletcher)
Falar Verdade a Mentir (Garrett)
Falecida (Rodrigues)
Fall (Saunders)
Fall and Repentance of Mary (Hrotsvitha)
Fall des Schülers Vehgesack (Kaiser)
Fall In Rookies! (Jones)
Fall of the House of Usher (Berkoff)
Fallen Angels (Coward)
Fallen Fairies (Gilbert)
Fallen Leaves (Kishida)

Fallit (Bjørnson)
Falsa alarma (Piñera)
Falsche Bewegung (s Handke)
False Admissions (Wertenbaker)
False Confessions (Marivaux)
False Count (Behn)
False Demetrius (Cumberland)
False Friend (Vanbrugh)
False Gods (Brieux)
False Impressions (Cumberland)
False One (Fletcher, Massinger)
False Scham (Kotzebue)
False Servant (Marivaux)
False Shame (Dunlap)
False Shame (Kotzebue)
False Step (Augier)
Falso drama (Usigli)
Falu rossza (Örkény)
Fam and Yam (Albee)
Fame (Miller)
Fame and the Poet (Dunsany)
Fame Comes Late (Dunsany)
Famiglia dell'Antiquario (Goldoni)
Familia cena en casa (Usigli)
Familie Schroffenstein (Kleist)
Familien Zwirn (Nestroy)
Familjens renhet (Bergman)
Famille Benoîton (Sardou)
Famille de l'horloger (Labiche)
Famille Lavolette (Brieux)
Family Album (Coward)
Family Charge (Turgenev)
Family Circles (Ayckbourn)
Family Continues (L. Wilson)
Family Man (Galsworthy)
Family of Love (Middleton)
Family Party (Colman the Younger)
Family Portrait (Coulter)
Family Reunion (Eliot)
Family Strife in Hapsburg (Grillparzer)
Family Talk (Terry)
Family Trappings (Pollock)
Family Voices (Pinter)
Family Voices (r Pinter)
Family Way (Leonard)
Famine (Murphy)
Fan (Goldoni)
Fanal de Messine (Pixérécourt)
Fanchon das Leiermädchen (Kotzebue)
Fancies, Chaste and Noble (Ford)
Fanciullo sconosciuto (Fabbri)
Fancy Free (Houghton)
Fancy Meeting You Again (Kaufman)
Fancy's Sketch (Planché)
Fanda et Lis (Arrabal)
Fanfari rapito (Fo)
Fanlights (Marqués)
Fanny (Behrman)
Fanny Otcott (Wilder)
Fanny's Consent (Fernández de Moratín)
Fanny's First Play (Shaw)
Fanshen (Hare)
Fantasio (Musset)
Fantasticks (Rostand)
Fantastiques (Maillet)
Fantoches (Solórzano)
Fantôme amoureux (Quinault)

Ferro (D'Annunzio)
Fest für Boris (Bernhard)
Festin de Pierre (T. Corneille)
Festino (Goldoni)
Festspiel in deutschen Reimen (Hauptmann)
Fête du cordonnier (Vinaver)
Fête noire (Audiberti)
Fêtes de l'amour et de Bacchus (Quinault)
Feu de cheminée (Labiche)
Feu la mère de Madame (Feydeau)
Feud (M. Anderson)
Feud of the Schroffensteins (Kleist)
Feudal Times (Colman the Younger)
Feudatario (Goldoni)
Feuer aus den Kesseln (Toller)
Feuerprobe (Kotzebue)
Fiaccola sotto il moggio (D'Annunzio)
Fiançailles (Maeterlinck)
Fiancée du bon coin (Labiche)
Fiancés de Loches (Feydeau)
Fiancés du Havre (Salacrou)
Fiancés en herbe (Feydeau)
Fianza satisfecha (Vega)
Fiddler's House (Colum)
Fidelio (Arden)
Fidlavačka (Tyl)
Field (Keane)
Field God (Green)
Field of Ermine (Benavente y Martínez)
Fields of Heaven (Hewett)
Fiera, el rayo y la piedra (Calderón)
Fieras afemina amor (Calderón)
Fiesco (Planché)
Fiesco (Schiller)
Fiesque de Lavagne (Dumas père)
Fiesta del hierro (Arlt)
Fiesta (Vian)
Fieste del mulato (Hernández)
Fifteen Million Fifteen-Year-Olds (Terry)
Fifteen Minute Hamlet (Stoppard)
Fifteen Years of a Drunkard's Life! (Jerrold)
Fifth Commandment (Houghton)
5th of July (L. Wilson)
Figaro Gets a Divorce (Horváth)
Figaro lässt sich scheiden (Horváth)
Fight for Barbara (Lawrence)
Fighting Cock (Anouilh)
Fighting the Waves (Yeats)
Figli d'arte (Fabbri)
Figli del Marchese Arturo (Giacosa)
Figlia dell'aria (Gozzi)
Figlia di Iorio (D'Annunzio)
Figlia obbediente (Goldoni)
Figlio d'Arlecchino perduto e ritrovato (Goldoni)
figlio di Pulcinella (De Filippo)
Figure of Fun (Colman the Younger)
Figuro in the Night (O'Casey)
Fil à la patte (Feydeau)
Filandre (Rotrou)
Filántropo (Piñera)
Filipa de Vilhena (Garrett)
Filippo (Alfieri)
Fill the Stage with Happy Hours (Wood)
Fille bien gardée (Labiche)
Fille de Duramé (Brieux)
Fille de l'exilé (Pixérécourt)
Fille de Mme. Angot (Byron)

Fille de Tabarin (Sardou)
Fille du régent (Dumas père)
Fille pour le vent (Obey)
Filles errantes (Regnard)
Filleul de Pompignac (Dumas fils)
Film (s Beckett)
Film Crew (Mamet)
Film d'art et d'aventures (Tardieu)
Filmen om Christiern den Anden (s Munk)
Filo (Giacosa)
Filosofo (Aretino)
Filosofo inglese (Goldoni)
Fils de Giboyer (Augier)
Fils de l'émigré (Dumas père)
Fils de personne (Montherlant)
Fils du brigadier (Labiche)
Fils naturel (Dumas fils)
Fils supposé (Scudéry)
Filth Hunt (Rudkin)
Filthy Rich (Walker)
Filumena Marturano (De Filippo)
Fin de partie (Beckett)
Fin de Siegfried (Giraudoux)
Fin Mot (Labiche)
Final de un idilio (Carballido)
Find Me (t Mercer)
Findling (Barlach)
Fine Coloured Easter Egg (Ringwood)
Fine Feathers (Byron)
Fine Wagon (Green)
Finestrina (Alfieri)
Fineza contra fineza (Calderón)
Fingida Arcadia (Tirso De Molina)
Fink und Fliederbusch (Schnitzler)
Finn Maccoul (Boucicault)
Finnegans Wake (Johnston)
Finsternisse (Hauptmann)
Finta ammalata (Goldoni)
Fiorella (Sardou)
Fiori del dolore (Fabbri)
Fiorina (Ruzante)
Fire-Bringer (Moody)
Fire in the Opera House (Kaiser)
Fire Raisers (Frisch)
Firebugs (Frisch)
Fired (Edgar)
Fireworks (Terry)
Firmeza en la hermosura (Tirso De Molina)
First Aid (Shiels)
First and Last (t Frayn)
First and the Last (Galsworthy)
First Brutus (Alfieri)
First Campaign (Planché)
First Course (Ayckbourn)
First Day's Entertainment at Rutland House (Davenant)
First Distiller (L. N. Tolstoy)
First Episode (Rattigan)
First Flight (M. Anderson)
First Lady (Kaufman)
First Love (Cumberland)
First Love (Fuller)
First Man (O'Neill)
First Printer (Reade, Taylor)
First, the Last, and the Middle (Horovitz)
First Warning (Strindberg)
Firstborn (Fry)
Fische (Hacks)

Fischerin (Goethe)
Fischzug (Brecht)
Fish in the Sea (McGrath)
Fisherman's Revenge (Cook)
Fit to Be Tried (Feydeau)
Fitting for Ladies (Feydeau)
Five Finger Exercise (Shaffer)
Five Minutes Too Late (Colman the Younger)
Five Unrelated Pices (Mamet)
Fixin's (Green)
Flaco y el gordo (Piñera)
Flag is Born (Hecht)
Flamingo Red (Wilder)
Flaminius à Corinthe (Pixérécourt)
Flare Path (Rattigan)
Flash of Lightning (Daly)
Flat in Afghanistan (Terry)
Flea in Her Ear (Feydeau)
Flea in Her Ear (Mortimer)
Fledermaus (Ludlam)
Fledermaus (Mortimer)
Flies (Sartre)
Flight (Bulgakov)
Flight into Egypt (Wilder)
Flight of the Queen (Dunsany)
Flight to the West (Rice)
Flight to Venice (Kaiser)
Flint (Mercer)
Floating World (Romeril)
Flood (Barlach)
Flood (Grass)
Floorshow (Churchill)
Flora and the Bandits (Jellicoe)
Florence (Childress)
Florence (Dubé)
Florence (t Dubé)
Florentine Tragedy (Wilde)
Floresta de Enganos (Vicente)
Florian Geyer (Hauptmann)
Florimonde (Rotrou)
Florindo und die Unbekannte (Hofmannsthal)
Floss der Medusa (Kaiser)
Flowering Cherry (Bolt)
Flowering Peach (Odets)
Flowers of the Forest (Van Druten)
Flowers of Virtue (Connelly)
Flüchtling (Hochwälder)
Flüchtling (Nestroy)
Fluch des Römers (Kotzebue)
Flucht nach Venedig (Kaiser)
Flussgott Niemen und Noch-Jemand (Kotzebue)
Flutter of Wings (Murray)
Flying Dutchman (Dunlap)
Flying Dutchman (Jerrold)
Flying Scud (Boucicault)
Första varningen (Strindberg)
Fog (O'Neill)
Foggerty's Fairy (Gilbert)
Foi (Brieux)
Foire de Guibray (Lesage)
Foire d'empoigne (Anouilh)
Foire des fées (Lesage)
Foire Saint-Germain (Regnard)
Foleys (Colum)
Folie d'Hugo van der Goes (r Ghelderode)
Folies amoureuses (Regnard)
Folkefiende (Ibsen)

Folkungasagen (Strindberg)
Folle de Chaillot (Giraudoux)
Folle Journée; ou, Le Mariage de Figaro (Beaumarchais)
Follia dell'oro (Chiarelli)
Follies of a Day (Holcroft)
Follies of a Night (Planché)
Folline (Daly)
Follow My Leader (Rattigan)
Follow the Girl (Connelly)
Followers (Brighouse)
Folly or Saintliness (Echegaray)
Fonda de las siete cabrillas (Carballido)
Fontainebleau (O'Keeffe)
Fontane Effi Briest (s Fassbinder)
Food (Mamet)
Food for the Millions (Tawfiq al-Hakim)
Fool (Bond)
Fool and His Money (Byron)
Fool for Love (Shepard)
Foolish Notion (Barry)
Fools (Simon)
Fool's Errand (Mackaye)
Fool's Revenge (Taylor)
Footfalls (Beckett)
For All Those Who Get Despondent (Barnes)
Før Cannae (Munk)
For Colored Girls . . . (Shange)
For Love (Robertson)
For Love of the King (Wilde)
For Services Rendered (Maugham)
For Tea on Sunday (t Mercer)
For the Defense (Rice)
For the Honour of Wales (Jonson)
Forbidden Fruit (Boucicault)
Force de l'amour (Lesage)
Force du sang (Hardy)
Force of Calumny (Dunlap)
Force of Calumny (Kotzebue)
Force of Habit (Bernhard)
Force of Ridicule (Holcroft)
Forced Marriage (Behn)
Forced Marriage (Molière)
Fordringsägare (Strindberg)
Foreigner (Dumas *fils*)
Forensic and the Navigators (Shepard)
Foreskin's Lament (McGee)
Forest (Galsworthy)
Forest (Ostrovsky)
Forest of Bondy (Pixérécourt)
Foresters (Daly)
Forestiers (Dumas *père*)
Forêt de Dodôre (Lesage)
Forêt de Sicilie (Pixérécourt)
Forêt mouillée (Hugo)
Forever Yours, Marie-Lou (Tremblay)
Forfeits (M. Anderson)
Forge des châtaigniers (Labiche)
Forget Him (Fierstein)
Forget Me Not (Robinson)
Forget-Me-Not Lane (Nichols)
Foriwa (Sutherland)
Form (Simpson)
Former One-on-One Basketball Champion (Horovitz)
Formosa (Boucicault)
Forrigan Reel (Bridie)
Fort Field (Shiels)
Forteresse de Danube (Pixérécourt)

Fortuna con l'effe maiuscola (De Filippo)
Fortuna in cerca di tasche (De Filippo)
Fortunas de Andrómeda y Perseo (Calderón)
Fortunat (Tieck)
Fortunate Isles (Planché)
Fortunato (Granville-Barker)
Fortune by Land and Sea (Heywood)
Fortune Hunter (Gilbert)
Fortune Mends (Calderón)
Fortunio and His Seven Gifted Servants (Planché)
49ers (Connelly, Kaufman)
Forty Thieves (Colman the Younger)
Forty Years On (Bennett)
Forvandlede Brudgrom (Holberg)
Fosgatókönyv (s Örkény)
Fossie for Short (Brighouse)
Fossil (Sternheim)
Foster Sisters (Robertson)
Foter und Zon (Ansky)
Fotografía en la playa (Carballido)
Foul Play (Boucicault, Reade)
Foundation (Buero Vallejo)
Foundations (Galsworthy)
Founders (Green)
Fountain (O'Neill)
Fountain of Self-Love (Jonson)
Fountainville Abbey (Dunlap)
4 A.M. (Mamet)
4-H Club (Shepard)
Four Portraits—of Mothers (Wesker)
Four Prentices of London (Heywood)
Four Seasons (Wesker)
Fourberies de Scapin (Molière)
Fourchambault (Augier)
Fourmi dans le corps (Audiberti)
Foursome (Ionesco)
Fourteen Days (Byron)
Fourteen Hundred Thousand (Shepard)
Fourth for Bridge (Johnston)
Fox and the Goose (Boucicault)
Fox Chase (Boucicault)
Fox Hunt (Boucicault)
Fra Diavolo (Scribe)
Fra Diavolo Travestie (Byron)
Fragment de Théâtre (Beckett)
Fragment of the Tragedy of Robert Guiscard (Kleist)
Frágoa de Amor (Vicente)
Frailty and Hypocrisy (Beaumarchais)
Frame all-dress (Barbeau)
Frana allo scalo Nord (Betti)
Française (Brieux)
Francesca da Rimini (Boker)
Francesca da Rimini (D'Annunzio)
Francillon (Dumas *fils*)
François Bigot (Coulter)
Francophile (Friel)
Frank V (Dürrenmatt)
Franklin (Walcott)
Franklin and the King (Green)
Franziska (Wedekind)
Französischen Kleinstädter (Kotzebue)
Fratello d'armi (Giacosa)
Fraternal Discord (Dunlap)
Fraternal Discord (Kotzebue)
Frau im Fenster (Hofmannsthal)
Frau mit dem Dolche (Schnitzler)
Frau ohne Schatten (Hofmannsthal)

Frauenopfer (Kaiser)
Fräulein Julie (Weiss)
Freaks (Pinero)
Fredegunde (Hacks)
Frédérick Lemaitre (Fitch)
Fredlöse (Strindberg)
Free and Clear (R. Anderson)
Freedom of the City (Friel)
Freedom's Plow (r Hughes)
Freeway (Nichols)
Frégonde (Hardy)
Frei Luís de Sousa (Garrett)
Freiheit für Clemens (Dorst)
Freiheit in Krähwinkel (Nestroy)
Freimaurer (Kotzebue)
Freischutz (Byron)
Freischütz (Jellicoe)
Freischütz (Planché)
Freiwild (Schnitzler)
Fremdenführerin (Strauss)
Fremde Mädchen (Hofmannsthal)
French Lieutenant's Woman (s Pinter)
French Without Tears (Rattigan)
Frénétiques (Salacrou)
Frenzy for Two (Ionesco)
Frères corses (Dumas *père*)
Frères ennemis (Dubé)
Freud Scenario (s Sartre)
Freunde machen den Philosophen (Lenz)
Freundin (Sudermann)
Freygeist (Lessing)
Friar Bacon (O'Keeffe)
Friar Bacon and Friar Bungay (Greene)
Friday (Claus)
Friday's Hiding (Arden)
Fridolinades (Gelinas)
Fridolinons (Gelinas)
Frieden (Hacks)
Friedenfest (Hauptmann)
Friedrich, Prinz von Korsika (Nestroy)
Friedrich und Anna (Kaiser)
Friend at Court (Planché)
Friendly King (Brighouse)
Friends (Wesker)
Friends at Court (Taylor)
Friends or Foes? (Sardou)
Friendship in Fashion (Otway)
Frisette (Labiche)
Frisky Mrs. Johnson (Fitch)
Frist (Dürrenmatt)
Fritzchen (Sudermann)
Frog Prince (Mamet)
Frogs (Aristophanes)
Fröhliche Weinberg (Zuckmayer)
Fröken Julie (Strindberg)
Frolique (Byron)
From an Abandoned Work (Beckett)
From an Odets Kitchen (van Itallie)
From Bad to Worse (Calderón)
From Morn to Midnight (Kaiser)
From Morning to Midnight (Kaiser)
From Okra to Greens (Shange)
From Zia, with Love (Soyinka)
Front Page (Hecht)
Front Porch (Hughes)
Front Room Boys (Buzo)
Frontière de Savoie (Scribe)

Frontiers of Farce (Barnes)
Frost at Midnight (Obey)
Frosted Glass Coffin (Williams)
Frou-Frou (Daly)
Frozen Lake (Planché)
Fru Inger til Østråt (Ibsen)
Fru Vendlas kedja (Bergman)
Fruen fra havet (Ibsen)
Frühere Verhältnisse (Nestroy)
Frühlings Erwachen (Wedekind)
Fruit (Brenton)
Fruits of Culture (L. N. Tolstoy)
Fruits of Enlightenment (Frayn)
Fruits of Enlightenment (L. N. Tolstoy)
Fruktansvärd lycka (Norén)
Frutos caídos (Hernández)
Fünf Köche (Grass)
Fürstliche Wildfang (Kotzebue)
Fuego de Dios en el querer bien (Calderón)
Fuenteovejuna (Vega)
Fuerza bruta (Benavente y Martínez)
Fuerza bruta (Benavente y Martínez)
Fuerza de arrastrarse (Echegaray)
Fuggitiva (Betti)
Fugitive (Betti)
Fugitive (Galsworthy)
Fugitive (O'Keeffe)
Fugitive (Tagore)
Fugitive Kind (Williams)
Fugitive Kind (s Williams)
Fugitivos (Usigli)
Fugl Fønix (Munk)
Fugue in a Nursery (Fierstein)
Fuhrmann Henschel (Hauptmann)
Full Circle (Clark)
Full Moon (Gregory)
Full Moon in March (Yeats)
Fulling Block (Zeami)
Fumed Oak (Coward)
Fun to Be Free (Hecht)
Función de despedida (Usigli)
Fundación (Buero Vallejo)
Funérailles de la foire (Lesage)
Funeral (Steele)
Funeral Games (t Orton)
Funk-Hole (Brighouse)
Funny Old Man (Różewicz)
Funnyhouse of a Negro (Kennedy)
Fuochi d'artificio (Chiarelli)
Furcht und Elend des Dritten Reiches (Brecht)
Furcht und Hoffnung der BRD (Kroetz)
Furies (Ringwood)
Furio Omocha (Kishida)
Fūrō (Kinoshita)
Fursteslickaren (Norén)
Fussy Man (Holberg)
Futari no onna (Kara)
Future is in Eggs (Ionesco)
Future Soap (Terry)
Fuyu no jidai (Kinoshita)
Fuzoku jihyo (Kishida)
40-tal (Dagerman)

Gabriel Lambert (Dumas *père*)
Gabriel Schilling's Flight (Hauptmann)
Gabriel Schillings Flucht (Hauptmann)
Gabrielle (Augier)

Gadfly (Shaw)
Gaie spose di Windsor (Chiarelli)
Gaiety Gulliver (Byron)
Galán de la membrilla (Vega)
Galán fantasma (Calderón)
Galant doublé (T. Corneille)
Galanteries du Duc d'Ossonne (Mairet)
Galas (Ludlam)
Galas del difunto (Valle-Inclán)
Galatag in Krähwinkel (Kotzebue)
Galathea (Lyly)
Galerie (Tardieu)
Galerie du Palais (P. Corneille)
Galileo (Brecht)
Gallant Cassian (Schnitzler)
Gallantee Showman (Jerrold)
Gallardo español (Cervantes)
Gallega Mari-Hernández (Tirso De Molina)
Gallicanus (Hrotsvitha)
Gallipoli (s Williamson)
Gallows Humor (Richardson)
Gambler (Betti)
Gamblers (Gogol)
Gamblers (Stoppard)
Game (Brighouse)
Game at Chess (Middleton)
Game of Adam and Eve (Bullins)
Game of Golf (Ayckbourn)
Game of Hearts (Molnár)
Game of Love and Chance (Marivaux)
Games (Saunders)
Game's a Bogey (McGrath)
Gamester (Centlivre)
Gamester (Shirley)
Ganaches (Sardou)
Ganar amigos (Ruiz de Alarcón)
Ganarse la vida (Benavente y Martínez)
Gang zum Weiher (Schnitzler)
Gangsters (Edgar)
Gant rouge (Rostand)
Gapi et Sullivan (Maillet)
Garage Sale (Ringwood)
Garantie dix ans (Labiche)
Garbus (Mrożek)
Garçon de chez Véry (Labiche)
Garde-Forestier (Dumas *père*)
Garde Nationale (Boucicault)
Garden (Wood)
Garden Party (r Behan)
Garden Party (Havel)
Garden Party (Jones)
Gardener's Dog (Vega)
Gardenia (Guare)
Gargantua (Brenton)
Garibaldi (Taylor)
Garibaldi Excursionists (Byron)
Garigari hakase no hanzai (Terayama)
Garrick Fever (Planché)
Garrochés en Paradis (Maillet)
Gars (Barbeau)
Gars de Québec (Tremblay)
Garside's Career (Brighouse)
Gärtner von Toulouse (Kaiser)
Gas I–II (Kaiser)
Gastronome sans argent (Scribe)
Gata de Angora (Benavente y Martínez)
Gates of Summer (Whiting)

Gather Ye Rosebuds (Howard)
Gats (Kaiser)
Gaudeamus (Andreyev)
Gauntlet (Bjørnson)
Gay Deceivers (Colman the Younger)
Gay Lord Quex (Pinero)
Gay White Way (Rice)
Gayden Chronicles (Cook)
Gde tonko, tam i rvetsya (Turgenev)
Gebildeter Hausknecht (Nestroy)
Gefährliche Nachbarschaft (Kotzebue)
Gefährtin (Schnitzler)
Gefangene (Kotzebue)
Gefesselte Phantasie (Raimund)
Gefühlvolle Kerkermeister (Nestroy)
Gegen Torheit gibt es keine Mittel (Nestroy)
Gegner den Daumen aufs Auge und das Knie auf die Brust (Dorst)
Geist der Antike (Kaiser)
Geisterbahn (Kroetz)
Geizige (Dorst)
Geizige (Sternheim)
Gelieven (Claus)
Geloso avaro (Goldoni)
Gemini (Kopit)
Gendarme (Chiarelli)
Gendre de M. Poirier (Augier)
Gendre en surveillance (Labiche)
Général inconnu (Obaldia)
Generalet (Díaz)
General's Tea Party (Vian)
Generations (Pollock)
Généreuse Ingratitude (Quinault)
Generous Tar (O'Keeffe)
Genesis (Reaney)
Génesis fue mañana (Díaz)
Geneva (Shaw)
Genevieve (Boucicault)
Gengangere (Ibsen)
Genius (Brenton)
Genius of Nonsense (Colman the Elder)
Genius, Schuster und Marqueur (Nestroy)
Gennariniello (De Filippo)
Genom öknar till arvland (Strindberg)
Génousie (Obaldia)
Genoveva (Hebbel)
Gens nerveux (Sardou)
Gente conocida (Benavente y Martínez)
Gente di spirito (Giacosa)
Gentilhomme de la montagne (Dumas *père*)
Gentle Island (Friel)
Gentle Jack (Bolt)
Gentleman Caller (Bullins)
Gentleman Dancing-Master (Wycherley)
Gentleman in Black (Gilbert)
Gentleman of Olmedo (Vega)
Gentleman of Venice (Shirley)
Gentleman Usher (Chapman)
Gentleness and Nobility (Rastell)
Gentlewoman (Lawson)
Genuine Grub Street Opera (Fielding)
Genuine Sedemunds (Barlach)
Genussmensch (Wedekind)
Geografi og kjaerlighed (Bjørnson)
Geography Match (Reaney)
Geography of a Horse Dreamer (Shepard)
Geôle (Barbeau)

Geôlier de soi-même (T. Corneille)
Georg Faust (Claus)
George à Greene, the Pinner of Wakefield (Greene)
George Cameron (Mitchell)
George Dandin (Dorst)
George Dandin (Molière)
George Darville (Boucicault)
George de Barnwell (Byron)
George Washington Slept Here (Kaufman)
Georgette (Sardou)
Gerade Weg ist der Beste (Kotzebue)
Geräusch eines Geräusches (r Handke)
Gerettet (Sperr)
Gerettete Alkibiades (Kaiser)
Gerettete Venedig (Hofmannsthal)
Gericht über Zarathustra (Sorge)
German Emigrants (Harrigan)
German Hotel (Holcroft)
Germania Tod in Berlin (Müller)
Germinal (Zola)
Gertie Maude (Van Druten)
Gertrude's Cherries (Jerrold)
Gervaise Skinner (Jerrold)
Gesang im Feuerofen (Zuckmayer)
Gesang vom lusitanischen Popanz (Weiss)
Geschichten aus dem Wiener Wald (Horváth)
Geschwister (Goethe)
Gesellschaft im Herbst (Dorst)
Gesichte des Simone Machard (Brecht)
Gésippe (Hardy)
Gespenst (Kotzebue)
Gespenst von Gattnau (r Walser)
Gespräch im Hause Stein über den abwesenden Herrn von Goethe (Hacks)
Geste pour un autre (Tardieu)
Gestern (Hofmannsthal)
Gesticulador (Usigli)
Gestiefelte Kater (Dorst)
Gestiefelte Kater (Tieck)
Gesundheit! (t Forte)
Get Away Old Man (Saroyan)
Get Out of My Hair! (Feydeau)
Getheilte Herz (Kotzebue)
Getting Married (Shaw)
Getting On (Bennett)
Getting Out (Norman)
Getuigen (Claus)
Geueux aux Paradis (Obey)
Gewehre der Frau Carrar (Brecht)
Gewürzkrämerkleeblatt (Nestroy)
Ghetto (Heijermans)
Ghost (Plautus)
Ghost Goes West (s Sherwood)
Ghost in the Garden (Brighouse)
Ghost of Yankee Doodle (Howard)
Ghost Sonata (Strindberg)
Ghost Trio (t Beckett)
Ghosts (Hampton)
Ghosts (Ibsen)
Ghosts (Kilroy)
Ghosts (Kopit)
Ghosts (Nowra)
Ghosts of Windsor Park (Brighouse)
Giara (Pirandello)
Gibier de potence (Feydeau)
Gideon (Chayefsky)
Gift of Friendship (t Osborne)

Gift of the Gorgon (Shaffer)
Giganti della montagna (Pirandello)
Gigantomachie (Hardy)
Gigli Concert (Murphy)
Gil Pérez the Galician (Calderón)
Gildet pa Solhaug (Ibsen)
Gilles! (Claus)
Gilles und Jeanne (Kaiser)
Gillets hemlighet (Strindberg)
Ginger (Houghton)
Ginger Tree (t Hampton)
Gingerbread Lady (Simon)
Gingham Dog (L. Wilson)
Giocatore (Betti)
Gioconda (D'Annunzio)
Giornata qualunque (Fo)
Giovanni the Vampire (Planché)
Gipfel auf der Messe (Kotzebue)
Gipsy of Derncleuch (Jerrold)
Giralda (Boucicault)
Giralda (Scribe)
Girl and the Judge (Fitch)
Girl and the Soldier (van Itallie)
Girl from Andros (Terence)
Girl from Hakata (Chikamatsu)
Girl from Samos (Menander)
Girl in Melaine Klein (Saunders)
Girl Who Came to Supper (Coward)
Girl Who Did Not Want to Go to Kuala Lumpur (Bridie)
Girl Who Has Everything (Fitch)
Girl Who Saw Everything (De Groen)
Girl with the Green Eyes (Fitch)
Girls (Byron)
Girls (Fitch)
Girls and Boys (Pinero)
Gisela (Kotzebue)
Giselle (Byron)
Gismonda (Sardou)
Giullarata (Fo)
Giullarate religiose (Fo)
Giuocatore (Goldoni)
Giuoco delle parti (Pirandello)
Give a Dog (Robinson)
Give Him a House (Shiels)
Giveaway (Jellicoe)
Glacier (Carballido)
Glad of It (Fitch)
Gladiador de Ravena (Echegaray)
Glass Cage (Priestley)
Glass Menagerie (Williams)
Glass of Bitter (Priestley)
Glass of Water (Petrushevskaya)
Glass of Water (Scribe)
Glass Slipper (Molnár)
Glaube, Liebe, Hoffnung (Horváth)
Glaucus (Boker)
Gleichheit der Jahre (Nestroy)
Glendalough (Colum)
Glengarry Glen Ross (Mamet)
Glimpse of Reality (Shaw)
Glittering Gate (Dunsany)
Gloaming (Terry)
Globales Interesse (Kroetz)
Gloire en images (Arrabal)
Gloria (D'Annunzio)
Gloriana (Lee)
Glorious First of June (Sheridan)

Glory in the Flower (Inge)
Glory of Columbia (Dunlap)
Gloucester Road (Mortimer)
Glück auf! (Heijermans)
Glück im Winkel (Sudermann)
Glück, Missbrauch und Rückkehr (Nestroy)
Glücklichen (Kotzebue)
Glücksgott (Müller)
Glum Victoria and the Lad with Specs (Leigh)
Gluttony (Guare)
Glycerine Tears (Hibberd)
Gnädiges Fräulein (Williams)
Gnome King (Colman the Younger)
Go Out and Move the Car (Terry)
Goal Gate (Gregory)
Goal (Jones)
Goat Island (Betti)
Gobernadora (Benavente y Martínez)
Go-Between (s Pinter)
Gobseck (Hasenclever)
God Bless Our Home (Barry)
God Rot Tunbridge Wells (t Osborne)
Goddess (s Chayefsky)
Godelieve (Ghelderode)
Gods Are Not to Blame (Rotimi)
God's Favorite (Simon)
Gods of the Lightning (M. Anderson)
Gods of the Mountain (Dunsany)
Godsend (Lawler)
Gody stranstviya (Arbuzov)
Gog and Magog (Bridie)
Goglu (Barbeau)
Goin' a Buffalo (Bullins)
Going Home (De Groen)
Going Home Again (Harrigan)
Going to Pot (Feydeau)
Going to the Bad (Taylor)
Gold (O'Neill)
Gold! (Reade)
Gold Piece (Hughes)
Gold Through the Trees (Childress)
Goldberg Street (Mamet)
Golden Accord (Soyinka)
Golden Age (Heywood)
Golden Age (Nowra)
Golden Age Restored (Jonson)
Golden Apple: (Gregory)
Golden Boy (Odets)
Golden Branch (Planché)
Golden Calf (Jerrold)
Golden Cherub (Guare)
Golden Cuckoo (Johnston)
Golden Doom (Dunsany)
Golden Dragon City (Dunsany)
Golden Fleece (Grillparzer)
Golden Fleece (Planché)
Golden Fleece (Priestley)
Golden Goose (Ringwood)
Golden Helmet (Yeats)
Golden Holden Show (Romeril)
Golden Legend of Shults (Bridie)
Golden Lions (Walcott)
Golden Oldies (Hewett)
Golden Ray (Brighouse)
Golden Six (M. Anderson)
Golden Thread (Carballido)
Golden Valley (Hewett)

Golden Widow (Daly)
Golden Years (r Miller)
Goldene Harfe (Hauptmann)
Goldene Vlies (Grillparzer)
Goldenhair the Good (Byron)
Goldmäulchen (Grass)
Golfo de las sirenas (Calderón)
Golgo (H. Barker)
Goly Korol (Shvarts)
Goncourt (Dorst)
Gondoliers (Gilbert)
Gone Out (Różewicz)
Gone with the Wind (s Howard)
Gonza the Lancer (Chikamatsu)
Good and Faithful Servant (t Orton)
Good Bargain (Dunsany)
Good Citizens of Piffelheim (Kotzebue)
Good Companions (Priestley)
Good Doctor (Simon)
Good Earth (s Connelly)
Good Fairy (Molnár)
Good Fellow (Kaufman)
Good for Evil (Augier)
Good Girl (Goldoni)
Good Girl is Hard to Find (Baraka)
Good Help is Hard to Find (Kopit)
Good Hope (Heijermans)
Good Little Wife (Musset)
Good Natured Man (Goldsmith)
Good Neighbor (Dunlap)
Good News (Byron)
Good Night Children (Priestley)
Good Night's Sleep (Feydeau)
Good Parts (Horovitz)
Good Person of Setzuan (Brecht)
Good Thing (Keane)
Good Thing or a Bad Thing (Jellicoe)
Good Woman in the Wood (Planché)
Good Woman of Setzuan (Brecht)
Goodbye (Green)
Goodbye Ted (Hibberd)
Goodbye to the Summer (Carroll)
Good-Humoured Ladies (Goldoni)
Goona Goona (Terry)
Goose and Tomtom (Rabe)
Goose-Pimples (Leigh)
Gordische Ei (Kaiser)
Gore ot uma (Griboyedov)
Gorge (t Nichols)
Gorod na zare (Arbuzov)
Goryachee serdtse (Ostrovsky)
Goryōkaku kessho (Kubo)
Gospel Glow (Hughes)
Gossip (Fitch)
Gossip (Walker)
Gösta Berling (Brecht)
Gotham Election (Centlivre)
Götter der Pest (s Fassbinder)
Götter, Helden, und Wieland (Goethe)
Götz von Berlichingen (Goethe)
Goudland (Claus)
Goûter des généraux (Vian)
Government Inspector (Gogol)
Government Property (Brenton)
Governor's Lady (Mercer)
Governor's Lady (r Mercer)
Governor's Wife (Benavente y Martínez)

Gown for His Mistress (Feydeau)
Grace Mary (Jones)
Grace of Mary Traverse (Wertenbaker)
Grace of Todd (Rudkin)
Gracia (Gambaro)
Graciosa and Percinet (Planché)
Gracques (Giraudoux)
Graf Benyowsky (Dunlap)
Graf Benyowsky (Kotzebue)
Graf Öderland (Frisch)
Graf von Burgund (Kotzebue)
Graf von Gleichen (Kotzebue)
Graf von Ratzeburg (Barlach)
Grafoman (Volodin)
Graft (Brighouse)
Grafted (Pirandello)
Grain de café (Labiche)
Grammaire (Labiche)
Grammar (Labiche)
Gran Cenobia (Calderón)
Gran circo del mundo (Usigli)
Gran duque de Gandía (Calderón)
Gran Galeoto (Echegaray)
Gran mercado del mundo (Calderón)
Gran principe de Fez (Calderón)
Gran sultana, doña Catalina de Oviedo (Cervantes)
Gran teatro del mundo (Calderón)
Grand Cérémonial (Arrabal)
Grand Chasseur (Pixérécourt)
Grand Duke (Gilbert)
Grand Duke's Opera House (Harrigan)
Grand et dernier Solyman (Mairet)
Grand Guignol (Arrabal)
Grand' Mère (Hugo)
Grand Poucet (Barbeau)
Grand Tarot (Ludlam)
Grand Tour (Rice)
Grand Vizir (Obaldia)
Grande et la Petite Manoeuvre (Adamov)
Grande magia (De Filippo)
Grande Muraille (Adamov)
Grande pantomima con bandiere e pupazzi piccoli e medi
   (Fo)
Grande Revue du XXe siècle (Arrabal)
Grande Tentation de Saint Antoine (r Ghelderode)
Grandes Chaleurs (Ionesco)
Grandes Vacances (Tremblay)
Grandhotel Nevada (Langer)
Grandpa and the Statue (r Miller)
Grangecolman (Martyn)
Grania (Gregory)
Granny (Fitch)
Granny Boling (Green)
Granny (Poliakoff)
Granny Welfare and the Wolf (Arden)
Grass and Wild Strawberries (Ryga)
Grasse matinée (r Obaldia)
Grasshopper (Colum)
Grateful Servant (Shirley)
Great American Goof (Saroyan)
Great Catherine (Shaw)
Great Dark (Brighouse)
Great Divide (Moody)
Great Duke of Florence (Massinger)
Great Expectations (Gilbert)
Great Fury of Philipp Hotz (Frisch)
Great Galeoto (Echegaray)

Great God Brown (O'Neill)
Great Goodness of Life (Baraka)
Great Harvest Festival (Cook)
Great Highway (Strindberg)
Great In-Toe-Natural Walking Match (Harrigan)
Great Labor Day Classic (Horovitz)
Great Lover (Dumas *père*)
Great Magoo (Hecht)
Great Middle Class (Usigli)
Great Nebula in Orion (L. Wilson)
Great Noise (Murrell)
Great Peace (Bond)
Great Stage of the World (Calderón)
Great Theatre of the World (Calderón)
Great Unknown (Daly)
Great Wall of China (Frisch)
Greek (Berkoff)
Greek Tragedy (Leigh)
Green Bird (Gozzi)
Green Cars Go East (Carroll)
Green Coat (Augier, Musset)
Green Cockatoo (Schnitzler)
Green-Eyed Monster (Planché)
Green Forms (t Bennett)
Green Helmet (Yeats)
Green Pastures (Connelly)
Green Pastures (s Connelly)
Green Stone (Fitzmaurice)
Greenland (Brenton)
Grekh da beda na kogo ne zhivyot (Ostrovsky)
Grenzenloser Nachmittag (r Walser)
Gretchen (Gilbert)
Gretna Green (O'Keeffe)
Grey Farm (Rattigan)
Griffith Gaunt (Daly)
Griffith Gaunt (Reade)
Grimaldi (Boucicault)
Grin Bushes (Byron)
Grindkopf (Dorst)
Grip Am (Rotimi)
Grip (Harrigan)
Griselda (Hauptmann)
Grist to the Mill (Planché)
Grogan and the Ferret (Shiels)
Groote vlucht (Heijermans)
Grooving (Terry)
Gros Mot (Labiche)
Gross und klein (Strauss)
Grossbürger Möller (Kaiser)
Gross-Cophta (Goethe)
Grosse Hofversammlung in Paris (Kotzebue)
Grosse Schmährede an der Stadtmauer (Dorst)
Grosse Szene (Schnitzler)
Grosse Wut des Philipp Hotz (Frisch)
Grosser Frieden (Braun)
Grossmama (Kotzebue)
Grotte (Anouilh)
Grotte de Versailles (Quinault)
Grouch (Menander)
Groupuscule of My Heart (Arrabal)
Groza (Ostrovsky)
Grüne Flöte (Hofmannsthal)
Grüne Kakadu (Schnitzler)
Grub Street Opera (Fielding)
Grumbler (Goldsmith)
Grupa Laokoona (Różewicz)
Guarda cuidadosa (Cervantes)

Guárdate del agua mansa (Calderón)
Guardian (Massinger)
Guardsman (r Miller)
Guardsman (Molnár)
Guèbres (Voltaire)
Guerillas (Hochhuth)
Guérite (Audiberti)
Guernica (Arrabal)
Guerra (Goldoni)
Guerra di popolo in Cile (Fo)
Guerras do Alecrim e Mangerona (Silva)
Guerre civile (Montherlant)
Guerre de mille ans (Arrabal)
Guerre de Troie n'aura pas lieu (Giraudoux)
Guerre des femmes (Dumas *père*)
Guest (Fugard)
Guest (s Pinter)
Guest-Friend (Grillparzer)
Guevara (Braun)
Guichet (Tardieu)
Guid Sisters (Tremblay)
Guigne (Labiche)
Guillaume Tell (Pixérécourt)
Guillermo Tell tiene los ojos tristes (Sastre)
Guillermo y el nahua (Carballido)
Guilty One (O'Neill)
Guinea Gold (Byron)
Gulf Between Us (Griffiths)
Gulzara (Mowatt)
Gum and Goo (Brenton)
Gun (Griffiths)
Gundling's Life Frederick of Prussia Lessing's Sleep Dream
    Scream (Müller)
Guns of Carrar (Brecht)
Guntwar (Sorge)
Gustav Adolf (Strindberg)
Gustav III (Strindberg)
Gustave III (Scribe)
Gustav Vasa (Strindberg)
Gustav Wasa (Kotzebue)
Gustavus III (Planché)
Gustavus the Third (Scribe)
Gustavus Vasa (Strindberg)
Gustos y disgustos son no más que imaginación (Calderón)
Gute Besserung (Kroetz)
Gute Besserung (r Kroetz)
Gute Mensch von Setzuan (Brecht)
Gute Ruf (Sudermann)
Gute Zeit (Barlach)
Gutgeschnittene Ecke (Sudermann)
Gutmütige Teufel (Nestroy)
Guy Fawkes (Byron)
Guy Fawkes (Taylor)
Guys (Barbeau)
Gyges and His Ring (Hebbel)
Gyges und sein Ring (Hebbel)
Gypsies Metamorphosed (Jonson)
Gypsy (Laurents)
Gypsy (M. Anderson)
Gyroscope (Reaney)
Gyubal Wahazar (Witkiewicz)

H (Wood)
H.I.D. (Hess is Dead) (Brenton)
H.M.S. Pinafore (Gilbert)
Ha llegado Don Juan (Benavente y Martínez)
Ha sonado la muerte (Sastre)

Händler der vier Jahreszeiten (s Fassbinder)
Häuptling Abendwind (Nestroy)
Häusliche Zwist (Kotzebue)
Haar van de hond (Claus)
Habeas Corpus (Bennett)
Habit vert (Augier, Musset)
Habladme en entrando (Tirso De Molina)
Habladores (Cervantes)
Hacia la verdad (Benavente y Martínez)
Hackett Gets Ahead (Romeril)
Hado y divisa de Leonido y Marfisa (Calderón)
Hærmændene på Helgeland (Ibsen)
Hagestolz und die Körbe (Kotzebue)
Hahnenschlag (Kotzebue)
Hai mai vista in scena . . .? (Fabbri)
Haine (Sardou)
Hairy Ape (O'Neill)
Haitian Air (Walcott)
Hakata Kojorō Namimakura (Chikamatsu)
Hakurakuten (Zeami)
Half an Hour (Barrie)
Half an Hour's Courtship (Planché)
Half Gods (Howard)
Half-Caste (Robertson)
Halifax (Dumas *père*)
Hall of Healing (O'Casey)
Hallelujah, Baby! (Laurents)
Hallmarked (Galsworthy)
Hallowed Ground (Brighouse)
Halte Hulda (Bjørnson)
Ham Funeral (White)
Hamlet (Buero Vallejo)
Hamlet (Claus)
Hamlet (Davenant)
Hamlet (Dumas *père*)
Hamlet (Fernández de Moratín)
Hamlet (Müller)
Hamlet (Shakespeare)
Hamlet in Wittenberg (Hauptmann)
Hamletmachine (Müller)
Hamletmaschine (Müller)
Han sidder ved Smeltedligen (Munk)
Han som fick leva om sitt liv (Lagerkvist)
Hanákné-ügy (t Örkény)
Hand of Siva (Hecht)
Hand of the Slain (Prevelakis)
Hand on the Rail (Mason)
Han-dan ji (Tang Xianzu)
Handcuffs (Reaney)
Handful of Friends (Williamson)
Hands Across the Sea (Coward)
Hands Around (Schnitzler)
Hands of God (Solórzano)
Handshakers (Saroyan)
Handsome Hernani (Byron)
Handsome is That Handsome Does (Taylor)
Hang of the Gaol (H. Barker)
Hanging of Emanuel (Horovitz)
Hangman (Lagerkvist)
Hanibal pred bránami (Karvaš)
Hanjo (Zeami)
Hannele (Hauptmann)
Hanneles Himmelfahrt (Hauptmann)
Hannetons (Brieux)
Hannibal (Grabbe)
Hanrahan's Oath (Gregory)
Hans Faust (Braun)

Hans Kohlhaas (Saunders)
Hans Max Giesbrecht von der Humpenberg (Kotzebue)
Hans nåds testamente (Bergman)
Hansel and Gretel (Rudkin)
Hanske (Bjørnson)
Hapgood (Stoppard)
Happy Arcadia (Gilbert)
Happy Days (Beckett)
Happy End (Brecht)
Happy Family (Kotzebue)
Happy Funeral (Saroyan)
Happy Hangman (Brighouse)
Happy Haven (Arden)
Happy Hunter (Feydeau)
Happy Journey (to Trenton and Camden) (Wilder)
Happy Land (Gilbert)
Happy Marriage (Fitch)
Happy Prince (Pollock)
Hard Hit (Jones)
Harding's Luck (Nichols)
Harem (Kotzebue)
Harlequin and the Giant Helmet (Planché)
Harlequin Beauty and the Beast (Byron)
Harlequin Bluebeard (Byron)
Harlequin Cock-Robin, and Jenny Wren (Gilbert)
Harlequin Columbus (Taylor)
Harlequin in Waterford (O'Keeffe)
Harlequin King Nutcracker (Planché)
Harlequin St. George and the Dragon (Byron)
Harlequin Teague (Colman the Elder)
Harlequin Teague (O'Keeffe)
Harlequinade (Granville-Barker)
Harlequinade (Rattigan)
Harmónia (Molnár)
Harmony (Jones)
Harold (van Itallie)
Harold Muggins is a Martyr (Arden)
Haroldo el Normando (Echegaray)
Harper's Daughter (Schiller)
Harry Dernier (Walcott)
Harry's Christmas (Berkoff)
Hartnäckig (Kroetz)
Harvest Festival (O'Casey)
Harvest (Fitch)
Harvest (Robinson)
Has "Washington" Legs? (Wood)
Hasenfellhändler (Sudermann)
Hasses und der Liebe Rache (Kotzebue)
Hast Thou Considered My Servant Job? (Wilder)
Haste to the Wedding (Gilbert)
Hate (Sewell)
Hatmanul Baltaq (Caragiale)
Hattyū (Molnár)
Haunted House (Plautus)
Haunted Houses (Byron)
Haunted Man (Robertson)
Hauptmann von Köpenick (Zuckmayer)
Haus der Temperamente (Nestroy)
Haute surveillance (Genet)
Haven (Saunders)
Having a Wonderful Time (Churchill)
Hawk Moon (Shepard)
Hay Fever (Coward)
Hayami onna-juku (Kishida)
Haydée (Scribe)
Haydn's Head (Murrell)
Hazakuru (Kishida)

Hazard of the Die (Jerrold)
Hazardous Ground (Daly)
Hazel Flagg (Hecht)
Hazel Kirke (Mackaye)
He and She (Crothers)
He Can Swagger Sitting Down (Romeril)
He Lies Like Truth (Scribe)
He Sits at the Melting Pot (Munk)
He Who Gets Slapped (Andreyev)
He Who Said Yes; He Who Said No (Brecht)
He Would if He Could (Bickerstaff)
Head, Guts, and Soundbone Dance (Cook)
Head of the Family (Fitch)
Heading Home (t Hare)
Headlights (Terry)
Headlines (Williams)
Heads (Brenton)
Healing Arch (Mason)
Healing Spring (Holberg)
Hear Both Sides (Holcroft)
Heart of a Tenor (Wedekind)
Heart of Gold (Jerrold)
Heart of Hearts (Jones)
Heart of Paddy Whack (Crothers)
Heart to Heart (t Rattigan)
Heartbreak House (Shaw)
Heartlanders (Edgar)
Heartpiece (Müller)
Hearts and Diamonds (Jerrold)
Hearts and Flowers (t Nichols)
Hearts and Hands (Taylor)
Hearts of Oak (Herne)
Hearts of Oak (Jones)
Heartsong (Laurents)
Heat of the Day (t Pinter)
Heather Field (Martyn)
Heauton Timorumenos (Terence)
Heavenly and Earthly Love (Molnár)
Heavenly Bodies (Parker)
Hebamme (Hochhuth)
Hebi-hime-sama (Kara)
Hebra de oro (Carballido)
Hebriana (Norén)
Hecabe (Euripides)
Hechicero (Solórzano)
Hecuba (Euripides)
Hecuba (Hernández)
Hecyra (Terence)
Hedda Gabler (Bridie)
Hedda Gabler (Hampton)
Hedda Gabler (Ibsen)
Hedda Gabler (Osborne)
Heerenhuis te koop (Heijermans)
Heidi (Simon)
Heike Nyogo no shima (Chikamatsu)
Heiland (Sternheim)
Heilige Experiment (Hochwälder)
Heilige Johanna der Schlachthöfe (Brecht)
Heilige Zeit (Sudermann)
Heimarbeit (Kroetz)
Heimat (Sudermann)
Heimat (t Kroetz)
Heimliches Geld, heimliche Liebe (Nestroy)
Heinrich (Dorst)
Heinrich and Pernille (Holberg)
Heinrich Reuss von Plauen (Kotzebue)
Heir at Law (Colman the Younger)

Heirat wider Willen (Hofmannsthal)
Heizi ershiba (Cao Yu)
Held der westlichen Welt (Hacks)
Heldenplatz (Bernhard)
Helen (Euripides)
Helen in Egypt (Hofmannsthal)
Helen of Troy, New York (Connelly, Kaufman)
Helena (Euripides)
Hell of a Mess (Ionesco)
Hellas (Strindberg)
Hellequin, Harlekin, Arlechino (Fo)
Hello and Goodbye (Fugard)
Hello from Bertha (Williams)
Hello, Out There (Saroyan)
Hellseherei (Kaiser)
Héloïse Paranquet (Dumas *fils*)
Helper (Bullins)
Helping Hands (Taylor)
Hemsöborna (Strindberg)
Henceforward (Ayckbourn)
Hengist, King of Kent (Middleton)
Henna for Endurance (Terry)
Henri Christophe (Walcott)
Henri Quatre and the Fair Gabrielle (Planché)
Henri III et sa cour (Dumas *père*)
Henrik og Pernille (Holberg)
Henry Dunbar (Taylor)
Henry Lumper (Horovitz)
Henry of Auë (Hauptmann)
Henry VIII (Fletcher, Shakespeare)
Henry V (Shakespeare)
Henry IV (Pirandello)
Henry IV (I–II) (Shakespeare)
Henry VI (I–III) (Shakespeare)
Henryk Pobozny (Wyspiański)
Her Great Match (Fitch)
Her Last Stake (Augier)
Her Own Enemy (Daly)
Her Own Way (Fitch)
Her Sister (Fitch)
Her Tongue (Jones)
Heracleidae (Euripides)
Heracles (Euripides)
Héraclius, Empereur d'Orient (P. Corneille)
Heraclius, Emperor of the East (P. Corneille)
Herakles (Wedekind)
Herakles 5 (Müller)
Herberge (Hochwälder)
Herbert Engelmann (Hauptmann, Zuckmayer)
Hercule mourant (Rotrou)
Hercules and the Augean Stables (Dürrenmatt)
Hercules Furens (Seneca)
Hercules Oetaeus (Seneca)
Here Come the Clowns (Barry)
Here Comes a Chopper (Ionesco)
Here (Frayn)
Heri tou Skotomenu (Prevelakis)
Heria tou Zontanou Theou (Prevelakis)
Héritier du village (Marivaux)
Héritiers Rabourdin (Zola)
Herkules und der Stall des Augias (Dürrenmatt)
Herkules und der Stall des Augias (r Dürrenmatt)
Hermann und Thusnelde (Kotzebue)
Hermannsschlacht (Grabbe)
Hermannsschlacht (Kleist)
Hermanos parecidos (Tirso De Molina)
Hermine (Anouilh)

Hermione (Strindberg)
Hernani (Hugo)
Herne's Egg (Yeats)
Hero (Kopit)
Hero and Leander (Grillparzer)
Hero of Santa Maria (Hecht)
Hero of the World (Saroyan)
Hero Rises Up (Arden)
Herod and Mariamne (Hebbel)
Herod the King (Munk)
Heroes (Poliakoff)
Heroes of Labour (t H. Barker)
Heroic Stubbs (Jones)
Héros de mon enfance (Tremblay)
Herr Bengts hustru (Strindberg)
Herr Gottlieb Merks (Kotzebue)
Herr Puntila und sein Knecht Matti (Brecht)
Herr Sleeman kommer (Bergman)
Herrer Dommere (Munk)
Herrnburger Bericht (Brecht)
Herzliche Grüsse aus Grado (Kroetz)
Herzog Theodor von Gothland (Grabbe)
Herzstück (Müller)
He's Much to Blame (Holcroft)
Hester's Mystery (Pinero)
Heure du spectacle (Sardou)
Heureuse Constance (Rotrou)
Heureux Naufrage (Rotrou)
Heureux Strategème (Marivaux)
Hexerie (Holberg)
Hey, Stay a While (Guare)
Hidalga del valle (Calderón)
Hidalla (Wedekind)
Hidden City (s Poliakoff)
Hidden Hand (Taylor)
Hidden Laughter (Gray)
Hier, Les Enfants dansaient (Gelinas)
Higaki (Zeami)
High, Low, Jack, and the Game (Planché)
High Summer (t Rattigan)
High Time Along the Wabash (Saroyan)
High Toby (Priestley)
High Tor (M. Anderson)
Highest House on the Mountain (Keane)
Highland Call (Green)
Highland Girl (Voltaire)
Highland Reel (O'Keeffe)
Highly Improbable (Gilbert)
Hija del aire I–II (Calderón)
¡Hija del alma! (Benavente y Martínez)
Hija del capitán (Valle-Inclán)
Hija del rey (Hernández)
Hijo de Don Juan (Echegaray)
Hijo de hierro y el hijo de carne (Echegaray)
Hijo de Polichinela (Benavente y Martínez)
Hijo del sol, Faetón (Calderón)
Hijo único de Guillermo Tell (Sastre)
Hijos de la fortuna: Teágenes y Cariclea (Calderón)
Hijos del capitán Grant (Carballido)
Hijos padres de sus padres (Benavente y Martínez)
Hikaeshitsu (Satoh)
Hilfe, ich werde geheiratet (Kroetz)
Hilfe kommt aus Bregenz (r Walser)
Hilferufe (Handke)
Hillarys (Brighouse, Houghton)
Himbeerpflücker (Hochwälder)
Himlens hemlighet (Lagerkvist)

Himmel über Berlin (s Handke)
Himmelrikets nycklar (Strindberg)
Himmelwärts (Horváth)
Hin und her (Horváth)
Hindle Wakes (Houghton)
Hinkemann (Toller)
Hint to Husbands (Cumberland)
Hinüber-herüber (Nestroy)
Hinze und Kunze (Braun)
Hiob (Kokoschka)
Hippolytus (Euripides)
Hippolytus (Rudkin)
Hippolytus (Seneca)
Hiroshima mon amour (s Duras)
His Excellency (Gilbert)
His Excellency—the Governor (Carroll)
His Grace de Grammont (Fitch)
His House in Order (Pinero)
His Majesty (Granville-Barker)
His Widow's Husband (Benavente y Martínez)
His Wife (Jones)
Histoire de cirque (Salacrou)
Histoire de l'Opéra-Comique (Lesage)
Histoire de rire (Labiche)
Histoire de rire (Salacrou)
Histoire de Tobie et de Sara (Claudel)
Historia de Otelo (Benavente y Martínez)
Historia de un anillo (Hernández)
Historia de una escalera (Buero Vallejo)
Historia (Gombrowicz)
Historical Register for the Year 1736 (Fielding)
History and Fall of Caius Marius (Otway)
History of Australia (Romeril)
History of Sir Francis Drake (Davenant)
History of the American Film (Durang)
Histriomastix (Marston)
Histrionics (Bernhard)
Hitler Dances (Brenton)
Hitting Town (Poliakoff)
Hlasy ptáků (Topol)
Hmlisté ráno (Karvaš)
Hob (Cibber)
Hobby-Horse (Pinero)
Hoberaute (Audiberti)
Hobson's Choice (Brighouse)
Hochwasser (Grass)
Hochzeit (Brecht)
Hochzeit der Sobeide (Hofmannsthal)
Hodina lásky (Topol)
Hofer (Planché)
Hofmeister (Brecht)
Hofmeister (Lenz)
Hohenstaufen I: Kaiser Friedrich Barbarossa (Grabbe)
Hohenstaufen II: Kaiser Heinrich der Sechste (Grabbe)
Höhere Leben (Sudermann)
Hold Your Tongue (Planché)
Hölderlin (Weiss)
Holding Talks (Rotimi)
Hold-Up (Dubé)
Holdup (Norman)
Hole (Simpson)
Holiday (Barry)
Holiday Song (t Chayefsky)
Hölle Weg Erde (Kaiser)
Höllenangst (Nestroy)
Hollywood Holiday (Van Druten)
Hollywood Pinafore (Kaufman)

Holtak hallgatása (Örkény)
Holy Ghostly (Shepard)
Holy Isle (Bridie)
Holy Manhatten (Coulter)
Holy Terror (Gray)
Holy Terrors (Cocteau)
Hölzerne Säbel (Kotzebue)
Hombre llamado Isla (Díaz)
Hombre negro (Echegaray)
Hombre pobre todo es trazas (Calderón)
Hombre sensible (Arlt)
Hombre y sus sueños (Marqués)
Hombrecito (Benavente y Martínez)
Hombres y sus hombres (Sastre)
Home (Augier)
Home (Duras)
Home (Mortimer)
Home (Robertson)
Home (Storey)
Home Again (Jones)
Home and Beauty (Maugham)
Home Boy (Bullins)
Home Chat (Coward)
Home Fires (Guare)
Home Free! (L. Wilson)
Home Front (Walser)
Home is Tomorrow (Priestley)
Home Leave (Wertenbaker)
Home of the Brave (Laurents)
Home of the Free (Rice)
Home on the Range (Baraka)
Homecoming (Pinter)
Homenaje a Hidalgo (Carballido)
Homework (Kroetz)
Homicide (s Mamet)
Homme à trois visages (Pixérécourt)
Homme assis dans le couloir (s Duras)
Homme atlantique (s Duras)
Homme aux sandales de caoutchouc (Yacine)
Homme aux valises (Ionesco)
Homme comme les autres (Salacrou)
Homme de bien (Augier)
Homme de paille (Labiche)
Homme du cendre (Obey)
Homme économe (Feydeau)
Homme est venu me voir (Duras)
Homme et son désir (Claudel)
Homme gris (Laberge)
Homme intègre (Feydeau)
Homme qui manque le coche (Labiche)
Homme sanguin (Labiche)
Honest Man's Fortune (Fletcher)
Honest to God Schnozzola (Horovitz)
Honest Whore (Dekker, Middleton)
Honeycomb (Green)
Honeymoon Scruple (Jerrold)
Hongi (Mason)
Honnete Ambition (Holberg)
Honnêtes Femmes (Becque)
Honneur est satisfait (Dumas *père*)
Honor of the Family (Fitch)
Honorable Lord and Lady of Huntingdon's Entertainment
    at Ashby (Marston)
Honors at Dawn (Miller)
Honour Before Titles (Reade)
Honourable Entertainments (Middleton)
Honra de los hombres (Benavente y Martínez)

Honradez de la cerradura (Benavente y Martínez)
Honroso atrevimiento (Tirso De Molina)
Hooded Terror (Nichols)
Hoodman Blind (Jones)
Hooligan (Gilbert)
Hop Signor! (Ghelderode)
Hop, Skip, and Jump (Horovitz)
Hopeless Passion of Mr. Bunyon (Dunsany)
Hopes of the Living-Dead (Rotimi)
Hoppla, wir leben! (Toller)
Hopscotch (Horovitz)
Horace (P. Corneille)
Horatian (Müller)
Horatians and the Curatians (Brecht)
Horatier (Müller)
Horatier und die Kuratier (Brecht)
Horatius (P. Corneille)
Horikawa Nami no tsuzami (Chikamatsu)
Horizon (Daly)
Horizonte (Müller)
Hormigas (Díaz)
Hornet's Nest (Byron)
Horsky hotel (Havel)
Hörspiel (r Handke)
Hörspiel 2 (r Handke)
Hörspiel 3 (r Handke)
Hörspiel 4 (r Handke)
Hortense a dit: "Je m'en fous!" (Feydeau)
Hosanna (Tremblay)
Hose (Sternheim)
Hospital at the Time of the Revolution (Churchill)
Hospital Play (Terry)
Host (Molnár)
Hostage (Behan)
Hostage (Claudel)
Hot Fudge (Churchill)
Hot Ice (Ludlam)
Hot Iron (Green)
Hot l Baltimore (L. Wilson)
Hôtel du commerce (Hochwälder)
Hôtel du Libre Échange (Feydeau)
Hôtel Godelot (Sardou)
Hotel in Amsterdam (Osborne)
Hotel Paradiso (Feydeau)
Hotel Universe (Barry)
Hothouse (Pinter)
Hothouse (Terry)
Hour Glass (Yeats)
Hour Town (R. Anderson)
House in Blind Alley (Rice)
House in the Quiet Glen (Coulter)
House Not Meant to Stand (Williams)
House of Bernarda Alba (García Lorca)
House of Bernarda Alba (Stoppard)
House of Blue Leaves (Guare)
House of Connelly (Green)
House of Darnley Court (Bulwer-Lytton)
House of Fourchambault (Augier)
House of Games (s Mamet)
House of Humors (Nestroy)
House of Mirth (Fitch)
House or the Home? (Taylor)
House Party (Bullins)
House That Burned (Strindberg)
House That Jack Built (Delaney)
House That Jack Built (t Delaney)
House with a View on the Field (Vampilov)

House with the Column (Pirandello)
House with Two Doors is Difficult to Guard (Calderón)
Housekeeper (Jerrold)
Housewarming (Tagore)
Hover Through the Fog (McGrath)
How a Man May Choose a Good Wife from a Bad
  (Heywood)
How Are They at Home? (Priestley)
How Beautiful with Badges (Brenton)
How Brophy Made Good (Hare)
How Do You Do (Bullins)
How He Lied to Her Husband (Shaw)
How Mr. Mockinpott Was Cured of His Sufferings (Weiss)
How Not to Write a Play (Ludlam)
How She Loves Him! (Boucicault)
How the Other Half Loves (Ayckbourn)
How the Weather is Made (Brighouse)
How to Die for Love (Kotzebue)
How to Try a Lover (J. N. Barker)
How's the King? (Connelly)
Hoy es fiesta (Buero Vallejo)
Hra o básnnikovi (Karvaš)
Hübsche kleine Putzmacherin (Kotzebue)
Hu-die meng (Guan Hanqing)
Hue and Cry (Inchbald)
Hue and Cry After Cupid (Jonson)
Huerta de Juan Fernández (Tirso De Molina)
Huéspedes reales (Hernández)
Huggy Bear (t Mercer)
Hughie (O'Neill)
Hugo Grotius (Kotzebue)
Huguenots (Scribe)
Huis clos (Sartre)
Huis van Labdakos (Claus)
Huissiers (Vinaver)
800 Mètres (Obey)
Huldigung der Künste (Schiller)
Human Cannon (Bond)
Human Voice (Cocteau)
Humbug (Jones)
Humildad coronada de las plantas (Calderón)
Humiliation of the Father (Claudel)
Humoristische Eilwagenreise durch die Theaterwelt
  (Nestroy)
Humorists (Shadwell)
Humorous Courtier (Shirley)
Humorous Day's Mirth (Chapman)
Humorous Lieutenant (Fletcher)
Humulus le muet (Anouilh)
Hunchback (Daly)
Hund des Generals (Kipphardt)
Hundred Thousand Pounds (Byron)
Hundred Years Old (Granville-Barker)
Hunger (Fornés)
Hunger and Thirst (Ionesco)
Hunger Artist Departs (Różewicz)
Hungerers (Saroyan)
Hunted Down (Boucicault)
Hunter and the Bird (van Itallie)
Hunter's Moon (Connelly)
Hunting of Cupid (Peele)
Hurluberlu (Anouilh)
Hurlyburly (Rabe)
Husband and Wife (Saroyan)
Hush-a-Bye Baby on the Tree Top (Gilbert)
Hussiten von Naumburg im Jahr 1432 (Kotzebue)
Hut 42 (Keane)

Hyacinth Halvey (Gregory)
Hyakuman (Zeami)
Hyakunen no kodoku (Terayama)
Hyde Park (Shirley)
Hygea (Kotzebue)
Hymenaei (Jonson)
Hymn to the Rising Sun (Green)
Hymne Veni Creator (Wyspiański)
Hyperboräische Esel (Kotzebue)
Hyperchonder (Strauss)
Hyperion en het geweld (Claus)
Hypochondriac (Molière)
Hypochondriac (Reade)
Hypochondriaque (Rotrou)
Hypocrite (Bickerstaff)
Hypocrites (Jones)
Hypothèse (Pinget)
Hypothesis (Pinget)
Hypsipyle (Euripides)

I Am a Camera (Van Druten)
I Am a Stranger Here (Priestley)
I Am Lucy Terry (Bullins)
I Can't Imagine Tomorrow (Williams)
I Can't Sleep (Odets)
I, Claudius (Mortimer)
I Don't Generally Like Poetry But Have You Read
  "Trees"? (Durang)
I Don't Know Who to Feel Sorry For (Romeril)
I Have Been Here Before (Priestley)
I Know My Love (Behrman)
I Never Sang for My Father (R. Anderson)
I Never Sang for My Father (s R. Anderson)
I Ought to Be in Pictures (Simon)
I Remember Mama (Van Druten)
I Rise in Flame, Cried the Phoenix (Williams)
I Rom (Strindberg)
I Selimus (Greene)
I Spy (Mortimer)
I svet vo tme svetit (L. N. Tolstoy)
I, the Parade (Reaney)
I Think it's Gonna Turn Out Fine (Bullins)
I, Too, Speak of the Rose (Carballido)
I vnov vstrecha s yunostyu (Arbuzov)
I Will Have a Wife! (Planché)
I Will Marry When I Want (Ngugi)
Ia za shvetsyu (Petrushevskaya)
Iascaire (Harrigan)
Iashcheritsa (Volodin)
Ibolya (Molnár)
Ibrahim (Scudéry)
Ibsen's Ghost (Barrie)
Icarus's Mother (Shepard)
Iceberg (r Parker)
Icecream (Churchill)
Iceman Cometh (O'Neill)
Ich, Feuerbach (Dorst)
Ichneutae (Sophocles)
Ici ou ailleurs (Pinget)
I'd Rather Be Right (Kaufman)
Ida Collaborates (Coward)
Ideal Husband (Wilde)
Idealist (Munk)
Idealistka (Volodin)
Idées de Madame Aubray (Dumas fils)
Identité (Pinget)
Idiot (Gray)

Idiot's Delight (Sherwood)
Idiots Karamazov (Durang)
Idyll of the Shops (Hecht)
Idylle de la paix (Racine)
Iero Sfayo (Prevelakis)
If (Dunsany)
If (Rotimi)
If Five Years Pass (García Lorca)
If It Be Not Good the Devil is in It (Dekker)
If Men Played Cards Like Women Do (Kaufman)
If Shakespeare Lived Today (Dunsany)
If You Know Not Me, You Know Nobody I–II (Heywood)
If You Want to Know the Time (McGrath)
If You're Glad I'll Be Frank (Stoppard)
If You're Glad I'll Be Frank (r Stoppard)
Ifestio (Prevelakis)
Iglesia sitiada (Calderón)
Ignoramus (Reaney)
Ignorant und der Wahnsinnige (Bernhard)
Igroki (Gogol)
Ikke, Ikke, Nye, Nye, Nye (L. Wilson)
Ikudama shinjū (Chikamatsu)
Il est de la police (Labiche)
Il est important d'être aimé (Anouilh)
Il faut qu'une porte soit ouverte ou fermée (Musset)
Il ne faut jurer de rien (Musset)
Il pleut dans ma maison (Willems)
Il y avait foule au manoir (Tardieu)
Ile (O'Neill)
Île de la raison (Marivaux)
Île des Amazones (Lesage)
Île des esclaves (Marivaux)
Île du Gougou (Lesage)
Îles de tempête (Dadié)
I'll Leave it to You (Coward)
I'll Tell You What (Inchbald)
Ill-Treated Il Trovatore (Byron)
Illumination (Murray)
Illusion (P. Corneille)
Illusion comique (P. Corneille)
Illustre Amazone (Rotrou)
Illustre Corsaire (Mairet)
Illustres ennemis (T. Corneille)
Ils étaient venus pour . . . (Laberge)
Im Dickicht der Städte (Brecht)
I'm for Sweden (Petrushevskaya)
I'm Really Here (van Itallie)
Im Spiel der Sommerlüfte (Schnitzler)
I'm Talking About Jerusalem (Wesker)
Image (Gregory)
Imaginary Invalid (Molière)
Imamiya shinjū (Chikamatsu)
'Imarat al-Mu'allim Kanduz (Tawfiq al-Hakim)
Imbecille (Pirandello)
Imbianchini non hanno ricordi (Fo)
Immanuel Kant (Bernhard)
Immunidad del sagrado (Calderón)
Imperio del humo (Díaz)
Impertinents (Molière)
Importance of Being Earnest (Wilde)
Imposter (Romeril)
Imposters (Cumberland)
Impostore (Goldoni)
Imposture (Shirley)
Impresario delle Smirne (Goldoni)
Impresario from Smyrna (Goldoni)
Impromptu de l'Alma (Ionesco)

Impromptu de Paris (Giraudoux)
Impromptu de Quebec (Dubé)
Impromptu de Versailles (Molière)
Impromptu d'Outremont (Tremblay)
Impromptu du Palais-Royal (Cocteau)
Impromptu of Outremont (Tremblay)
Impromptu pour la Duchesse de Windsor (Ionesco)
Improvisation (Ionesco)
Imprudence (Pinero)
Imsik Harami (Tawfiq al-Hakim)
In a Fine Castle (Walcott)
In a Garden (Barry)
In a Place Somewhere Else (Romeril)
In Abraham's Bosom (Green)
In allen Sätteln gerecht (Wedekind)
In allen Wassern gewaschen (Wedekind)
In Camera (Sartre)
In Celebration (Storey)
In Chancery (Pinero)
In de Jonge Jan (Heijermans)
In der Sache J. Robert Oppenheimer (Kipphardt)
In der Sache J. Robert Oppenheimer (t Kipphardt)
In een haven (Claus)
In Fireworks Lie Secret Codes (Guare)
In Goethes Hand (Walser)
In Good King Charles's Golden Days (Shaw)
In Holy Russia (Dunsany)
In Honour Bound (Scribe)
In Kolonos (Claus)
In licenza (De Filippo)
In Memorandum Günter Opperman (Kroetz)
In My Many Names and Days (Fuller)
In New England Winter (Bullins)
In Old Vermont (Mamet)
In Praise of Guynemer (Wilder)
In Praise of Love (Rattigan)
In Reasonable Shape (Simpson)
In Service (Fornés)
In Spite of All (Mackaye)
In the Bar of a Tokyo Hotel (Williams)
In the Boom Boom Room (Rabe)
In the City of Grand-Daughters (Sewell)
In the Company of Men (Bond)
In the Deepest Part of Sleep (Fuller)
In the Jungle of Cities (Brecht)
In the Mall (Mamet)
In the Matter of J. Robert Oppenheimer (Kipphardt)
In the Mesh (s Sartre)
In the Penal Colony (Berkoff)
In the Season (Mitchell)
In the Shadow of the Glen (Synge)
In the Wine Time (Bullins)
In the Zone (O'Neill)
In Two Minds (Mercerr)
In Two Minds (t Mercer)
Inacoma (Shepard)
Inadmissible Evidence (Osborne)
Inca of Perusalem (Shaw)
Incêndio (Andrade)
Incepem! (Caragiale)
Incident at the Standish Arms (Inge)
Incident at Twilight (Dürrenmatt)
Incident at Vichy (Miller)
Incident in the Park (Kopit)
Incident with a Paginator (Vampilov)
Incidental Music (Ayckbourn)
Incognita persequitata (Goldoni)

Incognito (Kotzebue)
Incompatibility of Temper (Ostrovsky)
Incompris (Montherlant)
Inconnu (T. Corneille)
Inconnue d'Arras (Salacrou)
Inconstant (Daly)
Inconstant (Farquhar)
Incontro al parco delle terme (Fabbri)
Increased Difficulty of Concentration (Havel)
Incrimination (Tawfiq al-Hakim)
Indecent Exposure of Anthony East (Williamson)
Independent Means (Houghton)
India Ship (O'Keeffe)
India Song (Duras)
Indian (Ryga)
Indian Emperor (Dryden)
Indian Princess (J. N. Barker)
Indian Queen (Dryden)
Indian Wants the Bronx (Horovitz)
Indianer in England (Kotzebue)
Indians (Kopit)
Indians in England (Dunlap)
Indifférence (Lesage)
Indipohdi (Hauptmann)
Indiscret (Voltaire)
Individual Fruit Pies (Leigh)
Indulto general (Calderón)
Industria y la suerte (Ruiz de Alarcón)
Industrie (Lesage)
Indyk (Mrożek)
Inez de Castro (Hugo)
Infancy (Wilder)
Infant (Fonvizin)
Infanzona (Benavente y Martínez)
Infernal Machine (Cocteau)
Inferno (Santareno)
Infidelities (Marivaux)
Inför döden (Strindberg)
Información para extranjeros (Gambaro)
Information for Strangers (Gambaro)
Informer (Murphy)
Inga ehon Nezumi Kozō Jirokichi (Satoh)
Ingen går fri (Dagerman)
Ingratitude of a Commonwealth (Tate)
Inhabitants of Pontarcy (Sardou)
Inheritors (Glaspell)
Initiation into Madness (Rotimi)
1 Aprilie (Caragiale)
Injured Love (Tate)
Injustice Done to Tou O (Guan Hanqing)
Injustice to Tou O (Guan Hanqing)
Inkle and Yarico (Colman the Younger)
Inklusive (r Kroetz)
Inmaculada de los Dolores (Benavente y Martínez)
Inn (Hochwälder)
Innamorati (Goldoni)
Inner Man (Brighouse)
Inner Temple Masque (Middleton)
Inner Voices (De Filippo)
Inner Voices (Nowra)
Inner Voices (Simpson)
Innesto (Pirandello)
Innocence at Home (Harrigan)
Innocente Infidélité (Rotrou)
Inocentes y la huida e Egipto (Marqués)
Inquiry (Betti)
Inquisición (Arrabal)

Inquisitor (Holcroft)
Inquisizione (Fabbri)
Insatiate Countess (Marston)
Insect Play (Čapek)
Inside Out (Hare)
Inside Out (Wertenbaker)
Inside the Island (Nowra)
Inspector Calls (Priestley)
Inspector General (Gogol)
Insurance Man (t Bennett)
Insurance Money (Shiels)
Insurrection (Baraka)
Intelligence Comes to Grief (Griboyedov)
Intensive Care (t Bennett)
Intereses creados (Benavente y Martínez)
Interieur (Claus)
Intérieur (Maeterlinck)
Interior (Maeterlinck)
Interlude (Carroll)
Interlude at the Playhouse (Shaw)
Intermediate Zone (Carballido)
Intermezzo (Giraudoux)
Intermezzo (Kotzebue)
Intermezzo (Schnitzler)
International (Lawson)
International Match (Daly)
International Stud (Fierstein)
Interrupted Act (Różewicz)
Intervention (Hugo)
Interview (van Itallie)
1 Aprilie (Caragiale)
Intimate Exchanges (Ayckbourn)
Intimate Relations (Cocteau)
Intimité (Adamov)
Intrighi d'amore (Tasso)
Intrighi eleganti (Giacosa)
Intrigue and Love (Schiller)
Intrigue et amour (Dumas père)
Intriguers (Houghton)
Intriguing Chambermaid (Fielding)
Introducción al elefante y otras zoologías (Díaz)
Intruder (Maeterlinck)
Intruse (Maeterlinck)
Inugami (Terayama)
Invalid Corps (Harrigan)
Invasão (Gomes)
Invasion (Adamov)
Invasion (McGrath)
Inventeur de la poudre (Labiche)
Invention (Soyinka)
Invention for Service of Edward Barkham (Middleton)
Investigation (Harrigan)
Investigation (Weiss)
Invisible Friends (Ayckbourn)
Invisible (Carballido)
Invisible Prince (Planché)
Invitation à la valse (Dumas père)
Invitation au château (Anouilh)
Invitation to a March (Laurents)
Invités du Bon Dieu (Salacrou)
Io, l'erede (De Filippo)
Iolanthe (Gilbert)
Ion (Euripides)
Ione (Walcott)
Ioulianos o Paravatis (Kazantzakis)
Iphigeneia Aulidensis (Euripides)
Iphigeneia Taurica (Euripides)

Iphigenia (Racine)
Iphigenia in Aulis (Euripides)
Iphigenia in Tauris (Euripides)
Iphigenie auf Tauris (Fassbinder)
Iphigenie (Goethe)
Iphigénie (Racine)
Iphigénie (Rotrou)
Iphigenie auf Tauris (Goethe)
Iphigénie Hôtel (Vinaver)
Iphigenie in Aulis (Hauptmann)
Iphigenie in Aulis (Schiller)
Iphigenie in Delphi (Hauptmann)
Iphigenie in Tauris (Goethe)
Ipocrito (Aretino)
Iranian Nights (Brenton)
Ircana in Ispahan (Goldoni)
Ircana in Julfa (Goldoni)
Ireland vs. Italy (Harrigan)
Irene (Buero Vallejo)
Irène (Voltaire)
Irene de Otranto (Echegaray)
Irene innocente (Betti)
Irene Vanbrugh's Pantomime (Barrie)
Iridion (Krasiński)
Iris (Pinero)
Iris (Zeami)
Iris de paz (Echegaray)
Irish Emigrant (Harrigan)
Irish Heiress (Boucicault)
Irish Masque (Jonson)
Irish Mimic (O'Keeffe)
Irish Post (Planché)
Irkutsk Story (Arbuzov)
Irkutskaya istoriya (Arbuzov)
Irma Natividade (Santareno)
Iron Age (Heywood)
Iron Chest (Colman the Younger)
Iron Cross (Rice)
Iron Will (Mackaye)
Ironhand (Arden)
Ironhand (Goethe)
Iron-Master (Pinero)
Irtamène (Hugo)
Irydion (Krasiński)
Is He Guilty? (Rice)
Is Life Worth Living? (Robinson)
Isabella, tre caravelle e un cacciaballe (Fo)
Isis (Quinault)
Isis (Tawfiq al-Hakim)
Isla desierta (Arlt)
Island (Fugard)
Island (Jerrold)
Island (Saunders)
Island of Jewels (Planché)
Island of the Mighty (Arden)
Island Princess (Fletcher)
Island Princess (Tate)
Isle is Full of Noises (Walcott)
Isle of the Dead (Strindberg)
Isle of the Hermaphrodites (Ludlam)
Isma (Sarraute)
Ismene (Satoh)
Ismeretlen lány (Molnár)
Isola meravigliosa (Betti)
Isolation Box (Petrushevskaya)
Ispezione (Betti)
Istoriya s metranpazhem (Vampilov)

István, a magyrok elso királya (Katona)
It Bees Dat Way (Bullins)
It Could Be Any One of Us (Ayckbourn)
It Depends What You Mean (Bridie)
It Happened in Irkutsk (Arbuzov)
It Happened in Venice (Goldoni)
It Has No Choice (Bullins)
It is So (If You Think So) (Pirandello)
It is the Law (Rice)
It is There (Sarraute)
It Will Be Fine Tomorrow (Kishida)
Italian Ballet Master (Harrigan)
Italian Father (Dunlap)
Italian Girl (Saunders)
Italian Husband (Ravenscroft)
Italian Junkman (Harrigan)
Italian Road (Leonard)
Italian Straw Hat (Labiche)
Italiener (s Bernhard)
Italienische Nacht (Horváth)
Ito hime (Kara)
It's a Family Affair (Ostrovsky)
It's a Gamble (Brighouse)
It's Beautiful (Sarraute)
It's Called the Sugar Plum (Horovitz)
It's Later Than You Think (Anouilh)
It's My Criminal (Brenton)
It's Never Too Late to Mend (Reade)
Ivan Vasilevich (Bulgakov)
Ivanhoe (Byron)
Ivanhoë (Dumas *père*)
Ivanov (Chekhov)
I've Got Sixpence (Van Druten)
Iwona, Księżniczka Burgunda (Gombrowicz)
Izutsu (Zeami)
Izzuma (Sarraute)

J. Arthur Maginnis Story (Murphy)
J. Arthur Prufrock Hour (Cook)
Jack (Ionesco)
Jack and the Beanstalk (Ludlam)
Jack and the Joker (Ringwood)
Jack Drum's Entertainment (Marston)
Jack Juan (Hibberd)
Jack Juggler (Udall)
Jack Sheppard (Boucicault)
Jack Straw (Maugham)
Jack the Giant Killer (Byron)
Jackdaw (Gregory)
Jackets I–II (Bond)
Jack-Jack (Terry)
Jackson's Dance (Shepard)
Jacob and Esau (Udall)
Jacob e o Anjo (Régio)
Jacob von Tyboe (Holberg)
Jacobin en mission (Pixérécourt)
Jacobite (Planché)
Jacobowsky and the Colonel (Behrman)
Jacob's Wake (Cook)
Jacques (Ionesco)
Jacques and His Master (Kundera)
Jacques Duval (Kaufman)
Jade Mirror-Stand (Guan Hanqing)
Jadwiga (Wyspiański)
Jagdgesellschaft (Bernhard)
Jagdszenen aus Niederbayern (Sperr)
Jahrmarktsfest (Goethe)

Jahrmarktsfest zu Plundersweilern (Hacks)
J'ai compromis ma femme (Labiche)
J'ai mal aux dents (monologue) (Feydeau)
Jail Diary of Albie Sachs (Edgar)
Jailbird (Shiels)
Jakub a pán (Kundera)
Jalousie du barbouillé (Molière)
James the Fogey (Jones)
James the Fourth (Greene)
Jamie, On a Flying Visit (t Frayn)
Jan Hus (Tyl)
Jan Maciej Karol Wścieklica (Witkiewicz)
Jana (Ringwood)
Jane (Behrman)
Jane Annie (Barrie)
Jane Shore (Rowe)
Janet Pride (Boucicault)
Jano es una muchacha (Usigli)
Janulka, córka Fizdejki (Witkiewicz)
Janyangtian (s Cao Yu)
Jar (Pirandello)
Jardín de Falerina (Calderón)
Jardin de la maison blanche (Barbeau)
Jardin des délices (Arrabal)
Jardinero y los párajos (Carballido)
Jarvis l'honnête homme (Dumas *père*)
Jasager (Brecht)
Jashūmon (Terayama)
Játék a kastélyban (Molnár)
Jaws of Death (Leigh)
Jazva (Karvaš)
Je croque ma tante (Labiche)
Je ne suis pas français (Adamov)
Je ne trompe pas mon mari (Feydeau)
Jealous Old Husband (Cervantes)
Jealous Old Man (Cervantes)
Jealous Wife (Colman the Elder)
Jean and Jeannette (Labiche)
Jean Bête à la foire (Beaumarchais)
Jean de France (Holberg)
Jean de Thommeray (Augier)
Jean Henry Dunant (Forte)
Jeanie Deans (Boucicault)
Jeanne d'Arc (Crommelynck)
Jeanne d'Arc (Maeterlinck)
Jeanne d'Arc au bûcher (Claudel)
Jeannil le Breton (Dumas *père*)
Jedefrau (Brenton)
Jeden za všecky (Tyl)
Jedermann (Hofmannsthal)
Jeeves (Ayckbourn)
Jehr (Hochwälder)
Jejich den (Topol)
Jello (Baraka)
Jenkinses (Planché)
Jenny Villiers (Priestley)
Jenofa Juncal (Sastre)
Jenseits (Hasenclever)
Jenusia (Obaldia)
Jèsus (Piñera)
Jeppe of the Hill (Holberg)
Jeppe på Bierget (Holberg)
Jeremiah's Place (Ryga)
Jérémie (Dubé)
Jerico-Jim Crow (Hughes)
Jero's Metamorphosis (Soyinka)

Jeruzsálem pusztulása (Katona)
Jery and Betty (Goethe)
Jery und Bätely (Goethe)
Jessica! (Claus)
Jessie Brown (Boucicault)
Jest of Hahalaba (Dunsany)
Jésuite (Pixérécourt)
Jeu de la feuillée (Adam de la Halle)
Jeu de l'amour et du hasard (Marivaux)
Jeu de Robin et Marion (Adam de la Halle)
Jeu de Saint Nicolas (Bodel)
Jeune Fille à marier (Ionesco)
Jeune Fille Violaine (Claudel)
Jeune Homme pressé (Labiche)
Jeune Vieillard (Lesage)
Jeunes Barbares d'aujourd'hui (Arrabal)
Jeunesse (Augier)
Jeunesse de Louis XIV (Dumas *père*)
Jeunesse des mousquetaires (Dumas *père*)
Jeunesse illustrée (Arrabal)
Jeux de massacre (Ionesco)
Jeux d'enfants sont faits (Maillet)
Jeux sont faits (s Sartre)
Jew (Cumberland)
Jew of Malta (Marlowe)
Jew of Mogadore (Cumberland)
Jewess (Planché)
Jewess (Scribe)
Jewess of Toledo (Grillparzer)
Jézabel (Anouilh)
Jezebe (Boucicault)
Jia (Cao Yu)
Jian-dan pian (Cao Yu)
Jill and Jack (Osborne)
Jilt (Boucicault)
Jim Dandy (Saroyan)
Jim, Sam, and Anna (Saroyan)
Jimmy Watt (Boucicault)
Jinen the Preacher (Zeami)
Jingo (Wood)
Jinriki hikoki soromon (Terayama)
J'invite le colonel (Labiche)
Jin-xian chi (Guan Hanqing)
J'irai cracher sur vos tombes (Vian)
Jiříkovo vidění (Tyl)
Jiskra v popelu (Langer)
Jitney (A. Wilson)
Jitta's Atonement (Shaw)
Jitters (French)
Jiu feng-chen (Guan Hanqing)
Jízdní hlídka (Langer)
Jo Anne!!! (Bullins)
Jó tündér (Molnár)
Joan (Hewett)
Joan (Reade)
Joan of Arc (s M. Anderson)
Joan of Arc (Taylor)
Joan of Lorraine (M. Anderson)
Joanna of Montfaucon (Cumberland)
João Cambão (Gomes)
Job (Kokoschka)
Jocelyne Trudel trouvée morte dans ses larmes (Laberge)
Jocko (Planché)
Jocrisse the Juggler (Robertson)
Joe Beef (Fennario)
Joe Turner's Come and Gone (A. Wilson)
Joel Brand: Die Geschichte eines Geschäfts (Kipphardt)

Joe's Drum (McGrath)
Johan Padan a la descoverta de le Americhe (Fo)
Johanna von Montfaucon (Kotzebue)
Johannes (Sudermann)
Johannisfeuer (Sudermann)
John (Barry)
John Brown's Body (McGrath)
John Bull (Boucicault)
John Bull (Colman the Younger)
John Bull's Other Island (Shaw)
John Gabriel Borkman (Ibsen)
John Knox (Bridie)
John of Bordeaux (Greene)
John Overy the Miser (Jerrold)
John Pierpont Morgan (Sternheim)
John Shirubaa: Ai no kojiki (Kara)
John Silver: The Beggar of Love (Kara)
Johnny Johnson (Green)
Johnson over Jordan (Priestley)
Joie de Vivre (Rattigan)
Joie imprévue (Marivaux)
Joker of Seville (Tirso De Molina)
Joker of Seville (Walcott)
Joking Apart (Ayckbourn)
Jolly (Chiarelli)
Jona (Hacks)
Jonah (Romeril)
Jonah and the Whale (Bridie)
Jonah 3 (Bridie)
José de las mujeres (Calderón)
Joseph Entangled (Jones)
Josephine (Barrie)
Josephs Legende (Hofmannsthal)
Joss Adams Show (De Groen)
Joualez-moi d'amour (Barbeau)
Joueur (Regnard)
Joueur de flûte (Augier)
Jourmard (Walcott)
Journalists (Wesker)
Journey of M. Perrichon (Labiche)
Journey of the Soul (Dunsany)
Journey to Jerusalem (M. Anderson)
Journey to London (Saunders)
Journeys Among the Dead (Ionesco)
Jovial Crew (Brome)
Joy (Galsworthy)
Joy of Living (Sudermann)
Joy to My Soul (Hughes)
Joya de las montañas (Tirso De Molina)
Joyeuse criée (Maillet)
Joyeux retour (Tardieu)
Joyous Season (Barry)
Joyzelle (Maeterlinck)
Józsi (Molnár)
Jüdin von Toledo (Grillparzer)
Jüdische Witwe (Kaiser)
Jüngling (Sorge)
Jüngste Tag (Horváth)
Juan Feldman (Richardson)
Juana (Kaiser)
Jubilee (Chekhov)
Jubilee (Heijermans)
Juda de Kérioth (Maeterlinck)
Judah (Jones)
Judas Ischarioth (Sternheim)
Judas Macabeo (Calderón)
Juden (Lessing)

Judeo (Santareno)
Judge (Gorky)
Judge (Mortimer)
Judge of the Divorce Court (Cervantes)
Judgement (Horváth)
Judgement Day (Rice)
Judgement of Paris (Congreve)
Judge's Wife (t Churchill)
Judith (Bickerstaff)
Judith (Fry)
Judith (Giraudoux)
Judith (H. Barker)
Judith (Hebbel)
Judith (Hochhuth)
Judith and Holofernes (Nestroy)
Judith, the Daughter of Merari (Daly)
Judith und Holofernes (Nestroy)
Jueces en la noche (Buero Vallejo)
Juerga de los polichinelas (Arlt)
Juez de los divorcios (Cervantes)
Jugement dernier (Maeterlinck)
Jugglers Three (Williamson)
Juguetes olvidados (Díaz)
Juive (Scribe)
Jule-stue (Holberg)
Julia (Hebbel)
Julius Caesar (Kroetz)
Julius Caesar (Shakespeare)
Juliusz II (Wyspiański)
Jumbo (Hecht)
Jumbo-Track (Kroetz)
Jumeaux (Hugo)
Jumeaux étincelants (Obaldia)
Jumpers (Stoppard)
June Moon (Kaufman)
Junge Gelehrte (Lessing)
Junge Medardus (Schnitzler)
Junge Welt (Wedekind)
Jungfrau vom Bischofsberg (Hauptmann)
Jungfrau von Orleans (Schiller)
Jungle of Cities (Brecht)
Junius Brutus (Bulwer-Lytton)
Junkies Are Full of (SHHH . . .) (Baraka)
Juno and the Paycock (O'Casey)
Juré (Feydeau)
Juristen (Hochhuth)
Just (Camus)
Just a Little Simple (Childress)
Just an Ordinary Person (Ryga)
Just Around the Corner (Hughes)
Just Assassins (Camus)
Just Before the Honeymoon (Hibberd)
Just Between Ourselves (Ayckbourn)
Just Italian (Davenant)
Justes (Camus)
Justice (Galsworthy)
Justice Without Revenge (Vega)

K.41 (Chiarelli)
K zvezdam (Andreyev)
Kabala sviatosh (Bulgakov)
Kabale und Liebe (Schiller)
Kaera shoten (Kinoshita)
Kaeraji-to (Kishida)
Kærlighed (Munk)
Kaffeehaus (Fassbinder)
Käficht (Kotzebue)

Kafka's Dick (Bennett)
Kagekiyo (Zeami)
Kainova pechat (Ne ubi) (Andreyev)
Kaiser Claudius (Kotzebue)
Kaiser Karls Geisel (Hauptmann)
Kaiser Oktavianus (Tieck)
Kaiser und die Hexe (Hofmannsthal)
Kaiserin von Neufundland (Wedekind)
Kakadu-Kakadu (Zuckmayer)
Kakitsubata (Zeami)
Kalbskopf (Bernhard)
Kalkutta 4 Mai (Brecht)
Kalldewey Farce (Strauss)
Kalte Licht (Zuckmayer)
Kamen, broshenny v vody (Sologub)
Kamenny gost (Pushkin)Kkamerschut (Heijermans)
Kami fūsen (Kishida)
Kami to hito to na aida (Kinoshita)
Kammersänger (Wedekind)
Kampl (Nestroy)
Kamraterna (Strindberg)
Kandidat (Sternheim)
Kantan (Zeami)
Kantaten auf der Kellertreppe (Walser)
Kanzlist Krehler (Kaiser)
Kaos år dagens med Gud (Norén)
Kaoyo Utragaruta (Chikamatsu)
Kapitän Belronde (Kotzebue)
Kapodhistrias (Kazantzakis)
Kappa (Kara)
Kara-ban kaze no Matasaburō (Kara)
Kara-ban taki no shiraito (Kara)
Karaluchy (Witkiewicz)
Kardinalen og Kongen (Munk)
Karikaturen-Charivari (Nestroy)
Karl Hetmann (Wedekind)
Karl XII (Strindberg)
Karl von Berneck (Tieck)
Karna and Kunti (Tagore)
Karol (Mrożek)
Kartenspieler (Bernhard)
Kartoteka (Różewicz)
Kasimir and Karoline (Horváth)
Kasimir und Karoline (Horváth)
Kaspar Hausers Tod (Forte)
Kaspar (Handke)
Kašpárek jako detektiv (Langer)
Kassette (Sternheim)
Kastruchcha (Volodin)
Kat (Zuckmayer)
Kate Peyton (Reade)
Kater und der Rosenstock (Kotzebue)
Katerina (Andreyev)
Katharina Knie (Zuckmayer)
Käthchen von Heilbronn (Kleist)
Katmandu (Terry)
Katzelmacher (Fassbinder)
Katzelmacher (s Fassbinder)
Kaukasische Kreidekreis (Brecht)
Kayoi Komachi (Zeami)
Kazanbaichi (Kubo)
Kazimierz Wielki (Wyspiański)
Kean (Dumas *père*)
Kean (Sartre)
Keep an Eye on Amélie (Feydeau)
Keep Tightly Closed in a Cool Dry Place (Terry)
Keep Your Own Secret (Calderón)

Keeping Barbara (Lawrence)
Kegawa no Mari (Terayama)
Kegger (Terry)
Keiner ist böse und keiner ist gut (r Fassbinder)
Keisei Hangoko (Chikamatsu)
Kejser og Galilæer (Ibsen)
Kelly Dance (Romeril)
Kenilworth Castle (Planché)
Kerry (Boucicault)
Key is on the Bottom (Terry)
Key Largo (M. Anderson)
Keys of Heaven (Strindberg)
Khochu rebenka (Tretyakov)
Kholostyak (Turgenev)
Kid Stakes (Lawler)
Kiddie (Crothers)
Kiktahan (Zuckmayer)
Kilde-reysen (Holberg)
Kill (Leonard)
Killdeer (Reaney)
Killer (Ionesco)
Killer Dove (Horovitz)
Killer's Head (Shepard)
Killing Game (Ionesco)
Killycreggs in Twilight (Robinson)
Kincora (Gregory)
Kind der Liebe (Kotzebue)
Kind Keeper (Dryden)
Kind (Heijermans)
Kind of Alaska (Pinter)
Kinder (Hacks)
Kinder und Narren (Wedekind)
Kindermörderin (Hacks)
Kinderspiel (Walser)
Kindred (Carroll)
Kindred (Kotzebue)
King (Bjørnson)
King (Lagerkvist)
King and No King (Beaumont, Fletcher)
King and the Queen (Tagore)
King Argimenes and the Unknown Warrior (Dunsany)
King Arthur (Dryden)
King Calico's Body Guard (Harrigan)
King Carrot (Daly)
King Charming (Planché)
King Christmas (Planché)
King Edgar and Alfreda (Ravenscroft)
King Edward the First (Peele)
King Edward the Fourth I–II (Heywood)
King Golgrutha (Sewell)
King Hunger (Andreyev)
King James His Royal and Magnificent Entertainment (Dekker, Jonson)
King John (Shakespeare)
King Lear (Colman the Elder)
King Lear (Shakespeare)
King Lear (Tate)
King Nicolo (Wedekind)
King Oedipus (Sophocles)
King Oedipus (Yeats)
King of Comedy (Ostrovsky)
King of Nowhere (Bridie)
King of the Alps (Raimund)
King of the Barna Men (Fitzmaurice)
King of the Dark Chamber (Tagore)
King of the Great Clock Tower (Yeats)
King of the Peacocks (Planché)

King of the United States (van Itallie)
King Ottokar, His Rise and Fall (Grillparzer)
King Richard III (Cibber)
King Richard the Second (Tate)
King Stag (Gozzi)
King, the Greatest Alcalde (Vega)
King Ubu (Jarry)
King Whistle! (Reaney)
King Who Could Not Laugh (Carroll)
Kingdom Come (Parker)
Kingdom of Earth (Williams)
Kingdom of God (Granville-Barker)
Kingdom of the Young (Colum)
King's Diversion (Hugo)
King's Edict (Hugo)
King's Entertainment at Welbeck (Jonson)
King's Maid (Molnár)
King's Rival (Reade, Taylor)
King's Threshold (Yeats)
King's Waistcoat (Brighouse)
Kinuta (Zeami)
Kipper (Braun)
Kirche, Küchen und Kinder (Williams)
Kiss for Cinderella (Barrie)
Kiss the One-Eyed Priest (Nowra)
Kissing Sweet (t Guare)
Kitchen (Wesker)
Kitchen Comedy (r Bridie)
Kitchen Table (Romeril)
Kiyotsune (Zeami)
Kjæmpehøjen (Ibsen)
Kjærlighedens komedie (Ibsen)
Klad (Shvarts)
Klag (Hibberd)
Klaras Mutter (t Dorst)
Klass (Arbuzov)
Klątwa (Wyspiański)
Klawitter (Kaiser)
Kleinbürgerhochzeit (Brecht)
Kleine Chaos (s Fassbinder)
Kleine Deklamator (Kotzebue)
Kleine Welttheater (Hofmannsthal)
Kleine Zigeunerin (Kotzebue)
Kleiner Mann, was nun? (Dorst)
Klettwitzer Bericht (r Muller)
Klop (Mayakovsky)
Kluge Frau vom Walde (Kotzebue)
Knack (Jellicoe)
Knacker's ABC (Vian)
Knackery for All (Vian)
Knave or Not? (Holcroft)
Knickerbocker Holiday (M. Anderson)
Knife (Hare)
Knife (Jones)
Knight from Olmedo (Vega)
Knight of Arva (Boucicault)
Knight of Guadalquiver (Dunlap)
Knight of Malta (Fletcher, Massinger)
Knight of the Burning Pestle (Beaumont)
Knight of the Rose (Hofmannsthal)
Knights (Aristophanes)
Knights (Foote)
Knight's Adventure (Dunlap)
Knights of the Round Table (Cocteau)
Knights of the Round Table (Planché)
Knightsbridge (t Mortimer)
Knock (Terayama)

Knock at the Door (Heijermans)
Knock at the Manor Gate (Berkoff)
Knuckle (Hare)
Kobold (Nestroy)
Kočka na kolejích (Topol)
Koi Hakkée Hashiragoyomi (Chikamatsu)
Koi no Omoni (Zeami)
Koi-koi karuta Nezumi Kozo Kirokichi (Satoh)
Kokhmal (Petrushevskaya)
Kokusenya Kassen (Chikamatsu)
Kollege Crampton (Hauptmann)
Kolportage (Kaiser)
Komachi at Sekidera (Zeami)
Komagata Maru Incident (Pollock)
Komedie z życia rodzinnego (Witkiewicz)
Komik XVII stoletiya (Ostrovsky)
Kommt ein Vogel geflogen (Hasenclever)
Komödiantin aus Liebe (Kotzebue)
Komödie der Verführung (Schnitzler)
Komödie der Worte (Schnitzler)
Kompromis Naib-Khana (Ivanov)
Komtesse Mizzi (Schnitzler)
Kon v senate (Andreyev)
Konec masopustu (Topol)
Konfuse Zauberer (Nestroy)
Kong Eynstejn (Bjørnson)
Kong Sverre (Bjørnson)
Kongen (Bjørnson)
Kongen (Munk)
Kongi's Harvest (Soyinka)
Kongs-Emnerne (Ibsen)
Koníčky (Langer)
König David (Sorge)
König Hahnrei (Kaiser)
König Johann (Dürrenmatt)
König Nicolo (Wedekind)
König Ödipus (Hofmannsthal)
König Ottokars Glück und Ende (Grillparzer)
Königsmark (Boker)
Konstantinos Paleologhos (Kazantzakis)
Kontrakt (Mrożek)
Konungen (Lagerkvist)
Koori Radio (Romeril)
Köpfe (Bernhard)
Koralle (Kaiser)
Koralle Meier (Sperr)
Korbes (Dorst)
Korion (Fonvizin)
Korol na ploschadi (Blok)
Korol, zakon i svoboda (Andreyev)
Korrektur (Müller)
Korrektur (r Muller)
Kosack und der Freiwillige (Kotzebue)
Kosciuszko (Grabbe)
Koshimaki Osen (Kara)
Köstlichste (Kotzebue)
Koulouf (Pixérécourt)
Kouros (Kazantzakis)
Kozma Zacharich Minin, Sukhoruk (Ostrovsky)
Kranichtanz (Zuckmayer)
Krapp's Last Tape (Beckett)
Krasavets-muzhchina (Ostrovsky)
Krasnaya Shapochka (Shvarts)
Krawiec (Mrożek)
Krechinsky's Wedding (Sukhovo-Kobylin)
Kreutzer Sonata (Mitchell)
Kreuzfahrer (Kotzebue)

Kreuzweg (Zuckmayer)
Kristina (Strindberg)
Krokhmal E Razmyshlenya u razbitogo koryta. . .
(Petrushevskaya)
Król Kazimierz Jagiellonczyk (Wyspiański)
Królowa polskiej korony (Wyspiański)
Kronbruden (Strindberg)
Krvavé křtiny (Tyl)
Księżniczka Magdalena (Witkiewicz)
Kto brat, kto sestra (Griboyedov)
Küffhäuser-Berg (Kotzebue)
Kühle Wampe (s Brecht)
Kukolny gorod (Shvarts)
Kulcskeresők (Örkény)
Kunst der Zähmung (Sperr)
Kurai hibana (Kinoshita)
Kureba (Zeami)
Kurka wodna (Witkiewicz)
Kuroi tulip (Kara)
Kurunmi (Rotimi)
Kurve (Dorst)
Kutnohorští havíři (Tyl)
Kvartira Kolumbiny (Petrushevskaya)
Kvetch (Berkoff)
Kwan-Hasshu Tsunagi (Chikamatsu)
Kynolog w rozterce (Mrożek)
Kyūketsuki (Kara)

L.E.F. (Chiarelli)
La! Somnambula (Byron)
La'bat al-Mawt (Tawfiq al-Hakim)
Laberinto de amor (Cervantes)
Laberinto de Creta (Silva)
Laberinto de Creta (Tirso De Molina)
Laberinto del mundo (Calderón)
Laboremus (Bjørnson)
Labour (Wood)
Laburnum Grove (Priestley)
Labyrinth (Arrabal)
Labyrinth (T. Corneille)
Labyrinth der Träume (Forte)
Labyrinthe (Arrabal)
Lackey's Carnival (Jones)
Lacrime e le stelle (Chiarelli)
Lacune (Ionesco)
Lad of the Hills (O'Keeffe)
Ladder of Fools (Brenton)
Laddie Boy (Ryga)
Ladies and Gentlemen (Hecht)
Ladies' Battle (Reade)
Ladies' Battle (Robertson)
Ladies' Battle (Scribe)
Ladies' Day (Aristophanes)
Ladies' Man (Feydeau)
Ladri, manichini e donne nude (Fo)
Lady (Benavente y Martínez)
Lady Belle Belle (Byron)
Lady Bird (Boucicault)
Lady Bountiful (Pinero)
Lady Caprice (Jones)
Lady Clancarty (Taylor)
Lady Frederick (Maugham)
Lady from Alfaqueque (Granville-Barker)
Lady from Dubuque (Albee)
Lady from Maxim's (Feydeau)
Lady from Maxim's (Mortimer)
Lady from the Sea (Ibsen)

Lady from the Sea (Jellicoe)
Lady Han (Zeami)
Lady in Difficulties (Planché)
Lady Inger of Ostraat (Ibsen)
Lady Jane Gray (Rowe)
Lady Julie (Strindberg)
Lady Killer (Jerrold)
Lady Nit-Wit (Vega)
Lady of Andros (Terence)
Lady of Belle Isle (Dumas père)
Lady of Larkspur Lotion (Williams)
Lady of Lions (Harrigan)
Lady of Luzon (Connelly)
Lady of Lyons (Bulwer-Lytton)
Lady of Lyons (Byron)
Lady of Pleasure (Shirley)
Lady of the Camellias (Durmas fils)
Lady of the Camellias (Nowra)
Lady of the Dawn (Casona)
Lady of the Lane (Byron)
Lady of the Rock (Holcroft)
Lady Othello (Wesker)
Lady Rose's Brazil Hide Out (Terry)
Lady und Schneider (Nestroy)
Lady Windermere's Fan (Wilde)
Lady's Last Stake (Cibber)
Lady's Not for Burning (Fry)
Lady's Trial (Ford)
Lady's Virtue (Crothers)
Lagos de San Vincente (Tirso De Molina)
Lai de Barabbas (Arrabal)
Laird de Dumbicky (Dumas père)
Lakeboat (Mamet)
Lakeyskaya (Gogol)
Lamb and the Beast (Strindberg)
Lame Lover (Foote)
Lament for Harmonica (Ringwood)
Lamentable Julie (Willems)
Lammet och vilddjuret (Strindberg)
Lámparas del cielo y de la tierra (Carballido)
Lancashire Lad (Kennedy)
Lancashire Lass (Byron)
Lancashire Witches (Shadwell)
Lancelo (Bridie)
Lances de amor y fortuna (Calderón)
Land (Colum)
Land is Bright (Kaufman)
Land of Heart's Desire (Yeats)
Land of Promise (Maugham)
Land of Volcanic Ash (Kubo)
Landed Gentry (Maugham)
Landhaus an der Heerstrasse (Kotzebue)
Landscape (Pinter)
Landscape (Rice)
Landscape of the Body (Guare)
Landshuter Erzählungen (Sperr)
Landslide (Betti)
Langrishe, Go Down (t Pinter)
Laodice, Reine de Cappadoce (T. Corneille)
Largo Desolato (Havel)
Largo Desolato (Stoppard)
Lark (Anouilh)
Lark (Fry)
Lark (Hellman)
Larmes de l'aveugle (r Obaldia)
Lascio all mie donne (Fabbri)
Lásky hra osudná (Čapek)

Last Act is a Solo (R. Anderson)
Last Carnival (Walcott)
Last Crusade of the Five Little Nuns (Leigh)
Last Day of the War (r Laurents)
Last Days—Pushkin (Bulgakov)
Last Night of Don Juan (Howard)
Last Night of Don Juan (Rostand)
Last of My Solid Gold Watches (Williams)
Last of the Dandies (Fitch)
Last of the Family (Cumberland)
Last of the Gladiators (Ryga)
Last of the Hogans (Harrigan)
Last of the Knights (Strindberg)
Last of the Lowries (Green)
Last of the Red Hot Lovers (Simon)
Last of the Wine (Bolt)
Last Pad (Inge)
Last Place on Earth (t Griffiths)
Last Sacrifice (Ostrovsky)
Last Summer in Chulimsk (Vampilov)
Last Supper (H. Barker)
Last Testament (Prevelakis)
Last Trump (Bridie)
Last Tycoon (s Pinter)
Last Word (Daly)
Last Yankee (Miller)
Lästigen (Hofmannsthal)
Låt människan leva (Lagerkvist)
Late Christopher Bean (Howard)
Late George Apley (Kaufman)
Late Lamented (Taylor)
Late Lancashire Witches (Brome, Heywood)
Latent Heterosexual (Chayefsky)
Latter Days of a Celebrated Soubrette (Williams)
Latude (Pixérécourt)
Laughing Mind (Brighouse)
Laughing Wild (Durang)
Laughter! (Barnes)
Laughter of the Gods (Dunsany)
Laune des Verliebten (Goethe)
Laure persécutée (Rotrou)
Laurel de Apolo (Calderón)
Lavender Bags (Hibberd)
Law Against Lovers (Davenant)
Law and Lions! (Jerrold)
Law of Java (Colman the Younger)
Lawsuit (Gogol)
Lawyer (Molnár)
Lay By (Brenton, Griffiths, Hare, Poliakoff)
Lay By (Hare)
Lay Off (McGrath)
Lay Out Letter (Fuller)
Lay This Body Down (Green)
Laying a Ghost (Boucicault)
Lazare (Obey)
Lazaretti (Hochwälder)
Lázaro en el laberinto (Buero Vallejo)
Lazaros (Prevelakis)
Lazarre (Zola)
Lazarus Laughed (O'Neill)
Lazarus (Pirandello)
Lazzaro (Pirandello)
Leader (Horovitz)
Leader (Ionesco)
League of Nations (Hibberd)
League of Youth (Ibsen)
Leah the Forsaken (Daly)

Lealtad contra la envidia (Tirso De Molina)
Léandre marchand d'Agnus (Beaumarchais)
Leap in the Dark (Leonard)
Lear (Bond)
Learned Ladies (Molière)
Learned Women (Molière)
Learning to Walk (Ionesco)
Leather Patch (Harrigan)
Leave Her to Heaven (Van Druten)
Leaving Home (French)
Leaving the Theater After a Performance of a New Comedy (Gogol)
Leavings (Bullins)
Lebedinaya pesnya (Chekhov)
Leben des Galilei (Brecht)
Leben des Horace A.W. Tabor (Zuckmayer)
Leben des schizophrenen Dichters Alexander März (t Kipphardt)
Leben Eduards des Zweiten von England (Brecht)
Leben Gundlings Friedrich von Preussen . . . (Müller)
Leben und Tod der heiligen Genoveva (Tieck)
Lebendige Stunden (Schnitzler)
Lebrel del cielo (Benavente y Martínez)
Lecciones de buen amor (Benavente y Martínez)
Leçon (Ionesco)
Leçons de français pour Américains (Ionesco)
Led Astray (Boucicault)
Leda und der Schwan (Hofmannsthal)
Lederköpfe (Kaiser)
Left Bank (Rice)
Left-Handed Liberty (Arden)
Left Out Lady (McGrath)
Legacy (Schnitzler)
Legami pure che tanto io spacco tutto lo stesso (Fo)
Légataire universel (Regnard)
Legend of Lovers (Anouilh)
Legend of "Norwood" (Daly)
Legend of Semimaru (Chikamatsu)
Legend of the Devil's Dyke (Boucicault)
Legenda I–II (Wyspiański)
Legends (Romeril)
Leggenda del ritorno (Fabbri)
Legger e scriveree (Chiarelli)
Leghorn Hat (Labiche)
Legion (Wyspiański)
Legion of Honour (Planché)
Legs Diamond (Fierstein)
Legs (Marivaux)
Leicester (Dunlap)
Leidende Weib (Sternheim)
Leineweber (Kotzebue)
Leiyu (Cao Yu)
Leka med elden (Strindberg)
Lelewel (Wyspiański)
Lemming (Terayama)
Lemon Sky (L. Wilson)
Lemons (Daly)
Lena (Ariosto)
Lend Me Your Wife (Boucicault)
Lenins Tod (Braun)
Lennon Play (Kennedy)
Lente maravillosa (Carballido)
Léo Burckart (Dumas *père*)
Léocadia (Anouilh)
Léocadia (r Wertenbaker)
Léocadia (Scribe)
Léocadie (Scribe)

Liolà (Pirandello)
Lion and the Jewel (Soyinka)
Lion and the Unicorn Were Fighting for the Crown (Byron)
Lion in Love (Delaney)
Lionel and Clarissa (Bickerstaff)
Lionnes pauvres (Augier)
Lions et renards (Augier)
Liquid Amber (Hibberd)
Lirio y la azucena (Calderón)
Lis aspirant (Mrożek)
Lis filozof (Mrożek)
Listen to the Wind (Reaney)
Listening (Albee)
Literatur (Schnitzler)
Literatura (Benavente y Martínez)
Litigants (Racine)
Litko (Mamet)
Little Bit to Fall Back On (Feydeau)
Little Carthaginian (Plautus)
Little David (Connelly)
Little Dick Whittington (Byron)
Little Doctor Faust (Byron)
Little Don Caesar de Bazan (Byron)
Little Don Giovanni (Byron)
Little Dream (Galsworthy)
Little Eyolf (Ibsen)
Little Foxes (Hellman)
Little Fraud (Harrigan)
Little French Lawyer (Fletcher, Massinger)
Little Ham (Hughes)
Little Hotel on the Side (Feydeau)
Little Hotel on the Side (Mortimer)
Little Hunch-Back (O'Keeffe)
Little Journey (Crothers)
Little Liberty (Brighouse)
Little Man (Galsworthy)
Little Me (Simon)
Little Minister (Barrie)
Little Miss Million (Daly)
Little Ocean (Shepard)
Little Old Lady (Wesker)
Little Red Hen (McGrath)
Little Red Riding Hood (Taylor)
Little Red Riding-Hood (Planché)
Little Red Shoes (Brighouse)
Little Theatre of the World (Hofmannsthal)
Liturgia para cornudos (Díaz)
Liturgiya nme (Sologub)
Live Corpse (L. N. Tolstoy)
Live Like Pigs (Arden)
Lives of the Great Poisoners (Churchill)
Living Corpse (L. N. Tolstoy)
Living for Show (Daly)
Living Hours (Schnitzler)
Living Quarters (Friel)
Living Skeleton (Jerrold)
Livre bleu (Labiche)
Livre de Christophe Colomb (Claudel)
Llamados y escogidos (Calderón)
Llave en el desvan (Casona)
Llegada de los dioses (Buero Vallejo)
Lo increíble (Benavente y Martínez)
Lo que hay que fiar del mundo (Vega)
Lo que no puede decirse (Echegaray)
Lo que va del hombre a Dios (Calderón)
Loan of a Lover (Planché)
Loaves and Fishes (Maugham)

Lobgesänge des Claudian (Sudermann)
Local Authority (De Filippo)
Local Boy Makes Good (Kaufman)
Locandiera (Goldoni)
Loco Dios (Echegaray)
Locomotive (Marinetti)
Locuturio (Díaz)
Lodge (Ringwood)
Lodgings to Let (Boucicault)
Lodgings to Let (Planché)
Logeuse (Audiberti)
Lohengrin (Nestroy)
Lohn der Wahrheit (Kotzebue)
Lohndrücker (Müller)
Loire (Obey)
Lois de Minos (Voltaire)
Lolah (Boucicault)
Lolita in the Garden (Fornés)
Lolita (Albee)
Lomonosov (Ivanov)
Londini Artium et Scientiarum Scaturigo (Heywood)
Londini Emporia (Heywood)
Londini Sinus Salutis (Heywood)
Londini Speculum (Heywood)
Londini Status Pacatus (Heywood)
London Assurance (Boucicault)
London Calling! (Coward)
London Characters (Jerrold)
London Cuckolds (Ravenscroft)
London Front (Brighouse)
London Hermit (O'Keeffe)
London Merchant (Lillo)
London Morning (Coward)
London Vertigo (Friel)
London Wall (Van Druten)
London's Jus Honorarium (Heywood)
London's Tempe (Dekker)
Lone Canoe (Mamet)
Lone Star (Green)
Lonely Lives (Hauptmann)
Lonely Man of Shiraz (Jerrold)
Lonely Road (Schnitzler)
Lonely Way (Schnitzler)
Lonesome-like (Brighouse)
Long Christmas Dinner (Wilder)
Long Day's Journey into Night (O'Neill)
Long Goodbye (Williams)
Long Mirror (Priestley)
Long Night (Green)
Long Strike (Boucicault)
Long Voyage Home (O'Neill)
Long Way Round (Handke)
Lönggången (Bergman)
Look After Lulu (Coward)
Look After Lulu (Feydeau)
Look Back in Anger (Osborne)
Look Behind You Neighbour (Ringwood)
Look Look (Frayn)
Looking Glass for London and England (Greene)
Loot (Orton)
Lord Adrian (Dunsany)
Lord Bateman (Byron)
Lord Byron's Love Letter (Williams)
Lord Dundreary Married and Done For (Byron)
Lord Halewyn (Ghelderode)
Lord Harry (Jones)
Lord Kuan Goes to the Feast (Guan Hanqing)

Lord Mayor's Day (O'Keeffe)
Lord Pengo (Behrman)
Lords and Commons (Pinero)
Lord's Will (Green)
Lorenzaccio (Musset)
Lorenzino (Dumas *père*)
Lorenzo (Richardson)
Lorgaire (Harrigan)
Lorlie's Wedding (Daly)
Loro peccati (Fabbri)
Los des Ossian Balvesen (Kaiser)
Losa de los sueños (Benavente y Martínez)
Loser Wins (Sartre)
Losing Game (Gregory)
Loss of a Teardrop Diamond (s Williams)
Loss of Memory (Laurents)
Loss of Roses (Inge)
Lost at Sea (Boucicault)
Lost at Sea (Byron)
Lost Child's Fireflies (Saroyan)
Lost Colony (Green)
Lost Husband (Reade)
Lost in a Mirror (Vega)
Lost in the Stars (M. Anderson)
Lost in Yonkers (Simon)
Lost Leader (Robinson)
Lost Letter (Caragiale)
Lost Saint (Gregory)
Lost Silk Hat (Dunsany)
Lost Weekend (Romeril)
Lotta fino all'alba (Betti)
Lottery (Fielding)
Lottery of Love (Daly)
Loud Boy's Life (H. Barker)
Loudspeaker (Lawson)
Louis XI (Boucicault)
Louise Bernard (Dumas *père*)
Louisiana Cavalier (Green)
Louisiana Territory (Kopit)
Louison (Musset)
Lounge Player (Horovitz)
Loup (Anouilh)
Loupežník (Čapek)
Love Affairs and Wedding Bells (Nestroy)
Love After All (Ayckbourn)
Love After Death (Calderón)
Love Among the Ruins (Rice)
Love and a Bottle (Farquhar)
Love and Ange (Walker)
Love and Fortune (Planché)
Love and Geography (Bjørnson)
Love and Honour (Davenant)
Love and How to Cure It (Wilder)
Love and Life (Taylor)
Love and Money (Boucicault)
Love and Money (Reade)
Love and War (O'Keeffe)
Love at a Venture (Centlivre)
Love Charm (Planché)
Love, Death and a Crown (Casona)
Love Death (Inge)
Love for Love (Congreve)
Love for Three Oranges (Stoppard)
Love Freed from Ignorance and Folly (Jonson)
Love Games (Schnitzler)
Love in a Camp (O'Keeffe)
Love in a Cottage (Maugham)

Love in a Maze (Boucicault)
Love in a Riddle (Cibber)
Love in a Sack (Boucicault)
Love in a Tub (Etherege)
Love in a Village (Bickerstaff)
Love in a Wood (Wycherley)
Love in Harness (Daly)
Love in Humble Life (Scribe)
Love in Idleness (Rattigan)
Love in Livery (Marivaux)
Love in Several Masques (Fielding)
Love in Tandem (Daly)
Love in the City (Bickerstaff)
Love is Like That (Behrman)
Love is Not to Be Trifled With (Musset)
Love is the Best Remedy (Molière)
Love is the Greatest Enchantment (Calderón)
Love Laughs at Locksmiths (Colman the Younger)
Love Letter from the Licensed Quarter (Chikamatsu)
Love Letters on Blue Paper (Wesker)
Love Makes a Man (Cibber)
Love Nest (Sherwood)
Love of a Good Man (H. Barker)
Love of Don Perlimpín and Belisa in the Garden (García
    Lorca)
Love of Hyppolita (Augier)
Love of King David and Fair Bethsabe (Peele)
Love of One's Neighbor (Andreyev)
Love of the Nightingale (Wertenbaker)
Love of Three Oranges (Gozzi)
Love on Crutches (Daly)
Love Passes By (Granville-Barker)
Love Restored (Jonson)
Love Revisited (R. Anderson)
Love Space Demands (Shange)
Love Story (Behrman)
Love Suicide at Amijima (Chikamatsu)
Love Suicides at Sonezaki (Chikamatsu)
Love Suicides in the Women's Temple (Chikamatsu)
Love Thy Neighbour (Andreyev)
Love Tiff (Molière)
Love Triumphant (Dryden)
Love vs. Insurance (Harrigan)
Love Yourself Above All Others (Díaz)
Loveliest Afternoon of the Year (Guare)
Lovely Sunday for Creve Coeur (Williams)
Lovely to Look At! (Arbuzov)
Lover (Pinter)
Lover by Proxy (Boucicault)
Lovers (Friel)
Lovers and Keepers (Fornés)
Lovers' Lane (Fitch)
Lovers Made Men (Jonson)
Lover's Melancholy (Ford)
Lover's Progress (Fletcher, Massinger)
Lovers' Quarrels (Molière)
Lovers' Resolutions (Cumberland)
Lovers' Vows (Dunlap)
Lovers' Vows (Inchbald)
Lovers' Vows (Kotzebue)
Lover's Whim (Goethe)
Love's Alarum (Planché)
Love's Comedy (Ibsen)
Love's Contrivance (Centlivre)
Love's Contrivance (Molière)
Love's Cruelty (Shirley)
Love's Cure (Beaumont, Fletcher, Massinger)

Love's Frailties (Holcroft)
Love's Labour's Lost (Auden)
Love's Labour's Lost (Daly)
Love's Labour's Lost (Shakespeare)
Love's Last Shift (Cibber)
Love's Metamorphosis (Lyly)
Love's Mistress (Heywood)
Loves of Cass McGuire (Friel)
Love's Old Sweet Song (Saroyan)
Love's Pilgrimage (Beaumont, Fletcher)
Love's Sacrifice (Ford)
Love's Tangled Webb (Ludlam)
Love's Triumph (Planché)
Love's Triumph Through Callipolis (Jonson)
Love's Welcome at Bolsover (Jonson)
Love's Young Dream (Daly)
Lovesick (r Churchill)
Love-Sick Court (Brome)
Low Life (Harrigan)
Low Water (Pinero)
Lower Depths (Gorky)
Loyal Brother (Southerne)
Loyal General (Tate)
Loyal Subject (Fletcher)
Loyalties (Galsworthy)
Lu Zhai-lang (Guan Hanqing)
Lubie (r Pinget)
Luca széke karácsony éjszakajan (Katona)
Luces de Bohemia (Valle-Inclán)
Luci veloci (Marinetti)
Lucia di Lammermoor (Byron)
Lucidor (Hofmannsthal)
Lucifer and the Lord (Sartre)
Lucius Junius Brutus (Lee)
Lucky Chance (Behn)
Lucky Finger (Robinson)
Lucky Pehr (Strindberg)
Lucky Per's Journey (Strindberg)
Lucky Peter's Travels (Strindberg)
Lucky Sam McCarver (Howard)
Lucky Spot (Henley)
Lucrèce (Hardy)
Lucrece (Obey)
Lucrèce (Wilder)
Lucrèce Borgia (Hugo)
Lucrécia (Garrett)
Lucretia Borgia (Hugo)
Lucrezia Borgia, M.D. (Byron)
Ludlow Fair (L. Wilson)
Luftmensch (Mamet)
Lugar donde mueren los mamíferos (Díaz)
Lugar y la hora (Carballido)
Lüge mit der gute Absicht (Kotzebue)
Lügenfeind (Kotzebue)
Lugre (Santareno)
Luis Pérez el gallego (Calderón)
Luisa (Giacosa)
Lulu (Barnes)
Lulu (Nowra)
Lulu (Wedekind)
Lumie di Sicilia (Pirandello)
Luminalia (Davenant)
Lunatics and Lovers (Kingsley)
Lunch Hour (Mortimer)
Lunch (Berkoff)
L'undia z našej ulice (Karvaš)
Lune à la recherche d'elle-même (Claudel)

Lusitania Songspiel (Durang)
Lust's Dominion (Dekker)
Lustspiel am Fenster (Kotzebue)
Lute Song (Howard)
Luther (Osborne)
Lux in Tenebris (Brecht)
Lycéenne (Feydeau)
Lycko-Pers resa (Strindberg)
Lydia Gilmore (Jones)
Lydie Breeze (Guare)
Lygdamon et Lidias (Scudéry)
Lying Lover (P. Corneille)
Lying Lover (Steele)
Lykkelige Skibbruid (Holberg)
Lysistrata (Aristophanes)
Lysistrata (Claus)
Lysistrata (Tremblay)
Lysistrate und die NATO (Hochhuth)
Lyubov (Petrushevskaya)
Lyubov i vernost (Sologub)
Lyubov k blizhnemu (Andreyev)
Lyubov nad bezdnami (Sologub)
Lyubvi (Sologub)

"M" is for Moon Among Other Things (r Stoppard)
M Le Modéré (Adamov)
M.P. (Robertson)
M.S.V. (Sastre)
Ma non è una cosa seria (Pirandello)
Ma Rainey's Black Bottom (A. Wilson)
Ma'a az-Zaman (Tawfiq al-Hakim)
Mabel's Life (Byron)
Macbeth (Davenant)
Macbeth (Maeterlinck)
Macbeth (Müller)
Macbeth (Schiller)
Macbeth (Shakespeare)
Macbett (Ionesco)
Machien (Heijermans)
Machine à écrire (Cocteau)
Machine infernale (Cocteau)
Machine Wreckers (Toller)
Macht der Gewohnheit (Bernhard)
Maciej Korbowa i Bellatrix (Witkiewicz)
Mackerel (Horovitz)
Mackinac (Mamet)
Macquarie (Buzo)
Macskajáték (Örkény)
Mad Couple Well Matched (Brome)
Mad Dog Blues (Shepard)
Mad Forest (Churchill)
Mad Lover (Fletcher)
Mad World, My Masters (Middleton)
Madam, Will You Walk? (Howard)
Madame Butterfly (Giacosa)
Madame Caverlet (Augier)
Madame de . . . (Anouilh)
Madame de . . . (Whiting)
Madame de Chamblay (Dumas père)
Madame est aux eaux (Labiche)
Madame est trop belle (Labiche)
Madame MacAdam Travelling Theatre (Kilroy)
Madame Sans-Gêne (Sardou)
Madame Sganarelle (Feydeau)
Madame Veuve Larifla (Labiche)
Madame Zenobia (r Barnes)
Madame Zoyka (Bulgakov)

Madcap (Kotzebue)
Mädchen aus der Feenwelt (Raimund)
Mädchenfreundschaft (Kotzebue)
Madelaine Morel (Daly)
Madeleine (Zola)
Mademoiselle de Belle-Isle (Benavente y Martínez)
Mademoiselle de Belle-Isle (Dumas *père*)
Mademoiselle Jaïre (Ghelderode)
Mademoiselle Julie (Vian)
Mademoiselle ma femme (Labiche)
Mademoiselle Marguerite (Tremblay)
Mademoiselle Zampa (Maugham)
Madheart (Baraka)
Madhouse in Goa (Sherman)
Madigan's Lock (Leonard)
Mädl aus der Vorstadt (Nestroy)
Madman and the Nun (Witkiewicz)
Madman or Saint (Echegaray)
Madman Theory of Deterrence (Hare)
Madmen and Specialists (Soyinka)
Madness of George III (Bennett)
Madness of Lady Bright (L. Wilson)
Madonna Dianora (Hofmannsthal)
Madras House (Granville-Barker)
Madre amorosa (Goldoni)
Madre Coraje y sus hijos (Buero Vallejo)
Madre (Fo)
Madres y los hijos (Usigli)
Madrid y en una casa (Tirso De Molina)
Madrina del cielo (Tirso De Molina)
Madrugada (Buero Vallejo)
Madwoman of Central Park West (Laurents)
Madwoman of Chaillot (Giraudoux)
Maestrazgo del Toisón (Calderón)
Maestro de danzar (Calderón)
Maeve (Martyn)
Magasin d'accessoires (Salacrou)
Magic Carpets of Antonio Angelini (Ringwood)
Magic Flute (t Auden)
Magic Flute (Planché)
Magic Glasses (Fitzmaurice)
Magic of an Hour (Benavente y Martínez)
Magic Realists (Terry)
Magic Tower (Williams)
Magico prodigioso (Calderón)
Magie rouge (Ghelderode)
Magische Eilwagenreise durch die Komödienwelt (Nestroy)
Magistrate (Pinero)
Magloire the Prestigitator (Robertson)
Magnetic Lady (Jonson)
Magnetic Martian (Romeril)
Magnificence (Brenton)
Magnus Garbe (Hauptmann)
Magot (Sardou)
Magotin (Lesage)
Magpie on the Gallows (Ghelderode)
Mahomet (Goethe)
Mahomet (Voltaire)
Maid and the Magpie (Byron)
Maid in the Mill (Fletcher)
Maid Marian (Planché)
Maid of Bath (Foote)
Maid of France (Brighouse)
Maid of Honour (Massinger)
Maid of Orleans (Schiller)
Maid of the Alps (Boucicault)
Maid of the Mill (Bickerstaff)

Maid the Mistress (Bickerstaff)
Maid the Mistress (O'Keeffe)
Maid to Marry (Ionesco)
Maidenhead Well Lost (Heywood)
Maiden's Consent (Fernández de Moratín)
Maidens of the Mount (Hauptmann)
Maids (Genet)
Maids (Rudkin)
Maid's Last Prayer (Southerne)
Maid's Revenge (Shirley)
Maid's Tragedy (Beaumont, Fletcher)
Mail vs. Female (Pollock)
Main leste (Labiche)
Main passe (Feydeau)
Mains blanches (Adamov)
Mains négatives (s Duras)
Mains sales (Sartre)
Mais n'te promène donc pas toute nue! (Feydeau)
Maison neuve (Sardou)
Maison suspendue (Tremblay)
Maître (Ionesco)
Maître de Santiago (Montherlant)
Maître Guérin (Augier)
Maitu Njugira (Ngugi)
Majak (Karvaš)
Majitelé klíču (Kundera)
Majlis al-'Adl (Tawfiq al-Hakim)
Major (Harrigan)
Major André (Fitch)
Major Barbara (Shaw)
Major Barbara (s Shaw)
Major Cravachon (Labiche)
Major Pendennis (Mitchell)
Makassar Reef (Buzo)
Make and Break (Frayn)
Make Way for Lucia (Van Druten)
Maker of Roads (Carroll)
Making History (Friel)
Making it Better (Saunders)
Making Money (Saroyan)
Making Money (t Saroyan)
Making of Muswell Hill (Arden)
Making Tracks (Ayckbourn)
Makropoulos Secret (Čapek)
Mal court (Audiberti)
Mal que nos hacen (Benavente y Martínez)
Mala nochebuena de don Etcétera (Díaz)
Malade imaginaire (Molière)
Maladie de la mort (Duras)
Malas herencias (Echegaray)
Malasangre (Gambaro)
Malatesta (Montherlant)
Malcochon (Walcott)
Malcolm (Albee)
Malcontent (Marston)
Malcontenti (Goldoni)
Malédictions d'une Furie (Tardieu)
Maleficio de la mariposa (García Lorca)
Malentendu (Camus)
Malhechores del bien (Benavente y Martínez)
Malheur passe (Maeterlinck)
Malia della voce (Gozzi)
Malini (Tagore)
Mall (Inge)
Malone's Night Off (Harrigan)
Malquerida (Benavente y Martínez)
Malvika and Agnimitra (Kalidasa)

Malvikagnimitra (Kalidasa)
Mama, kijk, zonder Handen (Claus)
Mama sensei to sono otto (Kishida)
Mamamouchi (Ravenscroft)
Maman Sabouleux (Labiche)
Mamelles de Tirésias (Apollinaire)
Mamz'elle fait ses dents (Labiche)
Man, a Dictionary (Kroetz)
Man About the Place (Brighouse)
Man and Boy (Rattigan)
Man and Superman (Shaw)
Man and the Masses (Toller)
Man and Wife (Colman the Elder)
Man and Wife (Daly)
Man, Beast and Virtue (Pirandello)
Man, Beast and Virtue (Wood)
Man Does Not Die By Bread Alone (Díaz)
Man Eating Tiger (Hecht)
Man Equals Man (Brecht)
Man for All Seasons (Bolt)
Man for the Ladies (Jerrold)
Man from Chicago (Romeril)
Man from Clare (Keane)
Man from Mukinupin (Hewett)
Man Full of Nothing (Nestroy)
Man Has Two Fathers (McGrath)
Man-Hater (Molière)
Man in a Side-Car (t Gray)
Man in Black (Echegaray)
Man Milliner (O'Keeffe)
Man of Business (Colman the Elder)
Man of Destiny (Shaw)
Man of Fortitude (Dunlap)
Man of Forty (Kotzebue)
Man of Honor (Boucicault)
Man of Honour (Maugham)
Man of Many Parts (Hibberd)
Man of Mode (Etherege)
Man of Ten Thousand (Holcroft)
Man of the Moment (Ayckbourn)
Man on the House (Green)
Man Only Dines (Edgar)
Man Outside (Borchert)
Man Who Came to Dinner (Kaufman)
Man Who Couldn't Talk (Kotzebue)
Man Who Died at Twelve O'Clock (Green)
Man Who Dug Fish (Bullins)
Man Who Forgot (Behrman)
Man Who Had All the Luck (Miller)
Man Who Had Three Arms (Albee)
Man Who Ignored the War (Brighouse)
Man Who Lived His Life Over (Lagerkvist)
Man Who Shot the Albatross (Lawler)
Man with Bags (Horovitz)
Man with Bags (Ionesco)
Man with the Flower in His Mouth (Pirandello)
Man with the Heart in the Highlands (Saroyan)
Man with the Luggage (Ionesco)
Man Without a Soul (Lagerkvist)
Manager in Distress (Colman the Elder)
Manager's Daughter (Boucicault)
Mañana será otro día (Calderón)
Mañanas de abril y mayo (Calderón)
Manantial que no se agota (Echegaray)
Mancha que limpia (Echegaray)
Manchettes d'un vilain (Labiche)
Mandarine (Anouilh)

Mandat (Erdman)
Mandate (Erdman)
Mandragola (Machiavelli)
Mandragola (Murrell)
Mandrake (Machiavelli)
Manganilla de Melilla (Ruiz de Alarcón)
Mangeront-ils? (Hugo)
Manifestación (Díaz)
Manivelle (Pinget)
Manivelle (r Pinget)
Mankind (Daly)
Mann, ein Wörterbuch (Kroetz)
Mann ist Mann (Brecht)
Mann von vierzig Jahren (Kotzebue)
Mannen utan själ (Lagerkvist)
Männersache (Kroetz)
Manny and Jake (Fierstein)
Manoeuvres of Jane (Jones)
Manoeuvring (Planché)
Manon Lastcall (Barbeau)
Manon Lescaut (Benavente y Martínez)
Manon Lescaut (Sternheim)
Manon/Sandra (Tremblay)
Manos de Dios (Solórzano)
Manos blancas no ofenden (Calderón)
Man's a Man (Brecht)
Man's an Ass (Jerrold)
Man's Best Friend (Saunders)
Man's the Master (Davenant)
Man's World (Crothers)
Mansaniello (Scribe)
Manuel (r Dubé)
Many Young Men of Twenty (Keane)
Manželství s.r.o. (Langer)
Map of the World (Hare)
Maple Sugaring (Mamet)
Mar sin orillas (Echegaray)
Marat-Sade (Sastre)
Marat/Sade (Weiss)
Marble Arch (Mortimer)
Marbrier (Dumas *père*)
Marc Antoine (Mairet)
Marcelle (Sardou)
March on Russia (Storey)
Marchand de regrets (Crommelynck)
Marchand de Venise (Vigny)
Marché des petites heures (Willems)
Marche royale (Arrabal)
Märchen (Granville-Barker)
Märchen (Schnitzler)
Marching Song (Lawson)
Marching Song (Whiting)
Marco Polo Sings a Solo (Guare)
Marco Spada (Scribe)
Marcolfa (Fo)
Marco's Millions (O'Neill)
Maréchale d'Ancre (Vigny)
Marescalco (Aretino)
Margaret Fleming (Herne)
Margarete in Aix (Hacks)
Margaret's Bed (Inge)
Margarita (Hugo)
Marginal Farm (Buzo)
Margot la folle (Maillet)
Margot (Sudermann)
Marguerite d'Anjou (Pixérécourt)
Marguerite (Salacrou)

Mari de la veuve (Dumas *père*)
Mari préféré (Lesage)
Mari qui lance sa femme (Labiche)
Mari qui prend du ventre (Labiche)
María Curia (Casona)
Maria, Jesu Moder (Bergman)
Mária királynő (Madách)
Maria Magdalene (Kroetz)
Maria Magdalena (Hebbel)
María Rosa (Echegaray)
Maria Stuarda (Alfieri)
Maria Stuart (Schiller)
Maria Stuart i Skotland (Bjørnson)
Mariaàgélas (Maillet)
Mariage au tambour (Dumas *père*)
Mariage Blanc (Różewicz)
Mariage dans un chapeau (Dumas *fils*)
Mariage de Barillon (Feydeau)
Mariage de Cambyse (Quinault)
Mariage d'Olympe (Augier)
Mariage forcé (Molière)
Mariage sous Louis XV (Dumas *père*)
Mariages de Canada (Lesage)
Mariamne (Hardy)
Mariamne (Voltaire)
Mariana (Echegaray)
Mariana (Marqués)
Mariana Pineda (García Lorca)
Marido de bronce (Benavente y Martínez)
Marido de la Téllez (Benavente y Martínez)
Marido de su viuda (Benavente y Martínez)
Marie (Kotzebue)
Marie Laveau (Walcott)
Marie le Misérable (Ghelderode)
Marie-Jeanne (Anouilh)
Marie-Magdeleine (Maeterlinck)
Marie Tudor (Hugo)
Marie-Victoire (Maeterlinck)
Maries Baby (Hacks)
Mariés de la tour Eiffel (Cocteau)
Marigolds in August (s Fugard)
Marina (Lillo)
Mário (Régio)
Marion Delorme (Hugo)
Mariposa que voló sobre el mar (Benavente y Martínez)
Mariscalito (Díaz)
Marito amante della moglie (Giacosa)
Marito e moglie (Betti)
Marius und Sulla (Grabbe)
Marjuana della mamma è la più bella (Fo)
Marks (t Bennett)
Markurells i Wadköping (Bergman)
Marmion (J. N. Barker)
Mar-Plot (Centlivre)
Marplot in Spain (Planché)
Marqués de Bradomín (Valle-Inclán)
Marqués de las Navas (Vega)
Marquesa Rosalinda (Valle-Inclán)
Marquis de Brunoy (Dumas *père*)
Marquis of Keith (Wedekind)
Marquis von Keith (Wedekind)
Marquise (Coward)
Marquise (Sardou)
Marquise de Sade et un lézard nommé King Kong (Barbeau)
Marquise von Arcis (Sternheim)
Marquises de la fourchette (Labiche)

Marranos (Mamet)
Marriage (Boucicault)
Marriage (Fitch)
Marriage (Gogol)
Marriage (Gombrowicz)
Marriage (Gregory)
Marriage (Mackaye)
Marriage a la Mode (Cibber)
Marriage à-la-Mode (Dryden)
Marriage by Moonlight (Herne)
Marriage Game (Fitch)
Marriage is no Joke (Bridie)
Marriage of Anansewa (Sutherland)
Marriage of Bette and Boo (Durang)
Marriage of Convenience (Dumas *père*)
Marriage of Figaro (Beaumarchais)
Marriage of Figaro (Planché)
Marriage of Maria Braun (s Fassbinder)
Marriage of Mr. Mississippi (Dürrenmatt)
Marriage of Olympe (Augier)
Marriage of Sobeide (Hofmannsthal)
Marriage of Zobeide (Hofmannsthal)
Marriage Play (Albee)
Marriage Proposal (Chekhov)
Marriages Are Made in Heaven (Maugham)
Marriages in the Making (Houghton)
Married in Haste (Byron)
Married Man (Inchbald)
Married Man (Lawrence)
Marrying Man (Brighouse)
Marrying of Ann Leete (Granville-Barker)
Marsall (Molnár)
Marseilles (Howard)
Marshal (Molnár)
Marta la piadosa (Tirso De Molina)
Martello Towers (Buzo)
Martha (Nestroy)
Martha Willis the Servant Maid (Jerrold)
Martin Luther und Thomas Münzer (Forte)
Marty (t Chayefsky)
Marty Malone (Harrigan)
Martyrdom of Piotr Ohey (Mrożek)
Martyrdom of the Holy Virgins Fides, Spes, and Karitas (Hrotsvitha)
Martyrdom of the Holy Virgins Irene, Agape and Chionia (Hrotsvitha)
Martyre de Saint Sébastien (D'Annunzio)
Martyred Soldier (Heywood)
Martyrs (Scribe)
Marvellous Melbourne (Hibberd)
Marvellous Melbourne (Romeril)
Marvellous Pageant (Cervantes)
Mary Baker Eddy (Toller)
Mary Barnes (Edgar)
Mary Goes First (Jones)
Mary of Scotland (M. Anderson)
Mary Read (Bridie)
Mary Rose (Barrie)
Mary Stuart (Alfieri)
Mary Stuart (Schiller)
Mary Stuart in Scotland (Bjørnson)
Mary the Third (Crothers)
Mary Warner (Taylor)
Marya (Hampton)
Mary's John (Brighouse)
Mary's Name (Arden)
März (Kipphardt)

Más allá de la meurte (Benavente y Martínez)
Más fuerte que el amor (Benavente y Martínez)
Mascarade (Holberg)
Maschera e il volto (Chiarelli)
Maschine (Kotzebue)
Maschinenstürmer (Toller)
Masir Sarsar (Tawfiq al-Hakim)
Mask and the Face (Chiarelli)
Mask and the Face (Maugham)
Mask of Moriarty (Leonard)
Mask of Virtue (Sternheim)
Maskarad (Lermontov)
Maske (Sternheim)
Masked Ball (Fitch)
Masked Ladies (Holberg)
Masken (Kotzebue)
Masks and Faces (Reade, Taylor)
Mason of Buda (Planché)
Masque (Reaney)
Masque of Augurs (Jonson)
Masque of Beauty (Jonson)
Masque of Blackness (Jonson)
Masque of Judgment (Moody)
Masque of Kings (M. Anderson)
Masque of Owls (Jonson)
Masque of Pedagogues (M. Anderson)
Masque of Queens (Jonson)
Masque of the Inner Temple and Gray's Inn (Beaumont)
Masquerade (Clark)
Masquerade (Holberg)
Masquerade (Lermontov)
Masqueraders (Jones)
Masques ostendais (Ghelderode)
Masrah al-Mujtama (Tawfiq al-Hakim)
Mass für Mass (Sperr)
Massachusetts Trust (Terry)
Massacre (Inchbald)
Massacre at Paris (Marlowe)
Massacre des innocents (r Ghelderode)
Massacre of Paris (Lee)
Massage (Berkoff)
Masscheroen (Claus)
Masse-Mensch (Toller)
Massere (Goldoni)
Masses and Man (Toller)
Massnahme (Brecht)
Master Builder (Ibsen)
"Master Harold" . . . and the Boys (Fugard)
Master of Santiago (Montherlant)
Master of the House (Houghton)
Mäster Olof (Strindberg)
Master Poisoner (Hecht)
Masterful Magician (De Filippo)
Mastro Don Gesualdo (Fabbri)
Mat Iyususa (Volodin)
Mata a tur prójimo como a ti mismo (Díaz)
Match Me in London (Dekker)
Matchmaker (Keane)
Matchmaker (Nestroy)
Matchmaker (Wilder)
Mate (Schnitzler)
Mater Imperatrix (Benavente y Martínez)
Maternité (Brieux)
Maternity (Brieux)
Matin comme les autres (Dubé)
Matka (Čapek)
Matka (Witkiewicz)

Matrimonial Ads (Harrigan)
Matrimonio per concorso (Goldoni)
Matrone de Charenton (Lesage)
Matsukaze (Zeami)
Matter of Dispute (Marivaux)
Matter of Honour (Dunsany)
Matwa (Witkiewicz)
Maures d'Espagne (Pixérécourt)
Maurice Harte (Murray)
Mauser (Müller)
Max (Grass)
Max Helfenstein (Kotzebue)
Maximian (T. Corneille)
May Day (Chapman)
Maya (Ringwood)
Maydays (Edgar)
Mayfair (Pinero)
Mayor desengaño (Tirso De Molina)
Mayor encanto, amor (Calderón)
Mayor general hablarí de teogonía (Triana)
Mayor monstruo los celos (Calderón)
Mayor of Garret (Foote)
Mayor of Zalamea (Calderón)
Mayordomo de la duquesa de Amalfi (Vega)
Maypole Morning (Brighouse)
Mąż (Wyspiański)
Mazeppa (Byron)
Mazourka (Byron)
McAllister's Legacy (Harrigan)
McDonough's Wife (Gregory)
McNooney's Visit (Harrigan)
McSorley's Inflation (Harrigan)
Me, I'm Afraid of Virginia Woolf (t Bennett)
Me, Myself, and I (Ayckbourn)
Me Times Me Times Me (Ayckbourn)
Mea culpa (Solórzano)
Meadows of St. Gervais (Sardou)
Meals on Wheels (Wood)
Mear contra el viento (Díaz)
Measure for Measure (Brenton)
Measure for Measure (Shakespeare)
Measures Taken (Brecht)
Męczenstwo Piotra Oheya (Mrożek)
Medea (Anouilh)
Medea (Euripides)
Medea (Fo)
Medea (Grillparzer)
Medea (Ludlam)
Medea (Sastre)
Medea (Seneca)
Medea (van Itallie)
Medea en el espejo (Triana)
Médecin malgré lui (Molière)
Médecin volant (Molière)
Médée (Anouilh)
Médée (P. Corneille)
Médée (T. Corneille)
Médée (t Dubé)
Medical Man (Gilbert)
Médico a palos (Fernández de Moratín)
Médico de su honra (Calderón)
Medico dei pazzi (De Filippo)
Medico olandese (Goldoni)
Medio tono (Usigli)
Medusa (Carballido)
Medved (Chekhov)
Meeres und der Liebe Wellen (Grillparzer)

Meeting (Petrushevskaya)
Meeting at Night (Bridie)
Mefistófela (Benavente y Martínez)
Mégère apprivoisée (Audiberti)
Meid (Heijermans)
Meido no Hikyaku (Chikamatsu)
Meier Helmbrecht (Hochwälder)
Mein Freund (Nestroy)
Meisje met de houten handen (Ghelderode)
Mejor alcalde, el rey (Vega)
Mejor espigadera (Tirso De Molina)
Mejor está que estaba (Calderón)
Mejor mozo de España (Vega)
Melampe (Holberg)
Melancólico (Tirso De Molina)
Meleager (Wyspiański)
Méléagre (Hardy)
Mélicerte (Molière)
Melindres de Belisa (Vega)
Melissa (Kazantzakis)
Mélite (P. Corneille)
Melky bes (Sologub)
Mellem slagene (Bjørnson)
Melodía del jazz-band (Benavente y Martínez)
Melodrama Play (Shepard)
Melon (Gray)
Melusina (Grillparzer)
Memoir (Murrell)
Mémoire d'Hortense (Labiche)
Memoirs of a Carlton Bohemian (Hibberd)
Memorable Masque of the Middle Temple and Lincoln's
    Inn (Chapman)
Memorandum (Havel)
Memorias de un madrileño (Benavente y Martínez)
Memory of Summer (Inge)
Memory of Two Mondays (Miller)
Men imorgen (Grieg)
Men in White (Kingsley)
Men on Women on Men (Ayckbourn)
Men Without Shadows (Sartre)
Menace (t Wesker)
Menaechmi (Chiarelli)
Menaechmi (Plautus)
Menaechmus Twins (Plautus)
Ménage de Caroline (Ghelderode)
Menagerie (Witkiewicz)
Ménages d'artistes (Brieux)
Menażeria (Witkiewicz)
Ménechmes (Regnard)
Ménechmes (Rotrou)
Meninas (Buero Vallejo)
Menocchio (r Saunders)
Men's Business (Kroetz)
Menschen (Hasenclever)
Menschen und Leidenschaften (Lermontov)
Menschenfreund (Walser)
Menschenhass und Reue (Kotzebue)
Mensch-Meier (Kroetz)
Mensonge (Sarraute)
Menteur (P. Corneille)
Menteur véridique (Scribe)
Menyegző (Molnár)
Mephisto (Wertenbaker)
Méprise (Marivaux)
Méprises de l'amour (Augier)
Mercatanti (Goldoni)
Mercator (Plautus)

Mercenaire (Vian)
Merchant Gentleman (Molière)
Merchant (Plautus)
Merchant (Wesker)
Merchant of Venice (Daly)
Merchant of Venice (Shakespeare)
Merchant of Yonkers (Nestroy)
Merchant of Yonkers (Wilder)
Merchant's Wedding (Planché)
Mercury Vindicated from the Alchemists (Jonson)
Mercy Dodd (Boucicault)
Mère (Becque)
Mère confidante (Marivaux)
Mère coquette (Quinault)
Mere Soup Songs (Ayckbourn)
Merlin (Dorst)
Mermaids Singing (Van Druten)
Merope (Alfieri)
Mérope (Garrett)
Mérope (Voltaire)
Merrily We Roll Along (Kaufman)
Merry Christmas (Norman)
Merry Gardener (Dunlap)
Merry-Go-Round (Becque)
Merry-Go-Round (Fitch)
Merry-Go-Round (Lawrence)
Merry-Go-Round (Schnitzler)
Merry Roosters' Panto (Shaffer)
Merry Sherwood (O'Keeffe)
Merry Wives of Windsor (Daly)
Merry Wives of Windsor (Shakespeare)
Merry Zingara (Gilbert)
Merton of the Movies (Connelly, Kaufman)
Merveilleuses (Sardou)
Mes (Claus)
Mesdames de Montenfriche (Labiche)
Meshchane (Gorky)
Message and Jehanne (Wilder)
Messe noir (Tremblay)
Messiah (Sherman)
Messidor (Zola)
Mestané a studenti (Tyl)
Mester Gert Westphaler (Holberg)
Mesyats v derevne (Turgenev)
Metafisico (Gozzi)
Metafizyka dwugłowego cielęcia (Witkiewicz)
Metamorozy (Różewicz)
Metamorphosis (Berkoff)
Metamorphosis (Murrell)
Metanoeite (Sorge)
Metaphysics of a Two-Headed Calf (Witkiewicz)
Metempsicosi (Goldoni)
Meteor (Behrman)
Meteor (Dürrenmatt)
Meteor (Karvaš)
Meu Caso (Régio)
Meuble (Tardieu)
Mezzetin aux Enfers (Regnard)
Mhil'daim (Kopit)
Mhoi-Ceul (Dadié)
Mia famiglia (De Filippo)
Michael (Bullins)
Michael and His Lost Angel (Jones)
Michael Kramer (Hauptmann)
Michael Strogoff (Byron)
Michaelmas Eve (Murray)
Michaelmas Term (Middleton)

Michel Angelo (Hebbel)
Michel Auclair (Howard)
Michel et Christine (Scribe)
Michel Pauper (Becque)
Michi's Blood (Kroetz)
Michis Blut (Kroetz)
Mick and Mick (Leonard)
Mickey's Moomba (Romeril)
Mid-Channel (Pinero)
Midas (Lyly)
Midas Connection (t Edgar)
Midday Sun (Churchill)
Middle-Class Gentleman (Molière)
Middle of the Night (Chayefsky)
Middleman (Jones)
Midnight Hour (Inchbald)
Midsommardröm i fattighuset (Lagerkvist)
Midsummer Dream in the Workhouse (Lagerkvist)
Midsummer Night's Dream (Daly)
Midsummer Night's Dream (Shakespeare)
Midwestern Manic (Inge)
Miedo (Gambaro)
Mientras amemos (Usigli)
Mi-figure, mi-raisin (Tardieu)
Mikado (Gilbert)
Milagre na Cela (Andrade)
Milagro en Egipto (Echegaray)
Miles Gloriosus (Plautus)
Milíony (Langer)
Military Tactics (Planché)
Milk Train Doesn't Stop Here Anymore (Williams)
Mill Hand's Lunch Bucket (A. Wilson)
Mill Hill (Mortimer)
Mille Francs de récompense (Hugo)
Miller and His Men (Byron)
Millionairess (Shaw)
Milye prizraki (Andreyev)
Mima (Molnár)
Mimi (Boucicault)
Mimi (Brighouse)
Mimos (Prevelakis)
Min adja-o (C'est mon héritage!) (Dadié)
"Mind the Paint" Girl (Pinero)
Mine at Falun (Hofmannsthal)
Mine Hostess (Goldoni)
Mines de Pologne (Pixérécourt)
Minetti (Bernhard)
Minglangde tian (Cao Yu)
Minick (Kaufman)
Minin i Pozharski (Bulgakov)
Minister (Schiller)
Minna von Barnhelm (Lessing)
Minnie (Byron)
Minor (Fonvizin)
Minor (Foote)
Minor Scene (Bullins)
Minute Men of 1774–1775 (Herne)
Miracle (Granville-Barker)
Miracle dans le fauborg (Ghelderode)
Miracle de Saint-Antoine (Maeterlinck)
Miracle en Alabama (Duras)
Miracle of the Corn (Colum)
Miracle of the Danube (r M. Anderson)
Miracle on the Pullman (Hecht)
Miracle on the Pullman (s Hecht)
Mirage (Ringwood)
Miraggi (Fabbri)

Miranda (Sewell)
Mirandolina (Goldoni)
Mirandolina (Gregory)
Miroir (Salacrou)
Miroirs d'Ostende (Willems)
Mirra (Alfieri)
Misa primera (Carballido)
Misalliance (Shaw)
Misanthrope et l'auvergnat (Labiche)
Misanthrope (Molière)
Misanthropy and Repentence (Kotzebue)
Mischief (Travers)
Miser (Fielding)
Miser (Gregory)
Miser (Shadwell)
Miseria e nobilità (De Filippo)
Miseries of Enforced Marriage (Heywood)
Miserly Knight (Pushkin)
Miser's Wedding (Dunlap)
Misfits (s Miller)
Misfortune of Being Clever (Griboyedov)
Misogyn (Lessing)
Miss Eily O'Connor (Byron)
Miss Firecracker Contest (Henley)
Miss Hewett's Shenanigans (Hewett)
Miss Hoyden's Husband (Daly)
Miss Jairus (Ghelderode)
Miss Julie (Strindberg)
Miss Julie Versus Expressionism (Berkoff)
Miss Liberty (Sherwood)
Miss Lucy in Town (Fielding)
Miss Lulu Bett (Gale)
Miss McCobb, Manicurist (Fitch)
Miss Sara Sampson (Lessing)
Miss Williams: A Turn (L. Wilson)
Mission (Müller)
Mississippi (Kaiser)
Mistake (Havel)
Mistake (Vanbrugh)
Mistaken Beauty; or, The Liar (P. Corneille)
Mistaken Husband (Dryden)
Mr. A's Amazing Maze Plays (Ayckbourn)
Mr. Big, the Big, Big Pig (Romeril)
Mr. Bolfry (Bridie)
Mr. Buckstone's Ascent of Mount Parnassus (Planché)
Mr. Buckstone's Voyage round the Globe (Planché)
Mr. Churchill of England (Coulter)
Mr. Faithful (Dunsany)
Mr. Gillie (Bridie)
Mr. Happiness (Mamet)
Mr. Leonida and the Reactionaries (Caragiale)
Mr. Livermore's Dream (Pinero)
Mr. Me (Tardieu)
Mr. Peter Piper (Boucicault)
Mister Pitt (Gale)
Mister Price (Witkiewicz)
Mr. Puntila and His Man Matti (Brecht)
Mr. Sleeman is Coming (Bergman)
Mr. Sliggen's Hour (Dunsany)
Mr. Somebody (Brighouse)
Mr. Whatnot (Ayckbourn)
Misterio de María Celeste (Casona)
Misterios de la misa (Calderón)
Misteriya-Buff (Mayakovsky)
Mistero Buffo (Fo)
Mistero Buffo (Tremblay)
Mistica y real Babilonia (Calderón)

Mistress (Wesker)
Mistress Betty (Fitch)
Mrs. Caudle's Curtain Lecture (Jerrold)
Mrs. Dane's Defence (Jones)
Mrs. Dot (Maugham)
Mrs. Grundy, Jr. (Fitch)
Mrs. John Hobbs (Crothers)
Mistress of the Inn (Goldoni)
Mrs. Porter and the Angel (Hewett)
Mrs. Scour and the Future of Western Civilisation
   (Saunders)
Mrs. Thally F (Romeril)
Mrs. Warren's Profession (Shaw)
Mrs. Waterbury's Millennium (Bridie)
Mit allen Hunden gehetzt (Wedekind)
Mit dem Kopf durch die Wand (Horváth)
Mithridate (Racine)
Mithridates (Racine)
Mithridates, King of Pontus (Lee)
Mitmacher (Dürrenmatt)
Mito (Buero Vallejo)
Mitschuldigen (Goethe)
Mitsuyama (Zeami)
Mituge Seefahrer (Kaiser)
Mixed Couple (Harrigan)
Mixed Doubles (Feydeau)
Mixed Doubles (Saunders)
Mladost (Andreyev)
Mob (Galsworthy)
Mock Doctor (Fielding)
Mock Doctor (Molière)
Modas (Benavente y Martínez)
Modern Antiques (O'Keeffe)
Modern Husband (Fielding)
Modern Match (Fitch)
Modern Tragedy (Foote)
Modern Wife (Gay)
Modernismo (Benavente y Martínez)
Moderskärlek (Strindberg)
Modet att döda (t Norén)
Mōdōken (Kara)
Modsommar (Strindberg)
Moe zaglyadenye (Arbuzov)
Moglie saggia (Goldoni)
Mogu of the Desert (Colum)
Mogu the Wanderer (Colum)
Mogul Tale (Inchbald)
Mohamed, prends ta valise (Yacine)
Mohicans de Paris (Dumas *père*)
Mohocks (Gay)
Mohrin (Dorst)
Moi (Labiche)
Mojigata (Fernández de Moratín)
Mojo (Childress)
Mole on Lincoln's Cheek (r Connelly)
Moliere (Goldoni)
Molinera de Arcos (Casona)
Moll (Keane)
Mollie Bailey's Traveling Family Circus (Terry)
Molly (Gray)
Molly's Dream (Fornés)
Molodye suprugi (Griboyedov)
Mombelli grófok (Katona)
Momies d'Égypte (Regnard)
Momolo cortesan (Goldoni)
Moms (Childress)
Mon Doux Royaume saccagé (Arrabal)

Mon Isménie (Labiche)
Mon Ours (Labiche)
Monaldi (Mackaye)
Monastère abandonné (Pixérécourt)
Monasterboice (Colum)
Monde renversé (Lesage)
Money (Bulwer-Lytton)
Money: A Jazz Opera (Baraka)
Money and Friends (Williamson)
Money Box (Sternheim)
Money Mad (Mackaye)
Money Makes the World Go Round (Marivaux)
Money Question (Dumas *fils*)
Money Spinner (Pinero)
Money the Mistress (Southerne)
Mongrel (Rice)
Mongrel Fox (Arden)
Monica's Blue Boy (Pinero)
Monna Vanna (Maeterlinck)
Monologi (Petrushevskaya)
Monostori Veronka (Katona)
Monsanto (Santareno)
Monsieur Alphonse (Daly)
Monsieur Alphonse (Dumas *fils*)
Monsieur Barnett (Anouilh)
Monsieur chasse (Feydeau)
Monsieur de Coyllin (Labiche)
Monsieur de Pourceaugnac (Molière)
Monsieur de Réboval (Brieux)
Monsieur de Saint-Cadenas (Labiche)
Monsieur D'Olive (Chapman)
Monsieur Garat (Sardou)
Monsieur Klebs et Rosalie (Obaldia)
Monsieur Moi (Tardieu)
Monsieur Nounou (Feydeau)
Monsieur Perrichon Goes Abroad (Labiche)
Monsieur Poirier's Son- (Augier)
Monsieur qui a brûlé une dame (Labiche)
Monsieur qui est condamné à mort (Feydeau)
Monsieur qui n'aime pas les monologues (monologue)
   (Feydeau)
Monsieur qui prend la mouche (Labiche)
Monsieur Thôgô-gnini (Dadié)
Monsieur Thomas (Fletcher)
Monsieur Vincent (s Anouilh)
Monsieur votre fille (Labiche)
Monster of Karlovy Vary (Mercer)
Monstres sacrés (Cocteau)
Monstruo de los jardines (Calderón)
Mont Sauvage (Pixérécourt)
Monte-Cristo I–II (Dumas *père*)
Month in the Country (Friel)
Month in the Country (s Gray)
Month in the Country (Turgenev)
Montserrat (Hellman)
Monument (Andreyev)
Monumento (De Filippo)
Monuments of Honour (Webster)
Moon for the Misbegotten (O'Neill)
Moon in the Yellow River (Johnston)
Moon of the Caribbees (O'Neill)
Moon Shines on Kylenamoe (O'Casey)
Moonlighter (Fitzmaurice)
Moonshine (Saunders)
Moonshot Tape (L. Wilson)
Moony's Kid Don't Cry (Williams)
Moppels Abenteuer im Viertel unter Wiener Wald

(Nestroy)
Mora (Boucicault)
Moral del divorcio (Benavente y Martínez)
Moralities (Auden)
Morals (Howard)
Moratória (Andrade)
(M)oratorium (Claus)
Morbinose (Goldoni)
Mord (Hasenclever)
Mordaza (Sastre)
Mordecai Lyons (Harrigan)
Mörder, Hoffnung der Frauen (Kokoschka)
More de Venise (Vigny)
More Dissemblers Besides Women (Middleton)
More Frightened Than Hurt (Jerrold)
More Sinned Against Than Sinning (Ostrovsky)
More Stately Mansions (O'Neill)
Morgens bis mitternachts (Kaiser)
Morgon (Gambaro)
Morir por no desperatar (Echegaray)
Morituri (Claus)
Morituri (Sudermann)
Moritz Tassow (Hacks)
Morning (Horovitz)
Morning After Optimism (Murphy)
Mornings of April and May (Calderón)
Moro di corpo bianco (Gozzi)
Morris and Joe (Mamet)
Morris Dance (Granville-Barker)
Morsa (Pirandello)
Mort d'Achille (T. Corneille)
Mort d'Achille (Hardy)
Mort d'Alexandre (Hardy)
Mort d'Annibal (T. Corneille)
Mort de César (Scudéry)
Mort de César (Voltaire)
Mort de Cyrus (Quinault)
Mort de Daïre (Hardy)
Mort de Danton (Adamov)
Mort de l'empereur Commode (T. Corneille)
Mort de Pompée (P. Corneille)
Mort de Tintagiles (Maeterlinck)
Mort du Docteur Faust (Ghelderode)
Mort regarde à la fenêtre (Ghelderode)
Morte accidentale di un anarchico (Fo)
Morte degli amanti (Chiarelli)
Morte e resurrezione di un pupazzo (Fo)
Morti non fanno paura (De Filippo)
Mortin pas mort (Pinget)
Morto da vendere (Fo)
Morts sans sépulture (Sartre)
Mosaisurs Zauberfluch (Raimund)
Moscas (Sastre)
Mosch (t Dorst)
Moscheta (Ruzante)
Moscow Gold (Brenton)
Moses and Aaron (Rudkin)
Most of the Game (Van Druten)
Mostellaria (Plautus)
Mostro turchino (Gozzi)
Mot pour un autre (Tardieu)
Motel (van Itallie)
Motet (Claus)
Moth and the Flame (Fitch)
Mothballs (Hibberd)
Mother (Arden)
Mother (Brecht)

Mother (Čapek)
Mother (Fo)
Mother (Jerrold)
Mother (t Chayefsky)
Mother (Witkiewicz)
Mother and Son (Boucicault)
Mother and Son (Esson)
Mother Bombie (Lyly)
Mother Carey's Chickens (Crothers)
Mother Courage and Her Children (Brecht)
Mother Courage and Her Children (Shange)
Mother Figure (Ayckbourn)
Mother Skipton (Colman the Elder)
Mother-in-Law (Terence)
Motherlove (Strindberg)
Mothers (Fornés)
Mother's Day (Priestley)
Mother's Day (Storey)
Mother's Dream (Jerrold)
Mother's Guilt (Beaumarchais)
Mother's Prayer (Tagore)
Motion of History (Baraka)
Motto: I Am All There (Byron)
Mouches (Sartre)
Mouchoir (monologue) (Feydeau)
Mouette (Duras)
Moulin des étangs (Pixérécourt)
Mound Builders (L. Wilson)
Mountain Dew (Shiels)
Mountain Giants (Pirandello)
Mountain Giants (Wood)
Mountain Hotel (Havel)
Mountain Hut (Planché)
Mountain Language (Pinter)
Mountaineers (Colman the Younger)
Mountebanks (Gilbert)
Mourning Becomes Electra (O'Neill)
Mourning Bride (Congreve)
Mousafirei sto Stepanchikovo (Prevelakis)
Mousquetaires (Dumas père)
Moutardier du pape (Jarry)
Mouthful of Birds (Churchill)
Mouton à l'entresol (Labiche)
Movie Man (O'Neill)
Movie Star Has to Star in Black and White (Kennedy)
Moving (Fennario)
Moving (Leonard)
Moving Clocks Go Slow (Churchill)
Moving Out (r Behan)
Möwe (Müller)
Moy bedny Marat (Arbuzov)
(Moya) starshaya sestra (Volodin)
Moytura (Colum)
Moza de Cántaro (Vega)
Mozart and Salieri (Pushkin)
Mozart and the Gray Steward (Wilder)
Mozart i Salieri (Pushkin)
Mózes (Madách)
Much Ado About Nothing (Daly)
Much Ado About Nothing (Shakespeare)
Mud (Fornés)
Mudarse por mejorarse (Ruiz de Alarcón)
Muddy Day (Harrigan)
Mueca (Pavlovsky)
Muero, luego existo (Díaz)
Muerte del ñeque (Triana)
Muerte en el barrio (Sastre)

Muerte en los labios (Echegaray)
Muerte hizo la luz (Solórzano)
Muerte no entrará en palacio (Marqués)
Muette de la forêt (Pixérécourt)
Muette de Portici (Scribe)
Mug (Brenton)
Muhammad (Tawfiq al-Hakim)
Mujer de malas (Carballido)
Mujer, llora y vencerás (Calderón)
Mujer no hace milagros (Usigli)
Mujer por fuerza (Tirso De Molina)
Mujer que manda en casa (Tirso De Molina)
Muktadhara (Tagore)
Mulato (Sastre)
Mulatto (Hughes)
Mulatto's Orgy (Hernández)
Mulcahey Twins (Harrigan)
Muldoon, The Solid Man (Harrigan)
Mule Bone (Hughes)
Muleteer of Toledo (Robertson)
Mulher sem Pecado (Rodrigues)
Müll, die Stadt und der Tod (Fassbinder)
Müller, Kohlenbrenner und Sesselträger (Nestroy)
Müller von Sanssouci (Hacks)
Mulligan Guard (Harrigan)
Mulligan Guard Ball (Harrigan)
Mulligan Guard Chowder (Harrigan)
Mulligan Guard Nominee (Harrigan)
Mulligan Guard Picnic (Harrigan)
Mulligan Guards' Christmas (Harrigan)
Mulligan Guards' Surprise (Harrigan)
Mulligans' Silver Wedding (Harrigan)
Mum's the Word (McGrath)
München-Athen (Norén)
Münchhausen (Hasenclever)
Münchner Freiheit (Sperr)
Münchner Kindl (Kroetz)
Mündel will Vormund sein (Handke)
Mundy Scheme (Friel)
Mura de ichi ban kuri no ki (Kishida)
Murder (Inge)
Murder in the Cathedral (Eliot)
Murder of Susan Parr (Fennario)
Murdered Woman (van Itallie)
Murderer Hope of Womankind (Kokoschka)
Murderer the Women's Hope (Kokoschka)
Murderers (Dunsany)
Murmuring Judges (Hare)
Musen (Hacks)
Museum of Science and Industry Story (t Mamet)
Music at Night (Priestley)
Music Lessons (Petrushevskaya)
Música cercana (Buero Vallejo)
Musica deuxième (Duras)
Musical Lady (Colman the Elder)
Music-Cure (Shaw)
Musik (Wedekind)
Mutilated (Williams)
Mutiny at the Nore (Jerrold)
Mutter (Brecht)
Mutter Courage und ihre Kinder (Brecht)
Muzeeka (Guare)
My Beatles (Satoh)
My Children! My Africa! (Fugard)
My Colleen (Herne)
My Daughter, Sir (Planché)

My First Interview (McGrath)
My First Play: Colman and Guaire (Gregory)
My Foot My Tutor (Handke)
My Friend the Governor (Planché)
My Great Aunt (Planché)
My Heart's Idol (Planché)
My Heart's in the Highlands (Saroyan)
My iz Kronstadta (s Vishnevsky)
My Lady Clara (Robertson)
My Lord and My Lady (Planché)
My Mother, My Father and Me (Hellman)
My Name is Aquilon (Barry)
My Name is Lisbeth (Pollock)
My Nightgown and Slippers (Colman the Younger)
My Old Man's a Tory (Arden)
My Parents Have Gone to Carlisle (Leigh)
My Son Dan (Harrigan)
My Son's My Son (Lawrence)
My Very Own Story (Ayckbourn)
My Wife's Diary (Robertson)
My Wife's Mother (Harrigan)
Myortvye dushi (Bulgakov)
Myrrha (Alfieri)
Myrsa Polagi (Lenz)
Myrtillo (Cibber)
Myself, Bettina (Crothers)
Mysl (Andreyev)
Mystère de la Passion de Notre Seigneur Jésus-Christ
   (Ghelderode)
Mystère de la rue Rousselet (Labiche)
Mystères de Marseille (Zola)
Mysterious Husband (Cumberland)
Mysterious Lady (Planché)
Mystery-Bouffe (Mayakovsky)
Mystery of Greenfingers (Priestley)
Mystery of Irma Vep (Ludlam)
Mystery of Phyllis Wheatley (Bullins)
Mystery Play (van Itallie)

Na bolshoy doroge (Chekhov)
Na boykom meste (Ostrovsky)
Na czworakach (Różewicz)
Na dne (Gorky)
Na pełnym morzu (Mrożek)
'Na santarella (De Filippo)
Na vsyakogo dovolno prostoty (Ostrovsky)
Na vsyakogo mudretsa dovolno prostoty (Tretyakov)
Na zapade boy (Vishnevsky)
Naar den ny vin blomstrer (Bjørnson)
Nabob (Foote)
Nachgedanken (Dürrenmatt)
Nacht, in der der Chef geschlachtet wurde (Kipphardt)
Nacht mit Gästen (Weiss)
Nacht und Träume (t Beckett)
Nächtliches Gespräch mit einem verachteten Mensch (r
   Dürrenmatt)
Nachtmütze des Propheten Elias (Kotzebue)
Nada que ver (Gambaro)
Nadie fie su secreto (Calderón)
Nadie sabe lo que quiere (Benavente y Martínez)
Nadobnisie i koczkodany (Witkiewicz)
Nagerl und Handschuh (Nestroy)
Nagy szerelem (Molnár)
Nahr al-Junun (Tawfiq al-Hakim)
Nahui Ollin (Carballido)
Naissance d'Amadis (Regnard)
Nakanune (Arbuzov)

Naked (Pirandello)
Naked King (Shvarts)
Nakhlebnik (Turgenev)
Näktergalen i Wittenberg (Strindberg)
Nameless Concern (Romeril)
Names and Nicknames (Reaney)
Nana (Zola)
Nance Oldfield (Reade)
Nancy and Company (Daly)
Nanette und Maria (Grabbe)
Nanine (Voltaire)
Nan-ke ji (Tang Xianzu)
Nannie's Night Out (O'Casey)
Naomi in the Living Room (Durang)
Năpasta (Caragiale)
Napoleon (Grabbe)
Napoléon Bonaparte (Dumas *père*)
Napoleon greift ein (Hasenclever)
Napoleon in New Orleans (Kaiser)
Napoleon's Old Guard (Boucicault)
Napoleons Reise-Abenteuer (Kotzebue)
Napoli milionaria! (De Filippo)
Napoli Milionaria (Simpson)
Nápolyi Endre (Madách)
Når vi døde vågner (Ibsen)
Narcisse (Taylor)
Narco Linguini Bust (Terry)
Naropa (van Itallie)
Narrow Road to the Deep North (Bond)
Nas gde-to zhdut (Arbuzov)
Nascuntur Poetae (Wilder)
Nashe gosteprymstvo (Shvarts)
Nashid al-Anshad (Tawfiq al-Hakim)
Natale in casa Cupiello (De Filippo)
Natchez (Pixérécourt)
Nathalie Granger (s Duras)
Nathan der Weise (Lessing)
Nathan der Weise (Schiller)
Nathan Hale (Fitch)
Nathan the Wise (Lessing)
National Guard (Planché)
National Health (Nichols)
National Interest (Edgar)
National Theatre (Edgar)
Natir Puja (Tagore)
Native Land! (Sardou)
Native Son (Green)
Nativity Play (Gregory)
Natten är dagens mor (Norén)
Nattvarden (Norén)
Natural Affection (Inge)
Natural Daughter (Dunlap)
Natural Daughter (Goethe)
Natural Son (Cumberland)
Natural Son (Kotzebue)
Nature and Purpose of the Universe (Durang)
Nature of the Four Elements (Rastell)
Naturels de Bordelais (Audiberti)
Natürliche Tochter (Goethe)
Nau de Amores (Vicente)
Naufragé (Dubé)
Naval Encounter (Goering)
Nave (D'Annunzio)
Nave del mercader (Calderón)
Navette (Becque)
Navio cargado de . . . (Usigli)
Návrat do Života (Karvaš)

Naznachenie (Volodin)
Ne bylo ni grosha, da vdrug sltyn (Ostrovsky)
Ne ot mira sego (Ostrovsky)
Ne Réveillez pas Madame (Anouilh)
Ne soshlis kharakterami (Ostrovsky)
Ne tak zhivi, kak khochetsya (Ostrovsky)
Ne v svoi sani ne sadis! (Ostrovsky)
Ne vse kot maslenitsa (Ostrovsky)
Neal Maquade (Shiels)
Nebbich (Sternheim)
Nebeneinander (Kaiser)
Nebiki no Kadomatsu (Chikamatsu)
Nebo-peklo (Karvaš)
Necromancer (Ariosto)
Ned McCobb's Daughter (Howard)
Nederlaget (Grieg)
Nedorosl (Fonvizin)
Needles and Pins (Daly)
Ne'er-Do-Weel (Gilbert)
Neffe als Onkel (Schiller)
Negersklaven (Kotzebue)
Negro Slaves (Kotzebue)
Negromante (Ariosto)
Neighbors (Vinaver)
Neighbours (Gale)
Neighbours (Saunders)
Neil and Tintinnabulum (Barrie)
Neil Cream (Fennario)
Neinsager (Brecht)
Neither Up Nor Down (Nichols)
Neizdannaya pesa (Chekhov)
Nejlepši rocky paní Hermanové (Havel)
Nekrassov (Sartre)
Nell Gwynne (Jerrold)
Nelligan (Tremblay)
NENAA (Leigh)
Nègres (Genet)
Neostorozhnost (Turgenev)
Neozhidanny sluchay (Ostrovsky)
Nephew as Uncle (Schiller)
Neporochnoye zachatiye (Tretyakov)
Neptune's Triumph for the Return of Albion. (Jonson)
Nero, Emperor of Rome (Lee)
Nero lässt grüssen (Walser)
Nesravnenny Nakonechnikov (Vampilov)
Nest (Kroetz)
Netherwood (White)
Nets and Snares (Petrushevskaya)
Nets and Traps (Petrushevskaya)
Neue Frauenschule (Kotzebue)
Neue Jahrhundert (Kotzebue)
Neue Menoza (Lenz)
Neue Prozess (Weiss)
1913 (Sternheim)
Neutral Ground (t Stoppard)
Never the Time and the Place (Robinson)
Neveu supposé (Lesage)
Nevolnitsy (Ostrovsky)
New Academy (Brome)
New Anatomies (Wertenbaker)
New Ark's a Moverin (Baraka)
New Brooms (Byron)
New Brooms! (Colman the Elder)
New Canadians (Pollock)
New Colony (Pirandello)
New Deliverance (Witkiewicz)
New Gossoon (Shiels)

New Hay at the Old Market (Colman the Younger)
New Haymarket Spring Meeting (Planché)
New House (Behan)
New Inn (Jonson)
New Leisure (Brighouse)
New Life (Rice)
New Marriage (Mitchell)
New Men and Old Acres (Taylor)
New Planet (Planché)
New Play (Saroyan)
New Regime (Shiels)
New Republican (Soyinka)
New River Entertainment (Middleton)
New Servant (Planché)
New System (Bjørnson)
New Tenant (Ionesco)
New Way to Pay Old Debts (Massinger)
New Word (Barrie)
New World (Murrell)
New World Order (Pinter)
New Year's Rhapsody (Kishida)
New York Comedy (Terry)
New York Idea (Mitchell)
New-found-land (Stoppard)
Newly Married Couple (Bjørnson)
News from Plymouth (Davenant)
News from the New World Discovered in the Moon
   (Jonson)
Next Door Neighbours (Inchbald)
Next Time (Bullins)
Next Time I'll Sing to You (Saunders)
Next Year in Jerusalem (Sherman)
Nezabyvayemy 1919–y (Vishnevsky)
Neznakomka (Blok)
Nezumi Kozō Jirokichi (Satoh)
Ngaahika Ndeenda (Ngugi)
Ni al amor ni al mar (Benavente y Martínez)
Ni Amor de libra de amor (Calderón)
Nibelungen (Hebbel)
Nice Firm (Taylor)
Nice People (Crothers)
Nice Valour (Fletcher, Middleton)
Nicht Fisch nicht Fleisch (Kroetz)
Nicomède (P. Corneille)
Nido ajeno (Benavente y Martínez)
Nieboska komedia (Krasiński)
Niece-Wife (Ionesco)
Niece of the Hermit Abraham (Bridie)
Nièce-Épouse (Ionesco)
Niels Ebbesen (Munk)
Niepodległość trójkątów (Witkiewicz)
Nietecito (Benavente y Martínez)
Nieve en Mayo (Benavente y Martínez)
Nigatsu to kinema (Satoh)
Night (Pinter)
Night and Day (Stoppard)
Night and Morning (Boucicault)
Night at an Inn (Dunsany)
Night Before Paris (Sherman)
Night-Blooming Cereus (Reaney)
Night Cap Bar (Laberge)
Night Clerk's Troubles (Harrigan)
Night in Rio and Other Bummerz (Romeril)
Night Life (Kingsley)
Night Like This (Travers)
'night, Mother (Norman)
Night Music (Odets)

Night of Mr. H. (Brighouse)
Night of the Beast (Bullins)
Night of the Day of the Imprisoned Writer (Hampton)
Night of the Iguana (Williams)
Night Off (Daly)
Night on Bald Mountain (White)
Night Out (Pinter)
Night over Taos (M. Anderson)
Night School (t Pinter)
Night the Prowler (s White)
Night Walker (Fletcher)
Night with Guests (Weiss)
Nightclass (McGrath)
Nightingale (Robertson)
Nightingale of Wittenberg (Strindberg)
Night's Adventure (Robertson)
Night's Lodging (Gorky)
Night's Work (Behrman)
Nightshade (Parker)
Nightwalk (Shepard, Terry, van Itallie)
Night-Walker (Shirley)
Nigilist (L. N. Tolstoy)
Nihilist (L. N. Tolstoy)
Nihon no kishō (Kubo)
Niklashauser Fahrt (s Fassbinder)
Nikoforos Fokas (Kazantzakis)
Nina (Dunlap)
Niña de Gómez Arias (Calderón)
Niña del cielo (Tirso De Molina)
Nina, c'est autre chose (Vinaver)
Nina, it's Different (Vinaver)
Nine (Kopit)
Nine Points of the Law (Taylor)
Nine Rivers from Jordan (Johnston)
1949 (French)
1913 [English version] (Sternheim)
99 (Boucicault)
Ninfa del cielo (Tirso De Molina)
Niño azul para esa sombra (Marqués)
Niño y la niebla (Usigli)
Ninon (Chiarelli)
Niños perdidos en la selva (Benavente y Martínez)
Nirvana (Lawson)
Nirwana (Hasenclever)
Nishikigi (Zeami)
Nito monogatari (Kara)
No Cards (Gilbert)
No 'Count Boy (Green)
No End of Blame: Scenes of Overcoming (H. Barker)
No Exit (Sartre)
No fumadores (Benavente y Martínez)
No-Good Friday (Fugard)
No hay burlas con el amor (Calderón)
No hay cosa como callar (Calderón)
No hay instante sin milagro (Calderón)
No hay mal que por bien no venga (Ruiz de Alarcón)
No hay más fortuna que Dios (Calderón)
No hay peor sordo (Tirso De Molina)
No hay que creer ni en la verdad (Calderón)
No Irish Wanted Here (Harrigan)
No juguéis con esas cosas (Benavente y Martínez)
No le arriendo la ganancia (Tirso De Molina)
No Limits of Love (Mercer)
No Man's Land (Pinter)
No Man's Son (Montherlant)
No More A-Roving (Whiting)
No More in Dust (Keane)

No More Peace (Toller)
No More Peace! A Thoughtful Comedy (Auden)
No Name (Daly)
No! No! No! (Pollock)
No One Knows How (Pirandello)
No One Was Saved (H. Barker)
No Prelude! (Colman the Younger)
¡No quiero, no quiero! (Benavente y Martínez)
No Room at the Inn (Arden)
No siempre lo peor es cierto (Calderón)
No, Sirree! (Connelly, Kaufman)
No Smoking (Benavente y Martínez)
No T.O. for Love (Chayefsky)
No Time (Fornés)
No Time for Comedy (Behrman)
No Time Like the Present (Hibberd)
No Title (Rudkin)
No Trespassing (L. Wilson)
No Trifling with Love (Musset)
No Villains (Miller)
No Why (Whiting)
No Wit, No Help Like a Woman's (Middleton)
Noah (Obey)
Noah's Flood (Lawrence)
Noapte furtunoasă (Caragiale)
Noble Gentleman (Beaumont, Fletcher)
Noble Peasant (Holcroft)
Noble Soldier (Dekker)
Noble Spaniard (Maugham)
Noble Spanish Soldier (Dekker)
Noble Vagabond (Jones)
Nobody Here But us Chickens (t Barnes)
Nobody Loves Me (Simon)
Noc (Langer)
Noc listopadowa (Wyspiański)
Noce et l'enterrement (Dumas père)
Noces de Bouchencoeur (Labiche)
Noch einen Löffel Gift, Liebling? (Hacks)
Noch-Jemands Reise Abenteuer (Kotzebue)
Noch nye plyaski (Sologub)
Noch zehn Minuten nach Buffalo (Grass)
Noche de Estío (Usigli)
Noche de los asesinos (Triana)
Noche de San Juan (Vega)
Noche del sábado (Benavente y Martínez)
Noche iluminada (Benavente y Martínez)
Nochnaya ispoved (Arbuzov)
Nočná návšteva (Karvaš)
Nocturne (Heijermans)
Nodo (Fabbri)
Noé (Obey)
Noémie (Robertson)
Noises Off (Frayn)
Noivado no Dàfundo (Garrett)
Noli me tangere (Kaiser)
Nomads (Whiting)
Nombre (Gambaro)
Nombril (Anouilh)
Nomori (Zeami)
Non dir quattro se non l'hai nel sacco (Giacosa)
Non è per scherzo che ti ho amato (Fabbri)
Non-Juror (Cibber)
Non si paga, non si paga (Fo)
Non si sa come (Pirandello)
Non-Stop Connolly Show (Arden)
Non ti pago! (De Filippo)
Non tutti i ladri vengono per nuocere (Fo)

None But the Lonely Heart (s Odets)
Nongogo (Fugard)
Nonne und das Kammermädchen (Kotzebue)
Nonomiya (Zeami)
Noonday Demons (Barnes)
Nora (Crothers)
Nora (Ibsen)
Norm and Ahmed (Buzo)
Norma (Ibsen)
Norma (Planché)
Norman Conquests (Ayckbourn)
Normandy Pippins (Byron)
North Shore Fish (Horovitz)
North Star (s Hellman)
Northern Lass (Brome)
Northern Star (Parker)
Northerners (Brighouse)
Northward Ho (Dekker, Webster)
Nos Bons villageois (Sardou)
Nos Intimes (Sardou)
Nosegay of Weeds (O'Keeffe)
Nosferatu (Gambaro)
Nostri sogni (Betti)
Not a Bad Judge (Planché)
Not as a Dream (Cook)
Not at All Jealous (Robertson)
Not by Bed Alone (Feydeau)
Not Christmas, But Guy Fawkes (Mason)
Not for Children (Rice)
Not I (Beckett)
Not If I Know It (Byron)
Not, Not, Not, Not, Not Enough Oxygen (r Churchill)
Not So Bad as We Seem (Bulwer-Lytton)
Not Such a Fool as He Looks (Byron)
Not with a Bang But a Whimper (Edgar)
Notaire à marier (Labiche)
Note of Hand (Cumberland)
Notebook of Trigorin (Williams)
Nothing But a Man (Ryga)
Nothing Sacred (Walker)
Nothing to Declare (Saunders)
Nothing to Lose (Fennario)
Noticias del día (Carballido)
Notoriety (Harrigan)
Notorious Mrs. Ebbsmith (Pinero)
Notre Futur (Feydeau)
Notruf (Sudermann)
Notte d'amore (Chiarelli)
Notte in casa del ricco (Betti)
Nottingham Captain (Wesker)
Nous n'irons plus au bois (Crommelynck)
Nouveau Locataire (Ionesco)
Novella (Brome)
Novelty Fair (Taylor)
Novia de nieve (Benavente y Martínez)
Novye Robinzony (Petrushevskaya)
Now I Ask You (O'Neill)
Now Playing Tomorrow (r Laurents)
Now the Servant's Name Was Malchus (Wilder)
Nowe Wyzwolenie (Witkiewicz)
Noyade des songes (Ghelderode)
Nubes (Aristophanes)
Nude with Violin (Coward)
Nudo ciego (Díaz)
Nue (Zeami)
Nuestra Natacha (Casona)
Nueva victoria de don Gonzalo de Córdoba (Vega)

Ohrfeige (Walser)
Oi for England (Griffiths)
Oil and Vinegar (Byron)
Oimatsu (Zeami)
Ointment Blue (Fitzmaurice)
Oiseau bleu (Maeterlinck)
Ojos de los muertos (Benavente y Martínez)
Okean (Andreyev)
Okinawa (Kinoshita)
Oktobertag (Kaiser)
Okujō teien (Kishida)
Olaf Liljekrans (Ibsen)
Old Acquaintance (Van Druten)
Old Bachelor (Congreve)
Old Broom (Shiels)
Old Cantankerous (Menander)
Old Christmas (Green)
Old Chums (Byron)
Old Clothesman (Holcroft)
Old Country (Bennett)
Old Crowd (t Bennett)
Old Debauchees (Fielding)
Old English (Galsworthy)
Old Flames (s Gray)
Old Folks of the Centuries (Dunsany)
Old Foolishness (Carroll)
Old Fortunatus (Dekker)
Old Friends (Barrie)
Old Guard (Boucicault)
Old Heads and Young Hearts (Boucicault)
Old King's Tale (Dunsany)
Old Lady Says "No!" (Johnston)
Old Lady Shows Her Medals (Barrie)
Old Lady 31 (Crothers)
Old Lavender (Harrigan)
Old Law (Middleton)
Old Man (Gorky)
Old Man of Edenton (Green)
Old Man Sleeps Alone (r Arden)
Old Man Taught Wisdom (Fielding)
Old Master (Jones)
Old Men (Ghelderode)
Old New Yorker (Harrigan)
Old Offender (Planché)
Old Ones (Wesker)
Old Pine Tree (Zeami)
Old Sailors (Byron)
Old School (Boucicault)
Old School Tie (Hibberd)
Old Score (Gilbert)
Old Soldiers (Byron)
Old Story (Byron)
Old Testament and the New (Houghton)
Old Times (Pinter)
Old Tune (r Beckett)
Old Wash Lucas (Green)
Old Wives Tale (Peele)
Old Woman Broods (Różewicz)
Old Woman Remembers (Gregory)
Old World (Arbuzov)
Oleanna (Mamet)
Olimpia (Molnár)
Olivier (Pixérécourt)
Olly's Prison (Bond)
Olympia (Howard)
Olympia (Molnár)
Olympia (Voltaire)

Olympians (Priestley)
Olympic Devils (Planché)
Olympic Revels (Planché)
Olympie (Voltaire)
Olympus in an Uproar (O'Keeffe)
Olyubvi, poezy i gosudarstvennoy sluzhbe (Blok)
Omai (O'Keeffe)
Ombligo para dos (Díaz)
Ombre de la foire (Lesage)
Ombre du cocher poète (Lesage)
Omelette à la Follembuche (Labiche)
Omon tota (Kinoshita)
Omoo (Boucicault)
Omphale (Hacks)
On a bien failli d'comprendre (Laberge)
On a String (Feydeau)
On Bail (Gilbert)
On Baile's Strand (Yeats)
On demande des culottières (Labiche)
On dira des bêtises (Labiche)
On Guard (Gilbert)
On ne badine pas avec l'amour (Musset)
On ne saurait penser à tout (Musset)
On purge bébé (Feydeau)
On the Eve of Publication (t Mercer)
On the Frontier (Auden)
On the Harmfulnes of Tobaccco (Chekhov)
On the High Road (Chekhov)
On the Highway (Chekhov)
On the Injurious Effects of Tobacco (Chekhov)
On the Inside (Murphy)
On the Job (Fennario)
On the Marry-Go-Wrong (Feydeau)
On the Outside (Murphy)
On the Pig's Back (McGrath)
On the Racecourse (Gregory)
On the Razzle (Nestroy)
On the Razzle (Stoppard)
On the Rim of the Curve (Cook)
On the Rocks (Shaw)
On the Run (Bulgakov)
On the Runway of Life (Kopit)
On Trial (Rice)
On va faire la cocette (Feydeau)
On with the Dance (Coward)
Onbekende (Heijermans)
Once a Hero (Brighouse)
Once a Year (Brighouse)
Once Around the Block (Saroyan)
Once in a Lifetime (Kaufman)
Once upon a Time There Were Two Kings (Planché)
Once upon a Time (Arbuzov)
Once upon a Time (Crothers)
Oncle Sam (Sardou)
Oncle Vania (Tremblay)
Onder het Melkewoud (Claus)
Ondine (Giraudoux)
Ondine (Pixérécourt)
One Arm (s Williams)
One Cannot Think of Everything (Musset)
One Crack Out (French)
One Day in October (Kaiser)
One Evening Gleam (Fitzmaurice)
One Fine Day (t Bennett)
One for the Road (Pinter)
100,001 Horror Stories of the Plains (Terry)
One-Man Masque (Reaney)

One Man's House (Ringwood)
One May Spin a Thread Too Finely (Turgenev)
One Minute Commercial (Bullins)
One More Little Drinkie (t Terry)
One More Ride on the Merry-Go-Round (Wesker)
One of Nature's Gentlemen (Hibberd)
One of These Days . . . (Usigli)
One of Those Letters (Brighouse)
One Thing More (Fry)
One Tiger to a Hill (Pollock)
One Was Nude and One Wore Tails (Fo)
One Way Pendulum (Simpson)
One-Way Ticket (Keane)
O'Neill (Kilroy)
Onì (Witkiewicz)
Onkel, Onkel (Grass)
Only a Woman (Daly)
Only Jealousy of Emer (Yeats)
Only Ten Minutes to Buffalo (Grass)
Onna Cyrano (Kara)
Onnagoroshi Abura Jigoku (Chikamatsu)
Onna-goroshi abura no jugoku (Satoh)
Onnyoro sisuiki (Kinoshita)
Onorevole Ercole Mallardi (Giacosa)
Op Hoop van Zegen (Heijermans)
Open Couple (Fo)
Open Door (Fry)
Open House (Byron)
Opéra-comique assiégé (Lesage)
Opera dello sghignazzo (Fo)
Opéra du monde (Audiberti)
Opera, Opera (Saroyan)
Opéra parlé (Audiberti)
Opera Wonyosi (Soyinka)
Operación quirúrgica (Benavente y Martínez)
Operaio conosce 300 parole, il padrone 1000: Per questo lui
    è il padrone (Fo)
Operation Iskra (Edgar)
Operation Sidewinder (Shepard)
Operationen (Munk)
Operetka (Gombrowicz)
Operetta (Gombrowicz)
Operette (Coward)
Opfer (Sudermann)
Opfertod (Kotzebue)
Opgaande zon (Heijermans)
Opportunity (Shirley)
Opportunity (Tirso De Molina)
Optimism (Guare)
Optimistecheskaya tragediya (Vishnevsky)
Optimistic Tragedy (Vishnevsky)
Opus (Saunders)
Ora et labora (Heijermans)
Oracle muet (Lesage)
Oracles of Apollo (Brighouse)
Oraison (Arrabal)
Orange sur le Mont de Vénus (Arrabal)
Orange Tree and the Humble Bee (Byron)
Oranges and Lemons (McGrath)
Orante (Scudéry)
Orators (Foote)
Orazia (Aretino)
Orbite (Fabbri)
Orchestra (Anouilh)
Orchestre (Anouilh)
Ordalie (Anouilh)
Orden de los factores (Hernández)

Orden de Melchisedech (Calderón)
Órdenes militares (Calderón)
Order (Hochwälder)
Ordet (Munk)
Ordinaire (Vinaver)
Ordinary Day (Fo)
Ordine! Per Dio.OOO.OOO.OOO (Fo)
Ördög (Molnár)
O'Reagans (Harrigan)
Oreste (Alfieri)
Oreste (Voltaire)
Oresteia (Aeschylus)
Orestes (Alfieri)
Orestes (Claus)
Orestes (Euripides)
Orestes (Fugard)
Orestes (Norén)
Orestes (Voltaire)
Orestes and Electra (Kennedy)
Orestie (Dumas père)
Orestie (Obey)
Organe des Schirms (Kotzebue)
Organist (Jones)
Organizer (Hughes)
Organs of the Brain (Kotzebue)
Orgástula (Díaz)
Orient Express (Daly)
Origen, pérdida y restauración de la Virgin del Sagrario
    (Calderón)
Originaux (Voltaire)
Orinoco (Carballido)
Orison (Arrabal)
Orlando Furioso (Greene)
Ornifle (Anouilh)
Oroonoko (Southerne)
Orphan (Otway)
Orphan (Rabe)
Orphan of China (Voltaire)
Orphans (Murphy)
Orphée (Cocteau)
Orphée (s Cocteau)
Orphelin de la Chine (Voltaire)
Orpheus (Bond)
Orpheus (Cocteau)
Orpheus (Planché)
Orpheus and Eurydice (Byron)
Orpheus Descending (Williams)
Orpheus und Euridike (Kokoschka)
Oscar XXVIII (Labiche)
Oscuro vuelo compartido (Díaz)
Osenny marafon (Volodin)
Oskar Wilde (Sternheim)
Osseny marafon (s Volodin)
Ossos do Barão (Andrade)
Osteria della posta (Goldoni)
Oswald et Zénaïde (Tardieu)
Osynlige (Lagerkvist)
Ot ney vse kachestva (L. N. Tolstoy)
Otage (Claudel)
Ôtez votre fille s'il vous plaît (Labiche)
Othello (Shakespeare)
Othelos Xanayirizi (Kazantzakis)
Other Days (Robertson)
Other Side of London (Simpson)
Other Son (Pirandello)
Other Times (Brighouse)
Other Times (Lawler)

Otherwise Engaged (Gray)
Othon (P. Corneille)
Otra honra (Benavente y Martínez)
Otra primavera (Usigli)
Otra vez el diablo (Casona)
Ottavia (Alfieri)
Ottō to yobareru nihonjin (Kinoshita)
Otyrok (Gogol)
Ouallou (Audiberti)
Oublier (Laberge)
Oude Piet (Ghelderode)
Ought We to Visit Her? (Gilbert)
Our American Cousin (Taylor)
Our Betters (Maugham)
Our Boys (Byron)
Our Century (Wilder)
Our Clerks (Taylor)
Our Country's Good (Wertenbaker)
Our Cranks (Harrigan)
Our English Friend (Daly)
Our Father's Failing (Horovitz)
Our Husband Has Gone Mad Again (Rotimi)
Our Irish Cousins (Harrigan)
Our Island Home (Gilbert)
Our Law Makers (Harrigan)
Our Lord of the Ship (Pirandello)
Our Own People (Edgar)
Our Power and Our Glory (Grieg)
Our Private Theatricals (Robertson)
Our Seamen (Boucicault)
Our Seamen (Reade)
Our Town (Wilder)
Our Winnie (t Bennett)
Ouragan (Zola)
Ours (Robertson)
Ours et la lune (Claudel)
Ourselves (Crothers)
Out at Sea (Mrożek)
Out Cry (Williams)
Out in the Cold (McGee)
Out of Our Heads (McGrath)
Out of Sight (McGrath)
Outer Edge of Society (Dumas *fils*)
Outlaw (Strindberg)
Outrageous Fortune (Travers)
Outside (Glaspell)
Outside Looking In (M. Anderson)
Outsider (Borchert)
Ouverture orang-outan (Arrabal)
Ováder (Strindberg)
Over the Wall (Saunders)
Over the Way (Robertson)
Over Ævne I–II (Bjørnson)
Overcoat (Hibberd)
Overland Route (Taylor)
Overnight (Inge)
Overruled (Shaw)
Oversight (Ionesco)
Ovonramwen Nogbaisi (Rotimi)
Owl Answers (Kennedy)
Owners (Churchill)
Oxcart (Marqués)
Oxonion in Town (Colman the Elder)
Oyster and the Pearl (t Saroyan)
Ozeanflug (Brecht)
Ozelenenie (Petrushevskaya)
Ozhidanie (Arbuzov)

Ozidi (Clark)

Pá Storhove (Bjørnson)
Pablo (Pavlovsky)
Pablo Neruda viena volando (Díaz)
Paces de los reyes y judía de Toledo (Vega)
Pächter Feldkümmel von Teippelskirchen (Kotzebue)
Pacient sto trinást' (Karvaš)
Pacific 1860 (Coward)
Pacifists (Jones)
Padlock (Bickerstaff)
Padre di famiglia (Goldoni)
Padre e Justiça e Misericórdia (Vicente)
Padre engañado (Vega)
Padre per amore (Goldoni)
Padrona (Betti)
Paese delle vacanze (Betti)
Pagador de Promessas (Gomes)
Pagnestreiche (Kotzebue)
Paid on Both Sides (Auden)
Pain dur (Claudel)
Painter of Ghent (Jerrold)
Painter of His Own Dishonour (Calderón)
Pair of Drawers (Sternheim)
Palabras comunes (Triana)
Palabras cruzadas (Carballido)
Palabras en la arena (Buero Vallejo)
Palabras y plumas (Tirso De Molina)
Palace of Truth (Gilbert)
Palacio confuso (Vega)
Paläophron und Neoterpe (Goethe)
Paličova dcera (Tyl)
Palm Sunday (Marqués)
Palo Duro (Green)
Paludi (Fabbri)
Pamela (Goldoni)
Paméla, marchande de frivolité (Sardou)
Pamela maritata (Goldoni)
Pamela's Prodigy (Fitch)
Pampered Menials (Byron)
Pan (Byron)
Pan comido en la mano (Benavente y Martínez)
Pan de todos (Sastre)
Pancarta (Díaz)
Pandämonium Germanicum (Lenz)
Pandora (Goethe)
Pandora (Hacks)
Pandora's Box (Byron)
Pandora's Box (Wedekind)
Pandora's Cross (Hewett)
Pandorens Büchse (Kotzebue)
Pani Marjánka, matka pluka (Tyl)
Pankraz erwacht (Zuckmayer)
Panna Tutli-Putli (Witkiewicz)
Panne (Dürrenmatt)
Panne (r Dürrenmatt)
Panoptikum (Molnár)
Pan's Anniversary (Jonson)
Pantagleize (Ghelderode)
Pantagruel (Jarry)
Pantaloon (Barrie)
Panthée (Hardy)
Pantomime (Walcott)
Pantsatte Bondedreng (Holberg)
Pantser (Heijermans)
Paolo and Francesca (Walcott)
Paolo Paoli (Adamov)

Paons (Tremblay)
Papa du prix d'honneur (Labiche)
Papa e la strega (Fo)
Papal Tyranny in the Reign of King John (Cibber)
Papegei (Kotzebue)
Paper Balloon (Kishida)
Paperhanger (Kaufman)
Paphian Bower (Planché)
Paphnutius (Hrotsvitha)
Papiere des Teufels (Nestroy)
Papiermühle (Kaiser)
Papiers d'Aspern (Duras)
Papillonne (Sardou)
Par de botas (Benavente y Martínez)
Par Instinct (Sardou)
Par la fenêtre (Feydeau)
Par la taille (Jarry)
Para el cielo y los altares (Benavente y Martínez)
Para tal culpa tal pena (Echegaray)
Para vencer amor, querer vencerle (Calderón)
Paracelsus (Schnitzler)
Paracelsus and the Hero (Ryga)
Parachute (t Mercer)
Parade (Cocteau)
Paradis perdu (Dubé)
Paradise Enow (Bridie)
Paradise Lost (Fry)
Paradise Lost (Odets)
Paralchimie (Pinget)
Parasit (Schiller)
Parásitas (Carballido)
Parasitaster (Marston)
Parasite (Schiller)
Paravents (Genet)
Par-dessus bord (Vinaver)
Paredes (Gambaro)
Paria (Strindberg)
Pariah (Strindberg)
Paris and London (Planché)
Paris Bound (Barry)
Paris by Night (s Hare)
Paris Comedy (Saroyan)
Paris Doctor (Brighouse)
Paris, Texas (s Shepard)
Paris varie (Vian)
Parish Clerk (Boucicault)
Parisienne (Becque)
Parisina (Bergman)
Parisina (D'Annunzio)
Park (Strauss)
Park Avenue (Kaufman)
Park Your Car in Harvard Yard (Horovitz)
Parlamento de Ruzante che iera vegnù de campo (Ruzante)
Parlate al portiere (De Filippo)
Parliament of Love (Massinger)
Parliamo di donne (Fo)
Parlor Magic (Lawson)
Parodie (Adamov)
Parodie de l'opéra de Télémaque (Lesage)
Parody of Private Lives (Coward)
Parque de la fraternidad (Triana)
Parricide (Daly)
Part du diable (Scribe)
Partage de midi (Claudel)
Parte del Leone (Fo)
Parte di Amleto (De Filippo)
Partisans (Planché)

Partita a scacchi (Giacosa)
Partners (Houghton)
Partners for Life (Byron)
Party (Griffiths)
Party for Boris (Bernhard)
Party Time (Pinter)
Party Wall (Kotzebue)
Parzifal (Dorst)
Pas de deux (Claus)
Paseo de Buster Keaton (García Lorca)
Pasiphaé (Montherlant)
Påsk (Strindberg)
Paso de dos (Pavlovsky)
Paso de Madraguda (Carballido)
Pasque Flower (Ringwood)
Pasquin (Fielding)
Passing By (Sherman)
Passing Day (Shiels)
Passing of Chow-Chow (Rice)
Passing Regiment (Daly)
Passion (Bond)
Passion de Narcisse Mondoux (Gelinas)
Passion Flower (Benavente y Martínez)
Passion Flowers (Robertson)
Passion in Six Days (H. Barker)
Passion of Josef D. (Chayefsky)
Passion of Peter Ginty (Leonard)
Passion Play (Nichols)
Passion Play (Shaw)
Passion, Poison, and Petrification (Shaw)
Passive Husband (Cumberland)
Passport to Romance (Brighouse)
Pastaga des loufs (Arrabal)
Pastor Ephraim Magnus (Brecht)
Pastor fido (Calderón)
Pastor Hall (Toller)
Pastor Sang (Bjørnson)
Pastoral Tragicomedy of the Strella da Estrella (Vicente)
Pastorale (Ruzante)
Pastorale comique (Molière)
Pastores de le ciudad, pastorela (Carballido)
Patchouli (Salacrou)
Patente (Pirandello)
Pathetic Prologue (Sastre)
Paths of Glory (Howard)
Patience (Gilbert)
Patient Grissel (Dekker)
Patients (Audiberti)
Pato Silvestre (Buero Vallejo)
Patrasket (Bergman)
Patrick Pearse Motel (Leonard)
Patrie! (Sardou)
Patriot Father (Kotzebue)
Patriot for Me (Osborne)
Patriot Game (Murphy)
Patriots (Kingsley)
Patriots (Robinson)
Patriottismo insetticida (Marinetti)
Patron (Foote)
Patte-en-l'air (monologue) (Feydeau)
Pattes de mouche (Sardou)
Pauken und Trompeten (Brecht)
Paul Bunyan (Auden)
Paul Forestier (Augier)
Paul Forrester (Augier)
Paul Jones (Dumas *père*)
Paul Kauvar (Mackaye)

Paul Lafarge (Boucicault)
Paul Lange and Tora Parsberg (Bjørnson)
Paul Lange og Tora Parsberg (Bjørnson)
Paul Pry (Jerrold)
Paul Schippel Esq. (Sternheim)
Paul Southman (Whiting)
Paul Twyning (Shiels)
Pauline (Dumas *père*)
Paura numero uno (De Filippo)
Pausanias (Quinault)
Pauvre Amour (Dubé)
Pauvre Bitos (Anouilh)
Pauvre Matelot (Cocteau)
Pauvrette (Boucicault)
Pavana de Aranzazú (Hernández)
Pavane (van Itallie)
Pavés de l'ours (Feydeau)
Pavilion of Masks (Priestley)
Pavillon des fleurs (Pixérécourt)
Pax (Aristophanes)
Pay to My Order (Planché)
Payable on Demand (Taylor)
Paying the Piper (Feydeau)
Payment as Pledged (Gomes)
Pays du dragon (Tremblay)
Paz ficticia (Hernández)
Pé-de-Cabra (Gomes)
Peace (Aristophanes)
Peace and Quiet (Granville-Barker)
Peace at Any Price (Robertson)
Peace in Our Time (Coward)
Pearl (r Arden)
Pearls (Houghton)
Peasant in Pawn (Holberg)
Peau de l'ours (Pixérécourt)
Peau d'ours (Willems)
Pecado de João Agonia (Santareno)
Pechos privilegiados (Ruiz de Alarcón)
Peculiar Position (Planché)
Peculiar Position (Scribe)
Pedagogue (Saunders)
Pedreira das Almas (Andrade)
Pedro Carbonero (Vega)
Pedro de Urdemalas (Cervantes)
Pedro the Artful Dodger (Cervantes)
Peeping Tom of Coventry (O'Keeffe)
Peer Gynt (Fry)
Peer Gynt (Green)
Peer Gynt (Ibsen)
Peer Gynt (Rudkin)
Peer Gynt (Strauss)
Peevish Man (Kotzebue)
Peg Woofington (Boucicault)
Peggy Sue (Hibberd)
Pei Du huan-dai (Guan Hanqing)
Peine du talion (Labiche)
Peking Man (Cao Yu)
Pélerine amoureuse (Rotrou)
Pélican (Adamov)
Pelican (Strindberg)
Pelikanen (Strindberg)
Pelléas and Mélisande (Maeterlinck)
Pelleas and Melisande (Wertenbaker)
Pelléas et Mélisande (Maeterlinck)
Pena de Francia (Tirso De Molina)
Penas sin importancia (Gambaro)
Penda's Fen (t Rudkin)

Penelope (Maugham)
Pénélope moderne (Lesage)
Penny for a Song (Whiting)
Penny That Beauty Spent (Wilder)
Pénombre et chuchotements (Tardieu)
Pensaci, Giacomino! (Pirandello)
Pentecost (Parker)
Penthesilea (Kleist)
Pentheus (Hofmannsthal)
Pèlerin blanc (Pixérécourt)
Pèlerins de la Mecque (Lesage)
Père (Adamov)
Père humilié (Claudel)
Père idéal (Dubé)
Père prodigue (Dumas *fils*)
Père prudent et équitable (Marivaux)
People (Glaspell)
People Are Living There (Fugard)
People at Sea (Priestley)
People in the Wind (Inge)
People of the Cave (Tawfiq al-Hakim)
People vs. Ranchman (Terry)
People with Light Coming Out of Them (r Saroyan)
People with Light Coming Out of Them (Saroyan)
People's Lives (Saroyan)
Peor está que estaba (Calderón)
Pepa Doncel (Benavente y Martínez)
Peppino Girella (t De Filippo)
Pequeno día de ira (Carballido)
Perdoa-me por Me Traíres (Rodrigues)
Peredes oyen (Ruiz de Alarcón)
Peregrine Pickle (Reade)
Perfect Analysis Given by a Parrot (Williams)
Perfect Cure (Houghton)
Perfect Gentleman (Maugham)
Perfect Happiness (Churchill)
Perfect Party (Fuller)
Perfecta casada (Carballido)
Perfectionist (Williamson)
Perfectly All Right (De Groen)
Peribañez and the Comendador of Ocaña (Vega)
Peribañez y el Comendador de Ocaña (Casona)
Peribáñez y el Comendador de Ocana (Vega)
Pericles (Shakespeare)
Pericolosamente (De Filippo)
Periferie (Langer)
Perikeiromene (Menander)
Perils of Bardfrod (Edgar)
Perils of Pippins (Jerrold)
Perinet Leclerc (Dumas *père*)
Period of Adjustment (Williams)
Perjured Husband (Centlivre)
Perkin Warbeck (Ford)
Perle de la Canebière (Labiche)
Perle noire (Sardou)
Perleberg (Sternheim)
Permettez, Madame! (Labiche)
Perníková chaloupka (Langer)
Pernilles korte Frøkenstand (Holberg)
Perolla and Izadora (Cibber)
Perplexed Lovers (Centlivre)
Perro del hortelano (Vega)
Perroquet de Charles Quint (r Ghelderode)
Persa (Plautus)
Persae (Aeschylus)
Persée (Quinault)
Persée et Démétrius (T. Corneille)

Persian (Plautus)
Persians (Aeschylus)
Personal Enemy (Osborne)
Personal Equation (O'Neill)
Pertharite, Roi des Lombards (P. Corneille)
Peruviana (Goldoni)
Pervaya konnaya (Vishnevsky)
Pervonte (Kotzebue)
Pervy vinokur (L. N. Tolstoy)
Pesnya sudby (Blok)
Peste de Marseille (Pixérécourt)
Peste de Otranto (Echegaray)
Pestro en claro (Gambaro)
Pete (Harrigan)
Peter and Paul (Planché)
Peter Bauer (Hauptmann)
Peter Pan (Barrie)
Peter the Great (Dunlap)
Petit Carillonneur (Pixérécourt)
Petit-Maître corrigé (Marivaux)
Petit Homme rouge (Pixérécourt)
Petit Ménage (monologue) (Feydeau)
Petit Page (Pixérécourt)
Petit Voyage (Labiche)
Petite Amie (Brieux)
Petite Molière (Anouilh)
Petite Révoltée (monologue) (Feydeau)
Petites Mains (Labiche)
Petits Auvergnats (Pixérécourt)
Petits bourgeois (Adamov)
Petits-maîtres (Lesage)
Petits Moyens (Labiche)
Petits Oiseaux (Labiche)
Petrified Forest (Sherwood)
Petruchcho (Volodin)
Pettigolezzi delle donne (Goldoni)
Petty Bourgeois (Gorky)
Peyrouse (Kotzebue)
Pfalzgraf Heinrich (Kotzebue)
Pferdewechsel (Kaiser)
Phädra (Schiller)
Phaedra (Claus)
Phaedra (Racine)
Phaedra (Seneca)
Phaethon (Euripides)
Phaéton (Quinault)
Phantasie (Bernhard)
Phantom (Boucicault)
Phantom (Kopit)
Phantom Lady (Calderón)
Phantom Lover (Kaiser)
Pharaoh's Daughter (Kotzebue)
Phèdre (Cocteau)
Phèdre (Racine)
Philadelphia, Here I Come! (Friel)
Philadelphia Story (Barry)
Philanderer (Shaw)
Philanthropist (Hampton)
Philaster (Beaumont, Fletcher)
Philaster (Colman the Elder)
Philemon (Dorst)
Philiberte (Augier)
Philip (Alfieri)
Philip Hotz's Fury (Frisch)
Philoctetes (Müller)
Philoctetes (Sophocles)
Philoktet (Müller)

Philosopher's Stone (Lagerkvist)
Philosopher's Stone (Taylor)
Philosophus udi egen indbilding (Holberg)
Philotas (Lessing)
Phipps (Houghton)
Phoenecian Women (Euripides)
Phoenissae (Euripides)
Phoenissae (Seneca)
Phoenix (Middleton)
Phoenix (Storey)
Phoenix Too Frequent (Fry)
Phormio (Terence)
Photograph: Lovers in Motion (Shange)
Photographs (van Itallie)
Phraarte (Hardy)
Phryne (Boucicault)
Physician (Jones)
Physician in Spite of Himself (Molière)
Physician of His Own Honour (Calderón)
Physiker (Dürrenmatt)
Piacere dell'onesta (Pirandello)
Piadoso aragonés (Vega)
Piano (Griffiths)
Piano Lesson (A. Wilson)
Piastowicze (Wyspiański)
Piccadilly Bushman (Lawler)
Piccolet (Labiche)
Piccolino (Sardou)
Piccolomini (Schiller)
Picket of Love (Cervantes)
Pickwick Papers (Daly)
Picnic (Green)
Picnic (Inge)
Picnic on the Battlefield (Arrabal)
Picture (Ionesco)
Picture (Massinger)
Picture (Molière)
Picture of Dorian Gray (Osborne)
Pictures in a Theatre (Robinson)
Pie-Dish (Fitzmaurice)
Pie sur le gibet (Ghelderode)
Piece of Monologue (Beckett)
Piece of My Mind (Nichols)
Pieces of Pleasantry . . . (Planché)
Pied dans le crime (Labiche)
"Piel contra piel" (Díaz)
Piel Gedeón (Calderón)
Piensa mal . . . y acertarás (Echegaray)
Pièce de Chambertin (Labiche)
Pierre de touche (Augier)
Pierre philosophale (T. Corneille)
Pierre the Foundling (Boucicault)
Pierrot Romulus (Lesage)
Pieszo (Mrożek)
Piet Bouteille (Ghelderode)
Piéton de l'air (Ionesco)
Piety in Pattens (Foote)
Pig in a Poke (t Gray)
Pig Pen (Bullins)
Pigeon (Galsworthy)
Pilatus (Munk)
Pilgrim (Fletcher)
Pilgrim (Vanbrugh)
Pilgrim of Love (Byron)
Pillsbury Muddle (Harrigan)
Pineapple Child (Sutherland)
Ping-pong (Adamov)

Ping-Pong Game (Saroyan)
Pining Wind (Zeami)
Pinprick of History (Arden)
Pintor de su deshonra (Calderón)
Pint's a Pound the World Around (Mamet)
Pioneer (Terry)
Pioneer (Terry)
Piovana (Ruzante)
Pi-Pa-Ki (Howard)
Pipe in the Fields (Murray)
Pique (Daly)
Pique-nique en campagne (Arrabal)
Piquillo (Dumas *père*)
Pir vo vremya chumy (Pushkin)
Pirate (Behrman)
Pirate (Planché)
Pirates of Penzance (Gilbert)
Pirueta y Voltereta (Díaz)
Pisanelle (D'Annunzio)
Piste (Sardou)
Pisti a vérzivatarban (Örkény)
Pit-a-Pat (Molnár)
Pitocchi fortunati (Gozzi)
Pitten (Heijermans)
Pity in History (H. Barker)
Più che l'amore (D'Annunzio)
Più due (Chiarelli)
Più forte (Giacosa)
Pizarre (Pixérécourt)
Pizarro (Sheridan)
Pizarro in Peru (Dunlap)
Pizarro in Peru (Kotzebue)
Pizzazz (Leonard)
Place Calling Itself Rome (Osborne)
Place du palais (Pixérécourt)
Place-Hunters (Martyn)
Place in the World (Sternheim)
Place Royale (P. Corneille)
Place Where the Mammals Die (Díaz)
Place with the Pigs (Fugard)
Plage aux anguilles (Willems)
Plaideurs (Racine)
Plain Dealer (Bickerstaff)
Plain-Dealer (Wycherley)
Plaintiffs and Defendants (t Gray)
Plaisirs de l'île enchantée (Molière)
Plantagenets (Wood)
Platonic Friendship (Barrie)
Platonic Lady (Centlivre)
Platonic Lovers (Davenant)
Platonov (Chekhov)
Play (Beckett)
Play (Robertson)
Play for Yesterday (Saunders)
Play House to Be Let (Davenant)
Play of Everyman (Hofmannsthal)
Play of Giants (Soyinka)
Play of Saint Nicolas (Bodel)
Play of the Play (Bullins)
Play Strindberg (Dürrenmatt)
Play Without a Title (García Lorca)
Play Without Words (Arden)
Playback 625 (Simpson)
Playboy of Seville (Tirso De Molina)
Playboy of the Western World (Synge)
Player Piano (Saunders)
Player Queen (Yeats)

Players (Williamson)
Playgoers (Pinero)
Playing for Time (Miller)
Playing for Time (t Miller)
Playing with Fire (Strindberg)
Playing with Love (Schnitzler)
Playing with Trains (Poliakoff)
Plays for Bleecker Street (Wilder)
Plays for England (Osborne)
Play's the Thing (Molnár)
Playwright and the Public (Saroyan)
Plaza Suite (Simon)
Pleasure of Honesty (Pirandello)
Pleasure Reconciled to Virtue (Jonson)
Plebeians Rehearse the Uprising (Grass)
Plebejer proben den Aufstand (Grass)
Pleito matrimonial del cuerpo y el alma (Calderón)
Plenty (Hare)
Plody prosvescheniya (L. N. Tolstoy)
Plot and Passion (Taylor)
Plough and the Stars (O'Casey)
Ploughmen of the Glacier (Ryga)
Plugged-in to History (McGrath)
Plunder (Travers)
Plus de Miracles pour Noël (Obey)
Plus Forte (Brieux)
Plus Heureux des trois (Labiche)
Pluto (Byron)
Plutus (Aristophanes)
Plutus (Holberg)
Plutus, the God of Riches (Fielding)
Pobeda smerti (Sologub)
Pobeditelnitsa (Arbuzov)
Pobre mujer (Benavente y Martínez)
Pochi (Alfieri)
Poczwórka (Mrożek)
Pod lipami Berlina (Shvarts)
Poder de la impotencia (Echegaray)
Poenulus (Plautus)
Poer nano ed altre storie (Fo)
Poet and the Rent (Mamet)
Poet and the Women (Aristophanes)
Poeta fanatico (Goldoni)
Poetaster (Jonson)
Poète et sa muse (Cocteau)
Poetic Situation in America (Saroyan)
Pogrzeb naturalny (Różewicz)
Pohutukawa Tree (Mason)
Point de mire (Labiche)
Point d'honneur (Lesage)
Point of Departure (Anouilh)
Point of View (Crothers)
Point Valaine (Coward)
Poire Acre (Maillet)
Poison and the Antidote (Calderón)
Poissons rouges (Anouilh)
Poivre de Cayenne (Obaldia)
Poker Session (Leonard)
Pokhozhdeniya zubnogo vracha (s Volodin)
Pokoušení (Havel)
Pole i doroga (Ivanov)
Police (Baraka)
Policeman (Mrożek)
Polichinelles (Becque)
Policja (Mrożek)
Policy (Robertson)
Polinice (Alfieri)

Politesse (Barrie)
Politesse inutile (Tardieu)
Political Tinker (Holberg)
Politician (Shirley)
Politique des restes (Adamov)
Politiske Kandstøber (Holberg)
Polly (Colman the Elder)
Polly (Gay)
Polly (Hacks)
Polly Honeycombe (Colman the Elder)
Polnočná omša (Karvaš)
Poloumny Zhurden (Bulgakov)
Polowanie na lisa (Mrożek)
Polter (Pixérécourt)
Polyeucte, Martyr (P. Corneille)
Polyeuctus (P. Corneille)
Polygon (Brighouse)
Polypheme (Cibber)
Pomme, Pomme, Pomme (Audiberti)
Pommes du voisin (Sardou)
Pompeji (Horváth)
Pompey the Great (Kyd)
Pompey the Great (P. Corneille)
Pont de l'Europe (Salacrou)
Poof (Salacrou)
Poor Bitos (Anouilh)
Poor Boy (Witkiewicz)
Poor Bride (Ostrovsky)
Poor Gentleman (Colman the Younger)
Poor Gentleman (Turgenev)
Poor Man's Friend (H. Barker)
Poor of Liverpool (Boucicault)
Poor of New York (Boucicault)
Poor Old Haymarket (Colman the Younger)
Poor Old Simon (Saunders)
Poor Soldier (O'Keeffe)
Poorhouse (Gregory)
Pope and the Witch (Fo)
Pope of Rome (Boucicault)
Pope's Wedding (Bond)
Poppy (Nichols)
Popul-Vuh (Hernández)
Popular Felons (Jerrold)
Por el sótano y el torno (Tirso De Molina)
Por la herida (Benavente y Martínez)
Por las nubes (Benavente y Martínez)
Por que se quitó Juan de la bebida (Benavente y Martínez)
Por salvar el amor (Benavente y Martínez)
Por ser con todos leal, ser para todos traidor (Benavente y Martinez)
Porque se ama (Benavente y Martínez)
Port-Royal (Montherlant)
Port Town (Hughes)
Porta Pietatis (Heywood)
Portable Yenberry (Connelly)
Portage to San Cristobal of A.H. (Hampton)
Portantina (Chiarelli)
Porton (Bergman)
Portrait (Colman the Elder)
Portrait (Robinson)
Portrait d'une femme (Vinaver)
Portrait of a Madonna (Williams)
Portrait of a Woman (Vinaver)
Portrait of Angelica (Ryga)
Porträt eines Nachmittags (r Forte)
Porträt eines Planeten (Dürrenmatt)
Portret (Mrożek)

Portret s dozhdem (Volodin)
Positive Man (O'Keeffe)
Poslednie (Gorky)
Posledniye dni Pushkin (Bulgakov)
Posledny resistelny (Vishnevsky)
Poslednyaya zhertva (Ostrovsky)
Possédés (Camus)
Possessed (Camus)
Possibilities (H. Barker)
Post-Inn (Goldoni)
Post-Mortem (Coward)
Post Office (Tagore)
Post-scriptum (Augier)
Poster of the Cosmos (L. Wilson)
Postfácio (Régio)
Posthaus in Treuenbrietzen (Kotzebue)
Postrer duelo de España (Calderón)
Pot-Bouille (Zola)
Pot of Broth (Yeats)
Pot of Gold (Plautus)
Potache (Feydeau)
Poteryanny syn (Arbuzov)
Potestad (Pavlovsky)
Pots of Money (Labiche)
Pott (Dorst)
Potter's Field (Green)
Poudre aux yeux (Labiche)
Poudre d'intelligence (Yacine)
Pound on Demand (O'Casey)
Poupée (Audiberti)
Poupées électriques (Marinetti)
Pour Lucrèce (Giraudoux)
Pour préparer un oeuf dur (Ionesco)
Pour un Oui ou pour un non (Sarraute)
Pourquoi pas moi? (Salacrou)
Poverty and Nobleness of Mind (Kotzebue)
Poverty and Pride (Reade)
Poverty is No Crime (Ostrovsky)
Poverty's No Vice (Ostrovsky)
Povest o molodykh suprugakh (Shvarts)
Power and Glory (Čapek)
Power and Principle (Schiller)
Power in the Blood (Murrell)
Power of Darkness (L. N. Tolstoy)
Power of the Dead (Maeterlinck)
Power of the Dog (H. Barker)
Power Outrage (Mamet)
Powrót Odysa (Wyspiański)
Pozdnyaya lyubov (Ostrovsky)
Pozo (Carballido)
Præsten i Vejlby (Munk)
Pragmatists (Witkiewicz)
Pragmatyści (Witkiewicz)
Prague Trial (Hampton)
Prairie du Chien (Mamet)
Präsident (Bernhard)
Präsident (Kaiser)
Prato (Fabbri)
Prato (r Fabbri)
Pratt's Fall (Parker)
Pravda khorosho, a schastye luchshe (Ostrovsky)
Pravda (Brenton, Hare)
Praxagora (Tawfiq al-Hakim)
Prayer Meeting (Green)
Prazdichny son—do obeda (Ostrovsky)
Pražský flamendr (Tyl)
Précieuses ridicules (Molière)

Précieux (Labiche)
Precious Damsels (Molière)
Precious Woman (Nowra)
Précipe (Pixérécourt)
Precipócio de Faetonte (Silva)
Predlozheniye (Chekhov)
Predmeste (Vampilov)
Preferido y los cenicientos (Echegaray)
Préjugé vaincu (Marivaux)
Premier Pas (Labiche)
Premier Prix de piano (Labiche)
Première Représentation (Lesage)
Premières Armes de Figaro (Sardou)
Près Saint-Gervais (Sardou)
Preparadise Sorry Now (Fassbinder)
Preparation of the Athenians for the Reception of Phocion
    (Davenant)
Present Laughter (Coward)
Preserving Mr. Panmure (Pinero)
President (Bernhard)
President (Howard)
President (Kaiser)
President (Molnár)
Presidente y el ideal (Usigli)
Preskasnye sabinyanki (Andreyev)
Press Cuttings (Shaw)
Press-Gang (Jerrold)
Presumptive Evidence (Boucicault)
Pretenders (Ariosto)
Pretenders (Ibsen)
Pretendiente al revés (Tirso De Molina)
Prétendus de Gimblette (Labiche)
Pretentious Young Ladies (Molière)
Pretty Boy (Poliakoff)
Pretty Druidess (Gilbert)
Pretty Esmeralda and Captain Phoebus of Ours (Byron)
Pretty Perfumeress (Byron)
Prexaspes (Hacks)
Price (Miller)
Price of Coal (Brighouse)
Price of Mercy (Walcott)
Prick Up Your Ears (s Bennett)
Pride (van Itallie)
Pride of the Market (Planché)
Priesterzögling (Hofmannsthal)
Prigioneri (Marinetti)
Priklyucheniya Gogenshtaufen (Shvarts)
Prima Ballerina (Hofmannsthal)
Prima Donna (Boucicault)
Primary English Class (Horovitz)
Primater (Blok)
Primer acto de un drama (Echegaray)
Primer flor del Carmelo (Calderón)
Primer refugio del hombre y probático piscina (Calderón)
Primero soy yo (Calderón)
Primero y segundo Isaac (Calderón)
Primícias (Gomes)
Primitive World (Baraka)
Primo Román (Benavente y Martínez)
Princ Kašpárek a jeho koníček (Langer)
Prince and the Showgirl (s Rattigan)
Prince déguisé (Scudéry)
Prince Dorus (Taylor)
Prince of Darkness (Mortimer)
Prince of Happy Land (Planché)
Prince of Homburg (Kleist)
Prince of Homburg (Nowra)

Prince of Naples (Walker)
Prince of Stamboul (Dunsany)
Prince travesti (Marivaux)
Prince Who Learned Everything Out of Books (Benavente
    y Martinez)
Prince Who Was a Piper (Brighouse)
Princesa Bebé (Benavente y Martínez)
Princesa sin corazón (Benavente y Martínez)
Princess (Gilbert)
Princess Royal (Daly)
Princess and the Butterfly (Pinero)
Princess Bebe (Benavente y Martínez)
Princess Far Away (Rostand)
Princess Ida (Gilbert)
Princess Ivona (Gombrowicz)
Princess Magdalena (Witkiewicz)
Princess of Burgundy (Gombrowicz)
Princess of Cleve (Lee)
Princess of Parma (Cumberland)
Princess Springtime (Byron)
Princess Sunshine (Tawfiq al-Hakim)
Princess Toto (Gilbert)
Princesse (Arrabal)
Princesse de Bagdad (Dumas *fils*)
Princesse de Charizme (Lesage)
Princesse de la Chine (Lesage)
Princesse de Navarre (Voltaire)
Princesse d'Élide (Molière)
Princesse Georges (Dumas *fils*)
Princesse Isabelle (Maeterlinck)
Princesse lointaine (Rostand)
Princesse Maleine (Maeterlinck)
Princess's Nose (Jones)
Príncipe constante (Calderón)
Príncipe despeñado (Vega)
Príncipe que todo lo aprendió en los libros (Benavente y
    Martinez)
Principessa filosofa (Gozzi)
Printemps 71 (Adamov)
Printer's Devil (Planché)
Printer's Measure (t Chayefsky)
Prinz Friedrich von Homburg (Kleist)
Prinz Friedrich von Homburg (Strauss)
Prinz Zerbino (Tieck)
Prinzessin von Cacambo (Kotzebue)
Prinzessin von Chimay (Hochwälder)
Priority Projects (Soyinka)
Prisoner at Large (O'Keeffe)
Prisoner of Second Avenue (Simon)
Prisoner of War (Jerrold)
Prisoners (Plautus)
Prisoners of the War (McGrath)
Prisonnier de la Bastille (Dumas *père*)
Pritvornaya nevernost (Griboyedov)
Privar contra su gusto (Tirso De Molina)
Private Ear (Shaffer)
Private Entertainment of the King and Queen at Highgate
    (Jonson)
Private Function (s Bennett)
Pvt. Jim Crow (r Hughes)
Private Life of the Master Race (Brecht)
Private Lives (Coward)
Private Parts (H. Barker)
Private Room (Pinero)
Private Rooms (Priestley)
Private View (Havel)
Privates on Parade (Nichols)

Privates on Parade (s Nichols)
Privilege of Place (Martyn)
Prix Martin (Augier, Labiche)
Pro Game (Terry)
Proba intermedy (Griboyedov)
Processional (Lawson)
Processo a Gesù (Fabbri)
Processo di famiglia (Fabbri)
Processo Karamazov (Fabbri)
Procris (Hardy)
Prodigal (Richardson)
Prodigal (Rotimi)
Prodigal (Scribe)
Prodigal Son (Daly)
Prodigal Son (Hughes)
Prodigious Magician (Calderón)
Prodigo (Goldoni)
Production of Mysteries (Ludlam)
Profecias de Bandarra (Garrett)
Professeur Taranne (Adamov)
Profession (Laberge)
Professional Foul (t Stoppardt)
Professor (Mrożek)
Professor Bernhardi (Schnitzler)
Professor Bedlam's Educational Punch and Judy Show
    (Ludlam)
Professor Storitsyn (Andreyev)
Professor Taranne (Adamov)
Professor Tim (Shiels)
Professor's Love Story (Barrie)
Profligate (Pinero)
Progress (Robertson)
Progress (Sardou)
Prohibido suicidarse en primavera (Casona)
Prokhodite v kukhnyu (Petrushevskaya)
Prólogo de un drama (Echegaray)
Prólogo patético (Sastre)
Prologue (Lesage)
Prologue to "King Lear" (Molnár)
Prom Night (Kaufman)
Promenade (Fornés)
Promenade (t Nichols)
Promessa (Santareno)
Prometheus (Goethe)
Prometheus (Müller)
Prometheus (Sorge)
Prometheus Bound (Aeschylus)
Prometheus Bound (Ryga)
Prometheus Vinctus (Aeschylus)
Promise (Arbuzov)
Promise (Santareno)
Promises, Promises (Simon)
Promitheas (Kazantzakis)
Promotion (Planché)
Prompter's Box (Byron)
Proper Gent (Molière)
Prophecy (Handke)
Prophet (Scribe)
Prophète (Scribe)
Prophetess (Fletcher, Massinger)
Prophets (Mrożek)
Propia estimación (Benavente y Martínez)
Proposal (Chekhov)
Proposal (Sutherland)
Proposal (Bridie)
Proserpina (Goethe)
Proserpina and the Devil (Wilder)

Proserpine (Quinault)
Proshchaniye v iyune (Vampilov)
Proshlym letom v Chulimske (Vampilov)
Próspera fortuna de Don Álvaro (Tirso De Molina)
Protagonist (Kaiser)
Protée (Claudel)
Protegée of the Mistress (Ostrovsky)
Protesilas i Laodamia (Wyspiański)
Protesilaus and Laodamia (Wyspiański)
Protest (Havel)
Protestación de la fe (Calderón)
Protivogazy (Tretyakov)
Protomastoras (Kazantzakis)
Proust Screenplay (s Pinter)
Proverb (Dunlap)
Providente Lucilla (Chiarelli)
Provincial Lady (Turgenev)
Provinciale (Marivaux)
Provintsialka (Turgenev)
Provody (Sologub)
Provoked Husband (Cibber, Vanbrugh)
Provoked Wife (Vanbrugh)
Prozess (Weiss)
Prozess der Jeanne d'Arc zu Rouen (Brecht)
Prozess der Jeanne d'Arc zu Rouen 1431 (r Brecht)
Prozess um des Esels Schatten (r Dürrenmatt)
Prude (Voltaire)
Prudence Corner (Brighouse)
Prudence in Women (Tirso De Molina)
Prudencia en la mujer (Tirso De Molina)
Prueba de amor (Arlt)
Prueba de las promesas (Ruiz de Alarcón)
Prueba de los amigos (Vega)
Prunella (Granville-Barker)
Prurient Prude (Reade)
Przyrost naturalny (Różewicz)
Pseudolus (Plautus)
Psiquis y Cupido (Calderón)
Psyché (P. Corneille, Molière, Quinault)
Psyche (Shadwell)
Psychic Pretenders (Bullins)
Ptákovina (Kundera)
Pubblico secreto (Gozzi)
Public (García Lorca)
Public Enemy (Ibsen)
Public Prosecutor (Hochwälder)
Público (García Lorca)
Publikumsbeschimpfung (Handke)
Puce à l'oreille (Feydeau)
Pucelle (Audiberti)
Pucelle pour un gorille (Arrabal)
Puchina (Ostrovsky)
Pudeur à la foire (Lesage)
Puente de Mantible (Calderón)
Puerta cerrada (Sastre)
Puisque je t'aime (Brieux)
Puissance des morts (Maeterlinck)
Pułapka (Różewicz)
Pulchérie (P. Corneille)
Pulchinella (Chiarelli)
Pullman Car Hiawatha (Wilder)
Půlnoční vítr (Topol)
Pum pum! Chi e? La polizia! (Fo)
Pumpkin (Dunsany)
Pumpkin Eater (s Pinter)
Punch (Barrie)
Punch (Byron)

Punch and Go (Galsworthy)
Punch for Judy (Barry)
Puñeta (Díaz)
Punho (Santareno)
Punizione nel precipizio (Gozzi)
Punk et punk Colégram (Arrabal)
Puntigli domestici (Goldoni)
Puntje (Heijermans)
Punto de la espada (Echegaray)
Puppenspieler (Schnitzler)
Puppet Play of Don Cristobál (García Lorca)
Puppet Show (Blok)
Pure in Heart (Lawson)
Purgatorio de San Patricio (Calderón)
Purgatory (Yeats)
Purgatory of St. Patrick (Calderón)
Purging (Feydeau)
Purification (Williams)
Purple Dust (O'Casey)
Púrpura de la rosa (Calderón)
Pusho (Santareno)
Puslespil (Munk)
Puss in a New Pair of Boots (Byron)
Puss in Boots (Planché)
Puss in Boots (Tieck)
Pussycat and the Expert Plumber Who Was a Man (r Miller)
Pustaky (Shvarts)
Put Yourself in His Place (Reade)
Putain respectueuse (Sartre)
Putta onorata (Goldoni)
Pyat vecherov (Volodin)
Pygmalion (Kaiser)
Pygmalion (Shaw)
Pygmalion (s Shaw)
Pygmalion (Tawfiq al-Hakim)
Pygmalion and Galatea (Gilbert)
Pyrate's Den (Bridie)
Pyrrhus, Roy d'Empire (T. Corneille)

Qiao (Cao Yu)
Qie-kuai dan (Guan Hanqing)
Quacks (Molière)
Quad (t Beckett)
Quadrille (Coward)
Quadrupeds of Quedlinburgh (Colman the Younger)
Quai West (Müller)
Quäker (Kotzebue)
Qualcuno fra voi (t Febbri)
Quality Street (Barrie)
Quando sarai povero sarai re (Fo)
Quando si e qualcuno (Pirandello)
Quanmin zongdongyuan (Cao Yu)
Quare Fellow (Behan)
Quare Medicine (Green)
Quartermaine's Terms (Gray)
Quartett (Müller)
Quasi per caso una donna: Elisabetta (Fo)
Quatre Éléments (Pixérécourt)
90° in the Shade (Labiche)
Quatres Cubes (Arrabal)
Queen (Ford)
Queen After Death (Montherlant)
Queen and Concubine (Brome)
Queen and the Rebels (Betti)
Queen Christina (Strindberg)
Queen for a Day (Scribe)

Queen Lucidora (Planché)
Queen Mab (Bickerstaff)
Queen Mary's Bower (Planché)
Queen of Corinth (Fletcher, Massinger)
Queen of Spades (Boucicault)
Queen of Spades (Scribe)
Queen of the Frogs (Planché)
Queen Was in the Parlour (Coward)
Queen's Champion (Scribe)
Queen's Comedy (Bridie)
Queen's Enemies (Dunsany)
Queen's Exchange (Brome)
Queen's Horse (Planché)
Queen's Husband (Sherwood)
Queens of France (Wilder)
Queer People (Gorky)
Quei figuri di trent'anni fa (De Filippo)
Quem Tem Farelos? (Vicente)
Quenouille de Barberine (Musset)
Querelle (s Fassbinder)
Querelle des théâtres (Lesage)
Questa sera si recita a soggetto (Pirandello)
Questi fantasmi! (De Filippo)
Question d'argent (Dumas fils)
Question of Attribution (Bennett)
Questioning of Nick (Kopit)
Queue de vérité (Lesage)
Qui est là? (Tardieu)
Quick, and the Dead (Leonard)
Quick Work (Pinero)
Quien calla ortorga (Tirso De Molina)
Quien da luego, da dos veces (Tirso De Molina)
Quien habló, pagó (Tirso De Molina)
¡Quién hallará mujer fuerte? (Calderón)
Quien mal anda en mal acaba (Ruiz de Alarcón)
Quien no cae, no se leyanta (Tirso De Molina)
Quiller (Cook)
Quiller Memorandum (s Pinter)
Quimera (García Lorca)
Quinas de Portugal (Tirso De Molina)
Quin's Secret (Shiels)
Quinto piano, ti saluto! (De Filippo)
Quits (Daly)
Quittance du diable (Musset)
Quitte pour la peur (Vigny)
Quoat-Quoat (Audiberti)
Quodlibet (Handke)
Quodlibet verschiedener Jahrhunderte (Nestroy)

RUR (Čapek)
Rabbit Race (Walser)
Rabegas (Sardou)
Race for Dinner (Scribe)
Rachel is Coming (Boucicault)
Rachel the Reaper (Reade)
Rächende Gewissen (Kotzebue)
Racing Demon (Hare)
Rack (Priestley)
Radical Cure (Boucicault)
Radio I (r Beckett)
Radio Play (r Saroyan)
Radio II (r Beckett)
Radio-Active Horror Show (Romeril)
Raffle (Dunsany)
Raffle for Mrs. Hennessey's Clock (Harrigan)
Raft (Clark)
Raft of Medusa (Kaiser)

Ragazza di Passaggio/La Femme du Gange (s Duras)
Raggiratore (Goldoni)
Ragione degli altri (Pirandello)
Railroad of Love (Daly)
Raimundo de Colibrados (Kotzebue)
Rain at the End of the Summer (Keane)
Rain from Heaven (Behrman)
Rainmaker (Ringwood)
Rainy Afternoon (Inge)
Raisin in the Sun (Hansberry)
Rajski ogródek (Różewicz)
Rake's Progress (Auden)
Rakhel (Bulgakov)
Ralph Roister Doister (Udall)
Rameaus Neffe (Dorst)
Ramée (Dorst)
Ramírez de Arellano (Vega)
Ramona and the White Slaves (Walker)
Ramonneurs (Hardy)
Ramzes (Blok)
Ranae (Aristophanes)
Rancid Pong (Leigh)
Rancore (Fabbri)
Randall's Thumb (Gilbert)
Random Happenings in the Hebrides (McGrath)
Random Moments in a May Garden (Saunders)
Rape of Lucrece (Heywood)
Rape of the Locks (Menander)
Rape upon Rape (Fielding)
Rapid Thaw (Robertson)
Rapparee (Boucicault)
Rappel de la foire à la vie (Lesage)
Rascatripa (Díaz)
Raschhoffs (Sudermann)
Raskinulos more shiroko (Vishnevsky)
Raspberry Picker (Hochwälder)
Rastro Atrás (Andrade)
Rat (Satoh)
Rat Trap (Coward)
Rat Trap (McGrath)
Rational Princess (Brighouse)
Rats (Hauptmann)
Rats (Horovitz)
Rat's Mass (Kennedy)
Ratten (Hauptmann)
Rattenfänger (Zuckmayer)
Ratto della Francesca (Fo)
Räuber (Schiller)
Räuber Mathias Kneissl (t Sperr)
Raven (Gozzi)
Ravenna (Schiller)
Ravissement de Proserpine (Hardy)
Ravissement de Scapin (Claudel)
Raymond de Toulouse (Pixérécourt)
Razgovor na bolshoi doroge (Turgenev)
Re Baldoria (Marinetti)
Re cervo (Gozzi)
Re de Ramos (Gomes)
Re Torrismondo (Tasso)
Reading Boy (Romeril)
Real Dreams (Griffiths)
Real envido (Gambaro)
Real Inspector Hound (Stoppard)
Real Long John Silver (Barnes)
Real Thing (Stoppard)
Real Thing at Last (Barrie)
Real World (Tremblay)

Realidad y el delirio (Echegaray)
Realm of Joy (Gilbert)
Rear Column (Gray)
Rearguard Action (Romeril)
Reason We Eat (Horovitz)
Reason Why (Miller)
Rebecca (s Sherwood)
Rebels (Ngugi)
Rebels (Priestley)
Rebirth Celebration of the Human Race (Saroyan)
Recent Killing (Baraka)
Recklessness (O'Neill)
Reckoning (Houghton)
Reckoning (Jellicoe)
Reckoning (O'Neill)
Reconciliation (Hauptmann)
Reconciliation (Kotzebue)
Reconstructie (Claus)
Reconstructing the Crime (Barrie)
Recruiting Officer (Daly)
Recruiting Officer (Farquhar)
Recruiting Serjeant (Bickerstaff)
Rector (Crothers)
Rector (Pinero)
Red, Black and Ignorant (Bond)
Red Burning Light (Fornés)
Red Cross (Shepard)
Red Devil Battery Sign (Williams)
Red Flag at Evening (Ringwood)
Red Letter Nights (Daly)
Red Madonna (Arrabal)
Red Magic (Ghelderode)
Red Mask (Planché)
Red Noses (Barnes)
Red Oleanders (Tagore)
Red Peppers (Coward)
Red Ribbon (Daly)
Red Riding Hood (Bridie)
Red River (Mamet)
Red Robe (Brieux)
Red Roses for Me (O'Casey)
Red Scarf (Daly)
Red Star (Wood)
Redaktøren (Bjørnson)
Redención de cautivos (Calderón)
Redevelopment (Havel)
Redevelopment (Saunders)
Reds (s Griffiths)
Redwood Curtain (L. Wilson)
Reed Cutter (Zeami)
Réformes (Feydeau)
Réformiste (Dubé)
Refusal (Cibber)
Régence (Brieux)
Regent (Planché)
Regent (Strindberg)
Régiment de la Calotte (Lesage)
Regina e gli insorti (Betti)
Regina (Hellman)
Regina (Sudermann)
Regina Eyre (Martyn)
Reginetta (Chiarelli)
Regular Army, O! (Harrigan)
Rehbock (Kotzebue)
Rehearsal (Anouilh)
Rehearsal (Gelber)
Rehearsal at Goatham (Gay)

Rehearsing the Tragedy (Daly)
Rei Sebastião (Régio)
Reigen (Schnitzler)
Reilly and the Four Hundred (Harrigan)
Reina de los reyes (Tirso De Molina)
Reine du Barostan (Lesage)
Reine d'un jour (Scribe)
Reine Margot (Dumas *père*)
Reine morte (Montherlant)
Reise (Sternheim)
Reise ins Glück (Kroetz)
Rejoice! (McGrath)
Rejolero de Córdoba (Carballido)
Rektor Kleist (Kaiser)
Rekviem (Andreyev)
Relapse (Vanbrugh)
Relative Values (Coward)
Relatively Speaking (Ayckbourn)
Reluctant Citizen (t Chayefsky)
Reluctant Tragedian (Chekhov)
Remarkable Rooming-House of Mme. Le Monde
    (Williams)
Remedio en la desdicha (Vega)
Remember Me (Tremblay)
Remembrance (Walcott)
Remembrance of Miracles (r Ringwood)
Rémouleur d'amour (Lesage)
Removalists (Williamson)
Remplaçantes (Brieux)
Renaud et Arminde (Cocteau)
Rencontre (Planché)
Rencorosa (Echegaray)
Rendez-vous de Senlis (Anouilh)
Rendez-vous du lendemain. (Dubé)
Renée (Zola)
Renegado (Massinger)
Rent (Edgar)
Rent Day (Jerrold)
Repas des fauves (Ghelderode)
Repeat Performance (Mrożek)
Répétition (Anouilh)
Repos du septième jour (Claudel)
Representative (Hochhuth)
República al revés (Tirso De Molina)
Republican (Soyinka)
Republiqven (Holberg)
Reputation (Planché)
Request Concert (Kroetz)
Requiem for a Futurologist (Soyinka)
Réquiem por un girasol (Díaz)
Requiem pour une nonne (Camus)
Resa a discrezione (Giacosa)
Rescued (Boucicault)
Rescued by a Coquette (Guan Hanqing)
Resistable Rise of Arturo Ui (Brecht)
Resounding Tinkle (Simpson)
Respectable Prostitute (Sartre)
Respectable Wedding (Brecht)
Respectful Prostitute (Sartre)
Respektabele Gesellschaft (Kotzebue)
Respetuosa (Sastre)
Respublica (Udall)
Restless Heart (Anouilh)
Restoration (Bond)
Restoration of Arnold Middleton (Storey)
Restos (Santareno)
Résultat des courses! (Brieux)

Resurrection (Yeats)
Resurrection in Life (Baraka)
Resurrection of Drusiana and Callimachus (Hrotsvitha)
Retablillo de Don Cristobál (García Lorca)
Retablo de las maravillas (Cervantes)
Retired from Business (Jerrold)
Retour d'Arlequin à la foire (Lesage)
Retour imprévu (Regnard)
Retribution (Taylor)
Retrievers (Shiels)
Retro (Terry)
Retrospect (Dunlap)
Retrouvailles (Adamov)
Retter (Goering)
Retter (Hasenclever)
Return Half (Van Druten)
Return Home (Clark)
Return of Odysseus (Wyspiański)
Return of the Soldier (Van Druten)
Return to a City (Saunders)
Return to Abyssinia (White)
Returned Killed (Planché)
Reunion (Mamet)
Reunion (s Pinter)
Réunion des amours (Marivaux)
Reunion in Vienna (Sherwood)
Rêve (Zola)
Revenge (Behn)
Revenge (Brenton)
Revenge of Bussy D'Ambois (Chapman)
Revenge of the Space Pandas (Mamet)
Revengers' Comedies (Ayckbourn)
Revenger's Tragedy (Middleton, Tourneur)
Reverend Griffith Davenport (Herne)
Reverse Psychology (Ludlam)
Review (Colman the Younger)
Revizor (Adamov)
Revizor (Gogol)
Revolt (Buzo)
Revolte auf Cote 3018 (Horváth)
Revolução dos Beatos (Gomes)
Revolutionary Witness (t Barnes)
Rey Don Pedro en Madrid (Tirso De Molina)
Rey Lear (Benavente y Martínez)
Rhampsinit (Dorst)
Rhesus (Euripides)
Rhinocéros (Ionesco)
Rhume onirique (Ionesco)
Ribbemont (Dunlap)
Ricardo III (Casona)
Ricco insidiato (Goldoni)
Rich and Famous (Guare)
Rich Jew of Malta (Marlowe)
Richard Darlington (Dumas *père*)
Richard of the Lion Heart (Byron)
Richard Savage (Barrie)
Richard II (Shakespeare)
Richard III (Shakespeare)
Richard III (Anouilh)
Richard III (Maillet)
Richard III (Obey)
Richard's Cork Leg (Behan)
Richelieu (Benavente y Martínez)
Richelieu (Bulwer-Lytton)
Richter von London (Dorst)
Richu (Cao Yu)
Riconstruire l'Italia con architettura futurista Sant'Elia

Rolling Home (t Bennett)
Roly Poly (Robinson)
Romagem de Agravados (Vicente)
Roman Actor (Massinger)
Roman d'Elvire (Dumas *père*)
Roman Fever (Leonard)
Romance de Dan y Elsa/ Romance en tres noches (Casona)
Romance de lobos (Valle-Inclán)
Romance in A Flat (Feydeau)
Romance of a Day (Planché)
Romancers (Rostand)
Romanesques (Rostand)
Romans in Britain (Brenton)
Romantic Idea (Planché)
Romantic Young Lady (Granville-Barker)
Romantics (Rostand)
Romany Road (Brighouse)
Rome Preserved (Voltaire)
Rome vaincue (Caragiale)
Romeo and Juliet (Shakespeare)
Roméo et Jeannette (Anouilh)
Roméo et Juliette (Cocteau)
Romeo und Juliet (Goethe)
Romera de Santiago (Tirso De Molina)
Romulus (Dumas *père*)
Romulus and Remus (Martyn)
Romulus der Grosse (Dürrenmatt)
Ronde (Schnitzler)
Roof (Galsworthy)
Roof Garden (Kishida)
Rookery Nook (Travers)
Room (Pinter)
Rooted (Buzo)
Roots (Wesker)
Rope (O'Neill)
Rope (Plautus)
Rosa (Pixérécourt)
Rosa, con otro nombre (Carballido)
Rosa de dos aromas (Carballido)
Rosa de papel (Valle-Inclán)
Rosalba y los llaveros (Carballido)
Rosalind (Barrie)
Rosamunde Floris (Kaiser)
Rosary (van Itallie)
Rosas de otoño (Benavente y Martínez)
Rosas rojas para mí (Sastre)
Rose (Bernhard)
Rose and the Cross (Blok)
Rose and the Crown (t Priestley)
Rose and the Nightingale (Pollock)
Rose Bearer (Hofmannsthal)
Rose Bernd (Hauptmann)
Rose blanche et la rose rouge (Pixérécourt)
Rose bleu (Brieux)
Rose Michel (Mackaye)
Rose Tattoo (Williams)
Rosebud of Stinging-nettle Farm (Byron)
Rosen (Sudermann)
Rosen by Any Other Name (Horovitz)
Rosen der Einöde (Bernhard)
Rosen des Herrn von Malherbes (Kotzebue)
Rosencrantz and Guildenstern (Gilbert)
Rosencrantz and Guildenstern Are Dead (Stoppard)
Rosenkavalier (Hofmannsthal)
Rosenmädchen (Kotzebue)
Roses (Sudermann)
Roses of Tralee (Keane)

Rosie träumt (Hacks)
Rosmersholm (Ibsen)
Rosmersholm (Jellicoe)
Rosmonda (Goldoni)
Rosmunda (Alfieri)
Ross (Rattigan)
Rosy Rapture (Barrie)
Rote Hahn (Hauptmann)
Rothmantel (Kotzebue)
Rotmord (t Dorst)
Roues d'infortune (Arrabal)
Rouge-gorge (Labiche)
Rough Crossing (Molnár)
Rough Crossing (Stoppard)
Rough for Radio I–II (r Beckett)
Roughing It! (Daly)
Round Dance (Schnitzler)
Round Table (Robinson)
Round the Clock (Daly)
Roundabout (Priestley)
Roundheads (Behn)
Roundheads and Peakheads (Brecht)
Routes du Monde (Lesage)
Rover I–II (Behn)
Row in the House (Robertson)
Roy Murphy Show (Buzo)
Royal Convert (Rowe)
Royal Family (Kaufman)
Royal Garland (Bickerstaff)
Royal Hunt of the Sun (Shaffer)
Royal King and the Loyal Subject (Heywood)
Royal Master (Shirley)
Royal Middy (Daly)
Royal Pardon (Arden)
Royal Shepherdess (Shadwell)
Royal Show (Nowra)
Royal Youth (Daly)
Roza i krest (Blok)
Rózsa (Katona)
Ruban (Feydeau)
Rübezahl (Kotzebue)
Rubin (Hebbel)
Rückkehr der Freiwilligen (Kotzebue)
Ruddigore (Gilbert)
Rudens (Plautus)
Rudera (Wyspiański)
Rudi Dutschke Must Stay (Arden)
Rudolph von Habsburg und König Ottkar von Böhmen (Kotzebue)
Rue de l'Homme-armé (Labiche)
Rue noire (Salacrou)
Ruf (Kotzebue)
Ruf des Lebens (Schnitzler)
Ruffian on the Stair (Orton)
Rufián dichoso, Cristóbal de Lugo (Cervantes)
Rufián viudo llamado Trampagos (Cervantes)
Rugged Path (Sherwood)
Rugged Path (Shiels)
Ruinen von Athen (Hofmannsthal)
Ruinen von Athen (Kotzebue)
Ruines de Babylone (Pixérécourt)
Ruins of Athens (Kotzebue)
Rule a Wife and Have a Wife (Fletcher)
Rule Britannia (H. Barker)
Rules of the Game (Hare)
Rules of the Game (Pirandello)
Ruling Class (Barnes)

Sandboy (Frayn)
Sanemori (Zeami)
Sang d'un poète (s Cocteau)
Sangre de Dios (Sastre)
Sani da legare (Fo)
Sanibel and Captiva (r Terry)
Sankthansnatten (Ibsen)
Santa Cruz (Frisch)
Santa Juana (Tirso De Molina)
Santa Juana II (Tirso De Molina)
Santa Rusia (Benavente y Martínez)
Santiago el Verde (Vega)
Säntis (r Walser)
Santo Inquérito (Gomes)
Santo rey Don Fernando (Calderón)
Santo y sastre (Tirso De Molina)
Sanyasi (Tagore)
Sapho (Augier)
Sapientia (Hrotsvitha)
Sapor (Regnard)
Sappho (Fitch)
Sappho (Grillparzer)
Sappho and Phao (Lyly)
Sarah and Abraham (Norman)
Sardanapale (Becque)
Sarita (Fornés)
Satiromastix (Dekker, Marston)
Saturday Night (Benavente y Martínez)
Saturday Night (Green)
Saturday Night (Ringwood)
Saturday, Sunday, Monday (De Filippo)
Saturday's Children (M. Anderson)
Satyr of La Villette (Obaldia)
Satyre de La Villette (Obaldia)
Satyros (Goethe)
Sauce for the Goose (Feydeau)
Saul (Alfieri)
Saül (Voltaire)
Sauspiel (Walser)
Sauvage (Anouilh)
Sauvagesse (Lesage)
Savage/Love (Shepard)
Savages (Hampton)
Savannah Bay (Duras)
Saved (Bond)
Saverio el cruel (Arlt)
Savonarola (Bergman)
Savoury Meringue (Saunders)
Savva (Andreyev)
Sawa-shi no futari musume (Kishida)
Saxon Shillin' (Colum)
Saxon Shore (Rudkin)
Say deKooning (L. Wilson)
Say Something Happened (t Bennett)
Sbohem Sokrate (Topol)
Scale di seta (Chiarelli)
Scamandro (Pirandello)
Scandalous Affair of Mr. Kettle and Mrs. Moon (Priestley)
Scapa Flow (Goering)
Scapin the Scamp (Molière)
Scaramanzia (Chiarelli)
Scaramouche a Philosopher . . . (Ravenscroft)
Scarf and the Flower (Calderón)
Scaring Off of Teddy Dawson (Brighouse)
Scatterbrains (Holberg)
Scavengers (Becque)
Scédase (Hardy)

Scénario (Anouilh)
Scénario Freud (s Sartre)
Scene One (Romeril)
Scenes from a Marriage (Barnes)
Scenes from an Execution (r H. Barker)
Scenes from Maps (Terry)
Scent of Flowers (Saunders)
Scène à quatre (Ionesco)
Schahabaham XLIV (Labiche)
Schakels (Heijermans)
Scharmante (Sternheim)
Schaste Kati Kozlovy (Vampilov)
Schastlivy den (Ostrovsky)
Schastlivye dni neschastlivogo cheloveka (Arbuzov)
Schatz (Lessing)
Schauspieler wider Willen (Kotzebue)
Schawl (Kotzebue)
Schein trügt (Bernhard)
Schellkönig (Kaiser)
Schelm von Bergen (Zuckmayer)
Schelmische Freier (Kotzebue)
Scherz, List und Rache (Goethe)
Scherz, Satire, Ironie und tiefere Bedeutung (Grabbe)
Schinderhannes (Zuckmayer)
Schism in England (Calderón)
Schlacht (Müller)
Schlacht bei Lobositz (Hacks)
Schlaue Witwe (Kotzebue)
Schleier der Pierette (Schnitzler)
Schleier von Beatrice (Schnitzler)
Schlimmen Buben in der Schule (Nestroy)
Schloss Wetterstein (Wedekind)
Schluck und Jau (Hauptmann)
Schlusschor (Strauss)
Schmetterlingsschlacht (Sudermann)
Schmitten (Braun)
Schmuckkästchen (Kotzebue)
Schnellmaler (Wedekind)
Schöne Helena (Hacks)
Schommelpaard (Claus)
School (Robertson)
School for Arrogance (Holcroft)
School for Buffoons (Ghelderode)
School for Fathers (Bickerstaff)
School for Friends (White)
School for Mothers-in-Law (Brieux)
School for Scandal (Boucicault)
School for Scandal (Daly)
School for Scandal (Sheridan)
School for Scheming (Boucicault)
School for Soldiers (Dunlap)
School for Widows (Cumberland)
School for Wives (Molière)
School of Compliment or, Love Tricks (Shirley)
School of Princesses (Benavente y Martínez)
Schoolboy (Cibber)
Schoolfellows (Jerrold)
Schoolmistress (Pinero)
Schoone slaapster (Heijermans)
Schreber's Nervous Illness (Churchill)
Schreibepult (Kotzebue)
Schreiner (Kotzebue)
Schuhu und der fliegende Prinzessin (Hacks)
Schule der Frauen (Kotzebue)
Schule von Uznach (Sternheim)
Schüler (Hofmannsthal)
Schuss in die Öffentlichkeit (Kaiser)

Schutzgeist (Kotzebue)
Schützlin (Nestroy)
Schwarze Schwan (Walser)
Schweik im zweiten Weltkrieg (Brecht)
Schweik in the Second World War (Brecht)
Schwestern (Schnitzler)
Schwierige (Hofmannsthal)
Science and Madness (Walker)
Sclerosis (Barnes)
Scoiattolo (Fabbri)
Scolastica (Ariosto)
Scornful Lady (Beaumont, Fletcher)
Scorpions (Leonard)
Scorzetta di limone (De Filippo)
Scott of the Antarctic (Brenton)
Scottish History of James the Fourth (Greene)
Scoundrel (Ostrovsky)
Scourers (Shadwell)
Scourge of Hyacinths (r Soyinka)
Scozzese (Goldoni)
Scrap of Paper (Sardou)
Scream (Laurents)
Screens (Brenton)
Screens (Genet)
Script (Wood)
Scrisoare pierdută (Caragiale)
Sculpteur de masques (Crommelynck)
Scuola del matrimonio (Giacosa)
Scuola di ballo (Goldoni)
Scuttled Ship (Boucicault)
Scuttled Ship (Reade)
Scythe and the Sunset (Johnston)
Scythes (Voltaire)
Se non cosi (Pirandello)
Sea (Bond)
Sea at Dauphin (Walcott)
Sea Battle (Goering)
Sea Captain (Bulwer-Lytton)
Sea Fever (Van Druten)
Sea Gull (van Itallie)
Sea Island Song (Childress)
Sea of Forms (Terry)
Sea of Ice (Robertson)
Sea Voyage (Fletcher, Massinger)
Seagull (Chekhov)
Seagull (Frayn)
Seagull (French)
Seagull (Jellicoe)
Seagull (Kilroy)
Seagull (McGrath)
Seagull (Murrell)
Seagulls (Churchill)
Sean O'Scrudu (Arden)
Séance de nuit (Feydeau)
Searching Satyrs (Sophocles)
Searching Wind (Hellman)
Seascape (Albee)
Seascape (Terry)
Season at Sarsaparilla (White)
Season in the Congo (Césaire)
Seasons (Taylor)
Season's Greetings (Ayckbourn)
Seat in the Park (Pinero)
Sea-Wife (M. Anderson)
Second Brutus (Alfieri)
Second Helping (Ayckbourn)
Second Man (Behrman)

Second Mrs. Tanqueray (Pinero)
Second Overture (M. Anderson)
Second Sentence (Wertenbaker)
Second Threshold (Barry, Sherwood)
(Seconde) Surprise de l'amour (Marivaux)
Secret Garden (Norman)
Secret Life (Granville-Barker)
Secret Lives of the Sexists (Ludlam)
Secret Love (Dryden)
Secret of Heaven (Lagerkvist)
Secret Rapture (Hare)
Secret Service (Planché)
Secret Spoken Aloud (Calderón)
Secret Vengeance for Secret Insult (Calderón)
Secrétaire de Madame (Labiche)
Secretario de sí mismo (Vega)
Secreto a voces (Calderón)
Secrets of the Rich (Kopit)
Secuestrados de Altona (Sastre)
Secular Masque (Dryden)
Sedanfeier (Kipphardt)
Sedtse (Arbuzov)
Seduced (Shepard)
Séducteur et le mari (Dumas *père*)
Seduction (Holcroft)
Seduttore (Fabbri)
Sędziowie (Wyspiański)
See Naples and Die (Rice)
See You Tomorrow at Maxim's (Hibberd)
Seelenwanderung (Kotzebue)
Seeschlacht (Goering)
Seeschlacht und die Meerkatze (Kotzebue)
Seger i mörker (Lagerkvist)
Segunda esposa y triunfar muriendo (Calderón)
Segundo Escipión (Calderón)
Sei personaggi in cerca d'autore (Pirandello)
Sejanus His Fall (Jonson)
Sejren (Munk)
Sekidera Komachi (Zeami)
Sel de la vie (Maeterlinck)
Selaginela (Carballido)
Selbstbezichtigung (Handke)
Selbstmörder (Kotzebue)
Selection of a Tutor (Fonvizin)
Self-Accusation (Handke)
Self-Immolation (Kotzebue)
Self-Tormentor (Terence)
Sélico (Pixérécourt)
Seltene Krankheit (Kotzebue)
Sembar en buena tierra (Vega)
Semejante a sí mismo (Ruiz de Alarcón)
Semele (Congreve)
Semeynaya kartina (Ostrovsky)
Semi-Monde (Coward)
Semilla y la cizaña (Calderón)
Semimaru (Chikamatsu)
Semimaru (Zeami)
Semíramis (Echegaray)
Semiramis (Hofmannsthal)
Sémiramis (Voltaire)
Señal que se espera (Buero Vallejo)
Senda del amor (Benavente y Martínez)
Séneca, ratón de biblioteca (Díaz)
Senecas Tod (Hacks)
Senhora dos Afogados (Rodrigues)
Senhora na Bôca do Lixo (Andrade)
Señor Galíndez (Pavlovsky)

Señor Laforgue (Pavlovsky)
Señora (Benavente y Martínez)
Señora Ama (Benavente y Martínez)
Señora Carrar's Rifles (Brecht)
Señora y la criada (Calderón)
Señorita se aburre (Benavente y Martínez)
Sens de la marche (Adamov)
Sens interdit (Salacrou)
Sensation Novel (Gilbert)
Sense and Sensation (Taylor)
Sense of Detachment (Osborne)
Sensitive (Labiche)
Sentinel (Boucicault)
Senza Alcun Sospetto (Walcott)
Separate Maintenance (Colman the Elder)
Separate Peace (t Stoppard)
Separate Tables (Rattigan)
Sepia Star (Bullins)
Sept Impromptus à loisir (Obaldia)
Sept Petits Sketches (Ionesco)
Sept Princesses (Maeterlinck)
Septem Contra Thebas (Aeschylus)
Séquestrés d'Altona (Sartre)
Seraphine (Boucicault)
Sérapine (Sardou)
Serapio y Yerbabuena (Díaz)
Serdtse ne kamen (Ostrovsky)
Serena Blandish (Behrman)
Serenada (Mrożek)
Serenade (Claus)
Sérénade (Regnard)
Serenade (Vicente)
Serenading Louie (L. Wilson)
Serenata (Green)
Serf (Taylor)
Serge Panine (Daly)
Sergeant Hickey (Harrigan)
Série blême (Vian)
Serinette (Reaney)
Serious Money (Churchill)
Serjeant Musgrave Dances On (McGrath)
Serjeant Musgrave's Dance (Arden)
Serment d'amour (Dadié)
Serments indiscrets (Marivaux)
Sermon (Mamet)
Serpent (van Itallie)
Serpent Woman (Gozzi)
Serpente (Rodrigues)
Serpiente de metal (Calderón)
Serra da Estrela (Vicente)
Serrure (Tardieu)
Sertorius (P. Corneille)
Serva amorosa (Goldoni)
Servant (s Pinter)
Servant-Master-Lover (Lawson)
Servant of Two Masters (Goldoni)
Servants' Hall (Gogol)
Servir a señor discreto (Vega)
Servitore di due padroni (Goldoni)
Servitude (O'Neill)
Sete Gatinhos (Rodrigues)
Seti i lovushki (Petrushevskaya)
Settimo, ruba un po'meno (Fo)
Settled Out of Court (Saroyan)
Settling Day (Taylor)
Seven Against Thebes (Aeschylus)
Seven Champions of Christendom (Planché)

Seven Deadly Sins of the Petty Bourgeoisie (Brecht)
Seven Deadly Virtues (Ayckbourn)
Seven Descents of Myrtle (Williams)
Seven Hours to Sundown (Ryga)
700,000 (Romeril)
Seven Impromptus for Leisure (Obaldia)
Seven Lears (H. Barker)
Seven Princesses (Maeterlinck)
7–20–8 (Daly)
Seven Women (Barrie)
Seventeenth Star (Green)
Seventh Symphony (Dunsany)
75th (Horovitz)
Severed Head (Priestley)
Sex is Between Two People (L. Wilson)
Sextet (Yes) (L. Wilson)
Sexual Perversity in Chicao (Mamet)
Sganarelle (Molière)
Sganarel's Journey to the Land of the Philosophers (Holberg)
Sganarels Reyse til de philosophiske Land (Holberg)
Shadow (Shvarts)
Shadow and Substance (Carroll)
Shadow of a Gunman (O'Casey)
Shadow Play (Coward)
Shadows of the Evening (Coward)
Shadow-Tree Shaft (Robertson)
Shadowy Waters (Yeats)
Shaga (Duras)
Shaharazad (Tawfiq al-Hakim)
Shajarat al-Hukm (Tawfiq al-Hakim)
Shakes Versus Shav (Shaw)
Shakespeare dringend gesucht (Kipphardt)
Shakespeare in Harlem (Hughes)
Shakespeare in Love (Boucicault)
Shakespeare's Legacy (Barrie)
Shakuntala (Kalidasa)
Shall We Join the Ladies? (Barrie)
Sham Biscayan (Cervantes)
Shams an-Nahar (Tawfiq al-Hakim)
Shams wa Qamar (Tawfiq al-Hakim)
Shamus O'Brien at Home (Harrigan)
Shanwalla (Gregory)
Shape of the Table (Edgar)
Sharon's Grave (Keane)
Sharpeville Crackers (McGrath)
Sharp's the Word (Boucicault)
Shattered Idol (Fitch)
Shaughraun (Boucicault)
Shaved Splits (Shepard)
Shawl (Mamet)
She Follows Me About (Travers)
She Gallant (O'Keeffe)
She Shall Have Music (Fry)
She Stoops to Conquer (Goldsmith)
She Stoops to Conquer (Murphy)
She Talks (Kennedy)
She Who Was Shorn (Menander)
She Would and She Would Not (Cibber)
She Would and She Would Not (Daly)
She Would if She Could (Etherege)
Sheep in Wolf's Clothing (Taylor)
Sheep Shearing (Colman the Elder)
Shell Shock (O'Neill)
Shellcove Road (Buzo)
Shelley (Jellicoe)
Sheltering Plaid (Green)

Shelty's Travels (Dunlap)
Shepherd on the Rocks (White)
Sheppey (Maugham)
Sherwood Forest (Planché)
She's Been Away (s Poliakoff)
She's Eloped (O'Keeffe)
Shestero lyubimykh (Arbuzov)
Shewing-Up of Blanco Posnet (Shaw)
Shield (Menander)
Shigosen no matsuri (Kinoshita)
Shilly Shally (Reade)
Shinjū Kasaneizutsu (Chikamatsu)
Shinjū Mannensō (Chikamatsu)
Shinjū nimai ezōshi (Chikamatsu)
Shinjū Ten no Amijima (Chikamatsu)
Shinnen kyōsō Kyoku (Kishida)
Shinsetsu Kokusenya gassen (Kubo)
Ship of Hell (Vicente)
Shipwreck (Dunlap)
Shitamachi no Hoffman (Kara)
Shitaya mannenchō monogatari (Kara)
Shivaree (Reaney)
Sho o suteyo machi ni deyō (Terayama)
Shoemakers (Witkiewicz)
Shoemaker's Holiday (Dekker)
Shoemaker's Prodigious Wife (García Lorca)
Shoemaker's Wonderful Wife (García Lorca)
Shoeshine (Mamet)
Shoeshine (Wesker)
Shōjo Kamen (Kara)
Shoki (Zeami)
Shoko (Kinoshita)
Shokugyo (Kishida)
Shooting Gallery (Horovitz)
Shooting the Chandelier (t Mercer)
Shore Acres (Herne)
Short Day's Anger (Carballido)
Short Play for a Small Theatre (Bullins)
Short Sharp Shock! (Brenton)
Shout Across the River (Poliakoff)
. . . Show (Edgar)
Show (Galsworthy)
Show-Booth (Colum)
Shrivings (Shaffer)
Shroud My Body Down (Green)
Shuang-fu meng (Guan Hanqing)
Shuibian (Cao Yu)
Shusse Kagekiyo (Chikamatsu)
Shutniki (Ostrovsky)
Shuttlecock (Byron)
Shūu (Kishida)
Shylock (Vigny)
Shylock (Wesker)
¡Si creerás tú que es por mi qusto! (Benavente y Martínez)
Sí de las niñas (Fernández de Moratín)
Si Jamais Je te pince! . . . (Labiche)
Si l'Été revenait (Adamov)
Si salvi chi può (De Filippo)
Siameses (Gambaro)
Síbila de Oriente (Calderón)
Sic vos no vobis (Echegaray)
Sicilian (Molière)
Sicilian Limes (Pirandello)
Sicilian Usurper (Tate)
Sicilien (Molière)
Sidi maître escroc (Dadié)
Sidnee Poet Heroical (Baraka)

Sidonie (Mairet)
Sie sollen ihn nicht (Nestroy)
Sieben Todsünden der Kleinbürger (Brecht)
Sieben Türen (Strauss)
Sieg des Christos (Sorge)
Siega (Vega)
Siege (Davenant)
Siege of Corinth (Planché)
Siege of Curzola (O'Keeffe)
Siege of Numancia (Cervantes)
Siege of Rhodes (Davenant)
Siegfried (Giraudoux)
Siegfried Frauenprotokolle deutsche Furor (Braun)
Siembra del Señor (Calderón)
Siempre ayuda la verdad (Ruiz de Alarcón)
Siempre ayuida la verdad (Tirso De Molina)
Siempre en ridiculo (Echegaray)
Sienna Red (Poliakoff)
Siete gritos en el mar (Casona)
Sightless (Maeterlinck)
Sign in Sidney Brustein's Window (Hansberry)
Sign No More (Coward)
Sign of the Prophet Jonah (r Bridie)
Signal Driver (White)
Signed and Sealed (Hampton)
Signora di Challant (Giacosa)
Signora è da buttare (Fo)
Signora Morli una e due (Pirandello)
Sigurd Jorsalfer (Bjørnson)
Sigurd Slembe (Bjørnson)
Sik-Sik, l'Artefice magico (De Filippo)
Sik-Sik, the Wonderful Magician (De Filippo)
Sikyonian (Menander)
Sikyonius (Menander)
Silas Marner (Mackaye)
Silberne Hochzeit (Kotzebue)
Silbersee (Kaiser)
Silence (Arden)
Silence (Pinter)
Silence (Sarraute)
Silencio de muerte (Echegaray)
¡Silencio, pollos pelones, ya les van a echar su maíz . . .!
  (Carballido)
Silènes (Jarry)
Silent Majority (Leigh)
Silent Night, Lonely Night (R. Anderson)
Silent Partner (Odets)
Silk Stockings (Kaufman)
Silver Age (Heywood)
Silver Box (Galsworthy)
Silver Cord (Howard)
Silver Face (Valle-Inclán)
Silver King (Jones)
Silver Tassie (O'Casey)
Silvia im "Stern" (Hofmannsthal)
Silvia (Lillo)
Simon (Hecht)
Simon Street Harvest (Horovitz)
Simone (Brieux)
Simoon (Strindberg)
Simple Hanrahans (Fitzmaurice)
Simple Life (Harrigan)
Simple Soldat (Dubé)
Simpleton of the Unexpected Isles (Shaw)
Simplex Deutsch (Braun)
Simply Heavenly (Hughes)
Simson (Wedekind)

Simultaneità (Marinetti)
Simultanina (Marinetti)
Sin (Hibberd)
Sin querer (Benavente y Martínez)
Sincères (Marivaux)
Sindaco del Rione Sanità (De Filippo)
Sinfonía doméstica (Carballido)
Sinfonía inacabada (Casona)
Sing a Rude Song (Bennett)
Sing All a Green Willow (Green)
Sing Sing (Harrigan)
Sing to Me Through Open Windows (Kopit)
Single Spies (Bennett)
Singleheart and Doubleface (Reade)
Singulier trépas de Messire Ulenspiegel (r Ghelderode)
Sink the Belgrano! (Berkoff)
Sinner (Tagore)
Sintetici a qualunque costa (De Filippo)
Sior Todero Brontolon (Goldoni)
Sir Anthony Love (Southerne)
Sir Giles Goosecap, Knight (Chapman)
Sir Harry Wildair (Farquhar)
Sir John van Olden Barnavelt (Fletcher, Massinger)
Sir Martin Mar-All (Dryden)
Sir Patient Fancy (Behn)
Sir Robert Sedley (Middleton)
Sir Roger de Coverley (Taylor)
Sir Thomas More (Shakespeare)
Sir Thomas Wyatt (Dekker, Heywood, Webster)
Sire Halewyn (Ghelderode)
Siren (Williamson)
Sirena (Giacosa)
Sirena varada (Casona)
Sirène (Scribe)
Sirocco (Coward)
Sista Mänskan (Lagerkvist)
Siste riddaren (Strindberg)
Sister Beatrice (Maeterlinck)
Sister Mary Ignatius Explains it All for You (Durang)
Sisterly Feelings (Ayckbourn)
Sisters (Sewell)
Sisters (Shirley)
Sisters (Storey)
Sister's Penance (Taylor)
Sister's Sacrifice (Daly)
Sitio de Bredá (Calderón)
Situation difficile (Dadié)
Sive (Keane)
Six Characters in Search of an Author (Johnston)
Six Characters in Search of an Author (Pirandello)
Six Degrees of Separation (Guare)
Six Florins (Pixérécourt)
Six Gentlemen in a Row (Granville-Barker)
Six Heures au plus tard (Tremblay)
Six in the Rain (Walcott)
Six Men of Dorset (McGrath)
Six of Calais (Shaw)
Sixtus V (Boucicault)
Sizilianische Vesper (Lenz)
Sizwe Bansi is Dead (Fugard)
Sjōjo toshi (Kara)
Skałka (Wyspiański)
Skandal in Assyrien (Hasenclever)
Skazka o poteryannom vremeni (Shvarts)
Skazki starogo Arbata (Arbuzov)
Skidmores (Harrigan)
Skin Game (Galsworthy)

Skin of Our Teeth (Wilder)
Skipper, and My Sister and I (H. Barker)
Skugga (Bergman)
Skuggen av Mart (Dagerman)
Skupoy (Bulgakov)
Skupoy rytsaw (Pushkin)
Sky-Blue Life (Brenton)
Sladek (Horváth)
Slag (Hare)
Slaughter of the Innocents (Saroyan)
Slaughterman (r Barnes)
Slave Island (Marivaux)
Slave Life (Taylor)
Slave Ship (Baraka)
Slave (Baraka)
Slavery Days (Harrigan)
Slavík na večerí (Topol)
Sleazing Towards Athens (Terry)
Sleep (Gelber)
Sleep My Pretty One (Coulter)
Sleep of Prisoners (Fry)
Sleep of Reason (Buero Vallejo)
Sleeping Beauty (Ringwood)
Sleeping Beauty in the Wood (Planché)
Sleeping Clergyman (Bridie)
Sleeping Dog (t Gray)
Sleeping Policemen (Brenton)
Sleeping Prince (Rattigan)
Sleepless City (Tardieu)
Slepý mládenec (Tyl)
Slice of Life 1910 (Barrie)
Slight Accident (Saunders)
Slight Ache (Pinter)
Slip Knot (Plautus)
Sloth (Durang)
Ślub (Gombrowicz)
Slyshish, Moskva?! (Tretyakov)
Small Craft Warnings (Williams)
Small Family Business (Ayckbourn)
Small Hours (Kaufman)
Small War on Murray Hill (Sherwood)
Smanie della villeggiatura (Goldoni)
Smelling a Rat (Leigh)
Smert Ioanna grotznogo (A. K. Tolstoy)
Smert Tarelkina (Sukhovo-Kobylin)
Śmierć Ofelji (Wyspiański)
Śmierć porucznika (Mrożek)
Śmieszny staruszek (Różewicz)
Smike (Boucicault)
Smile of Mona Lisa (Benavente y Martínez)
Smirnova's Birthday (Petrushevskaya)
Smith (Maugham)
Smoke-Screens (Brighouse)
Smoked Miser (Jerrold)
Smoking is Bad for You (Chekhov)
Smug Citizens (Gorky)
Snake Lady (Gozzi)
Sneeze (Frayn)
Snegurochka (Ostrovsky)
Snezhnaya Koroleva (Shvarts)
Sniper (O'Neill)
Snob (Sternheim)
Snödropparna (Bergman)
Snow Flower (Boucicault)
Snow in Midsummer (Guan Hanqing)
So ist das Leben (Wedekind)
So Long at the Fair (L. Wilson)

Soacră (Caragiale)
Soaps (Sherman)
Sobachy vals (Andreyev)
Sobowtór (Różewicz)
Sobresalienta (Benavente y Martínez)
Sobrinha do Marquês (Garrett)
Social Event (Inge)
Social Swim (Fitch)
Société Apollon (Tardieu)
Society (Robertson)
Socorro general (Calderón)
Socrate (Voltaire)
Socrates (Voltaire)
Sodhoma ke Ghomora (Kazantzakis)
Sodom and Gomorrah (Kazantzakis)
Sodome et Gomorrhe (Giraudoux)
Sodoms Ende (Sudermann)
Soeur (Rotrou)
Soeur Béatrice (Maeterlinck)
Sofonisba (Alfieri)
Soft or a Girl (McGrath)
Soft Targets (t Poliakoff)
Softcops (Churchill)
Soga Kaikeizan (Chikamatsu)
Soga Revenge (Chikamatsu)
Sogno di un tramonto d'autunno (D'Annunzio)
Sogno d'un mattino di primavera (D'Annunzio)
Sogno (ma forse no) (Pirandello)
Sohn (Hasenclever)
Soif et la faim (Ionesco)
Soir de pitié (Ghelderode)
Soirée des Champs-Élysées (Pixérécourt)
Sol que nace y un sol que muere (Echegaray)
Sol y los MacDonald (Marqués)
Solange (Barbeau)
Solar Spectrum (Wedekind)
Soldat (Kroetz)
Soldat Dioclès (Audiberti)
Soldat et la sorcière (Salacrou)
Soldat Tanaka (Kaiser)
Soldaten (Hochhuth)
Soldaten (Kipphardt)
Soldaten (Lenz)
Soldier of Fortune (Boucicault)
Soldier of '76 (Dunlap)
Soldiers (Lenz)
Soldier's Fortune (Otway)
Soldier's Play (Fuller)
Soldier's Tale (Arden)
Soleil se couche (Ghelderode)
Soleil sur la mer (Willems)
Solemn Communion (Arrabal)
Solid Gold Cadillac (Kaufman)
Solitaire (Planché)
Solitaire (Van Druten)
Solitaire de la Roche Noire (Pixérécourt)
Solitaire/Double Solitaire (R. Anderson)
Solitario en octobre (Carballido)
Solitary Thing (Sherman)
Sólo un aspecto (Gambaro)
Solo Voyages (Kennedy)
Some Kind of Love Story (Miller)
Some of My Best Friends Are Husbands (Leonard)
Some Problems for the Moose Lodge (Williams)
Somebody Else (Planché)
Somebody Knows (Van Druten)
Someone from Assissi (Wilder)

Someone in the House (Kaufman)
Somersaults (Barnes)
Something About a Soldier (Saroyan)
Something Cloudy, Something Clear (Williams)
Something I'll Tell You Tuesday (Guare)
Something Unspoken (Williams)
Somewhere in France (Zuckmayer)
Sommeil de la raison (Ghelderode)
Sommergäste (Strauss)
Somnambule (Scribe)
Somnambulist (Scribe)
Somnambulo and the Lively Little Alessio (Byron)
Somos (Pavlovsky)
Somov i drugiye (Gorky)
Son (Saroyan)
Son, Come Home (Bullins)
Son-in-Law (O'Keeffe)
Son of Don Juan (Echegaray)
Sonador para un pueblo (Buero Vallejo)
Sonata and the Three Gentlemen (Tardieu)
Sonata Belzebuba (Witkiewicz)
Sonate des spectres (Adamov)
Sonate et les trois messieurs (Tardieu)
Sonezaki Shinjū (Chikamatsu)
Song at Twilight (Coward)
Song of a Goat (Clark)
Song of the Lusitanian Bogey (Weiss)
Song of the Seals (Hewett)
Song Room (Nowra)
Songe du critique (Anouilh)
Sonne über dem Meer (Willems)
Sonnenjungfrau (Kotzebue)
Sonnenspektrum (Wedekind)
Sonntag (t Forte)
Sonrisa de Gioconda (Benavente y Martínez)
Sons and Lovers (t Griffiths)
Sons of Cain (Williamson)
Sons of Light (Rudkin)
Sons of Spain (Howard)
Sopha (Labiche)
Sophie et Sigismond (Lesage)
Sophisme et sadisme (Pinget)
Sophonisba (Lee)
Sophonisba (Marston)
Sophonisbe (P. Corneille)
Sophonisbe (Mairet)
Sophonisbe (Voltaire)
Sorcerer (Gilbert)
Sorceress (Daly)
Sorceries of Sin (Calderón)
Sorcière (Sardou)
Sordomudos (Hernández)
Sore Throats (Brenton)
Sorgen ohne Noth und Noth ohne Sorgen (Kotzebue)
Sorgen und die Macht (Hacks)
Sorina (Kaiser)
Sorprese notturne (Giacosa)
Sorrows of Belgium (Andreyev)
Sort-of-a-Prince (Brighouse)
Sortie de l'acteur (Ghelderode)
Sosies (Rotrou)
Sötét galamb (Örkény)
Soufflez-moi dans l'oeil (Labiche)
Souhaits (Regnard)
Soul Gone Home (Hughes)
Soulier de satin (Claudel)
Soul's Journey (Vicente)

Staroye po-novomu (Ostrovsky)
Starshy syn (Vampilov)
Start in Life (r Greene)
Starters (Gelber)
Stary drug luchshe novykh dvukh (Ostrovsky)
State of Emergency (Edgar)
State of Innocence and Fall of Man (Dryden)
State of Revolution (Bolt)
State of Siege (Camus)
State Office Bldg. Curse (Bullins)
Statements After an Arrest under the Immorality Act
    (Fugard)
States of Shock (Shepard)
Station Champbaudet (Labiche)
Statue Guest (Pushkin)
Statue Lover (Jerrold)
Statue merveilleuse (Lesage)
Steel (Walcott)
Stein der Weisen (Wedekind)
Stein unter Steinen (Sudermann)
Steinwurf (Hebbel)
Stella (Goethe)
Stella and Leatherlungs (Colman the Younger)
Stellvertreter (Hochhuth)
Stenio (Brieux)
Stephen D (Leonard)
Stephen Foster Story (Green)
Steps Must Be Gentle (Williams)
Sterne's Maria (Dunlap)
Sterntaler (Kroetz)
Sterrendief (Ghelderode)
Steve and Velma (Bullins)
Steve McQueen (Mamet)
Stichus (Plautus)
Sticks and Bones (Rabe)
Sticks and Stones (Reaney)
Stilicon (T. Corneille)
Still Alarm (Kaufman)
Still Life (Coward)
Still Life (Edgar)
Still Life (Molnár)
Still Stands the House (Ringwood)
Still Waters Run Deep (Taylor)
Stillheten (Norén)
Stingray (Buzo)
Stitch in Time (Connelly)
Stoffreste (Grass)
Stoker (Brighouse)
Stolen Heiress (Centlivre)
Stone (Bond)
Stone Guest (Pushkin)
Stopped Rocking (t Williams)
Stora landsvägen (Strindberg)
Storia delle tigre et altre storie (Fo)
Storia di un soldato (Fo)
Storia vecchia (Giacosa)
Storia vera di Piero d'Angera (Fo)
Stork (Hecht)
Storm (Ostrovsky)
Storm (Strindberg)
Storm in a Teacup (Bridie)
Storm Operation (M. Anderson)
Storm Song (Johnston)
Storming and Taking of Fort Omoa (Sheridan)
Stormy Night (Caragiale)
Stormy Weather (Strindberg)
Story Brought by Brigit (Gregory)

Story for Strangers (Connelly)
Story of Gus (r Miller)
Story So Far (Ayckbourn)
Story-Telling (Planché)
Storyville (Bullins)
Straight Road (Fitch)
Strains of Triumph (Inge)
Strakonický Dudák (Tyl)
Stramme Max (Kroetz)
Strandkinder (Sudermann)
Strange Case of Dr. Jekyll and Mr. Hyde (Edgar)
Strange Interlude (O'Neill)
Strange Lover (Dunsany)
Strange Occurrence on Ireland's Eye (Johnston)
Strange One (Lermontov)
Strange Rider (Ghelderode)
Stranger (Dunlap)
Stranger (Kotzebue)
Stranger (Ringwood)
Stranger (Sheridan)
Stranger's Birthday (Dunlap)
Strangest Kind of Romance (Williams)
Stranitzky und der Nationalheld (r Dürrenmatt)
Strapless (s Hare)
Strassenräuber aus kindlicher Liebe (Kotzebue)
Stratonice (Quinault)
Straw (O'Neill)
Strawberry Fields (Poliakoff)
Straż porządkowa (Różewicz)
Strazh velikogo tsarya (Sologub)
Streamers (Rabe)
Streber (Dagerman)
Street Play (Bullins)
Street Scene (Hughes, Rice)
Street Singer (Echegaray)
Street Sounds (Bullins)
Streetcar Named Desire (s Williams)
Streetcar Named Desire (Williams)
Streets of London (Boucicault)
Streets of New York (Boucicault)
Stretch of the Imagination (Hibberd)
Strife (Galsworthy)
Strike (Boucicault)
Strike Up the Band (Kaufman)
String (Childress)
Strings, My Lord, Are False (Carroll)
Striptease (Mrożek)
Strip-tease de la jalousie (Arrabal)
Stripwell (H. Barker)
Stroll in the Air (Ionesco)
Strong Are Lonely (Hochwälder)
Strong Box (Sternheim)
Strong Breed (Soyinka)
Stronger (Giacosa)
Stronger (Strindberg)
Struck Dumb (van Itallie)
Struggle Till Dawn (Betti)
Stseny iz rytsarskikh vryemen (Pushkin)
Stubbornness of Geraldine (Fitch)
Student (Griboyedov)
Students (Ariosto)
Students of Jena (Planché)
Stühle des Herrn Szmil (Kipphardt)
Stumme (Kotzebue)
Stunde des Erkennens (Schnitzler)
Stundesløe (Holberg)
Sturmgeselle des Sokrates (Sudermann)

Sturmgesellen (Sudermann)
Su amante esposa (Benavente y Martínez)
Sublime en lo vulgar (Echegaray)
Submerged (Gorky)
Suburb of Babylon (Leonard)
Suburban Strains (Ayckbourn)
Subway (Rice)
Subway Circus (Saroyan)
Success (Planché)
Success Story (Lawson)
Successful Life of Three (Fornés)
Successful Strategies (Wertenbaker)
Sucede lo que pasa (Gambaro)
Such Impossibilities (t Griffiths)
Such is the Law (Taylor)
Such Stuff as Dreams are Made of (Calderón)
Such Things Are (Inchbald)
Such Things Only Happen in Books (Wilder)
Sudden Shower (Daly)
Sudpolexpedition des Kapitän Scott (Goering)
Sueño de día (r Usigli)
Sueño de la razón (Buero Vallejo)
Sueño de una noche de verano (Casona)
Sueño del ángel (Solórzano)
Sueños hay que verdad son (Calderón)
Sufrimiento premiado (Vega)
Suggeritore nudo (Marinetti)
Suicide (Colman the Elder)
Suicide (Erdman)
Suicide (Pixérécourt)
Suicidé (Vinaver)
Suicide in B Flat (Shepard)
Suicide Prohibited in Springtime (Casona)
Suicidio de Lucerito (Benavente y Martínez)
Suiker (Claus)
Suil-a-mor (Boucicault)
Suitable Case for Treatment (t Mercer)
Suite du Menteur (P. Corneille)
Suite in Three Keys (Coward)
Suites d'un premier lit (Labiche)
Suitors (Racine)
Suivante (P. Corneille)
Súkromná oslava (Karvaš)
Sulayman al-Hakim (Tawfiq al-Hakim)
Sullen Lovers (Shadwell)
Sullied Hand (Wesker)
Sullivan (Robertson)
Sullivan's Christmas (Harrigan)
Sultan (Bickerstaff)
Sultan Bimbam (Kotzebue)
Sultan Wampum (Kotzebue)
Sultaness (Racine)
Sultan's Dilemma (Tawfiq al-Hakim)
Suma Genji (Zeami)
Sumidouro (Andrade)
Summer and Smoke (Williams)
Summer and Smoke (L. Wilson)
Summer (Bond)
Summer (Leonard)
Summer Brave (Inge)
Summer Day's Dream (Priestley)
Summer of the Aliens (Nowra)
Summer of the Seventeenth Doll (Lawler)
Summer Party (Poliakoff)
Summer Sports (Edgar)
Summerfolk (Gorky)
Summer's Tale (Cumberland)

Summertime (Betti)
Summit (Shiels)
Sun (Galsworthy)
Sun (Kennedy)
Sun and the Moon (Reaney)
Sun Do Move (Hughes)
Sun in Aries (Middleton)
Sun into Darkness (Rudkin)
Sunday Runners in the Rain (Horovitz)
Sündflut (Barlach)
Sunken Bell (Hauptmann)
Sunlight Sonata (Bridie)
Sunrise (Cao Yu)
Sunrise (Nowra)
Sunrise on Sarah (Ryga)
Sun's Darling: A Moral Masque (Dekker, Ford)
Sunset Boulevard (Hampton)
Sunsets and Glories (Barnes)
Sunshine Boys (Simon)
Supercoco (Díaz)
Superfluous Husband (Fitch)
Superior Residence (Goldoni)
Superstition (J. N. Barker)
Superstition Throu' the Ages (Pollock)
Superstitions (Shepard)
Suplicante (Carballido)
Supper for the Dead (Green)
Supplément au voyage de Cook (Giraudoux)
Suppliant Maidens (Aeschylus)
Suppliant Women (Aeschylus)
Suppliant Women (Euripides)
Suppliants (Aeschylus)
Supplice d'une femme (Dumas *fils*)
Supplices (Aeschylus)
Supplices (Euripides)
Supposit (Ariosto)
Suppressed Desires (Glaspell)
Sur la Lisière d'un bois (Hugo)
Sur le Fils (Arrabal)
Suréna, Général des Parthes (P. Corneille)
Surenas (P. Corneille)
Surgeon of His Honour (Calderón)
Surgeon of Honour (Calderón)
Surprise de l'amour (Marivaux)
Surprise! Surprise! (Tremblay)
Surrender of Calais (Colman the Younger)
Surrender to the Enemy (Green)
Survey (Connelly)
Susan and God (Crothers)
Susan Peretz at the Manhattan Theatre Club (Terry)
Susanna Andler (Duras)
Susannah and the Elders (Bridie)
Susannah's Dreaming (r Hewett)
Susto de la condesa (Benavente y Martínez)
Suttee (Tagore)
Suzette (Brieux)
Svadba (Chekhov)
Svadba Krechinskogo (Sukhovo-Kobylin)
Svanevit (Strindberg)
Svarta handksen (Strindberg)
Svaty Václav (Langer)
Svetit, da ne greyet (Ostrovsky)
Svoi sobaki gryzutsya (Ostrovsky)
Svoya semya (Griboyedov)
Svåra stunden (Lagerkvist)
Swamp Dwellers (Soyinka)
Swamp Hall (Jerrold)

Swan Song (Chekhov)
Swan Song (Hecht)
Swan Song (Mason)
Swanwhite (Strindberg)
Sweatproof Boy (De Groen)
Swedenhielms (Bergman)
Sweeney Agonistes (Eliot)
Sweeney in the Trees (Saroyan)
Sweet Bird of Youth (Williams)
Sweet Charity (Simon)
Sweet Lavender (Pinero)
Sweet Will (Jones)
Sweethearts (Gilbert)
Świadkwie (Różewicz)
Święty Stanislaw (Wyspiański)
Swing (Kishida)
Swings and Roundabouts (McGrath)
Switchback (Bridie)
Sword of Gideon (Jones)
Swords (Howard)
Sybil (Cumberland)
Sylvandire (Dumas *père*)
Sylvanine (Zola)
Sylvanire (Mairet)
Sylvester Daggerwood (Colman the Younger)
Sylvia Hears a Secret (Marivaux)
Sylvian (Mitchell)
Sylvie (Mairet)
Syren (Scribe)
Système Ribadier (Feydeau)
Szalona lokomotywa (Witkiewicz)
Szczesliwe wydarzenie (Mrożek)
Szewcy (Witkiewicz)
Szinház (Molnár)

T. (Braun)
TV (van Itallie)
Taberna fantástica (Sastre)
Tableau (Ionesco)
Tableau du mariage (Lesage)
Tabula rasa (Sternheim)
Tadanori (Zeami)
Taema (Zeami)
Tag (Barrie)
Tage des Kommune (Brecht)
Tahinta (Sutherland)
Tailleur pour dames (Feydeau)
Tailors (Colman the Elder)
Tailors (Foote)
Tain Bo Cuailgne (Johnston)
Taizanbukun (Zeami)
Takasago (Zeami)
Take a Deep Breath (van Itallie)
Take a Dream (Guare)
Take It (McGrath)
Take the Big Picture (Reaney)
Take the Fool Away (Priestley)
Take Two from One (Granville-Barker)
Taking of Miss Janie (Bullins)
Taking Off (s Guare)
Taking Steps (Ayckbourn)
Talanta (Aretino)
Talanty i poklonniki (Ostrovsky)
Talbot's Box (Kilroy)
Tale of a Tiger (Fo)
Tale of a Town (Martyn)
Tale of a Tub (Jonson)

Tale of Mystery (Holcroft)
Tale of the Wolf (Molnár)
Tale of Two Cities (Taylor)
Tale Told (L. Wilson)
Tales from Hollywood (Hampton)
Tales from Landshut (Sperr)
Tales from the Vienna Woods (Hampton)
Tales from the Vienna Woods (s Hampton)
Tales from the Vienna Woods (Horváth)
Talisman (Nestroy)
Talk to Me Like the Rain and Let Me Listen (Williams)
Talkative Barber (Holberg)
Talking Dog (Guare)
Talking Heads (Bennett)
Talking Heads (t Bennett)
Talking to You (Saroyan)
Tall Girls Have Everything (Parker)
Talley and Son (L. Wilson)
Talley Method (Behrman)
Talley's Folly (L. Wilson)
Tamar's Vengeance (Tirso De Molina)
Tamba Yosaku (Chikamatsu)
También hay duelo en las damas (Calderón)
Tambourines to Glory (Hughes)
Tamburlaine the Great I–II (Marlowe)
Tamburo di fuoco (Marinetti)
Tamerlane (Rowe)
Taming a Butterfly (Daly)
Taming of the Shrew (Daly)
Taming of the Shrew (Shakespeare)
Tamura (Zeami)
Tancred (Goethe)
Tancrède (Voltaire)
Tand om tand (Claus)
Tango (Mrożek)
Tango (Stoppard)
Tango Palace (Fornés)
Tannhäuser (Nestroy)
Tantalus (Lenz)
Tantara-Rara, Rogues All (O'Keeffe)
Tanto es lo de más como lo de menos (Tirso De Molina)
Tanya (Arbuzov)
Tapfere Cassian (Schnitzler)
Tarare (Beaumarchais)
Tardi ravveduta (Giacosa)
Tarelkins Tod (Müller)
Tartuffe (Anouilh)
Tartuffe (Gray)
Tartuffe (Hampton)
Tartuffe (Molière)
Taschenbuch (Kotzebue)
Task (Müller)
Taste (Foote)
Taste of Honey (Delaney)
Tatty Hollow Story (Hewett)
Tatyana Repin (Chekhov)
Taubstumme (Kotzebue)
1003 (Hochwälder)
Taverne des étudiants (Sardou)
Te juro, Juana, que tengo ganas (Carballido)
Tea and Sex and Shakespeare (Kilroy)
Tea and Sympathy (R. Anderson)
Tea Party (Pinter)
Tea Party (t Pinter)
Team (Williamson)
Tears and Smiles (J. N. Barker)
Teaser (Murrell)

Teatr niekonsekwencji (Różewicz)
Teatralny razyezd posle predstavleniya novoy komedy
    (Gogol)
Teatro comico (Goldoni)
Teatro feminista (Benavente y Martínez)
Teatro in fiamme (Chiarelli)
Tedderella (Edgar)
Teendreams (Edgar)
Teeth (t Stoppard)
Teeth 'n' Smiles (Hare)
Teja (Gregory)
Teja (Sudermann)
Tejador de Segovia I–II (Ruiz de Alarcón)
Tejedora de sueños (Buero Vallejo)
Tel chante le vieux coq! (Sardou)
Telarañas (Pavlovsky)
Téléki (Pixérécourt)
Telemachus (Planché)
Telephone (Harrigan)
Telescópio (Andrade)
Télévise-moi ça (Gelinas)
Tell Me Tell Me (McGrath)
Tell Truth and Shame the Devil (Dunlap)
Tell-Tale Heart (Berkoff)
Temnaya komnata (Petrushevskaya)
Température (Apollinaire)
Tempest (Césaire)
Tempest (Daly)
Tempest (Davenant)
Tempest (Dryden)
Tempest (Plautus)
Tempest (Shadwell)
Tempest (Shakespeare)
Tempesta (De Filippo)
Tempête (Césaire)
Temple Beau (Fielding)
Temple de la Gloire (Voltaire)
Temple de la Paix (Quinault)
Temple d'ennui (Lesage)
Temple du destin (Lesage)
Temple du mémoire (Lesage)
Temple of Independence (Dunlap)
Temple of Love (Davenant)
Templo de Apolo (Vicente)
Temps des lilas (Dubé)
Temps du verbe (Tardieu)
Temps tranquilles (Barbeau)
Temptation (Havel)
Tempter (Jones)
Ten (Shvarts)
Ten Blocks on the Camino Real (Williams)
Ten Million Ghosts (Kingsley)
10 Oxford-Snapshots (Munk)
Ten Times Table (Ayckbourn)
Tenants at Will (Shiels)
Tender Hands (Tawfiq al-Hakim)
Tender Husband (Steele)
Tenor (Wedekind)
Tent (McGrath)
Tentation de St. Antoine (Ghelderode)
Tenth Man (Chayefsky)
Tenth Man (Maugham)
Tents of the Arabs (Dunsany)
Tercera palabra (Casona)
Terence in English (Rastell)
Terenzio (Goldoni)
Térésa (Dumas *père*)

Teresa (Giacosa)
Teresa Desqueyroux (Fabbri)
Terra Australis (Esson)
Terre est ronde (Salacrou)
Terrible Baisht (Fitzmaurice)
Terrible Czar (A. K. Tolstoy)
Terrible Example (Harrigan)
Terrible Journey of Frederick Dunglass (r Cook)
Terror inmóvil (Buero Vallejo)
Teseo (Carballido)
Tesoro escondido (Calderón)
Tessa (Giraudoux)
Test (Marivaux)
Test Case (Daly)
Testament bizarre (Pinget)
Testament de César (Dumas *père*)
Testament d'Orphée (s Cocteau)
Testamento y el viudo (Usigli)
Testarium (Mrożek)
Testimoni (Fabbri)
Testőr (Molnár)
Tête de Méduse (Vian)
Tête d'or (Claudel)
Tête noir (Lesage)
Têtes de bois (Ghelderode)
Tethered Steed (Chikamatsu)
Tetsu kamen (Kara)
Teufels General (Zuckmayer)
Teufels Lustschloss (Kotzebue)
Texas (Green)
Thal von Almeria (Kotzebue)
Thanatos tou Medhikou (Prevelakis)
Thark (Travers)
That Good Between Us (H. Barker)
That Lass o' Lowrie's (Reade)
That Scoundrel Scapin (Molière)
That Summer (Edgar)
That They May Win (Miller)
That Time (Beckett)
That Worthless Fellow Platonov (Chekhov)
That's My Girl (Feydeau)
Théagène et Chariclée (Hardy)
Theaterg'schichten durch Liebe, Intrigue, Geld und Dumm-
    heit (Nestroy)
Theatermacher (Bernhard)
Théâtre (Anouilh)
Théâtre de la maintenance (Barbeau)
Théâtre 1970: Théâtre en marge (Arrabal)
Théâtre 1971: Les Monstres (Arrabal)
Theatre of the Film Noir (Walker)
Theatre I and II (Beckett)
Theatre Outside (Poliakoff)
Theatrical Illusion (P. Corneille)
Thébaïde (Racine)
Thebais (Seneca)
Theban Brothers (Racine)
Thebans (Wertenbaker)
Their Very Own and Golden City (Wesker)
Theme is Blackness (Bullins)
Then and Now (Mercer)
Théodat (T. Corneille)
Théodora (Sardou)
Théodore, vierge et martyre (P. Corneille)
Theodosius (Lee)
There Are Crimes and Crimes (Strindberg)
There Are Tragedies and Tragedies (Fitzmaurice)
There is One in Every Marriage (Feydeau)

There Shall Be No Night (Sherwood)
There's Always Juliet (Van Druten)
There's Nothing in It (Boucicault)
There's Something I Got to Tell You (Saroyan)
There's Something I Got to Tell (r Saroyan)
Therese (Boucicault)
Thérèse Raquin (Zola)
Therese's Creed (Cook)
Thermidor (Griffiths)
Thermidor (Przybyszewska)
Thermidor (Sardou)
These Our Actors (Priestley)
Thésée (Kazantzakis)
Thésée (Quinault)
Theseus (Carballido)
Theseus and Ariadne (Planché)
Thesmophoriazusae (Aristophanes)
Thespis (Gilbert)
They (Witkiewicz)
They Alone Knew (Tardieu)
They Are Dying Out (Handke)
They Came to a City (Priestley)
They Knew What They Wanted (Howard)
They're Knocking Down the Pie-Shop (McGrath)
They're Playing Our Song (Simon)
Thief of a Christmas (Murphy)
Thierna-na-Oge (Planché)
Thierry, King of France, and His Brother Theodoret
    (Beaumont, Fletcher, Massinger)
Thieves' Carnival (Anouilh)
Thing (Brenton)
Things Change (s Mamet)
Things That Are Caesar's (Carroll)
Things Went Badly in Westphalia (Sherman)
Third (Wertenbaker)
Third and Oak: The Laundromat (Norman)
Third and Oak: The Pool Hall (Norman)
Thirst (O'Neill)
Thirsting Heart (Green)
Thirteenth Night (Brenton)
Thirties Girl (Guare)
Thirty-First of June (Priestley)
39 East (Crothers)
Thirty Years (Dunlap)
This Declaration (Green)
This Great Gap of Time (Hibberd)
This Happy Breed (Coward)
This I Believe (Saroyan)
This is an Entertainment (Williams)
This is New York (Sherwood)
This is No Place for Tallulah Bankhead (Wertenbaker)
This is the Rill Speaking (L. Wilson)
This is Where We Came In (Ayckbourn)
This Old Man Comes Rolling Home (Hewett)
This Play is About Me (Horovitz)
This Property is Condemned (Williams)
This Time Tomorrow (r Ngugi)
This Was a Man (Coward)
This Year of Grace! (Coward)
Thomas and Sally (Bickerstaff(e))
Thomas à Becket (Jerrold)
Thomas More (s Anouilh)
Thomas Muskerry (Colum)
Thor und der Tod (Hofmannsthal)
Thor, with Angels (Fry)
Those the River Keeps (Rabe)
Thou Shalt Not Lie (Grillparzer)

Thoughts (Terry)
Thoughts on the Instant of Greeting a Friend (van Itallie)
Three Actors and Their Drama (Ghelderode)
Three Assassins (Walcott)
Three Birds Alighting on a Field (Wertenbaker)
Three Cheers for Paris (Labiche)
Three Daughters of Monsieur Dupont (Brieux)
Three Desks (Reaney)
Three-Dollar Day (Plautus)
Three for a Full Moon (Shange)
Three Girls in Blue (Petrushevskaya)
Three Graces (Travers)
Three Hours After Marriage (Gay)
Three Judgements in One (Calderón)
Three Judgments at a Blow (Calderón)
Three Men on a Horse (r Miller)
Three More Sleepless Nights (Churchill)
Three of Us (Crothers)
Three Old Friends (Hibberd)
Three Players of a Summer Game (Williams)
Three Sisters (Bond)
Three Sisters (Chekhov)
Three Sisters (Frayn)
Three Sisters (Friel)
Three Sisters (Hibberd)
Three Sisters (Mamet)
Three Sisters (van Itallie)
Three Sisters (L. Wilson)
Three Tall Women (Albee)
Three Views of Mount Fuji (Shange)
Three Wise Men (Vicente)
Three Wishes (Ringwood)
Three Woman Talking (Wesker)
Threepenny Opera (Brecht)
Threnodia Augustalis (Goldsmith)
Through Deserts to Ancestral Lands (Strindberg)
Through the Leaves (Kroetz)
Through the Night (t Griffiths)
Throwing Dust in People's Eyes (Labiche)
Thuis (Claus)
Thumbscrew (Byron)
Thunder (Ostrovsky)
Thunderbolt (Pinero)
Thunderstorm (Cao Yu)
Thunderstorm (Ostrovsky)
Thursday's Child (Fry)
Thwarting of Baron Bolligrew (Bolt)
Thyestes (Claus)
Thyestes (Seneca)
Thymus Vulgaris (L. Wilson)
Tía de Carlos (Triana)
Tianquis! (Carballido)
Tiao feng-yue (Guan Hanqing)
Tiberius in Capreae (Cumberland)
Tibetan Book of the Dead (van Itallie)
Ticket-of-Leave Man (Taylor)
Tickless Time (Glaspell)
Tide (Jellicoe)
Tidings Brought to Mary (Claudel)
Tie Up the Ballcock (Wood)
Tiempos oscuros (Díaz)
Tierra roja (Sastre)
Tierrabaja (Echegaray)
Tiger and the Horse (Bolt)
Tiger at the Gates (Fry)
Tiger at the Gates (Giraudoux)
Tiger Tail (Williams)

Ti-Jean and His Brothers (Walcott)
Tijl Uilenspiegel (Claus)
Tikhaya zavod (Vampilov)
Till Damaskus I–III (Strindberg)
Till Eulenspiegel (Wedekind)
Till the Day I Die (Odets)
Tiln (Cook)
Tiln (r Cook)
Time and the Conways (Priestley)
Time and the Place (Carballido)
Time and Time Again (Ayckbourn)
Time Flits Away, Lady (Hewett)
Time for a Gargle (Behan)
Time is Not Yet Ripe (Esson)
Time of the Barracudas (Barnes)
Time of the Cuckoo (Laurents)
Time of Wolves and Tigers (Leonard)
Time of Your Life (Saroyan)
Time Present (Osborne)
Time Remembered (Anouilh)
Time to Go (O'Casey)
Time Vindicated to Himself and to His Honours (Jonson)
Time Was (Leonard)
Time Works Wonders (Jerrold)
Times (Goldoni)
Times (Pinero)
Time's Joke (Dunsany)
Time's Triumph (Byron)
Timoclée (Hardy)
Timocrate (T. Corneille)
Timoleone (Alfieri)
Timon of Athens (Cumberland)
Timon of Athens (Shadwell)
Timon of Athens (Shakespeare)
Timothy to the Rescue (Byron)
Tin Can People (Bond)
Tinka (Braun)
Tinker's Wedding (Synge)
Tintock Cup (Bridie)
Tiny Alice (Albee)
Tiny Closet (Inge)
Tio Simplício (Garrett)
Tiote (Daly)
Tip and Run (Brighouse)
'Tis Pity She's a Whore (Ford)
Tis Well it's No Worse (Bickerstaff)
Tit-Coq (Gelinas)
Tit for Tat (Colman the Elder)
Titania (Benavente y Martínez)
Titanic (Durang)
Titanic chinbotsu (Satoh)
Tite et Bérénice (P. Corneille)
Titeres de Cachiporra: Tragicomedia de Don Cristobál y la
    señorita Rosita (García Lorca)
Tito y Berenice (Marqués)
Titus and Berenice (Otway)
Titus Andronicus (Dürrenmatt)
Titus Andronicus (Ravenscroft)
Titus Andronicus (Shakespeare)
To Be Young, Gifted and Black (Hansberry)
To Bobolink, for Her Spirit (Inge)
To Clothe the Naked (Pirandello)
To Damascus I–III (Strindberg)
To Die for Grenada (Walcott)
To Dwell in a Place of Strangers (Kopit)
To Find Oneself (Pirandello)
To Heaven in a Golden Coach (Williams)

To Marry, or Not to Marry (Inchbald)
To Oblige Benson (Taylor)
To Parents and Guardians (Boucicault)
To Parents and Guardians (Taylor)
To Quito and Back (Hecht)
To Sea in a Sieve (Fry)
To the Ladies! (Connelly, Kaufman)
To the Stars (Andreyev)
To Wally Pantoni, We Leave a Credenza (Guare)
Toadstool Boy (Guare)
Toast of the Town (Fitch)
Toast to Melba (Hibberd)
Tobias and the Angel (Bridie)
Tōboku (Zeami)
Tochter der Kathedrale (Hauptmann)
Tochter Pharaonis (Kotzebue)
Tod am Hochzeitstage (Nestroy)
Tod der Tizian (Hofmannsthal)
Tod eines Jägers (Hochhuth)
Tod und der Teufel (Wedekind)
Toda esta larga noche (Díaz)
Toda Nudez Será Castigada (Rodrigues)
Today, I am a Fountain Pen (Horovitz)
Today's a Holiday (Buero Vallejo)
Toddles (Fitch)
Todo es dar en una cosa (Tirso De Molina)
Todo es ventura (Ruiz de Alarcón)
Tog und Nacht (Ansky)
Toilet (Baraka)
Toison d'or (Lesage)
Toller (Dorst)
Tom (Buzo)
Tom Cobb (Gilbert)
Tom Jones (s Osborne)
Tom Thumb (Fielding)
Tombeau de Nostradamus (Lesage)
Tommaso D'Amalfi (De Filippo)
Tommy Allen Show (Terry)
Tomorrow and Tomorrow (Barry)
Tomorrow the Dawn (Montherlant)
Tongue-Lashing (Handke)
Tongues (Shepard)
Tonight at 8:30 (Coward)
Tonight We Improvise (Pirandello)
Tonin Bella Grazie (Goldoni)
Tonnere sans orage (Tardieu)
Tontine (Lesage)
Tony Lumpkin in Town (O'Keeffe)
Tony Lumpkin's Ramble Through Cork (O'Keeffe)
Too Clever by Half (Ostrovsky)
Too Curious by Half (Planché)
Too Late for Logic (Murphy)
Too Many Husbands (Maugham)
Too True to Be Good (Shaw)
Tooth and Claw (McGee)
Tooth and Consequence; or, Hortense Said: "No Skin Off
    My Ass!" (Feydeau)
Tooth of Crime (Shepard)
Toothache (Fitzmaurice)
Top End (Romeril)
Top Girls (Churchill)
Top Silk (s Williamson)
Top Silk (Williamson)
Topografía de un desnudo (Díaz)
Topsy-Turvydom (Gilbert)
Tor und der Tod (Hofmannsthal)
Torch Song Trilogy (Fierstein)

Tormentos y delicias de la carne (Arrabal)
Toronto (Fennario)
Torquato Tasso (Goethe)
Torquato Tasso (Goldoni)
Torquemada (Hugo)
Torre de Babilonia (Calderón)
Torrendal (Cumberland)
Tortue nommée Dostoievski (Arrabal)
Tōru (Zeami)
Tosca (Giacosa)
Tosca (Sardou)
Tot, kto poluchayet poshchechiny (Andreyev)
Total Eclipse (Hampton)
Tote Neffe (Kotzebue)
Tote Tag (Barlach)
Tóték (Örkény)
Toten-Insel (Strindberg)
Totentanz (Wedekind)
Totleben (Braun)
Tottles (Byron)
Tou O Was Wronged (Guan Hanqing)
Touch and Go (Lawrence)
Touch of the Poet (O'Neill)
Tough! (Walker)
Tour à terre (Salacrou)
Tour de Babel (Arrabal)
Tour de Babel (Dumas *père*)
Tour de Nestle (Dumas *père*)
Tour Saint-Jacques (Dumas *père*)
Tourist Guide (Strauss)
Tous ceux qui tombent (r Pinget)
Tous contre tous (Adamov)
Tout à Brown-Séquart! (Feydeau)
Tovarich (Sherwood)
Tower (Fry)
Tower (Hofmannsthal)
Tower (Wedekind)
Tower (Weiss)
Tower of Lochlain (Jerrold)
Town Fop (Behn)
Toy (O'Keeffe)
Toys in the Attic (Hellman)
Trachiniae (Sophocles)
Trachinian Maidens (Sophocles)
Tracings (Pollock)
Tragaluz (Buero Vallejo)
Tragedia fantástica de la gitana Celestina (Sastre)
Tragedian in Spite of Himself (Chekhov)
Tragédie chez Monsieur Grassot (Labiche)
Tragédie du roi Christophe (Césaire)
Tragedy a la Mode (Foote)
Tragedy of King Christophe (Césaire)
Tragedy of Man (Madách)
Tragedy of Tragedies (Fielding)
Tragic Muse (Bridie)
Tragic Role (Chekhov)
Tragik ponevole (Chekhov)
Traição do Padre Martinho (Santareno)
Train (Tremblay)
Train bleu (Cocteau)
Traitor (Shirley)
Traitors (Sewell)
Traître puni (Lesage)
Traktor (Müller)
Trampagos the Widower Bully (Cervantes)
Tramway nommé désir (Cocteau)
Transfiguration (Toller)

Transfiguration dans le cirque (Ghelderode)
Transformed Peasant (Holberg)
Transit Europa (Braun)
Transit of Leo (Daly)
Transit Through Fire (Coulter)
Transit Through Fire (r Coulter)
Translations (Friel)
Trap (Różewicz)
Traps (Churchill)
Trato de Argel (Cervantes)
Trauerspiel in Sizilien (Hebbel)
Traum ein Leben (Grillparzer)
Traumspiel (Weiss)
Travails of Sancho Panza (Saunders)
Travaux et les jours (Vinaver)
Traveler (Connelly)
Traveler (van Itallie)
Traveler in the Dark (Norman)
Traveller Without Luggage (Anouilh)
Traveller Without Luggage (Whiting)
Travellers (J. N. Barker)
Travelling Carriage (Planché)
Travelling Man (Gregory)
Travelling Man (Yeats)
Travelling North (Williamson)
Traversée de l'Empire (Arrabal)
Traversin et couverture (Labiche)
Travesties (Stoppard)
Tre brevi (Fo)
Tre cazune furtunate (De Filippo)
Tre del pra' di sopra (s Betti)
Tre mesi dopo (De Filippo)
Tread the Green Grass (Green)
Treasure on Pelican (Priestley)
Treats (Hampton)
Tree Climber (Tawfiq al-Hakim)
Trees Blew Down (Terry)
Trees in the Wind (McGrath)
13, Rue de l'Amour (Feydeau)
Trelawny of the "Wells" (Pinero)
Trelo Ema (Prevelakis)
Trembling Giant (McGrath)
Tren de los maridos (Benavente y Martínez)
Trente Millions de Gladiator (Labiche)
37 Sous de Monsieur Montaudoin (Labiche)
Trente Tombes de Judas (Salacrou)
Tres afectos de amor (Calderón)
Tres comedias impólicas (Usigli)
Tres diamantes y una mujer (Casona)
Tres justicias en una (Calderón)
Três Máscares (Régio)
Tres mayores prodigios (Calderón)
Tres perfectas casadas (Casona)
Tres sueños de Colilla (Echegaray)
Trescientos millones (Arlt)
Trety Yan (Arbuzov)
Treuer Diener seines Herrn (Grillparzer)
Treulose (Nestroy)
Tri devshki v golubom (Petrushevskaya)
Tri sestry (Chekhov)
Trial (Berkoff)
Trial by Jury (Gilbert)
Trial by Luck (Tagore)
Trial of Dedan Kimathi (Ngugi)
Trial of Effie Deans (Boucicault)
Trial of Joan of Arc (Brecht)
Trial of Joan of Arc on a Matter of Faith (Fornés)

Trial of Louis Riel (Coulter)
Trial of Lucullus (r Brecht)
Trial of Samuel Foote for a Libel on Peter Paragraph
  (Foote)
Trials of Brother Jero (Soyinka)
Triangle (Saunders)
Triángulo sutil (Carballido)
Tribute to Gallantry (Hecht)
Trick to Catch the Old One (Middleton)
Trickster (Plautus)
Trickster of Seville (Tirso De Molina)
Tricycle (Arrabal)
Trifles (Glaspell)
Trilogie des Wiedersehens (Strauss)
Trinummus (Plautus)
Trio (r Fabbri)
Trio (Saunders)
Triomphe d'amour (Hardy)
Triomphe d'amour (Quinault)
Triomphe de l'amour (Marivaux)
Triomphe de Plutus (Marivaux)
Triomphe des dames (T. Corneille)
Trionfo d'amore (Giacosa)
Trip Abroad (Labiche)
Trip to Brighton (Maugham)
Trip to Calais (Foote)
Trip to Kissingen (Taylor)
Trip to Niagara (Dunlap)
Trip to Scarborough (Ayckbourn)
Trip to Scarborough (Sheridan)
Trip to the Moon (s García Lorca)
Tripes à la mode de Caen (Chiarelli)
Tripes d'or (Crommelynck)
Tripez-vous Vous (Barbeau)
Triple porfía (Carballido)
Triptych (Frisch)
Triptychon (Frisch)
Tristi amori (Giacosa)
Tritschtratsch (Nestroy)
Triumph der Empfindsamkeit (Goethe)
Triumph der Zeit (Hofmannsthal)
Triumph of Beauty (Shirley)
Triumph of Death (Rudkin)
Triumph of Death (Sologub)
Triumph of Peace (Shirley)
Triumph of the Philistines (Jones)
Triumphant Widow (Shadwell)
Triumphs of Health and Prosperity (Middleton)
Triumphs of Honour and Industry (Middleton)
Triumphs of Honour and Virtue (Middleton)
Triumphs of Integrity (Middleton)
Triumphs of Love and Antiquity (Middleton)
Triumphs of the Prince d'Amour (Davenant)
Triumphs of Truth (Middleton)
Triunfo do Inverno (Vicente)
Troades (Euripides)
Troades (Seneca)
Tröpfen auf heisse Steine (Fassbinder)
Troas (Seneca)
Troia-Nova Triumphans, London Triumphing (Dekker)
Troilus and Cressida (Dryden)
Troilus and Cressida (Shakespeare)
Trois Acteurs, un drame (Ghelderode)
Trois Bons Amis (Brieux)
Trois Commères (Lesage)
Trois Coups de minuit (Obey)
Trois Entr'actes pour l'amour médecin (Dumas *père*)

Trois Filles de M. Dupont (Brieux)
Trois Justiciers (Maeterlinck)
Trois Moulins (Pixérécourt)
Trois Personnes entrées dans des tableaux (Tardieu)
Trois Petit Tours (t Tremblay)
Trojan War Will Not Take Place (Fry)
Trojan War Will Not Take Place (Giraudoux)
Trojan Women (Euripides)
Trojan Women (Sartre)
Trojan Women (Seneca)
Trommeln in der Nacht (Brecht)
Trompe-la-balle (Labiche)
Trompeur de Séville (Obey)
Trompeur puni (Scudéry)
Trop vieux! (monologue) (Feydeau)
Troppi (Alfieri)
Trotsky in Exile (Weiss)
Trotzki im Exil (Weiss)
Troubadours (Planché)
Trouble in Mind (Childress)
Troubled Island (Hughes)
Trovarsi (Pirandello)
Trovatore (Byron)
Troyennes (Sartre)
Truckline Cafe (M. Anderson)
Truculentus (Plautus)
Trudovoy khleb (Ostrovsky)
True History of Squire Jonathan and His Unfortunate
  Treasure (Arden)
True West (Shepard)
True Widow (Shadwell)
Truer Shade of Blue (Edgar)
Trumped Suit (Labiche)
Trumpet for Nap (Dorst)
Trumpet in the Land (Green)
Trumpet Shall Sound (Wilder)
Trumpets and Drums (Brecht)
Trumpets and Raspberries (Fo)
Trunkenboldt (Kotzebue)
Trust the People (Houghton)
Truth (Fitch)
Truth About the Russian Dancers (Barrie)
Truth Suspect (Ruiz de Alarcón)
Try it Again (Priestley)
Trying a Dramatist (Gilbert)
Tsar Boris (A. K. Tolstoy)
Tsar Fyodor Ioannovich (A. K. Tolstoy)
Tsar Fyodor Ivanovitch (A. K. Tolstoy)
Tsar golod (Andreyev)
Tsar Vodokrut (s Shvarts)
T'sé veux dire (Laberge)
Tsubasa o moyasu tenshi-tachi no butō (Satoh)
Tu étais si gentil quand tu étais petit (Anouilh)
Tu prójimo como a ti (Calderón)
Tu tare (Goldoni)
Tú una vez y el diablo diez (Benavente y Martínez)
Tündérálom (Madách)
Türkensklavin (Lenz)
Tueur sans gages (Ionesco)
Tumble-Down-Dick (Fielding)
Tumor Brainowicz (Witkiewicz)
Tumor Mózgowicz (Witkiewicz)
Túnel (Gomes)
Túnica amarilla (Benavente y Martínez)
Turandot (Brecht)
Turandot (Gozzi)
Turandot (Schiller)

Uncle Sam (Daly)
Uncle Snake (Horovitz)
Uncle Vanya (Chekhov)
Uncle Vanya (Fornés)
Uncle Vanya (Frayn)
Uncle Vanya (Hampton)
Uncle Vanya (Mamet)
Uncle Vanya (Murrell)
Uncle Vanya (van Itallie)
Und Pippa tanzt! (Hauptmann)
Under Cover (Harrigan)
Under Plain Cover (Osborne)
Under the Gaslight (Daly)
Under the Pylon (Brighouse)
Underbara leendet (Bergman)
Undercurrent (Daly)
Underground Lovers (Tardieu)
Underjordens leende (Norén)
Underneath (McGrath)
Underpants (Sternheim)
Undervud (Shvarts)
Undiscovered Country (Schnitzler)
Undiscovered Country (Stoppard)
Undivine Comedy (Krasiński)
Unequal Match (Taylor)
Unfortunate Lovers (Davenant)
Ung mands kjærlighet (Grieg)
Ungarns erster Wohlthäter (Kotzebue)
Unges forbund (Ibsen)
Unglücklichen (Kotzebue)
Unhappy Love (Giacosa)
Unheilbringende Krone (Raimund)
Unicorn from the Stars (Gregory)
Unicorn from the Stars (Yeats)
Uniform des Feldmarschalls Wellington (Kotzebue)
Universal Gallant (Fielding)
Unknown (Maugham)
Unknown General (Obaldia)
Unnatural Combat (Massinger)
Uno (Alfieri)
Unoha (Zeami)
Unsatisfactory Supper (Williams)
Unschuldige (Hochwälder)
Unseen Hand (Shepard)
Unser Fritz (Kotzebue)
Unshaven Cheek (Lawler)
Unsichtbare Mädchen (Kotzebue)
Unter den Pflaumenbäumen (Bernhard)
Unternehmen der Wega (r Dürrenmatt)
Untitled Play (L. Wilson)
Unto Such Glory (Green)
Unveiling (Havel)
Unverhofft (Nestroy)
Unvermählte (Kotzebue)
Unvernünftigen sterben aus (Handke)
Unwilling Doctor (Molière)
Unzusammenhängende Zusammenhang (Nestroy)
Uomo da rifare (Chiarelli)
Uomo dal fiore in bocca (Pirandello)
Uomo e galantuomo (De Filippo)
Uomo, la bestia, e la virtù (Pirandello)
Uomo nudo e l'uomo in frak (Fo)
Uomo prudente (Goldoni)
Up Against It (s Orton)
Up at the Hills (Taylor)
Up from Paradise (Miller)
Up Spaghetti Junction (Edgar)

Up the Flue (Boucicault)
Up to Thursday (Shepard)
Upper Crust (Byron)
Upptäcktsresanden (Dagerman)
Uprooted Tree (Chikamatsu)
Uranio 235 (Sastre)
Urbain Grandier (Dumas *père*)
Urbi et Orbi (r Obaldia)
Urfaust (Dürrenmatt)
Urfaust (Goethe)
Úridivat (Molnár)
Uroki muzyki (Petrushevskaya)
Urteil des Paris (Kotzebue)
Use of Man (Dunsany)
Used Up (Boucicault)
Ushiyama hoteru (Kishida)
Uspekh (Vampilov)
Usynlige (Holberg)
Ut de poitrine (Labiche)
Ut Pictura Poesis! or, The Enraged Musicians (Colman the Elder)
Utinaya okhota (Vampilov)
Utopia Incorporated (Ludlam)
Utopia (Limited) (Gilbert)
Utro delovogo cheloveka (Gogol)
Üvegcipő (Molnár)

V chuzhom piru pokhmelye (Ostrovsky)
V etom milom starom dome (Arbuzov)
V gostyakh i doma (Volodin)
Va et vient (Beckett)
Vacaciones I–II (Usigli)
Vacante general (Calderón)
Vaccaria (Ruzante)
Vacsora (Molnár)
Vægelsindede (Holberg)
Vagabond (Gilbert)
Vagabond Camp (Esson)
Valaki (Molnár)
Valentine and Orson (Taylor)
Valentine; ou, La Séduction (Pixérécourt)
Valentine; ou, Le Château et la ferme (Pixérécourt)
Valentinian (Fletcher)
Valiant One (Crothers)
Valle de la zarzuela (Calderón)
Valley Forge (M. Anderson)
Vals sin fin por el planeta (Carballido)
Valsa n. 6 (Rodrigues)
Valse des toréadors (Anouilh)
Values (Keane)
Vamos Soltar os Demônios (Gomes)
Vampire (Boucicault)
Vampire (Dumas *père*)
Vampyr (Planché)
Vampyre (Planché)
Van Ouds "De Morgenster" (Heijermans)
Vandaleur's Folly (Arden)
Vanity Fair (Boucicault)
Vanka klyuchnik i pazh Zhean (Sologub)
Vanka the Steward and Jehan the Page (Sologub)
Vår ære og vår makt (Grieg)
Vår lilla sommar (r Dagerman)
Vargas (Gomes)
Variaciones para muertos de percusión (Díaz)
Variation on a Theme (Rattigan)
Variedades de Proteu (Silva)
Varvary (Gorky)

Vasa Trilogy (Strindberg)
Vase (Ionesco)
Vasilisa Malentyeva (Ostrovsky)
Vassa Geleznova (Adamov)
Vassa Zheleznova (Gorky)
Vassal généreux (Scudéry)
Vater (Sternheim)
Vater (Weiss)
Vater von Ungefähr (Kotzebue)
Väterchen (Lenz)
Väterliche Erwartung (Kotzebue)
Vatzlav (Mrożek)
Vävaren i Bagdad (Bergman)
Vdokhnoveniye (Ivanov)
Věc Makropoulos (Čapek)
Vecchio bizzarro (Goldoni)
Vecher y Sorrente (Turgenev)
Vecherny svet (Arbuzov)
Vedova del Malabar (Gozzi)
Vedova scaltra (Goldoni)
Vedova spiritosa (Goldoni)
Veglia d'armi (Fabbri)
Veillée allemande (Dumas *père*)
Veland (Hauptmann)
Velbloud uchem jehly (Langer)
Velero en la botella (Díaz)
Velho da Horta (Vicente)
Ve'lká parachňa (Karvaš)
Venceslas (Rotrou)
Vendages (Regnard)
Vendages de la foire (Lesage)
Vendedores de Esperança (Santareno)
Veneno y la triaca (Calderón)
Venetian Night (Musset)
Venetian Outlaw (Pixérécourt)
Venetian Twins (Goldoni)
Venganza de Tamar (Tirso De Molina)
Venice Preserved (Boucicault)
Venice Preserved (Otway)
Vénitienne (Dumas *père*)
Ventaglio (Goldoni)
25 monologhi per una donna (Fo)
Vento notturno (Betti)
Ventre de Paris (Zola)
Ventriloquist's Wife (Ludlam)
Ventura con el nombre (Tirso De Molina)
Ventura te dé Dios, hijo (Tirso De Molina)
Venus (Crothers)
Vénus (Ghelderode)
Venus and Adonis (Cibber)
Venus and Adonis (Inge)
Venus and Adonis (Obey)
Vénus d'Emilio (Barbeau)
Vénus et Adonis (Obey)
Venus Observed (Fry)
Vera (Wilde)
Vera Baxter (s Duras)
Vera, Nadezhda, Lyubov (Arbuzov)
Verbannte Amor (Kotzebue)
Verbannung aus dem Zauberreiche (Nestroy)
Verbotene Garten (Dorst)
Verdad (Benavente y Martínez)
Verdad inventada (Benavente y Martínez)
Verdad sospechosa (Ruiz de Alarcón)
Verdadero Dios Pan (Calderón)
Verdict (Mason)
Vereda da Salvação (Andrade)

Verfassungsfeinde (Kroetz)
Verfolgung und Ermordung Jean Paul Marats . . . (Weiss)
Verge (Glaspell)
Verger (s Maugham)
Vergonzoso en palacio (Tirso De Molina)
Verhängnisvolle Faschingsnacht (Nestroy)
Verhör des Lukullus (Brecht)
Vernor des Lukullus (r Brecht)
Véritable Saint Genest (Rotrou)
Verkehrte Welt (Tieck)
Verkleidungen (Kotzebue)
Verkommenes Ufer Medeamaterial Landschaft mit
    Argonauten (Müller)
Verlegenheit und List (Kotzebue)
Verleumder (Kotzebue)
Verlorene Kind (Kotzebue)
Verloving (Heijermans)
Vermächtnis (Schnitzler)
Vermont Sketches (Mamet)
Vernisáž (Havel)
Vero amico (Goldoni)
Verre d'eau (Scribe)
Vérrokonok (Örkény)
Verrou de la reine (Dumas *père*)
Versailles Impromptu (Molière)
Verschweigene wider Willen (Kotzebue)
Verschwender (Raimund)
Verschwörung des Fiesko zu Genua (Schiller)
Verschwundene Mond (Hochwälder)
Versicherung (Weiss)
Versuchung (Kaiser)
Versunkene Glocke (Hauptmann)
Verteidigung von Friedrichshafen (r Walser)
Verveling (Heijermans)
Verwandtschaften (Kotzebue)
Verwickelte Geschichte (Nestroy)
Verwundete Bräutigam (Lenz)
Very Latest Edition of The Lady of Lyons (Byron)
Very Like a Whale (Osborne)
Very Woman (Fletcher, Massinger)
Vespae (Aristophanes)
Vesta (Daly)
Vestal de Occidente (Benavente y Martínez)
Vestido de Noiva (Rodrigues)
Vestire gl'ignudi (Pirandello)
Veterans (Wood)
Veuve (Becque)
Veuve (P. Corneille)
Veuve enragée (Maillet)
Viaducs de la Seine-et-Oise (Duras)
Viaducts of Seine-et-Oise (Duras)
Viaje alrededor de un pañuelo (Díaz)
Viaje de instrucción (Benavente y Martínez)
Viaje de invierno (Gambaro)
Viaje de Nocresida (Carballido)
Viaje infinito de Sancho Panza (Sastre)
Viático cordero (Calderón)
Vicar of Wakefield (Murphy)
Vicar of Wakefield (Taylor)
Vice Versa (Boucicault)
Vicere (Fabbri)
Vicki Madison Clocks Out (Buzo)
Victim (Racine)
Victimes du devoir (Ionesco)
Victims (Taylor)
Victims of Duty (Ionesco)

Victor (Anouilh)
Victor (Pixérécourt)
Victor and Hortense (Boucicault)
Victoria de la honra (Vega)
Victoria Station (Pinter)
Victors (Sartre)
Victors (Wilder)
Victory (Jones)
Victory (s Pinter)
Victory: Choices in Reaction (H. Barker)
Victory of Death (Sologub)
Vida alegre y muerte triste (Echegaray)
Vida Breve em 3 Fotografias (Santareno)
Vida do Grande D. Quixote de la Mancha (Silva)
Vida en verso (Benavente y Martínez)
Vida es sueño (Calderón)
Vida y muerte de Herodes (Tirso De Molina)
Vidas cruzadas (Benavente y Martínez)
Vidocq! The French Police Spy (Jerrold)
Vidularia (Plautus)
Vie en rose (Salacrou)
Vie publique de Pantagleize (Ghelderode)
Vie quotidienne d'Antoine X (Dubé)
Vieillards rajeunis (Lesage)
Vieillards (Ghelderode)
Viejo celoso (Cervantes)
Viejo matrimonio (Gambaro)
Viejo y la niña (Fernández de Moratín)
Viejos (Usigli)
Vielwisser (Kotzebue)
Viet Rock (Terry)
Vietnamese Wedding (Fornés)
Vietnamization of New Jersey (Durang)
Vieux Carré (Williams)
Vieux Garçons (Sardou)
Vieux Garon et la petite fille (Scribe)
Vieux Major (Pixérécourt)
Vieux Soudard (Ghelderode)
View from the Bridge (Miller)
View from the Obelisk (Leonard)
Vigilant Sentinel (Cervantes)
Vikings at Helgeland (Ibsen)
Vikrama-Urvashi (Kalidsa)
Vikramorvasiya (Kalidasa)
Vildanden (Ibsen)
Villa (Dorst)
Village: A Party (Fuller)
Village Fete (Cumberland)
Village Wooing (Shaw)
Villainous Squire and the Village Rose (Byron)
Villana de la Sagra (Tirso De Molina)
Villana de Vallecas (Tirso De Molina)
Villano en su rincón (Vega)
Ville (Claudel)
Ville à voile (Willems)
Ville dont le prince est un enfant (Montherlant)
Ville dont le prince était une princesse (Arrabal)
Villeggiatura (Goldoni)
Villes (Dadié)
Viña del señor (Calderón)
Vincent verkauft ein Bild (Kaiser)
Vindictive Man (Holcroft)
Vinegar Tom (Churchill)
29 degrés à l'ombre (Labiche)
Vingt-quatre février (Dumas *père*)
Vinovatye (Arbuzov)
Vint (Mamet)

Viol de Lucrèce (Obey)
Violaine la chevelue (Zola)
Violet (Boucicault)
Violet (Molnár)
Virgin Bride (Strindberg)
Virgin Martyr (Dekker, Massinger)
Virgin of the Sun (Dunlap)
Virgin of the Sun (Kotzebue)
Virginia (Alfieri)
Virginia (Hochwälder)
Virginie (Dubé)
Virginie (Mairet)
Virgin's Mask (Kara)
Virtud sospechosa (Benavente y Martínez)
Virtuoso (Shadwell)
Virtuous Island (Giraudoux)
Vise (Pirandello)
Vishnevy sad (Chekhov)
Vision of Delight (Jonson)
Visions (Nowra)
Visions of Simone Machard (Brecht)
Visit (Dürrenmatt)
Visit (Fornés)
Visit from Miss Prothero (t Bennett)
Visita del ángel (Triana)
Visitante (Solórzano)
Visite de noces (Dumas *fils*)
Visiteur (Dubé)
Vispera del degüello (Díaz)
Vita breve (Willems)
Vita che ti diedi (Pirandello)
Vítezové (Langer)
Vituvia (Kotzebue)
Viúva, Porém Honesta (Rodrigues)
Viva la muerte! (s Arrabal)
Vivacités du capitaine Tic (Labiche)
Vivandière (Gilbert)
Vivat! Vivat Regina! (Bolt)
Vive Henri IV (Anouilh)
Vizcaíno fingido (Cervantes)
Vizio assurdo (Fabbri)
Vladimir Mayakovsky (Mayakovsky)
Vlast Tmy (L. N. Tolstoy)
Vliegende Hollander (Heijermans)
Vögel (Goethe)
Vögel (Hacks)
Vörös malom (Molnár)
Vocations (De Groen)
Voces (Pavlovsky)
Voces de gesta (Valle-Inclán)
Voci di dentro (De Filippo)
Voesejacht (Claus)
Voevoda: Son na Volge (Ostrovsky)
Vogelscheuchen (Grass)
Voice of Nature (Dunlap)
Voice of the Turtle (Van Druten)
Voina i mir (Bulgakov)
Voisins (Vinaver)
Voitures (Vian)
Voix dans le vent (Dadié)
Voix humaine (Cocteau)
Voix sans personne (Tardieu)
Vole-moi un Petit Milliard (Arrabal)
Volki i ovtsy (Ostrovsky)
Volksbuch vom Herzog Ernst (Hacks)
Volontaire (Feydeau)
Volpone (Jonson)

Volunteers (Friel)
Volunteers (Shadwell)
Vom König und der Königin (Sternheim)
Vor dem Ruhestand (Bernhard)
Vor Sonnenaufgang (Hauptmann)
Vor Sonnenuntergang (Hauptmann)
Voronya roshcha (Vampilov)
Voronyezs (Örkény)
Vorrei morire anche stasera se dovessi pensare che non è
 servito a niente (Fo)
Vorspiel für ein Puppentheater (Hofmannsthal)
Vorstendroom (Heijermans)
Vortex (Coward)
Vospitannitsa (Ostrovsky)
Vospominanye (Arbuzov)
Vote by Ballot (Granville-Barker)
Vote for Them (t Edgar)
Voyage autour de ma marmite (Labiche)
Voyage de Monsieur Perrichon (Labiche)
Voyage en Chine (Labiche)
Voyage Round My Father (Mortimer)
Voyage to Tomorrow (Tawfiq al-Hakim)
Voyages chez les morts (Ionesco)
Voyageur sans bagage (Anouilh)
Voysey Inheritance (Granville-Barker)
Vragi (Gorky)
Vrai Monde? (Tremblay)
Vreemde jacht (Heijermans)
Vrijdag (Claus)
Vse ne kak u lyudei (Petrushevskaya)
Vstrecha (Gorky)
Vstrecha s yunostyu (Arbuzov)
Vudhas (Kazantzakis)
Vulcani (Marinetti)
Vulture! Vulture! (Sutherland)
Vultures (Becque)
Vybor (Arbuzov)
Vybor guvernyova (Fonvizin)
Výhoň Dub (Tyl)
Vyrozuměni (Havel)

W małym dworku (Witkiewicz)
Waddy Googan (Harrigan)
Wager (Giacosa)
Wages of Thin (Griffiths)
Wahl fürs Leben (Kroetz)
Wahl fürs Leben (r Kroetz)
Wail, Wind, Wail (Ringwood)
Wait and Hope (Byron)
Waiting for Godot (Beckett)
Waiting for Lefty (Odets)
Waiting for the Parade (Murrell)
Waiting in the Wings (Coward)
Waitress in Yellowstone (t Mamet)
Wake (Inge)
Wake of Jamey Foster (Henley)
Wake Up, Jonathan (Rice)
Waking Up (Fo)
Waldstück (Müller)
Walk in the Desert (t Whiting)
Walk on the Water (Leonard)
Walk on the Water (Stoppard)
Walker (Barrie)
Walkin' for Dat Cake (Harrigan)
Walking Through Walls (Terry)
Walled City (Wilder)
Wallenstein (Müller)

Wallenstein (Schiller)
Wallenstein's Camp (Schiller)
Wallenstein's Death (Schiller)
Wallensteins Lager (Schiller)
Wallensteins Tod (Schiller)
Walloons (Cumberland)
Walpole (Bulwer-Lytton)
Walsh (Pollock)
Waltz of the Dogs (Andreyev)
Waltz of the Toreadors (Anouilh)
Waltzing Matilda (Romeril)
Wand (r Forte)
Wanderer (Kotzebue)
Wandering: A Turn (L. Wilson)
Wandering Boys (Pixérécourt)
Wandering Heir (Reade)
Wandlung (Toller)
Wang Zhaojun (Cao Yu)
Wanted a Hermit (Taylor)
Wanted a Widow (Boucicault)
Wanton Countess (s Williams)
War (Robertson)
War Plays (Bond)
War (van Itallie)
War to the Knife (Byron)
Wariat i zakonnica (Witkiewicz)
Warna (Willems)
Warnings (O'Neill)
Warnung vor einer heiligen Nutte (s Fassbinder)
Warren Hastings (Brecht)
Warrior's Barrow (Ibsen)
Wars of Caesar and Pompey (Chapman)
Warszawianka (Wyspiański)
Warum läuft Herr R amok? (s Fassbinder)
Was He Anyone (Simpson)
Was kostet das Eisen (Brecht)
Washing (Fornés)
Wasps (Aristophanes)
Waste (Granville-Barker)
Waste Paper Guards (Leigh)
Wasted Weekend (t Mamet)
Watch it Come Down (Osborne)
Watch on the Rhine (Hellman)
Watch on the Rhine (s Hellman)
Watched Pot (Carroll)
Watching for Dolphins (McGrath)
Watchtower (Nowra)
Water Engine (Mamet)
Water Hen (Witkiewicz)
Waterloo Bridge (Sherwood)
Waters of Babylon (Arden)
Waters of Silence (Mason)
Waves of Sea and Love (Grillparzer)
Waves of the Sea (Fitzmaurice)
Wax (H. Barker)
Waxworks (Molnár)
Way of Lacross (Barbeau)
Way of the World (Congreve)
Way of the World (Fitch)
Way of the World (Planché)
Way Upstream (Ayckbourn)
Way We Live (Daly)
Ways and Means (Colman the Younger)
Ways and Means (Coward)
Wayward Saint (Carroll)
We Can Feed Everybody Here (Terry)
We Can't Be As Bad As All That! (Jones)

Winkelberg (Hecht)
Winner (Rice)
Winners (Terry)
Winslow Boy (Rattigan)
Winter Ballad (Hauptmann)
Winter, Daddykins (Brenton)
Winter Garden (Galsworthy)
Winter Journey (Odets)
Winterballade (Hauptmann)
Winter's Tale (Shakespeare)
Winterset (M. Anderson)
Wir werden schon noch handeln (Walser)
Wireless Can't Lie (Brighouse)
Wirrwarr (Kotzebue)
Wisdom of Solomon (Tawfiq al-Hakim)
Wisdom Tooth (Connelly)
Wise Child (Gray)
Wise Have Not Spoken (Carroll)
Wise Man of the East (Inchbald)
Wise Woman of Hogsdon (Heywood)
Wish Shop (Brighouse)
Wit at Several Weapons (Middleton)
Wit Without Money (Fletcher)
Wit Works Woe (Griboyedov)
Witch (Middleton)
Witch (Molnár)
Witch of Derncleugh (Planché)
Witch of Edmonton (Dekker, Ford)
Witch-Finders (Jerrold)
Witch's Daughter (Brighouse)
Within an Inch of His Life (Herne)
Within the Gates (O'Casey)
Without a Home (Byron)
Without a Parachute (Fennario)
Without Love (Barry)
Witnesses (Różewicz)
Wit's End (Mason)
Wits (Davenant)
Wittek geht um (Dorst)
Wittikind and His Brothers (Taylor)
Witty Fair One (Shirley)
Witwe und das Reitpferd (Kotzebue)
Wives as They Were and Maids as They Are (Inchbald)
Wives by Advertisement (Jerrold)
Wives' Excuse (Southerne)
Wives' Friend (Pirandello)
Wladimir Majakowski Tragödie (Müller)
Woe from Wit (Griboyedov)
Wohnung ist zu vermieten in der Stadt . . . (Nestroy)
Wolf (Molnár)
Wolfville (Fitch)
Wolokolamsker Chaussee I–V (Müller)
Wolves and Sheep (Ostrovsky)
Wolves! Wolves! (Valle-Inclán)
Woman (Bond)
Woman (Boucicault)
Woman Alone (Fo)
Woman and Whisky (Coward)
Woman-Captain (Shadwell)
Woman from Andros (Machiavelli)
Woman from Samos (Menander)
Woman Hater (Beaumont, Fletcher)
Woman in Mind (Ayckbourn)
Woman in the Case (Fitch)
Woman in the Moon (Lyly)
Woman Killed with Kindness (Heywood)
Woman Killer and the Hell of Oil (Chikamatsu)

Woman Never Vext (Planché)
Woman of No Importance (t Bennett)
Woman of No Importance (Wilde)
Woman of Paris (Becque)
Woman of Sumaria (Rostand)
Woman of Trachis (Sophocles)
Woman on Her Own (Brieux)
Woman Tamer (Esson)
Woman That Was a Cat (Scribe)
Woman Within the Cyprus Fence (Zeami)
Woman Without a Shadow (Hofmannsthal)
Woman Won't (Daly)
Woman's Honor (Glaspell)
Woman's Silence (Sardou)
Woman's Wit (Cibber)
Women! (Hibberd)
Women and Water (Guare)
Women at the Tomb (Ghelderode)
Women Beware Women (H. Barker)
Women Beware Women (Middleton)
Women Dandies (Sardou)
Women Do Things Like That (Brighouse)
Women Have Their Way (Granville-Barker)
Women in Parliament (Aristophanes)
Women in Power (Aristophanes)
Women in Power (McGrath)
Women of the Dunes (McGrath)
Women of Troy (Euripides)
Women Pleased (Fletcher)
Won at Last (Mackaye)
Won by a Head (Taylor)
Wonder! (Centlivre)
Wonder (Daly)
Wonder Hat (Hecht)
Wonder of a Kingdom (Dekker)
Wonder of Women (Marston)
Wonder Show (Cervantes)
Wonderful Travels of Gulliver (Byron)
Wonderful Water Cure (Boucicault)
Wonderful Wedding (Fitzmaurice)
Wonderworking Magician (Calderón)
Wood Demon (Chekhov)
Wooden Spoon (Daly)
Woods (Mamet)
Wooed and Viewed (Feydeau)
Woollen Stocking (Harrigan)
Word (Munk)
Words and Music (r Beckett)
Words and Music (Coward)
Words upon the Window Pane (Yeats)
Workhouse Donkey (Arden)
Workhouse Ward (Gregory)
Working Out (Romeril)
World a Mask (Boker)
World and His Wife (Echegaray)
World in a Village (O'Keeffe)
World is a Comedy (Tawfiq al-Hakim)
World is Round (Salacrou)
World of Fashion (Scribe)
World of Paul Slickey (Osborne)
World on a Hill (Childress)
World Tossed at Tennis (Middleton)
World We Live In (Čapek)
World We Make (Kingsley)
Worlds (Bond)
Worlds Apart (Triana)
Worship of the Dancing Girl (Tagore)

Worst is Not Always Certain (Calderón)
Would-Be Gentleman (Gregory)
Would-Be Gentleman (Molière)
Would-Be Invalid (Molière)
Wound in the Heart (Ngugi)
Woyzeck (Büchner)
Wrack P'int (Green)
Wrangling Lovers (Ravenscroft)
Wreck of the 5:25 (Wilder)
Wreck of the National Line Car (Pollock)
Wrecked Eggs (Hare)
Wreckers (Edgar)
Wrens (Gregory)
Wrinkles (Byron)
Writ of Inquiry on the Inquisitor General (Foote)
Writing Desk (Kotzebue)
Wrong Clothes Dream (Guan Hanqing)
Wrong Side of the Park (Mortimer)
Wrrraak! (Claus)
Wüste (Kotzebue)
Wudjesay? (Pollock)
Wu-hou-yan (Guan Hanqing)
Wunder in Amerika (Toller)
Wunschkonzert (Kroetz)
Wuthering Heights (s Hecht)
Wyszedł z domu (Różewicz)
Wyzwolenie (Wyspiański)

X.Y.Z. (Colman the Younger)
Xerxes (Cibber)
Xie Tianxiang (Guan Hanqing)
Ximena (Cibber)
Ximeroni (Kazantzakis)
Xmas in Las Vegas (Richardson)
Xmas v. Mastermind (Ayckbourn)
X-rayed-iate (Terry)

Y amargaba . . . (Benavente y Martínez)
Y va de cuento (Benavente y Martínez)
Ya anda la de Mazagatos (Vega)
Ya Tali' al-Shajara (Tawfiq al-Hakim)
Yamamba (Zeami)
Yamanami (Kinoshita)
Yankee Chronology (Dunlap)
Yard of Sun (Fry)
Yardsale (Wesker)
Yari no Gonza (Chikamatsu)
Yasha Kisō (Kara)
Yashima (Zeami)
Y'avait un prisonnier (Anouilh)
Year of the Duck (Horovitz)
Year of the Hiker (Keane)
Years of Wandering (Arbuzov)
Yegor Bulichoff and Others (Gorky)
Yegor Bulychov i drugiye (Gorky)
Yekaterina Ivanovna (Andreyev)
Yellow Dwarf (Byron)
Yellow Dwarf and the King of the Gold Mines (Planché)
Yellow Jack (Howard)
Yeomen of the Guard (Gilbert)
Yerma (García Lorca)
Yes (Mamet)
Yes, But So What (Mamet)
Yes, peut-être (Duras)
Yesterday the Children Were Dancing (Gelinas)
Yeux croisés (Vian)
Yevropeyskaya khronika (Arbuzov)

Yo también hablo de la rosa (Carballido)
Yoakemae (Kubo)
Yobbo Nowt (McGrath)
Yolimba (Dorst)
Yomei Tenno Shokunin Kagami (Chikamatsu)
Yonadab (Shaffer)
Yorick (Daly)
Yorimasa (Zeami)
Yoru to yoru no yoru (Satoh)
Yosaka from Tamba (Chikamatsu)
You and I (Barry)
You and Me and Him (t Mercer)
You Can't Just Live as You Please (Ostrovsky)
You Can't Take It with You (Kaufman)
You Gonna Let Me Take You Out Tonight, Baby?
   (Bullins)
You Know I Can't Hear You When the Water's Running
   (R. Anderson)
You Must Be Buried (Planché)
You Never Can Tell (Shaw)
You 'spute Me (Harrigan)
You Touched Me! (Williams)
You'll Never Guess (Jellicoe)
Young Actress (Boucicault)
Young Admiral (Shirley)
Young and Handsome (Planché)
Young and Old (Scribe)
Young Fra Diavolo, the Terror of Terracina (Byron)
Young Hopeful (Fonvizin)
Young Hypocrite (Foote)
Young Idea (Coward)
Young King (Behn)
Young King Louis (Dumas père)
Young Martin Luther King (Childress)
Young Men and Old Women (Inchbald)
Young Quaker (O'Keeffe)
Young Wisdom (Crothers)
Young Woodley (Van Druten)
Younger Brother (Behn)
Younger Generation (Houghton)
Youngest (Barry)
Your Fiery Furnace (Green)
Your Five Gallants (Middleton)
Your Navy (M. Anderson)
You're Not Watching Me Mummy (t Osborne)
Youth and the Peregrines (Fry)
Ytosuki Soga (Chikamatsu)
Yttersta dagen (Dagerman)
Yu jing-tai (Guan Hanqing)
Yuanye (Cao Yu)
Yubiley (Chekhov)
Yugiri Awa no Naruto (Chikamatsu)
Yuhi Shōsetsu (Kara)
Yura (Zeami)
Yuya (Zeami)
Yūzuru (Kinoshita)

Za chem poydesh, to i naydesh (Ostrovsky)
Zabawa (Mrożek)
Zacieranie rąk (Różewicz)
Zack (Brighouse)
Zadný vchod (Karvaš)
Zagadochny indus (s Volodin)
Zahradni slavnost (Havel)
Zaïre (Voltaire)
Zaïre (Wyspiański)

Zalozhniki zhizni (Sologub)
Zamoski (Planché)
Zampa del gatto (Giacosa)
Zampa der Tagdieb (Nestroy)
Zanina (Daly)
Zapatera prodigiosa (García Lorca)
Zapato (Solórzano)
Zar lässt sich photographieren (Kaiser)
Zarathustra (Sorge)
Zarazhennoye semeystvo (L. N. Tolstoy)
Zastrozzi, the Master of Discipline (Walker)
Zauberer Februar (Nestroy)
Zauberer Sulphurelektrimagnetikophosphoratus (Nestroy)
Zauberreise in die Ritterzeit (Nestroy)
Zauberschloss (Kotzebue)
Zavtrak upredvoditelya (Turgenev)
Zebra (Andrade)
Zebrácká opera (Havel)
Zeca Diabo (Gomes)
Zehn Tage, die die Welt erschütterten (Müller)
Zeidah (Ansky)
Zeim, re dei genii (Gozzi)
Zeit und das Zimmer (Strauss)
Zeitvertreib (Nestroy)
Zement (Müller)
Zémine et Almanzor (Lesage)
Zemlya dybom (Tretyakov)
Zensur (Wedekind)
Zentaur (Kaiser)
Zerbrochene Krug (Kleist)
Zeren Hoofzonden (Ghelderode)
Zerlina (Seneca)
Zerline (Scribe)
Zero Inn (Mason)
0–71 (Barbeau)
Zerrissene (Nestroy)
Zerstreuten (Kotzebue)
Zettelträger Papp (Nestroy)
Zevende gebod (Heijermans)
Zheng zai xiang (Cao Yu)
Zhenitba Belugina (Ostrovsky)
Zhenitba (Gogol)
Zhestokiye igry (Arbuzov)
Zhivoy trup (L. N. Tolstoy)
Zhizn cheloveka (Andreyev)

Zi-chai ji (Tang Xianzu)
Zimmerschlacht (Walser)
Ziska (Katona)
Zitherspieler (Kotzebue)
Zitti! Stiamo precipitando! (Fo)
Života hmyzu (Čapek)
Zi-xiao ji (Tang Xianzu)
Žižka z Trocnova (Tyl)
Zlá princezna a hodný drak (Langer)
Zmyrtvychvstanie deduska Kolomana (Karvaš)
Zobeide (Gozzi)
Zoia's Apartment (Bulgakov)
Zolushka (Shvarts)
Zona intermedia (Carballido)
Zone (Dubé)
Zoo Story (Albee)
Zooman and the Sign (Fuller)
Zorn einer Göttin (r Walser)
Zoroaster (Goldoni)
Zounds! (Frayn)
Zoykina kvartira (Bulgakov)
Zozo (Pixérécourt)
Zsugori uram (Örkény)
Ztížená možnost soustředění (Havel)
Zu ebener Erde und erster Stock (Nestroy)
Zug der Schatten (Schnitzler)
Zugemachte Fenster (Kotzebue)
Zulime (Voltaire)
Zum grossen Wurstel (Schnitzler)
Zur schönen Aussicht (Horváth)
Zurich Transit (t Frisch)
Züruckkunft des Vaters (Kotzebue)
Zusammengestoppelte Komödie (Nestroy)
Zwei ewige Juden für einen (Nestroy)
Zwei Krawatten (Kaiser)
Zwei Nichten für Eine (Kotzebue)
Zwei Schüsseln voll Faschingskrapfen (Nestroy)
Zweimal Amphitryon (Kaiser)
Zweimal Oliver (Kaiser)
Zweite (Goering)
Zwischenspiel (Schnitzler)
Zwölf Mädchen in Uniform (Nestroy)
Zygmunt August (Wyspiański)
Zykovs (Gorky)
Zykovy (Gorky)

NOTES ON ADVISERS AND CONTRIBUTORS

AARSETH, Asjbørn. Professor of Scandinavian Literature, University of Bergen, Norway. Former editor of *Edda: Scandinavian Journal of Literary Research*, 1986–90. Author of *Peer Gynt*, 1975, *"Peer Gynt" and "Ghosts"* (Text and Performance series), 1989, and of books in Norwegian on the Bergen National Theatre (1901–31), 1969, applied narratology, 1976, realism in Norwegian literary history, 1981, and Romanticism in Scandinavian literary history, 1985. **Essays:** Bjørnstjerne Bjørnson; Henrik Ibsen.

ADAMS, Elissa. Member of the Department of Theatre, University of California, La Jolla. **Essay:** Max Frisch.

ANDERMAN, Gunilla. Director of Centre for Translation and Language Studies and Head of Swedish, University of Surrey. Author of play reviews and articles on translation theory and theatre. Editor of *New Swedish Plays*, 1992. Translator of *The Changing Roles of Men and Women*, 1967, *Swedish Literature in the Post-War Period*, 1979, and *New Swedish Plays*, 1992. **Essay:** Lars Norén.

ANDREWS, Richard. Professor of Italian, University of Leeds. Author of articles on Ariosto, Calvino, Italian Renaissance comedy, community theatre in Tuscany, and a forthcoming book on 16th-century Italian comedy. **Essays:** Pietro Aretino; Ludovico Ariosto; Niccolò Machiavelli; Ruz(z)ante.

ARONSON, Arnold. Adviser. Professor in the Department of Theatre, Hunter College, City University of New York. Formerly Associate Professor of Drama, University of Virginia, and Professor of Drama, University of Michigan, Ann Arbor. Author of books and articles on American theatre and set design.

BANFIELD, Chris. Lecturer in Theatre Arts, University of Birmingham. **Essay:** John Mortimer.

BANHAM, Martin. Adviser. Professor of Drama and Theatre Studies, University of Leeds. Author of *Osborne*, 1969, and *African Theatre Today*, 1976. Editor of *Plays by Tom Taylor*, 1985, and *The Cambridge Guide to World Theatre*, 1988, revised 1992. Co-editor (with John Hodgson) of three volumes of *Drama in Education*, 1972, 1973, and 1975. **Essays:** Ama Ata Aidoo; Arthur Wing Pinero; Ola Rotimi; Wole Soyinka; Tom Taylor.

BARLOW, Judith E. Associate Professor of English and Women's Studies, State University of New York, Albany. Author of *Final Acts: The Creation of Three Late O'Neill Plays*, 1985, and many theatre reviews and articles on O'Neill, Crothers, Tina Howe, and other topics in American drama. Editor of *Plays by American Women (1900–30)*, 1981, and O'Neill centennial issue of *Theatre Survey*, 1988. **Essay:** Rachel Crothers.

BARNETT, Gene A. Professor of English and Comparative Literature, Fairleigh Dickinson University, Teaneck, New Jersey. Author of *Denis Johnston*, 1978, *Lanford Wilson*, 1987, and articles on modern drama and American literature. **Essay:** Hugh Leonard.

BASSNETT, Susan. Professor of Comparative Literature and Director, Centre for British and Comparative Cultural Studies, University of Warwick. Formerly lecturer in English Literature, University of Rome. Author of a number of books, including *Luigi Pirandello*, 1983, *Magdalena:*

Experimental Women's Theatre, 1988, the forthcoming *Shakespeare: The Elizabethan Plays*, and articles on theatre semiotics and women's theatre history. Co-author of *Bernhardt, Terry, Duse: The Actress in Her Time*, 1988. Compiler of *File on Pirandello*, 1989. Translator of plays, poems, and novels. **Essays:** Luigi Chiarelli; Gabriele D'Annunzio; Luigi Pirandello.

BEACHAM, Richard C. Senior Lecturer in Theatre Studies, University of Warwick. Author of *Adolphe Appia: Theatre Artist*, 1987, *Adolphe Appia: Essays, Scenarios and Designs*, 1989, *The Roman Theatre and Its Audience*, 1991, and articles on theatre history in *Theater*, *Theatre Research International*, *Maske und Kothurn*, *Opera Quarterly*, and *New Theatre Quarterly*. Editor of the video series *Ancient Theatre and Its Legacy*. Translator of Roman comedies. **Essays:** Menander; Plautus; Sophocles.

BENEDETTI, Jean. Adviser and consultant, School of Theatre, Manchester Polytechnic, Department of Performing Arts, Middlesex Polytechnic, and Academy of Theatre, Damascus, Syria. Formerly Principal, Rose Bruford College, Sidcup, Surrey, 1970–87; also actor and director. Author of *Gilles de Rais, A Biography*, 1972, *Stanislavski: An Introduction*, 1982, *Stanislavski: A Biography*, 1988, numerous articles on Stanislavski, and plays for radio and television. Editor of *The Moscow Art Letters*, 1992. Translator of Arrabal's *The Architect and the Emperor of Assyria*, 1971, and Brecht's *A Respectable Wedding*, 1980. **Essays:** Leonid Andreyev; A.K. Tolstoy.

BENNATHON, Joss. Freelance writer, drama teacher, actor, and community theatre worker. Contributor of articles to *Contemporary Dramatists*, 1988 and 1993. **Essays:** Shelagh Delaney; Mike Leigh.

BENNETT, Susan. Assistant Professor of English, University of Calgary, Alberta. Author of *Theatre Audiences: A Theory of Production and Reception*, 1990, and articles on contemporary British, Canadian, and American drama. **Essay:** Alice Childress.

BENSON, Eugene. Adviser. Professor of English, University of Guelph, Ontario; editor of the journal *Canadian Drama*. Former Chairman of the Writers' Union of Canada, 1983–84. Author of the plays *Joan of Arc's Violin*, 1972, *The Gunners' Rope*, 1973; the novels *The Bulls of Ronda*, 1976, *Power Game*, 1980; and the critical monograph *J.M. Synge*, 1980. Librettist of the operas *Heloise and Abelard*, 1973, *Everyman*, 1974, and *Psycho Red*, 1980. Co-editor (with L.W. Connolly) of *English-Canadian Theatre*, 1980, and *The Oxford Companion to Canadian Theatre*, 1989. **Essays:** John Coulter; John Murrell; James Reaney; Gwen Pharis Ringwood; John Millington Synge.

BENSON, Renate. Professor of German, University of Guelph, Ontario. Author of *Erich Kästner: Studien zu seinem Werk*, 1973, *German Expressionist Drama: Ernst Toller and Georg Kaiser*, 1985, and articles on Toller and Anne Hébert. Translator of Louis-H. Frechette's *Papineau*, 1982, M. Lescarbot's *The Theatre of Neptune*, 1982, E. Pacquin's *Riel*, and three plays by Anne Hébert. **Essays:** Wolfgang Borchert; Reinhard Goering; Walter Hasenclever; Georg Kaiser; Reinhard Sorge.

BERGHAUS, Günter. Lecturer in Drama, University of Bristol. Author of *Nestroy's Revolutionspossen*, 1978,

Gryphius' "Carolus Stuarolus", 1984, *The Reception of the English Revolution*, 1989, *Theatre and Film in Exile*, 1989, and articles on Italian Renaissance drama, German Baroque theatre, Austrian popular drama, and 20th-century avant-garde performance. **Essay:** Oskar Kokoschka.

BERKOWITZ, Gerald M. Professor of English, Northern Illinois University, DeKalb. Author of *David Garrick: A Reference Guide*, 1980, *Vanbrugh and the End of Restoration Comedy*, 1981, *New Broadways: Theatre Across America*, 1982, *American Drama of the 20th Century*, 1992, and articles on Shakespeare and modern British and American drama. Editor of *The Plays of David Garrick*, 1981. **Essays:** Robert Anderson; Ed Bullins; Paddy Chayevsky; Lorraine Hansberry; Neil Simon; Jean-Claude van Itallie; Thornton Wilder.

BILLINGTON, Michael. Adviser. Theatre Critic for *The Guardian* since 1971, and London Correspondent for *New York Times* since 1978; author and broadcaster. Formerly theatre, film, and television critic for *The Times*, 1965–71. Author of *The Modern Actor*, 1973, *How Tickled I am*, 1977, *Alan Ayckbourn*, 1983 (revised 1990), *Tom Stoppard: Playwright*, 1987, *Peggy Ashcroft*, 1988, and *One Night Stands*, 1993. Editor of *The Performing Arts*, 1980, *The Guinness Book of Theatre Facts and Feats*, 1982, and *Director's Shakespeare: "Twelfth Night"*, 1990. **Essay:** Alan Ayckbourn.

BISZTRAY, George. Professor of Hungarian Studies, University of Toronto; editor of *Hungarian Studies Review*. Author of *Marxist Models of Literary Criticism*, 1978, *Hungarian-Canadian Literature*, 1987, and numerous articles on Hungarian, Scandinavian, and comparative literature. Associate Editor, *National Theatre in Northern and Eastern Europe (1746–1900)*, 1991. **Essays:** József Katona; Imre Madách; Ferenc Molnár.

BLAHA, Franz G. Professor of English, University of Nebraska, Lincoln. Author of essays on Ludwig Anzengruber, Giraudoux, Beckett, Jack Gelber, Hammett, Parker, Leonard Sciascia, and popular literature. Translator of various works, including Peter Handke's *Kaspar*, 1969. **Essays:** Thomas Bernhard; Fritz Hochwälder.

BOOTH, Roy. Lecturer in English, Royal Holloway and Bedford New College, University of London. Author of articles on John Donne and Webster in *English*. **Essay:** John Lyly.

BRADBY, David. Adviser. Professor of Drama and Theatre Studies, Royal Holloway and Bedford New College, University of London. Formerly Reader in French Theatre Studies, University of Kent, Canterbury. Author of *Modern French Drama*, 1984 (revised 1991), *The Theatre of Robert Planchon* (Theatre in Focus series), *The Theatre of Michel Vinaver*, 1993 and various articles on French theatre. Co-author (with John McCormick) of *People's Theatre*, 1978, and (with David Williams) *Director's Theatre*, 1988. Editor of *Landmarks of French Classical Drama*, 1991. Co-editor (with Claude Schumacher) of *New French Plays*, 1989. Compiler of the bibliography *Adamov*, 1975. **Essay:** Arthur Adamov.

BRADISH, Gaynor F. Late Adjunct Associate Professor, Union College, Schenectady, New York. Director of many plays for drama workshops and university groups. Died 1989. **Essay:** Jack Richardson.

BRADY, Philip. Reader in German, Birkbeck College, University of London. Author of articles on German dramatists, German literature, and the literature, art, and photography of the 1920s. Co-editor of *Günter Grass's "Der Butt": Sexual Politics and the Male Myth of History*, 1990. **Essay:** Tankred Dorst.

BRAKE, Laurel. Lecturer in Literature, Centre for Extra-Mural Studies, Birkbeck College, University of London; co-editor, *Pater Newsletter*, Editor of *The Year's Work in English Studies*, from 1981, and *Investigating Victorian Journalism*, 1990. **Essay:** John Arden.

BRANDON, James. Adviser. Professor of Theatre, University of Hawaii, Honolulu. Previously taught at Michigan State University, East Lancing, 1961–68. Author of *Theatre in Southeast Asia*, 1967 and *Brandon's Guide to Theatre in Asia*, 1976. Advisory editor of *The Cambridge Guide to World Theatre*, 1988. Editor of *On Thrones of Gold: Three Javanese Shadow Plays*, 1970, *The Performing Arts in Asia*, 1971, *Traditional Asian Plays*, 1972, *Chushingura: Studies in Kabuki and the Puppet Theater*, 1982. Co-editor (with Tamako Niwa) of *Kabuki Plays*, 1966, and (with Rachel Baumer) *Sanskrit Drama in Performance*, 1981. Translator of *Kabuki: Five Classic Plays*, 1975.

BRIGGS, Anthony D.P. Professor of Russian Language and Literature, University of Birmingham. Author of *Mayakovsky: A Tragedy*, 1979, *Alexander Pushkin: A Critical Study*, 1983, *A Comparative Study of Pushkin's "The Bronze Horseman", Nekrasov's "Red-Nosed Frost" and Blok's "The Twelve"*, 1990, and the *Eugene Onegin*, 1993. Co- author of *A Wicked Story: The Rhetoric of "A Hero of Our Time"*, 1989. Editor of *Mikhail Lermontov: Commemorative Essays*, 1991. **Essays:** Mikhail Lermontov; Alexander Pushkin.

BRITZOLAKIS, Christina. Research Fellow in English Literature, St. Hilda's College, University of Oxford. Author of articles on the poetry of Ezra Pound, Eliot, and Yeats in *English Studies in Africa*, 1989, and on the literature of the 1930's in *CIEFL Bulletin*, 1989. **Essay:** T.S. Eliot.

BROOKS, William. Senior Lecturer in French, University of Bath. Author of *Bibliographie critique du théâtre de Quinault*, 1988, *Bellérophon*, 1990, *The Theatre in France Seen by Elizabeth Charlotte, Duchesse d'Orléans*, 1991, and articles on French theatre, the French *nouveau roman*, and British and French detective fiction for *Modern Language Review*, *Seventeenth-Century French Studies*, and other journals. **Essays:** Jean-François Regnard; Georges de Scudéry.

BROWN, John Russell. Adviser. Professor of Theatre, University of Michigan, since 1985. Formerly: Head of Drama, University of Birmingham, 1964–71; Professor of English, University of Sussex, 1971–82; Literary Manager and Associate of the National Theatre of Great Britain, 1973–88. Author of *Shakespeare and His Comedies*, 1957, *Shakespeare's "Macbeth"*, 1963, *Shakespeare's Plays in Performance*, 1966, *Effective Theatre*, 1969, *Shakespeare's "The Tempest"*, 1969, *Shakespeare's Dramatic Style*, 1970, *Theatre Language: A Study of Arden, Osborne, Pinter, Wesker*, 1972, *Free Shakespeare*, 1974, *Shakespeare in Performance*, 1976, *Discovering Shakespeare*, 1981, *Shakespeare and His Theatre*, 1982, *A Short Guide to Modern British Drama*, 1982, and *Shakespeares*, 1991. General Editor of the Stratford-upon-Avon Studies, 1960–67, and Theatre Production Studies. Editor of Shakespeare's *The Merchant of*

Venice, 1955, Webster's *The White Devil*, 1960, *The Duchess of Malfi*, 1965, and Shakespeare's *Henry V*, 1965.

BULL, John. Lecturer in English Literature and Drama, University of Sheffield. Author of *New British Political Dramatists*, 1984, *Stage Right: The Recovery of the Mainstream*, 1988, and articles on modern British drama. Editor of *Howard Brenton: Three Plays*, 1988, and *The Penguin Book of Pastoral Verse*, 1988. **Essays:** Edward Bond; Michael Frayn; Stephen Poliakoff.

BURGOYNE, Suzanne. Associate Professor of Theatre, University of Missouri, Columbia. Formerly Chair of Department of Fine and Performing Arts, Creighton University, Omaha, Nebraska. Author of articles in *Theatre Topics*, *Theatre Journal*, and *American Drama*. **Essay:** Paul Willems.

BURIAN, Jarka M. Adviser. Professor of Theatre, State University of New York, Albany. Author of *The Scenography of Josef Svoboda*, 1971, *Svoboda: Wagner*, 1983, and many articles on scenography, design, and Czechoslovakian theatre for *Theatre Journal*, *Theater Crafts*, *Drama Review*, *Modern Drama*, *American Theater*, and other journals. Contributor to *Contemporary Designers*, 1984, *Contemporary Dramatists* (fourth edition), 1988, and *The Cambridge Guide to World Theatre*, 1988.

BURNETT, Mark Thornton. Lecturer in English Literature, Queen's University, Belfast. Author of essays on Marlowe, Marston, and Renaissance literature for various publications, including *Studies in Philology*, *CIEFL Bulletin*, *L'Artiste témoin de son temps*, and *Criticism*. **Essays:** Thomas Dekker; Thomas Heywood.

BUTLER, Martin. Lecturer in English, University of Leeds. Author of *Theatre and Crisis (1632–42)*, 1984, *Volpone: A Critical Study*, 1987, and various articles on Tudor and Stuart theatre. Co-editor of *The Selected Plays of Ben Jonson 2*, 1989. **Essays:** Richard Brome; James Shirley.

CALANDRA, Denis. Professor of Theatre, University of South Florida, Tampa; playwright and theatre director. Formerly Senior Lecturer in Drama, Middlesex Polytechnic, London, and Lecturer in English and Drama at the University of Regensburg, West Germany. Author of *New German Dramatists*, 1983, and of articles on performance history, theory, and dramatic literature for *Theatre Quarterly*, *The Drama Review*, and *Modern Drama*. Translator and editor of *Rainer Werner Fassbinder: Plays*, 1985. **Essays:** Rainer Werner Fassbinder; Peter Handke.

CARLSON, Marvin A. Adviser. Sidney E. Cohn Professor of Theatre, Graduate School, City University of New York. Formerly taught at Cornell University, Ithaca, New York, 1961–79, and at Indiana University, Bloomington. Author of *The Theatre of the French Revolution*, 1966, *The French Stage in the Nineteenth Century*, 1972, *The German Stage in the Nineteenth Century*, 1972, *Goethe and the Weimar Theatre*, 1978, *The Italian Stage in the Nineteenth Century*, 1980, *Theories of the Theatre: A Historical and Critical Survey From the Greeks to the Present*, 1984, *The Italian Shakespearians: Performances by Ristori, Salvini and Rossi in England and America*, 1985, *Places of Performance: The Semiotics of Theatre Architecture*, 1989, *Theatre Semiotics*, 1990, and articles on theatre and drama in *Comparative Literature*, *Modern Drama*, *Educational Theatre Journal*, and other

periodicals. Translator of *André Antoine's Memories of the Théâtre-Libre*, 1964.

CARNEGIE, David. Senior Lecturer in Theatre and Film, Victoria University of Wellington, New Zealand. Author of articles on New Zealand theatre and Renaissance drama for various publications, including *Landfall*, *Australasian Drama Studies*, and *The Oxford Companion to the Theatre*. Editor of Shakespeare's *Henry IV, Part I*, 1970, Thomas Goffe's *The Raging Turke and the Courageous Turk*, 1974, and a forthcoming edition of the works of John Webster. **Essays:** Bruce Mason; Greg McGee; John Webster.

CARROLL, Dennis. Professor of Theatre, University of Hawaii, Manoa. Author of *Australian Contemporary Drama (1909–82): A Critical Introduction*, 1985, *David Mamet*, 1987, and articles on Australian and American theatre for *Modern Drama*, *Theatre Journal*, and essays collections. **Essays:** Alexander Buzol; Christopher Durang; John Guare; David Mamet; David Rabe; Sam Shepard; Patrick White.

CASCARDI, Anthony J. Associate Professor of Comparative Literature, Rhetoric, and Spanish, University of California, Berkeley. Author of *The Limits of Illusion: A Critical Study of Calderón*, 1984, *The Bounds of Reason: Cervantes, Dostoevsky, Flaubert*, 1986, and many essays on Lope de Vega, Tirso de Molina, Caldéron de la Barca, Cervantes, and literary theory, in *New Literary History*, *Modern Language Notes*, *Cervantes*, *The Review of Metaphysics*, and other publications. Editor of *Literature and the Question of Philosophy*, 1987. **Essays:** Pedro Calderón de la Barca; Miguel de Cervantes; Tirso de Molina; Lope de Vega Carpio.

CHAILLET, Ned. Producer, BBC Radio Drama, London. Formerly: staff member with the *Washington Star* and the *Times Literary Supplement*; deputy drama critic, *The Times*; London theatre critic, *The Wall Street Journal*, Europe. **Essay:** Steven Berkoff.

CLARKE, Janet. Part-time Lecturer in French, University of Lancaster. Formerly Lecturer, University of Exeter. Author of articles on the Evénégaud Theatre for *Seventeenth Century French Studies*. Editor of Thomas Corneille's *Circé*, 1989. **Essays:** Paul Claudel; René Guilbert de Pixérécourt.

CORBALLIS, Richard. Professor of English, Massey University, Palmerston North, New Zealand. Formerly theatre critic for *Dominion Sunday Times*. Author of *Stoppard: The Mystery and the Clockwork*, 1984, *"Rosencrantz and Guildenstern Are Dead", "Jumpers" and "Travesties": A Casebook*, 1990, and articles on English Renaissance drama and Tom Stoppard. Editor of *George Chapman's Minor Translations: A Critical Edition of His Renderings of Musaeus, Hesiod and Juvenal*, 1984. **Essays:** George Chapman; Lord Dunsany; Tom Stoppard.

COHN, Ruby. Adviser. Professor of Comparative Drama, University of California, Davis; on the editorial board of *Modern Drama*, *Theatre Journal*, and *Cambridge Guide to World Drama*. Author of *Samuel Beckett: The Comic Gamut*, 1962, *Currents in Contemporary Drama*, 1969, *Edward Albee*, 1969, *Dialogue in American Drama*, 1971, *Back to Beckett*, 1971, *Modern Shakespeare Offshoots*, 1976, *Just Play: Beckett's Theatre*, 1980, *From Desire to Godot*, 1987, *New American Dramatists 1960–1990*, 1991, and *Retreats from Realism*, 1992.

CORMAN, Brian. Associate Professor and Director of Graduate Studies in English, University of Toronto. Author of articles on Congreve, Etherege, Fielding, Shadwell, Samuel Johnson, Otway, Pope, Swift, Nahum Tate, and on genre theory and the history of drama and the novel (1660–1800). **Essays:** Susanna Centlivre; Colley Cibber; William Congreve; Thomas Shadwell; Nahum Tate; William Wycherley.

COTTIS, David. Freelance writer, director and lyricist; artistic director, Instant Classics Theatre Company. Formerly theatre critic for *City Wise* magazine, and part-time lecturer in drama and English Literature, University of East Anglia, Norwich. Author of several produced plays. **Essay:** Harvey Fierstein.

COUPE, W.A. Professor of German, University of Reading. Formerly Professor of German, University of Southampton. Publications include *The German Illustrated Broadsheet in the 17th Century* (2 vols.), 1966–67, *A 16th Century German Reader*, 1972, *German Political Satires (1918–45)*, 1985, *Germany Through the Looking Glass: A Cartoon Chronicle of the Federal Republic*, 1986, *German Political Satire (1849–1918)* (2 vols.), 1987, and various articles on German literature and the history of German cartoons. Co-author of *The Continental Renaissance*, 1971. **Essay:** Ludwig Tieck.

CRAIK, T.W. Emeritus Professor of English, University of Durham. Author of *The Tudor Interlude*, 1958, and *The Comic Tales of Chaucer*, 1964. Joint general editor of *The Revels History of Drama in the English Language*, editor of plays by Massinger, Marlowe, Beaumont and Fletcher, and Shakespeare, and co-editor of *Selected Poetry and Prose of Donne*, 1986. **Essay:** Nicholas Udall.

CRONACHER, Karen. Member of the School of Drama, University of Washington, Seattle. **Essay:** Ntozake Shange.

CROW, Brian. Lecturer in Drama and Theatre Arts, University of Birmingham. Previously taught drama at Ahmadu Bello University, Nigeria, and the University of Western Australia. Author of *Studying Drama*, 1983, and of articles on Ibsen, Soyinka, and African theatre for periodicals, including *Studies in Romanticism*, *The Journal of Commonwealth Literature*, *Theatre Research International*, and *Australasian Drama Studies*. **Essay:** Athol Fugard.

DACE, Tish. Adviser. Professor of English, Southeastern Massachusetts University, North Dartmouth; contributor to *Plays International*, *Plays and Players*, *Theater Week*, *Theatre Crafts*, *Other Stages*, *Village Voice*, New York *Times*, *American Theatre*, *Playbill*, and other periodicals. Author of *LeRoi Jones (Imamu Amiri Baraka): A Checklist of Works by and About Him*, 1971, *The Theatre Student: Modern Theatre and Drama*, 1973, and *Langston Hughes: Early Critical Responses*, 1991. **Essays:** Beth Henley; Charles Ludlam; Lanford Wilson.

DAVIS, Jim. Senior Lecturer in Theatre Studies, University of New South Wales, Sydney. Formerly Senior Lecturer in Drama, Roehampton Institute of Higher Education, London. Author of *John Liston Comedian*, 1985, and articles on 19th-century British theatre for *Theatre Notebook*, *New Theatre Quarterly*, and other publications. Editor of *Plays* by H.J. Byron, 1984. **Essays:** H.J. Byron; George Colman the Elder; W.S. Gilbert; Thomas Holcroft.

DAVISON, Peter. President of the Bibliographical Society. Former Professor of English, St. David's University College, Lampeter, and Professor of English & American Literature, University of Kent. Author of *Songs of the British Music Hall: A Critical Study*, 1971, *Popular Appeal in British Drama to 1850*, 1982, *Contemporary Drama and the Popular Dramatic Tradition in England*, 1983, *Hamlet* (Text and Performance series), 1985, *"Henry V": Masterguide*, 1987, and *"Othello": The Critical Debate*, 1988. Editor of *The Fair Maid of the Exchange*, 1963, Shakespeare's *Richard II*, 1964, *The Merchant of Venice*, 1967, *Henry IV, Part 1*, 1968, and *Henry IV, Part 2*, 1977, Marston's *The Dutch Courtesan*, 1968, *Facsimile of the Manuscript of Nineteen Eighty-Four*, 1984, *Sheridan: A Casebook*, 1986, *The Works of George Orwell* (20 vols.), 1986, and the forthcoming *The Word Encompassed: Studies for the Centenary of the Bibliographical Society, 1892–1992*. Contributing editor of *Theatrum Revivum*, 1972, *Literary Taste, Culture, and Mass Communication*, 1978–80, and *Year's Work in English Studies*, 1984–85, and has also contributed articles and reviews on bibliography, drama, and literature and society to many other periodicals. **Essay:** Samuel Foote.

DAWSON, Terence. Lecturer in English Literature, National University of Singapore. Has contributed articles on both English and French literature to numerous journals including *Modern Language Review*. **Essay:** Marguerite Duras.

DAY, Barbara. Freelance writer and translator; Secretary of the Jan Hus Educational Foundation. Author of articles and contributor to essay collections on Czech theatre. Translator of Ivan Klíma's *Games* (produced 1990) and the anthology *Czech Plays*, 1993. **Essays:** Karel Čapek; Václav Havel; Peter Karvaš; Milan Kundera; František Langer; Josef Topol; Josef Tyl.

DELETANT, Dennis. Senior Lecturer in Romanian Studies, School of Slavonic and East European Studies, University of London, Author of *Colloquial Romanian*, 1983. Editor of *Historians as Nation-Builders*, 1988. Translator of Marin Sorescu's *Vlad the Impaler*, 1987. **Essay:** Ion Luca Caragiale.

DELGADO, Maria M. Part-time tutor, Department of Spanish, University of Newcastle-on-Tyne. Formerly Special Lecturer in Drama, University of Hull. Author of articles on Spanish and Latin American theatre. Editor of *Three Plays* by Valle-Inclán, 1993. Translator of several produced Spanish plays. **Essay:** Alejandro Casona.

DIAMOND, Elin. Associate Professor of English, Rutgers University, New Brunswick, New Jersey. Author of *Pinter's Comic Play*, 1985, and articles on Pinter, Beckett, Churchill, Benmussa, and Duras in *Theatre Journal*, *Modern Drama*, *Comparative Drama*, and other journals. **Essay:** Adrienne Kennedy.

DiCENZO, Maria. Lecturer in English and Drama, Huron College, London, Ontario. Author of articles and reviews for *Canadian Theatre Review*, *Theatre History in Canada*, and *Theatre Journal*. **Essay:** John McGrath.

DOLBY, William. Lecturer in Chinese Studies, University of Edinburgh. Formerly Lecturer in Chinese, University of Malaysia, Kuala Lumpur. Author of *A History of Chinese Drama*, 1976, *Eight Chinese Plays*, 1978, and many other works on Chinese literature and theatre. **Essays:** Cao Yu; Tang Xianzu.

DOUCETTE, Leonard E. Professor of French, University of Toronto. Co-editor of *Theatre History in Canada*. Former Editor of *University of Toronto Quarterly*, and former Vice-President of the Association for Canadian Theatre History. Author of *Emery Bigot*, 1970, *Theatre in French Canada*, 1984, and many articles on French and French-Canadian theatre history, including major contributions to *The Canadian Encyclopaedia*, *The Cambridge Guide to World Theatre*, *The Oxford Companion to Canadian Literature*, and *The Dictionary of Literary Biography*. Co-editor (with Eugene Benson), *The Oxford Companion to Canadian Theatre*, 1989. **Essays:** Jean Barbeau; Marcel Dubé; Gratien Gélinas; Marie Laberge; Antonine Maillet; Michel Tremblay.

DOYLE, Peter. Lecturer in Russian Studies, University of Manchester. Author of several articles on Russian drama for *Journal of Russian Studies*, *Modern Language Review*, and other publications. **Essay:** Alexander Sukhovo-Kobylin.

DUNN, Tony. Senior Lecturer in Literature and Drama, University of Portsmouth (formerly Portsmouth Polytechnic); editor of the theatre journal *Gambit*. Author of articles on Howard Barker, Howard Brenton, and modern British theatre and society for various periodicals, including *Plays and Players*, *English-Amerikanische Studien*, *Toneel Teatraal*, and *Tribune*. **Essays:** Howard Brenton; David Mercer.

EDWARDS, Gwynne. Professor of Spanish, University College of Wales, Aberystwyth. Author of *Lorca: The Theatre Beneath the Sand*, 1980, *The Discreet Art of Luis Buñuel*, 1982, *Dramatists in Perspective: Spanish Theatre in the Twentieth Century*, 1985, and many articles on Spanish dramatists of the 17th and 20th centuries. Editor of *Lorca: Plays 1–3*, 1987–91, and *Calderón: Plays 1*, 1991. Translator of plays by Lorca for productions at the Bristol Old Vic, Battersea Arts Centre, London, and the Edinburgh Festival. **Essay:** Federico García Lorca.

EGAN, Robert G. Professor of Dramatic Art, University of California, Santa Barbara. Formerly Assistant Professor of English and Comparative Literature, Columbia University, New York, and director and actor for American regional and summer theatres. Author of *Drama Within Drama: Shakespeare's Sense of His Art*, 1975, a stage adaptation of Vonnegut's *Breakfast of Champions*, 1984, and articles on Shakespeare and other British dramatists. **Essay:** Sir George Etherege.

EILE, Stanislaw. Senior Lecturer in Polish, University of London. Formerly Associate Professor, University of Cracow, and Visiting Professor, University of Michigan. Author of the following books in Polish: a biography of Stefan Zeromski, 1961, *The Legend of Zeromski*, 1965, and *The Semantics of the Novel*, 1973, and of articles in English on Polish drama and literature for journals including *New Literary History*, *Soviet Jewish Affairs*, and the collection *Perspectives on Literature and Society in Eastern and Western Europe*, 1989. **Essay:** Stanisław Wyspiański.

FITZPATRICK, Peter. Senior Lecturer in English, Monash University, Clayton, Victoria. Author of *After the Doll: Australian Drama Since 1955*, 1979, *Williamson*, 1987,

and articles on Australian drama. **Essays:** Thomas Louis Esson; Stephen Sewell; David Williamson.

FLETCHER, Kathy. Visiting Assistant Professor of Theatre, University of Nebraska, Lincoln. Author of the play *Necessities*, and of many articles on Planché, pantomime, and Victorian popular theatre for *Women's Studies Encyclopaedia*, *Nineteenth Century Theatre*, *Victorian Britain: An Encyclopaedia*, *Theatre Studies*, and other publications. **Essays:** Susan Glaspell; Megan Terry.

FORSÅS-SCOTT, Helena. Tutor-Counsellor, Open University. Formerly Lector in Swedish, University of Aberdeen, and part-time tutor, Workers' Educational Association. Author of *Textual Liberation: European Feminist Writing in the Twentieth Century*, 1991, and articles on John Arden, Elin Wägner, Karin Boye, Sara Lidman, and Klara Johanson in *Modern Drama* and Scandinavian journals. **Essay:** August Strindberg.

FOSTER, Verna A. Professor of English, Loyola University, Chicago. Author of essays on Ford, Middleton, Fletcher, and Shakespeare for various journals including *Renaissance Drama*, *Renaissance Tragi-Comedy*, *Modern Language Quarterly*, and *Studies in English Literature*. **Essay:** John Ford.

FOULKES, Richard. Lecturer, Department of Adult Education, University of Leicester. Author of *The Shakespeare Tercentenary of 1864*, 1984, and articles on Samuel Phelp's *A Midsummer Night's Dream*, Helen Faucet, Ellen Terry, Terence Rattigan, The Royal Dramatic College, Charles Calvert's *Henry V*, and other topics for publications including *Theatre Notebook*, *Modern Drama*, *Theatrefile*, and *Shakespeare Survey*. Editor of *Shakespeare and the Victorian Stage*, 1986. **Essays:** Edward Bulwer-Lytton; Terence Rattigan.

GALE, Steven H. University Endowed Professor in Humanities, Kentucky State University. Formerly director of honours programme, Missouri Southern State College, and Fulbright Professor of British and American Literature and Drama. Author of *Butter's Going Up*, 1977, and *S.J. Perelman: A Critical Study*, 1987. Compiler of *Harold Pinter: An Annotated Bibliography*, 1978, and *S.J. Perelman: An Annotated Bibliography*, 1985. Editor of *Harold Pinter: Critical Approaches*, 1986, *Encyclopaedia of American Humorists*, 1988, *Critical Essays on Harold Pinter*, 1990, the forthcoming *S.J. Perelman: Critical Essays* and *Encyclopaedia of British Humorists*, and of many articles on modern British and American dramatists, Elizabethan and 19th-century theatre, poetry, and film. **Essays:** Jack Gelber; William Inge; Arthur Kopit; Harold Pinter.

GEROULD, Daniel. Adviser. Lucille Lortel Distinguished Professor of Theatre and Comparative Literature, Graduate School, City University of New York. Author of *Witkacy: Stanislaw Ignacy Witkiewicz as an Imaginative Writer*, 1981, and *Guillotine*, 1991. Co-author of *A Life of Solitude: Stanislaw Przybyszewska*, 1989. Editor of *America Melodrama*, 1983. Editor and translator of *Twentieth Century Polish Avant-Garde Drama*, 1977, *Gallant and Libertine: Divertissements & Parades of 18th Century France*, 1983, *Doubles, Demons and Dreamers: An International Collection of Symbolist Drama*, 1985, and *A Witkiewicz Reader*, 1991. **Essays:** Sławomir Mrożek; Stanisława Przbyszewska; Tadeusz Różewicz; Stanisław Witkiewicz.

GIANAKARIS, C.J. Professor of English and Theatre,

Western Michigan University, Kalamazoo. Co-founder and former co-editor of *Comparative Drama*, from 1966. Formerly Associate Dean, College of Arts and Sciences, Western Michigan University. Author of *Plutarch*, 1970, and *Foundations of Drama*, 1975. Editor of *Antony and Cleopatra*, 1969, *Peter Shaffer: A Casebook*, 1991. Co-editor (with Clifford Davidson and John H. Stroupe) of *Drama in the Middle Ages*, 1984, *Drama in the Twentieth Century*, 1985, and *Drama of the Renaissance*, 1986. Author of many essays for *Modern Drama*, *Drama Studies*, *Opera News*, *Theatre Journal*, *Comparative Drama*, *Theatre Week*, and other journals. **Essay:** Peter Shaffer.

GIBSON, Colin. Donald Collie Professor of English, University of Otago, Dunedin, New Zealand. Author of numerous articles on Massinger, Jonson, Ford, and Elizabethan drama for *Notes & Queries*, *Modern Language Review*, and *AUMLA Journal*. Editor of Shakespeare's *As You Like It*, 1965, *The Selected Plays of Philip Massinger*, 1978, *The Selected Plays of John Ford*, 1986, *Art and Society in the Victorian Novel: Essays on Dickens and His Contemporaries*, 1989, and *Witts Recreation (1640)*, 1989. **Essays:** Peter Barnes; Philip Massinger.

GILBERT, Reid. Professor of Drama, Capilano College, North Vancouver, British Columbia. Formerly director, Tamanhous Theatre. Author of the play *A Glass Darkly*, 1973, and numerous articles on Canadian and postmodern drama. **Essays:** Michael Cook; David Fennario; Sharon Pollock.

GILMAN, Donald. Professor and Co-Ordinator of French, Ball State University, Muncie, Indiana. Author of numerous articles in US and European journals on Ronsard, the theory of Renaissance dialogue, the moral play, Racine, Maeterlinck, Cocteau, Anouilh, and Mauriac. Editor of *Everyman and Company: Essays on the Theme and Structure of the European Moral Plays*, 1989. Co-editor of *Dialogues of Louis le Caron*, 1986. **Essay:** Jean Cocteau.

GÖMÖRI, George. Lecturer in Slavonic Studies, University of Cambridge. Author of *Polish and Hungarian Poetry 1945 to 1956*, 1966, *Cyprian Norwid*, 1974, and many articles on Polish, Hungarian, and comparative literature. Editor of *Forced March* by Miklós Radnóti, 1979, and *Night Song of the Personal Shadow* by György Petri, 1991. Co-editor of *Love of the Scorching Wind* by László Nagy, 1973. **Essays:** Witold Gombrowicz; Zygmunt Krasiński.

GONTARSKI, S.E. Professor of English, Florida State University; Editor of *The Journal of Beckett Studies*. Formerly Visiting Distinguished Professor of Comparative Literature, California State University, and Visiting Associate Professor of English, University of California, Riverside. Author of *The Intent of Undoing in Samuel Beckett's Dramatic Texts*, 1985. Editor of *Happy Days*, 1977, *On Beckett: Essays and Criticism*, 1986, and *The Theatrical Notebooks of Samuel Beckett: Endgame*, 1991. Co-editor (with Morris Beja and Pierre Astier) of *Samuel Beckett: Humanistic Perspectives*, 1983, and (with John Calder) *The Surrealist Reader*, 1991. Guest Editor of *Modern Fiction Studies*, 1983. **Essays:** Edward Albee; Samuel Beckett; Boris Vian.

GOODLIFFE, John. Senior Lecturer in Russian, University of Canterbury, Christchurch, New Zealand. **Essay:** Evgeny Shvarts.

GOODMAN, David G. Professor of Japanese and Comparative Literature, University of Illinois, Urbana-Champaign. Author of articles in *The Occupation of Japan: Arts and Culture*, 1988, and *The Cambridge Guide to World Theatre*, 1988. Editor of *After Apocalypse: Four Japanese Plays of Hiroshima and Nagasaki*, 1986, *Japanese Drama and Culture in the 1960s: The Return of the Gods*, 1988. Editor and Translator of *Land of Volcanic Ash* by Kubo Sakae, 1986, and *Five Plays by Kishida Kunio*, 1989. **Essays:** Kara Jūrō; Kinoshita Junji; Kishida Kunio; Kubo Sakae; Satoh Makoto; Terayama Shūji.

GORDON, Robert. Senior Lecturer in Drama, Goldsmiths' College, University of London; Co-director of Magna Carta Productions (theatre company). Formerly Lecturer in Drama and Theatre Studies, Royal Holloway College, University of London. Author of the plays *Red Earth* (produced 1985) and *Waterloo Road* (produced 1987), the critical study *Rosencrantz and Guildenstern Are Dead; Jumpers; The Real Thing* (Text and Performance series), 1991, and articles on Simon Gray, John Osborne, and the beginnings of the Avante-Garde. **Essay:** Joe Orton.

GORELL, Lynn Carbón. Assistant Professor and Curriculum Supervisor, Department of Spanish, Italian, and Portuguese, Pennsylvania State University, University Park. Former Editorial Assistant for *Latin American Theatre Review*, and President, Mid-American Association of Luso-Brazilianists. Author of *De lector a escritor: Desarrollo de la comunicación personal*, 1991, and articles on literature and foreign language study for *Modern Language Journal* and *Language Learning*. **Essays:** Jorge Andrade; Alfredo Dias Gomes.

GOSSIP, Christopher. Professor of French, University of New England, Armidale, New South Wales. Formerly Senior Lecturer, University College of Swansea, and Lecturer, University of Aberdeen. Author of *An Introduction to French Classical Tragedy*, 1981, and many articles on 17th-century French theatre. Editor of Thomas Corneille's *Stilicon*, 1974, and Cyrano de Bergerac's *La Mort d'Agrippine*, 1982. **Essay:** Thomas Corneille.

GOTTLIEB, Vera. Adviser. Professor of Drama, Goldsmiths' College, University of London; co-director of Magna Carta Productions (theatre company). Author of *Chekhov and the Vaudeville*, 1982, *Chekhov in Performance in Russia and Soviet Russia* (Theatre in Focus series), and articles on contemporary theatre, Chekhov, and farce for *Themes in Drama*, *New Theatre Quarterly*, and other periodicals. Translator and adaptor of *Chekhov Quartet* (produced London, Yalta, and Moscow, 1989). Co-director of *Red Earth* and *Waterloo Road*.

GRAHAM-WHITE, Anthony. Professor of Theatre, University of Illinois, Chicago. Former editor of *Educational Theatre Journal* (now *Theatre Journal*), 1972–75. Author of *The Drama of Black Africa*, 1974, and articles on traditional theatre, ritual in contemporary theatre, and Shakespeare's *Richard III* for *Yale/Theatre*, *Journal of Dramatic Theory and Criticism*, and other publications. **Essays:** John Pepper Clark; Bernard Dadié; Ann Jellicoe; George Lillo; Ngugi wa Thiong'o; George Peele; Efua Sutherland; Charles Wood; Kateb Yacine.

GRAVES, Peter. Head of Department of Scandinavian Studies, University of Edinburgh. Author of *Jan Fridegard: Lars Hard*, 1977, and articles on modern Swedish literature, particularly working-class writers of 1930s. Translator of

Linnaeus's *Lapland Journey* and Jacob Wallenberg's *My Son on the Galley*. **Essays:** Hjalmar Bergman; Stig Dagerman.

GRAY, Frances. Lecturer in Drama, University of Sheffield. Author of *John Arden*, 1982, *Noël Coward*, 1987, radio plays including *Mary*, 1983, *Neverland*, 1985, and *Dawnhorse*, 1991, and articles on radio drama, modern theatre, and women in comedy. Editor of *Second Wave at the Albany*. **Essay:** Caryl Churchill.

GROSVENOR MYER, Valerie. Lecturer in English, University of Sierra Leone. Author of *Margaret Drabble: Puritanism and Permissiveness*, 1974, *Jane Austen*, 1980, *Charlotte Brontë: Truculent Spirit*, 1987, *Culture Shock* (a novel), 1988, *A Victorian Lady in Africa: The Story of Mary Kingsley, 1989, Ten Great English Novelists*, 1990, *Margaret Drabble: A Reader's Guide*, 1991, and theatre and book reviews for *The Stage* and *Notes & Queries*. Editor of *Laurence Sterne: Riddles and Mysteries*, 1984, and *Samuel Richardson: Passion and Prudence*, 1986. **Essay:** Charles Reade.

GUTERRES, Maria. Lecturer in Portuguese, University of Liverpool; Assistant Editor, *Bulletin of Hispanic Studies*. Author of articles on the modern Portuguese novel and contemporary Portuguese drama. **Essays:** José Régio; Bernardo Santareno.

HALL, H. Gaston. Writer. Formerly: Reader in French, University of Warwick, Coventry; Professor of Romance Languages, City University of New York; and Lecturer in French Studies, Yale University, New Haven, Connecticut, University of Glasgow, and Monash University, Clayton, Victoria. Author of *Comedy in Context*, 1984, two other books on Molière, *Richelieu's Desmarets and the Century of Louis XIV*, 1990, two volumes of poetry, and numerous articles on French, English, Italian, and Spanish theatre and literature. Editor of *A Critical Bibliography of French Literature IIIA*, 1983, and of plays by Desmarets de Saint-Sorlin, Molière, Dorimond, and Cerou. Translator of *The French Renaissance* by F. Simone, 1970. **Essays:** Pierre Corneille; Alexandre Hardy; Jean Racine.

HANSFORD, James. Teacher of English, Royal Grammar School, Guildford; tutor in literature, Open University; tutor in literature, Surrey University Extra-Mural Department. Author of essays on Beckett for *The Journal of Beckett Studies* and *Studies in Short Fiction*, on Conrad for *The Conradian* and *Conradiana*, on Gabriel Josipovici and Alan Burns for *Prospice*, and a pamphlet on post-war British drama for the English Association. **Essay:** James Saunders.

HATTAWAY, Michael. Professor of English Literature, University of Sheffield. Formerly, Senior Lecturer in English, University of Kent. Author of *Elizabethan Popular Theatre*, 1982, and *Hamlet: The Critics Debate*, 1987. Editor of Jonson's *The New Inn*, 1985, and Shakespeare's *Henry VI (Parts 1 and 2)*, 1990–91. Co-editor (with A.R. Braunmuller) of *The Cambridge Companion to English Renaissance Drama*, 1990. **Essays:** John Fletcher; Ben Jonson; John Marston; Thomas Middleton.

HIDALGO CIUDAD, Juan Carlos. Research Fellow, University of Seville, Spain. Author of article on London Fringe theatre in the 1980's for *Nuevos mitos en la literatura Anglosajona*, 1990. **Essay:** [with Raphael Portillo] N.F. Simpson.

HOLLAND, Peter. Adviser. Judith E. Watson University Lecturer in Drama, Faculty of English, University of Cambridge. Author of *The Ornament of Action: Text and Performance in Restoration Comedy*, and of articles on Shakespeare, Chekhov, and contemporary theatre in *Shakespeare Survey*, *New Theatre Quarterly*, *Themes in Drama*, and other journals. Editor of *The Plays of Wycherley*, 1981. Co-editor (with Hanna Scolnicov) of *The Play out of Context*, 1988, and *Reading Plays*, 1991.

HOLT, Marion Peter. Professor of Theatre, City University of New York. Author of *The Contemporary Spanish Theatre: 1949–1972*, 1975, and numerous articles on modern Spanish drama and performance. Editor and translator of *Antonio Buero Vallejo: Three Plays*, 1985, and Buero's *Las Meninas*, 1987. Editor of *Drama Contemporary: Spain*, 1985. **Essay:** Antonio Buero Vallejo.

HOOVER, Marjorie L. Emeritus Professor of German and Russian, Oberlin College, Ohio. Formerly assistant Professor of German, Swarthmore College, Pennsylvania, and Honored Campbell Professor, Wells College, Aurora, New York. Author of *Meyerhold: The Art of Conscious Theater*, 1974, *Alexander Ostrovsky*, 1981, *Meyerhold and His Set Designers*, 1988, and articles and dictionary entries on Brecht, Russian theatre, and other topics. Editor of *Das Tagebuch der Anne Frank*, *Die Verwandlung* by Kafka, and *Two Plays* by Tankred Dorst. Translator (with George Genereux) of Erdman's *The Mandate* and *The Suicide*, 1975. **Essay:** Alexander Volodin.

HORTON, David. Senior Lecturer in German Studies, Manchester Metropolitan University (formerly Manchester Polytechnic). Author of *Grabbe und sein Verhältnis zur Tradition*, 1981, and articles on various aspects of modern German drama and short prose fiction. **Essay:** Dieter Forte.

HOUSE, Jane. Assistant Professor of Educational Theatre, New York University and Department of Drama, Vassar College, Poughkeepsie, New York. Formerly actress, and Director of the Institute on Western Europe Theatre Project, Columbia University, 1985–90. Author of articles on Italian theatre and translations for *Western European Theatre*, *LMDA Review*, and *Italian Journal*. Editor of *Political Theatre Today*, 1988. **Essays:** Ugo Betti; Diego Fabbri; Giuseppe Giacosa; F.T. Marinetti.

HOWARTH, William D. Adviser. Emeritus Professor of French, University of Bristol. Formerly Fellow and Tutor in Modern Languages, Jesus College, University of Oxford, 1948–66; Professor of Classical French Literature, Bristol University, 1966–88. Author of *Life and Letters in France: The Seventeenth Century*, 1965, *Sublime and Grotesque: A Study of French Romantic Drama*, 1975, *Molière: A Playwright and His Audience*, 1982, *Anouilh: Antigone*, 1983, *Corneille: Le Cid*, 1988, and many articles on French literature and theatre. Editor of *Comic Drama: The European Heritage*, 1978, and editions of works by Anouilh, Molière, La Chaussée, and Voltaire. Co-editor of *Molière: Stage and Study*, 1973. Member of the editorial board for the series *A Documentary History of the European Theatre* (15 vols.), 1989– . **Essays:** Alexandre Dumas *père*; Victor Hugo; Molière; Edmond Rostand; Alfred de Vigny.

HUGHES, Derek. Senior Lecturer in English, University of Warwick. Formerly Lecturer in English, Brock University, Ontario. Author of *Dryden's Heroic Plays*, 1981, and articles on Restoration drama in various journals, including *English*

Literary History, *Modern Language Review*, *Modern Language Quarterly*, and *Comparative Drama*. **Essay:** Thomas Otway.

HUNT, Hugh. Emeritus Professor of Drama, Manchester University. Formerly: Producer, Abbey Theatre, Dublin, 1935–38; Director, Bristol Old Vic, 1945–49; Artistic Director, Old Vic Company, London, 1949–53; Executive Director, Australian Elizabethan Trust, 1955–60; Professor of Drama, Manchester University, 1961–73; Artistic Director, Abbey Theatre, Dublin, 1969–71. Made Commander of the British Empire, 1971. Author of *Old Vic Prefaces*, 1954, *The Director in the Theatre*, 1954, *The Making of Australian Theatre*, 1960, *The Living Theatre*, 1961, *The Abbey: Ireland's National Theatre*, 1979, *Sean O'Casey*, 1980, various articles and contributions to collections of essays, and several plays, including *The Invincibles* and *In the Train*. **Essays:** Paul Vincent Carroll; Denis Johnston; Edward Martyn; Lennox Robinson; George Shiels.

HURRELL, John D. Emeritus Professor of English, University of Minnesota, Minneapolis; Advisory Editor, *Comparative Drama*, since 1966. Formerly: editor of *Drama Survey*, 1961–68; Associate Dean, College of Liberal Arts, 1964–68, and Associate Chair, English Department, 1981–84, University of Minnesota. Author of articles on Shakespeare, Ibsen, Chekhov, Whiting, medieval drama, and farce for various periodicals, including *Quarterly Journal of Speech*, *Educational Theatre Journal*, *College English*, and *Modern Drama*. Editor of *Two Modern American Tragedies*, 1961. **Essay:** T.W. Robertson.

IIZUKA, Naomi. Playwright. Author of several produced plays. **Essays:** Amiri Baraka; María Irene Fornés.

INNES, Christopher. Adviser. Professor of English, York University, North York, Ontario; general editor of the "Directors in Perspective" series for Cambridge University Press. Author of *Erwin Piscator's Political Theatre*, 1972, *Modern German Drama*, 1979, *Holy Theatre: Ritual and the Avant Garde*, 1981, *Edward Gordon Craig*, 1983, *Modern British Drama 1980–1990*, *Avant Garde Theatre*, 1993, and articles on drama and theatre.

JACK, R.D.S. Professor of Scottish and Medieval Literature, University of Edinburgh. Formerly Visiting Professor, University of Virginia, Charlottesville. Author of *The Italian Influence on Scottish Literature*, 1972, *Alexander Montgomerie*, 1985, *Scotland's Literary Debt to Italy*, 1986, *Patterns of Divine Comedy in Medieval Drama*, 1989, *Structured Thought: The Road to Never Land*, 1990, and many articles and reviews on Scottish literature for *Studies in Scottish Literature*, *Comparative Literature*, *Review of English Studies*, *Modern Language Review*, *Scottish Literary Journal*, and other periodicals. Editor of *Scottish Prose (1550–1700)*, 1971, *A Choice of Scottish Verse (1550–1660)*, 1978, and *The History of Scottish Literature: Volume 1, Origins to 1660*, 1988. Co-editor of *Robert Maclellan's "Jamie the Saxt"*, 1971, *The Art of Robert Burns*, 1982, *Sir Thomas Urquhart: "The Jewel"*, 1984, and *Leopardi: A Scottis Quair*, 1987. **Essay:** J.M. Barrie.

JOHNSON, Christopher. Lecturer in English, University of Winnipeg, Manitoba. **Essays:** David French; George F. Walker.

JOHNSON, Samantha. Researcher in 19th-century theatre and culture, Victoria Studies Centre, University of Leeds. **Essay:** Douglas Jerrold.

JORDAN, Robert. Professor of Theatre Studies, University of New South Wales, Kensington. Formerly Foundation Professor of Drama, University of Newcastle, Australia, and Reader in English, University of Queensland. Author of articles on Restoration theatre and society, and Jacobean, early 20th-century British, and Australian theatre and drama. Co-editor (with H.H.R. Love) of *The Works of Thomas Southerne* (2 vols.), 1988. **Essays:** George Farquhar; Thomas Southerne.

KEITH-SMITH, Brian. Senior Lecturer in German, University of Bristol. Author of *Johannes Bobrowski*, 1970, *Lothar Schreyer*, 1990, and essays on 20th-century writers, chiefly Hofmannsthal and Schreyer. Editor of *Essays on Contemporary German Literature*, 1966, *Anthologie neuerer deutscher Prosaerzählungen*, 1971, *German Men of Letters 6*, 1972, *Martin Luther*, 1983, *Das expressionistische Werk Lothar Schreyers*, 1985, *German Expressionism in the United Kingdom and Ireland*, 1986, *Büchner in Britain*, 1987, *Georg Büchner: Tradition and Innovation*, 1990, and *Bristol Austrian Studies*, 1990. **Essays:** Johann Wolfgang von Goethe; Heinar Kipphardt; Heinrich von Kleist; Carl Sternheim; Carl Zuckmayer.

KELLY, Veronica. Senior Lecturer in English, University of Queensland, Brisbane; co-editor of *Australasian Drama Studies*. Author of *Louis Nowra*, 1987, and articles on contemporary Australian drama for *Australasian Drama Studies*, *Kunapipi*, *Southerly*, and other periodicals. Editor of Garnet Walch's *Australia Felix; or, Harlequin, Laughing Jackass and the Magic Bat*, 1988. **Essay:** Louis Nowra.

KENDLE, Burton S. Professor of English, Roosevelt University, Chicago. Author of articles on D.H. Lawrence, John Cheever, William March, Tennessee Williams, Paul Bowles, and other writers, and on screenwriting. **Essay:** Simon Gray.

KENNEDY, Dennis. Professor of Theatre Studies, University of Pittsburgh; general editor of the series "Pittsburgh Studies in Theatre and Culture". Author of *Granville Barker and the Dream of Theatre*, 1985, *Looking at Shakespeare*, 1991, a number of plays, and essays on Shakespeare in performance and modern playwrights, including Shaw and Barker. Editor of *Plays by Harley Granville Barker*, 1987. **Essay:** Harley Granville-Barker.

KING, Adele. Professor of French, Ball State University, Muncie, Indiana. Formerly: Reader in French, Ahmadu Bello University, Nigeria; Lecturer in French, universities of Lagos and Ibadan, Nigeria. Author of *Camus*, 1964, *Proust*, 1968, *Paul Nizan: Écrivain*, 1976, *The Writings of Camara Laye*, 1980, *French Women Novelists: Defining a Female Style*, 1989, articles on women writers in France and the Third World, African literature in French, Camus, and study guides on Camus, Camara Laye, Ernest Hemingway, Graham Greene, and Ibsen. Editor *Camus's "L'Etranger": Fifty Years On*. **Essay:** Albert Camus.

KING, Bruce. Adviser. Adjunct Professor of English, University of Guelph, Ontario; general editor of the series "Modern Dramatists" and "English Dramatists". Formerly Professor and Visiting Professor of English at universities in the United States, Canada, Scotland, France, Israel, Nigeria, and New Zealand. Author of *Dryden's Major Plays*, 1966, *Marvell's Allegorical Poetry*, 1977, *The New English Literatures: Cultural Nationalism in a Changing World*, 1980, *History of Seventeenth Century English Literature*, 1988, *Modern Indian Poetry in English*, 1987/1989, *Coriolanus*, 1989, *Three Indian Poets: Ezekiel, Ramanujan and Moraes*, 1991, and *V.S. Naipaul*, 1993. Editor of *Twentieth Century Interpretations of "All for Love"*, 1968, *Dryden's Mind and Art*, 1969, *Introduction to Nigerian Literature*, 1971, *Literatures of the World in English*, 1974, *A Celebration of Black and African Writing*, 1976, *West Indian Literature*, 1979, *Contemporary American Theatre*, 1991, *The Commonwealth Novel Since 1960*, 1991, and *The Later Fiction of Nadine Gordimer*, 1993. **Essay:** Derek Walcott.

KING, Kimball. Member of the Department of English, University of North Carolina, Chapel Hill; managing editor of *Southern Literary Journal*. Author of the bibliographies *Ten Modern Irish Playwrights*, 1979, and *Ten Modern American Playwrights*, 1982, and of *Augustus Baldwin Longstreet*, 1984, and *Sam Shepard: A Casebook*, 1989. **Essay:** Lillian Hellman.

KING, Pamela M. Senior Lecturer in English and Director of the Centre for Medieval Studies, Queen Mary and Westfield College, University of London. Editor of *Church Monuments Society Newsletter*, 1985–88. Author of essays on Medieval drama and culture for various publications, including *Medieval English Theatre*, *Drama and Philosophy* (Themes in Drama series), *Studies in Scottish Literature*, as well as reviews for *The Times Higher Education Supplement*, *Theatre Notebook*, and *Medieval Theatre*. Co-editor (with Richard Beadle) of *York Mystery Plays: A Selection in Modern Spelling*, 1984. **Essay:** John Rastell.

KNOWLES, A.V. Senior Lecturer in Russian Studies, and Assistant Director of Combined Honours (Arts), University of Liverpool. Author of *Turgenev*, 1988, and articles on Russian literature, history, and drama. Co-author of *Anglescina za vsakogar*, 1962. Editor of *Tolstoy: The Critical Heritage*, 1978, *Turgenev's Letters*, 1983 and Ostrovsky's *The Storm*, 1988. **Essays:** Denis Fonvizin; Alexander Ostrovsky.

KREMER, Manfred K. Professor of German and Chair of Department of Languages and Literatures, University of Guelph, Ontario. Author of *Die Satire bei Johann Beer*, 1964, and articles on Günter Grass, Lessing, Thelens, Christian Weis, and satire for various publications including *German Quarterly*, *Lessing and the Enlightenment*, 1986, *Der moderne deutsche Schelmenroman*, 1986, *Absurda Comica*, 1988, and *Simpliciana*. Editor of Johann Beer's *Der kurtzweilige Bruder Blau-Mantel*, 1979. **Essays:** Günter Grass; Martin Walser.

LAMONT, Rosette C. Professor of French and Comparative Literature, Queen's College, and at the Graduate School of the City University of New York. Author of *The Life and Works of Boris Pasternak*, 1964, *De Vive Voix*, 1971, *Ionesco*, 1973, *The Two Faces of Ionesco*, 1978, and various articles on literature and drama. Editor, *Women on the Verge*, 1992, and (with Norman Simms) *New Literary Continents*, 1992. Contributing Editor for *Performing Arts Journal* and *Centrepoint*. **Essays:** Eugène Ionesco; Jean Tardieu; Michel Vinaver.

LANGE, Bernd-Peter. Professor of English, University of Oldenburg, Germany. Former Editor of *Gulliver* and *German-English Yearbook*. Author of *Charles Dickens*, 1969,

George Orwell, 1975, *The Theory of Genres*, 1979, *Orwell: 1984*, 1982, *Cultural Studies*, 1984, *The Spanish Civil War in British and American Literature*, 1988, *Classics in Cultural Criticism 1: Britain*, 1990, and essays on Edward Bond, Steve Gooch, George Orwell, and William Beckford. **Essay:** John Dryden.

LAWLEY, Paul. Senior Lecturer in English, University of Plymouth (formerly Polytechnic South West). Author of essays and reviews for *Contemporary Dramatists*, 1982 and subsequent editions, *The Journal of Beckett Studies*, *Modern Drama*, *Modern Fiction Studies*, *Theatre Journal*, *Modern Language Review*, and the collection *"Make Sense Who May": Essays on Samuel Beckett's Later Works*, 1988. **Essay:** Stewart Parker.

LAYERA, Ramón. Professor in the Department of Spanish and Portuguese, Miami University, Oxford, Ohio. **Essay:** Rodolfo Usigli.

LEACH, Robert. Lecturer in Drama and Theatre Arts, University of Birmingham. Formerly Director of Cannon Hill Community Theatre, Birmingham. Author of *Theatre For Youth*, 1970, *The Wellsbourne Tree: A Musical Documentary Play*, 1975, *How to Make a Documentary Play*, 1975, *Theatre Workshop Series*, 1977–83, *The Punch and Judy Show*, 1985, and *Vsevolod Meyerhold*, 1989. **Essays:** Alexander Blok; Vsevolod Ivanov; Sergei Tretyakov; Vsevolod Vishnevsky.

LEAVITT, Charles L. Emeritus Professor of English, College of Insurance, New York; Adjunct at Fairleigh Dickinson University, Teaneck, New Jersey; lifetime deputy governor, American Biographical Institute Research Association. Author of 10 literature study guides for Monarch Press, 1963–64. **Essay:** Langdon Mitchell.

LEWIS, Peter. Reader in English, University of Durham. Author of *John Gay: The Beggar's Opera*, 1976, *Orwell: The Road to 1984*, 1984, *John Le Carré*, 1985, *Fielding's Burlesque Drama*, 1987, *Eric Ambler*, 1990, and many articles on Restoration and 18th-century drama, and contemporary literature. Editor of *The Beggar's Opera*, 1973, *Poems '74*, 1974, *Papers of the Radio Literature Conference 1977*, 1978, and *Radio Drama*, 1981. Co-editor (with Nigel Wood) of *John Gay and the Scriblerians*, 1988. **Essays:** Henry Fielding; John Gay; Sir John Vanbrugh.

LEWIS, Tim. Director of Modern Languages Teaching Centre, University of Sheffield. **Essays:** Aimé Césaire; Robert Pinget.

LÖB, Ladislaus. Reader in German, University of Sussex, Brighton. Author of *Mensch und Gesellschaft bei J.B. Priestley*, 1962, (with E.R. Baer) *Der arme Millionär: A Radio Course in German*, 1967, 1977, and *From Lessing to Hauptmann: Studies in German Drama*, 1974. Editor of *Grabbe über seine Werke*, 1991. **Essay:** Christian Dietrich Grabbe.

LOMAX, Derek W. Late Emeritus Professor of Hispanic Studies, University of Birmingham. Author of *La orden de Santiago, 1170–1275*, 1965, and *The Reconquest of Spain*, 1978. Co-editor of *The English in Portugal* by Fernão Lopes, 1988, and *God and Man in Medieval Spain*, 1989. Died 1992. **Essays:** Jacinto Benavente y Martínez; José Echegaray.

LONDRÉ, Felicia Hardison. Adviser. Curators' Professor of Theatre, University of Missouri, Kansas City; dramaturg for Missouri Repertory Theatre. Author of *Tennessee Williams*, 1979, *Tom Stoppard*, 1981, *Federico García Lorca*, 1984, *The History of World Theatre 2*, 1991, and articles on European and American theatre history for essay collections, casebooks, and various journals including *Theatre Research International*, *Theatre History Studies*, *Theatre Journal*, *Theater Week*, *Slavic and East European Arts*, *Studies in Popular Culture*, and *Comparative Drama*. **Essay:** Christopher Hampton.

LOWE, N.J. Lecturer in Classics, Queen Mary and Westfield College, University of London. Author of the forthcoming *The Classical Plot*, and articles on Greek and Latin literature, especially comedy, for various journals, including *Themes in Drama*, *Bulletin of the Institute of Classical Studies*, and *Classical Quarterly*. **Essays:** Aristophanes; Terence.

LUCAS, Valerie. Lecturer in Drama, Roehampton Institute, London. **Essay:** Elizabeth Inchbald.

MacDONALD, James. Fellow in Drama, University of Exeter, and play-reader for Northcott Theatre, Exeter. Formerly Associate Editor of *The Freethinker*. Reviewer and author of articles on humanism and the arts for *The Freethinker*, 1977–81. **Essays:** George S. Kaufman; Sidney Kingsley; Arthur Laurents; John Van Druten.

MACKERRAS, Colin. Professor and Director, Key Centre for Asian Language Studies, Griffith University, Brisbane. Formerly Chairman, School of Modern Asian Studies, Griffith University, 1979–85, and Foreign Expert, Beijing Institute of Foreign Languages, 1964–66, 1986, and 1990. Author of *The Rise of Peking Opera*, 1972, *The Chinese Theatre in Modern Times*, 1975, *The Performing Arts in Contemporary China*, 1981, and numerous articles on China and Chinese theatre. Editor of *Chinese Theater from Its Origins to the Present Day*, 1983, and *Chinese Drama: A Historical Perspective*, 1990. **Essay:** Guan Hanqing.

MALLINSON, G. Jonathon. Lecturer in French and Fellow of Trinity College, University of Oxford. Formerly Fellow and Director of French Studies, Pembroke College, University of Cambridge. Author of *The Comedies of Corneille: Experiments in the Comic*, 1984, *Molière: L'Avare*, 1988, and articles on French 17th- and 18th-century theatre and prose fiction. **Essays:** Pierre-Augustin Beaumarchais; Pierre Marivaux; Voltaire.

MARKER, Frederick J. Adviser. Professor of English, University College, University of Toronto. Author of articles for *The Revels History of Drama in English, 1750–1800*, 1975, *Ibsen and the Theatre*, 1980, *Ibsen Yearbook*, *Theatre Survey*, *Theatre Notebook*, *Scandinavian Review*, *Modern Drama*, and other publications. Co-author (with Lise-Lone Marker) of *The Scandinavian Theatre: A Short History*, 1975, *Edward Gordon Craig and "The Pretenders": A Production Revisited*, 1981, *Ingmar Bergman: Four Decades in the Theatre*, 1982. Editor of *The Heibergs*, 1971, and Hans Christian Anderson's *Den nye Barselstue*, 1975. Co-editor and translator of *Ingmar Bergman: A Project for the Theatre*, 1983.

McCALLUM, John. Senior Lecturer in Theatre Studies and Director of the Australian Theatre Studies Centre, University of New South Wales, Kensington. Author of many articles on recent Australian drama. **Essays:** Ray Lawler; John Romeril.

McGILLICK, Paul. Lecturer in Applied Linguistics, University of Sydney; theatre critic for *Australian Financial Review*. Formerly Editor of *New Theatre Australia*. Author of *Jack Hibberd*, 1988, and numerous monographs and articles on theatre and the visual arts. **Essays:** Alma De Groen; Jack Hibberd.

McNAUGHTON, Howard. Reader in English, University of Canterbury, Christchurch, New Zealand. Author of *Bruce Mason*, 1976, *New Zealand Drama*, 1981, and the section on the novel in *The Oxford History of New Zealand Literature*, 1991. Editor of *Contemporary New Zealand Plays*, 1976, and *James K. Baxter: Collected Plays*, 1982. **Essays:** Maxwell Anderson; Brendan Behan; Dion Boucicault; Zona Gale; Ben Hecht; Hrotsvitha; Nathaniel Lee; Peter Nichols; Marsha Norman; Clifford Odets; Elmer Rice; Victorien Sardou; William Saroyan; Eugène Scribe.

McVAY, Gordon. Reader in Russian, University of Bristol. Author of *Esenin: A Life*, 1976, *Isadora and Esenin*, 1980, and of articles on Sergei Esenin, Chekhov, the peasant poets, and the Imaginists for journals, and play reviews for *Plays and Players*. **Essays:** Nikolai Erdman; Maxim Gorky.

MEECH, Anthony. Lecturer in Drama, University of Hull. Author of articles on German theatre (especially of the former DDR), and a forthcoming history of German theatre for Cambridge University Press. **Essays:** Ernst Barlach; Volker Braun; Georg Büchner; Gotthold Ephraim Lessing.

MEISSNER, Ulrich. Producer, BBC World Service (German Language Service). Formerly German Language Assistant, Queen Mary and Westfield College, University of London, and Lecturer, English Department, University of Mannheim. Author of articles on late 17th-century and modern British drama. Translator of Vincent O'Sullivan's *Shuriken: A Play*. **Essay:** William Davenant.

MESERVE, Walter J. Adviser. Distinguished Professor of Theatre and English, Graduate School, City University of New York; co-editor of *Journal of American Drama and Theatre*. Formerly Professor of Theatre and Drama and Director of the Institute for American Studies, Indiana University, Bloomington. Author of *An Outline History of American Drama*, 1965, *Robert Sherwood: Reluctant Moralist*, 1970, *An Emerging Entertainment: The Drama of the American People to 1828*, 1977, *American Drama* (Volume 8 of the *Revels History*), with others, 1977, *American Drama to 1900: A Guide to Reference Sources*, 1980, and *Heralds of Promise: The Drama of the American People During the Age of Jackson 1829–1849*, 1986. Editor of *The Complete Plays of William Dean Howells*, 1960, *Discussions of Modern American Drama*, 1966, *American Satiric Comedies*, 1969, *Modern Drama from Communist China*, 1970, *The Rise of Silas Lapham by Howells*, 1971, *Studies in Death of a Salesman*, 1972, and *Modern Literature from China*, 1974. Compiler of *Who's Where in the American Theatre*, 1990. **Essays:** James Nelson Barker; Philip Barry; George Henry Boker; Augustin Daly; Clyde Fitch; Edward Harrigan; James A. Herne; Sidney Howard; James Steele Mackaye; Robert Sherwood; Rabindranath Tagore.

MILES, Patrick. Senior Research Associate, Gonville and Caius College, University of Cambridge. Formerly Russian literary consultant and translator. National Theatre of Great Britain, 1977–80, and director of the Cambridge Young Chekhov Company, 1974–77. Author of *Chekhov on the*

British Stage, 1909–1987, 1987. Translator (with Harvey Pitcher) of *Chekhov: The Early Stories, 1883–87*. **Essays:** Lyudmila Petrushevskaya; Alexander Vampilov.

MILLS, Ken. Lecturer in German, University of Bristol. Formerly Assistant Lecturer in German, University of Cambridge, and Fellow, Downing College, Cambridge. Author of articles on 19th-century German and Austrian literature and drama. **Essay:** Friedrich Hebbel.

MITCHELL, Michael. Lecturer in German, University of Stirling. Author of *Peter Hacks: Drama for a Socialist Society*, 1990, and articles on German and Austrian drama and literature. **Essay:** Peter Hacks.

MOE, Christian H. Professor and Chair of Theatre, Southern Illinois University, Carbondale; member of the Dramatists Guild. Previously taught at Flinders University, South Australia, and Vita International Center, Luxembourg. Author of articles on dramatists and children's writers for *Twentieth-Century Children's Writers*, 1989, *Encyclopedia of Literary Characters*, 1990, *Twentieth-Century Romance and Historical Writers*, 1990, *Contemporary Dramatists*, 1988, and in various journals. Co-author of *Creating Historical Drama*, 1965, *The Strolling Players*, 1971, *When Santa Claus Came to Simpson's Crossing*, 1975, *Three Rabbits White*, 1979, *Tom Sawyer: An Adaptation*, 1979. Co-editor of *Six New Plays for Children*, 1971, and *Eight Plays for Youth*, 1991. **Essays:** S.N. Behrman; Paul Green; John Howard Lawson.

MORASH, Christopher. Lecturer in English, St. Patrick's College, Maynooth, Ireland. Author of *Thornton Wilder's "Our Town"* (York Notes series), 1988, *The Hungry Voice: The Poetry of the Irish Famine*, 1989, and articles on Irish literature. **Essays:** Thomas Kilroy; Thomas Murphy.

MORGAN, Margery. Emeritus Reader in English and Theatre Studies, University of Lancaster. Formerly Lecturer in English, Royal Holloway College (University of London), and Reader in English, Monash University, Australia. Author of *A Drama of Political Man: A Study of the Plays of Harley Granville Barker*, 1961, *The Shavian Playground*, 1972, *York Notes on "Pygmalion"*, 1980, *Bernard Shaw* (Writers and Their Work), 1982, *John Galsworthy* (Writers and Their Work), 1982, *York Notes on "Major Barbara"*, 1982, *August Strindberg*, 1985, *York Handbook on Drama*, 1987, and articles on Granville-Barker, Shaw, Wesker, Gregan McMahon, and other topics. Editor of Granville-Barker's *The Madras House*, 1977, and Shaw's *The Doctor's Dilemma*, 1981. Compiler of *File on Shaw*, 1989, and *File on Wilde*, 1990. **Essays:** John Galsworthy; John Osborne; George Bernard Shaw; David Storey; Arnold Wesker.

MULRYNE, J.R. Professor of English and Comparative Literary Studies, and Chairman of the Graduate School of Renaissance Studies, University of Warwick, Coventry. Formerly Reader in English Literature, University of Edinburgh, 1962–77. Author of essays of Middleton, Kyd, Shakespeare, Webster, Sir Thomas Browne, and W.B. Yeats. Editor of Middleton's *Women Beware Women*, Webster's *The White Devil*, Kyd's *The Spanish Tragedy*, and *An Honoured Guest: New Essays on W.B. Yeats*. Co-editor of *War Literature and the Arts in Sixteenth Century Europe*, *English and Italian Theatre of the Renaissance*, *Italian Renaissance Festival and Its European Influence*, and *Theatre and Government under the Early Stuarts*. Joint editor, compiler, and publisher (with Margaret Shewring) of *This Golden*

Round: The Royal Shakespeare Company at the Swan. **Essay:** William Shakespeare.

NICHOLSON, Steve. Lecturer in the Workshop Theatre, University of Leeds. Author of theatre reviews and articles on British political theatre for *New Theatre Quarterly*. **Essays:** Trevor Griffiths; David Hare.

NICOLAEFF, Ariadne. Freelance writer and translator. Translator of *Selected Plays of Aleksei Arbuzov*, 1982, and further plays by Chekhov, Arbuzov, Volodin, and other modern Russian playwrights. **Essay:** Alexei Arbuzov.

NIGRO, Kirsten F. Associate Professor of Spanish, University of Cincinnati, Ohio; member of editorial board of *Latin American Theatre Review*; editor, *Studies in Latin American, Chicano and U.S. Latino Theatre*. Former Associate Professor, Arizona State University and Assistant Provost, Washburn University of Topeka. Author of articles on modern Latin American theatre and literature, women writers and feminist theory, José Triana, Vicente Leñero, Griselda Gambaro, Luisa Josefina Hernández, Carlos Fuentes, José Ignacio Cabrujas, and Rosario Castellanos for *Latin American Theatre Review*, *Hispania*, *Revista de estudios hispánicos*, *Theatre Journal*, *Theatre Annual*, and other journals. **Essays:** Jorge Díaz, Luisa Josefina Hernández; José Triana.

Ó hAODHA, Micheál. Writer, critic, broadcaster, and playwright. Formerly productions director, then assistant director (Radio), RTE, and Director and Chair, Abbey Theatre, Dublin. Author of *Plays and Places*, 1961, *Dlína Feirme*, 1965, *The Abbey—Then and Now*, 1969, *Theatre in Ireland*, 1973, *The Abbey in Pictures*, 1983, *The Weaver's Grave*, 1984, and *The Importance of Being Micheál: A Portrait of MacLiammóir*, 1990. Editor of *The O'Casey Enigma*, 1980. **Essays:** Padraic Colum; George Fitzmaurice; John B. Keane; T.C. Murray.

OAKLEY, R.J. Lecturer in Spanish and Portuguese, University of Birmingham. Author of articles on Spanish drama and Luso-Brazilian prose fiction. Co-editor of *The English in Portugal* by Fernão Lopes, 1988. **Essays:** Leandro Fernández de Moratín; Juan Ruiz de Alarcón.

OSBORNE, John. Professor of German, University of Warwick, Coventry. Formerly: Alexander von Humboldt Research Fellow, University of Göttingen, 1972–73 and 1975–76; Visiting Professor, University of Metz, 1985–86. Author of *The Naturalist Drama in Germany*, 1971, *J.M.R. Lenz: The Renunciation of Heroism*, 1975, *Die Meininger: Texte zur Rezeption*, 1980, *The Meiningen Court Theatre (1866–90)*, 1988, and articles on German drama and theatre of the 18th and 19th centuries. **Essays:** Gerhart Hauptmann; Jakob Lenz; Hermann Sudermann.

PARKER, Dorothy. Associate Professor of English, Victoria College, University of Toronto; Editor of the journal *Modern Drama*. Editor of *Modern American Drama: Miller, Williams, Albee, and Shepard* (reprinted essays from *Modern Drama*), 1986. **Essay:** George Ryga.

PATTERSON, Michael. Adviser. Senior Lecturer in Theatre Studies, University of Ulster, Coleraine, since 1987. Formerly: Lecturer in German, Queens University of Belfast, 1965–70; Lecturer in Drama, University College of North Wales, Bangor, 1970–74; Senior Lecturer in Drama and

Theatre Arts, University of Leeds, 1974–87. Author of *German Theatre Today*, 1976, *The Revolution in German Theatre, 1900–1933*, 1981, *Peter Stein*, 1981. Editor of *Büchner: The Complete Plays*, 1987.

PERKINS, Juliet. Lecturer in Portuguese and Brazilian Studies, King's College, London. Author of *The Feminine in the Poetry of Herberto Helder*, 1991, and articles on Portuguese-African folk theatre and contemporary Portuguese poetry. **Essays:** Almeida Garrett; Antonio José da Silva; Gil Vicente.

PIASECKI, Andy. Freelance writer. Formerly Lecturer in Drama, Royal Holloway and Bedford New College, University of London, 1981–90. Author of articles on Elizabethan theatre for *The Shakespeare Handbook*, 1987, and on modern British drama for *The Bloomsbury Guide to English Literature*, 1989. Compiler of *File on Lorca*, 1991. Contributor to *Plays International*. **Essays:** Christopher Marlowe; Cyril Tourneur.

POPENHAGEN, Ludvika. Researcher and teacher of acting, formerly at University of California, Santa Barbara; also professional actress. Has previously taught acting in Australia, Lithuania, and France. **Essays:** Jacques Audiberti; Fernand Crommelynck.

POPENHAGEN, Ron. Member of the Department of Theatre and Film, University of Kansas, Lawrence; professional actor working in the United States and Australia. **Essays:** René de Obaldia; André Obey.

PORTILLO, Raphael. Lecturer in English, University of Seville. Author of many articles on the theory of drama, Medieval and Renaissance English theatre, and contemporary playwrights. Co-author (with Jesús Casado) of *English-Spanish, Spanish-English Dictionary of Theatre Terms*, 1986, and *Abecedario del teatro*, 1988. Co-author (with P. Hidalgo, A. Usandizaga, and B. Dietz) of *Historia crítica del teatro inglés*, 1988. Editor of *Estudios literarios ingleses: Shakespeare y el teatro de su epoca*, 1987. **Essay:** [with Juan Carlos Hidalgo Ciudad] N.F. Simpson.

PRATT, Karen. Lecturer in French, King's College, University of London. Formerly Lecturer in French, Goldsmiths' College, University of London, 1983–93. Author of *Meister Otte's "Eraclius" as an Adaptation of "Eracle" by Gautier d'Arras*, 1987, a critical study of *Mort Artu*, and articles on comparative literature, medieval translation and rhetorical theory, and late-medieval pro- and anti-feminist French texts. Editor of *Shifts and Transpositions in Medieval Narrative*, 1993. Co-editor of *Woman Defamed and Woman Defended*, 1992. **Essays:** Adam de la Halle; Jean Bodel.

PRONKO, Leonard C. Professor of Theatre, Claremont College, Pomona, California. Author of *The World of Jean Anouilh*, 1961, *Avant-Garde*, 1962, *Eugène Ionesco*, 1965, *Theatre East and West*, 1967, *Guide to Japanese Drama*, 1973, *Georges Feydeau*, 1975, *Eugène Labiche and Georges Feydeau*, 1982, and articles for many journals including *Tulane Drama Review*, *Bucknell Review*, *Educational Theatre Journal*, *Comparative Drama*, and *Japan Quarterly*. **Essays:** Georges Feydeau; Eugène Labiche.

RABEY, David Ian. Lecturer in Drama, University College of Wales, Aberystwyth. Formerly Lecturer in English and Drama, Trinity College, Dublin. Author of *British and*

Irish Political Drama in the Twentieth Century, 1986, *Howard Barker: Politics and Desire*, 1989, and articles on David Edgar, Shakespeare, and Timberlake Wertenbaker for *Modern Drama*, *Critical Quarterly*, and other publications. **Essays:** Howard Barker; David Rudkin; Timberlake Wertenbaker.

RADFORD, Colin. Professor of French and Director of the School of Modern and Medieval Languages, Queen's University, Belfast. Author of several books, articles, and reviews. **Essays:** Jean Anouilh; Jean Giraudoux; Armand Salacrou.

RANALD, Margaret Loftus. Professor of English, Queen's College, City University of New York. Author of *The Eugene O'Neill Companion*, 1984, *Shakespeare and His Social Context: Essays in Osmotic Knowledge and Literary Interpretation*, 1987, *John Webster*, 1989, and numerous articles and reviews on Shakespeare, Webster, O'Neill, research methodology, computer applications, historiography, bibliography, biography, and theatre history. Associate Editor of *International Bibliography of Theatre*, 1982–85. **Essay:** Eugene O'Neill.

RAYFIELD, Donald. Professor of Russian, Queen Mary and Westfield College, University of London. Author of *Chekhov: The Evolution of His Art*, 1975, *Nikolay Przhevalsky: Explorer of Central Asia*, 1976, and many articles on Russian literature and theatre. **Essays:** Fyodor Sologub; Leo Tolstoy.

READ, Leslie du S. Lecturer in Drama, University of Exeter, Devon. Contributor to *The Cambridge Guide to World Theatre*, 1988, *The Cambridge Encyclopaedia*, 1990, and to the forthcoming *Literature and Criticism: A New Century Guide*. **Essays:** Robert Greene; Thomas Kyd.

REYNOLDS, Bonnie Hildebrand. Professor of Latin American Literature, University of Louisville, Kentucky. Author of *Space, Time and Crisis: The Theatre of René Marqués*, 1988, and of articles on Marqués, Roberto-Ramos-Perea, and Latin American theatre. **Essay:** René Marqués.

RICHARDS, Francesca H.A. Freelance lecturer, writer, and translator. Formerly Lecturer at universities in Sardinia and Paris, 1986–89. **Essay:** Nathalie Sarraute.

RICHARDS, Kenneth. Adviser. Professor of Drama and Director of University Theatre, University of Manchester; previously taught at universities of Ljubljana (Yugoslavia), Trondheim (Norway), and Uppsala, and has been a Fellow of the Folger Shakespeare Library, Washington, DC, and the Huntington Library, California. Author of *Comedy*, 1977, many articles on drama and theatre for *The Oxford Companion to the Theatre*, *The Cambridge Guide to World Theatre*, 1988, and various journals. Co-author (with Laura Richards) of *The Commedia dell'Arte: A Documentary History*, 1991. Editor of *Nineteenth Century British Theatre*. Co-editor (with Peter Thomson) of *The Eighteenth Century English Stage*, 1973, and (with David Meyer) *Western Popular Theatre*, 1978. **Essays:** W.H. Auden (and Christopher Isherwood); James Bridie; Harold Brighouse; Noël Coward; Christopher Fry; Carlo Goldoni; Carlo Gozzi; Stanley Houghton; D.H. Lawrence; Somerset Maugham; J.B. Priestley; John Whiting.

RICHARDS, Laura. Lecturer in the Department of

Modern Languages, University of Salford. Co-author (with Kenneth Richards) of *Commedia dell'Arte: A Documentary History*, 1991. **Essays:** Vittorio Alfieri; Eduardo De Filippo; Dario Fo.

RICHARDS, Sandra L. Assistant Professor of Drama and Director of the Committee on Black Performing Arts, Stanford University, California. Author of the introduction to *Center Stage: An Anthology of Twenty-One Black American Plays*, 1981, and articles on Amiri Baraka, the actor Bert Williams, and Nigerian playwrights in *Theatre Journal*, *Mime*, and *San Francisco Theatre*. **Essay:** Charles Fuller.

RORRISON, Hugh. Senior Lecturer in German, University of Leeds. Author of *Erwin Piscator: Politics on the Stage in the Weimar Republic*, 1987, introductions to *Brecht: Plays* (3 vols. to 1993), regular play reviews for *Plays and Players*, *Drama*, and *Plays International*, and articles on Peter Handke, Wolfgang Bauer, Heiner Müller, Botho Strauss, Ernst Stern, Ibsen, and the Berliner Schaubühne. Editor of plays by Brecht, including *Mother Courage and Her Children*, 1983, *The Caucasian Chalk Circle*, 1984, and *Life of Galileo*, 1986. Translator of Piscator's *The Political Theatre*, 1978, Pavel Kohout's *The Maple Tree Game* (produced 1990), and Wedekind's *The Lulu Plays* (produced 1991). **Essays:** Bertolt Brecht; Heiner Müller; Botho Strauss; Ernst Toller.

ROTHENBERG, John. Lecturer in French, University of Leeds. Author of articles on Jean Anouilh, Rochefort, and Beckett for *Modern Languages* and other publications. **Essay:** Michel de Ghelderode.

ROY, Donald. Professor of Drama, University of Hull. Formerly Lecturer in French at the universities of Glasgow and St. Andrews. Author of articles on 17th- and 18th-century French theatre and 19th-century British theatre. Editor of *Molière: Five Plays*, 1982, and *Plays by James Robinson Planché*, 1986. **Essays:** Alain-René Lesage; James Robinson Planché.

SANDERS, Leslie C. Associate Professor of English, Atkinson College, York University, Toronto. Author of *The Development of Black Theater in America*, 1988, and articles on Langston Hughes, Ed Bullins, and black writers in Canada. **Essay:** Langston Hughes.

SARLÓS, Robert K. Professor of Dramatic Art, University of California, Davis. Author of *Jig Cook and the Provincetown Players: Theatre in Ferment*, 1982, and of many articles on O'Neill, the Provincetown Players, and European and American theatre history. **Essay:** István Örkény.

SCHRANK, Bernice. Professor of English Language and Literature, Memorial University of Newfoundland, St. Johns. Author of articles on Sean O'Casey, Denis Johnston, Brian Friel, and Mavis Gallant in *Modern Drama*, *Irish University Review*, and other publications. Co-editor of *Literature and Folk Culture: Ireland and Newfoundland*, 1977. **Essays:** Israel Horovitz; Sean O'Casey.

SCHUMACHER, Claude. Reader in Theatre Studies, University of Glasgow; editor of the journal *Theatre Research International*. Author of *Jarry and Apollinaire*, 1984, and articles on Dürrenmatt, Frisch, Appia, Zola, the theatre of the absurd, and other aspects of literature and theatre. Editor of *40 Years of Mise en Scène*, 1986, *Marivaux: Plays*, 1988,

and *Artaud on Theatre*, 1990. Co-editor (with David Bradby) of *New French Plays*, 1989. **Essays:** Guillaume Apollinaire; Fernando Arrabal; Alexandre Dumas *fils*; Alfred Jarry; Émile Zola.

SCOBBIE, Irene. Former Reader and Head of Department of Scandinavian Studies, University of Aberdeen. Author of *Pär Lagerkvist: An Introduction*, Stockholm, 1962, *Sweden: Nation of the Modern World*, 1972, *Pär Lagerkvist: Gäst hos verkligheten*, 1974, and many articles on Lagerkvist, Strindberg, and Swedish drama and literature. Editor of *Essays on Swedish Literature: From 1880 to the Present Day*, 1979, *An Anthology of Swedish Poetry from 1880 to the Present Day*, 1980, *Aspects of Modern Swedish Literature*, 1988, *Proceedings of the 8th Biennial Conference of Teachers of Scandinavian Studies, Edinburgh*, 1989. Translator of Stig Claesson's *Ancient Monuments*, 1980, and (with Susan Davies) B. Henriksson's *Not For Sale*, 1983. **Essay:** Pär Lagerkvist.

SCOTT, Virginia. Professor, Department of Theater, University of Massachusetts, Amherst. Formerly editor of *Theatre Journal*. Author of *The Commedia dell'Arte in Paris, 1644–1697*, 1990, and numerous articles on *commedia dell'arte*, pantomime, Molière, and other subjects. **Essays:** Jean Mairet; Philippe Quinault; Jean de Rotrou.

SENELICK, Laurence. Adviser. Fletcher Professor of Drama, Tufts University, Medford, Massachusetts. Formerly: member of the US-Soviet Commission on Theatre and Dance Studies; Fellow, Wissenschaftskolleg zu Berlin; Fellow, John Simon Guggenheim Foundation. Author of *Gordon Craig's Moscow Hamlet*, 1982, *Serf Actor: The Life and Art of Mikhail Shchepkin*, 1984, *Anton Chekhov*, 1985, *The Age and Stage of George L. Fox*, 1988, and *The Prestige of Evil: The Murderer as Romantic Hero*. Editor of *British Music-Hall, 1840–1923: A Bibliography*, 1981, *Russian Dramatic Theory from Pushkin to the Symbolists*, 1981, *Russian Satiric Comedy*, 1983, *Cabaret Performance in Europe, 1890–1920*, 1989, *National Theatre in Northern and Eastern Europe, 1743–1900*, 1991, and *Wandering Stars: Russian Emigré Theatre*, 1992.

SILVESTER, Robert. Visiting Professor, University of Southern Maine, and freelance researcher; formerly Head of Drama, King Alfred's College, Winchester. Compiler of *United States Theatre: A Bibliography from the Beginning to 1990*, published by Motley Press, 1993. **Essay:** Henry Arthur Jones.

SIMMONS, James. Writer in Residence, Queen's University, Belfast. Formerly Senior Lecturer in Drama and Anglo-Irish Literature, University of Ulster, 1968–84. Author of seven volumes of poetry, 1956–86, and *Sean O'Casey*, 1982. Founding editor of *The Honest Ulsterman*, 1968. Has made several recordings of songs. **Essay:** W.B. Yeats.

SINGH, G. Emeritus Professor of Italian, Queen's University, Belfast. Formerly Reader in English, Bocconi University, Milan, and Lecturer in English, Muslim University, Aligarh, India. Author of *Leopardi and the Theory of Poetry*, 1964, *Leopardi e L'Inghilterra*, 1968, *Poesie di Thomas Hardy*, 1968, *Eugenio Montale: A Critical Study*, 1973, *Ezra Pound*, 1979, *T.S. Eliot: Poeta, drammaturgo e critico*, 1985, and articles in various English and Italian journals and magazines. Translator (with Ezra Pound) of *Poesie di Kabir*, 1966. **Essays:** Kalidasa; Torquato Tasso.

SKLOOT, Robert. Professor of Theatre and Drama, University of Wisconsin, Madison. Formerly Fulbright Professor of American Drama in Israel, 1980–81, and Vienna, 1988–89. Author of *The Darkness We Carry: The Drama of the Holocaust*, 1988. Editor of *The Theatre of the Holocaust*, 1982. **Essay:** August Wilson.

SKRINE, Peter. Professor of German and Head of Department, University of Bristol. Formerly Senior Lecturer in German, University of Manchester. Author of *The Baroque*, 1978, *Hauptmann, Wedekind and Schnitzler*, 1989, and numerous articles on German and European drama in *Modern Language Review*, *German Life and Letters*, *Jahrbuch für internationale Germanistik*, *Wolfenbütteler Arbeiten zur Barockforschung*, and *Bristol Austrian Studies*. Co-author (with Lilian Furst) of *Naturalism*, 1971. **Essays:** August von Kotzebue; Friedrich von Schiller; Arthur Schnitzler; Frank Wedekind.

SMITH, Christopher. Senior Lecturer in French and Comparative Literature, University of East Anglia. Author of *Jean Anouilh: Life, Work and Criticism*; *Alabaster, Bikinis and Calvados*, 1985; and numerous articles on drama and translation. Editor of Jean de Taille's *Dramatic Works*, Jacques de la Taille's *Alexandre*, A. Montchrestien's *Two Tragedies*, and of the journal *Seventeenth-Century French Studies*. **Essays:** Isaac Bickerstaff; Robert Bolt; John O'Keeffe.

STANLEY, Noel. Freelance writer, specialising in Japanese history and culture. **Essay:** Chikamatsu Monzaemon.

STARKEY, Paul. Lecturer in Arabic, University of Durham. Author of *From the Ivory Tower: A Critical Study of Tawfiq al-Hakim*, 1987. **Essay:** Tawfiq al-Hakim.

STEWART, Mary E. Fellow and University Lecturer in German, Robinson College, University of Cambridge. Contributor to *Rejection and Emancipation: Writing in German-Speaking Switzerland 1945–91*, edited by M. Butler and M. Pender, 1991, and to *Beyond Realism*, edited by D. Midgley, 1993. **Essay:** Franz Xaver Kroetz.

STRANG, Ronald W. Lecturer in Drama and Theatre Studies, University of Kent, Canterbury. Formerly Lecturer in Drama, University College of North Wales, Bangor. Author of articles on Orton and British theatre, and reviewer of books for *Theatre Research International* and *Notes & Queries*. **Essays:** Alan Bennett; Ben Travers.

SWAIN, Elizabeth. Associate Professor of Theatre, Barnard College, New York, and professional actress. Has also taught at New York University and City College, New York. Author of *David Edgar: Playwright and Politician*, 1984, *Notable Women in American Theatre*, 1989, and articles for *Contemporary Dramatists*, 1988, and for various US publications. **Essays:** Aphra Behn; David Edgar.

SZOKA, Elzbieta. Writer and researcher on Latin American theatre. **Essay:** Nelson Rodrigues.

TAYLOR, Diana. Associate Professor of Spanish and Comparative Literature, Dartmouth College, Hanover, New Hampshire. Author of *Theatre of Crisis: Drama and Politics in Latin America*, 1990, and of numerous articles on modern theatre, especially that of Latin America, for *Theatre Journal*,

Performing Arts Journal, *Latin American Theatre Review*, *Gestos*, and other journals. Editor of books on Fernando Arrabal, and Griselda Gambaro and José Triana. **Essays:** Emilio Carballido; Griselda Gambaro; Eduardo Pavlovsky.

TAYLOR, Val. Lecturer in Drama, University of East Anglia; freelance theatre director. Formerly Lecturer in Drama, Roehampton Institute, London, 1988–92. Author of *Hamlet* (study guide), 1993, essays for *The Politics of Theatre and Drama*, 1992, and *Boxed Sets*, edited by Jeremy Ridgman (forthcoming), and articles on Timberlake Wertenbaker and Britain's National Theatre for *Critical Survey*. **Essay:** Martin Sherman.

THANIEL, George. Professor and Director of Modern Greek Studies, University of Toronto. Author of three books of poetry, *The Lepidopterist of Anguish, Nikos Kachtitsis*, 1981 (in Greek), *Homage to Byzantium: The Life and Work of Nikos Gabriel Pentzikis*, 1983, *Splendour and Anguish: The Work of Nikos Kachtitsis (1926–1970)*, 1986 (in Greek), and many articles on the Greek poet George Seferis. **Essays:** Nikos Kazantzakis; Pandelis Prevelakis.

THODY, Philip. Professor of French Literature, University of Leeds. Past positions include visiting professorships at the universities of Western Ontario, California (at Berkeley), Harvard, Adelaide, Canterbury (New Zealand), Western Australia, and Virginia. Author of *Albert Camus*, 1957, *Jean-Paul Sartre*, 1960, *Albert Camus, 1913–1960*, 1961, *Jean Anouilh*, 1968, *Jean Genet*, 1968, *Jean-Paul Sartre*, 1971, *Aldous Huxley*, 1973, *A True Life Reader for Children and Parents*, 1977, *Dog Days in Babel*, 1979, *Faux Amis and Keywords*, 1985, *Marcel Proust*, 1987, *Albert Camus*, 1989, *French Caesarism from Napoleon to Charles de Gaulle*, the forthcoming *Jean-Paul Sartre, Novelist*, many articles on French language and literature, and a series of teaching tapes on French authors. Editor of Sartre's *Les Séquestrés d'Altona*, 1965, Camus' *Caligula*, 1973, and Christiane Rochefort's *Les Petits Enfants du siècle*, 1982. Translator of works by Camus, Orwell, Lucien Goldmann, and Jacqueline de Romilly. **Essays:** Henry de Montherlant; Jean-Paul Sartre.

THOMSEN, Bjarne T. Lecturer in Scandinavian Studies, University of Edinburgh. **Essays:** Ludwig Holberg; Kaj Munk.

THOMSON, Peter. Adviser. Professor of Drama, University of Exeter, Devon. Author of *Shakespeare's Theatre*, 1983, revised 1992, *Shakespeare's Professional Career*, 1991, and articles on Shakespeare, 19th-century theatre, and other topics. Co-author (with Jan Needle) of *Brecht*, and (with Gāmini Salgādo) *The Everyman Companion to the Theatre*, 1985. Editor of Shakespeare's *Julius Caesar*, 1970, Malcolm Elwin's *Lord Byron's Family*, 1975, and *Plays by Dion Bouicicault*, 1984. Co-editor (with Kenneth Richards) of *Nineteenth Century British Theatre*, 1971, and *The Eighteenth Century English Stage*, 1973. **Essay:** George Colman the Younger.

TROIANO, James J. Professor of Modern Languages, University of Maine, Orono. Author of several articles on Arlt and Latin American literature and theatre. **Essay:** Roberto Arlt.

TRUSSLER, Simon. Senior Lecturer in Drama, Goldsmiths' College, University of London; editor of *New Theatre Quarterly*. Formerly editor of *Theatre Quarterly*. Author of *The Plays of John Osborne*, 1969, *The Plays of*

John Whiting, 1972, *The Plays of Harold Pinter: An Assessment*, 1973, *Edward Bond*, 1976, and articles on theatre bibliography and classification. Co-author (with Glenda Leeming) of *The Plays of Arnold Wesker*, 1971. General editor of Swan Theatre Plays and Writers on File series. Editor of *Burlesque Plays of the Eighteenth Century*, 1969, *Royal Shakespeare Company Yearbook* (annually since 1978), *New Theatre Voices of the Seventies*, 1982. **Essay:** Richard Cumberland.

TSUBAKI, Andrew T. Professor of Theatre, Film, East Asian Languages and Cultures, and Director of International Theatre Studies Centre, University of Kansas, Lawrence. Area Editor for *Asian Theatre Journal*. Former Chairman, East Asian Languages and Cultures, University of Kansas, and Chairman, Asian Theatre Programme of American Theatre Association. Author of articles on Japanese theatre for *The Journal of Aesthetics and Art Criticism*, 1971, and *Educational Theatre Journal*, 1977. Co-author of article for *Indian Theatre: Traditions and Performance*, 1990. Contributing editor for the Asian section of *Theatre Companies of the World*, 1986. Has directed many productions of Japanese, Classical Greek, and Shakespearian plays. **Essay:** Zeami.

VINCENT, Paul. Specialist in Dutch culture. Formerly Senior Lecturer in Dutch, University College, London University. Co-editor of *Modern Dutch Studies*, 1988. **Essay:** Herman Heijermans.

VISSER, Colin Wills. Professor and Associate Chairman, English Department, and Director of Graduate Center for the Study of Drama, University of Toronto. Formerly Director, University College Drama Programme. Author of articles on Restoration and 18th-century theatre for *Theatre Survey*, *Theatre Notebook*, and *Theatre Research International*. Contributor to *The London Theatre World*, 1980. **Essays:** Edward Ravenscroft; Nicholas Rowe; Sir Richard Steele.

WAAL, Carla. Professor of Theatre, University of Missouri, Columbia. Formerly Associate Professor of Theatre, University of Georgia, Athens. Author of *Johanne Dybwad: Norwegian Actress*, 1967, *Harriet Bosse: Strindberg's Muse and Interpreter*, 1990, and articles on Ibsen, and Scandinavian and American theatre, for publications including *Southern Speech Communication*, *Educational Theatre Journal*, *Theatre History Studies*, *Encyclopaedia of World Literature in the Twentieth Century*, and *Theatre Companies of the World*. Translator of some of Bjørg Vik's writings for *Scandinavian Studies*, *Scandinavian Review*, and the anthologies *An Everyday Story*, 1984, and *Scandinavian Women Writers*, 1987. **Essay:** Nordahl Grieg.

WALCOT, Peter. Professor in the School of History and Archaeology, University College of Wales, Cardiff; joint editor of the journal *Greece and Rome*. Formerly Visiting Professor, University of California, 1982, and Webster Lecturer, Stanford University, California, 1991. Author of *Hesiod and the Near East*, 1966, *Greek Peasants, Ancient and Modern*, 1970, *Greek Drama in Its Theatrical and Social Context*, 1976, *Envy and the Greeks, A Study of Human Behaviour*, 1978, and articles and reviews on Greek, Roman, and Near Eastern literature and culture for various periodicals, including *Journal of Hellenic Studies*, *Classical Quarterly*, *Times Literary Supplement*, and *Classical Review*. **Essay:** Seneca.

WALKER, David H. Professor of French, and Head of the Department of Modern Languages, University of Keele. Formerly assistant editor, *Theatre Research International*. Author of *André Gide*, 1990, and essays on Camus, Gide, Robbe-Grillet, and John Fowles. Editor of Genet's *Le Balcon*, 1982. Translator of French drama for BBC radio, and of Henry Becque's *The Scavengers*, 1986. **Essays:** Émile Augier; Henri Becque; Eugène Brieux; Jean Genet; Alfred de Musset.

WALTON, J. Michael. Reader in Theatre History, University of Hull; general editor, Methuen Classical Texts in Translation. Author of *Greek Theatre Practice*, 1980, *The Greek Sense of Theatre: Tragedy Reviewed*, 1984, *Living Greek Theatre: A Handbook of Classical Performance and Modern Production*, 1987, and of articles for *Theatre Research International*, *New Theatre Magazine*, *Asian Theatre Bulletin*, *Plays and Players* and other periodicals. Editor of *Craig on Theatre*, 1983, *Euripides: Plays 1* (also translator of *The Bacchae*), and *Sophocles: Plays 2* (also translator of *Women of Trachis*). **Essays:** Aeschylus; Euripides.

WARING, Alan G. Head of Department of Russian and Slavonic Studies, University of Sheffield. Author of *Science Russian Grammar*, 1967, *Comprehensive Russian*, 1985, and articles on Slavonic language and literature. Translator of works by Griboyedov and Mayakovsky. **Essay:** Alexander Griboyedov.

WEBER, Carl. Professor of Drama, Stanford University, California. Author of articles on Brecht, Müller, and other aspects of modern German theatre for *Performing Arts Journal*, *The Drama Review*, and other publications. Translator of plays by Müller. **Essay:** Martin Sperr.

WEINER, Jeremy. Freelance writer and historian. **Essay:** Solomon Ansky.

WELLAND, Dennis. Emeritus Professor, University of Manchester, and Chairman of Contact Theatre Company (since 1984). Formerly Professor of American Literature, University of Manchester, 1965–83, and founder-editor of *Journal of American Studies*, 1967. Author of *Wilfred Owen: A Critical Study*, 1960 (revised 1978), *Arthur Miller*, 1961 (several subsequent revisions), *Mark Twain in England*, 1978, and numerous articles on English and American literature. Editor of *The U.S.A.: A Companion to American Studies*, 1974 (revised 1977 and 1987). **Essays:** Marc Connelly; William Dunlap; Arthur Miller; William Vaughn Moody; Anna Cora Mowatt; Tennessee Williams.

WELLS, Stanley. Adviser. Professor of Shakespeare Studies, and Director of the Shakespeare Institute, University of Birmingham, since 1988; general editor (with Gary Taylor) of "The Oxford Shakespeare" series; editor of *Shakespeare Survey*, since 1981. Formerly: Reader in English, University of Birmingham, 1962–77; Senior Research Fellow, Balliol College, Oxford, 1980–88. Author of *Literature and Drama, Royal Shakespeare*, 1977, *Shakespeare: An Illustrated Dictionary*, 1978, *Shakespeare: The Writer and His Work*, 1978, and many articles on Shakespeare and Renaissance drama. Editor of *Thomas Nashe: Selected Writings*, 1964, Shakespeare's *A Midsummer Night's Dream*, 1967, *Richard II*, 1969, *Shakespeare: A Reading Guide*, 1969, *The Comedy of Errors*, 1972, the Select Bibliographical Guides *Shakespeare*, 1973 (revised as *Shakespeare: A Bibliographical Guide*, 1990) and *English Drama Excluding Shakespeare*, 1975, *The Cambridge Companion to Shakespeare Studies*, 1986, *The Oxford*

Anthology of Shakespeare, 1987. General editor, with Gary Taylor, of *The Complete Oxford Shakespeare*, 1986. Co-editor (with R.L. Smallwood) of Dekker's *The Shoemaker's Holiday*, 1979, and (with others) *William Shakespeare: A Textual Companion*, 1987.

WELLWARTH, George E.   Adviser. Professor of Theatre and Comparative Literature, State University of New York. Binghampton, since 1970; co-editor, *Modern International Drama*, since 1967. Author of *The Theatre of Protest and Paradox*, 1964, *Modern Drama and the Death of God*, 1986. Editor of *The New Wave Spanish Drama*, 1970, *German Drama Between the Wars*, 1972, *Themes of Drama*, 1972, *Spanish Underground Drama*, 1972, *New Generation Spanish Drama*, 1974, *Three Catalan Dramatists*, 1974. Co-editor of *Modern French Theatre*, 1964, *Modern Spanish Theatre*, 1968. Translator of *Concise Encyclopedia of the Modern Drama*, 1964.

WHITTON, Kenneth S.   Professor of European Cultural Studies and German, University of Bradford. Formerly: President, British Association of German Teachers; Chair, British Modern Languages Association, and Guest Professor, University of Hamburg. Author of *The Theatre of Friedrich Dürrenmatt*, 1980, *Dietrich Fischer-Dieskau: Mastersinger*, 1981, *Zusammen*, 1981, *Lieder: An Introduction to German Song*, 1984, *Dürrenmatt: Reinterpretation in Retrospect*, 1990, and many articles on German, Austrian, and Swiss literature and music. Translator of *Schubert: A Biographical Study of His Songs* by Dietrich Fischer-Dieskau, 1976. **Essay:** Friedrich Dürrenmatt.

WIECZOREK, John P.   Lecturer in German, University of Reading. Formerly Assistant Lecturer, University of Stirling, and Lecturer, University of St. Andrews and University College Galway. Author of several articles on German literature. **Essays:** Rolf Hochhuth; Ödön von Horváth; Peter Weiss.

WILLIAMS, Margaret.   Adviser. Senior Lecturer in Theatre Studies, University of New South Wales, Kensington, Australia. Author of *Drama* (Writers and Their Work series), *Australia on the Popular Stage, 1829–1929*, 1983, and many articles on Australian drama for *Contemporary Australian Drama*, 1981, *The Cambridge Guide to World Theatre*, 1988, and various periodicals. **Essay:** Dorothy Hewett.

WILLIAMS, Simon.   Professor of Dramatic Art, University of California, Santa Barbara. Previously taught at universities in Sweden, Austria, Libya, Iran, the universities of Regina and Alberta (Canada) and Cornell (USA). Author of *German Actors of the Eighteenth and Nineteenth Centuries: Idealism, Romanticism and Realism*, 1985, *Shakespeare on the German Stage, 1587–1914*, 1990, and articles on Irish theatre, 18th- and 19th-century theatre, acting, and opera. **Essay:** Ferdinand Raimund.

WILLINGER, David.   Professor of Theatre, City College and Graduate Center, City University of New York. Author of *Theatrical Gestures from the Belgian Avant-Garde*, 1987, *Ghelderode*, 1990, and many articles on modern and contemporary Belgian theatre. Editor of *An Anthology of Contemporary Belgian Plays*, 1984, and *A Theatre Anthology*, 1990. **Essay:** Hugo Claus.

WOODYARD, George.   Adviser. Professor of Spanish,

University of Kansas, Lawrence; editor of *Latin American Theatre Review*. Author of articles on Latin American theatre. Editor of *The Modern Stage in Latin America: Six Plays*, 1971. Co-editor (with Leon F. Lyday) of *Dramatists in Revolt: The New Latin American Theatre*, 1976, and *A Bibliography of Latin American Theatre Criticism, 1940–1974*, 1976. **Essays:** Virgilio Piñera; Carlos Solórzano.

WORRALL, Nick.   Principal Lecturer in English and Drama, Middlesex University (formerly Middlesex Polytechnic). Formerly Soviet correspondent for British centre of the International Theatre Institute; editor of Soviet Union section of *International Theatrelog*. Author of *Nikolai Gogol and Ivan Turgenev*, 1982, *Modernism to Realism on the Soviet Stage*, 1989, and many articles on Russian and Soviet drama. Compiler of *File on Chekhov*, 1986. **Essays:** Mikhail Bulgakov; Anton Chekhov; Nikolai Gogol; Vladimir Mayakovsky; Ivan Turgenev.

WORTH, Katharine.   Adviser. Emeritus Professor, University of London, and Visiting Professor at King's College, University of London. Formerly Professor of Drama and Theatre Studies, Royal Holloway and Bedford New College, until 1987. Author of *Revolutions in Modern English Drama*, 1973, *The Irish Drama from Yeats to Beckett*, 1978, *Oscar Wilde*, 1983, *Maeterlinck's Plays in Performance*, 1985, *"Waiting for Godot" and "Happy Days"* (Text in Performance series), 1990, *Sheridan and Goldsmith*, 1992, and many articles on Beckett, Yeats, and Irish and Noh drama for collections and periodicals. Editor, *Where There is Nothing* (plays by Yeats), 1991. Has co-directed (with David Clark) television versions of Beckett's *Eh Joe*, *Words and Music*, *Embers*, *Cascando*, and made an award-winning adaptation of Beckett's *Company* for the stage in 1987. **Essays:** Brian Friel; Oliver Goldsmith; Lady Gregory; Maurice Maeterlinck; Richard Brinsley Sheridan; Oscar Wilde.

YATES, W.E.   Professor of German, University of Exeter, Devon. Formerly Deputy Vice-Chancellor, University of Exeter, 1986–89, and Germanic editor for *Modern Language Review*, 1981–88. Author of *Grillparzer: A Critical Introduction* 1972, *Nestroy: Satire and Parody in Popular Viennese Comedy*, 1972, *Humanity in Weimar and Vienna: The Continuity of an Ideal*, 1973, *Tradition in the German Sonnet*, 1981, *Schnitzler, Hofmannsthal and the Austrian Theatre*, 1992, and various articles on Viennese cultural and theatrical history, German literature, and lyric poetry. Editor of Hofmannsthal's *Der Schwierige*, 1966, Grillparzer's *Der Traum ein Leben*, 1968, and five volumes of Nestroy's works, 1981–91. Co-editor of *Viennese Popular Theatre*, 1985, and *Grillparzer und die europäische Tradition*, 1987. **Essays:** Franz Grillparzer; Hugo von Hofmannsthal; Johann Nestroy.

ZATLIN, Phyllis.   Professor of Spanish, State University of New Jersey, Rutgers. Author of *Elena Quiroga*, 1977, *Victor Ruiz Iriarte*, 1980, *Jaime Salom*, 1982, and numerous articles on contemporary Spanish theatre. Co-author of *Lengua y lectura: Un repaso y una continuación*, 1970. Editor of Francisco Ayala's *El Rapto*, 1971, Iriarte's *El landó de seis caballos*, 1979, Salom's *La piel del limón*, 1980, Antonio Gala's *Noviembre y un poco de yerba; Petra Regalada*, 1981, and Francisco Nieva's *Combate de Opalos y Tasia; Sombra y quimera de Larra; La magosta*, 1990. Co-editor (with Martha T. Halsey) of *The Contemporary Spanish Theatre: A Collection of Critical Essays*, 1988. Translator of French and Spanish plays and short stories. **Essays:** Alfonso Sastre; Ramón del Valle-Inclán.

PICTURE ACKNOWLEDGEMENTS

photo Mike Abrahams / Network: Havel, Václav.

Australian Overseas Information Service, London: Hewett, Dorothy; White, Patrick.

(photo) Jerry Bauer: Beckett, Samuel.

Bibliothèque Municipale, Arras: Adam de la Halle.

Bibliothèque Nationale, Paris: Scribe, Eugène; Terence.

J. M. Burian: Čapek, Karel (photo Jaromir Svoboda).

Alexander Caminada / Select: Simon Neil.

Jean-Loup Charmet, Paris: Anouilh, Jean; Augier, Émile; Cocteau, Jean; Corneille, Pierre; Dumas *père*, Alexandre; Feydeau, Georges; Genet, Jean; Hugo, Victor; Jarry, Alfred; Labiche, Eugène; Molière; Musset, Alfred de; Racine, Jean; Sartre, Jean-Paul.

© **Donald Cooper / Photostage:** Barker, Howard; Berkoff, Stephen; Bond, Edward; Brenton, Howard; Fugard, Athol; Hare, David; Leigh, Mike; Mamet, David.

Culver Pictures Inc., New York: Rice, Elmer.

Deutsches Theater-Museum, Münich: Nestroy, Johann.

Drottningholms teatermuseum, Stockholm: Lagerkvist, Pär; Strindberg, August (photo University of Bristol Theatre Collection).

© **Jillian Edelstein:** Frayn, Michael.

(photo) Corrado Maria Falsini: Fo, Dario.

(photo) Mark Gerson: Hampton, Christopher; Rudkin, David.

Giraudon, Paris: Aeschylus; Beaumarchais, Pierre-Augustin (Lauros-Giraudon); Euripides; Menander (Alinari Anderson-Giraudon); Montherlant, Henry de (Lauros-Giraudon, Musée des Beaux-Arts, Rouen, © SPADEM); Quinault, Philippe; Sardou, Victorien (Archives Larousse-Giraudon, rights reserved); Sophocles.

Estate of Nikos Kazantzakis: Kazantzakis, Nikos.

Hulton-Deutsch Collection, London: Behan, Brendan; Hellman, Lillian; Miller, Arthur; O'Neill, Eugene; Pinter, Harold; Pirandello, Luigi; Planché, J.R.; Soyinka, Wole; Stoppard, Tom; Toller, Ernst; Wilder, Thornton; Williams, Tennesee.

© **Lipnitzki-Viollet, Paris:** Duras, Marguerite; Tardieu, Jean; Vinaver, Michel.

The Mander and Mitchenson Theatre Collection: Arden, John (photo Snowdon); Barrie, J.M.; Behn, Aphra; Congreve, William; Coward, Noël; Galsworthy, John; Gilbert, W.S.; Inge, William; Jonson, Ben; Lessing, Gottfried Ephraim; Marlowe, Christopher; Massinger, Philip; O'Casey, Sean; Orton, Joe (photo John Haynes); Pinero, Arthur Wing; Priestley, J.B.; Rattigan, Terence; Robinson, T.W.; Shadwell, Thomas; Shakespeare, William; Shaw, George Bernard; Synge, John Millington; Travers, Ben; Van Druten, John; Wilde, Oscar; Wycherley, William.

The Mansell Collection, London: Alfieri, Vittorio; Aristophanes; Brome, Richard; Cervantes, Miguel; Ibsen, Henrik; Kleist, Heinrich von; Kotzebue, August von; Machiavelli, Niccolò; Maeterlinck, Maurice; Rostand, Edmond; Schiller, Friedrich von; Seneca; Sheridan, Richard Brinsley; Vega Carpio, Lope de.

Mary Evans Picture Library: Calderón de la Barca, Pedro; Davenant, William; Echegaray, José; Gozzi, Carlo; Holberg, Ludvig.

Roger Mayne: Jellicoe, Ann.

Národní Divadlo, Prague: Tyl, Josef.

The National Gallery, London: Ariosto, Ludovico.

National Library of Ireland, Dublin: Farquhar, George.

National Portrait Gallery, London: Dryden, John; Eliot, T.S.; Granville-Barker, Harley; Yeats, W.B.

The New York Public Library at Lincoln Center, Astor and Tilden Foundations (Billy Rose Theatre Collection): Hecht, Ben.

Országos Szinháztörténeti Muzeum és Intézet, Budapest: Katona, József.

Österreichisches Nationalbibliothek, Vienna: Bernhard, Thomas; Grillparzer, Franz; Höchwalder, Fritz; Raimund, Ferdinand.

Nigel Parry / Katz: Walcott, Derek.

James Reaney: Reaney, James.

Royal Court Theatre, London: Churchill, Caryl.

Society for Co-operation in Russian and Soviet Studies: Chekhov, Anton; Gogol, Nikolai; Griboyedov, Alexander; Mayakovsky, Vladimir; Ostrovsky, Alexander; Tretyakov, Sergei.

Städelschen Kunstinstituts, Frankfurt: Goethe, Johann Wolfgang von (photo Ursula Edelmann).

Stadtarchiv, Zürich: Dürrenmatt, Friedrich; Frisch, Max.

Theatermuseum der Universität zu Köln: Brecht, Bertolt; Hauptmann, Gerhart; Kaiser, Georg; Wedekind, Frank; Zuckmayer, Carl.

University of Bristol Theatre Collection: Bickerstaff, Isaac; Boucicault, Dion; Cibber, Colley; Daly, Augustin; Gay, John; Steele, Sir Richard.

Yale Repertory Theatre: Wilson, August (photo Gerry Goodstein).

Phyllis Zatlin: Buero Vallejo, Antonio (photo Stan Sasowski).